Wyatt and Dashwood's European Union Law

First published 30 years ago, *Wyatt and Dashwood's European Union Law* was a landmark publication, designed and written for students taking degree-level courses in EU law. In the intervening years new editions have appeared at regular intervals, firmly establishing the book as a reliable and authoritative text. Besides introducing generations of students to the intricacies of European law, it has also been increasingly relied upon by scholars, practitioners and the courts as a valuable source of reference on this complex and ever-expanding body of law.

While the book cannot cover every aspect of the subject matter, it nevertheless offers comprehensive coverage of those aspects of EU law most commonly studied at degree level. Part I introduces the history and foundations of the Union's primary law. Part II looks at the Union's institutions, decision-making procedures and competences. It also deals with the Union judiciary, focusing on direct actions before the Union courts and preliminary references from national courts. The constitutional fundamentals of direct effect and supremacy, effective judicial protection before national courts, general principles of Union law and the Charter of Fundamental Rights are dealt with in Part III. Part IV covers the internal market: free movement of goods, Union citizenship, workers, establishment and services, the services directive, mutual recognition of qualifications, corporate establishment and company law harmonisation. Part V deals with competition law: Articles 101 and 102 TFEU, the enforcement of Union competition rules and other related competition law issues. Part VI then includes a brand new chapter concerned with the EU's external relations, together with treatment of the legal effects of international agreements entered into by the EU.

As with previous editions the aim is to provide an accurate, critical, pragmatic and original account of the subject, at times also offering unique insiders' insights. The book holds to its reputation as being both broad and profound, the ideal foundation for gaining a deep understanding of EU law.

This edition reflects the law post-Lisbon. It has also been restructured and redesigned, so as to facilitate ease of use. Its original authors, Derrick Wyatt and Alan Dashwood, continue to make a significant contribution. Michael Dougan, Eleanor Spaventa and Barry Rodger complete the team of authors working on this invaluable textbook and reference work.

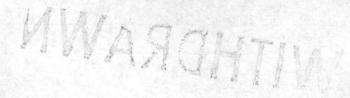

Wyatt and Dashwood's European Union Law

Alan Dashwood, Michael Dougan,
Barry Rodger, Eleanor Spaventa and
Derrick Wyatt

·HART·
PUBLISHING

OXFORD AND PORTLAND, OREGON
2011

Published in the United Kingdom by Hart Publishing Ltd
16C Worcester Place, Oxford OX1 2JW
Telephone: +44 (0)1865 517530
Fax: +44 (0)1865 510710
E-mail: mail@hartpub.co.uk
Website: http://www.hartpub.co.uk

Published in North America (US and Canada) by
Hart Publishing
c/o International Specialized Book Services
920 NE 58th Avenue, Suite 300
Portland, OR 97213-3786
USA
Tel: +1 503 287 3093 or toll-free: (1) 800 944 6190
Fax: +1 503 280 8832
E-mail: orders@isbs.com
Website: http://www.isbs.com

British Library Cataloguing in Publication Data
Data Available

ISBN: 978-1-84946-126-9

Typeset by Forewords, Oxford
Printed and bound in Great Britain by
TJ International Ltd, Padstow, Cornwall

Preface

The previous edition of this book appeared in 2006. Needless to say, a great many things have changed since then.

The first main change concerns our writing team. Alan Dashwood, Michael Dougan, Eleanor Spaventa and Derrick Wyatt have all remained very much on board. We were sad to say goodbye to Tony Arnull and Malcolm Ross, both of whom had contributed so much to previous editions but now felt obliged by other commitments to move on to fresh pastures, though not without graciously permitting us to continue using their past chapters as the basis for updating this 6th edition. But we were delighted to welcome a new author to the team: Barry Rodger from the University of Strathclyde took on responsibility for the competition law sections of the book.

The second main change concerns our publisher. After many editions working fruitfully with Sweet & Maxwell, we were nonetheless excited to enter into a new arrangement with Hart Publishing. All of the authors have previously worked closely with Richard and his first-rate team. We are truly indebted to everyone at Hart Publishing for their professionalism, efficiency, flexibility, dedication and warmth—attributes we have long associated with Hart Publishing, and which were once more displayed in abundance, as Richard and his team worked tirelessly to ensure that the finished book was delivered on schedule and to such a high standard of production.

The final main change, of course, concerns European Union law itself. It becomes ever more true to observe that EU law has become so vast in its scope and dynamic in its evolution that no scholar can hope to keep abreast even of the main developments in this fascinating and frustrating field of research. Lucky, then, that we are five. All the main changes since the last edition have been incorporated into the relevant chapters of this new edition—from the entry into force of the Treaty of Lisbon to the key judgments of the Court of Justice. We have endeavoured to provide a comprehensive overview of the main institutional and constitutional principles of EU law, together with several substantive topics which continue to dominate the degree-level study of EU law. The law is stated as on 1 January 2011; a few subsequent developments were incorporated (where possible) at proof stage.

Alan Dashwood was responsible for updating Chapters 6 and 7 and for writing the new Chapter 27 on the Union's external action. Michael Dougan updated Chapter 1, provided the new Chapter 2, and revised Chapters 3–5, 8 and 9. Barry Rodger undertook the updating to Part V on competition law, which now comprises Chapters 22–26. Eleanor Spaventa handled the myriad revisions to Chapters 10–16. Derrick Wyatt updated Chapters 17–21, which include a new chapter dedicated to the Services Directive; he also updated the section on intellectual property rights in Chapter 14, as well as revising and updating Chapter 28 on the legal effects of international agreements.

AD
MD
BR
ES
DW

Contents

Preface   v
Table of Cases   xxi
Table of Legislation   xcv

PART I: INTRODUCTION   1

1 From the Founding Treaties to the Treaty of Lisbon   3
   I   THE SCHUMAN PLAN AND THE ESTABLISHMENT OF THE ECSC   3
   II   THE EDC AND THE EPC: A FALSE DAWN   5
   III   THE SPAAK REPORT AND THE TWO TREATIES OF ROME   7
   IV   A SINGLE SET OF INSTITUTIONS   8
   V   ENLARGEMENT FROM SIX TO FIFTEEN   9
   VI   AMENDMENT AND DEVELOPMENT OF THE FOUNDING TREATIES UP
       TO 2004   11
       A   The Budgetary Treaties of 1970 and 1975   11
       B   Own Resources Decisions   12
       C   A Directly Elected European Parliament   12
       D   The Single European Act   12
       E   The Treaty on European Union   13
       F   The Treaty of Amsterdam   15
       G   The Treaty of Nice   16
   VII ENLARGEMENT FROM 15 TO 27 (PLUS . . .)   16
   VIII TREATY REFORM SINCE 2004: FROM THE CONSTITUTIONAL TREATY
       TO THE TREATY OF LISBON   18
       A   The Treaty Establishing a Constitution for Europe   18
       B   The Treaty of Lisbon   19
       C   Yet Further Treaty Reform . . .   21

2 An Overview of the Union's Primary Law   23
   I   INTRODUCTION   23
   II   THE TREATY ON EUROPEAN UNION   24
       A   Title I: Common Provisions   24
       B   Title II: Provisions on Democratic Principles   26
       C   Title III: Provisions on the Institutions   26
       D   Title IV: Provisions on Enhanced Co-operation   27
       E   Title V: General Provisions on the Union's External Action and Specific
          Provisions on the Common Foreign and Security Policy   27
       F   Title VI: Final Provisions   28
   III   THE TREATY ON THE FUNCTIONING OF THE EUROPEAN UNION   30
   IV   THE RELATIONSHIP BETWEEN TEU AND TFEU   33
   V   OTHER WRITTEN SOURCES OF PRIMARY LAW   34
   VI   UNWRITTEN SOURCES OF PRIMARY LAW   36

PART II: INSTITUTIONAL FUNDAMENTALS   39

3   The Institutions of the European Union   41
   I   ARTICLE 13 TEU   41
   II   THE EUROPEAN COUNCIL   43
   III   THE COUNCIL   46
   IV   THE COMMISSION   51
   V   A NOTE ON THE HIGH REPRESENTATIVE OF THE UNION FOR
        FOREIGN AFFAIRS AND SECURITY POLICY   54
   VI   THE EUROPEAN PARLIAMENT   56
   VII THE COURT OF JUSTICE OF THE EUROPEAN UNION   61
   VIII SOME CONCLUDING REMARKS: ON THE UNION'S 'INTER-
        INSTITUTIONAL BALANCE'   65

4   The Union's Decision-making Procedures   69
   I   A NEW DISTINCTION BETWEEN LEGISLATIVE AND NON-LEGISLATIVE
        ACTS   69
   II   ADOPTION OF LEGISLATIVE ACTS   71
        A   Initiation of Legislative Procedures   72
        B   Ordinary Legislative Procedure   73
        C   Special Legislative Procedures   77
        D   Passerelle Clauses   80
        E   Emergency Brakes   82
   III   ADOPTION OF NON-LEGISLATIVE ACTS   83
        A   Non-legislative Acts Adopted Directly Under the Treaties   83
        B   Non-legislative Acts Adopted as Delegated Acts   86
        C   Non-legislative Acts Adopted as Implementing Acts   87
   IV   SOME FURTHER ISSUES CONCERNING DECISION-MAKING
        INTERACTION BETWEEN THE UNION INSTITUTIONS   91
        A   The Commission's Right to Alter or Withdraw Its Proposal   91
        B   The Council's Power of Amendment   93
        C   The European Parliament's Participation   94
   V   SOME CONCLUDING REMARKS   95

5   The System of Union Competences   97
   I   THE FUNDAMENTAL PRINCIPLES OF UNION COMPETENCE IN
        ARTICLES 4 AND 5 TEU   97
   II   THE PRINCIPLE OF CONFERRAL   99
        A   Establishing the Existence of Union Competence   99
        B   Establishing the Nature of Union Competence   99
        C   The Problem of 'Competence Creep'   105
        D   The Problem of 'Legal Basis Disputes'   111
   III   THE PRINCIPLE OF SUBSIDIARITY   114
        A   The Meaning(s) of Subsidiarity   114
        B   Implementing Subsidiarity: The Role of the Union's Political Institutions   116
        C   Implementing Subsidiarity: The Role of the Union Courts   117
        D   Implementing Subsidiarity: The Role of the National Parliaments   119
   IV   THE PRINCIPLE OF PROPORTIONALITY   122

V   FLEXIBILITY   124
    A   Primary Flexibility: The Opt-out Provisions   125
    B   Secondary Flexibility: Enhanced Co-operation   127
VI SOME CONCLUDING REMARKS   131

6   **Direct Actions Before the Union Courts**   **135**
I   INFRINGEMENT ACTIONS AGAINST MEMBER STATES   135
    A   Introduction   135
    B   Procedure   137
    C   Substantive Issues in Infringement Proceedings   143
    D   Fines and Penalty Payments   149
II THE ACTION FOR ANNULMENT   153
    A   Introduction   153
    B   The Time Limit   155
    C   Acts Susceptible of Judicial Review   156
    D   Standing of Privileged and Semi-privileged Applicants   160
    E   Standing of Non-privileged Applicants   162
    F   Grounds of Review   177
    G   The Effects of Annulment   180
III THE ACTION FOR FAILURE TO ACT   182
    A   Introduction   182
    B   No Set Time Limit   183
    C   Failures to Act that May Be Challenged   183
    D   Standing   185
    E   Taking a Position   187
    F   The Effect of a Finding of Failure to Act   189
IV THE ACTION FOR DAMAGES   189
    A   Introduction   189
    B   'Traditional' Case Law and the *Schöppenstedt* Formula   191
    C   The Case Law after *Bergaderm*   195
    D   Concurrent Liability of the Union and the Member States   198
    E   Damage and Causation   198
    F   Limitation   199
V   THE PLEA OF ILLEGALITY AND NON-EXISTENCE OF AN ACT   200
VI INTERIM MEASURES   203
VII CONCLUDING REMARKS   205

7   **References for Preliminary Rulings**   **209**
I   GENERAL ISSUES   209
II QUESTIONS THAT MAY BE REFERRED   211
III COURTS AND TRIBUNALS OF THE MEMBER STATES   214
IV THE RELATIONSHIP BETWEEN THE COURT OF JUSTICE AND THE
    REFERRING COURT   216
V   REFERRAL: DISCRETION OR DUTY?   218
    A   The Discretion Conferred by Article 267(2) TFEU   218
    B   Mandatory References   222
    C   References on Validity   225
VI EFFECTS OF THE RULING BY THE COURT OF JUSTICE   228
VII CONCLUDING REMARKS   230

PART III: CONSTITUTIONAL FUNDAMENTALS   233

8   The Direct Effect and Supremacy of Union Law   235
I   INTRODUCTION: THE SYSTEM OF DECENTRALISED ENFORCEMENT   235
II   THE DUTY OF CONSISTENT INTERPRETATION   239
III   THE PRINCIPLE OF DIRECT EFFECT   244
   A   The Threshold Criteria for Direct Effect   245
   B   Who May Rely on Directly Effective Union Law?   248
   C   Against Whom May Directive Effective Union Law Be Enforced?   252
IV   THE PRINCIPLE OF SUPREMACY   270
V   THE RELATIONSHIP BETWEEN DIRECT EFFECT AND SUPREMACY   278
VI   CONCLUDING REMARKS   284

9   Judicial Protection of Union Rights before the National Courts   287
I   INTRODUCTION   287
II   THE FUNDAMENTAL RIGHT TO JUDICIAL PROCESS   289
III   THE PRINCIPLE OF EQUIVALENCE   292
IV   THE PRINCIPLE OF EFFECTIVENESS   294
   A   The Court's Early Period: Until the Mid-1980s   295
   B   The Court's Middle Period: Until 1993   296
   C   The Court's Most Recent Period: Since 1993   299
V   ACTIONS BASED DIRECTLY UPON UNION LAW   303
   A   The Right to Interim Relief   303
   B   The Right to the Recovery of Unlawfully Levied Charges   305
   C   The *Francovich* Right to Reparation   307
   D   A Private Law Right to Damages?   314
VI   UNION LEGISLATION CONCERNING REMEDIES AND PROCEDURAL
     RULES   316
VII   CONCLUDING REMARKS   318

10   General Principles of Union Law   321
I   FUNCTION AND SOURCES OF GENERAL PRINCIPLES   321
II   THE GENERAL PRINCIPLE OF SINCERE OR LOYAL CO-OPERATION   322
III   SUBSIDIARITY AS A GENERAL PRINCIPLE   324
IV   PROPORTIONALITY   325
   A   The Principle of Proportionality as a Limit to the Actions of the Institutions   325
   B   The Principle of Proportionality as a Limit to Member States Actions   327
V   LEGAL CERTAINTY AND LEGITIMATE EXPECTATION   328
VI   THE PRINCIPLE OF NON-DISCRIMINATION   332
VII   OTHER GENERAL PRINCIPLES   335

11   Fundamental Rights   337
I   EVOLUTION OF THE CONCEPT   337
II   THE RESPONSE OF THE POLITICAL INSTITUTIONS   339
   A   From the 1977 Political Declaration to the Nice Treaty   339
   B   The Treaty of Lisbon   340
III   THE SCOPE OF APPLICATION OF FUNDAMENTAL RIGHTS   343
   A   Fundamental Rights as a Limit to the Acts of the Institutions   343

	B	Fundamental rights and Member States' Implementing Powers	344
	C	Member States Acting within the Scope of Union law	346
	D	The Institutional Structure of the Union and Fundamental Rights	351
	E	Relationship between the European Union and the European Convention of Human Rights	354

12 The Charter of Fundamental Rights — 359

I	BACKGROUND TO THE DRAFTING OF THE CHARTER	359
II	THE CHARTER: STRUCTURE AND SUBSTANTIVE PROVISIONS	361
	A Structure of the Charter	361
	B Preamble	362
	C Substantive Provisions	363
III	THE HORIZONTAL PROVISIONS: INTERPRETATION AND SCOPE OF APPLICATION OF THE CHARTER	382
	A Article 51: The Charter's Field of Application	382
	B Article 52: Scope of the Charter's Provisions	383
	C Article 53: Level of Protection	385
	D Article 54: Abuse of Rights	385
IV	THE UK AND POLISH PROTOCOL	386

PART IV: THE INTERNAL MARKET — 389

13 Fiscal Barriers to the Free Movement of Goods — 391

I	THE FREE MOVEMENT OF GOODS	391
	A Customs Union and Charges Having Equivalent Effect	392
	B Customs Duties and Charges Having Equivalent Effect	393
	C Charges Falling Outside the Scope of Article 30 TFEU: Services Provided to the Importer and EU Law Obligations	394
II	PROHIBITION ON DISCRIMINATORY INTERNAL TAXATION	395
	A Discriminatory Taxation: Article 110(1) TFEU	396
	B Protectionist Taxation: Article 110(2) TFEU	399
	C The Importance of a Comparator	401
III	THE RELATIONSHIP BETWEEN ARTICLES 30 AND 110 TFEU	401
IV	THE RELATIONSHIP BETWEEN ARTICLES 30 AND 110 TFEU AND OTHER PROVISIONS OF THE TREATY	403
V	DISCRIMINATORY TAX TREATMENT OF EXPORTS	404
VI	THE COMMON CUSTOMS TARIFF AND EXTERNAL RELATIONS	405

14 The Free Movement of Goods: Quantitative Restrictions and Measures Having Equivalent Effect — 407

I	INTRODUCTION	408
II	QUANTITATIVE RESTRICTIONS ON IMPORTS AND EXPORTS	408
III	MEASURES HAVING EQUIVALENT EFFECT TO QUANTITATIVE RESTRICTIONS ON IMPORTS	409
	A The Inception of the Court's Case Law: *Dassonville* and *Cassis de Dijon*	409
	B The Application of the *Cassis* Ruling	413
	C The Sunday Trading Saga	415
	D The *Keck and Mithouard* Judgment	418
	E The Case Law after the *Keck* Judgment	422
	F The Member States' Positive Duties	430

	G	The Cross-border Element and Reverse Discrimination	431
IV		MEASURES HAVING EQUIVALENT EFFECT TO QUANTITATIVE RESRICTIONS ON EXPORTS	432
V		GENERAL REMARKS ABOUT ARTICLES 34 AND 35 TFEU	434
VI		DEROGATION FROM ARTICLES 34 AND 35 TFEU	435
	A	Grounds of Derogation	435
	B	Burden of Proof Lies with the National Authorities	440
	C	The Effect of Harmonisation Directives and Other EU Measures on Recourse to Article 36 TFEU	441
VII		MANDATORY REQUIREMENTS IN THE GENERAL INTEREST	441
	A	Mandatory Requirements	441
	B	The Principle of Proportionality	445
VIII		THE RELATIONSHIP BETWEEN ARTICLES 34–36 TFEU AND OTHER PROVISIONS OF THE TREATY	446
IX		ARTICLE 37 TFEU: STATE MONOPOLIES OF A COMMERCIAL CHARACTER	447
X		ARTICLES 34–36 TFEU AND INTELLECTUAL PROPERTY RIGHTS	449
	A	Intellectual Property and the Internal Market	449
	B	A Distinction between the Existence and Exercise of Intellectual Property Rights	451
	C	Free Movement of Goods: The Exhaustion of Rights Principle	452
	D	Exhaustion of Patent Rights	453
	E	Exhaustion of Trade Mark Rights	456
XI		CONCLUDING REMARKS	459

15   Union Citizenship and the Rights to Move and Reside in the European Union   **461**

I		THE ROAD TO CITIZENSHIP	461
II		THE EVOLUTION OF THE CASE LAW ON UNION CITIZENSHIP	463
III		THE RESIDENCE DIRECTIVE	467
	A	The Personal Scope of Directive 2004/38	468
	B	The Material Scope of the Directive: Right to Enter, Exit and Temporary Residence	471
	C	The Material Scope of the Directive: Right of Residence for more than Three Months	472
	D	Administrative Formalities	477
	E	Right of Permanent Residence	479
	F	Rights of Residents and Permanent Residents	481
	G	Derogations on the Right of Entry and Residence on the Grounds of Public Policy, Public Security and Public Health	482
	H	Abuse of Rights	488
IV		OTHER RIGHTS PERTAINING TO EU CITIZENS	489
	A	Right to Equal Treatment, Right to Move and Beyond	489
	B	Political Rights and Rights to Good Administration	492

16   Freedom of Movement for Workers   **497**

I		INTRODUCTION	497
II		THE AMBIT OF ARTICLE 45 TFEU	500
	A	The Cross-border Element	500
	B	Vertical, Semi-horizontal and Horizontal Effect	501
	B	Territorial Application	502

III THE PERSONAL SCOPE OF APPLICATION OF ARTICLE 45 TFEU: THE
CONCEPT OF 'WORKER' 503
    A The Definition of Worker 503
    B Retention of Status of Worker 505
    C Work-seekers 506
IV THE MATERIAL SCOPE OF ARTICLE 45 TFEU: ACCESS TO
EMPLOYMENT AND EQUAL TREATMENT 508
    A Right to Move and Reside in Member States 508
    B The Right to Equal Treatment 509
    C Equality in the Employment Context and Beyond 514
    D Equality in Social and Tax Advantages 517
V THE MATERIAL SCOPE OF ARTICLE 45 TFEU: NON-DISCRIMINATORY
RESTRICTIONS 520
VI THE WORKER'S FAMILY 525
    A Right to Education 525
    B Tax and Social Advantages 527
VII THE TRANSITIONAL ARRANGEMENT FOR THE NEW MEMBER STATES 528

17 The Right of Establishment and the Freedom to Provide Services 531
I ESTABLISHMENT AND SERVICES 532
    A Meaning of the Right of Establishment and Freedom to Provide Services 532
II THE SCOPE OF THE PRESENT CHAPTER 534
III THE RIGHT OF ESTABLISHMENT 534
    A General Scope 534
    B Evolution of the Court's Case Law on the Interpretation of Article 49 TFEU 535
    C Abolition of Restrictions on the Right of Establishment 541
    D Effect of the Direct Applicability of Article 49 TFEU on Harmonisation 543
    E Direct and Indirect Discrimination on Grounds of Nationality 545
    F Relationship between Article 18 TFEU and Articles 49 and 56 TFEU 547
    G Non-discriminatory Restrictions on the Right of Establishment 547
    H Parallel Interpretation of Articles 45, 49 and 56 TFEU and Horizontal Effect 552
IV FREEDOM TO PROVIDE SERVICES 554
    A General Scope 554
    B National Measures Affecting both Free Movement of Goods (Article 34
       TFEU) and Freedom to Provide Services (Article 56 TFEU) 558
    C Abolition of Discriminatory Restrictions: The General Programme and
       Secondary Legislation 558
    D Effect of the Direct Applicability of Article 56 TFEU on Harmonisation 559
    E Prohibition of Restrictions on Freedom to Provide Services: Evolution of the
       Court's Case Law 559
    F Prohibition of Non-discriminatory Restrictions on Freedom to Provide
       Services 565
V ESTABLISHMENT AND SERVICES: NATIONAL MEASURES TO PREVENT
CIRCUMVENTION, AND DEROGATION ON EXPRESS OR IMPLIED
GROUNDS 567
    A National Measures to prevent Circumvention of National Rules in the
       Context of the Right of Establishment and Freedom to Provide Services 567
    B Articles 51 TFEU and 62 TFEU: Exception for Activities connected with the
       Exercise of Official Authority 568
    C Articles 52 TFEU and 62 TFEU: The Public Policy Proviso 571
    D Imperative Requirements in the General Interest 573
VI NATIONAL TAX MEASURES AS RESTRICTIONS ON FUNDAMENTAL
FREEDOMS 581

A The Normal Principles Apply but Account is Taken of the Particular Features of Tax Law 581

B For Tax Purposes Residence and the Location of a Company's Seat Are Legitimate Connecting Factors but National Rules which Differentiate on these Grounds may Be Held to Be Discriminatory 582

C Tax Measures which Discriminate against Non-residents May Amount to Restrictions on the Right of Establishment 584

D Discrimination against Non-resident Parent Companies in their Dealings with Resident Subsidiaries 585

E National Tax Rules which Inhibit Individuals and Companies Established in a Member State from Extending their Activities to Another Member State 588

F Possible Justifications for National Tax Rules which Restrict the Exercise of Fundamental Freedoms 589

VII CONCLUDING REMARKS 596

18 The Directive on Services in the Internal Market **599**

I GENERAL 599

II SERVICES COVERED BY THE DIRECTIVE 600

III 'REQUIREMENTS' 601

IV FREEDOM OF ESTABLISHMENT FOR PROVIDERS 602
A General 602
B Authorisations 602
C Prohibited Requirements 604
D Requirements which Must Be Amended if They Cannot Be Justified 604

V THE FREE MOVEMENT OF SERVICES 605
A General 605
B Freedom for Providers to Provide Services 605
C Additional Derogations from the Freedom of Providers to Provide Services 607
D Case-by-case Derogations from the Freedom of Providers to Provide Services 607
E Rights of Recipients of Services 607

VI QUALITY OF SERVICES 609
A Information from Providers 609
B Professional Liability Insurance and Guarantees 610
C Advertising and Other Forms of Commercial Communications by the Regulated Professions 610

VII ADMINISTRATIVE CO-OPERATION 611
A General 611
B The Division of Supervisory Tasks 611
C Mutual Assistance: General Obligations 612
D Checks, Inspections and the Supply of Information by the Member State of Establishment 612
E Checks, Inspections and the Supply of Information by the Member State where the Service is provided 613
F Information on the Good Repute of Providers 613
G Mutual Assistance in the Event of Case-by-case Derogations 614
H Internal Market Information System 615

VIII ADMINISTRATIVE SIMPLIFICATION 616
A Simplification of Procedures 616
B Points of Single Contact: 'One-stop Shops' 617
C Procedures by Electronic Means 619

IX MUTUAL EVALUATION 619

X SOME PROVISIONS OF THE DIRECTIVE COVER INTERNAL AS WELL AS CROSS-BORDER SITUATIONS 621

XI		THE DIRECTIVE EXCLUDES CERTAIN JUSTIFICATIONS WHICH WOULD OTHERWISE BE AVAILABLE	622
XII		CONCLUDING REMARKS: ASSESSMENT OF THE SERVICES DIRECTIVE	623

19 Mutual Recognition of Diplomas, Training and Experience, and the Co-ordination of National Qualifications — 625

I		DIRECT APPLICABILITY OF ARTICLES 49 AND 56 TFEU (AND ARTICLE 45 TFEU)	626
	A	The Principles Applicable Where No Relevant Harmonisation Directives Have Been Adopted	626
	B	The Principles Applicable in the Absence of Harmonisation Directives Are Also Applicable after Harmonisation to Situations Not Covered by Relevant Directives	627
	C	A National Requirement that a Person Possess a Particular Qualification in Order to Carry on a Particular Occupational Activity is in Itself a Restriction on a Fundamental Freedom which Must Be Justified	628
II		MUTUAL RECOGNITION OF DIPLOMAS AND THE CO-ORDINATION OF NATIONAL QUALIFICATIONS BY EU RULES	630
	A	Introduction	630
	B	Freedom of Establishment: Recognition on the Basis of Co-ordination of Minimum Training Conditions—Chapter III of Title III of the PQ Directive	631
	C	Freedom of Establishment: Recognition of Professional Experience—Chapter II of Title III of the PQ Directive	631
	D	Freedom of Establishment: The General System—Chapter I of Title III of the PQ Directive	632
	E	Freedom to Provide Services: Pursuit of Activities under Home-Country title—Title II of the PQ Directive	634
	F	Right of Establishment under 'Home-country' Professional Title?	637
	G	Other Specific Arrangements for a Given Regulated Profession	638
III		LAWYERS: FREEDOM TO PROVIDE SERVICES	639
IV		LAWYERS: RIGHT OF ESTABLISHMENT	640
V		CONCLUDING REMARKS	644

20 Corporate Establishment, Cross-border Acquisitions and Golden Shares — 647

I		CORPORATE ESTABLISHMENT	647
	A	General	647
	B	Right of Primary and Secondary Establishment of Companies	649
	C	Parent Company May Implement a Uniform Advertising Concept at EU level through its Subsidiaries in Other Member States	658
	D	National Rules Making it More difficult for Subsidiaries to Compete with Existing Market Operators Hinder their Market Access and Must be Justified	659
	E	Harmonisation at EU Level to Achieve Freedom of Establishment	659
	F	Mergers and Acquisitions as Aspects of Freedom of Establishment	660
II		CROSS-BORDER ACQUISITIONS	661
	A	Free Movement of Capital	661
	B	Meaning of 'Capital Movement': 'Direct Investment' and 'Portfolio Investment'	662
	C	Cross-border Acquisitions Involve both the Free Movement of Capital and the Right of Establishment	663
	D	National Rules on Surveillance and Control of Cross-border Investments and the Free Movement of Capital	663

E Restrictions on Capital Movement Arising from 'Special Shares' or 'Golden Shares' 664

III CAN THE CORPORATE CONSTITUTION AND PRIVATE ACTION TAKEN PURSUANT TO IT AMOUNT TO RESTRICTIONS ON FUNDAMENTAL FREEDOMS? 670
A State Action Derogating from the Normal Rules of Company Law: Only Actions External to the Market Can Place Restrictions Upon It 670
B Actions of Private Operators under Private Law May Amount to Restrictions on Fundamental Freedoms 671

IV CONCLUDING REMARKS 673

21 Company Law Harmonisation 677

I COMPANY LAW HARMONISATION WAS DESIGNED TO PROMOTE FREEDOM OF ESTABLISHMENT 677

II OBSTACLES TO ESTABLISHMENT ADDRESSED BY COMPANY LAW HARMONISATION 679
A Summary 679
B Psychological Obstacles to Dealing with Foreign Companies, Unfamiliarity with Regimes Applicable to Foreign Companies, and Promoting Legal Certainty 679
C Differences between National Rules which Unless Harmonised Would Require Compliance with Further Requirements by Virtue of Establishment in Another Member State 681
D National Rules or Practices which (Whether or Not they Vary from State to State) Inhibit Cross-border Establishment 683

III HAS COMPANY LAW HARMONISATION MADE AN EFFECTIVE CONTRIBUTION TO THE INTERNAL MARKET? 684
A An Open Question 684
B Claims to Promote Cross-border Activity Have Not Always Been Made Good: The Example of EEIGs 685
C The Need for Empiricism: Evaluation and Feedback on European legislation 687

IV IMPROVING COMPETITIVENESS THROUGH COMPANY LAW HARMONISATION 688
A The Evolution of Law and Policy 688
B Reports of the High Level Group of Company Law Experts 688
C The Commission's Response: Modernising Company Law and Enhancing Corporate Governance in the European Union 689

V IS THE PROMISE OF MORE EMPIRICAL AND MORE PRO-COMPETITIVE EUROPEAN LEGISLATION BEING REALISED? 690
A Two Recent Initiatives 690
B The European Company Statute 691
C Directive 2004/25/EC on Takeover Bids 693

VI CONCLUDING REMARKS 700

PART V: COMPETITION LAW 703

22 Introduction to EU Competition Law 705

I EU COMPETITION LAW SOURCES 705
A The Principal Treaty Provisions 706
B Other Sources of EU Competition Law 708

II COMPETITION LAW AND POLICY IN AN EU CONTEXT 709
A The Early Focus Upon the Market 709

B Post-'Lisbon' Modernisation: Competitiveness, Consumer Welfare and
Efficiency 711
III THE SCOPE OF THE EU COMPETITION RULES 713
A 'Personal' Scope 713
B Material Scope 718
C Territorial Scope 718
IV COMPETITION LAW IN AN INTERNATIONAL CONTEXT 722
A Co-operation Agreements 722
B Developments Towards Global Regulation or Co-operation 724
V CONCLUDING REMARKS 725

23 Article 101: Cartels and Anti-competitive Agreements **729**
I INTRODUCTION: RATIONALE AND PURPOSE 729
II UNDERTAKINGS AND CONCURRENCE OF WILLS 731
III FORMS OF CO-OPERATION 734
A Decisions of Associations of Undertakings 734
B Agreements between Undertakings 735
C Concerted Practices 735
IV RESTRICTING COMPETITION 741
A 'By Object' Restrictions 742
B 'By Effect' Restrictions 744
C Information Exchange 750
D Appreciable Effects on Competition and on Trade between Member States 752
V THE LEGAL EXCEPTION UNDER ARTICLE 101(3) 754
A Efficiency Gains 756
B Benefit to Consumers 758
C No Restrictions That Are Not Indispensable 758
D No Possibility of Eliminating Competition 759
E Block Exemptions 760
VI CONCLUDING REMARKS 762

24 Abuse of Dominance: Article 102 **765**
I INTRODUCTION: THE PURPOSE OF ARTICLE 102 765
II ESTABLISHING THE RELEVANT
MARKET 768
A The Relevant Product or Service Market 768
B The Geographic Market 773
C The Temporal Market 775
III DOMINANCE 775
A Market Shares 776
B Barriers to Market Entry or Expansion by Rivals 777
C Conduct and Performance of the Undertaking 778
IV THE CONCEPT OF JOINT OR COLLECTIVE DOMINANCE 779
V THE CONCEPT OF AN ABUSE 781
A Recurring Conceptual Issues 782
B Commission Guidance on Enforcement Priorities 2009 785
C Types of Abuse 786
VI CONCLUDING REMARKS 806

25 Enforcement of Articles 101 and 102 **809**
I INTRODUCTION 809

II REGULATION 1/2003 AND EU COMPETITION LAW ENFORCEMENT 810
   A The Commission's Powers 811
   B The National Competition Authorities 812
   C The ECN in Operation 812
III THE CONDUCT OF PROCEEDINGS BY THE COMMISSION 814
   A Information and Evidence 815
   B The Right to a Hearing 820
   C Final Decision 823
IV PUBLIC ENFORCEMENT: FINES 826
   A Calculating Fines: The 2006 Guidelines Notice 827
   B Rights of the Defence, Fundamental Rights Protection and the Commission's
      Enforcement Processes: The Future 832
   C Uncovering Cartels: Leniency Incentives 833
   D Settlements 836
V PRIVATE ENFORCEMENT: REMEDIES BEFORE NATIONAL COURTS 838
   A Regulation 1/2003: Facilitating Private Enforcement? 838
   B *Crehan v Courage* and an EU-based Remedy for Private Parties? 840
   C Commission Reform Proposals 842
VI CONCLUDING REMARKS 843

26 State Aid and State Regulation 847
I INTRODUCTION: STATE AID AND THE MODERNISATION AGENDA 848
II THE STRUCTURE OF ARTICLE 107 TFEU 849
III DEFINING STATE AID: THE CONDITIONS OF ARTICLE 107(1) 850
   A Intervention by the State or Through State Resources 851
   B Liable to Affect Trade between Member States 852
   C Conferring an Advantage on the Recipient 853
   D Distortion of Competition 857
IV JUSTIFICATIONS FOR AID: MANDATORY EXCEPTIONS UNDER ARTICLE
   107(2) 857
V DISCRETIONARY EXCEPTIONS UNDER ARTICLE 107(3) 859
VI ARTICLE 107 AND SERVICES OF GENERAL ECONOMIC INTEREST 862
   A Aid or Compensation 862
   B Article 106(2) after Altmark 864
   C Legislation Post-*Altmark* in Relation to SGEIs 864
VII ENFORCEMENT OF STATE AID RULES: THE LEGISLATIVE MACHINERY 866
   A Notified Aid 867
   B Unlawful Aid 868
   C Misuse of Aid 870
   D Existing Aids 871
VIII RIGHTS OF INTERESTED PARTIES 871
IX THE ROLE OF NATIONAL COURTS 873
X INTRODUCTION TO ARTICLE 106 TFEU 874
XI ARTICLE 106(1): THE RESPONSIBILITY OF MEMBER STATES 877
   A The Categories of Undertaking in Article 106(1) 877
   B The Scope of the Obligation Imposed on Member States under Article 106(1) 880
XII ARTICLE 106(2): ENTRUSTED UNDERTAKINGS AND FISCAL
   MONOPOLIES 884
   A The Categories of Undertaking in Article 106(2) 884
   B Application of the Conditions in Article 106(2) 886

C   The Proviso to Article 106(2)   888
D   Direct Effect of Article 106(2)   889
E   Article 106(3): The Supervisory and Legislative Competence of the Commission 889
XIII NATIONAL LEGISLATION AND ARTICLE 101   890
A   Requiring or Favouring Anti-competitive Agreements, or Reinforcing their
     Effects   891
B   Legislation Deprived of its State Character by Delegation   892
XIV CONCLUDING REMARKS   893

PART VI: EXTERNAL RELATIONS   **897**

27 External Action   **899**

I   THE CONSTUTIONAL FRAMEWORK   899
A   External Action Under the New Treaty Structure   899
B   Part Five of the TFEU   900
C   The High Representative of the Union for Foreign Affairs and Security Policy 902
D   The General Treaty Provisions on the Union's External Action   903
E   Continuing Particularity of the CFSP   905
F   The Interface Between CFSP Competence and TFEU External Competences   907
II   EXPRESS AND IMPLIED EU EXTERNAL COMPETENCE   909
A   Two Fundamental Questions   909
B   The Pre-Lisbon Case Law on Implied External Competence   909
B   Article 216(1) TFEU   918
C   Summing Up: The TL's Answer to the Existence Question   922
III EXCLUSIVE EU EXTERNAL COMPETENCE   922
A   Exclusive External Competence Post-Lisbon   922
B   Article 3(2) TFEU and the Case Law on Supervening External Exclusivity   923
C   Article 3 (2) and Other Provisions of the Treaties   931
D   Lawful Member State Action in Areas of Exclusive EU Competence   932
IV   SHARED COMPETENCE AND THE DUTY OF CLOSE CO-OPERATION   933
V   THE PROCEDURAL CODE IN ARTICLE 218 TFEU   936
VI   MIXED AGREEMENTS   939
VII THE COMMON COMMERCIAL POLICY   941
A   Introduction   941
B   Scope of the CCP   943
C   Procedure   949
D   Summing Up on the CCP   950
VIII CONCLUDING REMARKS   950

28 The Legal Effects of International Agreements   **953**

I   THE DIRECT EFFECT OF INTERNATIONAL AGREEMENTS CONCLUDED
     BY THE EU   953
II   LIMITED LEGAL EFFECTS FOR THE GATT 1947 AND WTO AGREEMENTS   956
III REVIEW OF EU MEASURES ON THE BASIS OF DIRECTLY EFFECTIVE
     INTERNATIONAL AGREEMENTS   958
IV   THE *NAKAJIMA* EXCEPTION: REVIEW OF EU MEASURES ON THE BASIS
     OF NON-DIRECTLY EFFECTIVE INTERNATIONAL AGREEMENTS   961
V   EXTENSION OF THE *NAKAJIMA* EXCEPTION TO THE REVIEW OF EU
     MEASURES ON THE BASIS OF CUSTOMARY INTERNATIONAL LAW   963

VI INTERPRETATION OF EU MEASURES IN LIGHT OF INTERNATIONAL
AGREEMENTS AND CUSTOMARY INTERNATIONAL LAW   964
VII NATIONAL COURTS MUST INTERPRET NATIONAL LAW IN LIGHT
OF NON-DIRECTLY EFFECTIVE PROVISIONS OF INTERNATIONAL
AGREEMENTS BINDING ON THE EU   965
VIII THE JURISDICTION OF THE COURT OF JUSTICE TO INTERPRET MIXED
AGREEMENTS   966
IX CONCLUDING REMARKS   967

Index   969

Table of Cases

EU cases are presented first, grouped by instance (Court of Justice first, General Court/ CFI second, then Commission quasi-judicial decisions). For both Court of Justice and General Court, cases are presented in two sequences – case number order and alphabetical order by parties. International courts (notably the European Court of Human Rights) follow, with national cases listed last.

European Union

Court of Justice, Case Number Order

Case 3/54 ASSIDER v High Authority [1954-56] ECR 63 177
Joined Cases 7/56 and 3-7/57 Algera v Common Assembly [1957 and 1958] ECR 39 198
Case 1/58 Stork v High Authority [1959] ECR 17.................................337
Joined Cases 36-40/59 Geitling v High Authority [1960] ECR 425 337
Case 7/61 Commission v Italy [1961] ECR 317.....................................409, 435
Joined Cases 16 and 17/62 Producteurs de Fruits v Council [1962] ECR 471 163
Case 25/62 Plaumann v Commission [1963] ECR 95................. 163, 166–7, 169–70, 172, 175, 191, 872–3
Case 26/62 van Gend en Loos [1963] ECR 1 .... 37, 65–6, 235–8, 245, 248, 253, 262, 284
Joined Cases 28-30/62 da Costa en Schaake [1963] ECR 31 ....225, 229
Joined Cases 31 and 33/62 Wöhrmann v Commission [1962] ECR 501 200–1
Case 75/63 Hoekstra (neé Unger) [1964] ECR 177................................503
Joined Cases 90 and 91/63 Commission v Luxembourg and Belgium [1964] ECR 625 144
Joined Cases 90/63 and 91/63 Commission v Luxembourg and Belgium [1964] ECR 625 392
Case 6/64 Costa v Enel [1964] ECR 585............................. 37, 223, 237–8, 262, 270, 284, 447, 543
Case 40/64 Sgarlata v Commission [1965] ECR 215................................337
Case 45/64 Commission v Italy [1965] ECR 857.....................................396, 404
Joined Cases 56 and 58/64 Consten and Grundig v Commission [1966] ECR 299;
    [1966] CMLR 418 ....741, 743–4, 747, 753, 756
Case 10/65 Deutschmann v Federal Republic of Germany [1965] ECR 469.............................401
Case 32/65 Italy v Council and Commission [1966] ECR 389 .... 201–2, 706
Case 44/65 Maison Singer [1965] ECR 965 ....499, 621
Case 48/65 Lütticke v Commission [1966] ECR 19.................................141, 188
Joined Cases 52 and 55/65 Germany v Commission [1966] ECR 159....................................395
Case 56/65 Société Technique Minière v Maschinenbau Ulm [1966] ECR 235,
    [1966] CMLR 357 ....719, 741, 743, 747, 753–4, 843
Case 57/65 Lutticke v Hauptzollamt Saarlouis [1966] ECR 205 .... 396–7, 401
Case 61/65 Vaassen v Beamtenfonds Mijnbedrijf [1966] ECR 261.....................................215
Joined Cases 5, 7 and 13-24/66 Kampffmeyer v Commission [1967] ECR 245 .... 194, 198, 200
Case 7/67 Wohrmann v Hauptzollamt Bad Reichenhall [1967] ECR 177..............................402
Case 17/67 Neumann [1967] ECR 441 270
Case 24/67 Parke, Davis [1968] ECR 55 454
Case 25/67 Milch- Fett- und Eierkontor v Hauptzollamt Saarbrucken [1968] ECR 207.....................402
Case 27/67 Fink-Frucht [1968] ECR 223 402
Case 28/67 Molkerei-Zentrale v Hauptzollamt Paderborn [1968] ECR 143 .... 288, 396, 404
Case 34/67 Lück [1968] ECR 245...288
Case 7/68 Commission v Italy (Art Treasuries) [1968] ECR 423 393
Joined Cases 10 and 18/68 Eridania v Commission [1969] ECR 459...................................188
Case 13/68 Salgoil [1968] ECR 453 ....245, 288
Case 14/68 Walt Wilhelm [1969] ECR 1...101, 839, 922
Case 24/68 Commission v Italy [1969] ECR 193..395

Joined Cases 2 and 3/69 Sociaal Fonds etc v Brachfeld and Chougol Diamond Co
  [1969] ECR 211 . . . . 392–3, 395, 402
Case 4/69 Lütticke v Commission [1971] ECR 325 190
Case 5/69 Völk v Vervaecke [1969] ECR 295; [1969] CMLR 273 752
Joined Cases 6 and 11/69 Commission v France [1969] ECR 523; [1970] CMLR 43 856
Case 6/69 Commission v France [1969] ECR 523; [1970] CMLR 43 849
Case 9/69 Sayag v Leduc [1969] ECR 329 190–1
Case 15/69 Ugliola [1969] ECR 363 . . . . .514, 572
Case 29/69 Stauder [1969] ECR 419 . . . . .338, 343
Case 38/69 Commission v Italy [1970] ECR 47 145
Joined Cases 41, 44-45/69 ACF Chemiefarma v Commission [1970] ECR 661 . . . . 79, 169, 735
Case 45/69 Boehringer v Commission [1970] ECR 769 821
Case 47/69 France v Commission [1970] ECR 487 403
Case 48/69 ICI v Commission [1972] ECR 619; [1972] CMLR 557 . . . . 720, 736–7, 821, 830
Case 52/69 Geigy v Commission [1972] ECR 787 721
Case 54/69 Francolor v Commission [1972] ECR 851; [1972] CMLR 557 822
Case 69/69 Alcan v Commission [1970] ECR 385 165
Joined Cases 76 and 11/69 Commission v France [1969] ECR 523 141
Case 77/69 Commission v Belgium [1970] ECR 237 . . . . .145, 270
Case 9/70 Franz Grad [1970] ECR 825 268
Case 11/70 Internationale Handelsgesellschaft [1970] ECR 1125 . . . . 271, 273, 325, 338
Case 15/70 Chevalley v Commission [1970] ECR 975 . . . . .184, 186
Case 22/70 Commission v Council (AETR) [1971] ECR 263 . . . . 157, 542, 911–14, 916–17,
                                                                                        920–2, 924, 926–33, 940, 948
Case 25/70 Köster [1970] ECR 1161 88
Case 33/70 SACE v Italian Ministry of Finance [1970] ER 1213 392
Case 59/70 Netherlands v Commission [1971] ECR 639 183
Case 78/70 Deutsche Grammophon [1871] ECR 487 453
Case 5/71 Zuckerfabrik Schöppenstedt v Council [1971] ECR 975 . . . . .190, 193
Case 6/71 Rheinmühlen Düsseldorf [1971] ECR 719 334
Case 15/71 Mackprang v Commission [1971] ECR 797 186
Case 18/71 Eunomia v Italian Ministry of Education [1971] ECR 811 392
Case 20/71 Sabbatini [1972] ECR 345 332
Case 22/71 Béguelin Import Co v SA GL Import Export [1971] ECR 949; [1972] CMLR 81 731
Case 42/71 Nordgetreide v Commission [1972] ECR 105 188
Case 43/71 Politi v Italian Ministry of Finance [1971] ECR 1039 256–7
Case 48/71 Commission v Italy [1972] ECR 527 270
Joined Cases 51-54/71 International Fruit [1971] ECR 1107 410
Case 77/71 Gervais-Danone [1971] ECR 1127 329
Case 92/71 Interfood [1972] ECR 231 964
Case 93/71 Leonesio v Italian Ministry of Agriculture and Forestry [1972] ECR 287 257
Case 6/72 Europemballage and Continental Can v Commission
  [1973] ECR 215 . . . . .706, 721, 765, 767, 770–1, 782–3
Case 8/72 Cementhandelaren v Commission [1972] ECR 977, [1973] CMLR 7 719
Joined Cases 21-24/72 International Fruit Company [1972] ECR 1219 . . . . 942, 958–9
Case 39/72 Commission v Italy [1973] ECR 101 . . . . 140, 145, 189, 257
Case 44/72 Marsman [1972] ECR 1243 514
Joined Cases 63-69/72 Werhahn v Council [1973] ECR 1229 190
Case 70/72 Commission v Germany [1973] ECR 813; [1973] CMLR 741 869
Case 76/72 Michel S [1973] ECR 457 . . . . .498, 526
Case 77/72 Capolongo v Azienda Agricola Maya [1973] ECR 611 401–2
Case 79/72 Commission v Italy [1972] ECR 667 262
Case 81/72 Commission v Council [1973] ECR 575 . . . . .182, 822
Case 2/73 Geddo v Ente Nazionale Risi [1973] ECR 865 409
Case 4/73 Nold v Commission [1974] ECR I-491 . . . . 338–9, 368
Joined Cases 6-7/73 Istituto Chemioterapico Italiano SpA and
  Commercial Solvents Corpn v Commission [1974] ECR 223,
  [1974] 1 CMLR 309 . . . . 721, 754, 767, 772, 775, 779, 799, 802, 805, 824
Case 9/73 Schlüter [1973] ECR 1135 . . . . 956, 958–9
Case 34/73 Fratelli Variola v Italian Finance Ministry [1973] ECR 981 257
Joined Cases 37 and 38/73 Sociaal Fonds voor de Dimantarbeiders [1973] ECR 1609, ...405
Case 39/73 Rewe-Zentralfinanz v Landwirtschaftskammer [1973] ECR 1039 394

Joined Cases 40-48, 50, 54-56, 111, 113 and 114/73 Suiker Unie v Commission ('Sugar')
  [1975] ECR 1663; [1976] 1 CMLR 295 . . . . 731, 736, 774, 794
Case 120/73 Lorenz [1973] ECR 1471 . . . . 868, 873
Case 127/73 BRT v SABAM [1974] ECR 51 . . . . 254, 713, 838, 841, 885, 889
Case 134/73 Holtz v Council [1974] ECR 1 187
Case 146/73 Rheinmühlen-Düsseldorf v Einfuhr- und Vorratsstelle Getreide
  [1974] ECR 139 220
Case 152/73 Sotgiu [1974] ECR 153 . . . . 511, 515, 545, 569, 571–2, 583
Case 155/73 Sacchi [1974] ECR 409 . . . . 447, 555, 713, 875, 880, 887
Case 166/73 Rheinmühlen v Einfuhr- und Vorratsstelle Getreide [1974] ECR 33 . . . . 212, 220
Case 167/73 Commission v France [1974] ECR 359 . . . . 144, 508, 511
Case 169/73 Compagnie Continentale v Council [1975] ECR 117 199
Case 173/73 Italy v Commission [1974] ECR 709; [1974] 2 CMLR 593 850
Case 181/73 Haegeman v Belgium [1974] ECR 449 . . . . 212, 910
Case 2/74 Reyners [1974] ECR 631 . . . . 245–6, 248, 536, 543–4, 559, 569–71
Case 8/74 Procureur du Roi v Dassonville [1974] ECR 837 410
Case 9/74 Casagrande [1974] ECR 773 . . . . 498, 526
Case 15/74 Centrafarm v Sterling Drug [1974] ECR 1147 453–4
Case 16/74 Centrafarm v Winthrop [1974] ECR 1183 . . . . 454, 456
Case 17/74 Transocean Marine Paint v Commission [1974] ECR 1063; [1974] 2 CMLR 459 . . . . 178, 180, 821
Case 21/74 Airola [1972] ECR 221 332
Case 26/74 Roquette Frères [1976] ECR 677 . . . . 296, 302, 305
Case 27/74 Demag v Finanzamt Duisburg-Sud [1974] ECR 1037 401
Case 32/74 Haaga [1974] ECR 1205 680
Case 33/74 van Binsbergen [1974] ECR 1307 . . . . 559–60, 568, 577, 579
Case 35/74 Mutualités Chrétiennes v Rzepa [1974] ECR 1241 288
Case 36/74 Walrave and Koch [1974] ECR I-1405 . . . . 501–2, 553, 559–60, 608, 672
Case 41/74 van Duyn [1974] ECR 1337 . . . . 259, 483, 501, 508
Joined Cases 44, 46 and 49/74 ML Acton v Commission [1975] ECR 383 375
Case 48/74 Charmasson [1974] ECR 1383 449
Joined Cases 56-60/74 Kampffmeyer v Commission and Council [1976] ECR 711 199
Case 67/74 Bonsignore [1975] ECR 297 483
Case 68/74 Alaim [1975] ECR 109 526
Case 71/74 FRUBO v Commission [1975] ECR 563; [1975] 2 CMLR 123 734
Case 74/74 CNTA v Commission [1975] ECR 533 . . . . 194, 198, 330
Case 78/74 Deuka [1975] ECR 421 330
Case 94/74 IGAV v ENCC [1975] ECR 699 . . . . 402, 876
Case 100/74 CAM v Commission [1975] ECR 1393 . . . . 167–8, 171
Case 4/75 Rewe-Zentralfinanz v Landwirtschaftskammer [1975] ECR 843 . . . . 409, 437
Case 5/75 Deuka [1975] ECR 759 330
Case 7/75 F (Mr and Mrs) [1975] ECR 679 498
Case 26/75 General Motors Continental v Commission [1975] ECR 1367; [1976] 1 CMLR 95 776
Case 32/75 Cristini v SNCF [1975] ECR 1985 . . . . 518, 527
Case 36/75 Rutili [1975] ECR 1219 . . . . 259, 346, 481, 508
Case 39/75 Coenen [1975] ECR 1547 . . . . 535, 561
Case 43/75 Defrenne v Sabena (Defrenne II) [1976] ECR 455 . . . . 229, 254, 273, 331, 371, 672
Case 45/75 Rewe-Zentrale etc v Hauptzollamt Landau/Pfalz [1976] ECR 181 . . . . 396, 447
Case 48/75 Royer [1976] ECR 497 . . . . 478, 501, 503, 508, 544, 553
Case 52/75 Commission v Italy [1976] ECR 277 262
Case 59/75 Manghera [1986] ECR 91 448
Case 60/75 Russo [1976] ECR 45 296–7
Case 87/75 Bresciani [1976] ECR 129 . . . . 394, 954
Case 104/75 de Peijper [1976] ECR 613 438–40
Case 118/75 Watson and Belmann [1976] ECR 1185 . . . . 472, 509, 553
Case 119/75 Terrapin [1976] ECR 1039 452
Case 130/75 Prais v Council [1976] ECR 1589 371
Joined Cases 3, 4 and 6/76 Kramer [1976] ECR 1279 . . . . 100, 915, 933
Case 7/76 Thieffry [1977] ECR 765 . . . . 536, 542
Case 13/76 Dona v Mantero [1976] ECR 133 559
Case 20/76 Schottle & Sohne v Finanzamt Freudenstadt [1977] ECR 247 396
Case 26/76 Metro v Commission [1977] ECR 1875 . . . . 169, 710, 748
Case 27/76 The United Brands Company v Commission
  [1978] ECR 207; [1978] 1 CMLR 429 . . . . 767, 769–70, 775–6, 778, 786–7, 789–90, 799

Case 33/76 Rewe-Zentralfinanz v Landwirtschaftskammer für das Saarland
  [1976] ECR 1989 . . . . .272, 288, 292, 294–7, 305, 316
Case 35/76 Simmenthal [1976] ECR 1871 . . . . .394, 441
Case 41/76 Donckerwolcke [1976] ECR 1921 101
Case 45/76 Comet BV v Produktschap voor Siergewassen [1976] ECR 2043 . . . . .288, 292, 294–7, 303, 316
Case 46/76 Bauhuis v Netherlands [1977] ECR 5 . . . . .395, 435
Case 51/76 Verbond van Nederlandse Ondernemingen v Inspecteur der
  Invoerrechten en Accijnzen [1977] ECR 113 259
Case 52/76 Benedetti v Munari [1977] ECR 163 . . . . .228, 857
Joined Cases 54-60/76 Compagnie Industrielle du Comité de Loheac v Council and
  Commission [1977] ECR 645 198
Case 63/76 Inzirillo [1976] ECR 2057 . . . . .518, 527
Joined Cases 64 and 113/76, 167 and 239/78, 27, 28 and 45/79 Dumortier Frères v Council
  [1979] ECR 3091 199
Case 71/76 Thieffry [1977] ECR 765 626
Case 74/76 Iannelli & Volpi v Meroni [1977] ECR 557 . . . . .254, 396, 403, 409, 446–7
Case 77/76 Fratelli Cucchi v Avez [1977] ECR 987 402
Case 78/76 Firma Steinike und Weinlig v Germany [1977] ECR 595;
  [1977] 2 CMLR 688 . . . . 849, 862, 866
Case 85/76 Hoffmann-La Roche v Commission
  [1979] ECR 461 . . . . 192, 766, 769, 776, 778–9, 782, 784, 792–5, 821
Case 89/76 Commission v Netherlands [1977] ECR 1355 395
Case 90/76 Van Ameyde v UCI [1977] ECR 1091; [1977] 2 CMLR 478 . . . . .547, 886
Case 105/76 Interzuccheri v Ditta Rezzano e Cavassa [1977] ECR 1029 402
Case 107/76 Hoffmann-La Roche v Centrafarm [1977] ECR 957 . . . . .223, 225
Joined Cases 117/76 and 16/77 Ruckdeschel [1977] ECR 1753 333
Joined Cases 124/76 and 20/77 Moulins [1977] ECR 1795 333
Case 5/77 Tedeschi [1977] ECR 1556 438
Case 11/77 Patrick [1977] ECR 119 626
Case 13/77 INNO v ATAB [1977] ECR 2115; [1978] 1 CMLR 283 . . . . 776, 877, 879
Case 19/77 Miller Schallplatten v Commission [1978] ECR 131; [1978] 2 CMLR 334 741–2
Case 30/77 Bouchereau [1977] ECR 1999 483–4
Case 38/77 Enka [1977] ECR 2203 259
Case 52/77 Cayrol [1977] ECR 2261 663
Case 61/77 Commission v Ireland [1978] ECR 417 . . . . .204, 933
Case 65/77 Razanatsimba [1977] ECR 2229 626
Case 70/77 Simmenthal [1978] ECR 1543 405
Case 77/77 BP [1978] ECR 1513, [1978] 3 CMLR 174 800
Joined Cases 80 and 81/77 Commissionaires Reunis [1978] ECR 927 . . . . .392, 449
Joined Cases 83 and 94/76, 4, 15 and 40/77 HNL v Council and Commission [1978] ECR 1209 193–5
Case 102/77 Hoffmann-La Roche v Centrafarm [1978] ECR 1139 456
Case 106/77 Amministrazione delle Finanze dello Stato v Simmenthal [1978] ECR 629 . . . . 228, 271, 296, 303
Case 113/77 NTN Tokyo Bearing Company v Council [1979] ECR 1185 165
Joined Cases 116 and 124/77 Amylum v Council and Commission [1979] ECR 3497 194
Case 117/77 Pierik [1978] ECR 825 212
Case 148/77 Hansen v Hauptzollampt Flensburg [1978] ECR 1787 . . . . .397, 405
Case 149/77 Defrenne v Sabena [1978] ECR 1365 266
Case 156/77 Commission v Belgium [1978] ECR 1881 202
(Euratom) Ruling 1/78, Physical Protection of Nuclear Materials [1978] ECR 2151 933
Case 3/78 Centrafarm v American Home Products [1978] ECR 1823 . . . . .456, 459
Case 7/78 Thompson [1978] ECR 22247 436
Case 15/78 Koestler [1978] ECR 1971 559
Case 22/78 Hugin v Commission [1979] ECR 1869; [1979] 3 CMLR 345 . . . . .753, 772
Case 31/78 Bussone [1978] ECR 2429 257
Joined Cases 32/78, 36/78-82/78 BMW Belgium SA v Commission [1979] ECR 2435;
  [1980] 1 CMLR 370 742
Case 83/78 Redmond [1978] ECR 2347 449
Case 86/78 Grandes Distilleries [1979] ECR 897 . . . . .404, 448
Case 90/78 Granaria v Council and Commission [1979] ECR 1081 187
Case 91/78 Hansen II [1979] ECR 935 449
Case 92/78 Simmenthal v Commission [1979] ECR 777 201
Case 98/78 Racke [1979] ECR 69 329
Case 99/78 Decker [1979] ER 101 329

Case 100/78 Rossi [1979] ECR 831 331
Joined Cases 110 and 111/78 van Wesemael [1979] ECR 35 . . . . 559–61, 578
Case 115/78 Knoors [1979] ECR 399 . . . . 537–41, 567
Case 118/78 Meijer [1979] ECR 1387 409
Case 119/78 Grandes Distilleries [1979] ECR 975 448
Case 120/78 Rewe-Zentral AG v Bundesmonopolverwaltung für Branntwein
    ('Cassis de Dijon') [1979] ECR 649 . . . . 102, 254, 297, 407, 409, 411–15, 419,
                                                                                     441–2, 459, 540, 563
Case 128/78 Commission v United Kingdom [1979] ECR 419 334
Case 132/78 Denkavit Loire Sarl v France [1979] ECR 1923 402
Case 136/78 Auer [1979] ECR 437 . . . . 536–7, 542, 559
Case 141/78 France v United Kingdom [1979] ECR 2923 136
Case 148/78 Ratti [1979] ECR 1629 . . . . .246, 261
Case 153/78 Commission v Germany [1979] ECR 2555 438
Case 158/78 Biegi [1979] ECR 1103 329
Case 159/78 Commission v Italy [1979] ECR 3247 543
Case 166/78 Italy v Council [1979] ECR 2575 161
Case 168/78 Commission v France [1980] ECR 387 397
Case 170/78 Commission v UK [1983] ECR 2265 . . . . 396, 399–400
Case 175/78 Saunders [1979] ECR 1129 501
Case 177/78 Pigs and Bacon Commission v McCarren [1979] ECR 2161 . . . . 296, 305, 449
Case 179/78 Rivoira [1979] ECR 651 663
Case 182/78 Pierik [1979] ECR 1977 212
Case 207/78 Even [1979] ECR 2019 518–19
Joined Cases 209-215 and 218/78 Van Landewyck v Commission (FEDETAB)
    [1980] ECR 3125; [1981] 3 CMLR 134 . . . . .734, 822
Case 222/78 ICAP v Walter Beneventi [1979] ECR 1163 402
Case 230/78 Zuccheri [1979] ECR 2749 . . . . .257, 331
Case 231/78 Commission v United Kingdom [1979] ECR 1447 . . . . .334, 409
Case 232/78 Commission v France [1979] ECR 2729 144
Case 238/78 Ireks-Arkady v Council and Commission [1979] ECR 2955 . . . . .194, 199
Case 240/78 Atalanta [1979] ECR 2137 . . . . .36, 326
Joined Cases 241, 242 and 245 to 250/78 DGV v Council and Commission [1979] ECR 3017 199
Case 251/78 Denkavit [1979] ECR 3327 . . . . 394, 438–41
Joined Cases 253/78 and 1-3/79 Guerlain, Rochas, Lanvin and Nina Ricci ('Perfumes')
    [1980] ECR 2327; [1981] 2 CMLR 99 748–9
Joined Cases 261 and 262/78 Interquell Stärke v Council and Commission [1979] ECR 3045 199
Case 265/78 Ferwerda [1980] ECR 617 . . . . .296, 334
Case 15/79 Groenveld [1979] ECR 3409 433
Case 21/79 Commission v Italy [1980] ECR 1 397–8
Case 30/79 Land Berlin v Wigei [1980] ECR 1331 405
Case 34/79 Henn & Darby [1979] ECR 3795 . . . . 409, 436–7
Case 44/79 Hauer [1979] ECR 3727 368–9
Case 52/79 Debauve [1980] ECR 833 555
Case 55/79 Commission v Ireland [1980] ECR 481 397
Case 60/79 Producteurs de Vins de Table et Vins de Pays v Commission [1979] ECR 2429 187
Case 61/79 Amministrazione delle Finanze dello Stato v Denkavit Italiana [1980] ECR 1205 . . . . . . 229, 306, 850
Case 62/79 Coditel v Ciné Vog Films [1980] ECR 881 555
Case 68/79 Hans Just [1980] ECR 501 306
Case 73/79 Commission v Italy [1980] ECR 1547 403
Case 81/79 Sorasio [1980] ECR 3557 333
Case 91/79 Commission v Italy [1980] ECR 1099 145
Case 98/79 Pecastaing [1980] ECR 691 487
Case 102/79 Commission v Belgium [1980] ECR 1473 . . . . 241, 258, 329
Case 104/79 Foglia v Novello [1980] ECR 745 . . . . .212, 220
Case 130/79 Express Dairy Foods [1980] ECR 1887 . . . . .296, 306
Case 131/79 Santillo [1980] ECR 1585 484
Case 133/79 Sucrimex v Commission [1980] ECR 1299 198
Case 136/79 National Panasonic v Commission [1980] ECR 2033; [1980] CMLR 169 818
Case 138/79 Roquette Frères v Council [1980] ECR 3333 . . . . .79, 178
Case 140/79 Chemial Farmaceutici v DAF [1981] ECR 1 398
Case 149/79 Commission v Belgium (No 2) [1982] ECR 1845 512
Case 149/79 Commission v Belgium (No 1) [1980] ECR 3881 . . . . 512–13, 569

Case 155/79 AM & S v Commission [1982] ECR 1575; [1982] 2 CMLR 264 819–20
Case 157/79 Pieck [1980] ECR 2171 481
Case 730/79 Philip Morris Holland v Commission [1980] ECR 2671; [1981] 2 CMLR 321. . . . . .852, 859
Case 788/79 Gilli and Andres [1980] ECR 2071 413–14
Joined Cases 789 and 790/79 Calpak v Commission [1980] ECR 1949. 163
Case 804/79 Commission v UK [1981] ECR 1045 . . . . .101, 933
Case 811/79 Ariete [1980] ECR 2545 . . . . .296, 306
Case 826/79 MIRECO [1980] ECR 2559 . . . . .296, 306
Case 1253/79 Battaglia v Commission [1982] ECR 297. 79
Joined Cases 24 and 97/80 R Commission v France [1980] ECR 1319 204
Case 26/80 Schneider-Import [1980] ECR 3469 397
Case 27/80 Fietje [1980] ECR 3839 414
Case 30/80 Kelderman [1981] ECR 517 414
Case 31/80 L'Oréal v PVBA De Nieuwe AMCK [1980] ECR 3775; [1981] 2 CMLR 235. 768
Case 32/80 Officier van Justitie v Kortmann [1981] ECR 251. 402
Joined Cases 36 and 71/80 Irish Creamery Milk Suppliers Association v Ireland [1981] ECR 735. . . . . . . .212, 395
Case 46/80 Vinal v Orbat [1981] ECR 77 398
Case 53/80 Eyssen [1981] ECR 409 414
Case 61/80 Co-operatieve Stremsel-en-Kleurselfabriek v Commission [1981] ECR 851;
   [1982] 1 CMLR 240. 714
Case 66/80 International Chemical Corporation v Amministrazione delle Finanze dello Stato
   [1981] ECR 1191 229
Case 78/80 Deutsche Grammophon [1971] ECR 487. 453
Case 96/80 Jenkins v Kingsgate [1981] ECR 911. 265
Joined Cases 100-103/80 Musique Diffusion Française v Commission [1983] ECR 1825; [1983] 3 CMLR 221 .821
Case 113/80 Commission v Ireland [1981] ECR 1625 . . . . .435, 442
Case 127/80 Grogan [1982] ECR 869 331
Case 132/80 United Foods [1981] ECR 995. 402
Case 138/80 Borker [1980] ECR 1975. 215
Joined Cases 142 and 143/80 Essevi and Salengo [1981] ECR 1413. . . . . 137, 142, 273, 306, 397
Case 153/80 Rumhaus Hansen [1981] ECR 1165 401
Case 155/80 Oebel [1981] ECR 1993. . . . . .433, 443
Case 158/80 Rewe-Handelsgesellschaft Nord v Hauptzollamt Kiel [1981] ECR 1805. 296
Case 164/80 De Pasquale [1982] ECR 909 331
Case 167/80 Curtis [1982] ECR 931 331
Case 169/80 Gondrand Frères [1981] ECR 1931. 328
Case 172/80 Züchner [1981] ECR 2021; [1982] 1 CMLR 313 736
Case 187/80 Merck v Stephar [1981] ECR 2063 455–6
Joined Cases 188-190/80 France, Italy and the United Kingdom v Commission [1982] ECR 2545;
   [1982] 3 CMLR 144. 877–8
Case 196/80 Ango-Irish Meat [1981] ECR 1103 329
Joined Cases 212-217/80 Salumi [1981] ECR 2735 329
Case 244/80 Foglia v Novello [1981] ECR 3045. 212
Joined Cases 256, 257 and 267/80 and 5/81 Birra Wührer v Council and Commission [1982] ECR 85. 200
Case 258/80 Runi [1982] ECR 487. 329
Case 272/80 Frans-Nederlandse [1981] ECR 3277 439
Case 276/80 Pedana [1982] ECR 517 329
Case 279/80 Webb [1981] ECR 3305. . . . . 560–1, 578
Case 1/81 Pfizer [1981] ECR 2913 459
Case 8/81 Becker [1982] ECR 53 . . . . .241, 261
Case 15/81 Schul v Inspecteur de Invoerrechten en Accijnzen [1982] ECR 1409 8
Case 17/81 Pabst & Richarz KG v Hauptzollamt Oldenburg [1982] ECR 1331 . . . . 245, 403, 406, 954
Case 26/81 Oleifici Mediterranei v EEC [1982] ECR 3057. 199
Case 28/81 Commission v Italy [1981] ECR 2577. 140
Case 29/81 Commission v Italy [1981] ECR 2585. 140
Case 44/81 Commission v Germany [1982] ECR 1855 329
Case 51/81 De Franceschi v Council and Commission [1982] ECR 117. 200
Case 53/81 Levin [1982] ECR 1035. 503–4
Case 54/81 Fromme [1982] ECR 1449 . . . . .292, 296
Case 58/81 Commission v Luxembourg [1982] ECR 2175 544
Case 60/81 IBM v Commission [1981] ECR 2639. . . . . .159, 184
Joined Cases 62 and 63/81 Seco [1982] ECR 223 577–8
Case 65/81 Reina [1982] ECR 33 518

Case 75/81 Blegsen [1982] ECR 4575 416
Case 76/81 Transporoute [1982] ECR 417 561
Case 84/81 Staple Dairy Products [1982] ECR 1763...329
Case 95/81 Commission v Italy [1982] ECR 2187...435
Case 96/81 Commission v Netherlands [1982] ECR 1791.......................... 142, 258, 271
Case 102/81 Nordsee v Reederei Mond [1982] ECR 1095......................................215
Case 104/81 Kupferberg [1982] ECR 3641..245, 406, 954–5
Case 108/81 Amylum v Council [1982] ECR 3107............................... 182, 195, 329
Joined Cases 115/81 and 116/81 Adoui and Cornuaille [1984] ECR 1665 .... 484, 487–8
Case 144/81 Keurkoop [1982] ECR 2853...453
Joined Cases 152 etc/81 Ferrario [1983] ECR 2357..332
Case 152/81 Forcheri [1983] ECR 2323..498, 528
Case 211/81 Commission v Denmark [1982] ECR 4547 139
Case 220/81 Robertson [1982] ECR 2349..414, 435
Case 249/81 Commission v Ireland [1982] ECR 4005 .... 253, 447, 881
Case 255/81 Grendel [1982] ECR 2301...261
Case 261/81 Rau [1982] ECR 3961 .... 36, 414, 445
Case 266/81 SIOT [1983] ECR 731 395
Case 270/81 Felicitas [1982] ECR 2771..241
Case 271/81 Amélioration de l' Élevage v Mialocq [1983] ECR 2057 447–8
Case 283/81 CILFIT v Ministry of Health [1982] ECR 3415........................ 212, 224, 229
Case 286/81 Oosthoek's Uitqeversmaatschappij BV [1981] ECR 4575.......... 415, 433, 444
Joined Cases 292 and 293/81 Jean Lion [1982] ECR 3887 334
Case 322/81 NV Nederlandsche Banden-Industrie Michelin v Commission (Michelin I)
    [1983] ECR 3461; [1985] 1 CMLR 282.....................767–8, 771, 775, 778, 781, 793
Joined Cases 2-4/82 Le Lion [1983] ECR 2973 ....439, 441
Case 5/82 Maizena [1982] ECR 4601 331
Case 7/82 GVL v Commission [1983] ECR 483; [1983] 3 CMLR 645 ....713, 885
Case 8/82 Wagner [1983] ECR 271 333
Case 11/82 Piraiki-Patraiki v Commission [1985] ECR 207 .... 165, 168–9, 171
Joined Cases 35 and 36/82 Morson and Jhanjan v Netherlands [1982] ECR 3723.........223, 501
Case 40/82 Commission v United Kingdom [1984] ECR 283...................................437
Case 42/82 Commission v France [1983] ECR 1013...440
Joined Cases 43 and 63/82 VBVB and VBBB v Commission [1984] ECR 19; [1985] 1 CMLR 27.........756, 821
Case 66/82 Fromancais [1983] ECR 395..326
Case 74/82 Commission v Ireland [1984] ECR 317 141
Joined Cases 75/82 and 117/82 Razzouk and Beydoun [1984] ECR 1509.....................332
Case 84/82 Germany v Commission [1984] ECR 1451 867
Case 86/82 Hasselblad v Commission [1984] ECR 883; [1984] CMLR 559 748
Case 94/82 De Kikvorsch [1983] ECR 947...414
Joined Cases 96-102, 104, 105, 108 and 110/82 IAZ v Commission [1983] ECR 3369;
    [1984] 3 CMLR 276..735, 885
Case 107/82 AEG v Commission [1983] ECR 3151; [1984] 3 CMLR 325......................732, 749
Case 116/82 Commission v Germany [1986] ECR 2519..201
Case 132/82 Commission v Belgium [1983] ECR 1649 394
Case 145/82 Commission v Italy [1983] ECR 711..258
Case 155/82 Commission v Belgium [1983] ECR 531 438
Case 158/82 Commission v Denmark [1983] ECR 3573 402
Case 162/82 Cousin [1983] ECR 1101 333
Case 163/82 Commission v Italy [1983] ECR 3723...258
Case 172/82 Inter-Huiles [1983] ECR 555 433
Case 174/82 Sandoz [1983] ECR 2445 ....436, 440
Case 188/82 Thyssen [1983] ECR 3721..331
Case 198/82 Wirth [1993] ECR I-6447...555
Case 199/82 San Giorgio [1983] ECR 3595 .... 294, 298, 306
Joined Cases 205-215/82 Deutsche Milchkontor GmbH and others v Federal Republic of
    Germany [1983] ECR 2633 .... 296, 302, 332
Case 222/82 Apple and Pear Development Council [1983] ECR 4083..........................253, 446
Case 227/82 Leendert [1983] ECR 3883...440–1
Case 234/82 Ferriere di roe Volciano [1983] ECR 3921 333
Case 237/82 Jongeneel Kaas and Others v Netherlands [1984] ECR 483.....................433
Case 238/82 Duphar [1984] ECR 523 435
Joined Cases 239/82 and 273/82 Allied Corporation [1984] ECR 1005........................169

Case 264/82 Timex [1984] ECR 849 ....169, 182
Case 271/82 Auer [1983] ECR 2727 536
Joined Cases 286/82 and 26/83 Luisi and Carbone [1984] ECR 377 ....555, 557, 559
Joined Cases 296 and 318/82 The Netherlands and Leeuwarder Papierwaren fabriek BV v
    Commission [1985] ECR 809; [1985] 3 CMLR 380 854
Case 314/82 Commission v Belgium [1984] ECR 1543 395
Joined Cases 314-316/82 Waterkeyn [1986] ECR 1855 ....143, 432
Case 13/83 Parliament v Council [1985] ECR 1513 .... 184–6, 189
Case 14/83 Von Colson [1984] ECR 1891 ....25, 238–41, 288, 292, 297, 323
Case 15/83 Denkavit Nederland v Hoofdproduktschap voor akkerbouwprodukten
    [1984] ECR 2171..434–5
Case 16/83 Prantl [1984] ECR 1299 ....429, 444
Joined Cases 29/83 and 30/83 Compagnie Royale Asturienne des Mines SA (CRAM) v
    Commission [1984] ECR 1679; [1985] 1 CMLR 688 .... 737–8, 743
Case 41/83 Italy v Commission (British Telecom) [1985] ECR 873, [1985] 2 CMLR 368...............776, 885
Case 59/83 Biovilac v EEC [1984] ECR 4057...199
Case 72/83 Campus Oil Ltd v Minister for Industry and Energy [1984] ECR 2727;
    [1984] 3 CMLR 544.. 435, 441, 572, 886
Case 77/83 CILFIT [1984] ECR 1257 212
Case 79/83 Dorit Harz [1984] ECR 1921 239
Joined Cases 91 and 127/83 Heineken Brouwerijen [1984] ECR 2435; [1985] 1 CMLR 389 868
Case 94/83 Heijn [1984] ECR 3263 436
Case 97/83 Melkunie [1984] ECR 2367..438
Case 106/83 Sermide [1984] ECR 4209 332
Case 107/83 Klopp [1984] ECR 2971 .... 538, 542, 574–5
Case 120/83 R Raznoimport v Commission [1983] ECR 2573......................................199
Case 143/83 Commission v Denmark [1985] ECR 427..36
Case 145/83 Adams v Commission [1985] ECR 3539 .... 192, 199–200
Case 170/83 Hydrotherm [1984] ECR 2999...717–18
Case 177/83 Kohl [1984] ECR 3651..436
Case 180/83 Moser [1984] ECR 2539 501
Case 182/83 Fearon [1984] ECR 3677..542, 546
Case 220/83 Commission v France [1986] ECR 3663..578
Case 229/83 Leclerc v Sarl 'Au Blé Vert' [1985] ECR 1; [1985] 2 CMLR 286............. 435–6, 891
Case 231/83 H Cullet et Chambres Syndicale des réparateurs automobiles et détaillants
    de produits pétroliers v Centre Leclerc à Toulouse et Centre Leclerc à
    Saint-Orens-de-Gameville [1985] ECR 35..430, 440
Case 237/83 Prodest [1984] ECR 3153 502
Case 240/83 Bruleurs d'Huiles Usages [1985] ECR 532..443
Case 249/83 Hoecks [1985] ECR 973 518
Case 251/83 Eberhard Haug-Adrion [1984] ECR 4277 608
Case 252/83 Commission v Denmark [1986] ECR 3713 578
Case 253/83 Kupferberg [1985] ECR 157..401
Case 254/83 Commission v Italy [1984] ECR 3395..270
Case 261/83 Castelli [1984] ECR 3199 ....518, 528
Case 270/83 Commission v United Kingdom [1985] ECR 1201................... 442, 546, 582–4, 648–9
Case 272/83 Commission v Italy [1985] ECR 1057..257
Case 277/83 Commission v Italy [1985] ECR 2049..397, 403
Case 283/83 Racke [1984] ECR 3791..334, 370
Case 288/83 Commission v Ireland [1985] ECR 1761 435
Case 293/83 Gravier v City of Liège [1985] ECR 593 .... 105, 475, 528
Case 294/83 Les Verts v Parliament [1986] ECR 1339 .... 157–8, 165
Case 298/83 CICCE v Commission [1985] ECR 1105, [1986] 1 CMLR 486..........................776
Case 5/84 Direct Cosmetics [1985] ECR 617..261
Joined Cases 25-26/84 Ford v Commission [1985] ECR 2725; [1985] 3 CMLR 528 732
Case 29/84 Commission v Germany [1986] ECR 1661 ....147, 259
Case 41/84 Pinna v Caisse d'Allocations Familiales de la Savoie [1986] ECR 1 229
Case 42/84 Remia v Commission [1985] ECR 2545; [1987] 1 CMLR 1.............................747, 757
Case 52/84 Commission v Belgium [1986] ECR 89; [1987] 1 CMLR 710............................870
Joined Cases 60 and 61/84 Cinéthèque [1985] ECR 2605 ....415, 443
Case 67/84 Sideradria v Commission [1985] ECR 3983...332
Case 73/84 Denkavit [1985] ECR 1013..439
Case 75/84 Metro v Commission (No 2) [1986] ECR 3021; [1987] 1 CMLR 118 748

Case 94/84 Deak [1985] ECR 1873 518
Case 101/84 Commission v Italy [1985] ECR 2629. 143
Case 106/84 Commission v Denmark [1986] ECR 833 397
Case 112/84 Humblot [1985] ECR 1367. 400
Case 122/84 Scrivner [1985] ECR 1027 518
Case 137/84 Mutsch [1985] ECR 2681 518
Case 152/84 Marshall v Southampton and South-West Hampshire Area Health Authority
    [1986] ECR 723 . . . . .217, 261–4, 266–7, 281
Case 157/84 Frascogna [1985] ECR 1739. . . . . .518, 528
Case 161/84 Pronuptia de Paris v Schillgalis [1986] ECR 353; [1986] 1 CMLR 414 747–8
Case 169/84 COFAZ [1986] ECR 391 . . . . 169, 872–3
Case 175/84 Krohn v Commission [1986] ECR 753. . . . . .191, 198
Case 178/84 Commission v Germany [1987] ECR 1227 . . . . .308, 436
Case 179/84 Bozzetti [1985] ECR 2301. . . . . 288, 291, 296
Case 181/84 R v Intervention Board for Sugar ex parte Man (Sugar) [1985] ECR 2889 327
Case 197/84 Steinhauser [1985] ECR 1819. 543
Case 205/84 Commission v Germany [1986] ECR 3755 . . . . 532, 561, 568, 578, 648
Case 206/84 Commission v Ireland [1986] ECR 3817 578
Joined Cases 209-13/84 Ministère Public v Asjes [1986] ECR 1425. . . . . .718, 891
Case 222/84 Johnston v Chief Constable of the RUC [1986] ECR 1651 . . . . 263, 289–90, 338, 379
Case 243/84 John Walker [1986] ECR 875. 397
Case 249/84 Profant [1986] ECR 3237 402
Joined Cases 279, 280, 285 and 286/84 Rau v Commission [1987] ECR 1069 123
Case 298/84 Iorio [1986] ECR 247. 501
Case 307/84 Commission v France [1986] ECR 1725. 513
Case 311/84 Centre Belge d'Etudes de Marché Télémarketing v CLT [1985] ECR 3261;
    [1986] 2 CMLR 558 . . . . .783, 887
Case 15/85 Consorzio Cooperative d'Abruzzo v Commission [1987] ECR 1005. . . . . .181, 202
Case 20/85 Roviello [1988] ECR 2805. 79
Case 21/85 Maas v Bundesanstalt für Landwirtschaftliche Marktordnung [1986] ECR 3537 327
Case 28/85 Deghillage v Caisse Primaire d'Assurance Maladie [1986] ECR 991 217
Case 40/85 Re Boch: Belgium v Commission [1986] ECR 2321; [1998] 2 CMLR 301 854
Case 45/85 Verband der Sachversicherer [1987] ECR 405; [1988] 4 CMLR 264 734
Case 59/85 Reed [1986] ECR 1283 468
Case 66/85 Lawrie-Blum [1986] ECR 2121 . . . . 503–4, 513
Case 69/85 Wünsche v Germany [1986] ECR 947. 216
Case 72/85 Commission v Netherlands [1986] ECR 1219. 257
Case 79/85 Segers [1986] ECR 2375 . . . . 554, 572, 593, 648–50
Joined Cases 80 and 159/85 EDAH BV [1986] ECR 3359 432
Joined Cases 89, 104, 114, 116, 117 and 125-128/85 A Ahlström Oy v Commission
    ('Wood Pulp') [1988] ECR 5193; [1988] 4 CMLR 901 . . . . .181, 721–2, 735–6, 738–9, 821
Case 118/85 Commission v Italy [1987] ECR 2599. 878
Case 137/85 Maizena [1987] ECR 4587; C-210/00 Käserei Champignon Hofmeister [2002] ECR I-6453. 351
Case 139/85 Kempf [1986] ECR 1741 504
Case 193/85 Co-Frutta v Amministrazione delle Finanze dello Stato [1987] ECR 2085. . . . . .396, 402
Case 196/85 Commission v France [1987] ECR 1597. 397
Joined Cases 201 and 202/85 Klensch [1986] ECR 3466 322
Case 221/85 Commission v Belgium [1987] ECR 719 539
Case 223/85 Rijn-Schelde-Verolme (RSV) Maschinefabrieken en Scheepswerven NV v
    Commission [1987] ECR 4617; [1989] 2 CMLR 259 . . . . .332, 869
Case 225/85 Commission v Italy [1987] ECR 2625. 512–13
Joined Cases 227-230/85 Commission v Belgium [1988] ECR 1 143
Case 234/85 Keller [1986] ECR I-2897 368
Case 247/85 Commission v Belgium [1987] ECR 3029 258
Case 252/85 Commission v France [1988] ECR 2243. 258
Case 262/85 Commission v Italy [1987] ECR 3073. 258
Joined Cases 281, 283-85 and 287/85 Germany, France, Netherlands, Denmark and
    United Kingdom v Commission [1987] ECR 3203. 178
Case 293/85 Commission v Belgium [1988] ECR 305 . . . . .139, 141
Case 309/85 Bruno Barra [1988] ECR 355. 300
Case 311/85 VZW Vereniging van Vlaamse Reisbureaus v VZW Sociale Dienst [1987] ECR 3801;
    [1989] 4 CMLR para 10 891
Case 314/85 Foto-Frost v Hauptzollamt Lübeck-Ost [1987] ECR 4199. . . . . 201, 225–7, 304

Case 316/85 Lebon [1987] ECR 2811 ....507, 525
Joined Cases 331, 376 and 378/85 Bianco [1988] ECR 1099 306
Case 338/85 Pardini [1988] ECR 2041 330
Case 352/85 Bond van Adverteerders [1988] ECR 2085 .... 555, 578–80, 590
Case 355/85 Driancourt v Cognet [1986] ECR 3231 432
Case 356/85 Commission v Belgium [1987] ECR 3299 399
Case 406/85 Goffette [1987] ECR 2525...441
Case 407/85 Drei Glocken GmbH [1988] ECR 4233 414
Case 427/85 Commission v Germany [1988] ECR 1123 , , , , ... 562, 639–40
Case 433/85 Feldain [1987] ECR 3521 400
Case 12/86 Demirel [1987] ECR 3719...........................17, 901, 910, 938, 954, 966
Case 14/86 Pretore di Salò v Persons Unknown [1987] ECR 2545........................ 212, 215, 262, 269
Case 24/86 Blaizot v University of Liège [1988] ECR 379 .... 105, 229, 273
Case 26/86 Deutz und Geldermann v Council [1987] ECR 941 166
Joined Cases 31 and 35/86 Laisa v Council [1988] ECR 2285...193
Case 34/86 Council v Parliament [1986] ECR 2155 157
Case 39/86 Lair [1988] ECR 3161 505
Case 45/86 Commission v Council [1987] ECR 1493...........................161, 678, 944–5
Case 50/86 Grands Moulins de Paris v Council and Commission [1987] ECR 4833........................193
Case 53/86 Bouhelier [1977] ECR 197 433
Case 60/86 Commission v United Kingdom [1988] ECR 3921...102
Case 62/86 AKZO v Commission [1991] ECR I-3359; [1993] 5 CMLR 215................... 772, 776, 785–8
Case 63/86 Commission v Italy [1988] ECR 129...544
Case 63/86 Commission v Italy [1988] ECR 29...559
Case 66/86 Ahmed Saeed Flugreisen v Zentrale zur Bekampfung unlauteren Wettbewerbs
    [1989] ECR 803; [1990] 4 CMLR 102...787, 886
Case 77/86 Ex parte National Dried Fruit Association [1988] ECR 757 328
Case 80/86 Kolpinghuis [1987] ECR 3969 381
Case 80/86 Kolpinghuis Nijmegen [1987] ECR 3969 ....242, 283
Case 104/86 Commission v Italy [1988] ECR 1799...144, 306
Case 114/86 United Kingdom v Commission [1988] ECR 5289...158
Case 118/86 Nertsvoederfabriek Nederland BV [1987] ECR 3883...433, 448
Case 120/86 Mulder [1988] ECR 2321 ....36, 330
Case 157/86 Murphy v An Bord Telecom Eireann [1988] ECR 673...241
Joined Cases 166 and 220/86 Irish Cement Ltd v Commission [1988] ECR 6473 ....159, 188
Case 197/86 Brown [1988] ECR 3205...........................464, 504, 506
Case 198/86 Conradi [1987] ECR 4469 539
Case 222/86 Heylens and Others [1987] ECR 4097 .... 291, 379, 626
Case 249/86 Commission v Germany [1989] ECR 1263 499
Case 252/86 Bergandi [1988] ECR 1343...396
Case 257/86 Commission v Italy [1988] ECR 3249...258
Case 264/86 France v Commission [1988] ECR 973...178
Case 267/86 Van Eycke [1988] ECR 4769...24, 890
Case 286/86 Deserbais [1988] ECR 4907 549
Case 292/86 Gullung [1988] ECR 111...554
Case 300/86 Landschoot v Mera [1988] ECR 3443...333
Case 316/86 Hauptzollamt Hamburg-Jonas v Krucken [1988] ECR 2213........................322, 331
Case 18/87 Commission v Germany [1988] ECR 5427 395
Case 22/87 Commission v Italy [1989] ECR 143...307
Case 29/87 Denkavit [1988] ECR 2965...441
Case 30/87 Bodson v SA Pompes funèbres des regions liberées [1988] ECR 2479;
    [1989] 4 CMLR 984...........................731, 787, 880
Case 38/87 Commission v Greece [1988] ECR 4415 543
Case 42/87 Commission v Belgium [1988] ECR 5445 105
Case 45/87 Commission v Ireland [1988] ECR 4929 447
Joined Cases 46/87 and 227/88 Hoechst v Commission [1989] ECR 2859; [1991] 4 CMLR 410........818
Case 53/87 Maxicar v Renault [1988] ECR 6039...802
Joined Cases 62/87 and 72/87 Executif Regional Wallon and Glaverbel v Commission
    [1988] ECR 1573; [1989] 2 CMLR 771...860
Case 63/87 Commission v Greece [1988] ECR 2875; [1989] 3 CMLR 677 870
Case 70/87 Fediol [1989] ECR 1781 962
Case 81/87 Daily Mail [1988] ECR 3483...........................535, 538, 588, 651–2, 655, 657
Case C-142/87 Belgium v Commission ('Tubemeuse') [1990] ECR I-959 .... 851, 853, 870

Case 143/87 Stanton [1988] ECR 3877 . . . . 524, 538, 547, 574
Joined Cases 154 and 155/87 Wolf [1988] ECR 3897 . . . . 538, 547
Case 186/87 Cowan [1989] ECR 195. . . . . 333, 557
Case 190/87 Moormann BV [1988] ECR 4689 441
Case 196/87 Steymann [1987] ECR 6159 . . . . 532–3, 556
Case 204/87 Bekaert [1988] ECR 2029 535
Case 226/87 Commission v Greece [1988] ECR 3611 . . . . .202, 881
Case 238/87 Volvo v Erik Veng (UK) [1988] ECR 6211; [1989] 4 CMLR 122 802
Case 240/87 Deville [1988] ECR 3513. 300
Case 247/87 Star Fruit v Commission [1989] ECR 291 . . . . .139, 141
Case 254/87 Syndicat des Libraires de Normandie v L'Aigle Distribution [1988] ECR 4457 891
Case 265/87 Schrader [1989] ECR 2237 326
Joined Cases 266-267/87 Royal Pharmaceutical Society [1989] ECR 1295. 253
Case 301/87 France v Commission (Boussac) [1990] ECR I-307 869–70
Case 302/87 Parliament v Council [1988] ECR 5615 . . . . 89, 161, 184, 188
Case 305/87 Commission v Greece [1989] ECR 1461 . . . . 333, 544, 547, 559
Case C-308/87 Grifoni v EAEC [1994] ECR I-341 199
Case 344/87 Bettray [1989] ECR 1621 . . . . 498, 504–5
Case 374/87 Orkem v Commission [1989] ECR 3283; [1991] 4 CMLR 502. 816
Case 377/87 Parliament v Council [1988] ECR 4017 189
Case 378/87 Groener [1989] ECR 3967 510
Case 379/87 Groener [1989] ECR 3967 371
Case 382/87 Buet [1989] ECR 1235. 444
Joined Cases 389 and 390/87 Echternach [1989] ECR 723 . . . . 503, 512, 526
Case 395/87 Ministère Public v Tournier [1989] ECR 2521; [1991] 4 CMLR 248 787
Case C-2/88 Zwartveld [1990] ECR I-4405 . . . . 323, 839
Case C-3/88 Commission v Italy [1989] ECR I-4035 . . . . 545, 573
Case 5/88 Wachauf [1989] ECR 2609 344
Case 9/88 Lopes da Veiga [1989] ECR 2989. 502
Case 16/88 Commission v Council [1989] ECR 3457. 88–9
Case C-18/88 RTT v GB-Inno-BM [1991] ECR I-5941 . . . . 883, 885
Case 20/88 Roquette Frères v Commission [1989] ECR 1553. 198
Case 27/88 Solvay v Commission [1989] ECR 3255 816
Case 30/88 Greece v Commission [1989] ECR 3711 954
Case 33/88 Allué and Coonan [1989] ECR 1591. . . . . 513, 517
Case C-39/88 Commission v Ireland [1990] ECR I-4271. 145
Case C-47/88 Commission v Denmark (cars) [1990] ECR I-4509 . . . . 396, 401, 403, 421, 446
Case C-49/88 Al-Jubail Fertilizer Company v Council [1991] ECR I-3187. 178
Joined Cases C-54/88 Nino et al [1990] ECR I-3537 535
Case C-64/88 Commission v France [1991] ECR I-2727. 152
Case 68/88 Commission v Greece [1989] ECR 2965 . . . . .25, 88
Case C-69/88 H. Krantz GmbH & Co v Ontvanger der Directe Belastingen and Netherlands State
    [1990] ECR I-583. 428
Case C-70/88 Parliament v Council ('Chernobyl') [1990] ECR I-2041 . . . . .161, 188
Case 103/88 Fratelli Constanzo v Commune di Milano [1989] ECR 1839 . . . . 263–4, 272
Joined Cases 110 and 241-242/88 Lucazeau v SACEM [1989] ECR 2811; [1991] 4 CMLR 248. 787
Case C-119/88 Aerpo and Others v Commission [1990] ECR I-2189. 193
Case C-132/88 Commission v Greece [1990] ECR I-1567. 398
Joined Cases C-143/88 and C-92/89 Zuckerfabrik Süderditmarschen v Hauptzollamt Itzehoe
    [1991] ECR I-415. . . . . 225, 227, 304–5
Case 145/88 Torfaen BC v B&Q Plc [1989] ECR 3851. . . . . .416, 443
Case C-152/88 Sofrimport v Commission [1990] ECR I-2477. . . . . 169, 193–4, 196, 204, 330
Case 170/88 Ford España v Estado Español [1989] ECR 2305 . . . . .228, 395
Case C-175/88 Biehl [1990] ECR I-1779 515
Case C-177/88 Dekker [1990] ECR I-394. 377
Case C-200/88 Commission v Greece [1990] ECR I-4299. 141
Case C-202/88 France v Commission [1991] ECR I-1223; [1992] 5 CMLR 552 879
Case C-262/88 Barber [1990] ECR I-1889. . . . . 229, 273
Case C-265/88 Messner [1989] ECR I-4209. 328, 381, 472, 478, 509
Joined Cases C-297/88 and C-197/89 Dzodzi v Belgium [1990] ECR I-3763. . . . . .213, 219
Case C-303/88 Italy v Commission [1991] ECR I-1433; [1993] 2 CMLR 1. 854
Case C-304/88 Commission v Belgium [1990] ECR I-2801 441
Case C-306/88 Roschdale Borough Council v SJ Anders [1992] ECR I-6463. .416

Case 322/88 Grimaldi v Fonds des Maladies Professionnelles [1989] ECR 4407 . . . . .212, 244
Case C-323/88 Sermes [1990] ECR I-3027. 229
Case C-331/88 Ex Parte Fedesa [1990] ECR I-4023 326
Case C-337/88 SAFA [1990] ECR I-1 329
Case C-347/88 Commission v Greece [1990] ECR I-4747. . . . . .142, 448
Case C-362/88 GB-INNO-BM [1990] ECR I-667. 444
Case C-366/88 France v Commission [1990] ECR I-3571. 157
Case C-5/89 Commission v Germany [1990] ECR I-3437. 332
Case C-10/89 Hag GF [1990] ECR I-3711 452
Caoo C 23/89 Quiotlynn [1990] ECR I 3059 416
Case C-37/89 Weiser [1990] ECR I-2395 333
Case C-61/89 Bouchoucha [1990] ECR I-3551 . . . . 539, 541, 567
Case C-63/89 Assurances du Crédit v Council and Commission [1991] ECR I-1799. 193
Case C-69/89 Nakajima [1991] ECR I-2069. 962–3
Case C-79/89 Brown Boveri [1991] ECR I-1853 964
Case C-83/89 Openbaar Ministerie and the Minister for Finance v Vincent Houben [1990]
   ECR I-1161 392
Case C-93/89 Commission v Ireland [1991] ECR I-4569. 545
Case C-96/89 Commission v Netherlands [1991] ECR I-2461 142
Joined Cases C-104/89 and C-37/90 Mulder v Council and Commission (Mulder II) [1992]
   ECR I-3061 . . . . .193, 196
Case C-106/89 Marleasing [1990] ECR I-4135 . . . . 175, 238, 240–1, 292, 680
Case C-111/89 Hillegom [1990] ECR I-1735. 395
Case C-113/89 Rush Portuguesa [1990] ECR I-1417 . . . . 556, 578, 660
Case C-119/89 Commission v Kingdom of Spain [1991] ECR I-641. 396
Case C-152/89 Commission v Luxembourg [1991] ECR I-3171 404
Case C-153/89 Commission v Belgium [1991] ECR I-3171 404
Case C-154/89 Commission v France [1991] ECR I-4221. . . . . .562, 629
Case C-174/89 Hoche [1990] ECR I-2681 330
Case C-180/89 Commission v Italy [1991] ECR I-709. 578
Case C-188/89 Foster v British Gas [1990] ECR I-3313. 263
Case C-192/89 Sevince [1990] ECR I-3461 . . . . 938, 954–5
Case C-198/89 Commission v Greece [1991] ECR I-727. . . . . 558, 562–3, 578, 629
Case C-205/89 Commission v Greece [1991] ECR I-1361. 436
Case C-209/89 Commission v Italy [1991] ECR I-1575. 395
Case C-213/89 Factortame [1990] ECR I-2433 . . . . 212, 297–8, 303, 841
Case C-221/89 The Queen v Secretary of State for Transport, ex parte Factortame
   [1991] ECR I-3905. . . . . 212, 217, 308, 545
Case C-230/89 Commission v Greece [1991] ECR I-1909. 400
Case C-231/89 Gmurzynska-Bscher v Oberfinanzdirektion Köln [1990] ECR I-4003 213
Case C-234/89 Delimitis v Henninger Bräu [1991] ECR I-935; [1992] 5 CMLR 210 . . . . 744, 746, 839
Case 246/89 Commission v United Kingdom [1989] ECR 3125. 204
Case C-260/89 Elliniki Radiophonia Tiléorassi AE (ERT) v Dimotiki
   Etairia Pliroforissis and others [1991] ECR I-2925. . . . . 338, 346, 367, 383, 436, 440, 881, 883, 889
Case C-288/89 Gouda [1991] ECR I-4007 . . . . 367, 572, 578–80
Case C-292/89 Antonissen [1991] ECR I-745 506
Case C-292/89 R v Immigration Appeal Tribunal, ex parte Antonissen [1991] ECR I-745 36
Case C-294/89 Commission v France [1991] ECR I-3591. 640
Case C-300/89 Commission v Council [1991] ECR I-2867. . . . . .111, 113
Case C-305/89 Italy v Commission [1991] ECR I-1603. 854
Case C-306/89 Commission v Greece [1991] ECR I-5863. 569
Case C-309/89 Codorníu SA v Council of the European Union [1994] ECR I-1853. . . . . 164, 170, 333
Case C-312/89 Conforama [1991] ECR I-997 416
Case C-332/89 Andrè Marchandise [1991] ECR-1027 443
Case C-332/89 Merchandise and Others [1991] ECR 1027 416
Case C-340/89 Vlassopoulou [1991] ECR I-2357 . . . . .291, 626
Case C-345/89 Stoeckel [1991] ECR I-4047 252
Case C-357/89 Raulin [1992] ECR I-1027 462
Case C-358/89 Extramet Industrie v Council [1991] ECR I-2501 . . . . 171–2, 225
Case C-367/89 Richardt [1991] ECR I-4621 395
Case C-370/89 SGEEM and Etroy v EIB [1992] ECR I-6211. 190
Joined Cases C-1/90 and C-176/90 Aragonesa de Publicidad Exterior SA [1991] ECR I-4151 444
Case C-2/90 Commission v Belgium [1992] ECR I-4431 . . . . .393, 442

Case C-3/90 Bernini [1992] ECR I-1071 . . . . .504, 528
Joined Cases C-6/90 and C-9/90 Francovich [1991] ECR I-5357 . . . . 143, 150, 196, 212, 247, 267,
                                                            289, 292, 297–8, 303, 307–15, 318, 840–2, 874
Case C-18/90 Kziber [1991] ECR I-199 954
Case C-29/90 Commission v Greece [1992] ECR I-1971. 140
Case C-39/90 Denkavit [1991] ECR I-3069 441
Case C-41/90 Höfner v Macrotron [1991] ECR I-1979 . . . . .253, 713–14, 781, 882–3
Joined Cases C-46/90 and C-93/91 Procureur du Roi v Jean-Marie Lagauche and others
    [1993] ECR I-5267. 448
Case C-47/90 Etablissements Delhaize Frères et Compagnie Le Lion SA v Promalvin SA
    and AGE Bodegas Unidas SA [1992] ECR I-3669 433–4
Case C-52/90 Commission v Denmark [1992] ECR I-2187 142
Case C-55/90 Cato v Commission [1992] ECR I-2533. 191
Case C-58/90 Commission v Italy [1991] ECR I-4193. 144
Case C-65/90 European Parliament v Council [1992] ECR I-4593 79
Case C-72/90 Asia Motor France v Commission [1990] ECR I-2181 192
Case C-76/90 Säger [1991] ECR I-4221 . . . . 540, 563–5, 580, 629
Joined Cases C-78/90 etc, Compagnie Commerciale de l'Ouest and others v
    Receveur Principal des Douanes de La Pallice Port [1992] ECR I-1847 402–3
Joined Cases C-87-89/90 Verholen [1991] ECR I-3757 . . . . .212, 251
Joined Cases C-90/90 and C-91/90 Neu and Others [1991] ECR I-3617. 322
Case C-159/90 Grogan [1991] ECR I-4685 555
Case C-163/90 Legros and others [1992] ECR I-4625 . . . . .393, 405
Case C-179/90 Merci convenzionali porto di Genova SpA v Siderurgica Gabrielli SpA
    [1991] ECR I-5889. . . . . 447, 714, 775, 883, 886
Case C-195/90 R Commission v Germany [1990] ECR I-3351. 204
Case C-200/90 Dansk Denkavit [1992] ECR I-2217. 273
Case C-204/90 Bachmann [1992] ECR I-249. . . . . .516, 591
Case C-208/90 Emmott [1991] ECR I-4269. . . . . 291, 297–9
Case C-213/90 ASTI [1991] ECR 3507 519
Joined Cases C-228/90-234/90, C-339/90 and C-353/90 Simba SpA and others [1992] ECR I-3713 405
Joined Cases C-271, 281 and 289/90 Spain v Commission [1992] ECR I-5833 879
Case C-282/90 Vreugdenhil v Commission [1992] ECR I-1937. . . . . .194, 198
Case C-286/90 Poulsen and Diva Navigation [1992] ECR I-6019 964–5
Case C-295/90 Parliament v Council [1992] ECR I-4193 182
Case C-300/90 Commission v Belgium [1992] ECR I-305 591
Case C-313/90 CIRFS and Others v Commission [1993] ECR I-1125. 172
Joined Cases C-320/90, C-321/90 and C-322/90 Telemarsicabruzzo v Circostel [1993] ECR I-393 220–1
Case C-332/90 Steen [1992] ECR I-341 501
Case C-343/90 Manuel José Lourenço Dias v Director da Alfândega do Porto [1992] ECR I-4673 402
Case C-354/90 Fédération Nationale du Commerce Extérieur des Produits Alimentaires v France
    [1991] ECR I-5505. 873
Case C-358/90 Compagnia Italiana Alcool v Commission [1992] ECR I-2457 . . . . .191, 199
Case C-362/90 Commission v Italy [1992] ECR I-2353. 140
Case C-369/90 Micheletti and others [1992] ECR I-4239 . . . . .469, 534
Case C-370/90 Surinder Singh [1992] ECR I-4265. . . . . 471, 539, 541
Case C-2/91 Meng [1993] ECR I-5751 892
Case C-3/91 Exportur SA v LOR SA and Confiserie du Tech SA [1992] ECR I-5529. 445
Joined Cases C-13/91 and C-113/91 Criminal proceedings against Michel Debus [1992] ECR I-3617 440
Joined Cases C-15/91 and C-108/91 Buckl and Others v Commission [1992] ECR I-6061 188–9
Case C-16/91 Council of the City of Stoke-on-Trent and Norwich City Council v B&Q plc
    [1992] ECR I-6635. 416
Case C-17/91 Georges Lornoy en Zonen NV and others v Belgian State [1992] ECR I-6523 403
Case C-27/91 Union de Recouvrement des Cotisations de Sécurité Sociale et d'Allocations
    Familiales de la Savoie (URSSAF) v Hostellerie Le Manoir SARL [1991] ECR I-5531 . . . . .501, 517
Joined Cases C-31/91 to C-44/91 Lageder [1993] ECR I-1761 . . . . .36, 331
Case C-45/91 Commission v Greece [1992] ECR I-2509. 150
Joined Cases C-72-73/91 Firma Sloman Neptun Schiffahrts A-G v Seebetriebsrat Bodo Ziesmer,
    Sloman Neptun Schiffahrts AG [1993] ECR I-887; [1995] 2 CMLR 97. 851–2
Case C-83/91 Meilicke v ADV/ ORGA [1992] ECR I-4871. 220
Case C-97/91 Borelli [1992] ECR I-6313 291
Case C-104/91 Borrell [1992] ECR I-3003 291
Case C-106/91 Ramrath [1992] ECR I-3351 . . . . 553, 577, 579, 606

Case C-107/91 ENU v Commission [1993] ECR I-599 186
Case C-111/91 Commission v Luxembourg [1993] ECR I-817. 515
Case C-112/91 Hans Werner [1993] ECR I-429 535
Case C-113/91 Criminal proceedings against Michel Debus [1992] ECR I-3617. . . . . 436, 438–9
Case C-114/91 Criminal proceedings against Gérard Jerôme Claeys [1992] ECR I-6559. 401–2
Case C-144/91 Gilbert Demoor en Zonen NV and others v Belgian State [1992] ECR I-6613 401–3
Case C-146/91 KYDEP v Council and Commission [1994] ECR I-4199 192
Case C-148/91 Veronica [1991] ECR I-487 568
Joined Cases C-149/91 and C-150/91 Sanders Adour SNC and Guyomarc'h Orthez Nutrition
    Animale SA v Directeur des Services Fiscaux des Pyrénées-Atlantiques [1992] ECR I-3889 401–2
Case C-155/91 Commission v Council (Waste Directive) [1993] ECR I-939. 111–12
Case C-160/91 Poucet and Pistre [1993] ECR I-637. . . . . 715, 731, 876
Case C-169/91 Council of the City of Stoke-on-Trent and Norwich City Council v B&Q plc
    [1992] ECR I-6635. 427
Joined Cases C-181/91 and C-248/91 European Parliament v Council (Bangladesh) [1993] ECR I-3685. .104, 930
Case C-183/91 Commission v Greece [1993] ECR I-3131. 202
Case C-185/91 Reiff [1993] ECR I-5801 . . . . .890, 892
Case C-189/91 Kirsammer-Hack v Sidal [1993] ECR I-6185 851
Case C-198/91 Cook v Commission [1993] ECR I-2487. 873
Case C-220/91 Commission v Stahlwerke Peine-Salzgitter [1993] ECR I-2393. 196
Case C-225/91 Matra v Commission [1993] ECR I-3203 872–3
Case C-228/91 Commission v Italy [1993] ECR I-2701 439
Joined Cases C-241-242/91 RTE and ITP v Commission (Magill) [1995] ECR I-743, [1995] 4 CMLR 718 . . . 798,
    802–5
Case C-245/91 Ohra [1993] ECR 5851 892
Case C-266/91 Celulose Beira Industrial SA v Fazenda P·blica [1993] ECR I-4337 401–3
Joined Cases C-267 and C-268/91 Keck and Mithouard
    [1993] ECR I-6097. . . . . 407, 416, 418–22, 425–9, 443, 459, 522, 668, 892
Case C-271/91 Marshall II [1993] ECR I-4367 . . . . 288, 294, 297–8, 301
Case C-312/91 Metalsa Srl [1993] ECR I-3751 406
Case C-316/91 Parliament v Council [1994] ECR I-625 . . . . 104, 930, 940
Case C-320/91 Corbeau [1993] ECR I-2533, [1995] 4 CMLR 621 . . . . 883–5, 887–8
Case C-327/91 France v Commission [1994] ECR I-3641. . . . . .723, 939
Case C-330/91 Commerzbank [1993] ECR I-4017. . . . . .545, 573, 583, 588, 590, 593, 597, 648
Case C-338/91 Steenhorst-Neerings [1993] ECR I-5475 299
Joined Cases C-410/91 and C-402/92 Tankstaton 't Heukske vof [1994] ECR I-2199. 422
Case C-2/92 Bostock [1994] ECR I-955 . . . . .333, 344
Case C-19/92 Kraus [1993] ECR I-1663. . . . . 291, 500, 520, 524, 540–1
Case C-24/92 Corbiau v Administration des Contributions [1993] ECR I-1277. 215
Case C-41/92 Liberal Democrats v Parliament [1993] ECR I-3153 186
Case C-42/92 Thijssen [1993] ECR I-4047. 569
Case C-49/92 Commission v Anic [1999] ECR I-4125. . . . . 735–7, 739–40
Case C-53/92 Hilti A-G v Commission [1994] ECR I-667; [1994] 4 CMLR 614 . . . . 772, 778, 796–7
Case C-80/92 Commission v Belgium [1994] ECR I-1019 147
Case C-91/92 Faccini Dori [1994] ECR I-3325 . . . . 260, 262, 264, 267, 281, 310
Case C-93/92 CMC Motorradcenter GmbH v Pelin Baskiciogullari
    [1993] ECR I-5009. 428–9
Case C-114/92 Commission v Spain [1990] ECR I-6717. 570
Case C-128/92 Banks v British Coal Corporation [1994] ECR I-1209. 315
Case C-128/92 H Banks & Co Ltd v British Coal Corporation [1994] ECR I-1209;
    [1994] 5 CMLR 30 840
Case C-130/92 OTO SpA v Ministero delle Finanze [1994] ECR I-3281. 405
Case C-137/92 Commission v BASF and Others [1994] ECR I-2555 202
Case C-157/92 Banchero I [1993] ECR I-1085 221
Case C-188/92 TWD Textilwerke Deggendorf GmbH v Germany [1994] ECR I-833;
    [1995] 2 CMLR 145. . . . . 201, 225, 874
Case C-199/92 Hüls v Commission [1999] ECR I-4287; [1999] 5 CMLR 1016 . . . . 202, 737, 739
Case C-227/92 Hoechst v Commission [1999] ECR I-4443 202
Case C-234/92 Shell International Chemical Company v Commission [1999] ECR I-4501 202
Case C-235/92 Montecatini v Commission [1999] ECR I-4539 202
Case C-245/92 Chemie Linz v Commission [1999] ECR I-4643 202
Case C-250/92 Gottrup-Klim v Dansk Landbrugs [1994] ECR I-5641 776
Case C-275/92 Schindler [1994] ECR I-1039. . . . . 555, 558, 563, 580

Joined Cases C-278-80/92 Spain v Commission [1994] ECR I-4103 . . . . 851, 854, 857
Case C-292/92 Ruth Hünermund and others v Landesapothekerkammer Baden-Württemberg
    [1993] ECR I-6787 . . . . 253, 418, 420, 423
Case C-303/92 Commission v Netherlands [1993] ECR I-4739 270
Case C-315/92 Verband Sozialer Wettbewerb v Clinique Laboratories [1994] ECR I-317 . . . . . . 212, 254, 439, 443
Case C-319/92 Haim [1994] ECR I-425 628
Joined Cases C-332/92, C-333/92 and C-335/92 Eurico Italia and Others [1994] ECR I-711 217
Case C-334/92 Wagner Miret [1993] ECR I-6911 240
Case C-351/92 Manfred Graff v Hauptzollamt Köln Rheinau [1994] ECR I-3361 .344
Case C-360/92 Publishers Association v Commission [1995] ECR I-25; [1995] 5 CMLR 33 . . . . .756, 759
Case C-364/92 SAT Fluggesellschaft v Eurocontrol [1994] ECR I-43; [1994] 5 CMLR 208 . . . . 253, 714, 878
Case C-373/92 Commission v Belgium [1993] ECR I-3107 439
Case C-376/92 Metro v Cartier [1994] ECR I-15; [1994] 5 CMLR 331 748
Case C-379/92 Peralta [1994] ECR I-3453 429
Case C-383/92 Commission v UK [1994] ECR I-2435 375
Case C-386/92 Monin Automobiles I [1993] ECR I-2049 221
Case C-387/92 Banco Exterior de España [1994] ECR I-877; [1994] 3 CMLR 473 .874
Case C-391/92 Commission v Greece (processed milk for infants) [1995] ECR I-1621 421–2
Case C-393/92 Almelo [1994] ECR I-1477 . . . . 215, 780, 885
Case C-404/92 X v Commission [1994] ECR I-4737 364
Case C-410/92 Johnston II [1994] ECR I-5483 299
Case C-419/92 Scholz [1994] ECR I-505 . . . . 500, 515, 517, 541
Case C-431/92 Commission v Germany [1995] ECR I-2189 249
Case C-1/93 Halliburton Services [1994] ECR I-1137 . . . . 535, 545, 586, 597
Case C-5/93 DSM v Commission [1999] ECR I-4695 181
Case C-9/93 IHT Internationale Heiztechnik [1994] ECR I-2789 456
Case C-17/93 Van der Veldt [1994] ECR I-3537 . . . . .414, 436
Case C-19/93 Rendo NV v Commission [1995] ECR I-3319 885
Case C-23/93 TV10 [1994] ECR I-1963 . . . . .555, 557
Case C-32/93 Webb [1994] ECR I-3567 377
Case C-44/93 Namur-Les Assurances du Crédit SA v Office National du Ducroire and Belgium
    [1994] ECR I-3829 868
Joined Cases C-46 and 48/93 Factortame III and Brasserie du Pecheur
    [1996] ECR I-1029 . . . . 190, 195, 212, 308–13, 874
Case C-47/93 Commission v Belgium [1994] ECR I-1593 105
Case C-51/93 Meyhui NV v Schott Zwiesel Glaswerke AG [1994] ECR I-3879 435
Case C-56/93 Belgium v Commission [1996] ECR I-723 854
Case C-62/93 BP Supergas [1995] ECR I-1883 294
Case C-63/93 Duffand Others v Minister for Agriculture and Food, Ireland, and the Attorney General
    [1996] ECR I-569 328
Case C-65/93 European Parliament v Council [1995] ECR I-643 79
Joined Cases C-69/93 and C-258/93 Punto Casa Srl [1994] ECR I-2355 422
Case C-130/93 Lamaire v NDALTP [1994] ECR I-3215 395
Case C-131/93 Commission v Germany [1994] ECR I-3303 438–9
Case C-132/93 Steen [1994] ECR I-2715 501
Case C-143/93 Gebroeders van Es Douane Agenten BV v Inspecteur der Invoerrechten en Accijnzen
    [1996] ECR I-431 . . . . 36, 328–9
Case C-153/93 Delta Schiffahrts- und Speditionsgesellschaft [1994] ECR I-2517 890
Case C-187/93 Parliament v Council [1994] ECR I-2857 . . . . 111, 162, 943
Case C-279/93 Schumacker [1995] ECR I-225 . . . . 584–5, 596–7
Case C-280/93 Germany v Council [1994] ECR I-4973 . . . . 956, 958–9, 962
Case C-293/93 Houtwipper [1994] ECR I-4249 . . . . .414, 439
Case C-310/93 BPB Industries and British Gypsum v Commission [1995] ECR I-865;
    [1997] 4 CMLR 238 . . . . .783, 800
Case C-312/93 Peterbroeck [1995] ECR I-4599 . . . . .294, 300
Case C-316/93 Vaneetveld [1994] ECR I-763 . . . . .221, 262
Case C-320/93 Lucien Ortscheit GmbH [1994] ECR I-5243 424
Case C-323/93 Société Civile Agricole du Centre d'Insémination de la Crespelle v Coopérative
    d'Elevage et d'Insémination Artificielle du Département de la Mayenne
    [1994] ECR I-5077 . . . . 427, 438, 441, 775, 880, 882–3
Case C-324/93 R v Home Secretary, ex parte Evans Medical Ltd and Macfarlan Smith Ltd
    [1995] ECR I-563 . . . . 435, 437, 439

Joined Cases C-329/93 and C-62-63/95 Germany v Commission, Hanseatische Industrie
  Beteiligungen GmbH v Commission, Bremer Vulkan Verbund A-G v Commission
  [1996] ECR I-5151 854
Case C-346/93 Kleinwort Benson v City of Glasgow District Council [1995] ECR I-615 213
Case C-349/93 Commission v Italy [1995] ECR I-343 870
Joined Cases C-358/93 and C-416/93 Bordessa [1995] ECR I-361 663
Joined Cases C-363/93, etc, René Lancry SA [1994] ECR I-3957 394
Joined Cases C-367/93-377/93 Roders [1995] ECR I-2229 273
Case C-384/93 Alpine Investments [1995] ECR I-1141 . . . . 555, 563, 668
Case C-387/93 Banchero II [1995] ECR I-4663 . . . . 221, 423, 448
Case C-392/93 R v HM Treasury, ex parte British Telecommunications [1996] ECR I-1631 . . . . 267, 309–10
Case C-412/93 Leclerc-Siplec v TF1 Publicité and M6 Publicité [1995] ECR I-179 . . . . 221, 420, 424
Case C-415/93 Bosman [1995] ECR I-4921 . . . . .220–1, 273, 367, 501,
    521–4, 672–3
Case C-417/93 Parliament v Council [1995] ECR I-1185 . . . . .78, 89
Joined Cases C-418/93 etc, Semeraro Casa Uno [1996] ECR I-2975 552
Joined Cases C-422/93, C-423/93 and C-424/93 Zabala Erasun and Others [1995] ECR I-1567 . . . . 221, 450, 453,
    456–7, 459
Case C-426/93 Germany v Council [1995] ECR I-3723 123
Case C-428/93 Monin Automobiles II [1994] ECR I-1707 221
Joined Cases C-430-431/93 Van Schijndel [1995] ECR I-4705 . . . . .300, 302
Case C-441/93 Pafitis [1996] ECR I-1347 282
Case C-443/93 Ioannis Vougioukas [1995] ECR I-4033 500
Case C-446/93 SEIM [1996] ECR I-73 288
Case C-450/93 Kalanke [1995] ECR I-3051 372
Case C-465/93 Atlanta Fruchthandelsgesellschaft mbH v Bundesamt für Ernährung und
  Forstwirtschaft [1995] ECR I-3761 . . . . 228, 304–5
Case C-470/93 Mars [1995] ECR I-1923 443
Case C-473/93 Commission v Luxembourg [1996] ECR I-3207 514
Case C-479/93 Francovich [1995] ECR I-3843 212
Case C-484/93 Svensson [1995] ECR I-3955 . . . . .572, 579
Joined Cases C-485/93 and C-486/93 Maria Simitzi v Dimos Kos [1995] ECR I-2655 393–4
Case C-5/94 R v MAFF ex parte Hedley Lomas [1996] ECR I-2553 . . . . 144, 309, 313, 441
Case C-7/94 Lubor Gaal [1995] ECR I-1031 526
Case C-13/94 P v S Cornwall County Council [1996] ECR I-2143 . . . . 348, 371–2
Case C-25/94 Commission v Council (FAO) [1996] ECR I-1469 . . . . .100, 940
Case C-39/94 Syndicat Français de l'Express International (SFEI) and
  Others v La Poste and Others [1996] ECR I-3547 . . . . 323, 332, 848, 854, 866, 873
Case C-45/94 Cámara de Comercio, Industria y Navegación de Ceuta v
  Ayuntamiento de Ceuta [1995] ECR I-4385 396
Case C-55/94 Gebhard [1995] ECR I-4165 . . . . 503, 521, 532–3, 540, 547, 575–6, 635, 644, 665
Case C-61/94 Commission v Germany [1996] ECR I-3989 964
Case C-63/94 Groupement National des Négociants en Pommes de Terre de Belgique (Belgapom)
  [1995] ECR I-2467 . . . . .419, 430
Joined Cases C-68/94 and C-30/95 France and others v Commission [1998] ECR I-1375;
  [1998] 4 CMLR 829 780
Case C-70/94 Werner [1995] ECR I-3189 . . . . .944, 964
Joined Cases C-71/94, 72/94 and C-73/94 Eurim-Pharm [1996] ECR I-3603 459
Case C-80/94 Wielockx [1995] ECR I-2493 . . . . 545, 584, 592
Case C-83/94 Leifer [1995] ECR I-3231 . . . . 101, 944, 964
Case C-84/94 United Kingdom v Council (Working Time Directive) [1996] ECR I-5755 . . . . .118, 123
Case C-90/94 Haahr Petroleum Ltd v Åbenrå Havn and Others [1997] ECR I-4085 397
Case C-96/94 Centro Servizi Spediporto v Spedizioni Marittima del Golfo [1995] ECR I-2883;
  [1996] 4 CMLR 613 . . . . .429, 780
Case C-101/94 Commission v Italy [1996] ECR I-2691 . . . . .561, 573
Case C-105/94 Ditta A Celestini [1997] ECR I-2971 427
Case C-107/94 Asscher [1994] ECR I-1137 . . . . 541, 545, 553, 584
Case C-111/94 Job Centre [1995] ECR I-3361 215
Case C-122/94 Commission v Council [1996] ECR 881 862
Case C-125/94 Aprile Srl, in liquidation, v Amministrazione delle Finanze dello Stato [1995]
  ECR I-2919 405
Case C-126/94 Cadi Surgelés and others [1996] ECR I-5647 405
Case C-129/94 Ruiz Bernáldez [1996] ECR I-1829 282

Case C-137/94 ex parte Cyril Richardson [1995] ECR I-3407. 273
Joined Cases C-140, 141, 142/94 DIP v Commune di Bassano del Grappa [1995] ECRI-3257 . . . . .780, 892
Case C-152/94 Openbaar Ministerie v Geert Van Buynder [1995] ECR I-3981. 535
Case C-157/94 Commission v Netherlands [1997] ECR I-5699. . . . . 448, 875–6
Case C-158/94 Commission v Italy [1997] ECR I-5789. 419
Case C-159/94 Commission v France [1997] ECR I-5815. 885
Case C-175/94 Gallagher [1995] ECR I-4253 486
Joined Cases C-178-179 and 188-190/94 Dillenkofer [1996] ECR I-4845. . . . . 267, 309, 311
Case C-192/94 El Corte Inglés [1996] ECR I-1281 267
Case C-193/94 Skanavi and Chryssanthakopoulos [1996] ECR I-929. . . . . .328, 381
Case C-194/94 CIA Security [1996] ECR I-2201. 280–2
Joined Cases C-197/94 and C-252/94 Bautiaa and Société Française Maritime v
    Directeur des Services Fiscaux [1996] ECR I-505. 36
Case C-201/94 Medicines Control Agency [1996] ECR I-5819 . . . . 263–4, 281
Case C-209/94 Buralux and Others v Council [1996] ECR I-615. 168
Case C-212/94 FMC [1996] ECR I-389. 306
Case C-214/94 Boukhalfa [1996] ECR I-2253 502
Case C-232/94 MPA Pharma [1996] ECR I-3671 459
Case C-233/94 Germany v Parliament and Council (Deposit Guarantee Schemes Directive)
    [1997] ECR I-2405. . . . . 36, 118, 124, 267
Case C-237/94 O'Flynn [1996] ECR I-2617. . . . . 509, 516–18
Case C-241/94 France v Commission [1996] ECR 4551; [1997] 1 CMLR 983. 850
Case C-244/94 Fédération Française des Sociétés d'Assurance v Ministère de l'Agriculture
    et de la Pêche [1995] ECR I-4013 716
Case C-278/94 Commission v Belgium [1996] ECR I-4307 . . . . .507, 515
Joined Cases C-283/94, C-291/94 and C-292/94 Denkavit [1996] ECR I-5063 586
Case C-284/94 Spain v Council [1998] ECR I-7309 331
Case C-293/94 Brandsma [1996] ECR I-3159 427
Case C-315/94 de Vos [1996] ECR I-417 . . . . .515, 519
Joined Cases C-321/94, C-322/94, C-323/94, C-324/94 Jacques Pistre etc [1997] ECR I-2343 . . . . .432, 442
Case C-333/94 Tetra Pak v Commission (Tetra Pak II) [1996] ECR I-5951;
    [1997] 4 CMLR 662. . . . . 774, 784, 788, 797
Case C-336/94 Dafeki [1997] ECR I-6761 302
Case C-340/94 De Jaeck v Staatssecretaris van Financiën [1997] ECR I-461 328
Case C-3/95 Broede v Sandker [1996] ECR I-6511. 581
Case C-7/95 John Deere v Commission [1998] ECR I-3111; [1998] 5 CMLR 311. . . . . 736, 739, 750
Case C-10/95 Asocarne v Council [1995] ECR I-4149. 171
Case C-15/95 EARL [1997] ECR I-1961. 370
Case C-18/95 FC Terhoeve [1999] ECR I-345. 522
Case C-24/95 Alcan Deutschland [1997] ECR I-1591 302
Case C-28/95 Leur-Bloem v Inspecteur der Belastingdienst/Ondernemingen Amsterdam 2
    [1997] ECR I-4161. 213–14
Case C-29/95 Pastoors [1997] ECR I-285. . . . . .328, 381
Joined Cases C-34/95, C-35/95 and C-36/95 Konsumentombudsmannen (KO) v De Agostini
    and TV Shop [1997] ECR I-3843 425
Case C-51/95 Unifruit Hellas v Commission [1997] ECR I-727. 194
Case C-53/95 Kemmler [1996] ECR I-703. . . . . .538, 574
Case C-57/95 France v Commission [1997] ECR I-1627. 157
Joined Cases C-65/95 C-111/95 Shingara and Radiom [1997] ECR I-3343 488
Case C-66/95 ex parte Sutton [1997] ECR I-2163. 302
Case C-68/95 T Port v Bundesanstalt für Landwirtschaft und Ernährung [1996] ECR I-6065. . . . . 184–6, 228
Case C-70/95 Sodemare v Regione Lombardia [1997] ECR I-3395;
    [1998] 4 CMLR 291, 549, 557, 649, 780
Joined Cases C-71/95, C-155/95 and C-271/95 Belgium v Commission [1997] ECR I-687. 179
Case C-72/95 Kraaijeveld [1996] ECR I-5403 249
Case C-73/95 Viho Europe BV v Commission [1996] ECR I-5457 731
Joined Cases C-74/95 and C-129/95 Criminal Proceedings Against X [1996] ECR I-6609 242
Case C-84/95 Bosphorus [1996] ECR I-3953. 369
Case C-87/95 CNPAAP v Council [1996] ECR I-2003. 171
Case C-91/95 Tremblay v Commission [1996] ECR I-5574; [1997] 4 CMLR 211 838
Joined Cases C-94/95 and C-95/95 Bonifaci [1997] ECR I-3969 313
Case C-120/95 N Decker v Caisse de Maladie des Employés Privés [1998] ECR I-1831. . . . . 427, 435, 443
Case C-122/95 Germany v Council [1998] ECR I-973. . . . . .155, 939

Case C-126/95 Hallouzi-Choho [1996] ECR I-4807...273, 955
Case C-127/95 Norbrook Laboratories [1998] ECR I-1531..291
Case C-130/95 Giloy v Hauptzollamt Frankfurt am Main-Ost [1997] ECR I-4291.....................213–14
Case C-132/95 Jensen and Korn [1998] ECR I-2975 .... 293–4, 302
Case C-137/95 Vereniging van Samenwerkende Prijsregelende Organisaties in de Bouwnijverheid
    (SPO) v Commission [1996] ECR I-1611...756
Case C-138/95 Campo Ebro and Others v Council [1997] ECR I-2027 193
Case C-143/95 Commission v Socurte and Others [1997] ECR I-1...................................156
Case C-168/95 Criminal proceedings against Luciano Arcaro [1996] ECR I-4705.....................243
Case C-170/95 Wiljo [1997] ECR I 585 ....201, 225
Case C-185/95 Baustahlgewebe v Commission [1998] ECR I-8417...................................379, 821
Case C-188/95 Fantask [1997] ECR I-6783 .... 272, 289, 299, 306, 325
Case C-189/95 Criminal proceedings against Harry Franzén [1997] ECR I-5909............. 217, 427, 438, 448
Case C-191/95 Commission v Germany [1998] ECR I-5449...141
Joined Cases C-192-218/95 Comateb [1997] ECR I-165 306
Case C-219/95 Ferrière Nord SpA v Commission [1997] ECR I-4411, [1997] 5 CMLR 575 741
Case C-236/95 Commission v Greece [1996] ECR I-4459...258
Case C-241/95 The Queen v Intervention Board for Agricultural Produce, ex parte
    Accrington Beef and Others [1996] ECR I-6699...225
Case C-242/95 GT-Link A/S v De Danske Statsbaner [1997] ECR I-4449; [1997] 5 CMLR 601 886
Case C-250/95 Futura Participations [1997] ECR I-2471 595
Case C-259/95 Parliament v Council [1997] ECR I-5303 89
Case C-261/95 Palmisani [1997] ECR I-4025 .... 289, 293, 312–13
Case C-265/95 Commission v France [1997] ECR I-6959......................... 25, 144, 146, 430, 434, 673
Joined Cases C-267/95 and C-268/95 Merck v Primecrown [1996] ECR I-6285.........................456
Case C-270/95 Kik v Council and Commission [1996] ECR I-1987 167
Case C-272/95 Bundesanstalt für Landwirtschaft und Ernährung v Deutsches Milch-Kontor
    [1997] ECR I-1905...392
Case C-282/95 Guérin Automobiles v Commission [1997] ECR I-1503............................184, 186
Case C-284/95 Safety Hi-Tech [1998] ECR I-4301 36
Joined Cases C-286, 340 and 401/95 and C-47/96 Garage Molenheide [1997] ECR I-7281..............291
Case C-298/95 Commission v Germany [1996] ECR I-6747...259
Case C-299/95 Kremzow v Austria [1997] ECR I-2629 .... 214, 338, 501
Case C-300/95 Commission v United Kingdom [1997] ECR I-2649...................................147
Case C-321/95 Greenpeace [1998] ECR I-1651...167, 378
Case C-334/95 Krüger v Hauptzollamt Hamburg-Jonas [1997] ECR I-4517 227
Case C-337/95 Parfums Christian Dior v Evora [1997] ECR I-6013 223–4
Case C-338/95 Wiener v Hauptzollamt Emmerich [1997] ECR I-6495...............................219
Case C-341/95 Bettati [1998] ECR I-4355 36
Case C-343/95 Calì & Figli v SEPG [1997] ECR I-1547; [1997] 5 CMLR 484 715
Case C-344/95 Commission v Belgium [1997] ECR I-1035 506
Case C-347/95 Fazenda Pública v UCAL [1997] ECR I-4911.....................................401–3
Case C-349/95 Loenderloot [1997] ECR I-6227 ....456, 459
Case C-354/95 R v Minister of Agriculture, Fisheries and Food, ex parte National Farmers'
    Union and Others [1997] ECR I-4559..329, 332
Case C-355/95 TWD v Commission [1997] ECR I-2549...201
Case C-358/95 Tommaso Morellato v USL No 11, Prodenone [1997] ECR I-1431 414
Case C-360/95 Commission v Spain [1997] ECR I-7337...259
Case C-366/95 Steff-Houlberg [1998] ECR I-2661 302
Case C-367/95 Commission v Sytraval and Brink's Finance [1998] ECR I-1719 872–3
Case C-368/95 Familiapress [1997] ECR I-3689 .... 254, 346, 349, 367, 419, 422,
                                                                            440, 445–6, 673
Case C-369/95 Somalfruit SpA, Camar SpA v Ministero delle Finanze,
    Ministerio del Commercio con l'Estero [1997] ECR I-6619..................................326
Case C-373/95 Maso [1997] ECR I-4051 313
Case C-375/95 Commission v Greece [1997] ECR I-5981..398
Case C-388/95 Belgium v Spain (Rioja) [2000] ECR I-3123.....................................136, 434
Case C-390/95 Antillean Rice Mills and Others v Commission [1999] ECR I-769....................193–4
Case C-398/95 SETTG [1997] ECR I-3091 ....558, 566
Case C-408/95 Eurotunnel and Others v SeaFrance [1997] ECR I-6315.............................225
Case C-409/95 Marschall [1997] ECR I-6363 372–3
Case C-1/96 R v MAFF ex parte Compassion in World Farming Limited [1998] ECR I-1251 441
Case C-15/96 Schöning [1998] ECR I-47...517

Case C-35/96 Commission v Italy (Re CNSD) [1998] ECR I-3851, [1998] 5 CMLR 889 890–2
Case C-50/96 Deutsche Telekom AG v Lilli Schröder [2000] ECR I-743 . . . . .371, 431
Joined Cases C-51/96 and 191/97 Deliège [2000] ECR I-2549 . . . . .523, 566
Case C-53/96 Hermès v FHT [1998] ECR I-3603 . . . . .212–13, 940, 957, 965, 967
Case C-54/96 Dorsch Consult Ingenieurgesellschaft v Bundesbaugesellschaft Berlin
    [1997] ECR I-4961. . . . . .214–15, 240–1, 247, 292, 310
Case C-55/96 Job Centre Coop [1997] ECR I-7119 . . . . .781, 882
Case C-56/96 VT4 [1997] ECR I-3143 554
Case C-57/96 Meints v Minister van Landbouw [1997] ECR I-6689 516
Joined Cases C-64/96 and C-65/96 Uecker [1997] ECR I-3171 501
Case C-67/96 Albany International BV v Stichting Bedrijfspensioenfonds Textielindustrie
    [1999] ECR I-5751, [2000] 4 CMLR 446 . . . . .221, 716–17, 731, 876, 882, 888
Case C-85/96 Martínez Sala [1998] ECR I-2691 . . . . .464, 503
Case C-90/96 Petrie and Others [1997] ECR I-6527 501
Case C-92/96 Commission v Spain [1998] ECR I-505 151
Case C-108/96 Mac Quen [2001] ECR I-837 . . . . 577, 628–9
Case C-114/96 René Kieffer and Roman Thill [1997] ECR I-3629 . . . . .427, 435
Case C-122/96 Saldanha [1997] ECR I-5325 . . . . .534, 677
Case C-129/96 Inter-Environnement Wallonie [1997] ECR I-7411 . . . . 247–8, 259
Case C-149/96 Portugal v Council [1999] ECR I-8395 . . . . 24, 955, 957, 962
Case C-157/96 R v Minister of Agriculture, Fisheries and Food and Another
    ex parte National Farmers' Union and Others [1998] ECR I-2211 326
Case C-158/96 Kohll [1998] ECR I-1931 . . . . 564, 566, 572, 579, 581
Case C-161/96 Südzucker Mannheim/Ochsenfurt AG v Hauptzollamt Mannheim
    [1998] ECR I-281. 327
Case C-162/96 Racke [1998] ECR I-3655 . . . . .954, 963
Case C-163/96 Raso [1998] ECR I-533; [1998] 4 CMLR 737 . . . . 775–6, 882–3
Case C-170/96 Commission v Council [1998] ECR I-2763 908
Case C-176/96 Lehtonen [2000] ECR I-2681 523
Case C-177/96 Belgian State v Banque Indosuez and Others and European Community
    [1997] ECR I-659 328
Case C-180/96 United Kingdom v Commission [1998] ECR I-2265 158
Case C-184/96 Commission v France (paté de foie gras) [1998] ECR I-6197 . . . . .412, 422
Case C-203/96 Chemische Afvalstoffen Dusseldorp and Others v Minister van
    Volkshuisvesting, Ruimtelijke Ordering en Milieubeheer [1998] ECR I-4075 . . . . 442, 881–2, 888
Case C-207/96 Commission v Italy [1997] ECR I-6869 138
Case C-213/96 Outokumpu Oy [1998] ECR I-1777 . . . . .398, 404
Joined Cases C-215/96 and C-216/96 Carlo Bagnasco and others v Banco Polare di Navara and others [1999]
    ECR I-135 719
Case C-228/96 Aprile [1998] ECR I-7141 . . . . 293, 300, 305
Case C-230/96 Cabour SA and Nord Distribution Automobile SA v Automobiles Peugeot SA
    and Automobiles Citröen SA [1998] ECR I-2055; [1988] 5 CMLR 679 843
Case C-231/96 Edis [1998] ECR I-4951 . . . . .293, 305
Case C-233/96 Kingdom of Denmark v Commission [1998] ECR I-5759 328
Joined Cases C-239/96 and C-240/96 United Kingdom v Commission [1996] ECR I-4475 304
Case C-249/96 Grant v South West Trains Ltd [1998] ECR I-621 . . . . .348, 371
Case C-260/96 Spac [1998] ECR I-4997 293
Case C-264/96 ICI [1998] ECR I-4695 648
Case C-266/96 Corsica Ferries France SA v Gruppo Antichi Ormeggiatori del Porto di
    Genova Coop Arl et al [1998] ECR I-3949 . . . . 429, 875, 882, 886
Case C-274/96 Bickel and Franz [1998] ECR I-7637 . . . . 464, 472, 489
Joined Cases C-279-281/96 Ansaldo Energia [1998] ECR I-5025 . . . . .293, 305
Case C-284/96 Didier Tabouillet v Directeur des Services Fiscaux de Meurthe-et-Moselle
    [1997] ECR I-7471 405
Case C-298/96 Oelmühle Hamburg [1998] ECR I-4767 302
Case C-301/96 Germany v Commission [2003] ECR I-9919 860
Case C-318/96 SPAR Österreichische Warenhandels AG v Finanzlandesdirectktion für Salzburg
    [1998] ECR I-785. 325
Case C-319/96 Brinkmann [1998] ECR I-5255 311
Case C-326/96 Levez v Jennings (Harlow Pools) [1998] ECR I-7835 . . . . 291–4, 299
Case C-328/96 Commission v Austria [1999] ECR I-7479 140–1
Case C-336/96 Gilly [1998] ECR I-2793 . . . . 246, 500, 582
Case C-342/96 Spain v Commission [1999] ECR I-2459 855

Case C-343/96 Dilexport [1999] ECR I-579. . . . . 293, 300, 305–6
Case C-348/96 Calfa [1999] ECR I-11. 487
Case C-350/96 Clean Car Autoservice [1998] ECR I-2521 . . . . 251–2, 294, 302, 501
Case C-352/96 Italy v Council [1998] ECR I-6937 962
Case C-355/96 Silhouette International Schmied [1998] ECR I-4799 457
Joined Cases C-369 and 376/96 Arblade [1999] ECR I-8453. . . . . .578, 660
Case C-375/96 Galileo Zaninotto v Ispettorato Centrale Repressione FrodiùUfficio di
    ConeglianoùMinistero delle Risorse Agricole, Alimentari e Forestali [1998] ECR I-6629. . . . . 326, 330–1
Case C-389/96 Aher-Waggon GmbH v Germany [1998] ECR I-4473. 442
Case C 392/96 Commission v Ireland [1999] ECR I-5901 147
Joined Cases C-395/96 and C-396/96 Compagnie Maritime Belge Transports,
    Compagnie Maritime Belge SA and Dafra Lines A/S v Commission
    [2000] ECR I-1365; [2000] CMLR 1076. . . . . .766, 776–7, 779, 786, 789, 822–3
Case C-400/96 J Harpegnies [1998] ECR I-5121 427
Case C-404/96 Glencore Grain [1988] ECR I-2435 165
Case C-406/96 Sveriges Betodlares Centralförening and Henrikson [1997] ECR I-7531. 872
Case C-410/96 André Ambry [1998] ECR I-7875. 579
Case C-416/96 El-Yassini [1999] ECR I-1209 954–5
Case C-2/97 Borsana [1998] ECR I-8597 241
Case C-6/97 Commission v Italy [1999] ECR I-2981 870
Case C-7/97 Bronner [1998] ECR I-7791, [1999] 4 CMLR 112 . . . . 775, 782, 785, 798, 800–5
Joined Cases C-9/97 and C-118/97 Raija-Liisa Jokela [1998] ECR I-6267 329
Case C-10/97 IN.CO.GE. [1998] ECR I-6307 . . . . 271, 280, 288
Case C-33/97 Colim v Biggs [1999] ECR I-3175. . . . . .254, 413
Case C-35/97 Commission v France [1998] ECR I-5325 273
Joined Cases C-36/97 and C-37/97 Hilmar Kellinghusen v Amt für Land- und
    Wasserwirtschaft Kiel and Ernst-Detlef Ketelsen v Amt für Land- und Wasserwirtschaft
    Husum [1998] ECR I-6337. 323
Case C-42/97 Parliament v Council [1999] ECR I-869 943–4
Joined Cases C-52-54/97 Epifanio Viscido v Ente Poste Italiane [1998] ECR I-2629;
    [1998] 3 CMLR 184 851
Case C-61/97 FDV [1998] ECR I-5171. 452
Case C-67/97 Bluhme [1998] ECR I-8033 . . . . .429, 437
Case C-70/97 Kruidvat v Commission [1998] ECR I-7183 173
Case C-95/97 Région Wallonne v Commission [1997] ECR I-1787. . . . . .161, 856
Case C-111/97 EvoBus Austria [1998] ECR I-5411. 292
Case C-114/97 Commission v Spain [1998] ECR I-6717 514
Joined Cases C-115/97, C-116/97 and C-117/97 Brentjens v Stichting Bedrijfspensioenfonds
    voor de Handel in Bouwmaterialen [1999] ECR I-6025 221
Case C-120/97 Upjohn [1999] ECR I-223 291
Case C-126/97 Eco Swiss China Time v Benetton International [1999] ECR I-3055 215
Case C-140/97 Rechberger [1999] ECR I-3499. 311
Case C-158/97 Badek and others [2000] ECR I-1875. 372
Case C-162/97 Gunnar Nilsson [1998] ECR I-7477 423
Case C-174/97 FFSA v Commission [1998] ECR I-1303 . . . . .874, 887
Case C-180/97 Regione Toscana v Commission [1997] ECR I-5245 161
Case C-185/97 Coote v Granada Hospitality [1998] ECR I-5199. . . . . .291, 302
Case C-189/97 Parliament v Council [1999] ECR 4741 938
Case C-198/97 Commission v Germany [1999] ECR I-3257. 141
Case C-200/97 Ecotrade v AFS [1998] ECR I-7907; [1999] 2 CMLR 833 856
Case C-204/97 Portugal v Commission [2001] ECR I-3175 867
Case C-212/97 Centros [1999] ECR I-1458 . . . . 488, 554, 567, 573, 575–6, 648–54,
                                                                                    657, 681–2
Case C-217/97 Commission v Germany [1999] ECR I-5087. 147
Case C-222/97 Trummer [1999] ECR I-1661. 662
Case C-224/97 Ciola [1999] ECR I-2517 . . . . 271–2, 557, 572, 579, 590
Case C-226/97 Lemmens [1998] ECR I-3711 251
Case C-233/97 KappAhl Oy [1998] ECR I-8069 36
Case C-234/97 Bobadilla [1999] ECR I-4773. 627
Joined Cases C-253/96-258/97 Helmut Kampelmann [1997] ECR I-6907 263
Case C-254/97 Baxter and others [1999] ECR I-4809. . . . . 535, 576, 593
Case C-255/97 Pfeiffer Großhandel [1999] ECR I-2835. . . . . 574, 576, 658
Case C-256/97 DMT [1999] ECR I-3913 . . . . .220, 854

Case C-258/97 Hospital Ingenieure [1999] ECR I-1405. 292
Case C-262/97 Engelbrecht [2000] ECR I-7321. 241
Case C-269/97 Commission and Parliament v Council [2000] ECR I-2257. . . . . .113, 943
Case C-272/97 Commission v Germany [1999] ECR I-2175. 141
Case C-292/97 Karlsson [2000] ECR 2737. 370
Case C-295/97 Piaggio v IFITALIA and Others [1999] ECR I-3735 . . . . 217, 221, 856
Case C-298/97 Commission v Spain [1998] ECR I-3301. 270
Case C-302/97 Konle [1999] ECR I-3099. . . . . .313, 665
Case C-307/97 Saint-Gobain [1999] ECR I-6161 649
Case C-310/97 Commission v AssiDomän Kraft Products and Others [1999] ECR I-5363;
   [1999] 5 CMLR 1253. 181
Case C-311/97 Royal Bank of Scotland [1999] ECR I-2651. 548, 573, 579, 582
Case C-321/97 Andersson and Another v Swedish State [1999] ECR I-3551 212
Case C-341/97 Commission v Netherlands [2000] ECR I-6611 139
Case C-350/97 W Monsees v Unabhängiger Verwaltungssenat für Kärnten [1999] ECR I-2921 . . . . .427, 433
Case C-355/97 Landesgrundverkehrsreferent der Tiroler Landesregierung v Beck
   and Another [1999] ECR I-4977 221
Case C-365/97 Commission v Italy [1999] ECR I-7773. 142
Case C-378/97 Wijsenbeek [1999] ECR I-6207. . . . . 246, 464, 489
Case C-379/97 Pharmacia & Upjohn [1999] ECR I-6927 459
Case C-387/97 Commission v Greece [2000] ECR I-5047. 150
Case C-391/97 Gschwind [1999] ECR I-5451 585
Case C-394/97 Sami Heinonen [1999] ECR I-3599 101
Case C-412/97 ED Srl v I Fenocchio [1999] ECR I-3845. . . . . .429, 433
Case C-421/97 Tarantik v Directeur des Services Fiscaux de Seine-et-Marne [1999] ECR I-3633 . . . . .220, 400
Case C-424/97 Haim [2000] ECR I-5123 . . . . .311, 313
Case C-435/97 WWF and Others v Autonome Provinz Bozen and Others [1999] ECR I-5613 . . . . . . 216–17, 249
Case C-443/97 Spain v Commission [2000] ECR I-2415. 158
Case C-7/98 Krombach [2000] ECR I-1935. 289
Case C-17/98 Emesa Sugar Free Zone NV and Aruba, order of the Court, [2000] ECR I-665 352
Case C-22/98 Becu [1999] ECR I-5665, [2001] 4 CMLR 968 714
Case C-35/98 Verkooijen [2000] ECR I-4071 . . . . 590, 592, 596
Case C-44/98 BASF v Präsident des Deutschen Patentamts [1999] ECR I-6269 .429
Joined Cases C-49, 50, 52-54 and 68-71/98 Finalarte [2001] ECR I-7831. . . . . .103, 578
Case C-49/98 Finalarte and Others [2001] ECR I-7831 660
Case C-60/98 Butterfly Music Srl v CEMED [1999] ECR I-3939 220
Case C-78/98 Preston [2000] ECR I-3201 . . . . 292–4, 300
Case C-109/98 CRT France International SA [1999] ECR I-2237 405
Case C-156/98 Germany v Commission [2000] ECR I-6857. 859
Case C-165/98 Mazzoleni [2001] ECR I-2189 578
Case C-168/98 Luxembourg v Parliament and Council [2000] ECR I-9131. . . . . 623, 638, 642
Case C-173/98 Sebago [1999] ECR I-4103 457
Joined Cases C-174 and 189/98 Netherlands Van der Wal v Commission [2000] ECR I-1;
   [2002] 1 CMLR 16. 821
Joined Cases C-180-84/98 Pavlov [2000] ECR I-6451, [2001] 4 CMLR 30 . . . . .714, 876
Case C-187/98 Commission v Greece [1999] ECR I-7713. 142
Case C-190/98 Graf [2000] ECR I-493 522
Case C-192/98 ANAS [1999] ECR I-8583 215–16
Case C-195/98 OG v Austria [2000] ECR I-10497. 215
Case C-195/98 Österreichischer Gewerkschaftsbund [2000] ECR I-10497. 517
Case C-209/98 Entreprenørforeningens Affalds/ Miljøsektion (FFAD) v Københavns Kommune
   [2000] ECR I-3743. . . . . 434, 442, 880, 886
Case C-215/98 Commission v Greece [1999] ECR I-4913. 144
Case C-220/98 Estée Lauder v Lancaster [2000] ECR I-117 443–4
Case C-224/98 D'Hoop [2002] ECR I-6191. . . . . 465, 475, 507
Case C-228/98 Dounias [2000] ECR I-577. 289
Case C-238/98 Hocsman [2000] ECR I-6623. 627–8
Joined Cases C-240-4/98 Océano Grupo Editorial [2000] ECR I-4941 . . . . .248, 302
Case C-251/98 Baars [2000] ECR I-2787 661
Case C-254/98 Schutzverband gegen unlauteren Wettbewerb and TK-Heimdienst Sass GmbH
   [2000] ECR I-151. . . . . 323, 424, 432
Case C-281/98 Angonese [2000] ECR I-4131 . . . . 254, 315, 502, 510, 553, 672

Case C-286/98 Stora Kopparbergs Bergslags AB v Commission [2000] ECR I-9925;
   [2001] 4 CMLR 12...720
Case C-287/98 Linster [2000] ECR I-6917...249
Joined Cases C-300/98 and C-392/98 Parfums Christian Dior v Tuk Consultancy
   [2000] ECR I-11307...212, 958, 965
Case C-324/98 Telaustria [2000] ECR I-10745 547
Case C-343/98 Collino [2000] ECR I-6659 241
Case C-344/98 Masterfoods [2000] ECR I-11369 839
Case C-352/98 Bergaderm [2000] ECR I-5291 195-6
Case C-356/98 Kaba [2000] ECR I-2623..212
Case C-357/98 Yiadom [2000] ECR I-9265 ....483, 487
Case C-375/98 Epson Europe [2001] ECR I-4243.....................................586
Case C-376/98 Germany v Council and Parliament [2000] ECR I-8419...... 108, 178, 180, 678
Case C-377/98 Netherlands v Parliament and Council [2001] ECR I-7079 ......108-9, 116, 118, 180,
                                                                    324, 363-4, 960
Case C-379/98 Preussen Elektra [2001] ECR I-2099 ....442, 851
Case C-393/98 Gomes Valente [2001] ECR I-1327................................223, 401
Joined Cases C-397 and 410/98 Metallgesellschaft [2001] ECR I-1727 ....302, 305, 313, 590, 597
Case C-398/98 Commission v Greece (obligation to stock petroleum)
   [2001] ECR I-7915...436
Case C-403/98 Monte Arcosu [2001] ECR I-103......................................257
Case C-405/98 Gourmet International [2001] ECR I-1795....... 254, 425, 501, 552, 558, 564
Case C-440/98 RAI [1999] ECR I-8597 215
Joined Cases C-441 and 442/98 Mikhailidis [2000] ECR I-7145......................306, 393
Case C-443/98 Unilever Italia [2000] ECR I-7535.............................. 280-1, 605
Case C-448/98 Guimont [2000] ECR I-10663 432
Case C-451/98 Antillean Rice Mills [2001] ECR I-8949.............................169
Case C-456/98 Centrosteel v Adipol [2000] ECR I-6007.............................248
Case C-466/98 Commission v United Kingdom [2002] ECR I-9427.....................925
Case C-467/98 Commission v Denmark (Open Skies) [2002] ECR I-9519 ......920, 924-7, 948
Case C-468/98 Commission v Sweden [2002] ECR I-9575..............................925
Case C-469/98 Commission v Finland [2002] ECR I-9627.............................925
Case C-471/98 Commission v Belgium [2002] ECR I-9681 925
Case C-472/98 Commission v Luxembourg [2002] ECR I-9741 925
Case C-473/98 Toolex Alpha AB [2000] ECR I-5681 427
Case C-475/98 Commission v Austria [2002] ECR I-9797 925
Case C-478/98 Commission v Germany [2002] ECR I-9855............................925
Case C-1/99 Kofisa Italia v Ministero delle Finanze [2001] ECR I-207 ....213-14, 304, 318
Case C-9/99 EchirollesDistribution [2000] ECR I-8207..........................24, 99
Case C-33/99 Fahmi and Esmoris Cerdeiro-Pinedo Amado [2001] ECR I-2415............528
Case C-35/99 Arduino [2002] 4 CMLR 25.................................. 221, 890, 892-3
Case C-54/99 Église de Scientologie [2000] ECR I-1335.............................664
Case C-55/99 Commission v France (registration for reagents) [2000] ECR I-1149......142, 427
Case C-58/99 Commission v Italian Republic [2000] ECR I-3811.....................665
Case C-74/99 Imperial Tobacco [2000] ECR I-8599..................................108
Case C-87/99 Zurstrassen [2000] ECR I-3337.......................................519
Case C-88/99 Roquette Frères [2000] ECR I-10465 ....293, 305
Case C-89/99 Schieving-Nijstad [2001] ECR I-5851 965-6
Joined Cases C-122/99 and C-125/99 D and Sweden v Council [2001] ECR I-4319....... 332, 366, 371
Case C-127/99 Commission v Italy [2001] ECR I-8305..............................142
Case C-135/99 Elsen [2000] ECR I-10409 464
Case C-143/99 Adria-Wien Pipeline and Wietersdorfer & Peggauer Zementwerke
   [2001] ECR I-836...855-6
Case C-144/99 Commission v Netherlands [2001] ECR I-3541 148
Case C-145/99 Commission v Italy [2002] ECR I-2235..............................538
Case C-157/99 Geraets-Smits and Peerbooms [2001] ECR I-5473......291, 378, 555, 564, 566, 572, 608
Case C-163/99 Commission v Portugal [2001] ECR I-2613 775
Case C-164/99 Portugaia Construções Lda [2002] ECR I-787 ....578, 590
Case C-178/99 Salzmann [2001] ECR I-4421 216
Case C-184/99 Grzelczyk [2001] ECR I-6193 .... 26, 273, 464-5, 475, 507
Case C-192/99 Kaur [2001] ECR I-1237...469
Case C-194/99 Thyssen Stahl v Commission [2003] ECR I-10821......................751
Case C-205/99 Anilir [2001] ECR I-1271..564

Joined Cases C-216 and 222/99 Prisco [2002] ECR I-6761 . . . . .293, 305
Case C-226/99 Siples [2001] ECR I-277 . . . . .304, 318
Case C-230/99 Commission v France [2001] ECR I-1169 139
Case C-234/99 Niels Nygård and Svineafgiftsfonden [2002] ECR I-3657 403
Joined Cases C-238/99, C-244/99, C-245/99, C-247/99, C-250/99 to C-252/99 and
    C-254/99, PVC Cartel II [2002] ECR I-8375 816
Case C-239/99 Nachi Europe v Hauptzollamt Krefeld [2001] ECR I-1197 . . . . 181, 201, 225
Case C-268/99 Jany and others [2001] ECR I-8615 . . . . 484, 503, 553, 555, 954
Case C-269/99 Kühne [2001] ECR I-9517 291
Case C-274/99 Connolly v Commission [2001] ECR I-1611 367
Case C-294/99 Athinaïki Zythopoiia [2001] ECR I-2797 586
Case C-306/99 BIAO [2003] ECR I-1 214
Case C-307/99 OGT [2001] ECR I-3159 962
Case C-309/99 Wouters and others [2002] ECR I-1577, [2002] 4 CMLR 913 . . . . .714, 734, 749–50,
                                                                                              755, 757, 763, 893
Case C-334/99 Germany v Commission [2003] ECR I-1139 859
Case C-340/99 TNT Traco v Poste Italiana [2001] ECR I-4109 . . . . 224, 883, 888
Case C-381/99 Brunnhofer [2001] ECR I-4961 265
Case C-385/99 Müller Fauré and van Riet [2003] ECR I-4509 378
Case C-390/99 Canal Satélite Digital SL v Administracíon General del Estado [2002] ECR I-607 427
Case C-400/99 Italy v Commission [2005] ECR I-3657 867
Case C-413/99 Baumbast v Secretary of State [2002] 3 CMLR 23;
    [2002] ECR I-7091 . . . . 26, 221, 327, 347, 365, 373, 466, 475, 477, 527
Joined Cases C-414/99-416/99 Zino Davidoff and Levi Strauss
    [2001] ECR I-8691 458
Case C-424/99 Commission v Austria [2001] ECR I-9285 290
Case C-439/99 Commission v Italy [2002] ECR I-305 541
Case C-443/99 Mercke, Sharp & Dohme [2002] ECR I-3703 459
Case C-453/99 Courage v Crehan [2001] ECR I-6297; [2001] 5 CMLR 28 . . . . .212, 303, 315, 318, 840–2
Case C-454/99 Commission v United Kingdom [2002] ECR I-10323 144
Case C-459/99 MRAX [2002] ECR I-6591 471
Case C-462/99 Connect Austria Gesellschaft für Telekommunikation GmbH v
    Telekom-Control-Kommission [2003] ECR I-5197 . . . . 292, 881, 883
Case C-475/99 Ambulanz Glöckner [2001] ECR I-8089; [2002] 4 CMLR 726 . . . . .714, 878, 880, 882–4, 887
Case C-478/99 Commission v Sweden [2002] ECR I-4147 148
Case C-481/99 Heininger [2001] ECR I-9945 . . . . 299–300, 302
Case C-482/99 France v Commission ('Stardust Marine') [2002] ECR I-4397 . . . . 851–2, 854
Case C-483/99 Commission v France [2002] ECR I-4781 . . . . .664, 666
Case C-497/99 Irish Sugar v Commission [2001] ECR I-5333 . . . . .766, 777–8, 780, 783, 786, 791, 794
Case C-503/99 Commission v Belgium [2002] ECR I-4809 . . . . .662, 666
Case C-516/99 Schmid [2002] ECR I-4573 215
Case C-1/00 Commission v France [2001] ECR I-9989 . . . . .151, 204
Case C-3/00 Denmark v Commission [2003] ECR I-2643 178
Case C-11/00 Commission v European Central Bank [2003] ECR I-7147 . . . . 42, 147, 202
Case C-13/00 Commission v Ireland (Berne Convention) [2002] ECR I-2923 941
Case C-17/00 De Coster [2001] ECR I-9445 . . . . .215–16, 555, 564, 566
Case C-20/00 and C-64/00 Bokker Aquaculture Ltd et al v Scottish Ministers
    [2003] ECR I-7411 344
Case C-24/00 Commission v France [2004] ECR I-1277 440
Joined Cases C-27/00 and C-122/00 R v Secretary of State, ex parte Omega Air
    [2002] ECR I-2569 179
Case C-50/00 Unión de Pequeños Agricultores v Council [2002] ECR I-6677 . . . . .159, 164, 173–4, 177, 226
Case C-52/00 Commission v France [2002] ECR I-3827 147
Case C-53/00 Ferring v ACOSS [2001] ECR I-9067 862
Case C-60/00 Carpenter [2002] ECR I-6279 . . . . .347–8, 365, 485, 524, 566
Case C-62/00 Marks & Spencer [2002] ECR I-6325 . . . . 260, 300, 305
Case C-76/00 Petrotub [2003] ECR I-79 962
Case C-86/00 HSB-Wohnbau [2001] ECR I-5353 216
Case C-92/00 Hospital Ingenieure [2002] ECR I-5553 291
Case C-94/00 Roquette Frères [2002] ECR I-9011 . . . . .343, 818
Case C-99/00 Lyckeskog [2002] ECR I-4839 223
Case C-101/00 Tulliasiamies and Siilin [2002] ECR I-7487 401
Case C-112/00 Schmidberger [2003] ECR I-5659 . . . . 349, 367, 430, 434, 673

Case C-114/00 Spain v Commission [2002] ECR I-7657 860
Case C-118/00 Larsy [2001] ECR I-5063 311
Case C-129/00 Commission v Italy [2003] ECR I-14637 . . . . 145, 306, 314
Case C-136/00 Danner [2002] ECR I-8147 579
Case C-140/00 Commission v United Kingdom [2003] ECR I-10379 144
Case C-142/00 Commission v Netherlandse Antillen [2003] ECR I-3483 . . . . .169, 175
Case C-143/00 Boehringer Ingelheim KG and Others [2002] ECR I-3759 459
Case C-153/00 der Weduwe [2002] ECR I-11319 221
Case C-159/00 Sapod Audic v Eco-Emballages [2002] ECR I-5031 . . . . 253–4, 280
Case C 160/00 Leitner [2002] ECR I 2631 302
Joined Cases C-204/00, C-205/00, C-211/00, C-213/00, C-217/00 & C-219/00 Aalborg
    Portland A/S v Commission [2004] ECR I-123; [2005] 4 CMLR 4 . . . . 739–40, 823
Case C-208/00 Überseering [2002] ECR I-9919 . . . . 542, 651–7
Case C-210/00 Käserei Champignon Hofmeister [2002] ECR I-6453 351
Case C-218/00 Cisal [2002] ECR I-691, [2002] 4 CMLR 24 878
Case C-233/00 Commission v France [2003] ECR I-6625 147–8
Case C-253/00 Muñoz [2002] ECR I-7289 . . . . 249–52, 258
Case C-255/00 Grundig Italiana [2002] ECR I-8003 300
Case C-257/00 Givane [2003] ECR I-345 480
Case C-275/00 EC v First NV and Franex NV [2002] ECR I-10943 323
Case C-277/00 Germany v Commission [2004] ECR I-3925 859
Case C-278/00 Greece v Commission [2000] ECR I-8787 858
Case C-279/00 Commission v Italy [2002] ECR I-1425 579
Case C-280/00 Altmark GmbH v Nahverkehrsgesellschaft Altmark GmbH ('Altmark')
    [2003] ECR I-7747, [2003] 3 CMLR 12 . . . . 851, 853, 863–4
Case C-294/00 Gräbner [2002] ECR I-6515 . . . . .565, 628
Case C-312/00 Commission v Camar [2002] ECR I-11355 . . . . .175, 196
Case C-324/00 Lankhorst-Hohorst GmbH v Finanzamt Steinfurt [2002] ECR I-11779 . . . . .587, 597
Case C-327/00 Santex [2003] ECR I-1877 299
Case C-336/00 Huber [2002] ECR I-7699 302
Case C-338/00 Volkswagen v Commission [2003] ECR I-9189 831
Case C-340/00 Commission v Cwick [2001] ECR I-10269 367
Case C-355/00 Freskot [2003] ECR I-5263 501
Case C-378/00 Commission v European Parliament and Council [2003] ECR I-937 . . . . 89, 161, 178–9
Case C-389/00 Commission v Germany (shipment of waste) [2003] ECR I-2001 393
Case C-409/00 Spain v Commission [2003] ECR I-1487 . . . . .855, 857
Case C-416/00 Morellato [2003] ECR I-8343 . . . . .423, 427
Joined Cases C-418/00 and C-419/00 Commission v France [2002] ECR I-3969 .142
Case C-436/00 X and Y [2002] ECR I-829 590
Case C-440/00 Kühne and Nagel [2004] ECR I-887 374
Case C-442/00 Caballero [2002] ECR I-11915 255
Case C-453/00 Kühne & Heitz [2004] ECR I-837 . . . . .228, 272
Case C-458/00 Commission v Luxembourg [2003] ECR I-1553 142
Joined Cases C-463/00 Commission v Spain and C-98/01 Commission v United Kingdom
    [2003] ECR I-4581 878–9
Joined Cases C-465/00, C-138/01 and C-139/01 Österreichischer Rundfunk and others
    [2003] ECR I-4989 . . . . 108, 344, 366
Case C-466/00 Kaba (Kaba II) [2003] ECR I-2219 . . . . .212, 353
Case C-469/00 Ravil [2003] ECR I-5053 434
Case C-471/00 P(R) Commission v Cambridge Healthcare Supplies [2001] ECR I-2865 204
Case C-472/00 Commission v Fresh Marine [2003] ECR I-7541 196
Case C-473/00 Cofidis [2002] ECR I-10875 301–2
Joined Cases C-480/00-482/00, C-484/00, C-489/00-491/00 and C-497/00-499/00 Azienda Agricola
    Ettore Ribaldi v Azienda di Stato per gli interventi nel mercato agricolo (AIMA), Ministero
    del Bilancio e della Programma Economica [2004] ECR I-2943 327
Joined Cases C-2 and 3/01 Bundesverband der Arzneimittel-Importeure EV and Commission v
    Bayer AG [2004] ECR I-23, [2004] 4 CMLR 653 733
Joined Cases C-34/01 to C-38/01 Enirisorse Spa [2003] ECR I-14243 . . . . .403, 446
Case C-58/01 Océ Van der Grinten NV [2003] ECR I-9809 586
Case C-63/01 Evans [2003] ECR I-14447 . . . . 290, 295, 301
Case C-76/01 Eurocoton and Others v Council [2003] ECR I-10091 158
Joined Cases C-83/01, C-93/01 and C-94/01 Chronopost v Ufex [2003] ECR I-6993 854–5
Case C-98/01 Commission v United Kingdom [2003] ECR I-4641 . . . . .666, 668

Case C-100/01 Olazabal [2002] ECR I-10981 481–2
Case C-101/01 Lindqvist [2003] ECR I-12971. 242
Case C-103/01 Commission v Germany [2003] ECR I-5369. 325
Case C-108/01 Asda Stores [2003] ECR I-5121. 272
Case C-109/01 Akrich [2003] ECR I-9607 . . . . .347–8, 470, 485, 488, 504, 540
Case C-114/01 AvestaPolarit Chrome Oy [2003] ECR I-8725 325
Case C-117/01 KB [2004] ECR I-541 . . . . 348, 365, 371–2
Case C-125/01 Pflücke [2003] ECR I-9375. . . . . .300, 318
Case C-126/01 GEMO [2003] ECR I-13769. 863
Case C-135/01 Commission v Germany [2003] ECR I-2837. 137
Case C-147/01 Weber's Wine World [2003] ECR I-11365 306
Case C-159/01 Netherlands v Commission [2004] ECR I-4461 857
Case C-160/01 Mau [2003] ECR I-4791 250
Case C-167/01 Inspire Art [2003] ECR I-10155 . . . . 648–9, 652–5
Case C-168/01 Bosal [2003] ECR I-9409 . . . . 573, 586, 588, 590
Case C-187/01 Gözütok [2005] ECR I-1345 381
Case C-192/01 Commission v Denmark [2003] ECR I-9693 436
Case C-194/01 Commission v Austria [2004] ECR I-4579 147
Case C-198/01 Consorzio Industrie Fiammiferi (CIF) v Autorità Garante della Concorrenza
  e del Mercato [2003] ECR I-8055 . . . . .216, 890
Case C-207/01 Altair Chimica [2003] ECR I-8875 244
Case C-215/01 Schnitzer [2003] ECR I-14847. . . . . 533, 554, 556–7
Case C-222/01 BAT v Hauptzollamt Krefeld [2004] ECR I-4683 214
Case C-224/01 Köbler v Austria [2003] ECR I-10239. 145, 223–4, 277, 311, 314
Case C-241/01 National Farmers' Union v Secrétariat Général du Gouvernement
  [2002] ECR I-9079. . . . . .151, 202
Case C-243/01 Gambelli [2003] ECR I-13031 532
Case C-252/01 Commission v Belgium [2003] ECR I-11859 147
Case C-257/01 Commission v Council [2005] ECR I-345. 88
Joined Cases C-261/01 and C-262/01 Van Calster [2003] ECR I-12249 . . . . 864, 867, 874
Joined Cases C-264/01, C-306/01, C-354/01 and C-355/01 AOK Bundesverband
  [2004] ECR I-2493. . . . . 715–16, 731, 876
Case C-276/01 Steffensen [2003] ECR I-3735 . . . . .290, 302
Case C-278/01 Commission v Spain [2003] ECR I-14141. 151
Case C-281/01 Commission v Council (Energy Star) [2002] ECR I-12049 945
Case C-296/01 Commission v France [2003] ECR I-13909. 147
Case C-304/01 Spain v Commission [2004] ECR I-7655. 179
Case C-308/01 GIL Insurance [2004] ECR I-4777 . . . . .855, 857
Case C-313/01 Morgenbesser [2003] ECR I-13467. 639
Case C-322/01 Deutscher Apothekerverband eV v 0800 DocMorris NV, Jacques Waterval
  [2003] ECR I-4887. . . . . 254, 421, 425, 590
Case C-338/01 Commission v Council [2004] ECR I-4829. 112
Case C-358/01 Commission v Spain [2003] ECR I-13145. . . . . .139, 419
Case C-362/01 Commission v Ireland [2002] ECR I-11433 138–9
Case C-380/01 Schneider [2004] ECR I-1389 291
Case C-383/01 De Danske Billimportører [2003] ECR I-6065 . . . . 401, 403, 446
Case C-387/01 Weigel [2004] ECR I-4981 . . . . .397, 519
Case C-388/01 Commission v Italy [2003] ECR I-721 . . . . 573, 579, 608
Joined Cases C-397-403/01 Pfeiffer [2004] ECR I-8835. . . . . 241, 248, 250, 267, 283
Case C-405/01 Colegio de Oficiales de la Marina Mercante Española [2003] ECR I-10391. . . . . .513, 571
Case C-413/01 Ninni-Orasche [2003] ECR I-13187. . . . . 473, 504, 506
Case C-418/01 IMS Health v Commission [2004] ECR I-5039, [2004] 4 CMLR 1543 . . . . 798, 802–4
Case C-434/01 Commission v United Kingdom [2003] ECR I-13239. 142
Case C-439/01 Cipra and Kvasnicka v Bezirkshauptmannschaft Mistelbach [2003] ECR I-745 . . . . . 212, 217, 220
Case C-463/01 Commission v Germany (reusable containers) [2004] ECR I-11705. 431
Case C-476/01 Felix Kapper [2004] ECR I-5205. 222
Joined Cases C-482/01 and 493/01 Orfanopoulos and Olivieri [2004] ECR I-5257 . . . . 475, 483–5
Case C-491/01 R v Secretary of State, ex parte British American Tobacco
  [2002] ECR I-11453. . . . . 116, 118, 124, 180, 226, 326
Case C-9/02 de Lasteyrie du Saillant [2004] ECR I-2409. . . . . 588, 590, 597
Case C-12/02 Grilli [2003] ECR I-11585 434
Case C-14/02 ATRAL SA V Belgium [2003] ECR I-4431 . . . . .248, 427
Case C-25/02 Rinke [2003] ECR I-8349 266

Case C-34/02 Pasquini [2003] ECR I-6515 . . . . 292, 294–5, 318
Case C-36/02 Omega Spielhallen- und Automatenaufstellungs-GmbH v Oberbürgermeisterin
    der Bundesstadt Bonn [2004] ECR I-9609. . . . . 349, 363, 558, 572–3
Case C-41/02 Commission v Netherlands [2004] ECR I-11375 439
Case C-47/02 Anker and others [2003] ECR I-10447. 513
Case C-60/02 Criminal Proceedings Against X [2004] ECR I-651. 243
Case C-71/02 Karner [2004] ECR I-3025 . . . . .427, 558
Case C-115/02 Rioglass SA [2003] ECR I-12705. 452
Case C-138/02 Collins [2004] ECR I-2703. . . . . 291, 467, 474, 506–7
Case C-148/02 Garcia Avello [2003] ECR I-11613 . . . . 469, 489–90, 501
Case C-157/02 Rieser Internationale Transporte [2004] ECR I-1477. . . . . .248, 263
Case C-167/02 Rothley [2004] ECR I-3149 175
Case C-171/02 Commission v Portugal [2004] ECR I-5645 . . . . 534, 549, 556
Case C-174/02 Streekgewest Westelijk Noord-Brabant [2005] ECR I-85 . . . . 252, 867, 874
Case C-175/02 Pape [2005] ECR I-127. . . . . .867, 874
Joined Cases C-189/02, C-202/02, C-205-C-208/02 and C-213/02 Dansk Rørindustri v
    Commission [2005] ECR I-5425. . . . . .242, 827
Case C-196/02 Nikoloudi [2005] ECR I-1789 284
Case C-200/02 Chen [2004] ECR I-9925 534
Case C-200/02 Chen and others [2004] ECR I-9925 . . . . 373, 469, 474
Case C-201/02 Wells [2004] ECR I-723 . . . . 250, 263–4, 267, 281
Case C-209/02 Commission v Austria [2004] ECR I-1211 140
Case C-222/02 Peter Paul [2004] ECR I-9425 310
Case C-224/02 Pusa [2004] ECR I-5763. 489
Case C-234/02 European Ombudsman v Lamberts [2004] ECR I-2803 190
Case C-239/02 Douwe Egberts NV v Westrom Pharma NV and Christophe Souranis and
    Douwe Egberts NV v FICS-World BVBA [2004] ECR I-7007 . . . . 327, 426, 552
Case C-245/02 Anheuser-Busch v Budvar [2004] ECR I-10989 . . . . .212, 958
Case C-258/02 Bactria v Commission [2003] ECR I-15105 171
Case C-263/02 Jégo-Quéré v Commission [2004] ECR I-3425. 159
Case C-276/02 Spain v Commission [2004] ECR I-8091. 855
Case C-286/02 Bellio Flli [2004] ECR I-3465. 964
Case C-289/02 AMOK [2003] ECR I-15059 640
Case C-293/02 Jersey Produce Marketing Organisation Ltd [2005] ECR I-9543 393–4
Case C-299/02 Commission v Kingdom of the Netherlands [2004] ECR I-9761. 548
Case C-304/02 Commission v France [2005] ECR I-6263 151
Case C-309/02 Radlberger Getränkegesellschaft mbH & Co and S. Spitz KG [2004] ECR I-11763 431
Case C-313/02 Wippel [2004] ECR I-9483. 248
Case C-319/02 Manninen [2004] ECR I-7477. 596
Case C-334/02 Commission v France [2004] ECR I-2229. 593
Case C-345/02 Pearle v Hoofdbedrijfschap Ambachten [2004] ECR I-7139, [2004] 3 CMLR 9 851–2
Case C-350/02 Commission v Netherlands [2004] ECR I-6213 140
Case C-365/02 Lindorfs [2004] ECR I-7183. 519
Case C-377/02 Van Parys [2005] ECR I-1465 958
Case C-384/02 Allan Bang [2005] ECR I-9939 243
Case C-386/02 Baldinger [2004] ECR I-8411 . . . . .490, 519
Joined Cases C-387/02, C-391/02 and C-403/02 Berlusconi and others
    [2005] ECR I-3565. . . . . 243, 267, 283, 381
Case C-400/02 Merida [2004] ECR I-847. 501
Case C-416/02 Commission v Spain [2005] ECR I-7482. 381
Case C-429/02 Bacardi France [2004] ECR I-6613 572
Case C-434/02 Arnold André [2004] ECR I-11825. 124
Case C-438/02 Hanner [2005] ECR I-4551 . . . . 448, 876, 889
Case C-442/02 CaixaBank France [2004] ECR I-8961 . . . . 550–2, 591, 659
Case C-456/02 Trojani [2004] ECR I-7574. . . . . 466, 505, 532, 557
Case C-457/02 Niselli [2004] ECR I-10853 220
Case C-16/03 Peak Holding [2004] ECR I-11313 457
Case C-20/03 M Burmanjer and others [2005] ECR I-4133 424
Case C-53/03 Syfait v GlaxoSmithKline [2005] ECR I-4609 . . . . .215, 803
Case C-65/03 Commission v Belgium [2004] ECR I-6427 105
Case C-70/03 Commission v Spain [2004] ECR I-7999. 148
Case C-72/03 Carbonati Apuani Srl [2004] ECR I-8027 394

Case C-78/03 Commission v Aktionsgemeinschaft Recht und Eigentum [2005] ECR I-10737;
  [2006] 2 CMLR 48 871–2
Case C-94/03 Commission v Council (PIC Convention) [2006] ECR I-107 . . . . .112, 945
Case C-105/03 Pupino [2005] ECR I-5285. . . . . 241, 243, 269–70, 290
Case C-136/03 Dörr and Ünal [2005] ECR I-4759 487
Case C-140/03 Commission v Greece [2005] ECR I-3177. 576
Case C-143/03 Commission v Italy, 14 October 2004, unrep 419
Case C-147/03 Commission v Austria [2005] ECR I-5969 105
Case C-166/03 Commission v France [2004] ECR I-6535. 414
Case C-172/03 Heiser [2005] ECR I-1627 . . . . 850, 853, 855–6, 864
Case C-173/03 Traghetti del Mediterraneo [2006] ECR I-5177 314
Case C-176/03 Commission v Council (Criminal liability for offences against the environment)
  [2005] ECR I-7879. . . . . 112, 317, 381, 908
Case C-178/03 Commission v Parliament and Council [2006] ECR I-107. . . . . 112–13, 945
Case C-198/03 Commission v CEVA Santé Animale [2005] ECR I-6257. 196
Case C-205/03 FENIN v Commission [2006] ECR I-6295; [2006] 5 CMLR 7 . . . . 714, 717, 876
Case C-208/03 Le Pen v European Parliament, Judgment of 7 July 2005. .158
Case C-209/03 Bidar [2005] ECR I-2119 . . . . 273, 467, 476, 482
Case C-210/03 Swedish Match [2004] ECR I-11893. . . . . .108, 124
Case C-212/03 Commission v France (import licences for medicinal products)
  [2005] ECR I-4213. 438
Case C-213/03 Syndicat professionel coordination des pêcheurs de l'étang de
  Berre et de la région [2004] ECR I-7357 955
Case C-215/03 Oulane [2005] ECR I-1215. 471
Case C-231/03 Coname [2005] ECR I-7287. 546–7
Case C-235/03 QDQ Media [2005] ECR I-1937 . . . . .267, 284
Case C-239/03 Commission v France (Etang de Berre) [2004] ECR I-9325. 941
Case C-244/03 France v Parliament and Council [2005] ECR I-4021 180
Case C-266/03 Commission v Luxembourg [2005] ECR I-4805 934
Case C-276/03 Scott v Commission [2005] ECR I-8437 869
Case C-278/03 Commission v Italy (State Schools) [2005] ECR I-3747 .517
Case C-301/03 Italy v Commission (Judgment of 1 December 2005) 158
Case C-319/03 Briheche [2004] ECR I-8807 372
Case C-320/03 Commission v Austria (motorway ban) [2005] ECR I-9871. 431
Case C-350/03 Schulte [2005] ECR I-9215. . . . . .241, 284
Case C-380/03 Germany v Parliament and Council [2006] ECR I-11573. .108
Case C-397/03 Archer Daniels Midland v Commission [2006] ECR I-4429; [2006] 5 CMLR 4 828
Case C-403/03 Schempp [2005] ECR I-6421 519
Case C-408/03 Commission v Belgium (citizenship) [2006] ECR I-2647. .474
Case C-411/03 SEVIC Systems [2005] ECR 10805. 661
Case C-415/03 Commission v Greece [2005] ECR I-3875. 870
Case C-433/03 Commission v Germany [2005] ECR I-6985. 934
Case C-436/03 Parliament v Council [2006] ECR I-3733 . . . . .109, 678
Case C-443/03 Leffler [2005] ECR I-9611 302
Case C-445/03 Commission v Luxembourg [2004] ECR I-10191 . . . . .556, 660
Case C-446/03 Marks & Spencer [2005] ECR I-10837. . . . . 589, 592–5, 648
Case C-451/03 Servizi Ausiliari Dottori Commercialisti v Calafiori
  [2006] ECR I-2941. . . . . 549, 573, 863–4, 882
Case C-453/03 ABNA [2005] ECR I-10423 124
Case C-458/03 Parking Brixen [2005] ECR I-8585. 547
Case C-461/03 Gaston Schul Douane-expediteur BV [2005] ECR I-10513 .226
Case C-469/03 Miraglia [2005] ECR I-2009. 381
Case C-470/03 AGM-COS.MET [2007] ECR I-2749 . . . . .311, 313
Case C-495/03 Intermodal Transports (Judgment of 15 September 2005) .224
Case C-497/03 Commission v Austria (sale by mail), 18 November 2004, not published 425
Case C-503/03 Commission v Spain (Schengen Information System) [2006] ECR I-1097 . . . . .471, 484
Case C-511/03 Ten Kate [2005] ECR I-8979 . . . . .187, 310
Case C-514/03 Commission v Spain [2006] ECR I-963. . . . . 534, 549, 556
Case C-520/03 Olaso Valero [2004] ECR I-12065. 255
Case C-540/03 Parliament v Council (family reunification) [2006] ECR I-5769 373
Case C-551/03 General Motors BV v Commission [2006] ECR I-3173; [2006] 5 CMLR 1 743
Case C-3/04 Poseidon Chartering (Judgment of 16 March 2006). 214
Case C-15/04 Koppensteiner [2005] ECR I-4855 292

Case C-27/04 Commission v Council [2004] ECR I-6649...158
Case C-36/04 Spain v Council (Judgment of 30 March 2006).......................................180
Case C-49/04 Commission v Germany [2007] ECR I-6095..556
Case C-66/04 United Kingdom v Parliament and Council [2005] ECR I-10553 109
Case C-74/04 Commission v Volkswagen [2006] ECR I-6585; [2008] 4 CMLR 16.........................733
Joined Cases C-94/04 Cipolla v Fazari and C-202/04 Macrino, Capodarte v Meloni
    [2006] ECR I-11421; [2007] 4 CMLR 8 ....551, 605, 893
Case C-95/04 British Airways v Commission [2007] ECR I-2331; [2007] 4 CMLR 22.........766, 782, 793, 795
Case C-96/04 Standesamt Stadt Niebüll [2006] ECR I-3561 490
Case C-105/04 Nederlandse Federatieve Vereniging voor de Groothandel op Elektrotechnisch Gebied v
    Commission [2006] ECR I-8725; [2006] 5 CMLR 22.......................................743
Case C-109/04 Kranemann [2005] ECR I-493..522
Case C-114/04 Commission v Germany (parallel imports of phytosanitary products),
    14 July 2005, unpublished..431
Case C-119/04 Commission v Italy (pending)..152
Case C-122/04 Commission v Council and Parliament [2006] ECR I-2001.................................89
Case C-142/04 Aslanidou [2005] ECR I-7181 240
Case C-144/04 Mangold [2005] ECR I-9981 ....222, 248, 255–6, 265–7, 276, 284,
                                                            334, 339, 344–5, 371, 374, 608
Case C-145/04 Spain v United Kingdom [2006] ECR I-7917 ....58, 136, 356, 494
Case C-148/04 Unicredito Italiano Spa [2005] ECR I-11137..332
Joined Cases C-154/04 and 155/04 Alliance for Natural Health [2005] ECR I-6451 ....88, 116, 118
Case C-158/04 Alfa Vita [2006] ECR I-8135 427
Case C-168/04 Commission v Austria [2006] ECR I-9041 556
Case C-170/04 Rosengren [2007] ECR I-4071..409
Case C-194/04 Nevedi [2005] ECR I-10423..228
Case C-196/04 Cadbury Schweppes [2006] ECR I-7995 593
Case C-212/04 Adeneler [2006] ECR I-6057...241, 248
Case C-217/04 United Kingdom v Parliament and Council [2006] ECR I-3771 109
Case C-222/04 Ministero dell'Economia e delle Finanze v Cassa di Risparmio di Firenze SpA
    [2006] ECR I-289; [2008] 1 CMLR 28 ....713, 715
Case C-234/04 Kapferer [2006] ECR I-2585 ....228, 272
Case C-237/04 Enirisorse v Sotacarbo [2006] ECR I-2843 ....851, 856, 863, 878–80
Case C-244/04 Commission v Germany [2006] ECR I-885..556
Case C-258/04 Ioannidis [2005] ECR I-8275...467, 507
Case C-289/04 Showa Denko v Commission [2006] ECR I-5859.......................................832
Joined Cases C-295-298/04 Manfredi v Lloyd Adriatico Assicurazioni SpA
    [2006] ECR I-6619; [2006] 5 CMLR 17 ....293, 300–1, 315, 840, 842
Case C-300/04 Eman and Sevinger [2006] ECR I-8055..58, 302, 493
Case C-301/04 Commission v SGL Carbon [2006] ECR I-5915...816
Case C-308/04 SGL Carbon AG v Commission [2006] ECR I-5977; [2006] 5 CMLR 16...............829, 832
Case C-311/04 Algemene Scheeps Agentuur Dordrecht [2006] ECR I-609 964
Case C-313/04 Egenberger [2006] ECR I-633..962
Case C-316/04 Stichting Zuid-Hollandse Milieufederatie [2005] ECR I-9759..........................248
Case C-328/04 Vajnai [2005] ECR I-8577 214
Joined Cases C-338/04, C-359/04 and C-360/04 Placanica and Others [2007] ECR I-891..........549, 564, 580
Case C-341/04 Eurofood IFSC [2006] ECR I-3813..821
Case C-344/04 European Low Fares Airline Association [2006] ECR I-403.............75, 124, 226, 960
Case C-347/04 Rewe Zentralfinanz [2007] ECR I-2647..594–5
Case C-348/04 Boehringer Ingelheim [2007] ECR I-3391...459
Case C-355/04 Segi and Others v Council [2007] ECR I-1657..353, 907
Case C-366/04 Schwarz [2005] ECR I-10139..436
Case C-368/04 Transalpine Ölleitung in Österreich [2006] ECR I-9957...............................252
Case C-372/04 Watts [2006] ECR I-4325 ....378, 572
Case C-379/04 Dahms [2005] ECR I-8723...252
Case C-386/04 Stauffer [2006] ECR I-8203 559
Joined Cases C-392 and 422/04 i-21 Germany [2006] ECR I-8559 ....272, 294
Case C-406/04 De Cuyper [2006] ECR I-6947 489
Case C-411/04 Salzgitter Mannesmann GmbH (formerly Mannesmannrohren-Werke AG)
    v Commission [2007] ECR I-959; [2007] 4 CMLR 17 ....821, 823
Case C-421/04 Marazan Concord [2006] ECR I-2303 452
Case C-430/04 Finanzamt Eisleben v Feuerbesttungsverein Halle [2006] ECR I-4999...................252
Case C-441/04 A-Punkt Schmuckhandels GmbH v C Schmidt [2006] ECR I-2093 424

Case C-446/04 Test Claimants in the FII Group Litigation [2006] ECR I-11753 586
Case C-470/04 N v Inspecteur van de Belastingdienst Oost/kantoor Almelo [2006] ECR I-7409. 302
Case C-479/04 Laserdisken v Kulturministeriet [2006] ECR I-8089 24
Case C-506/04 Wilson [2006] ECR I-8613. . . . . .290, 643
Case C-519/04 Meca-Medina v Commission [2006] ECR I-6991; [2006] 5 CMLR 18 . . . . .750, 763
Case C-524/04 Test Claimants in the Thin Cap Litigation [2007] ECR I-2107. .582, 587
Case C-526/04 Laboratoires Boiron [2006] ECR I-7529 302
Case C-6/05 Medipac-Kazantzidis v Venizelio-Pananio [2007] ECR I-4557 263
Case C-10/05 Mattern and Cikotik [2006] ECR I-3145 476
Case C-20/05 Schwibbert [2007] ECR I-9447 280
Case C-54/05 Commission v Finland (transfer licence for cars) [2007] ECR I-2473. 427
Case C-64/05 Sweden v Commission [2007] ECR I-11389 119
Case C-77/05 United Kingdom v Council [2007] ECR I-11459 127
Case C-91/05 Commission v Council [2008] ECR I-3651. 908
Case C-97/05 Gattoussi [2006] ECR I-11917. 955
Case C-110/05 Commission v Italy (trailers) [2009] ECR I-519. 428
Case C-112/05 Commission v Germany [2007] ECR I-8995. . . . . .666, 668
Case C-119/05 Lucchini [2007] ECR I-6199 302
Case C-134/05 Commission v Italy [2007] ECR I-6251 603
Case C-137/05 United Kingdom v Council [2007] ECR I-11593 127
Case C-142/05 Mickelsson and Roos [2009] ECR I-4273 428
Case C-167/05 Commission v Sweden [2008] ECR I-2127 399–400
Case C-173/05 Commission v Italy (Sicilian environmental tax) [2007] ECR I-4917. .395
Case C-192/05 Tas-Hagen and Tas [2006] ECR I-10451 . . . . .489, 519
Case C-193/05 Commission v Luxembourg [2006] ECR I-8673 644
Case C-208/05 ITC Innovative Technology Centre [2007] ECR I-181 . . . . 251–2, 521
Case C-217/05 Confederación Española de Empresarios de Estaciones de Servicio
  [2006] ECR I-11987; [2007] 4 CMLR 5 732
Joined Cases C-222-225/05 van der Weerd [2007] ECR I-4233 302
Case C-231/05 OY AA [2007] ECR I-6373. . . . . 585, 589, 594–5
Case C-238/05 ASNEF-EQUIFAX Servicios de Informacion sobre Solvencia y Credito SL v
  Asociacion de Usuarios de Servicios Bancarios (AUSBANC) [2006] ECR I-11125;
  [2007] 4 CMLR 6 . . . . 719, 750–2
Case C-276/05 Wellcome Foundation [2008] ECR I-10479. 459
Case C-278/05 Robins [2007] ECR I-1059 311
Case C-297/05 Commission v Netherlands (road worthiness test for imported used cars)
  [2007] ECR I-7467. 427
Case C-303/05 Advocaten voor de Wereld [2007] ECR I-3633. 381
Case C-318/05 Commission v Germany [2007] ECR I-6952. 555
Case C-321/05 Kofoed [2007] ECR I-5795. . . . . .240, 266
Case C-341/05 Laval un Partneri [2007] ECR I-11767. . . . . .349–50, 375, 431, 501, 556, 581
Case C-379/05 Amurta [2007] ECR I-9569 . . . . .586, 592
Case C-389/05 Commission v France [2008] ECR I-5337. . . . . .541, 549
Case C-392/05 Alevizos [2007] ECR I-3505. 512
Case C-393/05 Commission v Austria [2007] ECR I-10195 . . . . .570, 580
Joined Cases C-402 and 415/05 Kadi [2008] ECR I-635 369
Case C-402/05 Kadi v Council and Commission [2008] ECR I-6321 907
Case C-403/05 Parliament v Commission [2007] ECR I-9045 86
Case C-404/05 Commission v Germany [2007] ECR I-10239 . . . . .570, 580
Case C-411/05 Palacios de la Villa [2007] ECR I-8531. 266
Case C-421/05 City Motors Groep [2007] ECR I-653 . . . . .302, 315
Case C-422/05 Commission v Belgium [2007] ECR I-4749 248
Case C-426/05 Tele2 Telecommunication [2008] ECR I-685 . . . . 251–2, 289
Case C-429/05 Rampion and Godard [2007] ECR I-8017. 302
Case C-431/05 Merck Genéricos [2007] ECR I-7001 966
Case C-432/05 Unibet [2007] ECR I-2271 . . . . 290, 295, 305
Case C-438/05 International Transport Workers' Federation and The Finnish
  Seamen's Union v Viking Line et al [2007] ECR I-10779. . . . . 349–50, 375, 387, 431, 434,
  501–2, 553, 577, 672
Case C-440/05 Commission v Council (Ship Source Pollution) [2007] ECR I-9097. . . . . 112, 317, 908
Case C-446/05 Doulamis v Union des Dentistes et Stomatologistes de Belgique (UPR)
  [2008] ECR I-1377; [2008] 5 CMLR 4 891
Joined Cases C-447/05 and C-448/05 Thomson and Vestel France [2007] ECR I-2049 964

Case C-465/05 Commission v Italy [2007] ECR I-11091 603
Case C-467/05 Dell'Orto [2007] ECR I-5557 243
Case C-2/06 Kempter [2008] ECR I-411 272
Case C-3/06 Group Danone v Commission, [2007] ECR I-1331; [2007] 4 CMLR 18 829
Joined Cases C-11 and 12/06 Morgan [2007] ECR I-9161 475
Joined Cases C-14/06 and C-295/06 Parliament and Denmark v Commission [2008] ECR I-1649 86
Case C-55/06 Arcor [2008] ECR I-2931 . . . . 252, 289, 302
Case C-80/06 Carp [2007] ECR I-4473 . . . . .256, 268
Joined Cases C-120 and C-121/06 FIAMM v Council and Commission [2008] ECR I-6513 197
Case C-125/06 Infront [2008] ECR I-1451 171
Case C-133/06 Parliament v Council [2008] ECR I-3189 88
Case C-143/06 Ludwigs-Apotheke [2007] ECR I-9623 424
Joined Cases C-147/06 and C-148/06 SECAP [2008] ECR I-3565 . . . . .547, 596
Case C-161/06 Skoma-Lux [2007] ECR I-10841 272
Case C-181/06 Deutsche Lufthansa [2007] ECR I-5903 . . . . .24, 99
Case C-199/06 CELF and Ministre de la culture et de la Communication v SIDE [2008] ECR I-469 . . . . .302, 873
Case C-205/06 Commission v Austria [2009] ECR I-1301 929
Case C-210/06 Cartesio [2008] ECR I-9641 . . . . .655, 657
Case C-220/06 Asociación Profesional de Empresas de Reparto y Manipulado de
   Correspondencia [2007] ECR I-12175 546
Case C-221/06 Stadtgemeinde Frohnleiten and Gemeindebetriebe Frohnleiten GmbH
   [2007] ECR I-9643 397
Case C-241/06 Lämmerzahl [2007] ECR I-8415 299
Case C-242/06 Sahin [2009] ECR I-8415 954
Case C-244/06 Dynamic Medien [2008] ECR I-505 419
Case C-249/06 Commission v Sweden [2009] ECR I-1335 929
Case C-250/06 United Pan-Europe Communications Belgium and Others [2007] ECR I-11135 564
Case C-265/06 Commission v Portugal (tinted car windows) [2008] ECR I-2245 .427–8
Case C-267/06 Maruko [2008] ECR I-1757 . . . . .266, 371
Case C-268/06 Impact [2008] ECR I-2483 . . . . .268, 295
Case C-279/06 CEPSA Estaciones de Servicios SA v LV Tobar e Hijos SL [2008] ECR I-6681;
   [2008] 5 CMLR 19 732
Case C-280/06 Autorita Garante della Concorrenza e del Mercato v Ente Tabacchi
   Italiani-ETI SpA [2007] ECR I-10893; [2008] 4 CMLR 11 721
Case C-284/06 Burda [2008] ECR I-4571 586
Case C-301/06 Ireland v Parliament and Council [2009] ECR I-593 108
Case C-303/06 Coleman [2008] ECR I-5603 371
Case C-308/06 'Intertanko' [2008] ECR I-4057 . . . . 960–1, 967
Case C-309/06 Marks & Spencer [2008] ECR I-2283 305
Case C-345/06 Heinrich [2009] ECR I-1659 272
Case C-352/06 Bosmann [2008] ECR I-3827 522
Case C-353/06 Grunkin and Paul [2008] ECR I-7639 490
Case C-409/06 Winner Wetten, 8 September 2010, nyr 273, 532
Case C-411/06 Commission v Parliament and Council (Waste Shipments) [2009] ECR I-7585 . . . . .112, 945
Case C-414/06 Lidl Belgium [2008] ECR I-3601 595
Case C-427/06 Bartsch [2008] ECR I-7245 . . . . .256, 265
Case C-445/06 Danske Slagterier [2009] ECR I-2119 . . . . 299–300, 312–13
Case C-450/06 Varec SA v Belgium [2008] ECR I-581 . . . . .290, 819
Case C-452/06 Synthon [2008] ECR I-7681 311
Case C-455/06 Heemskerk [2008] ECR I-8763 302
Case C-460/06 Paquay [2007] ECR I-8511 294
Case C-487/06 British Aggregates Associaton v Commission (BAA)[2009] 2 CMLR 10 872
Case C-499/06 Nerkowska [2008] ECR I-3993 . . . . .489, 519
Case C-500/06 Corporación Dermoestética SA v To Me Group Advertising Media
   [2008] ECR I-5785 565
Joined Cases C-501/06, C-513/06, C-515/06 and C-519/06 GlaxoSmithKline Services
   unlimited v Commission [2009] ECR I-9291; [2010] 4 CMLR 2 742–3
Case C-510/06 Archer Daniels Midland v Commission [2009] ECR I-1843; [2009] 4 CMLR 20 828
Case C-511/06 Archer Daniels Midland Co v Commission [2009] ECR I-5843; [2009] 5 CMLR 15 821–2
Case C-518/06 Commission v Italy [2009] ECR I-3491 . . . . .564, 602
Case C-531/06 Commission v Italy [2009] ECR I-4103 . . . . .549, 576
Case C-13/07 Commission v Council (Vietnam), 9 November 2010, nyr 930, 935, 938–9, 946
Case C-33/07 Jipa [2008] ECR I-5157 483

Case C-47/07 Masdar v Commission [2008] ECR I-9761 197
Case C-49/07 Motosykletistiki Omospondia Ellados Npid v Ellinko Dimosio [2008] ECR I-4863;
  [2008] 5 CMLR 11 . . . . 715, 883, 885
Case C-52/07 Kanal 5 Ltd v Foreningen Svenska Tonsattares Internationella Musikbyra
  (STIM) upa [2008] ECR I-9275 . . . . .787, 790
Case C-54/07 Feryn [2008] ECR I-5187 371
Joined Cases C-55 and C-56/07 Michaeler [2008] ECR I-3135 266
Case C-73/07 Satakunnan Markkinapörssi and Satamedia [2008] ECR I-9831 266
Case C-94/07 Raccanelli v Max-Planck- Gesellschaft zur Förderung der Wissenschaften eV
  [2008] ECR I-5939 502–3
Case C-101/07 Coop de France Betail et Viande (formerly Fédération Nationale de la
  Coopération Betail et Viande (FNCBV)) v Commission [2008] ECR I-10193;
  [2009] 4 CMLR 15 827
Case C-113/07 Selex sistemi Integrati SpA v Commission of the European Communities
  [2009] ECR I-2207 715
Case C-118/07 Commission v Finland [2009] ECR I-10889 929
Case C-121/07 Commission v France [2008] ECR I-9159 151
Case C-125/07 Erste Group Bank AG v Commission [2009] ECR I-8681; [2010] 5 CMLR 9 719
Case C-141/07 Commission v Germany (supply of medicinal products to hospitals)
  [2008] ECR I-6935 425
Joined Cases C-152/07-154/07 Arcor [2008] ECR I-5959 263
Case C-155/07 Parliament v Council (EIB Guarantee) [2008] ECR I-8103 112
Case C-157/07 Krankenheim Ruhesitz am Wannsee-Seniorenheimstatt [2008] ECR I-8061 592
Case C-158/07 Förster [2008] ECR I-8507 . . . . 467, 475–6, 482
Case C-161/07 Commission v Austria [2008] ECR I-671 545
Case C-166/07 Parliament v Council [2009] ECR I-7135 . . . . .24, 112
Case C-169/07 Hartlauer [2009] ECR I-1721 549
Joined Cases C-171/07 and C-172/07 Apothekerkammer des Saarlandes and Others
  [2009] ECR I-4171 . . . . .549, 576
Case C-202/07 France Télécom SA v Commission [2009] ECR I-2369; [2009] 4 CMLR 25 . . . . 785, 789, 792
Case C-205/07 Gysbrechts and Santurel Inter [2008] ECR I-4997 434
Case C-209/07 Competition Authority v Beef Industry Development Society Ltd [2008]
  ECR I-8637; [2009] 4 CMLR 6 742
Case C-246/07 Commission v Sweden (PFOS), 20 April 2010 934
Case C-260/07 Pedro IV Servicios SL v Total Espana SA [2009] ECR I-2437; [2009] 5 CMLR 1 761
Joined Cases C-261/07 and C-299/07 VTB-VAB [2009] ECR I-2949 248
Case C-269/07 Commission v Germany [2009] ECR I-7811 547
Case C-282/07 Truck Center [2008] ECR I-10767 585
Case C-303/07 Aberdeen Property Fininvest [2009] ECR I-5145 . . . . .586, 592
Case C-306/07 Ruben Andersen [2008] ECR I-10279 302
Case C-319/07 3F v Commission [2009] ECR I-5963; [2009] 3 CMLR 40 873
Case C-322/07 Papierfabrik August Koehler AG v Commission [2009] ECR I-7191;
  [2009] 5 CMLR 20 . . . . 815, 821–2
Case C-336/07 Kabel Deutschland [2008] ECR I-10889 580
Case C-350/07 Kattner Stahlbau GmbH v Maschinenbau- und Metall- Berufsgenossenschaft
  [2009] ECR I-1513; [2009] 2 CMLR 51 . . . . 581, 716, 876
Case C-369/07 Commission v Greece [2009] ECR I-5703 152
Case C-370/07 Commission v Council [2009] ECR I-8917 112
Case C-377/07 STEKO [2009] ECR I-299 587
Joined Cases C-378-380/07 Angelidaki [2009] ECR I-3071 . . . . .250, 268
Case C-388/07 Age Concern England [2009] ECR I-1569 371
Case C-404/07 Katz [2008] ECR I-7607 243
Case C-418/07 Papillon [2008] ECR I-8947 592
Case C-421/07 Damgaard [2009] ECR I-2629 242
Case C-429/07 Inspecteur van de Belastingdienst v X BV [2009] 5 CMLR 12 839
Case C-440/07 Schneider v Commission [2009] ECR I-6413 197
Case C-441/07 Commission v Alrosa Co Ltd [2011] All E.R. (EC) 1; [2010] 5 CMLR 11 . . . . .369, 825
Case C-465/07 Elgafaji [2009] ECR I-921 363
Case C-478/07 Budeinvcircjovický Budvar [2009] ECR I-7721 302
Case C-518/07 Commission v Germany (Judgment of 9 March 2010) 119
Case C-531/07 Fachverband der Buch- und Medienwirtschaft [2009] ECR I-3717 .428
Case C-550/07 Akzo Nobel Chemicals (Judgment of 14 September 2010) 101, 820, 923
Case C-555/07 Kücükdeveci (Judgment of 19 January 2010) 255, 265, 284, 334, 345, 371

Case C-558/07 SPCM [2009] ECR I-5783 124
Case C-562/07 Commission v Spain [2009] ECR I-9553. 323
Case C-567/07 Wongingstichting Sint Servatius [2009] ECR I-9021. 665
Case C-568/07 Commission v Greece [2009] ECR I-4505. 152
Joined Cases C-570 and 571/07 Blanco Pérez and Chao Gómez, 1 June 2010, nyr 349, 541
Case C-2/08 Fallimento Olimpiclub [2009] ECR I-7501 272
Case C-8/08 T-Mobile Netherlands BV v Raad van Bestuur van de Nederlandse
    Mededingingsautoriteit [2009] ECR I-4529; [2009] 5 CMLR 11 . . . . 735–7, 740, 743, 751
Case C-12/08 Mono Car Styling [2009] ECR I-6653 251
Case C-18/08 Foselev Sud-Ouest [2008] ECR I 8745. 268
Case C-19/08 Petrosian [2009] ECR I-495. 301
Joined Cases C-22/08 and 23/08 Vatsouras and Koupatantze [2009] ECR I-4585 . . . . 474, 482, 507–8
Case C-40/08 Asturcom [2009] ECR I-9579 272
Case C-46/08 Carmen Media Group, 8 September 2010, nyr 554
Case C-58/08 Vodafone and others, 8 June 2010, nyr. 108, 118, 124, 324
Case C-63/08 Pontin [2009] ECR I-10467 . . . . 294, 300, 302
Case C-64/08 Engelmann, 9 September 2010, nyr 546, 549, 574, 604, 649
Case C-69/08 Visciano [2009] ECR I-6741 300
Case C-73/08 Bressol, 13 April 2010, nyr 105, 475
Case C-75/08 Mellor [2009] ECR I-3799 291
Case C-97/08 Akzo Nobel v Commission [2009] ECR I-8237; [2009] 5 CMLR 23 . . . . .721, 731
Case C-101/08 Audiolux [2009] ECR I-9823. . . . . 255–6, 267
Case C-103/08 Gottwald [2009] ECR I-9117. 608
Case C-109/08 Commission v Greece [2009] ECR I-4657. 152
Case C-118/08 Transportes Urbanos y Servicios Generales, 26 January 2010, nyr 293, 313
Case C-127/08 Metock [2008] ECR I-6241 540
Case C-127/08 Metock and others [2008] ECR I-6241. 470
Case C-135/08 Rottmann, 2 March 2010, nyr 469
Case C-147/08 Römer, pending. 266
Case C-153/08 Commission v Spain [2009] ECR I-9735. 580
Case C-154/08 Commission v Spain, 12 November 2009, nyr 314
Case C-160/08 Commission v Germany, 29 April 2010, nyr. 570
Case C-171/08 Commission v Portugal, 8 July 2010, nyr. 669
Case C-182/08 Glaxo Wellcome [2009] ECR I-8591. . . . . .593, 663
Case C-227/08 Martín Martín, 17 December 2009. 267
Case C-237/08 Retuerta, 11 May 2010, nyr 964
Case C-243/08 Pannon [2009] ECR I-4713 302
Case C-263/08 Djurgården-Lilla Värtans Miljöskyddsförening [2009] ECR I-9967 251
Case C-303/08 Bozkurt, 22 December 2010, nyr. 346
Case C-304/08 Plus Warenhandelsgesellschaft, 14 January 2010, nyr 248
Case C-310/08 Ibrahim, 23 February 2010, nyr. 373, 477, 527
Case C-311/08 SGI, 21 January 2010, nyr. 593
Case C-314/08 Filipiak [2009] ECR I-11049 271–2
Joined Cases C-317/08, C-318/08, C-319/08 and C-320/08 Alassini, 18 March 2010, nyr 244
Case C-324/08 Makro Zelfbedieningsgroothandel and Others [2009] ECR I-10019 458
Case C-325/08 Olympique Lyonnais SASP v Bernard, 16 March 2010, nyr 521–2
Case C-333/08 Commission v France (processing aids), 28 January 2010, nyr 427
Case C-337/08 X Holding, 25 February 2010, nyr. 649
Case C-345/08 Krzysztof Pesacutela v Justizministerium Mecklenburg-Vorpommern
    [2009] ECR I-11677. 627
Case C-384/08 Attanasio, 11 March 2010, nyr. 552, 576, 604
Case C-386/08 Brita, 25 February 2010, nyr 392, 954
Case C-399/08 Commission v Deutsche Post AG [2011] 1 CMLR 14. . . . . .851, 864
Case C-406/08 Uniplex, 28 January 2010, nyr 300
Case C-407/08 Knauf Gips v Commission, 1 July 2010, nyr 379, 720, 832
Case C-413/08 Lafarge SA v Commission [2010] 5 CMLR 10 . . . . 739, 829, 831
Case C-428/08 Monsanto, 6 July 2010, nyr. 964
Case C-438/08 Commission v Portugal [2009] ECR I-10219 . . . . 549, 569–70
Case C-446/08 Solgar Vitamin France and others, 29 April 2010, nyr. 325
Case C-456/08 Commission v Ireland, 28 January 2010, nyr 300
Case C-458/08 Commission v Portugal,18 November 2010, nyr 606
Case C-470/08 van Dijk, 21 January 2010, nyr. 197
Case C-480/08 Teixeirai, 23 February 2010, nyr 373, 477, 527

Case C-482/08 United Kingdom v Council, 26 October 2010, nyr. 127
Case C-486/08 Zentralbetriebsrat der Landeskrankenhäuser Tirol, 22 April 2010, nyr .268
Case C-510/08 Mattner, 22 April 2010, nyr 596
Case C-515/08 Palhota and Others, 7 October 2010, nyr. 660
Case C-540/08 Mediaprint, 9 November 2010, nyr. 102
Case C-542/08 Barth, 15 April 2010, nyr 294, 299
Case C-543/08 Commission v Portugal, 11 November 2010, nyr. 589, 669
Case C-568/08 Combinatie Spijker Infrabouw-De Jonge Konstruktie, 9 December 2010, nyr 310
Case C-585/08 Pammer v Reederei Karl Schlüter GmbH & Co KG ECJ 10 December 2010, nyr. 762
Case C-1/09 CELF and Ministre de la culture et de la Communication v SIDE, 2010, nyr 874
Case C-34/09 Ruiz Zambrano, 8 March 2011, nyr 490–1
Case C-56/09 Zanotti, 20 May 2010, nyr 555
Joined Cases C-57 and 101/09 B, 9 November 2010, nyr. 382
Case C-70/09 Hengartner, 15 July 2010, nyr 954
Case C-81/09 Idrima Tipou, 21 October 2010, nyr. 661
Joined Cases C-92 and 93/09 Volker und Markus Scheke, 9 November 2010, nyr. 366
Case C-97/09 Schmelz, 26 October 2010, nyr 547
Case C-104/09 Álvarez, 30 September 2010, nyr. 266, 372
Case C-108/09 Ker-Optika, 2 December 2010, nyr. 426, 428
Case C-127/09 Coty Prestige, 3 June 2010, nyr 457
Case C-137/09 Josemans, 16 December 2010, nyr 483
Case C-137/09 Josemans v Burgemeester van Maastricht, 12 December 2010, nyr. 409
Case C-140/09 Fallimento Traghetti del Mediterraneo SpA v Presidenza del Consiglio dei Ministri
   [2010] 3 CMLR 46. 863–4
Case C-145/09 Tsakouridis, 23 November 2010, nyr 483, 485
Case C-160/09 Katsivardas, 20 May 2010, nyr. 954
Case C-162/09 Lassal, 7 October 2010, nyr 479
Case C-173/09 Elchinov, 5 October 2010, nyr 272, 590
Case C-197/09 RX-I and RX-II M v European Medicines Agency, 17 December 2009, nyr 64
Case C-208/09 Sayn-Wittgenstein, 22 December 2010, nyr 342, 347, 366, 370, 490
Case C-227/09 Accardo, 21 October 2010, nyr 262
Case C-233/09 Dijkman, 1 July 2010, nyr. 584
Case C-243/09 Günter Fuß, 14 October 2010, nyr 291
Case C-246/09 Bulicke, 8 July 2010,nyr 294, 300
Joined Cases C-250 and 268/09 Georgiev, 12 November 2010, nyr 371
Case C-279/09 DEB Deutsche Energiehandels- und Beratungsgesellschaft mbH,
   22 December 2010, nyr. 342, 379–80
Case C-291/09 Guarnieri e Cie, Opinion delivered on 14 September 2010, pending 429
Case C-304/09 Commission v Italy, 22 December 2010, nyr. 870
Case C-325/09 Dias, Opinion delivered 17 February 2011, case still pending 479
Case C-360/09 Pfleiderer AG v Bundeskartellamt, 16 December 2010, nyr 836
Case C-391/09 Runevicinvcirc-Vardyn and Wardyn, pending 490
Case C-421/09 Humanplasma, 9 December 2010, nyr. 428
Case C-434/09 McCarthy, Opinion delivered 25 November 2010, case still pending 468, 490
Case C-149/10 Chatzi, 16 September 2010, nyr. 377
Joined Cases C-188 and 189/10 Melki, 22 June 2010, nyr 272
Case C-211/10 Povse, 1 July 2010, nyr 373
Case C-287/10 Tankreederie, 22 December 2010, nyr 590
Case C-400/10 PPU J McB v LE, 5 October 2010, nyr 365, 373
Case C-424/10 Ziolkowski (pending) 479
Case C-425/10 Szeja (pending) 479
Case C-491/10 PPU Aguirre Zarraga v Pelz, 22 December 2010, nyr 373

Opinions

Opinion 1/75 [1975] ECR 1355. . . . . 101, 923, 942, 945
Opinion 1/76 [1977] ECR 741. . . . . 212, 912, 915–17, 920, 924–7, 930–1
Opinion 1/78 [1979] ECR 1045. . . . . 933, 942, 944–5
Opinion 1/91 [1991] ECR I-6079 . . . . 66, 927, 929–30, 954
Opinion 2/91 [1993] ECR I-1061 . . . . 913, 916–17, 927, 933
Opinion 2/92 [1995] ECR I-00521 . . . . .920, 924
Opinion 1/94 [1994] ECR I-5267 . . . . 109, 917, 920–1, 923–6, 933, 939, 942, 946, 950

Opinion 2/94 [1996] ECR I-1759 .... 99, 109–10, 338, 341, 909, 912, 916, 918
Opinion 2/00 [2001] ECR I-2793 943–5
Opinion 1/03 [2006] ECR I-1145 .... 920, 924, 928
Opinion 1/08 [2009] ECR I-11129 ....938, 946

Court of Justice, Name Order

3F v Commission [2009] ECR I-5963; [2009] 3 CMLR 40....................................873
Aalborg Portland A/S v Commission [2004] ECR I-123; [2005] 4 CMLR 4..................... 739–40, 823
Aberdeen Property Fininvest [2009] ECR I-5145 ....586, 592
ABNA [2005] ECR I-10423...124
Accardo, 21 October 2010, nyr...262
ACF Chemiefarma v Commission [1970] ECR 661 .... 79, 169, 735
Adams v Commission [1985] ECR 3539...192, 199–200
Adeneler [2006] ECR I-6057 ....241, 248
Adoui and Cornuaille [1984] ECR 1665... 484, 487–8
Adria-Wien Pipeline and Wietersdorfer & Peggauer Zementwerke [2001] ECR I-836...................855–6
Advocaten voor de Wereld [2007] ECR I-3633 381
AEG v Commission [1983] ECR 3151; [1984] 3 CMLR 325................................732, 749
Aerpo and Others v Commission [1990] ECR I-2189 193
Age Concern England [2009] ECR I-1569 371
AGM-COS.MET [2007] ECR I-2749 ....311, 313
Aher-Waggon GmbH v Germany [1998] ECR I-4473 442
Ahlström Oy v Commission ('Wood Pulp') [1988] ECR 5193;
   [1988] 4 CMLR 901.............................181, 721–2, 735–6, 738–9, 821
Ahmed Saeed Flugreisen v Zentrale zur Bekampfung unlauteren Wettbewerbs
   [1989] ECR 803; [1990] 4 CMLR 102...787, 886
Airola [1972] ECR 221..332
Akrich [2003] ECR I-9607 ....347–8, 470, 485, 488, 504, 540
Akzo Nobel Chemicals (Judgment of 14 September 2010) 101, 820, 923
Akzo Nobel v Commission [2009] ECR I-8237; [2009] 5 CMLR 23 ....721, 731
AKZO v Commission [1991] ECR I-3359; [1993] 5 CMLR 215........................ 772, 776, 785–8
Alaim [1975] ECR 109..526
Alassini, 18 March 2010, nyr..244
Albany International BV v Stichting Bedrijfspensioenfonds Textielindustrie
   [1999] ECR I-5751, [2000] 4 CMLR 446 ....221, 716–17, 731, 876, 882, 888
Alcan Deutschland [1997] ECR I-1591...302
Alcan v Commission [1970] ECR 385..165
Alevizos [2007] ECR I-3505..512
Alfa Vita [2006] ECR I-8135..427
Algemene Scheeps Agentuur Dordrecht [2006] ECR I-609...............................964
Algera v Common Assembly [1957 and 1958] ECR 39....................................198
Al-Jubail Fertilizer Company v Council [1991] ECR I-3187..............................178
Allan Bang [2005] ECR I-9939..243
Alliance for Natural Health [2005] ECR I-6451....................................... 88, 116, 118
Allied Corporation [1984] ECR 1005 169
Allué and Coonan [1989] ECR 1591...513, 517
Almelo [1994] ECR I-1477.. 215, 780, 885
Alpine Investments [1995] ECR I-1141 .... 555, 565, 668
Altair Chimica [2003] ECR I-8875 244
Altmark GmbH v Nahverkehrsgesellschaft Altmark GmbH ('Altmark')
   [2003] ECR I-7747, [2003] 3 CMLR 12 .... 851, 853, 863–4
Álvarez, 30 September 2010, nyr..266, 372
AM & S v Commission [1982] ECR 1575; [1982] 2 CMLR 264 819–20
Ambulanz Glöckner [2001] ECR I-8089; [2002] 4 CMLR 726 ....714, 878, 880, 882–4, 887
Amélioration de l' Élevage v Mialocq [1983] ECR 2057.................................447–8
Amministrazione delle Finanze dello Stato v Denkavit Italiana [1980] ECR 1205................... 229, 306, 850
Amministrazione delle Finanze dello Stato v Simmenthal [1978] ECR 629 .... 228, 271, 296, 303
AMOK [2003] ECR I-15059...640
Amurta [2007] ECR I-9569...586, 592
Amylum v Council [1982] ECR 3107 .... 182, 195, 329
Amylum v Council and Commission [1979] ECR 3497...................................194

ANAS [1999] ECR I-8583 215–16
Andersson and Another v Swedish State [1999] ECR I-3551 212
André Ambry [1998] ECR I-7875 579
Andrè Marchandise [1991] ECR-1027 443
Angelidaki [2009] ECR I-3071 . . . . .250, 268
Ango-Irish Meat [1981] ECR 1103 329
Angonese [2000] ECR I-4131 . . . . 254, 315, 502, 510, 553, 672
Anheuser-Busch v Budvar [2004] ECR I-10989 . . . . .212, 958
Anilir [2001] ECR I-1271 564
Anker and others [2003] ECR I-10447 513
Ansaldo Energia [1998] ECR I-5025 . . . . .293, 305
Antillean Rice Mills [2001] ECR I-8949 169
Antillean Rice Mills and Others v Commission [1999] ECR I-769 193–4
Antonissen [1991] ECR I-745 506
AOK Bundesverband [2004] ECR I-2493 . . . . 715–16, 731, 876
Apothekerkammer des Saarlandes and Others [2009] ECR I-4171 . . . . .549, 576
Apple and Pear Development Council [1983] ECR 4083 . . . . .253, 446
Aprile [1998] ECR I-7141 . . . . 293, 300, 305
Aprile Srl, in liquidation, v Amministrazione delle Finanze dello Stato [1995] ECR I-2919 405
A-Punkt Schmuckhandels GmbH v C Schmidt [2006] ECR I-2093 424
Aragonesa de Publicidad Exterior SA [1991] ECR I-4151 444
Arblade [1999] ECR I-8453 . . . . .578, 660
Arcaro [1996] ECR I-4705 243
Archer Daniels Midland Co v Commission [2009] ECR I-5843; [2009] 5 CMLR 15 821–2
Archer Daniels Midland v Commission [2006] ECR I-4429; [2006] 5 CMLR 4 .828
Archer Daniels Midland v Commission [2009] ECR I-1843; [2009] 4 CMLR 20 828
Arcor [2008] ECR I-2931 . . . . 252, 289, 302
Arcor [2008] ECR I-5959 263
Arduino [2002] 4 CMLR 25 . . . . 221, 890, 892–3
Ariete [1980] ECR 2545 . . . . .296, 306
Arnold André [2004] ECR I-11825 124
Asda Stores [2003] ECR I-5121 272
Asia Motor France v Commission [1990] ECR I-2181 192
Aslanidou [2005] ECR I-7181 240
ASNEF-EQUIFAX Servicios de Informacion sobre Solvencia y Credito SL v Asociacion
    de Usuarios de Servicios Bancarios (AUSBANC) ECJ [2006] ECR I-11125; [2007] 4 CMLR 6 . . . . 719, 750–2
Asocarne v Council [1995] ECR I-4149 171
Asociación Profesional de Empresas de Reparto y Manipulado de Correspondencia
    [2007] ECR I-12175 546
Asscher [1994] ECR I-1137 . . . . 541, 545, 553, 584
ASSIDER v High Authority [1954-56] ECR 63 177
Assurances du Crédit v Council and Commission [1991] ECR I-1799 193
ASTI [1991] ECR 3507 519
Asturcom [2009] ECR I-9579 272
Atalanta [1979] ECR 2137 . . . . .36, 326
Athinaïki Zythopoiia [2001] ECR I-2797 586
Atlanta Fruchthandelsgesellschaft mbH v Bundesamt für Ernährung und Forstwirtschaft
    [1995] ECR I-3761 . . . . 228, 304–5
ATRAL SA V Belgium [2003] ECR I-4431 . . . . .248, 427
Attanasio, 11 March 2010, nyr 552, 576, 604
Audiolux [2009] ECR I-9823 . . . . 255–6, 267
Auer [1979] ECR 437 . . . . 536–7, 542, 559
Auer [1983] ECR 2727 536
Autorita Garante della Concorrenza e del Mercato v Ente Tabacchi Italiani-ETI SpA
    [2007] ECR I-10893; [2008] 4 CMLR 11 721
AvestaPolarit Chrome Oy [2003] ECR I-8725 325
Azienda Agricola Ettore Ribaldi v Azienda di Stato per gli interventi nel mercato
    agricolo (AIMA), Ministero del Bilancio e della Programma Economica [2004] ECR I-2943 327
B, 9 November 2010, nyr 382
Baars [2000] ECR I-2787 661
Bacardi France [2004] ECR I-6613 572
Bachmann [1992] ECR I-249 . . . . .516, 591
Bactria v Commission [2003] ECR I-15105 171

Badek and others [2000] ECR I-1875 372
Baldinger [2004] ECR I-8411 . . . . .490, 519
Banchero I [1993] ECR I-1085 221
Banchero II [1995] ECR I-4663 . . . . 221, 423, 448
Banco Exterior de España [1994] ECR I-877; [1994] 3 CMLR 473 874
Banks v British Coal Corporation [1994] ECR I-1209 315
Barber [1990] ECR I-1889 . . . . .229, 273
Barth, 15 April 2010, nyr 294, 299
Bartsch [2008] ECR I-7245 . . . . .256, 265
BASF v Präsident des Deutschen Patentamts [1999] ECR I-6269 429
BAT v Hauptzollamt Krefeld [2004] ECR I-4683 214
Battaglia v Commission [1982] ECR 297 79
Bauhuis v Netherlands [1977] ECR 5 . . . . .395, 435
Baumbast v Secretary of State [2002] 3 CMLR 23; [2002] ECR I-7091 . . . . .26, 221, 327, 347, 365,
                                                                                        373, 466, 475, 477, 527
Baustahlgewebe v Commission [1998] ECR I-8417 . . . . .379, 821
Bautiaa and Société Française Maritime v Directeur des Services Fiscaux [1996] ECR I-505 36
Baxter and others [1999] ECR I-4809 . . . . 535, 576, 593
Becker [1982] ECR 53 . . . . .241, 261
Becu [1999] ECR I-5665, [2001] 4 CMLR 968 714
Béguelin Import Co v SA GL Import Export [1971] ECR 949; [1972] CMLR 81 731
Bekaert [1988] ECR 2029 535
Belgian State v Banque Indosuez and Others and European Community [1997] ECR I-659 328
Belgium v Commission [1996] ECR I-723 854
Belgium v Commission [1997] ECR I-687 179
Belgium v Commission ('Tubemeuse') [1990] ECR I-959 . . . . 851, 853, 870
Belgium v Spain (Rioja) [2000] ECR I-3123 . . . . .136, 434
Bellio Flli [2004] ECR I-3465 964
Benedetti v Munari [1977] ECR 163 . . . . .228, 857
Bergaderm [2000] ECR I-5291 195–6
Bergandi [1988] ECR 1343 396
Berlusconi and others [2005] ECR I-3565 . . . . 243, 267, 283, 381
Bernini [1992] ECR I-1071 . . . . .504, 528
Bettati [1998] ECR I-4355 36
Bettray [1989] ECR 1621 . . . . 498, 504–5
Bianco [1988] ECR 1099 306
BIAO [2003] ECR I-1 214
Bickel and Franz [1998] ECR I-7637 . . . . 464, 472, 489
Bidar [2005] ECR I-2119 . . . . 273, 467, 476, 482
Biegi [1979] ECR 1103 329
Biehl [1990] ECR I-1779 515
Biovilac v EEC [1984] ECR 4057 199
Birra Würhrer v Council and Commission [1982] ECR 85 200
Blaizot v University of Liège [1988] ECR 379 . . . . 105, 229, 273
Blanco Pérez and Chao Gómez, 1 June 2010, nyr 349, 541
Blegsen [1982] ECR 4575 416
Bluhme [1998] ECR I-8033 . . . . .429, 437
BMW Belgium SA v Commission [1979] ECR 2435; [1980] 1 CMLR 370 742
Bobadilla [1999] ECR I-4773 627
Boch, Re: Belgium v Commission [1986] ECR 2321; [1998] 2 CMLR 301 854
Bodson v SA Pompes funèbres des regions liberées [1988] ECR 2479; [1989] 4 CMLR 984 . . . . 731, 787, 880
Boehringer Ingelheim [2007] ECR I-3391 459
Boehringer Ingelheim KG and Others [2002] ECR I-3759 459
Boehringer v Commission [1970] ECR 769 821
Bokker Aquaculture Ltd et al v Scottish Ministers [2003] ECR I-7411 344
Bond van Adverteerders [1988] ECR 2085 . . . . 555, 578–80, 590
Bonifaci [1997] ECR I-3969 313
Bonsignore [1975] ECR 297 483
Bordessa [1995] ECR I-361 663
Borelli [1992] ECR I-6313 291
Borker [1980] ECR 1975 215
Borrell [1992] ECR I-3003 291
Borsana [1998] ECR I-8597 241

Bosal [2003] ECR I-9409 . . . . 573, 586, 588, 590
Bosman [1995] ECR I-4921 . . . . 220–1, 273, 367, 501, 521–4, 672–3
Bosmann [2008] ECR I-3827 522
Bosphorus [1996] ECR I-3953 369
Bostock [1994] ECR I-955 . . . . .333, 344
Bouchereau [1977] ECR 1999 483–4
Bouchoucha [1990] ECR I-3551 . . . . 539, 541, 567
Bouhelier [1977] ECR 197 433
Boukhalfa [1996] ECR I-2253 502
Bozkurt, 22 December 2010, nyr 346
Bozzetti [1985] ECR 2301 . . . . 288, 291, 296
BP [1978] ECR 1513, [1978] 3 CMLR 174 800
BP Supergas [1995] ECR I-1883 294
BPB Industries and British Gypsum v Commission [1995] ECR I-865; [1997] 4 CMLR 238 . . . . .783, 800
Brandsma [1996] ECR I-3159 427
Brentjens v Stichting Bedrijfspensioenfonds voor de Handel in Bouwmaterialen [1999] ECR I-6025 221
Bresciani [1976] ECR 129 . . . . .394, 954
Bressol, 13 April 2010, nyr 105, 475
Briheche [2004] ECR I-8807 372
Brinkmann [1998] ECR I-5255 311
Brita, 25 February 2010, nyr 392, 954
British Aggregates Associaton v Commission (BAA)[2009] 2 CMLR 10 872
British Airways v Commission [2007] ECR I-2331; [2007] 4 CMLR 22 . . . . 766, 782, 793, 795
Broede v Sandker [1996] ECR I-6511 581
Bronner [1998] ECR I-7791, [1999] 4 CMLR 112 . . . . 775, 782, 785, 798, 800–5
Brown [1988] ECR 3205 . . . . 464, 504, 506
Brown Boveri [1991] ECR I-1853 964
BRT v SABAM [1974] ECR 51 . . . . 254, 713, 838, 841, 885, 889
Bruleurs d'Huiles Usages [1985] ECR 532 443
Brunnhofer [2001] ECR I-4961 265
Bruno Barra [1988] ECR 355 300
Buckl and Others v Commission [1992] ECR I-6061 188–9
Budeinvcircjovický Budvar [2009] ECR I-7721 302
Buet [1989] ECR 1235 444
Bulicke, 8 July 2010,nyr 294, 300
Bundesanstalt für Landwirtschaft und Ernährung v Deutsches Milch-Kontor [1997] ECR I-1905 392
Bundesverband der Arzneimittel-Importeure EV and Commission v Bayer AG [2004] ECR I-23;
    [2004] 4 CMLR 653 733
Buralux and Others v Council [1996] ECR I-615 168
Burda [2008] ECR I-4571 586
Burmanjer and others [2005] ECR I-4133 424
Bussone [1978] ECR 2429 257
Butterfly Music Srl v CEMED [1999] ECR I-3939 220
Caballero [2002] ECR I-11915 255
Cabour SA and Nord Distribution Automobile SA v Automobiles Peugeot SA and Automobiles
    Citröen SA [1998] ECR I-2055; [1988] 5 CMLR 679 843
Cadbury Schweppes [2006] ECR I-7995 593
Cadi Surgelés and others [1996] ECR I-5647 405
CaixaBank France [2004] ECR I-8961 . . . . 550–2, 591, 659
Calfa [1999] ECR I-11 487
Calì & Figli v SEPG [1997] ECR I-1547; [1997] 5 CMLR 484 715
Calpak v Commission [1980] ECR 1949 163
CAM v Commission [1975] ECR 1393 . . . . 167–8, 171
Cámara de Comercio, Industria y Navegación de Ceuta v Ayuntamiento de Ceuta
    [1995] ECR I-4385 396
Campo Ebro and Others v Council [1997] ECR I-2027 193
Campus Oil Ltd v Minister for Industry and Energy [1984] ECR 2727; [1984] 3 CMLR 544 . . . 435, 441, 572, 886
Canal Satélite Digital SL v Administracíon General del Estado [2002] ECR I-607 427
Capolongo v Azienda Agricola Maya [1973] ECR 611 401–2
Carbonati Apuani Srl [2004] ECR I-8027 394
Carlo Bagnasco and others v Banco Polare di Navara and others [1999] ECR I-135 719
Carmen Media Group, 8 September 2010, nyr 554
Carp [2007] ECR I-4473 . . . . .256, 268

Carpenter [2002] ECR I-6279..347–8, 365, 485, 524, 566
Cartesio [2008] ECR I-9641 ....655, 657
Casagrande [1974] ECR 773..498, 526
Castelli [1984] ECR 3199 ....518, 528
Cato v Commission [1992] ECR I-2533 191
Cayrol [1977] ECR 2261 663
CELF and Ministre de la culture et de la Communication v SIDE [2008] ECR I-469.................302, 873
CELF and Ministre de la culture et de la Communication v SIDE, 2010, nyr.......................874
Celulose Beira Industrial SA v Fazenda P·blica [1993] ECR I-4337 401–3
Cementhandelaren v Commission [1972] ECR 977, [1973] CMLR 7 719
Centrafarm v American Home Products [1978] ECR 1823...................................456, 459
Centrafarm v Sterling Drug [1974] ECR 1147 453–4
Centrafarm v Winthrop [1974] ECR 1183 ....454, 456
Centre Belge d'Etudes de Marché Télémarketing v CLT [1985] ECR 3261; [1986] 2 CMLR 558.........783, 887
Centro Servizi Spediporto v Spedizioni Marittima del Golfo [1995] ECR I-2883;
    [1996] 4 CMLR 613..429, 780
Centros [1999] ECR I-1458 ....488, 554, 567, 573, 575–6,
                                                                        648–54, 657, 681–2
Centrosteel v Adipol [2000] ECR I-6007 248
CEPSA Estaciones de Servicios SA v LV Tobar e Hijos SL [2008] ECR I-6681; [2008] 5 CMLR 19 732
Charmasson [1974] ECR 1383 449
Chatzi, 16 September 2010, nyr..377
Chemial Farmaceutici v DAF [1981] ECR 1 398
Chemie Linz v Commission [1999] ECR I-4643...202
Chemische Afvalstoffen Dusseldorp and Others v Minister van Volkshuisvesting,
    Ruimtelijke Ordening en Milieubeheer [1998] ECR I-4075........................ 442, 881–2, 888
Chen [2004] ECR I-9925..534
Chen and others [2004] ECR I-9925....................................... 373, 469, 474
Chevalley v Commission [1970] ECR 975 ....184, 186
Chronopost v Ufex [2003] ECR I-6993..854–5
CIA Security [1996] ECR I-2201 280–2
CICCE v Commission [1985] ECR 1105, [1986] 1 CMLR 486 776
CILFIT [1984] ECR 1257 212
CILFIT v Ministry of Health [1982] ECR 3415 ....212, 224, 229
Cinéthèque [1985] ECR 2605 ....415, 443
Ciola [1999] ECR I-2517..271–2, 557, 572, 579, 590
Cipolla v Fazari Macrino, Capodarte v Meloni [2006] ECR I-11421; [2007] 4 CMLR 8 .... 551, 605, 893
Cipra and Kvasnicka v Bezirkshauptmannschaft Mistelbach [2003] ECR I-745............ 212, 217, 220
CIRFS and Others v Commission [1993] ECR I-1125 172
Cisal [2002] ECR I-691, [2002] 4 CMLR 24..878
City Motors Groep [2007] ECR I-653...302, 315
Claeys [1992] ECR I-6559..401–2
Clean Car Autoservice [1998] ECR I-2521.................................251–2, 294, 302, 501
CMC Motorradcenter GmbH v Pelin Baskiciogullari [1993] ECR I-5009 428–9
CNPAAP v Council [1996] ECR I-2003 171
CNTA v Commission [1975] ECR 533 .... 194, 198, 330
Coditel v Ciné Vog Films [1980] ECR 881 555
Codorníu SA v Council of the European Union [1994] ECR I-1853 .... 164, 170, 333
Coenen [1975] ECR 1547..535, 561
COFAZ [1986] ECR 391 ....169, 872–3
Cofidis [2002] ECR I-10875 301–2
Co-Frutta v Amministrazione delle Finanze dello Stato [1987] ECR 2085.......................396, 402
Colegio de Oficiales de la Marina Mercante Española [2003] ECR I-10391 ....513, 571
Coleman [2008] ECR I-5603 371
Colim v Biggs [1999] ECR I-3175 ....254, 413
Collino [2000] ECR I-6659..241
Collins [2004] ECR I-2703 .... 291, 467, 474, 506–7
Comateb [1997] ECR I-165..306
Combinatie Spijker Infrabouw-De Jonge Konstruktie, 9 December 2010, nyr......................310
Comet BV v Produktschap voor Siergewassen [1976] ECR 2043 .... 288, 292, 294–7, 303, 316
Commerzbank [1993] ECR I-4017 ....545, 573, 583, 588, 590, 593, 597, 648
Commission and Parliament v Council [2000] ECR I-2257 ....113, 943

Commission v Aktionsgemeinschaft Recht und Eigentum [2005] ECR I-10737;
  [2006] 2 CMLR 48 871–2
Commission v Alrosa Co Ltd [2011] All E.R. (EC) 1; [2010] 5 CMLR 11 . . . . .369, 825
Commission v Anic [1999] ECR I-4125 . . . . 735–7, 739–40
Commission v AssiDomän Kraft Products and Others [1999] ECR I-5363; [1999] 5 CMLR 1253 181
Commission v Austria [1999] ECR I-7479 140–1
Commission v Austria [2001] ECR I-9285 290
Commission v Austria [2002] ECR I-9797 925
Commission v Austria [2004] ECR I-1211 140
Commission v Austria [2004] ECR I-4579 147
Commission v Austria [2005] ECR I-5969 105
Commission v Austria [2006] ECR I-9041 556
Commission v Austria [2007] ECR I-10195 . . . . .570, 580
Commission v Austria [2008] ECR I-671 545
Commission v Austria [2009] ECR I-1301 929
Commission v Austria (motorway ban) [2005] ECR I-9871 431
Commission v Austria (sale by mail), 18 November 2004, not published 425
Commission v BASF and Others [1994] ECR I-2555 202
Commission v Belgium [1970] ECR 237 . . . . .145, 270
Commission v Belgium [1978] ECR 1881 202
Commission v Belgium [1980] ECR 1473 . . . . 241, 258, 329
Commission v Belgium [1983] ECR 531 438
Commission v Belgium [1983] ECR 1649 394
Commission v Belgium [1984] ECR 1543 395
Commission v Belgium [1986] ECR 89; [1987] 1 CMLR 710 870
Commission v Belgium [1987] ECR 719 539
Commission v Belgium [1987] ECR 3029 258
Commission v Belgium [1987] ECR 3299 399
Commission v Belgium [1988] ECR 1 143
Commission v Belgium [1988] ECR 305 . . . . .139, 141
Commission v Belgium [1988] ECR 5445 105
Commission v Belgium [1990] ECR I-2801 441
Commission v Belgium [1991] ECR I-3171 404
Commission v Belgium [1992] ECR I-305 591
Commission v Belgium [1992] ECR I-4431 . . . . .393, 442
Commission v Belgium [1993] ECR I-3107 439
Commission v Belgium [1994] ECR I-1019 147
Commission v Belgium [1994] ECR I-1593 105
Commission v Belgium [1996] ECR I-4307 . . . . .507, 515
Commission v Belgium [1997] ECR I-1035 506
Commission v Belgium [2002] ECR I-4809 . . . . .662, 666
Commission v Belgium [2002] ECR I-9681 925
Commission v Belgium [2003] ECR I-11859 147
Commission v Belgium [2004] ECR I-6427 105
Commission v Belgium [2007] ECR I-4749 248
Commission v Belgium (citizenship) [2006] ECR I-2647 474
Commission v Belgium (No 1) [1980] ECR 3881 . . . . 512–13, 569
Commission v Belgium (No 2) [1982] ECR 1845 512
Commission v Camar [2002] ECR I-11355 . . . . .175, 196
Commission v Cambridge Healthcare Supplies [2001] ECR I-2865 204
Commission v CEVA Santé Animale [2005] ECR I-6257 196
Commission v Council [1973] ECR 575 . . . . .182, 822
Commission v Council [1987] ECR 1493 . . . . 161, 678, 944–5
Commission v Council [1989] ECR 3457 88–9
Commission v Council [1991] ECR I-2867 . . . . .111, 113
Commission v Council [1996] ECR 881 862
Commission v Council [1998] ECR I-2763 908
Commission v Council [2004] ECR I-4829 112
Commission v Council [2004] ECR I-6649 158
Commission v Council [2005] ECR I-345 88
Commission v Council [2008] ECR I-3651 908
Commission v Council [2009] ECR I-8917 112

Commission v Council (AETR) [1971] ECR 263 . . . . .157, 542, 911–14, 916–17, 920–2, 924, 926–33, 940, 948
Commission v Council and Parliament [2006] ECR I-2001 89
Commission v Council (Criminal liability for offences against the environment)
  [2005] ECR I-7879. . . . . 112, 317, 381, 908
Commission v Council (Energy Star) [2002] ECR I-12049. 945
Commission v Council (FAO) [1996] ECR I-1469 . . . . .100, 940
Commission v Council (PIC Convention) [2006] ECR I-107. . . . . .112, 945
Commission v Council (Ship Source Pollution) [2007] ECR I-9097 . . . . 112, 317, 908
Commission v Council (Vietnam), 9 November 2010, nyr 930, 935, 938–9, 946
Commission v Council (Waste Directive) [1993] ECR I-939 111–12
Commission v Cwick [2001] ECR I-10269. 367
Commission v Denmark [1982] ECR 4547 139
Commission v Denmark [1983] ECR 3573 402
Commission v Denmark [1985] ECR 427 36
Commission v Denmark [1986] ECR 833 397
Commission v Denmark [1986] ECR 3713 578
Commission v Denmark [1992] ECR I-2187. 142
Commission v Denmark [2003] ECR I-9693. 436
Commission v Denmark (cars) [1990] ECR I-4509 . . . . 396, 401, 403, 421, 446
Commission v Denmark (Open Skies) [2002] ECR I-9519. . . . . 920, 924–7, 948
Commission v Deutsche Post AG [2011] 1 CMLR 14 . . . . .851, 864
Commission v European Central Bank [2003] ECR I-7147. . . . . 42, 147, 202
Commission v European Parliament and Council [2003] ECR I-937 . . . . 89, 161, 178–9
Commission v Finland [2002] ECR I-9627 925
Commission v Finland [2009] ECR I-10889 929
Commission v Finland (transfer licence for cars) [2007] ECR I-2473. 427
Commission v France [1969] ECR 523 141
Commission v France [1969] ECR 523; [1970] CMLR 43 . . . . .849, 856
Commission v France [1974] ECR 359. . . . . 144, 508, 511
Commission v France [1979] ECR 2729. 144
Commission v France [1980] ECR 387. 397
Commission v France [1980] ECR 1319. 204
Commission v France [1983] ECR 1013. 440
Commission v France [1986] ECR 1725. 513
Commission v France [1986] ECR 3663. 578
Commission v France [1987] ECR 1597. 397
Commission v France [1988] ECR 2243. 258
Commission v France [1991] ECR I-2727 152
Commission v France [1991] ECR I-3591 640
Commission v France [1991] ECR I-4221 . . . . .562, 629
Commission v France [1997] ECR I-5815 885
Commission v France [1997] ECR I-6959 . . . . 25, 144, 146, 430, 434, 673
Commission v France [1998] ECR I-5325 273
Commission v France [2001] ECR I-1169 139
Commission v France [2001] ECR I-9989 . . . . .151, 204
Commission v France [2002] ECR I-3827 147
Commission v France [2002] ECR I-3969 142
Commission v France [2002] ECR I-4781 . . . . .664, 666
Commission v France [2003] ECR I-6625 147–8
Commission v France [2003] ECR I-13909 147
Commission v France [2004] ECR I-1277 440
Commission v France [2004] ECR I-2229 593
Commission v France [2004] ECR I-6535 414
Commission v France [2005] ECR I-6263 151
Commission v France [2008] ECR I-5337 . . . . .541, 549
Commission v France [2008] ECR I-9159 151
Commission v France (Etang de Berre) [2004] ECR I-9325 941
Commission v France (import licences for medicinal products) [2005] ECR I-4213 438
Commission v France (paté de foie gras) [1998] ECR I-6197 . . . . .412, 422
Commission v France (processing aids), 28 January 2010, nyr. 427
Commission v France (registration for reagents) [2000] ECR I-1149 . . . . .142, 427
Commission v Fresh Marine [2003] ECR I-7541 196

Commission v Germany [1973] ECR 813; [1973] CMLR 741 869
Commission v Germany [1979] ECR 2555 438
Commission v Germany [1982] ECR 1855 329
Commission v Germany [1986] ECR 1661 . . . . .147, 259
Commission v Germany [1986] ECR 2519 201
Commission v Germany [1986] ECR 3755 . . . . 532, 561, 568, 578, 648
Commission v Germany [1987] ECR 1227 . . . . .308, 436
Commission v Germany [1988] ECR 1123 . . . . 562, 639–40
Commission v Germany [1988] ECR 5427 395
Commission v Germany [1989] ECR 1263 499
Commission v Germany [1990] ECR I-3351 204
Commission v Germany [1990] ECR I-3437 332
Commission v Germany [1994] ECR I-3303 438–9
Commission v Germany [1995] ECR I-2189 249
Commission v Germany [1996] ECR I-3989 964
Commission v Germany [1996] ECR I-6747 259
Commission v Germany [1998] ECR I-5449 141
Commission v Germany [1999] ECR I-2175 141
Commission v Germany [1999] ECR I-3257 141
Commission v Germany [1999] ECR I-5087 147
Commission v Germany [2002] ECR I-9855 925
Commission v Germany [2003] ECR I-2837 137
Commission v Germany [2003] ECR I-5369 325
Commission v Germany [2005] ECR I-6985 934
Commission v Germany [2006] ECR I-885 556
Commission v Germany [2007] ECR I-6095 556
Commission v Germany [2007] ECR I-6952 555
Commission v Germany [2007] ECR I-8995 . . . . .666, 668
Commission v Germany [2007] ECR I-10239 . . . . .570, 580
Commission v Germany [2009] ECR I-7811 547
Commission v Germany, 29 April 2010, nyr 570
Commission v Germany (Judgment of 9 March 2010) 119
Commission v Germany (parallel imports of phytosanitary products), 14 July 2005, unpublished 431
Commission v Germany (reusable containers) [2004] ECR I-11705 431
Commission v Germany (shipment of waste) [2003] ECR I-2001 393
Commission v Germany (supply of medicinal products to hospitals) [2008] ECR I-6935 425
Commission v Greece [1988] ECR 2875; [1989] 3 CMLR 677 870
Commission v Greece [1988] ECR 3611 . . . . .202, 881
Commission v Greece [1988] ECR 4415 543
Commission v Greece [1989] ECR 1461 . . . . 333, 544, 547, 559
Commission v Greece [1989] ECR 2965 . . . . .25, 88
Commission v Greece [1990] ECR I-1567 398
Commission v Greece [1990] ECR I-4299 141
Commission v Greece [1990] ECR I-4747 . . . . .142, 448
Commission v Greece [1991] ECR I-727 . . . . 558, 562–3, 578, 629
Commission v Greece [1991] ECR I-1361 436
Commission v Greece [1991] ECR I-1909 400
Commission v Greece [1991] ECR I-5863 569
Commission v Greece [1992] ECR I-1971 140
Commission v Greece [1992] ECR I-2509 150
Commission v Greece [1993] ECR I-3131 202
Commission v Greece [1996] ECR I-4459 258
Commission v Greece [1997] ECR I-5981 398
Commission v Greece [1999] ECR I-4913 144
Commission v Greece [1999] ECR I-7713 142
Commission v Greece [2000] ECR I-5047 150
Commission v Greece [2005] ECR I-3177 576
Commission v Greece [2005] ECR I-3875 870
Commission v Greece [2009] ECR I-4505 152
Commission v Greece [2009] ECR I-4657 152
Commission v Greece [2009] ECR I-5703 152
Commission v Greece (obligation to stock petroleum) [2001] ECR I-7915 436
Commission v Greece (processed milk for infants) [1995] ECR I-1621 421–2

Commission v Ireland [1978] ECR 417 . . . . .204, 933
Commission v Ireland [1980] ECR 481 397
Commission v Ireland [1981] ECR 1625 . . . . .435, 442
Commission v Ireland [1982] ECR 4005 . . . . 253, 447, 881
Commission v Ireland [1984] ECR 317 141
Commission v Ireland [1985] ECR 1761 435
Commission v Ireland [1986] ECR 3817 578
Commission v Ireland [1988] ECR 4929 447
Commission v Ireland [1990] ECR I-4271 145
Commission v Ireland [1991] ECR I 4569 545
Commission v Ireland [1999] ECR I-5901 147
Commission v Ireland [2002] ECR I-11433 138–9
Commission v Ireland, 28 January 2010, nyr 300
Commission v Ireland (Berne Convention) [2002] ECR I-2923 941
Commission v Italian Republic [2000] ECR I-3811 665
Commission v Italy [1961] ECR 317 . . . . .409, 435
Commission v Italy [1965] ECR 857 . . . . .396, 404
Commission v Italy [1969] ECR 193 395
Commission v Italy [1970] ECR 47 145
Commission v Italy [1972] ECR 527 270
Commission v Italy [1972] ECR 667 262
Commission v Italy [1973] ECR 101 . . . . 140, 145, 189, 257
Commission v Italy [1976] ECR 277 262
Commission v Italy [1979] ECR 3247 543
Commission v Italy [1980] ECR 1 397–8
Commission v Italy [1980] ECR 1099 145
Commission v Italy [1980] ECR 1547 403
Commission v Italy [1981] ECR 2577 140
Commission v Italy [1981] ECR 2585 140
Commission v Italy [1982] ECR 2187 435
Commission v Italy [1983] ECR 711 258
Commission v Italy [1983] ECR 3723 258
Commission v Italy [1984] ECR 3395 270
Commission v Italy [1985] ECR 1057 257
Commission v Italy [1985] ECR 2049 . . . . .397, 403
Commission v Italy [1985] ECR 2629 143
Commission v Italy [1987] ECR 2599 878
Commission v Italy [1987] ECR 2625 512–13
Commission v Italy [1987] ECR 3073 258
Commission v Italy [1988] ECR 29 559
Commission v Italy [1988] ECR 129 544
Commission v Italy [1988] ECR 1799 . . . . .144, 306
Commission v Italy [1988] ECR 3249 258
Commission v Italy [1989] ECR 143 307
Commission v Italy [1989] ECR I-4035 . . . . .545, 573
Commission v Italy [1991] ECR I-709 578
Commission v Italy [1991] ECR I-1575 395
Commission v Italy [1991] ECR I-4193 144
Commission v Italy [1992] ECR I-2353 140
Commission v Italy [1993] ECR I-2701 439
Commission v Italy [1995] ECR I-343 870
Commission v Italy [1996] ECR I-2691 . . . . .561, 573
Commission v Italy [1997] ECR I-5789 419
Commission v Italy [1997] ECR I-6869 138
Commission v Italy [1999] ECR I-2981 870
Commission v Italy [1999] ECR I-7773 142
Commission v Italy [2001] ECR I-8305 142
Commission v Italy [2002] ECR I-305 541
Commission v Italy [2002] ECR I-1425 579
Commission v Italy [2002] ECR I-2235 538
Commission v Italy [2003] ECR I-721 . . . . 573, 579, 608
Commission v Italy [2003] ECR I-14637 . . . . 145, 306, 314
Commission v Italy [2007] ECR I-6251 603

Commission v Italy [2007] ECR I-11091 603
Commission v Italy [2009] ECR I-3491 ....564, 602
Commission v Italy [2009] ECR I-4103 ....549, 576
Commission v Italy, 14 October 2004, unrep..419
Commission v Italy, 22 December 2010, nyr..870
Commission v Italy (Art Treasuries) [1968] ECR 423 393
Commission v Italy (pending) 152
Commission v Italy (Re CNSD) [1998] ECR I-3851, [1998] 5 CMLR 889 890–2
Commission v Italy (Sicilian environmental tax) [2007] ECR I-4917 395
Commission v Italy (State Schools) [2005] ECR I-3747................................517
Commission v Italy (trailers) [2009] ECR I-519 428
Commission v Kingdom of Spain [1991] ECR I-641 396
Commission v Kingdom of the Netherlands [2004] ECR I-9761 548
Commission v Luxembourg [1982] ECR 2175 544
Commission v Luxembourg [1991] ECR I-3171...404
Commission v Luxembourg [1993] ECR I-817...515
Commission v Luxembourg [1996] ECR I-3207..514
Commission v Luxembourg [2002] ECR I-9741 925
Commission v Luxembourg [2003] ECR I-1553..142
Commission v Luxembourg [2004] ECR I-10191....................................556, 660
Commission v Luxembourg [2005] ECR I-4805..934
Commission v Luxembourg [2006] ECR I-8673..644
Commission v Luxembourg and Belgium [1964] ECR 625........................144, 392
Commission v Netherlands [1977] ECR 1355..395
Commission v Netherlands [1982] ECR 1791...............................142, 258, 271
Commission v Netherlands [1986] ECR 1219..257
Commission v Netherlands [1991] ECR I-2461..142
Commission v Netherlands [1993] ECR I-4739..270
Commission v Netherlands [1997] ECR I-5699.............................448, 875–6
Commission v Netherlands [2000] ECR I-6611..139
Commission v Netherlands [2001] ECR I-3541..148
Commission v Netherlands [2004] ECR I-6213..140
Commission v Netherlands [2004] ECR I-11375..439
Commission v Netherlands (road worthiness test for imported used cars) [2007] ECR I-7467 427
Commission v Netherlandse Antillen [2003] ECR I-3483................................169, 175
Commission v Parliament and Council [2006] ECR I-107 ....112–13, 945
Commission v Parliament and Council (Waste Shipments) [2009] ECR I-7585 ....112, 945
Commission v Portugal [2001] ECR I-2613..775
Commission v Portugal [2004] ECR I-5645...........................534, 549, 556
Commission v Portugal [2009] ECR I-10219..........................549, 569–70
Commission v Portugal, 8 July 2010, nyr..669
Commission v Portugal, 11 November 2010, nyr....................................589, 669
Commission v Portugal (tinted car windows) [2008] ECR I-2245.....................427–8
Commission v Portugal,18 November 2010, nyr...606
Commission v SGL Carbon [2006] ECR I-5915 816
Commission v Socurte and Others [1997] ECR I-1 156
Commission v Spain [1990] ECR I-6717 570
Commission v Spain [1997] ECR I-7337 259
Commission v Spain [1998] ECR I-505 151
Commission v Spain [1998] ECR I-3301 270
Commission v Spain [1998] ECR I-6717 514
Commission v Spain [2003] ECR I-13145 ....139, 419
Commission v Spain [2003] ECR I-14141 151
Commission v Spain [2004] ECR I-7999 148
Commission v Spain [2005] ECR I-7482 381
Commission v Spain [2006] ECR I-963 ....534, 549, 556
Commission v Spain [2009] ECR I-9553 323
Commission v Spain [2009] ECR I-9735 580
Commission v Spain, 12 November 2009, nyr...314
Commission v Spain Commission v United Kingdom [2003] ECR I-4581...........................878–9
Commission v Spain (Schengen Information System) [2006] ECR I-1097....................471, 484
Commission v Stahlwerke Peine-Salzgitter [1993] ECR I-2393 196
Commission v Sweden [2002] ECR I-4147 148

Commission v Sweden [2002] ECR I-9575 925
Commission v Sweden [2008] ECR I-2127 399–400
Commission v Sweden [2009] ECR I-1335 929
Commission v Sweden (PFOS), 20 April 2010. 934
Commission v Sytraval and Brink's Finance [1998] ECR I-1719 872–3
Commission v UK [1981] ECR 1045. . . . . .101, 933
Commission v UK [1983] ECR 2265. . . . . 396, 399–400
Commission v UK [1994] ECR I-2435 375
Commission v United Kingdom [1979] ECR 419 334
Commission v United Kingdom [1979] ECR 1447. . . . . .334, 409
Commission v United Kingdom [1984] ECR 283 437
Commission v United Kingdom [1985] ECR 1201. . . . . 442, 546, 582–4, 648–9
Commission v United Kingdom [1988] ECR 3921. 102
Commission v United Kingdom [1989] ECR 3125. 204
Commission v United Kingdom [1997] ECR I-2649 147
Commission v United Kingdom [2002] ECR I-9427 925
Commission v United Kingdom [2002] ECR I-10323 144
Commission v United Kingdom [2003] ECR I-4641 . . . . .666, 668
Commission v United Kingdom [2003] ECR I-10379 144
Commission v United Kingdom [2003] ECR I-13239 142
Commission v Volkswagen [2006] ECR I-6585; [2008] 4 CMLR 16 733
Commissionaires Reunis [1978] ECR 927 . . . . .392, 449
Compagnia Italiana Alcool v Commission [1992] ECR I-2457. . . . . .191, 199
Compagnie Commerciale de l'Ouest and others v Receveur Principal des Douanes
   de La Pallice Port [1992] ECR I-1847. 402–3
Compagnie Continentale v Council [1975] ECR 117. 199
Compagnie Industrielle du Comité de Loheac v Council and Commission [1977] ECR 645 198
Compagnie Maritime Belge Transports, Compagnie Maritime Belge SA and
   Dafra Lines A/S v Commission [2000] ECR I-1365; [2000] CMLR 1076. . . . . .766, 776–7, 779, 786,
                                                                                                789, 822–3
Compagnie Royale Asturienne des Mines SA (CRAM) v Commission
   [1984] ECR 1679; [1985] 1 CMLR 688. . . . . 737–8, 743
Competition Authority v Beef Industry Development Society Ltd [2008] ECR I-8637;
   [2009] 4 CMLR 6. 742
Coname [2005] ECR I-7287 546–7
Confederación Española de Empresarios de Estaciones de Servicio [2006] ECR I-11987;
   [2007] 4 CMLR 5 732
Conforama [1991] ECR I-997 416
Connect Austria Gesellschaft für Telekommunikation GmbH v Telekom-Control-Kommission
   [2003] ECR I-5197. . . . . 292, 881, 883
Connolly v Commission [2001] ECR I-1611 367
Conradi [1987] ECR 4469. 539
Consorzio Cooperative d'Abruzzo v Commission [1987] ECR 1005 . . . . .181, 202
Consorzio Industrie Fiammiferi (CIF) v Autorità Garante della Concorrenza e del Mercato
   [2003] ECR I-8055. . . . . .216, 890
Consten and Grundig v Commission [1966] ECR 299; [1966] CMLR 418. . . . . .741, 743–4, 747, 753, 756
Cook v Commission [1993] ECR I-2487 873
Coop de France Betail et Viande (formerly Fédération Nationale de la Coopération
   Betail et Viande (FNCBV)) v Commission [2008] ECR I-10193; [2009] 4 CMLR 15. 827
Co-operatieve Stremsel-en-Kleurselfabriek v Commission [1981] ECR 851;
   [1982] 1 CMLR 240. 714
Coote v Granada Hospitality [1998] ECR I-5199 . . . . .291, 302
Corbeau [1993] ECR I-2533, [1995] 4 CMLR 621 . . . . 883–5, 887–8
Corbiau v Administration des Contributions [1993] ECR I-1277 215
Corporación Dermoestética SA v To Me Group Advertising Media [2008] ECR I-5785 565
Corsica Ferries France SA v Gruppo Antichi Ormeggiatori del Porto di Genova
   Coop Arl et al [1998] ECR I-3949. . . . . 429, 875, 882, 886
Costa v Enel [1964] ECR 585 . . . . 37, 223, 237–8, 262, 270,
                                                                                                284, 447, 543
Coty Prestige, 3 June 2010, nyr. 457
Council of the City of Stoke-on-Trent and Norwich City Council v B&Q plc
   [1992] ECR I-6635. . . . . .416, 427
Council v Parliament [1986] ECR 2155 157

Courage v Crehan [2001] ECR I-6297; [2001] 5 CMLR 28 ....212, 303, 315, 318, 840–2
Cousin [1983] ECR 1101...333
Cowan [1989] ECR 195..333, 557
Cristini v SNCF [1975] ECR 1985..518, 527
CRT France International SA [1999] ECR I-2237...405
Curtis [1982] ECR 931...331
D and Sweden v Council [2001] ECR I-4319..332, 366, 371
da Costa en Schaake [1963] ECR 31 ....225, 229
Dafeki [1997] ECR I-6761..302
Dahms [2005] ECR I-8723 252
Daily Mail [1988] ECR 3483...535, 538, 588, 651–2, 655, 657
Damgaard [2009] ECR I-2629 242
Danner [2002] ECR I-8147...579
Dansk Denkavit [1992] ECR I-2217 273
Dansk Rørindustri v Commission [2005] ECR I-5425..242, 827
Danske Slagterier [2009] ECR I-2119 ....299–300, 312–13
De Coster [2001] ECR I-9445..215–16, 555, 564, 566
De Cuyper [2006] ECR I-6947 489
De Danske Billimportører [2003] ECR I-6065..401, 403, 446
De Franceschi v Council and Commission [1982] ECR 117..200
De Jaeck v Staatssecretaris van Financiën [1997] ECR I-461...328
De Kikvorsch [1983] ECR 947 414
de Lasteyrie du Saillant [2004] ECR I-2409 ....588, 590, 597
De Pasquale [1982] ECR 909 331
de Peijper [1976] ECR 613 438–40
de Vos [1996] ECR I-417...515, 519
Deak [1985] ECR 1873 518
DEB Deutsche Energiehandels- und Beratungsgesellschaft mbH, 22 December 2010, nyr 342, 379–80
Debauve [1980] ECR 833 555
Debus [1992] ECR I-3617...436, 438–40
Decker [1979] ER 101 329
Decker v Caisse de Maladie des Employés Privés [1998] ECR I-1831 ....427, 435, 443
Defrenne v Sabena [1978] ECR 1365 266
Defrenne v Sabena (Defrenne II) [1976] ECR 455 ....229, 254, 273, 331, 371, 672
Deghillage v Caisse Primaire d'Assurance Maladie [1986] ECR 991 217
Dekker [1990] ECR I-394 377
Deliège [2000] ECR I-2549..523, 566
Delimitis v Henninger Bräu [1991] ECR I-935; [1992] 5 CMLR 210...........................744, 746, 839
Dell'Orto [2007] ECR I-5557 243
Delta Schiffahrts- und Speditionsgesellschaft [1994] ECR I-2517 890
Demag v Finanzamt Duisburg-Sud [1974] ECR 1037 401
Demirel [1987] ECR 3719...17, 901, 910, 938, 954, 966
Denkavit [1979] ECR 3327 ....394, 438–41
Denkavit [1985] ECR 1013..439
Denkavit [1988] ECR 2965..441
Denkavit [1991] ECR I-3069 441
Denkavit [1996] ECR I-5063 586
Denkavit Loire Sarl v France [1979] ECR 1923 402
Denkavit Nederland v Hoofdproduktschap voor akkerbouwprodukten [1984] ECR 2171 434–5
Denmark v Commission [2003] ECR I-2643..178
der Weduwe [2002] ECR I-11319 221
Deserbais [1988] ECR 4907 549
Deuka [1975] ECR 421 330
Deuka [1975] ECR 759 330
Deutsche Grammophon [1871] ECR 487..453
Deutsche Grammophon [1971] ECR 487..453
Deutsche Lufthansa [2007] ECR I-5903 ....24, 99
Deutsche Milchkontor GmbH and others v Federal Republic of Germany [1983] ECR 2633 ....296, 302, 332
Deutsche Telekom AG v Lilli Schröder [2000] ECR I-743..371, 431
Deutscher Apothekerverband eV v 0800 DocMorris NV, Jacques Waterval
      [2003] ECR I-4887...254, 421, 425, 590
Deutschmann v Federal Republic of Germany [1965] ECR 469...401
Deutz und Geldermann v Council [1987] ECR 941 166

Deville [1988] ECR 3513. 300
DGV v Council and Commission [1979] ECR 3017. 199
D'Hoop [2002] ECR I-6191 . . . . 465, 475, 507
Dias, Opinion delivered 17 February 2011, case still pending. 479
Didier Tabouillet v Directeur des Services Fiscaux de Meurthe-et-Moselle [1997] ECR I-7471 405
Dijkman, 1 July 2010, nyr 584
Dilexport [1999] ECR I-579 . . . . 293, 300, 305–6
Dillenkofer [1996] ECR I-4845 . . . . 267, 309, 311
DIP v Commune di Bassano del Grappa [1995] ECRI-3257. . . . . .780, 892
Direct Cosmetics [1985] ECR 617 261
Ditta A Celestini [1997] ECR I-2971. 427
Djurgården-Lilla Värtans Miljöskyddsförening [2009] ECR I-9967. 251
DMT [1999] ECR I-3913. . . . . .220, 854
Dona v Mantero [1976] ECR 133. 559
Donckerwolcke [1976] ECR 1921 101
Dorit Harz [1984] ECR 1921 239
Dörr and Ünal [2005] ECR I-4759. 487
Dorsch Consult Ingenieurgesellschaft v Bundesbaugesellschaft Berlin
   [1997] ECR I-4961. . . . . .214–15, 240–1, 247, 292, 310
Doulamis v Union des Dentistes et Stomatologistes de Belgique (UPR)
   [2008] ECR I-1377; [2008] 5 CMLR 4 891
Dounias [2000] ECR I-577 289
Douwe Egberts NV v Westrom Pharma NV and Christophe Souranis and
   Douwe Egberts NV v FICS-World BVBA [2004] ECR I-7007 . . . . 327, 426, 552
Drei Glocken GmbH [1988] ECR 4233. 414
Driancourt v Cognet [1986] ECR 3231. 432
DSM v Commission [1999] ECR I-4695. 181
Duff and Others v Minister for Agriculture and Food, Ireland, and the Attorney General
   [1996] ECR I-569. 328
Dumortier Frères v Council [1979] ECR 3091. 199
Duphar [1984] ECR 523 435
Dynamic Medien [2008] ECR I-505 419
Dzodzi v Belgium [1990] ECR I-3763. . . . . .213, 219
EARL [1997] ECR I-1961 370
Eberhard Haug-Adrion [1984] ECR 4277 608
EC v First NV and Franex NV [2002] ECR I-10943 323
EchirollesDistribution [2000] ECR I-8207 . . . . .24, 99
Echternach [1989] ECR 723 . . . . 503, 512, 526
Eco Swiss China Time v Benetton International [1999] ECR I-3055. 215
Ecotrade v AFS [1998] ECR I-7907; [1999] 2 CMLR 833 856
ED Srl v I Fenocchio [1999] ECR I-3845 . . . . .429, 433
EDAH BV [1986] ECR 3359. 432
Edis [1998] ECR I-4951. . . . . .293, 305
Egenberger [2006] ECR I-633. 962
Église de Scientologie [2000] ECR I-1335. 664
El Corte Inglés [1996] ECR I-1281 267
Elchinov, 5 October 2010, nyr 272, 590
Elgafaji [2009] ECR I-921 363
Elliniki Radiophonia Tiléorassi AE (ERT) v Dimotiki Etairia Pliroforissis and others
   [1991] ECR I-2925. . . . . 338, 346, 367, 383, 436, 440, 881, 883, 889
Elsen [2000] ECR I-10409. 464
El-Yassini [1999] ECR I-1209. 954–5
Eman and Sevinger [2006] ECR I-8055 . . . . 58, 302, 493
Emesa Sugar Free Zone NV and Aruba, order of the Court, [2000] ECR I-665. 352
Emmott [1991] ECR I-4269 . . . . 291, 297–9
Engelbrecht [2000] ECR I-7321. 241
Engelmann, 9 September 2010, nyr. 546, 549, 574, 604, 649
Enirisorse Spa [2003] ECR I-14243. . . . . .403, 446
Enirisorse v Sotacarbo [2006] ECR I-2843. . . . . 851, 856, 863, 878–80
Enka [1977] ECR 2203 259
Entreprenørforeningens Affalds/ Miljøsektion (FFAD) v Københavns Kommune
   [2000] ECR I-3743. . . . . 434, 442, 880, 886
ENU v Commission [1993] ECR I-599. 186

Epifanio Viscido v Ente Poste Italiane [1998] ECR I-2629; [1998] 3 CMLR 184 851
Epson Europe [2001] ECR I-4243 586
Eridania v Commission [1969] ECR 459 188
Erste Group Bank AG v Commission [2009] ECR I-8681; [2010] 5 CMLR 9.............................719
Essevi and Salengo [1981] ECR 1413 ....137, 142, 273, 306, 397
Estée Lauder v Lancaster [2000] ECR I-117...443–4
Etablissements Delhaize Frères et Compagnie Le Lion SA v Promalvin SA and AGE Bodegas
    Unidas SA [1992] ECR I-3669..433–4
Eunomia v Italian Ministry of Education [1971] ECR 811 392
Eurico Italia and Others [1994] ECR I-711 217
Eurim-Pharm [1996] ECR I-3603 459
Eurocoton and Others v Council [2003] ECR I-10091...158
Eurofood IFSC [2006] ECR I-3813 821
European Low Fares Airline Association [2006] ECR I-403 ....75, 124, 226, 960
European Ombudsman v Lamberts [2004] ECR I-2803...190
Europemballage and Continental Can v Commission [1973] ECR 215..........706, 721, 765, 767, 770–1, 782–3
Eurotunnel and Others v SeaFrance [1997] ECR I-6315 225
Evans [2003] ECR I-14447 ....290, 295, 301
Even [1979] ECR 2019...518–19
EvoBus Austria [1998] ECR I-5411 292
Executif Regional Wallon and Glaverbel v Commission [1988] ECR 1573; [1989] 2 CMLR 771 860
Exportur SA v LOR SA and Confiserie du Tech SA [1992] ECR I-5529 445
Express Dairy Foods [1980] ECR 1887..296, 306
Extramet Industrie v Council [1991] ECR I-2501....................................171–2, 225
Eyssen [1981] ECR 409 414
F (Mr and Mrs) [1975] ECR 679 498
Faccini Dori [1994] ECR I-3325...................................260, 262, 264, 267, 281, 310
Fachverband der Buch- und Medienwirtschaft [2009] ECR I-3717................................428
Factortame [1990] ECR I-2433 ....212, 297–8, 303, 841
Factortame III and Brasserie du Pecheur [1996] ECR I-1029 ....190, 195, 212, 308–13, 874
Fahmi and Esmoris Cerdeiro-Pinedo Amado [2001] ECR I-2415..................................528
Fallimento Olimpiclub [2009] ECR I-7501...272
Fallimento Traghetti del Mediterraneo SpA v Presidenza del Consiglio dei Ministri
    [2010] 3 CMLR 46 863–4
Familiapress [1997] ECR I-3689 ....254, 346, 349, 367, 419, 422,
                                                                           440, 445–6, 673
Fantask [1997] ECR I-6783..272, 289, 299, 306, 325
Fazenda Pública v UCAL [1997] ECR I-4911 401–3
FC Terhoeve [1999] ECR I-345 522
FDV [1998] ECR I-5171 452
Fearon [1984] ECR 3677...542, 546
Fédération Française des Sociétés d'Assurance v Ministère de l'Agriculture et de la Pêche
    [1995] ECR I-4013...716
Fédération Nationale du Commerce Extérieur des Produits Alimentaires v France
    [1991] ECR I-5505...873
Fedesa [1990] ECR I-4023...326
Fediol [1989] ECR 1781...962
Feldain [1987] ECR 3521 400
Felicitas [1982] ECR 2771 241
Felix Kapper [2004] ECR I-5205 222
FENIN v Commission [2006] ECR I-6295; [2006] 5 CMLR 7 ....714, 717, 876
Ferrario [1983] ECR 2357...332
Ferriere di roe Volciano [1983] ECR 3921 333
Ferrière Nord SpA v Commission [1997] ECR I-4411, [1997] 5 CMLR 575........................741
Ferring v ACOSS [2001] ECR I-9067 862
Ferwerda [1980] ECR 617...296, 334
Feryn [2008] ECR I-5187 371
FFSA v Commission [1998] ECR I-1303 ....874, 887
FIAMM v Council and Commission [2008] ECR I-6513..197
Fietje [1980] ECR 3839 414
Filipiak [2009] ECR I-11049..271–2
Finalarte [2001] ECR I-7831..103, 578
Finalarte and Others [2001] ECR I-7831 660

Finanzamt Eisleben v Feuerbesttungsverein Halle [2006] ECR I-4999 252
Fink-Frucht [1968] ECR 223 402
Firma Sloman Neptun Schiffahrts A-G v Seebetriebsrat Bodo Ziesmer, Sloman Neptun Schiffahrts AG
   [1993] ECR I-887; [1995] 2 CMLR 97 851–2
Firma Steinike und Weinlig v Germany [1977] ECR 595; [1977] 2 CMLR 688 . . . . 849, 862, 866
FMC [1996] ECR I-389 306
Foglia v Novello [1980] ECR 745. . . . . .212, 220
Foglia v Novello [1981] ECR 3045. 212
Forcheri [1983] ECR 2323. . . . . .498, 528
Ford España v Estado Español [1989] ECR 2305. . . . . .228, 395
Ford v Commission [1985] ECR 2725; [1985] 3 CMLR 528 732
Förster [2008] ECR I-8507 . . . . 467, 475–6, 482
Foselev Sud-Ouest [2008] ECR I-8745 268
Foster v British Gas [1990] ECR I-3313 263
Foto-Frost v Hauptzollamt Lübeck-Ost [1987] ECR 4199 . . . . 201, 225–7, 304
France, Italy and the United Kingdom v Commission [1982] ECR 2545; [1982] 3 CMLR 144 877–8
France and others v Commission [1998] ECR I-1375; [1998] 4 CMLR 829 780
France Télécom SA v Commission [2009] ECR I-2369; [2009] 4 CMLR 25 . . . . 785, 789, 792
France v Commission [1970] ECR 487. 403
France v Commission [1988] ECR 973. 178
France v Commission [1990] ECR I-3571 157
France v Commission [1991] ECR I-1223; [1992] 5 CMLR 552. 879
France v Commission [1994] ECR I-3641 . . . . .723, 939
France v Commission [1996] ECR 4551; [1997] 1 CMLR 983 850
France v Commission [1997] ECR I-1627 157
France v Commission (Boussac) [1990] ECR I-307 869–70
France v Commission ('Stardust Marine') [2002] ECR I-4397 . . . . 851–2, 854
France v Parliament and Council [2005] ECR I-4021. 180
France v United Kingdom [1979] ECR 2923 136
Francolor v Commission [1972] ECR 851; [1972] CMLR 557 822
Francovich [1991] ECR I-5357. . . . . 143, 150, 196, 212, 247, 267, 289, 292,
                                                                                              297–8, 303, 307–15, 318, 840–2, 874
Francovich [1995] ECR I-3843. 212
Frans-Nederlandse [1981] ECR 3277 439
Franz Grad [1970] ECR 825. 268
Franzén [1997] ECR I-5909 . . . . 217, 427, 438, 448
Frascogna [1985] ECR 1739 . . . . .518, 528
Fratelli Constanzo v Commune di Milano [1989] ECR 1839 . . . . 263–4, 272
Fratelli Cucchi v Avez [1977] ECR 987. 402
Fratelli Variola v Italian Finance Ministry [1973] ECR 981. 257
Freskot [2003] ECR I-5263 501
Fromancais [1983] ECR 395. 326
Fromme [1982] ECR 1449 . . . . .292, 296
FRUBO v Commission [1975] ECR 563; [1975] 2 CMLR 123 734
Futura Participations [1997] ECR I-2471 595
Galileo Zaninotto v Ispettorato Centrale Repressione FrodiùUfficio di Coneglianoù
   Ministero delle Risorse Agricole, Alimentari e Forestali [1998] ECR I-6629 . . . . 326, 330–1
Gallagher [1995] ECR I-4253. 486
Gambelli [2003] ECR I-13031 532
Garage Molenheide [1997] ECR I-7281 291
Garcia Avello [2003] ECR I-11613. . . . . 469, 489–90, 501
Gaston Schul Douane-expediteur BV [2005] ECR I-10513. 226
Gattoussi [2006] ECR I-11917 955
GB-INNO-BM [1990] ECR I-667 444
Gebhard [1995] ECR I-4165. . . . . 503, 521, 532–3, 540, 547,
                                                                                                    575–6, 635, 644, 665
Gebroeders van Es Douane Agenten BV v Inspecteur der Invoerrechten en Accijnzen
   [1996] ECR I-431. . . . . 36, 328–9
Geddo v Ente Nazionale Risi [1973] ECR 865. 409
Geigy v Commission [1972] ECR 787. 721
Geitling v High Authority [1960] ECR 425 337
GEMO [2003] ECR I-13769 863
General Motors BV v Commission [2006] ECR I-3173; [2006] 5 CMLR 1. 743

General Motors Continental v Commission [1975] ECR 1367; [1976] 1 CMLR 95 776
Georges Lornoy en Zonen NV and others v Belgian State [1992] ECR I-6523. 403
Georgiev, 12 November 2010, nyr 371
Geraets-Smits and Peerbooms [2001] ECR I-5473 . . . . .291, 378, 555, 564, 566, 572, 608
Germany, France, Netherlands, Denmark and United Kingdom v Commission
    [1987] ECR 3203 178
Germany v Commission [1966] ECR 159. 395
Germany v Commission [1984] ECR 1451 867
Germany v Commission [2000] ECR I-6857 859
Germany v Commission [2003] ECR I-1139 859
Germany v Commission [2003] ECR I-9919 860
Germany v Commission [2004] ECR I-3925 859
Germany v Commission, Hanseatische Industrie Beteiligungen GmbH v Commission,
    Bremer Vulkan Verbund A-G v Commission [1996] ECR I-5151 854
Germany v Council [1994] ECR I-4973 . . . . .956, 958–9, 962
Germany v Council [1995] ECR I-3723 123
Germany v Council [1998] ECR I-973 . . . . .155, 939
Germany v Council and Parliament [2000] ECR I-8419 . . . . .108, 178, 180, 678
Germany v Parliament and Council [2006] ECR I-11573 108
Germany v Parliament and Council (Deposit Guarantee Schemes Directive)
    [1997] ECR I-2405. . . . . .36, 118, 124, 267
Gervais-Danone [1971] ECR 1127 329
GIL Insurance [2004] ECR I-4777 . . . . .855, 857
Gilbert Demoor en Zonen NV and others v Belgian State [1992] ECR I-6613. 401–3
Gilli and Andres [1980] ECR 2071 413–14
Gilly [1998] ECR I-2793 . . . . .246, 500, 582
Giloy v Hauptzollamt Frankfurt am Main-Ost [1997] ECR I-4291 213–14
Givane [2003] ECR I-345 480
Glaxo Wellcome [2009] ECR I-8591 . . . . .593, 663
GlaxoSmithKline Services unlimited v Commission [2009] ECR I-9291; [2010] 4 CMLR 2 742–3
Glencore Grain [1988] ECR I-2435 165
Gmurzynska-Bscher v Oberfinanzdirektion Köln [1990] ECR I-4003. 213
Goffette [1987] ECR 2525 441
Gomes Valente [2001] ECR I-1327 . . . . .223, 401
Gondrand Frères [1981] ECR 1931 328
Gottrup-Klim v Dansk Landbrugs [1994] ECR I-5641. 776
Gottwald [2009] ECR I-9117 608
Gouda [1991] ECR I-4007 . . . . .367, 572, 578–80
Gourmet International [2001] ECR I-1795 . . . . .254, 425, 501, 552, 558, 564
Gözütok [2005] ECR I-1345 381
Gräbner [2002] ECR I-6515 . . . . .565, 628
Graf [2000] ECR I-493. 522
Granaria v Council and Commission [1979] ECR 1081. 187
Grandes Distilleries [1979] ECR 897. . . . . .404, 448
Grandes Distilleries [1979] ECR 975. 448
Grands Moulins de Paris v Council and Commission [1987] ECR 4833. 193
Grant v South West Trains Ltd [1998] ECR I-621 . . . . .348, 371
Gravier v City of Liège [1985] ECR 593 . . . . .105, 475, 528
Greece v Commission [1989] ECR 3711. 954
Greece v Commission [2000] ECR I-8787 858
Greenpeace [1998] ECR I-1651 . . . . .167, 378
Grendel [1982] ECR 2301 261
Grifoni v EAEC [1994] ECR I-341. 199
Grilli [2003] ECR I-11585. 434
Grimaldi v Fonds des Maladies Professionnelles [1989] ECR 4407 . . . . .212, 244
Groener [1989] ECR 3967. . . . . .371, 510
Groenveld [1979] ECR 3409. 433
Grogan [1982] ECR 869 331
Grogan [1991] ECR I-4685. 555
Group Danone v Commission, [2007] ECR I-1331; [2007] 4 CMLR 18 829
Groupement National des Négociants en Pommes de Terre de Belgique (Belgapom)
    [1995] ECR I-2467. . . . . .419, 430
Grundig Italiana [2002] ECR I-8003 300

Grunkin and Paul [2008] ECR I-7639...490
Grzelczyk [2001] ECR I-6193...26, 273, 464–5, 475, 507
Gschwind [1999] ECR I-5451..585
GT-Link A/S v De Danske Statsbaner [1997] ECR I-4449; [1997] 5 CMLR 601 886
Guarnieri e Cie, Opinion delivered on 14 September 2010, pending.......................429
Guérin Automobiles v Commission [1997] ECR I-1503 ....184, 186
Guerlain, Rochas, Lanvin and Nina Ricci ('Perfumes') [1980] ECR 2327; [1981] 2 CMLR 99.............748–9
Guimont [2000] ECR I-10663 432
Gullung [1988] ECR 111..554
Gunnar Nilsson [1998] ECR I-7477 423
Günter Fuß, 14 October 2010, nyr..291
GVL v Commission [1983] ECR 483; [1983] 3 CMLR 645 ....713, 885
Gysbrechts and Santurel Inter [2008] ECR I-4997 434
H Banks & Co Ltd v British Coal Corporation [1994] ECR I-1209; [1994] 5 CMLR 30.................840
H Cullet et Chambres Syndicale des réparateurs automobiles et détaillants de produits pétroliers v
    Centre Leclerc à Toulouse et Centre Leclerc à Saint-Orens-de-Gameville [1985] ECR 35...........430, 440
H. Krantz GmbH & Co v Ontvanger der Directe Belastingen and Netherlands State
    [1990] ECR I-583...428
Haaga [1974] ECR 1205 680
Haahr Petroleum Ltd v Åbenrå Havn and Others [1997] ECR I-4085.....................397
Haegeman v Belgium [1974] ECR 449 ....212, 910
Hag GF [1990] ECR I-3711...452
Haim [1994] ECR I-425..628
Haim [2000] ECR I-5123..311, 313
Halliburton Services [1994] ECR I-1137 ....535, 545, 586, 597
Hallouzi-Choho [1996] ECR I-4807 ....273, 955
Hanner [2005] ECR I-4551..448, 876, 889
Hansen II [1979] ECR 935 449
Hansen v Hauptzollampt Flensburg [1978] ECR 1787................................397, 405
Harpegnies [1998] ECR I-5121 427
Hartlauer [2009] ECR I-1721 549
Hasselblad v Commission [1984] ECR 883; [1984] CMLR 559 748
Hauer [1979] ECR 3727...368–9
Hauptzollamt Hamburg-Jonas v Krucken [1988] ECR 2213...........................322, 331
Heemskerk [2008] ECR I-8763 302
Heijn [1984] ECR 3263 436
Heineken Brouwerijen [1984] ECR 2435; [1985] 1 CMLR 389.........................868
Heininger [2001] ECR I-9945. ....299–300, 302
Heinrich [2009] ECR I-1659..272
Heiser [2005] ECR I-1627.................................850, 853, 855–6, 864
Helmut Kampelmann [1997] ECR I-6907 263
Hengartner, 15 July 2010, nyr..954
Henn & Darby [1979] ECR 3795 ....409, 436–7
Hermès v FHT [1998] ECR I-3603 ....212–13, 940, 957, 965, 967
Heylens and Others [1987] ECR 4097.........................291, 379, 626
Hillegom [1990] ECR I-1735 395
Hilmar Kellinghusen v Amt für Land- und Wasserwirtschaft Kiel and Ernst-Detlef
    Ketelsen v Amt für Land- und Wasserwirtschaft Husum [1998] ECR I-6337 323
Hilti A-G v Commission [1994] ECR I-667; [1994] 4 CMLR 614............772, 778, 796–7
HNL v Council and Commission [1978] ECR 1209...............................193–5
Hoche [1990] ECR I-2681..330
Hocsman [2000] ECR I-6623 627–8
Hoechst v Commission [1989] ECR 2859; [1991] 4 CMLR 410 818
Hoechst v Commission [1999] ECR I-4443...202
Hoecks [1985] ECR 973...518
Hoekstra (neé Unger) [1964] ECR 177..503
Hoffmann-La Roche v Centrafarm [1977] ECR 957..............................223, 225
Hoffmann-La Roche v Centrafarm [1978] ECR 1139................................456
Hoffmann-La Roche v Commission [1979] ECR 461.................192, 766, 769, 776, 778–9, 782,
                                                                      784, 792–5, 821
Höfner v Macrotron [1991] ECR I-1979.....................253, 713–14, 781, 882–3
Holtz v Council [1974] ECR 1 187
Hospital Ingenieure [1999] ECR I-1405 292

Hospital Ingenieure [2002] ECR I-5553 291
Houtwipper [1994] ECR I-4249. . . . . .414, 439
HSB-Wohnbau [2001] ECR I-5353 216
Huber [2002] ECR I-7699. 302
Hugin v Commission [1979] ECR 1869; [1979] 3 CMLR 345. . . . . .753, 772
Hüls v Commission [1999] ECR I-4287; [1999] 5 CMLR 1016. . . . . 202, 737, 739
Humanplasma, 9 December 2010, nyr 428
Humblot [1985] ECR 1367 400
Hydrotherm [1984] ECR 2999 717–18
i-21 Germany [2006] ECR I-8559 . . . . .272, 294
Iannelli & Volpi v Meroni [1977] ECR 557. 254, 396, 403, 409, 446–7
IAZ v Commission [1983] ECR 3369; [1984] 3 CMLR 276. . . . . .735, 885
IBM v Commission [1981] ECR 2639. . . . . .159, 184
Ibrahim, 23 February 2010, nyr 373, 477, 527
ICAP v Walter Beneventi [1979] ECR 1163 402
ICI [1998] ECR I-4695. 648
ICI v Commission [1972] ECR 619; [1972] CMLR 557 . . . . 720, 736–7, 821, 830
Idrima Tipou, 21 October 2010, nyr 661
IGAV v ENCC [1975] ECR 699 . . . . .402, 876
IHT Internationale Heiztechnik [1994] ECR I-2789. 456
Impact [2008] ECR I-2483 . . . . .268, 295
Imperial Tobacco [2000] ECR I-8599 108
IMS Health v Commission [2004] ECR I-5039, [2004] 4 CMLR 1543. . . . . 798, 802–4
IN.CO.GE. [1998] ECR I-6307. . . . . 271, 280, 288
Infront [2008] ECR I-1451 171
INNO v ATAB [1977] ECR 2115; [1978] 1 CMLR 283. . . . . 776, 877, 879
Inspecteur van de Belastingdienst v X BV [2009] 5 CMLR 12 839
Inspire Art [2003] ECR I-10155. . . . . 648–9, 652–5
Inter-Environnement Wallonie [1997] ECR I-7411 . . . . 247–8, 259
Interfood [1972] ECR 231. 964
Inter-Huiles [1983] ECR 555 433
Intermodal Transports (Judgment of 15 September 2005). 224
International Chemical Corporation v Amministrazione delle Finanze dello Stato
    [1981] ECR 1191 229
International Fruit [1971] ECR 1107. 410
International Fruit Company [1972] ECR 1219. . . . . 942, 958–9
International Transport Workers' Federation and The Finnish Seamen's Union v
    Viking Line et al [2007] ECR I-10779. . . . . 349–50, 375, 387, 431, 434,
                                                                                                         501–2, 553, 577, 672
Internationale Handelsgesellschaft [1970] ECR 1125. . . . . 271, 273, 325, 338
Interquell Stärke v Council and Commission [1979] ECR 3045. 199
'Intertanko' [2008] ECR I-4057 . . . . 960–1, 967
Interzuccheri v Ditta Rezzano e Cavassa [1977] ECR 1029 402
Inzirillo [1976] ECR 2057 . . . . .518, 527
Ioannidis [2005] ECR I-8275 . . . . .467, 507
Ioannis Vougioukas [1995] ECR I-4033 500
Iorio [1986] ECR 247. 501
Ireks-Arkady v Council and Commission [1979] ECR 2955. . . . . .194, 199
Ireland v Parliament and Council [2009] ECR I-593 108
Irish Cement Ltd v Commission [1988] ECR 6473. . . . . .159, 188
Irish Creamery Milk Suppliers Association v Ireland [1981] ECR 735 . . . . .212, 395
Irish Sugar v Commission [2001] ECR I-5333. . . . . .766, 777–8, 780, 783,
                                                                                                         786, 791, 794
Istituto Chemioterapico Italiano SpA and Commercial Solvents Corpn v
    Commission [1974] ECR 223, [1974] 1 CMLR 309 . . . . 721, 754, 767, 772, 775, 779,
                                                                                                         799, 802, 805, 824
Italy v Commission [1974] ECR 709; [1974] 2 CMLR 593 850
Italy v Commission [1991] ECR I-1433; [1993] 2 CMLR 1 854
Italy v Commission [1991] ECR I-1603 854
Italy v Commission [2005] ECR I-3657 867
Italy v Commission (British Telecom) [1985] ECR 873, [1985] 2 CMLR 368. . . . . .776, 885
Italy v Commission (Judgment of 1 December 2005). 158
Italy v Council [1979] ECR 2575 161

Italy v Council [1998] ECR I-6937...962
Italy v Council and Commission [1966] ECR 389.................................201–2, 706
ITC Innovative Technology Centre [2007] ECR I-181.........................251–2, 521
Jany and others [2001] ECR I-8615......................484, 503, 553, 555, 954
Jean Lion [1982] ECR 3887...334
Jégo-Quéré v Commission [2004] ECR I-3425....................................159
Jenkins v Kingsgate [1981] ECR 911..265
Jensen and Korn [1998] ECR I-2975...293–4, 302
Jersey Produce Marketing Organisation Ltd [2005] ECR I-9543..........393–4
Jipa [2008] ECR I-5157..483
Job Centre [1995] ECR I-3361...215
Job Centre Coop [1997] ECR I-7119..781, 882
John Deere v Commission [1998] ECR I-3111; [1998] 5 CMLR 311.........736, 739, 750
John Walker [1986] ECR 875...397
Johnston II [1994] ECR I-5483...299
Johnston v Chief Constable of the RUC [1986] ECR 1651.........263, 289–90, 338, 379
Jongeneel Kaas and Others v Netherlands [1984] ECR 483....................433
Josemans, 16 December 2010, nyr...483
Josemans v Burgemeester van Maastricht, 12 December 2010, nyr.........409
Just [1980] ECR 501...306
Kaba (Kaba II) [2003] ECR I-2219...212, 353
Kaba [2000] ECR I-2623...212
Kabel Deutschland [2008] ECR I-10889...580
Kadi [2008] ECR I-635...369
Kadi v Council and Commission [2008] ECR I-6321............................907
Kalanke [1995] ECR I-3051...372
Kampffmeyer v Commission [1967] ECR 245....................194, 198, 200
Kampffmeyer v Commission and Council [1976] ECR 711....................199
Kanal 5 Ltd v Foreningen Svenska Tonsattares Internationella Musikbyra (STIM) upa
    [2008] ECR I-9275..787, 790
Kapferer [2006] ECR I-2585...228, 272
KappAhl Oy [1998] ECR I-8069...36
Karlsson [2000] ECR 2737..370
Karner [2004] ECR I-3025..427, 558
Käserei Champignon Hofmeister [2002] ECR I-6453...........................351
Katsivardas, 20 May 2010, nyr..954
Kattner Stahlbau GmbH v Maschinenbau- und Metall- Berufsgenossenschaft
    [2009] ECR I-1513; [2009] 2 CMLR 51............................581, 716, 876
Katz [2008] ECR I-7607..243
Kaur [2001] ECR I-1237...469
KB [2004] ECR I-541..348, 365, 371–2
Keck and Mithouard [1993] ECR I-6097.............407, 416, 418–22, 425–9, 443,
                                                                        459, 522, 668, 892
Kelderman [1981] ECR 517...414
Keller [1986] ECR I-2897..368
Kemmler [1996] ECR I-703...538, 574
Kempf [1986] ECR 1741..504
Kempter [2008] ECR I-411..272
Ker-Optika, 2 December 2010, nyr...426, 428
Keurkoop [1982] ECR 2853...453
Kieffer and Thill [1997] ECR I-3629...427, 435
Kik v Council and Commission [1996] ECR I-1987..............................167
Kingdom of Denmark v Commission [1998] ECR I-5759.......................328
Kirsammer-Hack v Sidal [1993] ECR I-6185.......................................851
Kleinwort Benson v City of Glasgow District Council [1995] ECR I-615....213
Klensch [1986] ECR 3466...322
Klopp [1984] ECR 2971...538, 542, 574–5
Knauf Gips v Commission, 1 July 2010, nyr.................379, 720, 832
Knoors [1979] ECR 399...537–41, 567
Köbler v Austria [2003] ECR I-10239..........145, 223–4, 277, 311, 314
Koestler [1978] ECR 1971...559
Kofisa Italia v Ministero delle Finanze [2001] ECR I-207........213–14, 304, 318
Kofoed [2007] ECR I-5795...240, 266

Kohl [1984] ECR 3651 436
Kohll [1998] ECR I-1931 . . . . 564, 566, 572, 579, 581
Kolpinghuis [1987] ECR 3969 381
Kolpinghuis Nijmegen [1987] ECR 3969 . . . . .242, 283
Konle [1999] ECR I-3099 . . . . .313, 665
Konsumentombudsmannen (KO) v De Agostini and TV Shop [1997] ECR I-3843 .425
Koppensteiner [2005] ECR I-4855 292
Köster [1970] ECR 1161 88
Kraaijeveld [1996] ECR I-5403 249
Kramer [1976] ECR 1279 . . . . 100, 915, 933
Kranemann [2005] ECR I-493 522
Krankenheim Ruhesitz am Wannsee-Seniorenheimstatt [2008] ECR I-8061 592
Kraus [1993] ECR I-1663 . . . . 291, 500, 520, 524, 540–1
Kremzow v Austria [1997] ECR I-2629 . . . . 214, 338, 501
Krohn v Commission [1986] ECR 753 . . . . .191, 198
Krombach [2000] ECR I-1935 289
Krüger v Hauptzollamt Hamburg-Jonas [1997] ECR I-4517 227
Kruidvat v Commission [1998] ECR I-7183 173
Krzysztof Pesacutela v Justizministerium Mecklenburg-Vorpommern
     [2009] ECR I-11677 627
Kücükdeveci (Judgment of 19 January 2010) 255, 265, 284, 334, 345, 371
Kühne & Heitz [2004] ECR I-837 . . . . .228, 272
Kühne [2001] ECR I-9517 291
Kühne and Nagel [2004] ECR I-887 374
Kupferberg [1982] ECR 3641 . . . . 245, 406, 954–5
Kupferberg [1985] ECR 157 401
KYDEP v Council and Commission [1994] ECR I-4199 192
Kziber [1991] ECR I-199 954
Laboratoires Boiron [2006] ECR I-7529 302
Lafarge SA v Commission [2010] 5 CMLR 10 . . . . 739, 829, 831
Lageder [1993] ECR I-1761 . . . . .36, 331
Lair [1988] ECR 3161 505
Laisa v Council [1988] ECR 2285 193
Lamaire v NDALTP [1994] ECR I-3215 395
Lämmerzahl [2007] ECR I-8415 299
Land Berlin v Wigei [1980] ECR 1331 405
Landesgrundverkehrsreferent der Tiroler Landesregierung v Beck and Another
     [1999] ECR I-4977 221
Landschoot v Mera [1988] ECR 3443 333
Lankhorst-Hohorst GmbH v Finanzamt Steinfurt [2002] ECR I-11779 . . . . .587, 597
Larsy [2001] ECR I-5063 311
Laserdisken v Kulturministeriet [2006] ECR I-8089 24
Lassal, 7 October 2010, nyr 479
Laval un Partneri [2007] ECR I-11767 . . . . 349–50, 375, 431, 501, 556, 581
Lawrie-Blum [1986] ECR 2121 . . . . 503–4, 513
Le Lion [1983] ECR 2973 . . . . .439, 441
Le Pen v European Parliament, Judgment of 7 July 2005 158
Lebon [1987] ECR 2811 . . . . .507, 525
Leclerc v Sarl 'Au Blé Vert' [1985] ECR 1; [1985] 2 CMLR 286 . . . . 435–6, 891
Leclerc-Siplec v TF1 Publicité and M6 Publicité [1995] ECR I-179 . . . . 221, 420, 424
Leendert [1983] ECR 3883 440–1
Leffler [2005] ECR I-9611 302
Legros and others [1992] ECR I-4625 . . . . .393, 405
Lehtonen [2000] ECR I-2681 523
Leifer [1995] ECR I-3231 . . . . 101, 944, 964
Leitner [2002] ECR I-2631 302
Lemmens [1998] ECR I-3711 251
Leonesio v Italian Ministry of Agriculture and Forestry [1972] ECR 287 .257
Les Verts v Parliament [1986] ECR 1339 . . . . 157–8, 165
Leur-Bloem v Inspecteur der Belastingdienst/Ondernemingen Amsterdam 2 [1997] ECR I-4161 213–14
Levez v Jennings (Harlow Pools) [1998] ECR I-7835 . . . . 291–4, 299
Levin [1982] ECR 1035 503–4
Liberal Democrats v Parliament [1993] ECR I-3153 186

Lidl Belgium [2008] ECR I-3601 595
Lindorfs [2004] ECR I-7183 519
Lindqvist [2003] ECR I-12971 242
Linster [2000] ECR I-6917 249
Loenderloot [1997] ECR I-6227 .... 456, 459
Lopes da Veiga [1989] ECR 2989 502
L'Oréal v PVDA De Nieuwe AMCK [1980] ECR 3775; [1981] 2 CMLR 235 768
Lorenz [1973] ECR 1471 .... 868, 873
Lubor Gaal [1995] ECR I-1031 526
Lucazeau v SACEM [1989] ECR 2811; [1991] 4 CMLR 248 787
Lucchini [2007] ECR I-6199 302
Lucien Ortscheit GmbH [1994] ECR I-5243 424
Lück [1968] ECR 245 288
Ludwigs-Apotheke [2007] ECR I-9623 424
Luisi and Carbone [1984] ECR 377 .... 555, 557, 559
Lütticke v Commission [1966] ECR 19 .... 141, 188
Lütticke v Commission [1971] ECR 325 190
Lutticke v Hauptzollamt Saarlouis [1966] ECR 205 .... 396–7, 401
Luxembourg v Parliament and Council [2000] ECR I-9131 .... 623, 638, 642
Lyckeskog [2002] ECR I-4839 223
Maas v Bundesanstalt für Landwirtschaftliche Marktordnung [1986] ECR 3537 327
Mac Quen [2001] ECR I-837 .... 577, 628–9
McCarthy, Opinion delivered 25 November 2010, case still pending 468, 490
Mackprang v Commission [1971] ECR 797 186
Maison Singer [1965] ECR 965 .... 499, 621
Maizena [1982] ECR 4601 331
Maizena [1987] ECR 4587; C-210/00 Käserei Champignon Hofmeister [2002] ECR I-6453 351
Makro Zelfbedieningsgroothandel and Others [2009] ECR I-10019 458
Manfred Graff v Hauptzollamt Köln Rheinau [1994] ECR I-3361 344
Manfredi v Lloyd Adriatico Assicurazioni SpA [2006] ECR I-6619;
    [2006] 5 CMLR 17 .... 293, 300–1, 315, 840, 842
Manghera [1986] ECR 91 448
Mangold [2005] ECR I-9981 .... 222, 248, 255–6, 265–7, 276, 284, 334,
                                                   339, 344–5, 371, 374, 608
Manninen [2004] ECR I-7477 596
Manuel José Lourenço Dias v Director da Alfândega do Porto [1992] ECR I-4673 402
Marazan Concord [2006] ECR I-2303 452
Maria Simitzi v Dimos Kos [1995] ECR I-2655 393–4
Marks & Spencer [2002] ECR I-6325 .... 260, 300, 305
Marks & Spencer [2005] ECR I-10837 .... 589, 592–5, 648
Marks & Spencer [2008] ECR I-2283 305
Marleasing [1990] ECR I-4135 .... 175, 238, 240–1, 292, 680
Mars [1995] ECR I-1923 443
Marschall [1997] ECR I-6363 372–3
Marshall II [1993] ECR I-4367 .... 288, 294, 297–8, 301
Marshall v Southampton and South-West Hampshire Area Health Authority
    [1986] ECR 723 .... 217, 261–4, 266–7, 281
Marsman [1972] ECR 1243 514
Martín Martín, 17 December 2009 267
Martínez Sala [1998] ECR I-2691 .... 464, 503
Maruko [2008] ECR I-1757 .... 266, 371
Masdar v Commission [2008] ECR I-9761 197
Maso [1997] ECR I-4051 313
Masterfoods [2000] ECR I-11369 839
Matra v Commission [1993] ECR I-3203 872–3
Mattern and Cikotik [2006] ECR I-3145 476
Mattner, 22 April 2010, nyr 596
Mau [2003] ECR I-4791 250
Maxicar v Renault [1988] ECR 6039 802
Mazzoleni [2001] ECR I-2189 578
Meca-Medina v Commission [2006] ECR I-6991; [2006] 5 CMLR 18 .... 750, 763
Mediaprint, 9 November 2010, nyr 102
Medicines Control Agency [1996] ECR I-5819 .... 263–4, 281

Medipac-Kazantzidis v Venizelio-Pananio [2007] ECR I-4557..263
Meijer [1979] ECR 1387 409
Meilicke v ADV/ ORGA [1992] ECR I-4871 220
Meints v Minister van Landbouw [1997] ECR I-6689 516
Melki, 22 June 2010, nyr 272
Melkunie [1984] ECR 2367...438
Mellor [2009] ECR I-3799...291
Meng [1993] ECR I-5751 892
Merchandise and Others [1991] ECR 1027 416
Merci convenzionali porto di Genova SpA v Siderurgica Gabrielli SpA
    [1991] ECR I-5889.. 447, 714, 775, 883, 886
Merck Genéricos [2007] ECR I-7001 966
Merck v Primecrown [1996] ECR I-6285...456
Merck v Stephar [1981] ECR 2063...455–6
Mercke, Sharp & Dohme [2002] ECR I-3703...459
Merida [2004] ECR I-847 501
Messner [1989] ECR I-4209 .... 328, 381, 472, 478, 509
Metallgesellschaft [2001] ECR I-1727 .... 302, 305, 313, 590, 597
Metalsa Srl [1993] ECR I-3751...406
Metock [2008] ECR I-6241...540
Metock and others [2008] ECR I-6241 470
Metro v Cartier [1994] ECR I-15; [1994] 5 CMLR 331 748
Metro v Commission [1977] ECR 1875 .... 169, 710, 748
Metro v Commission (No 2) [1986] ECR 3021; [1987] 1 CMLR 118.................................748
Meyhui NV v Schott Zwiesel Glaswerke AG [1994] ECR I-3879 435
Michaeler [2008] ECR I-3135..266
Michel S [1973] ECR 457 ....498, 526
Micheletti and others [1992] ECR I-4239..469, 534
Mickelsson and Roos [2009] ECR I-4273 428
Mikhailidis [2000] ECR I-7145 ....306, 393
Milch- Fett- und Eierkontor v Hauptzollamt Saarbrucken [1968] ECR 207 402
Miller Schallplatten v Commission [1978] ECR 131; [1978] 2 CMLR 334 741–2
Ministère Public v Asjes [1986] ECR 1425...718, 891
Ministère Public v Tournier [1989] ECR 2521; [1991] 4 CMLR 248 787
Ministero dell'Economia e delle Finanze v Cassa di Risparmio di Firenze SpA
    [2006] ECR I-289; [2008] 1 CMLR 28 ....713, 715
Miraglia [2005] ECR I-2009 381
MIRECO [1980] ECR 2559...296, 306
ML Acton v Commission [1975] ECR 383..375
Molkerei-Zentrale v Hauptzollamt Paderborn [1968] ECR 143 .... 288, 396, 404
Monin Automobiles I [1993] ECR I-2049..221
Monin Automobiles II [1994] ECR I-1707...221
Mono Car Styling [2009] ECR I-6653..251
Monsanto, 6 July 2010, nyr 964
Monsees v Unabhängiger Verwaltungssenat für Kärnten [1999] ECR I-2921 ....427, 433
Monte Arcosu [2001] ECR I-103...257
Montecatini v Commission [1999] ECR I-4539..202
Moormann BV [1988] ECR 4689...441
Morellato [2003] ECR I-8343..423, 427
Morgan [2007] ECR I-9161..475
Morgenbesser [2003] ECR I-13467..639
Morson and Jhanjan v Netherlands [1982] ECR 3723 ....223, 501
Moser [1984] ECR 2539 501
Motosykletistiki Omospondia Ellados Npid v Ellinko Dimosio [2008] ECR I-4863;
    [2008] 5 CMLR 11.. 715, 883, 885
Moulins [1977] ECR 1795...333
MPA Pharma [1996] ECR I-3671..459
MRAX [2002] ECR I-6591...471
Mulder [1988] ECR 2321 ....36, 330
Mulder v Council and Commission (Mulder II) [1992] ECR I-3061..............................193, 196
Müller Fauré and van Riet [2003] ECR I-4509..378
Muñoz [2002] ECR I-7289 ....249–52, 258
Murphy v An Bord Telecom Eireann [1988] ECR 673 241

Musique Diffusion Française v Commission [1983] ECR 1825; [1983] 3 CMLR 221 821
Mutsch [1985] ECR 2681 518
Mutualités Chrétiennes v Rzepa [1974] ECR 1241 288
N v Inspecteur van de Belastingdienst Oost/kantoor Almelo [2006] ECR I-7409 302
Nachi Europe v Hauptzollamt Krefeld [2001] ECR I-1197 . . . . 181, 201, 225
Nakajima [1991] ECR I-2069 962–3
Namur-Les Assurances du Crédit SA v Office National du Ducroire and Belgium [1994] ECR I-3829 868
National Dried Fruit Association [1988] ECR 757 328
National Farmers' Union v Secrétariat Général du Gouvernement [2002] ECR I-9079 . . . . .151, 202
National Panasonic v Commission [1980] ECR 2033; [1980] CMLR 169 818
Nederlandse Federatieve Vereniging voor de Groothandel op Elektrotechnisch Gebied v
    Commission [2006] ECR I-8725; [2006] 5 CMLR 22. 743
Nerkowska [2008] ECR I-3993. . . . . .489, 519
Nertsvoederfabriek Nederland BV [1987] ECR 3883 . . . . .433, 448
The Netherlands and Leeuwarder Papierwaren fabriek BV v Commission [1985] ECR 809;
    [1985] 3 CMLR 380 854
Netherlands v Commission [1971] ECR 639 183
Netherlands v Commission [2004] ECR I-4461 857
Netherlands v Parliament and Council [2001] ECR I-7079 . . . . 108–9, 116, 118, 180, 324, 363–4, 960
Netherlands Van der Wal v Commission [2000] ECR I-1; [2002] 1 CMLR 16 821
Neu and Others [1991] ECR I-3617 322
Neumann [1967] ECR 441 270
Nevedi [2005] ECR I-10423 228
Niels Nygård and Svineafgiftsfonden [2002] ECR I-3657 403
Nikoloudi [2005] ECR I-1789. 284
Ninni-Orasche [2003] ECR I-13187 . . . . 473, 504, 506
Nino et al [1990] ECR I-3537. 535
Niselli [2004] ECR I-10853. 220
Nold v Commission [1974] ECR I-491 . . . . 338–9, 368
Norbrook Laboratories [1998] ECR I-1531 291
Nordgetreide v Commission [1972] ECR 105 188
Nordsee v Reederei Mond [1982] ECR 1095 215
NTN Tokyo Bearing Company v Council [1979] ECR 1185 165
NV Nederlandsche Banden-Industrie Michelin v Commission (Michelin I)
    [1983] ECR 3461; [1985] 1 CMLR 282. . . . . 767–8, 771, 775, 778, 781, 793
Océ Van der Grinten NV [2003] ECR I-9809 586
Océano Grupo Editorial [2000] ECR I-4941 . . . . .248, 302
Oebel [1981] ECR 1993. . . . . .433, 443
Oelmühle Hamburg [1998] ECR I-4767. 302
Officier van Justitie v Kortmann [1981] ECR 251 402
O'Flynn [1996] ECR I-2617 . . . . 509, 516–18
OG v Austria [2000] ECR I-10497. 215
OGT [2001] ECR I-3159. 962
Ohra [1993] ECR 5851 892
Olaso Valero [2004] ECR I-12065 255
Olazabal [2002] ECR I-10981. 481–2
Oleifici Mediterranei v EEC [1982] ECR 3057. 199
Olympique Lyonnais SASP v Bernard, 16 March 2010, nyr. 521–2
Omega Spielhallen- und Automatenaufstellungs-GmbH v Oberbürgermeisterin der
    Bundesstadt Bonn [2004] ECR I-9609 . . . . 349, 363, 558, 572–3
Oosthoek's Uitqeversmaatschappij BV [1981] ECR 4575. . . . . 415, 433, 444
Openbaar Ministerie and the Minister for Finance v Vincent Houben [1990] ECR I-1161 392
Openbaar Ministerie v Geert Van Buynder [1995] ECR I-3981 535
Orfanopoulos and Olivieri [2004] ECR I-5257 . . . . 475, 483–5
Orkem v Commission [1989] ECR 3283; [1991] 4 CMLR 502 816
Österreichischer Gewerkschaftsbund [2000] ECR I-10497 517
Österreichischer Rundfunk and others [2003] ECR I-4989. . . . . 108, 344, 366
OTO SpA v Ministero delle Finanze [1994] ECR I-3281 405
Oulane [2005] ECR I-1215 471
Outokumpu Oy [1998] ECR I-1777 . . . . .398, 404
OY AA [2007] ECR I-6373. . . . . 585, 589, 594–5
P v S Cornwall County Council [1996] ECR I-2143. . . . . 348, 371–2
Pabst & Richarz KG v Hauptzollamt Oldenburg [1982] ECR 1331 . . . . 245, 403, 406, 954

Pafitis [1996] ECR I-1347 282
Palacios de la Villa [2007] ECR I-8531 266
Palhota and Others, 7 October 2010, nyr 660
Palmisani [1997] ECR I-4025 . . . . 289, 293, 312–13
Pammer v Reederei Karl Schlüter GmbH & Co KG ECJ 10 December 2010, nyr 762
Pannon [2009] ECR I-4713 302
Pape [2005] ECR I-127 . . . . .867, 874
Papierfabrik August Koehler AG v Commission [2009] ECR I-7191; [2009] 5 CMLR 20 . . . . 815, 821–2
Papillon [2008] ECR I-8947 592
Paquay [2007] ECR I-8511 294
Pardini [1988] ECR 2041 330
Parfums Christian Dior v Evora [1997] ECR I-6013 223–4
Parfums Christian Dior v Tuk Consultancy [2000] ECR I-11307 . . . . 212, 958, 965
Parke, Davis [1968] ECR 55 454
Parking Brixen [2005] ECR I-8585 547
Parliament and Denmark v Commission [2008] ECR I-1649 86
Parliament v Commission [2007] ECR I-9045 86
Parliament v Council [1985] ECR 1513 . . . . 184–6, 189
Parliament v Council [1988] ECR 4017 189
Parliament v Council [1988] ECR 5615 . . . . 89, 161, 184, 188
Parliament v Council [1992] ECR I-4193 182
Parliament v Council [1992] ECR I-4593 79
Parliament v Council [1994] ECR I-625 . . . . 104, 930, 940
Parliament v Council [1994] ECR I-2857 . . . . 111, 162, 943
Parliament v Council [1995] ECR I-643 79
Parliament v Council [1995] ECR I-1185 . . . . .78, 89
Parliament v Council [1997] ECR I-5303 89
Parliament v Council [1999] ECR 4741 938
Parliament v Council [1999] ECR I-869 943–4
Parliament v Council [2006] ECR I-3733 . . . . .109, 678
Parliament v Council [2008] ECR I-3189 88
Parliament v Council [2009] ECR I-7135 . . . . .24, 112
Parliament v Council (Bangladesh) [1993] ECR I-3685 . . . . .104, 930
Parliament v Council ('Chernobyl') [1990] ECR I-2041 . . . . .161, 188
Parliament v Council (EIB Guarantee) [2008] ECR I-8103 112
Parliament v Council (family reunification) [2006] ECR I-5769 373
Pasquini [2003] ECR I-6515 . . . . 292, 294–5, 318
Pastoors [1997] ECR I-285 . . . . .328, 381
Patrick [1977] ECR 119 626
Paul [2004] ECR I-9425 310
Pavlov [2000] ECR I-6451, [2001] 4 CMLR 30 . . . . .714, 876
Peak Holding [2004] ECR I-11313 457
Pearle v Hoofdbedrijfschap Ambachten [2004] ECR I-7139, [2004] 3 CMLR 9 851–2
Pecastaing [1980] ECR 691 487
Pedana [1982] ECR 517 329
Pedro IV Servicios SL v Total Espana SA [2009] ECR I-2437; [2009] 5 CMLR 1 761
Peralta [1994] ECR I-3453 429
Peterbroeck [1995] ECR I-4599 . . . . .294, 300
Petrie and Others [1997] ECR I-6527 501
Petrosian [2009] ECR I-495 301
Petrotub [2003] ECR I-79 962
Pfeiffer [2004] ECR I-8835 . . . . 241, 248, 250, 267, 283
Pfeiffer Großhandel [1999] ECR I-2835 . . . . 574, 576, 658
Pfizer [1981] ECR 2913 459
Pfleiderer AG v Bundeskartellamt, 16 December 2010, nyr 836
Pflücke [2003] ECR I-9375 . . . . .300, 318
Pharmacia & Upjohn [1999] ECR I-6927 459
Philip Morris Holland v Commission [1980] ECR 2671; [1981] 2 CMLR 321 . . . . .852, 859
Physical Protection of Nuclear Materials [1978] ECR 2151 933
Piaggio v IFITALIA and Others [1999] ECR I-3735 . . . . 217, 221, 856
Pieck [1980] ECR 2171 481
Pierik [1978] ECR 825 212
Pierik [1979] ECR 1977 212

Pigs and Bacon Commission v McCarren [1979] ECR 2161...............................296, 305, 449
Pinna v Caisse d'Allocations Familiales de la Savoie [1986] ECR 1.....................................229
Piraiki-Patraiki v Commission [1985] ECR 207 ....165, 168–9, 171
Pistre etc [1997] ECR I-2343 ....432, 442
Placanica and Others [2007] ECR I-891..549, 564, 580
Plaumann v Commission [1963] ECR 95....................................163, 166–7, 169–70, 172, 175,
                                                                                      191, 872–3
Plus Warenhandelsgesellschaft, 14 January 2010, nyr..248
Politi v Italian Ministry of Finance [1971] ECR 1039...256–7
Pontin [2009] ECR I-10467..294, 300, 302
Portugaia Construções Lda [2002] ECR I-787...578, 590
Portugal v Commission [2001] ECR I-3175..867
Portugal v Council [1999] ECR I-8395..24, 955, 957, 962
Poseidon Chartering (Judgment of 16 March 2006)..214
Poucet and Pistre [1993] ECR I-637...715, 731, 876
Poulsen and Diva Navigation [1992] ECR I-6019..964–5
Povse, 1 July 2010, nyr...373
PPU Aguirre Zarraga v Pelz, 22 December 2010, nyr..373
PPU J McB v LE, 5 October 2010, nyr...365, 373
Prais v Council [1976] ECR 1589..371
Prantl [1984] ECR 1299...429, 444
Preston [2000] ECR I-3201..292–4, 300
Pretore di Salò v Persons Unknown [1987] ECR 2545 ....212, 215, 262, 269
Preussen Elektra [2001] ECR I-2099...442, 851
Prisco [2002] ECR I-6761...293, 305
Procureur du Roi v Dassonville [1974] ECR 837...410
Procureur du Roi v Jean-Marie Lagauche and others [1993] ECR I-5267..............................448
Prodest [1984] ECR 3153...502
Producteurs de Fruits v Council [1962] ECR 471 163
Producteurs de Vins de Table et Vins de Pays v Commission [1979] ECR 2429 187
Profant [1986] ECR 3237 402
Pronuptia de Paris v Schillgalis [1986] ECR 353; [1986] 1 CMLR 414.............................747–8
Publishers Association v Commission [1995] ECR I-25; [1995] 5 CMLR 33 ....756, 759
Punto Casa Srl [1994] ECR I-2355..422
Pupino [2005] ECR I-5285 ....241, 243, 269–70, 290
Pusa [2004] ECR I-5763 489
PVC Cartel II [2002] ECR I-8375 816
QDQ Media [2005] ECR I-1937 ....267, 284
Quietlynn [1990] ECR I-3059 416
R v HM Treasury, ex parte British Telecommunications [1996] ECR I-1631 ....267, 309–10
R v Home Secretary, ex parte Evans Medical Ltd and Macfarlan Smith Ltd [1995] ECR I-563 ...... 435, 437, 439
R v Immigration Appeal Tribunal, ex parte Antonissen [1991] ECR I-745...............................36
R v Intervention Board for Agricultural Produce, ex parte Accrington Beef and Others
    [1996] ECR I-6699..225
R v Intervention Board for Sugar ex parte Man (Sugar) [1985] ECR 2889 327
R v MAFF ex parte Compassion in World Farming Limited [1998] ECR I-1251.........................441
R v MAFF ex parte Hedley Lomas [1996] ECR I-2553................................. 144, 309, 313, 441
R v Minister of Agriculture, Fisheries and Food and Another ex parte National Farmers'
    Union and Others [1998] ECR I-2211 326
R v Minister of Agriculture, Fisheries and Food, ex parte National Farmers' Union
    and Others [1997] ECR I-4559 ....329, 332
R v Secretary of State, ex parte British American Tobacco [2002] ECR I-11453 ...... 116, 118, 124, 180, 226, 326
R v Secretary of State, ex parte Omega Air [2002] ECR I-2569...179
R v Secretary of State for Transport, ex parte Factortame [1991] ECR I-3905 ....212, 217, 308, 545
Raccanelli v Max-Planck- Gesellschaft zur Förderung der Wissenschaften eV
    [2008] ECR I-5939...502–3
Racke [1979] ECR 69..329
Racke [1984] ECR 3791...334, 370
Racke [1998] ECR I-3655 ....954, 963
Radlberger Getränkegesellschaft mbH & Co and S. Spitz KG [2004] ECR I-11763........................431
RAI [1999] ECR I-8597...215
Raija-Liisa Jokela [1998] ECR I-6267 329
Rampion and Godard [2007] ECR I-8017 302

Ramrath [1992] ECR I-3351 .... 553, 577, 579, 606
Raso [1998] ECR I-533; [1998] 4 CMLR 737 .... 775–6, 882–3
Ratti [1979] ECR 1629 ....246, 261
Rau [1982] ECR 3961 .... 36, 414, 445
Rau v Commission [1987] ECR 1069 123
Raulin [1992] ECR I-1027 462
Ravil [2003] ECR I-5053 434
Razanatsimba [1977] ECR 2229 626
Raznoimport v Commission [1983] ECR 2573 199
Razzouk and Beydoun [1984] ECR 1509 332
Rechberger [1999] ECR I-3499 311
Redmond [1978] ECR 2347 449
Reed [1986] ECR 1283 468
Région Wallonne v Commission [1997] ECR I-1787 ....161, 856
Regione Toscana v Commission [1997] ECR I-5245 161
Reiff [1993] ECR I-5801 ....890, 892
Reina [1982] ECR 33 518
Remia v Commission [1985] ECR 2545; [1987] 1 CMLR 1 ....747, 757
Rendo NV v Commission [1995] ECR I-3319 885
René Lancry SA [1994] ECR I-3957 394
Retuerta, 11 May 2010, nyr 964
Rewe Zentralfinanz [2007] ECR I-2647 594–5
Rewe-Handelsgesellschaft Nord v Hauptzollamt Kiel [1981] ECR 1805 296
Rewe-Zentral AG v Bundesmonopolverwaltung für Branntwein ('Cassis de Dijon')
    [1979] ECR 649 .... 102, 254, 297, 407, 409, 411–15, 419,
                                                                                            441–2, 459, 540, 563
Rewe-Zentrale etc v Hauptzollamt Landau/Pfalz [1976] ECR 181 ....396, 447
Rewe-Zentralfinanz v Landwirtschaftskammer [1973] ECR 1039 394
Rewe-Zentralfinanz v Landwirtschaftskammer [1975] ECR 843 ....409, 437
Rewe-Zentralfinanz v Landwirtschaftskammer für das Saarland
    [1976] ECR 1989 .... 272, 288, 292, 294–7, 305, 316
Reyners [1974] ECR 631 .... 245–6, 248, 536, 543–4, 559, 569–71
Rheinmühlen Düsseldorf [1971] ECR 719 334
Rheinmühlen Düsseldorf v Einfuhr- und Vorratsstelle Getreide [1974] ECR 139 220
Rheinmühlen v Einfuhr- und Vorratsstelle Getreide [1974] ECR 33 ....212, 220
Richardson [1995] ECR I-3407 273
Richardt [1991] ECR I-4621 395
Rieser Internationale Transporte [2004] ECR I-1477 ....248, 263
Rijn-Schelde-Verolme (RSV) Maschinefabrieken en Scheepswerven NV v Commission
    [1987] ECR 4617; [1989] 2 CMLR 259 ....332, 869
Rinke [2003] ECR I-8349 266
Rioglass SA [2003] ECR I-12705 452
Rivoira [1979] ECR 651 663
Robertson [1982] ECR 2349 ....414, 435
Robins [2007] ECR I-1059 311
Roders [1995] ECR I-2229 273
Römer, pending 266
Roquette Frères [1976] ECR 677 .... 296, 302, 305
Roquette Frères [2000] ECR I-10465 ....293, 305
Roquette Frères [2002] ECR I-9011 ....343, 818
Roquette Frères v Commission [1989] ECR 1553 198
Roquette Frères v Council [1980] ECR 3333 ....79, 178
Roschdale Borough Council v SJ Anders [1992] ECR I-6463 416
Rosengren [2007] ECR I-4071 409
Rossi [1979] ECR 831 331
Rothley [2004] ECR I-3149 175
Rottmann, 2 March 2010, nyr 469
Roviello [1988] ECR 2805 79
Royal Bank of Scotland [1999] ECR I-2651 .... 548, 573, 579, 582
Royal Pharmaceutical Society [1989] ECR 1295 253
Royer [1976] ECR 497 .... 478, 501, 503, 508, 544, 553
RTE and ITP v Commission (Magill) [1995] ECR I-743, [1995] 4 CMLR 718 .... 798, 802–5
RTT v GB-Inno-BM [1991] ECR I-5941 ....883, 885

Ruben Andersen [2008] ECR I-10279. 302
Ruckdeschel [1977] ECR 1753 333
Ruiz Bernáldez [1996] ECR I-1829 282
Ruiz Zambrano, 8 March 2011, nyr. 490–1
Rumhaus Hansen [1981] ECR 1165 401
Runevicinvcirc-Vardyn and Wardyn, pending. 490
Runi [1982] ECR 487. 329
Rush Portuguesa [1990] ECR I-1417. . . . . 556, 578, 660
Russo [1976] ECR 45. 296–7
Ruth Hünermund and others v Landesapothekerkammer Baden-Württemberg
    [1993] ECR I-6787. . . . . 253, 418, 420, 423
Rutili [1975] ECR 1219 . . . . 259, 346, 481, 508
RX-I and RX-II M v European Medicines Agency, 17 December 2009, nyr. 64
Sabbatini [1972] ECR 345. 332
Sacchi [1974] ECR 409 . . . . 447, 555, 713, 875, 880, 887
SACE v Italian Ministry of Finance [1970] ER 1213. 392
SAFA [1990] ECR I-1. 329
Safety Hi-Tech [1998] ECR I-4301. 36
Säger [1991] ECR I-4221. . . . . 540, 563–5, 580, 629
Sahin [2009] ECR I-8415 954
Saint-Gobain [1999] ECR I-6161. 649
Saldanha [1997] ECR I-5325 . . . . .534, 677
Salgoil [1968] ECR 453 . . . . .245, 288
Salumi [1981] ECR 2735. 329
Salzgitter Mannesmann GmbH (formerly Mannesmannrohren-Werke AG) v Commission
    [2007] ECR I-959; [2007] 4 CMLR 17 . . . . .821, 823
Salzmann [2001] ECR I-4421. 216
Sami Heinonen [1999] ECR I-3599. 101
San Giorgio [1983] ECR 3595. . . . . 294, 298, 306
Sanders Adour SNC and Guyomarc'h Orthez Nutrition Animale SA v Directeur des
    Services Fiscaux des Pyrenées-Atlantiques [1992] ECR I-3889 401–2
Sandoz [1983] ECR 2445. . . . . .436, 440
Santex [2003] ECR I-1877. 299
Santillo [1980] ECR 1585 484
Sapod Audic v Eco-Emballages [2002] ECR I-5031 . . . . 253–4, 280
SAT Fluggesellschaft v Eurocontrol [1994] ECR I-43; [1994] 5 CMLR 208 . . . . 253, 714, 878
Satakunnan Markkinapörssi and Satamedia [2008] ECR I-9831 266
Saunders [1979] ECR 1129 501
Sayag v Leduc [1969] ECR 329. 190–1
Sayn-Wittgenstein, 22 December 2010, nyr. 342, 347, 366, 370, 490
Schempp [2005] ECR I-6421 519
Schieving-Nijstad [2001] ECR I-5851. 965–6
Schindler [1994] ECR I-1039. . . . . 555, 558, 563, 580
Schlüter [1973] ECR 1135. . . . . 956, 958–9
Schmelz, 26 October 2010, nyr. 547
Schmid [2002] ECR I-4573. 215
Schmidberger [2003] ECR I-5659 . . . . 349, 367, 430, 434, 673
Schneider [2004] ECR I-1389. 291
Schneider v Commission [2009] ECR I-6413 197
Schneider-Import [1980] ECR 3469 397
Schnitzer [2003] ECR I-14847 . . . . 533, 554, 556–7
Scholz [1994] ECR I-505. . . . . 500, 515, 517, 541
Schöning [1998] ECR I-47 517
Schottle & Sohne v Finanzamt Freudenstadt [1977] ECR 247 396
Schrader [1989] ECR 2237 326
Schul v Inspecteur de Invoerrechten en Accijnzen [1982] ECR 1409. 8
Schulte [2005] ECR I-9215 . . . . .241, 284
Schumacker [1995] ECR I-225. . . . . 584–5, 596–7
Schutzverband gegen unlauteren Wettbewerb and TK-Heimdienst Sass GmbH
    [2000] ECR I-151. . . . . 323, 424, 432
Schwarz [2005] ECR I-10139 436
Schwibbert [2007] ECR I-9447. 280
Scott v Commission [2005] ECR I-8437. 869

Scrivner [1985] ECR 1027 518
Sebago [1999] ECR I-4103 457
SECAP [2008] ECR I-3565 . . . . .547, 596
Seco [1982] ECR 223 577–8
Segers [1986] ECR 2375 . . . . 554, 572, 593, 648–50
Segi and Others v Council [2007] ECR I-1657 . . . . .353, 907
SEIM [1996] ECR I-73 288
Selex sistemi Integrati SpA v Commission of the European Communities [2009] ECR I-2207 715
Scmeraro Casa Uno [1996] ECR I-2975 552
Sermes [1990] ECR I-3027 229
Sermide [1984] ECR 4209 332
Servizi Ausiliari Dottori Commercialisti v Calafiori [2006] ECR I-2941 . . . . 549, 573, 863–4, 882
SETTG [1997] ECR I-3091 . . . . .558, 566
SEVIC Systems [2005] ECR-10805 661
Sevince [1990] ECR I-3461 . . . . 938, 954–5
Sgarlata v Commission [1965] ECR 215 337
SGEEM and Etroy v EIB [1992] ECR I-6211 190
SGI, 21 January 2010, nyr 593
SGL Carbon AG v Commission [2006] ECR I-5977; [2006] 5 CMLR 16 . . . . .829, 832
Shell International Chemical Company v Commission [1999] ECR I-4501 202
Shingara and Radiom [1997] ECR I-3343 488
Showa Denko v Commission [2006] ECR I-5859 832
Sideradria v Commission [1985] ECR 3983 332
Silhouette International Schmied [1998] ECR I-4799 457
Simba SpA and others [1992] ECR I-3713 405
Simmenthal [1976] ECR 1871 . . . . .394, 441
Simmenthal [1978] ECR 1543 405
Simmenthal v Commission [1979] ECR 777 201
SIOT [1983] ECR 731 395
Siples [2001] ECR I-277 . . . . 304, 318
Skanavi and Chryssanthakopoulos [1996] ECR I-929 . . . . .328, 381
Skoma-Lux [2007] ECR I-10841 272
Sociaal Fonds etc v Brachfeld and Chougol Diamond Co [1969] ECR 211 . . . . 392–3, 395, 402
Sociaal Fonds voor de Dimantarbeiders [1973] ECR 1609, ...405
Société Civile Agricole du Centre d'Insémination de la Crespelle v Coopérative d'Elevage
      et d'Insémination Artificielle du Département de la Mayenne [1994] ECR I-5077 . . . . 427, 438, 441,
                                                                                                                                               775, 880, 882–3
Société Technique Minière v Maschinenbau Ulm [1966] ECR 235, [1966] CMLR 357 . 719, 741, 743, 747, 753–4,
      843
Sodemare v Regione Lombardia [1997] ECR I-3395; [1998] 4 CMLR 291, 549, 557, 649, 780
Sofrimport v Commission [1990] ECR I-2477 . . . . 169, 193–4, 196, 204, 330
Solgar Vitamin France and others, 29 April 2010, nyr 325
Solvay v Commission [1989] ECR 3255 816
Somalfruit SpA, Camar SpA v Ministero delle Finanze, Ministerio del Commercio con
      l'Estero [1997] ECR I-6619 326
Sorasio [1980] ECR 3557 333
Sotgiu [1974] ECR 153 . . . . 511, 515, 545, 569, 571–2, 583
Spac [1998] ECR I-4997 293
Spain v Commission [1992] ECR I-5833 879
Spain v Commission [1994] ECR I-4103 . . . . 851, 854, 857
Spain v Commission [1999] ECR I-2459 855
Spain v Commission [2000] ECR I-2415 158
Spain v Commission [2002] ECR I-7657 860
Spain v Commission [2003] ECR I-1487 . . . . .855, 857
Spain v Commission [2004] ECR I-7655 179
Spain v Commission [2004] ECR I-8091 855
Spain v Council [1998] ECR I-7309 331
Spain v Council (Judgment of 30 March 2006) 180
Spain v United Kingdom [2006] ECR I-7917 . . . . 58, 136, 356, 494
SPAR Österreichische Warenhandels AG v Finanzlandesdirectktion für Salzburg
      [1998] ECR I-785 325
SPCM [2009] ECR I-5783 124
Stadtgemeinde Frohnleiten and Gemeindebetriebe Frohnleiten GmbH [2007] ECR I-9643 397

Standesamt Stadt Niebüll [2006] ECR I-3561 490
Stanton [1988] ECR 3877 .... 524, 538, 547, 574
Staple Dairy Products [1982] ECR 1763.......................................329
Star Fruit v Commission [1989] ECR 291 ....139, 141
Stauder [1969] ECR 419 ....338, 343
Stauffer [2006] ECR I-8203..559
Steen [1992] ECR I-341...501
Steen [1994] ECR I-2715...501
Steenhorst-Neerings [1993] ECR I-5475..299
Steffensen [2003] ECR I-3735.......................................290, 302
Steff-Houlberg [1998] ECR I-2661.......................................302
Steinhauser [1985] ECR 1819.......................................543
STEKO [2009] ECR I-299..587
Steymann [1987] ECR 6159 ....532–3, 556
Stichting Zuid-Hollandse Milieufederatie [2005] ECR I-9759 248
Stoeckel [1991] ECR I-4047 252
Stora Kopparbergs Bergslags AB v Commission [2000] ECR I-9925; [2001] 4 CMLR 12 720
Stork v High Authority [1959] ECR 17.......................................337
Streekgewest Westelijk Noord-Brabant [2005] ECR I-85...................... 252, 867, 874
Sucrimex v Commission [1980] ECR 1299 198
Südzucker Mannheim/Ochsenfurt AG v Hauptzollamt Mannheim [1998] ECR I-281.............327
Suiker Unie v Commission ('Sugar') [1975] ECR 1663; [1976] 1 CMLR 295 ....731, 736, 774, 794
Surinder Singh [1992] ECR I-4265 ....471, 539, 541
Sutton [1997] ECR I-2163...302
Svensson [1995] ECR I-3955 ....572, 579
Sveriges Betodlares Centralförening and Henrikson [1997] ECR I-7531 872
Sweden v Commission [2007] ECR I-11389 119
Swedish Match [2004] ECR I-11893 ....108, 124
Syfait v GlaxoSmithKline [2005] ECR I-4609 ....215, 803
Syndicat des Libraires de Normandie v L'Aigle Distribution [1988] ECR 4457..................891
Syndicat Français de l'Express International (SFEI) and Others v La Poste and Others
        [1996] ECR I-3547.......................... 323, 332, 848, 854, 866, 873
Syndicat professionel coordination des pêcheurs de l'étang de Berre et de la région
        [2004] ECR I-7357...955
Synthon [2008] ECR I-7681 311
Szeja (pending)...479
T Port v Bundesanstalt für Landwirtschaft und Ernährung [1996] ECR I-6065 ....184–6, 228
Tankreederie, 22 December 2010, nyr.......................................590
Tankstaton 't Heukske vof [1994] ECR I-2199.......................................422
Tarantik v Directeur des Services Fiscaux de Seine-et-Marne [1999] ECR I-3633.........220, 400
Tas-Hagen and Tas [2006] ECR I-10451.......................................489, 519
Tedeschi [1977] ECR 1556 438
Teixeirai, 23 February 2010, nyr.......................................373, 477, 527
Telaustria [2000] ECR I-10745.......................................547
Tele2 Telecommunication [2008] ECR I-685.......................................251–2, 289
Telemarsicabruzzo v Circostel [1993] ECR I-393 220–1
Ten Kate [2005] ECR I-8979.......................................187, 310
Terrapin [1976] ECR 1039 452
Test Claimants in the FII Group Litigation [2006] ECR I-11753 586
Test Claimants in the Thin Cap Litigation [2007] ECR I-2107 ....582, 587
Tetra Pak v Commission (Tetra Pak II) [1996] ECR I-5951, [1997] 4 CMLR 662 ......774, 784, 788, 797
Thieffry [1977] ECR 765 ....536, 542, 626
Thijssen [1993] ECR I-4047 569
Thompson [1978] ECR 22247 436
Thomson and Vestel France [2007] ECR I-2049 964
Thyssen [1983] ECR 3721.......................................331
Thyssen Stahl v Commission [2003] ECR I-10821 751
Timex [1984] ECR 849 ....169, 182
T-Mobile Netherlands BV v Raad van Bestuur van de Nederlandse Mededingingsautoriteit
        [2009] ECR I-4529; [2009] 5 CMLR 11 .... 735–7, 740, 743, 751
TNT Traco v Poste Italiana [2001] ECR I-4109.......................... 224, 883, 888
Tommaso Morellato v USL No 11, Prodenone [1997] ECR I-1431 414
Toolex Alpha AB [2000] ECR I-5681 427

Torfaen BC v B&Q Plc [1989] ECR 3851 . . . . .416, 443
Traghetti del Mediterraneo [2006] ECR I-5177 314
Transalpine Ölleitung in Österreich [2006] ECR I-9957 252
Transocean Marine Paint v Commission [1974] ECR 1063; [1974] 2 CMLR 459 . . . . 178, 180, 821
Transporoute [1982] ECR 417 561
Transportes Urbanos y Servicios Generales, 26 January 2010, nyr .293, 313
Tremblay v Commission [1996] ECR I-5574; [1997] 4 CMLR 211. 838
Trojani [2004] ECR I-7574 . . . . 466, 505, 532, 557
Truck Center [2008] ECR I-10767 585
Trummer [1999] ECR I-1661 662
Tsakouridis, 23 November 2010, nyr 483, 485
Tulliasiamies and Siilin [2002] ECR I-7487 401
TV10 [1994] ECR I-1963 . . . . .555, 557
TWD Textilwerke Deggendorf GmbH v Germany [1994] ECR I-833; [1995] 2 CMLR 145 . . . . 201, 225, 874
TWD v Commission [1997] ECR I-2549 201
Überseering [2002] ECR I-9919 . . . . 542, 651–7
Uecker [1997] ECR I-3171 501
Ugliola [1969] ECR 363 . . . . .514, 572
Unibet [2007] ECR I-2271 . . . . 290, 295, 305
Unicredito Italiano Spa [2005] ECR I-11137 332
Unifruit Hellas v Commission [1997] ECR I-727 194
Unilever Italia [2000] ECR I-7535 . . . . 280–1, 605
Unión de Pequeños Agricultores v Council [2002] ECR I-6677 . . . . 159, 164, 173–4, 177, 226
Union de Recouvrement des Cotisations de Sécurité Sociale et d'Allocations Familiales
    de la Savoie (URSSAF) v Hostellerie Le Manoir SARL [1991] ECR I-5531 . . . . .501, 517
Uniplex, 28 January 2010, nyr 300
United Brands Company v Commission [1978] ECR 207; [1978] 1 CMLR 429 . . . . 767, 769–70, 775–6,
                                                                                          778, 786–7, 789–90, 799
United Foods [1981] ECR 995 402
United Kingdom v Commission [1988] ECR 5289 158
United Kingdom v Commission [1996] ECR I-4475 304
United Kingdom v Commission [1998] ECR I-2265 158
United Kingdom v Council [2007] ECR I-11459 127
United Kingdom v Council [2007] ECR I-11593 127
United Kingdom v Council, 26 October 2010, nyr 127
United Kingdom v Council (Working Time Directive) [1996] ECR I-5755 . . . . .118, 123
United Kingdom v Parliament and Council [2005] ECR I-10553 109
United Kingdom v Parliament and Council [2006] ECR I-3771 109
United Pan-Europe Communications Belgium and Others [2007] ECR I-11135 564
Upjohn [1999] ECR I-223 291
Vaassen v Beamtenfonds Mijnbedrijf [1966] ECR 261 215
Vajnai [2005] ECR I-8577 214
Van Ameyde v UCI [1977] ECR 1091; [1977] 2 CMLR 478 . . . . .547, 886
van Binsbergen [1974] ECR 1307 . . . . 559–60, 568, 577, 579
Van Calster [2003] ECR I-12249 . . . . 864, 867, 874
Van der Veldt [1994] ECR I-3537 . . . . .414, 436
van der Weerd [2007] ECR I-4233 302
van Dijk, 21 January 2010, nyr 197
van Duyn [1974] ECR 1337 . . . . 259, 483, 501, 508
Van Eycke [1988] ECR 4769 . . . . .24, 890
van Gend en Loos [1963] ECR 1 . . . . 37, 65–6, 235–8, 245, 248,
                                                                                          253, 262, 284
Van Landewyck v Commission (FEDETAB) [1980] ECR 3125; [1981] 3 CMLR 134 . . . . .734, 822
Van Parys [2005] ECR I-1465 958
Van Schijndel [1995] ECR I-4705 . . . . .300, 302
van Wesemael [1979] ECR 35 . . . . 559–61, 578
Vaneetveld [1994] ECR I-763 . . . . .221, 262
Varec SA v Belgium [2008] ECR I-581 . . . . .290, 819
Vatsouras and Koupatantze [2009] ECR I-4585 . . . . 474, 482, 507–8
VBVB and VBBB v Commission [1984] ECR 19; [1985] 1 CMLR 27 . . . . .756, 821
Verband der Sachversicherer [1987] ECR 405; [1988] 4 CMLR 264 734
Verband Sozialer Wettbewerb v Clinique Laboratories [1994] ECR I-317 . . . . 212, 254, 439, 443

Verbond van Nederlandse Ondernemingen v Inspecteur der Invoerrechten en Accijnzen
  [1977] ECR 113 259
Vereniging van Samenwerkende Prijsregelende Organisaties in de Bouwnijverheid (SPO) v
  Commission [1996] ECR I-1611 756
Verholen [1991] ECR I-3757 . . . . .212, 251
Verkooijen [2000] ECR I-4071 . . . . 590, 592, 596
Veronica [1991] ECR I-487 568
Viho Europe BV v Commission [1996] ECR I-5457 731
Vinal v Orbat [1981] ECR 77 398
Visciano [2009] ECR I-6741 300
Vlassopoulou [1991] ECR I-2357 . . . . .291, 626
Vodafone and others, 8 June 2010, nyr 108, 118, 124, 324
Völk v Vervaecke [1969] ECR 295; [1969] CMLR 273 752
Volker und Markus Scheke, 9 November 2010, nyr 366
Volkswagen v Commission [2003] ECR I-9189 831
Volvo v Erik Veng (UK) [1988] ECR 6211; [1989] 4 CMLR 122 802
Von Colson [1984] ECR 1891 . . . . 25, 238–41, 288, 292, 297, 323
Vreugdenhil v Commission [1992] ECR I-1937 . . . . .194, 198
VT4 [1997] ECR I-3143 554
VTB-VAB [2009] ECR I-2949 248
VZW Vereniging van Vlaamse Reisbureaus v VZW Sociale Dienst [1987] ECR 3801;
  [1989] 4 CMLR para 10 891
Wachauf [1989] ECR 2609 344
Wagner [1983] ECR 271 333
Wagner Miret [1993] ECR I-6911 240
Walrave and Koch [1974] ECR I-1405 . . . . .501–2, 553, 559–60, 608, 672
Waterkeyn [1986] ECR 1855 . . . . .143, 432
Watson and Belmann [1976] ECR 1185 . . . . 472, 509, 553
Watts [2006] ECR I-4325 . . . . .378, 572
Webb [1981] ECR 3305 . . . . 560–1, 578
Webb [1994] ECR I-3567 377
Weber's Wine World [2003] ECR I-11365 306
Weigel [2004] ECR I-4981 . . . . .397, 519
Weiser [1990] ECR I-2395 333
Wellcome Foundation [2008] ECR I-10479 459
Wells [2004] ECR I-723 . . . . 250, 263–4, 267, 281
Werhahn v Council [1973] ECR 1229 190
Werner [1993] ECR I-429 535
Werner [1995] ECR I-3189 . . . . .944, 964
Wielockx [1995] ECR I-2493 . . . . 545, 584, 592
Wiener v Hauptzollamt Emmerich [1997] ECR I-6495 219
Wijsenbeek [1999] ECR I-6207 . . . . 246, 464, 489
Wilhelm [1969] ECR 1 . . . . 101, 839, 922
Wiljo [1997] ECR I-585 . . . . .201, 225
Wilson [2006] ECR I-8613 . . . . .290, 643
Winner Wetten, 8 September 2010, nyr 273, 532
Wippel [2004] ECR I-9483 248
Wirth [1993] ECR I-6447 555
Wöhrmann v Commission [1962] ECR 501 200–1
Wohrmann v Hauptzollamt Bad Reichenhall [1967] ECR 177 402
Wolf [1988] ECR 3897 . . . . .538, 547
Wongingstichting Sint Servatius [2009] ECR I-9021 665
Wouters and others [2002] ECR I-1577, [2002] 4 CMLR 913 . . . . .714, 734, 749–50, 755,
                                                                                            757, 763, 893
Wünsche v Germany [1986] ECR 947 216
WWF and Others v Autonome Provinz Bozen and Others [1999] ECR I-5613 . . . . 216–17, 249
X (criminal proceedings against) [1996] ECR I-6609 242
X (criminal proceedings against) [2004] ECR I-651 243
X and Y [2002] ECR I-829 590
X Holding, 25 February 2010, nyr 649
X v Commission [1994] ECR I-4737 364
Yiadom [2000] ECR I-9265 . . . . .483, 487
Zabala Erasun and Others [1995] ECR I-1567 . . . . 221, 450, 453, 456–7, 459

Zanotti, 20 May 2010, nyr..555
Zentralbetriebsrat der Landeskrankenhäuser Tirol, 22 April 2010, nyr............................268
Zino Davidoff and Levi Strauss [2001] ECR I-8691 458
Ziolkowski (pending) 479
Zuccheri [1979] ECR 2749 ....257, 331
Züchner [1981] ECR 2021; [1982] 1 CMLR 313 736
Zuckerfabrik Schöppenstedt v Council [1971] ECR 975 ....190, 193
Zuckerfabrik Süderditmarschen v Hauptzollamt Itzehoe [1991] ECR I-415.............. 225, 227, 304–5
Zurstrassen [2000] ECR I-3337 519
Zwartveld [1990] ECR I-4405...323, 839

General Court/Court of First Instance, Case Number Order

Case T-7/89 Hercules Chemicals v Commission [1991] ECR II-1711; [1992] 4 CMLR 84 .... 822–3, 830
Case T-30/89 Hilti A-G v Commission [1991] ECR II-1439; [1992] 4 CMLR 16............... 772, 778, 796–7
Case T-48/89 Beltrante [1990] ECR II-493..333
Case T-65/89 BPB Industries and British Gypsum v Commission......................... 789, 794, 800
Joined Cases T-79/89 etc, BASF and Others v Commission [1992] ECR II-315......................202
Case T-121/89 X v Commission [1992] ECR II-2195...364
Case T-150/89 Martinelli v Commission [1995] ECR II-1165 827
Case T-24/90 Automec Srl v Commission ('Automec No 2') [1992] ECR II-2223; [1992] 5 CMLR 431.......838
Case T-28/90 Asia Motor France and Others [1992] ECR II-2285.................................184
Case T-39/90 Samenwerkende Electriciteits-produktiebedrijven (SEP) v Commission
    [1991] ECR II-1497; [1992] 5 CMLR 33...816
Case T-30/91 Solvay v Commission [1995] ECR II-1775; [1996] 5 CMLR 57 821
Case T-83/91 Tetra Pak v Commission (Tetra Pak I) [1994] ECR II-755, [1997] 4 CMLR 726 774
Case T-19/92 Groupement D'Achat Edouard Leclerc v Commission [1996] ECR II-1961;
    [1997] 4 CMLR 995..748
Case T-29/92 R SPO v Commission [1992] ECR II-2161...304
Case T-60/92 Noonan v Commission [1996] ECR II-215 332
Case T-114/92 BEMIM v Commission [1995] ECR II-147 172
Case T-5/93 Roger Tremblay and François Lucazeau and Harry Kestenberg v Commission
    [1995] ECR II-185 325
Case T-7/93 Langnese-Iglo v Commission [1995] ECR II-611; [1995] 5 CMLR 602...................753
Case T-12/93 CCE de Vittel v Commission [1995] ECR II-1246 169
Case T-17/93 Matra Hachette v Commission [1994] ECR II-595................................755, 758
Case T-49/93 SIDE v Commission [1995] ECR II-2501 861
Joined Cases T-244/93 and T-486/93 TWD v Commission ECR II-2265 201
Joined Cases T-447/93, T-448/93 and T-449/93 Associazione Italiana Tecnico Economica
    del Cemento (AITEC) and Others v Commission [1995] ECR II-1971 172
Case T-450/93 Lisrestal and Others v Commission [1994] ECR II-1177..........................178
Case T-472/93 Campo Ebro and Others v Council [1995] ECR II-421 ....167, 193
Joined Cases T-480/93 and T-483/93 Antillean Rice Mills [1995] ECR I-2305...................169, 177
Joined Cases T-481/93 and T-484/93 Exporteurs in Levende Varkens and Others v
    Commission [1995] ECR II-2941 .... 170, 193–4
Case T-482/93 Weber v Commission [1996] ECR II-609..171
Case T-489/93 Unifruit Hellas [1994] ECR I-1201 ....169, 194
Case T-504/93 Tiercé Ladbroke v Commission [1997] ECR II-923, [1997] 5 CMLR 309........... 774, 802, 853
Case T-514/93 Cobrecaf and Others v Commission [1995] ECR II-621 191
Case T-521/93 Atlanta and Others v European Community [1996] ECR II-1707 178
Joined Cases T-551/93, T-231/94, T-233/94 and T-234/94 Industria Pesdquera Campos and
    Others v Commission [1996] ECR II-247 332
Joined Cases T-576-582/93 M Browet and others v Commission [1994] ECR II-677 375
Case T-585/93 Greenpeace and Others v Commission [1995] ECR II-2205................... 166, 172, 378
Case T-99/94 Asocarne v Council [1994] ECR II-871 170
Case T-107/94 Kik v Council and Commission [1995] ECR II-1717..............................167
Case T-154/94 CSME v Commission [1996] ECR II-1377.......................................200–1
Case T-161/94 Sinochem Heilongjiang v Council [1996] ECR II-695...........................162
Joined Cases T-177/94 and T-377/94 Altmann and Others v Commission [1996] ECR II-2041.........200, 334
Case T-260/94 Air Inter v Commission [1997] ECR II-997; [1997] 5 CMLR 851 ....886, 888
Case T-275/94 CB v Commission [1995] ECR II-2169 159

Joined Cases T-305-307, 313-316, 318, 325, 328-29 and 335/94 Re the PVC Cartel II:
   Limburgse Vinyl Maatschappij v Commission [1999] ECR II-931;
   [1999] 5 CMLR 303 . . . . 381, 720, 739, 818, 822
Case T-334/94 Sarrió v Commission [1998] ECR II-1439; [1998] 5 CMLR 195 740
Case T-336/94 Efisol SA v Commission [1996] ECR II-1343 331
Case T-353/94 Postbank NV v Commission [1996] ECR I-921 323
Case T-358/94 Air France v Commission [1996] ECR II-2109; [1997] 1 CMLR 492 852
Joined Cases 1-374-75, 384 and 388/94, European Night Services and others v
   Commission [1998] ECR II-3141; [1998] 5 CMLR 710 . . . . . .   , , , ... 743–4, 753, 801, 803
Case T-390/94 Schröder and Others v Commission [1997] ECR II-501 . . . .   , , , 193
Case T-395/94 Atlantic Container Line AB v Commission [2002] ECR II-875 . . . . .759, 776
Joined Cases T-25, 26/95, 30-32, 34-39, 42-46, 48, 50-65, 68-71, 87, 88, 103 & 104/95
   Cimenteries CBR v Commission ('Cement') [2000] ECR II-491 740
Case T-73/95 Estabelecimentos Isidoro M Oliveira SA v Commission [1997] ECR II-381 . . . . .328, 332
Case T-81/95 Interhotel-Sociedade Internacional de Hotéis SARL v Commission
   [1997] ECR II-1265 331
Case T-105/95 WWF UK v Commission [1997] ECR II-313 138
Case T-145/95 Proderec v Commission [1997] ECR II-823 177
Case T-155/95 LPN and GEOTA v Commission [1998] ECR II-2751 156
Case T-184/95 Dorsch Consult v Council and Commission [1998] ECR II-667 197
Case T-194/95 Area Cova and Others v Council [1999] ECR II-2271 171
Joined Cases T-198/95, T-171/96, T-230/97, T-174/98 and T-225/99 Comafrica v
   Commission [2001] ECR II-1975 196
Joined Cases T-213/95 and 18/96 SCK and FNK v Commission [1997] ECR II-1739;
   [1998] 4 CMLR 259 821
Case T-214/95 Vlaams Gewest v Commission [1998] ECR II-717 . . . . .854, 857
Case T-219/95 Danielsson and Others v Commission [1995] ECR II-3051 166
Case T-227/95 Commission v AssiDomän Kraft Products and Others [1997] ECR II-1185 181
Case T-230/95 BAI v Commission [1999] ECR II-123 199
Case T-12/96 Area Cova and Others v Council and Commission [1999] ECR II-230 .171
Case T-14/96 BAI v Commission [1999] ECR II-139 155
Case T-16/96 Cityflyer Express v Commission [1998] ECR II-757; [1998] 2 CMLR 537 854
Case T-34/96 and T-163/96 Connolly v Commission [1999] ECR II-463 367
Case T-41/96 Bayer [2000] ECR II-3383; [2001] 4 CMLR 126 732
Case T-47/96 SDDDA v Commission [1996] ECR II-1559 141
Joined Cases T-79/96, T-260/97 and T-117/98 Camar and Tico v Commission [2000] ECR II-2193 186
Case T-82/96 ARAP and Others v Commission [1999] ECR II-1889 177
Case T-95/96 Gestevisión Telecinco v Commission [1998] ECR II-3407 . . . . .186, 869
Case T-102/96 Gencor Ltd v Commission [1999] 4 CMLR 971 . . . . .177, 722
Case T-111/96 ITT Promedia v Commission [1998] ECR II-2937; [1998] 5 CMLR 491 789
Case T-113/96 Dubois et Fils v Council and Commission [1998] ECR II-125 193
Case T-120/96 Lilly Industries v Commission [1998] ECR II-2571 188
Joined Cases T-121/96 and 151/96 Mutual Aid Administration Services NV v
   Commission [1992] ECR II-1335 156
Case T-122/96 Federolio v Commission [1997] ECR II-1559 172
Joined Cases T-125 and 152/96 BI Vetmedica and Another v Council and Commission
   [1999] ECR II-3427 . . . . 164, 170, 177, 188
Joined Cases T-132 and 143/96 Freistaat Sachsen and Volkswagen v Commission
   [1999] ECR II-3663 858
Case T-135/96 UEAPME v Council [1998] ECR II-2335 164
Joined Cases T-185 and 190/96 Riviera Auto Service Etablissements Dalmasso v
   Commission [1999] ECR II-93; [1999] 5 CMLR 31 843
Case T-5/97 Industrie des Poudres Sphériques v Commission [2000] ECR II-3755 792
Case T-26/97 Antillean Rice Mills v Commission [1997] ECR II-1347 177
Case T-80/97 Starway v Council [2000] ECR II-3099 165
Case T-109/97 Molkerei v Commission [1998] ECR II-3533 170
Case T-220/97 H & R Ecroyd Holdings Ltd v Commission [1999] ECR II-1677 .181, 229
Case T-231/97 New Europe Consulting v Commission [1999] 2 CMLR 1452 191
Case T-277/97 Ismeri Europa Srl v Court of Auditors [1999] ECR II-1825 198
Case T-288/97 Regione Autonoma Friuli-Venezia Giulia v Commission [1999] ECR II-1169 161
Case T-309/97 Bavarian Lager Co v Commission [1999] 3 CMLR 544 138
Case T-598/97 BSC Footware Supplies v Council [2002] ECR II-1155 172
Case T-613/97 Ufex v Commission [2000] ECR II-4055 854

Case T-62/98 Volkswagen v Commission [2000] ECR II-2707; [2000] 5 CMLR 948 767
Case T-65/98 Van den Bergh Foods v Commission [2003] ECR II-4653, [2004] 4 CMLR 1 . . . . 745–6, 797
Case T-112/98 Mannesmannröhren-Werke AG v Commission [2001] ECR II-729 816
Case T-127/98 UPS Europe v Commission [1999] ECR II-2633 184
Case T-155/98 SIDE v Commission [2002] ECR II-1179. . . . . .857, 861
Case T-166/98 Dolianova [2004] ECR II-3991 . . . . .188, 196
Joined Cases T-172 and 175-177/98 Salamander [2000] ECR II-2487. 164
Case T-173/98 Unión de Pequeños Agricultores v Council [1999] ECR II-3357 . . . . 159, 164, 173–4, 177, 226
Case T-178/98 Fresh Marine v Commission [2000] ECR II-3331. 196
Joined Cases T-202, T-204 and T-207/98 Tate & Lyle and Others v Commission
   [2001] ECR II-2035 719
Case T-18/99 Cordis v Commission [2001] ECR II-913 180
Case T-23/99 LR AF 1998 v Commission [2002] ECR II-1705 830
Case T-28/99 Sigma Tecnologie v Commission [2002] ECR II-1845. 830
Joined Cases T-38/99 to T-50/99 SAA and Others v Commission [2001] ECR II-585 .170
Case T-69/99 DSTV v Commission [2000] ECR II-4039. 165–6
Case T-82/99 Cwick v Commission [2000] ECR II-713. 367
Case T-112/99 Métropole Télévision (M6) v Commission [2001] ECR II-2459;
   [2001] 5 CMLR 1236. . . . . .746, 756
Case T-114/99 CSR Pampryl v Commission [1999] ECR II-3331 170
Case T-152/99 HAMSA v Commission [2002] ECR II-3049. 855
Case T-159/99 Dieckmann & Hansen v Commission [2001] ECR II-3143. 196
Case T-219/99 British Airways plc v Commission [2003] ECR II-5917 . . . . 773, 776, 783, 794
Case T-222/99 Martinez and others v Parliament [2001] ECR II-2823 368
Joined Cases T-228/99 and T-233/99 Westdeutsche Landesbank Girozentrale v
   Commission [2003] ECR II-435 . . . . .855, 857
Case T-319/99 FENIN [2003] ECR II-357 717
Case T-326/99 Olivieri [2003] ECR II-1985. 177
Case T-342/99 Airtours plc v Commission [2002] ECR II-2585. 781
Joined Cases T-346/99, T-347/99 and T-348/99 Disputación de álava [2002] ECR II-4259 857
Case T-48/00 Corus UK Ltd v Commission [2004] ECR II-2325; [2005] 4 CMLR 3. .740
Joined Cases T-67/00, T-68/00, T-71/00 and T-78/00 JFE Engineering v
   Commission [2004] ECR II-2501 . . . . .380, 827
Joined Cases T-69/00, T-151/00, T-301/00, T-320/00, T-383/00 and T-135/01 FIAMM v
   Council and Commission [2005] ECR II-5393 197
Case T-89/00 Europe Chemi-Con v Council [2002] ECR II-3651 . . . . .177, 181
Case T-98/00 Linde AG v Commission [2002] ECR II-3961. 854
Case T-114/00 Aktionsgemeinschaft Recht und Eigentum v Commission [2002] ECR II-5121 872
Case T-190/00 Regione Siciliana v Commission [2003] ECR II-5015 868
Case T-220/00 Cheil Jedang v Commission [2003] ECR II-2473 352
Case T-349/00 Lebedef v Commission [2001] ECR II-1031 375
Case T-353/00 Le Pen v European Parliament [2003] ECR II-125 159
Joined Cases T-377/00, T-379/00, T-380/00, T-260/01 and T-272/01 Philip Morris International
   and Others v Commission [2003] ECR II-1 . . . . 159, 174–5
Case T-26/01 Fiocchi Munizioni v Commission [2003] ECR II-3951 188
Case T-33/01 Infront [2005] ECR II-5897 171
Case T-109/01 Fleuren Compost [2004] ECR II-127 869
Joined Cases T-116/01 and T-118/01 P & O Ferries (Vizcaya) SA v Commission [2003] ECR II-2957 858
Case T-139/01 Comafrica v Commission [2005] ECR II-409 196
Case T-157/01 Danske Busvognmµnd v Commission [2004] ECR II-917 863
Case T-177/01 Jégo-Quéré v Commission [2002] ECR II-2365 174–6
Joined Cases T-195 and T-207/01 Government of Gibraltar v Commission [2002] ECR II-2309 . . . . .161, 853
Case T-203/01 Manufacture française des pneumatiques Michelin v Commission
   (Michelin II) [2003] ECR II-4071, [2004] 4 CMLR 923. . . . . 769, 778, 784, 793–5, 797
Case T-208/01 Volkswagen v Commission [2003] ECR II-5141, [2004] 4 CMLR 727 733
Case T-274/01 Valmont Nederland BV v Commission [2004] ECR. 863
Joined Cases T-297/01 and T-298/01 SIC v Commission [2004] ECR II-743. 189
Case T-315/01 Kadi v Council and Commission [2005] ECR II-3649. 907
Case T-15/02 BASF v Commission [2006] ECR II-497; [2006] 5 CMLR 2 . . . . 827, 829–30
Case T-64/02 Dr Hans Heubach GmbH & Co KG v Commission [2005] ECR II-5137 . . . . .351, 381
Case T-93/02 Confédération nationale du Crédit Mutuel [2005] ECR II-143 . . . . .857, 863

Joined Cases T-109/02, T-118/02, T-122/02, T-125/02, T-126/02, T-128/02, T-129/02,
    T-132/02 and T-136/02 Bollore et al v Commission ('Carbonless Paper Cartel')
    [2007] ECR II-947; [2007] 5 CMLR 2..721
Case T-193/02 Piau v Commission [2005] ECR II-209; [2005] 5 CMLR 2..........................734, 781
Case T-228/02 OMPI v Council [2006] ECR II-4665...907
Case T-253/02 Ayadi v Council [2006] ECR II-2139..907
Case T-282/02 Cementbouw Handel and Industrie BV v Commission [2006] ECR II-319..............330
Case T-313/02 Meca Medina and Majcen v Commission (Judgment of the CFI, 30 September 2004)........750
Case T-351/02 Deutsche Bahn v Commission [2006] ECR II-1047; [2006] 2 CMLR 54 ....850, 852
Case T-18/03 CD-Contact Data GmbH v Commission of the European Communities
    [2009] ECR II-1021; [2009] 5 CMLR 5..733, 831
Case T-53/03 BPB Plc v Commission [2008] ECR II-1333; [2008] 5 CMLR 18.......733, 735, 740, 742, 751, 829
Case T-141/03 Sniace [2005] ECR II-1197...177
Case T-189/03 ASM Brescia SpA v Commission..864
Case T-271/03 Deutsche Telekom, pending...792
Case T-289/03 BUPA Insurance Ltd v Commission [2008] ECR II-81; [2009] 2 CMLR 41..............863, 885
Case T-328/03 O2 v Commission [2006] ECR II-1231.......................................746, 756
Case T-351/03 Schneider v Commission [2007] ECR II-2257 197
Case T-364/03 Medici Grimm v Council [2006] ECR II-79 196
Case T-410/03 Hoechst GmbH v Commission [2008] ECR II-881; [2008] 5 CMLR 12 .... 822–3, 832
Case T-415/03 Cofradía de pescadores de 'San Pedro' de Bermeo v Council [2005] ECR II-4355 196
Case T-127/04 KME Germany and others v Commission of the European Communities
    [2009] ECR II-1167.. 827–8, 831
Case T-155/04 SELEX Sistemi Integrati SpA v Commission [2009] ECR I-2207;
    [2009] 4 CMLR 24..715
Case T-167/04 Asklepios Kliniken v Commission [2007] ECR II-2378.............................187
Case T-196/04 Ryanair Ltd v Commission [2008] ECR II-3643; [2009] 2 CMLR 7.................854
Case T-201/04 Microsoft v Commission [2007] ECR II-3601;
    [2007] 5 CMLR 11...................................766, 777, 784, 797–8, 803–5, 824
Case T-233/04 Netherlands v Commission [2008] ECR II-591..................................856
Joined Cases T-309/04, T-317/04, T-329/04 and T-336/04 TV 2/Danmark A/S v
    Commission [2008] ECR II-02935 862
Case T-339/04 France Telecom SA v Commission [2007] ECR II-521, [2008] 5 CMLR 6 ....792, 813
Case T-395/04 Air One v Commission [2006] ECR II-1343...................................187, 189
Case T-24/05 Alliance One International Inc v Commission, 27 October 2010, nyr.......................721
Case T-91/05 Sinara Handel v Commission [2007] ECR II-245................................198
Joined Cases T-101/05 & T-111/05 BASF and UCB v Commission [2007] ECR II-4949;
    [2008] 4 CMLR 13..741
Case T-112/05 Akzo Nobel v Commission [2007] ECR II-5049; [2008] 4 CMLR 12 731
Case T-161/05 Hoechst GmbH v Commission [2009] ECR II-3555; [2009] 5 CMLR 25...............721
Case T-452/05 Belgian Sewing Thread (BST) NV v European Commission [2010] 5 CMLR 16..........740, 830
Case T-170/06 Alrosa v Commission [2007] ECR II-2601; [2007] 5 CMLR 7 825
Case T-405/06 ArcelorMittal Luxembourg SA v Commission [2009] ECR II-771;
    [2010] 4 CMLR 6..721, 822
Case T-411/06 Sogelma v EAR [2008] ECR II-2771 Sogelma...............................157–8
Case T-335/08 BNP Paribas and Banca Nazionale del lavoro SpA (BNL) v Commission,
    1 July 2010, nyr...855
Case T-85/09 Kadi v Commission, 10 September 2010, nyr 369
Case T-18/10 Inuit Tapiriit Kanatami and Others v European Parliament (pending).....................175

General Court/Court of First Instance, Name Order

Air France v Commission [1996] ECR II-2109; [1997] 1 CMLR 492.................................852
Air Inter v Commission [1997] ECR II-997; [1997] 5 CMLR 851 ....886, 888
Air One v Commission [2006] ECR II-1343 ....187, 189
Airtours plc v Commission [2002] ECR II-2585..781
Aktionsgemeinschaft Recht und Eigentum v Commission [2002] ECR II-5121 872
Akzo Nobel v Commission [2007] ECR II-5049; [2008] 4 CMLR 12..............................731
Alliance One International Inc v Commission, 27 October 2010, nyr..............................721
Alrosa v Commission [2007] ECR II-2601; [2007] 5 CMLR 7 825
Altmann and Others v Commission [1996] ECR II-2041 ....200, 334
Antillean Rice Mills [1995] ECR I-2305 ....169, 177

Antillean Rice Mills v Commission [1997] ECR II-1347 177
ARAP and Others v Commission [1999] ECR II-1889 177
ArcelorMittal Luxembourg SA v Commission [2009] ECR II-771; [2010] 4 CMLR 6 . . . . .721, 822
Area Cova and Others v Council [1999] ECR II-2271 171
Area Cova and Others v Council and Commission [1999] ECR II-230. 171
Asia Motor France and Others [1992] ECR II-2285 184
Asklepios Kliniken v Commission [2007] ECR II-2378 187
ASM Brescia SpA v Commission 864
Asocarne v Council [1994] ECR II-871 170
Associazione Italiana Tecnico Economica del Cemento (AITEC) and Others v Commission
   [1995] ECR II-1971. 172
Atlanta and Others v European Community [1996] ECR II-1707 178
Atlantic Container Line AB v Commission [2002] ECR II-875 . . . . .759, 776
Automec Srl v Commission ('Automec No 2') [1992] ECR II-2223; [1992] 5 CMLR 431 838
Ayadi v Council [2006] ECR II-2139. 907
BAI v Commission [1999] ECR II-123 . . . . .155, 199
BASF and Others v Commission [1992] ECR II-315 202
BASF and UCB v Commission [2007] ECR II-4949; [2008] 4 CMLR 13 741
BASF v Commission [2006] ECR II-497; [2006] 5 CMLR 2 . . . . 827, 829–30
Bavarian Lager Co v Commission [1999] 3 CMLR 544 138
Bayer [2000] ECR II-3383; [2001] 4 CMLR 126 732
Belgian Sewing Thread (BST) NV v European Commission [2010] 5 CMLR 16 . . . . .740, 830
Beltrante [1990] ECR II-493 333
BEMIM v Commission [1995] ECR II-147 172
BI Vetmedica and Another v Council and Commission [1999] ECR II-3427. . . . . 164, 170, 177, 188
BNP Paribas and Banca Nazionale del lavoro SpA (BNL) v Commission, 1 July 2010, nyr 855
Bollore et al v Commission ('Carbonless Paper Cartel') [2007] ECR II-947; [2007] 5 CMLR 2. 721
BPB Industries and British Gypsum v Commission 789, 794, 800
BPB Plc v Commission [2008] ECR II-1333; [2008] 5 CMLR 18 . . . . .733, 735, 740, 742, 751, 829
British Airways plc v Commission [2003] ECR II-5917. . . . . 773, 776, 783, 794
Browet and others v Commission [1994] ECR II-677 375
BSC Footware Supplies v Council [2002] ECR II-1155 172
BUPA Insurance Ltd v Commission [2008] ECR II-81; [2009] 2 CMLR 41 . . . . .863, 885
Camar and Tico v Commission [2000] ECR II-2193 186
Campo Ebro and Others v Council [1995] ECR II-421 . . . . .167, 193
CB v Commission [1995] ECR II-2169. 159
CCE de Vittel v Commission [1995] ECR II-1246 169
CD-Contact Data GmbH v Commission of the European Communities [2009] ECR II-1021;
   [2009] 5 CMLR 5 . . . . .733, 831
Cementbouw Handel and Industrie BV v Commission [2006] ECR II-319 330
Cheil Jedang v Commission [2003] ECR II-2473 352
Cimenteries CBR v Commission ('Cement') [2000] ECR II-491 740
Cityflyer Express v Commission [1998] ECR II-757; [1998] 2 CMLR 537 854
Cobrecaf and Others v Commission [1995] ECR II-621 191
Cofradía de pescadores de 'San Pedro' de Bermeo v Council [2005] ECR II-4355 196
Comafrica v Commission [2001] ECR II-1975 196
Comafrica v Commission [2005] ECR II-409 196
Commission v AssiDomän Kraft Products and Others [1997] ECR II-1185 181
Confédération nationale du Crédit Mutuel [2005] ECR II-143. . . . . .857, 863
Connolly v Commission [1999] ECR II-463 367
Cordis v Commission [2001] ECR II-913. 180
Corus UK Ltd v Commission [2004] ECR II-2325; [2005] 4 CMLR 3. 740
CSME v Commission [1996] ECR II-1377. 200–1
CSR Pampryl v Commission [1999] ECR II-3331. 170
Cwick v Commission [2000] ECR II-713 367
Danielsson and Others v Commission [1995] ECR II-3051 166
Danske Busvognmµnd v Commission [2004] ECR II-917 863
Deutsche Bahn v Commission [2006] ECR II-1047; [2006] 2 CMLR 54. . . . . .850, 852
Deutsche Telekom, pending 792
Dieckmann & Hansen v Commission [2001] ECR II-3143 196
Disputación de álava [2002] ECR II-4259 857
Dolianova [2004] ECR II-3991. . . . . .188, 196
Dorsch Consult v Council and Commission [1998] ECR II-667 197

Dr Hans Heubach GmbH & Co KG v Commission [2005] ECR II-5137 ....351, 381
DSTV v Commission [2000] ECR II-4039...165–6
Dubois et Fils v Council and Commission [1998] ECR II-125 193
Efisol SA v Commission [1996] ECR II-1343 331
Estabelecimentos Isidoro M Oliveira SA v Commission [1997] ECR II-381 ....328, 332
Europe Chemi-Con v Council [2002] ECR II-3651 ....177, 181
European Night Services and others v Commission [1998] ECR II-3141;
    [1998] 5 CMLR 718............   ,,,,,,,,,,,,,,,,,.......... 743–4, 753, 801, 803
Exporteurs in Levende Varkens and Others v Commission [1995] ECR II-2941.................170, 193–4
Federolio v Commission [1997] ECR II-1559 172
FENIN [2003] ECR II-357 717
FIAMM v Council and Commission [2005] ECR II-5393...197
Fiocchi Munizioni v Commission [2003] ECR II-3951 188
Fleuren Compost [2004] ECR II-127 869
France Telecom SA v Commission [2007] ECR II-521, [2008] 5 CMLR 6 ....792, 813
Freistaat Sachsen and Volkswagen v Commission [1999] ECR II-3663................................858
Fresh Marine v Commission [2000] ECR II-3331..196
Gencor Ltd v Commission [1999] 4 CMLR 971 ....177, 722
Gestevisión Telecinco v Commission [1998] ECR II-3407 ....186, 869
Government of Gibraltar v Commission [2002] ECR II-2309......................................161, 853
Greenpeace and Others v Commission [1995] ECR II-2205 .... 166, 172, 378
Groupement D'Achat Edouard Leclerc v Commission [1996] ECR II-1961; [1997] 4 CMLR 995............748
H & R Ecroyd Holdings Ltd v Commission [1999] ECR II-1677 ....181, 229
HAMSA v Commission [2002] ECR II-3049..855
Hercules Chemicals v Commission [1991] ECR II-1711; [1992] 4 CMLR 84..................... 822–3, 830
Hilti A-G v Commission [1991] ECR II-1439; [1992] 4 CMLR 16..................... 772, 778, 796–7
Hoechst GmbH v Commission [2008] ECR II-881; [2008] 5 CMLR 12 .... 822–3, 832
Hoechst GmbH v Commission [2009] ECR II-3555; [2009] 5 CMLR 25 721
Industria Pesdquera Campos and Others v Commission [1996] ECR II-247..............................332
Industrie des Poudres Sphériques v Commission [2000] ECR II-3755 792
Infront [2005] ECR II-5897 171
Interhotel-Sociedade Internacional de Hotéis SARL v Commission [1997] ECR II-1265 331
Inuit Tapiriit Kanatami and Others v European Parliament (pending) 175
Ismeri Europa Srl v Court of Auditors [1999] ECR II-1825..198
ITT Promedia v Commission [1998] ECR II-2937; [1998] 5 CMLR 491 789
Jégo-Quéré v Commission [2002] ECR II-2365 174–6
JFE Engineering v Commission [2004] ECR II-2501 ....380, 827
Kadi v Commission, 10 September 2010, nyr 369
Kadi v Council and Commission [2005] ECR II-3649..907
Kik v Council and Commission [1995] ECR II-1717...167
KME Germany and others v Commission of the European Communities [2009] ECR II-1167 .... 827–8, 831
Langnese-Iglo v Commission [1995] ECR II-611; [1995] 5 CMLR 602................................753
Le Pen v European Parliament [2003] ECR II-125 159
Lebedef v Commission [2001] ECR II-1031 375
Lilly Industries v Commission [1998] ECR II-2571 188
Linde AG v Commission [2002] ECR II-3961...854
Lisrestal and Others v Commission [1994] ECR II-1177...178
LPN and GEOTA v Commission [1998] ECR II-2751...156
LR AF 1998 v Commission [2002] ECR II-1705...830
Mannesmannröhren-Werke AG v Commission [2001] ECR II-729 816
Manufacture française des pneumatiques Michelin v Commission (Michelin II)
    [2003] ECR II-4071;[2004] 4 CMLR 923...................................769, 778, 784, 793–5, 797
Martinelli v Commission [1995] ECR II-1165...827
Martinez and others v Parliament [2001] ECR II-2823 368
Matra Hachette v Commission [1994] ECR II-595...755, 758
Meca-Medina and Majcen v Commission (Judgment of the CFI, 30 September 2004) 750
Medici Grimm v Council [2006] ECR II-79...196
Métropole Télévision (M6) v Commission [2001] ECR II-2459, [2001] 5 CMLR 1236 ....746, 756
Microsoft v Commission [2007] ECR II-3601; [2007] 5 CMLR 11.......................766, 777, 784, 797–8,
                                                                                              803–5, 824
Molkerei v Commission [1998] ECR II-3533..170
Mutual Aid Administration Services NV v Commission [1992] ECR II-1335............................156
Netherlands v Commission [2008] ECR II-591..856

New Europe Consulting v Commission [1999] 2 CMLR 1452 191
Noonan v Commission [1996] ECR II-215 332
O2 v Commission [2006] ECR II-1231...746, 756
Olivieri [2003] ECR II-1985...177
OMPI v Council [2006] ECR II-4665 907
P & O Ferries (Vizcaya) SA v Commission [2003] ECR II-2957.......................................858
Philip Morris International and Others v Commission [2003] ECR II-1 ....159, 174–5
Piau v Commission [2005] ECR II-209; [2005] 5 CMLR 2 ....734, 781
Postbank NV v Commission [1996] ECR I-921 323
Proderec v Commission [1997] ECR II-823...177
Re the PVC Cartel II: Limburgse Vinyl Maatschappij v Commission [1999] ECR II-931;
    [1999] 5 CMLR 303..381, 720, 739, 818, 822
Regione Autonoma Friuli-Venezia Giulia v Commission [1999] ECR II-1169..........................161
Regione Siciliana v Commission [2003] ECR II-5015 868
Riviera Auto Service Etablissements Dalmasso v Commission [1999] ECR II-93; [1999] 5 CMLR 31........843
Roger Tremblay and François Lucazeau and Harry Kestenberg v Commission [1995] ECR II-185 325
Ryanair Ltd v Commission [2008] ECR II-3643; [2009] 2 CMLR 7......................................854
SAA and Others v Commission [2001] ECR II-585 170
Salamander [2000] ECR II-2487 164
Samenwerkende Electriciteits-produktiebedrijven (SEP) v Commission [1991] ECR II-1497;
    [1992] 5 CMLR 33..816
Sarrió v Commission [1998] ECR II-1439; [1998] 5 CMLR 195..740
Schneider v Commission [2007] ECR II-2257...197
Schröder and Others v Commission [1997] ECR II-501 193
SCK and FNK v Commission [1997] ECR II-1739; [1998] 4 CMLR 259 821
SDDDA v Commission [1996] ECR II-1559 141
SELEX Sistemi Integrati SpA v Commission [2009] ECR I-2207; [2009] 4 CMLR 24.....................715
SIC v Commission [2004] ECR II-743 189
SIDE v Commission [1995] ECR II-2501...861
SIDE v Commission [2002] ECR II-1179..857, 861
Sigma Tecnologie v Commission [2002] ECR II-1845...830
Sinara Handel v Commission [2007] ECR II-245 198
Sinochem Heilongjiang v Council [1996] ECR II-695 162
Sniace [2005] ECR II-1197 177
Sogelma v EAR [2008] ECR II-2771 Sogelma 157–8
Solvay v Commission [1995] ECR II-1775; [1996] 5 CMLR 57 821
SPO v Commission [1992] ECR II-2161..304
Starway v Council [2000] ECR II-3099..165
Tate & Lyle and Others v Commission [2001] ECR II-2035 719
Tetra Pak v Commission (Tetra Pak I) [1994] ECR II-755, [1997] 4 CMLR 726 774
Tiercé Ladbroke v Commission [1997] ECR II-923, [1997] 5 CMLR 309.....................774, 802, 853
TV 2/Danmark A/S v Commission [2008] ECR II-02935...862
TWD v Commission ECR II-2265...201
UEAPME v Council [1998] ECR II-2335..164
Ufex v Commission [2000] ECR II-4055 854
Unifruit Hellas [1994] ECR I-1201 ....169, 194
Unión de Pequeños Agricultores v Council [1999] ECR II-3357 ....159, 164, 173–4, 177, 226
UPS Europe v Commission [1999] ECR II-2633...184
Valmont Nederland BV v Commission [2004] ECR...863
Van den Bergh Foods v Commission [2003] ECR II-4653, [2004] 4 CMLR 1 ....745–6, 797
Vlaams Gewest v Commission [1998] ECR II-717...854, 857
Volkswagen v Commission [2000] ECR II-2707; [2000] 5 CMLR 948.................................767
Volkswagen v Commission [2003] ECR II-5141, [2004] 4 CMLR 727................................733
Weber v Commission [1996] ECR II-609...171
Westdeutsche Landesbank Girozentrale v Commission [2003] ECR II-435........................855, 857
WWF UK v Commission [1997] ECR II-313 138
X v Commission [1992] ECR II-2195..364

Commission

Aid to Buna [1996] OJ L239/1 858
Alrosa Decision COMP/B-2/38.381 825

Aluminium Imports from Eastern Europe [1985] OJ L92/1; [1987] 3 CMLR 813...........................714
ANSEAU-NAVEWA [1982] 2 CMLR 193 ....885, 887
AOIP/Beyrard [1976] OJ L6/8; [1976] 1 CMLR D14 714
AROW/BNIC [1982] OJ L379/1; [1983] 2 CMLR 240 734
ASPA [1970] OJ L148/9; [1970] CMLR D25 734
BBC [1976] 1 CMLR D89 713
British Midland/Aer Lingus Decision 92/213 [1992] OJ L96/34; [1993] 4 CMLR 596 778
CECED, Decision 2000/475 756–7
Discount on Landing Fees at Zaventem: Decision 95/364 [1995] OJ L216/8 883
Intel Case COMP/C-3/37.990...795
KSB/Goulds/Lowara/ITT, Decision 91/38 757
London European v Sabena Decision 88/589; [1988] OJ L317/47 801–2
Microsoft (24 March 2004), COMP/C-3/37.792..797, 824
Nuovo CEGAM [1984] OJ L99/29; [1984] 2 CMLR 484 734
Philips/Osram, Decision 94/986 757
Plasterboard Case COMP/E-1/37.152...839
Rennet [1980] OJ L51/19; [1980] 2 CMLR 402 714
Rolled Zinc Products and Zinc Alloys [1982] OJ L362/40 [1983] 2 CMLR 285...........................738
Scandlines v Port of Helsingborg, COMP/A.36.568 (23 July 2004) 787
Sea Containers v Stena Sealink Decision 94/19 [1994] OJ L15/8 800
Sundbusserne v Port of Helsingborg, COMP/A.36.570 (23 July 2004) 787
Synthetic Fibres [1984] OJ L207/17; [1985] 1 CMLR 787 757
Telespeed Services v United Kingdom Post Office [1982] OJ L360/36; [1983] 1 CMLR 457 885
Uniform Eurocheques [1985] OJ L35/43, [1985] 3 CMLR 434...885
Unitel [1978] OJ L157/39; [1978] 3 CMLR 306...714
Volkswagen, Decision 94/1068, [1994] OJ L385/1 858
Wanadoo Interactive, 16 July 2003, COMP/38.233...788–9
William Prym-Werke [1973] OJ L296/24; [1973] CMLR D250 714

International

EFTA Court

Case E-9/97 Sveinbjörnsdóttir (Judgment of 10 December 1998) 311

European Court of Human Rights

Achour v France (Judgment of 29 March 2006) 242
Aksoy v Turkey (Appl No 21987/93) (1997) 23 EHRR 553 364
Amuur v France (Appl No 19776/92) (1996) 22 EHRR 533 365
Bascedillkaya and Okçuoginvcirclu v Turkey, App Nos 23536/94 and 24408/94 (Judgment of 8 July 1999) 242
Bosphorus v Ireland (Appl. No. 45036/98), ECHR 2005-VI, noted (2005) EHRLR 649 356
Buscarini and others v San Marino (Appl No 24645/95) (2000) 30 EHRR 208 367
Cantoni v France (Judgment of 15 November 1996) 242
Coëme v Belgium (Judgment of 22 June 2000) 242–3
CR v United Kingdom, App No 20190/92 (Judgment of 22 November 1995) 242
D v UK (Appl No 30240/96) (1997) 24 EHRR 423 370
Dogan and others v Turkey (Appls Nos. 8803-11/02, 8813/02, 8815-19/02) (2005) 41 EHRR 15 368
Elsholz v Germany (Appl No 25735/94) (2002) 34 EHRR 58 365
Funke v France, Series A, No.256-A, (1993) 16 EHRR 297 818
Glass v UK (Appl No 61827/00) (2004) 39 EHRR 15 363
Goodwin v UK (Appl No 28957/95) (2002) 35 EHRR 18 ....348, 365
Handyside v UK (Appl No 5493/72) (1970-80) 1 EHRR 737 367
Hertel v Switzerland (Appl No 25181/94) (1999) 28 EHRR 534 368
Informationsverein Lentia v Austria (Appl Nos 13914/88, 15041/89, 15717/89, 15779/89 and
     17207/90) (1994) 17 EHRR 93..367
Ireland v UK (Appl No 5310/71) (1979-80) 2 EHRR 25...364
JB v Switzerland, App No 31827/96 (Judgment of 3 May 2001) 817
Kafkaris v Cyprus (Judgment of 12 February 2008) 242
Kokkinakis v Greece (Judgment of 25 May 1993)..242
Kress v France (Appl No 39594/98), ECHR Reports 2001-VI..352

Lawless v Ireland (No 3) (1979/80) 1 EHRR 15 386
Lilly France SA v France (Appl No 53892/00), Judgment of 3 December 2002 351
Matthews v UK (Appl No 24833/94), ECHR 1999-I 355–6, 494
Mellacher and others v Austria (Appl Nos 10522/83, 10011/84 and 11070/84)
    (1990) 12 EHRR 391 369
MSS v Belgium and Greece (Appl No 30696/09), Judgment of 21 January 2011 . . . . 354, 356, 370
Müller v Switzerland (Appl No 10737/84) (1991) 13 EHRR 485 368
National Union of Belgian Police v Belgium (Appl No 4464/70), (1979-80) 1 EHRR 578 374
Niemitz v Germany, Series A, No 251-B, (1993) 16 EHRR 97 818–19
NUT v Governing Body of St Mary's CoE Junior School [1997] 3 CMLR 630 263
Öcalan v Turkey (Appl No 46221/99) (2003) 37 EHRR 10 363
OOO Neste St Petersburg and others v Russia (Appl No 69042/01) 351
Peck v The United Kingdom no 44647/98, ECHR 2011-I 819
Posti and Rahko v Finland, App No 27824/95, Judgment of 24 September 2002 174
Rotaru v Romania (Appl No 28341/95), Judgment of 4 May 2000 366
Salgueiro da Silva Mouta v Portugal (Appl No 33290/96), (1999) EHRR 176 .371
Schmidt and Dahlström v Sweden (Appl No 5589/72) [1978-9] 1 EHRR 632 375
Scoppola v Italy (No 2) (Judgment of 17 September 2009) 242–3
Siliadin v France (Appl No 73316/01), Judgment of 26 July 2005 364
Smith and Grady v UK (Appl No 33895/96 and 33896/96) (2001) 31 EHRR 24 365
Societe Colas Est and Others v France, no 37971/97, üECHR 2002-III 819
Societé Stenuit v France (Appl No 11598/85) [1992] 14 EHRR 509 351
Soering v UK (Appl No 14038/88) (1989) 11 EHRR 439 370
Stenuit (1992) 14 EHRR 509 832
Streletz, Kessler and Krenz v Germany (Judgment of 22 March 2001) 242
SW v United Kingdom (Judgment of 22 November 1995) 242
Tyrer v UK (Appl No 5856/72) (1979-80) 2 EHRR 1 363
Veeber v Estonia (No 2) (Judgment of 21 January 2003) 242
Vermeulen v Belgium, Appl No 19075/91, Reports 1996-I 352
Vetter v France (Appl No 59842/00), Judgment of 31 May 2005 365
Wilson and National Union of Journalists v UK (Appl No 30668/96, 30671/96, 30678/96)
    [2002] 35 EHRR 20 375

PCIJ

Treatment of Polish Nationals in Danzig (1932) PCIJ Rep, Ser A/B, No 44, 24 270

National

France

Conseil Constitutionnel
    Decision No 98-400 (20 May 1998) 492
    Decision No 2004-496 (10 June 2004) 339
    Decision No 2004-497 (1 July 2004) 339
Conseil d'Etat
    Cohn-Bendit [1979] Dalloz Jur 155 259
Cour d'Appel de Paris
    Joseph Aim [1972] CMLR 901 259

Germany

Bananas, Federal Constitutional Court, decision 7/6/00 [2000] Human Rights Law
    Journal 251 339
Brunner, Federal Constitutional Court, [1994] 1 CMLR 57 . . . . 106–7, 110, 275–6, 339
Firma Baer Getreide BmbH [1972] CMLR 539, Hessischer Verwaltunggerichtschof .259
Honeywell, Federal Constitutional Court, 6 July 2010 276–7
Kloppenburg, Bundesfinanzhof, 25 April 1985) 259
Mangold, Federal Constitutional Court, 2 BvR 2666/06 339

Solange I, Federal Constitutional Court, [1974] 2 CMLR 540...................................275, 339
Solange II, Federal Constitutional Court, [1987] 3 CMLR 225.....................275–6, 297, 339–40
Treaty of Lisbon, Federal Constitutional Court, 30 June 2009.......................................276, 947

Italy

Constitutional Court
   Judgment 7/3/64, n 11..339
   Judgment 27/12/65, n 98..339

Poland

Constitutional Court
   judgment of 27.04.05, P 1/05, Dziennik Ustaw 2005.77.680.......................................339

United Kingdom

AAA and others v Secretary of State for the Home Department, [2006] 1 All ER 575 364
Attheraces Ltd v The British Horseracing Board Ltd [2007] EWCA Civ 38, CA 786
Chiron Corporation v Murex Diagnostics [1995] All ER (EC) 88, [1995] FSR 309.......................223
Commissioners of Customs and Excise v Samex ApS [1983] 3 CMLR 194 (HC) 218
Crehan v Inntrepreneur Pub Co [2007] 1 AC 333(HL) 839, 842
Criterion Properties plc v Stratford UK Properties LLC [2004] UKHL 28; [2004] 1 WLR 1846 (HL) 695
Factortame, ex parte (No 5) [2000] 1 AC 524 (HL)..311
Gouriet v Secretary of State for Foreign and Commonwealth Affairs [2003] EWCA Civ 384 275
Griffin v South-West Water Services Ltd [1995] IRLR 15 263
HP Bulmer Ltd v J Bollinger SA [1974] Ch 401...219
J Rothschild Holdings plc v Commissioners of Inland Revenue [1989] 2 CMLR 621......................218
M v Home Office [1994] 1 AC 377 ....298, 303
Macarthys Ltd v Smith [1979] 3 All ER 325..274
Madzimbamuto v Lardner-Burke [1969] 1 AC 645..274
O'Boyle and Plunkett [1999] NI 126 [2000] EuLR 637...513
Pickstone v Freemans plc [1987] 2 CMLR (CA) 218
Polydor Ltd v Harlequin Record Shops Ltd [1980] 2 CMLR 413 (CA) 212
R v chief Constable of Sussex, ex parte International Trader's Ferry Ltd (ITF) [1997] 2 All ER 65;
   [1999] 1 All ER 129...430
R v Inspectorate of Pollution, ex parte Greenpeace (No 2) [1994] 4 All ER 329......................167
R v Intervention Board for Agricultural Produce, ex parte ED and F Man (Sugar) Ltd
   [1986] 2 All ER 126 (QBD) 226
R v Minister of Agriculture, ex parte Fédération Européenne de la Santé Animale
   [1988] 3 CMLR 207 and 661 (DC) 226
R v Pharmaceutical Society of Great Britain, ex parte The Association of Pharmaceutical
   Importers [1987] 3 CMLR 951..218
R v Secretary of State, ex parte Duddridge [1996] 2 CMLR 361......................................223
R v Secretary of State for Employment, ex parte Equal Opportunities Commission [1995] 1 AC 1 274
R v Secretary of State for Transport, ex parte Factortame [1989] 2 CMLR 353 224
R v Secretary of State for Transport, ex parte Factortame (No 2) [1990] 3 WLR 818 274
R v Stock Exchange, ex parte Else (1982) Ltd [1993] 2 WLR 70; [1993] 1 All ER 420 (CA)................219
Thoburn v Sunderland City Council [2002] 4 All ER 156 274–5
Trinity Mirror PLC v Commissioners of Customs and Excise [2001] 2 CMLR 33.........................219
Woolwich Building Society v IRC [1993] AC 70...298

United States

Leegin Creative Leather Products Inc v PSKS Inc 127 S Ct 2705 US (2007)...........................746, 761
Timberlane Lumber Co v Bank of America 549 F2d 597 (1976) 721
US v Aluminium Co of America 148 F2d 416 (1945)...721
US v EI du Pont de Namours & Co 351 US 377, 76 S Ct 994 (1956) 769
Verizon Communications Inc v Law Offices of Curtis V Trinko, LLP 540 US 682 (2004) 800

Table of Legislation

European Union

Agreement between the European Communities and the Government of the United States of America
    on the application of positive comity principles in the enforcement of their competition laws 723
    Art III 723
Brussels Convention on jurisdiction and the recognition and enforcement of judgments in civil and
    commercial matters 213
Budgetary Treaty 1970..11
Budgetary Treaty 1975..11
Charter of Fundamental Rights (CFR) 20, 23, 25, 33–5, 359–61
    Preamble...361
    Art 1...363
    Art 2...363, 370
    Art 3..363–4, 384
    Art 4...364, 370
    Art 5...364
    Art 5(1) 364
    Art 5(2) 364
    Art 5(3) 364
    Art 6...365
    Art 7...365–6, 485
    Art 8...366
    Art 9...366
    Art 10...366–7
    Art 10(2) 367
    Art 11...367
    Art 11(2) 367, 494
    Art 12...367
    Art 12(2) 368
    Art 13...368
    Art 14...368
    Art 14(2) 368
    Art 14(3) 368
    Art 15...369
    Art 15(1) 368
    Art 15(2) 368
    Art 16...369
    Art 17...369
    Art 18...369–70
    Art 19...370
    Art 20...370
    Art 21...370–2, 377
    Art 21(2) 371
    Art 22...371
    Art 23...371–2, 377
    Art 23(2) 372–3
    Art 24...373
    Art 24(1) 373
    Art 24(2) 373
    Art 24(3) 373
    Art 25...373

Art 26. 374
Art 27. 374
Art 28. . . . . 350, 367, 375
Art 29. 375
Art 30. 376
Art 31. 376
Art 32. 376
Art 32(2) 376
Art 33. 377
Art 34. 377
Art 34(1) 377
Art 34(2) 377
Art 34(3) 377
Art 35. 377–8
Art 36. 378
Art 37. . . . . 378, 384
Art 38. 378
Art 39. 379
Art 40. 379
Art 41. 832
Arts 41–44. 379
Art 45. 379
Art 46. 379
Art 47. . . . . .159, 197, 289, 291, 351, 379–80
Art 47(1) 833
Art 47(2) 379, 833
Art 47(3) 380
Art 48. 380
Art 48(2) 833
Art 49. . . . . 326, 380–1
Art 49(1) 242, 381, 833
Art 49(2) 381
Art 49(3) 381
Art 50. . . . . .381, 833
Art 51. 382–3
Arts 51–54. 361
Art 52. . . . . 326, 353, 383–5
Art 52(1) 383, 832
Art 52(2) 368, 383
Art 52(3) 354, 362, 383, 832
Art 52(4) 384
Art 52(5) 371, 374, 384–5
Art 52(6) 385
Art 52(7) 341, 362–3, 385
Art 53. 385
Art 54. 385–6
Title I 363–4
Title II 365–70
Title III 370–4
Title IV 374–8
Title V 378–9
Title VI 379–82
Title VII. 382–6
Co-operation Agreement 1999 between the EC, ECSC and Canada 724
Common Position 2001/931. 353
Common Position 2002/402. 353
Convention Implementing the Schengen Agreement (CISA) 484
Art 5(1) 484
Art 5(2) 484
Art 54-58. 381
Arts 92 et seq 484
Art 96. 484
Convention on certain Institutions Common to the European Communities (25 March 1957). 9

Decision 70/243 12
Decision 76/787 . . . . .12, 56
Decision 87/373 88
Decision 88/591
　Art 3(1)(c) 708
Decision 93/569 375
Decision 94/94 945
Decision 94/800 957–8
Decision 95/1 11
Decision 95/145 723
Decision 95/553 494
　Art 5 494
Decision 1999/435 126
Decision 1999/436 126
Decision 1999/468 . . . . .88–9, 91
　Art 2(2) 90
　Art 3 89
　Art 4 89
　Art 5 89
　Art 5a 89
Decision 2000/402 945
Decision 2001/462 822
Decision 2002/772 57
Decision 2003/8 375
Decision 2004/752 64
Decision 2004/833 908
Decision 2005/380
　Recital (3) 690
Decision 2005/842 864–5
Decision 2005/902 46
Decision 2006/512 89
Decision 2007/436 12
Decision 2008/79 211
Decision 2009/857 . . . . .35, 50
Decision 2009/878 46
Decision 2009/880 56
Decision 2009/881 46–7
Decision 2009/882 . . . . .45, 59
Decision 2009/908 47
Decision 2009/937 . . . . .47, 49, 51, 59
　Art 5(2) 92
　Arts 7–9 51
　Art 8 51
Decision 2009/950 56
Decision 2010/80 53
Decision 2010/279 908
Decision 2010/405 131
Decision 2010/427 55
Decision 2010/594 46
Directive 64/221 . . . . .483, 486
Directive 64/223 . . . . .543, 559
　Art 3 543
　Art 4 543
　Art 6 543
Directive 68/151 679
Directive 68/360 . . . . .462, 508–9
Directive 69/335
　Art 2(1) 653
　Art 10(a) 653
Directive 70/50 409
　Art 2 409
　Art 3 409
Directive 73/148 . . . . .462, 470

Directive 75/34 480
Directive 75/117 . . . . .264, 544
Directive 76/207 . . . . .239, 251, 261, 288, 297, 371
    Art 2(2) 376
    Art 2(7) 377
Directive 77/91 682
    Art 6 682
    Art 6(3) 682
Directive 77/249 . . . . .554, 562, 568, 604, 607, 638, 641
    Recital (Final) 639
    Art 1(1) 639
    Art 1(2) 639
    Art 2 639
    Art 3 638–9
    Art 4 554
    Art 4(1) 639
    Art 4(2) 639
    Art 4(4) 640
    Art 5 639
Directive 77/780 921
Directive 78/660 . . . . .576, 680–1
Directive 80/723 878
Directive 80/987 307
Directive 83/189 . . . . .139, 280–2
    Art 8 280
    Art 9 280
Directive 83/349 680
Directive 85/337 . . . . .249–50, 263
Directive 85/374 316
Directive 88/301 879
Directive 88/361 662
    Ann I 662
Directive 89/48 642
    Art 4(1)(b) 642
Directive 89/104 . . . . .450, 456
Directive 89/391 376
Directive 89/646 921
    Recital (20) 921
Directive 89/665 . . . . .298, 316
Directive 89/666
    Art 3 681
    Art 4 681
Directive 90/364 . . . . .462, 466
Directive 90/365 . . . . .462, 466
Directive 90/388 . . . . .879, 890
Directive 90/435 585–6
    Art 4(1) 586
Directive 91/533 316
Directive 92/85 . . . . .316, 377
Directive 92/100 450
    Art 9 453
Directive 93/13 . . . . .148, 316
Directive 93/96 . . . . .462, 464–6, 475–6
Directive 93/104 . . . . .103, 117–18, 123, 282–3, 376
Directive 93/109 493
    Art 4 493
Directive 94/33 . . . . .316, 376
Directive 94/45 374
Directive 94/80 492
    Art 5(3) 492–3
    Art 12(4) 492
    Ann 492
Directive 94/96 879

Directive 95/46 . . . . .242, 366
Directive 95/51 890
Directive 96/2 890
Directive 96/9 450
Directive 96/30 492
Directive 96/71 . . . . .607, 660
  Art 1 529
Directive 98/5 . . . . 554, 568, 604, 623, 625, 638, 640, 642–4
  Art 1 641
  Art 1(1) 640
  Art 1(2) 641
  Art 1(2)(d) 638
  Art 2 641
  Art 3 554
  Art 3(1) 641
  Art 3(2) 641
  Art 5(1) 641
  Art 5(2) 641
  Art 6(1) 641
  Art 6(3) 641
  Art 7(1) 641
  Art 10 642
Directive 98/34 . . . . 280, 422, 605
Directive 98/43 107–8
  Art 3(1) 107
  Art 3(2) 101
  Art 3(5) 107
  Art 5 107
Directive 98/44 . . . . .118, 364
  Art 9 964
Directive 98/59 . . . . .316, 374
Directive 98/71 450
Directive 99/44 316
Directive 1996/43 85
Directive 1997/81 85
Directive 1999/70 85
Directive 2000/43 . . . . 214, 266, 371–2
  Art 2(3) 376
Directive 2000/78 . . . . 255, 265–6, 345, 371–2
  Art 2(3) 376
Directive 2001/23 . . . . .316, 376
  Art 7 374
Directive 2001/29 450
Directive 2001/37 118
Directive 2001/86 691
Directive 2002/14 374
Directive 2002/46 118
Directive 2002/58 365
Directive 2002/73 . . . . 371, 376–7
Directive 2002/77 879
  Art 1(5) 880
  Art 1(6) 880
Directive 2003/8 . . . . 317, 366, 376, 380
Directive 2003/9 369
Directive 2003/33 108
Directive 2003/35 . . . . .251, 316
Directive 2003/88 376
Directive 2004/17 . . . . .542, 546
  Art 3(a) 546
  Art 16 546
  Art 18 546
Directive 2004/18 . . . . 542, 546, 621
  Art 1(4) 546

Art 7..546
Art 17...546
Art 55...597
Directive 2004/25 693–701
  Recital (21) 695
  Art 3(c) 697–8
  Art 5...694
  Art 9...694–6
  Art 9(2) 673, 694–5, 697–8
  Art 11...694, 696
  Art 11(3) 695
  Art 12(1) 695
  Art 12(2) 695
  Art 12(3) 695
  Art 15...694
  Art 16...694
  Art 20...699
Directive 2004/34
  Art 7..373
  Art 13...373
Directive 2004/35 316
Directive 2004/38 ....366, 373, 461–2, 467–88, 491, 505–10, 518,
                                          525, 527–9, 534, 571–2
  Art 2...470, 528
  Art 3...366, 468, 471, 518, 525
  Art 4...471
  Art 4(3) 366
  Art 5...471
  Art 5(2) 478
  Art 5(4) 471
  Art 6...472, 506
  Art 7..472–3
  Art 7(1) 472
  Art 7(1)(b) 474
  Art 7(1)(c)..475
  Art 7(3) 473
  Art 7(3)(d) 505
  Art 8...478
  Art 8(4) 474
  Art 9...478
  Art 11...479
  Art 12...477, 481
  Art 12(3) 527
  Art 13...477, 481
  Art 14(1) 472
  Art 14(2) 475
  Art 14(3) 475, 477
  Art 14(4) 508
  Art 14(4)(b) 474, 506
  Art 15...475
  Art 16...479
  Art 16(3) 479
  Art 16(4) 479
  Art 17...479, 509
  Art 17(1) 480
  Art 17(2) 480
  Art 17(3) 480
  Art 17(4) 477, 480
  Art 19...481
  Art 20(2) 481
  Art 21...481
  Art 22...481
  Art 23...476, 482

Art 24. . . . . 474–5, 482, 507, 528
Art 24(1) 509
Art 24(2) 472, 474–6, 482, 506, 508, 525
Art 27. 483
Art 27(1) 483
Art 27(2) 483
Art 27(3) 484
Art 27(4) 486
Art 28. 485
Art 28(2) 479, 485
Art 28(3) 485
Art 28(3)(b) 485
Art 29. 485–7
Art 30. . . . . 475, 486
Art 31. . . . . 475, 486, 488
Art 31(1) 488
Art 31(3) 487
Art 31(4) 487–8
Art 32. 487–8
Art 33. 484
Art 35. 488
Art 37. 488
Directive 2004/48 316
Directive 2004/81 364
Directive 2004/83 364
Directive 2005/36 . . . . 599, 604, 607, 615–16, 624–5, 630–2,
                                                                        634, 637–9, 642, 645
Recital (5) 635
Recital (13) 632
Recital (42) 638
Art 1. 630
Art 2(1) 630
Art 2(3) 638
Art 3(1)(g) 633
Art 3(1)(h) 633
Art 3(2) 630, 634
Art 3(a) 630
Art 4(1) 631
Art 5(1)(h) 635
Art 5(2) 635
Art 5(3) 635
Art 6. 635–6
Art 7(3) 636
Art 7(4) 636–7
Art 10. 632
Art 11. 632
Art 13(1) 632
Art 14(1) 642
Art 14(2) 634
Art 14(3) 634
Art 14(4) 634
Art 14(5) 634
Art 14(a)-(c) 633
Art 16. 632
Art 21. 631
Art 21(6) 631
Art 24. 631
Art 24(2) 631
Art 24(3)(b) 631
Art 52(1) 634
Art 52(2) 634
Art 62(1) 642
Ann IV. 632

Directive 2005/56 . . . . .682, 684
   Art 4(1)(b) 683
Directive 2005/85 370
Directive 2006/24 365
Directive 2006/54 . . . . .239, 251, 261, 264, 288, 297, 316, 544
Directive 2006/111 . . . . .864, 878
Directive 2006/115 450
Directive 2006/123 599–624
   Recital (4) 603
   Recital (6) 600, 602
   Recital (9) 601–2
   Recital (21) 600
   Recital (33) 601
   Recital (49) 618
   Recital (52) 619
   Recital (97) 609
   Recital (100) 610
   Art 1(1) 600
   Art 2(1) 600
   Art 2(2) 600
   Art 2(2)(d) 600
   Art 2(3) 600
   Art 4(1) 600
   Art 4(7) 601, 612
   Art 5(1) 616
   Art 5(2) 617
   Art 5(3) 617
   Art 5(4) 617
   Art 6(1) 617
   Art 6(2) 617
   Art 7(1) 618
   Art 7(2) 618
   Art 7(3) 618
   Art 7(4) 618
   Art 7(5) 619
   Art 7(6) 618
   Art 8(1) 619
   Art 8(2) 619
   Art 9 603
   Art 9(1) 603, 612
   Art 9(2) 603
   Art 10(1) 603
   Art 10(2) 603
   Art 10(3) 603
   Art 10(4) 603
   Art 10(6) 603
   Art 11 603
   Art 11(1) 619
   Art 11(2) 619
   Art 12(1) and (2) 603
   Art 13 604
   Art 14 604
   Art 14(1) 604, 606
   Art 14(2) 604
   Art 15 . . . . .604, 620
   Art 15(1)-(3) 604
   Art 15(2)(a) 604
   Art 15(2)(b) 604
   Art 15(2)(d) 605
   Art 15(2)(g) 605
   Art 15(7) 605
   Art 16 . . . . 607, 611, 614, 620
   Arts 16-20 621

Art 16(1) 605–6
Art 16(1)(a)-(c) 605
Art 16(2) 606, 612
Art 16(2)(a) 606
Art 16(2)(b) 606
Art 16(2)(c) 606
Art 16(2)(f) 611
Art 16(3) 606, 612
Art 17 611
Art 17(1) 607
Art 17(2) 607
Art 17(4) 607
Art 17(5) 607
Art 17(6) 607
Art 18 ....606–7, 614
Art 19 607
Art 20 608
Art 21 ....608–9, 621
Art 22(1)(a) 609
Art 22(1)(b) 609
Art 22(1)(c)–(k) 609
Art 22(2) 609
Art 22(3) 609
Art 23 610
Art 23(1) 610
Art 23(2) 610
Art 24 621
Art 24(1) 610
Art 24(2) 610
Art 25(3) 620
Art 28(1) 612
Art 28(3) 612
Art 28(6) 612
Art 29(1) 613
Art 29(2) 613
Art 29(3) 613
Art 30(1) 612
Art 30(2) 612
Art 30(3) 613
Art 31(1) 611–12
Art 31(2) 613
Art 31(4) 613
Art 33(1) 613
Art 33(2) 614
Art 33(3) 614
Art 34(1) 615
Art 34(2) 615
Art 35 ....607, 614
Art 35(1) 614
Art 35(2) 614
Art 35(3) 614
Art 35(4) 614
Art 35(5) 614
Art 35(6) 615
Art 39 619
Art 39(1) 605
Art 39(1)(a) 619
Art 39(1)(b) 620
Art 39(1)(c) 620
Art 39(2) 620
Art 39(4) 620
Art 39(5) 620
Art 40(1) 620

Directive 2007/36 684
   Recital (5) 684
Directive 2008/95 450
   Arts 5-7 457
   Art 7 453
   Art 7(1) 456–8
Directive 2008/99 317
Directive 2009/22 . . . . .251, 316
Directive 2009/38 374
   Art 17 374
Directive 2009/42 87
Directive 2009/50 369
   Art 14 369
Directive 2009/101 679
Directive 2010/18 377
Directive 2010/76 87
EC Treaty (former) 13
   Art 2 . . . . .399, 705–6
   Art 3 705
   Art 3(1) 706
   Art 3(1)(g) 706
   Art 3(2) 706
   Art 5 . . . . .98, 117, 327
   Art 5(b) 114
   Art 8a 462
   Art 10 . . . . .239, 321–4, 706, 881, 890, 893
   Art 14 13
   Art 16 . . . . .876, 890
   Art 18 462
   Art 23 392
   Art 25 403
   Art 28 403
   Art 30 . . . . .369, 442–3
   Art 31 876
   Art 37 . . . . .77, 915, 949
   Art 39 714
   Art 40(2) 333
   Art 42 . . . . .76, 82
   Art 43 588
   Art 44 558
   Art 47(2) 76
   Art 52 558
   Art 65 928
   Art 71(1)(b) 185
   Art 81 . . . . .706, 729, 749
   Art 81(1) 181, 758
   Art 81(3) 742, 756, 760
   Art 82 . . . . .706, 765, 782–3, 789
   Art 83 755
   Arts 83-85 707
   Art 86 . . . . .707, 781, 847
   Art 86(2) 717
   Arts 87-89 . . . . .707, 847
   Art 89 866
   Art 90 . . . . .396, 403
   Art 94 108
   Art 95 . . . . .13, 91
   Art 99(5) 78
   Art 102(2) 78
   Art 103(2) 78
   Art 106(2) 78
   Art 113 946
   Art 114(4) 178

Art 133...77, 101, 946–7
Art 133(5)..935
Art 133(5) and (6)...950
Art 133(6)..949
Art 137(2)...81
Art 141..431
Arts 158-162...13
Arts 163-173...13
Arts 174-176...13
Art 175(2)...81
Art 189..21, 57–8
Art 190..21, 57–8
Art 200...12
Art 202..88, 90
Art 205...48
Art 213(1)..51–2
Art 226..145
Art 229..831
Art 230...158, 170, 187, 708
Art 232(3)..186
Art 233(2)..182
Art 234...215, 219, 223, 708
Art 241..202
Art 249...70
Art 252...77
Art 252(c)..77
Art 252(d) and (e)...77
Art 256..721
Arts 266-267..190
Art 281...910–11
Art 288(2)..182
Art 293...246, 657
Art 294(7)(c)..92
Art 300(3)..949
Art 305..8
Art 308...28, 109–10, 678–9
Art 309..340
Title IV, Pt 3...317
Protocol and Agreement on Social Policy..125
ECSC Treaty (former) see Treaty Establishing the European Coal and Steel Community (former)
EEA Agreement...66, 212, 216, 724
  Ann XVII...457
  Art 65(2)..457
EEC-Greece Association Agreement (former)
  Art 53(1)..954
EEC-Morocco Cooperation Agreement
  Art 41(1)..955
EEC-Portuguese Association Agreement (former)..955
  Art 21...954
EEC Treaty (former)...8–9, 13
  Preamble...7
  Art 5...322–3
  Art 9..392
  Art 12...392
  Art 13...401
  Art 13(2)..392
  Art 14...401
  Art 16...392
  Art 43...915
  Art 43(2)...78
  Art 53...543
  Art 75(1)(a)...914
  Art 95...401

Art 113..910, 942
Art 128..105
Art 130R(4)..114
Art 190(4)...12
Art 210..911
Art 228..910
Arts 229-231...910
Art 234..236
Art 238..910
Art 249..237
Art 269..12
EEC-Turkey Association Agreement..346, 966
Art 12...955
EEC-Yugoslavia Cooperation Agreement..963
Euratom Treaty see Treaty establishing the European Atomic Energy Community
Euro-Mediterranean Agreement
Art 64(1)..955
Europe Agreements..17, 901
European Council Decision 2009/879..45
European Council Decision 2009/881..46
European Council Decision 2009/882..45
European Economic Area (EEA) Agreement..457
Europol Convention
Art 2(1)...364
Framework Agreement on relations between the Parliament and Commission..........60–1
Framework Decision 2001/220...243, 317
Framework Decision 2001/500...317
Framework Decision 2002/475...317
Framework Decision 2002/584...317, 381
Arts 3 and 4...381
Framework Decision 2002/629...364
Framework Decision 2002/946...317
Framework Decision 2004/757...317
Framework Decision 2008/841...317
Framework Decision 2008/909...317
Framework Decision 2008/913...317
Inter-Institutional Agreement between the European Parliament, the Council and the
     Commission on budgetary discipline and sound financial management 2006.......12
Joint Action 2008/736...907–8
Joint Position 96/196...369
Lomé Convention
Art 62...626
Maastricht Treaty (see also Treaty on European Union)............13, 16, 26–7, 33, 73, 78, 104,
                                  114, 117, 125, 260, 340, 391, 461–3, 492, 858
Protocol amending the Europol Convention..364
Regulation 3/58
Art 52...499
Regulation 17/62.......................................351, 707, 730, 755, 810–11, 815–16, 818,
                                                               820, 844, 849
Regulation 99/63..184
Art 6..184
Regulation 67/67..717
Art 1(1)...717
Regulation 259/68
Art 17...367
Art 17a..367
Regulation 950/68...405
Regulation 1612/68.............................347, 375, 462, 464, 470, 476, 498–9,
                                                          509–11, 517, 526, 529
Preamble...526
Recital 5..498
Art 1(2)...510
Art 2..510

Art 3. . . . . .371, 510
Art 3(1) 510
Art 4. 511
Art 5. 506
Art 6(1) 511
Art 6(2) 511
Art 7. . . . . 511, 514–15, 527
Art 7(1) 514–15
Art 7(2) 504, 516–19, 522, 527–8
Art 7(3) 517
Art 7(4) 501, 553
Art 8. 519
Art 9(1) 520
Art 9(2) 520
Art 10. . . . . .525, 528
Art 11. . . . . .525, 529
Art 12. . . . . 476–7, 510, 525–7
Art 12(1) 526
Art 12(2) 526
Regulation 543/69 . . . . .911, 914
Regulation 2603/69 945
Regulation 1251/70 479–80
Regulation 1408/71 . . . . 464, 506, 518, 522
Regulation 2988/74 822–3
Regulation 2641/84
   Art 2(1) 962
Regulation 2137/85 . . . . 680, 685–6
   Art 21. 686
   Art 40. 686
Regulation 4056/86 718
Regulation 2658/87 405
Regulation 4064/89 780
Regulation 2913/92 318
   Arts 114 et seq 392
Regulation 2187/93 196
Regulation 40/94. . . . . 450, 964–5
   Art 99. 965
Regulation 3286/94 962
Regulation 384/96
   Art 6(9) 159
Regulation 994/98 849
Regulation 1154/98 377
Regulation 1540/98 861
Regulation 1638/98 177
Regulation 2679/98 . . . . .146, 430
Regulation 2842/98
   Art 6. 184
Regulation 659/1999 . . . . 849, 866–7, 869–71
   Art 1(f) 868
   Art 1(g) 871
   Art 2. 867
   Art 3. 867
   Art 4. 867
   Art 4(5) 868
   Art 4(6) 868, 871
   Art 6. 868
   Art 7. 868
   Art 7(3) 867
   Art 7(4) 868
   Art 7(6) 868
   Art 10(1) 869
   Art 10(3) 869
   Art 11(1) 869

Art 11(2) 869
Art 14(1) 869
Art 14(3) 870
Art 15(1) 869
Art 17 871
Art 18 871
Regulation 2790/1999 ....748, 755, 760–1
Regulation 2659/2000 755
Regulation 2667/2000
  Arts 13 and 13a 158
Regulation 44/2001 ....213, 317, 928
Art 15 762
Regulation 539/2001 471
Regulation 1049/2001 ....495, 836
Art 4 495
Art 9 495
Regulation 2157/2001 ....680, 691
Art 4(1) 691
Art 4(2) 691
Art 5 691
Art 38 692
Regulation 6/2002 ....450, 453
Regulation 178/2002 43
Regulation 881/2002 353
Regulation 1/2003 ....85, 316, 351, 705, 707–9, 718,
                                                                      725, 730, 762, 809–14, 816, 820,
                                                                      822–8, 838–40, 844, 849, 890

Recital (15) 811
Recital (23) 816
Art 1(3) 767
Art 2 756
Art 3 754
Art 3(1) 719
Art 5 ....709, 767, 812, 826
Art 6 ....709, 767, 838
Art 7 ....708, 811, 825–6, 837
Art 8 823
Art 9 ....811, 825–7
Art 10 ....708, 811, 823
Art 11 811
Art 11(3) 812
Art 11(4) 812
Art 11(6) 813
Art 12(1) 813
Art 12(3) 813
Art 14 837
Art 15(1) 839
Art 15(2) 831
Art 15(3) 839
Art 16 839
Art 18 815
Arts 18-21 815
Art 18(2) 815
Art 18(3) 815
Art 18(5) 815
Art 18(6) 815
Art 19 817
Art 20 817
Art 20(2) 817
Art 20(3) 818
Art 20(6) 818
Art 20(8) 818
Art 21 818–19

Art 21(3) 819
Art 23. ....708, 837
Art 23(1) 811
Art 23(2) 811, 827, 830
Art 23(3) 827
Art 23(5) 351, 832
Art 24. 708
Art 24(1) 824
Art 27. 821
Art 29(2) 762
Art 31. ....708, 831
Regulation 343/2003 370
Regulation 1435/2003 678
Regulation 2004/2003 58
Regulation 2201/2003 ....317, 373
Regulation 139/2004 .... 707, 722, 779–82
Regulation 261/2004 960
Regulation 772/2004 755
Regulation 773/2004 .... 809, 814, 820, 837
Art 3. 817
Art 3(2) and (3) 817
Art 10(1) 821
Art 10a(2) 837
Art 12. 822
Art 12(2) 837
Art 14. 822
Art 14(8) 822
Art 15. 822
Art 15(1a) 837
Art 16. 822
Regulation 794/2004 ....849, 866
Regulation 802/2004 779
Regulation 847/2004 948
Regulation 883/2004 .... 377–8, 464, 506, 518, 522
Art 20. 378
Regulation 1290/2005 366
Regulation 1184/2006 718
Regulation 1419/2006 718
Regulation 1998/2006 ....849, 853
Regulation 168/2007 ....43, 340
Regulation 717/2007 118
Regulation 1234/2007 718
Regulation 259/2008 366
Regulation 662/2008 837
Regulation 800/2008 .... 848–9, 861, 893
Regulation 207/2009 450
Art 13. 453
Regulation 401/2009 43
Regulation 428/2009 949
Regulation 987/2009 377
Regulation 1061/2009 101
Regulation 1225/2009 169
Regulation 1286/2009 353
Regulation 330/2010 .... 742, 755, 760–1
Art 1(a) 761
Art 2(1) 760
Art 4. 761
Art 4(a) 761
Art 4(b) 761
Art 4(b)(i) 761
Art 4(c) 761
Art 4(d) 761
Regulation 407/2010 21

Regulation 438/2010 87
Regulation 995/2010 87
Regulation 1080/2010 55
Regulation 1081/2010 55
Regulation 1090/2010 87
Regulation 1093/2010 87
Regulation 1094/2010 87
Regulation 1095/2010 . . . . . . , , , , ...87
Regulation 1231/2010 . . . . , , , ...377
Regulation 1236/2010 . . . . , , , , ...87
Regulation 2017/2010 755
Regulation 2018/2010 755
Rules of Procedure of the Court of Justice 154, 203
   Art 62a. 211
   Art 76. 380
   Art 80(1)(a). 156
   Art 81(1) 156
   Art 81(2) 156
   Arts 83-92. 203
   Art 83(1) 203
   Art 83(2) 204
   Art 85. 204
   Art 86. 204
   Art 92(1) 221
   Art 93. 136
   Arts 104-110. 203
   Art 104a. 211
   Art 104b 211
Rules of Procedure of the European Parliament
   Code of Conduct for negotiating in the context of the ordinary legislative procedure. 95
Rules of Procedure of the General Court
   Art 94. 380
   Arts 94 et seq 380
   Art 101(1) 156
   Art 102(1) 156
   Art 102(2) 156
   Arts 115-16. 136
Schengen Agreement. 126, 484
   see also Convention Implementing the Schengen Agreement (CISA)
Single European Act (SEA). 12–13, 19, 36, 43, 56, 63, 77–8, 88,
                                                                                                91, 106, 109, 114, 193,
                                                                                                297, 340, 360, 918–19

   Preamble 340
Statute of the Court of Justice of the European Union 62
   Art 9. 63
   Art 16. 62
   Art 20. 62
   Art 23. 216
   Art 23a. 211
   Art 37. 136
   Art 48. 63
   Art 49. 63
   Art 51. . . . . .64, 154
   Art 58. 64
   Arts 62-62b. 64–5
   Art 62-62b. 210
   Art 256(3) 210
   Ann I 64
Treaty establishing a Single Council and a Single Commission of the European Communities
   (Merger Treaty) 1965 . . . . .8–9, 11
   Art 10. 8
Treaty establishing the European Atomic Energy Community. 9, 23
   Art 96. 497

Art 101(1) 8, 919
Art 108(3) 12
Art 173. 12
Art 188(2) 191
Treaty establishing the European Coal and Steel Community (former) 4, 8–9, 12
Art 1. 4
Art 4. 5
Art 5. 5
Art 6(2) 910
Art 9. 8
Art 14. 8
Art 21(3) 12
Art 26. 8
Art 35. 183
Art 49. 8
Art 61. 8
Art 65. 8
Art 66. 8
Art 66(7) 768
Art 69. 497
Art 97. 4
Treaty of Accession 1972. . . . . .10, 18
Art 102. 915
Treaty of Accession 1985. 456
Treaty of Accession 2003. . . . . 16–17, 126, 528–9
Ann V-XV. 528
Treaty of Accession 2005. . . . . 16–17, 529
Ann VI and VII 529
Treaty of Amsterdam (TA) 12–13, 15–16, 19, 33,
72–3, 76–8, 98, 114, 124–7, 130–1, 143,
149, 164, 317, 340, 370, 372–3, 543,
858, 876, 900, 915, 928, 936
Treaty of Lisbon (TL). 3, 19–21, 26, 30, 32–5, 42, 44, 46,
48–50, 52, 54–5, 57–8, 62–3, 69–73, 77–8,
82, 84, 86–7, 90–1, 98–101, 108, 110–11, 114,
116, 119, 121–2, 125–7, 129, 137, 152, 154–8,
161–2, 164, 173, 175–6, 186, 190, 201, 205, 210–12,
222, 230, 268, 276–8, 290, 317, 323–4, 337, 340,
342–3, 351, 353–4, 359, 361, 364, 379,
381, 383, 460, 469, 657, 688, 706,
725, 859, 890, 899
see also Treaty on European Union (TEU); Treaty on the Functioning of the
European Union (TFEU)
Art 6(2) 20
Declaration No 4 . . . . .21, 57
Declaration No 5 . . . . .21, 57
Declaration No 7 35
Declaration No 10 52
Declaration No 17 . . . . 35–6, 268, 278
Declaration No 18 99–100
Declaration No 23 82
Declaration No 41 110
Declaration No 42 110
Declaration No 57 59
Declaration No 61 35
Declaration No 64 . . . . .35, 59
Treaty of Nice (TN) 16, 18–19, 48–51, 63, 76–7, 101, 109, 125, 127, 161, 186,
190, 340, 917, 942, 946, 950
Political Declaration 339
Treaty on European Union (TEU). 13–15, 19–21, 23–30, 33–4
see also Treaty of Lisbon (TL)
ex-Art 1 13
Art 1. . . . . .24, 33, 115

Art 1(1) 99
Art 1(3) 900
Art 2 . . . . 24–5, 30, 99, 499
Art 2(1) 128
ex-Art 3 14
Art 3 . . . . 24, 99, 128, 399, 706
Art 3(3) 371, 678
Art 3(6) 24, 99
Art 4 25
ex-Art 4 . . . . , , 43
Art 4 97–8
Art 4(2) 25, 115
Art 4(3) 25, 87, 239, 248, 270, 321, 323–4, 706, 847, 890, 933–5
Art 5 . . . . 25, 97–8, 117, 123–4, 322, 324–5, 327
Art 5(2) 99–100, 108, 128, 909
Art 5(3) 114–16, 118–19, 324
Art 5(4) 122–3
Art 6 . . . . .25, 214
ex-Art 6 340
Art 6 . . . . .341, 386
Art 6(1) 34, 290, 359
ex-Art 6(2) 340
Art 6(2) 341, 354
Art 6(3) 36, 342, 344
Art 7 25
ex-Art 7 340
Art 7 . . . . .360, 494
Art 7(1) 370
Art 7(2) 44, 370
Art 9 26
Art 10 . . . . .26, 58, 73
Art 10(4) 57, 368
Art 11 . . . . 26, 900, 950
Art 11(1) 904
Art 11(4) 72
Art 12 . . . . .26, 121
Art 13 . . . . .14, 41–3
Art 13(1) 26, 41, 190
Art 13(2) 26, 41, 66, 79
Art 14 . . . . 26, 726, 890, 894
ex-Art 14 907
Art 14(1) 59
Art 14(2) 21, 30, 44–5, 57–8
Art 14(3) 56
Art 15 26
ex-Art 15 907
Art 15(1) 44
Art 15(2) 45, 55
Art 15(3) 45
Art 15(4) 45
Art 15(5) 45
Art 15(6) 45, 55
Art 16 26
Art 16(1) 48
Art 16(2) 46
Art 16(3) 48
Art 16(4) 49–50
Art 16(5) 49
Art 16(6) 46
Art 16(7) 47
Art 16(8) 50, 71
Art 16(9) 46–7
Art 17 26

Art 17(1) 51, 54
Art 17(2) 72
Art 17(3) 51, 53
Art 17(4) 52
Art 17(5) 44–5, 52
Art 17(6) 53–4, 56
Art 17(7) 44–5, 52, 56
Art 17(8) 56, 60
Art 18. . . . . .27, 902
Art 18(1) 44–5, 54–5
Art 18(2) 55
Art 18(3) 47, 55, 902
Art 18(4) 53, 55, 902
ex-Art 18(4) 906
Art 19. . . . . 26, 255, 322
Art 19(1) 61, 157, 317
Art 19(2) 62–3
Art 19(3) 64
Art 20. . . . . .27, 83
Art 20(1) 127–9
Art 20(2) 128
Art 20(3) 128
Art 20(4) 30, 129
Arts 21-46 24
Art 22(1) 44, 906
Art 24. 88
ex-Art 24. . . . . .936, 939
Art 24(1) 28, 905, 907
Art 26. 88
Art 26(1) 906
Art 26(2) 906
Art 27. 902
Art 27(1) and (2) 906
Art 27(3) 55, 84, 903
Art 28. 907
Art 29. 907
Art 31. . . . . .28, 84, 907
Art 31(2) 938
Art 31(3) 84
Art 31(4) 84
ex-Art 34. 137
Art 34. 211
ex-Art 34. . . . . .269, 353
ex-Art 34(2) 72
Art 35. 211
ex-Art 35. 353
Art 35(6) 155
Art 36. 906
Art 37. 919
Art 38. 47
Art 39. 28
Art 40. . . . . 907–8, 932
Art 42. 45
Art 42(2) 44, 80
ex-Art 46. 340
Art 47. . . . . .28, 900
ex-Art 47. 908
Art 47. 911
ex-Art 48. 14
Art 48. . . . . 14, 28–9, 99, 121, 125
Art 48(2)-(5) 28
Art 48(4) 21, 57
Art 48(6) 29, 80

Art 48(7) 29, 81–4, 110, 129
Art 49 . . . . 14, 30, 80, 125, 129
ex-Art 49 340
Art 50 30
Art 50(2) 84
Art 50(2)-(4) 30
Art 50(5) 30
Art 51 34
Art 53 28
Art 55 20
Art 114 112
ex-Art 133 942
ex-Art F(2) 340
ex-Art L 340
ex-Art N(2) 15
Pt V 32
Title I 24, 933
Title II 24, 26
Title III 24, 26
Title IV 24, 27, 127
Title V 13–14, 27, 29, 55, 84, 900
Ch 1 . . . . 27, 903
Ch 2 . . . . 27–8, 34, 84, 906, 919, 932
Title VI 13–14, 28, 30
ex-Title VI 72, 317
Title VI 900
Protocol No 1 . . . . 29, 81, 84, 121, 324
Art 6 29
Protocol No 2 . . . . 34, 114, 116, 119, 122–3, 322, 324
Art 1 117
ex-Art 3 116
ex-Arts 4 and 5 116
Art 5 . . . . 117, 123
Art 6 120
ex-Arts 6 and 7 123
Art 7 120
Art 8 . . . . 121–2, 324
Art 9 117
Protocol No 3 62
Protocol No 7 98
Protocol No 8 . . . . 341, 354
Protocol No 14 . . . . 34, 125
Protocol No 15 . . . . 34, 126
Protocol No 16 126
Protocol No 19 127
Protocol No 20 127
Protocol No 21 . . . . 126, 370
Protocol No 22 127
Protocol No 24 370
Protocol No 25 100
Protocol No 27 706
Protocol No 30 386–7
Art 1 386
Art 1(1) 386
Art 1(2) 386
Art 2 386
Protocol No 32 34
Protocol No 36 . . . . 21, 34, 57, 65
Art 2 57
Art 3(2) 45, 49
Art 3(3) 49
Art 4 46
Art 9 269

Art 10(1) and (3) 137, 155, 211
Title VII..70
Protocol on enlargement of the EU (former) 52
Treaty on the Functioning of the European Union (TFEU)..........................9, 23, 30-2
Art 1(1) 30
Art 1(2) 33
Art 2...100, 105
Arts 2-6 922
Art 2(1) 100, 103, 922, 932
Art 2(2) 101, 931
Art 2(3) 105
Art 2(4) 105, 906, 932
Art 2(5) 104, 919
Art 2(6) 100
Art 3...100, 102, 105
Arts 3-6 706
Art 3(1) 100–1, 103, 922–3
Art 3(2) 908–9, 920, 923–32, 941
Art 4...100, 931
Art 4(1) 105, 932
Art 4(2) 102
Art 4(3) 103, 187, 250, 881, 914, 930
Art 4(4) 103, 930
Art 5...105
Art 5(4) 123–4
Art 6...100, 102, 104–5, 368, 378, 919
Art 6(2) 833
Art 8...371, 706
Art 13(1) 158
Art 14...378, 876
Art 15...495
Art 15(2) 51, 71
Art 15(3) 76
Art 16(2) 28, 76
Art 18...............31, 105, 321, 333, 371, 462–5, 489–90, 528, 547–8, 608
Art 18(2) 76
Art 19...31, 322, 334, 371
Art 19(1) 78
Art 19(2) 76
Art 20...463, 469, 489–91
Art 21.....................31, 327, 463–6, 482, 489, 493, 500, 519
Art 21(1) 462, 903
Art 21(2) 77, 903–5, 908
Art 21(3) 78, 904
Art 22...31, 78, 492–3, 904–5
Art 22(2) 58
Art 23...31, 78
Art 24...31, 73
Art 24(1) 494
Art 24(2) 494
Art 24(3) 495
Art 25...31, 80
Art 26..13, 127, 246
Art 27...124
Art 28...392–4
Arts 28-30 446
Arts 28-32 403
Art 29...392
Art 30.................................236, 245, 248, 391–5, 401–5
Art 31...392
Art 32(2) 449

Art 34 . . . . 245, 248, 253–5, 280, 327, 349, 401, 403,
407–14, 416–32, 434–41, 443–4, 446–8,
450–2, 558, 572, 874, 881, 886
Arts 34-36 . . . . .446, 450
Art 35 . . . . 327, 407–9, 430–41, 446, 451–2
Art 36 . . . . 101, 245, 346, 407–8, 410, 413, 431,
434–41, 451–3, 457
Art 37 . . . . 404, 447–9, 876
Art 37(1) 447–9
Art 37(2) 447, 449
Art 37(3) 449
Art 38(1) 449
Art 40(2) 194, 325, 333
Art 41 492
Art 41(1) 905
Art 41(2) 905
Art 42(1) 905
Art 43 . . . . 77, 113, 176, 346, 915
Art 43(2) 176–7
Art 43(3) 176, 949
Art 44 346
Art 45 . . . . .253–4, 315, 327, 368, 474, 498, 500–25, 529,
537, 548, 552–4, 571, 582, 584, 626–30, 672, 714
Arts 45-48 . . . . .499, 556
Arts 45-62 571
Art 45(1) 498, 520
Art 45(1)-(3) 512
Art 45(2) 507–10, 514, 516, 520
Art 45(3) 346, 482, 509, 571–2
Art 45(4) 492, 509, 511–14, 569, 571
Art 48 . . . . 76, 82, 498–9, 621
Art 49 . . . . 245, 248, 262, 308, 327, 349, 368, 434,
511, 532, 534–41, 543–9, 551–5, 559, 564,
583–4, 586–90, 597, 602–4, 622, 625–30, 638,
648–9, 651, 655–6, 659–61, 665, 672, 697–8
Arts 49-55 556
Art 50 . . . . .543, 684
Art 50(1) 536, 659, 661, 677–8, 697
Art 50(2) 544, 659
Art 50(2)(f) 541, 659–60
Art 50(2)(g) 657, 660, 677–9, 687
Art 51 . . . . 568–71, 580, 600
Art 52 . . . . 346, 571–3, 579, 590
Art 52(1) 482, 571–4, 577–8, 580
Art 52(2) 76
Art 53 . . . . 76–7, 537, 559, 626, 640
Art 53(1) 536, 542, 623, 626, 630
Art 53(2) 626, 630–1
Art 54 . . . . 532, 538, 582, 589, 597, 647–8,
651, 655–6, 661, 672, 677, 921
Art 56 . . . . 103, 327, 346–7, 368, 378, 427, 472, 489,
503, 511, 524, 532, 535, 537, 546–7, 552–4,
556–65, 568, 578, 597, 602–3, 606–8,
622, 625–30, 660
Arts 56-62 533
Art 56(1) 529
Art 57 . . . . 533, 554–7, 560–1, 600
Art 59 503
Art 60 83
Art 62 . . . . 559, 568–73, 579
Art 63 . . . . 327, 662, 664–5, 948
Arts 63-66 947
Art 63(1) 663

Art 64(2) and (3) 929, 948
Art 64(3) 78
Art 65(1)(a). 589, 595–6, 662
Art 65(1)(b) 662–3
Art 65(2) 662
Art 65(3) 595–6, 662
Art 66. . . . . 84, 929, 948
Art 68. 44
Art 70. 121
Art 71. . . . . .48, 121
Art 74. . . . . .83, 85
Art 75. . . . . .84, 369
Art 76. . . . . .72, 120
Art 77(3) 78
Art 78. 370
Art 78(3) 84
Art 79(4) 100
Art 81. . . . . .29, 81, 928
Art 81(3) 78, 121
Art 82(3) 82, 128
Art 83(2) 317
Art 83(3) 82, 128
Art 84. 100
Art 85. . . . . .43, 121
Art 86(1) 78, 128
Art 86(4) 44–5, 84
Art 87(3) 78, 128
Art 88. . . . . .43, 121
Art 88(2) 867
Art 88(3) 868
Art 89. 78
Art 91(1) 76
Art 91(1)(a). 914
Art 97. 83
Art 100. 76
Art 101. . . . . 85, 163, 253–4, 315, 705–10, 713, 716,
                                           718–20, 729–63, 765, 784, 809–44, 847, 849,
                                           865, 875, 881, 886, 890–3
Art 101(1) 712, 726, 729, 731–4, 738, 740–57,
                                           760, 762–3, 823, 825
Art 101(2) 843
Art 101(3) 709, 726, 729, 731, 741–2, 746,
                                           754–63, 783, 809, 811, 838
Art 102. . . . . 85, 163, 192, 253–4, 315, 705–10, 713,
                                           715–17, 730, 732, 753–4, 765–807, 809–44,
                                           849, 865, 875, 882–3, 886, 894
Art 102(b). 883
Art 102(c) 790
Art 102(d) 796
Art 103. . . . . .85, 708
Arts 103-105. 707
Art 105. 83
Art 106. . . . . .705–7, 713, 847, 874–7, 894
Art 106(1) 847, 875, 877–84, 886
Art 106(2) 707, 717, 726, 847, 862–5, 874–6, 883–90
Art 106(3) 864, 881, 889–90
Art 107. . . . . 403, 446–7, 449, 847–50, 862–6, 870
Arts 107-109. . . . . 705, 707, 847, 850, 876
Art 107(1) 849–58, 861, 863, 866–7
Art 107(2) 847, 849, 857–9, 866
Art 107(2)(b) 858
Art 107(2)(c). 859
Art 107(3) 847–9, 859–62, 866

Art 107(3)(a) 858, 860
Art 107(3)(b) 858, 860
Art 107(3)(c) 858, 860–1
Art 107(3)(d) 861
Art 107(3)(e) 861
Art 108 ....83, 403, 446–7, 449, 849, 866, 871
Art 108(1) 871
Art 108(2) 135, 861, 867, 870–3
Art 108(3) 252, 849, 866–8, 872–4, 894
Art 109 866
Art 110 ....391–2, 396–406, 446, 448
Art 110(1) 396–7
Art 110(2) 396, 399
Art 111 404
Art 113 ....78, 326
Art 114 ....13, 71, 76, 92, 102, 106–13, 116, 118–19, 132,
                                              162, 316, 441, 678, 684
Art 114(1) 106
Art 115 ....78, 102, 106, 108, 316, 441
Art 116 876
Art 117 876
Art 118 78
Art 121(6) 78
Art 125(2) 78
Art 126 ....94, 159
Art 126(8) and (9) 159
Art 128(2) 78
Art 132 83
Art 134 47
Arts 136-138 46
Art 139 126
Art 149 76
Art 151 ....118, 375
Art 153 ....85, 118, 268, 316, 375
Art 153(2) 29, 76, 81
Art 153(2)(b) 920
Art 153(4) 100
Art 155(2) 85, 268
Art 157 ....253–4, 262, 264, 300, 348, 371–2, 502, 544, 672
Art 157(3) 76
Art 157(4) 372
Art 164 76
Art 165 104
Art 165(3) 919
Art 166(3) 919
Art 166(4) 76
Art 167 77
Art 167(3) 919
Art 167(5) 76
Art 168 ....76, 107–8
Art 168(1) 378
Art 168(3) 919
Art 168(4) 76, 378
Art 169 ....76, 378
Art 169(4) 100
Art 171(3) 919
Art 172 76
Art 173 959
Arts 174-178 13
Art 178 76
Arts 179-190 13
Art 182 919
Art 182(1) 76

Art 186. 919
Art 188. 76
Art 191. 378
Arts 191-193. 13
Art 191(4). 919
Art 192. . . . . 111–13, 316, 919, 945
Art 192(1). 76
Art 192(2). 29, 81
Art 193. . . . . .100, 112
Art 194. 71
Art 207. . . . . 77, 113, 162, 901, 910–11, 942–5, 947–9
Art 207(1). 943, 946–7
Art 207(2). 949
Art 207(3). 94, 949
Art 207(4). 949
Art 207(5). 948
Art 207(6). 948
Arts 208-211. 901
Art 209. 76
Art 212. 901
Art 213. 901
Art 214. 901
Art 215. . . . . .901, 907
Art 216. 953
Art 216(1). 902, 909, 918–21, 923–4, 926, 931
Art 216(2). 953
Art 217. . . . . 901, 910, 953
Art 218. . . . . .902, 910, 936–9, 941, 949, 953
Art 218(2). 937
Art 218(3). 94, 937–8, 943
Art 218(4). 937
Art 218(5). 937, 940
Art 218(6). 937–8
Art 218(6)(v). 949
Art 218(8). 80, 938, 949
Art 218(9). 938
Art 218(10). 938
Art 218(11). 912, 938–9
Art 219. 901
Art 220. 910
Art 220(1). 901
Art 222. 32
Art 223(1). 56, 80
Art 223(2). 82
Art 224. . . . . .58, 76
Art 225. . . . . .59, 72
Art 226. . . . . .59, 82
Art 227. . . . . .60, 494
Art 228. . . . . .60, 494
Art 228(4). 82
Art 229. 79
Art 230(2). 59
Art 230(3). 59
Art 233. 59
Art 234. . . . . .56, 60
Art 235(1). 45
Art 235(2). 45
Art 235(4). 45
Art 236. . . . . .44–6, 84
Art 236(b). 46
Art 238(2). 49–50
Art 238(3). 128
Art 240. 47–8

Art 240(2) 47
Art 241. . . . . .59, 72
Art 244. . . . . .44, 52
Art 245. 51
Art 248. 53
Art 249(2) 59
Art 250. 51
Art 251. 62
Art 252. 62
Art 254. 63
Art 255. 63
Art 256(1) 64, 154
Art 256(2) 64
Art 256(3) 65, 210
Art 257. . . . . .63, 217
Art 257(4) 84
Art 258. . . . . 135–9, 142–3, 145–6, 149, 151–3, 155, 189,
                                                    192, 201, 204, 236, 439, 941
Arts 258-260. . . . . 64, 135, 271
Art 258(2) 139–40, 150
Art 259. . . . . 136, 145, 149, 236
Art 260. . . . . .149, 152
Art 260(1) 143
Art 260(2) 143, 149–52
Art 260(3) 152–3
Art 261. 831
Art 262. 80
Art 263. . . . . .135, 141, 153–8, 160–2, 164, 172, 175–6,
                                                    179–80, 182–8, 194, 199–203, 205, 225, 322,
                                                    379, 708, 832, 874, 907, 958–9, 962
Arts 263-264. 64
Art 263(1) 156, 160, 162
Art 263(2) 160, 162, 177, 180
Art 263(3) 160, 162
Art 263(4) 160, 162–4, 166, 173, 176–7, 205, 343
Art 264. . . . . .135, 331
Art 264(1) 153, 180
Art 264(2) 182
Art 265. . . . . .64, 135, 141, 159, 182–9, 199, 201
Art 265(1) 183, 186
Art 265(2) 187
Art 266. . . . . 64, 135, 177, 182, 189, 229
Art 266(1) 181, 189
Art 267. . . . . .64, 195, 201, 209, 211–17, 219, 227, 229–30,
                                                    236, 238–9, 250, 314, 708, 757, 874, 941, 953, 967
Art 267(1) 222, 225
Art 267(2) 218
Art 267(3) 223, 225
Art 268. . . . . .64, 135, 138, 182, 189–90, 196–9
Art 269. 65
Art 273(6) 156
Art 275. . . . . .65, 353
Art 275(2) 343
Art 276. . . . . .65, 343
Art 277. . . . . .135, 200–2
Art 278. . . . . 203, 227, 304
Art 279. . . . . 203–4, 304
Arts 282-284. 42
Art 282(3) 42
Arts 285-287. 42
Art 288. . . . . 70, 157, 163, 186, 193, 237, 239, 244,
                                                    256, 258–62, 268, 542
Art 288(5) 157

Art 289. . . . . .72, 157
Art 289(1)-(3). 71
Art 289(3). 156, 176
Art 289(4). 72
Art 290. . . . . 86–7, 91, 176, 256
Art 291. . . . . 86, 91, 258, 949
Art 291(1). 87
Art 291(2). 88, 153, 176, 949
Art 291(3). 90–1
Art 292. 83
Art 293(1). 93–4
Art 293(2). 91–2
Art 294. . . . . 73–6, 80, 92
Art 294(10). 93
Art 294(13). 93
Art 294(15). 73
Art 296. . . . . 117–18, 123, 178–9
Art 297. . . . . .155, 936
Art 299. 721
Art 300. 42
Art 301. 84
Arts 301-304. 42
Art 305. 84
Arts 305-307. 42
Arts 308-309. 42
Art 310. 93
Art 311. . . . . 29, 78, 80–2
Art 312. 93
Art 312(2). 29, 78, 81–2
Art 314. 93
Art 315(2). 93
Art 325(4). 76
Art 326. 128
Art 327. 129
Art 328(1). 129
Art 329. 83
Art 329(1). 83, 128
Art 329(2). 83, 128
Art 330. . . . . .46, 128
Art 331(1). 129
Art 331(2). 129
Art 333. . . . . .29, 81, 129
Art 333(3). 129
Art 334. 128
Art 338(1). 76
Art 340. . . . . 32, 36, 64, 189–90, 192, 196, 199
Art 340(2). 182, 190, 197–9, 308, 322
Art 340(2) and (3). 135
Art 340(3). 190
Art 341. 32
Art 342. . . . . .32, 83
Art 344. 940
Art 345. . . . . 452, 875, 879
Art 351. 32
Art 352. . . . . .28–9, 32, 78, 81–2, 84, 109–12, 316,
657, 678, 944
Art 352(1). 110
Art 352(2). 111
Art 352(3). 110
Art 352(4). 28
Art 353. . . . . 29, 81–2, 84, 110
Art 356. 32
Pt 1. 31

Pt 2...31
Pt 3...31–2
Title III...102
Title V...34, 77, 102, 126, 211, 269, 317
Title VI..102
Title X...102, 125
Title XII...104
Title XIII..104
Title XIV..104
Title XV...102
Title XVII...104
Title XVIII..109
Title XX..102, 109
Title XXI..102
Title XXII...104
Title XXIII..104
Title XXIV..104
Pt 4..32
Pt 5...32, 900–2, 919
Title III..109
Pt 6...32, 62
Title II...71
Title III..127
Pt 7..32
Protocols see Treaty on European Union (TEU), Protocols
Yaoundé Convention
Art 2(1)..954

International

Council of Europe

Convention against Trafficking in Human Beings (CETS 197)...384
Convention for the Protection of Human Rights and Dignity of the Human Being with regard to the application
    of Biology and Medicine (Oviedo Convention, ETS 164)......................................364
Additional protocol on the Prohibition of Cloning Human Beings 364
European Convention for the Prevention of Torture (ETS 126)...364
European Convention on Human Rights (ECHR) 7, 25, 36, 80, 242, 291, 337–9, 341–3,
                                                          346, 348–9, 354–5, 360–3, 367–8, 370,
                                                374, 379, 381, 383–5, 431, 485, 494, 708, 809–10,
                                                815, 818–19, 821, 823, 829, 832–3, 844
    Art 1..355
    Art 2..363
    Art 2(1)..363
    Art 2(2)..363
    Art 3..355, 364, 370
    Art 4..364
    Art 4(2)..364
    Art 5..365
    Art 5(1)..365
    Art 6..243, 291, 351–2, 379, 816–17, 832
    Art 6(1)..289–90, 353, 833
    Art 6(2)..381
    Art 6(2) and (3)..380
    Art 7..352
    Art 7(1)...242–3, 833
    Art 7(2)..381
    Art 8...343, 347–8, 363, 365, 817, 819
    Art 8(1)..818
    Art 8(2)..819

Art 9. 366–7
Art 10. . . . . 367–8, 445
Art 11. . . . . .367, 375
Art 12. . . . . .348, 366
Art 13. 379
Art 15. 370
Art 17. 385
Art 59. 341
Protocol 1 7
Protocol 1, Art 1. 368
Protocol 1, Art 1(1) 369
Protocol 1, Art 1(2) 369
Protocol 1, Art 2. 368
Protocol 1, Art 3. 494
Protocol 6 363
Protocol 7, Art 4. 382
Protocol 13 363
Protocol 14 341
European Social Charter. 340, 360, 374–5
Art 1(3) 375
Art 6. 375

Other

AETR Agreement. 212, 911–12, 914–15, 920, 926–32, 940
Agreement on Trade Related Aspects of Intellectual Property (TRIPS). 212–13, 246, 917,
939, 942, 946–7, 956–8, 964–6
Art 33. 966
Art 50. 965
Art 50(6) 958, 966
Convention on Biological Diversity 1992. 959–60
Convention on future multilateral co-operation in the North-East Atlantic fisheries. .87
Convention on the Grant of European Patents (European Patent Convention). 450
ERTA Agreement see AETR Agreement
General Agreement on Tariffs and Trade (GATT) 276, 408, 941–2, 955–9, 962, 964
Art XXIV(6) 962
General Agreement on Trade in Services (GATS). 917, 924, 939, 942, 946–7, 949, 956–7
Geneva Convention of 28 July 1951 relating to the status of refugees 370
Art 1. 369
ILO Convention No 170 on dangerous substances 927
ILO Declaration on Fundamental Principles and Rights at Work, June 1998. 375
International Dairy Agreement 964
Montreal Convention for the Unification of Certain Rules for International Carriage by Air 960
North Atlantic Treaty. 4–7
Protocol on the Accession of the Federal Republic of Germany. 7
Paris Agreements of 23 October 1954. 7
Stockholm Convention 1960 9–10
UN Charter 24, 359, 903
UN Convention on the Law of the Sea 939, 961, 964
UN International Covenant of 1966 359
Vienna Convention on the Law of Treaties 270, 963
Art 27. 270
Art 31. . . . . .944, 954
WTO Agreement 917, 938, 940, 955–60, 962–4

National

Austria

Constitution 349

Czech Republic

Constitution
  Art 27...375

France

Constitution
  Preamble, paras 8 and 9 375

Italy

Constitution
  Art 39...375

Portugal

Constitution
  Art 54...375

Spain

Constitution
  Art 28...375

United Kingdom

Airports Act 1986..667–8
Civil Jurisdiction and Judgments Act 1982....................................213
Consumer Protection Act 1987 148
  s 1(1) 148
Enterprise Act 2002 826
  s 204...826
European Communities Act 1972 274
  s 2 273–4
  s 3(1) 228
Human Rights Act 1998 ....274, 348
  s 4 348

United States

Clayton Anti-Trust Act
  Art 6..498
Sherman Act 1890
  s 1 745

Part I

Introduction

From the Founding Treaties to the Treaty of Lisbon

The modern European Union is a highly idiosyncratic entity, whose complexity can prove both confusing and offputting. But some of that complexity can be unravelled if one appreciates that it stems from a particular historical experience: understanding how the EU evolved can help clarify and explain much about its current nature and functioning. This chapter provides a brief overview of the development of European integration since the end of the Second World War. Beginning with the establishment, by the six founding Member States, of the three original 'European Communities', we will explore two major sets of subsequent developments. The first concerns the accession of new Member States, bringing the total number of participating countries to 27 (though with further enlargements in sight for the future). The second line of developments has been concerned rather with substantive reform of and additions to the original agreements. The main breakthrough was the Treaty on European Union (TEU) of 1992, which first created the modern European Union and regulated its relationship to the pre-existing Communities. The TEU was followed by a prolonged period of further reform, reflection and contestation, culminating in the Treaty of Lisbon (TL) of 2007, which proposed a thorough overhaul of the Union's primary law. The TL entered into force on 1 December 2009. There is general consensus that it will continue to provide the basic architecture for European integration into the forseeable future.

I – THE SCHUMAN PLAN AND THE ESTABLISHMENT OF THE ECSC

Although there was a certain ideological groundswell in favour of a 'United Europe' shortly after the Second World War[1]—as evidenced by the call of the 1948 Hague Congress for

---

[1] On the historical context, see A Milward, *The Reconstruction of Western Europe 1945–51* (Berkeley and Los Angeles, University of California Press, 1984). On the early history of the European Communities, see M Palmer et al, *European Unity* (London, Allen & Unwin, 1968) Introduction; Lord Gladwyn, *The European Idea* (New York, Frederick A Praeger, 1967) ch 4; AH Robertson, *European Institutions*, 3rd edn (New York, Praeger,

Western European economic and political union—the first concrete steps towards integration were prompted by the spectre of Soviet expansion. Within days of the signature by France and the United Kingdom of the Dunkirk Treaty, providing for mutual assistance in the event of a renewal of hostilities with Germany, the breakdown of the Moscow Conference over the future of occupied Germany was to set the pattern for future strained relations between the USSR on the one side, and the United States, Great Britain and France on the other. Despite the indispensable US defence commitment affirmed in the North Atlantic Treaty, Western Europe stood divided and vulnerable in the face of a Soviet Union whose wartime military potential had been scarcely diminished by demobilisation, and whose political influence had been enhanced by successful Communist Party coups in Bulgaria, Romania, Poland and Czechoslovakia.[2] It was in this context that Robert Schuman, the French Foreign Minister, made an historic proposal to a ministerial meeting in London on 9 May 1950.[3] His proposal was for nothing less than the fusion of the coal and steel industries of France and Germany, and any other countries wishing to participate, under a supranational High Authority. Not only would such a pooling of production make future conflict between France and Germany impossible, it would provide a sound basis for economic expansion. The implications of the scheme were clearly far-reaching, constituting, as Mr Schuman explained, 'the first concrete foundation for a European Federation which is indispensable for the preservation of peace'.

The Schuman Plan was enthusiastically endorsed by the Benelux countries, France, Germany and Italy, but the United Kingdom declined to participate, refusing to accept the supranational role of the projected High Authority. The Treaty Establishing the European Coal and Steel Community (ECSC) was signed in Paris on 18 April 1951, and came into force on 20 July of the following year. It was concluded for a period of 50 years from that date and thus expired in July 2002.[4]

The strategy of the Treaty, inspired by the Schuman Declaration, was to set limited and specific economic objectives as steps towards the long-term political objective of European unity. The preamble to the Treaty announced that Europe was to be built 'through practical achievements which will first of all create real solidarity, and through the establishment of common bases for economic development'. The economic community created pursuant to the Treaty was to constitute 'the basis for a broader and deeper community among peoples long divided by bloody conflicts' and the foundations were to be laid 'for institutions which will give direction to a destiny henceforward shared'.

The central economic mechanism of the ECSC was a common market for coal and steel.[5] Article 4 of the Treaty thus provided that various measures were to be recognised as incompatible with the common market and should accordingly be prohibited within the Community: for example, import and export duties, or charges having equivalent effect, and quantitative restrictions on the movement of products; measures or practices which discriminated between producers, between purchasers or between consumers, especially

1973) 5–17; DW Urwin, *The Community of Europe: A History of European Integration*, 2nd edn (Harlow, Pearson Education, 1995).

   [2] *NATO: Facts and Figures* (Brussels, 1971) ch 1.

   [3] For the French text, see *Documents on International Affairs* (1949–50) 315–17. An English translation (from which the quotations in the text are extracted) appears in 22 *Department of State Bulletin* 936–37.

   [4] Art 97 ECSC. Since no steps were taken to renew the ECSC Treaty, the coal and steel sectors now come within the purview of the TEU and TFEU (see below).

   [5] Art 1 ECSC proclaimed that the Community is 'founded upon a common market, common objectives and common institutions'.

in prices and delivery terms or transport rates and conditions; measures or practices which interfered with the purchaser's free choice of supplier; subsidies or aids granted by states, or special charges imposed by states, in any form whatsoever; and restrictive practices which tended towards the sharing or exploiting of markets.

Article 4 thus envisaged a Community-wide market for coal and steel free from interference by the Member States or by economic operators tending to impede the flow of trade or to distort the play of competition. The Community was empowered to carry out its task under the Treaty 'with a limited measure of intervention', inter alia, by placing financial resources at the disposal of undertakings for investment and by bearing part of the cost of readaptation.[6] Only when circumstances so required was it authorised to exert direct influence upon production or upon the market, for instance, by imposing production quotas.[7]

II – THE EDC AND THE EPC: A FALSE DAWN

Significant as the founding of the ECSC may have been, it contributed little of itself to the increasingly pressing problem of incorporating West Germany into the defence network established by the Brussels and North Atlantic Treaties.

While the United States was enthusiastic for German participation, France was naturally chary of seeing her recently vanquished enemy so soon rearmed. At the instigation of Sir Winston Churchill and Paul Reynaud,[8] the Consultative Assembly of the Council of Europe[9] called for the 'immediate creation of a unified European Army', under the authority of a European Minister of Defence, subject to proper European democratic control and acting in full co-operation with the United States and Canada'.[10]

After a French initiative known as the 'Pleven Plan', the Treaty Establishing the European Defence Community (EDC) was signed—subject to ratification—by the Benelux countries, France, Germany and Italy.[11] Once again the United Kingdom held aloof. If the ECSC had been calculated to bind Germany to France industrially, the EDC was to provide the framework for German rearmament.

The projected Defence Community had two significant characteristics. First, it was to be endowed with a supranational institutional structure not unlike that of the Coal and Steel Community. Secondly, its statute assumed that it would be of a transitional nature, and would give way to some more comprehensive form of federal or confederal European Union.

The EDC Treaty provided for a European Army, composed of units placed at the dis-

---

[6] Art 5 ECSC.

[7] ibid, second sub-para, third indent.

[8] Robertson, above n 1, 18.

[9] The Council of Europe is an intergovernmental organisation established in 1949. Its aim is to achieve greater unity among its members, and to this end it seeks agreement on common action 'in economic, social, cultural, scientific, legal and administrative matters and in the maintenance and further realisation of human rights and fundamental freedoms'.

[10] Resolution of the Consultative Assembly of the Council of Europe (11 August 1950); *Documents on International Affairs* (1949–50) 331. As is clear from the quotation cited in the text, the Council at times interprets the terms of its statute with some liberality. See Robertson, above n 1, 19.

[11] 27 May 1952. See *Documents on International Affairs* (1952) 116–62. See also E Furdson, *The European Defence Community: A History* (Macmillan, London, 1979).

posal of the Council of Ministers by the Member States. A Common Budget would be drawn up, and an executive body, the 'Commissariat', would lay down common programmes in the field of armaments, provisioning and military infrastructure. The objects of the Community were to be purely defensive, within the context of the North Atlantic Treaty.

The transitional nature of the proposed Community was evidenced by the terms of Article 8(2), which provided that the institutional structure laid down in the Treaty would remain in force until displaced by the establishment of the federal or confederal organisation envisaged by Article 38.

This latter Article required the Assembly of the EDC to make proposals to the governments of the Member States on the establishment of a directly elected Assembly, and the powers it should exercise. Particular regard was to be had to the principle that such a modified parliamentary body should be able to constitute one of the elements in a subsequent federal or confederal structure.

These proposals were to be presented to the governments of the six founding states after the Assembly of the EDC assumed its functions, but within days of the signature of the Treaty, the Consultative Assembly of the Council of Europe resolved that it would be

> of great advantage if the basic principles of a European supranational political authority and the nature and limits of its powers were defined within the next few months, without waiting for the entry into force of the Treaty instituting the European Defence Community.[12]

Despite the fact that the Assembly provided for in Article 38 of the EDC Treaty was not yet in existence, and that the Article only referred to the constitution of a future parliamentary body, the foreign ministers of the Member States of the Coal and Steel Community requested the members of the Coal and Steel Community Assembly to co-opt additional members, reorganise the distribution of seats laid down in the Paris Treaty in accordance with that prescribed for the Assembly of the proposed EDC, and draw up a draft Treaty for a European Political Community (EPC). On 10 March 1953, the 'Ad Hoc Assembly' presented the requested draft.[13]

The 'European Community' proposed by the Ad Hoc Assembly provided for the extensive political and economic integration of its Members. Its aims were as follows:

- to contribute towards the protection of human rights and fundamental freedoms in Member States;
- to co-operate with the other free nations in ensuring the security of Member States against all aggression;
- to ensure the co-ordination of the foreign policy of Member States in questions likely to involve the existence, the security or the prosperity of the Community;
- to promote the development of employment and the improvement of the standard of living in Member States, by means, in particular, of the progressive establishment of a common market.

To ensure the protection of human rights in the proposed Community, provision was

---

[12] Resolution of 30 May 1952. Texts Adopted (1952) and see *Report on the Constitutional Committee instituted to work out a Draft Treaty setting up a European Political Community* (Paris, 20 December 1952) 6.

[13] See *Information and Official Documents of the Constitutional Committee of the Ad Hoc Assembly* (Paris, 1953) 53 *et seq.* For a brief but informative account of the events surrounding the preparation of the draft Treaty and its ultimate demise, see RT Griffiths, 'Europe's First Constitution: The European Political Community, 1952–1954' in S Martin (ed), *The Construction of Europe* (Dordrecht, Kluwer, 1994).

made for the application—as part of the Community Statute—of the provisions of section I of the European Convention on Human Rights (ECHR), along with the first Protocol to that Convention, signed in Paris on 20 March 1952.

The institutions of the EPC were to comprise a bicameral legislature, a European Executive Council, a Council of National Ministers, a Court of Justice, and an Economic and Social Council. Financial resources would be derived from a combination of Community taxation and contributions from the Member States.

The hopes of those who saw the future of Western Europe in immediate federation were dashed when the French Parliament voted against ratification of the EDC Treaty. A change of government in France, and an easing of tension between East and West,[14] contributed to the rejection of the Treaty by the combined votes of Gaullists, Communists, socialists and radicals.[15]

In the event, Germany's participation in the defence of Western Europe was achieved by other means. The Paris Agreements of 23 October 1954 provided for the recognition of the Federal Republic of Germany as a sovereign state, and for its subsequent accession to the North Atlantic Treaty.[16]

III – THE SPAAK REPORT AND THE TWO TREATIES OF ROME

Despite the setback represented by the rejection of the EDC Treaty, the Six were still convinced of the need for closer integration. At a conference held in the Sicilian city of Messina in 1955, the foreign ministers of the ECSC countries expressed the belief that the time had come to make 'a fresh advance towards the building of Europe', but that this must be achieved 'first of all, in the economic field'.[17] The two objectives were agreed of developing atomic energy for peaceful purposes, and establishing a European common market. An intergovernmental committee under the chairmanship of the Belgian Foreign Minister, Paul-Henri Spaak, was entrusted with the task of making proposals to this end. The United Kingdom was invited to participate in the work of the committee, but although a Board of Trade official was initially dispatched, he was recalled after a few weeks.

The Spaak Report was published in April 1956.[18] In the light of its conclusions, two new treaties were negotiated, one providing for the establishment of a European Economic Community (EEC) and the other for the establishment of a European Atomic Energy Community (Euratom). The EEC and Euratom Treaties were signed in Rome on 25 March 1957 and came into force on 1 January 1958.

The preamble to the EEC Treaty expressed the determination of the High Contracting

[14] Robertson, above n 1, 21.

[15] Palmer et al, above n 1, Introduction.

[16] *NATO: Facts and Figures* (Brussels, 1971) 35. For the Protocol to the North Atlantic Treaty on the Accession of the Federal Republic of Germany, and the texts known collectively as the 'Paris Agreements', see Apps 9 and 10.

[17] *Documents on International Affairs* (1950) 163; Cmnd 9525.

[18] *Rapport des chefs de délégation aux ministres des affaires étrangères* (Brussels, 21 April 1956). A summarised translation of Part I of the Spaak Report, 'The Common Market', was published by *Political and Economic Planning* as Broadsheet No 405 of 17 December 1956.

Parties 'to lay the foundation of an ever closer union among the peoples of Europe', and, from 1958 to the present day, that Treaty (though much amended, not least in its name) has provided the core framework for the process of European integration.

The central mechanism of the original EEC was to create a common market covering all economic sectors other than those falling within the purview of the ECSC Treaty (while it remained in force) or the Euratom Treaty.[19] The construction and maintenance of that common market—the existence, on a Europe-wide scale, of economic conditions similar to those on the market of a single state[20]—remains for many the central responsibility of the modern European Union. The common market, as envisaged by the EEC Treaty, involved the establishment of a customs union, through the elimination of all customs duties and quantitative restrictions (quotas) in trade between the Member States and the erection of a common customs tariff (CCT), as well as the removal of barriers to the free movement of 'the factors of production'—labour, business and capital. In addition, the EEC Treaty introduced rules designed to prevent competition from being restricted by arrangements between private operators, or by government subsidies or the activities of state monopolies. Legal machinery was provided for the harmonisation of national legislation that may have a bearing on the smooth functioning of the common market. Other primordial features of the system were the common agricultural policy and the common transport policy, relating to sectors where a completely free market was thought impracticable; and provisions relating to the Community's external trade and the possibility of creating an 'association' with a third country or an international organisation.

IV – A SINGLE SET OF INSTITUTIONS

The ECSC Treaty had created four main institutions: a High Authority, a Special Council of Ministers, a Common Assembly and a Court of Justice. In accordance with the Schuman Plan, the leading role in the implementation of the Treaty was given to the supranational High Authority, whose members were under a duty to act with complete independence, in the Community interest.[21] The High Authority was empowered to take legally binding decisions;[22] and was authorised, inter alia, to procure funds,[23] to fix maximum and minimum prices for certain products,[24] and to fine undertakings in breach of the ECSC's rules on competition.[25] The Special Council of Ministers, a body composed of representatives of the Member States, was given the function of harmonising 'the action of the High Authority and that of Governments, which are responsible for the general economic policies of their countries'.[26] With limited exceptions, the role of the Council in the institutional system of the ECSC was confined to consultation with the High Authority and

---

[19] See ex-Art 305 EC.
[20] See the description of the common market in Case 15/81 *Schul v Inspecteur de Invoerrechten en Accijnzen* [1982] ECR 1409, 1431–32.
[21] Art 9 ECSC, replaced by Merger Treaty (see Art 10).
[22] Art 14 ECSC.
[23] Art 49 ECSC.
[24] Art 61 ECSC.
[25] Arts 65 and 66 ECSC.
[26] Art 26 ECSC.

the giving (or withholding) of its assent (*avis conforme*) to actions which the latter proposed to take.

According to the EEC and Euratom Treaties, the two later Communities were each to have, in their turn, four main institutions: an Assembly, a Council, a Commission and a Court of Justice; but, to avoid unnecessary proliferation, a Convention was signed contemporaneously with the Treaties of Rome providing for there to be a single assembly (now the European Parliament) and a single court to carry out the functions assigned to those institutions under the three Community Treaties.[27] For some years after 1957, however, in addition to the High Authority and the Special Council of Ministers of the ECSC, there was a separate EEC Council and Commission and a separate Euratom Council and Commission. That situation was brought to an end by the Treaty establishing a Single Council and a Single Commission of the European Communities (known as the 'Merger Treaty'), which was signed in April 1965 and came into force in July 1967.[28] From that time, the ECSC (while it remained in force), the EEC and Euratom were served by the same set of institutions, whose powers varied depending on the Treaty under which they acted for any given purpose.

As will be seen in Chapters 3 and 4, in the institutional structure of the Rome Treaties, and particularly of the EEC Treaty, decision-making power was concentrated in the hands of the Council, and the role of the Commission was principally that of the initiator, and subsequently the executant, of Council decisions.[29] This difference, as compared with the institutional structure of the old ECSC, may be explained by the fact that, whereas the rules applicable to the coal and steel sectors were spelt out in considerable detail in the ECSC Treaty itself, in many areas of EEC competence the Treaty merely established a framework for common action, leaving fundamental political choices to be made by the Community institutions. It was inevitable that the final say in respect of such choices be left to the Council, the institution in which Member States are directly represented.

V – ENLARGEMENT FROM SIX TO FIFTEEN

Largely in response to the creation of the EEC, Austria, Denmark, Norway, Sweden, Switzerland, Portugal and the United Kingdom signed the Stockholm Convention on 4 January 1960, and the European Free Trade Association (or EFTA) came into being in May of that year. The primary object of the 'Outer Seven' was to offset any detrimental effects to their trade resulting from the progressive elimination of tariffs inside the Community by a similar reduction within EFTA.

To a certain extent, EFTA was regarded as a stepping stone to possible future Community membership. As the White Paper that was published in July 1971 setting out the terms agreed, and the case for UK membership of the Communities explained: 'From the outset . . . it was recognised that some members of the EFTA might eventually wish to join, and others to seek closer trading arrangements with, the European

---

[27] Convention on certain Institutions Common to the European Communities (25 March 1957).
[28] Treaty Establishing a Single Council and a Single Commission of the European Communities.
[29] The Commission is also 'guardian of the Treaties', with powers to ensure that the Member States and other Union institutions comply with their obligations: see further chs 3 and 6.

Communities.'[30] Indeed, barely 14 months after the Stockholm Convention entered into force, the Macmillan government applied for EC membership. This was to be the first of two applications thwarted by the opposition of President de Gaulle of France. After lengthy negotiations had taken place with the Six, the French President made it clear, in January 1963, that he would not consent to British accession.

Applications in 1967 by the United Kingdom, Denmark, Ireland and Norway met with a similar rebuff. Nevertheless, these four countries left their applications 'lying on the table', and at the Hague Summit Conference of the Six in December 1969, summoned on the initiative of the new President of France, Georges Pompidou, it was agreed that

> The entry of other countries of the continent to the Communities . . . could undoubtedly help the Communities to grow to dimensions more in conformity with the present state of world economy and technology. . . . In so far as the applicant States accept the Treaties and their political objective . . . the Heads of State or Government have indicated their agreement to the opening of negotiations between the Community on the one hand and the applicant States on the other.[31]

Negotiations between the applicant states and the Six formally opened on 30 June 1970, and a Treaty of Accession was eventually signed on 22 January 1972. The provisions of the Treaty, and the detailed adaptations contained in the Act of Accession annexed to it, have served as a model, mutatis mutandis, for later enlargements. The only institutional changes required were those resulting from the need to accommodate the additional Member States. The elimination of customs duties and quotas between the prospective Member States and the Six, and the adoption of the Common External Tariff, were to be phased in between April 1973 and July 1977. A transitional period was also to be allowed for the adoption of the Common Agricultural Policy, and for the build up of contributions to the Community budget. Although the United Kingdom would be compelled to forego Commonwealth preference as such, special arrangements were agreed for the access of New Zealand dairy products and lamb, and the importation of sugar from Commonwealth suppliers. It was understood that association arrangements comparable with those already accorded to developing countries enjoying traditional relations with the original Six would be made with developing countries in the Commonwealth.[32]

On 1 January 1973, the Treaty of Accession entered into force, and Denmark, Ireland and the United Kingdom became Members of the three Communities. Norway, which had signed the Treaty on 22 January 1972, did not proceed to ratification, following an adverse result in a national referendum held on the issue of membership.

British membership of the Communities was briefly put in doubt by the election in February 1974 of a Labour government. Although the membership negotiations which were brought to a successful conclusion by the Conservative administration had been set in train by their predecessors, Labour in opposition declared themselves unable to accept the terms of entry finally agreed. When Labour returned to power, the government of Harold Wilson set out to 'renegotiate' the agreed terms in respect of agriculture, contributions to the Community budget, economic and monetary union, state aid to industry,

---

[30] See *The United Kingdom and the European Communities*, Cmnd 4715. After the accession of Denmark, Ireland and the United Kingdom to the European Communities, Austria, Finland, Norway, Portugal, Sweden and Switzerland entered into free trade agreements with 'the Nine'. See *Seventh General Report on the Activities of the European Communities* (1973) 400.

[31] *Third General Report on the Activities of the Communities* (1969) Annex: Documents on the Summit Conference, 497, 489.

[32] See [1973] OJ L2/1.

movement of capital, the Commonwealth and developing countries, and value added tax, and on 23 January 1975 it was announced that a national referendum would be held on the results of the renegotiation. The government declared itself satisfied with those results and felt able to recommend to the British people that they cast their votes in favour of continued membership of the European Communities.[33] This view was endorsed by an overwhelming majority of the votes in the referendum which followed on 5 June 1975.[34]

The transitional period for the accession of the three new Member States was barely half spent when a further application for membership was received from Greece. Negotiations commenced on 27 July 1976. The instruments relating to Greece's accession were signed in Athens on 28 May 1979 and Greece became the tenth Member State on 1 January 1981.[35]

Meanwhile, Spain and Portugal had also applied for membership. After long and sometimes difficult negotiations, the instruments of accession were signed in Madrid and Lisbon on 12 June 1985, and Spain and Portugal joined the Communities on 1 January 1986.[36]

The next enlargement, which took place on 1 January 1995, brought into the European Union (as it had by then become: see below) three states which had formerly belonged to EFTA: Austria, Finland and Sweden.[37] Norway had also applied for membership, and had taken part in the negotiations and signed the accession instruments; however, once again, as in 1972, the referendum in that country on ratification of the Treaty of Accession produced a negative result. So, by this stage, the original Six had become the Fifteen, comprising all the European states that escaped the imposition of Communist regimes protected by Soviet military power in the aftermath of the Second World War, with the exception of Iceland, Norway, Lichtenstein and Switzerland.

VI – AMENDMENT AND DEVELOPMENT OF THE FOUNDING TREATIES UP TO 2004

Apart from the amendments contained in the Merger Treaty and in the Accession Treaties referred to above, the texts of the three founding Treaties have been amended or developed over the years by a series of Treaties, Decisions or Acts, the most significant of which are identified below.

A – The Budgetary Treaties of 1970 and 1975

These two Treaties, which were signed, respectively, on 22 April 1970 and 22 July 1975, replaced the original budgetary procedure of the Communities with a new one giving important powers to the European Parliament.[38] The 1975 Treaty also created a new body, the Court of Auditors, to act as a financial watchdog for the Communities.

---

[33] See *Membership of the European Community*, Cmnd 5999; *Report on Renegotiation*, Cmnd 6003.
[34] See REM Irving, 'The United Kingdom Referendum' (1975–76) 1 *ELRev* 1.
[35] [1979] OJ L291.
[36] [1985] OJ L302.
[37] [1994] OJ C241/10. See also Council Decision 95/1 [1995] OJ L1/1, adjusting the instruments of accession in the light of Norway's failure to ratify.
[38] The text of the 1970 Treaty is published at [1971] OJ L2/1 and that of the 1975 Treaty at [1977] OJ L359/1.

B – Own Resources Decisions

In the early years of the EEC and Euratom, the Communities' revenue came from direct financial contributions by the Member States, according to scales that were laid down by the Treaties. However, Article 269 EEC and Article 173 Euratom looked forward to the replacement of financial contributions by a system giving the Communities their 'own resources'.[39] A legislative procedure was provided for the establishment of such a system by a unanimous decision of the Council, acting on the basis of proposals by the Commission and after consulting the European Parliament, with the additional step that the Council decision be recommended to the Member States for adoption in accordance with their respective national requirements. That especially solemn procedure gives the decisions to which it applies (in effect) a legal status only slightly inferior to the Treaties themselves.

A first own-resources Decision was adopted in 1970.[40] This has been replaced by a series of Decisions, forming part of the package of measures governing the Union's finances, which it became customary to renegotiate every seven years. The currently applicable own-resources Decision was adopted in June 2007;[41] it forms part of the multi-annual financial framework applicable during the period 2007–13.[42]

C – A Directly Elected European Parliament

Article 190(4) EEC and the corresponding provisions of the other Treaties[43] laid down a solemn procedure for the enactment of rules for direct elections to the European Parliament. Under that procedure, an Act concerning the election of the representatives of the European Parliament by direct universal suffrage was approved by the Council in September 1976 and recommended to the Member States for adoption in accordance with their respective constitutional requirements.[44] The first elections were held in June 1979 and these have been followed by elections in 1984, 1989, 1994, 1999, 2004 and 2009. Further discussion of these developments is found in the section relating to the European Parliament in Chapter 3.

D – The Single European Act

The Single European Act (SEA) was signed on 17 February 1986 and entered into force on 1 July 1987.[45] Its odd-seeming title is explained by the fact that, within a single legal instrument, there were juxtaposed provisions amending the three Community Treaties and provisions organising co-operation in the intergovernmental sphere of foreign policy.

---

[39] The relevant provision of the old EC Treaty, Art 200 EC, was deleted as being obsolete by the TA. Different financial arrangements applied under the ECSC Treaty: see Arts 49 ECSC *et seq*.

[40] Council Decision 70/243 [1970] OJ L94/19.

[41] Council Decision 2007/436 on the system of the European Communities' own resources [2007] OJ L163.

[42] See Inter-Institutional Agreement between the European Parliament, the Council and the Commission on budgetary discipline and sound financial management [2006] OJ C139.

[43] Art 21(3) ECSC; Art 108(3) Euratom.

[44] Council Decision 76/787 [1976] OJ L278/1.

[45] The SEA is published at [1987] OJ L169/1.

The amendments to the Treaties contained in Title II of the SEA were the most extensive adopted up to that time. They included the introduction of a new 'cooperation procedure' giving the European Parliament a significantly enhanced role in the legislative process: although important in the development of the Parliament's power within the EU, that 'cooperation procedure' is now defunct and thus of purely historical interest.[46] One of the principal objectives of the SEA was to ensure the completion of the EEC's internal market by the end of 1992.[47] The SEA also inserted into the EEC Treaty a number of specific new legal bases for Community action: for example, concerning economic and social cohesion;[48] research and technological development;[49] and the protection of the environment.[50]

Title III of the SEA contained the Treaty provisions on European co-operation in the sphere of foreign policy, known for short as 'European Political Cooperation' (EPC). Those provisions were superseded by Title V of the Treaty on European Union, which continues to provide the legal basis for the common foreign and security policy (see below).

E – The Treaty on European Union

The TEU[51] (often referred to by the name of the Dutch city, Maastricht, where it was signed in February 1992) entered into force on 1 November 1993.

The Treaty brought into being a new legal and political entity: the European Union. Article 1 of the TEU as adopted at Maastricht stated that '[t]he Union shall be founded on the European Communities, supplemented by the policies and forms of cooperation established by this Treaty'. That wording sought to capture the complex character of the new-born Union and the preponderant influence of the three Communities within it, ie the ECSC (while it remained in force), Euratom, and what was thenceforth known as the European Community (EC)—the word 'Economic' being dropped from the title, in recognition of the substantially extended and enhanced role of the Community in various fields of governmental activity. The TEU's clumsy phrase, 'policies and forms of co-operation', referred to the legal arrangements provided by Title V and Title VI of the Maastricht Treaty, which organised the activities of the common institutions in two fields of activity the Member States could not agree to bring within the purview of the EC Treaty. Title V concerned common foreign and security policy (CFSP). Broadly speaking, that covers the *political* aspect of external relations (diplomatic contacts, election monitoring and other forms of political assistance to third countries, security activities such as peace-keeping and peace-making, prospectively even defence), to be distinguished from external *economic* relations (such as trade, development co-operation and emergency aid) which fell within the competence of the EC.[52] In the TEU as originally concluded, Title VI grouped together, under the heading 'cooperation in the fields of justice and home affairs' (JHA), a variety of matters concerning the treatment of third-country nationals and aspects of

---

[46] See further Chapter 4.
[47] Ex-Arts 14 and 95 EC (see now Arts 26 and 114 TFEU).
[48] Ex-Arts 158–62 EC (see now Arts 174–78 TFEU).
[49] Ex-Arts 163–73 EC (see now Arts 179–90 TFEU).
[50] Ex-Arts 174–76 EC (now Arts 191–93 TFEU).
[51] [1992] OJ C191/1. Note that the numbering of the original TEU, like that of the old EC Treaty, was altered by the TA.
[52] See further Chapter 27.

law enforcement and the maintenance of public order. These included: aspects of the free movement of persons, such as asylum policy, the control of the Union's external frontiers, and immigration policy; combating drug addiction and international fraud; and co-operation between the Member States' judicial, customs and police authorities.

The image of a Greek temple façade, with three pillars joined by a pediment, was commonly used to illustrate the constitutional structure that was created by the original TEU.[53] The difference between the 'First Pillar' (comprising the pre-existing Communities) and the 'Second and Third Pillars' (respectively, Titles V and VI of the TEU) lay in the much lesser degree to which, in respect of the latter, the sovereign powers of the Member States were curtailed. The 'pediment' consisted of the elements common to the three components of the Union, notably that they were to be served by a single institutional framework,[54] and that there was common machinery for the amendment of the Treaties,[55] as well as for the enlargement of the Union.[56]

As well as establishing the Union structure, the TEU effected a number of significant reforms within the EC system (the First Pillar), two of which may briefly be noted here. First, an effort was made to tackle the problem of the 'democratic deficit' in the system, by changing the rules on the appointment of the Commission and by introducing a new legislative procedure, commonly referred to as 'co-decision', both measures being designed to enhance the role of the European Parliament: these are matters considered further in Chapters 3 and 4. Secondly, the Treaty contained detailed provisions on the organisation of economic and monetary union (EMU), and a timetable for its realisation in three stages. It was specifically provided that the third stage, involving the introduction of a single currency, must start, at the latest, on 1 January 1999; and so, in the event, it did, with the introduction on that date of the euro as the currency of 11 out of the then 15 Member States.

The ratification process of the TEU was thrown off course by the negative outcome of the referendum that was held in Denmark in June 1992. Subsequent referenda in Ireland in June, and in France in September 1992, brought votes in favour of ratification, although in the latter case by a narrow margin. Political and economic uncertainty increased as a result of turbulence in the international money markets during the period immediately preceding and following the French referendum, and this led to the suspension by Italy and the United Kingdom of their membership of the exchange rate mechanism of the European Monetary System and to the reintroduction of exchange rate controls by Spain and Ireland. However, at an extraordinary meeting of the European Council at Birmingham on 16 October 1992,[57] the heads of state or government reaffirmed their commitment to the TEU. It was agreed that the Community must develop together, on the basis of the TEU, while respecting, as the Treaty did, the identity and diversity of the Member States.[58]

---

[53] The structure created by the TEU was much criticised. See, in particular, U Everling, 'Reflections on the Structure of the Union' (1992) 29 *CMLRev* 1053; D Curtin, 'The Constitutional Structure of the Union: a Europe of Bits and Pieces' (1993) 30 *CMLRev* 17.

[54] See Art 3 of the original TEU (cp Art 13 TEU as it currently stands).

[55] See Art 48 of the original TEU (which remains Art 48 TEU).

[56] See Art 49 of the original TEU (which remains Art 49 TEU).

[57] The European Council was (at that time) not formally an institution of the EU, but nevertheless acted as the Union's supreme political body, since it brought together the highest political offices from across the Member States. The European Council is discussed in detail in Chapter 3.

[58] See Presidency Conclusions from the Birmingham European Council in October 1992, to which the text of the 'Birmingham Declaration' is annexed.

That positive development was confirmed by the European Council held in Edinburgh on 11–12 December 1992. Agreement was reached in Edinburgh on texts establishing interpretations of various provisions of the TEU which the Danish authorities announced would make it possible to hold a second referendum, with a good prospect that Denmark would be in a position to ratify the Treaty.[59] Nevertheless, there were more alarms and delays during 1993. Ratification of the TEU by the Parliament of the United Kingdom was achieved by the narrowest of margins; and in Germany the Treaty was the subject of a legal challenge before the Constitutional Court.[60] Thus, it was only on 1 January 1993 that the TEU finally entered into force, and the EU appeared as a new player on the international stage.

F – The Treaty of Amsterdam

To some of those who had been involved in the Intergovernmental Conference (IGC) on the TEU, the institutional reforms that were agreed seemed disappointing; and provision was made for a new IGC to be convened as early as 1996, in order to consider further changes.[61] However, the ambition to press ahead with further 'deepening' of European integration was overtaken by other aims which became the primary focus of the 1996 IGC: to counteract the alienation of public opinion from the whole EU enterprise, which had become painfully apparent during the process of ratifying the TEU; and to effect the changes in the composition and functioning of the institutions of the Union, necessary in order to pave the way for an enlargement, by then perceived as politically ineluctable, that would bring in many (and eventually perhaps all) the countries of central and eastern Europe, as well as other applicants from the Mediterranean area (see below).[62]

The IGC on the Treaty of Amsterdam (TA) completed its work in June 1997, and the Treaty was signed in October of that year.[63] The ratification process went more smoothly than that of the TEU, and the TA entered into force on 1 May 1999.[64]

A major achievement of the TA was the reform of the Community's legislative process (considered further in Chapter 4). The TA also brought about a significant shift of matters relating to the treatment of third-country nationals from the Third Pillar to the First Pillar: a new Title IV of Part Three of the EC Treaty dealt with 'visas, asylum, immigration and other policies related to free movement of persons', while also including provisions relating to cross-border judicial co-operation in civil matters. The reorganised Third Pillar was thereafter focused on 'police and judicial cooperation in criminal matters', with a notable extension in the scope of Union powers to take action in that field. Another reform, which will be examined in Chapter 5, was the adoption of the principle of 'closer cooperation'. The idea behind the latter principle remains the same today, even if the detailed rules governing its implementation have been much revised: it should be possible for a limited

---

[59] See Presidency Conclusions of the Edinburgh European Council in December 1992.

[60] See Bundesverfassungsgericht, Judgment of 12 October 1993, 2 BvR 2134 and 2 BvR 2153/92 [1994] 1 CMLR 57.

[61] See Art N(2) of the original TEU (deleted by the TA).

[62] On the task of the IGC, see A Dashwood (ed), *Reviewing Maastricht Issues for the 1996 IGC* (London, Sweet & Maxwell, 1996).

[63] See the text of the TA as published in [1997] OJ C340.

[64] On the TA, see eg A Duff, *The Treaty of Amsterdam* (London, Sweet & Maxwell, 1997); S Langrish, 'The Treaty of Amsterdam: Selected Highlights' (1998) 23 *ELRev* 3.

number of Member States to establish, within the institutional framework of the Union, rules in relation to a certain matter, which will apply only to themselves, and not to the non-participating Member States.

G – The Treaty of Nice

There were, however, two important issues, regarded as relevant to the impending enlargement of the Union, on which the IGC on the TA was unable to reach agreement: the size and composition of the Commission; and the distribution of votes between the Member States when the Council acts by a qualified majority (the so-called 'weighting' of votes in the Council).[65] Those matters, together with a possible extension of the policy areas in which the Council is empowered to act by a qualified majority (rather than by unanimity), were placed on the agenda of a new IGC which completed its work in December 2000. The Treaty of Nice (TN) was signed on 26 February 2001.[66] As with the Maastricht Treaty, the ratification process was thrown off course by a negative referendum result, this time in Ireland; but following a second popular vote in the Irish Republic, the TN finally entered into force on 1 February 2003.[67]

The TN carried through important reforms intended to adapt the institutional functioning of the Union to the challenges of further enlargement: for example, in relation to the scope of both qualified majority voting and the co-decision procedure;[68] the provisions on closer (renamed 'enhanced') co-operation between groups of Member States;[69] and the structure and jurisdiction of the Union courts.[70] Other major issues of institutional concern were also addressed: the size and composition of the Commission; the weighting of votes in Council; and also the composition of the European Parliament.[71] However, since the TN was finalised before it was decided when and in what order the various candidate countries would eventually accede to the Union, many of the relevant provisions on these issues sought merely to establish templates for future reform—the full details of which were subsequently finalised in the Treaties of Accession of 2003 and 2005 (see below).

VII – ENLARGEMENT FROM 15 TO 27 (PLUS . . .)

We have mentioned several times the pressure for internal reform of the Union's structure and functioning occasioned by its enlargement into central and eastern Europe. It was, in fact, the collapse of the Communist regimes across that region, symbolised by the dismantling of the Berlin Wall in 1989 and given concrete reality by the withdrawal of the Red Army behind the borders of what was once more to become Russia, which opened

---

[65] See further Chapter 3.

[66] See the text of the TN as published at [2001] OJ C80.

[67] On the TN, see eg K St Bradley, 'Institutional Design in the Treaty of Nice' (2001) 38 *CMLRev* 1095; A Dashwood, 'The Constitution of the European Union After Nice: Law-Making Procedures' (2001) 26 *ELRev* 215.

[68] See further Chapters 3 and 4, respectively.

[69] See further Chapter 5.

[70] See Chapter 3.

[71] See further on all those issues Chapter 3.

up the perspective of a much more challenging enlargement than the EU had ever previously experienced.

In the light of those historic events, so-called 'Europe Agreements' were concluded with a large number of central and eastern European countries (CEECs): Bulgaria, the Czech Republic, Hungary, Poland, Romania, Slovakia and Slovenia, together with Estonia, Latvia and Lithuania, the three Baltic Republics that had formerly been part of the Soviet Union. The Agreements established a close 'association' between the EU and each of those countries, and explicitly held out the prospect of eventual accession. They were bolstered by the adoption of pre-accession strategies to help each of the countries concerned prepare for membership, inter alia, by providing technical assistance on the harmonisation of their legislation and administrative structures and practices with those of the Union. Other candidates for membership of the Union included Cyprus, Malta and Turkey, with which the EC had long-standing association agreements.[72]

The European Council held in Luxembourg in December 1997 decided that accession negotiations should formally be opened with five of the CEECs, namely the Czech Republic, Estonia, Hungary, Poland and Slovenia, as well as with Cyprus. However, the Helsinki European Council in December 1999 reaffirmed 'the inclusive nature of the accession process, which now comprises 13 candidate States within a single framework'. Those states, it was said, 'are participating in the accession process on an equal footing'. Clearly, though, not all of the candidates were destined to fulfil the political and economic criteria for membership of the Union at the same time. The Helsinki Conclusions stated that 'the Union should be in a position to welcome new Member States from the end of 2002 as soon as they have demonstrated their ability to assume the obligations of membership and once the negotiating process has been successfully completed'.[73]

As events turned out, the Treaty of Accession 2003 provided for the accession to the Union of ten new Member States (Cyprus, the Czech Republic, Estonia, Hungary, Latvia, Lithuania, Malta, Poland, Slovakia and Slovenia) as from 1 May 2004.[74] This 'Big Bang' enlargement took effect subject to two main sets of legal provisions.[75] In the first place, the Treaty of Accession 2003 contained numerous transitional provisions intended to ensure the smooth assimilation of the new Member States into the Union (eg in the field of the free movement of workers and freedom to provide services); as well as to provide a realistic timetable for the full application of Union law within those countries (as with certain aspects of agricultural, environmental, transport and energy policies). In the second place, the Treaty of Accession 2003 provided for more permanent adjustments to the EU and EC Treaties so as to accommodate the new Member States: for example, as regards the allocation of seats within the European Parliament, and (as mentioned above) the weighting of votes within the Council of Ministers.

A further Treaty of Accession, signed on 25 April 2005, provided for the accession of Bulgaria and Romania on 1 January 2007.[76] That brought to 27 the number of Member States of the European Union. The 2005 Accession Treaty, like its 2003 predecessor, contained the necessary temporary and permanent adjustments to the existing body of EU

---

[72] 'Association' is a form of relationship involving 'special, privileged links with a non-member country': Case 12/86 *Demirel* [1987] ECR 3719, para 9.

[73] See Presidency Conclusions, paras 3–13.

[74] See the text of the Treaty of Accession 2003 as published at [2003] OJ L236.

[75] For analysis, see C Hillion, 'The European Union is Dead. Long Live the European Union . . . A Commentary on the Accession Treaty 2003' (2004) 29 *ELRev* 583.

[76] See the text of the Treaty of Accession 2005 as published at [2005] OJ L157.

law. There were some important differences, however, not least in the way that Bulgaria and Romania were subject to more intensive supervision by the Commission, for a transitional period following their accession to the Union, in fields such as cross-border criminal co-operation and as regards judicial co-operation in civil matters.[77]

The 2007 accessions are not intended to represent the end of the Union's enlargement programme. In October 2005, accession negotiations were formally opened with Croatia and Turkey (though in the latter case, the negotiations are expected to last a considerable period of time). The former Yugoslav Republic of Macedonia was officially recognised as a candidate country by the European Council in December 2005. Following the domestic economic instability generated by the world financial crisis which had erupted in 2008, Iceland submitted an application for EU membership in July 2009 and was accorded the status of candidate country in June 2010. Other countries in the Western Balkans— Albania, Bosnia Herzegovina, Serbia, Montenegro and Kosovo—are acknowledged to be potential candidates; while states such as the Ukraine have expressed their political ambition of becoming members of the EU in the future.

VIII – TREATY REFORM SINCE 2004: FROM THE CONSTITUTIONAL TREATY TO THE TREATY OF LISBON

A – The Treaty Establishing a Constitution for Europe

Even as they concluded the TN in December 2000, the Member States decided to adopt a 'Declaration on the Future of the Union', highlighting the need for a more thorough reflection upon the EU's constitutional framework. The Laeken European Council held in December 2001 then agreed a 'Declaration on the Future of the European Union', laying down more precisely the parameters for this process of constitutional reflection, and establishing a 'Convention on the Future of Europe' charged with preparing proposals for consideration at a future IGC. The Convention—composed of representatives of the Member States, the European Parliament, the national parliaments and the Commission— commenced its work in February 2002 and culminated in the presentation of a draft 'Treaty establishing a Constitution for Europe' to the European Council in July 2003.[78] That text provided the basis for further negotiations between the Member States, leading eventually to the signature of the Treaty establishing a Constitution for Europe (the Constitutional Treaty or CT) on 29 October 2004.[79]

The CT represented a very far-reaching set of proposals for reform of the Union's primary legal instruments. In the first place, the CT would have reconstituted the Union

---

[77] For analysis, see A Łazowski, 'And Then They Were Twenty-Seven . . . A Legal Appraisal of the Sixth Accession Treaty' (2007) 44 *CMLRev* 401.

[78] For analysis, see eg M Dougan, 'The Convention's Draft Constitutional Treaty: Bringing Europe Closer to its Lawyers?' (2003) 28 *ELRev* 763; J Kokott and A Ruth, 'The European Convention and its Draft Treaty Establishing a Constitution for Europe: Appropriate Answers to the Laeken Questions?' (2003) 40 *CMLRev* 1315.

[79] See the text of the CT as published at [2004] OJ C310. For analysis, see eg A Dashwood, 'The EU Constitution: What Will Really Change?' (2004/2005) 7 *CYELS* 33.

upon an entirely new (and much simplified) set of legal foundations. Most of the existing EU Treaties would have been repealed and replaced in their entirety (including the Treaties of Rome, Maastricht, Amsterdam and Nice). The pillar structure introduced at Maastricht would have been dismantled, and the European Community abolished as a distinct legal entity. Instead, there would have been a unitary European Union, based upon a single Constitutional Treaty, and possessing its own legal personality. In the second place, the CT would also have carried out a multitude of more detailed reforms to many aspects of the Union's functioning and activities: for example, as regards the structure of and relations between the institutions, the range of competences exercised by the Union, the types of legal instrument available to it, the protection of human rights and fundamental freedoms, and the arrangements for enhanced co-operation between groups of Member States.

B – The Treaty of Lisbon

The CT was to be ratified by the High Contracting Parties in accordance with their respective constitutional requirements, with a view to entering into force on 1 November 2006. At first, ratification by national parliaments (and, in the case of Spain, through a popular referendum) proved unproblematic. However, the ratification process descended into crisis following negative results in popular referenda in France (29 May 2005) and the Netherlands (1 June 2005). In the light of those events, the European Council meeting in June 2005 called for a 'period of reflection' across all Member States.[80] The outcome of that process was that the European Council, meeting in June 2007 under the presidency of Germany, agreed to declare the CT dead and approved the mandate for another IGC charged with drafting a new 'Reform Treaty'.[81] That Reform Treaty was to shed the form, language and symbols of a 'European Constitution', in favour of having another amending Treaty, similar in nature to the SEA, TA or TN; but within this new garb, to preserve as many as possible of the technical reforms proposed under the old CT which were intended to improve the Union's effectiveness, efficiency and accountability.

The IGC itself was convened by the Portuguese presidency in July 2007,[82] and reached political agreement on the text in October 2007. The Reform Treaty (known as the Treaty of Lisbon, or TL) was then signed by the Member States at a ceremony in Lisbon on 13 December 2007. Its contents closely followed the 2007 mandate. In particular, instead of repealing and replacing the existing Treaties entirely, the TEU would be extensively revised; the Treaty establishing the European Community would also be substantially amended and recast as the Treaty on the Functioning of the European Union (TFEU). But the European Community would still be abolished as a distinct legal entity and succeeded by a unitary European Union possessed of its own legal personality. In addition, the existing Third Pillar on police and judicial co-operation in criminal matters would

---

[80] See the Declaration by the Heads of State or Government of the Member States of the European Union on the Ratification of the Treaty establishing a Constitution for Europe (18 June 2005). The 'period of reflection' was extended by the European Council meeting in June 2006 (see Presidency Conclusions of 16 June 2006). Note also the Commission's 'Plan D for Democracy, Dialogue and Debate': COM(2005) 494 and COM(2006) 212.

[81] See Presidency Conclusions of 23 June 2007.

[82] 12004/07. The IGC was formally based on a proposal submitted by Germany (11222/07) reproducing the European Council mandate. Note the Commission's generally positive opinion on the IGC mandate (COM(2007) 412 Final); as well as the more ambivalent opinion of the European Parliament (Resolution of 11 July 2007).

be transferred out of the TEU and incorporated (with certain special provisions) into the TFEU.

The TL was intended to enter into force on 1 January 2009, before the European Parliament elections scheduled for June of that year.[83] However, that timetable was again thwarted when the population of Ireland—the only country to hold a popular referendum on the TL's ratification—voted 'no' in June 2008. A fresh period of uncertainty ensued: the Irish government undertook to investigate the reasons behind the negative referendum result;[84] the European Council then agreed on various 'guarantees' intended to address the concerns thus identified (though without formally amending the TL, which would have required its re-ratification by the other Member States).[85] The most important of those 'guarantees' was an agreement by the European Council to exercise its powers under the revised Treaties so as to retain the principle that the European Commission should contain one member per country—the potential loss of 'Ireland's Commissioner' being treated as a major factor behind the TL's unpopularity in that Member State.[86] On the strength of the European Council's guarantees, Ireland held a second referendum in October 2009; this time, just over 67 per cent of votes cast were in favour of the TL.

The Irish referendum saga was not, though, the only hurdle to implementation of the TL. Constitutional challenges to domestic ratification of the TL had been raised (ultimately unsuccessfully) before the supreme courts of several Member States.[87] The original Irish 'no' vote had also provided a rallying point for eurosceptic leaders in other countries, particularly Poland and the Czech Republic, to resist formal ratification of the TL.[88] Shortly after the second Irish referendum, the Polish President, Lech Kaczynski, finally gave up his resistance and signed off the TL. The Czech President, Vaclav Klaus, held out for longer, though even his bullish opposition eventually yielded, after the Czech Constitutional Court reaffirmed the compatibility of the TL with domestic law.[89] That was not before Klaus had secured the European Council's agreement that a controversial protocol agreed under the TL, seeking to qualify the application of the EU's Charter of Fundamental Rights within the United Kingdom and Poland, should be extended also to cover the Czech Republic at the time of the next accession treaty.[90]

All final obstacles overcome, the path was cleared for the TL to enter into force on 1 December 2009. Thus, after nearly a decade of complex negotiations and often bitter disputes, the outcome of the constitutional reform process initiated at Nice and Laeken is that the TEU and the TFEU (as revised by the TL) now provide the fundamental legal framework for the institutions and activities of the European Union.[91]

---

[83] See Art 6(2) TL.
[84] See, in particular, European Council Conclusions of 19–20 June 2008; and of 15–16 October 2008.
[85] See, in particular, European Council Conclusions of 11–12 December 2008; and of 18–19 June 2009.
[86] See further Chapter 3.
[87] eg in Germany, the Czech Republic and Latvia.
[88] Even though the TL had already received the necessary parliamentary assents in those Member States.
[89] See the Czech Constitutional Court's 'Second Lisbon Treaty Judgment' of 3 November 2009.
[90] See European Council Conclusions of 29–30 October 2009.
[91] For consolidated texts of the TEU and TFEU (as well as their Protocols and Declarations), see [2010] OJ C83.

C – Yet Further Treaty Reform . . .

With Lisbon's fate finally settled, many commentators argued that the Union should try to move on from what felt like interminable wrangling about treaty revisions, to focus instead on delivering concrete results as regards its substantive policy objectives, and on winning back support from an apparently disillusioned and disaffected public.

Nevertheless, further Treaty reform remains on the agenda. In the first place, elections to the European Parliament took place in 2009 on the basis of the pre-TL system of 736 MEPs;[92] yet the TL itself had envisaged a total of 751 MEPs, with some countries (such as Spain, France and the United Kingdom) gaining and one state (Germany) losing positions within the Parliament as compared to the 2009 figures.[93] The European Council decided that special provisions were needed to address this situation: all MEPs already elected to the Parliament should remain in office, but the additional MEPs provided for by Lisbon should also be able to take up their posts, thus raising the total number of MEPs to 754, at least for the remainder of the 2009–14 parliamentary term.[94] The amendments to Union primary law necessary to implement this solution were agreed upon at a brief IGC held in June 2010,[95] though the changes will only enter into force upon ratification by all 27 Member States.[96] In the second place, several Member States believed that the economic turmoil which followed the world financial crisis of 2008 had highlighted serious problems in the existing rules governing the operation of the EU's single currency. At its meeting in December 2010, the European Council formally initiated the 'simplified' procedure for revising the Treaties,[97] so as to provide for the establishment of a permanent crisis fund to assist individual members of the euro-zone and thereby guarantee the financial stability of the euro-area as a whole.[98]

Clearly, while Lisbon has not proven to be the last word on revision of the EU's main treaties, even in the short term, the changes now being proposed are relatively minor in comparison with the very thorough overhaul brought about by the TL itself. The next chapter will explain in greater detail the structure and contents of the TEU and TFEU, as well as the other legal sources which make up the primary law of the European Union.

---

[92] In accordance with ex-Arts 189 and 190 EC.
[93] See Art 14(2) TEU; Protocol No 36 on transitional provisions; Declarations No 4 and 5.
[94] See, in particular, European Council Conclusions of 11–12 December 2008; and of 18–19 June 2009.
[95] Published at [2010] OJ C263/1.
[96] See Art 48(4) TEU.
[97] On which, see further Chapter 2.
[98] See European Council Conclusions of 16–17 December 2010 (especially Annex I). Note the interim measures provided, eg, by Reg 407/2010 establishing a European financial stabilisation mechanism [2010] OJ L118/1.

An Overview of the
Union's Primary Law

This chapter seeks to provide an accessible overview of the EU's written and unwritten primary law: the Treaty on European Union, the Treaty on the Functioning of the European Union, the various Protocols and Annexes attached to the Treaties, the Charter of Fundamental Rights, the general principles of Union law and certain fundamental legal doctrines such as the direct effect and supremacy of EU law. The aim is to make readers familiar with the overall structure of the EU's core constitutional architecture, in preparation for exploring the more detailed institutional and substantive topics dealt with in subsequent chapters.

I – INTRODUCTION

The primary law of the European Union consists of several main sources: the TEU; the TFEU; the various Protocols and Annexes attached to the two Treaties; the Charter of Fundamental Rights of the European Union; and the general principles of Union law developed in the case law of the European Court of Justice, together with other judge-made principles (direct effect and supremacy) which are fundamental in defining the character of the Union legal order.[1] Together, those sources might well be referred to as the 'constitution' of the European Union—of course, using the concept of a 'constitution' not as it is associated with the foundational ordering of a sovereign state such as the United Kingdom or France, but in the broader sense of establishing the ground rules by which an organisation is constituted, and which stand at the apex of its hierarchy of legal norms. It is within the framework established by that body of primary law that the EU institutions carry out their myriad activities, including the adoption of legislative and other acts, and that the Union's complex legal order functions and evolves. This chapter is intended to offer an overview of the Union's primary law—familiarity with which will enable readers to navigate their way through the more detailed treatment of particular institutional and substantive topics provided in subsequent chapters.

---

[1] We will not specifically consider the Euratom Treaty. For a consolidated text of that Treaty, see [2010] OJ C84.

II – THE TREATY ON EUROPEAN UNION

In addition to its Preamble, the TEU consists of six Titles. Titles I–IV contain certain core 'constitutional principles' such as those setting out the Union's objectives, the limits of its competences and respect for fundamental rights (Title I); those identifying the democratic principles upon which the Union is founded (Title II); those dealing with the Union's institutions (Title III); and the possibility for groups of Member States to engage in 'enhanced co-operation' within the framework of the Treaties (Title IV). The bulk of the text of the TEU—in fact, Articles 21–46—is to be found in Title V: general provisions on the EU's external action and specific provisions on the common foreign and security policy. Title VI contains various 'final provisions' dealing with issues such as the EU's legal personality, the procedures for amendment of the Treaties and accession to/withdrawal from the Union.

A – Title I: Common Provisions

According to Article 1 TEU, the High Contracting Parties 'establish among themselves a European Union . . . on which the Member States confer competences to attain objectives they have in common', the Treaty marking 'a new stage in the process of creating an ever closer union among the peoples of Europe, in which decisions are taken as openly as possible and as closely as possible to the citizen'.

The remainder of Title I deals with four main issues. First, there is a statement of the Union's fundamental values and of its objectives. According to Article 2 TEU, the Union

> is founded on the values of respect for human dignity, freedom, democracy, equality, the rule of law and respect for human rights, including the rights of persons belonging to minorities. These values are common to the Member States in a society in which pluralism, non-discrimination, tolerance, justice, solidarity and equality between women and men prevail.

Article 3 then specifies the various objectives of the Union—ranging from issues such as the establishment of an internal market and an economic and monetary union, through the promotion of social justice and protection and equality between women and men, to the observance of international law and respect for the principles of the UN Charter. According to Article 3(6) TEU, the Union shall pursue its objectives 'by appropriate means commensurate with the competences which are conferred upon it in the Treaties'. Indeed, it is well established that the Union's values and objectives do not in themselves create any legally exercisable power for the Union institutions and cannot act as an independent source of directly binding rights and obligations.[2] In order to promote its values and achieve its objectives, the Union must rely on the specific competences conferred upon it elsewhere in the Treaties—though the values and objectives set out in Articles 2 and 3 TEU obviously perform an important and sometimes even decisive role when it comes to interpreting the nature and limits of the powers vested in the Union institutions.[3]

---

[2] eg Case C-9/99 *Echirolles Distribution* [2000] ECR I-8207; Case C-181/06 *Deutsche Lufthansa* [2007] ECR I-5903.

[3] Consider, eg, Case 267/86 *Van Eycke* [1988] ECR 4769; Case C-149/96 *Portugal v Council* [1999] ECR I-8395; Case C-479/04 *Laserdisken v Kulturministeriet* [2006] ECR I-8089; Case C-166/07 *Parliament v Council* [2009] ECR I-7135.

Secondly, Articles 4 and 5 enumerate some of the fundamental principles governing the existence and exercise of the Union's competences. Three key concepts are established: the principle of conferral (that the EU enjoys only those powers conferred upon it by the Member States and that it must act within the limits set out in the Treaties); the principle of subsidiarity (which seeks to insist upon the Union demonstrating some 'added value' to adopting collective action under the Treaties as compared to each Member State pursuing its own individual policy); and the principle of proportionality (limiting the content and form of Union action to what is necessary in order to realise its objectives). Those key concepts will be considered in greater detail in Chapter 5. In addition, Article 4(2) TEU obliges the Union to 'respect the equality of Member States before the Treaties as well as their national identities, inherent in their fundamental structures, political and constitutional, inclusive of regional and local self-government'; and also 'their essential State functions, including ensuring the territorial integrity of the State, maintaining law and order and safeguarding national security'. Conversely, Article 4(3) TEU deals with the principle of sincere co-operation—a mutual obligation for the Union and its Member States to assist each other in carrying out the tasks which flow from the Treaties—and elaborates on the duties this entails for the Member States, ie to take 'any appropriate measure, general or particular, to ensure fulfilment of the obligations arising out of the Treaties or resulting from the acts of the institutions of the Union' and to 'facilitate the achievement of the Union's tasks and refrain from any measure which could jeopardise the attainment of the Union's objectives'. As we shall see at various points in subsequent chapters, the principle of sincere co-operation is no piece of empty political rhetoric: it has provided the basis, in whole or in part, for the development of an entire series of much more specific, legally binding obligations incumbent upon the Member States, aimed at securing the effectiveness of Union law and policy.[4]

Thirdly, there are provisions which govern the Union's commitment to human rights and fundamental freedoms. Article 6 TEU contains three main points: the conferral of legally binding status upon the Union's Charter of Fundamental Rights (see below); a power and indeed obligation for the EU to accede to the ECHR; and recognition that fundamental rights also form part of the general principles of Union law which are developed by the Court of Justice in its case law (see below). Article 7 TEU deals with a rather different issue: the Union's power to monitor respect by the Member States for the Union's values as identified in Article 2 TEU, not only when the Member States are acting within the scope of the Treaties but also in situations which fall altogether outside the field of Union law; and (if necessary) to impose sanctions upon a delinquent Member State in the form of suspending certain of its rights under the Treaties. All of those issues will be dealt with in greater detail in Chapters 11 and 12.

Fourthly, a rather lonely provision, Article 8 TEU, obliges the Union to develop a 'special relationship' with neighbouring countries characterised by close and peaceful relations based on co-operation.

---

[4] eg on sanctions for the domestic enforcement of Union law: Case 68/88 *Commission v Greece* [1989] ECR 2965 (see also Chapter 4); eg on the duty to interpret national law in conformity with Union law: Case 14/83 *Von Colson* [1984] ECR 1891 (see also Chapter 8); eg on the obligation to take appropriate measures against private obstacles to the free movement of goods: Case C-265/95 *Commission v France* [1997] ECR I-6959 (see also Chapter 14).

B – Title II: Provisions on Democratic Principles

Title II contains various provisions which seek to explain the democratic basis of the Union and establish certain mechanisms for ensuring its accountability. For those purposes, Article 9 TEU contains a provision of crucial importance: the statement that every national of a Member State is also a citizen of the Union, such Union citizenship being additional to (rather than replacing) national citizenship. As we shall see elsewhere in this book, the introduction of Union citizenship under the Maastricht Treaty included a series of rights which are of increasing significance within the Union legal order, such as a general right to free movement between Member States and to equal treatment on grounds of nationality as regards all matters falling within the scope of the Treaties.[5] For present purposes, Union citizenship is noteworthy because it is expressly linked to the democratic legitimacy and accountability of the Union institutions.

Article 10 TEU clarifies that the Union is essentially a system of representative democracy wherein its citizens are represented both directly in the European Parliament and indirectly through the activities of their own Member State (particularly within the Council and the European Council). Article 11 TEU then deals with certain principles of participatory democracy within the EU—perhaps the most interesting of which is the new 'citizens' initiative', whereby at least one million citizens from a significant number of Member States are entitled to request the European Commission to submit proposals for Union action in implementation of the Treaties.[6] In addition, Article 12 TEU identifies the various means by which national parliaments—although they are obviously not institutions or bodies of the Treaties as such—can nevertheless contribute actively to the good functioning of the Union and thus provide an additional source of democratic legitimacy for/accountability in respect of the latter's activities: for example, by scrutinising draft Union legislation, particularly with a view to its compliance with the principle of subsidiarity; and by taking part in the procedures by which the Treaties can be formally amended. Such issues will be explored further below and also in subsequent chapters.[7]

C – Title III: Provisions on the Institutions

According to Article 13(1) TEU, the Union shall have an institutional framework which aims to promote its values, advance its objectives, serve its interests, those of its citizens and those of the Member States, and ensure the consistency, effectiveness and continuity of its policies and actions. As stated in Article 13(2) TEU, each institution 'shall act within the limits of the powers conferred on it in the Treaties, and in conformity with the procedures, conditions and objectives set out in them'.

The remainder of Title III lays down fundamental principles relating to the functions, powers and composition of the Union's most important institutions: the European Parliament (Article 14); the European Council (Article 15); the Council (Article 16); the Commission (Article 17); and the Court of Justice of the European Union (Article 19). Title III also deals with one of the main institutional novelties introduced by the TL: the

---

[5] eg Case C-184/99 *Grzelczyk* [2001] ECR I-6193; Case C-413/99 *Baumbast* [2002] ECR I-7091. See further Chapter 15.

[6] See further Chapter 4.

[7] In particular, see Chapter 5 on the subsidiarity monitoring mechanism.

post of High Representative of the Union for Foreign Affairs and Security Policy (Article 18), whose occupant is (uniquely) both a member of the Commission and closely associated with the Council. More detailed provisions concerning the main Union institutions, as well as provisions concerning the remaining two Union institutions (the European Central Bank and the Court of Auditors), are set out in the TFEU (see below). We will deal with the nature and roles of the European Parliament, European Council, Council and Commission in greater detail in Chapters 3 and 4. The structure and jurisdiction of the Court of Justice are considered further in Chapters 3, 6 and 7.

D – Title IV: Provisions on Enhanced Co-operation

Article 20 TEU refers to the possibility for Member States to engage in enhanced co-operation within the framework of the Treaties, ie to make use of the institutions, powers and instruments of the Union so as to enact additional policy measures that will be binding only upon those Member States which chose voluntarily to participate in the relevant initiative. Enhanced co-operation is an example of the phenomenon of 'flexible integration' which has become an increasingly important characteristic of the European Union particularly since the adoption of the Maastricht Treaty. Other notable instances of such flexible integration include mechanisms such as the opt-outs enjoyed by certain Member States from the adoption of the single currency; and the right of countries such as the UK and Ireland to remain outside or instead opt into measures adopted by the Union in fields such as asylum and immigration policy or cross-border co-operation in civil and criminal matters. Flexible integration in general, and the system of enhanced co-operation in particular, will be discussed further in Chapter 5.

E – Title V: General Provisions on the Union's External Action and Specific Provisions on the Common Foreign and Security Policy

Chapter 1 of Title V contains general provisions concerning the Union's external action: the principles and objectives which structure and guide the Union's relations with and policies towards the outside world, together with the placing of responsibility upon the European Council for defining the Union's overall strategic interests and objectives. Those principles and objectives, and that responsibility, extend across the full gamut of the Union's substantive powers to engage in various categories of external action—whether pursuant to the CFSP as dealt with in Chapter 2 of Title V itself; or in accordance with the specific external relations powers contained in the TFEU (eg as regards the common commercial policy or the grant of humanitarian aid to third countries); or as regards the external dimension of any other Union policy (in fields such as environmental protection or cross-border co-operation in civil and criminal matters). The Union's external action is considered in greater detail in Chapter 27. Suffice for now to offer some brief observations on the broader constitutional context of the CFSP provisions.

Chapter 2 of Title V is unusual in that it is the only section of the TEU which contains substantive provisions relating to a specific category of Union activity. That peculiarity is partly historical. The CFSP provisions have been contained in Title V of the TEU since the original Maastricht Treaty, when they made up the 'Second Pillar' of the European Union.

Even as the rest of the old pillar structure has been eroded and now effectively abolished (see below), the CFSP has retained its position within Title V of the TEU. But the peculiarity of Chapter 2 of Title V is not simply historical. The physical separation of the CFSP within the TEU, as distinct from the rest of the Union's substantive internal and external policies under the TFEU, is intended to emphasise and indeed reinforce the highly differentiated nature of the CFSP within the Union legal order: for example, the continued predominance of unanimous voting within the European Council and the Council; the express exclusion of any competence to adopt legislative acts; the special role of the High Representative for Foreign Affairs; the more marginal influence of the Commission and especially the European Parliament; and the virtual exclusion of the jurisdiction of the Court of Justice.[8] It is also widely assumed that decisions adopted specifically pursuant to the CFSP will remain distinct, as regards their potential effects within the national legal systems, from decisions adopted in any other field of Union activity, to the extent that CFSP acts should not generally be capable of having independent effects (such as direct effect and/or supremacy) within the domestic legal orders.[9]

F – Title VI: Final Provisions

Title VI TEU contains various provisions dealing with issues such as the EU's legal personality (Article 47); the fact that the Treaty is concluded for an unlimited period of time (Article 53); and the equal authenticity of the various language versions of the Treaty (Article 55). In the present context, several other provisions warrant specific mention.

First, Article 48 TEU deals with the procedures for amending the TEU and TFEU. The 'ordinary revision procedure' is contained in Articles 48(2)–(5) TEU. Any Member State, the European Parliament or the Commission may submit amendment proposals to the Council; those proposals shall be forwarded to the European Council and notified to the national parliaments. If the European Council, having consulted the European Parliament and the Commission, decides (by simple majority) in favour of examining the proposals, it may convene a Convention charged with drawing up recommendations for consideration by an IGC. The idea of using a Convention to deliberate on and recommend potential Treaty changes is based on an approach already used in the drafting of the Charter of Fundamental Rights and then employed again in the negotiation of the Constitutional Treaty.[10] It is intended to offer a more inclusive and transparent approach to revising the Treaties, since the Convention is to be composed of representatives not only of the Member States but also of the national parliaments, the European Parliament and the Commission, and can be assumed to operate in a more public and deliberative manner than the approach usually associated with a traditional IGC. Nevertheless, the European Council may decide, with the consent of the European Parliament, that the scale of the proposals does not warrant a Convention, and proceed to define for itself the terms of reference for the IGC. That power was invoked for the negotiation of the 2010

---

[8] See Art 24(1) TEU. Also Art 31 TEU. It is also expressly provided that the 'flexibility clause' contained in Art 352 TFEU (ex-Art 308 EC) cannot be used to attain CFSP objectives: see Art 352(4) TFEU. Note that the revised Treaties also envisage the adoption of specific data protection rules within the context of the CFSP: see Art 39 TEU and Art 16(2) TFEU.

[9] See further, eg, A Arnull, A Dashwood, M Dougan, M Ross, E Spaventa and D Wyatt, *Wyatt & Dashwood's EU Law*, 5th edn (London, Sweet & Maxwell, 2006) para 11-013.

[10] On which, see Chapters 12 and 1, respectively.

amendments concerning the composition of the European Parliament.[11] In either event, the IGC shall determine the amendments by common accord, and they will enter into force after being ratified by all the Member States in accordance with their respective constitutional requirements.[12]

In addition to that ordinary revision procedure, Article 48 TEU also provides for several types of 'simplified revision procedures'. In the first place, Article 48(6) TEU provides that the provisions of Part Three of the TFEU, containing the detailed legal bases governing internal Union policies, may be amended (on a proposal from any Member State, the European Parliament or the Commission) by unanimous decision of the European Council (after consulting the European Parliament and the Commission).[13] That decision must then be approved by all Member States in accordance with their respective constitutional requirements; and must not, in any case, increase the Union's existing competences under the Treaties. Article 48(6) TEU was the procedure chosen by the European Council in December 2010, so as to make provision in the Treaties for a new 'European Stability Mechanism' designed to safeguard the financial stability of the euro-area.[14] In the second place, Article 48(7) TEU contains two so-called 'passerelle clauses': one by which the requirement of unanimity among the Member States for approval of a decision in the Council (either under Title V of the TEU or within the TFEU)[15] may be converted into a requirement instead to secure merely a qualified majority of votes; the other by which provisions of the TFEU permitting the Council to adopt legislative acts according to a 'special legislative procedure' (involving a lower level of participation for the European Parliament) may be upgraded to the 'ordinary legislative procedure' (based upon full equality of power between the Council and European Parliament). The procedure in each of those passerelle situations is the same: the European Council must reach its decision by unanimity and with the consent of the European Parliament; the proposed decision must also be notified to the national parliaments, each of which has an effective right to veto the proposal within a six-month period.[16] The voting requirements within the Council, and the role of the European Parliament in adopting Union legislation, will be dealt with in greater detail in subsequent chapters.[17] For now, it should be noted that specific provisions of the TFEU are excluded from the potential scope of application of the general passerelle powers contained in Article 48(7) TEU.[18] Moreover, various provisions of the Treaties contain specific 'mini-passerelle clauses' of their own, permitting limited changes to Union primary law to be enacted without recourse to the ordinary or simplified revision procedures.[19] It is also worth bearing in mind that certain decisions of constitutional significance, which before the Treaty of Lisbon would have required a fully

---

[11] [2010] OJ C263/1. See further Chapters 1 and 3.

[12] If, after two years, four-fifths of the Member States have ratified the amendments and one or more Member States have encountered difficulties in ratification, the matter shall be referred to the European Council.

[13] And the ECB, in the case of institutional changes in the monetary area.

[14] See European Council Conclusions of 16–17 December 2010.

[15] Though not as regards decisions with military implications or those in the area of defence.

[16] cp Art 6 of the Protocol on the role of national parliaments in the European Union.

[17] See Chapters 3 and 4, respectively.

[18] See Art 353 TFEU: the relevant provisions are Art 311, third and fourth paras on Union own resources; Art 312(2), first para on the multiannual financial framework; and the Art 352 flexibility clause.

[19] eg Art 81 TFEU (family law); Art 153(2) TFEU (social policy); Art 192(2) TFEU (environment); Art 312(2) TFEU (multiannual financial framework). Note also the 'internal' enhanced co-operation passerelle clauses found in Art 333 TFEU (see further Chapter 5).

fledged Treaty amendment, may now be put into effect under the current Treaties through acts of the Union institutions alone.[20]

The second provision contained in Title VI of the TEU which deserves special mention is Article 49 TEU concerning the accession of new Member States to the EU: 'Any European State which respects the values referred to in Article 2 [TEU] and is committed to promoting them may apply to become a member of the Union.' The applicant country must address its application to the Council, with the European Parliament and the national parliaments being notified of the application. The Council may accept the applicant country as an official candidate for accession to the Union acting unanimously, after consulting the Commission and with the consent of the European Parliament. In reaching its decision, the Council must take into account the conditions of eligibility agreed upon by the European Council.[21] The actual conditions of admission and any adjustments to the Treaties which such admission would entail must be determined by agreement between the Member States and the candidate country. That accession treaty must then be ratified by all the contracting parties in accordance with their respective constitutional requirements.

The third provision worth considering is Article 50 TEU on the right of any Member State voluntarily to withdraw from the Union in accordance with its own constitutional requirements. The procedure for withdrawal is set out in Articles 50(2)–(4) TEU. It involves, in particular, the negotiation of an agreement between the Union and the Member State concerned, setting out the arrangements for the latter's withdrawal and the framework of its future relationship with the Union. The agreement shall be negotiated in accordance with guidelines established by the European Council; it is to be concluded by the Council, acting by qualified majority vote, with the consent of the European Parliament. The Treaties shall cease to apply to the relevant state as from the date of entry into force of the withdrawal agreement or (failing that) two years after the relevant state's original notification of its intention to withdraw (unless the European Council, in agreement with the relevant state, unanimously decides to extend this period). It is expressly provided that representatives of the withdrawing state shall not participate in the relevant discussions or decisions of the European Council or the Council, though it is perhaps curious that there is no express bar on Members of the European Parliament from the withdrawing state taking part in the European Parliament's vote to approve the withdrawal agreement. In any case, pursuant to Article 50(5) TEU, should the withdrawing state subsequently change its mind, its application for readmission will be treated like any other accession to the Union.

III – THE TREATY ON THE FUNCTIONING OF THE EUROPEAN UNION

The TFEU, according to its own Article 1(1), 'organises the functioning of the Union and determines the areas, delimitation of, and arrangements for exercising its competences'. Besides its Preamble, the TFEU consists of seven Parts.

---

[20] eg the European Council decision determining the future composition of the European Parliament as regards the allocation of MEPs between Member States: Art 14(2) TEU.

[21] Note also Art 20(4) TEU: enhanced co-operation measures are not part of the *acquis* which must be accepted by candidate countries.

Part One contains additional 'constitutional principles' which should be read, alongside the relevant provisions of the TEU, as part of the fundamental architecture of the EU legal system. In the first place, and building upon the principle of conferred powers established in the TEU, the various categories of competences attributed by the Member States to the Union are systematically identified and defined, together with indicative lists of the policy fields to which those categories primarily relate. However, the precise scope and nature of EU competence over any given regulatory sphere must still be determined in accordance with the detailed provisions found in subsequent provisions of the TFEU. That complex system of Union competences will be explored further in Chapter 5. In the second place, a range of so-called 'horizontal principles' are identified—principles which are intended to inform and guide the Union's activities across every policy field falling within its attributed competences pursuant to the Treaties. Those 'horizontal principles' include, inter alia, equality between men and women; combating other forms of discrimination on grounds such as race, disability, age or sexual orientation; environmental and consumer protection; the transparency of Union activities; and the protection of personal data.

Part Two is relatively short, but contains some of the most legally interesting and important provisions of the TFEU. Again, the relevant articles can be divided into two main categories. In the first place, there are provisions concerned with advancing equal treatment within the Union. Article 18 TFEU enshrines the fundamental rule that, within the scope of application of the Treaties, any discrimination on grounds of nationality shall be prohibited. As we shall see, that principle has played a central role in the development of Union law in many fields, not least the free movement of goods, persons and services.[22] Article 19 TFEU then confers upon the Union institutions the power to adopt measures to combat other forms of discrimination (based on race, religion, disability, age or sexual orientation). In the second place, there are the provisions dealing with Union citizenship and its associated rights: to move and reside freely across the Union territory (Article 21 TFEU); to vote and stand in local and European elections in the Member State of residence (Article 22 TFEU); to diplomatic protection from the Member States in the territory of third countries (Article 23 TFEU); to make various forms of petition and representation to the Union institutions (Article 24 TFEU); and such other rights as may be provided for in the future (Article 25 TFEU). Union citizenship and its associated rights form the subject of Chapter 15.

Part Three is by far the longest section of the TFEU. It contains the substantive provisions on Union policies and internal actions, which should be read alongside the generic categories of Union competence defined in Part One (see above). Some of the provisions in Part Three define the objectives and principles that are intended to govern Union activity in any given field of activity; others lay down directly binding rules which can form the basis for judicial control over the conduct of the Union institutions, Member States and/or private parties; others again empower the Union institutions to adopt a variety of legislative and non-legislative acts for the purposes of achieving the Treaties' objectives in the relevant field (as well as specifying the procedures by which such measures should be adopted). It is not our intention to explore the legal dimension of every single Union policy dealt under the Part Three: that would require a small library. Instead, this book will offer a detailed treatment of some of the most important of the Union's internal actions: the internal market provisions dealing with the free movement of goods, persons, services

---

[22] See further Part IV of this book.

and capital;[23] and Union competition policies.[24] Readers should refer to more specialist texts for knowledge of EU law in other fields such as economic and monetary policy,
employment and social rights, the Area of Freedom, Security and Justice, consumer protection or environmental policy.

Part Four of the TFEU governs the association with the Union of various overseas
countries and territories which have special relations with certain Member States.[25] Part
Five is then concerned with various aspects of the Union's external relations, within the
overall framework for external action established in Part V of the TEU: for example, the
Union's common commercial policy as regards economic relations with the outside world;
co-operation with developing countries and economic, financial and technical co-operation with other third countries; and the provision of humanitarian aid. Part Five also
sets out other rules relevant to the Union's external relations, such as the procedure for
the negotiation and conclusion of international agreements between the Union and third
countries or international organisations. Article 222 TFEU, introduced by the TL, deals
with the Union's response to a terrorist attack or other (natural or manmade) disaster
which befalls one of the Member States. Chapter 27 of this book offers further analysis of
the Union's external action.

From the point of view of EU constitutional law, Part Six of the TFEU is of crucial
importance. It contains more detailed provisions on the functioning of the Union's institutions, the arrangements governing Union finances, and the detailed rules on engaging in
enhanced co-operation. It is here that we find, in particular, the provisions dealing with
the Union judiciary: the composition of the various Union courts, how to identify the precise division of labour between them, and the various types of jurisdiction exercised by
the Union judges in respect of disputes involving the Union institutions, Member States
and/or private parties. Those issues are considered further in Chapters 3, 6 and 7. Part Six
also includes, inter alia, detailed rules on the various types of legal acts available to the
Union institutions in the exercise of their competences under the Treaties;[26] as well as a
full description of the Union's 'ordinary legislative procedure'.[27]

The 'general and final provisions' make up Part Seven of the TFEU. They include articles dealing with issues such as the Union's contractual and non-contractual liability
(Article 340 TFEU); the seat (Article 341 TFEU) and the languages (Article 342 TFEU)
of the Union institutions; the impact of Union membership upon pre-existing international agreements of the Member States (Article 351 TFEU); and the fact that the TFEU
is (like the TEU) concluded for an unlimited period of time (Article 356 TFEU). One
provision of particular importance is Article 352 TFEU—the so-called 'flexibility clause'—
which permits the Union institutions to take action to attain one of the Union's objectives
where the Treaties have not provided the necessary powers. As we shall see in Chapter 5,
this provision has historically been associated with allegations that the Union institutions
seek gradually to extend the scope of their existing competences in a manner that can
sometimes seem difficult to square with the fundamental principle of conferred powers.

---

[23] See Part IV of this book.
[24] See Part V of this book.
[25] In particular: Denmark, France, the Netherlands and the UK.
[26] On which, see further Chapters 4 and 8.
[27] See Chapter 4.

IV – THE RELATIONSHIP BETWEEN TEU
AND TFEU

Article 1, third paragraph TEU and Article 1(2) TFEU each state that the Union is founded on both Treaties, which shall have the same legal value. In other words, the TEU and TFEU (together with their various Protocols and Annexes, as well as the Charter of Fundamental Rights, all discussed further below) should be read as a seamless ensemble of written primary law for the Union.

At first glance, it might be difficult to identify any compelling reason why the Union should be founded upon two separate treaties. Moreover, the logic of apportioning provisions between the two texts is sometimes hard to fathom: for example, the principles of conferred powers, subsidiarity and proportionality, regulating the existence and exercise of Union competences, are located within Title I of the TEU, whereas the (closely related) provisions on the various types of Union competences are to be found in Part One of the TFEU.

The explanation for that 'two Treaty solution' is largely historical. The Maastricht Treaty of 1992 had created the new European Union, founded upon and incorporating but still constitutionally distinct from the existing European (Economic) Community, with two different Treaties for each of the Union and Community legal orders. The Treaty establishing a Constitution for Europe signed in 2004 had indeed sought to simplify and rationalise the system by proposing repeal of both the TEU and the EC Treaty, to be replaced with a single Constitutional Treaty (CT). The negative referenda on that CT in France and the Netherlands then led the European Council to rethink its approach: on the one hand, deciding to jettison the 'constitutional concept' which had underpinned the 2004 package; on the other hand, still seeking to preserve the many detailed reforms contained in the now-defunct CT. Part of that compromise was to accept that, if two Treaties were what the EU was already based upon, and the nature of the new agreement due to be finalised in Lisbon was merely to amend those Treaties in a primarily technical fashion, then two Treaties is what should emerge again at the end—even if that final product was not necessarily as straightforward or rational as the 2004 text.

Moreover, it is possible to identify a rough-and-ready division of labour between the two Treaty texts. Besides the detailed CFSP provisions, the TEU has more the character of a 'mission statement', coupled with some basic organising principles on issues such as the institutional architecture. By contrast, the TFEU seems more concerned with the nitty-gritty work of setting out the legal bases required to fulfil that mission statement, and fleshing out more of the details on the institutional framework. Indeed, the TEU contains no legal bases for the adoption of Union legislation; all Union legislative acts will be adopted pursuant to the TFEU.[28]

Lisbon's 'two Treaty solution' does nevertheless raise some interesting constitutional questions. The most important is perhaps whether the TL has finally abolished the 'pillar structure' according to which the EU was first constructed under the Maastricht Treaty (and which survived, albeit in a modified form, under the Treaties of Amsterdam and Nice). In our view, it now seems inappropriate to conceptualise the Union in terms of dis-

---

[28] However, the TEU does provide for the adoption of various non-legislative acts, especially as regards the functioning of the Union institutions, and in the field of the CFSP.

tinct 'pillars' each possessed of their own peculiar legal sub-orders. After all, the European Community which made up the old 'First Pillar' has been suppressed as an entity separate from the Union; at the same time, the provisions on cross-border co-operation in criminal matters which made up the old 'Third Pillar' have been absorbed (albeit with some special features) into Title V, Part Three TFEU on the Area of Freedom, Security and Justice.[29] Even as regards the CFSP, its physical separation in Chapter 2 of Title V TEU, as well as the various grounds for institutional differentiation provided for therein, should hardly warrant continuing to treat the CFSP effectively as a separate 'pillar'; to recognise the existence of such an autonomous subsystem would undermine the clear intention of the TL that the Union should constitute a unitary entity. Indeed, the degree of cross-fertilisation between the TEU and the TFEU, on issues such as the Union's objectives, competences and institutional framework, is such that pillar-talk becomes largely meaningless or even positively unhelpful. Across the great majority of legal bases on internal and external Union action, variations in the strength and scope of decision-making powers, the applicable decision-making procedures or the available legal instruments certainly exist—but they are not such as to call into question the essential unity of the Union's underlying legal order.

V – OTHER WRITTEN SOURCES OF PRIMARY LAW

Although the TEU and TFEU together provide the essential rulebook for the Union's constitutional functioning, it is important to bear in mind that they are not the only written sources of the Union's primary law.

In the first place, attached to the Treaties are a whole series of Protocols and Annexes which, according to Article 51 TEU, are to form an integral part thereof. Those Protocols and Annexes are not necessarily of a purely technical nature or marginal interest. Some contain important bodies of rules which directly implement or supplement core provisions of the Treaties themselves. Consider, for example: Protocol No 2 containing the procedure by which national parliaments may formally object to Union legislative proposals on the grounds that the latter are incompatible with the principle of subsidiarity; or Protocol No 36 containing the various transitional provisions which are designed to deal with the complex institutional and legal issues involved in amending the old TEU and EC Treaty in accordance with the TL. Other Protocols contain provisions which are of vital importance, albeit for only some of the Member States. Consider, for example: Protocol No 14 on provisions specific to the Member States which have adopted the euro, designed to reinforce their mutual co-operation and co-ordination; Protocol No 15 containing the UK's opt-out from any obligation to join the single currency; or Protocol No 32 permitting Denmark to maintain its existing legislation limiting the acquisition of second homes (notwithstanding the potential incompatibility of that legislation with the Treaty rules on the free movement of persons and capital).

In the second place, Article 6(1) TEU states that the Charter of Fundamental Rights of the European Union shall have the same legal value as the Treaties. The Charter was origi-

---

[29] Those special features are highlighted at appropriate points throughout this book.

nally adopted in 2000 in the form of a non-binding political declaration by the Council, Commission and Parliament.[30] The Convention on the Future of Europe subsequently proposed revising the text of the Charter and directly incorporating it into the draft Treaty establishing a Constitution for Europe so as to provide a legally binding bill of rights for the Union. The Member States agreed to that proposal in the final CT signed in 2004.[31] Again, however, in the light of the negative referenda in France and the Netherlands, the European Council decided that a different approach was necessary in order to cleanse the difficult process of Treaty reform of its overtly constitutional trappings: the Charter would indeed provide the Union with a legally binding bill of rights, but it should be incorporated into the Union's primary law by cross-reference rather than direct replication within the text of the Treaties; for that purpose, the Charter was 're-proclaimed' in 2007 by Council, Commission and Parliament in its revised form.[32] Chapter 12 will explore in greater detail the evolution and current legal value of the amended Charter.

In the third place, future Treaties, and the effects of certain decisions adopted pursuant to the existing Treaties, will also assume their rightful place among the sources of Union primary law. That applies, in particular, to Treaties adopted pursuant to the ordinary revision procedure for amendment of the TEU, TFEU, or their existing Protocols and Annexes; decisions of the European Council (or the Council) to amend the TEU or TFEU in accordance with the various simplified revision procedures (or under one of the other more specific 'mini-passerelle clauses' provided for under the existing Treaties); and Treaties providing for the accession of new Member States in accordance with Article 49 TEU.

It is worth noting that the Final Act of the IGC which adopted the TL is accompanied by a lengthy series of declarations. Some of those declarations were adopted by the entire IGC and are intended to reflect the collective understanding or views of the Member States at that time. For example, Declaration No 7 contained the draft text of a decision to be adopted by the Council, in accordance with the relevant provisions of the Treaties, concerning the detailed operation of qualified majority voting after the TL had entered into force.[33] Declaration No 17 is also noteworthy: the Member States recall (and thus politically endorse) the established case law of the Court of Justice concerning the principle of primacy for EU law over purely national law.[34] Other declarations were adopted by individual Member States or groups of Member States and are intended to represent only the views of that country or those countries: consider, for example, Declaration No 61 by Poland, setting out its understanding that the Charter of Fundamental Rights should not affect in any way the right of Member States to legislate in the sphere of public morality, family law or the protection of human dignity;[35] or Declaration No 64 by the UK, expressing the view that the amended Treaties are not intended to change the basis for the franchise for elections to the European Parliament.[36]

The important point, for present purposes, is that all the various Declarations annexed to the Final Act are essentially political in character; they do not form part of the

---

[30] [2000] OJ C364/1.
[31] See Art I-9 and Part II CT.
[32] [2010] OJ C83/389.
[33] See now Decision 2009/857 [2009] OJ L314/73.
[34] On which, see further Chapter 8.
[35] See further, on the Charter, Chapter 12.
[36] See further, on that issue, Chapter 3.

Union's primary law and are not directly legally binding.[37] That is not to say that all such Declarations are legally irrelevant. The view of the Member States on a given issue may well accurately reflect the current state of Union law, even if their Declaration to that effect does not provide the actual source of the relevant Union rules.[38] It may also be possible for Declarations adopted by the Member States collectively to be taken into consideration by the Union or national courts when interpreting provisions of Union law, though no Declaration by the Member States, whether made collectively or individually, may contradict or undermine the force of binding Union law.[39]

VI – UNWRITTEN SOURCES OF PRIMARY LAW

The Union's written primary law—made of the Treaties, their Protocols and Annexes, the Charter, and various instruments of amendment and/or accession—is supplemented by an important source of unwritten primary law: the so-called 'general principles of Union law'. In fact, various provisions of the Treaties make express reference to the existence and importance of such 'general principles': for example, Article 340 TFEU refers to the Union incurring non-contractual liability 'in accordance with the general principles common to the laws of the Member States'; similarly, Article 6(3) TEU states that fundamental rights, as guaranteed under the ECHR and as they result from the constitutional traditions common to the Member States, 'shall constitute general principles of the Union's law'. Despite such occasional Treaty references, however, the general principles of Union law are essentially the creation of the judges: they constitute an unwritten source of Union law, open to future development in a dynamic and flexible manner, forming part of the jurisprudence developed by the Union courts under their case law.

Some of those general principles of Union law contain directly binding rights and obligations which can provide a grounds for judicial review against Union acts and (in certain circumstances) also in respect of Member State conduct. That includes general principles such as proportionality, legal certainty and legitimate expectations.[40] Further general principles are more programmatic in character and seek to provide guidance as to the interpretation and application of other provisions of Union law. That would be the case, for example, with the Union's commitment to pursuing high standards of environmental or consumer protection.[41] In any event, the general principles of Union law are treated as being equivalent in their legal status to the written sources of Union primary law. Although there has been academic speculation about whether, in some circumstances, the general principles of Union law might even be considered to be legally superior to

---

[37] See further, eg, AG Toth, 'The Legal Status of the Declarations Annexed to the Single European Act' (1986) 23 *CMLRev* 803.

[38] As with Declaration No 17 on the principle of supremacy (mentioned above).

[39] eg Case C-233/97 *KappAhl Oy* [1998] ECR I-8069. Cp Case 143/83 *Commission v Denmark* [1985] ECR 427; Case C-292/89 *R v Immigration Appeal Tribunal, ex parte Antonissen* [1991] ECR I-745; Cases C-197/94 and C-252/94 *Bautiaa and Société Française Maritime v Directeur des Services Fiscaux* [1996] ECR I-505.

[40] On proportionality, eg Case 240/78 *Atalanta* [1979] ECR 2137; Case 261/81 *Rau* [1982] ECR 3961. On legal certainty, eg Case C-143/93 *Gebroeders van Es Douane Agenten BV v Inspecteur der Invoerrechten en Accijnzen* [1996] ECR I-431. On legitimate expectations, eg Case 120/86 *Mulder* [1988] ECR 2321; Cases C-31/91 to C-44/91 *Lageder* [1993] ECR I-1761. See further Chapter 10.

[41] cp Case C-233/94 *Germany v Parliament and Council (Deposit Guarantee Schemes Directive)* [1997] ECR I-2405; Case C-284/95 *Safety Hi-Tech* [1998] ECR I-4301; Case C-341/95 *Bettati* [1998] ECR I-4355.

the Treaties and Protocols themselves, there is as yet no persuasive legal authority to support such an analysis. The general principles of Union law are dealt with more fully in Chapters 10 and 11.

There are other strands in the jurisprudence of the Union courts which—even if they are not to be classified as 'general principles of Union law' in the strict technical sense just described—are nevertheless of such constitutional importance for the nature and functioning of the European Union that that jurisprudence surely deserves to be classified as another unwritten source of the Union's primary law. We refer, in particular, to the principles of direct effect and supremacy.[42] As we shall see in Chapter 8, the principles of direct effect and supremacy were developed relatively early in the case law of the Court of Justice in order to structure the relationship between the Union and national legal orders; in particular, to define the circumstances when Union measures should be recognised as a legitimate and indeed superior source of law by the competent domestic judicial and administrative authorities. Although in certain respects they remain even today a source of considerable doctrinal confusion and political controversy, the principles of direct effect and supremacy have long played a decisive role in the Union's overall development and surely make a unique, indeed inestimable, contribution to the constitutional nature of the Union legal order—permitting the Treaties and law made thereunder to penetrate deep into the domestic legal systems, and binding the Member States together in respect for the common rights and obligations embodied in Union law.

---

[42] See, in particular, Case 26/62 *van Gend en Loos* [1963] ECR 1 on direct effect and Case 6/64 *Costa v Enel* [1964] ECR 585 on supremacy.

Part II

Institutional Fundamentals

3

The Institutions of the European Union

This chapter provides an introduction to the four main political institutions of the European Union: the European Council (the supreme political organ, responsible for providing impetus to the Union's development and for defining its general strategic guidelines); the Council (composed of ministers from the Member States, through which the latter's interests find expression, and are able to be reconciled, at the Union level); the Commission (which is intended to represent the general interest of the Union, in complete independence from any government or body); and the European Parliament (the Union's only directly elected institution, exercising legislative and budgetary powers together with the Council, as well as being responsible for supervising the Commission's activities). We also outline the structure and functions, as well as stress the fundamental importance, of the Court of Justice of the European Union.

I – ARTICLE 13 TEU

According to Article 13(1) TEU, the Union's institutional framework shall aim to promote its values, advance its objectives, serve its interests, those of its citizens and those of the Member States, and ensure the consistency, effectiveness and continuity of its policies and actions. Article 13(1) TEU then goes on to identify the Union's seven formal institutions: the European Parliament; the European Council; the Council; the European Commission; the Court of Justice of the European Union; the European Central Bank (ECB); and the Court of Auditors. It is expressly provided in Article 13(2) TEU that each of the institutions shall act within the limits of the powers conferred on it in the Treaties and in conformity with the procedures, conditions and objectives set out therein. Thus, the Union's institutional system is founded upon the idea of conferred or attributed powers: the institutions have only those powers given to them expressly or impliedly by the Treaties.[1]

Most of this chapter will be devoted to a closer examination of the Union's four main political institutions: the European Council, the Council, the Commission and the European Parliament. We will also outline the broad structure and functions of the Court

---

[1] For further discussion of the legal implications of this principle, see Chapter 5.

of Justice of the European Union—made up of the Court of Justice, the General Court and the specialised courts—though it will quickly become evident throughout this book that the Court's role in the development and functioning of the Union legal order is all-pervasive. Only a few words need be said about the remaining two Union institutions. The Court of Auditors was created by the Financial Treaty of 1975 and 'promoted' to the status of a formal institution by the TEU. Its main responsibility is to carry out the Union's audit by examining the accounts of all Union revenue and expenditure, reporting as to the reliability of the Union's accounts and the legality and regularity of the underlying transactions.[2] For its part, the ECB was created under the TEU and subsequently 'promoted' to the status of a formal institution by the TL. Acting together with the national central banks of all the Member States—the 'European System of Central Banks'—the ECB's main task is to maintain price stability and otherwise to support the Union's general economic policies in order to contribute to the achievement of its objectives. Furthermore, acting together with the national central banks of those Member States whose currency is the euro, the ECB is responsible for conducting the Union's monetary policy.[3] Although Article 282(3) TFEU states that the ECB shall be independent in the exercise of its powers, the Court of Justice has confirmed that such independence does not have the consequence of separating the ECB entirely from the fundamental principles of the Union's institutional framework, including the obligation to act within the limits of the powers conferred upon the ECB through the Treaties.[4]

In addition to the seven Union institutions listed in the first paragraph of Article 13 TEU, paragraph 4 also mentions the Economic and Social Committee and the Committee of the Regions. The role of those two bodies is to assist the European Parliament, the Council and the Commission by giving advisory opinions. The Economic and Social Committee, which has been in existence since the establishment of the EEC and Euratom, consists of representatives of the different categories of economic and social life and of the general interest, while the Committee of the Regions, which was created by the TEU, consists of representatives of regional and local bodies.[5] The latter's establishment represented a response to political demands in certain Member States, particularly those with a federal structure, that regional and local interests be given a direct line of communication to the Union institutions. However, almost 20 years after it was established, it cannot be said that the Committee has become a significant political force.

In addition to the seven Union institutions and the two advisory committees, other important bodies are created directly by the Treaties. For example, the European Investment Bank—composed of the Member States—is charged with contributing to the balanced and steady development of the internal market by granting loans and giving guarantees on a non-profit-making basis which facilitate the financing of projects (for example) for developing the Union's less-developed regions.[6] Moreover, numerous additional bodies have been created pursuant to the Treaties through acts of Union secondary legislation. These include various Union agencies charged with executing technical, scientific or management tasks in particular fields of Union policy: for example, the European

---

[2] See further on the composition and powers of the Court of Auditors: Arts 285–87 TFEU.

[3] See further on the composition and powers of the ECB: Arts 282–84 TFEU.

[4] Case C-11/00 *Commission v European Central Bank* [2003] ECR I-7147.

[5] See Art 300 TFEU. See further on the Economic and Social Committee: Arts 301–04 TFEU. See further on the Committee of the Regions: Arts 305–07 TFEU.

[6] See further on the European Investment Bank: Arts 308–09 TFEU.

Environment Agency (which collects and disseminates information on the state of the European environment);[7] the European Food Safety Authority (which is responsible for providing independent scientific advice on all matters relevant to food safety);[8] and the EU Agency for Fundamental Rights (which provides the Union institutions and Member States with assistance and expertise on fundamental rights).[9] Other specialist bodies are provided for under the Treaties, with their activities regulated by Union secondary legislation: for example, Eurojust (which promotes co-operation between Member States as regards the investigation and prosecution of serious cross-border crime) and Europol (which facilitates cross-border co-operation between the national police and other law enforcement services).[10]

II – THE EUROPEAN COUNCIL

It was at the summit meeting of European Community leaders in Paris in December 1974 that the decision was taken to hold regular meetings at the highest political level, within a European Council (as distinct from 'the Council', considered below, composed of Ministers). The first European Council was held in Dublin in March 1975, and the series of meetings continued on an informal basis for some years thereafter. A more formal legal basis for the activities of the European Council was then introduced by the TEU: Article 4 of the pre-Lisbon TEU provided that the European Council brought together the heads of state or government of the Member States and the president of the Commission;[11] at least two meetings of the European Council were to be held each year, chaired by the head of state or government of the Member State holding the presidency of the Council for the time being, though it became established practice to hold four meetings of the European Council per year and for additional meetings to be called on an ad hoc basis.

Although the European Council was not foreseen by the original Treaties and for many years was not even treated as a formal Union institution, its strategic political influence within the EU was highly significant. To demonstrate the contribution various European Councils have made to the Union's strategic development, it is enough to recall: the meeting in Fontainebleau in June 1984 when work was set in train which eventually bore fruit in the institutional reforms of the SEA; the meeting in Hanover in June 1988 when the project of establishing an economic and monetary union was relaunched; and the series of meetings at which the criteria for, and the modalities of, the accession to the Union of the countries of central and eastern Europe were laid down, from Copenhagen in June 1993 to Helsinki in December 1999. The Fontainebleau meeting illustrates another function of the European Council: that of unravelling knotty political problems which have defeated the efforts of the institutions. It was at that meeting that a solution was found to the long-running dispute about the level of the United Kingdom's net contribution to the

---

[7] See Reg 401/2009 [2009] OJ L126/13.
[8] See Reg 178/2002 [2002] OJ L31/1.
[9] See Reg 168/2007 [2007] OJ L53/2.
[10] See Arts 85 and 88 TFEU, respectively.
[11] The formula 'Heads of State or Government' was designed to accommodate the constitutional position of the French President.

EEC budget.[12] More recently, the European Council has played a central role in mobilising the Union's response to many of the major challenges facing its Member States: for example, the fight against climate change; the problems with ratifying the CT and then the TL; and dealing with the consequences of the world financial crisis.[13]

With the TL, the European Council joined the fold of formal Union institutions; its organisation, powers and functions were also clarified and reformed. According to Article 15(1) TEU, the European Council shall provide the Union with the necessary impetus for its development and shall define the general political directions and priorities thereof. That overall political role is also given specific expression in various fields: for example, the European Council is to define the strategic interests and objectives of the Union in the field of external relations;[14] and its strategic guidelines for action within the Area of Freedom, Security and Justice.[15] Article 15(1) TEU also states that the European Council shall not exercise legislative functions. However, numerous provisions of the Treaties give the European Council power to take legally binding decisions of a 'quasi-constitutional' or 'high politics' nature: for example, on the Council's future configurations and system of rotating presidencies;[16] the future composition of the European Parliament as regards the allocation of MEPs between Member States;[17] the power to alter the number of Commissioners;[18] proposing the candidate for Commission President and final appointment of the Commission after its nominees have received the consent of the European Parliament;[19] and appointing the High Representative for Foreign Affairs and Security Policy.[20] As dealt with in greater detail elsewhere in this book, the European Council also plays an important role in issues such as mediating after the use by a Member State of an 'emergency brake' within the Council so as to prevent a majority vote being taken on certain sensitive policy questions;[21] or in situations where lack of unanimity within the Council could lead to a group of Member States being exceptionally authorised to embark upon an enhanced co-operation;[22] and also as regards accession to/withdrawal from the Union and amendment of the Treaties by the ordinary or various special revision procedures.[23]

One of the most important reforms to the European Council contained in the TL was to end the previous system of rotating the presidency of the European Council among the Member States. That system was deemed to create problems of consistency and continuity in defining the Union's political agenda; the tasks associated with the presidency had become too demanding to be discharged effectively by a person who acts at the

---

[12] The solution consisted of providing for an 'abatement' of the amount payable by the UK under the rules for the calculation of the 'own resources' which constitute the Union's revenue. Provision has been made for similar such abatements in successive Council Decisions on own resources.

[13] See further eg Editorial, 'An Ever Mighty European Council: Some Recent Institutional Developments' (2009) 46 *CMLRev* 1383.

[14] Art 22(1) TEU.

[15] Art 68 TFEU.

[16] Art 236 TFEU.

[17] Art 14(2) TEU.

[18] Art 17(5) TEU and Art 244 TFEU.

[19] Art 17(7) TEU.

[20] Art 18(1) TEU. See also eg Art 42(2) TEU on the decision to adopt a common defence policy; Art 86(4) TFEU on expanding the powers of a future European Public Prosecutor's Office; Art 7(2) TEU on determining that a Member State is guilty of a serious and persistent breach of the Union's core values.

[21] See further Chapter 4.

[22] See further Chapter 5.

[23] See further Chapter 2.

same time as his/her head of state or government; certain concerns were voiced about the potential for conflicts of interest between the President's role as impartial chair of the European Council and his/her duty to protect the national interests of the relevant Member State; moreover, the benefits of rotation in encouraging a sense of 'ownership' by all Member States over the European Council had become tenuous in a Union of 27 countries. After Lisbon, the European Council therefore acquired a more stable Presidency. Article 15(5) TEU provides that the President is to be elected by the European Council, acting by qualified majority vote (QMV), for a term of two and a half years (renewable once).[24] Article 15(6) TEU expressly states that he/she may not hold a national office. The European Council's first fixed President—Herman Van Rompuy, a former Prime Minister of Belgium—was duly elected in December 2009.[25]

According to Article 15(6) TEU, the President is responsible for chairing European Council meetings, ensuring the preparation and continuity of the European Council's work, facilitating cohesion and consensus within the European Council, presenting reports to the European Parliament after European Council meetings, and representing the EU externally at his/her level as regards the CFSP.[26] More detailed provisions governing the President's discharge of those functions, and indeed the internal functioning of the institution as a whole, are contained in the European Council's Rules of Procedure.[27]

As a result of the Lisbon reforms, the European Council is now composed of the heads of state or government of the Member States, together with its elected President and the President of the Commission.[28] Lisbon also formalised the established practice of holding European Council meetings twice every six months (with the possibility for the President to convene further meetings if the situation so requires).[29] According to Article 15(4) TEU, except where otherwise provided, the European Council shall reach decisions by consensus. True enough, some of the European Council's decisions are to be reached by unanimity,[30] certain others may be taken by QMV.[31] Where relevant, Article 235(1) TFEU provides that the definition of a qualified majority within the European Council is based on that applicable to the Council.[32] Where the European Council does decide an issue by voting (rather than by consensus), neither its own President nor the President of the Commission shall participate in the vote.[33]

---

[24] The President's term of office can be terminated according to the same procedure in the event of an impediment or serious misconduct.

[25] See European Council Decision 2009/879 [2009] OJ L315/48.

[26] Though without prejudice to the powers of the new High Representative for Foreign Affairs: see below.

[27] European Council Decision 2009/882 adopting its Rules of Procedure [2009] OJ L315/51. Note that, according to Art 235(4) TFEU, the European Council shall be assisted by the General Secretariat of the Council.

[28] The High Representative for Foreign Affairs takes part in the European Council's work but is not a formal member of the institution: see Art 15(2) TEU. Note also that the President of the European Parliament may be invited to be heard by the European Council: see Art 235(2) TFEU.

[29] Art 15(3) TEU.

[30] ie so that abstentions will not prevent adoption of the relevant decision: see Art 235(1) TFEU. Eg Arts 14(2), 17(5) and 42 TEU; Art 86(4) TFEU.

[31] eg Arts 15(5), 17(7) and 18(1) TEU; Art 236 TFEU.

[32] See further below. Note, however, that (unlike the situation within the Council) there does not appear to be any option, between 1 November 2014 and 31 March 2017, for members of the European Council to pick-and-choose between the old and new definitions of QMV: Art 3(2) of the Protocol on Transitional Provisions refers only to a member of the Council, not of the European Council.

[33] Art 235(1) TFEU.

III – THE COUNCIL

Article 16(2) TEU provides that the Council 'shall consist of a representative of each Member State *at ministerial level*, who may commit the government of the Member State in question and cast its vote' (emphasis added). It is therefore clear that each national representative within the Council must be a person holding political office, ie not a civil servant. The wording of Article 16(2) TEU does nevertheless allow Member States with a devolved structure to be represented, when the Council is dealing with matters falling within the competence of regional authorities, by a member of one of those authorities rather than by a minister in the central government.[34] In such a case, the regional minister concerned would have to be authorised to act on behalf of the Member State as a whole, so that his/her agreement to a matter on the Council agenda would bind that Member State both legally and politically.

In law, the Council is a unitary institution: in other words, it is the same institution with the same powers under the Treaties, whatever the particular national responsibilities of the ministers attending a given meeting. However, Article 16(6) TEU provides that the Council shall meet in different configurations. That provision expressly identifies two such configurations: the General Affairs Council (which ensures consistency in the work of the different Council configurations and both prepares for and follows-up meetings of the European Council) and the Foreign Affairs Council (which elaborates the Union's external action based on the strategic guidelines laid down by the European Council and ensures that such action is consistent). Eight other configurations were provisionally identified by the Council immediately following the entry into force of the TL;[35] that list was later approved with minor amendments by the European Council, exercising its powers under Article 236 TFEU to determine definitively the remaining Council configurations.[36] Among those formations, one might highlight the Economic and Financial Affairs (or Ecofin) Council; Agriculture and Fisheries; Competitiveness (including issues related to the internal market, industry, research and now also space); the Environment; and Employment, Social Policy, Health and Consumer Affairs. It is worth noting that, in some situations, the Treaties allow decisions to be taken by the Council without the participation of all 27 of its members: for example, certain decisions relating to Member States whose currency is the euro;[37] or where a group of Member States has been authorised to pursue 'enhanced co-operation' between themselves within a given field of Union activity.[38] Such different instances of 'flexibility' are considered further in Chapter 5.

Before the TL, the Presidency of the Council was held in turn by each of the Member States for periods of six months following an order laid down by the Council pursuant to ex-Article 203(2) EC.[39] However, Article 16(9) TEU now provides that the Presidency of Council configurations (other than the Foreign Affairs Council) shall be held by the Member States on the basis of equal rotation in accordance with conditions to be established by the European Council.[40] According to Decision 2009/881 of the European

---

[34] The UK could, for instance, be represented by a member of the Scottish Executive.
[35] See Decision 2009/878 [2009] OJ L315/46, based upon Art 4 of the Protocol on Transitional Provisions.
[36] See Decision 2010/594 [2010] OJ L263/12.
[37] See Arts 136–38 TFEU.
[38] See Art 330 TFEU.
[39] See eg Decision 2005/902 [2005] OJ L328/60.
[40] Acting by QMV under Art 236(b) TFEU.

Council, the Presidency should be held by pre-established groups of three Member States for a period of 18 months. Groups are to be made up on the basis of equal rotation, taking into account the diversity of Member States and their geographical balance. Unless they decide otherwise, each member of the group shall in turn chair for six months the relevant Council configurations, with the other members assisting the Chair on the basis of a common programme.[41] The first of the post-Lisbon 'team presidencies' consisted of Spain, Belgium and Hungary; they began their 18-month shared term on 1 January 2010.[42] The Presidency of the Foreign Affairs Council alone does not rotate; that configuration is presided over by the High Representative for Foreign Affairs and Security Policy (see below).[43] It is anticipated that those arrangements will facilitate greater coherence and continuity in the Council's multifarious activities.[44]

The duties of the Presidency, which are identified in greater detail in the Council's Rules of Procedure, include the convening of Council meetings, the establishment of the provisional agenda, taking the actual chair at meetings and ensuring the smooth conduct of discussions.[45] In particular, the Presidency has come to play an active role in managing the progress of Commission proposals through the Council. Negotiations between national delegations within the Council take place in relation to a series of compromise texts devised by the Presidency with a view to securing the necessary majority or unanimity for the adoption of the measure in question. A Presidency is expected to show objectivity in furthering proposals, without undue regard to its specific national interests.

The work of the Council is prepared by a Committee of Permanent Representatives of the Governments of the Member States (COREPER) who are senior national officials based in Brussels. The legal basis of COREPER's activities is Article 16(7) TEU read together with Article 240 TFEU. Its primary responsibility is to ensure consistency in the Council's work and to resolve various political and technical issues before draft decisions are presented to the Council for the latter's deliberation. COREPER's activities are prepared, in turn, by the work of a whole host of specialised committees and working parties made up of Member State delegates. The Council, COREPER and the various committees and working groups are assisted by an independent body of civil servants—the General Secretariat—under the responsibility of a Secretary-General appointed by the Council.[46]

In addition, with the extension of EU activity into new fields, the need was felt for the creation of various bodies capable of providing the Council with specialised back-up (also composed of senior national officials). Notable examples are the Economic and Financial Committee (concerned with supporting the co-ordination of national policies for the better functioning of the internal market);[47] the Political and Security Committee (concerned with the common foreign and security policy, including the political control and strategic direction of crisis management operations);[48] and the Standing Committee on Operational Cooperation on Internal Security (concerned with facilitating operational co-

---

[41] Decision 2009/881 [2009] OJ L315/50.

[42] See Council Decision 2009/908 [2009] OJ L322/28 for the list of 'team presidencies' envisaged up to 30 June 2020.

[43] See Arts 16(9) and 18(3) TEU.

[44] For a critical view of the Council's new system of rotating presidency teams within the post-TL Union, see Editorial, 'The Post-Lisbon Institutional Package: Do Old Habits Die Hard?' (2010) 47 *CMLRev* 597.

[45] Decision 2009/937 [2009] OJ L325/35.

[46] See Art 240(2) TFEU.

[47] See Art 134 TFEU.

[48] See Art 38 TEU.

ordination between the competent national authorities in the field of internal security).[49] The relationship between COREPER and these influential bodies is inevitably somewhat delicate; the contribution of the latter to the preparation of Council business is, however, stated by the relevant Treaty provisions to be 'without prejudice to Article 240' of the TFEU, thereby preserving the position of COREPER as the filter through which such business must pass. The principle is important because, with so many different formations of the Council, there is a danger that political coherence may be lost: COREPER is the only Council body able to take a horizontal view of the development of Union policies.

Turning from the composition and organisation of the Council to its powers, these are described in Article 16(1) TEU: the Council shall, jointly with the European Parliament, exercise legislative and budgetary functions; it shall also carry out policy-making and co-ordinating functions as laid down in the Treaties. For the purposes of this book, the Council's legislative powers are by far the most important and will be dealt with in greater detail in Chapter 4. Other functions, such as the Council's role in the opening and conclusion of agreements with third countries and international organisations, are also discussed in subsequent chapters.[50]

For now, it remains to discuss the rules by which the Council reaches its own decisions (whether of a legislative or non-legislative character).[51] The general rule is set out in Article 16(3) TEU: the Council shall act by QMV. Various provisions of the Treaties make exceptions to that general rule, usually by instructing that the Council shall act instead by unanimity.[52] The Treaties do, though, contain various mechanisms by which a requirement of unanimity within the Council can be converted to QMV without the need to adopt a formal Treaty amendment.[53]

The definition of QMV has long been highly problematic: its requires balancing the demographic weight of the larger Member States (which understandably wish to carry greater voting power in the Council, commensurate with their much larger proportion of the actual Union population) against the independence of the smaller Member States (which after all remain sovereign countries, even if their actual share of the overall Union population is very small). Before the entry into force of the TL, the Council operated under the so-called 'triple threshold' system established by the TN.[54] The *first* threshold was based upon a weighted allocation of votes among Member States: a qualified majority required at least 255 votes out of 345 (approximately 74 per cent), with the allocation of votes to the various Member States corresponding to differences in the size of their populations in a most rough and ready fashion.[55] The *second* threshold required that the votes in favour must, in any case, have been cast by a majority of Member States. This was intended to reassure the smaller countries that they could not be outvoted by a minority coalition of larger Member States, since (in theory) just 12 Member States could have had sufficient weighted votes to cross the first voting threshold.[56] The *third* threshold required

---

[49] See Art 71 TFEU.

[50] On the Union's external action, see Chapter 27.

[51] On the distinction between Union legislative and non-legislative acts, see Chapter 4.

[52] For examples, see Chapter 4.

[53] The so-called 'passerelle clauses': see Chapters 2 and 4.

[54] See ex-Art 205 EC.

[55] eg Germany, France, Italy and the UK had 29 votes each; Spain and Poland both had 27 votes; Belgium, Hungary, the Czech Republic, Greece and Portugal had 12 votes each; Denmark, Ireland, Lithuania, Finland and the Slovak Republic had 7 votes each; Estonia, Cyprus, Slovenia, Latvia and Luxembourg had 4 votes each.

[56] eg Belgium, Spain, Hungary, the Netherlands, Poland, the UK, the Czech Republic, Germany, Greece, France, Italy, plus any other Member State. It should be noted that, in the rather rare cases where the Council

that any member of the Council could request verification that the Member States who constituted the qualified majority on the basis of the previous two calculations further-more represented at least 62 per cent of the total Union population.[57] That requirement was intended to reassure the larger Member States that the Council could not be driven towards a particular decision by a coalition of small and medium sized countries.

Reforming that definition of QMV proved to be one of the main points of contention throughout the long process of constitutional reform which followed the Laeken European Council in December 2001. On the one hand, it was generally considered that the post-TN definition of QMV constituted an obstacle to efficient decision-making within the Council. On the other hand, the Member States were not prepared to swallow the rela-tively straightforward proposal made by the Convention on the Future of Europe, that a qualified majority should consist of a simple majority of Member States representing at least 60 per cent of the actual Union population.[58] Negotiations were further com-plicated by the determination of the incumbent Polish administration to preserve the highly favourable, if disproportionate, voting influence its country (together with Spain) had previously secured under the TN. The final package of reforms agreed under the TL are hardly a triumph of simplification. But they do succeed in consigning to the history books the idea of weighted votes, which gave disproportionate voting power to the smaller Member States and were increasingly unsustainable in the enlarged and enlarging Union, while retaining safeguards against the possibility that the larger Member States might, by the sheer size of their populations, find it too easy either to steamroll or scupper deci-sions within the Council.

The Lisbon reforms must be divided into three periods of time. The first runs, accord-ing to Article 16(5) TEU and Article 3(3) of the Protocol on Transitional Provisions, until 31 October 2014: the previous definition of QMV will continue to apply, the 'triple threshold' introduced by the TN requiring a weighted majority of votes from a simple majority of Member States representing at least 62 per cent of the actual Union popula-tion. The second period then runs from 1 November 2014 until 31 March 2017. According to Article 16(4) TEU, a new definition of QMV will come into play, ie consisting of at least 55 per cent of Member States, comprising at least 15 countries, representing at least 65 per cent of the actual Union population; furthermore, a blocking minority must include at least four Member States, failing which the qualified majority shall be deemed attained (a provision intended to reassure the smaller Member States that a few very large countries cannot form an automatic blocking minority solely on the basis of their populations).[59] However, during this period, pursuant to Article 16(5) TEU and Article 3(2) of the Protocol on Transitional Provisions, any Member State may instead request that the vote be taken in accordance with the old 'triple threshold' definition of a quali-

could act without a proposal from the Commission, the second threshold was raised to at least two-thirds of the Member States.

[57] For those purposes, the Council's Rules of Procedure contained the relevant population figures for each Member State, revised with effect from 1 January each year, in accordance with data provided by the Statistical Office of the European Communities.

[58] See Art 24(1) of the Convention's draft Constitutional Treaty; under Art 24(2), higher thresholds were to apply in respect of proposals not emanating from the Commission or the proposed Minister for Foreign Affairs.

[59] Higher thresholds apply where the Council does not act on a proposal from the Commission or the High Representative: see Art 238(2) TFEU.

fied majority as inherited from the TN. Finally, as from 1 April 2017, the new definition of QMV contained in Article 16(4) TEU alone will apply.[60]

To complicate matters yet further, Poland succeeded in securing an additional package of reforms—often referred to as 'the Ioannina Compromise'—intended to protect the interests of dissenting countries where the qualified majority made up by the other Member States is relatively slim. First, Decision 2009/857 (adopted by the Council shortly after the entry into force of the Lisbon Treaty on the basis of a text previously agreed by the IGC)[61] provides that, from 1 November 2014 until 31 March 2017, if countries representing at least three-quarters of the Member States or of the actual Union population necessary to constitute a blocking minority resulting from the application of Article 16(4) TEU[62] indicate their opposition to the adoption of an act by QMV, the Council must try to reach a satisfactory solution addressing their concerns, within a reasonable period and without prejudicing any mandatory deadlines. As from 1 April 2017, the same obligation will arise at the initiative of countries representing at least 55 per cent of the Member States or of the actual Union population necessary to constitute a blocking minority under Article 16(4) TEU.[63] Secondly, a new Protocol (No 9) on the Council decision relating to the implementation of the QMV rules provides that, before the Council should examine any proposal intended to amend or abrogate the Ioannina Decision or any of its provisions, or to modify indirectly its scope or meaning through the modification of another Union act, the European Council must hold a preliminary deliberation and reach a consensus on that proposal. Thus, while the Ioannina Compromise lacks any formal basis in Union primary law, the Ioannina Decision nevertheless enjoys a significant degree of constitutional protection against future alteration.

Although QMV is now the rule for Council decision-making, and unanimity is reserved for decisions of an especially sensitive character, there is a long tradition within the Council of seeking (wherever possible) to reach decisions through consensus—thus guaranteeing that all (or at least the great majority of) Member States feel able to subscribe to a given outcome. Many commentators had feared that enlargement of the Union into central and eastern Europe might lead to either prolonged stalemate and paralysis, or increasingly antagonistic majority voting, within the Council, but such fears do not seem to have been borne out in practice.[64] The Council still works towards achieving a broad consensus among the Member States; the important point is that, if such compromise is not forthcoming, QMV does permit the Council ultimately to override the objections of those Member States unable to muster a blocking minority.[65]

It is worth noting that, under Article 16(8) TEU, the Council shall meet in public when

---

[60] Again, with higher thresholds applicable where the proposal does not emanate from the Commission or the High Representative: see Art 238(2) TFEU.

[61] [2009] OJ L314/73.

[62] Or, where applicable, Art 238(2) TFEU.

[63] Or, where applicable, Art 238(2) TFEU.

[64] See the recent empirical study of voting patterns within the Council by R Dehousse and F Deloche-Gaudez, 'Voting in the Council of Ministers: The Impact of Enlargement' in A Ott and E Vos (eds), *Fifty Years of European Integration: Foundations and Perspectives* (The Hague, TMC Asser Press, 2009).

[65] The so-called 'Luxembourg Compromise'—seen in some quarters as an attempt to reintroduce a de facto veto even in areas subject to QMV and which was the subject of much critical discussion in past times—no longer deserves such detailed consideration. See the last edition of this textbook for further details: A Arnull, A Dashwood, M Dougan, M Ross, E Spaventa and D Wyatt, *Wyatt & Dashwood's EU Law*, 5th edn (London, Sweet & Maxwell, 2006) para 3-010.

it deliberates and votes on a draft Union legislative act.[66] That is an important step towards countering widespread criticism of the Council's perceived secrecy as a legislative chamber, and suspicions about cynical political horse-trading between Member States. In fact, thanks to reforms to the Council's Rules of Procedure enacted during the 'period of reflection' which followed the French and Dutch referenda rejecting the Constitutional Treaty, many of the Council's legislative deliberations and some of its non-legislative debates had already been opened up to the public.[67] Detailed rules for implementing the principle of openness in Council business are now to be found in the latter's post-TL Rules of Procedure.[68]

IV – THE COMMISSION

Unlike the Council, whose members directly represent the interests of their Governments, the Commission has a vocation to further the interests of the Union as a whole.[69] The members of the Commission are required to be persons 'whose independence is beyond doubt',[70] and in carrying out its responsibilities, the Commission 'shall be completely independent'.[71] Members of the Commission may neither seek nor take instructions from any government or other body; each Member State has undertaken to respect that principle and not to seek to influence Commissioners in the performance of their tasks.[72] The rule that the Commission acts by a majority of its members[73] provides a further guarantee that its decisions will not reflect, even inadvertently, particular national viewpoints.

As with the definition of QMV within the Council, so too the composition of the Commission has long proved to be a tricky institutional question for the Union. At the time of accession of Austria, Finland and Sweden to the EU, the number of members of the Commission was fixed at 20.[74] That followed the previous convention whereby one Commissioner be appointed from each of the smaller Member States, and two from each of the larger Member States (Germany, France, Italy, Spain and the United Kingdom). However, it became generally accepted, during preparations for the enlargement into central and eastern Europe, that a reduction in the number of Commissioners was necessary to prevent the institution from becoming unwieldy.[75] The issue was nevertheless fraught for both the larger Member States (who were under pressure to sacrifice their second Commissioner) and the smaller ones (who feared that any reduction in the number of Commissioners would mean their not being 'represented' in the College at all). A compromise agreement was reached under the TN: the Commission which took office in

---

[66] See also Art 15(2) TFEU. On Union legislative acts, see Chapter 4.

[67] See Art 8 of the Council's Rules of Procedure (as in force at that time) [2006] OJ L285/47. See further eg Editorial, 'In the Meantime . . . Further Progress in Transparency and Democracy while the Constitution is Dormant' (2006) 43 *CMLRev* 1243.

[68] See Arts 7–9 of the Council's Rules of Procedure (current version) [2009] OJ L325/35.

[69] See Art 17(1) TEU.

[70] Art 17(3) TEU.

[71] Art 17(3) TEU.

[72] Art 245 TFEU.

[73] Art 250 TFEU.

[74] See ex-Art 213(1) EC.

[75] On the pros and cons, see Justus Lipsius, 'The 1996 Intergovernmental Conference' (1995) 20 *ELRev* 265; A Dashwood, *Reviewing Maastricht: Issues for the 1996 IGC* (London, Sweet & Maxwell, 1996) 152 *et seq.*

November 2004 would comprise one national from each Member State; however, the Commission due to be appointed to office in November 2009 would have fewer members than the number of Member States.[76] The Council (acting unanimously) was to fix the precise number of Commissioners, as well as to lay down implementing arrangements for a rotation system between nationals of the different Member States, based on the principle of equality, reflecting satisfactorily the demographic and geographical range of all the Member States.[77]

Before those Nice reforms to reduce the size of the 2009 Commission took effect, however, a new system was introduced by the TL. According to Article 17(4) TEU, the Commission appointed between the date of entry into force of the TL and 31 October 2014 shall still consist of one national per Member State.[78] Thus, the Commission appointed (after a series of delays) in February 2010 (with a mandate to remain in office until 31 October 2014) does indeed contain 27 members, ie one from each of the Member States. According to Article 17(5) TEU, however, subsequent Commissions shall consist of a number of members equal to two-thirds of the number of Member States,[79] unless the European Council, acting unanimously, decides to alter this number. Those members are to be selected on the basis of equal rotation between the Member States, and must reflect the demographic and geographical range of all Member States. The detailed rotation system is to be established by the European Council, acting unanimously, and subject to the rule contained in Article 244 TFEU, whereby the difference between the total number of terms of office held by nationals of any given pair of Member States may never be more than one.[80]

Once more, however, events have overtaken plans to reduce the size of the Commission. As part of the deal to persuade the Irish government to hold a second referendum on ratification of the TL, and to persuade the Irish people to vote in the latter's favour, the European Council at its meetings in December 2008 and June 2009 agreed to exercise its powers under Article 17(5) TEU so as to reinstate the principle that the Commission should comprise one member from each Member State.[81] Thus, years of often difficult debates and two fully fledged Treaty timetables for shrinking the Commission have in the end come to nought: it seems that the Commission will remain with one-member-per-country well into the future, buying political acceptance for the remainder of the TL's reforms, albeit at the potential cost of a certain degree of unwieldiness in the functioning of the Commission itself.

The procedure for the appointment of the President and the other members of the Commission is found in Article 17(7) TEU. Amendments since the TEU have both enhanced the role of the European Parliament in the selection process, and given the President-designate a greater say in the composition of his/her 'team', as well as reducing the hurdles for decision-making by the Council. The first step in the procedure is the nomination by the European Council (acting by QMV) of a candidate for Commission President. The candidate then requires election by the European Parliament (acting by a majority of its component members). Next, the Council (acting by qualified majority

---

[76] See ex-Art 213(1) EC (as amended).
[77] See Art 4(3) of the Protocol on enlargement of the EU (now repealed).
[78] Including the President and the High Representative.
[79] Including the President and the High Representative.
[80] Note also Declaration No 10 annexed to the Final Act of the IGC which adopted the TL: [2010] OJ C83/342.
[81] See European Council Conclusions of 11–12 December 2008; and of 18–19 June 2009.

and in common accord with the President-elect) shall adopt the list of persons it proposes to appoint as the remaining members of the Commission—selected on the basis of suggestions made by the Member States, having regard to the stated criteria of general competence, European commitment and independence.[82] The whole slate of Commissioners is then subject to a vote of consent by the European Parliament.[83] The final step in the procedure is the formal appointment of the entire Commission by the European Council (acting by qualified majority).

The appointment procedure is designed to ensure both a more coherent Commission and one more politically accountable to the European Parliament. Thus, when proposing its candidate for Commission President, the European Council is expressly instructed to take into account the elections to the European Parliament—a reform that is meant both to increase the political influence of the MEPs and hence the incentive for citizens to vote at the European parliamentary elections, and also to bolster the Commission's own legitimacy by linking its complexion more closely to the popular will as represented in the European Parliament. Furthermore, the term of office for each Commission (five years)[84] has been aligned with that of the European Parliament: each new College of Commissioners will be vetted by MEPs newly elected in the previous June. That the Parliament intends to take its new responsibilities seriously was well illustrated by the difficulties encountered in securing approval for the Barroso Commission in autumn 2004. The affair was sparked by the highly controversial, indeed offensive, views of the Italian nominee to the Justice, Freedom and Security portfolio (which encompasses responsibility for the Union's anti-discrimination policy) on issues concerning homosexuality and the role of women in society. At one point, after the President-designate attempted a show of political strength by vowing support for his 'team' as nominated by the Member States, the scandal threatened to end in an unprecedented parliamentary rejection of the entire Commission. The matter was only resolved when both the Italian and Latvian nominees (the latter having also been severely criticised by MEPs) were replaced by figures more acceptable to the European Parliament. What was seen in some quarters as a crisis which had both delayed the appointment and damaged the credibility of the new Commission was interpreted by other commentators as a victory for democracy and accountability within the Union. A similarly robust approach to the scrutiny of proposed Commissioners was evident after the European parliamentary elections in summer 2009: the Parliament's rigorous approach to assessing the competence and suitability of individual nominees led directly to the withdrawal of the Bulgarian candidate, and was at least partly responsible for the delayed appointment of the new Commission as a whole only in February 2010.[85]

The Treaties have increasingly sought to bolster the powers of the President within the Commission. According to Article 17(6) TEU, the President shall lay down the guidelines within which the Commission is to work and decide upon the internal organisation of the Commission (ensuring that it acts consistently, efficiently and as a collegiate body). He/she shall structure and allocate the Commission's duties among its members and may reshuffle that allocation of responsibilities during the Commission's term of office.[86] The President

---

[82] See Art 17(3) TEU.
[83] Including the President and the High Representative.
[84] Art 17(3) TEU.
[85] See European Council Decision 2010/80 [2010] OJ L38/7.
[86] See Art 248 TFEU. Save for the responsibilities incumbent upon the High Representative by virtue of Art 18(4) TEU.

may also appoint Vice-Presidents from among the members of the Commission.[87] Furthermore, a Commissioner must resign if the President so requests.[88]

The Commission is assisted by a staff of permanent officials under a Secretary General, who are organised into Directorates General and various other services. In addition, each Commissioner has a small personal staff (or *cabinet*) composed partly of political associates and seconded national officials and partly of seconded Union officials. Meetings of the heads of these personal staffs (the *Chefs de Cabinet*) prepare the weekly meetings of the Commission.

The various elements that define the complex role of the Commission are described in Article 17(1) TEU in the following terms:

> The Commission shall promote the general interest of the Union and take appropriate initiatives to that end. It shall ensure the application of the Treaties, and of measures adopted by the institutions pursuant to them. It shall oversee the application of Union law under the control of the Court of Justice of the European Union. It shall execute the budget and manage programmes. It shall exercise coordinating, executive and management functions, as laid down in the Treaties. With the exception of the common foreign and security policy, and other cases provided for in the Treaties, it shall ensure the Union's external representation. It shall initiate the Union's annual and multiannual programming with a view to achieving inter-institutional agreements.

For the purposes of this book, however, only several key aspects of the Commission's functions will provide the subject for detailed consideration in subsequent chapters: for example, the Commission's power to initiate the Union legislative process by bringing forward proposals;[89] the Commission's responsibilities in implementing Union legislative acts once they have been adopted;[90] and the Commission's role as 'guardian of the Treaties' by bringing judicial procedures against the other institutions and especially against the Member States for breaching their obligations under Union law.[91]

V – A NOTE ON THE HIGH REPRESENTATIVE OF THE UNION FOR FOREIGN AFFAIRS AND SECURITY POLICY

Having discussed both the Council and the Commission, we should dwell briefly on one of the chief constitutional innovations of the Lisbon Treaty, which has created a novel bridge between those two otherwise very distinct institutions.

A principal objective of the reform process launched by the European Council at Nice in 2000, and continued in earnest after the European Council meeting in Laeken in 2001, was to furnish the Union with an institutional framework capable of executing its external policies more effectively and coherently. Both the Convention on the Future of Europe, and the IGC which agreed the doomed Constitutional Treaty, had proposed creating the

---

[87] Besides the High Representative, who is automatically a Vice-President.

[88] Art 17(6) TEU. In the case of the High Representative, the European Council must also agree to end his/her term of office (acting by QMV): see Arts 17(6) and 18(1) TEU.

[89] See Chapter 4.

[90] See Chapter 4.

[91] See Chapter 6.

post of 'Minister for Foreign Affairs'. That new post was designed to amalgamate two existing but institutionally entirely separate functions: first, that of the High Representative
for the Common Foreign and Security Policy (who was also the Secretary General of the
Council); and secondly, that of the Commissioner for External Relations (who was obviously a member of the Commission). The awkward division of powers, and potential for
institutional rivalry, between those two positions was widely seen as an undesirable source
of weakness in the Union's ability to realise its external policies. Following the negative
referenda on the CT in France and the Netherlands, and the 'period of reflection' insti-
gated by the European Council, the Member States came to feel that the title 'Minister'
was perhaps unhelpful in conveying the true nature of this institutional reform to the
wider public. The post itself was therefore retained under the TL, but renamed the High
Representative of the Union for Foreign Affairs and Security Policy.

According to Article 18(2) TEU, the High Representative shall conduct the Union's
common foreign and security policy.[92] In particular, he/she will enjoy a power of initiative as regards CFSP proposals; and will be responsible for implementing the CFSP under
mandate from the Council.[93] The High Representative will, moreover, preside over the
Foreign Affairs Council, whether it is considering CFSP or other external relations matters
such as the common commercial policy.[94] However, the chief constitutional novelty of the
High Representative is that he/she will simultaneously be associated with the Council *and*
a member of the Commission (in fact, one of its Vice-Presidents). In the latter capacity,
according to Article 18(4) TEU, the High Representative shall ensure the consistency of
the Union's external action, with responsibility within the Commission for external relations and co-ordinating other aspects of the Union's external action. Under Article 15(2)
TEU, the High Representative shall also take part in the work of the European Council,
though without formally becoming a member thereof.

When the Convention's original proposals were first published, doubts were expressed
about whether the same person could really owe their institutional loyalty to both the
Council and the Commission. However, the final text of the TL makes clear that the High
Representative should be bound by the Commission's procedures *only* when discharging
his/her responsibilities under Article 18(4) TEU, and *only* to the extent that this is consistent with his/her position within the Council. In other words, the High Representative
may well be 'double-hatted'—but his/her Council hat will sit on top of the Commission
one at the final stage of decision-making by the Foreign Affairs Council. In any event,
the Treaties provide for the High Representative to be assisted in his/her work by a new
'European External Action Service' (EEAS) made up of officials from relevant departments
within the Council's General Secretariat and the Commission as well as staff seconded
from the Member State's own diplomatic services.[95]

According to Article 18(1) TEU, the High Representative is to be appointed by the

---

[92] cf Art 15(6) TEU on external representation of the Union by the President of the European Council,
without prejudice to powers of the High Representative.

[93] See the detailed provisions on external action in general and the CFSP in particular contained in Title V
TEU. See further Chapter 27.

[94] Art 18(3) TEU.

[95] Art 27(3) TEU. After some difficult negotiations, the legal acts necessary to make the EEAS operational
were adopted during the course of 2010: see Council Decision 2010/427 establishing the organisation and functioning of the European External Action Service [2010] OJ L201/30; also Reg 1080/2010 [2010] OJ L311/1 and
Reg 1081/2010 [2010] OJ L311/9.

European Council (acting by QMV) with the agreement of the Commission President.[96] In December 2009, Catherine Ashton (a UK national and former member of the Commission) was appointed as the Union's very first new-style High Representative.[97] Since the High Representative is also one of the Commission's Vice-Presidents, he/she must be approved, collectively with the remainder of the College, by the European Parliament.[98] Moreover, as we shall see, in the event of a motion of censure being passed by the European Parliament against the Commission, the High Representative must resign from his/her duties within the Commission (but will remain in post for those responsibilities associated with the Council).[99]

VI – THE EUROPEAN PARLIAMENT

The European Parliament has undergone more fundamental changes in its history than any of the other Union institutions. First, as to its name: it was called the 'Assembly' in the founding Treaties, and continued to be referred to as such in Council acts until its change of name was officially recognised by the SEA. Secondly, as to its composition: originally a nominated body, its members drawn from the parliamentary institutions of the Member States, the European Parliament was transformed into a body of representatives directly elected by universal suffrage in June 1979 when the first elections were held under rules which had been laid down by an Act annexed to a Council decision of 1976.[100] Thirdly, as to its powers: described in the founding Treaties as exercising 'advisory and supervisory powers', the European Parliament has gradually acquired significant new powers, particularly in the legislative and budgetary spheres, thus becoming the equal of the Council in most (though not all) of the Union's policy fields.

The members of the European Parliament are to be elected for a fixed-term of five years by direct universal suffrage in a free and secret ballot.[101] The basic legal framework governing elections to the European Parliament remains that contained in the 1976 Act. The latter was approved by the Council under the procedure now prescribed in Article 223(1) TFEU. That procedure requires a proposal to be drawn up by the European Parliament 'for the election of its Members by direct universal suffrage in accordance with a uniform procedure in all Member States or in accordance with principles common to all Member States'; and empowers the Council (acting unanimously in accordance with a special legislative procedure and after obtaining the consent of the European Parliament) to lay down the necessary provisions.[102] However, the latter will only enter into force after their approval by the Member States in accordance with their respective constitutional requirements. It did not prove possible in 1976 to agree a uniform electoral procedure. However, the amended version of the 1976 Act requires that, in each Member State, members of the European Parliament must be elected on the basis of proportional representation (using

---

[96] The European Council may end his/her term of office by the same procedure. This applies also in situations where the Commission President requests the High Representative to resign: see Art 17(6) TEU.

[97] See European Council Decisions 2009/880 [2009] OJ L315/49 and 2009/950 [2009] OJ L328/69.

[98] Art 17(7) TEU.

[99] See Art 17(8) TEU and Art 234 TFEU.

[100] Decision 76/787 [1976] OJ L278/1.

[101] See Art 14(3) TEU.

[102] On the Union's 'special legislative procedures', see further Chapter 4.

either the list system or the single transferable vote).[103] Subject to the various provisions of the Act, the electoral procedure itself is to be governed in each Member State by its own national provisions—though such national provisions should not affect the essentially proportional nature of the voting system.[104]

Article 14(2) TEU states that the European Parliament shall be composed of representatives of the Union's citizens not exceeding 751 in number (including the President of the European Parliament). The allocation of seats between Member States should be degressively proportional, with a minimum of 6 and a maximum of 96 seats for any given country. On the basis of those principles, the European Council (acting unanimously on the initiative of the European Parliament and with the latter's consent) should decide on the Parliament's composition. This new system of allocating MEPs to Member States through secondary instruments is intended to offer greater flexibility, particularly in the light of future enlargements, as compared to the previous approach (whereby changes to the allocation of MEPs to Member States required formal amendment of the Treaty itself).

In this context too, however, the delays which arose in ratifying the TL created certain tricky problems. It had been anticipated that the revised Treaties would already be in force before the 2009 elections to the European Parliament. On the one hand, the entry into force of the TL was not to affect the composition of the European Parliament for the remainder of its 2004–09 term.[105] On the other hand, a draft decision on the new allocation of MEPs between Member States for the 2009–14 term stood ready for adoption by the European Council, under the revised Article 14(2) TEU, in good time before the elections due to be held in summer 2009. That draft decision envisaged one Member State (Germany) losing some of its MEPs, while others (such as Spain, France and the United Kingdom) were to gain additional seats.[106] But that neat transition never materialised: the 2009 elections were held while the TL was still in abeyance, and thus on the basis of the Treaty provisions as they then stood; only 736 MEPs were elected, including those Germany should have lost, and excluding the extra seats intended for other Member States.[107] The European Council decided that special provisions were needed to address this messy and unintended situation: all MEPs already elected to the European Parliament in summer 2009 should remain in office, but the additional MEPs provided for by the TL should also be able to take up their posts, thus raising the total number of MEPs to 754 for the remainder of the 2009–14 term, in derogation from the ceiling laid down in Article 14(2) TEU.[108] The complex amendments to Union primary law necessary to implement this solution were agreed upon at a brief IGC held in June 2010,[109] though the changes will only enter into force upon ratification by all 27 Member States.[110]

Once elected, MEPs are organised into cross-national *political groups*, broadly following the ideological divisions that are familiar in domestic politics. Thus, the two largest groups are the Group of the European People's Party (composed in the main of Christian Democrats from continental Member States) and the Group of the Progressive Alliance of Socialists and Democrats in the European Parliament. In addition, Article 10(4) TEU rec-

---

[103] Art 1 of the Act as amended by Decision 2002/772 [2002] OJ L283/1.
[104] Art 7 of the Act as amended by Decision 2002/772 [2002] OJ L283/1.
[105] Art 2 of the Protocol (No 36) on Transitional Provisions.
[106] See Art 14(2) TEU; Protocol (No 36) on transitional provisions; Declarations No 4 and 5.
[107] See ex-Arts 189 and 190 EC.
[108] See, in particular, European Council Conclusions of 11–12 December 2008; and of 18–19 June 2009.
[109] Published at [2010] OJ C263/1.
[110] See Art 48(4) TEU.

ognises that *political parties* at the European level contribute to forming European political awareness and to expressing the will of the Union's citizens. Against that background, Article 224 TFEU empowers the European Parliament and the Council to adopt Union legislation governing political parties at the European level, particularly as regards their funding.[111]

The scope of the franchise in elections to the European Parliament also raises some interesting questions. In principle, each Member State is obliged to offer voting rights for European Parliament elections to all Union citizens resident within its territory, on the same terms as own nationals.[112] However, in *Spain v United Kingdom*, the Court of Justice was asked to clarify whether *only* Union citizens were entitled to vote and stand in elections to the European Parliament, or whether those rights could *also* be extended to certain third-country nationals.[113] The Court noted that the relevant provisions of the pre-TL Treaties neither expressly defined who may vote/stand in the European Parliament elections, nor clearly excluded the possibility that a third-country national might be entitled to do so. In particular, the reference in ex-Articles 189 and 190 EC to the European Parliament representing the 'peoples of the Member States' had different meanings in different countries and languages and could not be taken as determinative of the issue. The Court concluded that, in the state of Union law as it then stood, the definition of the persons entitled to vote/stand in the European Parliament elections fell within the competence of each Member State.[114] However, the relevant provisions of the Treaties as revised by the TL now seem more precise about the European Parliament's democratic franchise. For example, Article 14(2) TEU states that the European Parliament 'shall be composed of representatives of the Union's citizens'; Article 10 TEU concerning the principle of representative democracy also refers repeatedly to 'citizens'.[115] It is therefore unclear whether the approach adopted by some Member States, of permitting certain third-country nationals to vote in elections to the European Parliament, remains compatible with Union law after the entry into force of the TL. One might feel somewhat uneasy at the prospect of disenfranchising whole classes of persons whose rights to vote/stand in the European Parliament elections have already been sanctioned under Union law. For its part, the Court may yet decide that, while the revised Treaty text undeniably leaves less room for manoeuvre, the changes agreed under the TL nevertheless fail to outweigh the other sorts of factor taken into consideration in reaching the conclusion in *Spain v United Kingdom*: for example, that an express principle of parliamentary representation for Union citizens does not necessarily exclude the recognition of limited electoral rights also for certain third-country nationals; or that, given the territorial basis upon which MEPs are allocated across Member States, the decision by one country to confer electoral

[111] On which, see Reg 2004/2003 on the regulations governing political parties at European level and the rules regarding their funding [2003] OJ L297/1.

[112] Art 22(2) TFEU. Union citizens are also entitled to stand for election as candidates for the European Parliament in their Member State of residence. See also Dir 93/109 laying down detailed arrangements for the exercise of the right to vote and stand as a candidate in elections to the European Parliament for citizens of the Union residing in a Member State of which they are not nationals [1993] OJ L329/34. See further eg J Shaw, *The Transformation of Union Citizenship: Electoral Rights and the Restructuring of Political Space* (Cambridge, Cambridge University Press, 2007).

[113] Case C-145/04 *Spain v United Kingdom* [2006] ECR I-7917. See further eg L Besselink, Annotation of *Spain v United Kingdom* etc (2008) 45 *CMLRev* 787.

[114] Albeit that that competence must be exercised 'in compliance with [Union] law'. For an indication of what this might require, see Case C-300/04 *Eman and Sevinger* [2006] ECR I-8055.

[115] That is true not only of the English version, but also eg the French, Italian, Spanish and German texts.

rights upon specific categories of third-country nationals has no effect upon the choice or number of MEPs elected in any other Member State.[116]

Article 14(1) TEU defines the functions of the European Parliament in the following terms:

> The European Parliament shall, jointly with the Council, exercise legislative and budgetary functions. It shall exercise functions of political control and consultation as laid down in the Treaties. It shall elect the President of the Commission.

The formal powers of the European Parliament are thus broadly of three kinds: it participates in the adoption of Union legislation; together with the Council, it constitutes the budgetary authority of the Union; and it exercises political supervision over the performance by the Commission of its tasks under the Treaties. Besides these formal powers, the European Parliament evidently considers that it is entitled, as the collective voice of the Union electorate, to express reactions to political events both within the Union and in the wider world. It does not have an independent right of initiative, but tends instead to bring its influence to bear on the Commission and (so far as it is able) also on the Council. For that purpose, the position of the European Parliament was strengthened by an amendment first introduced under the TEU: the power under Article 225 TFEU to request the Commission to submit any appropriate proposal on matters on which the Parliament considers that a Union act is required for the purpose of implementing the Treaties.[117]

The participation of the European Parliament in the Union's law-making process will be discussed further in Chapter 4. In the present chapter, we will confine our attention to the Parliament's role as political watchdog of the Commission.

Detailed supervision by the European Parliament over the activities of the Commission is made possible by the regular attendance of members of the Commission at part-sessions of the Parliament, and of Commissioners or their officials at meetings of Parliamentary committees. There is an express Treaty obligation on members of the Commission to reply to written and oral questions,[118] and, following the first enlargement of the Communities in 1973, a question time, clearly influenced by the British model, was introduced. The Treaty also requires the Commission to submit an annual general report to the Parliament,[119] and the practice has developed of publishing, in conjunction with that report, other reports of a more specialised character relating, for instance, to competition policy, which are an important source of information. It is worth noting that, although not formally obliged by the Treaty to do so, both the European Council and the Council also reply to questions from the European Parliament.[120]

The supervisory powers of the European Parliament were reinforced after the TEU in three ways. First, the Parliament was given the right, under Article 226 TFEU, to set up temporary Committees of Inquiry to investigate 'alleged contraventions or maladministration in the implementation of Union law' (except where the matter is *sub judice*). It is

---

[116] Note Declaration No 64 annexed to the Final Act, in which the UK expresses its understanding that the revised Treaties are not intended to change the basis for the franchise for EP elections; though the rather cryptic Declaration No 57, made by Italy, might seem to express a contrary understanding.

[117] cf the Council's right under Art 241 TFEU to request the Commission to undertake studies and to submit to it any appropriate proposals. Note also the 2003 inter-institutional agreement on 'better law-making' concluded between the Parliament, the Council and Commission [2003] OJ C321/1, para 9.

[118] Art 230(2) TFEU.

[119] Arts 233 and 249(2) TFEU.

[120] See Art 230(3) TFEU; Rules of Procedure of the European Council, Decision 2009/882 [2009] OJ L315/51; Rules of Procedures of the Council, Decision 2009/937 [2009] OJ L325/35.

interesting to note that the text does not explicitly limit the scope of such investigations to contraventions or maladministration for which Union institutions or bodies are allegedly responsible. Secondly, Article 227 TFEU gives any citizen of the Union, or any resident of a Member State, the right to petition the European Parliament on a matter falling within the Union's fields of activity and which affects him/her directly. Thirdly, under Article 228 TFEU, the European Parliament appoints an Ombudsman who is empowered to receive complaints concerning instances of maladministration in the activities of Union institutions or bodies (other than the Court of Justice of the European Union acting judicially). If the Ombudsman establishes a case of maladministration, he/she must give the institution or body concerned three months in which to inform him/her of its views; then forward a report to the European Parliament and to the relevant institution or body, while also informing the complainant of the outcome. The Ombudsman is appointed after each election to the European Parliament for the duration of the latter's term of office.

The effectiveness of the European Parliament's supervision of the Commission does not depend only on the moral authority of its democratic mandate: Article 234 TFEU puts into the hands of the Parliament the supreme political weapon of a motion of censure by which it can force the resignation of the College of Commissioners.[121] If a motion of censure is tabled, three days must elapse before a vote is taken; and, for the motion to be carried, there must be a two-thirds majority of the votes cast, representing a majority of the members of the European Parliament. In the past it was sometimes claimed that the power to dismiss the Commission by a vote of censure was too powerful a weapon ever to be used. Even if that claim was ever plausible, the events of March 1999 demonstrated that it should no longer be considered so: the Commission presided over by Jacques Santer resigned *en masse*, following an adverse report by a Committee of Experts which had been appointed to investigate claims of fraud, mismanagement and nepotism within certain Directorates General. The resignation was evidently precipitated by pressure from the European Parliament, where it had become clear that a motion of censure would otherwise, in all likelihood, be adopted. That episode, it has been said, marked the political coming of age of the Parliament.[122] Together with the more recent scrutiny surrounding the appointment of the Barroso Commission in 2004 and then again in 2009–2010, it suggests that the Parliament does indeed take its role of supervising the Commission seriously—even when the political stakes for the Union as a whole are very high.

However, the resignation of the Santer Commission also revealed a potential weakness in the Parliament's political supervision over the Commission: the power of censure can only be exercised against the entire Commission, not against any individual member(s) of the College. Successive European Parliaments have attempted to alleviate that potential weakness through the conclusion of inter-institutional agreements with the Commission. The Framework Agreement on relations between the Parliament and Commission agreed in 2000 provided that, where the Parliament expressed a lack of confidence in any given member of the College, the President of the Commission should seriously consider whether to request that member to resign.[123] Revisions to that Framework Agreement approved in 2005 further provided that, if the Commission President refused to request

---

[121] According to Art 17(8) TEU and Art 234 TFEU, if the motion of censure is carried, the members of the Commission shall resign as a body, while the High Representative for Foreign Affairs shall resign from his/her duties within the Commission.

[122] See Editorial Comment (1999) 36 *CMLRev* 270.

[123] [2001] OJ C121/122.

the relevant member's resignation, he/she should explain that decision before the European Parliament.[124] However, the Council soon expressed concerns that any such informal understanding between the Parliament and Commission in fact brought about an inappropriate shift in the institutional balance established under Article 234 TFEU.[125] After all, the Treaties did not intend to offer the European Parliament any power to force the resignation of an individual Commissioner. Nevertheless, the contested provisions were maintained in the latest version of the Framework Agreement, agreed by the European Parliament and the Commission in October 2010;[126] for its part, the Council has reiterated its opposition to provisions which have the effect of according the European Parliament prerogatives not provided for under the Treaties and of limiting the autonomy of the Commission President.[127]

VII – THE COURT OF JUSTICE OF THE EUROPEAN UNION

Article 19(1) TEU provides that the 'Court of Justice of the European Union' shall include the Court of Justice (widely referred to as the European Court of Justice or ECJ); the General Court (previously known as the Court of First Instance or CFI); and specialised courts (formerly known as Judicial Panels). Their role is to ensure that 'in the interpretation and application of the Treaties the law is observed'.

The Court of Justice, in particular, plays a central role in the system created by the Treaties and has made a vital contribution to the Union's development.[128] Some of the concepts which are fundamental to the way in which the Union functions are to be found, not in the Treaties themselves, but in the case law of the Court of Justice: for example, the doctrine that Union law may produce direct effect and thus act as an autonomous source of law within the national legal systems and, indeed, should as such enjoy primacy over any conflicting provisions of purely domestic law.[129] The Court's profound influence over the Union legal order has repeatedly led to allegations of 'judicial activism'—that the Court is stepping beyond its proper judicial function, by creating new law without any real mandate under the Treaties, and sometimes doing so even in apparent defiance of the Treaty texts themselves. However, the Court's many defenders are quick to stress the often selective nature of such critiques and to highlight the unique nature of the judicial role within the Union legal order—as well as to recall the many valuable interventions the Court has made in fields such as respect for fundamental rights, the free movement of goods and the rights of Union citizens.[130]

---

[124] [2006] OJ C117E/125.

[125] [2005] OJ C161/1.

[126] [2010] OJ L304/47.

[127] [2010] OJ C287/1.

[128] See further eg R Dehousse, *The European Court of Justice* (London, Palgrave Macmillan, 1998); G de Búrca and J Weiler (eds), *The European Court of Justice* (Oxford, Oxford University Press, 2001); A Arnull, *The European Union and its Court of Justice*, 2nd edn (Oxford, Oxford University Press, 2006).

[129] On which, see further Chapter 8.

[130] See further eg H Rasmussen, *On Law and Policy in the European Court of Justice* (Dordrecht, Martinus Nijhoff, 1986); M Cappelletti, 'Is the European Court of Justice "Running Wild"?' (1987) 12 *ELRev* 3; T Hartley, 'The European Court, Judicial Objectivity and the Constitution of the European Union' (1996) 112 *LQR* 95;

An extensive treatment of the institutional structure, procedural functioning or herme-neutic techniques of the Union judiciary falls beyond the scope of this chapter and indeed of this book.[131] For present purposes, we need only summarise the key features of the Union's judicial architecture. Detailed provisions concerning the Union courts are found in Part Six of the TFEU, in the Protocol (No 3) on the Statute of the Court of Justice of the European Union, and in the Rules of Procedure adopted by the Union courts.[132]

The Court of Justice consists of one judge from each Member State, ie currently 27 judges.[133] In accordance with Article 251 TFEU, the Court of Justice shall sit in chambers, or in a Grand Chamber, though it may also sit as a Full Court. Most cases are assigned to chambers of either three or five judges (according to the importance and complexity of the case). The Grand Chamber of 13 judges is required when a Member State or Union institution that is party to the proceedings so requests. In cases of exceptional impor-tance, a Full Court may be summoned; the Full Court is also required to sit in certain disputes, such as proceedings for removal of the Ombudsman or for disciplining a way-ward Commissioner or member of the Court of Auditors.[134]

In addition, the Court of Justice is assisted by Advocates General.[135] There are currently eight Advocates General: five posts are reserved for nominations from Germany, France, the United Kingdom, Italy and Spain; the remaining three posts rotate among the other 22 Member States. The Court of Justice may request the Council (acting unanimously) to increase the number of Advocates General.[136] Declaration No 38 annexed to the Final Act of the IGC which adopted the TL provides that, should the Court of Justice request that the number of Advocates General be increased by three, the Council will agree to such an increase; in that event, Poland will also acquire a permanent Advocate General, rather than continuing to take part in the rotation system.

In accordance with Article 252 TFEU, an Advocate General's duty is, acting with com-plete impartiality and independence, to make, in open court, reasoned submissions on disputes being considered by the Court. Article 20 of the Statute provides that, where it considers the case raises no new point of law, the Court may decide (after hearing the Advocate General) that the case shall be determined without a submission from the Advocate General. Otherwise, the Advocate General's Opinion is normally delivered after the parties have concluded their submissions and before the judges begin their delibera-tions; it is fully reasoned in the manner of a reserved judgment in the higher English courts—setting out any relevant facts and legislation, discussing the issues that have been raised, situating them in the evolving pattern of the Court's case law, and recommend-ing a decision to the judges. However, the Advocate General's Opinion is not binding on the judges; the latter may chose to follow his/her advice in whole, in part, or not at all.[137]

A Arnull, 'The European Court and Judicial Objectivity: A Reply to Professor Hartley' (1996) 112 *LQR* 411; Editorial, 'The Court of Justice in the Limelight—Again' (2008) 45 *CMLRev* 1571.

[131] Though see the last edition of this text for further discussion of issues such as judicial reasoning and precedent: Arnull et al, above n 65, ch 12.

[132] For the Court of Justice, see [2010] OJ C177/1. For the General Court, see [2010] OJ C177/37.

[133] See Art 19(2) TEU.

[134] See Art 16 of the Court's Statute.

[135] Art 19(2) TEU.

[136] Art 252 TFEU.

[137] See further eg T Tridimas, 'The Role of the Advocate General in the Development of Community Law: Some Reflections' (1997) 34 *CMLRev* 1349; R Greaves, 'Reforming Some Aspects of the Role of Advocates General' in A Arnull, C Barnard, M Dougan and E Spaventa (eds), *A Constitutional Order of States? Essays in EU Law in Honour of Alan Dashwood* (Oxford, Hart Publishing, 2011).

Article 253 provides that judges and Advocates General of the Court of Justice shall be chosen from persons whose independence is beyond doubt and who possess the qualifications required for appointment to the highest judicial offices in their respective countries or who are jurisconsults of recognised competence. The judges and Advocates General are appointed by common accord of the governments of the Member States for a term of six years (renewable).[138]

The SEA first made provision for the establishment of what is now the General Court, in an attempt to reduce pressure on the growing workload of the Court of Justice itself. Article 19(2) TEU provides that the General Court must include at least one judge per Member State. In accordance with Article 254 TFEU, the exact number of judges of the General Court shall be determined by the Statute. In fact, there are currently 27 judges of the General Court.[139] The Statute may also provide for the General Court to be assisted by Advocates General. For the time being, there are no dedicated Advocates General at the General Court; instead, members of the General Court may be called upon to perform the task of an Advocate General in certain cases.[140] The members of the General Court must be chosen from persons whose independence is beyond doubt and who possess the ability required for appointment to high judicial office. They shall be appointed by common accord of the governments of the Member States for a term of six years (renewable).[141]

In the case of judges and Advocates General of the Court of Justice, as well as judges of the General Court, the Member States should proceed to make appointments only after having consulted the panel provided for in Article 255 TFEU (an innovation introduced by the TL). That panel—composed of seven persons chosen from among former members of the Court of Justice and the General Court, members of national supreme courts and lawyers of recognised competence, one of whom shall be proposed by the European Parliament—must give an opinion on the candidates' suitability to perform the duties of judge or Advocate General. Although the panel's views will not be binding on the Council, it is anticipated that this new layer of scrutiny will dissuade Member States from nominating potentially inappropriate persons for senior judicial office, and thereby contribute to the maintenance of high levels of competence within the Union courts. In any case, the new appointments procedure should not be viewed with suspicion as a first step towards greater politicisation of the Union judiciary: the nature of the panel itself hardly harks in the direction of the US Senate's confirmation hearings for appointing Supreme Court justices; surely the constitutional culture of Europe in general, and the EU in particular, frowns upon the selection of Union judges on blatantly political grounds. If anything, the new panel should reinforce that culture still further.[142]

In addition to the Court of Justice and the General Court, the TN first introduced a legal basis for the creation of specialised courts, again in an attempt to provide extra resources to meet the increasing demands placed upon the Union judiciary arising from the continuing enlargement of the EU and the growing number of policy areas falling within the Union's fields of competence. Under Article 257 TFEU, the European Parliament and the Council (acting in accordance with the ordinary legislative procedure either on a proposal

---

[138] Every three years there shall be a partial replacement of the Judges and Advocates General. See further Art 9 of the Court's Statute.

[139] See Art 48 of the Court's Statute.

[140] See Art 49 of the Court's Statute.

[141] See Art 254 TFEU. That provision also states that the membership shall be partially renewed every three years.

[142] cp R Barents, 'The Court of Justice in the Draft Constitution' (2004) 11 *MJ* 121.

from the Commission after consultation of the Court of Justice; or at the request of the Court of Justice after consultation of the Commission) may adopt regulations to establish specialised courts attached to the General Court to hear and determine at first instance certain classes of action or proceeding brought in specific areas.[143] Decisions given by such specialised courts may be subject to a right of appeal on points of law only or, when provided for in the parent regulation, a right of appeal also on matters of fact, before the General Court. So far, only one specialised court has been established: the Civil Service Tribunal, which exercises first-instance jurisdiction over employment disputes between the Union and its civil servants.[144] Other ideas for specialised courts have been mooted: for example, in highly technical fields such as intellectual property disputes.

In order to discharge their constitutional function of ensuring that the law is observed within the Union legal system, the Treaties equip the Court of Justice of the European Union with a series of specific powers.[145] It is customary to divide the jurisdiction of the Union courts into two main types.

First, there are direct actions, which are brought directly before and finally settled by the Union courts themselves. Direct actions include actions for the annulment of a Union measure which is alleged to have been adopted in breach of a hierarchically superior provision of the Union legal order;[146] actions against a Union institution for allegedly failing to act when it was under a duty to do so;[147] actions for damages against the Union institutions based upon the latter's non-contractual liability;[148] and enforcement proceedings against a Member State for failing to fulfil its obligations under the Treaties, which may be brought by the Commission or another Member State.[149] Some of those direct actions fall directly within the jurisdiction of the Court of Justice; others are heard at first instance by the General Court, subject to a right of appeal to the Court of Justice on points of law.[150] As we have seen, staff disputes are heard at first instance by the Civil Service Tribunal and subject to a right of appeal to the General Court; in such cases, decisions given by the General Court may exceptionally be subject to review by the Court of Justice, where there is a serious risk of the unity or consistency of Union law being affected.[151] Chapter 6 will consider in greater detail the direct actions provided for under the Treaties.

The second main category of actions heard by the Union courts consists of preliminary rulings as governed by Article 267 TFEU. Those are cases referred to the Union judiciary by national courts for assistance with the resolution of domestic legal disputes involving the interpretation, application or validity of Union law. In such cases, the legal action commences and finishes at the national level: the role of the Union courts is to provide assistance to the domestic judges, during the course of the relevant proceedings, as far as concerns issues of Union law; having received an answer to their queries from the Union courts, it is the responsibility of the national courts to apply that answer to the facts of the

---

[143] On the Union's 'ordinary legislative procedure', see Chapter 4.

[144] Decision 2004/752 establishing the European Union Civil Service Tribunal [2004] OJ L333/7 (and see now Annex I to the Court's Statute). See further eg H Kraemer, 'The European Union Civil Service Tribunal: A New Community Court Examined after Four Years of Operation' (2009) 46 *CMLRev* 1873.

[145] See Art 19(3) TEU.

[146] See Arts 263–64 and 266 TFEU.

[147] See Art 265 and 266 TFEU.

[148] See Arts 268 and 340 TFEU.

[149] See Arts 258–60 TFEU.

[150] See Art 256(1) TFEU; Arts 51 and 58 of the Court's Statute.

[151] See Art 256(2) TFEU; Arts 62–62b of the Court's Statute. As to which, consider Case C-197/09 RX-I and RX-II *M v European Medicines Agency* (Review of 24 June 2009 and Judgment of 17 December 2009).

case. At present, all requests for a preliminary ruling from the national courts go directly to the Court of Justice. However, Article 256(3) TFEU states that the General Court may be granted jurisdiction to hear and determine questions referred for a preliminary ruling by the national courts in the specific areas identified under the Statute. So far, such jurisdiction has not been conferred upon the General Court. Nevertheless, it is worth noting that, in the event of the Statute being amended so as to confer jurisdiction over particular classes of preliminary references upon the General Court, the latter may still then refer the case to the Court of Justice where it considers that the case requires a decision of principle likely to affect the unity or consistency of Union law. Decisions given by the General Court on questions referred for a preliminary ruling may exceptionally be subject to review by the Court of Justice, where there is a serious risk of the unity or consistency of Union law being affected.[152] Chapter 7 will deal in greater detail with the system of preliminary rulings sought by national courts.

It is worth noting that special limitations are imposed upon the ordinary jurisdiction of the Court of Justice of the European Union in certain situations: for example, as regards the common foreign and security policy;[153] in the field of police and judicial co-operation in criminal matters;[154] and in respect of sanctions imposed upon Member States for violating the Union's core values.[155]

VIII – SOME CONCLUDING REMARKS: ON THE UNION'S 'INTER-INSTITUTIONAL BALANCE'

Having examined the European Union's four main political institutions, in particular, it should be evident that the EU is a rather unusual if not altogether unique organisation. It is perhaps worth reflecting briefly upon the broader constitutional significance of the Union's *sui generis* character.

On the one hand, the Union is clearly not a traditional state or federation: it is not a self-authenticating entity with inherent competences; its Member States remain full sovereign states under international law; the Union lacks general powers (for example) to levy taxes; and it possesses no coercive security apparatus (such as a European police force or a European army). Furthermore, it is undeniable that, for their own peoples, the Member States remain the principal focus of collective loyalty and the primary forum of democratic political activity. On the other hand, the EU is clearly much more than a traditional international organisation: it comprises supranational institutions endowed with real decision-making powers capable of binding the Member States across a wide range of policy fields; including a directly elected European Parliament and an influential Commission acting independently from the Member States. Moreover, as we shall see in Chapter 8, the Court of Justice in its case law since *Van Gend en Loos* has established the constitutional

---

[152] As regards which, see also Arts 62–62b of the Court's Statute.

[153] See Art 275 TFEU. Note also, as regards Union acts adopted under the ex-Second Pillar, the temporary limitations on the Court's jurisdiction provided for under the Protocol (No 36) on transitional provisions.

[154] See Art 276 TFEU. Note also, as regards Union acts adopted under the ex-Third Pillar, the temporary limitations on the Court's jurisdiction provided for under the Protocol (No 36) on transitional provisions.

[155] See Art 269 TFEU.

character of the order brought into being by the Treaties.[156] In adhering to the 'new legal order' resulting from the Treaties, the Member States have (in the words of the Court) 'limited their sovereign rights in ever wider fields'.[157]

Our attempt to capture the essence of the unique polity created by the Treaties lies in the phrase: 'a constitutional order of states'.[158] Indeed, it has become common to view the EU as part of a complex system of multi-level governance, whereby governmental power in Europe is dispersed across different types of public authorities, operating at different levels (the supranational, the national and also the regional), but each characterised by mutual interdependence in their activities.

For present purposes, the EU's *sui generis* nature is reflected most obviously in the fact that the Union does not possess a constitutional system based upon any traditional system of separation of powers, or any traditional model of checks and balances. One would look in vain to identify 'an institution' responsible for exercising either legislative or executive power within the EU. Instead, the EU possesses a constitutional system designed to meet the particular demands of its own historical circumstances: the desire to strike an appropriate balance between the competing claims of supranationalism and intergovernmentalism within the evolving process of European integration. Supranationalism refers to the idea of identifying and pursuing a collective European interest that overreaches the specific identities of each individual Member State. Institutions such as the Commission and the European Parliament most clearly embody this supranational ideal. Its natural tendency is to pull the Union towards some form of federal or confederal constitutional system. Intergovernmentalism, by contrast, refers to a more traditional model of international relations: the Member States interact *qua* nation states, and do so essentially in pursuit of their own individual national interests, albeit realised through joint action in the pursuit of collective goals. Institutions such as the European Council and the Council represent this persistent intergovernmental instinct within the process of European integration. Its natural tendency is centrifugal—pulling the Union towards looser forms of international co-operation firmly within the grip of the Member States.

One might argue that the overall integration process—and therefore the EU's general constitutional structure—seeks to find a delicate compromise between those two powerful forces: reconciling the need and desire for closer co-operation at the supranational level, against the need and desire to respect the prerogatives of individual Member States. The attempt under the Treaties to create a political and constitutional framework capable of striking that difficult compromise is usually referred to as the 'inter-institutional balance'. The inter-institutional balance has a political foundation: the different constituencies represented by various Union institutions, whereby the European Parliament acts as the directly elected representative of the entire citizen body, the European Council and the Council provide the fora for representatives drawn from the nation states, and the Commission acts as the even-handed guardian of the Treaties' overall goals and objectives. The inter-institutional balance also has a clear legal foundation: the instruction in Article 13(2) TEU that each institution shall act within the limits of the powers conferred upon

---

[156] Case 26/62 [1963] ECR 1, 12. See further eg F Mancini, 'The Making of a Constitution for Europe' (1989) 26 *CMLRev* 595.

[157] Opinion 1/91 *EEA Agreement* [1991] ECR I-6079, para 21.

[158] The description was first used in A Dashwood (ed), *Reviewing Maastricht: Issues for the 1996 IGC* (London, Sweet & Maxwell, 1996) 7. For critical reflections upon the Union as a 'constitutional order of states', see further Arnull et al, above n 137.

it by under the Treaties and in accordance with the procedures, conditions and objectives set out therein.

However, it is important to stress that, although the inter-institutional balance seeks to make the four main institutions interact in a way that balances out their competing constituencies of interest, the Treaties do not seek to strike the same balance across every field of EU activity. In fact, the Treaties require the institutions to interact in very different ways in different policy fields. In some especially sensitive areas, such as the common foreign and security policy and as regards national tax policies, the Council plays a more dominant role than the Commission or the European Parliament—thus ensuring that the intergovernmental interests of the Member States dominate Union decision-making. In other fields, such as environmental and consumer policies, the European Parliament plays a more equal role with the Council—thus ensuring that the interests of the Member States are combined with the interests of the Union's citizens as a whole. In other fields again, such as competition policy and the control of state financial aid, the Commission tends to take a leading position—so that Union decision-making becomes more 'apolitical' or 'non-majoritarian', with an emphasis rather on the protection of collective interests and the application of technical expertise.

The next two chapters will examine some of the most important constitutional implications of the Union's variegated 'inter-institutional balance' and more generally of its character as a 'constitutional order of states': first, when it comes to the procedures for adopting Union legislation and for the latter's implementation (Chapter 4); and secondly, as regards the complex system governing the existence and exercise of different types of Union competences (Chapter 5).

Further reading

Given the pace of Treaty reform, some of the following suggestions for further reading should be seen primarily as a means of understanding the context and development of the EU's current institutional framework.

A Arnull, *The European Union and its Court of Justice*, 2nd edn (Oxford, Oxford University Press, 2006).

G de Búrca and J Weiler (eds), *The European Court of Justice* (Oxford, Oxford University Press, 2001).

P Craig, 'The Lisbon Treaty: Process, Architecture and Substance' (2008) 33 *ELRev* 137.

——, 'Institutions, Power and Institutional Balance' in P Craig and G de Búrca (eds), *The Evolution of EU Law*, 2nd edn (Oxford, Oxford University Press, 2011).

A Dashwood, 'Decision-Making at the Summit' (2000) 3 *CYELS* 79.

A Dashwood and A Johnston (eds), *The Future of the Judicial System of the European Union* (Oxford, Hart Publishing, 2001).

R Dehousse, 'European Institutional Architecture after Amsterdam: Parliamentary System or Regulatory Structure?' (1998) 35 *CMLRev* 595.

M Dougan, 'The Treaty of Lisbon 2007: Winning Minds, Not Hearts' (2008) 45 *CMLRev* 617.

P Kapteyn, 'Reflections on the Future of the Judicial System of the European Union After Nice' (2001) 20 *YEL* 173.

K Lenaerts, 'Constitutionalism and the Many Faces of Federalism' (1990) 38 *AJCL* 205.

——, 'Some Reflections on the Separation of Powers in the European Community' (1991) 28 *CMLRev* 11.

A Moberg, 'The Nice Treaty and Voting Rules in the Council' (2002) 40 *JCMS* 259.

P Raworth, 'A Timid Step Forwards: Maastricht and the Democratisation of the European Community' (1994) 19 *ELRev* 16.

K St Clair Bradley, 'Institutional Design in the Treaty of Nice' (2001) 38 *CMLRev* 1095.

The Union's Decision-making Procedures

This chapter discusses the main procedures by which the Union institutions may adopt legally binding acts. Since the Treaty of Lisbon, the Union's legal acts are formally divided into 'legislative' and 'non-legislative' instruments. Legislative acts are generally adopted under the 'ordinary legislative procedure', wherein the Council and the European Parliament are treated as equal partners in the law-making process. However, certain Union legislation is created through 'special legislative procedures' in which one or other institution (usually the Council) assumes a more dominant role. Discussion then focuses on the Union's non-legislative acts—some of which are adopted directly under the Treaties; others consist of significant discretionary powers delegated to the Commission by legislative acts of the Council and/or the European Parliament; while others still are adopted for the purely executive implementation of Union law.

I – A NEW DISTINCTION BETWEEN LEGISLATIVE AND NON-LEGISLATIVE ACTS

Before the Lisbon reforms, the task of understanding how the Union institutions adopted their own secondary acts under the Treaties was complicated by the availability of a wide variety of both legal instruments and decision-making procedures. For those purposes, it should be observed that no formal distinction was drawn anywhere in the Treaties between *legislative* and *non-legislative* (executive) instruments or procedures. Only as a matter of practice could commentators agree that certain acts—by virtue of their nature and content as well as the procedure by which they had been adopted—should be considered 'legislative' in character; while other acts—again, having regard to their subject-matter and their legal basis under Union law—seemed better conceived as of a 'non-legislative' nature.[1]

---

[1] See further eg A von Bogdandy, F Arndt and J Bast, 'Legal Instruments in European Union Law and their Reform: A Systematic Approach on an Empirical Basis' (2004) 23 *YEL* 91; R Schütze, 'The Morphology of Legislative Power in the European Community: Legal Instruments and the Federal Division of Powers' (2006) 25 *YEL* 91.

In particular, the Union's pre-TL legal instruments and decision-making procedures varied according to which 'pillar' was at issue. Under the First Pillar, the Union institutions had at their disposal three types of legally binding instrument: regulations, directives and decisions.[2] In some situations, the adoption of those instruments was generally acknowledged to be of a legislative nature. But there was no single legislative procedure under the First Pillar. Instead, the EC Treaty contained a variety of legislative procedures in which the Commission, the Council and the European Parliament enjoyed varying powers and influence across different fields of Union activity. In other situations, the adoption of First Pillar regulations, directives or decisions was generally acknowledged to be of an executive character—but again, the procedure by which the relevant instrument might be adopted, especially the institution(s) involved in doing so, would vary from Treaty provision to Treaty provision. Under the Second Pillar, the Union employed a different set of legal instruments: common strategies, joint actions and common positions. Here, it was generally assumed that none of those instruments served a legislative purpose as such: the CFSP was essentially an executive activity. As we have already noted, the decision-making framework of the CFSP was also rather distinctive—being dominated by the activities of the Council, almost always acting unanimously, with only a marginal role for the Commission or the European Parliament. Finally, under the Third Pillar, yet another set of legal instruments was available: common positions, framework decisions, decisions and conventions. As with the First Pillar, it was possible informally to divide the Union's use of those instruments into broadly legislative and non-legislative activities—but the relevant decision-making procedures were again unique, dominated by the Council, with a somewhat greater role for the Commission, but still only a limited input from the European Parliament.[3]

One of the core objectives of the TL—and one of its most positive achievements—was to reform that highly complex system of Union legal instruments and decision-making procedures, so as to deliver for the Union's constitutional system some much-needed simplification, enhanced democratic legitimacy and increased decision-making efficiency.[4] The TL's approach here rests upon two important foundations. The first is abolition of the various bespoke legal instruments used in the old Second and Third Pillars in favour of a unified set of binding legal acts for the Union as a whole, based upon the regulations, directives and decisions traditionally used under the First Pillar.[5] The second foundation for the TL's reform package is the introduction, within that unified set of legal instruments, of a formal distinction between *legislative acts* and *non-legislative acts*. However, the basis for drawing that distinction throughout the revised Treaties is not a substantive one, ie based upon a qualitative assessment of the role and nature of the relevant legal

---

[2] There were also a range of non-binding instruments, especially recommendations and opinions (see ex-Art 249 EC).

[3] For more details on the legal instruments and decision-making procedures applicable under the old Second and Third Pillars, see A Arnull, A Dashwood, M Dougan, M Ross, E Spaventa and D Wyatt, *Wyatt & Dashwood's EU Law*, 5th edn (London, Sweet & Maxwell, 2006) ch 10.

[4] See further eg K Lenaerts and M Desomer, 'Towards a Hierarchy of Legal Acts in the European Union? Simplification of Legal Instruments and Procedures' (2005) 11 *ELJ* 744; J B Liisberg, 'The EU Constitutional Treaty and Its Distinction Between Legislative and Non-Legislative Acts', Jean Monnet Working Paper 01/06 (New York University School of Law).

[5] Note, however, that transitional provisions apply in respect of legal acts already adopted under the old Second and Third Pillars: see Title VII of Protocol (No 36) on transitional provisions [2010] OJ C83/322. Note also that the Treaties continue to place a range of non-binding instruments at the disposal of the Union institutions, especially recommendations and opinions: see Art 288 TFEU.

instrument. Rather, the approach adopted by the TL is to categorise legal instruments as either legislative or non-legislative according simply to the decision-making procedure by which the Treaties now specify they should be adopted. *Legislative acts* are regulations, directives or decisions which are described as being adopted through either the 'ordinary' or a 'special' legislative procedure as identified in the relevant legal basis.[6] *Non-legislative acts* comprise all other legal instruments, ie adopted under or pursuant to the Treaties (by default) through a non-legislative procedure. It is worth noting that that distinction, between legislative and non-legislative acts, has important consequences in various other fields: for example, the national parliaments' right to object to Union measures on the grounds of an alleged incompatibility with the principle of subsidiarity applies only as regards draft legislative acts;[7] similarly, the Council's obligation to deliberate and vote in public applies only to draft legislative acts;[8] the distinction between legislative and non-legislative measures may also prove crucial to the new rules on the standing of natural and legal persons to bring an action for the annulment of Union measures directly before the Union courts.[9] Such issues will be explored further below and in subsequent chapters.

The remainder of this chapter will deal with the Union's decision-making procedures as revised by the TL.[10] We will begin by considering legislative acts under the Treaties: the special role of the Commission in initiating the Union's legislative deliberations; the nature of the 'ordinary legislative procedure'; and the use of various 'special legislative procedures'. We will then move on to deal with non-legislative instruments: those provided for directly under the Treaties; those adopted by the Commission as 'delegated acts'; and finally the category of 'implementing acts'.

II – ADOPTION OF LEGISLATIVE ACTS

As observed before, there is no single institution that constitutes the Union's legislature. Three main Union institutions—the Commission, the Council and the European Parliament—are assigned their respective roles in a variety of more or less elaborate law-making procedures. A range of other bodies also participate in the Union's various legislative procedures, albeit in lesser ways. For example, the Council and/or the European Parliament are often obliged to consult the Economic and Social Committee and/or the Committee of the Regions before adopting a Union legislative act.[11] The TL also introduced a special mechanism by which national parliaments may participate in the Union's legislative procedures, by raising objections to proposed acts on the grounds that the latter do not comply with the principle of subsidiarity. That 'yellow card' mechanism will be considered further in Chapter 5.

---

[6] See Art 289(1)–(3) TFEU.

[7] The possibility for national parliaments, and the Committee of the Regions, to seek judicial review on subsidiarity grounds is also limited to Union legislative acts. See further Chapter 5.

[8] Art 16(8) TEU and Art 15(2) TFEU. See further Chapter 3.

[9] See further Chapter 6.

[10] Note that we will not consider the Union's budgetary process (an important but rather specialised and intricate topic): see Title II of Part Six TFEU.

[11] See eg Art 114 TFEU (consultation of the Economic and Social Committee as regards internal market harmonisation); Art 194 TFEU (consultation of both the Economic and Social Committee and the Committee of the Regions as regards energy policy).

A – Initiation of Legislative Procedures

According to Article 17(2) TEU, Union legislative acts may be adopted only on the basis of a Commission proposal, except where the Treaties provide otherwise.[12] That general rule can be seen as an express codification of the approach which had already become familiar under the old EC Treaty. It is designed to ensure that the Council and/or the European Parliament exercise their legislative powers only in relation to a text which has been formulated by the Union institution with a duty to act independently and without regard to any specific national interests. The main exception to the general principle that the Commission enjoys a monopoly over the initiation of Union legislation is contained in Article 76 TFEU: in the field of police and judicial co-operation in criminal matters, acts may also be adopted on the initiative of a quarter of the Member States.[13] That exception is a partial hangover from the old Third Pillar: there, proposals relating to police and judicial co-operation in criminal matters could be presented to the Council either by the Commission or by any (single) Member State.[14] Article 76 TFEU continues to reflect— though in a more diluted form—the relative sensitivity of Union action in the field of criminal law and the desire of the Member States to retain the ability to exercise particular influence over Union decision-making therein.[15]

Although neither institution is capable of initiating the Union's legislative procedure for itself, both the Council and the European Parliament are nevertheless entitled to request that the Commission should consider submitting a proposal on any given issue.[16] In practice, of course, many of the Commission's proposals originate from cross-institutional deliberations: there would be little point in the Commission bringing forward legislative ideas which it did not already know would secure significant support among the Member States and within the European Parliament. Moreover, the influence of the European Council here should not be overlooked: by identifying the Union's overall strategic interests and goals, based on preparatory input from the Commission and with the direct participation of the Commission President, the European Council is capable of exercising an important steer over the Union's legislative agenda; indeed, the formal conclusions of European Council meetings will sometimes call upon the Commission to exercise the latter's prerogatives so as to bring forward proposals for Union action on specified issues.[17]

Mention should also be made in this context of a further innovation introduced by the TL. According to Article 11(4) TEU, at least one million citizens from a significant number of Member States may invite the Commission, within the framework of its powers, to submit appropriate proposals on matters where those citizens consider that a Union legal act is required for the purpose of implementing the Treaties. The detailed procedures and conditions for exercising this 'citizens' initiative' (including the minimum number of

---

[12] See also Art 289 TFEU.

[13] Note the additional exceptions referred to in Art 289(4) TFEU.

[14] See ex-Art 34(2) TEU.

[15] On a historical note: a shared right of initiative was retained, on a temporary basis, for decision-making on the matters which were transferred by the TA from ex-Title VI TEU to ex-Title IV of Part Three of the EC Treaty (visas, asylum and immigration). Ex-Art 67(1) EC provided that, during a transitional period of five years from the entry into force of the TA, the Council should act, under most of the transferred legal bases, 'on a proposal from the Commission or on the initiative of a Member State'. That deviation having expired, the Commission has long since regained its monopoly of initiative for the purposes of the relevant provisions under the revised Treaties.

[16] See Arts 241 and 225 TFEU, respectively.

[17] Consider eg the European Council's Conclusions of 15–16 October 1999; or those of 19–20 June 2003.

Member States whose citizens must be involved) shall be laid down in regulations adopted by the European Parliament and the Council (in accordance with the 'ordinary legislative procedure') under Article 24 TFEU.[18] It will be interesting to see how far, and in what ways, this new 'citizens' initiative' might influence the exercise of the Commission's power of initiative and, indeed, the conduct of the Union's legislative procedures as a whole.[19]

B – Ordinary Legislative Procedure

Article 10 TEU contains a concise statement of the Union's dual basis of democratic legitimacy: *citizens* are directly represented at the Union level in the European Parliament; *Member States* are represented in the European Council and the Council, those representatives being themselves democratically accountable either to their national parliaments or their citizens. That dual democratic basis is best reflected in the Union's 'ordinary legislative procedure'—previously known as co-decision—since it is based on an equal say between the European Parliament and the Council.

The co-decision procedure was first introduced into the EC Treaty by the Maastricht Treaty (the TEU), then refined and streamlined by the TA, before being tweaked once more and renamed the 'ordinary legislative procedure' by the TL. The full process is described in Article 294 TFEU. It entails successive 'readings' of a proposal for legislation, offering a series of opportunities for interaction between the Commission, the Council and the European Parliament, all designed to channel the latter two institutions towards approval of a joint text. The various possible stages are outlined below, and are also illustrated in Figure 4.1.[20] We say 'possible' stages because the procedure does not have to run its full course, if agreement between the co-legislators can be reached earlier. In practice, it has become common for proposals to be adopted at first or second reading; only a minority need to be taken to the stage of compulsory conciliation. As we shall see further below, the texts of many draft Union legislative acts are now in fact agreed through informal meetings of representatives from the Council, the European Parliament and the Commission—so-called 'trilogues'—which inject extra speed and fluidity into the functioning of the ordinary legislative procedure (though some would say at the cost of its intended transparency and accountability).

The first reading commences with the submission of the Commission's proposal to the European Parliament and the Council. The Parliament adopts its position in relation to the proposal, which may or may not contain amendments. The Council then has a choice, to be exercised by qualified majority decision: it may definitively adopt the proposed act in conformity with the Parliament's position (ie incorporating the Parliament's amendments, if any); or, if it does not approve all of the amendments contained in the Parliament's position, or wishes to make others, it may adopt its own position, which must be communicated to the Parliament with a full explanation of the underlying reasons. The Commission, too, must inform the Parliament fully of its position.

At second reading, the Council's position replaces the Commission's proposal as the

---

[18] See Reg 211/2011 [2011] OJ L65/1.

[19] cp Editorial, 'Direct Democracy and the European Union . . . Is that a Threat or a Promise?' (2008) 45 *CMLRev* 929.

[20] We will not deal with the special provisions, applicable to legislative proposals emanating other than from the Commission, governed by Art 294(15) TFEU.

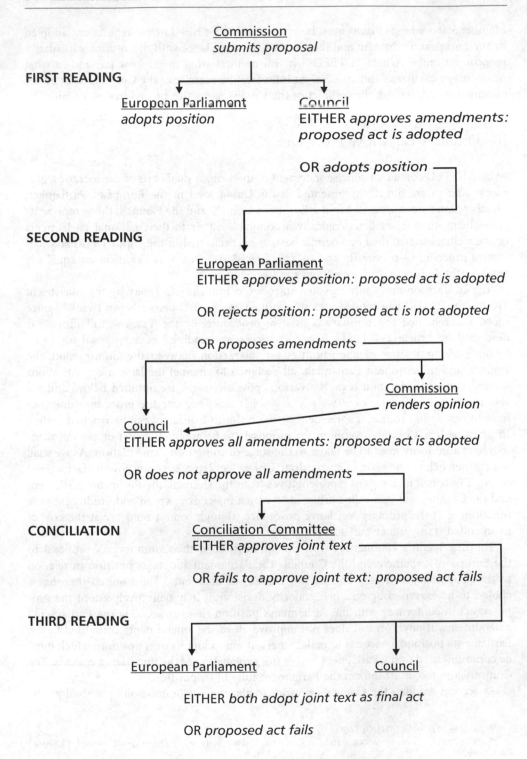

Figure 4.1 Ordinary legislative procedure: Article 294 TFEU

text which is the object of the interaction between the co-legislative institutions. The choice is now for the European Parliament between: (i) expressly approving the Council's position (or doing so tacitly by taking no decision within the prescribed period of three months); or (ii) rejecting the Council's position (this requires an absolute majority of MEPs, not merely of those voting); or (iii) proposing amendments to the Council's position (by the same majority). Approval or rejection by the Parliament at this stage has the effect of concluding the procedure one way or the other: the act in question is deemed to have been adopted in accordance with the Council's position; or, as the case may be, not to have been adopted. In the (more likely) eventuality that amendments are proposed, these must be forwarded to the Council; as well as to the Commission, which is required to deliver an opinion on them. The ball is then, once again, in the Council's court. It may, within three months, approve all of the proposed amendments (by a qualified majority, or by unanimity in respect of those on which the Commission has delivered a negative opinion), in which case the act will be deemed to have been adopted in the form of the Council's amended position. Otherwise, the President of the Council, in agreement with the President of the Parliament, must, within six weeks, convene a meeting of the 'Conciliation Committee'.

The procedure of the first and second readings involves interaction between the Council and the European Parliament at arm's length. As described in the preceding paragraphs, they will have had three separate opportunities for reaching agreement, but if they fail to do so, Article 294 TFEU provides the remedy of direct negotiation within the Conciliation Committee so as to try to break the deadlock. The Committee is composed of the members of the Council or their representatives (normally, the appropriate COREPER, depending on the subject-matter of the act in question) and an equal number of representatives of the European Parliament. Its task is, within six weeks, to reach agreement on a joint text, by a qualified majority on the Council side and by a majority on the Parliament side. The Commission has a role in the proceedings as honest broker. The negotiations within the Committee take place on the basis of the positions adopted by the Council and the European Parliament at second reading. However, the Court of Justice held in the *European Low Fares Airline Association* case that, so as to make the ordinary legislative procedure effective, the Conciliation Committee must enjoy a wide discretion: it is charged, not with coming to an agreement on the Parliament's proposed amendments to the Council's original position, but rather with reaching an agreement on a joint text; for these purposes, Article 294 TFEU does not include any restriction as to the content of the measures chosen by the Conciliation Committee to enable such agreement to be reached. In the case itself, the Conciliation Committee had not exceeded its powers by agreeing modifications to the Council's position on certain provisions of a draft regulation on air transport, as regards which the Parliament had not previously proposed any amendments.[21]

If conciliation is successful, the ordinary legislative procedure moves on to its third reading. The joint text agreed by the Committee is submitted to the co-legislators, who have a further six weeks in which formally to adopt the act in question, in accordance with that joint text, the European Parliament acting by a majority of votes cast and the Council acting by a qualified majority. Should either of them fail to do so, the act will fall.

---

[21] Case C-344/04 *European Low Fares Airline Association* [2006] ECR I-403.

That will also be the result if the Conciliation Committee is unable to agree a joint text within the six-week deadline.[22]

The various time limits prescribed by Article 294 TFEU are very important, to prevent the legislative process from becoming too lengthy, and to avoid a loss of political momentum. There is, however, provision for the periods of three months to be extended by a maximum of one month, and those of six weeks by a maximum of a fortnight, at the initiative of either the European Parliament or the Council.

The co-decision procedure was originally prescribed by the TEU for enacting Community legislation relating to the internal market.[23] It was also provided for under several of the new legal bases for Community activity introduced under the TEU.[24] The TA took matters still further: many more provisions of the EC Treaty were amended so as to provide for the co-decision procedure in place of either the now-defunct co-operation procedure,[25] or the procedure based upon mere consultation of the European Parliament (on both of which, see further below).[26] Co-decision was, moreover, the legislative procedure chosen by the authors of the TA for almost all the new legal bases established pursuant to that Treaty, including in areas of considerable political sensitivity.[27] Further (more modest) extensions of the co-decision procedure were implemented under the TN.[28] In a few matters, however, the extension of co-decision was purchased at the price of requiring the Council to act, throughout the procedure, by unanimity instead of the normal qualified majority.[29] That variant was unfortunate because it was liable to distort

---

[22] Note that under the co-decision procedure as originally introduced by the TEU, if the Conciliation Committee failed to approve a joint text, it remained possible for the Council to confirm unilaterally the position it had agreed prior to conciliation, with the option of including some or all of the European Parliament's amendments; the measure would then become law, unless it was rejected, within six weeks, by a majority of MEPs. By abolishing this possibility, the TA formally placed the Parliament on an equal footing with the Council, both being required to give their positive approval to any final legislation.

[23] Notably under the power of approximation conferred by Art 114 TFEU—a legal basis previously governed by the now-defunct co-operation procedure (referred to below).

[24] See eg the provisions which have now become Art 168 TFEU on various public health measures; Art 169 TFEU on consumer protection; Art 172 TFEU on trans-European networks. See also Art 167(5), first indent TFEU on culture; and Art 182(1) TFEU on the multiannual framework programmes for research. Under both of the latter, as provided for by the original TEU, the Council was required to act by unanimity (a situation referred to further below).

[25] eg the provisions which have now become Art 18(2) TFEU on discrimination on grounds of nationality; Art 91(1) TFEU on the common transport policy; Art 100 TFEU on sea and air transport; Art 153(2) TFEU on conditions of employment; Art 164 TFEU on implementation of the European Social Fund; Art 166(4) TFEU on vocational training; Art 178, first para, TFEU on implementing decisions for the purposes of the European Regional Development Fund; Art 188, second para, TFEU on the implementation of the research framework programme; Art 192(1) TFEU on the environment; Art 209 TFEU on development co-operation.

[26] eg the provisions which have now become Art 48 TFEU on social security for migrant workers; Art 52(2) TFEU on the co-ordination of national provisions derogating, on grounds of public policy, public sector or public health, from the right of establishment and the freedom to supply services; Art 53 TFEU on the co-ordination of provisions governing certain aspects of the taking up and pursuit of self-employed activities.

[27] eg the provisions which have now become Art 149 TFEU on incentive measures in the field of employment; Art 157(3) TFEU on equal opportunities and equal treatment for men and women in matters of employment and occupation; Art 168(4) TFEU on various public health measures; Art 15(3) TFEU on access to documents; Art 325(4) TFEU on countering fraud against the Union's financial interests; Art 338(1) TFEU on the production of Community statistics; Art 16(2) TFEU on data protection.

[28] eg the provisions which have now become Art 19(2) TFEU as regards incentive measures to combat various forms of discrimination; Art 153(2) TFEU concerned with soft-law measures designed to combat social exclusion and modernise social protection; Art 224 TFEU on the regulation and funding of political parties at the European level.

[29] eg as with ex-Art 42 EC (now Art 48 TFEU) and ex-Art 47(2) EC (now Art 53 TFEU). Similar requirements in what are now Art 182(1) TFEU on the adoption of the multinational framework programme for

the process of decision-making, and to diminish the ability of the European Parliament to influence the final outcome, since at second reading the Council could be found less willing than usual to shift from its position, which would have had to accommodate the particular viewpoints of all delegations. Nevertheless, a clear trend was evident towards the recognition of co-decision as the standard procedure for enacting Union measures which were genuinely legislative in character.[30]

That trend was confirmed by the TL, which extended co-decision, in its reincarnation as the Union's 'ordinary legislative procedure', across many more legal bases: for example, agricultural policy (previously subject to mere consultation of the European Parliament by the Council);[31] and the common commercial policy (as regards which the European Parliament was previously denied any formal right of participation).[32] Perhaps most significantly, the ordinary legislative procedure now applies across most of the Area of Freedom, Security and Justice.[33] In particular, most of the Union's legislative activities as regards police and judicial co-operation in criminal law matters—previously governed by the distinct institutional arrangements of the Third Pillar—are now conducted through the ordinary legislative procedure.[34] Furthermore, those variants of the co-decision procedure which had instructed the Council to act by unanimity throughout have now been abrogated so that the ordinary rule of qualified majority voting becomes fully applicable.[35]

C – Special Legislative Procedures

Despite its impressive expansion in the scope of the ordinary legislative procedure, the TL has still not bestowed upon the Union a uniform legislative process: certain legislative acts remain to be adopted under so-called 'special legislative procedures'.

As noted above, the Treaties have always been characterised by a wide variety of decision-making procedures. Some such procedures have gradually withered away and now disappeared—most notably the 'co-operation procedure'.[36] Like co-decision, of which it was the forerunner, the co-operation procedure involved a series of readings: the main differences were that it contained no procedure for compulsory conciliation; and, at the end of the day, the Council could not be prevented from adopting a text that ignored the European Parliament's wishes, although it could be required, in so doing, to act by unanimity.[37] The co-operation procedure was introduced by the SEA and is of historical

---

research, and in Art 21(2) TFEU on facilitating EU citizens' rights of free movement and residence, were dropped (respectively) by the TA and by the TN.

[30] For a positive assessment of the way in which the co-decision procedure (in the version provided for by the TEU) functioned in practice, see S Boyron, 'Maastricht and the Co-decision Procedure: A Success Story' (1996) 45 *ICLQ* 293; and, by the same author, 'The Co-decision Procedure: rethinking the constitutional fundamentals' in P Craig and C Harlow, *Lawmaking in the European Union* (The Hague, Kluwer, 1998).

[31] Art 43 TFEU. Cf ex-Art 37 EC.

[32] Art 207 TFEU. Cf ex-Art 133 EC.

[33] See Title V, Part Three TFEU.

[34] See Chapter 4, Title V, Part Three TFEU.

[35] eg what is now Art 53 TFEU on measures to facilitate the taking up and pursuit of self-employed activities; and also Art 167 TFEU on incentive measures in the field of culture.

[36] See ex-Art 252 EC.

[37] Unanimity was required in two situations: where the Parliament had formally rejected the common position (ex-Art 252(c), second para EC); or where the Commission, having re-examined its proposal by taking into account the Parliament's amendments, forwarded to the Council a text which the latter was unwilling to adopt without amendment (ex-Art 252(d) and (e) EC).

importance because it constituted the first step towards enhancing the legislative role of the European Parliament beyond the simple consultation provided for by the original EEC Treaty. In the SEA, the co-operation procedure was closely associated with the project of completing the internal market by the end of 1992. As we have seen, internal market measures were brought within the scope of co-decision by the Maastricht Treaty, but co-operation did survive for enacting EC legislation on, for example, transport, aspects of environment policy and development co-operation. The co-operation procedure was subsequently superseded in those policy areas too, eventually surviving after the TA only in a few provisions relating to economic and monetary policy.[38] The TL finally eliminated the co-operation procedure altogether.[39]

What remains after the TL are special legislative procedures based upon the Council acting by unanimity, sometimes after consulting,[40] sometimes with the consent of,[41] the European Parliament; however, a few such special legislative procedures do permit the Council to act by QMV.[42]

In the original EEC Treaty, the consultation procedure was the only procedure giving the European Parliament a guaranteed role in the enactment of legislation. The basic process is very simple: the European Parliament is consulted on the Commission's legislative proposal before the Council takes the final decision (acting either by a qualified majority or by unanimity, as laid down by the relevant provision of the Treaty).[43] However, the requirement of consultation must be strictly complied with. In practice, work on a Commission proposal begins immediately within Council bodies, without waiting for the Parliament's opinion: the Court of Justice has found that practice to be lawful, so long as the Council does not determine its position definitively before the Parliament's opinion is received.[44] The reason why the Council must normally await the opinion before taking its final decision was explained by the Court in the *Isoglucose* case:

> The consultation provided for [in ex-Article 43(2) EEC], as in other similar provisions of the Treaty, is the means which allows the Parliament to play an actual part in the legislative process of the Community. Such power represents an essential factor in the institutional balance intended by the Treaty. Although limited, it reflects at Community level the fundamental democratic principle that the peoples should take part in the exercise of power through the intermediary of a representative assembly. Due consultation of the Parliament in the cases provided for by the

---

[38] Ex-Arts 99(5), 102(2), 103(2) and 106(2) EC.

[39] Replacing it in one area with the ordinary legislative procedure (ex-Art 99(5) EC became Art 121(6) TFEU); in the rest by a non-legislative procedure involving mere consultation of the EP by the Council (ex-Arts 102(2) and 103(2) EC became Art 125(2) TFEU; ex-Art 106(2) EC became Art 128(2) TFEU).

[40] eg Art 21(3) TFEU on social measures for migrant Union citizens; Art 22 TFEU on electoral rights of Union citizens; Art 64(3) TFEU on regressive measures on the free movement of capital to/from third countries; Art 77(3) TFEU on border/residency documents for migrant Union citizens; Art 81(3) TFEU on cross-border family law; Art 87(3) TFEU on operational co-operation between national law enforcement agencies; Art 89 TFEU on cross-border operation of national law enforcement agencies; Art 113 TFEU on the harmonisation of indirect taxation; Art 115 TFEU on internal market harmonisation; Art 118 TFEU on language arrangements for European IPRs.

[41] eg Art 19(1) TFEU on general anti-discrimination measures; Art 86(1) TFEU on establishment of a European Public Prosecutor's Office; Art 312(2) TFEU on the Union's multiannual financial framework; the flexibility clause contained in Art 352 TFEU.

[42] eg Art 23 TFEU on diplomatic protection of Union citizens (after consulting the European Parliament); Art 311, fourth para TFEU on implementing the Union's own resources (with the EP's consent).

[43] Though depending also on whether the Council exercises its power of amendment (discussed further below).

[44] Case C-417/93 *European Parliament v Council* [1995] ECR I-1185.

Treaty therefore constitutes an essential formality disregard of which means that the measure concerned is void.[45]

In that case, the Court annulled an agricultural regulation which the Council had adopted without having received the opinion of the Parliament, which had been requested some months previously, as required under the provisions of the EEC Treaty then in force. The Court rejected the Council's argument that the Parliament, by its own conduct in failing to give an opinion on a measure it knew to be urgent, had made compliance with the consultation requirement impossible. The judgment laid emphasis on the fact that the Council had not formally invoked the emergency procedure for which the Parliament's own rules provide, nor had it taken advantage of its right, under what is now Article 229 TFEU, to request an extraordinary session of the Parliament: the implication seemed to be that, if the Council had exhausted all the procedural possibilities open to it, the adoption of the regulation, without waiting any longer for the opinion, might well have been justified. That was confirmed, some 15 years later, in a case relating to the Council regulation laying down the arrangements for granting generalised trade preferences to developing countries during the year 1993.[46] The regulation had to be adopted before the end of 1992, to avoid disrupting trade with the countries concerned. On that occasion, the Council had requested the application of the European Parliament's urgency procedure and, when an opinion was still not forthcoming, suggested that an extraordinary session be held in late December; having received a negative reply from the Office of the President of the Parliament, the Council proceeded without more ado to adopt the regulation. The action brought by the Parliament for the annulment of the regulation was rejected by the Court of Justice, on the ground that the failure punctually to render an opinion amounted, in the circumstances, to an infringement of the duty of loyal co-operation which binds the institutions.[47]

The consultation of the European Parliament takes place in relation to the Commission's original legislative proposal. If the Commission amends its proposal, or the Council intends to exercise its power of amendment, and this means that, considered as a whole, the substance of the text which was the subject of the first consultation will be altered, there is a duty to consult the Parliament a second time.[48] Reconsultation is not required if the change is one of method rather than of substance (eg the substitution, in a draft regulation relating to officials' pay, of updated exchange rates); or if the change goes in the direction of wishes expressed by the Parliament itself in its opinion.[49] Overall, although it is true to say that the European Parliament's power to shape Union legislation under the consultation procedure is very limited—certainly when compared to its role within the ordinary legislative procedure—empirical investigations nonetheless suggest that tactical use of the consultation process (eg so as to delay further progress of the Commission's proposal, giving more time for informal negotiations with the Council) can sometimes

---

[45] Case 138/79 *Roquette Frères v Council* [1980] ECR 3333, 3360.

[46] Case C-65/93 *European Parliament v Council* [1995] ECR I-643.

[47] See now Art 13(2) TEU.

[48] Case 41/69 *ACF Chemiefarma v Commission* [1970] ECR 661; Case 1253/79 *Battaglia v Commission* [1982] ECR 297; Case C-65/90 *European Parliament v Council* [1992] ECR I-4593. See also Opinion of Advocate General Mancini in Case 20/85 *Roviello* [1988] ECR 2805; Opinion of Advocate General Darmon in Case C-65/90 *European Parliament v Council* [1992] ECR I-4593.

[49] Case 1253/79 *Battaglia v Commission* [1982] ECR 297.

offer the European Parliament an appreciable influence over the Council's final legislative output.[50]

Under the consent (previously known as the assent) procedure, the Council acts on a legislative proposal by the Commission, after obtaining the consent of the European Parliament. This could be considered a form of co-decision, since the act in question can only pass into law if the Council and the Parliament both give their positive approval. The difference, as compared with the ordinary legislative procedure as laid down in Article 294 TFEU, is that there is no series of formal interactions between the two institutions: a common orientation is reached within the Council, and this is presented to the European Parliament, effectively, on a take-it-or-leave-it basis. The procedure might therefore appear less suited to the enactment of complex legislative measures than to deciding on matters that only require a 'yes' or 'no' answer from the Parliament. In that regard, it is worth noting that the consent procedure is used not only for the adoption of various Union legislative acts, but also for certain major decisions of constitutional importance, such as the accession of new Member States.[51]

A few of the Union's special legislative procedures also contain what has sometimes been termed an 'organic law' clause. Its unique feature is that the Council, having adopted a Union act according to the prescribed special legislative procedure, must then recommend that Union act for approval by the Member States in accordance with their respective constitutional requirements. The Union's own legislative act will only enter into force if those national ratification procedures result in a positive outcome. This relatively 'heavy' legislative procedure applies to issues which the Treaty authors have deemed to be of an importance just falling short of amendments to the Treaties themselves. It is used (in combination with the consent procedure, and with the Council having acted unanimously) for Union legislation strengthening or adding to the rights of Union citizens under the Treaties;[52] or laying down a uniform procedure or common principles for direct elections to the European Parliament.[53] The 'organic law' clause is also used (in combination with the consultation procedure, though with the Council still having acted unanimously) for Union legislation conferring jurisdiction on the Court of Justice in disputes involving Union acts which create European intellectual property rights;[54] or laying down the system of Union own resources.[55] Again, it is worth noting that the 'organic law' clause is used not only for the adoption of various Union legislative acts, but also for certain major decisions of constitutional importance which nevertheless fall short of a formal amendment to the Treaties.[56]

D – Passerelle Clauses

Although in many situations the Union therefore follows special legislative procedures,

---

[50] See R Kardasheva, 'The Power to Delay: The European Parliament's Influence in the Consultation Procedure' (2009) 47 *JCMS* 385.

[51] See Art 49 TEU.

[52] Art 25 TFEU.

[53] Art 223(1) TFEU.

[54] Art 262 TFEU.

[55] Art 311, third para TFEU.

[56] eg Art 42(2) TEU on the decision to adopt a common European defence; Art 48(6) TEU on simplified revisions to Part Three of the TFEU; Art 218(8) TFEU on the agreement concerning EU accession to the ECHR.

the Treaties also contain various 'passerelle clauses' (simplified revision processes) which may be used to alter some of those deviant legislative procedures without recourse to the full-blown drama of a Treaty amendment.[57]

First, there are passerelle clauses which provide for the extension of the ordinary legislative procedure. In particular, Article 48(7) TEU states that, as regards legal bases contained in the TFEU which provide for legislative acts to be adopted by the Council in accordance with a special legislative procedure, the European Council (acting unanimously and with the consent of the European Parliament) may decide to provide instead for the future application of the ordinary legislative procedure. Any such proposal must be notified to the national parliaments, each of which has an effective right to veto the proposal within a six-month period.[58] Specific provisions of the TFEU are excluded from the scope of application of this passerelle clause.[59] In addition, Article 81 TFEU contains a more specific passerelle clause whereby the Council may identify which aspects of family law having cross-border implications shall in the future be adopted by the ordinary legislative procedure (rather than by a special legislative procedure based on unanimity in the Council and consultation with the European Parliament); any such proposal to extend the ordinary legislative process must also be notified to the national parliaments, each of which has a right to veto the proposal within a six-month period.[60] The Council also enjoys specific passerelle powers—based in part on the previous provisions of the old EC Treaty—to convert the applicable legislative procedure from 'special' to 'ordinary' in respect of various aspects of the Union's social and environmental policies, though in those situations, the national parliaments hold no right of veto.[61]

Secondly, there are passerelle clauses which provide for the extension of QMV within the Council. In particular, Article 48(7) TEU provides that, as regards legal bases contained in the TFEU under which the Council acts by unanimity within the context of a special legislative procedure, the European Council (acting unanimously and with the consent of the European Parliament) may authorise the future use of QMV.[62] By these means, the Member States may decide that the legislative procedure should become more efficient within the Council while remaining 'special' as regards the participation of the European Parliament. Again, any such proposal must be notified to the national parliaments, each of which has an effective right to veto the proposal within a six-month period;[63] and again, specific provisions of the TFEU are excluded from the scope of application of this passerelle clause.[64] Among the latter is Article 312(2) TFEU on the adoption of the Union's multi-annual financial framework by the Council, acting unanimously

---

[57] See further Chapter 2 on the procedures for amending the Treaties.

[58] cp Art 6 of the Protocol on the role of national parliaments in the European Union.

[59] See Art 353 TFEU: the relevant provisions are Art 311, third and fourth paras TFEU on Union own resources; Art 312(2), first para TFEU on the multiannual financial framework; and the Art 352 TFEU flexibility clause.

[60] Note also the enhanced co-operation passerelle clause in Art 333 TFEU: if the legal basis to which an enhanced co-operation relates provides for the Council to legislate according to a special legislative procedure, then the Council (acting unanimously and in its restricted enhanced co-operation formation, after consulting the European Parliament) may decide instead to apply the ordinary legislative procedure. The national parliaments have no formal role here. See further Chapter 5.

[61] See Art 153(2) TFEU (social policy) and Art 192(2) TFEU (environment). Cf ex-Arts 137(2) and 175(2) EC (respectively).

[62] This passerelle clause may also be used in the context of certain legal bases for the adoption of non-legislative acts: see below.

[63] cp Art 6 of the Protocol on the role of national parliaments in the European Union.

[64] See Art 353 TFEU: the relevant provisions are Art 311, third and fourth paras TFEU on Union own

according to a special legislative procedure, with the consent of the European Parliament. However, that provision contains a specific passerelle clause of its own: the European Council may authorise the Council to act by QMV; that decision may be taken unilaterally, without the national parliaments having any right of veto.[65]

It is worth noting that other special legislative procedures under the revised Treaties involve different combinations of actors and decision-making rules. For example, legislative acts concerning the status of MEPs and the exercise of the European Parliament's supervisory prerogatives are to be adopted by the Parliament with limited participation from the Council and the Commission.[66] Such legal bases are not amenable to conversion into the ordinary legislative procedure by means of Article 48(7) TEU. As regards those legislative acts whose adoption occurs according to a special legislative procedure, but whose entry into force is subject to an 'organic law' clause, even where the passerelle powers of Article 48(7) TEU might be employed so as to convert the relevant legal basis into the ordinary legislative procedure, or to the use of QMV, pursuant to Article 48(7) TEU,[67] the requirement for approval by the Member States in accordance with their own constitutional requirements will remain inviolate.

E – Emergency Brakes

As regards a few legal bases based on the ordinary legislative procedure, the TL introduced a novel 'emergency brake' mechanism, deviating from the general rules applicable to QMV in the Council, by offering each Member State an effective right of veto (albeit one that is intended to be used only in special circumstances). Those emergency brakes can be divided into two variants.

The first variant applies to Union legislation governing the co-ordination of national social security systems. The old Article 42 EC used the co-decision procedure, but with the Council acting unanimously throughout. Article 48 TFEU now employs the ordinary legislative procedure, with the Council acting by QMV as normal. However, where a Member State declares that draft legislation would affect fundamental aspects, or the financial balance, of its social security system, it may refer the matter to the European Council, suspending the ordinary legislative procedure. Within four months, the European Council may (by consensus) refer the draft back to the Council, permitting the ordinary legislative procedure to resume; or instead kill off the draft, by either taking no action or requesting the Commission to submit a new proposal.[68]

The second 'emergency brake' variant applies to various legal bases for Union action to promote judicial co-operation in criminal matters and the definition of criminal offences and sanctions.[69] Here, where a Member State considers that draft legislation would affect

resources; Art 312(2), first para TFEU on the multiannual financial framework; and the Art 352 TFEU flexibility clause.

[65] Note also the enhanced co-operation passerelle clause in Art 333 TFEU: if unanimity applies under the legal basis to which an enhanced co-operation relates, then the Council (acting unanimously and in its restricted enhanced co-operation formation) may move instead to QMV. Again, the national parliaments have no role here. See further Chapter 5.

[66] See Arts 223(2), 226 and 228(4) TFEU.

[67] ie other than in the case of Art 311, third para TFEU: see Art 353 TFEU.

[68] Note Declaration No 23 annexed to the Final Act of the IGC which adopted the TL.

[69] See the detailed provisions of Arts 82(3) and 83(3) TFEU.

fundamental aspects of its criminal justice system, it may refer the matter to the European Council, again suspending the ordinary legislative procedure. This time, however, if the European Council fails to reach a consensus in favour of resuming the ordinary legislative procedure, and at least nine Member States wish to establish an enhanced co-operation on the basis of the draft act, authorisation to proceed with that enhanced co-operation shall automatically be deemed to have been granted (without having to comply with the usual procedural requirements applicable to the initiation of an enhanced co-operation, such as obtaining Commission support, Council approval and European Parliament consent).[70]

Since all those legal bases are explicitly described as using the ordinary legislative process, and decision-making within the Council is at no point formally subject to a requirement of unanimity, one assumes that the specifities of the 'emergency brake' mechanism—the de facto veto and (where applicable) the extraordinary authorisation to engage in enhanced cooperation—could not be suppressed pursuant to the passarelle clause contained in Article 48(7) TEU.

III – ADOPTION OF NON-LEGISLATIVE ACTS

Whereas the category of Union legislation refers to all those legal acts of the Union institutions adopted according to the ordinary or a special legislative procedure, as described above, the category of Union non-legislative acts comprises all the remaining instruments adopted by the Union institutions and other bodies created by or pursuant to the Treaties. In fact, Union non-legislative acts may be divided into three main categories: those adopted directly under the Treaties, where provided for by a specific legal basis; delegated acts in situations where the Commission has been authorised to supplement or amend 'non-essential elements' of a legislative act; and implementing acts of the Commission or the Council which are required for the uniform application of Union law.[71]

A – Non-legislative Acts Adopted Directly Under the Treaties

Myriad legal bases across the Treaties directly authorise the adoption of non-legislative acts: for example, the Commission adopts measures in the field of competition and state aids;[72] the ECB does so in the field of monetary policy.[73] The Council also adopts various non-legislative measures directly under the Treaties: sometimes by unanimity (eg rules governing the languages of the Union institutions,[74] and authorising enhanced co-operation within the CFSP);[75] sometimes by QMV (as with administrative co-operation between Member States within the Area of Freedom, Security and Justice,[76] and authorising enhanced co-operation in other fields of non-exclusive Union competence).[77] So too

---

[70] See Art 20 TEU and Art 329 TFEU. On enhanced co-operation, see further Chapter 5.
[71] Note also, on the adoption of recommendations, Art 292 TFEU. Also, eg Arts 60 and 97 TFEU.
[72] Arts 105 and 108 TFEU.
[73] Art 132 TFEU.
[74] Art 342 TFEU.
[75] Art 329(2) TFEU.
[76] Art 74 TFEU.
[77] Art 329(1) TFEU.

the European Council: for example, in establishing the list of Council configurations,[78] or extending the powers of a future European Public Prosecutor's Office.[79] One of the most important categories of non-legislative acts adopted directly under the Treaties are measures of the European Council and the Council in the field of the CFSP (where the use of legislative instruments is expressly precluded, and unanimity remains the general rule).[80] It should be noted that there is no general presumption that non-legislative acts may only be adopted upon a proposal from the Commission; each legal basis under the Treaties will identify, on a case-by-case basis, the institution or body that is entitled bring forward proposals for a non-legislative Union act.

As regards legal bases contained in the TFEU or Title V TEU, which provide for the Council to adopt non-legislative acts by unanimity, the passerelle clause contained in Article 48(7) TEU empowers the European Council (acting unanimously, with the consent of the European Parliament, and subject to a veto by each national parliament) to authorise the Council to act thenceforth by QMV.[81] As before, specific provisions of the TFEU are excluded from the scope of application of this simplified revision clause;[82] so too are the remaining provisions of the TEU, and any decisions with military implications or those in the area of defence. But in addition, Chapter 2, Title V TEU on the CFSP seems to contain its own passerelle clause: under Article 31(3) TEU, the European Council may unanimously decide to extend the use of QMV by the Council within this field (though again excluding decisions with military or defence implications).[83]

The European Parliament is able to exercise some influence over the adoption of certain non-legislative acts directly under the Treaties. That influence tends to take the form of ex ante input into the decision-making process through the consultation procedure;[84] though in a few cases, the European Parliament's supervisory powers are strengthened by a requirement to obtain its consent to the proposed measures.[85] There are still legal bases where the European Parliament exercises no direct control over the adoption of executive acts, though these generally concern individual administrative measures,[86] or the appointment of members to ancillary Union bodies.[87]

Just as important as understanding the institutional aspects of non-legislative acts adopted directly under the Treaties is to recognise that the distinction between legislative and non-legislative acts drawn under Union law is clearly not based on the sort of institutional criterion familiar to national legal systems which are organised according to a traditional separation of powers: with an institutional structure as complex as that of the

---

[78] Art 236 TFEU.

[79] Art 86(4) TFEU.

[80] See Chapter 2, Title V TEU, esp Art 31 TEU.

[81] Note Art 6 of the Protocol on the role of national parliaments in the European Union.

[82] See Art 353 TFEU: the relevant exclusions are non-legislative acts adopted under the Art 352 TFEU flexibility clause; and decisions to suspend Member State rights under Art 354 TFEU.

[83] Art 31(4) TEU. The relationship between Article 48(7) TEU and Article 31(3) TEU seems to give rise to certain problems: see further eg M Dougan, 'The Treaty of Lisbon 2007: Winning Minds, Not Hearts' (2008) 45 *CMLRev* 617, 645–46.

[84] eg Art 27(3) TEU on the organisation and functioning of the European External Action Service; Art 78(3) TFEU on emergency measures to cope with asylum influxes.

[85] eg Art 50(2) TEU on conclusion of agreements between the Union and withdrawing states; Art 352 TFEU on non-legislative measures adopted under the flexibility clause.

[86] eg Art 66 TFEU on urgent and exceptional safeguard restrictions on capital movements as regards third countries; Art 75, second para TFEU on the implementation of restrictive measures against natural and legal persons/groups.

[87] eg Arts 257(4), 301 and 305 TFEU on members of specialised courts, the Economic and Social Committee and the Committee of the Regions, respectively.

EU, it would have been difficult to state (for example) that *only* acts of the Council and the European Parliament, or *all* acts of the Council and/or the European Parliament, are to be considered legislative in nature. The Treaties settle instead on a purely formal criterion for distinguishing between legislative and non-legislative acts, based on the applicable decision-making procedures for their adoption, as they are identified in specific legal provisions and on an ad hoc basis under the Treaties. But could such a criterion ever hope to reflect any coherent underlying constitutional principle? It seems instead to emerge as a labelling exercise with an essentially pragmatic basis and some rather arbitrary consequences.[88]

After all, from the point of view of process, many 'special legislative procedures' (based on a Commission proposal, unanimity or QMV in Council, and consultation with or the consent of the European Parliament) appear identical to non-legislative procedures conducted in the same manner.[89] Moreover, as regards their substance, many measures identified as 'non-legislative' in nature will seem indistinguishable from 'legislative' ones in terms of their scope of application (in general terms across the entire Union territory) and subject-matter (regulating the rights and obligations of natural and legal persons). Consider, for example, regulations and directives adopted to give effect to the competition principles set out Articles 101 and 102 TFEU.[90] One might query whether a measure such as Regulation 1/2003 on competition enforcement is really any less 'legislative' in nature—in terms of the procedure for its adoption, or its substantive content—than many of the 'legislative acts' which would be adopted elsewhere under the Treaties.[91] Or again, consider Council measures implementing agreements between the social partners falling within the fields of social policy competence entrusted to the Union under Article 153 TFEU.[92] Are directives enacting binding Union-wide rules on issues such as parental leave,[93] part-time workers[94] or fixed-term workers[95] really best categorised as 'non-legislative' in character?

The desire to bestow upon the Union a clearer hierarchy of norms, for the sake of enhancing the transparency of its activities, may therefore be undermined by certain anomalies and controversies. In particular, the lack of a coherent distinction between legislative and non-legislative acts is likely to produce similarly arbitrary knock-on effects for other provisions premised on exactly the same distinction: for example, the national parliaments' right to object to legislative proposals on subsidiarity grounds;[96] the Council's obligation to deliberate and vote on legislative acts in public;[97] and the ability of natural and legal persons to bring actions for annulment without having to demonstrate 'individual concern'[98]—all issues that will be discussed further elsewhere in this book.

---

[88] See further eg M Dougan, 'The Convention's Draft Constitutional Treaty: Bringing Europe Closer to its Lawyers?' (2003) 28 *ELRev* 763, 783–84; J Kokott and A Ruth, 'The European Convention and its Draft Treaty Establishing a Constitution for Europe: Appropriate Answers to the Laeken Questions?' (2003) 40 *CMLRev* 1315, 1341–43.

[89] Consider eg Art 74 TFEU on administrative co-operation within the Area of Freedom, Security and Justice.

[90] ie adopted under Art 103 TFEU.

[91] [2003] OJ L1/1. On the enforcement of Union competition law, see further Chapter 25.

[92] ie as provided for under Art 155(2) TFEU.

[93] Directive 1996/43 [1996] OJ L145/4.

[94] Directive 1997/81 [1998] OJ L14/9.

[95] Directive 1999/70 [1999] OJ L175/43.

[96] And to seek the annulment of Union legislation on subsidiarity grounds. See further Chapter 5.

[97] See further Chapter 3.

[98] See further Chapter 6.

B – Non-legislative Acts Adopted as Delegated Acts

The second category of non-legislative Union instrument is governed by Article 290 TFEU: a legislative act may delegate to the Commission the power to adopt non-legislative acts of general application to supplement or amend certain 'non-essential elements' of the parent act. The latter must explicitly define the objectives, content, scope and duration of the Commission's delegated powers. It must also lay down the conditions to which the delegation is subject: the possibility of the delegated powers being revoked by the Council or the European Parliament; and/or of the delegated act entering into force only in the absence of objection from the Council or the European Parliament within a predefined period.

This category of 'delegated acts' is another innovation of the TL. The primary aim of Article 290 TFEU is to encourage the Union legislature to concentrate on defining only the central tenets of legislation, in the hope that this will make it easier for the Council and/or European Parliament to agree on any given regulatory package, and permit the latter to be adapted more quickly and effectively to changes in market behaviour or scientific technology. The introduction of delegated acts is also a useful attempt to divide the Union's executive activities more clearly between the quasi-legislative and the purely administrative—formally subjecting the former category of powers to various direct forms of scrutiny by the Union legislature itself, in a manner which is assumed to be commensurate with their greater constitutional and regulatory importance.

Some of the terms and conditions contained in Article 290 TFEU are obviously capable of giving rise to uncertainties and difficulties of interpretation.[99] Concepts such as what amounts to the Commission supplementing or amending, rather than merely implementing, a legislative measure will play a crucial part in dividing the scope of application of delegated acts under Article 290 TFEU from that of 'implementing acts' as dealt with under Article 291 TFEU (discussed further below).[100] Similarly, what constitutes the essential, as opposed to non-essential, elements of a legislative measure, for the purposes of dividing the delegated powers of the Commission from the primary powers of the Council and/ or the European Parliament, obviously cries out for further clarification through institutional practice and (eventually) judicial review.[101] Other uncertainties relate to the scope of the Council and/or the European Parliament's scrutiny powers over the Commission's delegated activities: are the possibilities of veto or revocation explicitly identified in Article 290 TFEU intended to be exhaustive or purely indicative?

Soon after the entry into force of the TL, the Commission sought to explain its understanding of how the new system of delegated acts under Article 290 TFEU should function in practice.[102] Perhaps unsurprisingly, the Commission focused much of its attention on the appropriate terms of any delegation of power, as well as on the scope for external control over its delegated activities. For example, on grounds of efficiency and speed of

---

[99] See further eg B Driessen, 'Delegated Legislation after the Treaty of Lisbon: An Analysis of Article 290 TFEU' (2010) 35 *ELRev* 837.

[100] Though some situations will be clear, eg if implementation relates to a non-legislative parent act, or is to be carried out by the Council, it must take the form of an implementing act under Art 291 TFEU (since delegated acts under Art 290 TFEU are only available as regards legislative parents acts and may only be adopted by the Commission).

[101] For recent examples of judicial review over the Commission's delegated powers, consider Case C-403/05 *Parliament v Commission* [2007] ECR I-9045; Cases C-14/06 and C-295/06 *Parliament and Denmark v Commission* [2008] ECR I-1649.

[102] Commission, *Communication on the implementation of Article 290 TFEU*, COM(2009) 673 Final.

action, the Commission argued that delegations of power under Article 290 TFEU should preferably be of indefinite duration, subject to a formal power of revocation at any time; rather than based on so-called 'sunset clauses', which set an automatic time limit for the lapse of delegated authority. The Commission also clearly believes that the powers of veto or revocation identified in Article 290 TFEU should be the only options available to the Council and/or Parliament for controlling the exercise of the Commission's delegated powers—vetoing an individual measure being the norm, revoking the entire delegated power constituting an exceptional measure. In particular, while the Commission seems happy to consult with national experts when preparing its delegated acts, it wishes to retain autonomy over its own decision-making prerogatives—thus excluding any more formal institutional role for national representatives in the preparation of delegated acts, as compared to the powers conferred upon the committees of national experts which form a familiar part of the 'comitology system' employed in respect of the category of Union 'implementing acts' (discussed further below).[103]

Legislative practice in the first year after the entry into force of the TL suggests that the Union legislature generally prefers to confer delegated powers upon the Commission for a fixed period of time which is nevertheless automatically renewable;[104] for the delegation to be subject to revocation by the Council and/or European Parliament at any time (though without affecting the validity of delegated acts already in force); and for the Council and/or European Parliament to enjoy a power of veto over any delegated act, to be exercised within a specific time period after the latter's notification by the Commission and before its possible entry into force.[105]

C – Non-legislative Acts Adopted as Implementing Acts

Article 291(1) TFEU reflects a basic fact which has long underpinned the system for implementing Union law: in the vast majority of situations, it falls to the Member States themselves to adopt all measures of national law necessary for the purely executive implementation of legally binding Union acts. For those purposes, the Member States are bound by the duty of loyal co-operation laid down in Article 4(3) TEU. The latter provision has been interpreted by the Court of Justice so as to impose various more specific obligations upon the Member States when discharging their function of implementing Union law within their respective territories. For example, in *Commission v Greece (Greek Maize)*, it was held that the Member States are obliged to take all the measures necessary to guar-

---

[103] However, on delegated acts in the field of financial services, see Declaration No 39 annexed to the Final Act of the IGC which adopted the TL [2010] OJ C83/350; and s 4.2 of the Commission's 2010 Communication, COM(2009) 673 Final. Consider eg Reg 1093/2010 establishing a European Banking Authority [2010] OJ L331/12; Reg 1094/2010 establishing the European Insurance and Occupational Pensions Authority [2010] OJ L331/48; Reg 1095/2010 establishing the European Securities and Markets Authority [2010] OJ L331/84.

[104] Subject to revocation by the Council and/or European Parliament.

[105] See eg Reg 438/2010 amending Reg 998/2003 on the animal health requirements applicable to the non-commercial movement of pet animals [2010] OJ L132/3; Reg 995/2010 laying down the obligations of operators who place timber and timber products on the market [2010] OJ L295/23; Reg 1090/2010 amending Dir 2009/42 on statistical returns in respect of carriage of goods and passengers by sea [2010] OJ L325/1; Dir 2010/76 amending Dirs 2006/48 and 2006/49 as regards capital requirements for the trading book and for resecuritisations, and the supervisory review of remuneration policies [2010] OJ L329/3; Reg 1236/2010 laying down a scheme of control and enforcement applicable in the area covered by the Convention on future multilateral co-operation in the North-East Atlantic fisheries [2010] OJ L348/17.

antee the application and effectiveness of Union law; for that purpose, whilst the choice of sanction for breaching Union law remains within their discretion, Member States must ensure that infringements of Union law are penalised under conditions equivalent to those applicable to infringements of comparable national law and which, in any event, make the penalty effective, proportionate and dissuasive.[106]

Nevertheless, Article 291(2) TFEU goes on to identify our third category of non-legislative Union instrument: where uniform conditions for implementing binding Union acts are needed, those acts shall confer implementing powers (the ability to adopt non-legislative measures) upon the Commission or, in duly justified specific cases, upon the Council. In addition, the Council is specifically mandated to adopt the non-legislative measures required for implementation of the CFSP.[107]

The principle now found in Article 291(2) TFEU—that the executive implementation of Union law, where required at the Union level, should generally fall to the Commission, and only exceptionally to the Council—is not a new one; interpretation of that provision will doubtless be aided through appropriate reference to the legal framework as it stood pre-TL. In particular, the SEA had amended ex-Article 202 EC so as to establish the general rule that power to implement acts of the Council should be conferred upon the Commission. The Council was allowed to reserve implementing power for itself in specific cases, though the Court of Justice came to insist that the Council must state in detail the grounds for such a decision.[108] In particular, the Council was obliged to explain properly, by reference to the nature and content of the basic instrument to be implemented, why an exception was being made to the rule that, when implementing measures need to be taken at Union level, it is the Commission which is normally to be responsible for exercising that power.[109] Where a conferral of implementing powers to the Commission did take place, the Court also stipulated that the essential elements of matters to be dealt with by the Commission under its derived powers had to be determined by the parent act of the Council itself.[110] Under that legal framework, the Commission came to exercise extensive powers for the executive implementation of Union legislation in fields such as agricultural policy, competition policy, research, and economic and social cohesion (including managing the resources made available through the Union's structural funds).

Ex-Article 202 EC also expressly recognised the Council's right to impose various procedural requirements upon the Commission's exercise of the powers of implementation granted to it under acts of the Council—provided that such requirements were 'consonant with principles and rules to be laid down in advance'. A closed catalogue of procedures was accordingly laid down, eventually contained in what is known as the Council's Second Comitology Decision.[111] Each procedure involves the submission of the Commission's draft implementing measures to a committee composed of national officials. However, the precise degree of constraint placed upon the Commission's freedom of action then

---

[106] Case 68/88 *Commission v Greece* [1989] ECR 2965. See further eg C Harding, 'Member State Enforcement of European Community Measures: The Chimera of 'Effective' Enforcement' (1997) 4 *MJ* 5.

[107] As provided for under Arts 24 and 26 TEU.

[108] See eg Case 16/88 *Commission v Council* [1989] ECR 3457, 3485.

[109] eg Case C-257/01 *Commission v Council* [2005] ECR I-345; Case C-133/06 *Parliament v Council* [2008] ECR I-3189.

[110] Case 25/70 *Köster* [1970] ECR 1161, 1170.

[111] Decision 1999/468 [1999] OJ L184/23. This replaced the First Comitology Decision 87/373 [1987] OJ L197/33. For general judicial observations on the relationship between the comitology system and the principle of good administration, see Joined Cases C-154/04 and 155/04 *Alliance for Natural Health* [2005] ECR I-6451.

varies from one procedure to another. For instance, under the 'advisory procedure', the Commission is required to take the utmost account of the opinion delivered by the committee, but is not bound by it.[112] However, under the 'management procedure', in the event of a negative opinion by the committee, the matter is referred to the Council, which may (within a prescribed time-limit) substitute its own decision for that of the Commission.[113] The 'regulatory procedure' is different again. There, the Commission may only adopt its proposed implementing measure if it gains the positive approval of the committee; in the event of a negative or no opinion, the Commission must submit a proposal to the Council. The latter may then either adopt the Commission's proposal for itself; or reject that proposal and oblige the Commission to carry out a re-examination; or do neither— only in which event may the Commission proceed to adopt the proposed implementing measure for itself.[114]

It is for the Council (and where relevant the European Parliament), when adopting an act conferring implementing powers upon the Commission, to determine which (if any) procedure should be attached to the exercise of that power. Article 2 of the Second Comitology Decision provides certain criteria on which type of procedure is appropriate for various categories of implementing powers, but the Court of Justice has held that these criteria are not strictly binding, though the Council (and where relevant the European Parliament) is obliged at least to state its reasons for deviating from the guidance laid down in Article 2.[115] Furthermore, the Court has rejected the argument that, where implementation involves no more than simply applying set rules to individual cases, the legislature should be legally obliged to impose only the relatively light-touch advisory procedure.[116]

The comitology system has frequently provoked discord among the Union institutions. In particular, following the introduction of the co-operation and then especially of the co-decision legislative procedures,[117] the European Parliament raised concerns that it was effectively being excluded from supervising the exercise of implementing powers devolved upon the Commission through parent legislation which the Parliament had been closely or even jointly involved in adopting—thus distorting the inter-institutional balance, as intended by the Treaties, in favour of the Council. This prompted a series of often acrimonious political and legal disputes between the European Parliament and the Council.[118] In 2006, the Second Comitology Decision was amended so as to make provision for a further procedure, the 'regulatory procedure with scrutiny', designed to address some of the European Parliament's concerns.[119] The latter is to be used where Union legislation has been enacted in accordance with the co-decision procedure, providing for the adoption of measures of general scope designed to amend non-essential elements of the

---

[112] See Art 3 of Decision 1999/468.

[113] See Art 4 of Decision 1999/468.

[114] See Art 5 of Decision 1999/468.

[115] Case C-378/00 *Commission v Parliament and Council* [2003] ECR I-937; Case C-122/04 *Commission v Council and Parliament* [2006] ECR I-2001.

[116] Case 16/88 *Commission v Council* [1989] ECR 3457.

[117] See above.

[118] On Parliament's judicial challenges to the comitology system, see eg Case 302/87 *Parliament v Council* [1988] ECR 5615; Case C-417/93 *Parliament v Council* [1995] ECR I-1185; Case C-259/95 *Parliament v Council* [1997] ECR I-5303.

[119] See Art 5a of Decision 1999/468 as amended by Decision 2006/512 [2006] OJ L200/11. Cf the agreement between Parliament and Commission on procedures for implementing Decision 1999/468 [2008] OJ C143/1. See further eg G Schusterschitz and S Kotz, 'The Comitology Reform of 2006' (2007) 3 *European Constitutional Law Review* 68.

parent instrument.[120] In such cases, even if the committee of national officials approves the Commission's draft implementing measure, either the European Parliament or the Council may still effectively veto its adoption on specified grounds.[121] Where the committee delivers a negative or no opinion on the draft implementing measure, the Commission must submit a proposal to the Council; as under the ordinary 'regulatory procedure', the latter may then either reject the proposal, or adopt it, or leave the Commission free to carry on for itself. The difference is that the European Parliament in this context still enjoys the right to veto adoption of the implementing measures—whether by Council or Commission—on specified grounds.[122]

The TL introduced a new legal basis for the adoption of future comitology provisions. Article 291(3) TFEU now provides that regulations adopted through the ordinary legislative procedure shall lay down in advance the rules and general principles concerning mechanisms for control by Member States of the Commission's exercise of implementing powers. On the one hand, that provision further enhances the influence of the European Parliament when it comes to establishing the general comitology framework: the necessary 'rules and general principles' are to be adopted according to the ordinary legislative procedure (rather than mere consultation as previously provided for under ex-Article 202 EC) as regards all situations in which the Commission exercises implementing powers (even under legislative acts originally adopted by a special legislative procedure; and also as regards non-legislative acts enacted without any participation by the European Parliament). On the other hand, it should be noted that Article 291(3) TFEU refers to control of the Commission's exercise of implementing powers only 'by Member States'—a wording that seems to contradict the trend to offer the European Parliament a greater say in the daily supervision of the exercise of the Commission's executive powers, and could indeed be construed as a challenge even to the Council's long-standing ability to intervene in the adoption of implementing acts, under the management procedure, regulatory procedure or regulatory procedure with scrutiny.

In that regard, it is worth noting that the Commission has, for its part, long found it difficult to love the comitology system—based upon its apparent self-perception as the Union's 'true' executive organ and a consequent sense that the intrusive power of the committees, and indeed of the other Union institutions, interferes with its rightful decision-making autonomy.[123] Already in 2002, the Commission had proposed amending the Second Comitology Decision so as to reduce the committees' power to block Commission proposals ex ante; and to permit the Council and the European Parliament to object to Commission implementing measures only ex post, by means of an action for annulment before the Court of Justice.[124] The entry into force of the Lisbon Treaty has offered the Commission an opportunity to make its case afresh. In the Commission's view, the revised Treaties—with their clear distinction between delegated acts under Article 290 TFEU and

---

[120] See Art 2(2) of the amended Decision 1999/468.

[121] ie that it exceeds the implementing powers provided for in the basic instrument or is not compatible with the aim or the content of the basic instrument or does not respect the principles of subsidiarity or proportionality.

[122] Again, that the draft act exceeds the implementing powers provided for in the basic instrument or is not compatible with the aim or the content of the basic instrument or does not respect the principles of subsidiarity or proportionality.

[123] See further, on the Commission's attitude, eg COM(2002) 728 Final/2.

[124] COM(2002) 719 Final. See also COM(2004) 324 Final. On judicial review of the acts of Union institutions before the Union courts, see Chapter 6.

mere implementing acts under Article 291 TFEU—call for a thorough re-examination of the entire comitology system. In particular, the scheme and text of those Treaty provisions suggest that control over the Commission's executive activities by the Council and European Parliament should be limited to the category of delegated acts; the Member States, and they alone, should be involved in scrutinising the adoption by the Commission of its implementing acts. The Commission has therefore proposed the adoption of a new Comitology Regulation based upon Article 291(3) TFEU but containing only two main committee procedures: a purely 'advisory procedure', which would be used in the majority of situations; and a more exceptional 'examination procedure', which could only be used in certain specified cases and whereby delivery by the committee of a negative opinion would block the Commission's draft implementing act but without further involving either the Council or the European Parliament.[125] It will be interesting to see whether the Commission succeeds in persuading the Council and the European Parliament thus to sacrifice their existing powers to scrutinise the exercise of purely executive implementing powers at the Union level.[126]

IV – SOME FURTHER ISSUES CONCERNING DECISION-MAKING INTERACTION BETWEEN THE UNION INSTITUTIONS

Having explained the main features of the Union's decision-making procedures—both legislative and non-legislative—we should now consider certain additional aspects of the interaction between the Commission, the Council and the European Parliament which count as important facets of the decision-making process at Union level.

A – The Commission's Right to Alter or Withdraw Its Proposal

The Commission is expressly empowered, as long as the Council has not acted, to alter its proposal at any time during the procedures leading to the adoption of a Union act (whether the latter is legislative or non-legislative in character).[127] There are various reasons why the Commission may choose to do so.

In the first place, the Commission may independently form the view that the proposal needs to be improved or completed; or perhaps to be updated, in order to keep abreast of scientific developments, especially if it has been lying on the table for some time. Or account may have to be taken of changes in the legal situation: for instance, after the entry into force of the SEA, the Commission substituted ex-Article 95 EC (now Article 114

---

[125] See COM(2010) 83 Final. The Commission envisages that references to existing comitology procedures under Decision 1999/468 should be converted into references to its new comitology procedures under the draft regulation; with the exception of references to the 'regulatory procedure with scrutiny', which would remain in force for existing measures which already utilise that procedure.

[126] Note that the European Parliament seems to accept the need, in principle, for an overhaul of the existing comitology system in the light of the TL: see Resolution on Parliament's new role and responsibilities in implementing the Treaty of Lisbon [2010] OJ C212E/37, paras 70–73.

[127] Art 293(2) TFEU.

TFEU) as the legal basis of a large number of proposals which had originally been based upon other provisions of the Treaty of Rome.

Secondly, the Commission may respond to an opinion rendered by the European Parliament under the consultation procedure, or at first reading under the ordinary legislative procedure, by incorporating into its proposal some or all of the amendments put forward by the Parliament. At second reading under the ordinary legislative procedure, the Commission indicates its acceptance (or otherwise) of the European Parliament's amendments, not by amending its own proposal, but by delivering an opinion, as required pursuant to Article 294(7)(c) TFEU.[128]

Thirdly, the Commission may alter its proposal in order to facilitate decision-making within the Council. Decisions are reached by the Council through negotiations between national delegations in working groups, in COREPER and at ministerial level. Those negotiations involve progressive adaptation of the Commission's proposal in order to take account of Member States' particular interests and difficulties. The process is managed by the Presidency, aided by the General Secretariat of the Council, with the aim of achieving a balanced compromise text, commanding the qualified majority or unanimity required for the adoption of the measure in question. The Commission is represented at meetings of Council bodies where its proposals are under discussion,[129] and it may play a vital part in the development of the Presidency compromise, both by providing technical assistance and by indicating amendments it is able to accept.

There is no explicit provision of the Treaties enabling the Commission to withdraw a proposal which it has already submitted to the Council. However, it seems generally agreed that, within certain limits, the Commission does indeed enjoy such a power.[130] One view is that withdrawal may be regarded as the extreme case of amendment, but perhaps the better view is that both amendment and withdrawal are corollaries of the Commission's right of initiative: the latter would be incomplete if the Commission, having put forward a proposal which it no longer considered appropriate, was then unable to remedy the situation. At the same time, the power of withdrawal should not be used to prevent other Union institutions from performing their envisaged decision-making roles under the Treaties. Thus, it might be considered an abuse of power for the Commission to withdraw a proposal which is already on the point of being adopted by the Council, simply in order to prevent the latter institution from exercising its own power of amendment (considered below). Similarly, under the ordinary legislative procedure, one might consider that the Commission has no right to withdraw its proposal once the Council has adopted its position at first reading. This seems to follow from the clear terms in which Article 294 TFEU specifies the options open to the European Parliament and to the Council at second reading, and the legal consequences that ineluctably follow from the course of action chosen.

---

[128] Art 293(2) TFEU, as the more general provision, must be read consistently with the specific requirements of the ordinary legislative procedure.

[129] Art 5(2) of the Council's Rules of Procedure [2009] OJ L325/35 provides: 'The Commission shall be invited to take part in meetings of the Council. . . . The Council may, however, decide to deliberate without the presence of the Commission.'

[130] For an early proponent of this view, see eg J Mégret et al, *Le droit de la CEE* (Brussels, Editions de l'Université de Bruxelles, 1979) vol 9, 135–36.

B – The Council's Power of Amendment

The Council has a general power under Article 293(1) TFEU to amend proposals of the Commission—for example, when adopting its position at first reading under the ordinary legislative procedure, or when adopting definitively a legislative act under a special legislative procedure—but in so doing, the Council must act unanimously. The rule requiring unanimity for the amendment of Commission proposals was of limited practical significance during the period when the Council was required to act unanimously anyway or habitually acted on the basis of consensus even when unanimity was not strictly required. Now, however, with the enormous extension in the range of matters that can be decided by a QMV, and with majority decisions actually taken more frequently in practice where the Treaties do so permit, the rule in Article 293(1) TFEU has come into its own as a pivotal element of the Council/Commission relationship. This is because, if the Council is unwilling to adopt a proposal without making certain changes, the only way of avoiding the unanimity rule is for a compromise to be negotiated that the Commission can make its own; that compromise will then have the legal status of an amended Commission proposal and be capable of being enacted by a qualified majority. The Commission is thus able to maintain direct influence over the progress of its own proposal, right up to the final outcome of the negotiations within the Council.

The right of the Council to amend the Commission's proposal by unanimity does not extend to the substitution of an entirely new proposal, since that would be to usurp the Commission's right of initiative.[131] Nonetheless, it should be the case that Council amendments, however radical, will not be ultra vires, as long as the subject-matter of the measure in question remains the same. For instance, in a draft directive concerning animal welfare, the Council may decide to establish different criteria of welfare from those proposed by the Commission; but it would not be entitled to transform the directive into one fixing quality standards for fresh meat.

Article 293(1) TFEU refers to certain exceptions to its own general requirement of unanimity—the most important of which concerns the stages of conciliation and third reading under the ordinary legislative procedure.[132] The Council is thus able to adopt by QMV a text representing the result of a successful conciliation, regardless of whether the Commission has altered its proposal accordingly; indeed, from the end of the first reading, the Commission's original proposal ceases to be relevant to the final outcome of the ordinary legislative procedure. In any case, the requirement of unanimity for the amendment of Commission *proposals* does not extend to cases where the decision-making process is initiated by the submission to the Council of a *recommendation* by the Commission.[133] That is the case, for example, where the Commission seeks authorisation to negotiate an international agreement with a third country or international organisation. The Commission makes a recommendation to the Council, which decides whether to authorise the opening of negotiations and, if so, whether any negotiating directives should be issued to the Commission; in so doing, the Council is free to act by a qualified major-

---

[131] Again, a view adopted early on, eg by Mégret et al, ibid, 133.

[132] ie under Arts 294(10) and (13) TFEU. The other exceptions involve certain decisions concerning the Union's finances, ie under Arts 310, 312, 314 and 315(2) TFEU.

[133] This follows from the very wording of Art 293(1) TFEU: 'Where, pursuant to the Treaties, the Council acts *on a proposal from the Commission*' (emphasis added).

ity, even if it departs from the Commission's recommendation as to what the parameters of the negotiations should be.[134]

C – The European Parliament's Participation

There is obviously a great difference between the ability of the European Parliament to influence the final shape of a legislative measure enacted under the ordinary legislative procedure, as compared to its position under a special legislative procedure, especially where the latter is based upon mere consultation. In particular, we have seen how, where consultation of the European Parliament is required by the legal basis of a legislative proposal, the Council must be formally seised of the opinion rendered by the European Parliament before proceeding to the adoption of the act in question (apart from in urgent cases, where all procedural possibilities for obtaining the opinion have been tried unsuccessfully); and that, if either the Commission or the Council is minded to amend a proposal in a way that would alter the substance of the text on which the Parliament has already been consulted, adoption may have to be postponed pending reconsultation. However, the Council, having considered the Parliament's opinion, is under no legal obligation to follow it. In practice, the most effective way for the European Parliament to influence the final shape of Union legislation on a matter for which a special legislative procedure is prescribed, based upon mere consultation, is by putting political pressure on the Commission to incorporate elements of the opinion into an amended proposal. If the Commission responds favourably, the Council will then be faced with a text which it will only be able to amend further by unanimity.[135]

It was often the case, at first reading under the ordinary legislative procedure in its early years of operation, that the traditional interplay between the Commission and the Council, based on the former's monopoly of initiative and the two institutions' respective powers of amendment, tended to dominate negotiations. However, the Commission and the Council would doubtless be aware of any major concerns harboured by the European Parliament—concerns which would have to be accommodated if the legislative act in question is ultimately to receive the approval of the co-legislators. Moreover, from the beginning of the second reading, we have noted that the Commission's proposal is effectively spent; the politically significant interaction becomes that between the European Parliament and the Council in relation to the latter's first reading position. Experience in the years after co-decision was first introduced by the TEU already provided reason for optimism that the give-and-take necessary to enable the procedure to function effectively would indeed be forthcoming between the co-legislators.[136] However, the ordinary legislative procedure has also witnessed moments of serious inter-institutional tension: for example, July 2005 saw the first occasion on which the European Parliament simply rejected a Council position by absolute majority at second reading, in the case of the proposed directive on the patentability of computer software, after many MEPs reacted

---

[134] See Art 207(3) TFEU on agreements in the field of the common commercial policy; and Art 218(3) TFEU on international agreements in general. Consider also eg Art 126 TFEU on the excessive deficit procedure.

[135] Under the rule in Art 293(1) TFEU (considered above). See further R Kardasheva, 'The Power to Delay: The European Parliament's Influence in the Consultation Procedure' (2009) 47 *JCMS* 385.

[136] See eg M Shackleton, 'The Politics of Co-Decision' (2000) 38 *JCMS* 325.

angrily to the perception that neither the Commission nor the Council had taken seriously the concerns expressed by the Parliament in its opinion at first reading.[137]

In more recent years, however, some commentators have worried that the pendulum may have swung too far in the other direction. A very significant proportion of Union legislative proposals adopted via the ordinary legislative procedure are now agreed at first reading stage through the medium of an informal mechanism known as 'trilogues'.[138] A trilogue is a tripartite meeting bringing together representatives from the Council, the European Parliament and the Commission with a view to reaching agreement on draft legislative texts. Such trilogues can take place at any stage of the ordinary legislative procedure, but they have proven particularly successful at the first reading stage, where their aim is to hammer out an early compromise text that can be signed up to by the Council and effectively rubber-stamped by the plenary session of the European Parliament, thus saving the ordinary legislative procedure from having to proceed any further. On the one hand, the trilogues are generally acknowledged to have made a valuable contribution to the speed and efficiency of the Union's ordinary legislative procedure. On the other hand, concerns have been expressed about whether the growing use of trilogues is entirely consonant with the desire for full and proper democratic scrutiny of Union legislative acts: the trilogue system offers significant influence to those MEPs who make up the relevant parliamentary committee, conducting the negotiations and agreeing to the compromise texts, which might be seen to undermine the ability of the European Parliament as a whole to engage with and shape the draft Union legislative act; along the same lines, one might query whether the use of trilogues effectively replaces open political debate within the European Parliament with closed technocratic negotiation between the three main Union institutions.[139] The European Parliament has responded to such concerns by adopting a Code of Conduct designed to increase the transparency and accountability of trilogues, especially at the early stages of the ordinary legislative procedure: for example, by ensuring the representative nature of the Parliament's negotiating team; insisting that trilogue meetings should in principle be announced; and setting out rules on the circulation of relevant documentation.[140]

V – SOME CONCLUDING REMARKS

The Union's myriad decision-making procedures for adopting legislative and non-legislative acts are a prime illustration of the fundamental constitutional notion of the Union's 'inter-institutional balance' in action. The Treaties have been carefully crafted so as to ensure that an appropriate combination of institutional actors, exercising a predetermined degree of power and influence, take part in the enactment of legally binding Union instruments. Fundamental considerations, such as the need for proper democratic legitimacy, the desire to safeguard national interests, the search for common objectives and values, protecting the interests of non-majoritarian stakeholders, securing adequate participation,

---

[137] See COM(2002) 92 Final.

[138] See Joint Declaration of the European Parliament, Council and Commission on practical arrangements for the co-decision procedure [2007] OJ C145/5.

[139] cp Editorial, 'European Elections: Is the European Parliament Important Today?' (2009) 46 *CMLRev* 767.

[140] See Annex XX (Code of Conduct for negotiating in the context of the ordinary legislative procedure) annexed to the European Parliament's Rules of Procedure (7th Parliamentary Term, adopted in December 2009).

expertise and consensus, etc—all are balanced against each other, though in very different ways across the various fields of Union activity.

The result is a decision-making system whose complexity can understandably confound the average citizen, and where the apparent triumph of one fundamental principle (eg the preservation of Member State power through and within the Council) can produce a sense that other competing interests (eg respecting the popular will as represented in the European Parliament) have been unduly neglected or even unjustly sacrificed. Nevertheless, such complex and often contested balancing exercises appear inevitable in an entity such as the European Union in its current state of development. Moreover, successive amendments to the Treaties have at least gradually promoted the emergence of an idealised template for law-making at the EU level of governance: the Commission proposes in the general interest, then the Council and the European Parliament adopt the final legislative text, representing and reconciling the interests of the Member States and of the citizens (respectively).

Having explained how the Union institutions reach their legally binding decisions, our next chapter will explore the closely related question of what sorts of decision-making powers the Union actually enjoys, as well as the various constitutional principles which structure the legitimate exercise of those powers. As we shall see, the topic of Union competences further illustrates and refines our understanding of the Union's complex and delicate 'inter-institutional balance'.

Further Reading

As before, the sheer pace and scale of EU reform means that some of the following suggestions for further reading are now of value primarily in understanding the context and development of the EU's current decision-making procedures.

M Andenas and A Türk (eds), *Delegated Legislation and the Role of Committees in the EC* (The Hague, Kluwer, 2000).

A Arnull and D Wincott (eds), *Accountability and Legitimacy in the European Union* (Oxford, Oxford University Press, 2003).

C F Bergström, *Comitology: Delegation of Powers in the European Union and the Committee System* (Oxford, Oxford University Press, 2005).

P Craig, *EU Administrative Law* (Oxford, Oxford University Press, 2006).

D Curtin, *Executive Power of the European Union: Law, Practices and the Living Constitution* (Oxford, Oxford University Press, 2009).

A Dashwood, 'Community Legislative Procedures in the Era of the Treaty on European Union' (1994) 19 *ELRev* 343.

——, 'Community Decision-Making After Amsterdam' (1998) 1 *CYELS* 25.

——, 'The Constitution of the European Union After Nice: Law-Making Procedures' (2001) 26 *ELRev* 215.

C Joerges and E Vos (eds), *EU Committees: Social Regulation, Law and Politics* (Oxford, Hart Publishing, 1999).

R Kardasheva, 'The Power to Delay: the European Parliament's Influence in the Consultation Procedure' (2009) 47 *JCMS* 385.

F Mancini, *Democracy and Constitutionalism in the European Union* (Oxford, Hart Publishing, 2000).

M Shackleton, 'The Politics of Co-Decision' (2000) 38 *JCMS* 325.

J Wouters, 'Institutional and Constitutional Challenges for the European Union: Some Reflections in the Light of the Treaty of Nice' (2001) 26 *ELRev* 342.

5

The System of Union Competences

This chapter outlines the legal framework underpinning the system of Union competences. According to the principle of conferral, the Union institutions enjoy only those powers conferred upon them by the Member States. Once the existence of Union competence is identified by reference to an appropriate legal basis within the Treaties, the principle of subsidiarity then seeks to guide the circumstances under which the Union should actually exercise that competence in practice (rather than leave the matter for the Member States to address). For its part, the principle of proportionality seeks to control the form and extent of Union action, which should not go beyond what is necessary to achieve its own objectives. Discussion closes with the phenomenon of flexibility: the possibility that certain Union acts will only apply to certain Member States, with other countries either unwilling or unable to participate in the relevant exercise of Union competence.

I – THE FUNDAMENTAL PRINCIPLES OF UNION COMPETENCE IN ARTICLES 4 AND 5 TEU

The system of Union competences—exactly which powers the EU possesses and the manner in which it should exercise them—is based upon three fundamental principles contained in Articles 4 and 5 TEU. The relevant provisions read as follows:

Article 4

1. In accordance with Article 5, competences not conferred upon the Union in the Treaties remain with the Member States.

2. The Union shall respect the equality of Member States before the Treaties as well as their national identities, inherent in their fundamental structures, political and constitutional, inclusive of regional and local self-government. It shall respect their essential State functions, including ensuring the territorial integrity of the State, maintaining law and order and safeguarding national security. In particular, national security remains the sole responsibility of each Member State.

3. . . . .

Article 5

1. The limits of Union competences are governed by the principle of conferral. The use of Union competences is governed by the principles of subsidiarity and proportionality.

2. Under the principle of conferral, the Union shall act only within the limits of the competences conferred upon it by the Member States in the Treaties to attain the objectives set out therein. Competences not conferred upon the Union in the Treaties remain with the Member States.

3. Under the principle of subsidiarity, in areas which do not fall within its exclusive competence, the Union shall act only if and in so far as the objectives of the proposed action cannot be sufficiently achieved by the Member States, either at central level or at regional and local level, but can rather, by reason of the scale or effects of the proposed action, be better achieved at Union level.

The institutions of the Union shall apply the principle of subsidiarity as laid down in the Protocol on the application of the principles of subsidiarity and proportionality. National Parliaments ensure compliance with the principle of subsidiarity in accordance with the procedure set out in that Protocol.

4. Under the principle of proportionality, the content and form of Union action shall not exceed what is necessary to achieve the objectives of the Treaties.

The institutions of the Union shall apply the principle of proportionality as laid down in the Protocol on the application of the principles of subsidiarity and proportionality.

The principles of conferral (or attribution, as it is sometimes called), subsidiarity and proportionality now enshrined in Articles 4 and 5 TEU have always been immanent in the Union's constitutional order, though they were introduced as express organising principles for the system of Union competences under the TEU, through the insertion of ex-Article 5 EC. A 'Protocol on the application of the principles of subsidiarity and proportionality' was annexed to the EC Treaty by the TA.[1] Both the main Treaty provisions on Union competences and the Protocol concerning subsidiarity and proportionality were then substantially revised by the TL. This chapter will explain in detail the core elements of the system of Union competences. We will begin with the principle of conferral, including the different 'categories' of Union competences as defined by the TL, as well some of the main problems which have arisen with enforcing the principle of conferral in practice. We will then continue to examine the principles of subsidiarity and proportionality, including the new system for monitoring the Union institutions' respect for the principle of subsidiarity through input from the national parliaments. Finally, we will consider the idea of 'flexibility' under the Treaties, whereby certain exercises of Union competence do not apply to all 27 Member States, since one or more countries is/are under no legal obligation to participate in the relevant instruments of Union law.

---

[1] Protocol No 7 to the Final Act of the IGC which adopted the TA. That Protocol was based largely upon an interpretation of ex-Art 5 EC agreed by the European Council at its Edinburgh meeting in December 1992: see Annex 1 to Part A of the Presidency Conclusions (Bull EC 12-1992, 13). Note also the Inter-Institutional Agreement between the European Parliament, the Council and the Commission on the procedure for implementing the principle of subsidiarity (Bull EC 10-1993, 128).

II – THE PRINCIPLE OF CONFERRAL

A – Establishing the Existence of Union Competence

The authors of the TL were keen to highlight the point that the Union is an organisation of derived and limited powers, 'on which the Member States confer competences to attain objectives they have in common'.[2] The key idea underlying the principle of conferral as set out in Article 5(2) TEU is that 'the Union shall act only within the limits of the competences conferred upon it by the Member States in the Treaties to attain the objectives set out therein'.[3] As the Court of Justice put it bluntly in Opinion 2/94, the Union 'has only those powers which have been conferred on it'.[4] To make the point another way, the Union order is not a self-authenticating one: new powers cannot be generated within the order itself, above and beyond those conferred by the constitution-making authority, acting in accordance with the procedure provided for by Article 48 TEU.[5]

The technique for attributing powers to the Union employed in the Treaties is (in most cases) highly specific.[6] It is true that Articles 2 and 3 TEU set out the Union's basic values and objectives. However, those provisions contain no power-conferring provision, and so cannot be used as legal bases for enacting particular measures. The Union can only take action to uphold its values and pursue its objectives where a more specific legal basis contained in the Treaties empowers it to do so—and only under the particular conditions laid down in that legal basis.[7]

The concept of legal basis therefore plays a key role in the system of Union competences. The characteristic approach is for the Treaties to group together several provisions relating to a given area of policy (eg the internal market, or environmental policy, or educational policy). Such provisions will identify, in more or less detail, the main principles guiding Union action in that field; and will define the decision-making powers offered to the Union institutions for the realisation of those activities. The powers thus conferred are exercisable, under the conditions specified, in that particular area and not elsewhere. Each legal basis will also lay down the precise decision-making procedure to be followed for enacting the relevant Union measures (eg whether legislative acts are to be adopted according to the ordinary or by a special legislative procedure). The legal basis may also prescribe the adoption of certain types of measure (eg only the harmonisation of national laws; or conversely, no harmonisation of national laws); and the form(s) of legal instrument that may be used (eg action only by means of directives or of decisions).

B – Establishing the Nature of Union Competence

Closely related to the question of whether Union competence actually exists for a given

---

[2] Art 1(1) TEU.

[3] See also Declaration No 18 annexed to the Final Act of the IGC which adopted the TL.

[4] Opinion 2/94 [1996] ECR I-1759, para 23.

[5] Because it is not a state, the Union lacks what German scholars call *Kompetenz Kompetenz*, the ability to pull itself up legally by its own bootstraps.

[6] Opinion 2/94 [1996] ECR I-1759, para 25.

[7] See Art 3(6) TEU. Cf Case C-9/99 *Echirolles Distribution* [2000] ECR I-8207; Case C-181/06 *Deutsche Lufthansa* [2007] ECR I-5903.

purpose in accordance with the principle of conferral under Article 5(2) TEU is that of the 'nature' of the competence that has been conferred upon the Union. This refers, more particularly, to the different sorts of legal consequences which the existence or the exercise of a Union competence may have upon national regulatory power in the policy area concerned. Before the entry into force of the TL, the Treaties themselves contained no systematic explanation of the different possible types of Union regulatory power: it was left to commentators to piece together (and argue over) various possible models for categorising the Union's available competences, based upon the more detailed provisions of the Treaties, the principles established in the caselaw of the Union courts, and the legislative practice of the other Union institutions.

However, in what is surely one of the TL's most successful exercises in clarification, the Treaties now offer—for the very first time—a general explanation for the nature of different Union competences. The system chosen is based upon identifying three main categories of Union regulatory power: exclusive Union competence; Union competence shared with the Member States; and Union competence to support, co-ordinate or supplement Member State action. Article 2 TFEU contains the generic definitions for understanding each of those three main categories of Union power.[8] Articles 3 (exclusive), 4 (shared) and 6 (supporting) TFEU then give an indicative list of the various fields of Union activity which are deemed to fall within each of the three main categories of competence. However, the precise scope of, and arrangements for exercising, the Union's competences are still determined by the individual legal bases contained elsewhere in the Treaties.[9] In particular, those legal bases may set out more elaborate rules on the impact of Union competence upon national regulatory powers: for example, whether Union harmonising measures adopted in fields of shared competence may be fully pre-emptive or should consist only in the setting of minimum standards;[10] and whether specific aspects of a field otherwise designated as one of shared competence do not in fact confer upon the Union any power to harmonise national laws, and thus exhibit the characteristics of a purely supporting competence.[11]

(i) Exclusive Competence

Article 2(1) TFEU states that, when the Treaties confer on the Union exclusive competence in a specific area, only the Union may legislate and adopt legally binding acts, the Member States being able to do so themselves only if so empowered by the Union or for the implementation of Union acts. In other words, in areas of exclusive Union competence, regulatory authority belongs to the Union institutions alone; the Member States have given up the right to act autonomously.

Exclusive Union competence is very much the exception under the Treaties. Article 3(1) TFEU states that the Union shall enjoy exclusive competence in the following fields: the customs union; establishing the competition rules necessary for the functioning of the internal market; monetary policy for the Member States whose currency is the euro; the conservation of marine biological resources under the common fisheries policy;[12] and

---

[8] Those definitions should be read in conjunction with the Protocol (No 25) on the exercise of shared competence; and also Declaration No 18 annexed to the Final Act of the IGC which adopted the TL.

[9] See Art 2(6) TFEU.

[10] See eg Arts 153(4) TFEU (social policy), 193 TFEU (environment) and 169(4) TFEU (consumer policy).

[11] eg Arts 79(4) and 84 TFEU on TCN integration and crime prevention measures, respectively.

[12] cp Joined Cases 3, 4 and 6/76 *Kramer* [1976] ECR 1279; Case C-25/94 *Commission v Council (FAO)* [1996] ECR I-1469.

the common commercial policy.[13] In each of those fields, the view was taken that the possibility for Member States to adopt independent regulatory initiatives would in practice be inherently incompatible with the realisation of the Union's objectives as defined under the Treaties. For the most part, the list of policy fields subject to exclusive Union competence in accordance with Article 3(1) TFEU represents a codification of the status quo.[14] Only the inclusion of competition law was seen as novel: the Court of Justice had previously asserted that Union competence in the field of competition law is shared with the Member States[15]—though since the TL's entry into force, the Court has accepted that competition has now been transformed into an area of exclusive Union competence.[16] Article 3(2) TFEU furthermore provides that the Union shall also have exclusive competence for the conclusion of an international agreement when its conclusion is provided for in a legislative act of the Union or is necessary to enable the Union to exercise its internal competence, or in so far as its conclusion may affect common rules or alter their scope. That provision—which represents a somewhat clumsy attempt to codify the previous case law defining when the Union's competence in the field of external relations is to be considered exclusive—shall be considered further in Chapter 27.

The crucial point about areas of exclusive Union competence is that the Member States are precluded from exercising any independent legislative initiative; they may only act if, and in so far as, the Union authorises them to do so. Such authorisation is usually express: for example, within the context of the common commercial policy, Regulation 1061/2009 provides that exports from the Union to third countries shall not be subject to any quantitative restrictions; but Article 10 of the Regulation grants the Member States the right to restrict external trade on grounds identical to those contained in Article 36 TFEU.[17] However, authorisation may also be implied, for instance, where the Union has failed to exercise its exclusive competence and a situation of urgency arises which demands some form of public action. The Court recognised in the *Fisheries Conservation* case that, in such situations, the Member States may be regarded as implicitly authorised by the Union to adopt necessary regulatory measures acting as 'trustees of the common interest'—provided that they act in close consultation and co-operation with the Commission.[18]

(ii) Shared Competence

The second main category of Union competence is defined by Article 2(2) TFEU: when the Treaties confer on the Union a competence shared with the Member States in a specific area, the Union and the Member States may legislate and adopt legally binding acts in that area. However, the Member States shall only exercise their competence to the extent that the Union has not exercised its competence. Conversely, the Member States

---

[13] cp Opinion 1/75 *Local Cost Standard* [1975] ECR 1255.

[14] Note that the TN had introduced certain qualifications to the exclusivity of Union competence in the field of the common commercial policy under ex-Art 133 EC: for details, see M Cremona, 'A Policy of Bits and Pieces? The Common Commercial Policy After Nice' (2001) 4 *CYELS* 61. The TL has since undone those qualifications.

[15] eg Case 14/68 *Walt Wilhelm* [1969] ECR 1.

[16] eg Case 550/07 P *Akzo Nobel Chemicals* (Judgment of 14 September 2010).

[17] Reg 1061/2009 establishing common rules for exports [2009] OJ L291/1. See Case C-83/94 *Peter Leifer* [1995] ECR I-3231. Also: Case 41/76 *Donckerwolcke* [1976] ECR 1921; Case C-394/97 *Sami Heinonen* [1999] ECR I-3599. Further: M Cremona, 'The External Dimension of the Single Market: Building (on) the Foundations' in C Barnard and J Scott (eds), *The Law of the Single European Market: Unpacking the Premises* (Oxford, Hart Publishing, 2002).

[18] Case 804/79 *Commission v UK* [1981] ECR 1045.

shall again exercise their competence to the extent that the Union has decided to cease exercising its competence.

In other words: in fields of shared competence, the Treaties recognise that both the Union and the Member States are competent to regulate the relevant sector; but the actual exercise of Union regulatory power is liable to curtail the scope for exercising national regulatory power with respect to the same matters. Such shared competence is the normal relationship between Union and Member State powers. According to Article 4(1) TFEU, shared competence applies by default to Union powers which are not categorised either as exclusive in accordance with Article 3 TFEU or as supporting in accordance with Article 6 TFEU. Article 4(2) TFEU then identifies the principal fields of shared competence: for example, the internal market;[19] the Area of Freedom, Security and Justice (AFSJ);[20] social policy;[21] environmental policy;[22] consumer protection;[23] agriculture and fisheries (excepting the preservation of marine biological resources);[24] transport;[25] and energy.[26]

Where the Union has not yet exercised its shared regulatory competence, the Member States remain free to exercise theirs—provided they comply with any obligations imposed upon them by directly effective provisions of the Treaties, such as in the field of free movement of goods, persons, services or capital. A good example is the famous decision in *Cassis de Dijon*, which concerned German rules on the alcohol content of fruit liqueurs. The Court held that, in the absence of Union secondary legislation addressing this issue, each Member State was free to adopt its own regulatory standards—provided that the applicable national measures did not create unjustified obstacles to the free movement of fruit liqueurs lawfully marketed in other Member States and imported into the national territory.[27]

Where the Union has already exercised its shared regulatory competence, the Member States in principle remain free to exercise theirs—but now they must respect not only the obligations resulting from primary Treaty provisions, but also any obligations imposed by the relevant Union legislation. This includes the possibility for Union measures to have so-called 'pre-emptive effects', ie to occupy the relevant regulatory field, and prevent Member States from legitimately exercising their own competence therein.

Such pre-emptive effects are sometimes total: they effectively prevent the Member State from lawfully adopting divergent national regulatory standards, unless and until the relevant Union legislation is revised or repealed. A good example is the *Dim-Dip Headlights* case, which concerned a Union directive seeking to promote the free movement of cars within the internal market by listing exhaustively the types of device which could lawfully be incorporated into car lighting systems.[28] The United Kingdom subsequently attempted to prohibit the use on British roads of any car which did not use dim-dip headlights— a lighting system which was considered to offer superior road safety standards, but was not actually referred to in the directive, since it had not been sufficiently commercially

---

[19] In particular, under Arts 114 and 115 TFEU.
[20] See Title V, Part Three TFEU.
[21] See Title X, Part Three TFEU.
[22] See Title XX, Part Three TFEU.
[23] See Title XV, Part Three TFEU.
[24] See Title III, Part Three TFEU.
[25] See Title VI, Part Three TFEU.
[26] See Title XXI, Part Three TFEU.
[27] Case 120/78 [1979] ECR 649.
[28] Case 60/86 *Commission v United Kingdom* [1988] ECR 3921. More recently eg Case C-540/08 *Mediaprint* (Judgment of 9 November 2010).

developed at the time that measure was adopted. The Court of Justice held that the directive had effected a total harmonisation of the relevant field. The United Kingdom was not
permitted unilaterally to deviate from the common standards agreed by the Union legislator, either by requiring cars to use dim-dip headlights instead of the headlights referred
to in the directive, or even by permitting cars to use dim-dip headlights instead of the
headlights referred to in the directive. To that extent, fully pre-emptive Union secondary
legislation appears similar, in terms of its impact upon national regulatory competence,
to the type of a priori exclusivity which applies under the Treaties themselves in accordance with Articles 2(1) and 3(1) TFEU to fields such as the common commercial policy
and the protection of marine biological resources. The difference is that, in the areas of
a priori exclusivity, autonomous action by the Member States is prohibited irrespective of
whether or not the Union has acted; whereas in areas of shared competence, the exercise
of national regulatory power is prohibited only to the extent of any incompatibility with a
particular legislative measure that has been adopted by the Union and remains in force.[29]

In other situations, the pre-emptive effects of Union legislation need only be partial:
while imposing certain obligations on Member States as to how they must exercise their
own regulatory competences, the Union measure nevertheless leaves the national authorities a margin of discretion to make their own independent policy choices, even within the
occupied field. This is the case, for example, with Union legislation which provides for
only minimum harmonisation: the Union act establishes a regulatory 'floor of rights', above
which the Member States remain competent to enact higher standards of protection (for
example) in favour of consumers, workers or the environment, provided that those more
stringent national measures continue to respect the primary rules contained within the
Treaties themselves. A good illustration is the dispute in *Finalarte*.[30] The Working Time
Directive provided that workers must enjoy a certain number of paid holidays per year,
but expressly stated that the measure lays down only minimum requirements, and preserved each Member State's right to apply more favourable rules for the protection of the
health and safety of workers.[31] On that basis, German legislation guaranteed longer paid
leave to employees, over and above the basic standards of the Working Time Directive.
In such circumstances, it was clear that any dispute must focus not on Germany's basic
freedom to enact more stringent standards of health and safety than the Union legislation;
but rather on whether the application of those national rules to workers posted within
Germany by foreign undertakings created unlawful obstacles to the freedom to provide
services within the domestic territory.[32]

Finally, in certain areas of shared competence, owing to the particular nature of the
authorised activity, the actual exercise of Union competence might have no pre-emptive
effect at all. Article 4(3) TFEU states that, in the areas of research, technological development and space, the Union shall have competence to carry out activities, in particular to
define and implement programmes; however, the exercise of that competence shall not
result in Member States being prevented from exercising theirs. Similarly, Article 4(4)
TFEU provides that, in the areas of development co-operation and humanitarian aid, the
Union shall have competence to carry out activities and conduct a common policy; how-

[29] This distinction may have important legal implications, eg for the Union institutions' obligation to respect
the principle of subsidiarity when amending a fully pre-emptive legislative regime (see further below).
[30] Cases C-49, 50, 52–54 and 68–71/98 *Finalarte* [2001] ECR I-7831.
[31] Dir 93/104 [1993] OJ L307/18.
[32] Under Art 56 TFEU. See further Chapter 17.

ever, the exercise of that competence shall not result in Member States being prevented from exercising theirs. Those provisions reflect previous case law particularly from the fields of humanitarian aid and development co-operation.[33] The explanation lies in the fact that, in such fields, the competences of the Union and the Member States are perfectly parallel: the exercise of either competence leaves open the full range of possibilities for the future exercise of the other. Thus, it would not interfere with the implementation of a Union regulation establishing a programme of financial and technical aid to a given developing country, if the United Kingdom, say, were to commence a similar programme of assistance to that country; nor would a pre-existing programme of Member State aid inhibit the Union from coming onto the scene as an additional donor.

(iii) Competence to Support, Co-ordinate or Supplement Member State Action

The third main category of Union competence is defined under Article 2(5) TFEU: in certain areas and under the conditions laid down in the Treaties, the Union shall have competence to carry out actions to support, co-ordinate or supplement the actions of the Member States, without thereby superseding their competence in these areas. In particular, legally binding acts of the Union adopted on the basis of the provisions of the Treaties relating to these areas shall not entail harmonisation of Member States' laws or regulations.

In such fields, the Union's role is typically to adopt broad guidelines or incentive measures, or to facilitate the exchange of information about best practice. Where it is given power to adopt legally binding acts, these are not capable of harmonising national laws or having pre-emptive effects vis-à-vis domestic competence. Regulatory power, therefore, remains in the Member States' hands; Union action merely complements domestic policies. A good illustration is Article 165 TFEU, first introduced by the Maastricht Treaty, which states that the Union shall contribute to the development of quality education by encouraging co-operation between Member States and, if necessary, by supporting and supplementing their action, while fully respecting the responsibility of the Member States for the content of teaching and the organisation of education systems and their cultural and linguistic diversity. The Council and the European Parliament, acting under the ordinary legislative procedure, are empowered to adopt incentive measures,[34] *excluding* any harmonisation of the laws and regulations of the Member States. Article 6 TFEU provides a full list of the areas subject to supporting Union competence: the protection and improvement of human health;[35] industry;[36] culture;[37] tourism;[38] education, vocational training, youth and sport;[39] civil protection;[40] and administrative co-operation.[41]

Nevertheless, the Court of Justice has held that, even in areas of supporting Union competence, Member States must still respect the 'horizontal' principles imposed under

---

[33] Cases C-181/91 and C-248/91 *European Parliament v Council and Commission* [1993] ECR I-3685; Case C-316/91 *European Parliament v Council* [1994] ECR I-625.

[34] eg Union programmes such as Erasmus and Leonardo da Vinci, which seek to encourage and facilitate cross-border mobility for education and training purposes.

[35] See Title XIV, Part Three TFEU.

[36] See Title XVII, Part Three TFEU.

[37] See Title XIII, Part Three TFEU.

[38] See Title XXII, Part Three TFEU.

[39] See Title XII, Part Three TFEU.

[40] See Title XXIII, Part Three TFEU.

[41] See Title XXIV, Part Three TFEU.

primary Union law (ie principles that apply to all the policy areas within the scope of the Treaties), such as those relating to the free movement of goods, persons, services and capital, and to non-discrimination on grounds of nationality. Consider, by way of illustration, the famous judgment in *Gravier*, which concerned Belgian rules requiring foreign students whose parents lived abroad to pay an additional enrolment fee in order to attend vocational training courses at universities and technical colleges; the fee was not levied on foreign students whose parents lived within Belgium, or on Belgian students regardless of their parents' domicile.[42] The Court observed that educational organisation and policy were not as such included in the spheres which the EEC Treaty had entrusted to the Community institutions. Indeed, since the case was pre-Maastricht, the EEC did not enjoy even the limited competence now contained in Article 165 TFEU; the only relevant Treaty provision was ex-Article 128 EEC empowering the Council to lay down general principles for implementing a common vocational training policy. That was treated by the Court as sufficient to establish that vocational training fell within the scope of application of the Treaty, thus bringing into play the principle of equal treatment on grounds of nationality now contained in Article 18 TFEU. By discriminating against students from other Member States as regards the conditions for admission to vocational training courses within its territory, Belgium was found to be in breach of its Treaty obligations. Subsequent authorities have extended the principle that the conditions of access must be the same for all Member State nationals to the whole of the higher-education sector.[43]

(iv) Specified Forms of Union Competence

Besides the three main categories of Union competence—exclusive, shared and supporting—described above, Article 2 TFEU identifies another two, more specific, types of Union power. In the first place, Article 2(3) TFEU states that the Member States shall co-ordinate their economic and employment policies within arrangements as determined by the TFEU, which the Union shall have competence to provide.[44] In the second place, Article 2(4) TFEU provides that the Union shall have competence, in accordance with the provisions of the TEU, to define and implement a common foreign and security policy, including the progressive framing of a common defence. Those powers may nonetheless be considered as variants within the more general category of shared competence,[45] whose particular political sensitivity for the Member States led the Treaty drafters to highlight their special character.

C – The Problem of 'Competence Creep'

It is now time to consider some of the main constitutional problems which arise with the principle of conferral—beginning with the phenomenon of 'competence creep'. Most of the legal bases contained within the Treaties define the purpose and nature of Union compe-

---

[42] Case 293/83 *Gravier v City of Liège* [1985] ECR 593.

[43] eg Case 24/86 *Blaizot* [1988] ECR 379; Case 42/87 *Commission v Belgium* [1988] ECR 5445; Case C-47/93 *Commission v Belgium* [1994] ECR I-1593; Case C-65/03 *Commission v Belgium* [2004] ECR I-6427; Case C-147/03 *Commission v Austria* [2005] ECR I-5969; Case C-73/08 *Bressol* (Judgment of 13 April 2010).

[44] See also Art 5 TFEU.

[45] Art 4(1) TFEU states that shared competence applies to all areas other than those listed in Arts 3 and 6 TFEU—thus including by implication the Union's co-ordinating powers and its competence as regards the CFSP.

tence as regards the relevant policy field in a relatively detailed manner. However, a few Treaty provisions are much more ambiguous and open-ended in their potential scope of application. Such provisions have given rise to accusations that the Union legislature, by exploiting such ambiguities, can extend the scope of Union action beyond the limits which were perhaps understood by the Treaty drafters. If so, the principle of conferral may well be maintained in principle—but its spirit is undermined in practice, since Union competences might be applied for unintended purposes and/or in unintended contexts. Two Treaty provisions have provided the source of particular controversy: Article 114 TFEU on the harmonisation of national laws for the completion of the internal market; and the 'flexibility clause' now contained in Article 352 TFEU.

(i) Article 114 TFEU

Article 114 TFEU was first introduced by the SEA to enable the Union to adopt the legislation necessary to complete the internal market using qualified majority voting in Council, rather than the unanimity required under the legal basis which had already been provided under Article 115 TFEU. In its current version, Article 114(1) TFEU states that the European Parliament and the Council shall, acting in accordance with the ordinary legislative procedure and after consulting the Economic and Social Committee, adopt the measures for the approximation of the provisions laid down by law, regulation or administrative action in Member States which have as their object the establishment and functioning of the internal market.

To some extent, the adoption of harmonising measures to complete the internal market—in other words, to eliminate obstacles to free movement across national borders and/or to eradicate distortions of competitive conditions between Member States—will always imply that the Union must simultaneously make choices about other policy objectives. After all, when adopting harmonisation measures intended to replace divergent national rules on product specifications or marketing practices, the Union must decide not merely to approximate but to do so at a particular pitch and taking account of competing societal concerns (for example) about protection of the environment, employees or consumers. By that process, Article 115 TFEU had already witnessed an inevitable form of 'competence creep' as the Union legislature adopted extensive legislation dealing not only with the internal market per se, but also with a broader range of social policy issues which quite naturally 'flanked' the process of economic integration. Since Article 115 TFEU required unanimity, such competence creep at least occurred with the consent of every Member State. Moreover, the pre-SEA Treaty of Rome did not provide any other legal bases determining the scope of or limits to Union action in those flanking policy fields.

Now, however, Article 114 TFEU operates in a very different political and constitutional environment. Since decisions in Council are taken by a qualified majority, there is no guarantee that a broad construction of the circumstances in which Union legislation can be considered to help complete the internal market will actually command support from all the Member States. Moreover, successive Treaty amendments have introduced many additional legal bases (in fields such as environmental, employment and consumer policies) which confer specific powers for Union action precisely in such fields. Controversy over the correct interpretation of the scope of the powers conferred upon the Union pursuant to Article 114 TFEU was made even more acute by the judgment of the German Federal Constitutional Court in *Brunner*, where it warned against the Union institutions claiming for themselves functions and powers which were not clearly specified in the Treaties.[46] In short: there was little tolerance left for the prospect that the Union institutions might rely upon Article 114 TFEU, not so as to advance the functioning of the internal market, or even to articulate those social policy choices which are inherent in the harmonisation of national laws for the purposes of promoting economic integration; but rather so as to achieve certain objectives which bore no real connection to the internal market per se, merely so as to evade whatever procedural and substantive constraints had been imposed by the Treaties upon Union action in such fields under their own dedicated legal bases.

This set the scene for the important dispute over the Tobacco Advertising Directive 98/43 (adopted under Article 114 TFEU, together with closely related legal bases on the freedom of establishment and freedom to provide services).[47] Article 3(1) of the Directive provided that all forms of advertising and sponsorship of tobacco be banned within the Union; while Article 3(2) gave Member States the option of excluding diversification products (such as jeans and shoes bearing the same name as well-known tobacco brands) from the scope of this general prohibition; and Article 3(5) excluded from the material scope of the Directive certain types of advertising (such as communications intended exclusively for professionals in the tobacco trade). Article 5 stated that the Directive shall not preclude Member States from laying down, in accordance with the Treaties, such stricter requirements concerning the advertising and sponsorship of tobacco products as they deem necessary to guarantee the health protection of individuals. Germany had voted against the measure in the Council, and subsequently brought an action for its annulment before the Court of Justice. The gist of the German government's complaint was that Directive 98/43 was not really designed to promote the operation of the internal market, but rather to regulate public health—a field of merely supporting Union competence as regards which Article 168 TFEU explicitly excludes any harmonisation of the laws and regulations of the Member States.

In its judgment in *Germany v Parliament and Council*, the Court held that Article 114 TFEU could not be construed as conferring upon the Union legislator a general power to regulate the internal market: measures that can be adopted under the Article must have the specific object of improving the conditions for the establishment and functioning of the internal market; they must be designed to remove genuine obstacles to free movement or appreciable distortions of competition, not purely abstract risks. Directive 98/43 could not be said to fulfil those criteria. By prohibiting tobacco advertising not only in media such as newspapers and magazines, which are traded between Member States, but also on articles such as hotel and restaurant posters, parasols and ashtrays, the Directive went beyond the scope of Article 114 TFEU. Moreover, the Directive did not ensure free movement for compliant products: it permitted the Member States to enact more stringent welfare provisions but failed to guarantee access to the entire single market for products conforming to the Union standards. Similarly, Directive 98/43 could not be said to contribute to the removal of appreciable distortions of competition. The competitive advantages enjoyed by advertising agencies and producers of advertising media established in Member States with fewer restrictions were too remote and indirect; and the admittedly appreciable distortions which arose in the field (say) of sports sponsorship could not justify the more

---

[46] [1994] 1 CMLR 57. See further Chapter 8.
[47] Dir 98/43 [1998] OJ L213/9.

extensive prohibition contained in the Directive. Furthermore, by imposing a wide-ranging ban on tobacco advertising, the Directive was not actually removing any distortion of competition between Member States, but simply restricting forms of competition across the Union by limiting the means available for economic operators to enter or remain in the market. The Court concluded that Directive 98/43 should be annulled on the grounds that it had been adopted on an incorrect legal basis and (implicitly) in breach of the principle of conferral contained in Article 5(2) TEU.[48]

The judgment in the *Tobacco Advertising* case provides a striking example of the judicial enforcement of the principle of conferral. By annulling the directive, the Court of Justice seemed to be signalling its intention to act as a true constitutional court whose role is to police the fine boundaries between Union and Member State competence established in the Treaties, and thus preserve the delicate system of checks and balances that is essential to the proper functioning of the Union. But the dispute that gave rise to the proceedings also reminds us of the role played by the Member States themselves in contributing to the problem of 'competence creep'. It was the Member States at the Maastricht IGC who drafted Article 168 TFEU in a way specifically designed to place strict limits on Union competence in the field of public health; but a majority of the Member States subsequently attempted to bypass exactly those same limits, through recourse to Article 114 TFEU, in order to achieve what they regarded as valuable social welfare objectives.

Some commentators have expressed concerns that the ruling in *Tobacco Advertising* was merely a flash in the pan: the Court in subsequent cases, it is argued, has permitted the Union institutions once more to make relatively liberal use of the powers conferred under Article 114 TFEU for purposes which have only a slight connection to the completion of the internal market.[49] It is certainly true that, in subsequent cases, the criteria set down in *Tobacco Advertising Directive* for legitimate use of Article 114 TFEU have been interpreted and/or applied in a manner which usually justifies, rarely constrains, the exercise of harmonising competences by the Union legislature: consider, for example, the ruling in the *Biotechnology Directive* case to the effect that potential future as well as actual current barriers to trade are amenable to regulation under Article 114 TFEU;[50] the finding in *Österreichischer Rundfunk* that internal market harmonisation measures could govern also situations which are wholly internal to one Member State and have no relevant cross-border implications;[51] and the judgment in *Swedish Match* affirming the Union's competence to enact a total ban on any given product or activity, even though this seemed only to eliminate markets rather than to integrate them.[52] Nevertheless, although there was much discussion during the post-Laeken constitutional reform process about how to overcome the problems of 'competence creep', the TL did not, in the end, make any significant amendments to Article 114 TFEU.[53]

---

[48] Case C-376/98 *Germany v Parliament and Council* [2000] ECR I-8419. Also: Case C-74/99 *Imperial Tobacco* [2000] ECR I-8599. A new Tobacco Advertising Directive was subsequently adopted, intended to comply with the ECJ's judgment: see Dir 2003/33 [2003] OJ L152/16. Germany's challenge to the latter measure was eventually rejected by the ECJ: see Case C-380/03 *Germany v Parliament and Council* [2006] ECR I-11573.

[49] eg D Wyatt, 'Community Competence to Regulate the Internal Market' in M Dougan and S Currie (eds), *50 Years of the European Treaties: Looking Back and Thinking Forward* (Oxford, Hart Publishing, 2009).

[50] Case C-377/98 [2001] ECR I-7079.

[51] Cases C-465/00, C-138/01 and C-139/01 [2003] ECR I-4989.

[52] Case C-210/03 [2004] ECR I-11893. Other recent (and controversial) rulings on the scope of Union competence under Art 114 TFEU include Case C-301/06 *Ireland v Parliament and Council* [2009] ECR I-593 and Case C-58/08 *Vodafone* (Judgment of 8 June 2010).

[53] Only its relationship to ex-Art 94 EC/Art 115 TFEU was revised.

(ii) Article 352 TFEU

The second legal basis which has given rise to persistent allegations of 'competence creep' is Article 352 TFEU (ex-Article 308 EC)—often referred to as the 'flexibility clause'.

Ex-Article 308 EC provided that, should action by the Community prove necessary to attain, in the course of the operation of the common market, one of the objectives of the Community and the EC Treaty had not provided the necessary powers, the Council could, acting unanimously on a proposal from the Commission and after consulting the European Parliament, take the appropriate measures. Ex-Article 308 EC has traditionally provided an appropriate legal basis for the enactment of Union secondary measures which do not seek to approximate (and thereby replace, at least partially) national laws affecting the functioning of the internal market in the sense of Article 114 TFEU; but rather to introduce new legal phenomena at the Union level (such as intellectual property or company forms) which will take effect alongside existing national legislation, whilst still promoting the sound operation of the internal market.[54]

However, there is no doubt that that flexibility clause—through a combination of textual ambiguity and institutional connivance—was also used historically so as to extend the scope of Community action beyond the limits apparently set by the express provisions of the EC Treaty. For example, policies in fields such as regional aid, environmental protection and development co-operation were all developed through recourse to ex-Article 308 EC; only subsequently was the EC Treaty amended so as to equip the Community with specific power-conferring provisions in those fields.[55] Ex-Article 308 EC was also used, not entirely appropriately, for providing technical assistance to countries other than developing countries (until the insertion of a dedicated legal basis for such measures under the TN).[56] On the one hand, such creative uses of ex-Article 308 EC might have appeared less controversial for the Member States: at least that legal basis still required unanimity within the Council. On the other hand, such unanimity surely felt like cold comfort (in particular) to domestic parliaments: national executives could sign up to Community action in fields not clearly envisaged under the EC Treaty in a way which still had a direct impact upon the exercise of national legislative competences.[57]

Again, the Court of Justice gradually came to recognise the need to prevent ex-Article 308 EC from being used so blatantly to undermine the principle of conferral. The leading case remains Opinion 2/94, where the Court was asked whether the European Community was competent to accede to the European Convention for the Protection of Human Rights and Fundamental Freedoms. It was found by the Court that '[n]o Treaty provision confers on the Community institutions any general power to enact rules on

---

[54] eg Opinion 1/94 [1994] ECR I-5267; Case C-377/98 *Netherlands v Parliament and Council* [2001] ECR I-7079; Case C-66/04 *United Kingdom v Parliament and Council* [2005] ECR I-10553; Case C-436/03 *Parliament v Council* [2006] ECR I-3733; Case C-217/04 *United Kingdom v Parliament and Council* [2006] ECR I-3771.

[55] See now Title XVIII (on Economic, Social and Territorial Cohesion) and Title XX (on Environment) of Part Three TFEU (both of which date from the SEA); and Chapter 1 of Title III (Development Cooperation) of Part Five TFEU (dating from the TEU).

[56] The unsuitability of ex-Art 308 EC as a legal basis for the latter category of measures was due to the difficulty of demonstrating a connection with 'the course of operation of the Common Market' as required by the pre-TL version of that provision.

[57] See further eg R Schütze, 'Organised Change Towards an "Ever Closer Union": Article 308 EC and the Limits to the Community's Legislative Competence' (2003) 22 *YEL* 79; A Dashwood, 'Article 308 EC as the Outer Limit of Expressly Conferred Community Competence' in C Barnard and O Odudu (eds), *The Outer Limits of European Union Law* (Oxford, Hart Publishing, 2009).

human rights or to conclude international conventions in this field'.[58] Was it, then, possible to fall back on ex-Article 308 EC? The Court stressed that ex-Article 308 EC 'cannot be used as a basis for the adoption of provisions whose effect could, in substance, be to amend the Treaty'.[59] The Article, said the Court, 'cannot serve as a basis for widening the scope of Community powers beyond the general framework created by the provisions of the Treaty as a whole and, in particular, by those that define the tasks and the activities of the Community'.[60] Recourse to ex-Article 308 EC was not possible in the instant case because accession to the European Convention would entail entry into 'a distinct international institutional system', with fundamental implications for both the Community and the Member States; such a modification of the EC system of human rights protection would be 'of constitutional significance', and thus could be brought about only by means of a formal Treaty amendment.[61]

Whereas Article 114 TFEU emerged from the Lisbon Treaty virtually unscathed, ex-Article 308 EC was substantially amended precisely with a view to minimising the risk of its abuse in contravention of the spirit of the principle of conferral. Article 352(1) TFEU now provides that, if action by the Union should prove necessary, within the framework of the policies defined in the Treaties, to attain one of the objectives set out in the Treaties, and the Treaties have not provided the necessary powers, the Council (still acting unanimously on a Commission proposal, though now with the European Parliament's consent) shall adopt the appropriate measures. Those measures may be legislative in character, in which case they are deemed to have been adopted according to a special legislative procedure.[62] On the one hand, the reference to action in furtherance of the Union's objectives in toto makes the potential scope of application of Article 352 TFEU much broader than that of ex-Article 308 EC, which referred only to action in furtherance of the common market. On the other hand, the comparatively restrictive wording of ex-Article 308 EC rarely acted in itself as a practical barrier to its liberal employment across a wide range of policy fields. It seems more likely that extensive recourse to Article 352 TFEU—and with it any further 'competence creep'—will be rendered unnecessary by the sheer range of sector-specific legal bases under which the Union is now empowered to act. In that regard, it is significant that measures based on Article 352 TFEU shall not entail harmonisation of national laws in cases where the Treaties exclude such harmonisation—thus preventing Article 352 TFEU being used to undermine the distinction between shared and supporting Union competences.[63] Furthermore, Article 352 TFEU cannot be used as the basis for attaining objectives pertaining to the CFSP, or in the implementation of other Union policies so as to affect the exercise of CFSP powers.[64]

---

[58] Opinion 2/94 [1996] ECR I-1759, para 27.

[59] Opinion 2/94 [1996] ECR I-1759, para 30. The same view has been firmly taken by the German Budesvervassungsgericht (Federal Constitutional Court). The Court indicated in its *Brunner* judgment that a measure based on ex-Art 308 EC which exceeded the scope of the democratic authorisation given in respect of the transfer of legislative competence to the Union would not be considered binding in Germany: see [1994] 1 CMLR 57.

[60] Opinion 2/94 [1996] ECR I-1759, para 30.

[61] Opinion 2/94 [1996] ECR I-1759, paras 34 and 35.

[62] Note that the requirement of unanimity/designation of a special legislative procedure cannot be converted to QMV/the ordinary legislative procedure by means of the 'passerelle clauses' contained in Art 48(7) TEU: see Art 353 TFEU (and see further Chapters 2 and 4).

[63] Art 352(3) TFEU.

[64] Art 352(4) TFEU. Note also Declaration Nos 41 and 42 annexed to the Final Act of the IGC which adopted the TL.

In any case, it is expressly provided under Article 352(2) TFEU that the Commission must draw national parliaments' attention to proposals made under the flexibility clause, using the new procedure for monitoring the subsidiarity principle (discussed below). However, it is unclear whether this provision is intended to act merely as an explicit cross-reference to the 'yellow card' system, which would in any case apply to all proposals for the adoption of *legislative* acts under Article 352 TFEU; or whether it is instead meant materially to extend the national parliaments' power to issue reasoned opinions, and the Union institutions' obligation to take them into consideration, so as also to cover proposals for the adoption of *non-legislative* measures under Article 352 TFEU (proposals which would not otherwise fall within the scope of the 'yellow card' procedure at all).

D – The Problem of 'Legal Basis Disputes'

If 'competence creep' is one of the main constitutional difficulties associated with a system of Union regulatory power based upon the principle of conferral, another significant problem worth investigating further in that regard is the phenomenon of 'legal basis disputes'.[65]

As we have seen, one of the striking characteristics of the Treaties is their multiplicity of legal bases, each conferring the necessary competence upon the Union institutions to adopt binding measures and undertake other action in the relevant field, but with each legal basis also setting out its own framework of principles and rules: for example, as regards the applicable decision-making procedure to be followed by the institutions; the nature and degree of competence conferred upon the Union institutions as well as its impact upon the Member States' power to adopt independent regulatory action; and other issues such as the precise range of legal instruments available to the Union institutions in the relevant field. Given that it is not always easy to identify a given policy proposal with a corresponding legal basis under the Treaties, or to associate a given initiative exclusively with one legal basis to the exclusion of all other Treaty provisions, disputes are liable to arise between the Union institutions, and between the Union institutions and the Member States, as to precisely which legal basis should be used for the adoption of a proposed Union measure. For example, in the early 1990s, there was a series of cases in which the Council found itself at odds with the Commission and/or the European Parliament over the correct legal basis for various measures regulating the disposal of industrial waste: should the basis for such measures be Article 114 TFEU, since disparities between national provisions could result in different levels of costs for industry in the different Member States, thus distorting competition on the internal market; or was the correct legal basis Article 192 TFEU, which confers law-making powers upon the Union institutions for the protection of the environment?[66]

Such legal basis disputes are not merely a matter of ensuring that the principle of conferral is complied with in some formal sense—ensuring that Union instruments are explicitly related to the correct empowering provision under the Treaties—though that

---

[65] See further eg N Emiliou, 'Opening Pandora's Box: The Legal Basis of Community Measures before the Court of Justice' (1994) *ELRev* 488; A Charlesworth and H Cullen, 'Diplomacy by Other Means: The Use of Legal Basis Litigation as a Political Strategy by the European Parliament and Member States' (1999) 36 *CMLRev* 1243; M Klamert, 'Conflicts of Legal Basis: No Legality and No Basis but a Bright Future under the Lisbon Treaty?' (2010) 35 *ELRev* 497.

[66] eg Case C-300/89 *Commission v Council* [1991] ECR 2867. Cf Case C-155/91 *Commission v Council* [1993] ECR I-939; Case C-187/93 *European Parliament v Council* [1994] ECR I-2857.

objective is in itself of the utmost constitutional importance; indeed, failure to identify the legal basis for a Union act will provide a grounds for its annulment by the Union courts.[67] Just as importantly, legal basis disputes often involve important questions of inter-institutional balance within the Union. For example, at the time of the legal basis disputes which arose over the disposal of industrial waste, the choice between Article 114 TFEU or Article 192 TFEU had a crucial impact upon the relative powers of the various institutions involved in the decision-making process: Article 114 TEU was based upon the ordinary legislative procedure, whereas Article 192 TFEU at that time employed the (now defunct) co-operation procedure. Furthermore, legal basis disputes may sometimes raise significant questions about the system of Union competences and their impact upon the regulatory power of the Member States. For example, returning again to legal basis disputes over the disposal of industrial waste, the choice between Article 114 TFEU or Article 192 TFEU could have a crucial impact upon the relative powers available to the Union and those reserved to its Member States: although both the internal market and environmental policy are categorised as areas of shared Union competence, Article 114 TEU permits the Union institutions to adopt legislative measures with fully pre-emptive legal effects, whereas Union measures adopted pursuant to Article 192 TFEU are only ever capable of carrying out a minimum harmonisation of domestic laws.[68]

The Court of Justice has frequently been called upon to resolve such legal basis disputes. The relevant principles have been established and worked out in a long line of rulings.[69] All Union measures must be based on the correct legal basis or they will be struck down as invalid. For those purposes, the choice of legal basis must be based on objective factors amenable to judicial review and, in particular, on the aim and content of the measure in question. Where the Treaties contain a more specific provision that is capable of constituting the legal basis for the relevant measure, the measure must be founded on that provision.[70] Otherwise, if the measure concerns two different policy areas, and it is possible to identify one policy as the main or predominant purpose, whereas the other is merely incidental, the measure should be based on the primary legal basis. Exceptionally, however, a measure may concern two different policy areas which are indissolubly linked, without one being secondary in relation to the other: in that event, the measure may be based on a dual legal basis under the Treaties;[71] unless the relevant procedures are incompatible with each other, for example, because one legal basis uses unanimity within the Council, whereas the other is based upon QMV.[72]

It is worth noting that some commentators relied on the *Titanium Dioxide* case as

[67] eg Case C-370/07 *Commission v Council* [2009] ECR I-8917.
[68] See Art 193 TFEU.
[69] See, in particular, C-155/91 *Commission v Council (Waste Directive)* [1993] ECR I-939. More recently eg Case C-155/07 *Parliament v Council (EIB Guarantee)* [2008] ECR I-8103; Case C-411/06 *Commission v Parliament and Council (Waste Shipments)* [2009] ECR I-7585.
[70] eg by its own terms, Art 352 TFEU can only be used as a default provision where recourse to another (sufficient) legal basis is not possible: see further eg Case C-166/07 *Parliament v Council* [2009] ECR I-7135. Note also the competence disputes which arose pre-TL, between the First (priority) and Third (default) Pillar as regards the adoption of certain harmonisation measures in the field of criminal law, eg Case C-176/03 *Commission v Council (Environmental Crimes)* [2005] ECR I-7879; Case C-440/05 *Commission v Council (Ship Source Pollution)* [2007] ECR I-9097.
[71] eg Case C-94/03 *Commission v Council* [2006] ECR I-1; Case C-178/03 *Commission v Parliament and Council* [2006] ECR I-107.
[72] eg Case C-338/01 *Commission v Council* [2004] ECR I-4829. Although it appears possible to have a joint legal basis which results in an obligation for the Council to act unanimously throughout the ordinary legislative procedure: see Case C-166/07 *Parliament v Council* [2009] ECR I-7135.

authority for the proposition that, where the dispute involved a choice between two legal basis with different legislative procedures, the Court would favour the legal basis which offered the greatest opportunity for the European Parliament to participate in the decision-making process, and which thus increased the democratic legitimacy of the Union system.[73] On the one hand, as regards the standard category of Union measures which are capable of being split into one primary and another incidental purpose, the Court has held that the task of determining the appropriate legal basis should ignore any consideration of granting greater powers to the European Parliament. For example, in the *Bovine Registration Regulation* case, the Court expressly rejected the Parliament's argument that the disputed measure should have been adopted under Article 114 TFEU (using the ordinary legislative procedure) rather than Article 43 TFEU (which at that time involved mere consultation of the European Parliament), when the internal market aspect of the disputed measure was clearly secondary to its character as an agricultural policy initiative, merely so as to ensure that directly elected MEPs were more closely involved in the adoption of protective measures against the spread of the BSE disease, which was then a matter of grave public concern across the Union.[74]

On the other hand, when it comes to the exceptional category of Union measures whose objectives cannot be separated out into primary/predominant and secondary/incidental, thus making recourse to a dual legal basis possible in principle, the Court does seem prepared to give greater weight to considerations of increasing democratic input from the European Parliament. In particular, the respective decision-making procedures of the two relevant legal bases will be considered compatible with each other, provided that the European Parliament is able to exercise the greatest possible legislative role. For example, in a dispute over the adoption of a regulation on the import and export of dangerous chemicals from/into the internal market, it was held that considerations related to the common commercial policy (under Article 207 TFEU) and to the Union's environmental policy (under Article 192 TFEU) were so inseparable that recourse to a dual legal basis might be possible. Although the legislative procedures used under those two legal bases were (at the time, pre-TL) entirely different, they were not actually incompatible with each other. In the first place, both involved QMV within the Council. In the second place, although the version of Article 207 TFEU in force at that time made no provision for the involvement of the European Parliament, whereas Article 192 TFEU was based upon the ordinary legislative procedure, the institutions should simply follow whichever of the two possible decision-making processes was most favourable to the European Parliament's participation in the adoption of the relevant act.[75]

With the progressive extension of both qualified majority voting and the ordinary legislative procedure, legal basis disputes—or at least those concerning the applicable voting rules within the Council or the correct level of participation for the European Parliament—have become less problematic than in previous years.[76] However, so long as the Union still adopts measures according to a variety of decision-making procedures, the potential for legal basis disputes remains. Moreover, legal basis disputes will still arise from time to time inspired by other important differences between the various articles

---

[73] Case C-300/89 *Commission v Council* [1991] ECR I-2867.
[74] Case C-269/97 *Commission and Parliament v Council* [2000] ECR I-2257.
[75] Case C-178/03 *Commission v Parliament and Council* [2006] ECR I-107.
[76] eg both internal market and environmental measures are now adopted, for most purposes, according to the ordinary legislative procedure.

of the Treaties (such as the degree of regulatory competence conferred upon the Union within a given policy field).

III – THE PRINCIPLE OF SUBSIDIARITY

The principle of subsidiarity, though not under that name, was first introduced as a principle of the Union legal order by the SEA. The latter created an Environmental Title within the (then) EEC Treaty and provided that the Community should take action to the extent to which environmental objectives 'can be attained better at Community level than at the level of the individual Member States'.[77] Subsidiarity was then elevated to the status of a fully fledged constitutional principle by the Maastricht Treaty.[78] Subsidiarity was widely seen as a response to the wide and expanding scope of Union law-making competence and to the increasing exercise of that competence (the latter being facilitated not least by the more widespread use of QMV within the Council). In the run up to the agreement on the Maastricht amendments, some Member States, including Spain, France and Italy, had sought a reference to subsidiarity in the preamble of the Treaty of Rome.[79] But the main advocates of subsidiarity as a legally binding principle inhibiting the exercise of Union competence had been Germany and the United Kingdom.[80] The TA subsequently introduced a Protocol on the application of the principles of subsidiarity and proportionality, containing various procedural requirements and legally binding criteria for the application of the principle of subsidiarity. The TL then slightly amended the definition of subsidiarity, now to be found in Article 5(3) TEU; and also replaced the Amsterdam Protocol with a new Protocol (No 2) on the application of the principles of subsidiarity and proportionality.[81]

A – The Meaning(s) of Subsidiarity

The broad idea underlying the principle of subsidiarity is a simple one: that public powers

---

[77] See what was Art 130R(4) EEC.

[78] Ex-Art 5(b) EC.

[79] See further A Estella, *The EU Principle of Subsidiarity and its Critique* (Oxford, Oxford University Press, 2002) 85.

[80] A Estella, *The EU Principle of Subsidiarity and its Critique* (Oxford, Oxford University Press, 2002) 85; J Cloos, D Reinesch, G Vinges and J Weyland, *Le Traité de Maastricht: Genèse, Analyse, Commentaires* (Brussels, Bruylant, 1993) 149. And see T Schilling, 'A New Dimension of Subsidiarity: Subsidiarity as a Rule and a Principle' (1994) 14 *YEL* 203, referring to D Cass, 'The Word that Saved Maastricht? The Principle of Subsidiarity and the Division of Powers within the European Community' (1992) 29 *CMLRev* 1107.

[81] There is an extensive literature on the principle of subsidiarity, much of it now overtaken by events. For a selection of views, see V Constantinesco, 'Who's Afraid of Subsidiarity?' (1991) 11 *YEL* 33; N Emiliou, 'Subsidiarity: An Effective Barrier against the Enterprises of Ambition?' (1992) 17 *ELRev* 383; AG Toth, 'The Principle of Subsidiarity in the Maastricht Treaty' (1992) 29 *CMLRev* 1079; D Cass, 'The Word that Saves Maastricht? The Principle of Subsidiarity and the Division of Powers within the European Community' (1992) 29 *CMLRev* 1107; E Mattina, 'Subsidiarité, Démocratie et Transparence' (1992) 4 *RMUE* 203; JP Gonzalez, 'The Principle of Subsidiarity' (1995) 20 *ELRev* 355; D Wyatt, 'Subsidiarity—Is it too Vague to be Effective as a Legal Principle?' in K Nicolaidis and S Weatherill (eds), *Whose Europe? National Models and the Constitution of the European Union* (Oxford University Press/European Studies at Oxford, 2003) 86 (available at www.europeanstudies.ox.ac.uk).

should normally be located at the lowest tier of government where they can be exercised effectively.[82]

In constitutional texts such as the TEU and TFEU, that broad idea can be seen at work in a variety of different contexts.[83] For example, it may serve as a general political value permeating the constitutional order: that is the significance of the reference in Article 1, second paragraph of the TEU, that the 'ever closer union among the peoples of Europe' is one in which 'decisions are taken . . . as closely as possible to the citizen'. It is also reflected in Article 4(2) TEU, according to which the Union shall respect the national identities of the Member States, inherent in their political and constitutional fundamental structures, including systems of regional and local self-government. Furthermore, the notion of subsidiarity may also guide the hand of the constitution-makers in allocating powers, within the Union's complex legal order, between the central authorities and the component entities. Thus, the division of Union power into the categories of exclusive, shared and supporting competences—the latter in particular exhibiting a strong preference for the preservation of domestic regulatory power and only limited supranational involvement in a supplementary or complementary capacity—can also be seen as a manifestation of the spirit of subsidiarity.[84] Finally, the idea of subsidiarity may be employed so as to influence the exercise of Union competences, particularly where the latter exist concurrently with those of the Member States. Its effect here is to require that, in matters where the constitutional texts allow action to be taken either by the central authorities or by the component entities, the choice should, other things being equal, fall on the latter.

That last-mentioned function of the subsidiarity principle is the one provided for by Article 5(3) TEU: in areas which do not fall within its exclusive competence, the Union shall act only if and in so far as the objectives of the proposed action cannot be sufficiently achieved by the Member States, either at central level or at regional and local level, but can rather, by reason of the scale or effects of the proposed action, be better achieved at Union level. In other words, once it is established that the Union enjoys competence in accordance with the principle of conferral, the principle of subsidiarity is then designed to assist in deciding whether or not the Union should exercise that competence in practice—based upon the criterion that, in cases where the Treaties leave the matter open, one should prefer action by the Member States acting individually, unless one can demonstrate a specific need for collective action at the Union level instead.

When it comes to applying the principle of subsidiarity as defined in Article 5(3) TEU, the first point to note is that the principle does not apply to areas falling within the Union's exclusive competence. On the one hand, to apply the subsidiarity principle in such situations would be pointless, since the option of leaving it to the Member States to pursue the objectives in question has been specifically disallowed by the Treaty system. On the other hand, in accordance with the definition of exclusivity given in Articles 2 and 3 TFEU, only a small number of fields of Union activity are thereby excluded from the potential application of the subsidiarity test. Thus, for example, the Court has expressly held that the test

---

[82] See the famous formulation of the principle by Pope Pius XI in his encyclical of 1931, *Quadragesimo Anno*, where he wrote, '[I]t is an injustice, a grave evil and a disturbance of the right order, for a larger and higher association to arrogate to itself functions which can be performed efficiently by smaller and lower societies' (London, Catholic Truth Society, 1936). On the historical background, see N Emiliou, 'Subsidiarity: An Effective Barrier against the Enterprises of Ambition?' (1992) 17 *ELRev* 383.

[83] See the analysis of G van Gerven, 'Les Principes de "Subsidiarité, Proportionnalité et Coopération" en Droit Communautaire Européen', a paper delivered in the author's capacity as President of the Académie royale des sciences, lettres et beaux-arts de Belgique, at the general meeting of the Academy on 21 December 1991.

[84] See above.

of subsidiarity applies to the exercise of the Union's power to harmonise national laws to further the completion the internal market, under Article 114 TFEU, since that is a field of shared (not exclusive) competence.[85] The same is true in situations where the Union has already exercised its shared competence to enact secondary legislation in the relevant field, with at least some pre emptive effects, and now wishes to repeal and replace that legislation with a revised regulatory code.[86]

For those fields of Union law characterised by shared or supporting competence, the test of subsidiarity prescribed by Article 5(3) TEU has a dual aspect: the impossibility of attaining the objectives in question 'sufficiently' by action at national or regional level; and the superior efficacy of taking action rather at Union level. The original Amsterdam Protocol on the application of the principles of subsidiarity and proportionality offered some useful guidelines for determining whether both limbs of that test had been satisfied in practice. Although those guidelines were repealed by the TL, they are nevertheless worth bearing in mind, since they surely still represent the sorts of considerations relevant to the subsidiarity assessment:[87] the issue under consideration has transnational aspects which cannot be satisfactorily regulated by action by Member States; action by Member States alone or lack of Union action would conflict with the requirements of the Treaties (such as the need to correct distortions of competition or to avoid disguised restrictions on trade or to strengthen economic and social cohesion) or would otherwise significantly damage Member States' interests; and/or action at Union level would produce clear benefits by reason of its scale or effects compared with action at the level of the Member States.[88]

Another point that was emphasised in the original Amsterdam Protocol, and again surely remains true today, is that subsidiarity is a dynamic concept, allowing action by the Union 'to be expanded where circumstances so require, and conversely, to be restricted or discontinued where it is no longer justified'.[89] Thus, the principle must not be applied crudely as a brake on the exercise of Union powers. On the one hand, events such as the BSE crisis, or the discovery of dioxins in certain foodstuffs, might well point to the need for a new Union programme of food safety measures.[90] On the other hand, a review of existing proposals might indicate that they need to be withdrawn, or existing legislation repealed, where those are found no longer to meet the test in Article 5(3) TEU.[91]

B – Implementing Subsidiarity: The Role of the Union's Political Institutions

According to Article 5(3) TEU, the Union institutions shall apply the principle of sub-

---

[85] eg Case C-377/98 *Netherlands v Parliament and Council* [2001] ECR I-7079; Cases C-154-155/04 *Alliance for Natural Health* [2005] ECR I-6451.

[86] eg Case C-491/01 *ex parte British American Tobacco* [2002] ECR I-11453.

[87] cp Commission, *17th Report on Better Lawmaking*, COM(2010) 547 Final.

[88] Amsterdam Protocol, Arts 4 and 5, read together.

[89] Amsterdam Protocol, Art 3.

[90] See eg the Commission's Report, 'Better Lawmaking 1999' COM(1999) 562 Final 2.

[91] Note that an extensive review of existing proposals and legislation was initiated by the Commission shortly after the entry into force of the TEU: see COM(94) 533 Final, pp 15 *et seq*. The Commission continues to organise periodic 'culls' of pending legislative proposals, eg COM(2005) 462 Final provided a relatively large-scale example (though that particular exercise was not specifically justified by reference to the principle of subsidiarity, but rather on grounds such as promoting greater economic competitiveness or having failed to undertake an appropriate impact assessment).

sidiarity as laid down in the Protocol on the application of the principles of subsidiarity and proportionality. Article 1 of the Lisbon Protocol then states that each Union institution 'shall ensure constant respect' for the principle of subsidiarity. In practice, primary responsibility for ensuring the effective application of the subsidiarity principle falls upon the Commission, the Council and the European Parliament, as the institutions with the leading roles in the Union's legislative process.

Under Article 5 of the Lisbon Protocol, all draft legislative acts of the Union shall be justified with regard to the principles of subsidiarity and proportionality. Any draft legislative act should contain a detailed statement making it possible to appraise compliance with the principles of subsidiarity and proportionality. This statement should contain some assessment of the proposal's financial impact and, in the case of a directive, of its implications for the rules to be put in place by Member States, including, where necessary, the regional legislation. The reasons for concluding that a Union objective can be better achieved at Union level shall be substantiated by qualitative and, wherever possible, quantitative indicators. Draft legislative acts shall take account of the need for any burden, whether financial or administrative, falling upon the Union, national governments, regional or local authorities, economic operators, and citizens, to be minimised and commensurate with the objective to be achieved. Moreover, pursuant to Article 296 TFEU, the Union institutions must state the reasons for adopting any legal act: as we shall see below, that general obligation implies also a binding requirement for the preamble to Union legislation to contain reasons sufficient to demonstrate the latter's compliance with the principle of subsidiarity.

Finally, Article 9 of the Lisbon Protocol places an obligation upon the Commission to submit an annual report on the application of Article 5 TEU to the European Council, the European Parliament, the Council and the national parliaments.[92]

C – Implementing Subsidiarity: The Role of the Union Courts

It was hotly debated, in the early days following the insertion of ex-Article 5 into the EC Treaty by the Maastricht Treaty, whether the principle of subsidiarity was justiciable.[93] As an eminent commentator pointed out, there was nothing in the text of ex-Article 5 EC to suggest the contrary, nor that the Court of Justice did not have power to interpret the Treaty provisions containing the principle of subsidiarity.[94] Any doubts should by now have been dissipated by the available case law—though in practice, many commentators remain sceptical of the Court's capacity to enforce respect for the principle of subsidiarity in anything other than a relatively light-touch or superficial manner.[95]

Earlier case law suggested that the Court was reluctant to get too deeply involved in what seemed to be essentially political rather than judicial questions about the appropriate need for Union regulation. For example, in the *Working Time Directive* case, the UK sought annulment of a Union directive adopted under the Treaty provisions concerning

---

[92] See eg COM(1999) 562 Final; COM(2005) 98 Final; COM(2010) 547 Final.

[93] See eg AG Toth, 'Is Subsidiarity Justiciable?' (1994) 19 *ELRev* 268.

[94] Lord Mackenzie-Stuart, 'Subsidiarity—A Busted Flush?' in D Curtin and D O'Keefe, *Constitutional Adjudication in European and National Law: Essays for the Hon Mr Justice TFO'Higgins* (London, Butterworths, 1992) 19.

[95] See the 'critical assessment' of the principle of subsidiarity offered in the last edition of this book: A Arnull, A Dashwood, M Dougan, M Ross, E Spaventa and D Wyatt, *Wyatt & Dashwood's EU Law*, 5th edn (London, Sweet & Maxwell, 2006) paras 4-018 to 4-021.

the health and safety of workers so as to lay down common rules on the maximum working week, minimum rest periods and minimum paid leave. In particular, the UK argued that the Union institutions had failed to demonstrate that the directive's aims could better be achieved at Union level rather than by action on the part of the Member States. However, the ECJ simply held that, once the Council has found that it is necessary to improve levels of protection as regards the health and safety of workers, achievement of that objective through the imposition of minimum common requirements necessarily presupposes Union-wide action.[96] In other words, it appeared that the simple political judgment of the Union legislature—that Union action was necessary, in the circumstances, to achieve the desired policy objectives—would be sufficient to satisfy the Court that the principle of subsidiarity had been respected. That approach hardly seemed sufficient, especially given that the relevant Treaty provisions clearly contemplated the possibility of pursuing those same objectives through action at Member State level.[97]

Nevertheless, at that time, the Court clearly preferred to enforce the principle of subsidiarity (if at all) through procedural means, in particular, through the duty of the Union institutions under Article 296 TFEU to state the reasons upon which their legal acts are based. Consider, for example, the *Deposit Guarantee Schemes Directive* ruling, which concerned a Union directive adopted under the internal market provisions requiring every Member State to establish a deposit guarantee scheme within its territory and to ensure that no credit institution could be authorised to take deposits from customers unless it was a member of such a deposit guarantee scheme. Germany brought an action for annulment of the directive, inter alia, on the grounds that it infringed the principle of subsidiarity: the Union legislature had failed to provide an explicit statement of reasons to explain why the directive's objectives could not be sufficiently attained by action at Member State level. However, the Court observed that the directive's preamble did state that, in the Union legislature's view, differences in national legislation concerning deposit guarantee schemes had repercussions outside the borders of each Member State; it was obvious that such cross-border effects could not be addressed sufficiently by the Member States acting alone. The Union legislature had therefore fulfilled its duty to state the reasons for compliance with the principle of subsidiarity—even if it had not actually referred to subsidiarity as such.[98]

In more recent cases, however, the Court of Justice seems to have become more confident about determining whether Union legislation complies with the substantive requirements of the principle of subsidiarity as laid down in Article 5(3) TEU. In a series of judgments concerning (for example) the validity of the Biotechnological Inventions Directive,[99] the Second Tobacco Labelling Directive,[100] the Food Supplements Directive[101] and the Roaming Regulation,[102] the Court has indeed assessed whether the exercise of Union competence under Article 114 TFEU was justified from the perspective of subsidiarity. In each case, the Court held that the purpose of the disputed measure was to eliminate obstacles to trade and distortions of competition within the internal market

[96] Case C-84/94 *United Kingdom v Council (Working Time Directive)* [1996] ECR I-5755.
[97] See Arts 151 and 153 TFEU.
[98] Case C-233/94 *Germany v Parliament and Council (Deposit Guarantee Schemes Directive)* [1997] ECR I-2405.
[99] Case C-377/98 *Netherlands v European Parliament and Council* [2001] ECR I-7079.
[100] Case C-491/01 *ex parte British American Tobacco* [2002] ECR I-11453.
[101] Cases C-154/04 and C-155/04 *Alliance for Natural Health* [2005] ECR I-6451.
[102] Case C-58/08 *Vodafone* (Judgment of 8 June 2010).

resulting from the multifarious development of national laws. It was evident that that objective could not satisfactorily be achieved by the Member States alone (after all, leaving the Member States to their own devices had created the obstacles and distortions in the first place), and in fact required action at the Union level.

Those cases are significant because, really for the first time, the Court engaged in judicial review based upon substantive (rather than purely procedural) compliance with the principle of subsidiarity. But, in some respects, they were 'easy cases' for the Court. As we have seen, the emergence of cross-border obstacles to trade and/or distortions of competition is a *sine qua non* for the very existence of Union competence under Article 114 TFEU, and equally, their emergence would seem to support the conclusion that only action coordinated under the auspices of the Union can provide an effective regulatory solution. Thus, compliance with the principle of conferral might plausibly be equated with satisfaction of the principle of subsidiarity. The Court has not yet revealed its attitude towards the subsidiarity test in other, more difficult, situations involving legislation adopted under the legal bases (for example) dealing with environmental or social policy measures, ie where the prior existence of Union competence is not dependent upon some cross-border trigger, and satisfaction of the principle of subsidiarity cannot automatically be inferred from compliance with the principle of conferral. In such situations, the Court will surely allow the political institutions a wide discretion in weighing up the pros and cons as to whether action should be taken at Union or at national level. Judicial review is likely to be confined to examining whether the assessment reached by the responsible institution has been vitiated by manifest error or abuse of powers, or whether the institution has manifestly exceeded the limits of its discretion.[103]

D – Implementing Subsidiarity: The Role of the National Parliaments

During the constitutional reform process which led to the drafting of the CT and then the TL, a general consensus emerged that the traditional mechanisms for enforcing the principle of subsidiarity—self-restraint by the Union's political institutions and judicial review via the Union courts—had proven insufficient to translate that principle into a more meaningful brake upon the exercise of Union competence. The perceived failure of subsidiarity was closely linked, in turn, to the Union's problems of winning popular acceptance and legitimacy: it was proving very difficult to shake off the image of an overbearing Union intervening excessively in matters which should rightly be left to its Member States. The solution advocated under the CT and implemented by the TL was to look elsewhere for a subsidiarity watchdog, to bodies which were external to the Union's institutional system, yet had a powerful interest in ensuring that the Union did not exercise its competences too enthusiastically: the national parliaments.[104]

Article 5(3) TEU states that national parliaments ensure compliance with the principle of subsidiarity in accordance with the procedure set out in the Protocol on the application of the principles of subsidiarity and proportionality. Article 4 of the Lisbon Protocol seeks

---

[103] As with the principle of proportionality: see below. For more recent (unsuccessful) attempts to rely on the subsidiarity principle, eg Case C-64/05P *Sweden v Commission* [2007] ECR I-11389; Case C-518/07 *Commission v Germany* (Judgment of 9 March 2010).

[104] See further eg G Davies, 'The Post-Laeken Division of Competences' (2003) 28 *ELRev* 686; S Weatherill, 'Better Competence Monitoring' (2005) 30 *ELRev* 23.

to increase the flow of information about the Union's legislative activities to the national parliaments. Thus, the Commission must notify all its legislative proposals to the national parliaments at the same time as to the Union institutions themselves. Similar obligations apply to the Union's other institutions and bodies: for example, the Council is obliged to notify national parliaments of draft legislative acts originating from a group of Member States in the field of police and judicial co-operation in criminal matters.[105] Legislative resolutions of the European Parliament and positions of the Council must also be forwarded to the national parliaments.[106]

Articles 6 and 7 of the Lisbon Protocol then implement the famous 'yellow card' system first proposed by CT. Each national parliament (or chamber thereof) has the power to object to any given legislative proposal by means of a 'reasoned opinion', specifically on the grounds that it infringes the principle of subsidiarity, within a deadline of eight weeks from the date of transmission of the draft.[107] The Union institutions (and other relevant bodies) are obliged to consider all such reasoned opinions; but if one-third or more of the national parliaments object, then the draft legislation must be formally reviewed. That threshold is lowered to one-quarter, in the case of drafts proposed by the Commission or a group of Member States in the field of police and judicial co-operation in criminal matters.[108] For these purposes, each national parliament has two votes: both votes may be used by a unicameral legislature; the votes are to be divided out between the chambers in a bicameral legislature.[109] After the necessary review, the Commission (or other institution/body from which the draft legislation originated) must give reasons for its decision either to maintain, amend or withdraw the proposal.

Despite support for the idea that a sufficient number of negative reasoned opinions from national parliaments should be capable of acting as a 'red card', the 2004 and 2007 IGCs refused to confer upon national parliaments any such formal veto powers over the progress of the Union's own legislative processes. After all, one assumes that, if a sufficient number of national parliaments were to register serious objections to a given legislative proposal on subsidiarity grounds, the political costs for the Union institutions of simply ignoring that opposition—or at least, of doing so on any sort of regular basis—would be severe, particularly for those ministerial representatives who remain accountable to their national parliaments in respect of how they cast their Council votes. Nevertheless, the final Lisbon Protocol does go further than previous versions of the 'yellow card' system, in particular, as regards proposals made under the ordinary legislative procedure, where negative reasoned opinions represent a simple majority of the votes cast by national parliaments. If, having carried out its formal review, the Commission nevertheless decides to maintain its proposal, the Commission must produce its own reasoned opinion, justifying why the draft does comply with the principle of subsidiarity. Before concluding the first reading of the ordinary legislative procedure, the Council and the European Parliament must consider the reasoned opinions of the national parliaments and the Commission. If 55 per cent of Council members, or a simple majority of voting MEPs, consider that the

[105] cp Art 76 TFEU and Chapter 4.

[106] Note also the provisions on greater transmission of information about the Union's activities, contained in the Protocol (No 1) on the role of national parliaments in the European Union.

[107] Under the CT, the deadline was 6 weeks; many thought this was too tight, so the European Council mandate for the 2007 IGC instructed that it be extended to 8 weeks.

[108] Under Art 76 TFEU.

[109] National parliaments may arrange on their own account for the consultation of regional parliaments with legislative powers: see Art 6, first para of the Protocol.

proposal does not comply with the principle of subsidiarity, the ordinary legislative procedure will be terminated.

The Protocol's 'yellow card' system reflects the widespread view that compliance with the principle of subsidiarity will be more effectively achieved through a system of ex ante political input into the legislative procedure as it unfolds, rather than ex post judicial review of legislation after it has already been adopted.[110] More fundamentally, giving teeth to the principle of subsidiarity by entrusting national parliaments with responsibility for monitoring its application could increase the accountability and legitimacy of the EU's law-making bodies, and enhance in an unprecedented way the sense of 'ownership' of the European project at national level. In that regard, the 'yellow card' system should be read in the broader context of Article 12 TEU, which summarises the various ways in which national parliaments can actively contribute to the good functioning of the Union: not only through monitoring the principle of subsidiarity, but also (for example) by participating in the evaluation of various Union policies within the AFSJ[111] and taking part in the ordinary and simplified procedures for revising the Treaties.[112] Indeed, it is arguable that the importance of the 'yellow card' system itself is secondary to the more general goal of facilitating the fruitful engagement of national parliaments with the Union institutions, with a view to enhancing scrutiny of the Union's activities by domestic as well as supranational representative assemblies.[113]

Nevertheless, there are doubts about just how well the 'yellow card' system will work—even assuming that national parliaments take their new role seriously and actually exercise their power to issue reasoned opinions in practice. For example, although the TL extended the deadline for responses to eight weeks, rather than the six weeks originally proposed under the CT, it is still uncertain whether such a tight timetable will offer sufficient opportunity for the national parliaments to formulate (and if desired, coordinate) their subsidiarity objections.[114] Moreover, the Protocol assumes that national parliaments will issue reasoned opinions specifically on grounds of subsidiarity. What happens if the grounds for objection actually relate to complaints about (say) the principle of proportionality, or the simple desirability of the proposed regulatory standards? Another potential problem relates to the procedure for activating the system of heightened scrutiny, where negative reasoned opinions account for half the votes cast by national parliaments, which depends on the Commission 'maintaining' rather than 'amending' the relevant proposal: what if the Commission indeed amends its draft, but not in a way that materially affects, or substantially meets, the objections originally made by the national parliaments—would this nevertheless absolve the Commission from any obligation to produce its own reasoned opinion, and the Council and European Parliament from any need to carry out a preliminary subsidiarity vote?

At the time of writing, it remains too early to tell what impact the enhanced role for national parliaments might have upon the Union's legislative process and, in particular,

---

[110] Though see below on Art 8 of the Protocol.

[111] See Arts 70, 71, 85 and 88 TFEU.

[112] See Art 48 TEU and Art 81(3) TFEU. See Chapter 2.

[113] See further eg B Crum, 'Tailoring Representative Democracy to the European Union: Does the European Constitution Reduce the Democratic Deficit?' (2005) 11 *ELJ* 452; G Barrett, 'The King Is Dead, Long Live the King: the Recasting by the Treaty of Lisbon of the Provisions of the Constitutional Treaty Concerning National Parliaments' (2008) 33 *ELRev* 66.

[114] Note the provisions on interparliamentary co-operation, contained in the Protocol (No 1) on the role of national parliaments in the European Union.

upon respect for the principle of subsidiarity. It is interesting to note that the Commission had already, since 2006, invited opinions from the national parliaments upon its legislative proposals. The Commission received 115 such opinions in 2007, rising to 250 in 2009, though only around 10 per cent of the opinions received in 2009 contained comments relevant to the principles of subsidiarity and/or proportionality. As for the period since the entry into force of the TL, the Commission had, by June 2010, transmitted 19 legislative proposals to the national parliaments and received four reasoned opinions in accordance with the 'yellow card' mechanism.[115] Clearly, any proper evaluation of the Lisbon Protocol must await the availability of further data and the conduct of more detailed research.

In any case, the new 'yellow card' system does raise some interesting questions about the future role of the Court of Justice in subsidiarity disputes. On the one hand, it could be argued that the emphasis placed by the TL on ex ante political monitoring by the national parliaments should be taken by the Court as an indication that it need no longer strain itself towards adopting a more rigorous substantive test for judicial review on grounds of subsidiarity. On the other hand, Article 8 of the Protocol expressly confers upon the Court of Justice jurisdiction to hear actions for the annulment of Union legislative acts based on the principle of subsidiarity, brought by Member States or notified by them 'in accordance with their legal order' on behalf of their national parliaments or a chamber thereof.[116] Overlooking the important interpretative question of whether national parliaments are thereby given an inalienable right of access to the Court, or remain dependent on the co-operation of their Member State to initiate action on their behalf,[117] this provision suggests that, if anything, ex post judicial review on subsidiarity grounds may be poised to take on a whole new potency. After all, the Treaties have deliberately enlarged the possibilities for judicial scrutiny specifically on subsidiarity grounds; thanks to the 'yellow card' system, the Court may be presented with a mass of 'reasoned opinions' detailing the substantive objections held by national parliaments. With such a wealth of material, argumentation over subsidiarity could metamorphose from the politically subjective into the readily justiciable.

IV – THE PRINCIPLE OF PROPORTIONALITY

Long before its importation into Article 5(4) TEU, the principle of proportionality had become a familiar tool of judicial review in the field of Union administrative law. In that field, as we shall see in a later chapter, the principle has been used mainly for two purposes: controlling the extent to which measures, adopted by the Union authorities in furtherance of objectives of the Treaties, are permitted to override the interests of particular individuals; and limiting the leeway Member States have been given to protect important public interests, through derogations from certain fundamental rules of the

---

[115] See Commission, *17th Report on Better Lawmaking*, COM(2010) 547 Final.

[116] Art 8 also permits the Committee of the Regions to seek annulment of Union legislative acts in respect of which the TFEU provides for its consultation, for alleged breach of the subsidiarity principle. On standing to bring annulment actions more generally, see further Chapter 6.

[117] See further eg M Dougan, 'The Convention's Draft Constitutional Treaty: Bringing Europe Closer to its Lawyers?' (2003) 28 *ELRev* 763, 768; J Kokott and A Ruth, 'The European Convention and its Draft Treaty establishing a Constitution for Europe: Appropriate Answers to the Laeken Questions?' (2003) 40 *CMLRev* 1315, 1335.

Union system.[118] The case law establishes that, in applying the principle of proportionality, it must be ascertained (i) whether the means employed by the competent authority are suitable for the purpose of achieving the desired objective; and (ii) whether they do not go beyond what is necessary to achieve that objective.[119]

In the context of Article 5(4) TFEU, the logic of the proportionality principle remains the same, though it is here operating on the constitutional plane as regards the exercise of the Union's law-making powers. Assuming that Union competence exists in accordance with the principle of conferral, and that the Union should legitimately exercise that competence in accordance with the principle of subsidiarity, the proportionality test provides an answer to the next question: 'what should be the intensity or nature of the Union's action?'[120] Proportionality, in effect, guides the Union legislator towards choosing the form of action which, while being well designed to achieve its objective, will intrude, to the smallest practicable extent, upon the powers of the Member States.

The old Amsterdam Protocol on the application of the principles of subsidiarity and proportionality went into some detail in describing the elements relevant to an evaluation of proportionality in this 'constitutional' context. Among other things, it stated that

> [t]he form of [Union] action must be as simple as possible, consistent with the satisfactory achievement of the objective of the measure and the need for effective enforcement. . . . Other things being equal, directives should be preferred to regulations and framework directives to detailed measures.

Care should be taken 'to respect well established national arrangements and the organisation and working of Member States' legal systems'.[121] Those criteria have largely been repealed, though in practice, they will doubtless retain their relevance in any proportionality assessment.[122] Now, Article 5(4) TEU provides that the Union institutions shall apply the principle of proportionality in accordance with the new Lisbon Protocol (No 2) on the application of the principles of subsidiarity and proportionality. Article 5 of the Lisbon Protocol—which, as we have seen, sets out the various formal obligations to be undertaken in respect of draft Union legislative acts—applies to the principle of proportionality as much as to the principle of subsidiarity. However, the potential for national parliaments to show a 'yellow card' to draft Union legislative acts is available only in respect of the principle of subsidiarity, not for enforcing the principle of proportionality.

As one of the instruments deployed by Article 5 TEU to help preserve the balance between the Union and its Member States, the principle of proportionality usually has a stronger political flavour than in its usual administrative law setting. Not surprisingly, therefore, when the principle was invoked by the United Kingdom in the *Working Time Directive* case,[123] the Court of Justice saw fit to adopt the technique of 'marginal review'[124]

---

[118] See Chapter 10.

[119] See eg Cases 279, 280, 285 and 286/84 *Rau v Commission* [1987] ECR 1069, para 34; cited with reference to Art 5 TEU in Case 426/93 *Germany v Council* [1995] ECR I-3723, para 42.

[120] See Bull EC 12–1992, point I.15.

[121] See Amsterdam Protocol, Arts 6 and 7.

[122] Note that, under Art 296 TFEU, where the Treaties do not specify the type of act (regulation, directive, etc) to be adopted, the Union institutions shall select it on a case-by-case basis, in compliance with the applicable procedures and with the principle of proportionality.

[123] Case C-84/94 *United Kingdom v Council* [1996] ECR I-5755.

[124] This term is used by H Schermers and D Waelbroek, *Judicial Protection in the European Communities*, 5th edn (The Hague, Kluwer, 1992), when discussing the use of the technique in the judicial control of decisions based on broad economic assessments.

(for manifest error, misuse of powers or manifest excess of jurisdiction) which, we have suggested, would also be appropriate in dealing with issues of subsidiarity.[125] A similar 'hands off' approach to judicial review based upon the principle of proportionality, in the sort of constitutional contexts envisaged by Article 5(4) TFEU, can be seen in many other judgments from the Court of Justice.[126] Nevertheless, the Court has (very occasionally) struck down elements of Union legislation on the grounds that they manifestly exceed the level of regulation necessary to achieve their own objectives.[127]

V – FLEXIBILITY

The principles contained in Article 5 TEU—of conferral, subsidiarity and proportionality—represent the backbone of the system of Union competences. Our discussion would not be complete, however, without considering another important feature of that system— flexibility—by which we mean legal arrangements under which the Treaties recognise that one or more of the Member States may, in principle, remain permanently outside certain activities or practices being pursued within the single institutional framework of the Union, either because they choose to do so or because they do not meet the criteria for participation.[128]

So understood, flexibility is to be distinguished from other instances of regulatory differentiation within the Union legal order: for example, the long-established practice of allowing a transitional period before new Member States are required to apply the whole body of EU law; or that of prescribing differential periods for the implementation of new legislation, taking account of the fact that a particular Member State may face special difficulties of adjustment.[129] Such derogations from the rules generally applicable under the Treaties differ from the flexibility principle in that they apply only on a temporary basis, and are accorded in recognition of objective socioeconomic factors, not merely the political preferences of the Member State concerned.[130]

Indeed, the principle of flexibility is meant to recognise the difficulty of maintaining a workable consensus between the Member States about how best to exercise the Union's regulatory competences, especially given the dramatic growth both in the fields of activity

---

[125] See above.

[126] eg Case C-233/94 *Germany v Parliament and Council* [1997] ECR I-2405; Case C-491/01 *ex parte British American Tobacco* [2002] ECR I-11453; Case C-434/02 *Arnold André* [2004] ECR I-11825; Case C-210/03 *Swedish Match* [2004] ECR I-11893; Case C-344/04 *European Low Fares Airline Association* [2006] ECR I-403; Case C-558/07 *SPCM* [2009] ECR I-5783; Case C-58/08 *Vodafone* (Judgment of 8 June 2010).

[127] eg Case C-453/03 *ABNA* [2005] ECR I-10423.

[128] The term 'variable geometry' is also found, especially in the older literature, in the sense of 'flexibility' used here. For an analysis of the flexibility principle, from a political science perspective, see G Edwards and E Philippart, *Flexibility and the Treaty of Amsterdam: Europe's New Byzantium?*, CELS Occasional Paper No 3 (Cambridge, 1997). See also A Stubb, 'A Categorisation of Differentiated Integration' (1996) 34 *JCMS* 238; H Kortenberg, 'Closer Co-operation in the Treaty of Amsterdam' (1998) 35 *CMLRev* 833; G Gaja, 'How Flexible Is Flexibility under the Amsterdam Treaty?' (1998) 35 *CMLRev* 855; F Tuytschaever, *Differentiation in European Union Law* (Oxford, Hart Publishing 1999); G de Búrca and J Scott (eds), *Constitutional Change in the EU: From Uniformity to Flexibility?* (Oxford, Hart Publishing 2000); B de Witte, D Hanf and E Vos (eds), *The Many Faces of Differentiation in EU Law* (Antwerp, Intersentia 2001).

[129] cf Art 27 TFEU.

[130] See the distinctions drawn in A Dashwood (ed), *Reviewing Maastricht: Issues for the 1996 IGC* (London, Sweet & Maxwell, 1996) 41–43.

in which the EU has become involved (including many sensitive policy areas such as the environment, education and public health), and in the simple number of Member States (thus representing a more heterogeneous body of political opinion about how best to tackle emerging economic and social problems). Rather than accept either that Union activity must proceed at the pace of the 'lowest common denominator', or that more integrationist Member States will pursue their ambitions through new institutional arrangements lying altogether outside the Union, flexibility embodies a compromise: those Member States that are determined to pursue deeper integration between themselves may do so, but they are encouraged to employ the institutional structure, regulatory competences and legislative tools of the Union's own legal order. The main challenge posed by this compromise is to ensure that no irreparable harm is done to the legal fabric of the Union, or to the good functioning of its institutions, through an excessive fragmentation or incoherence in the Union's activities.

The legitimation of flexibility as an organising principle of the Union's constitutional order was achieved by the Maastricht Treaty; the vital role that flexibility is and will be further called upon to play in an increasingly complex and differentiated Union has since been underlined by the TA, TN and TL. For ease of exposition, it is useful to distinguish between two main types of flexibility: primary and secondary.

A – Primary Flexibility: The Opt-out Provisions

In cases of what we refer to as 'primary flexibility', the relevant legal arrangements are to be found in primary provisions of Union law, ie the Treaties and their accompanying Protocols. Thus, the policy areas in which flexibility may operate, the decision-making procedures to be followed and the Member States that may benefit from 'opt-outs' are all determined at the level of the Union's constitutional authority. In other words, the matter will have been specifically negotiated within an IGC, and ratified in accordance with the Member States' respective constitutional requirements, as part of an accession or amendment exercise.[131]

The earliest examples of primary flexibility under EU law date from the TEU. Consider, for example, the Protocol and Agreement on Social Policy which the TEU annexed to the EC Treaty (as it then was).[132] The combined effect of those instruments was to enable the Member States, with the exception of the United Kingdom, to have recourse to the institutions, procedures and mechanisms of the EC Treaty, for the purpose of exercising certain powers going beyond those provided for in the Social Provisions Chapter of the Treaty itself. However, that example soon became of largely historical interest: a change of government in the United Kingdom in 1997 brought the abandonment of its social policy 'opt-out', so that the relevant provisions of the Protocol and Agreement could be fully incorporated into the EC Treaty by the TA.[133]

Of more lasting significance are the arrangements which excuse two classes of Member States from participation in the single currency, following the (otherwise obligatory) transition to the third stage of EMU at the beginning of 1999. One class comprises 'Member States with a derogation', ie those that do not yet fulfil the conditions for the adoption of

---

[131] Thus, on the basis of either Art 48 or Art 49 TEU.
[132] See Protocol No 14 to the Final Act of the IGC which adopted the original TEU.
[133] They are now found in Title X, Part Three TFEU.

a single currency.[134] The other class comprises Denmark and the United Kingdom, whose respective positions are governed by separate Protocols. Denmark was given the right, by notifying the Council that it would not be taking part in the third stage, to treatment corresponding, for most purposes, to that of Member States with a derogation.[135] It was expressly recognised 'that the United Kingdom shall not be obliged or committed to adopt the euro without a separate decision to do so by its government and parliament'.[136]

Another very important case of primary flexibility was first established by the TA and later amended and extended by the TL. As we have seen, justice and home affairs issues were originally included in the TEU as the 'Third Pillar' of EU activity. The TA then transferred many such competences (visas, asylum and immigration policies, plus cross-border judicial co-operation in civil matters) into the old 'First Pillar'. Issues related to cross-border police and judicial co-operation in criminal matters was left behind as a rump 'Third Pillar'. Moreover, the TA also provided for the incorporation into Union law of the 'Schengen *acquis*', a body of international agreements signed by various Member States (as well as certain third countries) which sought to secure the gradual abolition of border controls between the participating countries.[137] Some parts of the Schengen *acquis* were attributed to the First Pillar and others were assimilated to the Third Pillar.[138] The TL later completed the process of 'depillarisation' begun under the TA, by reuniting all justice and home affairs matters within what is now Title V of Part Three of the TFEU on the AFSJ.[139]

The significance of all this for present purposes lies in the flexibility arrangements made for two groups of Member States.[140] In the first place, Ireland and the United Kingdom enjoy a general opt-out from measures adopted under the Union's competences relating to the AFSJ. However, they also benefit from the possibility of opting into individual AFSJ instruments on a case-by-case basis (whether at the time of the adoption or thereafter). Ireland has also reserved the right to notify the Council that it no longer wishes to be covered by this arrangement and thus become fully engaged with the Union's AFSJ competences.[141] Furthermore, the same two Member States are, in principle, not bound by the provisions of the incorporated Schengen *acquis*, though either country may seek the

---

[134] See Art 139 TFEU. Greece was such a Member State, at the time of the transition to a single currency, though it later adopted the euro as its currency. Sweden, it seems, was allowed to deem itself to be unqualified. All of the Member States which joined the EU in 2004 and 2007 fell into the category of 'Member States with a derogation'; though several (Slovenia, Cyprus, Malta, Slovakia and Estonia) have subsequently proceeded to adopt the euro as their currency.

[135] See now Protocol (No 16) on certain provisions relating to Denmark.

[136] Opening recital to Protocol (No 15) on certain provisions relating to the United Kingdom of Great Britain and Northern Ireland.

[137] The Schengen *acquis* was defined in an Annex to the original (TA) Schengen Protocol as comprising: the Schengen Agreement itself, dated 1985; the Implementing Convention, signed in 1990; the series of Accession Protocols and Agreements with eight other Member States of the EU; and decisions and declarations adopted by the Schengen Executive Committee, as well as acts of the organs on which the Committee has conferred decision-making powers.

[138] Under the original (TA) Schengen Protocol, the Council was given the task of assigning appropriate legal bases to the provisions and decisions included in the *acquis*. See Decision 1999/435 concerning the definition of the Schengen *acquis* [1999] OJ L176/1; Decision 1999/436 determining the legal basis for each of the provisions or decisions which constitute the Schengen *acquis* [1999] OJ L176/17.

[139] Though while still preserving a degree of special treatment in respect of criminal law co-operation.

[140] On the transitional provisions applicable to the Member States which acceded to the Union in 2004, as contained in the Treaty of Accession 2003, see A Adinolfi, 'Free Movement and Access to Work of Citizens of the New Member States: The Transitional Measures' (2005) 42 *CMLRev* 469; and as regards the Member States which acceded to the Union in 2007, as contained in the Treaty of Accession 2005, see A Łazowski, 'And Then They Were Twenty-Seven . . . A Legal Appraisal of the Sixth Accession Treaty' (2007) 44 *CMLRev* 401.

[141] For full details, see Protocol (No 21) on the position of the United Kingdom and Ireland in respect of

Council's permission to take part in some (or indeed all) of the individual Schengen provisions.[142] Those complex Schengen arrangements have been the subject of various disputes before the Court of Justice, when the Council refused permission for the UK to join certain measures building upon the existing Schengen *acquis*, with the Court generally favouring the Council's restrictive stance towards non-participating Member States, rather than the desire for greater freedom to pick-and-choose advocated by the UK.[143] In the second place, Denmark also enjoys a general opt-out from Union measures adopted in the field of the AFSJ. Moreover, Denmark has the right to decide whether or not to implement Union measures designed to build upon the Schengen *acquis*; if so, those measures will create obligations for Denmark only under international (not EU) law. However, Denmark does enjoy the possibility of abandoning its existing opt-out system. Alternatively, Denmark may decide to replace the current system with a new regime whereby the Schengen *acquis*, and all measures adopted to build upon it, will become binding as a matter of Union (not merely international) law; in respect of all other measures adopted or proposed under the Union's AFSJ powers, the position of Denmark would be governed by an opt-out/out-in system equivalent to that already applicable to the UK and Ireland.[144] The sheer complexity of the provisions governing the AFSJ is perhaps testament to the dangers of excessive flexibility within the Union legal order—militating against sheer comprehension, let alone effective scrutiny, by the interested public and affected stakeholders.

B – Secondary Flexibility: Enhanced Co-operation

'Secondary flexibility' was an innovation of the TA, in the form of the mechanism there referred to as 'closer co-operation'. The novelty of that mechanism was to allow flexibility arrangements to be established by internal legislative procedures, and therefore not in policy areas which have been pre-selected for such treatment at the level of primary Union law. The general idea of the new closer co-operation system was that a sufficient number of Member States could choose, in the future and in respect of a range of Union activities, to pursue deeper integration between themselves using the institutional and legislative framework provided under the Treaties. The original Amsterdam provisions were significantly amended by the TN, which also renamed the mechanism as 'enhanced co-operation'. For its part, the TL reformed the entire enhanced co-operation system once again: the new rules are to be found in Title IV TEU and Title III, Part Six, TFEU. It is perhaps curious that the enhanced co-operation provisions were the subject of two major constitutional revisions before they were even put to use for the first time in 2010.

Article 20(1) TEU provides that Member States which wish to establish enhanced co-operation between themselves within the framework of the Union's non-exclusive competences may make use of its institutions and exercise those competences by applying the relevant provisions of the Treaties. That provision immediately identifies two important

the Area of Freedom, Security and Justice. Note also Protocol (No 20) on the application of certain aspects of Article 26 TFEU to the United Kingdom and Ireland (dealing specifically with border controls).

[142] For full details, see Protocol (No 19) on the Schengen *acquis* integrated into the framework of the European Union.

[143] See eg Case C-77/05 *United Kingdom v Council* [2007] ECR I-11459; Case C-137/05 *United Kingdom v Council* [2007] ECR I-11593; Case C-482/08 *United Kingdom v Council* (Judgment of 26 October 2010).

[144] For full details, see Protocol (No 22) on the position of Denmark.

substantive conditions for engaging in enhanced co-operation: it may not relate to an area of exclusive Union competence as defined in Article 2(1) and 3 TEU; and more generally, it must comply with the fundamental principle of conferral contained in Article 5(2) TEU, so that enhanced co-operation may not be used to pursue initiatives that could not be adopted by the Union as a whole. Other Treaty provisions lay down additional substantive criteria with which any proposed enhanced co-operation must abide. Any initiative must comply with the Treaties and Union law;[145] in particular, it must aim to further the Union's objectives, protect its interests and reinforce the integration process.[146] Enhanced co-operation cannot undermine the internal market or economic, social and territorial cohesion; nor may it constitute a barrier to or discrimination in trade between Member States; nor may it distort competition across the Union.[147] Any decision by the Council to authorise enhanced co-operation must be taken as a last resort, when it has established that the initiative's objectives cannot be attained within a reasonable period by the entire Union, and at least nine Member States must agree to participate in the enhanced co-operation measure.[148]

The Treaties further specify the procedural aspects of initiating an enhanced co-operation. As regards enhanced co-operation *outside* the scope of the CFSP, interested Member States must first address a request to the Commission. If the Commission chooses not to support the initiative, it must inform the Member States of the reasons for its decision. Otherwise, the Commission may submit a proposal to the Council, which then decides (by QMV) whether to authorise the requested enhanced co-operation, with the consent of the European Parliament.[149] As regards enhanced co-operation *within* the scope of the CFSP, the Member States' request is addressed directly to the Council. Both the High Representative and the Commission may give their opinion on the proposal before the Council reaches its decision (acting unanimously).[150] It is worth noting that, in a few exceptional situations, the Treaties provide that authorisation to proceed with an enhanced co-operation shall be deemed to have been granted automatically, where one Member State either pulls an 'emergency brake' so as to prevent the adoption of a Council decision by QMV,[151] or exercises its ordinary right to veto a Council decision which requires unanimity.[152]

The effect of an authorisation to engage in enhanced co-operation is that the participating Member States may make use of the Treaties for the purposes of pursuing the initiative(s) specified in the Council's initial decision. All members of the Council may participate in the deliberations concerning an enhanced co-operation initiative, but only representatives from the participating Member States may vote in any relevant decisions.[153] However, as regards the participation of the European Parliament in decisions

---

[145] Art 326 TFEU.

[146] Art 20(1) TEU. Note also Art 334 TFEU: the Council and Commission must ensure consistency in enhanced co-operation activities as well as the latter's consistency with wider Union policies.

[147] Art 326 TFEU.

[148] Art 20(2) TEU.

[149] Art 329(1) TFEU.

[150] Art 329(2) TFEU.

[151] eg Art 82(3) TFEU and Art 83(3) TFEU on the adoption of various Union measures to promote criminal co-operation between Member States. On the 'emergency brake' system, see further Chapter 4.

[152] eg Art 86(1) TFEU on establishing a European Public Prosecutor's Office; Art 87(3) TFEU on operational police co-operation.

[153] Art 20(3) TEU and Art 330 TFEU. Unanimity is constituted only by the votes of participating Member States. The definition of QMV is found in Art 238(3) TFEU.

taken within an enhanced co-operation initiative, all MEPs are entitled to vote—even those elected from non-participating countries. Any acts adopted within the framework of the enhanced co-operation are binding only upon the participating Member States.[154]

Article 328(1) TFEU expressly states that, when enhanced co-operation is being established, it must be open to all Member States (subject to compliance with any objective conditions for participation laid down in the Council's authorisation). It must also remain open to the other Member States at any time (subject to compliance with both the authorising instrument and any further acts already adopted within the enhanced co-operation). The Commission and participating Member States must promote involvement by as many other countries as possible.[155] In the meantime, any enhanced co-operation must respect the competences, rights and obligations of non-participating countries; conversely, the latter must not impede the implementation of a legitimate enhanced co-operation.[156] A Member State which wishes to join an existing enhanced co-operation *outside* the scope of the CFSP must notify the Council and the Commission. Authorisation must first be sought from the Commission, taking into account the objective conditions for participation; but if the latter institution twice refuses the request, the Member State may directly ask the Council (acting by QMV in its restricted formation) to sanction its participation.[157] Authorisation to join an existing enhanced co-operation *within* the scope of the CFSP is always granted by the Council (acting unanimously in its restricted formation) after consulting the High Representative.[158]

One of the most important changes to the system of enhanced co-operation introduced by the TL is found in Article 333 TFEU. If unanimity within the Council applies under the legal basis to which an enhanced co-operation relates, then the Council (acting unanimously in its restricted formation) may decide instead to act by QMV. Similarly, if the relevant legal basis uses a special legislative procedure, then the Council (again acting unanimously in its restricted formation, but this time after consulting the European Parliament) may decide to change to the ordinary legislative procedure.[159] These 'internal' passerelle clauses offer a way of partially expanding the use of QMV and/or the ordinary legislative procedure within the Union legal order, where a group of Member States are willing to move away from unanimity and/or a special legislative procedure, but cannot persuade the remaining countries to agree to amending the relevant legal bases for the Union as a whole.[160]

Whilst the operation of economic and monetary union, and of the provisions on justice and home affairs, mean that we have accrued a good deal of experience in dealing with flexibility as regards the organisation and exercise of certain Union competences,[161] one of the peculiarities of the enhanced co-operation system is that (until very recently) it was not actually used in practice. Several calls to invoke the enhanced co-operation regime, in the face of threats to use the veto by a given Member State as regards proposals requiring

---

[154] Art 20(4) TEU. Such acts are not to be regarded as part of the Union *acquis* which must be accepted by candidate countries for accession to the Union under Art 49 TEU.

[155] See also Art 20(1) TEU.

[156] Art 327 TFEU.

[157] Art 331(1) TFEU.

[158] Art 331(2) TFEU.

[159] Those powers do not apply to decisions with military or defence implications: Art 333(3) TFEU.

[160] ie pursuant to the simplified revision procedures contained in Art 48(7) TEU.

[161] See eg J Usher, 'Flexibility: The Experience So Far' (2000) 3 *CYELS* 479.

unanimity in the Council, came to nothing in the end.[162] Much of the debate about the potential significance of enhanced co-operation for the Union legal order has therefore remained hypothetical in nature.[163] For example, will enhanced co-operation measures tend simply, and modestly, to build upon an existing body of Union secondary legislation—in effect, operating like a large-scale version of minimum harmonisation, whereby those Member States wishing to enact higher standards than some general Union norm can do so, merely acting in concert through the Union's institutional framework rather than unilaterally as a matter of their respective domestic competences? Or will enhanced co-operation be used, more boldly, to launch initiatives in policy fields where the Union as a whole has not yet enacted secondary measures—marking it out as qualitatively different from any form of minimum harmonisation, since there is no basic Union norm binding on the Member States as a whole? Just as importantly, it also remains unclear whether enhanced co-operation will eventually prove to be a relatively rare occurrence, or instead become a much more regular phenomenon. And if enhanced co-operation indeed becomes more regular, will it result in constantly shifting groups of participating countries, engaged in closer co-operation for ad hoc policy purposes, or instead witness the emergence of a relatively stable 'avant garde' of Member States pressing ahead with greater integration in a systematic fashion across a predetermined range of policy fields? And if an 'avant garde' does emerge, will it risk a long-term fracture of the Union into an identifiable 'core' versus 'periphery'; or will the core exert such an 'integrationist pull' that the remaining Member States are eventually obliged to follow their lead, such that enhanced co-operation tends (paradoxically) to create greater uniformity across the Union?

Accepting that the debate about enhanced co-operation remains largely speculative in nature, at least for the time being, it is nevertheless possible to identify a range of viewpoints on the implications of secondary flexibility for the Union's constitutional order. On the one hand, many commentators accept that, if a sufficiently large group of Member States is determined to proceed with closer integration in a certain field, it is much better for them to do so within the relatively transparent framework of the EU rather than outside it, in the sphere of intergovernmental co-operation. On the other hand, many observers foresee difficult problems with the widespread use of enhanced co-operation. There is now the possibility that Member States will coalesce into shifting regulatory groupings, each legislating for wider and/or deeper integration on any given subject. One can therefore envisage the emergence of ever more complex regulatory patterns: instruments applying throughout the whole Union lay down certain common standards, while additional layers of obligation are added by new measures, each embracing different combinations of Member States. Such a model may well respond to the political need to accommodate greater diversity within the enlarged Union, but it could also have serious implications (for example) as regards the efficient functioning and democratic legitimacy of the Union's legislative process.[164] It is also possible that the greatest significance of the enhanced co-operation provisions will not be formal, but indirect, concerning how the Union institutions and the Member States manage the Treaties' more traditional decision-

---

[162] See eg D Thym, 'The Political Character of Supranational Differentiation' (2006) 31 *ELRev* 781.

[163] See further eg M Dougan, 'The Unfinished Business of Enhanced Cooperation: Some Institutional Questions and their Constitutional Implications' in A Ott and E Vos (eds), *Fifty Years of European Integration: Foundations and Perspectives* (The Hague, TMC Asser Press, 2009).

[164] eg J Shaw, 'The Treaty of Amsterdam: Challenges of Flexibility and Legitimacy' (1998) 4 *ELJ* 63; N Walker, 'Sovereignty and Differentiated Integration in the European Union' (1998) 4 *ELJ* 355.

making processes. For example, the existence of the enhanced co-operation mechanism may perhaps provide the impetus for compromise between conflicting national viewpoints within the Union's (ordinary and special) legislative procedures: Member States unconvinced of the wisdom of a given initiative may be persuaded to join in nevertheless, rather than suffer the inconvenience—not to say the loss of influence—involved in having to opt in at a later stage.[165]

Time will reveal which of those viewpoints (if any) best captures the reality of enhanced co-operation within the Union's constitutional order. At the time of writing, as mentioned above, the enhanced co-operation provisions have at least been put into use for the first time. In 2006, the Commission presented a proposal to the Council for Union legislation for the purposes of identifying the law applicable to matrimonial disputes, based on the principle of applying the law of the country with which the spouses have a close connection, rather than the law of the country whose courts were hearing the dispute.[166] The relevant legal basis under the Treaties required unanimity within the Council, but Sweden strongly objected to the Commission's proposal, on the grounds that the latter could lead, in certain situations, to Swedish courts applying foreign divorce laws. After several attempts to find an acceptable compromise, the Council eventually decided in 2008 that the objectives of the Commission proposal could not be attained within a reasonable period by the Union acting as a whole.[167] A group of 14 Member States subsequently requested authorisation to launch an enhanced co-operation in the area of the law applicable to divorce and legal separation. The Commission duly submitted a proposal in March 2010,[168] and the Council adopted the necessary decision in July 2010.[169] Both the Commission proposal and the Council decision shed some interesting light on how those institutions understand and intend to apply the various substantive and procedural criteria set out in the Treaties—though further examples of institutional practice as regards enhanced co-operation will surely be needed before any clearer picture emerges.

VI – SOME CONCLUDING REMARKS

Just as the Union's complex decision-making procedures reflect the delicate compromises involved in striking an 'inter-institutional balance' acceptable to the Member States in their capacity as 'masters of the Treaties', so too the system of Union competences built around the fundamental principles of conferral, subsidiarity, proportionality and flexibility help illustrate the unique character of the Union as a 'constitutional order of states'. The fact that the Union possesses no inherent or self-authenticating regulatory power, the necessity to demonstrate that Union action meets a pressing need which the Member States cannot fulfil by acting alone, the requirement that Union measures must actually be necessary to achieve their own objectives, and the possibility for certain Union acts

---

[165] eg G Edwards and E Philippart, *Flexibility and the Treaty of Amsterdam: Europe's New Byzantium?*, CELS Occasional Paper No 3 (Cambridge, 1997); W Wessels, 'Flexibility, Differentiation and Closer Cooperation: The Amsterdam Provisions in the Light of the Tindemans Report' in M Westlake (ed), *The European Union Beyond Amsterdam: New Concepts of European Integration* (London, Routledge, 1998).

[166] COM(2006) 399 Final.

[167] Document 10383/08 PV/CONS 36 JAI 311.

[168] COM(2010) 104 Final/2. Note also COM(2010) 105 Final/2.

[169] Council Decision 2010/405 [2010] OJ L189/12.

to bind only some of the Member States while others stand aside—all those factors demonstrate how the system of Union competences has been designed so as to preserve the character of the Member States *as states*, and to protect their interests against undue incursion by the Union institutions they have created together.

Of course, there are tensions in the system, and also sources of uncertainty. Many commentators remain unconvinced that the Court of Justice is prepared to adopt a sufficiently robust stance against the phenomenon of 'competence creep', particularly in relation to the Union's power to harmonise national laws for the purposes of the internal market as provided for under Article 114 TFEU. It remains to be seen whether the 'yellow card' system for monitoring compliance with the principle of subsidiarity will be exploited to its full potential by the national parliaments, and thereby help redress concerns that the Union institutions sometimes intervene in matters which are best left to its Member States. The ignition of the enhanced co-operation provisions in 2010 should not disguise the fact that the implications of greater flexibility within the Union legal order may well prove to create as many problems as the system was intended to address, particularly when it comes to issues such as democratic transparency and sheer legal complexity. But more broadly, the Union still struggles to communicate its special character (and value) to an increasingly sceptical public across the Member States. Perhaps one of the great virtues of our 'constitutional order of states'—its ability to marry the novel supranational character of European integration with the continued centrality of the still-sovereign Member States—is also one of its weaknesses, insofar as many of the Union's own citizens remain to understand, let alone make an informed decision about how far to identify with, the Union's fundamentally unique legal nature.

Further Reading

Once more, some of these suggestions for further reading should be understood in the context of the recent process of constitutional reform culminating the Treaty of Lisbon: readers should seek to appreciate their value in understanding the history of, and debates surrounding, the current system of EU competences.

G de Búrca, 'The Principle of Proportionality and its Application in EC law' (1993) 13 *YEL* 105.

G de Búrca and J Scott (eds), *Constitutional Change in the EU: From Uniformity to Flexibility?* (Oxford, Hart Publishing, 2000).

A von Bogdandy and J Bast, 'The Federal Order of Competences' in A von Bogdandy and J Bast (eds), *Principles of European Constitutional Law*, rev 2nd edn (Oxford, Hart Publishing, 2010).

A Dashwood, 'The Limits of European Community Powers' (1996) 21 *ELRev* 113.

——, 'States in the European Union' (1998) 23 *ELRev* 201.

G Davies, 'Subsidiarity: the Wrong Idea, in the Wrong Place, at the Wrong Time' (2006) 43 *CMLRev* 63.

A Estella, *The EU Principle of Subsidiarity and its Critique* (Oxford, Oxford University Press, 2002).

M Dougan, 'Minimum Harmonisation and the Internal Market' (2000) 37 *CMLRev* 853.

R Schütze, *From Dual to Cooperative Federalism: The Changing Structure of European Law* (Oxford, Oxford University Press, 2009).

J Shaw, 'The Treaty of Amsterdam: Challenges of Flexibility and Legitimacy' (1998) 4 *ELJ* 63.

PJ Slot, 'Harmonisation' (1996) 21 *ELRev* 378.

AG Soares, 'Pre-emption, Conflicts of Powers and Subsidiarity' (1998) 23 *ELRev* 132.

D Thym, 'The Political Character of Supranational Differentiation' (2006) 31 *ELRev* 781.

N Walker, 'Sovereignty and Differentiated Integration in the European Union' (1998) 4 *ELJ* 355.

S Weatherill, 'Competence Creep and Competence Control' (2004) 23 *YEL* 1.

B de Witte, D Hank and E Vos (eds), *The Many Faces of Differentiation in EU Law* (Antwerp, Intersentia, 2001).

6

Direct Actions Before the Union Courts

'Direct actions' is the term used to designate proceedings that take place entirely at the level of the Court of Justice of the European Union; in other words, they are commenced, conducted and brought to a conclusion in either the Court of Justice or the General Court ('the Union Courts'). The following are the forms of direct action available pursuant to the TFEU that are considered in this Chapter: infringement actions against Member States (Articles 258 to 260 TFEU; actions to review the legality of acts of EU institutions and for the annulment of those acts found to be unlawful (Articles 263, 264 and 266 TFEU); actions in respect of an unlawful failure by an EU institution to act (Articles 265 and 266 TFEU); and actions against the Union for damages in respect of its non-contractual liability (Article 268 and Article 340(2) and (3) TFEU). In addition, we consider the so-called 'defence of illegality' (Article 277 TFEU), which is not a free-standing remedy but may remove the impediment to obtaining a remedy that would otherwise result from the expiry of the two-month time-limit for bringing actions under Article 263. Direct actions are contrasted with references for preliminary rulings, whereby guidance may be sought from the Court of Justice on issues of EU law that have to be resolved in the course of national proceedings. Such references, which merely constitute an episode in the resolution of a dispute by a Member State court, are the subject of Chapter 7.

I – INFRINGEMENT ACTIONS AGAINST MEMBER STATES

A – Introduction

A feature of the EU legal order, which distinguishes it from other supranational orders (and has done so from the time of the primordial EEC) is the power given to the Commission to supervise compliance by the Member States with their obligations under the Treaties.[1] That power now derives principally from Article 258 TFEU,[2] which provides as follows:

---

[1] See A Dashwood and R White, 'Enforcement Actions under Articles 169 and 170 EEC' (1989) 14 *ELRev* 388.

[2] An expedited procedure is applicable in the context of state aid under Art 108(2) TFEU.

If the Commission considers that a Member State has failed to fulfil an obligation under the Treaties, it shall deliver a reasoned opinion on the matter after giving the State concerned the opportunity to submit its observations.

If the State concerned does not comply with the opinion within the period laid down by the Commission, the latter may bring the matter before the Court of Justice of the European Union.

Article 258 TFEU may be contrasted with Article 88 of the now-expired ECSC Treaty, which used to give the Commission the power to record in a binding decision the failure of the Member State concerned to fulfil its obligations. That Member State could then challenge the Commission's decision before the Court.

Article 258 is complemented by Article 259 TFEU, the first paragraph of which provides that '[a] Member State which considers that another Member State has failed to fulfil an obligation under the Treaties may bring the matter before the Court of Justice of the European Union'. A Member State wishing to institute proceedings under Article 259 TFEU must first bring the matter before the Commission, which is required to give each of the Member States concerned the opportunity to submit its own case and its observations on the other party's case, both in writing and orally. The Commission must then deliver a reasoned opinion on the matter. Whether or not the respondent Member State complies with the reasoned opinion, the applicant Member State then has the right to refer the matter to the Court; as it may also do if the Commission fails to deliver an opinion within three months of the date on which the matter was brought to its attention. In practice, the Member States have shown marked reluctance to commence proceedings under Article 259,[3] evidently preferring to leave enforcement to the Commission, though they will sometimes intervene in proceedings brought by the latter.[4]

In contrast to the situation of the Commission and of other Member States, there is no direct action that can be brought in the Union Courts by individuals whose interests have been adversely affected by a Member State's infringement of EU law. However, as we shall see, such persons may be able to seek redress in their national courts, with the possibility for the latter to obtain assistance in resolving any issue of EU law by way of a reference for a preliminary ruling[5]. A further alternative would be for the individual concerned to submit a complaint to the Commission (see below).

In its White Paper on European Governance issued in July 2001,[6] the Commission offered guidance on the types of suspected infringement to which it would attach priority. It announced that it would focus on:

— The effectiveness and quality of transposition of directives as the most effective way of avoiding individual problems arising at a later stage.
— Situations involving the compatibility of national law with fundamental Community principles.
— Cases that seriously affect the Community interest (eg cases with cross-border implications) or the interests that the legislation intended to protect.
— Cases where a particular piece of European legislation creates repeated implementation problems in a Member State.

---

[3] For rare examples, see: Case 141/78 *France v United Kingdom* [1979] ECR 2923; Case C-388/95 *Belgium v Spain* [2000] ECR I-3123; Case C-145/04 *Spain v United Kingdom* [2006] ECR I-7917.

[4] Intervention involves taking part voluntarily in proceedings before one of the Community Courts in support of the relief sought by one of the parties. See Statute, Art 37; Rules, Art 93; General Court Rules, Arts 115–16.

[5] See Chapter 7.

[6] COM(2001) 428, 25–26.

— Cases that involve Community financing.

In other cases, different forms of intervention would be explored before formal infringement proceedings were launched.

The Commission publishes an annual Report on Monitoring the Application of EU Law. The 27th Report, covering the year 2009, was published in October 2010.[7] The Commission noted that '[t]he infringement process plays an essential role in guaranteeing the correct application of the law'.[8] The Report provides evidence of the relative efficacy of the process: the mere threat of infringement proceedings is usually enough to persuade errant Member States to toe the line. Thus at the end of 2009, some 77 per cent of complaints were closed before the first formal step in an infringement proceeding, about 12 per cent more were closed before the issuing of a reasoned opinion, and a further 7 per cent before a ruling by the Court of Justice. The Commission was at that time handling around 2,900 complaint and infringement files. A major source of infringement proceedings remains the failure by Member States to implement directives punctually. It is stated in the 27th Report that there has been some improvement of the 'overall transposition deficit' but this continues to be a major concern.

During a transitional period of five years from the entry into force of the TL, the Commission's powers under Article 258 TFEU will continue to be inapplicable in respect of Union measures in the field of police and judicial co-operation in criminal matters that were adopted, in the pre-Lisbon era, under the decision-making arrangements of the then Third Pillar.[9] That disability will cease, even before the expiry of the five-year period, where such an act is amended, for those Member States to which the act applies.[10] On the exclusion of the jurisdiction of the Union Courts from the field of the common foreign and security policy (CFSP), see Chapter 29, below.

B – Procedure

The procedure laid down in Article 258 TFEU falls into two distinct phases, the administrative phase (or pre-litigation procedure, as it is sometimes called by the Court of Justice) and the judicial phase.

(i) The administrative phase

The administrative phase corresponds to the first paragraph of Article 258 TFEU, which specifies two steps to be taken by the Commission: it must give the Member State concerned 'the opportunity to submit its observations' and then, if the Commission is still not satisfied, it must consider whether to 'deliver a reasoned opinion on the matter'. The Court has said that the first paragraph of the Article

> pursues the following three objectives: to allow the Member State to put an end to any infringement, to enable it to exercise its rights of defence and to define the subject-matter of the dispute with a view to bringing an action before the Court.[11]

---

[7] COM(2010) 538/F. At the time of writing, this was the latest of the annual Reports.

[8] At para 2.2.

[9] See Protocol (No 36) on Transitional Provisions, Art 10(1) and (3). The Third Pillar decision-making arrangements were laid down by former Art 34 TEU.

[10] Ibid, para (2).

[11] Case C-135/01 *Commission v Germany* [2003] ECR I-2837, para 21. See also Joined Cases 142 and

(a) Detecting Infringements

The Commission may become aware of a possible breach by a Member State of its obligations under the Treaty either through its own monitoring of the application of Community
law or, more often, following a complaint by a private party.[12]

For a number of years there was criticism of Commission practice in dealing with
complaints brought to its attention by members of the public. This culminated in a finding, recorded in the Report of the European Ombudsman for 2001, that the handling
of a complaint relating to an alleged infringement by the Greek government amounted
to maladministration.[13] The Commission responded in the following year with the publication in the *Official Journal* of a Communication on relations with complainants in
cases of alleged infringements of Community law by Member States.[14] The Annex to the
Communication contains a detailed description of 'the administrative measures for the
benefit of the complainant with which [the Commission] undertakes to comply when
handling his/her complaint and assessing the infringement in question'. This covers such
matters as how to make a complaint, recording complaints, acknowledging receipt of
correspondence, keeping complainants informed of the steps taken in response to their
complaint and time limits. A standard complaint form is provided. Sensibly, potential
complainants are warned against expecting too much of this remedy. They are reminded
that, as the Court of Justice has recognised (see below), the Commission enjoys discretion
as to whether and when to commence infringement proceedings, and whether to refer
a case to the Court. The complaint form invites them to consider seeking redress from
the national courts and administrative authorities, who may be able to act more quickly
than the Commission, and to offer a more immediate remedy, such as damages or a ruling on the validity of the contested national measure. The form notes that 'any finding of
an infringement by the Court of Justice [under Article 258 TFEU] has no impact on the
rights of the complainant, since it does not serve to resolve individual cases'.

(b) The Letter of Formal Notice

When the Commission decides to pursue a possible breach of Community law by a
Member State, it will first raise the matter on an informal basis through the Permanent
Representative of the Member State concerned in Brussels. If it is not satisfied with the
response this evokes, it will launch the infringement procedure by sending a letter of
formal notice to the Member State, giving the latter the opportunity to express its com-
ments. The letter defines the subject-matter of the dispute and indicates the essence of the
Commission's case. It constitutes 'an essential formal requirement of the procedure under
Article [268 TFEU]'.[15] A reasonable period must be allowed for the Member State to reply.

143/80 *Amministrazione delle Finanze dello Stato v Essevi and Salengo* [1981] ECR 1413, para 15; Case C-207/96
Commission v Italy [1997] ECR I-6869, paras 17–18. The Court may be prepared to excuse a minor procedural
breach where it did not prevent any of those objectives from being achieved: see Case C-362/01 *Commission v
Ireland* [2002] ECR I-11433, paras 18–22. The Commission is entitled to refuse the public access to documents
connected with proceedings under Art 258 TFEU where disclosure might jeopardise the chances of a settlement:
see Case T-105/95 *WWF UK v Commission* [1997] ECR II-313; Case T-309/97 *Bavarian Lager Co v Commission*
[1999] 3 CMLR 544.

[12] According to the 27th Report, complaints accounted for 54% of the total case load, or 63% of cases concerned with issues other than the implementation of directives.

[13] European Ombudsman, *Annual Report 2001*, 116–19.

[14] [2002] OJ C244/5.

[15] Ibid, paras 8 and 9.

What is reasonable depends on the circumstances of the case; very short periods may sometimes be justified, particularly where there is an urgent need to remedy a breach or where the Member State concerned was aware of the Commission's view before the procedure started.[16] The Member State is not obliged to avail itself of the opportunity given to it by the letter of formal notice.[17] The Court has said that 'No provision of Community law penalises failure to respond to the letter of formal notice within the period fixed by the Commission by rendering the Member State's observations inadmissible.'[18]

The Court has rejected attempts by the Commission to treat as a letter of formal notice an opinion issued by it under Directive 83/189, the so-called 'technical standards' Directive.[19] This requires Member States to notify to the Commission, in draft form, national measures introducing new technical standards, so that the standards can be vetted, to ensure their conformity with EU law. In cases where regulations applying new technical standards were introduced without account having been taken of the Commission's observations, the Commission sought to have these treated as equivalent to a letter of formal notice under Article 258 TFEU. Subsequent infringement actions were rejected as inadmissible.[20] The Court declared that, in order for a letter of formal notice to be issued, a prior infringement of its obligations by the Member State concerned must be alleged; however, when a detailed opinion under Directive 83/189 was delivered by the Commission, the Member State to which it was addressed could not have infringed EU law, since the national measure to which the opinion related existed only in draft form.

(c) The Reasoned Opinion

The letter of formal notice may lead to a further round of discussions between the Commission and the Member State concerned in an attempt to reach a settlement. If this does not prove possible, the Commission may decide to deliver a reasoned opinion on the matter. Although the Treaty uses the word 'shall' in this context, it seems that the Commission is not obliged to take this step. In the first place, the Commission may only deliver a reasoned opinion where it 'considers' that a Member State is in breach of Community law, involving an assessment that is necessarily discretionary. Secondly, Article 258(2) TFEU makes it clear that, even if the Member State concerned fails to comply with the reasoned opinion, the Commission is not obliged, but merely empowered, to bring the matter before the Court.[21] So it would have made little sense for it to have no discretion at the earlier stage of the delivery of a reasoned opinion.[22]

In *Commission v Spain*[23] the Court gave the following explanation of the relationship between the reasoned opinion and the letter of formal notice:

> The letter of formal notice from the Commission to the Member State concerned and the reasoned opinion issued by the Commission delimit the subject-matter of the proceedings, so

---

[16] Case 293/85 *Commission v Belgium* [1988] ECR 305, para 14.

[17] Case 211/81 *Commission v Denmark* [1982] ECR 4547, para 9.

[18] Case C-362/01 *Commission v Ireland* [2002] ECR I-11433, para 19.

[19] Directive 83/189 has now been replaced by Directive 98/34/EC of the European Parliament and the Council [1988] OJ L204/37. On the relevance of the technical standards Directive to the issue of the direct effect of directives, see below.

[20] See Case C-341/97 *Commission v Netherlands* [2000] ECR I-6611; Case C-230/99 *Commission v France* [2001] ECR I-1169.

[21] See Case 247/87 *Star Fruit v Commission* [1989] ECR 291, paras 11 and 12.

[22] See further Evans, 'The Enforcement Procedure of Article 169 EEC: Commission Discretion' (1979) 4 *ELRev* 442; Dashwood and White, above n 1, 398–99.

[23] Case C-358/01 [2003] ECR I-13145, paras 27–29.

that it cannot thereafter be extended. Consequently, the reasoned opinion and the proceedings brought by the Commission must be based on the same complaints as those set out in the letter of formal notice initiating the pre-litigation procedure. . . .

However, that requirement cannot be carried so far as to mean that in every case the statement of complaints in the letter of formal notice, the operative part of the reasoned opinion and the form of order sought in the application must be exactly the same, provided that the subject-matter of the proceedings has not been extended or altered but simply limited. . . .

The Court has also held that, although the reasoned opinion must contain a coherent and detailed statement of the reasons which led the Commission to conclude that the State in question has failed to fulfil one of its obligations under the Treaty, the letter of formal notice cannot be subject to such strict requirements of precision, since it cannot, of necessity, contain anything more than an initial brief summary of the complaints. There is therefore nothing to prevent the Commission from setting out in detail in the reasoned opinion the complaints which it has already made more generally in the letter of formal notice.

In *Commission v Netherlands*[24] the Court declared inadmissible a complaint mentioned in the letter of formal notice but which the Commission appeared to abandon in its reasoned opinion. An attempt by the Commission to reintroduce this in its subsequent application to the Court was regarded as 'an extension of the subject-matter of the dispute as opposed to its extent as specified in the reasoned opinion'.[25] Its effect, in the view of the Court, was to deprive the defendant Member State of the opportunity of terminating the alleged infringement or explaining itself prior to the infringement action.

The Commission is not required to indicate in its reasoned opinion the steps which need to be taken to eliminate the alleged infringement. However, the opinion must specifically indicate to the Member State concerned that it needs to adopt a certain measure if it intends to make failure to adopt that measure the subject of the action.[26] It must also lay down a deadline for compliance by the Member State.[27] That deadline determines the relevant date for the purposes of any subsequent proceedings before the Court;[28] if the Member State concerned complies with its obligations after the deadline has passed, the Commission is not prevented from bringing an infringement action. Thus, in *Commission v Austria*[29] the Court held that the quashing of the contested national measure with retrospective effect after the expiry of the deadline did not prevent the Commission from continuing with the case. The Court has said that the Commission retains an interest in continuing with a case in these circumstances, since a judgment of the Court 'may be of substantive interest as establishing the basis of a responsibility that a Member State can incur as a result of its default, as regards other Member States, the Community or private parties'.[30]

As in the case of the letter of formal notice, the Commission must allow the Member State concerned a reasonable period within which to comply with the reasoned opinion. The Court does not have the power to substitute a different period for that laid down by the Commission,[31] but if it considers the period allowed to have been too short, it may

---

[24] Case C-350/02 [2004] ECR I-6213.

[25] Para 28.

[26] Case C-328/96 *Commission v Austria* [1999] ECR I-7479, para 39.

[27] See Art 258(2) TFEU.

[28] See eg Case C-362/90 *Commission v Italy* [1992] ECR I-2353.

[29] Case C-209/02 [2004] ECR I-1211.

[30] See Case 39/72 *Commission v Italy* [1973] ECR 101, para 11; Case C-29/90 *Commission v Greece* [1992] ECR I-1971, para 12. On the liability of Member States to private parties for breaches of EU law, see Chapter 10.

[31] Case 28/81 *Commission v Italy* [1981] ECR 2577, para 6; Case 29/81 *Commission v Italy* [1981] ECR 2585, para 6.

dismiss any subsequent application as inadmissible. In *Commission v Belgium*,[32] for example, Belgium was given eight days to reply to the letter of formal notice and 15 days to comply with the reasoned opinion. The Court ruled the Commission's application inadmissible. By contrast, in *Commission v Ireland*[33] Ireland was given five days to amend legislation which had been on the statute book for over 40 years. The Court made it clear that it disapproved of so short a deadline, but declined to rule the application inadmissible. Member States are usually allowed a month or two to take the necessary steps. In *Commission v Belgium*[34] the Court said that 'very short periods may be justified in particular circumstances, especially where there is an urgent need to remedy a breach or where the Member State concerned is fully aware of the Commission's views long before the procedure starts'.

None of the measures taken by the Commission during the administrative phase of the procedure under Article 258 has binding force and they may not, therefore, be the subject of annulment proceedings under Article 263 TFEU.[35] The legality of those measures may be reviewed only in the context of a subsequent infringement action by the Commission.[36] Moreover, as the General Court explained in *SDDDA v Commission*,[37] '[t]he Commission is not bound to initiate an infringement procedure against a Member State; on the contrary, it has a discretionary power of assessment, which rules out any right for individuals to require it to adopt a particular position'. It follows that no action for failure to act under Article 265 TFEU will lie against the Commission if it decides against taking further action.[38] It is not for the Court to determine whether the Commission's discretion was wisely exercised.[39]

The Court has been willing to allow the Commission a degree of flexibility in the internal procedure it follows in deciding whether proceedings should be brought. In *Commission v Germany*[40] it was argued that the proceedings were inadmissible because the issue of the reasoned opinion and the decision to commence proceedings before the Court had been delegated to a single Commissioner instead of having been the subject of a decision by the Commission acting as a college. The Commission explained that, because of the number of infringement proceedings, Commissioners did not have before them draft reasoned opinions when they decided to issue such measures. However, they did have available to them the facts of each case and details of the provisions of Community law which the Commission's services considered to have been breached. The decision to issue the reasoned opinion and to commence proceedings before the Court was therefore taken in full knowledge of the essential facts. Drafting of the reasoned opinion then took place at administrative level under the responsibility of the competent Commissioner. The Court ruled that this procedure was acceptable.

---

[32] Case 293/85 [1988] ECR 305.

[33] Case 74/82 [1984] ECR 317.

[34] Case 293/85 *Commission v Belgium* [1988] ECR 305, para 14. See also Case C-328/96 *Commission v Austria* [1999] ECR I-7479, paras 51–56.

[35] Case 48/65 *Lütticke v Commission* [1966] ECR 19. The action for annulment is discussed below.

[36] cf Joined Cases 76 and 11/69 *Commission v France* [1969] ECR 523, para 36.

[37] Case T-47/96 [1996] ECR II-1559, para 42.

[38] Case 247/87 *Star Fruit v Commission* [1989] ECR 291. The action for failure to act is discussed below.

[39] Case C-200/88 *Commission v Greece* [1990] ECR I-4299, para 9.

[40] Case C-191/95 [1998] ECR I-5449. See also Case C-272/97 *Commission v Germany* [1999] ECR I-2175; Case C-198/97 *Commission v Germany* [1999] ECR I-3257.

(ii) The Judicial Phase

(a) The Onus Upon the Commission

If the Member State fails to comply with the reasoned opinion within the prescribed deadline, the Commission has the power to bring the matter before the Court of Justice. In principle, the Commission is not obliged to do so within any specific period, although the Court has recognised that the rights of the defence might be infringed if the duration of the pre-litigation procedure is excessive.[41]

In *Commission v Italy* Advocate General Mischo suggested that, in a case of an isolated failure by a Member State to apply a directive correctly, the Commission should only bring proceedings under Article 258 TFEU where the situation is particularly flagrant and a sustained effort to induce the Member State concerned to act has proved unsuccessful.[42] That suggestion was not taken up by the Court. It should be noted that the Commission's attitude to whether or not to bring proceedings does not affect the substance of the Member State's obligations under the Treaty or the rights which individuals may derive from them.[43]

If the Commission decides to make an application to the Court, it is not required to show any specific interest in doing so,[44] but it will be required to prove its allegation that the obligation in question has not been fulfilled.[45] The burden on the Commission is not easy to discharge. The Court requires the Commission to indicate not merely the legal basis of its complaint but also to give details of the facts and circumstances which are said to give rise to the alleged failure by the Member State concerned to comply with its obligations.[46] Where a Member State is required by a directive to inform the Commission of the steps taken to comply with it, failure to satisfy that requirement may itself amount to a breach of Community law, but it will not entitle the Commission to assume that no implementing measures have in fact been adopted.[47] Moreover, the mere existence in a Member State of a situation which is inconsistent with a directive does not in itself entitle the Commission to conclude that the directive concerned has not been properly implemented. However, the persistence of such a situation may indicate a failure by the Member State concerned to comply with its obligations.[48]

(b) The Declaration of Failure to Fulfil an Obligation

If the Commission brings its case home, the Court of Justice will declare that the Member State in question has failed to fulfil its obligations under the Treaty. The Court will specify the act or omission giving rise to the failure, but it has no power to tell the Member State what it must do in order to remedy the breach; nor does it have power to quash

---

[41] See Case C-96/89 *Commission v Netherlands* [1991] ECR I-2461; Case C-187/98 *Commission v Greece* [1999] ECR I-7713.

[42] Case C-365/97 [1999] ECR I-7773. See para 64 of the Opinion.

[43] See Joined Cases 142 and 143/80 *Amministrazione delle Finanze dello Stato v Essevi and Salengo* [1981] ECR 1413, paras 16–18.

[44] Joined Cases C-418/00 and C-419/00 *Commission v France* [2002] ECR I-3969, para 29.

[45] See eg Case C-434/01 *Commission v United Kingdom* [2003] ECR I-13239.

[46] See eg Case C-347/88 *Commission v Greece* [1990] ECR I-4747; Case C-52/90 *Commission v Denmark* [1992] ECR I-2187; Case C-55/99 *Commission v France* [2000] ECR I-11499; Case C-127/99 *Commission v Italy* [2001] ECR I-8305; Case C-458/00 *Commission v Luxembourg* [2003] ECR I-1553, paras 44–45.

[47] See Case 96/81 *Commission v Netherlands* [1982] ECR 1791, paras 4–6.

[48] See Case C-365/97 *Commission v Italy* [1999] ECR I-7773, para 68.

any national measure which it may have found incompatible with an EU provision. The Member State is required by Article 260(1) TFEU 'to take the necessary measures to comply with the judgment of the Court'. If it fails to do so, it exposes itself to further proceedings under Article 260(2) TFEU. The conditions under which a financial penalty may be imposed upon a Member State found to have committed an infringement, which have been been amended by the Treaty of Amsterdam, are considered in section D, below.

(c) The Effect of the Court's ruling

Action by a Member State to comply with the ruling must be commenced as soon as it is delivered and completed as soon as possible.[49] The effect produced by a ruling of the Court of Justice under Article 258 TFEU in the legal order of the Member State concerned was considered in *Procureur de la République v Waterkeyn*,[50] where it was held that, if a Member State's legislation has been found in infringement proceedings to be incompatible with its EU obligations, the courts of that Member State are bound to draw the necessary inferences from the judgment; however, it must be understood that the rights accruing to individuals derive, not from the judgment itself, but from the relevant provisions of EU law, assuming that they have direct effect in the internal legal order. A ruling under Article 258 TFEU establishes conclusively that the provision in question has been breached. Moreover, the *Francovich*[51] judgment made clear that a finding under Article 258 TFEU that a Member State has failed to comply with a provision of EU law, even one that does not have direct effect, may render the Member State concerned liable to pay compensation to anyone who has suffered loss as a direct consequence.[52]

C – Substantive Issues in Infringement Proceedings

Under this heading we consider some of the substantive issues that have had to be resolved by the Court of Justice in infringement proceedings, including defences that have been put forward by Member States, usually with lack of success.

(i) Infringements in General

(a) The Essential Question

The essential question is whether, objectively speaking, the situation in the defendant Member State is consistent with the requirements of EU law. This may lead the Member State concerned to challenge the Commission's understanding of either EU law or the State's own national law. However, except in cases of *force majeure* (a concept which is construed narrowly),[53] the Court will not be interested in how any inconsistency may have arisen. The Commission is not required to show 'inertia or opposition on the part

---

[49] See eg Joined Cases 227–230/85 *Commission v Belgium* [1988] ECR 1, para 11.
[50] Joined Cases 314–316/81 and 83/82 [1982] ECR 4337.
[51] Joined Cases C-6/90 and C-9/90 [1991] ECR I-5357.
[52] See the discussion of state liability in Chapter 10.
[53] See Case 101/84 *Commission v Italy* [1985] ECR 2629.

of the Member State concerned'[54] or 'to draw distinctions based on the nature or gravity of the infringement'.[55]

Thus, it is no defence that national legislation, although technically incompatible with EU law, is in practice applied in accordance with the requirements of the Treaties. The Court has said that the mere retention in force of such legislation 'gives rise to an ambiguous state of affairs by maintaining, as regards those subject to the law who are concerned, a state of uncertainty as to the possibilities available to them of relying on Community law'.[56] The need to avoid this type of uncertainty has also led the Court to refuse to allow Member States to rely on the fact that the provisions of EU law which have been breached are directly effective and may therefore be invoked in the national courts, which would be bound to accord them precedence over inconsistent provisions of national law. The Court has stated that 'the primacy and direct effect of the provisions of Community law do not release Member States from their obligation to remove from their domestic legal order any provisions incompatible with Community law'.[57]

(b) Failures by EU Institutions

Member States may not rely, as a defence, upon a failure by the EU institutions to comply with their own obligations under the Treaty. In *Commission v Luxembourg and Belgium*[58] the Court said that

> the Treaty is not limited to creating reciprocal obligations between the different natural and legal persons to whom it is applicable. . . . [E]xcept where otherwise expressly provided, the basic concept of the Treaty requires that the Member States shall not take the law into their own hands. Therefore the fact that the Council failed to carry out its obligations cannot relieve the defendants from carrying out theirs.

The appropriate remedy for a Member State in such circumstances would be a direct action against the institution in question.

(c) Failures by Other Member States

Similarly, a Member State may not justify a breach of EU law on the ground that its object was to correct the effects of such a breach by another Member State. The Court made it clear in *Commission v France*[59] that

> [a] Member State cannot under any circumstances unilaterally adopt, on its own authority, corrective measures or measures to protect trade designed to prevent [ie obviate][60] any failure on the part of another Member State to comply with the rules laid down by the Treaty.

The Court pointed out that a Member State which considers the action of another Member

---

[54] Case C-215/98 *Commission v Greece* [1999] ECR I-4913, para 15.
[55] Case C-140/00 *Commission v United Kingdom* [2003] ECR I-10379, para 34; Case C-454/99 *Commission v United Kingdom* [2002] ECR I-10323, para 27.
[56] Case 167/73 *Commission v French Republic* [1974] ECR 359, para 41. See also Case C-58/90 *Commission v Italy* [1991] ECR I-4193, para 12.
[57] Case 104/86 *Commission v Italy* [1988] ECR 1799, para 12.
[58] Joined Cases 90 and 91/63 [1964] ECR 625, 631.
[59] Case 232/78 [1979] ECR 2729, para 9. See also Case C-5/94 *The Queen v MAFF, ex parte Hedley Lomas* [1996] ECR I-2553, para 20; Case C-265/95 *Commission v France* [1997] ECR I-6959, para 63.
[60] The French text reads 'destinées à obvier à une méconnaissance éventuelle, par un Etat membre, des règles du traité'.

State incompatible with EU law has the option of acting at the political level, or of inviting the Commission to bring proceedings against that Member State under Article 226 EC, or of or taking action itself under Article 259 TFEU.

(d) Minute Statements

Reservations or statements made by the Member State concerned in the course of the procedure leading to the adoption of an act, which is alleged to have been breached, will not be accepted as providing any excuse since, the Court has said, 'the objective scope of rules laid down by the common institutions cannot be modified by reservations or objections which Member States have made at the time the rules were being formulated'.[61]

(e) Internal Circumstances

As the Court pointed out in *Commission v Ireland*,[62]

> '[i]t is well established in the case-law of the Court . . . that a Member State may not plead internal circumstances in order to justify a failure to comply with obligations and time-limits resulting from Community law. Moreover, it has been held on several occasions... that practical difficulties which appear at the stage when a Community measure is put into effect cannot permit a Member State unilaterally to opt out of fulfilling its obligations.

In particular, it has been made clear that the obligations arising from the Treaty

> devolve upon States as such and the liability of a Member State under Article [226 EC] arises whatever the agency of the State whose action or inaction is the cause of the failure to fulfil its obligations, even in the case of a constitutionally independent institution.[63]

Thus, it is no defence that draft legislation intended to give effect to the requirements of EU law lapsed due to the dissolution of the national parliament.[64]

(f) Conduct of Member State Courts

It follows that proceedings under Article 258 TFEU could in principle be brought against a Member State if its courts failed to comply with their obligations under the Treaties, at least if the failure were deliberate or systematic. However, it might be less provocative to challenge the competent national authority's failure to introduce legislation which is sufficient to give effect to the requirements of Community law. In *Commission v Italy*[65] the Commission sought a declaration that Italy had failed to fulfil its Treaty obligations by maintaining in force a legislative provision which, as construed and applied by the domestic administrative authorities and courts, was producing a result that was contrary to Community law. The Court said that, although the contested legislative provision was not self-evidently incompatible with Community law, its effect had to be determined in

---

[61] Case 39/72 *Commission v Italy* [1973] ECR 101, para 22. See also Case 38/69 *Commission v Italy* [1970] ECR 47, para 12.

[62] Case C-39/88 [1990] ECR I-4271, para 11.

[63] Case 77/69 *Commission v Belgium* [1970] ECR 237, para 15.

[64] Ibid. See also eg Case 91/79 *Commission v Italy* [1980] ECR 1099.

[65] Case C-129/00 [2003] ECR I-14637. *cf* Case C-224/01 *Köbler v Austria* [2003] ECR I-10239, where the Court held that a Member State was obliged to make good damage caused to an individual by an infringement of EU law stemming from a decision of a national court. The *Köbler* case is discussed in Chapter 7.

the light of the way it was interpreted by the national courts. The Court acknowledged that 'isolated or numerically insignificant judicial decisions in the context of case-law taking a different direction, or still more a construction disowned by the national supreme court, cannot be taken into account'. However, a 'widely-held judicial construction' which, as here, had been confirmed by the supreme court, was relevant to the question whether the Member State concerned had failed to fulfil its obligations.[66] Where the case law on the meaning of national legislation was inconsistent, the Court held that, 'at the very least, such legislation is not sufficiently clear to ensure its application in compliance with Community law'.[67] The Court concluded that Italy had breached its obligations by failing to amend a provision 'which is construed and applied by the administrative authorities and a substantial proportion of the courts, including the Corte suprema di cassazione' in a way which resulted in a situation which was contrary to Community law.

To date, there has been no instance of an infringement action brought specifically on account of the conduct of a Member State court; however, it has been held that, in an extreme case, such conduct may give rise to a liability claim against the Member State concerned.[68]

(g) Actions of Individuals

A Member State may incur liability under Article 258 TFEU as a result of the actions of individuals, if the Court considers that it has not taken appropriate steps to prevent such actions from interfering with the rights of others under EU law. This was established in *Commission v France*,[69] where the Commission argued that France had breached its Treaty obligations by failing to take effective action to prevent imports of fruit and vegetables from other Member States from being disrupted by the violent protests of farmers. The Court held that the Treaty required the Member States to take all necessary and appropriate measures to ensure that the fundamental principle of the free movement of goods was respected on their territory. Although the Member States had a margin of discretion in determining what measures were most appropriate to eliminate barriers to imports in a given situation, it was the responsibility of the Court to ensure that that margin had not been exceeded. The Court concluded that

> in the present case the French Government has manifestly and persistently abstained from adopting appropriate and adequate measures to put an end to the acts of vandalism which jeopardize the free movement on its territory of certain agricultural products originating in other Member States and to prevent the recurrence of such acts.[70]

(ii) Failure to Implement Directives

The growth in the use of directives since the advent of the single market programme highlighted the importance of ensuring compliance by Member States with the obligations they lay down.

Many infringement actions concern the total failure by a Member State to imple-

---

[66] Para 32.
[67] Para 33.
[68] See Case C-224/01 *Köbler v Austria* [2003] ECR I-10239.
[69] Case C-265/95 [1997] ECR I-6959.
[70] Para 65. The Court's decision led to the adoption of Reg 2679/98 on the functioning of the internal market in relation to the free movement of goods among the Member States [1998] OJ L337/8. See further on this issue Chapter 15.

ment a directive. Such actions are often straightforward, the Member State concerned scarcely troubling to defend itself before the Court. Member States are not permitted in infringement proceedings to contest the validity of a directive they are accused by the Commission of having failed to implement properly.[71] This is because the Treaty provides a special remedy, the action for annulment, for challenging the validity of EU acts (see below). Member States do not have to satisfy any standing requirements in order to bring an annulment action.[72]

Actions for failure to implement directives properly do, however, sometimes give rise to difficult questions about the meaning of the measure concerned and the precise steps which need to be taken to give effect to it. Potential areas of dispute are apparent from the following summary of the obligations imposed by directives on Member States, which was offered by the Court in *Commission v France*:[73]

> While it is . . . essential that the legal situation resulting from national implementing measures is sufficiently precise and clear to enable the individuals concerned to know the extent of their rights and obligations, it is none the less the case that, according to the very words of the third paragraph of Article [249] of the Treaty, Member States may choose the form and methods for implementing directives which best ensure the result to be achieved by the directives, and that provision shows that the transposition of a directive into national law does not necessarily require legislative action in each Member State. The Court has thus repeatedly held that it is not always necessary formally to enact the requirements of a directive in a specific express legal provision, since the general legal context may be sufficient for implementation of a directive, depending on its content. In particular, the existence of general principles of constitutional or administrative law may render superfluous transposition by specific legislative or regulatory measures provided, however, that those principles actually ensure the full application of the directive by the national authorities and that, where the relevant provision of the directive seeks to create rights for individuals, the legal situation arising from those principles is sufficiently precise and clear and that the persons concerned are put in a position to know the full extent of their rights and, where appropriate, to be able to rely on them before the national courts.

In *Commission v Austria*[74] the Court emphasised that Member States were not released from their obligation to implement a directive 'where they consider that their national provisions are better than the Community provision concerned and that the national provisions are therefore better able to ensure that the objective pursued by the directive is achieved'.

The problems that may arise where national implementing legislation is regarded by the Commission as ambiguous were highlighted in *Commission v United Kingdom*.[75] In that

---

[71] A decision addressed to the Member State concerned is treated in the same way as a directive for this purpose: see Case C-52/00 *Commission v France* [2002] ECR I-3827, para 28; Case C-194/01 *Commission v Austria* [2004] ECR I-4579, para 41. The position may be different in the case of regulations, because the impact of such an act on a Member State may not initially be apparent: see further para 191 of the Opinion of AG Jacobs in Case C-11/00 *Commission v European Central Bank* [2003] ECR I-7147.

[72] The action for annulment is discussed below.

[73] Case C-233/00 [2003] ECR I-6625, para 76. See also Case 29/84 *Commission v Germany* [1985] ECR 1661, paras 22 and 23; Case C-217/97 *Commission v Germany* [1999] ECR I-5087, paras 31 and 32; Case C-296/01 *Commission v France* [2003] ECR I-13909, paras 54 and 55. A provision contained in a directive which concerns only relations between the Member States and the Commission does not, in principle, need to be transposed: Case C-296/01 *Commission v France* [2003] ECR I-13909, para 92.

[74] Case C-194/01 [2004] ECR I-4579, para 39.

[75] Case C-300/95 [1997] ECR I-2649. See also Case C-80/92 *Commission v Belgium* [1994] ECR I-1019, para 7. *cf* Case C-392/96 *Commission v Ireland* [1999] ECR I-5901; Case C-252/01 *Commission v Belgium* [2003] ECR I-11859.

case, the Commission argued that the United Kingdom Consumer Protection Act 1987 (CPA) failed to give proper effect to the EU Directive on liability for defective products. The United Kingdom pointed out that section 1(1) of the CPA made it clear that its purpose was to give effect to the Directive, and required the Act to be construed accordingly. It maintained that the relevant provision of the CPA (section 4(1)(e)) was capable of being interpreted consistently with the Directive. The Court held that the Commission had not succeeded in refuting that argument:[76]

> [T]he Court has consistently held that the scope of national laws, regulations or administrative provisions must be assessed in the light of the interpretation given to them by national courts. . . . Yet in this case the Commission has not referred in support of its application to any national judicial decision which, in its view, interprets the domestic provision at issue inconsistently with the Directive.[77]

The UK courts have, on the whole, a good record of interpreting national legislation consistently with directives it is designed to implement,[78] and this provided a further ground for rejecting the Commission's application:[79]

> [T]here is nothing in the material produced to the Court to suggest that the courts in the United Kingdom, if called upon to interpret section 4(1)(e), would not do so in the light of the wording and the purpose of the Directive so as to achieve the result which it has in view and thereby comply with the third paragraph of Article [249] of the Treaty. . . . Moreover, section 1(1) of the Act expressly imposes such an obligation on the national courts.

The Court concluded that the Commission had failed to make out its allegation that the Act was inadequate to give effect to the Directive.[80]

A Member State will not be able to avoid the necessity of adopting legislative measures through reliance on the principle of consistent interpretation.[81] In *Commission v Netherlands*[82] it was alleged that the Netherlands had failed to take the steps necessary to transpose certain provisions of Directive 93/13. The Netherlands claimed that specific implementing provisions had not been necessary, as its national law already achieved the aims of the directive. Advocate General Tizzano explained[83] that the principle of consistent interpretation

> does not solve the problem at issue here. It is designed to be of use pending the transposition of a directive into national law—or even after transposition if this is incorrect or incomplete—but it certainly cannot serve as an excuse for failure to transpose or for inadequate transposition.

The Court pointed out that, while legislative action on the part of each Member State was not necessarily required, it was essential that the legal position under national law should be sufficiently precise and clear, and that individuals should made fully aware of their rights. The Court declared that, even where the national courts were willing to

---

[76] Para 37.

[77] cf Case C-233/00 *Commission v France* [2003] ECR I-6625, paras 84–87.

[78] See generally A Arnull, 'Interpretation and Precedent in English and Community Law: Evidence of Cross-fertilisation?' in M Andenas (ed), *English Public Law and the Common Law of Europe* (1998).

[79] Para 38 of the judgment.

[80] For another example of a case where the Commission failed to bring home a claim of failure properly to implement a directive against a Member State, see Case C-478/99 *Commission v Sweden* [2002] ECR I-4147. See also Case C-70/03 *Commission v Spain* [2004] ECR I-7999.

[81] See Chapter 5.

[82] Case C-144/99 [2001] ECR I-3541.

[83] See [2001] ECR I-3541, 3555.

interpret national law in a manner which satisfied the requirements of a directive, that was not sufficient to meet the requirements of legal certainty. The Commission's application was therefore upheld. The circumstances were not the same as those of *Commission v United Kingdom*, discussed above, because there, specific implementing legislation had been adopted which said it was to be interpreted in the light of the directive in question.

D – Fines and Penalty Payments

Over the years, rulings of the Court in infringement proceedings that were adverse to the Member State concerned have normally been complied with, although sometimes only after considerable delay. With the increase in the number of infringements found by the Court during the 1980s, it came to be felt that the procedure needed to be strengthened by introducing a power to impose financial sanctions on recalcitrant Member States.[84] Accordingly, the TEU in its original Maastricht version added a paragraph (2) to the provision which is now Article 260 TFEU, laying down a procedure that could lead to the imposition by the Court of a lump sum or penalty payment on a Member State found to be in breach of its obligation to comply with a judgment given against it. The TA has simplified that procedure, and added a paragraph (3) to Article 260, which applies in the specific situation where proceedings are brought pursuant to Article 258 TFEU on the grounds that the Member State concerned has failed to fulfil its obligation to notify measures transposing a directive adopted under a legislative procedure. The conditions under which financial sanctions may be imposed under paragraph (2) and under paragraph (3) are separately considered below.

(i) The Sanctions Procedure for Failure to Comply with a Judgment

Article 260 (2) TFEU provides:

> If the Commission considers that the Member State concerned has not taken the necessary measures to comply with the judgment of the Court, it may bring the case before the Court, after giving that State the opportunity to submit its observations. It shall specify the amount of the lump sum or penalty payment to be paid by the Member State concerned which it considers appropriate in the circumstances.
>
> If the Court finds that the Member State concerned has not complied with its judgment it may impose a lump sum or penalty payment on it.
>
> This procedure shall be without prejudice to Article 259.

Under the pre-Lisbon version of Article 260 (2), the Commission was required to follow an administrative procedure corresponding to that laid down by Article 258 TFEU, which provided a further opportunity for prevarication by the Member State concerned. The amended paragraph (2) no longer requires the Commission to issue a second reasoned opinion. Having sent the Member State a letter of formal notice to enable it to submit observations, and after considering these, it may bring the case directly before the Court, specifying the amount of the lump sum or penalty payment it considers appropriate in the

---

[84] The explanation for this development may lie partly in the increased vigour with which the Commission, between the late 1970s and the early 1990s, pursued Member States which failed to comply with their Treaty obligations. See Dashwood and White, above n 1, 399–400.

circumstances. As previously, the Court is free, if it finds that its judgment has not been complied with, to determine the appropriate level of any penalty it imposes.

By the time the TEU was signed on 7 February 1992, the Court of Justice had held in the famous *Francovich* case,[85] decided the previous November, that there was a principle 'inherent in the system of the Treaty' that Member States were liable to compensate individuals for damage caused by breaches of Community law for which they were responsible. That principle deprived Article 258(2) of some of its significance, by exposing Member States in default to the risk of substantial damages claims. However, the principle of Member State liability as an incentive to compliance is dependent on the emergence of willing private litigants, with a good case and the means to pursue it. Therefore, there undoubtedly remains a place, to ensure effective enforcement of Member States' Treaty obligations, for the machinery of financial sanctions that was created by the TEU and has recently been strengthened.

In 1996, the Commission issued a first 'Memorandum' setting out its approach to the application of Article 260 (2).[86] This identified three criteria for determining the level of financial sanctions pursuant to that provision: (a) the seriousness of the infringement, (b) its duration and (c) the need to deter further infringements. In January 1997, further guidance was issued as to how the Commission proposed to calculate the appropriate penalty in particular case; the amount of any penalty payments proposed to the Court would be determined by multiplying coefficients reflecting the gravity and duration of the infringement by an 'invariable factor' based on the respective ability of Member States to pay, in line with the principles of proportionality and equality. [87]

The first judgment on the imposition of a financial penalty was rendered in July 2000.[88] The Court of Justice decided to subject Greece to a penalty of €20,000 for each day of delay in taking the measures necessary to comply with a ruling given as long before as 7 April 1992, in which Greece had been found to be in breach of its obligations under two directives on the disposal of waste.[89] The Court in that case endorsed the guidelines on the calculation of sanctions laid down by the Commission, while noting that it could not be bound by them. It observed: 'Those guidelines . . . help to ensure that [the Commission] acts in a manner which is transparent, foreseeable and consistent with legal certainty' and that they were 'designed to achieve proportionality in the amounts of the penalty payments to be proposed by it'.[90] The Court stated that the Commission's suggestion that account be taken of the defendant Member State's gross domestic product and the number of votes it had in the Council 'appears appropriate in that it enables that Member State's ability to pay to be reflected while keeping the variation between Member States within a reasonable range'.[91] The 'basic criteria' to be taken into account were 'the duration of the infringement, its degree of seriousness and the ability of the Member State to pay'; in applying them, regard must be had in particular to the effects of failure to comply on private and public interests and to the urgency of getting the Member State concerned to fulfil its obligations.[92]

---

[85] Joined Cases C-6/90 and C-9/90 [1991] ECR I-5357. See Chapter 9.
[86] [1996] OJ C242/6.
[87] See [1997] OJ C63/2.
[88] Case C-387/97 *Commission v Greece* [2000] ECR I-5047.
[89] Case C-45/91 *Commission v Greece* [1992] ECR I-2509.
[90] Para 87 of the judgment.
[91] Para 88.
[92] Para 92.

Consistently with the Commission's application, the penalty imposed by the Court was to run from the date of the second judgment rather than that of the first or the (subsequent) entry into force of the TEU. The judgment implies[93] that the date of the original judgment under Article 258 TFEU will normally be regarded as marking the starting date of the infringement for the purposes of fixing the amount of the penalty, not the date on which the underlying breach of the Treaty took place (in a case such as this, the expiry of the deadline for implementing the relevant directive).[94] Measures to give effect to the original ruling were finally adopted by the Greek authorities on 26 February 2001, who therefore paid a total penalty of €5,400,000 for the period between July 2000 and March 2001.

The Court imposed a penalty for a second time in *Commission v Spain*.[95] That case also involved a failure on the part of the Member State concerned to give effect to a directive on the protection of the environment, on this occasion by reducing the pollution of bathing water. Spain was found to have failed to comply with a judgment delivered on 12 February 1998[96] declaring it in breach of its obligation to implement the directive concerned. The Court thought that the amount of the penalty should take account of progress made by Spain in complying with the initial judgment against it and of the difficulty of complying fully with that judgment in a short time. It therefore imposed a lower penalty than the one proposed by the Commission; and, since the quality of bathing water was assessed on an annual basis, made this payable annually, from the first assessment following delivery of its (second) judgment, until the year in which its initial judgment was complied with.

The original practice of the Commission under Article 260(2) TFEU was to propose the imposition of penalty payments (rather than a lump sum) upon the defaulting Member State. However, an indication of a change in attitude came in the institution of the proceedings under Article 260(2) against France, which induced the latter Member State to lift its ban on the importation of British beef imposed during the BSE crisis, and declared unlawful by the Court in December 2001.[97] The Commission announced in November 2002 that it would not be pursuing its application to the Court for the imposition of a penalty,[98] but according to the 20th Report on Monitoring the Application of Community Law,[99]

> the British beef controversy prompted the Commission to consider the possibility of proposing that the Court of Justice should order not only a periodic penalty payment but also a fine, to give Member States an incentive to comply with judgments holding them to be in default.[100]

That was the course taken by the Court of Justice, on its own initiative, in another case involving France,[101] where the Commission had asked only for the imposition a daily

---

[93] See para 98.

[94] In the *Greece* case, the defendant should have implemented both Directives by 1 January 1981: see para 10 of the judgment.

[95] Case C-278/01 [2003] ECR I-14141.

[96] Case C-92/96 *Commission v Spain* [1998] ECR I-505.

[97] See Case C-1/00 *Commission v France* [2001] ECR I-9989.

[98] See Commission press releases IP/02/1086 and IP/02/1671.

[99] COM(2003) 669 final, 9.

[100] It should in any event be borne in mind that the Treaty gave those affected by the French ban a remedy in the French courts: see Case C-241/01 *National Farmers' Union v Secrétariat Général du Gouvernement* [2002] ECR I-9079.

[101] Case C-304/02 *Commission v France* [2005] ECR I-6263. See also Case C-121/07 *Commission v France* [2008] ECR I-9159.

penalty payment.[102] Advocate General Geelhoed took the view that the infringement[103] was so serious that the Court should impose both a lump sum and a penalty payment. As he pointed out:

> Where a Member State succeeds in complying with the obligations it neglected before such a penalty is payable, the final result may be that no sanction is imposed. Though effective in finally ensuring compliance, the imposition of a periodic penalty payment may not therefore always be an appropriate response to the infringement in question'.[104]

The Court noted that both a lump sum and penalty payments are intended to achieve the objective, pursued by Article 258 TFEU, of inducing a defaulting Member State to comply with a judgment establishing a breach of its obligations. Each measure is to be applied depending on its respective ability to meet that objective, according to the circumstances of each case: penalty payments seem particularly suited to inducing a Member State to put an end as soon as possible to a breach of obligations which would otherwise tend to persist; a lump sum is based more on an assessment of the effects on public and private interests of the failure of the Member State to comply with its obligations, in particular, where the breach has persisted for a long period since the judgment which initially established it. Recourse to both types of penalty in the same case is possible, especially where the breach of obligations both has continued for a long period and is inclined to persist. Moreover, the Court confirmed that it enjoys discretion, where appropriate, to depart from the Commission's suggestions: for example, to impose a lump sum on a Member State, even though the Commission did not propose doing so.[105] In the event, France was subjected to a penalty payment of €57,761,250, running from the date of this second judgment, for each period of six months at the end of which it had not yet complied with the Court's initial judgment, as well as to a lump sum fine of €20 million.[106]

The Commission's 1996 and 1997 Memoranda have been replaced by a Communication of 2005.[107] This adopts the three basic criteria originally identified in 1996 and updates the method of calculating sanctions to the enlarged Union, while drawing lessons from the case law; in particular, as to the appropriateness of proposing the imposition of both a penalty payment and a lump sum. This means that, where a Member State rectifies its infringement before the judgment under Article 260 TFEU, so that penalty payments have lost their purpose, the Commission may still proceed with the case on the basis of the lump sum payment, which retains its objective of penalising the infringement up to the time of its rectification.[108] The Commission has confirmed that its 2005 Communication remains fully applicable to the procedures governed by Article 260(2) TFEU, following the amendment of that provision by the TL.[109]

---

[102] Case C-64/88 *Commission v France* [1991] ECR I-2727.

[103] This involved failure to ensure compliance with Community measures on the conservation of fishery resources.

[104] Para 88 of his Opinion of 29 April 2004. A second Opinion was delivered on 18 November 2004, confirming his view that the Court was entitled to impose both a lump sum and a penalty payment, even where the Commission had only suggested a penalty payment.

[105] cp Case C-119/04 *Commission v Italy* (Opinion of 26 January 2006; Judgment pending).

[106] For recent examples of financial penalties imposed on a Member State pursuant to Art 260(2), see Case C-369/07 *Commission v Greece* [2009] ECR I-5703; Case C-568/07 *Commission v Greece* [2009] ECR I-4505; Case C-109/08 *Commission v Greece* [2009] ECR I-4657.

[107] SEC(2005)1658.

[108] Para 11 of the Communication.

[109] See para 4 of the Commission's Communication on the implementation of Art 260(3) TFEU, SEC(2010) 1371 final.

(ii) The Sanctions Procedure for Failure to Notify Measures Transposing a Directive

Article 260 (3) TFEU provides:

> When the Commission brings a case before the Court pursuant to Article 258 on the grounds that the Member State concerned has failed to fulfil its obligation to notify measures transposing a directive adopted under a legislative procedure, it may, when it deems appropriate, specify the amount of the lump sum or penalty payment to be paid by the Member State concerned which it considers appropriate in the circumstances.

> If the Court finds that there is an infringement it may impose a lump sum or a penalty payment on the Member State concerned not exceeding the amount specified by the Commission. The payment obligation shall take effect on the date set by the Court in its judgment.

This new mechanism is designed to speed up the disposal of cases involving the most blatant of infringements of their EU obligations by Member States, namely where they have failed to notify measures transposing a directive. The procedure applies only in the case of directives adopted under a legislative procedure—not, for instance, where the Commission exercises, by way of a directive, implementing powers that have been conferred upon it pursuant to Article 291(2) TFEU. A further restriction to note is that the lump sum or penalty payment decided on by the Court must not exceed the amount the Commission has specified.

The Commission has issued a Communication on the implementation of Article 260(3).[110] It is stated that the discretionary power conferred upon the Commission by paragraph (3) 'should be used as a matter of principle in all cases covered by this provision'.[111] The principles and the machinery governing the calculation of penalties will be those laid down by the 2005 Communication.[112]

II – THE ACTION FOR ANNULMENT

A – Introduction

It would have been incompatible with the legal traditions of the founding Member States and with the rule of law for the exercise by the EU institutions of their law-making powers to have escaped judicial review. Article 263 TFEU therefore permits direct actions for the review of the legality of acts of the institutions to be brought before the Union Courts. If the action is well founded, Article 264 (1) TFEU provides that the act concerned shall be declared void. As we shall see in Chapter 7, the validity of EU acts may also be raised as an issue before the Court of Justice by way of a reference for a preliminary ruling from a national court.

At the present stage in the development of the judicial system of the EU, the General Court has jurisdiction, at first instance, in all actions brought under Article 263 TFEU by natural or legal persons, and also in such actions when brought by Member States for the

---

[110] See n 109.
[111] At para 17.
[112] See paras 12–15 and 23.

annulment of acts of the Commission, and of certain acts of the Council that are executive in character; in the case of actions brought by Member States for the annulment of other Council acts or of acts of the European Parliament, and in all actions for annulment brought by one of the EU institutions against another, the Court of Justice has exclusive jurisdiction.[113] However, many of the leading cases on Article 263 belong to the period before the establishment of the General Court, or before its jurisdiction was extended. In the discussion that follows, references to 'the Court' with further qualification must be understood as relating to the Court of Justice.

Article 263 TFEU, as amended most recently by the TL, provides as follows:

> The Court of Justice of the European Union shall review the legality of legislative acts, of acts of the Council, of the Commission, and of the European Central Bank, other than recommendations and opinions, and of acts of the European Parliament and of the European Council intended to produce legal effects *viv-à-vis* third parties. It shall also review the legality of acts of bodies, offices or agencies of the Union intended to produce legal effects *viv-à-vis* third parties.
>
> It shall for this purpose have jurisdiction in actions brought by a Member State, the European Parliament, the Council or the Commission on grounds of lack of competence, infringement of an essential procedural requirement, infringement of the Treaties or of any rule of law relating to their application, or misuse of powers.
>
> The Court shall have jurisdiction under the same conditions in actions brought by the Court of Auditors, by the European Central Bank or by the Committee of the Regions for the purpose of protecting their prerogatives.
>
> Any natural or legal person may, under the conditions laid down in the first or second paragraphs, institute proceedings against an act addressed to that person or which is of direct and individual concern to them, and against a regulatory act which is of direct concern to them and does not entail implementing measures.
>
> Acts setting up bodies, offices and agencies of the Union may lay down specific conditions and arrangements concerning actions brought by natural or legal persons against acts of these bodies, offices or agencies intended to produce legal effects in relation to them.
>
> The proceedings provided for in this Article shall be instituted within two months of the publication of the measure, or of its notification to the plaintiff, or, in the absence thereof, of the day on which it came to the knowledge of the latter, as the case may be.

It can be seen from the text of Article 263 TFEU that there are four main issues that fall to be considered in determining whether an action for annulment lies in given circumstances:

— Is the acton being brought within the time limit prescribed by the sixth paragraph of the Article (as applied under the Rules of Procedure of the Court of Justice and the General Court)?
— Is the disputed act one that is susceptible of review?
— Does the applicant have standing (locus standi) to bring the action?

As we shall see, the conditions that govern standing vary, depending upon which of three

---

[113] See Art 256(1) TFEU and Statute, Art 51. The allocation of jurisdiction between the General Court and the Court of Justice is similar in respect of the action for a failure to act and the action for damages, which are discussed below.

classes—customarily referred to as 'privileged applicants', semi-privileged applicants and 'non-privileged applicants'—a given applicant belongs to.

— Are there grounds within the terms of the second paragraph of the Article on which the legality of the disputed act can be challenged?

The first three of those issues go the admissibility of an action for annulment and the fourth to the substance of the challenge to the validity of the disputed act. As we shall see, the most vexed issue in relation to Article 263 concerns the conditions governing the standing of natural and legal persons (private parties) to bring the action.

A final point by way of introduction concerns restrictions upon the scope of the jurisdiction of the Union Courts to entertain actions for annulment in certain fields of EU competence. During a transitional period of five years from the entry into force of the TL, jurisdiction to review the validity of pre-Lisbon acts adopted under the decision-making arrangements of the Third Pillar will continue to be restricted in the same way as previously under Article 35(6) TEU.[114] Like the disability of the Commission in respect of Article 258 TFEU, that restriction will cease, even before the expiry of the five-year period, where such an act is amended, for those Member States to which the act applies.[115] On the extremely narrow annulment jurisdiction applicable to certain acts in the field of the CFSP, see Chapter 27, below.

B – The Time Limit

Under the sixth paragraph of Article 263 TFEU, proceedings must be instituted 'within two months of the publication of the measure, or of its notification to the plaintiff, or, in the absence thereof, of the day on which it to the notice of the latter'. Article 297 TFEU requires all legislative acts and all regulations, as well as directives addressed to all Member States and decisions with no specific addressee, to be published in the *Official Journal*. Other directives and decisions are only required to be notified to those to whom they are addressed, but may in practice also be published.

Where a measure is published in the *Official Journal*, the date of publication is that on which the issue concerned actually becomes available, which may not be the same as the date on the cover. This is so, irrespective of whether publication was compulsory and whether the measure actually came to the knowledge of the applicant before it was published. In *Germany v Council*[116] the Court said that the wording of Article 263(6) TFEU made it clear 'that the criterion of the day on which a measure came to the knowledge of an applicant, as the starting point of the period prescribed for instituting proceedings, is subsidiary to the criteria of publication or notification of the measure'.

In a case where the disputed act has not been published in the *Official Journal* and the time limit runs from notification, it will be important to know precisely what that term

---

[114] See Protocol (No 36) on Transitional Provisions, Art 10(1) and (3). Pursuant to former Art 35(6) TEU, the Court of Justice had jurisdiction in actions brought by a Member State or the Commission for the review of the Third Pillar acts termed 'framework decisions' and 'decisions'.

[115] Ibid, para (2). As to the 'opt-out' secured by the United Kingdom, see pp 125–27 above.

[116] Case C-122/95 [1998] ECR I-973, para 35. See also Case T-14/96 *BAI v Commission* [1999] ECR II-139, paras 32–37.

entails. In *Commission v Socurte and Others*[117] the Court said that notification for these purposes

> necessarily involves the communication of a detailed account of the contents of the measure notified and of the reasons on which it is based. In the absence of such an account, the third party concerned would be denied precise knowledge of the contents of the act in question and of the reasons for which it was adopted, which would enable him to bring proceedings effectively against that decision.

That requirement could only be satisfied by sending the applicant the text of the measure in issue, not a brief summary of its contents. However, once aware of the existence of a measure concerning it, a party will be expected to request the text of the measure within a reasonable period. Once that period has expired, time will start running.[118]

Article 263(6) TFEU must be read in the light of the Rules of Procedure of the Union Courts. Under Article 80(1)(a) of the Rules of the Court of Justice, and Article 101(1)(a) of the Rules of the General Court, the day on which an event occurs is not counted as falling within the prescribed period of time. Furthermore, by virtue of Article 81(1) of the Court of Justice Rules and Article 102(1) of the General Court Rules, where the period of time allowed for commencing proceedings runs from publication of the contested measure, this is calculated 'from the end of the 14th day after publication thereof in the *Official Journal of the European Union*'. In addition, Article 81(2) of the Court's Rules and Article 102(2) of the CFI's Rules grant a 10-day extension of the prescribed time limits 'on account of distance'.[119]

In *Mutual Aid Administration Services NV v Commission* the General Court said:

> It is settled case-law that the time-limit prescribed for bringing actions under Article [263 TFEU] is a matter of public policy and is not subject to the discretion of the parties or the Court, since it was established in order to ensure that legal positions are clear and certain and to avoid any discrimination or arbitrary treatment in the administration of justice.[120]

Failure to observe the time limit therefore constituted 'an absolute bar' to the admissibility of an application.[121] The act in issue was a Commission Decision, which had been notified to the applicant, so the 14 days' grace from the date of publication allowed by Article 102(1) of the Rules was not available. On the other hand, the General Court made an allowance for the then applicable extension on account of distance.[122]

C – Acts Susceptible of Judicial Review

Article 263(1) TFEU identifies the following as acts that are reviewable under the Article:

— 'legislative acts': the category of legislative acts, newly introduced by the TL is defined by Article 289(3) TFEU as comprising '[l]egal acts adopted by legislative procedure'.

---

[117] Case C-143/95 P [1997] ECR I-1, para 31.
[118] See Case T-155/95 *LPN and GEOTA v Commission* [1998] ECR II-2751.
[119] Formerly, extensions on account of distance were of variable length, depending on the distance from Luxembourg of the Member State where the applicant was established. The extension has now been standardised as 10 days.
[120] Joined Cases T-121/96 and T-151/96 [1992] ECR II-1335, para 38.
[121] Para 39.
[122] Para 51.

Pursuant to, respectively, paragraphs (1) and (2) of Article 289, any act adopted by the ordinary legislative procedure or by a special legislative procedure must take the form of a regulation, a directive or a decision, which are the three forms of legally binding act defined by Article 288 TFEU.

— 'acts of the Council, of the Commission and of the European Central Bank, other than recommendations and opinions': the two excluded forms of act, recommendations and opinions, are stated by Article 288(5) TFEU to 'have no binding force'. Clearly, the category of reviewable acts identified here includes those adopted in the form of a regulation, a directive or a decision. However, as we shall see, the Court of Justice has interpreted the category as extending to any act of the institutions, whatever the form in which it may have been adopted, so long as it is intended to produce legal effects vis-à-vis third parties.

— 'acts of the European Parliament and of the European Council intended to produce legal effects *vis-à-vis* third parties': this wording, so far as it relates to acts of the European Parliament, was introduced into Article 263 by the TEU, in order to reflect developments in the case law.[123] The reference to acts of the European Council, which has been added by the TL, acknowledges the new status of that body as an institution of the Union with formal power to take decisions.

— 'acts of bodies, offices or agencies of the Union intended to produce legal effects *vis-à-vis* third parties': the final sentence Article 263(1) TFEU is a further addition by the TL. This, again, reflects developments in the case law.[124]

The question whether Article 263 TFEU can be used to challenge measures adopted by the EU institutions which produce legal effects, but which do not take any of the three forms of binding act referred to in Article 288 TFEU, was considered quite early in the development of EU law, in the *ERTA* case.[125] The Commission sought the annulment of Council 'proceedings' establishing that the negotiation and conclusion of a European road transport agreement would be undertaken by the Member States, rather than by the Commission acting on behalf of the then Community. One of the issues in a case that is also an important authority in the field of the Union's external action[126] was whether, in thus informally arriving at an agreed position, the Council had adopted an 'act' susceptible of judicial review. The Court of Justice said that 'Article [263 TFEU] treats as acts open to review by the Court all measures adopted by the institutions which are intended to have legal force.' It would be inconsistent with the purpose of Article 263, which was to ensure that the law was observed in accordance with Article 19(1) TEU, 'to limit the availability of this procedure merely to the categories of measures referred to by Article [288 TFEU]'. The Court concluded that '[a]n action for annulment must therefore be available in the case of all measures adopted by the institutions, whatever their nature or form, which are intended to have legal effects'.

Similarly, in *Les Verts v Parliament*[127] a French political grouping sought the annulment of two measures adopted by the European Parliament. At the material time, the

---

[123] See the *Les Verts* case, below n 175.
[124] See the *Sogelma* case, below n 130.
[125] Case 22/70 *Commission v Council* [1971] ECR 263, paras 39–42. See also Case C-366/88 *France v Commission* [1990] ECR I-3571.
[126] See Chapter 29, below.
[127] Case 294/83 [1986] ECR 1339. See also Case 34/86 *Council v Parliament* [1986] ECR 2155; Case C-57/95 *France v Commission* [1997] ECR I-1627.

Parliament was not mentioned in Article 263(1). The Court of Justice held that the then EC Treaty had established a complete system of legal remedies designed to allow the Court to review the legality of measures adopted by the institutions. It would be inconsistent with the spirit of the Treaty, and with its general scheme, for measures adopted by the Parliament that were intended to produce legal effects vis-à-vis third parties to be excluded from the scope of the action for annulment.[128]

The possibility, prior to the TL, of bringing an action for the annulment of an act of an EU body other than one of the formally identified institutions[129] was considered by the General Court in the *Sogelma* case.[130] The disputed act was a decision of the European Agency for Reconstruction (EAR) on the cancellation of a tendering procedure. There was express provision in the legislation under which EAR functioned[131] giving the General Court jurisdiction in disputes relating to compensation for the Agency's non-contractual liability, and in the matter of access to documents; but no jurisdiction was conferred with respect to annulment proceedings. The General Court said that the principle to be elicited from *Les Verts* was that 'any act of a Community body intended to produce legal effects vis-à-vis third parties must be open to judicial review'.[132] The Court went on:

> [T]he situation of Community bodies endowed with power to take measures intended to produce legal effects vis-à-vis third parties is identical to the situation which led to the *Les Verts* judgment; it cannot be acceptable, in a Community based on the rule of law, that such acts escape judicial review.

Accordingly, the disputed decision was an act open to challenge.

What renders an act susceptible of review under Article 263 TFEU is, therefore, the intention of an EU institution, or of any other entity established pursuant to the Treaties, to exercise their powers in a way that affects the legal situation of others.[133] Successive amendments to the first paragraph of the Article have been designed to give explicit effect to that principle.

Failure by an EU institution to adopt an act may, in certain circumstances, be assimilable to a positive decision against taking action, which is susceptible of review under Article 263. An example is found in *Eurocoton and Others v Council*,[134] a case relating to the non-adoption by the Council of a Commission proposal for a regulation imposing a definitive anti-dumping duty.[135] The non-adoption, it was held, possessed 'all the characteristics of a reviewable act within the meaning of Article [263 TFEU, in that it produced binding legal effects capable of affecting the appellants' interests'.[136] This was due to the

---

[128] For examples of acts which were not intended to produce legal effects, and therefore could not be challenged under Art 230 EC, see Case 114/86 *United Kingdom v Commission* [1988] ECR 5289; Case C-180/96 *United Kingdom v Commission* [1998] ECR I-2265; Case C-443/97 *Spain v Commission* [2000] ECR I-2415; Case C-208/03 P *Le Pen v European Parliament* (Judgment of 7 July 2005); Case C-301/03 *Italy v Commission* (Judgment of 1 December 2005).

[129] As now listed in Art 13(1) TFEU.

[130] Case C-411/06, *Sogelma v EAR* [2008] ECR II-2771.

[131] Council Regulation (EC) No 2667/2000, as amended, Arts 13 and 13a.

[132] Para 37.

[133] For a more recent example, see Case C-27/04, *Commission v Council* [2004] ECR I-6649.

[134] Case C-76/01 [2003] ECR I-10091.

[135] Dumping takes place when a product is imported into the Community from a non-member country at a price that is lower than its normal value in the exporting country, and this results in injury to a Community industry. Dumped products may be the subject of regulations imposing anti-dumping duties. Under the procedure applicable at the time of *Eurocoton*, a regulation providing for the replacement of a provisional anti-dumping duty by a definitive duty had to be taken by the Council on a proposal from the Commission.

[136] Para 67.

particular circumstance that a fixed time limit, within which given anti-dumping proceedings were required to be terminated, was about to expire;[137] 'determined definitively the Council's position in the final phase of the anti-dumping proceedings'.[138]

The Commission sought unsuccessfully to rely on *Eurocoton* in a subsequent case arising out of the Council's failure to adopt measures against France and Germany, which it had recommended within the framework of the machinery established by Article 126 TFEU to enable action to be taken against Member States running excessive budgetary deficits.[139] As the Court explained, the difference, as compared with the anti-dumping situation in *Eurocoton*, was that the excessive deficit procedure did not lay down any deadlines the expiry of which would prevent the Council from taking, at some later date, the action recommended by the Commission. It followed that 'failure by the Council to adopt acts provided for in Article [126(8) and (9) TFEU] that are recommended by the Commission cannot be regarded as giving rise to acts open to challenge for the purposes of Article 230 EC'. The proper remedy for the Commission in circumstances such as these was an action for failure to act under Article 265 TFEU[140] (though, in fact, the conditions laid down in that Article were not met in this case[141]).

Finally, it is important to note that annulment proceedings cannot be brought against certain types of act, which may nevertheless be thought to have legal consequences. That is true of the preparatory steps in a procedure involving several stages, such as the procedure leading to the adoption by the Commission of a decision that an undertaking is in breach of the rules on competition.[142] Only the final act under such procedures, definitively establishing the position of the adopting body, is susceptible of judicial review. Nor can proceedings be brought against an act that merely confirms a previous measure, which has not been challenged within the two-month time limit laid down in the last paragraph of Article 230 EC.[143]

Philip Morris International and Others v Commission[144] shows that the line between reviewable and non-reviewable acts may not always be easy to draw. The applicants, who were cigarette manufacturers, sought the annulment of two decisions of the Commission to commence legal proceedings against them in the United States as part of the Commission's efforts to combat the alleged smuggling of cigarettes into the EU. The General Court dismissed the action as inadmissible on the basis that a decision to commence legal proceedings did not in itself determine definitively the obligations of the parties or alter the legal position. The ruling seems inconsistent with the right to an effective remedy, which the General Court has strongly emphasised in other cases,[145] since one of the arguments of the applicants was that the Commission had exceeded its powers in launching the US

---

[137] Reg 384/96 on protection against dumped imports from countries not members of the European Community [1996] OJ L56/1, under Art 6(9) of which anti-dumping investigations had to be concluded within 15 months of initiation.

[138] Para 65.

[139] See Case C-27/04 *Commission v Council* [2004] ECR I-6649.

[140] See below.

[141] See para 25 of the judgment.

[142] Case 60/81 *IBM v Commission* [1981] ECR 2639.

[143] See eg Joined Cases 166 and 220/86 *Irish Cement Ltd v Commission* [1988] ECR 6473, para 16; Case T-275/94 *CB v Commission* [1995] ECR II-2169, para 27.

[144] Joined Cases T-377/00, T-379/00, T-380/00, T-260/01 and T-272/01 [2003] ECR II-1. See also Case T-353/00 *Le Pen v European Parliament* [2003] ECR II-125.

[145] See eg Case C-50/00 P *Unión de Pequeños Agricultores v Council* [2002] ECR I-6677; Case C-263/02 *Jégo-Quéré v Commission* [2004] ECR I-3425; Art 47 of the Charter of Fundamental Rights.

proceedings. Moreover, the commencement of proceedings in the United States would clearly alter the legal situation of the applicants (as defendants in those proceedings), by exposing them to the risk of having judgment given against them in default of appearance. The action for damages against the EU, [146] which the General Court mentioned as a possible remedy for the applicants, would necessarily only come into play once the action in the United States had been lost by the Commission, which might not become clear for several years, after the expenditure of quantities of time and money.

D – Standing of Privileged and Semi-privileged Applicants

In order to bring proceedings under Article 263 TFEU, applicants must show that they satisfy the conditions as to standing (or locus standi) laid down by the Article. As we have noted, those conditions differ as between three categories of possible applicants which, in the present version of Article 263, comprise the following:

— Member States, the European Parliament, the Council and the Commission ('privileged applicants'), as provided for by Article 263(2) TFEU;
— the Court of Auditors, the European Central Bank and the Committee of the Regions ('semi-privileged applicants'), as provided for by Article 263(3) TFEU; and
— natural and legal persons ('non-privileged applicants'), as provided for by Article 263(4) TFEU.

In the present section we consider the conditions governing the standing of so-called 'privileged applicants' and 'semi-privileged applicants'. The much more restrictive conditions applicable to 'non-privileged applicants' are discussed in section E, below.

It is worth remarking that the European Council, as well as 'bodies, offices and agencies of the Union', although liable to have their legally effective acts challenged pursuant to Article 263(1) TFEU, are not mentioned at all in the Article as possible applicants. In practice, it seems barely conceivable that the European Council, composed of heads of state or government, together with its own President and the President of the Commission, would ever find itself in a position where it felt compelled to seek judicial review of an act of one of the other institutions.[147] As for 'bodies, offices and agencies of the Union', these are normally endowed by their foundational instruments with legal personality; where this is so, the entity in question could seek the annulment of an act adopted by an institution that trespasses upon the area for which it has been given responsibility, assuming it were able to satisfy the conditions as to standing that are applicable to natural and legal persons.[148] History suggests, however, that the Court of Justice might well discover, in the jurisdictional system of the Treaties, a status for such entities similar to that of semi-privileged applicants, as it did for the European Parliament, prior to the formal conferral of such status on the Parliament by the TEU.[149]

---

[146] The action for damages is considered below.
[147] But see the contrary view expressed by P Craig, *The Lisbon Treaty* (Oxford, Oxford University Press, 2010) 127–28.
[148] Ibid.
[149] See below.

(i) Privileged Applicants

Applicants falling within the first category automatically have standing to bring proceedings and do not have to establish any particular interest.[150] To put the point another way, such applicants are presumed to have an interest in the legality of all Community acts.

The right of the Commission to bring proceedings is not affected by its position during the legislative procedure.[151] Similarly, where a Member State seeks the annulment of a measure adopted by the Council, its right to bring proceedings is not affected by whether or not it voted for the measure when it was adopted.[152] The term 'Member State' in this context means the governments of the Member States and does not include the governments of regions or autonomous communities, whatever their powers might be under national law. The Court has said that '[i]t is not possible for the European Communities to comprise a greater number of Member States than the number of States between which they were established'.[153] Regional governments constitute legal persons for the purposes of Article 263 TFEU and may only bring proceedings where the conditions set out in the fourth paragraph of that Article are satisfied.[154]

(ii) Semi-privileged Applicants

The category of semi-privileged applicant was initially recognised by the Court of Justice for the European Parliament. Prior to the TEU, the Parliament was not mentioned by Article 263 as a possible applicant, and in 1988 the Court of Justice held inadmissible an action it had brought for the annulment of a Council measure.[155] Two years later, however, in a case relating to the choice of legal basis for a measure adopted in the wake of the Chernobyl nuclear disaster, the Court held that the Parliament had the right to seek the annulment of acts adopted by the Council or by the Commission where the purpose of the proceedings was to protect its own prerogatives;[156] for instance, the role allocated to the Parliament in the legislative process prescribed for the adoption of the disputed act. Case 302/87 was distinguished on the highly artificial ground that the issue in that case was whether the Parliament had a right of action under Article 263, which (at the time) it had not; the right recognised in the Chernobyl case was said to be derived from the necessity of maintaining the institutional balance established by the Treaties. As we have seen, the TEU gave the Parliament the status of a semi-privileged applicant, and the TN that of a privileged applicant. The semi-privileged category now comprises the Court of Auditors, the European Central Bank and the Committee of the Regions, the last of these having been added by the TL.

Unlike privileged applicants, those that are semi-privileged are not deemed to have an interest in the legality of Community acts in general. To establish standing, they have to demonstrate that the act they wish to challenge impinges in some way on their particu-

---

[150] See Case 45/86 *Commission v Council* [1987] ECR 1493, para 3.

[151] Case C-378/00 *Commission v European Parliament and Council* [2003] ECR I-937, para 28.

[152] Case 166/78 *Italy v Council* [1979] ECR 2575, para 6.

[153] See Case C-95/97 *Région Wallonne v Commission* [1997] ECR I-1787, para 6; Case C-180/97 *Regione Toscana v Commission* [1997] ECR I-5245, para 6.

[154] See eg Case T-288/97 *Regione Autonoma Friuli-Venezia Giulia v Commission* [1999] ECR II-1169. Gibraltar is a quite frequent litigant in the Union courts. Its standing was recognised by the General Court in Joined Cases T-195 and T-207/01, *Government of Gibraltar v Commission* [2002] ECR II-2309. The conditions laid down in the fourth paragraph of Art 263 TFEU are considered below.

[155] See Case 302/87 *Parliament v Council* [1988] ECR 5615.

[156] Case C-70/88 *Parliament v Council* [1990] ECR I-2041.

lar prerogatives. For example, at the time when it still enjoyed this status, the European Parliament sought to challenge a Council Regulation governing shipments of waste,[157] which had been adopted under an environment legal basis; in the contention of the Parliament, the internal aspect of the measure ought to have been based on the provision that is now Article 114 TFEU (approximation measures relating to the establishment or functioning of the internal market) and the external aspect, on the provision that is now Article 207 TFEU (the common commercial policy). The action was ruled inadmissible, in so far as it related to the external aspect of the Regulation, since under the version of Article 207 then in force, the Parliament had no formal role in the adoption of measures of commercial policy.[158]

E – Standing of Non-privileged Applicants

Article 263(4) TFEU lays down the conditions governing the standing of '[a]ny natural or legal person' to bring an action for annulment. A natural person is an individual. According to the General Court,

> [A]n applicant is a legal person if, at the latest by the expiry of the period prescribed for proceedings to be instituted, it has acquired legal personality in accordance with the law governing its constitution . . . or if it has been treated as an independent legal entity by the Community institutions.[159]

The wording of Article 263 covers all natural and legal persons, regardless of their nationality or place of residence or establishment. For convenience in the discussion that follows, we refer to this class of applicants as 'private parties', to distinguish them from the Member States, institutions and other Union bodies whose standing is defined by Article 263(2) and (3) TFEU.

Private parties are described as 'non-privileged applicants', because the conditions they have to satisfy in order to establish standing to bring an action for annulment are somewhat restrictive. Article 263(4) as amended by the TL gives a private party the right to institute proceedings, under the conditions as to the reviewability of acts and the grounds of review laid down by Article 263(1) and (2), 'against an act addressed to that person or which is of direct and individual concern to them and against a regulatory act which is of direct concern to them and does not entail implementing measures'.

Thus, for their action to be admissible, non-privileged applicants must be able to show:

— either that the disputed act was addressed to them;
— or that it is of direct and individual concern to them;
— or that it is 'a regulatory act which is of direct concern to them and does not entail implementing measures'.

Those three possible ways for a non-privileged applicant to establish standing will be examined in order.

---

[157] Case C-187/93, *Parliament v Council* [1994] ECR I-2857.
[158] Paras 15 and 16.
[159] Case T-161/94 *Sinochem Heilongjiang v Council* [1996] ECR II-695, para 31.

(i) An Act Addressed to the Applicant

This is the most straightforward case. No question can be raised as to the standing of an applicant to challenge the legality of an act that was specifically addressed to that person. An example would be an action brought by an undertaking for the annulment of a Commission decision finding that it has infringed the rules on competition in Article 101 and/or Article 102 TFEU.

(ii) An Act of Direct and Individual Concern to the Applicant

(a) The Disputed 'Act'

There is no implication in the post-Lisbon version of Article 263(4) TFEU that the ability of an applicant to establish standing on the basis that the disputed act is of direct and individual concern to him/her may be dependent in any way upon the particular form in which the act was adopted—whether as a regulation, a directive or a decision, or indeed in none of the forms prescribed by Article 288 TFEU.

This is a significant change, as compared with the pre-Lisbon version of Article 263(4) TFEU, which referred to the institution of proceedings by a natural or legal person 'against a *decision* addressed to that person or against a *decision* which, although *in the form of a regulation* or a *decision* addressed to another person, is of direct and individual concern to the former'.[160] The italicised words appeared to express the wish of the authors of the Treaty that measures having the characteristics of true regulations be excluded in principle from review at the suit of private parties; the latter should have standing only to challenge an act that was, in substance at least, if not in form, a 'decision' as defined by Article 288, which in its then applicable version confined this category to acts addressed to specific persons.[161]

There is a considerable body of case law on the distinction between regulations and decisions, for the purposes of Article 263(4) in its former wording. In *Producteurs de Fruits v Council*[162] the Court deduced from the terms of Article 288 that '[t]he criterion for the distinction [between regulations and decisions] must be sought in the general "application" or otherwise of the measure in question'.[163] Thus, regulations were said to be essentially legislative in nature and to apply to 'categories of persons viewed abstractly and in their entirety'.[164] By contrast, the Court said in *Plaumann v Commission*[165] that 'decisions are characterized by the limited number of persons to whom they are addressed. In order to determine whether or not a measure constitutes a decision one must enquire whether that measure concerns specific persons'.[166] The consequence of a finding that an act must be considered a true regulation may be illustrated by *Calpak v Commission*.[167] The Court of Justice dismissed as inadmissible a challenge by two Italian companies to a regulation restricting the amount of aid payable to processors of Williams pears pre-

---

[160] Emphasis added.
[161] In its post-Nice version, Art 288 recognises that decisions may not necessarily have specific addressees.
[162] Joined Cases 16 and 17/62 [1962] ECR 471.
[163] At 478.
[164] Case 25/62 [1963] ECR 95
[165] Case 25/62 *Plaumann v Commission* [1963] ECR 95.
[166] At p107.
[167] Joined Cases 789 and 790/79 [1980] ECR 1949.

served in syrup. There were only 38 processors of Williams pears in the Community: 15 in France and 23 in Italy. None the less, the Court said that the contested regulation was

> by nature a measure of general application within the meaning of Article [288] of the Treaty. In fact the measure applies to objectively determined situations and produces legal effects with regard to categories of persons described in a generalized and abstract manner. The nature of the measure as a regulation is not called in question by the mere fact that it is possible to determine the number or even the identity of the producers to be granted the aid which is limited thereby.[168]

However, the inability of private parties to bring annulment proceedings in respect of true regulations came increasingly to be regarded as unsatisfactory; and, in some cases where regulations were challenged, the Court dealt with the issue of admissibility on the basis of the measure's direct and/or individual concern to the applicant, without first finding that the disputed act was in substance a decision. The final step was taken by the Court of Justice in the landmark case of *Codorniu v Council*,[169] which concerned a challenge to the validity of a regulation on the description and presentation of sparkling wines. The Court acknowledged that, according to the criteria applicable under the provision corresponding to Article 263(4) TFEU, the disputed act was 'by nature and by virtue of its sphere of application, of a legislative nature in that it applies to the traders concerned in general', but this did not prevent the act from being of individual concern to some of them.[170] Since the *Codorniu* judgment, it has been clear that, in spite of the pre-Lisbon drafting of Article 263(4), actions brought by private parties for the annulment of true regulations may in principle be admissible, provided that applicants are able to establish that the disputed act is of direct and individual concern to themselves.[171]

The pre-Lisbon text of Article 263(4) seemed also not to contemplate that private parties might have the right to challenge the validity of directives. However, once again the apparent intention of the authors of Article 263 has been overridden by the case law. In *UEAPME v Council*[172] and *Salamander AG and Others v Parliament and Council*[173] the General Court acknowledged that, notwithstanding the legislative character of the directives at issue in those cases, the admissibility of the claims should depend on whether the applicants were directly and individually concerned by them.

Those developments in the case law are now reflected in the wording of Article 163(4) TFEU, with its simple reference to 'an *act* . . . which is of direct and individual concern

---

[168] Para 9.

[169] Case C-309/89 [1994] ECR I-1853. See Waelbroeck and Fosselard (1995) 32 *CMLRev* 257; Usher (1994) 19 *ELRev* 636.

[170] Para 19. Direct concern was not at issue in the case.

[171] At para 33 of its judgment on appeal in Case C-50/00, *UPA* [2002] ECR I-6677, the Court observed that 'a measure of general application such as a regulation can, in certain circumstances, be of individual concern to certain natural or legal persons and is thus in the nature of a decision in their regard'. It seems unlikely this represented an intentional retreat from the position adopted in *Codorniu*. At all events, the matter has now been settled by the TL.

[172] Case T-135/96 [1998] ECR II-2335, paras 67–68. See Adinolfi, 'Admissibility of Action for Annulment by Social Partners and "Sufficient Representativity" of European Agreements' (2000) 25 *ELRev* 165. The directive at issue in *UEAPME* was adopted under the Agreement on Social Policy annexed to the Protocol on Social Policy agreed at Maastricht and itself annexed to the EC Treaty. The Protocol and Agreement were repealed by the TA.

[173] Cases T-172 and 175–177/98 *Salamander* [2000] ECR II-2487, paras 27–31. *cf* Joined Cases T-125/96 and T-152/96 *BI Vetmedica and Another v Council and Commission* [1999] ECR II-3427, para 143, where the General Court dismissed as unfounded a challenge by a private applicant to a directive without ruling on an objection of inadmissibility raised by the Council.

to [the applicant]'.[174] Cases such as *Producteurs de Fruit* and *Calpak* remain relevant as authorities on the distinguishing features of a regulation, as opposed to a decision, but no longer on the admissibility of annulment actions brought by private parties.

(b) Direct Concern

The Court stated in *Les Verts v Parliament* that a measure was of direct concern to an applicant where it constituted 'a complete set of rules which are sufficient in themselves and which require no implementing provisions', since in such circumstances the application of the measure 'is automatic and leaves no room for any discretion'. [175] Thus, in order to establish direct concern, it must be possible to demonstrate an unbroken causal link between the disputed act and the effect produced upon the applicant. Where the applicant is only affected by an EU measure because of the particular way in which a discretion conferred upon a third party has been exercised, and it was not possible for the author of the measure to tell in advance what the outcome was going to be, the applicant would not be able to establish direct concern. In *Alcan v Commission*,[176] for example, a decision addressed to two Member States refusing to grant them import quotas was held not to be of direct concern to an applicant, where the allocation of any quota would have been a matter for the discretion of the Member States concerned.

A measure requiring implementation by a third party may be of direct concern to an applicant if the third party has no discretion in the matter.[177] Similarly, an applicant may be able to establish direct concern if, at the time the contested measure was adopted, there was no real doubt how any discretion left to a third party would be exercised. In *Piraiki-Patraiki v Commission*,[178] for example, the applicants sought the annulment of a Commission decision authorising France to impose a quota system restricting imports of cotton yarn from Greece during a specific period shortly after Greek accession. The Commission argued that the applicants were not directly concerned by the contested decision, since it required implementation by the French authorities, which were free not to make use of the authorisation. That argument was rejected by the Court, since the contested decision had been adopted in response to a request from the French authorities for permission to impose an even stricter quota system. In those circumstances, the Court concluded that 'the possibility that the French Republic might decide not to make use of the authorization granted to it by the Commission decision was entirely theoretical, since there could be no doubt as to the intention of the French authorities to apply the decision'.[179]

Where the Commission pronounces ex post facto on the compatibility with EU law of a national measure which has already been adopted, the Commission's act will not be of direct concern to someone who objects to the national measure. This emerges from *DSTV v Commission*.[180] DSTV was a Danish television company which transmitted a satellite television service called 'Eurotica Rendez-Vous' to viewers in various Member

---

[174] Emphasis added.
[175] Case 294/83 *Les Verts* [1986] ECR 1339, para 31.
[176] Case 69/69 [1970] ECR 385.
[177] See eg Case 113/77 *NTN Tokyo Bearing Company v Council* [1979] ECR 1185.
[178] Case 11/82 [1985] ECR 207. *cf* Case C-404/96 P *Glencore Grain* [1988] ECR I-2435; Case T-80/97 *Starway v Council* [2000] ECR II-3099, para 68.
[179] Para 9 of the judgment.
[180] Case T-69/99 [2000] ECR II-4039.

States, including the UK. The UK authorities took the view that the service infringed a Directive on television broadcasting and made an order imposing restrictions on it. Under the Directive, the UK was required to notify the order to the Commission and it duly did so. Had the order been found incompatible with EU law, the UK would have been required to repeal it; in the event, however, the Commission found it to be compatible. In proceedings brought by DSTV to challenge this decision, the General Court held that DSTV was not directly concerned by it. The order existed independently of the decision by the Commission. That decision did not take the place of the UK order, nor did it retrospectively render the order valid, so it could not be said directly to affect the applicant's legal position.

(c) Individual Concern

The requirement of individual concern has always been a major hurdle to be overcome in establishing the admissibility of annulment actions brought by private parties.

1. The Plaumann Test

The starting point of an analysis of individual concern within the meaning of Article 263(4) TFEU remains the well-known test first formulated by the Court of Justice in *Plaumann* v *Commision*.[181] According to a more recent version of the test:

> In order for a measure to be of individual concern to the persons to whom it applies, it must affect their legal position because of a factual situation which differentiates them from all other persons and distinguishes them individually in the same way as a person to whom it is addressed.[182]

The essential idea is, therefore, that the effect produced upon the legal situation of the applicant results from factors in the latter's relationship to the disputed act, which single out that person in a similar way to a specific addressee.

In the *Plaumann* case itself, the applicant failed that test. Plaumann was a company that imported southern fruits into Germany; it sought the annulment of a decision by the Commission denying a request by the German government partially to suspend the general external tariff applicable to fresh clementines. The Court of Justice held that the applicant could not be considered to be individually concerned by the Commission's negative decision, because it was affected merely as an importer of clementines, that is to say, by reason of carrying on a commercial activity which was open to any person to practise at any time. The effect was not, therefore, such as to distinguish the applicant in relation to the disputed act as in the case of an addressee.[183]

The difficulty of satisfying the *Plaumann* test is further illustrated by *Greenpeace and Others v Commission*, where several individuals and three associations concerned with the protection of the environment sought the annulment of a Commission decision granting Spain financial assistance for the construction of two electric power stations in the Canary Islands.[184] The applicants invited the General Court to accept that standing could

---

[181] See Case 25/62 [1963] ECR 95, 107; Craig, 'Legality, Standing and Substantive Review in Community Law' (1994) 14 *OJLS* 507, 508–11.

[182] Case 26/86 *Deutz und Geldermann v Council* [1987] ECR 941, para 9.

[183] [1963] ECR at p 107.

[184] See Case T-585/93 [1995] ECR II-2205. See also Case T-219/95 *Danielsson and Others v Commission* [1995] ECR II-3051.

derive from a concern for the protection of the environment. The applicants claimed that in each Member State associations set up for the protection of the environment, which were sufficiently representative of the interests of their members, or which satisfied certain formalities, were entitled to challenge administrative decisions alleged to breach rules on environmental protection.[185] The General Court refused to accept that the standing of the applicants should be assessed by reference to criteria other than those laid down in the case law. It concluded that the individual applicants were affected by the contested measure in the same way as anyone living, working or visiting the area concerned and that they could not therefore be considered individually concerned. The same was true of the applicant associations, since they had been unable to establish any interest of their own distinct from that of their members, whose position was no different from that of the individual applicants. On appeal,[186] the Court declared that the approach taken by the General Court was 'consonant with the settled case-law of the Court of Justice'.[187]

On a strict application of the *Plaumann* test, that conclusion seems incontrovertible. The applicants in *Greenpeace*, and particularly the environmental groups involved, had a special kind of interest, of a semi-public and non-financial character, that would be affected by the Commission's decision to help finance the power stations in question; however, the effects liable to be felt were not the consequence of an individualising relationship between the applicants and the decision itself, analogous to the situation of an addressee. Over the years, the case law has helped to clarify the factors that will establish the necessary kind of relationship; though it also shows that there may be special considerations that will sometimes persuade the Union Courts to let in an action, where it cannot plausibly be claimed that the *Plaumann* test has been satisfied.

2. An Individualising Relationship

The factors that establish an individualising relationship sufficient to satisfy the *Plaumann* test are well brought out by the case of *CAM v Commission*.[188] The disputed act was a Commission Regulation on the detailed implementation of a Council Regulation increasing the threshold price of cereals and rice under the then applicable rules of the Common Agricultural Policy. The price support system included the granting of export refunds (in effect, a form of subsidy to cover the difference between internal EU prices and the much lower prices on the world market). Traders could obtain export licences with the amount of the refunds due to them fixed some months in advance, to enable them to judge what they could afford to pay their suppliers. In the event of such advance-fixing, refunds would normally be adjusted automatically to reflect changes in the price support system prior to the actual date of export. However, on this occasion it was stipulated in the Commission Regulation that there should be no change in the refunds payable to holders of export licences with advance-fixing that were still unused on the date the price increase took effect (7 October 1974). The applicant, a company in the business of exporting cereals, was a holder of such unused licences. Its action for the annulment of the Regulation was found by the Court of Justice to be admissible, though it failed on the merits. In the part

---

[185] In England, see eg *R v Inspectorate of Pollution, ex parte Greenpeace* (No 2) [1994] 4 All ER 329. For a comparison between the position in England and the United States, see Cane, 'Standing, Representation, and the Environment' in Loveland (ed), *A Special Relationship? American Influences on Public Law in the UK* (1995).

[186] Case C-321/95 P [1998] ECR I-1651.

[187] Para 27. See also eg Case T-472/93 *Campo Ebro and Others v Council* [1995] ECR II-421; Case T-107/94 *Kik v Council and Commission* [1995] ECR II-1717 (upheld on appeal: Case C-270/95 P [1996] ECR I-1987).

[188] Case 100/74 [1975] ECR 1393.

of the judgment relating to the individual concern of the applicant, the Court observed that the Regulation 'applies to a fixed and known number of cereal exporters as well as, in respect of each of them, to the amount of the transactions for which advance fixing had been requested'.[189] It observed further that, as indicated by the third recital of the preamble to the Commission Regulation, the distinction drawn in relation to that group of exporters was 'based on the presumption that they were already previously covered in respect of exports not yet effected on 7 October at prices not yet affected by the increase that was to take effect on that date'.[190] The Court concluded: 'By adopting those distinguishing criteria the contested measure affects a fixed number of traders identified by reason of the individual course of action which they pursued or are regarded as having pursued during a particular period'.[191]

The *CAM* case used to be regarded as an authority for the proposition that the requirement of individual concern could be satisfied by showing that the disputed act was only capable of affecting a finite group, or closed class, of which the applicant was a member. However, as the reference in the Court's conclusion to '*those* distinguishing criteria'[192] would suggest, being one of 'a fixed and known number of cereal exporters' holding export licences with advanced fixing on 7 October was not the only factor seen as tending to individualise CAM's relationship with the disputed act. It was equally relevant that the Commission had considered and set out to regulate the specific situation of that particular group of exporters.

Another example of an individualising relationship is provided by *Piraiki-Patraiki v Commission*,[193] where the applicants challenged a Commission decision authorising France to restrict imports of cotton yarn from Greece under the special transitional arrangements that applied during the period following that country's accession to the then Communities. The Court of Justice held that the contested decision was of individual concern to those of the applicants who, before it was adopted, had entered into contracts to be performed while it was in force and the execution of which would not now be possible. The Court found that the Commission had been in a position to discover the existence of contracts of that kind. Moreover, it noted that Article 130 of the Greek Act of Accession required the Commission to take account of the effect on the parties to such contracts of the measures it was proposing to authorise.

In *Buralux and Others v Council*[194] the Court of Justice dismissed an appeal against a decision of the General Court that a challenge to a Council Regulation enabling Member States to prohibit shipments of waste was inadmissible. The Regulation had the effect of legitimising a ban previously imposed by the French authorities on the importation of household waste. The applicants had been engaged in the disposal of waste originating in Germany, which had been exported to France, and one of them had concluded renewable five-year contracts for waste disposal with a number of German public bodies. The Court distinguished *Piraiki-Patraiki* on the ground (among others) of the Commission's existing obligation in that case to enquire into the negative effects of its decision on the undertakings concerned.[195] Clearly, there was no corresponding obligation necessarily bringing

---

[189] Para 15.
[190] Para 17.
[191] Para 18.
[192] Emphasis added.
[193] Case 11/82 [1985] ECR 207.
[194] Case C-209/94P [1996] ECR I-615.
[195] Paras 33 and 34.

the applicants in *Buralux* within the contemplation of the Council when it adopted the disputed Regulation.

Piraiki-Patraiki was again distinguished in *Commission* v *Nederlandse Antillen*.[196] The applicant was the government of a Dutch overseas territory enjoying a legal right under the Decision of 1991 on the association of the overseas countries and territories (OCTs) with the EU that, before certain measures were taken, the competent EU institution must enquire into the possible negative effects this might have on its economy. That obligation was not, the Court of Justice found, sufficient in itself to establish an individualising relationship for the purposes of the *Plaumann* test; applicants needed to show, in addition, that they were affected by the act 'by reason of a factual situation which differentiates them from all other persons'.[197] The Court recalled that only some of the applications in *Piraiki-Patraiki* had been declared admissible: applicants unable to show that, prior to the adoption of the disputed Commission decision, they had entered into contracts with customers in France for the delivery of cotton yarn during the period when the decision was in force, were held not to be individually concerned by it.

The lesson that can be drawn from those cases, confirmed by the similar reasoning of many other judgments of the Union Courts,[198] is that the *Plaumann* test of individual concern will be satisfied by a relationship between the applicant and the disputed act comprising two elements: first, the applicant belongs to a closed class of persons affected by the act in a way that singles them out from others to whom it may apply; and, secondly, the likely effect upon the situation of the applicant and other persons in that class either was actually, or ought to have been, taken into consideration by the competent EU institution when it adopted the act. Neither of those elements will normally be found sufficiently individualising on its own.[199] Together they establish a relationship placing the applicant in a position analogous to that of an addressee of the disputed act.

3. Procedural Participation

There are some particular contexts in which the Court has traditionally been willing to accord standing to natural and legal persons on the basis of their participation in the procedure leading to the adoption of an act adversely affecting them. The contexts in question all involve what have been termed 'quasi-judicial determinations'[200] made at the end of a procedure in the course of which interested parties are given the opportunity to express their views. Such procedures, which may begin with the lodging of a complaint, are particularly prominent in three fields: competition,[201] state aid[202] and dumping.[203]

---

[196] Case C-142/00 P [2004] 2 CMLR 41.

[197] Para 76.

[198] See eg Joined Cases 41–44/70 *International Fruit Company* v *Commission*[1971] ECR 4111; Case C-152/88, *Sofrimport* v *Commission* [1990] ECR I-2477; Case T-12/93 *CCE de Vittel* v *Commission* [1995] ECR II-1246; Joined Cases T-480/93 and T-483/93, *Antillean Rice Mills* [1995] ECR I-2305; Case T-489/93, *Unifruit Hellas* [1994] ECR I-1201; Case C-451/98, *Antillean Rice Mills* [2001] ECR I-8949.

[199] See, however, the exceptional cases discussed under (iv) and (v), below.

[200] See Hartley, *The Foundations of European Community Law*, 7th edn (2010) 382–86.

[201] eg Case 26/76 *Metro* [1977] ECR 1875 (complainant). See Bailey, 'Scope of Judicial Review under Article 81 EC' (2004) 41 *CMLRev* 1327; Völcker, 'Developments in EC Competition Law in 2003: An Overview' (2004) 41 *CMLRev* 1027, 1061–63 (judicial review in merger cases). On procedure in competition matters, see Chapter 26, below.

[202] eg Case 169/84 *COFAZ* [1986] ECR 391 (complainant).

[203] eg Joined Cases 239/82 and 273/82 *Allied Corporation* [1984] ECR1005 (exporters); Case 264/82 *Timex* [1984] ECR 849 (complainant). See Reg No 1225/2009 on protection against dumped imports from countries not members of the European Community [2009] OJ L343/51.

It appears to be recognised as a general rule that procedural participation will confer individual concern if—but only if—the person concerned enjoys specific procedural guarantees under the legal basis of the disputed act.[204] Thus sending a Community institution letters criticising a previous measure and seeking to influence its future conduct,[205] or commenting on proposed acts, will not in itself be enough to distinguish the correspondent individually, even if the institution replies.[206] This seems right, since otherwise anyone would be able to ensure that they would be individually concerned by contacting the competent EU institution with observations on draft measures. In the case of legislative instruments, the interests of those liable to be affected are 'deemed to be represented by the political bodies called upon to adopt those measures'.[207] In *CSR Pampryl v Commission* the General Court stated:

> [I]n the absence of expressly guaranteed procedural rights, it would be contrary to the wording and spirit of Article 230 EC to allow any individual, where he has participated in the preparation of a legislative measure, subsequently to bring an action against that measure.[208]

Individual concern as a corollary of a guaranteed right of participation in procedures leading to the adoption of a reviewable act should in our view be understood as a special case of compliance with the *Plaumann* test.

4. Specific Rights

Exceptionally, the Union Courts may be willing to recognise individual concern where the disputed act affects an applicant's so-called 'specific rights'. The leading case is *Codorniu*,[209] which we have already referred to as an authority on the point that true regulations may nevertheless be of direct and individual concern to some of those they affect.[210] The regulation in question provided for, among other things, the description *cremant* to be applied exclusively to wines produced in France and Luxembourg in accordance with a specified method. This would have prevented the applicant company, a Spanish producer, from continuing to use the description 'Gran Cremant de Cordoniu', which it had registered as a trade mark as long ago as 1924, and had traditionally used both before and after that date, for wine produced by a similar method. The effect of the regulation upon that 'specific right' was held by the Court of Justice to be enough to distinguish the applicant from all other traders affected by the regulation.

The first reference to 'specific rights' by the General Court seems to have been in *Asocarne v Council*,[211] where a Spanish trade association sought the annulment of a directive on the financing of health inspections and controls of meat and poultry. The General Court maintained that

> [u]nlike the regulation in question in Case C-309/89 [*Codorniu*] . . . the directive now under consideration has not affected *specific rights* of the applicant or its members. On the contrary, the applicant and its members are—like all traders in the Community operating in the sector in

---

[204] See eg Joined Cases T-125/96 and T-152/96 *BI Vetmedica and Another v Council and Commission* [1999] ECR II-3427.
[205] See Joined Cases T-481/93 and T-484/93 *Exporteurs in Levende Varkens and Others v Commission* [1995] ECR II-2941, para 59; Cases T-38/99 to T-50/99 *SAA and Others v Commission* [2001] ECR II-585, para 46.
[206] Case T-109/97 *Molkerei v Commission* [1998] ECR II-3533, para 67.
[207] Ibid, para 60.
[208] Case T-114/99 [1999] ECR II-3331, para 50.
[209] Case C-309/89 [1994] ECR I-1853.
[210] Above, p 164.
[211] Case T-99/94 [1994] ECR II-871.

question—subject to the national measures adopted for the purposes of transposing the directive.[212]

On appeal, that finding was endorsed by the Court of Justice, which repeated the expression 'specific rights', and there have been several such references in subsequent cases.[213]

In our view, the Court's reasoning in *Codorniu* represents an exception to the *Plamann* test, at least in the application given to it in *CAM* and *Piraiki-Patraiki*. Even if it was right to treat the applicant company as belonging to a closed class (those prevented by the disputed Regulation from continuing to use existing intellectual property rights), there was no basis for regarding the Council as having actually taken, or having been legally required to take, the specific situation of members of that class into consideration when it adopted the disputed Regulation.

The scope of the exception is unclear, however. It should probably be confined to cases where the disputed act prevents the exercise of a right of a proprietary nature, which had been acquired by the applicant prior to the act's adoption. The *Infront* case provides some support for this suggestion.[214] Infront was a broker of television broadcasting rights, which had purchased the exclusive rights for the 2002 and 2006 World Cup finals. It did so prior to the adoption of an EU Directive authorising Member States to take steps to ensure the availability on free television of live or deferred coverage of sporting events regarded as being of major importance for society. Member States were required to obtain Commission approval of their lists of such events. The case related to the approval which had been given on behalf of the Commission to the list of events submitted by the United Kingdom, which included the World Cup finals. On appeal from the General Court, the Court of Justice upheld the finding that the effect of that approval, which prevented the exploitation by Infront, with respect to the United Kingdom, of its pre-existing exclusive right, was sufficient to confer individual concern upon the company. Advocate General Bot, whose Opinion on the issue of individual concern was referred to with approval by the Court, observed that the disputed act affected 'Infront's right to property',[215] while also citing *Codorniu* as a precedent.[216]

5. Exceptional Circumstances Liable to Result in Particularly Serious Harm

In *Extramet v Council*[217] the Court of Justice accepted as sufficient to establish individual concern the existence of a set of exceptional circumstances which meant that the impact of the disputed act on the business activities of the applicant was liable to be particularly serious. The case concerned a Council Regulation imposing a definitive anti-dumping duty on imports of calcium metal into the then Community. For technical reasons connected with the method of determining anti-dumping duties, Extramet did not have the expressly guaranteed rights of a participant in the procedure, and so was outwith the category of applicants just considered. It was nevertheless held to be individually concerned by the Regulation, in view of three factors that were peculiar to its situation, namely: it

---

[212] Paras 20–21 (emphasis added).
[213] Case C-10/95 P [1995] ECR I-4149, para 43. See also Case C-87/95 P *CNPAAP v Council* [1996] ECR I-2003, para 36; Case T-482/93 *Weber v Commission* [1996] ECR II-609, para 69; Case T-194/95 *Area Cova and Others v Council* [1999] ECR II-2271, para 69; Case T-12/96 *Area Cova and Others v Council and Commission* [1999] ECR II-230, para 68; Case C-258/02P *Bactria v Commission* [2003] ECR I-15105, paras 48–52.
[214] Case C-125/06P [2008] ECR I-1451. At first instance, Case T-33/01 [2005] ECR II-5897.
[215] Para 98.
[216] Para 102.
[217] Case C-358/89 [1991] ECR I-2501.

was the largest importer of the product subject to the duty; it was, at the same time, the end-user of that product; and its business activities would be seriously affected by the Regulation, because of the difficulty of obtaining alternative supplies, more particularly in view of the fact that the sole Community producer was also its competitor on the market for the end-product.[218]

The decision in *Extramet* represents a clear exception to the *Plaumann* test. The applicant's standing depended purely and simply on the severity of the effect the Regulation was likely to have upon its commercial interests, as compared with those of other actual or potential importers of calcium metal. As later cases have shown, the particularity of Extramet's situation is likely to mean that the case will seldom, if ever, be invoked successfully as a precedent on the existence of individual concern.[219]

6. Individual Concern of Representative Bodies

Representative bodies, such as environmental groups or trade associations, are a special category of non-privileged applicants. The circumstances in which such bodies have standing to bring actions for annulment was one of the issues in the *Greenpeace* case.[220] In his Opinion Advocate General Cosmas counselled against treating environmental associations as a special case. Otherwise, he observed, '[n]atural persons without *locus standi* under the fourth paragraph of Article [263 TFEU] could circumvent that procedural impediment by setting up an environmental association'. Moreover, he said, 'the number of environmental associations capable of being created is, at least in theory, infinite'.[221]

Three types of situation in which actions brought by associations have been ruled admissible were identified by the General Court in the case of *Federolio v Commission*.[222] The applicant, a trade organisation representing undertakings active on the market for edible vegetable oils, was challenging a Commission regulation. From the context, it is clear that the General Court regarded the three situations as different sets of factors tending to establish that the disputed act was of individual concern to the association in question. These are:

> (a) where a legal provision expressly grants trade associations a series of procedural rights . . . ;
> (b) where the association represents the interests of undertakings which would be entitled to bring proceedings in their own right . . . ;
> (c) where the association is differentiated because its own interests as an association are affected, and especially where its position as negotiator is affected by the measure which it seeks to have annulled.

The General Court added that, in those situations, the Court of Justice and the General Court itself 'have also taken into account the participation of the associations in question in the procedure'. In *Federolio*, however, it was found that none of the three situations applied and the action was held to be inadmissible.

---

[218] Para 17.
[219] See eg Case T-598/97 *BSC Footware Supplies* v *Council* [2002] ECR II-1155.
[220] Case T-585/93 [1995] ECR II-2205.
[221] [1998] ECR I-1651, 1699.
[222] Case T-122/96 [1997] ECR II-1559, paras 59–61. *cf* Joined Cases T-447/93, T-448/93 and T-449/93 *Associazione Italiana Tecnico Economica del Cemento (AITEC) and Others* v *Commission* [1995] ECR II-1971, paras 58–62. See also Case T-114/92 *BEMIM* v *Commission* [1995] ECR II-147, paras 28–30. Where a number of applicants (eg an association and some of its members) make a single application, this will be treated as admissible if one of the applicants fulfils the conditions laid down in Art 263 TFEU: see Case C-313/90 *CIRFS and Others* v *Commission* [1993] ECR I-1125, para 31.

The fact that a representative body may have standing to challenge an EU act does not mean that all of its members will be in the same position. Whether an individual member of an association has standing will depend on its own particular circumstances.[223]

(iii) A Regulatory Act Which Is of Direct Concern to the Applicant and Does Not Entail Implementing Measures

The third basis for the admissibility of actions brought by private parties is an innovation of the TL. It may aid understanding of this addition to Article 263(4) TFEU for us briefly to recall the debate in the academic literature, and more importantly in the case law, of which it represents the outcome.

(a) The Debate: Should the Test of Individual Concern Be relaxed?

The difficulty which has been experienced by non-privileged applicants in satisfying the conditions of standing under Article 263(4) TFEU, more particularly that of individual concern, has sometimes been seen as incompatible with fundamental rights such as the right of access to a court or the right to a fair trial and to an effective remedy.[224] The stand-ard rebuttal is that private parties should seek relief by bringing proceedings in the courts of their Member State, from which a reference could be made to the Court of Justice for a preliminary ruling on the validity of the EU measure in question.[225] However, that may appear unpersuasive when there is no implementing act at Member State level that can be challenged in the national courts.

Such was the case in *Unión de Pequeños Agricultores v Council*,[226] where proceedings were brought by a trade association, UPA, representing small agricultural businesses in Spain for the annulment of a Council Regulation withdrawing aid granted to producers of olive oil. The General Court found that the applicant was not able to rely on any of the three situations identified above, in which an association may establish that an action for annulment is admissible: UPA had no rights of a procedural nature under the common organisation of the market in oils and fats; it had not established that its members were affected by the disputed Regulation by reason of certain attributes which were peculiar to them or by reason of factual circumstances in which they were differentiated from all other persons; and the contested regulation did not affect any specific interests or special protections enjoyed by UPA as an association distinct from the interests of its members.[227] The applicant had, however, put forward the additional argument that, because the dis-puted Regulation simply took away a benefit that oil producers had previously enjoyed, there was no call for any national measures of implementation and, therefore, no way of contesting the validity of the Regulation in national proceedings—denial of standing to bring annulment proceedings in the Union Courts would therefore deprive the applicant of its right to effective judicial protection. That argument, too, was rejected by the General Court, on the ground that access to the Union Courts by means of the action for annul-

---

[223] Case C-70/97 P *Kruidvat v Commission* [1998] ECR I-7183.

[224] See C Harlow, 'Access to Justice as a Human Right: The European Convention and the European Union' in Alston, Bustelo and Heenan (eds), *The EU and Human Rights* (1999).

[225] See Chapter 7, below.

[226] Case T-173/98 [1999] ECR II-3357. On appeal, Case C-50/00 P [2002] ECR I-6677. Hereinafter, *UPA*.

[227] So noted by AG Jacobs, when the case was appealed to the Court of Justice: para 14 of his Opinion. As to the latter, see further below.

ment could not be made dependent on the availability, or not, of a remedy at national level.

On appeal to the Court of Justice,[228] Advocate General Jacobs expressed his agreement with the General Court on that issue, noting that '[f]or the Community judicature to examine, on a case-by-case basis, the existence in national law of of procedures and remedies enabling individual applicants to challenge Community measures would . . . come perilously close to taking on a role not conferred by the Treaty'.[229] Instead, he urged the Court to adopt a new, more liberal, test of individual concern under Article 263, according to which a person would be regarded as individually concerned by a Community measure 'where, by reason of his particular circumstances, the measure has, or is liable to have, a substantial adverse effect on his interests'.[230]

That novel approach was taken up by the General Court in *Jégo-Quéré v Commission*,[231] a case decided before judgment had been given on appeal in *UPA*. The Commission Regulation at issue in *Jégo-Quéré* prohibited the use by fishing vessels of nets with mesh below a certain size; Member States would be required to enforce this prohibition, but they could do so by virtue of its direct application, no implementing measures being necessary. A five-judge formation of the General Court, headed by its President, abandoned its previous reluctance to relax the rules on standing to bring annulment proceedings. Citing with approval the Opinion of Advocate General Jacobs in *UPA*,[232] the General Court observed:

> The fact that an individual affected by a Community measure may be able to bring its validity before the national courts by violating the rules it lays down and then asserting their illegality in subsequent judicial proceedings brought against him does not constitute an adequate means of judicial protection. Individuals cannot be required to breach the law in order to gain access to justice.[233]

The General Court expressed the conviction that the strict existing test of individual concern ought to be reconsidered, and went on:

> [I]n order to ensure effective judicial protection for individuals, a natural or legal person is to be regarded as individually concerned by a Community measure of general application that concerns him directly if the measure in question affects his legal position, in a manner which is both definite and immediate, by restricting his rights or by imposing obligations on him. The number and position of other persons who are likewise affected by the measure, or who may be so, are of no relevance in that regard.[234]

That was a bold move, because the new test laid down by the General Court was clearly inconsistent with settled case law, from which the Court of Justice itself had not endorsed any departure;[235] and, indeed, when the Court gave judgment in *UPA*, it reaffirmed that

---

[228] See n 226, above.
[229] Opinion, para 52.
[230] Opinion, para 60.
[231] Case T-177/01 [2002] ECR II-2365.
[232] Judgment, para 43.
[233] Para 45. See *Posti and Rahko v Finland*, App No 27824/95, Judgment of 24 September 2002, para 64 (ECtHR).
[234] Para 51. The final sentence of that passage reiterated a point made by AG Jacobs in *UPA*: see para 59 of his Opinion.
[235] The departure from settled case law may not have been supported by all the members of the General Court. It is noteworthy that, notwithstanding its importance, the case was not referred to the plenary of the General Court and that, in Joined Cases T-377/00, T-379/00, T-380/00, T-260/01 and T-272/01 *Philip Morris*

case law. It was noted in the judgment that the appellant accepted that the disputed Regulation was of general application, that its specific interests were not affected by the Regulation and that it possessed no peculiar attributes which were such as to distinguish it from all other persons. For the Court of Justice, the question was therefore whether the appellant should be accorded standing 'on the sole ground that, in the alleged absence of any legal remedy before the national courts, the right to effective judicial protection requires it'.[236] The Court endorsed the view of Advocate General Jacobs that standing could not be accorded to an applicant on that ground. It would mean that, in every case, the Union Courts would have to examine and interpret national procedural law, which was outside their jurisdiction when reviewing the legality of EU measures.[237] The Court acknowledged that individuals were 'entitled to effective judicial protection of the rights they derive from the Community legal order';[238] however, it sought to demonstrate that the Treaty provided various means of challenging the validity of Community acts, devoting particular attention to the preliminary rulings procedure. The Court declared that it was the responsibility of the Member States 'to establish a system of legal remedies and procedures which ensure respect for the right to effective judicial protection'.[239] National courts were required, 'so far as possible, to interpret and apply national procedural rules governing the exercise of rights of action'[240] in a way that would enable claimants to challenge national measures applying EU measures of general application by contesting their validity. The Court ended by observing that, if reform of the system currently in force were considered desirable, that was a matter for the Member States.[241]

The Court of Justice subsequently upheld an appeal brought by the Commission against the judgment of the General Court in *Jégo-Quéré*.[242] The judgment on appeal contained strong criticism of the General Court for 'removing all meaning from the requirement of individual concern set out in the fourth paragraph of [Article 263 TFEU]'. The Court was silent on alternative tests, such as that put forward by Advocate General Jacobs in *UPA*, which offered a way of reconciling the open-textured language of Article 263 with the Union's values. Thus, the traditionally restrictive approach to the requirement of individual concern, pursuant to the *Plaumann* formula and notwithstanding all pressure for judicial reform, has been reaffirmed.[243]

(b) The New Basis for Standing

The concerns raised by the *UPA* and *Jégo-Quéré* litigation did not escape the attention of the authors of either the abortive CT or subsequently the TL. The solution devised for the former[244] and taken over into the latter was to leave intact the notion of individual

International and Others v Commission [2003] 1 CMLR 21, decided in January 2003, a differently constituted formation of the Court took a more restrictive approach. The *Philip Morris* case is discussed above.

[236] Para 33.

[237] Para 43. See also paras 50–53 of the Opinion of AG Jacobs.

[238] Para 39.

[239] Para 41.

[240] Para 42. *cf* Case C-106/89 *Marleasing* [1990] ECR I-4135.

[241] Para 45. The case was decided while the Convention on the Future of Europe was sitting.

[242] eg Case C-312/00 *Commission v Camar* [2002] ECR I-11355; Case C-142/00 *Commission v Netherlandse Antillen* [2003] ECR I-3483; Case C-167/02P *Rothley* [2004] ECR I-3149.

[243] Art III-365 (4).

[244] An opportunity to clarify the meaning of 'regulatory act' may be provided by a case that was pending before the General Court at the time of writing: Case T-18/10, *Inuit Tapiriit Kanatami and Others v European Parliament*. Two applications for interim measures were made in the case, both of them rejected by reasoned

concern, as it has been understood in the case law, and instead to introduce a new basis for the standing of private parties in annulment proceedings. They now have locus standi under Article 263(4) to seek the annulment of acts which are neither addressed to themselves nor of individual concern to them, if they are able to show that the disputed act is 'regulatory' in character, that it is of direct concern to them and that it does not entail implementing measures.

The term 'regulatory act' is not anywhere defined by the TFEU. As we have seen, the category of 'legislative acts' is defined by Article 289(3) TFEU as comprising 'legal acts adopted by legislative procedure'. Had it been the intention of the authors of the TL that such acts be included within the scope of the new basis for standing provided for by Article 263(4), they would surely have been mentioned there specifically. Another indication may lie in the distinction drawn in French legal terminology between *pouvoir legislatif* and *pouvior reglementaire*—in broad terms, the respective law-making powers of a parliament and of a government. It is inconceivable that a French reader of the TFEU would interpret the reference in Article 263 to '*actes reglementaires*' as capable of covering the '*actes legislatifs*' referred to in Article 289(3). Subject to that exclusion, however, it is submitted that the evident purpose of catering for the problem situation identified in *UPA* and *Jégo-Quéré* militates in favour of giving 'regulatory act' the widest possible interpretation. It seems most likely that the new basis for standing will be understood by the Union Courts to cover any legally binding act that is non-legislative, so long as it concerns the applicant directly and requires no implementing measures to be taken either by EU institutions or by Member States.[245]

We see no reason to restrict the category of 'regulatory acts' to delegated or implementing acts within the meaning of, respectively, Articles 290 and 291(2) TFEU. For instance, Article 43 TFEU, as amended by the TL, contains two separate legal bases: that in Article 43(2), relating to the establishment of the common organisation of agricultural markets, which requires action by the European Parliament and the Council under the ordinary legislative procedure; and that in Article 43(3) relating to the adoption by the Council, on a proposal from the Commission, of 'measures on fixing prices, levies, aid and quantitative limitations and on the fixing and allocation of fishing opportunities'. Despite being adopted under primary powers conferred by the Treaty itself, measures of the latter kind are clearly non-legislative. They may very well count as 'regulatory acts' for the purposes of Article 263(4).

On the other hand, it is hard to see how any non-legislative act that is a true directive would be able to satisfy the condition of not requiring implementation, such a requirement being inherent in the very nature of this form of instrument.

Assuming the foregoing analysis is correct, the addition made to Article 263(4) TFEU would have helped the applicant in *Jégo-Quéré* to get his case into Court, since the disputed Commission Regulation was a non-legislative act, adopted under implementing powers of the kind that would now be conferred pursuant to Article 291(2), while itself

---

Orders of the President of the General Court dated, respectively, 30 April 2010 and 25 October 2010. The Order of 30 April 2010 noted, at para 33, that the Parliament and the Council had argued that the regulatory acts referred to in Art 263(4) could not include legislative acts. The Order went on to state, at para 44, that the category of regulatory acts 'would probably have to be defined in relation to "legislative acts"'. While noting that the Union Courts had not yet had the opportunity to rule on that issue, among others (para 46), the President concluded that it was impossible, in the context of an application for interim measures, to exclude the admissibility of the main action brought by the applicants.

[245] See the discussion in Craig, above n 147, 130–31.

requiring no implementation by national authorities. In our view, the prosecution of a fisherman in breach of the rule on mesh size would entail the *application*, not the *implementation*, of the Regulation. In contrast, the amendment would not have helped the applicant association in *UPA*, since in the post-Lisbon era the Regulation there in issue, amending substantially the common organisation of the market in oils and fats, would have to have been adopted under Article 43(2) TFEU as a legislative act.[246]

(4) Interest in Bringing Proceedings

Aside from the criteria of locus standi in Article 263(4) TFEU, the defendant institution may argue that the applicant has no interest in challenging an act because annulment will not affect his/her rights or interests, notably where the disputed act has already been repealed or implemented. It does not, however, necessarily follow that an applicant has no interest in seeking the annulment of such an act, and arguments of this nature have rarely succeeded. The position was helpfully summarised by the General Court in *Antillean Rice Mills and Others v Commission*:[247]

> It is settled law that a claim for annulment is not admissible unless the applicant has an interest in seeing the contested measure annulled. . . . Such an interest can be present only if the annulment of the measure is of itself capable of having legal consequences. . . .
>
> In that regard, it must be borne in mind that, under Article [266 TFEU], an institution whose act has been declared void is required to take the necessary measures to comply with the judgment. Those measures do not concern the elimination of the act as such from the Community legal order, since that is the very essence of its annulment by the Court. They involve, rather, the removal of the effects of the illegalities found in the judgment annulling the act. The annulment of an act which has already been implemented or which has in the mean time been repealed from a certain date is thus still capable of having legal consequences. Such annulment places a duty on the institution concerned to take the necessary measures to comply with the judgment. The institution may thus be required to take adequate steps to restore the applicant to its original situation or to avoid the adoption of an identical measure.

That case may be compared with *Proderec v Commission*,[248] where the General Court held that the applicant had no interest in seeking the annulment of the contested act since it had by then been withdrawn with retroactive effect.

F – Grounds of Review

In order to succeed in an action for the annulment of an EU act, the applicant must establish that the disputed measure was unlawful. Article 263(2) TFEU mentions four possible grounds of review, which are derived from French administrative law.[249] These are:

---

[246] Reg 1638/98, [1998] OJ L210/32.

[247] Joined Cases T-480/93 and T-483/93 [1995] ECR II-2305, paras 59 and 60. See also Case T-102/96 *Gencor Ltd v Commission* [1999] 4 CMLR 971, paras 40–41; Case T-82/96 *ARAP and Others v Commission* [1999] ECR II-1889, paras 35–37; Joined Cases T-125/96 and T-152/96 *BI Vetmedica and Another v Council and Commission* [1999] ECR II-3427, paras 158–60; Case T-89/00 *Europe Chemi-Con v Council* [2002] ECR II-3651, paras 34–35.

[248] Case T-145/95 [1997] ECR II-823. See also Case T-26/97 *Antillean Rice Mills v Commission* [1997] ECR II-1347; Case T-326/99 *Olivieri* [2003] ECR II-1985; Case T-141/03 *Sniace* [2005] ECR II-1197.

[249] See AG Lagrange in Case 3/54 *ASSIDER v High Authority* [1954–56] ECR 63, a case decided under the ECSC Treaty.

— lack of competence;
— infringement of an essential procedural requirement;
— infringement of the Treaties or of any rule of law relating to their application; or
— misuse of powers.

In practice, those grounds overlap to a considerable extent and the Union Courts do not distinguish rigidly between them.

(i) Lack of Competence

A measure may be annulled for lack of competence, if the EU institution or body concerned lacked the legal authority to adopt it. This typically occurs where the legal basis under which the adopting institution purported to act is found by the Court not to cover the contested measure.[250]

(ii) Breach of an Essential Procedural Requirement

A particularly clear example of a breach of an essential procedural requirement is failure to consult the European Parliament prior to the adoption of an act where consultation is required by the Treaty.[251] Another example is failure to give a hearing to interested parties before a decision that affects them adversely is adopted.[252] In *Lisrestal and Others v Commission*,[253] an application for the annulment of a decision reducing financial assistance initially granted under the European Social Fund, the General Court stated:

> [I]t is settled law that respect for the rights of the defence in all proceedings which are initiated against a person and are liable to culminate in a measure adversely affecting that person is a fundamental principle of Community law which must be guaranteed, even in the absence of any specific rules concerning the proceedings in question. . . . That principle requires that any person who may be adversely affected by the adoption of a decision should be placed in a position in which he may effectively make known his views on the evidence against him which the Commission has taken as the basis for the decision at issue.

Thus, a person against whom administrative proceedings have been initiated has a right to a hearing; however, that requirement does not apply to the adoption of legislation of general application. In that context, the only obligations of consultation which the EU legislator must respect are those prescribed in the legal basis of the disputed act.[254]

Another important instance of an essential procedural requirement is contained in Article 296 TFEU, which requires EU legal acts to provide an adequate statement of the reasons on which they are based. The Court of Justice explained in *Commission v European Parliament and Council*[255] that

---

[250] See eg Joined Cases 281, 283–85 and 287/85 *Germany, France, Netherlands, Denmark and United Kingdom v Commission* [1987] ECR 3203; Case 264/86 *France v Commission* [1988] ECR 973; Case C-376/98 *Germany v Parliament and Council* (Tobacco Advertising) [2000] ECR I-8419.

[251] Case 138/79 *Roquette Frères v Council* [1980] ECR 3333.

[252] See eg Case 17/74 *Transocean Marine Paint Association v Commission* [1974] ECR 1063; Case C-49/88 *Al-Jubail Fertilizer Company v Council* [1991] ECR I-3187.

[253] Case T-450/93 [1994] ECR II-1177, para 42.

[254] See Case T-521/93 *Atlanta and Others v European Community* [1996] ECR II-1707, paras 70–74. The right to be heard does not apply to the Member States under Art 114(4) EC: Case C-3/00 *Denmark v Commission* [2003] ECR I-2643, paras 47–50.

[255] Case C-378/00 [2003] ECR I-937, para 34.

absence of reasons or inadequacy of the reasons stated goes to an issue of infringement of essential procedural requirements within the meaning of [Article263 TFEU], and constitutes a plea distinct from a plea relating to the substantive legality of the contested measure, which goes to infringement of a rule of law relating to the application of the Treaty within the meaning of that Article.

The disputed act in that case contained a brief statement of reasons on the point at issue, but this had been developed in a declaration made by the Council when the act was adopted, and which was published in the *Official Journal.* The Court held:

> First, the statement of reasons for a Community measure must appear in that measure . . . and, second, it must be adopted by the author of the measure . . . so that, in the present case, a declaration adopted by the Council alone cannot in any event serve as a statement of reasons for a regulation adopted jointly by the Parliament and the Council.[256]

The amount of detail required by Article 296 TFEU depends on the nature of the act and the context in which it is intended to operate. In *R v Secretary of State, ex parte Omega Air*[257] the Court of Justice summarised the effect of its case law on the Article:

> [I]t should be borne in mind that it is settled case-law that the statement of reasons required by [Article 296 TFEU] must be adapted to the nature of the act in question. It must disclose in a clear and unequivocal fashion the reasoning followed by the Community institution which adopted the measure in such a way as to make the persons concerned aware of the reasons for the measure and to enable the Court to exercise its power of review. It follows from the case-law that it is not necessary for details of all relevant factual and legal aspects to be given. The question whether the statement of the grounds for an act meets the requirements of [Article 296 TFEU] must be assessed with regard not only to its wording but also to its context and to all the legal rules governing the matter in question. . . .
>
> The Court has also held that if the contested measure clearly discloses the essential objective pursued by the institution, it would be excessive to require a specific statement of reasons for the various technical choices made.

The Court added that

> the statement of reasons in a regulation of general application cannot be required to specify the various facts, frequently very numerous and complex, on the basis of which the regulation was adopted, nor *a fortiori* to provide a more or less complete evaluation of those facts. . . . That is particularly the case where the relevant factual and technical elements are well known to the circles concerned.[258]

The Court concluded that the reasoning of the contested act was adequate to satisfy Article 296. The reasoning contained in the decisions is, however, expected to be more detailed.

(iii) Infringement of the Treaty or of Any Rule of Law Relating to its Application

The third ground, infringement of the Treaty or of any rule of law relating to its application, is the widest, and indeed is capable of subsuming the other three. As we have seen, it covers the substantive legality of the contested measure.[259] It may therefore be invoked

---

[256] Para 66.
[257] Joined Cases C-27/00 and C-122/00 [2002] ECR I-2569, paras 46–47. See also Joined Cases C-71/95, C-155/95 and C-271/95 *Belgium v Commission* [1997] ECR I-687, para 53; Case C-304/01 *Spain v Commission* [2004] ECR I-7655.
[258] Para 51.
[259] See Case C-378/00 *Commission v European Parliament and Council* [2003] ECR I-937, para 34.

if an act contravenes a provision of the Treaty or is inconsistent with a parent measure. It also covers infringements of general principles of law which have been recognised by the Court of Justice. The general principles constitute a body of unwritten rules to which the Community Courts have recourse in order to supplement the Treaties and acts made under them. They are discussed in more detail in Chapters 11 and 12.

An EU act may also be declared void on this ground if it infringes an international agreement to which the Union is a party (even if the provisions of the agreement do not produce direct effect within the Union).[260]

(iv) Misuse of Powers

The last ground of invalidity mentioned in Article 263(2) TFEU is misuse of powers. This is a particularly difficult ground to establish: it is concerned with the purpose of a measure, not just its content,[261] and therefore requires the applicant to establish that the intentions of the defendant institution were different from those stated in the contested measure. In *R v Secretary of State, ex parte British American Tobacco*[262] the Court stated:

> [A] measure is vitiated by misuse of powers only if it appears on the basis of objective, relevant and consistent evidence to have been taken with the exclusive or main purpose of achieving an end other than that stated or evading a procedure specifically prescribed by the Treaty for dealing with the circumstances of the case.

In that case, the applicants challenged a Directive on the manufacture, presentation and sale of tobacco products. The Directive purported to be one designed to improve the functioning of the internal market by ironing out differences between the laws of the Member States, but the applicants said it was in fact designed to protect public health, a field in which the Community's competence was more limited. The Court of Justice rejected that argument, taking the view that

> it has not in any way been established that [the Directive] was adopted with the exclusive, or at least decisive, purpose of achieving an end other than that of improving the conditions for the functioning of the internal market in the tobacco products sector.[263]

G – The Effects of Annulment

According to Article 264(1) TFEU, where the Court of Justice of the EU finds an action under Article 263 to be well founded, it 'shall declare the act concerned to be void'.[264] The Union Courts have no power to order the institution concerned to take any particu-

---

[260] Case C-377/98 *Netherlands v European Parliament and Council* [2001] 3 CMLR 49.

[261] See Case T-18/99 *Cordis v Commission* [2001] ECR II-913, para 56 (Community not guilty of misuse of powers in adopting regulation allegedly containing infringements of WTO rules).

[262] Case C-491/01 [2002] ECR I-11453. See also Joined Cases C-133/93, C-300/93 and C-362/93 *Crispoltoni* [1994] ECR I-4863, para 27.

[263] Para 191.

[264] Note that, where it is possible to sever and annul only the legally flawed elements of the relevant act, the remainder may be allowed to stand, eg Case 17/74 *Transocean Marine Paint* [1974] ECR 1063; *cf* Case C-376/98 *Germany v Parliament and Council* [2000] ECR I-8419. Conversely, a request for partial annulment, in the case of non-severable provisions, may be grounds for declaring the entire action inadmissible, eg Case C-244/03 *France v Parliament and Council* [2005] ECR I-4021; Case C-36/04 *Spain v Council* (Judgment of 30 March 2006).

lar steps,[265] but the institution is required by Article 266(1) TFEU to adopt the measures necessary to comply with the judgment.[266]

The scope of the defendant institution's obligations under Article 266(1) TFEU was considered in *Commission v AssiDomän Kraft Products and Others*.[267] That case was a sequel to the ruling of the Court of Justice in the so-called *Wood Pulp* case,[268] a competition proceeding in which a Decision of the Commission was partially annulled. In the disputed Decision, the Commission found that 43 undertakings, including the seven applicants in *AssiDomän* ('the Swedish addressees'), had infringed one of the competition provisions of the Treaty.[269] The Commission imposed fines on almost all the addressees of the Decision.[270] In annulment proceedings brought by 26 of the addressees, the Court quashed provisions finding that there had been an infringement of the Treaty and annulled or reduced the fines imposed on the applicants. The Swedish addressees had not sought the annulment of the Decision and had paid the fines imposed upon them. After the Court had given judgment, they asked the Commission to refund the fines they had paid in respect of findings which had now been quashed by the Court. The Commission refused on the basis that the Court had only annulled or reduced the fines imposed on the applicants in *Wood Pulp* and that the decision was unaffected in so far as it concerned the Swedish addressees.

After a ruling by the General Court in favour of the applicants,[271] an appeal by the Commission was upheld by the Court of Justice.[272] Although drafted and published in the form of a single instrument, the disputed Decision had been treated by the General Court as a bundle of individual decisions respectively affecting each of the addressees. The Court did not dissent from that approach. It made it clear that, while the defendant institution must ensure that any measure intended to replace the act annulled was not vitiated by the same defects, this did not mean that the institution was required to 're-examine identical or similar decisions allegedly affected by the same irregularity, addressed to addressees other than the applicant'.[273] A decision, which had not been challenged by persons to whom it was addressed within the time limit set by Article 263, became definitive as against those persons. The purpose of the time limit was 'to ensure legal certainty by preventing Community measures which produce legal effects from being called in question indefinitely'.[274] The Court explained that

> [w]here a number of similar individual decisions imposing fines have [*sic*] been adopted pursuant to a common procedure and only some addressees have taken legal action against the decisions concerning them and obtained their annulment, the principle of legal certainty . . .

---

[265] See eg Case 15/85 *Consorzio Cooperative d'Abruzzo v Commission* [1987] ECR 1005, para 18; Case C-5/93 P *DSM v Commission* [1999] ECR I-4695, para 36.

[266] See A Toth, 'The Authority of Judgments of the European Court of Justice: Binding Force and Legal Effects' (1984) 4 *YEL* 1.

[267] See also Case T-89/00 *Europe Chemi-Con v Council* [2002] ECR II-3651, para 32.

[268] Joined Cases C-89/85, C-104/85, C-114/85, C-116/85, C-117/85 and C-125/85 to C-129/85 *Ahlström Osakeyhtiö and Others v Commission* [1993] ECR I-1307.

[269] Art 81(1) EC: see Chapter 24.

[270] The Commission's power to impose fines on undertakings which infringe the Treaty competition rules is discussed in Chapter 26.

[271] Case T-227/95 [1997] ECR II-1185. See also Case T-220/97 *H & R Ecroyd Holdings Ltd v Commission* [1999] ECR II-1677.

[272] Case C-310/97 P [1999] 5 CMLR 1253. See also Case C-239/99 *Nachi Europe v Hauptzollamt Krefeld* [2001] ECR I-1197.

[273] Para 56.

[274] Para 61.

precludes any necessity for the institution which adopted the decisions to re-examine, at the request of other addressees, in the light of the grounds of the annulling judgment, the legality of the unchallenged decisions and to determine, on the basis of that examination, whether the fines paid must be refunded.[275]

Where Article 266 TFEU requires the adoption of a new measure to replace the one declared void, the principle of legal certainty will generally mean that the new measure cannot be made retrospective. However, in exceptional cases this is permitted, 'where the purpose to be achieved so demands and where the legitimate expectations of those concerned are duly respected'.[276] The Court's ruling may also lead to a claim for compensation against the Union in accordance with Articles 268 and 340(2) TFEU.[277]

While in principle a declaration by the Court under Article 263 TFEU that an act is void takes effect *erga omnes* and *ex tunc* (ie with regard to the whole world and with retrospective effect), Article 264(2) TFEU provides: 'However, the Court of Justice shall, if it considers this necessary, state which of the effects of the act which it has declared void shall be considered as definitive.' This enables the Court to minimise any disruption which might be caused by the gap left by the disappearance of the measure which has been quashed. For example, in a case where the Court declared void certain provisions of a Regulation relating to the remuneration of Community officials, it stated that those provisions should continue to have effect until they were replaced, 'to avoid discontinuity in the system of remuneration'.[278] In *Timex v Council* the Court annulled a provision in a Regulation imposing an anti-dumping duty. The aim of the action had been to have the rate of the duty increased and to secure the imposition of a duty on a wider range of products. The Court therefore ruled that the provision in question should remain in force until it had been replaced.[279] The Court's power under the second paragraph of Article 264 in its pre-Lisbon version was expressly conferred only in respect of 'regulations'. The amendment of the paragraph, with the substitution of the neutral term 'act', reflects developments in the case law. For instance, in a case in which a Directive was quashed, recourse to the paragraph was said to be justified by 'important reasons of legal certainty, comparable to those which operate in cases where certain regulations are annulled'.[280]

III – THE ACTION FOR FAILURE TO ACT

A – Introduction

The action for annulment is complemented by the action for failure to act, for which provision is made in Article 265 TFEU. That Article is in the following terms:

> Should the European Parliament, the European Council, the Council, the Commission or the European Central Bank, in infringement of the Treaties, fail to act, the Member States and the

---

[275] Para 63.
[276] See eg Case 108/81 *Amylum v Council* [1982] ECR 3107.
[277] See Art 233(2) EC. Art 288(2) EC is discussed below.
[278] Case 81/72 *Commission v Council* [1973] ECR 575, para 15.
[279] Case 264/82 [1985] ECR 849, para 32.
[280] Case C-295/90 *Parliament v Council* [1992] ECR I-4193, para 26.

other institutions of the Union may bring an action before the Court of Justice of the European Union to have the infringement established. This Article shall apply, under the same conditions, to bodies, offices and agencies of the Union that fail to act.

The action shall be admissible only if the institution, body, office or agency concerned has first been called upon to act. If, within two months of being so called upon, the institution, body, office or agency concerned has not defined its position, the action may be brought within a further period of two months.

Any natural or legal person may, under the conditions laid down in the preceding paragraphs, complain to the Court that an institution, body, office or agency of the Union has failed to address to that person any act other than a recommendation or an opinion.

The conditions governing the availability of this remedy will be considered under the following headings:

— no set time limit;
— failures to act that may be challenged;
— standing;
— taking a position; and
— the effect of a finding of failure to act.

B – No Set Time Limit

Article 265 TFEU does not specify how soon an action must be brought after the alleged failure to act has come to light. In a case decided under Article 35 ECSC, the counterpart of Article 265 TFEU, the Court of Justice held that proceedings for failure to act must be instituted within a reasonable period once it has become clear that the institution concerned has decided to take no action.[281] In the *Transport* case, however, the Court partially upheld an application made in January 1983, in respect of a failure to discharge an obligation which should have been fulfilled by the end of 1969, by which time the applicant (the European Parliament) was fully aware of the failure concerned. These cases may perhaps be distinguished on the ground that in the former the defendant (the Commission) had made it clear that it had decided not to take any action, whereas in the latter the defendant (the Council) accepted the need for it to take further steps. The conclusion may be drawn that it is only in the former type of case that proceedings must be brought within a reasonable period of the alleged failure to act having come to the applicant's attention.

C – Failures to Act that May Be Challenged

(i) Whose Failures to Act May Be Challenged?

The new drafting of Article 265(1) TFEU refers to the European Council and the European Central Bank, alongside the European Parliament, the Council and the Commission, as institutions of the Union in respect of whose failures to act proceedings may be brought. The second sentence of the paragraph follows the example of Article 263 in expressly

---

[281] Case 59/70 *Netherlands v Commission* [1971] ECR 639.

identifying the 'bodies, offices and agencies of the Union' as further potential defendants in such proceedings.

(ii) Failure to Adopt a Preparatory Act

The Court of Justice has occasionally emphasised the parallel between the action for failure to act and the action for annulment. In *Chevalley v Commission*,[282] for example, the Court said that Articles 263 and 265 TFEU 'merely prescribe one and the same method of recourse'. Similarly, in the so-called *Transport* case[283] the Court emphasised that 'in the system of legal remedies provided for by the Treaty there is a close relationship between the right of action given in Article [263 TFEU] . . . and that based on Article [265 TFEU]'. However, the analogy between the two Articles should not be pushed too far. In particular, the Court has accepted that the right to bring proceedings under Article 265 should not always be confined to failure to adopt an act having legal effects rendering it susceptible of review in annulment proceedings.

This can be seen clearly in the treatment of failures to adopt preparatory acts which, although not themselves reviewable under Article 263,[284] constitute an essential step in the process leading to the adoption of an act that produces legal effects. In the *Comitology* case,[285] for example, the Court of Justice observed that '[t]here is no necessary link between the action for annulment and the action for failure to act'. It pointed out that the European Parliament could bring proceedings against the Council under Article 265 if the latter failed to present a draft budget within the deadline laid down under the previously applicable budgetary procedure; however, as a preparatory measure, the draft budget could not, once established, be challenged under Article 263. If the Parliament had no right of action under Article 265 in these circumstances, it would be unable to challenge an unlawful failure by the Council to establish a draft budget, thus being prevented from exercising its power under the Treaty to adopt the budget.

In *Asia Motor France and Others v Commission*[286] the General Court held that, where the Commission declined to pursue a complaint by a natural or legal person of an infringement of the rules on competition, the complainant could bring an action for failure to act if it had not been informed beforehand of the Commission's reasons, and given the opportunity to submit further comments. The Commission was required to take that step by Article 6 of Regulation 99/63,[287] but where it did so the notification concerned would not be reviewable under Article 263 TFEU, because it was only a provisional measure designed to pave the way for the final decision.[288] Such a decision could not, however, be adopted in the absence of a notification under Regulation 99/63. If a complainant

---

[282] Case 15/70 [1970] ECR 975, para 6. See also Case C-68/95 *T Port v Bundesanstalt für Landwirtschaft und Ernährung* [1996] ECR I-6065, para 59.

[283] Case 13/83 *Parliament v Council* [1985] ECR 1513, para 36. The case is more fully considered below.

[284] See Case 60/81 *IBM v Commission* [1981] ECR 2639.

[285] Case 302/87 *Parliament v Council* [1988] ECR 5615, para 16.

[286] Case T-28/90 [1992] ECR II-2285, paras 29–30. *cf* Case T-127/98 *UPS Europe v Commission* [1999] ECR II-2633.

[287] [1963–1964] OJ English Sp Edn, 47. See now Art 6 Reg 2842/98 [1998] OJ L354/18, which replaced Reg 99/63 with effect from 1 February 1999.

[288] See Case C-282/95 P *Guérin Automobiles v Commission* [1997] ECR I-1503, paras 33–38. A definitive decision rejecting a complaint may be the subject of an action for annulment. Moreover, if the Commission fails to adopt such a decision within a reasonable time, the complainant may bring proceedings against it for failure to act. That is so even if he has already brought such proceedings in order to obtain the notification provided for by Art 6 Reg 2842/98.

were unable to challenge an unlawful failure to issue such a notification, it might not be able to challenge a failure by the Commission to adopt the final decision, because the Commission could say that, in the absence of the notification, it had no power to adopt such a decision.[289]

It may also be noted that, although a national court can use the preliminary rulings procedure to obtain a ruling from the Court of Justice on the (in)validity of a Union act,[290] the procedure is not available to obtain a ruling that an institution or body has failed to act. As the Court put it bluntly in *T Port*: 'Judicial review of alleged failure to act can be exercised only by the Community judicature.'[291]

(iii) Failure to Take Measures the Scope of Which Can Be Sufficiently Defined

In the *Transport* case[292] the Court of Justice stated that an action under Article 263 TFEU would only lie in respect of 'failure to take measures the scope of which can be sufficiently defined for them to be identified individually and adopted in compliance with the Court's judgment'. In that case, the Parliament brought proceedings for a declaration that the Council had infringed the Treaty by failing to introduce, before the end of the transitional period, a common policy for transport, dealing (among other things) with 'the conditions under which non-resident carriers may operate transport services within a Member State'.[293] The application was successful in part only. The Court made it clear that it was irrelevant how difficult it might be for the institution concerned to comply with its obligations, but found that under the Treaty the Council enjoyed a discretion with regard to the implementation of the common transport policy. Although that discretion was subject to certain limits, the Court said that it was for the Council to determine 'the aims of and means for implementing a common transport policy'.[294] The Court concluded that the absence of such a policy 'does not in itself necessarily constitute a failure to act sufficiently specific in nature to form the subject of an action under Article [263 TFEU]'.[295] The Commission, which intervened in support of the Parliament, had argued, however, that the common transport policy envisaged by the Treaty contained one element which was sufficiently well defined to be regarded as imposing on the Council a specific obligation, namely a requirement to ensure freedom to provide services; the scope of that requirement could be determined by reference to the Treaty rules on services and the relevant directives and case law.[296] That argument found favour with the Court, which ruled that, in so far as the obligations laid down in the Treaty related to freedom to provide services, they were sufficiently well defined to be the subject of a finding of failure to act.

D – Standing

Article 265 TFEU does not reproduce the distinction between privileged and semi-privi-

---

[289] Hartley, above n 200, 400.
[290] See Chapter 7.
[291] Case C-68/95 *T Port v Bundesanstalt für Landwirtschaft und Ernährung* [1996] ECR I-6065, para 53.
[292] Case 13/83 *Parliament v Council* [1985] ECR 1513, para 37.
[293] See Art 71(1)(b) EC.
[294] Para 49.
[295] Para 53.
[296] See Chapter 18.

leged applicants that is found in Article 263. However, the Member States, the institutions and 'bodies, offices and agencies of the Union' enjoy broader rights to bring proceedings for failure to act than the non-privileged class comprising natural and legal persons.

The phrase 'the other institutions' in Article 265(1) TFEU covers all of the institutions of the Union (including now the European Council and the European Central Bank), other than the one responsible for the failure to act. That phrase was interpreted in the *Transport* case as including the European Parliament within the class of potential applicants under Article 265, even before the amendment of the Article by the Treaty of Nice, which brought the Parliament within the group of institutions expressly identified as potential defendants.[297] It would seem to follow that the Court of Auditors must similarly be included, though it still does not figure on the list of those whose failures to act may be challenged. The drafting of the second sentence of Article 265(1) TFEU, as amended by the TL, places 'bodies, offices and agencies of the Union' on the same footing as the institutions.

Under Article 232(3) EC, any natural or legal person may complain to the Court 'that an institution of the Community has failed to address to that person any act other than a recommendation or an opinion'. Thus, in *Chevalley v Commission*[298] the Court held that a definition of the Commission's position on a question, which would have amounted in substance to an opinion within the meaning of Article 288 TFEU, was not capable of forming the subject-matter of an action under Article 265 TFEU. However, the decision in *Guérin Automobiles v Commission*[299] shows that a non-privileged applicant may bring proceedings under Article 265 TFEU where an institution fails to take a step which, although it could not itself have been challenged in annulment proceedings, constitutes a prerequisite for the adoption of an act that could be.

The wording of Article 265 TFEU suggests that a non-privileged applicant has to show that he/she would have been the addressee of the act that allegedly should have been adopted. If that requirement were applied strictly, however, there would be a significant gap in the system of remedies established by the Treaty: natural or legal persons would be unable to challenge a failure to adopt an act which, if it had been adopted, would have been of direct and individual concern to them, or a regulatory act of direct concern to them and not calling for implementing measures, and which they would, accordingly, have had standing to challenge in proceedings under Article 263 TFEU. The Court of Justice has avoided that result by a flexible interpretation of the word 'address'. In *T Port v Bundesanstalt für Landwirtschaft und Ernährung* the Court explained:

> [J]ust as the fourth paragraph of Article [263 TFEU] allows individuals to bring an action for annulment against a measure of an institution not addressed to them provided that the measure is of direct and individual concern to them, the third paragraph of Article [232 EC] must be interpreted as also entitling them to bring an action for failure to act against an institution which they claim has failed to adopt a measure which would have concerned them in the same way. The possibility for individuals to assert their rights should not depend upon whether the institution concerned has acted or failed to act.[300]

---

[297] Case 13/83 *Parliament v Council* [1985] ECR 1513, para 17.
[298] Case 15/70 [1970] ECR 975.
[299] Case C-282/95 P *Guérin Automobiles v Commission* [1997] ECR I-1503.
[300] Case C-68/95 *T Port v Bundesanstalt für Landwirtschaft und Ernährung* [1996] ECR I-6065, para 59. See also Case C-107/91 *ENU v Commission* [1993] ECR I-599; Case T-95/96 *Gestevisión Telecinco v Commission* [1998] ECR II-3407; Joined Cases T-79/96, T-260/97 and T-117/98 *Camar and Tico v Commission* [2000] ECR II-2193. cp AG Darmon in Case C-41/92 *Liberal Democrats v Parliament* [1993] ECR I-3153, 3172; AG Dutheillet de Lamothe in Case 15/71 *Mackprang v Commission* [1971] ECR 797, 807–808.

Notwithstanding earlier case law to the contrary,[301] it would seem to have follow that natural or legal persons may challenge a failure to adopt a regulation, or indeed a directive, that would have concerned them directly and individually, or that is regulatory in character and does not require implementation, in spite of the fact that regulations are not addressed to anyone, and directives can only be addressed to Member States. The parallelism between Articles 265 and 263 TFEU as regards the standing of non-privileged applicants to brings actions for failure to act has been confirmed in clear terms by recent judgments of the General Court.[302]

The Court clarified in the *Ten Kate* case that Article 265 TFEU does not impose any obligation on a Member State to bring an action for failure to act for the benefit of one of its citizens.[303] On the other hand, EU law does not, in principle, preclude national law itself from requiring the national authorities to take such action, or from making them liable if they fail to do so. However, Article 4(3) TFEU would require the Member State in such circumstances to enjoy a measure of discretion under national law as to the appropriateness of initiating proceedings under Article 265, so as to avoid the risk that the Union Courts might be inundated with actions, some patently unfounded, such as would jeopardise their proper functioning.

E – Taking a Position

According to Article 265(2) TFEU, an action for failure to act will only be admissible if the institution, body, office or agency concerned has first been 'called upon to act'. In the *Transport* case, the Council argued that that requirement had not been met. The Court of Justice disagreed, since the President of the European Parliament had sent a letter to the Council that referred to Article 265 and stated that the Parliament was calling on the Council to act pursuant to that provision. Moreover, annexed to the letter was a list of the steps which the Parliament considered necessary to remedy the failure. If the institution or other body concerned has not 'defined its position' within two months of having been called upon to act, an application may be made to the Court within a further period of two months. Thus, where the institution does define its position in time, for instance by indicating that, after due consideration, it does not consider the requested action to be appropriate, no proceedings will lie under Article 265. In *Transport* the Court declined to treat as a definition of its position the Council's reply to the letter from the Parliament calling upon it to act. The Court observed that the Council's reply

> was confined to setting out what action it had already taken in relation to transport without commenting 'on the legal aspects' of the correspondence initiated by the Parliament. The reply neither denied nor confirmed the alleged failure to act nor gave any indication of the Council's views as to the measures which, according to the Parliament, remained to be taken. [304]

The applicant will not normally be able to seek the annulment of the act by which the institution defines its position, unless he/she would have had standing to challenge the

---

[301] See eg Case 134/73 *Holtz v Council* [1974] ECR 1, para 5; Case 90/78 *Granaria v Council and Commission* [1979] ECR 1081, para 14 (from the final sentence of which the word 'not' has inadvertently been omitted in the English version); Case 60/79 *Producteurs de Vins de Table et Vins de Pays v Commission* [1979] ECR 2429.

[302] See Case T-95/04 *Air One v Commission* [2006] ECR II-1343, para 25; Case T-167/04 *Asklepios Kliniken v Commission* [2007] ECR II-2378, para 49.

[303] The same is true of Art 230 EC: see C-511/03 *Ten Kate* (Judgment of 20 October 2005).

[304] Para 25 of the Judgment.

measure requested under Article 263, had it been adopted. In *Nordgetreide v Commission*[305] the applicant, a private undertaking, sought the annulment of a refusal by the Commission to adopt an act which would have taken the form of a regulation. Since the measure requested 'would have affected the applicant only in so far as it belongs to a category viewed in the abstract and in its entirety', and could not, therefore, have been challenged in annulment proceedings, the application was declared inadmissible. However, the General Court takes a more liberal approach where an institution is requested to act but refuses to do so under a procedure laid down by regulation which places it under an obligation to rule on such requests.[306]

Some of the case law[307] suggests that the defendant institution may define its position sufficiently for the purposes of Article 265 TFEU by a mere refusal to adopt the act requested by the applicant. However, the Court of Justice took a more relaxed stance in the *Comitology* case.[308] One of the arguments put forward by the European Parliament in support of its claim to have standing to bring annulment proceedings, at a time when this was not expressly provided for by Article 263, was that it would otherwise be unable to challenge an express refusal by the Council or the Commission, after they had been called upon to act under Article 265. The Court replied: '[T]hat argument is based on a false premise. A refusal to act, however explicit it may be, can be brought before the Court under Article [265 TFEU] since it does not put an end to the failure to act.'[309] It is possible that the Court's statement in *Comitology* is limited to cases where the applicant would otherwise be deprived of a remedy because of being unable to challenge an express refusal to act under Article 263.[310] However, Article 265 cannot be used to challenge a refusal by an institution to revoke an act the annulment of which has not been sought within the deadline laid down in Article 263, since this would provide applicants 'with a method of recourse parallel to that of Article [263 TFEU], which would not be subject to the conditions laid down by the Treaty'.[311]

Where the failure to act is remedied within two months of the institution or other body's having been called upon to act, no action may be brought before the Court. The steps taken need not be the same as those requested by the applicant, for 'Article [265 TFEU] refers to failure to act in the sense of failure to take a decision or to define a position, and not the adoption of a measure different from that desired or considered necessary by the persons concerned.'[312] Thus, an institution which proposes a particular legal basis for a measure cannot use Article 265 to challenge the choice of a different legal basis by the adopting institution.[313]

If the defendant institution or other body takes the steps requested more than two

---

[305] Case 42/71 [1972] ECR 105. See also Case T-166/98 *Cantina sociale di Dolianova v Commission* (pending); Joined Cases C-15/91 and C-108/91 *Buckl and Others v Commission* [1992] ECR I-6061; Case 48/65 *Lütticke v Commission* [1966] ECR 19.

[306] See Case T-120/96 *Lilly Industries v Commission* [1998] ECR II-2571, paras 61–63; cf Joined Cases T-125/96 and T-152/96 *BI Vetmedica and Another v Council and Commission* [1999] ECR II-3427, paras 166–69.

[307] See eg Case 42/71 *Nordgetreide v Commission* [1972] ECR 105.

[308] Case 302/87 [1988] ECR 5615.

[309] Para 17 of the Judgment. cf the Opinion of AG Darmon at 5630–31.

[310] See O Due, 'Legal Remedies for the Failure of European Community Institutions to Act in Conformity with EEC Treaty Provisions' (1990–91) 14 *Fordham International Law Journal* 341, 356; Hartley (above n 200, 399) notes that the Court's statement in the *Comitology* case was made in a very special context.

[311] Joined Cases 10 and 18/68 *Eridania v Commission* [1969] ECR 459, para 17.

[312] Joined Cases 166 and 220/86 *Irish Cement Ltd v Commission* [1988] ECR 6473, para 17. Also eg Case T-26/01 *Fiocchi Munizioni v Commission* [2003] ECR II-3951.

[313] See Case C-70/88 *Parliament v Council* ('Chernobyl') [1990] ECR I-2041.

months after being called upon to do so but before judgment is given, the Court will decline to give a ruling on the basis that 'the subject-matter of the action has ceased to exist'.[314] As the Court explained in *Buckl and Others v Commission*:[315]

> [W]here the act whose absence constitutes the subject-matter of the proceedings was adopted after the action was brought but before judgment, a declaration by the Court to the effect that the initial failure to act is unlawful can no longer bring about the consequences prescribed by Article [2266 TFEU]. It follows that in such a case, as in cases where the defendant institution has responded within the period of two months after being called upon to act, the subject-matter of the action has ceased to exist.

The Court's approach may be contrasted with its attitude in proceedings brought by the Commission under Article 258 TFEU, where the Member State complies with its obligations after the expiry of the deadline laid down in the reasoned opinion.[316] Such cases are allowed to continue unless withdrawn by the Commission.

F – The Effect of a Finding of Failure to Act

Where an application under Article 265 TFEU is upheld, the Court declares that the failure of the institution concerned to act is contrary to the Treaties. The Court cannot remedy the failure itself or order the institution concerned to take any particular steps. In the *Air One* case, the General Court said: 'The Community judicature is not competent to issue directions to an institution in the context of an action based on Article [265 TFEU].'[317] However, the institution is required by Article 266(1) TFEU 'to take the necessary measures to comply with the judgment of the Court of Justice of the European Union'. The Court has said that those measures must be adopted within a reasonable period of the judgment.[318]

IV – THE ACTION FOR DAMAGES

A – Introduction

Article 268 TFEU gives the Union Courts jurisdiction in actions for damages brought under the second paragraph of Article 340 TFEU. The latter provides:

> In the case of non-contractual liability, the Union shall, in accordance with the general principles common to the laws of the Member States, make good any damage caused by its institutions or by its servants in the performance of their duties.[319]

In broad terms, 'non-contractual liability' corresponds to liability in tort. The combined

---

[314] See Case 377/87 *Parliament v Council* [1988] ECR 4017. Also eg Joined Cases T-297/01 and T-298/01 *SIC v Commission* [2004] ECR II-743.

[315] Joined Cases C-15/91 and C-108/91 *Buckl and Others v Commission* [1992] ECR I-6061, para 15.

[316] See eg Case 39/72 *Commission v Italy* [1973] ECR 101.

[317] Case T-395/04 [2006] ECR II-1343, para 24.

[318] See Case 13/83 *Parliament v Council* [1985] ECR 1513, para 69.

[319] See generally T Heukels and A McDonnell (eds), *The Action for Damages in Community Law* (1997).

effect of Articles 268 and 340 TFEU is to provide a remedy in damages, where wrongdoing by the Union or by its officials in the course of their duties causes financial harm to others.

Article 340(3) TFEU still makes separate provision for the European Central Bank to be subject to such liability, though it has enjoyed the formal status of an 'institution' since the TN. Indeed, such provision may never have been strictly necessary. The Court of Justice held in *SGEEM and Etroy v EIB*[320] that the term 'institutions' in Article 340(2) TFEU was not confined to the formal list of institutions (now found in Article 13(1) TEU) but extended to any body established under the Treaties and authorised to act in the Union's name and on its behalf;[321] thus, for example, the acts of the Ombudsman may, in principle, provide grounds for an action for damages.[322] It follows that the 'bodies, offices and agencies' whose acts or failures to act the Treaty of Lisbon has made explicitly clear may be the subject of legal proceedings must also be recognised as potential defendants in proceedings under Article 340 TFEU.

According to the Treaty, it is the Union as such whose liability is in issue in such proceedings. However, in *Werhahn v Council* the Court said that, 'where Community liability is involved by reason of the act of one of its institutions, it should be represented before the Court by the institution or institutions against which the matter giving rise to liability is alleged'.[323] Where the action relates to a legislative measure adopted by the Council on a proposal from the Commission, proceedings may be brought against both institutions jointly.[324]

The reference to the general principles common to the laws of the Member States in Article 340(2) TFEU does not mean that the Union Courts must search in cases on non-contractual liability for a solution favoured by a majority of the Member States, still less that they have to apply the lowest common denominator. It means simply that the Courts must look to the national systems for inspiration in devising a regime of non-contractual liability adapted to the specific circumstances of the Union.[325] The principles traditionally applied by the Union Courts have in fact been relatively strict, with the result that the number of successful damages claims over the years has been relatively small. However, the case law has recently undergone some significant changes, the stimulus for which has been the development of the doctrine of state liability for damage caused by breaches of EU law.[326] In *Brasserie du Pêcheur* and *Factortame* the Court of Justice said: 'The protection of the rights which individuals derive from Community law cannot vary depending on whether a national authority or a Community authority is responsible for the damage.'[327]

It is well established that the action for damages constitutes an independent or autonomous form of action. Its purpose is different from that of proceedings for annulment or failure to act and it is not necessary to have recourse to such proceedings before bringing an action under Article 340(2) TFEU.[328] However, a claim for damages will not be enter-

---

[320] Case C-370/89 [1992] ECR I-6211.
[321] Para 15. It therefore covered the European Investment Bank (on which see Arts 266–67 EC).
[322] Case C-234/02P *European Ombudsman v Lamberts* [2004] ECR I-2803.
[323] Joined Cases 63–69/72 [1973] ECR 1229, para 7.
[324] Ibid, para 8.
[325] See AG Gand in Case 9/69 *Sayag v Leduc* [1969] ECR 329, 339–40; AG Roemer in Case 5/71 *Zuckerfabrik Schöppenstedt v Council* [1971] ECR 975, 989.
[326] See Chapter 10.
[327] Joined Cases C-46/93 and C-48/93 [1996] ECR I-1029, para 42.
[328] See eg Case 4/69 *Lütticke v Commission* [1971] ECR 325; Case 5/71 *Zuckerfabrik Schöppenstedt v Council* [1971] ECR 975.

tained where its purpose is to secure exactly the same result as an action for annulment which has been found inadmissible.[329] In *Cobrecaf and Others v Commission*,[330] for example, the General Court dismissed as inadmissible both an application for annulment and a claim for damages. It found that

> the actual purpose of the applicants' alternative claim for damages is to secure payment of a sum corresponding exactly to the amount denied to it by reason of the disputed decision and that it is therefore designed to secure indirectly annulment of the individual decision rejecting the applicants' request for financial aid.

Where the applicant relies upon harm caused by by an EU official in the performance of his/her duties, the Court applies a strict, perhaps unduly strict, test. In *Sayag v Leduc*,[331] a case concerning the corresponding provision of the EURATOM Treaty,[332] the Court held that the Community was not liable for an accident caused by a servant while using his private car during the performance of his duties. According to the Court:

> Only in the case of *force majeure* or in exceptional circumstances of such overriding importance that without the servant's using private means of transport the Community would have been unable to carry out the tasks entrusted to it, could such use be considered to form part of the servant's performance of his duties.

Of much greater practical importance, and the main focus of this section, is the Union's potential liability in damages for loss caused by acts adopted by its institutions or other bodies. For these purposes, it is convenient to deal with the case law in two main phases: the 'traditional' case law, centred upon the restrictive *Schöppenstedt* formula; and the more recent case law, which is tending to align the rules relating to Union liability more closely upon those governing Member State liability.

B – 'Traditional' Case Law and the *Schöppenstedt* Formula

The older case law on the liability in damages of EU institutions drew a basic distinction between administrative measures and legislative measures.

(i) Administrative Measures

In this context, an administrative measure is an act not having general application, or a failure to adopt such an act. In such cases, it was enough for the applicant to establish illegality, damage and causation. As the General Court explained in *New Europe Consulting v Commission*: '[T]he conduct of the Community institutions in question must be unlawful; there must be real and certain damage; and a direct causal link must exist between the conduct of the institution concerned and the alleged damage.'[333] Liability can only be incurred as a result of an omission where the institution concerned had a legal obli-

---

[329] See Case 25/62 *Plaumann v Commission* [1963] ECR 95; Case 175/84 *Krohn v Commission* [1986] ECR 753.

[330] Case T-514/93 [1995] ECR II-621.

[331] Case 9/69 [1969] ECR 329.

[332] Art 188(2) Euratom.

[333] Case T-231/97 [1999] 2 CMLR 1452, para 29. See also Case C-358/90 *Compagnia Italiana Alcool v Commission* [1992] ECR I-2457, para 46; Case C-55/90 *Cato v Commission* [1992] ECR I-2533, para 18.

gation to act under a provision of EU law.[334] Thus, a failure by the Commission to bring proceedings against a Member State under Article 258 TFEU is not capable of fixing the Union with liability in damages because the Commission is not under any obligation to initiate such proceedings.[335]

The Stanley Adams saga provides a striking example of a successful damages claim arising out of both an act and an omission on the part of the Commission.[336] Stanley Adams was an employee of the Swiss pharmaceutical company, Hoffmann-La Roche. Believing that some of the company's practices were incompatible with the EU rules on competition, He alerted the Commission and supplied it with copies of a number of internal company documents. The Commission subsequently commenced an investigation into the company's activities, in the course of which it handed over to the company edited copies of some of the documents supplied by Adams. The Commission ultimately adopted a decision imposing a substantial fine on the company for breach of Article 102 TFEU.[337]

In the meantime, the company, realising the Commission must have had an informant, attempted to discover that person's identity. The company's lawyer told the Commission that it was considering taking criminal proceedings against the informant for economic espionage under the Swiss Penal Code. The company eventually succeeded in identifying Adams from the copies of its own documents which it had been handed by the Commission. Adams had by then left the company and moved to Italy, but he was arrested by the Swiss authorities as he attempted to enter Switzerland on a visit. While he was being held in custody, his wife committed suicide. He was subsequently released on bail, but was in due course found guilty of economic espionage and sentenced in his absence to a suspended term of one year's imprisonment. His conviction damaged his creditworthiness and led to the failure of a business he had established after leaving the company.

In proceedings against the Commission under the second paragraph of Article 340 TFEU,[338] the Court found that two aspects of the Commission's conduct gave rise to liability: first, the disclosure to the company of the documents which enabled Adams to be identified; secondly, the failure to warn Adams of the risk that he would be prosecuted if he returned to Switzerland, a risk of which the Commission should have been aware following its discussions with the company's lawyer. However, the Court took the view that Adams was partly to blame for his misfortunes: he had not, for example, warned the Commission that he could be identified from the documents he had supplied and he had returned to Switzerland without enquiring as to the risks involved in doing so. The Court therefore decided that responsibility for the damage he had suffered should be apportioned equally between himself and the Commission.

(ii) Legislative Measures

(a) The Schöppenstedt Formula

Legislative measures, in the sense of acts having general application, are also capable of

---

[334] See eg Case C-146/91 *KYDEP v Council and Commission* [1994] ECR I-4199, para 58.

[335] Case C-72/90 *Asia Motor France v Commission* [1990] ECR I-2181, para 13.

[336] The story is recounted by Stanley Adams in *Roche versus Adams* (1984). See also Hunnings, 'The Stanley Adams Affair or the Biter Bit' (1987) 24 *CMLRev* 65.

[337] The essence of the Commission's decision was upheld by the Court in Case 85/76 *Hoffmann-La Roche v Commission* [1979] ECR 461.

[338] Case 145/83 *Adams v Commission* [1985] ECR 3539.

giving rise to liability in damages on the part of the Union where these involved choices of economic policy; however, the Courts have traditionally applied a particularly stringent test of unlawfulness.[339] That test was laid down in *Zuckerfabrik Schöppenstedt v Council*,[340] in which the Court of Justice stated:

> Where legislative action involving measures of economic policy is concerned, the Community does not incur non-contractual liability for damage suffered by individuals as a consequence of that action . . . unless a sufficiently flagrant violation of a superior rule of law for the protection of the individual has occurred.

Since nearly all Union legislation of a type liable to give rise to a claim in damages is concerned in some way with economic policy, the test laid down in the *Schöppenstedt* case was broad in scope. It also applied in the case of an unlawful failure to adopt a legislative act.[341]

(b) Legislative Action

Applying the *Schöppenstedt* formula involved defining what exactly constituted 'legislative action'. The case law set out certain guidelines. First, the term did not cover instruments of primary EU law, such as Treaties concerning the accession of new Member States[342] or the Single European Act.[343] These are agreements concluded by the Member States, not acts of the institutions. Secondly, the General Court made it clear in *Schröder and Others v Commission*[344] that 'the concept of legislative measure within the meaning of the case-law may apply to all the measures referred to by Article [288 TFEU] and not only to regulations'. As in actions for annulment, the decisive question was not what the disputed act was called but whether it was of general application. In *Schröder* the General Court concluded that the disputed acts, even though they took the form of decisions, produced 'with regard to the applicants effects which are those of a measure of general application, in the same way as a regulation'.[345] The *Schöppenstedt* test was therefore applicable. The Court also applied that test in a claim for loss allegedly caused by a directive.[346] Conversely, the *Schöppenstedt* test did not apply where the contested act, although labelled a regulation, was not in fact a legislative measure of general application.[347] Because the action for damages and the action for annulment are independent remedies, the nature of a measure for the purposes of the former action was not affected by whether or not the applicant has standing to challenge it for the purposes of the latter action. Thus, in *Antillean Rice Mills and Others v Commission*,[348] a decision which had been found to be of direct and indi-

---

[339] See Case 50/86 *Grands Moulins de Paris v Council and Commission* [1987] ECR 4833, paras 7–8; AG van Gerven in Joined Cases C-104/89 and C-37/90 *Mulder v Council and Commission* [1992] ECR I-3061, 3103. It is not enough to establish liability that the measure in question has previously been declared void by the Court: see eg Joined Cases 83 and 94/76, 4, 15 and 40/77 *HNL v Council and Commission* [1978] ECR 1209, para 4.

[340] Case 5/71 [1971] ECR para 11.

[341] See Case T-113/96 *Dubois et Fils v Council and Commission* [1998] ECR II-125, para 60.

[342] See Joined Cases 31 and 35/86 *Laisa v Council* [1988] ECR 2285.

[343] See Case T-113/96 *Dubois et Fils v Council and Commission* [1998] ECR II-125, para 41.

[344] Case T-390/94 [1997] ECR II-501, para 54.

[345] Para 56. See also Case C-390/95 P *Antillean Rice Mills and Others v Commission* [1999] ECR I-769, para 60; Joined Cases T-481/93 and T-484/93 *Exporteurs in Levende Varkens and Others v Commission* [1995] ECR II-2941.

[346] See Case C-63/89 *Assurances du Crédit v Council and Commission* [1991] ECR I-1799.

[347] See Case C-119/88 *Aerpo and Others v Commission* [1990] ECR I-2189; Case T-472/93 *Campo Ebro and Others v Council* [1995] ECR II-421 (appeal dismissed: see Case C-138/95 P [1997] ECR I-2027).

[348] Case C-390/95 P *Antillean Rice Mills and Others v Commission* [1999] ECR I-769, para 62. See also Case C-152/88, *Sofrimport v Commission* [1990] ECR I-2477.

vidual concern to the applicants for the purposes of Article 263 TFEU was treated as a legislative measure in the context of a parallel claim for damages.

(c) A Superior Rule of Law for the Protection of Individuals

The *Schöppenstedt* formula also called for a definition of what constituted a 'superior rule of law for the protection of individuals'. Again, the case law established that this could include a provision of the Treaty, such as Article 40(2) TFEU prohibiting discrimination between producers and consumers in the Union in the context of the common organisation of agricultural markets,[349] or a provision contained in a regulation.[350] An applicant was required only to show that the rule in question was for the protection of individuals generally, not that it was for the protection of a particular class of which he/she was a member.[351] Thus, the category was held to include general principles of law, such as proportionality, equal treatment, the protection of legitimate expectations and the right to be heard. Misuse of powers by an institution was also covered.[352] However, failure to respect the institutional balance laid down in the Treaties was not sufficient to render the Union liable, since the division of powers among the institutions was not intended to protect individuals.[353]

(d) A Sufficiently Serious Breach

In order to succeed, the applicant was furthermore obliged to show that the superior rule of law in question had been breached in a manner that was sufficiently serious to fix the Union with liability. In *HNL v Council and Commission*[354] the Court of Justice said that, in a legislative field which involved the exercise of a wide discretion, such as that of the Common Agricultural Policy, non-contractual liability would not be incurred 'unless the institution concerned has manifestly and gravely disregarded the limits on the exercise of its powers'. Where the applicant was unable to show that such conduct had occurred, it was not possible to establish a sufficiently serious breach of a superior rule of law.[355] The Court went even further in *Amylum v Council and Commission*,[356] where it stated that a legal situation resulting from legislative measures involving choices of economic policy would only be sufficient to fix the Community with liability if the conduct of the institutions concerned 'was verging on the arbitrary'.

A consequence of that extremely strict test was that actions in respect of legislative measures conferring discretionary powers on the institutions have rarely been successful. The Court of Justice regarded the strictness of its approach as justified by two factors. The first was that, if liability were too easy to establish, the institutions would be unduly ham-

---

[349] See eg Joined Cases 83 and 94/76, 4, 15 and 40/77 *HNL v Council and Commission* [1978] ECR 1209, para 5; Case 238/78 *Ireks-Arkady v Council and Commission* [1979] ECR 2955, para 11.

[350] See Case 74/74 *CNTA v Commission* [1975] ECR 533; Case C-152/88 *Sofrimport v Commission* [1990] ECR I-2477.

[351] See Joined Cases 5, 7 and 13–24/66 *Kampffmeyer v Commission* [1967] ECR 245, 262–63.

[352] See Joined Cases T-481/93 and T-484/93 *Exporteurs in Levende Varkens and Others v Commission* [1995] ECR II-2941, para 102, with references to earlier case law. See also Case T-489/93 *Unifruit Hellas v Commission* [1994] ECR II-1201, para 42 (appeal dismissed: see Case C-51/95 P [1997] ECR I-727).

[353] Case C-282/90 *Vreugdenhil v Commission* [1992] ECR I-1937, paras 20–21.

[354] Joined Cases 83 and 94/76, 4, 15 and 40/77 *HNL v Council and Commission* [1978] ECR 1209, para 6.

[355] See Case C-390/95 P *Antillean Rice Mills and Others v Commission* [1999] ECR I-769, paras 64–70.

[356] Joined Cases 116 and 124/77 [1979] ECR 3497, para 19.

pered in the performance of the tasks conferred on them by the Treaty.[357] The second was that an individual who considered himself injured by a Union act which had been implemented by the national authorities could challenge the act's validity before the national courts, who could make a reference for a preliminary ruling under Article 267 TFEU. According to the Court, '[t]he existence of such an action is by itself of such a nature as to ensure the efficient protection of the individuals concerned'.[358]

C – The Case Law after *Bergaderm*

The Court's traditional case law on Union non-contractual liability attracted criticism, not only because of the restrictive nature of the *Schöppenstedt* formula, but also on other grounds. For example, it seemed odd that administrative acts could attract liability on the basis of illegality alone, without any further requirements as to fault or culpability, even where those acts might equally involve the exercise of wide discretionary powers. An EU institution might justifiably consider its ability to discharge its responsibilities in the general interest to be hampered by the prospect of wide-ranging liability, regardless of whether the act in question were considered to be administrative or legislative in nature. Furthermore, despite the Court's statement in *Brasserie du Pêcheur* and *Factortame* that the protection of the rights which individuals derive from Community law cannot vary depending on whether a national authority or an EU authority is responsible for the damage, it was evident that precisely such variations existed in the case law. In the case of Member State liability, the key factor in determining liability was the extent of the discretion involved, rather than the classification of the act as administrative or legislative in nature; the strict requirement of a 'manifest and grave disregard' of the limits of Member State powers applied to any situation in which the national authorities exercised appreciable discretion in the general interest.[359]

Perhaps in reaction to such criticisms, the Court of Justice in *Bergaderm* revised its approach to EU liability.[360] The case concerned a Commission directive amending the list of substances which, if contained in cosmetic products, would require Member States to prohibit the marketing of those products in accordance with Directive 76/768.[361] The claimant company argued that, since it was the only undertaking affected by the Commission's directive, the latter should be considered an administrative act and its illegality per se could found a damages action. However, the General Court held the act to be legislative in nature, and applied the *Schöppenstedt* formula. The company's appeal to the Court of Justice was based on, inter alia, an alleged error of law by the General Court in characterising the directive for the purposes of establishing damages liability. The Court of Justice noted that, regarding Member State liability, the right to reparation under EU law depends upon fulfilling three conditions: the rule of law infringed must be intended to confer rights on individuals; the breach must be sufficiently serious; and there must be a direct causal link between the breach and the damage sustained.[362] As to the require-

---

[357] See eg Joined Cases 83 and 94/76, 4, 15 and 40/77 *HNL v Council and Commission* [1978] ECR 1209, para 5.

[358] See Case 108/81 *Amylum v Council* [1982] ECR 3107, para 14.

[359] For full discussion, see Chapter 6.

[360] Case C-352/98P *Bergaderm* [2000] ECR I-5291.

[361] [1976] OJ L262/169.

[362] See Chapter 10.

ment of a sufficiently serious breach, liability depends on the Member State, or the Union institution, manifestly and gravely disregarding the limits of its discretion. Where the Member State or Union institution has considerably reduced, or even no, discretion, the mere infringement of EU law may be sufficient to establish the existence of a sufficiently serious breach. However, the general or individual nature of a measure adopted by the Union institution should not be a decisive factor.

It was, at first, uncertain how far the Court of Justice in *Bergaderm* had intended to revise its case law on Union liability; the judgment did not expressly reject the *Schöppenstedt* formula, no clear hint being given of a change of approach to Union liability in damages.[363] Nevertheless, subsequent cases have shown that the *Bergaderm* approach indeed represents the current law: the system of liability worked out in respect of the Member States under the *Francovich* case law (which was supposed, after all, to have been inspired by the jurisprudence relating to Articles 268 and 340 TFEU) now applies to the liability of the EU institutions themselves.[364] In some respects, this change might be seen as largely cosmetic: for example, the idea of a 'superior rule of law for the protection of the individual' will in most cases prove identical to the concept of a 'rule intended to confer rights on the individual'. But in other respects, the change is quite fundamental: in particular, the mere illegality of an administrative act will no longer suffice to establish liability, without taking into account the degree of discretion enjoyed by the institution when discharging its functions.[365]

This change of approach means that it has actually become *more* difficult for claimants to establish EU liability than under the older case law, in respect of acts which would previously have been categorised as administrative in nature. On the other hand, there were already signs in the pre-*Bergaderm* case law of a modest relaxation of the 'manifest and grave' test regarding unlawful legislative (discretionary) acts. For example, in *Commission v Stahlwerke Peine-Salzgitter*[366] the Court acknowledged that it was not necessary to establish 'conduct verging on the arbitrary' where liability for unlawful legislative acts was in issue. Similarly, in *Mulder v Council and Commission (Mulder II)*[367] the Court upheld claims arising out of unlawful legislative acts even though the consequence was to expose the Community to liability to large numbers of other claimants in a position similar to that of the applicants.[368] That case is particularly striking because it arose within the framework of the Common Agricultural Policy, where the institutions enjoy wide discretionary powers.

A recent illustration of a (partially) successful damages claim, in a case that would

---

[363] Consider also post-*Bergaderm* rulings such as Case T-178/98 *Fresh Marine v Commission* [2000] ECR II-3331.

[364] eg Joined Cases T-198/95, T-171/96, T-230/97, T-174/98 and T-225/99 *Comafrica v Commission* [2001] ECR II-1975; Case T-159/99 *Dieckmann & Hansen v Commission* [2001] ECR II-3143; Case C-472/00 P *Commission v Fresh Marine* [2003] ECR I-7541; Case T-166/98 *Dolianova* [2004] ECR II-3991; Case T-139/01 *Comafrica v Commission* [2005] ECR II-409; Case C-198/03 P *Commission v CEVA Santé Animale* [2005] ECR I-6257; Case T-415/03 *Cofradía de pescadores de 'San Pedro' de Bermeo v Council* [2005] ECR II-4355. For a clear example of case law on Member State liability being cited to illuminate the system of EU liability, see Case T-364/03 *Medici Grimm v Council* [2006] ECR II-79.

[365] eg Case C-312/00 P *Commission v Camar* [2002] ECR I-11355.

[366] Case C-220/91 P [1993] ECR I-2393, para 51.

[367] Joined Cases C-104/89 and C-37/90 [1992] ECR I-3061. See also Case C-152/88 *Sofrimport v Commission* [1990] ECR I-2477.

[368] Because of the number of those affected by the Court's judgment, the Council adopted a regulation to facilitate the settlement of claims: see Reg 2187/93 providing for an offer of compensation to certain producers of milk and milk products temporarily prevented from carrying on their trade [1993] OJ L196/6.

previously have fallen into the 'administrative' category, is *Schneider v Commission*.[369] The Court of Justice upheld the finding by the General Court[370] that a procedural defect in a competition matter, involving the infringement by the Commission of the rights of the defence, constituted a sufficiently serious breach of a rule intended for the protection of individuals. The first-instance judgment was overturned, however, on certain issues going to the existence of a direct causal link between the illegality and the damage suffered.

Under the laws of some Member States, the administration may incur liability in damages for loss caused by acts which are lawful. The idea, enshrined in the French doctrine of *égalité devant les charges publiques* and the German doctrine of *Sonderopfer*, is that it is unfair to make a limited group of individuals bear the financial burden of measures taken in the general interest.[371] In the previous edition of this book we noted the development of case law in the General Court recognising that non-contractual liability might exceptionally be incurred by the EU institutions, where undertakings were forced to bear a disproportionate burden resulting from *lawful* Union action.[372] That development has, however, been cut off by the Court of Justice, which has reaffirmed that the unlawfulness of the act leading to the damage complained of is a condition of liability pursuant to Articles 268 and 340(2) TFEU.[373]

At the same time, and perhaps not entirely consistently, the Court of Justice has held in *Masdar v Commission* that those provisions can be invoked as the basis for a claim of unjust enrichment, even though such claims do not require proof of unlawful conduct. [374] In the Court's own words, an unjust enrichment claim requires 'merely proof of enrichment on the part of the defendant for which there is no valid legal basis and of impoverishment on the part of the applicant which is linked to that enrichment'.[375] To deny a remedy based upon Articles 268 and 340(2) TFEU in cases of unjust enrichment would, the Court said, be contrary to the principle of effective judicial protection laid down in the case law and confirmed by Article 47 of the Charter of Fundamental Rights.[376] The Court noted that unjust enrichment was 'a source of non-contractual obligation common to the legal systems of the Member States'; [377] that could perhaps provide a point of distinction from liability for exceptional damage caused by lawful acts, which is recognised by only some of them. The proceedings in the *Masdar* case were brought by a company that had failed to obtain payment for work done under a contract with another company, but within the framework of the Union's TACIS Programme of assistance to former member countries of the Soviet Union. The action against the Commission was based on the premise that the Union had received the benefit of services rendered at the applicant's expense. It was dismissed by the Court of Justice, on appeal from the General Court where it had similarly failed, on the ground that the dispute was about obligations

---

[369] Case C-440/07P [2009] ECR I-6413.

[370] See Case T-351/03 [2007] ECR II-2257.

[371] See Bronkhorst, 'The valid legislative act as a cause of liability of the Communities' in Heukels and McDonnell (eds), above n 320, 156.

[372] See, in particular, Case T-184/95 *Dorsch Consult v Council and Commission* [1998] ECR II-667; Joined Cases T-69/00, T-151/00, T-301/00, T-320/00, T-383/00 and T-135/01 *FIAMM v Council and Commission* [2005] ECR II-5393.

[373] Joined Cases C-120 and C-121/06P *FIAMM v Council and Commission* [2008] ECR I-6513.

[374] Case C-47/07 P [2008] ECR I-9761, paras 46–50. See also Case C-470/08 *van Dijk*, Judgment of 21 January 2010.

[375] Case 47/07 P, para 46.

[376] Para 50.

[377] Para 47.

allegedly arising under a contract, and could not therefore be pursued by way of a non-contractual remedy.

D – Concurrent Liability of the Union and the Member States

Under the system established by the Treaties, it is common for EU legislation to require implementation by the authorities of the Member States. If a person suffers damage as a result of such implementation, the question may arise whether he should commence proceedings against the competent national authorities in the national courts (which might have to ask the Court of Justice for a preliminary ruling), or against the Union under Articles 268 and 340(2). It has been persuasively argued[378] that a claimant should in these circumstances have the right to choose whether to bring proceedings in the national courts or the Union Courts, but that solution would involve a departure from the case law.

The Court has held that, in some cases, actions for damages against the Union will only be admissible if the applicant has exhausted any cause of action he might have against the national authorities in the domestic forum.[379] It seems that such a cause of action must be pursued first where the actions of the national authorities, although based on EU legislation, are a more direct cause of the damage suffered by the applicant.[380] However, where the conduct in question is in fact the responsibility of an EU institution (eg where the national body was acting under its instructions), it is the Union Courts that have jurisdiction.[381] In any event, it is not necessary to exhaust any national rights of action that may be available where they are not capable of providing an effective means of protection for the applicant and compensating him for the damage he claims to have suffered.[382]

E – Damage and Causation

In proceedings under Articles 268 and 340(2) TFEU, an applicant may in principle recover actual financial loss[383] as well as loss of profits.[384] In order to succeed, the applicant must either quantify the loss which it claims to have suffered or point to evidence on the basis of which its nature and extent can be assessed.[385] It is also possible to recover damages for non-material injury, such as the effect on the applicant's integrity and reputation of defamatory remarks made by the defendant.[386] In staff cases, small amounts have been awarded for shock, disturbance and uneasiness.[387] Moreover, the Court has acknowledged that it may be asked 'to declare the Community liable for imminent damage foreseeable

---

[378] See Wils, 'Concurrent liability of the Community and a Member State' (1992) 17 *ELRev* 191, 204–06.

[379] See eg Case 175/84 *Krohn v Commission* [1986] ECR 753, para 27 .

[380] See eg Case 133/79 *Sucrimex v Commission* [1980] ECR 1299; Case C-282/90 *Vreugdenhil v Commission* [1992] ECR I-1937; Case T-91/05 *Sinara Handel v Commission* [2007] ECR II-245.

[381] See eg Case 175/84 *Krohn v Commission* [1986] ECR 753.

[382] Ibid, para 27; Case 20/88 *Roquette Frères v Commission* [1989] ECR 1553, para 15.

[383] See Joined Cases 5, 7 and 13–24/66 *Kampffmeyer v Commission* [1967] ECR 245; Case 74/74 *CNTA v Commission* [1975] ECR 533.

[384] See eg Joined Cases 5, 7 and 13–24/66 *Kampffmeyer v Commission* [1967] ECR 245. cf Joined Cases 54–60/76 *Compagnie Industrielle du Comité de Loheac v Council and Commission* [1977] ECR 645.

[385] See Case T-277/97 *Ismeri Europa Srl v Court of Auditors* [1999] ECR II-1825, para 67.

[386] See eg Case T-277/97 *Ismeri Europa Srl v Court of Auditors* [1999] ECR II-1825, paras 80–94.

[387] See eg Joined Cases 7/56 and 3–7/57 *Algera v Common Assembly* [1957 and 1958] ECR 39, 66–67.

with sufficient certainty even if the damage cannot yet be precisely assessed'.[388] However, the applicant must take steps to mitigate any damage[389] and will not be able to recover compensation where he could have passed the loss on to his customers.[390] The applicant must also show that the damage he has suffered 'exceeds the limits of the economic risks inherent in operating in the sector concerned'.[391]

Where a claim under Articles 268 and 340 TFEU is successful, the Court does not normally make a specific award of damages. Instead, the judgment will usually establish the acts or omissions giving rise to liability and, if appropriate, make an award of interest. It will then order the parties to attempt to reach an agreement, within a specified period, on the amount of compensation payable. The judgment will require the parties to transmit to the Court a statement of their views, with supporting figures, in case agreement cannot be reached.[392]

The Court has said that Article 340(2) TFEU does not require the Union 'to make good every harmful consequence, even a remote one, of unlawful legislation'.[393] The applicant must therefore establish that the damage is a 'sufficiently direct consequence of the unlawful conduct'.[394] In *Compagnia Italiana Alcool v Commission*[395] the Court said that there was no causal link between the damage allegedly suffered by the applicant and a deficiency in the statement of reasons contained in a Commission decision. As the Court explained, '[i]f that deficiency had not existed, the damage allegedly suffered by [the applicant] would have been the same'. The chain of causation may be broken by, for example, the actions of national authorities or by the behaviour of the applicant himself. In this respect, traders are expected to behave in a prudent manner and to apprise themselves of the conditions on the markets in which they operate. If they fall short of this standard, the Community will not be held responsible for any loss that ensues.[396]

F – Limitation

Unlike Articles 263 and 265 TFEU, Articles 268 and 340 TFEU do not specify any time limit within which the action for which they provide must be brought. However, Article 43 of the Statute of the Court of Justice provides that 'proceedings against the Union in matters arising from non-contractual liability "shall be barred after a period of five years

---

[388] Joined Cases 56–60/74 *Kampffmeyer v Commission and Council* [1976] ECR 711, para 6. *cf* Case T-230/95 *BAI v Commission* [1999] ECR II-123.

[389] See Case 120/83 R *Raznoimport v Commission* [1983] ECR 2573, para 14.

[390] See Joined Cases 64 and 113/76, 167 and 239/78, 27, 28 and 45/79 *Dumortier Frères v Council* [1979] ECR 3091, para 15; Case 238/78 *Ireks-Arkady v Council and Commission* [1979] ECR 2955, para 14; Joined Cases 241, 242 and 245 to 250/78 *DGV v Council and Commission* [1979] ECR 3017, para 15; Joined Cases 261 and 262/78 *Interquell Stärke v Council and Commission* [1979] ECR 3045, para 17 (the so-called *Gritz and Quellmehl* cases, after the products with which they were concerned). See Rudden and Bishop, 'Gritz and Quellmehl: Pass It On' (1981) 6 *ELRev* 243.

[391] Case 59/83 *Biovilac v EEC* [1984] ECR 4057, para 28.

[392] See eg the *Gritz and Quellmehl* cases, above; Case 145/83 *Adams v Commission* [1985] ECR 3539. *cf* Case C-308/87 *Grifoni v EAEC* [1994] ECR I-341, where the parties were unable to reach agreement and the Court had to quantify the precise amount of compensation to which the applicant was entitled.

[393] Joined Cases 64 and 113/76, 167 and 239/78, 27, 28 and 45/79 *Dumortier Frères v Council* [1979] ECR 3091, para 21.

[394] Ibid.

[395] Case C-358/90 [1992] ECR I-2457, para 47.

[396] See Case 169/73 *Compagnie Continentale v Council* [1975] ECR 117, paras 22–32; Case 26/81 *Oleifici Mediterranei v EEC* [1982] ECR 3057, paras 22–24.

from the occurrence of the event giving rise thereto'". The running of time is suspended if the aggrieved party brings proceedings for annulment or failure to act against the institution concerned.[397] The limitation period does not start to run 'before all the requirements governing an obligation to provide compensation for damage are satisfied and in particular before the damage to be made good has materialized'.[398] Thus where the liability of the Union derives from a legislative measure, the limitation period does not begin 'before the injurious effects of that measure have been produced'.[399] Where the cause of the damage suffered by the applicant is an administrative act or omission, the limitation period does not start to run until the person concerned becomes aware of it.[400]

V – THE PLEA OF ILLEGALITY AND NON-EXISTENCE OF AN ACT

Article 277 TFEU provides:

> Notwithstanding the expiry of the period laid down in Article 263, sixth paragraph, any party may, in proceedings in which an act of general application adopted by an institution, body, office or agency of the Union is at issue, plead the grounds specified in Article 263, second paragraph, in order to invoke before the Court of Justice of the European Union the inapplicability of that act.

Article 277 TFEU allows the illegality of an act to be pleaded indirectly in proceedings which are pending before the Union Courts under some other provision.[401] In particular, it mitigates to some extent the strict time limits and rules on standing laid down in Article 263 TFEU. Where, for instance, a natural or legal person seeks the annulment of a decision addressed to that person, which is based on a regulation, the validity of that latter may be put in question, even though the applicant would not have been able to seek its annulment directly under Article 263. The General Court has explained that

> [s]ince the legality of the individual measure contested must be assessed on the basis of the elements of fact and of law existing at the time when the measure was adopted . . . the legality of the legislative measure which forms its legal basis must also be assessed at that time rather than at the time of its own adoption.[402]

The plea of illegality, therefore, represents a compromise between the principle of legal certainty, which would rule out a challenge to a Community act once the deadline laid down in Article 263(6) had expired, and the principle of legality, which would preclude reliance on unlawful acts. It is important to emphasise, however, that Article 277 TFEU does not give rise to a separate remedy. As the General Court explained in *CSF and CSME v Commission*:

---

[397] See Joined Cases 5, 7 and 13–24/66 *Kampffmeyer v Commission* [1967] ECR 245, 260.
[398] Joined Cases 256, 257 and 267/80 and 5/81 *Birra Wührer v Council and Commission* [1982] ECR 85, para 10; Case 51/81 *De Franceschi v Council and Commission* [1982] ECR 117, para 10.
[399] Ibid.
[400] See Case 145/83 *Adams v Commission* [1985] ECR 3539, paras 50–51.
[401] See Joined Cases 31 and 33/62 *Wöhrmann v Commission* [1962] ECR 501.
[402] Joined Cases T-177/94 and T-377/94 *Altmann and Others v Commission* [1996] ECR II-2041, para 119.

The possibility afforded by Article [277 TFEU] of pleading the inapplicability of a measure of general application forming the legal basis of the contested decision does not constitute an independent right of action and recourse may be had to it only as an incidental plea. More specifically, Article [277 TFEU] may not be invoked in the absence of an independent right of action.[403]

Since the Article applies only in proceedings before the Union courts,[404] it does not affect the circumstances in which the validity of EU acts may be contested in the national courts. It seems, however, that a declaration of inapplicability made by the Court of Justice under Article 277 in a previous case would enable a national court to treat the act in question as invalid without referring the matter to the Court of Justice under Article 267 TFEU.[405]

Like Articles 263 and 265 TFEU, Article 277 has been amended by the TL so as make explicitly clear that it applies to measures adopted by all the institutions of the Union, as well as its 'bodies, offices and agencies'. Another amendment is the substitution of the term 'act of general application' for the term 'regulation', which was found in previous versions. This reflects long-standing case law. In *Simmenthal v Commission* the Court of Justice concluded that Article 277 extended to

> acts of the institutions which, although they are not in the form of a regulation, nevertheless produce similar effects and on those grounds may not be challenged under Article [263 TFEU] by natural or legal persons other than Community institutions and Member States.[406]

It seems to follow from *Simmenthal* that the plea of illegality may be invoked in relation to any act producing legal effects which natural and legal persons are unable to challenge directly under Article 263, for example, a decision addressed to a third party, which is not of direct and individual concern to the applicant. Conversely, in *TWD Textilwerke Deggendorf*[407] it was held that the validity of an EU act may not be challenged in a national court by an applicant who would undoubtedly have had standing to contest its validity in a direct action under Article 263 but who failed to do so in time. In *TWD v Commission*[408] the CFI said that, as a result,

> [t]he objection of illegality provided for by Article [241] of the Treaty cannot be raised by a legal or natural person who could have brought proceedings under the second paragraph of Article [263 TFEU] but who did not do so within the period prescribed therein.

According to its express terms, the plea of illegality may be invoked by 'any party', an expression which is clearly broad enough to cover Member States, notwithstanding their privileged status for the purpose of annulment proceedings. The case law suggests that a Member State may challenge the validity of a regulation indirectly in proceedings under both Articles 263[409] and 258 TFEU.[410] The rationale seems to be that 'defects appertaining to a general regulation often do not clearly emerge until the regulation is applied to

---

[403] Case T-154/94 [1996] ECR II-1377, para 16.
[404] See Joined Cases 31 and 33/62 *Wöhrmann v Commission* [1962] ECR 501, 507.
[405] See Case 314/85 *Foto-Frost v Hauptzollamt Lübeck-Ost* [1987] ECR 4199, para 16, where the Court refers to Art 241 ECR. The *Foto-Frost* case is discussed in Chapter 7.
[406] Case 92/78 [1979] ECR 777, para 40.
[407] Case C-188/92 [1994] ECR I-833. Also eg Case C-178/95 *Wiljo* [1997] ECR I-585; Case C-239/99 *Nachi Europe* [2001] ECR I-1197. See further Chapter 14.
[408] Joined Cases T-244/93 and T-486/93 [1995] ECR II-2265, para 103 (appeal dismissed: see Case C-355/95 P [1997] ECR I-2549).
[409] See Case 32/65 *Italy v Council and Commission* [1966] ECR 389.
[410] See Case 116/82 *Commission v Germany* [1986] ECR 2519.

a particular case'.[411] That rationale does not apply to acts addressed to a Member State and it is well established that a Member State may not challenge the validity of a decision addressed to it once the deadline laid down in Article 263 TFEU has expired.[412] It appears that other privileged applicants (including the Council, Commission and European Parliament) are in the same position, mututis mutandis, as the Member States. This is supported by the ruling in *Commission v European Central Bank*.[413] There, the ECB sought to rely on Article 277 TFEU so as to invoke the illegality of an anti-fraud regulation adopted by the Parliament and Council, within the context of an action for annulment brought by the Commission against an ECB act which was alleged to contravene that regulation. The Commission argued that the ECB should be prevented from relying on Article 277, since it had failed to challenge the regulation under Article 263 TFEU within the two-month time limit. The Court of Justice agreed that a regulation may become definitive as against any party as regards whom it must be considered an individual decision, where that party could have sought annulment of the regulation under Article 263; but here the disputed regulation was clearly of a legislative nature and could not be treated as a decision, or in any event, not as a decision of which the ECB was an addressee, so the plea of illegality under Article 241 EC was admissible.

When a plea of illegality is successful, the Court does not formally annul the measure in question, but simply declares it inapplicable. This has the effect of depriving any act adopted under it of its legal basis. Nevertheless, although the Court's ruling in relation to the first measure is technically limited to the case in which it is made, it is tantamount in practical terms to a declaration of invalidity, for the institutions will immediately cease to apply the measure and the Union Courts will thenceforth treat it as invalid.

In a case where the plea of illegality cannot be invoked, and the deadline for bringing annulment proceedings has expired, a party may nevertheless argue that an act, regardless of its nature, is vitiated by such fundamental defects that it should be considered non-existent[414] and thus incapable of producing any legal effects at all.[415] This test is extremely difficult to satisfy, as the judgment of the Court of Justice in *Commission v BASF and Others*[416] makes clear. That case was an appeal by the Commission against a ruling of the General Court[417] that a Commission Decision on the application of the Treaty competition rules was 'vitiated by particularly serious and manifest defects' and was to be considered non-existent. The General Court had taken the view that the defects in question made it impossible to be certain of the exact date on which the contested measure took effect, the precise terms of the statement of reasons it was required by the Treaty to contain, the extent of the obligations it imposed on its addressees, and the identity of

---

[411]   See AG Roemer in Case 32/65 *Italy v Council and Commission* [1966] ECR 389, 414.

[412]   See eg Case 156/77 *Commission v Belgium* [1978] ECR 1881; Case C-183/91 *Commission v Greece* [1993] ECR I-3131. cp Case C-241/01 *National Farmers' Union* [2002] ECR I-9079: a Member State is precluded from pleading before the national courts the illegality of a Community measure of which it is an addressee, once the time limit for bringing an action for annulment has expired.

[413]   Case C-11/00 *Commission v European Central Bank* [2003] ECR I-7147.

[414]   Case 226/87 *Commission v Greece* [1988] ECR 3611, para 16.

[415]   See Case 15/85 *Consorzio Cooperative d'Abruzzo v Commission* [1987] ECR 1005, para 10.

[416]   Case C-137/92 P [1994] ECR I-2555. See also Case C-199/92 P *Hüls v Commission* [1999] ECR I-4287; Case C-227/92 P *Hoechst v Commission* [1999] ECR I-4443; Case C-234/92 P *Shell International Chemical Company v Commission* [1999] ECR I-4501; Case C-235/92 P *Montecatini v Commission* [1999] ECR I-4539; Case C-245/92 P *Chemie Linz v Commission* [1999] ECR I-4643.

[417]   Joined Cases T-79/89 etc, *BASF and Others v Commission* [1992] ECR II-315.

those addressees or that of the authority which issued the definitive version of the act. The Court of Justice took a more lenient approach, observing:

> It should be remembered that acts of the Community institutions are in principle presumed to be lawful and accordingly produce legal effects, even if they are tainted by irregularities, until such time as they are annulled or withdrawn.
>
> However, by way of exception to that principle, acts tainted by an irregularity whose gravity is so obvious that it cannot be tolerated by the Community legal order must be treated as having no legal effect, even provisional, that is to say that they must be regarded as legally non-existent. The purpose of this exception is to maintain a balance between two fundamental, but sometimes conflicting, requirements with which a legal order must comply, namely stability of legal relations and respect for legality.
>
> From the gravity of the consequences attaching to a finding that an act of a Community institution is non-existent it is self-evident that, for reasons of legal certainty, such a finding is reserved for quite extreme situations.[418]

The Court of Justice concluded that the irregularities identified by the General Court were not serious enough to render the disputed Decision non-existent, although it went on to annul the Decision. Unlike the ruling of the General Court, the judgment of the Court of Justice, therefore, had no implications for the validity of earlier decisions suffering from similar defects, in respect of which any challenge under Article 263 TFEU would by then have been out of time.

VI – INTERIM MEASURES

There are two rather meagre provisions of the TFEU relating to interlocutory relief in direct actions before the Union Courts.

Article 278 TFEU provides:

> Actions brought before the Court of Justice of the European Union shall not have suspensory effect. The Court may, however, if it considers that circumstances so require, order that application of the contested act be suspended.

Article 279 TFEU provides:

> The Court of Justice of the European Union may in any case before it prescribe interim measures.

Those provisions are amplified by the Rules of Procedure of the Court of Justice.[419] Interim measures must be accessory to 'main' proceedings: an application pursuant to Article 278 TFEU to suspend the operation of a measure adopted by an institution is admissible only if the applicant is challenging that measure in proceedings before the Court; similarly, an application for the adoption of any other interim measure pursuant to Article 279 TFEU is admissible only if made by a party to a case before the Court and relating to that case.[420] The prescribed contents of the application identifies the elements of which the Court must be satisfied: the application must state the subject-matter of the proceedings, the cir-

---

[418] See paras 48–50 of the Judgment.
[419] See Rules, Arts 83–92. Corresponding provisions relating to proceedings before the General Court are found in its Rules, Arts 104–10.
[420] Rules, Art 83(1).

cumstances giving rise to urgency and the pleas of fact or law establishing a prima facie case for the interim measures that are being sought.[421] The President of the Court may decide upon the application him/herself or refer it to the Court.[422] The decision on the applications takes the form of a reasoned order, the enforcement of which may be made conditional upon the lodging by the applicant of security.[423]

Urgency is assessed 'in the light of the extent to which an interim order is necessary in order to avoid serious and irreparable damage to the party requesting the interim measure'.[424] It was found to be present in *Sofrimport*, where there was a risk that, without interim relief, the applicant might be faced with going out of business.[425] Damage of a purely pecuniary nature will only exceptionally be found to be irreparable.[426]

Interim relief can be obtained not only where a measure adopted by an EU institution is being challenged but also in connection with infringement proceedings brought against a Member State.[427] In the latter instance, the stage of referral to the Court of Justice must have been reached, owing to the rule that measures can be sought under Article 279 TFEU only in respect of pending proceedings (although both applications may be made simultaneously).[428] Interim measures are not available in proceedings against a Member State for failure to take the steps necessary to comply with a previous ruling of the Court under Article 258 TFEU, where the measures sought would merely repeat the substance of the earlier ruling.[429]

In *Commission v France*[430] the Commission brought proceedings against France for failing to comply with two decisions requiring it to allow some beef and beef products to be imported from the UK. The Commission had required France to reply to the letter of formal notice and the reasoned opinion within short time limits but had not applied to the Court for interim relief. It was argued that this amounted to an abuse of process because it put pressure on the French government without observing the procedural and substantive conditions governing proceedings for interim relief. The Court found that, having regard to the circumstances of the case, the time limits set by the Commission for replying to the letter of formal notice and the reasoned opinion were not unreasonable. The Commission had chosen the proceedings specifically envisaged by the Treaty for cases where it considered that a Member State had infringed the Treaty. The Treaty did not require the Commission to apply for interim relief in a case such as this.

---

[421] Rules, Art 83(2).
[422] Rules, Art 85.
[423] Rules, Art 86.
[424] Case C-152/88 R *Sofrimport v Commission* [1988] ECR 2931, para 26.
[425] Ibid, para 32.
[426] Case C-471/00 P(R) *Commission v Cambridge Healthcare Supplies* [2001] ECR I-2865.
[427] See Case 61/77 R *Commission v Ireland* [1977] ECR 937 and 1411 (note in particular the remarks of AG Reischl at 953–54); Case 246/89 R *Commission v United Kingdom* [1989] ECR 3125; Case C-195/90 R *Commission v Germany* [1990] ECR I-3351.
[428] See eg Case 246/89 R *Commission v United Kingdom* [1989] ECR 3125.
[429] Joined Cases 24 and 97/80 R *Commission v France* [1980] ECR 1319.
[430] Case C-1/00 [2001] ECR I-9989.

VII – CONCLUDING REMARKS

The different forms of direct action that have been discussed in this chapter enable remedies to be sought in the Union Courts. The legal wrongs the remedies are designed to put right are broadly of two kinds—those committed by Member States and those committed by the institutions, bodies, offices and agencies of the Union. Infringement actions provide one means of recalling to order the Member States, who are the mightiest subjects of EU law, when they break its rules. This is the principal weapon of the Commission in its role as guardian of the Treaties; and we have seen what a surprisingly effective weapon it has proved, and how it has been strengthened by the establishment of a system of financial sanctions for failure to comply with Court rulings, which has been further streamlined by the TL. Actions for annulment, for a failure to act and for damages are remedies of an administrative law nature. They are designed to ensure that EU law is observed by the institutions and other bodies entrusted with exercising the far-reaching powers that have been conferred upon the Union by the Treaties. Developments in the case law have been inspired by the principle of effective judicial protection against the wrongful acts or omissions of Union authorities, understood by the Union Courts as calling for the completion of the system of remedies, in respects where this has seemed deficient; and such developments have often been later enshrined in a Treaty provision, as successive changes to the text of Article 263 TFEU bear witness. Hence the disappointment of some commentators that the strict conditions of locus standi under that Article for private parties wishing to bring an action for annulment (and, therefore, also an action for failure to act) have not been relaxed by creative judicial interpretation. The revision of the language of Article 263(4) by the TL is the largest step towards relaxation that has so far been taken, though for the time being its precise scope and effect remain uncertain.

Whilst not wishing in any way to cast doubt on the importance of the direct actions available before the Union Courts, it must be stressed that they represent only half of the story of judicial protection in the European Union. The other half of that story is about the day-to-day application by courts in the Member States of rules that are derived directly or indirectly from EU law, and the enforcement of the rights to which they give rise, both as between private individuals and between individuals and their national authorities. The involvement of the Court of Justice in this process, as the source of authoritative guidance on the interpretation of the Treaties and the interpretation and validity of EU acts, is the subject of our next chapter.

Further Reading

Infringement proceedings against Member States

Dashwood and White, 'Enforcement Actions under Articles 169 and 170 EEC' (1989) 14 *ELRev* 388.

Evans, 'The Enforcement Procedure of Article 169 EEC: Commission Discretion' (1979) 4 *ELRev* 442.

Everling, 'The Member States of the European Community before their Court of Justice' (1984) 9 *ELRev* 215.

Kilbey, 'The Interpretation of Article 260 TFEU (ex Article 228 EC)' (2010) 35 *ELRev* 370.

Rawlings, 'Engaged Elites: Citizen Action and Institutional Attitudes in Commission Enforcement' (2000) 6 *ELJ* 4.

Snyder, 'The Effectiveness of European Community Law: Institutions, Processes, Tools and Techniques' (1993) 56 *MLR* 19.

Theodossiou, 'An Analysis of the Recent Response of the Community to Non-compliance with Court of justice Judgments: Article 228(2) EC' (2002) 27 *ELRev* 25.

Wennerås, 'A New Dawn for Commission Enforcement Under Articles 226 and 228 EC: General and Persistent (GAP) Infringements, Lump Sums and Penalty Payments' (2006) 43 *CML Rev* 31.

The action for annulment

Albors Llorens, *Private Parties in European Community Law: Challenging Community Measures* (Oxford, Clarendon Press, 1996).

——, 'The Standing of Private Parties to Challenge Community Measures: Has the European Court Missed the Boat?' [2003] *CLJ* 72.

Arnull, 'Private Applicants and the Action for Annulment Since *Codorniu*' (2001) 38 *CMLRev* 7.

Barents, 'The Court of Justice after the Treaty of Lisbon', (2010) 47 *CMLRev* 709.

Gormley, 'Judicial Review in EC and EU Law–Some Architectural Malfunctions and Design Improvements?' (2001) 4 *Cambridge Yearbook of European Legal Studies* 167.

Greaves, 'Locus Standi under Article 173 EEC when Seeking Annulment of a Regulation' (1986) 11 *ELRev* 119.

Joliet, 'The Reimbursement of Election Expenses: A Forgotten Dispute' (1994) 19 *ELRev* 243.

Lenaerts and Corthaut, 'Judicial Review as a Contribution to the Development of European Constitutionalism' (2003) 22 *YEL* 1.

Lenaerts and Vanhamme, 'Procedural Rights of Private Parties in the Community Administrative Process' (1997) 34 *CMLRev* 531.

Maselis and Gilliams, 'Rights of Complainants in Community Law' (1997) 22 *ELRev* 103.

Neuwahl, 'Article 173, Paragraph 4 EC: Past, Present and Possible Future' (1996) 21 *ELRev* 17.

Stein and Vining, 'Citizen Access to Judicial Review of Administrative Action in a Transnational and Federal Context' (1976) 70 *AJIL* 219.

Usher, 'Judicial Review of Community Acts and the Private Litigant' in Campbell and Voyatzi (eds), *Legal Reasoning and Judicial Interpretation of Community Law* (1996).

——, 'Direct and Individual Concern—An Effective Remedy or a Conventional Solution?' (2003) 28 *ELRev* 575.

Van Nuffel, 'What's in a Member State? Central and decentralized authorities before the Community Courts' (2001) 38 CMLRev 871

Ward, *Judicial Review and the Rights of Private Parties in EC Law* (Oxford, Oxford University Press, 2000).

——, 'Judicial Architecture at the Cross-roads—Private Parties and Challenge to EC Measures Post-Jégo-Quéré' (2001) 4 *Cambridge Yearbook of European Legal Studies* 413.

——, '*Locus standi* under Article 230(4) of the EC Treaty: Crafting a Coherent Test for a "Wobbly Polity"(2003) 22 *YEL* 45.

Other direct actions and the plea of illegality

Barav, 'The Exception of Illegality in Community Law: A Critical Analysis' (1974) 11 *CMLRev* 366.

Due, 'Legal Remedies for the Failure of European Community Institutions to Act in Conformity with EEC Treaty Provisions' (1990–91) 14 *Fordham International Law Journal* 341.

Heukels and McDonnell (eds), *The Action for Damages in Community Law* (1997).

Hilson, 'The Role of Discretion in EC Law on Non-Contractual Liability' (2005) 42 *CMLRev* 677.

Hunnings, 'The Stanley Adams Affair or the Biter Bit' (1987) 24 *CMLRev* 65.

Odudu, Annotation of *Commission v European Central Bank* (2004) *41 CMLRev* 1073.

Tridimas, 'Liability for Breach of Community Law: Growing Up and Mellowing Down?' (2001) 38 *CMLRev* 301.

Vogt, 'Indirect Judicial Protection in EU Law: The Case of the Plea of Illegality' (2006) 31 *ELRev* (forthcoming)

Wils, 'Concurrent Liability of the Community and a Member State' (1992) 17 *ELRev* 191.

7

References for Preliminary Rulings

This chapter considers the jurisdiction of the Court of Justice to render preliminary rulings under Article 267 TFEU. References for preliminary rulings are the means by which national judges are able to obtain guidance from the Court as to the correct interpretation of provisions of EU law, and the validity of acts of the institutions, bodies, offices or agencies of the Union, which they are called upon to apply within their domestic legal orders. Such references not only account for a substantial proportion of the Court's workload; they have also provided the Court with the opportunity to develop many of the fundamental principles of Community law (including direct effect and the primacy of EU law). Particular attention will be paid to the situations in which national courts have a discretion whether to make a reference, as distinct from those where there is a positive obligation upon them to do so. The latter class of case includes the use of Article 267 TFEU, not as a means to of better understanding an EU measure, but to challenge its validity; in this way, as noted in Chapter 6, the preliminary rulings procedure complements the direct action for annulment.

I – GENERAL ISSUES

As we noted at the end of Chapter 6, much of the responsibility for applying the rules laid down by the Treaties and in acts of the Union legislator lies with the national courts of the Member States. This would be problematic if it led to courts in different Member States interpreting the same set of rules in different ways. To help safeguard the uniform application of EU law, Article 267 TFEU lays down a procedure that enables, and in some circumstances requires, national courts to make a reference to the Court of Justice for a preliminary ruling on a question of EU law they are called upon to decide before giving judgment.

A reference to the Court of Justice under Article 267 TFEU may in principle be made at any stage in the proceedings pending before the national court. The ruling of the Court is interlocutory in that it constitutes a step in the proceedings before the national court, which must apply it to the facts of the case, and so reach a decision on the merits. It is in this sense that the ruling of the Court of Justice is 'preliminary'. As will be discussed below, the relationship between the referring court and the Court of Justice is not a hierarchical one. References for preliminary rulings are not a form of appeals procedure but an exercise in collaboration between courts to co-ordinate legal orders, to ensure the uniform application of a body of rules that are common to them.

It is hard to exaggerate the importance of this procedure in the development of the EU legal order. Courts can evidently only decide issues that are raised by cases before them. The reference procedure has brought before the Court of Justice a host of issues that it might not otherwise have had an opportunity to consider, and has enabled the Court to influence directly the application of EU law in the Member States. The Court has described the procedure as

> the veritable cornerstone of the operation of the internal market, since it plays a fundamental role in ensuring that the law established by the Treaties retains its Community character with a view to guaranteeing that the law has the same effect in all circumstances in all the Member States of the European Union.[1]

There is quite a wide variation in the number of references for preliminary rulings that come to the Court of Justice from different Member States. Once allowance has been made for length of membership, this would seem to be due, mainly if not exclusively, to differences between Member States in terms of the volume of economic activity in areas that are subject to EU law.[2]

Pursuant to Article 256(3) TFEU, the General Court could be given jurisdiction to hear and determine questions referred for a preliminary ruling 'in specific areas laid down by the Statute'. However, the opportunity offered by the TL to amend the Statute in this respect has not been taken.[3] For the time being, therefore, references for a preliminary ruling still go exclusively to the Court of Justice.

Article 267 TFEU provides:

> The Court of Justice of the European Union shall have jurisdiction to give preliminary rulings concerning:
>
> (a) the interpretation of the Treaties;
> (b) the validity and interpretation of acts of the institutions, bodies, offices and agencies of the Union;
>
> Where such a question is raised before any court or tribunal of a Member State, that court or tribunal may, if it considers that a decision on the question is necessary to enable it to give judgment, request the Court of Justice to give a ruling thereon.
>
> Where any such question is raised in a case pending before a court or tribunal of a Member State against whose decisions there is no judicial remedy under national law, that court or tribunal shall bring the matter before the Court.
>
> If such a question is raised in a case pending before a court or tribunal of a Member State with regard to a person in custody, the Court of Justice of the European Union shall act with the minimum of delay.

---

[1] See the Court's report on the application of the TEU: 'The Proceedings of the Court of Justice and Court of First Instance of the European Communities', 22–26 May 1995 (No 15/95) para 11.

[2] See Tridimas and Tridimas, 'National Courts and the European Court of Justice: A Public Choice Analysis of the Preliminary Reference Procedure' (2004) 24 *International Review of Law and Economics* 125, 132–33.

[3] In anticipation of the creation of a preliminary rulings jurisdiction for the General Court, procedures have been provided that would enable its decisions on questions referred to it to be reviewed by the Court of Justice, should there be 'a serious risk of the unity or consistency of Union law being affected': see the third subparagraph of Art 256(3) and Art 62–62(b) of the Statute.

The mention of acts of 'bodies, offices and agencies of the Union' under (b) in the first paragraph of the Article was added by the TL. Now that the European Council has been formally recognised as an institution of the Union, its acts may also be the subject of references for preliminary rulings.

The new fourth paragraph enshrines in Article 267 TFEU an obligation for the Court of Justice to act 'with the minimum of delay' in responding to a references for a preliminary ruling where the national proceedings relate to a person in custody. In practice, the only provisions of EU law liable to be in issue in such proceedings are those contained in, or derived from, Title V of Part Three of the TFEU on the area of freedom, security and justice (AFSA). The Statute of the Court of Justice was amended in 2008,[4] through the insertion of a new Article 23a establishing an 'accelerated procedure', available in respect of direct actions as well as references for preliminary rulings,[5] and an 'urgent procedure', available only in respect of references for preliminary rulings relating to the AFSA.[6] Under both of these special forms of procedure, the normally prescribed time-limits may be shortened and the presentation by the Advocate General of a formal opinion be dispensed with (though he/she will still be 'heard' by the Court). Under the urgent procedure, the written part of the proceedings may be omitted altogether 'in cases of extreme urgency', such as those to which Article 167(4) refers.[7]

Certain restrictions on the availability of the preliminary rulings jurisdiction, which previously applied to the matters now covered by the AFSA, have been swept away by the TL. However, under the transitional regime, the implications of which for direct actions we have noted in the previous chapter, the truncated jurisdiction provided for by the former Article 35 TEU is to be retained with respect to existing measures in the fields of police co-operation and judicial co-operation in criminal matters that were adopted by the Council using its pre-Lisbon Third Pillar powers.[8] The most startling difference, as compared with the normal regime of Article 267, is that it is for Member States to decide whether they will make a declaration accepting the jurisdiction of the Court of Justice to give preliminary rulings on the validity or interpretation of such measures; and also to decide whether that facility should be generally available to their courts and tribunals or confined to those against whose decisions no appeal lies. As we have seen, this transitional regime will apply for a maximum period of five years from the entry into force of the Lisbon Treaty, or until a given Third Pillar measure is amended.

II – QUESTIONS THAT MAY BE REFERRED

Any question of EU law may be referred to the Court of Justice for a preliminary ruling by any national court or tribunal which considers a decision on the question 'necessary to enable it to give judgment'. The question may be raised either by one of the parties or

---

[4] See Council Decision 2008/79/EC [2008] OJ L24/42.

[5] See Rules of Procedure, Arts 62a and 104a.

[6] Rules of Procedure, Art 104b. The urgent procedure is commonly referred to by its French acronym, PPU (*procedure prejudicial d'urgence*).

[7] For a critical assessment of the initial operation of the urgent procedure, see C Barnard, 'The PPU: Is it Worth the Candle? An Early Assessment' (2009) 34 *ELRev* 281.

[8] See Protocol (No 36) on Transitional Provisions, Art 10(1) and (3). The Third Pillar decision-making arrangements were laid down by former Art 34 TEU.

by the judge of his/her own motion.[9] A decision is 'necessary' for these purposes if the national court sees it as a step, which need not be the final one, in its strategy for disposing of the case. The EU point need not be conclusive.[10]

Questions referred under Article 267 may relate to the interpretation of provisions contained in the TEU[11] and the TFEU, or in amending or Accession Treaties, as well as to questions on the validity and interpretation of acts of EU institutions, bodies, offices or agencies, including recommendations.[12] References may also be made on the interpretation of the provisions of international agreements concluded by the EU with third states or international organisations; according to the analysis adopted by the Court of Justice, such an agreement has the status in the internal Union order of an act of the institution that concluded it.[13] Importantly, the issue whether a given provision of EU law produces direct effect (that is to say, whether it confers rights on individuals which national courts are called upon to recognise and enforce) has always been treated by the Court as going to the interpretation of the provision, and may accordingly be the subject of a reference.[14]

National courts are free to bring issues of EU law before the Court of Justice under Article 267 TFEU whenever they feel it necessary to do so, even if the point in question may be thought already to have been settled by the Court.[15] Indeed, a national court may, if it wishes, make more than one reference in the same proceedings. This was acknowledged in *Pretore di Salò v Persons Unknown*,[16] where the Court said that a second reference

> may be justified when the national court encounters difficulties in understanding or applying the judgment, when it refers a fresh question of law to the Court, or again when it submits new considerations which might lead the Court to give a different answer to a question submitted earlier.

In practice, more than one reference in the same case happens only exceptionally.[17]

---

[9] Case 166/73 *Rheinmühlen v Einfuhr- und Vorratsstelle Getreide* [1974] ECR 33. See also Joined Cases C-87/90, C-88/90 and C-89/90 *Verholen and Others* [1991] ECR I-3757.

[10] See eg Case C-453/99 *Courage v Crehan* [2001] 5 CMLR 28; Case C-315/92, *Verband Sozialer Wettbewerb v Clinique Laboratories and Estée Lauder* [1994] ECR I-317; Joined Cases 36 and 71/80 *Irish Creamery Milk Suppliers Association v Ireland* [1981] ECR 735; *Polydor Ltd v Harlequin Record Shops Ltd* [1980] 2 CMLR 413 (CA).

[11] Prior to the TL, the preliminary rulings procedure did not extend to the TEU. It is still restricted by the special rules limiting the Court's jurisdiction in the field of the common foreign and security policy: see Chapter 23 below.

[12] Case 322/88, *Grimaldi v Fonds des Maladies Professionnelles* [1989] ECR 4407.

[13] See Case 181/73 *Haegeman v Belgium* [1974] ECR 449; Opinion 1/76 [1977] ECR 741; Case C-321/97 *Andersson and Another v Swedish State* [1999] ECR I-3551. The Court has no jurisdiction under Art 267 to rule on the interpretation of the EEA Agreement as regards its application in the EFTA states, only to situations which come within the EU legal order. See also Case C-53/96 *Hermès v FHT* [1998] ECR I-3603; Joined Cases C-300/98 and C-392/98 *Parfums Christian Dior v Tuk Consultancy* [2000] ECR I-11307; Case C-245/02 *Anheuser-Busch v Budvar* [2004] ECR I-10989 (Court has jurisdiction to interpret TRIPs Agreement, to which both the Community and its Member States are parties); Case C-439/01 *Cipra and Kvasnicka v Bezirkshauptmannschaft Mistelbach* [2003] ECR I-745 (AETR Agreement forms part of Community law and Court has jurisdiction to interpret it). The effects of international agreements in the EU internal order are more fully considered in Chapter 28.

[14] This is attested by the leading cases on direct effect, which are discussed in Chapter 8.

[15] See Case 283/81 *CILFIT v Ministry of Health* [1982] ECR 3415, para 15.

[16] Case 14/86 [1987] ECR 2545.

[17] For examples, see *Pierik*, Case 117/77 [1978] ECR 825 and Case 182/78 [1979] ECR 1977; *Foglia v Novello*, Case 104/79 [1980] ECR 745 and Case 244/80 [1981] ECR 3045; *CILFIT*, Case 283/81 [1982] ECR 3415 and Case 77/83 [1984] ECR 1257; *Francovich*, Joined Cases C-6/90 and C-9/90 [1991] ECR I-5357 and Case C-479/93 [1995] ECR I-3843; *Factortame*, Case C-213/89 [1990] ECR I-2433, Case C-221/89 [1991] ECR I-3905 and Joined Cases C-46/93 and C-48/93 [1996] ECR I-1029; *Kaba*, Case C-356/98 [2000] ECR I-2623 and Case C-466/00 [2003] ECR I-2219.

In *Dzodzi v Belgium*[18] the Court of Justice held that it has jurisdiction under Article 267 TFEU to give preliminary rulings on the effect of provisions of EU law which are applicable in the action pending before the national court only because their scope has been extended by national law. The Court took the view that the proper functioning of the Union's legal order made it imperative that provisions of EU law be given a uniform interpretation regardless of the circumstances in which they fell to be applied. It proceeded to deal with the substance of the questions which had been put to it.[19] The Court seems to have been concerned that, had it declined jurisdiction in these circumstances, parallel lines of national case law might have developed, one concerning the interpretation of provisions of EU law applicable in their own right, the other concerning the interpretation of the same provisions when applicable solely by virtue of national law. The possibility that cases in the second category might have influenced cases in the first could in principle have jeopardised the uniform application of EU law.

Paradoxically, this point is perhaps best explained by looking at a case where doubt was cast on the continued applicability of the *Dzodzi* approach, namely *Kleinwort Benson v City of Glasgow District Council*.[20] In that case, the English Court of Appeal made a reference on the interpretation of the Brussels Convention on jurisdiction and the recognition and enforcement of judgments in civil and commercial matters.[21] In the United Kingdom, rules based on the Brussels Convention had been laid down by Act of Parliament (the Civil Jurisdiction and Judgments Act 1982) to provide for the allocation of civil jurisdiction between England and Wales, Scotland and Northern Ireland. In *Kleinwort Benson* the Court of Appeal asked the Court of Justice for guidance on the meaning of the Convention so that it could decide whether, under the 1982 Act, the dispute between the parties fell within the jurisdiction of the English or Scottish courts. The Court of Justice said it had no jurisdiction to answer. The national court had made the reference to enable it to apply, not the Convention, but its national law. Moreover, the relevant Act, although modelled on the Convention, did not wholly reproduce its terms. The Court concluded that the Act did not render the Convention applicable as such to cases which fell outside its scope. Moreover, the Act did not require UK courts to follow the interpretation of the Convention supplied by the Court of Justice, but merely to have regard to it when applying its national law. The preliminary rulings procedure did not, in the Court's view, envisage that it should give purely advisory rulings which lacked binding effect.

In two subsequent cases, the Court appeared to retreat from the line taken in *Kleinwort Benson*. The *Dzodzi* approach continued to apply where a Member State had chosen to align its domestic legislation with EU law so as to apply the same treatment to purely internal situations as that accorded to situations governed by EU law itself. The cases in question[22] involved domestic rules on the imposition of tax. The Court explained that:

---

[18] Joined Cases C-297/88 and C-197/89 [1990] ECR I-3763, followed in Case C-231/89 *Gmurzynska-Bscher v Oberfinanzdirektion Köln* [1990] ECR I-4003.

[19] Which concerned the rules on the free movement of persons.

[20] Case C-346/93 [1995] ECR I-615.

[21] The reference was not made under Art 267 TFEU but under a special Protocol on the interpretation of the Convention by the Court of Justice: see [1998] OJ C27/28. However, this does not detract from the relevance of the case for present purposes. The Brussels Convention has now been replaced by the so-called 'Brussels I Regulation', Regulation No 44/2001 of the European Parliament and the Council, [2001] OJ L372/31.

[22] Case C-28/95 *Leur-Bloem v Inspecteur der Belastingdienst/Ondernemingen Amsterdam 2* [1997] ECR I-4161; Case C-130/95 *Giloy v Hauptzollamt Frankfurt am Main-Ost* [1997] ECR I-4291. See also Case C-53/96 *Hermès v FHT* [1998] ECR I-3603, paras 32 and 33 (TRIPS); Case C-1/99 *Kofisa Italia v Ministero delle Finanze*

[W]here in regulating internal situations, domestic legislation adopts the same solutions as those adopted in Community law so as to provide for one single procedure in comparable situations, it is clearly in the Community interest that, in order to forestall future differences of interpretation, provisions or concepts taken from Community law should be interpreted uniformly, irrespective of the circumstances in which they are to apply.[23]

The Court's decision in *BIAO*[24] suggests that the decisive question is not whether the relevant EU provisions have been reproduced verbatim, but whether any interpretation given by the Court would be treated by the referring court as binding on it as a matter of national law. That decision (like those in *Leur-Bloem* and *Giloy*) was reached against the advice of Advocate General Jacobs, who pointed out[25] that it might mean that the Court has to take a view on questions of national law which are both complex and controversial. The Advocate General went on to explain that:

> The referring court will not as a matter of Community law be bound by the Court's judgment, which will thus inevitably be (again as a matter of Community law) purely advisory. Such a consequence clearly alters the function of the Court as envisaged in the Treaty. [26]

Despite its (perhaps questionable) approach in those cases, the Court has generally taken the firm position that it has no jurisdiction under Article 267 TFEU to deliver interpretative rulings concerning provisions of EU law, where the subject-matter of the dispute is not connected with any of the situations contemplated by the Treaties.[27] Thus, for example, in the *Vajnai* case, the Court dismissed a request for a preliminary ruling on the compatibility with Article 6 TEU of the Race Directive 2000/43,[28] and the Charter of Fundamental Rights,[29] of a rule of Hungarian criminal law penalising the public display of certain 'totalitarian symbols', where the proceedings in question (against a Hungarian national) were wholly unconnected with EU law.[30]

III – COURTS AND TRIBUNALS OF THE MEMBER STATES

The power to make a reference under Article 267 TFEU belongs to 'any court or tribunal of a Member State'. That notion has traditionally been interpreted broadly by the Court of Justice. In *Dorsch Consult Ingenieurgesellschaft v Bundesbaugesellschaft Berlin* the Court said:

> In order to determine whether a body making a reference is a court or tribunal for the purposes

---

[2001] ECR I-207; Case C-222/01 *BAT v Hauptzollamt Krefeld* [2004] ECR I-4683, paras 39–41; Case C-3/04 *Poseidon Chartering* (Judgment of 16 March 2006), paras 16–18.

[23] Case C-28/95 *Leur-Bloem v Inspecteur der Belastingdienst/Ondernemingen Amsterdam 2* [1997] ECR I-4161, para 32; Case C-130/95 *Giloy v Hauptzollamt Frankfurt am Main-Ost* [1997] ECR I-4291, para 28. The Court's conclusion was reached against the advice of AG Jacobs: see in particular I-4180 and I-4187.

[24] Case C-306/99 [2003] ECR I-1, para 92.

[25] Para 57 of the Opinion.

[26] Ibid, para 61.

[27] eg Case C-299/95 *Kremzow* [1997] ECR I-2629.

[28] [2000] OJ L180/22.

[29] [2000] OJ C364/1.

[30] Case C-328/04 *Vajnai* [2005] ECR I-8577.

of Article [234] of the Treaty, which is a question governed by Community law alone, the Court takes account of a number of factors, such as whether the body is established by law, whether it is permanent, whether its jurisdiction is compulsory, whether its procedure is *inter partes*, whether it applies rules of law and whether it is independent.[31]

Thus, in *Vaassen v Beamtenfonds Mijnbedrijf*[32] a Dutch social security tribunal, which gave 'non-binding opinions', and which did not consider itself a court or tribunal under Dutch law, was held to be a court or tribunal of a Member State for the purposes of Article 267 TFEU. The Court reached that conclusion because the members of the tribunal were appointed, its chairman designated and its rules of procedure laid down by the responsible minister. Moreover, the tribunal was a permanent body which heard disputes according to an adversarial procedure and it was bound to apply rules of law. By contrast, in *Corbiau v Administration des Contributions*[33] the Court held that the notion of a court or tribunal for the purposes of Article 267 was confined to authorities which had no connection with the body which had adopted the measure being challenged in the main action. In that case, the reference had been made by the head of Luxembourg's tax administration (Directeur des Contributions), to whom appeals lay under the relevant national legislation. Given his link with one of the parties to the proceedings, he was held not to be a court or tribunal within the meaning of Article 234 EC and the reference was found inadmissible.[34]

A body will not be considered a 'court or tribunal of a Member State' within the meaning of Article 267 TFEU unless it is closely linked to 'the organisation of legal remedies through the courts in the Member State in question'. That requirement was laid down in *Nordsee v Reederei Mond*,[35] where an arbitrator appointed under a private contract was held not to be entitled to make a reference. The public authorities of the Member State concerned had not been involved in the decision by the parties to the contract to opt for arbitration, nor were those authorities automatically called upon to intervene in the proceedings before the arbitrator. However, the Court made it clear that a court or tribunal hearing appeal against an arbitrator's award would have power to make a reference.[36]

A body may only make use of the facility for which Article 267 TFEU provides if its functions are judicial rather than administrative in nature; in other words, if it is responsible for settling disputes through the application of rules of law.[37] Where a body exercises both judicial and administrative functions, it may not request a preliminary ruling when performing its administrative tasks.[38] It is becoming increasingly common for the Court to dismiss references as inadmissible on the basis that they have been made by bodies exercising non-judicial functions, such as entering contracts for the sale of land

---

[31] Case C-54/96 [1997] ECR I-4961, para 23. The requirement that the procedure should be inter partes is not absolute: see Case C-17/00 *De Coster* [2001] ECR I-9445, para 14.

[32] Case 61/65 [1966] ECR 261. See also Case C-195/98 *OG v Austria* [2000] ECR I-10497.

[33] Case C-24/92 [1993] ECR I-1277. Cf Case C-516/99 *Schmid* [2002] ECR I-4573.

[34] See also eg Case C-53/03 *Syfait* [2005] ECR I-4609.

[35] Case 102/81 [1982] ECR 1095. See para 13.

[36] See also Case C-393/92 *Almelo* [1994] ECR I-1477. *cf* Case C-126/97 *Eco Swiss China Time v Benetton International* [1999] ECR I-3055.

[37] See eg Case C-111/94 *Job Centre* [1995] ECR I-3361, paras 9–11; Case 138/80 *Borker* [1980] ECR 1975, para 4.

[38] See Case C-192/98 *Ministero dei Lavori Pubblici and Another* [1999] ECR I-8583; Case C-440/98 *RAI* [1999] ECR I-8597. *cf* Case 14/86 *Pretore di Salò v Persons Unknown* [1987] ECR 2545.

in the land register,[39] or entering the transfer of a company's registered office in the commercial register.[40]

In the *de Coster* case[41] Advocate General Ruiz-Jarabo Colomer argued that the case law on what constituted a court or tribunal offered insufficient guidance to national bodies and was in need of rationalisation. He expressed concern about the number of entities that might seek to make references in an enlarged Union and proposed a new, stricter test, namely that 'the referring body must also act in the capacity or a court or tribunal and it must have a case pending before it, a dispute between litigants which it is called upon to settle by interpreting and applying legal rules'. He concluded that the body which had made the reference in that case was not a judicial one and was not, therefore, entitled to do so. The Court of Justice rejected the Advocate General's opinion and applied the criteria set out in *Dorsch Consult*, concluding that the reference was admissible. It seems, therefore, that the Court regards those criteria as striking the right balance between clarity and flexibility.

IV – THE RELATIONSHIP BETWEEN THE COURT OF JUSTICE AND THE REFERRING COURT

The relationship between the Court of Justice and the national court in proceedings under Article 267 TFEU is co-operative rather than hierarchical in nature. Both courts have distinct but complementary roles to play in finding a solution to the case which is in conformity with the requirements of EU law. A reference to the Court of Justice is not in any sense an appeal against the decision of the national court. There are technically no parties to the proceedings before the Court of Justice,[42] which may be regarded as a form of dialogue with the referring court. The parties to the action before the referring court have the right, along with the Member States and the Commission, to submit written and oral observations to the Court of Justice in accordance with Article 23 of the Statute of the Court. That right is also extended, where appropriate, to the institution, body, office or agency which adopted the act the validity or interpretation of which is at issue. Article 23 requires the Court to notify the reference to those entitled to submit observations,[43] but not any accompanying documents. The national court's order for reference should therefore be self-contained and self-explanatory.

The Court of Justice will not, in the context of a reference for a preliminary ruling, entertain a challenge to the jurisdiction of the referring court based on national law or to the facts set out by that court in its order for reference.[44] Nor will it rule upon the appli-

---

[39] Case C-178/99 *Salzmann* [2001] ECR I-4421.

[40] Case C-86/00 *HSB-Wohnbau* [2001] ECR I-5353. See also Case C-192/98 *ANAS* [1999] ECR I-8583.

[41] Case C-17/00 [2001] ECR I-9445.

[42] See Case 69/85 *Wünsche v Germany* [1986] ECR 947, para 14.

[43] As well as to the EFTA states which are parties to the EEA Agreement and the EFTA Surveillance Authority and sometimes non-Member States, who also have the right in certain cases to submit observations: see Art 23 of the Statute, third and fourth paragraphs.

[44] See Case C-435/97 *WWF and Others v Autonome Provinz Bozen and Others* [1999] ECR I-5613, paras 28 and 29; Case C-198/01 *Consorzio Industrie Fiammiferi v Autorità Garante* [2003] 5 CMLR 16, para 62.

cation of the law to the facts or the compatibility of national law with the requirements of EU law.[45] These are matters within the exclusive jurisdiction of the national court in proceedings under Article 257 TFEU. The questions referred should be couched in terms which pose a general question of EU law, rather than the concrete issue as it falls to be decided in the instant case; if they are not, the Court may reformulate them. Questions may also be reformulated if the Court of Justice considers this necessary to furnish the national court with all the elements of EU law which it requires to give judgment,[46] or to avoid an issue which the Court would prefer not to address.[47] The Court will not, at the request of one of the parties to the main proceedings, examine questions which have not been submitted to it by the national court,[48] but it may consider provisions which the national court has not cited in the text of its question.[49]

In *Arsenal Football Club v Matthew Reed* the referring court refused to follow the ruling given by the Court of Justice because it thought the Court had exceeded its jurisdiction under Article 267 TFEU. The case concerned an attempt by the Club to prevent Reed from selling souvenirs bearing official Arsenal logos outside its ground. It turned upon the effect of an EU Directive on trade marks, and that issue was referred to the Court of Justice by the High Court.[50] The Court of Justice made it clear that there was an infringement in circumstances such as those of the main action.[51] However, the High Court gave judgment for Reed,[52] on the footing that the Court had exceeded its jurisdiction under Article 267 TFEU by making findings of fact which were inconsistent with those made by the High Court prior to the reference.

The judgment of the High Court was later overturned by the Court of Appeal,[53] but the case illustrates the delicacy of the relationship between the Court of Justice and the national courts, and the care the Court needs to take when rendering preliminary rulings.[54] The Court of Justice clearly thought that the national judge had underestimated the risk that the essential function of a mark might be compromised in a case such as this. However, it failed to express that view in sufficiently objective terms, crucial passages of its judgment referring directly to the parties to the main action. That does not mean, however, that the referring court was justified in giving a judgment which effectively ignored the guidance it had been given. The remedy for a national court which is confronted with a preliminary ruling it thinks is based on a misunderstanding or misrepresentation of the facts is to make a further reference.[55] Why did the High Court reject that course, given

---

[45] See eg Joined Cases C-332/92, C-333/92 and C-335/92 *Eurico Italia and Others* [1994] ECR I-711; Case C-295/97 *Piaggio v IFITALIA and Others* [1999] ECR I-3735.

[46] See eg Case 28/85 *Deghillage v Caisse Primaire d'Assurance Maladie* [1986] ECR 991, para 13; Case C-221/89 *The Queen v Secretary of State for Transport, ex parte Factortame* [1991] ECR I-3905.

[47] eg the horizontal effect of directives before the *Marshall* case. See Chapter 8.

[48] See Case C-189/95 *Franzén* [1997] ECR I-5909, para 79; Case C-435/97 *WWF and Others v Autonome Provinz Bozen and Others* [1999] ECR I-5613, paras 28 and 29.

[49] See Case C-439/01 *Cipra and Kvasnicka v Bezirkshauptmannschaft Mistelbach* [2003] ECR I-745, para 22.

[50] See [2001] 2 CMLR 23.

[51] See [2003] 1 CMLR 12.

[52] See [2003] 1 CMLR 13.

[53] See [2003] 2 CMLR 25.

[54] See A Arnull (2003) 40 *CMLRev* 753.

[55] For a recent discussion, see T Tridimas, 'Knocking on Heaven's Door: Fragmentation, Efficiency and Defiance in the Preliminary Rulings Procedure' (2003) 40 *CMLRev* 1, 31–33.

that, as the judge, Laddie J, acknowledged, 'national courts do not make references to the ECJ with the intention of ignoring the result'?[56]

The authors of a leading text on the preliminary rulings procedure[57] divide cases in which national courts have resisted rulings given by the Court of Justice into three categories:

— those where there is a conflict between Community law and values enshrined in national constitutions;
— those where the national court takes the view that the Court of Justice has exceeded its jurisdiction; and
— those where the national court has disliked the ruling given by the Court of Justice and sought to avoid applying it to the case in hand.

The *Arsenal* case seems to fall into both the second and the third categories. Laddie J's sympathies were clearly with Reed, who would probably have won under the English law as it stood before the trade marks directive was implemented. Laddie J appears to have seized on an apparent excess of jurisdiction by the ECJ in order to avoid applying the guidance it gave.

V – REFERRAL: DISCRETION OR DUTY?

A – The Discretion Conferred by Article 267(2) TFEU

Under Article 267(2) TFEU, inferior national courts enjoy a discretion in deciding whether or not to ask for a preliminary ruling. The mere existence of the right to make a reference does not deprive them of the right to reach their own conclusions on questions of EU law it may be necessary for them to decide.[58] Indeed, where the point raised is reasonably clear, or it is possible to deduce from the case law of the Court of Justice a clear general approach to a particular question, it may be preferable for an inferior national court to decide the point itself.[59] However, where it seems likely that a reference will be made at some stage in the proceedings, it is sensible for that step to be taken sooner rather than later, for an early reference may well save time and costs.[60] Moreover, as Bingham J acknowledged in *Commissioners of Customs and Excise v Samex ApS*,[61] the Court of Justice is far better equipped than national courts to resolve issues of EU law:

> Sitting as a judge in a national court, asked to decide questions of Community law, I am very conscious of the advantages enjoyed by the Court of Justice. It has a panoramic view of the Community and its institutions, a detailed knowledge of the Treaties and of much subordinate

---

[56] [2003] 1 CMLR 11, para 28.
[57] Anderson and Demetriou, *References to the European Court* (London, Sweet & Maxwell, 2nd edn, 2002) 327–30.
[58] See Slade LJ in *J Rothschild Holdings plc v Commissioners of Inland Revenue* [1989] 2 CMLR 621, 645 (CA).
[59] See *Pickstone v Freemans plc* [1987] 2 CMLR 572, 591 (CA) *per* Purchas LJ.
[60] This was acknowledged by Kerr LJ in *R v Pharmaceutical Society of Great Britain, ex parte The Association of Pharmaceutical Importers* [1987] 3 CMLR 951, 972.
[61] [1983] 3 CMLR 194, 210–11 (HC).

legislation made under them, and an intimate familiarity with the functioning of the Community market which no national judge denied the collective experience of the Court of Justice could hope to achieve. Where questions of administrative intention and practice arise the Court of Justice can receive submissions from the Community institutions, as also where relations between the Community and non-Member States are in issue. Where the interests of Member States are affected they can intervene to make their views known. . . . Where comparison falls to be made between Community texts in different languages, all texts being equally authentic, the multi-national Court of Justice is equipped to carry out the task in a way which no national judge, whatever his linguistic skills, could rival. The interpretation of Community instruments involves very often not the process familiar to common lawyers of laboriously extracting the meaning from words used but the more creative process of applying flesh to a spare and loosely constructed skeleton. The choice between alternative submissions may turn not on purely legal considerations, but on a broader view of what the orderly development of the Community requires. These are matters which the Court of Justice is very much better placed to assess and determine than a national court.

The proper functioning of the preliminary rulings procedure, therefore, depends to a large extent upon the way in which inferior national courts exercise the discretion conferred on them by Article 267 TFEU. Since the scope of that discretion depends on the correct interpretation of Article 234, only the Court of Justice is competent to make authoritative pronouncements on the matter. Nonetheless, some national courts have purported to lay down guidelines of their own. An early attempt to do so was made by Lord Denning in *HP Bulmer Ltd v J Bollinger SA*.[62] Lord Denning's guidelines had a considerable influence on the practice of the English courts, but they attracted a certain amount of academic criticism because of their tendency to discourage references.[63] A more positive emphasis was given, once again by Sir Thomas Bingham MR, as he then was, in the later case of *R v Stock Exchange, ex parte Else (1982) Ltd*:

> I understand the correct approach in principle of a national court (other than a final court of appeal) to be quite clear: if the facts have been found and the Community law issue is critical to the court's final decision, the appropriate course is ordinarily to refer the issue to the Court of Justice unless the national court can with complete confidence resolve the issue itself. In considering whether it can with complete confidence resolve the issue itself the national court must be fully mindful of the differences between national and Community legislation, of the pitfalls which face a national court venturing into what may be an unfamiliar field, of the need for uniform interpretation throughout the Community and of the great advantages enjoyed by the Court of Justice in construing Community instruments. If the national court has any real doubt, it should ordinarily refer.[64]

It is well established in the case law of the Court of Justice that the national court is in principle the sole judge of whether a preliminary ruling is necessary, and of the relevance of the questions referred.[65] 'Consequently, where the questions submitted concern the interpretation of Community law, the Court of Justice is, in principle, bound to give a

---

[62] [1974] Ch 401.

[63] See eg A Dashwood and A Arnull, 'English Courts and Article 177 of the EEC Treaty' (1984) 4 *YEL* 255, 263.

[64] [1993] 2 WLR 70, 76; [1993] 1 All ER 420, 426 (CA). *cf Trinity Mirror PLC v Commissioners of Customs and Excise* [2001] 2 CMLR 33, paras 48–56, where the Court of Appeal, influenced by the Opinion of AG Jacobs in Case C-338/95 *Wiener v Hauptzollamt Emmerich* [1997] ECR I-6495, declined to make a reference on the basis that there was 'no real doubt' about the answer to the question of EU law that had arisen.

[65] See eg Case 297/88 *Dzodzi v Belgium* [1990] ECR I-3763.

ruling.'[66] The fact that the issue referred is the subject of a pending infringement action against the state concerned is irrelevant.[67] Moreover, the Court of Justice made it clear in *Rheinmühlen*[68] that a national court cannot be deprived of its power to make a reference by the rulings of superior national courts. The Treaty does not preclude a decision to refer from remaining subject to the remedies normally available under national law (such as appeal), but the Court will act on the decision to refer until it has been formally revoked.[69]

Nonetheless, the Court explained in *Cipra and Kvasnicka v Bezirkshauptmannschaft Mistelbach* that:[70]

> In exceptional circumstances, it can examine the conditions in which the case was referred to it by the national court, in order to assess whether it has jurisdiction. . . . The Court may refuse to rule on a question referred for a preliminary ruling by a national court only where it is quite obvious that the interpretation of Community law that is sought bears no relation to the actual facts of the main action or its purpose, where the problem is hypothetical, or where the Court does not have before it the factual or legal material necessary to give a useful answer to the questions submitted to it.

The decision in *Foglia v Novello*,[71] cited by the Court in *Cipra*, began a retreat from the more liberal attitude originally taken by the Court. In *Foglia*, the Court refused to entertain a reference made in the context of what it considered to be a collusive action brought in one Member State by parties who were not really in dispute with each other, in order to challenge the compatibility of another Member State's law with EU law. The decision in *Foglia* was heavily criticised[72] and was for many years applied with considerable restraint. However, it was given a new lease of life by the ruling in *Telemarsicabruzzo v Circostel*.[73] In that case, an Italian judge, the Vice Pretore di Frascati, referred two questions on the compatibility with the EC Treaty, and in particular the rules on competition, of provisions of Italian law restricting the right of private-sector television channels to use certain frequencies. The orders for reference contained very little information about the factual background to the cases or the relevant provisions of Italian law. The Court emphasised that the need to give a useful ruling in proceedings under Article 267 made it essential for the national judge to define the factual and legislative background to the case, or at least the factual hypotheses on which the questions referred were based. These requirements were particularly important in the field of competition, characterised as it was by complex legal and factual situations. The Court pointed out that the orders for reference in the present cases contained no information on these matters. The information the Court had been able to glean in the course of the proceedings was not sufficient to enable it usefully to respond to the questions put to it by the Vice Pretore.

---

[66] Case C-256/97 *DMT* [1999] ECR I-3913, para 10.
[67] Case C-457/02 *Niselli* [2004] ECR I-10853, para 27.
[68] Case 166/73 [1974] ECR 33, paras 3 and 4.
[69] See Case 146/73 *Rheinmühlen-Düsseldorf v Einfuhr- und Vorratsstelle Getreide* [1974] ECR 139, para 3.
[70] Case C-439/01 [2003] ECR I-745, para 19. See also Case C-60/98 *Butterfly Music Srl v CEMED* [1999] ECR I-3939, para 13; Case C-421/97 *Tarantik v Directeur des Services Fiscaux de Seine-et-Marne* [1999] ECR I-3633, para 33; Case C-415/93 *URBSFA and Others v Bosman and Others* [1995] ECR I-4921, para 61.
[71] Case 104/79 [1980] ECR 745.
[72] See eg A Barav, 'Preliminary Censorship? The Judgment of the European Court in *Foglia v Novello*' (1980) 5 *ELRev* 443; Bebr, 'The Existence of a Genuine Dispute: An Indispensable Precondition for the Jurisdiction of the Court under Article 177 EEC?' (1980) 17 *CMLRev* 525 and 'The Possible Implications of *Foglia v Novello II*' (1982) 19 *CMLRev* 421.
[73] Joined Cases C-320/90, C-321/90 and C-322/90 [1993] ECR I-393. See also Case C-83/91 *Meilicke v ADV/ORGA* [1992] ECR I-4871.

The judgment in *Telemarsicabruzzo* was delivered by the full Court and was clearly intended to emphasise that, if the background to the case is not clearly set out by the referring court, jurisdiction will be declined. That message was subsequently reinforced in a series of cases in which inadequately explained references were dismissed by reasoned order as manifestly inadmissible under the abbreviated procedure for which provision is made in Article 92(1) of the Rules of Procedure.[74] In one case,[75] the Court rejected a reference as inadmissible where the relevance of EU law depended on an interpretation by the referring court of the national law of another Member State, which the government of that state regarded as implausible. The Court said it was unable to establish from the information supplied to it whether answering the referring court's questions would serve a useful purpose. In another case, the Court refused even to give a ruling when it thought the reference should have been withdrawn by the national court in the light of developments since it had been made.[76]

However, there are some more recent cases where the Court of Justice has been willing to deal with questions it might have been expected to reject. In *Vaneetveld*,[77] for example, the order for reference contained no information about the facts of the case. Nonetheless, following the advice of Advocate General Jacobs, the Court observed:

> It is true that the Court has held that the need to arrive at an interpretation of Community law which is useful for the national court requires that court to define the factual and legislative context of the questions, or at least to explain the factual hypotheses on which they are based. . . . Nonetheless, that requirement is less pressing where the questions relate to specific technical points and enable the Court to give a useful reply even where the national court has not given an exhaustive description of the legal and factual situation.[78]

The Court concluded that it had enough information to enable it to give a useful answer.

The Court of Justice may also treat possible deficiencies in the information supplied by the national court as having been cured during later stages of the proceedings. An example is *Arduino*,[79] where the Court observed: 'The observations submitted by the governments of the Member States and the Commission . . . show that the information supplied in the order for reference enabled them effectively to state their views on the questions referred to the Court.' It continued:

> Furthermore, the information in the order for reference was supplemented by the written observations lodged before the Court. All that information, which was included in the Report for the Hearing, was brought to the notice of the governments of the Member States and the other

---

[74] See eg Case C-157/92 *Banchero I* [1993] ECR I-1085; Case C-386/92 *Monin Automobiles I* [1993] ECR I-2049. For the sequel to these cases, see Case C-428/93 *Monin Automobiles II* [1994] ECR I-1707; Case C-387/93 *Banchero II* [1995] ECR I-4663.

[75] Case C-153/00 *der Weduwe* [2002] ECR I-11319.

[76] See Joined Cases C-422/93, C-423/93 and C-424/93 *Zabala Erasun and Others* [1995] ECR I-1567.

[77] Case C-316/93 [1994] ECR I-763. See also Case C-412/93 *Leclerc-Siplec v TF1 Publicité and M6 Publicité* [1995] ECR I-179; Case C-415/93 *URBSFA and Others v Bosman and Others* [1995] ECR I-4921; Case C-295/97 *Piaggio v IFITALIA and Others* [1999] ECR I-3735; Case C-355/97 *Landesgrundverkehrsreferent der Tiroler Landesregierung v Beck and Another* [1999] ECR I-4977; Case C-67/96 *Albany International v Stichting Bedrijfspensioenfonds Textielindustrie* [1999] ECR I-5751; Joined Cases C-115/97, C-116/97 and C-117/97 *Brentjens v Stichting Bedrijfspensioenfonds voor de Handel in Bouwmaterialen* [1999] ECR I-6025; Case C-413/99 *Baumbast v Secretary of State* [2002] 3 CMLR 23, paras 31–34.

[78] Case C-316/93 [1994] ECR I-763, para 13.

[79] Case C-35/99 [2002] 4 CMLR 25, para 28.

interested parties for the purposes of the hearing, at which they had an opportunity, if necessary, to amplify their observations.[80]

The Court concluded that

> the information provided by the national court, supplemented where necessary by the abovementioned material, gives the Court sufficient knowledge of the factual and legislative background to the dispute in the main proceedings to enable it to interpret the relevant rules of the Treaty.[81]

The case law suggests therefore that, where the referring court sets out clearly what the case is about and gives a plausible explanation of why it needs an answer to the questions it has referred, the Court of Justice will normally proceed to answer them. However, it will not answer questions which are manifestly irrelevant,[82] nor will it respond where it takes the view that there is no real dispute between the parties to the main action.[83] Moreover, it will not normally spend time trying to identify what a case is about when this has not been properly explained by the national court. An exception is sometimes made where gaps in the information supplied are cured during subsequent stages of the proceedings, provided the dispute is genuine, the questions are relevant and those submitting observations have not been prevented from stating their views effectively.

In a series of Information Notes on references from national courts for preliminary rulings, the Court of Justice has summarised its case law and offered advice as to, inter alia, what references should contain, and at what point in the proceedings they should be made. The latest Note, issued in 2009 to take into account the entry into force of the TL, issued by the Court of Justice in 2005, states:

> A national court or tribunal may refer a question to the Court for a preliminary ruling as soon as it finds that a ruling on the point or points of interpretation or validity is necessary to enable it to give judgment; it is the national court which is in the best position to decide at what stage of the proceedings such a question should be referred.
>
> It is, however, desirable that a decision to seek a preliminary ruling should be taken when the national proceedings have reached a stage at which the national court is able to define the factual and legal context of the question, so that the Court of Justice has available to it all the information necessary to check, where appropriate, that European Union law applies to the main proceedings. It may also be in the interests of justice to refer a question for a preliminary ruling only after both sides have been heard.[84]

B – Mandatory References

Where a question of EU law, within the meaning of Article 267(1) TFEU, is raised in a case pending before a court or tribunal of a Member State against whose decisions there is no judicial remedy under national law, that court or tribunal is obliged, under Article 267(3), to refer the question to the Court of Justice. The obligation is not confined to

---

[80] Ibid, para 29. See also Case C-476/01 *Felix Kapper* [2004] ECR I-5205, paras 26–29.

[81] Ibid, para 30.

[82] See generally C Barnard and E Sharpston, 'The Changing Face of Article 177 References' (1997) 34 *CMLRev* 1113; D O'Keeffe, 'Is the Spirit of Article 177 under Attack? Preliminary References and Admissibility' (1998) 23 *ELRev* 509.

[83] Though consider the Court's perhaps surprising dismissal of the allegation of contrivance in Case C-144/04 *Mangold* [2005] ECR I-9981.

[84] [2009] OJ C297/1, paras 18 and 19.

courts whose decisions are always final, such as the House of Lords. It covers any court, even if not the highest court, against whose decision there is no judicial remedy in the instant case.[85] In *Köbler v Austria*[86] the Court held that non-compliance by a top national court with its obligations under Article 267(3) might render the state in which it was situated liable in damages to an individual who was thereby deprived of his/her rights under EU law.[87]

In the English legal system, a potential difficulty arises at the level of an appeal from the Court of Appeal to the Supreme Court. Such an appeal can only be brought with the leave of either the former or the latter. If leave is granted, there is no problem; but what is the position if the Court of Appeal refuses to grant leave? In *Chiron Corporation v Murex Diagnostics*[88] the Court of Appeal held that, where it refused leave, and the Supreme Court was subsequently presented with an application for leave to appeal, before refusing leave the Supreme Court should consider whether it needed to resolve an issue of EU law; and if it found that there was a question to be decided, and that the answer was unclear, it could either make a reference at that stage, or grant leave and consider at a later stage whether to make a reference. The Court of Appeal thought that the possibility of making an application to the Supreme Court for leave to appeal constituted a 'judicial remedy' within the meaning of Article 267(3) TFEU, so it could not itself be considered a court of last resort for the purposes of that provision. Nor would it have jurisdiction to make a reference if the Supreme Court refused leave, since by that stage it would be *functus officio*.

The approach of the Court of Appeal was subsequently endorsed by the Court of Justice in *Lyckeskog*,[89] a reference from the Court of Appeal for Western Sweden, which wanted to know if it was a court of last resort for the purposes of Article 267(3) TFEU. The referring court's decision in the main action would be subject to appeal to the Swedish Supreme Court, but only if the latter declared it admissible on grounds set out in the Swedish Code of Procedure. The Court of Justice ruled that the possibility of an appeal to the Supreme Court meant that the Court of Appeal could not be considered a court of last resort for these purposes, even where the merits of the appeal would only be examined by the Supreme Court after it had declared the appeal admissible. The Court said:

> If a question arises as to the interpretation or validity of a rule of Community law, the supreme court will be under an obligation, pursuant to the third paragraph of Article 234 EC, to refer a question to the Court of Justice for a preliminary ruling either at the stage of the examination of admissibility or at a later stage. [90]

The obligation to refer is not affected by the fact that the Commission may have discontinued infringement proceedings raising the same issue as that which the national court is called upon to decide.[91] However, although Article 267(3) states that a reference is mandatory 'where any such question is raised', this does not mean that the obligation arises wherever a party contends that a question of EU law needs to be decided. In *CILFIT*

---

[85] Case 6/64 *Costa v ENEL* [1964] ECR 585. See also Case 107/76 *Hoffmann-La Roche v Centrafarm* [1977] ECR 957 and Joined Cases 35 and 36/82 *Morson and Jhanjan v Netherlands* [1982] ECR 3723. *cf* Case C-337/95 *Parfums Christian Dior v Evora* [1997] ECR I-6013.

[86] Case C-224/01 [2003] ECR I-10239, para 55.

[87] On this issue, see Chapter 6.

[88] [1995] All ER (EC) 88, [1995] FSR 309. See Demetriou (1995) 20 *ELRev* 628. *cf R v Secretary of State, ex parte Duddridge* [1996] 2 CMLR 361.

[89] Case C-99/00 [2002] ECR I-4839.

[90] Ibid, para 18.

[91] Case C-393/98 *Gomes Valente* [2001] ECR I-1327.

v Ministry of Health[92] the Court of Justice held that final courts are in the same position as other national courts in deciding whether they need to resolve a question of EU law before giving judgment. A final court is not, therefore, obliged to seek a preliminary ruling where the answer to the question raised cannot affect the outcome of the case. The Court went to hold that, even where a question of EU law is relevant to the outcome, a final court is not under an obligation to make a reference if: (a) 'previous decisions of the Court have already dealt with the point of law in question'[93] (although in that event the national court remains free to refer, if it wishes to invite the Court of Justice to reconsider its earlier ruling);[94] or (b) the correct application of EU law is so obvious as to leave no scope for any reasonable doubt as to the manner in which the question raised is to be resolved. This is known as the doctrine of *acte claire*. However, before the national court reaches this conclusion, it must be convinced that the matter would be equally obvious to the courts of the other Member States and to the Court of Justice itself. In that regard, account must be taken of the characteristic features of EU law and the particular difficulties to which its interpretation gives rise.[95] These criteria may also be relevant where an inferior national court is called upon to interpret EU law. This is because, where the criteria are satisfied, such a court may properly refuse, in the exercise of its discretion, to make a reference.[96]

What is the relationship between the *CILFIT* criteria and the *Köbler* case? If a top national court relies on *CILFIT* to avoid a reference, and then in its judgment causes one of the parties to be deprived of rights under EU law, does that party have a claim for damages against the Member State concerned? The issue was addressed in *Köbler* itself.[97] The Court's judgment suggests that the Member State will not be liable where a national court mistakenly, but in good faith, concludes that the *CILFIT* criteria are satisfied and declines to make a reference. The Member State clearly would be liable, however, if it could be shown that the court in question had deliberately misconstrued the *CILFIT* criteria to avoid making a reference. However, that reasoning would appear inapplicable to lower courts: the correct remedy for a party who believes that such a court has deprived him/her of rights under EU law is to appeal to a higher court.

Some commentators take the view that the *CILFIT* criteria are too strict. The authors of a report published by the British Institute of International and Comparative Law observed: 'Compliance with these requirements for *acte clair* is virtually impossible. In practice this test is completely unworkable.'[98] In one English case, the criteria were even described as 'intimidating'.[99] That view perhaps gives insufficient weight to the Court's acceptance that the Treaty imposed no obligation to refer where the Court had already dealt in previous decisions with the point at issue. In a development of previous case law,[100] the Court made

---

[92] Case 283/81 [1982] ECR 3415. More recently, eg Case C-495/03 *Intermodal Transports* (Judgment of 15 September 2005).

[93] Ibid, para 14.

[94] This applies a fortiori 'when the question raised is substantially the same as a question which has already been the subject of a preliminary ruling in the same national proceedings': Case C-337/95 *Parfums Christian Dior v Evora* [1997] ECR I-6013, para 29.

[95] On methods of interpretation, see Chapter 12.

[96] *cf* Case C-340/99 *TNT Traco v Poste Italiana* [2001] ECR I-4109, para 35.

[97] See paras 118 and 123 of the Judgment.

[98] British Institute of International and Comparative Law, 'The Role and Future of the European Court of Justice' (1996) 76.

[99] Hodgson J in *R v Secretary of State for Transport, ex parte Factortame* [1989] 2 CMLR 353, 379.

[100] See Joined Cases 28–30/62 *Da Costa v Nederlandse Belastingadministratie* [1963] ECR 31.

it clear that this was so 'irrespective of the nature of the proceedings which led to those decisions, even though the questions at issue are not strictly identical'.[101] In circumstances such as these, there is no need to invoke the *acte clair* doctrine. The obligation laid down by Article 267(3) TFEU needs to be applied strictly, as a safeguard against the incorrect application of EU law by national courts.

It was held in *Hoffmann-La Roche v Centrafarm* that a national court is not under a duty to refer to the Court of Justice a question of interpretation which is raised in inter-locutory proceedings for an interim order, provided that each of the parties is entitled to institute proceedings (or to require proceedings to be instituted) on the substance of the case, and that during such proceedings the question provisionally decided at the inter-locutory stage may be re-examined and referred to the Court.[102] This is so even where the criteria laid down in the *CILFIT* case are not satisfied and no judicial remedy is available against the interlocutory decision itself.

C – References on Validity

Under Article 267(1) TFEU, the Court of Justice may be asked to give a preliminary rul-ing not only on the interpretation of acts of EU institutions, bodies, offices and agencies, but also on the validity of such acts. This jurisdiction complements the Court's jurisdic-tion to review the legality of EU acts under Article 263 TFEU.[103] A person affected by an EU act may sometimes, therefore, challenge its validity independently of the direct action for annulment provided for by Article 263, by way of proceedings before a national court, with the hope of securing a reference to Luxembourg. However, the Court of Justice has imposed limits on the availability of this alternative route. The effect of the decision in *TWD Textilwerke Deggendorf*[104] is that a natural or legal person who fails to challenge an EU measure under Article 263 TFEU, in spite of clearly having standing to do so, may not subsequently contest its validity in proceedings before a national court. The *TWD* case concerned the Treaty rules on state aid and there was initially some doubt as to whether it was confined to that context. The Court made clear that this was not so in *Wiljo v Belgian State*,[105] where it applied the *TWD* approach in a different context.[106]

The jurisdiction of the Court of Justice to rule on validity typically arises where a

---

[101] Ibid, para 14.

[102] Case 107/76 *Hoffmann-La Roche v Centrafarm* [1977] ECR 957. The *Hoffmann-La Roche* judgment also refers to questions of validity, but must be considered superseded on that point by *Foto-Frost*: see AG Lenz in *Zuckerfabrik Süderditmarschen* [1991] ECR I-415, 483–89.

[103] See Chapter 6.

[104] Case C-188/92 [1994] ECR I-833.

[105] Case C-178/95 [1997] ECR I-585. See also Case C-408/95 *Eurotunnel and Others v SeaFrance* [1997] ECR I-6315. *cf* Case C-241/95 *The Queen v Intervention Board for Agricultural Produce, ex parte Accrington Beef and Others* [1996] ECR I-6699; Case C-239/99 *Nachi Europe* [2001] ECR I-1197.

[106] The *TWD* ruling was not well received in some quarters. See eg D Wyatt, 'The Relationship between Actions for Annulment and References on Validity after *TWD Deggendorf*' in Lonbay and Biondi (eds), *Remedies for Breach of EC Law* (1997); AG Tesauro in Case C-408/95 *Eurotunnel and Others v SeaFrance* [1997] ECR I-6315, 6328. *cf* Tesauro, 'The Effectiveness of Judicial Protection and Co-operation between the Court of Justice and the National Courts' (1993) 13 YEL 1, 15–16. However, the preliminary rulings procedure is in several respects a less satisfactory mechanism for reviewing the legality of EU acts than the action for annulment. See AG Jacobs in Case C-188/92 *TWD* [1994] ECR I-833, 840-844 and Case C-358/89 *Extramet Industrie v Council* [1991] ECR I-2501, 2523–25; Waelbroeck and Verheyden, 'Les conditions de recevabilité des recours en annula-tion des particuliers contre les actes normatifs communautaires' (1995) 31 *CDE* 399, 433–36.

national measure is challenged before a Member State court on the ground that it is based upon an EU measure that is invalid. Indeed, the Court said in the *UPA* case[107] that national courts were under a duty to apply their national law in a way that enabled such challenges to be made.

In *R v Secretary of State, ex parte British American Tobacco*[108] the Court of Justice made clear that a claimant's right to plead the invalidity of a Community act of general application before a national court need not necessarily depend on the existence of national implementing measures. In that case, the applicants sought judicial review in the High Court of 'the intention and/or obligation' of the UK government to transpose a Directive on tobacco products into national law. The Court held that a reference by the High Court on the validity of the Directive was admissible, even though at the time of the application for judicial review the deadline for transposition of the Directive had not expired, and no implementing measures had yet been adopted. The judgment may be seen in part as a reflection of the duty imposed on national courts in *UPA*. In *BAT*, however, the applicants had been granted permission to seek judicial review. The Court's judgment does not address the problems that may face claimants where no national remedy is available to them and they lack standing to bring a direct action under Article 263.

The Treaty appears to confer on inferior national courts the same discretion, whether the question of EU law raised in the case is one of interpretation or of validity. However, in the controversial case of *Foto-Frost v Hauptzollamt Lübeck-Ost*[109] the Court of Justice held that, while national courts were entitled to find that acts adopted by the EU institutions were valid, they had no power to declare such acts invalid. This was because '[d]ivergences between courts in the Member States as to the validity of Community acts would be liable to place in jeopardy the very unity of the Community legal order and detract from the fundamental requirement of legal certainty'. The Court also pointed out that, if the matter were referred to it, the institution which adopted the contested act would be able to participate in the proceedings. This will rarely, if ever, be possible in proceedings before a national court.

The result is that, where a real and substantial doubt is raised in a national court as to the validity of an EU measure, and where it is clear that a decision on the validity of the measure is necessary for the resolution of the case, the issue must be referred to the Court of Justice. This is so even where similar provisions have been declared void by the Court in other cases,[110] and where the national court is not one of last resort. If the national court is a final one, the *acte clair* doctrine laid down in *CILFIT* cannot operate to relieve it of its obligation to refer: that doctrine applies only to questions of interpretation. Thus where in proceedings before a national court, whether or not it is one of last resort, there is a real possibility that an EU measure might be invalid, the matter must be referred to the Court of Justice.[111]

---

[107] Case C-50/00 P *Unión de Pequeños Agricultores v Council* [2002] 3 CMLR 1, para 42. The case is discussed in Chapter 6.

[108] Case C-491/01 [2002] ECR I-11453.

[109] Case 314/85 [1987] ECR 4199. See Bebr, 'The Reinforcement of the Constitutional Review of Community Acts under Article 177 EEC Treaty' (1988) 25 *CMLRev* 667.

[110] cf *R v Intervention Board for Agricultural Produce, ex parte ED and F Man (Sugar) Ltd* [1986] 2 All ER 126 (QBD); *R v Minister of Agriculture, ex parte Fédération Européenne de la Santé Animale* [1988] 3 CMLR 207 and 661 (DC).

[111] See Case C-461/03 *Gaston Schul Douane-expediteur BV* [2005] ECR I-10513; Case C-344/04 *European Low Fares Airline Association* [2006] ECR I-403.

Some commentators[112] have objected to the ruling in *Foto-Frost* on the basis that it is incompatible with the clear language of Article 267 TFEU, but the reasoning underlying the conclusion reached by the Court seems compelling.

The judgment in *Foto-Frost* suggested that national courts might have jurisdiction to declare EU acts invalid in interlocutory proceedings, where the urgency of the case rendered it impractical to wait for a ruling from the Court of Justice.[113] The powers of national courts in such proceedings were considered in more detail in *Zuckerfabrik Süderditmarschen v Hauptzollamt Itzehoe*.[114] The essential point at issue in that case was whether, and if so in what circumstances, a national court could suspend the operation of a national measure based on an EU Regulation, which was alleged to be invalid. The Court of Justice observed that the rights of individuals under EU law would be compromised if a regulation could not be suspended pending a preliminary ruling as to its validity, given that the Court's jurisdiction in the matter was exclusive.[115] A request for a preliminary ruling was one of the means provided by the Treaty for reviewing the validity of EU acts. Another means was the action for annulment brought directly before the Court pursuant to Article 263. In proceedings of the latter kind, the Court had power under Article 278 TFEU to order the suspension of the contested act. 'The coherence of the system of interim legal protection therefore requires that national courts should also be able to order suspension of enforcement of a national administrative measure based on a Community regulation, the legality of which is contested.'[116]

The Court of Justice observed that the suspension of administrative measures based on an EU regulation, whilst governed by national rules of procedure, had to be subject to conditions which were uniform throughout the Union, so far as the granting of relief was concerned.[117] Since the power of the national courts to suspend administrative measures in these circumstances corresponded to the jurisdiction of the Court itself to grant interim measures in actions for annulment, the national courts could only be permitted to provide such relief on the same conditions.[118] The Court concluded:

> [S]uspension of enforcement of a national measure adopted in implementation of a Community regulation may be granted by a national court only:
>
> (i) if that court entertains serious doubts as to the validity of the Community measure and, should the question of the validity of the contested measure not already have been brought before the Court, itself refers that question to the Court;
>
> (ii) if there is urgency and a threat of serious and irreparable damage to the applicant;
>
> (iii) and if the national court takes due account of the Community's interests'.[119]

In *Krüger v Hauptzollamt Hamburg-Jonas*[120] the Commission argued that, when considering the Union interest, a national court which was minded to grant interim relief must give the EU institution that adopted the contested act an opportunity to express its views. The Court of Justice was not prepared to impose such a requirement, simply observing

---

[112] See eg T Hartley, *Constitutional Problems of the European Union* (1999) 34–35.
[113] Para 19 of the Judgment.
[114] Joined Cases C-143/88 and C-92/89 [1991] ECR I-415. See also the discussion in Chapter 6.
[115] See Case 314/85 *Foto-Frost* [1987] ECR 4199.
[116] Ibid, para 18.
[117] Ibid, para 26.
[118] Ibid, para 27.
[119] Ibid, para 33.
[120] Case C-334/95 [1997] ECR I-4517.

that it was for the national court to decide on the most appropriate way of obtaining all the information it needed to assess the Community interest.

In *Atlanta Fruchthandelsgesellschaft v Federal Republic of Germany*[121] the Court offered further clarification of the conditions laid down in *Zuckerfabrik*. Where a national court had serious doubts about the validity of an EU act and made a reference to the Court of Justice on that issue, it had to explain why it thought the act in question might be invalid. If the Court had already dismissed as unfounded an action for annulment in respect of the disputed act, or had previously held on a reference for a preliminary ruling that no doubt had been cast on the act's validity, the national court was not entitled to grant interim measures; and any such measures which had already been granted would have to be revoked, unless the new grounds of illegality put forward differed from those which had been rejected by the Court. The same applied, mutatis mutandis, where a challenge to the validity of an act had been dismissed by the General Court in a decision which had become final and binding.

However, it was established in the *Nevedi* case that interim relief against the application of allegedly invalid Community measures may not be granted by national administrative authorities. These, it was held, are not in a position to comply with the conditions for granting interim relief, as defined by the Court in rulings such as *Zuckerfabrik* and *Atlanta*. In particular, the status of national administrative authorities is not generally such as to guarantee that they possess the same degree of independence and impartiality as national courts; and it is uncertain that they benefit from the exercise of the adversarial principle inherent to judicial proceedings, which allows account to be taken of the arguments put forward by the different parties before the necessary weighing of interests at stake in the dispute.[122]

VI – EFFECTS OF THE RULING BY THE COURT OF JUSTICE

A ruling on interpretation given by the Court of Justice under Article 267 TFEU 'is binding on the national court as to the interpretation of the Community provisions and acts in question'.[123] The referring court is under a duty to give full effect to the provisions of EU law as interpreted by the Court. This may require it to refuse to apply conflicting provisions of national law, even if adopted subsequently.[124] Moreover, other courts are entitled

---

[121] Case C-465/93 [1995] ECR I-3761. *cf* Case C-68/95 *T Port v Bundesanstalt für Landwirtschaft und Ernährung* [1996] ECR I-6065.

[122] Case C-194/04 *Nevedi* [2005] ECR I-10423.

[123] Case 52/76 *Benedetti v Munari* [1977] ECR 163, para 26. This obligation is reinforced for courts in the United Kingdom by s 3(1) of the European Communities Act 1972. For a detailed discussion of the effects of rulings given by the Court of Justice under Article 177, see Toth, 'The Authority of Judgments of the European Court of Justice: Binding force and Legal Effects' (1984) 4 1.

[124] See eg Case 106/77 *Amministrazione delle Finanze dello Stato v Simmenthal* [1978] ECR 629; Case 170/88 *Ford España v Estado Español* [1989] ECR 2305. However, on the relationship between preliminary rulings and the principle of *res judicata*, see Case C-453/00 *Kühne & Heitz* [2004] ECR I-837; Case C-234/04 *Kapferer* [2006] ECR I-2585.

to treat the ruling of the Court of Justice as authoritative and as thereby obviating the need for the same points to be referred to the Court again.[125]

A ruling under Article 267 declaring an act of one of the institutions void is also binding on the referring court.[126] Moreover, such a ruling entitles 'any other national court to regard that act as void'.[127] The consequences for the institutions of a preliminary ruling declaring an EU act void were considered by the General Court in *H & R Ecroyd Holdings Ltd v Commission*.[128] The Court observed:

[W]hen the Court of Justice rules in proceedings under Article [267 TFEU] . . . that an act adopted by the Community legislature is invalid, its decision has the legal effect of requiring the competent Community institutions to adopt the measures necessary to remedy that illegality. . . . In those circumstances, they are to take the measures that are required in order to comply with the judgment containing the ruling in the same way as they are, under Article 233 EC, in the case of a judgment annulling a measure or declaring that the failure of a Community institution to act is unlawful. . . . [W]hen a Community measure is held to be invalid by a preliminary ruling, the obligation laid down by Article [266] applies by analogy.[129]

This may mean that the institution concerned must not only adopt the legislative or administrative measures necessary to give effect to the Court's judgment but must also consider whether the unlawful measure caused harm to those affected by it, which has to be made good. On the other hand, where the Court in proceedings under Article 267 rejects a challenge to the validity of a measure, it will rule that consideration of the questions raised has disclosed no factor of such a kind as to affect the validity of the contested act.[130] The national court is not of course entitled to declare the act invalid on the grounds rejected by the Court, but the effect of the ruling is to leave open the possibility of a subsequent challenge on other grounds.

A preliminary ruling on the interpretation of a rule of EU law

clarifies and defines where necessary the meaning and scope of that rule as it must be or ought to have been understood and applied from the time of its coming into force. It follows that the rule as thus interpreted may, and must, be applied by the [national] courts even to legal relationships arising and established before the judgment ruling on the request for interpretation.[131]

Very exceptionally the Court of Justice may, in the interests of legal certainty, be led to limit the effects on past transactions of preliminary rulings on questions of both interpretation and validity.[132] Any such limitation will always be laid down in the ruling itself.[133]

---

[125] See Joined Cases 28-30/62 *da Costa en Schaake* [1963] ECR 31; Case 283/81 *CILFIT v Ministry of Health* [1982] ECR 3415.

[126] Case 66/80 *International Chemical Corporation v Amministrazione delle Finanze dello Stato* [1981] ECR 1191.

[127] Ibid, para 13.

[128] Case T-220/97 [1999] ECR I-1677.

[129] Ibid, para 49.

[130] See eg Case C-323/88 *Sermes* [1990] ECR I-3027.

[131] Case 61/79 *Amministrazione delle Finanze dello Stato v Denkavit Italiana* [1980] ECR 1205, para 16.

[132] See eg Case 43/75 *Defrenne v SABENA* [1976] ECR 455; Case 41/84 *Pinna v Caisse d'Allocations Familiales de la Savoie* [1986] ECR 1; Case 24/86 *Blaizot v University of Liège* [1988] ECR 379; Case 262/88 *Barber* [1990] ECR I-1889.

[133] See Case 61/79 *Amministrazione delle Finanze dello Stato v Denkavit Italiana* [1980] ECR 1205.

VII – CONCLUDING REMARKS

Article 267 TFEU has provided the conduit for the transmission to the Court of Justice of a vast range of legal issues, as they have arisen in the everyday life of EU Member States. The richness of this source has created opportunities for the Court to develop the concepts and principles that give the legal order of the Union its unique character. As will be apparent from other chapters in this volume,[134] it was in cases that came to the Court by way of references for preliminary rulings that the very idea that the Treaties have established something in the nature of an autonomous legal system, the principles governing the relationship between that system and the legal systems of the Member States, and the mechanisms protecting the interests of individuals and businesses against Union and Member State authorities when they exercise public powers under the Treaties, have been worked out. Although direct actions, especially the action for annulment, have played a significant part in this process, without the preliminary rulings procedure, EU law would undoubtedly have been a less highly articulated and mature system, and its impact on the lives of Union citizens less organised and coherent.

The open-door policy of earlier years, when the Court of Justice appeared to welcome all the references that came its way, has been replaced since *Foglia* v *Novello* by an alertness to the nature of the Article 267 jurisdiction, as one designed to enable the Court to assist in the resolution of genuine disputes, not simply to answer interesting legal questions. Cases such as *Telemarsicabruzzo* also show the Court requiring more active collaboration from referring courts, to help it exercise its jurisdiction effectively. There is a difficult balance to be struck between the principle, steadfastly maintained by the Court, that it is for the national court to decide whether it needs a ruling from Luxembourg to enable it to give judgment, and the risk that the volume of references may bring undue delay in dealing with them. Whether through its efforts to 'educate' national judges, or through practical measures such as disposing of straightforward cases by way of reasoned Orders, the recent statistical record shows an increase in the number of new references for preliminary rulings (up from 221 in 2005 to 302 in 2009) matched by a reduction in the average duration of cases (from 20.4 months in 2005 to 17.1 months in 2009).[135]

It remains to be seen how the Court of Justice will cope with the full Article 267 jurisdiction that it now enjoys (subject to transitional arrangements) in relation to the AFSJ, especially in the fields of police co-operation and judicial co-operation in criminal matters. The urgent procedure is an innovation showing the capacity of the Court to adapt to new challenges; though the disruption a proliferation of urgent proceedings would cause to the ordinary business of the Court is a matter of concern.

The fairly modest amendments to Article 267 TFEU instituted by the TL are an indication that the preliminary rulings procedure, as developed in the case law, is functioning in a manner regarded as broadly satisfactory. A big issue that remains is whether advantage will ever be taken of the possibility of assigning references on certain matters to the General Court. This will, presumably, depend on whether the volume of work increases markedly, as courts in the 12 new Member States develop the habit of referring questions to Luxembourg, and whether the Court of Justice is able to continue managing the flow of cases with its present success.

---

[134] See, in particular, Chapters 8–12 below.
[135] See Annual Report, 81 and 94.

Further Reading

Allott, 'Preliminary Rulings—Another Infant Disease' (2000) 25 *ELRev* 538

Anderson and Demetriou, *References to the European Court* (2nd edn, 2002).

Arnull, 'The Use and Abuse of Article 177 EEC' (1989) 52 *MLR* 622.

——, 'References to the European Court' (1990) 15 *ELRev* 375.

Barav, 'Preliminary Censorship? The Judgment of the European Court in *Foglia v Novello*' (1980) 5 *ELRev* 443.

Barnard and Sharpston, 'The Changing Face of Article 177 References' (1997) 34 *CMLRev* 1113.

Barnard, 'The PPU: Is it Worth the Candle? An Early Assessment' (2009) *ELRev* 281.

Bebr, 'The Existence of a Genuine Dispute: An Indispensable Precondition for the Jurisdiction of the Court under Article 177 EEC Treaty?' (1980) 17 *CMLRev* 525.

——, 'The Reinforcement of the Constitutional Review of Community Acts under Article 177 EEC Treaty' (1988) 25 *CMLRev* 667.

Dougan M, *National Remedies Before the Court of Justice* (Oxford, Hart Publishing, 2004) ch 6.

Kennedy, 'First Steps Towards a European Certiorari?' (1993) 18 *ELRev* 121.

Komarek, 'In the Court(s) We Trust. On the Need for Hierarchy and Differentiation in the Preliminary Ruling Procedure' (2007) 32 *ELRev* 467.

Lefevre, 'The Interpretation of Community Law by the Court of Justice in Areas of National Competence' (2004) 29 *ELRev* 501.

de la Mare T, 'Article 234 in Social and Political Context' in P Craig and G de Búrca (eds), *The Evolution of EU Law* (Oxford, Oxford University Press, 1999).

O'Keeffe, 'Is the Spirit of Article 177 under Attack? Preliminary References and Admissibility' (1998) 23 *ELRev* 509.

Snell, 'European Courts and Intellectual Property: A Tale of Hercules, Zeus and Cyclops' (2004) 29 *ELRev* 178.

Tridimas, 'Knocking on Heaven's Door: Fragmentation, Efficiency and Defiance in the Preliminary Rulings Procedure' (2003) 40 *CMLRev* 9.

Walsh, 'The Appeal of an Article 177 EEC Referral' (1993) 56 *MLR* 881.

Wyatt, 'The Relationship between Actions for Annulment and References on Validity after *TWD Deggendorf*' in Lonbay and Biondi (eds), *Remedies for Breach of EC Law* (1997).

Part III

Constitutional Fundamentals

8

The Direct Effect and Supremacy of Union Law

One of the defining characteristics of the European Union is the extraordinary degree to which it has penetrated the individual legal orders of its Member States: Union law is (for the most part) enforced in a decentralised manner though the medium of the domestic judicial systems, albeit in accordance with various fundamental principles established by the Court of Justice. This chapter explores some of the key building blocks in that system of decentralised enforcement: the principle of direct effect (through which Union law is capable of producing independent effects within the national legal orders), the principle of supremacy (whereby conflicting national provisions must be disapplied in favour of Union law), and the duty to interpret national law in conformity with the Treaties (which is a manifestation of the Member State's obligation of loyal co-operation towards the Union).

I – INTRODUCTION: THE SYSTEM OF DECENTRALISED ENFORCEMENT

Previous chapters have discussed the Union's primary law, and secondary acts adopted by the Union institutions within the framework of their competences, as well as the jurisdiction of the Court of Justice of the European Union to determine direct actions and to deliver preliminary rulings. It is now time to consider in greater detail the system of *decentralised* enforcement for Union law, ie the capacity of Union norms to produce independent legal effects within the *national* legal systems and to be enforced as such before the *domestic* courts.

The system of decentralised enforcement for Union law is built upon several main legal pillars. The two most important are the principles of direct effect and supremacy (which we have already mentioned on several previous occasions).[1]

The foundational ruling on direct effect is *van Gend en Loos*, delivered by the Court of Justice in 1963.[2] Dutch importers challenged the rate of import duty charged on a chemical product imported from Germany, alleging that reclassifying it under a different

---

[1] The principle of supremacy is often referred to also as the principle of primacy.
[2] Case 26/62 *van Gend en Loos* [1963] ECR 1.

heading of the Dutch customs tariff had resulted in an increase in duty that was prohibited under what is now Article 30 TFEU, which (in the version applicable at that time) provided that 'Member States shall refrain from introducing between themselves any new customs duties on imports . . . or any charges having equivalent effect, and from increasing those which they already apply in their trade with each other.' The Dutch administrative tribunal hearing the dispute asked the Court of Justice whether Article 30 TFEU had direct application within the territory of a Member State, in the sense that Member State nationals might, on the basis of those provisions, lay claim to rights which the domestic courts must protect. The Dutch government, in its submissions to the Court, argued that an infringement of the Treaty by a Member State could be submitted to the Court only under the procedure laid down by what are now Articles 258 and 259 TFEU, ie at the suit of the Commission or another Member State.[3] This general argument, to the effect that the provisions of the EEC Treaty simply gave rise to rights and obligations between Member States in international law, was rejected by Advocate General Roemer, who argued that anyone 'familiar with Community law' knew that 'in fact it does not just consist of contractual relations between a number of States considered as subjects of the law of nations'.[4] The Court's own reply is worth quoting in full.

> To ascertain whether the provisions of an international treaty extend so far in their effects it is necessary to consider the spirit, the general scheme and the wording of those provisions.
>
> The objective of the EEC Treaty, which is to establish a common market, the functioning of which is of direct concern to interested parties in the Community, implies that this treaty is more than an agreement which merely creates mutual obligations between the contracting states.
>
> This view is confirmed by the preamble to the Treaty which refers not only to governments but to peoples. It is also confirmed more specifically by the establishment of institutions endowed with sovereign rights, the exercise of which affects Member States and also their citizens.
>
> Furthermore, it must be noted that the nationals of the states brought together in the Community are called upon to co-operate in the functioning of this Community through the intermediary of the European Parliament and the Economic and Social Committee.
>
> In addition the task assigned to the Court of Justice under Article 234 EEC (now Article 267 TFEU), the object of which is to secure uniform interpretation of the Treaty by national courts and tribunals, confirms that the states have acknowledged that Community law has an authority which can be invoked by their nationals before those courts and tribunals.
>
> The conclusion to be drawn from this is that the Community constitutes a new legal order of international law for the benefit of which the states have limited their sovereign rights, albeit within limited fields, and the subjects of which comprise not only Member States but also their nationals. Independently of the legislation of Member States, Community law therefore not only imposes obligations on individuals but is also intended to confer upon them rights which become part of their legal heritage. These rights arise not only where they are expressly granted by the Treaty, but also by reason of obligations which the Treaty imposes in a clearly defined way upon individuals as well as upon the Member States and upon the institutions of the Community.

In other words, the EEC Treaty did not expressly deal with the legal effect of Community law within the Member States. In the absence of any express provision, the Court of Justice looked at the purpose and spirit of the Treaty. The purpose of the Community was to build a common market with common rules applying to Member States and private parties across the entire Community territory; that objective implied that all Community

[3] Case 26/62 [1963] ECR 1, 6. On these actions, see further Chapter 6.
[4] Case 26/62 [1963] ECR 1, 20.

rules had to be recognised and enforced effectively and uniformly by the national courts in every Member State, independently of any implementing measures taken by the Member States themselves. It followed that Community law must be capable of having direct effect and being enforced as such within the national legal systems—acting as a potential source of directly enforceable rights and obligations for individuals and public authorities.

It is difficult to overstate the importance of *van Gend en Loos*. One day, it was widely assumed that the Treaty of Rome was an ordinary international legal instrument entered into between contracting states and binding under ordinary international law—its relevance for individuals depending largely upon the approach and attitude of the Member States themselves towards incorporation of those international legal norms into their respective domestic legal systems. The next day, law created by or under the Treaty of Rome had in principle been emancipated into the legal order of every single Member State, becoming an independent source of rights and obligations—just like the Member State's own constitution, or primary legislation, or secondary legislation, or case law. But in that regard, *van Gend en Loos* raised an obvious next question: what happens if directly effective Community law conflicts with another provision of purely national law? Which should take priority, and which should be set aside? The answer came with the Court's ruling in *Costa v Enel*:[5]

> By contrast with ordinary international treaties, the EEC Treaty has created its own legal system which, on the entry into force of the Treaty, became an integral part of the legal systems of the Member States and which their courts are bound to apply.
>
> By creating a Community of unlimited duration, having its own institutions, its own personality, its own legal capacity and capacity of representation on the international plane and, more particularly, real powers stemming from a limitation of sovereignty or a transfer of powers from the states to the Community, the Member States have limited their sovereign rights, albeit within limited fields, and have thus created a body of law which binds both their nationals and themselves.
>
> The integration into the laws of each Member State of provisions which derive from the Community, and more generally the terms and the spirit of the Treaty, make it impossible for the states, as a corollary, to accord precedence to a unilateral and subsequent measure over a legal system accepted by them on a basis of reciprocity. Such a measure cannot therefore be inconsistent with that legal system. The executive force of Community law cannot vary from one state to another in deference to subsequent domestic laws, without jeopardizing the attainment of the objectives of the Treaty....
>
> The obligations undertaken under the Treaty establishing the Community would not be unconditional, but merely contingent, if they could be called in question by subsequent legislative acts of the signatories....
>
> The precedence of Community law is confirmed by Article 249 [EEC, now Article 288 TFEU], whereby a regulation 'shall be binding' and 'directly applicable in all Member States'. This provision, which is subject to no reservation, would be quite meaningless if a state could unilaterally nullify its effects by means of a legislative measure which could prevail over Community law.
>
> It follows from all these observations that the law stemming from the Treaty, an independent source of law, could not, because of its special and original nature, be overridden by domestic legal provisions, however framed, without being deprived of its character as Community law and without the legal basis of the Community itself being called into question.
>
> The transfer by the states from their domestic legal system to the Community legal system of the rights and obligations arising under the Treaty carries with it a permanent limitation of

---

[5] Case 6/64 *Costa v Enel* [1964] ECR 585.

their sovereign rights, against which a subsequent unilateral act incompatible with the concept of the Community cannot prevail.

In other words, we see the same concerns being used to justify the principle of supremacy as those which the Court had previously used to justify the doctrine of direct effect: it would be incompatible with attaining the Community's objective of creating a common market with common rules applying in all Member States, to tolerate a situation in which countries decide which rules they want to respect and which rules they do not; the existence of the common market, and therefore the existence of the Community itself, depends upon Treaty rules being applied effectively and uniformly across the Member States, and this implies the automatic and unconditional supremacy of directly effective Community over conflicting provisions of national law.

Through its rulings in *van Gend en Loos* and *Costa v Enel*, the Court of Justice laid the legal foundations for the European Union as we know it today: the addressees of Union law are not merely the Member States but also individuals, who can claim the benefits of Union law—and also bear its burdens—through a direct nexus with the Treaties themselves.

Fundamental as they are, the principles of direct effect and supremacy are not the only pillars supporting the system of decentralised enforcement for Union law. Three other key doctrines should be highlighted. The first is the duty of consistent interpretation as recognised in the case of *von Colson* and further developed in the ruling in *Marleasing*: national courts are obliged, so far as possible, to construe existing provisions of national law in conformity with relevant provisions of Union law.[6] In many ways, the duty of consistent interpretation might be seen as a first resort, as compared to the principles of direct effect and supremacy: many apparent conflicts between Union and national law might well be resolved by construing existing domestic rules so as to comply with the requirements laid down in Union law; only if such consistent interpretation is not possible does it become necessary to call upon the principles of direct effect and supremacy, so as to resolve the incompatibility between domestic and Union law in the latter's favour.[7] Next, there is the right to effective judicial protection: individuals relying upon provisions of Union law before the national courts are entitled to certain minimum standards of legal protection as regards the applicable remedies and procedural rules (eg when it comes to the availability of interim relief or the provision of compensatory damages; or as regards the imposition of time limits for bringing proceedings or the definition of admissible evidence). The right to effective judicial protection seeks to ensure that, even if the Member State respects the principles of direct effect and supremacy on paper, the effectiveness and uniformity of Union law are not undermined in practice by the more technical mechanics of decentralised enforcement via the domestic courts. Finally, there is the preliminary ruling procedure under Article 267 TFEU: national judges may (and sometimes must) seek guidance from the Court of Justice as regards the interpretation and application of Union law within the domestic legal system—thus providing an invaluable institutional channel for communication and co-operation between the Union's central and decentralised judicial authorities which further reinforces the effectiveness and uniformity of the Treaties.

Given its role as 'solution of first resort', this chapter begins within an examination of the duty of consistent interpretation. We continue by examining in greater detail the prin-

---

[6] Case 14/83 *von Colson* [1984] ECR 1891; Case C-106/89 *Marleasing* [1990] ECR I-4135.
[7] See further below.

ciples of direct effect and supremacy. Our analysis is completed by an exploration of the surprisingly contested relationship between those two doctrines. The remaining building blocks in the system of decentralised enforcement for Union law are dealt with elsewhere in this book: the right to effective judicial protection as regards remedies and procedural rules is considered in Chapter 9; the system of preliminary rulings under Article 267 TFEU was dealt with in Chapter 7.

II – THE DUTY OF CONSISTENT INTERPRETATION

Article 4(3) TEU (previously Article 10 EC) states that the Member States shall take any appropriate measure, general or particular, to ensure fulfilment of the obligations arising out of the Treaties or resulting from the acts of the Union institutions; the Member States shall facilitate the achievement of the Union's tasks and refrain from any measure which could jeopardise the attainment of the Union's objectives. The Court of Justice has divined from that general duty of loyal co-operation a whole series of more specific and legally binding obligations for the Member States designed to ensure the effective application of the Treaties—one of the most important of which is the duty of consistent interpretation between national and Union law.[8]

The Court first identified the duty of consistent interpretation in its ruling in *von Colson*.[9] The dispute concerned German rules purporting to implement Directive 76/207 on equal treatment between men and women in the field of employment.[10] The remedy provided for under national law in respect of a discriminatory refusal of employment in breach of the Directive seemed to consist merely of reimbursement of the claimant's costs in applying for the job, such as the travel expenses incurred in attending for interview—a purely nominal sum which fell short of the Directive's requirement that Member States should provide victims of unlawful discrimination with adequate judicial protection. Having found that the relevant provisions of the Directive were not sufficiently clear and precise to have direct effect in their own right (see further below), the Court nonetheless continued to state that:

> the Member States' obligation arising from a directive to achieve the result envisaged by the directive and their duty under Article [4(3) TEU] to take all appropriate measures, whether general or particular, to ensure the fulfilment of that obligation, is binding on all the authorities of Member States including, for matters within their jurisdiction, the courts. It follows that, in applying the national law and in particular the provisions of a national law specifically introduced in order to implement Directive 76/207, national courts are required to interpret their national law in the light of the wording and the purpose of the directive in order to achieve the result referred to in the third paragraph of Article [288 TFEU].[11]

---

[8]   On which, see further eg G Betlem, 'The Doctrine of Consistent Interpretation: Managing Legal Uncertainty' (2002) 22 *OJLS* 397; S Drake, 'Twenty Years After *von Colson*: The Impact of "Indirect Effect" on the Protection of the Individual's Community Rights' (2005) 30 *ELRev* 329.

[9]   Case 14/83 *von Colson* [1984] ECR 1891. See also Case 79/83 *Dorit Harz* [1984] ECR 1921.

[10]   [1976] OJ L39/40. See now Dir 2006/54 [2006] OJ L204/23.

[11]   Case 14/83 *von Colson* [1984] ECR 1891, para 26.

The Court qualified this statement two paragraphs later in its judgment:

> It is for the national court to interpret and apply the legislation adopted for the implementation of the directive in conformity with the requirements of Community law, *in so far as it is given discretion to do so under national law*.[12]

Although the Judgment in *von Colson* introduced the idea of consistent interpretation into Union law, it also suggested certain restrictions on the scope of that principle: first, that consistent interpretation applied only to national legislation specifically introduced to implement Union obligations; and secondly, that whether the domestic judge engaged in the process of consistent interpretation was a matter of discretion whose parameters were determined by national law itself. In the subsequent case of *Marleasing*, however, the Court rejected such restrictions.[13] The case concerned a Union directive which contained an exhaustive list of the grounds upon which Member States should treat companies as being legally null and void. However, Spanish law permitted the national courts to order companies a nullity on certain grounds not listed in the Union legislation. Unlike in *von Colson*, the relevant provisions of the directive could well be considered sufficiently clear and precise as to have direct effect in their own right, but the possibility of direct effect was precluded in this particular dispute because it involved two private parties and (as we shall see) directives cannot of themselves impose obligations upon an individual. Instead, the Court of Justice was asked to clarify the scope of the duty of consistent interpretation incumbent upon the Spanish courts. The Court held that, where a domestic court is called upon to interpret national law, whether the provisions in question were adopted before or after the directive concerned, it is required to do so, so far as possible, in the light of the wording and the purpose of the directive in order to achieve the result pursued by the latter. In other words: it is clear that the duty of consistent interpretation applies to all domestic legislation which is relevant to the subject-matter of the directive at issue, regardless of the date at or purpose for which that domestic legislation was introduced; furthermore, consistent interpretation is a duty imposed upon the national courts by Union law, which must be discharged regardless of the limits of their discretion under domestic law alone.[14]

The duty of national courts to interpret domestic law in conformity with Union law is a general one which applies regardless of the identity of the parties to the relevant proceedings. Thus, the duty of consistent interpretation must be respected (as in a case like *von Colson*) where the individual is seeking to enforce their Union law rights against the public authorities of a Member State.[15] Conversely, the duty of consistent interpretation applies also where the Member State is seeking to enforce Union law obligations against an individual. For example, in *Aslanidou*, Greece had failed correctly to implement a Union directive within the applicable time limit, but the competent public authorities nevertheless requested the national court to interpret existing Greek legislation in conformity with that directive, to the potential detriment of the other (private) party to the proceedings.[16] Furthermore, it is well established (by rulings such as *Marleasing* itself) that the duty of consistent interpretation will be activated within the context of disputes between

---

[12] Case 14/83 *von Colson* [1984] ECR 1891, para 28 (emphasis added).
[13] Case 106/89 *Marleasing* [1990] ECR 4135.
[14] Also eg Case C-334/92 *Wagner Miret* [1993] ECR I-6911.
[15] Also eg Case C-54/96 *Dorsch Consult* [1997] ECR I-4961.
[16] Case C-142/04 *Aslanidou* [2005] ECR I-7181. Also eg Case C-321/05 *Kofoed* [2007] ECR I-5795.

two purely private parties concerning their mutual rights and obligations.[17] The general nature of the duty of consistent interpretation is also reflected in the fact that it operates independently of the principles of direct effect and supremacy. Thus, the duty of consistent interpretation applies (as in a case such as *von Colson*) where the relevant provisions of Union law are incapable of having direct effect because they fail to fulfil the essential prerequisites of being sufficiently clear, precise and unconditional (see further below).[18] Similarly, the duty of consistent interpretation applies (as in a case such as *Marleasing*) where the relevant Union act cannot have direct effect because of the identity of the parties involved in the dispute, as when the provisions of a directive are invoked during litigation between two private individuals (see further below).[19] Indeed, the duty of consistent interpretation will apply even where the relevant provisions of Union law might in theory be fully capable of having direct effect and thus also of enjoying supremacy over any conflicting national measures. As mentioned above, if an apparent inconsistency between Union and national law can be resolved by purely interpretative means, then that path should be followed as the solution of first resort, without ever needing to have recourse to the principles of direct effect and supremacy at all. For example, in *Murphy v An Bord Telecom Eireann*, the Court regarded the duty to set aside national rules incompatible with the direct effect of Article 157 TFEU, concerning the right to equal pay between men and women, as arising *only* if it proved impossible to construe the disputed national rules in a way which accorded with the requirements of Union law.[20] Similarly, where a Union directive has been properly implemented by national measures—if necessary through the medium of consistent interpretation—then its effects will extend to individuals through those implementing measures.[21] It is not open to the individuals to side-step the appropriate provisions of national law and rely upon the direct effect of the provisions of the Union directive itself.[22]

Despite its far-reaching scope of application, Union law does nevertheless impose certain limits upon the duty of consistent interpretation, in particular, by reference to the general principles of Union law.[23] Two general principles of Union are especially relevant in this context. The first is the principle of legal certainty. As highlighted in *Marleasing* itself, the national courts are only obliged to interpret domestic legislation in conformity with Union law *in so far as it is possible to do so*.[24] As the Court confirmed in rulings such as *Pupino*, the duty of consistent interpretation does not require national courts to distort any reasonable meaning of the words, or to adopt a construction which is simply *contra legem*.[25] What is expected, as the Court explained in its ruling in *Pfeiffer*, is that the domestic courts will consider national law *as a whole* in order to assess to what extent it may be applied so as not to produce a result contrary to that sought by Union law.[26]

---

[17] Also eg Case C-2/97 *Borsana* [1998] ECR I-8597; Case C-343/98 *Collino* [2000] ECR I-6659; Cases C-397-403/01 *Pfeiffer* [2004] ECR I-8835; Case C-350/03 *Schulte* [2005] ECR I-9215.

[18] Also eg Case C-54/96 *Dorsch Consult* [1997] ECR I-4961.

[19] Also eg Case C-343/98 *Collino* [2000] ECR I-6659; Cases C-397–403/01 *Pfeiffer* [2004] ECR I-8835.

[20] Case 157/86 *Murphy v An Bord Telecom Eireann* [1988] ECR 673, para 11. Similarly eg Case C-262/97 *Engelbrecht* [2000] ECR I-7321, paras 39–40; Cases C-444/09 and C-456/09 *Gavieiro* (Judgment of 22 December 2010) para 73.

[21] eg Case 102/79 *Commission v Belgium* [1980] ECR 1473; Case 8/81 *Becker* [1982] ECR 53.

[22] Case 270/81 *Felicitas* [1982] ECR 2771.

[23] Note also the limitations which apply to the duty of consistent interpretation before the deadline (if any) for implementing Union law into the national legal system expires: see further below.

[24] Case 106/89 *Marleasing* [1990] ECR 4135, para 8.

[25] See Case C-105/03 *Pupino* [2005] ECR I-5285, para 47.

[26] Cases C-397–403/01 *Pfeiffer* [2004] ECR I-8835. Also eg Case C-212/04 *Adeneler* [2006] ECR I-6057.

The second general principle of Union law which is particularly relevant in this context is the principle of legality in the sphere of criminal law (a principle derived from Article 7(1) ECHR and now enshrined in Article 49(1) of the Charter of Fundamental Rights). The principle of legality requires that the criminal law must be clearly defined.[27] As the ECtHR held in *SW v United Kingdom*, Article 7(1) ECHR is an essential element of the rule of law which provides effective safeguards against arbitrary prosecution, conviction and punishment.[28] The ECtHR has developed an extensive body of case law on the definition and interpretation of criminal obligations: it requires, for example, that criminal rules must be clear and accessible; should not be interpreted extensively against the defendant; and the development of criminal law through case law interpretation should be consistent with the essence of the offence and should have been reasonably foreseeable by the defendant.[29]

The Court of Justice has sought to adapt those requirements under the ECHR to the particular context of EU law. On the one hand, it seems clear that national courts must refer to Union law where the latter is intended merely to act as a point of reference for the purposes of interpreting any relevant national implementing measures—even where the latter involve liabilities of a criminal nature. For example, in *Lindqvist*, the Court provided detailed guidance on the interpretation of the Data Protection Directive,[30] for the purposes of determining the criminal liability of a Swedish defendant, pursuant to the relevant national implementing legislation.[31] On the other hand, the principle of legality kicks in at the point where reliance upon Union law would tend rather to aggravate the defendant's criminal liabilities beyond the ordinary interpretation to be attributed to the applicable national criminal law.[32] Thus, the Court of Justice held in *Kolpinghuis Nijmegen* that the national court's obligation to refer to the content of a Union directive when interpreting its own domestic law reaches a limit where such an interpretation has the effect of determining or aggravating, on the basis of the directive and in the absence of a law enacted for its implementation, the liability in criminal law of persons who act in contravention of that directive's provisions.[33] For example, *Arcaro* concerned an Italian citizen charged before the criminal courts with having discharged dangerous substances into a local water system. The prosecution was based on Italian legislation adopted to implement a Union environmental protection directive but which had failed to do so correctly. The national court was unsure whether nevertheless to construe the Italian measure so as to conform with the directive and thereby criminalise the defendant's behaviour. The Court of Justice advised the national court that the duty of consistent interpretation reached its limit where this would lead to the imposition upon a private party of obligations laid

---

[27] ECtHR in *Kokkinakis v Greece* (Judgment of 25 May 1993).

[28] ECtHR in *SW v United Kingdom* (Judgment of 22 November 1995).

[29] See eg *SW v United Kingdom* (Judgment of 22 November 1995); *CR v United Kingdom* (Judgment of 22 November 1995); *Cantoni v France* (Judgment of 15 November 1996); *Başkaya and Okçuoğlu v Turkey* (Judgment of 8 July 1999); *Coëme v Belgium* (Judgment of 22 June 2000); *Streletz, Kessler and Krenz v Germany* (Judgment of 22 March 2001); *Veeber v Estonia (No 2)* (Judgment of 21 January 2003); *Achour v France* (Judgment of 29 March 2006); *Kafkaris v Cyprus* (Judgment of 12 February 2008); *Scoppola v Italy (No 2)* (Judgment of 17 September 2009).

[30] Dir 95/46 [1995] OJ L281/31.

[31] Case C-101/01 *Lindqvist* [2003] ECR I-12971. Also eg Case C-421/07 *Damgaard* [2009] ECR I-2629.

[32] Consider eg Cases C-74/95 and C-129/95 *Criminal Proceedings Against X* [1996] ECR I-6609. Also eg Cases C-189/02, C-202/02, C-205-C-208/02 and C-213/02 *Dansk Rørindustri v Commission* [2005] ECR I-5425.

[33] Case 80/86 *Kolpinghuis Nijmegen* [1987] ECR 3969.

down in an incorrectly implemented directive.[34] The principle of legality applies not only in respect of directives but as regards Union law more generally. Consider the ruling in *Criminal Proceedings Against X*.[35] Austrian legislation prohibiting the importation or sale of counterfeit goods on pain of criminal penalties failed to fully implement the relevant Union regulation, which also obliged the Member States to adopt appropriate sanctions in cases concerning the mere transit of counterfeit goods across the national territory. The Court held that, insofar as national law did not prohibit the mere transit of counterfeit goods, the general principles of Union law prohibited the imposition of criminal penalties—even if this meant accepting the existence of national rules which ran contrary to Union law.

There is an important qualification to the case law limiting the duty of consistent interpretation by reference to the principle of legality in the sphere of criminal law. *Pupino* concerned an alleged incompatibility between Italian rules permitting the cross-examination, during the adversarial stage of criminal proceedings, of evidence given by the child victims of non-sexual abuse; and the obligation under Framework Decision 2001/220 on the standing of victims in criminal proceedings,[36] adopted under the old Third Pillar, to ensure that particularly vulnerable victims benefit from specific treatment best suited to their circumstances.[37] The judgment was highly significant at the time of its delivery for having recognised that the duty of loyal co-operation applied to Member States also within the legal order established under the old Third Pillar; despite the lack of any possibility that framework decisions could produce direct effect, the national courts were nonetheless bound by the duty of consistent interpretation.[38] Having recalled that that duty was limited in accordance with the standards developed under the *Kolpinghuis Nijmegen* caselaw, the Court nevertheless went on to find that 'the provisions which form the subject-matter of this [preliminary ruling] do not concern the extent of the criminal liability of the person concerned but the conduct of the proceedings and the means of taking evidence'.[39] In such cases, the duty of consistent interpretation is qualified not by reference to the principle of legality as derived from Article 7(1) ECHR, but rather by the national court's duty to respect the defendant's other fundamental rights under Union law, in particular, the need to ensure that the relevant criminal proceedings (considered as a whole) are not rendered incompatible with the right to a fair trial in the sense of Article 6 ECHR.

The distinction drawn in *Pupino* between the relevance of the principle of legality for substantive rules of criminal liability, as compared to the rules of criminal procedure and evidence, has since been reinforced in subsequent rulings.[40] Although the position under Union law does not appear to be incompatible with the standards contained in Article 7(1) ECHR as construed by the ECtHR itself,[41] the Court's approach has nevertheless attracted considerable academic criticism: not only because it will often be difficult to distinguish between substantive and procedural rules (and such distinctions in any case are drawn very differently across the Member States); but also on the grounds that changes

---

[34] Case C-168/95 *Criminal proceedings against Luciano Arcaro* [1996] ECR I-4705. Also eg Cases C-387/02, C-391/02 and C-403/02 *Berlusconi* [2005] ECR I-3565; Case C-384/02 *Allan Bang* [2005] ECR I-9939.

[35] Case C-60/02 *Criminal Proceedings Against X* [2004] ECR I-651.

[36] [2001] OJ L82/1.

[37] Case C-105/03 *Pupino* [2005] ECR I-5285.

[38] See further below on the legal effects of ex-Third Pillar framework decisions.

[39] Case C-105/03 *Pupino* [2005] ECR I-5285, para 46.

[40] eg Case C-467/05 *Dell'Orto* [2007] ECR I-5557; Case C-404/07 *Katz* [2008] ECR I-7607.

[41] eg *Coëme v Belgium* (Judgment of 22 June 2000); *Scoppola v Italy (No 2)* (Judgment of 17 September 2009).

in the rules of procedure and evidence can still have significant detrimental effects for the defendant, amounting in practice to determining or aggravating his/her criminal liabilities, in a manner which undermines the spirit even if not the letter of the safeguards developed in the *Kolpinghuis Nijmegen* case law.[42]

As well as the limits to the duty of consistent interpretation imposed by reference to the general principles of Union law, it is worth pointing out that the *Marleasing* case law only applies as regards *legally binding* provisions of Union law. An appreciably weaker interpretative obligation applies in respect of other categories of Union act. That is true, in particular, of the recommendations referred to in Article 288 TFEU and described as having 'no binding force'. The Court held in *Grimaldi* that, even if recommendations are not intended to produce binding effects and are not capable of creating rights that individuals can rely on before a national court, they are not without any legal effect. The national courts are bound to take recommendations into consideration in order to decide disputes brought before them, in particular, where such recommendations cast light on the interpretation of national measures adopted in order to implement them, or where they are designed to supplement binding provisions of Union law.[43]

In summary: the duty of consistent interpretation is the first port of call for resolving apparent inconsistencies between national law and Union law. It applies in a wide range of situations and imposes a strong interpretative obligation upon the national courts. But the duty of consistent interpretation is not unlimited: the general principle of legal certainty, as well as the general principle of legality in the sphere of criminal law, mean that there will be many situations where domestic rules cannot be construed so as to conform to the Member State's obligations under the Treaties. In such situations, we must turn to the 'harder' tools of decentralised enforcement, so as to guarantee the effective application of Union law: the principles of direct effect and supremacy.

III – THE PRINCIPLE OF DIRECT EFFECT

We understand the principle of direct effect to refer to the capacity of Union law to produce independent legal effects within the national legal systems. As we shall see further below, that understanding would not go uncontested among certain commentators; nevertheless, it is the approach we feel best reflects the Court of Justice's case law and it is the one we shall adopt in the analysis which follows.

Before continuing, it may be useful to clarify a potentially confusing point of terminology: the description of provisions of Union law as being either 'directly applicable' or 'directly effective'. In theory, it is possible to draw a clear distinction between those two concepts. Direct applicability is the attribute expressly conferred by the Treaties upon regulations to ensure that the latter are assimilated into the national legal order without the need for specific incorporation by the Member State.[44] Direct effect refers to the capacity of any provision of Union law, provided it satisfies certain threshold criteria, to create legal

---

[42] See eg E Spaventa, 'Opening Pandora's Box: Some Reflections on the Constitutional Effects of the Decision in *Pupino*' (2006) 3 *European Constitutional Law Review* 5.

[43] Case C-322/88 *Grimaldi* [1989] ECR 4407. More recently, eg Case C-207/01 *Altair Chimica* [2003] ECR I-8875; Cases C-317/08, C-318/08, C-319/08 and C-320/08 *Alassini* (Judgment of 18 March 2010).

[44] See Art 288 TFEU and further below.

rights and/or obligations and/or powers which must be recognised and enforced within the domestic legal system. Establishing the existence of direct effect is therefore a matter of interpretation; specific provisions of the Treaties, regulations, directives and decisions may all be endowed with this quality. In practice, however, the expressions 'directly applicable' and 'directly effective' are often used interchangeably—even by the Court of Justice itself—usually so as to refer to the principle of direct effect.[45] The point is not a fundamental one, save in the cause of pedantry, and any confusion need go no deeper than the terminological, since the intended meaning will invariably be clear from the context.

A – The Threshold Criteria for Direct Effect

For any provision of Union law to have direct effect, and thus be recognised as capable of producing independent legal effects within the national legal system, it must satisfy certain threshold criteria: first, the relevant provision must be sufficiently clear and precise; secondly, the relevant provision must be unconditional and leave no room for discretion in its implementation by the Union or national institutions; and finally, the deadline (if any) for the application, implementation or transposition of the relevant Union provisions must already have expired.[46] If those three criteria are fulfilled, then the relevant Union act becomes capable of producing direct effect. Application of the threshold criteria for direct effect is essentially an interpretative task to be undertaken on a case-by-case basis. Unsurprisingly, there is an enormous jurisprudence testing whether particular provisions of countless Union acts satisfy the conditions for having direct effect. Some examples should suffice to illustrate the general approach adopted by the Court of Justice.

Consider some of the major judgments in which Union law was recognised as capable of having direct effect. For example, *van Gend en Loos* itself concerned Article 30 TFEU—a relatively straightforward provision which prohibits Member States from imposing customs duties or charges having equivalent effect on imported goods.[47] Such a provision is clear and precise, does not depend on any further implementation by the Union institutions or the Member States before it becomes 'legally perfect', and does not contain any exceptions or derogations. It is entirely apt for producing direct effect. *Salgoil* concerned the rather more complex provisions now found in Articles 34 and 36 TFEU, prohibiting quantitative restrictions and measures having equivalent effect upon imported goods, but also permitting Member States to derogate from that prohibition on certain specified grounds.[48] The Court nevertheless held that the relevant Treaty provisions could have direct effect, since the rules were clear and precise, and did not require further implementation by the Union institutions or the Member States, while the permitted derogations were themselves clear and precise, and their application by the Member States was amenable to judicial review before the Union and national courts. The provisions at issue in *Reyners* were different again: the original version of what is now Article 49 TFEU seemed to envisage that securing the freedom of establishment for self-employed persons depended upon the Union institutions adopting implementing legislation within a certain

---

[45] See the ruling in Case 2/74 *Reyners* [1974] ECR 631, to the effect that Art 49 TFEU is directly applicable. In similar vein, eg Case 17/81 *Pabst* [1982] ECR 1331; Case 104/81 *Kupferberg* [1982] ECR 3641.

[46] Note the Opinion of AG Mayras in Case 2/74 *Reyners* [1974] ECR 631.

[47] Case 26/62 *van Gend en Loos* [1963] ECR 1.

[48] Case 13/68 *Salgoil* [1968] ECR 453.

time period.[49] On that basis, one might have assumed that the relevant Treaty provision was conditional in nature and could not enjoy direct effect. However, the Court held that, once the deadline for Union action had passed, the freedom of establishment was still sufficiently clear and precise to have direct effect in its own right, even in the absence of specific implementing measures from the Union institutions.

Conversely, consider various judgments in which Union law was denied the capacity to produce direct effect of its own. For example, the Court in *Ratti* was asked to clarify the circumstances in which provisions of a directive might have direct effect.[50] As we shall see further below, directives always contain a deadline for their transposition by the Member State into national law. The Court held that provisions of a directive—even if they are clear and precise—cannot have direct effect until after that deadline for transposition has expired. During the period for transposition, individuals may never rely directly upon rights and obligations envisaged for them under Union law by the relevant directive. The dispute in *Gilly* concerned ex-Article 293 EC (now repealed), which set out an obligation for Member States to enter into negotiations with each other with a view to abolishing double taxation within the common market.[51] The question arose: could an individual, faced with possibility of being taxed by two Member States in respect of the same income, rely on ex-Article 293 EC so as to challenge that double taxation? The Court held that ex-Article 293 EC was purely programmatic: it created no more than an obligation for the Member States to begin negotiations so as to achieve its stated objective at some future point in time; ex-Article 293 EC was not intended to create any freestanding rules enforceable per se by individuals. Finally, consider the dispute in *Wijsenbeek*.[52] The original version of what is now Article 26 TFEU provided that the Union institutions should adopt measures with the aim of progressively establishing the internal market over a period expiring on 31 December 1992, that internal market being defined as an area without internal frontiers in which the free movement of goods, persons, services and capital is ensured in accordance with the provisions of the Treaty. A Dutch national who returned to the Netherlands from a trip to Belgium, and was fined by the national immigration authorities for crossing the border without possessing a valid passport or identity card, attempted to rely on Article 26 TFEU as a directly effective measure so as to challenge the existence of passport controls at the Union's internal borders. After all, the deadline of 31 December 1992 for establishing the area without internal frontiers had already passed and the Union institutions had failed to adopt the measures necessary to abolish border checks. By analogy with *Reyners*, Article 26 TFEU might have been capable of producing direct effect on its own two feet. However, the Court of Justice pointed out that the abolition of internal border checks between Member States was necessarily dependent upon the adoption of Union legislation establishing a common policy on border controls at the Member States' external frontiers; until such Union legislation had actually been passed, there could be no question of Article 26 TFEU having any direct effect of its own.

In those situations where Union measures do not meet the threshold criteria required to have direct effect, individuals may still be able to achieve a more limited degree of protection under Union law. However, it is necessary in this regard to distinguish between

---

[49]   Case 2/74 *Reyners* [1974] ECR 631.
[50]   Case 148/78 *Ratti* [1979] ECR 1629.
[51]   Case C-336/96 *Gilly* [1998] ECR I-2793.
[52]   Case C-378/97 *Wijsenbeek* [1999] ECR I-6207.

two different situations: where the deadline (if any) for implementation of the relevant Union measures into national has already expired; and where such a deadline remains active.

Where the deadline (if any) has already expired, the individual may seek to rely on two main forms of protection as an alternative to direct effect per se. The first is the duty of consistent interpretation: as we have seen, the national courts are obliged to construe existing domestic law, so far as possible, in conformity with Union law—even where the latter lacks direct effect because it is insufficiently clear, precise and unconditional. Consider, for example, the dispute in *Dorsch Consult*.[53] Germany had failed to implement a Union directive requiring the Member States to establish tribunals competent to hear disputes about the fairness of procedures for awarding public *service* contracts, though national tribunals did exist with jurisdiction to determine disputes about procedures for the award of public *supply* contracts. The Court held that the Union directive was incapable of having direct effect, since it left significant discretion to the Member State in its choice of which court or tribunal should be considered competent to exercise jurisdiction over the relevant category of disputes; but the German courts were still obliged to consider whether the provisions of the existing German legislation, establishing public supply tribunals, could be construed so as to give effect also to the directive on public service tribunals. The second avenue of redress—particularly where the duty of consistent interpretation is incapable of resolving the incompatibility between national law and non-directly effective Union law—is to bring an action for reparation against the Member State pursuant to the *Francovich* case law. The latter case law will be discussed more extensively in Chapter 9. Suffice for present purposes to summarise the ruling in *Francovich* itself, as a useful illustration of the action for damages being invoked as an alternative to the existence of direct effect per se.[54] A Union directive required the Member States to establish a guarantee body which would cover workers' unpaid wages in the event of their employer becoming insolvent. Italy had failed to implement the directive into its national legal system within the applicable deadline. A group of workers whose employer had gone into insolvency attempted to rely on the directive directly against the Italian state, but the Court of Justice held that the directive did not have direct effect: it left the Member States significant discretion about the identify and nature of the relevant guarantee institution. The Court nevertheless continued to find that Italy was obliged (in principle) to make reparation to the affected workers for the losses they had incurred as a result of the Member State's failure to comply with its obligation to implement the directive into national law within its deadline.

Where the deadline for implementing Union law into the national legal system remains active, the claimant's legal situation is more precarious. The Court of Justice is clearly more hesitant in such situations about interfering with the Member State's intended margin of discretion and therefore offers less effective standards of protection for affected individuals. On the one hand, the Court in *Inter-Environnement Wallonie* was prepared to impose certain negative obligations upon the Member State.[55] The very purpose of a transposition period is to offer Member States the necessary time to adopt implementation measures; Member States cannot be faulted for failing to implement Union measures into their domestic legal order before the expiry of such a period. However, it follows

---

[53] Case C-54/96 *Dorsch Consult* [1997] ECR I-4961.
[54] Cases C-6 and 9/90 *Francovich* [1991] ECR I-5357.
[55] Case C-129/96 *Inter-Environnement Wallonie* [1997] ECR I-7411.

from the duty of loyal co-operation contained in Article 4(3) TEU that, even during the period for transposition, Member States must refrain from taking any measures liable seriously to compromise the result prescribed by the directive.[56] On the other hand, the ruling in *Adeneler* shows how the Court is reluctant to go further and impose more positive obligations upon the Member State while the deadline for implementation remains active.[57] The case raised the question of whether the duty of consistent interpretation should apply in disputes arising before the deadline for implementing Union law has expired. Some commentators had argued that national courts should indeed be obliged to interpret national law, so far as possible, to comply with Union law regardless of any deadline for implementation.[58] However, the Court in *Adeneler* held that national courts are not actively obliged to construe domestic law in compliance with Union law before the deadline for transposition has expired; they too are bound only by the negative obligation under *Inter-Environnement Wallonie* to refrain from construing national law in a manner that might seriously compromise the attainment of the objectives pursued by the relevant Union measure.[59]

B – Who May Rely on Directly Effective Union Law?

Having established that any given provision of Union law is capable, in principle, of producing direct effect within the national legal system, one might consider an obvious next question to be: who may actually benefit from that direct effect, in the sense of being legally competent to invoke the relevant Union provisions before the national courts?

In many situations, the tendency of a given Union provision to produce direct effect can be equated with the creation of individual rights enforceable before the national courts by its intended beneficiary or any member of its intended class of beneficiaries. Thus, for example, the direct effect of Articles 30 or 34 TFEU on the free movement of goods (as recognised in *van Gend en Loos* and in *Salgoil*, respectively) necessarily implies an individual right for traders not to be burdened by unjustified hindrances to cross-border trade, and the ability of such traders to challenge national measures infringing that right before the domestic courts.[60] Similarly, the direct effect of Article 49 TFEU on the freedom of establishment (as recognised in *Reyners*) necessarily implies an individual right for migrant Union citizens not to be discriminated against on grounds of nationality as regards their self-employed activities, and the ability of such individuals to challenge public or private measures infringing that right before the national courts.[61]

That close association between direct effect and individual rights led some commentators to argue that a more fundamental legal interrelationship was at work here: direct

---

[56] See also eg Case C-14/02 *ATRAL* [2003] ECR I-4431; Case C-157/02 *Rieser Internationale Transporte* [2004] ECR I-1477; Case C-316/04 *Stichting Zuid-Hollandse Milieufederatie* [2005] ECR I-9759; Case C-144/04 *Mangold* [2005] ECR I-9981; Case C-422/05 *Commission v Belgium* [2007] ECR I-4749.

[57] Case C-212/04 *Adeneler* [2006] ECR I-6057. Note that previous authorities already pointed in a similar direction, eg Case C-456/98 *Centrosteel v Adipol* [2000] ECR I-6007; Cases C-240–4/98 *Océano Grupo Editorial* [2000] ECR I-4941; Cases C-397–403/01 *Pfeiffer* [2004] ECR I-8835.

[58] cf AG Kokott in Case C-313/02 *Wippel* [2004] ECR I-9483; AG Tizzano in Case C-144/04 *Mangold* [2005] ECR I-9981; AG Kokott in Case C-212/04 *Adeneler* [2006] ECR I-6057.

[59] See also eg Cases C-261/07 and C-299/07 *VTB-VAB* [2009] ECR I-2949; Case C-304/08 *Plus Warenhandelsgesellschaft* (Judgment of 14 January 2010).

[60] See further Chapters 13 and 14.

[61] See further Chapter 17.

effect was only possible in situations where the relevant Union provision could be said to create individual rights; conversely, recognition by the Court of direct effect must necessarily have implied the creation of some corresponding individual right.[62] However, the case law has gradually clarified that the Court's understanding of direct effect—at least when defined as the capacity of Union law to produce independent effects within the national legal systems—stretches beyond the creation of individual rights so as also to embrace legal proceedings initiated for the protection of more diffuse public interests. In such cases, it might appear that the claimant is vested not with any subjective personal right, but rather, with a right of standing to invoke the relevant provisions of Union law before the national courts.

Some situations have involved what might be considered an administrative law right to standing for the enforcement of directly effective Union law in the general interest. Consider, for example, the Member State's obligation to carry out environmental impact assessments under Directive 85/337.[63] The dispute in *Kraaijeveld* concerned an action brought by a local business challenging the legality of the decision of a Dutch local authority to approve certain dyke reinforcement works without conducting the necessary assessment. The Court held that, where the Union has imposed on Member States the obligation to pursue such a course of conduct, the useful effect of that directive would be weakened if individuals were prevented from relying on it before their national courts, and if the latter were prevented from taking it into consideration in order to rule whether the national legislature had kept within the limits of its discretion.[64] Other situations have involved what might better be thought of as a private law right to standing for the enforcement of directly effective Union law, albeit still in the general interest. Consider, for example, the judgment in *Muñoz*. The claimant alleged that a rival undertaking was selling grapes in the United Kingdom in breach of certain Union regulations on quality standards for fruit and vegetables. Under English law, enforcement of those regulations was reserved exclusively to a public authority, which refused to exercise its monopoly powers in this particular dispute. The claimant therefore initiated its own proceedings before the domestic courts, arguing that the Union regulations were directly effective and could be enforced not only by the competent public authorities but also by interested individuals. The Court of Justice held that the purpose of the regulations was to keep unsatisfactory products off the market, for the protection of both consumers and rival undertakings. The full effectiveness of those quality standards implied that it must be possible to enforce obligations contained in the regulations by means of civil proceedings brought against a trader by one of its competitors—thus supplementing enforcement by the Member State itself.[65]

However, the dividing line within the concept of direct effect, between the narrow sense of creating individual rights, and a broader understanding which embraces also the mere invocability of Union law, is not always an easy one to maintain. For example, the

---

[62] For a good example of this argument in practice, consider Case C-431/92 *Commission v Germany* [1995] ECR I-2189. See further eg A Downes and C Hilson, 'Making Sense of Rights: Community Rights in EC Law' (1999) 24 *ELRev* 121.

[63] Dir 85/337 on the assessment of the effects of certain public and private projects on the environment [1985] OJ L175/40.

[64] Case C-72/95 *Kraaijeveld* [1996] ECR I-5403. Similarly eg Case C-435/97 *World Wildlife Fund* [1999] ECR I-5613; Case C-287/98 *Linster* [2000] ECR I-6917. See further eg S Prechal and L Hancher, 'Individual Environmental Rights: Conceptual Pollution in EU Environmental Law?' (2001) 2 *Yearbook of European Environmental Law* 89.

[65] Case C-253/00 *Muñoz* [2002] ECR I-7289.

Court of Justice in *Wells* suggested that individuals whose interests are adversely affected by the Member State's failure to carry out an environmental impact assessment under Directive 85/337 must be entitled to seek damages before the national courts in respect of their losses—a remedy that is more usually associated with the vindication of personal rights than with the protection of wider public interests,[66] Similarly, it is unclear whether the claimant in *Muñoz* was merely granted a right of standing to invoke the relevant Union regulations before the national courts in the general interest; or was instead vested with an individual right to compete under fair economic conditions (and, by implication, perhaps also to some form of compensatory remedy in respect of any losses which may have been incurred).[67]

Similar points arise when one considers those provisions of Union law which simply authorise public authorities to take action which they would not otherwise be authorised to take. Again, it would appear difficult to describe such provisions as directly effective in any narrow sense focused around the creation of individual rights; but such provisions do undoubtedly produce independent legal effects within the Member States and thus qualify as directly effective in the broader sense advocated here. Consider, for example, Article 267 TFEU directly bestowing upon national courts the competence to refer questions to the Court of Justice for a preliminary ruling. National rules may establish the relevant details of procedure for making such references, but they neither create nor condition the capacity to make a reference, which flows directly from Article 267 TFEU itself.[68] The latter provision does not give rise to rights in individuals which the national courts are bound to safeguard, but it may nevertheless be considered directly effective in the sense that it produces independent effects within the national legal order.[69] The same would appear true of the duty of consistent interpretation derived from Article 4(3) TFEU. There is no doubt that that provision creates binding obligations for the national courts as regards their approach to the construction of domestic law. More recent cases go so far as to state that the duty of consistent interpretation must be considered to be 'inherent in the system of the Treaty'.[70] But it seems difficult to describe the duty of consistent interpretation in terms of the creation of individual rights (whether to a personal benefit, or of standing and invocability).[71] The duty of consistent interpretation is another provision of Union law that is directly effective only in the broader sense of producing independent effects within the national legal system, through the imposition of an autonomous obligation upon the domestic judges.

There now seems to be greater consensus around the proposition that the doctrine of direct effect is capable of applying, in principle, to any provision of Union law (regardless of whether it creates personal individual rights, merely rights to standing, or indeed no rights at all).[72] That point clarified, we can return to our original question—of determining

---

[66] Case C-201/02 *Wells* [2004] ECR I-723.

[67] See further eg A Biondi, Annotation of *Muñoz* (2003) 40 *CMLRev* 1241.

[68] See further Chapter 7.

[69] Particularly in circumstances where Art 267 TFEU imposes a *duty* on national courts to make a reference: see Chapter 7 for further discussion.

[70] eg Case C-160/01 *Mau* [2003] ECR I-4791, para 34; Cases C-397/01–403/01 *Pfeiffer* [2004] ECR I-8835, para 114; Cases C-378–380/07 *Angelidaki* [2009] ECR I-3071, para 198.

[71] Especially where the duty of consistent interpretation works against the individual, within the context of litigation brought by the defaulting Member State: see above.

[72] See further eg D Edwards, 'Direct Effect: Myth, Mess or Mystery?' in J M Prinssen and A Schrauwen (eds), *Direct Effect: Rethinking a Classic of EC Legal Doctrine* (Groningen, Europa Law Publishing, 2002); S Prechal, 'Member State Liability and Direct Effect: What's the Difference After All?' [2006] *European Business*

exactly which range of persons should be recognised as legally competent to enforce any given provision of Union law before the domestic courts—knowing that that is actually a separate inquiry from the issue of whether the relevant Union act is capable of producing direct effect in the first place.

Defining the precise range of persons entitled to enforce any given provision of Union law is a task that falls primarily to the Court of Justice.[73] A detailed consideration of the Court's approach falls outside the scope of this chapter.[74] However, the broad principles may be summarised as follows. The starting point for the Court's analysis of exactly who may rely upon a directly effective provision of Union law is to ascertain the protective scope of the relevant Union instrument based upon an interpretation of its legislative text.[75] For those purposes, Union secondary legislation sometimes establishes relatively clear parameters for determining the capacity to enforce any given provision: consider, for example, Directive 2003/35 on public participation and access to justice as regards environmental protection in fields such as environmental impact assessments;[76] or Directive 2009/22 on the public and private entities that should be entitled to seek injunctions for the protection of collective consumer interests.[77] In addition to the legislative text per se, however, the ECJ also considers significant the broader regulatory context and objectives of the relevant measure—whilst furthermore taking into account certain more general policy factors, especially those that secure the effective enforcement of Union law within each national legal order.[78] In particular, it appears that the Court will usually be persuaded to transform a mere factual involvement in any given situation into a concrete legal capacity to enforce the applicable Union law, based on an analysis of the claimant's direct interest in the subject-matter of the relevant provisions, and of his/her 'added value' in securing the effective enforcement of Union law.[79] For those purposes, the available case law suggests that the Court will carry out such a transformation from factual interest into legal capacity based on one of two main factors.

The first factor is whether the claimant's interest can be assimilated to that of the primary beneficiary under the relevant Union instrument, so that recognising capacity to enforce for the claimant directly advances the legal position of the primary beneficiary—assuming that it is possible to identify a sufficiently close relationship between the claimant and the primary beneficiary, and to demonstrate a sufficiently consistent alignment of their respective interests. For example, in *Stockel*, an employer was entitled to rely on the provisions of the Equal Treatment Directive,[80] as a defence to his own criminal prosecution under domestic legislation, where the latter discriminated against his female

---

Law Review 299; M Dougan, 'When Worlds Collide! Competing Visions of the Relationship Between Direct Effect and Supremacy' (2007) 44 *CMLRev* 931. But contrast with eg K Lenaerts and T Corthaut, 'Of Birds and Hedges: The Role of Primary in Invoking Norms of EU Law' (2006) 31 *ELRev* 287.

[73] Though with some input from the Member States: consider rulings such as Cases C-87–89/09 *Verholen* [1991] ECR I-3757; Case C-263/08 *Djurgården-Lilla Värtans Miljöskyddsförening* [2009] ECR I-9967.

[74] For further analysis, see M Dougan, 'Who Exactly Benefits from the Treaties? The Murky Interaction Between Union and National Competence Over the Capacity to Enforce EU Law' (2009–10) 12 *CYELS* 73.

[75] eg Case C-350/96 *Clean Car Autoservice* [1998] ECR I-2521; Case C-208/05 *ITC Innovative Technology Centre* [2007] ECR I-181; Case C-426/05 *Tele2 Telecommunication* [2008] ECR I-685; Case C-12/08 *Mono Car Styling* [2009] ECR I-6653.

[76] Dir 2003/35 [2003] OJ L156/17.

[77] Dir 2009/22 [2009] OJ L110/30.

[78] cp AG Geelhoed in Case C-253/00 *Muñoz* [2002] ECR I-7289.

[79] cp AG Fennelly in Case C-226/97 *Lemmens* [1998] ECR I-3711, paras 28 *et seq* of the Opinion.

[80] Dir 76/207 [1976] OJ L39/40. See now Dir 2006/54 [2006] OJ L204/23.

employees on grounds of their sex.[81] Similarly, an employer in *Clean Car Autoservice* and a work placement agency in *ITC Innovative Technology Centre* were able to invoke the Treaty provisions on the free movement of workers so as to query the lawfulness of domestic rules discriminating against migrant workers on grounds of their nationality.[82]

The second factor is whether the claimant is otherwise acting as a 'private policeman' in the enforcement of certain Union regulatory obligations, most commonly against a commercial rival operating on the same market, and the claimant's own interests might be adversely affected by any relevant distortion in the conditions of competition. Consider, for example, rulings such as *Muñoz*: for the purposes of recognising the claimant's capacity to enforce Union secondary legislation, the Court emphasised the valuable role performed by undertakings operating in the relevant market in identifying and pursuing infringements of applicable regulatory standards committed by their commercial rivals.[83] The 'private policemen' analysis may apply even where the claimant is not arguing that any distortion of competition directly affects his/her own interests. Consider the judgment in *Streekgewest Westelijk Noord-Brabant*, where the Court alluded to the valuable contribution made to the effective enforcement of the Treaty provisions on state aid by claimants seeking to rely upon the direct effect of Article 108(3) TFEU in order to obtain the reimbursement of a national tax or levy, the revenue from which had been used to fund an unlawful state subsidy for the benefit of third-party undertakings.[84] The interest of a disgruntled taxpayer there acted as an alternative trigger for coming within the protective scope of Article 108(3) TFEU, as compared to the more traditional grounds of being a market competitor whose commercial interests are adversely affected by the market-distorting impact of the disputed aid measures.[85]

C – Against Whom May Directive Effective Union Law Be Enforced?

Having determined that the relevant provisions of Union law satisfy the threshold criteria for producing direct effect in principle, and having considered the range of persons entitled to invoke those provisions before the national courts, the next issue to be discussed is precisely *who* the relevant Union measure may be enforced *against*. At a substantive level, answering that question is again a matter of interpretation: upon which class of persons does the Union act, properly construed, seek to impose obligations (and does the relevant party to the dispute actually fall within that class)? However, there is also an important constitutional dimension to this issue: regardless of identifying the class of persons upon whom Union law seeks to impose binding legal obligations, in the absence of full and correct implementation by the Member State into national law, certain Union acts are *by their very nature* only capable of being directly enforced against certain parties and not

---

[81] Case C-345/89 *Stoeckel* [1991] ECR I-4047.

[82] Case C-350/96 *Clean Car Autoservice* [1998] ECR I-2521; Case C-208/05 *ITC Innovative Technology Centre* [2007] ECR I-181.

[83] Case C-253/00 *Muñoz* [2002] ECR I-7289. Also eg Case C-379/04 *Dahms* [2005] ECR I-8723; Case C-430/04 *Finanzamt Eisleben v Feuerbesttungsverein Halle* [2006] ECR I-4999; Case C-426/05 *Tele2 Telecommunication* [2008] ECR I-685.

[84] Case C-174/02 *Streekgewest Westelijk Noord-Brabant* [2005] ECR I-85. Consider also eg Case C-55/06 *Arcor* [2008] ECR I-2931.

[85] eg as in Case C-368/04 *Transalpine Ölleitung in Österreich* [2006] ECR I-9957.

against others. In other words: some Union acts may project their direct effect only in particular types of situation.

Two main variables are at work here. The first variable concerns the type of Union act in question: whether we are dealing with provisions of Union primary law (the Treaties themselves or the general principles of Union law); or with regulations; or with directives; or with decisions. The second variable concerns the type of dispute at issue. Some disputes are 'vertical' in nature in the sense that they involve an individual seeking to enforce Union law against the Member State. Other disputes are 'horizontal' in character in the sense that they involve an individual seeking to enforce Union law against another private party. Yet further disputes involve a Member State seeking to enforce Union law against an individual—the dispute being vertical in form but horizontal in substance, since it still involves the purported enforcement of Union law against a private party. As we shall see, some Union acts (including primary Union law, regulations and decisions) are *by their very nature* capable of projecting their direct effect in both vertical and horizontal disputes. However, other Union acts (primarily directives) are *by their very nature* only capable of producing direct effect when the dispute is vertical in form and substance, and thus cannot of themselves be enforced against private parties.

(i) Treaty provisions

As we have seen, the judicial source of the principle that certain provisions of the Treaties may be invoked by individuals in national courts is the judgment in *van Gend en Loos*.[86] The Court's finding that the Community constituted a new legal order of international law, for the benefit of which the Member States have limited their sovereign rights, provided the basis for the entire doctrine of direct effect and laid the foundations for the future evolution of the Union legal order.

At the substantive level, individual Treaty provisions might seek to impose obligations upon the Member States, or upon individuals, or upon both public and private bodies. That choice depends entirely upon interpretation of the relevant Treaty provision, having regard not only to its text and objectives, but also to its place within the scheme of the Treaties as a whole. For example, Article 34 TFEU on the free movement of goods creates substantive obligations only for the Member States and other entities which can be assimilated to the exercise of state power.[87] It does not seek to impose substantive obligations upon purely private actors.[88] By contrast, Articles 101 and 102 TFEU on competition law create substantive obligations which are directed primarily against private economic undertakings engaged in anticompetitive agreements or conduct.[89] Other Treaty provisions—such as Article 45 TFEU on equal treatment on grounds of nationality for migrant workers, or Article 157 TFEU on equal pay between men and women—are intended to regulate the conduct of both public and private entities. Even if those Treaty provisions only refer expressly to the conduct of the Member States, the Court has construed them as implicitly applying also to private individuals, since the objective of securing equal

[86] Case 26/62 *van Gend en Loos* [1963] ECR 1.

[87] eg Case 249/81 *Commission v Ireland* [1982] ECR 4005; Case 222/82 *Apple and Pear Development Council* [1983] ECR 4083; Cases 266–267/87 *Royal Pharmaceutical Society* [1989] ECR 1295; Case C-292/92 *Hünermund* [1993] ECR I-6787.

[88] eg Case C-159/00 *Sapod Audic v EcoEmballages* [2002] ECR I-5031.

[89] Contrast eg Case C-41/90 *Höfner* [1991] ECR I-1979 with Case C-364/92 *Eurocontrol* [1994] ECR I-43. See further the detailed analysis provided in Part V of this book.

treatment on grounds of nationality or of sex would be jeopardised if private employers remained free to engage in discriminatory practices.[90]

At the constitutional level, Treaty provisions will always be capable of being enforced in litigation against their substantive obligation-holder: obligations directed against the Member State can be enforced in vertical disputes, those directed instead (or also) against individuals can be enforced in horizontal litigation (as well as in proceedings brought by the Member State against the relevant private party). Thus Article 34 TFEU can be enforced directly against the Member State whose legislation creates unjustified obstacles to the free movement of goods;[91] Articles 101 and 102 TFEU can be invoked directly against the private undertakings which engage in anti-competitive practices;[92] Articles 45 and 157 TFEU can be relied upon directly against any employer (public or private) who discriminates on grounds of nationality or of sex, respectively.[93]

It is worth observing, however, that the potential for Treaty provisions to project their own direct effect is not necessarily limited to litigation involving the substantive obligation-holder. For example, it may well be true that (at a substantive level) Article 34 TFEU on the free movement of goods imposes obligations only upon the Member State and other public bodies; but (at a constitutional level) those obligations can still be invoked also in horizontal disputes involving two private parties, where the outcome hinges upon the compatibility of the relevant public measures with Union law.[94] In other words, when it comes to the decentralised enforcement of primary Treaty provisions, the Court draws no practical distinction between situations where Union law creates only public law duties for the Member State which can nevertheless be invoked also collaterally during the course of horizontal proceedings between two private parties; and situations where Union law instead imposes private law obligations directly upon an individual which may be apt for enforcement in litigation before the national courts.

(ii) General Principles of Union Law

The Court's approach to the direct effect of the general principles of Union law is essentially the same as that adopted in respect of express provisions of the Treaties themselves: having established that the relevant general principle is sufficiently clear, precise and unconditional to enjoy direct effect at all, one should define—at a substantive level—the range of bodies upon whom the relevant obligation has been imposed. In the context of the general principles of Union law, that choice is usually quite straightforward. In the present state of Union law, the general principles act as administrative law obligations binding only upon the Union institutions; and also upon the Member States when the latter are acting within the scope of the Treaties. As we shall see in a subsequent chapter, it may not always be easy to define exactly when a Member State is acting 'within the scope of the Treaties' for those purposes.[95] But in no case so far has the Court of Justice

---

[90] See Case C-281/98 *Angonese* [2000] ECR I-4131 and Case 43/75 *Defrenne v Sabena* [1976] ECR 455, respectively.

[91] From countless rulings, eg Case 120/78 *'Cassis de Dijon'* [1979] ECR 649; Case C-368/95 *Familiapress* [1997] ECR I-3689; Case C-405/98 *Gourmet International* [2001] ECR I-1795.

[92] Case 127/73 *BRT v SABAM* [1974] ECR 51.

[93] Case C-281/98 *Angonese* [2000] ECR I-4131; Case 43/75 *Defrenne v Sabena* [1976] ECR 455.

[94] eg Case 74/76 *Iannelli & Volpi v Meroni* [1977] ECR 557; Case C-315/92 *Verband Sozialer Wettbewerb v Clinique Laboratories* [1994] ECR I-317; Case C-33/97 *Colim v Biggs* [1999] ECR I-3175; Case C-159/00 *Sapod Audic v Eco-Emballages* [2002] ECR I-5031; Case C-322/01 *Deutscher Apothekerverband* [2003] ECR I-14887.

[95] See Chapters 10–12.

held that a general principle of Union law imposes substantive obligations directly upon a private party.[96]

Nevertheless—at a constitutional level—it is now clearly established that the general principles of Union law may project their direct effect in both vertical and horizontal disputes. As with Treaty provisions such as Article 34 TFEU, therefore, the incompatibility of Member State action within the scope of the Treaties (on the one hand) with a directly effective general principle of Union law (on the other hand) might be relied upon by an individual in litigation involving the Member State itself;[97] or instead in the context of a dispute against another private party, whose outcome hinges upon the legality of the relevant national measures.

The main authority for the latter proposition is *Mangold*.[98] The case involved Directive 2000/78, which was adopted under Article 19 TFEU and lays down a general framework for combating discrimination, inter alia, on grounds of age in the field of employment and occupation.[99] Germany was given until 2 December 2006 to transpose the Directive's provisions into national law. *Mangold* involved the German legislation for protecting workers employed under fixed-term contracts of employment: as a general rule, such contracts may only be concluded if there were 'objective grounds' for doing so; but thanks to a derogation taking effect on 1 January 2003 and running until 31 December 2006, fixed-term contracts could be concluded without showing any 'objective grounds' where the worker was aged 52 or above. The Court of Justice found that the German rules amounted to unjustified discrimination within the terms of Directive 2000/78. However, there were two obstacles to the potential direct effect of the unimplemented Directive within the national legal system. First, the deadline for transposition of the Directive into German law had not yet expired; as we know, directives cannot have direct effect until such deadlines have elapsed. Secondly, the actual dispute in *Mangold* was horizontal insofar as it involved a purely private employer who discriminated against his employee (albeit in accordance with the disputed German legislation); as we have already mentioned, and shall explore in greater detail below, directives cannot of themselves be relied upon against individuals. To overcome those twin obstacles, the Court observed that the principle of non-discrimination on grounds of age must in fact be regarded as a general principle of Union law; Directive 2000/78 does not in itself lay down the principle of equal treatment as regards employment and occupation. As such, observance of the general principle of equal treatment on grounds of age cannot be made conditional upon expiry of the implementation period in respect of Directive 2000/78; it is the responsibility of national courts to provide the legal protection which individuals derive from Union law by setting aside, if necessary, any incompatible provision of domestic law.

As we shall see further below, *Mangold* has proved a rather controversial judgment: the Court seemed to be using the direct effect of a general principle of Union law in order to evade the limitations imposed upon the direct effect of unimplemented directives. For present purposes, however, the ruling in *Mangold* is simply an illustration of the propo-

---

[96] Consider, in particular, Case C-101/08 *Audiolux* [2009] ECR I-9823 contrasting the Opinion with the Judgment. See further eg X Groussot and H H Lidgard, 'Are There General Principles of Community Law Affecting Private Law?' in U Bernitz, J Nergelius and C Cardner (eds), *General Principles of EC Law in a Process of Development* (The Hague, Kluwer Law International, 2008).

[97] eg Case C-442/00 *Caballero* [2002] ECR I-11915; Case C-520/03 *Olaso Valero* [2004] ECR I-12065.

[98] Case C-144/04 *Mangold* [2005] ECR I-9981. Also: Case C-555/07 *Kücükdeveci* (Judgment of 19 January 2010).

[99] Dir 2000/78 [2000] OJ L303/16.

sition that a general principle of Union law—provided it is sufficiently clear, precise and unconditional; and also that the Member State's conduct falls within the scope of the Treaties—is capable of having certain legal effects in relations between two private parties. The general principle of Union law concerning equal treatment on grounds of age does indeed seem to be sufficiently clear, precise and unconditional.[100] The German rules in *Mangold* did indeed fall within the scope of the Treaties, since Germany was implementing another Union directive concerning fixed-term workers.[101] From there, it was hardly objectionable for the Court to find that public law acts tainted by illegality in accordance with the standards of administrative conduct laid down under Union law may be impugned, not only directly in an action for judicial review against the delinquent public authorities themselves, but also indirectly where such public law acts are challenged collaterally in a dispute between two private individuals.[102]

(iii) Regulations

Article 288 TFEU states that '[a] regulation shall have general application. It shall be binding in its entirety and directly applicable in all Member States'. We saw in Chapter 4 that some regulations are legislative in character (where they are adopted by an ordinary or special legislative procedure); the remainder are non-legislative in nature (eg when adopted by the Commission as delegated regulations pursuant to Article 290 TFEU).

At first sight, the description of regulations contained in Article 288 TFEU appears automatically to attribute them with the characteristics of those Treaty provisions capable of giving rise to independent legal effects which the national courts are bound to recognise and enforce. Even a cursory scrutiny of the *Official Journal*, however, reveals that each and every provision of each and every regulation does not give rise to directly effective rights and obligations within the domestic legal system.[103] The reference to 'direct applicability' in Article 288 TFEU is best understood as referring to the process by which regulations are generally incorporated into the national legal order. National courts must take cognisance of regulations as legal instruments the validity and recognition of which is not inherently conditioned upon national procedures of incorporation or transposition into the domestic legal order. But whether or not particular provisions of any given regulation in fact give rise to rights or obligations which national courts must safeguard is a matter of interpretation of the provisions concerned, in light of the same criteria established by the Court of Justice with respect to the direct effect of other provisions of Union law, such as primary Treaty provisions.[104]

This approach is entirely consistent with the decided cases. In earlier rulings, it is true that the Court hardly went out of its way to clarify the matter. For example, in *Politi v Italian Ministry of Finance*, an Italian court asked the Court of Justice whether certain

---

[100] Though contrast the views of M Dougan, 'In Defence of *Mangold*?' in A Arnull, C Barnard, M Dougan and E Spaventa (eds), *A Constitutional Order of States? Essays in EU Law in Honour of Alan Dashwood* (Oxford, Hart Publishing, 2011), with those of P Craig, 'The Legal Effect of Directives: Policy, Rules and Exceptions' (2009) 34 *ELRev* 349.

[101] Dir 1999/70 giving effect to the Framework Agreement on Fixed Term Work [1999] OJ L175/43.

[102] cp AG Sharpston in Case C-427/06 *Barstch* [2008] ECR I-7245, especially at paras 79–85 of the Opinion. Also eg AG Trstenjak in Case C-80/06 *Carp* [2007] ECR I-4473 and in Case C-101/08 *Audiolux* Case C-101/08 *Audiolux* [2009] ECR I-9823.

[103] cp R Král, 'National Normative Implementation of EC Regulations: An Exceptional or Rather Common Matter?' (2008) 33 *ELRev* 243.

[104] See above on the relationship between direct applicability and direct effect.

provisions of an agricultural regulation were directly applicable, and if so, whether they created rights for individuals which national courts were bound to safeguard. The question presented to the Court reflected neatly the distinction indicated above—but the Court's response did not. 'Under the terms of the second paragraph of Article [288 TFEU]', it declared,

> regulations 'shall have general application' and 'shall be . . . directly applicable in all Member States.' Therefore, by reason of their nature and their function in the system of the sources of Community law, regulations have direct effect and are as such capable of creating individual rights which national courts must protect.[105]

Advocate General Roemer in *Leonesio v Italian Ministry of Agriculture and Forestry* was more willing to separate the issues of direct applicability and direct effect. He pointed out that simply to acknowledge the status of a Union legal instrument as a regulation did not solve the problem of whether certain of its provisions bestowed enforceable rights on individuals as against the Member State—the solution to which 'depends on the questions whether an area of discretion was left to the national authorities in the matter of implementation and in what manner the national provisions were to supplement the measures adopted'.[106] That approach has since been vindicated by the Court of Justice itself. For example, it was held in *Monte Arcosu* that although, by virtue of the very nature of regulations, their provisions generally have immediate effect in the national legal systems without it being necessary for the national authorities to adopt measures of application, some of their provisions may nonetheless necessitate, for their implementation, the adoption of such measures by the Member States. In such situations, given the discretion enjoyed by the Member States, it cannot be held that individuals may derive rights from the relevant provisions of the regulation, in the absence of measures adopted by the national authorities.[107]

The circumstances in which national provisions might properly supplement a Union regulation have given rise to a considerable case law. For example, in principle, the corollary of the proposition that regulations must be recognised as legal instruments without the need for their terms to be transposed into national law by national implementing measures is that such transposition, unless otherwise authorised by the particular regulation,[108] is impermissible, in as much as it tends to disguise from those subject to the law the Union source of their rights and obligations.[109] This is not to deny that regulations will never require supplementary national rules to be adopted so as to ensure the effective application of the relevant provisions within the Member States.[110] Where Union regulations do require implementation by national measures, the incorporation of the texts of such regulations may be justified for the sake of coherence and in order to make them comprehensible to the persons to whom they apply.[111]

The important point for now is that the mere status of an instrument *qua* regulation cannot determine whether any of its provisions in fact enjoy direct effect—that is a ques-

---

[105] Case 43/71 [1971] ECR 1039, para 9.
[106] Case 93/71 [1972] ECR 287, 300.
[107] Case C-403/98 *Monte Arcosu* [2001] ECR I-103.
[108] eg Case 31/78 *Bussone* [1978] ECR 2429; Case 230/78 *Zuccheri* [1979] ECR 2749.
[109] eg Case 39/72 *Commission v Italy* [1973] ECR 101; Case 34/73 *Fratelli Variola v Italian Finance Ministry* [1973] ECR 981.
[110] eg Case 72/85 *Commission v Netherlands* [1986] ECR 1219.
[111] Case 272/83 *Commission v Italy* [1985] ECR 1057, para 27.

tion dependent upon detailed interpretation of each specific provision. Where a given regulation does satisfy the threshold criteria for producing direct effect, the framework for its enforcement is analogous to the position as regards primary Treaty provisions and general principles of Union law: having identified the actor(s) subject to the substantive obligations contained in the relevant provisions of the regulation, the latter can in principle project its direct effect into both vertical and horizontal disputes.[112] Consider, for example, the ruling in *Muñoz* (discussed above): the Union regulations concerning quality standards for agricultural products could be enforced directly by one undertaking against its commercial rival—a dispute where the regulation's substantive obligations were directed against the latter private party, and the regulation's direct effect was invoked in the context of a purely horizontal dispute.[113]

(iv) Directives

Article 288 EC states that '[a] directive shall be binding, as to the result to be achieved, upon each Member State to which it is addressed, but shall leave to the national authorities the choice of form and methods'. Again, some directives are legislative in character (where they are adopted by an ordinary or special legislative procedure); the remainder are non-legislative in nature (eg when adopted by the Commission as implementing acts pursuant to Article 291 TFEU).[114]

By contrast with regulations, the Treaties might seem to have envisaged that directives are by their very nature an 'incomplete' form of Union measure: having set out the objectives to be achieved by the Member State, a directive will become fully effective only when transposed into the domestic legal order, through the adoption of the necessary implementing measures, which must be achieved within the deadline prescribed under the directive itself. As before, the precise circumstances under which national provisions will be considered correctly to have implemented a Union directive have given rise to a considerable case law.[115] For example, although Member States enjoy the freedom to choose the most appropriate legislative format for implementing the directive into national law,[116] and the transposition measures adopted need not use exactly the same words as the directive itself,[117] the national implementing rules should nevertheless give the persons concerned a clear and precise understanding of their rights and obligations and enable national courts to ensure that those rights and obligations are observed.[118] Moreover, implementation of a directive requires transposition by binding measures of national law; neither the adoption of administrative practices, which by their nature may be altered at the whim of the authorities and lack the appropriate publicity, nor the publication of administrative circulars, which do not have binding effects, will be enough to satisfy the requirements of Article 288 TFEU.[119] Problems at the national level, such as an

---

[112] Which would include the ability of one individual to invoke a breach by the Member State of its Union law obligations within the context of a dispute with another individual by way of collateral challenge.

[113] Case C-253/00 *Muñoz* [2002] ECR I-7289.

[114] See further Chapter 4.

[115] See further eg S Prechal, *Directives in EC Law*, 2nd edn (Oxford, Oxford University Press, 2005).

[116] Case 163/82 *Commission v Italy* [1983] ECR 3723, 3286–87.

[117] Case 247/85 *Commission v Belgium* [1987] ECR 3029, para 9; Case 262/85 *Commission v Italy* [1987] ECR 3073, para 9; Case 252/85 *Commission v France* [1988] ECR 2243, para 5.

[118] Case 257/86 *Commission v Italy* [1988] ECR 3249, 3267; Case C-236/95 *Commission v Greece* [1996] ECR I-4459.

[119] Case 102/79 *Commission v Belgium* [1980] ECR 1473; Case 96/81 *Commission v Netherlands* [1982] ECR 1791; Case 145/82 *Commission v Italy* [1983] ECR 711.

overcrowded legislative timetable, cannot justify the Member State's failure to comply with the deadline for implementation.[120] However, the Court has held that directives do not require legislative implementation where there exist general principles of constitutional or administrative law which render specific legislation superfluous, provided that those principles guarantee the application of the directive, are clear and precise, are made known to those subject to the law, and are capable of being invoked by the courts.[121] Many directives require that legislative measures of transposition refer to the underlying directive: in such a case, failure to include a reference to the directive in national implementing legislation will amount to a distinct breach of Union law.[122]

As we have seen, during the period for adopting the necessary implementing measures offered to the Member State by each directive, the national authorities are required to refrain from conduct liable seriously to compromise the results prescribed by Union law.[123] But the question arises: what if the deadline for transposition of the directive has indeed passed, yet the Member State has still failed (or at least failed correctly) to carry out the transposition required under Article 288 TFEU?

For some time, it was widely assumed that directives gave rise exclusively to rights and obligations as between the Member States and the Union institutions.[124] However, the Court signalled a different approach in its decision in *van Duyn v Home Office*.[125] The case concerned a provision of a Union directive allowing the deportation of a worker from another Member State on public policy grounds based exclusively on the personal conduct of the individual concerned. The Court noted that the directive laid down an obligation which was not subject to any exception or condition and which, by its very nature, did not require the intervention of any act on the part either of the Union institutions or of the Member States—thus concluding that the provision conferred upon individuals rights which were enforceable before the national courts and which the latter were bound to protect. Similar reasoning was adopted in later cases.[126] It was soon well established that not only individual discretionary decisions of the national authorities, but also legislative provisions, may be challenged by individuals relying upon the direct effect of Union directives whose deadline for transposition had already expired.[127] Indeed, the Court in its (much more recent) *Marks & Spencer* ruling rejected any absolute proposition that, if a Member State has correctly implemented the provisions of a Union directive into its domestic law, individuals are thereby deprived of any possibility of relying before the national courts on the rights which they may derive from those provisions. In fact, the adoption of national measures correctly implementing a Union directive does not necessarily exhaust the effects of the latter measure; Member States remain bound *actually* to ensure full application of the directive *even after* the adoption of implementing measures. Individuals are therefore entitled to rely before national courts on the precise and unconditional provisions of a directive whenever the full application of the directive is

---

[120] Case C-298/95 *Commission v Germany* [1996] ECR I-6747 (citing previous case law).
[121] Case 29/84 *Commission v Germany* [1986] ECR 1661.
[122] Case C-360/95 *Commission v Spain* [1997] ECR I-7337.
[123] In accordance with the Case C-129/96 *Inter-Environnement Wallonie* [1997] ECR I-7411 case law: see above.
[124] See eg *Joseph Aim* [1972] CMLR 901 (Cour d'Appel de Paris); *Firma Baer Getreide BmbH* [1972] CMLR 539 (Hessischer Verwaltunggerichtschof); and even after the development of the ECJ's case law, *Cohn-Bendit* [1979] Dalloz Jur 155 (Conseil d'Etat); and *Kloppenburg* (Bundesfinanzhof Judgment of 25 April 1985).
[125] Case 41/74 [1974] ECR 1337.
[126] See eg Case 36/75 *Rutili* [1975] ECR 1219; Case 51/76 *Verbond van Nederlandse Ondernemingen v Inspecteur der Invoerrechten en Accijnzen* [1977] ECR 113; Case 38/77 *Enka* [1977] ECR 2203.
[127] Case 41/74 *van Duyn* [1974] ECR 1337; Case 36/75 *Rutili* [1975] ECR 1219.

not in fact secured, ie not only where the directive has not been implemented or has been implemented incorrectly, but also where the national measures correctly implementing the directive are not being applied in such a way as to achieve the result sought by it—for example, because the national administrative authorities are in fact applying the domestic implementing legislation in a manner which is inconsistent with the parent directive.[128]

Although the case law generally concerned challenges to Member State action which was incompatible with an unimplemented directive, and were raised in vertical proceedings between an individual and the defaulting public authorities, there was nothing in the Court's earlier case law to suggest that the legal effects of a directly effective directive would be much different from those of a directly effective Treaty provision or regulation. One might therefore have assumed that directives were capable of being invoked *not only* against the Member State *but also* against a private individual. However, several arguments were levelled against any such assumption.[129]

First, at least under the original Treaty of Rome, there was no legal requirement to publish directives; it might have seemed unfair to individuals if directives could give rise to binding obligations when they were not publicly accessible as of right. But it should be pointed out that that argument became much less persuasive after the Maastricht Treaty amendments to the EC Treaty (which did introduce a publication requirement also for directives).[130] Secondly, it was arguable that to allow directives to be pleaded against individuals would assimilate directives to regulations in contravention of Article 288 TFEU, since the latter provision seemed to envisage that regulations were the appropriate instrument by which the Union institutions might impose obligations directly upon private parties.[131] Again, though, such an argument was not overwhelmingly persuasive. On the one hand, as we have seen, many regulations leave enough discretion to the Member States as to require the adoption of national implementing measures and are thus incapable of having direct effect. On the other hand, many directives are sufficiently detailed that their provisions easily satisfy the threshold criteria of being clear, precise and unconditional, the only material discretion left to the Member State being the time limit for implementation; if that time limit has expired, there seems little reason to deny that the relevant provisions should not be capable of having full direct effect. In other words: institutional practice has already blurred the distinction between regulations and directives, so that it hardly seems a good reason to distort the latter's potential for decentralised enforcement. Thirdly, there was an argument that to allow directives to be pleaded against individuals would be contrary to the principle of legal certainty, since those subject to obligations contained in directives might be unsure whether to rely upon national implementing legislation or upon the underlying directives. That argument seemed somewhat more compelling than the others. After all, individuals should not be placed in unreasonable doubt as to their obligations by requiring the scrutiny of overlapping texts at both the national and Union level as a prerequisite to a complete appreciation of the law. The fact that individuals may be bound by primary Treaty provisions or by regulations does not give rise to the same risk of uncertainty: the Treaties are a contained set of documents with a limited number

---

[128] Case C-62/00 *Marks & Spencer* [2002] ECR I-6325.

[129] See further eg AJ Easson, 'Can Directives Impose Obligations on Individuals?' (1979) 4 *ELRev* 67. More recently, eg P Craig, 'Once Upon a Time in the West: Direct Effect and the Federalisation of EEC Law' (1992) 12 *OJLS* 453; T Tridimas, 'Horizontal Effect of Directives: A Missed Opportunity?' (1994) 19 *ELRev* 621.

[130] cp AG Lenz in Case C-91/92 *Faccini Dori* [1994] ECR I-3325.

[131] See the ECJ's own arguments in Case C-91/92 *Faccini Dori* [1994] ECR I-3325.

of provisions capable of directly binding individuals; as for regulations, it has always been clear that they constitute direct Union legislation and are only subject to national implementation where they so provide.

While none of those arguments could be described as particularly conclusive of the issue, there was perhaps a further consideration—albeit of a political, rather than a legal, nature—which may have played strongly upon the Court's mind, particularly during the 1980s, when the case law on the direct effect of directives was being thrashed out. The courts in some Member States were having difficulty in accepting that directives could have direct effect at all; for the Court of Justice to go even further and recognise horizontal direct effect for directives might further diminish the credibility of the Court of Justice in such Member States, and lead to the uneven enforceability of directives across the Union.[132]

Against the background of such concerns, the Court laid the conceptual foundations for the current law in 1979, in the *Ratti* case, where it held that 'a Member State which has not adopted the implementing measures required by the directive in the prescribed period *may not rely, as against individuals, on its own failure to perform the obligations which the directive entails*'.[133] Although the Court went on to confirm its jurisprudence on the potential vertical direct effect of directives in a consistent case law, the 'estoppel argument' first raised in *Ratti* soon became the Court's main rationale for permitting individuals to rely on the directly effective provisions of Union directive against the Member State.[134] However, that 'estoppel argument' soon led to an important converse conclusion, fully articulated in the judgment in *Marshall*.[135] The latter dispute concerned an employee of an Area Health Authority (AHA) in the United Kingdom who was dismissed at the age of 62, having already passed the ' normal retirement age' of 60 applicable to female employees (whereas the normal retirement age for male employees was 65). The claimant instituted proceedings against the AHA alleging sex discrimination contrary to the Equal Treatment Directive.[136] The AHA argued before the Court of Justice that the directive could not be relied upon against private parties; in dismissing the claimant, the AHA, although a public authority, was not acting in its capacity as an emanation of the state, but merely in its capacity as an employer. The Court held that, since a directive under Article 288 TFEU was binding only upon 'each Member State to which it was addressed', such a measure could not of itself impose obligations upon an individual. However, this did not preclude an individual from relying upon a directive against the Member State, regardless of the capacity in which the latter was acting, whether as an employer or as a public authority.

In other words, the principles governing the decentralised enforcement of Union directives differ fundamentally from those applicable to primary Treaty provisions, general principles of Union law or Union regulations. While unimplemented directives may be invoked against the Member State in vertical disputes, they cannot of themselves be relied upon against private individuals. That is true in the context of horizontal disputes, ie where one private party seeks to rely on the provisions of an unimplemented directive against another individual. That position was strongly affirmed by the Court in rulings

---

[132] See further eg P Pescatore, 'The Doctrine of Direct Effect: an Infant Disease of Community Law' (1983) 8 *ELRev* 155.

[133] Case 148/78 *Criminal proceedings against Tullio Ratti* [1979] ECR 1629, para 22 (emphasis added).

[134] Case 8/81 *Becker* [1982] ECR 53; Case 255/81 *Grendel* [1982] ECR 2301; Case 5/84 *Direct Cosmetics* [1985] ECR 617.

[135] Case 152/84 *Marshall v Southampton and South-West Hampshire Area Health Authority* [1986] ECR 723.

[136] Dir 76/207 [1976] OJ L39/40. See now Dir 2006/54 [2006] OJ L204/23.

such as *Faccini Dori*: the claimant there was unable to rely on the provisions of an unimplemented Union directive so as to enforce her (intended) right to cancel a consumer contract, which had been concluded away from a private seller's business premises, within the 'cooling-off period' provided for under Union law.[137] The position is the same where the relevant dispute is vertical in form but horizontal in substance, ie where a Member State itself seeks to rely on the provisions of an unimplemented directive against a private party. For example, *Pretore di Salò* concerned dams built across an Italian river which had caused sudden and significant changes in the water level, resulting in the death of many of the river's fish. No offence had been committed under Italian criminal law alone, but the prosecuting magistrate sought to bring criminal charges based directly on a Union directive concerning the quality of fresh water for the purposes of protecting fish life. The Court of Justice affirmed that a Union directive which had not been properly transposed into the national legal order could not give rise to such obligations as against private individuals.[138]

The distinction drawn in *Marshall* and affirmed in rulings such as *Faccini Dori* continues to attract considerable controversy.[139] For example, the Court says that directives bind the Member State and therefore cannot be invoked against individuals. Yet, as we have seen, this very argument failed to prevent Treaty provisions such as Article 49 TFEU on the free movement of workers, or Article 157 TFEU on equal pay for men and women, from being construed as imposing obligations upon private parties as well as the public authorities. What is true of the Treaties should also, one might assume, be true of directives: after all, the obligation to comply with a Union directive is itself a primary Treaty obligation, under Article 288 TFEU, and the Court has held that directives have an effect no less binding than that of any other rule of Union law.[140] Moreover, the position laid down in rulings such as *Marshall* and *Faccini Dori* is capable of giving rise to some undesirable consequences: for example, one victim of sex discrimination may well be able to enforce her right to equal treatment under Union law, by invoking the provisions of an unimplemented directive against her public sector employer, whereas another victim of sex discrimination who finds herself in almost entirely comparable circumstances may well be left without legal protection, simply because her employer is a private undertaking. And all of that is besides the adverse implications of the *Marshall/Faccini Dori* case law for the fundamental imperatives of effectiveness and uniformity in the application and enforcement of Union law which supposedly inspired the system of decentralised enforcement from its very origins in *van Gend en Loos* and *Costa v Enel*.

Perhaps in recognition of some of the adverse consequences that might result from its case law, the Court of Justice has sought to expand the range of situations which can be classified as 'vertical' for the purposes of recognising the direct effect of unimplemented directives. As we have seen, it was held in *Marshall* that disputes will be treated as 'vertical' even if the relevant public body is not exercising state power as such, but acting in a private capacity, eg as an employer or purchaser. *Marshall* also illustrates how the concept of public authorities is not limited to the central authorities: it will also embrace, for exam-

---

[137] Case C-91/92 *Faccini Dori* [1994] ECR I-3325.

[138] Case 14/86 *Pretore di Salò* [1987] ECR 2545. More recently eg Case C-227/09 *Accardo* (Judgment of 21 October 2010).

[139] See further eg AG van Gerven in Case C-271/91 *Marshall v Southampton and South-West Hampshire Area Health Authority* [1993] ECR I-4367; AG Jacobs in Case C-316/93 *Vaneetveld* [1994] ECR I-763.

[140] Case 79/72 *Commission v Italy* [1972] ECR 667; Case 52/75 *Commission v Italy* [1976] ECR 277.

ple, an area health authority responsible for the organisation and delivery of healthcare services;[141] local and regional authorities;[142] and constitutionally independent authorities responsible for the maintenance of public order and safety.[143] The leading case remains *Foster v British Gas*, where the Court held that:

> a body, whatever its legal form, which has been made responsible, pursuant to a measure adopted by the state, for providing a public service under the control of the state and which has for that purpose special powers beyond those which result from the normal rules applicable in relations between individuals is included in any event among the bodies against which the provisions of a directive capable of having direct effect may be relied upon.[144]

In that ruling, it was found that the provisions of an unimplemented directive could be enforced against a nationalised public utility. The Court has applied a similarly broad approach to the concept of an 'emanation of the state' in subsequent cases concerning public services.[145] If anything, some national courts have gone even further in their willingness to classify disputes as being vertical in character and thus within the scope of an unimplemented directive's permissible direct effect.[146] Yet such generosity towards the intended beneficiaries of Union directives is not without its drawbacks: after all, local authorities, police forces or public utilities might seem as much (or rather, as little) responsible for the Member State's own default in failing to adopt the measures necessary to transpose a Union directive into the national legal system as a purely private individual—thus undermining the Court's very rationale for advocating the vertical, while excluding the horizontal, direct effect of Union directives in the first place.

In another line of cases, the Court has clarified that the attempt by an individual to rely upon an unimplemented Union directive against the defaulting public authorities will not cease to be categorised as 'vertical' in nature merely because the practical effects of enforcing the directly effective provisions of the directive will be borne in practice by a third (private) party. Consider, for example, an action for judicial review of a national authority's decision to grant planning permission for certain mining works to be carried out, on the grounds that that decision was adopted without the Member State having conducted an environmental impact assessment as required under Directive 85/337.[147] On its face, such an action is clearly based on the vertical direct effect of the Directive by the claimant against the public body; but it is readily apparent that, should the action succeed, it will adversely affect the interests of the third (private) party which was granted the flawed planning permission. The Court in *Wells* held that, in such circumstances, the fact that a third (private) party will suffer certain adverse repercussions for its rights cannot justify preventing an individual from invoking the provisions of the Directive against the delinquent Member State.[148] Consider, along similar lines, the *Medicines Control Agency*

---

[141] As in Case C-271/91 *Marshall v Southampton and South-West Hampshire Area Health Authority* [1993] ECR I-4367. Also eg Case C-6/05 *Medipac-Kazantzidis v Venizelio-Pananio* [2007] ECR I-4557.

[142] eg Case 103/88 *Fratelli Constanzo v Commune di Milano* [1989] ECR 1839.

[143] eg Case 222/84 *Johnston v Chief Constable of the RUC* [1986] ECR 1651.

[144] Case C-188/89 *Foster v British Gas* [1990] ECR I-3313, para 20.

[145] eg Cases C-253/96–258/97 *Helmut Kampelmann* [1997] ECR I-6907; Case C-157/02 *Rieser Internationale Transporte* [2004] ECR I-1477.

[146] From the UK courts, consider eg *Griffin v South-West Water Services Ltd* [1995] IRLR 15; *NUT v Governing Body of St Mary's CoE Junior School* [1997] 3 CMLR 630.

[147] [1985] OJ L175/40.

[148] Case C-201/02 *Wells* [2004] ECR I-723. See also Cases C-152/07–154/07 *Arcor* [2008] ECR I-5959.

case.[149] This involved an action for judicial review of a decision of the Medicines Control Agency granting a marketing authorisation to a company in respect of a proprietary medicinal product, initiated by a competing undertaking which held an original marketing authorisation for a proprietary medicinal product bearing the same name, on the grounds that the authorisation had been granted by the Agency contrary to the provisions of a Union directive. The Court of Justice held that the holder of the original marketing authorisation could rely upon the relevant provisions of the directive in proceedings before a national court in order to challenge the validity of an authorisation issued by the competent national authority to one of its competitors. Or again, an undertaking which tenders for a public contract and has its tender rejected on grounds inconsistent with the directly effective provision of a Union directive may rely upon that directive to challenge the rejection of its tender, and it seems that this is the case even if the public contract has been awarded to a third party.[150]

It is true that rulings such as *Wells* or *Medicines Control Agency* can be reconciled, in a formal sense, with the principle in *Marshall* and *Faccini Dori* that an unimplemented Union directive cannot of itself impose obligations upon an individual. However, for the Court to accept so willingly that the enforcement of an unimplemented directive vertically against the Member State may legitimately produce 'incidental effects' for a third (private) party does threaten to make its reasoning appear rather more formalistic than deeply principled. In any case, it is worth noting that rulings such as *Wells* and *Medicines Control Agency* are linked to another line of case law—discussed not here, but further below—in which certain unimplemented Union directives appear to have produced various 'incidental effects' against private parties, not in the context of disputes which were undoubtedly vertical in form, but even as regards litigation that was clearly horizontal between two individuals. Consideration of that case law is best deferred until after we have explored not only the principle of direct effect, but also that of supremacy, since we shall see that the rulings in question are as much concerned with the broader relationship between those two doctrines, as they are with the question of when precisely unimplemented Union directives might produce certain legal effects for private parties.

In the meantime, other recent judgments have shown the Court adept at finding new ways to qualify (though still without formally overruling) its rulings in *Marshall* and *Faccini Dori*. The Court has occasionally held that a Union directive merely embodies the substantive rights and obligations already contained in primary provisions of the Treaties themselves—and can thus be enforced as against a private individual, even if the relevant directive has not itself been correctly implemented by the Member State. For example, it was held in cases such as *Brunnhofer* that the Equal Pay Directive merely clarifies the intended meaning of Article 157 TFEU on the right of equal pay between men and women, by emphasising that equal pay applies not only to equal work but also to work of equal value.[151] As such, the Equal Pay Directive may be 'enforced' within the context of purely private relationships; Article 157 TFEU provides the true source of the relevant

---

[149] Case C-201/94 [1996] ECR I-5819.

[150] Case 103/88 *Fratelli Costanzo* [1989] ECR 1839. The question nevertheless arises of the extent to which Union law recognises that individuals who have ostensibly derived rights under national law from legislative or administrative measures which have been adopted in contravention of the terms of a directive may have legitimate expectations which may or must be respected by national courts and other authorities which are subsequently called upon to disapply the national measure in question.

[151] Dir 75/117 [1975] OJ L45/19. See now Dir 2006/54 [2006] OJ L204/23.

rights and obligations, and there is no doubt that that provision can be invoked in both vertical and horizontal disputes.[152]

The Court extended that idea further (and more controversially) in the case of *Mangold*, by finding that certain Union directives may instead merely embody a general principle of Union law, with the latter considered enforceable in its own right within the context of litigation between two private parties, even if the relevant directive itself has not been correctly implemented by the Member State.[153] As we saw before, *Mangold* itself concerned Directive 2000/78 laying down a general framework for combating discrimination, inter alia, on grounds of age in the field of employment and occupation.[154] Germany had enacted rules concerning the treatment of certain older workers employed on fixed-term contracts that were in breach of Directive 2000/78. However, the dispute arose before the deadline for implementation of Directive 2000/78 had expired, and within the context of a horizontal relationship between a private employer and one of his employees, thus making it doubly difficult to argue that Directive 2000/78 should be capable of having direct effect in the case. The Court of Justice nevertheless managed to side-step both those limitations by finding that Directive 2000/78 merely embodied a general principle of Union law guaranteeing the right to equal treatment on grounds of age; since the disputed German legislation fell within the scope of the Treaties, having been adopted in order to implement another Union directive concerning the treatment of fixed-term workers, the relevant general principle of Union law was capable of being invoked by the claimant employee before the national courts.

The legal essentials of the ruling in *Mangold* have been affirmed by the Court in subsequent rulings—most notably in *Kücükdeveci*.[155] The latter case involved German rules concerning calculation of the notice period for dismissal from employment which were alleged to discriminate on grounds of age. The Court held that those German rules fell within the scope of the Treaties because (unlike in *Mangold*) the deadline for implementation of Directive 2000/78 had already expired and (furthermore) the latter measure expressly regulated employment conditions such as those on dismissal. Having brought the disputed German rules within the scope of the Treaties, the path lay open for the claimant employee to invoke the general principle of Union law guaranteeing equal treatment on grounds of age—even though the incompatibility between German law and Union law had been raised in the course of a horizontal dispute with her (private) employer.

The Court's ruling in *Mangold* has provoked some fierce criticism. Much of that criticism has focused on the fact that the legal basis for the Court's 'discovery' of a general principle of Union law guaranteeing equal treatment on grounds of age appeared rather weak—though that is a criticism which relates more to the Court's methodology for identifying the general principles of Union law, than it does to the potential for those general principles to produce independent legal effects before the national courts.[156] Other objections have concerned the finding in *Kücükdeveci* that national rules may fall within the

---

[152] Case C-381/99 *Brunnhofer* [2001] ECR I-4961. See also Case 96/80 *Jenkins v Kingsgate* [1981] ECR 911.
[153] Case C-144/04 *Mangold* [2005] ECR I-9981.
[154] Dir 2000/78 [2000] OJ L303/16.
[155] Case C-555/07 *Kücükdeveci* (Judgment of 19 January 2010). Note also Case C-427/06 *Bartsch* [2008] ECR I-7245.
[156] eg Editorial, 'Horizontal Direct Effect—A Law of Diminishing Coherence?' (2006) 43 *CMLRev* 1; E Muir, 'Enhancing the Effects of Community Law on National Employment Policies: The *Mangold* Case' (2006) 31 *ELRev* 879; J Jans, 'The Effect in National Legal Systems of the Prohibition of Discrimination on Grounds of Age as a General Principle of Community Law' (2007) 34 *LIEI* 53. See further Chapters 10–12.

scope of the Treaties, and thus trigger the potential application of the general principles of Union law, when the link between Member State action and the constitutional need to respect Union administrative law seems rather tenuous—though, again, that is a criticism directed principally against the Court's approach to defining the proper scope of application of Union law (a problem which properly belongs in another chapter and is not directly relevant to the present discussion).[157] However, the Court has also been attacked for permitting the general principle of Union law guaranteeing discrimination on grounds of age to be enforced between two private parties, even though Directive 2000/78 (containing exactly the same substantive rights and obligations and also potentially applicable to the subject-matter of the relevant disputes) was itself prohibited from producing any independent legal effects—a situation which appears difficult to reconcile with exactly those considerations of legal certainty for private individuals that have long justified the exclusion of horizontal direct effect for unimplemented Union directives in the first place.[158]

Future case law will doubtless explore such problems and tensions in greater detail—as well as clarify the important question of precisely which other Union directives might be considered merely to embody some general principle of Union law, with the latter capable of being invoked in litigation between two private parties, so as to alter the framework of rights and obligations which would otherwise apply as a matter of purely national law. Moving beyond the prohibition on age discrimination, the Court of Justice in *Mangold* seemed to anticipate that its ruling should apply also to the other forms of equal treatment referred to in Directive 2000/78 (religion or belief, disability and sexual orientation).[159] In fact, although the Court passed over the opportunity to recognise the prohibition of discrimination on grounds of sexual orientation as a general principle of Union law in *Maruko*,[160] Advocate General Jääskinen in the *Römer* dispute has since urged the ECJ to do precisely that.[161] In any event, there is surely a strong case for arguing that the principle of equal treatment on grounds of sex should be recognised as a general principle of Union law capable of giving rise to enforceable rights, within the scope of the Treaties, à la *Mangold*, even in horizontal disputes where the Equal Treatment Directive has not been correctly implemented into national law.[162] Familiar disputes of the sort highlighted in *Marshall*—about whether the employer can be treated as an 'emanation of the state' for the purposes of enforcing the unimplemented directive—would thus become a thing of the past.[163] By contrast, one can readily imagine various propositions which—even if

---

[157] eg G Thüsing and S Horler, Annotation of *Kücükdeveci* (2010) 47 *CMLRev* 1161; Editorial, 'The Scope of Application of the General Principles of Union Law: An Ever Expanding Union?' (2010) 47 *CMLRev* 1589. See further Chapters 10–12.

[158] eg AG Kokott in Case C-321/05 *Kofoed* [2007] ECR I-5795; AG Mazák in Case C-411/05 *Palacios de la Villa* [2007] ECR I-8531; AG Colomer in Cases C-55 and C-56/07 *Michaeler* [2008] ECR I-3135; AG Kokott in Case C-73/07 *Satakunnan Markkinapörssi and Satamedia* [2008] ECR I-9831.

[159] See paras 74 and 76 of the ruling in *Mangold*; cp AG Mazák in Case C-411/05 *Palacios de la Villa* [2007] ECR I-8531. One assumes that the same would be true for the prohibition on race discrimination as regulated by Dir 2000/43 [2000] OJ L180/22.

[160] Case C-267/06 *Maruko* [2008] ECR I-1757; though note AG Colomer at para 78 (footnote 82) of the Opinion.

[161] Case C-147/08 *Römer* (Opinion of 15 July 2010; judgment pending).

[162] Equal treatment on grounds of sex has long been recognised as a general principle of Union law by the ECJ, eg Case 149/77 *Defrenne v Sabena* [1978] ECR 1365; more recently eg Case C-25/02 *Rinke* [2003] ECR I-8349. There is as yet no post-*Mangold* authority, though note the rather reticent approach of AG Kokott in Case C-104/09 *Roca Álvarez* (Opinion of 6 May 2010; Judgment of 30 September 2010).

[163] cp Case 152/84 *Marshall* [1986] ECR 723.

they were to be treated as general principles of Union law—would surely not be considered sufficiently clear, precise and unconditional as to be capable of producing their own direct effect within the national legal systems.[164] Consider, for example, a principle such as consumer protection: it is surely too nebulous to be capable of creating justiciable individual rights and obligations, independently of the various instruments of secondary legislation adopted by the Union institutions to deal with specific categories of consumer disputes, and thus seems destined to perform a primarily interpretative role within the Union legal order.[165]

In the face of whatever criticism, the Court continues to adhere to the principle laid down in *Marshall* and affirmed in *Faccini Dori* that unimplemented directives cannot, of themselves, impose obligations upon private individuals.[166] It is possible the claimant may demonstrate that his/her adversary in litigation is indeed an 'emanation of the state' in the sense of *Foster v British Gas* against which vertical direct effect is constitutionally permitted. It may also be open to the claimant to frame his/her action directly against the national authorities, so that the burden which falls upon any third (private) party is considered to be merely incidental and hence acceptable (as in cases like *Wells*). Some individuals may instead be able to demonstrate that the substantive rights they wish to claim under an unimplemented Union directive merely embody some higher provision of the Treaties or general principles of Union law, capable in their own right of producing direct effect within the context of a horizontal dispute (as in rulings such as *Mangold*).

But otherwise, once those avenues for judicial protection under the doctrine of direct effect itself have been exhausted, it remains for the claimant to pursue two alternative sources of potential relief—though it must be stressed that neither is guaranteed to produce a favourable result. In the first place, the national court remains under its general obligation to construe national law, so far as possible, in conformity with any relevant Union directive. As we have seen, that duty arises whether the dispute is to be classed as vertical or horizontal in nature; but it is limited by the need to respect the general principles of Union law, for example, as regards the principles of legal certainty and of legality in the sphere of criminal law.[167] In the second place, the claimant may always seek to obtain reparation from the Member State, in accordance with the *Francovich* case law, in respect of losses suffered through the Member State's failure to implement the relevant Union directive correctly and within the applicable deadline.[168] The *Francovich* right to reparation will be considered in Chapter 9. Suffice for now to point out that the possibility of compensation does not flow automatically from the Member State's failure to implement, but depends on demonstrating that the Member State committed a 'seriously serious breach' of its obligations under Article 288 TFEU, taking into account a range of factors and considerations relevant to determining the requisite degree of culpability under Union law.[169]

---

[164] cp Case C-101/08 *Audiolux* [2009] ECR I-9823.

[165] Consider eg Case C-233/94 *Germany v Parliament and Council* [1997] ECR I-2405.

[166] Important rulings such as Cases C-397/01–403/01 *Pfeiffer* [2004] ECR I-8835 and Cases C-387/02, C-391/02 and C-403/02 *Berlusconi* [2005] ECR I-3565 are discussed further below.

[167] eg Case C-91/92 *Faccini Dori* [1994] ECR I-3325; Case C-192/94 *El Corte Inglés* [1996] ECR I-1281; Case C-235/03 *QDQ Media* [2005] ECR I-1937; Case C-227/08 *Martín Martín* (Judgment of 17 December 2009). See further above.

[168] Cases C-6 and 9/90 *Francovich* [1991] ECR I-5357.

[169] eg contrast Cases C-178–179 and 188–190/94 *Dillenkofer* [1996] ECR I-4845 with Case C-392/93 *R v HM Treasury, ex parte British Telecommunications* [1996] ECR I-1631.

(v) Decisions

The final category of Union secondary instrument is the decision. According to Article 288 TFEU, '[a] decision shall be binding in its entirety'; while '[a] decision which specifies those to whom it is addressed shall be binding only on them'. The Court has long held that decisions are capable of having direct effect against their addressees.[170] If the latter is a private party, then the decision should be capable of being enforced against that addressee in just the same way as would a provision of the Treaties or a Union regulation. However, if the addressee is a Member State, then the legal effects of the relevant decision will be assimilated to that of a Union directive.[171]

It is worth noting the widely held assumption that the potential legal effects of decisions should be curtailed where the latter are adopted by the European Council or the Council acting within the particular sphere of the common foreign and security policy under Chapter 2 of Title V of the TEU. In particular, the deletion from the TL of any express provision that Union acts per se have primacy over national law,[172] coupled with the IGC's declaration recalling the principle of supremacy of *Community* law,[173] as opposed to the legal provisions which made up the old Second Pillar, supports the view that—even today—CFSP decisions should not generally be capable of having independent effects (based on the principles of direct effect and supremacy) within the domestic legal orders.[174]

(vi) A Note on Ex-Third Pillar Framework Decisions and Decisions

In any event, it seems beyond doubt that acts previously adopted under the old Second Pillar, as regards the common foreign and security policy, were always incapable of having direct effect within the national legal systems. Article 9 of the Protocol (No 36) on transitional provisions states that the legal effects of such acts should be preserved, despite the entry into force of the TL, until those acts are repealed, annulled or amended in implementation of the Treaties in their current form.

The same provisions of the Protocol on transitional measures refer also to acts adopted under the old Third Pillar concerning cross-border police and judicial co-operation in criminal matters. Given the number and importance of such Third Pillar acts which are still in existence, it is worth recalling what their legal effects were under Union law as it stood before the Lisbon reforms, and thus as they shall remain until they are eventually repealed, annulled or amended in accordance with the revised Treaties.

As we mentioned in Chapter 4, the old Third Pillar furnished the Union institutions

---

[170] Case 9/70 *Franz Grad* [1970] ECR 825. Contrast with eg Case C-18/08 *Foselev Sud-Ouest* [2008] ECR I-8745.

[171] Case C-80/06 *Carp* [2007] ECR I-4473. That would appear to be the case, in particular, with decisions adopted by the Council under Art 155(2) TFEU so as to give effect to agreements between the social partners as regards matters falling with the Union's social policy competences under Art 153 TFEU. Before the Treaty of Lisbon, such agreements were implemented at the Union level in the form of directives: see eg Case C-268/06 *Impact* [2008] ECR I-2483; Cases C-378–380/07 *Angelidaki* [2009] ECR I-3071; Case C-486/08 *Zentralbetriebsrat der Landeskrankenhäuser Tirol* (Judgment of 22 April 2010); Cases C-444/09 and C-456/09 *Gavieiro* (Judgment of 22 December 2010).

[172] See further below.

[173] Declaration No 17 annexed to the Final Act of the IGC which adopted the TL (referring to an opinion of the Council Legal Service and the caselaw of the Court of Justice): see further below.

[174] See further the discussion in last edition of this book: A Arnull, A Dashwood, M Dougan, M Ross, E Spaventa and D Wyatt, *Wyatt & Dashwood's EU Law*, 5th edn (London, Sweet & Maxwell, 2006) para 11-013.

with a different set of legal instruments than the ordinary regulations, directives and deci-sions available as regards Community action under the First Pillar. Ex-Article 34 TEU provided for four types of legal act specific to Union action in the field of criminal law: common positions defining the approach of the Union to a particular matter; framework decisions, for approximating national laws, which were binding upon the Member States as to the result to be achieved, while leaving the national authorities the choice of form and methods; decisions, for achieving binding purposes other than the approximation of national law; and conventions, the provisions of which were to be recommended to the Member States for adoption in accordance with their respective constitutional require-ments.

While it seemed evident that Third Pillar common positions and conventions were sim-ply not apt by their very nature to enjoy direct effect, Third Pillar framework decisions and decisions appeared at first glance closely similar in form to First Pillar directives and deci-sions, respectively. However, ex-Article 34 TEU expressly stated that neither framework decisions nor decisions should be capable of having direct effect—thus ensuring that the potential legal effects of Third Pillar instruments within the national legal systems were severely curtailed. Nevertheless, we have already noted how the Court of Justice estab-lished in *Pupino* that the absence of direct effect for framework decisions and decisions did not mean that such instruments were devoid of any legal relevance before the national courts.[175] In particular, the Court held that, even though the Treaty on European Union (in its pre-TL version) contained no expression provisions on the matter, the duty of loyal co-operation between the Union and its Member States nevertheless applied also to the Third Pillar. The national courts were thus bound by the duty of consistent interpretation as regards framework decisions and decisions adopted under the Third Pillar—though the strength of that obligation remained limited by reference to the general principles of Union law (eg the principle of legal certainty, the principle of legality in the sphere of criminal law, and respect for human rights and fundamental freedoms more generally).[176]

Thus, when it comes to Third Pillar framework decisions and decisions whose legal effects have been upheld pursuant to Article 9 of the Protocol on transitional provisions, there remains no possibility of them having direct effect (whether vertical or horizontal); but the national courts are obliged to construe existing domestic law, so far as possible, in conformity with any relevant ex-Third Pillar instruments. Once those Third Pillar frame-work decisions and decisions are repealed, annulled or amended in accordance with the current Treaties—and in any case, as regards those measures now adopted by the Union institutions in the field of criminal law within the framework provided for under Title V of Part Three of the TFEU—they will be governed by the same principles as are applicable to all ordinary Union secondary measures. In principle, that includes the possibility of hav-ing direct effect, as well as attracting the duty of consistent interpretation. But in practice, it should be recalled that the potential for Union directives in the field of criminal law to produce direct effect will inherently be limited by the exclusion of the possibility that such measures may of themselves impose obligations upon individuals;[177] while their relevance to the interpretation of existing national legislation will necessarily be conditioned by the

---

[175] Case C-105/03 *Pupino* [2005] ECR I-5285.
[176] See further eg S Peers, 'Salvation Outside the Church: Judicial Protection in the Third Pillar after the *Pupino* and *Segi* Judgments' (2007) 44 *CMLRev* 883.
[177] Case 14/86 *Pretore di Salò* [1987] ECR 2545. See above.

need to respect the principle of legality as regards substantive criminal law obligations/the right to a fair trial as regards the rules of criminal procedure and evidence.[178]

IV – THE PRINCIPLE OF SUPREMACY

International law by its nature binds the state in its executive, legislative and judicial activities, and no international tribunal would permit a respondent state to plead provisions of its law or constitution as a defence to an alleged infringement of an international obligation.[179] The same is true of Union law, 'over which no appeal to provisions of internal law of any kind whatever can prevail'.[180] The Court of Justice has always declined to accept a plea of force majeure where a Member State has attempted to comply with Union obligations, but failed as a result of delays in the legislative process.[181] Similarly, the Court has consistently held that a Member State may not plead provisions, practices or circumstances existing in its internal legal order to justify a failure to comply with the obligations and time-limits laid down in a directive.[182]

As mentioned before, the obligation of Member States to take all appropriate measures to ensure the fulfilment of obligations arising under the Treaties is laid down explicitly in Article 4(3) TEU. The most significant manifestation of the duty of loyal co-operation contained in Article 4(3) TEU is surely the principle of supremacy as established in *Costa v Enel*.[183] As we saw at the outset of this chapter, the Court of Justice there affirmed that, by contrast with ordinary international treaties, the EEC Treaty created its own legal system which, on the entry into force of the Treaty, became an integral part of the legal systems of the Member States and which their courts became bound to apply. By creating a Community of unlimited duration, having powers stemming from a limitation of sovereignty, or a transfer of powers from the Member States to the Community, the Member States limited their sovereign rights, albeit within limited fields, and thus created a body of law which binds both their nationals and themselves.

That the duty of national courts to give precedence to Union law over national law extends to national legislation adopted after the incorporation of the relevant Union rules into the national legal order was made clear in *Simmenthal*:

> Furthermore, in accordance with the principle of the precedence of Community law, the relationship between provisions of the Treaty and directly applicable measures of the institution on the one hand and the national law of the Member States on the other is such that those provisions and measures not only by their entry into force render automatically inapplicable any conflicting provision of current national law but—in so far as they are integral part of, and take precedence in, the legal order applicable in the territory of each of the Member States—also preclude the valid adoption of new national measures to the extent to which they would be incompatible with Community provisions. . . . It follows from the foregoing that every national court must, in a case

---

[178]   Case C-105/03 *Pupino* [2005] ECR I-5285. See above.

[179]   *Treatment of Polish Nationals in Danzig* (1932) PCIJ Rep, Ser A/B, No 44, 24. Vienna Convention on the Law of Treaties 1969, Art 27.

[180]   Case 48/71 *Commission v Italy* [1972] ECR 527, 535.

[181]   eg Case 77/69 *Commission v Belgium* [1970] ECR 237; Case 254/83 *Commission v Italy* [1984] ECR 3395.

[182]   See eg Case C-303/92 *Commission v Netherlands* [1993] ECR I-4739, para 9; Case C-298/97 *Commission v Spain* [1998] ECR I-3301, para 14.

[183]   Case 6/64 [1964] ECR 585. Note also Case 17/67 *Neumann* [1967] ECR 441, 453.

within its jurisdiction, apply Community law in its entirety and protect rights which the latter confers on individuals and must accordingly set aside any provision of national law which may conflict with it, whether prior or subsequent to the Community rule.[184]

However, contrary to what that passage might seem to suggest, the principle of supremacy does not render national provisions which conflict with Union law null and void, or otherwise render them somehow 'invalid', within the national legal system. The principle of supremacy merely requires that the national courts 'disapply' the conflicting domestic rules insofar as they are incompatible with Union law. That point was made clear by the Court in its ruling in *IN.CO.GE.*[185] In the latter case, the Commission relied upon the above-quoted passage in *Simmenthal* to argue that a Member State had no power whatsoever to adopt a fiscal provision that is incompatible with Union law, with the result that such a provision and the corresponding fiscal obligation must be treated as legally nonexistent. However, the Court rejected this argument, saying:

> In *Simmenthal*, the issue facing the Court related in particular to the consequences of the direct applicability of a provision of Community law where that provision was incompatible with a subsequently adopted provision of national law. . . . It cannot . . . be inferred from the judgment in *Simmenthal* that the incompatibility with Community law of a subsequently adopted rule of national law has the effect of rendering that rule of national law non-existent. Faced with such a situation, the national court is, however, obliged to disapply that rule, provided always that this obligation does not restrict the power of the competent national courts to apply, from among the various procedures available under national law, those which are appropriate for protecting the individual rights conferred by Community law.[186]

One important consequence of the idea that the principle of supremacy merely requires the disapplication (rather than the outright nullity) of national provisions which conflict with Union law is that the enforcement of the principle of supremacy by the national courts does not excuse the Member State from its underlying responsibility formally to amend that conflicting domestic legislation so as to conform with its Union obligations (failing which the Member State may still suffer enforcement proceedings before the Union courts pursuant to Articles 258–60 TFEU).[187]

The Court of Justice expects the national courts to enforce the principle of supremacy of Union law as against all conflicting provisions of national law—from the most fundamental provisions of the Member State's written constitution,[188] right down to individual administrative decisions adopted by the lowest public authorities.[189] Moreover, the duty to disapply conflicting national law in cases falling within its jurisdiction applies to every domestic court or tribunal, regardless of its place within the Member State's judicial hierarchy, and without (for example) having to await a ruling from the supreme constitutional or administrative court establishing the existence of an incompatibility between the relevant national legislation and Union law.[190] In fact, the Court in rulings such as *Fratelli*

---

[184] Case 106/77 [1978] ECR 629, 643–44.

[185] Case C-10/97 *IN.CO.GE.* [1998] ECR I-6307.

[186] *Ibid*, paras 20–21. See further eg R Schütze, 'Supremacy Without Pre-emption: The Very Slowly Emergent Doctrine of Community Pre-emption' (2006) 43 *CMLRev* 1023.

[187] Case 96/81 *Commission v Netherlands (Bathing Water Directive)* [1982] ECR 1791. On enforcement proceedings against Member States, see further Chapter 6.

[188] eg Case 11/70 *Internationale Handelsgesellschaft* [1970] ECR 1125.

[189] eg Case C-224/97 *Erich Ciola* [1999] ECR I-2517.

[190] See Case 106/77 *Simmenthal* [1978] ECR 629. More recently eg Case C-314/08 *Filipiak* [2009] ECR

Costanzo and *Erich Ciola* went further—asserting that the principle of supremacy is binding not only upon the Member State's judicial but also its administrative bodies.[191]

However, despite its prima facie unconditional nature, there are certain limitations to the practical effect of the principle of supremacy. Such limitations derive from two very different sources: Union law itself; and the constitutional framework of individual Member States.

Dealing first with Union law itself, it seems clear from the Court's case law that the principle of supremacy is not in fact totally unconditional. In certain situations, the imperative of disapplying national rules which are incompatible with provisions of Union law must be balanced against other equally fundamental principles of the Union legal order—such as the need to respect the principle of legal certainty or to protect legitimate expectations.

For example, *Kühne and Heitz* raised the question under which circumstances the principle of supremacy might require national authorities to reopen decisions which have become final following an unsuccessful challenge before the domestic courts, where it becomes apparent from a subsequent judgment of the Court of Justice that those decisions were based on a misinterpretation of Union law. It was held that legal certainty is one of the general principles of Union law, and implies that administrative bodies should not be required, in principle, to reopen a decision which has become final upon the expiry of reasonable limitation periods or the exhaustion of available legal remedies—even if that decision is incompatible with certain provisions of Union law. However, in the special circumstances of the case (where the national court of last instance had refused to make a reference to the Court of Justice under Article 267 TFEU, the claimants had complained to the Dutch authorities as soon as they became aware of the subsequent Court of Justice judgment, and Dutch law did actually give administrative bodies the power to reopen final decisions), Union law could indeed require the national authorities to revisit their apparently final decision.[192]

Subsequent rulings have explored in greater detail the circumstances in which respect for the principle of legal certainty will lead the Court of Justice to tolerate breaches of Union law, where a wayward administrative decision has become final,[193] or an erroneous judgment of a national court has acquired the force of *res judicata*.[194] But there are other important lines of case law which illustrate the same phenomenon: for example, where the Court refuses to sanction the enforcement against individuals of (perfectly valid) Union legislation which has not been adequately published;[195] or respects the integrity of national decisions which have become final through the expiry of reasonable limitation periods, even if those decisions do not fulfil the Member State's Treaty obligations;[196] or exceptionally limits the temporal effects of its own rulings on the interpretation of Union

---

I-11049; Cases C-188 and 189/10 *Melki* (Judgment of 22 June 2010); Case C-173/09 *Elchinov* (Judgment of 5 October 2010).

[191] Case 103/88 *Fratelli Costanzo* [1989] ECR 1839; Case C-224/97 *Erich Ciola* [1999] ECR I-2517. See further eg M Claes, *The National Courts' Mandate in the European Constitution* (Oxford, Hart Publishing, 2006) ch 10.

[192] Case C-453/00 *Kühne & Heitz* [2004] ECR I-837.

[193] eg Case C-2/06 *Kempter* [2008] ECR I-411.

[194] eg Case C-234/04 *Kapferer* [2006] ECR I-2585; Cases C-392 and 422/04 *i-21 Germany* [2006] ECR I-8559; Case C-2/08 *Fallimento Olimpiclub* [2009] ECR I-7501; Case C-40/08 *Asturcom* [2009] ECR I-9579.

[195] eg Case C-108/01 *Asda Stores* [2003] ECR I-5121; Case C-161/06 *Skoma-Lux* [2007] ECR I-10841; Case C-345/06 *Heinrich* [2009] ECR I-1659.

[196] eg Case 33/76 *Rewe-Zentralfinanz v Landwirtschaftskammer für das Saarland* [1976] ECR 1989; Case C-188/95 *Fantask* [1997] ECR I-6783. See further Chapter 9.

law—on imperative grounds of legal certainty—so that the legal effects of the Court's judg-ments will apply only to future legal relationships, rather than as from the prior date of entry into force of the relevant Union instrument.[197] Furthermore, in its ruling in *Winner Wetten*, the Court left open the possibility of recognising a decentralised judicial power to suspend the full supremacy of Union law over conflicting national legislation, on a purely temporary basis and under conditions defined by the Court itself, where disappli-cation of the relevant domestic rules would create a dangerous legal vacuum threatening the public interest.[198]

The important point is that, in all such situations, Union law itself determines the scope and limits of the principle of supremacy, by examining the role of that principle relative to other basic tenets of the Union legal order, and determining whether the Union's interest in securing the effective and uniform enforcement of its own legal norms is outweighed by the need to respect competing values such as legal certainty or legitimate expectations. By contrast, it is in principle impermissible for national courts or tribunals to condition the supremacy of Union provisions unilaterally upon the requirements of purely domestic law (however fundamental).[199] Yet this brings us precisely to our second type of limita-tion on the principle of supremacy: however well established in the jurisprudence of the Court of Justice, supremacy may well be denied its full practical effect by national courts, which sometimes feel constrained to temper the rigour of the Treaties' requirements. In such situations, discharge of the national courts' primary responsibility—to maintain the integrity of their own domestic legal order—may lead them to defy their obligation under the Treaties to ensure the supremacy of Union law.

In fact, the judicial authorities in the great majority of Member States have encoun-tered constitutional difficulties in incorporating the principle of supremacy into their own national legal systems, at least in the unconditional form articulated by the Court of Justice. Across the European Union, the principle of supremacy may well be recog-nised and applied in everyday practice—but it is rarely as securely embedded in national constitutional theory as the Court of Justice might demand. Many national courts leave open the possibility (sometimes rather remote, but sometimes more tangible) of refus-ing to enforce the supremacy of Union law under certain circumstances.[200] Those precise circumstances differ from country to country, according to the distinct constitutional structures and values of each Member State. It would clearly fall beyond the scope of this chapter to survey the reception of the principles of supremacy in all 27 national legal sys-tems. We will content ourselves with a brief outline of the judicial attitude adopted in two Member States—the United Kingdom and Germany—whose very different approaches to the supremacy of Union law may nevertheless be taken as illustrative of our broader point.

Dealing first with the United Kingdom, section 2 of the European Communities Act 1972 provides for the recognition of all directly enforceable Union law, and its applica-

---

[197] eg Case 43/75 *Defrenne v Sabena* [1976] ECR 455; Case 24/86 *Blaizot* [1988] ECR 379; Case C-262/88 *Barber* [1990] ECR I-1889; Case C-415/93 *Bosman* [1995] ECR I-4921. Contrast with eg Cases 142 and 143/80 *Essevi and Salengo* [1981] ECR 1413; Case C-200/90 *Dansk Denkavit* [1992] ECR I-2217; Cases C-367/93–377/93 *Roders* [1995] ECR I-2229; Case C-137/94 *ex parte Cyril Richardson* [1995] ECR I-3407; Case C-126/95 *Hallouzi-Choho* [1996] ECR I-4807; Case C-35/97 *Commission v France* [1998] ECR I-5325; Case C-184/99 *Grzelczyk* [2001] ECR I-6193; Case C-209/03 *Bidar* [2005] ECR I-2119.

[198] Case C-409/06 *Winner Wetten* (Judgment of 8 September 2010).

[199] See, in particular, Case 11/70 *Internationale Handelsgesellschaft* [1970] ECR 1125.

[200] For extensive analysis and discussion, eg K Alter, *Establishing the Supremacy of European Law* (Oxford, Oxford University Press, 2001); M Claes, *The National Courts' Mandate in the European Constitution* (Oxford, Hart Publishing, 2006).

tion in preference to any Act of Parliament 'passed or to be passed'. That was a clear attempt to give legislative force, within the United Kingdom, to the principle of supremacy. However, this attempt appeared to clash with certain fundamental principles of British constitutional law: the sovereignty of the institution of Parliament, which prevents any given Parliament from curtailing the fullest legislative prerogatives of any subsequent Parliament, and implies that any measure passed after 1972 which conflicts with the requirements of Union law should have the effect of (impliedly) repealing the European Communities Act.[201] Under traditional constitutional doctrine, the latest expression of parliamentary will must always prevail—yet that risked bringing the United Kingdom into semi-perpetual breach of the principle of supremacy under Union law. The House of Lords (now the Supreme Court) resolved this dilemma in the *Factortame* and *Equal Opportunities Commission* litigation through the fiction of the 'implied supremacy clause': every Act of Parliament passed since 1972 is deemed to incorporate a section to the effect that its provisions are without prejudice to any directly effective requirements of Union law.[202] By this expedient, the House of Lords reached a compromise whereby, for most practical purposes, the principle of supremacy will be respected and enforced by the English courts; but its justification under British constitutional law remains the sovereignty of Parliament, as expressed in the 1972 Act with sufficient force as to abrogate the normal doctrine of implied repeal in respect of that particular legislation.[203] However, this compromise logically requires that, if Parliament were *expressly* to derogate from section 2 of the European Communities Act 1972, the English courts would be obliged be give effect to that subsequent provision of national law, rather than enforce the unconditional supremacy of Union law.[204] In any case, Parliament remains entitled ultimately to repeal the European Communities Act 1972 altogether (as would happen in the event of the UK's voluntary withdrawal from the EU).[205] Short of such steps, however, the British courts will assume that Parliament did not intend to repudiate the UK's obligations under Union law; and will thus pursue the appropriate interpretation or, if that is not possible, the necessary disapplication of the relevant domestic legislation.[206]

Within the space which lies between faithful implementation of the European Communities Act 1972 (on the one hand) and the theoretical possibility of a future Parliamentary derogation from Union law (on the other hand), some UK judges have explored the constitutional implications of rulings such as *Factortame* when viewed in their broader context alongside other major domestic legal developments (such as enactment of the Human Rights Act and of the Devolution Acts for Scotland and Wales). For example, Laws LJ in *Thoburn v Sunderland City Council* suggested drawing a distinction between 'ordinary' statutes and a special class of 'constitutional statutes', with the latter being exempt from the usual doctrine of implied repeal, so that the relevant measures can only be abrogated by clear and express parliamentary language.[207] However, such an

---

[201] cp *Madzimbamuto v Lardner-Burke* [1969] 1 AC 645.

[202] *R v Secretary of State for Transport, ex parte Factortame (No 2)* [1990] 3 WLR 818; and *R v Secretary of State for Employment, ex parte Equal Opportunities Commission* [1995] 1 AC 1.

[203] For a view on the constitutional implications of these cases, see P Craig, 'Supremacy of the United Kingdom Parliament after *Factortame*' (1991) 11 *YEL* 221.

[204] cp Lord Denning in *Macarthys Ltd v Smith* [1979] 3 All ER 325.

[205] On voluntary withdrawal from the EU, see further Chapter 2.

[206] For further analysis of Supreme Court case law concerning the application of EU law, see A Arnull, 'The Law Lords and the European Union: Swimming with the Incoming Tide' (2010) 35 *ELRev* 57.

[207] *Thoburn v Sunderland City Council* [2002] 4 All ER 156.

analysis—even if one accepted it to reflect the current state of the common law—does not significantly affect the underlying status of Union law within the UK. Indeed, as Laws LJ stated, '[t]he fundamental legal basis of the United Kingdom's relationship with the EU rests with the domestic, not the European, legal powers'.[208] The Coalition Government which took office in the UK after the 2010 general election seems keen to clarify the same point: clause 18 of the European Union Bill introduced in the House of Commons on 11 November 2010 states that '[i]t is only by virtue of an Act of Parliament that directly applicable or directly effective EU law... falls to be recognised and available in law in the United Kingdom';[209] that clause is apparently intended

> to address concerns that the doctrine of Parliamentary sovereignty may in the future be eroded
> by decisions of the courts. . . . [It will provide] clear authority which can be relied upon to
> counter arguments that EU law constitutes a new higher autonomous legal order derived from
> the EU Treaties . . . which has become an integral part of the UK's legal system independent of
> statute.[210]

The tensions which arise between the principle of supremacy as conceived by the Court of Justice (on the one hand) and its reception into the national constitutional environment (on the other hand) is, if anything, even better illustrated by the German experience. Prompted by concerns about the level of fundamental rights protection guaranteed within the Union legal system against acts adopted pursuant to the Treaties, the Federal Constitutional Court in its so-called *Solange I* judgment of 1974 suggested that, in the event of a conflict between Union law and the basic rights contained in the German constitution, the latter would prevail.[211] However, in the light of the evolution of the Court of Justice's case law on fundamental freedoms as general principles of Union law and the affirmation by the Union institutions of the importance of human rights within the Treaty system, the Federal Constitutional Court moderated its position in the so-called *Solange II* ruling: so long as the Union generally ensures an effective protection of fundamental rights, substantially similar to the level guaranteed under German law, the national courts should refrain from exercising their jurisdiction to review the legality of Union acts according to the German constitution.[212]

However, views appeared to harden again when the Federal Constitutional Court was called upon to assess the constitutional legality of German ratification of the TEU. The famous *Brunner* judgment affirmed that the supremacy of Union law within the German legal system is not unconditional. In particular, the Federal Constitutional Court asserted its ultimate jurisdiction to police the compatibility of Union measures with the German constitution, not only as regards the protection of fundamental rights ('fundamental rights review'), but also as concerns the principle that the Union enjoys merely attributed and limited competences ('ultra vires review').[213] The *Brunner* judgment was followed by one of the most dramatic illustrations of how national attitudes can determine the practical

---

[208] At para 69 of his judgment in *Thoburn*. If anything, some UK judges have left open the (albeit hypothetical) possibility of recognising limits to the degree that Parliament has authorised, or may in the future authorise, the supremacy of Union law within the UK, eg *Thoburn v Sunderland City Council* [2002] 4 All ER 156; *Gouriet v Secretary of State for Foreign and Commonwealth Affairs* [2003] EWCA Civ 384.

[209] Bill 106.

[210] Bill 106-EN (Explanatory Notes) para 106.

[211] [1974] 2 CMLR 540.

[212] [1987] 3 CMLR 225.

[213] [1994] 1 CMLR 57. See further eg M Herdegen, 'Maastricht and the German Constitutional Court: Constitutional Restraints for an 'Ever Closer Union' (1994) 31 *CMLRev* 235.

effectiveness of the principle of supremacy. The 'Bananas litigation' concerned a Union regulation establishing a common organisation of the market in bananas, the legality of which under both Union law and the GATT was challenged and upheld before the Court of Justice. Disgruntled German banana importers, however, continued their battle before the national tribunals—leading to a series of rulings in which the German administrative and tax courts, relying on the *Brunner* judgment, declared the Union regulations unlawful and thus inapplicable within the domestic territory. The crisis culminated in the *Bananas* judgment of the Federal Constitutional Court in 2000, in which that institution ultimately refused to exercise its reserved jurisdiction to review the legality of the relevant Union measures: given that the general level of fundamental rights protection under the Treaties remained substantially similar to that guaranteed under the German constitution, the conditions for recognising the principle of supremacy as established in *Solange II* and *Brunner* had been respected.[214]

The next major development occurred in 2009, when the Federal Constitutional Court delivered its ruling on the compatibility of the TL with the German constitution.[215] According to the Federal Constitutional Court, even after Lisbon, the EU remains an association of sovereign states founded upon international law. The Member States continue to provide the primary focus of democratic expression for their own citizens, on whose behalf the domestic authorities retain primary responsibility for the European integration process. The Federal Constitutional Court sent a clear warning that this 'union of nation states' must be taken seriously in practice as well as on paper, by reasserting its ultimate right to ensure that the Union does not abuse the limits of its own competences in an ultra vires sense. The terms of that 'ultra vires review' were subsequently developed by the Federal Constitutional Court in the 2010 *Honeywell* judgment.[216] The latter case involved a challenge to the authority of the Court of Justice's *Mangold* ruling within Germany, based upon some of the criticisms we noted above, for example, concerning the plausibility of finding that the right to equal treatment on grounds of age constituted a general principle of Union law.[217] The Federal Constitutional Court clarified that its 'ultra vires review' would be based upon the notion of a 'sufficiently serious' violation by the Union institutions of their own competences, taking into account how far that violation was 'obvious', and whether it would lead to a structurally important shift in power to the detriment of the Member States. The Federal Constitutional Court did not feel that that (relatively high) threshold had in fact been crossed by the Court of Justice itself in the *Mangold* ruling.

In addition to the established heads of 'fundamental rights review' and 'ultra vires review', the Lisbon Ruling of the Federal Constitutional Court also asserted the ultimate jurisdiction of the domestic courts to ensure that Union action (even if it remains prima facie within the competences defined by the Treaties) should not compromise the fundamental constitutional identity of the German state, which must retain sufficient room for

---

[214] (2000) 21 HRLJ 251. See further eg U Everling, 'Will Europe Slip on Bananas? The Bananas Judgment of the Court of Justice and National Courts' (1996) 33 *CMLRev* 401; C U Schmid, 'All Bark and No Bite: Notes on the Federal Constitutional Court's Bananas Decision' (2001) 7 *ELJ* 95.

[215] BVerfG Judgment of 30 June 2009. Note also the ruling on the *German European Arrest Warrant Law*: see further (2005) *30 ELRev* 605 and (2006) 43 *CMLRev* 583.

[216] BVerfG Judgment of 6 July 2010. See further eg M Payandeh, 'Constitutional Review of EU Law After *Honeywell*: Contextualising the Relationship Between the German Constitutional Court and the EU Court of Justice' (2011) 48 *CMLRev* 9.

[217] Case C-144/04 *Mangold* [2005] ECR I-9981. See further above.

the political formation of the economic, social and cultural destiny of its own population. In particular, the Federal Constitutional Court signalled that it expects a strict interpretation to be given to Union powers which touch upon fields such as the administration of criminal law; the civil and military monopoly over the use of force; fundamental fiscal decisions over revenue and expenditure; shaping the circumstances of life by social policy; and important decisions on cultural issues such as education, the media and religion. The conditions for exercising that novel head of 'constitutional identity review' remain to be worked out in future case law. In the meantime, the combined effect of the Federal Constitutional Court's 2009 ruling on the Lisbon Treaty and its judgment in the *Honeywell* case send a clear signal to the Union in general, and to the Court of Justice in particular: the German judges remain open and indeed friendly towards the process of European integration; but the principle of supremacy is very much a conditional one and its continued enforcement within Germany should not be taken for granted.[218]

Academic views differ on the seriousness of such difficulties surrounding the reception of the principle of supremacy into national law. On the one hand, many commentators view the supremacy debate as a process of constructive dialogue between the Union and national judges about the Union's evolving legal order—reminding the Court of Justice of the importance of protecting fundamental rights against potential infringements by the Union institutions, or of enforcing the limits to Union competences which are intended to safeguard national sovereignty.[219] On the other hand, some commentators warn against the dangers of recognising (let alone encouraging) the right of national courts to dictate the course of Union policy under the threat of rebellion against the principle of supremacy; and indeed, question the legitimacy of a 'dialogue' in which the domestic judges unilaterally reject Treaty obligations freely entered into by their elected politicians.[220] In any event, one might wonder whether the Court of Justice has, for its part, also adopted a somewhat more aggressive approach towards those national courts that might defy their obligation to disapply provisions of domestic law conflicting with directly effective Union law. As we shall see in Chapter 9, the ruling in *Köbler* established that Member States may be obliged to make reparation to individuals for losses incurred by a sufficiently serious breach of the Treaties perpetrated by the national supreme court.[221] Given the unconditional nature of the principle of supremacy, it is arguable that any refusal to respect that obligation would cross the high threshold required for establishing liability—thus increasing the political pressure upon national courts to think long and hard before taking the drastic step of refusing to enforce provisions of Union law adjudged valid according to the Treaties themselves.

By and large, the system of decentralised enforcement of Union law was left untouched by the TL. However, one interesting development did emerge from the Union's long process of constitutional reflection and reform. Against the background of the long-running

---

[218] See further eg D Thym, 'In the Name of Sovereign Statehood: A Critical Introduction to the *Lisbon* Judgment of the German Constitutional Court' (2009) 46 *CMLRev* 1795; D Doukas, 'The Verdict of the German Federal Constitutional Court on the Lisbon Treaty: Not Guilty, But Don't Do It Again!' (2009) 34 *ELRev* 866.

[219] Consider eg N MacCormick, 'The Maastricht-Urteil: Sovereignty Now' (1995) 1 *ELJ* 259; J Weiler and U Haltern, 'Constitutional or International? The Foundations of the Community Legal Order' in A-M Slaughter, A Stone Sweet and J Weiler (eds), *The European Court and National Courts: Doctrine and Jurisprudence* (Oxford, Hart Publishing, 1998).

[220] eg N Reich, 'Judge-made "Europe à la carte"' (1996) 7 *European Journal of International Law* 103. Consider also the analysis of J Baquero Cruz, 'The Legacy of the Maastricht-Urteil and the Pluralist Movement' (2008) 14 *ELJ* 389.

[221] Case C-224/01 *Köbler* [2003] ECR I-10239.

tension between the Court's assertion of the unconditional supremacy of Union over national law and the refusal by many domestic courts to accept any such conception of supremacy within their own legal systems, the drafters of the CT had proposed introducing an express clause whereby '[t]he Constitution and law adopted by the institutions of the Union in exercising competences conferred on it shall have primacy over the law of the Member States'.[222] That provision was widely criticised on the grounds that, compared to the myriad nuances which embellish the Court's case law, the CT offered a simplistic and potentially misleading statement of the relationship between Union and national law. Nevertheless, the CT's primacy clause offered clear political endorsement of the Court's case law and could have increased the pressure on national courts to pay more fulsome obeisance to the supremacy of Union law.[223]

However, the European Council's mandate for the 2007 IGC agreed that the idea of an express primacy clause should be dropped. Instead, the Member States adopted a simple declaration recalling the existing jurisprudence of the Court of Justice on the principle of supremacy of Union over national law 'under the conditions laid down by the said case law', and referring to an opinion of the Council's Legal Service delivered on 22 June 2007, according to which '[t]he fact that the principle of primacy will not be included in the future treaty shall not in any way change the existence of the principle and the existing case-law of the Court of Justice'.[224] That approach is arguably preferable from the perspective of capturing better the subtlety of the Court's own case law, but the question nevertheless arose: would the removal of the express primacy clause encourage certain national courts to continue their previous approach of accepting the principle of supremacy only under the conditions deemed acceptable within their own domestic legal order? The evidence of the German rulings from 2009 and 2010, at least, suggests that that may indeed have proved to be the case.

V – THE RELATIONSHIP BETWEEN DIRECT EFFECT AND SUPREMACY

So far, we have discussed the principle of direct effect in terms of the process by which Union provisions (provided they satisfy certain threshold criteria) are capable of acting as an independent source of law within the national legal system; and the principle of supremacy in terms of the obligation of national courts (as part of their duty of loyal co operation) to disapply domestic rules which conflict with Union law. But we have deliberately avoided engaging in any greater detail with one crucial issue—until now at least—namely the nature of the relationship between the principles of direct effect and supremacy. In particular, does the national court's obligation to disapply domestic law apply only where the latter is incompatible with *directly effective* provisions of Union law? Or are the national courts also obliged to enforce the principle of supremacy even in situ-

---

[222] Art I-6 CT.

[223] See further eg P Cramér, 'Does the Codification of the Principle of Supremacy Matter?' (2004–05) 7 *CYELS* 57. For a broader discussion of national sovereignty and the CT, see A Albi and P van Elsuwege, 'The EU Constitution, National Constitutions and Sovereignty: an Assessment of a European Constitutional Order' (2004) 29 *ELRev* 741.

[224] Declaration No 17 annexed to the Final Act of the IGC which adopted the TL.

ations where the relevant Union measure *fails to satisfy* the threshold criteria for having direct effect?

Attempting to answer those important questions highlights an important division within the academic literature on the principles of direct effect and supremacy. For ease of exposition, it is possible to identify two main theories, which we shall refer to as the 'primacy' and 'trigger' models.[225]

The 'primacy' model treats supremacy as a 'constitutional fundamental' of the European Union and reasons forwards, from that overarching starting point, to elucidate the consequences of the supremacy principle for the settlement of disputes pending before the national courts. This model has gained a considerable academic following in recent years.[226] Its basic outlines can be summarised as follows. Supremacy is capable of producing certain legal effects within the national systems, independently of the principle of direct effect, and without reference to the latter's threshold criteria (such as the need for the relevant Union norm to be clear, precise and unconditional). In particular, the principle of supremacy is capable, in itself, of producing *exclusionary effects* within the domestic legal order—understood as the mere setting aside of national rules which are incompatible with a hierarchically superior norm of Union law, and thus amounting to judicial review of the validity of domestic rules judged against the obligations imposed upon the Member States under the Treaties. For these purposes, the principle of direct effect is neither necessary nor even relevant: its threshold criteria have no particular function to perform, since the question is not whether the relevant Union norm is clear, precise and unconditional, but merely whether there exists an incompatibility between Union and domestic law. However, that category of situation is conceptually distinct from the phenomenon of *substitutionary effects*—understood as the direct and immediate application of Union law, so as to create new rights or obligations derived from the Treaties which do not already exist within the national legal system. This is the proper domain of the principle of direct effect: here, the threshold criteria of clarity, precision and unconditionality serve to identify which norms of Union law are apt for direct and immediate application within the domestic legal system (though supremacy still has a role to play, of course, should national law prove incompatible with the novel rights or obligations just deduced from the relevant Union measure).

By contrast, the 'trigger' view sees supremacy, at the outset, as little more than a remedy to be administered by the domestic courts in the resolution of disputes involving Union law, reasoning backwards from that quotidian function to draw very different conclusions about the juridicial nature of the supremacy principle. In particular, the practical remedy afforded by supremacy is available in those individual cases involving a conflict between Union law and national law; but that remedy can only be invoked when Union law has been rendered cognisable before the domestic courts, by satisfying the threshold criteria for enjoying direct effect. Under this model, direct effect encompasses *any and every* situation in which Union norms produce independent effects within the national legal systems. In other words, direct effect enjoys a monopoly over rendering Union norms justiciable before the national courts; its threshold criteria act as a trigger, and thus a necessary precondition, for the principle of supremacy. Readers might well realise upon reflection that

---

[225] See further Dougan, above n 72.
[226] eg M Lenz, D Sif Tynes and L Young, 'Horizontal What? Back to Basics' (2000) 25 *ELRev* 509; T Tridimas, 'Black, White and Shades of Grey: Horizontality of Directives Revisited' (2002) 21 *YEL* 327; Lenaerts and Corthaut, above n 72.

that is the approach which we have adopted (at least implicitly) throughout this chapter.[227] By contrast, for the 'primacy' model to postulate the freestanding potency of the supremacy principle, in situations demanding no more than the exclusionary effect of Treaty norms, seems to short-circuit this entire theoretical framework.

In many contexts, these two very different understandings of the relationship between the principles of direct effect and supremacy lie dormant and unnoticed in the academic literature, since they either reach the same conclusions about a given issue,[228] or are equally incapable of offering any firm solutions to a particular problem.[229] However, there are certain situations in which the 'primacy' and 'trigger' models pull in very different directions—and the choice between the two acquires real constitutional relevance.

Perhaps the most famous situation in which the 'primacy' and 'trigger' models have clashed head-on concerns the Court's case law on the legal effects of (what was) Directive 83/189 concerning the notification of draft technical regulations.[230]

Directive 83/189 was designed to protect the free movement of goods through a system of preventive control.[231] Article 8 required Member States to notify all draft technical regulations (as defined in the Directive) to the Commission; Article 9 then provided that such regulations could not enter into force during certain specified periods. That was intended to give the Commission an opportunity to prevent unlawful obstacles to free movement from arising in the first place, by persuading the Member State to amend its proposed regulations; the Commission also had the option of proposing centralised harmonisation measures which would reduce or eliminate even lawful obstacles to free movement. The Court held in *CIA Security* (as regards Article 8) and *Unilever Italia* (as regards Article 9) that the effectiveness of the Directive's system of preventive control would be greater if breach of the obligation either to notify or to suspend constituted a 'substantial procedural defect' such as to render the relevant technical regulations inapplicable to individuals.[232] However, both cases involved horizontal disputes. In *CIA Security*, one party claimed that its rival had marketed alarm systems which did not comply with domestic law; that rival brought an action under national rules prohibiting unfair trading practices, claiming that the domestic regulations had themselves been adopted by Belgium in breach of Article 8 Directive 83/189. Thanks to their substantial procedural defect, the domestic regulations were to be treated as inapplicable to the claimant—even within the context of its horizontal litigation against another private undertaking. *Unilever Italia* concerned a contract for the supply of olive oil by one party to another. When the latter refused to accept delivery because the oil did not comply with labelling requirements imposed by recent Italian legislation, the supplier initiated legal proceedings, claiming that the domestic rules were themselves adopted in breach of Article 9 Directive 83/189. Thanks again to their substantial procedural defect, the Italian specifications were to be treated as inapplicable to the supplier—even within this private law dispute between two economic undertakings.

---

[227] See also eg Dougan, above n 72; A Dashwood, 'From *van Duyn* to *Mangold* via *Marshall*: Reducing Direct Effect to Absurdity?' (2006–07) 9 *CYELS* 81.

[228] eg neither model need commit the Commission's *IN.CO.GE.* sin of confusing the disapplication of national law (in an enforceability sense) with its alleged invalidity (in a competence sense): see above.

[229] eg neither model offers any resolution of the sovereignty problem, defining the circumstances (if any) in which national courts are entitled to refuse to recognise the supremacy of Union law: see above.

[230] [1983] OJ L109/8. Dir 83/189 was repealed and replaced by Dir 98/34 [1998] OJ L204/37.

[231] Thus supplementing the more traditional system whereby the Commission and private parties can challenge trade barriers erected by Member States *ex post* by relying on Art 34 TFEU. See further Chapter 14.

[232] Case C-194/94 *CIA Security* [1996] ECR I-2201; Case C-443/98 *Unilever Italia* [2000] ECR I-7535. Also eg Case C-159/00 *Sapod Audic* [2002] ECR I-5031; Case C-20/05 *Schwibbert* [2007] ECR I-9447.

Those judgments—clearly involving horizontal litigation about the rights and obligations of private parties inter se—seemed to fly directly in the face of the fundamental rule in *Marshall* and *Faccini Dori* that unimplemented directives cannot of themselves impose obligations upon private parties. Moreover, it seemed difficult to explain the Directive 83/189 case law by reference to authorities such as *Wells* or *Medicines Control Agency* (discussed above): the litigation in *CIA Security* and *Unilever Italia* was clearly horizontal (not vertical); the legal effects of the unimplemented directive bore directly (not merely incidentally) upon the private party.

The Court in *Unilever Italia* clearly recognised that tensions existed between its approach to Directive 83/189 and its broader case law on the legal effects of unimplemented directives. Its attempt to resolve this tension was reasoned as follows. Whilst it is true that a directive cannot of itself impose obligations on an individual and cannot therefore be relied on as such against an individual, that case law does not apply where non-compliance with Directive 83/189, which constitutes a substantial procedural defect, renders a technical regulation inapplicable. In such circumstances, Directive 83/189 does not in any way define the substantive scope of the legal rule on the basis of which the national court must decide the case before it. In fact, the Directive creates neither rights nor obligations for individuals.[233]

For advocates of the 'trigger' model of direct effect and supremacy, the Court's reasoning in *Unilever Italia* seems to be suggesting an exception to the general rule in *Marshall* and *Faccini Dori* that directives cannot of themselves impose obligations upon individuals: in the case of purely procedural directives, which define a course of conduct for the Member State to follow in its relations with the Union institutions, breach of such a directive can indeed be raised as a directly effective point of Union law, even within the context of horizontal litigation between two private parties. That is not to say that such an exception is particularly compelling in terms of its legal reasoning. On one level, it is of course true that Directive 83/189 did not provide for a traditional regulatory code, aimed at governing relations between private individuals, such as one usually finds in fields such as consumer or employment law. Thus, it is also true that the black letter of the Directive did not define the substantive legal rules for determining disputes under national law about unfair trading or contractual performance. In that sense, the Court was correct to observe that the Directive did not seek to create rights or obligations for individuals. But surely the consequence of rendering the Belgian or Italian technical regulations inapplicable was precisely to transform Directive 83/189 into a measure which determined the substantive legal rules applicable to each case: the effect of the Directive *as construed by the Court* was to create rights and obligations for private parties, to the extent that one undertaking could enforce claims and another undertaking was bound by duties not recognised as such under existing Belgian or Italian law.[234] Nevertheless, even if the Court's reasoning was unpersuasive, the rulings in *CIA Security* and *Unilever Italia* could still be fitted into the conceptual framework of the 'trigger' model: Directive 83/189 can (exceptionally) have direct effect so as to impose, of itself, obligations upon an individual, ie through the disapplication of conflicting national legislation.

For advocates of the 'primacy' model of direct effect and supremacy, however, the rulings in *CIA Security* and *Unilever Italia* were no flash in the pan whose legal relevance

---

[233] Case C-443/98 *Unilever Italia* [2000] ECR I-7535, paras 50–51.
[234] See further M Dougan (2001) 38 *CMLRev* 1503.

should be limited to the exceptional category of 'procedural' measures such as Directive 83/189. The true explanation for those rulings lay in the fact that, since the Belgian and Italian technical regulations were inconsistent with Directive 83/189, the exclusionary effect of the principle of supremacy *in and of itself* could require the national courts to set aside those conflicting domestic laws, even in the context of private litigation, without amounting to any form of horizontal direct effect of the Directive per se. Moreover, that interpretation of *CIA Security* and *Unilever Italia* seemed to find support in other judgments where the Court appeared to sanction the horizontal application of an unimplemented directive, and the latter measure was clearly not of an exceptional 'procedural' character but did clearly seek to regulate the rights or obligations of private parties inter se. For example, in *Ruiz Bernáldez*, the Court suggested that an obligation to compensate third-party victims of car accidents, derived from a Union directive, could be imposed upon insurers even in the face of inadequate national implementing measures.[235] Similarly, in *Pafitis*, the Court ruled that the duty to hold a general meeting of shareholders before raising company capital, again derived from a Union directive, could be enforced in litigation between two groups of private parties so as to set aside incompatible provisions of domestic law.[236] Whereas supporters of the 'trigger' model must assume that the Court in such rulings either believed the national judges would resolve any apparent conflict between Union and domestic rules through the duty of consistent interpretation, or felt that it had not been asked by the national tribunal to rule explicitly on the direct effect issue,[237] supporters of the 'primacy' model could argue that there was growing evidence to demonstrate the existence of a clear division of labour between the principle of supremacy (which could always produce mere exclusionary effects) and the principle of direct effect (which was required in order to achieve more complex substitutionary effects).

But more recent case law appears to have undermined the persuasiveness of the 'primary model'. In the first place, consider the *Pfeiffer* dispute. This involved German legislation which, by and large, correctly implemented the Working Time Directive rules concerning the maximum 48-hour working week.[238] However, the national legislation also contained a derogation permitting collective agreements to prescribe longer working hours in the case of contracts involving significant periods of 'duty time' (*in casu*, emergency workers required to make themselves available to their employer at the place of employment and able to act as and when the need arose). Having established that this derogation was incompatible with the requirements imposed under the Working Time Directive, the next question concerned the potential legal effects of the misimplemented Directive for the purposes of a horizontal dispute involving two private parties. The Court of Justice (sitting as a Grand Chamber) reopened oral proceedings and sought further observations in response to a structured series of questions on precisely this issue. One view would have been to argue that the Working Time Directive could legitimately be invoked so as to set aside the conflicting rule of German law, creating an exception in favour of certain collective agreements: that would not involve horizontal direct effect for the Directive, since the employees are not seeking to substitute any new rule derived from the Directive which does not already exist under German law; it would merely be an example of the exclusionary effects vis-à-vis incompatible domestic norms which flow

---

[235] Case C-129/94 *Ruiz Bernáldez* [1996] ECR I-1829.
[236] Case C-441/93 *Pafitis* [1996] ECR I-1347.
[237] See further M Dougan, 'The Disguised Vertical Direct Effect of Directives?' [2000] *CLJ* 586.
[238] Dir 93/104 [1993] OJ L307/18.

inexorably from the overarching supremacy of Union law. But the Court, having affirmed that the relevant provisions of the Working Time Directive were sufficiently clear, precise and unconditional to enjoy direct effect in principle, affirmed that directives cannot of themselves impose obligations upon individuals and cannot therefore be relied upon as such against individuals. Instead, it was for the national court to interpret existing German law so far as possible to achieve an outcome consistent with the objectives pursued by the Working Time Directive.[239]

In the second place, consider the ruling in *Berlusconi*.[240] The case concerned a criminal prosecution for false corporate accounting, commenced in 1999, relating to the defendant's earlier business activities, in accordance with the Italian legislation applicable at that time. Luckily for the defendant, he had since become the prime minister of Italy and, in 2002, the Italian legislature found itself minded to pass new and significantly more lenient false accounting laws. Under the Italian criminal code, the courts must always apply the legislation which is most favourable to the defendant, even if that legislation was adopted subsequent to the allegedly criminal behaviour. On that basis, Berlusconi argued that his prosecution for false accounting should be halted. However, Union law threw an inconvenient spanner into the smooth running of the defendant's works. Italian legislation on false accounting fell within a regulatory field occupied by various EU company law directives: whereas the original Italian rules were assumed adequately to have implemented those directives, it was argued that the new rules adopted in 2002 breached the Member State's obligation to impose effective and dissuasive sanctions upon those who infringe their Union law responsibilities. The question arose: were the national courts obliged to set aside the (non-compliant) 2002 legislation, and permit the defendant's criminal prosecution to proceed in accordance with the original (compliant) Italian rules? Once again, the 'primacy' model suggested one solution to this problem: there was, in principle, no bar to the public authorities seeking to rely on a misimplemented Union directive against Berlusconi; this was not a case of substituting new rules derived from that directive which did not already exist under Italian law; it was rather a case of excluding certain provisions of national law which did not comply with the Union directive. Indeed, that was the analysis recommended to the Court by Advocate General Kokott.[241] However, as in *Pfeiffer*, the Court in *Berlusconi* rejected this line of analysis. The Court accepted that the principle of the retroactive application of a more lenient criminal penalty represents a general principle of Union law which national courts must respect when applying national legislation adopted for the purpose of implementing Union law. Difficulties arise in a situation (such as the present dispute) where the more lenient penalty is itself alleged to be incompatible with Union law. But the Court did not consider it necessary to address this difficulty as a matter of principle: the obligation to impose effective and dissuasive sanctions for false accounting derived from a Union directive; yet directives cannot of themselves impose obligations on an individual and cannot as such be relied on against private parties; more specifically, a directive cannot of itself have the effect of determining or aggravating the criminal liability of persons who act in contravention of that directive.[242] Here, reliance on the First Companies Directive so as to set aside the incompatible provisions of the 2002

---

[239] Cases C-397/01–403/01 *Pfeiffer* [2004] ECR I-8835.

[240] Cases C-387/02, C-391/02 and C-403/02 *Berlusconi* [2005] ECR I-3565.

[241] See Opinion of 14 October 2004. Note also A Biondi and R Mastroianni, Annotation of *Berlusconi* (2006) 43 *CMLRev* 553.

[242] cp Case 80/86 *Kolpinghuis Nijmegen* [1987] ECR 3969. See further above.

Italian legislation would have the effect of rendering applicable to the defendant the manifestly more severe regime contained in the original national legislation—and that would be contrary to the limits which flow from the essential nature of any directive.

Berlusconi affirmed the Court's understanding in *Pfeiffer* about the proper scope of the direct effect of unimplemented directives, and (more fundamentally) the interrelationship between the principles of direct effect and supremacy. Taken together, the two rulings clearly suggest that the 'primacy' model is out of favour with the Court itself.[243] That is not to say that its rival 'trigger' model paints an entirely convincing portrait of the case law either. But on balance, we feel that the 'trigger' model—whereby the disapplication of national measures pursuant to the principle of supremacy may only follow from a finding that the relevant Union law satisfies the conditions for producing direct effect—better reflects the current state of the Court's jurisprudence.

VI – CONCLUDING REMARKS

Although controversy over the 'primacy' and 'trigger' approaches to Union law rumbles on,[244] the very existence of such debates is a useful reminder that—even half a century after the foundational rulings in *van Gend en Loos* and *Costa v Enel*—many important facets of the system for the decentralised enforcement of Union law remain deeply contested and/or relatively unexplored.

Suffice to recall, from the analysis presented in this chapter alone, the precise strength of the national court's duty of consistent interpretation (particularly in cases involving criminal law); the nature of the Member State's duty of loyal co-operation before the deadline for implementing Union into national law has expired; the complex relationship between the principle of direct effect and the creation of individual rights and/or rights of standing to protect the general interest; the task of identifying precisely who should be recognised as competent to invoke any given provision of Union law before the national courts; the interminable controversy surrounding the capacity of unimplemented directives to impose obligations upon private individuals; the scope for general principles of Union law to produce direct effect of their own, particularly where they are supplemented by a directive which should incapable of having direct effect; the nature of the limits to the principle of supremacy recognised under Union law on grounds such as legal certainty; and the sometimes awkward reception of the principle of supremacy into the national constitutional systems.

But despite such problems, one should not lose sight of the fact that—in the great majority of situations—the system of decentralised enforcement for Union law works incredibly well: national courts all across the Member States are daily busy at work interpreting national law so as to conform to the Treaties, recognising the direct effect of myriad instruments of Union law, and disapplying irreconcilable provisions of domestic legislation.

---

[243] The ECJ expressly affirmed its *Marshall/Faccini Dori* case law in other rulings delivered around the same time, eg Case C-235/03 *QDQ Media* [2005] ECR I-1937; Case C-196/02 *Nikoloudi* [2005] ECR I-1789; Case C-350/03 *Schulte* [2005] ECR I-9215.

[244] Particularly in the light of the rulings in Case C-144/04 *Mangold* [2005] ECR I-9981 and Case C-555/07 *Kücükdeveci* (Judgment of 19 January 2010). Consider eg K Lenaerts and JA Gutiérrez-Fons, 'The Constitutional Allocation of Powers and General Principles of EU Law' (2010) 47 *CMLRev* 1629; E Muir, 'Of Ages In—And Edges of—EU Law' (2011) 48 *CMLRev* 39.

The next chapter will address the right to effective judicial protection before the national courts, as regards the applicable remedies and procedural rules, for individuals who seek to rely upon their rights under the Treaties—another important pillar in the system for the decentralised enforcement of Union law.

Further Reading

K Alter, *Establishing the Supremacy of European Law* (Oxford, Oxford University Press, 2001).

A Arnull, 'The Law Lords and the European Union: Swimming with the Incoming Tide' (2010) 35 *ELRev* 57.

G Betlem, 'The Doctrine of Consistent Interpretation: Managing Legal Uncertainty' (2002) 22 *OJLS* 397.

M Claes, *The National Courts' Mandate in the European Constitution* (Oxford, Hart Publishing, 2006).

J Coppel, 'Rights, Duties and the End of *Marshall*' (1994) 57 *MLR* 859.

P Craig, 'Once Upon a Time in the West: Direct Effect and the Federalisation of EEC Law' (1992) 12 *OJLS* 453.

——, 'The Legal Effect of Directives: Policy, Rules and Exceptions' (2009) 34 *ELRev* 349.

A Dashwood, 'From *van Duyn* to *Mangold* via *Marshall*: Reducing Direct Effect to Absurdity?' (2006-2007) 9 *CYELS* 81.

M Dougan, 'When Worlds Collide! Competing Visions of the Relationship Between Direct Effect and Supremacy' (2007) 44 *CMLRev* 931.

——, 'Who Exactly Benefits from the Treaties? The Murky Interaction Between Union and National Competence Over the Capacity to Enforce EU Law' (2009–10) 12 *CYELS* 73.

S Drake, 'Twenty Years After *von Colson*: the Impact of `Indirect Effect' on the Protection of the Individual's Community Rights' (2005) 30 *ELRev* 329.

K Lenaerts and T Corthaut, 'Of Birds and Hedges: The Role of Primary in Invoking Norms of EU Law' (2006) 31 *ELRev* 287.

M Lenz, D Sif Tynes and L Young, 'Horizontal What? Back to Basics' (2000) 25 *ELRev* 509.

N MacCormick, 'The Maastricht--Urteil: Sovereignty Now' (1995) 1 *ELJ* 259.

F Mancini, 'The Making of a Constitution for Europe' (1989) 26 *CMLRev* 595.

S Prechal, 'Does Direct Effect Still Matter?' (2000) 37 *CMLRev* 1047.

——, *Directives in EC Law*, 2nd edn (Oxford, Oxford University Press, 2005).

JM Prinssen and A Schrauwen, *Direct Effect: Rethinking a Classic of EC Legal Doctrine* (Groningen, Europa Law Publishing, 2002).

D Thym, 'In the Name of Sovereign Statehood: A Critical Introduction to the *Lisbon* Judgment of the German Constitutional Court' (2009) 46 *CMLRev* 1795.

T Tridimas, 'Horizontal Effect of Directives: A Missed Opportunity?' (1994) 19 *ELRev* 621.

——, 'Black, White and Shades of Grey: Horizontality of Directives Revisited' (2002) 21 *YEL* 327.

S Weatherill, 'Breach of Directives and Breach of Contract' (2001) 26 *ELRev* 177.

B de Witte, 'Direct Effect, Primacy, and the Nature of the Legal Order' in P Craig and G de Búrca (eds), *The Evolution of EU Law*, 2nd edn (Oxford, Oxford University Press, 2011).

9

Judicial Protection of Union Rights before the National Courts

In most situations, Union law is enforced through the national courts according to the latter's own system of remedies and procedural rules. However, the Court of Justice has imposed three main limits to Member State competence over the standards of judicial protection applicable in disputes based upon the Treaties. First, beneficiaries of Union law enjoy a fundamental right of access to the courts for the purposes of asserting their legal claims. Secondly, the principle of equivalence requires that Union law actions cannot be treated less favourably than comparable actions derived from purely domestic law. Thirdly, the principle of effectiveness demands that national remedies and procedural rules cannot in any case render the exercise of Union law rights virtually impossible or excessively difficult. This chapter also considers some of the specific forms of redress guaranteed to claimants under Union law: interim relief against allegedly invalid national or Union measures; the recovery of charges imposed contrary to Union law; the Francovich action for damages against a Member State for breaching the Treaties; and the possibility of private law damages against individuals who infringe a Union law obligation. We also offer some remarks on the Union's increasing tendency to enact secondary legislation harmonising the standards of judicial protection applicable within the Member States.

I – INTRODUCTION

As we saw in Chapter 8, the system for the decentralised enforcement of Union law is built around the principles of direct effect and supremacy. By insisting that Union provisions may be cognisable before the national courts as an autonomous source of law, and should take priority over any conflicting domestic legislation, the Court of Justice has made a major contribution to ensuring the effective and uniform application of Union law within and across the Member States. However, the principles of direct effect and supremacy cannot achieve those objectives alone. In the great majority of situations, the Union creates rights and obligations without specifying any further how precisely they are to be enforced in practice. Union law must therefore be actualised through the medium of each national legal system—which includes the latter's own system of remedies (the forms of relief actually provided under domestic law for the vindication of the claimant's rights) and procedural rules (the requirements which structure the assertion of one's legal rights and regulate the conduct of judicial proceedings). Indeed, it is often said that the Treaties operate on the basis of a presumption of 'national procedural autonomy': save insofar as Union law requires otherwise, it is for each Member State to design its own system of judicial protection in respect of the exercise of Union rights within its territory.[1] For example, it is for the Member State to designate the particular court or tribunal having jurisdiction to adjudicate over a given category of claim derived from Union law.[2] Similarly, it lies within the discretion of the domestic legislature to decide upon the appropriate remedy for discriminatory employment practices that constitute a breach of the Equal Treatment Directive.[3]

That presumption of national procedural autonomy is often seen as problematic because it will not necessarily safeguard the effective and uniform application of Union law. In the first place, weaknesses in the domestic standards of judicial protection could *in themselves* endanger the effectiveness of substantive Union rules within any given country: for example, if Union law prohibits the Member State from imposing a given tax, but national law either fails to provide a right to reimbursement of unlawfully levied charges, or subjects the exercise of such a right to highly onerous restrictions. In the second place, significant differences in the systems of judicial protection provided by the Member States could *in themselves* undermine the uniform application of the Treaties: for example, if the remedy for a discriminatory dismissal from employment in breach of Union law in one Member State is compensation capped at a statutory ceiling, while compensation in another Member State is for unlimited damages, and the relief provided in yet another country consists of reinstatement in post.[4]

Requests for preliminary rulings, seeking clarification of the nature of judicial protection that national courts should provide in respect of Union law rights, first began to reach the Court of Justice in the 1960s and early 1970s. The Court's initial answer was almost invariably to leave each dispute to be determined solely in accordance with the applicable domestic law.[5] However, the Court changed track in 1976 with its twin rulings in *Rewe-Zentralfinanz eG and Rewe-Zentral AG v Landwirtschaftskammer für das Saarland* and *Comet BV v Produktschap voor Siergewassen*.[6] Those judgments established the basic framework that (with certain modifications) has consistently served the Court ever since when addressing issues relating to the decentralised enforcement of Union law: in the absence of any relevant Union legislation, the enforcement of Treaty-based rights and

---

[1] Though the true nature of that 'autonomy' is rather contested: consider eg CM Kakouris, 'Do the Member States Possess Judicial Procedural "Autonomy"?' (1997) 34 *CMLRev* 1389.

[2] eg Case 179/84 *Bozzetti* [1985] ECR 2301; Case C-446/93 *SEIM* [1996] ECR I-73; Cases C-10–22/97 *IN.CO.GE.* [1998] ECR I-6307.

[3] Dir 76/207 [1976] OJ L39/40. See now Dir 2006/54 [2006] OJ L204/23. eg Case 14/83 *von Colson* [1984] ECR 1891; Case C-271/91 *Marshall II* [1993] ECR I-4367.

[4] For early analyses eg T Hartley, 'The Effects in National Law of Judgments of the European Court' (1980) 5 *ELRev* 366; J Bridge, 'Procedural Aspects of the Enforcement of European Community Law through the Legal Systems of the Member States' (1984) 9 *ELRev* 28.

[5] eg Case 28/67 *Molkerei-Zentrale* [1968] ECR 143; Case 34/67 *Lück* [1968] ECR 245; Case 13/68 *Salgoil* [1968] ECR 661; Case 35/74 *Mutualités Chrétiennes v Rzepa* [1974] ECR 1241.

[6] Case 33/76 *Rewe-Zentralfinanz v Landwirtschaftskammer für das Saarland* [1976] ECR 1989; Case 45/76 *Comet BV v Produktschap voor Siergewassen* [1976] ECR 2043.

obligations is presumed to take place in accordance with existing national remedies and procedural rules, but subject to certain overarching requirements imposed by Union law.[7]

This chapter will consider the three most important of the Court's tools for scrutinising the domestic standards of judicial protection: the fundamental right of access to judicial process (which guarantees that beneficiaries under Union law are able to assert their rights before the Member State's courts); the principle of equivalence (whereby rights derived from Union law may not be treated less favourably than comparable rights of purely national origin); and the principle of effectiveness (which requires that, in any case, national remedies and procedural rules should not render the exercise of Union rights virtually impossible or excessively difficult in practice).[8] Moreover, the Court has identified certain actions which are properly to be considered as Union (not merely national) remedies: for example, the provision of interim relief in respect of alleged violations of one's Union rights; the recovery of charges levied in contravention of Union law; and most famous of all, the *Francovich* right to reparation in respect of losses caused by a breach of Union law for which the Member State can be held responsible.[9] As we shall see, the related question of whether Union law directly provides for a private law action in damages, against individuals who breach their obligations under the Treaties, remains in something of a state of legal flux. This chapter goes on to discuss the growing contribution of the Union legislature to the system of decentralised enforcement, through the adoption of legislation laying down harmonised rules on remedies and procedural rules within each Member State.

II – THE FUNDAMENTAL RIGHT TO JUDICIAL PROCESS

Article 6(1) ECHR provides that, in the determination of his/her civil rights and obligations or of any criminal charge against him/her, everyone is entitled to a fair and public hearing within a reasonable time by an independent and impartial tribunal established by law. As the Court of Justice first recognised in the *Johnson* ruling from 1986, this fundamental right of access to judicial process forms part of the general principles of Union law binding upon the Member States when acting within the scope of the Treaties, and thus applies for the benefit of all individuals whose Union rights are implemented through the national systems of judicial protection.[10] The *Johnson* ruling is now reflected in Article 47 of the Charter of Fundamental Rights,[11] the indirect legal status of which had already been

---

[7] See further eg J Lonbay and A Biondi (eds), *Remedies for Breach of EC Law* (Chichester, Wiley, 1997); C Kilpatrick, T Novitz and P Skidmore (eds), *The Future of Remedies in Europe* (Oxford, Hart Publishing, 2000); M Dougan, *National Remedies Before the Court of Justice* (Oxford, Hart Publishing, 2004).

[8] Note that the terms 'equivalence' and 'effectiveness' first emerged into common usage during 1997: eg Case C-261/95 *Palmisani* [1997] ECR I-4025; Case C-188/95 *Fantask* [1997] ECR I-6783.

[9] Cases C-6 and 9/90 *Francovich* [1991] ECR I-5357.

[10] Case 222/84 *Johnston* [1986] ECR 1651. Affirmed on many occasions since, eg Case C-228/98 *Dounias* [2000] ECR I-577; Case C-7/98 *Krombach* [2000] ECR I-1935; Case C-426/05 *Tele2* [2008] ECR I-685; Case C-55/06 *Arcor* [2008] ECR I-2931.

[11] [2010] OJ C83/389.

recognised by the Court in judgments such as *Unibet*,[12] even before it became directly legal binding (with the entry into force of the TL) in accordance with Article 6(1) TEU.[13]

The case law following *Johnson* has been largely preoccupied with addressing familiar questions about the detailed application of the fundamental right of access to judicial process. Thus, Union law requires Member States to provide claimants with access to an independent and impartial tribunal. For example, *Johnson* itself concerned UK legislation which permitted derogations from the principle of equal treatment between men and women in relation to acts intended to safeguard national security or protect public safety; and provided that a certificate issued by the national authorities should constitute conclusive evidence that the act in question complied with the terms of such derogations. The Court of Justice held that such an ouster clause permitted the national authorities to deprive individuals of the opportunity of asserting their right to equal treatment and was therefore contrary to the general principles of Union law.[14] Similarly, *Commission v Austria* concerned the system for challenging decisions by the competent domestic authority to reject applications for inclusion in the list of medicinal products covered by the national health insurance system. Austrian legislation provided that, at the applicant's request, such decisions should be referred to an independent advisory board consisting of technical experts, which could then issue recommendations to the competent domestic authority (if appropriate) urging the latter to reconsider its refusal. The Court of Justice held that redress before an administrative body without true decision-making powers was clearly incapable of satisfying the principle of access to judicial process.[15]

Moreover, Union law requires Member States to ensure that claimants enjoy a fair hearing before the relevant tribunal. For example, *Steffensen* concerned analyses conducted by the national authorities which indicated that certain foodstuffs failed to comply with domestic rules on labelling, but as regards which the relevant manufacturer had been unable to exercise its right under Union law to obtain a second opinion. The question arose whether such analyses could be admitted as evidence before the competent German court during the manufacturer's appeal against an administrative decision imposing financial penalties. The Court of Justice observed that Article 6(1) ECHR does not lay down any rules on evidence as such; but the requirement of a fair hearing, which implies that the parties enjoy an adequate opportunity to participate in proceedings before the competent court, covers also the manner in which evidence was taken. In particular, parties must be afforded a real opportunity to comment effectively upon evidence submitted to the court, especially where that evidence pertains to a technical field beyond the knowledge of the judges. If the German court found that, in the circumstances of this case, admitting the analyses would infringe the right to a fair hearing, Union law would then require the evidence to be excluded.[16]

Other lines of case law have explored additional facets of the fundamental right of access to judicial process: for example, when courts of first instance and/or appeal can be said to exercise full jurisdiction over a dispute so as to guarantee an adequate level of

---

[12] Case C-432/05 *Unibet* [2007] ECR I-2271.

[13] As regards which, consider Case C-279/09 *DEB Deutsche Energiehandels- und Beratungsgesellschaft* (Judgment of 22 December 2010). See further Chapter 12.

[14] Case 222/84 *Johnston* [1986] ECR 1651.

[15] Case C-424/99 *Commission v Austria* [2001] ECR I-9285. Also eg Case C-506/04 *Wilson* [2006] ECR I-8613.

[16] Case C-276/01 *Steffensen* [2003] ECR I-3735. Also eg Case C-63/01 *Evans* [2003] ECR I-14447; Case C-105/03 *Pupino* [2005] ECR I-5285; Case C-450/06 *Varec* [2008] ECR I-581.

judicial scrutiny;[17] or the circumstances in which provisional acts adopted by the national authorities must also be subject to judicial review.[18] However, the *Johnson* case law is not merely a mirror image of the protection individuals would in any case be entitled to expect under the ECHR; the Union's fundamental right of access to judicial process also offers certain specific advantages. For example, *Johnson* applies to the exercise of *all* rights derived from Union law, including those of a purely administrative character, which would not ordinarily fall within the scope of Article 6 ECHR per se.[19] Furthermore, the Court has divined from *Johnson* certain supplementary rights, intended to safeguard the practical effects of Article 6 ECHR within the Union legal order, particularly in respect of conduct designed to deter the claimant from pursuing his/her entitlements under the Treaties through the national courts. First, individuals have a right to know the reasoning behind adverse administrative decisions of a final character.[20] For example, the Court in *Heylens* decreed that the right of access to judicial procedure in respect of restrictions on the free movement of persons implies a duty upon the competent authority to disclose the reasons for its decision, without which the citizen could not decide whether there was any point in bringing legal proceedings in the first place.[21] Secondly, individuals enjoy a degree of protection against harassment or retribution intended to deter them from exercising their Treaty rights. For example, the Court held in *Coote v Granada Hospitality* that the right of access to the courts to protest about a breach of the principle of equal treatment between men and women necessarily implies an ancillary guarantee of protection against retaliatory measures taken by an employer aimed at deterring the victim of discriminatory action from pursuing her grievances by judicial means.[22]

One difficult problem for the Court, however, concerns the balance between guaranteeing respect for the fundamental right of access to judicial process (on the one hand) and respecting the Member State's competence to designate the courts and tribunals having jurisdiction over particular categories of Union action (on the other hand).[23] Clearly, where the competent court finds its jurisdiction improperly inhibited by the presence of an ouster clause (in situations such as *Johnson*), or the fairness of its hearing distorted by certain evidential rules (in cases such as *Steffensen*), such domestic legislation must

---

[17] eg Case C-120/97 *Upjohn* [1999] ECR I-223; Case C-92/00 *Hospital Ingenieure* [2002] ECR I-5553; Case C-380/01 *Schneider* [2004] ECR I-1389.

[18] eg Case C-97/91 *Borelli* [1992] ECR I-6313; Cases C-286, 340 and 401/95 and C-47/96 *Garage Molenheide* [1997] ECR I-7281; Case C-269/99 *Kühne* [2001] ECR I-9517.

[19] See Art 47 Charter of Fundamental Rights. Cf. *Schouten and Meldrum* [1994] 19 EHRR 432. Further eg EG de Enterría, 'The Extension of the Jurisdiction of National Administrative Courts by Community Law: The Judgment of the Court of Justice in *Borelli* and Article 5 of the EC Treaty' (1993) 13 *YEL* 19; C Harlow, 'Access to Justice as a Human Right: The European Convention and the European Union' in P Alston (ed), *The EU and Human Rights* (Oxford, Oxford University Press, 1999).

[20] This duty applies only to final decisions, not to merely preparatory or intermediate stages in the overall decision-making process: Case C-127/95 *Norbrook Laboratories* [1998] ECR I-1531. Moreover, the duty to provide reasons applies only to administrative decisions adversely affecting individuals, not national measures of general scope: Case C-70/95 *Sodemare* [1997] ECR I-3395.

[21] Case 222/86 *Heylens* [1987] ECR 4097. Also eg Case C-340/89 *Vlassopoulou* [1991] ECR I-2357; Case C-104/91 *Borrell* [1992] ECR I-3003; Case C-19/92 *Kraus* [1993] ECR I-1663; Case C-75/08 *Mellor* [2009] ECR I-3799. cp other rulings linking the transparency of national procedures to effective judicial review, eg Case C-157/99 *Smits and Peerbooms* [2001] ECR I-5473; Case C-138/02 *Collins* [2004] ECR I-2703.

[22] Case C-185/97 *Coote v Granada Hospitality* [1998] ECR I-5199. See also Case C-243/09 *Günter Fuß* (Judgment of 14 October 2010). Consider also eg Case C-208/90 *Emmott* [1991] ECR I-4269 and Case C-326/96 *Levez* [1998] ECR I-7835 (defendant engaged in misleading conduct which effectively prevented claimant from initiating claim within the applicable time-limits): these rulings are discussed further below.

[23] eg as in Case 179/84 *Bozzetti* [1985] ECR 2301 (noted above).

simply be set aside as incompatible with the binding requirements of Union law. But what if the Member State has failed to designate *any* tribunal competent to adjudicate upon the claimant's rights? The case law suggests that, unless such a gap in jurisdiction can be resolved through recourse to the duty of consistent interpretation derived from *von Colson* and *Marleasing*,[24] the Court will be reticent about obliging national courts to assume jurisdiction in entirely novel situations which lie beyond their prima facie field of competence.[25] The claimant's only real recourse in such situations is to bring an action for damages against the Member State, under the *Francovich* case law, on the basis that the latter has breached its Union law obligation to provide access to effective judicial protection.[26]

III – THE PRINCIPLE OF EQUIVALENCE

The principle of equivalence was first introduced by the Court in its 1976 rulings in *Rewe* and *Comet*.[27] The principle of equivalence requires that actions based upon Union law brought before the domestic courts should not be furnished with less favourable remedies and procedural rules than those available in respect of similar actions based upon purely national law.[28] For example, a Member State may not levy interest on the recovery of wrongly paid Union subsidies at a higher rate than that which applies to the recovery of comparable wrongly paid domestic monies.[29] After many years of neglect, the principle of equivalence has increasingly become the focus of interest by litigants keen to exploit its full potential to improve the levels of protection offered by the national courts in respect of Union law rights. The Court has responded by making clear that the principle of equivalence is not so broad as to oblige the Member States to extend to Union actions any more favourable remedial or procedural rules available in respect of domestic claims falling simply within the same policy field.[30] The test in fact consists of two main stages.

The first stage concerns when a Union and domestic claim will be considered 'sufficiently similar' to found the basis of an appropriate comparison. This is, in principle, a matter to be determined by the national court. However, the latter's deliberations should be guided by the 'objective' or 'purpose' of the actions in question, determined in the light of their 'essential characteristics'.[31] So, for example, a *Francovich* action for Member State liability in damages seeks to compensate the claimant for losses incurred through a breach

---

[24] Case 14/83 *von Colson* [1984] ECR 1891; Case C-106/89 *Marleasing* [1990] ECR I-4135. See further Chapter 8.

[25] eg Case C-54/96 *Dorsch Consult* [1997] ECR I-4961; Case C-111/97 *EvoBus Austria* [1998] ECR I-5411; Case C-258/97 *Hospital Ingenieure* [1999] ECR I-1405. cf Case C-462/99 *Connect Austria* [2003] ECR I-5197; Case C-15/04 *Koppensteiner* [2005] ECR I-4855.

[26] Further eg M Dougan, 'The *Francovich* Right to Reparation: Reshaping the Contours of Community Remedial Competence' (2000) 6 *EPL* 103.

[27] Case 33/76 *Rewe-Zentralfinanz v Landwirtschaftskammer für das Saarland* [1976] ECR 1989; Case 45/76 *Comet BV v Produktschap voor Siergewassen* [1976] ECR 2043.

[28] Note that the principle of equivalence applies not only to procedural rules before the national courts (such as limitation periods), but also to those applied by the national authorities in reaching administrative decisions, eg Case C-34/02 *Pasquini* [2003] ECR I-6515.

[29] Case 54/81 *Fromme* [1982] ECR 1449.

[30] eg Case C-326/96 *Levez* [1998] ECR I-7835, para 42.

[31] eg Case C-326/96 *Levez* [1998] ECR I-7835, paras 39–41 and 43; Case C-78/98 *Preston* [2000] ECR I-3201, paras 49 and 56–57.

of Union law perpetrated by the national authorities; its appropriate comparator is therefore a domestic action for the non-contractual liability of public authorities which have committed an unlawful act in the exercise of their powers.[32] Similarly, an action for the recovery of financial charges levied by a Member State in breach of Union rules should be compared to a claim for the refund of taxes wrongly collected by a public authority under purely domestic rules. Such an action need not be considered 'similar' to a claim for the restitution of monies wrongly demanded by a private individual, in respect of which it is therefore permissible for the Member State to apply different limitation periods than those found in relation to public bodies.[33] The principle of equivalence becomes relevant only where conditions for the repayment of charges levied by the Member State in breach of Union law are less favourable than those applicable to the repayment of other taxes raised by a public body contrary to purely domestic law.[34]

It is possible that no appropriate national comparator can be located in respect of the relevant Union action. In such cases, the principle of equivalence is deemed to have been fulfilled.[35] But if a particular domestic action is considered sufficiently similar to found the basis of comparison, the second question is whether there has been 'less favourable treatment' of the Union claim. For these purposes, the national courts are obliged to conduct a contextual assessment—considering the place of the disputed rule within the relevant domestic procedure, examining that procedure as a whole and taking account of its special features.[36] On that basis, less favourable treatment can arise not only from patent differences in, for example, the availability of punitive damages as between comparable Union and national actions,[37] but also from less obvious factors such as the degree of formality involved in bringing proceedings, which might cause the Union claim to be more expensive and less convenient to pursue than its domestic comparator.[38] However, it is also possible that a contextual analysis will reveal apparent differences in the regulation of comparable claims to be in fact objectively justified by factors unrelated to their Union or domestic provenance.[39]

The basic aim of the principle of equivalence is therefore to embed Union rights into the domestic legal orders on an equal basis with comparable national rights. But despite the recent growth in case law, the Court's guidance on the full scope and precise application of the principle of equivalence remains far from comprehensive. In particular, a test of comparability based on the 'objectives' and 'essential characteristics' of the relevant claims is capable of operating at several different levels of abstraction. For example, a claim for financial benefits wrongly withheld from an employee in breach of the principle of equal pay between men and women might be said to have the purpose of enforcing the general principle of non-discrimination, and thus to be comparable to domestic claims based on other forms of unlawful prejudice. Alternatively, such a claim might be

---

[32] eg Case C-261/95 *Palmisani* [1997] ECR I-4025. Also eg Case C-118/08 *Transportes Urbanos y Servicios Generales* (Judgment of 26 January 2010).

[33] eg Case C-231/96 *Edis* [1998] ECR I-4951; Case C-260/96 *Spac* [1998] ECR I-4997; Case C-228/96 *Aprile* [1998] ECR I-7141; Case C-343/96 *Dilexport* [1999] ECR I-579; Case C-88/99 *Roquette Frères* [2000] ECR I-10465.

[34] Consider eg Cases C-216 and 222/99 *Prisco* [2002] ECR I-6761. cf Cases C-279–281/96 *Ansaldo Energia* [1998] ECR I-5025.

[35] Case C-261/95 *Palmisani* [1997] ECR I-4025, para 39.

[36] Case C-326/96 *Levez* [1998] ECR I-7835, para 44; Case C-78/98 *Preston* [2000] ECR I-3201, paras 60–62.

[37] eg Cases C-295–298/04 *Manfredi* [2006] ECR I-6619.

[38] eg Case C-78/98 *Preston* [2000] ECR I-3201.

[39] eg Case C-132/95 *Jensen and Korn* [1998] ECR I-2975, paras 50–51.

understood to pursue the objective of recovering remuneration properly due to a worker by his/her employer, and thus properly to be compared with domestic actions for arrears of wages or breach of the employment contract. Conflicting advice on the appropriate level of abstraction to be pursued under the principle of equivalence has been offered by the Advocates General.[40] For its part, the Court of Justice often seems reluctant to rule definitively on matters of equivalence, preferring to leave the final decision to the referring judges, particularly in the absence of detailed information about the structure of the national judicial system, and about the procedural rules applicable to various purely domestic legal actions.[41] In other cases, however, the Court has indeed offered relatively detailed analysis of whether it believes a given national rule to fall foul of the principle of equivalence.[42]

The more robust the Court's guidance on the principle of equivalence, the greater its potential to shine an unflattering light upon the dark corners of the national legal systems: particularly where a given Union claim might well be compared to several distinct national actions, each of which attracts rather different standards of judicial protection, the equivalence assessment can challenge each Member State to revisit the inherited but possibly rather incoherent structures of its own legal system.[43] Moreover, the Court's 2007 ruling in *Paquay* has opened up another dimension to this process of promoting more rational and cohesive standards of judicial protection: the principle of equivalence requires that the Member State guarantee equal treatment in the remedies and procedural rules applicable not only to comparable Union and national actions, but also to Union rights inter se where the latter are themselves of similar nature and importance (as might be the case, for example, with discrimination based on sex as compared to race, age or sexual orientation).[44]

IV – THE PRINCIPLE OF EFFECTIVENESS

The principle of effectiveness was also recognised by the Court of Justice for the first time in its *Rewe* and *Comet* judgments from 1976.[45] It requires that national remedies and procedural rules should not render the exercise of Union rights virtually impossible or excessively difficult.[46] The principle of effectiveness is distinct from that of equivalence: whereas the latter seeks to ensure that existing standards of domestic judicial protection

---

[40] Consider the Opinions in eg Case 199/82 *San Giorgio* [1983] ECR 3595; Case C-271/91 *Marshall II* [1993] ECR I-4367; Case C-62/93 *BP Supergas* [1995] ECR I-1883; Case C-312/93 *Peterbroeck* [1995] ECR I-4599; Case C-132/95 *Jensen and Korn* [1998] ECR I-2975; Case C-326/96 *Levez* [1998] ECR I-7835; Case C-78/98 *Preston* [2000] ECR I-3201.

[41] eg Case C-326/96 *Levez* [1998] ECR I-7835; Case C-78/98 *Preston* [2000] ECR I-3201; Case C-472/99 *Clean Car Autoservice* [2001] ECR I-9687.

[42] For examples of relatively detailed guidance: Case C-34/02 *Pasquini* [2003] ECR I-6515; Cases C-392 and 422/04 *i-21 Germany* [2006] ECR I-8559; Case C-63/08 *Pontin* [2009] ECR I-10467; Case C-542/08 *Barth* (Judgment of 15 April 2010); Case C-246/09 *Bulicke* (Judgment of 8 July 2010).

[43] T Tridimas, 'Liability for Breach of Community Law: Growing Up and Mellowing Down?' (2001) 38 *CMLRev* 301, 321.

[44] Case C-460/06 *Paquay* [2007] ECR I-8511.

[45] Case 33/76 *Rewe-Zentralfinanz v Landwirtschaftskammer für das Saarland* [1976] ECR 1989; Case 45/76 *Comet BV v Produktschap voor Siergewassen* [1976] ECR 2043.

[46] The rulings in *Rewe* and *Comet* themselves used only the formulation 'virtually impossible'; the additional wording of 'or excessively difficult' emerged in Case 199/82 *San Giorgio* [1983] ECR 3595.

are extended to Union law on an equal footing with comparable domestic law claims, the principle of effectiveness addresses itself to the possibility that those national remedies and procedural rules may well fall short of the minimum standards required for the adequate enforcement of the Treaties within each Member State.[47] The principle of effectiveness is also distinct from the fundamental right of access to judicial process: for example, even if the Member State's allocation of jurisdiction to a given national tribunal is adequate to satisfy the minimum standards expected under the *Johnson* caselaw, the detailed provisions governing the operation of that national tribunal, or the interaction between its jurisdiction and that of other domestic courts, might still prove sufficiently complex, costly and inconvenient as to render the exercise of the claimant's substantive Union rights excessively difficult for the purposes of the principle of effectiveness.[48]

It is perfectly possible that certain domestic remedies or procedural rules will (for reasons of historical accident or deliberate obstructionism) be considered plainly inadequate to the task of enforcing Union law. However, in most situations, even if aspects of the national systems of judicial protection could somehow prejudice the effective and/or uniform application of Union law, it must be admitted that such rules nevertheless serve some entirely rational and indeed valuable purpose, and not always merely of a technical nature of interest only to lawyers and court administrators, but often of a constitutional stature directly or indirectly reflecting fundamental conceptions about relations between state and citizen, or between private citizens themselves, or concerning appropriate standards of fairness in the administration of justice.[49] The major challenge facing the Court in applying the principle of effectiveness is therefore to strike an appropriate balance between (on the one hand) legitimate Union concerns about its own legal effectiveness and uniformity and (on the other hand) equally legitimate national conceptions about the organisation and functioning of the administration of justice. In meeting that challenge, the Court has (since 1976) delivered an enormous body of jurisprudence concerning the principle of effectiveness—though it goes without saying that the Court has not followed any clear or consistent pathway. Commentators usually try to make sense of the voluminous case law on effectiveness by dividing it into three main historical periods.

A – The Court's Early Period: Until the Mid-1980s

The early period of the Court's case law can be summarised quite simply: domestic standards of judicial protection remained the rule; Union interference proved to be an ill-defined and rarely practised exception. For example, the Court held in *Rewe* and *Comet* that domestic limitation periods regulating the initiation of proceedings before the national courts may also apply to Union cases. In order to satisfy the principle of effectiveness, the relevant time limit must be reasonable in duration; a 30-day limitation period in respect

---

[47] Which may well result in Union rights benefiting from higher standards of judicial protection than comparable national rights: see eg Case C-432/05 *Unibet* [2007] ECR I-2271.

[48] eg Case C-268/06 *Impact* [2008] ECR I-2483. Note, however, that the ECJ itself sometimes fails to distinguish clearly between the fundamental right of access to judicial process and the ordinary the principle of effectiveness: contrast Case C-34/02 *Pasquini* [2003] ECR I-6515 with Case C-63/01 *Evans* [2003] ECR I-14447.

[49] See further eg R Craufurd Smith, 'Remedies for Breaches of EU Law in National Courts: Legal Variation and Selection' in P Craig and G de Búrca (eds), *The Evolution of EU Law*, 1st edn (Oxford, Oxford University Press, 1999).

of actions for the recovery of unlawfully levied charges passed that test.[50] Moreover, in the *Butter Buying Cruises* case, it was bluntly stated that the Treaty of Rome was not intended to create any new forms of relief not already available under national law.[51] Thus, for example, the ruling in *Russo* held that the availability of compensatory damages against a Member State for its breach of Union law was to be determined by domestic rules;[52] while the judgment in *Roquette Frères* established that the Member States were entitled to apply their own rules regarding the payment of statutory interest in cases concerning the reimbursement of unlawfully levied charges.[53]

Such judicial restraint might be explained by various factors: for example, the possibility that the Court was mindful of its own institutional limitations and therefore hesitant about further alienating those national courts which were still encountering difficulties with the principles of direct effect and supremacy, let alone any more developed system of decentralised enforcement;[54] and perhaps also an assumption on the part of the Court that what was good for the national goose must be good enough too for the Union gander, so that the brunt of Union scrutiny could be carried by the principle of equivalence, whilst reserving intervention on grounds of the principle of effectiveness for those rare occasions when ordinary national remedies might indeed prove to be patently deficient.[55] Nevertheless, it might be worth noting that, even in this early period in the Court's case law, there were already some signs of the potential for a more interventionist approach. Consider, for example, the Court's insistence that, where the Member State has levied charges contrary to Union law, the payor must in principle be entitled to seek reimbursement through the national courts.[56] Similarly, consider the finding in *Simmenthal* that any domestic judge must be in a position to disapply a provision of national legislation in breach of the Treaty, without having to refer the dispute to some higher tribunal—a ruling with significant implications for the procedural conduct of cases, and indeed, for the distribution of jurisdiction within certain Member States.[57]

B – The Court's Middle Period: Until 1993

In any event, the Court's middle period jurisprudence was, by contrast, dominated by the increasing frequency and vitality of Union intervention in the national systems of judicial protection, achieved almost entirely through a renewed conception and application of the principle of effectiveness. That renewed conception can be seen in the changing language of the Court: the language of negative scrutiny derived from *Rewe* and *Comet* was supplemented by a more positive obligation upon the national courts to guarantee the 'effective protection' of rights derived from Union law.[58] As for the renewed application

---

[50] Case 33/76 *Rewe-Zentralfinanz v Landwirtschaftskammer für das Saarland* [1976] ECR 1989; Case 45/76 *Comet BV v Produktschap voor Siergewassen* [1976] ECR 2043.

[51] Case 158/80 *Rewe-Handelsgesellschaft Nord v Hauptzollamt Kiel* [1981] ECR 1805.

[52] Case 60/75 *Russo* [1976] ECR 45.

[53] Case 26/74 *Roquette Frères* [1976] ECR 677.

[54] Consider eg Case 265/78 *Ferwerda* [1980] ECR 617; Case 130/79 *Express Dairy Foods* [1980] ECR 1887; Case 54/81 *Fromme* [1982] ECR 1449; Cases 205–215/82 *Deutsche Milchkontor* [1983] ECR 2633. On national resistance to the principles of direct effect and supremacy, see further Chapter 8.

[55] Consider eg Case 811/79 *Ariete* [1980] ECR 2545; Case 826/79 *MIRECO* [1980] ECR 2559.

[56] Case 177/78 *Pigs and Bacon Commission v McCarren* [1979] ECR 2161.

[57] Case 106/77 *Simmenthal* [1978] ECR 629.

[58] Case 179/84 *Bozzetti* [1985] ECR 2301.

of the principle of effectiveness, that is borne witness in a series of rulings which rank among the best known in the whole of EU law. For example, the Court held in *Emmott* that, even if a domestic limitation period complies with the requirement of reasonableness set out in *Rewe* and *Comet*, it must nevertheless be set aside in cases where the Member State has failed correctly to implement a Union directive within the prescribed deadline, and the individual would otherwise be deprived of the opportunity to rely on rights based on that directive.[59] Moreover, despite the *Butter Buying Cruises* ruling, the judgment in *Factortame* established that national courts must be able to offer interim protection to claimants seeking to assert their Union rights by judicial process—even if such relief is not ordinarily available under domestic rules.[60] Similarly, despite the *Russo* case, the Court in *Francovich* held that it is inherent in the system of the Treaties that individuals are entitled to seek compensation in respect of losses suffered through a Member State's breach of their intended Union rights—and went on to specify the substantive conditions that must be fulfilled in order to exercise that right to reparation.[61] Another good illustration is *Marshall II*, which established that where the Member State chooses to protect victims of discriminatory dismissal from employment, contrary to the provisions of the Equal Treatment Directive,[62] through the award of compensation, such compensation should be full; notwithstanding the judgment in *Roquette Frères*, full compensation must include the payment of interest to represent losses suffered through the effluxion of time.[63]

This change in judicial policy has been attributed to a number of factors.[64] First, confidence in the legal fundamentals of the system of decentralised enforcement had increased, as the principles of direct effect and supremacy became less controversial with previously sceptical national courts.[65] Secondly, it was clear that, if the Court had indeed placed its faith in the underlying adequacy (and therefore equivalent application) of domestic rules, that faith had been overly optimistic: in fact, as disputes such as *Factortame* demonstrated, national law often offered less than satisfactory levels of protection. Thirdly, there was a growing feeling that such challenges to the effectiveness and uniform application of Union law were indeed a serious problem and deserved to be treated as such. In particular, the renewed impetus towards the creation of an internal market following the ruling in *Cassis de Dijon*,[66] and especially after the Single European Act,[67] fuelled concerns that, without greater Union intervention, the benefits of closer economic integration would be dissipated as the rules on free movement and fair competition were filtered through the national systems of judicial protection.[68] Fourthly, the character of the challenge to effectiveness and uniformity was itself changing significantly. The Court of Justice was increasingly being called upon not only by big business to assist in enforcing the rules of

---

[59] Case C-208/90 *Emmott* [1991] ECR I-4269.

[60] Case C-213/89 *Factortame* [1990] ECR I-2433.

[61] Cases C-6 and 9/90 *Francovich* [1991] ECR I-5357.

[62] Dir 76/207 [1976] OJ L39/40. See now Dir 2006/54 [2006] OJ L204/23.

[63] Case C-271/91 *Marshall II* [1993] ECR I-4367. cp Case 14/83 *von Colson* [1984] ECR 1891; Case C-177/88 *Dekker* [1990] ECR I-3941.

[64] Further: A Ward, 'Effective Sanctions in EC Law: A Moving Boundary in the Division of Competence' (1995) 1 *ELJ* 205.

[65] Consider eg the judgment of the German Federal Constitutional Court known as *Solange II* (1987) 3 CMLR 225. See further Chapter 8.

[66] Case 120/78 '*Cassis de Dijon*' [1979] ECR 649. See further Chapter 14.

[67] [1987] OJ L169. See further Chapter 1.

[68] Further: M Bronckers, 'Private Enforcement of 1992: Do Trade and Industry Stand a Chance Against the Member States?' (1989) 26 *CMLRev* 513; D Curtin, 'Directives: The Effectiveness of Judicial Protection of Individual Rights' (1990) 27 *CMLRev* 709.

the common market, but also by ordinary citizens asserting their right to enjoy the social benefits of Union membership—for example, as consumers or workers. That change may well have increased the Court's inclination to bolster the levels of judicial protection guaranteed by Union law.[69] Finally, despite numerous hints from the Court itself, legislative intervention by the Union's political institutions to address the problems posed by national remedies and procedural rules remained patchy and limited.[70] The initiative for action therefore lay firmly with the judiciary.

However, the Court's newfound confidence in scrutinising the effectiveness of the national systems of judicial protection, and increasingly in substituting its own solutions for those of the Member States, also drew growing criticism. First, there were concerns about the practical effects of the Court's case law on values such as legal certainty, and for the financial interests of the Member States. In particular, it was argued that the Court's creative but also unpredictable application of the principle of effectiveness was making it increasingly difficult for legal practitioners to advise their clients, and conduct their cases, when no one really knew whether the relevant domestic limitation period, or rules on evidence, or limits on damages, would remain in place. For their part, the Member States were evidently increasingly alarmed at the newfound costs of failing to comply with their obligations under Union law: rulings such as *Emmott*, *Marshall II* and *Francovich* seemed to be systematically dismantling the safeguards against 'excessive liability' built into the domestic systems of judicial protection. Secondly, such practical concerns were accompanied by constitutional reservations about what many commentators felt to be blatant judicial law-making. The ruling in *Francovich*, for example, was seen in certain quarters as little more than legislation without a legislature, motivated by woolly concerns about effectiveness with an almost limitless potential to justify (or rather excuse) the exercise of judicial power.[71] Moreover, the adoption of a directive specifically addressing the question of remedies in the field of public procurement raised the prospect of a more considered intervention in the field of judicial protection by the Union legislature—thus putting the Court under further pressure to defer to the competent political institutions.[72] Thirdly, the gradual 'Europeanisation' of national remedies and procedural rules implied the creation of a dual system of judicial protection within each Member State—with one standard reserved for EU-based rights and another (lower) standard applying to purely national rights—contradicting basic values such as equality between citizens and undermining the internal coherence of the national legal system.[73] The only solution was for Member States to permit Union standards of judicial protection to 'spill over' into wholly internal structures—though that was far from guaranteed to happen in practice.[74]

---

[69] Further: AP Tash, 'Remedies for European Community Law Claims in Member State Courts: Toward a European Standard' (1993) 31 *Columbia Journal of Transnational Law* 377; E Szyszczak, 'Making Europe more Relevant to its Citizens: Effective Judicial Process' (1996) 21 *ELRev* 351.

[70] See further below.

[71] See further below.

[72] Dir 89/665 [1989] OJ L395/33. See further below on Union legislation concerning remedies and procedural rules.

[73] Further: R Caranta, 'Judicial Protection Against Member States: A New *Jus Commune* Takes Shape' (1995) 32 *CMLRev* 703; and 'Learning from our Neighbours: Public Law Remedies, Homogenisation from Bottom Up' (1997) 4 *MJ* 220.

[74] For examples of 'spill-over' from Union situations into purely domestic ones, consider the House of Lords (now Supreme Court) in *M v Home Office* [1994] 1 AC 377 (in the light of Case C-213/89 *Factortame* [1990] ECR I-2433); and in *Woolwich Building Society v IRC* [1993] AC 70 (in the light of Case 199/82 *San Giorgio* [1983] ECR 3595).

C – The Court's Most Recent Period: Since 1993

By the early 1990s, the case law on effective judicial protection had therefore both accumulated a considerable following and provoked a significant body of critical reaction. Against that background, during the course of 1993, the Court of Justice seems to have suffered a crisis of confidence.[75] Perhaps the most high-profile casualty was the ruling in *Emmott*, which concerned the national court's obligation to set aside even reasonable limitation periods where the dispute involved the Member State's failure properly to implement a Union directive—an approach which seemed to have particularly serious consequences for legal certainty, evidential reliability and Member State budgets. The Court held in *Steenhorst-Neerings* that that obligation did not apply in the case of national rules limiting back-claims for the payment of wrongly withheld social security benefits—even though the rationale for extending the *Emmott* ruling to such analogous disputes seemed entirely applicable.[76] The Court then stated in *Johnson II* that, even as regards limitation periods for the commencement of proceedings, the ruling in *Emmott* had been justified by the particular circumstances of that dispute, whereby the competent Irish ministry had actively dissuaded the claimant from enforcing her Union rights within the relevant limitation period.[77] Subsequent rulings confirm that *Emmott* has indeed been distinguished down to a much narrower principle: where one party misleads another as to the latter's rights under Union law, thus causing him/her to exceed the applicable domestic time limit, the national court should (exceptionally) disapply that procedural rule and permit the action to proceed.[78] Consider, in particular, the ruling in *Levez*: a national rule restricting entitlement to arrears of remuneration to the two years preceding the date on which proceedings for equal pay were instituted was not in itself open to criticism; however, it appeared that the claimant was late in bringing her claim only because of inaccurate information provided by the employer regarding the level of remuneration received by her male comparator. The Court of Justice considered that to allow an employer to rely on a national time limit would, in such circumstances, be manifestly incompatible with the principle of effectiveness.[79]

However, it soon became clear that the Court's intention was not to abandon, merely to refine, the commitment to effective judicial protection for Union rights, by seeking to strike a better balance between the Union's legitimate concerns about effectiveness and uniformity (on the one hand) and respect for each Member State's choices concerning the administration of justice (on the other hand). Again, the case law on limitation periods provides an instructive case-study. Just as the Court was engineering the demise of its own broad and bothersome *Emmott* ruling, the case law witnessed the growth of other important dimensions to the principle of effectiveness insofar as it applies to national time limits. For example, the Court used its previous rulings in *Bruno Barra* and *Deville* to build on the idea that Member States cannot reduce the duration of their limitation periods so as specifically to disadvantage the exercise of Treaty rights which have been

---

[75] A 'hasty retreat': see A Ward, 'Effective Sanctions in EC Law: A Moving Boundary in the Division of Competence' (1995) 1 *ELJ* 205.

[76] Case C-338/91 *Steenhorst-Neerings* [1993] ECR I-5475.

[77] Case C-410/92 *Johnston II* [1994] ECR I-5483.

[78] eg Case C-188/95 *Fantask* [1997] ECR I-6783; Case C-445/06 *Danske Slagterier* [2009] ECR I-2119.

[79] Case C-326/96 *Levez v Jennings (Harlow Pools)* [1998] ECR I-7835; cf Case C-542/08 *Barth* (Judgment of 15 April 2010). In similar vein, consider eg Case C-481/99 *Heininger* [2001] ECR I-9945; Case C-327/00 *Santex* [2003] ECR I-1877; Case C-241/06 *Lämmerzahl* [2007] ECR I-8415.

the subject of proceedings before the Union courts;[80] while also establishing that Member States cannot in any case shorten the duration of the limitation period applicable to the exercise of a Union right in a manner which has retroactive effects, without including adequate transitional provisions respecting the principle of legitimate expectations.[81] Meanwhile, in judgments such as *Preston*, the Court considerably strengthened its once laissez-faire scrutiny of domestic time limits under the original *Rewe* and *Comet* rulings, by finding that the 'reasonableness' of a limitation period should be examined not merely in the abstract but within its specific legal and factual context, including by reference to the particular circumstances of each individual dispute.[82] *Preston* itself concerned United Kingdom legislation which provided for a six-month time limit, running from the end of their employment contract, within which women could challenge a discriminatory refusal of membership of an occupational pension scheme as prohibited under Article 157 TFEU. The Court noted that this time limit was not in itself objectionable. However, the claimants in *Preston* were employed on a continuous series of short-term contracts. Under English law, the six-month time limit was deemed to run from the end of each individual contract, thus placing severe temporal restrictions on the claimants' ability to seek redress in respect of past exclusion from the relevant benefits. In such circumstances, the Court ruled that the principle of effectiveness requires domestic limitation periods to run from the end of the parties' overall employment relationship.[83]

It is now common to regard the Court of Justice's approach to questions of national judicial protection as akin to a form of 'objective justification', not dissimilar to that developed in other Union law contexts such as free movement or equal treatment: national procedural rules which restrict the exercise of Union rights must be analysed by reference to their purpose within the domestic legal order, and an appropriate balance must be struck against the extent of their restrictive effects upon the full application of Union law.[84] This idea of applying the principle of effectiveness in a more contextual manner was most famously (if rather obtusely) expressed by the Court in *Peterbroeck*:

> [E]ach case which raises the question whether a national procedural provision renders application of Community law impossible or excessively difficult must be analysed by reference to the role of that provision in the procedure, its progress and its special features, viewed as a whole, before the various national instances. In the light of that analysis the basic principles of the domestic judicial system, such as protection of the rights of the defence, the principle of legal certainty and the proper conduct of procedure, must, where appropriate, be taken into consideration.[85]

Moreover, the Court now applies the principle of effectiveness in not only a contextual but

---

[80] Case 309/85 *Bruno Barra* [1988] ECR 355; Case 240/87 *Deville* [1988] ECR 3513. eg Case C-228/96 *Aprile* [1998] ECR I-7141; Case C-343/96 *Dilexport* [1999] ECR I-579.

[81] eg Case C-228/96 *Aprile* [1998] ECR I-7141; Case C-343/96 *Dilexport* [1999] ECR I-579; Case C-62/00 *Marks & Spencer* [2002] ECR I-6325; Case C-255/00 *Grundig Italiana* [2002] ECR I-8003.

[82] Case C-78/98 *Preston* [2000] ECR I-3201.

[83] On application of the principle of effectiveness to national limitation periods, consider also eg Case C-481/99 *Heininger* [2001] ECR I-9945; Case C-125/01 *Pflücke* [2003] ECR I-9375; Cases C-295–298/04 *Manfredi* [2006] ECR I-6619; Case C-445/06 *Danske Slagterier* [2009] ECR I-2119; Case C-69/08 *Visciano* [2009] ECR I-6741; Case C-63/08 *Pontin* [2009] ECR I-10467; Case C-456/08 *Commission v Ireland* (Judgment of 28 January 2010); Case C-406/08 *Uniplex* (Judgment of 28 January 2010); Case C-246/09 *Bulicke* (Judgment of 8 July 2010).

[84] Further eg S Prechal, 'Community Law in National Courts: The Lessons From *Van Schijndel*' (1998) 35 *CMLRev* 681.

[85] Case C-312/93 *Peterbroeck* [1995] ECR I-4599, para 14. Also: Cases C-430–431/93 *Van Schijndel* [1995] ECR I-4705, para 18.

also an ad hoc manner, wary of setting out generic rules, and keen to stress the factors at work in specific disputes. As was stated in *Cofidis*, judgments on national remedies and procedures are 'merely the result of assessments on a case by case basis, taking account of each case's own factual and legal context as a whole, which cannot be applied mechanically in fields other than those in which they were made'.[86]

The scholarly reaction to such developments has been largely positive: the pragmatic goal of striking a fair balance between Union interests and Member State competences is generally viewed as preferable to the previous extremes of either neglecting altogether to safeguard the effectiveness and uniform application of Union law or riding roughshod over domestic concerns such as legal certainty and the coherence of the judicial system.[87] But there have still been voices of dissent. On the Union side, some commentators have expressed concerns about whether the Court's contextual and ad hoc case law is really sufficient to guarantee the effectiveness of the Treaties against the restrictions which result from the dependence of Union law upon national remedies and procedural rules.[88] Others have argued that the Court's current approach of establishing only minimum standards of judicial protection has all but sacrificed the fundamental goals of equalising the conditions of competition for economic actors and promoting common standards of social rights for the Union's own citizens;[89] though that analysis has not gone uncontested among those who believe that the EU's increasing political heterogeneity and regulatory differentiation actually renders many traditional concerns about the uniform application of Union law more rhetorical than real.[90]

On the Member State side, too, the Court's post-1993 case law has hardly received unanimous praise. National courts and tribunals may often appear to be enthusiastic accomplices, even procurers, in the Court's case law on effective judicial protection; but if anything, practical concerns about the adverse implications of legal certainty for litigants, and intellectual reservations about preserving the coherence of the national legal systems, seem to have increased.[91] It would certainly be fair to admit that the Court's contextual and ad hoc approach to the principle of effectiveness has sometimes given rise to serious difficulties of predictability and consistency—a point well illustrated if one were to explore the haphazard case law following *Marshall II* 'clarifying' how far the principle of effectiveness requires the payment of statutory interest.[92] On the one hand, the Court has affirmed that, as regards compensatory remedies, the principle of effectiveness indeed requires the payment of interest so as to preserve the value of the claimant's damages against losses suffered through the effluxion of time.[93] On the other hand, the Court held in rulings such as *ex parte Sutton* that the inclusion of statutory interest is not called for when the claim-

---

[86] Case C-473/00 *Cofidis* [2002] ECR I-10875, para 37.

[87] For a recent example of the ECJ giving 'due weight' to considerations of national procedural economy, consider Case C-19/08 *Petrosian* [2009] ECR I-495.

[88] Further: B Fitzpatrick and E Szyszczak, 'Remedies and Effective Judicial Protection in Community Law' (1994) 57 *MLR* 434; W van Gerven, 'Of Rights, Remedies and Procedures' (2000) 37 *CMLRev* 501.

[89] Further: MP Chiti, 'Towards a Unified Judicial Protection in Europe(?)' (1997) 9 *European Review of Public Law* 553; C Himsworth, 'Things Fall Apart: The Harmonisation of Community Judicial Procedural Protection Revisited' (1997) 22 *ELRev* 291.

[90] Further: M Dougan, *National Remedies Before the Court of Justice* (Oxford, Hart Publishing, 2004).

[91] Further: M Hoskins, 'Tilting the Balance: Supremacy and National Procedural Rules' (1996) 21 *ELRev* 365; Himsworth, above n 89; A Biondi, 'The European Court of Justice and Certain National Procedural Limitations: Not Such a Tough Relationship' (1999) 36 *CMLRev* 1271.

[92] Case C-271/91 *Marshall II* [1993] ECR I-4367.

[93] eg Case C-63/01 *Evans* [2003] ECR I-14447; Cases C-295–298/04 *Manfredi* [2006] ECR I-6619.

ant's action relates to the payment or recovery of a fixed sum (such as a social security benefit wrongly withheld, or a tax wrongly levied, contrary to Union law).[94] That seems a rather arbitrary and unconvincing distinction: insofar as interest is intended to reflect the inevitable losses suffered by a claimant who is unable to enjoy his/her rights at the intended time, such losses can clearly arise as much with fixed sums as with compensatory damages.[95] Moreover, the case law shows that the Court has sometimes found it difficult to maintain a clear distinction between compensatory remedies and fixed-sum remedies when it comes to applying the principle of effectiveness to questions of statutory interest.[96]

Whatever its limitations, the Court's contextual and ad hoc approach to the principle of effectiveness remains the primary framework for assessing the adequacy of national remedies and procedural rules—of which there seems to be an inexhaustible supply, waiting to be tested under Union law for the first time, or judged afresh in the light of new legal and/or factual circumstances.[97] Moreover, one consequence of the Court's more nuanced application of the principle of effectiveness has been to create space for the emergence of distinct sectoral trends in the case law: certain categories of disputes appear deserving of more (or at least rather different) 'effective judicial protection' than others. Consider the imposition upon national judges of a duty to raise of their own motion unfair terms in consumer contracts, which goes much further than the standard of effectiveness applicable to the ex officio application of Union law in other contexts.[98] The unfair terms case law is motivated by the Court's concern over the particularly vulnerable position of consumers, and the importance attached to the protection of their economic interests by the Union legislature—a line of reasoning which could readily extend to other categories of consumer disputes,[99] and thereby provide the basis for a distinct conception of the principle of effectiveness in that policy field.[100] Increasingly diffuse understandings of effectiveness can also be seen in other sectors of Union law: for example, the Court is particularly strict about how far national procedural autonomy might frustrate the Member State's obligation to secure the recovery of subsidies granted by the national authorities in breach of the Union rules on state aids.[101]

---

[94] Case C-66/95 *ex parte Sutton* [1997] ECR I-2163. The Court held that the claimant in such situations should pursue a *Francovich* claim against the Member State for his/her losses. cp Case C-470/04 *N* [2006] ECR I-7409.

[95] eg M Dougan, 'Cutting Your Losses in the Enforcement Deficit: A Community Right to the Recovery of Unlawfully Levied Charges?' (1998) 1 *CYELS* 233.

[96] Consider eg Cases C-397 and 410/98 *Metallgesellschaft* [2001] ECR I-1727.

[97] Consider eg Case C-336/94 *Dafeki* [1997] ECR I-6761; Case C-132/95 *Jensen and Korn* [1998] ECR I-2975; Case C-472/99 *Clean Car Autoservice* [2001] ECR I-9687; Case C-276/01 *Steffensen* [2003] ECR I-3735; Case C-443/03 *Leffler* [2005] ECR I-9611; Case C-526/04 *Laboratoires Boiron* [2006] ECR I-7529; Case C-300/04 *Eman and Sevinger* [2006] ECR I-8055; Case C-421/05 *City Motors Groep* [2007] ECR I-653; Case C-55/06 *Arcor* [2008] ECR I-2931; Case C-478/07 *Budějovický Budvar* [2009] ECR I-7721.

[98] Contrast eg Cases C-240–4/98 *Océano Grupo Editorial* [2000] ECR I-4941, Case C-473/00 *Cofidis* [2002] ECR I-10875 and Case C-243/08 *Pannon* [2009] ECR I-4713; with eg Cases C-430–431/93 *Van Schijndel* [1995] ECR I-4705, Cases C-222–225/05 *van der Weerd* [2007] ECR I-4233 and Case C-455/06 *Heemskerk* [2008] ECR I-8763.

[99] Consider Case C-429/05 *Rampion and Godard* [2007] ECR I-8017.

[100] Consider also eg Case C-481/99 *Heininger* [2001] ECR I-9945; Case C-168/00 *Leitner* [2002] ECR I-2631. Note also decisions concerning vulnerable employees, eg Case C-185/97 *Coote v Granada Hospitality* [1998] ECR I-5199; Case C-306/07 *Ruben Andersen* [2008] ECR I-10279; Case C-63/08 *Pontin* [2009] ECR I-10467.

[101] eg Case C-24/95 *Alcan Deutschland* [1997] ECR I-1591; Case C-119/05 *Lucchini* [2007] ECR I-6199; Case C-199/06 *CELF* [2008] ECR I-469. Contrast with case law on the recovery of wrongly paid Union monies, eg Case 26/74 *Roquette Frères* [1976] ECR 677; Cases 205–215/82 *Deutsche Milchkontor* [1983] ECR 2633; Case C-366/95 *Steff-Houlberg* [1998] ECR I-2661; Case C-298/96 *Oelmühle Hamburg* [1998] ECR I-4767; Case C-336/00 *Huber* [2002] ECR I-7699.

V – ACTIONS BASED DIRECTLY UPON UNION LAW

In addition to the general case law on the principle of effectiveness, the Court of Justice has identified various causes of action or specific forms of remedy, the legal origin of which is deemed to derive from the Treaties themselves, inherently and directly, without being initially mediated through the usual presumption of national procedural autonomy. We shall discuss three main examples: the right to interim relief for the protection of putative Union law rights; the right to the recovery of unlawfully levied charges; and the right to reparation against Member States under *Francovich*. We will then consider how far Union law confers a right to damages in respect of private law obligations imposed pursuant to the Treaties (based upon the important ruling in *Courage v Crehan*).[102]

A – The Right to Interim Relief

The main case concerning the availability of interim relief against Member State action alleged to infringe one's rights under the Treaties remains *Factortame*.[103] The House of Lords (now the UK Supreme Court) asked the Court of Justice whether Union law either obliged or authorised a national court to grant interim relief against a domestic measure alleged to be compatible with Union law, in circumstances where that national court would ordinarily have no power to provide interim protection to the claimant's putative rights by, for example, suspending the application of the disputed domestic legislation.[104] The Court of Justice, having referred to the principle of the supremacy of Union law, and to the duty of national courts to ensure the legal protection which individuals derive from the direct effect of Union provisions, went on to observe that:

> The Court has also held that any provision of a national legal system and any legislative, administrative or judicial practice, which might impair the effectiveness of Community law by withholding from the national courts having jurisdiction to apply such law the power to do everything necessary at the moment of its application to set aside national legislative provisions which might prevent, even temporarily, Community rules from having full force and effect are incompatible with those requirements, which are the very essence of Community law. … Consequently, the reply to the question raised should be that Community law must be interpreted as meaning that a national court which, in a case before it concerning Community law, considers that the sole obstacle which precludes it from granting interim relief is a rule of national law must set aside that rule.[105]

The *Factortame* judgment confirmed that interim relief must be available, in principle, so

---

[102] Case C-453/99 *Courage v Crehan* [2001] ECR I-6297.

[103] Case C-213/89 *R v Secretary of State for Transport, ex parte Factortame* [1990] ECR I-2433.

[104] The House of Lords proceeded on the basis that no injunctive relief could be made available under English law; but see *M v Home Office* [1994] 1 AC 377.

[105] Case C-213/89 *R v Secretary of State for Transport, ex parte Factortame* [1990] ECR I-2433, paras 20 and 23. Interestingly, the Court made no reference to cases such as Case 45/76 *Comet v Produktschap voor Siergewassen* [1976] ECR 2043 on the principle of effectiveness; but instead relied upon its judgment in Case 106/77 *Simmenthal v Amministrazione dello Stato* [1978] ECR 629 on the supremacy and direct effect of Union law (discussed in Chapter 8).

as to secure the effectiveness of rights derived from Union law.[106] However, the Court in *Factortame* did not address the question of the *criteria* to be applied in granting or with-holding such interim relief. One might have assumed that the substantive conditions for obtaining interim protection would be defined by national law—subject to the Union principles of equivalence and effectiveness—thus creating a hybrid remedy' of Union der-ivation but national content.

However, the Court adopted a more interventionist approach when the issue arose again, in the cases of *Zuckerfabrik* and *Atlanta*, though this time concerning the availability of interim relief in respect of Union acts (or their national implementing measures) which are themselves alleged to be incompatible with higher provisions of the legal order estab-lished under the Treaties.[107] As we have seen in a previous chapter, the Court of Justice held in *Foto-Frost* that a national court does not have jurisdiction to invalidate a Union act, such jurisdiction being reserved exclusively to the Union courts themselves.[108] But the ruling in *Foto-Frost* also noted that different considerations might apply if an applicant sought to suspend a Union act pending a ruling on its invalidity by the Court. It might have been assumed that, as in *Factortame*, the criteria for suspending the application of the disputed Union act would be determined by national law (subject to the principles of equivalence and effectiveness). However, the consequence of such an approach could have been the *over*protection of individual rights at the expense of the uniform application of Union law: in those Member States where interim relief is very readily granted against the administration, the practical consequence of the presumption of national procedural autonomy might be the paralysis of a Union legal regime as a result of the (albeit tempo-rary) suspension of the relevant Union legislation.

For those reasons, the Court in *Zuckerfabrik* and *Atlanta* decided to specify in detail the substantive criteria to be applied by national courts when considering whether to suspend the application or implementation of Union acts. In that regard, the Court drew upon the test for obtaining interim relief in direct actions before the Union courts them-selves in accordance with Articles 278 and 279 TFEU.[109] In such direct actions, the Union courts will suspend the relevant Union act where there is a prima facie case, and urgency resulting from the likelihood of irreparable damage to the applicant; where those condi-tions are satisfied, the urgency is balanced against the possibility of irreparable damage to the Union should the act be suspended but the applicant's case fail.[110] However, in *Zuckerfabrik*, instead of the requirement to show a prima facie case, the Court held that a national court must be satisfied that *serious doubts* exist as to the validity of the Union act in question. Moreover, in *Atlanta*, as regards the balancing stage, the Court stressed the need to take into account the Union interest; and for the national court to have regard to the potential cumulative effect of a large number of other courts also adopting interim measures. Such additional hurdles for the grant of interim relief against allegedly invalid

---

[106] See also Case C-1/99 *Kofisa Italia* [2001] ECR I-207 and Case C-226/99 *Siples* [2001] ECR I-277 (dis-cussed further below).

[107] Cases C-143/88 and C-92/89 *Zuckerfabrik Süderdithmarschen and Zuckerfabrik Soest* [1991] ECR I-415; Case C-465/93 *Atlanta Fruchthandelsgesellschaft mbH v Bundesamt für Ernährung und Forstwirtschaft* [1995] ECR I-3761.

[108] Case 314/85 *Foto-Frost v Hauptzollamt Lubeck-Ost* [1987] ECR 4199. See Chapters 6 and 7.

[109] See Chapter 6.

[110] eg Case T-29/92 R *SPO v Commission* [1992] ECR II-2161, para 34; Joined Cases C-239/96 R and C-240/96 R *United Kingdom v Commission* [1996] ECR I-4475, paras 51–53 and 61. While the test for prima facie case is not onerous, it seems that some account may be taken of the strength of the applicant's case, eg Joined Cases C-239/96 R and C-240/96 R *United Kingdom v Commission* [1996] ECR I-4475, para 70.

Union acts by the national courts, as compared to the principles which apply regarding interim relief directly before the Union courts, no doubt reflect the Court's concerns that the over-hasty grant of interim measures by domestic judges might prejudice the uniform application of Union law.

The rulings in *Zuckerfabrik* and *Atlanta* raised the question whether the substantive criteria for the grant of interim relief against allegedly invalid Union measures would also be extended so as to cover *Factortame*-style situations where the claimant is challenging purely national measures allegedly adopted in breach of Union law. After all, the Court in *Zuckerfabrik* and *Atlanta*, referring to *Factortame*, stated that the interim legal protection which Union law ensures for individuals before national courts must remain the same, irrespective of whether they contest the compatibility of national legal provisions with Union law or the validity of secondary Union law, in view of the fact that the dispute in both cases is based on Union law itself.[111] However, that argument was refuted by the Court itself in the more recent case of *Unibet*: the substantive conditions under which interim relief is to be granted by the national courts, in respect of allegedly unlawful national measures, are indeed to be determined in accordance with the usual *Rewe/Comet* framework of national procedural autonomy, equivalence and effectiveness.[112] It would thus appear, in the eyes of the Court, that the uniform application of Union law is placed in greater jeopardy by challenges to the validity of Union law itself, than by the adoption of national measures in breach of the Treaties.

B – The Right to the Recovery of Unlawfully Levied Charges

The Court of Justice established relatively early, in its ruling in *Pigs and Bacon Commission v McCarren*, that Union law confers directly upon individuals the right to recover charges levied by the national authorities in breach of the Treaties.[113] That position has been confirmed many times since, with the Court stressing that the right to recover unlawfully levied charges should be seen as inherent in the substantive provisions of Union law which prohibit the relevant charges in the first place.[114] However, the Court has also consistently held that the conditions under which that Union right to recovery must be exercised in practice are a matter for national law—subject (of course) to the principles of equivalence and effectiveness.

In certain respects, for example, as regards issues such as the payment of interest and the imposition of limitation periods, that approach remains true in both letter and spirit.[115] But in other respects, it is perhaps true to say that the Court now pays little more than lip-service to the idea of national procedural autonomy in regulating exercise of the Union right to recovery. Indeed, Union intervention through the principle of effectiveness

---

[111] Cases C-143/88 and C-92/89 *Zuckerfabrik Süderdithmarschen and Zuckerfabrik Soest* [1991] ECR I-415, para 20; Case C-465/93 *Atlanta Fruchthandelsgesellschaft mbH v Bundesamt für Ernährung und Forstwirtschaft* [1995] ECR I-3761, para 24.

[112] Case C-432/05 *Unibet* [2007] ECR I-2271.

[113] Case 177/78 *Pigs and Bacon Commission v McCarren* [1979] ECR 2161.

[114] eg Case C-343/96 *Dilexport* [1999] ECR I-579; Cases C-397 and 410/98 *Metallgesellschaft* [2001] ECR I-1727; Case C-62/00 *Marks & Spencer* [2002] ECR I-6325; Case C-309/06 *Marks & Spencer* [2008] ECR I-2283

[115] As regards interest, eg Case 26/74 *Roquette Frères* [1976] ECR 677; Cases C-279–281/96 *Ansaldo Energia* [1998] ECR I-5025; Cases C-397 and 410/98 *Metallgesellschaft* [2001] ECR I-1727. As regards limitation periods, eg Case C-231/96 *Edis* [1998] ECR I-4951; Case C-228/96 *Aprile* [1998] ECR I-7141; Case C-88/99 *Roquette Frères* [2000] ECR I-10465; Cases C-216 and 222/99 *Prisco* [2002] ECR I-6761.

has reached such an extent as to amount de facto to positive harmonisation of the circumstances in which Member States may legitimately resist claims for reimbursement.[116] For example, the Court in judgments such as *FMC* and *Fantask* made clear that liability to repay is imposed upon the defaulting Member State on the basis of illegality per se; national rules cannot require proof of the existence of fault or unreasonableness on the part of the relevant public authorities.[117]

In fact, the only defence available to the Member State faced within an action for recovery is to argue that the quantum due for reimbursement should be reduced to the extent that the claimant would otherwise be unjustly enriched, having already passed on a proportion of the charge to his/her customers.[118] Successful reliance upon this defence is subject to strict conditions concerning the allocation of the burden of proof. Consider the ruling in *San Giorgio*.[119] The case concerned a national rule which precluded the repayment of unlawfully levied taxes where such taxes had been passed by the payor onto third parties. However, taxes were presumed to have been passed on whenever the goods, in respect of which the charge had been levied, were transferred to third parties, unless the payor could adduce documentary proof to the contrary. The Court of Justice confirmed that national courts might legitimately take into account the fact that unlawfully levied charges had been incorporated into the price of goods and thus passed on to purchasers—but a reversal in the burden of proof which required the taxpayer to establish that the charges had not been passed on, and the exclusion of any kind of evidence other than documentary evidence for that purpose, would have the effect of making it virtually impossible, or excessively difficult, to secure the repayment of charges levied contrary to Union law. Once it was established that the levying of the charge was incompatible with Union law, the national court must be free to decide whether or not the burden of the charge had been passed on (in whole or in part) to other persons.

Indeed, so strict is the case law concerning allocation of the burden of proof that the Court now seems to expect the national authorities (in effect) to demonstrate on a case-by-case basis the existence of both passing on by and unjust enrichment of the payor; the Court has limited the claimant's possible obligations to co-operating with the national authorities as regards access to relevant documentation (such as the undertaking's balance sheets).[120] In any event, if it transpires that the burden of the unlawful charge was passed on only in part, the national authorities remain obliged to reimburse the trader the amount which has not been passed on.[121] Furthermore, if the payor suffers damage to his/her business as a result of the unlawfully levied charges (eg through a fall in turnover attributable to the passing on of the higher costs resulting from the illegal taxation), it will

---

[116] Further: M Dougan, 'Cutting Your Losses in the Enforcement Deficit: A Community Right to the Recovery of Unlawfully Levied Charges?' (1998) 1 *CYELS* 233. Also eg LJ Smith, 'A European Concept of Condictio Indebiti' (1982) 19 *CMLRev* 269; K Magliveras, 'Unjust Enrichment and Restitution in Community Law' (1997) 6 *IJEL* 190; A Biondi and L Johnson, 'The Right to Recovery of Charges Levied in Breach of Community Law: No Small Matter' (1998) 4 *EPL* 313.

[117] Case C-212/94 *FMC* [1996] ECR I-389; Case C-188/95 *Fantask* [1997] ECR I-6783.

[118] In particular: Case 68/79 *Hans Just* [1980] ECR 501. Also eg Case 61/79 *Denkavit* [1980] ECR 1205; Case 130/79 *Express Dairy Foods* [1980] ECR 1887; Case 811/79 *Ariete* [1980] ECR 2545; Case 826/79 *MIRECO* [1980] ECR 2559; Cases 142–3/80 *Essevi and Salengo* [1981] ECR 1413.

[119] Case 199/82 *San Giorgio* [1983] ECR 3595.

[120] eg Case 104/86 *Commission v Italy* [1988] ECR 1799; Cases 331, 376 and 378/85 *Bianco* [1988] ECR 1099; Cases C-192–218/95 *Comateb* [1997] ECR I-165; Case C-343/96 *Dilexport* [1999] ECR I-579; Cases C-441 and 442/98 *Mikhailidis* [2000] ECR I-7145; Case C-147/01 *Weber's Wine World* [2003] ECR I-11365; Case C-129/00 *Commission v Italy* [2003] ECR I-14637.

[121] Cases C-192/95–218/95 *Comateb* [1997] ECR I-165.

be possible to bring an action not only for recovery of the relevant charge itself, but also for compensation from the Member State in accordance with the *Francovich* case law.[122]

C – The *Francovich* Right to Reparation

In *Francovich*,[123] the Court delivered a judgment which 'caused a minor legal earthquake, perhaps comparable to that caused by the ruling of the House of Lords in *Donogue v Stevenson*.[124]

The *Francovich* case concerned a directive on the protection of employees in the event of the insolvency of their employer,[125] which had not been implemented by Italy within the time limit specified, a default which had been established by the Court in previous enforcement proceedings brought by the Commission against that Member State.[126] The Court held that the principle of Member State liability for harm caused to individuals by breaches of Union law for which the Member State can be held responsible is inherent in the scheme of the Treaties. The Court stated in succinct terms the conditions for liability in a case such as that in issue:

> Although State liability is thus required by Community law, the conditions under which that liability gives rise to a right to reparation depend on the nature of the breach of Community law giving rise to the loss and damage. Where, as in this case, a Member State fails to fulfil its obligation under the third paragraph of Article [288 TEU] to take all the measures necessary to achieve the result prescribed by a directive, the full effectiveness of that rule of Community law requires that there should be a right to reparation provided that three conditions are fulfilled. The first of those conditions is that the result prescribed by the directive should entail the grant of rights to individuals. The second condition is that it should be possible to identify the content of those rights on the basis of the provisions of the directive. Finally, the third condition is the existence of a causal link between the breach of the State's obligation and the loss and damage suffered by the injured parties. Those conditions are sufficient to give rise to a right on the part of individuals to obtain reparation, a right founded directly on Community law.[127]

The judgment in *Francovich* was undoubtedly a bold and significant development of the law. The principle of Member State liability which it propounded could not be explained as a corollary or adjunct of the direct effect of a provision of Union law (as, for example, with the right to recover sums of money levied contrary to Union law).[128] After all, the provision of the directive relied upon by the plaintiff in *Francovich* was held by the Court not to be directly effective; liability was based upon the failure to bring into existence an enforceable right in national law by way of transposition of the directive. But *Francovich* also raised many questions about the future scope of this right to damages: for example, whether *Francovich* liability was actually confined to breach of the duty to implement non-directly effective norms derived from directives; or, if the action for damages was

---

[122] Ibid.
[123] Cases C-6/90 and C-9/90 *Francovich* [1991] ECR I-5357.
[124] D Wyatt, 'Injunctions and Damages against the State for Breach of Community Law: A Legitimate Judicial Development' in M Andenas and F Jacobs (eds), *European Community Law in the English Courts* (Oxford, Clarendon Press, 1998) 93.
[125] Dir 80/987 [1980] OJ L283/23.
[126] Case 22/87 *Commission v Italy* [1989] ECR 143.
[127] Cases C-6/90 and C-9/90 *Francovich* [1991] ECR I-5357, paras 38–41.
[128] As discussed above.

indeed potentially more far-reaching, whether liability would follow automatically from the Member State's breach of Union law (as appeared to be the case in *Francovich* itself), or might be conditional on the existence of fault or culpability of one kind or another.[129]

Important guidance on these issues came as a result of the requests for preliminary rulings in *Factortame III* and *Brasserie du Pêcheur*.[130] Proceedings in the former case arose from the adoption of UK rules which had sought to reserve the British flag for vessels owned by British nationals. That these rules amounted to an infringement of the right of establishment of Spanish fishermen under Article 49 TFEU had been established by a judgment of the Court of Justice.[131] The fishermen had from the start claimed damages for the losses they had sustained. The *Brasserie du Pêcheur* proceedings resulted from the application of German rules which had had the effect of excluding from the German market beer produced other than in accordance with German 'beer purity' requirements. The German rules were held by the Court to be contrary to Article 34 TFEU in enforcement proceedings brought by the Commission.[132] A French brewery sought compensation for alleged loss of profits which would have been made on exports to Germany, but for the exclusionary effects of the German rules. These proceedings were, if anything, more controversial than the judgment in *Francovich*. The German government argued before the Court of Justice that

> an extension of Community law by judge-made law going beyond the bounds of the legitimate closure of lacunae would be incompatible with the division of competence between the Community institutions and the Member States laid down by the Treaty, and with the principle of the maintenance of institutional balance.[133]

This came close to arguing that the Court would exceed its competence if it developed Union law in the way in which, in the event, it actually did.

The national courts in *Factortame III* and *Brasserie du Pêcheur* asked the Court of Justice to specify the conditions under which a right to reparation of loss or damage caused to individuals by breaches of Union law attributable to a Member State was guaranteed by Union law. In its response, the Court drew a parallel between liability of the Member State and liability of the Union institutions themselves under Article 340(2) TFEU.[134] Where the Union acted in a legislative context characterised by the exercise of a wide discretion, the Union only incurred liability if the institution concerned had manifestly and gravely disregarded the limits on its powers. This strict approach was justified by the need to ensure that the legislative process was not unduly hindered by the prospect of actions for damages. Where national authorities had a wide discretion, comparable to that of the Union institutions in implementing common policies, the conditions under which the Member State might incur liability must in principle be the same as for

---

[129] For discussion eg P Craig, '*Francovich*, Remedies and the Scope of Damages Liability' (1993) 109 *LQR* 595; J Steiner, 'From Direct Effects to *Francovich*: Shifting Means of Enforcement of Community Law' (1993) 18 *ELRev* 3; M Ross, 'Beyond *Francovich*' (1993) 56 *MLR* 55.

[130] Cases C-46 and 48/93 [1996] ECR I-1029. For discussion eg P Craig, 'Once More Unto the Breach: The Community, the State and Damages Liability' (1997) 113 *LQR* 67; N Emiliou, 'State Liability Under Community Law: Shedding More Light on the *Francovich* Principle?' (1996) 21 *ELRev* 399; E Deards, 'Curiouser and Curiouser? The Development of Member State Liability in the Court of Justice' (1997) 3 *EPL* 117.

[131] Case C-221/89 *Factortame II* [1991] ECR I-3905.

[132] Case 178/84 *Commission v Germany* [1987] ECR 1227.

[133] Report for the Hearing in Joined Cases C-46 and 48/93, para 32.

[134] On damages under Art 340(2) TFEU (including the converse influence of the *Francovich* case law upon the jurisprudence on Union liability) see further Chapter 6.

the Union itself. The Court considered, as regards the proceedings at issue, that both the United Kingdom and Germany had a wide discretion in adopting the national rules in question and, accordingly, they would be liable only if three conditions were satisfied: first, the rule of law relied upon must be intended to confer rights on individuals; secondly, the breach must be sufficiently serious; and thirdly, there must be a direct causal link between the breach and the damage suffered. As regards the question whether the breach was sufficiently serious, the Court said that the test for liability was whether the Member State had 'manifestly and gravely disregarded the limits on its discretion'.[135] The Court went on to indicate the factors which should be taken into consideration by a national court in determining whether a breach of Union law was to be regarded as sufficiently serious to ground liability:

> The factors which the competent court may take into consideration include the clarity and precision of the rule breached, the measure of discretion left by that rule to the national or Community authorities, whether the infringement and the damage caused was intentional or involuntary, whether any error of law was excusable or inexcusable, the fact that the position taken by a Community institution may have contributed towards the omission, and the adoption or retention of national measures or practices contrary to Community law, On any view, a breach of Community law will clearly be sufficiently serious if it has persisted despite a judgment finding the infringement in question to be established, or a preliminary ruling or settled case-law of the Court on the matter from which it is clear that the conduct in question constituted an infringement.[136]

The ruling in *Factortame III* and *Brasserie du Pêcheur* thus made clear: (i) that the potential scope of *Francovich* liability was not limited to a failure to implement the non-directly effective provisions of a directive, but could be incurred on the basis of *any* breach by the Member State of its Treaty obligations; and (ii) that considerations of culpability would be relevant to determining whether such liability had been engaged—at least as regards disputes involving legislation adopted by the Member State in breach of directly effective Treaty provisions. The Court subsequently applied its *Factortame III* and *Brasserie du Pêcheur* conditions to other categories of dispute: for example, those concerning decisions of the national administration taken in breach of the Treaties;[137] and cases involving the incorrect implementation (rather than total non-implementation) of directives by the Member State.[138] Yet that merely raised a new question: why did the Member State's simple failure to implement a directive (as in *Francovich*) seem to be governed by different substantive conditions than every other type of infringement of Union law?

The situation became clearer in the light of *Dillenkofer*, which (like *Francovich*) involved a claim for damages against a Member State for having failed to take any measures to transpose a directive within the prescribed deadline. The Court held that, in substance, the two sets of substantive conditions set out in *Francovich* and *Factortame III/Brasserie du Pêcheur* were the same; the requirement of a sufficiently serious breach, although not expressly mentioned in *Francovich*, was nevertheless evident from the circumstances of that case.[139]

---

[135] Cases C-46 and 48/93 [1996] ECR I-1029, para 55.
[136] Cases C-46 and 48/93 [1996] ECR I-1029, paras 56 and 57.
[137] Case C-5/94 *ex parte Hedley Lomas* [1996] ECR I-2553.
[138] Case C-392/93 *ex parte British Telecommunications* [1996] ECR I-1631.
[139] Cases C-178–179 and 188–190/94 *Dillenkofer* [1996] ECR I-4845. Similarly, the ECJ has held that actions for damages against the Member State specifically provided for under Union secondary legislation, in fields such as public procurement which are of a public law nature, merely give concrete expression to the *Francovich* case

Dillenkofer therefore generalised the three substantive conditions required in *Factortame III* and *Brasserie du Pêcheur* for imposing liability upon the Member States. Subsequent case law has explored each of these conditions in greater detail. First, the claimant must demonstrate that the relevant provisions of Union law were intended to confer rights on individuals. The important point here is that, although directly effective provisions will often fulfil this criterion,[140] so too may non-directly effective Union law. For example, in *Francovich* itself, the provisions of the directive requiring Member States to establish a guarantee institution for workers' wages in the event of the insolvency of their employer were not capable of having direct effect because they were insufficiently clear, precise and unconditional; the directive was nevertheless clearly meant to confer identifiable rights upon an identifiable class of beneficiaries and was therefore capable of providing the basis for an action for damages against the defaulting Member State.[141] Similarly, we saw in Chapter 8 that an important function of *Francovich* liability is to provide a means of redress to individuals where they are unable to rely on the provisions of an unimplemented directive against another private party—so that holding the Member State responsible in damages for its failure to transpose correctly into national law provides an alternative to the possibility of direct effect per se.[142] However, not every provision of Union law is intended to confer rights on individuals for the purposes of obtaining damages against the Member State. For example, the Court held in *Peter Paul* that various Union directives in the field of banking law were not intended to confer rights upon individual depositors, in the event of their deposits becoming unavailable as a result of defective supervision by the competent national regulatory authorities, over and above the compensation guaranteed by the directives themselves, since the purpose of the relevant Union measures was to ensure the stability of the banking sector in the broader public interest.[143]

Secondly, the Member State must have committed a sufficiently serious breach of its obligations under Union law. For those purposes, rulings such as *Factortame III* and *Brasserie du Pêcheur*, and *Dillenkofer*, suggested that there was a fundamental distinction between two categories of situation. On the one hand, where the Member State had an appreciable degree of discretion in complying with its Treaty obligations, the claimant had to demonstrate that the Member State perpetrated a manifest and grave disregard of the limits on its powers—taking into account the various factors listed in *Factortame III* and *Brasserie du Pêcheur* (such as the clarity and precision of the rule breached, the measure of discretion left to the national authorities, whether the infringement was intentional or involuntary, whether any error of law was excusable and whether the position adopted by the Union institutions had contributed towards the breach).[144] On the other hand, where the Member State had no appreciable degree of discretion in complying with the Treaties, the mere breach of Union law should be considered sufficiently serious, without further ado: that would be the case (for example) with the obligation to transpose a Union direc-

---

law and should be governed by the same principles/conditions (at least in the absence of more specific guidance from the Union legislature): consider eg Case C-568/08 *Combinatie Spijker Infrabouw-De Jonge Konstruktie* (Judgment of 9 December 2010).

[140] As in *Factortame III* and *Brasserie du Pêcheur* themselves.

[141] Also eg Case C-54/96 *Dorsch Consult* [1997] ECR I-4961.

[142] eg Case C-91/92 *Faccini Dori* [1994] ECR I-3325.

[143] Case C-222/02 *Peter Paul* [2004] ECR I-9425. Consider also eg Case C-511/03 *Ten Kate* [2005] ECR I-8979.

[144] As in Cases C-46 and 48/93 *Factortame III* and *Brasserie du Pecheur* [1996] ECR I-1029 and Case C-392/93 *ex parte British Telecommunications* [1996] ECR I-1631.

tive into national law within a fixed deadline.[145] However, subsequent judgments, such as *Haim* and *Larsy*, suggested that, even in the latter category of situation, it is still necessary for national courts to take into account the full range of factors listed in *Factortame III* and *Brasserie du Pêcheur*.[146] Thus, there might well be an insufficiently serious breach, even though the Member State had no real discretion in discharging its Treaty obligations, for example, because the relevant Union provisions were ambiguous and the Member State had acted reasonably and in good faith. Indeed, Advocate General Léger in *Köbler* argued that, in the light of such case law, the decisive factor for establishing *Francovich* liability seems simply to be whether the error of law at issue can be considered excusable or inexcusable.[147] The Court's more recent case law seems to have affirmed its preference for a 'unitary' assessment of whether the Member State's conduct amounted to a sufficiently serious breach of Union law: the degree of discretion left to the national authorities is an important (but not necessarily the only or even the overriding) criterion in determining the existence of a sufficiently serious breach of Union law; after all, it is only possible to calculate the degree of discretion left to the Member State by reference to other *Brasserie* factors such as the clarity and precision of the relevant Union obligations.[148] In any case, a breach of Union law will be treated as sufficiently serious if it persisted despite a judgment from the Union courts finding the infringement to be established; or a preliminary ruling or settled line of case law from which it was clear that the conduct indeed constituted an infringement of the Treaties.[149]

Thirdly, the claimant must demonstrate that there is a causal link between the Member State's breach of Union law and the damage sustained by the claimant. The Court in *Factortame III* and *Brasserie du Pêcheur* seemed to envisage that the Member States would retain a significant degree of influence over this particular substantive condition. It was simply stated that 'it is for the national courts to determine whether there is a direct causal link between the breach of the obligation borne by the State and the damage sustained by the injured parties'.[150] This was widely interpreted to mean that causation should be determined (at least in principle) on the basis of national (not Union) law. That position was criticised based on fears that domestic discretion over the test of causation might be exploited so as to limit the practical impact of the *Francovich* case law, by providing a loophole through which Member States with relatively restrictive principles of causation could escape liability.[151] The Court seems to have responded to such fears by tightening its grip over the direct causal link requirement—continuing to acknowledge that it is, in principle, for the national courts to determine whether causation exists, but sometimes deciding that the Court itself has sufficient information to judge whether a causal link should, in fact, be found in a particular dispute.[152] It therefore seems useful to consider

---

[145] As in Cases C-178–179 and 188–190/94 *Dillenkofer* [1996] ECR I-4845.

[146] Case C-424/97 *Haim* [2000] ECR I-5123; Case C-118/00 *Larsy* [2001] ECR I-5063.

[147] Case C-224/01 *Köbler* [2003] ECR I-10239, para 139 Opinion. cp the approach of the EFTA Court in Case E-9/97 *Sveinbjörnsdóttir* (Judgment of 10 December 1998); and the approach of the House of Lords (now Supreme Court) in *ex parte Factortame (No 5)* [2000] 1 AC 524.

[148] eg Case C-278/05 *Robins* [2007] ECR I-1059; Case C-452/06 *Synthon* [2008] ECR I-7681.

[149] Cases C-46 and 48/93 *Factortame III* and *Brasserie du Pecheur* [1996] ECR I-1029, para 57.

[150] Ibid, para 65.

[151] Consider eg the judgment of the German Federal Constitutional Court in *Brasserie du Pêcheur* [1997] 1 CMLR 971. Further: E Deards, '*Brasserie du Pêcheur*: Snatching Defeat from the Jaws of Victory?' (1997) 22 *ELRev* 620.

[152] eg Case C-319/96 *Brinkmann* [1998] ECR I-5255; Case C-140/97 *Rechberger* [1999] ECR I-3499; Case C-470/03 *AGM-COS.MET* [2007] ECR I-2749.

that causation rules remain within the presumptive competence of the Member State, subject to the Union law principles of equivalence and effectiveness.[153]

The Court has held that the three substantive conditions set out above are sufficient to found a right in individuals to obtain redress.[154] National rules may not impose more rigorous requirements for the exercise of the right to reparation. Thus, the requirement under English law that public authorities must have been guilty of malice before incurring liability under the tort of misfeasance in a public office is relevant to *Francovich* liability only insofar as bad faith has already been incorporated into the test for a manifest and grave disregard by the Member State of the limits of its powers.[155] Similarly, the Court observed that the test in *Factortame III* and *Brasserie du Pêcheur* does take into account certain objective and subjective factors connected with the concept of fault under the national legal systems; but ruled that the Member State's obligation to make reparation cannot depend upon any concept of fault (whether intentional or negligent) going beyond that of a sufficiently serious breach of Union law, since the imposition of any such supplementary condition would be tantamount to calling in question the right to reparation founded upon the Union legal order.[156] However, the three substantive conditions laid down by Union law are merely minimum standards of judicial protection for the individual. Member States remain free to grant relief under more generous conditions than those laid down by Union law itself.[157] Indeed, by virtue of the principle of equivalence, any less stringent standards of liability, applicable to comparable domestic law claims against public authorities for having exceeded the limits of their powers, must be extended also to the *Francovich* right to reparation.[158]

Assuming liability has been established in accordance with the substantive conditions laid down by Union law, 'it is in accordance with the rules of national law on liability that the State must make reparation for the consequences of the harm caused',[159] subject to the proviso that any conditions laid down by national law remain governed by the principles of equivalence and effectiveness.[160] For example, in a case concerning Italian legislation designed to facilitate damages actions pursuant to the *Francovich* ruling, the Court held that a one-year time limit for such actions was consistent with Union law from the point of view of the principle of effectiveness, though the national court still had to verify that the Italian legislation also satisfied the requirement of equivalence.[161]

As regards the actual quantum of damages, the Court in *Factortame III* and *Brasserie du Pêcheur* set out the principle that reparation for losses caused to individuals as a result of breaches of Union law must be commensurate with the damage sustained so as to ensure the effective protection of their rights.[162] That said, in the absence of relevant Union provisions, it is again for the domestic legal system of each Member State to set the criteria for determining the extent of reparation, subject to the principles of equivalence

---

[153] Similarly eg C Kremer, 'Liability for Breach of European Community Law: An Analysis of the New Remedy in the Light of English and German Law' (2003) 22 *YEL* 203.

[154] Cases C-46 and 48/93 *Factortame III* and *Brasserie du Pecheur* [1996] ECR I-1029, para 66.

[155] Ibid, paras 66–73.

[156] Ibid, paras 75–80.

[157] Ibid, para 66.

[158] See further above.

[159] Cases C-6/90 and C-9/90 *Francovich* [1991] ECR I-5357, para 42.

[160] Ibid, paras 42–43.

[161] Case C-261/95 *Palmisani* [1997] ECR I-4025. See also eg Case C-445/06 *Danske Slagterier* [2009] ECR I-2119.

[162] Cases C-46 and 48/93 *Factortame III* and *Brasserie du Pecheur* [1996] ECR I-1029, para 82.

and effectiveness. For example, a national rule which totally excluded loss of profit as a head of recoverable damage cannot be accepted in cases concerning a breach of Union law; especially in the context of economic or commercial litigation, such a total exclusion of lost profits would be such as to make reparation of the damage suffered by the claimant practically impossible.[163] The Court in *Factortame III* and *Brasserie du Pêcheur* noted that the national court may enquire whether the injured person showed reasonable diligence in order to avoid the loss or damage or limit its extent and whether, in particular, they had availed themselves in time of all the legal remedies available.[164] Subsequent rulings have clarified, however, that the duty to mitigate one's own losses through the exhaustion of alternative remedies applies only where those remedies can be considered adequate: for example, it would not be reasonable to deny the award of damages to an undertaking whose Union rights were infringed by the application of unlawful national tax provisions, on the grounds that the undertaking should have simply refused to comply with the disputed domestic legislation, then raised the breach of Union law as a defence in civil or administrative proceedings brought against it by the Member State.[165]

Finally, it is necessary to consider the range of bodies whose infringement of Union law may lead the Member State to incur liability under the *Francovich* case law. The basic principle was established by the Court in *Factortame III* and *Brasserie du Pêcheur*: the right to reparation applies to any case in which a Member State breaches Union law, whichever is the authority of the Member State whose act or omission was responsible for the breach. The Court justified this principle by the fact that, under international law, a Member State which incurs liability for breach of an international commitment is viewed as a single entity, irrespective of whether the breach is attributable to the legislature, the judiciary or the executive. According to the Court, that principle must apply a fortiori in the Union legal order since all national authorities are bound in performing their tasks to comply with the rules laid down by Union law which directly govern the situation of individuals. In addition, the Court observed that, having regard to the fundamental requirement that Union law be uniformly applied, the obligation to make good damage caused to individuals by breaches of the Treaties should not depend upon domestic rules as to the division of powers between constitutional authorities.[166] *Francovich* liability may therefore be attributed to the Member State on the basis of acts of the national legislature;[167] acts of the national executive (eg administrative decisions taken by central government departments);[168] acts of local or regional authorities (eg within a federal system);[169] and acts adopted by autonomous bodies governed by public law (eg professional regulatory agencies).[170]

---

[163] Case C-470/03 *AGM-COS.MET* [2007] ECR I-2749. On the duty to make adequate reparation, see further eg Cases C-94/95 and C-95/95 *Bonifaci* [1997] ECR I-3969; Case C-373/95 *Maso* [1997] ECR I-4051; Case C-261/95 *Palmisani* [1997] ECR I-4025.

[164] Cases C-46 and 48/93 *Factortame III and Brasserie du Pecheur* [1996] ECR I-1029, para 84.

[165] Cases C-397 and 410/98 *Metallgesellschaft* [2001] ECR I-1727. Also eg Case C-445/06 *Danske Slagterier* [2009] ECR I-2119. Note too Case C-118/08 *Transportes Urbanos y Servicios Generales* (Judgment of 26 January 2010) on application of the principle of equivalence as regards the duty to exhaust alternative remedies.

[166] Cases C-46 and 48/93 *Factortame III and Brasserie du Pecheur* [1996] ECR I-1029, paras 31 *et seq.*

[167] eg as in Cases C-46 and 48/93 *Factortame III and Brasserie du Pecheur* [1996] ECR I-1029 themselves.

[168] eg Case C-5/94 *ex parte Hedley Lomas* [1996] ECR I-2553. Note also Case C-470/03 *AGM-COS.MET* [2007] ECR I-2749 on the conditions for holding a Member State liable in respect of acts of individual civil servants ostensibly acting within their legitimate powers under national law.

[169] eg Case C-302/97 *Konle* [1999] ECR I-3099. Further eg G Anagnostaras, 'The Allocation of Responsibility in State Liability Actions for Breach of Community Law: A Modern Gordian Knot?' (2001) 26 *ELRev* 139.

[170] eg Case C-424/97 *Haim* [2000] ECR I-5123.

Perhaps most controversially, the ruling in *Köbler* established that decisions of a national supreme court may, in certain circumstances, also give rise to a right to reparation against the Member State.[171] In particular, the Court of Justice found that the full effectiveness of the Treaties would be called into question, and the protection of rights derived from Union law would be weakened, if individuals were unable to obtain reparation in respect of infringements resulting from judicial decisions delivered at last instance as regards which there could be no further possibility of correction. In reaching that conclusion, the Court dismissed arguments that *Francovich* liability might undermine either the principle of *res judicata* or the independence of the judiciary. The Court also noted that the principle of liability for judicial decisions was accepted by the legal orders of most Member States and was well-established under the case law of the European Court of Human Rights. However, when applying the substantive conditions for reparation, liability in respect of an infringement of the Treaties resulting from a judicial decision delivered at last instance should be incurred only in exceptional cases where the national court has manifestly breached Union law—taking into account the usual *Brasserie* factors, but also whether the domestic court had abrogated its obligation to seek a preliminary ruling under Article 267 TFEU. Indeed, the judgment seems to suggest that *Francovich* liability for judicial decisions will be incurred only in extreme and really rather unlikely circumstances—for example, where the claimant can demonstrate that the judges of the national supreme court were motivated by improper purposes.[172] In any case, it remains to be seen whether (and if so under what circumstances) infringements of the Treaties perpetrated via decisions delivered by lower courts and tribunals might furnish the basis for Member State liability under *Francovich*.[173]

D – A Private Law Right to Damages?

That discussion leads on to another important topic: the availability of damages under Union law in respect of the conduct of purely private parties who have contravened an enforceable obligation imposed by or pursuant to the Treaties. Such individuals cannot be treated as public bodies whose actions are attributable to the Member State for the purposes of bringing a *Francovich* action. Nor does it seem possible to bring an action for reparation directly against a private party on the basis of the *Francovich* case law (which is, after all, tailored to the administrative law liabilities of public authorities exercising their powers in the general interest).[174] Nevertheless, Advocate General van Gerven in *Banks*

---

[171] Case C-224/01 *Köbler* [2003] ECR I-10239. See also Case C-173/03 *Traghetti del Mediterraneo* [2006] ECR I-5177. Note too Case C-154/08 *Commission v Spain* (Judgment of 12 November 2009): the Member State's breach of Union law was established in enforcement proceedings (for the first time) purely on the basis of a judgment delivered by its national supreme court.

[172] See further eg B Beutler, 'State Liability for Breaches of Community Law by National Courts: Is the Requirement of a Manifest Infringement of the Applicable Law an Insurmountable Obstacle?' (2009) 46 *CMLRev* 773. On the relationship between Member State liability under *Köbler* and national court resistance to the principle of supremacy, see the discussion in Chapter 8.

[173] Especially bearing in mind the duty to exhaust available remedies (such as rights of appeal). Consider the position as regards enforcement proceedings against the Member State, eg Case C-129/00 *Commission v Italy* [2003] ECR I-14637. See further eg L S Rossi and G Di Federico, Annotation of *Commission v Italy* (2005) 42 *CMLRev* 829; G Anagnostaras, Annotation of *Traghetti del Mediterraneo* (2006) 31 *ELRev* 735.

[174] See further M Dougan, 'What is the Point of *Francovich*?' in T Tridimas and P Nebbia (eds), *European Union Law for the Twenty-First Century: Rethinking the New Legal Order*, vol I (Oxford, Hart Publishing, 2004).

suggested that the Court of Justice should adapt the *Francovich* case law to the context of private law relations, such as those created in the field of competition law, so as to permit those whose rights are infringed by another individual to bring an action for damages in accordance with substantive conditions laid down by Union (rather than domestic) law.[175]

This question was presented to the Court of Justice in *Courage v Crehan*,[176] which concerned a beer tie agreement between a brewery and a publican alleged to contravene Article 101 TFEU on anticompetitive agreements. The publican's action for damages against the brewery was dismissed by the English courts on the grounds that anticompetitive agreements are to be treated as unlawful, and, under domestic law, the parties to an unlawful contract cannot seek compensation or restitution inter se. Asked to determine whether this restriction on the availability of damages was compatible with Union law, the Court of Justice observed that the full effectiveness of Article 101 TFEU would be jeopardised if it were not open to any individual to claim damages for loss caused to him/her by a contract liable to restrict competition. There should not therefore be any absolute bar to an action for damages being brought by a party to a contract which is held to violate the competition rules; but in the absence of relevant Union rules, national law must lay down the detailed rules governing such actions, subject to the principles of equivalence and effectiveness.

Courage v Crehan was therefore a very significant but also rather ambiguous judgment. On the one hand, the Court of Justice did not go so far as the Advocate General had suggested in *Banks*: there was no bold attempt to create a 'private *Francovich*' with its own substantive conditions for incurring liability as a matter of Union law. On the other hand, the Court made clear that the proper enforcement of certain Treaty provisions would require national courts to ensure the availability in principle of damages actions; and Union law would supervise the detailed conditions for awarding such compensation in accordance with the standards of equivalence and effectiveness. Subsequent rulings, such as *Manfredi* and *City Motors*, have affirmed the existence in principle of a Union right to compensation, to be exercised under controlled conditions, though it is noteworthy that the relevant rulings have been delivered still in the field of competition law.[177] However, there seems no inherent reason to confine the possibility of a Union law action for private damages to the competition provisions contained in Articles 101 and 102 TFEU, even if the sorts of substantive conditions for liability appropriate to competition law will not necessarily prove transposable to other policy contexts.[178] The Court should also be prepared to guarantee the effective judicial protection, for example, of a Union citizen who suffers discrimination on grounds of nationality by his or her private employer, in breach of Article 45 TFEU on the free movement of workers, where national law imposes unduly restrictive conditions for the award of compensation.[179]

---

[175] Case C-128/92 *Banks v British Coal Corporation* [1994] ECR I-1209.

[176] Case C-453/99 *Courage v Crehan* [2001] ECR I-6297.

[177] Cases C-295–298/04 *Manfredi* [2006] ECR I-6619; Case C-421/05 *City Motors Groep* [2007] ECR I-653. See further Chapter 25.

[178] Further: A Komninos, 'New Prospects for Private Enforcement of EC Competition Law: *Courage v Crehan* and the Community Right to Damages' (2002) 39 *CMLRev* 447; W van Gerven, 'Harmonization of Private Law: Do We Need It?' (2004) 41 *CMLRev* 505; S Drake, 'Scope of *Courage* and the Principle of 'Individual Liability' for Damages' (2006) 31 *ELRev* 841; D Leczykiewicz, 'Private Party Liability in EU Law: In Search of the General Regime' (2009–2010) 12 *CYELS* 257.

[179] Art 45 TFEU having been established as capable of producing horizontal direct effect against private employers: Case C-281/98 *Angonese* [2000] I-4139. See further Chapters 8 and 16.

VI – UNION LEGISLATION CONCERNING REMEDIES AND PROCEDURAL RULES

The Court of Justice, right from the 1976 rulings in *Rewe* and *Comet*, envisaged that its framework of national autonomy, equivalence and effectiveness should provide only the default approach to Union control over the national systems of judicial protection, in the absence of Union legislation specifically adopted for the purposes of harmonising the remedies and procedural rules applicable in disputes based upon the Treaties. Indeed, the Court expressly suggested the use of legal bases such as (what are now) Articles 115 and 352 TFEU for the purpose of removing distortions of competition and other obstacles to the proper functioning of the common market attributable to differences in the levels of judicial protection provided by each Member State.[180]

In practice, the Union legislature has responded to the Court's call to reinforce the effectiveness and uniform application of Union law—whether for the benefit of the internal market,[181] or for the sake of any other substantive Union policy[182]—only occasionally and often through relatively marginal intrusions into the presumption of national autonomy.[183] To be sure, there are a small number of secondary measures which address the decentralised enforcement of Union law in significant detail for specific sectors: for example, the Public Procurement Remedies Directive has given rise to a considerable jurisprudence in its own right;[184] and important measures have been adopted dealing with the burden of proof in sex discrimination cases,[185] injunctions in consumer disputes,[186] implementation of the Århus Convention on access to justice in environmental matters,[187] environmental liability with regard to the prevention and remedying of environmental damage,[188] and the enforcement of intellectual property rights.[189] For the most part, however, the Union legislature has confined itself either to tinkering with limited procedural issues,[190] or including general clauses about enforcement which do no more than codify or recall the Member States' existing obligations under the *Rewe* and *Comet* case law.[191] Any systematic programme for the harmonisation of the national systems of judicial protection in cases involving the enforcement of substantive Treaty rules has yet to emerge, despite the considerable effort devoted to the issue through projects such as the Storme Report.[192] For their part, the Member States, in their capacity as 'masters of the Treaties',

---

[180] Case 33/76 *Rewe-Zentralfinanz v Landwirtschaftskammer für das Saarland* [1976] ECR 1989; Case 45/76 *Comet BV v Produktschap voor Siergewassen* [1976] ECR 2043 at paras 5 and 14, respectively.

[181] eg under Art 114 TFEU.

[182] eg under Art 153 TFEU on social policy or Art 192 TFEU on environmental policy.

[183] Further: T Heukels and J Tib, 'Towards Homogeneity in the Field of Legal Remedies: Convergence and Divergence' in in P Beaumont, C Lyons and N Walker (eds), *Convergence and Divergence in European Public Law* (Oxford, Hart Publishing, 2002).

[184] Dir 89/665 [1989] OJ L395/33.

[185] Dir 2006/54 [2006] OJ L204/23.

[186] Dir 2009/22 [2009] OJ L110/30.

[187] Dir 2003/35 [2003] OJ L156/17.

[188] Dir 2004/35 [2004] OJ L143/56.

[189] Dir 2004/48 [2004] OJ L157/45.

[190] Consider: Dir 85/374 [1985] OJ L210/29; Dir 93/13 [1993] OJ L95/29; Dir 99/44 [1999] OJ L171/12; Reg 1/2003 [2003] OJ L1/1.

[191] Consider: Dir 91/533 [1991] OJ L288/32; Dir 92/85 [1992] OJ L348/1; Dir 94/33 [1994] OJ L216/12; Dir 98/59 [1998] OJ L225/16; Dir 2001/23 [2001] OJ L82/16.

[192] M Storme (ed), *Approximation of Judiciary Law in the European Union* (Dordrecht, Martinus Nijhoff, 1994).

appear basically content with the status quo: Article 19(1) TEU now states merely that Member States shall provide remedies sufficient to ensure effective legal protection in the fields covered by Union law.[193]

However, in the period since the TEU, and especially following the TA, the interest of the Union legislature in issues concerning judicial enforcement within the Member States has been kindled in a rather different way: the goal of developing the Union into an Area of Freedom, Security and Justice (AFSJ).[194] Through the legal bases previously provided for under Title IV, Part Three EC (which included judicial co-operation in civil matters) and Title VI TEU (which covered judicial co-operation in criminal matters)—now to be found all together in Title V, Part Three TFEU—the Union legislature has adopted a series of measures which impact upon national remedies, sanctions and procedural rules in a variety of ways: sometimes pursuant to the objective of facilitating mutual recognition in certain fields of civil and criminal law,[195] but also through the straightforward approximation of selected substantive and procedural rules.[196]

Building the AFSJ has thereby resulted in significant interventions into the ordinary functioning of the domestic legal systems—often with controversial results. For example, the Union's considerable efforts at approximating the type and level of criminal sanctions which Member States should impose for a wide range of offences, some of which are primarily intended to bolster the effective enforcement of particular substantive Union policies,[197] while others are considered necessary for the purposes of facilitating closer cross-border police and judicial co-operation within the specific context of the AFSJ,[198] have led to accusations that the Union is promoting excessive resort to the criminal justice system and encouraging reliance upon repressive punishments such as incarceration.[199] Again, however, the products of this newfound legislative activity remain, for the time being, too targeted in scope and limited in content as to presage the construction of a unified system of judicial protection in Europe. Reform of the primary law governing the AFSJ as contained in the TL does not in itself signal any significant change in this regard; indeed, if the warnings contained in the judgment of the German Federal Constitutional Court concerning ratification of the TL are taken seriously, Union action, particularly in the field of criminal law and procedure, should if anything become more targeted and restrained.[200]

In any case, it is worth pointing out that the Court's case law on effective judicial protection should not be considered entirely displaced merely by the adoption of Union legislation dealing with remedies and procedural rules in particular categories of disputes. After all, the fundamental right of access to the courts, as well as the principles of

---

[193] Similarly, the introduction of Art 83(2) TFEU on the Union's competence to impose criminal sanctions in areas already subject to harmonisation measures builds on the existing position under Case C-176/03 *Commission v Council* [2005] ECR I-7879 and Case C-440/05 *Commission v Council* [2007] ECR I-9097.

[194] On the historical context, see Chapter 1.

[195] On civil law, eg Reg 44/2001 [2001] OJ L12/1; Reg 2201/2003 [2003] OJ L338/1. On criminal law, eg Framework Dec 2002/584 [2002] OJ L190/1; Framework Dec 2008/909 [2008] OJ L327/27.

[196] eg Framework Dec 2001/220 [2001] OJ L82/1; Framework Dec 2002/475 [2002] OJ L164/3; Dir 2003/8 [2003] OJ L26/41; Dir 2008/99 [2008] OJ L328/28.

[197] eg Framework Dec 2001/500 [2001] OJ L182/1; Framework Dec 2002/946 [2002] OJ L328/1; Dir 2008/99 [2008] OJ L328/28.

[198] eg Framework Dec 2002/475 [2002] OJ L164/3; Framework Dec 2004/757 [2004] OJ L335/8; Framework Dec 2008/841 [2008] OJ L300/42; Framework Dec 2008/913 [2008] OJ L328/55.

[199] eg P Asp, 'Harmonisation and Cooperation Within the Third Pillar: Built In Risks' (2001) 4 *CYELS* 15; E Herlin-Karnell, '*Commission v Council*: Some Reflections on Criminal Law in the First Pillar' (2007) 13 *EPL* 69.

[200] See Chapter 8 for a full discussion of those developments.

equivalence and effectiveness, are all general principles of Union law which rank alongside the Treaties themselves within the Union's hierarchy of norms.[201] Union secondary acts must therefore respect those principles, or risk being rendered unlawful themselves. For example, the Court in *Kofisa Italia* and *Siples* considered provisions of Regulation 2913/92 which purported to confer the power to suspend implementation of contested customs decisions exclusively upon the national customs authorities.[202] It was held that a Union regulation could not restrict the fundamental right to effective judicial protection, and therefore could not deprive the domestic courts of their general jurisdiction to grant interim relief as recognised in rulings such as *Factortame*.[203]

VII – CONCLUDING REMARKS

Notwithstanding the increasing interest and activity of the Union legislature, the Court of Justice retains its central position in determining the balance between national procedural autonomy (on the one hand) and Union control over the standards of judicial protection applicable in cases concerning rights derived from the Treaties (on the other hand). As we have seen, the Court's basic approach has evolved and changed over time. Its current preference is to guarantee the fundamental right of access to judicial process, and ensure respect for the principle of equivalence between comparable Union and national actions; but otherwise to apply the principle of effectiveness in a measured and context-sensitive manner, which ensures that national remedies and procedural rules do not render the exercise of Union rights excessively difficult, yet refrains from making grand gestures that might unduly upset the fair and efficient administration of justice within each Member State. The slow and piecemeal development of the law on private liability in damages after *Courage v Crehan* is perhaps emblematic of that essentially pragmatic approach to the principle of effectiveness: whereas the creation of a Union right to interim relief under *Factortame*, and to reparation against the Member State under *Francovich*, were dramatic and far-reaching developments, the Court seems to prefer addressing the issue of individual liability for infringing the Treaties in a considered and understated manner which intertwines concerns about the effectiveness and uniformity of Union law with respect for differing Member State traditions and approaches.

Of course, pragmatism and restraint need not be mistaken for a lack of interesting legal questions. This topic continues to provide a fruitful source of academic research as well as practical challenges: we have mentioned issues such as the Court's creative use of the right to judicial process so as to generate derived rights to good administration and protection from harassment; the way in which the principle of equivalence forces Member States to think critically about the internal coherence of their own systems of judicial protection; the emergence of increasingly distinctive sectoral approaches to the implications of the principle of effectiveness; the degree to which claimants can seek damages from the Member States under *Francovich* based upon erroneous judicial decisions; and how far the Court may be prepared to extend damages actions against individuals beyond the

---

[201] eg Case C-34/02 *Pasquini* [2003] ECR I-6515; Case C-125/01 *Pflücke* [2003] ECR I-9375. See further Chapters 10–12.

[202] Reg 2913/92 establishing the Community customs code [1992] OJ L302/1.

[203] Case C-1/99 *Kofisa Italia* [2001] ECR I-207; Case C-226/99 *Siples* [2001] ECR I-277.

established category of competition disputes into other private law relationships regulated by Union law. The case law on effective judicial protection is surely a never-ending work-in-progress. What should be clear from our discussion is that that case law constitutes an essential pillar in the system of decentralised enforcement for Union law—working alongside the principles of direct effect and supremacy to ensure that the Treaties are effectively integrated into the domestic legal systems and that Union law translates into meaningful practical benefits for individuals.

Further Reading

B Beutler, 'State Liability for Breaches of Community Law by National Courts: Is the Requirement of a Manifest Infringement of the Applicable Law an Insurmountable Obstacle?' (2009) 46 *CMLRev* 773.

A Biondi, 'The European Court of Justice and Certain National Procedural Limitations: Not Such a Tough Relationship' (1999) 36 *CMLRev* 1271.

P Craig, 'Once More Unto the Breach: The Community, the State and Damages Liability' (1997) 113 *LQR* 67.

M Dougan, *National Remedies Before the Court of Justice* (Oxford, Hart Publishing, 2004).

S Drake, 'Scope of *Courage* and the Principle of "Individual Liability" for Damages' (2006) 31 *ELRev* 841.

W van Gerven, 'Of Rights, Remedies and Procedures' (2000) 37 *CMLRev* 501.

C Himsworth, 'Things Fall Apart: The Harmonisation of Community Judicial Procedural Protection Revisited' (1997) 22 *ELRev* 291.

M Hoskins, 'Tilting the Balance: Supremacy and National Procedural Rules' (1996) 21 *ELRev* 365.

CM Kakouris, 'Do the Member States Possess Judicial Procedural "Autonomy"?' (1997) 34 *CMLRev* 1389.

C Kilpatrick, T Novitz and P Skidmore (eds), *The Future of Remedies in Europe* (Oxford, Hart Publishing, 2000).

A Komninos, 'New Prospects for Private Enforcement of EC Competition Law: *Courage v Crehan* and the Community Right to Damages' (2002) 39 *CMLRev* 447.

J Lonbay and A Biondi (eds), *Remedies for Breach of EC Law* (Chichester, Wiley, 1997).

S Prechal, 'Community Law in National Courts: The Lessons From *Van Schijndel*' (1998) 35 *CMLRev* 681.

E Szyszczak, 'Making Europe More Relevant to its Citizens: Effective Judicial Process' (1996) 21 *ELRev* 351.

T Tridimas, 'Liability for Breach of Community Law: Growing Up and Mellowing Down?' (2001) 38 *CMLRev* 301.

A Ward, *Individual Rights and Private Party Judicial Review in the EU*, 2nd edn (Oxford, Oxford University Press, 2007).

10

General Principles of Union Law

This chapter examines the general principles of Union law, unwritten principles deriving from the common constitutional traditions of the Member States and developed by the Court of Justice. The general principles are binding upon the Union institutions as well as on the Member States when they implement Union law or when they act within the scope of Union law. This chapter analyses the principle of loyal co-operation, proportionality, legal certainty, and legitimate expectations and non-discrimination. Subsidiarity is only dealt with briefly as it is fully analysed in Chapter 5. Fundamental rights, also general principles of Union law and now codified in the Charter, are of such constitutional importance that they deserve more thorough analysis and are therefore the subject of the two following chapters.

I – FUNCTION AND SOURCES OF GENERAL PRINCIPLES

In the EU context, general principles of law are written or unwritten principles that supplement the Treaties and guide their interpretation. General principles operate at two levels. They define and limit the scope of the competences of the Union Institutions to adopt binding acts. They also place obligations on Member States when they are implementing Union legislation through the adoption of national rules or administrative acts, and when they are acting within the scope of Union obligations, ie when Member States invoke exceptions to fundamental Treaty freedoms.

The EEC Treaty, as it was then, had from the outset expressly laid down certain general legal principles, such as the duty of co-operation which binds both Member States and Union institutions in ensuring fulfilment of the obligations arising from the Treaty;[1] and the principle of non-discrimination on grounds of nationality.[2] Some general principles, such as proportionality, equality and legitimate expectation, are wholly or mainly the product of judicial development, though the principle of proportionality is now expressly

---

[1] ex Art 10 EC, now repealed but replaced in substance by Art 4(3) TEU, see below.
[2] Now Art 18 TFEU, see below.

recognised in the Treaty as a constitutional principle of the Union legal order,[3] and the Union has been given competence to legislate to fight discrimination other than that on grounds of sex and nationality.[4] Fundamental rights travelled a similar road to proportionality; first recognised by the Court's case law, then endorsed by declarations of the institutions, and finally written into the fundamental law of the European Union.[5] General principles such as these have important legal effects. They place limits on the administrative and legislative competence of the Union institutions, they govern the interpretation of provisions of Union law,[6] and they bind the Member States when the latter act within the scope of operation of Union law.

The Court can hardly be said to have exceeded its jurisdiction by its recourse to the general principles of law. No Treaty regime, let alone the 'new legal order' of the Union, could be interpreted and applied in a legal vacuum. International tribunals have long been regarded as competent to draw upon the general principles of municipal law as a source of international law,[7] and the competence of the Court of Justice in the interpretation and application of Union law could surely have been intended to be no less. The Treaty might be said to imply as much. Article 19 TEU provides that the Court of Justice 'shall ensure that in the interpretation and application of this Treaty the law is observed'. While this formulation implies commitment to the rule of law, it has been argued that this implies a *corpus juris* outwith the express Treaty texts.[8] Other provisions are consistent with the proposition that the general principles of law constitute a source of Union law. Article 263 TFEU includes among the grounds of invalidity of Union acts infringement of 'any rule of law' relating to the Treaties' application, an expression wide enough to encompass the principles under consideration. Furthermore, Article 340(2) TFEU provides that the non-contractual liability of the Union shall be determined 'in accordance with the general principles common to the laws of the Member States', which amounts to express recognition of the role of the general principles of Union law. In the following sections of this chapter, particular principles will be examined.

II – THE GENERAL PRINCIPLE OF SINCERE OR LOYAL CO-OPERATION

The principle of sincere or loyal co-operation in its original version (Article 5 EEC and then 10 EC) provided that Member States shall take all appropriate measures, whether general or particular, to ensure fulfilment of the obligations arising out of the Treaty or resulting from action taken by the institutions of the then Community. They are obliged

---

[3] See Art 5 TEU and Protocol 2 on the Application of the Principles of Subsidiarity and Proportionality.

[4] Art 19 TFEU.

[5] See Chapters 12 and 13 below.

[6] Case 316/86 *Hauptzollamt Hamburg-Jonas v Krucken* [1988] ECR 2213, para 22; Joined Cases 201 and 202/85 *Klensch* [1986] ECR 3466, para 10; Joined Cases C-90/90 and C-91/90 *Neu and Others* [1991] ECR I-3617, para 12.

[7] See D Wyatt, 'New Legal Order, or Old?' (1982) 7 *ELRev* 147, 157. cf Art 38 of the Statute of the International Court of Justice, which lists as a source of international law, 'the general principles of law recognized by civilized nations'.

[8] See P Pescatore, 'Fundamental Rights and Freedom in the System of the European Communities' (1970) *AJIL* 343, 348.

to facilitate the achievement of the Community's tasks, and to abstain from any measure that could jeopardise the attainment of the objectives of the Treaty. The Treaty of Lisbon retains, substantially unaltered, this formulation. However, it also adds the following starting paragraph:

> Pursuant to the principle of sincere cooperation, the *Union* and the Member States shall, in full mutual respect, assist each other in carrying out tasks which flow from the Treaties.
>
> (Article 4(3) TEU, emphasis added)

The extension of the duty of sincere co-operation to the Union, whilst expressly introduced only by the Treaty of Lisbon, is nothing new since it had already been imposed by the Court in the *Hilmar Kellinghusen* case:

> As to Article 5 [EEC then 10 EC] of the Treaty, it should be born in mind that, according to the case-law of the Court, the relations between the Member States and the Community institutions are governed, under that provision, by a principle of sincere cooperation. That principle not only requires the Member States to take all the measures necessary to guarantee the application and effectiveness of Community law, but also imposes on the Community institutions reciprocal duties of sincere co-operation with the Member States.[9]

The principle of sincere, or loyal[10] co-operation requires the Union institutions, and above all the Commission, which is entrusted with the task of ensuring application of the provisions of the Treaty, to give active assistance to any national judicial authority dealing with an infringement of Union rules. That assistance, which takes various forms, may, where appropriate, consist in disclosing to the national courts documents acquired by the institutions in the discharge of their duties.[11] The Commission is obliged to respond as quickly as possible to requests from national courts.[12] The Court also considers itself bound by the duty of loyal co-operation and, in preliminary references, it might accept jurisdiction when it deems the answer to be useful to the national court even when the situation appears to be outside the scope of Union law.[13]

As far as the Member States are concerned, it is the principle of loyal co-operation upon which the Court has built the entire European Union constitutional architecture, since it binds national courts as well as the other organs of the state. For instance, in *Von Colson*, the Court held:

> However, the Member States' obligation arising from a directive to achieve the result envisaged by the directive and their duty under Article 5 [EEC] of the Treaty to take all appropriate measures, whether general or particular, to ensure the fulfillment of that obligation, is binding on all the authorities of member states including, for matters within their jurisdiction, the courts.[14]

---

[9] Joined Cases C-36/97 and C-37/97 *Hilmar Kellinghusen v Amt für Land- und Wasserwirtschaft Kiel* and *Ernst-Detlef Ketelsen v Amt für Land- und Wasserwirtschaft Husum* [1998] ECR I-6337, para 31; Case C-275/00 *EC v First NV and Franex NV* [2002] ECR I-10943, para 49.

[10] The French text refers to the obligation of 'loyauté' or to 'loyale' co-operation. The English text has sometimes rendered this as 'sincere' co-operation, and sometimes as 'loyal' co-operation.

[11] Case C-2/88 *Imm JJ Zwartveld and Others* [1990] ECR I-3365, para 17; Case T-353/94 *Postbank NV v Commission* [1996] ECR I-921, para 64.

[12] Case C-39/94 *Syndicat Français de l'Express International (SFEI) and Others v La Poste and Others* [1996] ECR I-3547, para 50; Case C-275/00, n 6, para 49; the Court has also made clear that Member States cannot invoke the principle of loyal co-operation in order to escape infringement proceedings brought by the Commission, eg Case C-562/07 *Commission v Spain* [2009] ECR I-9553.

[13] eg Case C-254/98 *Schutzverband gegen unlauteren Wettbewerb and TK-Heimdienst Sass GmbH* [2000] ECR I-151.

[14] Case 14/83 *Von Colson* [1984] ECR 1891, para 26.

As we have seen in Chapters 8 and 9, Article 10 EC (now 4(3) TFEU) has been directly or indirectly instrumental to establishing the doctrine of supremacy, direct effect, the duty of consistent interpretation, as well as the general principles of equivalence and effectiveness in relation to national procedural autonomy and *Francovich* damages.

III – SUBSIDIARITY AS A GENERAL PRINCIPLE

Subsidiarity has been discussed in detail in Chapter 5, on union competences. As we have seen in that chapter, the principle of subsidiarity provides a constitutional limit to the EU's ability to act so that in spheres which do not fall within the Union's exclusive competence, the EU can act only insofar as the proposed objectives cannot be sufficiently achieved by the Member States.[15] We have also seen that the Treaty of Lisbon has introduced a new ex ante 'political' mechanism to monitor compliance with the principle of subsidiarity,[16] as well as recognising the jurisdiction of the Court for post-fact scrutiny.[17] Regardless of the protocol, subsidiarity is a general principle since, however unwilling the Court of Justice has been to enforce application of the principle through the mechanism of judicial review of Union acts,[18] the fact remains that subsidiarity lays down conditions for the exercise of Union competence, and non-compliance with subsidiarity may in principle lead to the annulment of a Union act.

This is accepted by the Court of Justice, which has on a number of occasions considered claims that Union acts should be annulled on grounds of compliance with subsidiarity.[19] Subsidiarity is not a general principle derived from the common constitutional traditions of the Member States; it is derived from Article 5 TEU.[20] And whereas general principles of law proper bind not only the Union institutions, but also the Member States when they implement Union law,[21] subsidiarity by its nature binds only the Union to defer in certain circumstances to Member State action.

In principle, subsidiarity would seem relevant to the interpretation of Union acts, at least those adopted after the principle took effect within the Union legal order. Since the Union institutions take account of the principle in framing Union legislation, it would seem logical to apply the principle in interpreting that legislation. Furthermore, if two interpretations are possible, one consistent with subsidiarity, and the other not, one would expect the Court to prefer the former—that is the normal approach of the Court where

---

[15] Art 5(3) TEU.

[16] See Protocol (No 1) on the Role of National Parliaments in the European Union and Protocol (No 2) on the Application of the Principle of Subsidiarity; on the debate as to the best way to monitor the principle of subsidiarity, see generally the documents produced by the European Convention, Working Group I on the Principle of Subsidiarity, available on http://european-convention.eu.int/doc_register.asp?lang=EN&Content=WGI, and in particular the Conclusions of the Working Group, document CONV 286/02 (23 September 2002), available on http://register.consilium.europa.eu/pdf/en/02/cv00/cv00286.en02.pdf.

[17] See Protocol on the Application of the Principle of Subsidiarity (No 2), in particular Art 8.

[18] So far the Court has never annulled an Act or part thereof for infringement of the principle of subsidiarity, although it has discussed it, albeit briefly, in a number of cases, eg Case C-377/98 *Netherlands v Parliament and Council* (biotechnology) [2001] ECR I-7079; Case C-58/08 *Vodafone and others*, judgment of 8 June 2010, nyr.

[19] See Chapter 5, section III.

[20] It is true that it has always been possible to argue that proportionality was also derived from the Treaty, even before it was given a specific Treaty basis, along with subsidiarity, in what is now Art 5 TEU, see below section IV.

[21] See above at p 321.

there is a risk of conflict between a provision of Union law and a general principle of law. Differing views on this point have been expressed by Advocates General,[22] but it now seems clear from the judgment of the Court of Justice *AvestaPolarit Chrome Oy*[23] that the principle of subsidiarity may be invoked as a guide to the interpretation of Union secondary legislation. It also seems that the Commission takes into account subsidiarity along with the other circumstances of the case when deciding whether to dismiss a complaint for want of sufficient Union interest; this is surely correct in principle.[24]

IV – PROPORTIONALITY

The principle of proportionality as codified by Article 5 TEU provides that 'Union action shall not exceed what is necessary to achieve the objectives of the Treaty'. [25] As a general principle of Union law, the principle applies also to Member States when they implement Union law;[26] and to the acts of the Member States when they act within the field of Union law, for instance when they seek to limit one of the rights conferred on individuals by the Treaty.[27]

A – The Principle of Proportionality as a Limit to the Actions of the Institutions

The Union's institutions are bound to comply with the principle of proportionality (Article 5 TEU), and indeed breach of such obligation constitutes one of the grounds for annulment of the contested act. The duty for the institutions to act in a proportionate way—when legislating but also when taking decisions which affect individuals—originally found recognition in the express words of the Treaty only in specific contexts. Thus, for example, the Treaty has always provided, in connection with the establishment of a common organisation of agricultural markets, that such common organisation may include all measures *required* to attain the objectives specified by the Treaty;[28] and the provision made for the harmonisation of indirect taxation is for 'such harmonization as is *necessary* to ensure the

---

[22] eg in Case C-188/95 *Fantask* [1997] ECR I-6783, AG Jacobs rejects the argument that the text should be interpreted in light of the principle of subsidiarity, see para 28 of Opinion (although in that case the Directive pre-dated the incorporation of subsidiarity into the Union legal order); AG Alber in C-318/96 *SPAR Österreichische Warenhandels AG v Finanzlandesdirectktion für Salzburg* [1998] ECR I-785, at para 59 of his Opinion, implies that subsidiarity is relevant to the interpretation of the directive under consideration. In Case C-103/01 *Commission v Germany* [2003] ECR I-5369, at para 40 of his Opinion, AG Ruiz-Jarabo Colomer observes that the Commission's interpretation does not breach the principle of subsidiarity.

[23] C-114/01 [2003] ECR I-8725, paras 55–57.

[24] Case T-5/93 *Roger Tremblay and François Lucazeau and Harry Kestenberg v Commission* [1995] ECR II-185, para 61.

[25] Case 11/70 *Internationale Handelsgeselklschaft* [1970] ECR 1125, 1127 AG Dutheillet de Lamothe gave the following definition of proportionality 'the individual should not have his freedom of action limited beyond the degree necessary for the public interest'.

[26] eg recently Case C-446/08 *Solgar Vitamin France and others*, judgment of 29 April 2010, nyr.

[27] On the different standards of review according to when the principle is invoked, see G de Búrca 'The Principle of Proportionality and its application in EC Law' (1993) 13 *YEL* 105.

[28] Art 40(2) TFEU.

establishment and the functioning of the internal market'.[29] Notwithstanding the sectorial references to the principle in the Treaty, the Court from a very early stage found that the principle of proportionality was one of the general principles of (then) Community law which applied regardless of the field in which action was taken, even though the intensity with which it is applied might vary according to the amount of discretion enjoyed by the institutions.[30] Where a Union institution has a wide discretionary power, eg in the context of common agricultural policy, the Court of Justice will only interfere if a measure is manifestly inappropriate having regard to the objective that the competent institution is seeking to pursue.[31]

The Court has given a number of different formulations of the principle of proportionality; one more or less standard formulation is as follows:

> In order to establish whether a provision of Community law is consonant with the principle of proportionality it is necessary to establish, in the first place, whether the means it employs to achieve the aim correspond to the importance of the aim, and, in the second place, whether they are necessary for its achievement.[32]

A somewhat fuller formulation of the principle is to the effect that

> the principle of proportionality, which is one of the general principles of Community law, requires that measures adopted by Community institutions do not exceed the limits of what is appropriate and necessary in order to attain the objectives legitimately pursued by the legislation in question; when there is a choice between several appropriate measures recourse must be had to the least onerous, and the disadvantages caused must not be disproportionate to the aims pursued.[33]

The principle has operated, inter alia, to invalidate a provision of a regulation providing for the forfeiture of a security for any failure to perform a contractual undertaking, irrespective of the gravity of the breach.[34] The Court held that the:

> Absolute nature . . . of the above-mentioned regulation is contrary to the principle of proportionality in that it does not permit the penalty for which it provides to be made commensurate with the degree of failure to implement the contractual obligations or with the seriousness of the breach of those obligations.[35]

Thus where Union legislation makes a distinction between a primary obligation (eg the export of a commodity from the Union), compliance with which is necessary in order to attain the objective sought, and a secondary obligation (eg the duty to apply for an export licence), essentially of an administrative nature, it cannot, without breaching the principle

---

[29] Art 113 TFEU; see also Art 49 (proportionality of penalties for criminal offences) and Art 52 (general principle of proportionality of limits to rights) Charter of Fundamental Rights .

[30] See generally de Búrca, above n 27.

[31] Case 265/87 *Schrader* [1989] ECR 2237, paras 21, 22; Case 331/88, *Ex Parte Fedesa* [1990] ECR I-4023, para 14; Case C-375/96 *Zaninotto v Ispettorato Centrale Repressione Frodi—Ufficio di Conegliano—Ministero delle risorse agricole, alimentari e forestali* [1998] ECR I-6629, para 64.

[32] Case 66/82 *Fromancais* [1983] ECR 395, para 8; Case C-369/95 *Somalfruit SpA, Camar SpA v Ministero delle Finanze, Ministerio del Commercio con l'Estero* [1997] ECR I-6619; in a different context, see eg C-491/01 *British American Tobacco (Investments) and Imperial Tobacco* [2002] ECR I-11453, paras 122 and ff.

[33] Case C-157/96 *R v Minister of Agriculture, Fisheries and Food and Another ex parte National Farmers' Union and Others* [1998] ECR I-2211, para 60; Case C-375/96 *Galileo Zaninotto v Ispettorato Centrale Repressione Frodi—Ufficio di Conegliano—Ministero delle Risorse Agricole, Alimentari e Forestali* [1998] ECR I-6629, para 63.

[34] Case 240/78 *Atalanta* [1979] ECR 2137.

[35] Ibid, 2151.

of proportionality, penalise failure to comply with the secondary obligation as severely as failure to comply with the primary obligation.[36]

If the principle was to start with of jurisprudential derivation, however, it was incorporated in an express provision of the Treaty at Maastricht (Article 5 EC) and, as mentioned above, it is now codified in Article 5 TEU.

B – The Principle of Proportionality as a Limit to Member States Actions

When Member States are implementing Union law, eg by enacting legislation pursuant to a Directive, they must exercise whatever discretion they have in compliance with the general principle of Union law, including proportionality. Thus, for example, the Court found that the power left to the Member States to derogate from harmonised labelling rules on grounds of public health and consumer protection needs to be exercised consistently with the principle of proportionality. National rules which absolutely, and without exceptions, precluded any reference to 'slimming' and 'medical recommendations' in product labels were found to be not proportionate as there were less restrictive means to ensure that buyers would not be mislead and that those statements would not be used in a fraudulent way.[37] The same reasoning applies in the case in which a Regulation leaves some discretion to the Member State—since the Member State here acts as a 'delegated power' it has to comply with the general principles of Union law, including the principle of proportionality.[38]

Furthermore, Member States are also bound by the general principles of Union law, including proportionality, when acting within the field of Union law. This is particularly the case when the national authorities seek to limit the free movement rights enshrined in Articles 34, 35, 45, 49, 56 and 63 TFEU by relying on the mandatory requirements doctrine or on the Treaty derogations. In this context, the Court has consistently held that a rule which impacts on one of those rights not only has to pursue an interest consistent with Union law, but has also to be proportionate to that end.[39] Furthermore, following the direct effect of the provisions on Union citizenship contained in Article 21 TFEU, the principle of proportionality also applies to the limits imposed on the right to reside and move of non-economically active Union citizens. In this field, and as we shall see in Chapter 15 below, the principle of proportionality acts as an hermeneutic principle which might call into question national rules which, even though consistent with secondary legislation enacted at Union level, produce results that are out of proportion with the aim sought. Thus in *Baumbast*,[40] the Court found that to deprive a Union citizen who had resided for several years in another Member State of his right to reside only because he lacked cover for emergency treatment was out of proportion with the legitimate aim of

---

[36] Case 181/84 *R v Intervention Board for Sugar ex parte Man (Sugar)* [1985] ECR 2889, para 20; Case 21/85 *Maas v Bundesanstalt für Landwirtschaftliche Marktordnung* [1986] ECR 3537, para 15; Case C-161/96 *Südzucker Mannheim/Ochsenfurt AG v Hauptzollamt Mannheim* [1998] ECR I- 281, para 31.

[37] Case C-239/02 *Douwe Egberts NV v Westrom Pharma NV and Christophe Souranis* and *Douwe Egberts NV v FICS-World BVBA* [2004] ECR I-7007.

[38] Joined Cases C-480/00–482/00, C-484/00, C-489/00–491/00 and C-497/00–499/00 *Azienda Agricola Ettore Ribaldi v Azienda di Stato per gli interventi nel mercato agricolo (AIMA), Ministero del Bilancio e della Programma Economica* [2004] ECR I-2943 (also authority for legal certainty and legitimate expectations).

[39] See Chapters 14–18 below.

[40] Case C-413/99 [2002] ECR I-7091.

ensuring that he would not become an 'unreasonable burden' on the welfare system of that state. Following this case law an increasing number of national rules are subjected to the proportionality scrutiny, and the principle has become even more central in the assessment of the compatibility of national legislation with Union law.

Furthermore, and even though it is for the Member State to decide the penalties imposed for breaches of its rules, the principle of proportionality also applies to criminal and administrative sanctions imposed for breach of rules in any way connected with the exercise of a Union right. This is the case in relation, for instance, to penalties imposed to secure compliance with formalities relating to establishing a right of residence under Union law,[41] or providing evidence of entitlement to drive based on recognition of a valid driving licence issued in another Member State.[42]

V – LEGAL CERTAINTY AND LEGITIMATE EXPECTATION

The principle of legal certainty requires that those subject to the law should be able clearly to ascertain their rights and obligations. The related concept of legitimate expectation constitutes what has been described as a corollary[43] to this principle: those who act in good faith on the basis of the law as it is or as it seems to be should not be frustrated in their expectations.

The principle of legal certainty requires that EU rules must enable those concerned to know precisely the extent of the obligations which are imposed upon them.[44] In one case the Court appears to say that the latter principle requires that the Commission must adhere to the interpretation of a Regulation which is dictated by the normal meaning of the words used, but it is certainly not an invariable principle of interpretation that the normal meaning be attributed to the words in a text.[45] Nevertheless, the Court of Justice in a consistent case law has held that ambiguity or lack of clarity in measures alleged to impose charges should be resolved in favour of the taxpayer. For instance, in *Gondrand Frères* the Court declared 'The principle of legal certainty requires that rules imposing charges on the taxpayer must be clear and precise so that he may know without ambiguity what are his rights and obligations and may take steps accordingly.'[46]

It seems, however, that rules may present some difficulties of interpretation without

---

[41] Case C-265/88 *Messner* [1989] ECR 4209.

[42] Case C-193/94 *Skanavi and Chryssanthakopoulos* [1996] ECR I-929, paras 35–38; Case C-29/95 *Pastoors* [1997] ECR I-285 (higher penalty for non-resident permissible in principle but must not be disproportionately higher).

[43] Case C-63/93 *Duff and Others v Minister for Agriculture and Food, Ireland, and the Attorney General* [1996] ECR I-569, para 20; Case T-73/95 *Estabelecimentos Isidoro M Oliveira SA v Commission* [1997] ECR II-381, para 29.

[44] Case C-233/96 *Kingdom of Denmark v Commission* [1998] ECR I-5759, para 38.

[45] Ibid. In interpreting a provision of Union law it is necessary to consider not only its wording but also, where appropriate, the context in which it occurs and the objects of the rules of which it is part, see,in particular, Case C-340/94 *De Jaeck v Staatssecretaris van Financiën* [1997] ECR I-461, para 17.

[46] Case 169/80 [1981] ECR 1931, 1942. See also Case C-143/93 *Gebroeders van Es Douane Agenten BV v Inspecteur der Invoerrechten en Accijnzen* [1996] ECR I-431, para 27; Case C-177/96 *Belgian State v Banque Indosuez and Others and European Community* [1997] ECR I-659, para 27. However, where a regulation authorises the total or partial suspension of imports, a power to impose charges, as a less drastic measure, may be implied, Case 77/86 *Ex parte National Dried Fruit Association* [1988] ECR 757.

thereby infringing the principle of legal certainty, at any rate where the difficulties result from the complexity of the subject matter, and where a careful reading of the rules in question by one professionally involved in the area allows the sense of the rules to be grasped.[47] The failure of the Commission to amend a Regulation concerning tariff nomenclature where it was required to do so, and which resulted in uncertainty on the part of individuals as to their legal obligations, had the consequence that the Regulation could not thereafter be applied.[48] The principle is also capable of operating in favour of Member States, and a provision laying down a time-limit, particularly one which may have the effect of depriving a Member State of the payment of financial aid, application for which has been approved and on the basis of which it has already incurred considerable expenditure, should be clearly and precisely drafted so that the Member States may be made fully aware of the importance of complying with the time limit.[49]

The principle of legal certainty also applies when Member States adopt rules when required or authorised to do so pursuant to Union law. Thus, Member States are bound to implement directives in a way which meets the requirements of clarity and certainty, by enacting appropriate national rules, and mere administrative practices will be inadequate for this purpose.[50] In *Raija-Liisa Jokela*, a case involving Finnish legislation adopted in accordance with a Regulation, the Court described the principle of legal certainty as requiring that 'legal rules be clear and precise, and aims to ensure that situations and legal relationships governed by Community law remain foreseeable'.[51]

The principle of legal certainty militates against administrative and legislative measures taking effect without adequate notice to persons concerned. As the Court declared in *Racke*, 'A fundamental principle in the Community legal order requires that a measure adopted by the public authorities shall not be applicable to those concerned before they have the opportunity to make themselves acquainted with it.'[52]

This principle also militates against the retroactive application of Union measures, and this is indeed the general principle, but it is not invariable. As the Court explained in *Decker*:

> Although in general the principle of legal certainty precludes a Community measure from taking effect from a point in time before its publication, it may exceptionally be otherwise where the purpose to be achieved so demands and where the legitimate expectations of those concerned are duly respected.[53]

---

[47] Case C-354/95 *R v Minister of Agriculture, Fisheries and Food, ex parte National Farmers' Union and Others* [1997] ECR I-4559, para 57.

[48] Case C-143/93 *Gebroeders van Es Douane Agenten BV v Inspecteur der Invoerrechten en Accijnzen*. [1996] ECR I-431.

[49] Case 44/81 *Commission v Germany* [1982] ECR 1855.

[50] Case 102/79 *Commission v Belgium* [1980] ECR 1473, 1486. And see above at p 144.

[51] Joined Cases C-9/97 and C-118/97 [1998] ECR I-6267, para 48.

[52] Case 98/78 [1979] ECR 69, 84. And see Case 84/81 *Staple Dairy Products* [1982] ECR 1763, 1777; Case 108/81 *Amylum* [1982] ECR 3107, 3130. Case 77/71 *Gervais-Danone* [1971] ECR 1127; Case 158/78 *Biegi* [1979] ECR 1103; Case 196/80 *Ango-Irish Meat* [1981] ECR 1103. A regulation is deemed to be published throughout the Union on the date appearing on the issue of the *Official Journal* containing the text of the regulation, unless the date of the actual issue was later, Case C-337/88 *SAFA* [1990] ECR I-1; Union legislation which has not been translated in one of the official languages of the EU cannot impose obligations upon individuals in that state, see Case C-161/06 *Skoma-Lux* [2006] ECR I-10841.

[53] Case 99/78 [1979] ER 101, 111. See also Case 276/80 *Pedana* [1982] ECR 517, 541; Case 258/80 *Runi* [1982] ECR 487, 503. Procedural rules are generally held to apply to all proceedings pending at the time when they enter into force, while substantive rules are usually interpreted as applying to situations existing before their entry into force only insofar as it clearly follows from the terms, objectives or general scheme that such an effect must be given to them: Cases 212–217/80 *Salumi* [1981] ECR 2735.

Thus, for instance, a public statement of intention to alter monetary compensatory amounts justifies a later regulation altering the rate retrospectively to the earlier date.[54]

The principle of legitimate expectations, which may be invoked against Union rules only to the extent that the Union has previously created a situation which can give rise to a legitimate expectation,[55] operates in particular to protect individuals where they have acted in reliance upon measures taken by Union institutions, as the *Mulder* case illustrates. In order to stabilise milk production, (then) Community rules provided for dairy farmers to enter into non-marketing agreements for a period of five years, in return for which they received a money payment. In 1984 milk quotas were introduced, whereby milk producers would pay a super-levy on milk produced in excess of a quota determined by reference to their production during the 1983 marketing year. No provision was made for the grant of a quota to those who did not produce during 1983, because of the existence of a non-marketing agreement. Having been urged to suspend milk production under Community rules, farmers were then excluded from milk production when their non-marketing period came to an end. One such farmer challenged the regulations in this regard. The Court of Justice held that the relevant regulation was invalid to the extent that no provision for allocation of quota was made in such cases. The basis of the ruling was the principle of legitimate expectations. As the Court explained:

> [W]here such a producer, as in the present case, has been encouraged by a Community measure to suspend marketing for a limited period in the general interest and against payment of a premium he may legitimately expect not to be subject, upon the expiry of his undertaking, to restrictions which specifically affect him because he availed himself of the possibilities offered by the Community provisions.[56]

On the basis of the same principle, if an undertaking purchases grain for denaturing with a view to qualifying for an EU subsidy, it is not permissible to discontinue or reduce the subsidy without giving the interested party a reasonable opportunity to denature the grain in question at the old rate.[57] Again, if the Union induces prudent traders to omit to cover their transactions against exchange risk, by establishing a system of compensatory amounts, which in practice eliminate such risks, it must not withdraw such payments with immediate effect, without providing appropriate transitional measures.[58] Similar reasoning protected certain former Community officials in receipt of pensions which had increased in value over a number of years as a result of the Council's failure to adjust the exchange rates used to calculate the amounts due. The Council sought to rectify the situation and phase out, over a ten-month period, the advantages that had accrued. The Court held that

---

[54] Case 338/85 *Pardini* [1988] ECR 2041, 24–26.

[55] Case C-375/96 *Zaninotto v Ispettorato Centrale Repressione Frodi—Ufficio di Conegliano—Ministero delle risorse agricole, alimentari e forestali.* [1998] ECR I-6629, para 50. Three essential conditions in order to claim legitimate expectations: (i) precise, consistent and unconditional assurances given by the institution to the individual; (ii) those assurances must be as such as to create a legitimate expectation; (iii) the assurances must comply with the applicable rules, eg Case T-282/02 *Cementbouw Handel and Industrie BV v Commission* [2006] ECR II-319, para 77.

[56] Case 120/86 [1988] ER 2321, para 24. For a survey of the case law of the Court, see E Sharpston, 'Legitimate Expectation and Economic Reality' (1990) 15 *ELRev* 103.

[57] Case 48/74 *Deuka* [1975] ECR 421; Case 5/75 *Deuka* [1975] ECR 759.

[58] Case 74/74 *CNTA* [1975] ECR 533; and prudent traders are deemed to know the contents of the *Official Journal*, see Case C-174/89 *Hoche* [1990] ECR I-2681, para 35. But an overriding public interest may preclude transitional measures from being adopted in respect of situations which arose before the new rules came into force but which are still subject to change: Case 74/74 *CNTA*, para 44; Case 152/88 *Sofrimport* [1990] ECR I-2477, paras 16 and 19.

respect for the legitimate expectations of those concerned required a transitional period twice as long as that laid down by the Council.[59] Moreover, if the Commission brings about a situation of uncertainty for an individual, and the individual in consequence does not comply with certain requirements, the Commission may be precluded from relying upon those requirements without notifying the individual and clarifying the situation.[60]

Considerations of both legal certainty and legitimate expectations may argue in favour of modifying the temporal effects of judicial and administrative decisions which would normally apply with retroactive effect. It has already been noted that in exceptional circumstances considerations of legal certainty may preclude the retroactive effect of a judgment of the Court of Justice concerning the direct effect of a provision of Union law.[61] Similar considerations explain Article 264 TFEU, which allows the Court of Justice to determine which of the legal effects of an EU act declared to be void by the Court shall nevertheless be considered as definitive.

Respect for vested rights is itself an aspect of the principles of certainty and legitimate expectations. In *Rossi* the Court stressed that:

> The Community rules could not, in the absence of an express exception consistent with the aims of the Treaty, be applied in such as way as to deprive a migrant worker or his dependents of the benefit of a part of the legislation of a Member State.[62]

Yet traders may not rely upon legitimate expectations to insulate them from changes in legal regimes subject to constant adjustments. As the Court explained in *Eridania*, in the context of the common agricultural policy: 'an undertaking cannot claim a vested right to the maintenance of an advantage which is obtained from the establishment of a common organization of the market and which it enjoyed at a given time'.[63]

The Court has said on numerous occasions that a wrongful act on the part of the Commission or its officials, and likewise a practice of a Member State which does not conform with Union rules, is not capable of giving rise to legitimate expectations on the part of an economic operator who benefits from the situation thereby created.[64] But it is possible that the broad scope of this proposition may be limited by the conclusion which is often drawn from it in the case law to the effect that it follows that the principle of the protection of legitimate expectations cannot be relied upon against a *precise*[65] provision of Union law, or an *unambiguous*[66] provision of Union law. Another limitation on recourse to the principle of legitimate expectations is to the effect that 'the principle of the protection

---

[59] Case 127/80 *Grogan* [1982] ECR 869; Case 164/80 *De Pasquale* [1982] ECR 909; Case 167/80 *Curtis* [1982] ECR 931.

[60] Case T-81/95 *Interhotel–Sociedade Internacional de Hotéis SARL v Commission* [1997] ECR II-1265, paras 49–58.

[61] eg Case 43/75 *Defrenne v SABENA* [1976] ECR 455.

[62] Case 100/78 [1979] ECR 831, 844.

[63] Case 230/78 [1979] ECR 2749, 2768. See also Case C-375/96 *Zaninotto v Ispettorato Centrale Repressione Frodi—Ufficio di Conegliano—Ministero delle risorse agricole, alimentari e forestali.* [1998] ECR I-6629, para 50 (common agricultural policy). The same principle has been stated in the context of the common commercial policy, Case C-284/94 *Spain v Council* [1998] ECR I-7309, para 43.

[64] Case 188/92 *Thyssen* [1983] ECR 3721; Case 5/82 *Maizena* [1982] ECR 4601, 4615; Case 316/86 *Hauptzollamt Hamburg-Jonas v Firma P. Krücken* [1988] ECR 2213, 2239; Joined Cases C-31/91–44/91 *SpA Alois Lageder and others* [1993] ECR I-1761, para 34; Case T-336/94 *Efisol SA v Commission* [1996] ECR II-1343, para 36.

[65] Case 316/86 *Firma P Krücken* [1988] ECR 2213.

[66] Joined Cases C-31/91–44/91 *SpA Alois Lageder and others* [1993] ECR I-1761, para 35.

of legitimate expectations may not be relied upon by an undertaking which has committed a manifest infringement of the rules in force'.[67]

Where EU or national subsidies are paid to undertakings in contravention of Union law, the principle of legitimate expectations may preclude recovery.[68] This will not be the case, however, where a beneficiary was in a position to appreciate that the state aid was paid contrary to mandatory provisions of Union law.[69] Circumstances in which legitimate expectations may preclude recovery of state aid include long delay on the part of the Commission in taking a decision, and aid comprising measures which do not self-evidently constitute state aid and which could not readily be identified as such by the beneficiary.[70]

VI – THE PRINCIPLE OF NON-DISCRIMINATION

A further principle binding upon the Union in its administrative and legislative activities is that prohibiting discrimination, whereby comparable situations must not be treated differently, and different situations must not be treated in the same way, unless such treatment is objectively justified.[71]

The principle is applied in the relationships between the Union institutions and its officials. As the Court stated in the *Ferrario* case: 'According to the Court's consistent case law the general principle of equality is one of the fundamental principles of the law of the Community civil service.'[72]

On this basis in *Sabbatini* and *Airola* the Court invalidated differentiation between (then) Community officials on grounds of sex in the payment of expatriation allowances.[73] Furthermore, in *Noonan* the Court said that it would only be lawful to treat candidates with a university qualification differently to those who had none where there were essential differences between the situations in law and in fact of the two categories.[74] However, the Union cannot be called to account for inequality in the treatment of its officials for which it is not itself responsible. In *Sorasio* it was alleged that a Community dependent child tax allowance paid only once in respect of each child, even where both parents were

---

[67] Case 67/84 *Sideradria v Commission* [1985] ECR 3983, para 21; Joined Cases T-551/93, T-231/94, T-233/94 and T-234/94 *Industria Pesdquera Campos and Others v Commission* [1996] ECR II-247, para 76; Case T-73/95 *Estabelecimentos Isidoro M Oliveira SA v Commission* [1997] ECR II-381, para 28.

[68] Joined Cases 205–215/82 *Deutsche Milchkontor GmbH and others v Federal Republic of Germany.* [1983] ECR 2633, paras 30–33; Case 5/89 *Commission v Germany* [1990] ECR I- 3437, paras 13–16.

[69] Case 5/89 *Commission v Germany* [1990] ECR I-3437.

[70] Case 223/85 *Rijn-Schelde-Verolme (RSV) Machinefabrieken en Scheepswerven NV v Commission* [1987] ECR 4617; Case C-39/94 *Syndicat Français de l'Express International (SFEI) and Others v La Poste and Others* [1996] ECR I-3547, para 70, and paras 73–77 of the AG's Opinion; Case C-148/04 *Unicredito Italiano Spa* [2005] ECR I-11137.

[71] Case 106/83 *Sermide* [1984] ECR 4209, para 28; and a consistent case law, see eg Case C-354/95 *R v Minister for Agriculture, Fisheries and Food, ex parte, National Farmers' Union and Others* [1997] ECR I-4559, para 61; Art 21 Charter of Fundamental Rights prohibits discrimination on several grounds, see below Chapter 12.

[72] Joined Cases 152 etc/81 [1983] ECR 2357, 2367.

[73] Case 20/71 *Sabbatini* [1972] ECR 345; Case 21/74 *Airola* [1972] ECR 221; see also *Razzouk and Beydoun* [1984] ECR 1509; however, the Court has so far refused to include in the principle of non-discrimination the right not to be discriminated against on grounds of sexual orientation and found that registered partnerships are not comparable to marriages: Cases C-122/99 and C-125/99 *D and Sweden v Council* [2001] ECR I-4319.

[74] Case T-60/92 *Noonan v Commission* [1996] ECR II-215, para 32.

employed by the Community, was contrary to the principle of equality, since it did not take into account tax allowances which might be claimed by a spouse who did not work for the Community, under national law. The Court rejected this argument: 'The principle of equality does not require account to be taken of possible inequalities which may become apparent because the Community and national systems overlap'.[75]

The principle of non-discrimination provides a basis for the judicial review of measures adopted by the Union in all its various activities. Thus the Court has invalidated a Regulation which provided substantially more severe criteria for the determination of the origin of cotton yarn than for the determination of the origin of cloth and fabrics.[76] The Court has also required consistency in the Commission's policy of imposing fines upon undertakings for the infringement of production quotas for steel.[77]

The principle of non-discrimination has been held to add a gloss to Article 40(2) TFEU, which provides that the common organisations of the agricultural markets 'shall exclude any discrimination between producers or consumers within the Union'. In *Codorniu* the Court held the foregoing principle includes the prohibition of discrimination on grounds of nationality laid down in the first paragraph of Article 18 TFEU,[78] which states that '[w]ithin the scope of application of this Treaty, and without prejudice to any special provisions contained therein, any discrimination on grounds of nationality shall be prohibited'.[79] In *Ruckdeschel*[80] and *Moulins*[81] proceedings arose from challenges in national courts to the validity of the Council's action in abolishing production refunds on maize used to make quellmehl and gritz, while continuing to pay refunds on maize used to make starch, a product in competition with both quellmehl and gritz. Producers of the latter product argued that they had been placed at a competitive disadvantage by the Council's discriminatory, and hence unlawful, action. Their pleas were upheld. Referring to what is now Article 40(2) TFEU, the Court observed:

> While this wording undoubtedly prohibits any discrimination between producers of the same product it does not refer in such clear terms to the relationship between different industrial or trade sectors in the sphere of processes agricultural products. This does not alter the fact that the prohibition of discrimination laid down in the aforesaid provision is merely a specific enunciation of the general principle of equality which is one of the fundamental principles of Community law. This principle requires that similar situations shall not be treated differently unless differentiation is objectively justified.[82]

The *Wagner* case[83] affords a helpful illustration of objective criteria justifying differentia-

---

[75] Case 81/79 *Sorasio* [1980] ECR 3557, para 18.

[76] Case 162/82 *Cousin* [1983] ECR 1101.

[77] Case 234/82 *Ferriere di roe Volciano* [1983] ECR 3921.

[78] Case C-309/89 *Codorníu SA v Council of the European Union* [1994] ECR I-1853, para 26.

[79] The reference to 'without prejudice to any special provisions contained therein' refers particularly to other provisions of the Treaty in which the application of the general principle of non-discrimination on grounds of nationality is given concrete form in respect of specific situations, such as free movement of workers, the right of establishment and the freedom to provide services: see Case C-186/87 *Cowan* [1989] ECR 195, para 14. Art 18 TFEU 'applies independently only to situations governed by Community law in regard to which the Treaty lays down no specific prohibition of discrimination': see Case 305/87 *Commission v Greece* [1989] ECR 1461, para 13.

[80] Joined Cases 117/76 and 16/77 *Ruckdeschel* [1977] ECR 1753.

[81] Joined Cases 124/76 and 20/77 *Moulins* [1977] ECR 1795.

[82] Joined Cases 117/76 and 16/77 *Ruckdeschel* [1977] ECR 1753, para 7; Joined Cases 124/76 and 20/77 [1977] *Moulins* ECR 1795, paras 14–17. And see Case 300/86 *Landschoot v Mera* [1988] ECR 3443; Case C-37/89 *Weiser* [1990] ECR I-2395; Case C-2/92 *Bostock* [1994] ECR I-955, para 23. The principle applies as between identical or comparable situations, Case T-48/89 *Beltrante* [1990] ECR II-493, para 34.

[83] Case 8/82 *Wagner* [1983] ECR 271.

tion between apparently similar situations. Community rules provided for reimbursement of storage costs in respect of sugar in transit between two approved warehouses situated in the same Member State, but not in respect of sugar in transit between two approved warehouses in different Member States. The Court rejected the argument that this was discriminatory, since the difference in treatment was based on requirements of supervision which could be objectively justified. The Court's ruling is a reminder that the principle of non-discrimination is only infringed by differences in treatment where the Union legislator treats *comparable* situations in different ways[84] (or non-comparable situations in the same way). It follows that an allegation of discrimination cannot be based on differences in treatment of products subject to different market organisations which are not in competition with each other.[85]

The principle whereby Union rules may treat differently apparently similar situations where objective justification exists for such differentiation allows a challenge to the validity of the rules in question once the circumstances constituting objective justification have ceased to obtain.[86] Pending such challenge, the Union institutions are bound to continue to apply the measure in question.[87] However, it would seem to follow that even in the absence of a challenge, the Union institutions are bound to take steps to amend the rules in question.

The principle of non-discrimination has also been invoked in the budgetary context,[88] and the 'equality of states' has been resorted to as a general principle of the interpretation of the Treaties.[89]

As is the case with the other general principles, the Court has found that it applies also to the Member States when they act within the scope of Union law. As we have seen in Chapter 8, in *Mangold* the Court found the principle of non-discrimination on grounds of age to be a general principle of Union law.[90] The Court did not give much explanation as to why discrimination on grounds of age should be elevated to the rank of general principle, although the fact that it is codified in the Charter might have contributed to this finding; in any event, it is likely that all the areas in which the European Union can act to fight discrimination according to Article 19 TFEU now constitute general principles of EU law. Furthermore, according to the *Mangold* ruling, and as confirmed in the case of *Kücükdeveci*,[91] such general principles are also of horizontal application, ie they can be invoked, at least to a certain extent, against a private party regardless of whether or not there is national legislation in place.[92]

---

[84] See eg, Case 6/71 *Rheinmühlen Düsseldorf* [1971] ECR 719; Case 283/83 *Racke* [1984] ECR 3791.

[85] Cases 292 and 293/81 *Jean Lion* [1982] ECR 3887.

[86] Case T-177/94 and T-377/94 *Henk Altmann and Margaret Casson v Commission* [1996] ECR II-2041, paras 121–23.

[87] Ibid.

[88] Case 265/78 *Ferwerda* [1980] ECR 617.

[89] Case 128/78 *Commission v United Kingdom* [1979] ECR 419; Case 231/78 *Commission v United Kingdom* [1979] ECR 1447, 1462.

[90] Case C-144/04 *Mangold* [2005] ECR I-9981.

[91] See also Case C-555/07 *Kücükdeveci*, judgment of 19 January 2010, nyr.

[92] See Chapter 12 below and E Spaventa, 'The Horizontal Application of Fundamental Rights as General Principles' in A Arnull, C Barnard, M Dougan and E Spaventa (eds), *A Constitutional Order of States? Essays in EU Law in Honour of Alan Dashwood* (Oxford, Hart Publishing, 2011) 199.

VII – OTHER GENERAL PRINCIPLES

The Court has recognised several other general principles which have now been codified in the Charter of Fundamental Rights. Accordingly, and as mentioned at the beginning of this chapter, we will analyse those in Chapter 13.

Further Reading

G de Búrca, 'The Principle of Proportionality and its Application in EC Law' (1993) 13 *YEL* 105.

PP Craig, 'Substantive Legitimate Expectations in Domestic and Community Law' (1996) 55 *CLJ* 289.

E Ellis (ed) *The Principle of Proportionality in the Laws of Europe* (Oxford, Hart Publishing 1999).

K Lenaerts and JA Gutierrez-Fons, 'The Constitutional Allocation of Powers and General Principles of EU Law' (2010) 47 *CMLRev* 1629.

E Sharpston, 'Legitimate Expectations and Economic Reality' (1990) 15 *ELRev* 103.

T Tridimas, *The General Principles of EU Law*, 2nd edn (Oxford, Oxford University Press, 2007).

JA Usher, 'The Reception of General Principles of Community Law in the United Kingdom' (2005) *EBLRev* 489.

11

Fundamental Rights

Fundamental rights form part of the general principles of Union law and, because of their importance, deserve separate space. This chapter examines the evolution of the case law of the Court of Justice, whilst the Charter of Fundamental Rights will be the subject of next chapter. We will start by examining the case law of the Court of Justice where it was held that fundamental rights formed part of the general principles of Union law which it would guarantee. We will then look at the scope of application of fundamental rights which apply not only to the Union institutions but also to the Member States when they act within the field of Union law. Next, this chapter analyses some problems concerning fundamental rights protection arising from the Union institutional framework. We will then examine the relationship between the European Court of Justice and the European Court of Human Rights (ECtHR). Whilst the European Convention of Human Rights (ECHR) is not yet part of Union law, the Court of Justice has recognised its primary importance as a source in identifying the rights protected at Union level as general principles, and it has looked at the case law of the ECtHR to establish the appropriate level of protection of those rights. However, the protection afforded at Union level has been deemed not always appropriate: this has led to a lively doctrinal debate as well as to a ruling of the ECtHR which held that, at least in some cases, it can hold the Member States collectively responsible for a breach of the Convention provoked by an act of the Union institutions. As a result of this debate, the Treaty of Lisbon provides for the duty for the Union to accede to the ECHR and negotiations for accession are now underway.

I – EVOLUTION OF THE CONCEPT

Unlike the abortive Treaty for the establishment of a European Political Community, which provided explicitly for the application of section I of the ECHR,[1] the EEC Treaty made no provision for the protection of human rights as such. Nevertheless, after some initial hesitation,[2] probably due to the way the questions had been phrased by the referring national courts,[3] the Court of Justice made it clear that fundamental rights were

---

[1] One of the initiatives which pre-dated the EEC Treaty but which failed to secure the support of all potential signatories.

[2] Case 1/58 *Stork v High Authority* [1959] ECR 17; Case 36-40/59 *Geitling v High Authority* [1960] ECR 425; Case 40/64 *Sgarlata v Commission* [1965] ECR 215.

[3] In *Stork*, *Geitling* and *Sgarlata* the Court of Justice had been asked to rule as to the compatibility of ECSC and Community decisions with national constitutional law; not surprisingly the Court held that national constitutional law (and the fundamental rights guarantees contained therein) was not relevant.

implicitly recognised by (then) Community law, and that they were capable of limiting the competence of the (then) Communities.

In the case of *Stauder*,[4] the claimant argued that a Commission Decision which conditioned the distribution of butter at reduced prices on the disclosure of the name of the recipient breached his right to dignity as protected by the German Constitution. The German court made a reference to the Court of Justice, enquiring whether such rules conflicted 'with the general principles of Community law in force'. In other words the national court enquired not whether the Community decision was compatible with the German Constitution, but rather whether there were general principles of *Community* law which could be applied in the case in hand to the advantage of the applicant. Put in this way, the question did not affect nor threaten the principle of supremacy. The Court replied that on its true construction the Decision in question did not require the disclosure of the names of beneficiaries to retailers, and added that: 'Interpreted in this way the provision at issue contains nothing *capable of prejudicing the fundamental rights . . . protected by the Court*.'[5] The Court of Justice thus recognised that even though fundamental rights were not mentioned in the original Treaties, they were nonetheless part of the general principles of Community law. This was then confirmed in the *Internationale Handelsgesellschaft* case, in which the Court stated:

> In fact, respect for fundamental rights forms an integral part of the general principles of law protected by the Court of Justice. The protection of such rights, whilst inspired by the constitutional traditions common to the Member States, must be ensured within the framework of the structure and objectives of the Community.[6]

In *Internationale*, the Court not only restated its intention to review the acts of the (then) Community institutions in relation to fundamental rights, but it also identified in the 'common constitutional traditions' one of the sources to ascertain the content of those rights. In *Nold*, whilst restating the importance of national constitutions, it also held that 'international treaties for the protection of human rights on which the Member States have collaborated or of which they are signatories' would supply useful guidelines.[7] It was always clear that of the Treaties referred to, the ECHR was of special significance in this respect and the Court has said as much in a consistent case law.[8]

The readiness of the Court of Justice to interpret what was then Community law as containing implicit human rights guarantees which operated as limits on the permissible scope of Community action has generally been attributed to a desire to persuade national constitutional courts that it was not necessary to subject Community acts to scrutiny pursuant to national constitutional provisions guaranteeing human rights and fundamental freedoms. If the Court had not guaranteed fundamental rights protection national courts (and especially the German and Italian constitutional courts) would have had reservations in accepting the principle of supremacy. After all, the memory of the gross violations that occurred during the Second World War was all too recent and it would have been pointless to have introduced ring-fenced constitutional guarantees for funda-

---

[4] Case 29/69 *Stauder* [1969] ECR 419.

[5] Para 7, emphasis added.

[6] Case 11/70 [1970] ECR 1125, para 4.

[7] Case 4/73 [1974] ECR 491, para 13.

[8] Case 222/84 *Johnston v Royal Ulster Constabulary* [1986] ECR 1651, para 18; Case C-260/89 *Elliniki Radiophonia Tiléorassi AE (ERT) v Dimotiki Etairia Pliroforissis and others* [1991] ECR I-2925, para 41; Opinion 2/94 [1996] ECR I-1759, para 33; Case C-299/95 *Kremzow v Austria* [1997] ECR I-2629, para 14.

mental rights, and to have provided a safety-net through the ECHR, only for Member States to escape their fundamental rights obligations by acting at (then) Community level. That said, the early case law on fundamental rights is better seen as a dialogue between the Court of Justice and national courts: the judges sitting in the former had the same legal and cultural background as those sitting in the latter and it is difficult to imagine that they would have been unconcerned about a potential fundamental rights gap. Furthermore, notwithstanding the Court's prompt response to the national constitutional courts' concerns, it took some time before the latter, and especially the German Constitutional Court (Bundesverfassungsgericht), renounced their case-by-case jurisdiction over fundamental rights compliance of Union acts. Thus, as we have seen in Chapter 8, in the so-called *Solange I* case,[9] delivered a few weeks after the case of *Nold*, the German court held that in the 'hypothetical case' of a conflict between a provision of Union law and the fundamental rights contained in the German Constitution, the latter would take precedence so long as (*solange*) the Union institutions would not remove the conflict. It was only in 1987, in the so-called *Solange II* case,[10] that the Bundesverfassungsgericht declared itself satisfied with the general level of fundamental rights protection afforded by the European Court of Justice and held that it would not exercise its jurisdiction to review acts of the Union institutions in relation to the German Constitution. This, as long as (*solange*) the Union institutions, and especially the Court of Justice, were to guarantee the effective protection of fundamental rights.[11] More recently, debates about the relationship between supremacy and fundamental rights protection have focused on the field of co-operation in criminal matters, as well as on specific action enacted by the Union in order to fight terrorism.[12]

II – THE RESPONSE OF THE POLITICAL INSTITUTIONS

A – From the 1977 Political Declaration to the Nice Treaty

The Court's case law was endorsed by the European Parliament, the Council and the Commission in their Joint Declaration of 5 April 1977, where they declared themselves

---

[9] *Internationale Handelsgesellschaft* . . . [1974] 2 CMLR 540 (*Solange I*); see also *Steinike und Weinling* . . . [1980] 2 CMLR 531; and cf also the Italian Constitutional Court rulings Sentenza 7/3/64, n 14 (in F Sorrentino, *Profili Costituzionali dell'Integrazione Comunitaria*, 2nd edn (Giappichelli Editore, 1996) 61 *et seq*) and *Società Acciaierie San Michele v. High Authority* (27/12/65, n 98), [1967] CMLR 160.

[10] *Wünsche Handelsgesellschaft* . . . [1987] 3 CMLR 225 (*Solange II*).

[11] See discussion on supremacy in Chapter 8; as noted above, the Maastricht decision (*Brunner and others v EU Treaty* [1994] 1 CMLR 57) subsequently cast some doubts as to whether the German Constitutional Court would continue to refuse jurisdiction in such cases; however, this was confirmed in the decision following the banana litigation, see Federal Constitutional Court, decision 7/6/00 [2000] Human Rights Law Journal 251. See also the French Conseil Constitutionnel, Decision No 2004-496 (10 June 2004); Decision No 2004-497 (1 July 2004); the Polish Constitutional Court ruling in *Trybunal Konstytucyjny, arrêt du 27.04.05, P 1/05, Dziennik Ustaw 2005.77.680*, as reported by *Réflets-Informations rapides sur les développements juridiques présentant un intérêt communautaire*, no 2/2005, 16, also available on http://curia.eu.int/en/coopju/apercu_reflets/lang/index. htm; for an interesting ruling by the German Constitutional Court on the *Mangold* case, see 2 BvR 2666/06 and press release in English, both available on http://www.bundesverfassungsgericht.de/pressemitteilungen/bvg10-069en.html.

[12] See generally V Mitsilegas, *EU Criminal Law* (Oxford, Hart Publishing, 2009) ch 3.

bound by fundamental rights as general principles of (then) Community law.[13] Treaty endorsement came later, first in the preamble to the Single European Act[14] and then more forcefully in the Maastricht Treaty. The latter provided that the Union has to respect fundamental rights, as guaranteed by the European Convention and as they result from the constitutional traditions common to the Member States, as general principles of Community law,[15] although, at the time, such obligation did not fall within the jurisdiction of the Court of Justice.[16] The Treaty of Amsterdam[17] extended the Court's jurisdiction to 'Article 6(2) [the fundamental rights obligation] with regard to action of the institutions, insofar as the Court has jurisdiction under the Treaties establishing the European Communities and under this Treaty'.[18] It also added a new procedure in cases in which a Member State is found to be in serious and persistent breach of fundamental rights.[19] In this case the rights of the Member State in question, including the voting rights, may be suspended by the Council acting with unanimity but without taking into account the vote of the Member State in question.[20] The Treaty of Nice added a new paragraph to this Article, according to which the Council acting with a majority of four-fifths can make a recommendation to one Member State when there is a *clear risk* of a serious breach of the principles contained in then Article 6 TEU (respect for liberty, freedom, democracy, rule of law and fundamental rights). Finally, following the Treaty of Amsterdam, respect for the aforementioned principles is also a precondition for accession to the European Union.[21] Finally, in 2000, the Commission, Council and European Parliament, proclaimed the Charter of Fundamental Rights (see next chapter); at the time at which it was proclaimed the Charter was a non-legally binding catalogue of fundamental rights recognised by the European Union.[22] It has now become legally binding following the entry into force of the Lisbon Treaty.

B – The Treaty of Lisbon

The TL introduces important changes in relation to fundamental rights protection, both in general terms and because of the (positive) effects which derive from changes in the detailed provisions of the Treaties. We will mention only the most important changes.

---

[13] [1977] OJ C103/1. Note that the declaration was referred to by the German Constitutional Court in the ruling in *Solange II* as one of the indications that the fundamental rights protection in the EC had reached a satisfactory level and that they would as a result cease to exercise their power of scrutiny over EC law.

[14] The Preamble to the Single European Act stated, inter alia, 'Determined to work together to promote democracy on the basis of the fundamental rights recognized in the constitutions and laws of the Member States, in the Convention for the Protection of Human Rights and Fundamental Freedoms and the European Social Charter, notably freedom, equality and social justice.'

[15] Art F(2) TEU (Maastricht version).

[16] Art F(2) appeared in Title I of the TEU and under Art L it would not be subject to the jurisdiction of the Court of Justice.

[17] Art F(2) remained unaltered but was renumbered Art 6(2) by the TA.

[18] Art 46 TEU (Amsterdam version) which amended Art L.

[19] Art 7 TEU (Amsterdam version).

[20] There is a corresponding provision in the EC Treaty (also added by the TN), Art 309 TEC.

[21] Art 49 TEU (Amsterdam version).

[22] Charter of Fundamental Rights [2000] OJ C364/1; other initiatives in the field of fundamental rights include the establishment of a Fundamental Rights Agency, Regulation 168/2007 establishing a European Union Agency for Fundamental Rights [2007] OJ L53/1; see generally P Alston and O de Schutter (eds), *Monitoring Fundamental Rights in the EU* (Oxford, Hart Publishing, 2005).

(i) Article 6 TEU

Probably the single most important change is brought about by the new Article 6 TEU, which provides:

> 1. The Union recognises the rights, freedoms and principles set out in the Charter of Fundamental Rights of 7 December 2000, as adapted at Strasbourg, on 12 December 2007, which shall have the same legal value as the Treaties.
>
> The provisions of the Charter shall not extend in any way the competences of the Union as defined in the Treaties.
>
> The rights, freedoms and principles in the Charter shall be interpreted in accordance with the general provisions in Title VII of the Charter governing its interpretation and application and with due regard to the explanations referred to in the Charter, that set out the sources of those provisions.
>
> 2. The Union shall accede to the European Convention for the Protection of Human Rights and Fundamental Freedoms. Such accession shall not affect the Union's competences as defined in the Treaties.
>
> 3. Fundamental rights, as guaranteed by the European Convention for the Protection of Human Rights and Fundamental Freedoms and as they result from the constitutional traditions common to the Member States, shall constitute general principles of the Union's law.

Paragraph 1 gives full legal effect to the Charter, which is now officially legally binding. The provisions of the Charter are subject of detailed analysis in the next chapter. For the time being, it is important to recall two issues concerning the Charter: first of all, the scope of application of the Charter is more limited than that of the general principles and this also explains why Article 6(3) TEU also refers to the latter; secondly, the adoption of the Charter has provoked debate and raised fears of excessive Union interference with national sovereignty in some Member States, especially in the United Kingdom. For this reason, the second indent of Article 6(1) makes clear that the provisions of the Charter do not extend the competences of the Union. These same fears are at the origin also of the third indent of Article 6(1), which both states the obvious by restating that the Charter must be interpreted in accordance with the rules contained therein in relation to its scope of application and interpretation; and requires the interpreter to have due regard to the explanations to the Charter, reproducing a (debatable) provision of the Charter itself.[23] The anxieties that led to such cautious drafting also led to the adoption of a Protocol on the position of the United Kingdom and Poland on the Charter. This will be subject of detailed analysis in the next chapter.

Article 6(2) TEU provides for an obligation for the Union to accede to the ECHR.[24] Accession negotiations have started and raise complex institutional issues relating in particular to the modalities for the participation of a non-state entity to the ECHR; to the jurisdiction of the ECtHR and its relationship with the Court of Justice of the European

---

[23] Art 52(7) Charter of Fundamental Rights.

[24] See also Protocol (no 8) Relating to Art 6(2) of the Treaty on European Union on the Accession of the Union to the European Convention on the Protection of Human Rights and Fundamental Freedoms ([2010] OJ C83/273). An express legal basis was necessary following Opinion 2/94 (Accession to the ECHR), [1996] ECR I-1759, paras 34 and 35; and see CELS Occasional Paper no 1 'The Human Rights Opinion of the ECJ and its Constitutional Competence' (Cambridge, 1996); S O'Leary 'Accession by the European Community to the European Convention on Human Rights—The Opinion of the ECJ' [1996] *EHRLR* 362. As far as the Council of Europe is concerned, accession to the ECHR has been made possible by the entry into force of Protocol 14 to the Convention which amends Art 59 ECHR so as to provide the legal basis for accession by the EU.

Union; to the representation of the EU in the Court and to the repartition of responsibility between Member States and EU.[25] Despite the unavoidable complexities which need to be addressed before accession, the fact that the ECHR will become binding on the European Union is a positive step forward for two reasons: first of all, the EU has been accused of hypocrisy and double standards since in its international relations it often adopts human rights conditionality clauses and it imposes human rights compliance as a precondition to accession. In other words, pre-Charter, it required international partners to comply with rules and principles which bound it only because of the jurisprudence of the Court of Justice. Secondly, lack of membership to the ECHR determined also an internal discrepancy since Member States are bound by the Convention (even though they also possess constitutional fundamental rights guarantees), whilst the EU is not, thus potentially compromising the very safety-net that the ECHR aims to provide. We shall see in more detail below how the ECtHR has dealt with these problems.

Finally Article 6(3) TEU restates that fundamental rights must be considered general principles of Union law. This provision indicates that the jurisprudence of the Court in relation to the scope of application, and level of protection, of fundamental rights as general principles of EU law, and especially in relation to their application in national law, is left unaltered by the TL. Taken at face value, the more limited scope of the Charter together with the application of fundamental rights through the general principles determines a dichotomy in fundamental rights protection so that when the EU acts, the standard is that provided for in the Charter; whilst when the Member States act within the field of Union law, the standard is that provided for by the Court of Justice through its interpretation of the general principles. Whether from a practical viewpoint this dichotomy will actually be maintained (apart from a different application of the margin of discretion) is too early to say.[26] We shall return to these problems towards the end of this chapter.

(ii) Other Changes Relevant for Fundamental Rights Protection

As we have seen in Chapter 1, the TL has introduced significant changes in the institutional and constitutional structure of the Union, as well as modifying several substantive provisions in the Treaties. From a fundamental rights perspective the most significant changes—which are the subject of detailed analysis elsewhere in this book—are the following:

— The changes in the jurisdiction of the Court of Justice and in particular:

[25] For the accession negotiations, see Press Release IP/10/906, 10 July 2010 and Justice and Home Affairs Council Press Release, 3–4 June 2010, 10630/1/10/REV 1; and Draft Council Decision authorising the Commission to negotiate the Accession Agreement of the European Union to the European Convention for the Protection of Human Rights and Fundamental Freedoms, *Involvement of the ECJ regarding the Compatibility of Legal Acts of the Union with Fundamental Rights*, Doc no 10568/10 (2 June 2010); and *Co-Respondent Mechanism*, Doc No 10569 (2 June 2010). The Draft Council Decision authorising the Commission to negotiate is classified (Doc No 9689/10—request for access denied). See also *Discussion Document of the Court of Justice of the European Union on certain aspects of the accession of the European Union to the European Convention for the protection of Human Rights and Fundamental Freedoms*, document of 5 May 2010 (unnumbered), available at http://curia.europa.eu/jcms/upload/docs/application/pdf/2010-05/convention_en_2010-05-21_12-10-16_272.pdf.

[26] Although see eg Case C-208/09 *Ilonka Sayn-Wittgenstein*, Judgment of 22 December 2010, nyr, esp paras 52 and 89, where the Court refers to the Charter even though the case concerned the application of fundamental rights to a Member State when acting within, rather than implementing, EU law. See also Case C-279/09 *DEB Deutsche Energiehandels- und Beratungsgesellschaft mbH*, Judgment of 22 December 2010, nyr, where the Court seems to interpret 'when implementing EU law' in a loose way; see next chapter.

- the extension of (almost) full jurisdiction of the Court in relation to co-operation in criminal matters;[27]
- the creation of jurisdiction for the judicial review of legality of CFSP measures providing for restrictive measures against natural or legal persons;[28]
- the changes in the conditions for locus standi in relation to regulatory acts which do not entail implementing measures.[29]

— The changes in the democratic structure of the EU, including:
- the extension of co-decision;
- the communitarisation of co-operation in criminal matters;
- possibly (depending on how it will work in practice) the new role for national parliaments in relation to subsidiarity;
- possibly (again depending on how it will work in practice) the possibility for direct petition by EU citizens.

We shall now turn our attention to fundamental rights as general principles of Union law.

III – THE SCOPE OF APPLICATION OF FUNDAMENTAL RIGHTS

As with the other general principles, fundamental rights apply in three different situations. First of all, they apply to the acts of the Union institutions; secondly, they apply to acts of the Member States when they implement Union law; and thirdly, they apply to acts of the Member States in fields which fall within the scope of Union law.

A – Fundamental Rights as a Limit to the Acts of the Institutions

As noted above, despite the lack of any mention of fundamental rights in the original Treaties, the Court has since *Stauder* held Union institutions to be bound by fundamental rights as general principles of Union law.[30] As also noted above, the institutions, in turn, accepted this obligation. As a result of the Court's case law, then, breach of fundamental rights is one of the grounds of review that might lead to the annulment of any measure having legal effects adopted by Union institutions.[31] It has already been stressed that in determining the existence and the content of fundamental rights, the Court has always taken particular account of the ECHR, and of the jurisprudence of the ECtHR.[32] Following the entry into force of the TL, the Charter of Fundamental Rights has become the main point of reference (and yardstick) against which to assess the acts of Union institutions. The Charter will be the subject of detailed examination in the next chapter and the

---

[27] The Court does not have jurisdiction to assess the validity or proportionality of operations carried out by law enforcements services, law and order and internal security, see Art 276 TFEU.

[28] Art 275(2) TFEU.

[29] Art 263(4) TFEU.

[30] Case 29/69 *Stauder* [1969] ECR 419.

[31] See Chapter 6 above.

[32] eg Case C-94/00 *Roquette Frères* [2002] ECR I-9011, where the Court of Justice 'updated' its interpretation of the scope of Art 8 ECHR in order to take into account subsequent case law of the ECtHR.

relevant pre-Charter case law will be discussed there. In any event, it should be remembered that, as unlikely as this might appear to be, the reference to the general principles of Union law in Article 6(3) Charter means that the Court, if need be, could go beyond the protection afforded by the Charter (but never below).

B – Fundamental rights and Member States' Implementing Powers

Fundamental rights as general principles of Union law apply to the acts of the Member States when they are implementing Union law, ie when they are enacting administrative acts in order to enforce a Regulation, or when they enact administrative and legislative acts to implement a Directive. In those cases, the Member States are acting as 'delegated powers' and are therefore bound by the general principles of Union law.

An instructive example of the applicability of general principles of Union law to national authorities when they implement Union rules is to be found in the *Wachauf* case.[33] Under (then) Community regulations concerned with milk quotas it was provided that the milk quota should be transferred when the holding to which the quota related was transferred. A producer acquired a quota in the first place by virtue of his having produced milk during the applicable reference year. The issue in *Wachauf* was whether a transfer of quota from lessee to lessor on the expiry of the lease in accordance with the applicable regulation would be consistent with the general principles of (then) Community law where it had been the lessee's milk production which had secured entitlement to the milk quota. The Court of Justice referred to the *Hauer* case to support applicability of fundamental rights in the (then) Community system, subject to such proportionate restrictions as might be imposed in the general interest. The Court stated:

> Having regard to those criteria, it must be observed that Community rules which, upon the expiry of the lease, had the effect of depriving the lessee, without compensation, of the fruits of his labour and of his investments in the tenanted holding would be incompatible with the requirements of the protection of fundamental rights in the Community legal order. Since those requirements are also binding on the Member States when they implement Community rules, the Member States must, as far as possible, apply those rules in accordance with those requirements.[34]

The same principle has been affirmed in the case of directives: in exercising their discretion when implementing a directive, Member States must, so far as possible, respect fundamental rights as general principles of Union law.[35] This principle is now established case law and, as we shall see in the next chapter, has been codified by the Charter which applies to the Member States when they are implementing Union law. Furthermore, recent case law seems to suggest that in those cases in which the Member State is implementing Union law, the general principles/fundamental rights obligations might stretch so as to apply also to private parties. As has been mentioned in the previous chapter, in the case of *Mangold* the Court found that given that the situation fell within the scope of Union law (by virtue of a directive other than the framework discrimination directive), general

---

[33] Case 5/88 [1989] ECR 2609.

[34] [1989] ECR 2609, para 19. See also Case C-2/92 *Bostock* [1994] ECR I-955, and Case C-351/92 *Manfred Graff v Hauptzollamt Köln Rheinau* [1994] ECR I-3361.

[35] C-20/00 and C-64/00 *Bokker Aquaculture Ltd et al v Scottish Ministers* [2003] ECR I-7411, para 88; see Joined Cases C-465/00, C-138/01 and C-139/01 *Österreichischer Rundfunk and others* [2003] ECR I-4989.

principles were applicable. The Court then found that the principle of non-discrimination on grounds of age was a general principle of Union law. In relation to the case at issue, this meant that Mr Mangold could invoke that principle in litigation with his employer, a private party. Following *Mangold*, the extent to which the principle of non-discrimination on grounds of age, and general principles (including fundamental rights), applied to private parties was uncertain. However, following the ruling in *Kücükdeveci*,[36] it seems that in cases following within the scope of Union law by virtue of a piece of secondary legislation, private parties might be bound by the general principles of Union law, regardless of whether the provision which brought the case within the scope of application of Union law is horizontally applicable. In that case, German legislation provided for a reduced notice period for dismissal for younger workers so that work undertaken before the age of 25 would not be taken into account when calculating the period of notice to which the worker had a right. As a consequence of this legislation, Ms Kücükdeveci received a notice period of about 40 days rather than the 4 months she would have been entitled to had her period of service before she turned 25 been taken into account. She therefore brought proceedings against her employer (a private company), arguing that she had been a victim of age discrimination. The framework directive on discrimination was of little help since the litigation was horizontal, ie between two private parties, and the Court restated its previous case law to the effect that directives cannot have horizontal direct effect.[37] The principle of consistent interpretation, according to which national law must be interpreted insofar as possible so as to comply with Union law,[38] was also of little help since the German legislation at issue was phrased in a way that left no space for interpretative discretion. The Court then found that since Directive 2000/78 simply gave effect to the general principle of non-discrimination on grounds of age, the national court was under a duty to ensure the effectiveness of such principle, if need be by disapplying the conflicting legislation even in proceedings between private parties.[39]

The ruling in *Kücükdeveci* thus opens the possibility for the horizontal applicability of some general principles, at least in those cases in which setting aside conflicting national law might help the claimant. Furthermore, this case law also raises questions as to whether it applies only to the principle of non-discrimination or also to other general principles, including the other rights listed in the Charter. Indeed, one of the reasons that led the Court to find that non-discrimination on grounds of age was a general principle of Union law, despite it not being part of common constitutional traditions, was its inclusion in the Charter, which, as we shall see in the next chapter, codifies existing rights rather than creating new ones. Whilst the Charter per se should not be horizontally applicable, since it is addressed to the institutions and the Member States, the rights contained therein could be considered as general principles and be subjected to the *Kücükdeveci* approach. Whether this would be at all sensible is open to debate.[40]

---

[36] Case C-555/07 *Kücükdeveci*, Judgment of 19 January 2010, nyr.
[37] Ibid, para 46 and case law therein cited. See also Chapter 8 above.
[38] See Chapter 8 above.
[39] *Kücükdeveci*, above n 36, esp paras 51 and 54.
[40] See E Spaventa 'The Horizontal Application of Fundamental Rights as General Principles of EU Law' in A Arnull, C Barnard, M Dougan and E Spaventa (eds), *A Constitutional Order of States? Essays in Honour of Alan Dashwood* (Oxford, Hart Publishing, 2011); for a more favourable view, see S Peers 'Supremacy, Equality and Human Rights: Comment on *Kücükdeveci*' (2010) 35 *ELRev* 849.

C – Member States Acting within the Scope of Union law

Fundamental rights as general principles of Union law bind the Member States also when the latter are acting 'within the scope' of Union law, ie where the state's action limits or has an impact on one of the rights guaranteed by the Treaty[41] and in particular when the Member States seek to limit the enjoyment of one of the free movement provisions either by relying on the mandatory requirements doctrine[42] or on one of the express Treaty derogations contained in Articles 36,[43] 45(3)[44] and 52 TFEU.[45] When an individual is exercising one of the rights conferred by the Treaty, she/he falls within the scope of Union law and therefore any interference with the Treaty right must not only be justified, but must also be consistent with the general principles of Union law, and in particular with fundamental rights. Accordingly, a national rule which limits a free movement right, maybe for a legitimate policy reason, but which infringes fundamental rights as guaranteed by the general principles of Union law, must be set aside by the national court (see section (i) below). Furthermore, fundamental rights as general principles of EU law might be relevant in determining the limits of other Treaty rights in those cases where there is a clash of rights so that the enjoyment of the latter and the former are mutually exclusive (see section (ii) below).

(i) Fundamental Rights and Derogations, Limitations and Interpretations of Union Law Rights

In *Rutili* the French authorities granted to Mr Rutili, an Italian national working in France, a resident permit which allowed him to reside only in one part of the French territory because of his political and trade union activities. The French government pleaded that such restrictions were justified according to the public policy derogation contained in Article 45(3) TFEU. In adopting a restrictive interpretation of the public policy derogation, the Court expressly referred to the ECHR.[46] Some years later, in *ERT*,[47] the Court was more explicit. In this case, a company complained against the Greek national monopoly on broadcasting (a service covered by Article 56 TFEU), arguing that the impossibility for private operators to provide broadcasting services was a limitation on the free movement of services which also affected freedom of expression as guaranteed by Article 10 ECHR. In examining the Greek government's contention that such rules were justified under Article 52 TFEU, the Court held that national rules can be justified by one of the Treaty derogations 'only if they are compatible with the fundamental rights the observance of which is ensured by the Court.'[48] The Court later extended this doctrine to all limitations to the free movement provisions, and not only those justified by the Treaty derogations.

---

[41] This doctrine also applies to the EEC–Turkey Association Agreement, see eg Case C-303/08 *Bozkurt*, Judgment of 22 December 2010, nyr, esp para 60.

[42] Case C-368/95 *Familiapress* [1997] ECR I-3689, para 24.

[43] Case C-260/89 *Elliniki Radiophonia Tiléorassi AE (ERT) v Dimotiki Etairia Pliroforissis and others* [1991] ECR I-2925, para 42.

[44] Case 36/75 *Rutili v French Minister of the Interior* [1975] ECR 1219.

[45] Case C-260/89 *Elliniki Radiophonia Tiléorassi AE (ERT) v Dimotiki Etairia Pliroforissis and others* [1991] ECR I-2925, para 42.

[46] Case 36/75 *Rutili* [1975] ECR 1219, para 32.

[47] Case C-260/89 *Elliniki Radiophonia Tiléorassi AE (ERT)* [1991] ECR I-2925.

[48] Case C-260/89 *Elliniki Radiophonia Tiléorassi AE (ERT)* [1991] ECR I-2925, para 43.

The extension of the scope of fundamental rights as general principles of Union law to cover Member States acts that merely limit (or regulate) a free-movement right has been criticised since it expands significantly the scope of Union law by allowing for the direct effect of fundamental rights in all those situations which have an even remote link with Union law. A good example of such expansion can be found in the case of *Carpenter*.[49] Here Mrs Carpenter, a third-country national, married a British national after having overstayed her leave to enter the United Kingdom. She then applied for, but was refused, leave to remain in the United Kingdom as the spouse of a British national. A deportation order had also been made. Her husband ran a business selling advertising space in medical and scientific journals and offering various services to the editors of those journals. A significant proportion of the business was conducted with advertisers established in other Member States and as a result Mr Carpenter travelled occasionally to other Member States for the purposes of his business.

The Court held that since Mr Carpenter was providing services within the meaning of Article 56 TFEU[50] it was clear 'that the separation of Mr and Mrs Carpenter would be detrimental to their family life and, therefore, to the conditions under which Mr Carpenter exercises a fundamental freedom'.[51] The Court went on:

> A Member State may invoke reasons of public interest to justify a national measure   which   is likely to obstruct the exercise of the freedom to provide services only if that measure is compatible with the fundamental rights whose observance the Court ensures . . .

> The decision to deport Mrs Carpenter constitutes an interference with the exercise by Mr Carpenter of his right to respect for his family life within the meaning of Article 8 of the [ECHR], which is among the fundamental rights which . . . are protected in Community law.[52]

The Court, referring to the case law of the ECtHR, concluded that a decision to deport Mrs Carpenter in circumstances such as those in the main proceedings did not strike a fair balance between the competing interests—namely, on the one hand, the right of Mr Carpenter to respect for his family life and, on the other hand, the maintenance of public order and public safety.[53]

The *Carpenter* case is a good example of the expansion of Union law arising from the Court's case law on fundamental rights: the rule in itself would have been justified according to the mandatory requirements doctrine, since control of migration is clearly a matter of public interest consistent with Union law. However, since the application of the rule did interfere with Mr Carpenter's right to family life in a way that the Court of Justice deemed disproportionate, it needed to be set aside. As a result, through the medium of Union law, fundamental rights become directly effective even in situations where they

---

[49] Case C-60/00 *Carpenter* [2002] ECR I-6279. For interpretation of Regulation 1612/68 on freedom of movement for workers in light of respect for family life, see Case C-413/99 *Baumbast, R v Secretary of State for the Home Department* [2002] ECR I-7091, para 72.

[50] See below Chapter 17.

[51] The reference to a fundamental freedom is a reference to a fundamental internal market freedom, see Part IV below.

[52] Paras 40, 41.

[53] On the right to family life see also Case C-109/01 *H Akrich* [2003] ECR I-9607 where the Court confusingly excludes the possibility to apply Community law to then nonetheless impose on the national court a duty to have due regards to fundamental rights as general principles of Union law; see further E Spaventa, 'Annotation on *Akrich*' (2005) *CMLRev* 225. On restrictions to fundamental rights that might also be qualified as restrictions to movement rights see recently Case C-208/09 *Ilonka Sayn-Wittgenstein*, Judgment of 22 December 2010, nyr.

would not be so according to national law. Take the case of the United Kingdom by way of example: here a statutory rule which is inconsistent with the Human Rights Act 1998 is valid and enforceable against an individual until when Parliament or the minister responsible, using the fast-track procedure provided under the Act, amends the rule.[54] However, if the situation falls within the scope of Union law, then the national court is under a duty not to apply that rule to the case at issue without having to wait for Parliament to change the law.

A further significant feature of the *Carpenter* case was that the Court of Justice defined in this case the scope of right to family life as a general principle of Union law by reference to the case law of the ECtHR.[55] Any distinction in principle or difference in practice between Convention rights inspiring and influencing the content of general principles of Union law, on the one hand, and the Court of Justice applying the European Convention, and the case law of the ECtHR, on the other, would seem to have disappeared. This is even more visible in the case of *KB*.[56] KB attacked UK legislation which prevented those who had undergone gender reassignment from amending their birth certificates to reflect their change of sex. As a result, post-operative transsexuals were effectively prevented from marrying a person of the other sex, since only their sex of birth would be taken into account. The Court of Justice had already ruled that, unlike discrimination on grounds of sexual orientation,[57] discrimination against transsexuals fell within the scope of application of Article 157 TFEU (equal pay for men and women).[58] KB argued that the fact that she could not marry her partner, who was a post-operative man, constituted discrimination on grounds of sex since her partner would be deprived of a widower's pension in the event of KB's death on the grounds that the couple was not married. Since the reason why the couple could not marry was because of the UK legislation preventing KB's partner from amending his birth certificate to reflect his change of sex, KB attacked the UK rules under Article 157 TFEU (employment pension is considered 'pay' for the purposes of Article 157 TFEU). The British registration rules preventing those who had undergone gender reassignment from amending their birth certificate had just been declared inconsistent with the ECHR.[59] The European Court of Justice put great weight on the Strasburg's Court ruling and held that:

> Article [157 TFEU], in principle, precludes legislation, such as that at issue before the national court, which, in breach of the European Convention for the Protection of Human Rights and Fundamental Freedoms . . . prevents a couple such as KB and R from fulfilling the marriage requirement which must be met for one of them to be able to benefit from part of the pay of the other.[60]

It is clear that a broad interpretation of the scope of the Treaty in the free movement cases, and of the meaning of what constitutes sex discrimination falling within the scope of Article 157 TFEU, come to the benefit of individuals, who see their fundamental rights recognised through the medium of Union law. However, such case law also has the effect

---

[54] See s 4 HRA 1998; and see also s 10.

[55] Case C-60/00 *Carpenter* [2002] ECR I-6279, para 42; Case C-109/01 *H Akrich* [2003] ECR I-9607, para 60.

[56] Case C-117/01 *KB* [2004] ECR I-541.

[57] Case C-249/96 *Grant v South West Trains Ltd* [1998] ECR I-621.

[58] Case C-13/94 *P v S Cornwall County Council* [1996] ECR I-2143.

[59] *Goodwin v UK* (Appl No 28957/95) (2002) 35 EHRR 18; the ECtHR found that the British legislation at issue breached the right to respect for private life enshrined in Art 8 of the Convention, and the right to marry enshrined in Art 12.

[60] Case C-117/01 *KB* [2004] ECR I-541, operative part of the ruling.

of reducing Member States' regulatory autonomy and relocating the balancing exercise between fundamental rights and competing interests in the hands of the Court of Justice, a step not necessarily welcomed by all of the Member States.[61]

(ii) Clash of Rights—Economic Treaty Rights v Non-economic Rights

Another, related problem, occurs when the rights guaranteed by the Treaty directly clash with (non-economic) rights guaranteed by the common constitutional traditions and the ECHR. In those cases, the Court has been willing to admit that the need to protect fundamental rights constitutes a legitimate aim justifying a restriction to Treaty rights;[62] however, the limitation must be proportionate and the balance between conflicting interests is a matter for Union rather than national law. For instance, and as we shall see in more detail in the chapter relating to the free movement of goods, in Schimidberger,[63] a trader attacked the Austrian government's decision not to block a demonstration on the motorway which had the effect of interrupting the flow of road-borne goods for several days. The trader's right to transport goods guaranteed by Article 34 TFEU therefore directly clashed with the demonstrators' right to freedom of expression, a right recognised and guaranteed by the Austrian Constitution as well as by the ECHR. The Court held that fundamental rights might take precedence even over the Treaty free-movement provisions, and found that in the case at stake the interference with the traders' right to free movement was proportionate.

A more complex case of clash between Treaty and fundamental rights arose when the exercise of collective labour rights, conferred by national law, came into conflict with Treaty free-movement rights. In the case of Viking,[64] Viking Line was a Finish company seeking to reflag its ship in Estonia in order to benefit from lower labour costs.[65] To prevent this from happening, the Finish trade union contacted the International Transport Workers' Federation (ITF), whose aim is to fight flags of convenience and to protect the conditions of seafarers. ITF instructed all of its members (including the Estonian ones) not to negotiate with Viking, thus rendering reflagging impossible. The Finnish trade union then took industrial action in order either to prevent the reflagging, or to force the company to employ its crew under Finnish employment law subsequent to the reflagging (which would have made reflagging essentially pointless). Viking brought proceedings against the trade union to prevent it from taking industrial action on the grounds that such action constituted a restriction on its freedom, granted by Article 49 TFEU, to establish itself in any of the Member States. The trade union, on the other hand, claimed it had a fundamental right to strike and take industrial action which it was exercising in conformity with the applicable legislation. A similar issue arose in the case of Laval,[66] this

---

[61] See the discussion about the horizontal provisions of the Charter in the next Chapter.

[62] Case C-368/95 Familiapress [1997] ECR I-3689; more recently Case C-36/02 Omega Spielhallen- und Automatenaufstellungs-GmbH v Oberbürgermeisterin der Bundesstadt Bonn [2004] ECR I-9609; Joined Cases C-570 and 571/07 Blanco Pérez and Chao Gómez, Judgment of 1 June 2010, nyr .

[63] Case C-112/00 Schmidberger [2003] ECR I-5659.

[64] Case C-438/05 International Transport Workers' Federation and The Finnish Seamen's Union v Viking Line et al [2007] ECR I-10779.

[65] The flag of a ship determines its nationality and therefore the rules to which the ship its subject; this gives rise to the 'flag of convenience' phenomenon where owners might seek to re-flag their ships in a place with which they have no connection because it offers the most convenient (and cheaper) regulatory practice, sometime at the expenses of the seamen working on the ship (social dumping).

[66] Case C-341/05 Laval un Partneri [2007] ECR I-11767.

time in relation to a Latvian company that posted its workers to Sweden to work in one of its companies (incorporated under Swedish law but owned by Laval) which had entered into a contract of services to build a school in Sweden. Laval entered into negotiations with the local trade unions in order to determine the contractual conditions applicable to its posted workers; however, the negotiations broke down and as a result the Swedish trade union engaged in collective action, which, eventually, resulted in the bankruptcy of Laval's subsidiary. Laval sued the trade union for damages arguing that the latter's action was a violation of its free movement rights.[67] Both cases then raised two fundamental issues: first of all, and as we shall see later in Chapter 17, whether the Treaty provisions for free movement of persons might apply horizontally so as to impose obligations on private (or semi-private) parties. Secondly, if the trade unions were indeed bound by the Treaty, how the clash between a Treaty right and a non-Treaty right should be assessed. Having found that the Treaty free-movement provisions applied, the Court also found that the right to strike is a fundamental right protected by the general principles of Union law.[68] It then construed the exercise of the collective rights as a potentially legitimate limitation to the Treaty rights; as such, the collective action at stake had to be scrutinised to assess whether it had been exercised in a proportionate way, even though such action had been undertaken in compliance with the national legislation applicable. In *Viking* the Court left it to the national court to determine the proportionality of the collective action (although it indicated that it might be compatible with Union law), whilst in *Laval* it declared that the collective action was inconsistent with Union law.[69] These two rulings gave rise to a significant academic debate, both for their impact on labour law and the law of industrial relations;[70] and for their significance for fundamental rights protection.[71] In relation to the latter, it should be noted that this case law has a centralising effect, so that the balancing act inherent in assessing clashes of fundamental rights might now be relocated from national to supranational level. Given that the Court of Justice has by its nature an integration bias, this relocation might have the effect of creating (at least implicitly) a hierarchy of fundamental rights where the free-movement rights constitute the starting point (as was the case in both *Viking* and *Laval*) and competing rights are construed as barriers which might, or might not, be justified in the case at issue. Furthermore, in an area as complex as that of labour relations, the wisdom of determining the lawfulness of industrial action

---

[67] There were also issues about the posted-workers directive as well as the Swedish legislation on trade union action which was discriminatory in that it differentiated between action taken against Swedish-based companies and foreign companies.

[68] See also Art 28 Charter; for a detailed account of the submissions of the parties in *Viking*, see B Bercusson, 'The Trade Union Movement and the European Union: Judgment Day' (2007) 13 *ELJ* 279.

[69] The case of *Viking* was settled after the ruling of the ECJ; the case of *Laval* has now reached a final ruling and the trade unions had to pay €55,000 in punitive damages: see M Ronmar 'Laval Returns to Sweden: The Final Judgment of the Swedish Labour Court and Swedish Legislative Reforms' (2010) 39 *ILJ* 280.

[70] See eg S Giubboni, 'Social Rights and Market Freedoms in the European Constitution: A Re-appraisal' (2010) 1 *ELLJ* 161; S Sciarra, 'Notions of Solidarity in Times of Economic Uncertainty' (2010) 39 *ILJ* 223; C Kilpatrick, 'Laval's Regulatory Conundrum: Collective Standard Setting and the Court's New Approach to Posted workers' (2009) 34 *ELRev* 844; C Barnard, 'Social Dumping or Dumping Socialism?' (2008) 67 *CLJ* 262, as well as 'Fifty Years of Avoiding Social Dumping? The EU's Economic and Not So Economic Constitution' in M Dougan and S Currie (eds), *50 years of the European Treaties: Looking Back and Thinking Forward* (Oxford, Hart Publishing, 2009) 311. For a more theoretical and broader perspective see S Giubboni, *Social Rights and Market Freedom in the European Constitution: A Labour Law Perspective* (Cambridge, Cambridge University Press, 2009).

[71] P Sirpis and T Novitz, 'Economic and Social Rights in Conflict: Political and Judicial Approaches to their Reconciliation' (2008) 33 *ELRev* 411; E Spaventa, 'Federalisation versus Centralisation: Tensions in Fundamental Rights Discourse in the EU' in Dougan and Currie, above n 70, 343.

through a case-by-case ex post judicial assessment, rather than through an ex ante regulatory framework, might well be questioned.[72]

D – The Institutional Structure of the Union and Fundamental Rights

Despite the Court's willingness to protect fundamental rights in the Union system, some concerns have been raised in relation to the compatibility of certain features of the Union system with fundamental rights, and in particular with the right to fair trial and effective judicial protection enshrined in Article 6 of the ECHR (and now also in Article 47 Charter). In particular, problems arise in relation (i) to some characteristics of the competition law enforcement system; and (ii) to the role of the Advocate General in direct proceedings. Before the entry into force of the TL, there were also serious concerns about the reduced jurisdiction of the Court over instruments adopted under the co-operation in criminal matters pillar (Third Pillar). The TL solves this problem since it 'communitarises' the Third Pillar although it will take five years for the Court to gain full jurisdiction also in this field (see (iii) below).

(i) Fundamental Rights and Competition Law

In relation to competition law proceedings, and as we shall see in the relevant chapters below, the Commission is responsible both for carrying out the investigation on competition law breaches, and imposing a fine should it find that a breach of competition law has occurred. According to Regulation 1/2003, such a fine—which can be very high (up to 10 per cent of global turnover for the preceding year)—is not of a criminal nature.[73] However, the ECtHR, in deciding whether proceedings are of a criminal nature, adopts a substantial rather than a formal criterion. Thus, if the national legal system qualifies the offence as criminal in nature, Article 6 ECHR is automatically applicable. Otherwise the ECtHR will look at several factors in order to decide whether a 'charge' is a 'criminal charge' for the purposes of the Convention. Amongst these factors are the nature of the offence and the severity of the penalty imposed. If a fine is substantial, punitive in nature and aimed at deterring future breaches, it might be qualified as a criminal sanction.[74] If European competition law fines were to be qualified as criminal sanctions, then the fine-imposing powers of the Commission might be problematic in relation to Article 6 ECHR. The General Court has so far refused to consider competition law fines as criminal sanctions,[75] even though both it and the Court of Justice have held that the guarantees

---

[72] Furthermore, it should be noticed that whilst the free-movement provisions have an impact on national rules concerning collective action, there is no competence for those rules to be harmonised so that a situation of legal uncertainty is likely to remain as to the liability of trade unions and the boundaries to collective action imposed by Union law.

[73] Art 23(5) Reg 1/2003 on the implementation of the rules on competition laid down in Arts 81 and 82 of the Treaty, [2003] OJ L1/1; Reg 17 also provided that the fine was not a criminal sanction. The Court has held that penalties/fines imposed in relation to the CAP are not of a criminal nature: see eg Case 137/85 *Maizena* [1987] ECR 4587; C-210/00 *Käserei Champignon Hofmeister* [2002] ECR I-6453.

[74] A fine for breach of competition law was qualified as a criminal sanction by the European Commission of Human Rights in *Societé Stenuit v France* (Appl No 11598/85) [1992] 14 EHRR 509; also see obiters in *Lilly France SA v France* (Appl No 53892/00), Judgment of 3 December 2002, and *OOO Neste St Petersburg and others v Russia* (Appl No 69042/01).

[75] eg Case T-64/02 *Dr Hans Heubach GmbH & Co KG v Commission* [2005] ECR II-5137.

provided for in Articles 6 and 7 ECHR also apply, to a certain extent, to the Commission's investigatory power.[76]

(ii) Fundamental Rights and the Role of the Advocate General

A further problem with the institutional organisation of the European Union relates to the role of the Advocate General in court proceedings, at least in direct proceedings. Here, the rules of procedure of the Court do not allow the parties to reply to the Advocate General's opinion. In *Emesa*, another competition law case, Emesa sought leave to submit observations on the Advocate General's opinion. It relied on a ECtHR case, *Vermeulen*,[77] in which the Strasbourg Court held that the fact that the parties could not reply to the submissions of the Belgian Procureur Général in proceedings before the Cour de Cassation, infringed the right to adversarial proceedings and thus Article 6 ECHR. The European Court of Justice distinguished the role of the Advocate General from that of the Procureur General. It held:

> [T]he Opinion of the Advocate General brings the oral procedure to an end. It does not form part of the proceedings between the parties, but rather opens the stage of deliberation by the Court. It is not therefore an opinion addressed to the judges or to the parties which stems from an authority outside the Court or which 'derives its authority from that of the Procureur Général's department [in the French version, 'ministère public']'. . . . Rather, it constitutes the individual reasoned opinion, expressed in open court, of a Member of the Court of Justice itself.[78]

Whilst the reasoning of the Court of Justice seems persuasive in distinguishing the role of the Procureur_from that of the Advocate General, a subsequent ruling of the ECtHR cast some doubts on the compatibility with Article 6 ECHR of the lack of rebuttal to the Advocate General's Opinion. In *Kress*,[79] a case concerning the French Commissaire du Government, whose role is very similar to that of the Advocate General,[80] the ECtHR held:

> [T]he concept of a fair trial also means in principle the opportunity for the parties to a trial to have knowledge of and comment on all evidence adduced or observations filed, even by an independent member of the national legal service, with a view to influencing the court's decision.[81]

In the case at issue the ECtHR found that there was no breach of Article 6 ECHR since the parties could ask the Commisaire to indicate the general tenor of her/his submissions; and it was open to the parties to reply to the Commissaire's submissions. This is not possible, however, in the Union legal system.

As a result of the *Kress* ruling, the institution of the Advocate General came under attack again. In *Kaba II* the applicant claimed that the fact that in the first ruling concerning his situation he was not able to rectify some allegedly wrong factual assessment reached by the Advocate General in his opinion was a breach of Article 6(1) of the Convention

---

[76] eg T-220/00 *Cheil Jedang v Commission* [2003] ECR II-2473, para 44, on non-retroactivity of sanctions.

[77] *Vermeulen v Belgium*, Appl No 19075/91, Reports 1996-I.

[78] Case C-17/98 *Emesa Sugar Free Zone NV and Aruba*, order of the Court, [2000] ECR I-665, para 14.

[79] *Kress v France* (Appl No 39594/98), ECHR Reports 2001-VI.; see also *Martinie v France* (Appl No 59675/00).

[80] In fact the French government, resisting the application, held that were the ECtHR to apply the *Vermeulen* ruling to the Commisaire du Government it would be 'condemning' the European Community judicial system, cf para 62.

[81] *Kress v France* (Appl No 39594/98) para 74.

as interpreted by the ECtHR in *Kress*. Advocate General Ruiz-Jarabo Colomer unsurprisingly defended the role of the Advocate General and attacked the ECtHR for its *Kress* ruling.[82] The Court of Justice avoided the issue by inverting the order of the questions and thus limiting itself to examining the issue of substance. Whilst it could be argued that in the case of preliminary rulings the problem is much reduced by the fact that the case is decided by the national court which can therefore ensure that the ruling of the Court of Justice is not based upon a misunderstanding of the facts or of the national rules applicable and, if that is the case, can refer a new question to the Court of Justice, the issue is more delicate in relation to direct proceedings. Here, the fact that the parties are unable to reply to the Advocate General's submissions seems to be in direct conflict with the ECtHR assessment of the scope of Article 6(1) ECHR. This might be a problem given that, according to Article 52 of the Charter, the Union's standard of protection of those rights which derive from the Convention cannot fall below the Convention's standard.[83] It is to be seen whether the issue will be addressed by the ECtHR once the Union accedes to the Convention.

(iii) Measures Adopted in the Field of Co-operation in Criminal Matters and Counter-terrorism

Before the entry into force of the TL certain areas of Union law were excluded from the jurisdiction of the European judicature even though instruments adopted therein could have serious effects on individual rights. This was the case in relation to instruments adopted in the area of co-operation in criminal matters when the Court did not have jurisdiction, either because the Member State had failed to agree to the jurisdiction of the Court (which in the Third Pillar was voluntary), or because the instrument adopted was a Common Position which was altogether excluded from the Court's jurisdiction by virtue of the Treaty.[84] Furthermore, as part of its counter-terrorism strategy the Union also adopted measures targeting individuals using CFSP competence, an area where again the Court did not have jurisdiction.[85]

The lack of jurisdiction of the Union judicature has been remedied by the TL which, as mentioned before, provides for full jurisdiction in relation of instruments adopted in the field of co-operation in criminal matters, as well as in relation to those CFSP measures providing for restrictive measures against natural and legal persons.[86] The only problem concerning the institutional structure of the EU in this field therefore relates to the tran-

---

[82] Case C-466/00 *Kaba* (Kaba II) [2003] ECR I-2219, Opinion, esp paras 104–07.

[83] See Chapter 12, section III below.

[84] See Arts 34 and 35 TEU pre-Lisbon.

[85] Common Position 2002/402/CFSP concerning restrictive measures against Usama bin Laden, members of the Al-Qaida organization and the Taliban and other individuals, groups, undertakings and entities associated with them and repealing Common Positions 96/746/CFSP, 1999/727/CFSP, 2001/154/CFSP and 2001/771/CFSP, [2002] OJ L169/4, implemented by Reg 881/2002 imposing certain specific restrictive measures directed against certain persons and entities associated with Usama bin Laden, the Al-Qaida network and the Taliban ... [2002] OJ L139/9, recently modified by Reg 1286/2009 [2009] OJ L346/42; and Common Position 2001/931/CFSP on the application of specific measures to combat terrorism [2001] OJ L344/93, partially implemented by Council Reg 2580/2001 on specific restrictive measures directed against certain persons and entities with a view to combating terrorism, [2001] OJ L344/70. The Regulations were subject to the full jurisdiction of the Court since they are Community measures; however, the Common Positions had effects on individuals regardless of the Regulation since to be defined as a terrorist has per se detrimental effects. See Case C-355/04 P *Segi and Others v Council* [2007] ECR I-1657; and E Spaventa, 'Remembrance of Principles Lost: On Fundamental Rights, the Third Pillar and the Scope of Union Law' (2007) 26 *YEL* 153.

[86] Art 275 TFEU.

sitional period during which the pre-Lisbon arrangements will continue to operate for those Acts that had been adopted before the entry into force of the latter Treaty.[87] And, as we shall see further below, in respect to those, the ECtHR has now made clear that the presumption of equivalent protection does not apply.[88]

E – Relationship between the European Union and the European Convention of Human Rights

As we have seen above, the ECHR does not directly apply to the European Union since it has yet to be ratified by it. Thus, the Convention merely serves as a source (the main one until the Charter came into force) for the identification of those rights which are to be considered protected as general principles of Union law; and the case law of the ECtHR is looked at to determine the appropriate minimum level of protection, which, in any event, according to Article 52(3) of the Charter, can never fall below that determined by the ECHR. However, the fact that the EU is not part to the Convention has given rise to some controversy, in that some commentators, as well as some claimants, have argued that the protection of fundamental rights afforded by the Court of Justice through the general principles (or the Charter) might on some occasions fall below that afforded by the ECtHR. Should that be the case, the applicant is left with no remedy since she cannot bring a complaint in front of the ECtHR as would be possible were the situation a domestic rather than a EU one. Furthermore, and as we have seen, the institutional framework of the Union might fall short of fundamental rights guarantees. In those cases, membership of the EU might have the effect of weakening the protection of fundamental rights by removing that minimum floor of rights which should be a common denominator for all Member States. It is in order to address these criticisms that, as we have seen above, the TL provides in Article 6(2) TEU a duty for the EU to accede to the Convention, and the accession negotiations have now started.[89] As we have mentioned above, there are several issues that need solving before accession can be completed, such as the modalities of interaction between the Court of Justice of the EU and the ECtHR; the problem of representation of EU's interest (including the problem of whether a judge should be nominated by the Union); and the definition of 'exhaustion of legal remedies' in cases concerning EU legislation when the Court of Justice has not had the chance to adjudicate on the matter for lack of a preliminary reference. Until accession has been completed, however, the existing case law of the ECtHR on EU law will continue to be relevant. It is to this case law that we now turn our attention.

(i) The European Court of Human Rights and EU Law

It has been mentioned above that the fact that the EU is not (yet) a signatory to the ECHR

---

[87] This said, there might be concerns about the actual level of protection guarantee by the Court in these cases: see generally E Spaventa, 'Counter-Terrorism and Fundamental Rights: Judicial Challenges and Legislative Changes after the Rulings in *Kadi* and *PMOI*' in A Antoniadis, R Schütze and E Spaventa (eds), *The EU and Global Emergencies* (Hart Publishing, Oxford, 2011).

[88] *MSS v Belgium and Greece* (Appl No 30696/09), Judgment of 21 January 2011, especially paras 330–40.

[89] See also Protocol (no 8) Relating to Art 6(2) of the Treaty on European Union on the Accession of the Union to the European Convention on the Protection of Human Rights and Fundamental Freedoms ([2010] OJ C83/273). The negotiations for accessions have now started: above n 25.

has created a fracture in the system of fundamental rights protection in Europe. The European Convention was intended to be a safety net to ensure a minimum level of fundamental rights protection in its contracting parties; however, in theory, the EU Member States could escape their Convention obligations by acting at Union rather than at national level. In this way, membership of the EU might have created some loopholes in the safety net provided by the Convention. Bearing this in mind, it is not surprising that some claimants have argued that the fact that the Convention does not bind the European Union does not deprive it of its effects since the Member States and the national authorities are always bound by the ECHR, even when they are enforcing/implementing an EU decision. According to this view, national authorities would be under an obligation to refuse to apply/implement a piece of Union law if it conflicted with one of the Convention rights. It is clear that this approach would place a limit on the doctrine of supremacy of Union law and that there is an inherent tension between such principle and the need to ensure that Member States do not escape their Convention obligations through the medium of Union law. It is for the ECtHR to strike the balance between these two potentially conflicting interests, and with time the ECtHR has taken a more interventionist stance.

The first case in which the relationship between (then) Community/national and Convention law was examined is *M & Co*.[90] There the claimant tried to rely on the reasoning outlined above in attacking the acts of the German authorities which were enforcing a European Commission's decision taken within the field of competition law. In that occasion, the European Commission of Human Rights (then in charge of deciding on the admissibility of the case in front of the ECtHR) partially rejected such reasoning. It first noted that, according to Article 1 of the Convention, Member States are responsible for *any* violation of the Convention, whether it is a consequence of domestic or international law. However, it also found that the Community system both secured and controlled compliance with fundamental rights. To require the Member State to check whether the Convention rights had been respected in each individual case would be contrary to the very idea of transferring powers to an international organisation. The *M & Co* ruling lays down the doctrine of equivalent protection (not dissimilar from that espoused by national constitutional courts): since the (then) Community system affords fundamental rights protection as well as the possibility to enforce such rights in front of the Union judiciary, the national courts/authorities do not need to check case by case whether such protection is adequate, and the ECtHR will refuse jurisdiction.[91]

Some years later, however, in the *Matthews* ruling,[92] the ECtHR allowed for the Convention to have some effect in a field occupied by Union law. In this case, Ms Matthews was a Gibraltar national who complained about the fact that Gibraltar nationals did not have the right to vote in European Parliament elections. She argued that, even though the exclusion from the right to vote followed from a Council decision rather than a unilateral act of the United Kingdom, the UK was still responsible for the effect of the decision which deprived her of the right to vote guaranteed by Article 3 of Protocol No 1.[93] The main question for the ECtHR was whether, notwithstanding the fact that the European

---

[90] (1990) 64 ECmHR 138.

[91] The ECtHR had no problem asserting jurisdiction when the national rule under attack was reproducing Community law, Case *Cantoni v France* (1997-V) ECHRR 1614.

[92] *Matthews v UK* (Appl No 24833/94), ECHR 1999-I.

[93] Art 3 recites 'The High Contracting Parties undertake to hold free elections at reasonable intervals by secret ballot, under conditions which will ensure the free expression of the opinion of the people in the choice of the legislature.'

Parliament was an organ of the Community, the United Kingdom was under an obligation to 'secure' elections to it. The ECtHR found that even though the Council decision
could not be challenged in front of it, since the Community itself was not party to the
Convention and its Protocols, the Member States' responsibility to secure the rights in the
Convention continued even after the transfer of sovereignty to an international organisation. Noting that in this case the Court of Justice did not have jurisdiction to review the
Council decision, as this was primary law having the same status of the Treaty, the ECtHR
held that the United Kingdom, together with all the other Members States of the EU, was
responsible for possible violations of the Protocol. It then found that such Protocol had
been violated and as a result the UK subsequently amended its rules to allow Gibraltar
citizens to vote in European Parliament elections.[94]

The ruling in *Matthews* signalled the ECtHR's willingness to intervene at least in those
cases in which the Court of Justice lacked jurisdiction since in those cases the protection
afforded by the EU is not equivalent to that afforded by the Convention. In *Bosphorus*,[95]
the ECtHR further curtailed the scope of the doctrine of equivalent protection. Here the
case at issue related to a Community Regulation implementing a UN Security Council
Resolution; consistently with the Regulation, the Irish authorities impounded the claimant's aircraft on the grounds that it was owned by a company established in Serbia, which
was the target of the UN sanctions. The claimant argued that since it leased the aircraft
from the Serbian company before the sanctions came into force, the impoundment constituted a disproportionate interference with its right to property. The Court of Justice
found that the public interest of securing a resolution to the Serbian conflict outweighed
the claimant's right to property, and that therefore the impoundment was consistent
with fundamental rights. When the claimant seized the ECtHR, the preliminary question was whether the ECtHR had jurisdiction over the issue: after all the case related
to a Community measure over which the Court of Justice had jurisdiction. The ECtHR
restated the doctrine of equivalent protection; however, it added that:

> any such presumption [of equivalence] can be rebutted if, in the circumstance of a *particular
> case*, it is considered that the protection of Convention rights was *manifestly deficient*. In such
> cases, the interest of international co-operation would be outweighed by the Convention's role
> as a 'constitutional instrument of European public order' in the field of fundamental rights.[96]

Following the rulings in *Matthews* and *Bosphorus*, it is clear that despite the fact that the
Union was and is not yet part to the Convention, the ECtHR is willing to assert jurisdiction to ensure that Union law does not fall systematically below the standards required
by the Convention. However, if it is true that the ECtHR now allows for the possibility
that claimants rebut the presumption of equivalent protection, the threshold for successfully doing so is set at a high level since a mere infringement of Convention's rights is
not enough to trigger the ECtHR's intervention: rather the protection must be 'manifestly
deficient'. In a more recent case, *MSS*,[97] the ECtHR has had the chance to clarify that the
doctrine of equivalent protection only applies to the 'First Pillar', ie to areas which are fully
subjected to the jurisdiction of the Court of Justice. Thus, it is to be presumed that, even

---

[94] Such change was then the subject of an action by Spain against the UK based on the fact that the new UK
rules allowed non-EU citizens resident in Gibraltar to vote for the European Parliament elections, Case C-145/04
Spain v United Kingdom [2006] ECR I-7917.
[95] *Bosphorus v Ireland* (Appl No 45036/98), ECHR 2005-VI, noted (2005) EHRLR 649.
[96] *Ibid*, para 156.
[97] *MSS v Belgium and Greece* (Appl No 30696/09), Judgment of 21 January 2011, especially paras 330–40.

pending accession, the ECtHR might be willing to assert jurisdiction in relation to areas were the jurisdiction of the Court of Justice is either reduced or altogether absent, such as it is the case in co-operation in criminal matters in the transitional period, and in common foreign and security policy. Furthermore, in *MSS* the ECtHR also clarified that if a Member State retains any discretion under Union law, then its actions are fully subjected to the jurisdiction of the ECtHR.

Further Reading

P Alston (ed), *The EU and Human Rights* (Oxford, Oxford University Press, 1999).

P Alston and JHH Weiler 'An "Ever Closer Union" in Need of a Human Rights Policy: The European Union and Human Rights', Jean Monnet Working Paper 1/99.

EM Ameye, 'The Interplay between Human Rights and Competition Law in the EU' (2004) 25 *ECLR* 332.

N Banforth, 'Sexual Orientation after *Grant v South West Trains*' (2000) 63 *MLR* 694.

G de Búrca, 'The Language of Rights and European Integration' in J Shaw and G More (eds), *New Legal Dynamics of European Integration* (Oxford, Clarendon Press, 1995) 29.

A Coppel and O'Neill, 'The European Court of Justice: Taking Rights Seriously?' (1992) 12 *Legal Studies* 227.

R Harmsen, 'National Responsibility for European Community Acts under the European Convention on Human Rights: Recasting the Accession Debate' (2001) *EPL* 625.

FG Jacobs, 'Human Rights in the European Union: The Role of the Court of Justice' (2001) 26 *ELRev* 331.

T King, 'Ensuring Human Rights of Inter-governmental Acts in Europe' (2000) *ELRev* 79.

R Lawson, 'Confusion and Conflict? Diverging Interpretation of the European Convention on Human Rights in Strasbourg and Luxembourg' in R Lawson and M de Bloijs (eds), *The Dynamics of the Protection of Human Rights in Europe. Essays in Honour of G Schermers* (Dordrecht, Kluwer, 1994).

NA Neuwhal and A Rosas (eds), *The European Union and Human Rights* (The Hague and London, Martinus Nijhoff, 1995).

P Sirpis and T Novitz, 'Economic and Social Rights in Conflict: Political and Judicial Approaches to Their reconciliation' (2008) 33 *ELRev* 411.

E Spaventa, 'Federalisation versus Centralisation: Tensions in Fundamental Rights Discourse in the EU' in M Dougan and S Currie, *50 Years of the European Treaties: Looking Back and Thinking forward* (Oxford, Hart Publishing, 2009) 343

E Spaventa, 'The Horizontal Application of Fundamental Rights as General Principles of EU Law' in A Arnull, C Barnard, M Dougan and E Spaventa (eds), *A Constitutional Order of States? Essays in Honour of Alan Dashwood* (Oxford, Hart Publishing, 2011).

J Weiler and N Lockhart '"Taking Rights Seriously" Seriously: The European Court of Justice and its Fundamental Rights Jurisprudence' (1995) 51 *CMLRev* 579.

A Williams, *EU Human Rights Policies. A Study in Irony* (Oxford, Oxford University Press, 2004).

B de Witte, 'The Past and Future Role of the European Court of Justice in the Protection of Human Rights' in P Alston (ed), *The EU and Human Rights* (Oxford, Oxford University Press, 1999) 859.

12

The Charter of Fundamental Rights

The Charter of Fundamental Rights of the European Union was officially proclaimed by the Council, the Parliament and the Commission in December 2000. It was then included in the Constitutional Treaty with a few amendments. It has now been added to the Treaty of Lisbon and according to Article 6(1) TEU has the same value as the Treaties. This chapter examines the Charter's substantive provisions as well as its scope and legal value. The Charter is narrower in scope than the general principles and it applies only to the acts of the Union institutions and to the Member States when they implement Union law. Thus, the Charter (in theory), unlike the general principles, does not apply to the Member States when they act within the scope of Union law. This could potentially create a dichotomy in the application of fundamental rights. However, as we shall see below, this is most likely to be just a formal dichotomy.

I – BACKGROUND TO THE DRAFTING OF THE CHARTER

In the previous chapter we saw that in the absence of any written catalogue of rights, the task of identifying the fundamental rights applicable at Union level fell primarily upon the Court of Justice. As a result of the Court's case law, the issue of fundamental rights protection in the (then) European Economic Community became a matter of political discussion. The first resolution inviting the Commission to elaborate proposals on fundamental rights in the light of the UN International Covenant of 1966, and of the political and civil rights contained in the UN Charter, was issued in 1977 a few months after the institutional endorsement by the Parliament, Council and Commission of the Court's case law.[1] The issue of fundamental rights was further discussed in relation to the draft European Union Treaty adopted by the European Parliament in 1984,[2] Article 4 of that

---

[1] Joint declaration of European Parliament, the Council and the Commission Concerning the Protection of Fundamental Rights and the European Convention for the Protection of Human Rights and Fundamental Freedoms, [1977] OJ C103/1.

[2] Draft European Union Treaty adopted by the European Parliament on 14 February 1984 (the Spinelli draft); see F Capotorti, M Hilf, F Jacobs, and JP Jacqué, *The European Union Treaty. Commentary on the Draft Adopted by the European Parliament on 14 February 1984* (Oxford, Clarendon Press, 1986) esp 39 *et seq*.

draft providing for an express fundamental rights guarantee, as well as for a procedure for breach of fundamental rights not dissimilar from that currently contained in Article 7 TEU. As we saw in the previous chapter, each Treaty amendment after the Single European Act also included new provisions relevant to fundamental rights. Eventually in 1999 it was decided that the Union should equip itself with its own fundamental rights document,[3] and the Cologne European Council in its Conclusions held that 'at the present stage of development of the European Union, the fundamental rights applicable at Union level should be consolidated in a Charter and thereby made more evident'.[4] This declaration was complemented by an Annex IV, which detailed the mandate as well as outlining the composition of the body which would be entrusted with the drafting of the Charter.

According to the Cologne mandate, the Charter was to contain: the fundamental rights contained in the ECHR and in the constitutional traditions common to the Member States (ie the general principles of Union law), together with the fundamental rights pertaining to Union citizens (eg political representation, consular protection, as well as free movement). In addition, the mandate stated that account should be taken of the economic and social rights contained in the European Social Charter[5] and in the Community Charter of the Fundamental Social Rights of Workers.[6]

As far as the composition of the body entrusted with the drafting of the Charter was concerned, Annex IV of the Cologne Conclusions stated that it should be comprised of representatives of the heads of state and government and of the President of the Commission, as well as representatives of the European Parliament and of the national parliaments. The Cologne Council, however, left it to the following European Council to be held in Tampere to decide the precise composition of the body. The Tampere Council set up a 'Convention' composed of 62 people:[7] 15 representatives of the heads of states or government of the Member States, 1 representative of the Commission, 16 representatives of the European Parliament, and 30 representatives of the national parliaments (2 for each Member State). The number of European Parliament representatives was set so as to counterbalance the number of representatives of the (then) Community executive (15 + 1); whilst the number of representatives of national parliaments was set at 2 for each Member State so as to ensure that those Member States which have a bicameral system could have a representative from each chamber. The inclusion of representatives from national parliaments, which had previously been excluded from any direct participation to the legislative and political processes of the European Union, was by far the biggest innovation. This move was aimed at providing the Convention with stronger democratic legitimacy than the traditional intergovernmental process adopted in drafting primary Union legislation. For the same reason, the Convention proceedings were to be as transparent as possible,

---

[3] For an analysis of the reason which might have led to this decisions, see E Paciotti 'La Carta: I contenutu e gli autori' in A Manzella, P Melograni, E Paciotti, S Rodotà, *Riscrivere i diritti in Europa* (Bologna, Il Mulino, 2001).

[4] Cologne European Council, 3 and 4 June 1999, Presidency Conclusions, 150/99 REV 1, para 44.

[5] The European Social Charter is an instrument adopted by the Council of Europe (the body which adopted the ECHR) in 1961 and revised in 1996. Whilst the ECHR focuses on civil and political rights, the Social Charter focuses on economic and social rights (housing, education, employment, etc). The enforcement mechanisms for the latter are different from those provided for in relation to the ECHR and the ECtHR has no jurisdiction over the Social Charter.

[6] This is a non-binding instrument adopted at Community level by 11 out of the then 12 Member States (the UK was the exception). In 1999 the UK signed the Charter.

[7] Tampere European Council, 15 and 16 October 1999, Annex to the Presidency Conclusions, http://ue.eu.int/ueDocs/cms_Data/docs/pressData/en/ec/00200-r1.en9.htm.

with all documents published on the internet. Furthermore, the Convention accepted representations from a number of institutions, including non-governmental organisations, as well as from the then applicant countries, and there were also two observers from the European Court of Justice and two from the ECtHR.

The introduction of the Convention method was seen as a revolutionary step in European governance and it was reproduced in the drafting of a Treaty establishing a Constitution for Europe.[8] The Convention met for the first time on 17 December 1999, and delivered the completed Charter on 2 October 2000. The Charter was then solemnly proclaimed by the European Parliament, the Commission and the Council at the Nice European Council on 7 December 2000.[9] As a result the Charter was not, until the entry into force of the TL, legally binding. The CT incorporated the entire Charter (including the Preamble) in its second part; it also amended the numbering and the provisions on its interpretation and application. It is this later version that has been given full legal effect by the TL.

II – THE CHARTER: STRUCTURE AND SUBSTANTIVE PROVISIONS

A – Structure of the Charter

The structure of the Charter is innovative in that it departs from the traditional division between civil and political rights on the one hand, and economic and social rights on the other. Instead, it adopts a 'horizontal' approach to fundamental rights, placing them (at least theoretically) all at the same level, thus highlighting the indivisible nature of fundamental rights.[10] For this reason the Charter is divided in Titles according to six fundamental values:[11]

— Dignity (Articles 1–5)
— Freedom (Articles 6–19)
— Equality (Articles 20–26)
— Solidarity (Articles 27–38)
— Citizenship (Articles 39–46)
— Justice (Articles 47–50)

These are complemented by the Preamble and by the general provisions (so-called horizontal provisions, Articles 51–54) which set out the scope of application of the Charter. As we shall see below, the Charter—unlike the ECHR—contains a general derogating provision which theoretically applies to all Charter provisions; however, when Charter rights derive from Convention rights, the scope of the former cannot be less extensive that the

---

[8] See Chapter 1; on the significance of the Convention process, G de Búrca 'The Drafting of the European Union Charter of Fundamental Rights' (2001) *ELRev* 126.

[9] Charter of Fundamental Rights (2000) OJ C364/1.

[10] On indivisibility of fundamental rights, cp J Kenner, 'Economic and Social Rights in the EU Legal Order: The Mirage of Indivisibility' in T Hervey and J Kenner (eds), *Economic and Social Rights under the EU Charter of Fundamental Rights—A Legal Perspective* (Oxford, Hart Publishing, 2003) 1.

[11] The Nice version of the Charter was divided in Chapters rather than Titles.

scope of the latter. In order to understand the scope of some of the Charter rights it is therefore necessary to look at the ECHR.

As said above, the mandate of the Convention was to codify existing rights, not to create new ones. Whilst the main sources of such rights had been identified by the Cologne Council, the list therein provided was not considered exhaustive and the Convention drew extensively from the case law of the Court of Justice of the European Union and of the ECtHR, and from secondary and primary Union legislation, as well as from other international conventions and treaties. As we shall see, this allowed the Convention also to codify the so-called new generation of rights. The fact that the Charter aims to be a comprehensive document of the rights recognised by the Union entailed a substantial degree of duplication with rights contained in other Treaty provisions as well as internal duplication. The reason for these duplications was to ensure that *all rights* which are recognised by the Union would be clearly visible. It is not obvious, however, that such duplication has not come at the expense of clarity, especially since Article 52(2) provides that those rights which duplicate rights contained elsewhere in the Treaties have the same scope as the latter.

The Charter is accompanied by 'explanations' which clarify both the scope of each of the Charter rights/provisions and where they are derived from.[12] The source of the rights is especially important for those rights deriving from the ECHR since, as we said above and as we shall see in more detail below, Article 52(3) makes clear that the meaning and scope of the rights corresponding to Convention rights must be at least the same as those laid down by the ECHR. Article 52(7) makes clear that the explanations must be given 'due regard' by the courts of the Union and of the Member States. As we mentioned in the previous chapter, the reference to the explanations is of dubious utility, both because the duty of the courts is limited to an obligation to take those into account; and because the explanations reflect a status quo which in due time will be outdated and supplanted by the Court's own vision of EU fundamental rights. The best way to look at Article 52(7) is then to interpret it as a minimum standard guarantee so that when the Charter rights reflect rights derived from other instruments the former cannot fall below the standard set by the latter.

B – Preamble

The Preamble reaffirms the Union values as well as its founding principles and its aims. It then states that it is necessary to 'strengthen the protection of fundamental rights in the light of the changes in society, social progress and scientific and technological developments by making those rights *more visible* in a Charter'.[13] The Preamble therefore stresses the non-innovative nature of the Charter, so that rights are not created by the Charter but simply made visible by it (which rendered much of the debate about the legal value of the Charter pre-Lisbon rather redundant). The Preamble then identifies, in a non-exhaustive manner, the sources of such fundamental rights. It mentions the common constitutional traditions, international obligations common to the Member States, the

---

[12] The original explanations can be found on the Council's documents website (www.europa.eu.int), or as an official publication of the European Communities (ISBN 92-824-1955-X, 2001); the amended explanations can be found in Explanations relating to the Charter of Fundamental Rights, [2007] OJ C303/02.

[13] Emphasis added.

ECHR, the European Union and Council of Europe Social Charters, as well as the case law of the European Court of Justice and the ECtHR. Furthermore, the Preamble duplicates Article 52(7) by explicitly referring to the explanations which accompany the Charter and indicating that they must be used as a guide to its interpretation. It also makes clear that enjoyment of the rights contained in the Charter also entails responsibilities and duties towards other persons, the human community and future generations. The Preamble then concludes by stating that the Union recognises the rights, freedoms and principles set out in the Charter.

C – Substantive Provisions

(i) Title I—Dignity

The first Title of the Charter deals with those rights which are essential in order to enjoy any fundamental right.

Article 1 provides that *human dignity* is inviolable and that it shall be respected and protected. Human dignity is generally seen as the basis for enjoyment of any fundamental right. Thus, according to the explanations to the Charter, no provision of the Charter may be used to harm the dignity of another person, and dignity is part of the substance of the Charter rights, and therefore has *always* to be respected even when Charter rights are limited. The Court of Justice had recognised that the right to human dignity is a general principle of Union law in the biotechnology case (see below).[14]

Article 2 provides for the *right to life* as well as for the *prohibition of the death penalty and execution*. It substantially reproduces the right to life as enshrined in Article 2(2) ECHR and in Protocol No 6 on the death penalty, and it has at least the same scope as the Convention rights.[15] Thus, even though this is not explicitly stated in the Charter, the right to life can be limited only in (exhaustively) listed circumstances, ie defence from unlawful violence, to make a lawful arrest or to prevent someone lawfully detained from escaping, or in order to quell a riot or insurrection. The prohibition on the death penalty can be derogated from in time of war or in time of imminent threat of war.

Article 3, entitled right to the *integrity of the person*, contains the so-called new generation rights.[16] Thus, as well as providing for a general right to physical and mental integrity, Article 3 prescribes limits to be respected in the fields of medicine and biology, such as the principle of informed consent,[17] the prohibition of eugenic practices, the prohibition on making the human body or its parts a source of financial gain, as well as the prohibition

---

[14] Case C-377/98 *Netherlands v Council* (Biotechnology Directive) [2001] ECR I-7079; see also Case C-36/02 *Omega* [2004] ECR I-9609, esp para 34. Even though it is not expressly mentioned in the Convention, the right to dignity informs the interpretation of all Convention rights, eg *Tyrer v UK* (Appl No 5856/72) (1979–80) 2 EHRR 1.

[15] Art 2(1) ECHR provides for the possibility of death penalty; however, the ECtHR has revisited its previous case law and held that following the adoption of the Protocol, and changes in attitudes towards the death penalty, the exception in Art 2 is no longer applicable and capital punishment is no longer admissible, cp *Öcalan v Turkey* (Appl No 46221/99) (2003) 37 EHRR 10. See also Protocol 13 ECHR on the abolition of death penalty in all circumstances, signed by all Member States but not yet ratified by Poland. In the EU context, see Case C-465/07 *Elgafaji* [2009] ECR I-921, in relation to the notion of serious harm in asylum cases.

[16] They are called new generation rights because they result from scientific developments; however, it should be remembered that they are inherent in other rights: thus, for instance, the principle of informed consent is inherent in Art 8 ECHR (respect for private life), eg *Glass v UK* (Appl No 61827/00) (2004) 39 EHRR 15.

[17] The principle of informed consent to medical practices had been recognised by the Court of Justice in

on reproductive cloning.[18] It is open to the legislature to afford more extensive protection: thus, and as highlighted by the explanations, it would be open to the legislature to prohibit other forms of cloning. The prohibition on the marketability of the human body and its parts has already given rise to litigation in the case of *Netherlands v Council*.[19] Here, the Netherlands sought the annulment of the biotechnology directive,[20] inter alia, on the grounds that by allowing for the patentability of elements isolated from the human body or otherwise produced by means of a technical process, including the sequence or partial sequence of a gene, it breached the principle of human dignity and of non-marketability of the human body and its parts. The Court drew a distinction between inventions which combine a natural element with a technical process, which can be patented, and mere discoveries of DNA sequences which are not as such patentable. The Court then found that given the safeguards provided for in the Directive, the patentability of DNA-based inventions did not conflict with the principle of human dignity and non-commercialisation of the human body.

Article 4 prohibits *torture* and *inhuman or degrading treatment* and *punishment*. It reproduces exactly the wording of Article 3 of the Convention and it is an *absolute* right that can never be derogated from, not even in time of war.[21] Thus, even though the horizontal provisions theoretically apply to all Charter rights, because of the Convention floor guarantee, the Charter derogations cannot be validly invoked in relation to Article 4.[22]

Article 5 prohibits *slavery and forced labour*. Article 5(1) provides that no one shall be held in slavery (which is a legal condition) and servitude (which is a de facto status);[23] since it reproduces Article 4 of the ECHR it has to be construed accordingly and cannot therefore be derogated for any reason, not even in time of war. Article 5(2) prohibits forced and compulsory labour, and again shall be construed in relation to Article 4(2) of the Convention that excludes from the definition of 'forced and compulsory labour' work done in the course of lawful detention; military service or service done instead of military service; work required in the case of public emergencies or calamities; and work which forms part of normal civic obligations. Article 5(3) adds an explicit prohibition on trafficking in human beings that reflects both the Europol Convention as well as the framework decision on human trafficking.[24]

Case C-404/92 *X v Commission* [1994] ECR I-4737 (AIDS test case) overruling Case T-121/89 *X v Commission* [1992] ECR II-2195.

[18] Those principles are contained in the Convention for the Protection of Human Rights and Dignity of the Human Being with regard to the application of Biology and Medicine (Oviedo Convention, ETS 164); and in its additional protocol on the Prohibition of Cloning Human Beings.

[19] Case C-377/98 *Netherlands v Council* (Biotechnology Directive) [2001] ECR I-7079.

[20] Directive 98/44/EC on the legal protection of biotechnological inventions [1998] OJ L213/13.

[21] Of course, it is then a matter of interpretation to decide what is to be defined as 'torture', 'inhuman' and 'degrading'. See eg *Ireland v UK* (Appl No 5310/71) (1979–80) 2 EHRR 25; and *Aksoy v Turkey* (Appl No 21987/93) (1997) 23 EHRR 553. See also European Convention for the Prevention of Torture (ETS 126). The House of Lords, reversing a ruling of the Court of Appeal, has stated that evidence obtained through torture or inhuman and degrading treatment is not admissible in British courts, *A and others v Secretary of State for the Home Department*, [2006] 1 All ER 575. In the EU context, this provision is of relevance in relation to the interpretation of the Asylum Directive (2004/83).

[22] See below Section III.

[23] cp *Siliadin v France* (Appl No 73316/01), Judgment of 26 July 2005.

[24] Art 2(1) Europol Convention ([1995 P] C313/2) as amended by the Protocol amending the Europol Convention [2003] OJ C2/01; cf also Framework Decision 2002/629/JHA on combating trafficking in human beings (2002) OJ L203/1 (the Commission had put forward a new proposal, see COM (2009) 136 final, although this has now been caught by the changed to co-operation in criminal matters brought about by the TL) and Council Directive 2004/81 on the residence permit issued to third-country nationals who are victims of traffick-

(ii) Title II—Freedoms

Title II of the Charter is devoted to freedoms ranging from traditional Convention rights to social rights. It includes principles which pursuant to Article 52(5) are not judicially enforceable (apart from for the assessment of legality of acts implementing them).

Article 6 provides for the right to *liberty and security* and it reproduces the first sentence of Article 5 of the ECHR. In order to understand the scope of Article 6 it is necessary to look at the Convention. Thus, Article 5(1) ECHR contains an exhaustive list of exceptions to the right to liberty which, in order to be consistent with the Convention, have to be prescribed by law.[25] Accordingly, the right to liberty might be limited because of detention following conviction by a court and lawful arrest (and there are further conditions for the detention/arrest to be consistent with the Convention); detention of a minor for educational supervision or lawful detention to bring her/him in front of the competent authority; lawful detention for medical purposes (to avoid the spreading of infectious diseases; or detention of mentally ill people, alcoholics and drug addicts and vagrants). Article 5 of the Convention also contains minimum procedural guarantees as well as the principle of compensation for unlawful detention. The explanations provide that Article 6 should be respected 'in particular' in the exercise of Union competences in criminal matters (and by Member States when they implement Union measures adopted in that field).

Article 7 provides for the right to respect for *private and family life, home and communications*. It reproduces the first sentence of Article 8 ECHR apart from using the word 'communications' rather than 'correspondence', so as to reflect technological developments.[26] Again it is impossible to understand the scope of this provision without looking at the list of legitimate limitations contained in the Convention article. Thus public authorities can interfere with the right to privacy only in accordance with the law and for listed reasons (national security, public safety; economic well-being of the country; prevention of disorder and crime; protection of health, morals or the rights and freedoms of others); the interference must in any event be limited to what is necessary in a democratic society. Article 8 ECHR has been broadly construed by the ECtHR to include interferences as diverse as the prohibition to rectify a birth certificate following gender reassignment,[27] to the right not to be separated from one's family,[28] from the right not to be subject to audio surveillance,[29] to matters relating to sexuality.[30] The Court of Justice has found that

---

ing in human beings or who have been the subject of an action to facilitate illegal immigration, who co-operate with the competent authorities [2004] OJ L261/19. The Directive does not apply to the UK, Ireland and Denmark. For a critique of the Union's approach to trafficking, see H Cullen, 'The EU and Human Trafficking: Framing a Regional Response to a Global Emergency' in A Antoniadis, R Schütze and E Spaventa (eds), *The EU and Global Emergencies* (Hart Publishing, Oxford, 2011) 225.

[25] And in order to decide whether a derogation has been prescribed by law, the ECtHR has recourse to a substantial assessment aimed at guaranteeing the rule of law and dispose of any arbitrariness, eg *Amuur v France* (Appl No 19776/92) (1996) 22 EHRR 533.

[26] cp also Case 400/10 PPU *J McB v LE*, Judgment of 5 October 2010, nyr, para 53.

[27] eg *Goodwin v UK* (2005) 35 EHRR 18; the same right was recognised by the Court of Justice in Case C-117/01 *KB* [2004] ECR I-541.

[28] eg *Elsholz v Germany* (Appl No 25735/94) (2002) 34 EHRR 58; and cf eg Case C-60/00 *Mary Carpenter* [2002] ECR I-6279; Case C-413/99 *Baumbast and R* [2002] ECR I-7091.

[29] eg *Vetter v France* (Appl No 59842/00), Judgment of 31 May 2005.

[30] eg *Smith and Grady v UK* (Appl No 33895/96 and 33896/96) (2001) 31 EHRR 24. The EU commitment to the right to privacy might well be called into question by Directive 2006/24/EC on the retention of data generated or processed in connection with the provision of publicly available electronic communications services or of public communications networks and amending Directive 2002/58/EC, [2006] OJ L105/54.

a person's name is a constituent element of her/his identity and of her/his private life, the protection of which is enshrined in Article 7.[31]

Article 8 provides for the right to the protection of *personal data*, and is a new generation right (albeit implicit in the right to privacy)[32] deriving from the TFEU and the data protection directives.[33] It provides that personal data have to be processed fairly, either for legitimate reasons provided by law or with the consent of the person concerned who shall also have access to such data and the right to have it rectified. It also provides for an independent authority that shall ensure compliance with these rules; the Union has its own authority, the European Data Protection Supervisor.

Article 9 provides for the right to *marry and the right to found a family*, in accordance with national laws. It is a modernised version of Article 12 ECHR, which states that 'men and women have a right to marry and to found a family'. By severing the right to found a family from the right to marry, and omitting any reference to the sex of the partners, Article 9 seeks to leave open the door for recognition of other types of partnerships (such as civil partnerships) and for same-sex marriages.[34] Of course, for the time being, the definition and regulation of marriage is entirely for the Member States. However, Article 9 might still be relevant when Member States implement Union law. Thus, for example, it is not clear how the right in Article 9 will relate to the Citizenship Directive,[35] which does not impose on Member States any obligation to recognise civil partnerships contracted in another Member State unless there is a domestic equivalent. The Directive does, however, impose a duty to 'facilitate' the entry of Union citizens' partners: refusing entry to a registered partner (without there being a public policy/security/health reason) could then be construed as an interference with Article 9 of the Charter that applies when Member States are implementing Union law.

Article 10 provides for freedom of *thought, conscience and religion*, and the right to change belief or religion as well as the freedom to manifest, alone or with others, religion or belief 'in worship, teaching, practice and observance'. This provision corresponds to Article 9 ECHR, and therefore the limitations provided for therein apply also in relation to Article 10 of the Charter. As a result those rights can be derogated from only when prescribed by law and to the extent to which a limitation is necessary in a democratic society

---

[31] Case C-208/09 *Ilonka Sayn-Wittgenstein*, Judgment of 22 December 2010, nyr, para 52. Note that the case concerned the application of fundamental rights to a Member State when acting within, rather than implementing, Union law. The Court has also annulled part of Regulation 1290/2005 ([2005] OJ L205/1, as later amended) and Regulation 259/2008 ([2008] OJ L76/28) which provided for the publication of the names of beneficiaries of agricultural aid of for breach of Arts 7 and 8 of the Charter, see Joined Cases C-92 and 93/09 *Volker und Markus Scheke*, Judgment of 9 November 2010, nyr.

[32] eg *Rotaru v Romania* (Appl No 28341/95), Judgment of 4 May 2000; and see Joined Cases C-465/00 and C-138 and 139/01 *Rechnungshof and others v Osterreichischer Rundfunk* [2003] ECR I-4989.

[33] Directive 95/46 on the protection of individuals with regard to the processing of personal data and on the free movement of such data [1995] OJ L281 (as amended, consolidated version available on http://eur-lex.europa.eu/LexUriServ/LexUriServ.do?uri=CONSLEG:1995L0046:20031120:EN:PDF); and Directive 2002/58 concerning the processing of personal data and the protection of privacy in the electronic communications sector [2002] OJ L201/37 (as amended, consolidated version available on http://eur-lex.europa.eu/LexUriServ/LexUriServ.do?uri=CONSLEG:2002L0058:20091219:EN:PDF).

[34] The Court of Justice refused to equate the situation of a same-sex partnership to that of a marriage in Joined Cases C-122/99 and C-125/99 *D and Sweden v Council* [2001] ECR I-4319.

[35] Directive 2004/38 on the right of citizens of the Union and their family members to move and reside freely within the territory of the Member States [2004] OJ L229/35, Art 3 and see below Chapter 16, section x; even more problematic is Directive 2003/86 on the right to family reunification [2003] OJ L251/12 which merely authorises Member States to allow long-term unmarried partners in the country for family reunification purposes (Art 4(3)).

in order to protect public safety, public order, health or morals, and for the protection of the freedom of others. Article 10(2) provides for the 'recognition' of the right of conscientious objection in accordance with national law. It is derived from national legislation and constitutional practices, and the use of the word 'recognises' suggests that the right to conscientious objection is entirely dependent upon the right provided for in domestic contexts. Article 10 has been criticised because it fails to recognise expressly the right 'not to hold a religious belief',[36] despite the fact that the ECtHR has recognised such right to be inherent in Article 9 ECHR.[37]

Article 11 provides for the right to *freedom of expression and information* which includes the right to hold opinions as well as to impart information and ideas without interference from public authorities. It corresponds to Article 10 ECHR and so any limitation to the right of expression must be prescribed by law and be limited to what is necessary in a democratic society for the protection of national security, territorial integrity, public safety, prevention of disorder and crime, protection of health and morals, reputation or rights of others (ie libel), for preventing breaches of confidence and for maintaining the authority and impartiality of the judiciary.[38] Freedom of expression entails any form (written, oral, artistic, pictorial, broadcasting, etc) and type of expression: thus, it encompasses not only freedom of the press, the freedom to hold opinions, including political opinions, but also commercial expression (and advertising in particular).[39] The General Court and the Court of Justice in the past have adjudicated on the matter in relation to publications of European Union officials that the institutions considered prejudicial to the reputation of the European Union.[40]

Article 11(2) provides that freedom and pluralism of the media shall be respected, a principle which, even though not expressly provided for in the ECHR, has been recognised as inherent in freedom of expression by both the ECtHR[41] and the Court of Justice.[42] Article 10 ECHR also recognises the possibility of licensing of broadcasting, televisions and cinemas; the explanations make clear that such possibility remains but shall be exercised consistently with Union competition law.[43]

Article 12 provides for the right to freedom of *peaceful assembly* and to *freedom of association* at all levels,[44] and in particular in *political, trade union and civic matters*, which also implies the right for everyone to join trade unions.[45] This provision corresponds to Article 11 ECHR and therefore those rights can be limited only according to the Convention's derogations. As usual those must be prescribed by law, and be necessary in a democratic

---

[36] cf Amnesty International Comments on the Draft Charter, CHARTE 4446/00, CONTRIB 300.

[37] *Buscarini and others v San Marino* (Appl No 24645/95) (2000) 30 EHRR 208.

[38] On Art 10 ECHR, cp *Handyside v UK* (Appl No 5493/72) (1970-80) 1 EHRR 737.

[39] In the Community context, see eg Case C-368/95 *Familiapress* [1997] ECR I-3689.

[40] eg Case T-34/96 and T-163/96 *Connolly v Commission* [1999] ECR II-463, [1999] ECR-SC I-A-87, upheld in Case C-274/99 P *Connolly v Commission* [2001] ECR I-1611; T-82/99 *Cwick v Commission* [2000] ECR II-713, upheld in Case C-340/00 P *Commission v Cwick* [2001] ECR I-10269; Art 17 of the Commission's Staff Regulations was amended in 2004 to guarantee a more effective right to freedom of expression (see new Art 17 and 17a which have substituted the system of prior authorisation for publication with a system of notification and silence/assent).

[41] eg *Informationsverein Lentia v Austria* (Appl Nos 13914/88, 15041/89, 15717/89, 15779/89 and 17207/90) (1994) 17 EHRR 93.

[42] cp eg Case C-288/89 *Gouda* [1991] ECR I-4007, para 23; Case C-368/95 *Familiapress* [1997] ECR I-3689, para 24.

[43] cp eg Case C-260/89 *Elliniki Radiophonia Tiléorassi AE (ERT)* [1991] ECR I-2925.

[44] cp eg Case C-112/00 *Schmidberger* [2003] ECR I-5659; Case C-415/93 *Bosman* [1995] ECR I-4921, para 79.

[45] See also Art 28 below.

society in the interest of national security, public safety, the prevention of disorder or crime, the protection of health or morals; or for the protection of the rights and freedoms of others. Lawful restrictions can be imposed on members of the armed forces, the police or the administration of the state. Article 12(2) provides that 'Political parties at Union level contribute to expressing the political will of the citizens of the Union.'[46] This provision corresponds to Article 10(4) TEU, although the latter is phrased slightly differently, mentioning also the political parties' role in forming European political awareness.

Article 13 provides that the *arts and scientific research* shall be free of constraint and that *academic freedom* shall be respected. This right is not explicitly spelled out in the Convention, but it has always been interpreted as part of freedom of expression.[47] The explanations indicate that this right shall be exercised having regard to the principle of human dignity and it shall be subject to the same limitations as contained in Article 10 ECHR.

Article 14 provides for the *right to education,* and the right to have *access to vocational and continuing training.* This corresponds to the common constitutional traditions as well as to Article 2 of the first Protocol to the ECHR. The reference to vocational and continuing training is new to the Charter. Article 14(2) provides that the right to education includes the 'possibility to receive free compulsory education'. According to the explanations, this provision means that compulsory education shall be provided free of charge by the state, and that children (and their parents) shall have the right to choose whether to take advantage of such education. Article 14(3) provides that the right to found educational establishments with due respect for democratic principles shall be recognised; the same goes for the right of the parents to choose their children's education in conformity with their religious, philosophical and pedagogical beliefs. This article is of limited importance given that the Union has only supplementary competences in the field of education.[48] Thus, it is mostly aimed at guaranteeing that the Union in its policies respects the principles enshrined in this article.

Article 15(1) provides for the right to *engage in work* and to *pursue a freely chosen* or *accepted occupation.*[49] This right has been recognised by the Court of Justice from the very first cases concerning fundamental rights protection: thus, in both *Nold* and *Hauer* the Court recognised that the (then) Community protected the right to choose an occupation, even though that right was not unfettered and could be limited in the public interest provided the substance of the right was left untouched.[50]

Article 15(2) provides for the Union citizens' right to engage in an economic activity (either in an employed or self-employed capacity) and to seek work in any of the Member States; it reproduces existing economic free movement rights contained in Articles 45, 49 and 56 TFEU, and therefore according to Article 52(2) Charter shall be exercised under the conditions and within the limits provided for in the Treaties.[51]

---

[46] cp eg Case T-222/99 *Martinez and others v Parliament* [2001] ECR II-2823.

[47] eg *Hertel v Switzerland* (Appl No 25181/94) (1999) 28 EHRR 534; *Müller v Switzerland* (Appl No 10737/84) (1991) 13 EHRR 485.

[48] Art 6 TFEU.

[49] This right is not expressly included in the ECHR but the ECtHR has included the right to pursue economic activities in the right to property provided by Art 1 of the Protocol to the ECHR, cp *Dogan and others v Turkey* (Appls Nos 8803-11/02, 8813/02, 8815-19/02) (2005) 41 EHRR 15.

[50] Case 4/73 *Nold v Commission* [1974] ECR I-491; Case 44/79 *Hauer* [1979] ECR 3727; also eg Case 234/85 *Keller* [1986] ECR I-2897.

[51] cf relevant chapters on free movement in Part IV below.

The third paragraph of Article 15 provides that third-country nationals who lawfully work in the Union are entitled to conditions of employment 'equivalent' to those of Union citizens.[52]

Article 16 (II-76) provides for the recognition of the *freedom to conduct a business* in accordance with Union law, and national law and practices.[53] Thus, Articles 15 and 16 substantially deal with the freedom to exercise an economic activity, recognised in the case law of both the Court of Justice and the ECtHR as well as in national constitutional traditions. In assessing whether a limitation to those rights is justified (eg a piece of secondary legislation that prohibits trade in a certain substance), the principle of proportionality is of particular importance.

Finally, Article 17 (II-77) provides for the right to *property* (long recognised by the Court of Justice),[54] and substantially reproduces the provisions of Article 1(1) of the first Protocol to the ECHR,[55] including the possibility of expropriation on public interest grounds subject to due compensation.[56] Furthermore, the Charter adds an express recognition of intellectual property, which shall be protected.[57] Article 17 also provides that the use of property can be *regulated* by law insofar as this is necessary for the general interest, thus codifying the case law of the Court of Justice[58] as well as common constitutional traditions and the case law of the ECtHR.[59]

As pointed out above, the Charter disposes of the traditional partition between civil and political rights on the one hand, and socioeconomic rights on the other. Thus having dealt with economic freedoms, it leaps to the right to *asylum*.[60] Article 18 provides that

---

[52] In 2001, the Commission put forward a proposal relating to the conditions of employment for third-country nationals which provided also for the right to equal treatment of lawfully resident third-country nationals: see Proposal for a Council Directive on the conditions of entry and residence of third-country nationals for the purposes of paid employment and self-employed economic activities, COM(2001) 386 final, Art 11(1)(f); however, the proposal failed to gain Council approval and was dropped. Subsequently Directive 2009/50 on the conditions of entry and residence of third-country nationals for the purposes of highly qualified employment [2009] OJ L155/17 (the so-called 'blue card directive') was adopted and Art 14 provides for equal treatment in relation to conditions of employment. This Directive does not apply to the UK, Denmark and Ireland; see also Commission Proposal for a directive on the entry and residence of third country nationals for the purposes of seasonal employment, COM(2010) 379 final.

[53] AG Kokott has interpreted the freedom to contract as part of the freedom to conduct a business in Case C-441/07 P *Commission v Alrosa*, Opinion of 17 September 2009, nyr.

[54] cf Case 44/79 *Hauer* [1979] ECR 3727.

[55] It is interesting to note that the Charter departs from the ECHR Protocol in not limiting the enjoyment of the right of property to 'peaceful enjoyment' and not mentioning the general principles of international law. Art 1(2) of the protocol explicitly provided for the right of the state to regulate property and to impose taxes, other contributions and penalties.

[56] The extent to which the right to property can be limited for reasons of public (international) interest has become very relevant following the EU implementation of UN Security Council Resolutions; see eg Case C-84/95 *Bosphorus* [1996] ECR I-3953; Case C-402 and 415 P *Kadi* [2008] ECR I-635; and Case T-85/09 *Kadi v Commission*, Judgment of 10 September 2010, nyr, where the General Court finally calls into question whether the freezing of assets of Mr Kadi, which had been in operation for 10 years, could be truly considered as a mere precautionary measure which did not affect the very substance of the right to property of the applicant. There is also a broader question as to whether such a freezing order can truly be qualified as mere administrative measures (see Art 75 TFEU); on these points, see E Spaventa 'Counter-Terrorism and Fundamental Rights: Judicial Challenges and Legislative Changes after the Rulings in *Kadi* and *PMOI*' in A Antoniadis, R Schütze and E Spaventa (eds), *The EU and Global Emergencies* (Oxford, Hart Publishing, 2011, forthcoming).

[57] cf also Art 30 TEC.

[58] eg Case 44/79 *Hauer* [1979] ECR 3727.

[59] Eg *Mellacher and others v Austria* (Appl Nos 10522/83, 10011/84 and 11070/84) (1990) 12 EHRR 391.

[60] cp also Joint Position 96/196/JHA on the harmonised application of the definition of the term 'refugee' in Art 1 of the Geneva Convention of 28 July 1951 relating to the status of refugees, [1996] OJ L63/2; Council Directive 2003/9 laying down minimum standards for the reception of asylum seekers [2003] OJ L31/18 (the

such a right shall be guaranteed with due respect to the rules of the Geneva Convention on refugees and in accordance with the TEU and the TFEU. Respect for the Geneva Convention is already a precondition for the exercise of Union competence pursuant to Article 78 TFEU.[61] According to the Protocol on Asylum,[62] Member States' nationals cannot, as a matter of principle, obtain asylum in any of the Member States, since the Member States are satisfied that the level of fundamental rights protection within the Union is adequate and therefore each Member State constitutes a 'safe country of origin' for asylum purposes. The only cases in which an asylum request from a national of a Member State can be taken into account is when (i) the Member State of origin is derogating from the ECHR pursuant to Article 15 ECHR; (ii) the procedure provided for in Article 7(1) TEU (procedure relating to a clear risk of a serious breach of fundamental rights) has been initiated; (iii) the Council has determined the existence of a clear risk of a serious breach of fundamental rights pursuant Article 7(1) TEU or of a serious and persistent breach pursuant to Article 7(2) TEU; (iv) the Member State so decides unilaterally, in which case the Council shall be informed immediately and the application shall be dealt with on the basis of the presumption of being 'manifestly unfounded' (although the receiving Member State retains the final decision on the matter).

Finally, Article 19 provides for protection in the event of *removal, expulsion* and *extradition*. It prohibits collective expulsions, as well as deportation in cases in which there is a serious risk that the person removed would be subjected to the death penalty, or to torture or inhuman and degrading treatment or punishment. This is consistent with the prohibition of the death penalty contained in Article 2 and the prohibition on torture and inhuman treatment contained in Article 4, as well as with the case law of the ECtHR.[63] As a result the Union would not be able to enter into extradition agreements with countries which practise the death penalty, without inserting appropriate safeguards.

(iii) Title III— Equality

Title III is concerned with equality, and accordingly Article 20 provides that *everyone is equal before the law*. The principle of equality requires that comparable situations should be treated equally, and that non-comparable situations should be treated in different ways; it corresponds to established constitutional traditions in all of the Member States, and has been recognised by the case law of the Court of Justice.[64]

Article 21 provides for the more general prohibition of *discrimination*. The provision

---

UK has opted in this directive); Council Regulation 343/2003 establishing the criteria and mechanisms for determining the Member State responsible for examining an asylum application lodged in one of the Member States by a third-country national [2003] OJ L50/1 (the UK and Ireland have both opted in); and Council Directive 2005/85 on minimum standards on procedures for granting and withdrawing refugee status [2005] OJ L326/13.

[61] On the position of the UK and Ireland, see Protocol (No 21) of the United Kingdom and Ireland in respect of the Area of Freedom, Security and Justice. For a partial blow to the EU Asylum policy, see the ECtHR ruling in *MSS v Belgium and Greece* (Appl No 30696/09), Judgment of 21 January 2011.

[62] Protocol (No 24) on Asylum for Nationals of Member States of the European Union (originally added by the Treaty of Amsterdam).

[63] eg *Soering v UK* (Appl No 14038/88) (1989) 11 EHRR 439; in *D v UK* (Appl No 30240/96) (1997) 24 EHRR 423, the ECtHR accepted the applicant's contention that his removal from the UK would constitute inhuman treatment prohibited by Art 3 ECHR since he was terminally ill with AIDS and he would not receive adequate treatment and care in his country of origin.

[64] eg Case 283/83 *Racke* [1984] ECR 3791; Case C-15/91 *EARL* [1997] ECR I-1961; Case C-292/97 *Karlsson* [2000] ECR 2737; post-Charter, see eg Case C-208/09 *Ilonka Sayn-Wittgenstein*, Judgment of 22 December 2010.

contains a non-exhaustive list of prohibited grounds of discrimination, ie sex, race,[65] colour, ethnic or social origin, genetic features, language,[66] religion or belief,[67] political or any other opinion, membership of a national minority, property, birth, disability,[68] age[69] and sexual orientation.[70] It is thus slightly broader in scope than Article 19 TFEU which provides for competence to adopt measures intended to fight discrimination on grounds of sex, racial or ethnic origin, religion or belief, disability, age or sexual orientation.[71] Surprisingly, Article 21 does not explicitly mention gender discrimination, which is a broader concept than sex discrimination and encompasses in a clearer way also discrimination against transsexuals. Discrimination against transsexuals has been to a certain extent equated by the Court of Justice to sex discrimination and therefore Article 21, which in any case is not exhaustive,[72] prohibits also that type of discrimination. It could be argued, however, that, given that the Charter should make rights more visible to the citizen, it would have been appropriate for Article 21 to state this explicitly.

Article 21(2) prohibits discrimination on grounds of nationality: however, like Article 18 TFEU, this applies only within the scope of the Treaties, and subject to the conditions contained therein;[73] it is thus mainly a right pertaining to Union citizens.

Article 22 requires the Union to respect *cultural, religious* and *linguistic* diversity. It is a very likely example of a 'principle' which, according to Article 52(5), is judicially cognisable only in interpreting acts of the Union institutions and acts of the Member States implementing Union law, and in assessing the validity of such acts. In other words Article 22, differently from Article 21, seems not to constitute a free standing right.

Article 23 is based on, and substantially duplicates, existing TEU and TFEU provisions.[74] It provides for additional protection against *sex discrimination*: thus, despite the

---

[65] eg Case C-54/07 *Feryn* [2008] ECR I-5187.

[66] But in the field of employment conditions relating to linguistic knowledge required by the nature of the post are allowed, see Art 3 Regulation 1612/68 on freedom of movement for workers within the Community (as amended) [1968] OJ Sp Edn L257/2, and the Treaty does not prohibit a policy for the protection and the promotion of a language of a Member State, see Case 379/87 *Groener* [1989] ECR 3967.

[67] See Case 130/75 *Prais v Council* [1976] ECR 1589.

[68] See Case C-303/06 *Coleman* [2008] ECR I-5603.

[69] On discrimination on grounds of age, see eg Case C-144/04 *Mangold* [2005] ECR I-9981; Case C-388/07 *Age Concern England* [2009] ECR I-1569; Case C-55/07 *Kücükdeveci*, judgment Of 19 January 2010, nyr; Joined Cases C-250 and 268/09 *Georgiev*, Judgment of 12 November 2010, nyr .

[70] See eg Case C-267/06 *Maruko* [2008] ECR I-1757; pre-Directive 2000/78 establishing a general framework for equal treatment in employment and occupation [2000] OJ L303/16, discrimination on grounds of sexual orientation was excluded from the scope of the prohibition of discrimination on grounds of sex (and therefore from the scope of the Treaty) in Case C-249/96 *Grant v South West Trains Ltd* [1998] ECR I-621 and the Court had given a restrictive interpretation, arguably inconsistent with ECHR case law (*Salgueiro da Silva Mouta v Portugal* (Appl No 33290/96), (1999) EHRR 176), also in relation to the EU institutions, see Joined Cases C-122/99 and C-125/99 *D and Sweden v Council* [2001] ECR I-4319. Following the adoption of Art 19 TFEU and the ruling in Case C-144/04 *Mangold* [2005] ECR I-9981and Case C-55/07 *Kücükdeveci*, Judgment of 19 January 2010, nyr, it is possible that discrimination on grounds of sexual orientation is also prohibited as a general principle of Union law, see Chapter 11 above.

[71] Two Directives have so far been adopted using the competence conferred in Art 19 TFEU: Directive 2000/43 implementing the principle of equal treatment between persons irrespective of racial or ethnic origin [2000] OJ L180/22; and Directive 2000/78 establishing a general framework for equal treatment in employment and occupation [2000] OJ L303/16.

[72] Case C-13/94 *P v S Cornwall County Council* [1996] ECR I-2143; Case C-117/01 *K.B.* [2004] ECR I-541.

[73] See Chapter 15, esp section IV.A, and Chapters 16 and 17.

[74] cf Art 3(3) TEU, and Arts 8 and 157 TFEU, implemented through Directive 76/207 on the implementation of the principle of equal treatment for men and women as regards access to employment, vocational training and promotion, and working conditions [1976] OJ L39/40, as amended by Directive 2002/73 [2002] OJ L269/15 (see in particular Art 2(8), previously Art 2(4)); see eg Case 43/75 *Defrenne v Sabena* (Defrenne II) [1976] ECR 455, and Case C-50/96 *Deutsche Telekom AG v Lilli Schröder* [2000] ECR I-743, where the Court clarified that the

fact that discrimination on grounds of sex is already prohibited by Article 21, Article 23 provides that 'equality between women and men must be ensured in all areas, including employment, work and pay'. Article 23 is broader in scope than Article 157 TFEU, since it applies also beyond the field of employment.

Article 23(2) provides that 'the principle of equality shall not prevent the maintenance or the adoption of measures providing for specific advantages for the under represented sex'.[75] Therefore, consistently with Article 157(4) TFEU,[76] the Union and the Member States when implementing Union law are allowed to enact 'positive discrimination', ie measures aimed at achieving substantive rather than just formal equality between the sexes. In the context of employment, the Court has imposed two conditions which must be satisfied if positive discrimination measures are to be compatible with the general principle of equality: such measures cannot give priority automatically and uncondition-ally to the underrepresented sex; and they must also allow for an objective assessment of the specific personal situations of all candidates.[77] This is the case since such measures derogate from the (formal) principle of equality, and therefore have to comply with the principle of proportionality, ie remain within the limits of what is necessary to achieve the purported aim (substantive equality). Thus, for instance, a measure that provides that if men and women are equally qualified for a job, precedence should be given to the woman if women are underrepresented in that job, is inconsistent with Union law since it is 'absolute' and 'unconditional' in its application.[78] However, rules that provide that when women are underrepresented and a woman and a man candidate are equally qualified, the woman shall be granted preferential treatment unless there are other considerations that might tilt the balance in favour of the male candidate, are compatible with the principle of equal treatment.[79] In other words, in order to be compatible with Union law, a positive discrimination policy must always allow for an objective assessment of the specific per-sonal circumstances of all candidates. Since, as said above, Article 23 partially reproduces existing TFEU provisions, it must be exercised under the conditions and according to the limits provided therein.

It could well be questioned whether Article 23 was really necessary: on the one hand, by singling out sex discrimination, it weakens the general prohibition on discrimination contained in Article 21. On the other hand, the relationship between Articles 21 and 23 is made more difficult because, unlike Article 23, Article 21 does not contain a provision authorising 'positive action'. Such positive action, however, is authorised by the race and ethnic origin anti-discrimination directive,[80] and by the framework anti-discrimination directive.[81] The result is thus confusing, also given that the anti-discrimination direc-

---

economic aim of sex equality is secondary to its social aim, which constitutes the expression of a 'fundamental human right' (para 57). As mentioned above, discrimination on grounds of gender reassignment has been held to constitute discrimination on grounds of sex, see Case C-13/94 *P v S Cornwall County Council* [1996] ECR I-2143 and Case C-117/01 *KB* [2004] ECR I-541.

[75] Emphasis added.

[76] This provision was introduced with the Treaty of Amsterdam.

[77] cf recently Case C-319/03 *Briheche* [2004] ECR I-8807, esp paras 22–24; for an interesting ruling on sub-stantial equality, see also Case C-104/09 *Álvarez*, Judgment of 30 September 2010, nyr.

[78] Case C-450/93 *Kalanke* [1995] ECR I-3051; more recently in a different context Case C-104/09 *Álvarez*, Judgment of 30 September 2010, nyr.

[79] See Case C-158/97 *Badek and others* [2000] ECR I-1875; and Case C-409/95 *Marschall* [1997] ECR I-6363.

[80] Directive 2000/43 implementing the principle of equal treatment between persons irrespective of racial or ethnic origin [2000] OJ L180/22.

[81] Directive 2000/78 establishing a general framework for equal treatment in employment and occupation [2000] OJ L303/16.

tives pre-date both the completion and the proclamation of the Charter. Thus, it could be argued that the fact that the Charter refers to the possibility to enact positive measures to achieve substantive equality in relation only to sex discrimination precludes the possibility of enacting such measures in relation to other form of discrimination (and eventually would even invalidate the positive action clauses in the directives). Or, which is preferable and consistent with existing case law,[82] it could be argued that Article 23(2) is redundant since the principle of equal treatment must always be interpreted as aimed at achieving substantive and not only formal equality.[83]

Article 24 provides for the *rights of the child*. Article 24(1) provides that children

> shall have the right to such protection and care as it is necessary for their well-being. They may express their views freely. Such views shall be taken into consideration on matters which concern them in accordance to their age and maturity.

Article 24(2) lays down the general principle that public authorities and private institutions must take the child's best interests as the primary consideration. Article 24(3) provides that children shall have a right to maintain a personal relationship and contact with both parents, unless that is contrary to the child's interests.[84] Whilst family law falls primarily within the competence of the Member States, this Article is relevant in relation to cases of cross-border divorce, ie when the parents end up living in different countries.[85] In relation to Union citizenship, the Court had already found that a third-country national who is the primary carer of a Union citizen who has not reached the age of majority and who has the right to reside in the host Member State, derives from his/her child a right to reside in the same Member State.[86] The Charter provision is broader since it refers to the right of the child to maintain contact with both parents, and not only with the carer. Consistently, Article 13 of Directive 2004/34 provides for the right of residence of both the parent who has custody of a child having the right of residence pursuant to the Directive, and of the parent who has access to a minor child.[87]

Article 25 deals with the *rights of the elderly*, and provides that the Union recognises and respects the rights of the elderly to lead a life of 'dignity and independence and to participate in social and cultural life'. According to the explanations, this is a mere prin-

---

[82] The Court of Justice has accepted the compatibility of positive action with equal treatment even before the TA entered into force, see Case C-409/95 *Marschall* [1997] ECR I-6363.

[83] See generally E Ellis, *EU Anti-Discrimination Law* (Oxford, Oxford University Press, 2005); S Fredman, *Discrimination law* (Oxford, Oxford University Press, 2001).

[84] The Court has found that legislation that automatically grants custody of the children to the natural mother whilst the father must apply for a court judgment in order to obtain rights of custody is not incompatible with Art 24, see Case 400/10 PPU *J McB v LE*, Judgment of 5 October 2010, nyr. A rather restrictive interpretation of this right was given in Case C-540/03 *Parliament v Council* (family reunification) [2006] ECR I-5769, where the Court found that Art 24 together with Art 7 (right to family life) do not create for the members of a family the right to enter the territory of a Member State (para 59).

[85] See also Council Regulation 2201/2003 concerning jurisdiction and the recognition and enforcement of judgments in matrimonial matters and the matters of parental responsibility, repealing Regulation (EC) No 1347/2000, [2003] OJ L338/1; and see Case C-211/10 *Povse*, Judgment of 1 July 2010, nyr; Case C-491/10 PPU *Aguirre Zarraga v Pelz*, Judgment of 22 December 2010, nyr. The Court has been criticised for its rigid adherence to principles concerning conflict of jurisdiction/*lis pendens* which might come at the expense of the best interests of the child; see generally H Stalford, 'EU Law and Children's Rights: A Case Study of EU Family Law' (2010) 10 *Contemporary Issues in Law* 25.

[86] eg Case C-413/99 *Baumbast and R* [2002] ECR I-7091; Case C-200/02 *Chen and others* [2004] ECR I-9925; Case C-310/08 *Ibrahim*, Judgment of 23 February 2010, nyr; Case C-480/08 *Teixeirai*, Judgment of 23 February 2010, nyr. See Chapter 16 below.

[87] Directive 2004/38 on the right of citizens of the Union and their family members to move and reside freely within the territory of the Member States [2004] OJ L229/35.

ciple rather than a free-standing right; however, as we saw in the previous chapter, the right not to be discriminated against on grounds of age has been elevated to the status of a general principle of Union law by the European Court of Justice.[88]

Article 26 provides for the *integration of persons with disabilities*, according to which the 'Union recognises and respects the right of people with disabilities to benefit from measures designed to ensure their independence, social and occupational integration and participation in the life of the community.' The explanations to the Charter clarify that Article 26 constitutes a principle rather than a right.

(iv) Title IV—Solidarity

Title IV is concerned with solidarity, and most of the rights listed therein are in fact 'principles' that must inspire the Union's legislative action rather than free-standing rights.[89] As mentioned above, Article 52(5) clarifies that in the case of 'principles', judicial proceedings can be brought only to challenge Union action, or its implementation by the Member States, on the grounds that the Union/implementing Member State failed to comply with one of the stated principles. Solidarity rights are in most cases merely inspirational, ie they are not free-standing rights. Most of the rights/principles listed in this part derive from the European Social Charter, like the ECHR an instrument of the Council of Europe,[90] and from the Community charter on the rights of workers, a soft law instrument adopted through a declaration by all of the Member States.[91]

Article 27 provides for *workers' right to information and consultation* within the undertaking. The Charter does not detail the extent of workers' right to be informed, rather referring to Union law and national laws and practices. There is an extensive body of Union secondary legislation which provides for workers' right to consultation, and the basic principle is that workers (or their representatives) should be informed and/or consulted in relation to all events relating to the undertaking that might have an impact on the workers' employment situation. These include the economic situation and the development of the undertaking; structural developments and changes especially when there is a threat to employment or when it is likely that there are going to be substantial changes in the organisation of the work or in contractual relations;[92] when there is a transfer of undertaking;[93] or when the employer is contemplating collective redundancies.[94]

---

[88] Case C-144/04 *Mangold* [2005] ECR I-0000.

[89] For the position of the UK and Poland (and the Czech Republic in due course) see the discussion on the UK and Polish Protocol in Section IV below.

[90] The ECtHR does not have jurisdiction over the Social Charter, and the mechanisms for enforcement are different from those relating to the ECHR.

[91] Originally the UK did not sign up to the Charter; however, it did so in 1998.

[92] Council Directive 2002/14 establishing a general framework for informing and consulting employees in the European Community [2002] OJ L80/29. In relation to Union scale undertakings and Union scale groups of undertakings, see Directive 2009/38 on the establishment of European Works Council or a procedure in Community-scale undertakings or Community-scale groups of undertakings for the purposes of informing and consulting employees [2009] OJ L122/28 (Art 17 of which repeals Directive 94/45 [1994] OJ L254/64 as from the 11 June 2011), and Case C-440/00 *Kühne and Nagel* [2004] ECR I-887. The ECtHR has held that Art 11 ECHR (freedom of association) encompasses a right for trade unions to be heard, but not the right for trade unions to be treated in a particular way, and leaves it to the Member States to decide the means by which to secure the right to be heard; see *National Union of Belgian Police v Belgium* (Appl No 4464/70), (1979–80) 1 EHRR 578.

[93] cf Art 7 Directive 2001/23 on the approximation of the laws of the Member States relating to the safeguarding of employees' rights in the event of transfer of undertakings, business, or parts of undertakings or business [2001] OJ L82/16.

[94] Directive 98/59 on the approximation of the laws of the Member States relating to collective redundan-

Generally speaking, the promotion of dialogue between employers and labour, of which the Union secondary legislation is clearly an expression, is one of the aims of EU social policy (Article 151 TFEU), and Article 153 TFEU expressly confers on the Union complementary competence in relation to information and consultation of workers.[95]

Article 28 provides for the right of *collective bargaining and action*: thus workers and employers have the right to negotiate and enter into collective agreements as well as the right to collective action, including the right to strike. Those rights must be exercised in accordance with Union and national law, and it is the latter which regulates the conditions for the right to strike; thus, at least in theory, for the time being this provision is directly relevant only in relation to the duties of the Union institutions as employers.[96] Whilst the right to strike is not recognised explicitly by the ECHR (since this is concerned with civil and political rights), Article 11 on freedom of association recognises the right to form and join trade unions,[97] and the ECtHR has recognised that, at least to a certain extent, the right to strike is inherent in Article 11.[98] Furthermore the right to collective bargaining and action are also recognised by the European Social Charter, the Community Social Charter,[99] several International Labour Organisation instruments,[100] as well as several of the national constitutions.[101] As we have seen in the previous chapter, the right to take collective action might interfere with other Union fundamental rights and, in particular, with the free-movement provisions.[102]

Article 29 provides for *free access to placement services*. The right to placement services, based on existing provisions of the European and Community Social Charters,[103] is seen as a condition for the effective exercise of the right to work, and in order to increase workers' mobility (and their chances of finding employment) the Commission has established the European Employment Services (EURES),[104] a network for the exchange of

cies [1998] OJ L225/16; on the extent to which the trade unions must be involved in those circumstances, see eg Case C-383/92 *Commission v UK* [1994] ECR I-2435.

[95] See Chapter 5 above.

[96] Case C-438/05 *International Transport Workers' Federation and The Finnish Seamen's Union v Viking Line et al* [2007] ECR I-10779; and Case C-341/05 *Laval un Partneri* [2007] ECR I-11767, discussed in the previous chapter, were concerned with the right to strike as a general principle of EU law since the Member State was not implementing Union law. For the right to strike against Union institutions, see Joined Cases 44, 46 and 49/74 *ML Acton v Commission* [1975] ECR 383; Joined Cases T-576–582/93 *M Browet and others v Commission* [1994] ECR II-677, IA-191. On the rights of trade unions see Case T-349/00 *Lebedef v Commission* [2001] ECR II-1031, IA-225, where the CFI annulled the new operational rules because one of the trade unions had been left out of the negotiations.

[97] And the Member States' positive obligation to protect those rights include an obligation to prohibit employers from providing financial incentives to employees who forfeit their right to be represented by trade unions: see *Wilson and National Union of Journalists v UK* (Appl No 30668/96, 30671/96, 30678/96) [2002] 35 EHRR 20.

[98] *Schmidt and Dahlström v Sweden* (Appl No 5589/72) [1978-9] 1 EHRR 632.

[99] Art 6 and paras 12–14, respectively.

[100] eg ILO Declaration on Fundamental Principles and Rights at Work, June 1998.

[101] eg Art 39 of the Italian Constitution; Art 27 of the Czech Constitution; Art 28 of the Spanish Constitution; paras 8 and 9 of the Preamble to the French Constitution; Art 54 of the Portuguese Constitution.

[102] Case C-438/05 *International Transport Workers' Federation and The Finnish Seamen's Union v Viking Line et al* [2007] ECR I-10779; Case C-341/05 *Laval un Partneri* [2007] ECR I-11767..

[103] Art 1(3) European Social Charter; point 13 of the Community Charter of the Fundamental Social Rights of Workers.

[104] Commission Decision 2003/8 implementing of Council Regulation (EEC) No 1612/68 as regards the clearance of vacancies and applications for employment [2003] OJ L5/16; this repealed the original Commission Decision 93/569 on the implementing of Council Regulation (EEC) No 1612/68 on freedom of movement for workers within the Community as regards, in particular, as regards the clearance of vacancies and applications for employment, establishing a network entitled EURES (European Employment Services) [1993] OJ L274/32.

information in relation to employment services aimed at increasing workers' mobility.[105] There has been considerable debate as to whether such right should have been included in a fundamental rights Charter, and indeed it is not clear that this is a free-standing right rather than a principle.

Article 30 provides for the right to *protection in the event of unjustified dismissal*; this right must be exercised in accordance with Union and national laws. Article 30 thus provides that the worker has a right to a judicial remedy, ie the right to review, as well as the right to compensation or reinstatement, in relation to unjustified dismissal. This right is enshrined in several of the workers' protection directives.[106]

Article 31 provides for the right to *fair and just working conditions*. This encompasses the right to working conditions that respect health, safety and dignity of the worker, as provided in Directive 89/391 on safety and health at work;[107] and the right to maximum working hours, the right to daily and weekly rest periods, and the right to an annual period of paid leave, as guaranteed by the working time Directive.[108] The right to dignity at work encompasses the right not to be harassed, especially, but not only, sexually and racially (also provided by secondary legislation),[109] as well as the right not to be discriminated against.

Article 32 deals with the rights of children and young people in the context of employment. Thus, it lays down a general prohibition of *child labour*, and establishes that the minimum age for admission to employment should not be lower than the minimum school leaving age, except for limited derogations. Directive 94/33 on the protection of young people at work[110] provides that in any event the minimum age for work shall be no less than 15 (or higher if the leaving school age is higher), although Member States may provide for limited exceptions for children of at least 14 and 13 years of age (Article 4). The derogations concern employment for the purposes of cultural, sporting or advertising activities. Article 32(2) provides for the protection of *young people at work*; thus minors admitted to work need to be afforded working conditions appropriate to their age and need to be protected against economic exploitation as well as from any work which would harm their safety, their health or their physical, mental, moral or social development or interfere with their education. Article 32 might be relevant in informing the Union's external policy: thus, for instance, the Union provides for a system of bonus tar-

---

[105] See EURES Charter, [2003] OJ C106/03.

[106] eg Directive 2001/23 relating to the safeguarding of employees' rights in the event of transfers of undertakings, business or parts of undertakings or businesses [2001] OJ L82/16.

[107] Directive 89/391 on the introduction of measures to encourage improvements in the safety and health of workers at work [1989] OJ L183/1, as amended, consolidated version http://eur-lex.europa.eu/LexUriServ/LexUriServ.do?uri=CONSLEG:1989L0391:20081211:EN:PDF; see also Communication from the Commission 'Adapting to Change in Work and Society: A New Community Strategy on Health and safety at Work 2002–2006' COM(2002) 118 final.

[108] Directive 2003/88 concerning certain aspects of the organization of working time (which repealed Directive 93/104) [2003] OJ L299/9.

[109] See Directive 2000/43 implementing the principle of equal treatment between persons irrespective of racial or ethnic origin [2000] OJ L180/22, Art 2(3); and Directive 2000/78 establishing a general framework for equal treatment in employment and occupation [2000] OJ L303/16, Art 2(3); Directive 76/207 on the implementation of the principle of equal treatment for men and women as regards access to employment, vocational training and promotion, and working conditions [1976] OJ L39/40, as amended by Directive 2002/73 [2002] OJ L269/15, Art 2(2) third indent.

[110] Directive 94/33 on the protection of children at work [1994] OJ L216/12, as amended, consolidated version: http://eur-lex.europa.eu/LexUriServ/LexUriServ.do?uri=CONSLEG:1994L0033:20070628:EN:PDF.

iffs for developing countries which respect given ILO Conventions, including Convention 138 on the minimum age for work.[111]

Article 33 provides for the right to *family and professional life*, and it states that the family shall enjoy legal, economic and social protection. Paragraph 2 details this by providing that, in order to reconcile family and professional life, everyone has the right to protection from dismissal for reasons connected with maternity, as well as the right to paid maternity leave and to parental leave following the birth or adoption of a child.[112] This maternity and parental protection is based on existing Union legislation;[113] it should be remembered that dismissal on grounds of pregnancy constitutes direct discrimination on grounds of sex and is therefore also prohibited by Articles 21 and 23.[114] Parental leave is available to men as well as women, although it does not need to be paid. It is interesting to note that the Ombudsman relied also on this provision of the Charter to initiate an investigation on the Commission's failure to provide for parental leave.[115]

Article 34 provides for the right to *social security and social assistance*. Article 34(1) provides for the recognition of entitlement to several social security benefits, whilst Article 34(2) provides that everyone (ie not only Union citizens) residing and moving legally within the Union is entitled to social benefits and social advantages. Union migrant workers are entitled to social advantages and benefits at the same level as host country citizens and are also entitled to export some social security benefits to the Member State they move to in order not to lose entitlement because of their migration.[116] As for third-country nationals, they are also, to a certain extent, protected by Union law.[117]

Article 34(3) recognises the right to social assistance and housing, so as to ensure a decent existence for those who lack sufficient resources; this right is to be exercised in accordance with Union and national law. As we shall see in Chapter 15, Union citizens who are not economically active have only limited entitlement to draw on the social assistance system of a Member State other than that of their nationality.

Article 35 provides for the right to *health care* and states that everyone has the right to access preventive health care and medical treatment under the conditions established by national law and practices. It should be recalled that the Union has only supplementary

---

[111] Regulation 1154/98 applying the special incentive arrangements concerning labour rights and environmental protection provided for in Arts 7 and 8 of Regulations No 3281/94 and No 1256/96 applying multi-annual schemes of generalised tariff preferences in respect of certain industrial and agricultural products originating in developing countries [1998] OJ L160/1; on the possible problems arising from imposing Charter values in the EU external policis, see J Wounters 'The EU Charter of Fundamental Rights—Some Reflections on its external dimension' (2001) *MJ* special issue on the Charter, 3.

[112] The Court has clarified that this right does not entail a right to double parental leave in the case of birth of twins, see Case C-149/10 *Chatzi*, Judgment of 16 September 2010, nyr.

[113] See Directive 92/85 on the introduction of measures to encourage improvements in the safety and health of work of pregnant workers and workers who have recently given birth or are breast-feeding [1992] OJ L348/91, as amended, consolidated version: http://eur-lex.europa.eu/LexUriServ/LexUriServ.do?uri=CONSLEG:1992L00 85:20070627:EN:PDF; Council Directive 2010/18 implementing the revised Framework Agreement on parental leave concluded by BUSINESSEUROPE, UEAPME, CEEP and ETUC and repealing Directive 96/34/EC, [2010] OJ L68/13.

[114] See eg Case 177/88 *Dekker* [1990] ECR I-394; Case C-32/93 *Webb* [1994] ECR I-3567; and also Art 2(7) Directive 76/207, as amended by Directive 2002/73.

[115] See European Ombudsman press release 19/2001, and decision OI/4/2001/ME.

[116] Regulation 883/2004 on the co-ordination of social security systems [2004] OJ L166/1; see generally Chapter 16 below.

[117] Regulation 1231/2010 extending Regulation 883/2004 and Regulation 987/2009 to nationals of third countries who are not already covered by these Regulations solely on the ground of their nationality [2010] OJ L344/1.

competence in relation to the protection and improvement of health (Article 6 TFEU).[118] Thus, the first part of Article 35 is of very limited application, and might be primarily relevant in the interpretation of secondary Union legislation.[119] The second part of the same article reproduces Article 168(1) TFEU by providing that a high level of health protection shall be ensured in the definition and implementation of all health policies.[120]

Article 36 recognises *access to services of general economic interest as provided by* national law and practices and in accordance with the Treaties, in order to promote the social and territorial cohesion of the Union. This provision draws on Article 14 TFEU which also provides that Member States and the Union shall take care that 'such services operate on the basis of principles and conditions which enable them to fulfil their mission'. Services of general economic interest include postal and telecommunication services, water and electricity, transportation services, etc. It should be noted that Article 36 does not provide a right to such services: rather, like Article 14 TFEU, it is aimed at informing Union policy and at ensuring that liberalisation of such services does not come at the expense of citizens' access to them.

Article 37 provides that a *high level of environmental protection* and the improvement of the environment must be integrated into the policies of the Union and ensured in accordance with the principle of sustainable development. This provision is based on existing Treaty provisions, in particular Article 191 TFEU, and, like the preceding two Articles, is a good example of a 'principle', ie it is not a free-standing right but is 'judicially cognisable' only in assessing the validity of Union secondary legislation and Member States' implementing measures.

Finally, Article 38 provides that Union policies shall ensure a *high level of consumer protection*. This 'principle' draws on Article 169 TFEU. The inclusion of the provisions relating to services of general economic interest, environmental protection and consumer protection in a fundamental rights document has been criticised as not relevant to such document. Thus, it could be argued that the main interests that those Articles seek to achieve are already protected elsewhere in the Treaties; and that a repetition is confusing and, in many respects, misleading since those principles are of very limited application as far as citizens are concerned.[121] As we have seen, this is a criticism that applies throughout the Charter.

(v) Title V—Citizens' rights

Title V deals with Union citizens' rights. It reproduces existing rights contained in the Treaties, in secondary legislation or emerging from the Court's case law. Those rights are

---

[118] There are some very limited exceptions, see Art 168(4) TFEU. This does not mean that Union law does not impact on health-care provision; apart from Art 20 Regulation 883/2004, the Court has interpreted Art 56 TFEU as granting a (limited) right to seek treatment abroad at the expenses of the state of origin, eg Case C-157/99 *Geraets-Smits* and *Peerbooms v Stichting* [2001] ECR I-5473; Case C-385/99 *Müller Fauré* and *van Riet* [2003] ECR I-4509; Case C-372/04 *Watts* [2006] ECR I4325. See also Proposal for a Directive on patients' rights to cross-border healthcare, COM(2008) 414. See Chapter 17 below.

[119] eg Art 20 Regulation 883/2004.

[120] See Commission Communication on the Precautionary Principle, (2000) COM 1 final.

[121] Not least because of the restrictive rules on standing; the requirement to prove individual concern makes it impossible to bring actions at Union level for the protection of diffuse interests, such as environmental protection; cp Case T-585/93 *Greenpeace* [1995] ECR II-2205 upheld in appeal Case C-321/95 P *Greenpeace* [1998] ECR I-1651.

dealt with extensively in Chapter 15; for this reason it is sufficient to provide a brief list of the rights contained in the Charter. The latter lists as citizens' rights: electoral rights (the right to vote and to stand as a candidate at elections of the European Parliament and at municipal elections);[122] rights to good administration (good administration, access to documents, European ombudsman, right to petition);[123] rights to free movement and residence;[124] and the right to diplomatic and consular protection.[125] Those rights have the same scope as the rights contained in the TFEU.

(vi) Title VI—Justice

Title VI deals with rights concerning the administration of justice. It draws primarily on the ECHR, the common constitutional traditions and the case law of the Court of Justice of the European Union.

Article 47 provides for the right to *an effective remedy and to a fair trial*, and is based on Articles 6 and 13 of the ECHR.[126] Consistently with the Charter's scope, its application is limited to violation of rights and freedoms guaranteed by Union law, and it provides that in relation to the latter, everyone has the right to an effective remedy before a tribunal (which is here used in the continental sense of any court of law, not in the more limited English sense).[127]

The explanations to the Charter make clear that this Article does not 'intend' to change the system of judicial review laid down in the Treaties and in particular the rules on standing (Article 263 TFEU). As we have seen in Chapter 6, those are rather strict, even after the amendments introduced by the TL.

Article 47(2) provides for the right to a fair and public hearing within a reasonable time, by an independent tribunal previously established by law, and for the right to be advised, defended and represented. This is a codification of existing case law, since the Court of Justice has been called on several times, especially in competition law proceedings,[128] to adjudicate as to the compatibility of the Union system of judicial protection with the principles of a fair trial. However, and as we saw in the previous chapter, there are open questions regarding the extent to which some of the features of the Union institutional framework satisfy the standard required to guarantee the right to effective judicial protection. This might be the case for the role of the Commission in administering heavy fines for breaches of competition law; and for the lack of a right to respond to the Advocate General's opinion in direct proceedings.

---

[122] Arts 39 and 40 Charter.

[123] Arts 41–44 Charter.

[124] Art 45 Charter.

[125] Art 46 Charter.

[126] The right to an effective remedy has been long recognised by the Court, especially in relation to national rules implementing Union legislation or national rules relating to rights conferred by Union law; eg Case 222/84 *Johnston v Chief Constable of Royal Ulster* [1986] ECR 1651; Case 222/86 *Heylens* [1987] ECR 4097. The Court has held that Art 47 Charter prevents an interpretation according to which a business cannot raise objections at the judicial stage of competition proceedings if those had not been raised at the administrative stage, Case C-407/08 P *Knauf Gips v Commission*, Judgment of 1 July 2010, nyr.

[127] On the scope of Art 47, see Case C-279/09 *DEB Deutsche Energiehandels- und Beratungsgesellschaft mbH*, Judgment of 22 December 2010, nyr.

[128] See Chapter 1, section I above; eg Case C-185/95 P *Baustahlgewebe v Commission* [1998] ECR I-8417.

Article 47(3) provides that 'legal aid shall be made available for those who lack sufficient resources insofar as such aid is necessary to ensure effective access to justice'. Article 94 of the rules of procedure of the General Court provides that legal aid shall be granted to those who, because of their economic circumstances, are unable to meet, wholly or in part, the costs of the procedure, unless the action is manifestly unfounded or manifestly inadmissible.[129] The application for legal aid suspends the passing of time for bringing an action, and the decision as to the availability of legal aid is taken by the President of the Court by means of an order, which cannot be appealed. For proceedings before the Court of Justice of the European Union the decision concerning legal aid is taken by a formation of the Court after having heard the Advocate General and the Judge Rapporteur's proposal. The Court decides by means of an order and takes into consideration whether there is 'manifestly no cause of action'.[130] Since the Charter applies to Member States when they implement Union law, legal aid shall be available as a matter of Union law in relation to litigation concerning Member States' implementation of Directives and Regulations, as well as in relation to cross-border litigation following the adoption of Directive 2003/8.[131] For instance, in the case of *DEB Deutsche Energiehandels- und Beratungsgesellschaft mbH*,[132] the issue related to an action against the state for liability for breach of EU law, and specifically for the delay in transposition of some Directives. The Court found that Article 47 of the Charter was relevant in determining whether a national rule excluding legal persons from legal aid was compatible with EU law.

Article 48 provides for the *presumption of innocence and right of defence*, according to which a person charged shall be presumed innocent until proved guilty according to law, and for the rights of the defence of anyone who has been charged.[133] It draws on Article 6(2) and (3) of the ECHR, and accordingly must be construed as encompassing the guarantees contained therein. Thus, according to Article 6(3), everyone charged shall have, as minimum rights, the right to be informed promptly and in a language she or he understands of the nature and cause of the accusation against her/him; to have adequate time and facilities for the preparation of her/his defence; to defend him/herself in person or through legal assistance (and to have legal aid as detailed above); to have witnesses against her/him cross-examined as well as to have the right to have witnesses on his/her behalf give evidence under the same conditions as witnesses against him/her; and to have an interpreter free of charge when she/he cannot understand or speak the language used in court. These are minimum procedural rights, and national legislation would often provide for a more generous regime. Given that, at least for the time being, the Union does not have direct criminal competence (ie it does not have the power to prosecute and adjudicate on individuals' criminal liability), Article 49 is relevant for assessing the validity of

---

[129] Arts 94 *et seq* of the Consolidated Version of the Rules of Procedure of the General Court [2010] OJ C177/37.

[130] Art 76 of the Consolidated Version of the Rules of Procedure of the Court of Justice [2010] OJ C177/1.

[131] Council Directive 2003/8 to improve access to justice in cross-border disputes by establishing minimum common rules relating to legal aid for such disputes [2003] OJ L26/41. The Directive appeared as Directive 2002/8 but a corrigendum ([2003] OJ L32/15) rectified the mistake.

[132] Case C-279/09 *DEB Deutsche Energiehandels- und Beratungsgesellschaft mbH*, Judgment of 22 December 2010, nyr.

[133] The presumption of innocence applies also to competition law proceedings; cf eg Joined Cases T-67/00, T-68/00, T-71/00, T-78/00 *JFE Engineering v Commission* [2004] ECR II-2501, esp para 178.

legislative acts of the Union[134] and of the Member States when they prosecute individuals as a result of breaches of measures implementing Union law.[135]

Article 49 provides for the *principles of legality and proportionality of criminal offences and penalties*. Article 49(1) states that no one can be held guilty of a criminal offence which was not a crime at the time it was committed (*nullum crimen sine lege*);[136] that the penalty cannot be heavier than that which was applicable at the time when the offence was committed;[137] and that if, after a criminal offence has been committed, the law is amended so as to provide for a lighter penalty than that in force when the act was committed, the lighter penalty shall be applicable (this principle is not contained in the ECHR).[138] Article 49(2) provides that that Article does not prejudice trial and punishment for crimes that when committed were criminal according to the general principles recognised by the community of nations. Thus, like Article 7(2) ECHR, this exception allows for the prosecution of crimes against humanity. Article 49(3) provides that 'the severity of penalties must not be disproportionate to the criminal offence', and results from the general principle of proportionality that applies in all areas of Union law as well as to Member States when implementing or acting within the scope of Union law.[139] The Court has held that the principle of proportionality also applies in relation to Member States' penalties for breaches of rules in any way connected with the exercise of Treaty rights.[140]

Article 50 provides for the right not to be *tried or punished twice* in criminal proceedings for an offence for which one has already been finally acquitted or convicted within the Union in accordance with the law.[141] It is the so-called *ne bis in idem* rule codified in

---

[134] eg Case C-303/05 *Advocaten voor de Wereld* [2007] ECR I-3633 where the Belgian Court of Arbitration enquired, inter alia, as to the compatibility of Framework Decision 2002/584/JHA on the European Arrest Warrant [2002] OJ L190/1 with Art 6(2) ECHR insofar as the Framework decision disposes of the requirement of double criminality (ie the principle according to which in cases of extradition the offence must be a criminal offence in both the requesting and requested State). The Court found that the Framework decision was valid

[135] This is going to become more relevant following the depillarisation of criminal law as a result of the TL; furthermore, Community law measures could require Member States to impose a criminal sanction for breaches of the obligations imposed in Union law. See eg Case C-176/03 *Commission v Council* (Criminal liability for offences against the environment) [2005] ECR I-7879.

[136] And, accordingly, a Directive cannot be interpreted in a way that would create or aggravate criminal liability: see eg Case 80/86, *Kolpinghuis* [1987] ECR 3969; Joined Cases C-387/02, C-391/02 and C-403/02 *Berlusconi and others* [2005] ECR I-3565, and Chapter 8 above.

[137] The Commission is bound by the principle of non-retroactivity of criminal sanctions when acting in its administrative capacity in competition law proceedings; however, that principle does not prevent it from raising the level of fines after the behaviour has taken place, cf Case T-64/02 *Dr Hans Heubach GmbH & Co KG v Commission* [2005] ECR II-5137. Were the fines to be qualified as criminal penalties, this would not be possible.

[138] AG Kokott found that this was a general principle of Community law in Joined Cases C-387/02, C-391/02 and C-403/02 *Berlusconi and others* [2005] ECR I-3565, Opinion paras 154 *et seq*; the Court did not examine the issue.

[139] Thus penalties provided by Union law must be proportionate, eg Case C-356/97 *Molkereigenossenschaft Wiedergeltingen* [2000] ECR I-5461.

[140] eg Case C-265/88 *Messner* [1989] ECR 4209; Case C-193/94 *Skanavi and Chryssanthakopoulos* [1996] ECR I-929, paras 35–38; Case C-29/95 *Pastoors* [1997] ECR I-285.

[141] In Union law the principle is provided in several pieces of legislation, eg Arts 3 and 4 of Council Framework Decision 2002/584/JHA on the European arrest warrant and the surrender procedure between Member States, [2002] OJ L190/1; Arts 54–58 of the Schengen Convention; and see Case C-187/01 *Gözütok* [2005] ECR I-1345 and Case C-469/03 *Miraglia* [2005] ECR I-2009. The no *bis in idem* principle applies beyond the confines of criminal law; thus, for instance, it applies also to competition law proceedings: cf Joined Cases T-305/94, T-306/94, T-307/94, T-313/94, T-314/94, T-315/94, T-316/94, T-318/94, T-325/94, T-328/94, T-329/94 and T-335/94 *Limburgse Vinyl Maatschappij NV and others v Commission* [1999] ECR II-931; and to Commission proceedings for infringement of Community law against Member States, Case C-416/02 *Commission v Spain* [2005] ECR I-7482.

Article 4 of Protocol 7 of the ECHR which allows for the reopening of the case if there is new evidence or newly discovered facts or if there has been a fundamental defect in the previous proceedings which could affect the outcome of the case.

III – THE HORIZONTAL PROVISIONS: INTERPRETATION AND SCOPE OF APPLICATION OF THE CHARTER

Title VII contains the general provisions on the interpretation and application of the Charter (commonly referred to as horizontal provisions). Title VII is, legally speaking, the most complex part of the Charter, and the horizontal provisions have been criticised because of their lack of clarity. The aim of the drafters was to ensure that the Charter would not be used to encroach on Member States' competence and that the balancing exercise inherent in such matters would not be relocated in the hands of the Court of Justice except when the Member States were implementing Union law. The result is far from satisfactory, highlighting a degree of political schizophrenia in relation to fundamental rights policy which results in a dichotomy in the sources of fundamental rights: when the Member States implement Union law, the applicable standard is that set by the Charter. However, when the Member States act within the field of Union law, the applicable standard is that set through the case law on the general principles. It is too early to say whether this distinction will be respected by the Court; and whether it will amount to much more than a broader margin of discretion been left to the Member States when they are acting within the scope of Union law rather than implementing it.

A – Article 51: The Charter's Field of Application

According to Article 51, the Charter is addressed to the Union's institutions, bodies (offices and agencies),[142] with due regard to the principle of subsidiarity and to the Member States only when they *implement* Union law.[143] The European Union and the Member States shall respect the rights, observe the principles and promote the application of the Charter in accordance with their respective powers (and respecting the limits of the Union's powers as conferred by the Treaties). The second paragraph of Article 51, provides that the Charter does not extend the field of application of Union law beyond the powers of the Union or establish any new power or task for the Union, or modify powers and tasks defined in the Treaties.

It is clear that the main concern of the drafters was to ensure that the Charter would not be used to expand the competences of the EU, and that it would not become a vehicle through which the Court of Justice would acquire general human rights jurisdiction. For this reason, the Charter is narrower in its application than the general principles: thus it applies to Member States only when they *implement* Union law, rather than when

---

[142] The reference to offices and agencies has been added by the Constitutional Treaty.
[143] The Charter also works as an aid to interpretation of secondary (and primary legislation) in the same way as general principles, see eg Joined Cases C-57 and 101/09 *B*, Judgment of 9 November 2010, nyr, esp para 78.

they 'act within the scope' of Union law. Thus, the Charter, at least in theory, applies only when the Member States are implementing a directive or taking measures to implement a Regulation, and not when an individual simply falls within the scope of Union law by virtue of, for instance, having exercised one of the Treaties' rights. However, the distinction might not be so clear cut not only because, as mentioned before, it is slightly artificial to have two different sources of fundamental rights (Charter and General Principles) to cover the same rights, but also because the explanations to the Charter refer to the fact that 'the requirement to respect fundamental rights defined in the context of the Union is only binding on the Member States when *they act in the scope of Union Law*', inter alia quoting as authority for this statement the *ERT* case,[144] which is a free-movement case and not one where the Member State was implementing Union law.

The reference to the principle of subsidiarity and the distinction between rights and principles are similarly confusing. As to the former, the Charter does not confer new competences on the Union and therefore cannot be used as a legal basis for any Union action. Since the principle of subsidiarity is aimed at regulating the exercise of Union competences, it is not clear what its significance in relation to the Charter is. The most likely explanation is that it is a political statement, with no real legal significance, aimed at reinforcing the fact that the Charter cannot be used to extend the competences of the Union. As for the latter, the distinction between rights (to be respected) and principles (to be observed), a distinction that is also present in Article 52, is, as we shall see, more confusing than helpful. The idea behind such a distinction is to clarify that some of the provisions in the Charter are purely inspirational, ie are yardsticks against which to measure the Union's legislative activity rather than free-standing rights. This is not unusual in constitutional documents (and therefore not particularly surprising) although regrettably the language in the Charter is not always consistent with that distinction (rights are sometimes referred to as principles, and vice versa).

B – Article 52: Scope of the Charter's Provisions

Article 52 deals with the *scope* of the Charter and was substantially amended by the CT, in that the latter added four new paragraphs, whilst the first three paragraphs remained the same as in the original version. The TL maintained the CT version.

Article 52(1) contains the general derogation clause, according to which any limitation on the rights and freedoms recognised in the Charter shall respect the *essence* of those rights; shall be proportionate; and must be necessary to 'genuinely meet objectives of general interest recognised by the Union or the need to protect the rights and freedoms of others'.[145] Article 52(2) clarifies that rights recognised in the Treaties shall be exercised under the conditions and within the limits defined in the Treaties. And Article 52(3) provides the minimum floor guarantee, according to which insofar as the Charter rights correspond to rights guaranteed by the ECHR, their meaning and scope shall be the same as those laid down by the Convention (which shall be interpreted as also including its Protocols).[146] The Union is, however, entitled to provide more extensive protection. The

---

[144] Case C-260/89 [1991] ECR I-2925.

[145] In contrast, the general principles can be limited also to protect an interest of the Member State, provided such interest is compatible with Union law, see Chapter 11 above.

[146] See explanation to the Charter; the Protocols to the Convention are an integral part of the Convention over which the ECtHR has jurisdiction.

general derogation clause constitutes a significant departure from the structure followed in the ECHR. The Convention provides for possible grounds of limitation on an Article-by-Article basis: this means that some rights (eg torture, slavery) can never be derogated from; some rights can be limited only in exhaustively listed situations (eg right to life; right to fair trial); and some Articles can be limited in order to pursue legitimate public interests, which are also listed (eg right to private life, freedom of expression). The scheme of the Convention achieves therefore two aims: first, the scope of the rights and their possible limitations is made clearer to the individual; secondly, it defines when and how those rights can be limited, therefore curtailing legislative discretion. The Charter unfortunately does not achieve either aim: having a general clause means that the citizen is not able to assess the possible limitations without referring to the Convention. Furthermore, it means that the absolute nature of some of the rights is disguised; and that new generation rights that should be absolute are not so clearly defined since they are not contained in the Convention. Take, for instance, the prohibition on trafficking: short of slavery and forced labour, trafficking is not explicitly prohibited by the Convention.[147] Of course it is not a right which can be derogated from since any limitation of it would undermine the very *essence* of the prohibition.[148] However, it would have been preferable to have this expressly set out. As to the second aim, that of clearly curtailing legislative discretion by listing interests and occasions in which rights can be derogated from, Article 52 not only does not achieve this, but fails to mention that any limitation must be necessary in a 'democratic society' in order to be legitimate. So, overall, the choice of a general derogation clause is unsatisfactory; however, it is possible that the inclusion of such a provision is due in part to the fact that the Charter is much broader in scope than the Convention. In other words, whilst in relation to some of the more clearly defined rights (civil and political as well as social) it would have been easy to provide for article-by-article limitations, that might have been more difficult for statement of principles (eg environmental and consumer protection).

As noted above, the CT added another four paragraphs to Article 52 which, unfortunately, do nothing to increase visibility and clarity. The new Article 52(4) provides that insofar as the Charter rights result from the constitutional traditions common to the Member States, they have to be interpreted in 'harmony' with those traditions. The explanations state that this is a codification of the Court's case law, which, as we have seen, refers to the common constitutional traditions as a *source* of rights. Thus, Article 52(4) seems not to codify the Court's case law: rather it seems more aimed at curtailing the Court's hermeneutic autonomy in interpreting the Charter.

Article 52(5) reaffirms the distinction between principles and rights and spells out the consequence of such distinction by stating that principles may be implemented through legislative/executive acts of the Union, and by acts of the Member States when they are implementing Union law; and that they are judicially cognisable only in the interpretation of such acts and in the ruling of their validity. Thus, for instance, whilst the principle of environmental protection contained in Article 37 does not give rise to a free-standing right, if the Union were to adopt an act in blatant defiance of such a principle, such act

---

[147] It is prohibited by the Council of Europe Convention against Trafficking in Human Beings (CETS 197), but since this is a Convention and not a Protocol to the ECHR, it is not relevant in assessing the scope of Charter's rights.

[148] The same problem—if not even more pronounced—arises in relation to the prohibition of eugenic practices in Art 3 Charter.

could be held invalid by the Court. And, if the Union act were to be drafted in uncertain terms, then the interpretation which enhances environmental protection would have to be favoured.

Article 52(6) provides that 'full account shall be taken of national law and practice as specified in this Charter', and seems a rather redundant provision probably dictated by political needs rather than by legal necessities.

Finally, Article 52(7) provides that the explanations to the Charter shall be given due regard by Union and national courts. In this way, the explanations acquire a hybrid status: they are not 'legally binding' and yet they seem to aim to curtail the judiciary's hermeneutic freedom.[149]

C – Article 53: Level of Protection

Article 53 reinforces the minimum floor guarantees; thus it states that nothing in the Charter shall be interpreted as

> restricting or adversely affecting human rights and fundamental freedoms as recognised, in their respective fields of application, by Union law and international law and by international agreements to which the Union, the Community or all of the Member States are party, including the European Convention on Human Rights, and by the Member States' Constitutions.

The reference to the Member States' constitutions rather than to the common constitutional traditions has raised fears as to the consistency of this provision with the principle of supremacy according to which Union law shall always take precedence even over conflicting national constitutional law.[150] Take the *Biotechnology Directive* case where the Dutch government challenged the validity of said Directive on the grounds, inter alia, that it infringed human dignity as guaranteed by the Dutch Constitution. Would Article 53 require the Court of Justice to apply the higher Dutch standard? And how is Article 53 going to apply when different national constitutions privilege different conflicting interests (eg right to life/right to dignity, right to health/right of the unborn)?

D – Article 54: Abuse of Rights

The final provision states:

> Nothing in the Charter shall be interpreted as implying any right to engage in any activity or to perform any act aimed at the destruction of any of the rights and freedoms recognised in the Charter or at their limitation to a greater extent than is provided for therein.

This provision is almost identical to Article 17 ECHR and therefore should be construed in a similar way: thus, it is aimed at ensuring that individuals/groups and states do not

---

[149] The explanations to the Charter state that 'Although they do not as such have the status of law, they are a valuable tool of interpretation intended to clarify the provisions of the Charter.'

[150] This problem has been extensively analysed by JB Liisberg, 'Does the EU Charter of Fundamental Rights Threaten the Supremacy of Community Law?' (2001) 38 *CMLRev* 1171, who gives a negative answer to the question. The explanations merely refer to national law, a concept much broader than national Constitutions.

use the Convention to destroy rights contained therein; it is not aimed at depriving individuals of the rights conferred by the Convention.[151]

IV – THE UK AND POLISH PROTOCOL

It has been mentioned above that the adoption of the Charter as a legally binding document has been politically a very sensitive step. The drafting of both Article 6 TEU and the horizontal provisions of the Charter can only be properly understood having regard to the level of scepticism existing in some of the EU countries, and particularly, but not only, in the UK, in relation to both a fundamental rights document and the fear of 'competence creep'. It is in this context that *Protocol No 30 on the application of the Charter of Fundamental Rights of the European Union to Poland and the United Kingdom* should be understood.[152] This document, aimed at 'clarifying the application of the Charter' in relation to laws and administrative actions of the UK and Poland, provides the following:

> Article 1
>
> 1. The Charter does not *extend* the ability of the Court of Justice of the European Union, or any court or tribunal of Poland or the United Kingdom, to find that the laws, regulations or administrative provisions, practices or action of Poland and of the United Kingdom are inconsistent with fundamental rights, freedoms and principles that it reaffirms.
>
> 2. In particular, and for the avoidance of doubt, nothing in Title IV of the Charter [Solidarity] *creates* justiciable rights applicable to Poland or the United Kingdom except in so far as Poland or the United Kingdom has provided for such rights in its national law. [emphasis added]
>
> Article 2
>
> To the extent that a provision of the Charter refers to national laws and practices, it shall only apply to Poland or the United Kingdom to the extent that the right or principles that it contains are recognised in the law or practices of Poland or of the United Kingdom.

The significance (and the meaning) of the Protocol are far from clear; from a strictly formal legal perspective it has the same value as EU primary legislation, ie the same value as the Treaties and the Charter. However, the wording is so carefully drafted as to be nebulous: Article 1(1) seems really to be a clarifying statement rather than a normative one. The Charter is not aimed at extending rights or the jurisdiction of the European courts since it is only a codifying document, hence not creative of rights; rather, if anything, it applies in a more limited way than the existing case law of the Court of Justice since, as said above, it only applies to Member States when *implementing* EU law. On the other hand Article 1(2) does seem, at first sight, to have normative value in excluding the justiciability of Title IV in Poland and the UK. This is true unless we interpret the reference to 'creating' justiciable rights as meaning that the Charter, as noted above, does not have per se creative effects but only codifying effects, in which case this paragraph too would simply be declarative rather than normative. Equally unclear, but possibly more prescriptive is Article 2. Even should Article 2 have true legal effects, however, the case law of the

---

[151] See eg *Lawless v Ireland* (No 3) (1979/80) 1 EHRR 15.
[152] The Protocol will also be extended to the Czech Republic, see the Presidency Conclusions, Brussels European Council (Doc 15265/09 CONCL 3).

Court on the general principles might make it redundant. Take the cases of *Viking* and *Laval*: it might be recalled that in those cases the Court found that the right to strike is a general principle of Union law. As such, even though it is a right contained in *Title IV*, it is justiciable in the UK through the general principles of Union law.

The significance of the Protocol seems to be uncertain also in the eyes of the UK government. For instance, the UK Secretary of State for the Home Department, in a recent case, made clear that he did not agree with a judicial finding that the Charter could not be relied upon against the UK; rather it held that 'the Secretary of State accepts, in principle, that fundamental rights set out in the Charter can be relied on as against the United Kingdom'.[153] The case has now been referred to the Court of Justice and the national court has explicitly enquired about the effect of Protocol No 30.[154]

It is clear that the Protocol, whatever its significance will turn out to be, highlights a certain caution as to the extent to which fundamental rights should be pursued through claims anchored in EU law. The same caution, and possibly confusion, arises in relation to the dual system created as a result of the dichotomy between the Charter and the general principles of Union law. Yet, and this notwithstanding, the codification of EU fundamental rights is a positive step forward: for all its shortcomings, the Charter will have positive effects not least in making the European judiciary more confident in developing its own fundamental rights jurisprudence and holding the EU institutions to proper account.

Further Reading

AA, VV (2001) *MJ* 1, Special Issue on the Charter

Arnull, 'From Charter to Constitution and Beyond: Fundamental Rights in the New European Union' (2003) *PL* 774.

Ashiagbor, 'Economic and Social Rights in the European Charter of Fundamental Rights' (2004) *EHRLR* 62.

Basselink, 'The Member States, the National Constitutions and the Scope of the Charter' (2001) *MJ* 69.

de Búrca and de Witte (eds) *Social Rights in Europe* (Oxford, Oxford University Press, 2005).

de Búrca, 'The Drafting of the European Union Charter of Fundamental Rights' (2001) *ELRev* 126.

——, 'Human Rights: The Charter and Beyond', Jean Monnet Working Paper No 10/01.

Curtin and R Van Ooik, 'The String is Always in the Tail. The Personal Scope of Application of the EU Charter of Fundamental Rights' (2001) *MJ* 103

Eechout, 'The EU Charter of Fundamental Rights and the Federal Question' (2002) *CMLRev* 945.

Heringa and Verhey, 'The EU Charter: Text and Structure' (2001) *MJ* 11.

Hervey and Kenner (eds), *Economic and Social Rights under the EU Charter of Fundamental Rights—A Legal Perspective* (Oxford, Hart Publishing 2003).

Knook, 'The Court, the Charter and the Vertical Division of Powers in the EU' (2005) *CMLRev* 367.

Lanaerts and de Smijter, 'The Charter and the Role of the European Courts' (2001) *MJ* 90.

Lemmens, 'The Relationship between the Charter of Fundamental Rights of the European Union and the European Convention on Human Rights—Substantive Aspects' (2001) *MJ* 49.

---

[153] See *R (NS) v the Secretary of State for the Home Department* [2010] ECWA 990 (available on http://www.bailii.org/ew/cases/EWCA/Civ/2010/990.html) para 7.

[154] Case C-411/10 *R (NS) v the Secretary of State for the Home Department*, case pending; see esp Question no 7.

Liisberg, 'Does the EU Charter of Fundamental Rights Threaten the Supremacy of Community Law?' (2001) 38 *CMLRev* 1171.

Peers and Ward (eds), *The Charter of Fundamental Rights* (Oxford, Hart Publishing, 2004).

Wounters, 'The EU Charter of Fundamental Rights—Some Reflections on its External Dimension' (2001) *MJ.*

de Witte, 'The Legal Status of the Charter: Vital Question or Non-Issue?' (2001) *MJ* 81.

Part IV

The Internal Market

Fiscal Barriers to the Free Movement of Goods

13

One of the main aims of the European integration project is that of market integration. Thus the Treaty sought from the outset to ensure the free movement of goods, persons and services within the European Union. With time, the Treaty also included in its aims the free movement of capital and a single currency for some of its Member States. Furthermore, the Maastricht Treaty introduced a new, and possibly revolutionary, concept: that of Union citizenship. In this part we will look at some of these developments. In particular we will consider the 'traditional' four freedoms (goods, workers, establishment and services) together with Union citizenship.

We start with the free movement of goods, and in this chapter we analyse fiscal barriers to intra-European Union trade (customs duties and discriminatory taxation); in the next chapter we will look at quantitative restrictions and measures having equivalent effect to quantitative restrictions to imports and exports. Fiscal barriers, prohibited by Article 30 TFEU, are customs duties and charges having equivalent effect to customs duties. Those are charges imposed for the sole reason that the goods have crossed a frontier. Customs duties and charges having equivalent effect can never be justified; this said, the Court has held that some charges which might at first sight seem charges having equivalent effect do not fall within the scope of Article 30 TFEU if they represent consideration for a service provided to the importer or if they represent the cost of mandatory inspections required by Union law. Discriminatory or protectionist taxation is prohibited by Article 110 TFEU. Discrimination arises when similar goods are taxed in a different way so as to benefit domestic products at the expense of imported ones. Protectionist taxation arises when products which are in competition with each other are taxed in such a way so as to afford an advantage to domestic products. As we shall see, the assessment of whether internal taxation is compatible with Article 110 TFEU might require complex economic analysis, and in some cases taxes which appear at first sight to have a more burdensome effect on imported products might be objectively justified by legitimate public policy aims.

I – THE FREE MOVEMENT OF GOODS

One of the main aims of the internal market is to ensure the free movement of goods within the territory of the Union; in order to achieve these aims the Treaty prohibits EU

Member States from imposing restrictions on the flow of goods. Typically restrictions on trade in goods are aimed at protecting domestic production and take the form of customs duties (which artificially inflate the price of imports); discriminatory taxation (which imposes an extra fiscal burden on imports, so as to advantage domestic production); and trade restrictions (typically quotas and/or prohibition on imports to shelter domestic production from competition). It is not surprising, then, that the Treaty prohibits all three forms of trade restrictions, as well as establishing a customs union. We will start by the prohibition on customs duties and charges having equivalent effect to customs duties (Article 30 TFEU), and then turn to discriminatory taxation (Article 110 TFEU).

A – Customs Union and Charges Having Equivalent Effect

(i) Establishment of a Customs Union

Whereas a free trade area comprises a group of customs territories in which duties are eliminated on trade in goods originating in such territories, a customs union represents a further step in economic integration, since a common tariff is adopted in trade relations with the outside world. Article 28 TFEU provides that:

> The Union shall comprise a customs union which shall cover all trade in goods and which shall involve the prohibition between Member States of customs duties on imports and exports and of all charges having equivalent effect, and the adoption of a common customs tariff in their relations with third countries.[1]

The abolition as between the Member States of customs duties and charges having equivalent effect constitutes a fundamental principle of the common market applicable to all products and goods with the result that any exception, which in any event must be strictly interpreted, must be clearly laid down.[2] Furthermore, the TFEU makes provision in Article 31 for a Common Customs Tariff, a common tariff applicable to all imports in the territory of the Union; once a product from a third country has lawfully entered the Union territory, and has complied with all import formalities, it is considered to be in free circulation (Article 29 TFEU) and the free movement of goods provisions apply also to those products.[3]

The Treaty free movement of goods provisions (including those prohibiting quantitative restrictions and measures having equivalent effect) apply to all products which 'can

---

[1] Former Art 9 EEC (ex 23 EC) was held to be directly applicable in conjunction with other Treaty Articles: see eg Cases 2 and 3/69 *Sociaal Fonds etc v Brachfeld and Chougol Diamond Co* [1969] ECR 211 (ex Art 9 and 12 EEC); Case 33/70 *SACE v Italian Ministry of Finance* [1970] ER 1213 (ex Arts 9 and 13(2) EEC); Case 18/71 *Eunomia v Italian Ministry of Education* [1971] ECR 811 (ex Arts 9 and 16 EEC); the decision as to which status non-EU goods should enjoy might be both complex and politically charged: see eg Case C-386/08 *Brita GmbH* [2010] ECR I-000; and G Harpaz and E Rubinson, 'The Interface between Trade, Law and Politics and the Erosion of Normative Power in Europe: Comment on Brita' (2010) 35 *ELRev* 551.

[2] Joined Cases 90/63 and 91/63 *Commission v Luxembourg and Belgium* [1964] ECR 625; Joined Cases 80/77 and 81/77 *Commissionaires Réunis and Another v Receveur des Douanes* [1978] ECR 927, para 24; Case C-272/95 *Bundesanstalt für Landwirtschaft und Ernährung v Deutsches Milch-Kontor* [1997] ECR I-1905, para 36.

[3] The Court has made clear that products which are in free circulation are 'definitively and wholly assimilated to products originating in Member States', see Case C-83/89 *Openbaar Ministerie and the Minister for Finance v Vincent Houben* [1990] ECR I-1161, para 10; Art 29 TFEU does not apply to goods which have benefited from a total or partial drawback, ie when goods are imported for the purposes of processing followed by re-export; see Regulation 2913/92 establishing the Community Customs Code [1992] OJ L302/1, Arts 114 *et seq.*

be valued in money and which are capable as such of forming the subject of commercial transactions'.[4]

B – Customs Duties and Charges Having Equivalent Effect

Article 30 TFEU contains an outright prohibition on customs duties and charges having equivalent effect to customs duties on imports and exports (CEEs). Customs duties are taxes, no matter how small, levied on imports and exports,[5] whilst

> *any* pecuniary charge, however small and whatever its designation and mode of application, which is imposed unilaterally on domestic or foreign goods by reason of the fact that they cross a frontier, and which is not a customs duty in the strict sense, constitutes a *charge having equivalent* effect within the meaning of Articles [28, 30, . . . TFEU], even if it is not imposed for the benefit of the state, is not discriminatory or protective in effect and if the product on which the charge is imposed is not in competition with any domestic product.[6]

In the case at issue, Italy charged a very small fee for gathering statistical data on exports. The Court made clear that both the amount and the purpose of the charge was immaterial: any charge, however small and whatever its purpose, is a charge having equivalent effect to a customs duty if it is imposed by reason of goods crossing a frontier.

The irrelevance of protectionist intent was confirmed in *Sociaal Fonds*.[7] Here, Belgium had instituted a social fund for workers in the diamond industry which would be financed by a charge levied on imported diamonds. Belgium did not produce any diamonds, therefore excluding any protectionist effect or intent; the charge was minimal compared to the value of the imported diamonds; and the aim was to ensure the protection of particularly vulnerable workers. This notwithstanding, and consistently with the definition given in the statistical levy case, the Court found that the charge represented a CEE.

Overall, the interpretation of the prohibition on customs duties and CEEs has not been particularly controversial. However, in more recent years, the Court stretched the interpretation of Article 30 TFEU to encompass also charges imposed within Member States' internal/administrative borders in apparent contradiction with the above-mentioned definition which refers to charges imposed 'by reason of the fact that goods cross a frontier'. Thus, in *Legros* the Court held that the description of CEEs covered dock dues (comprising *ad valorem* duties on goods) imposed on the import of goods into the Réunion region of France from another Member State, even though the dock dues in question also applied to goods entering Rèunion from Metropolitan France. The Court stated:

> A charge levied at a regional frontier by reason of the introduction of products into a region of a Member State constitutes an obstacle to the free movement of goods which is at least as serious

---

[4] Case 7/68 *Commission v Italy* (Art Treasuries) [1968] ECR 423, 428; even waste can constitute 'goods' for the purposes of the Treaty free movement of goods provisions, see Case C-2/90 *Commission v Belgium* (Walloonian Waste) [1992] ECR I-4431.

[5] See eg Case 7/68 *Commission v Italy* (Art Treasuries) [1968] ECR 423.

[6] Case 24/68 *Commission v Italy* (Statistical Levy) [1969] ECR 193 (emphasis added).

[7] Joined Cases 2 and 3/69 *Sociaal Fonds voor de Diamantarbeiders* [1969] ECR 211; more recently see eg Joined Cases C-441/98 and C-442/98 *Michailidis* [2000] ECR I-7145; Case C-389/00 *Commission v Germany* (shipment of waste) [2003] ECR I-2001; the same reasoning applies if the charge is not levied for the benefit of the State: eg Case C-293/02 *Jersey Produce Marketing Organisation Ltd* [2005] ECR I-9543, para 55.

as a charge levied at the national frontier by reason of the introduction of the products into the whole territory of a Member State.[8]

The same system of dock dues as was in issue in *Legros* was the subject of a preliminary ruling in *Lancry*, but this time the question posed was whether the imposition of the dues on goods from the same Member State, France, also amounted to charges having equivalent effect prohibited by the Treaty. The Court rejected the argument of the Council to the effect that the Treaty's prohibition on CEEs to customs duties did not apply to charges internal to a Member State, as follows:

> The unity of the EU customs territory is undermined by the establishment of a regional customs frontier just the same, whether the products on which a charge is levied by reason of the fact that they cross a frontier are domestic products or come from other Member States.
>
> Furthermore, the obstacle to the free movement of goods created by the imposition on domestic products of a charge levied by reason of their crossing that frontier is no less serious than that created by the collection of a charge of the same kind on products from another Member State.
>
> Since the very principle of a customs union covers all trade in goods, as provided for by Article [28 TFEU], it requires the free movement of goods generally, as opposed to inter-State trade alone, to be ensured within the Union. Although Article [28 TFEU] et seq makes express reference only to trade between Member States, that is because it was assumed that there were no charges exhibiting the features of a customs duty in existence within the Member States. Since the absence of such charges is an essential precondition for the attainment of a customs union covering all trade in goods, it follows that they are likewise prohibited by Article [28 TFEU] et seq.[9]

Similarly, in *Simitzi* the Court held that charges imposed on goods dispatched from one region of a Member State to another region of that same Member State amounted to CEEs to customs duties on exports.[10] In *Carbonati Apuani*,[11] the Court found that a charge imposed on marble leaving the district territory of Carrara (the town where it was excavated) was a CEE even though it applied also to marble destined to other parts of Italy, and in *Jersey* the Court adopted similar reasoning with respect to charges imposed on Jersey potatoes exported to the UK.[12]

C – Charges Falling Outside the Scope of Article 30 TFEU: Services Provided to the Importer and EU Law Obligations

A charge falling within the scope of Article 30 TFEU can never be justified; however, in some cases (narrowly interpreted) a charge might fall altogether outside the scope of the Treaty prohibition. This is the case in relation to charges imposed on traders to cover the costs of services actually rendered to the importer/exporter,[13] and in relation to charges imposed to fulfil an obligation imposed by Union law.

In relation to the former the Court has usually rejected the 'consideration for services' argument in the case of unilateral measures, either because the services in question were

---

[8] Case 163/90 *Legros and others* [1992] ECR I-4625, para 16; see also Joined Cases C-485/93 and C-486/93 *Maria Simitzi v Dimos Kos* [1995] ECR I-2655, para 17.

[9] Joined Cases C-363/93, etc, *René Lancry SA* [1994] ECR I-3957, esp paras 27–29.

[10] Joined Cases C-485/93 and C-86/93 *Maria Simitzi v Dimos Kos* [1995] ECR I-2655, paras 26 and 27.

[11] Case C-72/03 *Carbonati Apuani Srl* [2004] ECR I-8027.

[12] Case C-293/02 *Jersey Produce Marketing Organisation Ltd* [2005] ECR I-9543.

[13] eg Case 132/82 *Commission v Belgium* [1983] ECR 1649.

rendered in the general interest (eg health inspections),[14] rather than in the interests of traders themselves or, if the services did benefit traders, because they benefited them as a class in a way which was impossible to quantify in a particular case (eg compilation of statistical data).[15] Furthermore, in order to fall outside the scope of Article 30 TFEU the charge imposed as consideration for a service must reflect the actual cost of the service provided. Therefore a charge calculated according to the value of the good necessarily falls within the scope of Article 30 TFEU, since it bears no relation to the actual cost of the service provided.[16]

On the other hand, the position is rather different if charges are imposed to cover the cost of procedures (such as inspections) mandated by Union law. Such charges will not amount to CEEs prohibited by Article 30 TFEU,[17] provided the fee charged does not exceed the actual cost of the operations involved.[18] However, if the inspection/procedure is merely authorised by Union law, but is not mandatory, then the Member State cannot charge for it without contravening Article 30 TFEU.[19]

As regards CEEs on exports, the Court has held that an internal duty which falls more heavily on exports than on domestic sales amounts to a CEE to a customs duty.[20] Fees for inspections of plants charged only in respect of exported product, and not in respect of those intended for the home market, constitute CEEs on exports, even if those inspections are carried out to meet the requirements of international conventions affecting only exported products. The contrary would be true only if it were established that the products intended for the home market derived no benefit from the inspections.[21] Finally it should be noted that the Court has made clear that the Treaty also prohibits charges to be imposed on goods in transit, whether EU produced or in free circulation.[22]

II – PROHIBITION ON DISCRIMINATORY INTERNAL TAXATION

The elimination of customs duties and CEEs would be of little consequence if the Member States were then allowed to impose internal taxation on imports in excess of what imposed

---

[14] eg Case 39/73 *Rewe-Zentralfinanz v Landwirtschaftskammer* [1973] ECR 1039; Case 87/75 *Bresciani* [1976] ECR 129; Case 35/76 *Simmenthal* [1976] ECR 1871; Case 251/78 *Firma Denkavit Futtermittel Gmbh* [1979] ECR 3369 (fees to offset the costs of compulsory and sanitary inspections).

[15] Joined Cases 52 and 55/65 *Germany v Commission* [1966] ECR 159 (charge by national intervention agency for import licences); Case 24/68 *Commission v Italy* [1969] ECR 193, 201 (fee to defray the costs of compiling statistical data).

[16] Case 170/88 *Ford España* [1989] ECR 2305.

[17] Case 46/76 *Bauhuis* [1977] ECR 5; Case 18/87 *Commission v Germany* [1988] ECR 5427; Case C-130/93 *Lamaire v NDALTP* [1994] ECR I-3215, para 19.

[18] Case C-209/89 *Commission v Italy* [1991] ECR I-1575, para 10. Similarly, measures taken by a Member State under an international Treaty to which all Member States are parties, and which encourage the free movement of goods, may be assimilated to EU measures, and fees covering costs may be charged accordingly: see Case 89/76 *Commission v Netherlands* [1977] ECR 1355.

[19] Case 314/82 *Commission v Belgium* [1984] ECR 1543.

[20] Joined Cases 36 and 71/80 *Irish Creamery Milk Suppliers Assn v Govt of Ireland* [1981] ECR 735.

[21] Case C-111/89 *Hillegom* [1990] ECR I-1735.

[22] eg Case 266/81 *SIOT* [1983] ECR 731 where it was likely that the goods in question (oil) were not in free circulation (see the questions referred in para 10); see also Case C-367/89 [1991] *Richardt* ECR I-4621 and more recently Case C-173/05 *Commission v Italy* (Sicilian environmental tax) [2007] ECR I-4917, esp para 15.

on domestic products.[23] It is therefore not surprising that Article 110 TFEU prohibits discriminatory and protectionist taxation.[24]

The purpose of the Article has been explained as follows in a consistent line of cases:

> Article [110 TFEU] supplements the provisions on the abolition of customs duties and charges having equivalent effect. Its aim is to ensure free movement of goods between the Member States in normal conditions of competition by the elimination of all forms of protection which may result from the application of internal taxation that discriminates against products from other Member States. Thus Article [110 TFEU] must guarantee the complete neutrality of internal taxation as regards competition between domestic products and imported products.[25]

The rule prohibiting discriminatory internal taxation on imported goods constitutes an essential basic principle of the common market,[26] and is directly applicable.[27] It should be noted, however, that it is only discriminatory and protectionist taxation that is prohibited by the Treaty; in other words, Member States remain free to establish both the system and the level of taxation that they deem suitable.

A – Discriminatory Taxation: Article 110(1) TFEU

Article 110(1) TFEU provides that:

> No Member State shall impose, directly or indirectly,[28] on the products of other Member States any internal taxation of any kind in *excess* of that imposed directly or indirectly on *similar* domestic products. (emphasis added)

Thus, in order for Article 110(1) to apply, the goods in question (i) must be similar, and (ii) there must be a difference in taxation. We shall look at those two requirements in turn.

(i) The goods must be similar

In order for discrimination to be established, there must be a 'similar' domestic prod-

---

[23] Joined Cases 2 and 3/62 *Commission v Belgium and Luxembourg* [1962] ECR 425, 431.

[24] Art 110 TFEU has been held to include products from third countries which are in free circulation in Member States: see eg Case 193/85 *Co-Frutta* [1987] ECR 2085, para 25; furthermore, once a product has been imported from another Member State and placed on the market, it becomes a domestic product for the purposes of comparison of its tax position with an import from another Member State under Art 90 EC: Case C-47/88 *Commission v Denmark* (cars) [1990] ECR I-4509, para 17.

[25] Case 252/86 *Bergandi* [1988] ECR 1343, para 24; Case C-45/94 *Cámara de Comercio, Industria y Navegación de Ceuta v Ayuntamiento de Ceuta* [1995] ECR I-4385, para 29.

[26] Case 57/65 *Lütticke* [1966] ECR 205, 214.

[27] Case 57/65 *Lütticke* [1966] ECR 205; Case 28/67 *Molkerei-Zentrale v Hauptzollamt Paderborn* [1968] ECR 143; Case 45/75 *Rewe-Zentrale etc v Hauptzollamt Landau/Pfalz* [1976] ECR 181; Case 74/76 *Iannelli & Volpi v Paolo Meroni* [1977] ECR 557; Case C-119/89 *Commission v Kingdom of Spain* [1991] ECR I-641, para 5.

[28] Indirect taxation includes charges levied on raw materials and semi-finished products incorporated in the goods in question, eg Case 45/64 *Commission v Italy* [1965] ECR 857. Whilst taxation of undertakings manufacturing products will not in general be regarded as constituting taxation of the products themselves, the taxation of specific activities of an undertaking which has an 'immediate effect' on the cost of the national imported product must by virtue of Art 110 TFEU be applied in a manner which is not discriminatory to imported products. Thus taxation imposed indirectly upon products within the meaning of Art 110 TFEU must be interpreted as including charges imposed on the international transport of goods by road according to the distance covered on the national territory and the weight of the goods in question, see eg Case 20/76 *Schottle & Sohne v Finanzamt Freudenstadt* [1977] ECR 247; and also as including a tax on use, where imported products are intended for such use and were imported solely for that purpose, see eg Case 252/86 *Bergandi* [1988] ECR 1343.

uct which is treated more favourably than the imported product. In order to determine whether two products are similar the Court will have regard to whether the products have similar characteristics and whether they meet the same needs from the viewpoint of the consumer. So, for instance, in *Commission v Denmark* the Court found that fruit wine and wine made from grapes, the former almost exclusively home-produced, whilst the latter almost exclusively imported, were similar products for the purposes of Article 110(1) TFEU. Thus, both products were produced from agricultural produce through fermentation; their taste and alcohol content were also similar. The Court also found that the products under consideration could meet the same needs from the viewpoint of the consumers: both products could be used to quench thirst, as refreshments and at meal times. The Court also specified that, in order to assess whether two products meet the same needs from the perspective of the consumers regard should be had not (only) to existing consumer habits (since those might be determined also by the tax regime in as much as price might shape consumer preferences)[29] but to the 'prospective development of those habits and, essentially, on the basis of objective characteristics which ensure that a product is capable of meeting the same needs as another product from the point of view of certain categories of consumers'.[30]

(ii) Imports Must Be Directly or Indirectly Discriminated Against

Article 110(1) TFEU prohibits both direct and indirect discrimination. Direct discrimination is discrimination in law, ie where the foreign product is treated differently to a similar domestic product.[31] This might be because of a different rate of taxation; or because of the fact that the detailed rules on how a tax is levied differ. Thus, for instance, in *Commission v Ireland* the Court found that tax rules which allowed domestic producers of alcoholic beverages to defer tax payment for six weeks whilst the tax on imported beverages would be levied immediately discriminated against imports. The Court found that:

> the decisive criterion of comparison for the purposes of the application of article [110 TFEU] is the actual effect of each tax on national production on the one hand and on imported products on the other, since even where the rate of tax is equal the effect of that tax may vary according to the detailed rules for the basis of assessment and levying thereof applied to national production and imported products respectively.[32]

Discrimination might occur also when the Member State refuses to extend tax advantages or concessions to imports. Thus, for instance, in the *Hansen* case[33] the question arose whether an importer of spirits into Germany was entitled to take advantage of tax relief available, inter alia, in respect of spirits made from fruit by small businesses and collective farms. The Court acknowledged that advantages of this kind could serve legiti-

---

[29] See in the case of Art 110(2) TFEU, Case 170/78 *Commission v UK* [1983] ECR 2265.

[30] Case 106/84 *Commission v Denmark* [1986] ECR 833, para 15; see also eg Case 168/78 *Commission v France* [1980] ECR 387; Case 243/84 *John Walker* [1986] ECR 875; more recently eg Case C-387/01 *Weigel and Weigel* [2004] ECR I-4981, paras 85 *et seq.*

[31] eg Case 57/65 *Lütticke* [1966] ECR 205; see also Case C-90/94 *Haahr Petroleum Ltd v Åbenrå Havn and Others* [1997] ECR I-4085.

[32] Case 55/79 *Commission v Ireland* [1980] ECR 481, para 8.

[33] Case 148/77 *H Hansen v Hauptzollampt Flensburg* [1978] ECR 1787. See also Case 21/79 *Commission v Italy* [1980] ECR 1; Case 26/80 *Schneider-Import* [1980] ECR 3469; Joined Cases 142 and 143/80 *Italian Finance Administration v Essevi SpA* [1981] ECR 1413; Case 277/83 *Commission v Italy* [1985] ECR 2049, para 17; Case 196/85 *Commission v France* [1987] ECR 1597; Case C-221/06 *Stadtgemeinde Frohnleiten and Gemeindebetriebe Frohnleiten GmbH* [2007] ECR I-9643.

mate economic or social purposes, such as the use of certain raw materials, the continued production of particular spirits of high quality, or the continuance of certain classes of undertakings such as agricultural distilleries. However, Article 110 TFEU required that such preferential systems must be extended without discrimination to spirits coming from other Member States.[34] It is not always easy to distinguish between direct and indirect discrimination (or between discriminatory and protectionist taxation) and yet it might be important to do so since direct discrimination can never be justified.[35]

On the other hand, indirect discrimination (much more common) occurs when a rule that appears neutral in its formulation places a heavier (and unjustified) burden on imports.

Indirect discrimination can be objectively justified, since taxation might be used not only to raise revenues but also to pursue public policy objectives. If those are compatible with EU law, and the aim of the tax is not to discriminate or pursue a protectionist policy, then taxation that affects imports more than domestic products might be legitimate regardless of the different impact.

Thus, for instance, in *Commission v Greece*[36] the Court accepted a system of taxation for cars which increased having regard to cylinder capacity, an objective criterion, since the Treaty does not prevent Member States from pursuing social policy objectives (in this case a heavier tax burden on luxury goods) through taxation. This was the case even though all of the cars in the higher tax band were imported since those would be competing with cars in the band immediately lower which were both imported and domestically produced so excluding any protectionist effect. The issue of justification is an important one, and the Court has made clear that technical or practical difficulties are not sufficient justification for indirect discrimination. In another action brought by the Commission against Greece, the Greek government claimed that extending to imported cars the reduced rate of special consumer tax payable in respect of domestic cars using 'anti-pollution technology' would require a technical test to be carried out on each import, which was not practical. The Court held that such considerations could not justify tax discrimination against imports, and held the tax contrary to Article 110 TFEU.[37] In *Outokumpu Oy* the Court considered a Finnish tax regime whereby domestic electricity was subject to rates varying with the method of production and energy sources used, whereas imported electricity was subject to a flat-rate tariff which in certain cases exceeded the lowest rate applicable to domestic electricity. The Court noted that while the characteristics of electricity may indeed make it extremely difficult to determine precisely the method of production of imported electricity and hence the energy sources used for that purpose,

> the Finnish legislation at issue does not even give the importer the opportunity of demonstrating that the electricity imported by him has been produced by a particular method in order to qualify for the rate applicable to electricity of domestic origin produced by the same method.[38]

The Court concluded that the tax was contrary to Article 110 TFEU.

---

[34] Ibid.
[35] Case 21/79 *Commission v Italy* [1980] ECR 1. See also Case 140/79 *Chemial Farmaceutici v DAF* [1981] ECR 1; Case 46/80 *Vinal v Orbat* [1981] ECR 77.
[36] Case C-132/88 *Commission v Greece* [1990] ECR I-1567.
[37] Case C-375/95 *Commission v Greece* [1997] ECR I-5981, esp para 47.
[38] Case C-213/96 [1998] ECR I-1777, para 39.

B – Protectionist Taxation: Article 110(2) TFEU

Article 110(2) TFEU provides that

> Furthermore, no Member State shall impose on the products of other Member States any internal taxation of such a nature as to afford *indirect protection* to other products. (emphasis added)

Article 110(2) TFEU is designed to prevent Member States from imposing higher taxes on imported products which, whilst not technically similar, are in competition with domestic products so as to afford protection to the latter.

(i) Products in Competition with One Another

In order to determine whether two products are in competition with one another the Court will mainly focus on the extent to which consumers might substitute one for the other. Thus, for instance, in *Commission v UK*[39] the issue related to whether beer and wine (the former taxed at a significantly lower rate than the latter) were products in competition with one another. The Court held that Article 110(2) TFEU concerned products which are, even only potentially, in competition with one another. It then continued:

> In order to determine the existence of a competitive relationship under the second paragraph of Article [110 TFEU], it is necessary to consider not only the present state of the market but also the *possibilities* for development within the context of free movement of goods at the Community level and the further potential for the substitution of products for one another which may be revealed by intensification of trade, so as fully to develop the complementary features of the economies of the Member States in accordance with the objectives laid down by Article 2 [TEC].[40]

In order to determine whether there is a competitive relationship (even just potential, partial or indirect)[41] between products, the degree of substitution between two products is one of the most important factors. In very simple terms, this requires an analysis as to whether consumers would, at least potentially, be willing to switch from one product to the other (because the product satisfies similar needs). The analysis cannot be based on the 'consumer habits in one Member State or in a given region',[42] not least since tax policies, by impacting on prices, might crystallise such habits. In the case at issue, and in the many cases regarding wine and beer that followed,[43] the Court found that only more common and cheaper wines were in competition with beer.

(ii) Protectionist Effect

Once products have been found to be in competition, the investigation focuses on whether the tax system has protectionist effects. Unlike Article 110 TFEU a different rate of taxation is not conclusive; rather it must be proven that the effect on price is such as to afford protection to domestic products. For instance, whilst in *Commission v UK* the tax on

---

[39] Case 170/78 [1980] ECR 417, interlocutory ruling; the Court delivered the final ruling a few years later [1983] ECR 2265.

[40] Case 170/78 *Commission v UK* (wine and beer) [1980] ECR 417, para 6 (emphasis added). Note that Art 2 TEC (and EEC) has been repealed and that the objectives of the Union are now contained in Art 3 TEU. Because of the changes it was deemed inappropriate to refer to the new provision in the quote.

[41] See eg Case 356/85 *Commission v Belgium* [1987] ECR 3299, para 7.

[42] Case 170/78 *Commission v UK* (wine and beer) [1980] ECR 417, para 14.

[43] eg Case 356/85 *Commission v Belgium* [1987] ECR 3299; and more recently Case C-167/05 *Commission v Sweden* [2008] ECR I-2127.

cheap (imported) wine was so high as to afford protection to beer, mainly domestically produced,[44] in *Commission v Sweden* the Court found that the difference in price between beer and wine pre-tax and after tax was very similar: hence even though taxes for wine were higher, such difference was not capable of influencing consumer behaviour in the sector concerned.[45]

It is not always easy to determine whether products are similar or in competition, and indeed it might be of little practical relevance if the tax regime is at least protectionist. In *Commission v Greece* the Court considered Greek rules imposing the general VAT rate of 16 per cent on certain spirits (including ouzo, brandy, liqueurs), while imposing a higher rate of 36 per cent on others (including whisky, gin, vodka and rum). Spirits in the former category were produced in Greece, while those in the latter category were not, or to no significant extent. The Court proceeded on the basis that all the spirits in the former category were either similar products within the meaning of the first paragraph of Article 110 TFEU, or were partly or potentially in competition with products in the second category, and considered that the tax regime in question contravened Article 110 TFEU. The Court made the following observation:

> The tax system established by the Greek legislation displays undeniably discriminatory or protective features. Although it does not establish any formal distinction according to the origin of the products, it is arranged in such a way that all the national production of spirits falls within the most favoured tax category. Those features of the system cannot be cancelled out by the fact that a fraction of imported spirits benefits from the most favourable rate. . . . It therefore appears that the tax system benefits national production and puts imported spirits at a disadvantage.[46]

In *Humblot*,[47] the case arose from a challenge to a French special car tax payable by reference to 'fiscal horsepower' or CV. Cars were subject in the first place to a tax which rose uniformly in proportion to increases in CV, and in the second place to a special tax levied at a single and considerably higher rate on cars rated at more than 16CV. No cars of more than 16CV were manufactured in France; all were imported. The Court emphasised that Member States were free to subject products such as cars to a system of tax which increases progressively in amount depending on an objective criterion, such as the power rating for tax purposes, which might be determined in various ways. Such a system of domestic taxation would only be compatible with Article 110 TFEU, however, if it were free of any discriminatory or protective effect. France denied any protective effect, arguing that there was no evidence that a consumer who might have been dissuaded from buying a vehicle of more than 16CV would purchase a car of French manufacture of 16CV or less. The Court of Justice rejected this argument, noting that cars on each side of the 16CV line were in competition with each other. The substantial additional increase in tax on cars of more than 16CV was liable to cancel out advantages which certain cars imported from other Member States might have in consumers' eyes over comparable cars of domestic manufacture. 'In that respect', said the Court, 'the special tax reduces the amount of competition to which cars of domestic manufacture are subject and hence is contrary to the principle of neutrality with which domestic taxation must comply.'[48]

---

[44] Case 170/78 [1983] ECR 2265.

[45] Case C-167/05 *Commission v Sweden* [2008] ECR I-2127, esp para 57.

[46] Case C-230/89 [1991] ECR I-1909, para 10.

[47] Case 112/84 [1985] ECR 1367.

[48] Case 112/84 *Humblot* [1985] ECR 1367, para 15; see also Case 433/85 *Feldain* [1987] ECR 3521; Case C-421/97 *Yves Tarantik v Direction des Services Fiscauz de Seine-et-Marne* [1999] ECR I-3633. Rules on taxation of used vehicles must take into account depreciation of imported vehicles and legislation cannot be drafted in

C – The Importance of a Comparator

The object of Article 110 TFEU is to abolish direct or indirect discrimination against imported products, but not to place them in a privileged tax position.[49] Internal taxation may therefore be imposed on imported products, even in the absence of a domestically produced counterpart. Indeed, if there is no similar domestic product, or product in competition with the imported product, there cannot be any discrimination or protectionist effect and Article 110 TFEU cannot be applied. In *Commission v Denmark*,[50] the Commission objected, inter alia, to what it considered excessively high taxation on registration of new cars. However, the Court found that since Denmark did not produce any goods which were similar or in competition with cars, Article 110 TFEU could not be applied.[51] However, in the rather remote situation in which taxation was charged at such a high rate to impede the free movement of goods, then Article 34 TFEU might be applicable.[52]

III – THE RELATIONSHIP BETWEEN ARTICLES 30 AND 110 TFEU

The prohibitions of Article 30 TFEU on the one hand, and Article 110 TFEU on the other, have often been contrasted by the Court. Article 30 TFEU applies to all charges exacted at the time of or by reason of importation which are imposed specifically on an imported product to the exclusion of the similar domestic product.[53] Article 110 TFEU, on the other hand, applies to financial charges levied within a general system of internal taxation applying systematically to domestic and imported goods.[54] The application of these respective prohibitions has been held to be mutually exclusive, not only because one and the same charge could not have been both removed during the transitional period (as had originally been provided under Articles 13 and 14 of the EEC Treaty for customs duties and CEEs), and by no later than the beginning of the second stage (as had originally provided for discriminatory internal taxation under Article 95 of the EEC Treaty),[55] but also because the requirement for customs duties and CEEs is that they are abolished,

---

general and abstract terms unless it ensures that any discriminatory effect be excluded, eg Case C-393/98 *Gomes Valente* [2001] ECR I-1327; Case C-101/00 *Tulliasiamies and Siilin* [2002] ECR I-7487.

[49] Case 153/80 *Rumhaus Hansen* [1981] ECR 1165; Case 253/83 *Kupferberg* [1985] ECR 157.

[50] Case C-47/88 *Commission v Denmark* [1990] ECR I-4509.

[51] Case C-47/88 *Commission v Denmark* [1990] ECR I-4509, esp paras 10 and 11 ; see also Case C-383/01 *De Danske Billimportører* [2003] ECR I-6065, para 38.

[52] See Case C-383/01 *De Danske Billimportører* [2003] ECR I-6065, para 40. See Chapter 14.

[53] See above Section I, and eg Case 77/82 *Capolongo v Azienda Agricola Maya* [1973] ECR 611; Joined Cases C-149/91 and C-150/91 *Sanders Adour SNC and Guyomarc'h Orthez Nutrition Animale SA v Directeur des Services Fiscaux des Pyrenées-Atlantiques* [1992] ECR I-3889, para 15 where it was also been held that pecuniary charges intended to finance the activities of an agency governed by public law can constitute charges having equivalent effect; see also Case C-114/91 *Criminal proceedings against Gérard Jerôme Claeys* [1992] ECR I-6559, para 13; Case C-144/91 *Gilbert Demoor en Zonen NV and others v Belgian State* [1992] ECR I-6613, para 15; Case C-266/91 *Celulose Beira Industrial SA v Fazenda Pública* [1993] ECR I-4337, para 10.

[54] eg Case 77/82 *Capolongo v Azienda Agricola Maya* [1973] ECR 611; Case C-347/95 *Fazenda Pública v UCAL* [1997] ECR I-4911.

[55] Case 10/65 *Deutschmann v Federal Republic of Germany* [1965] ECR 469. And see Case 57/65 *Lutticke v Hauptzollamt Saarlouis* [1966] ECR 205; Case 27/74 *Demag v Finanzamt Duisburg-Sud* [1974] ECR 1037.

while the requirement for discriminatory internal taxation is the elimination of any form of discrimination between domestic products and products originating in other Member States.[56] The Court has explicitly rejected the argument that an equalisation tax on an imported product which exceeds the charges applied to similar domestic products takes on the character of a CEE as to the difference.[57] It is thus established that 'provisions relating to charges having equivalent effect and those relating to discriminatory internal taxation cannot be applied together, so that under the system of the Treaty the same imposition cannot belong to both categories at the same time'.[58]

A charge which is imposed both on imported products and on domestic products, but in practice applies almost exclusively to imported products because domestic production is extremely small, does not amount to a CEE if it is part of a general system of internal dues applied systematically to categories of products in accordance with objective criteria irrespective of the origin of the products. It therefore constitutes internal taxation within the meaning of Article 110 TFEU.[59] Indeed, a charge comprises internal taxation even where there are no comparable domestic products at all, where the charge in question applies to whole classes of domestic or foreign products which are all in the same position irrespective of origin.[60]

To fall within the scope of Article 110 TFEU, however, a charge must be levied at the same marketing stage on both domestic goods and imports, and the chargeable event giving rise to the duty must be identical in each case.[61] If there is an insufficiently close connection between the charges levied on domestic goods, and those levied on imports, in that they are determined on the basis of different criteria, they will fall to be classified under Article 30 TFEU, rather than Article 110 TFEU.[62] In *Interzuccheri v Ditta Rezzano e Cavassa*,[63] the Court considered a charge imposed on sales of sugar, whether home pro-

---

[56] Case 94/74 *IGAV v ENCC* [1975] ECR 699.

[57] Case 25/67 *Milch- Fett- und Eierkontor v Hauptzollamt Saarbrucken* [1968] ECR 207; Case 32/80 *Officier van Justitie v Kortmann* [1981] ECR 251.

[58] Joined Cases C-78/90 etc, *Compagnie Commerciale de l'Ouest and others v Receveur Principal des Douanes de La Pallice Port* [1992] ECR I-1847, para 22; Joined Cases C-149/91 and C-150/91 *Sanders Adour SNC and Guyomarc'h Orthez Nutrition Animale SA v Directeur des Services Fiscaux des Pyrenées-Atlantiques* [1992] ECR I-3889, para 14; Case C-114/91 *Criminal proceedings against Gérard Jerôme Claeys* [1992] ECR I-6559, para 12; Case C-144/91 *Gilbert Demoor en Zonen NV and others v Belgian State* [1992] ECR I-6613, para 14; Case C-266/91 *Celulose Beira Industrial SA v Fazenda Pública* [1993] ECR I-4337, para 9; Case C-347/95 *Fazenda Pública v UCAL* [1997] ECR I-4911, para 17.

[59] Case 193/85 *Co-Frutta v Amministrazione delle Finanze dello Stato* [1987] ECR 2085, para 14; Case C-343/90 *Manuel José Lourenço Dias v Director da Alfândega do Porto* [1992] ECR I-4673, para 53.

[60] Joined Cases 2 and 3/69 *Chougol Diamond Co* [1969] ECR 211; a limited number of products as 'groundnuts, groundnut products and Brazil nuts' cannot fall within the concept of such whole classes of products, a concept which implies a much larger number of products determined by general and objective criteria; see Case 27/67 *Fink-Frucht* [1968] ECR 223; Case 158/82 *Commission v Denmark* [1983] ECR 3573.

[61] Case 132/78 *Denkavit Loire Sarl v France* [1979] ECR 1923; Joined Cases C-149/91 and C-150/91 *Sanders Adour SNC and Guyomarc'h Orthez Nutrition Animale SA v Directeur des Services Fiscaux des Pyrenées-Atlantiques* [1992] ECR I-3889, para 17. However, VAT levied on imports does not amount to a charge having equivalent effect, Case 249/84 *Profant* [1986] ECR 3237.

[62] Case 132/80 *United Foods* [1981] ECR 995; but *in the absence of any protective purpose*, an internal tax could not be regarded as a charge having equivalent effect to a customs duty, see Case 7/67 *Wohrmann v Hauptzollamt Bad Reichenhall* [1967] ECR 177.

[63] Case 105/76 [1977] ECR 1029. See also eg Case 77/72 *Capolongo* [1973] ECR 611; Case 94/74 *IGAV* [1975] ECR 699; Case 77/76 *Fratelli Cucchi v Avez* [1977] ECR 987; Case 222/78 *ICAP v Walter Beneventi* [1979] ECR 1163; Joined Cases C-78/90 etc, *Compagnie Commerciale de l'Ouest and others v Receveur Principal des Douanes de La Pallice Port* [1992] ECR I-1847, paras 24 and 26; Case C-266/91 *Celulose Beira Industrial SA v Fazenda Pública* [1993] ECR I-4337, paras 12–14; Case C-347/95 *Fazenda Pública v UCAL* [1997] ECR I-4911, paras 20-24; Case C-234/99 *Niels Nygård and Svineafgiftsfonden* [2002] ECR I-3657, para 23.

duced or imported, the proceeds of which were used for the exclusive benefit of national sugar refineries and sugar beet producers. The Court held that such a charge, on the face of it internal taxation, could only be considered a CEE if:

— it had the sole purpose of financing activities for the specific advantage of the taxed domestic product;
— the taxed product and the domestic product benefiting from it were the same;
— the charges imposed on the domestic product were made good in full.

IV – THE RELATIONSHIP BETWEEN ARTICLES 30 AND 110 TFEU AND OTHER PROVISIONS OF THE TREATY

Where national measures are financed by a discriminatory internal tax, Article 110 TFEU is applicable to the latter, despite the fact that it forms part of a national aid, subject to scrutiny under Articles 107 and 108 TFEU.[64] Equally, Article 30 TFEU on the one hand, and Articles 107 and 108 TFEU on the other, are cumulatively applicable in such circumstances.[65] Articles 30 and 110 TFEU do not, however, overlap with the prohibition on quantitative restrictions and measures having equivalent effect contained in Article 34 TFEU. The Court held in *Ianelli & Volpi v Paolo Meroni* that:

> However wide the field of application of Article [34 TFEU] may be, it nevertheless does not include obstacles to trade covered by other provisions of the Treaty. Thus obstacles which are of a fiscal nature or have equivalent effect and are covered by Articles [28–32 TFEU] and [110 TFEU] . . . do not fall within the prohibition of Article [34 TFEU].[66]

However, the Court has also indicated that very high taxation *might*, in the absence of discrimination, constitute a barrier to the free movement of goods caught by Article 34 TFEU.[67] Given the fact that Member States remain free to decide upon the level of taxation, it is only in the most extreme of cases that a tax would be construed as a measure having equivalent effect.[68]

The relationship between Article 37 TFEU on state monopolies, and Article 110 TFEU,

---

[64] Case 47/69 *France v Commission* [1970] ECR 487; Case 73/79 *Commission v Italy* [1980] ECR 1547; Case 17/81 *Pabst and Richarz v Hauptzollamt Oldenburg* [1982] ECR 1331; Case 277/83 *Commission v Italy* [1985] ECR 2049; Case C-266/91 *Celulose Beira Industrial SA v Fazenda Pública* [1993] ECR I-4337, para 21. Arts 25 and 90 EC are relevant even when the state aid has been authorised by the Commission, eg Case C-234/99 *Niels Nygård and Svineafgiftsfonden* [2002] ECR I-3657, operative part of the ruling.

[65] Joined Cases C-78/90 etc, *Compagnie Commerciale de l'Ouest and others v Receveur Principal des Douanes de La Pallice Port* [1992] ECR I-1847, para 32; Case C-144/91 *Gilbert Demoor en Zonen NV and others v Belgian State* [1992] ECR I-6613, para 24; Case C-266/91 *Celulose Beira Industrial SA v Fazenda Pública* [1993] ECR I-4337, para 21.

[66] Case 74/76 [1977] ECR 557; Joined Cases C-78/90 etc, *Compagnie Commerciale de l'Ouest and others v Receveur Principal des Douanes de La Pallice Port* [1992] ECR I-1847, para 20; Case C-17/91 *Georges Lornoy en Zonen NV and others v Belgian State* [1992] ECR I-6523, para 14. But if Art 110 TFEU is inapplicable because an import lacks a domestic counterpart, Art 34 TFEU may apply to the tax in question: see Case C-47/88 *Commission v Denmark* I-4509.

[67] Case C-383/01 *De Danske Billimportører* [2003] ECR I-6065; Joined Cases C-34/01–38/01 *Enirisorse Spa* [2003] ECR I-14243.

[68] See Chapter 14 below.

was considered by the Court in *Grandes Distilleries Peureux*.[69] Whereas Article 37 TFEU was acknowledged to have provided an exception to certain rules of the Treaty—in casu Article 110 TFEU—during the transitional period, this was declared to be no longer the case. Where internal taxation is concerned, Article 110 TFEU apparently constitutes a *lex specialis*, even it seems in the case of activities which would otherwise qualify for scrutiny under Article 37 TFEU.

V – DISCRIMINATORY TAX TREATMENT OF EXPORTS

The system adopted for taxing products in intra-EU trade is based on the 'destination principle', ie goods exported from a Member State receive a rebate of internal taxation paid, and are in turn subjected to internal taxation in the country of destination.[70] The purpose of Article 110 TFEU is to prevent this process being used to place a heavier burden on imports than on domestic goods, but the system is vulnerable to another, equally damaging abuse: the repayment to exporters of an amount exceeding the internal taxation in fact paid, which would amount to an export subsidy for domestic production. It is to counteract this possibility that Article 111 TFEU provides that where products are exported to the territory of any Member State, any repayment of internal taxation shall not exceed the internal taxation imposed on them, whether directly or indirectly.

The Court laid down guidelines as to the extent of repayments permissible under this Article in *Commission v Italy*,[71] where the Commission alleged excessive repayment of taxes levied on certain engineering products. The Commission claimed that the repayment of duties paid on licenses, concessions, motor vehicles and advertising, in connection with the production and marketing of the products in question, were ineligible for repayment under Article 111 TFEU. The Court ruled that the words 'directly or indirectly' referred to the distinction between taxes which had been levied on the products themselves (directly), and taxes levied on the raw materials and semi-finished goods used in their manufacture (indirectly).[72] It followed that the charges referred to by the Commission could not be repaid consistently with Article 111 TFEU, for the simple reason that they were not taxes imposed on the products at all, but 'upon the producer undertaking in the very varied aspects of its general commercial and financial activity'.[73] The Court has also held that when a Member State employs a flat-rate system for determining the amount of internal taxation which can be repaid on exportation to another Member State, it is for that former Member State to establish that such a system remains *in all cases* within the mandatory limits of Article 111 TFEU.[74]

---

[69] Case 86/78 [1979] ECR 897.

[70] Case C-213/96 *Outokumpu Oy* [1998] ECR I-1777, Opinion of AG Jacobs, para 46.

[71] Case 45/64 [1965] ECR 857. For infringements of Art 111 TFEU, see Case C-152/89 *Commission v Luxembourg* [1991] ECR I-3171; Case C-153/89 *Commission v Belgium* [1991] ECR I-3171.

[72] On the similar wording in Art 110, see above at section II.A, and Case 28/67 *Molkerei-Zentrale* [1968] ECR 143, 155.

[73] Case 45/64 [1965] ECR 857, 866.

[74] Case 152/89 *Commission v Luxembourg* [1991] ECR I-3171, para 36.

VI – THE COMMON CUSTOMS TARIFF AND EXTERNAL RELATIONS

The preceding exposition has been concerned with the elimination of customs duties and other financial charges on trade between the Member States, but brief mention must be made of imports and exports between the EU and third countries.

Neither the relevant Articles of the Treaty, nor Regulation 950/68 on the Common Customs Tariff,[75] explicitly provided for the regulation of CEEs in trade relations between the Member States and third countries. Nevertheless, the Court held in *Sociaal Fonds voor de Dimantarbeiders*[76] that the unilateral imposition of such charges after the adoption of the Common Customs Tariff was inconsistent with the aim of the Treaty that Member States adopt a common policy in their trade relations with the outside world. The Court has confirmed this position in a consistent case law,[77] but has indicated that the Treaty does not preclude the levying of a CEE to a customs duty on imports which, having regard to all its essential characteristics, must be regarded as a charge already in existence on 1 July 1968, provided that the level at which it is levied has not been raised, and where the level has been raised, only the amount by which it has been raised must be regarded as incompatible with the Treaty.[78]

The Treaty itself has no provision analogous to Article 110 TFEU applying to imports from non-member countries.[79] International agreements between the EU and third countries, and the provisions of agricultural regulations, may prohibit customs duties, CEEs and discriminatory internal taxation on trade between the EU and third countries. It cannot be assumed without more that such provisions as these are to be construed as strictly as analogous provisions governing intra-European trade, though a provision in an international agreement prohibiting CEEs will be construed in the same way as the same term appearing in the TFEU if to give it more limited scope would deprive the agreement in question of much of its effectiveness.[80] But even where a provision of a regulation prohibits CEEs on trade with third countries, and the Court takes the view that the concept is the same as that embodied in Article 30 TFEU, the requirement may be subject to derogation authorised by the Union institutions in a way that would not be possible were intra-Union trade involved.[81] And where health inspections are permitted by Union regulations on imports from third countries, the inspections may be stricter, and the fees charged higher, than in intra-Union trade, since Union law does not require Member States to show the same degree of confidence towards non-member countries as they are required to show other Member States.[82]

Where an international agreement prohibits discriminatory internal taxation on

---

[75] OJ Sp Edn 1969(1), 275, repealed with effect from 31 December 1987 by Reg 2658/87, [1987] OJ L256/1.

[76] Joined Cases 37 and 38/73 [1973] ECR 1609.

[77] Case C-125/94 *Aprile Srl, in liquidation, v Amministrazione delle Finanze dello Stato* [1995] ECR I-2919, paras 35–37; Case C-109/98 *CRT France International SA* [1999] ECR I-2237, para 22.

[78] Case C-126/94 *Cadi Surgelés and others* [1996] ECR I-5647.

[79] Case 148/77 *Hansen* [1978] ECR 1787; Joined Cases C-228/90–234/90, C-339/90 and C-353/90 *Simba SpA and others* [1992] ECR I-3713, para 14; Case C-130/92 *OTO SpA v Ministero delle Finanze* [1994] ECR I-3281, paras 18 and 19; Case C-284/96 *Didier Tabouillet v Directeur des Services Fiscaux de Meurthe-et-Moselle* [1997] ECR I-7471, para 23.

[80] Case C-163/90 *Legros and others* [1992] ECR I-4625, para 26.

[81] Case 70/77 *Simmenthal* [1978] ECR 1543.

[82] Case 30/79 *Land Berlin v Wigei* [1980] ECR 1331.

imports from third countries, it will be a matter of interpretation whether or not the provision in question is intended to fulfil the same purpose in relations between the EU and third countries as Article 110 TFEU fulfils in respect of intra-Union trade.[83]

Further Reading

L Gormley, *EU Law of Free Movement of Goods and Customs Union* (Oxford, Oxford University Press, 2009).

BJM Terra and PJ Wattel, *European Tax Law*, 5th edn (Alphen aan den Rijn, Kluwer Law International, 2008).

---

[83] Compare Case 17/81 *Pabst & Richarz KG v Hauptzollamt Oldenburg* [1982] ECR 1331, with Case 104/81 *Hauptzollamt Mainz v Kupferberg* [1982] ECR 3641; see also Case C-312/91 *Metalsa Srl* [1993] ECR I-3751.

14

The Free Movement of Goods: Quantitative Restrictions and Measures Having Equivalent Effect

In the previous chapter we considered fiscal barriers to trade. This chapter is concerned with non-fiscal barriers to trade. Articles 34 and 35 TFEU prohibit quantitative restrictions and measures having equivalent effect to quantitative restrictions om imports, exports and goods in transit. Article 36 TFEU allows the Member States to retain such measures in order to protect listed interests. The definition of quantitative restrictions did not give rise to problems: the concept was already known in international trade law before the establishment of the EEC, and aims at prohibiting quotas on imports/exports. The definition of measures having equivalent effect to a quantitative restriction on imports proved to be more complex. In the seminal case of *Dassonville*, the Court gave a broad interpretation of the concept that encompasses any direct or indirect, actual or potential obstacle to intra-EU trade. However, such a broad interpretation may lead to significant problems. First, the narrow grounds for justification contained in Article 36 TFEU proved inadequate to strike the correct balance between the legitimate regulatory needs of the Member States and the demands of the Treaty. In order to solve this problem, the Court held in the *Cassis de Dijon* ruling that Member States could rely on broader grounds of public interest—so-called mandatory requirements—to justify non-directly discriminatory restrictions to intra-Community trade. Secondly, the broad *Dassonville* formula, even if coupled with the *Cassis de Dijon* mandatory requirements doctrine, led to further problems when almost any trading rule was found to constitute an obstacle to intra-Community trade in need of justification. As a result, the Court revisited its own case law in the *Keck* ruling, and introduced a distinction based on the 'type' of rules: rules regulating the physical qualities of a product (product requirements) automatically fall within the scope of Article 34 TFEU. However, rules that merely discipline the *way* a product is sold (selling arrangements) in principle fall outside the scope of Article 34 TFEU, unless directly or indirectly discriminatory. The *Keck* ruling brought much-needed clarification; however, it also reignited the debate as to the appropriate scope of Article 34 TFEU. Furthermore, the application of the *Keck* ruling has not been without its problems and, as we shall see, the boundaries of Article 34 TFEU are still not so clearly defined as it might appear at first sight. This chapter deals with these issues, as well as with the scope of Articles 35 and 36 TFEU; the scope of the mandatory requirements doctrine; the relationship between the free movement of goods provisions and other Treaty provisions; and the relationship between Article 36 TFEU and Intellectual property rights. The coexistence of different national systems of intellectual property law is capable of conflicting with the objective of creating a single market. For example, a company holding patent or trade mark rights protected under the law of two Member States might use its rights in each to prevent products which it itself had placed on the market in one of the Member States being imported into the other. Articles 34–36 TFEU have been interpreted as preventing holders of intellectual property rights from using them to prevent the import of goods into one Member State from the territory of another where the holder of the rights in question has consented to their being placed on the market. This principle is known as 'exhaustion' of intellectual property rights, and is examined in some detail in this chapter. Harmonisation of intellectual property rights is considered in outline by way of introduction and reference is made to specific harmonising legislation where appropriate.

I – INTRODUCTION

The elimination of fiscal barriers to trade would be of little consequence if Member States could then impose restrictions on the actual flow of goods; for this reason the Treaty prohibits Member States from imposing quantitative restrictions (ie quotas) and measures having equivalent effect to quantitative restrictions on imports, exports and goods in transit.[1] Although the concept of quota is both easy to define and was already known in international trade law,[2] the concept of a 'measure having equivalent effect' to a quantitative restriction was new to the (then) EEC Treaty and was undefined therein. As we shall see in the following sections, the latter gave rise to intense academic and jurisprudential debate touching upon issues of wider constitutional significance, and especially on the respective scopes of Union and national law, and the extent to which the interpretation of the scant provisions in the Treaty could legitimately have wide-ranging effects on national regulatory autonomy.

II – QUANTITATIVE RESTRICTIONS ON IMPORTS AND EXPORTS

The notion of a quantitative restriction is well understood, and its definition poses little difficulty. As the Court explained in *Geddo*, 'The prohibition on quantitative restrictions covers measures which amount to a total or partial restraint of, according to the cir-

---

[1] Given the trade-restrictive effects of quotas, the authors of the Spaak Report considered their elimination as a 'fundamental element' in the creation of a common market, see *Rapport des Chefs de Délégation aux Ministres des Affaires Etrangères* (1956) 35.

[2] J Jackson, *World Trade and the Law of GATT* (Indianapolis, Bobbs-Merrill, 1969) 305.

cumstances, imports, exports, or goods in transit.'[3] Thus, when the Italian authorities suspended imports of pork into Italy from other Member States in June 1960, the Court ruled that such a measure amounted to an infringement of the 'standstill' provision of then Article 31(1) EEC, as the text of the Treaty stood at the time.[4] A total prohibition on imports is considered a zero quota, and therefore is qualified as a quantitative restriction. For instance, in *Henn and Darby* a statutory prohibition in the United Kingdom on the import of pornographic material was held to amount to a quantitative restriction contrary to Article 34 TFEU, subject to possible justification under Article 36 TFEU,[5] and a restriction in the United Kingdom on imports of main crop potatoes was held to amount to a quantitative restriction.[6] Articles 34 and 35 TFEU can be invoked by individuals in relation to personal imports.[7]

III – MEASURES HAVING EQUIVALENT EFFECT TO QUANTITATIVE RESTRICTIONS ON IMPORTS

A – The Inception of the Court's Case Law: *Dassonville* and *Cassis de Dijon*

As mentioned above, the concept of a measure having equivalent effect to a quantitative restriction on imports was not defined in the Treaty and is almost entirely of jurisprudential derivation. In 1969 the Commission adopted Directive 70/50/EEC,[8] which provides valuable guidance on the meaning of measures having equivalent effect even though it has seldom been referred to by the Court.[9] The Directive identifies as measures having equivalent effect both those that apply only to imported products (Article 2) and those that apply to both domestic and imported products but that are likely to affect the latter in a specific way. Amongst those, Article 3 identifies rules concerning, inter alia, weight, shape, composition and size of products where the effects of those rules on the free movement of goods exceeds the effects intrinsic to trade rules. This would be the case where the effects are out of proportion to the aim of the rules and where such aims could be achieved with means that are less trade-restrictive. As mentioned above, the Court only very seldom referred to Directive 70/50/EEC, rather developing its own independent definition of a measure having equivalent effect to a quantitative restriction on imports.

---

[3] Case 2/73 *Geddo v Ente Nazionale Risi* [1973] ECR 865, 879; however, Arts 34 and 35 TFEU cannot be invoked if the trade in goods is illegal throughout the EU, see Case C-137/09 *Josemans v Burgemeester van Maastricht*, judgment of 12 December 2010.

[4] Case 7/61 *Commission v Italy* [1961] ECR 317.

[5] Case 34/79 *Henn and Darby* [1979] ECR 3795.

[6] Case 118/78 *Meijer* [1979] ECR 1387; Case 231/78 *Commission v United Kingdom* [1979] ECR 1447.

[7] eg Case C-170/04 *Rosengren* [2007] ECR I-4071.

[8] OJ Sp Edn 1970(I), 17. While strictly this measure applies to measures in force at the end of the transitional period, it provides valuable guidance on the meaning of measures having equivalent effect.

[9] eg Art 2 Directive 70/50 was referred to in Case 4/75 *Rewe-Zentralfinanz v Landwirtschaftskammer* [1975] ECR 843; Case 74/76 *Ianelli & Volpi SpA v Meroni* [1977] ECR 557.

(i) The Dassonville Case

It was clear from the Court's early case law that a national rule requiring import licences for the import of goods from other Member States would amount to a measure having equivalent effect to a quantitative restriction, even if the requirement was a formality.[10] This was consistent with the view that it was a characteristic of such measures that they applied specifically to imports and burdened them in some way. However, it was in the judgment in *Procureur du Roi v Dassonville* that one finds the first attempt to lay down a general definition of measures having equivalent effect to quantitative restrictions on imports. The defendants in the national proceedings imported into Belgium Scotch whisky which they had purchased from French distributors. Belgian legislation required such goods to be accompanied by a certificate of origin made out in the name of the Belgian importer, and the goods in question were without such certificates, which could have been obtained only with the greatest difficulty once the goods had been previously imported into France. The importers argued that the Belgian requirement amounted to a measure having equivalent effect and was therefore contrary to Article 34 TFEU. On a reference for a preliminary ruling the Court of Justice provided the definition (still valid) of a measure having equivalent effect to a quantitative restriction:

> 5. All trading rules enacted by Member States which are capable of hindering, *directly or indirectly, actually or potentially*, intra-Community trade are to be considered as measures having an effect equivalent to quantitative restrictions.
>
> 6. In the absence of a Community system guaranteeing for consumers the authenticity of a product's designation of origin, if a Member State takes measures to prevent unfair practices in this connection, it is however subject to the condition that these measures should be reasonable and that the means of proof required should not act as a hindrance to trade between member states and should, in consequence, be accessible to all community nationals.
>
> 7. Even without having to examine whether or not such measures are covered by [Article 36] TFEU, they must not, in any case, by virtue of the principle expressed in the second sentence of that Article, constitute a means of arbitrary discrimination or a disguised restriction on trade between Member States.
>
> 8. That may be the case with formalities, required by a Member State for the purpose of proving the origin of a product, which only direct importers are really in a position to satisfy without facing serious difficulties.[11]

The definition of measures having equivalent effect in paragraph 5 of the above judgment is stated in very broad terms, and indeed this, in time, will lead to problems in defining the boundaries of the free movement of goods. However, the national measure in issue in *Dassonville* had a real and significant impact on intra-European trade: as the Court indicates in paragraphs 7 and 8 of its judgment set out above, the national measure in issue in that case imposed a considerably greater burden on one category of imports (imports from a Member State into which the goods had already been imported—so-called parallel imports) than on another category of imports (imports directly from the country of origin). Furthermore it is important to note that the *Dassonville* formula does not mention discrimination: thus, in order for a national measure to fall within the scope of Article 34 TFEU, there is no need to prove that it affects imports more than it affects domestic

---

[10] Joined Cases 51–54/71 *International Fruit* [1971] ECR 1107.
[11] Case 8/74 *Procureur du Roi v Dassonville* [1974] ECR 837, paras 5–8, emphasis added.

goods. Rather, what matters is an effect, actual or potential, direct or indirect, on intra-European trade.

(ii) The Cassis Ruling

The *Cassis*[12] case involved the intended importation into Germany of a consignment of the alcoholic beverage 'Cassis de Dijon'. Under German legislation fruit liqueurs such as 'Cassis' could only be marketed if they contained a minimum alcohol content of 25 per cent, whereas the alcohol content of the product in question was between 15 and 20 per cent. A German court asked the Court of Justice whether legislation such as that in issue was consistent with Article 34 TFEU. Before the Court of Justice, the German government argued that the legislation in question was discriminatory in neither a formal nor a material sense; any obstacle to trade resulted simply from the fact that France and Germany had different rules for the minimum alcohol contents of certain drinks. The Court's judgment makes no reference at all to the issue of discrimination. Rather it regards incompatibility with Article 34 TFEU as flowing from the very fact that the 'Cassis' could not be placed lawfully on the German market, and addresses itself at once to the question whether there existed any justification for the restriction.

> 8. In the absence of common rules relating to the production and marketing of alcohol . . . it is for the Member States to regulate all matters relating to the production and marketing of alcohol and alcoholic beverages on their own territory.
>
> Obstacles to movement within the Community resulting from disparities between the national laws relating to the marketing of the products in question must be accepted in so far as those provisions may be recognized as being necessary in order to satisfy mandatory requirements relating in particular to the effectiveness of fiscal supervision, the protection of public health, the fairness of commercial transactions and the defence of the consumer.[13]

The Court rejected the arguments of the German government relating to the protection of public health and to the protection of the consumer against unfair commercial practices, and continued:

> 14. It is clear from the foregoing that the requirements relating to the minimum alcohol content of alcoholic beverages do not serve a purpose which is in the general interest and such as to take precedence over the requirements of the free movement of goods, which constitutes one of the fundamental rules of the Community.[14]

In the paragraphs which follow the Court describes the restrictive effect of national rules such as those at issue in terms which seem to make the existence of an element of discrimination irrelevant in establishing violation of Article 34 TFEU, or to presume it to exist from the very fact of exclusion of products lawfully produced and marketed in one of the Member States.

> [14 cont] In practice, the principal effect of requirements of this nature is to promote alcoholic beverages having a high alcohol content by excluding from the national market products of other Member States which do not answer that description.

---

[12] Case 120/78 *Rewe-Zentral AG v Bundesmonopolverwaltung für Branntwein* ('Cassis de Dijon') [1979] ECR 649.

[13] Ibid, para 8, emphasis added.

[14] Ibid, para 14.

> It therefore appears that the unilateral requirement imposed by the rules of a Member State of a minimum alcohol content for the purposes of the sale of alcoholic beverages constitutes an obstacle to trade which is incompatible with the provisions of Article [34TFEU]. . . . There is therefore no valid reason why, *provided that they have been lawfully produced and marketed in one of the Member States, alcoholic beverages should not be introduced into any other Member State*; the sale of such products may not be subject to a legal prohibition on the marketing of beverages with an alcohol content lower than the limit set by the national rules.[15]

The judgment in this case was one of the great formative events in the establishment of the internal market. The ruling in *Cassis* is notable for two main reasons: first of all, it lays down the principle of mutual recognition;[16] and secondly, it lays down the mandatory requirements doctrine.

(a) The Principle of Mutual Recognition: Positive and Negative Integration

According to the principle of mutual recognition, a Member State must recognise (and trust) regulatory standards in other Member States so that once the goods have been lawfully produced in one of the Member States they should be able to circulate freely in the European Union, and be marketed everywhere in the EU, *unless* there is a valid reason to stop them. The importing Member State can impose its own rules on imported products only to the extent to which that is necessary to protect a mandatory requirement of public interest, such as consumer protection, fiscal supervision, etc.[17]

The mutual recognition principle has been one of the founding stones of the internal market: it allowed the free movement of goods, whilst at the same time leaving in place the regulatory differentiation, an aspect also of cultural diversity, that characterises the European Union. The Commission immediately understood the beneficial potential of the mutual recognition principle: if Member States had a duty in Union law to allow goods lawfully produced elsewhere to be marketed in their territory, and could not impose unnecessary regulation, then the need for common standards set through harmonising legislation would be greatly reduced. In its communication on the *Cassis de Dijon* ruling, the Commission hence clarified that in the future

> The Commission's work of harmonization will henceforth have to be directed mainly at national laws having an impact on the functioning of the common market where barriers to trade to be removed arise from national provisions which are admissible under the criteria set by the Court.[18]

As a result of the *Cassis* ruling, then, the need for positive integration (the setting of one standard for all of the EU) is reduced to the minimum due to the fact that market integration in significant areas can be achieved via mutual recognition (negative integration). An example might serve to illustrate this point: take, for instance, the case of blue cheese; this is traditionally produced in many Member States according to different rules—Gorgonzola in Italy, Stilton in the UK, Roquefort in France, etc. If each of the Member States were allowed to impose its own rules on blue cheese, so as to prevent import of blue cheese produced according to rules different from its own, there would be 27 different markets

---

[15] Ibid, para 14, emphasis added.

[16] The Court has held that the lack of a mutual recognition clause in rules on product requirements (composition, etc) is per se a breach of Union law: Case C-184/96 *Commission v France* (paté de foie gras) [1998] ECR I-6197.

[17] See below section VII.

[18] [1980] OJ C256/2.

in blue cheese since each producer would have to comply with the rules of the Member State of destination in order to market and sell its products in that country. The only way to achieve a single market would then be to have only *one* EU standard for blue cheese (positive integration), with the consequent loss of both regulatory and product diversity. On the other hand, thanks to Article 34 TFEU, as interpreted by the Court, there is no need to impose *one* standard: different regulatory traditions, and different products, can coexist since each product can gain access to the other Member States' markets without having to be modified (negative integration). Thus, it is only when the Member States successfully invoke a justification for imposing their own rules on imported products (ie when they successfully rely on the mandatory requirements doctrine) that there will be the need to remove such barriers through positive harmonisation.

(b) The Mandatory Requirements Doctrine

If the principle of mutual recognition is one of the foundation stones of the internal market, the mandatory requirements doctrine is hardly less important. The broad interpretation given to Article 34 TFEU would have given rise to significant problems if the Court had not accepted that the Member States could still impose their own rules on imported products when there was a mandatory requirement of public interest which justified such rules. Take, for instance, labelling requirements (which are measures having equivalent effect falling within the scope of Article 34 TFEU): it is clearly in the interest of consumer protection that product labels can be easily understood by consumers and therefore Member States should be allowed to require that labels are in the official language or at least in a language widely spoken in their territory.[19] However, consumer protection is not mentioned in Article 36 TFEU as one of the interests that allows Member States to derogate from Articles 34 and 35 TFEU. The mandatory requirements doctrine addresses this problem: as we shall see in more detail later, it allows a Member State to invoke broader public interest grounds to justify the imposition of its rules on imported products. However, such grounds of public interest can be invoked only if the rules are not directly discriminatory, ie if they apply in law to domestic and imported products alike; furthermore, such rules must also be necessary to the achievement of the stated aim as well as proportionate (see below).

B – The Application of the *Cassis* Ruling

The ruling in *Cassis* was confirmed in later case law; for instance, in *Gilli & Andres*,[20] Italian rules prohibited the marketing of vinegar containing acetic acid derived otherwise than from the acetic fermentation of wine; the defendants in the national proceedings were prosecuted for being in possession of apple vinegar for sale for gain. In this case the Court slightly modified one of its observations in *Cassis*:

> In practice, the principal effect of provisions of this nature is to protect domestic production by prohibiting the putting on to the market of products from other Member States which do not answer the descriptions laid down by the national rules.[21]

---

[19] Case C-33/97 *Colim* [1999] ECR I-3175, para 44.
[20] Case 788/79 *Gilli and Andres* [1980] ECR 2071.
[21] Case 788/79 *Gilli and Andres* [1980] ECR 2071, para 10.

If discrimination was the distinguishing feature of national measures prima facie contrary to Article 34 TFEU before the *Cassis* judgment, emphasis after that case was placed upon the protective effect of national rules which excluded from the market of one Member State goods lawfully produced and marketed in the territory of another. As the Commission stated in its above-mentioned communication on *Cassis*:

> Any product imported from another Member State must in principle be admitted to the territory of the importing Member State if it has been lawfully produced, that is, conforms to rules and processes of manufacture that are customarily and traditionally accepted in the exporting country, and is marketed in the territory of another.[22]

There is a rich body of case law applying the *Cassis* ruling to national rules of the importing Member State, and the Court was vigilant in ensuring that only rules truly necessary for the achievement of a mandatory requirement survived scrutiny. On the other hand, rules that simply reflected cultural traditions, or reinforced consumer habits and prejudices, especially in the field of food and beverages, would usually fall foul of Article 34 TFEU and would therefore not be applicable to imported products. Thus, for instance, in the above-mentioned case of *Gilli and Andres* the Court made clear that Italian rules which provided that only vinegar obtained only from the fermentation of wine could be sold (to the exclusion of vinegar made from cider) could not be applied to imported products.[23] In *Glocken*,[24] the Court found that rules that prohibited the sale of dry pasta not made with 100 per cent durum wheat could not be applied to imports from other Member States. The Court disposed of the Italian Government's submission concerning the importance of high-quality pasta to the Italian consumer, who would expect pasta to be made only with durum wheat, and held that the consumer could be informed through labelling. In *Rau*, similar reasoning was applied to rules which required margarine to be sold in cube-shaped packets.[25] Overall, in the Court's view, the consumer can be easily informed of the fact that an imported product has been produced according to different standards by means of labelling, and for this reason there is no need to exclude a product which has been manufactured according to a different set of rules.

As noted above, neither the *Dassonville* nor the *Cassis* rulings mention discrimination. If a national rule places imports at a disadvantage, it will of course be caught by Article 34 TFEU; however, the importer/claimant does not need to prove discrimination in order to trigger the protection of the Treaty.[26] If the product has been lawfully produced and marketed in another Member State, there is a presumption that it should be free to circulate within the EU unless further regulation is necessary to protect a mandatory requirement of public interest. The absence of a test of discrimination eventually led to some confusion in relation to the boundaries of the free movement of goods provisions: if a difference in

---

[22] [1980] OJ C 256/2.

[23] Case 788/79 *Gilli and Andres* [1980] ECR 2071.

[24] Case 407/85 *Drei Glocken GmbH* [1988] ECR 4233.

[25] Case 261/81 *Rau* [1982] ECR 3961; other examples of rules found to infringe Art 34 TFEU are: national rules imposing a labelling requirement (eg Case 27/80 *Fietje* [1980] ECR 3839; Case 94/82 *De Kikvorsch* [1983] ECR 947); national rules prohibiting use of the additives in cheese (Case 53/80 *Eyssen* [1981] ECR 409); national rules regulating the dry matter content, moisture content, and salt content, of bread (eg Case 30/80 *Kelderman* [1981] ECR 517; Case C-358/95 *Tommaso Morellato v USL No 11, Prodenone* [1997] ECR I-1431; Case C-17/93 *Van der Veldt* [1994] ECR I-3537); national rules requiring silver products to be hall-marked (eg Case 220/81 *Robertson* [1982] ECR 2349; Case C-293/93 *Houtwipper* [1994] ECR I-4249; Case C-166/03 *Commission v France* [2004] ECR I-6535).

[26] This is not to belittle the importance of discrimination as a conceptual framework for the internal market.

treatment between imported and domestic goods was not necessary to trigger the Treaty, would any rule regulating the marketing (even indirectly) of products be caught by the Treaty? The question is of fundamental importance because each time the Treaty applies, the Member States see their regulatory choices scrutinised by the judiciary so that not only must their rules pursue a public interest compatible with Union law, but they also have to do so in a proportionate way. However, the proportionality assessment always carries the risk of substituting the assessment and the preferences of the (elected) regulator with that of the (unelected) judiciary. Whilst this is more than legitimate if the rules actually place imports at a disadvantage (since discrimination is incompatible with the internal market), the question is more sensitive when the national rules under scrutiny apply in the same way to imported and domestic products. This problem became apparent in the so-called Sunday Trading cases, to which we shall now turn our attention.

C – The Sunday Trading Saga

It has been said above that neither *Dassonville* nor *Cassis* mention discrimination; in the case of *Cinéthèque*[27] it became apparent that the *Cassis* formulation was not limited in its application to national measures which are proved to have or are assumed to have some discriminatory purpose or effect. The case concerned French rules which provided that videotapes of films could not be distributed within one year of the release of the films in question at the cinema. The Court made the following observations:

> [S]uch a system, if it applies without distinction to both video-cassettes manufactured in the national territory and to imported video-cassettes, does not have the purpose of regulating trade patterns; its effect is not to favour national production as against the production of other Member States, but to encourage cinematograph production as such.
> *Nevertheless*, the application of such a system may create barriers to intra-Community trade in video-cassettes because of the disparities between the systems operated in the different Member States and between the conditions for the release of cinematographic works in the cinemas of those States. In those circumstances a prohibition of exploitation laid down by such a system is not compatible with the principle of the free movement of goods provided for in the Treaty unless any obstacle to intra-Community trade thereby created does not exceed what is necessary in order to ensure that attainment of the objective in view and unless that objective is justified with regard to Community law.[28]

The stage was reached where a wide range of commercial and marketing rules applied by national authorities in the Member States were potentially covered by the prohibition on measures having equivalent effect to quantitative restrictions, even if the national rules in question did not differentiate between domestic goods and imports, and were not intrinsically more difficult for imports to comply with than for domestic goods. Thus, for instance, national rules on advertising and promotion were regarded as being capable of amounting to measures having equivalent effect if there was a possibility that they might affect the prospects of importing products from other Member States. As the Court explained in *Oosthoek's Uitqeversmaatschappij BV*:[29]

---

[27] Joined Cases 60 and 61/84 *Cinéthèque* [1985] ECR 2605.
[28] Ibid, paras 21 and 22, emphasis added.
[29] Case 286/81 *Oosthoek's Uitqeversmaatschappij BV* [1981] ECR 4575.

Legislation which restricts or prohibits certain forms of advertising and certain means of sales promotions may, although it does not directly affect imports, be such as to restrict their *volume* because it affects marketing opportunities for the imported products. The possibility cannot be ruled out that to compel a producer either to adopt advertising or sales promotion schemes which differ from one Member State to another or to discontinue a scheme which he considers to be particularly effective may constitute an obstacle to imports even if the legislation in question applies to domestic products and imported products without distinction. [30]

The focus on the mere reduction of volume of sales led eventually to the so-called Sunday Trading saga. In *Torfaen BC v B&Q Plc*,[31] B&Q a chain of shops selling DIY material attacked British rules prohibiting Sunday trading. The claimants argued that such rules had the effect of reducing the overall volume of trade (by 23 per cent); since 10 per cent of the products sold by B&Q were imported, the retailer argued that the reduction in the volume of trade also determined a reduction in the sale of imported products. As a result, it was argued, the rules fell within the scope of Article 34 TFEU and were a disproportionate interference with the free movement of goods. The UK government, on the other hand, claimed that, since the rules were general in purpose and had no discriminatory effect, they fell altogether outside the scope of Article 34 TFEU. The Advocate General also found that the rules fell outside the scope of Article 34 TFEU since they were not of such a nature as to restrict intra-EU Trade.[32] The Court, however, relied on the *Cinéthèque* ruling to find that the rules fell in principle within the scope of Article 34 TFEU and needed to be justified by a mandatory requirement of public interest. Whilst the Court accepted that the rules at issue pursued a public interest compatible with Union law (the determination of working hours), it left the assessment as to their proportionality to the national court. This approach was confirmed in later cases[33] and created significant problems since different courts reached different conclusions as to the proportionality of the rules at issue.[34]

Following the *Cinéthèque* and Sunday Trading interpretation the concept of non-discriminatory trade restriction developed by the Court covered (subject to justification) national measures defining not only the composition of products, and their labelling and packaging, but also methods of advertising and sales promotion, and indeed all manner of terms and conditions under which goods were marketed in Member States.

(i) The Debate Following the Sunday Trading Cases

This is perhaps an appropriate point at which to analyse the problems arising from an over-broad interpretation of Article 34 TFEU (or of the other free-movement provisions).

---

[30] Ibid, para 15, emphasis added; advertising falls now within the *Keck* selling arrangements exemption, see below section E(ii). the Court's case law on the application of the above-mentioned principles was not entirely consistent; see eg Case 75/81 *Blegsen* [1982] ECR 4575, para 15, where the Court considered that a legislative provision that concerned only the sale of strong spirits for consumption on the premises in all places open to the public and did not concern other forms of marketing the same drinks had in fact no connection with the import of the products and for that reason was not of such a nature as to impede trade between Member State; see also Case C-23/89 *Quietlynn* [1990] ECR I-3059 in relation to restrictions on the sale of sex articles.

[31] Case 145/88 *Torfaen BC v B & Q Plc* [1989] ECR 3851.

[32] AG Van Gerven's Opinion, Case 145/88 *Torfaen BC v B&Q Plc* [1989] ECR 3851, esp para 25.

[33] See Case C-332/89 *Conforama* [1991] ECR I-997; Case C-306/88 *Roschdale Borough Council v SJ Anders* [1992] ECR I-6463; Case C-16/91 *Council of the City of Stoke-on-Trent and Norwich City Council v B&Q plc* [1992] ECR I-6635. See also Case C-332/89 *Merchandise* [1991] ECR 1027 where the Court found that a prohibition on the employment of workers in retail shops on Sundays after 12 noon might have negative repercussions on the volume of sales and hence on the volume of imports (though the Court regarded any such restrictions as being justified).

[34] See A Arnull, 'What Shall We Do on Sunday' (1991) *ELRev* 112.

The Sunday trading interpretation is problematic because it leads to national courts and the Court of Justice deciding whether national legislative bodies have excessively burdened trade by enacting and maintaining in force national rules, which, while neutral from an intra-EU trade perspective, nevertheless tend to reduce the overall level of sales of domestic goods and imports alike, or to inconvenience producers or traders who might, for example, have chosen to adopt a sales promotion scheme under the law of one Member State and to seek to extend it to the territory of another Member State where such schemes are subject to restrictions not applicable in the first Member State (such as the rules referred to by the Court in the *Oosthoek's* case). Judicial resolution of the question of whether any impact on imports caused by such measures is justified by the purpose of the measure in question (whether it be protection of shop-workers or consumer protection) involves making value judgments on broad policy questions, and places judges at the outer limits of their legitimate judicial role, where the judiciary risks substituting its assessment for that of the legislature.[35] Whilst in the case where there is a clear impact on intra-EU trade (either because the measure is directly or indirectly discriminatory or because it specifically affects imports or exports), the judiciary is entitled, and indeed required, to balance different interests, this might be more contentious in relation to measures that do not have a specific impact on intra-EU trade and that merely express societal and cultural preferences.

Given the above, it is not surprising that following the ruling in *Torfaen* there was a lively scholarly debate as to the appropriate scope of Article 34 TFEU. Some authors suggested that the latter should be construed as encompassing only a prohibition on discriminatory (in law or in fact) restrictions. Most of the case law, it was argued, could be reconciled with such an approach since the concept of indirect discrimination is broadly construed to encompass all measures that might place imports at a disadvantage, such as composition requirements, labelling requirements, etc. Other authors suggested a more careful assessment of the 'effect on intra-Community trade', which is in any case required by the *Dassonville* formula. Thus, the problem did not lie with the original definition of a measure having equivalent effect, but with the Court's misunderstanding that measures which merely reduce the volume of sales could have such an effect.[36] Finally, other authors proposed a distinction according to the type of rules at issue;[37] in particular, White[38] suggested differentiating between rules concerning the physical characteristics of the products, which should always be caught by Article 34 TFEU and rules concerning the *way* a product is sold. The former are an obstacle to intra-EU trade since they require producers to modify their product in order to comply with the rules imposed by the country of destination. However, rules concerning how and when a product can be sold do not have any specific effect on intra-EU trade, unless they are directly or indi-

---

[35] See also N Bernard, *Multilevel Governance in the European Union* (The Hague, Kluwer Law International, 2002), esp ch 2.

[36] L Gormley, '"Actually or Potentially, Directly or Indirectly?" Obstacles to the Free Movement of Goods' (1989) 9 *YEL* 197; 'Some Reflections on the Internal Market and Free Movement of Goods' (1989) 12 *LIEI* 9; 'Recent Case Law on the Free Movement of Goods: Some Hot Potatoes' (1990) 27 *CMLRev* 825, and to a certain extent J Steiner, 'Drawing the line: Uses and Abuses of Article 30 EEC' (1992) 29 *CMLRev* 749, and WPJ Wils 'The Search for the Rule in Article 30 EEC: Much Ado About nothing?' (1993) 18 *ELRev* 475.

[37] K Mortelmans, 'Article 30 of the EEC Treaty and Legislation Relating to Market Circumstances: Time to Consider a New Definition?' (1991) 28 *CMLRev* 115, 129–31; EL White, 'In Search of the Limits to Article 30 of the EEC Treaty'(1989) 26 *CMLRev* 235.

[38] White, ibid.

rectly discriminatory.[39] It is this distinction that was embraced by the Court in the ruling in *Keck*, which we shall now consider.

D – The *Keck and Mithouard* Judgment

In *Keck and Mithouard*,[40] Mr Keck and Mr Mithouard were prosecuted for reselling products in an unaltered state at prices lower than their actual purchase price contrary to French legislation. In their defence, they contended that a general prohibition on resale at a loss was incompatible with, inter alia, Article 34 TFEU, and a reference on that question was made to the Court of Justice. In its judgment, the Court redefined its *Cassis* case law as follows:

> 12. National legislation imposing a general prohibition on resale at a loss is not designed to regulate trade in goods between Member States.
>
> 13. Such legislation may, admittedly, restrict the volume of sales, and hence the volume of sales of products from other Member States, in so far as it deprives traders of a method of sales promotion. But the question remains whether such a possibility is sufficient to characterize the legislation in question as a measure having equivalent effect to a quantitative restriction on imports.
>
> 14. In view of the increasing tendency of traders to invoke Article [34 TFEU] as a means of challenging any rules whose effect is to limit their commercial freedom even where such rules are not aimed at products from other Member States, the Court considers it necessary to re-examine and clarify its case-law on this matter.
>
> 15. It is established by the case-law beginning with 'Cassis de Dijon' . . . that, in the absence of harmonization of legislation, obstacles to free movement of goods which are the consequence of applying, to goods coming from other Member States where they are lawfully manufactured and marketed, rules that lay down requirements to be met by such goods (such as those relating to designation, form, size, weight, composition, presentation, labelling, packaging) constitute measures of equivalent effect prohibited by Article [34 TFEU]. This is so even if those rules apply without distinction to all products unless their application can be justified by a public-interest objective taking precedence over the free movement of goods.
>
> 16. By contrast, contrary to what has previously been decided, the application to products from other Member States of national provisions *restricting or prohibiting certain selling arrangements* is *not such as to hinder directly or indirectly, actually or potentially, trade between Member States* within the meaning of the *Dassonville* judgment . . ., so long as those provisions a*pply to all relevant traders operating within the national territory and so long as they affect in the same manner, in law and in fact, the marketing of domestic products and of those from other Member States.*
>
> 17. Provided that those conditions are fulfilled, the application of such rules to the sale of products from another Member State meeting the requirements laid down by that State is not *by nature* such as *to prevent their access to the market or to impede access any more than it impedes the access of domestic products.* Such rules therefore fall outside the scope of Article [34 TFEU]. (emphasis added)

The above passages from the judgment of the Court contrast on the one hand, national rules laying down requirements to be met by goods themselves (product requirements),

---

[39] And see AG Tesauro's opinion in Case C-292/92 *R Hünnermund and others v Landesapothekerkammer Baden-Wurttemberg* [1993] ECR I-6787, which was the opinion on which the Court based its *Keck* ruling.

[40] Joined Cases C-267 and C-268/91 *Keck and Mithouard* [1993] ECR I-6097.

and on the other hand, rules which lay down 'certain selling arrangements'. The former continue to be governed by the *Cassis* case law and have therefore always to be justified by the mandatory requirements/Treaty derogations.[41] The latter, notwithstanding the previous case law of the Court, are no longer held to hinder trade and to require justification provided that they apply to all relevant traders operating within the national territory, and so long as they affect in the same manner, in law and in fact, the marketing of domestic products and of those from other Member States.

In paragraph 17 of its *Keck* ruling the Court gives some indication as to why certain selling arrangements should be caught by the Treaty only when directly or indirectly discriminatory: in the Court's view, provided they are not discriminatory, selling arrangements neither prevent the access of imports to the market nor impede the access of imports more than that of domestic products.[42] Non-discriminatory selling arrangements only restrict imports to the extent that they restrict the overall volume of sales of both domestic goods and imports,[43] and it may be questioned whether such measures could ever be said to impede the *access* of products to the market at all. Rather, such measures deprive traders of a sales opportunity which affects equally all products which have secured access to the market and are the subject of transactions on that market. The Court also indicates, in the first of the paragraphs cited from its judgment above, that its reference to 'certain selling arrangements' does not cover measures which are designed to regulate trade in goods between Member States.[44] The Court in *Keck* concluded that Article 34 TFEU did not apply to legislation of a Member State imposing a general prohibition on resale at a loss, which the Court clearly regarded as comprising 'selling arrangements' of the type referred to above.[45]

Given that product requirements always fall within the scope of Article 34 TFEU and must therefore always be justified, whilst selling arrangements are in need of justification only if they are directly or indirectly discriminatory, it is important to distinguish the two. In *Familiapress*,[46] the Court held that a rule which prohibited the marketing of magazines containing prize competitions fell within the scope of Article 34 TFEU without there be any need to assess whether it was discriminatory. Even though the rule concerned a method of sale promotion, ie a selling arrangement, it also bore on the content of the product, and was therefore to be considered as a product requirement. The trader could not in fact import its magazines in Austria, the country of destination, without altering the content of the periodicals. Thus, if a rule can be qualified at the same time as a product requirement and as a selling arrangement, it will fall automatically within the scope of Article 34 TFEU by virtue of being a product requirement.

(i) The Academic Debate on the Keck Ruling: Market Access vis-à-vis Discrimination

We saw above that the scholarship was highly critical of the turn taken by the Court in the

---

[41] Consistent case law, eg Case C-358/01 *Commission v Spain* [2003] ECR I-13145; Case C-143/03 *Commission v Italy* [2004] ECR I-0000.

[42] Para 17 of Judgment.

[43] Para 13 of Judgment.

[44] Case C-158/94 *Commission v Italy* [1997] ECR I-5789, para 31.

[45] For an analogous case concerning sales at low profit margins, see Case C-63/94 *Groupement National des Négociants en Pommes de Terre de Belgique (Belgapom)* [1995] ECR I-2467.

[46] Case C-368/95 *Familiapress* [1997] ECR I-3689; see also Case C-244/06 *Dynamic Medien* [2008] ECR I-505.

Sunday Trading cases; however, not everyone welcomed the Court's chosen solution to the problem. In particular, it was feared that the Court might have gone a step too far in the opposite direction and might have chosen too narrow an approach to Article 34 TFEU.

The case in favour of rethinking the *Keck* ruling was forcefully made by Advocate General Jacobs in *Leclerc Siplec*,[47] where he proposed an alternative to the *Keck* test Advocate General Jacobs argued that the ruling in *Keck* produced two main shortcomings. First of all, it was not appropriate to introduce a rigid distinction between different categories of rules and to impose different tests. In his opinion, the difference in the effect that selling arrangements might have on intra-EU trade is one of degree, not one of quality. Thus, if some selling arrangements might well have little impact (such as the prohibition on advertising outside pharmacies in *Hünermund*),[48] other rules (such as rules severely limiting the outlets in which a product can be sold) might have a very restrictive impact on intra-EU trade. Secondly, in Mr Jacobs' opinion, it was inappropriate to introduce a discriminatory test, since an obstacle to intra-EU trade does not cease to exist merely because the rules affect domestic producers to the same extent as importers. A discriminatory test would lead to fragmentation of the single market across national borders, since traders would have to adapt their arrangements to meet the demands of different Member States. Restrictions to trade should not be tested against local conditions, but against the aim 'of access to the entire Community market'.[49] In his opinion, the guiding principle which provides the appropriate test for the scope of Article 34 TFEU should be that

> all undertakings which engage in a legitimate economic activity in a Member State should have unfettered access to the whole of the Community market, unless there is a valid reason for denying them full access to a part of that market.[50]

In order to limit the breadth of this principle, and to avoid a new Sunday Trading trap, Advocate General Jacobs suggested the introduction of a form of de minimis test. Thus, in his opinion, only rules which impose a *substantial* restriction on access should be scrutinised in relation to the mandatory requirements doctrine. Of course, the de minimis test would not apply to directly discriminatory rules, since in that case the Treaty provides for an outright prohibition. Similarly, product requirements always have a substantial effect on intra-EU trade and thus would always be scrutinised since they always affect market access.

As we shall see below, Advocate General Jacobs' suggestion was not immediately taken on board by the Court; however, it gained favour with part of the scholarship who, with a few modifications, argued that a market access test would be better apt at ensuring that Article 34 TFEU catches all barriers to intra-EU trade, regardless of discrimination.[51] Moreover, a market access test would bring the case law on goods in line with the case

---

[47] Case C-412/93 *Société d'importation Éduard Leclerc-Siplec v TF1 Publicité SA* [1995] ECR I-179.
[48] Case C-292/92 *R Hünnermund and others v Landesapothekerkammer Baden-Wurttemberg* [1993] ECR I-6787.
[49] Ibid, para 40 of the Opinion.
[50] Ibid, para 41 of the Opinion.
[51] S Weatherill, 'After *Keck*: Some Thoughts on How to Clarify the Clarification' (1996) 33 *CMLRev* 885, 897, also criticising the *Keck* distinction based on the type rather than on the effect of the rules, suggested that non-discriminatory measures should escape scrutiny if they impose 'no direct or substantial hindrance to the access of imported goods or services'. On almost the same lines C Barnard, 'Fitting the Remaining Pieces into the Goods and Persons Jigsaw?' (2001) 26 *ELRev* 34, with the only difference that the test would apply also to discriminatory rules since those always either prevent or substantially impede market access.

law on the other free-movement provisions, where the Court has accepted that barriers to market access fall within the scope of the Treaty and therefore need to be justified.[52]

Other authors, however, have favourably received the *Keck* ruling, and in particular the return to a discriminatory approach.[53] Thus, some argue that the scope of Article 34 TFEU, and indeed of the other free-movement provisions, should be confined to a prohibition on discriminatory rules since the Treaty does not contain any indication as to the preferred level/type of regulation. In other words, all that the Treaty requires is that Member States do not create obstacles to the free flow of goods (and to the other free-movement provisions) by having rules which are directly or indirectly discriminatory. Provided this condition is satisfied, it is for the Member States, not for the judiciary, to decide the appropriate level of regulation. For those reasons, those who support a discriminatory approach welcomed the *Keck* ruling as a step in the right direction.

They argued that following the *Keck* ruling the scope of Article 34 TFEU has been narrowed down to a prohibition on discrimination. Product requirements are always caught by Article 34 TFEU since they are inherently indirectly discriminatory: the imposition of rules concerning the physical qualities of a product on imported goods have a heavier effect on the latter than on domestic products. This is the case because the imported product has already been regulated in the country of production and in order to comply with further product rules the importer would have to modify its product (and thus face a double regulatory burden). On the other hand, goods produced and sold in the domestic market have to comply with only the domestic regulatory standard. Selling arrangements are caught only when directly or indirectly discriminatory. So, according to this view, and even though the Court has not expressly said so, Article 34 TFEU post-*Keck* would be limited to a prohibition of discriminatory restrictions.

As we shall see below, neither the market access view nor the discriminatory view is entirely supported by the case law. The latter disregards the fact that some rules (residual rules) are caught regardless of discrimination; and that product requirements are always caught by Article 34 TFEU even when there is no domestic production of similar or competing goods, therefore excluding discrimination.[54] The market access theory is also not entirely convincing: though it is certainly true that product requirements also constitute a barrier to market access and might be seen to fall within the scope of Article 34 TFEU for that reason, other rules (eg restrictions on internet sales) that clearly affect market access have so far been found to fall outside its scope unless discriminatory.[55] This said, more recent case law seems to indicate a shift towards a market access approach.

---

[52] See Chapters 16 and 17.

[53] N Bernard, 'Discrimination and Free Movement in EC Law' (1996) 45 *ICLQ* 83; N Bernard, 'La libre circulation des marchandises, des personnes et des services dans le Traité CE sous l'angle de la compétence' (1998) 33 *CDE* 11, 34–35; N Bernard, *Multi Level Governance in the European Union* (London, Kluwer Law International, 2002), 168; and J Snell, *Goods and Services in EC Law* (Oxford, Oxford University Press, 2002).

[54] In relation to discriminatory taxation, the Court has clearly held that in the absence of similar or comparable domestic production, there cannot be any discrimination: eg Case C-47/88 *Commission v Denmark* [1990] ECR I-4509. See Chapter 13, p 401. And in Case C-391/92 *Commission v Greece* (processed milk for infants) [1995] ECR I-1621, para 17, the Court, against the advice of AG Lenz, has excluded that the absence of domestic production, a 'purely fortuitous factual circumstance', is enough for there to be a finding of discrimination.

[55] Case C-322/01 *Deutscher Apothekerverband eV v 0800 DocMorris NV, Jacques Waterval* [2003] ECR I-4887, and see below pp 425–26.

E – The Case Law after the *Keck* Judgment

(i) Product Requirements

Product requirements, ie those rules which concern the physical qualities of a product (eg composition, packaging, labelling requirements), continue to be automatically caught by Article 34 TFEU also after the *Keck* ruling, and therefore cannot be imposed on imports unless the Member State can invoke a mandatory requirement of public interest. The trader does not need to prove any discrimination, either direct or indirect; thus, for instance, in *Commission v France* the Court made clear in relation to rules on foie gras that failure to include a mutual recognition clause in relation to product requirements is a breach of Article 34 TFEU and needs to be justified even when the Member State is virtually the only producer/regulator of the product in question.[56] Generally speaking, product requirements are considered very trade restrictive and therefore will be subjected to a strict proportionality test. As said above, if a rule can be qualified as both a product requirement and a certain selling arrangement it will fall within Article 34 TFEU as a product requirement.[57]

(ii) Certain Selling Arrangements

As explained above, following the *Keck* ruling, certain selling arrangements (ie rules concerning when and how a product should be sold) are caught by Article 34 TFEU only in so far as they are directly or indirectly discriminatory. However, as we shall see in more detail below, with time the Court relaxed, at least to a certain extent, the concept of indirect discrimination as well as introducing some market access jargon, so that it is now easier for some selling arrangements to be brought within the scope of Article 34 TFEU.[58]

From the very beginning, and not surprisingly given the 'Sunday trading' saga, rules relating to opening and closing times were included in the certain selling arrangements category so that they are caught by Article 34 TFEU, and need to be justified, only if they are directly or indirectly discriminatory. For instance, in *Punto Casa SpA* the Court considered Italian rules restricting the Sunday opening hours of shops; the Court held that Article 34 TFEU did not apply to national legislation on the closure of shops which applies to all traders operating within the national territory and which affects in the same manner, in law and in fact, the marketing of domestic products and of those from other Member States.[59] The Court has applied the 'selling arrangements' analysis also to national rules which restrict the distribution of certain products to certain types of outlet. Thus in *Commission v Greece*[60] the Court considered Greek rules which required processed milk

---

[56] C-184/96 *Commission v France* (foie gras) [1998] ECR I-6197; technical standards must be communicated to the Commission, see Directive 98/34 laying down a procedure for the provision of information in the field of technical standards and regulations [1998] OJ L24/37, subsequently amended, consolidated version available at http://eur-lex.europa.eu/LexUriServ/LexUriServ.do?uri=CONSLEG:1998L0034:20070101:EN:PDF; the Commission has now proposed a new directive, see COM(2010) 179 final.

[57] Case C-368/95 *Familiapress* [1997] ECR I-3689.

[58] See generally E Spaventa, 'The Outer Limit of the Treaty Free Movement Provisions: Some Reflections on the Significance of *Keck*, Remoteness and Deliège' in C Barnard and O Odudu (eds), *The Outer Limits of European Law* (Oxford, Hart Publishing, 2009) 245.

[59] Joined Cases C-69/93 and C-258/93 *Punto Casa Srl* [1994] ECR I-2355. See also Joined Cases C-410/91 and C-402/92 *Tankstaton 't Heukske vof* [1994] ECR I-2199.

[60] Case C-391/92 *Commission v Greece* [1995] ECR I-1621.

for infants to be sold exclusively by pharmacies. The Court took the view that the legislation,

> the effect of which is to limit the commercial freedom of traders irrespective of the actual characteristics of the product referred to, concerns the selling arrangements of certain goods, inasmuch as it prohibits the sale, other than exclusively by pharmacies, of processed milk for infants and thus generally determines the points of sale where they may be distributed.

Since the legislation applied without distinction according to the origin of the products in question to all of the traders operating within the national territory, and did not affect the sale of products originating in other Member States any differently from that of domestic products, the Court concluded that it did not fall within Article 34 TFEU. The Court noted that this conclusion was not affected by the fact, pointed out by the Commission, that Greece did not itself produce processed milk for infants, and the Court added that the situation would be different 'only if it was apparent that the legislation in issue protected domestic products which were similar to processed milk for infants from other Member States or which were in competition with milk of that type'. However, the Commission had not shown this to be the case.[61] Similar reasoning has been applied in the case of national rules confining tobacco sales to authorised retailers,[62] and national rules which require authorisation for the distribution of bovine semen.[63]

However useful the *Keck* distinction between selling arrangements and product requirements is, the case law needed some fine tuning. The main problem, identified already in 1995 by Advocate General Jacobs, and widely commented upon by the scholarship, concerns advertising restrictions and selling techniques that are particularly useful, and effective, for long-distance transactions. As mentioned above, in *Hünermund* the Court qualified rules regulating advertising as selling arrangements.[64] This might well have been a mistake, albeit unintentional, that had more to do with the fact that the rules at issue in that case (a prohibition of advertising just outside pharmacies) clearly did not have any effect on intra-EU trade. However, other advertising rules might well have important effects on intra-EU trade. First of all, advertising is crucial to penetrate new markets, since without it the consumer might not be aware of a new product/brand. Take the example of alcopops or MP3 players: if the producers of such products were not allowed to advertise them, it would be almost impossible, and probably not economically viable, to penetrate a new market (or indeed create a new demand for a product that was previously not there). Secondly, in relation to heavily branded products, advertising might be as, if not more, important than the physical qualities of the products. Take, by way of example, the case of perfumes: branding is crucial, much more so than the scent itself might be. The effect of forcing a producer to devise different advertising campaigns for each of the Member States might be as market partitioning as the imposition of domestic product requirements on imported goods. In other words, in the case of heavily branded products, advertising, the image of the product, the perception that the consumer has of a particular brand, might be more important than the intrinsic qualities of the product itself. For this reason, to

---

[61] Ibid, paras 15–19.
[62] Case C-387/93 *Banchero* [1995] ECR I-4663, paras 37 and 44.
[63] Case C-162/97 *Gunnar Nilsson* [1998] ECR I-7477; see also Case C-416/00 *Morellato* [2003] ECR I-8343.
[64] Case C-292//92 *Ruth Hünermund and others v Landesapothekerkammer Baden-Württemberg* [1993] ECR I-6787, para 23.

exclude advertising from the scope of Article 34 TFEU unless it is discriminatory in fact or in law might have the effect to leave in place significant barriers to intra-EU trade.

A similar problem arises in relation to rules that determine the way a product is sold (a selling arrangement) when such way is especially useful in penetrating new markets. That would be the case, for instance, in relation to internet sales where producers have a means to penetrate a new market without having to bear the commercial risks inherent in doing so. Thus, even a small producer can attempt to penetrate a foreign market through the internet because it does not have to bear the costs and the risk of setting up a distribution system, or a retail network. It is especially in relation to those cases that the *Keck* distinction based on the type of rules, rather than on their effects, has proven to be inadequate. For this reason, as we saw above, Advocate General Jacobs,[65] as well as several authors, have suggested that the determinant factor in order to decide whether a rule falls within or outside the scope of Article 34 TFEU should be whether the rule restricts market access in a significant way. Whilst the Court has so far refused to depart from the *Keck* product requirement/selling arrangement distinction, it has, as said above, tuned its approach to deal with these problems.

The first indication of a less rigid approach to selling arrangements came in the case of *TK-Heimdienst*.[66] Here, Austrian rules restricted the possibility to do sales on rounds of given groceries to those traders who had an establishment in the administrative district where the sale on rounds took place or in a district bordering with it. The Court was asked by the national court whether those rules were to be considered restrictions falling within the scope of Article 34 TFEU. For the purposes of the case, it was accepted that traders established in bordering districts in other Member States would be allowed to do sales on rounds under the same conditions as the Austrian traders. The rules were clearly selling arrangements and the issue was whether they were indirectly discriminatory or not. Advocate General La Pergola found that there was no discrimination since traders established in bordering states could do sales on rounds under the same conditions as Austrian traders; furthermore, the rules had no effect on intra-EU trade since it was not realistic to think that a baker established in Paris would want to go and sell her/his bread in Austria. Having taken a substantial and realistic approach to the question of discrimination, the Advocate General found that there was no way the rules at issue could have an effect on intra-EU trade. The Court, however, favoured a purely abstract assessment of the rules at issue: since a residence/establishment requirement is always indirectly discriminatory (national traders being more likely than foreign traders to have an establishment within the national territory),[67] the Austrian rules were to be so qualified. Furthermore, the Court found that the rules were not justified and were therefore incompatible with Article 34 TFEU.[68]

---

[65] See Opinion in Case C-412/93 *Société d'importation Éduard Leclerc-Siplec v TF1 Publicité SA* [1995] ECR I-179 and text and footnotes above section III.D(i).

[66] Case C-254/98 *TK-Heimdienst Sass GmbH* [2000] ECR I-151; in Case C-320/93 *Lucien Ortscheit GmbH* [1994] ECR I-5243, para 9, advertising rules fell within the scope of Article 34 TFEU because discriminatory (see also in relation to the same rules Case C-143/06 *Ludwigs-Apotheke* [2007] ECR I-9623).

[67] An establishment requirement is always considered to be indirectly discriminatory, see Chapter 17 on the free movement of services.

[68] A more reasonable approach was taken in Case C-441/04 *A-Punkt Schmuckhandels GmbH v C Schmidt* [2006] ECR I-2093, where the Court left it to the national court to determine whether a prohibition on doorstep sales of silver jewellery affected market access for imported products more than market access for domestic products. See also Case C-20/03 *M Burmanjer and others* [2005] ECR I-4133.

In *Gourmet*,[69] Swedish legislation imposed an almost complete ban on the advertising of alcoholic products. The question for the Court was whether, as contended by the Swedish government, the advertising ban fell within the *Keck* exception since it was a selling arrangement that applied to domestic and imported products alike, or whether, as contended by *Gourmet*, it instead fell within the scope of Article 34 TFEU. The Court held:

> 18. It should be pointed out that, according to paragraph 17 of its judgment in *Keck and Mithouard*, if national provisions restricting or prohibiting certain selling arrangements are to avoid being caught by [Article 34 TFEU], they must not be of such a kind as to prevent access to the market by products from another Member State or to impede access any more than they impede the access of domestic products.
>
> . . .
>
> 21. . . . in the case of products like alcoholic beverages, the consumption of which is linked to traditional social practices and to local habits and customs, a prohibition of all advertising directed at consumers in the form of advertisements in the press, on the radio and on television, the direct mailing of unsolicited material or the placing of posters on the public highway is liable to impede access to the market by products from other Member States more than it impedes access by domestic products, with which consumers are instantly more familiar.

The Court then found that the advertising ban was caught by Article 34 TFEU, and left it to the national court to determine whether it constituted a proportionate measure to safeguard the legitimate aim of protecting the population from the harmful effects of alcohol abuse.

It should be noted that the Court's reasoning is ambiguous in that it is based both on a market access rationale and on an the potential discriminatory effects of an outright ban of advertising that might render access to the market of foreign alcoholic products more difficult than access to the market of domestic products with which consumers are more familiar. Thus, the ruling can be interpreted in two ways: first, restrictions that *prevent* market access are caught by Article 34 TFEU without there be any need to prove a discriminatory effect. A total ban on advertising always has the effect of preventing access to a market. Or, alternatively, a total ban on advertising by its nature puts imported products at a disadvantage and therefore is caught by Article 34 TFEU. No matter which reading of the case is chosen, it is clear that in the case of a total ban on advertising there is no need to prove a discriminatory effect. The case might be usefully compared with the *De Agostini* ruling where the Court held that in the case of a partial ban on advertising, a ban on television advertising directed at children, where other means of advertising are allowed (billboard, advertising on publications, etc), discrimination needs to be established before the rule can be held to fall within the scope of Article 34 TFEU and therefore be in need of justification.[70] This said, subsequent case law seems to indicate that the Court has not accepted a market access test in relation to selling arrangements.

In *DocMorris*,[71] the main defendant was a company established in the Netherlands

---

[69] Case C-405/98 *Gourmet International Products* [2001] ECR I-1795; see A Biondi, 'Advertising Alcohol and the Free Movement Principle: The *Gourmet* Decision' (2001) 26 *ELRev* 616. See also Chapter 17, esp section IV.B.

[70] Joined Cases C-34/95, C-35/95 and C-36/95 *Konsumentombudsmannen (KO) v De Agostini and TV Shop* [1997] ECR I-3843.

[71] Case C-322/01 *Deutscher Apothekerverband eV v 0800 DocMorris NV, Jacques Waterval* [2003] ECR I-4887; see also Case C-497/03 *Commission v Austria* (sale by mail), not published, available on http://curia.europa.eu/; and Case C-141/07 *Commission v Germany* (supply of medicinal products to hospitals) [2008] ECR I-6935.

which sold medicinal products over the internet. The company sold both prescription and non-prescription drugs. In relation to the former it would sell the drugs only on production of a prescription. In order to determine whether a drug was a prescription-only drug it would have regard to both the Dutch legislation and the rules of the place where the consumer was established, always applying the strictest rule. As a result, it would not sell a drug without prescription if such prescription was required in the Netherlands, and it would not sell a drug without prescription if prescription was required in the place where the consumer was located, even if Dutch law did not require such prescription. The dugs would either be posted by courier or could be collected in a pharmacy located in the Netherlands. The company also provided advice through the internet, by telephone and by post. The company sold its drugs also to German consumers. *Deutscher Apothekerverband*, a German association protecting the interests of pharmacists, therefore brought proceedings on the grounds that the internet sale of drugs breached German legislation. The national court requested a preliminary ruling from the Court as to the compatibility with Article 34 TFEU of the German legislation which, inter alia, prohibited the sale of medicinal products outside pharmacies, therefore prohibiting postal and internet sales of drugs. The Court found that the rules were selling arrangements; it then turned to the question of discrimination. After having acknowledged that the ban applied in law in the same way to German and foreign pharmacies, it held:

> 72. A prohibition such as that at issue in the main proceedings is more of an obstacle to pharmacies outside Germany than to those within it. Although there is little doubt that as a result of the prohibition, pharmacies in Germany cannot use the extra or alternative method of gaining access to the German market consisting of end consumers of medicinal products, they are still able to sell the products in their dispensaries. However, for pharmacies not established in Germany, the internet provides a more significant way to gain direct access to the German market. A prohibition which has a greater impact on pharmacies established outside German territory could impede access to the market for products from other Member States *more* than it impedes access for domestic products. (emphasis added)

The Court then examined whether the rules at issue were justified and found that a ban on sale outside pharmacies of prescription drugs was justified by public health concerns, whilst in the case of non-prescription drugs such ban was disproportionate.[72]

The ruling in *DocMorris* clarified the ruling in *Gourmet*: it is clear that were the Court to have moved to a clear market access test it should have not assessed the discriminatory effect of the rules, since a prohibition on the marketing of a product over the internet clearly restricts market access. Instead, the Court decided to restate the *Keck* approach: selling arrangements are caught by Article 34 TFEU only in so far as they affect in law or in fact imported products more than domestic products.[73] We have seen above that a total ban on advertising is to be qualified as inherently indirectly discriminatory. Rules banning internet sales should also be so qualified: by nature foreign producers which do not have a network of retail outlets in the market of destination are more affected than domestic producers by a ban on sale over the internet.

That said, given the importance of advertising and its effect on market penetration it

---

[72] See also Case C-108/09 *Ker-Optika*, judgment of 2 December 2010, esp para 55 where the Court found that a ban on the internet sale of contact lenses was caught by Article 34 TFEU since it affected foreign traders more than domestic ones (although the ruling is not the clearest in terms of reasoning).

[73] See also the rather confusing Case C-239/02 *Douwe Egberts NV and others* [2004] ECR I-7007, where the Court first refers to pre-Keck case law in relation to advertising rules to then revert to a *Keck* assessment, see esp paras 52 and 53.

would have been preferable if rules concerning advertising had not been included in the category of 'certain selling arrangements' that are caught only if discriminatory. In any event, however, cases such as *Gourmet* and *DocMorris*[74] demonstrate that the *Keck* distinction between product requirements and selling arrangements is not as rigid as some authors feared:[75] the Court is willing to look at whether the rules might put foreign traders at a disadvantage and therefore have a specific effect on intra-EU trade. If that is the case, then such rules fall within the scope of Article 34 TFEU and have to be justified. Furthermore, the fine-tuning of the *Keck* distinction between product requirements and selling arrangements is complemented by Article 56 TFEU which guarantees the free movement of services within the European Union. As we shall see in Chapter 17, the scope of Article 56 TFEU is broader than that of Article 34 TFEU, in that the former catches any hindrance/discouragement to the provision of cross-border services. As it happens, advertising and internet provision are also services since both imply the sell/ purchase of services from a third person (the advertising agency, the internet provider, etc). Thus, the rules in *Gourmet* were scrutinised also having regard to Article 56 TFEU: even had they been found not to be indirectly discriminatory under Article 34 TFEU, they would have still required justification as a restriction to the provision of cross-border services. In this way, even if an advertising/internet restriction were to fall outside Article 34 TFEU, it might be caught by Article 56 TFEU, and therefore need to be justified.[76]

(iii) Residual Rules: Other Rules that Might Be Caught by Article 34 TFEU

Not all national measures which affect intra-EU trade can be classified as either rules relating to the goods themselves on the one hand, or selling arrangements, on the other: bans on sale or use;[77] inspections;[78] registration[79] and authorisation requirements;[80] licence requirements;[81] restrictions on transport;[82] obligations to provide data for statistics;[83] non-

---

[74] See also Case C-158/04 *Alfa Vita* [2006] ECR I-8135.

[75] See also P Koutrakos 'On Groceries, Alcohol and Olive Oil: More on the Free Movement of Goods after *Keck*' (2001) 26 *ELRev* 391.

[76] This provided the service provision is not entirely ancillary to the sale of goods; *cf* Case C-71/02 *Karner* [2004] ECR I-3025, para 46.

[77] Case C-293/94 *Brandsma* [1996] ECR I-3159; Case C-400/96 *J Harpegnies* [1998] ECR I-5121; Case C-473/98 *Toolex Alpha AB* [2000] ECR I-5681; Case C-265/06 *Commission v Portugal* (tinted car windows) [2008] ECR I-2245.

[78] Case C-105/94 *Ditta A Celestini* [1997] ECR I-2971; see also Case C-297/05 *Commission v Netherlands* (road worthiness test for imported used cars) [2007] ECR I-7467.

[79] Case C-55/99 *Commission v France* (registration for reagents) [2000] ECR I-1149; Case C-390/99 *Canal Satélite Digital SL v Administración General del Estado* [2002] ECR I-607. In this case the Court excluded that the *Keck* ruling could apply because of 'the need in certain cases to adapt the products in question to the rules in force in the Member State in which they are marketed' (para 30); to the same effect also Case C-14/02 *ATRAL SA V Belgium* [2003] ECR I-4431.

[80] Case C-120/95 *N Decker v Caisse de Maladie des Employés Privés* [1998] ECR I-1831; Case C-333/08 *Commission v France* (processing aids) [2010] ECR I-000.

[81] Case C-189/95 *Franzén* [1997] ECR I-5909; a transfer licence is also caught by Art 34 TFEU Case C-54/05 *Commission v Finland* (transfer licence for cars) [2007] ECR I-2473. It is not clear whether or not an obligation to store semen in authorised centres is a selling arrangement, *cf* Case C-323/93 *Société Civile Agricole du Centre d'Insémination de la Crespelle v Coopérative d'Elevage et d'Insémination Artificielle du Département de la Mayenne* [1994] ECR I-5077, where the Court unusually refers to Case C-169/91 *Council of the City of Stoke-on-Trent and Norwich City Council v B&Q plc* [1992] ECR I-6635 (one of the Sunday trading cases) rather than to *Keck*. Similarly rules relating to bake-off products have been assessed in a different way in Case C-416/00 *Morellato* [2003] ECR I-9343, where they were considered as certain selling arrangements; and in Case C-158/04 *Alfa Vita* [2006] ECR I-8135, where they were considered as rules hindering trade. See further Spaventa, above n 58, 245.

[82] Case C-350/97 *W Monsees v Unabhängiger Verwaltungssenat für Kärnten* [1999] ECR I-2921.

[83] Case C-114/96 *René Kieffer and Roman Thill* [1997] ECR I-3629.

profit/no-payment requirements for blood purchases,[84] cannot be comfortably categorised under either heading. Whilst, however, product requirements are always deemed to have an (at least potential) effect on intra-EU trade, and directly and indirectly discriminatory restrictions always fall within the scope of application of Article 34 TFEU (whether selling arrangements or not), in the case of 'residual' rules, an investigation might be necessary as to the (at least potential) effect of the measure on intra-EU trade. Before the rulings in *Commission v Italy* and *Mickelsson and Roos*,[85] the Court simply relied on the *Dassonville* formula to determine whether such an effect was present (excluding rules the effect of which is too uncertain and indirect to be caught by the Treaty, see below). However, in the above-mentioned cases, the Court introduced a market access assessment, at least in relation to rules disciplining the way a product should be used. In *Commission v Italy*, the Commission brought proceedings against the Italian government alleging an infringement of Article 34 TFEU in relation to rules prohibiting motorbikes and the like to tow trailers; in *Mickelsson and Roos*, the contested rules restricted the use of personal watercraft to navigable waterways. In both cases the Court could have relied on previous case law to find that the rules were caught by the *Dassonville* formula and proceed to assess the issue of justification.[86] Instead, the Court relied on the market access concept to find that those measures fell within the scope of Article 34 TFEU and needed to be justified.[87] As a result of those two cases there was some confusion as to whether the *Keck* ruling should now be considered outdated; however, more recent rulings have maintained the distinction between certain selling arrangements and other rules[88] so that it is likely that the significance of *Commission v Italy* and *Mickelsson and Roos* is limited to residual rules (in which case, from a practical viewpoint, very little has changed).

(a) The Doctrine of Effect Too Uncertain and Indirect

As said above, although product requirements always have effects on intra-Union trade, and certain selling arrangements are deemed to have such an effect only when discriminatory or preventing market access, residual rules might have effects on intra-Union trade which are negligible and therefore do not trigger the application of Article 34 TFEU. Thus, when the measure does not distinguish according to the origin of the goods, and its purpose is not to regulate trade in goods with other Member States, the restrictive effects which it might have on the free movement of goods might be *too uncertain and indirect* for the obligation which it imposes to be regarded as being capable of hindering trade between Member States.[89] This is not, however, to say that there is a de minimis test, but

---

[84] Case C-421/09 *Humanplasma*, judgment of 9 December 2010.

[85] Case C-110/05 *Commission v Italy* (trailers) [2009] ECR I-519; and C-142/05 *Mickelsson and Roos* [2009] ECR I-4273; see further E Spaventa, 'Leaving *Keck* behind? The Free Movement of Goods after the rulings in *Commission v Italy* and *Mickelsson and Roos*' (2009) 34 *ELRev* 914; P Wennerars and K Boe Moen 'Selling Arrangements, Keeping Keck' (2010) 35 *ELRev* 387; J Snell 'The Notion of Market Access: a Concept or a Slogan?' (2010) 47 *CMLRev* 437.

[86] eg Case C-265/06 *Commission v Portugal* (tinted car windows) [2008] ECR I-2245.

[87] See Case C-110/05 *Commission v Italy* (trailers) [2009] ECR I-519, esp paras 34, 37 and 56; and C-142/05 *Mickelsson and Roos* [2009] ECR I-4273, esp para 24.

[88] See esp Case C-108/09 *Ker-Optika*, judgment of 2 December 2010; see also Case C-531/07 *Fachverband der Buch- und Medienwirtschaft* [2009] ECR I-3717.

[89] The 'effect to uncertain and indirect' doctrine has been referred to, for example, in Case C-69/88 *H. Krantz GmbH & Co v Ontvanger der Directe Belastingen and Netherlands State* [1990] ECR I-583, in relation to the tax collector's seizure powers, para 11; Case C-93/92 *CMC Motorradcenter GmbH v Pelin Baskiciogullari* [1993] ECR I-5009, in relation to rules establishing a duty to communicate relevant information to the counter-party

rather—as explained by Advocate General La Pergola[90]—that in these cases, the causal link between the rule and an effect on intra-EU trade might be lacking.

The investigation of the Court will thus be directed at assessing whether the link between rule and intra-EU effect, necessary in any case in order to trigger the application of Article 34 TFEU, exists at all, ie whether the effect of the rule is not 'too uncertain and indirect' to exclude the application of the free movement of goods provisions. On the other hand, a de minimis test, often rejected by the Court, would imply the exclusion of the applicability of Article 34 TFEU when the measure would have 'non-appreciable' effects on intra-EU trade.[91] In the latter case, there is *an* effect—however small or potential—on intra-EU trade. In the former case, there is *no* effect at all. This could be because, for instance, the effect does not depend on the rules at issue, but rather on the unforeseeable decisions of economic operators;[92] because the impact of the rule on the price of the goods is so minimal as not to be able to affect intra-EU trade;[93] or because there is not even a risk that the rules might affect intra-EU trade.[94]

The 'effect too uncertain and indirect doctrine' creates some confusion as to the relationship between this doctrine and selling arrangements that escape scrutiny under Article 34 TFEU. Thus, it is not clear whether non-discriminatory selling arrangements fall outside the scope of the Treaty because there is no effect on intra-EU trade; or because they fall outside the definition of a measure having equivalent effect in that they are recognised as falling within the inherent regulatory competence of the Member States. The latter is a more convincing explanation for two reasons. First of all, the 'effect too uncertain and indirect' doctrine pre-dates the ruling in *Keck*. Thus, if non-discriminatory selling arrangements had no effect on intra-EU trade, the Court would have had no need to impose a different test for this type of rules. The focus in the case of selling arrangements is on the *type* of rule, not on its *effect*. Secondly, and more importantly, it would be difficult to maintain that a restriction on advertisement has only a remote effect on intra-EU trade, since it might considerably affect the volume of sales. In that case, there might not be a *specific* effect on intra-EU trade, but there is *an* effect. On the other hand, rules which benefit from the effect too uncertain and indirect doctrine do not even lead to a

---

to a contract, para 12; Case C-379/92 *Peralta* [1994] ECR I-3453, in relation to an obligation for vessels to carry costly equipment, para 24; Case C-96/94 *Centro Servizi Spediporto Srl v Spedizioni Marittima del Golfo Srl* [1995] ECR I-2883 on road haulage tariffs; Case C-266/96 *Corsica Ferries France SA v Gruppo Antichi Ormeggiatori del Porto di Genova Coop Arl et al* [1998] ECR I-3949 on mooring tariffs; Case C-44/98 *BASF v Präsident des Deutschen Patentamts* [1999] ECR I-6269, in relation to an obligation to translate patents in order to benefit of the exclusive right. The doctrine applies also to Art 29, Case C-412/97 *ED Srl v I Fenocchio* [1999] ECR I-3845 in relation to a rule prohibiting the issue of a summary payment to be served outside the national territory; see also AG Sharpston's Opinion in Case C-291/09 *Guarnieri e Cie*, opinion delivered on 14 September 2010, case still pending at the time of writing, in relation to security for costs. Generally see further, Spaventa, above n 58, 245.

[90] Opinion in Case C-44/98 *BASF v Präsident des Deutschen Patentamts* [1999] ECR I-6269. See also AG Fenelly's Opinion in Case C-67/97 *Bluhme* [1998] ECR I-8033, para 19. AG Fenelly in his opinion in Case C-266/96 *Corsica Ferries France SA v Gruppo Antichi Ormeggiatori del Porto di Genova Coop Arl et al* [1998] ECR I-3949, has identified in the fact that the measure must have some 'protective effect' the necessary element in order to trigger Art 34 TFEU. This is lacking when the effects on the cost of importing goods is entirely incidental. However, the definition of what is to be considered as protective effect is not necessarily easy. It is debatable whether any protectionist effect or intent is needed in order to trigger Article 34 TFEU.

[91] Case 16/83 *Prantl* [1984] ECR 1299, para 20.

[92] Case C-44/98 *BASF v Präsident des Deutschen Patentamts* [1999] ECR I-6269.

[93] Case C-266/96 *Corsica Ferries France SA v Gruppo Antichi Ormeggiatori del Porto di Genova Coop Arl et al* [1998] ECR I-3949.

[94] Case C-93/92 *CMC Motorradcenter GmbH v Pelin Baskiciogullari* [1993] ECR I-5009.

contraction on the volume of sales.[95] This is not to say, however, that the Court could not have chosen a test capable of accommodating both types of rules. But it has not and for the reasons outlined above it seems more consistent to consider the two tests as distinct.

F – The Member States' Positive Duties

So far we have focused on a Member State's duty to refrain from introducing barriers to intra-EU trade. However, in certain cases, Article 34 (and 35) TFEU might impose a duty on Member States to act in a given way. This is in particular the case in relation to Member States' active duty to protect the fundamental freedoms conferred by the Treaty; and to Member States' duty to enact regulation in a *way* that allows traders time to adapt to regulatory changes.

(i) The Member States' Duty to Protect the Rights Conferred by Article 34 TFEU

Member States might be infringing Article 34 TFEU not only when imposing rules which are liable to affect intra-EU trade, but also when failing to take appropriate steps to ensure that obstacles to free movement created by actions of individuals are removed. In *Commission v France*, the Commission brought proceedings against France, alleging that the latter's failure to take any action against the unlawful behaviour of French farmers, who repeatedly engaged in violent actions to prevent imports of Spanish strawberries, constituted a breach of the Treaty.[96] The Court accepted the Commission's plea, although it recognised that, in these cases, Member States retain a wide margin of discretion as to the action needed to deal with obstacles to free movement created by private actions. Article 34 TFEU[97] imposes not only a duty of non-interference upon Member States, but also a positive duty to ensure that the Treaty freedom may—in practice—be enjoyed by its right-holders. This approach is entirely consistent with fundamental rights theory, according to which states have not only a negative duty of non-interference with individuals' fundamental rights, but might also have a positive duty to guarantee the effective enjoyment of those rights.[98]

This principle was confirmed in the following case of *Schmidberger*.[99] Here, an Austrian

---

[95] Contrast AG Cosmas' Opinion in C-63/94 *Groupement National des Négociants en Pommes de Terre de Belgique v ITM Belgium Sa and Vocarex SA* [1995] ECR I-2467, esp para 26.

[96] Case C-265/95 *Commission v France* (Riots) [1997] ECR I-6959. The ECJ has in principle accepted that, if the Member State is unable to use the means at its disposal to deal with possible public order, public security problems caused by its citizens, then it can rely on the Treaty derogations, Case 231/83 *H Cullet et Chambres Syndicale des réparateurs automobiles et détaillants de produits pétroliers v Centre Leclerc à Toulouse et Centre Leclerc à Saint-Orens-de-Gameville* [1985] ECR 35. For an application of this case law by the English courts, see *R v chief Constable of Sussex, ex parte International Trader's Ferry Ltd (ITF)* [1997] 2 All ER 65, also in [1997] 2 CMLR 164, upheld in the HL, [1999] 1 All ER 129, and [1999] 1 CMLR 1320. For a critical assessment of *Commission v France* and *ITF*, C Barnard and I Hare 'The Right to Protest and the Right to Export: Police Discretion and the Free Movement of Goods' (1997) 60 *MLR* 394; G Orlandini 'The Free Movement of Goods as a Possible "Community" Limitation on Industrial Conflict' (2000) 6 *ELJ* 341.

[97] It is likely that the reasoning in Case C-265/95 *Commission v France* (Riots) [1997] ECR I-6959 could be applied also to the other free movement provisions.

[98] The outcome of the ruling was later codified in Council Regulation 2679/98 on the functioning of the internal market in relation to the free movement of goods among the Member States [1998] OJ L337/8; the Regulation also clarifies that it does not affect fundamental rights as recognised in the Member States.

[99] Case C-112/00 *Schmidberger* [2003] ECR I-5659; and see A Biondi, 'Free Trade, a Mountain Road and the Right to Protest: European Economic Freedoms and Fundamental Individual rights' [2004] *EHRLR* 51.

court made a preliminary reference in order to ascertain the compatibility with Article 34 TFEU of a decision authorising a demonstration on the Brenner motorway, a major transit route between Italy and the rest of continental Europe. The claimants argued that the demonstration was an obstacle to the free movement of goods since it impeded road transport of goods coming from Italy. The Court found that the demonstration, which resulted in the closure of the motorway, was capable of restricting intra-EU trade and was thus a measure having equivalent effect. It then turned to assess whether such a restriction could be justified, and whether the free movement provisions should be construed as taking precedence over fundamental rights as enshrined in the ECHR and recognised by national constitutions (in this case, freedom of expression and assembly). The Court held that, since fundamental rights are general principles of Union law which bind both the EU and the Member States, the protection of those rights justifies a restriction of 'the obligations of EU law, even under a fundamental freedom guaranteed by the Treaty'.[100] The scope of the free movement provisions might be, not surprisingly, *inherently limited* by the proportionate enjoyment by others of their (not necessarily economic) rights.[101]

(ii) The Member States' Duty to Leave Time to Traders to Adjust to Regulatory Changes

Even when the rules enacted by a Member State are in principle compatible with the Treaty because they are justified by a mandatory requirement of public interest or by a Treaty derogation, they might fall foul of Article 34 TFEU because of the *way* they have been enacted. Thus, the Court has found that Article 34 TFEU imposes on Member States constraints on *how* to regulate The principle of proportionality, always to be complied with when acting within the scope of Union law, requires that when Member States introduce important changes in their regulatory system, they allow enough time to traders to adapt to the changes; this might well require a transitional period before the changes can be brought to effect. Thus, for instance, a Member State must provide for such a transitional period when introducing a mandatory deposit scheme for drinks containers aimed at maximising reuse of such containers and thus protecting the environment;[102] and a Member State must leave traders time to adapt if it wishes to ban transport on wheels of given goods on a part of its territory in order to reduce pollution and shift transport from wheels to trains.[103]

G – The Cross-border Element and Reverse Discrimination

It has been held that the inconsistency of national rules with Articles 34–36 TFEU is a point which can only be taken in respect of goods imported or to be imported from

---

[100] Ibid, para 74. *cf* Case C-50/96 *Deutsche Telekom AG v Lilli Schroder* [2000] ECR I-743, para 57, where the Court held that the economic aim pursued by Art 141, is secondary to the social aim pursued by that provision which is the expression of a fundamental right (of equality between men and women).

[101] In the context of the free movement of persons provisions, see the more contested Case C-438/05 *Viking* [2007] ECR I-10779; and Case C-341/05 *Laval un Partneri* [2007] ECR I-11767; see Chapter 17 below.

[102] eg Case C-309/02 *Radlberger Getränkegesellschaft mbH & Co and S. Spitz KG* [2004] ECR I-11763. esp para 81, and the same issue in Case C-463/01 *Commission v Germany* (reusable containers) [2004] ECR I-11705.

[103] Case C-320/03 *Commission v Austria* (motorway ban) [2005] ECR I-9871; on a similar problem see Case C-114/04 *Commission v Germany* (parallel imports of phytosanitary products), 14 July 2005, unpublished.

another Member State.[104] Where Article 34 TFEU precludes the application of national law to imports, the result may be that domestic products are placed at a disadvantage in comparison with imports. However, this is consistent with Union law.[105] It is a consequence of, on the one hand, the choice of the national legislator and, on the other hand, the fact that the prohibition of quantitative restrictions and measures having equivalent effect applies exclusively to imported products. That said, in *Pistre* the Court considered the compatibility with Article 34 TFEU of national rules restricting use of the description 'mountain' to products having links with a specific region of national territory.[106] The reference arose from national criminal proceedings against French nationals prosecuted for marketing French products wrongly bearing the designation in question. The Court rejected the argument that Article 34 TFEU could have no application since imports were not involved. It noted that nevertheless

> the application of the national measure may also have effects on the free movement of goods between Member States, in particular when the measure in question facilitates the marketing of goods of domestic origin to the detriment of imported goods. In such circumstances, the application of the measure, even if restricted to domestic producers, in itself creates and maintains a difference of treatment between those two categories of goods, hindering, at least potentially, intra-Community trade.

Since the legislation in issue in the national proceedings discriminated against goods from other Member States, Article 34 TFEU precluded the application of the rules in question. The ruling in *Pistre* lead to some confusion as to whether Article 34 TFEU could apply to purely internal situations. However, the ruling in *Guimont* clarified that Article 34 TFEU does not apply to purely internal situations. The fact that the Court is nonetheless willing to accept jurisdiction also in cases which do not have an intra-EU element[107] seems to be due to the spirit of co-operation with national courts that characterises the relationship between European and domestic judiciary. Thus, since in order to apply their domestic law (usually the Constitutional guarantee of equal treatment) national courts need to assess the extent to which Article 34 TFEU would apply if it was a cross-border case, the Court is willing to reply to the questions referred so as to allow national courts to settle the (purely domestic) dispute before them.[108]

IV – MEASURES HAVING EQUIVALENT EFFECT TO QUANTITATIVE RESRICTIONS ON EXPORTS

Article 35 TFEU provides that quantitative restrictions on exports, and all measures having equivalent effect, shall be prohibited between Member States. Quite naturally, there is substantially less case law relating to Article 35 TFEU than to Article 34 TFEU: not only

---

[104] See eg Joined Cases 314–316/82 *Waterkeyn* [1986] ECR 1855.

[105] Case 355/85 *Driancourt v Cognet* [1986] ECR 3231; Cases 80 and 159/85 *EDAH BV* [1986] ECR 3359.

[106] Joined Cases C-321/94, C-322/94, C-323/94, C-324/94 *Jacques Pistre etc* [1997] ECR I-2343.

[107] Case C-448/98 *Guimont* [2000] ECR I-10663 esp paras 15 *et seq*. Case C-254/98 *Schutzverband gegen unlauteren Wettbewerb and TK-Heimdienst Sass GmbH* [2000] ECR I-151 also involved a purely internal situation.

[108] For an extensive analysis of these issues, see E Spaventa, 'Annotation of *TK-Heimdiest*' (2000) 37 *CMLRev* 1265.

do Member States have little interest in restricting exports, but also the very principle of mutual recognition rests on the idea that the country where the goods are produced has full regulatory autonomy and can impose the regulatory standards it wishes over such goods. As a result, the notion of measure having equivalent effect to a quantitative restriction to exports is narrower that its counterpart in imports. Obviously, the notion of measure having equivalent effect to export clearly embraces measures that formally differentiate between domestic trade on the one hand, and the export trade on the other, as the *Bouhelier* case illustrates.[109] In order to ensure quality control, French legislation authorised a public authority to inspect pressed lever watches and watch movements made in France and destined for export to other Member States. If the watches or movements complied with the relevant quality standards, a certificate was issued to that effect. The export of such watches and movements was subject to the grant of a licence, except in the case of consignments in respect of which a standards certificate had been issued. The Court held that Article 35 TFEU precluded both export licensing and the imposition of quality controls on exports. Since the latter controls were not required in the case of products for the domestic market, their imposition amounted to arbitrary discrimination and constituted an obstacle to intra-EU trade.

As noted above, the evolution of the case law on measures having equivalent effect to quantitative restrictions on exports has not mirrored that on imports. Notwithstanding developments in the *Cassis* doctrine, the Court has consistently required a national measure to have discriminatory effects before it could be held to comprise a prohibited restriction on exports. As the Court explained in *Groenveld*:

> That provision [ie Article 35 TFEU] concerns the national measures which have as their specific object or effect the restriction of patterns of exports and thereby the establishment of a difference in treatment between the domestic trade of a Member State and its export trade in such a way as to provide a particular advantage for national production or for the domestic market of the State in question at the expense of the production or of the trade of other Member States. This is not so in the case of a prohibition like that in question which is applied objectively to the production of goods of a certain kind without drawing a distinction depending on whether such goods are intended for the national market or for export.[110]

The Court has repeated this formulation on numerous occasions.[111] For instance, an obligation on producers to deliver poultry offal to their local authority has been held to involve by implication a prohibition of exports and to fall accordingly within the scope of application of Article 35 TFEU.[112] Similarly, an obligation to transport animals for short maximum periods and distances combined with an obligation for all such transport to end at the nearest suitable abattoir in national territory for slaughter was held to amount to a measure having equivalent effect to a quantitative restriction on both imports and exports.[113] And an obligation to bottle the wine in the region of production in order to be able to benefit from the certified denomination of origin also constituted a restriction prohibited by Article 35 TFEU.[114] As noted above, until recently, the Court had found

---

[109] Case 53/86 [1977] ECR 197.

[110] Case 15/79 [1979] ECR 3409, para 7.

[111] See eg,Case 155/80 *Oebel* [1981] ECR 1993, para 15; Case 286/81 *Oosthoek's* [1982] ECR 4575, para 13; Case 172/82 *Inter-Huiles* [1983] ECR 555, para 12; Case 237/82 *Jongeneel Kaas and Others v Netherlands* [1984] ECR 483, para 22; Case C-412/97 *ED Srl v Italo Fenocchio* [1999] ECR I-0000, para 10.

[112] Case 118/86 *Nertsvoederfabriek Nederlandse* [1987] ECR 3883.

[113] Case C-350/97 *Wilfried Monsees* [1999] ECR I-2921.

[114] Case C-47/90 *Etablissements Delhaize Frères et Compagnie Le Lion SA v Promalvin SA and AGE Bodegas*

that the scope of Article 35 TFEU was limited to a prohibition on directly discriminatory restrictions and hence only the derogations contained in Article 36 TFEU could be used to justify measures falling within its scope.[115] However, in the case of *Gysbrechts and Santurel Inter*[116] the Court accepted that a rule which did not explicitly distinguish between domestic and export trade fell within the scope of Article 35 TFEU since it had a greater effect on exports. The issue related to a rule which prevented them from requiring payment or credit card data from customers before the expiry of the seven-working-day period allowed for withdrawal from the contract. The claimants complained that the rule affected their ability to sell goods abroad over the internet since, in case of default of the buyer, recovery of the sums owed would become excessively difficult. The Court found that given the difficulties in recovering sums from customers based abroad the rule affected exports more than domestic trade; however, it also found that the rule was justified on consumer protection grounds, thus clarifying that the mandatory requirements also apply to (non-directly discriminatory) restrictions on exports.

As it is the case in relation to Article 34 TFEU, Article 35 TFEU binds the Union institutions as well as the Member States.[117]

V – GENERAL REMARKS ABOUT ARTICLES 34 AND 35 TFEU

Unlike the free movement of persons provisions,[118] Articles 34 and 35 TFEU apply only vertically, ie to the state and its emanations, not to private individuals.[119] The concept of state includes regional as well as local and municipal entities, even when the rules penalise not only imports/exports but also trade from other regions. The reason why the free movement of goods provisions do not apply to private parties are twofold: first of all, the free movement of goods would otherwise come at the expense of contractual freedom, so that, for instance, a trader would have to justify its decision to stock only products from a given Member State. Secondly, in order to safeguard both internal market and consumers from the abusive conduct of commercial operators, the Treaty contains specific provisions to ensure fair competition.

Unidas SA [1992] ECR I-3669; the Court changed its mind as to whether such rules were justified in Case C-388/95 *Belgium v Spain* (Rioja) [2000] ECR I-3123, noted E Spaventa (2001) 38 *CMLRev* 211. See also Case C-12/02 *Grilli* [2003] ECR I-11585; see also Case C-469/00 *Ravil* [2003] ECR I-5053, paras 44 *et seq*.

[115] Although the case law is not entirely consistent in this respect: see eg C-209/98 *Entreprenørforeningens Affalds/Miljøsektion (FFAD) v Københavns Kommune* [2000] ECR I-3743, and see discussion about the problems inherent in the fact that Art 36 TFEU does not expressly mention environmental protection as one of the grounds which allows a Member State to derogate from Art 34 TFEU, below section VI.

[116] Case C-205/07 [2008] ECR I-4997.

[117] eg Case 15/83 *Denkavit* [1984] ECR 2171.

[118] See Chapters 16 and 17 below.

[119] In Case C-438/05 *Viking* [2007] ECR I-10779, AG Maduro considered the free movement of goods provisions capable of binding individuals in certain circumstances, see Opinion at paras 31–43. The Court in *Viking* regarded Case C-265/95 *Commission v France* [1997] ECR I-6959, para 30, and C-112/00 *Schmidberger* [2003] ECR I-5659, paras 57 and 62, as supporting the proposition that Art 49 TFEU could be invoked horizontally against trade unions, see paras 61, 62. For the possible horizontal effect of Art 34 TFEU, see D Wyatt, 'Horizontal Effect of Fundamental Freedoms and the Right to Equality after *Viking* and *Mangold*, and the Implications for Community Competence' (2008) 4 *Croatian Yearbook of European Law and Policy* 1, 19–25.

As mentioned above, in order for the Treaty provisions to apply there must be a cross-border element, at least potentially (although loosely interpreted and not always actually present). This notwithstanding, the Court accepts to deliver rulings in purely internal situations when it deems the answer to be of use to the national court. Finally, as in the case of the other internal market provisions, Articles 34 and 35 TFEU apply not only to national measures but also to measures adopted by the EU institutions.[120]

VI – DEROGATION FROM ARTICLES 34 AND 35 TFEU

Article 36 TFEU provides:

> The provisions of Articles 34 and 35 shall not preclude prohibitions or restrictions on imports, exports or goods in transit justified on grounds of public morality, public policy or public security; the protection of health and life of humans, animals or plants; the protection of national treasures possessing artistic, historic or archaeological value; or the protection of industrial and commercial property. Such prohibitions or restrictions shall not however, constitute a means of arbitrary discrimination or a disguised restriction on trade between Member States.

A – Grounds of Derogation

Article 36 TFEU is the only available justification for quantitative restrictions and directly discriminatory measures; it constitutes an exception to the fundamental rule that all obstacles to the free movement of goods between Member States shall be abolished and therefore must be interpreted strictly.[121] It follows that the list of exceptions is exhaustive.[122] Thus the Court has held that Article 36 TFEU does not justify derogation from Article 34 TFEU on the grounds of the protection of consumers or the fairness of commercial transactions,[123] economic policy,[124] or the protection of creativity and cultural

---

[120] Case 15/83 *Denkavit Nederland v Hoofdproduktschap voor akkerbouwprodukten* [1984] ECR 2171, para 15; Case C-51/93 *Meyhui NV v Schott Zwiesel Glaswerke AG* [1994] ECR I-3879, para 11; Case C-114/96 *RenJ Kieffer and Romain Thill* [1997] ECR I-3629, para 27.

[121] Case 46/76 *Bauhuis v Netherlands* [1977] ECR 5; Case 113/80 *Commission v Ireland* [1981] ECR 1625; Case 95/81 *Commission v Italy* [1982] ECR 2187.

[122] Case 95/81 *Commission v Italy* [1982] ECR 2187.

[123] Ibid; Case 220/81 *Robertson* [1982] ECR 2349; Case 229/83 *Leclerc* [1985] ECR 2. Such considerations may, however, in the case of non-discriminatory restrictions, amount to mandatory requirements justifying reasonable restrictions on the free movement of goods in the general interest, see below section VII.

[124] Case 7/61 *Commission v Italy* [1961] ECR 317; Case 95/81 *Commission v Italy* [1982] ECR 2187; Case 238/82 *Duphar* [1984] ECR 523; Case 72/83 *Campus Oil* [1984] ECR 2727; Case 288/83 *Commission v Ireland* [1985] ECR 1761; Case C-324/93 *R v Home Secretary,ex parte Evans Medical Ltd and Macfarlan Smith Ltd.* [1995] ECR I-563, para 36. But non-discriminatory measures designed to limit the costs of a state health insurance scheme are compatible with Union law: see Case 238/82 *Duphar* [1984] ECR 523, at para 17; see also Case C-120/95 *Nicholas Decker v Caisse de Maladie de Employés Privés* [1998] ECR I-1831, para 39, 'aims of a purely economic nature cannot justify a barrier to the fundamental principle of the free movement of goods. However, it cannot be excluded that the risk of seriously undermining the financial balance of the social security system may constitute an overriding reason in the general interest capable of justifying a barrier of that kind'.

diversity,[125] since none of the foregoing are referred to in the Article. While the Court has accepted that the expression 'public policy' is capable of embracing a national ban on the export of coins no longer constituting legal tender,[126] it has refused to accept that the expression includes the protection of consumers.[127] In the absence of harmonised rules at the EU level, recourse to Article 36 TFEU may entail the application of different standards in different Member States, as a result of different national value-judgments, and different factual circumstances. Thus the Court has stated that: 'In principle, it is for each Member State to determine in accordance with its own scale of values and in the form selected by it the requirements of public morality in its territory.'[128]

Similarly, in the absence of harmonisation at EU level, it is for each Member State to determine the appropriate level of protection which they wish to accord to the protection of human health, whilst taking account of the free movement of goods within the EU.[129] As the Court explained in *Heijn*:

> In so far as the relevant Community rules do not cover certain pesticides, Member States may regulate the presence of residues of those pesticides in a way which may vary from one country to another according to the climatic conditions, the normal diet of the population and their state of health.[130]

Nevertheless, while a public health risk to consumers is capable of justifying national rules under Article 36 TFEU, 'the risk must be measured, not according to the yardstick of general conjecture, but on the basis of relevant scientific research',[131] and the discretion of the Member States to decide, in the case of a food additive, on the degree of protection of the health and life of humans to be adopted, is one which is retained 'in so far as there are uncertainties in the present state of scientific research with regard to the harmfulness' of the additive in question.[132] Thus, Article 36 TFEU does not have the effect of imposing on Member States a minimum common standard in health protection, and indeed scientific uncertainty regarding the effect of a product is enough for the Member State to be able to invoke the public health derogation (the so-called precautionary principle).[133]

While Article 36 TFEU leaves a margin of discretion in the national authorities as to the extent to which they wish to protect the interests listed therein, the discretion is limited by two important principles. First, that any discrimination between imports and domestic products must not be arbitrary. Secondly, that national measures must not restrict trade any more than is necessary to protect the interest in question. Furthermore, the Court has held that Article 36 TFEU can never be invoked to protect purely economic interests,[134] and that the Member States are under an obligation to respect fundamental rights as general principles of Union law when invoking Article 36 TFEU (or the mandatory requirement doctrine).[135]

---

[125] Case 229/83 *Leclerc* [1985] ECR 2.
[126] Case 7/78 *Thompson* [1978] ECR 22247.
[127] Case 177/83 *Kohl* [1984] ECR 3651.
[128] Case 34/79 *Henn & Darby* [1979] ECR 3795.
[129] Case C-205/89 *Commission v Greece* [1991] ECR I-1361, para 8.
[130] Case 94/83 [1984] ECR 3263; more recently eg Case C-366/04 *Schwarz* [2005] ECR I-00000.
[131] Case C-17/93 *JJJ Van der Veldt* [1994] ECR I-3537, para 17; Case 178/84 *Commission v Germany* [1987] ECR 1227.
[132] Case C-113/91 *Criminal proceedings against Michel Debus* [1992] ECR I-3617, para 13.
[133] Case 174/82 *Sandoz* [1983] ECR 2445; C-192/01 *Commission v Denmark* [2003] ECR I-9693.
[134] eg Case C-398/98 *Commission v Greece* (obligation to stock petroleum) [2001] ECR I-7915.
[135] Mutatis mutanda Case C-260/89 *ERT* 2925.

Article 36 TFEU expressly permits restrictions justified on grounds of 'the protection of industrial or commercial property'—or 'intellectual property' as it is more commonly referred to. The relationship between national intellectual property rights and the free movement of goods is explained in the final section of this chapter.

(i) Arbitrary Discrimination or a Disguised Restriction on trade

Article 36 TFEU provides that prohibitions or restrictions permitted under that Article shall not, however, constitute a means of arbitrary discrimination or a disguised restriction on trade between Member States. The purpose of this proviso was described by the Court in *Henn & Darby* as being to

> prevent restrictions on trade based on the grounds mentioned in the first sentence of [Article 36 TFEU] from being diverted from their proper purpose and used in such a way as either to create discrimination in respect of goods originating in other Member States or indirectly to protect certain national products.[136]

In determining whether or not discrimination against imported goods is arbitrary, an important yardstick will be a comparison with measures taken vis-à-vis domestic goods. As a precaution against transmission of the destructive San José scale insect, German legislation provided for the phyto-sanitary examination of certain imported fruit and vegetables at point of entry. On a reference for a preliminary ruling, the Court held that such measures must be considered to be justified in principle under Article 36 TFEU, provided that they did not constitute a means of arbitrary discrimination. This would not be the case where effective measures were taken to prevent the distribution of contaminated domestic products, and where there was reason to believe that there would be a risk of the harmful organism spreading if no inspections were held on importation.[137]

A measure which discriminates against imports, and indeed excludes imports, may nevertheless be justified if it is the only way to achieve the objective of protection for the health and life of humans. Thus in *Evans Medical Ltd and Macfarlan Smith Ltd*, the Court of Justice held that a Member State was entitled to refuse a licence for importation of narcotic drugs from another Member State on the ground that such importation threatened the viability of the sole licensed manufacturer in the former Member State and jeopardised reliability of the supply of diamorphine for medical purposes, provided that the latter objective could not be achieved as effectively by measures less restrictive of intra-EU trade.[138] If a Member State seeks to preserve an indigenous animal population with distinct characteristics by banning imports of other species which might mate with the indigenous population and endanger its survival, this can be justified under Article 36 TFEU as a measure to protect the life of animals.[139]

(ii) Proportionality and Necessity: National Measures Are Only Justified if They Are No More Restrictive than Is Strictly Necessary

The Court has emphasised that Article 36 TFEU is not designed to reserve certain matters

---

[136] Case 34/79 *Henn & Darby* [1979] ECR 3795, para 21; Case 40/82 *Commission v United Kingdom* [1984] ECR 283, para 36.

[137] Case 4/75 *Rewe-Zentralfinanz v Landwirtschaftskammer* [1975] ECR 843.

[138] Case C-324/93 *R v Home Secretary, ex parte Evans Medical Ltd and Macfarlan Smith Ltd* [1995] ECR I-563, paras 35–39.

[139] Case C-67/97 *Ditlev Bluhme* [1998] ECR I-8033.

to the exclusive jurisdiction of Member States, but only permits national laws to derogate from the principle of the free movement of goods to the extent to which such derogation is and continues to be justified for the attainment of the objectives referred to in that Article.[140] The word 'justified' is to be construed as meaning 'necessary'.[141] Application of the Article is thus to be conditioned upon compliance with the principle of proportionality.[142] As the Court explained in *Commission v Belgium*:

> However [public health] measures are justified only if it is established that they are necessary in order to attain the objective of protection referred to in [Article 36 TFEU] and that such protection cannot be achieved by means which place less of a restriction on the free movement of goods within the Community.[143]

Thus, in *de Peijper*,[144] the Court considered the argument that restrictive provisions of Netherlands legislation which favoured imports by dealers securing the co-operation of the manufacturer were justified on the basis that they were necessary for the protection of the health and life of humans. While the Court acknowledged that this interest ranked first among the interests protected by Article 36 TFEU, it emphasised that national measures did not fall within the exception if the health or life of humans could be as effectively protected by means less restrictive of intra-EU trade. In particular, Article 36 TFEU did not justify restrictions motivated primarily by a concern to facilitate the task of the authorities, or reduce public expenditure, unless alternative arrangements would impose unreasonable burdens on the administration.

Where a measure having equivalent effect has but a slight impact on trade, this will be relevant in assessing the proportionality of the national measures in question. As the Court explained in *Société Civile Agricole du Centre d'Insémination de la Crespelle*:

> In order to ascertain that the restrictive effects on intra-Community trade of the rules at issue do not exceed what is necessary to achieve the aim in view, it must be considered whether those effects are direct, indirect or purely speculative and whether those effects do not impede the marketing of imported products more than the marketing of national products.[145]

Judicial assessment of the proportionality of a measure may well involve a review of possible alternative means of achieving the aim in question,[146] and determining the compatibility with Article 36 TFEU of, for example, a national measure limiting the sulphur dioxide content of beer can entail a detailed consideration of available scientific evidence as regards the qualities and effects of the additive in question.[147] There can be no doubt that claims to restrict the free movement of goods on public health grounds are not beyond judicial scrutiny, and such matters as the burden of proof,[148] or, in cases on food additives, the tolerated levels of the additive in question in other beverages or foodstuffs, or other

---

[140] Case 5/77 *Tedeschi* [1977] ECR 1556; Case 251/78 *Denkavit* [1979] ECR 3327.

[141] Case 153/78 *Commission v Germany* [1979] ECR 2555, para 8; Case 251/78 *Denkavit* [1979] ECR 3327, para 21.

[142] As to which, see also below section VII.B.

[143] Case 155/82 [1983] ECR 531. And a consistent case law to this effect, see eg Case 97/83 *Melkunie* [1984] ECR 2367, para 12; Case C-189/95 *Harry Franzén*, [1997] ECR I-5909, para 75; Case C-212/03 *Commission v France* (import licences for medicinal products) [2005] ECR I-4213.

[144] Case 104/75 [1976] ECR 613.

[145] Case C-323/93 [1994] ECR I-5077, para 36.

[146] Case C-131/93 *Commission v Germany* [1994] ECR I-3303, para 25.

[147] Case C-113/91 *Criminal proceedings against Michel Debus* [1992] ECR I-3617, paras 17–29.

[148] Ibid, paras 18 and 24; Case C-131/93 *Commission v Germany* [1994] ECR I-3303, para 26; Case C-189/95 *Harry Franzén* [1997] ECR I- 5909, para 76.

conduct of the relevant national authorities which suggests that alternative measures less restrictive of trade would be adequate to achieve the aims in question,[149] may play a large part in the outcome of a case.[150] In adversarial proceedings under Article 258 TFEU it will be for the Court of Justice to decide whether or not a national measure is proportionate.[151] On a reference for a preliminary ruling the Court of Justice may consider it has enough information to allow it to determine itself whether the requirement of proportionality is satisfied, and do so,[152] or it may leave it to the national court to decide.[153]

As long as the rules relating to health protection in a particular sector have not been harmonised, it is open to the Member States to carry out any necessary inspections at national frontiers.[154] However, the free movement of goods is facilitated by the carrying out of health inspections in the country of production, and the health authorities of the importing Member State should co-operate in order to avoid the repetition, in the importing country, of checks that have already been carried out in the country of production.[155] Similar considerations apply to approval by national authorities of products that have been approved on health grounds in other Member States. Whilst a Member State is free to require such products to undergo a fresh procedure of examination and approval, the authorities of that Member State are bound to assist in bringing about a relaxation of the controls applied in intra-EU trade,[156] and are not entitled unnecessarily to require technical or chemical analyses or tests where those analyses or tests have already been carried out in another Member State and their results are available to those authorities, or may at their request be placed at their disposal.[157] The same principles apply to checking for other purposes, for example to confirm the precious metal content of articles.[158]

(iii) Disguised Restrictions, Arbitrary Discrimination and Proportionality

The requirements that measures taken by Member States under Article 36 TFEU must not constitute a means of arbitrary discrimination, nor a disguised restriction on trade, and must comply with the principle of proportionality, must overlap, and should not be considered in isolation. Thus, infringement of the principle of proportionality may lead to a measure being categorised as a disguised restriction on trade.[159] Furthermore, discrimination between imports and domestic products as regards frequency of testing may

---

[149] Case C-131/93 *Commission v Germany* [1994] ECR I-3303, para 27; also eg Case C-41/02 *Commission v Netherlands* [2004] ECR I-11375, where the Court found that the Netherlands had failed to fulfil its obligation under Art 34 TFEU because it had not carried out an in-depth assessment of given nutrients before banning the imports of products containing them.

[150] Case C-113/91 *Criminal proceedings against Michel Debus* [1992] ECR I-3617, para 25.

[151] See eg Case C-131/93 *Commission v Germany* [1994] ECR I-3303, paras 25–27.

[152] Case 315/92 *Verband Sozialer Wettbewerb eV v Clinique Laboratories SNC* [1994] ECR I-317, paras 20–23; though the Advocate General thought that the national court should decide the matter, Opinion of Mr Gulmann, esp para 26.

[153] Case C-324/93 *R v Home Secretary, ex parte Evans Medical Ltd and Macfarlan Smith Ltd* [1995] ECR I-563, where the Court left it to the referring court to determine whether it was necessary to refuse licences for the import of drugs from other Member States to ensure a reliable supply of drugs for essential medical purposes.

[154] Case 73/84 *Denkavit* [1985] ECR 1013.

[155] Case 251/78 *Denkavit* [1979] ECR 3327; Case 73/84 *Denkavit* [1985] ECR 1013; Case C-228/91 *Commission v Italy* [1993] ECR I - 2701.

[156] Case 104/75 *de Peijper* [1976] ECR 613; Case 272/80 *Frans-Nederlandse* [1981] ECR 3277.

[157] Case 272/80 *Frans-Nederlandse* [1981] ECR 3277; Case C-373/92 *Commission v Belgium* [1993] ECR I-3107; Case C-228/91 *Commission v Italy* [1993] ECR I-2701.

[158] Case C-293/93 *Houtwipper* [1994] ECR 3159.

[159] Case 272/80 *Frans-Nederlandse* [1981] ECR 3277, paras 13, 14; Joined Cases 2–4/82 *Le Lion* [1983] ECR 2973, para 12.

lead to the conclusion that the level of scrutiny of imports is disproportionate. Thus in deciding in *Commission v France*[160] whether or not the frequency of French frontier tests of Italian wine complied with the principle of proportionality, the Court of Justice took into account not only the fact that similar checks on Italian wine were carried out by the Italian authorities, but also the fact that the frequency of the French frontier inspections was distinctly higher than the occasional checks carried out on the transportation of French wine within France.

B – Burden of Proof Lies with the National Authorities

It is for the national authorities of the Member States to prove that their restrictive trading rules may be justified under Article 36 TFEU.[161] Thus in *Cullet* the French government attempted to defend national rules fixing retail selling prices for fuel on grounds of public order and security represented by the violent reactions which would have to be anticipated on the part of retailers affected by unrestricted competition. The Court rejected this argument summarily:

> In that regard, it is sufficient to state that the French Government has not shown that it would be unable, using the means at its disposal, to deal with the consequences which an amendment of the rules in question...would have upon public order and security.[162]

The burden of proving that Article 36 TFEU applies accordingly entails:

(i) showing that the national measures in question fall within one of the categories (eg public health, public policy or public morality) referred to in Article 36 TFEU;[163]
(ii) establishing that the measure does not constitute a means of arbitrary discrimination, ie that if it differentiates between domestic products and imports, it does so on objective and justifiable grounds;[164]
(iii) establishing that the measure does not constitute a disguised restriction on trade, that is to say, that any restrictive effect on the free movement of goods is limited to what is necessary to protect the interest in question.[165]

The requirement that national authorities must prove the consistency of national legislation with Article 36 TFEU may be incapable of application if no national authorities are party to the proceedings in question.[166] Finally, and as mentioned above, Member States must comply with fundamental rights as general principles of Union law whenever they are derogating from a Treaty provision.[167]

---

[160] Case 42/82 [1983] ECR 1013, paras 51–57.
[161] Case 227/82 [1983] *Leendert van Bennekom* ECR 3883, para 40; see also Case 104/75 *de Peijper* [1976] ECR 613; Case 251/78 *Denkavit* [1979] ECR 3369, para 24; Case 174/82 *Sandoz* [1983] ECR 2445, para 22; Joined Cases C-13/91 and C-113/91 *Criminal proceedings against Michel Debus* [1992] ECR I-3617, para 18.
[162] Case 231/83 [1985] ECR 306, paras 32, 33.
[163] Above at section A.
[164] Above at section A(i).
[165] Above at section A(ii). But in direct proceedings if the national authority/government puts forward convincing reasons why Art 36 TFEU should apply, it falls upon the Commission to challenge the soundness of such reasons (including scientific opinion): eg Case C-24/00 *Commission v France* [2004] ECR I-1277, paras 68 *et seq*.
[166] *cf* Case C-368/95 *Familiapress* [1997] ECR I-3689, a case involving mandatory requirements where it seems the national court was obliged to resolve the matter on the basis of a study of the market in question.
[167] Mutatis mutanda Case C-260/89 ERT 2925.

C – The Effect of Harmonisation Directives and Other EU Measures on Recourse to Article 36 TFEU

Recourse to Article 36 TFEU is no longer justified if EU rules provide for the necessary measures to ensure protection of the interests set out in that Article.[168] This may be the case, for example, when directives enacted under Articles 114 and 115 TFEU or otherwise provide for the full harmonisation of the measures necessary for the protection of animal and human health, and establish the procedures to check that they are observed.[169] Thus, if such a directive places the responsibility for public health inspections of a product upon the Member State of export, the national authorities of the importing Member State will no longer be entitled to subject the product to systematic inspection upon importation; only occasional inspections to check compliance with the EU standards will be permissible.[170] But procedures for checking imports authorised under Union law must not entail unreasonable cost or delay.[171] Where harmonization is not complete, however, Member States may continue to rely upon Article 36 TFEU.[172]

VII – MANDATORY REQUIREMENTS IN THE GENERAL INTEREST

A – Mandatory Requirements

Although the Court has stated repeatedly that the exceptions listed in Article 36 TFEU are exhaustive,[173] it could be said that in effect it established further grounds of justification for limiting Article 34 TFEU in the *Cassis* case, in which it held that obstacles to the free movement of goods in the EU resulting from disparities between national marketing rules must be accepted in so far as they were necessary to satisfy mandatory requirements relating in particular to the effectiveness of fiscal supervision, the protection of public health, the fairness of commercial transactions and the defence of the consumer.[174] One explanation for this apparent inconsistency is that the *Cassis* list does not so much provide grounds for derogating from Article 34 TFEU as define the circumstances in which national measures fall within Article 34 TFEU in the first place.[175] Another explanation is that the indistinctly applicable measures described in the *Cassis* case and in subsequent case law as amounting to measures having equivalent effect are in truth indirectly discrim-

---

[168] Case 72/83 *Campus Oil* [1984] ECR 2727, para 27.
[169] Case 251/78 *Denkavit* [1979] ECR 3369, para 14; Case 227/82 *Leendert* [1983] ECR 3883, para 35; Case 29/87 *Denkavit* [1988] ECR 2965; Case 190/87 *Moormann BV* [1988] ECR 4689; Case C-304/88 *Commission v Belgium* [1990] ECR I–2801; *R v MAFF ex parte Hedley Lomas* [1996] ECR I-2553, para 18; *R v MAFF ex parte Compassion in World Farming Limited* [1998] ECR I-1251, para 47.
[170] Case 35/76 *Simmenthal* [1976] ECR 1871; Cases 2–4/82 *Le Lion* [1983] ECR 2973.
[171] Case 406/85 *Goffette* [1987] ECR 2525.
[172] Case C-323/93 *Société Civile Agricole du Centre d'Insémination de la Crespelle* ECR I-5077, para 35; Case C-39/90 *Denkavit* [1991] ECR I-3069, para 19.
[173] Above at section VI.A.
[174] See above at section VI.A.
[175] *cf* also E Spaventa, 'On Discrimination and the Theory of Mandatory Requirements' (2000) 3 *CYELS* 457.

inatory, and the mandatory requirements amount to grounds which objectively justify the discrimination in question.[176]

In any event it should be noted that mandatory requirements cannot be invoked to justify directly discriminatory measures, and/or quantitative restrictions.[177] Thus in the case of national rules requiring certain imported products but not their domestically produced counterparts to bear an indication of country of origin, the Court held that considerations of consumer protection and the fairness of commercial transactions could have no application.[178] In the case of national rules requiring both domestic goods and imports to bear an indication of country of origin, the Court again refused to consider arguments based on considerations of consumer protection on the grounds that the national rules were in fact discriminatory:

> The requirements relating to the indication of origin of goods are applicable without distinction to domestic and imported products only in form because, by their very nature, they are intended to enable the consumer to distinguish between those two categories of products, which may thus prompt him to give his preference to national products.[179]

Thus, mandatory requirements are only available for measures that, at least in law, apply to imported and domestic products alike. That said, there have been some exceptions to this principle, and environmental protection (a mandatory requirement of public interest not included in Article 36 TFEU) has been successfully invoked in some cases which related to discriminatory measures.[180] In order to allow for such justification to be invoked in cases relating to discriminatory measures, the Court has relied also on the fact that a high level of the protection of the environment constitutes one of the objectives of the Treaty. Nevertheless, such cases represent a threat to the consistency of the Court's case law on the respective scope of Treaty derogations and mandatory requirements. For this reason, Advocate General Jacobs has called on the Court to dispose of such distinction and just consider the mandatory requirements as additional grounds of justification for any type of measure, including discriminatory ones.[181] The Court has not taken the suggestion on board. It could be argued that that is the correct approach and that in any event measures taken to protect the environment could be justified on the grounds of being aimed at protecting the life of humans, animals and plants from a long-term threat.[182]

A further difference between the Treaty derogations and the mandatory requirements is that the former cannot pursue economic aims, whilst in relation to the latter economic aims can be taken into consideration, even though they may not be the only reason why

---

[176] See above at section III.A(ii) for the view that the restrictions such as that involved in *Cassis* are indirectly discriminatory.

[177] Case 113/80 *Commission v Ireland* [1981] ECR 1625, paras 8 and 11; Joined Cases C-321/94, C-322/94, C-323/94, C-324/94 *Jacques Pistre etc* [1997] ECR I-2343, para 52.

[178] Case 113/80 *Commission v Ireland* [1981] ECR 1625.

[179] Case 270/83 *Commission v United Kingdom* [1985] ECR 1201.

[180] Case C-2/90 *Commission v Belgium* [1992] ECR I-4431; Case C-389/96 *Aher-Waggon GmbH v Germany* [1998] ECR I-4473; Case C-203/96 *Chemische Afvalstoffen Dusseldorp and Others v Minister van Volkshuisvesting, Ruimtelijke Ordering en Milieubeheer* [1998] ECR I-4075; Case C-209/98 *Entreprenørforeningens Affalds/ Miljøsektion (FFAD) v Københavns Kommune* [2000] ECR I-3743; Case C-379/98 *PreussenElektra AG v Schleswag AG* [2001] ECR I-2099.

[181] Case C-379/98 *PreussenElektra AG v Schleswag AG* [2001] ECR I-2099, para 226; see also P Oliver, 'Some Further Reflections on the Scope of Article 28–30 (ex 30–36) EC' (1999) 36 *CMLRev* 783, 804 *et seq*; and C Barnard, 'Fitting the Remaining pieces into the Goods and Persons Gigsaw' (2001) 26 *ELRev* 35, 54.

[182] See further Spaventa, above n 175.

the measure was adopted.[183] The categories of justification under the *Cassis* formulation are not closed, as appears from the formulation itself, which refers to four categories 'in particular'. The categories of justification expanded during the period prior to the limitation imposed on the *Cassis* doctrine by *Keck and Mithouard*.[184] While some of the restrictions identified by the pre-*Keck* case law would no longer be regarded as falling within the scope of Article 34 TFEU unless directly or indirectly discriminatory, the categories of justification upheld in such cases would seem to remain good law. The Court has added to the original *Cassis* list of mandatory requirements, inter alia, environmental protection[185] and the encouragement of film-making, upholding on this latter ground national rules providing that videocassettes of films could not be distributed until one year after the release of the films at the cinema.[186] In *Oebel* the Court stated that legitimate interests of economic and social policy, consistent with the Treaty, might similarly justify impediments to the free movement of goods.[187] In addition, the Court has held that restrictions on imports which result from national rules governing the opening hours of retail premises, in particular as regards Sunday trading, may be justified by reference to national or regional sociocultural characteristics.[188]

(i) Consumer Protection

By far the most invoked requirement of public interest to justify restrictions to intra-EU trade is that of consumer protection. This is natural having regard to the fact that different regulatory environments and mutual recognition might allow into the market products unfamiliar to consumers. Whilst the Court recognises that consumer protection is a valid ground of justification, it scrutinises carefully national measures as to their proportionality. This means that in most cases concerning product requirements, the Court is satisfied that a labelling requirement is enough to ensure that the consumer is not going to be mislead. Furthermore, in deciding whether the measures are necessary to protect the consumer, the Court has had regard to the 'reasonably well informed consumer'.[189] This majoritarian approach, whereby the Court would accept measures directed at protecting the majority of consumers (the reasonably well informed ones), but not those directed at protecting the more vulnerable consumers (the non-reasonably informed) has led to some criticism.[190]

In *Mars*,[191] the defendant launched a campaign to promote some ice-cream bars. Those were packaged with a wrapping bearing the statement '+10%'. An association fighting unfair competition brought proceedings to restrain Mars from marketing its products in that way arguing, inter alia, that the packaging was misleading since the proportion of the wrapping where the '+10%' statement appeared was significantly bigger than 10 per cent

---

[183] This is probably the reason why in Case C-120/95 *N Decker v Caisse de Maladie des Employés Privés* [1998] ECR I-1831, the Court relied on the mandatory requirement of public health rather than on Art 36 TFEU.
[184] See above at section III.B.
[185] Case 240/83 *Bruleurs d'Huiles Usages* [1985] ECR 532.
[186] Joined Cases 60 and 61/84 *Cinéthèque* [1985] ECR 2605.
[187] Case 155/80 *Oebel* [1981] ECR 1993, para 12.
[188] Case 145/88 *Torfaen BC v B&Q Plc* [1989] ECR 3851, para 14; Case C-332/89 *Andrè Marchandise* [1991] ECR-1027, para 12.
[189] eg Case C-315/92 *Clinique* [1994] ECR I-317; Case C-470/93 *Mars* [1995] ECR I-1923; this was somehow relaxed in Case C-220/98 *Estée Lauder v Lancaster* [2000] ECR I-117.
[190] eg S Weatherill, 'Recent Case Law Concerning the Free Movement of Goods: Mapping the Frontiers of Market Deregulation' (1999) 36 *CMLRev* 51.
[191] Case C-470/93 *Mars* [1995] ECR I-1923.

of the wrapping, thus giving the impression that the product had been increased by a bigger proportion. The Court was seized of the question whether German legislation which would have prevented Mars from wrapping its products in such a way could be justified on consumer protection grounds. After having held that the rules fell within the scope of Article 34 TFEU, the Court found that they were not justified on consumer protection grounds since: 'Reasonably circumspect consumers may be deemed to know that there is not necessarily a link between the size of publicity markings relating to an increase in a product's quantity and the size of that increase'.[192] In *Estée Lauder* the Court adopted a more nuanced approach and in relation to the possible misleading effects of the indication 'lifting' in relation to a firming cream, it held that whilst the 'reasonably circumspect consumer' should not be mislead, the national court could investigate whether German consumers would be mislead. It held:

> In particular, it must be determined whether social, cultural or linguistic factors may justify the term 'lifting', used in connection with a firming cream, meaning something different to the German consumer as opposed to consumers in other Member States, or whether the instructions for the use of the product are in themselves sufficient to make it quite clear that its effects are short-lived, thus neutralising any conclusion to the contrary that might be derived from the word 'lifting'.[193]

Other rules might be easier to assess. In *Oosthoek's Uitgeversmaatschaapij BV* the Court upheld national measures restricting the giving of gifts as a means of sales promotion, on the grounds of the fairness of commercial transactions and the defence of the consumer, in the following terms:

> It is undeniable that the offering of free gifts as a means of sales promotion may mislead consumers as to the real prices of certain products and distort the conditions on which genuine competition is based. Legislation which restricts or even prohibits such commercial practices for that reason is therefore capable of contributing to consumer protection and fair trading.[194]

In *GB-INNO-BM*, however, the Court took a different view of the need for state intervention in the interests of consumer protection. A Belgian company had distributed advertising leaflets in Luxembourg as well as in Belgium allegedly contrary to Luxembourg rules, according to which sales offers involving a temporary price reduction may not state the duration of the offer or refer to previous prices. The Court held that under EU law concerning consumer protection the provision of information to the consumer is considered one of the principal requirements. It followed that Article 34 TFEU could not be interpreted as meaning that national legislation which denies the consumer access to certain kinds of information might be justified by mandatory requirements concerning consumer protection.[195]

Consumer protection and fair trading also raise issues which extend beyond the market of the importing Member State. In *Prantl*[196] the Court considered trading rules reserving to national wine producers the use of the characteristically shaped *Bocksbeutel* bottle.

---

[192] Ibid, para 24.

[193] Case C-220/98 *Estée Lauder v Lancaster* [2000] ECR I-117, para 29.

[194] Case 286/81 *Oosthoek's Uitgeversmaatschaapij BV* [1982] ECR 4575, para 18. And in Cases C-1/90 and C-176/90 *Aragonesa de Publicidad Exterior SA* [1991] ECR I-4151. The Court upheld on public health grounds restrictions on advertising of certain alcoholic beverages. See also Case 382/87 *Buet* [1989] ECR 1235 (prohibition of door-to-door canvassing of educational material justified).

[195] Case C-362/88 *GB-INNO-BM* [1990] ECR I-667.

[196] Case 16/83 [1984] ECR 1299.

Consumer protection and fair trading were pleaded in support of the national rules. The Court noted, however, that in the common market, consumer protection and fair trading as regards the presentation of wines must be guaranteed 'with regard on all sides for the fair and traditional practices observed in the various Member States'.[197] It followed that an exclusive right to use a certain type of bottle granted by national legislation in a Member State could not be used to bar imports of wines originating in another Member State put in bottles of the same or similar shape in accordance with a fair and traditional practice in that Member State.[198]

B – The Principle of Proportionality

Recourse to mandatory requirements is subject to the principle of proportionality, as the Court made clear in the *Rau* case:

> It is also necessary for such rules to be proportionate to the aim in view. If a Member State has a choice between various measures to attain the same objective it should choose the means which least restrict the free movement of goods.[199]

The Court of Justice, or the competent national court, must determine whether the least-restrictive measure has in fact been selected by the national legislature; this can in some cases lead to an extensive review of the rules at issue. For example, the *Familiapress*[200] case concerned a national prohibition on the sale of periodicals containing prize puzzle competitions or games, which the Court of Justice regarded as impairing access of imported periodicals to the market of the Member State in question and as constituting in principle a measure having equivalent effect. Nevertheless, the Court held that 'Maintenance of press diversity may constitute an overriding requirement justifying a restriction on the free movement of goods', noting that 'Such diversity helps to safeguard freedom of expression as protected by Article 10 of the European Convention on Human Rights and Fundamental Freedoms, which is one of the fundamental rights guaranteed by the Community legal order.' The Court went on to examine in detail how the national court should go about assessing the proportionality of the matter in issue. This involved a detailed study by the national court of the economic conditions prevailing on the Austrian press market. The Court stated, inter alia:

> In carrying out that study, it will have to define the market for the product in question and to have regard to the market shares of individual publishers or press groups and the trend thereof.
>
> Moreover, the national court will also have to assess the extent to which, from the consumer's standpoint, the product concerned can be replaced by papers which do not offer prizes, taking into account all the circumstances which may influence the decision to purchase, such as the presence of advertising on the title page referring to the chance of winning a prize, the likelihood

---

[197] Ibid, para 27.

[198] The principle may be confined to cases involving similar indirect indications of national provenenance, and the problem in *Prantl* is explained in Case C-3/91 *Exportur SA v LOR SA and Confiserie du Tech SA* [1992] ECR I-5529, para 34, as being 'how to reconcile user of an indirect indication of national provenance with concurrent user of an indirect indication of foreign provenance', which was 'not comparable to the use of names of Spanish towns by French undertakings, which raises the problem of the protection in one State of the names of another State'.

[199] Case 261/81 [1982] ECR 3961, para 12.

[200] Case C-368/95 *Vereinigte Familiapress Zeitungsverlags- und vertriebs GmbH* [1997] ECR I-3689.

of winning, the value of the prize or the extent to which winning depends on a test calling for a measure of ingenuity, skill or knowledge.[201]

The ruling in *Familiapress* also clarified that whenever Member States invoke a mandatory requirement to justify a restriction to intra-EU trade, they have to respect fundamental rights as guaranteed by the general principles of Union law since the situation falls within the scope of Union law.[202]

VIII – THE RELATIONSHIP BETWEEN ARTICLES 34–36 TFEU AND OTHER PROVISIONS OF THE TREATY

However wide the field of application of Articles 34 and 35 TFEU may be, it does not include obstacles to trade covered by other provisions of the Treaty, such as Articles 28–30 TFEU (customs duties and charges having equivalent effect), Article 110 TFEU (discriminatory internal taxation), and Articles 107 and 108 TFEU (state aids).[203] Where national taxes are imposed on an import which lacks a domestic counterpart, the rate of tax must not be so high as to impede the free movement of goods. Such an impediment to free movement would fall to be governed by Articles 34–36 TFEU, rather than within the framework of Article 110 TFEU.[204] The extent to which fiscal charges not falling within the scope of Articles 30 or 110 TFEU might fall within the scope of Article 34 TFEU was clarified in *De Danske Billimportører*.[205] Here the claimant argued that a very high registration duty for new cars was an obstacle to trade prohibited by Article 34 TFEU. Denmark does not produce cars or any product in competition with cars and so there was no issue of discrimination for Article 110 TFEU purposes. After having found that the charge was of a fiscal nature, the Court held that if such charges are of such an amount as to represent an obstacle to the free movement of goods within the Common Market, they might be caught by Article 34 TFEU. However, in the case at issue, the Court found that the figures communicated by the national court in relation to the number of new vehicles registered in Denmark (and thus imported therein) did not in any way show that free movement of cars between Denmark and other Member States had been impeded. The Court has also clarified that the non-applicability of Articles 30 and 110 TFEU by no means triggers the automatic applicability of Article 34 TFEU.[206] Thus, it is very likely that only in the most extreme of circumstances would a non-discriminatory/non-protectionist tax be qualified as an obstacle to intra-EU trade within the meaning of Article 34 TFEU (and subject to justifications).

National measures which fail to be scrutinised by the Commission under Articles 107 and 108 TFEU cannot be categorised as measures having equivalent effect simply by virtue

---

[201] Case C-368/95 [1997] ECR I-3689, paras 30, 31.
[202] See Chapter 11 above.
[203] Case 74/76 *Iannelli & Volpi* [1977] ECR 557; Case 222/82 *Apple and Pear Development Council* [1983] ECR 4083, para 30.
[204] Case C-47/88 *Commission v Denmark* [1990] ECR I-4509.
[205] Case C-383/01 *De Danske Billimportører* [2003] ECR I-6065, and see Chapter 13, section IV above.
[206] Joined Cases C-34/01 to C-38/01 *Enirisorse Spa* [2003] ECR I-14243.

of their effects upon trade, unless the aid in question produces 'restrictive effects which exceed what is necessary to enable it to attain the objectives permitted by the Treaty'.[207] This may be the case where aid is granted to traders who obtain supplies of imported products through a state agency but is withheld when the products are imported direct, if this distinction is not clearly necessary for the attainment of the objectives of the said aid or for its proper functioning.[208] Furthermore, the Court has held that the possibility that state subsidies to a campaign designed to favour domestic products might fall within Articles 107 and 108 TFEU does not mean that the campaign itself thereby escapes the prohibitions laid down in Article 34 TFEU.[209] The fact that a public works contract relates to the provision of services cannot remove a clause in an invitation to tender restricting the material that may be used from the scope of the prohibitions set out in Article 34 TFEU.[210] Moreover, a national measure which facilitates an abuse of a dominant position will generally infringe Article 34 TFEU.[211]

IX – ARTICLE 37 TFEU: STATE MONOPOLIES OF A COMMERCIAL CHARACTER

Article 37 TFEU provides, in part:

1. Member States shall adjust any State monopolies of a commercial character so as to ensure that no discrimination regarding the conditions under which goods are procured and marketed exists between nationals of Member States.

The provisions of this Article shall apply to any body through which a Member State, in law or in fact, either directly or indirectly supervises, determines or appreciably influences imports or exports between Member States. These provisions shall likewise apply to monopolies delegated by the State to others.

2. Member States shall refrain from introducing any new measure which is contrary to the principles laid down in paragraph 1 or which restricts the scope of the Articles dealing with the abolition of customs duties and quantitative restrictions between Member States. [212]

3. . . . .

The State monopolies in question are those enjoying exclusive rights in the procurement and distribution of goods, not services,[213] and Article 37 TFEU applies to monopolies over provision of services only in so far as such a monopoly contravenes the principle of the free movement of goods by discriminating against imported products to the advan-

---

[207] Case 74/76 *Iannelli & Volpi* [1977] ECR 557.
[208] Case 74/76 *Iannelli & Volpi* [1977] ECR 557.
[209] Case 249/81 *Commission v Ireland* [1982] ECR 4005, para 18.
[210] Case 45/87 *Commission v Ireland* [1988] ECR 4929.
[211] Case C-179/90 *Merci convenzionali porto di Genova SpA v Siderurgica Gabrielli SpA* [1991] ECR I- 5889, para 21.
[212] Art 37(2) was declared directly applicable in Case 6/64 *Costa v ENEL* [1964] ECR 585; Art 37(1) was held to be directly effective in Case 45/75 *Pubblico Ministero v Flavia Manghera and Rewe-Zentrale des Lebensmittel-Grosshandels v Hauptzollamt Landau/Pfalz* [1976] ECR 91.
[213] Case 155/73 *Sacchi* [1974] ECR 409; Case 271/81 *Societe d'Insemination Artificielle* [1983] ECR 2057. In the latter case the Court recognised the possibility that a monopoly over the provision of services might have an indirect influence on trade in goods.

tage of products of domestic origin.[214] However, the existence of national rules requiring the licensing of particular activities is not sufficient to amount to a state monopoly of a commercial character.[215] Moreover, Article 37 TFEU has no application to national legislation which reserves the retail sale of manufactured tobacco products to distributors authorised by the state, provided that the state does not intervene in the procurement choices of retailers.[216]

By the end of the transitional period every national monopoly of a commercial character must have been adjusted so as to eliminate the exclusive right to import from other Member States.[217] Exclusive import rights give rise to discrimination prohibited by Article 37 TFEU against exporters established in other Member States, and such rights directly affect the conditions under which goods are marketed only as regards operators or sellers in other Member States.[218] However, for the prohibition of all discrimination between nationals of Member States provided for in Article 37(1) TFEU to be applicable, it is not necessarily a requirement that the exclusive rights to import a given product relate to all imports; it is sufficient if those rights relate to a proportion such that they enable the monopoly to have an appreciable influence on imports.[219] However, the Court has repeatedly stated that Article 37 TFEU does not require national monopolies having a commercial character to be abolished but requires them to be adjusted in such a way as to ensure that no discrimination regarding the conditions under which goods are procured and marketed exists between nationals of Member States.[220] The purpose of Article 37 TFEU is to reconcile the possibility for Member States to maintain certain monopolies of a commercial character as instruments for the pursuit of public interest aims with the requirements of the establishment and functioning of the common market. It aims at the elimination of obstacles to the free movement of goods, save, however, for restrictions on trade which are inherent in the existence of the monopolies in question.[221] Thus Article 37 TFEU only applies to activities intrinsically connected with the specific business of the monopoly and is irrelevant to national provisions which have no connection with such specific business.[222] While, during the transitional period, Article 37 TFEU suspended the operation of Article 110 TFEU, prohibiting discriminatory internal taxation,[223] once the the transitional period ended, the position of internal taxes has been subject exclusively to Article 110 TFEU.[224] Furthermore, while Article 37 TFEU permits the continuation of the obligation to deliver goods to the monopoly, and a corresponding obligation upon the monopoly to purchase such goods, Article 34 TFEU applies so as to ensure equal treatment of domestic goods and imports.[225] It thus seems that Article 37 TFEU is cumu-

---

[214] Case 271/81 *Amélioration de l' Élevage v Mialocq* [1983] ECR 2057; Joined Cases C-46/90 and C-93/91 *Procureur du Roi v Jean-Marie Lagauche and others.* [1993] ECR I-5267, para 33.

[215] Case 118/86 *Nertsvoederfabriek Nederland BV* [1987] ECR 3883.

[216] Case C-387/93 *Banchero.* [1995] ECR I-4663, para 31.

[217] Case 59/75 *Manghera* [1986] ECR 91.

[218] Case C-157/94 *Commission v Netherlands* [1997] ECR I-5699, para 15.

[219] Case C-347/88 *Commission v Greece* [1990] ECR I-4747, para 44; Case C-157/94 *Commission v Netherlands* [1997] ECR I-5699, para 18.

[220] Case C-189/95 *Criminal proceedings against Harry Franzén* [1997] ECR I-5909, para 38 and cases cited therein; see also Case C-438/02 *Hanner* [2005] ECR I-4551.

[221] Case C-189/95 *Criminal proceedings against Harry Franzén* [1997] ECR I-5909, para 39.

[222] Case 86/78 *Grandes Distilleries* [1979] ECR 897.

[223] As to which, see above at Chapter 13, section IV.

[224] Case 86/78 *Grandes Distilleries* [1979] ECR 897.

[225] Case 119/78 *Grandes Distilleries* [1979] ECR 975.

latively applicable with the provisions of the chapter on the elimination of quantitative restrictions, and the provisions on customs duties and charges having equivalent effect.

In the second *Hansen* case,[226] arising from the operation of the German alcohol monopoly, the Court held:

(i)   that after the end of the transitional period, Article 37 TFEU remained applicable wherever the exercise by a state monopoly of its exclusive rights entailed a discrimination or restriction prohibited by that Article;

(ii) that Article 37 TFEU prohibited a monopoly's right to purchase and resell national alcohol from being exercised so as to undercut imported products with publicly subsidised domestic products; and

(iii) that Articles 37 and 107 and 108 TFEU were capable of cumulative application to one and the same fact situation.

In *Pigs and Bacon Commission v McCarren*[227] the Court held that Article 38(1) TFEU[228] gave priority to the rules for the organisation of the agricultural markets over the application of Article 37 TFEU. The better view is that this means merely that Article 37 TFEU cannot be pleaded by way of derogation from rules imposed by a common organisation: the positive obligations of the Article are surely to be implied into the framework of a common organisation and it is established that common organisations can derogate only in exceptional circumstances from the free-movement provisions of the Treaty.[229]

Article 37(3) TFEU provides:

> If a State monopoly of a commercial character has rules which are designed to make it easier to dispose of agricultural products or obtain for them the best return, steps should be taken in applying the rules contained in this Article to ensure equivalent safeguards for the employment and standard of living of the producers concerned.

In *Charmasson*[230] the Court held that Article 37(3) TFEU had never allowed any derogation from Article 37 TFEU, and that the 'equivalent safeguards' referred to in Article 37(3) TFEU must themselves be compatible with the provisions of Article 37(1) and (2) TFEU.

X – ARTICLES 34–36 TFEU AND INTELLECTUAL PROPERTY RIGHTS

A – Intellectual Property and the Internal Market

The coexistence of separate systems of protection for intellectual property rights in the different Member States is capable of conflicting with the objective of creating a single internal market. For example, if one hypothetically considers for a moment national law in isolation from EU law, and supposes that a company holds a patent protected under the

---

[226] Case 91/78 [1979] ECR 935.
[227] Case 177/78 [1979] ECR 2161.
[228] Art 32(2) provides: 'Save as otherwise provided in Articles 33 to 38, the rules laid down for the establishment of the common market shall apply to agricultural products.'
[229] Cases 80 and 81/77 *Commissionaires Reunis* [1978] ECR 927; Case 83/78 *Redmond* [1978] ECR 2347.
[230] Case 48/74 [1974] ECR 1383.

law of two Member States, A and B, that company might be entitled to rely upon that patent in Member State B to oppose the import into that state of an article manufactured and placed on the market under the patent in Member State A, and vice versa, even though it was the company itself, or a licensee, which had placed that article on the market in the first place. Similarly, if a company held the rights to a trade mark in each Member State, it might oppose the import into Member State A of an article bearing the trade mark and placed on the market in Member State B, and vice versa, even though, once again, it was the company itself, or a licensee, which had placed that article on the market in the first place. In fact, national patent and trade mark rights do not operate in isolation from EU law, and EU law has addressed the above problem from two perspectives. The first is that of the application of Articles 34–36 TFEU, which have been interpreted by the Court as preventing holders of patents, trade marks, or copyright or other intellectual property rights from using those rights to prevent the import of goods covered by those rights into one Member State from the territory of another where the holder of the rights in question has consented to their being placed on the market. The second perspective has been the harmonisation of laws. Thus, for example, there has been harmonisation of national trade mark rules under Directive 2008/95/EC to approximate the laws of the Member States relating to trade marks,[231] while under Regulation (EC) No 207/2009 on the Community Trade Mark,[232] trade mark owners may apply for a single registered trade mark for the whole of the European Union from the Office for Harmonisation in the Internal Market (OHIM), which is located in Alicante, Spain. It is also possible to apply to the OHIM for a design right for one area comprising all Member States under Regulation (EC) No 6/2002 on Community designs.[233] Such harmonisation does not, however, render the case law of the Court of Justice on the free movement of goods provisions redundant, since EU secondary legislation must be interpreted in the light of the Treaty rules on the free movement of goods and in particular Article 34 TFEU.[234] Reference may also be made to other examples of harmonisation of intellectual property rights (eg rental and lending rights, legal protection of databases, certain aspects of copyright and related rights, and the protection of designs).[235]

In the field of patent law there has to date been co-ordination at the level of processing applications for patent protection in the various Member States, within the framework of the European Patent Convention. The Convention on the Grant of European Patents, or European Patent Convention, came into force on 7 October 1977. The European Patent Office, which processes patent applications, is in Munich, with a branch in the Hague, sub-offices in Berlin and Vienna, and a bureau in Brussels. An applicant for a European patent specifies the contracting states in which protection is sought, and if an application is granted, the patent has the same effect as a national patent in each of those states. The

---

[231] [2008] OJ L299/25, codifying Directive 89/104/EEC, as amended.

[232] [2009] OJ L78/1, codifying Regulation (EC) No 40/94, as amended.

[233] [2002] OJ L3/1, as amended, see Eurlex consolidated version 2007-01-01.

[234] Joined Cases C-427/93, C-429/93 and C-436/93 *Bristol-Myers Squibb and Others* [1996] ECR I-3457, para 27.

[235] See eg Directive 2006/115/EC on rental right and lending right and on certain rights related to copyright in the field of intellectual property [2006] OJ L376/28, codifying Directive 92/100/EEC [1992] OJ, as amended; Directive 96/9/EC on the legal protection of databases [1996] OJ L77/20; Directive 2001/29/EC on the harmonisation of certain aspects of copyright and related rights in the information society [2001] OJ L167/10, as amended, see Eurlex consolidated version 2001-06-22; Directive 98/71/EC on the legal protection of designs [1998] OJ L289/28.

Convention is not confined to EU Member States and there are approximately 40 contracting states.

The 1975 Luxembourg Convention on a Community Patent, which would have provided for a unitary Community patent, superseding national patents after a transitional period, has never come into force, because it has not been ratified by a sufficient number of Member States, and it is not expected that this initiative will be pursued. The Commission put forward in August 2000 a proposal for a Council Regulation on the Community patent.[236] Under this proposal, Community Patents would be issued by the European Patent Office. National and European Patents would coexist with the Community Patent system, so that inventors would be free to choose which type of patent protection best suited their needs. The patent would be valid as granted by the European Patent Office in one of the three EPO languages (English, French and German), with translations of the claims in the other two languages published for information. However, disagreement over the language rules has prevented progress on this proposal. On 14 December 2010 the Commission proposed a Council Decision authorising enhanced co-operation[237] in the area of the creation of unitary patent protection.[238] This followed a formal request to this effect from 12 Member States, namely Denmark, Estonia, Finland, France, Germany, Lithuania, Luxembourg, the Netherlands, Poland, Slovenia, Sweden and the United Kingdom.

The following sections of this chapter deal with the relationship between intellectual property rights and the provisions of the Treaty on the free movement of goods, rather than with harmonising legislation relating to intellectual property, though reference to the latter is made where appropriate.

B – A Distinction between the Existence and Exercise of Intellectual Property Rights

A question which arose at the outset for the Court in the present context was how far it was bound to recognise rights conferred by national laws on holders of intellectual property ('industrial and commercial property' in the language of Article 36 TFEU), even if the exercise of those rights could lead in certain circumstances to impeding the movement of goods between Member States. The answer to this question, on a superficial reading of the relevant Treaty texts, appeared, and indeed appears, to be that effect must be given to intellectual property rights, even if the result is indeed to prevent imports in certain cases. A general Treaty provision of obvious relevance is Article 345 TFEU, which provides: 'This Treaty shall in no way prejudice the rules in Member States governing the system of property ownership.'

On the face of it, this might appear to uphold the rights of holders of intellectual property rights to exercise those rights, even if the result were to be some interference with the free movement of goods. Indeed, Article 36 TFEU provides, in relevant part:

The provisions of Articles [34 and 35 TFEU] shall not preclude prohibitions or restrictions on imports, exports or goods in transit justified on grounds of . . . the protection of industrial and

---

[236] COM(2000) 412 final.
[237] For an explanation of enhanced co-operation, see Chapter 5 at p 127.
[238] COM(2010) 790 final.

commercial property. Such prohibitions or restrictions shall not, however, constitute a means of arbitrary discrimination or a disguised restriction on trade between Member States.

While restrictions on imports that are necessary for the protection of industrial and commercial property are exempted from the prohibitions in Articles 34 and 35 TFEU, it is made clear in the second sentence of the Article that there may be circumstances where, regardless of the rights existing under national law, the prohibition will apply. But where is this line to be drawn as regards intellectual property rights? The judicial answer to this question involves drawing a distinction between the *existence* of intellectual property rights, which remains intact, and the *exercise* of those rights, which must be modified in order to ensure the free movement of goods. This solution is formulated as follows in *Terrapin*:

> [W]hilst the Treaty does not affect the existence of rights recognized by the legislation of a Member State in matters of industrial and commercial property, yet the exercise of those rights may nevertheless, depending on the circumstances, be restricted by the prohibitions in the Treaty. Inasmuch as it provides an exception to one of the fundamental principles of the common market, Article [36 TFEU] in fact admits exceptions to the free movement of goods only to the extent to which such exceptions are justified for the purposes of safeguarding the rights which constitute the specific subject-matter of that property. [239]

The distinction drawn by the Court between the existence of rights and their exercise is evidently inspired by a wish to remain at least within the letter of Article 345 TFEU. It invites the criticism that a form of property is the bundle of rights recognised by national law under a particular designation, and if EU law prevents any rights in the bundle from being exercised, the property is to that extent diminished. Yet such a criticism is not really convincing since if taken to its logical conclusion it would argue that, for example, the Treaty's prohibition of discrimination on grounds of nationality could have no application to the exercise of property rights, so that a municipal authority offering public housing to workers could charge nationals of other Member States a higher rent than nationals, or even exclude non-nationals altogether. What the Court has done, in reality, emerges from the second sentence in the quoted passage. The derogation in Article 36 TFEU has been confined to rights which, the Court considers, constitute the essential core or 'specific subject-matter' of the property in question. The exercise of the 'specific subject-matter' of such rights is permitted by EU law, even if it impedes trade or competition, because otherwise it would no longer be possible to say that the property was receiving protection. On the other hand, rights which the Court regards as merely incidental to the property are not allowed to be used to partition the market.

C – Free Movement of Goods: The Exhaustion of Rights Principle

The exclusive right of an owner of intellectual property to put into circulation for the first time goods that are subject to that property is likely to be understood in the law of the Member State concerned (leaving aside EU law considerations) as applying to sale in that Member State's territory. Sales elsewhere will not count as an exercise of the right—in the

---

[239] Case 119/75 *Terrapin* [1976] ECR 1039, para 5; Case C-10/89 *Hag GF* [1990] ECR I-3711, para 12, Case C-61/97 *FDV* [1998] ECR I-5171, para 13; Case C-115/02 *Rioglass SA* [2003] ECR I-12705, para 23; Case C-421/04 *Marazan Concord* [2006] ECR I-2303, para 28.

jargon of the subject, they are not considered to 'exhaust' that right. This means that, as a matter of national law alone, it would be open to the owner of intellectual property to oppose the sale by other traders of imported products covered by that property where the products have been acquired in another Member State where they have been marketed by the owner himself, or by a licensee of the owner. It should be noted that there would be an incentive for such so-called 'parallel' importing if, for some reason, the products in question were significantly cheaper in the Member State of initial distribution than in the one from which it was sought to exclude them.

On the other hand, the Court of Justice has repeatedly stated that, as a general principle:

> [T]he proprietor of an industrial or commercial property right protected by the legislation of a Member State may not rely on that legislation in order to oppose the importation of a product which has lawfully been marketed in another Member State by, or with the consent of, the proprietor of the right himself or a person legally or economically dependent on him.[240]

Whatever the position in national law, the proprietor's exclusive right is deemed in EU law to be exhausted by putting products into circulation anywhere in the internal market. The rationale of the principle is to be found in the limitation of the exception in Article 36 TFEU by reference to the case law derived concept of the specific subject-matter of the intellectual property in question. Where exhaustion occurs it is because the right to exclude imports originally marketed in another Member State is not seen as part of the specific subject-matter of the property in question. The exercise of the right would, therefore, not be 'justified' within the meaning of Article 36 TFEU as being necessary for the protection of the industrial and commercial property right in question.[241] The principle of exhaustion has been applied by the Court of Justice to most of the important forms of intellectual property (patents, trade marks, copyright and related rights,[242] and industrial designs[243]) and since the principle is derived from the Treaty itself, it is applicable to EU intellectual property rights, and has been incorporated into the EU Regulations establishing such rights.[244] In order to illustrate application of the principle of exhaustion of rights, reference will be made to the case law on the relationship between the free movement of goods and patent and trademark rights.

D – Exhaustion of Patent Rights

The leading case on the application of the exhaustion of rights principle to patents is *Centrafarm v Sterling Drug*.[245] Patents for a drug used in the treatment of urinary tract

---

[240] Case 144/81 *Keurkoop* [1982] ECR 2853, para 25; the principle appears in numerous cases, see eg Joined Cases C-427/93, C-429/93 and C-436/93 *Bristol-Myers Squibb and Others* [1996] ECR I-3457, para 45.

[241] This analysis was applied by the Court for the first time in Case 78/80 *Deutsche Grammophon* [1971] ECR 487. It is more fully developed in Case 15/74 *Centrafarm* [1974] ECR 1147.

[242] The earliest case in which the exhaustion principle was applied concerned a right akin to copyright: see Case 78/70 *Deutsche Grammophon* [1871] ECR 487.

[243] Case 144/81 *Keurcoop* [1982] ECR 2853.

[244] Art 13 of Regulation (EC) No 207/2009 (Community trade mark); Art 21 of Regulation (EC) No 6/2002 (Community design). It is also to be found in Directives harmonising national rules on intellectual property, see eg Directive 2008/95/EC on trade marks, Art 7, and Directive 92/100/EEC on rental right and lending right, Art 9.

[245] Case 15/74 *Centrafarm v Sterling Drug* [1974] ECR 1147.

infections were held by Sterling Drug, a US company, in the United Kingdom and the Netherlands. The case originated in the proceedings brought for the infringement of the Dutch patent against Centrafarm, a company famous in the annals of European Court litigation as a parallel importer of pharmaceutical products.[246] Centrafarm's alleged infringement consisted of importing into the Netherlands and offering for sale there quantities of the patented product which had been lawfully marketed by licensees of Sterling Drug in the United Kingdom. This was commercially attractive for Centrafarm, because the price of the drug on the United Kingdom market was only about half the price on the Dutch market. The Court of Justice defined the specific subject-matter of a patent as

> the guarantee that the patentee, to reward the creative effort of the inventor, has the exclusive right to use an invention with a view to manufacturing industrial products and putting them into circulation for the first time, either directly or by the grant of licences to third parties as well as the right to oppose infringements.[247]

The essential function of a patent is here acknowledged to be the rewarding of (and hence encouragement of) creative effort. The reward comes from the patentee's ability to earn a monopoly profit through an exclusive right to manufacture the protected product and put it into circulation for the first time. That right may be exploited directly or by appointing licensees. It has, as a corollary, a right to oppose manufacturing or first marketing of the product by third parties.

In the light of that definition the Court went on to consider the circumstances in which the use of a patent to block the importation of protected products from another Member State might be justified. Two cases of possible justification were mentioned: where the product is not patentable in the Member State of origin and has been manufactured there by a third party without the consent of the patentee in the Member State of importation;[248] and where a patent exists in each of the Member States in question but the original proprietors of the patents are legally and economically independent. On the other hand, there could be no justification for opposing importation 'where the product has been put onto the market in a legal manner, by the patentee himself or with his consent, in the Member State from which it has been imported, in particular in the case of parallel patents'.[249] If a patent could be used in this way, the patentee would be able to cordon off national markets, thereby restricting trade between Member States, 'where no such restriction was necessary to guarantee the essence of the exclusive rights flowing from the parallel patents'.[250] The objection that national patents were unlikely to be truly parallel, with the result that levels of protection would vary between Member State, was brushed aside. 'It should be noted here', the Court said, 'that, in spite of divergences which remain in the absence of any unification of national rules concerning industrial property the identity of the protected invention is clearly the essential element of the concept of parallel patents which it is for the courts to assess'.[251] The Court concluded that

> the exercise, by a patentee, of the right which he enjoys under the legislation of a Member State

---

[246] There were parallel proceedings for the infringement of the Dutch trademark: Case 16/74 *Centrafarm v Winthrop* [1974] ECR 1183.

[247] [1974] ECR 1162.

[248] This was the situation in Case 24/67 *Parke, Davis* [1968] ECR 55. The questions put to the Court were, however, formulated with reference to the competition rules.

[249] [1974] ECR 1163.

[250] Ibid.

[251] Ibid.

to prohibit the sale, in that State, of a product protected by the patent which has been marketed in another Member State by the patentee or with his consent is incompatible with the rules of the EEC Treaty concerning the free movement of good within the common market.[252]

The basis of the ruling was not made altogether clear. On the one hand, it might be thought that the existence of parallel patents was a crucial factor: a right to oppose the importation of protected products could be regarded as superfluous, because the patentee would already have received the monopoly profit, which was his due, in the Member State where the products were first put on the market.

On the other hand, the general terms in which the ruling was expressed, taken with other hints in the judgment,[253] strongly suggested the principle of exhaustion would apply, even where the initial marketing occurred without the benefit of patent protection. If that were so, then the explanation could only lie in the patentee's consent to the market- ing. That such was indeed the Court's meaning was shown in the later case of *Merck v Stephar*.[254] The plaintiff in the national proceedings, Merck and Co Inc, was the holder in the Netherlands of patents relating to a drug used mainly in the treatment of high blood pressure. The proceedings arose because Stephar BV had imported the drug into the Netherlands from Italy where, although it was not patentable, it had been put into circulation by Merck. On Merck's behalf it was argued that the function of rewarding an inventor's creative effort would not be fulfilled if, owing to the impossibility of patenting a product, its sale in the Member State in question did not take place under monopoly conditions. To this the Court replied:

> That right of first placing a product on the market enables the inventor, by allowing him a monopoly in exploiting his product, to obtain the reward for his creative effort, without, how- ever, guaranteeing that he will obtain such a reward in all circumstances.
>
> It is for the proprietor of the patentee to decide, in the light of all the circumstances, under what conditions he will market his product, including the possibility of marketing it in a Member State where the law does not provide patent protection for the product in question. If he decides to do so he must accept the consequences of his choice as regards the free movement of the product within the Common Market, which is a fundamental principle forming part of the legal and economic circumstances which must be taken into account by the proprietor of the patent in determining the manner in which his exclusive right will be exercised.[255]

This approach seems wrong in principle. The justification for 'exhaustion' of patent rights by first sale in a Member State is surely that the patent holder is entitled to exercise the specific subject-matter of his right only once in the internal market; but in the case of a sale in one Member State of a product not patented there, but entitled to patent protection in other Member States, there has been no exercise of the patent right at all, and the effect of holding that the right cannot be subsequently exercised to prevent parallel imports in the Member States where the product is covered by patent protection is to extinguish the right entirely. The conclusion that it is for the patent holder to make the choice whether or not to market patented products in a Member State where the product is not patent- able, and must accept the consequences of that decision, rather begs the question as to whether this an appropriate dilemma to impose upon patent holders in the first place.

---

[252] Ibid.

[253] See, in particular, the reference, ibid , to non-patentable goods 'manufactured by third parties without the consent of the patentee'.

[254] Case 187/80 [1981] ECR 2063.

[255] Case 187/80 [1981] ECR 2063, 2081–82.

The occasion for the Court to reconsider *Merck v Stephar* arose in *Merck v Primecrown*,[256] which concerned the application of transitional arrangements in the Act of Accession of Spain and Portugal to parallel imports into the United Kingdom from the latter countries. Merck argued that the Court should overrule *Merck v Stephar*. Advocate General Fennelly agreed.[257] But the Court did not. The Court noted that the transitional measures provided for in the Act of Accession were adopted in light of the ruling in *Merck* and indicated that upon expiry of those transitional arrangements, the free movement of goods provisions of the Treaty, as interpreted in *Merck*, should apply in full to trade between Spain and Portugal. That is a defensible ground for adhering to the result in *Merck* even if the reasoning underlying the original decision was unsatisfactory.

E – Exhaustion of Trade Mark Rights

The Court described the principle of exhaustion of rights as regards trade marks as follows in *IHT Internationale Heiztechnik* :

> That principle, known as the exhaustion of rights, applies where the owner of the trade mark in the importing State and the owner of the trade mark in the exporting State are the same or where, even if they are separate persons, they are economically linked. A number of situations are covered: products put into circulation by the same undertaking, by a licensee, by a parent company, by a subsidiary of the same group, or by an exclusive distributor.[258]

In a much earlier case, *Centrafarm v Winthrop*,[259] the specific subject-matter of a trade mark was said to be

> the guarantee that the owner of the trade mark has the exclusive right to use that trade mark, for the purpose of putting products protected by the trade mark into circulation for the first time, and is therefore intended to protect him against competitors wishing to take advantage of the status and reputation of the trade mark by selling products illegally bearing that trade mark.[260]

The emphasis here is on what makes a trade mark valuable—the reservation to the owner, through his exclusive right to put trade-marked products into circulation, of the goodwill associated with the mark. The Court did not on this occasion examine the reason why such a right should be given, the question of the 'essential function' of a trade mark, but it did so in later cases, in which it described that essential function as being to guarantee the identity of the trade marked product to the consumer or ultimate user.[261]

The exhaustion of rights conferred by a trade mark is covered by Article 7(1) of the Trade Mark Directive,[262] which states in relevant part:

> The trade mark shall not entitle the proprietor to prohibit its use in relation to goods which have been put on the market in the Community under that trade mark by the proprietor or with his consent.

---

[256] Joined Cases C-267/95 and C-268/95 [1996] ECR I-6285.
[257] This lengthy Opinion is erudite and convincing
[258] Case C-9/93 [1994] ECR I-2789, para 34.
[259] Case 16/74 *Centrafarm v Winthrop* [1974] ECR 1183.
[260] [1974] ECR 1194.
[261] See Case 102/77 *Hoffmann-La Roche v Centrafarm* [1978] ECR 1139; Case 3/78 *Centrafarm v American Home Products* [1978] ECR 1823; Joined Cases C-427/93, C-429/93 and C-436/93 *Bristol-Myers Squibb and Others* [1996] ECR I-3457; Case C-349/95 *Loenderloot* [1997] ECR I-6227.
[262] Directive 2008/95/EC [2008] OJ L299/25, codifying Directive 89/104/EEC, as amended.

The text refers to goods put on the market in the Community, but to accommodate the European Economic Area (EEA) Agreement this reference is to be read as a reference to a contracting party in situations to which that agreement applies.[263] The EEA comprises the EU, Iceland, Liechtenstein and Norway. In *Peak Holding*[264] the Court was called upon to interpret the reference in Article 7(1) of the Directive to 'goods which have been put on the market', and in particular to decide whether goods bearing a trade mark are regarded as having been put on the market in the EEA where the proprietor has imported them with a view to selling them there, or where he/she has offered them for sale to consumers in the EEA, in his own shops or those of an associated company, but without actually selling them. The Court held that where a proprietor merely imports his goods with a view to selling them in the EEA or offers them for sale in the EEA, he does not put them on the market within the meaning of Article 7(1) of the Directive, since such acts do not transfer to third parties the right to dispose of the goods bearing the mark, and do not allow the proprietor to realise the economic value of the trade mark. 'Even after such acts', declared the Court, 'the proprietor retains his interest in maintaining complete control over the goods bearing his trade mark, in order in particular to ensure their quality.'[265]

In *Bristol Myers-Squibb and Others*[266] the Court held that Article 7 comprehensively regulates the question of the exhaustion of trade mark rights for products traded in the Community, and that national rules must be assessed in the light of that Article, but added that 'the directive must be interpreted in the light of the Treaty rules on the free movement of goods and in particular Article [36 TFEU]'.[267] Citing Article 7(1), the Court stated:

> That provision is framed in terms corresponding to those used by the Court in judgments which, in interpreting Articles [34 and 36 TFEU] have recognized in Community law the principle of the exhaustion of the rights conferred by a trade mark. It reiterates the case-law of the Court to the effect that the owner of a trade mark protected by the legislation of a Member State cannot rely on that legislation to prevent the importation or marketing of a product which was put on the market in another Member State by him or with his consent.[268]

It follows from the foregoing that the concept of exhaustion of trade mark rights under Article 7(1) of the Directive and the concept of exhaustion under Articles 34 and 36 TFEU are one and the same concept.

The principle of exhaustion of trade mark rights referred to above is of course a concept applicable to the marketing of trade-marked goods *within* the EEA. The issue which arose in *Silhouette International Schmied*[269] was whether national rules providing for exhaustion of trade mark rights in respect of products put on the market outside the EEA were contrary to Article 7(1) of the Directive. The Court concluded that Articles 5–7 of the Directive must be considered as embodying a complete harmonisation of the rules relating to the rights conferred by a trade mark, and that accordingly national rules providing for the exhaustion of trade mark rights put on the market *outside* the EEA under that mark by

---

[263] EEA Agreement, Art 65(2) and Annex XVII [1994] OJ L1/482.
[264] C-16/03 *Peak Holding* [2004] ECR I-11313; see S Enchelmaier, 'The Peak Holding Case: The Notion of Exhaustion of Intellectual Property Rights in the Internal Market Clarified' (2005) *European Current Law* Part 5 'Focus', xi–xv.
[265] Ibid, para 42; and see Case C-127/09 *Coty Prestige* (CJEU Judgment of 3 June 2010).
[266] Joined Cases C-427/93, C-429/93 and C-436/93 *Bristol-Myers Squibb and Others* [1996] ECR I-3457.
[267] Ibid, paras 25–27.
[268] Ibid, para 31.
[269] Case C-355/96 *Silhouette International Schmied* [1998] ECR I-4799. See also Case C-173/98 *Sebago* [1999] ECR I-4103.

the proprietor or with his consent were contrary to Article 7(1) of the Directive. The Court considered a somewhat different but related issue in *Zino Davidoff and Levi Strauss*,[270] which arose from proceedings in an English court by proprietors in the UK of various trade marks, including Levi's, against various retailers, including Tesco and Costco, who had sold in the UK products originally placed on the market in various countries outside the EEA, including the United States. In favour of the UK retailers it was argued that the proprietor of the trade mark of goods placed on the market *outside* the EEA might nevertheless have consented, expressly or impliedly, to those goods being placed on the market *inside* the EEA, that such consent should be presumed unless the trade mark proprietor proved the contrary, and that a trade mark proprietor wishing her/his exclusive rights to be reserved within the EEA must ensure that the goods bearing the trade mark carry a clear warning of the existence of such reservations, and that the reservations must be stipulated in the contracts for the sale and resale of those goods. These were far-reaching arguments indeed, and were largely rejected by the Court of Justice. The starting point for the Court was that if the concept of consent were a matter for the national laws of the Member States, trade mark protection for proprietors would vary according to the legal system concerned, and this would be contrary to the objective of Directive 89/104 of achieving the same protection under the legal systems of all the Member States. In the Court's view, it fell to it to supply a uniform interpretation of the concept of consent to the placing of goods on the market within the EEA as referred to in Article 7(1) of the Directive. In view of its serious effect in extinguishing the exclusive rights of the proprietors of trade marks, the Court considered that consent must be so expressed that an intention to renounce those rights be unequivocally demonstrated. Such intention would normally be gathered from an express statement of consent, but it was conceivable that consent might, in some cases, be inferred from facts and circumstances prior to, simultaneous with or subsequent to the placing of the goods on the market outside the EEA.[271] The Court did not, however, consider that implied consent could be inferred from the mere silence of a trade mark proprietor; it was for the trader alleging consent to prove it, and not for the trade mark proprietor to demonstrate its absence. Nor could consent be inferred (a) from the fact that the trade mark proprietor had not communicated his opposition to marketing within the EEA, (b) from the fact that the goods did not carry any warning that it was prohibited to place them on the market within the EEA, (c) from the fact that the trade mark proprietor transferred ownership of the goods bearing the mark without imposing contractual reservations, nor (d) from the fact that, according to the law governing the contract, the property right transferred included, in the absence of such reservations, an unlimited right of resale, or, at the very least, a right to market the goods subsequently within the EEA.[272] The Court concluded that: 'A rule of national law which proceeded upon the mere silence of the trade mark proprietor would not recognise implied consent but rather deemed consent. This would not meet the need for consent positively expressed required by Community law.'[273]

One of the boldest aspects of the case law of the Court of Justice in the trade mark field

---

[270] Joined Cases C-414/99–416/99 *Zino Davidoff and Levi Strauss* [2001] ECR I-8691; see GT Petursson and P Dryberg, 'What Is Consent?' (2002) 27 *ELRev* 464; Case C-324/08 *Makro Zelfbedieningsgroothandel and Others* [2009] ECR I-10019.

[271] Ibid, paras 45, 46.

[272] Ibid, paras 53–57.

[273] Ibid, para 58.

has been its acceptance that there are exceptions to the principle that the proprietor of a trade mark right which is protected in two Member States is entitled to prevent a product to which the trade mark has lawfully been applied in one of those Member States from being marketed in the other Member State after it has been repackaged in new packaging to which the trade mark appearing on the original packaging has been reaffixed by a third party. The exceptions apply where use of the trade mark right by the owner will contribute to the artificial partitioning of the market; where the repackaging cannot adversely affect the original condition of the product; where the owner of the mark receives prior notice before the repackaged product is put on sale; and where it is stated on the new packaging by whom the product has been repackaged. There is considerable case law on the meaning and scope of these exceptions.[274] The exceptions may apply not only to cases where the parallel importer reaffixes the original trade mark on the new packaging, but also to cases where the parallel importer replaces the original trade mark used by the proprietor in the Member State of export by the trade mark which the proprietor uses in the Member State of import.[275]

XI – CONCLUDING REMARKS

The Court's approach to the interpretation of the Treaty's prohibition of quantitative restrictions and measures having equivalent effect on imports was from the outset a broad approach, as the *Dassonville* formulation shows. That formulation, however, was and is too broad and too general to provide solutions to concrete cases, and that is why the later rulings in *Cassis* and *Keck* have been of such significance. *Keck* in the first place confirmed that the *Cassis* ruling required product requirements in all cases to be justified, and in the second place held that this was not the case for what it described as 'selling arrangements', which need only be justified if they directly or indirectly discriminate against imported products. On the face of it, that has remained the position to the present day, though the Court's case law on national restrictions on advertising is prone to detect discrimination against imported products when any discrimination that is present is as much discrimination against new market entrants as discrimination against importers. In such cases the distinction between a discrimination test and a market access test all but disappears. Recent cases on restrictions on use have been resolved by reference to market access analysis, though later case law suggests that this analysis will be applied only to such 'residual' cases, rather than foreshadowing a replacement of the *Keck* approach to selling arrangements. As regards measures having equivalent effect on exports, the Court has at last done what it has long been thought that it would do—it has accepted that it is not only national rules which directly discriminate against exports which require justification, but also those which indirectly do so. Although the substance of the Treaty rules

---

[274] Case 102/77 *Hoffmann-La Roche* [1978] ECR 1139; Case 3/78 *Centrafarm v American Home Products* [1978] ECR 1823; Case 1/81 *Pfizer* [1981] ECR 2913; Joined Cases C-427/93, C-429/93 and C-436/93 *Bristol-Myers Squibb* [1996] ECR I-3457; Joined Cases C-71/94, 72/94 and C-73/94 *Eurim-Pharm* [1996] ECR I-3603; Case C-232/94 *MPA Pharma* [1996] ECR I-3671; Case C-349/95 *Frits Loenderloot* [1997] ECR I-6227; Case C-143/00 *Boehringer Ingelheim KG and Others* [2002] ECR I-3759; Case C-443/99 *Mercke, Sharp & Dohme* [2002] ECR I-3703;Case C-348/04 *Boehringer Ingelheim* [2007] ECR I-3391; Case C-276/05 *Wellcome Foundation* [2008] ECR I-10479.

[275] Case C-379/97 *Pharmacia & Upjohn* [1999] ECR I-6927.

which prohibit quantitative restrictions and measures having equivalent effect on imports and exports have no more been changed by the TL than by any other of the numerous large-scale adjustments to the founding Treaties which have preceded it, it cannot quite be said that the law has stood still.

Further Reading

N Bernard, 'Discrimination and Free Movement in EC Law' (1996) 45 *ICLQ* 82.

S Enchelmaier, 'Moped Trailers, Michelsson & Roos, Gysbrechts: The ECJ's Case Law on Goods Keeps on Moving' (2010) 29 *YEL* 190.

DT Killing, *Intellectual Property Rights in EU Law*, Vol I: *Free Movement and Competition Law* (Oxford, Oxford University Press, 2004).

P Koutrakos, 'On Groceries, Alcohol and Olive Oil: More on the Free Movement of Goods after *Keck*' (2001) 26 *ELRev* 391.

M Poiares Maduro, *We, the Court* (Oxford, Hart Publishing, 1998).

J Snell 'The Notion of Market Access: A Concept or a Slogan?' (2010) 47 *CMLRev* 437.

E Spaventa, 'Leaving *Keck* Behind? The Free Movement of Goods after the Rulings in *Commission v Italy* and *Mickelsson and Roos*' (2009) 34 *ELRev* 914.

——, 'The Outer Limit of the Treaty Free Movement Provisions: Some Reflections on the Significance of *Keck*, Remoteness and Deliège' in C Barnard and O Odudu (eds), *The Outer Limits of European Law* (Oxford, Hart Publishing, 2009) 245.

P Wenneras and K Boe Moen, 'Selling Arrangements, Keeping Keck' (2010) 35 *ELRev* 387.

E White, 'In Search of the Limits to Article 30 of the EEC Treaty' (1989) 26 *CMLRev* 235.

15

Union Citizenship and the Rights to Move and Reside in the European Union

The original European Economic Community Treaty granted a right to reside in other Member States, together with a right to equal treatment with host-state nationals, only to those nationals of the Member States who migrated in order to pursue an economic activity. As a result, non-economically active migrants were not protected by (then) Community law. With time, however, this changed. First, three residence directives were adopted which granted a conditional right of residence to those who had sufficient means to support themselves, including students and pensioners. Secondly, and more importantly, the Maastricht Treaty introduced the notion of Union citizenship: according to Article 21 TFEU, Union citizens have a right to move and reside freely within the territory of any of the Member States subject to the limitations and conditions contained in the Treaties and secondary legislation. The Court of Justice then defined Union citizenship as the 'fundamental status' of Union citizens. As a result of these legislative changes, Union citizens previously excluded from the scope of Union law have gained directly enforceable rights, including a (still) conditional right of residence and a limited right to equal treatment. Furthermore, in 2004 Council and Parliament adopted a new directive (2004/38) detailing the right of Union citizens, previously contained in several sectorial pieces of secondary legislation. In this chapter we will consider the evolution of the case law on Union citizenship, and then turn to the regime established by the Union Citizenship Directive. This analysis focuses on Union citizens' rights of residence and equal treatment. We will then conclude with a brief analysis of the other rights that Union citizens derive from the Treaty.

I – THE ROAD TO CITIZENSHIP

Economic migrants, ie those who move to another Member State to exercise there an economic activity as an employed or self-employed person, or to receive a service, have always had the right to enter and reside in that Member State. Those rights derive directly

461

from the Treaty, and are further detailed in secondary legislation.[1] Furthermore, economically active migrants, as we shall see in the following chapters, have always enjoyed the right to equal treatment in respect of most benefits.

On the other hand, non-economic migrants, ie those who moved for reasons not related to an economic activity, originally did not derive rights from the EEC Treaty. In other words, those who were not economically active, such as pensioners and students, did not have a right to move and reside in other Member States bestowed by the Treaty, and would be thus subject to the national migratory regime. However, in 1990 three residency directives were adopted:[2] those conferred a conditional right of residence to pensioners, students and other non-economic migrants. The right of residence was conditional upon two criteria: first of all, the non-economic migrant needed to have comprehensive medical insurance; secondly, she/he needed to have sufficient resources so as not to become a burden on the social security system of the host Member State.[3] If those two conditions were fulfilled, the migrant would have a right to reside in any of the Member States bestowed by (then) Community secondary legislation. In 1992, the Maastricht Treaty created Union citizenship (Article 20 TFEU) and, amongst other provisions, introduced a new provision referring to a general right to move and reside anywhere in the European Union. Article 21(1) TFEU[4] provides that:

> Every citizen of the Union shall have the right to move and reside freely within the territory of the Member States, subject to the limitations and conditions laid down in the Treaties and the measures adopted to give it effect.

In the aftermath of the Maastricht Treaty, it was unclear whether this provision was capable of having direct effect, ie whether it could be relied upon in order to establish a right of residence independent from that provided for by another Treaty provision or by secondary legislation. The Court eventually decided that what is now Article 21 TFEU bestowed on Union citizens a directly effective right to move and reside in the EU, although subject to some 'limitations and conditions'.

The introduction of Union citizenship, together with the evolution of the Court's case law, rendered the secondary legislation on free movement of both economic and non-economic citizens rather outdated. Moreover, the fact that a Union citizen should negotiate his/her way through a plurality of different legal instruments to understand her/his rights was considered highly unsatisfactory. For this reason, in April 2004 a new residence direc-

---

[1] Then Directive 68/360 on the abolition of restrictions on movement and residence within the Community for workers of Member States and their families [1968(I)] OJ Sp Edn 485; Directive 73/148 on the abolition of restrictions on movement and residence within the Community for nationals of Member States with regard to establishment and the provision of services [1973] OJ L172/14; both directives have now been repealed by, and subsumed in, Directive 2004/38 on the right of citizens of the Union and their family members to move and reside freely within the territory of the Member States amending Regulation (EEC) No 1612/68 and repealing Directives 64/221/EEC, 68/360/EEC, 72/194/EEC, 73/148/EEC, 75/34/EEC, 75/35/EEC, 90/364/EEC, 90/365/EEC and 93/96/EEC [2004] OJ L229/35, hereinafter Directive 2004/38.

[2] Directive 90/364 on a general right to residence [1990] OJ L180/26 (hereinafter Directive 90/364); Directive 90/365 on retired persons [1990] OJ L180/28 (hereinafter Directive 90/365); Directive 93/96 on students [1993] OJ L317/59 (hereinafter Directive 93/96). The Court had already held that students may derive residency rights directly from Art 18 TFEU, eg Case C-357/89 *Raulin* [1992] ECR I-1027. The students' directive was first adopted in 1990 together with the other directives, but it had to be readopted in 1993 following a successful challenge to its legal basis.

[3] Directives 90/365 and 90/364: the claimant must have sufficient resources to avoid becoming a burden on the state's social assistance. Directive 93/96: the student need only assure the national authorities that he/she has sufficient resources to avoid becoming a burden on the state.

[4] At the time Art 8a, then Art 18 TEC.

tive was adopted: this repealed and replaced most of the relevant secondary legislation, so as to provide a single and coherent framework detailing the Union citizens' rights of residence in Member States other than that of their nationality; and codifying the existing case law.

In this chapter we are going to look at the evolution of the case law on citizenship, and then consider in detail the new residency directive, and the other rights pertaining to Union citizens (eg to vote in local and European elections). The rights which are particular to economic migrants will then be analysed in detail in the chapters on free movement of workers, the right to establishment and the freedom to provide services.

II – THE EVOLUTION OF THE CASE LAW ON UNION CITIZENSHIP

We have said above that before the adoption of the three residency directives only economically active migrants derived rights from (then) Community law.[5] Those who were not engaged in an economic activity, however generously construed this notion was, would be subject to ordinary national migration policies. The three residency directives provided for a Community right of residence in any of the Member States for students, retired people, and those who could afford it. However, this right of residence was conditional upon the fulfilment of two criteria: comprehensive medical insurance; and sufficient resources so as not to become a burden on the host welfare system. Those two conditions were included to ensure that the right to reside in any of the Member States would not give rise to so-called 'welfare tourism', ie movement undertaken for the sole purpose of exploiting a more generous welfare system of another Member State.[6] By making the right to reside conditional, Member States would protect their welfare provision: on the one hand, medical care would not be a problem since the non-active migrant would in any event have medical insurance; on the other hand, the fact that the migrant needed to have 'sufficient resources' would disqualify him/her from means-tested benefits. Migration of non-economically active people would therefore incur no expense for the host Member State's public purse. This framework, however, came under attack, and very much under strain, after the introduction of Union citizenship. As said above, Union citizenship was established in 1992 with the Maastricht Treaty.

Article 20 TFEU, which established Union citizenship, provides that 'every person holding the nationality of a Member State shall be a citizen of the Union'. Article 21 TFEU provides that all Union citizens have the right to move and reside freely within any of the Member States, subject to the limitations and conditions contained in the Treaty and in secondary legislation. Furthermore, Article 18 TFEU provides that within the scope of the Treaties, 'and without any prejudice to any special provisions contained therein, any discrimination on grounds of nationality shall be prohibited'. The main question for the

---

[5] Including work-seekers; see Chapter 16, section III below; as we shall see further below the rights of economically active migrants also include the right to have their family with them. As a result some of the family members of the migrant (ie spouse and children) also acquire rights in Union law.

[6] On the impact of EU law on national welfare systems, see generally M Dougan and E Spaventa (eds), *Social Welfare and EU law* (Oxford, Hart Publishing, 2005); G de Búrca (ed), *EU Law and the Welfare State* (Oxford, Oxford University Press, 2005).

Court was then whether Article 21 TFEU granted a right to reside independently from the three residency directives; and whether, as a result of the combined effect of Articles 21 and 18 TFEU, any Union citizen had the right to be treated equally, especially in relation to welfare provision.

In the case of *Martínez Sala*,[7] a Spanish citizen living in Germany was denied a child-raising allowance on the grounds that she was not a German national, and did not have a residence permit. It was not entirely clear whether Mrs Martínez Sala, who had been previously employed, could be considered a worker and thus be entitled to equal treatment in respect of social advantages pursuant to Regulation 1612/68,[8] and family benefits pursuant to Regulation 1408/71.[9] The Court relied partially on the citizenship provisions in order to find that Mrs Martínez Sala was protected by the principle of non-discrimination in respect of the allowance, even were she not to be considered a worker. However, the Court preferred not to address the issue of the direct effect of Article 21 TFEU, rather relying on the fact that Mrs Martínez Sala was in any case lawfully resident in Germany under national law (albeit without a residence permit). Since Germany had granted her residency rights, it could not exclude her from the principle of equal treatment. Hence, as a result of the ruling in *Martínez Sala*, once a Union citizen is lawfully resident (even independently from Union law) in one of the Member States she/he can rely on the principle of equal treatment to claim welfare benefits.[10] However, following *Martínez Sala*, it was unclear exactly which rights were conferred by Union citizenship.[11] In particular it was not clear whether a Union citizen could derive a right to reside directly from Article 21 TFEU; whether a Union citizen could rely on the non-discrimination obligation when he/she was residing in the host-Member State by virtue of one of the three residency directives; and if yes how far the principle of non-discrimination would stretch. In particular, the key issue was, and is, how far can a Union citizen rely on her/his rights under the Treaties in order to demand welfare provision from the host Member State. Those issues were clarified in subsequent case law.

In *Grzelczyk*[12] a French citizen who was studying in Belgium applied, during the last year of his studies, for the minimex, a non-contributory benefit reserved for Belgian nationals and other Member States' citizens covered by Regulation 1612/68.[13] As a student, Mr Grzelczyk derived his right of residence from Directive 93/96, which provided that those enrolled in a recognised educational establishment had a right to reside in the host-Member State provided they had sufficient resources and comprehensive health insurance. Mr Grzelczyk worked throughout his studies to support himself; however, in his last year he was unable to work due to the demands of his degree; he therefore applied for the minimex, a non-contributory benefit, which was denied on the grounds that he was not a Belgian national. The issue was clearly one of discrimination on grounds of

---

[7] Case C-85/96 *Martínez Sala* [1998] ECR I-2691.

[8] Regulation 1612/68 on freedom of movement for workers within the Community [1968(I)] OJ Eng Sp Edn 475 (hereinafter Regulation 1612/68).

[9] Regulation 1408/71 on the application of social security schemes to employed persons, to self-employed persons and to members of their families, as amended, Consolidated text in Annex A Regulation 118/97 [1997] OJ L28/1 (hereinafter Regulation 1408/71); the Regulation has now been replaced by Regulation 883/2004 on the co-ordination of social security systems [2004] OJ L166/1 (hereinafter Regulation 883/2004).

[10] See also Case C-135/99 *Elsen* [2000] ECR I-10409;

[11] cp also Case C-274/96 *Bickel and Franz* [1998] ECR I-7637; Case C-378/97 *Wijsenbeek* [1999] ECR I-6207.

[12] Case C-184/99 R *Grzelczyk* [2001] ECR I-6193.

[13] This was consistent with a previous ruling of the Court, Case 197/86 *SM Brown* [1988] ECR 3205.

nationality and the problem was whether or not Mr Grzelczyk fell within the scope of the Treaty by virtue of the citizenship provisions. Only if he fell within the scope of the Treaty would he be able to rely on the general prohibition of discrimination on grounds of nationality contained in Article 18 TFEU. The Court held that since he was a lawfully resident Union citizen he fell within the scope of the Treaty and was therefore protected by the prohibition of non-discrimination on grounds of nationality. It stated:

> Union citizenship is destined to be the *fundamental status* of nationals of the Member States, enabling those who find themselves in the same situation to enjoy the same treatment in law irrespective of their nationality, subject to such exceptions as are expressly provided for.[14]

The Court then acknowledged that the right to move and reside granted by Article 21 TFEU was subject to the limitations and conditions contained in the Treaty and in secondary legislation, and especially in the residency directives. Thus, Member States could legitimately require students to fulfil the conditions contained in Directive 93/96, ie availability of sufficient resources not to become an unreasonable burden on the welfare system of the host Member State and comprehensive health insurance. However, this did not mean that the Member State could refuse a welfare benefit to the Union citizen: the only thing that the host Member State could do was to consider whether, because of a change in circumstances, the Union citizen was no longer fulfilling the conditions provided for in the Directive and thus either withdraw the residence permit or refuse to renew it. But in no event could such action be taken automatically, without taking into consideration the citizen's individual circumstances.

The ruling in *Grzelczyk* confirmed that Union citizens who have moved in another country fall within the scope *rationae personae* of the Treaty, and thus, provided they also fall within the scope *rationae materiae* of the Treaty, they can rely on Article 18 TFEU to claim equal treatment also in relation to welfare benefits.[15] However, *Grzelczyk* also clarified the scope of the *Sala* ruling: the rights conferred by Article 21 TFEU can be limited if the citizen becomes an 'unreasonable' burden. This was further elaborated in *D'Hoop*,[16] where the issue was whether a Union citizen could rely on Articles 21 and 18 TFEU in order to obtain a tide-over allowance for young people seeking their first employment. One of the conditions to be satisfied in order to be eligible was to have received secondary education in Belgium.[17] Ms D'Hoop was a Belgian national who, having received her secondary education in France, failed to fulfil that condition, even though she had received her university education in Belgium. The Court, consistently with *Grzelczyk*, found that movement together with citizenship is enough to bring oneself within the scope *rationae materiae* and *personae* of the Treaty. Ms D'Hoop fell within the scope of the Treaty because she had moved first to France and then back to Belgium. The rule was clearly putting those who move, and therefore exercise their Treaty rights, at a disadvantage since if Ms D'Hoop had stayed in Belgium for her secondary education she would have now been eligible for the benefit. The Court held that a difference in treatment between those who have exercised their free movement rights and those who have not, can be accepted only in so far as it is based on objective reasons and it is proportionate to the legitimate aim of the

---

[14] Case C-184/99 *R Grzelczyk* [2001] ECR I-6193, para 31, emphasis added.
[15] On the scope of Union citizenship, see generally E Spaventa 'Seeing the Wood Despite the Trees? On the Scope of Union Citizenship and its Constitutional Effects' (2008) *CMLRev* 13.
[16] Case C-224/98 *D'Hoop* [2002] ECR I-6191.
[17] An exception is made for children of migrant workers.

national rules. In the case at issue, the purpose of the restriction was to ensure that there was a *real link* between the applicant and the geographic employment market concerned. However, the rules at issue went beyond what was necessary to ensure this link, since the fact that a person completed her secondary education abroad was not in itself representative of the connection between applicant and geographical labour market.

In the cases examined above, the Court linked Union citizenship rights to lawful residency, to find that once a Union citizen was lawfully resident in the host Member State, she/he could rely on the principle of non-discrimination to claim welfare benefits (subject to the possibility that the Member States could rely on imperative grounds of public interest to justify discrimination). In *Baumbast*[18] the Court found that Article 21 TFEU granted a directly effective (albeit conditional) right to reside in any of the Member States. Here, Mr Baumbast, a German national living in the UK, was denied renewal of his residency permit on the grounds that he did not fulfil the conditions set out in Directive 90/364, which make the right to reside in another Member State conditional upon having sufficient resources and comprehensive health insurance. Although Mr Baumbast had sufficient resources and health insurance in Germany, where he and his family would go to receive health treatment, he did not have insurance for emergency treatment in the UK and thus was not insured for *all* health risks as required by Directive 90/364. The issue was then whether Article 21 TFEU granted a free-standing right to residency. Further, the Court had to consider what weight should be given to the specification contained in Article 21 TFEU that the right to move and reside is subject to the limitations contained in the Treaty and by the measures adopted to give it effect. The Court stated that Article 21 TFEU had conferred 'on every citizen the right to move and reside freely within the territory of the Member States'.[19] This right is subject to the limitations contained in secondary legislation, ie sufficient resources and comprehensive health insurance so as not to become a burden on the host welfare system. However, the Court also found that these limitations and conditions had to be applied consistently with the general principles of Union law and in particular with the principle of proportionality. To deny Mr Baumbast's right to reside in the UK only because he was not covered by emergency treatment insurance would be a disproportionate interference with the substance of the right of residence which he derived directly from the Treaty.

Following these developments, the situation for economically inactive citizens was (and is) as follows.[20] First of all, Union citizens who lawfully reside in another Member State are entitled to equal treatment in respect of all benefits. However, excessive reliance on this right might be grounds for the host Member State to terminate the right to residency itself, subject, however, to the general principles of Union law, and in particular to the principle of proportionality.[21] Secondly, Member States are not prevented from introducing criteria which, whilst distinguishing between Union citizens, are objectively justified and proportionate to the legitimate aim the rules pursue. Thus, the ruling in *D'Hoop* suggests that the Member States might be entitled to make some benefits conditional on a

---

[18] Case C-413/99 *Baumbast and R* [2002] ECR I-7091.
[19] Case C-413/99 *Baumbast and R* [2002] ECR I-7091, para 81.
[20] These issues have been thoroughly examined in M Dougan and E Spaventa, 'Educating Rudy and the (non-)English patient: A Double-Bill on Residency Rights under Article18 EC' (2003) 28 *ELRev* 699, and the conclusions in the text draw from that analysis.
[21] *cf* Case C-456/02 *Trojani* [2004] ECR I-7574.

link between the claimant and the territory.[22] Thirdly, Union citizens now derive their right to residency (and movement) directly from Article 21 TFEU, before deriving it from secondary legislation. That right to residency might be subject to conditions as contained in secondary legislation, and especially the sufficient resources and comprehensive health insurance requirements. Thus, in principle, Union citizenship does not entitle the individual to become an 'unreasonable' burden on the welfare system of the host Member State. However, what is to be considered 'unreasonable' will very much depend on the case at issue, and in any event the Member States have to comply with the principle of proportionality, and arguably also with fundamental rights as general principles of Union law.

The introduction of Union citizenship has therefore changed the European Union landscape: whilst before only those who actively contributed to the host society by engaging in economic activity as either employed or self-employed derived rights from the Treaty, following the introduction of citizenship, economically inactive citizens derive a right to move, and to participate in, and benefit from, at least to a certain extent, to the host welfare society. In this way, the Union becomes much more than an economic enterprise: without calling into question the strongest bond arising from national citizenship, Union citizenship creates a link between European citizens that is quite independent of their economic contribution. Thus, even though the Union citizen is not necessarily entitled to claim full solidarity with her/his fellow citizens, she/he can expect some solidarity, in the form of welfare provision, should the need arise. Whilst most Member States initially resisted the turn that the case law was taking, they eventually agreed to codify much of it in the new residence directive, which replaces the previous residence directives, together with other secondary legislation. We shall now look in detail at the rights contained in the new directive. The reader should in any event remember that most of these rights remain conferred directly by the Treaty.

III – THE RESIDENCE DIRECTIVE

In May 2001 the Commission proposed a directive on the 'right of citizens of the Union and their family members to move and reside freely' within the Union. The basic concept underlying the Commission's proposal was that:

> Union citizens should . . . be able to move between Member States on similar terms as nationals of a Member State moving around or changing their place of residence or job in their own country. Any additional administrative or legal obligations should be kept to the bare minimum required by the fact that the person in question is a non-national.[23]

To this effect, the proposed directive sought to replace the plethora of existing legislation with one single document, as well as to enhance the rights to move and reside of Union citizens and their families.

---

[22] See also Case C-138/02 *Collins* [2004] ECR I-2703; Case C-209/03 *Bidar* [2005] ECR I-2119; Case C-258/04 *Ioannidis* [2005] ECR I-8275; in Case C-158/07 *Förster* [2008] ECR I-8507, the Court accepted that a period of five years in order to qualify for study-related benefits (as prescribed by Directive 2004/38) is a reasonable way of ascertaining the existence of a real link. See below.

[23] Proposal for a European Parliament and Council Directive on the right of citizens of their Union and their family members to move and reside freely within the territory of the Member States, COM(2001) 257 final, [2001] OJ C270 E 23/150, para 13 of the explanatory memorandum.

In this respect, the original proposal was more ambitious than the text which was eventually approved. Thus, the Commission had proposed a six-month period of unconditional temporary residence for all Union citizens and their family members (so that even economically inactive citizens would have a right to reside regardless of resources and health insurance), as well as the right to permanent residency (ie the right to stay in the host country unconditionally) after four years for all Union citizens and their families. The Commission also broadened the definition of family member to include unmarried partners when the legislation of the host Member State treats unmarried couples in a similar way to married ones. This represented a positive step forward in recognising, at least to a limited extent, the right to family life of those who do not want or cannot enter into marriage, and especially of same-sex couples. It also removed the oddity in the case law where, in order to afford protection to non-married couples in those countries where some advantages where recognised to the latter, the Court had defined the right to have a partner reside with the migrant worker as a 'social advantage' and therefore covered by the principle of non-discrimination.[24]

The European Parliament went further, and sought to include in the scope of the directive registered partners and unmarried partners in a durable relationship irrespective of their sex, provided that *either* the home *or* the host Member State recognised their rights in a corresponding manner to those of married couples.[25] In this way, the Union citizen would have been able to be accompanied by his/her unmarried partner even if the host Member State did not recognise rights corresponding to those of married couples to partnerships. However, the Council successfully watered down the proposal: thus, as we shall see, Directive 2004/38 grants an unconditional right to reside for three months only, a right to permanent residence after five rather than four years, and adopts a definition of family member narrower than both the one proposed by the European Parliament and that proposed by the Commission.[26]

A – The Personal Scope of Directive 2004/38

(i) Union Citizens

Directive 2004/38 governs the *exercise* of the right to move and reside within the territory of Member States by Union citizens and their family members. As noted above, the Directive is not constitutive of such rights, since these are bestowed on Union citizens directly by the Treaty. This means that the Court is not prevented from taking a more generous view as to citizens' rights than those contained in the Directive. According to Article 3 of the Directive, the latter applies only to Union citizens who move and reside in a Member State other than that of their nationality.[27]

---

[24] Case 59/85 *Reed* [1986] ECR 1283.

[25] European Parliament Report A5-0009/2003, final.

[26] Unfortunately, however, implementation of the Directive has so far been disappointing; see Report from the Commission on the application of Directive 2004/38, COM(2008) 840 final; see also European Parliament Resolution on the implementation of Directive 2004/38 (P6_PA 2009 (206) 0203) [2010] OJ C137/E02. See also Communication from the Commission to the European Parliament and the Council on guidance for better transposition and application of Directive 2004/38, COM(2009)313 final.

[27] At the time of writing is still unclear whether the Directive applies to those who have dual nationality and want to rely on the Directive against the Member State of one of their nationalities by exploiting the other nationality; See AG Kokott's Opinion in Case C-434/09 *McCarthy*, opinion delivered 25 November 2010, case

A Union citizen is any person having the nationality of one of the Member States since, as provided by Article 20 TFEU, Union citizenship is additional to, and does not replace, national citizenship.[28] It is exclusively for the Member State to decide the conditions upon which nationality is granted, and other Member States cannot interfere with that decision. Thus, for instance, in *Chen*[29] a baby was born in Northern Ireland to Chinese parents who had gone to Northern Ireland with the sole intention of gaining Irish nationality for their baby. Apart from having born there, neither the baby nor her family had any connection to the United Kingdom or to the Republic of Ireland. However, at the time, the Republic of Ireland granted Irish nationality to anyone born in the Irish island, including those born in Northern Ireland. Ms Chen therefore acquired Irish citizenship without ever having set foot in the Republic. She then moved to Wales arguing that she (as well as her mother as her primary carer) had a right to reside there because she was a Union citizen. The Court accepted the contention and stated that it was immaterial that Ms Chen had never been in the Republic of Ireland: since she held the nationality of one of the Member States, she was a Union citizen and as such was protected by the Treaty when residing in a Member State other than that of her nationality.

On the other hand, if a Member State refuses to grant full rights to its nationals, Union citizenship is of no help. In *Kaur* Ms Kaur was a British national who had no right to reside in the United Kingdom since she was born in Kenya and gained British nationality as a result of the post-colonial settlement. Ms Kaur attempted to rely on (then) Community law to obtain a right to reside in the United Kingdom. The Court held that it was for the United Kingdom to decide the conditions under which its nationals gained the right to reside in the United Kingdom. Since the UK had made a declaration to the effect that *only* British nationals with full rights to reside were to be considered as Union citizens, the situation fell outside the scope of Union law.[30]

This said, even though it is for Member States to decide on the conferral of nationality, Union law might still impose some obligations upon the exercise of the Member State's discretion. In *Rottmann*[31] Mr Rottmann was an Austrian national who, facing a criminal investigation in Austria, moved to Germany, where he acquired German nationality and lost his Austrian nationality as a consequence. However, his German nationality was later retroactively withdrawn on the grounds that he had failed to disclose the criminal proceedings pending against him in Austria. Mr Rottmann brought an action for annulment of the decision to withdraw naturalisation, arguing, inter alia, that it would be inconsistent with Union law because it would have the effect of rendering him stateless and hence of depriving him of his Union citizenship. The German and Austrian governments, together with the Commission, argued that the matter fell outside the scope of Union law since it concerned the conditions for acquisition of national citizenship; and that the situation

---

still pending, for a negative answer; however, Case C-148/02 *Garcia Avello* [2003] ECR I-11613 seemed to suggest that, at least for the purposes of primary Treaty provisions, dual nationality is enough to bring oneself within the scope, and reap the benefits, of Union law.

[28] The TL slightly changed the wording of Art 20 TFEU which previously stated that Union citizenship *complemented* national citizenship. This, if the political will were ever to emerge, would allow for the possibility to confer Union citizenship on third-country nationals.

[29] Case C-200/02 *Chen and others* [2004] ECR I-9925; see also Case C-369/90 *Micheletti and others* [1992] ECR I-4239.

[30] Case C-192/99 *Kaur* [2001] ECR I-1237.

[31] Case C-135/08 *Rottmann*, Judgment of 2 March 2010, nyr, noted D Kochenov (2010) 47 *CMLRev* 1831; and T Konstadinides 'La fraternité européene? The Extent of National Competence to Condition the Acquisition and Loss of Nationality from the Perspective of EU Citizenship' (2010) 35 *ELRev* 401.

was in any event purely internal since it concerned an administrative act directed at one of their own citizens. The Court disagreed. It held that the decision fell within the scope of Union law since, if confirmed, it would entail the loss of Union citizenship and the rights deriving from it. The Court then proceeded to assess whether withdrawal of naturalisation was justified and found that whilst, in principle, such sanction was compatible with Union law, in practice, and given the severity of the consequence (statelessness), the national court would have to assess whether it was proportionate. As a result, and as it happens in many other fields, a reserve of national sovereignty does not entail a total shelter from scrutiny under EU rules.

(ii) Family Members

A Union citizen's willingness to move to another Member State would be greatly reduced if she/he had to leave his/her family behind. For this reason, from the very early stages of (then) Community integration, Regulation 1612/68 provided that the worker's spouse and descendants (ie offspring) under the age of 21 or dependent upon the worker, together with dependent relatives on the ascending line (ie the parents/grandparents of both workers and their spouses) had a right to install themselves in the host Member State with the worker, regardless of their nationality (ie even if they were third country nationals).[32] Moreover, Member States had to facilitate the admission of any other family member dependent on the worker, or living with her/him in the country whence she came. The worker's spouse and the worker's children also had a right to work and the children had a right to be educated under the same conditions as nationals of the host Member State. Directive 73/148 provided for almost identical rights for the family members of self-employed persons (ie service providers and those taking advantage of the freedom of establishment).[33]

Article 2 of the new residence Directive adds to those already listed in the above-mentioned secondary legislation, the 'partner with whom the Union citizen has contracted a *registered* partnership' if the legislation of the host Member State treats registered partnership as '*equivalent*' to marriage and in accordance with the host Member State's legislation. Thus, the rights granted to non-married couples are not as extensive as the European Parliament had proposed, since only 'registered' partnerships produce rights, and only if the host Member State treats those partnerships as equivalent to marriage. It is likely that the assessment of equivalence will give rise to some questions of interpretation, since treatment of registered partnerships, whilst often similar to that of marriages, is seldom identical. In many respects, this limitation on the rights of non-married couples is disappointing, especially having regard to emerging case law of the ECtHR which is increasingly critical of discrimination on grounds of sexual orientation.[34] The Court has made clear in *Metock*,[35] de facto reversing its prior ruling in *Akrich*,[36] that the migration status of the third country national spouse of a Union migrant is irrelevant for the

---

[32] Regulation 1612/68 on freedom of movement for workers within the Community [1968] OJ Sp Edn L257/2, 475.

[33] Council Directive 73/148 on the abolition of restrictions on movement and residence within the Community for nationals of Member States with regard to establishment and the provision of services [1973] OJ L172/14.

[34] cp the minority opinion of Mr Turco and Mr Capato (MEPs) in the European Parliament Recommendation for the Council's Second Reading, A5-0090/2004, final.

[35] Case C-127/08 *Metock and others* [2008] ECR I-6241.

[36] Case C-109/01 *Akrich* [2003] ECR I-9607.

purposes of the Directive. Hence, provided the marriage is genuine, the spouse acquires a right to reside even though she/he was illegally present in the territory of the Member State at the time when the marriage was contracted. Furthermore, it is irrelevant whether the spouses arrived together in the host Member State or rather whether they met there.[37]

Article 3 extends the duty of the Member States to *facilitate* the entry and residence of dependent family members also to the partner with whom the Union citizen has a durable relationship duly attested. Moreover, the Directive also provides for the duty of the Member State to facilitate entrance and residence of a Union citizen's family member who, even though not dependent, requires, on serious health grounds, the personal care of the Union citizen. The obligation to 'facilitate' admission is also more stringent than was previously the case: the Member State shall take into account the personal circumstances of the applicant and shall justify any denial of entry and residence of non-protected family members. Thus, it is clear that, in the drafters' view, denial of the right to entry and reside should be the exception rather than the rule.

B – The Material Scope of the Directive: Right to Enter, Exit and Temporary Residence

(i) Right to Exit and Right to Enter

Article 4 provides that Union citizens have a right to leave the territory of a Member State on production of a valid identity card or passport; and their family members who are not Union nationals have a right to leave on production of a valid passport. No additional formality can be imposed. Similarly, an identity card or valid passport is all that a Union citizen needs to enter the territory of any Member State (Article 5). A third-country national family member might be required to have an entry visa according to the provisions of Union or national law.[38] An entry visa shall not be required if the third-country national family member has a residence card, ie a document attesting the family member's right to establish him/herself in one of the Member States with the Union citizen. An important innovation is contained in Article 5(4) which, codifying previous case law,[39] provides that if a Union citizen or his/her family member lack the necessary travel documents or the necessary visa, the Member State has to give them every opportunity to prove identity and/or family ties before turning them away.[40] In practice, then, Union citizens and their family members cannot be turned back at the frontier except for reasons of public policy/security/health (see below).[41] Once in the territory of the Member

---

[37] It should be recalled that since the Directive applies only to those who are in the territory of a Member State other than that of their nationality, the *Singh* ruling (Case C-370/90 [1992] ECR I-4265), according to which own nationals coming back to their Member State of origin after having moved, have to be treated as if they were Union migrants from other Member States in relation to the advantages conferred by Union law, is not relevant for its application. Yet, the ruling is still relevant for the application of the primary Treaty provisions.

[38] cp for the Schengen zone, Regulation 539/2001 listing the third countries whose nationals must be in possession of visas when crossing the external border and those whose nationals are exempt from such requirement [2001] L81/1, as amended, consolidated version: http://eur-lex.europa.eu/LexUriServ/LexUriServ.do?uri=CONSLEG:2001R0539:20091219:EN:PDF.

[39] Case C-459/99 *MRAX* [2002] ECR I-6591.

[40] Similarly, Member States cannot make recognition of the right of residence for a Union citizen conditional upon the Union citizen producing an identity card or a passport when the Union citizen can prove his/her identity unequivocally by other means: see Case C-215/03 *Oulane* [2005] ECR I-1215.

[41] *cf* Case C-503/03 *Commission v Spain* (Schengen Information System) [2006] ECR I-1097.

State, Union citizens and their family members might be asked to report their presence to the authorities within a reasonable and non-discriminatory period of time, and Member States might impose sanctions for failure to do so.[42] As always in relation to sanctions for behaviour in any way linked to the exercise of a Treaty right, the sanction must be proportionate and non-discriminatory.

(ii) Right of Temporary Residence

Article 6 of Directive 2004/38 provides for an unconditional right of residence for *all* Union citizens for up to three months. Prior to the Directive, the right to reside even on a temporary basis was conditional upon exercising an economic activity, looking for a job, or satisfying the sufficient resources/health insurance requirement. De facto, however, such right was easily gained by any Union citizen by relying on Article 56 TFEU, arguing that she/he was a recipient of services in the host Member State. This was the case, for instance, for tourists, but also for those who were just passing through a country since they would always receive services of some sort (hotels, restaurants, etc).[43]

Following the adoption of Directive 2004/38, however, such right is codified and cannot be made subject to any condition other than the requirement to hold a valid identity card or passport; furthermore, the right to temporary residence is granted also to the Union citizen's family. Union citizens and their families temporarily resident in a Member State other than that of the Union citizen's nationality enjoy a right to equal treatment with the nationals of the host Member State. The Commission had originally proposed that the right to equal treatment should be absolute.[44] However the Council, concerned about the possibility of welfare tourism, modified the Commission's proposal, and Article 24(2) of the Directive now provides that the host Member State is not obliged to confer entitlement to social assistance to those who are residing only temporarily in their territory pursuant to Article 6. Furthermore, according to Article 14(1), the right of temporary residence pursuant to Article 6 is retained only as long as the Union citizen and her/his family do not become an unreasonable burden on the social assistance of the host Member State. This means that even if the host Member State confers some social assistance to temporary residents, it is open to that state to terminate temporary residence should the Union migrant rely excessively on social assistance.

C – The Material Scope of the Directive: Right of Residence for more than Three Months

If the right to residence for up to three months is unconditional, Article 7 provides that the right to reside in another Member State for more than three months is conditional upon satisfaction of listed requirements. Those, roughly speaking, reflect the requirements contained in pre-existing legislation, or elaborated by the Court of Justice.

Article 7(1) provides that:

---

[42] See eg Case 118/75 *Eatson and Belmann* [1976] ECR 1185; Case C-265/88 *Messner* [1989] ECR I-4209.

[43] eg Case C-274/96 *Bickel and Franz* [1998] ECR I-7637.

[44] Proposal for a European Parliament and Council Directive on the right of citizens of their Union and their family members to move and reside freely within the territory of the Member States, COM(2001) 257 final, [2001] OJ C270/150, Art 21. As mentioned above, the original proposal also provided for the right of temporary residence to be for up to six rather than three months (Art 6).

All Union citizens shall have the right of residence on the territory of another Member State for a period longer than three months if they:

(a) are workers or self-employed persons in the host Member State; or

(b) have sufficient resources for themselves and their family members not to become a burden on the social assistance system of the host Member State during their period of residence and have comprehensive sickness insurance cover in the host Member State; or

(c)—are enrolled at a private or public establishment, accredited or financed by the host Member State on the basis of its legislation or administrative practice, for the principle purpose of following a course of study, including vocational training; and

—have comprehensive sickness insurance cover in the host Member State and assure the relevant national authority, by means of a declaration or by such equivalent means as they may choose, that they have sufficient resources for themselves and their family members not to become a burden on the social assistance system of the host Member State during their period of residence; or

(d) are family members accompanying or joining a Union citizen who satisfies the conditions referred to in points (a), (b) or (c).'

The second paragraph of Article 7 provides that the right of residence for family members extends also to those members of the family who are not nationals of a Member State. Article 7(3) provides that, in certain circumstances, the status of worker/self-employed (with all the advantages deriving from such status) is retained even if the Union citizen is no longer exercising an economic activity. We shall now look more closely at the conditions required for each of the different categories of Union citizens.

(i) Economically Active Citizens

As we shall see in more detail in the following chapters, economically active citizens derive extensive rights from the Treaty. In particular, once a Union citizen is engaged in an economic activity either as an employed or a self-employed person, she/he has, upon production of evidence as to their economic activity,[45] a right to reside in the host Member State, provided only that the economic activity is genuine and not on such a small scale so as to be marginal and ancillary. Economically active citizens enjoy a right to be treated equally with own nationals in relation to almost all welfare benefits; furthermore, they retain their status in certain circumstances even once they have ceased their economic activity. Article 7(3) provides that the status of economically active citizen is retained when the Union migrant is (i) unable to work because of illness or an accident; (ii) he/she is in recorded involuntary unemployment after having been employed for more than one year and has registered as a work-seeker with the relevant employment office; (iii) he/she is recorded in involuntary unemployment after having been employed (in a fixed-term or indefinite-term capacity) for less than one year and has registered as a work-seeker[46]— in this case the status of worker is retained for at least six months; or (iv) when she/he has embarked on vocational training related to the previous employment (if the worker is involuntarily unemployed the training can be in any area). The possibility of retaining the status of economically active citizen is important because it means that the Union citi-

---

[45] In the case of workers, this takes the form of a confirmation of engagement from the employer; in the case of self-employed, proof of activity.

[46] See also Case C-413/01 *Ninni-Orasche* [2003] ECR I-13187.

zen can continue to reside in the host Member State without having to satisfy any other condition; and that she/he is entitled to welfare provision. We shall look at those issues in more detail in the chapters dealing with economically active citizens.

Furthermore, and as we shall see more in detail in Chapter 16, Union citizens who move to look for a job in another Member State are also protected by Article 45 TFEU and by Directive 2004/38. They can stay beyond the initial three months without having to satisfy any additional requirement (ie sufficient resources/health insurance) provided that they can demonstrate that they are continuing to seek employment and have a 'genuine chance' of being engaged (Article 14(4)b). According to Article 24(2), however, Member States are not obliged to confer entitlement to social assistance to work-seekers. As we shall see in Chapter 16, following the rulings in *Collins* and *Vatsouras*,[47] it is not clear how far this exemption applies.

(ii) Economically Independent Citizens

The second category of Union citizens who have a right to reside for more than three months in a Member State other than that of their nationality are those who have (i) 'sufficient resources' for themselves and their family members not to become a burden on the social assistance system of the host Member State; and (ii) comprehensive health insurance. Article 7(1)(b) Directive 2004/38 thus unifies in one category both pensioners and those who are self-sufficient, previously dealt with in two separate directives. The Member State cannot lay down a fixed amount to be considered as 'sufficient resources' and must have due regard to the applicant's individual circumstances. Furthermore, in no event can the amount required be higher than the threshold below which nationals of the host Member State receive social assistance; or higher than the minimum social security pension.[48] The Court has clarified that the economic resources do not need to be the Union citizen's own: thus resources provided by a family member,[49] or by a third party even when there is no legal link between the Union citizen and the person who supplies the resources,[50] have to be taken in the same account as if they were the Union citizen's own resources.

As for the comprehensive sickness insurance requirement, it is worth recalling the ruling in *Baumbast* where the Court held that the fact that the Union citizen is only partially insured cannot justify the Member State's refusal to renew his/her residence permit. Thus, both conditions—medical insurance and resources—have to be assessed with due regard to the individual circumstances and the principle of proportionality, and the Member State cannot have a rule which requires automatic expulsion of Union citizens who do not produce the relevant evidence within the prescribed time.[51]

Whilst Article 24 does not exclude economically inactive Union citizens from the scope of the principle of equal treatment, this is more limited than in the case of economically active citizens. This is so since, as we have seen above, should a Union citizen who is not economically active rely excessively on the host Member State's welfare system, he/she could become an 'unreasonable burden' and lose her/his right to reside in the host state.

---

[47] Case C-138/02 *Collins* [2004] ECR I-2703; Joined Cases C-22 and C-23/08 *Vatsouras and Koupatantze* [2009] ECR I-4585; see also M Dougan, 'Free Movement: The Workseeker as a Citizen' (2001) 4 *CYELS* 94.

[48] Art 8(4).

[49] Case C-200/02 *Chen and others* [2004] ECR I-9925.

[50] Case C-408/03 *Commission v Belgium* (citizenship) [2006] ECR I-2647.

[51] Ibid.

However, and as we also saw above, the Court has made clear that before terminating the Union citizen's right to reside in its territory, a Member State must look at the individual circumstances of the citizen; must act proportionally; and must respect fundamental rights including the right to family life.[52] This principle has been codified in Article 14(3) of the Directive which clarifies that 'an expulsion measure shall not be the automatic consequence of a Union citizen's or his/her family member's recourse to the social assistance of the host Member State'. Should the Member State want to terminate the right to reside of a Union citizen on those grounds, it has to respect the procedural safeguards detailed in relation to the public policy/security/health derogations (ie notification, judicial review, etc—see below).

As we shall see below, Article 24(2) provides that Member states are not obliged to confer maintenance grants and the likes to economically inactive citizens who are not permanent resident.[53]

(iii) Students

Finally, students enrolled in a private or public establishment accredited or financed by the host Member State, have a right to reside in the host state if they have comprehensive sickness insurance as well as sufficient resources for themselves and their family members. Article 7(1)(c) Directive 2004/38, like Directive 93/96 before it, provides that students do not need to provide evidence of their financial situation, but merely need to assure the relevant authorities by means of a declaration or by such equivalent means as they may choose. As is the case for economically independent citizens, students are not in principle excluded from the right of equal treatment provided for in Article 24,[54] although excessive reliance on the host welfare system might transform them into 'unreasonable burdens', and entitle the Member State to terminate (but not automatically) or refuse to renew their residence permit (Article 14(2)).[55] Furthermore, Member States might make entitlement to welfare provision conditional upon the Union citizen showing that he/she has a real link with the employment market in the host Member State.[56] On the other hand, Article 24(2) does allow Member States to refuse maintenance grants and maintenance loans to economically inactive Union citizens (including students) who are not permanent residents. In its ruling in *Förster*,[57] the Court has confirmed that such exclusion is compatible with the Treaty provisions on Union citizenship.

---

[52] *cf* Case C-413/99 *Baumbast and R* [2002] ECR I-7091; Joined Cases C-482/01 and 493/01 *Orfanopoulos and Olivieri* [2004] ECR I-5257.

[53] Art 24(2) also limits the right to equal treatment in relation to social assistance for temporary residents and work-seekers. For the latter, see Chapter 16 below.

[54] Since the ruling in Case 293/83 *Gravier* [1985] ECR 593 (decided long before citizenship) students have had a right to equal treatment in relation to access to education; however, this right has been recently called into doubt in the ruling in Case C-73/08 *Bressol*, Judgment of 13 April 2010, where the Court found that discriminatory conditions on access to some university degree courses could in principle be justified. The Treaty also impacts on the ability of Member States to limit the right of students to study abroad: see Case Joined Cases C-11 and 12/06 *Morgan* [2007] ECR I-9161.

[55] And, according to Art 15 Directive 2004/38, the procedural safeguards provided for in Arts 30 and 31 of the Directive apply to termination and refusal to renew residence permits.

[56] Case C-184/99 *R Grzelczyk* [2001] ECR I-6193; Case C-224/98 *D'Hoop* [2002] ECR I-6191.

[57] Case C-158/07 *Förster* [2008] ECR I-8507, noted O Golynker (2009) 46 *CMLRev* 2021; S O'Leary, 'Equal Treatment and EU Citizens: A New Chapter on Cross-border Educational Mobility and Access to Student Financial Assistance' (2009) 34 *ELRev* 612.

Ms Förster was a German national who enrolled for a teaching training course in the Netherlands; during her course she was in paid employment save for a short period of time. As a worker she was granted a maintenance grant; however, the Dutch authorities later asked for the repayment of the grant for the period during which Ms Förster was not employed since according to Dutch rules economically inactive Union citizens qualified for such grants after five years of residence,[58] whilst Ms Förster had lived in the Netherlands for three and a half years. The national court enquired as to the compatibility of the Dutch legislation with the Treaty provisions on Union citizenship. In particular, whilst the rules seemed compatible with Article 24(2) Directive 2004/38 (already enacted but not yet applicable to the case) as well as with its predecessor Directive 93/96, it was not clear whether Articles 21 and 18 TFEU as interpreted by the Court in the case of *Bidar* would grant Union citizens additional rights. In *Bidar*[59] the Court found that a French student who had been living in England for three years had a right to equal treatment in respect of a maintenance loan. Whilst the Court acknowledged that England could limit the award of such loans to Union citizens who had shown a certain degree of integration, it could not altogether exclude them from such benefits. Following *Bidar* then, and as argued by Ms Förster, there was an expectation that Union citizens might be entitled to maintenance grants and the like if they could show a genuine degree of integration in the host Member State. Since Ms Förster has lived in the Netherlands for longer than Mr Bidar had lived in England, she had a reasonable expectation that, having shown a sufficient degree of integration, she should be entitled to the maintenance grant on equal footing with Dutch nationals. However, the Court found that the Dutch rules were compatible with the Treaty since a period of five years was a proportionate and legitimate way of guaranteeing that the Union citizen would have achieved a sufficient degree of integration in the host Member State. Furthermore, this requirement was compatible with Article 24(2) Directive 2004/38 and had the benefit of providing legal certainty. The Court distinguished the case at issue form the *Bidar* case by pointing out that the rules in the latter case made it altogether impossible for students ever to qualify for a maintenance grant or loan, regardless of their degree of integration.

(iv) The Union Citizen's Family

As we have seen above, the Union citizen's spouse, registered partner (if the host Member State recognises registered partnerships), children and ascendants (ie parents) have a right to install themselves with the Union citizen, regardless of whether they themselves are Union citizens. However, students do not have a right to bring their parents with them, although the Member State has a duty to facilitate their entry and residence.

Once they are lawfully resident in the host Member State, the Union citizen's spouse/ partner and children have a right to pursue an economic activity.[60] Whilst the right to

---

[58] It is open to debate whether Ms Förster should have been qualified as economically inactive at all: see O'Leary, ibid.

[59] Case C-209/03 *Bidar* [2005] ECR I-2119; see C Barnard, 'Annotation on *Bidar*' (2005) 42 *CMLRev* 1465; M. Dougan, 'Fees, Grants, Loans and Dole Cheques: Who Covers the Costs of Migrant Education Within the EU?' (2005) 42 *CMLRev* 943.

[60] Art 23 of Directive 2004/38 (and previously Art 11 of Regulation 1612/68). However, they have the right to pursue an economic activity only in the state where they have a right to reside, ie a cross-border element needs to be present; see Case C-10/05 *Mattern and Cikotik* [2006] ECR I-3145. Family members of economically active citizens benefit from slightly more favourable conditions, eg maintenance grants and student grants/loans; *cf* Art 24(2) of Directive 2004/38. They also still benefit from Art 12 of Regulation 1612/68 which has not been

reside of family members is dependent upon the right to reside of the Union citizen, Directive 2004/38 has provided that in certain circumstances the family members retain an independent right of residence.

This will be the case first, if the Union citizen dies (Article 12). In this case, her/his family retains the right of residence, provided that, if they are not Union citizens, they have resided in the host Member State for at least a year before the Union citizen's death.[61]

Secondly, family members retain the right to reside in the host Member State if the Union citizen leaves the host state, provided they are Union citizens. In any event, however, the Union citizen's children and the parent who has custody retain the right to reside in the host Member State as long as the children are in education (Article 14(3)).[62]

Thirdly, Article 13 provides that the spouse/partner of the Union citizen maintains the right to reside in the host Member State upon divorce, annulment of the marriage or termination of the partnership. However, if the spouse/partner is not a Union citizen, maintenance of the right to reside is conditional upon certain requirements. Thus, in order to retain the right to reside, the marriage must have lasted for at least three years, including one in the host Member State; or the spouse/partner has custody of the children; or she/he has a right to access the children and a court has ruled that such access shall be exercised in the host Member State; or this is warranted by particularly difficult circumstances such as having been the victim of domestic violence.[63]

In any event, the family member who retains the right of residence after termination of the relationship with the main right-holder (ie after the death of the spouse, or after the divorce or annulment of the marriage/partnership) has to satisfy the conditions that are imposed on Union citizens in order to gain residence. Thus, they must be either economically active (employed or self-employed), or possess sufficient resources and comprehensive health insurance so as not to become a burden on the social assistance of the host Member State.

D – Administrative Formalities

(i) Administrative Formalities for Union Citizens

As we have seen above, Union citizens have a right, conferred directly upon them by the Treaty, to reside in any of the Member States, provided they satisfy the conditions detailed by Directive 2004/38. This does not mean, however, that Member States cannot impose administrative formalities upon Union citizens: the Court had already ruled in the past that such formalities are justified by the imperative need for Member States to know

---

repealed; following the rulings in Case C-480/08 *Teixeira*, and Case C-310/08 *Ibrahim*, Judgments of 23 February 2010, nyr; the right of the children of a worker to continue their education pursuant to Art 12 of Regulation 1612/68 entitle the parent who is the carer of the children to remain in the host Member State without having to satisfy the conditions provided for in Directive 2004/38; Art 12 therefore still grants more extensive rights than the more general equal treatment obligation provided in Art 24 of Directive 2004/38.

[61] The prior regime naturally confined the family's right to stay to families of economically active people; this right is still present in its original formulation, see Art 17(4).

[62] See Case C-413/99 *Baumbast and R* [2002] ECR I-7091.

[63] This represents a welcomed, and very necessary, improvement on the prior regime where rights of non-EU national spouses would be terminated upon dissolution of the marriage; this was a case of concern particularly in cases of domestic violence since it potentially gave the abusive partner the additional weapon of blackmailing the abused partner not to report the violence.

who is present in their territory.[64] Not surprisingly, then, Article 8 of Directive 2004/38 authorises Member States to require Union citizens residing in their territory for longer than three months to register their presence with the relevant authorities. Since, as we saw above, the right of residence of the Union citizen for the first three months is unconditional, the Member States must allow for a minimum period of at least three months from the date of arrival in their territory for Union citizens to register. Furthermore, the registration certificate has to be issued immediately, stating the date of registration (which is important to evidence length of stay in order to gain permanent residency), as well as the name and address of the applicant.

It should be remembered that the registration certificate is mere evidence of the right to stay in the host Member State: it is not constitutive of such right. Accordingly, failure to register can give rise to sanctions; however, these need to be proportionate and non-discriminatory, ie not different from sanctions imposed upon nationals for a comparable breach (such as the breach of the obligation to carry identity cards at all times). It is thus very unlikely that the Member States would be able to impose a custodial sentence for a breach of the registration requirement, since that would be disproportionate. In any event, the Member States cannot deport a Union citizen for her/his failure to comply with administrative formalities.[65]

Article 8(3) provides that in order to obtain the certificate, a Union citizen needs only to demonstrate that she/he satisfies the conditions laid down in the Directive in order to gain residence. Thus if he/she is the main right-holder, she/he has to provide proof of employment or economic activity; or sufficient resources and health insurance and, where applicable, student status as detailed above. If a Union citizen is seeking residence by virtue of being a family member of an economically active or financially independent citizen, then she/he has merely to prove identity and the family (or partnership) tie with the main right-holder.

(ii) Administrative Formalities for Family Members Who Are Not Union Citizens

Third-country nationals who derive their right of residence in one of the Member States by virtue of being a family member of a Union citizen are in a more vulnerable position than Union citizens. Whilst Union citizens (whatever their status) are always protected by the Treaty and are therefore not subjected to ordinary immigration law, third-country nationals are subject to migration law unless they can prove that they have a link with a Union citizen entitling them to claim protection under Union law. For this reason, Article 9 provides that Member States must provide the third-country national family member with a residence card, as evidence of their right to stay in the host Member State; a residence card also allows third-country nationals to travel within the EU without having to obtain a visa, where such a visa is usually required.[66] Differently from ordinary migration law, the Member State retains no discretion in issuing a residence card to a third-country national who is a protected family member of a migrant Union citizen (exception given for the derogations expressly provided for in the Directive that we shall consider in detail below); and the residence card must be valid for at least five years or for the envisaged period of residence of the Union citizen if that is less that five years. Furthermore,

---

[64] eg Case C-265/88 *Messner* [1989] ECR 4209.
[65] eg Case 48/75 *Royer* [1976] ECR 497.
[66] Art 5(2) of Directive 2004/38.

temporary absences do not affect the validity of the residence card. Those are absences not exceeding six months a year, or absences for a longer duration due to compulsory military service, or an absence for a maximum of twelve months for important reasons 'such as childbirth, pregnancy, serious illness, study or vocational training, or a posting in another Member State or a third country' (Article 11). The list is clearly not exhaustive and it would be open to the third-country national family member to prove that a long absence was due to another, not listed, important reason. As in the case of Union citizens, the third-country national only needs to prove identity and entitlement (family tie and dependency where required). However, identity must be proven by means of a passport, rather than just an identity card.

E – Right of Permanent Residence

One of the most significant innovations of Directive 2004/38 is the introduction of the right of permanent residence for Union citizens and their family members. Article 16 provides that the right of permanent residence is acquired after five years of continuous legal residence in the host Member State.[67] Permanent residency differs in a very important respect from the right of residence for more than three months, since after the Union citizen or his/her family have acquired the right to permanent residence, the host Member State cannot impose any additional requirement, ie it cannot require the Union citizen and her/his family to be either economically active or financially independent. After five years of continuous residence, then, the Union migrant is deemed to have established a sufficient link with the host society to become almost akin to a national of that state, and has a full right to equal treatment in respect of social assistance. In this respect, it is immaterial whether the period of five years' residence was completed before the deadline for transposition of the Directive has expired (ie 30 April 2006),[68] exactly because the rationale behind the right to permanent residence is an integration rationale. As we shall see more in detail below, Member States can deport permanent residents only on 'serious grounds of public policy and public security' (Article 28(2)); and permanent residents lose their right to residence only if they are absent from the host Member State's territory for more than two years (Article 16(4)).

For the purposes of the Directive, continuity of residence is not affected by temporary absences not exceeding six months a year, or for longer absences due to compulsory military service. Furthermore, and as we have seen already in relation to third-country national family members, an absence of a maximum of twelve consecutive months does not affect continuity of residence if it is due to 'important reasons' such as pregnancy and childbirth, serious illness, study or vocational training or posting to another country (Article 16(3)).

(ii) More Favourable Conditions for Formerly Economically Active People

Consistently with pre-existing EU legislation,[69] Article 17 provides a more favourable

---

[67] On how to calculate periods of residence, see Case C-325/09 *Dias*, Opinion delivered 17 February 2011, case still pending at the time of writing; Case C-424/10 *Ziolkowski*, and Case C-425/10 *Szeja*, both pending at the time of writing.

[68] See Case C-162/09 *Lassal*, Judgment of 7 October 2010, nyr.

[69] Commission Regulation 1251/70 on the right of workers to remain in the territory of a Member State after

treatment for those who have reached pensionable age; for those who have had to stop working because of a permanent incapacity; and for 'frontier workers'.

Those who stop working because they have reached the age that entitles them to an old-age pension (or the age of 60 if there is no right to an old-age pension) or because they have taken early retirement, have a right to permanent residence provided they have worked in the host Member State for at least a year, and have resided there for more than three years.

Those who stop working as a result of a permanent incapacity to work acquire the right of permanent residence provided they have resided in the host Member State for more than two years. However, if the incapacity is the result of an accident at work or of an occupational disease entitling the person concerned to a benefit payable in full or in part by one of the host Member State's institutions, there is no requirement as to length of residence.

Frontier workers, ie those who live in a Member State but work in another, do not have to satisfy any additional length of residence if they have worked in the host Member State where they reside for at least three years before starting to work in another Member State, and provided they retain their residence in the host Member State, to which they return as a rule at least once a week.

Continuity of employment is not affected by involuntary unemployment duly recorded; periods not worked for reasons not of the person's own making; and absences from work or cessation of work due to illness or accident (Article 17(1)).

Finally, the worker or self-employed who is married/partnered with a national of the host Member State, or with someone who has lost the nationality of that Member State through marriage to the worker/self-employed, does not have to satisfy any length of residence since the required connection with the host state is provided by family ties rather than residence (Article 17(2)).

(iii) Right of Permanent Residence of the Citizen's Family Members

As we have said above, the right of permanent residence accrues also to family members, even if they are third-country nationals, once the main right-holder has gained such right. Moreover, family members who have remained in the host Member State after the death of the main right-holder, or after the divorce or annulment of their marriage/registered partnership, have a right to acquire permanent residence after five years of continuous lawful residence.

Moreover, if the main right-holder was economically active and died whilst still working, but before he/she acquired the right to permanent residence, her/his family members residing with her/him in the host Member State acquire the right of permanent residence provided that (a) the main right-holder had at the time of death resided in the host Member State for a continuous period of two years;[70] or (b) the death resulted from an accident at work or an occupational disease; or (c) the surviving spouse has lost the nationality of that Member State following the marriage to the worker or self-employed

having been employed in that State [1970] OJ L142/24; and Directive 75/34 concerning the right of nationals of a Member State to remain in the territory of another Member State after having pursued therein an activity in a self-employed capacity [1975] OJ L14/10; the latter has been repealed by Directive 2004/38. However, and for unclear reasons, Regulation 1251/70 has not been repealed. Note also that Art 17 (3) and (4) are not gender neutral; an oversight of drafting no doubt, but a rather unfortunate one.

[70] This condition was interpreted narrowly in Case C-257/00 *Givane* [2003] ECR I-345.

person. If the above conditions are not satisfied, and provided the conditions in Articles 12 or 13 are satisfied, the family members retain the right of residence provided they satisfy the conditions of economic activity or economic independence. After five years of continuous residence they will gain the right to permanent residence.

(iv) Permanent Residence Cards

The right of the Union citizen to permanent residence is evidenced by a document that must be issued as soon as possible after the Member State has verified the duration of residence. This document must be of indefinite duration (Article 19).

Member States have also to issue a permanent residence card to thirdcountry national family members; this needs to be issued within six months from submission of the application and is renewable automatically every ten years. Article 20(2) makes it a duty for the third-country national family member to apply for the permanent residence card before the (normal) residence card expires, and provides that failure to comply with such provision might give rise to proportionate and non-discriminatory sanctions. The third-country national can also, without affecting the validity of her/his permanent residence card, interrupt her/his residence for a maximum of two consecutive years.

As always, the documents attesting residence are merely evidence of the right, which is conferred directly by the Treaty, through the Directive.[71] The host Member State can impose on the Union citizen, and on the citizen's family members, an obligation to carry the residence card with them at all times, but only if it also imposes upon its citizens a duty to carry an identity card at all times. The Member State cannot charge for such documents more than it would charge its own nationals for a similar document.

In order to prove continuity of residence the Union citizen and/or his/her family members can rely on any means of proof in use in the host Member State. This would typically be evidence of employment or gainful activity, rent receipts, etc. Continuity of residence is interrupted in the case of an expulsion decision duly enforced against the person concerned (Article 21).

F – Rights of Residents and Permanent Residents

The right to reside in the host territory shall cover the entire of the Member State's territory. Article 22 provides that territorial restrictions can be imposed only where the same restrictions apply to a Member State's own nationals. This provision clearly seeks to codify the ruling in *Rutili*,[72] where the Court held that France could not impose a territorial restriction on Mr Rutili, an Italian trade unionist, if such restriction could have not been imposed on a French citizen for similar reasons. However, some 30 years later, the Court changed its case law and in *Olazabal*[73] upheld the same French legislation which it had found inconsistent with (then) Community law in *Rutili*. In this case, the French authorities imposed a territorial restriction on a convicted ETA sympathiser, Mr Olazabal, who could not reside in any of the districts bordering Spain, and who could not leave the district where he was residing without previously warning the police authorities.

---

[71] See Case 157/79 *Pieck* [1980] ECR 2171.
[72] Case 36/75 *Rutili* [1975] ECR 1219.
[73] Case C-100/01 *Olazabal* [2002] ECR I-10981.

Notwithstanding the fact that such a restriction could have not been imposed on a French national, the Court found that it was justified on public policy grounds and therefore was compatible with Community law. Following the adoption of the Directive, however, the ruling in *Olazabal* should no longer be considered good law, and Member States will not be able to impose territorial restrictions on Union citizens and their family members unless they would be able to do so in relation to their own nationals.

As said above, pursuant to Article 24, all Union citizens who are lawfully resident in another Member State have a right to be treated equally with the nationals of the host Member State.[74] However, Member States may exclude the right to equal treatment in relation to social assistance during the first three months of residence; and for work-seekers, although the Court has held that benefits aimed at facilitating access to the employment market are not to be qualified as social assistance for the purposes of Article 24(2) Directive 2004/38 (we shall look at the regime provided for work-seekers in detail in the next chapter).[75] Furthermore, the right of equal treatment does not encompass, before the acquisition of permanent residence, the grant of maintenance aid for studies to economically inactive citizens and their families. As mentioned above, before the entry into force of Directive 2004/38 there were some doubts as to how this provision would actually be interpreted by the Court since in its ruling in *Bidar* it had held that lawfully resident Union citizens might be entitled to maintenance loans once they had established a real link with the host Member State.[76] The blank exclusion of maintenance grants and the like from the principle of equal treatment for non-economically actively Union citizens up until that time in which they had become permanent resident seemed therefore to be inconsistent with the Court's ruling. However, in the case of *Förster* the Court held that a rule that made the award of such benefits conditional upon prior residence for five years was compatible with Union law in that such a length of residence is a means to ensure that the claimant has established a real link with the host society.[77] The Court distinguished that case from *Bidar* by pointing out that the English rules at issue in the latter made it impossible for a student *ever* to establish the length of residence required to qualify for full access to student support.

Third-country national family members have a right to work, both as employed and as self-employed, as well as the right to equal treatment, as long as they have a right to residence or permanent residence (ie with the exclusion of the first three months of residence) (Article 23).

G – Derogations on the Right of Entry and Residence on the Grounds of Public Policy, Public Security and Public Health

Articles 45(3) and 52(1) TFEU provide for the possibility for Member States to derogate from the Treaty provisions free movement of workers, establishment and free movement of services provisions on the grounds of public policy, public security and public health. Even though there is no similar express derogation for the rights contained in Article 21 TFEU, the reference in that Article to the limitations and conditions contained in the

---

[74] See above section II.
[75] Joined Cases C-22 and C-23/08 *Vatsouras and Koupatantze* [2009] ECR I-4585.
[76] Case C-209/03 *Bidar* [2005] ECR I-2119.
[77] Case C-158/07 *Förster* [2008] ECR I-8507.

Treaty and in secondary legislation clearly means that the derogations apply also to Union citizens' rights.[78] Directive 2004/38, as Directive 64/221 before it, details the modalities according to which Member States can rely on such derogations, partially codifying the Court's case law. Article 27(1) clarifies that the derogations can never be invoked to serve economic ends. It should also be remembered that in fields governed by the Directive, Member States are bound by the Charter of Fundamental Rights since they are implementing Union law.

(i) Public Policy and Public Security

The possibility of derogating from the Treaty free movement provisions is extremely limited and in 40 years of case law Member States have very seldom succeeded in invoking the derogations,[79] although in more recent years (and peculiarly post-citizenship) the Court has been more open to accept the pleadings of Member States.[80]

Article 27 provides that measures (typically deportation or refusal of residence) taken on grounds of public policy/security shall comply with the principle of proportionality and be based 'exclusively on the personal conduct of the individual concerned'.

In *Bonsignore,* for instance, Carmelo Bonsignore was an Italian worker resident in Germany, who unlawfully acquired a Beretta pistol, with which he accidentally shot his younger brother Angelo. He was fined for unlawful possession of a firearm, and deportation was ordered by the Chief Administrative Office of the City of Cologne. The national court referred a question to the Court of Justice enquiring whether the equivalent provision in Directive 64/221 were to be interpreted as excluding deportation of a national of a Member State for the purpose of deterring other foreign nationals for such offences, or whether expulsion was only permissible when there were clear indications that an (E)EC national, who had been convicted of an offence, would himself commit further offences or in some other way disregard public security or public policy. 'As departures from the rules concerning the free movement of persons constitute exceptions which must be strictly construed', declared the Court, 'the concept of "personal conduct" expresses the requirement that a deportation order may only be made for breaches of the peace and public security which might be committed by the individual affected.'[81] This principle has now been codified in Article 27(2) of Directive 2004/38 which states that consideration of general prevention cannot be accepted to justify deportation. Furthermore, previous criminal convictions do not constitute in themselves grounds for an expulsion order, although they might be evidence of the fact that the individual poses a 'present threat' to public policy/security. Thus, in *Bouchereau,*[82] the Court held that

> the existence of a previous criminal conviction can therefore only be taken into account in so far as the circumstances which gave rise to that conviction are evidence of personal conduct constituting a present threat to the requirements of public policy.
>
> Although, in general, a finding that such a threat exists implies the existence in the individual

---

[78] cf Case C-357/98 *Yiadom* [2000] ECR I-9265; Joined Cases C-482/01 and 493/01 *Orfanopoulos and Olivieri* [2004] ECR I-5257, para 47.

[79] A public policy derogation was successfully invoked in Case 41/74 *Van Duyn* [1975] ECR 1337.

[80] eg Case C-33/07 *Jipa* [2008] ECR I-5157; Case C-145/09 *Tsakouridis*, judgment of 23 November 2010; Case C-137/09 *Josemans*, judgment of 16 December 2010.

[81] Case 67/74 *Bonsignore* [1975] ECR 297, 307.

[82] Case 30/77 *Bouchereau* [1977] ECR 1999.

concerned of a propensity to act in the same way in the future, it is possible that past conduct alone may constitute such a threat to the requirements of public policy.[83]

Directive 2004/38 also codifies the case law in relation to the definition of the conduct which might justify recourse to the public policy derogation: the conduct of the individual concerned must 'represent a genuine, present and sufficiently serious threat affecting one of the fundamental interests of society'. In order to pose such a threat the conduct must lead to serious sanctions if performed by own nationals: thus it is very likely that Member States would not be able to invoke the public policy/security derogation if the same conduct would not give rise to criminal liability when performed by own nationals.[84] That said, criminal behaviour in itself is not determinant, since the Member States cannot issue a deportation order as a penalty or legal consequence of a custodial penalty (Article 33) unless the individual poses a genuine and present threat to public policy or public security.[85] Thus, exclusion orders can never be an automatic consequence of a breach of law.[86] Furthermore if more than two years have elapsed between when the expulsion order was issued as a penalty or the result of a custodial penalty and its execution, the Member State must check that the individual concerned is at that time still a current and genuine threat to public policy/security, and whether there has been any material change in the circumstances (such as family circumstances) since the order was first issued.[87]

In order to ascertain whether the individual represents a genuine, present and sufficient threat to public policy/security, the Member State can exceptionally, and if it considers it essential, request information from the person's state of nationality, or from any other state (Article 27(3)). The Court has also clarified that the safeguards provided by Union law to Union citizens and their family members apply also in relation to the Schengen Information System.[88] The latter is a system whereby Member States participatory to the Schengen agreement can issue an alert against a non-Union national on grounds of public policy/security, which are more loosely defined than the same concepts in relation to Directive 2004/38.[89] Once the alert has been issued, the other Member States parties to the Schengen agreement must refuse a visa (save for limited circumstances) to the Schengen area.[90] In *Commission v Spain*[91] the Commission brought proceedings against Spain because the latter had refused visas/entry to spouses of Union nationals against whom a Schengen Information System alert had been issued. The Court held that even though inclusion in the Schengen Information System constitutes evidence that there are reasons to refuse the person concerned entry/visa, such evidence must be corroborated by information that enables the Member State to ascertain whether the individual is a

---

[83] Ibid, paras 28 and 29.

[84] *cf* Joined Cases 115/81 and 116/81 *Adoui and Cornuaille* [1984] ECR 1665; Case C-268/99 *Jany and others* [2001] ECR I-8615.

[85] Case 131/79 *Santillo* [1980] ECR 1585.

[86] Art 33; and *cf* also Case 30/77 *Bouchereau* [1977] ECR 1999.

[87] *cf* Case 131/79 *Santillo* [1980] ECR 1585; Joined Cases C-482/01 and 493/01 *Orfanopoulos and Olivieri* [2004] ECR I-5257.

[88] Convention Implementing the Schengen Agreement (CISA) [2000] OJ L239/19, Title IV, Arts 92 and ss.

[89] *cf* Art 96 CISA, and see Declaration of the Executive Committee established by the CISA of 18 April 1996 defining the concept of alien [2000] OJ L239/458.

[90] Art 5(1) CISA; Art 5(2) provides for the possibility for a Member State to derogate from the obligation to refuse entry/visa on humanitarian grounds, on grounds of national interest, or because of international obligations. However, in this case, the geographic validity of the visa must be limited to the area of the Member State issuing the visa.

[91] Case C-503/03 *Commission v Spain* (Schengen Information System) [2006] ECR I-1097.

present and *sufficiently serious* threat affecting one of the fundamental interests of society. In other words, the Schengen Information System cannot be used to circumvent the guarantees and the rights that Union citizens' family members derive from EU law, and entry/visa can be denied only if the narrower definition of public policy/security is met.

Furthermore, before issuing an expulsion order, the Member State has to take into due consideration the personal situation of the Union citizen or her/his family members. In particular, Article 28 of the Directive instructs Member States to take into account the length of stay in the host state; the individual's age; state of health; family and economic situation; social and cultural integration in the host Member State; and the extent of her/his links with the country. Those requirements are clearly an aspect of the proportionality and fundamental rights scrutiny which is always required when a Member State seeks to limit a Union citizen's right.[92] Thus, the more the individual is integrated into the host-state society, the less likely it is for the Member State to be able to invoke successfully the derogations; that would be especially the case when the individual has established ties (family, friends, work) in the host country. In this respect, a deportation order might also conflict with the right to family life as guaranteed by Article 7 of the Charter of Fundamental rights (as well as by the general principles of Union law and the European Convention on Human Rights).[93] It is not by coincidence, then, that Article 28 (2) provides that those who have a right to permanent residence, and are therefore more integrated in the host-state society, cannot be deported from the host state's territory except on 'serious grounds of public policy and security'; and that Article 28(3) provides that those who have resided in the host state for at least ten years can be deported only for 'imperative grounds of public security'. Given that the public policy and security derogations are already very narrowly defined, it is only in the most serious of cases that an individual who has lived in the host country for more than five years should be lawfully deported. That said, in a recent case the Court seems to have taken a more lenient view of the state's right to invoke the public security/policy derogation. In *Tsakouridis*[94] the Court accepted, at least in theory, that Germany could invoke the stricter Article 28(3) (imperative grounds of) public security/policy derogation, and Article 28(2), against a Greek national born and raised in Germany in relation to drugs-related offences. However, it should be noted that the Court left the final assessment of the proportionality and fundamental rights compliance of a deportation order to the national court.

Finally, concern towards the family rights of Union citizens and their family members also inspired the more protective regime set out for minors, who, pursuant to Article 28(3)(b) can only be deported on 'imperative grounds of public security' or if the expulsion is necessary for the best interests of the child as provided by the UN Convention on the Rights of the Child. In any event, the child's right to family life has to be respected, and if her/his family is in the host Member State, an expulsion order is very unlikely to succeed.

(ii) Public Health

Article 29 provides that Member States can refuse entry as well as refuse to issue the

---

[92] See Chapter 11 above.

[93] See Joined Cases C-482/01 and 493/01 *Orfanopoulos and Olivieri* [2004] ECR I-5257; and by analogy Case C-60/00 *Carpenter* [2002] ECR I-6279; Case C-109/01 *Akrich* [2003] ECR I-9607.

[94] Case C-145/09 *Tsakouridis*, Judgment of 23 November 2010.

first residence permit on grounds of public health in relation to diseases with epidemic potential (as defined by the World Health Organisation), and other infectious or contagious parasitic diseases if they are subject to protection provisions also in relation to own nationals. In this respect, and only if there are very serious indications that that is necessary, the host Member State can require the individual (within three months of their arrival) to undergo a medical examination, free of charge; those examinations can never be imposed as a matter of routine. The health derogation can be invoked only during the first three months of stay; after that time the individual cannot be made subject to an expulsion order since, of course, if this time has elapsed the individual would have either caught the disease in the host country or have already had the chance to spread it, so that an expulsion would become meaningless. In any event it is very unlikely that a Member State would invoke the health derogation against a given individual (and in fact there is no case law on the issue); rather it is more likely that if such measures were to be necessary, they would be adopted in relation to individuals coming from, or having recently visited, a region (whether within or outside Europe) stricken by an epidemic disease.

If a person is validly excluded from the host Member State on any ground, he/she shall be allowed to re-enter the territory of the state of origin even if his/her document is no longer valid or if the holder's nationality is disputed (Article 27(4)).

(iii) Procedural Requirements

Directive 2004/38, like its precursor Directive 64/221, provides for essential procedural guarantees for those whose right to movement and residence is limited on public policy, security or health grounds.

Article 30 provides that the individual concerned must be notified in writing of the decision to exclude/expel him/her, in such a 'way that they are able to comprehend its content and the implication for them'. This suggests a possible obligation upon the host Member State's authorities to write in the individual's language, as well as to write in clear (and not excessively bureaucratic) terms. The written communication needs to state, precisely and in full, the grounds upon which the decision is based unless that would be contrary to the interests of state security. Furthermore, since the individual has a right to appeal granted directly by Union law (cp Article 31), Article 30 states that the written communication must also provide the details of the competent judicial or (independent) administrative authority to hear the appeal, the time limit for the appeal, and the time allowed for the person to leave the territory.[95] Such time cannot be less than a month unless there are substantiated cases of urgency. The individual seeking judicial review/ appealing (according to the host state's rules) might also ask for an interim order to suspend removal pending the judicial/administrative court's decision on the substance of the matter. In this case, pursuant to Article 31, the host state's authorities cannot execute the expulsion order until the competent authority has adjudicated on the interim order, unless the expulsion is based on a previous judicial decision (such as, for instance, as a result of previous criminal proceedings), or where the person has already had access to judicial review, or when expulsion is based on an imperative requirement of public security in the case of long-term and permanent residents. Therefore, even though the appeal

---

[95] *cf* also Case C-175/94 *Gallagher* [1995] ECR I-4253; the authority can be appointed by the same authority that takes the decision provided it is truly independent from it.

might not have automatic suspensory effects,[96] ie might not stop repatriation, the Member State has a duty (apart from the narrowly defined exemptions) to wait at least until the competent court or administrative authority has had the chance to assess the prima facie strength of the host state claim.[97] After that, and if the court/authority has not granted the interim order, the host state might exclude the individual, pending the appeal. However, it has to allow the individual to come back in order to allow her/him the possibility to submit her/his defence in person, unless his/her appearance may cause serious troubles to public policy or security; or unless judicial review concerns a denial of entry to the territory (Article 31(4)). Denial of entry is narrowly defined, and the Court in *Yiadom* has held that if the person has been allowed temporarily in the host state's territory pending a decision following investigation of his/her case, as to whether she/he should be allowed leave to enter; and, at least when presence in the territory has been of not inconsiderable length (in the case at issue seven months), the decision refusing leave to enter cannot be considered as a decision concerning entry and therefore full procedural guarantees apply, and the claimant has the right to submit her/his defence in person.[98]

As for the appeal proper, Article 31(3) codifies the case law by requiring that the competent authority review not only the legality of the measure (ie whether the measure is formally correct) but also, and much more importantly, the substance of the issue, and in particular whether deportation is a proportionate reaction to the actual threat that the individual might pose to the requirements of public policy, security or health.[99] Thus, the Directive ensures that exclusion of Union citizens and their family members from the territory of any of the Member States can occur only because of objective (and thus reviewable) considerations, and not as a matter of political (and thus not reviewable) discretion.[100]

(iv) Duration and Modalities

As already established by the Court,[101] an exclusion order can never be of permanent duration since that would violate the very requirement that a derogation can be invoked only in relation to individual conduct constituting an 'actual' threat to public policy/security, and that past conduct alone is not conclusive to that effect. Furthermore, permanent exclusions would run against the principle of proportionality. In the case of public health it is only when the individual is actually carrying a disease that an exclusion might be justified (Article 29).

It is not surprising, then, that Article 32 limits the possibility to exclude a person protected by the Directive from the host territory for a given amount of time to cases relating to public policy or public security. After a reasonable amount of time, the person so

---

[96] cf also Case 98/79 *Pecastaing* [1980] ECR 691.

[97] And a rule which provides for the possibility to assess only the prima facie legality of the measure, but not the substantive grounds for the measure, is incompatible with Union law, Case C-136/03 *Dörr and Ünal* [2005] ECR I-4759.

[98] Case C-357/98 *Yiadom* [2000] ECR I-9265.

[99] Joined Cases 115/81 and 116/81 *Adoui and Cornuaille* [1984] ECR 1665, para 15; and also Case C-136/03 *Dörr and Ünal* [2005] ECR I-4759.

[100] National immigration rules in relation to third-country nationals not covered by the Directive are usually significantly more restrictive of the procedural rights of individuals; see eg the British rules: http://www.ind.homeoffice.gov.uk/.

[101] cf Case C-348/96 *Calfa* [1999] ECR I-11.

excluded has a right to submit an application for lifting of the exclusion order;[102] what is reasonable will depend on the circumstances of the particular case. In any event, though, after three years from enforcement of the final exclusion order the person excluded can put forward arguments to demonstrate that there has been a change in the material circumstances which justified the decision ordering the exclusion. The Member State then has six months to reach a decision on the application for the lifting of the exclusion order. During this time, the person concerned has no right of entry into the territory of the Member State. Article 32 does not specify that the individual has a right to judicial review in those cases; however, it is clear that Article 31 would apply also in these circumstances, since a decision refusing to lift the exclusion order is still a decision taken on grounds of public policy or security according to Article 31(1). Since the decision would be concerning a denial of entry, the person concerned would not have, according to Article 31(4), the right to enter to submit his/her defence in person.

H – Abuse of Rights

Article 35 explicitly provides that Member States are entitled to refuse, terminate or withdraw any right conferred by the Directive in the case of abuse of rights or fraud, such as marriages of convenience.

The extent to which a Member State will be able to invoke the abuse of rights doctrine seems to be rather limited:[103] the Court has on several occasions refused to consider the exercise of Union rights for a purpose different from the one for which the right was originally granted as an abuse of right.[104] Thus, the fact that a Union citizen moves to another Member State with the sole intention of triggering the Treaty, and therefore benefit from the often more generous EU law regime in relation to the rights of partners and spouses, is immaterial.[105] Finally, it should be noted that any right in the Directive is subject to compliance with the general principles of Union law. Thus procedural provisions cannot be less favourable than those available to own nationals for similar claims and cannot deprive the rights in the directive of their effectiveness.[106] Sanctions imposed for breach of the directive must be proportionate and are subject to the principle of non-discrimination and must therefore be equivalent to sanctions imposed on nationals for comparable breaches of law (Article 35). Furthermore, since the Directive is a minimum measure, it is open to the Member States to provide for a more favourable regime (Article 37).

---

[102] See also Joined Cases C-65/95 C-111/95 *Shingara and Radiom* [1997] ECR I-3343.

[103] See K Ziegler in R De La Feria and S Vogenauer (eds), *Prohibition of Abuse of Law: A New General Principle of EU Law* (Oxford, Hart Publishing, forthcoming).

[104] *cf* Case C-212/97 *Centros* [1999] ECR I-1459, paras 24 *et seq*; Case C-109/01 *Akrich* [2003] ECR I-9607.

[105] eg Case C-109/01 *Akrich* [2003] ECR I-9607; the same is true in relation to those citizens who seek to return to their Member State of origin after having taken advantage of their free movement right. Upon returning to their Member State of origin they, and their family members, are protected by primary Union law (Directive 2004/38 does not apply) even if the only reason why they left in the first place was to be able to rely on the more favourable EU law regime upon returning to their state of origin.

[106] eg Joined Cases 115/81 and 116/81 *Adoui and Cornuaille* [1984] ECR 1665, and see Chapter 9 above.

IV – OTHER RIGHTS PERTAINING TO EU CITIZENS

A – Right to Equal Treatment, Right to Move and Beyond

So far, we have focused on the Union citizens' right to reside and on the right to equal treatment in relation to welfare provision. However, the rights granted by the Treaty go further than that, and indeed Articles 20 and 21 TFEU (read together with Article 18 TFEU) encompass a more general right to equal treatment, as well as a more general right not to be hindered in one's ability to move.[107] In *Bickel and Franz* an Austrian and a German national undergoing trial in the bilingual South Tyrol region in Italy claimed a right to have the proceedings conducted in German. Residents in the province had such a right, but non-residents had to face trial in Italian. Given that a residence requirement always amounts to indirect discrimination, the issue for the Court was whether the situation fell within the scope of application of the Treaty so that the principle of non-discrimination would apply. In deciding that it did, the Court preferred to find in Article 56 TFEU the trigger for Article 18 TFEU to apply, rather than to rely directly on the citizenship provisions, which it nevertheless mentioned in order to strengthen its reasoning.[108]

In *Garcia Avello*[109] the right to equal treatment of Union citizens in respect of all matters having an even remote connection with movement rights was more clearly established. The dispute related to Belgian rules on how to determine a child's surname. Mr Garcia Avello was a Spanish national married to a Mrs Weber, a Belgian national. The couple resided in Belgium and had two children, who were born in Belgium and had dual nationality (Belgian and Spanish); following Belgian practice, the children were registered under their father's last name, Garcia Avello. The couple then requested the competent authority to change the surname of the children into Garcia Weber, following established Spanish practice whereby the children's last name results from the father's last name followed by the mother's last name. In the meanwhile, the couple also registered the children at the Spanish embassy as Garcia Weber. The Belgian authorities rejected the couple's request, merely changing the last name to Garcia, on the grounds that, according to Belgian law, children bear their father's last name. Mr Garcia Avello, acting as legal representative for the children, brought proceedings challenging the Belgian authorities' decision; the Belgian Court referred a question to the Court of Justice to enquire as to whether Articles 20 and 21 TFEU prevented the Belgian authorities from rejecting the requested change of name.

The preliminary question for the Court was whether the Treaty had been triggered. The Belgian Government argued that the situation was purely internal since the children were born and had always resided in Belgium. In examining the question, the Court focused on

---

[107] cp Case C-224/02 *Pusa* [2004] ECR I-5763; see also AG Geelhoed's Opinion in Case C-406/04 *De Cuyper* [2006] ECR I-6947. Any residence requirement is always construed as a barrier to movement, also when imposed by the Member State of origin in respect of the award of benefits (although of course it is open to the Member States to justify it); eg Case C-192/05 *Tas-Hagen and Tas* [2006] ECR I-10451; Case C-406/04 *De Cuyper* [2006] ECR I-6947; Case C-499/06 *Nerkowska* [2008] ECR I-3993. However, in the absence of harmonising legislation (ie for non-Schengen countries), Member States retain the right to have border controls to establish identity and entitlement of those entering their territory: Case C-378/97 *Wijsenbeek* [1999] ECR I-6207.

[108] Case C-274/96 *Bickel and Franz* [1998] ECR I-7637, para 15.

[109] Case C-148/02 *Garcia Avello* [2003] ECR I-11613.

the fact that the children were Spanish nationals residing in Belgium; therefore the cross-border element had been triggered. Having found that the situation fell within the scope of the Treaty, the Court turned to the substantive issue, and in particular to whether the Belgian rules entailed any discrimination prohibited by Article 18 TFEU, read in conjunction with Article 20 TFEU. It restated the principle according to which non-discrimination requires that comparable situations should be treated equally; and that non-comparable situations should be treated differently. The Belgian rules, however, treated citizens having dual nationality (objectively in a different situation than Belgian citizens) in the same way as it treated Belgian nationals having only Belgian nationality. The Court therefore found that the refusal to allow the Garcia Avello children to register with their father's and mother's last name constituted discrimination caught by Article 18 TFEU. In bringing the rules on names (in principle within the exclusive competence of the Member States) within the scope of the Treaty,[110] the Court relied on the fact that the prohibition on having the same last name as that registered in the Spanish documents might have affected the children's right to move in the future, and especially their right to return to Spain, since all of the Belgian official documents would be drawn using the Belgian surname. The Court found then that the strict practice concerning authorisation to change names was unnecessary to protect risks of confusion as to parentage, as well as being disproportionate.

As a consequence, the ruling in *Garcia Avello* is important for two reasons: first of all the Court seems to suggest that dual nationality is per se, and regardless of actual movement, enough to trigger the Treaty.[111] Secondly, the link with the material scope of the Treaty was rather remote, and not entirely convincing: on the one hand, it was based on purely potential factors (ie the children's willingness to move in the future); on the other hand, nothing, besides cultural reasons, would have prevented the children from using their Belgian name so as to avoid future confusion. Thus, the ruling in *Garcia Avello* not only further restricts the scope of the 'purely internal situation', according to which the Treaty free movement provisions apply only when there is a cross-border element,[112] but also suggests that the effect of the introduction of Union citizenship is to subject an increasing number of national rules to the proportionality assessment,[113] even when those rules only remotely affect their Treaty rights.[114]

The expansion of the scope of the Treaty, to the detriment of an absolute reserve of national sovereignty in cases which have a more remote, if not only entirely potential, link with movement has been confirmed in recent case law. In the above-mentioned case of *Rottman* the Court found that withdrawal of German nationality from a German naturalized citizen fell within the scope of Union law so that the general principle of proportionality applied. More strikingly, in *Ruiz Zambrano* the Court applied the Treaty provisions on Union citizenship to a situation which traditionally would have been judged

---

[110] See also Case C-353/06 *Grunkin and Paul* [2008] ECR I-7639; Case C-208/09 *Sayn-Wittgenstein*, Judgment of 22 December 2010; Case C-391/09 *Runevič-Vardyn and Wardyn*, Opinion delivered 16 December 2010, case still pending at the time of writing.

[111] But see, partially in contradiction with this statement, the Opinion of AG Kokott in Case C-434/09 *McCarthy*, delivered 25 November 2010, case still pending at the time of writing.

[112] See also N Nic Shuibhne, 'Free Movement of Persons and the Wholly Internal Rule: Time to Move On?' (2002) 39 *CMLRev* 731.

[113] But not all of them, *cf* Case C-386/02 *Baldinger* [2004] ECR I-8411, where the Court did not follow AG Ruiz-Jarabo Colomer's Opinion and refused to bring within the scope of Treaty rules concerning compensation for ex-prisoners of war.

[114] See also AG Jacobs' Opinion in Case C-96/04 *Standesamt Stadt Niebüll* [2006] ECR I-3561; the Court denied jurisdiction; it then examined the issue in Case C-353/06 *Grunkin and Paul* [2008] ECR I-7639.

as purely internal.[115] In that case, two Columbian nationals migrated to Belgium and applied for asylum, which was refused. However, Mr and Mrs Ruiz Zambrano remained in Belgium,[116] where Mr Ruiz Zambrano found employment and where they had two children who were accorded Belgian nationality. The couple's legal situation in relation to their residence right was complex, and eventually Mr and Mrs Ruiz Zambrano argued that they should gain a right of residence in Belgium directly from Union law since they were the parents (and carers) of two Union citizens. In order to argue their case they relied both on the provisions of Directive 2004/38 and on the ruling in *Chen*, where the Court accepted that carers of (foreign) Union citizens derive a right of residence from Union law by virtue of their children right to move and reside in the European Union. However, in this case, and differently from *Chen*, the children had not moved and had the nationality of the state of residence. In other words, there was no obvious intra-European Union link, and hence Directive 2004/38 was found not to be applicable. The question for the Court was therefore whether Union citizenship was at all relevant in this case; or whether this was a purely internal situation, as argued by all intervening governments and by the Commission. In a very short ruling the Court found that 'Article 20 TFEU precludes national measures which have the effect of depriving citizens of the Union of the genuine enjoyment of the *substance* of the rights conferred by virtue of their status as citizens of the Union.'[117] It then held that refusal of a residence and a work permit to the children's parents would interfere with the substance of the rights granted by Union citizenship since it would lead to a situation where the children would have to leave the territory of the EU in order to follow their parents.[118] As a result, Belgium was prevented by Article 20 TFEU from refusing a residence and work permit to Mr and Mrs Ruiz Zambrano.

The ruling in *Ruiz Zambrano* can be interpreted in two ways: a narrow reading of it (supported by the Court's reference to the ruling in *Rottmann*) is to consider it authority for the establishment of an outer limit to national sovereignty in relation to matters concerning EU citizens. In this respect, it could be argued that the Court is willing to interfere in prima facie internal situation only when the effect of national rules would be to *deprive* Union citizenship of any meaningful effect (thus affecting the very substance of the rights granted by it). Read in this way both *Rottmann* and *Ruiz Zambrano* might be less controversial – it is only in cases with extraordinary factual circumstances that Union law is of relevance in relation to the way a Member State treats its own citizens.

A broader reading would be to consider *Ruiz Zambrano* as a clear endorsement of a more rounded vision of the effect of Union citizenship, which also provides a basic level of protection for citizens against their own state regardless of any (sometimes entirely artificial) desire to move. After all, the converse of the right to move should be the right *not to move* without being unduly penalised for doing so.

---

[115] Case C-34/09 *Ruiz Zambrano*, Judgment of 8 March 2011.

[116] It was accepted that they could not return to Columbia because of a civil war and hence the Belgian court's order included a non-refoulement clause according to which the couple could not be returned to Columbia.

[117] Case C-34/09 *Ruiz Zambrano*, Judgment of 8 March 2011, para 42, emphasis added.

[118] This is actually slightly inaccurate since the children (and their parents as carers) had a Union law right conferred by the Treaty and detailed in Directive 2004/38 to move to any other EU Member State.

B – Political Rights and Rights to Good Administration

(i) Right to Vote

As noted above, the Maastricht Treaty established Union citizenship; whilst it was not clear at the time whether Article 21 TFEU was a mere codification of the status quo, or whether it was going to create more extensive rights of movement and residence than those granted by the three residence directives, the Maastricht Treaty also established new rights.

In particular, Article 22 TFEU provides that Union citizens residing in a Member State other than that of nationality have the right to vote and to stand in the local elections of the Member State where she/he resides under the same conditions as nationals of that state. This right is to be exercised subject to detailed arrangements adopted by the Council, which may provide for derogations 'where warranted by problems specific to a Member State'. Such arrangements have been laid down by Directive 94/80.[119]

The municipal elections concern representative councils and the local government units listed in the Annex to the Directive[120]—parishes, districts, counties, county boroughs, communities, regions, etc.

Article 5(3), first paragraph, of the Directive provides:

> Member States may provide that only their own nationals may hold the office of elected head, deputy or member of the governing college of the executive of a basic local government unit if elected to hold office for the duration of his mandate.

This provision is worthy of remark. The right of a citizen of the Union to 'stand as a candidate . . . under the same conditions as nationals of that State' would be worthless if he/she were not entitled, if elected, to carry out all the functions and exercise all the prerogatives of an elected member of the nationality of the Member State in question. It is true that Article 22 TFEU permits derogations, but these must be 'warranted by problems specific to a Member State', and the issue addressed by Article 5(3) could not be so described. It appears from the preamble to the Directive that the justification for Article 5(3) is to be found by analogy with Article 41 TFEU, which provides that the right of establishment for self-employed persons does not apply to activities connected, even occasionally, with the exercise of official authority.[121] This latter provision is the counterpart of Article 45(4) TFEU, which provides that the right of freedom of movement of workers does not apply

---

[119] Council Directive 94/80 laying down detailed arrangements for the exercise of the right to vote and to stand as a candidate in municipal elections by citizens of the Union residing in a Member State of which they are not nationals, [1994] OJ L368/38, as amended, consolidated version: http://eur-lex.europa.eu/LexUriServ/LexUriServ.do?uri=CONSLEG:1994L0080:20070101:EN:PDF. See also Commission Report on granting a derogation pursuant to Article 19(1) of the Treaty, presented under Art 12(4) of Directive 94/80 on the right to vote and stand as a candidate in municipal elections, COM(2005)382 final. On the compatibility of the legislation transposing Directive 94/80 with the French Constitution, see Conseil Constitutionnel, Decision 98-400, 20/5/98.

[120] As amended by Directive 96/30.

[121] See Chapter 17, section V.B. The preamble of the Directive states in relevant part: 'Whereas, since the duties of the leadership of basic local government units may involve taking part in the exercise of official authority and in the safeguarding of the general interest, Member States should be able to reserve these offices for their nationals; whereas Member States should also be able to take appropriate measures for that purpose; whereas such measures may not restrict more than is necessary for the achievement of that objective the possibility for other Member States' nationals to be elected.'

to 'employment in the public service'.[122] It is true that the 'public service/authority proviso' comprises one of the 'limitations and conditions laid down in this Treaty and by the measures adopted to give it effect' within the meaning of Article 21 TFEU which defines the right of movement and residence referred to in that Article. But it does not follow that a principle based on the official authority/public service proviso may be invoked to limit the right to vote and stand in municipal elections which is laid down in Article 22 TFEU. The official authority/public service proviso is concerned with access to certain remunerated posts in the public service, and seeks to distinguish economic activity from the exercise of powers of governance. However, the right to hold elected office in a local government authority intrinsically involves the right to exercise official authority, by way of participation in the exercise of powers conferred by public law (eg decisions on licensing, planning permission). Even an allegedly limited and proportionate application of the official authority/public service proviso in the context in question appears to take back by secondary legislation some part of the very right which the Treaty has bestowed. The application of the official authority/public service proviso by way of Article 5(3) of Directive 94/80 appears to be as much an exercise in second thoughts on the part of the Council as regards the implications of bestowing the right to stand for office in the first place, as a laying down of detailed arrangements for the exercise of the right in question.

Union citizens also have the right to participate in the elections of the European Parliament: as a result, every citizen of the Union residing in a Member State of which she/he is not a national must be given the right to vote and to stand as a candidate in elections to the European Parliament in which she/he resides, under the same conditions as nationals of that Member State. Council Directive 93/109 lays down detailed arrangements for the exercise of this right.[123] It is to be noted that the Directive provides that voters shall exercise their right to vote either in the Member State of residence or in their home Member State.[124] No person may vote more than once at the same election, and no person may stand as a candidate in more than one Member State at the same election.[125]

Whilst it is for the Member State to decide the modalities for the exercise of the right to vote for the European Parliament, such as conditions relating to age, residence, etc, such power is not unfettered. In *Eman and Sevinger*[126] two Dutch citizens residing in Aruba, a Dutch oversea territory, challenged their exclusion from the right to vote in the European Parliament. According to Dutch rules, residents in the territories could not vote for the political elections in the mainland and consequently could also not vote for the European Parliament. The Court of Justice found that the matter fell within the scope of Union law so that the general principles of Union law applied. Whilst the conditions to vote and stand for the European Parliament fell to be defined by the Member States, the general principle of equality applied. Since Dutch citizens residing anywhere else in the world were entitled to vote for the European Parliament, whilst Dutch citizens residing in one of the Dutch overseas territories were not, the principle of equality had been breached since comparable situations were treated in different ways. In the case of *Spain v UK* the Court confirmed that it is for Member States to decide who is entitled to vote for the

---

[122] Chapter 16, section IV.B(ii)(a).
[123] [1993] OJ L329/34.
[124] Ibid, Art 4.
[125] Ibid, Art 4; Union citizens of course have the right to vote for the European Parliament in their home state.
[126] Case C-300/04 *Eman and Sevinger* [2006] ECR I-8055.

European Parliament.[127] The case followed from a successful challenge brought in front of the European Court of Human Rights by a Gibraltar resident claiming that her inability to vote for the European Parliament was inconsistent with Article 3 Protocol 1 which guarantees the right to democratic participation.[128] In order to comply with the ruling of the European Court of Human Rights the United Kingdom amended its rules; consistently with the electoral rules in the UK mainland, the right to vote was extended to British and Commonwealth citizens resident in Gibraltar, hence granting the electoral franchise also to non-EU citizens. Spain brought proceedings against the UK, arguing that the extension of the right to vote for the European Parliament to non-EU citizens was inconsistent with the Treaty. The Court found that it was for the Member State to decide eligibility to vote, and that the UK was not prevented from extending such right to Commonwealth citizens consistently with its own constitutional traditions.

(ii) Diplomatic and Consular Protection and Other Citizens' Rights

Citizenship of the Union also bestows advantages for individuals as regards diplomatic and consular protection in the territory of third countries. Every citizen of the Union shall, in the territory of a third country in which the Member State of which he/she is a national is not represented, be entitled to protection by the diplomatic or consular authorities of any Member State, on the same conditions as the nationals of that Member State. Member States are obliged to establish the necessary rules among themselves and start the international negotiations required to secure this protection. In accordance with this obligation, the representatives of the governments of the Member States meeting within the Council adopted a Decision regarding protection for citizens of the European Union by diplomatic and consular representations.[129] The Decision, inter alia, defines the diplomatic protection to be extended to citizens of the Union, as follows:

(a) assistance in cases of death;
(b) assistance in cases of serious accident or serious illness;
(c) assistance in cases of arrest or detention;
(d) assistance to victims of violent crime;
(e) the relief and repatriation of distressed citizens of the Union.

In addition, Member States' diplomatic representations or consular agents serving in a non-Member State may, in so far as it is within their powers, also come to the assistance of any citizen of the Union who so requests in other circumstances.[130]

Further rights enjoyed by citizens of the Union are the right of initiative and the right to petition the European Parliament,[131] the right to apply to the Ombudsman established under Article 228 TFEU,[132] and the right to write to the Union institutions or the

---

[127] Case C-145/04 *Spain v UK* [2006] ECR I-7917.
[128] *Matthews v UK* (Appl No 24833/94), ECHR 1999-I. See Chapter 11 above.
[129] Decision 95/553 [1995] OJ L314/73.
[130] Ibid, Art 5.
[131] Art 24(1) TFEU and Art 227 TFEU, which grants the right to petition to all EU residents, and not only to EU citizens. See, for instance, with reference to a possible violation of the media pluralism in Italy, the Report of the European Parliament the on the risks of violation, in the EU and especially in Italy, of freedom of expression and information (Art 11(2) of the Charter of Fundamental Rights) 2003/2237(INI)) which was drafted following a private citizens' petition. The report, though clearly scathing about the situation in Italy, stopped short of requesting the Council to activate the Art 7 TEU procedure.
[132] Art 24(2) TFEU.

Ombudsman in any of the EU's official languages and to receive an answer in the same language.[133]

As mentioned in Chapter 13, the Charter of Fundamental Rights reproduces these rights in its Title V; furthermore the Charter also includes, as Union citizens' rights, the right to good administration, which is not limited to Union citizens; and the right of access to documents, which is available to Union residents as well as to Union citizens. The latter is provided for in Article 15 TFEU, and is detailed in Regulation 1049/2001 on public access to Parliament, Council and Commission documents.[134] Article 4 of the Regulation provides for exceptions to the principle of open access: those, not surprisingly, concern the Union public interest (such as security, defence, etc), and the protection of commercial interests, court proceedings, the purpose of investigations, etc. Article 9 provides for treatment of sensitive documents, ie those that the institution classifies as secret, top secret or confidential. Each institution must make the rules concerning sensitive documents public and a refusal of access must be reasoned.

Further Reading

C Barnard, 'EU Citizenship and Social Solidarity' in Dougan and Spaventa (eds), *Social Welfare and EU Law* (Oxford, Hart Publishing, 2005).

M Dougan, 'The Constitutional Dimension to the Case Law on Union Citizenship' (2006) 31 *ELRev* 613.

M Dougan and E Spaventa, 'Educating Rudy and the (non-)English Patient: A Double-bill on Residency Rights under Article18 EC' (2003) 28 *ELRev* 699.

——, '"Wish You Weren't Here . . .": New Models of Social Solidarity in the European Union' in M Dougan and E Spaventa (eds), *Social Welfare and EU Law* (Oxford, Hart Publishing, 2005).

M Everson, 'The Legacy of the Market Citizen' in J Shaw and G More (eds), *New Legal Dynamics of European Union* (Oxford, Clarendon Press, 1995).

M Ferrara, 'Towards an "Open" Social Citizenship? The New Boundaries of Welfare in the European Union' in G de Búrca (ed), *EU Law and the Welfare State* (Oxford, Oxford University Press, 2005).

E Meehan, *Citizenship and the European Community* (London, Sage, 1993),

N Nic Shuibhne, 'The Resilience of Market Citizenship' (2010) 47 *CMLRev* 1597.

C O'Brien, 'Real Links, Abstract Rights and False Alarms: The Relationship between the ECJ's "Real Link" Case Law and National Solidarity' (2008) 33 *ELRev* 643.

S O'Leary, *The Evolving Concept of Community Citizenship* (The Hague, Kluwer, 1996).

E Spaventa, 'Seeing the Wood Despite the Trees? On the Scope of Union Citizenship and its Constitutional Effects' (2008) 45 *CMLRev* 13.

J Shaw, *The Transformation of Citizenship in the European Union—Electoral Rights and the Restructuring of Political Space* (Cambridge, Cambridge University Press, 2007).

---

[133] Art 24(3) TFEU.
[134] Regulation 1049/2001 regarding public access to European Parliament, Council and Commission documents [2001] OJ L145/43.

16

Freedom of Movement for Workers

The original EEC Treaty provided for a right to move and reside across the then Community only for those who were economically active (workers and self-employed). In this chapter we are going to look at the rights of workers; in Chapters 17, 18 and 19 we will focus on self-employed and corporate actors. Even though the right to free movement was provided with an economic rationale in mind, so that workers could migrate from areas of the Union where there was unemployment to areas where there were jobs available, workers were never treated as mere factors of production. Thus, secondary legislation provided not only for an extensive right to equal treatment, including a right to welfare provision, but also for the right to be joined by one's family, who also derived rights from Union law, for the right to stay in the host Member State when involuntarily unemployed, for protection from deportation, and so on. The Court of Justice not surprisingly interpreted the Treaty provisions and the relevant secondary legislation in a generous and purposive way, protecting the worker as a person as well as a 'factor of production'. In this chapter we will focus on those rights that are peculiar to workers, whilst just recalling the rights that we have already analysed in the previous chapter. In particular we will focus on the personal scope (who is protected) and on the material scope (what constitutes a barrier to movement) of Article 45 TFEU.

I – INTRODUCTION

The Treaties establishing the original European Communities each contained provisions designed to facilitate the movement of workers between Member States. The signatories to the Treaty establishing the European Coal and Steel Community undertook in Article 69 to remove any restrictions based on nationality upon the employment in the coal and steel industries of workers holding the nationality of one of the Member States and having recognised qualifications in coal-mining or steel-making,[1] and a similar provision appeared in Article 96 of the Treaty establishing the European Atomic Energy Community, declaring the right of nationals of the Member States to take skilled employment in the field of nuclear energy.[2] Acting under this latter Article, the Council issued a Directive in

---

[1] The ECSC Treaty is no longer on force: see Chapter 1 above.
[2] This Article remains unaltered: see EURATOM consolidated version [2010] OJ C84/1.

1962[3] defining the scope of skilled employment and requiring that Member States adopt all necessary measures to ensure that any authorisation required for taking up employment in the field specified should be automatically granted.

As Treaties concerned only with limited economic integration, the ECSC and Euratom Treaties naturally only dealt with workers in their respective sectors. The EEC Treaty first, and the EC and EU Treaties later, on the other hand, sought to promote comprehensive economic integration, and its provisions requiring that 'freedom of movement for workers shall be secured within the Union' are applicable to all workers of the Member States regardless of occupation.[4] It is with the provision of the TFEU, and the implementing legislation made thereunder, that we shall be hereafter concerned.

Since a common market requires the removal of all obstacles to the free movement of the factors of production, as well as of goods and services, the free movement of workers in the EU may be seen simply as a prerequisite to the achievement of an economic objective. Support for this view may be found in the Spaak Report,[5] and in the texts of Articles 45, 46 and 48 TFEU. Under Article 45 TFEU, workers of the Member States are to be free to accept offers of employment actually made, and to remain in a Member State for the purposes of carrying on employment. Article 46 TFEU authorises legislation to eliminate administrative procedures likely to impede the movement of workers, and to set up machinery for matching offers of employment in one Member State with available candidates in another. The provisions of Article 48 TFEU establish the legal basis for legislative action in the field of social security and at first sight might appear to apply only to measures necessary for safeguarding the rights of the migrant worker stricto sensu.

Yet such a functional economic approach to the interpretation of the free movement provisions would have been inadequate for two reasons. First, in the graphic words of Article 6 of the Clayton Anti-Trust Act, because of the notion that 'the labour of a human being is not a commodity or article of commerce', or as Advocate General Trabucchi has put it: 'The migrant worker is not regarded by Community law—nor is he by the internal legal system—as a mere source of labour but is viewed as a human being.'[6] A similar sentiment may be discerned in the fifth recital to the preamble to Regulation 1612/68 of the Council,[7] which speaks of the exercise of workers' rights in 'freedom and dignity', and describes freedom of movement for workers as a 'fundamental right' and 'one of the means by which the worker is guaranteed the possibility of improving his living and working conditions and promoting his social advancement, while helping to satisfy the requirements of the economies of the Member States'. As Advocate General Jacobs has observed, 'The recital makes it clear that labour is not, in Community law, to be regarded as a commodity and notably gives precedence to the fundamental rights of workers over satisfying the requirements of the economies of the Member States.'[8]

But for another reason a purely economic approach is likely to be deficient. The EEC was established after the failure of rather more ambitious attempts to institute a Western

---

[3] [1962] OJ 1650.

[4] Art 45(1) TFEU.

[5] *Rapport des chefs de délégation aux ministres des affaires étrangères* (Brussels, 21 April 1956).

[6] Case 7/75 *Mr and Mrs F* [1975] ECR 679, 696.

[7] [1968] OJ L257/2. The Court has referred to the fifth recital both as a guide to the interpretation of the Regulation, and as an indication of the scope of the application of the Treaty: Case 76/72 *Michel S* [1973] ECR 457; Case 9/74 *Casagrande* [1974] ECR 773 (interpretation of Regulation 1612/68); Case 152/81 *Forcheri* [1983] ECR 2323 (scope of application of the Treaty).

[8] Case 344/87 *Bettray* [1989] ECR 1621, 1637.

European military and political union, and it represented an attempt to achieve a similar political aim by means of economic integration. Thus the first recital to the preamble of the (now) TFEU records the determination of the signatories to lay the foundation of an ever closer union among the peoples of Europe, and the eighth records their resolve to strengthen peace and liberty by a pooling of their respective resources. The closing words of Article 2 TEU lays down as one of the Union's allotted tasks that of promoting economic and social cohesion and solidarity among the Member States. To this extent, there may be said to be a larger objective contained in the provisions relating to the free movement of persons. It is to be noted that the Declaration issued after the Summit Conference of October 1972 included the words: 'The Member States re-affirm their resolve to base their Community's development on democracy, freedom of opinion, *free movement of men and ideas* and participation by the people through their elected representatives.'[9]

The Court of Justice has sometimes interpreted the provisions of Articles 45–48 TFEU, and the implementing legislation made thereunder, in a rather more liberal manner than would be dictated by a purely functional view of the Treaty based on its economic objectives. The case of *Maison Singer*[10] arose following the death in a road accident of a German national on holiday in France. His dependants were paid benefit by a German social security institution, which then brought an action in France against the employer of the driver of the other vehicle, claiming that the French court was bound to recognise the subrogation that German law allowed, by virtue of Article 52 of Regulation 3.[11] In the course of the proceedings before the Court of Justice, it was argued that to apply Article 52 of the Regulation in circumstances such as those before the national court would be incompatible with Article 48 TFEU, inasmuch as that provision only allowed the Council to adopt such measures as were necessary to provide freedom of movement for workers qua workers, not qua holidaymakers. The Court responded:

> Since the establishment of as complete as possible a freedom of movement of labour is among the 'foundations' of the Community, it is the ultimate goal of [Article 48 TFEU] and, therefore, governs the exercise of the power it confers upon the Council. It would not be in keeping with such a concept to limit the idea of 'worker' to migrant workers strictly speaking or to travel connected with their employment. Nothing in [Article 48 TFEU] requires such a distinction; moreover, such a distinction would make the application of the contemplated rules unfeasible. On the other hand, the system adopted for Regulation No 3, which consists in removing, as much as possible, the territorial limitations for applying the various social security systems, is quite in keeping with the objectives of [Article 48 TFEU].[12]

It was in a similar spirit that the Court of Justice considered the purpose and effect of Regulation 1612/68[13] in *Commission v Germany*[14] in the following terms:

> It is apparent from the provisions of the regulation, taken as a whole, that in order to facilitate the movement of members of workers' families the Council took into account, first, the importance for the worker, from a human point of view, of having his entire family with him, and secondly,

---

[9] Emphasis added. EC Bull 10/72, 15.
[10] Case 44/65 [1965] ECR 965.
[11] [1958] OJ 561.
[12] [1965] ECR 965, 971.
[13] [1968] OJ L257/2.
[14] Case 249/86 *Commission v Germany* [1989] ECR 1263.

the importance, from all points of view, of the integration of the worker and his family into the host Member State without any difference in treatment in relation to nationals of that State.[15]

More recently, the introduction of Union citizenship, which clearly transcends the economic requirements of the common market, is in line with the interpretation given by the Court to Article 45 TFEU, and with the very idea of considering economic migrants as persons rather than mere factors of production.[16] As we said before, the economic free movement provisions take precedence over Article 21 TFEU, both because they confer more extensive rights and because they are *lex specialis*. This is not to say, however, that the notion of Union citizenship is not relevant to economic migrants: first of all, and as we shall see below, the Court of Justice has partially amended its interpretation of Article 45 TFEU in the light of the introduction of Union citizenship; secondly, citizenship of the Union gives rights other than residence and equality, and in particular the right to vote for local and European elections in the host country, thus strengthening the link between migrant and host community.

II – THE AMBIT OF ARTICLE 45 TFEU

A – The Cross-border Element

Article 45 TFEU aims to secure freedom of *movement* for workers. This provision, along with the other provisions of the Treaty relating to freedom of movement for persons, are intended to facilitate the pursuit of occupational activities of all kinds throughout the European Union and preclude national legislation which might place EU nationals at a disadvantage when they extend their activities beyond a single Member State.[17]

In order for Article 45 TFEU to apply there needs to be a cross-border element. This is present when (i) the worker moves to another Member State to work and reside there; (ii) when the worker resides in a Member State but is employed in another one (a so-called 'frontier worker'); (iii) when the worker returns to her/his Member State of origin after having exercised his/her Article 45 TFEU rights by working in another Member State. In the latter case, the worker benefits of the protection of EU law against her/his Member State as if she/he were a national of another Member State.[18] Thus, a national who has undertaken a course of study in another Member State and then returned to his/her Member State of origin may rely upon Article 45 TFEU against that Member State to uphold his/her right to use the postgraduate academic title acquired in that other Member State.[19]

---

[15] [1989] ECR 1263, para 11.

[16] Indeed the free movement provisions, and in particular the regime for workers, has been identified as an embryonic form of European citizenship: see E Meehan, *Citizenship and the European Community* (London, Sage, 1993).

[17] Case C-443/93 *Ioannis Vougioukas* [1995] ECR I-4033, para 39.

[18] Case C-419/92 *Scholz* [1994] ECR I-505, para 9; Case C-443/93 *Ioannis Vougioukas* [1995] ECR I-4033, para 38. A worker working in her state of origin (Germany) who acquired French nationality by marriage (retaining her German nationality) and resided in France is to be regarded as having exercised her right of free movement in order to work in a Member State other than that in which she resides: see Case C-336/96 *Gilly* [1998] ECR I-2793, paras 20 and 21.

[19] Case C-19/92 *Kraus* [1993] ECR I-1663.

It should be remembered, however, that a cross-border element is always necessary, and Article 45 TFEU does not extend to situations wholly internal to a Member State,[20] for example the binding over of a person charged within theft on condition that he proceed to Northern Ireland and not return to England or Wales for three years.[21] A worker cannot rely upon Article 45 TFEU unless he/she has exercised the right to freedom of movement within the EU,[22] or is genuinely seeking to exercise that right. The purely hypothetical possibility that an individual may at some time in the future seek work in another Member State is not sufficient.[23] Thus, whilst a custodial sentence clearly limits the possibility to move, it cannot of itself be considered as a restriction to one of the free movement provisions since a 'purely hypothetical' prospect of exercising a Treaty right is not sufficient to trigger the necessary cross-border element.[24]

B – Vertical, Semi-horizontal and Horizontal Effect

Article 45 TFEU is directly effective.[25] It can be relied upon by the worker, even in a case in which the adverse effects on a worker result from obligations imposed by national law upon the employer,[26] as well as by an employer who wishes to employ, in a Member State in which she is established, a worker who is a national of another Member State.[27] As the Court said in *Clean Car Autoservice*:

> While those rights are undoubtedly enjoyed by those directly referred to—namely, workers— there is nothing in the wording of [Article 45 TFEU] to indicate that they may not be relied upon by others, in particular employers.[28]

As any directly effective provision, Article 45 TFEU applies to all rules, acts and practices of public authorities. Furthermore, it also applies to rules of any other nature aimed at regulating gainful employment in a collective manner.[29] Otherwise, the effect of the Treaty

---

[20] Case 175/78 *Saunders* [1979] ECR 1129; Case 298/84 *Iorio* [1986] ECR 247; Case C-332/90 *Steen* [1992] ECR I-341; Case C-132/93 *Steen* [1994] ECR I-2715; Joined Cases C-64/96 and C-65/96 *Uecker* [1997] ECR I-3171.

[21] Case 175/78 *Saunders* [1979] ECR 1129.

[22] Joined Cases 35 and 36/82 *Morson* [1982] ECR 3723.

[23] Case 180/83 *Moser* [1984] ECR 2539; however, as we have seen in Chapter 15 above, a purely hypothetical intention to move might be enough to trigger the citizenship provisions: see Case C-148/02 *Garcia Avello* [2003] ECR I-11613, although in that case the dual nationality of the applicants was the determinant factor. In the case of the free movement of services a potential cross-border element is enough: see eg Case C-405/98 *Gourmet International (GIP)* [2001] ECR I-1795; Case C-355/00 *Freskot* [2003] ECR I-5263; on this point see E Spaventa, *Free Movement of Persons in the EU: Barriers to Movement in their Constitutional Context* (Alphen aan den Rijn, Kluwer Law International, 2007) ch 3.

[24] Case C-299/95 *Kremzow* [1997] ECR I-2629.

[25] eg Case 48/75 *Royer* [1977] ECR 497, para 23; Case 41/74 *Van Duyn v Home Office* [1974] ECR 1337; Case C-90/96 *Petrie and Others* [1997] ECR I-6527, para 28.

[26] Case C-27/91 *Union de Recouvrement des Cotisations de Sécurité Sociale et d'Allocations Familiales de la Savoie (URSSAF) v Hostellerie Le Manoir SARL.* [1991] ECR I-5531, para 9.

[27] Case C-350/96 *Clean Car* [1998] ECR I-2521.

[28] Ibid, para 19.

[29] Art 7(4) Regulation 1612/68; eg Case 36/74 *Walrave* [1974] ECR 1405, para 17; Case C-415/93 *Bosman* [1995] ECR I-4921, para 82; and more recently Case C-400/02 *Merida* [2004] ECR I-847; in the field of establishment and services the Court has made clear that the Treaty applies also to industrial action: see Case C-438/05 *International Transport Workers' Federation and The Finnish Seamen's Union v Viking Line et al* [2007] ECR I-10779; Case C-341/05 *Laval un Partneri* [2007] ECR I-11767; see also Chapter 11 above and Chapter 17 below.

would have been greatly reduced since, especially in the continent, a significant proportion of labour relations is regulated by means of collective agreements.

Moreover, the Court has expanded the scope of Article 45 TFEU to apply (at least partially) also in horizontal situations, ie when the claim involves private parties. In *Angonese* the Court held that the prohibition on discrimination on grounds of nationality contained in Article 45 TFEU applies also to private employers. The Court drew a parallel with the prohibition of discrimination on grounds of sex (Article 157 TFEU) which also binds private employers: both provisions, the Court held, are designed to ensure that there is no discrimination in relation to the labour market, and therefore bind private as well as state parties.[30] In *Angonese* the Court was quite careful in delimiting the possibility of relying on Article 45 TFEU against a private party to claims relating to discrimination on grounds on nationality. To extend the horizontal application of Article 45 TFEU also to non-discriminatory barriers (see below) would in fact be a step too far in that it would risk unduly limiting the contractual freedom of private parties.[31]

B – Territorial Application

The application of Article 45 TFEU is not conditional upon all conduct pertaining to an economic relationship or activity occurring within the territory of the Member States: it applies in judging all legal relationships which can be localised within the EU, by reason either of the place where they were entered into, or the place where they take effect.[32] In *Boukhalfa* the Court held that the latter principle must be deemed to extend to cases in which there was a sufficiently close link between the employment relationship, on the one hand, and the law of a Member State and thus the relevant rules of Union law, on the other. The Court concluded that Article 45 TFEU applied where a national of a Member State (a Belgian) permanently resident in a non-Member country (Algeria) was employed by another Member State (Germany) in its embassy in that non-Member country, where that person's contract of employment was entered into and permanently performed in that latter country, and where the plaintiff's situation was subject to the law of the employing state in several respects. The consequence was that the prohibition of discrimination laid down in the Treaty applied to all aspects of the employment relationship which were governed by the law of the employing Member State.[33]

---

[30] Case C-281/98 *Angonese* [2000] ECR I-4139, esp paras 34–36; Case C-94/07 *Raccanelli v Max-Planck-Gesellschaft zur Förderung der Wissenschaften eV* [2008] ECR I-5939.

[31] eg a clause providing for a penalty for termination of a fixed-term contract could be construed as a barrier to movement. In *Viking* and *Laval*, above n 29, the Treaty provisions on services and establishment were applied horizontally to direct barriers to movement.

[32] Case 36/74 *Walrave* [1974] ECR 1405; Case 237/83 *Prodest* [1984] ECR 3153; Case 9/88 *Lopes da Veiga* [1989] ECR 2989.

[33] Case C-214/94 *Boukhalfa* [1996] ECR I-2253.

III – THE PERSONAL SCOPE OF APPLICATION OF ARTICLE 45 TFEU: THE CONCEPT OF 'WORKER'

A – The Definition of Worker

The definition of 'worker' (and self-employed) was of paramount importance before the introduction of Union citizenship since until then, and as noted in the previous chapter, EU law conferred free movement rights only on economic migrants and their families. Even after the introduction of Union citizenship, however, the correct identification of the legal basis for the exercise of EU rights is highly relevant. As we have seen in the previous chapter, workers (and economically active migrants in general) benefit from more extensive rights than non-economically active Union migrants. In particular, economic migrants have an unconditional right of residence (ie not dependent upon resources/insurance), as well as a right to access most welfare benefits as if they were nationals of the host-Member State. Thus, it will be in the interest of the Union citizen to be defined, whenever possible, as a 'worker' (or self-employed),[34] rather than just as a Union citizen.

Given the fact that non-economically active migrants were not protected by then Community law, it is not surprising that the Court gave a broad and purposive interpretation to who was to be defined as a worker and therefore come within the personal scope of application of Article 45 TFEU. Thus, the term cannot be defined according to the national laws of the Member States, as otherwise the meaning would vary from state to state, but has a EU meaning.[35] The Court has in its case law held that the essential characteristic of the employment relationship is that for a certain period a person performs services for and under the direction of another person in return for which she/he receives remuneration.[36] Since the concepts of worker and employed person define the field of application of one of the fundamental freedoms guaranteed by the Treaty, they must not be interpreted restrictively.[37] For this reason the Court has held that part-time workers whose activity is genuine and not ancillary are also protected by Article 45 TFEU. Otherwise a large number of those who seek to improve their living conditions through part-time work would be excluded from the scope of the Treaty.[38] Thus, the Court held in *Levin*:

> Since part-time employment, although it may provide an income lower that what is to be considered to be the minimum required for subsistence, constitutes for a large number of persons an effective means to improve their living conditions, the effectiveness of Community law would be impaired and the achievement of the objectives of the Treaty would be jeopardised if the

---

[34] The difference between workers and self-employed is less crucial since the Court has clarified that Arts 45, 59 and 56 TFEU are based on the same principles: see Case 48/75 *Royer* [1969] ECR 197, and more recently Case C-55/94 *Gebhard* [1995] ECR I-4165. However, the distinction might still be relevant in determining the proportionality of restrictions, as well as in relation to the transitional arrangements for new Member States: see Case C-268/99 *Jany amd others* [2001] ECR I-8615, and see below section VII.

[35] Case 75/63 *Hoekstra (neé Unger)* [1964] ECR 177; Case 53/81 *Levin* [1982] ECR 1035.

[36] Case 66/85 *Lawrie-Blum* [1986] ECR 2121, paras 16 and 17; Case 85/96 *Martinez Sala* [1998] ECR I-2691, para 32; in Case C-94/07 *Raccanelli v Max-Planck- Gesellschaft zur Förderung der Wissenschaften e V* [2008] ECR I-5939 the Court gave very little guidance as to whether doctoral students should be defined as workers.

[37] Case 53/81 *Levin* [1982] ECR 1035; Joined Cases 389 and 390/87 *Echternach* [1989] ECR 723.

[38] Furthermore since in most industries women form most of the part-time workforce, to exclude part-timers from the scope of Art 45 TFEU would have had sex discrimination implications.

enjoyment of rights conferred by the principle of freedom of movement of workers were reserved solely to persons engaged in full time employment earning, as a result, a wage at least equivalent to the guaranteed minimum wage in the sector under consideration.[39]

This is the case even when the part-time worker works just a few hours a week and his/her pay falls below the minimum wage so that she/he has to rely on welfare provision to supplement his/her earnings. Thus, for instance, in *Kempf* a German piano teacher giving 12 lessons a week in Belgium was held to be a worker and for this reason was entitled to welfare provision to supplement his salary as well as benefits when he found himself incapable to work for health reasons.[40] This is the case also for a person engaged in preparatory training in the course of occupational training, who has to be regarded as a worker if the training period is completed under the conditions of genuine and effective activity as an employed person, even if the trainee's productivity is low, and he/she works only a small number of hours per week and consequently receives limited remuneration.[41]

The fact that a worker has worked for only a short period of time in a fixed-term contract does not exclude her/him from the scope of Article 45 TFEU, provided that the activity was not purely marginal and ancillary. In *Ninni-Orasche*[42] the issue under consideration was whether the claimant, who had worked for just two and a half months, could nonetheless be considered a worker, and therefore have a right not to be discriminated against on grounds of nationality in relation to study finance for a university course (Article 7(2) Regulation 1612/68—see below). The Court instructed the national court to have sole regard to the nature of the activity, ie whether it was genuine and not purely ancillary, in order to determine the status of Ms Ninni-Orasche, and to disregard any other consideration, including the fact that she had taken up the job years after having first entered the host territory; that soon after taking up the job she obtained a qualification which made her eligible for university enrolment; and the that she was looking for a job in between finishing her short fixed-term employment and enrolling at university.

The reason why an individual moves to seek work in another Member State is immaterial to her/his qualification as a worker. Thus, it is irrelevant that a person has moved for the sole purpose of triggering the Treaty and therefore benefit of rights granted by EU law, provided that he/she pursues or wishes to pursue an effective and genuine activity.[43] However, in *Brown* the Court held that if the primary purpose for which the person has moved is to undertake university education, and the employed activity, whilst being genuine, is purely ancillary to the studies, then the rights to equal treatment in relation to social advantages might be of more limited application, and the worker/student will not be entitled to maintenance grants otherwise available to workers who, after having worked, decide to pursue training relevant to their previous occupation.[44]

Furthermore, even though the concept of worker is generously construed, it still covers only the pursuit of *effective* and *genuine* activities, and not activities on such a small scale as to be regarded as 'marginal and ancillary'.[45] Work cannot be regarded as an effective and genuine economic activity if it constitutes merely a means of rehabilitation or reintegra-

---

[39] Case 53/81 *Levin* [1982] ECR 1035.
[40] Case 139/85 *Kempf* [1986] ECR 1741.
[41] Case 66/85 *Lawrie-Blum* [1986] ECR 2121, paras 19–21; Case 344/87 *Battray* [1989] ECR 1621, para 15; Case C-3/90 *Bernini* [1992] ECR 1071, paras 15 and 16.
[42] Case C-413/01 *Ninni-Orasche* [2003] ECR I-13187, para 32.
[43] Case 53/81 *Levin* [1982] ECR 1035; Case C-109/01 *Akrich* [2003] ECR I-9607.
[44] Case 197/86 *Brown* [1988] ECR 3205; Case C-3/90 *Bernini* [1992] ECR I-1071, paras 20 and 21.
[45] Case 53/81 *Levin* [1982] ECR 1035; case C-413/01 *Ninni-Orasche* [2003] ECR I-13187.

tion for the persons concerned and the purpose of the paid employment, which is adapted to the physical and mental capabilities of each person, is to enable those persons sooner or later to recover their capacity to take ordinary employment or to lead as normal as possible a life.[46] In the case of *Trojani*[47] a French citizen living in Belgium worked about 30 hours a week for the Salvation Army as part of a personal socio-occupational reintegration scheme; in return for his work he received board, lodging and some pocket money. He then claimed subsistence benefits, which were denied on the grounds that he was not a worker within the meaning of Article 45 TFEU and was therefore not entitled to social assistance. In a preliminary ruling, the Court of Justice held that in deciding whether work is to be regarded as an 'effective and genuine' economic activity the national court

> must in particular ascertain whether the services actually performed by Mr Trojani are capable of being regarded as forming part of the normal labour market. For that purpose, account may be taken of the status and practices of the hostel, the content of the social reintegration programme, and the nature and details of performance of the services.[48]

B – Retention of Status of Worker

We have seen in the previous chapter that an economically active Union citizen might retain her/his status as worker or self-employed when she/he is unable to work as a result of illness and accident; she/he is duly recorded in involuntary unemployment having been employed for more than one year and having registered as a work-seeker; if a worker has been employed for less than a year, her/his status as a worker is retained for no less than six months; or she/he embarks in vocational training related to the previous employment—in the case of involuntarily unemployment the latter condition does not apply, and the worker can choose any vocational training.[49] The retention of the status of worker is important both in order to establish unconditional residence, and for entitlement to welfare benefits. In relation to vocational training, welfare benefits include maintenance grants during education, and Directive 2004/38 codifies, seemingly in a slightly more generous way, pre-existing case law.

In the case of *Lair*[50] the Court—relying on the fact that secondary legislation provided for rights for workers who are no longer active either because of involuntary unemployment, illness or retirement—held that migrant workers 'are guaranteed certain rights linked to the status of worker even when they are no longer in an employment relationship'.[51] It then specified that concerning maintenance grants for education, there should be either some continuity between the previous occupational activity and the studies undertaken; or involuntary unemployment, combined with job market conditions, has obliged the worker to retrain in another field. As we have seen above, in relation to involuntarily unemployed workers, Article 7(3)(d) of Directive 2004/38 does not link the possibility to retrain in another field to the conditions of the job market.

What constitutes 'involuntary unemployment' depends on the circumstances. Thus the

---

[46] Case 344/87 *Bettray* [1989] ECR 1621.
[47] Case C-456/02 *Trojani* [2004] ECR I-7574.
[48] Ibid, para 24.
[49] Art 7(3) Directive 2004/38.
[50] Case 39/86 *Lair* [1988] ECR 3161.
[51] Ibid, para 36.

Court has clarified that a worker might be qualified as involuntarily unemployed even when she/he is unemployed as a result of the expiry of a fixed-term contract,[52] ie when the unemployment is not caused by dismissal. Whether in such cases the worker is involuntarily unemployed depends on several circumstances and in particular the structure of the labour market in that sector, ie whether the fixed-term contract is usual practice in the sector concerned, whether it is imposed on the worker, etc. Finally, in order to avoid abuses of EU law directed at exploiting the welfare provision of the host Member State, the Court has clarified that the 'worker' does not retain her/his status in relation to maintenance grants when the employment is purely ancillary to the studies about to be undertaken.[53] Again, Directive 2004/38 does not contain this caveat.

C – Work-seekers

Article 45 TFEU would lose much of its effect if Union citizens were not entitled to move in order to seek work, as it can be difficult to locate employment opportunities in one country while living in another. For this reason, the Court had no hesitation in holding that Article 45 TFEU also applies to work-seekers, who have a right to move to another Member State to seek employment.[54] As we have seen in the previous chapter, Directive 2004/38 has codified the case law and work-seekers have an unconditional right of stay for three months, and are entitled to stay beyond that time if they can prove that they are looking for employment and that they have a genuine chance of being engaged.[55]

Originally, the Court had excluded work-seekers from the right to equal treatment in relation to social and tax advantages, and limited their right to equal treatment to access to the labour market. Thus, even though Union citizens could move to any of the Member States in order to look for a job, they could not claim social assistance from the authorities of the host Member State. Rather, the work-seeker was (and is) entitled under Regulation 883/2004[56] to 'export', where possible, to the host Member State such benefits as she/he would have been entitled to in her/his home Member State. This system was clearly inspired by the desire to avoid welfare tourism, ie the instrumental use of the free movement provisions for the sole purpose of exploiting the most generous welfare system available, and, prima facie has been maintained in Directive 2004/38 since Article 24(2) provides that Member States are not obliged to grant social assistance to work-seekers. That said, the Court's case law significantly curtails the extent to which the exclusion from the right to equal treatment can validly be invoked.

In the case of *Collins*[57] Mr Collins was an Irish citizen who went to the United Kingdom, and whilst looking for a job claimed unemployment benefits. He was denied the benefit on the grounds that he was not habitually resident in the United Kingdom; since he was not

---

[52] Case C-413/01 *Ninni-Orasche* [2003] ECR I-13187, para 32, and see Art 7(3)(c) Directive 2004/38.

[53] Case 197/86 *Brown* [1988] ECR 3205.

[54] Case C-292/89 *Antonissen* [1991] ECR I-745; Case C-344/95 *Commission v Belgium* [1997] ECR I-1035. In *Antonissen*, the Court held that six months was to be considered a 'reasonable time', and in *Commission v Belgium* it held that even three months would be enough. Art 5 Regulation 1612/68 makes clear that work-seekers have a right to receive the same assistance from the host Member State as that granted to own nationals.

[55] Arts 6 and 14(4)(b) Directive 2004/38. See also Chapter 15 above.

[56] Regulation 883/2004 [2004] OJ L200/1 and Regulation 1408/71 beforehand.

[57] Case C-138/02 *Collins* [2004] ECR I-2703.

a worker but a work-seeker he was not, according to the Court's own previous case law,[58] entitled to equal treatment in relation to welfare benefits. The case reached the Court before the adoption of Directive 2004/38, so that the latter was not legally relevant; however, the Court was aware of the draft provisions on the exclusion of work-seekers from the right to equal treatment in relation to social assistance since those had been discussed in the Opinion of the Advocate General.[59] This notwithstanding, the Court decided that the time was ripe for a change in its interpretation of Article 45 TFEU in the light of the introduction of Union citizenship. Since Union citizens are entitled to equal treatment in regard to all matters falling within the material scope of the Treaty,[60] it was no longer possible to exclude from the scope of application of Article 45(2) TFEU (which provides for the general right to equal treatment of workers) benefits of a financial nature for work-seekers. Thus, following the ruling, work-seekers became fully protected by Article 45 TFEU, and would be entitled to equal treatment in the host Member State, even in relation to welfare benefits. However, the Court also made clear that Member States could justify indirect discrimination (a residence requirement is always to be so considered), in particular by claiming the necessity to ensure that a genuine link exists between claimant and labour market, therefore limiting, if not eliminating, the possibility of welfare tourism. The Court then recognised that a residence requirement is, in principle, an appropriate way of ensuring that the claimant is genuinely seeking work (although, the length of residence required must not go beyond what is necessary).[61]

The ruling in *Collins* created a prima facie tension between the Court's interpretation of Article 45 TFEU and the provisions of Directive 2004/38 which allowed Member States to exclude work-seekers from the right to equal treatment in relation to social assistance. Since secondary legislation must comply with the Treaty, there was a danger that the *Collins* interpretation might lead to the (partial) annulment of Article 24 Directive 2004/38; otherwise, the Court would have had to revisit its case law. The occasion for clarification manifested itself in the case of *Vatsouras*,[62] where a German court inquired as to the relationship between Article 45 TFEU and Directive 2004/38. The case related to two Greek nationals who were denied a job-seeker benefit. The Court confirmed that:

> [I]n view of the establishment of citizenship of the Union and the interpretation of the right to equal treatment enjoyed by citizens of the Union, it is no longer possible to exclude from the scope of [Article 45(2) TFEU] a benefit of a financial nature intended to facilitate access to employment in the labour market of a Member State.[63]

The Court then restated that it was legitimate for Member States to limit the grant of such benefits to claimants having established a real link with the employment market,[64] and such a link can be determined having regard to the fact that the claimant has genuinely sought work in the host Member State for a reasonable time. After having clarified that

---

[58] Case 316/85 *Lebon* [1987] ECR 2811; Case C-278/94 *Commission v Belgium* [1996] ECR I-4307.

[59] See AG Ruiz-Jarabo Colomer's Opinion, Case C-138/02 *Collins* [2004] ECR I-2703, para 69.

[60] See in particular Case C-184/99 *Grzelcyk* [2001] ECR I-6193 and Case C-224/98 *D'Hoop* [2002] ECR I-6191, and the discussion in the previous chapter.

[61] The ruling in *Collins* was confirmed in Case C-258/04 *Ioannidis* [2005] ECR I-8275 (again Directive 2004/38 was not relevant in that case).

[62] Joined Cases C-22/08 and 23/08 *Vatsouras and Koupatantze* [2009] ECR I-4585.

[63] Ibid, para 37.

[64] On the notion of real link, see C O'Brien, 'Real Links, Abstract Rights and False Alarms: The Relationship between the ECJ's "Real Link" Case Law and National Solidarity' (2008) 33 *ELRev* 643.

Article 24(2) of Directive 2004/38 had to be interpreted consistently with Article 45(2) TFEU, the Court then held that:

> Benefits of a financial nature which, independently of their status under national law, are intended to facilitate access to the labour market cannot be regarded as constituting 'social assistance' within the meaning of Article 24(2) of Directive 2004/38.[65]

In this way the Court reconciled the letter of the Directive with its interpretation in *Collins*: nevertheless, the case has been criticised since the Court betrayed the legislature's intentions, which was clearly to ensure that work-seekers would be welcomed only in so far as they do not represent a burden on the public purse. In any event, it should be remembered that not *all* work-seekers are entitled to benefits facilitating access to the labour market: a real link between claimant and host state is still required. Furthermore, Article 14(4) makes the right to stay in the host Member State beyond the first three months conditional upon evidence that the work-seeker is continuing to look for employment; *and* that she has a genuine chance of finding a job. Finally, it is only those benefits which have a link with the employment market that are covered by the Court's interpretation; other benefits, such as housing or disability allowances, continue to be reserved to permanent residents and economically active citizens.

IV – THE MATERIAL SCOPE OF ARTICLE 45 TFEU: ACCESS TO EMPLOYMENT AND EQUAL TREATMENT

The Treaty provides that freedom of movement for workers shall entail the right to move freely within the Member States for the purpose of accepting offers of employment actually made, as well as a right not to be discriminated against on grounds of nationality. The provisions of Article 45 TFEU are directly effective,[66] as were those of Directive 68/360, and now of Directive 2004/38.[67]

A – Right to Move and Reside in Member States

As we have seen in the previous chapter, Directive 2004/38—like Directive 68/360 before it—grants the worker a right to enter any Member State in order to seek or take up employment; to move freely within the territory of that Member State; and to reside there. Moreover, the right to enter, move and reside can be limited only by invoking grounds of public policy, public security or public health. Those are narrowly construed as they are derogations from a fundamental EU right.[68] After five years of lawful residence, the worker (and her/his family) can obtain a right to reside permanently in the host Member

---

[65] Joined Cases C-22/08 and 23/08 *Vatsouras and Koupatantze* [2009] ECR I-4585, para 45.
[66] Case 167/73 *Commission v France* [1974] ECR 359; Case 41/74 *Van Duyn* [1974] ECR 1337.
[67] Case 36/75 *Rutili* [1975] ECR 1219; the Court explained in Case 48/75 *Royer* [1976] ECR 497 that 'the directives concerned [including 68/360] determined the scope and detailed rules for the exercise of rights conferred directly by the Treaty'.
[68] See above Chapter 15.

State, and, as we have seen in the previous chapter, in certain cases (retirement and incapacity) the right of permanent residence can be acquired before five years.[69]

Article 45 TFEU does not exclude the right of Member States to adopt reasonable measures to keep track of the movement of aliens within their territory.[70] On the other hand, while Member States may impose penalties for failure to comply with the requirements of Union law relating to migrants, such penalties must be comparable to those attaching to the infringement of provisions of equal importance by nationals, and such punishment must be proportionate to the gravity of the offences involved. [71]

B – The Right to Equal Treatment

(i) General

Article 45(2) TFEU provides that freedom of movement for workers shall entail the abolition of any discrimination based on nationality between workers of Member States as regards employment, remuneration, and other conditions of work and employment. According to the Court's case law, the prohibition on discrimination on grounds of nationality encompasses both direct and indirect discrimination.

Direct discrimination occurs when the national and the non-national are treated differently in law; as we shall see below, such discrimination can only be justified on one of the grounds listed in Article 45(3) and (4) TFEU. Indirect discrimination occurs when an apparently neutral rule affects non-nationals more heavily than nationals—for example, a residence requirement is indirectly discriminatory since nationals are more likely than non-nationals to be resident in the national territory.[72] Indirect discrimination can be justified by imperative requirements of public interest, ie when it pursues an aim compatible with Union law (an interest worthy of protection); and when the restriction it imposes on the enjoyment of the right granted by Union law is necessary to achieve that aim, as well as proportionate. Furthermore, and as seen in Chapter 11, when the Member States invoke either a Treaty derogation or an imperative requirement to justify a rule, the situation falls within the scope of Union law and the rule must also respect fundamental rights as general principles of Union law.

Whereas Directive 2004/38 ensures entry and residence for Union workers,[73] as well as a general right to equal treatment (Article 24(1)), the right to equal treatment in respect of job opportunity and conditions of employment is detailed by Regulation 1612/68 on freedom of movement for workers within the EU.[74] Part I of the Regulation is divided into three Titles:

— Eligibility for employment.

---

[69] Art 17 Directive 2004/38, see Chapter 15.

[70] Case 118/75 *Watson and Belmann* [1976] ECR 1185; but a requirement that nationals of other Member States make a declaration of residence within three days of arrival is unreasonable and contrary to Union law: Case 265/88 *Messner* [1989] ECR 4209.

[71] Case 118/75 *Watson and Belmann* [1976] ECR 1185, para 21.

[72] See generally Case C-237/94 *O'Flynn* [1996] ECR I-2617.

[73] And such rights were previously ensured by Directive 68/360.

[74] [1968] OJ L257/2, OJ Sp Edn (II), 475. The right to equal treatment is of course granted directly by Art 45 TFEU and the Court has made clear that Regulation 1612/68 is therefore not constitutive of rights granted directly by the Treaty. This means that the fact that a given right is not mentioned in the Regulation is immaterial if that right is seen as to be conferred directly by Art 45 TFEU.

— Employment and equality of treatment.
— Workers' families.

The Title concerning the workers' family has been moved to Directive 2004/38, with the exception of Article 12 which provides for equal treatment regarding education of workers' children. It is convenient to adopt the scheme of the Regulation for the purposes of exposition of its terms and discussion of the case law of the Court.

(ii) Eligibility for Employment

Regulation 1612/68 guarantees to workers the right to take up employment in the territory of a Member State with the same priority as the nationals of the Member State in question.[75] Employees and employers are entitled to exchange their applications for, and offers of, employment and to conclude and perform contracts in accordance with 'the provisions in force laid down by law, regulation or administrative action, without any discrimination resulting therefrom'.[76]

National provisions, whether the result of legal regulation or administrative action, are stated to be inapplicable if they limit explicitly or implicitly the right of workers to take up and pursue employment.[77] An exception is made in the case of linguistic requirements necessitated by the nature of the post to be filled.[78] In the *Groener* case[79] the Court considered the compatibility with Regulation 1612/68 of national rules making appointment to a permanent full-time post as a lecturer in public vocational educational institutions conditional upon proof of an adequate knowledge of the Irish language. Knowledge of the Irish language was not required for the performance of the duties which teaching of the kind at issue specifically entailed. The Court held, however, that the post justified the requirement of linguistic knowledge, provided that the requirement in question was imposed as part of a policy for the promotion of the national language which was the first official language; and provided that the request was applied in a proportionate and non-discriminatory manner. A language requirement is considered indirectly discriminatory also when imposed by the employer rather than by legislation. Whilst in this case Article 3 of Regulation 1612/68 is not relevant, in the above-mentioned case of *Angonese* the Court held that the requirement to possess a certificate of bilingualism issued by a local authority, without the applicant being allowed to prove language proficiency by alternative means, infringed the principle of equal treatment as provided for in Article 45(2) TFEU (nationals being more likely to reside in the region and therefore to have acquired the regional language certificate).[80]

Article 3 of Regulation 1612/68 itemises, as particular instances of the provisions declared inapplicable by the foregoing, those that:

(a) prescribe a special recruitment procedure for foreign nationals;
(b) limit or restrict the advertising of vacancies in the press or through any other medium or subject it to conditions other than those applicable in respect of employers pursuing their activities in the territory of that Member State;

---

[75] Art 1(2).
[76] Art 2.
[77] Art 3(1).
[78] Article 3(1), last sub-para.
[79] Case 378/87 [1989] ECR 3967.
[80] Case C-281/98 *Angonese* [2000] ECR I-4139.

(c) subject eligibility for employment to conditions of registration with employment offices or impede recruitment of individual workers where persons who do not reside in the territory of that Member State are concerned.

Article 4 of the Regulation provides that national rules restricting by number or percentage the employment of foreign nationals are to be inapplicable to nationals of the Member States. In *Commission v France*[81] the Court held that France had infringed Article 45 TFEU and Article 4 of Regulation 1612/68 by providing for a maximum ratio of one foreigner to three Frenchmen in certain jobs on sea vessels. Faced with the French government's objection that it had given instructions that such provision should not apply to EU nationals, and that in practice it was not applied to them, the Court acknowledged that whilst the objective legal situation was clear—namely that Article 45 TFEU and Regulation 1612/68 were directly applicable in France—the fact that the non-discriminatory application of the offending rules appeared to be a matter of grace, not of law, brought about an ambiguous situation creating uncertainty for those subject to the law.

Regulation 1612/68 further provides that the engagement or recruitment of a national of one Member State for a post in another Member State shall not depend on medical, vocational or other criteria which are discriminatory by comparison with those applied in the case of national workers.[82] Nevertheless, when an employer actually offers a job to a national of another Member State, she/he may expressly make this offer conditional on the candidate undergoing a vocational test.[83] An issue not addressed by Regulation 1612/68 is that of national requirements to the effect that those carrying on certain activities be in possession of certain qualifications. Such requirements also affect self-employed activities, and the exercise of the right of establishment and the freedom to provide services. The compatibility of such requirements with Articles 45, 49 and 56 TFEU, and the effect of directives on mutual recognition of qualifications on the exercise of employed and self-employed activities, are considered in some detail in Chapter 19.

(a) The Public Service Proviso

As we have seen, Member States cannot impose nationality conditions for access to employment. However, there is an exception to this rule, and Member States are entitled to reserve some posts in the public service to their own nationals. Article 45(4) TFEU provides that the 'provisions of this Article shall not apply to employment in the public service'. The provision does not apply to all employment in the public service, nor does it allow discrimination in the terms and conditions of employment once appointed. This much is clear from the judgment in *Sotgiu*,[84] in which the referring court sought a ruling from the Court of Justice on the question whether or not Article 7 of Regulation 1612/68 (the right to equal treatment) was applicable to employees in the German postal service in view of this proviso. The Court replied that since the exception contained in Article 45(4) TFEU could not be allowed a scope extending beyond the object for which it was included, the provision could be invoked to restrict the admission of foreign nationals

---

[81] Case 167/73 *Commission v France* [1974] ECR 359.
[82] Art 6(1).
[83] Art 6(2).
[84] Case 152/73 [1974] ECR 153.

to *certain activities* in the public service, but *not* to justify discrimination once they had been admitted.[85]

The Court further clarified the scope of Article 45(4) TFEU in *Commission v Belgium* (No 1), holding that that provision

> removes from the ambit of Article [45(1) to (3) TFEU] a series of posts which involve direct or indirect participation in the exercise of powers conferred by public law and duties designed to safeguard the general interests of the State or of other public authorities. Such posts in fact presume on the part of those occupying them the existence of a special relationship of allegiance to the State and reciprocity of rights and duties which form the foundation of the bond of nationality.[86]

Thus not all posts in the public service fall within the public service proviso. In the Court's view, to extend Article 45(4) TFEU to posts which, while coming under the purview of the state or other organisations governed by public law, still do not involve any association with tasks belonging to the public service properly so called, would be to remove a considerable number of posts from the ambit of the principles set out in the Treaty and to create inequalities between the Member States according to the different ways in which the state and certain sectors of economic life are organised.

Nevertheless, classification of particular posts can cause difficulty. In *Commission v Belgium* (No 2)[87] the Court approved the Commission's concession that the following posts fell within the ambit of Article 45(4) TFEU: head technical office supervisor; principal supervisor; works supervisor; stock controller; and nightwatchman, with the municipalities of Brussels and Auderghem. The Court also upheld the Commission's view that a number of other jobs with Belgian National Railways, Belgian Local Railways, the city of Brussels, and the commune of Auderghem fell outside Article 45(4) TFEU. These jobs included railway shunters, drivers, platelayers, signalmen and nightwatchmen, and nurses, electricians, joiners and plumbers employed by the municipality of Auderghem.

Participation in the exercise of powers conferred by public law would clearly cover the exercise of police powers not exercisable by the ordinary citizen, and the exercise of other binding powers such as the grant or refusal of planning permission. A Commission notice has stated that:

> [T]he derogation in [Article 45(4) TFEU] covers specific functions of the State and similar bodies such as the armed forces, the police and other forces for the maintenance of order, the judiciary, the tax authorities and the diplomatic corps. . . . The derogation is also seen as covering posts in State Ministries, regional government authorities, local authorities and other similar bodies, central banks and other public bodies, where the duties of the post involve the exercise of State authority, such as the preparation of legal acts, the implementation of such acts, monitoring of their application and supervision of subordinate bodies.[88]

---

[85] On the point that Art 45(4) TFEU cannot justify discrimination if non-nationals are admitted to the public service, see also Case 225/85 *Commission v Italy* [1987] ECR 2625, and Cases 389 and 390/87 *Echternach* [1987] ECR 723. The Northern Ireland Court of Appeal has held that admission of non-nationals to a post in the public service within the meaning of Art 45(4) TFEU does not preclude subsequent reliance on the public service proviso as regards the post in question: *In the Matter of an Application by Edward Michael O'Boyle for Judicial Review; In the matter of an Applicaton by Suzanne Plunkett for Judicial Review*, Judgment of 19 February 1999, unreported.

[86] Case 149/79 [1980] ECR 3881, para 10.

[87] Case 149/79 [1982] ECR 1845.

[88] [1988] OJ C72/2; in Case C-392/05 *Alevizos* [2007] ECR I-3505, the Court held that a position in NATO could fall within the concept of public service (para 69).

The nature of some of the posts held in *Commission v Belgium* above to fall within the public service proviso seems to suggest that the reference to participation in the exercise of powers conferred by public law includes the exercise of senior managerial powers over state resources. This is confirmed by the judgment of the Court in *Commission v Italy*,[89] in which the Court rejected the proposition that research posts at the national research centre (CNR) could be reserved to Italian nationals, and stated:

> Simply referring to the general tasks of the CNR and listing the duties of all its researchers is not sufficient to establish that the researchers are responsible for exercising powers conferred by public law or for safeguarding the general interests of the state. Only the duties *of management or of advising the state on scientific and technical questions could be described as employment in the public service within the meaning of* [Article 45(4) TFEU]. However, it has not been established that these duties were carried out by researchers.[90]

The italicised words in the above extract of the Court's judgment certainly suggest that managerial activities and advice to the state are regarded by the Court as falling within the scope of Article 45(4) TFEU, as interpreted by the Court in *Commission v Belgium*.

Whereas access to the public service posts in question will often be direct, it might also be by promotion from other posts which could not be classified along with those 'certain activities' to which access may be limited. It would seem to follow that Article 45(4) TFEU should be read as permitting discrimination against EU nationals already holding posts in the public service, insofar as promotion to 'sensitive' posts is concerned. This consideration was argued by the German Government in *Commission v Belgium*[91] to militate against construing Article 45(4) TFEU as only applying to certain posts within the public service, rather than to the public service at large. The Court's reply was that applying Article 45(4) TFEU to all posts in the public service would impose a restriction on the rights of nationals of other Member States which went further than was necessary to achieve the aims of the proviso.[92]

The public service exception can be relied upon even if the employer is a private person/company, provided that the worker would be exercising public law powers (such as the maintenance of law and order on a vessel). However, the Court has clarified that in order for the derogation in Article 45(4) TFEU to be relied upon, public law powers linked to a given position must be exercised on a regular basis and must not represent a 'very minor' part of the worker's activities.[93]

The Court of Justice has held that the following posts do not qualify for application of the public service proviso: a nurse in a public hospital;[94] a trainee teacher;[95] a foreign-language assistant at a university;[96] researchers at a national research centre;[97] and numerous public-sector posts covering teaching, research, inland transport, posts and telecommu-

---

[89] Case 225/85 [1987] ECR 2625.
[90] Ibid, para 9 (emphasis added).
[91] Case 149/79 [1980] ECR 3881.
[92] Applying the tests laid down by the Court of Justice, the Court of Appeal of Northern Ireland in the *O'Boyle* and *Plunkett* cases [1999] NI 126 [2000] EuLR 637, has found the post of Deputy Chief Fire Officer of Northern Ireland, and the post of Inland Revenue Claims Examiner, to be posts falling within the public service within the meaning of Art 45(4) TFEU.
[93] Case C-47/02 *Anker and others* [2003] ECR I-10447; see also Case C-405/01 *Colegio de Oficiales de la Marina Mercante Española* [2003] ECR I-10391.
[94] Case 307/84 *Commission v France* [1986] ECR 1725.
[95] Case 66/85 *Lawrie-Blum* [1986] ECR 2121.
[96] Case 33/88 *Allué and Coonan* [1989] ECR 1591.
[97] Case 225/85 *Commission v Italy* [1987] ECR 2625.

nications, and water, gas and electricity—posts such as these do not involve the direct or indirect participation in the exercise of powers conferred by public law and duties to safeguard the general interests of the state.[98] Article 45(4) TFEU cannot be relied upon by private security undertakings which do not as such comprise part of the public service.[99]

C – Equality in the Employment Context and Beyond

Article 45(2) TFEU provides for the abolition of discrimination based on nationality in terms and conditions of employment, and this prohibition is reiterated and expanded in Article 7(1) of the Regulation as follows:

> A worker who is a national of a Member State may not, in the territory of another Member State, be treated differently from national workers by reason of his nationality in respect of any conditions of employment and work, in particular as regards remuneration, dismissal, and should he become unemployed, re-instatement or re-employment.

Infringement of the principle of equality will occur where national legislation expressly attaches different terms to the conditions of employment of national workers and workers from other Member States. In *Marsman*[100] a Dutch national resident in the Netherlands was employed in Germany. After becoming incapacitated as a result of an accident at work, he was dismissed by his employer. German legislation provided that seriously disabled workers could not be dismissed without the approval of the main public assistance office. While this protection extended to nationals resident outside Germany, it applied only to non-nationals within the jurisdiction. Mr Marsman challenged the legality of his dismissal before a German court, which sought a ruling from the Court of Justice as to whether a (then) Community national in the position of Mr Marsman was entitled to the same protection against dismissal as that afforded to German nationals. The Court replied in the affirmative, emphasising that the social law of the then Community was based on the principle that the laws of every Member State were obliged to grant nationals of the other Member States employed in its territory all the legal advantages that it provided for its own citizens.

A slightly more complex situation arises when legislation makes certain advantages conditional upon criteria which, although theoretically applicable to nationals and non-nationals alike, will in practice be fulfilled only by nationals. The point is illustrated in *Ugliola*.[101] The respondent in the main suit was an Italian national employed by the appellant in Germany. He performed his military service in Italy between May 1965 and August 1966, and claimed the right to have this period taken into account in calculating his seniority with his employer. German legislation provided that military service in the German Army was to be taken into account for such purposes, but made no similar provision for services in the forces of other Member States. The German court seised of the dispute sought a preliminary ruling from the Court of Justice on the question whether Article 7 of Regulation 1612/68 entitled Mr Ugliola to have military service in his home country

---

[98] Case C-473/93 *Commission v Luxembourg* [1996] ECR I-3207.
[99] Case C-114/97 *Commission v Spain* [1998] ECR I-6717, para 33.
[100] Case 44/72 [1972] ECR 1243.
[101] Case 15/69 [1969] ECR 363.

taken into account for the purposes of the German legislation in question. In its observation to the Court, the German Government argued that the Job-protection Law was not discriminatory, since the possibility to have the period spent in the military taken into account (a) did not apply to nationals who served in the forces of other Member States and (b) applied to non-nationals who served in the German forces. Advocate General Gand regarded such an argument as tempting, but was not convinced, since performance of military service in the army of a Member State other than the one whose nationality one possessed was a hypothesis which the German Government conceded was quite theoretical. The Court agreed. The provisions of (then) Community law in question prohibited Member States from 'indirectly establishing discrimination'[102] in favour of their own nationals in such a way.[103]

The Court was faced with the problem of allegedly indirect discrimination once more in *Sotgiu*.[104] The plaintiff, an Italian whose family lived in Italy, was employed by the German postal service. He received a separation allowance at 7.50 DM per day, on the same basis as workers of German nationality. In accordance with a government circular the allowance paid to workers residing within Germany at the time of their recruitment was increased to 10 DM per day, while those workers residing abroad at the time of their recruitment—German and foreign alike—continued to receive the allowance at the old rate. Mr Sotgiu invoked Regulation 1612/68 before a German court, which sought a ruling, inter alia, on whether Article 7(1) of the Regulation could be interpreted as prohibiting discrimination on the basis of residence as well as on the basis of nationality. In the course of the arguments before the Court it became apparent that although workers residing within Germany at the time of the recruitment indeed received a larger allowance, it was conditional on their willingness to move to their place of work, and in any event was no longer paid after two years. No such conditions were attached to payment of the allowance to workers residing abroad at the time of the recruitment. The Court affirmed that Article 7 prohibited all covert forms of discrimination which, by the application of criteria other than nationality, nevertheless led to the same result.[105] Such an interpretation was consonant with the fifth recital to the Regulation, which required that equality of treatment for workers to be established in fact as well as in law. Application of criteria such as place of origin or residence, reasoned the Court, could, in appropriate circumstances, have a discriminatory effect in practice that would be prohibited by the Treaty and the Regulation. This would not, however, be the case where the payment of a separation allowance was made on conditions which took account of objective differences in the situation of workers, which differences could involve the place of residence of a worker when recruited. Similarly, the fact that in the case of one group of workers allowances were only temporary, while in the case of another they were of unlimited duration, could be a valid reason for differentiating between the amounts paid.

In *Biehl*[106] the Court considered a national rule whereby overpaid tax deducted from

---

[102] Ibid, para 6.

[103] But see Case C-315/94 *die Vos* [1996] ECR I-1417.

[104] Case 152/73 [1974] ECR 153.

[105] The Court has consistently held that Art 45 TFEU prohibits not only overt discrimination by reason of nationality, but also all forms of discrimination which, by the application of other distinguishing criteria, lead in fact to the same result: see eg Case 111/91 *Commission v Luxembourg* [1993] ECR I-817, para 9; Case C-419/92 *Ingetraut Scholz v Opera Universitaria di Cagliari* [1994] ECR I-505, para 7; Case 278/94 *Commission v Belgium* [1996] ECR I-4307, para 27.

[106] Case C-175/88 *Biehl* [1990] ECR I-1779.

salaries and wages was not repayable to taxpayers resident during only part of the year in the relevant Member State. The national tax administration argued that a difference in treatment between two distinct categories of taxpayers did not constitute discrimination if it was objectively justified, and that the rule prevented taxpayers from avoiding the effects of progressive taxation by spreading their tax liability between different Member States. The Court noted that there was a risk that the criterion of permanent residence in the national territory would work in particular against taxpayers who were nationals of other Member States. The Court rejected the justification offered by the national tax authorities since a national rule such as that at issue was liable to infringe the principle of equal treatment in various situations—in particular where no income arose during the year of assessment to the temporarily resident taxpayer in the country which he had left or in which he had taken up residence. In such a situation, the taxpayer would be treated less favourably than a residence taxpayer because he would lose the right to repayment of the over-deduction of tax which a residence taxpayer would always enjoy. It followed in the Court's view that such a measure was contrary to Article 45(2) TFEU. In *Bachmann*[107] the Court clarified that while a national rule making pension contributions tax deductible but confining this advantage to contributions made in the national territory was in principle contrary to Article 45 TFEU, it could be justified where the counterpart of making such contributions tax deductible was subjecting the resulting pensions to tax liability.

Unless it is objectively justified and proportionate to its aim, a provision of national law must be regarded as *indirectly* discriminatory if it is intrinsically liable to affect migrant workers more than national workers and if there is a consequent risk that it will place the former at a particular disadvantage.[108] As is clear from the cases referred to above, the Court has given a broad interpretation of the principle of indirect discrimination—and the best formulation of the concept has been given in the case of *O'Flynn*. In that case an Irish national working in the UK applied for a grant to cover the funeral expenses of his son. The British authorities refused to grant the benefit on the grounds that the funeral was taking place outside the UK territory. Mr O'Flynn claimed that such refusal was inconsistent with Article 7(2) Regulation 1612/68, as the grant was to be considered a social advantage which could not be made conditional upon directly or indirectly discriminatory criteria. The Court agreed. It held that:

> [C]onditions imposed by national law must be regarded as indirectly discriminatory where, although applicable irrespective of nationality, they affect essentially migrant workers . . . or the great majority of those affected are migrant workers . . ., where they are indistinctly applicable but can more easily be satisfied by national workers than by migrant workers . . . or where there is a risk that they may operate to the particular detriment of migrant workers.[109]

Thus the Court made clear that any rule that even only risks putting foreigners or migrants at a disadvantage has to be considered indirectly discriminatory and needs to be justified by an imperative requirement. Furthermore, the Court also clarified that, unlike sex discrimination law, it is enough for a rule 'potentially' to affect more migrants than nationals for it to be considered discriminatory. As a result, the claimant does not need to prove, via statistical means or otherwise, that the rule imposes a heavier burden on migrants.

---

[107] Case C-204/90 *Bachmann* [1992] ECR I-249.
[108] Case C-237/94 *O'Flynn* [1996] ECR I-2617, para 20; Case 57/96 *H Meints v Minister van Landbouw* [1997] ECR I-6689, para 45.
[109] Case C-237/94 *O'Flynn* [1996] ECR I-2617, para 18.

The mere likelihood of a rule so doing is enough to bring it within the scope of the prohibition on discrimination. Not surprisingly, then, the Court held that the rule in *O'Flynn* was indeed indirectly discriminatory since foreigners are more likely to want to have their relatives buried in their country of origin. Nor could the rule be justified by an imperative requirement. The United Kingdom sought to justify the rule having regard to the 'prohibitive costs and practical difficulties' of paying for a burial taking place outside the United Kingdom. The Court was not persuaded: the cost of transport was not reimbursed, and so the higher costs faced in relation to intra-state transport was not an issue; and, as far as the cost of the burial was concerned, the Court simply reminded the United Kingdom that it could adopt other, non-discriminatory, cost containing measures, such as fixing a lump sum or limiting the amount of the reimbursement to a given amount having regard to the normal cost of burial in the United Kingdom.

The Court seems willing to assume, on a common sense basis, that certain distinguishing criteria, especially if they contain a territorial element, such as a period of practical training administered by the authorities of the Member State in question, will in the vast majority of cases operate to the advantage of nationals rather than non-nationals.[110] The same reasoning imposes upon the Member States the duty to take into account employment in the public service of other Member States if they take into account experience gained in their own public service.[111]

D – Equality in Social and Tax Advantages

In order to ensure equality for EU workers in the employment context, Regulation 1612/68 provides that they shall have 'by virtue of the same right and under the same conditions as national workers . . . access to training in vocational schools and retraining centres'.[112] Freedom from discrimination for EU workers, although limited explicitly to the employment context in the Treaty, could not be achieved without requiring appropriate adjustments to all fields of national law and practice which might be likely to have an effect on the conditions under which migrants take up and pursue employment. For this reason, Article 7(2) of the Regulation provides that a national of one Member State employed in another 'shall enjoy the same social and tax advantages as national workers'. The wording and context of the Article suggest that it might be restricted to social and tax advantages conferred by national law on workers as such, but the Court of Justice has taken a more liberal view, as its judgment in *Cristini* illustrates. French legislation provided that in families of three or more children under the age of 18 years, the father, mother and each child under 18 years should receive a personal identity card entitling them to a reduction of between 30 and 75 per cent of the scheduled fare charged by

---

[110] Case C-27/91 *Union de Recouvrement des Cotisations de Sécurité Sociale et d'Allocations Familiales de la Savoie (URSSAF) v Hostellerie Le Manoir SARL* [1991] ECR I-5531, para 11. The Court will sometimes be in a position to make an assessment based on an actual numerical estimate of the relative numbers of nationals and non-nationals involved: eg Case 33/88 *Allué and Coonan* [1989] ECR 1591, in which the Court found indirect discrimination where 'only' 25% of persons affected were nationals of the host Member State: see para 32 of judgment. However, as mentioned above, a numerical estimate is not a precondition to establishing indirect discrimination.

[111] Case C-419/92 *Scholz* [1994] ECR I-505; Case C-15/96 *Schöning* [1998] ECR I-47; Case C-195/98 *Österreichischer Gewerkschaftsbund* [2000] ECR I-10497; Case C-278/03 *Commission v Italy* (State Schools) [2005] ECR I-3747.

[112] Art 7(3). For education and vocational training, see Chapter 19.

French railways, the SNCF. A French court sought a preliminary ruling from the Court of Justice on the question whether the reduction card issued by the SNCF to large families constituted for Member State workers a 'social advantage' within the meaning of Article 7(2) of the Regulation. The SNCF, in its observations to the Court, argued that Article 7(2) referred exclusively to advantages attaching to the nationals of Member States by virtue of their status as workers, and accordingly had no application to a benefit such as the reduction cards issued by the SNCF. The Court rejected this view, reasoning as follows:

> Although it is true that certain provisions in this article refer to relationships deriving from the contract of employment, there are others, such as those concerning reinstatement and re-employment should a worker become unemployed, which have nothing to do with such relationships and even imply the termination of a previous employment.
>
> It therefore follows that, in view of the equality of treatment which the provision seeks to achieve, the substantive area of application must be delineated so as to include all social and tax advantages, whether or not attached to the contract of employment, such as reductions in fares for large families.[113]

The Court has subsequently held that Article 7(2) applies to any benefit payable by virtue of an individual's status as a worker, or residence in national territory, where the extension of the benefit to nationals of other Member States seems suitable to facilitate free movement of workers.[114] Thus, Article 7(2) has been held to cover seven-year, interest-free, means-tested loans to families in respect of newly born children, even though the loans were of a discretionary nature;[115] an allowance to handicapped adults covered by Regulation 1408/71 on Social Security;[116] a guaranteed minimum subsistence allowance;[117] the possibility of using one's own language in court proceedings;[118] a special unemployment benefit for young persons falling outside the ambit of Regulation 1408/71;[119] an old-age benefit for those lacking entitlement to a pension under the national social security system;[120] a guaranteed minimum income for old persons;[121] and a grant to cover funeral expenses.[122] Finally, in *Reed*, faced with a national rule which provided that nationals could obtain a residence permit for their (unmarried) partners, whilst foreigners could not, the Court held that the right to have one's partner was a social advantage falling within the scope of Article 7(2) and it was thus covered by the principle of non-discrimination.[123] Admittedly, the ruling is rather far fetched; however, it shows the Court's willingness to stretch the provisions of EU law to the maximum in order to foster and ensure free movement. That said, the term 'social advantage' does not extend to cover benefits awarded because of the 'special link of nationality'. This would be the case for most benefits awarded as compensation for services rendered to one's country during wartime, or as compensation for military service. This type of benefit is not awarded to the individuals for reason of their being workers; rather, it is awarded because of the special link of nationality that requires

---

[113] Case 32/75 *Cristini v SNCF* [1975] ECR 1985, 1094 and 1095.
[114] Case 207/78 *Even* [1979] ECR 2019.
[115] Case 65/81 *Reina* [1982] ECR 33.
[116] Case 63/76 *Inzirillo* [1976] ECR 2057, now Regulation 883/2004.
[117] Case 249/83 *Hoecks* [1985] ECR 973; Case 122/84 *Scrivner* [1985] ECR 1027.
[118] Case 137/84 *Mutsch* [1985] ECR 2681.
[119] Case 94/84 *Deak* [1985] ECR 1873, now Regulation 883/2004.
[120] Case 157/84 *Frascogna* [1985] ECR 1739
[121] Case 261/83 *Castelli* [1984] ECR 3199.
[122] Case C-237/94 *John O'Flynn v Adjudication Officer* [1996] ECR I-2617.
[123] The ruling has now been codified in Art 3 of Directive 2004/38.

individuals to serve in the armed forces. For instance, an early retirement on full pension for those in receipt of an invalidity pension granted by an Allied Power in respect of war-time service;[124] an advantage comprising partial compensation for national workers for the consequences of the obligation to perform military service;[125] and an allowance for former prisoners of war[126] are not considered to be social advantages within the meaning of Article 7(2).[127]

Article 7(2) also requires non-discrimination in relation to tax advantages; here the assessment of the existence of indirect discrimination might well be more complicated since taxes (and tax advantages) are inherently territorial. This means that in some cases a residence requirement in order to benefit from tax advantages, a requirement which would normally be considered indirectly discriminatory, might be compatible with the Treaty since residents and non-residents are in non-comparable situations in relation to direct taxation. That said, the Court is always willing to scrutinise tax regimes to ensure that there is no discrimination: in *Zurstrassen*, for instance, Luxembourg legislation provided that spouses could make a joint tax declaration, which was more convenient from a tax viewpoint, only if both spouses were resident in the national territory. Mr Zurstrassen was a Belgian national working and residing in Luxembourg. His wife and children continued to reside in Belgium and, as his wife was not earning, she was not liable to tax in Belgium. Mr Zurstrassen was prevented from making a joint tax declaration, and instead was treated as a single person, because of the fact that his wife was resident in Belgium. The Court held that, even though residence might be relevant for tax benefits, in the case at stake the Luxembourg legislation was incompatible with Article 45 TFEU and Article 7(2) of the Regulation since Mr Zurstrassen received almost all his income in Luxembourg, and was therefore taxed in Luxembourg. To prevent him from declaring his wife as a dependant on the sole ground that she did not reside in Luxembourg constituted indirect discrimination on grounds of nationality since Luxembourg nationals were more likely to reside in Luxembourg.[128]

Article 8 of the Regulation provides that a worker who is a national of a Member State and who is employed in the territory of another Member State shall enjoy equality of treatment as regards membership of trade unions and the exercise of rights attaching thereto, including the right to vote and to be eligible for the administration and management posts of a trade union. He/she may, however, be excluded from taking part in the management of bodies governed by public law and from holding an office governed by public law. In *ASTI*,[129] a case concerning 'occupational guilds' from which non-nationals

---

[124] Case 207/78 *Even* [1979] ECR 2019.

[125] Case C-315/94 *de Vos* [1996] ECR I-417.

[126] Case C-386/02 *Baldinger* [2004] ECR I-8411

[127] This does not mean, however, that such benefits fall altogether outside the scope of Union law since the Court has made clear that the right to free movement provided for by Art 21 TFEU precludes a Member State granting a war-related benefit from making it conditional upon a residence requirement unless such condition is objectively justified: see eg Case C-192/05 *Tas-Hagen and Tas* [2006] ECR I-10451; Case C-499/06 *Nerkowska* [2008] ECR I-3993.

[128] Case C-87/99 *Zurstrassen* [2000] ECR I-3337. In relation to a case brought under Art 21 TFEU, the Court has made clear that 'the Treaty offers no guarantee to a citizen of the Union that transferring his activities to a Member State other than that in which he previously resided will be neutral as regards taxation. Given the disparities in the tax legislation of the Member States, such a transfer might be to the citizen's advantage in terms of indirect taxation or not, according to the circumstances': Case C-365/02 *Lindorfs* [2004] ECR I-7183, para 34. See also Case C-403/03 *Schempp* [2005] ECR I-6421; and in relation to Art 45 TFEU, see Case C-387/01 *Weigel* [2004] ECR I-4981, para 55.

[129] Case C-213/90 [1991] ECR 3507.

were excluded, it was denied that the bodies in question comprised trade unions for the purpose of the above-mentioned provision. The Court held that this Article constitutes a particular expression of the principle of non-discrimination in the specific field of workers' participation in trade-union organisation and activities, and could not be limited by reference to the legal form of the body in question. 'On the contrary', stated the Court,

> the exercise of the trade-union rights referred to in that provision extends beyond the bounds of trade-union organizations in the strict sense and includes, in particular, the participation of workers in bodies which, while not being, in law, trade-union organizations, perform similar functions as regards the defence and representation of workers' interests.[130]

Once more we are reminded of the interrelation between the secondary legislation in this field and the fact that it is designed to facilitate the enjoyment of rights conferred directly by the Treaty, and is to be interpreted accordingly.

The Regulation recognises the importance of freely available housing to the migrant worker when it provides that he/she shall 'enjoy all the rights and benefits accorded to national workers in matters of housing, including ownership of the housing he needs'.[131] She/he may also, 'with the same right as nationals, put his name down on the housing lists in the region in which he is employed, where such lists exist; he shall enjoy the resultant benefits and priorities'.[132] If the worker's family have remained in the country whence he/she came, they must be considered, for the purposes of priority on housing lists, as residing in the area where the worker is employed, where national workers benefit from a similar presumption.[133]

V – THE MATERIAL SCOPE OF ARTICLE 45 TFEU: NON-DISCRIMINATORY RESTRICTIONS

Article 45(1) TFEU states that 'freedom of movement shall be secured within the Union' and Article 45(2) TFEU states that such freedom 'shall entail the abolition of any discrimination based on nationality' between workers of the Member States. While this formulation makes it clear that freedom of movement *includes* the abolition of discrimination based on nationality, it also leaves room for the possibility that non-discriminatory restrictions to the freedom of movement are also prohibited by the Treaty. Until the early 1990s the Court had limited the scope of Article 45 TFEU to encompass only directly and indirectly discriminatory restrictions;[134] it then broadened the scope of the free movement of workers provisions to encompass also a prohibition on (certain) non-discriminatory barriers.

In *Kraus*[135] the Court of Justice considered the situation of a German national who went to the United Kingdom, where he took an LLM at Edinburgh University. After returning to Germany, he objected to a German legal requirement that as a precondition to using his

---

[130] Ibid, para 16.
[131] Art 9(1).
[132] Art 9(2).
[133] Article 9(2), second sub-para.
[134] And, of course, direct barriers to movement which would prevent individuals from leaving or entering or moving within the national territory.
[135] Case C-19/92 *Dieter Kraus* [1993] ECR I-1663.

Scottish academic title he must obtain authorisation from the competent German authority. The Court noted that a postgraduate academic title was not usually a prerequisite for
access to a profession, either as an employee or on a self-employed basis, but that the possession of such a title nevertheless constituted, for the person entitled to make use of it,
an advantage for the purpose both of gaining entry to such a profession and of prospering
in it.[136] The Court held that Article 45 TFEU precluded any national measure governing
the conditions under which an academic title obtained in another Member State might
be used, where that measure, even though it was applicable without discrimination on
grounds of nationality, was liable to hamper or to render less attractive the exercise by
EU nationals, including those of the Member State which enacted the measure, of fundamental freedoms guaranteed by the Treaty.[137] The situation would be different only if such
a measure pursued a legitimate objective compatible with the Treaty and was justified by
pressing reasons of public interest.[138] It is to be noted that the Court's recourse to a very
general test of whether a national measure was 'liable to hamper or render less attractive'
the exercise of free movement was in circumstances in which a national rule in effect governed the conditions of access (as regards the use of the title) of the worker concerned to
the labour market of the Member State in question.

This was confirmed in the case of *Bosman*[139] where the Court considered the consistency with Article 45 TFEU of rules laid down by sporting associations under which a professional footballer who is a national of one Member State could not, on the expiry of his
contract with a club, be employed by another club unless the latter club had paid to the
former a transfer, training or development fee. The rules applied to all transfers regardless of whether the footballer moved clubs within the same Member State or between
different Member States. The Court held that the rules in question, although they did not
discriminate on grounds of nationality, constituted an obstacle to freedom of movement
for workers. The Court's reasoning was straightforward. It noted that nationals of Member
States have in particular the right, which they derived directly from the Treaty, to leave
their country of origin to enter the territory of another Member State and reside there
in order to pursue an economic activity.[140] And it added that provisions which preclude
or deter a national of a Member State from leaving her/his country of origin in order to
exercise her/his freedom of movement constitute an obstacle to that freedom even if they
apply without regard to the nationality of the workers concerned.[141] This was the effect

---

[136] Ibid, para 18.

[137] In Case C-55/94 *Gebhard* [1995] ECR I-4165, a case relating to the freedom of establishment, the Court
referring to *Kraus* held: 'It follows, however, from the Court's case-law that national measures liable to hinder or
make less attractive the exercise of fundamental freedoms guaranteed by the Treaty must fulfil four conditions:
they must be applied in a non-discriminatory manner; they must be justified by imperative requirements in the
general interest; they must be suitable for securing the attainment of the objective which they pursue; and they
must not go beyond what is necessary in order to attain it' (para 37), hence extending its interpretation also to
the other free movement of persons provisions.

[138] Ibid, para 32. In the event, the Court of Justice held that the national measure in question might be so
justified.

[139] Case C-415/93 *Bosman* [1995] ECR I-4921; see also Case C-208/05 *ITC* [2007] ECR I-181 in relation
to national legislation which provided that the fees due to private-sector employment agencies would be reimbursed by the state only if the employment was subject to compulsory social security contribution in that state;
and Case C-325/08 *Olympique Lyonnais SASP v Bernard*, Judgment of 16 March 2010, nyr, noted J Lindholm
(2010) 47 *CMLRev* 1187.

[140] Case C-415/93 *Bosman* [1995] ECR I-4921, para 95.

[141] Ibid, para 96.

of the rules at issue in the national proceedings in the cases in point, even if similar rules also governed transfers between clubs within a single Member State. The Court stated:

> It is sufficient to note that, although the rules in issue in the main proceedings apply also to transfers between clubs belonging to different national associations within the same Member State and are similar to those governing transfers between clubs belonging to the same national association, they still directly affect players' *access to the employment market* in other Member States and are thus capable of impeding freedom of movement for workers.[142]

The Court concluded that the transfer rules constituted an obstacle to freedom of movement for workers prohibited in principle by Article 45 TFEU. It could only be otherwise if the rules pursued a legitimate aim compatible with the Treaty and were justified by pressing reasons of public interest. In order to be so justified they would have to be appropriate to ensure achievement of the aim in question, and not go beyond what was necessary for that purpose.[143]

In *Terhoeve*[144] the Court considered the position of a migrant worker who transferred his residence from one Member State to another. The latter subjected Mr Terhoeve to a heavier social security burden than would have been the case if he, in otherwise identical circumstances, had continued to reside throughout the whole year in the Member State in question. The Court, taking a very similar approach to that in *Bosman*, held that a national of a Member State could be deterred from leaving the Member State in which she resides in order to pursue an activity as an employed person in the territory of another Member State if she were required to pay greater social security contributions than if she had not moved, without thereby being entitled to additional social benefits such as to compensate for that increase.[145] It followed, in the view of the Court, that national legislation of the kind at issue in the main proceedings constituted an obstacle to freedom of movement for workers, prohibited in principle by Article 45 TFEU, and it was therefore unnecessary to consider whether there was indirect discrimination on grounds of nationality, prohibited by the Treaty or by Article 7(2) of Regulation 1612/68.[146]

The breadth of the *Bosman* formula, which includes mere discouragement to the willingness to move within the definition of obstacles relevant for free movement purposes, led to a rather imaginative attack on national rules regulating compensation for termination of an employment contract. In *Graf*[147] Mr Graf quit his employment in Austria to take up a position in Germany. The Austrian legislation provided for compensation for termination of employment when such termination resulted from a decision not attrib-

---

[142] Ibid, para 103 (emphasis added); the Court thus distinguishes the 'selling arrangements' referred to in the context of the free movement of goods in Joined Cases C-267/91 and C-268/91 *Keck and Mithouard* [1993] ECR I-6097, as to which see above Chapter 14.

[143] Ibid, para 104; in Case C-325/08 *Olympique Lyonnais SASP v Bernard*, Judgment of 16 March 2010, nyr, the Court indicated that a contractual clause providing for reimbursement for training costs for a football player moving to another club after his training despite having been offered a contract from the club who trained him is compatible with Art 45 TFEU provided it is proportionate. In the case at issue the Court found that the fee was not proportionate because it was calculated in terms of damages rather than the actual cost of training. For the proportionality of national measures in the similar contexts of the right of establishment, and freedom to provide services.

[144] Case C-18/95 *FC Terhoeve* [1999] ECR I-345. For another example of an 'exit' restriction, see Case C-109/04 *Kranemann* [2005] ECR I-493; see also Case C-352/06 *Bosmann* [2008] ECR I-3827; on the difficult interaction between Regulation 1408/71 (now 883/2004) and Art 45 TFEU, see R Babayev (2011) 1 *EJSL* 76.

[145] Case C-18/95 *FC Terhoeve* [1999] ECR I-345, para 40.

[146] Ibid, para 41.

[147] Case 190/98 *Graf* [2000] ECR I-493.

utable to the employee. Since Mr Graf had voluntarily quit his occupation, he was not entitled to any compensation. Relying on a literal interpretation of the *Bosman* ruling, Mr Graf argued that the rule constituted an obstacle to his right to move to take up employment in another Member State, since the prospect of losing the right to be compensated discouraged him from moving. The Court was not impressed by the submission: having found that the rule did not put migrant workers at a disadvantage, it turned to the question as to whether nonetheless the rule could be considered an obstacle to movement. The Court found that that could not be the case, since in order to be considered an obstacle to movement, the rule has to affect '*access of the worker to the labour market*'.[148] In the case at issue, that was not so since the compensation for involuntary dismissal was not

> dependent upon the worker's choosing whether or not to stay with his current employer but on a future and hypothetical event, namely the subsequent termination of his contract without such termination being at his own initiative or attributable to him.[149]

Such an event was 'too uncertain and indirect' for such a rule to be regarded as an obstacle to free movement falling within the scope of the Treaty. In *Graf* the Court defined more precisely the boundaries of Article 45 TFEU: not any rule which might potentially discourage movement is an obstacle caught by that Article. Rather, the rule needs to affect access to the employment market in a way that is not too uncertain and indirect.

A few months later, the Court delivered two other important rulings. In *Lehtonen*[150] the Court held that a rule which imposed a deadline in order to field players for the basketball championship was an obstacle falling within the scope of Article 45 TFEU. Even though the rule applied regardless of the nationality of the player, the Court found that it restricted the possibility of engaging players from other Member States where they have been engaged after the specified date. The Court accepted that in principle a rule prohibiting late transfers is aimed at ensuring that the strength of the teams does not change substantially just before the end of the championship, and is therefore aimed at pursuing the legitimate aim of ensuring the proper functioning of sporting competition. However, when the Court turned its attention to assessing the proportionality of the rule, it found that it went beyond what was necessary, since players from a federation outside the EU benefited from a later deadline. Thus, if non-EU players could be engaged at a later date without affecting the proper functioning of the championship, then there was no reason why players from the EU could not also benefit from the extended deadline. In *Deliège*[151] the Court was once again seised with the question of the compatibility with Community law of rules regulating sporting activity. Even though the case related to the free movement of services, the rationale of the case can be easily transposed to the scope of Article 45 TFEU. Here, the claimant attacked the selection process for taking part in an international judo championship. If the *Bosman* ruling were to be applied mechanically, it could be agued that such rules constituted an obstacle to movement, since the fact that Ms Deliège had not been selected meant that she could not go to another Member State to take part in the championship. The Court, however, wisely avoided such interpretation. It held that even though the rules at issue inevitably limited the possibility of taking part in

---

[148] Ibid, para 23 (emphasis added).
[149] Ibid, para 24.
[150] Case C-176/96 *Lehtonen* [2000] ECR I-2681.
[151] Joined Cases C-51/96 and 191/97 *Deliège* [2000] ECR I-2549.

sporting competitions, they 'were inherent in the conduct of an international high-level sports event'.[152]

The above case law shows the limits of the *Bosman* formula: not *all* non-discriminatory rules are to be considered as an obstacle to the free movement of workers, as otherwise all rules regulating any aspect of employment activity would have to be justified according to the imperative requirements doctrine. Rather, the above case law is consistent with the proposition that national measures which apply to the entry and residence of migrants, to their access to the employment market, or apply in any other way specifically to the transfer of the migrant from one Member State to another for the purposes of employment, will be prohibited by Article 45 TFEU if they restrict or impede freedom of movement for workers, even if they do not discriminate, directly or indirectly, on grounds of nationality. National measures that discriminate, not on grounds of nationality, but by placing at a disadvantage those who have exercised their right of free movement as compared to those who have not, will also be regarded as impeding the exercise of freedom of movement.[153] However, once a migrant worker has secured entry and residence in a Member State, and gained access to the employment market of a Member State, and is pursuing employed activities in that Member State, it will not be possible to object to national rules concerning, for example, the terms of conditions and employment, or the tax treatment of residents, solely on the ground that they might be described as excessively burdensome to those subject to them. Once integrated into the economic and social life of the host Member State, the migrant worker's fundamental right derived from Article 45 TFEU is the right to equality of treatment, in law and in fact.[154]

This proposition is not entirely straightforward, however. The argument against drawing a distinction between national rules which might hinder access to the market, and those which do not, is that such a distinction is difficult to draw in practice, since rules which relate to, say, the terms and conditions of employment, or to the tax treatment of residents, might, if unduly burdensome, be said to deter workers of other Member States from entering the employment market of the host Member State. Furthermore, it cannot be said that all the Court's case law is consistent with the proposition that non-discriminatory rules need only be justified if they hinder access to the employment market. In *Carpenter*[155] the Court held that a UK national residing in the United Kingdom and selling advertising space to advertisers in other Member States could rely on Article 56 TFEU to resist the deportation of his wife, a third-country national illegally resident in the United Kingdom, since their separation would be detrimental to their family life, and therefore to the conditions under which the UK national was exercising a fundamental

---

[152] Ibid, para 64.

[153] The Court has held that the provisions of the Treaty relating to the free movement of persons are thus intended to facilitate the pursuit by Union citizens of occupational activities of all kinds throughout the EU, and preclude national legislation which might place Union citizens at a disadvantage when they wish to extend their activities beyond the territory of a single Member State: see Case 143/87 *Christopher Stanton and SA belge d'assurances 'L'Étoile 1905' v Inasti (Institut national d'assurances sociales pour travailleurs indépendants)* [1988] ECR 3877, para 13.

[154] If a restriction on access to the market is imposed on a migrant after his/her integration into the economic and social life of the host Member State, this does not of course preclude it being regarded as a restriction on access to the market, and it will required to be justified even if non-discriminatory. Thus a restriction such as that at issue in Case C-19/92 *Kraus* [1993] ECR I-1663 is by its nature a restriction on access to the market, and it is immaterial whether it is invoked against a new market entrant, or against a person already pursuing the relevant economic activity.

[155] Case C-60/00 *Carpenter* [2002] CR I-6279.

freedom.[156] While this case is concerned with the provision of services by a self-employed person rather than with the rights of a migrant worker, the proposition that a national measure which is detrimental to the conditions under which an individual exercises a fundamental freedom must be justified would seem capable to be of general application. Moreover, as we shall see in the next chapter, there are other examples of an expansive interpretation of the free movement provisions, which might well go beyond the 'access to the market' criterion.

VI – THE WORKER'S FAMILY

We have seen in the previous chapter that Union citizens have a right to bring their families into the host Member State to which they are migrating. For economically active citizens this right is unconditional, ie not dependent upon sufficient resources and health insurance. We have also seen that the spouse, the registered partner when registered partnerships are recognised in the host Member State, and children under the age of 21 or children who are dependent upon the worker/spouse (regardless of whether they are children of the couple or of only one of the spouses),[157] as well as dependent relatives in the ascending line, come within the definition of 'family member' for Union law purposes.[158] All these have a right to enter and install themselves with the Union citizen worker, as well as a right to take up an economic activity and a right not to be discriminated against on grounds of nationality in respect of all matters, including welfare benefits.

Article 3 of Directive 2004/38 further provides that the Member State shall facilitate admission of, and justify any denial of entry for, other members of the family who are dependent on the Union citizen worker or, even though not dependent, require for serious health grounds the personal care of said worker; or who were living under his/her roof in the country whence she/he came; or the partner with whom the Union citizen has a stable and duly attested relationship.[159]

A – Right to Education

As mentioned in the previous chapter, Directive 2004/38 repealed earlier legislation, including Articles 10 and 11 of Regulation 1612/68 which dealt with the worker's family. However, Directive 2004/38 did not repeal Article 12 of Regulation 1612/68,[160] which provides that the children of a worker residing in the territory of a Member State must be admitted to that Member State's general educational, apprenticeship and vocational

---

[156] Ibid, para 39. For a critical analysis of *Carpenter*, see (2000) 340 *CMLRev* 537–43; for analysis of related issues, see E Spaventa, 'From Gebhard to Carpenter: Towards a (non)-Economic European Constitution' (2004) 41 *CMLRev* 743–73.

[157] The status of dependency is a result of a factual situation, namely the provision of support by the worker, without there being any need to determine the reasons for recourse to such support: see Case 316/85 *Lebon* [1987] ECR 2811.

[158] See above Chapter 15.

[159] See above Chapter 15.

[160] As we have seen in Chapter 15, Art 24(2) of Directive 2004/38 also grants the right to maintenance aids for students to economically active citizens and their families.

training courses under the same conditions as nationals of that Member State. This provision clearly bestows rights directly upon such children, although Article 12(2), which states that 'Member States shall encourage all efforts to enable such children to attend courses under the best possible conditions', is not directly effective, and provides merely an admonition to Member States as to the spirit in which they should apply Article 12(1), and a guide to courts about its interpretation.

The Court of Justice has had cause to interpret Article 12 on several occasions. In *Michel S*[161] the plaintiff in the main suit was the mentally handicapped son of a deceased Italian national who had worked as a wage-earner in Belgium. Michel S was refused benefits from a national fund established to assist persons of Belgian nationality whose chances of employment had been seriously diminished by physical or mental handicap. The Court held that the 'integration' contemplated by the preamble of Regulation 1612/68 presupposed that the handicapped child of a foreign worker would be entitled to take advantage of benefits provided by the law of the host country for rehabilitation of the handicapped on the same basis as nationals in a similar position. No conclusion to the contrary could be drawn from the failure of the Council explicitly to mention such benefits in the text of the Article; rather, this omission could be explained by the difficulty of including all possible hypotheses.

The Court's liberal approach to the text of Article 12 in *Michel S* was followed in *Casagrande*,[162] in which the son of a deceased Italian national who had worked as a wage-earner in the Federal Republic of Germany was refused, on grounds of nationality, a means-tested educational grant under a Bavarian statute. A German court sought a ruling from the Court of Justice on the consistency of such discriminatory provisions with Article 12 of Regulation 1612/68. The Court resorted once again to the fifth recital of the Regulation's preamble. Read with the words of Article 12(2), it became apparent that the Article guaranteed not simply access to educational courses, but all benefits intended to facilitate educational attendance. In the *Lubor Gaal* case[163] the Court held that Article 12 also covers financial assistance for those students who are already at an advanced stage in their studies, even if they are already 21 years of age or older and are no longer dependants of their parents.[164] In *Echternach*[165] the Court held that Article 12 of Regulation 1612/68 refers to any form of education, including university courses in economics and advanced vocational studies at a technical college. The Court also accepted that a child of a worker of a Member State, which latter has been in employment in another Member State, retains the status of member of a worker's family within the meaning of the Regulation when that child's family returns to the Member State of origin and the child remains in order to continue his studies, which she could not pursue in the Member State of origin. Furthermore, in *Baumbast and R* the Court held that since the worker's children have a right to remain to complete their education in the host Member State even when the worker has returned to her/his country of origin or when the Union citizen has lost his/her right of residence, the (divorced) parent who is the children's guardian/primary carer derives a right to residence from her children's right to stay. If the primary carer (in the case of divorce) or the parents were not allowed to stay in the host country, the children

---

[161] Case 76/72 [1973] ECR 457.
[162] Case 9/74 [1974] ECR 773, and see Case 68/74 *Alaim* [1975] ECR 109.
[163] Case C-7/94 *Lubor Gaal* [1995] ECR I-1031.
[164] For education and vocational training, see Chapter 28.
[165] Case 389/87 [1989] ECR 723.

might be deprived of their EU right to be educated in the host Member State.[166] The Court's interpretation was clearly purposive and aimed at guaranteeing that the worker's children's rights under Union law would not be compromised by a change in their parents' circumstances. As we have seen in the previous chapter, the ruling in *Baumbast* has now been codified in Article 12(3) of Directive 2004/38. Furthermore the *Baumbast* interpretation has been confirmed and expanded in the cases of *Ibrahim* and *Texeira*.[167] In those cases the Court had to decide whether a third-country national parent could derive an unconditional right to reside (ie not dependent upon being economically active or independent pursuant to Directive 2004/38) from their children's right to education. In *Ibrahim* a Danish citizen (Mr Yusuf) had moved to the UK with his third-country national spouse (Ms Ibrahim) and his children. When the marriage broke down, Mr Yusuf left the United Kingdom whilst Ms Ibrahim and their children, who were in education in the UK, remained there. Ms Ibrahim was not economically active; and did not have sufficient resources and health insurance. The question arose as to whether she could rely on Article 12 of Regulation 1612/68 to gain a right to reside (and consequently a right to equal treatment) in the United Kingdom. In *Texeira* a Portuguese family migrated to the United Kingdom; eventually, following the breakdown of the marriage, Ms Texeira, who was neither economically active nor economically independent, sought to rely on Article 12 of Regulation 1612/68 to establish her right to reside in the UK based on the fact that her daughter, who was in education in the UK, was living with her. In both cases the Court found that Article 12 of Regulation 1612/68 has not been affected by Directive 2004/38: hence parents can derive an unconditional right of residence based on the fact that their children are in education in the host Member State. This right can be invoked even when the migrant worker is no longer in the country; or is no longer in employment; and even when the children have reached the age of majority, but only if they need the presence and care of the parent in order to pursue and complete their education.

B – Tax and Social Advantages

As mentioned above, Article 7 of Regulation 1612/68, which provides for equal treatment in relation to social and tax advantages, has been interpreted also as applying, at least to a certain extent, to the worker's family. In *Cristini*, it will be recalled that the widow of a deceased Italian national applied for a reduced fare card on French national railways. The Court of Justice held that Article 7(2) must be interpreted as meaning

> that the social advantages referred to by that provision include fares reduction cards issued by a national railway authority to large families and that this applies, even if the said advantage is only sought after the worker's death, to the benefit of his family remaining in the same Member State.[168]

In *Inzirillo*[169] the Court observed that the protection of Article 7(2) of Regulation 1612/68 extended to handicapped, dependent adult children of a worker who have installed them-

---

[166] Case C-413/99 *Baumbast and R* [2002] ECR I-7091, esp para 71.
[167] Case C-310/08 *Ibrahim* and Case C-480/08 *Texiera*, both decided on 23 February 2010, nyr, noted O'Brien (2011) 48 *CMLRev* 203; MJ Elsmore (2010) 35 *ELRev* 571.
[168] Case 32/75 *Cristini v SNCF* [1975] ECR 1985, 1095.
[169] Case 63/76 [1976] ECR 2057.

selves with the worker in accordance with Article 10 of Regulation 1612/68.[170] And in *Castelli*[171] and *Frascogna*[172] the Court has held that Article 7(2) is intended to protect, as well as workers themselves, their dependent relatives in the ascending line who have installed themselves with the worker. It follows from the above cases that any member of a worker's family who is entitled to, and does, install himself with the worker is also entitled to treatment equal to that afforded to nationals of the host Member State in the grant of all social and tax advantages.[173] In *Bernini*[174] the Court held that finance provided for the purposes of study by a Member State to the children of workers constitutes a social advantage within the meaning of Article 7(2) of Regulation 1612/68, where the worker continues to support the children,[175] but that the child may himself or herself rely on that Article in order to obtain the financing if under national law it is granted directly to the student. Furthermore, and in any event, Article 24 of Directive 2004/38 grants a general equal treatment right to the workers' family members, and Article 18 TFEU provides for a general right of equal treatment in all matters falling within the scope of the Treaty.[176]

VII – THE TRANSITIONAL ARRANGEMENT FOR THE NEW MEMBER STATES

As we have seen in Chapter 1, in 2004 the European Union increased its population by 75 million people with the accession of 10 new Member States (A 10).[177] The 2004 enlargement was the largest and most ambitious enlargement in the history of the Union; its magnitude and disparities in the economic conditions between new and old Member States raised concerns about its possible impact on the labour markets of existing Member States,[178] especially at a time when the rate of unemployment in several Member States was very high.[179] For this reason, the Treaty of Accession 2003 established transitional arrangements,[180] contained in annexes to the Treaty, which allowed for the free movement of workers to be deferred for a maximum period of seven years following accession.[181]

---

[170] Art 10 has been repealed and substituted by Directive 2004/38 (Art 2).

[171] Case 261/83 [1984] ECR 3199.

[172] Case 157/84 [1985] ECR 1739.

[173] In this respect see also Art 24 of Directive 2004/38, which extends the equal treatment right to family members of the Union citizen, provided they have the right of residence or of permanent residence.

[174] Case C-3/90 *Bernini* [1992] ECR 1071, paras 25 and 26.

[175] Art 7(2) cannot be relied upon to claim study finance for the worker's children if the worker has ceased his/her occupational activity in the host Member State and has moved back to the Member State of origin: see Case C-33/99 *Fahmi and Esmoris Cerdeiro-Pinedo Amado* [2001] ECR I-2415.

[176] 152/82 *Forcheri* [1983] ECR 2323. See also Case 293/83 *Gravier* [1985] ECR 593.

[177] The 'new' Member States are commonly referred to as A 10, whilst the 'old' Member States are referred to as EU 15. A 8 refers to the new Member States minus Malta and Cyprus; A 2 refers to Bulgaria and Romania.

[178] According to Eurostat, the difference in GDP per capita at the moment of accession varied between 35% (Latvia) and 74% (Slovenia) of the EU 15 average; see the Commission's Communication, *More Unity and More Diversity. The Europe Union's Biggest Enlargement* (NA-47-02-389-EN-C) http://www.europa.eu.int/comm/publications/booklets/move/41/index_en.htm.

[179] eg Germany's unemployment rate in 2003 was 9%; Italy's 8.4%; France's 9.5%; Spain's 11.5%. The average unemployment rate in 2003 for the EU 25 was 9%, and 8% for the EU 15. These rates increased to 9.1% and 8.1%, respectively, in 2004, and dropped to 8.7% and 7.9%, respectively, in 2005 (source: Eurostat).

[180] Annexes V–XV of the Accession Treaty, [2003] OJ 236/803 *et seq*.

[181] See generally, S Currie, *Migration Work and Citizenship in the Enlarged European Union* (Farnham, Ashgate, 2008); A Adinolfi, 'Free Movement and Access to Work of Citizens of the New Member States: The

The limitation to free movement applied to all the new Member States (A 8) apart from Malta and Cyprus, whose citizens benefited from full free movement rights from the very beginning.[182] Similar arrangements have then been included in the Treaty of Accession of Bulgaria and Romania (2007).[183] The transitional arrangements for the A 8 countries expired on 30 April 2011; those for Bulgaria and Romania will expire on 31 December 2013.

According to the transitional arrangements, Member States can limit access to their employment market.[184] However, once the worker has gained access to the employment market, equal treatment applies in full, apart from a further derogation from Article 11 of Regulation 1612/68 (now subsumed in Directive 2004/38), in relation to the protected family members' right to work. The transitional agreements also provide for a stand-still obligation, whereby the Member States wishing to derogate from Article 45 TFEU cannot impose conditions more restrictive than those existing at the date of the signature of the Accession Treaty; and that Member States must give precedence to workers of the Member States to which the arrangements apply over third-country nationals in relation to access to their labour market.

Further Reading

N Bernard, 'Discrimination and Free Movement in EC Law' (1996) 45 *ICLQ* 82.

A Castro Oliveira, 'Workers and Other Persons: Step-by-Step from Movement to Citizenship—Case Law 1995–2001' (2002) 39 *CMLRev* 77.

L Daniele, 'Non-discriminatory Restrictions to the Free Movement of Persons' (1997) 22 *ELRev* 191.

C O'Brien, 'Social Blind Spots and Monocular Policy Making: The ECJ's Migrant Worker Model' (2009) 46 *CMLRev* 1107.

S O'Leary, 'Free Movement of Persons and Services' in P Craig and G de Búrca (eds), *The Evolution of EU Law*, 2nd edn (Oxford, Oxford University Press, 2011).

E Spaventa, 'From Gebhard to Carpenter: Towards a (non)-Economic European Constitution' (2004) 41 *CMLRev* 743.

——, *Free Movement of Persons: Barriers to Movement in their Constitutional Context* (Alphen aan den Rijn, Kluwer Law International, 2007).

Transitional Measures' (2005) 42 *CMLRev* 469; and M Dougan 'A Spectre is Haunting Europe . . . Free Movement of Persons and the Eastern Enlargement' in C Hillion (ed), *EU Enlargement: A Legal Approach* (Oxford, Hart Publishing, 2004). A similar framework is provided in the Treaty of Accession for Bulgaria and Romania. For a UK-focused analysis, see B Ryan, 'The Accession (Immigration and Worker Authorisation) Regulations 2006' (2008) 37 *ILJ* 75.

[182] Although Malta benefits from special arrangements.

[183] Treaty of Accession Annexes VI and VII [2005] OJ L157/104 and 138; see generally Commission Communication, *Report on the Functioning of the Transitional Arrangements Set Out in the 2003 Accession Treaty (period 1 May 2004–30 April 2006)* COM(2006) 48 final; and Commission Communication, *The Impact of Free Movement of Workers in the Context of EU Enlargement: Report on the First Phase (1 January 200 –31 December 2008) of the Transitional Arrangements Set Out in the 2005 Accession Treaty and as Requested According to the Transitional Arrangement Set Out in the 2003 Accession Treaty* COM(2008) 765 final.

[184] Art 45 TFEU applies apart from Arts 1–6 of Regulation 1612/68 which regulate access to the employment market. Germany and Austria can derogate from Art 56(1) TFEU in respect of posting workers according to Art 1 of Directive 96/71 concerning the posting of workers in the framework of the provision of services [1997] OJ L18/1; the derogation applies only to listed service sectors (as listed in para 13 of the transitional arrangements).

17

The Right of Establishment and the Freedom to Provide Services

The right of establishment and the freedom to provide services are for individuals the self-employed equivalent of the free movement of workers. Self-employed individuals are entitled to carry on economic activities in other Member States on a temporary or permanent basis. The temporary pursuit of a trade or business in another Member State is covered by the Treaty provisions on services; if the economic activities are permanent, and from a fixed place of business, the provisions on establishment apply. The right of establishment covers the right to set up and manage businesses, including companies, in other Member States. Companies and firms, as well as individuals, are entitled to freedom of establishment and freedom to provide services. Detailed consideration is given to corporate establishment in Chapter 20. This chapter deals generally with the right of establishment and the freedom to provide services, though some specific treatment is necessary as regards national tax provisions which operate as restrictions on freedom of movement. The case law on establishment and services has seen changes in the Court's approach to the interpretation of the relevant Treaty provisions over the years, and this chapter explains this evolution. Perhaps the most important change has been judicial recognition that non-discriminatory restrictions on the right of establishment and the freedom to provide services, as well as discriminatory restrictions, will be prohibited unless justified. Justification may be possible on the basis of express provisions in the TFEU, for example on grounds of public policy, or where an activity involves the exercise of official authority. It may also be possible on grounds of imperative or overriding requirements in the general interest—a category recognised by case law but without any explicit Treaty base.

I – ESTABLISHMENT AND SERVICES

A – Meaning of the Right of Establishment and Freedom to Provide Services

As well as ensuring the free movement of workers, the Treaty guarantees the right of establishment, and the freedom to provide services between Member States: what Article 45 TFEU provides for the employee, Articles 49 and 56 TFEU provide for the employer, the entrepreneur and the professional. The employed and self-employed activities covered by the foregoing provisions are not confined to typical commercial activities, and may include, for example, work done by members of a community based on religion or another form of philosophy, as part of the commercial activities of that community, and as a quid pro quo for services provided by it.[1]

The right of establishment is granted to natural and legal persons,[2] and subject to relevant exceptions, it allows all types of self-employed activity to be taken up and pursued on the territory of any other Member State, undertakings to be formed and operated, and agencies, branches and subsidiaries to be set up.[3] It follows that a person may be established, within the meaning of the Treaty, in more than one Member State—in particular, in the case of companies, through the setting up of agencies, branches or subsidiaries, and in the case of the members of professions, by establishing a second professional base.[4]

The concept of establishment within the meaning of the Treaty is a very broad one, allowing an EU national to participate, on a stable and continuous basis, in the economic life of a Member State other than his or her state of origin and to profit therefrom, so contributing to economic and social interpenetration within the Union, in the sphere of activities of self-employed persons.[5] The Court has held that an undertaking of one Member State which maintains a permanent presence in another is covered by the provisions on establishment

> even if that presence does not take the form of a branch or agency, but consists merely of an office managed by the undertaking's own staff or by a person who is independent but authorised to act on a permanent basis for the undertaking as would be the case with an agency.[6]

In the context of betting and gaming, an undertaking established in one Member State is also established in another where it has a presence which takes the form of commercial agreements with operators or intermediaries, relating to the creation of data transmission centres which make electronic means of communication available to users, collect and register intentions to bet and forward them to the undertaking in the first Member State.[7]

---

[1] Case 196/87 *Steymann* [1987] ECR 6159, paras 14 and 16; and *cf* Case C-456/02 *Trojani* [2004] ECR I-7574, paras 20–24, for the question whether a person is a 'worker' where he performs, for the Salvation Army and under its direction, various jobs for approximately 30 hours a week, as part of a personal reintegration programme, in return for which he receives benefits in kind and some pocket money.
[2] As defined in Art 54 TFEU. For corporate establishment, see Chapter 20.
[3] Case C-55/94 *Gebhard* [1995] ECR I-4165, para 23.
[4] Ibid, para 24.
[5] Ibid, para 25.
[6] Case 205/84 *Commission v Germany* [1986] ECR 3755, para 21.
[7] Case C-243/01 *Gambelli* [2003] ECR I-13031, paras 14 and 46; Case C-409/06 *Winner Wetten* (CJEU 8 September 2010) para 47.

The right of establishment is to be contrasted with the freedom to provide services. The former entails settlement in a Member State for economic purposes, and permanent integration into the host state's economy, being generally exercised either by a shift of a sole place of business, or by the setting up of agencies, branches or subsidiaries. The latter entails a person or undertaking established in one Member State providing services in another on a temporary basis, as in the case of a doctor established in France visiting a patient in Belgium. The distinction may not always be clear-cut, because the provision of services may involve temporary residence in the host Member State, as in the case of a German firm of business consultants which advises undertakings in France, or a construction company which erects buildings in a neighbouring country. As long as such residence is temporary the activities in question will fall within the ambit of Articles 56–62 TFEU, on freedom to provide services.[8] If the activities are carried out on a permanent basis, or without a foreseeable limit to their duration, and from a fixed place of business in the host Member State, they will not fall within the provisions of the Treaty on the provision of services, and will be regulated by the provisions on the right of establishment.[9] But the fact that the provision of services is temporary does not mean that the provider of services may not equip himself with some form of infrastructure in the host Member State, such as an office, chambers or consulting room.[10] The fact that both an established person and a person providing services may carry on business from such an office, consulting room or other place of business means that it may in practice be difficult to distinguish activities subject to the Treaty provisions on establishment from those subject to the Treaty provisions on services. As will be seen in subsequent sections of the present chapter, the interpretation of the respective provisions of the Treaty on establishment and services by the Court of Justice has reduced, though not eliminated, the significance of such a distinction being drawn. In any event, whether the activities in question are to be regarded as temporary, and so subject to the Treaty provisions on services, rather than on establishment, has to be determined in the light, not only of the duration of the provision of the service, but of its regularity, periodicity or continuity.[11] The Court has admitted that no provision of the Treaty provides a means of determining, in an abstract manner, the duration or frequency beyond which the supply of a service or of a certain type of service in another Member State can no longer be regarded as the provision of services within the meaning of the Treaty.[12] In addition, the Court has held that services may comprise services within the meaning of the Treaty even if supplied over an extended period to persons established in one or more other Member States, eg the giving of advice or information for remuneration.[13] It seems that the provision of services from one Member State to another on a regular basis, accompanied by use of an office or similar facility in the host state, may shade imperceptibly into establishment. But offering the services from an established professional base in the host Member State is essential if a person is to be

---

[8] Art 57 TFEU, third para provides: 'Without prejudice to the provisions of the Chapter relating to the right of establishment, the person providing a service may, in order to do so, temporarily pursue his activity in the State where the service is provided, under the same conditions as are imposed by that State on its own nationals.'

[9] Case 196/87 *Steymann* [1987] ECR 6159, para 16.

[10] Case C-55/94 *Gebhard* [1995] ECR I-4165, para 27; Case C-215/01 *Schnitzer* [2003] ECR I-14847, para 28.

[11] Ibid.

[12] Case C-215/01 *Schnitzer* [2003] ECR I-14847, para 31.

[13] Ibid, para 30.

regarded as established in that Member State;[14] the difficulty with insisting on this latter requirement is discussed later.[15]

II – THE SCOPE OF THE PRESENT CHAPTER

The right of establishment and the freedom to provide services may be invoked by companies and firms as well as by individuals. The present chapter will deal generally with the right of establishment and the freedom to provide services. Detailed consideration is given to corporate establishment in Chapter 20. As regards individuals, the rights of movement and residence of Union Citizens who are self-employed, and of members of their families, and limitations on those rights, are specified in Directive 2004/38/EC, and are covered in Chapter 15 on Union citizenship. The Court's case law on the general development of the right of establishment and freedom to provide services, and the limitations on those rights, are covered in the present chapter, as is the Court's case law on the effect of the right of establishment on the application of national tax rules. The direct effect of the Treaty provisions on the right of establishment and the freedom to provide services on national rules which require that those pursuing certain activities hold certain professional qualifications is dealt with in Chapter 19, as are EU rules on the mutual recognition of diplomas, and the co-ordination of national qualifications, along with the directives on the provision of services by lawyers, and the right of establishment of lawyers. It is to be noted that the EU rules on qualifications are applicable to employed as well as to self-employed persons.

III – THE RIGHT OF ESTABLISHMENT

A – General Scope

Article 49 TFEU draws a distinction between the right of establishment of nationals of Member States and the right of establishment of nationals *already established* in the territory of a Member State. The former are entitled to establish themselves in any Member State, that is to say to set up their main establishment, while the latter are entitled to set up agencies and branches. A Member State cannot refuse to accord rights under Article 49 TFEU to a national of another Member State on the ground that that national also holds the nationality of a third country.[16]

Freedom of establishment includes a number of distinct rights. One is the right of a natural or legal person to leave his/her/its Member State of origin or establishment in order to accomplish a shift in primary establishment, or to set up a secondary establish-

---

[14] Ibid, para 32; Case C-171/02 *Commission v Portugal* [2004] ECR I-5645, para 25; Case C-514/03 *Commission v Spain* [2006] ECR I-963, para 22.

[15] Below, at p 556.

[16] Case C-369/90 *Micheletti* [1992] ECR I-4239; see also Case C-122/96 *Saldanha* [1997] ECR I-5325; Case C-200/02 *Chen* [2004] ECR I-9925.

ment, in another Member State.[17] Another is the right to have more than one place of business in the EU.[18] A third is the right to carry on business under the conditions laid down for its own nationals by the law of the host Member State.[19] The fourth is a much broader right. It is the right to resist the application of national measures which are liable to hinder or make less attractive the exercise of the right of establishment guaranteed by the Treaty, unless such measures can be justified.[20] This latter broader right might be said to be confined to situations where national measures comprise a restriction of one sort or another on *access to the relevant market* by nationals of Member States, though it is questionable whether any concept of access to the market operates as a significant limit on the ability of an individual or firm to challenge national rules which hinder or make less attractive the exercise of a fundamental freedom.[21] All the foregoing rights are of course subject to the exceptions and derogations recognised by the EU.[22] It must be noted, however, that Article 49 TFEU can have no application in a situation which is purely internal to a Member State.[23] The right of establishment guaranteed by Article 49 TFEU is directly applicable.[24]

B – Evolution of the Court's Case Law on the Interpretation of Article 49 TFEU

The interpretation by the Court of Justice of Article 49 TFEU has been the subject of a quite significant evolution in two respects. Firstly, as regards the extent to which the provision may be relied upon by a national of a Member State when returning to his or her Member State of origin and against his or her own national authorities; the Court's early approach, relying upon a literal approach to the text, largely ruled out such reliance, but that approach has not been followed in later case law. The second respect concerns the type of national rule regarded by the Court as comprising a restriction prohibited by Article 49 TFEU. The Court's case law until the early 1990s was to the effect that only rules which discriminated against foreign nationals could be so regarded, apart from measures which prevented nationals from leaving their own Member States, or prevented them from having a place of business in more than one Member State, or placed individuals at a disadvantage by virtue of having exercised their right of free movement. More recently, however, the Court has adopted a broader approach, which holds that Article 49 TFEU covers all national measures which are liable to hinder or make less attractive (one formulation) or prohibit, impede or render less attractive (another formulation) the exercise of

---

[17] Below at p 538.
[18] Below at p 538.
[19] Below at pp 536, 545–47.
[20] Below at pp 540, 547 et seq.
[21] As to which, see below at pp 548–51.
[22] As to which see below at pp 567–81.
[23] Case 204/87 *Bekaert* [1988] ECR 2029; Cases C-54/88 et al *Nino* [1990] ECR I-3537; Case C-152/94 *Openbaar Ministerie v Geert Van Buynder* [1995] ECR I-3981. It appears that a person qualified in a Member State who carries on all his professional activity there may not rely upon Art 49 TFEU solely because he resides in another Member State, Case C-112/91 *Hans Werner* [1993] ECR I-429, but the Court has treated a similar situation as being governed by Art 56 TFEU: see Case 39/75 *Coenen* [1975] ECR 1555.
[24] Case 81/87 *Daily Mail* [1988] ECR 3483, para 15; Case C-1/93 *Halliburton Services* [1994] ECR I-1137, para 16; Case C-254/97 *Baxter and others* [1999] ECR I-4809, para 11.

the right of establishment. It is appropriate to consider first the text of Article 49 TFEU, and then to trace the major developments in the Court's interpretation of that text.

Article 49 TFEU provides that '[w]ithin the framework of the provisions set out below, restrictions on the freedom of establishment of *nationals of a Member State* in the territory of *another Member State* shall be prohibited' (emphasis added). It is to be noted that the words in italics indicate that the Article covers a national of one Member State exercising self-employed activities in the territory of another, but there is no indication that the scope of the Article extends to the case of a national of a Member State returning to his or her Member State of origin. The wording is, however, apt to cover restrictions imposed by a Member State of origin on the right of establishment of its own nationals in another Member State. Article 49 TFEU goes on to say that

> freedom of establishment shall include the right to take up and pursue activities as self-employed persons . . . [etc] . . . under the conditions laid down for its own nationals by the law of the country where such establishment is effected.

The use of the word 'include' in the latter formulation would seem to be consistent with the proposition that the 'restrictions' on freedom of establishment referred to in the first sentence of the Article, which are to be prohibited, are not confined to discriminatory restrictions. It is also to be noted that the 'restrictions' referred to in the first sentence of the Article refer to the 'framework of the provisions set out below', and the provisions in question authorise the adoption of directives in order 'to attain freedom of establishment as regards a particular activity',[25] and in order 'to make it easier for persons to take up and pursue activities as self-employed persons' by providing for the 'mutual recognition of diplomas, certificates and other evidence of formal qualifications'.[26]

In *Reyners* the Court of Justice held that the prohibition of discrimination contained in Article 49 TFEU was directly applicable, despite the reference in that Article to the prohibition of restrictions on the right of establishment 'within the framework' of subsequent Articles of the Treaty providing for the adoption of secondary legislation. This judgment was of considerable significance, and it is referred to further below.[27] Other judgments on the applicability of the prohibition on discrimination followed.[28] In the first *Auer* case,[29] however, the Court felt it necessary to address an important issue of principle as to the scope of Article 49 TFEU. The national proceedings which gave rise to a reference to the Court of Justice involved a Mr Vincent Auer, originally of Austrian nationality, who studied veterinary medicine first in Austria, then in France, and then in Italy, at the University of Parma, where he was awarded in 1956 the degree of doctor of veterinary medicine, and in March 1957 a provisional certificate to practise as a veterinary surgeon. Mr Auer took up residence in France and in 1961 acquired French nationality by naturalisation. He then applied, pursuant to a provision of French law allowing veterinary surgeons who have acquired French nationality to be authorised to practise in France despite the absence of a French doctorate. The competent French authority refused to recognise the equivalence of Mr Auer's Italian qualification, but he practised in France nevertheless, and he

---

[25] Art 50(1) TFEU.

[26] Art 53(1) TFEU.

[27] Case 2/74 *Reyners* [1974] ECR 631, see below at p 543.

[28] See eg Case 7/76 *Thieffry* [1977] ECR 765 (refusal of access to the Paris Bar of a Belgian national, on the ground that he did not possess a French law degree, despite the fact that he possessed a Belgian law degree, recognised by the University of Paris as equivalent to a French law degree, held discriminatory).

[29] Case 136/78 *Auer* [1979] ECR 437; see also Case 271/82 *Auer* [1983] ECR 2727.

was prosecuted on several occasions for doing so. One such prosecution led to a reference to the Court of Justice, asking whether the person concerned was in a position to claim in France the right to practise the profession of veterinary surgeon which he had acquired in Italy. The Court might have proceeded on the basis that a person in the situation of Mr Auer could not rely upon the right of establishment because he had never, as a national of a Member State, exercised his right of free movement. But it did not, it proceeded instead on the basis that the only relevant right under Article 49 TFEU in such circumstances was the right of non-discrimination, and that right could only be invoked by a national of one Member State in the territory of another. The Court, citing the text of the Treaty, including the reference to 'establishment of nationals of one Member State in the territory of another' stated:

> In so far as it is intended to ensure, within the transitional period, with direct effect, the benefit of national treatment, Article [49 TFEU] concerns only—and can concern only—in each Member State the nationals of other Member States, those of the host Member State coming already, by definition, under the rules in question.[30]

The Court went on to explain that in order to ensure complete freedom of establishment, the Treaty provided for directives to be adopted on mutual recognition of qualifications, and that such directives could be invoked both by nationals of one Member State in the territory of another, and by the nationals of a Member State in that Member State.[31]

The above judgment supported three related propositions. The first was that the direct effect of Article 49 TFEU was confined to a guarantee of national treatment; the second was that that guarantee could only by definition be invoked by a national of one Member State in the territory of another; and the third was that any restrictions on freedom of movement caused to nationals of a Member State by national rules on qualifications could be removed by the adoption of directives on mutual recognition of qualifications. Only the last of these propositions was to be confirmed by subsequent case law.

In a judgment given on the same day as *Auer*, in the *Knoors* case,[32] the Court explained the justification for allowing a national of a Member State, who had secured in another Member State a qualification which had been the subject of a directive issued under Article 53 TFEU to rely upon the terms of that directive. Referring to the free-movement provisions of the Treaty, Articles 45, 49 and 56 TFEU, the Court stated:

> In fact, these liberties, which are fundamental in the Community system, could not be fully realized if the Member States were in a position to refuse to grant the benefit of the provisions of Community law to those of their nationals who have taken advantage of the facilities existing in the matter of freedom of movement and establishment and who have acquired, by virtue of such facilities, the trade qualifications referred to by the directive in a Member State other than that whose nationality they possess.[33]

This rationale was well suited to the case in point; the plaintiff in the national proceedings was a Netherlands national who had resided in Belgium and there acquired the practical experience as a plumber which, pursuant to the directive, was to be accorded recognition by other Member States. The Court went on:

[30] Case 136/78 *Auer* [1979] ECR 437, para 20.
[31] Ibid, paras 22–26.
[32] Case 115/78 *Knoors* [1979] ECR 399.
[33] Ibid, para 20.

Although it is true that the provisions of the Treaty relating to establishment and the provision of services cannot be applied to situations which are purely internal to a Member State, the position nevertheless remains that the reference in Article [49 TFEU] to 'nationals of a Member State' who wish to establish themselves 'in the territory of another Member State' cannot be interpreted in such a way as to exclude from the benefit of Community law a given Member State's own nationals when the latter, owing to the fact that they have lawfully resided on the territory of another Member State and have there acquired a trade qualification which is recognised by the provisions of Community law, are, with regard to their State of origin, in a situation which may be assimilated to that of any other person enjoying the rights and liberties guaranteed by the Treaty.[34]

The effect of the judgment in *Knoors* is that nationals of a Member State may rely upon an 'establishment' directive even in their own Member State, where they have acquired a qualification covered by that directive in the territory of another Member State. The justification is that otherwise such nationals would be deprived of the advantages of the exercise of the right of establishment, in those cases where the qualification in question had in fact been secured by the exercise of the right of establishment in the first place.

In *Klopp*[35] the Court held that the right referred to in Article 49 TFEU to set up agencies and branches was a specific statement of a general principle, applicable equally to the liberal professions, according to which the right of establishment includes the freedom to set up and maintain, subject to observance of the professional rules of conduct, more than one place of work within the EU.[36] It was thus incompatible with freedom of establishment to deny to a national of another Member State the right to enter and to exercise the profession of advocate solely on the ground that he maintained chambers in another Member State, even if the national rules in question applied without discrimination on grounds of nationality. This case provides a good example of a non-discriminatory restriction which falls within the ordinary meaning of the words used in the text of the Treaty. It is thus incompatible with the right of establishment if national rules place at a disadvantage a person who has a place of business in more than one Member State, as compared to a person whose business activities are located within a single Member State.[37]

In the *Daily Mail* case the Court made it clear that Article 49 TFEU prohibited restrictions imposed by a Member State on its own nationals, or on companies incorporated under its legislation, seeking to establish themselves in the territory of another Member State. The Court stated:

Even though those provisions are directed mainly to ensuring that foreign nationals and companies are treated in the host Member State in the same way as nationals of that State, they also prohibit the Member State of origin from hindering the establishment in another Member State of one of its nationals or of a company incorporated under its legislation which comes within the definition contained in Article [54 TFEU].[38]

The foregoing case law indicated that the right of establishment gave to the nationals of a Member State the right to leave that Member State in order to take up self-employed

---

[34] Ibid, para 24.

[35] Case 107/83 *Klopp* [1984] ECR 2971.

[36] The context makes it clear that the Court is referring to a place of business in more than one Member State.

[37] For cases where national rules place at a disadvantage a person who has a place of business in more than one Member State, see eg Case 143/87 *Stanton* [1988] ECR 3877; Cases 154 and 155/87 *Wolf* [1988] ECR 3897; Case C-53/95 *Kemmler* [1996] ECR I-703; Case C-145/99 *Commission v Italy* [2002] ECR I-2235.

[38] Case 81/87 *Daily Mail* [1988] ECR 3483, para 16.

activities elsewhere, the right to set up a place of business in more than one Member State, and the right to carry on self-employed activities in another Member State under the same conditions as those laid down for nationals of that Member State. That the right to equality of treatment was the 'core' guarantee of Article 49 TFEU, and that that guarantee did not extend to a general prohibition on non-discriminatory measures which might be held to restrict the exercise of the right of establishment in some way was made clear in *Commission v Belgium*,[39] in which the Commission alleged that non-discriminatory Belgian rules governing the activities of clinical biology laboratories were incompatible with Article 49 TFEU, on the ground that the rules in question were excessively restrictive, and that the latter Article prohibited not only discriminatory measures, but also 'measures which apply to both nationals and foreigners without discrimination where they constitute an unjustified constraint for the latter'.[40] The Court rejected this approach to the right of establishment, emphasising that the text of Article 49 TFEU guaranteed equality of treatment for nationals and non-nationals, and stating:

> [P]rovided that such equality of treatment is respected, each Member State is, in the absence of Community rules in this area, free to lay down rules for its own territory governing the activities of laboratories providing clinical biology services.[41]

It will be recalled that in *Knoors* the proposition that a national in his or her own Member State might rely upon the terms of a directive adopted to secure the implementation of the right of establishment was justified by the fact that such a person might have brought himself or herself within the situation contemplated by the directive by prior exercise of the right of establishment. The Court took the proposition in *Knoors* a small step further in *Bouchoucha*, in that it described the scope of a case of a French national practising in France, while holding a professional diploma issued in another Member State, as 'not purely national' and noted that 'the applicability of the EEC Treaty provisions on freedom of establishment must be considered'.[42]

It fell to the Court in *Surinder Singh*[43] to consider whether a spouse (the husband) of a national of a Member State who had exercised her right of freedom of movement as an employed person in another Member State, and then returned to her own Member State to carry on self-employed activities, was entitled to install himself in the latter Member State. If his wife had been taking up self-employed activities in another Member State, it seemed that he would have derived that right from the applicable secondary legislation. It was argued, however, by the Member State of origin that the position was different where a national returned to her own Member State; such a situation was, it said, governed by national law. The Court replied as follows:

> However, this case is concerned not with a right under national law but with the rights of movement and establishment granted to a Community national by Articles [45] and [49] of the Treaty. These rights cannot be fully effective if such a person may be deterred from exercising them by obstacles raised in his or her country of origin to the entry and residence of his or her spouse. Accordingly, when a Community national who has availed himself or herself of those rights returns to his or her own country of origin, his or her spouse must enjoy at least the same

---

[39] Case 221/85 [1987] ECR 719.

[40] Ibid, para 5.

[41] Ibid, para 9. The Court confirmed this view of the scope of freedom of establishment in Case 198/86 *Conradi* [1987] ECR 4469.

[42] Case C-61/89 *Bouchoucha* [1990] ECR I-3551, para 11.

[43] Case C-370/90 *Surinder Singh* [1992] ECR I-4265.

rights of entry and residence as would be granted to him or her under Community law if his or her spouse chose to enter and reside in another Member State.[44]

This reasoning is worthy of remark. The Court appears disinclined to assert that the Treaty bestows directly on nationals of a Member State the right to enter that Member State—such a right is normally inherent in citizenship and arises under national law. So the Court asserts that an individual may be deterred from exercising his/her right to *leave* his/her own Member State in order to carry on economic activities in another Member State by the prospect of being treated less favourably on his/her return (as regards the right to be accompanied by his/her spouse) than he/she would be treated if he/she sought admission to another Member State instead. In *Akrich*, the Court made it clear that the right referred to in *Singh* arises where the national concerned returns to his Member State of origin in either an employed or self-employed capacity.[45]

In 1979 the Court in the *Cassis* case interpreted the free movement of goods provisions as covering non-discriminatory national measures which made the import of goods more difficult or costly,[46] and in 1991 in the *Säger* case the Court interpreted the provisions of the Treaty on the provision of services as applying to national rules which applied without distinction to nationals and non-nationals but nevertheless restricted the provision of services.[47] In 1993 the Court held in the *Kraus* case[48] that the right to freedom of movement for workers applied where a German national who had secured an academic title in the United Kingdom returned to his country of origin, it being the case that the possession of such a title constituted for the person entitled to make use of it an advantage for the purpose both of gaining entry to such a profession, and of prospering within it. The Court held, moreover, that Article 45 TFEU on the free movement of workers precluded any national measure governing the conditions under which an academic title obtained in another Member State might be used, where that measure, even though it was applicable without discrimination on grounds of nationality, was liable to hamper or to render less attractive the exercise by Community nationals, including those of the Member State which enacted the measure, of fundamental freedoms guaranteed by the Treaty. The situation would be different only if such a measure pursued a legitimate objective compatible with the Treaty and was justified by pressing reasons of public interest.[49] That this latter principle was also applicable in the context of Article 49 TFEU was made clear in *Gebhard*:[50]

[N]ational measures liable to hinder or make less attractive the exercise of fundamental freedoms guaranteed by the Treaty must fulfil four conditions: they must be applied in a non-discriminatory manner; they must be justified by imperative requirements in the general interest; they must be suitable for securing the attainment of the objective which they pursue; and they must not go beyond what is necessary in order to attain it (see Case C-19/92 *Kraus* . . ., para 32).[51]

---

[44] Ibid, para 23.

[45] Case C-109/01 *Akrich* [2003] ECR I-9607, paras 47 and 48. But for the rights of family members of a national of a Member State residing in the territory of another, see Case C-127/08 *Metock* [2008] ECR I-6241, and Chapter 15, at p 471.

[46] Chapter 14 at p 411.

[47] Below at p 563.

[48] Case C-19/92 *Kraus* [1993] ECR I-1663.

[49] Ibid, para 32. The Court of Justice in the event held that the national measure in question might be so justified. That a national of a Member State could rely upon the Treaty against his or her Member State of origin was justified in the terms referred to in *Knoors*, above, p 538.

[50] Case C-55/94 *Gebhard* [1995] ECR I-4165.

[51] Ibid, para 37.

The 'hinder or make less attractive' formulation continues to be used by the Court to describe restrictions on the exercise of the right of establishment which require justification if they are to be regarded as compatible with EU law,[52] but the Court also uses the formulation 'prohibit, impede or render less attractive (or advantageous)'[53] to describe such restrictions.[54]

In *Asscher* the Court considered whether a national of a Member State pursuing an activity as a self-employed person in another Member State, in which he/she resides, may rely on Article 49 TFEU against his/her Member State of origin, on whose territory he/she pursues another activity as a self-employed person. The Court stated:[55]

> It is settled law that, although the provisions of the Treaty relating to freedom of establishment cannot be applied to situations which are purely internal to a Member State, Article [49 TFEU] nevertheless cannot be interpreted in such a way as to exclude a given Member State's own nationals from the benefit of Community law where by reason of their conduct they are, with regard to their Member State of origin, in a situation which may be regarded as equivalent to that of any other person enjoying the rights and liberties guaranteed by the Treaty.

It appears from the foregoing survey of the case law that the Court's approach to the interpretation of the Treaty provisions on the right of establishment has been the subject of considerable development, both as regards the right of a national of a Member State, and members of the family deriving rights through that person, to invoke the right of establishment against the authorities of that Member State, and as regards the application of Article 49 TFEU to non-discriminatory national measures capable of restricting the right of establishment. It will be examined in a subsequent section of this chapter to what extent the formulation of the Court set out in *Gebhard* above is to be taken literally, since it implies that any national regulation of economic activity will have to be justified on grounds compatible with EU law, and in terms of proportionality, lest such regulation burden cross border economic activity.

C – Abolition of Restrictions on the Right of Establishment

(i) The General Programme and Secondary Legislation

The Treaty in its original text provided for the abolition of restrictions on freedom of establishment in progressive stages *during the transitional period*.[56] Such abolition was, and is, to be facilitated by secondary legislation abolishing restrictions on freedom of establishment,[57] ensuring the mutual recognition of 'diplomas and certificates, and other

---

[52] Joined Cases C-570/07 and C-571/07 *Pérez & Gómez* (CJEU 1 June 2010), para 53.

[53] The word 'attrayant' in the French version of a judgment may appear as 'attractive' or 'advantageous' in the English text: see eg Case C-389/05 *Commission v France* [2008] ECR I-5337, paras 52 and 57.

[54] The formulation appears to have been first used to describe restrictions on both the right of establishment and freedom to provide services in Case C-439/99 *Commission v Italy* [2002] ECR I-305.

[55] Case C-107/94 *Asscher* [1994] ECR I-1137, para 32, citing Case 115/78 *Knoors* [1979] ECR 399; Case C-61/89 *Bouchoucha* [1990] ECR I-3551; Case C-19/92 *Kraus* [1993] ECR I-1663; Case C-419/92 *Scholz* [1994] ECR I-505. This formulation may also provide the true explanation of Case C-370/90 *Surinder Singh* [1992] ECR I-4265.

[56] The words are omitted from the current text because they are now superfluous.

[57] See Art 50(2)(f) TFEU referring to 'effecting the progressive abolition of restrictions on freedom of establishment in every branch of activity under consideration'.

evidence of formal qualifications',[58] and co-ordinating national requirements concerning the pursuit of self-employed activities.[59] Legislation on the abolition of restrictions was to be preceded by a General Programme, which was to be drawn up by the Council before the end of the first stage. The Programme[60] was adopted in December 1961,[61] and provided the basis for the Council's subsequent legislative activities in this area.

(ii) Abolition of Discriminatory Restrictions by Secondary Legislation

Title III of the General Programme called for the abolition of discriminatory measures which might impair access to the non-wage-earning activities of nationals of the Member States, such as measures which:

— conditioned the access to or exercise of a non-wage earning activity on an authorisation or on the issuance of a document, such as a foreign merchant's card or a foreign professional's card;
— made the access to or exercise of a non-wage earning activity more costly through the imposition of taxes or other charges such as a deposit or surety bond paid to the receiving country;
— barred or limited membership in companies, particularly with regard to the activities of their members.

In addition to measures primarily likely to discriminate against nationals of the Member States with respect of access to non-wage-earning activities, the General Programme condemned specific national practices discriminating against such persons in the exercise of these activities, such as those limiting the opportunity:

— to enter into certain types of transactions, such as contracts for the hire of services or commercial and farm leases;
— to tender bids or to participate as a co-contractor or subcontractor in public contracts or contracts with public bodies;[62]
— to borrow and to have access to various forms of credit;
— to benefit from aids granted by the Member State.

Subsequently, the Council issued a series of Directives implementing the General Programme, and dealing with the right of establishment in a wide variety of commercial callings, from the wholesale trade to the provision of electricity, gas, water and sanitary services.[63] Many such Directives were applicable to both establishment and the provision

---

[58] Art 53(1) TFEU.

[59] Ibid.

[60] The General Programme constitutes neither a Regulation, Directive nor Decision within the meaning of Art 288 TFEU. For the view that it bound the Community institutions, but not the Member States, see W van Gerven (1966) 3 *CMLRev* 344, 354. There seems to be no reason why it could not bind the Member States, see Case 22/70 *ERTA* [1971] ECR 263.

[61] [1974] OJ Sp Edn, Second Series, IX, 7. The Court has referred to the General Programme in its case law, see eg Case 7/76 *Thieffry* [1977] ECR 765; Case 136/78 *Auer* [1979] ECR 452; Case 182/83 *Fearon* [1984] ECR 3677; Case 107/83 *Klopp* [1984] ECR 2971, Case C-208/00 *Überseering* [2002] ECR I-9919, at paras 74 and 75.

[62] There has been substantial harmonisation in this field, see in particular Directive 2004/17/EC of the European Parliament and of the Council, coordinating the procurement procedures of entities operating in the water, energy, transport and postal services sectors, [2004] OJ L134/1; Directive 2004/18/EC of the European Parliament and of the Council, on the coordination of procedures for the award of public works contracts, public supply contracts and public service contracts, [2004] OJ L134/114.

[63] The documents are too numerous to list.

of services, emphasising again the close practical relationship between the two. Directive 64/223 (which is no longer in force),[64] concerning the attainment of freedom of establishment and freedom to provide services in respect of activities in the wholesale trade, may be considered for illustrative purposes. Under the Directive, Member States were required to abolish the restrictions listed in Title III of the General Programmes with respect to the commercial activities concerned. Specific legislative provisions in effect in the Member States were singled out for prohibition, such as the obligation under French law to hold a *carte d'identité d'étranger commerçant*,[65] while Member States were obliged to ensure that beneficiaries of the Directive had the right to join professional or trade organisations under the same conditions, and with the same rights and obligations as their own nationals.[66] Where a host Member State required evidence of good character in respect of its own nationals taking up the commercial activities concerned, provision was made for accepting appropriate proof from other Member States, and for the taking of a solemn declaration by self-employed persons from such states, where the state in question did not issue the appropriate documentation.[67]

D – Effect of the Direct Applicability of Article 49 TFEU on Harmonisation

Although Article 53 of the EEC Treaty,[68] which prohibited Member States from introducing any new restrictions on the right of establishment of nationals of other Member States, was held by the Court to be directly applicable in *Costa v ENEL*,[69] the Council's extensive legislative scheme, based on the General Programme, appears to have been adopted on the basis that the prohibition of discrimination contained in Article 49 TFEU was ineffective in the absence of implementation. That this was not the case was made clear by the Court of Justice in *Reyners*.[70] The plaintiff in the main suit was a Dutch national resident in Belgium. He had been born in Belgium, educated there, and taken his *docteur en droit belge*, only to be finally refused admission to the Belgian bar on the ground of his Dutch nationality. On a reference for a preliminary ruling, the Court held that the prohibition on discrimination contained in Article 49 TFEU was directly applicable as of the end of the transitional period, despite the opening words of the text of that Article, which referred to the abolition of restrictions 'within the framework of the provisions set out below.' These provisions—the General Programme and the Directives provided for in Article 50 TFEU—were of significance 'only during the transitional period, since the freedom of establishment was fully attained at the end of it'. According to the Court, the aim of Article 49 TFEU was intended to be facilitated by the Council's Legislative programme, but not made dependent upon it.

---

[64] OJ Sp Edn [1963–64(I)] 123.
[65] Art 3.
[66] Art 4.
[67] Art 6.
[68] This Article appeared in the original text of the EEC Treaty, but was repealed as superfluous by the TA.
[69] Case 6/64 [1964] ECR 585.
[70] Case 2/74 [1974] ECR 631. For a discriminatory provision remaining on the statute book contrary to Art 49 TFEU, see Case 159/78 *Commission v Italy* [1979] ECR 3247. See also Case 38/87 *Commission v Greece* [1988] ECR 4415. For discriminatory conditions of tender contrary to Art 49 TFEU, see Case 197/84 *Steinhauser* [1985] ECR 1819.

The Court's decision had immediate repercussions. The Commission undertook, at a meeting of the Permanent Representatives, to report to the Council its view of the implications of the *Reyners* case for the implementation of the right of establishment. In its promised memorandum,[71] the Commission expressed the view that all the rules and formalities cited in the Directives on the abolition of restrictions were no longer applicable to nationals of the Member States, though in the interests of legal certainty, the Member States should formally bring their legislation into line with the requirements of Article 49 TFEU. In view of this, the Commission considered that it was no longer necessary to adopt Directives on the abolition of restrictions, and furthermore, since Directives were by their nature constitutive, that the adoption of such instruments having only declaratory effect would create confusion and protract the work of the Council unnecessarily. The latter view is open to question. Several Directives in the field of free movement of persons have been stated by the Court to give rise to no new rights, but merely to give closer articulation to rights bestowed directly by the Treaty.[72] This would also appear to be the case with Directive 75/117[73] on equal pay, which clarifies but does not add to the material scope of Article 157 TFEU. It was on this ground that Advocate General Verloren van Themaat urged the Court to hold a Member State in breach of Article 157 TFEU, rather than the Directive, in infringement proceedings brought by the Commission under Article 258 TFEU. The Court nonetheless held the Member State in default for failing to implement the Directive.[74] As the Court commented in *Reyners* itself, Directives already issued under Article 50(2) TFEU would not lose all interest, since they would 'preserve an important scope in the field of measures intended to make easier the effective exercise of the right of freedom of establishment'.[75] The Court was no doubt mindful of the value to the individual litigant before a national tribunal of some more precise formulation of his/her rights than the general prohibitions of the Treaty. In any event, the Commission formally withdrew a large number of proposed Directives on abolition of restrictions on freedom of establishment. A recent example of a Directive which contains some provisions declaratory of Treaty provisions on the right of establishment and freedom to provide services is the Directive on Services in the Internal Market (the Services Directive) which comprises the subject-matter of Chapter 18.

The prohibition in Article 49 TFEU of discrimination on grounds of nationality is not concerned solely with the specific rules on the pursuit of occupational activities but also with the rules relating to the various general facilities which are of assistance in the pursuit of those activities, including access to housing, and to the facilities provided by national authorities to alleviate the financial burden of acquiring housing.[76] For further discussion of the rights of economically active persons and members of their families to equal access to such benefits and facilities in the Member States, see Chapter 16.

---

[71] Commission Communication, SEC (74) Final, Brussels.

[72] Case 43/75 *Royer* [1976] ECR 497.

[73] [1975] OJ L45/19; repealed and replaced by Directive 2006/54/EC on the implementation of the principle of equal opportunities and equal treatment for men and women in matters of employment and occupation (recast) [2006] OJ L204/23.

[74] Case 58/81 *Commission v Luxembourg* [1982] ECR 2175.

[75] [1974] ECR 631, 652.

[76] See eg Case 63/86 *Commission v Italy* [1988] ECR 129; Case 305/87 *Commission v Greece* [1989] ECR 1461.

E – Direct and Indirect Discrimination on Grounds of Nationality

Article 49 TFEU has been interpreted as prohibiting both direct and indirect discrimination on grounds of nationality. Direct discrimination takes place when individuals or undertakings are treated differently by reference to their nationality.

Examples of direct discrimination are:

— a requirement that nationals *of other Member States* set up a company incorporated in the host Member State before obtaining a licence to fish at sea;[77]
— a requirement that in order for a ship to qualify for the nationality of a Member State, it must be *owned by nationals of that Member State;*[78]
— a requirement *applying only to nationals of certain new Member States* that such nationals wishing to register a partnership or limited company prove that they will not be working as employees by presenting a certificate prescribed by national law.[79]

In such cases the reference to nationality as a ground for differentiation is express, and such discrimination is described as 'direct' or 'overt'.

The Court has held that Article 49 TFEU prohibits not only direct, or overt discrimination by reason of nationality, but also all covert forms of discrimination which, by the application of other criteria of differentiation, lead in fact to the same result.[80] In *Commission v Italy* a national measure providing that only companies in which all or a majority of the shares are either directly or indirectly in public or state ownership may conclude agreements for the development of data-processing systems for public authorities was held to be contrary to Article 49 TFEU.[81] The Court held that although the rules in issue applied without distinction to all companies, they *essentially favoured* domestic companies, and observed that no data-processing companies from other Member States qualified under the criteria in question at the material time.[82] In the *Asscher* case the Court identified as being potentially discriminatory legislation which was 'liable to act mainly to the detriment of nationals of other Member States'.[83] Criteria that have been identified as potential sources of indirect discrimination include the place of residence of self-employed persons or the principal place of establishment of companies.[84]

However, differentiation between situations on objective grounds consistent with the Treaty does not amount to prohibited discrimination. Although residence requirements may amount in certain cases to indirect discrimination,[85] the Court has held that a national law exempting rural land from compulsory acquisition if the owners have lived on or near the land for a specified period is consistent with Article 49 TFEU, where the purpose of the law is to ensure as far as possible that rural land belongs to those who work it, and where the law applies equally to its own nationals and to the nationals of

---

[77] Case C-93/89 *Commission v Ireland* [1991] ECR I-4569.
[78] Case C-221/89 *Factortame* [1991] ECR I-3905.
[79] Case C-161/07 *Commission v Austria* [2008] ECR I-671, paras 29 and 30.
[80] Case C-3/88 *Commmission v Italy* [1989] ECR 4035.
[81] Ibid.
[82] [1989] ECR 4035, paras 9 and 10.
[83] Case C-107/94 *Asscher* [1994] ECR I-1137, para 38.
[84] Case C-1/93 *Halliburton Services* 1994] ECR I-1137; Case C-330/91 *Commerzbank* [1993] ECR I-4017; Case C-80/94 *Wielockx* [1965] ECR I-2493.
[85] Case C-80/94 *Wielockx* [1995] ECR I-2493; and see Case 152/73 *Sotgiu* [1974] ECR 153.

other Member States.[86] Again, in *Commission v France* the Court acknowledged the possibility that a distinction based on the location of the registered office of a company or the place of residence of a natural person might under certain conditions be justified in an area such as tax law.[87] National tax rules are increasingly held to amount to restrictions on freedom of establishment and other fundamental freedoms, and this topic is covered in some detail in section VI of the present chapter.

The principle that Article 49 TFEU prohibits discrimination against undertakings located in other Member States requires national authorities to accord sufficient publicity to the award of public contracts to allow such undertakings to express an interest in such contracts. EU public procurement directives[88] impose detailed and specific requirements for the advertisement and award of public contracts of various kinds, such as public works contracts, public supply contracts and public service contracts.[89] However, not all contracts with public authorities are subject to the requirements of these directives. Contracts below a minimum value are excluded,[90] and public concessions are excluded.[91] Nevertheless, when a contract or concession may be of interest to an undertaking located in a Member State other than that of the contracting or concession-granting authority, that authority is bound to comply with the obligation of transparency. This obligation requires the authority to ensure, for the benefit of a potential tenderer, a degree of publicity sufficient to enable the contact or concession to be opened up to competition and the impartiality of the award procedures to be reviewed.[92] Thus, in *Coname* the Court of Justice considered whether the direct award by a public authority of a management concession for a gas distribution service was compatible with Articles 49 and 56 TFEU.[93] The direct award of the concession to the Padania company was challenged before an Italian court by Coname, an undertaking which had previously held the concession in question. The Italian court asked whether it was consistent with Articles 49 and 56 TFEU to award such a concession without an invitation to tender. The Court held that in so far as the contract might also have been of interest to an undertaking located in another Member State, lack of transparency in the award of the contract would amount to a difference in treatment to the detriment of the undertaking located in the other Member State. The Court considered that:

> Unless it is justified by objective circumstances, such a difference in treatment, which, by excluding all undertakings located in another Member State, operates mainly to the detriment of the latter undertakings, amounts to indirect discrimination on the basis of nationality, prohibited under Articles [49 TFEU and 56 TFEU] . . .
>
> In those circumstances, it is for the referring court to satisfy itself that the award of the concession . . . complies with transparency requirements which, without necessarily implying an obligation to hold an invitation to tender, are, in particular, such as to ensure that an undertak-

---

[86] Case 182/83 *Fearon* [1984] ECR 3677.

[87] Case 270/83 [1986] ECR 273, para 19.

[88] Directive 2004/17/EC coordinating the procurement procedures of entities operating in the water, energy, transport and postal services sectors [2004] OJ L134/1; Directive 2004/18/EC on the coordination of procedures for the award of public works contracts, public supply contracts, and public service contracts [2004] OJ L134/14.

[89] Directive 2004/18/EC, ibid.

[90] Directive 2004/17/EC, Art 16; Directive 2004/18/EC, Art 7.

[91] Directive 2004/17, Art 3(a) and 18; Directive 2004/18/EC, Arts 1(4) and 17.

[92] Case C-64/08 *Engelmann* (CJEU 9 September 2010), para 50 (concession); Case C-220/06 *Asociación Profesional de Empresas de RepArt o y Manipulado de Correspondencia* [2007] ECR I-12175, paras 71–76 (contract below threshold for procurement directive).

[93] Case C-231/03 *Coname* [2005] ECR I-7287.

ing located in the territory of a Member State other than that of the Italian Republic can have access to appropriate information regarding that concession before it is awarded, so that, if the undertaking had so wished, it would have been in a position to express its interest in obtaining that concession.[94]

If the national court found that this was not the case, it would have to be concluded that there was a difference in treatment to the detriment of an undertaking located in another Member State. In such an event, the Court of Justice ruled out the possibility that such a difference in treatment could be objectively justified.

F – Relationship between Article 18 TFEU and Articles 49 and 56 TFEU

Article 18 TFEU prohibits discrimination on grounds of nationality within the scope of operation of the TEU and TFEU. This general prohibition of discrimination has been implemented as regards freedom of establishment and the provision of services by Articles 49 and 56 TFEU.[95] The Court has held that any rules incompatible with the latter Articles are also incompatible with Article 18 TFEU.[96] However, non-discriminatory rules which disadvantage a person by virtue of the fact that he has more than one place of business within the Community may be consistent with Article 18 TFEU but inconsistent with Article 49 TFEU.[97] And non-discriminatory rules which amount to restrictions on the provision of services may be incompatible with Article 56 TFEU, but consistent with Article 18 TFEU.[98] Furthermore, Article 18 TFEU 'applies independently only to situations governed by Community law in regard to which the Treaty lays down no specific prohibition of discrimination'.[99]

G – Non-discriminatory Restrictions on the Right of Establishment

It has been noted in section III.B above on the evolution of the Court's case law on Article 49 TFEU that in the *Gebhard* case[100] the Court adopted the concept of the non-discriminatory restriction on the right of establishment. That approach has been maintained and developed in a considerable subsequent case law. For convenience, the present writer will describe as the '*Gebhard* approach' the analysis which defines as restrictions on the right of establishment those national measures which hinder or make less attractive the exercise of that right, or prohibit impede or render less attractive the exercise of that right. A

---

[94] Case C-231/03, paras 19 and 21. See also Case C-324/98 *Telaustria* [2000] ECR I-10745; Case C-458/03 *Parking Brixen* [2005] ECR I-8585; Commission Interpretative Communication on the Community law applicable to contract awards not or not fully subject to the provisions of the Public Procurement Directives [2006] OJ C179/2; Joined Cases C-147/06 and C-148/06 *SECAP SpA* [2008] ECR I-3565 (automatic exclusion of tenders considered to be abnormally low as regards contracts of cross-border interest may constitute indirect discrimination and restrict access to the market).

[95] And as regards freedom of movement for workers by Art 45 TFEU.

[96] Case 90/76 *van Ameyde* [1977] ECR 1091, 1126, para 27; Case 305/87 *Commission v Greeece* [1989] ECR 1461, para 12.

[97] Case 143/87 *Stanton* [1988] ECR 3877; Joined Cases 154 and 155/87 *Wolf* [1988] ECR 3897.

[98] For the scope of Art 56 TFEU, see below at pp 554–58.

[99] Case 305/87 *Commission v Greece* [1989] ECR 1461, para 13; Case C-269/07 *Commission v Germany* [2009] ECR I-7811, at para 98; Case C-97/09 *Schmelz* (CJEU 26 October 2010) para 44.

[100] Case C-55/94 *Gebhard* [1995] ECR I-4165, above at p 540.

question yet to be resolved is whether the *Gebhard* approach is to be taken at face value, that is to say, as requiring to be justified *all* non-discriminatory measures likely to hinder or make less attractive the exercise of the right of establishment. An alternative possibility is that although all discriminatory restrictions have to be justified, non-discriminatory restrictions only require justification if they restrict access to the market. There were still signs in post-*Gebhard* case law that the Court regarded the main aim of Article 49 TFEU as being to prohibit discriminatory restrictions on establishment; thus in the *Royal Bank of Scotland* case, the Court states:

> It is common ground that the essential aim of Article [49] of the Treaty is to implement, in the field of self-employment, the principle of equal treatment laid down in Article [18] of the Treaty.[101]

Yet this emphasis on the significance of the principle of equal treatment in the scheme of Article 49 TFEU is not repeated in subsequent case law. There has already been some discussion in Chapter 16, on the scope of the prohibition on non-discriminatory restrictions laid down by Article 45 TFEU.[102] That analysis is in principle applicable to Article 49 TFEU, and the reader is accordingly referred to the relevant passages in that chapter, but it is nevertheless appropriate to consider cases specific to Article 49 TFEU in which the Court has had recourse to the *Gebhard* approach.

The *Gebhard* approach has led the Court to conclude that nationality requirements as to companies, shareholders and directors, defined by reference to the nationality of *any* Member State, rather than the nationality of the host state, may nevertheless constitute restrictions on freedom of establishment. In *Commission v Netherlands*[103] the Court considered Netherlands rules which conditioned registration of a ship in the Netherlands on the shareholders and directors of a 'Community' company owning the ship being of 'Community' nationality, and required local representatives in the Netherlands to be of 'Community' nationality.[104] The Court noted that if ship-owning companies wishing to register their ships in the Netherlands did not satisfy the conditions in issue, their only course of action would be to alter the structure of their share capital or of their boards of directors, and that such changes might entail serious disruption within a company and also require the completion of numerous formalities having financial consequences. The Court considered that the requirements amounted to restrictions which could not be justified. The Court's analysis is consistent with the conclusion that the rules in issue had discriminatory effects; yet the starting point is that even non discriminatory rules which hinder or make less attractive the exercise of a fundamental freedom must be justified.[105]

In *Pfeiffer Großhandel*[106] the Court considered the compatibility with Article 49 TFEU of a restraining order which prevented an Austrian subsidiary of a German parent operating discount stores in Austria from using a trade name used by the German parent in Germany and other Member States. The Court referred to the *Gebhard* test and held that the order in question was 'liable to constitute an impediment to the realization by those undertakings of a uniform advertising concept at Community level since it might force

---

[101] Case C-311/97 *Royal Bank of Scotland* [1999] ECR I-2651, para 21.
[102] Above at p 520.
[103] C-299/02 *Commission v Kingdom of the Netherlands* [2004] ECR I-9761.
[104] EEA nationality was a permissible alternative for shareholders, directors and local representatives.
[105] C-299/02 *Commission v Kingdom of the Netherlands* [2004] ECR I-9761, para 15.
[106] Case C-255/97 *Pfeiffer Großhandel* [1999] ECR I-2835.

them to adjust the presentation of the businesses they operate according to the place of establishment'.[107]

It is possible to see in this judgment the basis of a potentially far-reaching principle that any national measure which might constitute an impediment to the realisation by a company of a 'uniform advertising concept at Community level' is to be treated as prima facie contrary to Article 49 TFEU and must accordingly be justified. A narrower proposition is that preventing a national of one Member State or a company with its seat in one Member State from carrying out economic activities in another Member State under a title or trade name which it is entitled to use in the first Member State is to be regarded as in principle a restriction on *access* to the market of that Member State. This might be seen as analogous to case law holding incompatible with the free movement of goods national rules preventing the marketing of imported goods under their home country designation.[108] Restrictions on advertising the products or services provided by a subsidiary can amount to a restriction on the right of establishment of the parent. The Court held in *Corpoación Dermoestética*[109] that national rules prohibiting television advertisements for medical and surgical treatments provided by private health care establishments constituted, for companies established in other Member States, a serious obstacle to the pursuit of their activities by means of a subsidiary established in that Member State, and were therefore liable to make it more difficult for such economic operators to gain access to that market.

In *Commission v France*, which concerned the activities of bovine artificial insemination centres, the grant of an exclusive right to an economic operator for a particular geographical area was held to constitute a restriction on the right of establishment of other operators from other Member States.[110] And a requirement that any person wishing to operate a gaming establishment adopt the legal form of a public limited company was held in *Engelmann* to be a restriction on freedom of establishment which required justification. The Court's reasoning was that such a condition prevented operators—whether these were natural persons or undertakings—which, in the country in which they were established, had chosen a different corporate form, from setting up a secondary establishment in the Member State in question.[111] More broadly, the Court has held that non-discriminatory national rules which make establishment in the Member State in question subject to the issue of a licence or other prior authorisation, and allow business activities to be pursued only by certain economic operators who satisfy predetermined requirements, constitute a restriction on establishment which must be justified.[112] A criterion for the grant of a licence involving discretion requires justification since it may open the way for an arbitrary use of the discretion on the part of the competent authorities.[113] In *Hartlauer*, the

---

[107] Ibid, para 20.

[108] See eg Case 286/86 *Deserbais* [1988] ECR 4907 (German Edam could be marketed as such in the Netherlands despite not meeting the fat content requirements of Dutch Edam).

[109] Case C-500/06 *Corpoación Dermoestética* [2008] ECR I-5785, para 33.

[110] Case C-389/05 *Commission v France* [2008] ECR I-5337, para 53.

[111] Case C-64/08 *Engelmann* (CJEU 9 September 2010); Case C-70/95 *Sodemare* [1997] ECR I-3395 (healthcare activities confined to non-profit-making bodies); Case C-451/03 *Servizi Ausiliari Dottori Commercialisti* [2006] ECR I-2941 (certain tax advice activities reserved to tax advice centres); Case C-514/03 *Commission v Spain* [2006] ECR I-963 (private security undertaking must be constituted as a legal person), citing Case C-171/02 *Commission v Portugal* [2004] ECR I-5645, paras 41–44.

[112] Joined Cases C-338/04, C-359/04 and C-360/04 *Placanica and Others* [2007] ECR I-891, para 42; Case C-531/06 *Commission v Italy* [2009] ECR I-4103, para 44; Case C-531/06 *Commission v* Italy [2009] ECR I-4103, paras 44 and 45; Joined Cases C-171/07 and C-172/07 *Apothekerkammer des Saarlandes* [2009] ECR I-4171, paras 23 and 24 (right to operate a pharmacy restricted to pharmacists).

[113] Case C-438/08 *Commission v Portugal* [2009] ECR I-10219, para 30.

Court held that where the pursuit of an activity (*in casu* that of a private outpatient dental clinic) is subject to a condition linked to the economic or social need for that activity, that condition constitutes a restriction on the right of establishment, since it tends to limit the number of providers of that service, and deters or even prevents undertakings from other Member States from pursuing that activity in the Member State in question through a fixed place of business.[114] If a licencing scheme is to be justified, it must be based on objective, non-discriminatory criteria known in advance, in such a way as to circumscribe the exercise of the national authorities' discretion so that it is not used arbitrarily.[115]

In cases such as those referred to above, the measure which is described by the Court as a restriction on the right of establishment of economic operators from other Member States is a restriction which applies equally in law to economic operators originating in the Member State which is applying the contested measure. It might be said that in some cases, for example a requirement that an operator adopt a particular legal form to carry out a particular economic activity, there is some added burden *in fact* for an operator located in another Member State, which is already carrying on that same activity through a different legal form. However, a requirement such as that in issue in *Hartlauer*, that new places of business may only be set up if it is considered that there is an economic or social need for it, would seem to place the same restriction in fact, as well as in law, upon a domestic economic operator wishing to open a new outlet, as it places upon an economic operator based in another Member State wishing to do the same. The real mischief of such measures seems to be that they place restrictions of one kind or another upon economic operators seeking new business outlets or marketing opportunities rather than placing a particular burden upon economic operators from other Member States; though it is only, of course, market operators from other Member States who can claim infringement of the right of establishment.

In the *CaixaBank France* case[116] the Court considered whether national rules of a Member State prohibiting the remuneration of 'sight' current accounts in euros constituted restrictions on the freedom of establishment prohibited by Article 49 TFEU in so far as they apply to the subsidiary formed in that Member State by a legal person from another Member State. Advocate General Tizzano attempted to 'unravel the case law'.[117] He found it difficult to accept that national measures could be restrictions contrary to the Treaty for the sole reason that they reduced the economic attractiveness of pursuing an economic activity, if those measures did not directly affect access to that activity and did not discriminate on grounds of nationality. If such measures were restrictions, it would enable economic operators, both national and foreign, to oppose all national regulation, and would create a market in which 'rules are prohibited as a matter of principle, except for those necessary and proportionate to meeting imperative requirements in the general interest'. For that reason he did not consider that that was the right road to take.[118] In his view:

> [W]here the principle of non-discrimination is respected—and hence the conditions for the taking up and pursuit of an economic activity are equal both in law and in fact—a national measure

---

[114] Case C-169/07 *Hartlauer* [2009] ECR I-1721, paras 36–38.
[115] Case C-64/08 *Engelmann* (CJEU 9 September 2010) para 55.
[116] Case C-442/02 *CaixaBank France* [2004] ECR I-8961.
[117] Ibid, Opinion of AG, para 58.
[118] Ibid, paras 62 and 63.

cannot be described as a restriction on the freedom of movement of persons unless, in the light of its purpose and effects, the measure in question *directly affects market access*.[119]

In the Court's view, the prohibition in issue constituted for companies from Member States other than France 'a serious obstacle to the pursuit of their activities via a subsidiary in the latter Member State, affecting their access to the market'.[120] The prohibition deprived out-of-state companies of the possibility of competing more effectively with the banks traditionally established in France, which had an extensive network of branches and therefore greater opportunities for raising capital from the public. It is to be noted that the prohibition in issue discriminated against out-of-state banks seeking to enter the market in France because it reinforced a barrier to market entry in the sector in question (the cost of acquiring an extensive network of branches). It may be that where a national rule reinforces a barrier to market entry, and is accordingly likely to make it difficult for new market entrants to compete with established market entrants, this is enough to attract the application of Article 49 TFEU, since at the very least some new market entrants will or may be out-of-state operators. However, the Court's judgment is not to be confined to situations where national rule reinforces a barrier to market entry, such as the existence of a branch network, since the Court makes an observation which seems to be of more general application:

> Where credit institutions which are subsidiaries of foreign companies seek to enter the market of a Member State, competing by means of the rate of remuneration paid on sight accounts constitutes one of the most effective means to that end. Access to the market by those establishments is thus made more difficult by such a prohibition.[121]

This passage supports the proposition that national rules which deprive a new market entrant of what would be an effective means of competing with established market operators restricts access to the market and hinders the exercise of the right of establishment. National rules which make it more difficult for market operators to compete with each other might well be said to restrict market access even if the rules themselves regulate the conduct of business activities rather than market access as such. Advocate General Poiares Maduro has said that this case illustrates the principle 'that any national policy that results in treating transnational situations less favourably than purely national situations constitutes a restriction on the freedoms of movement'.[122] He goes on:

> The less favourable treatment of transnational situations may take various forms. Often it manifests itself as an obstacle to access to the national market, either by protecting positions acquired on that market or by making it more difficult for cross-border service providers to participate in the market.[123]

The present writer does not agree that national rules which protect positions acquired on the market are treating transnational situations less favourably than purely national situations. Any protection for established market positions is at the expense of new market entrants, including those originating in the Member State applying the contested rules, rather than in particular new market entrants from other Member States. If it is assumed that those holding established positions on the market are domestic operators, then the

---

[119] Ibid, para 66.
[120] Case C-442/02 *CaixaBank France*, [2004] ECR I-8961, para 12 .
[121] Ibid, para 14.
[122] Joined Cases C-94/04 and C-202/04 *Cipolla* [2006] ECR I-11421, Opinion, paras 57 and 58.
[123] Ibid, para 59.

protection afforded those operators from competition from new market entrants from other Member States would amount to indirect discrimination on grounds of nationality.[124] But the Court's analysis is framed in terms of market access, rather than indirect discrimination on grounds of nationality. Even if a market analysis in *Caixabank* would have shown that French banks dominate the French retail banking market, no such analysis was undertaken.

The Court applied the *Caixabank* case, 'by way of analogy', in the *Attanasio* case, in which the Court concluded that a requirement that there be a minimum distance between roadside petrol stations amounted to a restriction under Article 49 TFEU, since it made access to the activity of fuel distribution subject to conditions, and, by being more advantageous to operators already present on the Italian market, was liable to deter, or even prevent, access to the Italian market by operators from other Member States.[125]

It seems that national measures which make it difficult for market operators from other Member States to compete, from fixed places of business in the host Member State, with established market operators in that Member State, amount to restrictions on access to the market, and to restrictions on the exercise of the right of establishment, which must be justified, if they are to be regarded as compatible with Article 49 TFEU. This conclusion does not resolve at the level of principle all questions of demarcation between regulatory provisions which restrict access to the market, and those which do not. National rules requiring retail shops to close on Sundays and public holidays might be said to deprive market operators from other Member States of an effective method of competing with undertakings already established on the market. Yet the Court has taken a similar approach to Sunday closing rules in the context of the right of establishment to that it has taken in the context of the free movement of goods. It has rejected the argument that such rules require justification under Article 49 TFEU, reasoning that 'any restrictive effects which [such rules] might have on freedom of establishment are too uncertain and indirect' to be capable of hindering that freedom.[126] It seems that deciding whether national rules require justification because they make it more difficult for market operators from other Member States to compete with operators already established on the market in question, or do not require justification because any effect on the right of establishment is to be regarded as too uncertain and indirect, will involve questions of fact and degree, and indeed an impressionistic element.

H – Parallel Interpretation of Articles 45, 49 and 56 TFEU and Horizontal Effect

Theoretically, problems may arise in differentiating between the employed and the self-

---

[124] The Court has treated advertising bans as discriminating against imported products on the basis that such bans place imports at a disadvantage because consumers are familiar with domestic products. In Case C-405/98 *Gourmet International* [2005] ECR I-1795, para 21, the Court suggests that, in light of the characteristics of the product market in question, a ban on advertising is liable to impede access to the market by imports more than by domestic products, with which consumers are instantly more familiar. In Case C-239/02 *Douwe Egberts* [2004] ECR I-7017, para 53, the Court makes no mention of the characteristics of the product market in question, and simply repeats the proposition that a ban on advertising is liable to impede access to the market of imports more than domestic products.

[125] In Case C-384/08 *Attanasio* (CJEU 11 March 2010) para 45.

[126] Joined Cases C-418/93 etc, *Semeraro Casa Uno* [1996] ECR I-2975, para 32.

employed, and between instances of establishment and provision of services, but it will in many cases be unnecessary to make any hard and fast classification because the applicable principles will be the same in any event. Thus, in *Royer*,[127] the Court of Justice, considering a request for a preliminary ruling from a national court which was uncertain whether the subject of the proceedings before it was to be considered as falling within Article 45, Article 49 or Article 56 TFEU, observed:

> [C]omparison of these different provisions shows that they are based on the same principles both in so far as they concern the entry into and residence in the territory of Member States of persons covered by Community law and the prohibition of all discrimination between them on grounds of nationality.[128]

The distinction between employed and self-employed persons may, however, be important in relation to migrants from new Member States. Transitional arrangements may allow for temporary derogation from the rules guaranteeing non-discriminatory access for workers to the labour market, while freedom of movement for the self-employed is fully guaranteed.[129] The distinction between employed and self-employed persons will thus be significant in this context.

An important corollary of the statement of principle in the *Royer* case quoted above is that Article 49 TFEU, like Article 56 TFEU, must be construed as prohibiting discrimination by private parties as well as by public authorities. In *Walrave*[130] the Court expressed the opinion that Article 45 TFEU (free movement of workers) extended to agreements and rules other than those emanating from public authorities, citing in support of its view the text of Article 7(4) of Regulation 1612/68, which nullifies discriminatory clauses in individual or collective employment agreements. A similar conclusion was justified in the case of Article 56 TFEU, since the activities referred to therein were 'not to be distinguished by their nature from those in Article [45], but only by the fact that they are performed outside the ties of a contract of employment'.[131] That Article 49 TFEU has a similar ambit was confirmed by the Court in the *Viking* case.[132] Viking was a Finnish operator of ferry services between Finland and Estonia, which wished to change its place of establishment to Estonia in order to benefit from lower wage levels and provide its services from there. A Finnish trade union, supported by an international association of trade unions, sought to prevent this from happening and threatened strike action and boycotts if the company were to move without maintaining its current wage levels. The Court held that a private-sector operator such as Viking could rely on Article 49 TFEU against private bodies such as a trade union and an international association of trade unions, where the latter took collective action which restricted the right of establishment of the ferry operator concerned. The Court also held that the trade union bodies involved could justify such collective action on grounds of overriding reasons of public interest, in particular the protection of workers, providing that the jobs or conditions of employment at issue were jeopardised or under serious threat, and providing that the collective action in issue was

---

[127] Case 48/75 *Royer* [1976] ECR 497. And see Case 118/75, *Watson & Belmann* [1976] ECR 1185.

[128] [1976] ECR 497, 509. For parallel interpretation of Arts 45 and 49 TFEU, see Case C-106/91 *Ramrath* [1992] ECR I-3351, para 17; and Case C-107/94 *PH Asscher* [1994] ECR I-1137, para 29.

[129] The distinction may be relevant to the application of an association agreement prior to the accession of the state concerned: see Case C-268/99 *Jany* [2001] ECR I-8615.

[130] Case 36/74 *Walrave* [1974] ECR 1405.

[131] [1974] ECR 1405, 1419; and see Case C-281/98 *Angonese* [2000] ECR I-4139 (Art 45 TFEU binding on employers)

[132] Case C-438/05 *Viking* [2007] ECR I-10779.

suitable for achievement of the objective pursued and did not go beyond what was necessary to attain that objective.

While Articles 45, 49 and 56 TFEU might have similar effects in certain circumstances, this will not be so in all cases (quite apart from the special position of migrants from new Member States) Application in particular of the principle of proportionality may yield different results according to whether or not a particular individual or undertaking is providing services or is established in a Member State whose legislation Is called in question. Thus, for examplem, national rules requiring registration with an appropriate trade or professional body are presumptively not applicable to those providing services, but applicable to those established in the Member State in question.[133]

IV – FREEDOM TO PROVIDE SERVICES

A – General Scope

Article 56 TFEU provides that

> [w]ithin the framework of the provisions set out below, restrictions on freedom to provide services within the Community shall be prohibited in respect of nationals of Member States who are established in a State of the Community other than that of the person for whom the services are intended.

It will be noted that in order to invoke this provision, nationals must be 'established' in a Member State. In the case of companies whose registered office is situated inside the EU, but whose central management or principal place of business is not, this requirement is stated by the General Programme on Services to be satisfied by their activities having

> a real and continuous link with the economy of a Member State, excluding the possibility that this link might depend on nationality, particularly the nationality of the partners or the members of the managing or supervisory bodies, or of persons holding the capital stock.[134]

Yet it is not necessary for an undertaking to provide services in the Member State in which it is established in order to invoke its right to provide services in another Member State under Article 56 TFEU.[135] It is to be noted that a company registered in a Member State may be established in that Member State even if it conducts all its business through an agency branch or subsidiary in another Member State.[136]

'Services' are defined in Article 57 TFEU, and are considered as such when they are 'normally provided for remuneration'. The essential characteristic of remuneration lies in

---

[133] Case C-215/01 *Schnitzer* [2003] ECR I-14847; Case 292/86 *Gullung* [1988] ECR 111. Thus, Art 4 of Directive 77/249/EEC on provision of services by lawyers, exempts service providers from registration in the host Member State, while Art 3 of Directive 98/5/EC on the establishment of lawyers provides for such registration.

[134] General Programme (Services), [1974] OJ Sp Edn, 2nd Series, IX, 3.

[135] Case C-56/96 *VT4* [1997] ECR I-3143, para 22 (UK broadcaster's transmissions aimed exclusively at a Flemish audience); Case C-46/08 *Carmen Media Group* (CJEU 8 September 2010) para 43 (Gibraltar operator licensed exclusively to cover bets offered, via the internet, to persons located outside Gibraltar).

[136] Case 79/85 *Segers* [1986] ECR 2375; Case C-212/97 *Centros* [1999] ECR I-1458, below at p 650.

the fact that it constitutes consideration for the service in question.[137] One would expect the remuneration to be provided by the receiver of services, but this is not essential. In the *Debauve* and *Coditel* cases, Advocate General Warner expressed the opinion that the purpose of the definition of 'services' in Article 57 TFEU was to exclude those that are normally provided gratuitously. Television broadcasting thus in his view fell within the definition whether it was financed by licence fee or by advertising. The deciding factor was that the broadcasting was remunerated in one way or another.[138] *Bond van Adverteerders*[139] concerned, inter alia, the provision of services by cable television operators in one Member State to broadcasters in another by relaying to network subscribers in the first Member State television programmes transmitted to them by the broadcasters. The Court held that these services were provided for remuneration. The cable network operators were paid, in the form of the fees which they charged their subscribers for the service which they provided to the broadcaster, and it was irrelevant that the broadcasters generally did not themselves pay the cable network operators for relaying their programmes.[140] Similarly, the fact that hospital medical treatment is financed directly by sickness insurance funds on the basis of agreements and pre-set scales of fees does not remove such treatment from the sphere of services within the meaning of Article 57 TFEU.[141]

A non-exhaustive list of services in Article 57 TFEU specifies activities of an industrial character, activities of a commercial character, activities of craftsmen, and activities of the professions. Where a particular activity falls within the provisions of the Treaty relating to the free movement of goods, capital or persons, however, these latter provisions govern. The Court has held that the broadcasting of television signals,[142] cable transmission,[143] tourism, medical treatment[144] (including the termination of pregnancy[145] and in-patient hospital treatment[146]), education at school and university (where privately rather than publicly funded),[147] the importation of lottery advertisements and tickets into a Member State,[148] and unsolicited telephone calls to potential clients[149] are covered by the provisions on the freedom to provide services. In a different, but it seems analogous, context the Court has held that prostitution is a provision of services for remuneration.[150]

Without prejudice to the right of establishment, a person providing a service may, in order to do so, 'temporarily pursue his activity in the State where the service is pro-

---

[137] Case C-157/99 *Smits and Peerbooms* [2001] ECR I-5473, para 58.
[138] Case 52/79 *Debauve* [1980] ECR 833; Case 62/79 *Coditel v Ciné Vog Films* [1980] ECR 881 Opinion at 876.
[139] Case 352/85 [1988] ECR 2085.
[140] Ibid, para 16.
[141] Case C-157/99 *Smits and Peerbooms* [2001] ECR I-5473, para 56.
[142] Case 155/73 *Sacchi* [1974] ECR 490, para 6.
[143] Case 52/79 *Debauve* [1980] ECR 833, para 8; Case C-23/93 *TV10* [1994] ECR I-1963, para 13; Case C-17/00 *De Coster* [2001] ECR I-9445, para 28.
[144] Case C-157/99 *Smits and Peerbooms* [2001] ECR I-5473.
[145] Case 159/90 *Grogan* [1991] ECR I-4685, para 18.
[146] Case C-157/99 *Smits and Peerbooms* [2001] ECR I-5473.
[147] Joined Cases 286/82 and 26/83 *Luisi and Carbone* [1984] ECR 377; C-198/82 *Wirth* [1993] ECR I-6447, paras 15 and 16; Case C-56/09 *Zanotti* (CJEU 20 May 2010) (university courses financed by persons seeking training or professional specialisation constitute services within the meaning of Art 57 TFEU); Case C-318/05 *Commission v Germany* [2007] ECR I-6952 (school fees for privately funded schools even if funding not principally provided by the parents of pupils).
[148] Case C-275/92 *Schindler* [1994] ECR I-1039, para 37.
[149] Case C-384/93 *Alpine Investments* [1995] ECR I-1141.
[150] Case C-268/99 *Jany* [2001] ECR I-8615, para 49 (interpretation of provision of EC–Poland Association Agreement having the same meaning as Art 49 TFEU).

vided, under the same conditions as are imposed by that State on its own nationals'.[151] The Court of Justice in *Rush Portuguesa* concluded from these words that an undertaking could accordingly take with it its staff to the territory of another Member State to provide services there:

> Articles [56 and 57 TFEU] therefore preclude a Member State from prohibiting a person providing services established in another Member State from moving freely in its territory with all his staff and preclude that Member State from making the movement of staff in question subject to restrictions such as a condition as to engagement *in situ* or an obligation to obtain a work permit.[152]

As observed above,[153] the pursuit of economic activities on a permanent basis in a host Member State, would amount to establishment, rather than to the provision of services. As the Court explained in *Steymann*:

> It is clear from the actual wording of [Article 57] that an activity carried out on a permanent basis or, in any event, without a foreseeable limit to its duration does not fall within the Community provisions concerning the provision of services. On the other hand, such activities may fall within the scope of Articles [45–48] or Articles [49–55] of the Treaty, depending on the case.

The Court deduced from this proposition that:

> Consequently, . . . Articles [56 and 57 TFEU] do not cover the situation where a national of a Member State goes to reside in the territory of another Member State and establishes his principal residence there in order to provide or receive services there for an indefinite period.[154]

Since the permanent pursuit of economic activities cannot be covered by the Treaty provisions on freedom to provide services, and falls in principle within the chapter on establishment, it would seem to follow that an individual or company established in one Member State and carrying on all his her or its business in another Member State should be regarded as established in the latter Member State, even in the absence of any place of business in the latter Member State. Yet the Court's case law indicates that in order to be established in a Member State, the person concerned must have an established professional base in that Member State.[155] On the other hand, the Court's 'anti-circumvention' case law holds that if an undertaking is established in one Member State, and directs its activities entirely or principally to the territory of another, without having a place of business in the latter Member State, the latter state may either treat the chapter on establishment as applicable, or treat the person concerned as a domestic undertaking.[156] This case law certainly applies where an undertaking seeks to avoid the application of the national rules of the Member State where its economic activities are carried on by being established in a

---

151 Art 57 TFEU, third para.
152 Case C-113/89 *Rush Portuguesa Ldc* [1990] ECR I-1417, para 12; Case C-445/03 *Commission v Luxembourg* [2004] ECR I-10191; Case C-244/04 *Commission v Germany* [2006] ECR I-885 (prior declaration may be required for posted workers who are nationals of third countries); Case C-168/04 *Commission v Austria* [2006] ECR I-9041; Case C-49/04 *Commission v Germany* [2007] ECR I-6095 (documentary requirements relating to the social protection of posted workers a justified restriction on freedom to provide services); Case C-341/05 *Laval* [2007] ECR I-11767, para 56.
153 At p 533.
154 Case 196/87 *Steymann* [1987] ECR 6159, paras16 and 17.
155 Case C-215/01 *Schnitzer* [2003] ECR I-14847, para 32; Case C-171/02 *Commission v Portugal* [2004] ECR I-5645, para 25; Case C-514/03 *Commission v Spain* [2006] ECR I-963, para 22.
156 See below at pp 567–68.

another Member State.[157] In the *Schnitzer* case,[158] which concerned a Portuguese plastering firm engaged to carry out large-scale plastering work in Bavaria between November 1994 and November 1997, the Court admitted that no provision of the Treaty provided a means of determining, in an abstract manner, the duration or frequency beyond which the supply of a service or of a certain type of service in another Member State could no longer be regarded as the provision of services within the meaning of the Treaty,[159] and indicated that the Portuguese firm (which did not have an established professional base in Bavaria) should be regarded as providing services. The Court also noted that services may comprise services within the meaning of the Treaty even if supplied over an extended period to persons established in one or more other Member States, for example the giving of advice or information for remuneration,[160] but the Court does not go so far as to suggest that services may be provided indefinitely. Indeed, in a subsequent case, *Trojani*, the Court confirms the general proposition that 'an activity carried out on a permanent basis, or at least without a foreseeable limit to its duration, does not fall within the Community provisions concerning the provision of services', citing both *Steymann* and *Schnitzer*.[161] One difficulty with the Court's case law is that it seems to suggest that permanent service provision in a Member State without an established professional base comprises neither establishment nor the provision of services. This is hardly satisfactory. It is submitted that an undertaking established in one Member State carrying on economic activity in the territory of another, on a permanent basis, but without a place of business in the latter Member State, should be regarded as being in principle covered by the chapter on establishment; subject to the Court's case law on circumvention,[162] which would, if necessary, allow the host Member State to treat the situation as if it were a purely internal one.

A literal interpretation of Articles 56 and 57 TFEU would guarantee freedom to provide cross-frontier services, in circumstances where provider and recipient remain in their respective Member States, as in the case of financial advice given by UK advisers based in the United Kingdom to French clients in France. It would similarly uphold the right of a person established in one Member State to provide services in situ in the territory of another, as in the case of a French doctor practising in France making a house call on a patient in Luxembourg. The text also implies that a potential recipient of services would be entitled to visit another Member State so that those services could be provided there, as in the case of the hypothetical Luxembourg patient referred to above calling at the surgery in France of his or her French doctor. The Court has held that the right freely to provide services may be relied on by an undertaking against the Member State in which it is established if the services are provided for persons established in another Member State,[163] and that the right includes the freedom for recipients of services to go to another Member State in order to receive a service there, without being obstructed by restrictions.[164] The Court has furthermore given a rather generous interpretation to the text, in holding that Article 56 TFEU

---

[157] See eg Case C-23/93 *TV10* [1994] ECR I-4795, paras 20–22.
[158] Case C-215/01 *Schnitzer* [2003] ECR I-14847.
[159] Ibid, paras 30 and 31.
[160] Ibid, para 30.
[161] Case C-456/02 [2004] ECR I-7573, para 28.
[162] Below, at pp 567–68.
[163] Case C-70/95 *Sodemare*[1997] ECR I-3395, para 37; Case C-224/97 *Ciola* [1999] ECR I-2517, para 11.
[164] Joined Cases 286/82 and 26/83 *Luisi and Carbone* [1984] ECR 377, para 16; Case 186/87 *Cowan* [1989] ECR 195, para 15.

applies not only where a person providing services and the recipient thereof are established in different Member States, but also in cases where the person providing services offers those services in a Member State other than that in which he is established, wherever the recipients of those services may be established.[165]

Thus Article 56 TFEU could be invoked, for example, by a German tourist guide alleging that Greek rules comprised an obstacle to his or her provision of services, in Greece, to German tourists.

B – National Measures Affecting both Free Movement of Goods (Article 34 TFEU) and Freedom to Provide Services (Article 56 TFEU)

The cross-border provision of services and movement of goods may as a matter of fact be linked, and it may be necessary to determine whether either or both of the provisions of Article 34 TFEU, on the free movement of goods, or Article 56 TFEU, on the freedom to provide services, apply. Where a national measure affects both the freedom to provide services and the free movement of goods, the Court will, in principle, examine it in relation to just one of those two fundamental freedoms if it is clear that, in the circumstances of the case, one of those freedoms is secondary to the other and may be attached to it for the purposes of legal analysis.[166] Thus, the Court has held that sending advertisements and application forms, and tickets, on behalf of a lottery operator, from one Member State to another, are covered by the freedom to provide services, since they are only steps in the organisation or operation of a lottery and cannot, under the Treaty, be considered independently of the lottery to which they relate, so as to attract the application of Article 34 TFEU. The Court noted that the importation and distribution of the items referred to were not ends in themselves, and that their sole purpose was to enable residents of the Member States where the advertisements and forms, etc, were imported and distributed to participate in the lottery.[167] However, a national measure may affect both Article 34 TFEU and Article 56 TFEU, without the application of one being subordinate to the other, and it may accordingly be necessary to assess the compatibility of the measure with each. This may be the case, as in *Gourmet International*,[168] where a national rule prohibits advertising of various kinds; the rule in question may amount to a restriction on the free movement of goods, and on the provision of services, and require justification in respect of both Article 34 TFEU and Article 56 TFEU.

C – Abolition of Discriminatory Restrictions: The General Programme and Secondary Legislation

Like the original text of Article 44 EC, the original text of Article 52 EC provided for the drawing up of a General Programme for the abolition of restrictions on freedom to pro-

---

[165] Case C-198/89 *Commission v Greece* [1991] ECR I-727, paras 8–10; Case C-398/95 *SETTG* [1997] ECR I-3091, para 8.

[166] Case C-36/02 *Omega* [2004] ECR I-9609, para 26; Case C-71/02 *Karner* [2004] ECR I-3025, para 46.

[167] Case C-275/92 [1994] ECR I-1039, paras 21–25.

[168] Case C-405/98 *Gourmet International* [2001] ECR I-1795.

vide services within the Community. The Programme was adopted in December 1961,[169] and closely resembles the General Programme for the abolition of restrictions on the right of establishment.[170] Thus, for example, Title III calls for the abolition of restrictions such as those which 'condition the provision of services on an authorisation or on the issuance of a document, such as a foreign merchant's card or a foreign professional's card'.[171] As indicated earlier, most of the Directives issued to abolish restrictions on the right of establishment applied in addition to freedom to provide services. Thus Directive 64/223, used for illustrative purposes in the context of establishment,[172] also applied, in relation to the wholesale trade, to freedom to provide services. Furthermore, Article 53 TFEU, which provides for the harmonisation of national rules governing the pursuit of self-employed activities, is applied to the chapter on services by Article 62 TFEU. Further reference is made to this below.[173]

D – Effect of the Direct Applicability of Article 56 TFEU on Harmonisation

Just as the Court's decision in *Reyners* on the direct applicability of Article 56 TFEU reduced significantly the importance of Directives requiring the abolition of particular discriminatory restrictions, so its later decision in *van Binsbergen*, upholding the direct effect of Article 56 TFEU, first paragraph, and 57 TFEU, third paragraph, entailed similar consequences for the provisions of Directives concerned with the abolition of restrictions on the supply of services.[174]

The Court has held that Article 56 TFEU, like Article 49 TFEU, is concerned not only with the specific rules on the pursuit of occupational activities but also with the rules relating to the various general facilities which are of assistance in the pursuit of those activities, including the right to equal access to housing, and financial facilities to acquire housing.[175]

E – Prohibition of Restrictions on Freedom to Provide Services: Evolution of the Court's Case Law

It has already been noted that the Court's interpretation of the Treaty provisions on the free movement of goods, on freedom of movement for workers, and on the right of establishment has undergone a considerable evolution in the last two decades or so, and that

---

[169] [1974] OJ Sp Edn, 2nd Series IX, 3. The programme has been referred to by the Court in a number of cases, see eg Case 15/78 *Koestler* [1978] ECR 1971; Case 136/78 *Auer* [1979] ECR 452; Cases 286/82 and 26/83 *Luisi* [1984] ECR 377; Case 63/86 *Commission v Italy* [1988] ECR 29; Case 305/87 *Commission v Greece* [1989] ECR 1461.

[170] See above at p 542.

[171] [1974] OJ Sp Edn 2nd Series IX, 4.

[172] See above at p 543.

[173] See below at p 630.

[174] Case 33/74 [1974] ECR 1299; and see Case 36/74 *Walrave* [1974] ECR 1405; Case 13/76 *Dona v Mantero* [1976] ECR 133; Cases 110 and 111/78, *van Wesemael* [1979] ECR 35.

[175] Case 63/86 *Commission v Italy* [1988] ECR 29. For the view that the case law on free movement of capital supersedes such cases, see Case C-386/04 *Stauffer* [2006] ECR I-8203, AG Stix-Hackl at fn 6 of her Opinion.

the Court has given increased prominence in its judgments to the concept of the non-discriminatory restriction on free movement in the latter contexts.[176] This observation is also true of the case law on freedom to provide services, and the significant stages in that evolution are indicated below. The survey which follows will concentrate principally on Identifying restrictions on freedom to provide services which will conflict with the Treaty unless justified, referring only *en passant* to possible justifications for such restrictions; justifications for restrictions, and the application of the principle of proportionality, will be considered separately below.[177]

The starting point is the judgment in *van Binsbergen*.[178] The case involved a Netherlands national who acted as a legal representative in proceedings in the Netherlands where representation by an *advocaat* was not obligatory. As a result of moving house to Belgium (he practised from home[179]) his right to practise before a Netherlands court was called into question by a provision of Netherlands law under which only persons established in the Netherlands could act as legal representatives before that court. The Court identified the national measures covered by the prohibition in these Articles as follows:

> The restrictions to be abolished pursuant to Articles [56 and 57 TFEU] include all requirements imposed on the person providing the service by reason in particular of his nationality or of the fact that he does not habitually reside in the state where the service is provided, which do not apply to persons established within the national territory or which may prevent or otherwise obstruct the activities of the person providing the service.
>
> In particular, a requirement that the person providing the service must be habitually resident within the territory of the state where the service is to be provided may, according to the circumstances, have the result of depriving Article [56 TFEU] of all useful effect, in view of the fact that the precise object of that article is to abolish restrictions on freedom to provide services imposed on persons who are not established in the state where the service is to be provided.

The Court's judgment thus identifies discrimination on grounds of nationality and by reference to residence outside national territory as being characteristics of national measures prohibited by the Treaty. It appears from the text and context that the reference to the incompatibility with the Treaty of the residence requirement in issue was not based on the premise that such a requirement amounted to indirect discrimination *on grounds of nationality*. As regards the text, this follows from the terms of the Court's ruling on the direct effect of Articles 56 and 57 TFEU, to the effect that those Articles

> have direct effect . . . at least in so far as they seek to abolish any discrimination against a person providing a service by reason of his nationality *or of the fact that he resides in a Member State other than that in which the service is to be* provided.[180]

As regards the context, it will be noted that the plaintiff in the national proceedings was a Netherlands national, and so no question of discrimination against him on grounds of nationality in the Netherlands arose. The statement by the Court that a residence requirement would deprive Article 56 TFEU of all useful effect has been endorsed in a consistent subsequent case law. In *Commission v Germany* the Court described the requirement of

---

[176] See Chapter 14, pp 411–15, Chapter 16, pp 520–25 and this chapter at pp 547–52 above.

[177] See the section on the public policy proviso, at p 571 and that on mandatory requirements in the general interest, at p 573.

[178] Case 33/74 *van Binsbergen* [1974] ECR 1307.

[179] AG Mayras [1974] ECR 1314.

[180] For further rulings on direct effect, see eg Case 36/74 *Walrave* [1974] ECR 1405; Joined Cases 110 and 111/78 *van Wesemael* [1979] ECR 35; Case 279/80 *Webb* [1981] ECR 3305.

a permanent establishment as 'the very negation' of freedom to provide services. 'It has', said the Court,

> the result of depriving Article [56 TFEU] of the Treaty of all effectiveness, a provision whose very purpose is to abolish restrictions on the freedom to provide services of persons who are not established in the State in which the service is to be provided.[181]

In *van Wesemael*[182] the Court had to consider, inter alia, the extent to which national rules of one Member State could impose a licensing requirement on an employment agency established in another Member State placing employees in the first Member State. The Court repeated the proposition that Articles 56 and 57 TFEU 'abolish all discrimination against the person providing the service by reason of his nationality or the fact that he is established in a Member State other than that in which the service is to be provided'.[183] As regards the application of the licensing requirement, the Court held that it would be incompatible with the Treaty for a Member State to impose a licensing requirement on an employment agency established in another Member State, which was supervised and licensed in its home Member State, unless the requirement was objectively justified by the need to ensure observance of professional rules of conduct or the protection of the entertainers placed by the agency.[184] In the event, the Court held that such a requirement was not justified when the service was provided by an employment agency which was licensed in its home Member State under conditions comparable to those applicable in the host Member State and subject to the supervision of its home Member State authorities as regards all its activities in the Member State.[185] It follows from the reasoning in the latter case that it might be discriminatory to apply to a service provider established in another Member State all the requirements of host Member State law, and in the later case of *Webb*[186] (involving a 'manpower' agency licensed in one Member State providing services in another) the Court, confirming that the Treaty provisions on provision of services prohibited all discrimination against the person providing the service by reason of his or her nationality or the fact that he or she is established in a Member State other than that in which the service is provided, added that the reference in Article 57 TFEU, paragraph 3 to equality of treatment with nationals did not mean 'that all national legislation applicable to nationals of that State and usually applied to the permanent activities of undertaking established therein may be similarly applied in its entirety to the temporary activities of undertakings which are established in another Member State'.[187]

In *Commission v Germany*[188] the Court considered the compatibility with Article 56 TFEU of German rules requiring, inter alia, that insurance companies established in other Member States, and authorised and supervised in those Member States, obtain a separate German authorisation for their activities in Germany. The Court held that Articles 56 and 57 TFEU require the removal of not only of all discrimination against a provider of a service on the grounds of his nationality but also all restrictions on his freedom to pro-

---

[181] Case 205/84 *Commission v Germany* [1988] ECR 3755, para 52, citing Case 39/75 *Coenen* [1975] ECR 1547, and Case 76/81 *Transporoute* [1982] ECR 417. See also Case C-101/94 *Commission v Italy* [1996] ECR I-2691, para 31; and Case C-222/95 *Parodi* [1997] ECR I-3899, para 31.

[182] Joined Cases 110 and 111/78. *van Wesemael* [1979] ECR 35.

[183] Ibid, para 27.

[184] Ibid, para 29.

[185] Ibid, para 30

[186] Case 279/80 *Webb* [1981] ECR 3305.

[187] Ibid, para 16.

[188] Case 205/84 *Commission v Germany* [1988] ECR 3755.

vide services imposed by reason of the fact that he is established in a Member State other than that in which the service is to be provided.[189] It reiterated the proposition stated in *Webb* to the effect that national rules could not necessarily be applied in their entirety to a service provider established in another Member State, but added that specific requirements could nevertheless be imposed on such a provider if the provisions in question were justified in the public interest, to the extent that the relevant public interest was not safeguarded by the provisions to which the provider was subject in the Member State of establishment. The Court said that, '*In addition* such requirements must be objectively justified by the need to ensure that professional rules of conduct are complied with and that the interests which such rules are designed to safeguard are protected'.[190] The above formulation is significant, since it indicates that even national supervisory requirements which do not duplicate those applied in the Member State of establishment may only be applied to the out-of-state provider if they are objectively necessary. This is borne out by the Court's observation that the requirement of authorisation may not be justifiable on grounds relating to the protection of policy-holders and insured persons in all fields of insurance, and its suggestion that in the field of commercial insurance the policy-holders might simply not need the protection of mandatory rules of national law.[191] Whether the proposition can be said to emerge from the prior case law or not, the proposition emerges from this case that to impose national supervisory requirements on service providers who are established in other Member States where they are authorised to provide the service in question will be regarded as a restriction on freedom to provide services if *the need for the supervisory requirements of the host Member State* cannot be objectively justified. Nevertheless, the underlying logic of the Court's case law still appears to be that of discrimination. The reference in *Commission v Germany* and in other cases to restrictions on freedom to provide services imposed by reason of the fact that the provider is established in a Member State other than that in which the service is to be provided appear to be a restatement of the reference in *van Wesemael* and *Webb* to discrimination by reason of the fact of establishment in a Member State other than that where the service was to be provided. In a later infraction proceeding against Germany in relation to transposition of Directive 77/249/EEC on provision of services by lawyers, the Court refers again to the prohibition of discrimination on grounds of nationality or by reference to establishment in a Member State other than that in which the service is to be provided.[192]

In *Commission v Greece* the Court held that Article 56 TFEU prohibits not only discrimination on grounds of nationality, but also requires the abolition of any restriction imposed on the ground that the person providing the service is established in another Member State. The Court concludes that for one Member State (Greece) to insist that tourist guides established in another Member State and accompanying groups of foreign tourists possess the qualifications of the first Member State amounts to a restriction incompatible with Article 56 TFEU.[193]

The explanation of this evolution is that the Court had developed a broad concept of discrimination by reference to nationality, or by reference to establishment in another

---

[189] Ibid, para 25.
[190] Ibid, para 27 (emphasis added).
[191] Ibid. para 49.
[192] Case C-427/85 *Commission v Germany* [1988] ECR 1123, para 11.
[193] Case C-198/89 [1991] ECR I-727, paras 16 and 18. And see Case C-154/89 *Commission v France* [1991] ECR I-4221.

Member State, which had begun to evolve into a prohibition of non-discriminatory restrictions on economic operators established in other Member States. The Court was soon to acknowledge this evolution in explicit terms.

Very shortly after *Commission v Greece*, referred to above, the Court decided *Säger v Dennemeyer & Co Ltd*.[194] The national proceedings arose from a legal action by a patent agent in Munich against a company incorporated in England and Wales. The plaintiff was a specialist in patent renewal services who claimed that the provision of such services by the defendant was contrary to German rules reserving such activities exclusively to persons possessing the relevant professional qualification. The provision of patent renewal services was not subject to regulation in the United Kingdom. The German court seised of the dispute asked the Court of Justice whether rules such as those in issue were compatible with Article 56 TFEU. It is to be noted that the reasoning adopted by the Court of Justice in *Commission v Germany* and *Commission v Greece*, above, would have pointed towards the German rules in issue being treated as being incompatible with Article 56 TFEU, unless they could by justified by reference to the need to protect the interests asserted to be at stake. The Court indeed reached that conclusion, but abandoned its previous mode of analysis and adopted one rather closer to that adopted in the *Cassis* case,[195] as follows:

> It should first be pointed out that Article [56 TFEU] requires not only the elimination of all discrimination against a person providing services on the ground of his nationality but also the abolition of any restriction, even if it applies without distinction to national providers of services and to those of other Member States, when it is liable to prohibit or otherwise impede the activities of a provider of services established in another Member State where he lawfully provides similar services.[196]

The Court adopted the same approach to justification as it had adopted in *Commission v Greece*, above.[197] If Article 56 TFEU is read as laying down a general prohibition on non-discriminatory restrictions, then national rules prohibiting certain services outright will be subject to judicial scrutiny to determine whether such a general ban can be justified, taking account of the aims of the measure, and its proportionality.[198] Even in a case where most Member States banned a particular service, it seems that the final decision as to the sustainability of such a ban would lie in the hands of the judges, rather than national legislative authorities. In *Schindler*[199] the Court considered national rules which prohibited (with certain exceptions) lotteries in the United Kingdom, and prohibited the import of lottery tickets. The Court applied the *Säger* formulation, which meant that it was necessary to address the issue of objective justification, and proportionality. The Court noted that the regulation of lotteries raised wide issues, including moral, religious and cultural issues, and the risk of crime and fraud.[200] Instead of applying an objective test, the Court adopted a subjective test, allowing Member States 'to assess not only whether it is necessary to restrict the activities of lotteries but also whether they should be prohibited, providing that those restrictions are not discriminatory'.[201] The Court referred to the 'peculiar nature

---

[194] Case C-76/90 *Säger* [1991] ECR I-4221.
[195] Chapter 14, at p 411.
[196] Case C-76/90 *Säger* [1991] ECR I-4221, para 12.
[197] Case C-198/89 [1991] ECR I-727.
[198] As to justification, see below at p 577.
[199] Case C-275/92 *Schindler* [1994] ECR I-1039.
[200] Ibid, para 60.
[201] Ibid, para 61.

of lotteries, which has been stressed by many Member States'.[202] Significantly, the Court made no mention of the principle of proportionality. It is tempting to speculate that the Court, having embraced the concept of the non-discriminatory restriction, found that its strict application might lead to a result which was inappropriate, and found it expedient to adjust its reasoning accordingly in the sensitive context of gambling. In the later case of *Placanica*, however, the Court referred to *Schindler*, and noted that while moral, religious and cultural factors might justify a margin of appreciation for the national authorities in the context of betting and gaming, the restrictive measures they impose must nevertheless satisfy the requirement of proportionality.[203]

It of course remains the case that demonstrating some element of discrimination against service providers established in other Member States may be decisive in demonstrating a restriction on freedom to provide services. Thus the Court has held that Article 56 TFEU precludes the application of any national rules which have the effect of making the provision of services between Member States more difficult than the provision of services purely within one Member State.[204] In *Smits and Peerbooms* the Court held that restrictions in the latter category include rules of a Member State to the effect that reimbursement of the cost of hospital treatment from a sickness insurance fund be subject to prior authorisation where the hospital treatment is received in another Member State, where such authorisation is unnecessary where the hospital treatment is received in the first Member State.[205] In *De Coster* the Court made a similar finding as regards a municipal tax on satellite dishes in Belgium. The tax did not apply to the reception of programmes transmitted by cable. Since broadcasters established in Belgium enjoyed unlimited access to cable distribution for their programmes in that Member State, while broadcasters established in certain other Member States did not, the Court regarded the tax as impeding more the activities of operators established in other Member States than those of operators established in Belgium.[206]

The Court has increasingly used the wording 'prohibit, impede or render less attractive' to describe restrictions on the freedom to provide services, and on the right of establishment, stating, for example, in *Commission v Italy*, that '[i]t is settled case-law that the term "restriction" within the meaning of Articles [49 TFEU and 56 TFEU] covers all measures which prohibit, impede or render less attractive the freedom of establishment or the freedom to provide services'.[207] This wording appears to be a synthesis of that used in the *Säger* and *Gebhard*[208] cases.

In *Gourmet International*[209] the Court considered a ban on advertising of alcoholic beverages on TV and radio and in periodicals and other publications other than publications distributed solely at point of sale. The Court held that this ban was a restriction under Article 56 TFEU because it restricted the right of advertisers to offer advertising space to potential advertisers in other Member States.[210] This is an extension of the prin-

---

[202] Ibid, para 59; 11 Member States intervened in the proceedings.

[203] Joined Cases C-338/04, C-359/04 and C-360/04 [2007] ECR I-1891, paras 47 and 48.

[204] See eg Case C-158/96 *Kohll* [1998] ECR I-1931, para 33.

[205] Case C-157/99 *Smits and Peerbooms* [2001] ECR I-5473, para 61; Case C-250/06 *United Pan-Europe Communications Belgium and Others* [2007] ECR I-11135, para 30.

[206] Case C-17/00 *De Coster* [2001] ECR I-9445, paras 30–35.

[207] Case C-518/06 *Commission v Italy* [2009] ECR I-3491, para 62. The formulation was first applied to services in Case C-205/99 *Anilir* [2001] ECR I-1271, para 21.

[208] See above at p 547.

[209] Case C-405/98 *Gourmet International* [2001] ECR I-1795.

[210] Ibid, paras 37 and 38. The Court held the restriction could be justified on grounds of public health, subject to the principle of proportionality, which was a matter for the national court, see paras 40 and 41.

ciple recognised in *Säger* which dealt with restrictions on the cross-frontier provision of *services lawfully provided in the Member State of origin.*[211] For the principle in *Gourmet* to apply, it is necessary only to hypothesise that a service would be provided in a Member State, were it not for the existence of a restriction on the provision of that service, and that there are potential customers for such a service in other Member States. It is true that the Court observed in *Gourmet* that a measure such as that in issue 'even if it is non-discriminatory, has a particular effect on the cross-border supply of advertising space, given the international nature of the advertising market in the category of products to which the prohibition relates', but it is difficult to read this as placing much in the way of a limit on the general proposition that Article 56 TFEU applies where a national rule can be shown to prevent a potential in-state service provider from supplying a potential out-of-state customer. This ruling erodes the distinction between those restrictions on the supply of services which are purely internal to a Member State, and those which affect the freedom to provide services to customers across national borders.

F – Prohibition of Non-discriminatory Restrictions on Freedom to Provide Services

National measures which amount to restrictions on the right of establishment will invariably also amount to restrictions on freedom to provide services, and the discussion of the case law on the right of establishment earlier in this chapter will apply by analogy to freedom to provide services.[212] The formulation in *Säger*, covering as it does both discriminatory and non-discriminatory restrictions, has been applied on numerous occasions by the Court, and there are few signs that the Court acknowledges that a class of cases exists to which it does not apply.

Yet it is nevertheless possible that the test is only applicable to national rules which restrict access to the market, or, to put it another way, that a category of cases exists in which national rules will not be regarded as restricting access to the market and will be compatible with Article 56 TFEU provided they do not discriminate on grounds of nationality or by reference to establishment in another Member State. In *Alpine Investments*[213] the Court of Justice considered whether rules of a Member State prohibiting providers of services established in its territory from making unsolicited telephone calls to potential clients established in other Member States in order to offer their services constituted a restriction on freedom to provide services covered by Article 56 TFEU. The Court held that a prohibition such as that in issue 'directly affects *access to the market* in services in the other Member States and is thus capable of hindering intra-Community trade in services'.[214] The Court has subsequently held that a prohibition on advertising in one Member State of services available in the territory of another amounts to a restriction on the freedom to provide services.[215] The Court also continues to rely on the principle that Article 56 TFEU precludes the application of any national rules which have the effect of making the provision of services between Member States more difficult than the provision of serv-

---

[211] Case C-76/90 *Säger* [1991] ECR I-4221, para 12.
[212] See above at pp 547–52.
[213] Case C-384/93 *Alpine Investments* [1995] ECR I-1141.
[214] Ibid, para 38 (emphasis added).
[215] Case C-294/00 *Gräbner* [2002] ECR I-6515, para 68. See also Case C-500/06 *Corporación Dermoestética* [2008] ECR I-5785, para 33.

ices purely within one Member State.[216] Equally, cases in which the latter formulation is invoked more often than not concern national measures which are discriminatory, and/or amount to restrictions on access to the market.[217] In *Delière*, the Court rejected the proposition that certain selection rules applicable to sporting activities comprised restrictions on freedom to provide services, observing, in particular, that

> the selection rules at issue . . . do not determine the conditions governing *access to the labour market* by professional sportsmen and do not contain nationality clauses limiting the number of nationals of other Member States who may participate in a competition.[218]

However, in *Carpenter* the Court considered a decision to deport the wife (a national of a third country) of a UK national resident in the United Kingdom who provides services to customers in other Member States, and declared that 'it is clear that the separation of Mr and Mrs Carpenter would be detrimental to their family life and, therefore, to the conditions under which Mr Carpenter exercises a fundamental freedom'.[219] This approach seems inconsistent with the proposition that non-discriminatory restrictions on freedom to provide services only require justification if they restrict access to the market. Restrictions on access to the market are generally contrasted with those alleged restrictions which arise solely from the unattractiveness of the regulatory conditions under which a particular activity is exercised. One apparent difficulty with seeking to draw this distinction is that unattractive conditions for the carrying on of a particular activity might be held to deter operators from taking up the activity, and thereby to restrict access to the market. Yet to go so far would amount to the pursuit of general regulatory harmonisation through litigation rather than through the law-making process. Consideration of the case law on the right of establishment suggests that national rules which make it difficult for market operators from other Member States to compete with market operators already established on the market of the host Member State are to be regarded as affecting access to the market, and as amounting to restrictions on the exercise of a fundamental freedom.[220] The same considerations apply to freedom to provide services, and the present writer considers that national measures which make it difficult for market operators from other Member States to compete with established market operators in the host Member State amount to restrictions on access to the market, and to restrictions on freedom to provide services, which must be justified, if they are to be regarded as compatible with Article 49 TFEU.

It has been noted above that the Court has held that restrictions on Sunday trading are not caught by Article 49 TFEU because any effects on the right of establishment would be too 'uncertain and indirect',[221] and it would seem to follow that analogous principles also apply to ensure that such national measures are not covered by Article 56 TFEU. As in the analogous case of establishment, it seems that deciding whether national rules require justification because they make it more difficult for economic operators from other

---

[216] Case C-158/96 *Kohll* [1998] ECR I-1931, para 33; Case C-157/99 *Smits and Peerbooms* [2001] ECR I-5473; para 61; Case C-17/00 *De Coster* [2001] ECR I-9445, paras 30–35; Case C-211/08 *Commission v Spain* (CJEU 15 June 2010), para 55.

[217] Case C-272/94 *Guiot* [1996] ECR I-1905; Case C-3/95 *Broede* [1996] ECR I-6511; Case C-398/95 *SETTG* [1997] ECR I-3091; Case C-157/99 *Smits and Peerbooms* [2001] ECR I-5473, para 69.

[218] Case C-51/96 *Delière* [2000] ECR I-2549, para 61.

[219] Case C-60/00 *Carpenter* [2002] CR I-6279, para 39; see (2003) 40 *CMLRev* 537; for an analysis of related issues, see E Spaventa, 'From Gebhard to Carpenter: Towards a (non)-Economic European Constitution' (2004) 41 *CMLRev* 743.

[220] See above at p 551.

[221] See above at p 552.

Member States to compete with operators already established on the market in question, or do not require justification because any effect on the freedom to provide services is to be regarded as too uncertain and indirect, will involve questions of fact and degree, and indeed an impressionistic element.

V – ESTABLISHMENT AND SERVICES: NATIONAL MEASURES TO PREVENT CIRCUMVENTION, AND DEROGATION ON EXPRESS OR IMPLIED GROUNDS

A – National Measures to prevent Circumvention of National Rules in the Context of the Right of Establishment and Freedom to Provide Services

The Court of Justice has indicated in a number of cases that provisions of EU law should not be interpreted in such a way as to facilitate the wrongful avoidance of national rules.[222] It will be noted that in the *Centros* case[223] Danish nationals resident and carrying on business in Denmark incorporated a company to carry on that business and incorporated that company in England rather than Denmark in order to avoid the relatively high minimum capital requirement attendant upon incorporation in Denmark. The Danish authorities argued that those nationals could not rely upon the Treaty provisions on the right of establishment, since the sole purpose of the company formation in England was to circumvent the application of the Danish rules governing formation of private limited companies and therefore constituted abuse of the freedom of establishment.[224] The Court referred to its case law on wrongful circumvention of national rules,[225] and explained it as follows. That case law allowed national courts to take account, case by case, and on the basis of objective evidence, of abuse or fraudulent conduct on the part of the persons concerned in order, where appropriate, to deny them the benefit of provisions of EU law on which they relied. But it was nevertheless necessary to assess such conduct in the light of the objectives pursued by the provisions of EU law in question.[226] The Court noted that in the case in point, 'the provisions of national law, application of which the parties concerned have sought to avoid, are rules governing the formation of companies and not rules concerning the carrying on of certain trades, professions or businesses'.[227] The Court went on to note that the provisions of the Treaty on freedom of establishment were intended specifically to enable companies of one Member State to pursue activities in other Member States through an agency branch or subsidiary, and held that that being so, the fact that a national of a Member State who wished to set up a company chose to

---

[222] Case 115/78 *Knoors* [1979] ECR 399, para 25; Case C-61/89 *Bouchoucha* [1990] ECR I-3557, para 14.
[223] Case C-212/97 *Centros* [1999] ECR I-1458, see below at p 649.
[224] Case C-212/97 *Centros* [1999] ECR I-1458, para 23.
[225] Ibid, para 24.
[226] Ibid, para 25.
[227] Ibid, para 26.

form it in the Member State whose rules of company law seemed to him or her the least restrictive, and to set up branches in other Member States could not, in itself constitute an abuse of the right of establishment.[228]

From the outset the case law on freedom to provide services indicated that the Treaty did not prohibit Member States from taking appropriate steps to prevent the wrongful circumvention of national rules. The Court in *van Binsbergen* stated.

> Likewise, a member state cannot be denied the right to take measures to prevent the exercise by a person providing services whose activity is entirely or principally directed towards its territory of the freedom guaranteed by [Article 56 TFEU] for the purpose of avoiding the professional rules of conduct which would be applicable to him if he were established within that State; such a situation may be subject to judicial control under the provisions of the chapter relating to the right of establishment and not of that on the provision of services.[229]

It is to be noted that the Court clearly presupposed that control under the provisions of the chapter relating to the right of establishment would involve a greater ability to impose requirements on economic operators than would be possible under the chapter on the provision of services. While such a difference exists today in principle, it seems that the extent of that difference has diminished,[230] and this perhaps explains why the Court's formulation of national anti-circumvention competence has evolved over the years. Thus in *Veronica*[231] the Court of Justice repeated the above formulation, but omitted the reference to the situation being subject to judicial control under the provisions of the chapter relating to the right of establishment, and in *TV10 SA* the Court repeated the latter formulation, but added that it would therefore be compatible with the provisions of the Treaty on freedom to provide services to treat such organisations *as domestic organisations*. It is argued above that the better view is to regard an undertaking established in one Member State carrying on economic activity in the territory of another, on a permanent basis, but without a place of business in the latter Member State, as being covered in principle by the chapter on establishment, though this should not displace the Court's case law on circumvention in appropriate cases should supervision under the chapter on establishment be inadequate, and require supervision as if the situation were a purely internal one.[232]

B – Articles 51 TFEU and 62 TFEU: Exception for Activities connected with the Exercise of Official Authority

Article 51 TFEU provides that the provisions of the chapter on establishment shall not

---

[228] Ibid, paras 26 and 27; and see below at p 650.

[229] Case 33/74 *van Binsbergen* [1974] ECR 1307, para 13. This formulation was repeated verbatim by the Court in Case 205/84 *Commission v Germany* [1986] ECR 3755, para 22.

[230] The main, if not the only, difference would seem to be as regards application of the principle of proportionality. It will be more difficult to justify regulation of service providers than established undertakings. The reason it was necessary in the *Schnitzer* case (above at p 557) to decide whether the out-of-state plastering undertaking was established or a service provider was that the contested registration requirement could lawfully be applied to the former, but not the latter, category. For example, national rules on registration with professional bodies are presumptively applicable as regards those who are exercising the right of establishment, but not as regards those providing services. Thus, Art 4 of Directive 77/249/EEC on provision of services by lawyers, exempts service providers from registration in the host Member State, while Art 3 of Directive 98/5/EC on the establishment of lawyers provides for such registration.

[231] Case C-148/91 *Veronica* [1991] ECR I-487, para 12.

[232] Above at p 557.

apply, 'so far as any given Member State is concerned, to activities which in that State are connected, even occasionally, with the exercise of official authority'. Pursuant to Article 62 TFEU, this latter provision also applies to the chapter on freedom to provide services. This exception constitutes a derogation from a fundamental Treaty rule, and must be interpreted strictly, so as not to exceed the purpose for which it was inserted.[233]

In *Reyners*[234] it was argued that the profession of *avocat* was exempted from the chapter on establishment because it involved the exercise of official authority. The Court held that Article 51 TFEU applied only to those activities which, taken on their own, involved a direct and specific connection with the exercise of official authority,[235] and added that:

> Professional activities involving contracts, even regular and organic, with the courts, including even compulsory co-operation in their functioning, do not constitute, as such, connexion with the exercise of official authority. The most typical activities of the profession of *avocat*, in particular, such as consultation and legal assistance and also representation and the defence of parties in court, even when the intervention or assistance of the *avocat* is compulsory or is a legal monopoly, cannot be considered as connected with the exercise of official authority. The exercise of these activities leaves the discretion of judicial authority and the free exercise of judicial power intact.[236]

This latter observation certainly implies that the exercise of a judicial function by an advocate would amount to the exercise of official authority, which is in any event self-evident. Advocate General Mayras described official authority as 'that which arises from the sovereignty and majesty of the State; for him who exercises it, it implies the power of enjoying the [*sic*] prerogatives outside the general law, privileges of official power and powers of coercion over citizens'.[237] This is consistent with the approach of the Court of Justice in *Commission v Belgium*, on the ambit of Article 45(4) TFEU.[238] In the latter case the Court held that Article 45(4) TFEU covers posts which involve direct or indirect participation in the exercise of powers conferred by public law and duties designed to safeguard the general interests of the Member State.[239] Article 45(4) TFEU and Article 51 TFEU have essentially the same aim, and should be interpreted in an analogous way. As indicated at the outset, as an exception to a fundamental principle, Article 51 TFEU is given a strict construction.[240] Thus the Court has held that the activity of a traffic accident expert does not involve the exercise of official authority where the reports of these experts are not binding on the courts, leaving the discretion of the judiciary and the exercise of judicial power intact.[241] Similarly, the Court has held that the 'auxiliary and preparatory functions' of an 'approved commissioner' vis-à-vis an 'Insurance Inspectorate', which latter body was a body exercising official authority by taking the final relevant decision, could not be regarded as having a direct and specific connection with the exercise of official authority.[242] The Court has considered whether private bodies which conduct inspections

---

[233] Case 2/74 *Reyners* [1974] ECR 631; Case 152/73 *Sotgiu* [1974] ECR 153, see p 511.
[234] Case 2/74 *Reyners* [1974] ECR 631.
[235] Ibid, para 45.
[236] Ibid, paras 51–53.
[237] [1974] ECR 631, 664.
[238] Case 149/79 [1980] ECR 3881.
[239] Ibid, para 10. See in general Chapter 16, at p 511.
[240] Case 2/74 *Reyners* [1974] ECR 631, para 43; Case C-438/08 *Commission v Portugal* [2009] ECR I-10219, para 46.
[241] Case C-306/89 *Commission v Greece* [1991] ECR I-5863, para 7.
[242] Case C-42/92 *Thijssen* [1993] ECR I-4047, para 22.

relating to the organic production of agricultural products, and in so doing exercise the powers of a public body, by drawing conclusions from the inspections which they carry out, can be regarded as falling within the scope of Article 51 TFEU. The Court held that such activities could not be regarded as 'connected directly and specifically with the exercise of official authority', where the applicable legislation provided that the private bodies concerned were to be supervised by a public authority, which was responsible, ultimately, for the inspections and decisions of those bodies.[243] The Court drew the same conclusion as regards private vehicle roadworthiness testing bodies subject to supervision by public authorities. Security undertakings and security staff lacking legal powers of constraint cannot be described as exercising official authority because they make a contribution to the maintenance of public security, which any individual may be called upon to do.[244] The Court employed analogous reasoning when rejecting a claim by Germany that emergency ambulance services fell within the scope of Article 51 TFEU, noting that making a contribution to public health, which any individual may be called upon to make, in particular by assisting a person whose life or health are in danger, is not sufficient for there to be a connection with the exercise of official authority. As regards the right of ambulance service providers to use equipment such as flashing blue lights or sirens, and their right of way with priority under the German highway code, they certainly reflected the overriding importance which the national legislature attached to public health as against general road traffic rules. However, the Court considered that such rights could not, as such, be regarded as having a direct and specific connection with the exercise of official authority in the absence, on the part of the providers concerned, of official powers or of powers of coercion falling outside the scope of the general law, for the purposes of ensuring that those rights are observed.[245]

Article 51 TFEU refers to 'activities' connected with the exercise of official authority, rather than 'to professions'. The Court of Justice in *Reyners* made it clear that while certain 'activities' forming part of a particular profession might fall within Article 51 TFEU, the profession as a whole might nevertheless be subject to the right of establishment. This would be the case wherever the activities could be 'severed' from the profession concerned, as they could be so severed, it would seem, in the case of an advocate called upon to perform occasional judicial functions. The Court took the view that the exception allowed by Article 51 TFEU could only be extended to a whole profession where the activities in question 'were linked with that profession in such a way that freedom of establishment would result in imposing on the Member State concerned the obligation to allow the exercise, even occasionally, by non-nationals of functions appertaining to official authority'.[246] It is certainly the case that the text of Article 51 TFEU seems to rule out requiring a Member State to tolerate even the occasional exercise of official authority. It is interesting to consider by way of contrast the Court's interpretation of Article 45(4) TFEU in *Colegio de Oficiales de la Marina Mercante Española*; the Court held that the posts of master and chief mate in the Spanish merchant navy are posts in which the exercise of rights under powers conferred by public law is, in practice, only occasional, and it would be disproportionate to exclude those posts from the scope of Article 45 TFEU if the rights

---

[243] Case C-438/08 *Commission v Portugal* [2009] ECR I-10219, para 37; Case C-393/05 *Commission v Austria* [2007] ECR I-10195, paras 35–45; Case C-404/05 *Commission v Germany* [2007] ECR I-10239, paras 36–48.

[244] Case C-114/92 *Commission v Spain* [1990] ECR I-6717, para 37.

[245] Case C-160/08 *Commission v Germany* (CJEU 29 April 2010) paras 75–86.

[246] Case 2/74 *Reyners* [1974] ECR 631, para 46.

in question were exercised only exceptionally by nationals of other Member States.[247] On the face of it, it would seem that employment will not be excluded from the scope of Article 45 TFEU solely because it entails the occasional exercise of powers under public law by foreign nationals, while in the case of Article 51 TFEU even the occasional exercise of official authority will wholly exclude the activity in question, while leaving open the possibility that that activity might be severed from the relevant profession or overall self-employed activities carried on by the individual in question. While Article 45(4) TFEU is to be interpreted and applied in an analogous way to Article 51 TFEU, the outcome in comparable cases will not always be the same.

In view of the Court's decision in *Sotgiu* (concerning an employed person) it would seem that Article 51 TFEU should be interpreted by analogy as applying only to *access* to activities connected with the exercise of official authority, not as authorising discriminatory conditions of self-employed work once a person had been allowed to take up such activities.[248]

The second paragraph of Article 51 TFEU provides that the European Parliament and Council may, acting in accordance with the ordinary legislative procedure, 'rule that the provisions of this Chapter shall not apply to certain activities'. It seems that these words must be construed subject to the text of the previous paragraph, ie as involving activities connected with the exercise of official authority. The authority bestowed thereby upon the Council would thus seem to be rather limited. In applying Article 51 TFEU to a particular profession, it is necessary to establish the ambit of the 'activities' which 'taken on their own, constitute a direct and specific connection with the exercise of official authority'.[249] While the 'exercise of official authority' is a concept of Union law, the question of 'direct and specific connection' with such exercise is one of fact which, unresolved, can lead to uncertainty on the part of those subject to the law. It seems that the Council's function under this provision is limited to establishing that certain activities do indeed have a 'direct and specific connection' with the exercise of official authority. The Council has not exercised the power conferred by this provision.

C – Articles 52 TFEU and 62 TFEU: The Public Policy Proviso

Article 52(1) TFEU provides that the provisions of the chapter on establishment and measures taken in pursuance thereof shall not prejudice the applicability of provisions providing for special treatment for foreign nationals on grounds of public policy, public security or public health; Article 62 TFEU makes the same provision as regards the chapter on provision of services. The scheme of Articles 45–62 TFEU, the parallel interpretation given to these provisions in relation to discrimination, entry and residence,[250] and the fact that the public policy provisos of Article 45(3) TFEU and Article 52(1) TFEU are implemented by one and the same Directive—Directive 2004/38/EC—suggests that Article 52(1) TFEU is to be interpreted in an analogous manner to that of Article 45(3) TFEU.[251] Thus, for instance, it would seem to follow that Article 52(1) TFEU must be

---

[247] Case C-405/01 [2003] ECR I-10391, paras 44 and 45.
[248] Case 152/73 *Sotgiu* [1974] ECR 153.
[249] Case 2/74 *Reyners* [1974] ECR 631, para 45.
[250] Above at p 552.
[251] As indicated in Chapter 15, Directive 2004/38/EC lays down (a) the conditions governing the exercise of

interpreted as permitting derogation from the chapter on establishment only in respect of entry and residence—not in respect of the terms and conditions under which occupational activities are carried on.[252] For a detailed analysis of the terms of Directive 2004/38/EC, and an examination of the Court's jurisprudence on the public policy proviso in Article 45(3) TFEU, the reader is referred to Chapter 15.[253]

In the context of the right of establishment, the Court has said that while the need to combat fraud may justify a difference in treatment on grounds of nationality in certain circumstances, the mere risk of tax avoidance cannot justify discriminatory treatment.[254] Article 52(1) TFEU permits derogation from the right of establishment in the case of foreign nationals, but since this provision, by virtue of Article 62 TFEU, also applies as an exception to the Treaty's prohibition on restrictions to provide services, and since the latter prohibition covers national measures which discriminate not only on grounds of nationality, but also by reference to the fact that the place of establishment of a service provider,[255] or the place of residence of a service recipient,[256] is located in another Member State, discrimination in these latter cases may also be justified by reference to this provision.

The Court held in the *Omega* case that the concept of public policy includes respect for human dignity as a general principle of law, and may justify prohibiting the commercial exploitation of games (and thereby placing restrictions on the freedom to provide services) which involve the simulated killing of human beings.[257]

In *Kohll*[258] the Court noted that the Treaty allowed Member States to limit freedom to provide services on grounds of public health, but added that that did not permit them to exclude the public health sector, as a sector of economic activity and from the point of view of the freedom to provide services, from the application of the fundamental principle of freedom of movement. It did, however, permit Member States to restrict the freedom to provide medical and hospital services in so far as the maintenance of a treatment facility or medical service on national territory is essential for the public health and even the survival of the population.[259] Public health considerations justify a Member State in prohibiting television advertising for alcoholic beverages marketed in that Member State, in the case of indirect television advertising resulting from the appearance on screen of hoardings visible during the retransmission of bi-national sporting events taking place in other Member States.[260]

It is established that economic aims do not constitute grounds of public policy within the meaning of Article 52(1) TFEU.[261] Nor do the aims of reinforcing the financial sound-

the right of free movement and residence within the territory of the Member States by Union citizens and their family members, (b) the right of permanent residence in the territory of the Member States for Union citizens and their family members, and (c) the limits placed on the rights set out in (a) and (b) on grounds of public policy, public security or public health; see Art 1.

[252] Case 152/73 *Sotgiu* [1974] ECR 153; Case 15/69 *Ugliola* [1969] ECR 363.
[253] Chapter 15, at p 482.
[254] Case 79/85 *Segers* [1986] ECR 2375, para 17.
[255] Case C-484/93 *Svensson* [1995] ECR I-3955, para 15.
[256] Case C-224/97 *Ciola* [1999] ECR I-2517, para 16.
[257] Case C-36/02 *Omega* [2004] ECR I-9609.
[258] Case C-158/96 *Kohll* [1998] ECR I-1931, para 46.
[259] Ibid, para 51; the Court refers by analogy to Case 72/83 *Campus Oil* [1984] ECR 2727, paras 33–36, which deals with public security within the meaning of Art 34 TFEU; see also Case C-157/99 *Smits and Peerbooms* [2001] ECR I-5473, paras 72–74; and Case C-372/04 *Watts* [2006] ECR I-4325, paras 104–05.
[260] Case C-429/02 *Bacardi France* [2004] ECR I-6613.
[261] Case C-288/89 *Gouda* [1991] ECR I-4007, para 11; Case C-484/93 *Svensson* [1995] ECR I-3955, para 15.

ness of companies in order to protect public and private creditors.[262] Nor have the aims of avoiding diminution in tax revenue and erosion of the tax base been regarded as falling within Article 52(1) TFEU in the cases in which the argument to the contrary has been put.[263]

In order to justify a national measure on the basis of Article 52(1) TFEU, it is necessary to demonstrate that it is indispensable for achieving one of the aims referred to.[264] In upholding the right of a Member State, on grounds of public policy and respect for human dignity, to prohibit the commercial exploitation of games involving the simulated killing of human beings, the Court emphasised the requirement of proportionality and noted that by prohibiting only the variant of the laser game, the object of which was to fire on actual human targets and thus 'play at killing' people, the national measure did not go beyond what was necessary to attain the objective pursued by the competent national authorities.[265]

D – Imperative Requirements in the General Interest

(i) General

It has been noted in the last section that restrictions on the right of establishment and the freedom to provide services may be justified on grounds of public policy, public security or public health. However, these are not the only grounds upon which measures which hinder the exercise of fundamental freedoms may be justified. The Court has interpreted the relevant Treaty provisions in such a way that restrictions based on considerations described as imperative requirements, or overriding requirements, in the general interest, are not regarded as comprising prohibited obstacles to the right of establishment or the freedom to provide services. At first sight the admissibility of implied imperative/overriding requirements, in addition to express derogations on grounds of public policy, etc, seems to contradict the proposition that exceptions to general principles must be construed narrowly. However, a plausible theory underlying the concept of imperative/overriding requirements which justify derogation from fundamental freedoms (the theory is also applicable in the field of free movement of goods) is that the relevant Treaty provisions identify as restrictions and prohibit some national measures per se, subject to application of the express exceptions in the Treaty, while other national measures can only be said to comprise restrictions if their restrictive effects cannot be justified on grounds compatible with EU law, and consistently with the principle of proportionality. Thus, for example, direct discrimination on grounds of nationality is prohibited per se, and can be justified only in accordance with express derogations in the Treaty, such as Articles 45(3), 45(4), 51 and 52(1) TFEU (these latter two Articles in conjunction as appropriate with Article 62 TFEU).[266] For example, the Court has held that the obligation under national law for a company holding a concession to operate a gaming establishment to have its seat

---

[262] Case C-212/97 *Centros* [1999] ECR I-1458, paras 32–34.

[263] See eg Case C-330/91 *ICI* para 28; Case C-168/01 *Bosal* [2003] ECR I-9409, para 42.

[264] Case C-3/88 *Commission v Italy* [1989] ECR 4035, para 15; Case C-101/94 *Commission v Italy* [1996] ECR I-2691, para 26.

[265] Case C-36/02 *Omega* [2004] ECR I-9609, para 39.

[266] Case C-388/01 *Commission v Italy* [2003] ECR I-721, para 19; Case C-311/97 *Royal Bank of Scotland* [1999] ECR I-2651, para 32; Case C-451/03 *Servizi Ausiliari Dottori Commercialisti* [2006] ECR I-2941, para 36.

in national territory is to be regarded as a discriminatory restriction which can be justified only on the basis of an express derogating provision such as Article 52(1) TFEU.[267] Alleged indirect discrimination can, however, be justified on objective grounds consistent with EU law (a concept akin to that of imperative/overriding requirements in the general interest), and non-discriminatory restrictions on fundamental freedoms alleged to hinder or make less attractive the exercise of fundamental freedoms can similarly be justified on the basis of imperative/overriding requirements. It is accordingly appropriate to consider below, inter alia, the evolution of the Court's case law in this regard; the categories of imperative or overriding requirements in the general interest, which may justify restrictions; and the application of the principle of proportionality.

(ii) The Court's Case Law on Imperative Requirements in the General Interest in the Context of the Right of Establishment

In the context of the right of establishment, it has only been with the development of the concept of the non-discriminatory restriction on this right that recourse to imperative requirements has become a matter of some significance. That is not to say that the question of justification of restrictions otherwise than under express derogating Treaty provisions did not arise before the advent of the non-discriminatory restriction, but that it arose in the context of alleged indirect discrimination on grounds of nationality, which would not be prohibited by the provisions of the Treaty if objectively justified.[268] The concept of objective justification, and the concept of imperative requirements, are clearly closely related. Where national rules have been held to comprise a restriction on the right of establishment, not by discrimination on grounds of nationality, nor by prohibiting cross-frontier activities or transactions, but by placing at a disadvantage those with a place of business in more than one Member State, or hindering the right of establishment, the Court accepts that justification on grounds of imperative requirements is in principle possible.[269] Where national rules have the effect of prohibiting cross-border activities or transactions (even if the rules are non-discriminatory), it is less clear that imperative requirements should be held to justify such a restriction, since in such a case there is a flat incompatibility between the freedom that is guaranteed, and the national measure comprising the restriction, which would seem to indicate that the measure is prohibited, unless it can be justified under one of the express derogations provided in the Treaty. Reference has already been made to the *Klopp* case,[270] in which the Court considered a non-discriminatory national rule requiring an advocate to practise from a single set of chambers. The Court noted that Article 49 TFEU entitles a person established in one Member State to establish an agency or branch in another, and held that for an advocate this meant being entitled to practise from chambers in more than one Member State. It is true that the Court refers to a host State having the right to require that lawyers enrolled at a bar in its territory practise in such a way as to maintain sufficient contact with their clients and the judicial authorities and abide by the rules of their profession, but the Court adds that 'such requirements must not prevent the nationals of other Member States

[267] Case C-64/08 *Engelmann* (CJEU 9 September 2010) paras 32–34.
[268] See this chapter, at p 545 above.
[269] Case 143/87 *Stanton* [1988] ECR 3877, para 15; Case C-53/95 *Kemmler* [1996] ECR I-703, para 13; C-255/97 *Pfeiffer Großhandel* [1999] ECR I-2835, para 21.
[270] Case 107/83 *Klopp* [1983] ECR 2971; see above, p 538.

from exercising properly the right of establishment guaranteed them by the Treaty'.[271] A restriction such as that in issue in *Klopp* should probably be regarded as being capable of justification only on the basis of an express derogating provision in the Treaty.

With the development of the concept of the non-discriminatory restriction on the right of establishment has come the 'rolled up' formulation, in which the definition of the restriction and the possibilities for its justification are presented in a simple, apparently straightforward formulation, as the following statement of the Court in the *Gebhard* case indicates:

> [N]ational measures liable to hinder or make less attractive the exercise of fundamental freedoms guaranteed by the Treaty must fulfil four conditions: they must be applied in a non-discriminatory manner; they must be justified by imperative requirements in the general interest; they must be suitable for securing the attainment of the objective which they pursue; and they must not go beyond what is necessary in order to attain it.[272]

Application of the above criteria for justification can involve some fairly intensive proportionality review, as is illustrated by the Court's analysis in the *Centros* case.[273] In this case it was argued for the Danish authorities that they were justified in refusing to register a branch of an English company in Denmark, where the English company carried on no business in England, and did not meet the minimum capital requirements laid down for Danish companies. The share capital of the English company was £100, and the sole reason the Danish nationals set up a company in the United Kingdom rather than Denmark was to secure the advantages of limited liability without having to meet the cost of the £20,000 minimum capital requirement then prevailing in Denmark. The Danish authorities emphasised that had the company done any business at all in England, they would have registered the branch in Denmark, and argued that refusing to register the branch was the least restrictive means available of reinforcing the financial soundness of companies so as to protect the interests of public and private creditors (ie tax authorities), and in particular the latter, who, unlike private creditors, were not in a position to secure their debts by obtaining personal guarantees from the directors of debtor companies.[274]

The Court did not deny that interests such as those referred to might in principle justify measures such as those in issue, but rejected the arguments made on proportionality grounds. In the first place, the Court held that the refusal to register the branch was not appropriate to attain the objective of protecting creditors, since, if the company concerned had conducted business in the United Kingdom, its branch would—as the Danish authorities had indicated—have been registered in Denmark, even though Danish creditors might have been equally exposed to risk. Thus the Danish measure failed to satisfy the third of the conditions listed in the *Gebhard* formulation—the requirement that a national measure be *suitable* to achieve its aim. The Court next emphasised that the English company held itself out as such, and not as a company governed by Danish law, and that it followed that its creditors were on notice that it was covered by laws different from those governing Danish companies. The Court clearly attached significance to this, and added that creditors could refer to certain rules of EU law which protected them. These latter rules were disclosure rules designed to enable third parties to be able to check on the

---

[271] Ibid, paras 20 and 21.
[272] Case C-55/94 *Gebhard* [1995] ECR I-4165, para 37.
[273] Case C-212/97 *Centros* [1999] ECR I-1458.
[274] Ibid, para 32. See also Chapter 20, p 650.

financial position of companies, and in particular branches of foreign companies.[275] The Court concluded that it was possible to adopt measures which were less restrictive, or which interfered less with fundamental freedoms, by, for example, making it possible in law for public creditors to obtain the necessary guarantees.[276] The Danish measures thus also failed to satisfy the fourth condition stipulated in the *Gebhard* formulation—that in order to be justified, a national measure must go no further than is necessary to achieve its aim. The present writer agrees with the Court's conclusion, but would emphasise that in coming to it the Court is engaging in fairly intensive proportionality review.

In order for a national measure restricting the exercise of the right of establishment to be considered to be *suitable* to achieve its aim, the Court held in the *Attanasio* case that it must genuinely reflect a concern to attain it in 'a consistent and systematic manner'.[277] Applying a restrictive rule exclusively to new operators, while exempting existing operators, casts doubt on the consistency and therefore the suitability of such a rule.[278]

In assessing the proportionality of national measures which restrict freedom of movement, including freedom of establishment, account must be taken of the fact that the health and life of humans rank foremost among the assets and interests protected by the Treaty and that it is for the Member States to determine the level of protection which they wish to afford to public health and the way in which that level is to be achieved. Since the level may vary from one Member State to another, Member States must be allowed discretion in the matter.[279] The Court has accordingly upheld the right of Member States to require that pharmacies be owned and operated only be pharmacists, despite the restrictive effects of such a requirement.[280] The appropriately deferential approach in cases involving health protection is to be contrasted with the considerably more intense review which is often undertaken in other types of case, as illustrated by the Court's approach in *Centros*, discussed above. The difference, however, is one of fact and degree, and does not by any means exclude close judicial scrutiny of the proportionality of national measures which restrict the right of establishment on health grounds. Although the Court upheld the rule referred to above concerning the ownership and operation of pharmacies, it distinguished an earlier case in which it held a similar national rule applying to opticians to be disproportionate.[281]

Industrial and commercial property has been held to justify a restriction on the right of establishment,[282] and the effectiveness of fiscal supervision constitutes an 'overriding requirement of general interest' capable of justifying a restriction on the exercise of fundamental freedoms guaranteed by the Treaty.[283] In the context of the exercise of the right

---

[275] The Court refers to the Fourth Council Directive 78/660/EEC on the annual accounts of certain types of companies [1978] OJ L222/1, and to the Eleventh Council Directive 89/666/EEC concerning disclosure requirements in respect of branches opened in a Member State by certain types of company governed by the law of another State [1989] OJ L395/36.

[276] Case C-212/97 *Centros* [1999] ECR I-1458, para 37.

[277] Case C-384/08 *Attanasio* (CJEU 11 March 2010) para 51, citing case law.

[278] Ibid, para 53.

[279] Case C-531/06 *Commission v Italy* [2009] ECR I-4103, para 36; Joined Cases C-171/07 and C-172/07 *Apothekerkammer des Saarlandes and Others* [2009] ECR I-4171, para 19.

[280] Case C-531/06 *Commission v Italy* [2009] ECR I-4103, paras 49–88; Joined Cases C-171/07 and C-172/07 *Apothekerkammer des Saarlandes and Others* [2009] ECR I-4171.

[281] Case C-140/03 *Commission v Greece* [2005] ECR I-3177, distinguished in Case C-531/06 *Commission v Italy* [2009] ECR I-4103, at paras 89 and 90, and in Joined Cases C-171/07 and C-172/07 *Apothekerkammer des Saarlandes and Others* [2009] ECR I-4171, paras 59 and 60.

[282] Case C-255/97 *Pfeiffer Großhandel* [1999] ECR I-2835, para 21.

[283] Case C-254/97 *Baxter* [1999] ECR I-4809, para 18.

of establishment by a ferry-operating company against trade union bodies—the *Viking* case—the Court has confirmed the proposition that 'the right to take collective action for the protection of workers is a legitimate interest which, in principle, justifies a restriction of one of the fundamental freedoms guaranteed by the Treaty'.[284] As regards the categories of mandatory requirement which may be invoked to justify national rules that might restrict the exercise of the right of establishment, reference by analogy may be made in particular to the case law on the free movement of goods,[285] and on freedom to provide services. Protection of public health may justify restrictions resulting pursuant to the express derogation in Article 52(1) TFEU, and is therefore in principle also capable of justifying national measures which are indistinctly applicable, such as a measure reserving to persons holding certain qualifications the right to carry out certain medical procedures.[286]

(iii) The Court's Case Law on Overriding Reasons in the General Interest in the Context of Freedom to Provide Services

In the *van Binsbergen* case the Court of Justice stated that restrictions on freedom to provide services would not be prohibited by the Treaty where they had the purpose of applying

> professional rules justified by the general good—in particular rules relating to organisation, qualifications, professional ethics, supervision and liability—which are binding upon any person established in the state in which the service is provided, where the person providing the service would escape from the ambit of those rules being established in another Member State.[287]

It should be noted that the Court did not make any reference to Article 52(1) TFEU, and seemed to countenance that, in principle, and in an appropriate case, a Member State might insist on establishment within national territory to ensure application of national rules such as those referred to. In *Ramrath*[288] the Court held that a requirement that auditors maintain an establishment in national territory was justified in order to secure the application of national rules in the public interest designed to uphold the integrity and independence of those practising the profession in question. This latter case is the only one in which the Court has upheld such a requirement, and may be wrongly decided. In *van Binsbergen* the national rules identified as comprising restrictions on the freedom to provide services comprised those discriminating on grounds of nationality and those which discriminated by reference to the place of establishment of the service provider[289]—a formulation to be repeated in the Court's subsequent case law.[290]

In *Seco*[291] the Court considered an obligation imposed by national law on employers to pay social security contributions on behalf of their employees, which was also applicable to employers who were established in other Member States and temporarily providing services in the host State, and who were already liable to make similar contributions under the legislation of the Member States where they were established. The Court held that this amounted to indirect discrimination on grounds of nationality, which could not be jus-

---

[284] Case C-438/05 *Viking* [2007] ECR I-10779, para 77, and see cases cited.
[285] Chapter 14, at p 441.
[286] Case C-108/96 *Mac Queen* [2001] ECR I-837, para 28
[287] Case 33/74 *van Binsbergen* [1974] ECR 1307, para 12.
[288] Case C-106/91 *Ramrath* [1992] ECR I-3351.
[289] See above at p 560.
[290] See above at p 561.
[291] Joined Cases 62 and 63/81 *Seco* [1982] ECR 223, paras 8–10.

tified on account of the general interest in providing workers with social security, since no benefits were payable to the employees in such circumstances. It will be noted that in this case the examination of justification in the general interest is in fact an assessment of whether or not the indirect discrimination can be objectively justified. Later case law treated the application of national measures of social protection in such cases of posted workers as restrictions on the provision of services without the need to establish that the measures were indirectly discriminatory, and considered justification by reference to overriding requirements in the general interest.[292]

In *Bond van Adverteerders*[293] the Court stated that national rules which 'are not applicable to services without distinction as regards their origin and which are therefore discriminatory are compatible with Community law only if they can be brought within the scope of an express derogation', such as Article 52(1) TFEU. In *Gouda* the Court repeated and expanded upon this earlier statement. While national rules which discriminated against services by reference to their origin could only be justified if brought within an express provision of the Treaty, such as Article 52(1) TFEU,[294] the position was different for national rules which restricted the freedom to provide services by virtue of their effects on service providers established in the territory of another Member State who already had to satisfy the requirements of that State's legislation.[295] As regards restrictions in this latter category:

> [S]uch restrictions come within the scope of Article [56 TFEU] if the application of the national legislation to foreign persons providing services is not justified by overriding reasons relating to the public interest or if the requirements embodied in that legislation are already satisfied by the rules imposed on those persons in the Member State in which they are established.[296]

The Court goes on to list overriding reasons relating to the public interest which the Court had recognised to date.[297] It appears from that list that the Court regards the second category to which it has referred, which covers restrictions which need not be justified by reference to Article 52(1) TFEU (in conjunction with Article 62 TFEU), as covering both national rules which discriminate indirectly on grounds of nationality (where the overriding reasons in the general interest in effect amount to objective justification),[298] and national rules which discriminate indirectly by reference to the fact that the service

---

[292] See eg Joined Cases C-369 and 376/96 *Arblade* [1999] ECR I-8453, paras 46, 53 and 54; Case C-165/98 *Mazzoleni* [2001] ECR I-2189; see also Case C-164/99 *Portugaia Construções Lda* [2002] ECR I-787; Joined Cases C-49/98 etc *Finalarte et al* [2001] ECR I-7831.

[293] Case 352/85 *Bond van Adverteerders* [1988] ECR 2085, para 32.

[294] Case C-288/89 *Gouda* [1991] ECR I-4007, para 11.

[295] Ibid, para 12.

[296] Ibid, para 13.

[297] The Court listed professional rules intended to protect recipients of the service (Joined Cases 110/78 and 111/78 *Van Wesemael* [1979] ECR 35, para 28); protection of intellectual property (Case 62/79 *Coditel* [1980] ECR 881); the protection of workers (Case 279/80 *Webb* [1981] ECR 3305, para 19; Joined Cases 62/81 and 63/81 *Seco v EVI* [1982] ECR 223, para 14; Case C-113/89 *Rush Portuguesa* [1990] ECR I-1417, para 18); consumer protection (Case 220/83 *Commission v France* [1986] ECR 3663, para 20; Case 252/83 *Commission v Denmark* [1986] ECR 3713, para 20; Case 205/84 *Commission v Germany* [1986] ECR 3755, para 30; Case 206/84 *Commission v Ireland* [1986] ECR 3817, para 20; Case C-180/89 *Commission v Italy* [1991] ECR I-709, para 20; and Case C-198/89 *Commission v Greece*, [1991] ECR I-727, para 21), the conservation of the national historic and artistic heritage (*Commission v Italy*, cited above, para 20); turning to account the archaeological, historical and artistic heritage of a country and the widest possible dissemination of knowledge of the artistic and cultural heritage of a country (*Commission v France*, cited above, para 17; *Commission v Greece*, cited above, para 21).

[298] Note that the Court refers to the *Seco* case, which, as shown above, concerns in reality the question of objective justification for indirect discrimination.

provider is established in another Member State. The Court of Justice applied the *Gouda* reasoning in subsequent cases, holding that national rules which were directly discriminatory as regards the place of business of a service provider in another Member State, or as regards the residence of a service recipient in another Member State, could be justified only by an express derogation such as Article 52(1) TFEU.[299]

However, the case law is not really consistent. In *van Binsbergen* and *Ramrath* the Court held that national rules requiring an economic operator established in another Member State and providing services in the first Member State maintain a place of business in that Member State might be justified on grounds of overriding requirements in the general interest. In *Bond van Adverteerders* and *Gouda* the Court held that such a requirement, discriminating as it did against the out-of-state origin of a service, could only be upheld if the considerations of public interest could be regarded as falling within the scope of Article 52 TFEU. In support of the latter proposition, it might be said that prohibiting the provision of services on the sole ground that the service provider is not established in the same Member State as the service recipient is as much the very mischief at which Article 56 TFEU is in terms aimed, as the direct discrimination on grounds of nationality, prohibited by the Treaty, which the Court has emphasised can only be justified by reference to express derogating provisions in the Treaty.[300] The Court's 'realignment' of its case law in *Bond van Adverteerders* and *Gouda* thus seems in principle to have been correct. However, the Court continued to consider possible justifications of national measures which discriminate against out-of-state providers by reference to mandatory requirements.[301] Thus in *Commission v Italy*[302] the Court considered Italian rules requiring, inter alia, undertakings engaged in the provision of temporary labour established in other Member States to maintain their registered office or a branch office on Italian territory. Relying on *Gouda*, the Commission argued that these requirements could only be justified under Articles 52 and 62 TFEU, and that no such justification could be made out. The Court noted that it followed from the Court's case law (citing, inter alia, and surprisingly, *Gouda*) that 'the protection of workers is among the overriding reasons of public interest capable of justifying a restriction on the freedom to provide services', though it held, predictably, on proportionality grounds, that this could not justify the Italian requirements in issue.[303] The Court is, it seems, more attached to flexibility than to legal principle or consistency. In *Danner*[304] Advocate General Jacobs noted the existence of two inconsistent lines of case law on the question whether national rules which discriminate as regards the origin of a service can be justified by reference to imperative requirements or solely by reference to Articles 51 and 52(1) TFEU. He considered the state of uncertainty to be unsatisfactory, advocated a solution whereby all restrictions on the provision of services should be capable of justification on grounds of imperative requirements, and expressed the view that

---

[299] Case C-484/93 *Svensson* [1995] ECR I-3955, para 15 (discrimination as regards place of residence of service provider, though the Court goes on to examine whether the measure may nevertheless be justified by the need to maintain cohesion of the tax system, para 16); Case C-224/97 *Ciola* [1999] ECR I-2517, para 16 (discrimination as regards place of residence of service recipient).

[300] Case C-388/01 *Commission v Italy* [2003] ECR I-721, para 19; Case C-311/97 *Royal Bank of Scotland* [1999] ECR I-2651, para 32; and see above at p 573.

[301] Case C-158/96 *Kohll* 1998] ECR I-1931, paras 34 and 41; Case C-410/96 *André Ambry* [1998] ECR I-7875, paras 28–31; Case C-484/93 *Svensson* [1995] ECR I-3955.

[302] Case C-279/00 [2002] ECR I-1425.

[303] Ibid, paras 16–25.

[304] Case C-136/00 [2002] ECR I-8147, paras 34–40.

the Court should clarify the position. The Court in *Danner* did not do so. But the present position seems to be close in practice to that urged by Advocate General Jacobs, in that national rules which discriminate as to the origin of a service by requiring a fixed place of business in national territory may be justified either by reference to an express derogation such as Article 51 or 52(1) TFEU, or by reference to overriding requirements in the general interest.[305] *Bond van Adverteeders* and *Gouda* no longer seem to be cited for the contrary proposition, though they are cited on other points.[306] The Court still requires measures which restrict the provision of services by discriminating on grounds of nationality to be justified by reference to an express derogation in the Treaty, and discrimination against operators established in other Member States may amount to direct discrimination on grounds of nationality. Thus in *Commission v Spain* the Court held that a tax exemption for winnings from lotteries and games of chance which applied to winnings paid by certain Spanish public or non-profit-making charitable bodies, but not to winnings paid by similar bodies in other Member States, discriminated on grounds of nationality, and accordingly could only be justified under an express derogating provision such as Article 52(1) TFEU.[307]

The Court in *Gouda*, after listing the categories of public interest referred to above, ended with a reference to the need for national measures to be appropriate and proportionate in order to be justified:

> Lastly, as the Court has consistently held, the application of national provisions to providers of services established in other Member States must be such as to guarantee the achievement of the intended aim and must not go beyond what is necessary in order to achieve that objective. In other words, it must not be possible to obtain the same result by less restrictive rules.[308]

As regards the application of the proportionality test, the discussion of case law on this issue in the context of the right of establishment discussed above is equally applicable in the context of the freedom to provide services.

The Court's analysis of 'overriding reasons in the general interest' continued to follow the pattern established prior to the development of the concept of the non-discriminatory restriction in the *Säger* case.[309] The categories of 'overriding reasons' recognised to date at the time of the *Gouda* case, shortly before the ruling in *Säger*, have already been referred to.[310] More recently, the Court has upheld national rules which regulate lotteries on grounds of consumer protection and the maintenance of order in society,[311] and national rules which confine the judicial recovery of debts to members of the legal profession on the grounds of consumer protection and safeguarding the proper administration of justice.[312] The Court has acknowledged that the risk of seriously undermining the financial

---

[305] Case C-393/05 *Commission v Austria* [2007] ECR I-10195 (requirement of permanent infrastructure in the Member State where services provided a restriction on provision of services which cannot be justified either under Art 51 TFEU or on grounds of consumer protection); in the same vein, Case C-404/05 *Commission v Germany* [2007] ECR I-10239.

[306] See eg Case C-336/07 *Kabel Deutschland* [2008] ECR I-10889.

[307] C-153/08 [2009] ECR I-9735.

[308] Case C-288/89 *Gouda* [1991] ECR I-4007, para 15.

[309] Case C-76/90 *Säger* [1991] ECR I-4221.

[310] Above p 578.

[311] Case C-275/92 *Schindler* [1994] ECR I-1039, para 61; but see eg Joined Cases C-338/04, C-359/04 and C-360/04 *Placanica and Others* [2007] ECR I-891, esp paras 48 and 49, in which the Court shows itself ready to apply the principle of proportionality in the context of gambling in an appropriate case.

[312] Case C-3/95 *Broede v Sandker* [1996] ECR I-6511.

balance of the social security system may constitute an overriding reason in the general interest capable of justifying a Member State requiring authorisation for dental treatment in another Member State, where no such authorisation was required for treatment in the first Member State.[313] And the Court held in the *Laval* case, in which a building company invoked Article 56 TFEU against trade unions, on the ground that their collective action constituted a restriction on its freedom to provide services, that

> the right to take collective action for the protection of the workers of the host State against possible social dumping may constitute an overriding reason of public interest within the meaning of the case-law of the Court which, in principle, justifies a restriction of one of the fundamental freedoms guaranteed by the Treaty.[314]

VI – NATIONAL TAX MEASURES AS RESTRICTIONS ON FUNDAMENTAL FREEDOMS

A – The Normal Principles Apply but Account is Taken of the Particular Features of Tax Law

National tax rules are capable of constituting restrictions on the free movement of persons, services and capital.[315] The same principles apply to all the relevant Treaty provisions as regards the concept of a restriction on a fundamental freedom, and as regards the possibility of justifying derogation. This section of this chapter is mainly concerned with tax rules as restrictions on freedom of establishment, but reference is made where appropriate to case law on free movement of workers or capital. The guiding principles are that direct or indirect discrimination on grounds of nationality amounts to a restriction on freedom of movement, and that national measures which hinder or make less attractive the exercise of a fundamental freedom must be justified. In the context of the freedom of establishment these principles have been discussed earlier in the present chapter.[316] That said, the application by the Court of Justice of these principles in the context of restrictions resulting from national tax provisions and the justification for such restrictions has necessitated account being taken of the particular features of tax law.

The case law on national tax measures operating as restrictions on fundamental freedoms is extensive and often involves complicated national tax provisions. This section of this chapter does not aim to provide a comprehensive exposition of the compatibility with freedom of establishment of national tax rules, but rather to provide examples of the

---

[313] Case C-158/96 *Kohll* [1998] ECR I-1931, para 41; and see eg Case C-350/07 *Kattner Stahlbau* [2009] ECR I-1513 (risk of serious harm to financial equilibrium of a social security scheme can in principle justify compulsory affiliation of undertakings covered by the scheme at issue to the employers' liability insurance associations entrusted by the law with providing such insurance, subject to verification of the proportionality of the requirement by the national court).

[314] Case C-341/04 *Laval* [2007] ECR I-11767, para 103.

[315] For an explanation of the provisions on capital movement, see Chapter 20 at pp 661–62.

[316] See above at pp 545–52.

type of restriction which may result from national tax rules, and to indicate possible justifications for such restrictions.

B – For Tax Purposes Residence and the Location of a Company's Seat Are Legitimate Connecting Factors but National Rules which Differentiate on these Grounds may Be Held to Be Discriminatory

In *Commission v France* the Court endorsed three propositions of considerable importance as regards the relationship between the right of establishment of companies and the application of national tax legislation.

The first proposition is that as regards the exercise of the right of establishment by companies, it is the location of their registered office, or central administration, or principal place of business, which serves as the connecting factor with the legal system of a particular state, like nationality in the case of natural persons, and for a company seeking to establish itself in another Member State to be treated differently solely by reason of the fact that its registered office, etc, is situated in another Member State would deprive the right of establishment of all meaning.[317] In other words, it is the registered office, central administration or principal place of business which determines the seat of the company, in accordance with relevant national rules; and it is the location of the seat which comprises the relevant connecting factor with a national legal system: discrimination solely by reference to the fact that a company's seat is in another Member State is contrary to Article 49 TFEU.[318] Freedom of establishment thus aims to guarantee the benefit of national treatment in the host Member State, by prohibiting any discrimination based on the place in which companies have their seat.[319]

The second proposition endorsed by the Court is that notwithstanding the first proposition, nevertheless the possibility cannot 'altogether be excluded' that a distinction based 'on the location of the registered office of a company or the place of residence of a natural person may, under certain conditions, be justified in an area such as tax law'.[320] It is explained below that this way of putting it somewhat understates the significant role played by the connecting factors of residence and corporate seat in tax law.

The third proposition is that where national tax rules treat two forms of establishment in the same way for the purposes of taxing their profits (in the case in point, companies with a registered office in France on the one hand, and branches in France of companies with a registered office in another Member State on the other), that amounts to an admission that there is no objective difference between their positions as regards the detailed rules and conditions relating to that taxation which could justify different treatment.[321]

---

[317] Case 270/83 *Commission v France* [1986] ECR 273, para 18.

[318] Case C-311/97 *Royal Bank of Scotland* [1999] ECR I-2651, para 23.

[319] Case C-524/04 *Test Claimants in the Thin Cap Litigation* [2007] ECR I-2107, para 37.

[320] Ibid, para 19. The better view is that this amounts to justification of indirect discrimination on grounds of nationality, rather than justification of direct discrimination, since the connecting factors referred to in Art 54 TFEU, ie registered office, etc, not only comprise a link analogous to that of nationality, but may also be indicative of residence for tax purposes. Even if it is the case that direct discrimination on grounds of nationality cannot normally be justified, differentiation on grounds of residence may be so justified, perhaps particularly in the tax context, and it is to this latter possibility that the Court is referring in para 19. It might be added that the Court has accepted that it is consistent with Art 45 TFEU for Member States to define nationality as one of the criteria for allocating their powers of taxation as between themselves, with a view to eliminating double taxation, see Case C-336/96 *Gilly* [1998] ECR I-2793, para 30.

[321] Case 270/83 *Commission v France* [1986] ECR 273, para 20.

Even those with but the briefest familiarity with the intricacies of tax law will be aware that it frequently lays down different rules for residents and non-residents, whether they be individuals or companies. Yet it has been noted above that national rules which distinguish between individuals on the basis of their residence may amount to indirect discrimination on grounds of nationality, contrary to the provisions of the Treaty on the free movement of workers or right of establishment.[322] And it will be noted that the criteria referred to in the second and third propositions derived from the judgment of the Court in *Commission v France*, which allot to a company a status akin to that of the nationality, are also criteria used to determine the residence of a company. The result is that the application to individuals and companies of the residence or seat criteria which are such a commonplace of the national tax regimes seem almost intrinsically to raise a question as to compatibility with Article 49 TFEU or other fundamental freedoms. The case law certainly holds that the fact that a residence criterion is applied in the tax context is no guarantee of immunity from successful challenge under the Treaty.

Thus in *Commerzbank*[323] the Court of Justice considered a national tax rule which restricted repayment supplement (a payment analogous to an interest payment) on overpaid tax to companies resident for tax purposes in the Member State in question. In the case in which the question arose a non-resident company had received a repayment of overpaid tax by virtue of non-residence, pursuant to a double-tax convention, but been denied repayment supplement pursuant to the contested rule. The Court considered the rule was discriminatory, as follows:

> Although it applies independently of a company's seat, the use of the criterion of fiscal residence within national territory for the purpose of granting repayment supplement on overpaid tax is liable to work more particularly to the disadvantage of companies having their seat in other Member States. Indeed, it is most often those companies which are resident for tax purposes outside the territory of the Member State in question.[324]

The Member State in question argued that non-resident companies in the position of the claimant in the national proceedings, far from being discriminated against, enjoyed privileged treatment. They were exempt from tax normally payable by resident companies. In such circumstances there was no discrimination with respect to repayment supplement: resident companies and non-resident companies were treated differently because, for the purposes of corporation tax, they were in different situations.[325] The Court, however, did not accept that argument. The rule the benefit of which the non-resident company was denied was a rule allowing repayment supplement when tax was overpaid; the fact that the exemption from tax which gave rise to the refund was available only to non-resident companies could not justify a rule of a general nature withholding the benefit.[326]

It is appropriate to organise discussion of the impact of national tax rules on the internal market in a way which distinguishes between types of restriction on fundamental freedoms, and to examine the scope for justification of such restrictions. As regards

---

[322] See above at p 545. For the proposition that differentiating between individuals on grounds of residence will amount to indirect discrimination on grounds of nationality unless justified, in the contest of freedom of movement for workers, see Case 152/73 *Sotgiu* [1974] ECR 153; it is a case cited by the Court in support of the same proposition as regards companies in the context of Art 49 TFEU, see Case C-330/91 *Commerzbank* [1993] ECR I-4017, para 14.

[323] Case C-330/91 *Commerzbank* [1993] ECR I-4017.

[324] Ibid, para 15.

[325] Ibid, para 16.

[326] Ibid, paras 18 and 19.

restrictions, there will be discussion of discrimination against non-residents generally; of discrimination against out-of-state parent companies as regards their dealings with their subsidiaries; and of restrictions which inhibit persons established in a Member State from extending their activities to another Member State.

C – Tax Measures which Discriminate against Non-residents May Amount to Restrictions on the Right of Establishment

The second of the three propositions referred to above as having been endorsed by the Court of Justice in *Commission v France*, to the effect that the possibility could not 'altogether be excluded' that a distinction based 'on the location of the registered office of a company or the place of residence of a natural person may, under certain conditions, be justified in an area such as tax law',[327] seems to understate the significance of individual or corporate residence as a connecting factor with a Member State for tax purposes, and in later cases the Court allowed that

> in relation to direct taxes, the situations of residents and of non-residents in a given State are not generally comparable, since there are objective differences between them from the point of view of the source of the income and the possibility of taking account of their ability to pay tax or their personal and family circumstances.[328]

The Court has observed that, 'according to well-established case law, although direct taxation falls within their competence, the Member States must none the less exercise that competence consistently with European Union law',[329] and this in turn means examining in detail the distinctions drawn between resident and non-resident tax-payers to establish whether they are indeed compatible with EU law.

While the situations of residents and of non-residents are not generally comparable, if they are in fact comparable, and yet the non-resident is treated less favourably than the resident, this will amount to discrimination, and be contrary to Article 49 TFEU.[330] Thus in *Schumacker*[331] the Court held that it will not be discriminatory to deny to a non-resident certain tax benefits paid to a resident, where the major part of the income of the resident is concentrated in the Member State of residence, and the latter Member State has available all the information needed to assess the taxpayer's overall ability to pay, while this is not so in the case of the non-resident. But the Court added that the position will be different where the non-resident receives no significant income in the Member State of his or her residence and obtains the major part of his or her taxable income from an activity performed in the Member State of employment, with the result that the Member State of his or her residence is not in a position to grant him or her the benefits resulting from the taking into account of his or her personal and family circumstances.[332] The

---

[327] Case 270/83 *Commission v France* [1986] ECR 273, para 19.

[328] Case C-279/93 *Schumacker* [1995] ECR I-225, para 31; Case C-80/94 *Wielockx* [1995] ECR I-2493, para 18; Case C-107/94 *Asscher* [1994] ECR I-1137, para 41.

[329] Case C-233/09 *Dijkman* (CJEU 1 July 2010) para 20.

[330] See eg Case C-279/93 *Schumacker* [1995] ECR I-225 (the case concerns Art 45 TFEU); Case C-80/94 *Wielockx* [1995] ECR I-2493 (Art 49 TFEU).

[331] Case C-279/93 *Schumacker* [1995] ECR I-225, paras 33–35.

[332] Ibid, para 36. *Schumacker* is distinguished in Case C-391/97 *Gschwind* [1999] ECR I-5451.

Court concluded that there was no objective difference between the situations of such a non-resident and a resident engaged in comparable employment, such as to justify different treatment as regards the taking into account for taxation purposes of the taxpayer's personal and family circumstances.[333]

The Court applied the principles laid down in *Schumacker* and in its subsequent case law in *Truck Center*,[334] in which it considered national rules which charged withholding tax on interest on a loan given by a non-resident parent company to its resident subsidiary. Withholding tax would not have been charged if the interest had been payable to another resident company, which would have been taxed as regards the interest by means of the corporation tax to which it would be subject in the Member State of residence. The Court noted that the procedure for the charging of the tax in question depended on the place where the company receiving the interest had its registered office. But the Court concluded that the situations of a resident and non-resident company in such circumstances were not objectively comparable. This conclusion followed, inter alia, from the consideration that the payment of interest by one resident company to another resident company and the payment of interest by a resident company to a non-resident company gave rise to two distinct charges rested on separate legal bases. Furthermore, such companies were in different situations as regards the recovery of the relevant tax. While resident companies in receipt of interest payments were directly subject to the supervision of the tax authorities of the Member States of residence, that was not the case with regard to non-resident companies receiving interest, since in their case, recovery of the tax required the assistance of the tax authorities of the other Member State.[335]

D – Discrimination against Non-resident Parent Companies in their Dealings with Resident Subsidiaries

It is not uncommon for national tax rules to subject relations between resident subsidiaries and non-resident parent companies to less favourable treatment than relations between resident subsidiaries and resident parent companies. The Court has maintained in a consistent case law that:

> A difference in treatment between resident subsidiary companies according to the seat of their parent company constitutes an obstacle to the freedom of establishment if it makes it less attractive for companies established in other Member States to exercise that freedom and they may, in consequence, refrain from acquiring, creating or maintaining a subsidiary in the State which adopts that measure.[336]

It was to combat such discrimination that Directive 90/435/EEC on the common system of taxation applicable in the case of parent companies and subsidiaries of different Member States was adopted.[337] This Directive aims to prevent profits made by a subsidiary being taxed both in the Member State of the subsidiary, as income of the subsidiary,

---

[333] Ibid, para 37.

[334] Case C-282/07 *Truck Center* [2008] ECR I-10767.

[335] Ibid, paras 41–48. The case is criticised by A Cordewener, G Kofler and S van Thiel, 'The Clash between European Freedoms and National Direct Tax Law; Public Interest Defences Available to the Member States' (2009) 46 *CMLRev* 1951, 1996, n 226.

[336] Case C-231/05 *OY AA* [2007] ECR I-6373, para 39, and cases cited.

[337] [1990] OJ L225/6; see now amended and consolidated text of 01.01.2007 (Eurlex).

and in the Member State of the parent company, as dividends. The aims of the measure are described in the preamble, which refers to the need for the grouping together of companies of different Member States in order to create conditions analogous to those of an internal market. The preamble notes that such grouping together may result in the formation of groups of parent companies and subsidiaries, but adds that national tax provisions which govern the relations between parent companies and subsidiaries of different Member States vary and 'are generally less advantageous than those applicable to parent companies and subsidiaries of the same Member State'. The preamble concludes that 'it is necessary to eliminate this disadvantage by the introduction of a common system'. Under the common system for which the Directive provides, where a parent company by virtue of its association with its subsidiary receives distributed profits, the Member State of the parent company must either refrain from taxing such profits, or tax such profits while authorising the parent company to deduct from the amount of tax due that fraction of the corporation tax paid by the subsidiary and any lower-tier subsidiary which relates to those profits.[338] The Court of Justice has explained the rationale of the Directive in the following terms:

> The need for the Directive results from the double taxation to which groups comprising companies established in a number of States may be subject.
>
> If there is no specific exemption granted by States either unilaterally or under bilateral agreements, profits made by a subsidiary are liable to be taxed both in the State of the subsidiary, as operating income of the subsidiary, and in the State of the parent company, as dividends.[339]

Outside of the scope of the above Directive, national tax provisions discriminating against non-resident parent companies may be contrary to the Treaty provisions on establishment or capital movement.

In *Halliburton Services*[340] the Court considered the compatibility with Article 49 TFEU of an exemption from property transfer tax applicable in the case of an internal reorganisation of public limited companies and private limited companies, subject to the proviso that the companies party to the transfer were incorporated under the law of the Member State in question. The effect of the application of the Netherlands law in the national proceedings was that a transfer of property in the Netherlands from a German subsidiary of a US company to a Netherlands subsidiary of the same US company involved the liability of the latter subsidiary to the tax which would not have been payable if the transferor had also been a Netherlands company.

The Netherlands government argued that no discrimination was involved because the person liable to pay the tax was not the Germany company but the Netherlands company, which meant that the situation was purely internal to the Netherlands, and Community law was not involved. The Court rejected this argument, noting that 'payment of a tax on the sale of immovable property constitutes a burden which renders the conditions of sale of the property more onerous and thus has repercussions on the position of the transferor'.[341]

---

[338] Art 4(1) of the Directive.

[339] Case C-294/99 *Athinaïki Zythopoiia* [2001] ECR I-2797, paras 5 and 6. See also on the interpretation of the Directive, Joined Cases C-283/94, C-291/94 and C-292/94 *Denkavit* [1996] ECR I-5063; Case C-375/98 *Epson Europe* [2001] ECR I-4243; Case C-168/01 *Bosal* [2003] ECR I-9409; Case C-58/01 *Océ Van der Grinten NV* [2003] ECR I-9809; Case C-446/04 *Test Claimants in the FII Group Litigation* [2006] ECR I-11753; Case C-379/05 *Amurta* [2007] ECR I- 9569; Case C-284/06 *Burda* [2008] ECR I-4571; Case C-303/07 *Aberdeen Property Fininvest* [2009[ECR I-5145.

[340] Case C-1/93 *Halliburton Services* [1994] ECR I-1137.

[341] Ibid, para 19.

The Court concluded that although 'the difference in treatment has only an indirect effect on the position of companies constituted under the law of other Member States, it constitutes discrimination on grounds of nationality' prohibited by Article 49 TFEU.[342] The Netherlands government argued that the restriction of the exemption to companies constituted under national law was necessary because the competent tax administration was unable to check whether the legal forms of entities constituted in other Member States were equivalent to those of public and private limited companies within the meaning of the relevant national legislation. The Court rejected this argument because information relating to the characteristics of the forms in which companies can be constituted in other Member States could be obtained pursuant to EU legislation on mutual assistance by the competent authorities of the Member States in the field of direct taxation.[343]

Another example of national tax rules treating relations between resident subsidiaries and non-resident parent companies less favourably than relations between resident subsidiaries and resident parent companies were those at issue before the referring court in *Lankhorst-Hohorst*.[344] German rules on corporation tax ('thin capitalisation rules') provided that repayments in respect of loan capital which a company limited by shares subject to unlimited taxation had obtained from a shareholder not entitled to corporation tax credit, which had a substantial holding in its share capital, should be regarded as a covert distribution of profits. The reference to a shareholder 'not entitled to corporation tax credit' did apply to *some* German companies but applied to *all* non-resident companies. The essential facts of the case before the referring court were that a Netherlands company, LT BV, owned all the shares in the Netherlands company LH BV, which in turn owned all the shares in the German company Lankhorst-Hohorst GmbH (LH). LT BV gave a loan to LH repayable with interest over 10 years in annual instalments. The loan, which was intended as a substitute for capital, was accompanied by a 'letter of support' under which LT BV waived repayment if third-party creditors made claims against LH. The competent German tax authority took the view that interest paid to LT BV under the loan agreement was equivalent to a covert distribution of profits. Before the Court of Justice the German tax authority argued that the distinction drawn by the German rules between persons who are entitled to tax credit and those who are not did not amount to disguised discrimination on the basis of nationality, since those rules also excluded several categories of German taxpayers from entitlement to tax credit. The Court of Justice rejected this argument, on ground that in 'the large majority of cases, resident parent companies receive a tax credit, whereas, as general rule, non-resident parent companies do not'.[345] The Court concluded:

> Such a difference in treatment between resident subsidiary companies according to the seat of their parent company constitutes an obstacle to the freedom of establishment which is, in principle, prohibited by Article [49 TFEU]. The tax measure in question in the main proceedings makes it less attractive for companies established in other Member States to exercise freedom of establishment and they may, in consequence, refrain from acquiring, creating or maintaining a subsidiary in the State which adopts that measure.[346]

---

[342] Ibid, para 20.
[343] Ibid, para 22.
[344] Case C-324/00 *Lankhorst–Hohorst* [2002] ECR I-11779.
[345] Ibid, para 28.
[346] Ibid, para 32; see also Case C-524/04 *Test Claimants in the Thin Cap Group Litigation* [2007] ECR I-2107, para 61; Case C-377/07 *STEKO* [2009] ECR I-299, para 24.

E – National Tax Rules which Inhibit Individuals and Companies Established in a Member State from Extending their Activities to Another Member State

It is established that Article 49 TFEU prohibits 'exit' restrictions, ie restrictions which deter natural or legal persons from extending their activities to other Member States.[347] National tax rules which have this tendency amount to restrictions on the right of establishment.

In *de Lasteyrie du Saillant*[348] the Court of Justice considered national tax rules which provided that taxpayers intending to transfer their residence for tax purposes outside France were to be subject to immediate taxation on increases in value that had not yet been realised, and which would not be taxed if those taxpayers retained their residence in France. The Court noted that even if the rules in question did not prevent a French tax-payer from exercising his or her right of establishment, they were nevertheless of such a kind as to restrict the exercise of that right, having at the very least a dissuasive effect on taxpayers wishing to establish themselves in another Member State.[349] The Court held that the national rules in question amounted to an inappropriate and disproportionate means of achieving their alleged aim—to prevent temporary transfers of tax residence outside France exclusively for tax reasons.[350]

In *Bosal*[351] the issue before the national court was the compatibility with Article 49 TFEU of Netherlands tax rules which when determining the tax on profits of a parent company established in the Netherlands made the deductibility of costs in connection with the company's holding in the capital of a subsidiary established in another Member State subject to the condition that such costs were indirectly instrumental in making profits which were taxable in the Netherlands. The Court of Justice held that these rules constituted a hindrance to the establishment of subsidiaries in other Member States. A parent company might be dissuaded from carrying on its activities through the intermediary of a subsidiary established in another Member State since, normally, such subsidiaries do not generate profits that are taxable in the Netherlands.

In *ICI*[352] the Court considered whether Article 49 TFEU precluded UK legislation which, in the case of companies resident in that Member State belonging to a consortium which controls a holding company, makes a particular form of tax relief ('consortium relief') subject to the requirement that the holding company's business consist *wholly or mainly* in the holding of shares in subsidiaries that have their seat in the Member State concerned. The effect of the tax rules in question was that the setting up of a consortium company in another Member State could deprive a resident consortium company of relief on losses of another resident consortium company. The logic of placing a limit on the number of non-resident subsidiaries was from the United Kingdom's point of view, inter alia, to prevent charges being shifted to resident companies and profits being shifted to non-resident companies.[353] The Court considered that the requirement that the

---

[347] See eg Case 81/87 *Daily Mail* [1988] ECR 3483, para 16.
[348] Case C-9/02 *de Lasteyrie du Saillant* [2004] ECR I-409.
[349] Ibid, para 45.
[350] Ibid, paras 50–58.
[351] Case C-168/01 *Bosal* [2003] ECR I-9409.
[352] Case C-330/91 *ICI* [1998] ECR I-4695.
[353] Ibid, para 25.

above-mentioned subsidiaries be wholly or mainly UK resident subsidiaries could inhibit exercise of the right of establishment by the holding company in a Member State other than the United Kingdom.

In *Marks & Spencer*[354] the Court of Justice considered UK tax rules on group relief. These rules allowed transfers of losses from a resident subsidiary to a resident parent company, but did not allow such transfers from a non-resident subsidiary. Through the intermediary of a holding company established in the Netherlands, Marks and Spencer plc (M&S), resident in the United Kingdom, had subsidiaries in Germany, Belgium and France. From the middle of the 1990s, those subsidiaries began to record losses. During 2001, M&S divested itself of its continental European activities. M&S submitted group relief claims to the competent tax authority in respect of losses incurred by certain of its EU subsidiaries for the years 1998–2001. These claims were rejected on the ground that the group relief scheme did not apply to subsidiaries which were neither resident nor economically active in the United Kingdom. The Court of Justice noted that group relief such as that at issue constituted a tax advantage for the companies concerned, and added that:

> The exclusion of such an advantage in respect of the losses incurred by a subsidiary established in another Member State which does not conduct any trading activities in the parent company's Member State is of such a kind as to hinder the exercise of that parent company of its freedom of establishment by deterring it from setting up subsidiaries in other Member States.
>
> It thus constitutes a restriction on freedom of establishment within the meaning of Articles [49 and 54 TFEU], in that it applies different treatment for tax purposes to losses incurred by a resident subsidiary and losses incurred by a non-resident subsidiary.[355]

F – Possible Justifications for National Tax Rules which Restrict the Exercise of Fundamental Freedoms

(i) The Normal Principles Apply

As regards justification of national tax rules which restrict freedom of establishment or the free movement of capital, the normal principles apply, to the effect that a restriction must be justified by an overriding reason in the public/general interest, the measure must be appropriate to ensuring the attainment of the objective in question, and must not go beyond what is necessary to attain it.[356] That said, there are a number of distinct considerations applicable to national tax rules which merit specific mention. As regards free movement of capital, Article 65(1)(a) TFEU reserves the right of Member States to apply provisions of their tax law which differentiate between taxpayers on objective grounds. It follows that certain restrictions may be justified on this ground. The scope of these provisions is also discussed below. While the following is concerned with possible justifications for restrictions which have been recognised by the Court, it is appropriate to begin by examining a potential justification which has been advanced in argument before the Court on a number of occasions but which has nevertheless not been recognised by the Court as justifying restrictions on fundamental freedoms.

---

[354] Case C-446/03 *Marks & Spencer* [2005] ECR I-10837.
[355] Ibid, paras 33 and 34.
[356] Case C-231/05 *OY AA* [2007] ECR I-6373, para 44 (establishment); Case C-543/08 *Commission v Portugal* (CJEU 11 November 2010) para 83.

(ii) Avoiding a Reduction in Tax Revenue Cannot Justify Restrictions on Fundamental Freedoms.

In the *ICI* case, referred to above, one of the UK's arguments by way of justification for the rule that the majority of relevant subsidiaries must be resident companies was that revenue lost through the granting of tax relief on losses incurred by resident subsidiaries could not be offset by taxing the profits of non resident companies. The Court rejected that argument, pointing out

> that diminution of tax revenue occurring in this way is not one of the grounds listed in Article [52 TFEU] and cannot be regarded as a matter of overriding general interest which may be relied upon in order to justify unequal treatment that is, in principle, incompatible with Article [49 TFEU].[357]

In the *Bosal* case, referred to above,[358] the Court rejected an argument of the Netherlands and the Commission that the limitation on deductibility in issue in that case was justified by the aim of avoiding an erosion of the tax base going beyond mere diminution of tax revenue, concluding that such a justification did not differ in substance from that concerning the risk of diminution of tax revenue.[359] The Court has subsequently confirmed that the need to prevent a reduction in tax revenues is not an overriding reason in the public interest which can justify a restriction on a fundamental freedom.[360] The Court of Justice has never offered a satisfactory explanation of why diminution of revenue should not qualify as a matter of overriding general interest which might justify restrictions on fundamental freedoms. In *X and Y*[361] the Court stated that the aim of avoiding a reduction in tax revenue was 'purely economic' and could not, according to settled case law, constitute an overriding reason in the general interest. This analysis is not completely convincing. It is true that economic aims, in the sense of protectionist aims,[362] have been rightly ruled out as justifying restrictions on fundamental freedoms, but it does not follow that national measures aiming to avoid reduction in tax revenue should also be ruled out in this context.[363] The Court has held that it is not impossible that the risk of seriously undermining the financial balance of the social security system may constitute an overriding reason in the general interest.[364] This is as much an 'economic' aim as avoiding a reduction in tax revenues. Again, the Court has referred to, without ruling out, the possibility that the concern of a Member State to encourage long-term saving might justify a restriction on the

[357] Case C-330/91 *ICI* [1998] ECR I-4695, para 28. The point is reiterated in a consistent case law: see eg Case C-397/98 *Metallgesellschaft* and Case C-410/89 *Hoechst* [2001] ECR I-1727, para 59.

[358] Case C-168/01 *Bosal* [2003] ECR I-9409.

[359] Ibid, para 42. The Court rejected an argument concerning erosion of the tax base in similar terms in Case C-9/02 *de Lasteyrie du Saillant* [2004] ECR I-2409, para 59.

[360] Case C-287/10 *Tankreederie* (CJEU 22 December 2010), para 27.

[361] Case C-436/00 [2002] ECR I-829. The case involves the Treaty provisions on capital movement.

[362] In this (protectionist) sense, see eg Case 352/85 *Bond van Adverteerders* [1988] ECR I-2085, para 34; Case C-224/97 *Ciola* [1999] ECR I-2517, para 16; Case C-164/99 *Portugaia Construções Lda* [2002] ECR I-787, para 26.

[363] In *X and Y* at para 50 the Court supports its reference to 'economic aims' by reference to para 48 of its judgment in Case C-35/98 *Verkooijen* [2000] ECR I-4071. In fact the reference in the latter case to 'aims of a purely economic nature' is a reference to an argument of the UK that a provision such as that in issue might be justified by the intention to promote the economy of the Netherlands by encouraging investment in the Netherlands. This is an argument which can correctly be described as supporting an economic, in the sense of protectionist, objective.

[364] See eg Case C-322/01 *DocMorris* [2003] ECR I-14887, para 122; Case C-173/09 *Elchinov* (CJEU 5 October 2010) para 42.

right of establishment.[365] The aim of encouraging long-term saving would also seem to be an economic aim. To exclude absolutely from the category of mandatory requirements in the general interest national measures which have the aim of avoiding a reduction in tax revenue simply on the basis that such an aim is 'economic' aim is unconvincing.[366]

(ii) The Principle of 'Cohesion of the Tax System' May Justify Restrictions on Fundamental Freedoms.

In the *Bachmann* case[367] the Court introduced what seemed like a potentially significant ground of justification for national tax rules restricting the exercise of fundamental freedoms—'the need to preserve the cohesion of the tax system'. In the case in question a German national employed in Belgium, who made payments in respect of sickness invalidity and life insurance in Germany under arrangements made prior to his arrival in Belgium, challenged Belgian tax rules whereby contributions to sickness and invalidity and life insurance contracts were only tax deductible if paid to insurers based in Belgium. The Court noted that workers who have carried on an occupation in one Member State and who are subsequently employed in another Member State will normally have concluded their pension and life assurance contracts or invalidity and sickness insurance contracts with insurers established in the first Member State. It followed that there was 'a risk that the provisions in question may operate to the particular detriment of those workers who are, as a general rule, nationals of other Member States'. The Court, however, found that the restriction on freedom of movement involved could be justified, since there existed under Belgian law a connection between the deductibility of contributions and the liability to tax of sums payable by insurers under pension and life assurance contracts; under the tax system in question the loss of revenue resulting from the deduction of contributions was offset by the taxation of pensions, annuities or capital sums payable by the insurers. The Court stated:

> The cohesion of such a tax system, the formulation of which is a matter for each Member State, therefore presupposes that, in the event of a State being obliged to allow the deduction of life assurance contributions paid in another Member State, it should be able to tax sums payable by insurers. [368]

Since it was not possible to guarantee that sums payable in other Member States could be subject to such tax to compensate for the tax deductibility of the contributions, the rules in question comprised the least restrictive rules possible, compatible with maintaining the cohesion of the tax system in question.

The *Bachmann* case seemed to recognise that loss of revenue to the national exchequer amounted to a legitimate justification for placing restrictions on the exercise of a fundamental freedom. As the Court observed, '[I]n such a tax system the loss of revenue resulting from the deduction of life assurance contributions from total taxable income . . . is offset by the taxation of pensions . . . payable by the insurers'.[369] Subsequent case law on the scope of the 'cohesion of the tax system' justification indicated that its scope was

---

[365] Case C-442/02 *CaixaBank France* [2004] ECR I-8961, para 23.
[366] Yet the Court's approach is endorsed by Cordewener et al, above n 335, 1957–63.
[367] Case C-204/90 *Bachmann* [1992] ECR I-249; see also Case C-300/90 *Commission v Belgium* [1992] ECR I-305.
[368] Ibid, para 23.
[369] Case C-204/90, para 22.

very limited indeed. In the first place, the Court of Justice has held that for an argument based on such a justification to succeed, a direct link had to be established between the tax advantage concerned and the offsetting of that advantage by a particular deduction, and that such a direct link required that the advantage and the deduction relate to the same tax and the same taxpayer.[370] The decision in *Bachmann* itself has been criticised on the ground that the aim of the rules in question could have been achieved by less restrictive means.[371]

In *Marks & Spencer*, referred to above, the Court of Justice held that allowing group relief in respect of resident subsidiaries while refusing such relief in respect of non-resident subsidiaries amounted to a restriction on freedom of establishment. Advocate General Maduro suggested that the criteria for application of the principle of cohesion of the tax system should be relaxed. 'Cohesion must first and foremost be adjudged', he argued, 'in light of the aim and logic of the tax regime at issue.' The aim of the UK system of group relief was to ensure fiscal neutrality by permitting the circulation of losses within a group. It followed in the view of the Advocate General that it would be necessary to take account of the treatment applicable to losses of subsidiaries in the Member State in which they were resident, and that justification based on cohesion of the system of relief could be accepted only if the foreign losses could be accorded equivalent treatment in the Member State in which the losses arose. The Court of Justice came to a conclusion similar to that of the Advocate General, but did not base that analysis on the principle of fiscal cohesion.

The Court continues to apply the principle of cohesion in a very strict way. Arguments that restrictions on the right of establishment or freedom of capital movement can be justified on the ground of cohesion of the relevant tax system are rejected, either on the ground that no direct link has been established,[372] or on the ground that although a direct link has been established, the national measure in question is disproportionate since it goes beyond what is necessary to attain its objective.[373]

However, the principle of cohesion of the tax system is not a dead letter.[374] In *Krankenheim Ruhesitz am Wannsee-Seniorenheimstatt*[375] the German tax rules in issue in the national proceedings allowed a company established in Germany to take into account losses of a branch established in Austria in to calculate its tax liability, subject to those losses being offset by any future profits of the branch (the Court refers to the 'reintegration' of the losses). In the case of a branch established in Germany, by way of contrast, its losses could always be taken into account by the company concerned. The Court held that the rules in question favoured a Germany company with a branch in Germany over a Germany company with a branch in Austria, and might discourage a German company from operating a branch in Austria. But the Court accepted that the rules were justified by the principle of cohesion of the tax system. The Court held that there was a 'direct, personal and material link' between taking account of the losses of a branch on the one hand, and offsetting future profits of that branch against those losses on the other.[376] The

---

[370] Case C-35/98 *Verkooijen* [2000] ECR I-4071, paras 57 and 58. The case involves the Treaty provisions on capital movement.
[371] Case C-80/94 *Wielockx* [1995] ECR I-2493, Opinion at para 37; Cordewener et al, above n 335, 1970.
[372] Case C-379/05 *Amurta* [2007] ECR I- 9569, para 50; Case C-303/07 *Aberdeen Property Fininvest* [2009] ECR I-5145, para 74.
[373] Case C-418/07 *Papillon* [2008] ECR I-8947, paras 50–61.
[374] Cordewener et al, above n 335, 1972 and 1973.
[375] Case C-157/07 *Krankenheim Ruhesitz am Wannsee-Seniorenheimstatt* [2008] ECR I-8061.
[376] Ibid, para 42.

Court added that the restriction was appropriate to achieve its objective, in that it operated in a 'perfectly symmetrical manner', with 'only deducted losses being reintegrated', and the restriction was 'entirely proportionate to the objective pursued' since the reintegrated losses are reintegrated only up to the amount of the profits made.[377]

(iii) Avoiding Tax Fraud, the Risk of Tax Avoidance, the Double Counting of Losses, and Safeguarding a Balanced Allocation of the Power to Tax between the Various Member States

The Court has held that while the need to combat fraud may justify a difference in treatment on grounds of nationality in certain circumstances, the mere risk of tax avoidance cannot justify discriminatory treatment.[378] The prevention of tax avoidance and the need for effective fiscal supervision may be relied upon to justify restrictions on the exercise of fundamental freedoms guaranteed by the Treaty,[379] but a general presumption of tax avoidance or fraud is not sufficient to justify a fiscal measure which compromises the objectives of the Treaty.[380] The Court has refused to accept arguments of justification based on avoiding the risk of tax avoidance where the national legislation did not have 'the specific purpose of preventing wholly artificial arrangements'.[381] On the other hand, a national measure restricting freedom of establishment, may be justified where it specifically relates to wholly artificial arrangements aimed at circumventing the application of the legislation of the Member States concerned,[382] and where the legislation in question does not go beyond what is necessary to achieve that purpose.[383] This is a difficult test for national legislation to pass. The 'wholly artificial arrangements' referred to by the Court are those which 'do not reflect economic reality and whose only purpose is to obtain a tax advantage'.[384]

The risk of tax avoidance may also justify restrictions on freedom of movement, at any rate where it operates in conjunction with another public interest consideration. In *Marks & Spencer*, referred to above, the Court accepted that the UK rules identified as restrictive pursued legitimate objectives and constituted overriding reasons in the public interest, and that they were apt to achieve the attainment of those objectives. The Court, however, considered that the rules were disproportionately restrictive if applied in certain cases.[385] The reasoning offered by the Court relies on three justifications, in combination.

> First, in tax matters profits and losses are two sides of the same coin and must be treated symmetrically in the same tax system in order to protect a balanced allocation of the power to impose taxes between the different Member States concerned. Second, if the losses were taken into consideration in the parent company's Member State they might well be taken into account

---

[377] Ibid, paras 44 and 45.
[378] Case 79/85 *Segers* [1986] ECR 2375, para 17.
[379] C-254/97 *Baxter* [1999] ECR I4809, para 18,
[380] C-334/02 *Commission v France* [2004] ECR I-2229, para 27.
[381] Case C-330/91 *ICI* [1998] ECR I-4695, para 26.
[382] Case C-330/91 *ICI* [1998] ECR I-4695, para 26; Case C-446/03 *Marks & Spencer* [2005] ECR I-10637, para 57; Case C-196/04 *Cadbury Schweppes* [2006] ECR I-7995, para 51.
[383] Case C-196/04 *Cadbury Schweppes* [2006] ECR I-7995, paras 57 and 61.
[384] Case C-182/08 *Glaxo Wellcome* [2009] ECR I-8591, para 89. For a national tax measure which seems to satisfy the Court's requirements, see Case C-311/08 *SGI* (CJEU 21 January 2010) paras 65–75. See also generally, *Communication from the Commission to the Council, the European Parliament and the European Economic and Social Committee—The application of anti-abuse measures in the area of direct taxation—within the EU and in relation to third countries*, COM(2007) 0785 final.
[385] Case C-446/03 *Marks & Spencer* [2005] ECR I-10637, para 55.

twice. Third, and last, if the losses were not taken into account in the Member State in which the subsidiary is established there would be a risk of tax avoidance.[386]

The Court's reliance upon three connected public interest considerations in this case made it difficult to predict the extent to which this ruling would affect the outcome of cases in which the context was not identical but might be argued to be analogous. The Court has provided some clarification of its judgment in *Marks & Spencer* in subsequent cases.

As regards the need to safeguard a balanced allocation of the power to tax between Member States, the Court has held that that need cannot justify a Member State systematically refusing to grant a tax advantage to a resident subsidiary on the ground that the income of the parent company, having its establishment in another Member State, is not capable of being taxed in the first Member State.[387] That element of justification may be allowed, however, where the system in question is designed to prevent conduct capable of jeopardising the right of the Member States to exercise their taxing powers in relation to activities carried on in their territory.[388]

In *OY AA* the Court considered the compatibility with the freedom of establishment of national rules of a Member State allowing a subsidiary established in that Member State to deduct from its taxable income an intra-group financial transfer which it makes in favour of its parent company only if the latter is established in that same Member State.[389]

The Court noted that if such a deduction were allowed in the case of a cross-border transfer, groups of companies would be free to choose the Member State in which the profits of a subsidiary would be taxed, by removing the amounts in question from the basis of assessment of the subsidiary, and incorporating them in the basis of assessment of the parent company. The Court concluded that that would undermine the system of the allocation of the power to tax between Member States because, according to the choice made by the group of companies, the Member State of the subsidiary would be forced to renounce its right, in its capacity as the Member State of residence of that subsidiary, to tax the profits of that subsidiary in favour of the Member State in which the parent company has its establishment.[390]

As regards the prevention of tax avoidance, the Court accepted that the possibility of transferring the taxable income of a subsidiary to a parent company with its establishment in another Member State created a risk that, by means of purely artificial arrangements, income transfers might be organised within a group of companies in favour of those companies established in the Member States applying the lowest rates of taxation or in which such income is not taxed.[391]

Having regard to the combination of these two factors, concerning the need to safeguard the balanced allocation of the power to tax between the Member States and the need to prevent tax avoidance, the Court concluded that national rules which confined the right of deduction to transfers to a parent established in the same Member State as

---

[386] Ibid, para 43. The risk of tax avoidance is the risk that within a group of companies losses will be transferred to companies established in the Member States which apply the highest rates of taxation and in which the tax value of the losses is therefore the highest (para 49).

[387] Case C-347/04 *Rewe Zentralfinanz* [2007] ECR I-2647, para 41.

[388] Ibid, para 42.

[389] Case C-231/05 *OY AA* [2007] ECR I-6373.

[390] Ibid, para 56.

[391] Ibid, para 58.

the subsidiary were justified. The rules pursued legitimate objectives, were appropriate to attain those objectives, and did not go further than was necessary.[392]

In *Marks & Spencer* the Court referred to the combination of three factors to justify the restriction in issue, while in *OY AA* the Court referred to a combination of two of those factors to justify the restriction in issue in that case. In *Lidl Belgium* the Court confirmed that it was not necessary for all three of the factors referred to in *Marks & Spencer* to be present to justify a restriction, and upheld the national rules in issue on the basis of the need to safeguard the allocation of the power to tax between the Member States, and the need to prevent the danger that the same losses will be taken into account twice.[393]

(iv) The Principle of Territoriality May Justify Differentiation between Residents and Non-Residents

In *Futura Participations*[394] a non-resident taxpayer complained that Luxembourg rules allowing the carrying forward of tax losses limited this possibility to profits and losses arising from Luxembourg activities as regards non-residents, but imposed no such limitation in respect of residents. The Court held that 'such a system, which is in conformity with the fiscal principle of territoriality, cannot be regarded as entailing any discrimination, overt or covert, prohibited by the Treaty'. The Court means by its reference to the principle of territoriality that a Member State is entitled to tax residents on worldwide income but only to tax non-residents on income arising in its territory. In *Marks & Spencer* the Court of Justice referred to the principle of territoriality in these terms, but rejected the proposition that the fact that the United Kingdom does not tax the profits of the non-resident subsidiaries of a parent company might justify restricting group relief to losses incurred by resident companies.[395]

(v) Article 65(1)(a) TFEU as a Justification for Restrictions on Capital Movement

Article 65(1)(a) TFEU provides that Article 63 TFEU, which provides that all restrictions on capital movement between Member States and between Member States and third countries shall be prohibited, shall be without prejudice to the right of Member States 'to apply the relevant provisions of their tax law which distinguish between taxpayers who are not in the same situation with regard to their place of residence or with regard to the place where their capital is invested'. In *Manninen* the Court rejected the argument of the Finnish, French and UK governments that Article 65(1)(a) TFEU showed that Member States are entitled to reserve the benefit of a tax credit for in respect of dividends for dividends paid by companies established in their territory. The Court noted (a) that Article 65(1)(a) must be interpreted strictly, and (b) that Article 65(1)(a) is qualified by Article 65(3), which provides that national provisions referred to in Article 65(1) 'shall not constitute a means of arbitrary discrimination or a disguised restriction on the free movement of capital and payments as defined in Article 63'. It followed in the Court's view that a 'distinction must therefore be made between unequal treatment which is permitted under Article [65(1)(a) TFEU] and arbitrary discrimination which is prohibited by

---

[392] Ibid, paras 60–65.

[393] Case C-414/06 *Lidl Belgium* [2008] ECR I-3601, paras 38–42.

[394] Case C-250/95 *Futura Participations* [1997] ECR I-2471.

[395] Case C-446/03 *Marks & Spencer* [2005] ECR I-10837, paras 39 and 40. See also Case C-347/04 *Rewe Zentralfinanz* [2007] ECR I-2647, paras 68 and 69.

Article [65(3)]'. This meant in turn that any difference in treatment must concern situations which are not objectively comparable or are justified by overriding reasons in the general interest, such as the cohesion of the tax system.[396] In truth, the Court's interpretation of Article 65(1)(a) TFEU treats it as simply declaratory of principles developed in cases such as *Schumacker* (different treatment of objectively different situations) and *Bachmann* (different treatment justified by overriding reasons in the general interest, in particular in relation to cohesion of the tax system).[397]

VII – CONCLUDING REMARKS

As noted at the outset, perhaps the main development in the case law on establishment and services in recent years has been the development of the concept of the non-discriminatory restriction on the exercise of a fundamental freedom. The concept of discrimination nevertheless remains important. A generous approach to the concept of indirect discrimination has placed an obligation on national authorities, wishing to award contracts falling outside the scope of EU public procurement rules, but likely to be of cross-border interest, to ensure that such contracts receive appropriate publicity.[398] Thus if a contract to be awarded by a public authority falls within the scope of the public procurement rules, those rules specify obligations as to the advertising and award of the contract. Even if the contract falls outside the scope of those rules, it seems that some publicity must be given to contracts likely to be of cross border interest, to avoid discriminating against out-of-state providers. There are indications that the duty not to discriminate against out-of-state businesses which are interested in such contracts might go further than merely advertising those contracts, and might, in conjunction with the 'access to the market' principle, require an outcome similar to that which would result from the application of other EU rules on public procurement. Thus in the *SECAP* case, which involved the award of a contract falling below the threshold for application of the relevant public procurement directive, the Court held that applying a national rule requiring the automatic exclusion of tenders considered to be abnormally low to contracts of certain cross-border interest might constitute indirect discrimination. This was because, in practice, it placed at a disadvantage operators from other Member States, which might be in a position to make a bid that was competitive, and at the same time genuine and viable, but which the contracting authority would not be able to consider as a result of the national rule in issue. The Court added that:

> Accordingly, the application of the rule requiring the automatic exclusion of abnormally low tenders to contracts of certain cross-border interest could deprive economic operators from other Member States of the opportunity of competing more effectively with operators located in the Member State in question and thereby affect their access to the market in that State, thus impeding the exercise of freedom of establishment and freedom to provide services.[399]

---

[396] Case C-319/02 *Manninen* [2004] ECR I-7477, paras 27–29; Case C-510/08 *Mattner* (CJEU 22 April 2010) para 34.

[397] This is made clear in Case C-35/98 *Verkooijen* [2000] ECR I-4071, paras 43 and 44, cited by the Court in *Manninen* at para 29.

[398] See above at p 546.

[399] Joined Cases C-147/06 and C-148/06 *SECAP* [2008] ECR I-3565, paras 26 and 28.

The effect of this approach is to require national authorities to apply to contracts of potential cross-border interest but below the threshold for application of EU public procurement rules, a rule analogous to that contained in those very rules,[400] to the effect that public authorities must request further information regarding abnormally low tenders rather than rejecting them outright.

Yet as the above comment on the *SECAP* case shows—a comment which began by emphasising the continuing importance of the concept of discrimination—the Court's recourse to the principle that national measures must not restrict access to the market is all pervasive, and it is the Court's emphasis on that principle which remains most worthy of remark. And it will be recalled that the real mischief of many of the measures regarded by the Court as infringing Articles 49 or 56 TFEU, unless justified, is that they place restrictions of one kind or another upon economic operators seeking to enter the market or exploit new outlets or opportunities, rather than placing a particular burden upon economic operators from other Member States; though it is only of course market operators from other Member States who can claim infringement of fundamental freedoms under the TFEU.

Almost as important for the effective exercise of the right of establishment and the freedom to provide services as the Court's development of the concept of the non-discriminatory national measure which restricts access to the market, has been the Court's insistence upon rigorous application of the principle of proportionality. This has resulted in intense scrutiny both of the appropriateness of national measures to achieve their aims (which must of course be consistent with EU law), and of any claim that the aims of the national rules in question cannot be achieved by means less restrictive of cross-border activities.

In the case law on national tax provisions which operate as restrictions on the right of establishment, and indeed on other fundamental freedoms, the Court has taken a strict view not only as regards proportionality, but also (in contrast with its approach in other contexts) as regards the public interest considerations which might justify such restrictions. Even if the Court did adopt a more positive approach to possible justifications for restrictions resulting from the application of national tax rules, it is likely that the outcome in the great majority of cases would be the same. In many cases Member States have had difficulty in formulating convincing grounds for differential treatment of non-residents, either in general, or in the case in point, and the 'blanket' approach of some such rules would rule out justification on proportionality grounds.[401] And in terms of overall outcome, the Court's case law in this field, as in others, is having a positive and beneficial impact in removing obstacles to the cross-frontier activity of individuals and companies.

The Court's general approach, both as regards the concept of 'restrictions', and as regards the scope for justification of such restrictions, has evolved as much for policy reasons as for legal reasons. It is an approach which tends to increase competitiveness and consumer choice. If that approach is to be criticised, it is on the ground that it has

---

[400] Directive 2004/18/EC, Art 55.

[401] eg Case C-279/93 *Finanzamt Köln-Alstadt v Schumacker* [1995] ECR I-225; Case C-330/91 *R v Inland Revenue Commissioners ex parte Commerzbank AG* [1993] ECR I-4017; Case C-1/93 *Halliburton Services BV v Staatssecretaris van Financiën* [1994] ECR I-1137; Case C-397/98 *Metallgesellschaft Ltd* and Case C-410/89 *Hoechst AG, Hoechst UK Ltd* [2001] ECR I-1727; Case C-324/00 *Lankhorst-Hohorst GmbH v Finanzamt Steinfurt* [2002] ECR I-11779; Case C-9/02 *Hughes de Lasteyre du Saillant* [2004] ECR I-409.

narrowed both the regulatory options available to national authorities, and the regulatory options open to the EU authorities.

Further Reading

C Barnard, *The Substantive Law of the EU, The Four Freedoms*, 3rd edn (Oxford, Oxford University Press 2010) chs 10, 11 and 13.

A Brown, 'EU Primary law Requirements in Practice: Advertising, Procedures and Remedies for Public Contracts outside the Procurement Directives' [2010] *Public Procurement Law Review* 169.

A Cordewener, G Kofler and S van Thiel, 'The Clash between European Freedoms and National Direct Tax Law; Public Interest Defences Available to the Member States' (2009) 46 *CMLRev* 1951.

ACL Davies, 'One Step Forward, Two Steps Back? The Viking and Laval Cases in the ECJ' (2008) 37 *Industrial Law Journal* 126.

L Hancher and W Sauter, 'One Step Beyond? From Sodemare to Docmorris: The EU's Freedom of Establishment Case Law Concerning healthcare' (2010) 47 *CMLRev* 117.

J Hörnle, 'Country of Origin Regulation in Cross-border Media: One Step Beyond the Freedom to Provide Services?' (2005) 54 *ICLQ* 89.

E Spaventa, 'Caixa-Bank France' (2005) 42 *CMLRev* 1151.

18

The Directive on Services in the Internal Market

The Directive on Services in the Internal Market (the Services Directive) aims to improve the operation of the internal market in services by a combination of substantive and procedural innovations. The Directive does not apply to all services, but as regards the numerous services to which it does apply, it seeks, in the first place, to codify elements of the Court's case law on the right of establishment and the freedom to provide services, and identifies a number of restrictions which are either prohibited, or which must be justified if they are to be retained. Member States are required to review relevant national rules for compliance, and to make a detailed report to the Commission, which circulates such reports to other Member States, and then itself reports to the Council and Parliament, in a process known as 'mutual evaluation'. The Directive contains provisions designed to improve the quality of services, mainly by requiring providers to make relevant information available to potential customers, and prohibiting discrimination against recipients of services. Administrative co-operation between Member States is made obligatory to ensure supervision of service providers, and this is facilitated by the online Internal Market Information system, covering (so far) enquiries under the Services Directive and the Professional Qualifications Directive. Administrative simplification is a major aim of the Directive, and includes provision for 'points of single contact' or 'one-stop shops' in Member States to assist service providers to complete the procedures and formalities for starting up a business or a new branch of an existing business. It must be possible to complete all such procedures and formalities by electronic means across borders.

I – GENERAL

Directive 2006/123/EC on services in the internal market (hereafter 'the Directive')[1] is designed to have major beneficial effects on the exercise of the right of establishment and the freedom to provide services in the enlarged European Union. The Directive establishes 'general provisions facilitating the exercise of the freedom of establishment for service

---

[1] [2006] OJ L376/36. The Commission's 'Handbook on the Implementation of the Services Directive' (hereafter 'the Handbook') provides a helpful commentary on the Directive, and is available online at: http://ec.europa. eu/internal_market/services/docs/services-dir/guides/handbook_en.pdf. For excellent critical analyses of the Directive, see S Weatherill, 'Promoting the Consumer Interest in an Integrated Services Market', Europa Institute, Mitchell Working Paper Series, 2/2007; C Barnard, 'Unravelling the Services Directive' (2008) 45 *CML Rev* 323.

providers and the free movement of services, while maintaining a high quality of services'.[2] Part of the rationale of the Directive is revealed in its preamble, which reasons that barriers to the freedom of establishment for service providers in Member States, and barriers to the free movement of services between Member States, cannot be removed solely by relying on the direct application of Articles 49 and 56 TFEU. Addressing these obstacles on a case-by-case basis through infringement procedures against the Member States concerned would be extremely complicated for national and EU institutions—especially following enlargement. And the removal of many barriers requires prior co-ordination of national legal schemes, including the establishment of administrative co-operation.[3] The main provisions of the Directive deal with freedom of establishment for service providers, free of movement of services, the quality of services, administrative simplification and co-operation, and the mutual evaluation of restrictive provisions. This chapter addresses major features of the Directive but does not claim to provide comprehensive coverage.

II – SERVICES COVERED BY THE DIRECTIVE

The Directive applies in principle to 'services supplied by providers established in a Member State',[4] and the definition of services is essentially the same definition as that contained in Article 57 TFEU.[5] However, a substantial number of services are excluded,[6] most because they would otherwise fall within the definition of 'services', and others it would seem for the purposes of emphasis. The services excluded are non-economic services of general interest,[7] financial services, transport services (including air transport, rail transport, urban transport, taxis and ambulances as well as ports services),[8] electronic communication services and networks, services of temporary work agencies, healthcare services, social services relating to social housing, childcare and support of families and persons permanently or temporarily in need (to the extent that these services are provided by the state, by providers mandated by the state, or by charities recognised as such by the state), audiovisual and radio broadcasting services, gambling, activities which are connected with the exercise of official authority as set out in Article 51 TFEU, private security services, and services provided by notaries, who are appointed by an official act of government. Nor does the Directive apply to the field of taxation.[9] However, the Directive applies to any service unless that service is expressly excluded.

The Commission suggests a non-exhaustive list of services covered by the Directive which is based on a similar list in recital (33) of the preamble and which comprises: the activities of most of the regulated professions (eg legal and fiscal advisers, architects,

---

[2] Art 1(1).
[3] Recital (6) to the preamble.
[4] Art 2(1).
[5] Art 4(1).
[6] Art 2(2)
[7] This is a superfluous exclusion since such 'services' do not fall within the definition of the services to which the Directive applies in Art 2(2).
[8] Art 2(2)(d) and recital (21) to the preamble. The Handbook notes that 'the exclusion of transport services does not cover services which are not transport services as such like driving schools services, removal services, car rental services, funeral services or aerial photography services' (11).
[9] Art 2(3).

engineers, accountants, surveyors), craftsmen, business-related services (eg office maintenance, management consultancy, the organisation of events (trade fairs are specified in
the preamble), recovery of debts, advertising and recruitment services, distributive trades
(including retail and wholesale of goods and services), services in the field of tourism
(eg services of travel agencies), leisure services (eg services provided by sports centres
and amusement parks), construction services, services in the area of installation and
maintenance of equipment, information services (eg web portals, news agency activities, publishing, computer programming activities), accommodation and food services
(eg hotels, restaurants, catering services), services in the area of training and education,
rental (including car rental) and leasing services, real estate services, certification and
testing services, household support services (eg cleaning services, private nannies or gar-
dening services), etc. The preamble adds that the activities concerned may involve services
requiring the proximity of provider and recipient, services requiring travel by the recipient
or the provider, and services which may be provided at a distance, including the internet.[10]

III – 'REQUIREMENTS'

A number of the provisions of the Directive are concerned with prohibiting outright or
subjecting to justification 'requirements' relating to the access to or exercise of a service
activity. The definition of 'requirement' is wide and on the face of it covers almost any
legal rule, or administrative practice, of national authorities or professional bodies.[11] The
preamble (9th recital) states:

> This Directive applies only to requirements which affect the access to, or the exercise of, a service
> activity. Therefore, it does not apply to requirements, such as road traffic rules, rules concern-
> ing the development or use of land, town and country planning, building standards as well as
> administrative penalties imposed for non-compliance with such rules which do not specifically
> regulate or specifically affect the service activity but have to be respected by providers in the
> course of carrying out their economic activity in the same way as by individuals acting in their
> private capacity.

Nevertheless, the preamble also states (recital (59)) that 'environmental protection may
justify the requirement to obtain an individual authorisation for each installation on the
national territory'. As Barnard points out '[p]resumably, this means that some planning
requests are prohibited by the Directive, despite the wording of the 9th recital, unless they
can be justified'.[12] The Commission takes the same view, reasoning as follows:

> [I]t is clear that the mere fact that rules are labelled in a specific way, for example as town
> planning rules, or that requirements are formulated in a general way, ie are not specifically
> addressed to service providers, is not sufficient to determine that they are outside of the scope
> of the Services Directive. In fact, the actual effect of the requirements in question needs to be

---

[10] Recital (33).
[11] Art 4(7): '"requirement" means any obligation, prohibition, condition or limit provided for in the laws,
regulations or administrative provisions of the Member States or in consequence of case-law, administrative
practice, the rules of professional bodies, or the collective rules of professional associations or other professional organisations, adopted in the exercise of their legal autonomy; rules laid down in collective agreements
negotiated by the social partners shall not as such be seen as requirements within the meaning of this Directive'.
[12] Barnard, above n 1, 338.

assessed to determine whether they are of a general nature or not. Thus, when implementing the Directive, Member States need to take account of the fact that legislation labelled as 'town planning' or 'building standards' may contain requirements which specifically regulate service activities and are thus covered by the Services Directive. For instance, rules on the maximum surface of certain commercial establishments, even when contained in general urban planning laws, would come under the Services Directive and, as a result, will be covered by the obligations in the establishment chapter of the Directive.[13]

It appears from the preamble (recital (9)) that relevant requirements are those which specifically regulate or specifically affect access to or exercise of a service activity. Since the aim of the Directive is to remove barriers to the freedom of establishment and freedom to provide services[14] it would seem to follow that the concept of requirements having such a specific effect on service activities should be construed in the light of the concept of national measures which amount to restrictions on the right of establishment or freedom to provide services and infringe Articles 49 or 56 TFEU unless justified. As the Court stated in *Commission v Italy*, '[i]t is settled case-law that the term "restriction" within the meaning of Articles [49 TFEU and 56 TFEU] covers all measures which prohibit, impede or render less attractive the freedom of establishment or the freedom to provide services.'[15]

IV – FREEDOM OF ESTABLISHMENT FOR PROVIDERS

A – General

Chapter III of the Directive provides for freedom of establishment for providers. These provisions apply to all cases where a business seeks to establish itself in a Member State, irrespective of whether a provider intends to start a new business or whether an existing business seeks to open a new establishment, for example a subsidiary or a branch.[16] Chapter III covers both the situation where a service provider seeks to establish itself in another Member State and the situation where a provider seeks to establish itself in its own Member State,[17] in contrast with Chapter IV, on free movement of services, which does not prevent Member States from maintaining restrictive requirements for their own national operators.[18]

B – Authorisations

Section I of Chapter III of the Directive deals with 'authorisations', but this section has no application to those aspects of authorisation schemes which are governed directly or

---

[13] Handbook, 14. This is cited by Barnard, ibid.
[14] Preamble, recital (6).
[15] Case C-518/06 *Commission v Italy* [2009] ECR I-3491, para 62. And see Barnard, above n 1, 338–40.
[16] Handbook, 24.
[17] Ibid,
[18] Below at p 621, Handbook, 36.

indirectly by other EU acts.[19] Article 9 deals in particular with 'authorisation schemes', and reflecting and to some extent codifying the Court's case law, the latter Article provides that Member States shall not make access to a service activity or the exercise thereof subject to an authorisation scheme unless specified conditions are satisfied.[20] These conditions are that the authorisation does not discriminate against the provider in question; that the need for an authorisation scheme is justified by an overriding reason relating to the public interest;[21] and that the objective pursued cannot be attained by means of a less restrictive measure, 'in particular because an a posteriori inspection would take place too late to be genuinely effective'.[22]

'Conditions for the granting of authorisation' are regulated by Article 9 of the Directive. Authorisation schemes must be based on criteria which preclude the competent authorities from exercising their power of assessment in an arbitrary manner, and these criteria shall be non-discriminatory; justified by an overriding reason relating to the public interest; proportionate to that public interest objective; clear and unambiguous; objective; made public in advance; and transparent and accessible.[23] The Directive adds that the conditions for granting authorisation for a new establishment shall not duplicate requirements and controls which are equivalent or essentially comparable as regards their purpose to which the provider is already subject in another Member State or in the same Member State.[24]

An authorisation shall enable the provider to have access to the service activity, or to exercise that activity, throughout the national territory, except where an authorisation for each individual establishment or a limitation of the authorisation to a certain part of the territory is justified by an overriding reason relating to the public interest.[25] By way of procedural protection, the Directive provides that decisions refusing or withdrawing an authorisation shall be fully reasoned and be open to challenge before the courts.[26]

Where the number of authorisations available for a given activity is limited because of the scarcity of available natural resources or technical capacity, Member States shall apply a selection procedure to potential candidates which provides full guarantees of impartiality and transparency, including, in particular, adequate publicity about the launch, conduct and completion of the procedure. In such cases, authorisation shall be granted for an appropriate limited period, and may not be open to automatic renewal nor confer any other advantage on the provider whose authorisation has just expired.[27] In other cases, an authorisation granted to a provider shall not be for a limited period, unless this can be justified.[28]

Authorisation procedures and formalities are subject to requirements relating to clar-

---

[19] Art 9(2).

[20] Chapter 17, at p 549.

[21] There is a convenient non-exhaustive list of overriding requirements in recital (4) of the preamble to the Directive.

[22] Art 9(1). The wording is of course similar to that used in the *Gebhard* formulation: see Chapter 17, at p 540.

[23] Art 10(1) and (2).

[24] Art 10(3). *cf* Case C-465/05 *Commission v Italy* [2007] ECR I-11091 (territorial limitation of a licence, and a licensing procedure which fails to take account of controls and verifications already carried out in Member State of origin, are contrary to Art 56 TFEU).

[25] Art 10(4). *cf* Case C-134/05 *Commission v Italy* [2007] ECR I-6251, paras 56–65 (non-discriminatory Italian rules whereby an undertaking licensed for extrajudicial debt recovery in one province must seek a further licence to pursue that activity in another province contrary to Arts 49 and 56 TFEU).

[26] Art 10(6).

[27] Art 12(1), (2).

[28] Art 11.

ity and publicity, simplicity, speed of process, the consequences of authorities failing to respond to applications, acknowledgement of applications, and informing applications of the need for further information, and of the fact that their application has been rejected.[29]

C – Prohibited Requirements

Article 14 of the Directive prohibits outright certain requirements relating to access to, or the exercise of a service activity.[30] Discriminatory requirements based directly or indirectly on nationality, or, in the case of companies, the location of the registered office, are included in this list,[31] as is a prohibition on having an establishment in more than one Member State, or on being entered in the registers or enrolled with professional bodies of more than one Member State.[32] Other prohibited requirements include the case-by-case application of an economic test making the granting of authorisation subject to proof of the existence of an economic need or market demand.[33] In all these cases the lack of any reference even to the theoretical possibility of justification on grounds of public policy, or overriding requirements in the general interest, is worthy of note. It seems that the legislature has made an assessment that these types of restrictions simply could not, and perhaps should not, be justified on the grounds mentioned in the context of the services covered by the Directive.

D – Requirements which Must Be Amended if They Cannot Be Justified

Article 15 of the Directive lists requirements which one commentator has described as 'suspect',[34] and which must be examined by Member States to ensure they can be justified. These are certain requirements relating to access to a service activity or the exercise of it which must be appropriately amended unless they are found to be neither directly nor indirectly discriminatory, to be justified by overriding reasons relating to the public interest, and to be proportionate.[35] These requirements include

— quantitative or territorial restrictions, in particular in the form of limits fixed according to population or of a minimum geographical distance between providers;[36]
— obligations for a provider to take on a specific form;[37]
— requirements (other than those concerning matters covered by Directive 2005/36/EC on professional qualifications,[38] or provided for in other EU instruments[39]) which

---

[29] Art 13.
[30] The Handbook notes that these requirements 'are discriminatory or are in other ways particularly restrictive and thus cannot be maintained. In many cases the ECJ has already found them to be incompatible with Article [49 TFEU]' (28).
[31] Art 14(1).
[32] Art 14(2).
[33] Art 14(5).
[34] Barnard, above n 1, 357.
[35] Art 15(1)–(3).
[36] Art 15(2)(a). cf Case C-384/08 *Attanasio Group* (CJEU 11 March 2010); Chapter 17, at p 552.
[37] Art 15(2)(b). cf Case C-64/08 *Engelmann* (CJEU 9 September 2010); Chapter 17, at p 549.
[38] See below, Chapter 19, at p 650.
[39] eg the Lawyers' Services Directive and the Lawyers' Establishment Directive; Chapter 19, at pp 639 and 640.

reserve access to the service activity to particular providers by virtue of the specific nature of the activity;[40] and

— requirements fixing minimum and/or maximum tariffs with which the provider must comply.[41]

Requirements which Member States intend to maintain and the reasons why they consider that those requirements can be justified, along with requirements which have been abolished or made less stringent, are to be specified in the mutual evaluation report to be forwarded to the Commission in accordance with Article 39(1).[42] In addition, Member States shall notify the Commission of any new national rules which set requirements such as those referred to, and provide the Commission with the reasons for those requirements.[43] The Commission shall communicate the provisions concerned to the other Member States. Such notification shall not, however, prevent Member States from adopting the provisions in question.[44]

V – THE FREE MOVEMENT OF SERVICES

A – General

Chapter IV of the Directive, which deals with free movement of services, comprises two sections, the first of which covers freedom to provide services and related derogations, and the second of which covers rights of recipients of services.

B – Freedom for Providers to Provide Services

As regards section I, Member States must, under Article 16(1) of the Directive, respect the right of providers to provide services in a Member State other than that in which they are established, while the Member State in which the service is provided shall ensure free access to and free exercise of a service activity within its territory.[45] Accordingly, Member States shall not make access to or exercise of a service activity in their territory subject to compliance with any requirements which do not respect the principle of non-discrimination, and the principles that the requirement must be justified for reasons of public policy, public security, public health or the environment, must be suitable for attaining the objective pursued, and must not go beyond what is necessary to achieve that objective.[46] It is noteworthy that the Directive makes no mention of other overriding requirements in the

---

[40] Art 15(2)(d).

[41] Art 15(2)(g). *cf* Joined Cases C-94/04 and C-202/04 *Cipolla* [2006] ECR I-11421.

[42] As to which, see p 619.

[43] Art 15(7).

[44] The reason for this provision seems to be to make it clear that exclusionary effects analogous to those which arise for measures notified under Directive 98/34/EC on information on technical standards, as a result of Case C-443/98 *Unilever Italia* [2000] ECR I-7535, do not arise, as Barnard notes, above n 1, 359.

[45] Art 16(1), subparas 1 and 2.

[46] Art 16(1)(a)–(c).

general interest, and on the face of it the Directive excludes reliance upon any ground of derogation other than those specified.[47] The Court has noted that

> in particular, the general obligation set out in Article 16(1) of Directive 2006/123, according to which the Member States are to ensure access to and exercise of a service activity within their territory by making that access or exercise subject only to non discriminatory and objectively justified requirements, stems directly from Article [56 TFEU].[48]

These provisions do not require Member States to repeal existing requirements but only oblige them to refrain from applying them to service providers established in other Member States. Unlike the position as regards the right of establishment, Member States are not in principle precluded from maintaining their requirements for their national operators.[49]

Article 16(2) of the Directive appears at first sight to prohibit certain requirements outright, since it states that Member States may not restrict the freedom to provide services of a provider established in another Member State by imposing any of the requirements listed. These include an obligation on a provider to have an establishment in the territory of the Member State where the service is to be provided.[50] They also include an obligation for the provider to obtain an authorisation from the competent authorities in the Member State where the services are to be provided, including entry in a register or registration with a professional body or association in their territory. The only exceptions to this are those provided for in the Directive itself (presumably in particular case-by-case derogations under Article 18, as to which see below), or in other instruments of EU law.[51] Another prohibited requirement is a ban on the provider setting up a certain form or type of infrastructure in their territory, including an office or chambers which the provider needs in order to supply the service in question.[52] As noted above, at first sight the above requirements are prohibited outright. However, it will be noted that Article 16(2) states that Member States 'may' not restrict the freedom to provide services—in contrast with the wording of Article 14(1) to the effect that Member States 'shall' not make access to or the exercise of a service activity subject to certain requirements. Furthermore, Article 16(3) provides that the Member State to which the provider moves shall not be prevented from imposing requirements with regard to the provision of a service activity, where they are justified for reasons of public policy, public health or the protection of the environment in accordance with Article 16(1). The Commission comments that the 'list of requirements in Article 16(2) contains examples of requirements which in principle cannot be imposed by a Member State in the case of services provided in its territory by a provider established in another Member State.'[53]

---

[47] The Handbook states that this provision 'excludes Member States from invoking other public interest objectives' (37).

[48] Case C-458/08 *Commission v Portugal* (CJEU 18 November 2010) para 88.

[49] Handbook, 36.

[50] Art 16(2)(a). The present writer agrees that it is difficult to imagine a situation in which such restrictions can genuinely be justified and the view is expressed above that the *Ramrath* case might have been wrongly decided; Chapter 17, at p 577.

[51] Art 16(2)(b).

[52] Art 16(2)(c). Such a ban would be incompatible with the right of a service provider to have such infrastructure, as recognised by the Court in the *Gebhard* case, Chapter 17, at p 533.

[53] Handbook, 39.

C – Additional Derogations from the Freedom of Providers to Provide Services

The foregoing provisions are laid down in Article 16 of the Directive, but this Article is subject to a fairly long list of 'additional derogations' set out in Article 17. In the first place, there are services of general economic interest which are provided in another Member State, and comprising, inter alia, postal services, electricity services and gas services, to the extent the foregoing are covered by the relevant directives, along with water distribution and supply services and waste water services, and the treatment of waste.[54] Other 'additional derogations' include those covering matters covered by Directive 96/71/EC, the posted workers directive;[55] matters covered by Council Directive 77/249/EEC, the legal services directive;[56] the activity of the judicial recovery of debts;[57] and matters covered by Title II of Directive 2005/36/EC, on professional qualifications.[58]

D – Case-by-case Derogations from the Freedom of Providers to Provide Services

Provision is also made in Article 18 of the Directive for case-by-case derogations from the application of Article 16. In 'exceptional circumstances only', a Member State may, in respect of a provider established in another Member State, take measures relating to the safety of services, subject to compliance with several specified conditions, including compliance with the mutual assistance procedure specified in the Directive,[59] and with the principle of proportionality.

E – Rights of Recipients of Services

(i) Prohibited Restrictions and Non-discrimination

Section 2 of Chapter IV deals with the rights of recipients of services. Article 19 provides that Member States may not impose requirements on a recipient which restrict the use of a service supplied by a provider established in another Member State, and in particular any obligation to obtain authorisation from or to make a declaration to their competent authorities, as well as discriminatory limits on the grant of financial assistance by reason of the fact that the provider is established in another Member State or by reason of the location of the place at which the service is provided.[60] Since such restrictions seem to be not uncommon in the field of healthcare, it is perhaps appropriate to recall that the Directive excludes healthcare from its scope, though Article 56 TFEU, along with applica-

---

[54] Art 17(1).
[55] Art 17(2).
[56] Art 17(4), as to which, see Chapter 19, at p 639.
[57] Art 17(5).
[58] Art 17(6), as to which, see Chapter 19, at p 630.
[59] Art 35 of the Directive provides for mutual assistance in the event of case-by-case derogations.
[60] The Commission observes in the Handbook (44, n 142) that 'authorisation requirements imposed on service providers (rather than on recipients) should normally no longer be imposed on service providers from other Member States on the basis of Article 16. Article 19 complements Article 16 from the recipient's point of view.'

ble derogations, applies directly to cross-border provision of healthcare services, including hospital services.[61]

Recipients of services are also protected from discrimination on grounds of nationality, or of place of residence, pursuant to Article 20 of the Directive. This covers both action by public authorities and by private-sector service providers. The Handbook notes that recipients of services are sometimes confronted with discrimination based on their nationality or their place of residence, for instance in the form of higher tariffs for entering museums and parks. As regards non-discrimination by public authorities, the Commission notes that even though differences of treatment based on the place of residence in general constitute discrimination, in exceptional cases, such differences might not amount to discrimination if and in so far as they reflect relevant and objective differences in the situations of the recipients. The Commission suggests as an example reduced tariffs for residents of a given town, for instance, for the use of a public swimming pool run by the local authority and financed by local taxes.[62] This outcome would accord with common sense, but it cannot yet be said to follow clearly from the Court's case law.[63]

As regards non-discrimination by private operators providing services, Member States are required to ensure that the general conditions for access to a service, which are made available to the public at large by the provider, 'do not contain discriminatory provisions relating to the nationality or place of residence of the recipient, but without precluding the possibility of providing for differences in the conditions of access where those differences are directly justified by objective criteria'. Thus, for example, discrimination on grounds of nationality or residence on the part of hotels, restaurants and car-hire operators must be prohibited. In the event of failure correctly to transpose the Directive in this respect, it is tempting to speculate whether the *Mangold* case law might be applicable by analogy, so that the general principle of equality might be invoked within the framework of Article 20, at least to exclude the application of discriminatory national rules applicable to a recipient.[64] In any event Article 18 TFEU, which prohibits any discrimination on grounds of nationality within the scope of application of the Treaty, would seem to be horizontally directly applicable to situations falling within the scope of Article 20, and this may also be the case for Article 56 TFEU.[65]

(ii) Assistance for Recipients by Way of Provision of Information by the Member State of Residence

Chapter IV of the Directive also makes provision for assistance for recipients, and Article 21 requires Member States to ensure that recipients can obtain, in their Member States of residence, certain information, including general information on the requirements applicable in other Member States relating to access to, and exercise of, service activities, in

---

[61] See eg Case C-157/99 *Geraets-Smits* [2001] ECR I-5473.

[62] Handbook, 45.

[63] See eg Case C-338/01 *Commission v Italy* [2003] ECR I-721 (preferential rates for admission to museums parks and gardens for local residents granted by local or decentralised state authorities contrary to Arts 18 and 56 TFEU); *cf* Case C-103/08 *Gottwald* [2009] ECR I-9117 (free annual road toll disc for disabled persons resident in national territory consistent with Art 18 TFEU).

[64] Case C-144/04 *Mangold* [2005] ECR I-9981.

[65] Case 36/74 *Walrave and Koch* [1974] ECR I-1405, paras 16 and 25 (Art 18 TFEU capable of horizontal application); Case 251/83 *Eberhard Haug-Adrion* [1984] ECR 4277 (allegedly discriminatory tariff of premiums by insurance provider justifiable on actuarial grounds but Court does not rule out application of Arts 18 and 56 TFEU).

particular requirements relating to consumer protection. Also covered is information on the means of redress available in the case of a dispute between a provider and a recipient. Where appropriate, advice from the competent authorities shall include a simple step-by-step guide. Information and assistance shall be provided in a clear and unambiguous manner, shall be easily accessible at a distance, including by electronic means, and shall be kept up to date.

The Commission comments that Article 21 does not require information bodies to have at hand all the relevant information about other Member States' legislation that recipients of services could request from them or to have detailed knowledge on other Member States' legislation or to set up new databases. It is sufficient if Member States, if so requested by a recipient, gather the requested information, if necessary by contacting the relevant body of the Member State concerning which information is required. The information should be provided within a reasonable period of time by the Member State of residence of the recipient. It is not sufficient merely to refer the recipient to the necessary point of single contact in the other Member State.[66] It remains to be seen whether the provision of information of this kind by the Member State of residence will be provided sufficiently speedily and accurately to cater for the needs of potential cross-frontier shoppers for services.

VI – QUALITY OF SERVICES

A – Information from Providers

Chapter V covers the quality of services, and according to the preamble, the rules laid down should apply both to cases of cross-border provision of services between Member States and to cases of services provided in a Member State, without imposing unnecessary burdens on small and medium sized enterprises.[67] Member States are obliged to ensure that providers make certain information available to recipients, including the name of the provider, his legal status and form, and his address and the details which enable him to be contacted rapidly and communicated with directly.[68] Where the provider is registered in a trade or other similar public register, he must make available to a recipient the name of that register and the provider's registration number, or equivalent means of identification in the register.[69] A substantial list of further items of information must also be provided, including such matters as general conditions of business, and the existence or not of after-sales guarantees.[70] There are detailed provisions as to the means by which the information is provided.[71] Certain additional information must be provided at the recipient's request.[72]

---

[66] Handbook, 46. For points of single contact, see below at p 617.
[67] Recital (97).
[68] Art 22(1)(a).
[69] Art 22(1)(b).
[70] Art 22(1)(c)–(k).
[71] Art 22(2).
[72] Art 22(3).

B – Professional Liability Insurance and Guarantees

Professional liability insurance is at least indirectly relevant to the quality of a service, and Article 23 of the Directive provides that Member States *may* ensure that providers whose services present a direct and particular risk to the health or safety of the recipient or a third person, or to the financial security of the recipient, subscribe to professional liability insurance appropriate to the nature and extent of the risk, or provide a guarantee or similar arrangement which is equivalent or essentially comparable as regards its purpose.[73] The Commission comments that encouraging insurance for all providers of services which may potentially pose a risk to the consumer has the aim of enhancing consumer confidence in services from other Member States.[74]

When a provider establishes himself in their territory, Member States may not require professional liability insurance or a guarantee from the provider where he is already covered by a guarantee which is equivalent, or essentially comparable as regards its purpose and the cover it provides. Where equivalence is only partial, Member States may require a supplementary guarantee to cover those aspects not already covered.[75] Where a Member State requires a provider established in its territory to subscribe to professional liability insurance or to provide another guarantee, that Member State shall accept as sufficient evidence attestations of such insurance cover issued by credit institutions and insurers established in other Member States.[76]

C – Advertising and Other Forms of Commercial Communications by the Regulated Professions

Member States must remove all total prohibitions on commercial communications by the regulated professions,[77] and shall ensure that commercial communications by the regulated professions comply with professional rules, in conformity with EU law. The requirement may require removal of bans in any given medium, since the preamble gives as an example of a ban which must be removed one 'on all advertising in one or more given media'.[78] The professional rules in question are those which relate, in particular, to the independence, dignity and integrity of the profession, as well as professional secrecy. The Commission comments that respect for the obligation of professional secrecy will normally prevent providers from mentioning their clients in commercial communications without their explicit consent.[79] Professional rules on commercial communications shall be non-discriminatory, justified by an overriding reason relating to the public interest, and proportionate.[80] It follows from these requirements that Member States will have to screen their legislation, adapt it when necessary and also take appropriate measures to ensure that relevant rules of professional bodies and organisations are adapted where necessary.[81]

---

[73] Art 23(1).
[74] Handbook, 48.
[75] Art 23(2), first subpara.
[76] Art 23(2), second subpara.
[77] Art 24(1); Case C-119/09 *Société fiduciaire national d'expertise comptable* (CJEU 5 April 2011).
[78] Preamble, recital (100); the point is made by Barnard, above n 1, 378.
[79] Handbook, 49.
[80] Art 24(2).
[81] Handbook, 49.

VII – ADMINISTRATIVE CO-OPERATION

A – General

Chapter VI of the Directive deals with administrative co-operation. The Commission explains what it considers to be the rationale of administrative co-operation in the Handbook, and argues that administrative co-operation is essential to make the internal market in services work properly.[82] In the Commission's view, lack of trust in the legal framework and in supervision in other Member States has resulted in a multiplication of rules and duplication of controls for cross-border activities, which the Commission considers is one of the main reasons why the internal market in services has not functioned well to date.[83]

B – The Division of Supervisory Tasks

In fact a key element in and rationale of the chapter on administrative co-operation are the provisions on what the Commission calls the 'division of supervisory tasks' between Member States.[84] The Member States concerned in any given case are the Member State where a commercial operator is established, on the one hand, and the Member State where cross-border services are to be provided, on the other. Under Article 31(1) of the Directive the Member State where a service is provided is responsible for the supervision of the activity of the provider in its territory as regards national requirements which may be imposed pursuant to Articles 16 and 17.[85] An example of such supervision under Article 16 would be supervision of requirements necessary for health and safety at work affecting the use of equipment comprising an integral part of the service provided (eg scaffolding, diggers, cranes, etc, used in the provision of construction services).[86] This supervision would cover the actual use of the equipment, such as ensuring that scaffolding is properly erected, and a crane safely positioned and carefully operated. It would also cover requirements that such equipment be subject to periodic maintenance checks, but such requirements might have been carried out in the Member State of establishment, and such checks must be taken into account by national authorities applying their requirements in a non-discriminatory way. The Internal Market Information System (IMI) (discussed below) was designed to make it possible for a national authority in one Member State to secure a speedy response from a national authority in another in precisely such circumstances. Indeed, one of the hypothetical questions provided in the brochure for illustrative purposes is as follows: 'A German construction company will build a new shopping centre in our city. I'm not sure if the crane they brought has passed all the necessary technical checks in Germany.'[87] Another example of requirements subject to supervision under Article 16 by the Member State where the service is provided would be those relating to

---

[82] Handbook, 52.

[83] Handbook, 52; citing the Commission Report on 'The State of the Internal Market for Services' COM(2002) 441 final.

[84] Handbook, 55.

[85] Art 31(1).

[86] Art 16(2)(f); Handbook, 55, at 9.4.1.

[87] Brochure, 2; http://ec.europa.eu/internal_market/imi-net/docs/imi_brochure_en.pdf.

protection of the environment—an example might be use of equipment on a building site which is causing excessive emissions, or making too much noise.[88]

As regards cases not covered by Article 31(1) of the Directive, the Member State of establishment shall ensure that compliance with its requirements is supervised in conformity with the powers of supervision provided for in its national law, in particular through supervisory measures at the place of establishment of the provider.[89] One example would be ensuring that a service provider was in possession of necessary authorisations to carry on the activity in question.[90] In this connection, it will be recalled that Article 16(2) in principle prohibits the imposition of an authorisation requirement by the Member State where services are provided, while Article 9(1) requires that such requirements be justified in the Member State of establishment.[91] Another example would be ensuring that a service provider was in compliance with a requirement to be in possession of appropriate professional liability insurance. The Member State of establishment shall not refrain from taking supervisory or enforcement measures in its territory on the grounds that the service has been provided or caused damage in another Member State.[92] Since the definition of requirements covers rules of professional bodies,[93] it would seem to follow that national authorities are bound to ensure that such bodies undertake responsibilities as regards supervision of and enforcement in respect of their members in other Member States.

C – Mutual Assistance: General Obligations

Member States are obliged to give each other mutual assistance and to put in place measures for effective co-operation with one another, in order to ensure the supervision of providers and the services they provide.[94] Information requests and requests to carry out any checks, inspections and investigations under Chapter VI shall give reasons, in particular the reason for the request. Information exchanged shall be used only in respect of the matter for which it was requested.[95] Member States shall supply the information requested by other Member States or the Commission by electronic means and within the shortest possible period of time.[96]

D – Checks, Inspections and the Supply of Information by the Member State of Establishment

With respect to providers providing services in another Member State, the Member State of establishment shall supply information on providers established in its territory when requested to do so by another Member State and, in particular, confirm that a provider is established in its territory and, to its knowledge, is not exercising its activities in an unlaw-

---

[88] Art 16(3).
[89] Art 30(1).
[90] Handbook, 55, at 9.4.1.
[91] Above, pp 603, 606.
[92] Art 30(2).
[93] Art 4(7).
[94] Art 28(1).
[95] Art 28(3).
[96] Art 28(6).

ful manner.[97] The Member State of establishment shall undertake the checks, inspections and investigations requested by another Member State and shall inform the latter of the results, and, as the case may be, of the measures taken.[98] Upon gaining actual knowledge of any conduct or specific acts by a provider established in its territory which provides services in other Member States, that, to its knowledge, could cause serious damage to the health or safety of persons or to the environment, the Member State of establishment shall inform all other Member States and the Commission within the shortest possible period of time.[99]

E – Checks, Inspections and the Supply of Information by the Member State where the Service is provided

The Member State of establishment is not, however, obliged to carry out factual checks and controls in the territory of the Member State where the service is provided. Such checks and controls shall be carried out by the authorities of the Member State where the provider is temporarily operating, at the request of the authorities of the Member State of establishment.[100] On their own initiative, the competent authorities of the Member State where the service is provided may conduct checks, inspections and investigations on the spot, provided that such checks, etc, are not discriminatory, are not motivated by the fact that the provider is established in another Member State and are proportionate.[101]

F – Information on the Good Repute of Providers

Member States shall, at the request of a competent authority in another Member State, supply information, in conformity with their national law, on disciplinary or administrative actions or criminal sanctions and decisions concerning insolvency or bankruptcy involving fraud taken by their competent authorities in respect of the provider which are directly relevant to the provider's competence or professional reliability. A request for such information must be duly substantiated, in particular as regards the reasons for the request for information. The Member State which supplies the information shall inform the provider thereof.[102]

The criminal sanctions and disciplinary or administrative actions against a provider referred to shall only be communicated if a final decision has been taken. With regard to the other enforceable decisions referred to, the Member State which supplies the information shall specify whether a particular decision is final or whether an appeal has been lodged in respect of it, in which case the Member State in question should provide an indication of the date when the decision on appeal is expected. That Member State shall

---

[97] Art 29(1).
[98] Art 29(2).
[99] Art 29(3).
[100] Art 30(3); and see Art 31(2).
[101] Art 31(4).
[102] Art 33(1).

specify the provisions of national law pursuant to which the provider was found guilty or penalised.[103]

Implementation of these various obligations must comply with rules on the provision of personal data and with rights guaranteed to persons found guilty or penalised in the Member States concerned, including those penalised by professional bodies. Any information in question which is public shall be accessible to consumers.[104]

G – Mutual Assistance in the Event of Case-by-case Derogations

It will be recalled that Article 18 of the Directive provides for case-by-case derogations, in exceptional circumstances only, from the provisions of Article 16 of the Directive, by a Member State in respect of a provider established in another Member State. The Member State concerned may take measures relating to the safety of services, subject to a number of conditions, including compliance with the principle of proportionality. One of those conditions is compliance with the mutual assistance procedure in Article 35 of the Directive.

Article 35(1) provides that where a Member State intends to take a measure pursuant to Article 18, a specified procedure shall apply. The Member State where the service is provided shall ask the Member State of establishment to take measures with regard to the provider, supplying all relevant information on the service in question and the circumstances of the case.

The Member State of establishment shall check, within the shortest possible period of time, whether the provider is operating lawfully and verify the facts underlying the request. It shall inform the requesting Member State within the shortest possible period of time of the measures taken or envisaged or, as the case may be, the reasons why it has not taken any measures.[105]

Following this latter communication by the Member State of establishment, the requesting Member State shall notify the Commission and the Member State of establishment of its intention to take measures, indicating the reasons why it believes the measures taken or envisaged by the Member State of establishment are inadequate, and the reasons why it believes the measures it intends to take fulfil the conditions laid down in Article 18.[106] The measures may not be taken until 15 working days after the date of notification referred to.[107]

Without prejudice to the possibility for the requesting Member State to take the measures in question upon expiry of the 15-day period specified, the Commission shall, within the shortest possible period of time, examine the compatibility with EU law of the measures notified.[108] Where the Commission concludes that the measure is incompatible with EU law, it shall adopt a decision asking the Member State concerned to refrain from taking the proposed measures or to put an end to the measures in question as a matter of urgency.[109]

In cases of urgency, a Member State which intends to take a measure may derogate

---

[103] Art 33(2).
[104] Art 33(3).
[105] Art 35(2).
[106] Art 35(3).
[107] Art 35(4).
[108] Art 35(5).
[109] Art 35(5).

from the above procedure. In such cases, the measures shall be notified within the shortest possible period of time to the Commission and the Member State of establishment, stating the reasons for which the Member State considers that there is urgency.[110]

H – Internal Market Information System

Under the heading 'accompanying measures', and within the framework of administrative co-operation under Chapter VI of the Directive, Article 34(1) provides that the Commission, in co-operation with Member States, shall establish an electronic system for exchange of information between Member States, taking into account existing information systems. Provision is also made for Member States, with the assistance of the Commission, to take steps to facilitate the exchange of officials in charge of the implementation of the mutual assistance and the training of such officials, including language and computer training.[111]

In 2007 the Commission described the Internal Market Information System (IMI) as a horizontal tool to support the body of internal market legislation containing obligations of administrative co-operation. It would thus apply not only to administrative co-operation under the Services Directive, but also such co-operation under, for example, Directive 2005/36/EC on professional qualifications ('the Professional Qualifications Directive'). IMI, at that time still under development, would make the electronic exchange of information between competent authorities possible and would enable those authorities easily to find the relevant interlocutor in other Member States and to communicate with each other in a fast and efficient way.[112]

IMI has in fact been operational since December 2009.[113] More than 5,000 authorities from all EU countries are already registered with the IMI for the area of services. IMI currently covers the Professional Qualifications Directive[114] as well as the Services Directive. The IMI brochure explains[115] that IMI it is a multilingual electronic tool that makes it easier and faster for national, regional and local authorities to co-operate, reducing the costs caused by delays. Examples are given of the types of questions which IMI can answer. One hypothetical example of a question relevant to the application of the Services Directive is as follows: 'A German construction company will build a new shopping centre in our city. I'm not sure if the crane they brought has passed all the necessary technical checks in Germany.' Another is: 'I have asked Norwegian[116] colleagues if an electrician who is providing his services here is established in Norway. When can I expect a reply?' One example of a question relevant to the Professional Qualifications Directive is: 'A Portuguese doctor applied for a job in our local hospital. I don't know if she is qualified because her diploma is in Portuguese.'

---

[110] Art 35(6).

[111] Art 34(2).

[112] Handbook, 53, at 9.2.2.

[113] The development of IMI was funded under the IDABC programme (Interoperable Delivery of European eGovernment Services to public administrations, businesses and citizens) with a total budget of €1,300,000 over a period of five years (2005–09).

[114] Covered in Chapter 19.

[115] Brochure, at http://ec.europa.eu/internal_market/imi-net/docs/imi_brochure_en.pdf.

[116] An example which reminds us that the Services Directive applies to EFTA with a compliance date of 1 May 2010.

Competent authorities make and receive requests, and respond to requests, in their own language, and the IMI ensures translation. IMI undertakes to put a competent authority in one Member State in touch with the right partner authority in another Member State, and to track the progress of requests. 'By checking in IMI, you can follow all stages the request goes through. In the IMI pilot phase, 75% of all requests were answered within two weeks.'[117] Statistics for 2010 show that 77 per cent of requests under both the Services and Professional Qualifications Directive were answered within two weeks, and, indeed, 65 per cent of requests were answered within one week.[118] It must be said, however, that the absolute numbers of requests remain very modest overall, in particular as regards the Services Directive, though this is to be expected, since its provisions are novel, and its implementation date was 28 December 2009.

The total number of requests sent and received for the Services Directive in the period January–October 2010 amounted to 153. For the Professional Qualifications Directive there were 1,569 requests sent and received. As regards the latter Directive, the United Kingdom alone was responsible for 34 per cent of all requests, followed by Germany, which made 11 per cent of all requests, and the Netherlands, which was responsible for a further 10 per cent. The principal recipients of requests for information were Romania (16 per cent), Poland (15 per cent) and Germany (9 per cent), followed by Greece (8 per cent) and the UK (7 per cent). For the Services Directive, absolute numbers are, as noted above, still very modest; Germany made 42 per cent of all requests, while Spain and Poland each received 14 per cent of all requests. It remains to be seen to what extent demand increases for use of IMI, and to what extent response times can be maintained and improved. On the face of it, IMI is likely to prove an invaluable tool in improving the practical operation of the internal market.

VIII – ADMINISTRATIVE SIMPLIFICATION

A – Simplification of Procedures

The provisions on administrative simplification are to be found in Chapter II of the Directive, though their significance may be more readily understood in light of the provisions designed to facilitate freedom of establishment, freedom to provide services and the rights of recipients of services, and for this reason those matters have been considered prior to that of administrative simplification.

Member States are required to examine the procedures and formalities applicable to access to a service activity and to the exercise thereof, and where those procedures and formalities are not sufficiently simple, Member States 'shall simplify them'.[119] As the Commission observes, this 'requires Member States to undertake a real effort of administrative simplification' and suggests that 'Member States could take into consideration simplified administrative procedures used in other Member States and exchange best

---

[117] Brochure, 2.
[118] http://ec.europa.eu/internal_market/imi-net/docs/statistics_2010_en.pdf.
[119] Art 5(1).

practice'. The Commission says it will use its best endeavours to facilitate this,[120] and notes that, in practical terms, Member States will have to assess whether their administrative requirements are indeed necessary or whether some procedures or parts of those procedures can be abolished or replaced by alternatives which are less burdensome.[121] The Commission may introduce harmonised forms at EU level, and these forms shall be equivalent to certificates, attestations and other documents required of a provider.[122]

Where a Member State requires a provider or recipient to supply a certificate, attestation or any other document proving that a requirement has been satisfied, they shall accept any document from another Member State which serves an equivalent purpose or from which it is clear that the requirement in question has been satisfied. They may not require a document from another Member to be produced in its original form, or as a certified copy or as a certified translation, save in the cases provided for in other EU instruments or where such a requirement is justified by an overriding reason relating to the public interest, including public order or security. Nevertheless, these obligations do not affect the right of Member States to require non-certified translations of documents in one of their official languages.[123]

As regards the duty of Member States to refrain from seeking original documents or certified copies unless essential, the Commission points out that the mere doubt as to the authenticity of a given document, or its exact content, can be addressed by appropriate contacts between competent authorities, in particular with the authority which has issued the document, notably through administrative co-operation. The Commission adds that this should not be particularly burdensome since the IMI—discussed above—will allow for documents to be easily uploaded and checked remotely.[124]

B – Points of Single Contact: 'One-stop Shops'

Member States must ensure that it is possible for providers to complete certain procedures and formalities through 'points of single contact'. These procedures and formalities are all those needed for access to the provider's service activities, and in particular, all declarations, notifications or applications necessary for authorisation from the competent authorities, including applications for inclusion in a register, a roll or a database, or for registration with a professional body of association. Also included are procedures and formalities relating to any application for authorisation needed to exercise the provider's service activities.[125]

The establishment of points of single contact does not change the allocations of functions and powers among the authorities within national systems.[126] The Commission observes that the objective of setting up one-stop shops for businesses has been pursued by Member States for several years and the 'points of single contact' obligation is therefore in line with, and complementary to (as well as being broader than), the aims of European

---

[120] Handbook, 17.
[121] Ibid.
[122] Art 5(2).
[123] Art 5(3). Art 5(4) excludes certain documents covered by certain EU instruments.
[124] Handbook, 17.
[125] Art 6(1).
[126] Art 6(2).

initiatives, in particular the commitment taken by the European Council to put in place one-stop shops for start-ups by the end of 2007.[127]

The concept of 'points of single contact' does not mean that Member States have to set up one single centralised body in their territory. Member States may decide to have several points of single contact within their territory. The point of single contact must, however, be 'single' from the individual provider's perspective (ie the service provider should be able to complete all procedures by using only one such point of contact).[128] Member States may choose to set up single points of contact on an electronic basis only, without putting in place a specific physical infrastructure which service providers can actually visit.[129] However, the Commission cautions that it would not be sufficient for Member States to provide a mere list or compilation of web links on a central website, and adds that if points of single contact are to be set up on an electronic basis only, it will be necessary to establish a helpline which service providers can contact in case of difficulties.[130] It seems that reasonable and proportionate fees may be charged for use of points of single contact, since reference to this is made in the preamble.[131]

Member States shall ensure that specified categories of information are easily accessible to providers and recipients through the points of single contact. These categories include requirements concerning the procedures and formalities to be completed in order to access and to exercise service activities; the contact details of competent authorities enabling them to be contacted directly; and the contact details of the associations or organisations, other than the competent authorities, from which providers or recipients may obtain practical assistance.[132] It must be possible for providers and recipients to receive, at their request, assistance from the competent authorities, consisting in information on the way in which the requirements relating to the access and exercise of service activities are generally interpreted and applied. Where appropriate, such advice shall include a simple step-by-step guide. The information shall be provided in plain and intelligible language,[133] though it is only information which must be provided, and there is no obligation to provide legal advice.[134]

The information and assistance referred to must be provided in a clear and unambiguous manner, be easily accessible at a distance and by electronic means, and be kept up to date.[135] Points of single contact and competent authorities must respond as quickly as possible to any request for information or assistance, and in cases where the request is faulty or unfounded, inform the applicant accordingly without delay.[136]

The Directive does not require points of single contact to make information available in the language of other EU Member States, but it does provide for Member States and the Commission to take 'accompanying measures' in order to encourage points of single contact to make relevant information available in languages of other Member States, without

---

[127] Handbook, 18, at 5.2.
[128] Ibid.
[129] Ibid.
[130] Handbook, 19.
[131] Recital (49).
[132] Art 7(1).
[133] Art 7(2).
[134] Art 7(6).
[135] Art 7(3).
[136] Art 7(4).

interfering with Member States' legislation on the use of languages.[137] The Commission comments that Member States could consider making information available in the languages of the neighbouring Member States or in languages most commonly used by business in the EU.[138]

C – Procedures by Electronic Means

A further highly significant aspect of administrative simplification is the requirement that Member States shall ensure that all procedures and formalities relating to access to a service activity and to the exercise thereof may be easily completed, at a distance and by electronic means, through the relevant point of single contact and with the relevant competent authorities.[139] Predictably enough, this does not apply to the inspection of premises on which the service is to be provided, nor does it apply to inspection of equipment used by the provider or to physical examination of the capability or of the personal integrity of the provider or of his responsible staff.[140]

As the Commission points out, electronic procedures have to be available not only for service providers resident or established in the Member State of the administration concerned, but also for service providers resident or established in other Member States. This means that service providers should be able to complete procedures and formalities by electronic means across borders, and this point is made in the preamble to the Directive.[141]

IX – MUTUAL EVALUATION

Several provisions of the Directive which have been mentioned provide for mutual evaluation of national rules, and Article 39 of the Directive provides the procedure for such evaluation.

It will be recalled that Member States are precluded from making access to a service activity subject to an authorisation scheme unless it is non-discriminatory, and unless the need for the scheme is justified by an overriding reason relating to the public interest, and is proportionate.[142] Member States were required to identify their authorisation schemes and give reasons showing their compatibility with the foregoing requirements, in a report to be made to the Commission not later than 28 December 2009.[143]

Non-discriminatory requirements relating to the access to or exercise of a service activity, such as those imposing quantitative or territorial restrictions, must be examined by Member States to ensure they are justified by reference to overriding requirements in the

---

[137] Art 7(5).
[138] Handbook, 21, at 5.3.3.
[139] Art 8(1).
[140] Art 8(2).
[141] Handbook, 22, at 5.4.1; recital (52) of preamble.
[142] Art 11(1).
[143] Art 11(2); Art 39(1)(a).

general interest and the principle of proportionality, and Member States were required to specify in a report made to the Commission not later than 28 December 2009 both the requirements which they intended to maintain and the reasons why they considered that these requirements were compatible with the Directive, and the requirements which had been abolished or made less stringent.[144]

The Commission is required to forward these reports to the Member States, which shall submit their observations on each of the reports within six months of receipt, and within the same period, the Commission shall consult interested parties on the reports.[145] The Commission shall present the reports and the Member States observations to the Committee referred to in Article 40(1) of the Directive to assist the Commission, and this Committee may make observations.[146] In light of the observations of Member States, and the Committee, the Commission shall, by 28 December 2010 at the latest, present a summary report to the European Parliament and to the Council, accompanied where appropriate by proposals for additional initiatives.[147]

There is also provision for mutual evaluation of two categories of requirements applicable to service providers providing services in a Member State other than that in which they are established. These are requirements covered by Article 16, the first category of which are requirements which cannot be justified by reference to non-discrimination, overriding requirements in the general interest, and proportionality. The second category are requirements imposing obligations such as the obligation to have an establishment in the territory in which the service is to be provided, which can be justified only by reference to public policy, public security, public health or the protection of the environment. By 28 December 2009 at the latest Member States were required to present a report to the Commission on the national requirements requiring justification under the foregoing provisions and giving reasons why they considered that such requirements could be justified. The Commission refers by way of example to a Member State which considers that it needs to apply a national rule limiting noise levels for certain activities for reasons of environmental protection; in such a case that rule needs to be specified together with the reasons for its application.

Thereafter (that is to say, after 28 December 2009), Member States shall transmit to the Commission any changes in their requirements, including new requirements, together with the reasons for them. The Commission is to communicate the transmitted requirements to other Member States. This transmission does not prevent the adoption by Member States of the provisions in question. The Commission shall on an annual basis thereafter provide 'analyses and orientations' on the application of these provisions in the context of the Directive.[148] The Commission indicates that the aim of the latter process is to 'enhance transparency and legal certainty for service providers'.

---

[144] Art 15; Art 39(1)(b). For mutual evaluation of multidisciplinary activities, not addressed in this chapter, see Arts 25(3) and 39(1)(c).

[145] Art 39(2).

[146] Art 39(4).

[147] Art 39(4).

[148] Art 39(5).

X – SOME PROVISIONS OF THE DIRECTIVE COVER INTERNAL AS WELL AS CROSS-BORDER SITUATIONS

It is clear from the discussion of the Services Directive in this chapter that some of its provisions cover both internal and cross-border situations, while others cover only cross-border situations. Thus, for example, Chapter III on 'Freedom of Establishment for Providers', lays down requirements for authorisation procedures, etc, which are clearly of general application and are not confined to cross-border situations. In this way, meeting the needs of the internal market also improves the competitive position of market operators carrying on business in the Member State in question whose relevant activities have no cross-border element. The fact that provisions of the Directive bestow rights on commercial operators in internal situations as a means of ensuring the right of establishment for commercial operators from other Member States does not call in question the competence of the Union institutions to adopt the provisions in question. In an early case, *Maison Singer*,[149] the Court rejected the argument that an EEC Regulation adopted to implement Article 48 TFEU, which provides for 'such measures in the field of social security as are necessary to provide freedom of movement for workers', must be confined in its application to migrant workers, or to situations which are work related. The Court considered that removing the territorial limitations on the application of the national social security schemes was an appropriate means of achieving the objectives of Article 48 TFEU, and noted that confining the application of the EEC Regulation in issue to migrant workers and work-related situations 'would tend to make the application of the rules in question impracticable'.[150] That is the general position as regards competence today, and it allows considerable latitude to the EU law-making institutions.

This is not the first time that EU legislation designed to facilitate the exercise of the right of establishment and the freedom to provide services has also improved the competitive position of market operators whose relevant transactions are entirely internal to a Member State. EU legislation on public procurement is a case in point. The procedures which are put in place to implement freedom of establishment and freedom to provide services by adopting common rules on the advertising and award of public works contracts can be invoked by all commercial operators, including those for whom bids for the contract in question would be internal transactions falling wholly outside the scope of the Treaty provisions on establishment or services.[151]

Certainly, other provisions of the Directive are specifically concerned with cross-border situations, such as Articles 16–20, which deal with cross-border provision of services. Article 21, on assistance for recipients, would seem to cover actual and potential recipients of cross-border services, and therefore everybody. Article 24, requiring the removal of all total prohibitions on advertising and other commercial communications by the regulated professions, clearly cannot be confined to advertising in respect of cross-border transactions and is good example of how improving conditions for cross-border activity can

---

[149] Case 44/65 *Maison Singer* [1965] Eng Sp Edn 965.
[150] Ibid, 971.
[151] See Directive 2004/18/EC of the European Parliament and of the Council on the coordination of procedures for the award of public works contracts, public supply contracts and public service contracts [2004] OJ L134/114. A similar point is made by Barnard, above n 1, 351, 352.

contribute to greater competitiveness for all market operators. Whether or not a particular provision of the Directive applies solely to cross-border situations, or applies generally, is a matter of interpretation, rather than an issue calling in question the competence of the law-maker.

XI – THE DIRECTIVE EXCLUDES CERTAIN JUSTIFICATIONS WHICH WOULD OTHERWISE BE AVAILABLE

In Chapter III on 'Freedom of Establishment for Providers', Article 14 prohibits certain requirements, without allowing for even the possibility that a Member State might seek to show justification on grounds of public policy, public security or public health, or by reference to overriding requirements in the general interest, despite the fact that the possibility of arguing such justifications would in principle be available if the requirements in question were called in question directly under Article 49 TFEU. Again, in Chapter IV on 'Free Movement of Services', Article 16 prohibits certain requirements and restrictions unless they are both non-discriminatory and justified on grounds of public policy, public security, public health or the protection of the environment, but excludes the possibility of a Member State seeking to justify a requirement by reference to overriding reasons in the general interest.[152]

There are two possible explanations of the above. The first is that the law-maker has made the necessary assessment of the requirements in question, and concluded either that they cannot be justified at all, or that the justifications admissible under the Directive are the only justifications which are in law available.

Another possibility is that whatever the position would be as regards possible arguments as to justification if this or that requirement were challenged directly under Article 49 or 56 TFEU, it is within the competence of the law-maker to limit or remove the scope for justifying particular requirements in the Directive, and that that is what the law-maker has done in any case where the scope for justification is more limited under the Directive than it would be in the case of a direct challenge under the Treaty itself to the national rule in question.

Derogations from fundamental freedoms do not comprise uniform exclusions from those freedoms, but rather opportunities for Member States to make exceptions in accordance with their conceptions of the public interest, within the limits laid down by the Treaty. It follows that in a given set of circumstances a fundamental freedom may be exercised in full in one Member State, yet curtailed in another, because the first Member State makes no claim to derogate from the freedom in question on grounds permitted by EU law, while the second Member State does do so. It also follows that when EU rules seek to eliminate the disparities between national laws which arise from these differing applications of express and implied derogations from fundamental freedoms, the EU legislature will have to make choices applicable to all Member States as regards the legal

---

[152] Barnard sees the explanation of the inclusion of environmental protection but the exclusion of consumer protection as explained by recital (32) of the preamble, which asserts that the Directive is consistent with EU legislation on consumer protection: see Barnard, above n 1, 367.

standard to be applied, including the extent of any exceptions to or limitations on, freedom of movement. That standard will then be binding on all Member States, even if prior to the adoption of the common rules some Member States may have applied national rules placing greater restrictions on freedom of movement than would be permissible under the common rules. Nevertheless, the EU legislature is bound to have regard to the public interest in matters such as consumer protection in adopting common rules. The Court described the legal position as follows, in the context of a challenge by Luxembourg to Directive 98/5/EC, which was designed to facilitate the establishment of lawyers qualified in one Member State in the territory of other Member States:

> In that regard, the Court observes that, in the absence of coordination at Community level, the Member States may, subject to certain conditions, impose national measures pursuing a legitimate aim compatible with the Treaty and justified on overriding public interest grounds, which include the protection of consumers. They may thus, in certain circumstances, adopt or maintain measures constituting a barrier to freedom of movement. Article [53(1) TFEU] authorises the Community to eliminate obstacles of that kind in order to make it easier for persons to take up and pursue activities as self-employed persons. When adopting measures to that end, the Community legislature is to have regard to the public interest pursued by the various Member States and to adopt a level of protection for that interest which seems acceptable in the Community. . . . It enjoys a measure of discretion for the purposes of its assessment of the acceptable level of protection.[153]

The approach adopted in the Services Directive, of excluding the possibility in certain cases for Member States to seek to justify restrictions on the right of establishment or freedom to provide services on grounds which would in principle be available were those restrictions challenged directly on the basis of the relevant Treaty provisions, might in theory be open to challenge on the grounds that in one or other of the cases in point, the Council and Parliament had manifestly exceeded the bounds of its discretion, but that that is actually the case should not be too lightly assumed.

XII – CONCLUDING REMARKS: ASSESSMENT OF THE SERVICES DIRECTIVE

Forecasting the extent of any positive contribution of the Services Directive to the internal market in services is still largely a matter of impression. There is certainly no unanimity on the subject. Weatherill declares that the Directive 'scores badly on many counts' and views it as

> a peculiar mix of minor adjustment to regulatory competences, a great deal of what may or may not be codification of the Court's case law, new and awkward demarcations between the terrain occupied by the Directive and the application of the general rules of free movement of the Treaty, supported by exhortations to simplify and to cooperate.[154]

Snell observes that the 'certainty that the Directive could have provided has been lost, largely due to poor drafting', and adds that 'the credibility of the EU has been undermined

---

[153] Case C-168/98 *Luxembourg v Parliament and Council* [2000] ECR I-9131, para 32.
[154] Weatherill, above n 1, 19.

and its capacity to provide answers to the challenges facing Europe has been cast into further doubt'.[155] Davies is also critical.[156] Barnard is a more optimistic, arguing that the screening provisions are particularly important, and an improvement on leaving Member States simply to wait for enforcement proceedings to be brought against them on an ad hoc basis. She also sees advantages in codification, which gives to service providers a legal document setting out their legal rights to 'wave under the noses of obstructive bureau-crats'.[157] The present writer has in the past noted the advantages of duplicating Treaty obligations in Directives,[158] arguing (in the context of the free movement of goods) that 'rights created or confirmed by EC Directives and implemented by national rules are in practice more accessible and enforceable than directly applicable rights arising solely from the provisions of the Treaty'.[159] One advantage of the Directive is that it applies a number of its provisions to internal as well as cross-border situations; since the measures in question are designed to reduce unnecessary regulation of business, this is likely to make at least some contribution to the general competitiveness of service industries in the EU. The requirement that all procedures and formalities relating to the access to and exercise of a service activity may be completed at a distance and by electronic means through a point of single contact has the capability of reducing 'red tape' and the duplication of require-ments, and thus of making a contribution to competitiveness. Even if the provisions of the Directive on the quality of services are implemented sporadically and by degrees, some advantages to consumers are likely to accrue. The IMI alone has considerable potential for enhancing administrative co-operation in support of the application of the Services Directive, and the Professional Qualifications Directive, and, in due course other internal market legislation. While it is as yet too early to assess the actual impact of the Services Directive, it does not seem unduly optimistic to forecast some beneficial results as regards reduction of unnecessary regulation, enhanced competitiveness, and improvements for consumers in the quality and price of services covered by the Directive. Quantification of all this will be for the future, and it will be a matter for economists, rather than lawyers.

Further Reading

C Barnard, 'Unravelling the Services Directive' (2008) 45 *CMLRev* 323.

G Davies, 'The Services Directive: Extending the Country of Origin Principle and Reforming Public Administration' (2007) 32 *ELRev* 232.

M Klamert, 'Of Empty Glasses and Double Burdens: Approaches to Regulating the Services Market A Propos the Implementation of the Services Directive' (2010) 37 *Legal Issues of Economic Integration*, 111.

U Neergaard, L Nielsen and R Roseberry (eds), ***The Services Directive: Consequences for the Welfare State and the European Social Model*** (Copenhagen, DJØF Publishing, 2008).

S Weatherill, 'Promoting the Consumer Interest in an Integrated Services Market', Europa Institute, Mitchell Working Paper Series, 2/2007.

---

[155] U Neergaard, L Nielsen and R Roseberry (eds), *The Services Directive: Consequences for the Welfare State and the European Social Model* (Copenhagen, DJØF Publishing, 2008), 194, 195.

[156] G Davies, 'The Services Directive: Extending the Country of Origin Principle and Reforming Public Administration' (2007) 32 *ELRev* 232, 245.

[157] Barnard, above n 1, 393, 394.

[158] A Arnull, A Dashwood, M Dougan, M Ross, E Spaventa and D Wyatt, *Wyatt and Dashwood's European Union Law*, 5th edn (London, Sweet and Maxwell, 2006) 766, 767, 954, 955.

[159] Ibid, 955, 959.

19

Mutual Recognition of Diplomas, Training and Experience, and the Co-ordination of National Qualifications

National requirements as to professional qualifications may amount to discriminatory or non-discriminatory restrictions on the right of establishment and the freedom to provide services, and in this chapter such issues are considered from the perspective of the Court's case law on Articles 49 TFEU and 56 TFEU, and in the light of the Professional Qualifications Directive (2005/36/EC), and the Directives on Provision of Services (77/249/EEC), and Establishment (98/5/EC), by lawyers qualified in a Member State. In principle, a national of one Member State who wishes to carry on a professional activity in another Member State which requires the possession of qualifications is obliged to obtain those qualifications. But even on that basis the question arises as to the extent of a host Member State's duty to take account of skills and qualifications which might have been obtained in other Member States. The solution adopted for some qualifications (doctors, nurses, dentists and several other professions) has been to harmonise the content of qualifications at EU level, and to oblige Member States to recognise the qualifications in question irrespective of the Member State in which they have been obtained. However, extending this approach beyond a handful of professions has not proved to be practical, and a number of other methods have been adopted to make it possible for individuals to carry on cross-border activities without being obliged to requalify in every Member State in which they carry on commercial activities.

I – DIRECT APPLICABILITY OF ARTICLES 49 AND 56 TFEU (AND ARTICLE 45 TFEU)

A – The Principles Applicable Where No Relevant Harmonisation Directives Have Been Adopted

Article 53(1) TFEU provides that the Council shall issue directives for the mutual recognition of diplomas, certificates and other evidence of formal qualifications. Article 53(2) TFEU provides that in the case of the medical and allied and pharmaceutical professions, the progressive abolition of restrictions shall be dependent upon co-ordination of the conditions for their exercise in the various Member States. However, even in the absence of directives under Article 53 TFEU, recognition of foreign diplomas may be required by the prohibitions on discrimination contained in Articles 49 and 56 TFEU, and indeed Article 45 TFEU, on the free movement of workers. *Thieffry*,[1] concerning the application of Article 49 TFEU, is illustrative. A Belgian national held a Belgian law degree recognised by the University of Paris as equivalent to a French law degree. He acquired the qualifying certificate for the profession of advocate, but the Paris Bar Council refused to allow him to undergo practical training on the ground that he did not possess a French law degree. The Court of Justice held that such a refusal could amount to indirect discrimination prohibited by Article 49 TFEU. As the General Programme for the abolition of restrictions on freedom of establishment made clear in Title III(B), the Council proposed to eliminate not only overt discrimination, but also any form of disguised discrimination, including

> Any requirements imposed . . . in respect of the taking up or pursuit of an activity as a self-employed person where, although applicable irrespective of nationality, their effect is exclusively or principally to hinder the taking up or pursuit of such activity by foreign nationals.[2]

It would be for the competent national authorities, taking account of the requirements of EU law, to judge whether a recognition granted by a university authority could, in addition to its academic effect, constitute valid evidence of a professional qualification.

The Court emphasised in *Vlassopoulou* that a Member State, dealing with a request for authorisation to practise a profession access to which is under national legislation subject to the holding of a diploma or professional qualification, is obliged to take into account qualifications acquired in another Member State, by carrying out a comparison between the skills evidenced by those diplomas and the knowledge and qualifications required by national rules.[3] In the context of that review a Member State might take into consideration objective differences relating to the legal context of the profession concerned in the Member State or origin and its field of activity.[4] If such a comparison indicates the possession of a qualification equivalent to that required by the national law of the host state, the Member State is bound to accept the person concerned as being qualified. If the comparison shows only partial equivalence, the host state has the right to require that the person concerned should demonstrate that he or she has acquired the additional

---

[1] Case 71/76 *Thieffry* [1977] ECR 765. See Case 11/77 *Patrick* [1977] ECR 119; Case 65/77 *Razanatsimba* [1977] ECR 2229 (Lomé Convention, Art 62).
[2] [1974] OJ Eng Sp Edn, Second Series, IX, 8.
[3] Case C-340/89 *Vlassopoulou* [1990] ECR I-2327; citing Case 222/86 *Heylens and Others* [1987] ECR 4097.
[4] Case C-340/89 *Vlassopoulou* [1990] ECR I-2327, para 18.

knowledge and qualifications needed.[5] Comparison of the national qualifications must be carried out according to a procedure complying with the requirements of EU law relating to the effective protection of fundamental rights conferred by the Treaty on nationals of Member States.[6] It follows that it must be possible for any decision to be made the subject of judicial proceedings in which its legality under EU law can be reviewed and it must be possible for the person concerned to ascertain the reasons for the decision.[7]

In *Bobadilla*,[8] a case involving Article 45 TFEU, the Court added that, where no general procedure for official recognition has been laid down at national level by the host Member State, or where that procedure does not comply with the requirements of EU law, it is for a public body seeking to fill the post itself to investigate whether the diploma obtained by the candidate in another Member State, together, where appropriate, with practical experience, is to be regarded as equivalent to the qualification required. In the case in point, the public body in question (the Prado Museum, Madrid) had made a grant to the candidate to enable him to pursue his studies in another Member State and had already employed him on a temporary basis in the post to be filled. The Court of Justice held that in such a case, the public body was ideally placed to assess the candidate's actual knowledge and abilities compared to the knowledge and abilities of holders of the national diploma.[9]

In *Peśla*, a case concerning a claim under Article 45 TFEU by a Polish national for access to a German legal traineeship without having undertaken the first state examination, the Court confirmed that in carrying out the examination of equivalence required by the Treaty, national authorities were not required to accept a lower level of legal knowledge than that which could be regarded as essential for a traineeship, and which was attested by the first state examination, though the Treaty did not deprive national authorities of the possibility of relaxing the relevant qualification requirements.[10] The Court added that it was important in practice that the possibility of partial recognition of the required standard should be more than merely notional.[11]

B – The Principles Applicable in the Absence of Harmonisation Directives Are Also Applicable after Harmonisation to Situations Not Covered by Relevant Directives

In *Hocsman*[12] the Court rejected the argument that the above principles were only applicable in the absence of harmonisation of relevant qualifications, and thus had no application to the free movement of doctors, whose qualifications were exhaustively regulated by Directive 93/16/EEC.[13] Where requirements such as those set out in Directive 93/16/EEC were satisfied, mutual recognition of the diplomas in question rendered superfluous their recognition under the general principles developed by the Court. However, those principles remained relevant in situations not covered by such directives. In the case in

---

[5] Ibid, para 19.
[6] Ibid, para 22.
[7] Ibid, para 22.
[8] See Case C-234/97 *Bobadilla* [1999] ECR I-4773.
[9] Ibid, paras 34 and 35.
[10] Case C-345/08 *Peśla* [2009] ECR I -11677, paras 55–57.
[11] Ibid, para 58.
[12] Case C-238/98 *Hocsman* [2000] ECR I-6623.
[13] [1993] OJ L165/24; see now Dir 2005/36/EC, at pp 630, 631 below.

point, Dr Hocsman, of Argentine origin, acquired Spanish nationality in 1986, and French citizenship in 1998. He had been refused authorisation to practise medicine in France on the ground that he did not hold qualifications obtained in a Member State. He held an Argentine medical diploma recognised in Spain as equivalent to the Spanish university degree in medicine and surgery, so allowing him to practise medicine in Spain and train there as a specialist. The Court held that the authorities of the Member State to which Dr Hocsman had applied were bound to carry out the comparative assessment referred to in *Vlassopoulou* and *Bobadilla*. In particular, it would be necessary to verify whether recognition in Spain of Dr Hocsman's diploma from Argentina as equivalent to the Spanish degree in medicine and surgery was given on the basis of criteria comparable to those whose purpose, in the context of Directive 93/16/EEC, was to ensure that Member States may rely on the quality of the diplomas in medicine awarded by the other Member States.[14]

C – A National Requirement that a Person Possess a Particular Qualification in Order to Carry on a Particular Occupational Activity is in Itself a Restriction on a Fundamental Freedom which Must Be Justified

Failure to recognise that a foreign national has qualifications equivalent to national qualifications may thus hinder or make less attractive the exercise of a fundamental freedom. But it is also the case that national rules requiring that certain activities be reserved to those with certain qualifications are themselves regarded as hindering or making less attractive the exercise of the right of establishment or freedom to provide services, and require justification. The Court has subjected claims of justification to fairly searching scrutiny as regards proportionality, though unsurprisingly accords rather more deference to claims based on the protection of public health than to claims based on other grounds.

Thus in *Mac Quen*[15] national rules reserving to ophthalmologists the right to carry out certain eyesight operations was held to be a restriction on the right of establishment, though one which could in principle be justified on grounds of protection of public health. The Court noted, however, that the national rule in issue was not expressly provided for in legislation, but resulted from national judicial interpretation 'based on an assessment of the risks to public health which might result if opticians were authorised to carry out certain eyesight operations'.[16] The Court observed that an assessment of this kind was liable to change with the passage of time, particularly as a result of scientific and technical progress, and concluded that it was for the national court to assess, in the light of the Treaty requirements relating to freedom of establishment and the demands of legal certainty and the protection of public health, whether the interpretation of domestic law adopted by the competent national authorities in that regard remained valid.[17]

The occupational activity considered by the Court in *Gräbner*[18] was that of *Heilpraktiker* (or 'lay health practitioner') under German law, which was a professional or commer-

---

[14] Ibid, esp paras 33–39; see also Case C-319/92 *Haim* [1994] ECR I-425.
[15] Case C-108/96 *Mac Quen* [2001] ECR I-837.
[16] Ibid, para 35.
[17] Ibid, 36 and 37.
[18] Case C-294/00 *Gräbner* [2002] ECR I-6515.

cial activity involving the diagnosis, treatment or alleviation of illness, pain or physical injury. Austrian law recognised no such category, reserving all these latter activities to doctors. It was undisputed that the Austrian rules constituted a restriction on the exercise of the right of establishment and freedom to provide services; the main issue was whether the Austrian prohibition was a necessary and proportionate means of protecting human health. The Court repeated its observation in *Mac Quen* that assessments such as that made by the Austrian legislature are liable to change over time, but concluded without more that the Austrian rule did not go beyond what was necessary to protect public health.[19]

In *Commission v Greece* the Court considered a national rule of one Member State requiring that tourist guides travelling with a group of tourists from another Member State to show them around places of interest and historic sites have a licence requiring specific training evidenced by a diploma. The Court held that this was a restriction on the freedom to provide services which could not be justified by a Member State's general interest in the proper appreciation of its artistic and archaeological heritage, since the requirements imposed were disproportionate, in view of the fact that the tourist guides in question provided their services to a closed group with whom they travelled from the Member State of establishment to the Member State to be visited.[20]

In *Säger v Dennemeyer* the Court considered the application to service providers established in other Member States of a national rule requiring providers of patent renewal services (monitoring patents by a computerised system and advising them when renewal payments are due) to hold a special professional qualification, such as patent agent. The Court held that the rule in question was a restriction on the freedom to provide services, which could not be justified on grounds of protecting clients, since the services provided comprised advising clients on when renewal fees had to be paid in order to prevent a patent from lapsing, requesting them to state whether they wish to renew the patent, and paying the fees on their behalf if they so desired. These tasks were essentially of a straightforward nature and did not call for specific professional aptitudes, as was indicated by the high level of computerisation which appeared to have been attained by the defendant in the main proceedings. The Court added that the risk for the holder of a patent of the failure by a company entrusted with monitoring German patents to fulfil its obligations was very limited, since two months after the date for renewal, the German patent office sends a reminder to the holder of a patent pointing out that, failing payment of the fee, increased by a surcharge of 10 per cent, the patent will expire four months after the sending of the reminder.

Where national requirements reserving a particular occupational activity to those holding a particular qualification can be justified, nationals of other Member States can be required to hold that qualification or its equivalent. That may in turn raise the question whether a particular individual, qualified or experienced in one Member State, may rightly claim to be appropriately qualified or experience in another Member State. The Treaty rules on establishment and services may be directly invoked in such cases, as discussed above. Increasingly, EU legislation lays down specific rules on the mutual recognition of qualifications for particular professions, or general rules for assessing the compatibility of qualifications or experience gained in one Member State with the lawful requirements for

---

[19] Ibid, para 50.
[20] Case C-198/89 *Commission v Greece* [1991] ECR I-727, paras 16 and 18. And see Case C-154/89 *Commission v France* [1991] ECR I-4221.

pursuit of occupational activities in another. The most important EU legislation in this field is discussed below.

II – MUTUAL RECOGNITION OF DIPLOMAS AND THE CO-ORDINATION OF NATIONAL QUALIFICATIONS BY EU RULES

A – Introduction

Article 53(1) TFEU provides for the 'mutual recognition of diplomas, certificates, and other evidence of formal qualifications', and for 'the coordination of the provisions laid down by law, regulation or administrative action in Member States concerning the taking up and pursuit of activities as self-employed persons'. Article 53(2) TFEU provides that in the case of the medical and allied and pharmaceutical professions, the progressive abolition of restrictions shall be dependent upon co-ordination of the conditions for their exercise in the various Member States. By far the single most important piece of legislation adopted under Article 53(1) TFEU is Directive 2005/36/EC of the European Parliament and of the Council on the recognition of professional qualifications.[21] This Directive supersedes more than a dozen prior directives, and lays down the framework for application of a number of others. It will be referred to in the subsequent discussion as 'the PQ Directive'. This Directive does not prescribe a single approach or blueprint for dealing with mutual recognition, but combines a number of approaches, which vary according to the types of qualification, training or experience involved, and according to whether individuals are seeking mutual recognition in the context of exercise of the right of establishment, or the freedom to provide services. The aim of the following treatment is to give some indication of the scheme of the PQ Directive, and of its central principles, rather than to offer a comprehensive handbook on its detailed provisions. The PQ Directive establishes rules according to which a Member State which makes access to a pursuit of a regulated profession[22] in its territory contingent upon possession of specific professional qualifications (referred to in the Directive as the host Member State), shall recognise professional qualifications obtained in another Member State (referred to as the home Member State), and which allow the holder of these qualifications to pursue the same profession there, for access to and pursuit of that profession.[23] The Directive applies to all nationals of a Member State wishing to pursue a regulated profession in a Member State, including those belonging to the liberal professions, *other than that in which they obtained their professional qualifications*, on either a self-employed or employed basis.[24] The recognition of

---

[21] [2005] OJ L255/22; see Eurlex consolidated text 27 April 2009.

[22] Art 3(a) of the PQ Directive defines 'regulated profession' as 'a professional activity or group of professional activities, access to which, the pursuit of which, or one of the modes of pursuit of which is subject, directly or indirectly, by virtue of legislative, regulatory or administrative provisions to the possession of specific professional qualifications; in particular, the use of a professional title limited by legislative, regulatory or administrative provisions to holders of a given professional qualification shall constitute a mode of pursuit.' Other professional activities are treated as regulated professions, see Art 3(2) of the PQ Directive.

[23] PQ Directive, Art 1.

[24] Art 2(1).

professional qualifications by the host Member State allows the person concerned to gain access in that Member State to the same profession as that for which he is qualified in the home Member State and to pursue it in the host Member State under the same conditions as its nationals.[25]

B – Freedom of Establishment: Recognition on the Basis of Co-ordination of Minimum Training Conditions—Chapter III of Title III of the PQ Directive

It has been noted above that Article 53(2) TFEU requires that, for certain professions, the abolition of restrictions shall be dependent upon co-ordination of the conditions for their exercise. Chapter III of Title III of the PQ Directive deals with those professional activities for which mutual recognition has proceeded on the basis of the co-ordination of minimum training conditions. The activities covered are those of doctor (with basic training and specialised), nurse (general care), midwife, dental practitioner (and specialised dental practitioner), veterinary surgeon, pharmacist and architect. Under the principle of automatic recognition laid down in the PQ Directive,[26] detailed rules are laid down which identify the qualifications awarded in Member States which other Member States are bound to recognise. Each Member State is obliged to make access to and pursuit of the professional activities of all those referred to above (except architects) subject to possession of evidence of the formal qualifications referred to, attesting that the person concerned has acquired, over the duration of his or her training, and where appropriate, the knowledge and skills which are spelled out in the Directive.[27] Without underestimating their significance, it must be said that the requirements laid down in the PQ Directive are of necessity spelled out in fairly general terms. Thus the specification for 'basic medical training' in Article 24 of the PQ Directive specifies a combination of minimum periods of study and practical training,[28] and requirements such as 'sufficient understanding of the structure, functions and behaviour of healthy and sick persons, as well as relations between the state of health and physical and social surroundings of the human being'.[29] Apart from the periods of training specified, requirements of the generality of the example above are close to non-justiciable, and it seems that co-ordination of minimum training conditions based on such requirements is based on an implicit assumption that the quality and intensity of medical training in the various Member States is and will remain essentially comparable. The present writer is not qualified to judge whether or not this is a realistic assumption.

C – Freedom of Establishment: Recognition of Professional Experience— Chapter II of Title III of the PQ Directive

Chapter II of Title III of the PQ Directive deals with situations where access to or pursuit

---

[25] Art 4(1).
[26] Art 21.
[27] Art 21(6).
[28] Art 24(2).
[29] Art 24(3)(b).

of one the activities listed in Annex IV of the Directive is in a Member State contingent upon possession of general commercial or professional knowledge and aptitudes. In such a case, the Member State shall recognise previous pursuit of the activity in another Member State as sufficient proof of such knowledge and aptitudes.[30] Chapter II deals with activities covered by a dozen or so earlier directives which provide for recognition of commercial or professional activity in other Member States. Chapter II groups the activities into three lists in Annex IV, the purpose of the groupings being to distinguish, as appropriate, the requisite period of experience, or combination of experience and training, required in each case, for self-employed activities in one Member State to qualify for recognition in another.

D – Freedom of Establishment: The General System—Chapter I of Title III of the PQ Directive

(i) Introduction

Chapter I of Title III applies to all professions which are not covered by Chapters II and III and to certain cases in which a person, for specific and exceptional reasons, does not satisfy the conditions laid down in those Chapters.[31] The component parts of the mechanism of the general system should be seen as a whole; taking any one part out of context can be misleading. Particular note must be taken of (a) the different levels of qualification; (b) the conditions for recognition; and (c) compensation measures.

(a) The Different Levels of Qualification

The different levels of qualification 'are established only for the purpose of the operation of the general system, have no effect upon the national education and training structures nor upon the competence of Member States'.[32] There are five levels of qualification identified in the PQ Directive, ranging from an attestation of competence (level (a)), to three- or four-year university or equivalent degrees, combined with the professional training which might be required in addition to those courses (levels (d) and (e)).[33]

(b) The Conditions for Recognition

As regards the conditions for recognition, the general principle is that if access to or pursuit of a regulated profession in a host Member State is contingent upon possession of specific professional qualifications, the competent authority of that Member State shall permit access to and pursuit of that profession, under the same conditions as apply to its nationals, to applicants possessing the attestation of competence or evidence of formal qualifications required by another Member State in order to gain access to and pursue that profession in its territory.[34] It must, however, be emphasised that that is the general principle, and that the general principle is applied in a way which takes account of differ-

---

[30] Art 16.
[31] Art 10.
[32] Preamble, recital (13).
[33] Art 11.
[34] Art 13(1), first sub-para.

ences in the duration and content of different qualifications in different Member States, and provides for adaptation periods and aptitude tests to compensate for such differences.

(c) Compensation Measures—Adaptation Period or Aptitude Test

In principle, compensation measures are an exception to a general principle of recognition, and must be construed and applied strictly, in accordance with the principle of proportionality. In practice, and in view of the diversity of national systems of qualification and training, compensation measures operate in conjunction with the general principle of recognition, to make what would otherwise be an unworkable principle in many, if not most cases, workable in practice.

The general principle of recognition referred to above does not preclude the host Member State from requiring, in certain circumstances, the person concerned to complete an adaptation period of up to three years or to take an aptitude test. It is appropriate to offer a brief explanation of these requirements. By 'adaptation period' is meant the pursuit of the regulated profession in the host Member State under the responsibility of a qualified member of that profession, such period of supervised practice possibly being accompanied by further training. The period of supervised practice shall be the subject of an assessment. The detailed rules governing the adaptation period and its assessment, as well as the status of the migrant under supervision, shall be laid down by the competent authority in the host Member State.[35] The 'aptitude test' referred to is a test limited to the professional knowledge of the person concerned, set by the competent authorities of the host Member State with the aim of assessing the ability of the person concerned to pursue a regulated profession in that Member State. In order to permit this test to be carried out, the competent authorities shall draw up a list of subjects which, on the basis of a comparison between the education and training required in the Member State and that received by the person concerned, are not covered by the evidence of formal qualifications possessed by the latter.[36]

The Member State is entitled to require the person concerned to complete an adaptation period, or to take an aptitude test, in three situations. The first is where the duration of the training of which he or she provides evidence is at least one year shorter than that required by the host Member State. The second is where the training received by the person concerned covers substantially different matters than those covered by the evidence of formal qualifications required in the host Member State. The third is where the regulated profession in the host Member State comprises one or more regulated professional activities which do not exist in the corresponding profession in the home Member State of the person concerned, and that difference consists in specific training which is required in the host Member State and which covers substantially different matters from those covered by the attestation of competence or evidence of formal qualifications of the person concerned.[37] The reference in the second and third cases just mentioned to 'substantially different matters' means matters of which knowledge is essential for pursuing the profession and with regard to which the training received by the migrant shows important differences in terms of duration or content from the training required by the host Member

---

[35] Art 3(1)(g).
[36] Art 3(1)(h).
[37] Art 14 (a)(b)(c).

State.[38] Furthermore, recourse by a Member State to the possibility of requiring the person concerned to complete an adaptation period or to take an aptitude test is to be applied with due regard to the principle of proportionality. In particular, if the host Member State intends to impose such a requirement, it must first ascertain whether the knowledge acquired by the person concerned in the course of his or her professional experience in a Member State or in a third country, is of a nature to cover, in full or in part, the 'substantial difference' already referred to.[39]

(ii) Extent of Migrant's Choice between an Adaptation Period and an Aptitude Test

If the host Member State makes use of the option to require an adaptation period or aptitude test, it must in principle offer the person concerned a choice between the two.[40] However, where a Member State considers, with respect to a given profession, that it is necessary to derogate from the requirement that it offer the person concerned a choice, it shall inform the other Member States and the Commission in advance and provide sufficient justification for the derogation.[41] If, after receiving all necessary information, the Commission considers that such derogation is inappropriate or that it is not in accordance with EU law, it shall, within three months, ask the Member State in question to refrain from taking the envisaged measure. In the absence of a response from the Commission within the above-mentioned deadline, the derogation may be applied.

Quite apart from the possibility of a Member State seeking to override the choice of the migrant on the above basis, Member States are entitled to stipulate either an adaptation period or an aptitude test, for professions 'whose pursuit requires precise knowledge of national law and in respect of which the provision of advice and/or assistance concerning national law is an essential and constant aspect of the professional activity'.[42]

(iii) Use of Professional Titles

If, in a Member State, the use of a professional title relating to one of the activities of the profession in question is regulated, nationals of the other Member States who are authorised to practise a regulated profession on the basis of Title III shall use the professional title of the host Member State, which corresponds to that profession in that Member State, and make use of any associated initials.[43]

E – Freedom to Provide Services: Pursuit of Activities under Home-Country title—Title II of the PQ Directive

(i) Principle of the Free Provision of Services

For services, Title II of the PQ Directive declares the principle that Member States shall

---

[38] Art 14(4).
[39] Art 14(5).
[40] Art 14(2), first sub-para.
[41] Art 14(2), second sub-para.
[42] Art 14(3), first sub-para.
[43] Art 52(1). For the position where a profession is regulated by an association or organisation within the meaning of Art 3(2) of the PQ Directive, see Art 52(2).

not restrict, for any reason relating to professional qualifications, the free provision of services in another Member State: (a) if the service provider is legally established in a Member State for the purpose of pursuing the same profession there (the Member State of establishment), and (b) where the service provider moves. As regards the movement of the service provider, the Directive draws a distinction between regulated professions and others. If the profession is not regulated in the Member State of establishment, the person concerned must have pursued that profession in that State for at least two years during the ten years preceding the provision of services; but this condition does not apply when either the profession or the education and training leading to the profession is regulated.[44] The provisions of Title II apply only where the service provider moves to the territory of the host Member State to pursue the profession in question, on a temporary and occasional basis, and the temporary and occasional nature of the provision of services shall be assessed case by case, in particular in relation to its duration, its frequency, its regularity and its continuity.[45] The latter formulation is clearly derived from the *Gebhard* case.[46] The preamble to the Directive notes that in view of 'the different systems established for the cross border provision of services on a temporary and occasional basis on the one hand, and for establishment on the other, the criteria for distinguishing between these two concepts in the event of the movement of the service provider to the territory of the host State should be clarified'.[47] Simple repetition of the wording in the *Gebhard* case does not, however, amount to such clarification. Moreover, it is to be noted that for a service provider to equip himself or herself with an office or consulting room is not incompatible with the temporary and occasional nature of service provision.[48] Where a service provider moves, he or she is subject to those rules applicable in the host Member State to professionals who pursue the same profession in that Member State, which are of a professional, statutory or administrative nature and which are directly linked to professional qualifications, such as the definition of the profession, the use of titles, and serious professional malpractice which is directly and specifically linked to consumer protection and safety, as well as disciplinary provisions.[49]

(ii) Exemptions

The host Member State shall exempt service providers established in another Member State from the requirements which it places on professionals established in its territory relating to authorisation by, registration with or membership of a professional organisation of body. However, in order to facilitate the application of disciplinary provisions in force on their territory, Member States may provide either for automatic temporary registration with or for pro forma membership of such a professional organisation or body, provided that such registration or membership does not delay or complicate in any way the provision of services and does not entail any additional costs for the service provider.[50] The host Member State shall also exempt service providers established in another Member State from the requirement it places on professionals established in its territory relating to

---

[44] Art 5(1)(b).
[45] Art 5(2).
[46] Case C-55/94 *Gebhard* [1995] ECR I-4165; see above, at p 533.
[47] Recital (5) of preamble of the PQ Directive.
[48] Above, at p 533.
[49] PQ Directive, Art 5(3).
[50] Art 6, first subpara (a).

registration with a public social security body for the purpose of settling accounts with an insurer relating to activities pursued for the benefit of insured persons.[51] This provision is particularly relevant for the provision of medical and social services. The service provider shall, however, inform in advance—or in an urgent case afterwards—a public social security body such as that referred to above.[52]

(iii) Services Provided under the Professional Title of the Member State of Establishment

The services under discussion shall be provided under the professional title of the Member State of establishment, in so far as such a title exists in that Member State for the professional activity in question. That title shall be indicated in the official language or one of the official languages of the Member State of establishment in such a way as to avoid any confusion with the professional title of the host Member State. Where no such professional title exists in the Member State of establishment, the service provider shall indicate his or her formal qualification in the official language or one of the official languages of that Member State. By way of exception, the service shall be provided under the professional title of the *host Member State* for cases referred to Chapter III of Title III—the logic of this is that the qualifications in question (doctors, nurses, dentists, etc) are considered to be equivalent in all the Member States because the conditions for award of such qualifications have been harmonised.[53]

(iv) Regulated Professions Having Public Health or Safety Implications

For the first provision of services, in the case of regulated professions having public health or safety implications, which do not benefit from automatic recognition under Chapter III of Title III, the competent authority of the host Member State may check the professional qualifications of the service provider prior to the first provision of services. Such a prior check shall be possible only where the purpose of the check is to avoid serious damage to the health or safety of the service recipient due to a lack of professional qualification of the service provider and where this does not go beyond what is necessary for that purpose.[54] Within a maximum of one month of receipt of a service provider's declaration of intention to provide services and accompanying documents, the competent authority shall endeavour to inform the service provider either of its decision not to check his or her qualifications or of the outcome of such check. Where there is a difficulty which would result in delay, the competent authority shall notify the service provider within the first month of the reason for the delay and the timescale for a decision, which must be finalised within the second month of receipt of completed documentation.[55]

Where there is a substantial difference between the professional qualifications of the service provider and the training required in the host Member State, to the extent that that difference is such as to be harmful to public health or safety, the host Member State shall give the service provider the opportunity to show, in particular by means of an aptitude test, that he or she has acquired the knowledge or competence lacking. In any case,

---

[51] Art 6, first subpara (b).
[52] Art 6, second sub-para.
[53] Art 7(3).
[54] Art 7(4), first subpara.
[55] Art 7(4), second subpara.

it must be possible to provide the service within one month of a decision being taken in accordance with the timescale referred to above.[56] In the absence of a reaction of the competent authority within the deadlines referred to above, the service may be provided.[57]

It is to be noted that where qualifications have been verified under the requirements referred to above, the service shall be provided under the professional title of the host Member State.[58]

F – Right of Establishment under 'Home-country' Professional Title?

The rights of individuals under the PQ Directive, as regards establishment on the one hand, and service provision on the other, are in some cases similar, and in others markedly dissimilar. As regards a doctor or nurse qualified within the meaning of Chapter III of Title III, the main difference as regards service provision and establishment would be that in the former case the person concerned would be exempt from authorisation by or registration with or membership of a professional organisation or body, and from registration with any relevant public social security body, but would be subject to obligations as regards relevant declaratory, documentary and information requirements; in the latter case (establishment) the same conditions as apply to nationals would apply to the person concerned. In either case the activities would be carried out under the professional title of the host Member State.

In the case of a person engaged in a regulated profession having public health or safety implications, the person concerned would be subject to the exemptions and requirements just referred to in the case of service provision, but his or her qualifications would be subject to verification, including an aptitude test if there were a substantial difference between his or her professional qualifications and the training required in the host Member State. If such a person were to exercise the right of establishment, the substantial difference referred to would enable the host Member State to require the migrant to undertake an aptitude test or adaptation period, with the migrant having the right to choose, unless grounds existed to derogate from the requirement of choice. In the case of service provision or establishment, the activities would be carried out under the professional title of the host Member State.

There are a number of cases, however, where the PQ Directive implies that a person carrying on a professional activity in one Member State who wishes to extend those activities to another Member State will be able to do so under the professional title of the Member State of establishment by way of provision of services, but will have to undertake an aptitude test or adaptation period in order to exercise the right of establishment, and thereby to carry on their activities under the professional title of the host Member State. This would appear to be the case for a person whose training in his or her home Member State is shorter, or substantially different, from that of the intended host Member State. A point that the Directive does not directly address is whether an individual who is entitled under Title II of the PQ Directive to carry on professional activities under the professional title of the Member State of establishment by way of provision of services can operate *on a permanent basis* in the host Member State, and become established there, under the

---

[56] Art 7(4), third subpara.
[57] Art 7(4), fourth subpara.
[58] Art 7(4), fifth subpara.

professional title of the Member State of original and perhaps continuing establishment, complying only with relevant non-discriminatory rules regarding registration with professional bodies, etc, and relying not on the Directive, but directly on Article 49 TFEU. It would seem that the answer is in principle in the affirmative. The PQ Directive does not guarantee such a right, but nor does it, nor could it, exclude it. It has already been noted that to insist on a qualification for a particular activity is in principle a restriction on the right of establishment, which has to be justified by imperative requirements in the general interest.[59] It is difficult to see how a Member State could justify restricting the permanent exercise of professional activities under the professional title of another Member State by a person entitled to provide the services in question under that same professional title on a temporary and occasional basis. Transition from service provision to establishment might in any event be gradual and difficult to determine with certainty, particularly if professional activities are carried on from an office or consulting room, which, as noted above, is in itself compatible with both service provision and establishment. It may be difficult in many cases to determine whether a person established in one Member State and engaged in professional activities under home title in another Member State, is doing so on a temporary or occasional basis, or has become established in the second Member State as well as the first. This should not necessarily cause difficulty; the main consequence of becoming established is likely to be a duty to register with relevant professional bodies. Whether established or providing services, the person concerned will be subject to at least certain rules of professional conduct of both the home Member State and host Member State.

G – Other Specific Arrangements for a Given Regulated Profession

Other specific arrangements directly related to the recognition of professional qualifications may apply instead of the arrangements in the PQ Directive.[60] In particular, the Directive does not affect the operation of Council Directive 77/249/EEC to facilitate the effective exercise by lawyers of freedom to provide services (hereafter the Lawyers' Services Directive),[61] or of Directive 98/5/EC of the European Parliament and of the Council to facilitate practice of the profession of lawyer on a permanent basis in a Member State other than that in which the qualification was obtained (hereafter the Lawyers' Establishment Directive).[62] As indicated below, these Directives provide in each case for practice under home-country professional title,[63] and in the case of the latter Directive, it is provided that practice under home-country professional title may amount to an adaptation period for the purposes of acquiring the qualification of the host Member State. However, the recognition of professional qualifications for lawyers for the purpose of immediate estab-

---

[59] Above, at p 628.

[60] Art 2(3), recital (42) of preamble.

[61] [1977] OJ L78/17; Eurlex consolidated text 1 January 2007.

[62] [1998] OJ L77/36; Eurlex consolidated text 1 January 2007.

[63] The Lawyers Establishment Directive defines 'home-country professional title' as 'the professional title used in the Member State in which a lawyer acquired the right to use that title before practising the profession of lawyer in the host Member' (Art 1(2)(d)). The Lawyers Services Directive requires a lawyer providing cross-border services to 'adopt the professional title used in the Member State from which he comes' (Art 3). AG R-J Colomer rightly describes this latter formulation as requiring practice under home-country professional title, in Case C-168/98 *Commission v Luxembourg* [2000] ECR I-9131, Opinion at para 3.

lishment under the professional title of the host Member State is covered by the PQ Directive.

III – LAWYERS: FREEDOM TO PROVIDE SERVICES

Under the Lawyers' Services Directive, Member States must recognise designated legal practitioners as 'lawyers' for the purpose of pursuing 'the activities of lawyers pursued by way of provision of services'.[64] Since the substantive content of legal training differs in the Member States, and the Directive contains no provisions for the mutual recognition of diplomas, a designated legal practitioner must adopt the professional title used in the Member State from which he or she comes, expressed in the language of that Member State, and with an indication of the professional organisation by which he or she is authorised to practise.[65] Member States may reserve to prescribed categories of lawyers the preparation of formal documents for obtaining title to administer estates of deceased persons, and the drafting of formal documents creating or transferring interests in land.[66]

Activities relating to the representation of a client in legal proceedings or before public authorities shall be pursued in each host Member State under the conditions laid down for lawyers established in that Member State, with the exception of any conditions requiring residence, or registration with a professional organisation, in that Member State.[67] A lawyer pursuing these activities shall observe the rules of professional conduct of the host Member State, without prejudice to his or her obligations in the Member State from which he or she comes.[68] For the pursuit of these activities a Member State may require the lawyers to which the Directive applies (a) to be introduced, in accordance with local rules or customs, to the presiding judge and, where appropriate, to the President of the relevant Bar in the host Member State; and (b) to 'work in conjunction with' a lawyer who practises before the judicial authority in question and who would, where necessary, be answerable to that authority, or with an *avoué* or *procuratore*[69] practising before it.[70] The Court has held that the purpose of the requirement that a lawyer providing services 'work in conjunction with' a local lawyer is intended to provide him or her with the support necessary to enable him or her to act within a judicial system different from that to which he or she is accustomed and to assure the judicial authority concerned that the lawyer providing services actually has that support and is thus in a position fully to comply with the procedural and ethical rules that apply.[71] But national implementing measures must not lay down disproportionate requirements in this regard, such as a requirement that a local lawyer be present throughout the oral proceedings, or a requirement that the

---

[64] Art 1(2), 2.
[65] Final recital to preamble, and Art 3.
[66] Art 1(1), second sub-para.
[67] Art 4(1).
[68] Art 4(2).
[69] No longer relevant; this profession was abolished in 1997; see Case C-313/01 *Morgenbesser* [2003] ECR I-13467, para 9.
[70] Art 5.
[71] Case 427/85 *Commission v Germany* [1988] ECR 1123, para 23.

local lawyer be the authorised representative or defending counsel.[72] The German government sought to justify such requirements on the not implausible ground that a foreign lawyer practising under home title might not be familiar with German law. The Court's response was that any problem of possibly inadequate knowledge of German law forms part of the responsibility of the lawyer providing services vis-à-vis his client, who is free to entrust his interests to a lawyer of his choice.[73] The Court held in *AMOK* that national rules which preclude a successful litigant from recovering the costs of the local lawyer in addition to that of the foreign lawyer are incompatible with Article 56 TFEU, since such a rule 'is liable to make the transfrontier provision by a lawyer of his services less attractive. Such a solution may have a deterrent effect capable of affecting the competitiveness of lawyers in other Member States.'[74]

A lawyer pursuing activities other than those relating to the representation of a client in legal proceedings shall remain subject to the conditions and rules of professional conduct of the Member State from which he or she comes without prejudice to respect for the rules, whatever their source, which govern the profession in the host Member State, especially those concerning the incompatibility of the exercise of the activities of a lawyer with the exercise of other activities in that Member State, professional secrecy, relations with other lawyers, the prohibition on the same lawyer acting for parties with mutually conflict interests, and publicity.[75] The latter rules are applicable only if they are capable of being observed by a lawyer who is not established in the host Member State and to the extent to which their observance is objectively justified to ensure, in that Member State, the proper exercise of a lawyer's activities, the standing of the profession and respect for the rules concerning incompatibility.[76]

IV – LAWYERS: RIGHT OF ESTABLISHMENT

Perhaps the most interesting directive adopted under Article 53 TFEU, in terms of the techniques which it uses to remove obstacles to freedom of movement of those engaged in a profession, and to secure 'integration into the profession of lawyer in the host Member State', is the Lawyers' Establishment Directive.[77] The Directive provides two options for lawyers: the first is permanent practice under home title; the second is acquisition of the professional title of the host Member State after a period of practice under home title, which serves as an adaptation period for the purposes of securing qualification in the latter State. The Directive applies to both the self-employed and employed activities of lawyers.[78]

The Directive lists lawyers qualified under the laws of the Member States, and provides that any such lawyer shall be entitled to pursue on a permanent basis, in any other Member State under his home-country professional title, the activities specified in the

---

[72] Ibid, para 26, and see Case C-294/89 *Commission v France* [1991] ECR I-3591.
[73] Case C-427/85 *Commission v Germany* [1988] ECR 1123, para 27.
[74] Case C-289/02 *AMOK* [2003] ECR I-15059, para 36.
[75] Art 4(4).
[76] Art 4(4).
[77] [1998] OJ L77/36; Eurlex consolidated text 1 January 2007.
[78] Art 1(1).

Directive.[79] These activities are described as the same professional activities as a lawyer practising under the relevant professional title used in the host Member State and may, inter alia, give advice on the law of his home Member State, on EU law, on international law and on the law of the host Member State.[80] There are two exceptions or qualifications to the foregoing. The first applies where a Member State authorises in its territory a prescribed category of lawyers to prepare deeds for obtaining title to administer estates of deceased persons and for creating or transferring interests in land which, in other Member States are reserved for professions other than that of lawyer. In such a case the Member State may exclude from such activities lawyers practising under a home-country professional title conferred in one of the latter Member States.[81] The second qualification to the right to practise under home-country title applies to the pursuit of activities relating to the representation or defence of a client in legal proceedings where the law of the host Member State reserves such activities to lawyers practising under the professional title of that Member State. In such circumstances the host Member State may require lawyers practising under their home-country professional title to work in conjunction with a lawyer who practises before the judicial authority in question and who would, where necessary, be answerable to that authority or with an *avoué* practising before it. It will be noted that the latter safeguards are the same as those applicable under the Lawyers' Services Directive.

A lawyer who wishes to practise on a permanent basis in a Member State other than that in which he or she obtained his or her professional qualification shall register with the competent authority in that Member State.[82] The latter authority shall register the lawyer upon presentation of a certificate attesting to his or her registration with the competent authority in the home Member State. It may require that, when presented by the competent authority of the home Member State, the certificate be not more than three months old. It shall inform the competent authority in the home Member State of the registration.[83] Irrespective of the rules of professional conduct to which he or she is subject in his or her home Member State, a lawyer practising under his home-country professional title shall be subject to the same rules of professional conduct as lawyers practising under the relevant professional title of the host Member State in respect of all the activities he or she pursues in its territory.[84] The host Member State may require such a lawyer either to take out professional indemnity insurance or to become a member of a professional guarantee fund in accordance with the rules which that Member State lays down for professional activities pursued in its territory, unless he or she already has equivalent cover in accordance with the rules of the home Member State.[85] In the event of failure by a lawyer practising under his or her home-country professional title to fulfil the obligations in force in the host Member State, the rules of procedure, penalties and remedies provided for in the host Member State shall apply.[86]

Integration into the profession of lawyer in the host Member State is achieved, inter

[79] Arts 1(2), 2.
[80] Art 5(1).
[81] Art 5(2).
[82] Arts 1 and 3(1).
[83] Art 3(2).
[84] Art 6(1).
[85] Art 6(3).
[86] Art 7(1).

alia, as follows. A lawyer practising under his or her home-country professional title who has

> effectively and regularly pursued for at least three years an activity in the host Member State in the law of that State including Community law shall, with a view to gaining admission to the profession of lawyer in the host Member State, be exempted from the conditions set out [in Article 14(1) of the PQ Directive].[87]

The conditions referred to are those relating to the requirement of an adaptation period or aptitude test, as explained above, in the context of discussion of the PQ Directive. It is for the lawyer concerned to furnish the competent authority in the host Member State with proof of effective regular pursuit for a period of at least three years of an activity in the law of the host Member State.[88]

It is at first sight curious that a lawyer qualified in, say, Germany, and working with a law firm in Berlin, could transfer to that firm's London office, spend three years there working on mergers and acquisitions, or, for that matter, UK and EU competition law, and emerge as a solicitor, fully qualified to draw up a will or defend a client in criminal proceedings before a magistrates' court. It certainly must be doubted whether three years of specialised legal practice of the kinds referred to could provide overall knowledge and understanding of the laws and legal system of England and Wales. Related but slightly different misgivings were expressed by Luxembourg in a vigorously argued challenge to the validity of Directive 98/5/EC. The Court of Justice considered these arguments in *Luxembourg v Parliament and Council*.[89] It is to be noted that Spain, the Netherlands and the United Kingdom intervened in support of the Parliament and Council, as, predictably, did the Commission. Luxembourg's main concern was that the Directive allowed migrant lawyers to set up permanent practice under home title despite lack of knowledge of host Memnber State law—a situation that failed to protect the interests of consumers and the proper administration of justice. However, the Court held that consumer protection and the administration of justice were adequately protected by various provisions of the Directive. The Court emphasised that a lawyer practising under his or her home-country professional title is required to do so under that title, so that consumers are informed that the professional to whom they entrust the defence of their interests has not obtained his or her qualification in the host Member State and that his or her initial training did not necessarily cover the host Member State's national law.[90] The Court also referred to the possibility of the host Member State requiring (a) that certain activities be reserved to host Member State lawyers, and/or (b) that the migrant 'work in conjunction' with an appropriately qualified host Member State lawyer when representing a client in legal proceedings.[91] The Court added, inter alia, that the Directive makes a lawyer practising under home title subject not only to the rules of professional conduct applicable in his home Member State, but also to the same rules of professional conduct as lawyers practising under host Member State title,[92] and that the host Member State was entitled

---

[87] Art 10, first subpara. Art 10 refers to Art 4(1)(b) of Directive 89/48. Art 62(1) of the PQ Directive repeals Directive 89/48 with effect from 20 October 2007, and provides that references to Directives repealed by Art 62 shall be understood as references to the PQ Directive.

[88] Art 10, second subpara.

[89] Case C-168/98 *Luxembourg v European Parliament & Council* [2000] ECR I-9131.

[90] Ibid, para 34.

[91] Ibid, para 35.

[92] Ibid, para 36.

to require appropriate professional indemnity cover.[93] The final point made by the Court related to rules of professional conduct. Those rules applicable to lawyers generally entail, observed the Court,

> like Article 3.1.3 of the Code of Professional Conduct adopted by the Council of the Bars and Law Societies of the European Union (CCBE), an obligation, breach of which may incur disciplinary sanctions, not to handle matters which the professionals concerned know or ought to know they are not competent to handle.

The Court concluded that the arguments of Luxembourg as regards consumer protection and the administration of justice should be rejected.

However, this ruling did not, it seems, adequately reassure the Luxembourg authorities. In 2003, the Commission received a complaint concerning the existence of obstacles to European lawyers practising the profession of lawyer on a permanent basis under their home-country professional titles in Luxembourg. The obstacles complained of arose from Luxembourg rules (a) making the registration of such European lawyers on the register of one of the Bar Associations in Luxembourg subject to a language test, (b) making the maintenance of that registration subject to the production each year of a certificate of registration with the competent authority of the home Member State, and (c) prohibiting such European lawyers from being persons authorised to accept service on behalf of companies in Luxembourg. These rules were the subject of infraction proceedings by the Commission, and the requirement of a language test was the subject of a challenge before the Luxembourg courts by an English barrister, one Graham Wilson, which led to a reference to the Court of Justice. In the *Wilson* case[94] the Court held that a Member State was not entitled to make it a prior condition of exercising the right of establishment under home-country title that the person concerned pass a test of proficiency in the languages of that Member State (in casu French, German and Luxembourgish). The Court emphasised, as regards court work, the duty of the foreign lawyer to work in conjunction with a lawyer practising before the judicial authority in question.[95] The Court also refers to the requirement of the Directive to comply with home and host state rules of professional conduct, one of which is an obligation, says the Court, not to handle matters that the professionals concerned know or ought to know they are not competent to handle, for instance owing to lack of linguistic knowledge. In this regard, communication with clients, the administrative authorities and the professional bodies of the host Member State, like compliance with the rules of professional conduct laid down by the authorities of that Member State, requires a European lawyer to have sufficient linguistic knowledge, or recourse to assistance where that knowledge is insufficient.[96] The Court also points out that one of the objectives of the Lawyers' Establishment Directive is to meet the needs of consumers of legal services doing business across national borders, for whom international law, EU law and domestic laws overlap. The Court observed that:

> Such international cases, like those to which the law of a Member State other than the host Member State is applicable, may not require a degree of knowledge of the languages of the latter

---

[93] Ibid, para 37.
[94] Case C-506/04 *Wilson* [2006] ECR I-8613.
[95] Ibid, para 73.
[96] Ibid, para 74.

Member State as high as that required to deal with matters in which the law of that Member State is applicable.[97]

The Court concluded that the linguistic requirement imposed by the Luxembourg rules was incompatible with the requirements of the Directive.[98] In the infraction proceedings initiated by the Commission the other features of the Luxembourg rules referred to above as being the subject matter of a complaint to the Commission were also held to be incompatible with the Directive.[99]

The Lawyers' Establishment Directive is certainly a significant initiative in promoting freedom of movement both for self-employed and salaried lawyers, and a possible model for transition from service provision to establishment for other professional activities. The difficulties which it appears to pose, both as regards practice under home-country title, and as regards acquisition of host Member State title after three years' practice under home title, probably loom rather larger in theory than in practice. The hypothetical example of the German lawyer practising in mergers and acquisitions, and then emerging to draft a will or defend a client in criminal proceedings, is more rhetorical than realistic. Those engaging in specialised legal practice, whatever their original qualifications and training, become speedily unfit for unprepared forays into other specialist fields, including those of the high street solicitors' practice. Furthermore, the discipline imposed by professional bodies, the need to secure insurance, and the imperatives of the market place, are, as the Court of Justice implies, not to be underestimated. In many, if not most, cases, a lawyer qualified in one Member State wishing to join a legal practice in another Member State, in which the laws differ substantially from that of the first, will find it essential to prepare for and to take an aptitude test in host Member State law; the legal practice or law firm he or she wishes to join will simply insist on that for obvious reasons. In other cases, to return to our hypothetical German lawyer with a flair for mergers and acquisitions, the adaptation period of practice under home title under the Lawyers' Establishment Directive can provide for convenient and appropriate transition to the acquisition of a second legal qualification; not least for those whose practice is in fields of law containing a substantial element of EU law.

V – CONCLUDING REMARKS

In the *Gebhard* case the Court stated that where national rules in one Member State require qualifications for the pursuit of a particular activity, a national of another Member State wishing to carry on that activity must in principle comply with those rules.[100] However, the present chapter has demonstrated that EU law recognises more than one means by which that principle may be satisfied. Harmonisation of the contents of qualifications at EU level is the solution adopted for doctors and dentists, and a handful of other professions, and the result is a deemed equality of status for such qualifications irrespective of the Member State of award. For most professional activities which require qualifications,

---

[97] Ibid, para 75.
[98] Ibid, para 77.
[99] Case C-193/05 *Commission v Luxembourg* [2006] ECR I-8673.
[100] Case 55/94 *Gebhard* [1995] ECR I-4165, paras 35 and 36.

a Member State is entitled to stipulate that those with qualifications gained in another Member State must in fact possess knowledge and skills equivalent to those which it stipulates for its own nationals. But it must provide a procedural framework in which it is possible for individuals to demonstrate the extent of the knowledge and skills which they have acquired in other Member States, and this evidence must be taken into account in assessing their fitness to carry on the activity in question. In the case of professions covered by the 'general system' of the Professional Qualifications Directive, the mechanics of measuring equivalence, and the permitted means for rectifying deficiencies in qualifications on the part of skilled persons and professionals from other Member States, are specified in some detail. All the foregoing is in accordance with the spirit of the *Gebhard* proposition that if national rules require that pursuit of a particular activity requires qualifications of one kind or another, then a national of another Member State is bound in principle to comply with that requirement. Not all the possibilities afforded by EU law for cross-border pursuit of commercial activities requiring qualifications can, however, be explained by reference to that proposition. In particular, the possibility of carrying on cross-border activities, either by way of establishment or provision of services, on the basis of home-country professional title, side-steps the issue of equivalence, and for consumer protection purposes places its trust in a combination of qualification to carry on the activity in question in a Member State other than the host Member State, and full disclosure of that fact to consumers. This alternative approach in effect allows consumers in one Member State to 'shop abroad' for certain services provided by qualified professionals, while remaining in their own Member State. This might not be an approach for all types of service in all situations, but it may well be an option which will be welcomed by some service providers and some customers in at least some situations—for example specialist lawyers providing services in two or more Member States, and a whole range of professionals with a client base on both sides of a national frontier.

Further Reading

RG Lee, 'Liberalisation of Legal Services in Europe: Progress and Prospects' (2010) 30 *Legal Studies* 186.

J Lonbay, 'Assessing the European Market for Legal Services: Development in the Free Movement of Lawyers in the European Union' (2010) 33 *Fordham International Law Journal* 2629 (free download from SSRN http://papers.ssrn.com/sol3/papers.cfm?abstract_id=1712495##)

20

Corporate Establishment, Cross-border Acquisitions and Golden Shares

This chapter considers two distinct but related topics. The first is the application of the Treaty provisions on establishment to legal persons—companies and firms—and the significance of the case law of the Court of Justice on the interpretation of the relevant Treaty provisions. The right of establishment includes the right of undertakings to incorporate in a Member State of choice, and to engage in mergers and acquisitions across national frontiers. This leads into the second topic: cross-border acquisitions. Holding or acquiring shares in a company across national frontiers can involve exercise both of the right of establishment and the right of capital movement where the shareholding gives the investor definite influence over the company's decisions and allows the investor to determine its activities; where the cross-frontier investment does not give to the investor such influence it is known as 'portfolio' investment and falls solely within the scope of the Treaty provisions on capital movement. It is the former aspect which is addressed in particular in this chapter and there is discussion of the compatibility with EU law of 'special' or golden' shares which grant national authorities powers of intervention in the decision-making of corporate bodies—often formerly state-owned and recently privatised companies providing services in fields such as energy or transport. A further issue for consideration in the context of cross-border acquisitions is whether action taken by shareholders or directors under the corporate constitution can ever amount to restrictions on capital movement or freedom of establishment in the absence of state intervention.

I – CORPORATE ESTABLISHMENT

A – General

The right of establishment is enjoyed by companies and firms, as well as by natural persons. Article 54 TFEU, first paragraph, provides:

Companies or firms formed in accordance with the law of a Member State and having their registered office, central administration or principal place of business within the Community shall, for the purposes of this Chapter, be treated in the same way as natural persons who are nationals of Member States.

Article 54 TFEU further provides that:

'Companies or firms' means companies or firms constituted under civil or commercial law, including co-operative societies, and other legal persons governed by public or private law, save for those which are non-profit making.

A company formed in accordance with the law of a Member State is entitled to exercise the right of establishment if it has its registered office, its central administration, or its principal place of business within the Community.

The Court has said that the 'immediate consequence' of Article 54 TFEU is that 'those companies are entitled to carry on their business in another Member State through an agency, branch of subsidiary', and that the location of their registered office, central administration or principal place of business 'serves as the connecting factor with the legal system of a particular State in the same way as does nationality in the case of a natural person'.[1]

The Court has also held that Articles 49 and 54 TFEU confer a 'right of exit' on corporate bodies:

Even though those provisions are directed mainly to ensuring that foreign nationals and companies are treated in the host Member State in the same way as nationals of that State, they also prohibit the Member State of origin from hindering the establishment in another Member State of one of its nationals or of a company incorporated under its legislation which comes within the definition contained in [Article 54 TFEU].[2]

As the Court has observed:

In the case of a company, the right of establishment is generally exercised by the setting up of agencies, branches or subsidiaries, as is expressly provided for in the second sentence of the first paragraph of [Article 49 TFEU].[3]

An undertaking of one Member State which maintains a permanent presence in another comes within the scope of the provisions of the Treaty on the right of establishment, even if that presence does not take the form of a branch or agency, but consists merely of an office managed by the undertaking's own staff or by a person who is independent but authorised to act on a permanent basis for the undertaking, as would be the case with an agency.[4]

The Court has held that to allow a Member State in which a company carried on its business to treat that company in a different manner solely because its registered office was in another Member State would deprive Articles 49 and 54 TFEU of all meaning.[5]

---

[1] Case C-212/97 *Centros* [1999] ECR I-1459, para 20, citing Case 79/85 *Segers* [1986] ECR 2375, para 13; Case 270/83 *Commission v France* [1986] ECR 273, para 18; Case C-330/91 *Commerzbank* [1993] ECR I-4017, para 13; Case C-264/96 *ICI* ECR I-4695, para 20; Case C-167/01 *Inspire Art* [2003] ECR I-10155, para 97.

[2] Case 81/87 *Daily Mail* [1988] ECR 5483, para 16.

[3] Ibid, para 17.

[4] Case 205/84 *Commission v Germany* [1986] CCR 3755, para 21.

[5] Case 79/85 *Segers* [1986] ECR 2375, para 14, citing Case 270/83 *Commission v France* [1986] ECR 273, para 18 (referring to Art 54 TFEU); Case C-446/03 *Marks & Spencer* [2005] ECR I-10837, para 37 (referring to Art 49 TFEU).

Furthermore, discriminatory tax treatment as between companies of the host Member State and branches of companies registered in other Member States is contrary to Article 49 TFEU, and such discrimination cannot be justified on the ground that companies registered in other Member States are at liberty to establish themselves by setting up a subsidiary in order to have the benefit of the tax treatment in question.[6] As the Court has explained:

> The second sentence of the first paragraph of [Article 49 TFEU] expressly leaves traders free to choose the appropriate legal form in which to pursue their activities in another Member State and that freedom of choice must not be limited by discriminatory tax provisions.[7]

The *Sodemare* case indicates that even non-discriminatory restrictions on the legal form in which a company incorporated in another Member State may carry on business in the host Member State will require justification if they are to be compatible with Article 49 TFEU.[8]

B – Right of Primary and Secondary Establishment of Companies

Article 49 TFEU draws a distinction between setting up a primary establishment in another Member State, and setting up a secondary establishment, in the form of a branch or a subsidiary. In the former case the only qualifying characteristic is the nationality of a Member State, while in the latter there must be an existing establishment in one of the Member States.[9] The General Programme construed this qualification as requiring, in the case of companies having only the seat prescribed by their statutes in the Community, a 'real and continuous link with the economy of a Member State'.[10]

In *Segers*[11] the Court of Justice regarded a company registered in one Member State and undertaking *all* its business through a subsidiary in another Member State as entitled to exercise its right of establishment in the second Member State. Thus registration of a company in a Member State of itself amounts to establishment in that Member State, even if the company does no business in that Member State, and all its shareholders are nationals of the Member State in which it transacts all its business through an agency branch or subsidiary (for such was the position in *Segers*).

In *Centros*[12] the Court considered a situation in which Danish nationals resident in Denmark and carrying on business in Denmark set up a limited liability company in England whose only business activities would be carried out by a branch in Denmark. The share capital of the English company was £100, and the sole reason the Danish nationals set up a company in the United Kingdom rather than Denmark was to secure the advantages of limited liability without having to meet the cost of the £20,000 minimum capital

---

[6] Case 270/83 *Commission v France* [1986] ECR 273; and see Case C-307/97 *Saint-gobain,* [1999] ECR I-6161.

[7] Case 270/83 *Commission v France* [1986] ECR 273, para 22; Case C-337/08 *X Holding* (CJEU 25 February 2010) para 39.

[8] Case C-70/95 *Sodemare* [1997] ECR I-3395; and see Case C64/08 *Engelmann* (CJEU 9 September 2010), paras 28–31.

[9] The second sentence of Art 49 TFEU refers to the setting up of agencies, branches or subsidiaries by nationals of any Member State *established* in any Member State (emphasis added).

[10] Title I, [1974] OJ Sp Edn, Second Series, IX, 7.

[11] Case 79/85 *Segers* [1986] ECR 2375.

[12] Case C-212/97 *Centros* [1999] ECR I-1458. See also C-167/01 *Inspire Art* [2003] ECR I-10155.

requirement then prevailing in Denmark. When the Danish nationals sought to register the Danish branch of the company, the Danish authorities refused to do so, since that branch would be the principal establishment of the English company, which would do no business in the United Kingdom, and since the sole purpose of setting up the English company was the avoidance of Danish minimum capital requirements. The Danish authorities regarded the situation as in reality being internal to Denmark, but made it clear that they would have registered the branch if the company had also been carrying on business in the United Kingdom.

The Court of Justice referred to *Segers*, confirming that a company formed in one Member State, for the sole purpose of establishing itself in another, where its main or even sole business activities were to be carried on, could rely on the right of establishment, and added that the fact that the company was set up by nationals of the latter Member State resident in that Member State for the sole purpose of avoiding the minimum capital requirements of that Member State was immaterial.[13] The Court's judgment is most worthy of remark for its strong endorsement of the rights of individuals to choose the least restrictive corporate form of those available in the Member States as the vehicle of their entrepreneurial ambitions. The Court stated:

> The provisions of the Treaty on freedom of establishment are intended specifically to enable companies formed in accordance with the law of a Member State and having their registered office, central administration or principal place of business within the Community to pursue activities in other Member States through an agency, branch or subsidiary.
>
> That being so, the fact that a national of a Member State who wishes to set up a company chooses to form it in the Member State whose rules of company law seem to him the least restrictive and to set up branches in other Member States cannot, in itself, constitute an abuse of the right of establishment. The right to form a company in accordance with the law of a Member State and to set up branches in other Member States is inherent in the exercise, in a single market, of the freedom of establishment guaranteed by the Treaty.[14]

The Court held that the refusal in such circumstances of the national authorities in which the branch was to be formed to register that branch amounted to an infringement of the right of establishment, which could not be justified by mandatory requirements in the public interest, or on the ground of improper circumvention of national rules.[15] The Danish authorities argued that refusing to register the branch was the least restrictive means available of reinforcing the financial soundness of companies so as to protect the interests of public and private creditors, and in particular public creditors, who, unlike private creditors, were not in a position to secure their debts by obtaining personal guarantees from the directors of debtor companies.[16] The Court did not deny that interests such as those referred to might in principle justify measures such as those in issue, but rejected the argument on the ground that it was possible to adopt measures which were less restrictive, or which interfered less with fundamental freedoms, by, for example, making it possible in law for public creditors to obtain the necessary guarantees.[17]

It seemed initially that enjoyment in practice of the right of establishment endorsed by the Court in *Centros* might be subject to limitation vis-à-vis those Member States which

---

[13] Ibid, paras 17 and 18.
[14] Ibid, paras 26 and 27.
[15] As to the argument alleging improper circumvention of national rules, see Chapter 17, at p 567.
[16] Ibid, para 32.
[17] Ibid, para 37.

do not recognise that a company may be validly incorporated in a Member State other than that of its company headquarters or central administration. While the *Centros* case nominally involved a 'branch' of the company in question, that 'branch' comprised its sole place of business and its central administration.

A change of primary establishment involving a transfer of company headquarters or central management may be hindered by national legal provisions to the effect: (a) that a company transferring its central administration out of the jurisdiction loses its corporate personality; or (b) that a company incorporated elsewhere wishing to establish its central administration within the jurisdiction must be newly constituted there. This principle is described as the 'real seat' doctrine.[18] On the view taken in Germany the 'real seat' would be located in the place 'where the fundamental governance decisions are effectively transferred into ongoing managerial acts'.[19] A Member State applying the 'real seat' doctrine would be likely to refuse to recognise the legal personality of a company incorporated in a Member State other than that in which its actual central administration was located.

It had always been arguable that to deny recognition to a company satisfying the requirements of the first paragraph of Article 54 TFEU amounts to a denial of that company's right of establishment.[20] However, in *Daily Mail* the Court held that the differences in national legislation concerning the required connecting factor between a company and the Member State under which it is incorporated, and the question whether—and if so how—the registered office or real head office of a company incorporated under national law may be transferred from one Member State to another, were problems which were not resolved by the Treaty rules concerning the right of establishment, but were to be dealt with by future legislation or conventions.[21] It seemed to follow that Articles 49 and 54 TFEU could not be interpreted as conferring on companies incorporated under the law of a Member State a right to transfer their central management and control and their central administration to another Member State while retaining their status as companies incorporated under the legislation of the first Member State.[22] Did the *Daily Mail* ruling imply that the corporate establishment rights upheld by the Court in *Centros* could be resisted if asserted against a host Member State subscribing to the 'real seat' doctrine?

The Court gave a negative response to this question in *Überseering*.[23] In this case the Court considered a situation in which a company incorporated under Netherlands law, Überseering BV, acquired land in Düsseldorf, engaged NCC to undertake work on the site, then subsequently sued NCC in Düsseldorf for breach of contract in relation to that work. Prior to initiation of the legal proceedings in question, German nationals residing in Düsseldorf had acquired all the shares in Überseering BV. The central administration of the company thus became established in Germany. Under German law a company could

---

[18] See R Drury, 'Migrating Companies' (1999) 24 *ELRev* 354; for a discussion of 'incorporation theory jurisdictions' and 'real seat jurisdictions' see E Wymeersch, 'The Transfer of the Company's Seat in European Company Law' (2003) 40 *CMLRev* 661, 666–73.

[19] K Baelz and T Baldwin, 'The End of the Real Seat Theorie (Sitztheorie): The European Court of Justice Decision in Ueberseering of 5 November 2002 and its Impact on German and European Company Law' (2002) 3 *German Law Journal*, available at http://www.germanlawjournal.com/index.php?pageID=11&artID=214, para 5.

[20] U Everling, *The Right of Establishment in the Common Market* (CCH, Chicago, 1964) 71.

[21] *Daily Mail* [1988] ECR 5483, para 23.

[22] Ibid, para 24. Tridimas argued with foresight that the *Daily Mail* limitation on the scope of Art 49 TFEU only applied to restrictions imposed by the Member State of origin on the right of establishment and did not authorise a Member State of destination to refuse to recognise a transfer of primary establishment by a company authorised so to do by rules of the Member State of origin: 'Case Law on Corporate Entities' (1993) 13 *YEL* 335.

[23] Case C-208/00 *Überseering)* [2002] ECR I-9919.

only be recognised if it was incorporated under the law applicable in the place where its actual central administration was located. The Bundesgerichtschof considered whether, in view of the *Centros* case, the Treaty provisions on freedom of establishment precluded application of the German 'real seat' doctrine when the consequence would be to refuse to recognise the legal capacity of a company validly incorporated in another Member State and to deny its capacity to bring legal proceedings in Germany.

On a reference for a preliminary ruling, the Court of Justice regarded the *Daily Mail* case as concerning only the compatibility with Article 49 TFEU of restrictions imposed by the law of the Member State of incorporation of a company, and did not resolve the question raised in *Überseering* as to whether a Member State was entitled to refuse to recognise the legal personality of a company validly incorporated under the law of another Member State. The Court held that the companies and firms referred to in Article 54 TFEU which were formed in accordance with the law of a Member State and had their registered office, central administration or principal place of business within the Community, were 'entitled to carry on their business in another Member State',[24] and added that '[a] necessary precondition for the exercise of the freedom of establishment is the recognition of those companies by any Member State in which they wish to establish themselves'.[25]

The German rules in issue left a company in the position of Überseering BV with no choice but to reincorporate in Germany if it wished to enforce before a German court its rights under a contract entered into with a company incorporated under German law. It followed in the Court's view that the refusal by the German courts to recognise the legal capacity and capacity to be a party to legal proceedings of a company validly incorporated in another Member State constituted a restriction on freedom of establishment.[26] While the Court accepted that it was 'not inconceivable' that overriding requirements relating to the general interest, such as the protection of the interests of creditors, minority shareholders, employees and even the taxation authorities might, in certain circumstances and subject to certain conditions, justify restrictions on freedom of establishment, such objectives could not justify a denial of legal capacity and capacity to bring legal proceedings, which was tantamount to 'an outright negation of the freedom of establishment conferred on companies by [Articles 49 and 54 TFEU]'.[27]

The Court's approach in *Centros* was confirmed in the subsequent case of *Inspire Art*,[28] decided shortly after *Überseering*, in which the Court considered Netherlands rules which, inter alia, imposed minimum paid-up capital requirements (of €18,000) on 'formally foreign companies', which were defined as companies which carried on their activities entirely or almost entirely in the Netherlands and did not have any real connection with the Member State within which the law under which the company was formed applied. Until the conditions relating to paid-up share capital had been satisfied, the directors were jointly and severally liable with the company for all legal acts carried out during their directorship. The directors of a formally foreign company were likewise jointly and severally responsible for the company's acts if the capital subscribed and paid up fell below the minimum required, having originally satisfied the minimum capital requirement. The

---

[24] Ibid, paras 56 and 57.
[25] Ibid, para 59.
[26] Ibid, paras 78–82.
[27] ibid, para 93.
[28] Case C-167/01 *Inspire Art* [2003] ECR I-10155.

Court repeated the reasoning which it had adopted in *Centros* and held that such rules were contrary to Articles 49 and 54 TFEU.

These were radical judgments. *Centros* and *Inspire Art* might be said to imply the Court's lack of faith in the efficacy of or need for minimum capital requirements, at any rate for private companies, and these cases made it possible for businesses to avoid such requirements in their own Member State by incorporating in another. *Überseering* guaranteed this possibility even when the Member State where business was conducted did not recognise the possibility of a company being registered in a Member State other than that of the company's real seat. These three judgments seem to have contributed both to a considerable migration of private limited companies to the United Kingdom, and, perhaps more significantly, to a general tendency to reduce or eliminate capital requirements for private companies. Empirical research by Brecht, Mayer and Wagner indicates that the judgments in *Centros*, *Überseering* and *Inspire Art* were directly associated with a trend towards the incorporation of private companies in the United Kingdom by businesses located in other Member States. Between 2003 and 2006 over 67,000 new private limited companies were established in the United Kingdom from other EU Member States.[29] These figures refer to true 'Centros-type' incorporations, namely firms that incorporated in the United Kingdom without carrying on any business activity there. In absolute terms the largest flows of incorporations were from Germany, France, the Netherlands and Norway, with over 41,000 firms from Germany alone.[30] Brecht et al note that small differences in set-up costs and capital requirements between countries have surprisingly large effects on the probability that an entrepreneur will choose to incorporate in the United Kingdom rather than in his or her home country. Legal uncertainty, language and stronger enforcement of disclosure standards do not appear to be barriers to foreign incorporations. They argue that the 'evidence supports a simple model of choice of legal form dictated by relative costs of incorporation in different jurisdictions rather than a broader set of non-price considerations'.[31] It seems that one of the reasons why price is such an important consideration is the large-scale presence on the market of registration agents. These agents 'function as incorporation intermediaries and minimise the costs of shifting between legal jurisdictions' and by doing so 'they reduce the significance of non-price considerations and reduce the transaction costs of uninformed entrepreneurs'.[32] Brecht et al note that 'corporate mobility of the Centros type generally has no tax consequences' for the companies concerned, and that incorporation in the United Kingdom does not affect application of the legislation of the Member State in which the company operates as regards cases of insolvency.[33] Nor does the United Kingdom receive tax revenues in respect of such incorporations.[34] Brecht et al argue, however, that there is a political cost of loss of control in the case of entrepreneurs choosing to incorporate abroad. If corporate law is a means of implementing a political agenda, then politicians have an incentive to keep entrepreneurs from incorporating their companies abroad.[35]

---

[29] See M Becht, C Mayer and H Wagner, 'Where Do Firms Incorporate? Deregulation and the Cost of Entry' European Corporate Governance Institute (ECGI), Law Working Paper No 70/2006 (2008) 14 *Journal of Corporate Finance*. Free download at http://papers.ssrn.com/sol3/papers.cfm?abstract_id=906066.

[30] Ibid, 2.

[31] Ibid, 3.

[32] Ibid, 16.

[33] Ibid, 16

[34] Ibid, 6, referring to Arts 2(1) and 10(a) of Dir 69.335/EEC.

[35] Ibid, 3.

They find evidence that the judgments referred to above are leading to regulatory competition[36] between EU Member States to provide 'low-cost corporate law', and say:

In line with our hypothesis we find that following [the judgments in *Centros*, *Überseering* and *Inspire Art*] France, Spain, Germany and the Netherlands all have eliminated or lowered minimum capital requirements or are in the process of doing so. Both the Dutch and German consultation documents explicitly state as a reason for change the necessity to compete with more attractive UK company law and incorporation procedures. According to our results, reforms in France and Spain aimed at make domestic incorporations significantly cheaper have stopped the rapid growth in incorporation abroad.[37]

As regards the potential 'regulatory competition' effects of the Court's judgments, it should be added that the Commission proposal for a Council Regulation on the Statute for a European Private Company (to be known as an SPE) stipulated a minimum capital requirement of €1. The explanatory memorandum states:

In order to facilitate start-ups, the Regulation sets the *minimum capital* requirement at €1. The proposal departs from the traditional approach that considers the requirement of a high minimum of legal capital as a means of creditor protection. Studies show that creditors nowadays look rather at aspects other than capital, such as cash flow, which are more relevant to solvency. Director-shareholders of small companies often offer personal guarantees to their creditors (eg to banks) and suppliers also use other methods to secure their claims, eg providing that ownership of goods only passes upon payment. Moreover, companies have different capital needs depending on their activity, and thus it is impossible to determine an appropriate capital for all companies. The shareholders of a company are the best placed to define the capital needs of their business.[38]

As regards formation, the Explanatory Memorandum states (referring to Article 7 of the proposal):

The SPE is required to have its registered office and its central administration or principal place of business in the territory of the Member States. However, in accordance with the Centros judgment of the European Court of Justice, the SPE may be set up with its registered office and central administration or principal place of business in different Member States. Shareholders may also decide to transfer the registered office of the company to another Member State.[39]

The European Parliament Resolution on the Proposal indicated that the €1 minimum capital requirement would only be acceptable if the articles of association required executive management to sign a solvency certificate certifying that the company would be able to pay its debts in the following year; if there were no such requirement in the articles the minimum capital should be €8,000.[40] The 'Centros' provision in Article 7 of the proposal[41] was maintained subject to a new mandatory 'cross-border' element to comprise one of the following: a cross-border business intention or corporate object; an objective to be signifi-

---

[36] 'Regulatory competition' is a phenomenon which may occur where individuals and companies are free to move across jurisdictional boundaries, and choose the most 'business friendly' environment. National and regional law-makers may modify rules to attract and keep businesses, thus 'competing' with each other. Where the EU provides optional corporate forms for businesses, such as the European Company (see Chapter 19), the EU may engage in a form of regulatory competition.

[37] Becht et al, above n 29, 4.

[38] COM(2008) 396/3, 7.

[39] Ibid, 6, and Art 7 of proposal.

[40] European Parliament legislative resolution of 10 March 2009 on the proposal for a Council regulation on the Statute for a European private company (COM(2008)0396) [2010] OJ C87E/300, 311.

[41] Ibid, 306.

cantly active in more than one Member State; establishments in different Member States; or a parent company registered in another Member State. Such a cross-border element would deprive the SPE of much of the flexibility of a true 'Centros-type' company. Other amendments were also proposed. Negotiations in the Council broke down in December 2009 and it seems the outstanding issues related to the minimum capital requirement, employee participation rights and, in connection with the latter, the possibility of main taining the principal place of business and the registered office of the SPE in two different countries.[42]

A question increasingly asked after *Überseering* was whether application by a Member State of the 'real seat' doctrine to deny to companies incorporated under its law the right to move their primary establishment to another Member State without dissolution under the law of the first Member State and reincorporation under the law of the second, amounted to a restriction on the right of establishment.[43] As noted above, *Überseering* distinguished the *Daily Mail* case and did not call into question the reasoning or ruling in the latter case. Ebke nevertheless argued that it was 'inconceivable' that the Court would treat an 'emigration' or 'exit' case (such as that under discussion) more restrictively than an 'immigration' or 'entry' case such as *Überseering*—in other words the Court of Justice would be bound to modify its ruling in the *Daily Mail* case, or its interpretation of that ruling.[44] Wymeersch considered that 'emigration should, from the angle of free movement, be dealt with along the same lines as immigration'.[45]

The question was resolved in *Cartesio*,[46] in which the Court of Justice was called upon to consider whether Articles 49 and 54 TFEU must be interpreted as meaning that legislation of a Member State which precludes a company incorporated under the law of that Member State from transferring its seat to another Member State, while retaining its status as a company governed by the law of incorporation, is incompatible with EU law. Advocate General Maduro considered that the case law on the right of establishment of companies had developed since the ruling in *Daily Mail* and *General Trust* and that the Court's approach had become more refined.[47] He thought it impossible to argue in the then current state of EU law that Member States enjoyed an absolute freedom to determine the 'life and death' of companies constituted under their domestic law, irrespective of the consequences for the freedom of establishment.[48] He concluded that '[Articles 49 and 54 TFEU] preclude national rules which make it impossible for a company constituted under national law to transfer its operational headquarters to another Member State.'[49] The Court, however, disagreed.[50] It recalled that in *Daily Mail* it had held that Article 54 TFEU placed on the same footing, as connecting factors with the territory of a Member State, the registered office, central administration and principal place of business of a company. The Court added that it had inferred from this in *Überseering* that the ques-

---

[42] Deutsche Bank Research 19 July 2010, http://www.dbresearch.de/PROD/DBR_INTERNET_EN-PROD/PROD0000000000260277.PDF

[43] See eg E Wymeersch, 'The Transfer of the Company's Seat in European Company Law' (2003) 40 *CMLRev* 661, 690.

[44] W Ebke, 'The European Conflict-of-Corporate-Laws Revolution: *Überseering, Inspire Art,*and Beyond' [2005] 16 *EBLR* 13, 23.

[45] Wymeersch, above n 43, 677.

[46] Case C-210/06 *Cartesio* [2008] ECR I-9641.

[47] Ibid, Opinion at para 27.

[48] Ibid, Opinion at para 31.

[49] Ibid, Opinion at para 35.

[50] Case C-210/06 *Cartesio* [2008] ECR I-9641, paras 99–124.

tion whether a company formed in accordance with the legislation of one Member State can transfer its registered office to another Member State without losing its legal personality under the law of the Member State of incorporation, was to be determined by the national law of that Member State. The Court reasoned that in the absence of a uniform EU law definition of the companies which may enjoy the right of establishment on the basis of a single connecting factor determining the national law applicable to a company, the question whether Article 49 TFEU applies to a company which seeks to rely on the fundamental freedom enshrined in that article—like the question whether a natural person is a national of a Member State, hence entitled to enjoy that freedom—is a preliminary matter which, as EU law now stands, can only be resolved by the applicable national law. It followed that the question whether a company is faced with a restriction on the freedom of establishment, within the meaning of Article 49 TFEU, can arise only if it has been established, in the light of the conditions laid down in Article 54 TFEU, that the company actually has a right to that freedom. The Court concluded that

> Thus a Member State has the power to define both the connecting factor required of a company if it is to be regarded as incorporated under the law of that Member State and, as such, capable of enjoying the right of establishment, and that required if the company is to be able subsequently to maintain that status. That power includes the possibility for that Member State not to permit a company governed by its law to retain that status if the company intends to reorganise itself in another Member State by moving its seat to the territory of the latter, thereby breaking the connecting factor required under the national law of the Member State of incorporation.[51]

It followed that Articles 49 and 54 TFEU did not preclude legislation of a Member State under which a company incorporated under the law of that Member State may not transfer its seat to another Member State whilst retaining its status as a company governed by the law of the Member State of incorporation.

The Court's conclusion is clearly defensible, given the wording of the Treaty Articles in question, but the end result is not completely satisfactory. National systems of company law which apply the real seat principle place restrictions not only on the right of establishment of companies incorporated under their laws, but also on the rights of individuals and companies seeking to acquire control of companies incorporated under their laws. It is explained later that an individual or company acquiring a controlling stake in the shares of a company registered in another Member State is exercising the right of establishment—and indeed the right to free movement of capital.[52] Denial of Überseering BV's right to sue was assessed by the Court of Justice in terms of a restriction on the right of establishment of the latter company, but that denial operated no less as a restriction on the right of establishment of the German nationals residing in Düsseldorf, who had acquired all the shares in that company, thereby precipitating a shift in its central administration from the Netherlands to Germany, and resulting in the loss of the company's right to sue in a German court.

As the proceedings in *Überseering* illustrate, one consequence of investors residing in one Member State buying most or all of the shares in a company from shareholders residing in another Member State may be a shift in the real seat of that company from the second Member State to the first. If such a purchase of shares results in a transfer to another Member State of the real seat of a company incorporated under the law of a

---

[51] Para 110.
[52] Below at p 663, and see Case C-208/00 *Überseering* [2002] ECR I-9919, para 77.

Member State applying the real seat doctrine, the effect may be that acquisition of the company results in its non-existence. Since the principles applied in *Überseering* and *Cartesio* apply to 'immigration' or 'entry' situations but not to 'emigration' or 'exit' situations, it means that German shareholders precipitating a shift of the real seat of a Netherlands company by acquiring all its shares would be able to exercise the right of establishment, whereas Netherlands shareholders precipitating a shift of the real seat of a German company by acquiring all its shares would not.

But noting the above disparity of treatment does not amount to a criticism of the reasoning and conclusion of the Court in *Cartesio*. The Court of Justice cannot be expected to solve all problems which arise relating to cross-border activities simply by adopting ever more inventive interpretations of the Treaties. In *Cartesio*, it repeated an observation which it had made previously in *Daily Mail* and *Überseering*, to the effect that mechanisms provided by the Treaty for company law harmonisation,[53] and for agreements between Member States 'on the retention of legal personality in the event of transfer of their seat from one country to another'[54] had yet to be utilised to address the differences between the legislation of the various Member States which give rise to the problem under discussion.[55]

The judgments of the Court of Justice in *Centros* and *Überseering* were bold initiatives of the Court. It is not inconceivable that *Centros* might have been decided differently. The reference in Article 49 TFEU to the right to set up secondary establishments in other Member States being reserved to nationals of Member States *established* in a Member State could have been interpreted as requiring more of a limited company than that it be *registered* in a Member State, while undertaking its entire business elsewhere. Nor is it inconceivable that *Überseering* might have been decided differently, as the *Daily Mail* judgment suggested that it would or might be. But in each case such an alternative reading of the Treaty would have been unfortunate, because these judgments go a long way towards giving reality to corporate establishment in the internal market, and to promoting regulatory competition, as the research by Brecht et al, referred to above, indicates.

The Court's case law nevertheless leaves unresolved the issue of the transfer of the operational headquarters, or head office, of a company from one Member State to another. As has been noted above, where the company is incorporated in and thus has its registered office in a Member State applying the 'real seat' doctrine, such a transfer will involve the transfer of the company's registered office to the second Member State, to dissolution under the law of the first Member State, and reincorporation under the law of the second Member State. This problem is described as and has been addressed by the Commission as that of transfer of the registered office of the company. The Commission accepts that allowing a company to transfer its registered office to another Member State, and to change its legal personality, may enable it to increase its productivity and exercise its freedom of establishment, but notes that such a transfer has so far not been the subject of any harmonisation or coordination at EU level. The Commission adds that '[t]he highly diverse laws of the Member States on the matter sometimes prohibit it and in most cases render it impossible in practice unless the company is wound up'.[56] The Commission

---

[53] Art 50(2)(g).

[54] Art 293 EC. It was repealed by the TL, no doubt on the basis that it was unnecessary in view of the provision made for EU legislation in the field of company law by Arts 50(2)(g) and 352 TFEU.

[55] Case C-210/06 *Cartesio* [2008] ECR I-9641, para 114.

[56] 'The Current Framework', http://ec.europa.eu/internal_market/company/seat-transfer/2004-consult_en.htm#frame.

outlined a proposal for a 14th Company law Directive, which it described as follows in a press release of 26 February 2004:

> The planned Directive would enable companies to transfer their registered office from the Member State where they are registered (the 'home' Member State) to another Member State (the 'host' Member State), under an appropriate procedure providing legal certainty A company transferring its registered office would be registered in the host Member State and would acquire a legal identity there, while at the same time being removed from the register in its home Member State and giving up its legal identity there.[57]

The Commission undertook a public consultation on the outline of its proposal which closed on the 15 April 2004. The Commission subsequently carried out an impact assessment.[58] Commissioner McCreevy concluded there was no need for action at EU level on this issue,[59] and as a result DG Internal Market and Services discontinued work in this area. It is not, however, impossible that the issue will be revisited in the future.

C – Parent Company May Implement a Uniform Advertising Concept at EU level through its Subsidiaries in Other Member States

In *Pfeiffer*[60] the Court considered the compatibility with Article 49 TFEU of a restraining order pursuant to national law which prevented an Austrian subsidiary of a German parent operating 139 discount stores in Austria from using a trade name owned by the parent company which the subsidiary had begun to use to market its goods. The parent company was active in the discount store sector in Germany, Italy, Spain, the Czech Republic and Hungary under the trade name in question and the parent company's aim was for all its stores throughout Europe to adopt the same style of presentation, making it possible to use the same advertising material across Europe and to go on to develop a 'corporate identity'. The Court stated:

> A restraining order of the type sought by the plaintiff in the main proceedings operates to the detriment of undertakings whose seat is in another Member State where they lawfully use a trade name which they would like to use beyond the boundaries of that State. Such an order is liable to constitute an impediment to the realization by those undertakings of a uniform advertising concept at Community level since it may force them to adjust the presentation of the businesses they operate according to the place of establishment.[61]

It is possible to see in this judgment the basis of a potentially far-reaching principle that any national measure which might constitute an impediment to the realisation by a company of a 'uniform advertising concept at Community level' is to be treated as prima facie contrary to Article 49 TFEU and must accordingly be justified by imperative requirements in the public interest (the restriction in issue in *Pfeiffer* was in fact held to be justified on intellectual property grounds).[62]

---

[57] IP/04/270.
[58] SEC (2007) 1707; for Impact Assessment Board Opinion see D(2007) 974.
[59] Speech/07/59 by Commissioner McCreevey at the Eruopean Parliament's Legal Affairs Committee.
[60] Case C-255/97 *Pfeiffer* [1999] ECR I-2835.
[61] Ibid, para 20.
[62] For a narrower analysis, see Chapter 17, at p 549.

D – National Rules Making it More difficult for Subsidiaries to Compete with Existing Market Operators Hinder their Market Access and Must be Justified

In the *CaixaBank France* case[63] the Court was asked to indicate whether national rules of a Member State prohibiting the remuneration of 'sight' current accounts in euros constitute restrictions on the freedom of establishment prohibited by Article 49 TFEU in so far as they apply to a subsidiary formed in that Member State by a parent company from another Member State. The Court's analysis was as follows:

> That prohibition hinders credit institutions which are subsidiaries of foreign companies in raising capital from the public, by depriving them of the possibility of competing more effectively, by paying remuneration on sight accounts, with the credit institutions traditionally established in the Member State of establishment, which have an extensive network of branches and therefore greater opportunities than those subsidiaries for raising capital from the public.
>
> Where credit institutions which are subsidiaries of foreign companies seek to enter the market of a Member State, competing by means of the rate of remuneration paid on sight accounts constitutes one of the most effective methods to that end. Access to the market by those establishments is thus made more difficult by such a prohibition.[64]

There seem to be two distinct strands to this reasoning. One is that the national rule in question reinforces a barrier to market entry. The barrier to market entry is the existence of an extensive network of branches, and the rule prohibiting the payment of interest reinforces that barrier by prohibiting a potential means of competing with established market operators. The second (wider) strand or proposition is simply that prohibiting a potential means of effectively competing with established market operators is a restriction on access to the market which must be justified. On this latter basis the Court concluded in *Corporación Dermoestética*[65] that national rules of a Member State (Italy) prohibiting advertisements for medical and surgical treatments provided by private healthcare establishments on national television networks constituted, for companies established in other Member States, a serious obstacle to the pursuit of their activities by means of a subsidiary established in that Member State. These rules, held the Court, referring 'by analogy' to *Caixabank France*, were 'liable to make it more difficult for such economic operators to gain access to the Italian market'.[66]

E – Harmonisation at EU Level to Achieve Freedom of Establishment

(i) Article 50(1) and 50(2)(f) TFEU

Article 50(1) TFEU provides that in order to attain freedom of establishment as regards a particular activity, the Council, acting in accordance with the ordinary legislative procedure and after consulting the Economic and Social Committee, shall act by means of directives. Under Article 50(2) TFEU the responsibilities of the European Parliament, the Council and the Commission are more specifically defined.

Article 50(2)(f) EC (which refers to every branch of activity) provides lawmaking com-

---

[63] Case C-442/02 *CaixaBank France* [2004] ECR I-8961.
[64] Ibid, paras 13–14.
[65] Ibid, para 33.
[66] See Chapter 17.

petence for, inter alia, the abolition of restrictions on the transfer of personnel from the main establishment to managerial or supervisory posts in its branches or subsidiaries. In the event of such personnel holding the nationality of a Member State, they will, of course, be entitled to assert an independent right of entry and residence under the provisions of the Treaty guaranteeing freedom of movement for workers.[67] The implication is that certain senior personnel may be transferred under Article 50(2)(f) TFEU who would not otherwise be entitled to a right of residence under the Treaty. The principal reason for such lack of entitlement is likely to be that they are nationals of third countries. An undertaking providing services in another Member State, rather than being established there, may bring its workforce with it, irrespective of whether the employees concerned enjoy an independent right of free movement.[68] It would seem to follow that in principle a national of a third country may be posted from the main establishment to a *senior* post in a branch or subsidiary in another Member State, and that workers employed by an undertaking established in a Member State may, *irrespective of status*, be posted on a temporary basis to another Member State under Article 56 TFEU. This distinction between the scope of Articles 49 and 56 TFEU as regards the status of employees who may be entitled to residence as a result of a posting would seem to reflect the permanent nature of establishment as against the temporary and sporadic nature of the provision of services, and the intent of the draftsman of the Treaty to place a clear limit on the duty of Member States to grant a right of residence to nationals of third countries. It might be questioned, however, whether it is necessary to adopt rules under Article 50(2)(f) TFEU in order to abolish the restrictions on the transfer of the staff referred to, since the objective in question would seem achievable by means of the direct effect of Article 49 TFEU.

(ii) Company Law Harmonisation to Facilitate Freedom of Establishment

The prospect of firms incorporated under the law of one Member State being free to establish themselves in another led those who drafted the original Treaty to insert what is now Article 50(2)(g) TFEU, which requires the co-ordination of the provisions of national company law which safeguard the position of investors and 'others'. The rationale of such harmonisation appears to be that in its absence the existence of different national rules could discourage the exercise of the right of establishment, and deter third parties from dealing with companies having their seats in other Member States. This provision provides the legal basis for company law harmonisation, which is considered in the next chapter.

F – Mergers and Acquisitions as Aspects of Freedom of Establishment

The Court has held that a national of a Member State who has a holding in the capital of a company established in another Member State which gives him definite influence over the company's decisions and allows him to determine its activities is exercising his right of

---

[67] Case C-113/89 *Rush Portugesa Ldc* [1990] ECR I-1417; *Arblade* [1999] ECR I-8453; Case C-49/98 *Finalarte and Others* [2001] ECR I-7831; Case C-445/03; *Commission v Luxemburg* [2004] ECR I-10191; Case C-515/08 *Palhota and Others* (CJEU 7 October 2010); and see Directive 96/71 on the posting of workers in the framework of the provision of services [1996] OJ L18/1.

[68] Case C-113/89 *Rush Portugesa Ldc* [1990] ECR I-1417; *Arblade* [1999] ECR I-8453; Case C-49/98 *Finalarte and Others* [2001] ECR I-7831; Case C-445/03; *Commission v Luxemburg* [2004] ECR I-10191; Case C-515/08 *Palhota and Others* (CJEU 7 October 2010); and see Directive 96/71 on the posting of workers in the framework of the provision of services [1996] OJ L18/1.

establishment'.[69] It follows that an individual or company seeking to acquire such a holding would also fall within the scope of the right of establishment, and this is consistent with the adoption of a directive on takeovers under Article 50(1) TFEU, which is considered in the next chapter. It might also follow that certain activities of the board of a target company which have the aim of frustrating a takeover bid might amount to restrictions on the freedom of establishment of the bidding company, and this possibility is considered later in the present chapter.

The Court of Justice has confirmed that mergers fall within the scope of Articles 49 and 54 TFEU. In *SEVIC Systems*[70] the Court of Justice considered a reference from a national court in which a German company had challenged the refusal of the competent German authority to register in the national commercial register the merger between the German company in question and a company established in Luxembourg. The ground for refusal was that the German law on company transformations provided only for mergers between companies established in Germany. The merger contract concluded in 2002 between the German and Luxembourg company provided for the dissolution without liquidation of the latter company and the transfer of the whole of its assets to the former, without any change in the name of the transferee. The Court of Justice rejected contentions of the German government and the Netherlands government that Article 49 TFEU had no application to a merger situation such as that in issue in the national proceedings, in the following terms:

> Cross-border merger operations, like other company transformation operations, respond to the needs for co-operation and consolidation between companies established in different Member States. They constitute particular methods of exercise of the freedom of establishment, important for the proper functioning of the internal market, and are therefore amongst those economic activities in respect of which Member States are required to comply with the freedom of establishment laid down by [Article 49 TFEU].[71]

The Court considered that since under national rules recourse to such a means of transformation was not possible where one of the companies was established in a Member State other than the Federal Republic of Germany, German law established a difference in treatment between companies according to the internal or cross-border nature of the merger, which was likely to deter the exercise of the freedom of establishment laid down by the Treaty.[72] The Court also rejected the argument that such a blanket restriction was justified on proportionality grounds.[73]

II – CROSS-BORDER ACQUISITIONS

A – Free Movement of Capital

In considering cross-border investment issues as they affect acquisition it is necessary to

---

[69] Case C-251/98 *Baars* [2000] ECR I-2787, paras 21 and 22; Case C-81/09 *Idrima Tipou* (CJEU 21 October 2010), para 47.

[70] Case C-411/03 *SEVIC Systems* [2005] ECR-10805

[71] Ibid, paras 18–19.

[72] Ibid paras 22–23.

[73] Ibid paras 24–30.

consider the Treaty provisions on capital movement as well as those on the right of establishment. Within the framework of the chapter on capital and payments, all restrictions on the movement of capital and on payments between Member States and between Member States and third countries are prohibited.[74] These provisions are without prejudice to the right of Member States to apply relevant provisions of their tax law which distinguish between taxpayers who are not in the same situation with regard to their place of residence or with regard to the place where their capital is invested.[75] Member States may also take all requisite measures to prevent infringements of national law and regulations, in particular in the field of taxation and the prudential supervision of financial institutions, or to lay down procedures for the declaration of capital movements for purposes of administrative or statistical information, or to take measures which are justified on grounds of public policy or public security.[76] The provisions of the chapter on capital and payments are stated to be without prejudice to the applicability of restrictions on the right of establishment which are compatible with the Treaty.[77] The rights of Member States to apply the foregoing national measures shall not, however, constitute a means of arbitrary discrimination or a disguised restriction on the free movement of capital and payments.[78]

B – Meaning of 'Capital Movement': 'Direct Investment' and 'Portfolio Investment

Although the Treaty does not define the terms 'movement of capital' and 'payments', the case law of the Court of Justice has indicated that Directive 88/361/EEC,[79] together with the nomenclature annexed to it, may be used for the purposes of defining what constitutes a capital movement.[80] Capital movements comprising 'direct investment' may be contrasted with 'portfolio investment'. Direct investment is defined as follows by the Court of Justice in *Commission v Belgium*:[81]

> Points I and III in the nomenclature set out in Annex I to Directive 88/361, and the explanatory notes appearing in that annex, indicate that direct investment in the form of participation in an undertaking by means of a shareholding or the acquisition of securities on the capital market constitute capital movements within the meaning of Article [63 TFEU]. The explanatory notes state that direct investment is characterised, in particular, by the possibility of participating effectively in the management of a company or in its control.

Referring to the same Directive, the Commission describes 'portfolio investment' as follows in its 1997 Communication on Certain Legal Aspects concerning intra-EU Investment:[82]

> In the Directive, the heading 'Acquisition . . . of domestic securities . . .' includes, among others, the transaction 'acquisition by non-residents' of shares and bonds in domestic companies on

---

[74] Art 63 TFEU.
[75] Art 65(1)(a) TFEU; Chapter 17, at p 595.
[76] Art 65(1)(b) TFEU.
[77] Art 65(2) TFEU.
[78] Art 65(3) TFEU.
[79] [1988] OJ L178/5.
[80] Case C-222/97 *Trummer* [1999] ECR I-1661, paras 20 and 21.
[81] Case C-503/99 *Commission v Belgium* [2002] ECR I-4809, para 38.
[82] [1997] OJ C220/15. See also the Commission's 2005 Communication on Intra-EU investment in the financial services sector [2005] OJ C293/2.

pure financial investment grounds, that is, without the aim of exerting any influence in the management of the company. Thus, this transaction is considered as a form of capital movement. It is also usually known in the financial literature as 'portfolio investment'.

The position was concisely summarised in *Glaxo Welcome* as follows:

Movements of capital for the purposes of Article 63(1) TFEU thus include in particular direct investments in the form of participation in an undertaking through the holding of shares which confers the possibility of participating effectively in its management and control ('direct' investments) and the acquisition of shares on the capital market solely with the intention of making a financial investment without any intention to influence the management and control of the undertaking ('portfolio' investments).[83]

C – Cross-border Acquisitions Involve both the Free Movement of Capital and the Right of Establishment

In the present context, that is to say, cross-border acquisitions, it is direct investment which will be considered, without losing sight of the parallel application of the right of establishment. As indicated above, the Court's case law confirms that mergers and acquisitions fall within the scope of the right of establishment. In its 1997 Communication referred to above, the Commission described the position as follows:[84]

[T]he acquisition of controlling stakes in a domestic company by an EU investor, in addition to being a form of capital movement, is also covered under the scope of the right of establishment. . . . Thus, nationals of other EU Member States should be free to acquire controlling stakes, exercise voting rights and manage domestic companies under the same conditions laid down in a given Member State for its own nationals (ie the application of the 'national treatment' principle to other EU investors).

D – National Rules on Surveillance and Control of Cross-border Investments and the Free Movement of Capital

National rules requiring the prior declaration of capital movements amount in principle to restrictions on capital movement but may be justified for the purposes of administrative or statistical information, or to take measures which are justified on grounds of public policy or public security.[85]

National rules requiring prior declarations must not be subject to disproportionate penalties, nor require those concerned to provide more information than they can reasonably be expected to have.[86] In the case of direct foreign investments which constitute a genuine and sufficiently serious threat to public policy or public security, a system of prior declaration may prove to be inadequate to counter such a threat, and call for a system

---

[83] Case C-182/08 *Glaxo Welcome* [2009] ECR I-8591, para 40.
[84] Ibid, para 4.
[85] Art 65(1)(b) TFEU; Joined Cases C-358/93 and C-416/93 *Bordessa* [1995] ECR I-361.
[86] Case 52/77 *Cayrol* [1977] ECR 2261; Case 179/78 *Rivoira* [1979] ECR 651.

of prior authorisation.[87] National rules which make a direct investment subject to prior authorisation require justification, even if consent is deemed to be given if no objection is made after the lapse of a time limit.[88] In the case of direct foreign investments, the difficulty in identifying and blocking capital once it has entered a Member State may make it necessary to prevent, at the outset, transactions which would adversely affect public policy or public security.[89]

Systems of prior authorisation must comply with the principle of legal certainty. A system of prior authorisation which does not make it clear which investments require authorisation will not comply with the principle of legal certainty.[90] Nor will a system of prior authorisation which indicates which transactions require authorisation but which gives 'no indication whatever as to the specific objective circumstances in which prior authorisation will be granted or refused. Such lack of precision does not enable individuals to be apprised of the extent of their rights and obligations deriving from [Article 63 TFEU]'.[91] The Court has observed that '[s]uch a wide discretionary power constitutes a serious interference with the free movement of capital, and may have the effect of excluding it altogether'.[92]

E – Restrictions on Capital Movement Arising from 'Special Shares' or 'Golden Shares'

(i) Introduction

In relatively recent years a definite trend has been discernible in the Member States—the tendency to move wholly or partly into the private sector undertakings previously owned and controlled by the state and carrying on economic activities of public importance, eg energy supply, airlines, telecommunications, etc. With the reduction in equity participation by the state in the undertakings carrying on such activities came a reduction in the control exercised by the state both in the strategic direction and the day-to-day management of these undertakings. A second and linked trend has been to set up in place of public undertakings new undertakings in which public authorities and private investors provide investment and participate to greater or lesser extent according to circumstances in corporate governance. Because of national perceptions of the importance of the services provided by such undertakings, safeguards of various kinds have been adopted when privatisations have taken place or when joint public and private ventures have been established.

(ii) The Commission's 1997 Communication

The safeguards referred to above have sometimes taken the form of 'special' or 'golden' shares, for example rights of the government of a Member State to appoint directors and/ or veto certain decisions of the company relating to the mortgage or transfer of important

---

[87] Case C-54/99 *Église de Scientologie* [2000] ECR I-1335.
[88] Ibid, paras 14, 15.
[89] Ibid, para 20.
[90] Ibid, paras 21–22.
[91] Case C-483/99 *Commission v France* [2002] ECR I-4781, para 50.
[92] Ibid, para 51.

assets of the company in question, and/or to restrict acquisition of a controlling interest in the company.

In the 1997 Communication mentioned above, the Commission referred to certain types of national arrangements which amounted in its view to unlawful restrictions on the free movement of capital/right of establishment. The arrangements included:

— a prohibition on investors from another EU country acquiring more than a limited amount of voting shares in domestic companies . . .

— measures applied without distinction to all investors, . . . in particular general authorisation procedures whereby, for example, any investor (EU and national alike) wanting to acquire a stake in a domestic company above a certain threshold . . . [must be authorised]

— the rights given to national authorities, in derogation of company law, to veto certain major decisions to be taken by the company, as well as the imposition of a requirement for the nomination of some directors as a means of exercising the right of veto, etc.

The first category of measure referred to above is discriminatory on grounds of nationality. Measures of this kind clearly infringe Article 49 TFEU. The second category covers restrictions on access to the market, which are incompatible with Article 49 TFEU in the absence of justification, while a requirement of a general authorisation for the acquisition of property or shares is in principle contrary to Article 63 TFEU.[93] The third category referred to is less obviously, or was less obviously at the time, a restriction requiring justification as regards either the movement of capital or the right of establishment. The basis for this proposition in the Commission's document is that such a power hindered or made less attractive the exercise of fundamental freedoms within the meaning of the *Gebhard* formulation.[94] However, the proposition that the power of a national authority to intervene in the decision making of a company is itself a restriction on capital movement/freedom of establishment was not clearly established at the time of the issue of the Commission's Communication. Subsequent infraction proceedings launched by the Commission were to confirm that the analysis of the Commission contained in its 1997 Communication was correct.

(iii) A Test Case Strategy

The Commission adopted what was in effect a test case strategy to combat the 'special share' phenomenon which it saw as a threat to cross-border acquisitions. Its first action was against Italy and challenged Italian rules providing for the reservation of special powers to the state and public bodies in privatised companies in the defence, transport, telecommunications, energy and other public-service sectors. The special powers included a power to grant express approvals, a power to appoint a minimum of one or several directors and an auditor, and the right to veto certain decisions. The Commission relied on its Communication of 1997 before the Court of Justice, citing relevant parts of it as established law, which the Commission considered it to be. The Italian rules challenged by the Commission proved to be something of a 'soft target', since Italy conceded the case, and the Court held the contested measures to be incompatible with the provisions on capital movement and establishment.[95] Since important issues in the case had been conceded,

---

[93] See eg Case C-302/97 *Klaus Konle* [1999] ECR I-3099; Case C-567/07 *Wongingstichting Sint Servatius* [2009] ECR I-9021, para 22.

[94] Case C-55/94 *Gebhard* [1995] ECR I-4165, para 37.

[95] Case C-58/99 *Commission v Italian Republic* [2000] ECR I-3811.

the Court's judgment was not as convincing a vindication of the legal position of the Commission on 'special shares' as it might have been. The Advocate General in subsequent 'special share' cases, Mr D Ruiz-Jarabo Colomer, described the ruling as 'disturbing' since it seemed to accept that the parties were free to decide how an action for failure to fulfil obligations under the Treaty was to be disposed of. He suggested that the Court of Justice attribute no significance to this precedent.[96]

Perhaps the most significant of the 'special share' cases were those brought against France, Belgium, the United Kingdom and Germany.[97] In all four cases the Commission was successful in upholding its view of the ways in which 'special shares' amounted to restrictions on capital movement, though in the proceedings against Belgium the Court accepted that the restrictions in issue were justified.

(a) France's 'Golden Share' in Elf-Aquitaine

In the proceedings against France the Commission challenged French rights attached by legislation to the French state's 'golden share' in the energy company Elf-Aquitaine. These rights in the first place required prior approval of the relevant French minister whenever certain percentage thresholds were reached for holdings in the capital of the company. In the second place they allowed the French state to oppose decisions to transfer or use as security or collateral the majority of the capital of four subsidiaries of Elf. The Court held that these rights were incompatible with the free movement of capital:

> Even though the rules in issue may not give rise to unequal treatment, they are liable to impede the acquisition of shares in the undertakings concerned and to dissuade investors in other Member States from investing in the capital of those undertakings. . . . They are therefore liable, as a result, to render the free movement of capital illusory.[98]

Although the reference in the passage cited is to investors in general the Court refers in a previous paragraph to direct investment in particular, and to the fact that it is characterised by the possibility of participating effectively in the management of a company or in its control.[99] What is particularly significant is that it seems that the rights of a state under a 'golden share' will amount to a restriction on capital movement on the sole ground that the state has reserved a right to interfere with the managerial decision making of the company. The reasoning is that since investors seeking a controlling stake in the company are seeking control, placing restrictions on that control will deter them and amount to a restriction on capital movement which must be justified. And the Court rejected France's arguments that the special rights in issue were justified. The Court accepted that the objective pursued by the legislation at issue, namely the safeguarding of supplies of petroleum products in the event of a crisis, amounted to a legitimate public interest. But the rights conferred wide discretionary powers, lacked precision and were disproportionate.

---

[96] See Case C-483/99 *Commission v France* [2002] ECR I-4781, paras 76–77 of Opinion; Case C-503/99 *Commission v Belgium* [2002] ECR I-4809, paras 76–77 of Opinion.

[97] See Case C-483/99 *Commission v France* [2002] ECR I-4781; Case C-503/99 *Commission v Belgium* [2002] ECR I-4809; Case C-98/01 *Commission v United Kingdom* [2003] ECR I-4641; Case C-112/05 *Commission v Germany* [2007] ECR I-8995.

[98] See Case C-483/99 *Commission v France* [2002] ECR I-4781, paras 41–42.

[99] See Case C-483/99 *Commission v France* [2002] ECR I-4781, para 37.

(b) Belgium's 'Golden Shares' in SNTC and Distrigaz

In the proceedings against Belgium, the Court considered that the rules vesting in the Kingdom of Belgium 'golden shares' in SNTC and Distrigaz, entitling that Member State to oppose, first, any transfer, use as security or change in the intended destination of lines and conduits or of certain other strategic assets and, second, certain management decisions regarded as contrary to the guidelines for the country's energy policy, constituted a restriction on the movement of capital between Member States. Noting that the Belgian government did not deny, in principle, that the restrictions to which the legislation in issue gave rise fell within the scope of the free movement of capital, the Court turned its attention to justification; and on justification the Court found for Belgium. The aim of the rules was compatible with EU law—to ensure a minimum level of energy supplies in the event of a genuine and serious threat to those supplies. The regime was not one of prior authorisation, but of ex post facto opposition by the government subject to a strict timetable. The regime was limited to certain decisions concerning the strategic assets of the companies in question and to such specific management decisions relating to those assets as might be called in question in any given case. Finally, the minister could only intervene where there was a threat to the objectives of national energy policy, any such intervention had to be supported by a formal statement of reasons, and could be made the subject of effective judicial review.

The rulings in the above proceedings against France and Belgium were significant. The Court adopts a wide view of restrictions on capital movement. Interfering with the managerial prerogatives of the company is seen as a restriction on capital movement, since direct investment involves the right to participate in the management of the company. And justification is given the usual narrow construction. In particular, it seems that a precondition of relying on justification in any analogous future case would be (a) the publication in advance of sufficiently precise criteria for the exercise of special powers, and (b) an ex post facto system of challenge by a reasoned decision of the state subject to judicial review.

(c) The United Kingdom's Special Share in BAA

The proceedings against the United Kingdom differed in one respect from those against Italy, France and Belgium, which is worthy of remark. In the latter cases the actions challenged provisions of national legislation. In the former case the action against the United Kingdom challenged provisions in the Articles of Association of the British Airports Authority (BAA). The Airports Act 1986 privatised BAA, which used to own and operate seven international airports in the United Kingdom. Under that Act, the Secretary of State had power to approve with or without modifications the Articles of Association of the company nominated to take over BAA's functions. BAA was formed for that purpose in 1987. A £1 Special Share was created and was held by the Secretary of State for Transport. This Special Share allowed the Secretary of State to veto (a) the winding up of BAA and (b) the sale of a 'designated airport' (Heathrow, Gatwick, etc). The articles also prohibited any shareholder holding more than 15 per cent of the equity of BAA. The Court of Justice held that the foregoing veto power and the equity limitation amounted to restrictions on capital movement. Two arguments advanced by the United Kingdom were rejected by the Court. The first was that the rights exercisable by the Secretary of State under the Special Share were not discriminatory and did not amount to restrictions on access to the market.[100] The Court dismissed this argument in the same terms as those used in its judgment in respect of the French golden share in Elf-Aquitaine, adding that the restrictions in question were 'liable to deter investors from other Member States from making such investments and, consequently, affect access to the market'.[101] The second argument of the United Kingdom rejected by the Court of Justice was that the alleged restrictions did not fall within the scope of the Commission's 1997 Communication, since they were all provisions contained in the Articles of Association of BAA, and were not 'in derogation of company law' as were restrictions in the third category referred to by the Commission in its Communication. The Court responded as follows:

> The United Kingdom Government's argument that what is concerned here is solely the application of private company-law mechanisms cannot be accepted. The restrictions at issue do not arise as the result of the normal operation of company law. BAA's Articles of Association were to be approved by the Secretary of State pursuant to the Airports Act 1986 and that was what actually occurred. In those circumstances, the Member State acted in this instance in its capacity as a public authority. . . . Consequently, the rules at issue constitute a restriction on the movement of capital for the purposes of [Article 63 TFEU].

The possible distinction to be drawn between private law mechanisms and national measures was also an issue in the case of the 'Volkswagen Law'.

(d) *Commission v Germany* – The 'Volkswagen Law'[102]

The Commission alleged infringement of both the provisions on establishment and capital movement but advanced no distinct arguments as regards establishment. The Commission alleged that the 'Volkswagen Law' (Law of 21 July 1960 on the privatisation of equity in the Volkswagenwerk limited company, hereafter the 'VW Law') was contrary to EU law because of:

(a) a 'capping provision' which limited the voting rights of any shareholder to 20 per cent of total voting rights, irrespective of the value of its shareholding (contrary to the normal rule in German company law);

(b) the right of the Federal Republic of Germany (FRG) and the Land of Lower Saxony to appoint two members of the supervisory board as long as they held shares in the company and irrespective of the value of those shares;

(c) a 'blocking minority rule' whereby resolutions of the general meeting required more than 80 per cent of the votes cast, despite the normal rule in German company law requiring only 75 per cent, though shareholders were always free to apply a higher minority.

The Commission argued that these rules were likely to deter investment and amounted to restrictions on capital movement, noting that the 80 per cent plus voting rule allowed the Land of Lower Saxony to block resolutions of the general meeting.

Germany argued that when it created and privatised the public limited company Volkswagen, the VW Law merely expressed the will of the shareholders and other persons and groups which had laid claim to private rights over that undertaking. This Law

---

[100] The argument was based by analogy on Joined Cases C-267 and C-268/91 *Keck and Mithouard* [1993] ECR I 6097, and Case C-384/93 *Alpine Investments* [1995] ECR I-1141.

[101] Case C-98/01 *Commission v United Kingdom* [2003] ECR I-4641, para 47.

[102] Case C-112/05 *Commission v Germany* [2007] ECR I-8995.

should therefore be treated in the same way as a private agreement. The Court rejected this argument. Even if the VW Law did no more than reproduce an agreement which should be classified as a private law contract, the fact that the agreement had become the subject of a Law sufficed for it to be considered as a national measure for the purposes of the free movement of capital.

The Court noted that the blocking minority rule 'derogating from general law, and imposed by way of specific legislation, thus affords any shareholder holding 20% of the share capital a blocking minority'. The Court accepted that the capping and blocking minority provisions 'may operate both to the benefit and to the detriment of any share-holder in the company'. However, when the VW Law was adopted, the FRG and the Land of Saxony were the two main shareholders in the recently privatised VW company, and each had 20 per cent of the capital. While the FRG had parted with its interest in the capital of VW, the Land of Lower Saxony still retained an interest in the region of 20 per cent. The provision in issue thus enabled the federal and state authorities to procure for themselves a blocking minority enabling them to oppose important resolutions, on the basis of a lower level of investment than would be required under general company law. The capping provision enabled the federal and state authorities to exercise considerable influence on the basis of a reduced investment. The Court concluded that by limiting the possibility for other shareholders to participate effectively in the management of the company, the situation was liable to deter direct investors from other Member States. The power of the FRG and Lower Saxony to appoint two directors irrespective of the scale of their shareholdings, also a derogation from general company law, enabled them to partici-pate in a more significant manner in the activity of a supervisory board than their status as shareholders would normally allow. This was also liable to deter direct investors from other Member States from investing in the company's capital. The Court rejected argu-ments that these restrictions could be justified on grounds of the protection of workers and minority shareholders, since it had not been established that the restrictions were appropriate or necessary to achieve these objectives.

An interesting sequel to the above proceedings is provided by a decision of the gen-eral meeting of VW of 3 December 2009 which adopted the right to appoint directors and the 80 per cent plus rule (features (b) and (c) set out above) as part of the articles of association of VW quite independently of the VW Law.[103] It is to be noted that any deterrent effect for investors from other Member States resulting from these features of the VW corporate constitution would be likely to be the same, irrespective of whether the source of such a restriction was to be found in national rules, or in the action of the shareholders of the company.

(iv) Reflections on the Golden Shares Case Law[104]

A core general objection to golden or special shares is that they allow to national author-ities a say over corporate management which is disproportionate to the shareholding which they hold—at any rate from the point of view of the normal application of the rules of company law in the Member State in question. More specific objections are that national authorities have the right to approve share acquisitions above a certain threshold,

---

[103] W-G Ringe 'Company Law and Free Movement of Capital' (2010) *CLJ* 378, 408.
[104] Not all the case law is discussed. See eg Case C-171/08 *Commission v Portugal* (CJEU 8 July 2010); Case C-543/08 *Commission v Portugal* (CJEU 11 October 2010).

to approve important management decisions, such as those concerning key assets, to lay down a limit on shareholdings or voting rights (or veto a change in such a limit), or to appoint directors, at any rate where this right is not the normal consequence of any state shareholding. The Court appears to proceed on the basis that the various mechanisms adopted in the various cases are examples of regulation by the state of certain aspects of the conduct of the company in question, and that this regulation either prevents the acquisition of a controlling shareholding in the company by private investors from other Member States, or hinders the exercise of any controlling shareholding which such private investors might acquire.

In the BAA and VW cases, it was argued by way of defence that the provisions objected to should have been regarded as essentially mechanisms of private law rather than state measures. The Court did not accept those arguments. It clearly took the view that any participation by the state in the activities of the companies concerned was participation in the capacity of regulator, rather than market operator. It is perhaps worth considering the extent to which this is a crucial distinction to make, or, to put it another way, to ask whether or not restrictions such as those under discussion in for example the BAA case—restrictions according special rights to a particular class of shares, and/or prohibiting any shareholder from holding a controlling proportion of the equity shares in the company—might amount to restrictions on freedom of establishment or free movement of capital, even if put in place by, for example, founding shareholders, without any prompting by the state. It has been noted above that as regards the corporate constitution of VW, shareholders in general meeting actually put in place two of the three features of the corporate constitutiion of VW found by the Court of Justice to amount to restrictions on capital movement. These considerations prompt the broader question whether action taken by shareholders or directors under the corporate constition, and indeed the corporate constitution itself, can ever amount to restrictions on capital movement or freedom of establishment in the absence of state intervention. This question is considered below.

III – CAN THE CORPORATE CONSTITUTION AND PRIVATE ACTION TAKEN PURSUANT TO IT AMOUNT TO RESTRICTIONS ON FUNDAMENTAL FREEDOMS?

A – State Action Derogating from the Normal Rules of Company Law: Only Actions External to the Market Can Place Restrictions Upon It

An argument can be made for the position taken by the Commission in its 1997 Communication, to the effect that it is only powers of veto over corporate decision making which are 'in derogation of company law' which amount to restrictions on capital movement or the right of establishment; despite the unfortunate imprecision of the latter expression. The argument is essentially as follows. In the first place, standard formulations in the Court's case law define restrictions on fundamental freedoms as 'national measures' which hinder or make less attractive the exercise of those freedoms; the exercise of rights under private law will not normally amount to restrictions on fundamental freedoms. In the second place, the right of establishment, the freedom to provide services and the free movement of capital are freedoms of market operators to carry on economic activities. The fact that the Treaty prohibits restrictions on these freedoms indicates that a distinction is to be drawn between the activities of operators *in the market*, who are the beneficiaries of fundamental freedoms, and activities *external* to the market, which are prohibited by the Treaty, unless they can be justified.

In this scheme of things, it might be said to be necessary to distinguish between rights of national authorities to veto corporate decisions, and nominate directors in accordance with company law (where they are acting as commercial operators), and rights of national authorities to do so 'in derogation of' company law. For example, a national authority owning all the shares in a company may be entitled to veto corporate decisions or nominate directors, and that national authority may resolve to maintain its shareholding rather than to place a controlling stake on the market. This state of affairs cannot be said in itself to amount to a restriction on the fundamental freedoms of potential investors in the company—at any rate as long as Member States are entitled to participate in economic activities on the market through the corporate forms of private law. Where, by way of contrast, a national authority holds special shares which, irrespective of their value, grant to it the power to veto corporate decisions or nominate directors, with a view to ensuring that the company concerned acts in accordance with the public interest, the position is different, even if the special shares are derived from, and exercisable via mechanisms of private law. In the latter case the Court's case law makes it clear that the existence of the special shares and the powers of the national authority derived therefrom may amount to a restriction on the exercise of fundamental freedoms.

The essential difference between the two situations is that in the former the state's powers are intrinsic to its activities as a market participant, while in the latter case its powers are a means of regulating the market, rather than participating in it. This is the distinction which it seems the Commission was seeking to draw in its reference in its 1997 Communication to powers to veto corporate decisions and to nominate directors *in derogation of company law* and this is the distinction which the Court of Justice seems to endorse in the passage in its BAA judgment, cited above, in which it refers to the Secretary of State acting in his capacity as a public authority when he endorsed the Articles of Association of BAA which created the rights under the Special Share and limited any single shareholding in BAA to 15 per cent.

This line of argument seems essentially correct, and it prevents a Member State from relying on the fact that its regulatory powers are derived from, and exercisable via, mechanisms of private law, such as the corporate constitution, in order to deny that such powers may amount to restrictions on a fundamental freedom. It is not, however, a line of argument which excludes the possibility that the actions of private operators under private law, may amount to restrictions on fundamental freedoms in certain exceptional circumstances.

B – Actions of Private Operators under Private Law May Amount to Restrictions on Fundamental Freedoms

The Court's case law holds that the collective regulation of economic activities by private operators under private law may amount to a restriction on fundamental freedoms, including non-discriminatory restrictions on access to the market.[105] In such circumstances private operators act as regulators, and are accordingly subject to the Treaty's prohibition of restrictions on fundamental freedoms. It cannot, however, necessarily be assumed that the activities of private regulatory bodies comprise the sole activities of private operators which might be regarded as external to the market and be capable of amounting to a restriction on fundamental freedoms.

Certainly, non discriminatory activities by or on behalf of market operators to improve their market position vis-à-vis their competitors or their suppliers or customers would not seem in principle and in general capable of amounting to restrictions on the fundamental freedoms of others. However, discriminatory conduct on the part of market operators, or action which restricts access to the market of other market operators, would seem capable of amounting to a restriction on a fundamental freedom. If this line of argument is correct, it is possible that, for example, certain action taken by shareholders, or by the directors of a company, to prevent foreign bidders, or a particular bidder acquiring a controlling stake in a company, might amount to a restriction on a fundamental freedom.[106]

In the first place it seems clear that provisions of the corporate constitution which discriminate on grounds of nationality (eg by prohibiting non-nationals from acquiring shares) are incompatible with the right of establishment—Article 49 TFEU is capable of horizontal application, and there seems no reason to exclude that horizontal application in such a case.[107] Moreover, Article 55 TFEU provides that:

> Member States shall accord nationals of the other Member States the same treatment as their own nationals as regards participation in the capital of companies or firms within the meaning of Article 54, without prejudice to the application of the other provisions of the Treaties.

This would seem to impose an obligation on Member States to adopt legislation prohibiting discrimination on grounds of nationality as regards participation in the capital of companies. While Article 49 TFEU applies only to shareholders seeking to acquire control or influence in the management of the company, Article 55 TFEU applies to all potential investors. The possibility that this provision might be horizontally directly effective cannot be excluded.[108] Moreover account must also be taken of the general prohibition on discrimination on grounds of nationality laid down in Article 18 TFEU.[109]

It is clear that an equity limitation such as that involved in the BAA Special Share case, discussed above, has restrictive *effects* which may hinder the right of establishment. The question which arises is whether those restrictive effects nevertheless fall outside the scope of the Treaty if such a provision is adopted without the prompting or endorsement of the authorities of a Member State.[110] It is to be noted that such a limitation does not enable

---

[105] Case 36/74 *Walrave* [1974] ECR 1405; Case C-415/93 *Bosman* [1995] ECR I-4921; Case C-438/05 *Viking* [2007] ECR I-10779.

[106] Art 49 TFEU is capable of direct application to private parties; the provisions of the Treaty on free movement of capital bind Member States, but probably do not bind private parties.

[107] Case C-438/05 *Viking* [2007] ECR I-10779.

[108] Art 157 TFEU on equal pay is addressed to Member States yet it has been held to bind employers; Case 43/75 *Defrenne* [1976] ECR 455.

[109] Art 45 TFEU directly binds employers as regards its prohibition of discrimination on grounds of nationality, see Case C-281/98 *Angonese* [2000] ECR I-4139, esp paras 34–36. It is difficult to avoid the conclusion that the prohibition of discrimination in Art 49 TFEU applies directly to the terms of a corporate constitution, whether its securities are traded on a regulated market or not.

[110] It is not suggested that such arrangements are likely to be encountered in practice; the point is addressed as a matter of principle.

potential bidders, shareholders or the company itself to maintain or improve their position on the market; it entrenches the position of the board of the company, and denies access to the market in corporate control by preventing such a market from operating. It would seem to amount to a serious restriction on the right of establishment, and would require to be justified by a mandatory requirement in the general interest. [111] In such circumstances it would be necessary to consider the rationale of the corporate structure. Suppose the company concerned published a newspaper and that the equity limitation backed by the special share had been established as part of a scheme to ensure editorial independence for the newspaper in question.[112] Any restrictions on freedom of establishment might be justified by the public interest in press diversity.[113]

A similar argument might well apply to provisions of a corporate constitution, or to measures permitted by or adopted under a corporate constitution, or to agreements applicable in connection with the exercise of the right of shareholders, which are intended to and do restrict access to the market in corporate control. Into this category might fall certain conduct of the kind referred to in Article 9(2) of Directive 2004/25/EC on takeover bids, taken to frustrate a bid, without the consent of the general meeting, where a Member State has opted out of the latter provision.[114] It might be objected that such a conclusion would be inconsistent with the regime established by the latter Directive, which authorises certain measures by the board which might frustrate a bid, where a Member State has exercised its right to opt out of Article 9(2) of the Directive. That is a point meriting further comment in the following chapter on company law harmonisation.[115]

It should be added that conduct of the board of the kind referred to would also seem to have restrictive effects on the free movement of capital. Whatever limitations may exist in this context on the horizontal effect of the Treaty provisions on capital movement, or indeed freedom of establishment, it is established that Member States are obliged to take all appropriate measures to ensure that private individuals do not interfere with the effective exercise of fundamental freedoms.[116] This obligation would seem to require each Member State to ensure that its national system of company law contains rules to ensure that company boards do not engage in conduct which might prevent shareholders from accepting an advantageous bid.

IV – CONCLUDING REMARKS

The Court's case law on corporate establishment has been fairly radical. It holds that an individual or company is entitled to choose the law of a Member State to provide the legal form in which to conduct its business activities, even if no business activities are to be

---

[111] Where rules of private law regulate economic activity mandatory requirements in the general interest may in principle be pleaded by way of justification, see Case C-415/93 *Bosman* [1995] ECR I-4921, paras 86, 104.

[112] The present writer is conscious of the loose parallel with the arrangements applicable to Reuters when it was floated in 1984.

[113] *cf* Case C-368/95 *Familiapress* [1997] ECR I-3689.

[114] See below at p 694.

[115] See below at p 697.

[116] Case C-26595 *Commission v France* [1997] ECR I-6959; Case C-112/00 *Schmidberger* [2003] ECR I-5659. These cases involve private action interfering with the free movement of goods, but para 62 of the latter case refers to 'restrictions on the exercise of a fundamental freedom'.

conducted in the Member State of incorporation, and all business activities are to be conducted elsewhere, provided only that this is permitted under the law of the Member State of incorporation. If it is permitted, then other Member States cannot refuse to recognise the existence of the company in question, though Member States remain entitled to apply the real seat doctrine, and thereby to place limits on the extent to which companies incorporated under their laws can 'export' the location and control of their business activities. The present writer considers that these developments have been positive developments, because they have increased flexibility for businesses, and reduced their costs, thus making some contribution to the overall competitiveness of businesses in the EU.

The Court's case law in the matter of 'golden shares' has been equally radical, and also beneficial. This case law has prevented Member States from retaining strategic business control over privatised companies without retaining the level of equity stake which would make this possible under the normally applicable rules of company law. Golden shares are designed to enable Member States to take key business decisions for the company—and indeed in some cases for the subsidiaries of the company—without being exposed to a commensurate share of the business risks. This is not business, it is regulation, and it deserves to be treated as such. That is why this case law has been beneficial: it has ensured that what is in substance regulation by the state, is identified as such, and is subject to the normal Treaty rules on justification for restrictions on fundamental freedoms. That said, the Court's interpretation of the fundamental freedoms in this context has in itself been fairly radical. The Court has treated the possibility of state intervention in the management of the company as being a restriction on capital movement (and it seems clear it is also a restriction on the right of establishment) because that possibility deters direct investors from other Member States who would otherwise be willing to pay the going rate for control, providing that they could then exercise it. Although the Court refers to deterring direct investors from other Member States, any deterrence would appear to affect direct investors generally, rather than particularly affecting direct investors from other Member States. In effect, the Court has held that the state must not place restrictions on access to the market in corporate control, unless perhaps (by implication) the state does this by retaining control through shareholdings maintained in accordance with the normal rules of company law applicable in the Member State in question.

Finally, this chapter has posed the question whether purely private conduct by shareholders or directors under the corporate constitution can ever amount to restrictions on establishment or capital movement. Where the corporate constitution discriminates on grounds of nationality, the answer should surely be 'yes'. The answer is much less clearly affirmative in cases where individuals seek business advantage from special classes of shares or other commercial arrangements which might be said to have the effect of restricting the access of others to the market in corporate control. But that is not to say that the answer must definitely be no. It is certainly legitimate—in the sense of being compatible with fundamental freedoms—for commercial operators to compete in the market. It is less obviously legitimate for commercial operators to seek to structure the market—including the market in shares of a particular company—in a way which favours current players and restricts the access of new market entrants. Such market behaviour begins to look like regulation of the market, and may deserve to be treated as such.

Further Reading

M Becht, C Mayer and H Wagner, 'Where Do Firms Incorporate? Deregulation and the Cost of Entry', European Corporate Governance Institute (ECGI), Law Working Paper No 70/2006 (2008) 14 *Journal of Corporate Finance*. Free download at http://papers.ssrn.com/sol3/papers.cfm?abstract_id=906066

W Ebke, 'The European Conflict-of-Corporate-Laws Revolution: *Überseering, Inspire Art*, and Beyond' [2005] *EBLR* 13.

C Gerner-Beuerle and M Schillig, 'The Mysteries of Freedom of Establishment after Cartesio' (2010) 59 *ICLQ* 303.

A Johnston and P Surpis, 'Regulatory Competition in European Company Law after Cartesio' (2009) 34 *ELRev* 378.

W-G Ringe, 'Case C-112/05 Commission v Germany ("VW law"), Judgment of the Grand Chamber of 23 October 2007' (2008) 45 *CMLRev* 537.

W-G Ringe 'Company Law and Free Movement of Capital' (2010) *CLJ* 378.

W H Roth, 'From *Centros* to *Uberseering*: Free Movement of Companies, Private International Law, and Community Law' (2003) 52 *ICLQ* 177.

E Szyszczak, 'Golden Shares and Market Governance'(2002) 29(3) *Legal Issues in European Integration* 255.

E Wymeersch, 'The Transfer of the Company's Seat in European Company Law' (2003) 40 *CMLRev* 661.

Company Law Harmonisation

21

The aim of company law harmonisation is to facilitate freedom of establishment, and such measures have always claimed to facilitate cross-border establishment in one way or another, for example by removing psychological obstacles to cross-border activity, or removing differences between national rules which necessitate compliance with further requirements by virtue of establishment in another Member State. A question which is tempting to ask but difficult to answer is whether company law harmonisation has in practice as well as in theory contributed to the internal market. In recent years a more empirical approach has been adopted by the Commission to this question, and more emphasis placed on the improvement of competitiveness of the European market, the modernisation of company law, and the improvement of corporate governance. In this context, particular attention is paid to two relatively recent initiatives, the European Company Statute, and the Takeover Bids Directive, and a tentative assessment made of their contribution to the internal market.

I – COMPANY LAW HARMONISATION WAS DESIGNED TO PROMOTE FREEDOM OF ESTABLISHMENT

Article 50(2)(g) TFEU provides for the adoption of legislation designed to co-ordinate the

> safeguards which, for the protection of the interests of members and others, are required by Member States of companies or firms within the meaning of the second paragraph of Article 54 with a view to making such safeguards equivalent throughout the Union.

The aim of this legislation is made clear in Article 50(1) TFEU; it is to 'attain freedom of establishment'. Edwards has argued that

> [w]hile company law harmonisation is not an end in itself, so that [Article 50(2)(g)] undoubtedly requires a link between the legislation adopted thereunder and the facilitation of companies' right of establishment,[1] that goal calls for a generous construction in accordance with the general

---

[1] See eg Case C-122/96 *Saldanha* [1997] ECR I-5325, where the Court of Justice stated that Art 50(2)(g) 'empowers the Council and the Commission, for the purpose of giving effect to the freedom of establishment, to coordinate to the necessary extent the safeguards' (para 23).

approach developed by the Court of Justice over the last three decades to the interpretation of Treaty provisions.[2]

Nevertheless, a slightly stricter approach to the Treaty base may be necessary today. The Court of Justice has emphasised that legislation adopted to improve the functioning of the internal market must genuinely have as its object the improvement of the conditions for the establishment and functioning of the internal market. This means, in the present context, that such legislation must remove barriers to cross-frontier business activity and/or eliminate appreciable distortions of competition.[3] Today, such legislation should also aim to reduce the transaction costs involved in cross-border business activity, and thus contribute to the overall competitiveness of the European market, in order to contribute to the 'highly competitive social market economy' which it is the task of the Union to promote.[4]

The provisions of Article 50(1) and 50(2)(g) TFEU are not the only legal basis for EU legislation regulating the structure of corporate bodies at European level. When the Council adopted Regulations for a European Economic Interest Grouping (EEIG), and for the European Company Statute, it did so on the basis of Article 352 TFEU (ex Article 308 EC)—a provision which can be used as a basis for legislation only when no other legal basis is available.[5] These regulations made provision for European corporate entities operating in parallel with existing national legal regimes. Use of Article 352 TFEU in such cases was put to the test when the European Parliament challenged the validity of the Council Regulation adopting a Statute for a European Cooperative Society—another European legal regime which would leave intact parallel national arrangements.[6] The European Parliament argued that the Statute could have been adopted by a regulation based on Article 114 TFEU, which provided for the harmonisation of national provisions to improve the functioning of the internal market, and the European Parliament concluded from this that recourse to Article 352 TFEU was accordingly excluded. It is not difficult to see why the European Parliament would have preferred Article 114 TFEU to have been used in such cases, since it provided for participation in the legislative process by the European Parliament through the co-decision procedure, whereas the text of Article 308 EC provided at that time only for consultation of the European Parliament. Advocate General Stix-Hackl considered that since the regulation in issue related to a particular form of co-operative society, and thus incorporated rules of company law, it was Article 50 TFEU which should first of all be taken into consideration, though she noted that the European Parliament had not raised that Article as a possible basis for the Statute, and in the event she reached the same conclusion as the Court.[7] The Court held that the Statute was rightly based on Article 352 TFEU, since it created a new legal form which left unchanged the different national laws already in existence, and could not be regarded as aiming to approximate the laws of the Member States applicable to co-operative societies.[8] This approach has the convenient political result of requiring unanimous agreement in Council. It should, however, be noted that the wording of Article 352 TFEU, which

---

[2] V Edwards, *EC Company Law* (Oxford, Oxford University Press 1999) 7.
[3] Case C-376/98 *Germany v Council and Parliament* [2000] ECR I-8419.
[4] Art 3(3) TEU.
[5] Case 45/86 *Commission v Council* [1987] ECR 1493, para 13.
[6] Reg (EC) No 1435/2003 on the Statute for a European Cooperative Society (SCE) [2003] OJ L207/1. Case C-436/03 *European Parliament v Council* [2006] ECR I-3733.
[7] Ibid, Opinion, paras 40–45.
[8] Ibid, Judgment, paras 44–46.

replaced Article 308 EC, now provides for the adoption of legislation with the consent of, rather than simply after consulting, the European Parliament.

Edwards has argued that company law harmonisation measures 'which prima facie have little immediate impact on cross-border establishment will in any event normally be found on closer scrutiny indirectly to smooth the path of cross-border establishment'.[9] This observation was probably not intended to damn with faint praise, but it might be questioned whether it should be regarded as appropriate today for the EU institutions to adopt measures of company law harmonisation unless direct gains to the internal market are likely to result. As Edwards indicates, however, company law harmonisation measures can at least be rationalised in terms of making some contribution to freedom of establishment.

II – OBSTACLES TO ESTABLISHMENT ADDRESSED BY COMPANY LAW HARMONISATION

A – Summary

The obstacles to establishment of companies addressed by harmonisation measures can be broadly grouped into three categories:

— Differences between national rules which deter cross-border activity to the extent that economic operators in one Member State are unfamiliar with rules in another (psychological obstacles).
— Differences between national rules which necessitate compliance with further requirements by virtue of establishment in another Member State.
— National rules which (whether or not they vary from state to state) inhibit establishment in another Member State.

B – Psychological Obstacles to Dealing with Foreign Companies, Unfamiliarity with Regimes Applicable to Foreign Companies, and Promoting Legal Certainty

The First Council Directive 68/151[10] concerned publicity requirements relating to companies, the circumstances in which company transactions would be valid, and the rules relating to the nullity of companies. The preamble of the directive is not particularly informative as regards the cross-frontier advantages likely to result from the directive, though these might have seemed obvious. The preamble refers to the co-ordination referred to in Article 50(2)(g) TFEU and states that that co-ordination and that provided for in the General Programme for the abolition of restrictions on freedom of establish-

---

[9] Edwards, above n 2, 7.
[10] [1968] OJ English Sp Edn, Series I, 41; codified and replaced by Directive 2009/101/EC [2009] OJ L258/11.

ment 'is a matter of urgency, especially in regards to companies limited by shares or otherwise having limited liability, since the activities of such companies often extend beyond the frontiers of national territories'.

The Court of Justice considered the rationale of the disclosure requirements to be as follows:

> [T]he objective of the directive, . . . is to guarantee legal certainty in dealings between companies and third parties in view of the intensification of trade between Member States following the creation of the common market.[11]

The Court makes the same legal certainty point about the nullity provisions in the *Marleasing* case.[12] It is indeed possible that third parties might be deterred from doing business with or investing in foreign companies by uncertainty as to the requirements applicable to such companies. This might have an adverse effect on the right of establishment of companies, or on the right of establishment of investors seeking a controlling stake in foreign companies. Third parties might be concerned as to whether they might be afforded a lesser degree of legal protection in dealings with foreign companies than in dealings with companies incorporated in their own Member States, and information about foreign companies might not dispel such concerns if published in an unfamiliar format, or if compiled on the basis of different rules. Such considerations, as well providing a case, in terms of promoting freedom of establishment, for the First Directive, also provide a justification for other measures of company law harmonisation, such as the Fourth Council Directive 78/660/EEC on the annual accounts of certain types of companies.[13] The preamble of this Directive refers to it being necessary to 'establish in the Community minimum equivalent legal requirements as regards the extent of the financial information that should be made available to the public by companies that are in competition with another.' The Fourth Directive was supplemented by the Seventh Council Directive 83/349/EEC on Consolidated Accounts.[14]

It should be noted that disparities between disclosure requirements could also comprise obstacles falling with the second category referred to above if not harmonised—disparities between national company law rules which might result in further, and perhaps varying, requirements being imposed on a company extending its activities beyond its state of origin. Edwards points out, as regards the Eleventh Council Directive on disclosure by branches, that 'certain Member States had imposed their own disclosure requirements on branches, which differed between Member States, leading to further discrepancies within the Community'.[15]

The Council Regulation establishing EEIGs[16] aims to promote cross-border co-operation between individuals and companies, and its preamble refers to 'legal, fiscal or *psychological* difficulties' (emphasis added) in the way of such co-operation, which would be addressed by the Regulation. The preamble of the Council Regulation on the statute for a European Company (SE)[17] similarly argues that restructuring and co-operation operations involving companies from different Member States 'give rise to legal and psy-

---

[11] Case 32/74 *Haaga* [1974] ECR 1205, para 6.
[12] Case C-106/89 [1990] ECR I-4135, para 12.
[13] [1978] OJ L222/11; Eurlex consolidated text 2009-07-16.
[14] [1983] OJ L193/1; Eurlex consolidated text 2009-07-16.
[15] Edwards, above n 2, 212.
[16] Council Reg 2137/85 [1985] OJ L199/1.
[17] Council Reg 2157/2001 [2001] OJ L294/1; Eurlex consolidated text 2007-01-01.

chological difficulties'. These references to psychological difficulties seem to be references to the unfamiliarity and uncertainty which might arise when dealing with foreign companies and legal regimes, which are discussed above.

C – Differences between National Rules which Unless Harmonised Would Require Compliance with Further Requirements by Virtue of Establishment in Another Member State

Reference has already been made to the Eleventh Directive on disclosure by branches. The preamble to this Directive refers to the First, Fourth, Seventh and Eighth Directives, and notes that whereas these Directives apply to companies as such, they do not apply to their branches. The preamble points out that this lack of co-ordination as regards branches, in particular concerning disclosure, leads to disparities in the protection of shareholders and third parties, and between companies which operate in other Member States by opening branches and those which operate there by creating subsidiaries. The preamble adds that differences in the laws of the Member States might interfere with the exercise of the right of establishment. As indicated above, the case for this Directive in terms of promoting the right of establishment is twofold. In the first place it assists companies wishing to set up branches in other Member States by countering the unfamiliarity of third parties with disclosure requirements in the country in which the branch is established. In the second place it assists such companies by laying down uniform disclosure requirements to be fulfilled by their branches in the Member States in which they are established. The compulsory disclosure is limited to documents specified, including the accounting documents of the company as drawn up, audited and disclosed pursuant to the law of the Member State by which the company is governed in accordance with Third, Fourth and Seventh Directives.[18] The Member State in which the branch has been opened may stipulate that the documents relating to the activities of the company and its accounting documents must be published in another official language of the Community (no doubt the Member State would specify its own language) and that the translation of such documents must be certified.[19] In the *Centros* case, discussed above, the Court of Justice found support in the Fourth and Eleventh Directives for its rejection of the arguments of the Danish authorities that refusing to register the Danish branch of an English company had been justified by the need to protect the interests of public and private creditors of the company:

> Since the company concerned in the main proceedings holds itself out as a company governed by the law of England and Wales and not as a company governed by Danish law, its creditors are on notice that it is covered by laws different from those which govern the formation of private limited companies in Denmark and they can refer to certain rules of Community law which protect them, such as the Fourth Council Directive 78/660/EEC . . . on the annual accounts of certain types of companies . . ., and the Eleventh Council Directive 89/666/EEC . . . concerning disclosure requirements in respect of branches opened in a Member State by certain types of company governed by the law of another State.[20]

Another company law directive whose Treaty basis can be justified, at least in part, by the

---

[18] Eleventh Directive, Art 3.
[19] Ibid, Art 4.
[20] Case C-212/97 *Centros* [1999] ECR I-1458, para 36.

need to remove obstacles to corporate establishment resulting from disparities between national laws is the Second Council Directive 77/91/EEC, which deals with the formation of public limited liability companies and the maintenance and alteration of their capital.[21] Article 6 of the Directive provides that the laws of the Member States shall require that, in order that a company may be incorporated or obtain authorisation to commence business, a minimum capital shall be subscribed the amount of which shall not be less than 25,000 European units of account. Edwards notes that the original Member States had minimum capital requirements ranging from 20,000 to 160,000 units of account, and that the United Kingdom and Ireland had no such requirement. As she points out, such wide divergences in the requirement were capable of affecting freedom of establishment, and distorting competition, for example by discouraging companies from setting up cross-border subsidiaries in Member States with higher limits. It should be added that such disparities might also encourage Member States to refuse to allow branches of companies incorporated in Member States with lower capital requirements to carry on business in their territory, or to subject such activity of branches to similar capital requirements as were applicable to the formation of companies. Considerations such as these gave rise to the proceedings in the *Centros* case.[22] In the latter case the Court held that a Member State could not justify placing restrictions on the activities of a 'branch' of a private company incorporated in another Member State on grounds of protection of public and private creditors. One of the Court's reasons for rejecting this justification was that arrangements might be made for public creditors to obtain guarantees from the proprietors of the company. Such considerations would not be applicable to public companies. The amount of paid up capital provided for under the Second Directive is, however, a minimum requirement, and has never been increased in the three decades since the Directive was adopted, though there is provision for review every five years.[23] As Edwards comments, 'The figure is unquestionably on the small side if the purpose is to ensure that the company's capital is a genuine guarantee for third parties and to reserve the public company for undertakings of a certain scale.'[24]

Directive 2005/56/EC of the European Parliament and Council on cross-border mergers of limited liability companies[25] seeks to overcome 'the many legislative and administrative difficulties' which mergers between companies registered in different Member States encounter in the EU. The obstacles facing companies were described by the Commission in the explanatory memorandum accompanying its proposal in the following terms:

> At present, as Community law now stands, such mergers are possible only if the companies wishing to merge are established in certain Member States. In other Member States, the differences between the national laws applicable to each of the companies which intend to merge are such that the companies have to resort to complex and costly legal arrangements. These arrangements often complicate the operation and are not always implemented with all the requisite transparency and legal certainty. They result, moreover, as a rule in the acquired companies being wound up—a very expensive operation.[26]

---

[21] [1977] OJ L26/1; Eurlex consolidated text 2009-10-22.

[22] Case C-212/97 *Centros* [1999] ECR I-1458.

[23] Second Directive, Art 6(3).

[24] Edwards, above n 2, 60, 61.

[25] Directive 2005/56 of the European Parliament and Council on cross-border mergers of limited liability companies, [2005] OJ L310/1; Eurlex consolidated text 2009-10-22.

[26] COM(2003) 0703 final, 2.

In order to facilitate cross-border merger operations, the Directive provides that each company taking part in a cross-border merger, and each third party concerned, remains subject to the provisions and formalities of the national law which would be applicable in the case of a national merger.[27] Employee participation in the newly created company will be subject to negotiations based on the model of the European Company Statute, which is discussed below. The proposal was designed in particular to benefit 'small and medium-sized enterprises, which stand to benefit because of their smaller size and lower capitalisation compared with large enterprises and for which, for the same reasons, the European Company Statute does not provide a satisfactory solution.'[28]

D – National Rules or Practices which (Whether or Not they Vary from State to State) Inhibit Cross-border Establishment

Some national rules, whether contained in legislation, or in the articles of association of companies, may inhibit the right of establishment. Such restrictions do not result from disparities between national rules in one or more Member States, but from the fact that the rules in question, or practices authorised by such rules, are intrinsically capable of inhibiting cross-frontier establishment. Restrictions falling within this category were the target of one of the provisions of the proposed directive on takeover bids. Article 9(2) of the Commission's proposal of 2002 provided as follows:

> During the [relevant period][29] . . . the board of the offeree company must obtain the prior authorisation of the general meeting of shareholders given for this purpose before taking any action other than seeking alternative bids which may result in the frustration of the bid and in particular before issuing any shares which may result in a lasting impediment to the offeror in obtaining control over the offeree company.[30]

The Commission's explanatory memorandum says of this part of the proposal:

> Where control of the offeree company is at stake, it is important to ensure that its fate is decided by its shareholders. The authorisation of the general meeting must therefore be given explicitly with a view to responding to a specific bid. . . . The Directive does not define the measures which can frustrate a bid. In general, such measures may be all operations which are not carried out in the normal course of the company's business or not in conformity with normal market practices.[31]

Such action as that referred to is clearly capable of inhibiting cross-frontier merger. The Commission's proposal was finally adopted in modified form as Directive 2004/25, and is discussed below.[32]

---

[27] Directive 2005/56 of the European Parliament and Council on cross-border mergers of limited liability companies, [2005] OJ L310/1, Eurlex consolidated text, esp Art 4(1)(b).

[28] COM(2003) 0703 final, 2.

[29] From the time the board of the offeree company receives information concerning the bid and until the result of the bid is made public or the bid lapses; see Art 9(2) of the proposal.

[30] COM(2002) 534 final.

[31] Ibid, 8.

[32] Below, at p 693.

III – HAS COMPANY LAW HARMONISATION MADE AN EFFECTIVE CONTRIBUTION TO THE INTERNAL MARKET?

A – An Open Question

Assessing the effectiveness of the contribution of harmonisation to the internal market is difficult in this area as it is in others. Even if legislation in principle can be said to address obstacles to establishment, it is difficult to establish that the net effect of harmonisation will be or has been increased cross-frontier activity, or less costly cross-frontier activity. The press release accompanying the adoption of Directive 2005/56/EC of the European Parliament and Council on cross-border mergers of limited liability companies,[33] stated that the Directive 'is expected to reduce costs, while guaranteeing the requisite legal certainty and enabling as many companies as possible to benefit. It is one of the key actions for growth and employment under the Lisbon agenda.' However, the Commission acknowledged in an earlier published memo that there had been no economic analysis quantifying the likely benefits of the Directive, adding that 'EU companies have been calling for many years for such a measure to be adopted, so clearly they believe it will benefit them even if it would be very difficult to quantify these benefits.'[34] In fact it seems a fair assessment of the Directive in question that it will reduce the future costs of cross-border mergers, at any rate for companies registered in Member States whose legislation previously excluded the possibility of such cross-border mergers.[35]

A recent proposal for harmonisation demonstrates a rigorous approach both to analysing the problems which can arise for cross-border activities, and to the search for cost-effective solutions. The preamble of Directive 2007/36/EC of the European Parliament and of the Council on the exercise of certain rights of shareholders in listed companies[36] declares that:

> Non-resident shareholders should be able to exercise their rights in relation to the general meeting as easily as shareholders who reside in the Member State in which the company has its registered office. This requires that existing obstacles which hinder the access of non-resident shareholders to the information relevant to the general meeting and the exercise of voting rights without physically attending the general meeting be removed. The removal of these obstacles should also benefit resident shareholders who do not or cannot attend the general meeting.[37]

The Commission Staff Working Document/Impact Assessment annexed to the Commission's proposal for this Directive was a detailed and lengthy document which sought to identify the problems facing shareholders who might wish to vote in cross-border situations (based on empirical evidence), and possible solutions to those problems.[38] On the basis of answers to an ad-hoc questionnaire submitted to qualified issuers and intermediaries (and

---

[33] [2005] OJ L310/1; see press release IP/05/1487, Brussels, 29 November, 2005.
[34] MEMO/03/233 Brussels, 18 November, 2003.
[35] According to MEMO/03/233, the countries referred to are the Netherlands, Sweden, Ireland, Greece, Germany, Finland, Denmark and Austria.
[36] [2007] OJ L184/17. The Directive is based on Arts 50 and 114 TFEU.
[37] Recital (5) of the preamble.
[38] SEC(2006) 181.

included in the Working Document), one conclusion reached was that the removal of the obstacles identified to cross-border voting would significantly increase the cross-border voting record of institutional shareholders and would make cross-border voting for small individual shareholders a real possibility. The success in practice of legislation can never be completely accurately forecast in advance, but this sort of approach seems more likely than not to produce positive results.

On the other hand, economic operators have always had to negotiate differences between national laws, and negotiating such differences does not always impose substantial costs, particularly where the law of the host Member State is relatively business friendly. The adverse impact of psychological obstacles or uncertainty factors is difficult to measure. So is the beneficial impact of adopting measures designed to counteract such considerations. Furthermore, if harmonisation takes place at the level of the more highly regulated Member States, the net cost of economic activity in Europe, including the cost of cross-frontier activity, might be more after harmonisation, than before. Until recently, the extent to which measures of company law harmonisation might promote freedom of establishment was approached more as a matter of principle, than of detailed empirical analysis. The results of some company law harmonisation initiatives have at least left doubts as to their practical contribution to the internal market. A perhaps over-cited statistic is that applicable to the Fourth Directive on annual accounts which left no fewer than 41 options to the Member States in addition to 35 options to the business enterprises themselves.[39] The significance of multiple options in a measure of harmonisation is that it places in doubt the extent to which the harmonisation in question is worthy of the name, and might be said to imply that the objective of achieving regulation of one sort or another at European level has overshadowed the aim of promoting cross-border business activity.[40] One reason why the effectiveness or not of measures of company law harmonisation to promote freedom of establishment has proved difficult to assess is that until recently it has not been thought appropriate to put in place mechanisms to attempt to evaluate the contribution by the legislation in question to the internal market. It is clear, however, that at least some initiatives designed to promote cross-frontier establishment of firms and corporate bodies have proved less successful than hoped.

B – Claims to Promote Cross-border Activity Have Not Always Been Made Good: The Example of EEIGs

(i) Characteristics of EEIGs

Council Regulation 2137/85 on European Economic Interest Groupings (EEIGs)[41] was adopted on the basis of Article 352 TFEU. According to its preamble, it aims to provide the means for natural persons, companies, firms and other legal bodies to co-operate effectively across frontiers. The preamble notes that co-operation of this nature can encounter legal, fiscal or psychological difficulties, and that the creation of an appropriate

---

[39] Edwards, above n 2, 117.
[40] Though Edwards argues that 'the achievement of the Fourth Directive in imposing certain common minimum standards should not be underestimated', ibid, 117.
[41] [1985] OJ L199/1.

Community legal instrument in the form of an EEIG would contribute to such co-operation.

An EEIG is based on a written contract, which contains its name, its official address, the names of its members and the duration of the contract. An EEIG must comprise at least two persons, natural or legal, from at least two Member States. EEIG activities must be ancillary to the main businesses of its members, it must not make profits for itself and it cannot practise a profession. The organs of an EEIG are its members, acting collectively, and its manager or managers. The grouping shall be registered in the country in which it has its official address and in each country in which it has an establishment. The official address must be in the EU and either be where the EEIG has its central administration or where one of its members has its central administration or principal place of business. Registration involves filing of information about the grouping, eg the contract, the managers and their powers. The law applying to the internal organisation of an EEIG is the law of the state in which the official address is situated. However, an EEIG is subject to the law of the relevant host state as regards its day-to-day activities and relations with third parties in that country, eg employment of staff and insolvency.

Profits or losses resulting from the activities of an EEIG shall be taxable only in the hands of its members.[42] Profits resulting from a grouping's activities shall be deemed to be the profits of its members and shall be apportioned among them in the proportions laid down in the contract for the formation of the grouping or in the absence of any such provision in each equal shares.[43]

(ii) Drawbacks of EEIGs

The Regulation claims that creation of EEIGs will remove obstacles to cross-frontier business co-operation. Yet it is not clear that it does so. The preamble refers to the fact that cross-frontier business co-operation of the kind envisaged can encounter legal and psychological difficulties. Clearly such difficulties include the need for participants from different Member States to deal with the legal systems of other Member States. Yet the first thing the members have to do is to choose which national law will govern the internal organisation of their EEIG, and hence their legal relationship, just as would be the case if parties from different Member States were seeking more ad-hoc joint-venture arrangements. However, the EEIG is not in other respects a particularly attractive framework for business co-operation. In particular, an EEIG cannot make profits for itself, which significantly reduces its attractiveness as a vehicle for cross-frontier business co-operation. It is difficult to avoid the impression that Member States only agreed to the creation of EEIGs on terms which excluded any possibility that it might compete in any significant way with national alternatives.

The Commission has sought to find niche uses for EEIGs, such as encouraging their use for consortia bidding for European projects. Yet the Economic and Social Committee[44]

---

[42] Art 40.

[43] Art 21.

[44] See the Opinion of the Economic and Social Committee on the 'Communication from the Commission to the Council, the European Parliament, the Economic and Social Committee and the Committee of the Regions on Public–Private Partnerships in Trans-European Transport Network projects' [1998] OJ C129/14: 'The European Economic Interest Grouping (EEIG) statute is a good instrument in the early phases of a project, but it is not well adapted to the requirements of the construction and operation phases.'

and the Court of Auditors have been critical of EEIGs even in such specialist contexts. The Court of Auditors observed:

> The Commission promotes the possibility of using a European Economic Interest Grouping (EEIG) as a mechanism for participating in RTD programmes. . . . Out of the 17 audited JOULE projects, six were coordinated by three different EEIGs. Although the consortium partners were satisfied that the administrative tasks were delegated to a separate entity,which in two cases was located close to the Commission, in none of the cases had the use of an EEIG resulted in easier or faster contract negotiations. On the contrary, there were several additional problems.[45]

(iii) Positive Aspect of EEIGs as an Additional Option Contributing to Regulatory Competition

An important positive feature of EEIGs was that they represented a new approach to European law-making in this field. They offered an additional *option* which did not limit in any way existing options which might be available under national law. This was in terms of technique a contrast to measures of company law harmonisation under Article 50(2)(g) TFEU which have replaced the diversity of national rules with a uniform, or at any rate more uniform, solution. Such additional European options as that offered by the EEIG Regulation contribute to regulatory competition, even if in the event they do not compete very effectively. It is also possible to evaluate whether such initiatives promote cross-frontier activity by monitoring the take-up by businesses of the opportunities they offer.

C – The Need for Empiricism: Evaluation and Feedback on European legislation

Today, more empiricism is regarded as necessary in the legislative process than has been the case in the past, both in general and in the company law harmonisation area in particular. In the Commission's 'White Paper on European Governance',[46] the Commission declares itself committed to an efficient and empirical approach to regulation:

> The European Union will rightly continue to be judged by the impact of its regulation on the ground. It must pay constant attention to improving the quality, effectiveness and simplicity of regulatory acts . . .
>
> — First, proposals must be prepared on the basis of an effective analysis of whether it is appropriate to intervene at EU level and whether regulatory intervention is needed. If so, the analysis must also assess the potential economic, social and environmental impact, as well as the costs and benefits of that particular approach. A key element in such an assessment is ensuring that the objectives of any proposal are clearly identified. . . .
>
> — Sixth, a stronger culture of evaluation and feedback is needed in order to learn from the successes and mistakes of the past. This will help to ensure that proposals do not over-regulate and that decisions are taken and implemented at the appropriate level.[47]

---

[45] Special Report No 17/1998 on support for renewable energy sources in the shared-cost actions of the JOULE-THERMIE Programme and the pilot actions the Altener Programme together with the Commission's replies (Submitted pursuant to Art 188c(4)(2) of the EC Treaty) [1998] OJ C356/03.

[46] Brussels, COM(2001) 428 final, 25 July, 2001.

[47] Ibid, 22.

IV – IMPROVING COMPETITIVENESS THROUGH COMPANY LAW HARMONISATION

A – The Evolution of Law and Policy

The constitutional framework for harmonisation has not stood still. New legal values have taken their place in the EU legal system. After ratification of the Maastricht amendments it was for the first time a declared aim of the European project to strengthen the competitiveness of Community industry. With the Amsterdam amendments in 1997 came an addition to the tasks of the Community—to achieve a high level of competitiveness. With the TL came, instead, a commitment to a 'highly competitive social market economy.' These textual changes have been reflected in the ostensible political direction of the European Union. In 2000 the Lisbon summit committed the European Union to the aim of being the most competitive knowledge-based economy in the world by 2010[48]—though in fact this ambition has not been realised. The Lisbon agenda has been replaced by 'Europe 2020', a 'new strategy for jobs and smart, sustainable and inclusive growth'.[49] This strategy 'will help Europe recover from the crisis and come out stronger, both internally and at the international level, by boosting competitiveness, productivity, growth potential, social cohesion and economic convergence'.[50] It seems that competitiveness is still a central part of Europe's economic strategy. The Council adopted on 13 July 2010 economic policy guidelines in support of the Europe 2020 strategy for jobs and growth, and these emphasise what they describe as 'smart growth', which is growth driven by knowledge and innovation.[51] It must be said that 'smart growth' and the aim of the reforms referred to seem remarkably similar to the ideals of the competitive knowledge-based economy proposed in 2000 in Lisbon. The Council's economic policy guidelines for Europe 2020 also stress the key importance of competitiveness.[52]

These legal, policy and political signals may have some significance. There are signs that in the last decade or so there has been a shift in emphasis, from a model of the internal market in which the price of freedom of movement might be harmonisation, bringing with it uncompetitive levels of regulation, towards a model of the internal market in which freedom of movement, regulatory competition and overall competitiveness play a more significant role.

B – Reports of the High Level Group of Company Law Experts

Some evidence of a shift of the kind referred to above came with the decision of the European Commission to appoint a High Level Group of Company Law Experts (hereafter the HLG) which was to prove a positive factor as regards the future direction of proposals

---

[48] Presidency Conclusions of the Lisbon European Council of 23 and 24 March 23, 2000, Press release nr: 100/1/00, 24/3/2000, published on the website of the Council of the European Union (http://ue.eu.int).

[49] Conclusions of the European Council of 17 June 2010: http://ec.europa.eu/eu2020/pdf/council_conclusion_17_june_en.pdf

[50] Ibid, 3, I.1.

[51] Ibid, point 8 of the Council Recommendation.

[52] Ibid, point 12.

for company law harmonisation. Internal Market Commissioner Frits Bolkestein referred to the setting up of the HLG as facilitating the goal set by the Lisbon Summit of restructuring the European economy to make it the most competitive in the world by 2010[53] The First Report of the HLG was on the proposed Take-over Directive and was presented in January 2002. The market-oriented approach of the HLG is revealed in the opening words of the Report's Summary:

> An important goal of the European Union is to create an integrated capital market in the Union by 2005. The regulation of takeover bids is a key element of such an integrated market.
>
> In the light of available economic evidence the Group holds the view that the availability of a mechanism for takeover bids is basically beneficial. Takeovers are a means to create wealth by exploiting synergies and to discipline the management of listed companies with dispersed ownership, which in the long term is in the best interests of all stakeholders, and society at large. These views also form the basis for the Directive.[54]

The Final Report of the HLG was on 'A Modern Regulatory Framework for Company Law in Europe' and was presented in November 2002.[55] In order to include in its work the broadest possible spectrum of opinions, the Group published a Consultative Document in April 2002, in which it asked those interested in and concerned with company law in Europe to comment on issues relating to modernising the regulatory framework for company law in Europe. The HLG's commitment to competitiveness and empiricism is demonstrated in the following extract from Chapter 2 of its Second Report:

> Company law should first of all facilitate the running of efficient and competitive business enterprises. This is not to ignore that protection of shareholders and creditors is an integral part of any company law. But going forward the Group believes that an important focus of the EU policy in the field of company law should be to develop and implement company law mechanisms that enhance the efficiency and competitiveness of business across Europe. Part of the focus should be to eliminate obstacles for cross-border activities of business in Europe. The European single market is more and more becoming a reality and business will have to become competitive in this wider arena. In order to do so, it will have to be able to efficiently restructure and move across-borders, adapt its capital structures to changing needs and attract investors from many Member States and other countries.

C – The Commission's Response: Modernising Company Law and Enhancing Corporate Governance in the European Union

In May 2003 the Commission gave a strong endorsement to the HLG's approach in a Communication to the Council and European Parliament entitled 'Modernising Company Law and Enhancing Corporate Governance in the European Union—A Plan to Move Forward'.[56] The Commission opens its Communication with a reference to the need for competitiveness:

---

[53] See Annex I of the First Report on Takeover Bids, containing the terms of reference laid down by the Commission for the HLG; see the following note for reference.

[54] Report of the High Level Group of Company Law Experts on issues related to takeover bids, Brussels, 10 January 2002, 2: http://europa.eu.int/comm/internal-market/company/docs/takeoverbids/2002-01-hlg-report-en.pdf.

[55] http://europa.eu.int/comm/internal-market/company/docs/modern/report-en.pdf.

[56] COM(2003) 284 final.

Good company law, good corporate governance practices throughout the EU will enhance the real economy:

An effective approach will foster the global efficiency and competitiveness of businesses in the EU.[57]

And in defining guiding political criteria for its company law Action Plan the Commission gives pride of place to subsidiarity.

In developing this Action Plan, the Commission has paid particular attention to the need for any regulatory response at European level to respect a number of guiding criteria:

— It should fully respect the subsidiarity and proportionality principles of the Treaty and the diversity of many different approaches to the same questions in the Member States, while at the same time pursuing clear ambitions (strengthening the single market and enhancing the rights of shareholders and third parties).[58]

The Action Plan recognises the importance of expert and public consultation as an integral part of the development of company law and corporate governance at Community level, and in April 2005 the Commission established a group of non-governmental experts on corporate governance and company law, 'to serve as a body for reflection, debate and advice to the Commission . . . in particular in connection with the measures foreseen in the Action Plan'.[59] At the fourth meeting of the Advisory Group in January 2006,

[T]he general view was that the new Action Plan should bring about initiatives that are more flexible, leave more choice to the Member States and companies and remove barriers that hinder entrepreneurship . . . the EU should, instead of regulating, lay down principles that Member States would follow or promote, . . . let the market regulate more and intervene only if this mechanism fails.[60]

V – IS THE PROMISE OF MORE EMPIRICAL AND MORE PRO-COMPETITIVE EUROPEAN LEGISLATION BEING REALISED?

A – Two Recent Initiatives

It is nevertheless worth asking the question whether the promise of more empirical and pro-competitive legislation at European level is actually being kept. It is possible to attempt a tentative answer by considering two recent initiatives which were claimed to be designed to make significant contributions to promoting cross-border business activity: the European Company Statute, and the Takeover Bids Directive.

---

[57] A Modern Regulatory Framework for Company Law in Europe: http://europa.eu.int/comm/internal-market/company/docs/modern/report-en.pdf, 3.

[58] Ibid, 4.

[59] Commission Decision 2005/380/EC [2005] OJ L126/40, see in particular, preamble, recital (3).

[60] Minutes of the Meeting of 27 January 2006 of the Advisory Group on Corporate Governnance and Company Law, MARKT/F2/LZ/MFS: D(2005) http://ec.europa.eu/internal_market/company/docs/advisory-committee/minutes4_en.pdf.

B – The European Company Statute

(i) Features of the European Company

Council Regulation 2157/2001 provides the basis for the Statute for a European Company (SE).[61] The Statute is supplemented by Council Directive 2001/86 on the involvement of employees.[62] The Regulation and Directive were adopted by unanimity under Article 352 TFEU and securing agreement on these instruments took many years; the project for a European Company was first subject to a Commission proposal in 1970[63] and was referred to in the Internal Market White Paper of 1985. The European Company Statute (ECS) is a measure designed to contribute to the internal market, and provides an option for companies wishing to merge, create a joint subsidiary or convert a subsidiary into an SE. The SE is a corporate form only available to existing companies incorporated in different Member States. The ECS does not identify in a very specific way, in its preamble, the obstacles which it seeks to remove, though it implies that it will help to counter 'legal and psychological difficulties'. It was originally intended that the ECS would comprise a self-contained European regime, but that aim proved impossible to achieve. While an SE must comply with mandatory rules laid down in the ECS, it has been noted that the latter refers on 84 occasions to the laws of the Member States.[64] Once an SE is established, it will be able to transfer its head office to another Member State without winding up.

The HLG refers to the SE in the following terms in their Final Report:

> The SE represents a major breakthrough, especially because it makes it possible for European companies to merge across-borders and to transfer their seat from one Member State to another. Moreover, it may be important for a company to do business as a European company and not as an Italian, German or French company. This latter objective of the SE, however, is only partly achieved, as the Statute often refers to the law of the Member State of incorporation and, as a result, different types of SEs will come to exist depending on where they have been incorporated.[65]

The SE has a number of mandatory European elements, though many features of the SE remain determined by national company law. The subscribed capital of an SE shall not be less than €120,000.[66] The laws of a Member State requiring a greater subscribed capital for companies carrying on certain types of activity shall apply to SEs with registered offices in that Member State.[67] Subject to the foregoing, the capital of the SE, its maintenance and changes thereto, together with its shares, bonds and other similar securities, shall be governed by the provisions which would apply to a public limited liability company with a registered office in the Member State in which the SE is registered.[68] Article 7 of the ECS provides that the registered office of an SE shall be located within the EU, in the same

---

[61] [2001] OJ L294/1; SE is an acronym for 'Societas Europaea'.

[62] [2001] OJ L294/22.

[63] V Edwards, 'The European Company—Essential Tool or Eviscerated Dream' (2003) 40 *CMLRev* 443, 444.

[64] M Siems, 'The Impact of the European Company (SE) on Legal Culture' (2005) 30 *ELRev* 431, 432.

[65] A Modern Regulatory Framework for Company Law in Europe: http://europa.eu.int/comm/internal-market/company/docs/modern/report-en.pdf, 3, 113.

[66] Council Reg 2157/2001, Art 4(1).

[67] Ibid, Art 4(2).

[68] Ibid, Art 5.

Member State as its head office, thus applying the 'real seat' doctrine to the SE. The ECS gives SEs the choice of opting for a one-tier or two-tier board system.[69]

The ECS and the Directive on the involvement of employees at board level provides for the protection of the rights of employees. Davies has summarised the position as follows:

> In general, one can say that no SE will be formed without either some special employee involvement provisions in place or an explicit decision on the part of the representatives of the employees that they do not want to have special involvement provisions for the SE.[70]

Board-level participation is required, as the default position in an SE, ie in default of agreement by the representatives of employees, only where such requirements are part of the mandatory national law governing a substantial part of the workforce who will be employed by the SE after it is formed.[71] These provisions have led to suggestions that companies registered in Member States whose laws provide for high levels of employee participation will not prove attractive partners to companies registered in Member States that do not provide for employee participation at board level.[72] Unlike the board-level rules, the information and consultation provisions are effectively mandatory for all SEs.[73]

(ii) Assessment of the European Company

A key question is whether the features of the SE make it a sufficiently attractive option to secure significant numbers of registrations. Edwards, writing in 2003 considered 'that the balance sheet is not obviously favourable, and time alone will tell whether the European Company will prove to have been worth the long wait'.[74] The fact that the ECS is a parallel optional regime is an important feature; it makes the regime self-evaluating. The pattern of registrations, and non-registrations, will reveal the perceptions of economic operators as to when the ECS is more cost-effective or otherwise attractive than compliance with national corporate forms. The ECS is in truth an example of regulatory competition. But not regulatory competition between the Member States; the EU has entered the market in competition between legal orders and is in competition with the systems of company law of the Member States.

While it is possible to be enthusiastic about a *method* of company law harmonisation which provides new European options without limiting the number of existing national options, it is appropriate to recall why it took so long to secure agreement on the ECS. While regulatory competition promotes competitiveness, relatively heavily regulated Member States tend to see relatively less heavily regulated regimes as a form of 'unfair' competition, and as providing possibilities for circumvention of elements of national law which are considered to be essential, eg particular schemes for the protection of employees. It was putting in place mechanisms to limit the possibility of such circumvention that prolonged discussion of the ECS for so long.

Research by Eidenmüller et al[75] on SE incorporations between October 2004 and February 2009 has shown that, '[s]ince 2004, the new corporate form has been increas-

---

[69] Ibid, Art 38.
[70] P Davies, 'Workers on the Board of the European Company?' (2003) 32 *Indus LJ* 75, 79.
[71] Ibid, 76.
[72] Ibid; Siems, above n 64, 441.
[73] Davies, above n 70, 81.
[74] Edwards, above n 63, 464.
[75] H Eidenmüller, A Engert and L Hornuf, 'How Does the Market React to the Societas Europaea?' (2010) 11 *European Business Organization Law Review* 35.

ingly used by European firms. . . . While the number of SEs is still in the hundreds, it has so far shown exponential growth.'[76] The authors note that 'the SE has become more and more popular as a corporate form, and the EU must be viewed as an emerging competitor in the market for corporate charters'.[77] Their research reveals 'strong evidence' that the SE is chosen as a means of avoiding national rules which impose mandatory co-determination. They find that the SE

> is popular especially in countries with mandatory co-determination on the board level, and firms seek to reduce this effect or even avoid mandatory co-determination altogether by choosing the SE corporate form. We also find that the use of the SE seems to be motivated at least in part by enhanced corporate mobility with a view to corporate tax savings. . . . Our survey evidence from Germany also suggests that the SE may be preferred to a domestic public company because of the choice between a one-tier and a two-tier board that it offers. Finally, incorporation costs seem to have hampered SE growth.[78]

Eidenmüller et al then sought to establish whether and to what extent the alleged benefits of the SE corporate form actually materialise.[79] They proceeded on the basis that if markets are at least reasonably efficient, the share price should reflect the quality of the corporate governance structure in so far as it has an effect on profitability and the position of shareholders in the firm. They undertook two successive studies in which they considered, essentially, the effect on the share price of the news of reincorporation as an SE. The first study (of 30 firms) indicated significant abnormal increases. The second study included a further eight firms, and still showed some abnormal increases but at a level that was no longer statistically significant.[80] The research leaves unresolved the question whether or not the reasons why incorporation as an SE appeal to firms and their managers, also appeal to diversified shareholders of public companies.[81]

Given the 'exponential growth' in registrations of European Companies recorded by Eidenmüller et al, and the positive market response which this represents, the provisional conclusion must be that the SE meets a need previously unmet by purely national corporate forms, and is accordingly to that extent a success.

C – Directive 2004/25/EC on Takeover Bids[82]

(i) Features of the Directive

Reference has been made to the Commission proposal for a Directive on takeover bids.[83] The Council and the European Parliament failed to adopt the Directive in the form advocated by the Commission. In the form proposed by the Commission the Directive would have had distinctive pro-market and pro-competitive features; these features survive but

---

[76] Ibid, 38. There were 23 registrations Jan 2005–Jan 2006; 40 in 2006–2007; 87 in 2007–2008; and 176 in 2008–2009.

[77] H Eidenmüller, A Engert and L Hornuf, 'Incorporating under European Law: The Societas Europaea as a Vehicle for Legal Arbitrage' (2009) 10 *European Business Organization Law Review* 1.

[78] Ibid, 32.

[79] Eidenmüller et al, above n 75.

[80] Ibid, 47.

[81] Ibid, 48.

[82] Directive 2004/25/EC of the European Parliament and of the Council on takeover bids, [2004] OJ L108/38; Eurlex consolidated text 2009-04-20.

[83] Above at p 683.

are made subject to arrangements which reduce their effectiveness. The main features of the Directive are as follows.[84] There is provision for a mandatory bid, at an equitable price, which must be made to all shareholders, once a natural or legal person acquires a controlling interest in a company. This is designed to protect minority shareholders.[85] When an offeror has acquired at least 90 per cent of the capital carrying voting rights he/she/it is entitled to require all the holders of the remaining securities to sell those securities to him/her/it at a fair price—this is known as 'the right of squeeze-out'.[86] Equally, a holder of remaining securities may require the offeror to buy his/her/its securities at a fair price.[87] Supposedly central features of the Directive are the requirement of board neutrality,[88] and the 'breakthrough rule'.[89] The requirement of board neutrality is in reality more of a requirement of non-frustration, and holds that the board should not take action to frustrate a bid which shareholders might wish to accept.[90] The 'breakthrough' rule is designed to facilitate takeovers, and overrides the voting rights of multiple-vote securities and those provided for in contractual arrangements which might block a bid. Yet while the non-frustration requirement and the breakthrough rule were mandatory in the Commission's original proposal, they were diluted in the course of the legislative process, and made subject to a regime of opt-outs and reciprocity. It is appropriate to consider these rules as they stand in a little more detail.

The Directive provides that during the period when a bid is pending, the board of an offeree company shall obtain the prior authorisation of the general meeting of shareholders given for this purpose before taking any action, other than seeking alternative bids, which may result in the frustration of a bid and in particular before issuing any shares which may result in a lasting impediment to the offeror's acquiring control of the offeree company (Article 9(2)). Mention has already been made of this provision in draft.[91] It is a significant feature of the Directive, and merits further remark.

Various steps might be taken by a board (subject to company law and practice in the relevant Member State) to frustrate a bid.[92] One step is to seek an alternative bid from a more acceptable bidder, sometimes known as the 'white knight' defence, and as noted above this is permitted by Article 9(2) without recourse to the general meeting. Another step to frustrate a bid is identified in Article 9(2), but this does require the consent of the general meeting—the issuing of shares to frustrate a bid. But other steps which may result in a lasting impediment to a successful bid are not listed, and examples are as follows. The 'poison pill' is a rights plan that entitles existing shareholders to securities or cash if a hostile bidder takes control, while being redeemable at the option of the board, should a friendly acquirer take control;[93] the 'sale of crown jewels' is selling valuable assets of the company; 'lock-up' options involve granting preferential options over shares or assets to

[84] For an excellent explanation and discussion, see T Papadopoulos, *EU Law and the Harmonization of Takeovers in the Internal Market* (Alphen aan den Rijn, Kluwer, 2010) ch 11.
[85] Art 5.
[86] Art 15.
[87] Art 16.
[88] Art 9.
[89] Art 11.
[90] Papadopoulos, above n 84, ch 11, 119.
[91] Above at p 683.
[92] See C Kirchner and R Painter, 'Takeover Defenses under Delaware Law, the Proposed Thirteenth EU Directive and the New German Takeover Law: Comparison and Recommendations for Reform' (2002) 50 *Am J Comp L* 451.
[93] Ibid, 452.

white knights or other persons; 'green mail' involves paying the hostile bidder to withdraw its bid; the 'Pac Man defence' involves launching a bid for the bidder itself; while 'golden parachutes' involve contractually binding the target company to make large severance payments to incumbent managers in the event of a change of control.[94] The effect of Article 9(2) is that, apart from seeking alternative bids, the board is precluded from adopting any of the foregoing 'defensive' measures without the prior consent of the general meeting, if they may result in the frustration of the bid.

The Directive further provides that any restrictions on the transfer of securities provided for in the articles of association of the offeree company, or provided for in contractual arrangements between the offeree company and holders of its securities, or in contractual arrangements between holders of the offeree company's securities entered into after the adoption of the Directive, shall not apply vis-à-vis the offeror during the time allowed for acceptance of the bid (Article 11(2)). Furthermore, multiple voting rights shall carry only one vote each, and restrictions on voting rights provided for in the articles of association of the offeree company, or provided for in contractual agreements between the offeree company and the holders of its securities, or in contractual agreements between holders of the offeree company's securities entered into after the adoption of the Directive, shall not apply, at any general meeting which decides on defensive measures in accordance with Article 9 (Article 11(3)).

These provisions of the Directive, if not subject to opt-out arrangements, would have improved conditions for takeovers in the internal market by preventing at least some self-serving defensive measures by company boards—though it must be admitted that the definition of multiple voting shares does not cover certain categories of share which have considerable potential for frustrating takeover bids. One example is that of ceiling or time-lapse voting securities, which are common in France, and which are only fully enfranchised after a specific holding period. The defensive potential of this kind of share is to discourage any potential bidder by ensuring that the offeror acquiring such a share obtains a diluted control right unless he/she/it is able to wait for up to four years for the shares to be fully enfranchised.[95]

In any event, pressure from the European Parliament and certain Member States led to the draft provisions of the Takeover Directive on non-frustration and breakthrough being considerably weakened in the course of the legislative process.[96] The result was that in the version actually adopted, Article 12(1) of the Directive allows Member States to opt out of the rules on defensive measures/voting rights in Articles 9 and/or 11 of the Directive for companies registered in their territories. Companies registered in those Member States which have opted out must nevertheless be allowed to opt into the regime of Articles 9 and/or 11 if they wish (Article 12(2)). And Member States may authorise companies which apply Articles 9 and/or 11 not to apply these Articles if they are the subject of a takeover by a company which does not apply that regime (Article 12(3)). The text of Article 12(3), which refers to companies 'which apply' the Articles in question, and recital (21), which refers to allowing reciprocity to companies which 'apply those provi-

---

[94] The definitions and descriptions are from Kirchner and Painter, ibid, 452; but the terms are widely used in commercial and academic literature and in judicial decisions: see eg *Criterion Properties plc v Stratford UK Properties LLC* [2004] UKHL 28; [2004] 1 WLR 1846 (HL) ('poison pill' agreement).

[95] Papadopoulos, above n 84, ch 11, 129, 130, citing Rickford.

[96] J Rickford, 'Takeovers in Europe, etc' in J Grant (ed), *European Takeovers—The Art of Acquisition* (London, Euromoney Books, 2005) ch 4.

sions in accordance with the optional arrangements', may be read as indicating that it is only companies which voluntarily opt into the application of those Articles which can be allowed to take advantage of the reciprocity rule. The present writer agrees with Rickford that this reading is not inevitable, and produces illogical results.[97] It seems that a number of Member States which apply Articles 9 and/or 11 have nevertheless exempted their companies from applying those Articles if they become the subject of an offer launched by a company which does not apply those Articles.[98]

On the view that reciprocity can be invoked only by a company opting into Articles 9 and/or 11 in a Member State which has opted out of those Articles, target boards of such companies can frustrate bids by home companies, unless those companies have opted in, and will be entitled to frustrate bids by companies subject to the law of a Member State which has opted out of Articles 9 and/or 11, unless the bidding company in question has opted into the latter regime. On the view that reciprocity can be invoked by any company applying the Articles in question (rather than only by companies which have opted in), against any company which does not, reciprocity can be applied by all companies registered in those Member States which have decided against opting out of the Articles in question, against all companies subject to the law of a Member State which has opted out of application of the Articles, unless the company in question has opted in. Whichever view is taken of the category of companies which may invoke reciprocity, reciprocity may lead to a bid from a company in the same Member State being subject to Articles 9 and/or 11 (either because those articles apply to all companies in that Member State or because the company in question has opted in), while a bid from a company registered in another Member State is not (because that Member State has opted out and the bidding company has not opted in); this might seem at first sight to amount to indirect discrimination on grounds of 'nationality' or corporate residence contrary to Article 49 TFEU. Yet any such difference in treatment is not based on the Member State of registration of the company, but results from differences in the legal regimes which may be applicable in different Member States, and indeed within the same Member State; differences moreover which reflect not only Member State choices but also the choices of individual companies. Such differences would seem to be consistent with Article 49 TFEU.

(ii) Assessment of the Takeover Bid Directive

The Commission's proposal was for a European wide takeover regime that would on the face of it have made for a rather more competitive Europe, even if the drafting of the breakthrough rule did not catch voting regimes under all categories of share with the capacity to frustrate a bid. It was modified in the course of the legislative process into a regime which allows Member States to adopt protectionist opt-outs, and target companies to invoke reciprocity against bidders, both of which seem difficult to reconcile with the aims of the Chapter on establishment.

Rickford has argued strongly against the 'international trade policy' logic which underlies reciprocity, saying that:

---

[97] J Rickford, 'The Emerging European Takeover Law from a British Perspective' (2004) 15 *EBLRev* 1379, 1397–98.

[98] France, Greece, Portugal, Slovenia and Spain; see P Davies, E-P Schuster and E van de Walle de Ghelcke, 'The Takeover Directive as a Protectionist Tool', ECGI Working Paper No 141/2010, 22 and note 100. A free download is available at http://ssrn.com/abstract=1554616.

At national company law level the main argument in favour of the provision appears to be that it is somehow legitimate for directors of a target company to inhibit a commercial transaction which would otherwise properly proceed, because . . . the bidder would not be open to a similar bid itself. . . . This general policy argument is likely to be completely irrelevant to the merits of the bid, and not a matter which should be of concern to the target board.[99]

A possible legal objection to the opt-out and reciprocity provisions of the Directive is that they authorise or appear to authorise at least *some* defensive conduct by the board of an offeree company which might amount to an infringement of the right of establishment of a bidding company.[100] The rationale of the takeover Directive, referring in its preamble first and foremost to Article 50(1) TFEU, which has as its aim freedom of establishment, is clearly to achieve freedom of establishment, and the assumption underlying Article 9(2) of the Directive, which prohibits conduct likely to frustrate a bid without the prior authority of the general meeting, seems to be that such defensive conduct, unless taken with the prior authorisation of the general meeting, constitutes an obstacle to the freedom of establishment.

Yet the fact that Article 9(2) is drafted so as to cover all defensive conduct of the board likely to hinder exercise of the right of establishment does not necessarily mean that *all* conduct incompatible with the latter Article would also be incompatible with the right of establishment of a bidder. Article 9(2) is a prophylactic rule which protects the interests of bidder and shareholders by requiring the consent of the general meeting in all cases to action of the kind referred to.

So if the general meeting of a company gives authority to the board, in advance of any bid being made, to adopt certain defensive measures to protect shareholders from inadequate offers, and on the basis that such defensive measures are likely to increase the ability of the target company to negotiate a higher premium, it will be inconsistent with Article 9(2) for the board to take such defensive measures. Yet it is not at all clear that action taken by the board in such circumstances should be considered to amount to an infringement of Article 49 TFEU.

It is suggested above[101] that non-discriminatory activities by or on behalf of market operators to improve their market position vis-à-vis their competitors or their suppliers or customers, are not in principle and in general to be regarded as restrictions on the fundamental freedoms of others, though discriminatory conduct on the part of market operators, or activities which restrict the access to the market of other market operators, would seem capable of amounting to such restrictions. If this analysis is correct, conduct of the kind described above; that is to say, defensive measures authorised in advance of a bid but with a view to protecting shareholders from inadequate bids, cannot be regarded as a restriction on the right of establishment.[102]

On the other hand, Article 49 TFEU would seem to impose some limits on the consequences of opting out of Article 9(2), as would Article 3(c) of the Directive, and the latter provision might be read as aiming in part to ensure that opting out of Article 9(2)

---

[99] Rickford, above n 97, 1402.

[100] See above at p 673.

[101] Above at p 672.

[102] Kirchner and Painter, above n 92, 458, citing C Bergström et al, 'Regulation of Corporate Acqusitions' (1995) *Colum Bus L Rev* 495, 510: 'A conclusion that defensive measures should be prohibited is too simplistic. The matter is complicated because defensive measures also increase a target company's ability to negotiate a higher premium', and adding that 'The higher premiums paid for US companies than for their European counterparts support this observation.'

remains compatible with Article 49 TFEU. Opting out of Article 9(2) does not suspend or create an exception to application of the general principle laid down in Article 3(c) of the Directive, to the effect that 'the board of an offeree company must act in the interests of the company as a whole and *must not deny the holders of securities the opportunity to decide on the merits of the bid*' (emphasis added).

Opting out of Article 9(2) thus does not authorise defensive action by a board which frustrates a bid by pre-empting decisions of shareholders, thereby denying them the opportunity to decide on the merits of the bid. To read Article 9(2) otherwise would be incompatible with Article 3(c) and with Article 49 TFEU. It follows that, in the view of the present writer, opting out of Article 9(2) will still leave certain conduct caught by the latter Article prohibited by the Directive, because it would place the board in default of Article 3(c) and of Article 49 TFEU.

An example of such conduct would be action taken by the board, without the authorisation of the general meeting, to break up the offeree company, in order to frustrate the hostile bid, and prevent shareholders of the target company acting on the favourable assessment the board considered they were likely to make of the bid.[103]

The Directive was to have been implemented by 20 May 2006, and shortly afterwards the Commission published a Staff Document reporting on its Implementation.[104] The Commission recalls at the outset that its proposal for a Directive was based on the assumption that takeovers offer a number of benefits for companies, investors and ultimately for the European economy as a whole. They 'may be effective drivers for value creation', they 'facilitate corporate restructuring and consolidation and provide a means for companies to achieve an optimal scale', and they 'discipline managements and stimulate competition'.

The Commission acknowledges that takeovers are not always beneficial for all, or any, of the parties concerned, but argue that, in the long run, takeovers are in the best interests of stakeholders and companies.[105] The Commission notes that the final text of the Directive allowed considerable deviation at national level from its key provisions, and that the impact of the Directive would therefore depend largely on the way it is implemented in the Member States.[106] The Commission's conclusions are largely negative. While accepting that it is difficult to predict the Directive's effects, and acknowledging that some provisions are likely to bring better protection for minority shareholders, the Commission warns:

> However, there is a risk that the board neutrality rule, as implemented in Member States will hold back the emergence of a European market for corporate control, rather than facilitate it. It is unlikely that the breakthrough rule, as implemented in Member States would bring any significant benefits in the short term. A large number of Member States have shown strong reluctance to lift takeover barriers. The new board neutrality regime may even result in the emergence of new obstacles on the market of corporate control. The number of Member States implementing the Directive in a seemingly protectionist way is unexpectedly large.[107]

In view of the potentially negative effects of the new takeover rules on the European market, the Commission indicates its intention to monitor closely the way in which the

---

[103] The example is taken from Kirchner and Painter, above n 92, 468, though they are commenting on the scope of the German takeover code which came into force on 1 January 2002, rather than on the issues discussed in the text.

[104] Commission Staff Working Document, Report on the Implementation of the Directive on Takeover Bids, SEC(2007) 268.

[105] Ibid, 3.

[106] Ibid, 3.

[107] Ibid, 10.

Directive's rules are applied and work in practice, and to evaluate their effects, as well as analysing the reasons why Member States are so reluctant to endorse the fundamental rules of the Directive.[108]

The Directive requires the Commission to examine the Directive in the light of the experience acquired in applying it and, if necessary, to propose its revision. This examination shall take place five years after the date fixed for transposition, that is to say, in May 2011.[109]

One analysis confirms the assessment of the Commission, and considers that 'overall' the Member States takeover rules are now located 'somewhat further away' from the Commission's ideal of a comprehensive, mandatory, 'board neutrality rule' than was the case before the adoption of the Directive.[110] Yet this same analysis concludes that this might be a good policy outcome, arguing that there is more than one way of organising efficient production in a capitalist system, and that different Member States have made difference choices. From this perspective, imposing rules reflecting one model of organisation of the firm across all Member States, 'is likely to impose significant costs on those Member States which have adopted a different model, while conferring only modest gains on those which have already adopted the preferred model'.[111]

Another study argues that research on the advantage to shareholders resulting from corporate acquisitions fails to demonstrate that it is essential either to implement a board neutrality rule generally, or to negate the possibility of defensive measures in order to protect the interests of shareholders.[112] This study concludes that the opt-out possibilities have in practice in been popular with Member States, and that a consensus has emerged regarding the effectiveness of the Directive and that any change would 'upset the balance and lead to a sub-optimal outcome'.[113]

The Commission's proposal for a Takeover Bid Directive was designed to put in place a single 'efficient' and transparent model for takeovers in Europe, with a board neutrality rule, and a breakthrough rule, at its heart. The inclusion of opt-out provisions, and the fairly enthusiastic use of those provisions by Member States, has produced a legal landscape for takeovers in which it is, overall, as easy or even easier than it was, rather than more difficult than it was, for boards of target companies to frustrate bids if they wish to do so. This confirms that no consensus exists for implementation of the model proposed by the Commission. Furthermore, real question marks must arise as to whether a 'one-size-fits-all' model would in any event provide the overall benefits which advocates of that model would wish to see. On balance, it cannot be said with any degree of confidence that the Takeover Bids Directive has made any contribution at all to the wellbeing of companies and their stakeholders, or to the overall competitiveness of the European economy.

---

[108] Ibid, 10 and 11.

[109] Directive, Art 20.

[110] Davies et al, above n 98, 48 and 49.

[111] Ibid, 55.

[112] JA McCahery and EPM Vermeulen, 'Does the Takeover Bids Directive Need Revision', Tilburg Law and Economics Center (TILEC) Law and Economics Discussion Paper 2010-006, 16; a free download is available at http://papers.ssrn.com/sol3/papers.cfm?abstract_id=1547861.

[113] Ibid, 17.

VI – CONCLUDING REMARKS

It has always been possible to rationalise measures of company law harmonisation in terms of promotion of cross-border business activity. It is more difficult to confirm the effectiveness in practice of such measures. The Commission's approach to company law harmonisation has, however, changed—perhaps more than that of the European Parliament and the Member States. The Commission has sought to utilise company law harmonisation as a means of promoting cross-border business activity to a greater extent than in the past, which accords with the logic of the Treaty basis for harmonisation being the chapter on establishment. The Commission has also embraced an approach to the internal market which lays greater emphasis on global competitiveness than has been the case in the past. All this is consistent with the emphasis placed on competitiveness in the EC Treaty post-Maastricht, and with the current commitment post Lisbon in the TEU to a 'highly competitive social market economy'. The change in the Commission's approach is also explicable on broader policy and political grounds, reflected in the conclusions of the Lisbon Presidency 2000, with their stated aim of making the EU the most competitive knowledge-based economy in the world, and in the successors of the Lisbon strategy, in the form of 'Europe 2020' and 'smart growth'.

Not all Member States, nor indeed the European Parliament, have responded favourably to Commission proposals designed to strengthen the internal market by liberalising it. Negotiation of the ECS was heavily influenced by the desire of some Member States to prevent circumvention of their national rules on employee participation at board level. Interestingly enough, one reason identified in the literature for opting for the form of a European Company has been to secure precisely such circumvention. As regards both the EEIG, and more recently, the ECS, the preoccupation of some Member States with preventing European joint venture or corporate models from effectively competing with their own national corporate forms has in each case reduced the attractiveness of the European model which has emerged from the negotiating process. Nevertheless, the steady increase in registrations of companies formed under the ECS indicates that the market sees it as meeting a need so far unmet by other available options. The verdict on the ECS must accordingly be—so far so good.

The changes made to the proposed Statute for a European Private Company during the legislative process—discussed in the previous chapter—show a potentially popular alternative to national corporate forms being progressively subjected to the very regulation the absence of which inspired the Commission to propose it, and confined to niche cross-border activities.

One procedural advantage of the EEIG and the SE (and of the European Cooperative Society and of any future European Private Company) is that they are or would be freestanding European initiatives which do not limit the options open to businesses under the various national laws of the Member States. The European legal order has in such cases entered into competition (a little timidly perhaps) with the national legal orders, rather than harmonising national options out of existence. Where the Commission has proposed that certain national options should be harmonised out of existence, because it considered that those options stood in the way of cross-border takeovers, it has failed to secure the support of the European Parliament and the Member States. The Commission's proposal for a Directive on Takeover Bids, if it had been adopted without its opt-out and reciprocity provisions, would almost certainly have had more impact on market behaviour than any other measure of company law harmonisation which has ever been adopted to date. In that case, was its dilution by opt-out and reciprocity arrangements a major set back for the internal market? Or was it a reminder that European proposals which insist that 'one size fits all' may simply reinforce the status quo in some Member States, while causing unwanted and costly adjustment in others? That question, it seems, must remain open.

Further Reading

P Davies, E-P Schuster, E van de Walle de Ghelcke, 'The Takeover Directive as a Protectionist Tool', ECGI Working Paper No 141/2010. A free download is available at http://ssrn.com/abstract=1554616.

H Eidenmüller, A Engert and L Hornuf, 'How does the Market React to the Societas Europaea?' (2010) 11 *European Business Organization Law Review* 35.

J A McCahery and EPM Vermeulen, 'Does the Takeover Bids Directive Need Revision', Tilburg Law and Economics Center (TILEC) Law and Economics Discussion Paper 2010-006. A free download is available at http://papers.ssrn.com/sol3/papers.cfm?abstract_id=1547861.

T Papadopoulos, *EU Law and the Harmonisation of Takeovers in the Internal Market* (Alphen aan den Rijn, Kluwer, 2010) ch 11.

Part V

Competition Law

22

Introduction to
EU Competition Law

This chapter assesses the objectives and functions of competition law in its specific EU context, distinguishing between its early focus upon buttressing the single market and its more modern place in the post-Lisbon competitiveness agenda. The chapter will outline the primary EU competition rules, contained in Articles 101 and 102 TFEU, together with the system for enforcement, primarily identified in Regulation 1/2003. The application of these rules together with the rules on state aid and state regulation, in Articles 107–09 and 106 TFEU, respectively, will be detailed in subsequent chapters, but it is important in this chapter to note the modernisation agenda which has affected the scope and application of each of these sets of rules. The chapter will then focus on the personal and territorial scope of the competition rules. In relation to the former, the chapter will outline the central concept of an 'undertaking', especially when applied to state organisation of healthcare and other activities. The territorial dimensions of the competition rules are also discussed with attention paid to the extra-territorial application of EU law and the increasing importance of bilateral and multilateral competition agreements and global co-operation networks, notably the International Competition Network (ICN).

I – EU COMPETITION LAW SOURCES

The primary Treaty provisions in which the substantive law on competition is to be found are Articles 101–09 TFEU. Together, these form the framework for EU competition law applicable to private undertakings, public enterprises and states. In addition, EU secondary legislation provides the detailed substance for merger control and enforcement action. The whole scheme of competition law is increasingly supplemented by 'soft law' devices, such as Guidelines, Notices and Communications, which provide important signals to business and legal communities as to the Commission's thinking and operation of key ideas such as market definition, fines and leniency policies and a framework for public service compensation.[1] However, the preamble and the general provisions of Articles 2

---

[1] See eg HCH Hofmann, 'Negotiated and Non-Negotiated Administrative Rule-Making—The Example of EC Competition Policy' (2006) 43 *CMLRev* 153.

and 3 EC played a significant part in the development of the case law on competition.[2] Articles 2 and 3(1) EC have been replaced in substance by Article 3 TEU and Articles 3–6 TFEU, respectively, and Article 3(2) EC is now Article 8 TFEU. The most significant provision in this context was Article 3(1)(g) EC, which required 'the institution of a system ensuring that competition in the internal market is not distorted'. However, following ratification of the TL, Article 3(1)(g) was effectively removed from the Treaty (at the instigation of the French delegation in the Treaty negotiations), and the 'competition principle' was downgraded from a Treaty provision to a protocol (No 27) annexed to the Treaties.[3] The removal of the competition principle from Treaty objective status has been criticised on the basis that although it may have played a minimal role in straightforward cartel and abuse of dominance cases under Articles 101 and 102, the Court relied on the provision in a wide array of cases involving the duties of Member States to ensure competitive markets, under the state aid rules, in the application of Article 106 TFEU, or in the combined application of Article 101 with Article 10 EC (now Article 4(3) TEU). Accordingly there is concern that the scope and application of these rules in particular may be emasculated following ratification of the TL.[4]

A – The Principal Treaty Provisions

So far as the behaviour of undertakings is concerned, EU law adopts a distinction which is familiar in competition law (or, to use the US term, 'antitrust law'[5]) between two types of problem that may arise. The first concerns restrictive agreements or practices involving a degree of collusion between undertakings that are economically independent of each other—the practice of forming 'cartels'. Examples can be found in agreements between A and B to keep out of each other's markets or to fix prices. Article 101 TFEU (ex Article 81 EC) is designed to deal with such situations. It is considered in Chapter 23. The second type of problem arises where a single undertaking (or a group of undertakings acting collectively) has reached a position of such strength in a given market that the normal constraints of the competitive process no longer apply to it. This is known in EU law as a 'dominant position'. Dominant undertakings represent a danger to other operators in the same market and to their customers or suppliers. They may, for example, drive the remaining participants in the same market out of business or charge unreasonably high prices for their products. Article 102 TFEU (ex Article 82 EC) is designed to deal with such abuses of dominance, and is discussed in Chapter 24. Here regulatory power is used primarily as a constraining influence, to compensate for the absence of effective competition. Another way of averting the problems of market power is to attack the fact of dominance itself, by seeking to prevent the growth of undertakings beyond a certain point, and by taking power to break up any that may succeed in doing so. This latter,

---

[2] See eg Case 32/65 *Italy v Council and Commission* [1966] ECR 389, 405; Case 6/72 *Europemballage and Continental Can v Commission* [1973] ECR 215, 243–44.

[3] For further discussion, see A Riley, 'The EU Reform Treaty and the Competition Protocol: Undermining EC Competition Law [2007] *ECLR* 703; R Lane, 'EU Law: Competition' (2010) 59 *ICLQ* 489.

[4] Ibid.

[5] In the nineteenth century anti-competitive arrangements were often carried out in the USA through trusts, hence this term.

structural, issue will now normally fall within the Merger Regulation,[6] at least where there is the requisite Community dimension in turnover and geographical terms. The Merger Regulation, and the Commission's supervisory role in relation to merger control, are not considered further in this book.[7]

Provision for the application of the substantive rules in Articles 101 and 102 is made by Articles 103–05 TFEU (ex Articles 83–85 EC). Article 103 empowers the Council, on a proposal from the Commission and after consulting the European Parliament, to adopt implementing regulations or directives. This power was used for the enactment of, inter alia, Regulation 17/62, which established the basic machinery for the execution of EU competition policy, giving primary responsibility to the Commission in a system originally contemplating ex ante notification.[8] This enforcement regime was dismantled and replaced by a new, decentralised regime in the form of Council Regulation 1/2003,[9] which became effective from 1 May 2004. Following Regulation 1/2003, national competition authorities (NCAs) have assumed an important role, alongside the Commission, as part of the European Competition Network (ECN) in enforcing EU competition law across the Member States of the Union. These arrangements, discussed further in Chapter 25 below, rely on ex post facto control of anti-competitive conduct. Furthermore, Chapter 25 will discuss the increasing significance of national courts in applying the EU competition rules to private litigation.

Under Articles 107–09 TFEU (ex Articles 87–89 EC) the EU institutions, and in particular the Commission, have supervisory powers over the granting of aids to industry in the various Member States. The general principle is that aid must not be granted if it distorts, or threatens to distort, competition by favouring certain undertakings or forms of production, in so far as trade between Member States may be affected. However, exceptions are permitted in relation to a number of economic, regional, social and cultural concerns, enabling the Commission to take account of the various pressures to which the Member States are subject. These provisions are discussed in Chapter 26.

Problems arising from the relationships between governments, on the one hand, and public undertakings or undertakings which have been entrusted with the performance of certain tasks in the public interest, on the other, are the subject of Article 106 TFEU (ex Article 86 EC). This relationship, although clearly liable to affect the conditions of competition, has a wider significance for the operation of the internal market. In particular, Article 106(2) provides an opportunity for entrusted undertakings to escape the application of 'normal' Treaty rules.[10] A particular issue which has arisen in recent years has been the provision of state support to undertakings charged with the operation of services of general economic interest (SGEIs). The significance of Article 106 and its interaction with other Treaty rules are also discussed in Chapter 26.

---

[6] Council Regulation 139/2004 [2004] OJ L24/1.

[7] For further reading, see M Rosenthal and S Thomas, *European Merger Control* (Oxford, Hart Publishing, 2010). See also A Weitbrecht, 'Horizontals Revisited—EU Merger Control in 2010' [2011] *ECLR* 126.

[8] [1962] JO 204; [1959–62] OJ 87.

[9] [2003] OJ L1/1.

[10] See J Baquero Cruz, 'Beyond Competition: Services of General Interest and European Community Law' in G de Búrca (ed), *EU Law and the Welfare State—In Search of Solidarity* (Oxford, Oxford University Press, 2005); also T Prosser, *The Limits of Competition Law, Markets and Public Services* (Oxford, Oxford University Press, 2005) esp chs 6–8. See further discussion in Chapter 26.

B – Other Sources of EU Competition Law

In addition to the Treaty provisions discussed above, the principal sources of EU competition law are regulations pursuant to Article 103 TFEU, the case law of the Court of Justice and the General Court (formerly the Court of First Instance (CFI)), and the administrative practice of the Commission.

Regulations on competition have been adopted by both the Council and the Commission, the latter acting under delegated powers. Regulation 1/2003, the general implementing Regulation for the enforcement of Articles 101 and 102 TFEU, has already been mentioned. The Court of Justice has played a vital part in the development of the rules on competition, as with other areas of EU law. Competition matters normally come to the European Courts by way of proceedings under Article 263 TFEU (ex Article 230 EC) for the review of decisions of the Commission applying the rules, or through references under Article 267 TFEU (ex Article 234 EC) from national courts before which the rules have been invoked.[11] In addition, the Court of Justice has unlimited jurisdiction to hear appeals against the imposition by the Commission of fines or periodic penalty payments for infringements of the rules.[12] Proceedings under Article 263 relating to the implementation of the competition rules of the EU must be brought before the General Court.[13] Appeal to the Court of Justice from the General Court can be made only on points of law. As a result of this realignment of responsibilities, the Court of Justice no longer has quite the same opportunities to influence the development of competition law as it once had,[14] although its exclusive role in providing preliminary rulings under Article 267 TFEU (ex Article 234 EC) remains, at least for the foreseeable future.[15] The role of the General Court and the Court of Justice, and the extent to which the potential for judicial review and annulment shores up deficiencies of the Commission decision-making process in relation to human rights law principles and the ECHR, will be considered in Chapter 25.

The Commission is the authority with primary responsibility for the administration and enforcement of EU competition rules. For this purpose it has been empowered to take decisions, inter alia, to order termination of infringements,[16] to make findings of inapplicability[17] and to impose fines[18] or periodic penalty payments.[19] In addition to its decisions in individual cases, the Commission's policy and practice can also be discerned from its Annual Reports on Competition Policy. Moreover, in recent years the Commission has increasingly made greater use of 'soft law' mechanisms such as Notices and Guidelines. These have covered a variety of topics, including market definition, de minimis rules, the 'allocation' of cases within the ECN network, fines and leniency, and enforcement priorities in relation to Article 102. Notices and Guidelines are influential in the areas

---

[11] See B Rodger, *Article 234 and Competition Law: An Analysis* (The Hague, Kluwer Law International, 2007).
[12] See Art 31 of Regulation 1/2003.
[13] Art 3(1)(c) of Council Decision 88/591, Establishing an EC Court of First Instance [1988] OJ L319/1. See Chapter 3 for a fuller discussion of the respective roles of the Court of Justice and General Court.
[14] See generally D Gerber, *Law and Competition in Twentieth Century Europe: Protecting Prometheus* (Clarendon Press, Oxford, 1998).
[15] See Rodger, above n 11.
[16] Art 7 of Regulation 1/2003.
[17] Art 10.
[18] Art 23.
[19] Art 24.

they cover, offering guidance and an element of certainty for the business community, and although not technically binding they create legitimate expectations as to how the Commission will act.[20]

Finally, the national courts and NCAs are increasingly important sources for the application and development of EU competition law. The directly effective provisions of Articles 101 and 102 invite recourse to national courts for the application of EU competition law. This is particularly true since the modernisation reforms of 2004 removed the Commission's previously exclusive power over Article 101(3) individual exemptions. National courts may accordingly now apply all of the provisions of Articles 101 and 102.[21] As part of the same reform package, NCAs are now also an integral part of the enforcement mechanism for EU competition law. Acting on their own initiative or on a complaint, such authorities may take decisions requiring infringements to be brought to an end, and impose a range of remedial measures and penalties provided for in their national law.[22]

II – COMPETITION LAW AND POLICY IN AN EU CONTEXT

Competition, at least in a commercial context, describes a struggle for superiority in the marketplace. It is an essential aspect of the market mechanism because the availability of choice between goods and services establishes a link between the success of an undertaking and its ability to satisfy consumers' wishes. The abstract, neoclassical perfect competition model is based on the presumption that society is better off when a state of perfect competition exists in a market—a market with infinite buyers and sellers, identical products and full information available to all buyers and sellers: in this type of market, efficiency is maximised. Like all modern competition (or 'antitrust') systems, EU law has adapted this theoretical economic paradigm to develop competition law in the light of the evolving policies and priorities of the European Union. Following a sustained period where the focus was upon the relationship between EU competition law and the single market, more recently the modernisation agenda has led to a reorientation in the application of the EU competition rules, primarily by the adoption of a more economics-based,[23] and efficiency-driven, consumer welfare approach.

A – The Early Focus Upon the Market

In the introduction to its *First Report on Competition Policy* the Commission wrote:

> Competition is the best stimulant of economic activity since it guarantees the widest possible freedom of action to all. An active competition policy pursued in accordance with the provi-

[20] See Hofmann, above n 1.

[21] Art 6 of Regulation 1/2003. See Chapter 25 for a fuller discussion regarding private enforcement.

[22] Art 5. See fuller discussion on Regulation 1/2003, the ECN and the role of the NCAs in Chapter 25.

[23] See J Drexl, L Idot and J Moneger (eds), *Economic Theory and Competition Law* (Cheltenham, Edward Elgar, 2009); S Bishop and M Walker, *The Economics of EC Competition Law: Concepts, Application and Measurement*, 3rd edn (London, Sweet & Maxwell, 2009).

sions of the Treaties establishing the Communities makes it easier for the supply and demand structure continually to adjust to technological development. Through the interplay of decentralized decision making machinery, competition enables enterprises continuously to improve their efficiency, which is the sine qua non for a steady improvement in living standards and employment prospects within the countries of the Community. From this point of view, competition policy is an essential means for satisfying to a great extent the individual and collective needs of our society.[24]

This early statement clearly portrayed competition policy as ensuring that the common market envisaged by the Treaty functioned as a genuine *market*. The importance of this focus was equally reflected in the emphasis placed by the Court of Justice upon the notion of *workable* competition. This expresses the 'degree of competition necessary to ensure the observance of the basic requirements and attainment of the objectives of the Treaty, in particular the creation of a single market achieving conditions similar to those of a domestic market'.[25] The idea of workable competition, not being anchored in any particular economic doctrine, permitted pragmatic responses to diverse and complex issues. Among the disparate areas which competition policies might address are the following: consumer welfare, the redistribution of wealth, the protection of small and medium-sized enterprises, regional, social or industrial considerations, and the integration of the single market. These concerns are not necessarily mutually compatible or easily reconciled in any given situation. Questions as to how they are to be balanced or, indeed, whether they are legitimate elements in competition policy at all, remain controversial for lawyers and economists alike.[26]

Many factors affecting competition and competition policy, such as industrial or social policy, are not peculiar to the European context. The exception, of course, is the influence wrought by the drive to create a single internal market.[27] Here, competition policy reinforces other EU provisions aiming at the removal of barriers between the economies of the Member States. Dismantling those (mainly) public obstacles to trade will hardly be effective if they are simply replaced by private ones. It would be futile to attempt to create a single market without internal frontiers in goods, persons, services and capital, if the isolation of national markets could effectively be maintained by restrictive practices on the part of undertakings, or by state aid policies giving competitive advantages to national industries. As will be seen in the discussion of Articles 101 and 102 in succeeding chapters, market partitioning is a particularly serious infringement of the rules on competition. Nevertheless, it is clear that EU competition policy's preoccupation with market integration has diminished in the last ten years at least, and the modernisation agenda has brought different considerations and conflicts to the fore.

---

[24] (1971) Comp Rep 11.

[25] Case 26/76 *Metro v Commission* [1977] ECR 1875, 1904.

[26] See, inter alia, the discussion of so-called Harvard and Chicago School economic theories by ? Burton, 'Competition over Competition Analysis: A Guide to Some Contemporary Economics Disputes' in J Lonbay (ed), *Frontiers of Competition Law* (London, Wiley Chancery Law, 1994) ch 1. Also R Bork, *The Antitrust Paradox: A Policy at War with Itself* (New York, Basic Books, 1978, reprinted with new Introduction and Epilogue, 1993); D Hildebrand, 'The European School in EC Competition Law' (2002) 25 *World Competion* 3; C Townley, *Article 81 EC and Public Policy* (Oxford, Hart Publishing, 2009).

[27] See C-D Ehlermann, 'The Contribution of EC Competition Policy to the Single Market' (1992) 29 *CMLRev* 257.

B – Post-'Lisbon' Modernisation: Competitiveness, Consumer Welfare and Efficiency

As the internal market came closer to realisation, so its position as the pre-eminent driver of competition policy diminished.[28] The so-called Lisbon strategy,[29] adopted in 2000, committed Member States to make the EU 'the world's most competitive and dynamic knowledge-based economy' by 2010. In 2004 the Commission set out its ideas for a 'proactive competition policy',[30] characterised by:

— improvement of the regulatory framework for competition which facilitates vibrant business activity, wide dissemination of knowledge, a better deal for consumers, and efficient restructuring throughout the internal market; and

— enforcement practice which actively removes barriers to entry and impediments to effective competition that most seriously harm competition in the internal market and imperil the competitiveness of European enterprises.

The goal of such a policy 'is to support the competitive process in the internal market and to induce firms to engage in competitive and dynamically efficiency-enhancing behaviours'.[31] The instrumentalism of competition law and policy is clear, as the Commission explicitly acknowledged: '[C]ompetition is not an end in itself. It is a vital market process which rewards firms offering lower prices, better quality, new products, and greater choice.'[32]

More recently, the Commission has focused its enforcement effort on international cartels affecting the EU market and consumers. It is instructive to read the foreword to the Report on Competition Policy 2006 by Neelie Kroes, as it provides a flavour of how she was developing the competition law agenda during her period as Competition Commissioner:

> The experience of the past fifty years of European integration shows that fair and undistorted competition in a single market works to the benefit of everyone in terms of prosperity, consumer choice, and sustainable employment.
>
> 'Free competition' is not an end in itself—it is a means to an end. When we strive to get markets working better, it is because competitive markets provide citizens with better goods and better services, at better prices. Competitive markets provide the right conditions for companies to innovate and prosper, and so to increase overall European wealth. More wealth means more money for governments to use to sustain the fabric of our societies and to guarantee social justice and a high-quality environment for generations to come.
>
> When companies fix prices in markets like beer or elevators, customers pay higher prices and the economy at large picks up the bill. When companies abuse a dominant position, they not only exclude competitors but also dampen innovation since other companies know that however good their products are, they cannot compete on the merits. So our European anti-trust rules outlaw such behaviour throughout the Union, to the benefit of consumers.
>
> European companies need to be able to take advantage of an open internal market, by creating efficiencies of scale and diversifying. Our merger control rules allow European champions to grow on their merits, developing into global players, provided that consumers are not harmed through reduced competition.
>
> Our properly balanced state aids discipline prevents undue state intervention which would

---

[28] T Frazer, 'Competition Policy after 1992: The Next Step' (1990) 53 *MLR* 609.
[29] An agenda first adopted in March 2000, then relaunched in March 2005.
[30] See *A Proactive Competition Policy for a Competitive Europe*, COM(2004) 293 final.
[31] Ibid, para 2.2.
[32] Ibid, para 2.1.

distort competition on the merits, but also increasingly helps Member States to target support where it is most effective in filling genuine gaps in the overall public interest, and so get real added value for tax-payers' money.

The spirit and objectives underlying the European competition rules, and the need to enforce them effectively, remain as pertinent today as ever before. But of course the environment in which competition policy functions changes and develops over time. European companies, employees and consumers are increasingly part of a global economy, and are having to adjust to reap the benefits globalisation has to offer.[33]

Despite this clear statement on overall objectives and priorities, it is evident that EU competition policy has been in a state of transition in recent years, visible in various aspects of the modernised application of its fundamental rules. Indeed, the reforms of 2004, together with Court case-law, have had a significant impact on the modern view of Article 101, which has become a more sophisticated instrument, assessing collusive arrangements in the light of their effects in the relevant market, an approach more firmly based in economics and market analysis. Nonetheless, there has also been a development in the recognition of other public-interest objectives which may ensure that an agreement falls outside the scope of the prohibition in Article 101(1), demonstrating the need to balance competition law with other policy objectives. Furthermore, there has been considerable debate and academic discussion regarding the rationale underlying Article 102 and the extent to which it should be predicated upon demonstrable consumer harm, as opposed to a more ordoliberal-inspired vision of open and competitive markets resulting in a more formalistic and interventionist application of Article 102.[34] It will be interesting to note the extent to which the Commission's 2009 Guidelines on Enforcement Priorities,[35] and the purported emphasis on an effects-based approach, will alter the Commission's approach to Article 102, which in recent years has attracted considerable critique as overly protecting competitors.[36] The key issues at the forefront of the debate, which derive to a great extent from the US antitrust tradition following the Chicago School, are the use of economics to guide the application of competition law and the extent to which competition law should be founded on the goal of consumer welfare, predicated on efficiency.[37] Nonetheless, consumer welfare Chicago-style (otherwise known as total welfare) is a different concept from consumer welfare in an EU context, where the consumer interest, and the associated protection of consumers from anti-competitive abuses by cartels and firms with market power has been stressed as the key factor in EU competition policy generally,[38] bolstered by the appointment of a Consumer Liaison Officer within DG Comp, and more recently by the focus in the debate on private enforcement in ensuring adequate collective redress for consumers.[39] As discussed in greater detail in Chapter 26, the Commission launched a comprehensive reform of state aid rules and procedures in its State Aid Action Plan in

---

[33] Available at http://ec.europa.eu/comm/competition/annual_reports/2006/en.pdf.

[34] See, in particular, P Akman 'Searching for the Long-Lost Soul of Art 82 EC' [2009] *OJLS* 267; T Eilmansberger, 'How to Distinguish Good from Bad Competition Under Article 82 EC: In Search of Clearer and More Coherent Standards for Anti-Competitive Abuses' (2005) 42 *CMLRev* 129.

[35] See Chapter 24.

[36] See eg B Sher, 'The Last of the Steam-Powered Trains: Modernizing Article 82' [2004] *ECLR* 243.

[37] See above n 26, and see also F Maier-Rigaud, 'On the Normative Foundations of Competition Law, Efficiency, Political Freedom and the Freedom to Compete', ASCOLA Competition Law Series (Cheltenham, Edward Elgar, forthcoming).

[38] See P Marsden and P Whelan, '"Consumer Detriment" and its Application in EC and UK Competition Law' [2007] *ECLR* 569

[39] See Chapter 25.

June 2005.[40] The state aid reform measures subsequently introduced reflect many of the themes developed in relation to Articles 101 and 102, notably an increased reliance on economic analysis of market failures. On the other hand, in relation to state aid, and the limits imposed on governmental market participation and regulation by Article 106, the concept of SGEIs has been particularly significant, with attention devoted to the ways and the extent to which Member States regulate the provision of public service obligations, as discussed in Chapter 26.

Despite a temporary relaxation of the state aid rules in response to the economic and financial crisis since 2008, the current Competition Commissioner, Joaquin Alumina, has stressed the need for more effective competition law enforcement, in particular in relation to cartels, as opposed to protectionism, to ensure the EU economy overcomes the crisis.[41] Furthermore, he has emphasised the multiple (and potentially conflicting) goals and objectives underpinning EU competition law, in particular identifying the relationships between EU competition policy and the social market, the internal market, competitiveness and international co-operation, respectively.[42]

III – THE SCOPE OF THE EU COMPETITION RULES

A – 'Personal' Scope

The rules in Articles 101 and 102 apply to 'undertakings'. No definition of this concept for the purposes of competition law is provided by the Treaties. However, the Court has taken an expansive and functional view of the notion, holding that it 'encompasses every entity engaged in an economic activity, regardless of the legal status of the entity and the way in which it is financed'.[43] The requirement of participation in economic activities must be understood in a wide sense. It covers not only the production and distribution of goods but also the provision of services.[44] A body that exists for a non-economic purpose but engages in certain operations of a commercial nature will be, to that extent, an undertaking:[45] for example a public service broadcasting establishment when it licenses the manufacture of toys based on a popular children's series.[46] Nor is there any need for the body in question to be motivated by the pursuit of profits. Thus, societies that manage the rights of authors and performing artists on a non-profit-making basis qualify as undertakings because they provide a commercial service.[47]

The entities accepted as undertakings by the Court of Justice and the Commission

---

[40] State Aid Action Plan, Less and Better Targeted State Aid: A Roadmap for State Aid Reform 2005–2009, COM(2005) 107 final, Commission press release IP/05/680, 7 June 2005.

[41] See Commission website, speech/11/96, 11 February 2011.

[42] See Commission website, speech/11/17, 14 January 2011.

[43] Case C-41/90 *Höfner v Macrotron* [1991] ECR I-1979, para 21.

[44] Case 155/73 *Sacchi* [1974] ECR 409; [1974] 2 CMLR 177.

[45] ibid.

[46] *Re BBC* [1976] 1 CMLR D89.

[47] Case 127/73 *BRT v SABAM* [1974] ECR 51 and 313; [1974] 2 CMLR 238; Case 7/82 *GVL v Commission* [1983] ECR 483; [1983] 3 CMLR 645. See also Case C-222/04 *Ministero dell'Economia e delle Finanze v Cassa di Risparmio di Firenze SpA* [2006] ECR I-289; [2008] 1 CMLR 28.

exhibit a wide range of legal forms. They include companies, partnerships,[48] co-operatives[49] and foreign trade associations.[50] Individuals may be undertakings, not just self-employed professionals[51] but also inventors who grant licences for the use of their patents[52] or opera stars who contract to perform for a television company.[53] However, individuals who are 'workers' within the meaning of Article 45 TFEU (ex Article 39 EC) will not be undertakings. Thus in *Becu*[54] 'recognised dockers' were found to perform their work for and under the direction of undertakings, thus satisfying the definition of 'worker'.[55] Since they were, for the duration of that relationship, incorporated into the undertakings concerned and formed an economic unit with each of them, the dockers did not in themselves constitute undertakings within the meaning of EU competition law.[56] Nor could the recognised dockers viewed collectively in a port area be regarded as an undertaking.[57]

The broad approach taken by the Court in *Höfner v Macrotron*[58] has not proved sufficient on its own to resolve complex situations which may arise in relation to the application of the competition rules to activities carried on by a state or state entity. As Advocate General Poiares Maduro has observed,[59] in this area 'the Court is entering dangerous territory, since it must find a balance between the need to protect undistorted competition on the common market and respect for the powers of the Member States'. One explanatory formulation often adopted by the Court is the notion of market participation or at least the exercise of functions in a market context, expressed in a number of cases in the proposition that 'any activity consisting in offering goods and services on a given market is an economic activity'.[60] A line is accordingly drawn between market, economic engagement and the exercise of public authority for regulatory functions.

Thus, in *SAT v Eurocontrol*[61] the body involved was an international organisation charged with supervising air traffic control services within the airspace of the states party to the convention under which it was established, and to collect the charges levied for those services. In the Court's view, Eurocontrol was carrying out, on behalf of the contracting states, tasks in the public interest aimed at contributing to the maintenance and improvement of air navigation safety. Collection of route charges, the subject of the dispute in the case, could not be separated from the organisation's other activities as they were merely the consideration, payable by users, for the obligatory and exclusive use of air navigation control facilities and services. Thus, taken as a whole, Eurocontrol's activities were connected with the exercise of powers relating to the control and supervision of air-

[48] eg *Re William Prym-Werke* [1973] OJ L296/24; [1973] CMLR D250.

[49] eg *Re Rennet* [1980] OJ L51/19; [1980] 2 CMLR 402. The decision was upheld by the Court in Case 61/80 *Co-operatieve Stremsel-en-Kleurselfabriek v Commission* [1981] ECR 851; [1982] 1 CMLR 240.

[50] Even if under their domestic law they have no identity separate from the state: *Re Aluminium Imports from Eastern Europe* [1985] OJ L92/1; [1987] 3 CMLR 813.

[51] Case C-309/99 *Wouters and others* [2002] ECR I-1577, [2002] 4 CMLR 913.

[52] See eg *Re AOIP/Beyrard* [1976] OJ L6/8; [1976] 1 CMLR D14.

[53] *Re Unitel* [1978] OJ L157/39; [1978] 3 CMLR 306.

[54] Case C-22/98 *Becu* [1999] ECR I-5665, [2001] 4 CMLR 968.

[55] See Case C-170/90 *Merci Convenzionali v Porto di Genova* [1991] ECR I-5889.

[56] *Becu*, above n 54, para 26.

[57] Ibid, para 27.

[58] *Höfner v Macrotron*, above n 43.

[59] Case C-205/03P *FENIN v Commission* [2006] ECR I-6295; [2006] 5 CMLR 7 (Opinion, para 26)

[60] Joined Cases C-180–84/98 *Pavlov* [2000] ECR I-6451; [2001] 4 CMLR 30, para 75; Case C-475/99 *Ambulanz Glöckner* [2001] ECR I-8089; [2002] 4 CMLR 726, para 19; Case C-309/99 *Wouters* [2002] ECR I-1577; [2002] 4 CMLR 913, para 47.

[61] Case C-364/92 *SAT Fluggesellschaft v Eurocontrol* [1994] ECR I-43; [1994] 5 CMLR 208.

space, which are typically those of a public authority. They were not of an economic nature justifying the application of the EU competition rules.[62] Similarly, charges levied by a body made responsible by the state for pollution surveillance at a particular port were held to be integral to its general surveillance activities and outside the scope of Article 102.[63]

There is perhaps a whiff of circularity in some of these arguments. The capacity to undermine the goals of competition policy can itself become the 'economic' character that leads to application of the Treaty provisions. This purposive approach has its champions. As Advocate General Jacobs has argued:[64]

> In assessing whether an activity is economic in character, the basic test appears to me to be whether it could, at least in principle, be carried on by a private undertaking in order to make profits. If there were no possibility of a private undertaking carrying on a given activity, there would be no purpose in applying the competition rules to it.[65]

In short, this is an effectiveness argument based on the need to avoid any distortions of competition in the market caused by the conduct of any entity, whether public or private.[66] Accordingly, more recent case law has examined closely the activities of legal parties, to ascertain whether they are purely exercising public powers or if they also have other activities which could be classified as economic.[67] For instance, in *Motosykletistiki Omospondia Ellados NPID (MOTOE) v Greece*[68] the exercise of public powers to give consent to applications for authorisation to organise motorcycle competitions did not preclude that legal person from being an undertaking in the organisation and commercial exploitation of motorcycle events as these constituted economic activities.

Healthcare and pensions have generated many of the refinements in the case law determining the point at which competition rules apply. The focus of the Court's tests, explicitly or implicitly, is the extent to which the schemes and systems in question exhibit dimensions of solidarity. This notion is likely to be demonstrated on a number of levels,[69] particularly by reference to the characterisation of a system in terms of its membership, funding and benefits. Thus, in *Poucet and Pistre*[70] the Court held that the concept of undertaking did not encompass organisations charged with the management of certain compulsory social security schemes. Indicators were provided by the fact that the sickness and maternity benefits involved were the same for all beneficiaries, regardless of

---

[62] Ibid, para 30. *cf* Case T-155/04 *SELEX Sistemi Integrati SpA v Commission* [2009] ECR I-2207; [2009] 4 CMLR 24. In that case, the Court of First Instance held that Eurocontrol was not an undertaking in relation to its technical standard or research and development activities, but its advice to national administrations constituted economic activities as it was a market in which private undertakings could offer their services. However, the latter finding was rejected by the Court of Justice. See J Nowag 'Selex sistemi Integrati SpA v Commission of the European Communities (C-113/07 P) [2009] ECR I-2207: Redefining the Boundaries between Undertaking and the Exercise of Public Authority' [2010] 12 *ECLR* 483.

[63] Case C-343/95 *Calì & Figli v SEPG* [1997] ECR I-1547; [1997] 5 CMLR 484.

[64] Opinion, at para 27, in Joined Cases C-264/01, C-306/01, C-354/01 and C-355/01 *AOK Bundesverband* [2004] ECR I-2493.

[65] See also *SELEX Sistemi Integrati SpA v Commission*, above n 62.

[66] Noted expressly by AG Jacobs in *Ministero dell'Economia e delle Finanze v Cassa di Risparmio di Firenze SpA*, above n 47, Opinion, para 79.

[67] See *SELEX Sistemi Integrati SpA v Commission*, above n 62

[68] Case C-49/07 *Motosykletistiki Omospondia Ellados NPID (MOTOE) v Greece* [2008] ECR I-4863; [2008] 5 CMLR 11.

[69] See V Hatzopoulos, 'Health Law and Policy: The Impact of the EU' in de Búrca, above n 10. See also JW Van de Gronden, 'Financing Health Care in EU Law: Do the European State Aid Rules Write Out an Effective Prescription for Integrating Competition Law with Health Care? (2009) 6 *Comp L Rev* 5.

[70] Case C-160/91 *Poucet and Pistre* [1993] ECR I-637.

contributions. The retirement pensions also operated on the basis that entitlements were not proportional to contributions paid into the scheme. Finally, schemes with a surplus contributed to the financing of those with structural financial difficulties. Consequently, taking all considerations together, the Court concluded that 'those schemes pursue a social objective and embody the principle of solidarity'.

In contrast, a non-profit-making organisation which managed a pension scheme intended to supplement a basic compulsory scheme, established by law as an optional scheme and operating according to the principles of capitalisation, was held to be an undertaking.[71] Benefits depended solely on the amount of the contributions paid by the beneficiaries and on the financial results of the investments made by the managing organisation, thus implying that the organisation carried on an economic activity in competition with life assurance companies. A similar result was reached in *Albany International*,[72] even though affiliation in that case was compulsory for workers in the relevant industrial sector.[73]

Solidarity is a matter of degree, and it is the measurement of its predominance that will decide whether an entity's activities are deprived of their economic nature to render competition law inapplicable. For example, in *AOK*[74] the dispute at issue concerned the way in which German sickness funds were authorised to set maximum amounts to be paid for medicinal products. Pharmaceutical companies who objected to these limits argued that the sickness funds were in fact competing strongly with each other in relation to the amount of contributions, the benefits offered, and the management and organisation of their services. Having noted that the sickness funds were obliged by national law to offer essentially identical obligatory benefits which did not depend on the amount of contributions, the Court then observed:

> The latitude available to the sickness funds when setting the contribution rate and their freedom to engage in some competition with one another in order to attract members does not call this analysis into question. As is apparent from the observations submitted to the Court, the legislature introduced an element of competition with regard to contributions in order to encourage the sickness funds to operate in accordance with principles of sound management, that is to say in the most effective and least costly manner possible, in the interests of the proper functioning of the German social security system. Pursuit of that objective does not in any way change the nature of the sickness funds' activity.[75]

The Court thus concluded that the sickness funds did not constitute undertakings within the meaning of Articles 101 and 102 TFEU. However, it also acknowledged that the funds might engage in operations that would step outside their social functions. But this was not the case in relation to the setting of maximum amounts, which was held by the Court to be inseparable from the exclusively social objective of the sickness funds.

The extent of severability of functions is thus highly relevant to any assessment of the

---

[71] Case C-244/94 *Fédération Française des Sociétés d'Assurance v Ministère de l'Agriculture et de la Pêche* [1995] ECR I-4013.

[72] Case C-67/96 *Albany International BV v Stichting Bedrijfspensioenfonds Textielindustrie* [1999] ECR I-5751; [2000] 4 CMLR 446.

[73] See also Case C-350/07 *Kattner Stahlbau GmbH v Maschinenbau- und Metall- Berufsgenossenschaft* [2009] ECR I-1513; [2009] 2 CMLR 51 where it was held that an employers' liability insurance association, with compulsory affiliation in relation to accidents at work and occupational diseases, was not an undertaking for the purposes of Articles 101 and 102 as it fulfilled an exclusively social function, and accordingly it appeared that the scheme applied the principle of solidarity and was subject to state control.

[74] *AOK Bundesverband*, above n 64.

[75] Ibid, para 56.

economic character of an entity. The state cannot shelter behind the pretext of solidarity in order to avoid economic operators being subject to competition law.[76] But whether activities can be neatly demarcated is not an easy task, as shown by the *FENIN* case involving alleged abuses of Article 102 by public bodies responsible for the management of the Spanish national health system ('the SNS'). FENIN, an association of undertakings which marketed medical goods and equipment used in Spanish hospitals, complained that the 26 bodies, including three ministries, running the SNS only paid sums invoiced after considerable delays (around 300 days on average). The Commission's rejection of the complaint was upheld by the Court of First Instance,[77] which held that purchasing activities linked to a non-economic, solidarity-based entity were to be classified in the same way. On subsequent appeal to the Court of Justice, FENIN claimed that the Court of First Instance had erred in law by taking too narrow a view of economic activity and too wide a view of solidarity.

Advocate General Poiares Maduro took the Court of First Instance to task over its analysis of FENIN's complaint. In particular, it had adopted a single, global, classification of the SNS instead of distinguishing between its activities. On the one hand, SNS managed the health insurance system in Spain. On the other, it was also responsible for providing healthcare services to its members. According to the Advocate General, the Court of First Instance had simply taken the solidarity case law relevant to the first activity and subsumed the second within it without identifying the different factors which might apply. Nonetheless, the Court of Justice affirmed the approach of the Court of First Instance that the nature of the purchasing activity had to be determined according to whether the subsequent use of the purchased goods amounted to an economic activity.[78]

As will be seen in Chapter 26 below, determining that an entity is not an undertaking by virtue of its lack of economic character is a different task to relieving an undertaking with special responsibilities of the full rigour of the competition rules by reference to the derogation for SGEIs set out in Article 106(2) TFEU (ex Article 86(2) EC). Thus, in *Albany International* the Court acknowledged that the pursuit of a social objective, the presence of solidarity features in the scheme and various restrictions on investments made by the sectoral fund might make its service less competitive than comparable services rendered by insurance companies. Although these considerations did not prevent the fund being an undertaking, they could be taken into account when applying Article 106(2).[79]

A final aspect of the meaning of 'undertaking' concerns the application of the rules on competition to groups of companies. Here the Court of Justice does not hesitate to go behind the façade of separate corporate personality. This pragmatic approach is illustrated by the *Hydrotherm* case[80] which concerned the block exemption granted by Regulation 67/67[81] to certain categories of exclusive dealing agreements. The exemption was expressly limited to agreements 'to which only two undertakings are party'.[82] That condition was held to be fulfilled where the parties to a contract were, on the distribution side, a German company, and on the manufacturing side, the Italian developer of a product and two legally independent firms controlled by him. The Court explained that 'In competition

---

[76] AG Poiares Maduro in *FENIN v Commission*, above n 59.
[77] Case T-319/99 *FENIN v Commission* [2003] ECR II-357.
[78] *FENIN v Commission*, above n 59.
[79] *Albany International*, above n 72, para 86.
[80] Case 170/83 *Hydrotherm* [1984] ECR 2999.
[81] Regulation 67/67 [1967] OJ 849; [1967] OJ 10.
[82] Art 1(1) of Regulation 67/67.

law, the term "undertaking" must be understood as designating an economic unit for the purpose of the subject-matter of the agreement in question even if in law that economic unit consists of several persons, natural or legal.'[83] In practice, the main impact of the 'enterprise entity' doctrine has been in relation to two issues: the assertion of jurisdiction against a parent company established in a third country which has subsidiaries within the common market; and the application of Article 101 to agreements and practices between parent companies and subsidiaries. These issues are examined further below.

B – Material Scope

The EU rules on competition apply generally, to all sectors of the economy, except where express derogations are provided in other Articles of the Treaty.[84] The expiry of the ECSC Treaty on 23 July 2002 saw the coal and steel industries fall within the EU regime of competition law.

The approach taken by the Union historically in relation to agriculture reflects the potential tension between the objectives of the common agricultural policy and the notion of undistorted competition. The extent to which the competition rules apply to the agriculture sector is specified in Regulation 1184/2006[85] and Regulation 1234/2007,[86] also commonly known as the 'Single Common Market Organisation (CMO) Regulation'.

Special mention should also be made of the transport sector. The Treaty provisions on competition apply,[87] and Regulation 1/2003 also now provides the arrangements for enforcement in this sector. Furthermore, a number of exemptions in relation to the transport sector have now been repealed, including the block exemption in relation to maritime conferences,[88] but there are certain specific rules on state aid granted to the transport sector.

C – Territorial Scope

The prohibition in Article 101 applies to arrangements between undertakings 'which may affect trade between Member States and which have as their object or effect the prevention, restriction or distortion of competition within the internal market', and that in Article 102 to any abuse of a dominant position 'within the internal market or in a substantial part of it . . . in so far as it may affect trade between Member States'. This wording makes it clear that the target of the prohibitions is behaviour having an actual or intended impact on the conditions of competition in the territory over which the internal market extends, ie the territory of the Union as defined by Article 52 TEU.

The requirement for trade between Member States to be affected demarcates the jurisdictional scope of the EU competition rules. The Court of Justice set out the basic test

---

[83]   *Hydrotherm*, above n 80, 3016.
[84]   Joined Cases 209–13/84 *Ministère Public v Asjes* [1986] ECR 1425.
[85]   [2006] OJ L352M/463.
[86]   [2007] OJ L299/1
[87]   See eg *Ministère Public v Asjes*, above n 84.
[88]   Regulation 4056/86 was repealed by Regulation 1419/2006, [2006] OJ L352M/486.

for the effect on inter-state trade in *Société Technique Minière v Maschinenbau Ulm* as follows:

> [I]t must be possible to foresee with a sufficient degree of probability on the basis of an objective set of factors of law or fact that the agreement in question may have an influence, direct or indirect, actual or potential, on the pattern of trade between Member States.[89]

This test has been given an expansive interpretation in the Commission Guidelines Notice on the effect on inter-state trade,[90] and also by the Court. Even agreements between undertakings based in the same Member State may satisfy this threshold test, where for instance the agreement compartmentalises the market and discourages undertakings from other Member States from entering the market,[91] a position reaffirmed more recently by the Court.[92] In *Erste Group Bank AG v Commission*[93] the Court stated that:

> On the other hand, the Court of Justice has already held that the fact that a cartel relates only to the marketing of products in a single Member State is not sufficient to preclude the possibility that trade between Member States might be affected. A cartel extending over the whole of the territory of a Member State has, by its very nature, the effect of reinforcing the partitioning of markets on a national basis, thus impeding the economic interpenetration which the EC Treaty is designed to bring about.[94]

Accordingly, in that case, where eight Austrian banks had engaged in agreements and concerted practices contrary to Article 101 TFEU by holding regular meetings relating to interest rates and fees and charges, the cartel had a cross-border effect as the very existence of the 'Lombard network' impeded free access to the Austrian market. It should also be noted that Article 3(1) of Regulation 1/2003 essentially requires NCAs to apply Articles 101 and 102 in addition to national competition law in dealing with any anti-competitive agreements or abuses of dominance which may affect inter-state trade.

On the other hand, undertakings carrying on business in the Union are free under the EU rules on competition to participate in agreements or practices that may interfere with the functioning of the market mechanism in third countries, so long as the consequences are unlikely to spill back into the internal market.[95] Thus, in its *VVVF* Decision[96] the Commission allowed a Dutch association of paint and varnish manufacturers to continue a system of minimum prices and uniform conditions of sale in respect of exports by its members outside the internal market, after securing the abolition of the system in respect of intra-EU trade.

The converse case is where undertakings not physically present on EU territory behave in ways that are liable to affect competition on the internal market. How far does the Union claim extraterritorial jurisdiction in competition matters? In addressing this question it is useful to bear in mind the distinction drawn by international lawyers between

---

[89] Case 56/65 *Société Technique Minière v Maschinenbau Ulm* [1966] ECR 235, 249 [1966] CMLR 357.
[90] [2004] OJ C101/81. See also the discussion in Chapter 23 regarding the requirement for an 'appreciable effect on trade between Member States' in the context of Art 101.
[91] Case 8/72 *Cementhandelaren v Commission* [1972] ECR 977, [1973] CMLR 7. See also Cases T-202, T-204 and T-207/98 *Tate & Lyle and Others v Commission* [2001] ECR II-2035. *cf* Cases C-215/96 and C-216/96 *Carlo Bagnasco and others v Banco Polare di Navara and others* [1999] ECR I-135.
[92] Case C-238/05 *ASNEF-EQUIFAX Servicios de Informacion sobre Solvencia y Credito SL v Asociacion de Usuarios de Servicios Bancarios (AUSBANC)* ECJ [2006] ECR I-11125; [2007] 4 CMLR 6
[93] Case C-125/07 P *Erste Group Bank AG v Commission* [2009] ECR I-8681; [2010] 5 CMLR 9.
[94] Ibid, para 38.
[95] However, the application of bilateral and multilateral agreements containing rules analogous to EU law may of course reduce the scope of such freedom.
[96] [1969] JO L168/22; [1970] CMLR D1.

'prescriptive jurisdiction' (the power to make rules and to take decisions under them) and 'enforcement jurisdiction' (the power to give effect to such rules or decisions through executive action).[97] The assertion of either form of jurisdiction, but especially the latter, against an undertaking located on another state's territory raises legal and political issues of some delicacy. Three possible bases for the application of the EU rules in such cases fall to be considered.

First, it is generally accepted in international law that a state is entitled to jurisdiction where activity which was commenced abroad is brought to consummation on its territory. This is known as the 'objective territorial principle'. It would, for example, allow the Commission to apply Article 101 to a contract made in a third country but substantially performed, at least on one side, within the EU.

Secondly, and more controversially, the Court of Justice has developed a doctrine of enterprise entity as a basis of jurisdiction against a parent company which has subsidiaries inside the EU, though situated itself on the outside. Under the doctrine, where material aspects of the subsidiary's commercial policy are controlled by the parent company, behaviour of the former in contravention of the rules on competition may be imputed to the latter. The leading case remains *Dyestuffs*,[98] which concerned a decision by the Commission that a group of major manufacturers of aniline dyes had been guilty on three separate occasions of concerted price fixing. The addressees of the decision included ICI (at that time the United Kingdom was not a Member State) and certain Swiss companies. Objections by these companies to the jurisdiction of the Commission were dismissed by the Court on the ground that all of them had subsidiaries within the common market for whose decisions on pricing they could be held responsible.

The circumstances in which liability for an EU competition law infringement by a subsidiary undertaking can be imputed to a parent undertaking has been the subject of considerable case law in recent years.[99] It should be stressed that this issue arises irrespective of any attempt to enforce the EU competition rules extraterritorially, and is important because in imposing a fine, the 10 per cent fine ceiling will apply to the turnover of the parent undertaking, and fine increases for recidivism are more likely.[100] The starting point is that separate legal entities may form a single economic unit, and therefore an undertaking for the purposes of EU competition law enforcement, where they do not determine their course of conduct on the market independently.[101] The key issue is the extent to which the parent company exercises decisive influence over the subsidiary,[102]

---

[97] See M. Shaw, *International Law*, 6th edn (Cambridge, Cambridge University Press, 2008) ch 12.

[98] There was, in fact, a group of cases brought by different addressees of the decision in question, to which this collective designation is given. See, in particular, Case 48/69 *ICI v Commission* [1972] ECR 619; [1972] CMLR 557.

[99] For earlier case law, see eg Joined Cases T-305–07, T-313–16, T-318, 325, T-328–29 and T-335/94 *Re the PVC Cartel II: Limburgse Vinyl Maatschappij NV v Commission* [1999] ECR II-931; [1999] 5 CMLR 303, para 984. In that case, the Court of First Instance ruled that since the subsidiary was wholly owned by the parent it was superfluous to inquire whether the latter was able to exercise a decisive influence on the former's commercial behaviour.

[100] See the discussion on the calculation of fines in Chapter 25.

[101] See eg Case C-286/98P *Stora Kopparbergs Bergslags AB v Commission* [2000] ECR I-9925; [2001] 4 CMLR 12, at para 26: '[A]s the Court of Justice has held on several occasions, the fact that a subsidiary has separate legal personality is not sufficient to exclude the possibility of its conduct being imputed to the parent company, especially where the subsidiary does not independently decide its own conduct on the market, but carries out, in all material respects, the instructions given to it by the parent company.' For discussion, see A Riesenkampf and U Krauthausen, 'Liability of Parent Companies for Antitrust Violations of their Subsidiaries' [2010] *ECLR* 38.

[102] See Case C-407/08 P *Knauf Gips KG v Commission* [2010] 5 CMLR 12.

and it has been confirmed by the Court of Justice that there is a rebuttable presumption that where a parent company has a 100 per cent shareholding in a subsidiary, it exercises a decisive influence over that wholly owned subsidiary.[103] Furthermore, in this context the EU courts have applied the economic continuity test in increasingly complicated contexts to ascertain whether liability may be imputed where all or part of the economic activities of a legal entity have been transferred to a new operator.[104]

The enterprise entity doctrine has been used by the Court and the Commission to found not only prescriptive but also enforcement jurisdiction. Thus competition proceedings may be validly initiated against the foreign parent of an EU subsidiary by sending it a statement of objections through the post,[105] and the final decision finding the company guilty of an infringement of the rules may be similarly served.[106] Fines may be imposed on the parent company for the infringement, and it may be ordered to take remedial action. In *Commercial Solvents*,[107] for example, a US multinational corporation was found to have abused its dominant position under Article 102 by refusing, through its Italian subsidiary, to supply a customer with a product in which it held the world monopoly. The Court did not question the power of the Commission, besides fining Commercial Solvents, to require the corporation to make an immediate delivery of a specified quantity of the product in question to the customer and to submit proposals for longer-term supply arrangements. Of course, if fines are not paid, they can only be enforced by levying execution on property of the parent or subsidiary which is on the territory of a Member State.[108]

A third, and still more controversial, basis for the extraterritorial application of competition law is the so-called 'effects doctrine'. Broadly, the doctrine holds that a state is entitled to assert jurisdiction in respect of non-nationals abroad, where these produce effects within the state's own territory. In EU law, the question is whether the Court of Justice has followed the approach of US courts in constructing a principle of jurisdiction based on direct, substantial and foreseeable effects.[109] The leading case is *Wood Pulp*,[110] where the Commission imposed fines on various US and Scandinavian producers of wood pulp for concertation on the fixing of prices at which they supplied the paper industry in the common market. The activities regarded by the Commission as constituting the concertation took place in the producers' home countries, and several of those involved had no establishment and no subsidiaries within the EU.

When the applicants challenged the Commission's decision before the Court, Advocate

---

[103] Ibid. See in particular the Court of Justice in Case C-97/08P *Akzo Nobel v Commission* [2009] ECR I-8237; [2009] 5 CMLR 23. *cf* the Court of First Instance in Joined Cases T-109/02, T-118/02, T-122/02, T-125/02, T-126/02, T-128/02, T-129/02, T-132/02 and T-136/02 *Bollore et al v Commission* ('Carbonless Paper Cartel') [2007] ECR II-947; [2007] 5 CMLR 2. Note that the relationship between parent and subsidiary for these purposes can also be indirect, via an intermediary subsidiary: Case T-24/05 *Alliance One International Inc v Commission* [2010] ECR (nyr).

[104] See Case T-161/05 *Hoechst GmbH v Commission* [2009] ECR II-3555; [2009] 5 CMLR 25. See also eg Case T-405/06 *ArcelorMittal Luxembourg SA v Commission* [2009] ECR II-771; [2010] 4 CMLR 6 and Case C-280/06 *Autorita Garante della Concorrenza e del Mercato v Ente Tabacchi Italiani-ETI SpA* [2007] ECR I-10893; [2008] 4 CMLR 11.

[105] See eg Case 52/69 *Geigy v Commission* [1972] ECR 787.

[106] *Continental Can*, above n 2.

[107] Joined Cases 6 and 7/73 *Commercial Solvents Corporation v Commission* [1974] ECR 223.

[108] See Art 299 TFEU (ex Art 256 EC).

[109] The classic US statement can be found in *US v Aluminium Co of America* 148 F2d 416 (1945), where it was said that 'any state may impose liabilities, even upon persons not within its allegiance, for conduct outside its borders that has consequences within its borders which the state reprehends'. This was modified in later cases such as *Timberlane Lumber Co v Bank of America* 549 F2d 597 (1976).

[110] Joined Cases 89, 104, 114, 116, 117 and 125–29/85 *Åhlström v Commission* [1988] ECR 5193.

General Darmon proposed the adoption of a qualified-effects doctrine of the type used in American competition law. However, the Court did not grasp this particular nettle, instead expressing its view in terms of an 'implementation' test as follows:

> If the applicability of prohibitions laid down under competition law were made to depend on the place where the agreement, decision or concerted practice was formed, the result would obviously be to give undertakings an easy means of evading those prohibitions. The decisive factor is therefore the place where it is implemented.
>
> The producers in this case implemented their pricing agreement within the common market. It is immaterial in that respect whether or not they had recourse to subsidiaries, agents, sub-agents or branches within the Community in order to make their contacts with purchasers within the Community.
>
> Accordingly the Community's jurisdiction to apply its competition rules to such conduct is covered by the territoriality principle as universally recognised in public international law.[111]

The scope of this concept of implementation, and its relationship to any effects doctrine, is still not entirely free from doubt.[112] In particular, it may be asked whether it applies to situations where the distortion to intra-EU trade is caused by the parties diverting their goods away from the Union as distinct from, say, fixing the prices at which those goods will eventually be sold on Union territory. It might be hard to see how refraining from trade would amount to an 'implemented' agreement, although it might equally well be said that this would also produce insufficiently direct consequences to be caught by an effects doctrine. Thus there may be little difference in real outcomes, despite the different language used by the Court.

In the later *Gencor* case,[113] decided in relation to the Merger Regulation, the Court of First Instance took the view that the *Wood Pulp* implementation criterion was satisfied by mere sale within the EU, irrespective of the sources of supply and the production plant, both based in South Africa. Moreover, the Court of First Instance also noted that application of the Merger Regulation was 'justified under public international law when it is foreseeable that a proposed concentration will have an immediate and substantial effect in the Community'.[114]

IV – COMPETITION LAW IN AN INTERNATIONAL CONTEXT

A – Co-operation Agreements

Ultimately, the delicate issues raised in cases with extra-territorial dimensions are perhaps best solved by international co-operation over the allocation of jurisdiction, rather than unilateral assertions of extensive jurisdiction. Certainly, it is one thing to claim juris-

---

[111]   Ibid, Judgment, paras 16–18.

[112]   See DGF Lange and JB Sandage, 'The *Woodpulp* Decision and its Implications...' (1989) 26 *CMLRev* 137. *cf* FA Mann, 'The Public International Law of Restrictive Trade Practices in the ECJ' (1989) 38 *ICLQ* 375.

[113]   Case T-102/96 *Gencor v Commission* [1999] ECR II-753; [1999] 4 CMLR 971. For discussion, see MP Broberg, 'The European Commission's Extraterritorial Powers in Merger Control: The Court of First Instance's Judgment in Gencor v. Commission' [2000] 49 *ICLQ* 172.

[114]   *Gencor v Commission*, ibid, para 90.

diction over particular activities, but quite another to exercise it. That decision may be influenced by considerations relating to the impact it would have on the relationship with authorities of another jurisdiction. Vigorous pursuit of an effects doctrine, for example, might provoke harmful retaliatory action by the home state of a parent company. Self-restraint may therefore be a preferable course in the light of these factors of comity. Comity considerations can be given a more formal status by the adoption of agreements between the EU and individual states. A prime example is the two agreements drawn up between the EU and the USA, originally adopted in 1991[115] and subsequently elaborated in 1998.[116] The 1991 Agreement provides for the competition authorities of the parties to notify each other where enforcement activities affect important interests of the other. It also seeks to avoid conflicts over enforcement by adoption of a so-called 'negative comity' clause.[117] This states that:

> [E]ach party shall consider important interests of the other party in decisions as to whether or not to initiate an investigation or proceeding, the scope of an investigation or proceeding, the nature of the remedies or penalties sought, and in other ways, as appropriate.

Use of this provision was made in the controversy surrounding the Boeing/McDonnell Douglas merger.[118] The concentration in question reduced the number for manufacturers of large commercial aircraft from three to two, leaving Airbus Industrie (the European producer) up against a single dominant US competitor. The merger was cleared by the US authorities, but authorisation was only given by the European Commission after last-minute assurances as to Boeing's future conduct.[119]

According to the 1998 EU–USA Positive Comity Agreement,[120] the competition authorities of one party may request the competition authorities of the other to investigate and, if warranted, to remedy anti-competitive activities in accordance with the requested party's competition laws. Such a request may be made regardless of whether the activities also violate the requesting party's competition laws, and regardless of whether the competition authorities of the requesting party have commenced, or are contemplating taking, enforcement activities under their own competition laws. Article IV sets out the conditions on which the competition authorities of the requesting party will normally defer or suspend their own enforcement activities in favour of those of the requested party. Inter alia, these require that the adverse effects on the interests of the requesting party can be and are likely to be fully and adequately investigated and, as appropriate, eliminated or adequately remedied. The competition authorities of the requested party must devote adequate resources to the investigation, carry it out promptly and use their best efforts to pursue all reasonably available sources of information, including such sources of information as may be suggested by the competition authorities of the requesting party.

---

[115] [1991] 4 CMLR 823 but struck down by the Court of Justice in Case C-327/91 *France v Commission* [1994] ECR I-3641. It was then readopted with proper ratification by the Council as Decision 95/145, [1995] OJ L95/45, corrected by [1995] OJ L131/38, and taking effect from its original date.

[116] *Agreement between the European Communities and the Government of the United States of America on the application of positive comity principles in the enforcement of their competition laws* OJ 1998 L173/28; [1999] 4 CMLR 502.

[117] Art VI of the 1991 Agreement.

[118] [1997] OJ L336/16.

[119] *cf* the position in relation to the GE/Honeywell proposed merger, blocked by the European Commission. For discussion of that issue, see A Burnside, 'GE, Honey, I Sunk the Merger' [2002] *ECLR* 107.

[120] Above n 116, Art III.

As well as bilateral agreements of this type,[121] multilateral arrangements also provide for the application of competition rules akin to EU provisions in other territories. The EEA Agreement was concluded[122] between the EU and the EFTA states, with the exception of Switzerland. It applies the fundamental freedoms and some of the horizontal policies of the EU, such as competition and social policies, to the EEA. As a number of former members of EFTA have since become full members of the EU, the importance of the EEA agreement has declined.

B – Developments Towards Global Regulation or Co-operation

The trends in EU competition law should not be considered in isolation, despite the rather incohate state of globalised competition regulation and policy co-operation. Competition policy was not included in the original remit of the World Trade Organization (WTO),[123] but a Working Group on the interaction between trade and competition policy was established at the Singapore Ministerial Conference in December 1996, producing a report in December 1998.[124] The 2001 Doha Ministerial Declaration listed the interaction between trade and competition policy as part of its work programme. However, following deadlock at the 2003 Cancún Ministerial Conference, the WTO General Council dropped this item from the work programme in August 2004 for the remainder of the Doha Round. Even though WTO discussion concerned neither the creation of some supranational antitrust agency nor the harmonisation of national competition laws,[125] competition developments remain stalled within the WTO framework.

A much more visible, distinctive but entirely different form of co-operation can be seen in the development of the International Competition Network (ICN),[126] launched in October 2001. The ICN's mission and activities are as follows:

(i) The International Competition Network ('ICN') is a project-oriented, consensus-based, informal network of antitrust agencies that addresses antitrust enforcement and policy issues of common interest and formulates proposals for procedural and substantive convergence through a results-oriented agenda and structure.

(ii) The ICN encourages the dissemination of antitrust experiences and best practices, promotes the advocacy role of antitrust agencies, and seeks to facilitate international cooperation.

(iii) The ICN's activities take place on a voluntary basis and rely on a high level of goodwill and cooperation among members, as well as effective working relationships with Non-

---

[121] See also the 1999 Co-operation Agreement 1999 between the EC, ECSC and Canada [1999] OJ L175, [1999] 5 CMLR 713. See J Galloway, 'Moving Towards a Template for Bilateral Antitrust agreements' (2005) 28 *World Competition* 589.

[122] [1994] OJ L1/3.

[123] For documentation on developments in relation to trade and competition policy, see the WTO's website: www.wto.org.

[124] Including matters such as the impact of anti-competitive practices of enterprises and associations on international trade; the impact of state monopolies and exclusive rights; the relationship between the trade-related aspects of intellectual property rights and competition policy; the relationship between investment and competition policy and the impact of trade policy on competition.

[125] See F Souty, 'Is There a Need for Additional WTO Competition Rules Promoting Non-Discriminatory Competition Laws and Competition Institutions in WTO Members?' in E-U Petersmann (ed), *Reforming the World Trading System* (Oxford, Oxford University Press, 2005).

[126] See www.internationalcompetitionnetwork.org.

Governmental Advisors ('NGAs') and other international bodies working in the same field.

(iv) The work of ICN is project-driven. During its regularly scheduled meetings, the ICN decides which projects it will pursue and adopts a work plan for each project. The ICN is not intended to replace or coordinate the work of other organizations, nor does it exercise any rule-making function.

(v) The ICN provides the opportunity for its members to maintain regular contacts, in particular, through an Annual Conference and regular workshops.

(vi) Where the ICN reaches consensus on recommendations arising from a project, it is left to its members to decide whether and how to implement the recommendations, for example, through unilateral, bilateral or multilateral arrangements.[127]

The European Commission, alongside the competition authorities of the Member States, is a member of the ICN. The ICN's goals are to achieve better competition enforcement and better competition advocacy, ie the promotion of competition culture among governments, the private sector and public awareness. The emphasis is on exchanging experience and best practice in procedures, systems and techniques.[128] Although there is no aspiration to harmonisation of competition law and policies throughout the world, the ICN has moved away from an initial focus on procedure and systems, and there is the possibility for gradual substantive convergence of competition laws through the auspices of the ICN, for instance via the working group established in relation to unilateral conduct.

V – CONCLUDING REMARKS

As the instrument to give effect to competition policies, competition law is hardly neutral.[129] It is different from the negative integration which flows from the implementation of fundamental freedoms. By curtailing or accepting the freedom of action of particular parties, competition law makes judgments about the content of notions of consumer welfare and other objectives, and the best means of promoting them within the Union. The ongoing debate regarding the appropriate objectives of EU competition law has not, as yet, crystallised, although we have witnessed an intense period of modernisation and reinterpretation of the primary competition rules in Articles 101 and 102 in recent years, as discussed in greater detail in Chapters 23 and 24. The EU competition law enforcement framework has changed dramatically with the introduction of Regulation 1/2003 and the enforcement role for NCAs as part of the European Competition Network, and an increasingly important role for the national courts. The Commission has inevitably prioritised enforcement resources on hard-core cartels, although, as discussed in Chapter 25, the compatibility with ECHR case law of various aspects of the EU competition law enforcement process is even more likely to be challenged in the aftermath of the ratification of the TL. Despite differences in approach on the two sides of the Atlantic, EU competition

---

[127] www.internationalcompetitionnetwork.org/about/operational-framework.aspx.

[128] See eg I Maher, 'Competition Law in the International Domain: Networks as a New Form of Governance' [2002] *Journal of Law and Society* 111.

[129] See generally G Amato, *Antitrust and the Bounds of Power* (Oxford, Hart Publishing, 1997). See also DJ Gerber, *Law and Competition in Twentieth Century Europe—Protecting Prometheus* (Oxford, Oxford University Press, 1998); DJ Gerber, *Global Competition: Law, Markets, and Globalization* (Oxford, Oxford University Press, 2010).

law and its reform has been greatly inspired by a number of fundamental aspects of US antitrust law and its enforcement, namely the prominence of private enforcement; the dramatic increase in fines imposed on cartels; and the adoption of antitrust leniency programmes for cartel 'whistleblowers'.

As already seen in parts of this chapter, competition law meets state sovereignty head-on in a number of situations. Most obviously, EU law may restrict the freedom of states to act as market regulators, facilitators (eg through providing state aid) or participants. More subtly, the notion of 'undertaking' is ultimately not about form but instead requires analysis of why it should be the case that the activity in question falls within the scope of EU competition law competence. The asymmetries between competition law and free movement reflect a somewhat inconsistent stance towards the choices to be made—variously represented as state/market, economic/non-economic, public/private or EU/national divisions. Furthermore, the extent to which competition concerns can be trumped by other, often non-economic, values surfaces not just in the explicit context of Article 106(2) (and Article 14 TEU) but also in relation to Article 101(1) and (3). In this sense, analysis of the competition rules is every bit as revealing about the state of EU evolution as other developments covered in this book, such as fundamental rights and citizenship.

Further Reading

P Akman, 'Searching for the Long-lost Soul of Art 82 EC' (2009) *Oxford Journal of Legal Studies* 267.

G Amato, *Antitrust and the Bounds of Power* (Oxford, Hart Publishing, 1997).

A Andreangeli, *EU Competition Enforcement and Human Rights* (Cheltenham, Edward Elgar, 2008).

J Drexl, L Idot and J Moneger (eds), *Economic Theory and Competition Law* (Cheltenham, Edward Elgar, 2009).

J Drexl, W Kerber and R Podszun (eds), *Competition Policy and the Economic Approach, Foundations and Limitations* (Cheltenham, Edward Elgar, 2011).

CD Ehlermann, 'The Modernisation of EC Antitrust Policy: A Legal and Cultural Revolution' (2000) 37 *CMLRev* 537.

A Ezrachi (ed), *Article 82 EC: Reflections on its Recent Evolution* (Oxford, Hart Publishing, 2009).

T Frazer, 'Competition Policy after 1992: The Next Step' (1990) 53 *MLR* 609.

J Galloway, 'Moving Towards a Template for Bilateral Antitrust Agreements' (2005) 28 *World Competition* 589.

DJ Gerber, *Law and Competition in Twentieth Century Europe—Protecting Prometheus* (Oxford, Oxford University Press, 1998).

DJ Gerber, *Global Competition: Law, Markets, and Globalization* (Oxford, Oxford University Press, 2010).

A Jones, 'Left Behind by Modernisation? Restrictions by Object under Article 101(1)' (2010) *European Competition Journal* 649.

I Maher, 'Competition Law in the International Domain: Networks as a New Form of Governance' [2002] *Journal of Law and Society* 111.

P Marsden and P Whelan, '"Consumer Detriment" and its Application in EC and UK Competition Law' [2007] *ECLR* 569.

C Noonan, *The Emerging principles of International Competition Law* (Oxford, Oxford University Press, 2008).

O Odudu, 'The Meaning of Undertaking within 81 EC' (2004–05) 7 *CYELS* 211.

T Prosser, *The Limits of Competition Law, Markets and Public Services* (Oxford, Oxford University Press, 2005).

C Townley, *Article 81 EC and Public Policy* (Oxford, Hart Publishing, 2009)

W Von Meibom and A Geiger, 'A World Competition Law as an Ultima Ratio' [2002] *ECLR* 445.

A Weitbrechht, 'From Freiburg to Chicago and Beyond—The First 50 Years of European Competition Law' [2008] *ECLR* 81.

WJ Wils, *Efficiency and Justice in European Antitrust Enforcement* (Oxford, Hart Publishing, 2008).

23

Article 101: Cartels and Anti-competitive Agreements

This chapter deals with collusive behaviour between undertakings, covering agreements between undertakings, decisions of associations of undertakings and concerted practices. The overlap between these concepts is illustrated by reference to the tests of concurrence of wills and the necessary evidentiary proof. The other constituent elements of the prohibition contained in Article 101(1) are analysed in the case law, secondary legislation, Commission Guidelines and other forms of practice Notices. In particular, the notion of a 'restriction on competition' is assessed in the context of whether any 'rule of reason' arguments about the balancing of pro- and anti-competitive concerns or non-competition values are recognised in an Article 101(1) analysis. The case law and legislative developments reveal an increasing emphasis upon market impact and economic analysis in the application of all stages of an Article 101 assessment. Horizontal and vertical agreements attract differential treatment as a result, with the latter being given a lighter regulatory touch except for 'hard-core' restrictions. The legal exception criteria set out in Article 101(3) are examined in outline, together with the umbrella block exemption in favour of vertical restraints.

I – INTRODUCTION: RATIONALE AND PURPOSE

Article 101 TFEU (ex Article 81 EC, hereinafter referred to as Article 101) seeks to address the problem of restricted competition resulting from collusion between market participants over their business decisions. Article 101 basically prohibits anti-competitive agreements subject to the possibility of justification, where, on balance, they are judged to be economically beneficial.

Article 101 provides:

1. The following shall be prohibited as incompatible with the internal market: all agreements between undertakings, decisions by associations of undertakings and concerted practices which

may affect trade between Member States and which have as their object or effect the prevention, restriction or distortion of competition within the internal market, and in particular those which:

(a) directly or indirectly fix purchase or selling prices or any other trading conditions;

(b) limit or control production, markets, technical development, or investment;

(c) share markets or sources of supply;

(d) apply dissimilar conditions to equivalent transactions with other trading parties, thereby placing them at a competitive disadvantage;

(e) make the conclusion of contracts subject to acceptance by the other parties of supplementary obligations which, by their nature or according to commercial usage, have no connection with the subject of such contracts.

2. Any agreements or decisions prohibited pursuant to this Article shall be automatically void.

3. The provisions of paragraph 1 may, however, be declared inapplicable in the case of:
— any agreement or category of agreements between undertakings;
— any decision or category of decisions by associations of undertakings;
— any concerted practice or category of concerted practices;
which contributes to improving the production or distribution of goods or to promoting technical or economic progress, while allowing consumers a fair share of the resulting benefit, and which does not:

(a) impose on the undertakings concerned restrictions which are not indispensable to the attainment of these objectives;

(b) afford such undertakings the possibility of eliminating competition in respect of a substantial part of the products in question.

The scope of paragraph (1) is potentially wide indeed. Its list of examples of prohibited arrangements is non-exhaustive and there is no attempt to distinguish between so-called horizontal and vertical arrangements (ie between economic operators at the same or different stages of the economic chain, respectively). However, as we shall see, a more lenient view has generally been taken of vertical restrictions between, for example, producer and distributor. Paragraph (1) is also silent on the meaning of its primary elements, allowing controversy to develop as to the degree of distortion of competition required and the scope for weighing the pros and cons of particular arrangements or the relevance of non-competition criteria. Accordingly, to put it in the language familiar from other areas of EU law and particularly in US antitrust law, a key debate has been the extent to which a 'rule of reason' applies under paragraph (1).

Paragraph (2) of Article 101 identifies a particular consequence for breach of the prohibition, although additional remedies may be available in national law.[1] Paragraph (3) sets out the criteria that must be met by arrangements prima facie within paragraph (1), in order to benefit from the legal exception to the prohibition. The power to exempt agreements under paragraph (3) from the prohibition was previously reserved exclusively by Regulation 17[2] to the Commission, but following the modernisation of EU competition law enforcement in Regulation 1/2003,[3] since 2004 parties are required to self-assess the compatibility of their arrangements with Article 101(3), and national courts may resolve contractual disputes by applying the legal exception in that paragraph.

---

[1] Enforcement of both Arts 101 and 102 is discussed further in Chapter 25, below.

[2] Regulation 17/62 [1962] OJ 204; [1959–62] OJ 87.

[3] Regulation 1/2003, On the Implementation of the Rules on Competition Laid Down in Articles 81 and 82 of the Treaty [2003] OJ L1/1, which came into force on 1 May 2004 following the *White Paper on Modernisation of the Rules Implementing Articles 85 and 86 of the EC Treaty*, 28 April 1999.

Indeed, the reforms of 2004, together with Court case law, have had a significant impact on the problems and priorities that form the modern view of Article 101. What was once perhaps a sweeping prohibition subject to narrow and tightly controlled exceptions has become a more sophisticated instrument which permits pragmatic assessments of collusive arrangements to be made in the light of their effects in the relevant market. These assessments are more firmly anchored in economics and market analysis, and there has also been a development in the recognition of other public-interest objectives which may ensure that an agreement falls outside the scope of the prohibition in Article 101(1). The scope of Article 101(1) and its relationship with Article 101(3) will be discussed further later in this chapter. Alongside this more flexible and economics-based test for various commercial arrangements, it should be stressed there has been a clear focus in enforcement action by the Commission since the late 1990s on horizontal hard-core cartels, notably price-fixing and market-sharing cartels, and a dramatic increase in fines imposed in this context. Aspects of the Commission's enforcement powers, penalties and processes in particular in relation to cartels will be considered in further detail in Chapter 25.

II – UNDERTAKINGS AND CONCURRENCE OF WILLS

The target of the prohibition in Article 101(1) is co-operative or collusive market behaviour between undertakings. As discussed in Chapter 22, the notion of 'undertakings' as independent economic entities limits the scope of Article 101 inter alia in relation to parent–subsidiary relationships,[4] some acts of public authorities[5] and the delivery of solidarity-based schemes.[6] Similarly, agreements within a pure agency relationship may fall outside the provision where the agent acts in the name and for the account of his principal, taking none of the risks of a transaction upon himself.[7] Such an agent, the Court of Justice has said, when working for his principal can be regarded 'as an auxiliary organ forming an integral part of the latter's undertaking bound to carry out the principal's instructions and thus, like a commercial employee, forms an economic unit with this undertaking'.[8] An agreement by the agent not to trade in goods competing with the products of his principal would not in these circumstances fall within Article 101(1).[9]

---

[4] There will be no agreement between undertakings for the purposes of Art 101 where the subsidiary enjoys no real freedom to determine its course of action on the market: Case 22/71 *Béguelin Import Co v SA GL Import Export* [1971] ECR 949; [1972] CMLR 81; Case C-73/95P *Viho Europe BV v Commission* [1996] ECR I-5457; [1997] 4 CMLR 419. See also Case T-112/05 *Akzo Nobel v Commission* [2007] ECR II-5049; [2008] 4 CMLR 12 and Case C-97/08 P *Akzo Nobel v Commission* [2009] ECR I- 8237; [2009] 5 CMLR 23.

[5] The key question being whether such a body is acting as a public authority at the time: see Case 30/87 *Bodson v Pompes Funèbres* [1988] ECR 2479; [1989] 4 CMLR 984.

[6] Case C-160/91 *Poucet and Pistre* [1993] ECR I-637. See also Cases C-264/01 C-306/01, C-354/01 and C-355/01 *AOK Bundesverband v Ichthyol-Gesellschaft Cordes, Hermani & Co and Others* [2004] ECR I- 2493, [2006] 4 CMLR 22; cf Case C-67/96 *Albany International BV v Stichting Bedrijfspensioenfonds Textielindustrie* [1999] ECR I-5751; [2000] 4 CMLR 446 .The issue was discussed more fully in Chapter 22, above.

[7] Joined Cases 40–48, 50, 54–56, 111, 113 and 114/73 *Suiker Unie v Commission* ('*Sugar*') [1975] ECR 1663; [1976] 1 CMLR 295.

[8] Ibid, [1975] ECR 1663, 2007.

[9] Ibid. In the instant case the relationship between a German sugar producer and its trade representatives was found not to be such as to escape the prohibition.

There has been more recent case law in relation to the application of Article 101 to principal–agent relationships, with two significant rulings by the Court of Justice, both in the context of contracts between service-station operators and their supplier. In *Confederación Española de Empresarios de Estaciones de Servicio (CEEES)*[10] the Court ruled that the decisive factor for determining if the former was an independent economic operator was the agreement, and clauses of that agreement, express or implied, relating to the assumption of the financial and commercial risks linked to sales of goods to third parties, to be assessed on a case-by-case basis.[11] Where the operator only assumes a negligible share of the risks, Article 101 is not applicable as the relationship is akin to that between an agent and a principal.[12] Accordingly, only where the operator under an exclusive supply contract assumes to a non-negligible extent the financial and commercial risks linked to the sale of products to third parties, will any anti-competitive clauses fixing the retail price in such an exclusive supply contract fall within Article 101(1), but the exclusivity and noncompetition clauses in that agreement will be caught by the prohibition.[13]

Another question concerns the extent to which ostensibly unilateral conduct might be caught by the Article. At first sight, the obvious source available to combat anti-competitive acts by single undertakings is Article 102. However, this is limited to firms occupying dominant positions, implying that unilateral conduct by non-dominant individual firms was not seen as a threat to competition by the drafters of the Treaty. But this does not mean that acts in furtherance of a contract escape prohibition under Article 101(1) merely because they are performed by a single party. In the *AEG* case[14] the Court of Justice was called upon to assess the compatibility with that Article of a system of selective distribution. Under such a system the resale of goods is limited to a network of 'approved' dealers. One of the arguments put forward by AEG was that refusal to admit prospective dealers to its network was a unilateral act and therefore not within the scope of the prohibition. The argument was rejected by the Court on the ground that refusals of approval were acts performed in the context of AEG's contractual relations with approved dealers.[15]

However, the European Courts have resisted attempts by the Commission to stretch the boundaries of tacit acceptance or acquiescence. Thus, in *Bayer AG v Commission*[16] the Court of First Instance overturned the Commission's finding of an agreement in the system operated by Bayer's subsidiaries in Spain and France in relation to supplies of the heart drug Adalat. In order to prevent the high prices which could be charged in the United Kingdom from being threatened by quantities of parallel imports through wholesalers located in Spain and France, Bayer's subsidiaries restricted supplies of Adalat to the latter to the amounts needed to satisfy domestic demand. There was evidence that the wholesalers had tried different tactics to obtain extra supplies, but that these were detected and countered by Bayer. The Commission had taken the view that the monitoring and supply restrictions constituted an agreement between Bayer's subsidiaries and the wholesalers to restrict exports. According to the Commission, an agreement for the purposes

---

[10] Case C-217/05 *Confederación Española de Empresarios de Estaciones de Servicio* [2006] ECR I-11987; [2007] 4 CMLR 5. See also Case C-279/06 *CEPSA Estaciones de Servicios SA v LV Tobar e Hijos SL* [2008] ECR I-6681; [2008] 5 CMLR 19.

[11] *Confederación Española*, ibid, para 46.

[12] Ibid, paras 61–63.

[13] *CEPSA*, above n 10, paras 41–44.

[14] Case 107/82 *AEG v Commission* [1983] ECR 3151; [1984] 3 CMLR 325.

[15] See also Joined Cases 25-26/84 *Ford v Commission* [1985] ECR 2725; [1985] 3 CMLR 528.

[16] Case T-41/96 *Bayer* [2000] ECR II-3383; [2001] 4 CMLR 126.

of Article 101(1) required an interest of two parties in concluding an agreement, without there being any need for that interest to be held in common. In this case Bayer's interest was in preventing, or at least reducing, parallel imports. The wholesalers' interest was to avoid a reduction in supplies of Adalat.

In forcefully rejecting the Commission's approach, the Court of First Instance underlined the need for a 'concurrence of wills' to exist in order to support the finding of an agreement within Article 101(1). Whilst this would be satisfied where an 'apparently' unilateral measure adopted by a manufacturer was shown to receive at least tacit acquiescence by the wholesalers, there was no evidence in the case to show that the latter had aligned themselves to Bayer's policy designed to reduce parallel imports. The Court of Justice subsequently endorsed the Court of First Instance's ruling, observing:

> [T]he mere fact that a measure adopted by a manufacturer, which has the object or effect of restricting competition, falls within the context of continuous business relations between the manufacturer and its wholesalers is not sufficient for a finding that . . . an agreement exists.[17]

The Court proceeded to distinguish the earlier *AEG* and *Ford* decisions on the basis that the *existence* of an agreement had not been at issue in those cases. Instead, they had been decided on whether the measures adopted by the manufacturers concerned fell within the scope of the agreement.

Proof of acquiescence is required to defeat 'apparent' unilateral conduct. This is not altogether surprising given the financial consequences for firms on the wrong end of Article 101(1) proceedings. A fine of €30.96 million was overturned in *Volkswagen v Commission*[18] in relation to the 'strict price discipline' alleged to have been the subject of agreement between the car manufacturer and its German dealers. The Commission sought to persuade the Court of First Instance that, in a selective distribution system such as this, the dealers agreed when signing up in the first place to any subsequent calls by the manufacturer in relation to dealers' activity. However, the Court of First Instance made it clear that 'a concurrence of wills must cover particular conduct, which must, therefore, be known to the parties when they accept it'.[19] The Court of Justice set aside the judgment of the Court of First Instance but agreed with its conclusion that the Commission had failed to establish an agreement.[20]

More recently, following an investigation into the video games market, the Commission fined Nintendo and various exclusive territorial distributors on the basis that they had breached Article 101(1) by participating in agreements and concerted practices designed to limit parallel trade in games consoles and cartridges. The distributor for Belgium and Luxembourg appealed, but the Court of First Instance rejected the appeal on the basis that there was correspondence between the parties aimed at an exchange of information to limit parallel trade and that this was sufficient to establish an agreement under Article 101(1).[21]

---

[17] Cases C-2 and 3/01P, *Bundesverband der Arzneimittel-Importeure EV and Commission v Bayer AG* [2004] ECR I-23, [2004] 4 CMLR 653.

[18] Case T-208/01 *Volkswagen v Commission* [2003] ECR II-5141, [2004] 4 CMLR 727.

[19] Ibid, para 56.

[20] Case C-74/04 P *Commission v Volkswagen* [2006] ECR I-6585; [2008] 4 CMLR 16. See also Case T-53/03 *BPB Plc v Commission* [2008] ECR II-1333; [2008] 5 CMLR 18.

[21] Case T-18/03 *CD-Contact Data GmbH v Commission of the European Communities* [2009] ECR II-1021; [2009] 5 CMLR 5.

III – FORMS OF CO-OPERATION

For Article 101(1) to be applicable, one of the following three forms of co-operation must be shown: agreements between undertakings; decisions of associations of undertakings; or concerted practices. There is substantial practical overlap between them and it is important to remember that the real borderline is between unlawful collusion evidenced by any of these forms and independently determined behaviour that will not be caught by Article 101(1) at all. We shall start by outlining what constitute decisions of associations of undertakings, and then deal with agreements and concerted practices, given the particularly close links between the latter two concepts.

A – Decisions of Associations of Undertakings

A typical example would be a resolution of a trade association laying down standard terms on which its members are required to do business. The express reference to 'decisions of associations of undertakings' makes it possible, in an appropriate case, for the Commission to impose a fine on the trade association itself.[22] The Court of Justice is inclined to brush aside technical arguments about the precise legal character of acts of trade associations. Its attitude is summed up by the remark in the *FRUBO* judgment[23] that Article 101(1) 'applies to associations in so far as their own activities or those of the undertakings belonging to them are calculated to produce the results to which it refers'.[24] For example, the constitution of an association has sometimes been treated as a decision[25] and sometimes as an agreement.[26] A Regulation issued by the Netherlands Bar in relation to the terms on which partnerships could be established between members of the Bar and other professions was deemed to be a decision adopted by an association of undertakings.[27]

There is no more need for 'decisions' than for 'agreements' to be legally binding. In *Re Fire Insurance*[28] the Commission applied Article 101 to a 'recommendation' by an association of insurers in Germany that premiums for various classes of policy be raised by a stipulated percentage. Although described in its title as 'non-binding' the recommendation was found to constitute a decision within the meaning of the first paragraph. 'It is sufficient for this purpose', the Commission said, 'that the recommendation was brought to the notice of members as a statement of the association's policy provided for, and issued in accordance with, its rules.'[29] In other cases a pattern of past compliance with recommendations has been emphasised.[30] The conclusive factor, it is submitted, is the ability of

---

[22] See eg *Re AROW/BNIC* [1982] OJ L379/1; [1983] 2 CMLR 240.

[23] Case 71/74 *FRUBO v Commission* [1975] ECR 563; [1975] 2 CMLR 123.

[24] [1975] ECR 563, 583. See also Case T-193/02 *Piau v Commission* [2005] ECR II-209; [2005] 5 CMLR 2, paras 68–79.

[25] *Re ASPA* [1970] OJ L148/9; [1970] CMLR D25.

[26] *Re Nuovo CEGAM* [1984] OJ L99/29; [1984] 2 CMLR 484.

[27] Case C-309/99 *Wouters* [2002] ECR I-1577, [2002] 4 CMLR 913, para 71. Ultimately, there was no infringement of Art 101 as the prohibition on multi-disciplinary partnerships did not amount to a 'restriction'; see discussion below.

[28] [1985] OJ L35/20. The Decision was upheld by the Court of Justice in Case 45/85 *Verband der Sachversicherer* [1987] ECR 405; [1988] 4 CMLR 264.

[29] [1985] OJ at L35/20, 24.

[30] See, in particular, Joined Cases 209-215 and 218/78 *Van Landewyck v Commission (FEDETAB)* [1980]

the association, in fact if not in law, to influence its members' conduct. However, where an association plays no distinguishable role in the implementation of an anti-competitive arrangement, or where its acts are not severable from those of its members, it may escape liability or the imposition of fines.[31]

B – Agreements between Undertakings

There is no need for an arrangement to be legally binding for it to be treated as an agreement for the purposes of Article 101(1). In the *Quinine* cases,[32] for instance, the Court had to consider the application of the rules to arrangements between European producers of quinine and quinidine contained in an 'export agreement' and a 'gentlemen's agreement': the former, which was signed and made public, purported to apply only to trade with third countries but its provisions were extended by the latter, which remained unsigned and secret, to trade within the EU. In view of its clandestine character, let alone its name, the gentlemen's agreement cannot have been intended to be legally enforceable. The parties had, however, made clear that it faithfully expressed their joint intention as to their conduct and that they considered themselves no less bound by it than by the export agreement. The Court accepted it as an agreement. The decisive test, that there has been an expression by the participating undertakings of their joint intention to conduct themselves on the market in a specific way, has been consistently relied upon by the Court in subsequent cases.[33] As expressed by the Court of First Instance, the requirement is for 'a concurrence of wills between at least two parties, the form in which it is manifested being unimportant so long as it constitutes the faithful expression of the parties' intention'.[34] Nonetheless, in many cases the Commission will simply state that the co-operation between undertakings amounts to an agreement and/or concerted practice, and the important issue is whether there is some form of collusion between the parties.[35]

C – Concerted Practices

The concept of a concerted practice has been given a particularly broad interpretation by the European Courts. This is necessary to catch looser forms of arrangement or co-operation between parties and to limit the possibility for parties to avoid the prohibition, but it has created some difficulties in relation to the evidence necessary to establish that a concerted practice exists. In any event, a rigid categorisation of particular circumstances as either agreements or concerted practices is not required. Indeed, where a number of firms are engaged to varying degrees in complex infringements, it is possible to treat those patterns of conduct as manifestations of a single infringement, made up partly of agreements

ECR 3125; [1981] 3 CMLR 134; Joined Cases 96–102, 104, 105, 108 and 110/82 *IAZ v Commission* [1983] ECR 3369; [1984] 3 CMLR 276.

[31] Joined Cases 89, 104, 114, 116, 117 and 125–128/85 *A Ahlström Oy v Commission* ('*Wood Pulp*') [1988] ECR 5193; [1988] 4 CMLR 901, para 27.

[32] See Joined Cases 41, 44-45/69 *ACF Chemiefarma v Commission* [1970] ECR 661.

[33] eg Case C-49/92 P *Commission v Anic Partecipazioni SpA* [1999] ECR I-4125; [2001] 4 CMLR 17, para 130.

[34] *Bayer*, above n 16. See also *BPB Plc v Commission*, above n 20.

[35] *Commission v Anic*, above n 33; Case C-8/08 *T-Mobile Netherlands BV v Raad van Bestuur van de Nederlandse Mededingingsautoriteit* [2009] ECR I-4529; [2009] 5 CMLR 11, paras 23–24.

and partly of concerted practices without having to specify exact borderlines between them.[36] According to the Court, agreements and concerted practices 'are intended to catch forms of collusion having the same nature and are only distinguishable from each other by their intensity and the forms in which they manifest themselves'.[37] As the Court of Justice stressed recently in *T-Mobile*:[38]

> It follows . . . that the criteria laid down in the Court's case law for the purpose of determining whether conduct has as its object or effect the prevention, restriction or distortion of competition are applicable irrespective of whether the case entails an agreement, a decision or a concerted practice.[39]

The Court's first attempts at defining a concerted practice treated it as 'a form of coordination between undertakings which, without having been taken to a stage where an agreement properly so called has been concluded, knowingly substitutes practical co-operation between them for the risks of competition'.[40] These criteria of co-ordination and co-operation are to be understood in the light of the concept inherent in the provisions of the Treaty relating to competition, according to which each economic operator must determine independently the policy which he intends to adopt on the market.[41] According to the Court:

> [A]lthough that requirement of independence does not deprive economic operators of the right to adapt themselves intelligently to the existing and anticipated conduct of their competitors, it does however strictly preclude any direct or indirect contact between such operators, the object or effect whereof is either to influence the conduct on the market of an actual or potential competitor or to disclose to such a competitor the course of conduct which they themselves have decided to adopt or contemplate adopting on the market, where the object or effect of such contact is to create conditions of competition which do not correspond to the normal conditions of the market in question, regard being had to the nature of the products or services offered, the size and number of the undertakings and the volume of the said market.[42]

This approach makes the question of 'contact', whether direct or indirect, central to the idea of a concerted practice. An example of how such contact may be established can be seen from the various infringements known collectively as the *Polypropylene* cases.[43] Following its investigations into the relevant market, the Commission had concluded that between 1977 and 1983 producers had regularly set target prices by way of a series of price initiatives and brought about a system of annual volume control to share out the available market between them according to agreed percentage or tonnage targets. The Commission cited the following evidence to support its allegations of agreements and concerted practices: contact through regular meetings in secret to discuss and determine commercial policies; the setting of target or minimum prices for sales in each Member State; the exchange of detailed information on deliveries; a system of 'account management' designed to implement price rises to individual customers; simultaneous price

---

[36] *Commission v Anic*, above n 33.

[37] Ibid, para 131. See also *T-Mobile Netherlands*, above n 35, para 23.

[38] *T-Mobile Netherlands*, ibid.

[39] Ibid, para 24.

[40] Case 48/69 *ICI v Commission* [1972] ECR 619, 655; [1972] CMLR 557; reiterated in *Sugar*, above n 7; *Wood Pulp*, above n 31, [1993] ECR I-1307; [1993] 4 CMLR 407, para 63; *Commission v Anic*, above n 33.

[41] *Sugar*, above n 7, para 173; Case 172/80 *Züchner* [1981] ECR 2021; [1982] 1 CMLR 313, para 13; Case C-7/95P *John Deere v Commission* [1998] ECR I-3111; [1998] 5 CMLR 311, para 86.

[42] *Commission v Anic*, above n 33, para 117, citing the cases listed in n 41, above.

[43] For the Commission's original Decision, see [1986] OJ L230/1; [1988] 4 CMLR 347.

increases implementing the said targets; and a limitation on monthly sales by reference to some previous period. The ensuing protracted litigation focused, inter alia, upon whether the Commission had been entitled to characterise the infringements as agreements *and* concerted practices, the requisite levels of intention and market effect for each and the extent to which each party could be responsible for the acts of others.

The Court of Justice held that:

[S]ubject to proof to the contrary, which it is for the economic operators concerned to adduce, there must be a presumption that the undertakings participating in concerting arrangements and remaining active on the market take account of the information exchanged with their competitors when determining their conduct on that market, particularly when they concert together on a regular basis over a long period.[44]

The presumption of a causal connection between concerted action and market conduct was subsequently confirmed by the Court of Justice in *T-Mobile Netherlands BV v Raad van Bestuur van de Nederlandse Mededingingsautoriteit*.[45]

(i) Proof and Responsibility

Proving that a concerted practice exists may be a complicated task. It will be especially difficult in those cases that tread the key borderline between co-ordinated market behaviour prohibited by Article 101(1) and parallel behaviour resulting from decisions independently arrived at by undertakings. Since it will often be the existence of parallel conduct that gives rise to the suspicion of concertation, it may become a matter of fine judgment as to whether what is going on is simply the right of a party to 'adapt intelligently' to the decisions of competitors or whether collusion has indeed been present. In the latter case, as discussed in Chapter 25, the Commission's leniency policy has to a great extent incentivised cartel participants to come forward and 'confess' and this has facilitated the discovery and proof of many cartels in recent years.

In the absence of information derived from a leniency application, direct evidence of relevant contact between the parties may be available in the form of letters, faxes, emails, or records of telephone conversations or meetings. Where direct evidence of concertation is lacking or inconclusive, the Commission has to rely on circumstantial evidence, ie on the inferences that can be drawn from the behaviour of the alleged parties, in the light of an analysis of conditions on the market in question.[46] In such cases the Commission, and ultimately the Court, must be satisfied that there can be no reasonable explanation of the parties' behaviour other than the existence of a concerted practice between them.

The point is well illustrated by the *Zinc Products* case.[47] The concerted practice in issue was allegedly designed to protect the German market for rolled zinc products, where prices were higher than elsewhere in the Community, against parallel imports. A French producer, CRAM, and a German producer, Rheinzink, had delivered quantities of zinc products to a Belgian dealer, Schiltz, under contracts which stipulated that the products be exported to Egypt. Schiltz, however, relabelled them and sent them back to Germany, where they were sold below the normal price. It was common ground that employees

---

[44] *Commission v Anic*, above n 33, para 121.
[45] Case C-8/08, [2009] ECR I-4529; [2009] 5 CMLR 11. See Case C-199/02 P *Hüls AG v Commission* [1999] ECR I-4287; [1999] 5 CMLR 1016; and *Commission v Anic*, above n 33.
[46] *ICI v Commission*, above n 40, 655.
[47] Joined Cases 29 and 35/83 *CRAM and Rheinzink v Commission* [1984] ECR 1679; [1985] 1 CMLR 688.

of Rheinzink found out about the reimports towards the end of October 1976 and that CRAM and Rheinzink discontinued their deliveries to Schiltz on, respectively, the 21st and 29th of that month. In its Decision[48] the Commission had taken the view that the cessation of deliveries by CRAM and Rheinzink could only be explained as the result of an exchange of information for the purpose of preventing imports into Germany. 'Faced with such an argument', the Court said, 'it is sufficient for the applicants to prove circumstances which cast the facts established by the Commission in a different light and which thus allow another explanation of the facts to be substituted for the one adopted by the contested decision.'[49] In the event, CRAM was able to point to two such circumstances: the fact that, when it ceased deliveries on 21 October, it had completed a particular order from Schiltz; and the fact that there had been difficulties over obtaining payment for products supplied to Schiltz in September (and there were similar difficulties in respect of the October delivery). The Court concluded that the Commission had failed to provide 'sufficiently precise and coherent proof' of a concerted practice.[50]

Oligopolistic markets present particular difficulties for the application of the prohibition in Article 101(1). Such markets[51] are typically characterised by small numbers of participants with roughly equal shares and, crucially, a mutual dependence that invites parallel conduct. There is likely to be transparency in market information and little incentive to compete on price. Changes in market strength are likely to arise from either investment in advertising or acquisition of competitors. In the absence of collusive agreements between the parties, any application of Article 101(1) will require proof that they have gone beyond independently acting in parallel to a point where concertation has been reached.

The *Wood Pulp* saga[52] indicates the problems in policing this particular line. At the heart of this epic[53] was an alleged concertation on prices between wood pulp producers mainly located in Finland, Sweden, Canada and the United States. In the Commission's view, concertation could be found in the virtually simultaneous and identical quarterly price announcements made by the producers. These announcements, though made to customers, circulated quickly through the trade press and agents who acted for more than one producer. Having ruled out the Commission's documentary evidence,[54] the Court of Justice considered the nature of the market in the light of the evidence provided by experts it had appointed.

According to the Court, the Commission had failed to establish a 'firm, precise and consistent body of evidence'.[55] In particular, it had not excluded other plausible explanations for the parallel conduct of the producers. Pulp buyers tended to spread their sources and habitually disclosed to producers the prices of competitors. Market transparency was further enhanced by rapid communication and a dynamic trade press. The net result was that the Court relied on the experts' evidence that the features of the market were at least as likely an explanation of price movements as any alleged concertation. Contrary to the

[48] *Re Rolled Zinc Products and Zinc Alloys* [1982] OJ L362/40 [1983] 2 CMLR 285.

[49] [1984] ECR 1679, 1704.

[50] Ibid.

[51] See R Whish and B Sufrin, 'Oligopolistic Markets and EC Competition Law' (1992) 12 *YEL* 59. See S Stroux, *US and EC Oligopoly Control* (The Hague, Kluwer Law International, 2004).

[52] *Wood Pulp*, above n 31.

[53] The Commission's original contested Decision was issued in 1984 but the Court's judgment on the merits was only given in 1993, having made a separate ruling on jurisdictional matters in 1988: see n 31 above.

[54] Inadmissible on several grounds, including the Commission's failure to identify all the parties adequately.

[55] Para 127 of the Judgment.

inferences drawn by the Commission, the system of price announcements was a rational response to the fact that the pulp market constituted a long-term market and to the need felt by both buyers and sellers to limit commercial risks. The coincidence of timing in announcements could be attributed to market transparency and the parallelism of the prices could be satisfactorily explained by the oligopolistic tendencies of the market.[56] Article 1(1) of the Commission's decision in relation to collusion was therefore annulled by the Court.

The Court's approach in *Wood Pulp* reflects the position suggested by Advocate General Cosmas that parallelism of conduct is an evidential issue, not an element of the concept of concerted practice.[57] As expressed subsequently by the Court of First Instance, where the Commission relies upon bare parallelism it is sufficient for the parties to prove circumstances which cast the facts established by the Commission in a different light, allowing another explanation of the facts to be substituted for the one adopted by the Commission.[58] The burden is different in cases where other documented evidence of concertation is available. As the Court of Justice indicated in *Lafarge SA v Commission*,[59] in most cases, the existence of an anti-competitive arrangement could be inferred from a number of coincidences and indicia which, taken together, may, in the absence of another plausible explanation, constitute evidence of a breach of Article 101(1).[60] In those circumstances, the onus is on the parties not merely to submit an alternative explanation for the facts found by the Commission but to challenge the existence of those facts established on the basis of the documents produced by the Commission.[61] Once the Commission establishes that undertakings have participated in regular meetings exchanging information with other producers, a presumption is created that the undertakings participating in those sessions and remaining active on the market take account of the information exchanged with their competitors when determining their conduct, especially when the concertation has taken place on a regular basis over a long period.[62] It is therefore for the economic operators to adduce evidence to rebut that presumption.

Almost inevitably, cases which arouse suspicions of concerted practices are likely to involve multiple parties and thus give rise to questions as to the extent of collective responsibility. Not every party will always have attended every meeting or received every circular or fax. In one of the appeals arising from the *Polypropylene* cases, the Court of Justice set out the relevant test as follows:

> [T]he Commission must, in particular, show that the undertaking intended to contribute by its own conduct to the common objectives pursued by all the participants and that it was aware of

---

[56] But *cf* the outcome in *John Deere v Commission*, above n 41. Here the information exchanged was between only the main suppliers on the relevant market instead of to purchasers. The information went beyond price announcements and amounted to business secrets enabling traders to know the market positions and strategies of their competitors. Unlike the situation in *Wood Pulp*, such exchanges lessened each undertaking's uncertainty as to the future attitude of its competitors.

[57] Para 188 of the Opinion.

[58] Joined Cases T-305-307, 313-316, 318, 325, 328-329 and 335/94 *Re PVC Cartel II: Limburgse Vinyl Maatschapij NV v Commission* [1999] ECR II-931, [1999] 5 CMLR 303, para 725.

[59] Case C-413/08 P *Lafarge SA v Commission* [2010] 5 CMLR 10

[60] Ibid, para 22. See Cases C-204/00 P, C-205/00 P, C-211/00 P, C-213/00 P, C-217/00 P & C-219/00 P *Aalborg Portland A/S v Commission* [2004] ECR I-123; [2005] 4 CMLR 4.

[61] *Lafarge SA v Commission*, para 728.

[62] *Commission v Anic*, above n 33, para 121. To the same effect, see Case C-199/92P *Hüls v Commission* [1999] ECR I-4287; [1999] 5 CMLR 1016, para 162. The parties in these cases failed to provide the necessary rebuttal.

the actual conduct planned or put into effect by other undertakings in pursuit of the same objectives or that it could reasonably have foreseen it and that it was prepared to take the risk.[63]

In the Court's view, the findings of fact made by the Court of First Instance supported the fixing of responsibility upon Anic for conduct followed by other undertakings in the period after it had stopped participating in meetings mid-1982. Anic was perfectly aware of all the elements of the single infringement by virtue of its participation in regular meetings over a period of years and must have assumed that they would continue after mid-1982.[64]

There has been considerable case law concerning the required degree of participation in a concerted practice in order for an undertaking to be in breach of Article 101(1). For instance, the General Court has stressed that an undertaking can be liable even if it participated only in some aspects of an overall cartel if it knew or must have known that the collusion was part of an 'overall plan' even if the role played by different undertakings in pursuit of a common objective were different.[65] The number, frequency and form of meetings required to establish concerted action may vary according to the type of collusion and the market conditions, and a single meeting between competitors may suffice for these purposes.[66] Where an undertaking participates in meetings where collusive behaviour is agreed upon, it cannot escape liability unless it manifestly opposes the agreed behaviour by making it clear to its competitors that it is distancing itself from the unlawful agreement and was participating in the meeting in a spirit different to that exhibited by those competitors.[67] In relation to a cartel established by the Commission in the plasterboard market, the Court of First Instance held that even where an undertaking participated in meetings with knowledge of their object, giving the impression that it would act in conformity with the outcomes of those meetings but did not take an active part in meetings, nor in fact consequently implement any of the agreed measures, it had breached Article 101(1).[68] Furthermore, the concept of a 'single continuous breach' has been developed by the European Courts to allow the Commission to find a continuous single breach of Article 101(1) constituted by separate acts which could also constitute, in isolation, breaches of Article 101(1) where they formed part of an overall plan and objective to distort competition.[69] A single continuous breach may be established even if there is a break of several months between separate cartel activity,[70] but whether separate infringements qualify as a single and continuous breach will depend on such factors as

---

[63] *Commission v Anic*, above n 33, para 87. See also the views of the Court of First Instance in Case T-334/94 *Sarrió v Commission* [1998] ECR II-1439; [1998] 5 CMLR 195 arising from a cartonboard cartel, paras 164–71.

[64] *Commission v Anic*, above n 33, 206. However, it is clear that the Court of Justice sees marginal participation as relevant to a reduction in any fine. See further, Chapter 25 below.

[65] Case T-452/05 *Belgian Sewing Thread (BST) NV v European Commission* [2010] 5 CMLR 16, paras 32–33; see also Case T-48/00 *Corus UK Ltd v Commission* [2004] ECR II-2325; [2005] 4 CMLR 3.

[66] *T-Mobile Netherlands*, above n 35.

[67] See *Aalborg Portland v Commission*, above n 60, para 81; Case C-510/06 P *Archer Daniels Midland Co v Commission* [2009] ECR I-1843; [2009] 4 CMLR 20 at paras 119–20.

[68] *BPB Plc v Commission*, above n 20. See earlier Cases C 238, 244, 245, 247, 250–252 & 254/99 P *Limburgse Vinyl Maatschappij NV (LVM) v Commission* [2002] ECR I-8375; [2003] 4 CMLR 10; Case T-99 *HFB Holding für Fernwärmetechnik Beteiligungsgesellschaft mbH & Co KG v Commission* [2002] ECR II-1487; Cases C 189, 202, 205–208 & 213/02 P *Dansk Rørindustri A/S v Commission* [2005] ECR I-5425; [2005] 5 CMLR 17.

[69] *Aalborg Portland v Commission*, above n 60; Cases T-25, 26/95, 30–32, 34–39, 42–46, 48, 50–65, 68–71, 87, 88, 103 & 104/95 *Cimenteries CBR v Commission* ('*Cement*') [2000] ECR II-491; [2000] 5 CMLR 204; see also *BPB Plc v Commission*, above n 20.

[70] See *BPB Plc v Commission*, above n 20.

the overlap of periods of activity, the similarities in methods and the identity of the anti-competitive objective.[71] Finally, the issue of the attribution of liability for infringements, in particular the liability of a parent company for the cartel activity of a subsidiary, was discussed in Chapter 22.

IV – RESTRICTING COMPETITION

Article 101(1) refers to agreements, etc,[72] 'which have as their object or effect the prevention, restriction or distortion of competition within the internal market'. This phrase has proved to be the very nub of the provision, its deceptive simplicity conflating a bundle of fundamental issues relating not just to the scope of the prohibition but also the methodology of investigation. These questions include whether the same test should be applied to all types of agreements, the nature and extent of economic market analysis required, the thresholds of scale and foreseeability to determine anti-competitive effects and the relevance of any offsetting benefits. Interpretative approaches to these problems have evolved over time in response to changes in the economic and political context in which Article 101 must operate. On the one hand, the advancing process of market integration and economic reappraisal of certain types of activity have led to some of the strictest applications of the prohibition being relaxed—for example, in relation to vertical restraints. On the other, workload pressures facing the Commission and changes in European Court approaches to the interpretation of Article 101 have influenced the conceptual development of Article 101 and also arguably the relationship between the prohibition in paragraph (1) and the legal exception in paragraph (3).

The phrase 'object or effect' must be read disjunctively.[73] The precise purpose of the agreement must first be ascertained by examining its terms in the particular context in which they will have to be performed. Where it can be seen that the purpose, if achieved, will entail the prevention, restriction or distortion of competition to an appreciable degree,[74] there will be no need to go on and show that such has in fact been the outcome. Where, however, the implications an agreement may have for competition are less clear-cut, it will be necessary to undertake an analysis of economic conditions on the relevant market to assess the extent of any adverse impact.[75] This, however, is not a matter of measuring actual effects on trade between Member States but a question of whether the agreement is capable of such effects.[76] Nothing turns on the distinction between 'prevention', 'restriction' and 'distortion' of competition. The *Consten and Grundig* judgment,[77] for instance, describes the agreement in question as being 'such as to *distort* competition

---

[71] See Joined cases T-101/05 & T-111/05 *BASF and UCB v Commission* [2007] ECR II-4949; [2008] 4 CMLR 13.

[72] References hereinafter to 'agreements' should be understood as applying also to decisions and concerted practices unless the context indicates otherwise.

[73] Case 56/65 *Société Technique Minière v Maschinenbau Ulm* [1966] ECR 235, [1966] 1 CMLR 357; confirmed in Case C-219/95P *Ferrière Nord SpA v Commission* [1997] ECR I-4411, [1997] 5 CMLR 575. In the latter case the Court held that the Italian version of the Treaty, referring to object *and* effect, could not prevail over the unambiguous and express use of the disjunctive in all the other language versions.

[74] On the de minimis rule, see below.

[75] *Société Technique Minière*, above n 73, 249.

[76] Case 19/77 *Miller Schallplatten v Commission* [1978] ECR 131; [1978] 2 CMLR 334.

[77] Joined Cases 56 and 58/64 *Consten and Grundig v Commission* [1966] ECR 299; [1966] CMLR 418.

in the common market', while a few lines later it refers to 'the above-mentioned *restrictions*'.[78] The three terms express, with varying emphasis, the basic idea of a change in the state of competition.

A – 'By Object' Restrictions

In assessing restrictions, the Commission has come to use the language of 'hard-core' restraints to describe their most objectionable forms.[79] Such restrictions are generally considered by the Commission to constitute restrictions by *object*.[80] For horizontal agreements, these will include price-fixing, limitation of output, and the sharing of markets or customers. For instance, a meeting between competitors had an anti-competitive object where it was intended to end a price war by raising prices and reducing the intensity of competition between the undertakings concerned.[81] As evidenced by block exemptions,[82] hard-core restraints in vertical relationships are most likely to be found in resale price maintenance or excessive territorial restraints. For instance, agreements aimed at prohibiting or limiting parallel trade have consistently been held to have as their object the prevention of competition,[83] without the need to prove any final consumers have been disadvantaged.[84]

The Commission's Guidelines on Horizontal Co-operation Agreements sets out the approach to be adopted in relation to by object restrictions as follows:

> 24. Restrictions of competition by object are those that by their very nature have the potential to restrict competition within the meaning of Article 101(1). It is not necessary to examine the actual or potential effects of an agreement on the market once its anti-competitive object has been established.[85]

An excellent, recent example to highlight the approach to be taken in relation to 'by object' restrictions is the Court of Justice's preliminary ruling in *Competition Authority v Beef Industry Development Society Ltd.*[86] In that case, due to perceived overcapacity in the Irish beef-processing industry, processors formed the so-called Beef Industry Development Society Ltd (BIDS), which purchased cattle from breeders, slaughtered and deboned them, and then sold the beef in Ireland and abroad. The processors wished to reduce the over-

---

[78] Ibid, [1966] ECR 299, 343 (emphasis added).

[79] See *Guidelines on the Application of Article 81(3) of the Treaty* [2004] OJ C101/08 for the Commission's position on the scope and application of Art 101(1) as well as the exemption provisions that provide the somewhat misleading title to this Notice.

[80] Ibid, para 23.

[81] *BPB Plc v Commission*, above n 20.

[82] See eg Vertical Agreements Regulation 330/2010 on the application of Art 101(3) of the Treaty on the Functioning of the European Union to categories of vertical agreements and concerted practices [2010] OJ L102/1.

[83] Case 19/77 *Miller International Schallplaten GmbH v Commission* [1978] ECR 131; [1978] 2 CMLR 334, paras 7 and 18 and Cases 32/78, 36/78–82/78 *BMW Belgium SA v Commission* [1979] ECR 2435; [1980] 1 CMLR 370 at paras 20–28 and 31; applied most recently in Joined cases C-501/06 P, C-513/06 P, C-515/06 P and C-519/06 P *GlaxoSmithKline Services unlimited v Commission* [2009] ECR I-9291; [2010] 4 CMLR 2

[84] *GlaxoSmithKline Services unlimited v Commission*, ibid, paras 63–64.

[85] *Guidelines on the Applicability of Article 101 of the Treaty on the Functioning of the European Union to Horizontal co-Operation Agreements* [2011] OJ C11/1; [2011] OJ C33/20. See Commission Press release IP/10/1702, 14 December 2010, para 24.

[86] Case C-209/07 *Competition Authority v Beef Industry Development Society Ltd* [2008] ECR I-8637; [2009] 4 CMLR 6.

capacity through agreed arrangements and set up arrangements where effectively those remaining in the industry ('the stayers') compensated those leaving the industry ('the goers'). The Court, in its preliminary ruling, confirmed that where an agreement's object was to prevent, restrict or distort competition, it was prohibited by Article 101(1) without any need to take into account any anti-competitive effects on the market.[87] In order to determine if an agreement came within the prohibition, close attention should be given to its wording and the objectives it seeks to attain.[88] In this case, the object of the agreement was to change appreciably the structure of the market by encouraging the withdrawal of competitors, thereby replacing a process of rivalry with a process of co-operation, patently conflicting with the purpose of Article 101.[89] Nonetheless, it is arguable that 'by object' restrictions cannot be equated with US antitrust-style 'per se' infringements, which are 'irredeemably unlawful'.[90] Indeed, in contrast with the approach set out in *European Night Services*,[91] the Court in *BIDS* looked beyond the objectively 'hard-core' nature of the infringement, stressing that the assessment under Article 101(1) is to be made in the light of the agreement's 'economic context',[92] a more contextual and economic-based approach to by object restrictions,[93] assessing the arrangement in the context of the nature of the particular industry and rivalry involved.[94] Indeed, this modernised approach is outlined in the 2011 Commission Guidelines on Horizontal Co-operation Agreements:

> 25. According to the settled case-law of the Court of Justice of the European Union, in order to assess whether an agreement has an anti-competitive object, regard must be had to the content of the agreement, the objectives it seeks to attain, and the economic and legal context of which it forms part. In addition, although the parties' intention is not a necessary factor in determining whether an agreement has an anti-competitive object, the Commission may nevertheless take this aspect into account in its analysis.[95]

If an agreement is not restrictive by object, then it must be examined according to whether there are restrictive *effects* on competition. This means that the agreement 'must affect actual or potential competition to such an extent that on the relevant market negative

---

[87] Ibid, paras 15–17. See *Société Technique Minière*, above n 73. See also *T-Mobile Netherlands*, above n 35, paras. 28 and 30; and *GlaxoSmithKline Services unlimited v Commission*, above n 83, para 55.

[88] *Competition Authority v BIDS*, above n 86, paras 18–21. See Case C-551/03 P *General Motors BV v Commission* [2006] ECR I-3173; [2006] 5 CMLR 1.

[89] *Competition Authority v BIDS*, above n 86, paras 24–37.

[90] Ibid, paras 40–41; see also Whish and Sufrin, above n 51, 150. We will discuss the extent to which a US-style 'rule of reason' approach has (or can be) transposed to the EU context under Art 101(1) further below. See A Andreangeli 'From Mobile Phones to Cattle: How the Court of Justice is Reframing the Approach to Article 101 (Formerly 81 EC Treaty) of the EU Treaty' (2011) *World Competition*, forthcoming.

[91] See Case T-374–75, 384 and 388/94, *European Night Services and others v Commission* [1998] ECR II-3141; [1998] 5 CMLR 718, para 136.

[92] *BIDS*, above n 86, para 17. See Cases 56/64 and 58/64 *Etablissements Consten Sarl v Commission* [1966] ECR 299; [1966] CMLR 418 ; Case C-105/04 P *Nederlandse Federatieve Vereniging voor de Groothandel op Elektrotechnisch Gebied v Commission* [2006] ECR I-8725; [2006] 5 CMLR 22; Cases 29/83 and 30/83 *Compagnie Royale Asturienne des Mines SA (CRAM) v Commission* [1984] ECR 1679; [1985] 1 CMLR 688.

[93] See Andreangeli, above n 90. See also O Odudu, 'Restriction of Competition by Object—What Is the beef?' (2008) 8 *Competition Law Journal* 11, 13. See the ECJ's preliminary ruling in *T-Mobile Netherlands*, above n 35.

[94] See Andreangeli, above n 90, and also A Andreangeli, 'Modernising the Approach to Article 101 TFEU in Respect to Horizontal Agreements: Has the Commission's Interpretation "Come of Age"?' (2011) *Competition and Regulation* 195.

[95] *Guidelines on the Applicability of Article 101*, above n 85, para 25.

effects on prices, output, innovation or the variety or quality of goods and services can be expected with a reasonable degree of probability'.[96]

B – 'By Effect' Restrictions

As summarised by the Court of First Instance, in assessing the effect of an agreement under Article 101(1),

> the examination of conditions of competition is based not only on existing competition between undertakings already present on the relevant market but also on potential competition, in order to ascertain whether, in the light of the structure of the market and the economic and legal context within which it functions, there are real concrete possibilities for the undertakings concerned to compete among themselves or for a new competitor to penetrate the relevant market and compete with the undertakings already established.[97]

This market-based analysis has not always been the basis for applying Article 101(1). Certainly, back in the 1960s, a much more abstract view of the potential for competition to be restricted was visible in judicial reasoning.[98] However, it is now clear that an 'effects' approach requires the agreement or practice to be situated within the market in which it operates. Particular guidance on the so-called 'network' effect of agreements can be seen from the Court's judgment in *Delimitis*,[99] a case concerning 'tie' arrangements between brewers and café-owners whereby the latter were committed to purchases from the former. A single agreement of this type might not be especially significant, but the overall impact of many similar tied contracts in a market could effectively foreclose competition. The Court of Justice ruled that such a beer-supply agreement infringed Article 101(1) if two cumulative conditions were met:

> The first is that, having regard to the economic and legal context of the agreement at issue, it is difficult for competitors who could enter the market or increase their market share to gain access to the national market for the distribution of beer in premises for the sales and consumption of drinks. . . . The second condition is that the agreement in question must make a significant contribution to the sealing-off effect brought about by the totality of those agreements in their economic and legal context. The extent of the contribution made by the individual agreement depends on the position of the contracting parties in the relevant market and on the duration of the agreement.[100]

In its Article 101(3) Guidelines of 2004, the Commission noted that when analysing restrictive effects, besides having to define the relevant market:

> It is normally also necessary to examine and assess, *inter alia*, the nature of the products, the market position of the parties, the market position of competitors, the market position of buyers, the existence of potential competitors and the level of entry barriers. In some cases, however, it may be possible to show anti-competitive effects directly by analysing the conduct of the parties to the agreement on the market. It may for example be possible to ascertain that an agreement has led to price increases.[101]

---

[96] *Guidelines on the Application of Article 81(3)*, above n 79, para 24.
[97] *European Night Services v Commission*, above n 91, paras 136–37.
[98] *Consten and Grundig*, above n 77.
[99] Case C-234/89 *Delimitis v Henninger Bräu* [1991] ECR I-935; [1992] 5 CMLR 210.
[100] Ibid, para 27.
[101] *Guidelines on the Application of Article 81(3) of the Treaty*, above n 79, para 27.

In *Van Den Bergh v Commission*[102] the legality of certain exclusive purchasing commitments was considered by the Court of First Instance in a dispute related to 'impulse ice cream'—wrapped ice creams for immediate consumption. Freezers were supplied by HB to retailers free or at nominal rent and the agreements could be terminated with two months' notice. The freezers were to be used exclusively for products supplied by HB and at least 40 per cent of all outlets in the relevant market only had freezers supplied on this basis by HB. The Court of First Instance stressed that the 'contractual restrictions on retailers must be examined not just in a purely formal manner from the legal point of view, but also by taking into account the specific economic context within which the agreements in practoce operate'.[103] The Court of First Instance considered that the HB network had a 'considerably dissuasive effect on retailers' and 'operate *de facto* as a tie on sales outlets' such that 'the effect of the exclusivity clause in practice is to restrict the commercial freedom of retailers to choose the products they wish to sell in their sales outlets'.[104]

(i) A Rule of Reason under Article 101(1)?

The fact that the possibility of a 'rule of reason' in Article 101(1) has remained a long-standing question[105] for both scholars and practitioners reflects the confluence of a number of rather different considerations and circumstances. As a term, 'rule of reason' has a different pedigree according to which side of the Atlantic has legal jurisdiction. In the EU context, it is tempting to equate the concept with its more familiar historic attachment to the single market and the fundamental freedoms. Further complication is added by the fact that the specific character of Article 101 involves the separation of the prohibition in paragraph (1) from the legal exception in paragraph (3), unlike the rule in section 1 of the Sherman Act 1890. Furthermore, there have been important developments in recent years in relation to the interpretation of Article 101(1) and the factors that may be considered in applying the prohibition. It should be stressed that the interpretation of Article 101 must ultimately be a teleological one based on its position within the competition rules and the wider Treaty context, rather than any notion transplanted from elsewhere.

As applied to competition law, the use of 'rule of reason' can be traced to US antitrust law,[106] where this idea arose to mitigate the rigour of the prohibition in section 1 of the Sherman Act against contracts in restraint of trade.[107] The rule of reason applies to agreements other than those, such as horizontal price-fixing agreements, which are treated by the US courts as illegal per se. Essentially, a court is required under the rule to consider the overall impact of the agreement in question on competition within the relevant market. This involves, in particular, identifying any pro-competitive effects the agreement may have and weighing them against its anti-competitive effects. However, the

---

[102] Case T-65/98 *Van den Bergh Foods v Commission* [2004] CMLR 1.
[103] Ibid, para 84.
[104] Ibid, para 98.
[105] See eg R Wesseling, 'The Rule of Reason and Competition Law: Various Rules, Various Reasons' in A Schrauwen (ed), *Rule of Reason, Rethinking Another Classic of European Legal Doctrine* (Groningen, Europa Law Publishing, 2005) ch 4. See C Callery, 'Should the European Union Embrace or Exorcise Leegin's "Rule of Reason"?' [2011] *ECLR* 42.
[106] See J Peeters, 'The Rule of Reason Revisited: Prohibition on Restraints of Competition in the Sherman Act and EEC Treaty' [1989] *AJ Comp Law* 521; IS Forrester and C Norall, 'The Laïcization of Community Law: Self-help and the Rule of Reason: How Competition Law Is and Could Be Applied' (1984) 21 *CMLRev* 11.
[107] The rule is summarised by R Whish and B Sufrin (1987) 7 *YEL* 1, 4–12. See also O Black, 'Per Se Rules and Rules of Reason: What Are They?' [1997] *ECLR* 145.

importance in US antitrust law of the rule of reason is explained by the absence of any 'gateway' through which a restrictive agreement which is considered, nevertheless, to be economically beneficial, may escape prohibition. Where application of the rule leads to a favourable assessment of an agreement under the Sherman Act, that will be because the agreement is judged, on balance, not to be restrictive of competition. The rule of reason test was controversially extended to vertical resale price maintenance by the Supreme Court in 2007 in *Leegin Creative Leather Products Inc v PSKS Inc.*[108]

In EU law, on the other hand, an agreement that restricts competition within the meaning of Article 101(1) may still qualify for the legal exception under Article 101(3). At first sight, therefore, it might be assumed that pro-competitive aspects of an agreement will only be taken into account in assessing the economic benefits in applying the legal exception, especially now that national courts and competition authorities are competent to take decisions under Article 101(3). Certainly, in earlier case law[109] the Court of First Instance expressly rejected the existence of a rule of reason in this 'weighing up' sense. In particular, it observed that much of the effectiveness of Article 101(3) as a precision framework would be lost if pro- and anti-competitive factors were to be balanced under paragraph (1). However, the Court of First Instance conceded that other case law[110] signalled a broader treatment of Article 101(1) to the extent that account needed to be taken of the actual context in which any agreement functioned.

At its narrowest, the potential for 'rule of reason' type arguments extends to the economic context of the agreement, and excludes a balancing of the pro- and anti-competitive features of the agreement. In fact, the 'economic context' case law, such as *Van den Bergh* and *Delimitis*, has tended to look at the economic effects of an agreement (or network of agreements) in order to confirm the existence of anti-competitive behaviour infringing Article 101(1).

However, despite expressly disavowing the adoption of a rule of reason approach involving an assessment of the pro- and anti-competitive effects of an agreement, the General Court's analysis of the counterfactual situation in *O2*,[111] ie the examination of competition in the absence of the agreement, led the Court to quash the Commission's finding of an infringement on the basis that the reduced freedom of action resulting from the network sharing agreement actually resulted in an increase in competition as O2 would now be able to enter the market and compete effectively, which it could not have done otherwise.[112] Although the General Court does not advocate a rule of reason approach as such, the counterfactual approach does appear to be wider than an in-context legal assessment,[113]

---

[108] 127 S Ct 2705 US (2007). See Callery, above n 105.

[109] Case T-112/99 *Métropole Télévision (M6) v Commission* [2001] ECR II-2459, [2001] 5 CMLR 1236 and Case T-65/98 *Van den Bergh Foods v Commission* [2003] ECR II-4653, [2004] 4 CMLR 1.

[110] eg *Delimitis*, above n 99; also the 'ancillary restraints' cases, discussed further below.

[111] Case T-328/03 *O2 v Commission* [2006] ECR II-1231, especially paras 68–69, 71–72, 75–79; M Marquis, 'O2 (Germany) v Commission and the Exotic Mysteries of Article 81(1)' (2007) 32 *ELRev* 29; see B Robertson, 'What Is a Restriction of Competition? The Implications of the CFI's Judgment in O2 Germany and the Rule of Reason' [2007] *ECLR* 252.

[112] See Andreangeli, above n 90, for fuller discussion.

[113] This approach is supported by the *Guidelines on the Applicability of Article 101*, above n 85, para 29:

The assessment of whether a horizontal co-operation agreement has restrictive effects on competition within the meaning of Article 101(1) must be made in comparison to the actual legal and economic context in which competition would occur in the absence of the agreement with all of its alleged restrictions (that is to say, in the absence of the agreement as it stands (if already implemented) or as envisaged (if not yet implemented) at the time of assessment). Hence, in order to prove actual or potential restrictive effects on competition, it is necessary to take into account competition between the parties and competi-

which in turn has implications for the relationship between Article 101(1) and the legal exception in Article 101(3) under the bifurcated approach to anti-competitive arrangements, and for the range of issues to be considered in relation to the latter.[114]

This leaves at least two further possibilities. The first engages a legal context expressed in terms of necessary or inherent elements of an agreement which must survive in order to make it work—sometimes known as the 'ancillary restraints' doctrine. It would perhaps seem curious to use the term 'rule of reason' here, although the case law discussed below clearly supports this margin of appreciation within Article 101(1). A second possibility, and much more redolent of the balancing characteristics of EU free-movement 'rule of reason' applications,[115] is that Article 101(1) permits or requires the balancing of competition and non-competition concerns as part of the 'actual context' of the agreement.

To illustrate the first group, the Court has held in a number of cases that contractual provisions giving a measure of protection against competition do not fall within Article 101(1) if they are genuinely necessary to enable a partner to be found in a business transaction. The earliest reference to this 'indispensable inducement' rationale was in *Société Technique Minière v Maschinenbau Ulm*[116] which concerned an exclusive distribution agreement. Under the agreement the supplier promised not to appoint another distributor in the concession territory or to sell the goods there itself, but no protection was provided against parallel imports. The Court said that 'it may be doubted whether there is an interference with competition if the said agreement seems really necessary for the penetration of a new area by an undertaking'.[117] The case is distinguishable from *Consten and Grundig*,[118] where the absolute territorial protection sought by the parties could not be regarded as 'really necessary' to secure access for Grundig products to the French market. A further example is *Remia*,[119] where the Court accepted that the seller of a business could be put under an obligation not to compete with the buyer, while emphasising that 'such clauses must be necessary to the transfer of the undertaking concerned and their duration and scope must be strictly limited to that purpose'.[120] The Court refused to interfere with the Commission's finding that four years' protection for the buyer of a sauce-manufacturing business would have been enough to cover the introduction of a new trademark and to win customer loyalty, instead of the ten-year period which had been agreed.

In a rather different vein, the Court held in *Pronuptia*[121] that various provisions in an agreement forming part of a distribution franchise system did not restrict competition within the meaning of Article 101(1) because they were necessary to the successful functioning of the system. This approach goes beyond the analysis of the cases just referred to: the issue is not whether, apart from the provisions in question, a bargain could have been struck, but whether the essential aims of the transaction (considered to be one that competition law ought not to disfavour) could have been realised. As applied by the

---

tion from third parties, in particular actual or potential competition that would have existed in the absence of the agreement. This comparison does not take into account any potential efficiency gains generated by the agreement as these will only be assessed under Article 101(3).

[114] See Andreangeli, above n 90, and Andreangeli, above n 94.
[115] See generally, Schrauwen (ed), above n 105.
[116] *Société Technique Minière*, above n 73.
[117] Ibid, 250.
[118] *Consten and Grundig*, above n 77.
[119] Case 42/84 *Remia v Commission* [1985] ECR 2545; [1987] 1 CMLR 1.
[120] See para 20 of the Judgment.
[121] Case 161/84 *Pronuptia de Paris v Schillgalis* [1986] ECR 353; [1986] 1 CMLR 414.

Court, the analysis comprised four logical steps: (i) definition of the salient features of the transaction; (ii) finding that the transaction is not in itself restrictive of competition; (iii) identification of the conditions that have to be met to enable such a transaction to be satisfactorily performed; and (iv) identification of the contractual terms indispensable to the fulfilment of those conditions. In other words, the Court's approach acknowledged an ancillary restraints element in the assessment of restrictions.

Distribution franchising, the Court explained, is a marketing system under which an established distributor whose success is associated with a certain trademark and certain commercial methods (the franchisor) puts his mark and methods at the disposal of independent traders (the franchisees) in return for the payment of a royalty. This has the advantage to the franchisor of enabling him to exploit his know-how without having to commit his own capital; and to the franchisees of giving them access to methods they could otherwise only have acquired through prolonged effort and research, while also allowing them to profit from the reputation of the mark. The success of such a system depends on two things: the franchisor must be able to communicate his know-how to the franchisees and help them in putting his methods into practice without running the risk that his competitors might benefit, even directly; and he must be able to take appropriate measures to preserve the identity and reputation of the network symbolised by the mark. Under the agreement in question the franchisee had undertaken not to open a shop selling competing goods and not to dispose of the franchise premises except with the prior consent of the franchisor. These terms imposed quite severe restraints on the running of the franchisee's business but they were found to be indispensable to the fulfilment of the first condition and so were outwith Article 101(1). Among the terms excluded from Article 101(1) by the second condition was the franchisee's obligation to obtain stock only from the franchisor or from suppliers chosen by him. This helped to protect the reputation of the network by ensuring that the public would find goods of uniform quality in all Pronuptia shops. Given the character of the franchise products (wedding dresses and formal wear), it would, in the Court's view, have been impossible to achieve that result by formulating a set of objective quality specifications.

The *Pronuptia* case, representing at the time a new form of business model for evaluation against competition rules, followed earlier judgments by the Court that had similarly focused upon the merit and purpose of another business method, selective distribution. Although now largely overtaken by block exemption legislation,[122] a series of cases established that selective distribution agreements based on objective quality criteria which are applied in a non-discriminatory way are compatible with Article 101(1).[123] Under such a system, for example, a manufacturer may limit the outlets for a product which is expensive and technically complex to dealers able and willing to promote it effectively and to provide pre-sales advice, and an after-sales maintenance and repair service, for customers.[124] Selectivity is likely, on the one hand, to result in higher prices. On the other, opportunities are created for competition between manufacturers in respect of the customer services

---

[122] Regulation 330/2020 [2010] OJ L102/1 discussed further below.

[123] See, in particular, Case 26/76 *Metro* [1977] ECR 1875, [1978] 2 CMLR 1; Joined Cases 253/78 and 1-3/79 *Guerlain, Rochas, Lanvin and Nina Ricci ('Perfumes')* [1980] ECR 2327; [1981] 2 CMLR 99; Case 86/82 *Hasselblad v Commission* [1984] ECR 883; [1984] CMLR 559; Case 75/84 *Metro v Commission (No 2)* [1986] ECR 3021; [1987] 1 CMLR 118; Case C-376/92 *Metro v Cartier* [1994] ECR I-15; [1994] 5 CMLR 331; Case T-19/92 *Groupement D'Achat Edouard Leclerc v Commission* [1996] ECR II-1961; [1997] 4 CMLR 995.

[124] The *Perfumes* cases, ibid, illustrate selective distribution of another kind of product thought to require special handling, namely luxury items.

associated with their brands. The rationale of the Court's approach to selective distribution can be seen from the *AEG* case,[125] where it said:

> [T]here are legitimate requirements, such as the maintenance of a specialist trade capable of providing specific services as regards high-quality and high-technology products, which may justify a reduction of price competition in favour of competition relating to factors other than price. Systems of selective distribution, in so far as they aim at the attainment of a legitimate goal capable of improving competition in relation to factors other than price, therefore constitute an element of competition which is in conformity with Article [101(1)].[126]

In essence, the Court's approach to franchising and selective distribution exhibits a willingness to weigh the pros and cons of different *forms* of competition against each other (in the sense of quality versus price). This could be seen as a rather sophisticated application of a 'rule of reason', buttressed by an application of the ancillary restraints idea to ensure that the merit of the business technique is rendered operational. Thus the Court still refused to uphold *quantitative* conditions, such as limits on numbers of outlets, resale price maintenance[127] or export bans,[128] without specific exemption even though, arguably,[129] the purpose of their inclusion in an agreement may be to ensure a sufficient turnover for the dealer to support the desired range of customer services.

Perhaps the most modern evidence of the 'rule of reason' in its EU competition context is provided by the cases in which the 'context' surrounding an agreement extends beyond economic analysis or ancillary requirements. Instead, the Court treats Article 101(1) as inapplicable because of some other public interest consideration that trumps the restrictive element of the agreement. The most potentially far-reaching example is provided by *Wouters*,[130] a case concerning regulations issued by the Netherlands Bar which prohibited multidisciplinary partnerships between members of the Bar and other professions, including accountants. The Court of Justice first decided that members of the Bar were undertakings carrying on an economic activity and that the Bar itself was an association of undertakings when it adopted regulations of the type in question. The Court then observed the adverse effect on competition that resulted from the prohibition against partnerships with accountants,[131] particularly in terms of preventing a wider range of services, maybe even new ones, from emerging in a one-stop shop structure for business clients. However, the Court proceeded to override this limitation of production and development[132] as follows:

> [N]ot every agreement between undertakings or every decision of an association of undertakings which restricts the freedom of action of the parties or of one of them necessarily falls within the prohibition laid down in [Article 101 TFEU]. For the purposes of application of that provision to a particular case, account must first of all be taken of the *overall context in which the decision of the association of undertakings was taken or produces its effects*. More particularly, account must be taken of its objectives, which are here connected with the need to make rules

---

[125] *AEG v Commission*, above n 14.

[126] Ibid, 3194.

[127] Ibid.

[128] See *Perfumes* cases, above n 123.

[129] See Chard, 'The Economics of the Application of Article 85 to Selective Distribution Systems' (1982) 7 ELRev 83.

[130] *Wouters*, above n 27.

[131] Described by the Dean of the Bar as a marriage between a mouse and an elephant in the light of the gigantic size of accountants' firms compared with Bar practices.

[132] A specific example of anti-competitive practice listed in Art 101(1).

relating to organisation, qualifications, professional ethics, supervision and liability, in order to ensure that the ultimate consumers of legal services and the sound administration of justice are provided with the necessary guarantees in relation to integrity and experience. . . . *It has then to be considered whether the consequential effects restrictive of competition are inherent in the pursuit of those objectives.*[133]

In conclusion, the Court held that the Regulation in issue could therefore 'reasonably be considered to be necessary in order to ensure the proper practice of the legal profession, as it is organised in the Member State concerned'.[134] Accordingly, the prohibition of multidisciplinary practices was regarded as necessary to ensure the proper exercise of the legal profession in the public interest, and this assessment took place within the confines of Article 101(1).[135]

The novelty of the *Wouters* judgment is that it clearly found a negative effect on competition but discounted it because of wider public-interest concerns. This balancing is not a purely competition-led inquiry. The *Wouters* case was subsequently adopted by the Commission as part of its alternative reasoning in relation to anti-doping rules applicable to professional sport. The Commission had rejected a complaint which sought to challenge the compatibility of certain regulations adopted by the International Olympic Committee and implemented by the governing body of swimming, the Fédération Internationale de Natation Amateur, relating to doping control, with the EU rules on competition and freedom to provide services. The Court of Justice, in *Meca-Medina v Commission*,[136] confirmed the *Wouters* broader 'rule of reason' approach in considering if the anti-doping rules were restrictive of competition and thereafter assessing if those effects were inherent in, and proportionate to, the sporting objectives pursued by those rules.[137]

The controversy about which test to use to mark the outer limits of application of the Treaty's competition rules thus persists. As seen in Chapter 22, above, the notion of 'undertaking' has increasingly performed this role in relation to healthcare systems or pension arrangements. *Wouters* and *Meca-Medina* appears to offer the opportunity to develop a convergence with free-movement case law by allowing for general public-interest justifications for particular rules and arrangements, and this may be important for bodies performing delegated public functions.[138]

C – Information Exchange

The European Courts have reiterated in a line of case law that agreements on the exchange of information 'are incompatible with the rules on competition if they reduce or remove the degree of uncertainty as to the operation of the market in question with the result that competition between undertakings is restricted'.[139] The Commission Guidelines on

---

[133] *Wouters* judgment, above n 27, para 97 (emphasis added).

[134] Ibid, para 107.

[135] See C Townley, *Article 81 EC and Public Policy* (Hart Publishing, Oxford, 2009) 148–53.

[136] Case C-519/04 P *Meca-Medina v Commission* [2006] ECR I-6991; [2006] 5 CMLR 18. See Case T-313/02 *Meca-Medina and Majcen v Commission* (Judgment of the CFI, 30 September 2004), criticised by S Weatherill, 'Anti-Doping Rules and EC Law' [2005] *ECLR* 416.

[137] *Meca-Medina and Majcen v Commission*, ibid, criticised by Weatherill, ibid.

[138] See E Szyszczak, 'Competition and Sport' (2007) *ELRev* 95.

[139] Case C-238/05 *ASNEF-EQUIFAX Servicios de Informacion sobre Solvencia y Credito SL v Asociacion de Usuarios de Servicios Bancarios (AUSBANC)* [2006] ECR I-11125; [2007] 4 CMLR 6, para 51; *John Deere Ltd v*

Horizontal Co-operation Agreements[140] provide further details on the approach to be adopted to information exchange agreements. The sharing of disaggregated, non-publicly available confidential information on future intentions is likely to be regarded as an object infringement, whereas the exchange of aggregated, historic and non-commercially sensitive information will be regarded on an effects basis, by comparison with the competitive situation which would prevail in the absence of the shared information.[141] Accordingly, an exchange of information is more likely to be prohibited if it involves the exchange of commercially sensitive data, particularly in relation to prices and quantities, in comparison with exchanges of more publicly available information. Relevant factors to be taken into account also include the level of detail and age of the information exchanged, the frequency of the information exchange and the market characteristics. Exchanges of information in markets with homogeneous products and high market concentration are more likely to restrict competition, particularly in oligopolistic markets.[142] The approach to be adopted was confirmed by the Court of Justice, in a preliminary ruling in relation to a register established in Spain which made available solvency and credit information provided by lending and credit organisations, as follows:

> 54 Accordingly, as follows from para [49] of this judgment, the compatibility of an information exchange system, such as the register, with the Community competition rules cannot be assessed in the abstract. It depends on the economic conditions on the relevant markets and on the specific characteristics of the system concerned, such as, in particular, its purpose and the conditions of access to it and participation in it, as well as the type of information exchanged—be that, for example, public or confidential, aggregated or detailed, historical or current—the periodicity of such information and its importance for the fixing of prices, volumes or conditions of service.

> . . .

> 58 In that regard, first of all, if supply on a market is highly concentrated, the exchange of certain information may, according in particular to the type of information exchanged, be liable to enable undertakings to be aware of the market position and commercial strategy of their competitors, thus distorting rivalry on the market and increasing the probability of collusion, or even facilitating it. On the other hand, if supply is fragmented, the dissemination and exchange of information between competitors may be neutral, or even positive, for the competitive nature of the market (see, to that effect, Thyssen Stahl at [84] & [86]). In the present case, it is common ground, as may be seen from para [10] of this judgment, that the referring court premised its reference for a preliminary ruling on the existence of 'a fragmented market', which it is for that court to verify.

> 59 Secondly, in order that registers such as that at issue in the main proceedings are not capable of revealing the market position or the commercial strategy of competitors, it is important that the identity of lenders is not revealed, directly or indirectly. In the present case, it is apparent from the decision for referral that the *Tribunal de Defensa de la Competencia* imposed on Asnef-Equifax, which accepted it, a condition that the information relating to lenders contained in the register not be disclosed.

> 60 Thirdly, it is also important that such registers be accessible in a non-discriminatory manner,

---

Commission, above n 40, paras 88 and 90; Case C-194/99 P *Thyssen Stahl v Commission* [2003] ECR I-10821, para 81.

[140] *Guidelines on the Applicability of Article 101*, above n 85. See Commission Press release IP/10/1702, 14 December 2010.

[141] See discussion above regarding the distinctive approaches to by object and effects infringements under Art 101(1).

[142] See eg *BPB Plc v Commission*, above n 20; and *T-Mobile Netherlands*, above n 35.

in law and in fact, to all operators active in the relevant sphere. If such accessibility were not guaranteed, some of those operators would be placed at a disadvantage, since they would have less information for the purpose of risk assessment, which would also not facilitate the entry of new operators on to the market.

61 It follows that, provided that the relevant market or markets are not highly concentrated, the system does not permit lenders to be identified and that the conditions of access and use by financial institutions are not discriminatory, an information exchange system such as the register is not, in principle, liable to have the effect of restricting competition within the meaning of Art [101(1)] .

62 While in those conditions such systems are capable of reducing uncertainty as to the risk that applicants for credit will default, they are not, however, liable to reduce uncertainty as to the risks of competition. Thus, each operator could be expected to act independently and autonomously when adopting a given course of conduct, regard being had to the risks presented by applicants. Contrary to Ausbanc's contention, it cannot be inferred solely from the existence of such a credit information exchange that it might lead to collective anti-competitive conduct, such as a boycott of certain potential borrowers.[143]

D – Appreciable Effects on Competition and on Trade between Member States

For Article 101(1) to apply, the agreement must restrict competition to an appreciable extent. This de minimis rule is a further illustration that the prohibition contained in the Article must be adapted to practical contexts. Given the instrumentalism of competition law, discussed in Chapter 22 above, there would be little point in regulating potential infringements of Article 101 which had no real impact on the internal market or the free play of competition. At the same time, there will be no breach of Article 101 without an appreciable effect on trade between Member States. This notion serves a jurisdictional role, since if it is not satisfied, then any regulation of the agreement will flow from national competition rules rather than the EU regime. These two applications of appreciability are discussed in turn below.

(i) The De Minimis Rule Applied to Restrictions on Competition

The de minimis rule was first laid down by the Court of Justice in *Völk v Vervaecke*,[144] where the manufacturer in question held only around 0.2 per cent of the market. Following the Court's lead, the Commission adopted, and periodically revised, guidance Notices for businesses on when agreements will be deemed to lack the appreciable effect necessary for the purposes of a restriction under Article 101(1). The 2001 Notice[145] is built upon market share criteria, the relevant figures being 10 per cent for agreements between competitors and 15 per cent for those between non-competitors.[146] Where there is doubt as to which category applies, the 10 per cent figure is to be used. For agreements with network effects the figures across the board are reduced to 5 per cent.[147] But in any event, the de minimis

---

[143] *ASNEF-EQUIFAX*, above n 139, paras 54 and 58–62.
[144] Case 5/69 *Völk v Vervaecke* [1969] ECR 295; [1969] CMLR 273.
[145] *Notice on Agreements of Minor Importance* [2001] OJ C368/13, [2002] 4 CMLR 699.
[146] Ibid, para 7.
[147] Ibid, para 8. However, the same provision notes that a cumulative foreclosure effect is unlikely to exist if less than 30% of the relevant market is subject to parallel network agreements having similar effects.

thresholds do not apply to agreements containing any of the hard-core restrictions identified in paragraph 11 of the Notice, such as price-fixing or market-partitioning.

Some care must be exercised when seeking to apply the Notice. As a piece of 'soft' law, it is not legally binding and, in particular, is subject to the jurisprudence of the Court.[148] Market shares above the thresholds of the Notice will not inevitably mean an appreciable effect is established.[149] The Notice does, however, drive the Commission's thinking and conduct. Thus in cases covered by it, the Commission will not institute proceedings either upon application or upon its own initiative. Where undertakings assume in good faith that an agreement falls within the Notice, the Commission will not impose fines.[150]

(ii) Appreciable Effect on Trade between Member States

The purpose of the condition in Article 101(1) relating to the effect of an agreement on trade between Member States is, in the words of the Court of Justice, 'to define, in the context of the law governing competition, the boundary between the areas respectively covered by Community law and the law of the Member States'.[151] The line of demarcation is the same under both Articles 101 and 102.[152] The test in the case law, first formulated in *Société Technique Minière*, is that

> it must be possible to foresee with a sufficient degree of probability on the basis of a set of objective factors of law or of fact that the agreement in question may have an influence, direct or indirect, actual or potential, on the pattern of trade between Member States.[153]

The crucial element is the diversion of trade flows from the pattern they would naturally follow in a unified market. Where trade has been so diverted, it is immaterial that the agreement may have led to an increase in the volume of goods or services reaching the market in other Member States. Thus in *Consten and Grundig*[154] trade was held to be affected in the necessary sense, regardless of any increase in imports of Grundig products into France, because not only were all such imports to be channelled through Consten but their re-exportation to the Member States was prohibited.

As part of the switch to decentralised enforcement of Article 101, the Commission issued an expansive Notice in 2004 on the meaning of the effect on trade requirement.[155] Building on the case law elaboration of the test, the Notice stresses that the concept of 'trade' is not limited to traditional exchanges of goods and services across borders. Instead, it is a wider concept, covering all cross-border activity including establishment.[156] Trade will also be affected where the competitive structure of the market is put at risk by the

---

[148] Ibid, para 6.

[149] Ibid, para 2. See also Case T-7/93 *Langnese-Iglo v Commission* [1995] ECR II-611; [1995] 5 CMLR 602. In *European Night Services v Commission*, above n 91, the Commission disputed the claims of the parties that their market shares fell below the then threshold figure of 5%. The Court of First Instance ruled that the Commission had failed to provide adequate reasoning, but that in any event a slight excess over the 5% Notice threshold would not in itself indicate an appreciable effect.

[150] *Notice on Agreements of Minor Importance*, above n 145, para 4.

[151] Case 22/78 *Hugin v Commission* [1979] ECR 1869, 1899; [1979] 3 CMLR 345.

[152] [1979] ECR 1869, 1899.

[153] *Société Technique Minière*, above n 73, 249.

[154] *Consten and Grundig*, above n 77.

[155] *Guidelines on the Effect on Trade Concept Contained in Articles 81 and 82 of the Treaty* [2004] OJ C101/7.

[156] Ibid, para 19.

elimination or threatened elimination of a competitor.[157] The impact on trade is to be measured against the *Société Technique Minière*[158] test of 'direct or indirect, actual or potential' effects. However, the Notice makes it clear that this does not mean that the analysis can be based on remote or hypothetical effects.[159]

The Notice focuses on the concept of appreciability, setting out some general principles before providing examples of their application to particular types of agreement.[160] Whilst acknowledging that the assessment of appreciability depends on the circumstances of each individual case, the Notice sets out a negative rebuttable presumption expressed somewhat inelegantly as the Non-Appreciable Affectation of Trade (NAAT) rule.[161] This applies to all agreements within the meaning of Article 101(1) irrespective of the nature of the restrictions contained in the agreement, including hard-core restraints.[162] Thus, an agreement will not be capable of appreciably affecting trade where the following cumulative conditions are met:

(a) the aggregate market share of the parties on any relevant market within the EU affected by the agreement does not exceed 5 per cent, and

(b) in the case of horizontal agreements, the aggregate annual EU turnover of the undertakings concerned in the products covered by the agreement does not exceed €40 million; in the case of vertical agreements the aggregate annual EU turnover of the supplier in the products covered by the agreement does not exceed €40 million.[163]

Where the agreement is one which by its very nature is capable of affecting trade, for example by governing imports and exports or covering several Member States, the Commission will apply a positive presumption that trade is affected once the above thresholds are met.[164]

The Notice assumes particular importance for national courts and competition authorities now charged with the enforcement of Articles 101 and 102. According to Article 3 of Regulation 1/2003, such bodies, when applying national competition rules, must also apply Articles 101 and 102 where the agreement or abuse affects trade between Member States.

V – THE LEGAL EXCEPTION UNDER ARTICLE 101(3)

Agreements that appreciably affect competition may nevertheless bring significant economic advantages. Accordingly, the prohibition of Article 101(1) is tempered by the

---

[157] Ibid, para 20. This is most likely in the context of abuses of dominance, discussed in Chapter 24 below. See Joined Cases 6-7/73 *Commercial Solvents Corporation v Commission* [1974] ECR 223; [1974] 1 CMLR 309.

[158] *Société Technique Minière*, above n 73.

[159] *Notice on Agreements of Minor Importance*, above n 145, para 43.

[160] In particular, distinguishing between agreements and abuses that cover several Member States and those which are confined to a single Member State or part thereof. The detail is omitted here; see paras 58–109 of the Notice.

[161] Ibid, para 50.

[162] Ibid.

[163] Ibid, para 52, with further refinements to the tests in paras 53–57.

[164] Ibid, para 53.

possibility of legal exception under Article 101(3). According to the latter, the provisions of Article 101(1) may be declared inapplicable to 'any agreement or category of agreements'. The power to grant individual exemptions was originally reserved by Regulation 17/62 to the Commission, but this was removed by the reforms implemented in 2004. There is no longer any requirement for exemptions to be obtained in advance, so national courts and competition authorities may now simply apply the legal exception in paragraph (3) where the validity of an agreement is at stake. However, the 2004 changes do not alter the position regarding so-called 'block' exemptions, which are regulations of the Commission adopted under powers delegated by the Council in accordance with Article 103 TFEU and applicable to categories of agreement. Such categories include: vertical agreements,[165] specialisation,[166] research and development,[167] and technology transfer.[168] Revised block exemptions were adopted in 2010 in relation to vertical agreements, specialisation, and research and development. The detailed contents of these block exemptions are not examined in this work, although their principles are discussed further below after consideration of the specific elements of Article 101(3). Together with the revised block exemptions adopted in 2010, the Commission published a revised set of Guidelines for dealing with Horizontal Co-operation Agreements,[169] providing a framework to analyse most types of commercial horizontal co-operation. In particular, they promote standards-setting in relation to the licensing costs for intellectual property rights and they also provide guidance on the compatibility of information exchanges.[170]

In principle, any agreement, no matter how restrictive of competition, is capable of being justified under Article 101(3).[171] From interpretative and policy perspectives, the function of paragraph (3) must be seen against the 'rule of reason' discussed earlier in this chapter in the context of paragraph (1).[172] Accordingly, given that assessment of the anti-competitive nature of arrangements is considered under the two-pronged approach of Article 101, the scope of the legal exception is directly related to the nature of the prohibition and the interpretation of what constitutes a restriction of competition. As seen from cases such as *Wouters*,[173] the Court appears to accept that non-competition, public-interest-based criteria can be deployed as part of the 'overall context' of an agreement when measuring the limits of application of the prohibition in paragraph (1). The question therefore arises whether a similar degree of contextual breadth attaches to consideration of the legal exception criteria set out in paragraph (3). In its guidance Communication,[174] the Commission firmly rejects this by stating that paragraph (3) deals with the assessment

---

[165] Vertical Agreements Regulation 330/2010 on the Application of Article 101(3) of the Treaty on the Functioning of the European Union to Categories of Vertical Agreements and Concerted Practices [2010] OJ L102/1 replacing Regulation 2790/1999 [1999] OJ L336/21, [2000] 4 CMLR 398.

[166] Commission Regulation 2018/2010 of 14 December 2010 on the Application of Article 101(3) of the Treaty on the Functioning of the European Union to Categories of Specialisation Agreements [2010] OJ L335/43 replacing Regulation 2659/2000 [2000] OJ L304/3, [2001] 4 CMLR 800.

[167] Commission Regulation 2017/2010 of 14 December 2010 on the Application of Article 101(3) of the Treaty on the Functioning of the European Union to Categories of Research and Development Agreements, 2010 OJ L335/36 replacing Regulation 2659/2000 [2000] OJ L304/7, [2001] 4 CMLR 808.

[168] Regulation 772/2004 [2004] OJ L123/18.

[169] *Guidelines on the Applicability of Article 101*, above n 85. See Commission Press release IP/10/1702, 14 December 2010.

[170] See further below.

[171] Case T-17/93 *Matra Hachette v Commission* [1994] ECR II-595.

[172] See text accompanying n 105, above.

[173] See *Wouters*, above n 27.

[174] *Guidelines on the Application of Article 81(3)*, above n 79.

of the positive *economic* effects of restrictive agreements.[175] However, in contrast with 'by object' restrictive agreements,[176] the counterfactual approach set out in *O2*,[177] in relation to 'by effect' restrictive agreements, whereby enhanced efficiency is subsumed within the paragraph (1) assessment, suggests that the scope of Article 101(3)[178] may require to be reappraised to extend to wider public policy goals/non-economic objectives which further broader Treaty objectives,[179] such as, for instance environmental policy.[180]

Article 101(3) sets out two positive criteria and two negative ones. To qualify for the legal exception an agreement must satisfy all the criteria, so that if it fails on one there is no need to go on and examine the others.[181] The burden of proof lies on the parties seeking the protection of Article 101(3).[182] The benefits required do not necessarily have to occur within the territory of the Member State or States in which the undertakings party to the agreement are established.[183] The four criteria for exemption under Article 101(3) are discussed in turn below.

A – Efficiency Gains

The first of the positive criteria identifies in broad terms a number of economic benefits that provide the rationale for refraining from applying Article 101(1). The agreement must contribute 'to improving the production or distribution of goods or to promoting technical or economic progress'. Only one from this list of efficiency gains needs to be satisfied. Although the reference is explicitly to goods, the Commission treats the provision as applicable by analogy to services.[184]

It is not sufficient merely that the parties themselves may secure advantages in their production and distribution activities.[185] As set out in the Commission's Guidelines, all efficiency claims must be substantiated so that the following can be verified:[186] (a) the *nature* of the claimed efficiencies; (b) the *link* between the agreement and the efficiencies; (c) the *likelihood* and *magnitude* of each claimed efficiency; and (d) *how* and *when* each claimed efficiency would be achieved. In essence, efficiencies flow from an integration of economic activities whereby undertakings combine their assets to achieve what they could not achieve as efficiently independently or whereby they entrust another undertaking with tasks that can be performed more efficiently by the latter.[187] Benefits from efficiencies may

---

[175] Ibid, para 32. In para 11 the Commission alludes to the balancing of pro-competitive and anti-competitive effects being conducted 'exclusively' within the framework of Art 81(3).

[176] See discussion re *Competition Authority v BIDS*, above n 86, and Andreangeli, above nn 90 and 94.

[177] *O2 v Commission*, above n 111. See also the *Guidelines on the Applicability of Article 101(3)*, above n 85, para 29.

[178] See *Métropole Télévision v Commission*, above n 109, and the Commission's *Guidelines on the Applicability of Article 101(3)*, above n 85.

[179] See Townley, above n 135.

[180] See eg Commission decision 2000/475/EC of 24 January 1999, *CECED*, [2000] OJ C47, especially paras 47–51.

[181] Case C-137/95P *Vereniging van Samenwerkende Prijsregelende Organisaties in de Bouwnijverheid (SPO) v Commission* [1996] ECR I-1611.

[182] Joined Cases 43, 63/82 *VBVB and VBBB v Commission* [1984] ECR 19, [1985] 1 CMLR 27. Now legislatively enshrined in Art 2 of Regulation 1/2003.

[183] Case C-360/92P *Publishers Association v Commission* [1995] ECR I-25; [1995] 5 CMLR 33.

[184] *Guidelines on the Applicability of Article 101*, above n 85, para 48.

[185] *Consten and Grundig*, above n 77.

[186] *Guidelines on the Applicability of Article 101*, above n 85, para 51.

[187] Ibid, para 60.

broadly be divided into cost and qualitative categories, both of which are given extensive elaboration in the Commission's Guidelines.[188]

'Economic progress' seems at first sight to be the widest of the four criteria identified in the first positive condition of Article 101(3). Indeed, there is evidence from early case law that it, rather than Article 101(1), incorporates any 'rule of reason' that might be legitimately invoked. In particular, some older decisions paid particular attention to crisis cartels, formed to enable an industry to adapt in an orderly way to adverse economic conditions such as a decline in the overall market for its products. In *Re Synthetic Fibres*[189] an agreement providing for joint measures to cut capacity, in an industry where the trend in demand had not kept pace with increased output resulting from rapid technical advances, was considered eligible for exemption. The advantages identified by the Commission included the shedding of the financial burden of keeping under-utilised capacity open, the achievement of optimum plant size and specialisation in the development of products adapted to user's requirements. 'The eventual result', the Commission said, ' should be to raise the profitability and restore the competitiveness of each party.'[190]

Social factors, too, have occasionally fallen within the heading of 'economic progress'.[191] Among the elements mentioned in support of the *Synthetic Fibres* exemption was the possibility of cushioning the social effects of restructuring by making suitable arrangements for the retraining and redeployment of redundant workers. Environmental concerns might also seem arguable as economic benefits, but the Commission's older practice appeared to place them within the second positive criterion, benefit to consumers. As it noted in *Philips/Osram*,[192] 'The use of cleaner facilities will result in less air pollution, and consequently in direct and indirect benefits for consumers from reduced negative externalities. This positive effect will be substantially reinforced when R&D in the field produces lead-free materials.'

The key question as yet not fully resolved is whether the Commission's narrow, economic approach in its 2004 Guidelines to the criteria of Article 101(3) will withstand any future judicial scrutiny. The Court's judgment in *Wouters*,[193] using wider public-interest tests to discount the restrictive elements of Article 101(1), gave an implicit green light to the Commission's view of the narrower balancing exercise to be undertaken for the purposes of Article 101(3).[194] Nonetheless, as outlined above, more recent developments in relation to 'by effect' restrictions, notably the *O2* ruling by the Court, suggest that for the bipartite structure of Article 101 to remain and for Article 101(3) to maintain a key role, one may have to interpret its scope as extending to broader non-economic objectives which are in line with EU policy objectives. Until such time as a national court chooses to refer the matter under Article 267 TFEU, it may be safer to assume that any 'rule of reason' is best argued within the parameters of the prohibition of Article 101(1).

---

[188] Ibid, paras 64–68 (cost) and 69–72 (qualitative).

[189] *Re Synthetic Fibres* [1984] OJ L207/17; [1985] 1 CMLR 787.

[190] Ibid, at para 36.

[191] The creation of employment is mentioned by the Court in *Metro*, above n 123, para 43. Also *Remia*, above n 119.

[192] Decision 94/986, para 27. See also Decision 91/38 *KSB/Goulds/Lowara/ITT* [1991] OJ L19/25; Decision 2000/475 *CECED* [2000] OJ L187/47, [2000] 5 CMLR 635.

[193] n 27 above and discussed above.

[194] *cf* AG Léger in *Wouters*, who had noted that 'Professional rules which . . . produce economic effects which are positive, taken as a whole, should therefore be eligible for exemption under [Art 101(1)]'.

B – Benefit to Consumers

The second positive benefit is that consumers must receive a fair share of the benefit resulting from the restriction of competition. At first sight, the use of the term 'consumer' suggests that only the consuming public, or end consumer, is meant. Such a construction, however, would have the effect of severely limiting the scope of the legal exception, because in many cases the parties to the agreement cannot by themselves do anything to ensure that the condition is met. It is not therefore surprising that the Commission has taken the view that consumers are the customers of the parties to the agreement and subsequent purchasers.[195]

According to the Commission's Guidelines[196]:

> The concept of *'fair share'* implies that the pass-on of benefits must at least compensate consumers for any actual or likely negative impact caused to them by the restriction of competition found under Article 81(1). In line with the overall objective of Article [101] to prevent anti-competitive agreements, the net effect of the agreement must at least be neutral from the point of view of those consumers directly or likely affected by the agreement.

Thus, pursuing this idea of compensation, if an agreement is likely to lead to higher prices, then consumers must be compensated through increased quality or other benefits.[197] A benefit now is worth more than one in the future, so that in calculating the compensatory effects a discount will be applied to future benefits.[198] The detailed Guidelines express the commitment of the Commission to economic analysis, fleshing out an analytical framework for the assessment of pass-on gains. Thus, in establishing the extent to which cost efficiencies are likely to be passed on to consumers, all of the following factors must normally be considered: (a) the characteristics and structure of the market; (b) the nature and magnitude of the efficiency gains; (c) the elasticity of demand; and (d) the magnitude of the restriction of competition.[199]

Where the purported benefits of an agreement are qualitative, the application of Article 101(3) is much more of a value judgment since the obtaining of a new or improved product is less susceptible to precise measurement.[200] Careful scrutiny will be required in situations where such qualitative benefits are needed to offset price increases.

C – No Restrictions That Are Not Indispensable

Turning to the negative criteria of Article 101(3), the first is that the legal exception cannot apply to restrictions of competition which are not indispensable to the attainment of the efficiency gains. In other words, the adverse effects on competition must be proportionate to the benefits made out for the agreement.[201] During the days of its exclusive powers

---

[195] *Guidelines on the Applicability of Article 101*, above n 85, para 84. In any event, the term 'consumer' in English may have a narrower connotation than the term used in other language texts: the French text uses the term *utilisateur*.

[196] Ibid, para 85.

[197] Ibid, para 86.

[198] Ibid, para 88.

[199] Ibid, para 96.

[200] Ibid, para 103.

[201] *Matra Hachette*, above n 171, para 135.

in relation to exemption, the Commission adopted a robust approach to this particular requirement in order to extract modifications to agreements before granting authorisation. The new, decentralised, ex post facto system of enforcement gives less opportunity for this particular strategy.

The Commission's 2004 Guidelines indicate that the indispensability condition amounts to a twofold test. First, the restrictive agreement as such must be reasonably necessary in order to achieve the efficiencies.[202] In other words, taking a market assessment and a realistic view of the parties' position, were there no other economically practicable and less restrictive means of achieving the benefits? The second stage is to ask whether individual restrictions within the agreement are reasonably necessary to achieve the efficiencies. The more restrictive the restraint, the more difficult it will be for the parties to establish its indispensability. Hard-core restrictions, such as those prohibited by block exemptions, are unlikely to gain protection.[203] However, for example, where the success of the product is uncertain, a restriction may be more likely to be seen as indispensable in order to secure gains.[204]

D – No Possibility of Eliminating Competition

The final criterion is that the agreement must not afford the parties the possibility of eliminating competition in respect of a substantial part of the products in question. Its presence in the assessment process underlines a key point of competition policy. As the Commission's Guidelines observe:

> Ultimately the protection of rivalry and the competitive process is given priority over potentially pro-competitive efficiency gains which could result from restrictive agreements. . . . When competition is eliminated the competitive process is brought to an end and short-term efficiency gains are outweighed by longer term losses stemming *inter alia* from expenditures incurred by the incumbent to maintain its position (rent seeking), misallocation of resources, reduced innovation and higher prices.[205]

Elimination of competition has its own meaning within Article 101(3),[206] and will depend on the degree of competition existing prior to the agreement and the reduction brought about by the agreement.[207] A 'realistic' market analysis is required, establishing the various sources of competition, the level of competitive constraint that they impose on the parties to the agreement, and the impact of the agreement on this competitive restraint. Both actual and potential competition should be considered.[208]

---

[202] *Guidelines on the Applicability of Article 101*, above n 85, para 73.

[203] Ibid, paras 79–80.

[204] See eg *Publishers Association v Commission*, above n 183. In the Court's view the Commission (and indeed the Court of First Instance) had failed to address properly the parties' claim that a collective system of fixed prices for books was indispensable.

[205] *Guidelines on the Applicability of Article 101*, above n 85, para 105.

[206] See Case T-395/94 *Atlantic Container Line* [2002] ECR II-875, [2002] 4 CMLR 28, para 330: '[T]he prohibition on eliminating competition is a narrower concept than that of the existence or acquisition of a dominant position, so that an agreement could be regarded as not eliminating competition within the meaning of Article [101](3)(b) of the Treaty, and therefore qualify for exemption, even if it established a dominant position for the benefit of its members.'

[207] *Guidelines on the Applicability of Article 101*, above n 85, para 107. Hypothetical examples of the analysis required are given in para 116.

[208] Ibid, para 108.

An agreement which clearly satisfies the other criteria in Article 81(3) is unlikely to fail under this one.

E – Block Exemptions

An agreement that would otherwise be liable to prohibition under Article 101(1) will automatically escape this fate if it fulfils the terms of a block exemption regulation. The use of block exemptions proliferated under the pre-2004 notification regime because parties to qualifying agreements were saved the uncertainty and delay of seeking individual exemption. The price to be paid for those advantages was that the regulations often imposed a degree of *dirigisme*, since the parties to a prospective agreement were inevitably under pressure to conduct their affairs so as to meet the terms and conditions tolerated or outlawed by a block exemption. However, even prior to the 2004 enforcement reforms, the style of block exemptions changed to promote a more flexible and market-based analysis.

The 'new' approach is typified by the Regulation on vertical restraints, first adopted in 1999,[209] and revised in 2010.[210] The treatment of vertical agreements between market participants at different levels of economic activity has always been more lenient in EU law than that of horizontal agreements between competitors. In a typical arrangement between producer and distributor, the producer can concentrate on the efficiencies of production whilst the marketing of the product or service is undertaken by a specialist. The classic economic problems created by such systems (eg exclusive or selective distribution models) reflect their different effects on inter-brand and intra-brand competition. Depending on the amount of territorial protection provided, intra-brand competition can almost be wiped out as the privileged distributor will be the outlet for most customers. On the other hand, inter-brand competition may be stimulated by the efforts made by the distributor to promote the product. Vertical restraints may well encourage non-price competition and improved quality in services. There may, however, be a question as to whether the efficiency savings of distribution agreements are passed on to customers. With these issues in mind, the Commission adopted the Vertical Agreements Regulation in 1999, and both it and the revised Regulation 330/2010[211] declare that Article 101(1) does not apply to any vertical agreement,[212] defined as

> an agreement or concerted practice entered into between two or more undertakings each of which operates, for the purposes of the agreement, at a different level of the production or distribution chain, and relating to the conditions under which the parties may purchase, sell or resell certain goods or services.[213]

---

[209] Regulation 2790/1999 on the application of Art 81(3) to categories of vertical agreements and concerted practices [1999] OJ L336/21. It expired on 31 May 2010.

[210] Vertical Agreements Regulation 330/2010 on the Application of Article 101(3) of the Treaty on the Functioning of the European Union to Categories of Vertical Agreements and Concerted practices [2010] OJ L102/1.

[211] See G De Stefano, 'The New EU Vertical Restraints Regulation: Navigating the Vast seas beyond Safe Harbours and Hardcore Restrictions' [2010] *ECLR* 487; C Hatton and D Cardwell, 'New Rules on Supply and Distribution Agreements: Main Changes of the New System' [2010] *ECLR* 439.

[212] Art 2(1).

[213] Art 1(a).

In essence,[214] Regulation 330 creates a presumption of legality for vertical agreements generally,[215] subject to two fundamental limitations. First, the 'safe harbour' protection is lost if a particular market share is exceeded. This is set at 30 per cent and the main change following the adoption of Regulation 330 is that the safe harbour requires both parties, ie supplier and buyer, to have a market share of less than 30 per cent, as opposed to simply that of the supplier as under Regulation 2790/1999. Secondly, there is no protection for hard-core restraints. According to Article 4, the exemption does not apply to vertical agreements which 'directly or indirectly, in isolation or in combination with other factors under the control of the parties, have as their object' a list of particular restraints. In line with the Commission's policy view of the risks attached to vertical agreements outlined above, the main targets are those restrictions which most significantly affect intra-brand competition. Thus provisions that impose resale price maintenance or seek to restrict the territory into which, or the customers to whom, the buyer may sell will be treated as hard-core restraints.[216] So too will particular restrictions in selective distribution agreements.[217] Regulation 330 continues to provide that resale price maintenance is a hard-core restriction,[218] although it is recognised that in limited circumstances, eg where necessary to promote a new product, this may generate efficiencies.[219]

The nuanced approach taken by the block exemption can be demonstrated by a more detailed examination of the way in which the territorial and customer hard-core restrictions operate. As the Commission's Guidelines[220] explain, the hard-core restraint set out in Article 4(b) seeks to prevent market partitioning by territory or by customer and covers not just direct limitations but also indirect measures aimed at inducing the distributor not to sell to certain customers. However, the Regulation identifies four exceptions, the first of which allows

> the restriction of active sales into the exclusive territory or to an exclusive customer group reserved to the supplier or allocated by the supplier to another buyer, where such a restriction does not limit sales by the customers of the buyer.[221]

In other words, the key idea behind this exception is that some degree of parallel trade in the goods or services in question must be possible. As the Commission makes clear in its Guidelines,[222] the essential distinction is between 'active' and 'passive' sales. Examples of the first, prohibited, group are direct mail shots to individual customers in another exclusive distributor's territory or establishing a warehouse or distribution outlet in such a territory. On the other hand, passive, permitted, sales mean responding to unsolicited requests from individual customers or general advertising which reaches customers in other exclusive territories but which is a reasonable way of reaching customers outside

[214] For a more detailed view of the 1999 Regulation, which is in broad terms identical to regulation 330/2010, see SM Colino, *Vertical Agreements and EC Competition Law* (Oxford, Hart Publishing, 2010) ch 3.

[215] Thus addressing objections to the Commission's previous practice of drawing up Regulations for specific types of agreement. Notably, the umbrella protection of Regulation 330 covers selective distribution, a form of dealing not previously exempted by legislation.

[216] Art 4(a) and (b), although the latter also identifies exceptions.

[217] Art 4(c) and (d).

[218] See Case C-260/07 *Pedro IV Servicios SL v Total Espana SA* [2009] ECR I-2437; [2009] 5 CMLR 1 regarding when a recommended sale price may constitute an imposed fixed or minimum sale price.

[219] *cf* the Supreme Court in *Leegin Creative leather Products Inc v PSKS Inc* 127 S Ct 2705 (2007).

[220] Commission, *Guidelines on Vertical Restraints* [2010] OJ C130/01 revising the earlier published Guidelines in relation to Regulation 2790/1999 [2000] OJ C291/1, See Commission press release IP/10/445, 20 April 2010.

[221] Art 4(b)(i).

[222] *Guidelines on the Applicability of Article 101*, above n 85, para 50.

those territories. Every distributor must be free to use the internet to advertise or to sell products.[223] In the Commission's view, the fact that such advertising will have effects outside the distributor's territory is a result of the technology and should not be classed as 'active'. The 2010 Guidelines deal in particular with online distribution and stress that the use of the internet is a form of passive sales, unless it specifically targets certain groups of customers.[224] However, a hard-core restriction would exist if a distributor is required to prevent customers in another exclusive territory from viewing its website or rerouting them to the manufacturers or another distributors' site; or where there is a limitation on overall internet sales and any requirement placed on a distributor to pay a higher price for goods to be sold online. In the case of exclusive distribution, the supplier may require the distributor not to target actively online customer groups or customers in areas exclusively reserved for another distributor of the supplier, but the distributor is free to sell if customers contact on their own initiative—this would constitute passive sales. In relation to selective distribution, a safe harbour is given to companies requiring resellers to have 'one or more brick and mortar shops or showrooms' to avoid free-riding by pure online companies.

As a final observation on block exemptions more generally, it must be stressed that the validity and enforceability of block exemptions is not called into question by the shift to the new institutional arrangements post-2004. National competition authorities, by virtue of Article 29(2) of Regulation 1/2003 may withdraw the benefit of a block exemption in respect of its territory (or part thereof) if that territory has all the characteristics of a distinct geographic market. National courts have no such power. Nor, obviously, can they modify the scope of a block exemption so as to extend them to agreements not within the exemption.[225]

VI – CONCLUDING REMARKS

Article 101 has developed considerably over the last ten years and there is ongoing debate regarding the future interpretation and application of the provision in a number of respects. The White Paper of 1999 followed by Regulation 1/2003 introduced important reforms to the system, notably in abolishing notification and the exclusive exemption power of the Commission. In relation to cartels, the law has changed little in substance, and the increasing importance of the leniency programme merely reflects the difficulties in proving the existence of a concerted practice in many cases. The major developments have been in the interpretation of Article 101(1) and arguably the rule has undergone substantive modernisation, effectively reducing the hitherto very broad catch of the prohibition. The *Competition Authority v BIDS* preliminary ruling has suggested that a more context-based assessment should be adopted in relation to by object restrictions. Furthermore, the *O2* ruling has arguably widened the scope for consideration of 'by effect' restric-

---

[223] Ibid, para 51.

[224] One may make the comparison with the ECJ's ruling in *Pammer* (Case C-585/08 *Pammer v Reederei Karl Schlüter GmbH & Co KG* ECJ 10 December 2010 [2011] OJ C55/4 (nyr)) albeit in the different context of the interpretation of what constitutes 'directing activities' under the protective consumer jurisdiction rule in Art 15 of the Brussels I Regulation.

[225] See *Guidelines on the Application of Article 81(3)*, above n 79, para 37.

tions by requiring consideration of the counterfactual approach. Both these developments, together with the *Wouters* and *Meca-Medina* line of cases allowing public interest objectives to be considered under Article 101(1), question the traditional bifurcated approach to restrictive agreements under paragraphs (1) and (3) of Article 101, respectively. It will be interesting to see how this case law develops and the extent to which this impacts on the interpretation of the scope of Article 101(3) arguments. The modernisation of Article 101 has also been evidenced by the newer style block exemptions, the revision of the Vertical Agreements Regulation and Guidelines, and the adoption of revised block exemptions in relation to Specialisation and Research and Development agreements together with the more enlightened policy concerning horizontal co-operation agreements generally set out in the 2011 Guidelines. Commission enforcement priorities and public attention will focus on horizontal price-fixing cartels in particular, but the ongoing modernisation of the interpretation of Article 101 will have a considerable impact on the legality of a wide range of horizontal and vertical agreements which proliferate in commercial practice.

Further Reading

A Andreangeli, 'Modernising the Approach to Article 101 TFEU in Respect to Horizontal Agreements: Has the Commission's Interpretation "Come of Age"?' (2011) *Competition and Regulation* 195.

A Andreangeli, 'From Mobile Phones to Cattle: How the Court of Justice is Reframing the Approach to Article 101 (Formerly 81 EC Treaty) of the EU Treaty' (2011) *World Competition*, forthcoming.

A Capobianco, 'Information Exchange under EC Competition Law' (2004) 41 *CMLRev* 1247.

G De Stefano, 'The New EU Vertical Restraints Regulation: Navigating the Vast Seas beyond Safe Harbours and Hardcore Restrictions' (2010) 12 *ECLR* 487.

A Jones, 'Analysis of Agreements under US and EC Antitrust Law—Convergence or Divergence?' (2006) 51 *Antitrust Bulletin* 691.

A Jones, 'Resale Price Maintenance: A Debate About Competition Policy in Europe' (2009) *European Competition Journal* 425

A Jones, 'Left behind by Modernisation? Restrictions by Object under Article 101(1)' (2010) *European Competition Journal* 649.

M Marquis, 'O2 (Germany v Commission) and the Exotic Mysteries of Article 81(1)' (2007) 32 *ELRev* 29.

G Monti, 'Article 81 EC and Public Policy' (2002) 39 *CMLRev* 1057.

R Nazzini, 'Article 81 between Time Present and Time Past: A Normative Critique of "Restriction of Competition" in EU Law' (2006) 43 *CMLRev* 497.

O Odudu, 'Interpreting Article 81(1): Object as Subjective Intention' (2001) 26 *ELRev* 60.

O Odudu, 'Interpreting Article 81(1): Demonstrating Restrictive Effect' (2001) 26 *ELRev* 261.

O Odudu, *The Boundaries of EC Competition Law: The Scope of Article 81* (Oxford, Oxford University Press, 2006).

O Odudu, 'Restriction of Competition by Object – What Is the Beef?' (2008) 8 *Comp LJ* 11.

C Townley, *Article 81 EC and Public Policy* (Oxford, Hart Publishing, 2009).

24

Abuse of Dominance: Article 102

Article 102 TFEU (formerly Article 82 EC, and hereinafter referred to as Article 102) prohibits abuses by dominant firms, individually or collectively. This chapter broadly adopts the three-stage analysis that has tended to prevail in the Commission's decisions and the case law of the European Courts. First, the relevant market is defined, using tests from the case law and the Commission's 1997 Notice. Secondly, dominance is discussed, exploring the range of possible criteria and the particular significance of market shares. Thirdly, the concept of abuse as non-justifiable behaviour prejudicial to competition is examined in the light of a number of commercial practices. These include pricing policies, rebates, tying arrangements and refusals to supply. The Commission's Guidance on Enforcement Priorities, adopted in 2009, following its earlier discussion paper of 2005 and lengthy consultation period, heralding the introduction of a more effects-based approach, will be outlined. Where appropriate, implications of the Commission's 2009 Guidance for the application of the existing body of law under Article 102 are incorporated throughout the chapter, together with brief concluding remarks on some key ongoing themes.

I – INTRODUCTION: THE PURPOSE OF ARTICLE 102

The Court of Justice has said that Articles 101 and 102 'seek to achieve the same aim on different levels, *viz*, the maintenance of effective competition within the common market'.[1] In that context, Article 102 effectively focuses on restraining market power. Explaining the balance between the two leading Treaty competition provisions, the Court has observed:

> [Article 101] of the Treaty applies to agreements, decisions and concerted practices which may appreciably affect trade between Member States, regardless of the position on the market of the undertakings concerned. [Article 102] of the Treaty, on the other hand, deals with the conduct of one or more economic operators consisting in the abuse of a position of economic strength which enables the operator concerned to hinder the maintenance of effective competition on the

---

[1] Case 6/72 *Europemballage and Continental Can v Commission* [1973] ECR 215, 244; [1973] CMLR 199. For an excellent recent treatise on the scope of this provision, see A Ezrachi (ed), *Article 82 EC: Reflections on its Recent Evolution* (Oxford, Hart Publishing, 2009).

relevant market by allowing it to behave to an appreciable extent independently of its competitors, its customers and, ultimately, consumers.[2]

The rationale of Article 102 has been expressed in the following terms by Advocate General Kokott:

> Article [102], like the other competition rules of the Treaty, is not designed only or primarily to protect the immediate interests of individual competitors or consumers, but to protect the *structure of the market* and thus *competition as such (as an institution)*, which has already been weakened by the presence of the dominant undertaking on the market. In this way, consumers are also indirectly protected. Because where competition as such is damaged, disadvantages for consumers are also to be feared.[3]

The Court of First Instance in *Microsoft v Commission*[4] stressed the importance of maintaining competitive market structures as underlying the application of Article 102:

> Lastly, it must be borne in mind that it is settled case law that Art [102] covers not only practices which may prejudice consumers directly but also those which indirectly prejudice them by impairing an effective competitive structure (Hoffmann-La Roche v Commission (85/76) [1979] ECR 461 at [125], and Irish Sugar v Commission, at [229] above, at [232]). In this case, Microsoft impaired the effective competitive structure on the work-group server operating systems market by acquiring a significant market share on that market.[5]

Nonetheless, there has been considerable debate and academic discussion regarding the rationale underlying Article 102 and the extent to which it should be predicated upon demonstrable consumer harm, as opposed to a more ordoliberal-inspired vision of open and competitive markets resulting in a more formalistic and interventionist application of Article 102.[6] Criticism of the European authorities' approach to the application of Article 102 led the Commission to undertake a review of Article 102.[7] The Commission's Guidance on enforcement priorities in applying Article 102 was published in December 2008[8] and adopted in February 2009, advocating an effects-based approach focusing on conduct most harmful to consumers.[9] The extent to which the Guidance is likely to revise existing practice under Article 102 will be examined later in this chapter.

Article 102 provides as follows:

> Any abuse by one or more undertakings of a dominant position within the internal market or in

---

[2] Joined Cases C-395/96P and C-396/96P *Compagnie Maritime Belge Transports, Compagnie Maritime Belge SA and Dafra Lines A/S v Commission* [2000] ECR I-1365, para 34; [2000] CMLR 1076.

[3] Case C-95/04P *British Airways v Commission* [2007] ECR I-2331; [2007] 4 CMLR 22 (Opinion 23 February 2006, para 68) (emphasis original, citations omitted).

[4] Case T-201/04 *Microsoft v Commission* [2007] ECR II-3601; [2007] 5 CMLR 11.

[5] Ibid, para 664.

[6] See, in particular, P Akman 'Searching for the Long-Lost Soul of Art 82 EC' [2009] *Oxford Journal of Legal Studies* 267; T Eilmansberger, 'How to Distinguish Good from Bad Competition Under Article 82 EC: In Search of Clearer and More Coherent Standards for Anti-competitive Abuses' (2005) 42 *CMLRev* 129.

[7] Commissioned by the Chief Economist of DG Competition, the Economic Advisory Group for Competition Policy produced a report ('the EAGCP Report'—'An Economic Approach to Art 82') in July 2005. The thinking therein underpinned a speech by the Competition Commissioner, Neelie Kroes, to the Fordham Corporate Law Institute in New York on 23 September 2005. The Commission published a staffing paper in December 2005, *DG Competition Discussion Paper on the Application of Art 82 of the Treaty to Exclusionary Abuses*, open for public consultation.

[8] See Commission Press release IP/08/1977, 3 December 2008.

[9] Communication from the Commission, *Guidance on the Commission's Enforcement Priorities in Applying Article 82 of the EC Treaty to Abusive Exclusionary Conduct by Dominant Undertakings* [2009] OJ C45/02.

a substantial part of it shall be prohibited as incompatible with the internal market in so far as it may affect trade between Member States. Such abuse may, in particular, consist in:

(a) directly or indirectly imposing unfair purchase or selling prices or other unfair trading conditions;

(b) limiting production, markets or technical development to the prejudice of consumers;

(c) applying dissimilar conditions to equivalent transactions with other trading parties, thereby placing them at a competitive disadvantage;

(d) making the conclusion of contracts subject to acceptance by the other parties of supplementary obligations which, by their nature or according to commercial usage, have no connection with the subject of such contracts.

The provision accordingly only prohibits abuse, not dominance itself. The abuses listed are purely illustrative, and not exhaustive.[10] Article 102 is directly effective and can be applied by national courts and competition authorities.[11]

Dominant undertakings may conduct their business efficiently, keeping down prices and maintaining or improving the quality of their product; indeed, the existence of a dominant position may have positive economic advantages, for example enabling the undertaking in question to pursue an adventurous research and development policy. On the other hand, insulation from competitive pressure is liable to encourage bad habits: for example, an undertaking may choose to limit its output and charge higher prices. The function of Article 102 is to ensure that the market conduct of dominant undertakings remains consistent with the objectives of the European Union. As the Court explained in the original *Michelin* case:

A finding that an undertaking has a dominant position is not in itself a recrimination but simply means that, irrespective of the reasons for which it has such a dominant position, the undertaking concerned has a special responsibility not to allow its conduct to impair genuine undistorted competition on the common market.[12]

Moreover, whilst the fact that an undertaking is in a dominant position cannot deprive it of its entitlement to protect its own commercial interests when they are attacked, and whilst such an undertaking must be allowed the right to take such reasonable steps as it deems appropriate to protect those interests, such behaviour will not be allowed if its purpose is to strengthen that dominant position and thereby abuse it.[13] Dominant undertakings are thus subject to legal obligations which are not incumbent on those with less economic power.

Investigation under Article 102 classically follows three stages: first, defining the relevant market as the precondition[14] for the second stage, establishing dominance, followed by the final (and determinative) issue of whether there has been an abuse. This will also be the pattern followed for analysis in this chapter. Other key elements of Article 102, such as the meaning of 'undertaking' and the notion of affecting inter-state trade, have been dealt with earlier in Chapter 22.

---

[10] *Continental Can*, above n 1, para 26; Joined Cases 6-7/73 *Istituto Chemioterapico Italiano SpA and Commercial Solvents Corpn v Commission* [1974] ECR 223, [1974] 1 CMLR 309.

[11] Regulation 1/2003, Arts 1(3), 5, 6.

[12] Case 322/81 *NV Nederlandsche Banden-Industrie Michelin v Commission* [1983] ECR 3461, 3511; [1985] 1 CMLR 282 (known as *Michelin I*).

[13] Case 27/76 *The United Brands Company v Commission* [1978] ECR 207, para 189; [1978] 1 CMLR 429.

[14] Case T-62/98 *Volkswagen v Commission* [2000] ECR II-2707, para 230; [2000] 5 CMLR 948.

II – ESTABLISHING THE RELEVANT MARKET

Article 102 defines neither markets nor dominance,[15] but the meaning and scope of these concepts have been clarified by the approach of the Commission and the case law of the Court of Justice. The Commission adopted a Market Definition Notice[16] in 1997 which has become an established reference point for day-to-day practice. The point of a market assessment, and dominance within it, is to establish the extent to which a firm is subject to competitive pressure and restraint. The three main questions to be answered are how wide a range of products, and what geographical area and period of reference, should be covered by the evaluation. These three criteria of relevance—product, geographic and temporal—are examined separately below.

A – The Relevant Product or Service Market

The definition of the product market is not always an easy matter because, on the one hand, things which are physically dissimilar may be in competition with regard to a particular application (eg oil and gas domestic heating systems), while, on the other hand, things which are physically similar may not be in competition (eg tyres for heavy vehicles and tyres for vans or motor cars).[17] It will usually be an advantage for the undertaking in question to have the product market defined as widely as possible, since the greater the variety of products involved, the more difficult it will be to make out the existence of a dominant position.

In the case law, the fundamental test for product differentiation is that of the interchangeability of product X and product Y as to their end uses. In the words of the European Court:

> [T]he possibilities of competition must be judged in the context of the market comprising the totality of the products which, with respect to their characteristics, are particularly suitable for satisfying constant needs and are only to a limited extent interchangeable with other products.[18]

The Court has stressed, however, that examination should not be limited to the objective characteristics of the products in question: '[T]he competitive conditions and the structure of supply and demand on the market must also be taken into consideration'.[19] In essence, the test involves 'cross-elasticity of demand'. By this is meant the degree to which sales of X increase in response to an increase in the price of Y; high elasticity, ie a substantial increase in the quantity of X sold when the price of Y rises only slightly, provides a clear indication of competition between the two products. There is also the narrower

---

[15] *cf* Art 66(7) ECSC which spoke of undertakings holding or acquiring 'a dominant position shielding them against effective competition in a substantial part of the common market'.

[16] [1997] OJ C372/5; [1998] 1 CMLR 177.

[17] See *Michelin I*, above n 12, and the discussion, below, of the issue of the relevant product market in that case.

[18] Case 31/80 *L'Oréal v PVBA De Nieuwe AMCK* [1980] ECR 3775, 3793; [1981] 2 CMLR 235.

[19] *Michelin I*, above n 12, 3505.

test in the case law of 'peculiar characteristics and uses', which makes the common-sense point that highly specialised products are likely to be found on a separate market.[20]

The Commission's Market Definition Notice of 1997[21] starts from the premise that there are three main sources of competitive restraints: demand substitution, supply substitutability and potential competition. It adopts the cross-elasticity approach, treating demand substitution as the 'most immediate and effective disciplinary force on the suppliers of a given product, in particular in relation to their pricing decisions'.[22] In an attempt to provide firms with transparency and certainty of guidance, the Commission's test[23] is whether the parties' customers would switch to readily available substitutes or to suppliers located elsewhere in response to a hypothetical small but significant (in the 5–10 per cent range) non-transitory increase in the price of products (the so-called SSNIP test). This test does not as such contradict the Court's case law and should be seen more as a refinement of it to enable a more robust economic measurement. It is not always applied strictly by the Commission.[24]

The SSNIP test to measure substitutability carries its own difficulties. Foremost among these is the so-called 'cellophane fallacy'.[25] This problem arises because the SSNIP approach normally assumes that the benchmark price for the analysis of substitutes comes from prevailing prices. In Article 102 cases, the prevailing price may already be high because the existence of dominance has allowed it to be significantly increased. The danger, therefore, is that the market may be assessed too widely as it might include products or geographic areas which only provide competitive restraints because the prevailing price is already above competitive levels. The Commission has recognised this issue[26] and notes that in most cases a market decision will have to be based on the consideration of a number of criteria and different items of evidence.[27] Paragraphs 38–43 of the Market Definition Notice develop a number of factors which might be relevant to determining whether two products are demand substitutes: evidence of substitution in the recent past; quantitative econometric tests; views of customers and competitors; consumer preferences and marketing studies; barriers and costs associated with switching demand to potential substitutes; and different categories of customers and price discrimination.

The Court's position may be illustrated by its attitude to interchangeability in the *United Brands*[28] case on the supply of bananas to certain of the Member States. The proceedings arose out of the condemnation of the supplier concerned, the United Brands Company (UBC), by the Commission on four counts of abusive conduct. According to the Commission, the product market consisted of 'bananas of all varieties, where branded or unbranded'. On the other hand, UBC argued that bananas formed part of the general mar-

---

[20] eg the different groups of vitamins in Case 85/76 *Hoffmann-La Roche v Commission* [1979] ECR 461; [1979] 3 CMLR 211.

[21] [1997] OJ C372/5; [1998] 1 CMLR 177.

[22] Ibid, para 13.

[23] Ibid, para 17.

[24] It was not used, for example, by the Commission in *Michelin II*, [2002] 5 CMLR 388. Michelin did not challenge the definition of market on appeal: Case T-203/01 *Manufacture française des pneumatiques Michelin v Commission* [2003] ECR II-4071, [2004] 4 CMLR 923.

[25] Taking its name from a US case involving a producer of cellophane: *United States v EI du Pont de Namours & Co* 351 US 377, 76 S Ct 994 (1956).

[26] See Market Definition Notice, above n 21, para 19; also see *DG Competition Discussion Paper*, above n 7, paras 13–17.

[27] Market Definition Notice, above n 21, para 25.

[28] *United Brands*, above n 13.

ket for fresh fruit: in other words, customers make their choice freely between bananas and other varieties of fruit on the basis of availability and relative prices. If this were so, even a very large supplier of bananas like UBC would not be at liberty to set prices within a wide range, since allowance would have to be made for the risk of potential customers altering their preferences (assuming, of course, that the same company did not control the supply of other fruits). The Court said that:

> For the banana to be regarded as forming a market which is sufficiently differentiated from other fruit markets it must be possible for it to be singled out by such special features distinguishing it from other fruits that it is only to a limited extent interchangeable with them and it is only exposed to their competition in a way that is hardly perceptible.[29]

In the Court's view, the test was satisfied. It noted, in particular, the year-round excess of banana supplies over demand, which enabled marketing to be adapted to the seasonal fluctuations of other fruits. There was no evidence of 'significant long term cross-elasticity', or of 'seasonal substitutability in general between the banana and all the seasonal fruits', the latter occurring only in Germany in respect of peaches and table grapes. Bananas also had characteristics enabling them to play an important part in the diet of a large section of the population comprising the very old, the very young and the sick. The constant needs of such consumers, and the limited and sporadic nature of the competition, justified recognition of the separate entity of the banana market.

Interchangeability may also be considered on the supply side of the market. This will certainly be the case where, according to the Market Definition Notice, its effects are equivalent to those of demand substitution in terms of effectiveness and immediacy.[30] It will be relevant, for example,[31] in situations where companies market a wide range of qualities or grades of one product; even if for a given final customer or group of consumers, the different qualities are not substitutable, the different qualities will be grouped into one product market, provided that most of the suppliers are able to offer and sell the various qualities immediately and without incurring significant additional costs or risks. The Commission cites paper[32] as a practical example: standard writing paper and high-quality artwork paper might not be interchangeable in terms of demand yet would still fall within the same product group on the basis that paper plants are prepared to switch swiftly, with negligible costs and no particular difficulties of distribution, between the different qualities.

Supply-side considerations were responsible for the Court's quashing of the Commission's Decision in *Continental Can*.[33] The Commission had found that the acquisition of a Dutch packaging firm, TDV, by the Continental Can subsidiary, Europemballage Corporation, amounted to an abuse of the dominant position which the US firm enjoyed, through its German subsidiary, SLW, on the market in Germany for meat tins, fish tins and metal closures for glass jars. The abuse consisted of an unacceptable strengthening of SLW's position on the markets concerned, since, in the Commission's view, TDV had been a potential competitor of SLW. The main ground for the annulment of the Decision was that the Commission had not shown convincingly why manufacturers of, for example, tins for vegetables, condensed milk, olive oil or fruit juice could not, by making some adap-

---

[29] Ibid, [1978] ECR 207, 272.
[30] Market Definition Notice, above n 21, para 20.
[31] Ibid, para 21.
[32] Ibid, para 22.
[33] *Continental Can*, above n 1.

tation to their product, enter the field as serious competitors to SLW, if the latter raised its prices unduly. The Commission was also criticised for not dealing adequately with the possibility that SLW's major customers might begin to manufacture the relevant types of container themselves. The essence of these objections was that potential competition from new products or new producers ('elasticity of supply') had not been ruled out.

On occasions it may be necessary to combine demand and supply substitution tests in order to define the relevant market. This was the case in *Michelin I*,[34] concerning a Decision of the Commission that NBIM, the Dutch subsidiary of the Michelin tyre group, was guilty of infringing the predecessor of Article 102 because of certain terms included in the contracts under which it supplied dealers. The Court of Justice approved the Commission's definition of the market as that in new 'replacement' tyres for heavy vehicles. This market was distinguishable from: (a) the market in 'original equipment' tyres; (b) the market in tyres for cars and light vans; and (c) the market in retreads. As to (a), it was common ground that the structure of demand for replacements was entirely different from that for original equipment tyres, although they were identical products: while the former were supplied to dealers for retail sale, the latter were supplied to manufacturers to be fitted to new vehicles. As to (b), besides the lack of interchangeability at user level between car and van tyres and heavy vehicle tyres, there was again a difference of demand structures. For car and van drivers the purchase of tyres was an occasional event; whereas buyers of heavy vehicle tyres were normally haulage undertakings for which tyres represented an important business cost and which expected specialised advice and services from dealers. Nor was there elasticity of supply between tyres for light and heavy vehicles: the time and expenditure needed to switch production from one to the other made this impracticable as a way of responding to fluctuations in demand.[35] As to (c), the Court acknowledged that retreads were to some extent interchangeable, and hence in competition, with new tyres, but not sufficiently to undermine a dominant position on the market for the latter. Some consumers had reservations, whether rightly or wrongly, about the safety and reliability of retreads. In addition, a significant proportion of retreads used by transport undertakings were made to order from their own tyre carcasses. These would not compete with new tyres, since their production involved the provision of a service directly by retreading firms to the tyre owners. A further consideration was the dependence of the market for retreads, with respect to price and supply, on the market for new tyres. Every retread must have started life as a new tyre; and there was a limit to the number of times retreading could be done. A dominant supplier of new tyres would therefore have a privileged position vis-à-vis retreading undertakings.

Prior economic choices by a consumer may narrow the range of offers from which future demands have to be met, a phenomenon sometimes referred to as 'lock-in'. It operates where the opportunity cost of reversing a choice is considered to outweigh the advantages in the longer term of doing so. For instance, oil, gas and other domestic fuels may form a single market from the point of view of a person contemplating the installation of a new central heating system, but not after one or other system has been installed.

---

[34] *Michelin I*, above n 12.

[35] The Court noted that in 1977, when there was a shortfall in the supply of heavy-vehicle tyres, Nederlandsche Banden-Industrie Michelin chose to grant an extra bonus rather than use surplus car-tyre capacity to meet demand; [1983] ECR 3461, 3506. *cf Continental Can*, above n 1, where the Decision of the Commission adverted to the barriers to market entry confronting possible competitors, notably the size of the necessary investments, but the Court did not think the burden of proof had been discharged.

Similar reasoning may apply to so-called 'aftermarkets' where a product or service follows on from another. An obvious example is where spare parts for a consumer durable are available only from the manufacturer. In such situations the spare parts from another product may be wholly useless for the durable in question. Moreover, supply-side substitution may be impossible because of the existence of intellectual property rights. In *Hugin*[36] the Court found that most of the spare parts for Hugin cash registers were not interchangeable with parts made to fit any other type of machine, so that the operator of an independent maintenance, repair or reconditioning business was entirely dependent on Hugin for supplies. The relevant market was, accordingly, that for Hugin spare parts required by such businesses. This was a crucial issue in the case, since the share held by Hugin of the market for cash registers as such was very modest.[37] A similarly restricted view of the relevant market was taken in *Hilti*,[38] where nails and cartridges were seen as distinct markets from the nail guns in which they were to be used as fastenings in the construction industry. This finding was based not on classes of user, as in *Hugin*, but primarily on the existence of independent suppliers of nails and cartridges for use in Hilti nail guns, together with the fact that nails and nail guns are not necessarily purchased together.

Market definition may also prove problematic in relation to raw materials which yield derivative or end products competing on wider markets. The Court first had to grapple with this question in *Commercial Solvents*.[39] The case arose from a complaint to the Commission by the Italian pharmaceutical firm, Zoja, that CSC, through its Italian subsidiary, Istituto, had refused to supply it with aminobutanol, the base product for the manufacture of the drug ethambutol, which was used in the treatment of tuberculosis. CSC contended, inter alia, that the relevant market could not be that for aminobutanol, on which its dominance was relatively easy to prove, since the derivative, ethambutol, formed part of a wider market for anti-tubercular drugs. With this the Court disagreed:

> [I]t is in fact possible to distinguish the market in raw material necessary for the manufacture of a product from the market on which the product is sold. An abuse of a dominant position on the market in raw materials may thus have effects restricting competition in the market on which the derivatives of the raw material are sold and these effects must be taken into account when considering the effects of an infringement, even if the market for the derivative does not constitute a self-contained market.[40]

Thus, according to the Court, the raw material may constitute a relevant market in its own right; but it may still be valid, in determining whether a dominant position on that market has been abused, to take into account any anti-competitive effects which may have been felt on the market for the derivative. This problem of the relevance of potentially separate markets is especially acute in the context of vertically integrated organisations, whose behaviour in one market may produce or be directed towards effects in others.[41]

---

[36] Case 22/78 *Hugin Kassaregister AB v Commission* [1979] ECR 1869; [1979] 3 CMLR 345. For criticism, see Baden Fuller, 'Article 86 EEC: Economic Analysis of the Existence of a Dominant Position' (1979) 4 *ELRev* 423, 426–27.

[37] Hugin had a market share of 12% in the common market as a whole and 13% in the UK. Its largest competitor, the US company National Cash Register, had shares of 36% and 40%, respectively.

[38] Case C-53/92P *Hilti A-G v Commission* [1994] ECR I-667; [1994] 4 CMLR 614, upholding the findings of the Court of First Instance in Case T-30/89 [1991] ECR II-1439; [1992] 4 CMLR 16.

[39] *Commercial Solvents*, above n 10.

[40] Ibid, 249–50.

[41] See also Case C-62/86 *AKZO v Commission* [1991] ECR I-3359; [1993] 5 CMLR 215, discussed further, below, in relation to abusive predatory pricing.

Although much of the case law concerns dominance held by producers or suppliers, it should be remembered that *buyer* power may also lead to abuses under Article 102. A leading example is provided by a case involving British Airways (BA). Following a complaint by Virgin Atlantic, the Commission investigated the allegedly abusive terms on which BA bought services from travel agents. The market here was therefore not BA's own services in operating air routes for passengers but, in the Commission's view, the services which airlines purchased from travel agents for the purposes of marketing and distributing their airline tickets. As the Court of First Instance concluded, upholding the Commission's findings:

> That specific nature of the services provided to airlines by travel agents, without any serious possibility of the airlines substituting themselves for the agents in order to carry out the same services themselves, is corroborated by the fact that, at the time of the events of which complaint is made, 85 per cent of air tickets sold in the territory of the United Kingdom were sold through the intermediary of travel agents.
>
> The Court therefore considers that the services of air travel agencies represent an economic activity for which, at the time of the contested decision, airlines could not substitute another form of distribution of their tickets, and that they therefore constitute a market for services distinct from the air transport market.[42]

The emergence of new products, services and forms of competition test the utility and robustness of market definition criteria. As an example, 'new economy' markets based on technological change can be seen as driven by competition over innovation rather than price—in which case the SSNIP test, discussed above, may be less than a precision tool.[43]

Finally, it may be noted that *potential* competition does not usually feature in assessment of the relevant product market. As the Commission observes in its Market Definition Notice, although potential competition is a source of competitive restraint, it will normally only come into consideration 'once the position of the companies involved in the relevant market has already been ascertained, and when such position gives rise to concerns from a competition point of view'.[44]

B – The Geographic Market

It is necessary in defining a relevant market for the purpose of Article 102 to identify the specific territory within which the interplay of supply and demand is to be considered. Once the relevant geographic market has been established, a further question arises as to whether it constitutes a sufficiently 'substantial part of the internal market' as specifically mentioned in Article 102.

The approach to the opening question is well settled. In the *British Airways* case[45] the Court of First Instance stated:

> [C]onsistent case law shows that it may be defined as the territory in which all traders operate in

---

[42] Case T-219/99 *British Airways plc v Commission* [2003] ECR II-5917, paras 99–100; [2004] 4 CMLR 19; BA's further appeal, above n 3, related only to the abuses, not market definition or dominance—see below.

[43] See J. Lücking, 'B2B E-Marketplaces: A New Challenge to Existing Competition Law Rules?' in C Graham and F Smith (eds), *Competition, Regulation and the New Economy* (Oxford, Hart Publishing, 2004) ch 4.

[44] Market Definition Notice, above n 21, para 24.

[45] *British Airways*, above n 42.

the same or sufficiently homogeneous conditions of competition in so far as concerns specifically the relevant products or services, without it being necessary for those conditions to be perfectly homogeneous.[46]

In its Market Definition Notice[47] the Commission lists the type of evidence relevant to determine a geographic market as follows: past evidence of diversion of orders to other areas, basic demand characteristics (such as preferences for national brands, language, culture and lifestyle), views of customers and competitors, current geographic pattern of purchases, trade flows/patterns of shipments (where statistics are sufficiently detailed for the relevant products), and barriers and costs connected with switching orders to companies in other areas. The impact of transportation costs is particularly relevant for the last-mentioned consideration, especially in relation to bulky, low-value products.

It might have been expected that the significance of distinct national geographic markets would diminish as integration continued in the context of an evolving single EU-wide internal market.[48] Nevertheless, numerous examples can still be found of geographic markets which present sufficiently distinctive national conditions. In *Tiercé Ladbroke*[49] the Court of First Instance found that the conditions existing on the market in sound and pictures for horse races taking place in France had to be considered in relation to betting outlets. This was because the latter constituted the demand-side for sound and pictures for retransmission to final consumers (the punters), with the result that the conditions in which the downstream market in sound and pictures operated were determined by the conditions under which the main betting market was conducted.[50] The conditions in which the main betting market operated were characterised by close geographical links between punters and betting outlets, in so far as the mobility of punters is necessarily limited and marginal. The effect of that proximity was that competition between betting outlets developed within geographical areas which, considered as a whole, could not in any event extend beyond national boundaries, even though pictures of the races were available in France, Germany and Belgium. Since the geographic betting market was national, ie Belgium in this case, this also had to be the case for the ancillary market in sound and pictures.[51]

Having identified the appropriate geographic area, it must then be considered whether it amounts to a 'substantial part' of the internal market. The test to be applied is not the geographic extent of the territory in question but the economic importance of the market situated there. This was made clear in the *Sugar* judgment, where the Court said:

> For the purpose of determining whether a specific territory is large enough to amount to 'a substantial part of the common market' . . . the pattern and volume of the production and consumption of the said product as well as the habits and economic opportunities of vendors and purchasers must be considered.[52]

---

[46] Ibid, para 108, citing Case T-83/91 *Tetra Pak v Commission (Tetra Pak I)* [1994] ECR II-755, [1997] 4 CMLR 726, confirmed on appeal in Case C-333/94P *Tetra Pak v Commission (Tetra Pak II)* [1996] ECR I-5951, [1997] 4 CMLR 662.
[47] Market Definition Notice, above n 21, paras 44–52.
[48] Indeed, the whole of the EC was taken to be the geographical market in *Tetra Pak I*, above n 46.
[49] Case T-504/93 *Tiercé Ladbroke v Commission* [1997] ECR II-923, [1997] 5 CMLR 309.
[50] Ibid, para 103.
[51] Ibid, paras 106–07.
[52] Joined Cases 40-48, 50, 54-56, 11, 113 and 114/73 *Suiker Unie v Commission* [1975] ECR 1663, 1977; [1976] 1 CMLR 295.

On this basis the Belgo-Luxembourg market and the southern part of Germany were considered a substantial part of the internal market.

A market amounting to a substantial part of the internal market may cover a number of Member States or a single Member State[53] or parts of one or more Member States. In a number of cases single ports or other economic hubs have been held to satisfy the 'substantial' criterion. Thus, in *Merci Convenzionali Porto di Genova*[54] the Court held that regard must be had to the volume of traffic in the port in question and its importance in relation to maritime import and export operations as a whole in the Member State concerned.

C – The Temporal Market

Market power will only give a dominant position if it is capable of enduring for a considerable time. The prospect of substitutes becoming available in the short run limits freedom of action because of the risk of future defections by customers.[55] The market on which an undertaking operates may fluctuate from time to time with respect both to the range of products and the geographical area covered. For example, if the view had been taken in *United Brands* that the demand for bananas was seriously affected by the availability of various seasonal fruits, it might have been concluded that bananas formed part of a series of different markets at different times of the year; and it would have followed that the position of UBC must be examined in relation to each of these markets. Another example is provided by *Commercial Solvents*, where it had been argued by CSC that the manufacture of ethambutol was possible by processes other than that involving aminobutanol. However, the Court held that the processes in questions were still of an experimental nature and incapable at the material time of being used for production on an industrial scale. They, therefore, did not constitute a realistic alternative for the customer, Zoja.[56]

III – DOMINANCE

This central element of Article 102 refers to the economic power of the undertaking concerned, which frees it from the constraints normally imposed by competing on the merits. This liberation is qualified, since the Court speaks of the 'power to behave *to an appreciable extent* independently'.[57] So understood, a dominant position is compatible with the

---

[53] *Michelin I*, above n 12; Case C-323/93 *Centre d'Insémination de la Crespelle* [1994] ECR I-5077; Case C-7/97 *Bronner* [1998] ECR I-7791, [1999] 4 CMLR 112.

[54] Case C-179/90 *Merci Convenzionali Porto di Genova* [1991] ECR I-5889, para 15; [1994] 4 CMLR 422. See also Case C-163/96 *Raso* [1998] ECR I-533; [1998] 4 CMLR 737, where the port of La Spezia was also held to be a substantial part of the common market, being the leading Mediterranean port for container traffic. In Case C-163/99 *Commission v Portugal* [2001] ECR I-2613 the three mainland airports of Portugal (Lisbon, Oporto and Faro) were taken together as a substantial part of the common market as regards the provision of intra-Community services.

[55] Gyeselen and Kyriazis, 'Art 86: Monopoly Power Measurement Issue Revisited' [1986] *ELRev* 134, stress that market power only gives cause for concern if it is a long-term phenomenon.

[56] *Commercial Solvents*, above n 10, 248.

[57] Used by the Court of Justice in *Michelin I*, above n 12, and reiterated routinely since.

survival of some competition.[58] It will be sufficient if the undertaking in question is able 'at least to have an appreciable influence on the conditions under which that competition will develop, and in any case to act largely in disregard of it so long as such conduct does not operate to its detriment'.[59] In its 2009 Guidance, the Commission explained dominance as follows:

> Dominance entails that these competitive constraints are not sufficiently effective and hence that the undertaking in question enjoys substantial market power over a period of time. This means that the undertaking's decisions are largely insentive to the actions and reactions of competitors, customers and, ultimately, consumers.[60]

Dominant positions often relate to the supply of goods or services, but they may also exist on the demand side.[61] Dominance may arise in relation to one undertaking or collectively[62] in relation to two or more undertakings.

The existence of dominance may derive from several factors which, taken separately, are not necessarily decisive. The most frequently used indicators are discussed below.

A – Market Shares

The most important factor is the size of the undertaking's share of the relevant market. According to the Court, extremely large market shares are in themselves, save in exceptional circumstances, evidence of the existence of a dominant position.[63] Not surprisingly, monopolies will be in a dominant position even where that position is the result of statute or other legal means.[64] A market share of over 50 per cent has been held in itself to give rise to dominance.[65] Where the share of the market held by the undertaking is smaller, other factors take on increased significance. Thus, in *United Brands*, the European Court cited as a consideration affording evidence of 'preponderant strength' the fact that UBC's percentage of the market was several times greater than that of its nearest competitor (16 per cent), with the remaining market participants well behind.[66] Similarly, market shares below 40 per cent may be considered dominant, depending on the strength and numbers of competitors.[67]

---

[58] *Hoffman-La Roche*, above n 20. Also, Case T-395/94 *Atlantic Container Line AB v Commission* [2002] ECR II-875.

[59] *Hoffman-La Roche*, above n 20, 520.

[60] *Guidance on the Commission's Enforcement Priorities in Applying Article 82*, above n 9, para 10.

[61] See Case 298/83 *CICCE v Commission* [1985] ECR 1105, [1986] 1 CMLR 486; also *British Airways*, above n 42.

[62] Collective dominance is discussed further below. See *Compagnie Maritime Belge*, above n2.

[63] *Hoffmann-La Roche*, above n 20; *AKZO*, above n 41.

[64] Case 26/75 *General Motors Continental v Commission* [1975] ECR 1367; [1976] 1 CMLR 95; Case 13/77 *INNO v ATAB* [1977] ECR 2115; [1978] 1 CMLR 283; Case 41/83 *Italy v Commission (British Telecom)* [1985] ECR 873; [1985] 2 CMLR 368; *Raso*, above n 54.

[65] *AKZO*, above n 41, para 60.

[66] *United Brands*, above n 13, [1978] ECR 207, 282–83. See also *Hoffmann-La Roche*, above n 20, where the smallness of its competitors' market shares helped to establish the dominance of Roche on the markets for vitamins A, C and E.

[67] The relevant market share in *British Airways*, above n 42, was 39.7% with BA having more than seven times the share of Virgin, its nearest competitor. In Case C-250/92 *Gottrup-Klim v Dansk Landbrugs* [1994] ECR I-5641 the Court treated shares of 36% and 32% as insufficient on their own to constitute conclusive evidence of dominance. Nonetheless in its 2009 *Guidance on the Commission's Enforcement Priorities in Applying Article 82*, above n 9, para 14, the Commission indicated that dominance is unlikely if an undertaking's market share is less than 40%.

In its 2009 Guidance on Enforcement Priorities, the Commission stressed the importance, in assessing dominance and the significance of market shares, of the relevant market conditions 'and, in particular, the dynamics of the market and the extent to which the products are differentiated'.[68] The longer the period over which a high market share is held, the stronger is the indication of market dominance.[69]

A tendency has also emerged towards the use of 'super-dominance'[70] to describe market shares in some cases. The significance of this development seems to be that there may be either more types of conduct that become abusive at that threshold or that an abuse is more easily inferred.[71] Nonetheless, the Commission's Guidance on Enforcement Priorities makes no explicit reference to the concept of 'super-dominance'.

B – Barriers to Market Entry or Expansion by Rivals

Even a very large market share can be rapidly eroded when the market is penetrated by lively new competitors. A careful analysis of a dominant position should, therefore, refer to any advantages enjoyed by the undertaking in question, or to any difficulties in the way of potential market entrants, making it unlikely that the structure of the market will change radically in the shorter run. Barriers should also be considered in relation to the scope for expansion by existing rivals. In its 2009 Guidance on Enforcement Priorities, the Commission observed that:

> Competition is a dynamic process and an assessment of the competitive constraints on an undertaking cannot be based solely on the existing market situation. The potential impact of expansion by actual competitors or entry by potential competitors, including the threat of such expansion or entry, is also relevant. An undertaking can be deterred from increasing prices if expansion or entry is likely, timely and sufficient. For the Commission to consider expansion or entry likely it must be sufficiently profitable for the competitor or entrant, taking into account factors such as the barriers to expansion or entry, the likely reactions of the allegedly dominant undertaking and other competitors, and the risks and costs of failure. For expansion or entry to be considered timely, it must be sufficiently swift to deter or defeat the exercise of substantial market power. For expansion or entry to be considered sufficient, it cannot be simply small-scale entry, for example into some market niche, but must be of such a magnitude as to be able to deter any attempt to increase prices by the putatively dominant undertaking in the relevant market.[72]

Barriers to entry and expansion may accordingly require examination of the history of the industry in question, and consideration of such issues as legal barriers, economies of scale, technological, distribution or other advantages, costs and network effect impediments.[73]

The presence of barriers can be found across a wide spectrum of situations. Thus, it may be that an undertaking controls essential patents or know-how; or because, like United

---

[68] Guidance on the Commission's Enforcement Priorities in Applying Article 82, above n 9, para 13.

[69] Ibid, para. 15. Maintaining prices above the competitive level for a significant period of time would indicate dominance, and a two-year period would suffice for these purposes (para 11).

[70] See Compagnie Maritime Belge, above n 2, where AG Fennelly expressly uses this term at para 137 of his Opinion. The Court's Judgment, para 119, pointedly refers to the fact that there was dominance amounting to 90% with only one competitor. See also Case C-497/99P Irish Sugar v Commission [2001] ECR I-5333 and Microsoft, above n 4.

[71] Discussed further, below, in relation to the concept of abuse and its application.

[72] Guidance on the Commission's Enforcement Priorities in Applying Article 82, above n 9, para 16.

[73] Ibid, para 17. In relation to network effects, see eg Microsoft, above n 4.

Brands, it is vertically integrated, with privileged access to supplies, means of transport and distribution outlets;[74] or because, like Michelin, it has a well-developed network of commercial representatives providing continuous contact with customers;[75] or because of its technical superiority,[76] its range of products[77] or a strong brand image resulting from advertising.[78] Established consumer preferences may also act as barriers, as in *British Midland/Aer Lingus*[79] where the Commission noted that Irish nationals preferred to use the national flagship airline.

From the point of view of a potential competitor the chief difficulty in overcoming such advantages would be that of cost. Very large resources may be needed, for example, to finance independent research or countervailing advertising. These are often sunk costs that cannot be recovered in the case of exit and therefore may make entry more risky. The crucial consideration will be the range within which the undertaking is free to fix its prices without making it commercially attractive for others to risk the investment required in order to mount a challenge. It is also important in the present context to bear in mind the time factor. The possibility that, at the end of a very long period of development, another undertaking may succeed in establishing itself as a serious competitor would not normally be sufficient to impair an existing dominant position.[80]

C – Conduct and Performance of the Undertaking

Market shares and barriers to entry and expansion are indicative of the structure of the market and the state of competition in it. A rather less clear issue in relation to the criteria for measuring dominance concerns the relevance of an undertaking's conduct or performance. Certainly, there is a real risk of circularity if the fact that particular behaviour, alleged to be abusive, could occur at all becomes the rationalisation for the existence of dominance.

Nevertheless, there is evidence that conduct or performance can affect decisions in relation to market power under Article 102. For example, the Court of First Instance in *Hilti*[81] endorsed the Commission's view that it was highly improbable that a non-dominant undertaking would have acted in the way that Hilti did in terms of its intellectual property rights. The Commission also claimed in *Michelin II*[82] that the firm's behaviour was strong evidence of dominance. The Court has also rejected arguments that tried to plead the absence of dominance on the basis of poor profitability.[83] Indeed, in its view, the ability to weather losses, at least temporarily, might suggest the exact opposite, ie that the undertaking has the economic strength to absorb them.

[74] *United Brands*, above n 13, 278–80.
[75] *Michelin I*, above n 12, 3511. See also the reference to 'a highly developed sales network' in *Hoffmann-La Roche*, above n 20, 524.
[76] *Hilti*, above n 38.
[77] *Michelin I*, above n 12.
[78] *United Brands*, above n 13.
[79] Decision 92/213 [1992] OJ L96/34; [1993] 4 CMLR 596. Aer Lingus's market share was also high, being 75% of the London Heathrow–Dublin route.
[80] See the very full analysis of those features of UBC's banana operation which the European Court regarded as contributing to its retention of a large market share: [1978] ECR 207, 278–81.
[81] *Hilti*, above n 38.
[82] *Michelin II*, above n 24.
[83] eg both *Michelin I*, above n 12, and *United Brands*, above n 13; also *Irish Sugar*, above n 70.

IV – THE CONCEPT OF JOINT OR COLLECTIVE DOMINANCE

The concept of an undertaking was examined in Chapter 22. It will be remembered that legally distinct companies may be regarded as forming a single undertaking, if in practice they are subject to common control. The importance of this principle in the context of Article 102 is that, in determining whether the conduct of one member of a group constitutes an abuse of a dominant position on a relevant market within the common market, it may be possible to take into account the economic strength of other members of the group, some or all of them established in third countries. For example, in *Commercial Solvents*[84] it was CSC's control over world supplies of aminobutanol that gave Istituto a dominant position on the common market; CSC was legally answerable for Istituto's refusal to supply Zoja.

The more controversial use of the phrase 'one or more undertakings' in Article 102 involves its attachment to so-called joint or collective dominance by non-connected firms. After early resistance by the European Court to the idea,[85] it is now clear that collective dominance may fall within Article 102. The first real judicial endorsement came from the Court of First Instance in *Italian Flat Glass*,[86] where it stated:

> There is nothing, in principle, to prevent two or more independent economic entities from being, on a specific market, united by such economic links that, by virtue of that fact, together they hold a dominant position *vis-à-vis* the other operators on the same market. This could be the case, for example, where two or more independent undertakings jointly have, through agreements or licences, a technological lead affording them the power to behave to an appreciable extent independently of their competitors, their customers and ultimately of their consumers.[87]

On the facts, the Commission had failed to adduce sufficient evidence to make out its claim. Nevertheless, the principle of collective dominance was subsequently developed by the Court of Justice in the context both of Article 102 and the Merger Regulation.[88]

The leading statement by the Court is found in the *Compagnie Maritime Belge* cases:[89]

> [T]he expression 'one or more undertakings' in Article [102] of the Treaty implies that a dominant position may be held by two or more economic entities legally independent of each other, provided that from an economic point of view they present themselves or act together on a particular market as a collective entity.[90]

To establish such a collective entity it is necessary to examine the economic links or factors which give rise to a connection between the undertakings concerned. The existence

---

[84] *Commercial Solvents*, above n 10.

[85] See *Hoffmann-La Roche*, above n 20; also Case 247/86 *Alsatel* [1988] ECR 5987; [1990] 4 CMLR 434, where the Court did not take up the Commission's arguments.

[86] Joined Cases T-68, 77 and 78/89 *SIV v Commission* [1992] ECR II-1403; [1992] 5 CMLR 302.

[87] Ibid, para 358.

[88] Regulation 139/2004 on the control of concentrations between undertakings [2004] OJ L24/1; supplemented by implementing Regulation 802/2004 [2004] OJ C77/1 together with Notices on the interpretation of provisions.

[89] *Compagnie Maritime Belge*, above n 2.

[90] Ibid, para 36.

of an agreement or concerted practice within Article 101 is not of itself sufficient to establish such a link. However:

> The existence of a collective dominant position may . . . flow from the nature and terms of an agreement, from the way in which it is implemented and, consequently, from the links or factors which give rise to a connection between undertakings which result from it. Nevertheless, the existence of an agreement or of other links in law is not indispensable to a finding of a collective dominant position; such a finding may be based on other connecting factors and would depend on an economic assessment and, in particular, on an assessment of the structure of the market in question.[91]

These cases confirm that a joint dominant position consists in a number of undertakings being able together, in particular because of factors giving rise to a connection between them, to adopt a common policy on the market.[92] In *Almelo*, for example, the issue left to be determined by the national court was whether the requisite links between the regional electricity suppliers in question were 'sufficiently strong'. One such factor was that the contracts between the regional distributors and local purchasers had common exclusive purchasing conditions. The links allegedly present in the *Flat Glass* case included structural ties relating to production in the form of systematic exchange of products between the three producers. In *Irish Sugar*[93] the Court of First Instance did not disturb the Commission's findings that Irish Sugar occupied a joint dominant position on the Irish granulated sugar market with Sugar Distribution Holdings (SDH), the latter being the parent company of the principal distributor (SDL) in that market. The factors relied upon by the Commission were Irish Sugar's 51 per cent shareholding in SDH, its representation on the boards of SDH and SDL, the policy-making structure of the companies and the communication process established to facilitate it, and the direct economic ties constituted by SDL's commitment to obtain its supplies exclusively from Irish Sugar and the latter's financing of all consumer promotions and rebates offered by SDL to its customers.

The precise application of collective dominance for the purposes of Article 102 is complicated by the fact that the case law, at least prior to the revised Merger Regulation of 2004, was intertwined with that developed in relation to concentrations. The essential difference between the provisions in this context is that whereas Article 102 is concerned only with abuses of market power, the rationale of the Regulation is based on the curbing of prospective concentrations which would undermine an effective market structure. This might explain any apparent divergence in the language used in the case law from the two areas. In *France and others v Commission*,[94] the first case to uphold the application of joint dominance under the Merger Regulation,[95] the Court of Justice referred to the need to establish an impediment to effective competition arising in particular from 'correlative factors' existing between the undertakings involved in the concentration.

---

[91]   Ibid, para 46.

[92]   Case C-393/92 *Almelo* [1994] ECR I-1477, para 42; Case C-96/94 *Centro Servizi Spediporto v Spedizioni Marittima del Golfo* [1995] ECR I-2883, paras 32–33; [1996] 4 CMLR 613; Joined Cases C-140-142/94 *DIP* [1995] ECR I-3257, para 26; [1996] 4 CMLR 157; Case C-70/95 *Sodemare v Regione Lombardia* [1997] ECR I-3395, paras 45–46; [1998] 4 CMLR 667.

[93]   Case T-228/97 *Irish Sugar plc v Commission* [1999] ECR II-2969; upheld by the ECJ in *Irish Sugar*, above n 70.

[94]   Joined Cases C-68/94 and C-30/95 *France and others v Commission* [1998] ECR I-1375, para 221; [1998] 4 CMLR 829.

[95]   Regulation 4064/89 [1989] OJ L395/1, prior to being revised in 2004.

In the *Airtours*[96] case, also brought in relation to the Merger Regulation prior to its 2004 amendment, the Court of First Instance fleshed out the conditions for collective dominance as follows:

> As the applicant has argued and as the Commission has accepted in its pleadings, three conditions are necessary for a finding of collective dominance as defined:
>
> — first, each member of the dominant oligopoly must have the ability to know how the other members are behaving in order to monitor whether or not they are adopting the common policy. As the Commission specifically acknowledges, it is not enough for each member of the dominant oligopoly to be aware that interdependent market conduct is profitable for all of them but each member must also have a means of knowing whether the other operators are adopting the same strategy and whether they are maintaining it. There must, therefore, be sufficient market transparency for all members of the dominant oligopoly to be aware, sufficiently precisely and quickly, of the way in which the other members' market conduct is evolving;
>
> — second, the situation of tacit coordination must be sustainable over time, that is to say, there must be an incentive not to depart from the common policy on the market. As the Commission observes, it is only if all the members of the dominant oligopoly maintain the parallel conduct that all can benefit. The notion of retaliation in respect of conduct deviating from the common policy is thus inherent in this condition. In this instance, the parties concur that, for a situation of collective dominance to be viable, there must be adequate deterrents to ensure that there is a long-term incentive in not departing from the common policy, which means that each member of the dominant oligopoly must be aware that highly competitive action on its part designed to increase its market share would provoke identical action by the others, so that it would derive no benefit from its initiative . . .
>
> — third, to prove the existence of a collective dominant position to the requisite legal standard, the Commission must also establish that the foreseeable reaction of current and future competitors, as well as of consumers, would not jeopardise the results expected from the common policy.[97]

Although the Merger Regulation appraisal criteria were revised in 2004,[98] these conditions continue to be applied in the determination of the existence of a collective dominant position under Article 102, as evidenced in *Laurent Piau v Commission*.[99]

V – THE CONCEPT OF AN ABUSE

The wording of Article 102 makes clear that the existence of a dominant position is not in itself prohibited.[100] Whilst not unlawful, however, it is clear that dominance creates special obligations for the undertakings concerned,[101] so that they must not abuse their power.

---

[96] Case T-342/99 *Airtours plc v Commission* [2002] ECR II-2585.

[97] Ibid, para 62.

[98] See M Rosenthal and S Thomas, *European Merger Control* (Oxford, Hart Publishing, 2010).

[99] Case T-193/02 *Laurent Piau v Commission* [2005] ECR II-209; [2005] 5 CMLR 42.

[100] *cf* Art 106 TFEU (Chapter 26 below), where the Court at one point developed an 'inevitable abuse' doctrine in relation to certain situations involving the creation and exercise of exclusive rights; see principally Case C-41/90 *Höfner v Macrotron* [1991] ECR I-1979; [1993] 4 CMLR 306; also Case C-55/96 *Job Centre Coop* [1997] ECR I-7119, paras 34–35; [1998] 4 CMLR 708.

[101] See *Michelin I*, above n 12.

There is no definition of abuse in the Art 102, and the instances listed in Article 102 (such as unfair pricing or limiting production) are only non-exhaustive examples. However, the Court of Justice gave what has become a benchmark test of abuse in *Hoffmann-La Roche*:

> The concept of abuse is an objective concept relating to the behaviour of an undertaking in a dominant position which is such as to influence the structure of a market where, as a result of the very presence of the undertaking in question, the degree of competition is weakened and which, through recourse to methods different from those which condition normal competition in products or services on the basis of the transactions of commercial operators, has the effect of hindering the maintenance of the degree of competition still existing in the market or the growth of that competition.[102]

A – Recurring Conceptual Issues

A number of general observations may be made from this starting point and its later applications.

First, there is a potential tension in the notion of abuse in so far as it is not expressly directed at the protection of one particular set of interests.[103] So-called exploitative abuses, such as excessive pricing, tend to harm consumers. On the other hand, anti-competitive conduct, such as predatory pricing, tying contracts or refusals to supply,[104] may more directly affect other actual or potential firms in the market (whilst having repercussions for consumers). Both types of abuse are caught by Article 102. In addition, it was made clear at an early stage in the case law that the provision was not confined to behavioural abuses but could also cover the strengthening of dominance by structural means such as the acquisition of competitors.[105] Indeed, this dichotomy reflects the core debate underlying the critique and review process relating to Article 102.[106] Exploitative abuses, notably excessive pricing, have featured to a minor extent in the enforcement activity of the Commission, and the case law of the Court of Justice, which has predominantly focused on anti-competitive or exclusionary abuses, such as predatory pricing and refusals to supply, where such abuses directly harm the competitive process and competitors, and may harm the consumer indirectly or in the long run. Criticism has been directed at the formalistic treatment of certain abuses, and more particularly that the EU authorities have been more concerned with the protection of competitors rather than with the interests of consumers and whether they have been harmed. The Commission's Guidance on Enforcement Priorities seeks, partially, to redress this perceived imbalance in the focus of Article 102, though, perhaps ironically, it does not address its enforcement priorities in relation to exploitative abuses.

---

[102] *Hoffmann-La Roche*, above n 20, 541.

[103] Although in *Bronner*, above n 53, AG Jacobs observed that the 'primary' purpose of Art 82 was to protect consumers, rather than safeguarding the position of particular competitors. See also AG Kokott's observations in *British Airways*, quoted at text accompanying n 3 above.

[104] These examples are also often referred to as 'exclusionary' abuses; this group exclusively forms the target of the Commission's 2005 *Discussion Paper* for reform, above n 7.

[105] *Continental Can*, above n 1. However, this application of Art 102 has been effectively superseded by the creation of merger control at EU level, at least where concentrations having a community dimension within the meaning of Regulation 139/2004 are concerned; see n 98 above.

[106] See, in particular, Akman, above n 6; P Akman, 'The European Commission's Guidance on Article 102 TFEU: From Inferno to Paradise?' (2010) 73 *MLR* 605.

Secondly, abuse is an objective concept, generally requiring neither an intention to harm nor any morally reprehensible dimension. However, intent may be of real significance in relation to specific abuses, such as predatory pricing.[107] Nonetheless, conduct may escape condemnation as abuse if it can be objectively justified. For example, there is considerable room for debate whether particular conduct is a firm's rational response to meet the challenge of competition or if it is abusive. This problem is particularly highlighted in developments concerning discriminatory pricing,[108] discussed below. Other potential justifications may arguably stem from efficiencies, at least for some types of abuse that are non-exploitative. There is no formal exception incorporated in to the text of Article 102 that corresponds to Article 101(3). However, the Commission's Guidance on Enforcement Priorities, may justify conduct which may foreclose competitors on the ground of efficiencies such that no net harm to consumers is likely.[109]

A third thread of difficulty relates to the question of causation. Must the undertaking have used its power as the means of achieving the result which is regarded as abusive? Ever since *Continental Can* it has been clear that the Court does not require a strict causal relationship of this type. As a result, an allegation of abuse cannot be negated by evidence that the same conduct is pursued by non-dominant firms or is a normal practice in the market concerned. Moreover, the abuse does not necessarily have to be committed in the same market as the one in which the firm is dominant. It may affect downstream or neighbouring markets, as in the *CBEM* case,[110] where action by an undertaking dominant on the television broadcasting market had abusive effects in the telemarketing services market. Conversely, conduct on a different market which strengthens the undertaking's position in the dominated market will also be caught.[111] In some situations the reach of Article 102 may go even further, so long as there are some 'associative' links between the markets in which the dominance and abuse are found.

The extent of this more controversial notion was tested in the *Tetra Pak* litigation. The Court of First Instance[112] had upheld a Commission decision fining Tetra Pak for abusing its dominant position in the markets for aseptic liquid repackaging machinery and aseptic cartons. The abusive conduct included predatory pricing and tying contracts undertaken on the non-aseptic machinery and carton markets in which Tetra Pak had not been established as dominant. According to the Court of First Instance, application of Article 102 was justified by the situation on the different markets and the close associative links between them, noting that Tetra Pak occupied a 'leading position' in the non-aseptic market whilst holding a quasi-monopolistic 90 per cent share of the aseptic sector, and that its customers in one sector were also potential customers in the other. On appeal, the Court of Justice observed:

It is true that application of Article [102] presupposes a link between the dominant position and the alleged abusive conduct, which is not normally present where conduct on a market distinct

---

[107] Discussed further below.

[108] eg Case T-228/97 *Irish Sugar*, [1999] ECR II-2969.

[109] Four cumulative criteria, similar to Art 101(3), require to be satisfied according to *Guidance on the Commission's Enforcement Priorities in Applying Article 82*, above n 9, para 30.

[110] Case 311/84 *Centre Belge d'Etudes de Marché Télémarketing v CLT* [1985] ECR 3261; [1986] 2 CMLR 558.

[111] Case C-310/93P *BPB Industries and British Gypsum v Commission* [1995] ECR I-865; [1997] 4 CMLR 238. See also *British Airways*, above n 43; although the case was brought in relation to a loyalty reward system operated in the market of airline travel agency services, the 'real' fruits of that conduct would be for the benefit of BA (especially vis-à-vis Virgin) in the different market of passenger air travel.

[112] Above n 46.

from the dominated market produces effects on that distinct market. In the case of distinct, but associated, markets, as in the present case, application of Article [102] to conduct found on the associated, non-dominated, market and having effects on that associated market can only be justified by special circumstances.[113]

However, it then adopted the 'associative' approach of the Court of First Instance to find that such special circumstances existed, concluding that Tetra Pak was placed in a situation 'comparable to that of holding a dominant position on the markets in question as a whole'.[114] It is indeed arguable that a significant proportion of the Commission practice and Court case-law in relation to abuse concerns leveraging of a dominant position from one market to another related, eg downstream, market.[115]

Fourthly, the notion of abuse has come under increasing scrutiny in the context of the economics and effects-led arguments which have dominated reforms elsewhere in EU competition law. In the extract from *Hoffman-La Roche* quoted at the start of this section, the Court of Justice referred to abuses being judged against 'normal' competition, an arguably question-begging view that perhaps chimes with rather loose notions of 'workable' or 'unfair' competition that might emanate from lawyers rather than economists. One of the key areas of economic debate has concerned the extent to which there must be a real anti-competitive effect on the market before an abuse should be considered established. The case law at present is not entirely unequivocal. In one of the fullest discussions of the point, the Court of First Instance in *Michelin II*[116] observed:

> Unlike Article [101], Article [102] contains no reference to the anti-competitive aim or anti-competitive effect of the practice referred to. However, in the light of the context of Article [102], conduct will be regarded as abusive only if it restricts competition.[117]

This might be seen as offering comfort to those seeking to prevent Article 102 applying to only foreseeable or potential harm. However, the Court of First Instance then recapitulated on this by stating:

> [I]t is sufficient to show that the abusive conduct of the undertaking in a dominant position tends to restrict competition *or, in other words*, that the conduct is *capable of* having that effect.[118]

The Court of First Instance's subsequent conclusion did little to kill off the doubts about the role of intent and effect in the measurement of abuse:

> It follows that, for the purposes of applying Article [102], establishing the anti-competitive object and the anti-competitive effect are one and the same thing. . . . If it is shown that the object pursued by the conduct of an undertaking in a dominant position is to limit competition, that conduct will also be liable to have such an effect.[119]

Apart from indicating that object and effect have a close correlation, this formulation unfortunately does not explain whether it is a general rule for all abuses, whether object or intent are necessary conditions, or whether there are such things as per se abuses. This issue has particular resonance in the light of the Commission's Guidance on Enforcement

---

[113] *Tetra Pak II*, above n 46, para 27.
[114] Ibid, para 31.
[115] See eg *Microsoft*, above n 4. See B Ong, 'Building Brick Barricades and Other Barriers to Entry: Abusing a Dominant Position by Refusing to Licence Intellectual Property Rights' [2005] *ECLR* 213.
[116] *Michelin II*, above n 24.
[117] Ibid, para 237.
[118] Ibid, para 239 (emphasis added).
[119] Ibid, para 241.

priorities. A number of the questions raised by these recurrent themes are reflected in the Commission's Guidance and will also be revisited below in the course of a more detailed view of conduct frequently treated as abusive in the case law.

B – Commission Guidance on Enforcement Priorities 2009

After a longer than anticipated period of consultation, the Commission's Guidance on Enforcement priorities under Article 102 was officially adopted on 9 February 2009[120] as part of the broader, more economic approach to its enforcement of competition law generally. The Guidance notes at paragraph 3: 'This document is not intended to constitute a statement of the law and is without prejudice to the interpretation of Article 82 by the Court of Justice or the Court of First Instance of the European Communities.' Therefore, the Commission's Guidance is important in terms of enforcement priorities but one must still look primarily to the jurisprudence of the Court of Justice in determining what type of behaviour may constitute an abuse under Article 102.

The Guidance sets out its approach to exclusionary conduct in four parts: Part I—introduction; Part II—statement of purpose; Part III—general approach to exclusionary conduct; and Part IV—specific forms of abuse.[121] Part III is the crucial part dealing with foreclosure leading to consumer harm, ie 'anticompetitive foreclosure'. Basically the Commission will normally intervene where, on the basis of cogent and convincing evidence, the conduct is likely to lead to anti-competitive foreclosure having an adverse impact on consumer welfare,[122] ie where the conduct has been or is capable of hampering competition from competitors which are considered as efficient as the dominant undertaking. The efficient competitor test was adopted by the Court of Justice in *AKZO*, and was implicit in *Oscar Bronner*.[123] It has been explicitly referred to more recently by the Court of Justice,[124] and in effect the equally efficient competitor test is a reformulation of the existing *AKZO* rule based on the costs of the dominant undertaking, revised to adopt the AAC and LRAIC cost benchmarks.[125] These general foreclosure criteria

---

[120] *Guidance on the Commission's Enforcement Priorities in Applying Article 82*, above n 9. For critique, see eg A Witt, 'The Commission's Guidance Paper on Abusive Exclusionary Conduct—More Radical than It Appears? (2010) 35 *ELRev* 214.

[121] See above in relation to various types of abusive conduct.

[122] *Guidance on the Commission's Enforcement Priorities in Applying Article 82*, above n 9, paras 19–20.

[123] Akman, above n 106 (2010), 616.

[124] *Deutsche Telekom* [2009] ECR I-2369; [2009] 4 CMLR 25.

[125] *Guidance on the Commission's Enforcement Priorities in Applying Article 82*, above n 9, paras 24–27. Witt, above n 120, considers at 228 that the test and cost benchmarks make for a 'hazy legal rule'. Long-run average incremental cost (LRAIC) is the average of all the (variable and fixed) costs that a company incurs to produce a particular product. LRAIC and average total cost (ATC) are good proxies for each other, and are the same in the case of single-product undertakings. If multi-product undertakings have economies of scope, LRAIC would be below ATC for each individual product, as true common costs are not taken into account in LRAIC. In the case of multiple products, any costs that could have been avoided by not producing a particular product or range are not considered to be common costs. In situations where common costs are significant, they may have to be taken into account when assessing the ability to foreclose equally efficient competitors.

Average avoidable cost (AAC) is the average of the costs that could have been avoided if the company had not produced a discrete amount of (extra) output, in this case the amount allegedly the subject of abusive conduct. In most cases, AAC and the average variable cost (AVC) will be the same, as it is often only variable costs that can be avoided. However, in circumstances where AVC and AAC differ, the latter better reflects possible sacrifice: for example, if the dominant undertaking had to expand capacity in order to be able to predate, then the sunk costs of that extra capacity should be taken into account in looking at the dominant undertaking's losses. Those costs would be reflected in the AAC, but not the AVC.

are supplemented by specific criteria in relation to individual types of abuse, particularly price-based exclusionary conduct which focus on cost benchmarks and below-cost pricing, outlining a revised form of the cost benchmark from those set out by the Court in AKZO. However, the application of the equally efficient competitor test is dependent on sufficient reliable date being available (in relation to costs and prices) and is also not a completely safe harbour. It should be stressed that there is no mention in the Guidance whatsoever of the *Irish Sugar* and *Compagnie Maritime Belge* jurisprudence in relation to selective above-cost pricing strategies, which indicates that this type of pricing strategy will not be an enforcement priority (and in any event, the circumstances of those cases were 'exceptional'.) The Guidance confirms that a dominant undertaking can demonstrate that its conduct is objectively justified or produces substantial efficiencies which outweigh the anti-competitive effects on consumers, measured by the Commission on the basis of the conduct's indispensability and proportionality to the goal.[126] This is consistent with a more economic effects-based approach, and it will remain difficult to establish such efficiencies to the Commission's satisfaction.[127]

C – Types of Abuse

The following, non-exhaustive, examples represent the most frequent or important manifestations of abuses in the case law. The subdivisions therefore reflect a variety of different commercial practices rather than a typology of conceptual categories such as exploitative versus exclusionary or anti-competitive abuses.

(i) Excessively High Prices

This is probably the first example of an abuse of a dominant position which would occur to most people, because of the direct impact borne by consumers. However, competition authorities are not usually over-anxious to intervene on high prices alone. In particular, it is not easy to formulate theoretically adequate and practically useful criteria for determining where the line between fair and unfair prices should be drawn in a given case.[128]

Nevertheless, the Court of Justice in its *United Brands* judgment spoke of a price being excessive 'because it has no reasonable relation to the economic value of the product supplied'.[129] It went on to approve as one test of excess over economic value, a comparison between the selling price of a product and its cost of production, which would disclose the size of the profit margin. As the Court said, the question was 'whether the difference between the costs actually incurred and the price actually charged is excessive' and, if so, 'whether a price has been imposed which is either unfair in itself or when compared to competing products'.

Such a test may attract criticism. High profits may be the result of a firm's efficiency which deserves to be rewarded (although it is reasonable to require some element of cost saving to be handed on to consumers); while low profits may be the result of inefficiency, in which case prices may still be excessive. The task of assessing how efficiently a domi-

---

[126] *Guidance on the Commission's Enforcement Priorities in Applying Article 82*, above n 9, paras 28–31.
[127] See Akman, above n 106 (2010), 620–23.
[128] See *Attheraces Ltd v The British Horseracing Board Ltd* [2007] EWCA Civ 38, CA.
[129] *United Brands*, above n 13, [1978] ECR 207, 301, echoing the Court's judgment in *General Motors*, above n 64.

nant undertaking employs its resources is likely to be a formidable one.[130] There is also the question of the proportion of indirect costs and general expenditure which should be allocated to the cost of putting a particular product on the market. The structure of the undertaking, the number of subsidiaries and their relationship with each other and with their parent company may cause further complications. However, it is clear that the Court was aware of these problems and intended the test to be applied sensitively, with due regard to its limitations. In the case of the banana market, the Court was of the opinion that a satisfactory estimate could have been arrived at.

From *United Brands* it seems that any attempt to establish an abuse in the form of unfairly high prices should normally proceed by way of an analysis of the cost structure of the undertaking concerned. However, other methods of proving unfairness will continue to be acceptable if the Court is satisfied of their appropriateness in the specific circumstances of the case.[131] For example, in *Bodson*[132] the Court noted that since in more than 30,000 communes in France the provision of the relevant funeral services was unregulated or operated by the communes themselves, there would be comparisons available to provide a basis for assessing whether the prices charged by the holders of exclusive concessions for those services were indeed excessive.[133] Legislation may also on occasion lend assistance to the evaluative task.[134] Nonetheless, excessively high prices are clearly not a priority of the enforcement authorities and do not feature in the Commission Guidance on Enforcement Priorities.

(ii) Predatory Prices

A dominant seller may adopt a tactic of pricing its goods very low, or even below cost, in order to drive out of business competitors with more limited resources who cannot for long sustain the losses occasioned by matching the terms it is offering. Consumers, of course, benefit from price reductions in the short run but risk finding themselves even more at the mercy of the dominant undertaking after it has captured a larger share of the market.

The application of Article 102 to predatory price cutting was first clearly established in *AKZO*.[135] AKZO was the EU's major supplier of a chemical substance, benzoyle peroxide, which is used in the manufacture of plastics and in the bleaching of flour.[136] The Commission found that, in order to deter ECS, a small competitor in the market in flour additives, from expanding its business into the market in organic peroxides for plastics,

---

[130] See Commission Decisions COMP/A.36.568 *Scandlines v Port of Helsingborg* and COMP/A.36.570 *Sundbusserne v Port of Helsingborg* (both 23 July 2004), where the Commission rejected complaints lodged by ferry operators alleging abuses involving excessive port fees. The Commission cited insufficient evidence and the lack of useful benchmarks for establishing excessive levels.

[131] See Case C-52/07 *Kanal 5 Ltd v Foreningen Svenska Tonsättares Internationella Musikbyra (STIM) upa* [2008] ECR I-9275 in relation to the determination of whether the method of calculating royalties relating to the television broadcast of musical works protected by copyright was abusive.

[132] Case 30/87 *Bodson v SA Pompes funèbres des regions liberées* [1988] ECR 2479; [1989] 4 CMLR 984.

[133] See also Case 395/87 *Ministère Public v Tournier* [1989] ECR 2521; [1991] 4 CMLR 248 and Cases 110 and 241–242/88 *Lucazeau v SACEM* [1989] ECR 2811, paras 38 and 25, respectively, of the Court's Judgments; [1991] 4 CMLR 248.

[134] Case 66/86 *Ahmed Saeed* [1989] ECR 803; [1990] 4 CMLR 102, in which a Directive on air fares was used as a reference point, albeit with criteria not unlike the judicial approach in *United Brands*.

[135] *AKZO*, above n 41.

[136] AKZO estimated its share of the relevant market as 50% or more; this was equivalent to those of all the remaining producers put together.

AKZO had first threatened and later implemented a campaign of price cuts aimed at important customers of ECS in the former market. If successful, the campaign would not only have eliminated ECS as a competitor in the supply of organic peroxides; it would also have discouraged other potential challenges to AKZO's established position. AKZO's appeal against the decision was dismissed [137]

Having indicated that not all forms of price competition were legitimate, the Court proceeded to set out a twofold test for determining whether an undertaking has practised predatory pricing, stating:

> Prices below average variable costs (that is to say, those which vary depending on the quantities produced) by means of which a dominant undertaking seeks to eliminate a competitor must be regarded as abusive. A dominant undertaking has no interest in applying such prices except that of eliminating competitors so as to enable it subsequently to raise its prices by taking advantage of its monopolistic position, since each sale generates a loss, namely the total amount of the fixed costs (that is to say, those which remain constant regardless of the quantities produced) and, at least, part of the variable costs relating to the unit produced. Moreover, prices below average total costs, that is to say, fixed costs plus variable costs, but above average variable costs, must be regarded as abusive if they are determined as part of a plan for eliminating a competitor.[138]

This approach was affirmed by the Court in *Tetra Pak*,[139] together with the additional observation that it was not necessary for the purposes of establishing predatory pricing to prove that the company had a realistic chance of subsequently recouping its losses. According to the Court, it must be possible to penalise predatory pricing whenever there is a risk that competitors will be eliminated. The aim pursued, which is to maintain undistorted competition, rules out waiting until such a strategy leads to the actual elimination of competitors.[140]

These principles have been criticised, especially the need for a plan to eliminate competition before predatory pricing can be established under the second limb of the *AKZO* test. The requisite element of intention can only be inferred from the surrounding evidence, such as the duration, continuity and scale of the losses made.[141] Commentators[142] have argued that the emphasis on intention is arbitrary, and fails to take account of a firm's rational economic behaviour. Instead, contrary to the Court's position in *Tetra Pak*, it is argued that any assessment should first entail a structural analysis with a view to establishing whether market conditions favour the undertaking being able to recoup its losses, since it is only the latter prospect which would rationally induce the undertaking to engage in predatory activity.[143] As the Commission has recognised,[144] predatory pricing is a risky strategy because the self-inflicted losses may not be regained if the predator

---

[137] After considerable delay, the Commission's Decision being in 1985 and the Court's Judgment in 1991. The fine was reduced for several reasons, and allegations of discrimination were held to be unfounded.

[138] *AKZO*, above n 41, paras 71–72.

[139] *Tetra Pak II*, above n 46.

[140] Ibid, para 44.

[141] Not all companies will be so obliging as AKZO, which had committed its plans to paper.

[142] eg EP Mastromanolis, 'Predatory Pricing Strategies in the European Union: A Case for Legal Reform' [1998] *ECLR* 211; J Temple Lang and R O'Donoghue, 'Defining Legitimate Competition: How to Clarify Pricing Abuses under Art 82 EC' (2002) 26 *Fordham Int LJ* 83.

[143] See COMP/38.233 *Wanadoo Interactive*, 16 July 2003, for an example of the Commission engaging in the attempt to assess recoupment.

[144] *DG Competition Discussion Paper on the Application of Art 82 of the Treaty to Exclusionary Abuses*, above n 7, para 97.

makes a mistake about the market conditions. Nonetheless, in *France Telecom*,[145] where the Commission had found that Wanadoo Interactive SA (WIN), a part of the France Telecom Group, had abused its dominant position by predatory pricing on the French internet access market, the Court held that the Commission was not required to prove possible recoupment of losses, and that the Court of First Instance had been right to establish that recoupment was not a necessary precondition for a finding of predatory pricing.[146] Furthermore, this case confirmed that a dominant undertaking does not even have the right to align its prices with those of competitors where that was part of a plan to eliminate effective competition and thereby constituted abusive conduct.[147] The limitations on the commercial conduct of a dominant undertaking were stressed by the Court of First Instance in that case as follows:

> 185 It should be recalled that, according to established case law, although the fact that an undertaking is in a dominant position cannot deprive it of the right to protect its own commercial interests if they are attacked and such an undertaking must be allowed the right to take such reasonable steps as it deems appropriate to protect those interests, such behaviour cannot be countenanced if its actual purpose is to strengthen this dominant position and abuse it (United Brands v Commission, cited above, at [189]; BPB Industries and British Gypsum v Commission (T-65/89) [1993] ECR II-389; [1993] 5 CMLR 32 at [117]; and Compagnie Maritime Belge Transports v Commission, cited above, at [146]).

> 186 The specific obligations imposed on undertakings in a dominant position have been confirmed by the case law on a number of occasions. The court stated in ITT Promedia v Commission (T-111/96) [1998] ECR II-2937; [1998] 5 CMLR 491 at [139] that it follows from the nature of the obligations imposed by Art 82 EC that, in specific circumstances, undertakings in a dominant position may be deprived of the right to adopt a course of conduct or take measures which are not in themselves abuses and which would even be unobjectionable if adopted or taken by non-dominant undertakings.

> 187 WIN cannot therefore rely on an absolute right to align its prices on those of its competitors in order to justify its conduct. Even if alignment of prices by a dominant undertaking on those of its competitors is not in itself abusive or objectionable, it might become so where it is aimed not only at protecting its interests but also at strengthening and abusing its dominant position.[148]

In the Commission's Guidance on Enforcement Priorities, the test and approach to be adopted in relation to predation is broadly similar to existing practice but there are subtle differences. Predatory conduct is where a dominant undertaking engages in conduct by

> deliberately incurring losses or foregoing profits in the short term (referred to hereafter as 'sacrifice'), so as to foreclose or be likely to foreclose one or more of the actual or potential competitors with a view to strengthening or maintaining its market power, thereby causing consumer harm.[149]

Normally, but not always, AAC will be the starting point for determining sacrifice. However, unlike the existing *AKZO*-based approach, whereby AVC and ATC are alternative tests based on the existence or absence of intention, under the Guidance the equally efficient competitor test for ascertaining conduct capable of foreclosure and harming com-

---

[145] Case C-202/07 P, *France Télécom SA v Commission*, [2009] ECR I-2369; [2009] 4 CMLR 25,
[146] Ibid, paras 110–13.
[147] CFI judgment [2007] ECR II-107; [2007] 4 CMLR 21, paras 176–87, and the ECJ judgment at paras 43–47.
[148] Ibid, paras 185–87.
[149] *Guidance on the Commission's Enforcement Priorities in Applying Article 82*, above n 9, para 63.

petitors utilises the LRAIC cost benchmark. In any event the Commission's Guidance confirms that it does not require to show likely recoupment[150] nor that competitors have actually exited the market.[151]

(iii) Discriminatory Prices

A dominant undertaking may fall foul of Article 102 by charging different prices in respect of equivalent transactions without objective justification. If the customers concerned are 'trading parties', ie the purchase is made for the purposes of an economic activity in which they are engaged, the objectionable feature of such a pricing policy is found in the competitive disadvantage suffered by those called upon to pay the higher prices, and the case falls precisely within Article 102(c).[152] However, even in transactions with ultimate consumers, discriminatory pricing may be abusive, if incompatible with any aims of the Treaty.

An abuse may take the form of discriminating between customers within the same market or of following different pricing policies on different markets, although in the latter case objective justification may be more readily available. It should be noted that the customers concerned need not be in competition with each other: the one paying the higher price suffers a 'competitive disadvantage' simply because he is, to that extent, less well equipped to meet competition, whatever quarter it may come from.

The *United Brands* case highlighted the particular problem of how far it is permissible for dominant undertakings to adapt their pricing policies to take account of the diversity of marketing conditions in the various Member States.[153] For instance, there may be significant disparities in rates of taxation, freight charges or the wages paid to workers for assembling or finishing the product, which may influence costs; or in other factors relevant to a marketing strategy, such as consumer preferences or the intensity of competition. In addition, price differences may result from government action over which a supplier has no control—eg the imposition of a price freeze on certain products. Some convergence of these conditions may be expected as progress to the single market and economic and monetary union develops, but markets within the EU are bound to retain a degree of territorial specificity (although not necessarily along national lines) due, for example, to climate, geography and cultural differences.

UBC had put forward, as objective justification for its policy of charging different prices for its bananas depending on the Member State where the ripened fruit was to be sold, the continuing division of the market for bananas along national lines. Each of the national markets had its own internal characteristics, and accordingly different price levels; and the prices to the ripener/distributors in a given week were intended to reflect as accurately as possible the prices which ripened bananas were expected to fetch on the individual markets during the following week. The defect which the European Court found in this argument was that UBC did not operate directly on the retail markets. It was not, therefore, entitled to take account of market pressures which were only evidenced at the retail

---

[150]   Ibid, paras 70–71.

[151]   Ibid, para 69.

[152]   *Kanal 5*, above n 131, in relation to the determination that the adoption of different methods of calculating royalties relating to the television broadcast of musical works protected by copyright according to whether the broadcast is by a commercial company or a public service undertaking was abusive.

[153]   *United Brands*, above n 13, 294 *et seq.* The Commission found that UBC's differential pricing policy amounted to a separate head of abuse, and this part of the Decision was upheld by the Court of Justice.

stage. However, not all commentators find this convincing,[154] resisting in particular the suggestion that a producer can be immune from the risks of demand conditions at the retail level.

Attempts have been made by dominant firms to justify discriminatory pricing on the basis of the need to meet competition. Thus, in *Irish Sugar*[155] the dominant party granted discounts to customers in the Republic of Ireland situated near the border with Northern Ireland in order to counter the effects of cheap imports into the Republic from across that border. Irish Sugar accused the Commission of failing properly to take account of the fact that price competition in the United Kingdom had widened the gap in prices between Northern Ireland and the Republic, that part of the border trade was illegal and that, at that time, Irish Sugar was incurring considerable losses. Irish Sugar also asserted that it had the right to defend its market position by meeting competition through selective, but non-predatory, pricing tactics.

The Court of First Instance gave short shrift to these arguments. Firstly, the influence of the pricing differential in the United Kingdom was 'of the very essence'[156] of an internal market, so that obstacles to its enjoyment raised by a dominant firm were abusive. This was all the more so since the lower prices outside Ireland were not themselves below cost. Secondly, Irish Sugar could not use its financial situation in the way it claimed without making a 'dead letter'[157] of the Treaty rule. Thirdly, on the question of defensive pricing, the Court of First Instance noted that Irish Sugar was defeated by its own arguments. By claiming that it did not have the financial resources to offer discounts and rebates throughout the Irish territory, the undertaking was in effect admitting that it was subsidising the discounts for border customers from the high prices being charged in the rest of the country. This practice was preventing the development of free competition on the market and distorting its structures, in relation to both purchasers and consumers.[158] If 'meeting competition' was available as an argument to a dominant firm in Irish Sugar's position at all then, at the very least, it would have to satisfy criteria of economic efficiency and be consistent with the interests of consumers.[159] The position adopted by the Court of First Instance[160] is a further example of how difficult it is to mount a defence to discriminatory pricing where the core values of market integration are threatened by that policy, in particular the inhibition of parallel imports. However, commentators[161] have taken issue with the general aversion to price discrimination adopted by the European Courts.

(iv) Margin Squeezing

Margin squeezing typically occurs in situations where a firm is dominant in one market but can use a pricing strategy to squeeze out competitors in downstream markets. The

---

[154] See W Bishop, 'Price Discrimination under Art 86: Political Economy in the European Court' (1981) 44 *MLR* 282.

[155] Case T-228/97, *Irish Sugar*, above n 93.

[156] Ibid, para 185.

[157] Ibid, para 186.

[158] Ibid, para 188.

[159] Ibid, para 189.

[160] The Court of Justice dismissed Irish Sugar's appeal without discussing the discrimination point: see Case C-497/99P, above n 7.

[161] See Bishop, above n 154; D Ridyard, 'Exclusionary Pricing and Price Discrimination Abuses under Art 82: An Economic Analysis' [2002] *ECLR* 286; Eilmansberger, above n 6, 139; Temple Lang and O'Donoghue, above n 142.

product price is set 'at such a level that those who purchase it do not have a sufficient profit margin on the processing to remain competitive on the market for the processed product'.[162] Vertically integrated firms are thus particularly able to squeeze out non-integrated rivals. This behaviour is often to be construed as a constructive refusal to supply or termination of a supply relationship. An example is *British Sugar/Napier Brown*,[163] where British Sugar was dominant in the industrial sugar market but also operated in the downstream, retail, market. The margin between its two prices was below its own repackaging and selling costs. Napier, a retail competitor, depended on supplies from British Sugar and could not viably operate against British Sugar's low pricing tactics.

A more recent example shows the squeeze at the upstream point. In *Deutsche Telekom*[164] the dominant firm (DT) in the wholesale broadband market charged such high prices that competitors could not then supply retail access at prices below those charged by the dominant firm itself. Part of the importance of the Commission's decision is in its methodology,[165] whereby it asserted that DT would not be able to offer its own retail services without incurring a loss if it needed to pay its own wholesale prices. According to the Commission, a margin squeeze, and therefore an abuse, occurred when the spread between DT's retail and wholesale prices was either negative or at least insufficient to cover DT's own downstream costs. DT's wholesale prices were actually higher than its retail levels. The Commission decision was confirmed on appeal by the General Court[166] and the Court of Justice.[167] The latter confirmed that it was sufficient to demonstrate that a combination of the wholesale and retail prices would exclude an 'as efficient competitor', determined according to the dominant undertaking's own costs,[168] irrespective of whether any final consumer had been harmed.[169] The protection of the competitive process, and hence competitors, to ensure consumer choice between alternative suppliers was vital.[170] The Commission's Guidance on Enforcement Priorities considers refusals to supply and margin squeezes together, as discussed below.

(v) Rebates, Single Branding and Discounts

Rebates, discounts and other 'incentives' come in a multitude of forms.[171] They will often be part of a wider range of strategies and so their market impact may not always be uniform or easily demarcated. Single-branding obligations require the buyer to concentrate its purchases to a large degree with one supplier. Such obligations also embrace 'English clauses', whereby the buyer has to report any better offer to the supplier and can only take it up if the latter does not match it.[172] Rebates may be unconditional or conditional. The former, whilst granted to some customers and not others, are applied without reference

---

[162] Case T-5/97 *Industrie des Poudres Sphériques v Commission* [2000] ECR II-3755.

[163] [1988] OJ L284/41, [1990] 4 CMLR 196.

[164] [2003] OJ L263/9, now under appeal as Case T-271/03.

[165] See also *Notice on the Application of Competition Rules to Access Agreements in the Telecommunications Sector* [1998] OJ C265/2.

[166] [2007] ECR II-521; [2008] 5 CMLR 6.

[167] [2009] ECR I-2369; [2009] 4 CMLR 25.

[168] Ibid at paras 197–202.

[169] Ibid, eg para 176.

[170] Ibid at paras 253–55.

[171] See D Ridyard, 'Exclusionary Pricing and Price Discrimination Abuses under Article 82—An Economic Analysis' [2002] *ECLR* 286.

[172] See *Hoffmann-La Roche*, above n 20. Moreover, if the buyer has to disclose the identity of the better offer, this will reinforce the knowledge of the dominant party about the market.

to customer behaviour—for example, to customers in border regions who might otherwise be tempted to seek foreign suppliers. Conditional rebates reward certain (purchasing) behaviour by customers—such as on the basis of previous amounts purchased or percentages of requirements taken from that supplier. As Advocate General Kokott observed in the *British Airways* case:

> [L]oyalty rebates and loyalty bonuses can in practice bind business partners so closely to the dominant undertaking (the 'fidelity-building effect'), that its competitors find it inordinately difficult to sell their products ('exclusionary' or 'foreclosure' effect), with the result that competition itself can be damaged and, ultimately, the consumer can suffer.[173]

In the sense that they are likely to target particular customers, or apply differently to selected traders, discounts and rebates also often imply discrimination.[174]

Nevertheless, there may be benefits to be derived. Simple 'quantity' discounts are not likely to be seen as anti-competitive where these correlate to cost savings for the supplier. The use of rebates in vertical relationships may induce efficient behaviour by retailers insofar as increased retail margins on additional volumes encourage retailers to promote the product. By allowing high- and low-demand elasticity consumers to be treated differently, rebates will impact upon margins. The result is that there is at least an open question as to whether the net effect on consumer welfare is positive or negative.[175] However, general economic intuition is that pure quantity rebates are more likely to be motivated by efficiency considerations than fidelity rebates.[176]

Accordingly, it had traditionally been considered, following the *Hoffman-La Roche* ruling, that quantity discounts, linked directly to actual volume of purchases, could not constitute an abuse under Article 102, on the basis that they were assumed to be in direct correlation with costs savings and thereby objectively justifiable. As the Court noted in that case:

> This method of calculating the rebates differs from the granting of quantitative rebates, linked solely to the volume of purchases from the producers concerned in that the rebates at issue are not dependent on quantities fixed objectively and applicable to all possible purchasers.[177]

Nonetheless, even so-called quantity discounts may be caught by the Article 102 prohibition, as demonstrated by the *Michelin II* case,[178] involving a scheme which was based on volume purchases without discrimination between identical customers. The case involved what the Commission identified as 'a complex system of rebates, discounts and/or various financial benefits whose main objective was to tie resellers to it and to maintain its market shares'—essentially individualised target rebates. The Court of First Instance held that 'the mere fact of characterising a discount system as quantity rebates does not mean that the grant of such discounts is compatible with Article [102]'.[179] The following passages of the Court of First Instance's ruling are significant in laying out the law in relation to discounts and rebates:

---

[173] Case C-95/04P, *British Airways*, above n 3.
[174] Although discrimination is not a precondition for a rebate or bonus to constitute an abuse: see *Michelin I*, above n 12, para 120.
[175] See EAGCP Report, above n 7, 36.
[176] Ibid.
[177] See *Hoffmann-La Roche*, above n 20, para 100.
[178] Case T-203/01 *Manufacture française des pneumatiques Michelin v Commission* [2003] ECR II-4071; [2004] 4 CMLR 18.
[179] Ibid, para 62.

56. With more particular regard to the granting of rebates by an undertaking in a dominant position, it is apparent from a consistent line of decisions that a loyalty rebate, which is granted in return for an undertaking by the customer to obtain his stock exclusively or almost exclusively from an undertaking in a dominant position, is contrary to Article [102]. Such a rebate is designed through the grant of financial advantage, to prevent customers from obtaining their supplies from competing producers (Joined Cases 40/73 to 48/73, 50/73, 54/73 to 56/73, 111/73, 113/73 and 114/73 Suiker Unie and Others v Commission [1975] ECR 1663, paragraph 518; Hoffmann-La Roche v Commission, cited at paragraph 54 above, paragraphs 89 and 90; Michelin v Commission, cited at paragraph 54 above, paragraph 71; and Case T-65/89 BPB Industries and British Gypsum v Commission, cited at paragraph 55 above, paragraph 120).

58. Quantity rebate systems linked solely to the volume of purchases made from an undertaking occupying a dominant position are generally considered not to have the foreclosure effect prohibited by Article [102] (see Michelin v Commission, cited at paragraph 54 above, paragraph 71). 60. In determining whether a quantity rebate system is abusive, it will therefore be necessary to consider all the circumstances, particularly the criteria and rules governing the grant of the rebate, and to investigate whether, in providing an advantage not based on any economic service justifying it, the rebates tend to remove or restrict the buyer's freedom to choose his sources of supply, to bar competitors from access to the market, to apply dissimilar conditions to equivalent transactions with other trading parties or to strengthen the dominant position by distorting competition (see Hoffmann-La Roche v Commission, cited at paragraph 54 above, paragraph 90; Michelin v Commission, cited at paragraph 54 above, paragraph 73; and Irish Sugar v Commission, cited at paragraph 54 above, paragraph 114).[180]

It is clear that the particular circumstances in which a discount is granted must be investigated with care. Most notable in relation to Michelin's quantity discounts, as stressed by the Court of First Instance, were that they were calculated on the dealer's entire turnover over a one-year period. Therefore the structure of the scheme may be an important factor, and, following *Michelin II*, above-cost rebates can clearly be unlawful if they produce a loyalty-inducing/market-foreclosing effect, particularly where the rebate is made on a discretionary or arbitrary basis.

The principle enunciated in *Hoffman-La Roche* and developed in the *Michelin* rulings was reaffirmed in *British Airways v Commission*, which additionally confirmed that rebates and bonuses can also operate in relation to buyer power. Thus, in *Virgin/British Airways*,[181] the Commission fined BA for its systems of financial incentives in relation to travel agencies providing airline ticket and promotional services. All the schemes were geared to meeting targets for sales growth and shared one key characteristic: the commission increased in relation to *all* tickets sold by an agent in the reference period, not just the ones sold after the target was reached. This meant that whenever a travel agent was close to reaching the trigger sales threshold for an increase in commission rates, selling relatively few extra BA tickets could have a significant impact on commission income. Any competitor (such as Virgin) would therefore have to pay a much higher rate of commission to an agent to divert some of its sales to the competitor's tickets in order to overcome that effect. The Court of First Instance, upholding the Commission's findings, accepted that this 'very noticeable effect at the margin'[182] would also mean that an agent could suffer significant financial losses for even a small drop in turnover in BA tickets.

---

[180] Ibid, paras 56, 58 and 60.
[181] Decision 2000/74 [2000] OJ L30/1.
[182] Case T-219/99, *British Airways*, above n 42, para 272.

On appeal to the Court of Justice, the Court of First Instance ruling was upheld.[183] The Court of Justice outlined its approach to the determination of the abusive nature of discounts as follows:

63. In Michelin, unlike in Hoffmann-La Roche, Michelin's co-contractors were not obliged to obtain their supplies wholly or partially from Michelin. However, the variable annual discounts granted by that undertaking were linked to objectives in the sense that, in order to benefit from them, its co-contractors had to attain individualised sales results. In that case, the Court found a series of factors which led it to regard the discount system in question as an abuse of a dominant position. In particular, the system was based on a relatively long reference period, namely a year, its functioning was non-transparent for co-contractors, and the differences in market share between Michelin and its main competitors were significant (see, to that effect, Michelin, paragraphs 81 to 83).

65. In that respect, Michelin is particularly relevant to the present case, since it concerns a discount system depending on the attainment of individual sales objectives which constituted neither discounts for quantity, linked exclusively to the volume of purchases, nor fidelity discounts within the meaning of the judgment in Hoffmann-La Roche, since the system established by Michelin did not contain any obligation on the part of resellers to obtain all or a given proportion of its supplies from the dominant undertaking.

68. It follows that in determining whether, on the part of an undertaking in a dominant position, a system of discounts or bonuses which constitute neither quantity discounts or bonuses nor fidelity discounts or bonuses within the meaning of the judgment in Hoffmann-La Roche constitutes an abuse, it first has to be determined whether those discounts or bonuses can produce an exclusionary effect, that is to say whether they are capable, first, of making market entry very difficult or impossible for competitors of the undertaking in a dominant position and, secondly, of making it more difficult or impossible for its co-contractors to choose between various sources of supply or commercial partners.[184]

The Court of Justice confirmed that the Court of First Instance had examined the relative competitive position of BA and its competitors in assessing whether the bonus schemes had a fidelity-building effect which could produce an exclusionary effect and that it would not, on an appeal limited to questions of law, substitute its own assessment for that of the Court of First Instance.[185] BA's claim that the performance rewards were objectively justified was also rejected by the Court of Justice on the basis that the Court of First Instance had concluded that there was no economic objective justification for the bonus schemes based on the high level of fixed costs in air transport and the importance of aircraft occupancy rates.[186]

The Commission adopted the more modern terminology of conditional rebates, and the complicated procedure for determining their legality, in its *Intel* decision in 2009 in which it fined Intel €1.06 billion for infringement of Article 102 by abusing its dominant position on the x86 central processing unit (CPU) market.[187] The Commission found inter alia that Intel gave wholly or partially hidden rebates to computer manufacturers on condition that they bought all, or nearly all, their x86 computers with Intel x86CPUs, a worldwide

---

[183] *British Airways*, above n 3.
[184] Ibid, paras 63, 65 and 68. At para 69 the Court acknowledges that exclusionary effects of similar practices should be analysed in light of any efficiency enhancing effects they may have.
[185] Ibid, paras 76–79.
[186] Ibid, para 88.
[187] Case COMP/C-3/37.990 *Intel*, See Commission website at http://ec.europa.eu/competition/elojade/isef/case_details.cfm?proc_code=1_37990. Summary of Commission decision, [2009] OJ C227/13.

market in which Intel had a dominant position of at least 70 per cent market share. The Commission noted that the conditional rebates granted constituted fidelity rebates satisfying the conditions of the *Hoffman La Roche* case law, but the Commission applied the equally efficient competitor test, utilising the assessment outlined in its Guidance, in particular by considering the contestable share of the market and average avoidable cost benchmark.

The methodology for calculating and identifying illegal and abusive conditional rebates as set out in the Commission Guidance on Enforcement Priorities is complex and complicated.[188] The Guidance notes that conditional rebates are

> rebates granted to customers to reward them for a particular form of purchasing behaviour. The usual nature of a conditional rebate is that the customer is given a rebate if its purchases over a defined reference period exceed a certain threshold, the rebate being granted either on all purchases (retroactive rebates) or only on those made in excess of those required to achieve the threshold (incremental rebates).[189]

The Commission Guidance indicates that they are not uncommon in practice, and may stimulate demand and benefit consumers, but they may also have potential foreclosure effects similar to exclusive purchasing obligations. The Commission Guidance proposes a complicated calculation, where feasible, of the effective price over the relevant range of products—and the lower the estimated price is over the relevant range compared to the average price of the dominant supplier, the stronger will be the loyalty-enhancing effect.

(vi) Tying and Bundling

The illustrative abuses listed in Article 102(d) specifically include 'tying' arrangements, where a person is required to accept, as a condition of entering into a contract, 'supplementary obligations which, by their nature or according to commercial usage, have no connection with the subject of such contracts'.[190] In simple terms this can mean that to order X (the tying good) the customer must also take quantities of Y (the tied good). X and Y may be complementary, independent or substitutes. Similarly, services may be tied so that the purchase of a heating system may include an obligation to sign up for a five-year service contract. Tying thus makes the sale of one item conditional upon the purchase of another. Bundling, however, describes the situation where two or more products are sold together. It may be 'pure' (the component goods can only be bought together) or 'mixed' (where the components are also available separately but the bundle comes at a discount on the price of the separate components).

The main objection to tying, the so-called leverage argument, is that it enables a dominant position in one market to be used in order to gain a competitive advantage in another. It may also be directly oppressive to consumers in the first market. Thus, in *Hilti*[191] it was held to be an abuse for Hilti to supply cartridge strips to certain end-users or distributors on terms that the requisite complement of nails was purchased as well. Hilti claimed as an objective justification that its policy was based on safety grounds, alleging

---

[188] *Guidance on the Commission's Enforcement Priorities in Applying Article 82*, above n 9, paras 37–46. R Whish (*Competition Law*, 6th edn (Oxford, Oxford University Press, 2009) noted the complexity in relation to the Commission's earlier Discussion Paper at paras 151–71.

[189] Ibid, para 37.

[190] See J Langer, *Tying and Bundling as Leveraging Concern Under EC Competition* Law (The Hague, Kluwer Law International, 2008).

[191] *Hilti*, above n 38.

that other manufacturers' nails were dangerous when used in the Hilti system. This argument was forcefully rejected by the Court of First Instance, noting that it was not for Hilti to take unilateral action in that way; safety issues could be referred to the relevant public authorities. Even in relation to products where tied sales are part of commercial usage, the possibility of such practice being an abuse cannot be ruled out.[192]

Bundling is a common phenomenon and is by no means confined to dominant firms. It can often be used as a means to increase the appeal of the product with which the second component is bundled.[193] However, when adopted by dominant firms, bundling may produce abusive leveraging effects. This was the Commission's claim in relation to Microsoft's bundling of its Windows Media Player (WMP) with its PC operating systems.[194] Customers could not obtain Windows without WMP. Nor were there any ready means to uninstall WMP. In the Commission's view, even though customers obtained WMP 'for free', alternative suppliers of media players were put at a disadvantage by Microsoft's bundling. Citing recent Court of First Instance judgments[195] in relation to the requisite burden of proof in relation to anti-competitive effects, the Commission claimed that the bundling was liable to foreclose competition in the market for media players. The Commission considered, essentially, that the presence of WMP in all Microsoft's PC operating systems gave content providers and applications manufacturers an incentive to design their products on the basis of WMP. In other words, the detriment to competition would result from these indirect network effects. The Commission also rejected Microsoft's arguments that it had in fact created a single integrated product (rather than a bundle). Microsoft further claimed that consumers benefited from having a set of default options in a personal computer 'out of the box' ready to run. However, in the Commission's view, the benefit of pre-installation needed to be distinguished from Microsoft making that selection itself. Microsoft appealed against the Commission's Decision.

The Court of First Instance[196] relied on earlier case law, according to which tying is abusive when four conditions are satisfied: (i) there are two separate products; (ii) the undertaking is dominant on the tying product market; (iii) there is coercion in that customers cannot obtain the tying product without the tied product; and (iv) the practice must be able to foreclose competition. Each of these requirements was satisfied in this case. In particular, in relation to the fourth requirement, Microsoft had achieved a level of penetration of the media player market, an adjunct of the operating system market in which it was dominant, and this could not be matched by competing suppliers, without Microsoft having to compete on the merits. Customers would be less likely to switch due to consumer confusion regarding different media functionalities, and furthermore the Court of First Instance concluded that other methods of acquiring and installing computer software did not constitute viable alternatives to pre-installation. Accordingly, Microsoft had abused its position on the operating system market as its practice conferred an 'unparalleled advan-

---

[192]   *Tetra Pak II*, above n 46, para 37.

[193]   See Eilmansberger, above n 6, 154. He uses the example of a sports section to boost sales of a newspaper.

[194]   COMP/C-3/37.792 *Microsoft* (24 March 2004). The interoperability aspect of the Decision is dealt with below in the section on refusals to supply. See also J Appeldoorn, 'He Who Spareth His Rod, Hateth His Son? Microsoft, Superdominance and Art 82 EC' [2005] *ECLR* 653.

[195]   In particular, Case T-65/98 *Van den Bergh Foods* [2003] ECR II-4653, *Michelin II*, above n 24, and *British Airways*, above n 42.

[196]   *Microsoft*, above n 4.

tage' on the tied product WMP, without any requirement to compete on quality,[197] and the CFI supported the Commission finding that the market had been foreclosed given the trend in such markets towards tipping in favour of a certain program.[198]

Its Guidance on Enforcement Priorities indicates that the Commission will normally take action in relation to tying 'where an undertaking is dominant in the tying market and where, in addition, the following conditions are fulfilled: (1) the typing and tied products are distinct products, and (ii) the tying practice is likely to lead to anti-competitive foreclosure'.[199] Anti-competitive foreclosure is more likely where the strategy adopted is a lasting one, for instance through technical tying, as evidenced in *Microsoft*.

(vii) Refusals to Supply

Freedom of contract implies that any economic operator should be able to determine whom to supply, or not, as the case may be.[200] Dominant firms enjoy that presumption too, but it is also the case that discontinuations, refusals or threats of refusals to supply may constitute abuse when dominant firms' special responsibilities are considered in particular circumstances. The notion of refusal to supply has become something of an umbrella term and can embrace 'constructive' refusals which at first sight take different forms, such as delaying tactics or pricing practices.[201]

The line of case law with the longest pedigree concerns termination of existing supply. However, more recent developments have seen abuses against first-time customers, especially where the refusal amounts to a form of leveraging which prevents access to a supply (or, in economic terms, an input) which is necessary for a downstream market. The case law is complex because the developments in this area are drawn from two rather different factual contexts which have become cross-referenced. On the one hand, there are refusals to license intellectual property rights (IPRs), particularly the *Magill*,[202] *IMS Health*[203] and *Microsoft*[204] cases. On the other, in cases such as *Bronner*[205] which do not entail IPRs, there are denials of access to inputs allegedly indispensable to downstream activities which have been argued, explicitly or by analogy, in support of a so-called 'essential facilities doctrine'. The policy undercurrents in these two modern strands of case law are not the same.[206] In relation to IPRs the issue is whether competition concerns can trump legally conferred monopoly rights. The problem posed by any imposition of a duty to share essential facilities lies in the interference with freedom of contract and (arguably) the potential protection of competitors rather than competition. The challenge for competition enforcement agencies and the European Courts is thus whether the competitive

---

[197] See generally ibid, paras 1038–58 re this fourth requirement.

[198] See A Andreangeli, 'Case T-201/04, *Microsoft v Commission*' (2008) 45 *CMLRev* 863, in particular at 887, where she accepts that the CFI conclusions are consistent with the principles developed in *Tetra Pak*, but queries whether the 'approach adopted by the ECJ in respect of "traditional" types of tying is suitable to cases of "technological integration"' (887).

[199] *Guidance on the Commission's Enforcement Priorities in Applying Article 82*, above n 9 para 50.

[200] See in particular the Opinion of AG Jacobs in *Bronner*, above n 53, paras 58–62.

[201] eg margin squeezes, discussed above.

[202] Joined Cases C-241-242/91P *RTE and ITP v Commission* [1995] ECR I-743, [1995] 4 CMLR 718.

[203] Case C-418/01 *IMS Health v Commission* [2004] ECR I-5039, [2004] 4 CMLR 1543.

[204] *Microsoft*, above n 4.

[205] *Bronner*, above n 53.

[206] See eg A Andreangeli, 'Interoperability as an "Essential Facility" in the Microsoft Case—Encouraging Competition or Stifling Innovation?' (2009) 34 *ELRev* 584.

harm in all these cases should be treated identically or whether the policy values involved demand differential treatment.

With the necessary caveat that the Court has never been inhibited from drawing upon all strands of case law to analyse any particular context, the discussion below first examines terminations of existing supply before looking at essential facilities and the intellectual property cases.

(a) Termination of Existing Supply

The case law suggests a distinction between termination of an existing relationship and a refusal to start dealing with a new customer. The earliest case on refusal to deal was *Commercial Solvents*.[207] The refusal from the end of 1970 to supply Zoja with aminobutanol required for the manufacture of the derivative, ethambutol, was the result of a policy decision by the CS group to manufacture and sell the derivative on its own account. According to the Court:

> [A]n undertaking being in a dominant position as regards the production of raw material and therefore able to supply to manufacturers of derivatives, cannot, just because it decides to start manufacturing these derivatives (in competition with its former customers) act in such a way as to eliminate their competition which in the case in question, would amount to eliminating one of the principal manufacturers of ethambutol in the common market.[208]

Three main points emerge from this passage. In the first place, Zoja was an established customer of CSC. Admittedly, at the beginning of 1970 Zoja had cancelled its orders under the current supply contract, but the Court regarded this as irrelevant because CSC had anyway decided to cut off the supplies once deliveries under the contract had been completed. Secondly, the effect of withholding supplies of the raw material was likely to be serious, namely the elimination of a major producer from the market for the derivative. Thirdly, the reason for driving Zoja out of the market was to smooth CSC's own entry. The Court made it clear that the conduct in question could not be justified as a legitimate competitive tactic.

The *United Brands* judgment contains an even more forthright condemnation of refusal to supply:

> [I]t is advisable to assert positively from the outset that an undertaking in a dominant position for the purpose of marketing a product—which cashes in on the reputation of a brand name known to and valued by the consumers—cannot stop supplying a long standing customer who abides by regular commercial practice, if the orders placed by that customer are in no way out of the ordinary.[209]

The victim was the Danish ripener/distributor, Olesen, which UBC had refused to supply with 'Chiquitas' bananas after it had taken part in a sales campaign mounted by a rival supplier, Castle and Cooke. That collaboration was not regarded by the Court as justifying the refusal. Even a dominant undertaking may act in defence of its commercial interests, but such action must be reasonable and proportional to the threat, which that taken against Olesen had not been.

The apparent importance of distinguishing carefully between different categories

---

[207] *Commercial Solvents*, above n 10.
[208] Ibid, 250–51.
[209] *United Brands*, above n 13, 292.

of customer was highlighted by the *BP*[210] judgment, in which the Court annulled the Decision of the Commission that BP had abused the dominant position which it enjoyed in relation to its Dutch customers during the oil supply crisis of 1973–74 by reducing deliveries of motor spirit to a particular customer, ABG, more drastically than to others. The Court found that BP had given notice of the termination of its supply contract with ABG in November 1972, and that at the time when the crisis broke, ABG's relationship with BP, so far as concerned supplies of motor spirit, was that of a casual customer. BP could not, therefore, be blamed for treating ABG less favourably than its regular customers, since the latter would have received a substantially smaller quantity than they were entitled to expect, if a standard rate reduction had been applied.[211] However, not all prioritising of customers will be objectively justified. In *BPB Industries*[212] the Court of First Instance found that British Gypsum was abusing its dominance in the plasterboard market by favouring customers who were not importers of plasterboard from other sources. It accordingly dismissed British Gypsum's argument that this was justified prioritisation for the benefit of regular customers in times of shortage. Whilst selection criteria can be adopted in such circumstances, they must be objectively justified and observe the rules governing fair competition between economic operators.

This older case law in relation to treatment of existing customers may seem rather removed from a close economic analysis of effects. They contain at the very least a nod in the direction of more nebulous notions of fair dealing.

(b) Essential Facilities

As with some other developments in EU competition law, such as the rule of reason,[213] the concept of essential facilities has a counterpart originating in the United States.[214] Put shortly, the idea requires that dominance over key facilities, such as transport or other infrastructure, requires access to be opened up to other users in particular circumstances. The US case law, as discussed by Advocate General Jacobs in *Bronner*, contains five conditions. First, an essential facility is under the control of a monopolist. Secondly, a competitor is unable practically or reasonably to duplicate the essential facility. Thirdly, the use of the facility is denied to a competitor, even on reasonable terms. Fourthly, it is feasible for the facility to be provided. Fifthly, there is no legitimate business reason for refusing access to the facility.

The term 'essential facilities' has been expressly adopted in EU law by the Commission, although the Court's position is less clear. In *Sea Containers v Stena Sealink*[215] the Commission decided that Sealink's refusal, as operator of the port of Holyhead, to allow access on reasonable and non-discriminatory terms to a potential competitor on the market for ferry services was an abuse of a dominant position. A facility will be essential if

---

[210] Case 77/77 [1978] ECR 1513, [1978] 3 CMLR 174.

[211] As AG Warner pointed out, a legal and moral right to security of supplies is the counterpart, for a contractual customer, of his loss of freedom to seek the best available bargain at a given moment, and the loyalty of regular, though non-contractual, customers also merits special consideration.

[212] Case T-65/89 *BPB Industries and British Gypsum v Commission* [1993] ECR II-389; [1993] 5 CMLR 32; this aspect of the case was not dealt with on appeal in Case C-310/93P, [1995] ECR I-865.

[213] See Chapter 23 above.

[214] Although its existence even in the US is now viewed with scepticism: see *Verizon Communications Inc v Law Offices of Curtis V Trinko, LLP* 540 US 682 (2004). See U Muller and A Rodenhausen, 'The Rise and Fall of the Essential Facility Doctrine' [2008] *ECLR* 310.

[215] Decision 94/19 [1994] OJ L15/8.

the handicap to a new entrant resulting from denial of access is one that can reasonably be expected to make competitors' activities in the market in question either impossible or permanently, seriously and unavoidably uneconomic.[216]

In *Bronner* the claimant, a small newspaper, sought access to the national home-delivery network for newspapers established by Mediaprint, which held 40 per cent of the Austrian newspaper market. Advocate General Jacobs emphasised the policy context which might discourage extensive resort to any 'essential facilities' notion. In particular, he pointed to the right to choose one's trading partners and freely to dispose of one's property as generally recognised principles in the laws of the Member States, in some cases with constitutional status. Furthermore, from a competition perspective, the long-term interests of consumers might be better served by allowing the undertaking to keep its facilities. Otherwise, automatic rights for new entrants would act as a disincentive to those parties to develop competing facilities. Short-term gains by opening access might well thus be offset by longer-term disadvantages. In relation to the specific circumstances of the case, Advocate General Jacobs noted that although the applicant might be unable to duplicate that network, it still had a variety of other distribution options open to it. The case thus fell 'well short' of the type of situation in which it might be appropriate to impose an obligation on a dominant undertaking to allow access to a facility which it has developed for its own use.

The Court of Justice, notably, reformulated the question in *Bronner* in terms of a refusal to supply and did not expressly articulate an essential facilities doctrine. However, it took a narrow view of the requirements necessary to make out a breach of Article 102, observing that not only would the refusal of access have to be likely to eliminate all competition in the daily newspaper market on the part of the person requesting the service and that such refusal be incapable of being objectively justified, but that the service must also be indispensable to carrying on that person's business. The last requirement was not satisfied in the particular case since Bronner could choose other methods of distributing its newspapers besides home delivery. The Court also emphasised that in order to demonstrate that it had no realistic alternatives, the applicant could not just assert that it would not be economically viable to set up its own distribution network for the small circulation of its newspapers. This view acknowledges criticisms prior to the judgment expressing fears about the rising tide of essential facilities doctrine.[217]

The indispensability requirement in *Bronner* thus displays twin features.[218] In addition to the generic question of whether home delivery as such was indispensable to the distribution of newspapers, it was also necessary to assess the specific question of whether Mediaprint's facility could be duplicated. In a judgment[219] delivered after the Opinion in *Bronner*, the Court of First Instance had also ruled that a facility could only be essential if there were no substitutes. This more rigorous standard casts doubt on the Commission's previous approach in cases such as *London European v Sabena*,[220] where the refusal to

---

[216] J Temple Lang, 'Defining Legitimate Competition: Companies Duties' to Supply Competitors, and Access to Essential Facilities' (1994) 18 *Fordham Int LJ* 245, quoted by AG Jacobs in *Bronner*, above n 53.

[217] eg D Ridyard, 'Essential Facilities and the Obligation to Supply Competitors under UK and EC Competition Law' [1996] *ECLR* 438.

[218] See B Doherty, 'Just What Are Essential Facilities?' (2001) 38 *CMLRev* 397.

[219] Cases T-374, 375, 384 and 388/94 *European Night Services v Commission* [1998] ECR II-3141, [1998] 5 CMLR 718, (although in relation to Art 81, not Art 82).

[220] Decision 88/589; [1988] OJ L317/47.

allow access to a computer reservation system was condemned without a particularly rigorous assessment of Sabena's market position.

The message from *Bronner*, if not all its ramifications, is clear: imposing a duty to share facilities will be an exceptional, not a routine, event.[221]

(c) Intellectual Property: Licensing and Interoperability Issues

In its *Bronner* judgment the Court of Justice carefully avoided commenting on whether its previous case law on refusal to license IPRs was of general application. The key previous decision was *Magill*,[222] a saga concerning access to rights protected by copyright. The three television companies involved had previously reproduced advance weekly listings of their programmes in separate magazines. Magill, which wanted to launch a single publication containing all the listings, was refused access to this information by the various copyright-holding companies. The Commission treated this refusal as an abuse, a view upheld by the Court of First Instance on the basis that preventing the emergence of a new product for which there was potential consumer demand went further than was necessary for protection of the essential function of copyright. The Court of Justice endorsed this conclusion, adding a direct reference to *Commercial Solvents*[223] and treating the programme scheduling as the indispensable raw material for the compilation of a new final magazine product.

Critics of the *Magill* judgment claimed that it took insufficient account of the rights and interests of holders of IPRs, to the point of undermining the Court's own often-stated position that a refusal to license such rights was not itself an abuse.[224] However, subsequent cases have allayed these early fears. First, the Court of First Instance in *Tiercé Ladbroke*[225] expressly rejected the application of the *Magill* judgment on the footing that the copyright holders who were refusing to license their television rights for transmission in Belgium were not themselves already exploiting them on the Belgian market. In his *Bronner* Opinion, Advocate General Jacobs described the *Magill* judgment as having special circumstances: the existing weekly guides were inadequate, the provision of copyright protection for television listings was hard to justify in any event, and, since the shelf-life of listings was short, any refusal to supply the information was bound to act as a permanent barrier to a new product.

The limits to *Magill* were confirmed by the Court's judgment in *IMS Health*,[226] a case that, like *Magill*, concerned copyright protection. IMS was dominant in the production of data on deliveries by wholesalers of pharmaceuticals in Germany. It had developed, with its customers (pharmaceutical companies), a so-called brick structure—1,860 blocks based on postcodes which contained data on pharmacies and drug prescription levels to track regional sales. Newcomers introduced modified versions of the 1,860-brick structure, which were then challenged by IMS as breach of its copyright. Having first affirmed that indispensability would only be satisfied by showing that alternatives would not be

---

[221] M Bergman, 'The Bronner Case—A Turning Point for the Essential Facilities Doctrine' [2000] *ECLR* 59.

[222] *Magill*, above n 202.

[223] *Commercial Solvents*, above n 10.

[224] Case 238/87 *Volvo v Erik Veng (UK)* [1988] ECR 6211; [1989] 4 CMLR 122; Case 53/87 *Maxicar v Renault* [1988] ECR 6039.

[225] *Tiercé Ladbroke*, above n 49.

[226] *IMS Health*, above n 203. See E Derclaye, 'The *IMS Health* Decision and the Reconciliation of Copyright and Competition Law' (2004) 29 *ELRev* 687.

viable for production on a scale comparable to that of IMS, the Court turned to the particular context of IPR licensing. Basing its argument on *Magill* and *Bronner*, the Court observed:

> It is clear from that case law that, in order for the refusal by an undertaking which owns a copyright to give access to a product or service indispensable for carrying on a particular business to be treated as abusive, it is sufficient that three cumulative conditions be satisfied, namely, that the refusal is preventing the emergence of a new product for which there is a potential consumer demand, that it is unjustified and such as to exclude any competition on a secondary market.[227]

The shift, or clarification, here is the statement that these three elements are cumulative.

Moreover, the first condition, the emergence of a new product, suggests a distinguishing requirement additional to cases about IPRs but absent from other putative claims involving essential facilities. The new product, and its demand, were clearly available in *Magill* in the form of the all-in-one television listings journal. However, in *IMS Health* the Court of Justice left to the national court the task of deciding whether an undertaking requesting an IPR licence was merely 'limiting itself essentially to duplicating the goods or services already offered on the secondary market' or whether there would indeed be a new product. It seems clear from *IMS Health* that the 'new product' requirement was expressly inserted as the means of balancing the interests of IPR holders against detriments to consumers.

As regards the exclusion of competition on a secondary market, several points may be noted. Firstly, this condition confirms the requirement that there must be an upstream and (secondary) downstream market before there can be a possible abuse in relation to a refusal to grant access. However, this can still be satisfied where there is no separate marketing of one of them (as was the case in *Bronner*, for example). Indeed, the Court in *IMS Health* specifically stated that 'it is sufficient that a potential market or even hypothetical market can be identified'.[228] What is required is that they are interconnected, insofar as the upstream product is indispensable for the downstream one. The breadth of this leaves some doubts about the parameters of *IMS Health*. After all, the brick structure (which in effect became an industry standard) was only developed to provide the data reports for sale. In this sense the case is very different from both *Magill* and *Bronner* where the secondary markets were not central to the dominant firms.

The remaining condition identified, but not explored, by the Court was objective justification. Arguments made by dominant firms will tend to rely on the substantial investments (and risks) involved in securing their IPRs or in establishing their hold on what turns out to be an essential facility. At the very least, such arguments might support a sufficient period of protection from competition in order to obtain an adequate return on investment.[229] This view also chimes with that expressed by Advocate General Jacobs in *Bronner* about the need to preserve incentives for innovation.[230]

Issues of justification were at the heart of the appeal arising from the Commission's investigation of Microsoft. The point at issue of importance at this juncture[231] concerned

---

[227] *IMS Health*, above 203, para 38.

[228] Ibid, para 44.

[229] See *European Night Services*, above n 219.

[230] See also his Opinion in Case C-53/03 *Syfait v GlaxoSmithKline* [2005] ECR I-4609; the Court, however, declined to accept jurisdiction under Art 267 TFEU.

[231] The bundling aspects relating to the WMP were discussed above.

the ways in which Microsoft had restricted the interoperability between its Windows operating system and other work-group server operating systems. In its Decision, the Commission had emphasised that Microsoft had changed its practices in relation to the disclosure of interoperability information, ie the complete and accurate specifications for all the protocols implemented in Windows workpgroup server operating systems. In the early 1990s competitors (such as Novell) had established a distinct technological lead in relation to group networks that contained non-Microsoft work-group servers. Thus, according to the Commission, for that period Microsoft had an incentive to have its client PC operating system interoperate with non-Microsoft work-group server systems. However, once its own work-group server operating system had gained acceptance, holding back information relating to interoperability with the Windows environment began to make sense. Microsoft accordingly reduced the release of information pertaining to core tasks expected from work-group systems, especially in relation to the provision of group and user administration services.

The Court of First Instance emphasised the limited review of complex economic appraisals made by the Commission in the appeal process and that it would focus on whether the Commission had complied with procedural rules, that the facts had been accurately stated and if there had been a manifest error of assessment or misuse of powers by the Commission.[232] The Court of First Instance reiterated the existing case law and exceptional circumstances criteria set forth in *Magill*, and subsequent case law. In relation to the indispensability criterion, the Court noted that the ability of non-Microsoft work-group operating systems to 'participate in the Windows domain architecture . . . on an equal footing' was necessary to ensure their viability and attractiveness to consumers,[233] and the absence of interoperability would reinforce Microsoft's dominant position to the detriment of its competitors. This is clearly a watered-down formulation of indispensability as understood in *Oscar Bronner*.[234] The Court also widened the scope of the 'new product' requirement to embrace refusals which hampered technical development[235] in line with Article 102(d). In any event, as *IMS* demonstrated, there are difficulties in identifying what constitutes a 'new product' for these purposes. The Court also rejected the argument that the Commission had applied the wrong test (of a 'risk' of elimination of competition) in assessing whether the refusal had excluded all competition from the secondary market. The Court dismissed this argument as based on semantics and that Article 102 envisaged intervention by the Commission before the elimination of competition on the market had become a reality.[236] The Commission had rejected any objective justification on the grounds that the possible negative impact of an order to supply on Microsoft's incentives to innovate was outweighed by its positive impact on the level of innovation of the whole industry (including Microsoft) and this was supported by the Court.[237]

By way of conclusion to this section, the question might be posed as to whether the Microsoft saga is best discussed in terms of *IMS Health* and *Bronner* at all.[238] Part of the

---

[232] *Microsoft*, above n 4, para 87.
[233] Ibid, paras 389–90.
[234] See Andreangeli, above n 206.
[235] *Microsoft*, above n 4, para 647.
[236] Ibid, paras 519 and 561.
[237] cf S Vezzoso, 'The Incentives Balance Test in the EU Microsoft Case: A Pro-Innovation "Economics Based" Approach' [2006] *ECLR* 382.
[238] See J Killick, '*IMS* and *Microsoft* Judged in the Cold light of *IMS*' (2004) 1 *CompLR* 23, available at http://www.clasf.org/CompLRev/Issues/Vol1Issue2Article2.pdf.

nub of the Commission's objections stemmed from Microsoft changing its policy to one of not providing information. In other words, was this exclusionary conduct closer to the termination of existing supply as demonstrated in *Commercial Solvents*? It may be recalled that the Court itself used the latter case as the foundational analogy for its analysis in *Magill*. On the other hand, the approach adopted by the Commission and Court in *Microsoft* has been criticised as inappropriate in the context of software (and other highly technological) markets characterised by network effects and the emergence of de facto industry standards. These factors imply competition for the market as opposed to on the market and the need not to disincentivise innovation and development in such high-technology markets.[239] Although the *Microsoft* ruling has been widely criticised, it could be understood in the context of the aggressive attitude of a particular super-dominant company and its attempts to leverage that power into neighbouring markets.[240] However, the *Microsoft* case clarifies further that each case should be considered on its merits and although there are guidelines from the existing case law, they will be applied flexibly: for instance, the Magill 'new product requirement' can be viewed as a response to a particular situation involving unmet consumer demand.

In relation to refusal to supply and margin squeeze, the Commission's inevitable starting point in its Guidance on Enforcement priorities is that undertakings are free to choose their business partners and that obligations to supply may reduce incentives to invest and innovate. However, typically on 'downstream' markets, refusals to supply may be unlawful and an enforcement priority, even where the refused product has not already been traded[241] where:

— the refusal relates to a product or service that is objectively necessary to be able to compete effectively in a downstream market;
— the refusal is likely to lead to the elimination of effective competition in the downstream market; and
— the refusal is likely to lead to consumer harm.

The Commission position here is clearly influenced by the *Microsoft* case. Objective necessity appears to be a lower threshold than *Oscar Bronner* indispensability and as set out in the 2005 Discussion paper,[242] and although the Guidance refers to whether an input is indispensable, this would be satisfied where it could not effectively be duplicated. Further, in assessing consumer harm, the new product requirement is abandoned and consumer harm may arise where competitors are 'prevented from bringing innovative goods or services to the market and/or where follow-on innovation is likely to be stifled'.[243] The relaxation of these requirements would appear to make it easier for the Commission to establish an abuse than under the pre *Microsoft* line of case law.

---

[239] See eg Andreangeli, above n 198, 869; R Pardolesi and A Renda, 'The European Commission's Case against Microsoft: Kill Bill?' (2004) 27 *World Competition* 513.

[240] See Andreangeli, above n 198.

[241] *Guidance on the Commission's Enforcement Priorities in Applying Article 82*, above n 9, para 79.

[242] See Andreangeli, above n 206, 605–06.

[243] *Guidance on the Commission's Enforcement Priorities in Applying Article 82*, above n 9, again this is influenced by the CFI ruling in *Microsoft*. Note the critique of the Guidance by Andreangelini, ibid, particularly at 606–11, criticising the Commission for focusing on the short-term impact of refusals to supply, and that this would would jeopardise incentives to innovate (see 610–11).

VI – CONCLUDING REMARKS

The scope of Article 102 and its application to what many perceive as legitimate commercial practices is controversial and contested. The abuse doctrine has certainly been applied in a more interventionist way by the EU authorities, in contrast with its US Sherman Act section 2 monopolising trade counterpart. This partly reflects different views of market structures and market fairness in the European Union but there are moves towards convergence in the treatment of unilateral conduct, under the auspices of the International Competition Network,[244] and the Commission has reviewed its practice in this area. Many critics see reform as long overdue.[245] For example, the claims that abuses have hitherto been too much determined by legal pigeonholes rather than anti-competitive effects might justifiably point to demarcation lines that have emerged in case law between types of transaction rather than impact on the market. Similarly, the apparent new category of super-dominance[246] fuels criticism that the proliferation of legal conceptual layers obscures the proper issues: competition on merit and restraint on market power. Indeed, some critics have posed the question whether a 'dominance' test is required at all.[247]

The Competition Commissioner, launching the review, claimed that the eventual outcome was not meant to be a radical shift in enforcement policy.[248] However, the Commission did not issue Guidance on the application of Article 102 but merely 'Guidance on the Enforcement Priorities'. The key issue is the Commission-endorsed effects-based approach and the extent to which consumer harm must be an essential element of abusive conduct. This follows considerable critique in recent years of the Commission's approach to Article 102 as protecting competitors.[249] Nonetheless, Akman,[250] in the context of a wider debate about the role of Article 102 and the extent to which it has its foundations and adheres to the ordoliberal school of thought emphasising the economic freedom of market actors,[251] considers that the consumer welfare approach, based on direct harm to consumers, rather than competition and competitors, has 'not been undisputed or unchallenged'.[252] There is a legitimate debate as to whether the Guidance actually goes far enough to establish an effects-based approach.[253] It aims to establish enforcement priorities;[254] it is not intended to constitute a statement of the law and is without prejudice to the interpretation of Article

---

[244] Note speech by Joaquin Almunia, 'Converging Paths in Unilateral Conduct', ICN Unilateral Conduct Workshop, Brussels, 3 December 2010, Commission website.

[245] See B Sher, 'The Last of the Steam-Powered Trains: Modernizing Article 82' [2004] *ECLR* 243.

[246] Above n 194. The Commission stressed the 'extraordinary' market strength of Microsoft: above n 194, para 586.

[247] D Ridyard, 'The Agenda for Art 82 Reform—Eight Key Economic and Policy Issues' (2005 Autumn) *Lawyers' Europe* 10; also A Majumdar, 'Whither Dominance?' [2006] *ECLR* 161.

[248] Neelie Kroes, speech 23 September 2005, text on Commission website.

[249] See eg Sher, above n 245.

[250] See Akman, above n 106 (2010).

[251] See eg Eilmansberger, above n 6; H Schweitzer, 'The History, Interpretation and Underlying Principles of Section 2 Sherman Act and Article 82 EC' in CD Ehlermann and M Marquis (eds), *European Competition Annual 2007: A Reformed Approach to Article 82 EC* (Oxford, Hart Publishing, 2008) 119. See also Akman, above n 6, where she criticised the conventional view that Art 102 was influenced by and is a product of ordoliberal views by focusing on the *travaux préparatoires* of the EC Treaty competition rules, in order to justify a more economic efficiency-based approach.

[252] Akman, above n 106 (2010), 608.

[253] See Akman, above n 106 (2010). *cf* LL Gormsen 'Why the European Commission's Enforcement Priorities on Article 82 EC Should Be Withdrawn' [2010] *ECLR* 45.

[254] Akman, above n 106 (2010), 609–10.

102 by the Court of Justice or General Court. Moreover in general terms, given the purported focus on consumers, it is strange that the Guidance is silent on exploitative abuses, nor is actual proof of harm to consumers actually required.

There is clearly a tension between the soft law nature of the Guidance and the jurisprudence of the EU courts,[255] and although the Commission, as an administrative body responsible for the implementation of the competition rules, is justified in setting priorities, the relationship between the Guidance and existing case law may create problems in relation to legitimate expectations and legal certainty.[256] Although arguably incompatible with the case law of the EU Courts, Akman considers that 'The Guidance may actually provide the Court with the perfect opportunity to reconsider its jurisprudence in Article 102 TFEU.'[257] Nonetheless, it is arguable that in publishing the Guidance the Commission has satisfied critics by promulgating an effects-based approach without in effect proposing any radical change in the application of Article 102 to the range of specific abuses considered—*plus ca change!* In any event, in some recent decisions, the Courts have stressed that Article 102 prohibits conduct which harms consumers indirectly as well as directly.[258]

Further Reading

P Akman, 'Searching for the Long-Lost Soul of Art 82 EC' (2009) *Oxford Journal of Legal Studies* 267.

——, 'The European Commission's Guidance on Article 102TFEU: From Inferno to paradise?' (2010) 73 *MLR* 605.

A Andreangeli, 'Microsoft v Commission' (2008) 45 *CMLRev* 863.

——, 'Interoperability as an "Essential Facility" in the Microsoft Case—Encouraging Competition or Stifling Innovation?' (2009) 34 *ELR* 584

M Bergman, 'The Bronner Case—A Turning Point for the Essential Facilities Doctrine' [2000] *ECLR* 59.

T Eilmansberger, 'How to Distinguish Good from Bad Competition Under Article 82 EC: In Search of Clearer and More Coherent Standards for Anti-competitive Abuses' (2005) 42 *CMLRev* 129.

A Ezrachi (ed), *Article 82 EC: Reflections on its Recent Evolution* (Oxford, Hart Publishing, 2009).

MS Gal, 'Below-Cost Price Alignment: Meeting or Beating Competition? The France Telecom Case' [2007] *ECLR* 382.

M Kellerbauer, 'The Commission's New Enforcement Priorities in Applying Article 82 EC to Dominant Companies' Exclusionary Conduct: A Shift Towards a More Economic Approach?' [2010] *ECLR* 175.

L Lovdahl Gormsen, 'Why the European Commission's Enforcement Priorities on Article 82 EC Should Be Withdrawn' [2010] *ECLR* 45.

U Muller and A Rodenhausen, 'The Rise and Fall of the Essential facility Doctrine' [2008] *ECLR* 310.

B Ong, 'Building Brick Barricades and Other Barriers to Entry: Abusing a Dominant Position by Refusing to Licence Intellectual Property Rights' [2005] *ECLR* 213.

---

[255] See Akman, above n 106 (2010), 624–30; see HCH Hoffmann, 'Negotiated and Non-negotiated Administrative Rule-Making: The Example of EC competition Policy' (2006) 43 *CMLRev* 158.

[256] See Akman, above n 106 (2010); Witt, above n 120; Gormsen, above n 253.

[257] Akman, above n 106 (2010), 627. *cf* Gormsen, above n 253.

[258] *British Airways*, above n 42, para 106 and also Joined Cases C-501/06P, C-513-06 P, C-515-06 P and C-519/06 P *GlaxoSmithKline Services Unlimited v Commission* [2010] 4 CMLR 2, para 63.

D Ridyard , 'Exclusionary Pricing and Price Discrimination Abuses under Article 82—An Economic Analysis' [2002] *ECLR* 286.

O Odudu, 'British Airways v Commission' (2007) 44 *CMLRev* 1781.

S Vezzoso, 'The Incentives Balance Test in the EU Microsoft Case: A Pro-Innovation "Economics Based" Approach' [2006] *ECLR* 382.

A Witt, 'The Commission's Guidance Paper on Abusive Exclusionary Conduct—More Radical than It Appears?' (2010) 35 *ELRev* 214.

25

Enforcement of Articles 101 and 102

This chapter examines the enforcement of Articles 101 and 102 in the light of Regulation 1/2003, Guidance Notices, fundamental rights protection and the general norms of effectiveness developed by the case law of the European Courts. Discussion concentrates on four principal areas: the distribution of responsibilities between Commission, national courts and national competition authorities under the umbrella of the European Competition Network; the main stages of a Commission investigation, including information-gathering and inspections and the extent to which the Commission is required to observe the rights of the defence; the decision-making powers of the Commission, notably the power to fine infringing companies, taking into account its Guidelines on fines and its Leniency Notice; and, finally, the increasing emphasis being put upon private enforcement by competitors and other injured parties in the pursuit of civil remedies in national courts. The post-2004 enforcement regime, centred upon Regulation 1/2003, offers a much more decentralised model of EU competition law enforcement than previously. However, arguably of greater significance in practical terms to EU competition law enforcement, is the potential impact of the Charter of Fundamental Rights (CFR) and the impending accession of the EU to the European Convention on Human Rights (ECHR) on challenges to the Commission's investigation and decision-making processes, and this will be examined where appropriate throughout the chapter.

I – INTRODUCTION

The enforcement system for EU competition law underwent a major overhaul with the introduction of Regulation 1/2003[1] in May 2004. This ended the Commission's exclusive powers of granting exemptions under Article 101(3) and marked a significant shift in both the institutional distribution of enforcement powers and in the ethos and assumptions underpinning the effective application of Articles 101 and 102. In short, the new system is characterised by decentralisation and privatisation. National Competition Authorities (NCAs) became lynchpins in the enforcement system alongside the Commission. At the

---

[1] Council Regulation 1/2003, *On the Implementation of the Rules on Competition Laid Down in Articles 81 and 82 of the Treaty* [2003] OJ L1/1. More detailed rules for the conduct of proceedings by the Commission are set out in Commission Regulation 773/2004 [2004] OJ L123/18.

same time, the new arrangements assumed and sought to encourage a change in competition culture by anticipating a much greater willingness among competitors and consumers to resort to litigation in national courts to obtain remedies such as damages for breaches of EU competition rules. These changes can be seen as representing a closer alignment than previously between competition law enforcement and the 'usual' rules of effective protection of EU law rights through national processes and remedies. Nevertheless, the Commission remains at the apex of the EU competition law enforcement system, still retains considerable powers and, crucially, is enabled (in theory, at least) to focus its resources in pursuit of the most pernicious and significant cartels.[2]

This chapter does not purport to describe in detail every aspect of the procedures for the investigation and hearing of complaints, or the voluminous case law that has been generated by appeals alleging infringements by the Commission of the rights of the defence or errors in the gathering of evidence and calculations of fines. Instead, it first sets out the basic tenets for the functioning of the European Competition Network (ECN) and the distribution of enforcement powers between the relevant institutions, namely the Commission and the NCAs, with a view to signposting some of the potential tensions or difficulties. The chapter will then proceed on the assumption that the Commission will be the enforcement authority, and the core stages in an investigation will be identified, together with the protections available to undertakings, particularly in the light of fundamental principles derived from general EU law and in the context of the provisions of the Charter of Fundamental Rights (CFR) and the European Convention on Human Rights (ECHR). The chapter moves on to address the sanctions and remedies available to the Commission, highlighting the importance of the fining sanction available to the Commission, together with consideration of the Commission's updated policy of leniency to encourage cartel whistleblowers. Consideration will also be given to two more recent Commission enforcement developments: the use of binding commitments and the introduction of a settlement process, loosely akin to plea bargaining, to expedite and simplify the Commission's administrative enforcement process. Finally, the chapter considers the increasing significance of the availability of private enforcement, involving parties harmed by an alleged infringement seeking a private remedy (most likely, but not exclusively, for compensation in damages) through national courts, a possibility that the Commission is seeking to facilitate in order to enhance deterrence and, in particular, encourage consumer redress.

II – REGULATION 1/2003 AND EU COMPETITION LAW ENFORCEMENT

Regulation 1/2003 builds an enforcement regime around three key centres of authority: the Commission, the NCAs and national courts. We shall return to the role of the national courts later in this chapter. An important change from the Regulation 17/62 system is

---

[2] The ability to prioritise its work was one of the explicit rationales adopted by the Commission in 1999 when putting forward the precursor of change, its White Paper on Modernisation [1999] OJ C132/1. The reasoning is also included in Recital (3) of Regulation 1/2003, above n 1. See WJ Wils, 'Discretion and Prioritisation in Public Antitrust Enforcement' [2011] *World Competition* forthcoming.

that the notion of advance notification under Article 101 has disappeared, along with the Commission's exclusive power of exemption under Article 101(3). The exception contained in the latter provision may now be applied by any of the enforcement agencies. The most striking change is the sharing of enforcement powers between the Commission and the NCAs, with the Commission no longer effectively the sole enforcer of Articles 101 and 102, as under Regulation 17/62. The (ECN) was established between the Commission and the various NCAs of the Member States, with provision for the exchange of information between enforcement authorities. Under Article 11 of Regulation 1/2003, the Commission and the NCAs shall apply the EU competition rules 'in close co-operation', by forming a network of public authorities,[3] known as the ECN. The mechanisms for operating this network were fleshed out in a Commission Notice (the 'Network Notice'),[4] which describes the ECN as the 'basis for the creation and maintenance of a common competition culture in Europe'.[5] The Network Notice also stresses that the ECN 'should ensure both an efficient division of work and an effective and consistent application of [EU] competition rules'.[6]

A – The Commission's Powers

The Commission is able to act on a complaint or on its own initiative and may determine that an infringement of Articles 101 or 102 has occurred. It may by decision require the undertaking(s) concerned to bring such infringement to an end and for this purpose may impose any 'behavioural or structural remedies which are proportionate to the infringement committed and necessary to bring the infringement effectively to an end'.[7] The Commission is also able to accept commitments given by undertakings after a preliminary assessment by the Commission that it intends to adopt a decision requiring an infringement to be brought to an end. In such a case the Commission can by decision make those commitments binding on the undertaking.[8] Regulation 1/2003 also empowers the Commission to adopt, on its own initiative, a decision such that Articles 101 or 102 are not applicable to an agreement, decision or conduct.[9] However, this latter provision has not hitherto been exercised and any fears that it might tend towards old-style 'negative clearance' appear unfounded.[10] As under the pre-2004 system, the Commission retains the power to impose fines. These may not exceed 10 per cent of total turnover of the undertaking in the case of intentional or negligent infringements of Articles 101 and 102 or failure to comply with commitments.[11] In relation to the supply of incorrect or misleading information and similar defaults, the maximum for an intentional or negligent failure is 1 per cent of total turnover in the preceding business year.[12] The investigation and decision-making practice of the Commission, including consideration of its leniency policy and settlement process, will be considered in further detail later in the chapter.

---

[3] Recital (15).
[4] *Commission Notice on Co-operation within the Network of Competition Authorities* [2004] OJ C101/43 ('Network Notice').
[5] Ibid, para 1.
[6] Ibid, para 3.
[7] Art 7 of Regulation 1/2003.
[8] Art 9.
[9] Art 10.
[10] The Commission also retains its ability to adopt block exemptions.
[11] Art 23(2).
[12] Art 23(1).

B – The National Competition Authorities

Article 5 of Regulation 1/2003 confers on NCAs the power to apply Articles 101 and 102 of the Treaty in individual cases. Acting on their own initiative or on a complaint they may take the following decisions:

— requiring that an infringement be brought to an end;
— ordering interim measures;
— accepting commitments;
— imposing fines, periodic penalty payments or any other penalty provided for in their national law.

The principal procedural obligation of NCAs is that when acting under Articles 101 or 102 they must inform the Commission in writing before or without delay after commencing the first formal investigative measure. This information may also be made available to the competition authorities of the other Member States.[13] Similarly, not later than 30 days before adopting a decision about infringement, accepting commitments or withdrawing the benefit of a block exemption, an NCA must inform the Commission.[14] Again, this information may be made available to the NCAs of other Member States. There is a general power for NCAs to consult the Commission on any case involving the application of EU law.

C – The ECN in Operation

As stated above, the ECN[15] consists of the Commission and the NCAs. Although the need for a network is recognised in Regulation 1/2003 and its operation is detailed in the Network Notice, the ECN is in many ways a remarkably informal arrangement.[16] In particular, there is no specific tool or authority to determine case allocation between the different potential arms of enforcement. Instead, the Network Notice refers to 'principles of allocation'[17] which might result in an investigation either being undertaken by one NCA, or by several NCAs acting in parallel or by the Commission. The key criterion is the notion of which institution is 'well placed' to undertake an investigation. These are not formal rules of jurisdiction and in effect provide for the possibility of reallocation of a case after an investigation has been commenced by one or more authority.[18]

According to paragraph 8 of the Network Notice, an authority can be considered well placed if the following three cumulative conditions are met:[19]

---

[13] Art 11(3).
[14] Art 11(4).
[15] Note that the ECN is not to be confused with the ICN, discussed briefly in Chapter 22, above.
[16] See http://ec.europa.eu/competition/ecn/index_en.html for the ECN website, nested within the Commission's Competition site. See F Cengiz, 'Multi-level Governance in Competition Policy: The European Competition Network' (2010) 35 *ELRev* 660.
[17] 'Network Notice', above n 4, para 5.
[18] See further S Brammer, 'Concurrent Jurisdiction under Regulation 1/2003 and the Issue of Case Allocation' (2005) 42 *CMLRev* 1383; B Rodger, 'The ECN and Co-ordination of Public Enforcement of EU Law—Can Lessons Be Learned from International Private Law Jurisdiction Rules and Vice-Versa?' in J Basedow, S Franca and L Idot (eds), *International Antitrust Litigation. Conflict of Laws and Coordination* (Oxford, Hart Publishing, 2011).
[19] The Network Notice goes on to give illustrations of how these tests might apply: see paras 10–14.

— the agreement or practice has substantial direct or foreseeable effects on competition within its territory, is implemented within or originates from its territory;

— the authority is able effectively to bring to an end the entire infringement, ie it can adopt a cease-and-desist order, the effect of which will be sufficient to bring an end to the infringement, and it can, where appropriate, sanction the infringement adequately;

— it can gather, possibly with the assistance of other authorities, the evidence required to prove the infringement.

The Notice provides that the Commission will be 'particularly well placed' to deal with a case where

it is closely linked to other Community provisions which may be exclusively or more effectively applied by the Commission, if the Community interest requires the adoption of a Commission decision to develop Community competition policy when a new competition arises or to ensure effective enforcement.[20]

Where, however, the Commission itself initiates proceedings for the adoption of a decision, this shall relieve the competition authorities of the Member States of their competence to apply Articles 101 and 102.[21] If a competition authority is already acting on a case, the Commission shall only initiate proceedings after consulting with that NCA.[22]

Paragraph 7 of the Network Notice indicates a preference for a single, well-placed authority as often as possible. However, there is no final arbiter in the case of a number of NCAs being concerned and none willing to withdraw. Since each ECN member retains 'full discretion' in deciding whether to pursue a case, there could be parallel proceedings in up to three Member States.[23] It has been suggested[24] that there may be competition between NCAs in the light of differences in legal culture and traditions, expertise, experience, staffing and reputation. NCAs looking to build up and enhance experience and reputation may encourage parallel investigations at the expense of efficient case allocation.

The Commission and the NCAs have the power to provide one another with and use in evidence any matter of fact or of law, including confidential information.[25] There are restrictions as to use, so that the information exchanged can only be used for the purpose of applying Articles 101 or 102 and in respect of the subject-matter for which it was collected by the transmitting authority. Further limitations apply if the exchanged information is to be used to impose sanctions on natural persons. Here the law of both the transmitting and receiving ECN authority must foresee penalties of 'a similar kind' for infringements of the Treaty rules. Failing that, the information must have been collected in such a way as to respect the same level of protection of the rights of the defence of natural persons as provided for under the rules of the receiving authority.[26] Although

---

[20] Ibid, para 15.

[21] Art 11(6) of Regulation 1/2003. See Case T-339/04 *France Telecom SA v Commission* [2007] ECR II-521, [2008] 5 CMLR 6, paras 77–91 regarding the system for allocating competences under Regulation 1, and the leading role for the Commission in the investigation of infringements, in particular under Art 11(6).

[22] Ibid.

[23] Where more than three Member States are affected the expectation must be that the Commission takes action since Art 14 of the Network Notice identifies it as 'best placed' in this scenario.

[24] Brammer, above n 18, 1404.

[25] Art 12(1) of Regulation 1/2003.

[26] Art 12(3).

there was concern expressed that the exchange arrangements may prove detrimental to undertakings and other parties, especially in relation to confidentiality,[27] the Commission Report on the functioning of Regulation 1/2003, published in April 2009,[28] suggested that to date the provisions for co-operation and work-sharing have been successful, and there have been no reported case allocation conflicts to date.[29] Furthermore, the Regulation appears to have been successful in terms of its central premise that more cases should be dealt with at the national level.[30] Nonetheless, the allocation (or reallocation) of competence to deal with a case may have significant importance in terms of the outcome of the case. When applying Articles 101 or 102, the NCA must rely upon the powers granted to it by domestic law as neither Regulation 1/2003 nor the Network Notice sought to harmonise domestic rules on enforcement procedures and powers of the various NCAs. At one stage there was a possibility that a future Modernisation II package, involving some form of harmonisation of national NCA powers, procedures and remedies in cases of EU competition law infringements, would be proposed. The Commission Report and Staff Working Paper recognised the potential problem of divergent procedures and sanctions;[31] and accordingly, the 'selection' of an NCA to deal with a case will have important repercussions on the legal processes involved and the types and range of sanctions likely to be imposed—resulting in divergent outcomes depending on which NCA is 'allocated' jurisdiction. As yet there have been no proposals to harmonise procedures, powers and sanctions for all NCAs enforcing EU competition law, but the ability to exchange information and engage in dialogue within the ECN has already facilitated a certain degree of convergence,[32] particularly in relation to leniency: all Member States (with the exception of Malta) now have some form of leniency programme, and the ECN has developed a Model Leniency Programme,[33] discussed later in this chapter.

III – THE CONDUCT OF PROCEEDINGS BY THE COMMISSION

Investigations are carried out within the legislative framework provided by Regulation 1/2003 and Regulation 773/2004,[34] together with the detailed guidance set out in the Commission's Notices.[35] Of course, the general principles of EU law developed by the

---

[27] eg D Reichelt, 'To What Extent Does the Co-operation within the European Competition Network Protect the Rights of Undertakings?' (2005) 42 *CMLRev* 745.

[28] Commission, 'Communication from the Commission to the European Parliament and the Council: Report on the functioning of Regulation 1/2003' COM (2009) 206 final.

[29] Ibid, paras 29–31. There have been unsubstantiated accounts of conflict at the Commission/NCA level regarding case allocation.

[30] This is borne out by the statistics published on the Commission's website at http://ec.europa.eu/competition/ecn/statistics.html.

[31] Commission Communication, above n 28, paras 36–38.

[32] See in particular the ECN Working Group on Cooperation Issues, Questionnaire Results in relation to Member State national laws as at April 2008, available at http://ec.europa.eu/competition/ecn/ecn_convergencequest_April2008.pdf.

[33] The ECN model leniency programme, available at http://ec.europa.eu/competition/ecn/model_leniency_en.pdf and see report on assessment of the state of convergence at http://ec.europa.eu/competition/ecn/model_leniency_programme.pdf.

[34] Above n 1.

[35] See especially the *Notice on the Handling of Complaints by the Commission under Articles 81 and 82* [2004] OJ C101/5.

Court of Justice and Court of First Instance also need to be taken into account and followed by the Commission. The discussion below broadly divides an investigation into two stages: first, the gathering of information and evidence, where the Commission has a range of weapons available to combat reluctant undertakings; and secondly, the rights of the defence once the Commission has moved to a formal statement of objections. It should be stressed that a significant proportion of the case law before the European Courts in recent years has concerned a range of challenges to the Commission's investigation, decision-making and sanctioning powers based on the rights of the defence[36] and concerns related to, inter alia, fairness, due process, equal treatment and the *non bis in idem* principle. These will be examined in the following sections where relevant and appropriate. More generally, there has been considerable debate and commentary on the extent to which specific aspects of the Commission's investigative processes meet the standards required under the ECHR according to the interpretation of its provisions by the ECtHR— the European Courts have to date emphasised that in applying EU law, the ECHR is not binding but a source of inspiration in the determination of the right to a fair trial.[37] This shall be examined subsequently together with the implications for EU competition law enforcement of the adoption of the CFR and the imminent accession of the European Union to the ECHR.[38]

A – Information and Evidence

The Commission is enabled to seek information and establish evidence in a variety of ways. Its powers under Articles 18–21 of Regulation 1/2003 broadly correspond to, but go further than, its former position under Regulation 17/62.

(i) Requests for Information and Power to Take Statements

By virtue of Article 18, the Commission may, by simple request or by decision, require undertakings and associations to provide all 'necessary' information. This is now a choice for the Commission and not, as was previously the case, a two-stage procedure. A failure to respond to a simple request will not lead to a penalty, although supplying false or misleading information will.[39] If, however, the request is by decision, then penalties may be imposed for non-compliance.[40] The Commission must forward copies of any request to the NCA of the Member State in whose territory the seat of the undertaking is located and the NCA of the Member State whose territory is affected.[41] At the request of the Commission, governments of the Member States and NCAs shall provide the Commission with all necessary information to carry out its duties under the Regulation.[42]

Case law from the similar provisions of the previous regime of Regulation 17/62 has

---

[36] See eg Case C-322/07 P *Papierfabrik August Koehler AG v Commission* [2009] ECR I-7191; [2009] 5 CMLR 20, para 34.

[37] See eg ibid, para 143.

[38] See WJ Wils, 'EU Antitrust Enforcement Powers and Procedural rights and Guarantees: The Interplay between EU law, national law, the Charter of Fundamental Rights of the EU and the European convention on Human Rights' [2011] *World Competition* forthcoming. See also W Weiß, 'Human Rights and EU Antitrust Enforcement: News from Lisbon' [2011] *ECLR* 186.

[39] Art 18(2) of Regulation 1/2003.

[40] Art 18(3).

[41] Art 18(5).

[42] Art 18(6).

been influential in shaping the current position under Regulation 1/2003. For example, the information to be supplied must not be disproportionate to the requirements of the investigation.[43] More fundamentally, in *Orkem*[44] the undertaking claimed that it had been forced into giving answers of a self-incriminating nature pursuant to an order under Regulation 17. The Court of Justice, whilst apparently denying the existence of any rule against self-incrimination as such in EU law, nevertheless held that the Commission could not compel an undertaking 'to provide it with answers which might involve an admission on its part of the existence of an infringement which it is incumbent upon the Commission to prove'.[45] The Court of First Instance in a later ruling indicated that the acknowledgement of any absolute right to silence would constitute an unjustified hindrance to the Commission's performance of its duty to ensure that the rules on competition within the common market are observed.[46] This case law seems to be captured by Recital 23 of Regulation 1/2003, which provides:

> When complying with a decision of the Commission, undertakings cannot be forced to admit that they have committed an infringement, but they are in any event obliged to answer factual questions and to provide documents, even if this information may be used to establish against them or against another undertaking the existence of an infringement.

However, the Court's position in *Orkem* has been criticised on the basis that it is incompatibile with Article 6 ECHR and the right to silence as part of a fair trial.[47] Nevertheless, the Court, whilst acknowledging developments in the jurisprudence of the ECtHR, has not seen the need to reverse its own case law.[48] This stance was defended by Advocate General Geelhoed,[49] arguing that subsequent ECtHR rulings offered no cogent reasons to change the *Orkem* position:

> First, it must be borne in mind that that case law concerned natural persons in the context of `classical' criminal procedures. Competition law concerns undertakings. The Commission is only allowed to impose fines on undertakings and associations of undertakings for violations of Articles 81 EC and 82 EC. It is not possible simply to transpose the findings of the [European Court of Human Rights] without more to legal persons or undertakings . . .
>
> Second, there is no dispute that the [European Court of Human Rights] extended certain rights and freedoms to companies and other corporate entities. The same is true under Community law and under the Charter of Fundamental Rights of the European Union. That being said, the [European Court of Human Rights] also makes a distinction between the level of protection

---

[43] Case T-39/90 *Samenwerkende Electriciteits-produktiebedrijven (SEP) v Commission* [1991] ECR II-1497; [1992] 5 CMLR 33.

[44] Case 374/87 *Orkem v Commission* [1989] ECR 3283; [1991] 4 CMLR 502.

[45] Ibid, [1989] ECR 3283, para 35. See also Case 27/88 *Solvay v Commission* [1989] ECR 3255 (summary publication).

[46] Case T-112/98 *Mannesmannröhren-Werke AG v Commission* [2001] ECR II-729, para 66.

[47] See eg KPE Lasok, 'The Privilege Against Self-incrimination in Competition Cases' [1990] *ECLR* 90; WBJ Van Overbeek, 'The Right to Remain Silent in Competition Investigations: The *Funke* Decision of the Court of Human Rights Makes Revision of the ECJ's Case Law Necessary' [1994] *ECLR* 127; A Riley, 'Saunders and the Power to Obtain Information in Community and United Kingdom Competition Law' [2000] *ECLR* 264; A Riley, 'The ECHR Implications of the Investigation Provisions of the Draft Competition Regulation' (2002) 51 *ICLQ* 55; WJ Wils, 'Self-incrimination in EC Antitrust Enforcement: A Legal and Economic Analysis' (2003) 26 *World Competition* 567; A MacCulloch, 'The Privilege against Self-incrimination in Competition Investigations: Theoretical Foundations and Practical Implications' (2006) 26 *Legal Studies* 211.

[48] Joined Cases C-238/99P, C-244/99P, C-245/99P, C-247/99P, C-250/99P to C-252/99P and C-254/99P, *PVC Cartel II* [2002] ECR I-8375.

[49] Case C-301/04P *Commission v SGL Carbon*, [2006] ECR I-5915; [2006] 5 CMLR 15.

conferred on natural persons on the one hand and legal persons on the other. That may be inferred from other fundamental rights in the Convention, such as Article 8. . . .

Third, what is decisive, however, so far as Article 6 of the Convention is concerned, is that a request for documents is not contrary to the right to remain silent. The [European Court of Human Rights] did not recognise an absolute right to remain silent. It held in *Saunders* that '[t]he right not to incriminate oneself is primarily concerned, however, with respecting the will of an accused person to remain silent. As commonly understood in the legal systems of the Contracting Parties the Convention and elsewhere, it does not extend to the use in criminal proceedings of material which may be obtained from the accused through the use of compulsory powers but which has an existence independent of the will of the suspect such as, *inter alia*, *documents* acquired pursuant to a warrant, breath, blood and urine samples and bodily tissues for the purpose of DNA testing.' That finding has been recently confirmed in *JB v Switzerland*.

Thus, the right not to make self-incriminating statements does not extend to information which exists independently of the will of the suspect such as, *inter alia*, documents. The production of those documents may be requested and they may be used as evidence. In that regard, I would refer in particular to documented information relating to and used in the internal processing and decision making of an undertaking, such as, for example, marketing or pricing strategies. Such information, available for internal use, may be requested. Possibly, it may reveal the likelihood of a cartel or concerted practice, but that as such is not self-incriminating. It is still possible to rebut that likelihood. To go further would be to take away the objective element of the Courts' case law, which would disturb the balance of enforcement.[50]

The Advocate General's robust endorsement of the existing case law, subsequently endorsed by the Court of Justice,[51] insists that the balance between effective enforcement of competition law and the rights of the defence is currently correctly drawn.

A new power introduced by Article 19 of Regulation 1/2003, and elaborated upon in Article 3 of Regulation 773/2004, allows the Commission to take statements from persons who give their consent to interview for the purpose of collecting information relating to the subject-matter of an investigation. The interview may be conducted by any means, including telephone or electronic, it may be recorded in any form and a copy made available to the person interviewed for approval.[52] This kind of consensual interview will most likely apply to competitors or customers giving information about cartels or abuses.

(ii) Inspections

The power to inspect premises has always been the most invasive of the Commission's weapons, giving rise to the notorious, but temporally misleading, epithet of the 'dawn raid'. Article 20 of Regulation 1/2003 authorises Commission officials to conduct all necessary inspections of undertakings and associations of undertakings. In particular,[53] they may enter any premises, land and means of transport of the undertaking, examine books and other records irrespective of the medium in which they are stored, take copies, seal any premises or records, and ask any representative or member of staff of the undertaking for explanations. Undertakings are required to submit to inspection ordered by decision of

---

[50] Ibid, paras 63–66.
[51] Ibid, particularly para 44.
[52] Art 3(2) and (3) of Regulation 773/2004.
[53] Art 20(2) of Regulation 1/2003. See also See DG Competition Best Practices on the Conduct of proceedings concerning Articles 101 and 102 TFEU, available at http://ec.europa.eu/competition/consultations/2010_best_practices/best_practice_articles.pdf.

the Commission.[54] Where an undertaking opposes an inspection, the Member State concerned must provide the Commission officials with necessary assistance, including the assistance of the police or equivalent authority.[55]

If such assistance requires authorisation from a judicial authority according to national rules, that authorisation shall be applied for. According to Article 20(8), that national judicial authority

> shall control that the Commission decision is authentic and that the coercive measures envisaged are neither arbitrary nor excessive having regard to the subject-matter of the inspection. In its control of the proportionality of the coercive measures, the national judicial authority may ask the Commission, directly or through the Member State competition authority, for detailed explanations in particular on the grounds the Commission has for suspecting infringement of Articles 81 and 82 of the Treaty, as well as on the seriousness of the suspected infringement and on the nature of the involvement of the undertaking concerned. However, the national authority may not call into question the necessity for the inspection nor demand that it be provided with the information in the Commission's file. The lawfulness of the Commission decision shall be subject to review only by the Court of Justice.

Authorisation from the national judicial authority must be sought if the Commission wishes to inspect *other* premises, land or means of transport on the basis of a reasonable suspicion that books or other records may be kept there which may be relevant to prove a serious violation of Articles 101 or 102. This extends to the homes of directors, managers and other members of staff, but with additional conditions.[56]

Not surprisingly, inspections conducted by the Commission have provoked defences based on fundamental rights protection, in particular by reference to the impact of the ECHR. At an early stage in the case law, the Court of Justice held[57] that the unannounced nature of a dawn raid of business premises under Regulation 17/62 did not infringe Article 8(1) of the ECHR relating to the protection of private and family life, home and correspondence. This was developed further in *Hoechst*,[58] where the Court explicitly stated that the protective scope of Article 8(1) ECHR was concerned with the development of man's personal freedom and could not be extended to business premises.[59] However, *Hoechst* was decided at a time when there was no direct interpretation on this issue by the ECtHR. Its subsequent ruling in *Niemitz*[60] determined that Article 8(1) included certain professional or business activities or premises since self-employed persons could engage in business activities at home and private activities at their place of work.

Despite *Niemitz* and other ECtHR rulings,[61] the Court of First Instance stated in *PVC Cartel II*,[62] for example, that those developments did not directly affect the solutions adopted in *Hoechst*. The issue was raised again in *Roquette Frères*,[63] a request for a preliminary ruling made by a French court in relation to the authorisation of assistance by

---

[54] Art 20(3) of Regulation 1/2003.
[55] Art 20(6).
[56] Art 21. This provision did not exist under the old regime of Regulation 17/62.
[57] Case 136/79 *National Panasonic v Commission* [1980] ECR 2033; [1980] CMLR 169.
[58] Joined Cases 46/87 and 227/88 *Hoechst v Commission* [1989] ECR 2859; [1991] 4 CMLR 410.
[59] Ibid, para 18.
[60] *Niemitz v Germany*, Series A, No 251-B, (1993) 16 EHRR 97, para 31.
[61] *Funke v France*, Series A, No.256-A, (1993) 16 EHRR 297.
[62] Joined Cases T-305-307, 313-316, 318, 325, 328-329 and 335/94 *Limburgse Vinyl Maatschappij v Commission* [1999] ECR II-931; [1999] 5 CMLR 303.
[63] Case C-94/00 *Roquettes Frères SA v Directeur général de la concurrence, de la consommation et de la répression des fraudes* [2002] ECR I-9011; [2003] 5 CMLR 53.

national authorities for an inspection. Advocate General Mischo carefully analysed the *Niemitz* reasoning and understood it to accept that the professional sphere does not nec-essarily, or, in every respect, deserve protection as extensive as that enjoyed by the private sphere.[64] In his view, inspections properly made pursuant to the competition rules of the Treaty and its own protections were therefore subject to safeguards equivalent to those inferred by the ECtHR from Article 8 ECHR. The Court of Justice dealt with the matter by recalling its own *Hoechst* ruling, which had established that:

> the need for protection against arbitrary or disproportionate intervention by public authorities in the sphere of the private activities of any person, whether natural or legal, constitutes a general principle of Community law. . . .
>
> For the purposes of determining the scope of that principle in relation to the protection of business premises, regard must be had to the case law of the European Court of Human Rights subsequent to the judgment in *Hoechst*. According to that case law, first, the protection of the home provided for in Article 8 of the ECHR may in certain circumstances be extended to cover such premises (see, in particular, the judgment of April 16, 2002 in *Colas Est and Others v France*) and, second, the right of interference established by Article 8(2) of the ECHR might well be more far-reaching where professional or business activities or premises were involved than would otherwise be the case (*Niemietz v Germany*).[65]

The attempt at reconciliation of the ECHR and EU competition law positions indicates that Article 8 ECHR considerations are relevant in assessing whether the Commission is entitled to exercise its power to make dawn raids seeking evidence for breach of EU com-petition law.[66] Article 21 of Regulation 1/2003 provides for additional procedural hurdles beyond 'normal' inspections in relation to the exercise of inspections at private premises, in particular the requirement of authorisation from the national judicial authority for the execution of the Commission's decision. The national court's control role includes consid-eration of the seriousness of the suspected infringement, the importance of the evidence sought, the involvement of the undertaking concerned and the reasonable likelihood that business records relating to the subject-matter of the inspection are kept in the premises for which authorisation is requested.[67]

(iii) Professional Privilege

A final concern in gathering information is that the Commission may be denied access to documents protected by professional privilege, the principle of the confidentiality of communications between lawyer and client. This principle was recognised by the Court of Justice in the *AM&S* case.[68] Protection of confidentiality was held to be subject, in effect, to three conditions. First, the communication must be 'made for the purposes and

---

[64] Ibid, Opinion, para 38.
[65] Ibid, paras 27 and 29.
[66] See also Case C-450/06 *Varec SA v Belgium* [2008] ECR I-581 at para 48:

> 48. . . . It follows from the case-law of the European Court of Human Rights that the notion of 'pri-vate life' cannot be taken to mean that the professional or commercial activities of either natural or legal persons are excluded (see *Niemietz v Germany*, judgment of 16 December 1992, Series A no 251-B, §29; *Société Colas Est and Others v France*, no 37971/97, §41, ECHR 2002-III; and also *Peck v The United Kingdom* no 44647/98, §57, ECHR 2003-I). Those activities can include participation in a contract award procedure.

[67] Art 21(3) of Regulation 1/2003.
[68] Case 155/79 *AM & S v Commission* [1982] ECR 1575; [1982] 2 CMLR 264.

in the interests of the client's rights of defence'. That extended, in particular, to 'all written communications exchanged after the initiation of the administrative procedure under Regulation 17 [as it was] which may lead to a decision on the application of [Articles 101 and 102] or to a decision imposing a pecuniary sanction on the undertaking',[69] as well as to 'earlier written communications which have a relationship to the subject-matter of that procedure'.[70] Secondly, the communication must 'emanate from independent lawyers, that is to say, lawyers who are not bound to the client by a relationship of employment'.[71] Thirdly, the lawyers in question must be entitled to practise their profession in one of the Member States. There are therefore two classes of lawyers communications with whom are outside the privilege: in-house lawyers, even in those Member States where they are subject to professional ethics and discipline; and lawyers from non-EU countries in the absence of any reciprocal arrangements with the EU.

The *AM&S* rule has been heavily criticised, particularly in the context of the advent of the 2004 changes to the enforcement system.[72] In *Akzo Nobel Chemicals v Commission*[73] the Court of Justice supported the General Court's refusal to extend the scope of legal professional privilege to cover documents emanating from in-house lawyers registered at the national Bar and subject to that Bar's disciplinary regime:

> 47 . . . [A]n in-house lawyer cannot, whatever guarantees he has in the exercise of his profession, be treated in the same way as an external lawyer, because he occupies the position of an employee which, by its very nature, does not allow him to ignore the commercial strategies pursued by his employer, and thereby affects his ability to exercise professional independence.

> 48 It must be added that, under the terms of his contract of employment, an in-house lawyer may be required to carry out other tasks, namely, as in the present case, the task of competition law coordinator, which may have an effect on the commercial policy of the undertaking. Such functions cannot but reinforce the close ties between the lawyer and his employer.

> 49 It follows, both from the in-house lawyer's economic dependence and the close ties with his employer, that he does not enjoy a level of professional independence comparable to that of an external lawyer.

> 50 Therefore, the General Court correctly applied the second condition for legal professional privilege laid down in the judgment in *AM & S Europe v Commission*.[74]

B – The Right to a Hearing

Before it adopts a decision applying Articles 101 or 102 the Commission is required, pursuant to Article 27 of Regulation 1/2003, to give the undertakings concerned the opportunity of being heard on the matters to which the Commission has taken objection. The exercise of the right to be heard is set out in more detail in Regulation 773/2004 on the conduct of proceedings.[75] These provisions implement in the sphere of competition

---

[69] Ibid, [1982] ECR 1575, 1611.

[70] Ibid.

[71] Ibid.

[72] See representations made on the White Paper on Modernisation, above n 1. See also M Frese, 'The Development of General Principles for EU Competition Law Enforcement—The Protection of Legal Privilege' [2001] *ECLR* 196.

[73] Case C-550/07 P *Akzo Nobel Chemicals Ltd v Commission* 14 September [2010] ECR I, nyr.

[74] Ibid, paras 47–50. Note, following *AKZO*, the 'sealed envelope' procedure for the Commission to take documents allegedly covered by the principle of professional privilege.

[75] Above n 1.

the general principle of law that a person whose interests are liable to be adversely affected by an individual decision of a public authority has a right to make his views known to the authority before the decision is taken.[76] The key stages, and the issues about protection which they raise, are briefly discussed below. The Court has repeatedly stressed the general principle of EU law that everyone is entitled to a fair legal process, a principle inspired by the common constitutional principles of the Member States and by the ECHR.[77]

(i) The Statement of Objections and the Hearing Officer

In order for a person effectively to exercise his right to a hearing, he must be informed of the facts and considerations on the basis of which the responsible authority is minded to act.[78] Article 10(1) of Regulation 773/2004 places the Commission under a duty to inform the parties in writing of the objections raised against them. The issuing of a 'statement of objections' marks the formal initiation of proceedings that may culminate in a finding that Articles 81 or 82 have been infringed. Article 27 of Regulation 1/2003 provides that the Commission can only base its decisions on objections on which the parties concerned have been able to comment.[79]

The statement of objections thus provides the boundaries of the case and it is a core aspect in ensuring the right to a fair hearing.[80] The Court of Justice has repeatedly affirmed that it must set forth clearly all the essential facts upon which the Commission relies against the respondent undertakings.[81] A fairly succinct summary may be judged adequate for this purpose,[82] although the Commission must identify in the objections each of the infringements which it alleges to have occurred.[83] The final decision need not be an exact replica of the statement of objections, since the Commission must take into account factors which emerge during the administrative proceedings: some objections may be abandoned altogether, and different arguments may be put forward in support of

[76] See eg Case C-511/06 P *Archer Daniels Midland Co v Commission* [2009] ECR I-5843; [2009] 5 CMLR 15, paras 85 and 88.

[77] See eg Case C-411/04 P *Salzgitter Mannesmann GmbH (formerly Mannesmannrohren-Werke AG) v Commission* [2007] ECR I-959; [2007] 4 CMLR 17, paras 40–41. See also Case C-185/95 P *Baustahlgewebe v Commission* [1998] ECR I-8417; [1999] 4 CMLR 1203, para 21; Case C 174 and 189 P *Netherlands Van der Wal v Commission* [2000] ECR I-1; [2002] 1 CMLR 16, para 17; and Case C-341/04 *Eurofood IFSC* [2006] ECR I-3813, para 65.

[78] Case 17/74 *Transocean Marine Paint v Commission*, [1974] ECR 1063; [1974] 2 CMLR 459.

[79] The undertakings may waive their right to a hearing: Joined Cases T-213/95 and 18/96 *SCK and FNK v Commission* [1997] ECR II-1739; [1998] 4 CMLR 259. However, this must be unambiguously done if the Commission is to be able to omit the communication of documents: Case T-30/91 *Solvay v Commission* [1995] ECR II-1775, para 57; [1996] 5 CMLR 57.

[80] See eg Case C-322/07 P *Papierfabrik August Koehler AG v Commission* [2009] ECR I-7191; [2009] 5 CMLR 20; Case C-511/06 P *Archer Daniels Midland Co v Commission* [2009] ECR I-5843; [2009] 5 CMLR 15 at paras 86–87.

[81] See eg Case 45/69 *Boehringer v Commission* [1970] ECR 769; Case 85/76 *Hoffmann-La Roche v Commission* [1979] ECR 461; [1979] 3 CMLR 211; Joined Cases 43 and 63/82 *VBVB and VBBB v Commission* [1984] ECR 19; [1985] 1 CMLR 27.

[82] Case 48/69 *ICI v Commission* [1972] ECR 619, 650-651; [1972] CMLR 557; Joined Cases 100-103/80 *Musique Diffusion Française v Commission* [1983] ECR 1825; [1983] 3 CMLR 221.

[83] Joined Cases C-89/85 etc *Ahlström Oy v Commission* ('*Wood Pulp*') [1993] ECR I-1307; [1993] 4 CMLR 407. Furthermore, the rights of the defence are not satisfied where crucial documents are merely annexed to the Statement of Objections: see Case C-511/06 P *Archer Daniels Midland Co v Commission* [2009] ECR I-5843; [2009] 5 CMLR 15, paras 89 and 93.

those which are maintained.[84] Where, however, the Commission wishes to introduce fresh objections, a supplementary statement should be sent to the respondents.[85]

Once the statement of objections has been issued, the parties have a right of access to the Commission's file. The Commission must give the addressees of the statement of objections the opportunity to develop their arguments at an oral hearing, if they so request.[86] Hearings are conducted by a Hearing Officer 'in full independence'.[87] The principal task of the Hearing Officer is to ensure that the effective exercise of the right to be heard is respected in competition proceedings before the Commission. Hearing Officers report to the Competition Commissioner but are not part of the Competition Directorate. The Hearing Officer may allow the parties to whom the statement of objections has been addressed, the complainants, other persons invited to the hearing, the Commission services and NCAs to ask questions during the hearing.[88] The right to a fair legal process requires a hearing to take place within a reasonable period of time.[89]

(ii) Access to the File

One of the most frequently contested aspects of the rights of defence in competition cases down the years has concerned access to the Commission's file. The evolution of principle in this area again displays the tensions between efficient and effective enforcement on the one hand, and fundamental rights and due process on the other. Establishing clear rules is not made any easier by the confidential and commercially sensitive nature of many documents in competition cases. According to Article 27(2) of Regulation 1/2003:

> The rights of defence of the parties concerned shall be fully respected in the proceedings. They shall be entitled to have access to the Commission's file, subject to the legitimate interest of undertakings in the protection of their business secrets. The right of access to the file shall not extend to confidential information and internal documents of the Commission or the competition authorities of the Member States.

These requirements are developed in Articles 15 and 16 of Regulation 773/2004 and largely reflect the significant contributions of the case law in formulating the content of the rights of the defence.

Thus, for example, the Court of First Instance had held in *Hercules*[90] that the Commission

---

[84] Joined Cases 209-215 and 218/78 *Van Landewyck v Commission* [1980] ECR 3125; [1981] 3 CMLR 134, paras 68–70. See also Joined Cases T-305-307, 313-316, 318, 325, 328–29 and 335/94 *Re the PVC Cartel II: Limburgse Vinyl Maatschappij v Commission* [1999] ECR II-931; [1999] 5 CMLR 303. Moreover, the Commission is not required to indicate the level of contemplated fines in the Statement of Objections: see Case C-511/06 P *Archer Daniels Midland Co v Commission* [2009] ECR I-5843; [2009] 5 CMLR 15, para 69

[85] Case 54/69 *Francolor v Commission* [1972] ECR 851; [1972] CMLR 557.

[86] Art 12 of Regulation 773/2004.

[87] Art 14. For the terms of reference for Hearing Officers, see Commission Decision 2001/462, [2001] OJ L162/21.

[88] Art 14(8) of Regulation 773/2004.

[89] Case C-322/07 P *Papierfabrik August Koehler AG v Commission* [2009] ECR I-7191; [2009] 5 CMLR 20, paras 143–45; Note that a longer period may be justified by the complexity of the proceedings: ibid, paras 147–49. The burden of proof rests with the undertaking to demonstrate that it experienced difficulties in defending itself as a result of the excessive duration of the procedure: see Case T-405/06, *ArcelorMittal Luxembourg SA v Commission* [2009] ECR II-771; [2010] 4 CMLR 6. See also Case T-276/04 *Compagnie Maritime Belge SA v Commission* [2008] ECR II-1277, [2009] 4 CMLR 21, para 39. The limitation period of five years for the imposition of sanctions (and the possibility of suspension of that period), set out in Regulation 2988/74, was also considered in that case and in Case T-410/03 *Hoechst GmbH v Commission* [2008] ECR II-881; [2008] 5 CMLR 12.

[90] Case T-7/89 *Hercules Chemicals v Commission* [1991] ECR II-1711; [1992] 4 CMLR 84, para 53, relying on Case 81/72 *Commission v Council* [1973] ECR 575; [1973] CMLR 639.

was not able to depart from the standards it had voluntarily set for itself in its Twelfth Report on Competition Policy. As a result, the Commission was obliged to make available to the undertakings involved in proceedings under Article 101(1) all documents, whether in their favour or otherwise,[91] which it had obtained during the course of the investigation, save where the business secrets of other undertakings, the internal documents of the Commission or other confidential information were involved.[92]

The Court of Justice has always refrained from holding the right of access to the file to be absolute. Instead, it has concentrated on the need for effective defence. It has summarised its case law as follows:[93]

> A corollary of the principle of respect for the rights of the defence, the right of access to the file means that the Commission must give the undertaking concerned the opportunity to examine all the documents in the investigation file which may be relevant for its defence. . . . Those documents include both incriminating evidence and exculpatory evidence, save where the business secrets of other undertakings, the internal documents of the Commission or other confidential information are involved . . .
>
> It may be that the undertaking draws the Commission's attention to documents capable of providing a different economic explanation for the overall economic assessment carried out by the Commission, in particular those describing the relevant market and the importance and the conduct of the undertakings acting on that market.
>
> The European Court of Human Rights has none the less held that, just like observance of the other procedural safeguards enshrined in Article 6(1) of the ECHR, compliance with the adversarial principle relates only to judicial proceedings before a tribunal and that there is no general, abstract principle that the parties must in all instances have the opportunity to attend the interviews carried out or to receive copies of all the documents taken into account in the case of other persons.
>
> The failure to communicate a document constitutes a breach of the rights of the defence only if the undertaking concerned shows, first, that the Commission relied on that document to support its objection concerning the existence of an infringement and, second, that the objection could be proved only by reference to that document.[94]

C – Final Decision

The Commission has a number of powers at its disposal once it has concluded that there has been an infringement of Articles 101 or 102, and we shall consider the fines which may be imposed further below.[95] Article 7 of Regulation 1/2003 provides that the Commission may by decision order an infringement to be brought to an end. Termination may involve

---

[91] See also Case T-410/03 *Hoechst GmbH v Commission* [2008] ECR II-881; [2008] 5 CMLR 12, regarding the right to examine exculpatory evidence.

[92] *Hercules Chemicals*, above n 90, [1991] ECR II-1711, at para 54.

[93] Joined Cases C-204/00 P, C-205/00 P, C-211/00 P, C-213/00 P, C-217/00 P and C-219/00 P *Aalborg Portland A/S v Commission* [2004] ECR I-123.

[94] Ibid, paras 68–71(citations omitted). See also Case C-411/04 P *Salzgitter Mannesmann GmbH (formerly Mannesmannrohren-Werke AG) v Commission* [2007] ECR I-959; [2007] 4 CMLR 17.

[95] Note the limitation period of five years for the imposition of sanctions (and the possibility of suspension of that period), set out in Regulation 2988/74 considered in Case T-276/04 *Compagnie Maritime Belge SA v Commission* [2008] ECR II-1277, [2009] 4 CMLR 21, para 39 and also in Case T-410/03 *Hoechst GmbH v Commission* [2008] ECR II-881; [2008] 5 CMLR 12, paras, 220–27. The Commission also has the power to impose interim measures and make a declaration of inapplicability under Arts 8 and 10 of Regulation 1/2003, respectively.

positive action on the part of the addressee or addressees, and the decision may specify the steps to be taken. Thus in *Commercial Solvents*,[96] a case involving an abuse of a dominant position, the Commission imposed on CSC and Istituto an obligation to deliver an initial quantity of aminobutanol to Zoja within 30 days and to submit within two months a plan for making supplies available in the longer term. A periodic penalty payment may be attached to the order to ensure that it is complied with.

The *Microsoft* saga[97] illustrates the extent to which positive action may be required. It will be recalled[98] that the Commission found two abuses under Article 102, one relating to Microsoft's refusal to disclose information which would allow interoperability, and one concerning the bundling of Windows Media Player (WMP) with its Windows PC operating system. The Commission imposed positive obligations on Microsoft to disclose accurate interface documentation and to offer to PC manufacturers a version of its operating system without WMP. The Commission added:

> As a result of the Commission's remedy, the configuration of such bundles will reflect what consumers want, and not what Microsoft imposes. Microsoft retains the right to offer a version of its Windows client PC operating system product with WMP. However, Microsoft must refrain from using any commercial, technological or contractual terms that would have the effect of rendering the unbundled version of Windows less attractive or performing. In particular, it must not give PC manufacturers a discount conditional on their buying Windows together with WMP.
>
> The Commission believes the remedies will bring the antitrust violations to an end, that they are proportionate, and that they establish clear principles for the future conduct of the company.
>
> To ensure effective and timely compliance with this decision, the Commission will appoint a Monitoring Trustee, which will, *inter alia*, oversee that Microsoft's interface disclosures are complete and accurate, and that the two versions of Windows are equivalent in terms of performance.

Those obligations were suspended pending the Court of First Instance's consideration of Microsoft's request for interim measures. After these were rejected, the Commission market-tested the interoperability 'solutions' before issuing a further decision on 10 November 2005 pursuant to Article 24(1) of Regulation 1/2003. This warned that if Microsoft did not comply by 15 December 2005 with its obligations (i) to supply complete and accurate interoperability information; and (ii) to make that information available on reasonable terms, it would face a daily fine of up to €2 million. Further significant sanctions were imposed on Microsoft for non-implementation of the Commission's decision, including a penalty payment of €899 million on 27 February 2008.[99] The most significant development in relation to the Commission's remedies was the Court of First Instance's finding that the Commission lacked power to delegate a proactive role to the monitoring trustee beyond that of reporting to the Commission.[100] It should be remembered that Article 7 of Regulation 1/2003 now refers to 'any behavioural or structural remedies' necessary to

---

[96] Joined Cases 6 and 7/73 *Commercial Solvents Corporation v Commission* [1974] ECR 223, [1974] 1 CMLR 309. The abuse consisted of a refusal to supply; see further, Chapter 24.

[97] COMP/C-3/37.792 *Microsoft* (24 March 2004); Case T-201/04 *Microsoft v Commission* [2007] ECR II-3601; [2007] 5 CMLR 11.

[98] Chapter 24, above.

[99] For fuller details of the Microsoft saga, see http://ec.europa.eu/competition/sectors/ICT/microsoft/index. html.

[100] See Case T-201/04 *Microsoft v Commission* [2007] ECR II-3601; [2007] 5 CMLR 11. See also D Howarth and K MacMahon, 'Windows Has Performed an Illegal Operation: The Court of First Instance's Judgment on Microsoft v Commission' [2008] *ECLR* 117; see also A Andreangeli, 'Between Economic Freedom and Effective

bring the infringement to an end, and that these can apply to either Article 101 or Article 102, although, particularly following *Microsoft*, the task of monitoring behavioural commitments may be difficult.[101]

(i) Commitments

The ability to accept binding commitments was a new enforcement mechanism formally introduced by Regulation 1/2003, intended to ensure the effective enforcement of the EU competition rules by delivering a quicker and more efficient solution to the competition problems identified by the Commission instead of requiring a formal finding of an infringement. It would allow undertakings to participate in the procedure by proposing the solutions they considered to be most appropriate for dealing with the competition concerns of the Commission. Accordingly, this was an important additional competition law enforcement tool at the Commission's disposal, and the scope and nature of the commitment remedy and process were examined by the Court of Justice in *Commission v Alrosa Co Ltd*.[102] Alrosa and De Beers were both active in the world market for rough diamonds. As part of a long-standing commercial arrangement, in 2002 the parties entered into a supply agreement whereby Alrosa undertook to sell De Beers rough diamonds produced in Russia to the value of $800 million a year and De Beers undertook to buy those diamonds from Alrosa. They notified the Commission, which subsequently sent a statement of objections to both parties, alleging that the notified agreement infringed Article 101(1) TFEU, and also opened parallel proceedings against De Beers under Article 102 TFEU. The parties offered joint commitments but the Commission required revised commitments, effectively requiring the parties to end their trading relationship. At a later stage De Beers offered unilateral commitments to reduce progressively their purchase of rough diamonds from Alrosa. These were accepted by the Commission, which, after providing Alrosa with a copy and receiving comments, adopted a decision to make the commitments binding.[103] Alrosa appealed that decision to the General Court, which annulled the decision[104] on the basis that the Commission had breached the principle of proportionality in accepting commitments that were more onerous than necessary to address the competition problem. The General Court also held that the Commission had breached Alrosa's right to be heard. The Commission appealed the judgment to the Court of Justice. The Court of Justice set aside the General Court's judgment. In assessing the application of the proportionality principle, the Court of Justice stressed the different objectives and contexts of decisions under Articles 7 and 9 of Regulation 1/2003, respectively:

> 41 Application of the principle of proportionality by the Commission in the context of art 9 of Regulation 1/2003 is confined to verifying that the commitments in question address the concerns it expressed to the undertakings concerned and that they have not offered less onerous commitments that also address those concerns adequately. When carrying out that assessment, the Commission must, however, take into consideration the interests of third parties.

> 47 There is therefore no reason why the measure which could possibly be imposed in the context of art 7 of Regulation 1/2003 should have to serve as a reference for the purpose of assess-

Competition Enforcement: The Impact of the Antitrust Remedies under the Modernisation Regulation on Investigated Parties Freedom to Contract and to Enjoy Property' (2010) 6 *Comp L Rev* 225.

[101] See Howarth and MacMahon, above n 100.
[102] Case C-441/07 P *Commission v Alrosa Co Ltd* [2011] All ER (EC) 1; [2010] 5 CMLR 11.
[103] Decision COMP/B-2/38.381.
[104] Case T-170/06 *Alrosa v Commission* [2007] ECR II-2601; [2007] 5 CMLR 7.

ing the extent of the commitments accepted under art 9 of the Regulation, or why anything going beyond that measure should automatically be regarded as disproportionate. Even though decisions adopted under each of those provisions are in either case subject to the principle of proportionality, the application of that principle nonetheless differs according to which of those provisions is concerned.[105]

Given the consensual nature of commitment proceedings, in comparison with the adversarial context of Article 7 decisions, proportionality in relation to commitments did not require the Commission to seek less onerous or more moderate solutions. Furthermore, the Commission was entitled to conduct separate proceedings in relation to the potential infringement of Articles 101 and 102, and although Alrosa had more extensive rights as an undertaking concerned in the Article 101 proceedings, it enjoyed less extensive rights of a third party in relation to the Article 102 proceedings,[106] and these had been satisfied during the Commission's process.[107]

IV – PUBLIC ENFORCEMENT: FINES

This section will concentrate on the powers of the Commission to impose fines on undertakings and restraints on their exercise arising either from the Commission's own guidelines or review by the European Courts. It should also be noted that Article 5 of Regulation 1/2003 also authorises NCAs to impose fines, penalty payments 'or any other penalty provided for in their national law'. The latter may result in stricter regimes in some cases. Indeed, one of the controversial issues with the ECN is that Regulation 1 did not introduce harmonised remedial or sanction powers for NCAs, and accordingly the punishment may vary according to which NCA is taking enforcement action. For example, the Enterprise Act 2002 in the United Kingdom provides for disqualification from office as a director on certain conditions.[108] The Commission's fining powers, on the other hand, are restricted to the undertaking committing the infringement.[109]

It may, of course, be asked why there is such a heavy reliance on fining as a sanction. There is a considerable literature[110] on the pros and cons of fining as a deterrent in relation to anti-competitive conduct. Without discussing these in detail, recurring questions address issues such as whether it is undertakings or individuals who should be the subject of penalties, whether fines are passed on in terms of prices or if they are budgeted for anyway in advance; and whether undertakings positively measure the risks of detection against benefits to be obtained in the short term and conduct themselves accordingly.

---

[105] Ibid, paras 41 and 47.

[106] Ibid, paras 89–91.

[107] For further discussion, see M Kellerbauer, 'Playground Instead of Playpen: The Court of Justice of the European Union's Alrosa Judgment on Art 9 of Regulation 1/2003' [2011] ECLR 1.

[108] Enterprise Act 2002 s 204.

[109] This may in itself be problematic. 'Undertaking' is construed widely (see Chapter 22 above) for the purposes of establishing a breach of the EU competition rules, but enforcement must be against a legal personality.

[110] See, inter alia, M Ermann and R Lundmann (eds), Corporate and Governmental Deviance (Oxford, Oxford University Press, 1978); WJ Wils, 'EC Competition Fines; To Deter or Not To Deter' (1995) 15 YEL 17; WJ Wils, 'The European Commission's 2006 Guidelines on Antitrust Fines: A Legal and Economic Analysis' (2007) 30 World Competition 197.

Regardless of the criminological, economic or sociological answers to these questions, it is clear that fines represent a major element of the Commission's enforcement policy.

A – Calculating Fines: The 2006 Guidelines Notice

Fines under Article 23(2) of Regulation 1/2003 relate to intentional or negligent infringements of Articles 101 or 102, contravention of interim measures or failing to comply with binding commitments.[111] The ceiling for each infringing undertaking is 10 per cent of turnover in the preceding business year.[112] With regard to the amounts and calculation of fines, Article 23(3) of Regulation 1/2003 stipulates only that 'regard shall be had both to the gravity and to the duration of the infringement'. In 1998 the Commission adopted a Guidelines Notice[113] to establish a 'new method' of determining fines with enhanced transparency and certainty, although this has since been replaced by a revised Guidelines Notice in 2006. Although Guidelines create 'soft law' and do not constitute EU legislative measures, case law makes it clear that they generate legitimate expectations.[114] In the *Pre-Insulated Pipes* cartel case,[115] the Court of Justice expressed the position as follows:

> In adopting such rules of conduct and announcing by publishing them that they will henceforth apply to the cases to which they relate, the institution in question imposes a limit on the exercise of its discretion and cannot depart from those rules under pain of being found, where appropriate, to be in breach of the general principles of law, such as equal treatment or the protection of legitimate expectations. It cannot therefore be excluded that, on certain conditions and depending on their conduct, such rules of conduct, which are of general application, may produce legal effects.[116]

Thus, whilst the Commission has a discretion when determining the amount of each fine and is not required to apply a precise mathematical formula,[117] it may not depart from the rules that it has imposed on itself. As the Court of First Instance has also observed:

> Since the Guidelines are an instrument intended to define, while complying with higher-ranking law, the criteria which the Commission proposes to apply in the exercise of its discretion when determining fines, the Commission must in fact take account of the Guidelines when determining fines, in particular the elements which are mandatory under the Guidelines.[118]

At the heart of the old 1998 Guidelines was the idea that gravity and duration of the infringement should be used to determine a basic amount for the fine, which can then

---

[111] ie decisions under Art 9 of Regulation 1/2003, discussed above.

[112] In relation to the determination of fines on associations of undertakings, see Case (C-101/07 P) *Coop de France Betail et Viande (formerly Fédération Nationale de la Coopération Betail et Viande (FNCBV)) v Commission* [2008] ECR I-10193; [2009] 4 CMLR 15.

[113] *Guidelines on the Method of Setting Fines* [1998] OJ C9/3 (1998 Guidelines).

[114] For a wider discussion, see HCH Hofmann, 'Negotiated and Non-negotiated Administrative Rule-Making: The Example of EC Competition Policy' (2006) 43 *CMLRev* 153.

[115] Joined Cases C-189/02P, C-202/02P to C-208/02P and C-213/02P *Dansk Rørindustri*, [2005] ECR I-5425.

[116] Ibid, para 211. Note that this is in relation to the 1998 Guidelines, above n 113, although the same principle applies to the revised 2006 Guidelines: *Guidelines on the Method of Setting Fines Imposed Pursuant to Article 23(2) of Regulation 1/2003* [2006] OJ C210/2 (2006 Guidelines).

[117] Case T-150/89 *Martinelli v Commission* [1995] ECR II-1165, para 59.

[118] Case T-15/02 *BASF v Commission* [2006] ECR II-497; [2006] 5 CMLR 2, para 119, citing Joined Cases T-67/00, T-68/00, T-71/00 and T-78/00 *JFE Engineering v Commission* [2004] ECR II-2501. See also Case T-127/04 *KME Germany and others v Commission of the European Communities* [2009] ECR II-1167, para 33.

be increased or reduced in the light of the aggravating or attenuating circumstances of the particular case. The guidelines divided both gravity and duration into three categories. Thus, in relation to gravity, infringements could be 'minor', 'serious' or 'very serious', examples respectively being vertical restraints with limited market impact, vertical or horizontal restrictions with more extensive effects, and horizontal cartels engaging in price-fixing or market-sharing. The basic element of the fine for these three types of gravity was likely to comprise up to €1 million for minor infringements, up to €20 million for serious ones, and above that for the very serious category. The three categories which made up duration were 'short', 'medium' and 'long', representing periods of, respectively, up to one year, up to five years, or longer. There has been considerable case law in recent years regarding the calculation of fines under the 1998 Guidelines, but these will not be considered in any detail here; it is more important to consider the position under the revised fining Guidelines published by the Commission in 2006.

The 1998 Notice was revised in 2006 in three principal ways to further increase deterrence and enhance certainty and predictability.[119] The 2006 Guidelines are applied in all cases where the Statement of Objections was notified to addressees after 1 September 2006. The first key change concerns the methodology used to determine the basic level of a fine. Accordingly, the fine will be based on the yearly sales in the relevant market for each undertaking participating in the infringement, multiplied by the years of participation.[120] The general rule is that the starting point will be set at up to 30 per cent of the relevant sales,[121] and in determining the appropriate percentage, the Commission will take a number of factors into account in assessing gravity, such as the nature of the infringement and its geographic scope,[122] with fines for secret horizontal cartel arrangements being set at the higher end of the 30 per cent scale.[123] This is a shift from a more crude methodology for assessing gravity to an approach designed, at least from its starting point, to reflect the market harm caused by the infringement.[124] It also embodies a greater emphasis on the infringement's duration. The second principal change is that the Commission may impose an additional 'entry fee' of 15–25 per cent of yearly relevant sales for serious infringements, notably horizontal price-fixing, market-sharing and output-limitation agreements. Thirdly, the most significant change to the detailed guidance on what constitutes aggravating factors concerns recidivists, providing for increases in fines of up to 100 per cent for each prior infringement by a repeat offender.[125]

Having determined the basic amount of the fine, the Commission also takes into

---

[119] *Guidelines on the Method of Setting Fines Imposed Pursuant to Article 23(2) of Regulation 1/2003* [2006] OJ C210/2. See WJ Wils, 'The European Commission's 2006 Guidelines on Antitrust Fines: A Legal and Economic Analysis' (2007) 30 *World Competition* 197.

[120] 2006 Guidelines, above n 116, para 19. Under previous practice, the Commission rarely referred to the relevant affected market (see also case law: eg Case C-510/06 P *Archer Daniels Midland v Commission* [2009] ECR I-1843; [2009] 4 CMLR 20, which stressed, at paras 74–75, that the penalty was not required to be proportionate to the undertaking's turnover from the sales in relation to which the anti-competitive breach had taken place), and in relation to duration, each year of participation in an infringement led to a 10% increase in the fine.

[121] 2006 Guidelines, above n 116, para 21.

[122] Ibid, paras 20 and 22.

[123] Ibid, para 23.

[124] See Case T-127/04 *KME Germany and others v Commission of the European Communities* [2009] ECR II-1167, para 93; Case C-397/03 P *Archer Daniels Midland v Commission* [2006] ECR I-4429; [2006] 5 CMLR 4, para 101.

[125] 2006 Guidelines, above n 116, para 28. See JM Connor, 'Has the European Commission Become More Severe in Punishing Cartels? Effects of the 2006 Guidelines' [2011] *ECLR* 27.

account aggravating and mitigating circumstances in coming to the final amount to be imposed.[126] The Guidelines note the following as potentially aggravating factors:[127] continued or repeated similar infringements of Articles 101 or 102; refusal to co-operate with, or obstruction of, the Commission in carrying out its investigations; any role as leader or instigator of the infringement, in particular by coercing participation of others or taking retaliatory measures to enforce any anti-competitive practices. Previously, the Commission could only increase fines by up to 50 per cent where undertakings were involved in similar previous infringements.[128] Under the 2006 Notice, the Commission can take account of prior NCA decisions and each prior infringement may support an increase.[129]

In *BASF*, the Court of First Instance emphasised that 'instigator' and 'leader' are two different concepts: whereas instigation is concerned with the establishment or enlargement of a cartel, leadership is concerned with its operation.[130] To be classified as an instigator

> an undertaking must have persuaded or encouraged other undertakings to establish the cartel or to join it. By contrast, it is not sufficient merely to have been a founding member of the cartel. Thus, for example, in a cartel created by two undertakings only, it would not be justified automatically to classify those undertakings as instigators. That classification should be reserved to the undertaking which has taken the initiative, if such be the case, for example by suggesting to the other an opportunity for collusion or by attempting to persuade it to do so.[131]

Leadership may be joint, and for that purpose does not have to be equal in degree with other members of the cartel. This will obviously be a matter of detailed investigation, and individual acts are not as such determinative. For example, in the part of the *BASF* decision relating to restrictions applied to vitamin C production by BASF, Roche, Takeda and others, the Court of First Instance rejected the Commission's finding that BASF had been the leader. A number of proposals about production quotas had been put forward; the fact that the proposal finally adopted was that of BASF as a compromise between the positions or Roche and Takeda did not make BASF a leader.[132] Roche, on the other hand, was the only undertaking which could conceivably be classified as a leader—it had organised a significant number of meetings, had met separately with cartel members in order to represent them in other further meetings, collected the sales figures of cartel members and reported to them overall results by undertaking.[133]

The 2006 Guidelines provide that mitigating circumstances include:[134] prompt termination of the violation as soon as the Commission intervenes; non-implementation

---

[126] 2006 Guidelines, above n 116, paras 28–29.

[127] Ibid, para 28.

[128] In relation to what constitutes recidivism for these purposes, see eg Case C-3/06 P *Group Danone v Commission*, [2007] ECR I-1331; [2007] 4 CMLR 18; Case C-308/04 P *SGL Carbon AG v Commission* [2006] ECR I-5977; [2006] 5 CMLR 16; Case T-53/03 *BPB plc v Commission* [2008] ECR II-1333, [2008] 5 CMLR 18.

[129] For a discussion of the ECHR issues in relation to increased fines for recidivism, see K Nordlander, 'The Commission's Policy on Recidivism: Legal Certainty for Repeat Offenders' [2005] *Comp L Rev* 55. The Court of Justice held in Case-C-413/08 P *Lafarge v Commission* [2010] 5 CMLR 10, paras 65–67, albeit in relation to the 1998 Guidelines, that treating recidivism as an aggravating circumstance did not breach the *nulla poena sine lege* principle, even in the absence of any prescribed maximum period for taking into account prior breaches. However, where the earlier decision was subsequently annulled by the courts, the Commission was required to take appropriate measures to ensure that the later decision no longer took account of the earlier 'breach' (ibid, paras 87–89).

[130] *BASF*, above n 118, para 316.

[131] Ibid, para 321.

[132] Ibid, para 392.

[133] Ibid, para 404.

[134] 2006 Guidelines, above n 116, para 29.

in practice of any anti-competitive agreement; negligent breaches; effective co-operation beyond the scope of the Leniency Notice;[135] and authorisation or encouragement by public authorities or legislation to commit the anti-competitive activity. In *BASF*, the Court of First Instance rejected the applicant's attempt to make any mitigating circumstance out of the measures it had taken after the infringements had come to an end. The company had dismissed senior executives, adopted internal competition compliance programmes and instituted staff awareness training. These steps, it argued, reduced the risk of future infringement and accordingly should reduce the need for a deterrence component in the fine. The Court of First Instance ruled that the preventive measures placed 'no duty whatsoever'[136] on the Commission to reduce the fine, even though it had taken compliance programmes into account in other previous cases.[137]

The 2006 Guidelines stress the importance of the deterrent impact of fines; paragraphs 30 and 31 provide as follows:

> 30. The Commission will pay particular attention to the need to ensure that fines have a sufficiently deterrent effect; to that end, it may increase the fine to be imposed on undertakings which have a particularly large turnover beyond the sales of goods or services to which the infringement relates.
>
> 31. The Commission will also take into account the need to increase the fine in order to exceed the amount of gains improperly made as a result of the infringement where it is possible to estimate that amount.'

Nonetheless, the Commission must always ensure that the proposed fine does not exceed the legal maximum of 10 per cent of the undertaking's worldwide annual turnover as required by Article 23(2) of Regulation 1.[138] Finally, paragraph 35 of the Notice provides that in exceptional cases the Commission can take into account an undertaking's inability to pay in a specific social and economic context, a flexibility utilised by the Commission on various occasions during the financial crisis period.[139]

As indicated, the intention behind the 2006 Guidelines was to treat hard-core cartel infringements more severely. As part of the Commission's emphasis on hard-core cartels, fines imposed in individual cases and overall have increased dramatically since the late 1990s. Research has indicated that Commission fines have been considerably higher under the 2006 Guidelines than under the 1998 Guidelines and compared to those imposed by the Department of Justice under US antitrust law, with particularly significant upward fine adjustments in recent years for recidivism.[140] The Commission website provides useful cartel statistics which demonstrate the significant uplift in fines during the 2006–10 period,[141] during which the Commission imposed the largest fines to date in an Article 101 case, of over €1.3 billion in the car glass producers cartel,[142] and of €1.06 billion in the

---

[135] Discussed further below.

[136] *BASF*, above n 118, para 266.

[137] eg Case T-7/89 *Hercules Chemicals v Commission* [1991] ECR II-1711; Case T-13/89 *ICI v Commission* [1992] ECR II-1021; Case T-28/99 *Sigma Tecnologie v Commission* [2002] ECR II-1845 and Case T-23/99 *LR AF 1998 v Commission* [2002] ECR II-1705.

[138] 2006 Guidelines, above n 116, para 32. See further in Chapter 22 regarding the attribution of liability for infringements.

[139] cf Case T-452/05 *Belgian Sewing Thread (BST) NV v Commission* [2010] 5 CMLR 16.

[140] Connor, above n 125. See also C Veljanovski, 'Penalties for Price Fixers: An Analysis of Fines Imposed on 39 Cartels under EC Antitrust' [2006] *ECLR* 510 and C Veljanovski, 'Cartel Fines in Europe' (2007) 30 *World Competition* 65; M Motta, 'On Cartel Deterrence and Fines in the European Union' [2008] *ECLR* 209.

[141] http://ec.europa.eu/competition/cartels/statistics/statistics.pdf.

[142] Commission press release IP/08/1685; Summary Decision, [2009] OJ C173/13.

Intel Article 102 infringement decision.[143] In 2010 alone, in cartel cases, the Commission fined six liquid crystal display panel producers €64 million for a price-fixing cartel; 11 air cargo carriers €799 million; animal feed phosphates cartel participants over €175m (in the first hybrid settlement case); pre-stressed steel cartel producers €458 million; 17 bathroom equipment manufacturers €622 million; and a price-fixing cartel of DRAM (dynamic random access memory computer chip) producers €331 million (in the first settlement case).[144] The question of the attribution of liability for fines, in particular as between subsidiary and parent undertakings, was considered in Chapter 22.

The Guidelines aim to be transparent and predictable, and the principle of legal certainty requires that the offence and sanction be clearly defined to satisfy the requirement of foreseeability.[145] However, the European Courts recognise the considerable discretion held by the Commission,[146] albeit that is constrained by Article 15(2) of Regulation 1, the Leniency Notice and fining Guidelines.[147] The General Court's review is confined to the legality of the Commission's decision. It is therefore only possible for the Court to exercise its unlimited jurisdiction under Article 261 TFEU (ex Article 229 EC) and Article 31 of Regulation 1/2003 if it makes a finding of illegality affecting that decision and accordingly moves to annul or adjust the fine if necessary. Moreover, where the Commission retains discretion, review of the legality of the Commission's decision is limited to manifest errors of assessment.[148] The Court of Justice, in turn, will not interfere with the General Court's assessment:

> [I]t is not for the Court, when ruling on questions of law in the context of an appeal, to substitute, on grounds of fairness, its own assessment for that of the [General Court] exercising its unlimited jurisdiction to rule on the amount of fines imposed on undertakings for infringements of Community law. The Court cannot therefore, at the appeal stage, examine whether the amount of the fine fixed by the [General Court], in the exercise of its unlimited jurisdiction, is proportionate in relation to the gravity and duration of the infringement as established by the [General Court] on completion of its appraisal of the facts.[149]

Proportionality and the right to equal treatment are, of course, key principles of EU law which can be invoked in order to contest the legality of the Commission's original fining decision.[150] Furthermore, the *non bis in idem* principle is a plea to the effect that undertakings should not be fined twice for effectively the same infringement. This plea has been raised on numerous occasions in recent years, particularly by parties involved in global cartels which have been sanctioned by various authorities. The Court of Justice has stressed that the principle may apply subject to satisfaction of three cumulative requirements: identity of the facts, unity of the defender and of the legal interest protected under

---

[143] http://ec.europa.eu/competition/sectors/ICT/intel.html.

[144] http://ec.europa.eu/competition/cartels/cases/cases.html.

[145] See Case- C-413/08 P *Lafarge v Commission*, [2010] 5 CMLR 10, para 94, Note this does not require the trader to know in advance the precise level of fine to be imposed. See F Dethmers and H Engelen, 'Fines under Article 102 of the Treaty on the Functioning of the European Union' [2011] *ECLR* 86, and the argument that a shift to an effects-based approach under Art 102 arguably makes satisfaction of the *nulla poena sina lege certa* principle under EU law, to the effect that fines can only be imposed if they have a clear and unambiguous legal basis, more difficult,

[146] See eg Case T-127/04 *KME Germany AG v Commission* [2009] 5 CMLR 8, para 35.

[147] Ibid. See also Case- C-413/08 P *Lafarge v Commission*, [2010] 5 CMLR 10, para 95,

[148] See eg Case T-127/04 *KME Germany AG v Commission* [2009] 5 CMLR 8, paras 36–37.

[149] Case C-338/00 *Volkswagen v Commission* [2003] ECR I-9189, para 151.

[150] In relation to the principle of equal treatment, see eg Case T-18/03 *CD-Contact data GmBH v Commission* [2009] ECR II-1021; [2009] 5 CMLR 5; Case T-127/04 *KME Germany AG v Commission* [2009] 5 CMLR 8 .

the separate proceedings.[151] Accordingly, the principle does not apply in relation to EU competition law infringements established by the Commission where non Member-States' authorities have also intervened in their own jurisdiction.[152]

B – Rights of the Defence, Fundamental Rights Protection and the Commission's Enforcement Processes: The Future

The development of the rights of the defence in EU competition law enforcement has been a notable feature of the Court's jurisprudence. The European Human Rights Commission (EHRC) in *Stenuit*[153] considered that competition law proceedings, which may lead to the imposition of a fine, are criminal in nature and that Article 6 ECHR is applicable to them, irrespective of the purported classification in Article 23(5) of Regulation 1/2003.[154] It has been made clear in Court jurisprudence that the principle in Article 6, providing for a fair and public hearing within a reasonable time by an independent and impartial tribunal, is to be indirectly respected. However, administrative decisions by the Commission are considered not to be contrary to this general right because of the existence of a full and independent review, involving due process, before an independent tribunal: the General Court or the Court of Justice.[155] There has been considerable academic criticism and critique of the Commission's enforcement processes, partly on the basis that the fining sanction is criminal in nature and the EU court review process is limited, and therefore any initial determination of the existence of an EU competition law violation should take place before an independent tribunal.[156] This general debate on the nature of the EU competition law proceedings and the implications for various aspects of the investigation and decision-making processes is likely to come into even sharper focus in the next few years, given that the entry into force of the TFEU made the CFR binding, and under Article 52(3) CFR, rights thereunder are to be granted the same meaning and scope as under the ECHR.[157] Article 41 CFR guarantees a 'right to good administration' as follows:

---

[151] Case T-410/03 *Hoechst GmbH v Commission* [2008] ECR II-881; [2008] 5 CMLR 12.

[152] See case C-289/04 P *Showa Denko v Commission* [2006] ECR I-5859, paras 60–61; Case C-308/04 P *SGL Carbon v Commission* [2006] ECR I-5977, paras 26–37. In Case T-410/03 *Hoechst GmbH v Commission* [2008] ECR II-881; [2008] 5 CMLR 12 the principle was not applicable in relation to action taken by the US Department of Justice, as the Commission's action was to safeguard free competition within the EU, and this was not the purpose of the decision taken by the US authority.

[153] *Stenuit* (1992) 14 EHRR 509.

[154] The distinction between natural and legal persons may also be important in relation to the level of protection: see M Emberland, *The Human Rights of Companies: Exploring the Structure of ECHR Protection* (Oxford, Oxford University Press, 2006).

[155] Under Art 263 TFEU, albeit appeal to the Court of Justice is on a point of law only. See WJ Wils, 'The Increased Level of EU Antitrust fines, Judicial Review and the ECHR' (2010) 33 *World Competition* 5.

[156] See IS Forrester, 'Due Process in EC Competition Cases: A Distinguished Institution with Flawed Procedures' (2009) 34 *ELRev* 817. See also A Riley, 'The Modernisation of EU Anti-Cartel Enforcement: Will the Commission Grasp the Opportunity?' [2010] *ECLR* 191. For a contrary view, based on the distinction between criminal penalties and the 'hard core of criminal law' (per *Jussila v Finland*, 23 November 2006 Application No 73053/01) and that accordingly in relation to competition law enforcement by the Commission involving administrative penalties Art 6 ECHR guarantees do not apply with 'full stringency', see Wils, above n 155.

[157] Art 52(1) CFR provides that 'any limitation on the exercise of the rights and freedoms recognised by this Charter must be provided for by law and respect the essence of these rights and freedoms. Subject to the principle of proportionality, limitations may be made only if they are necessary and genuinely meet objectives of general interest recognised by the Union or the need to protect the rights and freedoms of others'. See Case C-407/08 P *Knauf Gips KG v Commission* [2010] 5 CMLR 12.

1. Every person has the right to have his or her affairs handled impartially, fairly and within a reasonable time by the institutions, bodies, offices and agencies of the Union.

2. This right includes:
(a) the right of every person to be heard, before any individual measure which would affect him or her adversely is taken;
(b) the right of every person to have access to his or her file, while respecting the legitimate interests of confidentiality and of professional and business secrecy;
(c) the obligation of the administration to give reasons for its decisions.'

Article 47(1) CFR guarantees anyone whose EU law rights have been violated the right to an effective remedy before a national or EU tribunal, while Article 47(2) CFR specifies that 'everyone is entitled to a fair and public hearing within a reasonable time by an independent and impartial tribunal previously established by law' in terms which reflect Article 6(1) ECHR. Article 48(2) CFR requires 'respect for the rights of the defence of anyone who has been charged' and Article 49(1) CFR, reflecting Article 7(1) ECHR, expresses the EU 'principle of legality'. Article 49(3) CFR requires penalties to be proportionate to the offence. Finally, Article 50 CFR affirms the principle of *non bis in idem* by providing, that 'no one shall be liable to be tried or punished again in criminal proceedings for an offence for which he or she has already been finally acquitted or convicted within the Union in accordance with the law'.

Furthermore, Article 6(2) TFEU requires EU accession to the ECHR. Accordingly, the procedural requirements imposed under the general principles of EU law, Regulations, and Commission policy and practice, will in future have to be consistent with the due process rights developed by the ECHR jurisprudence; this will have direct application in the field of competition law.[158] Potential areas of tension and divergence with the ECHR case law include the right to silence and the scope of review of Commission decisions and processes by the EU courts.

C – Uncovering Cartels: Leniency Incentives

Obviously, enforcement of the competition rules will be less effective so long as cartels remain secret. The Commission's desire to detect as well as deter has led to its adoption of a leniency policy,[159] which seeks to reward (by immunity or reduced fines) cartel participants who 'blow the whistle' about the existence of the cartel. The adoption of a leniency policy was inspired by the success of the US Department of Justice Corporate Leniency Policy of 1993.[160] The theory, which has proven to be highly successful in practice, is that the existence of a leniency programme creates incentives for cartel participants to

---

[158] For a fuller discussion, see WJ Wils, 'EU Antitrust Enforcement Powers and Procedural Rights and Guarantees: The Interplay between EU Law, National Law, the Charter of Fundamental Rights of the EU and the European Convention on Human Rights' [2011] *World Competition* forthcoming. See also W Weiß, 'Human Rights and EU Antitrust Enforcement: News from Lisbon' [2011] *ECLR* 186.

[159] The current version applies to leniency applications after 8 December 2006: *Notice on Immunity from Fines and Reduction of Fines in Cartel Cases* [2006] OJ C298/17 ('2006 Leniency Notice'); this replaced the 2002 ('Valentine's Day') Notice: *Notice on Immunity from Fines and Reduction of Fines in Cartel Cases* [2002] OJ C45/3; which had replaced the original Notice [1996] OJ C207/4. For discussion, see WJ Wils, 'Leniency in Antitrust Enforcement: Theory and Practice' (2007) 30 *World Competition* 25.

[160] For a discussion of the US Corporate Leniency Policy, see C Harding and J Joshua, *Regulating Cartels in Europe—A Study of legal Control of Corporate Delinquency* (Oxford, Oxford University Press, 2000) ch VIII. See also eg A Riley, 'Cartel Whistleblowing: Toward an American Model' [2002] *MJECL* 67.

confess and thereby destabilises the trust mechanisms required for successful cartelisa-
tion, creating a 'race to the courthouse' (a misnomer under EU law, and also under US
law, as in both cases applications are made to the enforcing authority—the Commission
and the Department of Justice, respectively) to achieve the highest leniency reward possible, in terms of fine immunity or reduction. Not surprisingly, such an attractive carrot
comes with conditions, explained more fully below. The position is complicated by the
fact that virtually all NCAs[161] also run their own leniency programmes. As these can differ from each other, and from the scheme contained in the Commission's Notice, there
is a practical issue about whether multiple applications are necessary or desirable in the
absence of a 'one-stop shop' for leniency.[162] Certainly, the Network Notice indicates than
an application to one ECN authority is not to be considered as an application for leniency to any other authority, and underlines that it is for the applicant to take the steps
which it considers appropriate to protect its position.[163] Nonetheless, the difficulties have
been ameliorated to a great extent by the adoption of a Model Leniency Programme,[164]
which sought to harmonise key elements of leniency policies which Member State NCAs
should seek to implement. A subsequent ECN Report in 2009 noted a further degree of
convergence of NCA leniency programmes which was ongoing following the adoption of
the Model Leniency Programme.[165] The discussion below is confined to the Commission's
leniency policy.

The 2006 Leniency Notice concerns

> secret cartels . . . between two or more competitors aimed at co-ordinating their competitive
> behaviour on the market and/or influencing the relevant parameters of competition through
> practices such as the fixing of purchase or selling prices or other trading conditions, the alloca-
> tion of production or sales quotas, the sharing of markets including bid-rigging, restrictions of
> imports or exports and/or anti-competitive actions against other competitors.[166]

The requirements for obtaining leniency differ according to whether the undertaking is
seeking immunity or a reduction in fines. The 2006 Notice generally seeks to refine the
earlier practice by increasing the predictability and transparency of the scheme.[167] In the
case of immunity applications, the undertaking must be either the first to submit evidence
which in the Commission's view may enable it (a) to carry out a targeted inspection in
connection with the alleged cartel;[168] or (b) to find an infringement of Article 101 TFEU
in connection with the alleged cartel.[169]

In order to be able to carry out a targeted inspection, the Commission will require a
corporate statement comprising: a detailed description of the alleged cartel arrangement,
including, for instance, its aims, activities and functioning; the names and address of the

---

[161] This has increased considerably in recent years and at the time of writing, Malta was the only Member
State without a leniency programme.

[162] See M Reynolds and D Anderson, 'Immunity and Leniency in EU Cartel Cases: Current Issues' [2006]
ECLR 82.

[163] Network Notice, above n 4, para 38.

[164] DG Comp, ECN Model Leniency Programme, 29 September 2006, http://ec.europa.eu/competition/ecn/
documents.html. See C Gauer and M Jaspers, 'Designing a European Solution for a "One Stop Leniency Shop"'
[2006] *ECLR* 685.

[165] ECN, Model Leniency Programme, Report on the State of Convergence, see Commission press release,
MEMO 09/456, 15 October 2009.

[166] 2006 Leniency Notice, above n 159, para 1. See Wils, above n 159.

[167] See Riley, above n 156.

[168] 2006 Leniency Notice, above n 159, para 8(a).

[169] Ibid, para 8(b).

leniency applicant and all other undertakings that participate(d) in the alleged cartel; information in relation to other existing or potential leniency applications to other competition authorities, inside or outside the EU, in relation to the alleged cartel; and any other evidence in possession of the applicant or available to it relating to the alleged cartel.[170] The second category is used in practice to deal with requests for immunity made after an inspection has already occurred. This route is subject to additional requirements, namely that the Commission did not already have sufficient evidence to establish an infringement of Article 101 and that no conditional immunity has already been given to an undertaking on the basis of the first path.[171] Immunity either way is subject to the following cumulative conditions: (a) that the undertaking co-operates fully, on a continuous basis and expeditiously throughout the Commission's administrative procedure; (b) that the undertaking ends its involvement in the suspected infringement immediately following its application, except in so far as necessary to ensure the inspections could proceed;[172] and (c) that the undertaking did not take steps to coerce other undertakings to participate in the infringement.[173] The major innovation in the 2006 Notice was the introduction of a 'marker' system.[174] This allows undertakings who are intending to make a leniency application, but have not as yet gathered all the necessary information and evidence, effectively to hold their place in the leniency queue by confirming basic details about the cartel, subject to the provision of the evidence required to meet either of the thresholds in paragraph 8 discussed above within a specified period set by the Commission.

Undertakings that do not meet the conditions for immunity may nevertheless still benefit from a reduction in the fine that would otherwise be imposed. The basic requirement here is that an undertaking 'must supply the Commission with evidence of the suspected infringement which represents significant added value with respect to the evidence already in the Commission's possession' and must also meet the cumulative conditions set out in paragraph 12 of the Notice, outlined above—essentially by co-operating fully and terminating involvement in the infringement.[175] In any final decision adopted at the end of the administrative procedure, the Commission will determine whether the evidence indeed represented significant added value and set out the level of reduction to be applied. The benefit, in the form of a reduction relative to the fine which would otherwise be imposed, is 30–50 per cent for the first undertaking, 20–30 per cent for the second undertaking and up to 20 per cent for subsequent undertakings.[176]

According to the Notice, the concept of 'added value' refers to the extent to which the evidence strengthens, by its very nature and/or its level of detail, the Commission's ability to prove the facts in question.[177] The question of whether it is 'significant' will of course have to be measured in the context of specific case circumstances. However, the fact that undertakings are able to apply for both immunity and a reduction in fines under the Leniency Notice suggests that a reduction may be available for information which, whilst not sufficient to gain immunity, satisfies the significance test for a reduction. Particular

---

[170] Ibid, para 9.

[171] Ibid, para 11.

[172] Ibid, para 12.

[173] Ibid, para 13. Note that the latter criterion does not preclude the possibility of a reduction in the fine to be imposed.

[174] Ibid, para 15.

[175] Ibid, para 24.

[176] Ibid, para 26.

[177] Ibid, para 25.

possibilities include the corroboration of other evidence, identifying a larger geographical application or wider range of activities of the cartel than hitherto believed, or allowing the Commission to prove that the cartel has been in operation for longer than it could previously demonstrate. However, as it is the Commission that will decide what is 'significant', and, moreover, only do so at the end point of the administrative process, an application for leniency carries its own risks. Some firms may take the view that a possibility of securing, say, 10 per cent off an as-yet unquantified fine is not a gamble worth taking.

There are other problems associated with the operation of leniency applications. A particular criticism was made in relation to the possibility that corporate statements given to the Commission in the course of a leniency application could become more widely available through discovery procedures in later civil proceedings (especially in third countries, such as the United States).[178] The Commission has sought to address this by providing a special procedure for oral corporate statements to be provided to the Commission under the 2006 Notice.[179] These would be recorded and kept by the Commission, although private parties seeking damages in national courts may seek access to these documents under transparency laws or on the basis of the right to an effective remedy and fair trial.[180]

Despite the perceived bad publicity associated with confessing to cartel participation, and the uncertainty as to whether an application is likely to be fully or partially successful, depending on whether the undertaking is the first to approach the authority and satisfies the various threshold criteria, the Commission's Leniency Notice has been extremely successful in uncovering secret cartels, with virtually all cartel enforcement processes in recent years emanating from leniency applications. The success of the leniency programme has been self-perpetuating in further encouraging new leniency applications and destabilising ongoing cartels, although the danger, perhaps, is that requests for immunity and/or reductions clog up the very system that is intended to assist the targeting of the most objectionable anti-competitive practices. In any event, the 2006 Leniency Notice does not affect the civil liability of an undertaking for breach of Article 101, and we shall turn to the private enforcement of infringements of the competition rules, following, first discussion of the settlement procedure, which seeks to ameliorate the Commission's cartel enforcement burden, and, second, a review of the compatibility with fundamental rights requirements of the Commission's administrative enforcement regime.

D – Settlements

A further significant recent development, as part of the Commission's desire to enhance the effectiveness of its cartel enforcement strategies, was the adoption of a settlement procedure for cartel cases in 2008. The general notion is loosely akin to plea-bargaining in the US antitrust regime, and allows the Commission to negotiate settlement with cartel

---

[178] For a fuller discussion, see I Vandenborre, 'The Confidentiality of EU Commission Cartel Records in Civil Litigation: The Ball is in the EU Court' [2011] *ECLR* 116; C Cauffman, 'The Interaction of Leniency Programmes and Actions for Damages' (2011) 8 *CompLR* forthcoming.

[179] 2006 Leniency Notice, above n 159, para. 32.

[180] See the discussion by Vandenborre, above n 178. In relation to the former, see EU Transparency Regulation 1049/2001 [2001] OJ L145/43; and in relation to the latter see the Opinion of AG Mazak in Case C-360/09, *Pfleiderer AG v Bundeskartellamt*, 16 December 2010, paras 46–49. This was a case where a party sought access to a leniency corporate statement received by a Member State competition authority, and the Advocate General's view was that access should not be granted, and the aim of effective cartel enforcement justified the limitation on the rights guaranteed by the CFR.

members more quickly, thereby devoting less resources to individual cases, allowing it to take action against a greater number of cartels and consequently further enhance the deterrent effect of the enforcement system. The Competition Commissioner at the time, Neelie Kroes, noted the benefits of the introduction of a streamlined procedure for the Commission and undertakings as follows:

> This new settlements procedure will reinforce deterrence by helping the Commission deal more quickly with cartel cases, freeing up resources to open new investigations. Companies which are convinced that the Commission can prove their involvement in a cartel, will also benefit from quicker decisions and a fine reduction.[181]

A Regulation was adopted in 2008 introducing the settlement procedure,[182] and a Commission explanatory Notice was also published,[183] outlining how the Commission envisaged that the procedure would operate. There is no right to settle, and the Commission retains a broad discretion as to the cases which may be suitable for the settlement procedure given that procedural efficiencies are more likely to be achieved where there is a likelihood of achieving a common understanding with the various parties involved.[184] The first stage in the process is for the parties to request settlement discussions and introduce a formal request to settle in the form of a settlement submission.[185] The settlement submission should contain:

> (a) an acknowledgement in clear and unequivocal terms of the parties' liability for the infringement summarily described as regards its object, its possible implementation, the main facts, their legal qualification, including the party's role and the duration of their participation in the infringement in accordance with the results of the settlement discussions;

> (b) an indication of the maximum amount of the fine the parties foresee to be imposed by the Commission and which the parties would accept in the framework of a settlement procedure.[186]

The Commission will issue a statement of objections as is normal practice, and if the parties then confirm their commitment to settle, the Commission can proceed, without the requirement to take any other procedural steps,[187] to adopt a final decision under Articles 7 and/or 23 of Regulation 1/2003.[188] The incentive or reward for the settling parties in return for the procedural economies afforded the Commission is that, if the Commission accedes to the request, it will reduce by 10 per cent the amount of the fine to be imposed, taking into account its Fine Guidelines, discussed above. It is clear that the Commission considers this alternative, more informal, enforcement process to be an important and

---

[181] Commission Press Release IP/08/1056. See also Commission Notice on the conduct of settlement procedures in view of the adoption of Decisions pursuant to Article 7 and Article 23 of Council Regulation (EC) No 1/2003 in cartel cases [2008] OJ C167/1, para 1.

[182] Commission Regulation (EC) No 662/2008 of 30 June 2008 amending Regulation (EC) No 773/2004 as regards the conduct of settlement procedures in cartel cases [2008] OJ L171/3. For discussion, see A Ortega Gonzalez, 'The Cartel Settlement Procedure in Practice' [2011] *ECLR* 170.

[183] Commission Notice on the conduct of settlement procedures in view of the adoption of Decisions pursuant to Article 7 and Article 23 of Council Regulation (EC) No 1/2003 in cartel cases [2008] OJ C167/1.

[184] Ibid, para 5. See eg 19 May 2010 DRAM producers, IP 10/586. *cf* the hybrid settlement in the animal feed phosphates cartel, 20 July 2010, Commission Press Release IP/10/1985.

[185] Art 10a(2) of Regulation (EC) No 773/2004.

[186] Ibid, para 20.

[187] Accordingly there will be no final hearing or access to the file. See Arts 12(2) and 15(1a) of Regulation (EC) No 773/2004.

[188] After consultation with the Advisory Committee, under Art 14 of Regulation 1/2003.

efficient way of enhancing its cartel enforcement strategy. The first settlement was agreed in May 2010 in the DRAM case,[189] involving a cartel between ten producers of memory chips which were sold to manufacturers of personal computers or servers. The process was used more controversially in July 2010, in relation to the animal feed phosphates cartel,[190] a hybrid settlement whereby one undertaking withdrew from the settlement process. Although the remainder were entitled to a 10 per cent fine reduction, arguably any procedural savings were lost as the formal enforcement process was required for the non-settling undertaking.

V – PRIVATE ENFORCEMENT: REMEDIES BEFORE NATIONAL COURTS

A – Regulation 1/2003: Facilitating Private Enforcement?

The point has already been made that the modernisation reforms adopted in 2004 were premised on the view that more use could and should be made of private remedies by complainants/party litigants in their local national courts.[191] This argument was not confined to the perceived benefits to be achieved from freeing up the Commission's time to devote to hard-core cartels. After all, a competitor, customer or consumer injured by an undertaking in breach of Articles 101 or 102 does not derive any great or direct benefit from seeing the perpetrator fined by the Commission or NCA. For a considerable period prior to the 1999 White Paper on Modernisation,[192] the Commission had pointed to the value of private action with increasing frequency[193] and had successfully invoked the availability of alternative redress to justify refusals to take complaints forward.[194]

Under Article 6 of Regulation 1/2003, national courts shall have the power to apply Articles 101 and 102. In one sense this is not wholly new, since the Court of Justice first ruled in the 1970s that the prohibitions of those provisions were directly applicable by national courts.[195] The key difference is that, in addition to application of the prohibitory aspects, the exception of Article 101(3) now also falls within the jurisdiction of national courts for the first time.

As part of the 2004 modernisation 'package', the Commission also issued a Notice in relation to co-operation with national courts.[196] For obvious and understandable reasons

---

[189]   See above n 184.

[190]   See above n 184.

[191]   *cf* WJ Wils, 'Should Private Enforcement Be Encouraged in Europe' (2003) 26 *World Competition* 473. See criticism of these views by C Jones, 'Private Anti-trust Enforcement in Europe: A Policy Analysis and Reality Check' (2004) 27 *World Competition* 13.

[192]   White Paper on Modernisation, above n 2.

[193]   See eg 1993 Co-operation Notice [1993] OJ C39/6.

[194]   eg Case C-91/95 *Tremblay v Commission* [1996] ECR I-5574; [1997] 4 CMLR 211, where the CFI referred to the Commission being able to reject a complaint 'provided that the rights of the complainant . . . can be adequately safeguarded, in particular, by the national courts'. See also Case T-24/90 *Automec Srl v Commission* ('*Automec No 2*') [1992] ECR II-2223; [1992] 5 CMLR 431.

[195]   Case 127/73 *BRT and SABAM* [1974] ECR 51, para 16.

[196]   *Commission Notice on the Co-operation Between the Commission and the Courts of the EU Member States in the Application of Articles 81 and 82 EC Treaty* [2004] OJ C101/54. This replaced the previous such Co-operation Notice [1993] OJ C39/6.

relating to the function and independence of the judiciary, national courts cannot be members of the ECN[197] with the Commission and NCAs. Nor can the Cooperation Notice bind national courts. However, it does set out useful guidance which in part draws upon established case law[198] of the Court of Justice but also explains the Commission's view of the new arrangements under Regulation 1/2003.

As will be discussed further below, the value of the national court in competition law enforcement is in providing a decentralised opportunity for injured competitors and consumers (and, in some cases, even parties to the unlawful activity) to obtain remedies for infringements of Articles 101 and 102. This private aspect of enforcement, in parallel with the fining powers of the public authorities, sets up a system of dual enforcement that matches more closely the wider development of EU law as a result of the general principles established by the Court of Justice.[199] The latter, specifically the principles of equivalence and effectiveness, are underlined in the Cooperation Notice.[200]

As part of the need to secure uniform application of EU competition law, Article 16 of Regulation 1/2003 requires that national courts must avoid giving decisions which would conflict with a decision contemplated by the Commission in proceedings it has initiated.[201] To that effect, the national court may assess whether it is necessary to stay its proceedings. As a further device to enhance consistency and co-operation, NCAs, on their own initiative, may submit written observations to the national courts of their Member State on issues relating to the application of Articles 101 and 102.[202] With the permission of the court in question, NCAs may also make oral observations. The Commission enjoys similar powers, except that its observations are confined to situations 'where the coherent application of Article 101 or Article 102 so requires'. This, the Commission states, means that it will limit its observations 'to an economic and legal analysis of the facts underlying the case pending before the national court'.[203] Nonetheless, the ECJ has affirmed[204] that Article 15(3) provided the Commission with competence to intervene *amicus curiae* in proceedings in the Dutch courts concerning the tax deductibility of fines imposed by the Commission in relation to the plasterboard cartel[205] as the outcome of the dispute was capable of impairing the effectiveness of the penalty that had been imposed.[206]

National courts dealing with proceedings for the application of Articles 101 or 102 may also ask the Commission for information or its opinion on questions concerning the EU competition rules.[207] This power is, of course, without prejudice to any national court's ability to seek a preliminary ruling from the Court of Justice using the Article 267 TFEU procedure.[208]

Nevertheless, the encouragement of this privatisation tendency within the EU law

---

[197] Although it is possible for a national court to be designated as a national competition authority: Art 35(1) of Regulation 1/2003. In such a case, the court (qua NCA) would be covered by the Network Notice, above n 4.

[198] Especially Case 14/68 *Walt Wilhelm* [1969] ECR 1; Case C-2/88 *Zwartveld* [1990] ECR I-4405; Case C-234/89 *Delimitis* [1991] ECR I-935; Case C-344/98 *Masterfoods* [2000] ECR I-11369.

[199] See Chapter 10, above.

[200] Co-operation Notice, above n 196, para 10.

[201] See *Crehan v Inntrepreneur Pub Co* [2007] 1 AC 333(HL).

[202] Ibid, Art15(3).

[203] Co-operation Notice, above n 196, para 32.

[204] Case C- 429/07 *Inspecteur van de Belastingdienst v X BV* [2009] 5 CMLR 12.

[205] Case COMP/E-1/37.152—*Plasterboard* .

[206] See above n 204, paras 30–40, in particular para 39.

[207] Art 15(1) of Regulation 1/2003.

[208] See Chapter 7, above.

enforcement framework since 2004[209] still represents a significant leap of faith. As Advocate General Geelhoed observed in *Manfredi*, in relation to a number of cases referred by Italian courts on whether damages were available to consumers injured by concerted practices adopted by insurance companies:

> [P]rivate enforcement in Europe is still in its infancy, or at least it is clearly not practised on the scale familiar from other jurisdictions, especially that of the United States, where some 90 per cent of antitrust proceedings are initiated by private parties. In the European Union the emphasis has traditionally lain on public enforcement, both by the European Commission and by national authorities.[210]

The Advocate General summarised the arguments in favour of private enforcement thus:

> Besides the sanction of invalidity ensuing from Article 81(2) EC, an advantage mentioned in this context is that national courts may award damages. A court should also give a ruling in any dispute brought before it, and it should protect the rights of individuals. As public enforcers, on the other hand, act in the general interest, they often have certain priorities, and not every complaint is therefore considered as to its substance. Furthermore, civil actions may have a deterrent effect on (potential) offenders against the prohibition of cartels and so contribute to the enforcement of that prohibition and to the development of a culture of competition among market operators.[211]

However, the Advocate General also added a word of caution:

> The growth in private enforcement may, however, vary from one Member State to another, depending on procedural culture, the restrictions imposed on jurisdiction, rules on the burden of proof, the possibility of class actions, etc. The effectiveness of that enforcement is, of course, partly determined by the accessibility of the national courts.[212]

B – *Crehan v Courage* and an EU-based Remedy for Private Parties?

In purely doctrinal terms, it is important to clarify the exact basis of such claims. More specifically, the question to be examined is whether a *Francovich*-type[213] autonomous remedy exists, or should exist, at the private level for damages against undertakings in breach of Articles 101 or 102, or whether the enforcement mechanism amounts to a set of disparate (albeit perhaps converging) national remedies and claims regulated or supervised within the 'usual' twin themes of equivalence and effectiveness.

The case in favour of an EU right to damages against individuals who infringe Treaty rules had been forcefully presented by Advocate General van Gerven in *H Banks & Co Ltd v British Coal Corporation*,[214] a case following shortly on the heels of *Francovich*. The Advocate General pointed to the remedy as both the logical consequence of horizontal direct effect and an important step in the more effective enforcement of decentralised

---

[209] See the *Commission Notice on the Handling of Complaints by the Commission under Articles 81 and 82 of the EC Treaty* [2004] OJ C101/65.

[210] Joined Cases C-295-298/04 *Manfredi v Lloyd Adriatico Assicurazioni SpA* [2006] ECR I-6619; [2006] 5 CMLR 17, para 29.

[211] Ibid, para 30.

[212] Ibid, para 31.

[213] Joined Cases C-6 and 9/90 *Francovich v Italy* [1991] ECR I-5357; [1993] 2 CMLR 66; discussed above, Chapter 9.

[214] Case C-128/92 *H Banks & Co Ltd v British Coal Corporation* [1994] ECR I-1209; [1994] 5 CMLR 30.

competition law. However, the Court of Justice avoided the need to discuss these questions by finding that the rules of the ECSC Treaty at issue in that case were not directly effective in the first place. This particular discussion was only kick-started again by the Court's judgment in *Courage v Crehan*,[215] a decade after it had decided *Francovich*.

The case arose from a preliminary reference made by the English Court of Appeal in the context of a tied-pub contract. Two key aspects of the case formed the context for the request: first, it was one of the parties to the contract who was seeking to claim damages on the basis that it infringed Article 101; secondly, as presented by the referring court, English law treated contracts in breach of Article 101 as illegal and, consequently, parties to an illegal contract could not recover damages as a matter of English law. The answers given by the Court of Justice spawned a critical literature[216] which principally engaged with whether the Court had created a right to damages for breach of Article 101 as a matter of EU law, or whether it had, more narrowly, applied its general effectiveness principles to the particular context of Article 101. If the latter, then damages might be seen as the usual expectation as a national remedy but not mandated by EU law as such.

The key passages of principle are, indeed, strikingly reminiscent of the Court's reasoning earlier when unveiling state liability in damages to individuals in *Francovich*. Having referred to its *SABAM* ruling[217] in relation to national courts and the EU competition rules, the Court continued:

> It follows . . . that *any individual* can rely on a breach of [Article 81(1)] of the Treaty before a national court even where he is a party to a contract that is liable to restrict or distort competition within the meaning of that provision. . . .
>
> The full effectiveness of [Article 101] of the Treaty and, in particular, the practical effect of the prohibition laid down in [Article 101(1)] would be put at risk if it were not open to any individual to claim damages for loss caused to him by a contract or by conduct liable to restrict or distort competition.
>
> Indeed, *the existence of such a right* strengthens the working of the Community competition rules and discourages agreements or practices, which are frequently covert, which are liable to restrict or distort competition. From that point of view, *actions for damages before the national courts can make a significant contribution to the maintenance of effective competition* in the Community.
>
> There should not therefore be any absolute bar to such an action being brought by a party to a contract which would be held to violate the competition rules.[218]

Clearly, this passage can be read very widely if so desired. The italicised parts were couched in more general terms than required by the circumstances of the case. Moreover, as was also the case in the *Francovich* ruling, the structure of the *Courage* judgment is to set out general observations and then move to the particular context.

It is at this second stage that the *Courage* judgment could be read as a marginal retreat from a full-blown endorsement of any autonomous EU-law-based entitlement to damages. The final sentence in the above extract is much more redolent of the *Factortame*[219]

---

[215] Case C-453/99 *Courage v Crehan Ltd* [2001] ECR I-6314.

[216] See in particular A Komninos, 'New Prospects for the Private Enforcement of EC Antitrust Rules before National Courts' (2002) 39 *CMLRev* 447; O Odudu and J Edelman, 'Compensatory Damages for Breach of Art 81' (2002) 27 *ELRev* 327; N Reich, 'The "Courage" Doctrine: Encouraging or Discouraging Compensation for Antitrust Injuries?' (2005) 42 *CMLRev* 53.

[217] *SABAM*, above n 195.

[218] *Courage*, above n 215, paras 24–28 (citations omitted; emphasis added).

[219] Case C-213/89 *R v Secretary of State for Transport, ex p Factortame* [1990] ECR I-2433; [1990] 3 CMLR 375.

dispute, where a particular remedy in English law was also unavailable[220] at the time of the request for an interpretation under the preliminary ruling procedure. Indeed, in the later passages of *Courage*, the Court restricted the discussion to the effectiveness of the national (lack of) remedy in protecting an individual's enjoyment of his rights under the EU competition rules. The Court specifically acknowledged that there could be circumstances where the right to damages could be limited in relation to a party responsible for the restriction on competition.

The broader sense of the *Courage* judgment gained currency, and the Cooperation Notice, for example, puts *Courage* and *Francovich* together as examples where individuals should, under certain conditions, be able to ask a national court for damages.[221] More forcefully, the Commission's Green Paper of 2005[222] declared that 'individuals who have suffered a loss arising from an infringement of Articles [101 or 102] have the right to claim damages'. However, the ECJ in *Manfredi*,[223] emphasised that in the absence of EU rules, it was for the Member States' domestic legal systems to provide the rules governing the existence of the right to compensation, subject to the principles of equivalence and effectiveness being observed. Accordingly, a key problem for the development of private enforcement of EU competition law lies in the deference to national procedural autonomy by the Court of Justice combined with the range of national procedural obstacles to a coherent and developed system of private competition litigation, recognised by the Ashurst report,[224] produced for the Commission in 2004.

C – Commission Reform Proposals

Subsequently, the Commission published a Green Paper[225] which advocated damages claims as a way of boosting both the remedies for consumers and injured firms whilst improving the efficiency and effectiveness of competition law more generally. However, the Commission acknowledged that many obstacles still existed to the pursuit of claims in domestic courts—a very different situation to the United States, where antitrust litigation is commonplace as a result of a combination of factors, primarily the availability of class actions, 'treble damages', contingency fees and liberal discovery rules,[226] as well as a more litigious culture generally. The White Paper published in 2008 made a number of proposals which would require reform of civil procedure within Member States, based on the principle that all EU citizens who suffer damages through competition law infringements

---

[220] ie interim relief against the Crown.

[221] *Commission Notice on the Co-operation Between the Commission and the Courts*, above n 196, para 10. Note the discussion of the EU ruling and the decision in favour of Crehan by the Court of Appeal following that ruling, in *Crehan v Inntrrpreneur Pub Co* [2004] EWCA Civ 637 (CA). This was overturned on other grounds by the House of Lords, see [2007] 1 AC 333(HL).

[222] Green Paper, *Damages Actions for Breach of the EC Antitrust Rules*, COM(2005) 672 final.

[223] Joined Cases C-295-298/04 *Manfredi v Lloyd Adriatico Assicurazioni SpA* [2006] ECR I-6619; [2006] 5 CMLR 17.

[224] 'Study on the Conditions of Claims for Damages in Case of Infringement of EC Competition Rules', available at http://ec.europa.eu/comm/competition/antitrust/others/actions_for_damages/study.html. See also S Kon and A Maxwell, 'Enforcement in National Courts of the EC and New UK Competition Rules: Obstacles to Effective Enforcement' [1998] *ECLR* 443.

[225] Green Paper, *Damages Actions for Breach of the EC Antitrust Rule*, above n 222.

[226] See eg RH Lande and JP Davis, 'Of Myths and Evidence: An Analysis of 40 US Cases for Countries Considering a Private Right of Action for Competition Law Violations' [2009] *GCLR* 126.

should be able to claim full compensation.[227] The White Paper proposals included: guaranteed standing for all indirect purchasers, potentially through representative and opt-in collective actions; a minimum level of disclosure inter partes; the binding effect of NCA decisions across the EU; a non-binding framework to facilitate the calculation of damages; the availability of the passing-on defence to defendants, but a rebuttable presumption that damage had been passed on to indirect purchasers; and protection for leniency applicants. To date no EU legislation has been adopted in relation to the issues raised by the White Paper, but the Commission is consulting in 2011 on the need for a coherent European approach to collective redress,[228] and this may ultimately lead to improved and harmonised collective-redress mechanisms to facilitate consumer claims for competition law infringements at least. In the absence of a harmonised system of remedies for competition law infringements, the normal principles of equivalence and effectiveness are likely to come under further scrutiny in a competition context. On a more positive note, despite the dearth of reported cases where final damages have been awarded,[229] there is evidence of increasing resort to litigation,[230] and one must also bear in mind the 'hidden story' of actions that are settled before any final hearing.[231] Furthermore, damages actions are not the only way in which parties can exercise their rights in a competition law context. In the case of Article 101, the civil consequences of infringement are spelt out by the second paragraph, which provides: 'Any agreements or decisions prohibited pursuant to this Article shall be automatically void.' The automatic nullity in Article 101(2) 'applies to those parts of the agreement affected by the prohibition, or to the agreement as a whole if it appears that those parts are not severable from the agreement itself'.[232] Whether any offending clauses can be severed, leaving the main part of the agreement intact, falls to be determined under the law of the Member State concerned.[233]

VI – CONCLUDING REMARKS

The EU competition law enforcement framework has changed beyond recognition over the last 20 years, through evolving Commission policies, changes in the legislative framework and the seemingly never-ending Court jurisprudence in response to numerous challenges to the enforcement processes and sanctions deployed by the Commission. The

---

[227] White Paper on Damages Actions for Breach of the EC Antitrust Rules, COM(2008) 165 final. See also Commission Staff Working paper accompanying the White Paper on damages actions for breach of the EC antitrust rules, SEC(2008) 404, both available at http://ec.europa.eu/competition/antitrust/actionsdamages/index.html. For discussion, see F Bulst, 'Of Arms and Armour—The European Commission's White Paper on Damages Actions for Breach of EC Antitrust Law' [2008] *Bucerius Law Journal* 81; JS Kortmann and ChRA Swaak, 'The EC White Paper on Antitrust Damages Actions: Why the Member States Are (Right To Be) Less than Enthusiastic' [2009] *ECLR* 340.

[228] See http://ec.europa.eu/competition/antitrust/actionsdamages/index.html.

[229] See the *Crehan* litigation saga discussed above.

[230] See eg B Rodger, 'Competition Law Litigation in the UK Courts: A Study of All Cases 2005–2008' [2009] GCLR 91 (part I) and 136 (part II).

[231] See B Rodger, 'Private Enforcement of Competition law, the Hidden Story: Competition Litigation Settlements in the UK 2000–2005' [2007] *ECLR* 96.

[232] Case 56/65 *Société Technique Minière v Maschinenbau Ulm* [1966] ECR 235; [1966] CMLR 357.

[233] Case C-230/96 *Cabour SA and Nord Distribution Automobile SA v Automobiles Peugeot SA and Automobiles Citröen SA* [1998] ECR I-2055; [1988] 5 CMLR 679. See also Joined Cases T-185 and 190/96 *Riviera Auto Service Etablissements Dalmasso v Commission* [1999] ECR II-93; [1999] 5 CMLR 31.

Commission remains at the apex of EU competition law enforcement but the landscape has changed dramatically with the introduction of Regulation 1/2003 and the enforcement role for NCAs as part of the ECN. Decentralised enforcement by the NCAs has reduced the burden on the Commission and to date there appears to have been no jurisdictional case allocation conflicts between NCAs. Regulation 1 retained broadly similar investigative and decision-making powers for the Commission as under the old Regulation 17 regime, but with the addition of a more informal commitments remedy which has been utilised by the Commission on a number of occasions. The Commission has prioritised its enforcement resources on hard-core cartels, and as part of this so-called 'cartel-busting revolution' the Commission has introduced, revised and upgraded its leniency policy to encourage whistleblowers, and also dramatically increased the fines imposed for cartel participation. The success of its anti-cartel strategy has, nonetheless further stretched the enforcement capacity of the Commission and led to the introduction of a streamlined settlement procedure. There has been voluminous European Court case law in relation to the rights of defence generally, involving issues such as due process, equal treatment and double jeopardy. There has been sustained criticism of the compatibility of various aspects of the enforcement process with ECHR case law, and with the entry into force of the CFR and the imminent accession of the EU to the ECHR, the Court of Justice may be required to reconsider some of its existing case law: the clamour for reform of the administrative enforcement process is likely to increase. Finally, it is anticipated that in the coming years we will witness a substantial increase in competition law litigation in the national courts, further decentralising and privatising EU competition law enforcement, with or without any Commission-led harmonisation measures.

Further Reading

O Armengol and A Pascual, 'Some Reflections on Article 9 Commitment Decisions in the Light of the Coca-Cola Case' [2006] *ECLR* 124.

A Andreangeli, *EU Competition Enforcement and Human Rights* (Cheltenham, Edward Elgar Publishing, 2008).

S Brammer, 'Concurrent Jurisdiction under Regulation 1/2003 and the Issue of Case Allocation' (2005) 42 *CMLRev* 1383.

——, *Co-operation Between National Competition Agencies in the Enforcement of EC Competition Law* (Oxford, Hart Publishing, 2009).

F Bulst, 'Of Arms and Armour—The European Commission's White Paper on Damages Actions for Breach of EC Antitrust Law' [2008] *Bucerius Law Journal* 81.

F Cengiz, 'Multi-level Governance in Competition Policy: The European Competition Network' (2010) 35 *ELRev* 660.

K Dekeyser and M Jaspers, 'A New Era of ECN Co-operation' (2007) 30 *World Competition* 3.

C Hodges, *The Reform of Class and Representative Actions in European Legal systems* (Oxford, Hart Publishing, 2008).

I Forrester, 'Due Process in EC Competition Cases: A Distinguished Institution with Flawed Procedures' (2009) 34 *ELRev* 817

A Komninos, 'New Prospects for Private Enforcement of EC Competition Law: Courage v Crehan and the Community Right to Damages' (2002) 39 *CMLRev* 447.

——, *EC Private Enforcement: Decentralized Application of EC Competition Law by National Courts* (Oxford, Hart Publishing, 2008).

S Kon and A Maxwell, 'Enforcement in National Courts of the EC and New UK Competition Rules: Obstacles to Effective Enforcement' (1998) 7 *ECLR* 443.

JS Kortmann and ChRA Swaak, 'The EC White Paper on Antitrust Damages Actions: Why the Member States Are (Right To Be) Less than Enthusiastic [2009] *ECLR* 340.

M Motta, 'On Cartel Deterrence and Fines in the European Union' [2008] *ECLR* 209.

A Riley, 'The Modernisation of EU Anti-cartel Enforcement: Will the Commission Grasp The opportunity?' [2010] *ECLR* 191.

——, 'The Consequences of the European Cartel-Busting Revolution' (2005) 12 *Irish Journal of European Law* 5.

J Venit, 'Brave New World: The Modernization and Decentralization of Enforcement under Articles 81 and 82 of the EC Treaty' (2003) 40 *CMLRev* 537.

WJ Wils, 'The European Commission's 2006 Guidelines on Antitrust Fines: A Legal and Economic Analysis' (2007) 30 *World Competition* 197.

——, 'Leniency in Antitrust Enforcement: Theory and Practice' (2007) 30 *World Competition* 25.

——, *Efficiency and Justice in European Antitrust Enforcement* (Oxford, Hart Publishing, 2008).

——, 'The Increased Level of EU Antitrust Fines, Judicial Review and the European Convention on Human Rights' (2010) 33 *World Competition* 6.

——, 'Discretion and Prioritisation in Public Antitrust enforcement' (2011) 34 *World Competition* forthcoming.

——, 'EU Antitrust Enforcement Powers and Procedural Rights and Guarantees: The Interplay between EU Law, National Law, the Charter of Fundamental Rights of the EU and the European Convention on Human Rights' (2011) 34 *World Competition* forthcoming.

26

State Aid and State Regulation

This chapter deals with various EU competition rules related to state involvement in, and regulation of, markets. The chapter first examines the rules and enforcement of Articles 107–109 TFEU (ex Articles 87–89 EC) in relation to state aid, modernised to a great extent in recent years following the adoption of the State Aid Action plan in 2005. These provisions apply to advantages, such as subsidies, preferential loans and other support, conferred upon selected undertakings by the state or through state resources and which distort competition. The essential features of the system are that Member States should notify new aid to the Commission for approval against criteria set out in the Treaty. Only the Commission can declare aid incompatible with the Treaty, although national courts have been given an increasing role in upholding the procedural safeguards of the Treaty rules and ensuring that individuals are protected against failures by Member States to comply. The chapter begins by discussing the concept of aid for the purposes of Article 107, focusing on the case law relating to its requisite constituent elements. It then moves to an overview of the justifications for aid under the mandatory and discretionary exceptions of Article 107(2) and (3), respectively. The particular controversies surrounding state support to services of general economic interest are explored against recent case and legislative developments, including the relationship of the aid rules with Article 106(2). The procedural requirements for supervising and enforcing the state aid rules are summarised, with particular attention being paid to obstacles to the recovery of unlawful aid and the extent to which private remedies are available against states or beneficiaries of aid. The chapter then considers Article 106 TFEU (ex Article 86 EC), which is a complex provision governing the extent to which the usual competition rules apply to Member States and to undertakings given special rights or privileges by states. After a brief discussion of the general policy issues affecting the relationship between states, markets and public services, the chapter then analyses the three separate paragraphs of Article 106. It discusses the conditions upon which states will be legally responsible under Article 106(1) for infringements by undertakings of other rules of the Treaty. Article 106(2), which allows undertakings entrusted with services of general economic interest to escape the full rigour of the Treaty rules, is shown to have evolved from a strict derogation to a mechanism for balancing of competition and public-interest concerns. The Commission's special supervisory and legislative powers under Article 106(3) are also briefly examined. The chapter concludes with a discussion of the Court's limited use of Article 101 TFEU (ex Article 81 EC) in conjunction with Article 4(3) TEU (ex Article 10 EC) where Member States reinforce anti-competitive agreements or delegate their legislative powers to private economic operators.

I – INTRODUCTION: STATE AID AND THE MODERNISATION AGENDA

By curtailing the freedom of Member States to pursue unilateral industrial strategies, state aid control has been described as 'clearly the most original of the EU's competition policies'.[1] The unfettered grant of state aid would be liable to cause serious difficulties in a system which has as a primary objective the creation and maintenance of a single internal market. As the Court of Justice has observed:

> The aim of [Article 107] of the Treaty is to prevent trade between Member States from being affected by advantages granted by public authorities.[2]

The evolution of state aid regulation must be seen in the context of the developments already discussed in relation to the general competition rules.[3] In particular, the competitiveness agenda set out in the so-called Lisbon strategy also drove the reform of state aid policy.

The Commission launched a comprehensive reform of state aid rules and procedures in its State Aid Action Plan in June 2005.[4] The aim was to ensure that the state aid rules focus aid measures in order to contribute to the Lisbon strategy to enhance the competitiveness of EU industry and create sustainable jobs. The overall policy goal can be defined as 'less and better targeted state aid' but it also included the following elements: a more refined economic approach; more streamlined and efficient procedures; better enforcement; greater predictability; and enhanced transparency. Since the adoption of the Plan, a number of measures have been introduced, and other measures have been revised or are under revision with a view to completing the modernisation process by 2009. A key objective of the State Aid Action Plan was to create a coherent and user-friendly set of rules to apply to aid which fulfilled the compatibility criteria in Article 107(3). Accordingly, the Commission consolidated the existing Block Exemption Regulations into a single instrument, the General Block Exemption (GBER). The GBER was adopted in July 2008,[5] with a view to achieving less and better targeted aid. It covers certain types of horizontal aid already provided for by existing block exemption Regulations, such as training and regional aid, but also integrated into the GBER aid in the form of risk capital, and further enlarged the scope of existing BERs by extending the R&D aspect to large enterprises. The most significant inclusion was in relation to environmental aids, largely drawn from experience under the environmental guidelines published in 2001.

The state aid reform measures are strongly resonant of developments in relation to Articles 101 and 102: more economic analysis of distortions and market failures; more networking between EU and national agencies; more guidance documentation from the Commission; and greater participation in enforcement from private parties and national courts.

Certainly, it may be said that the operation and effectiveness of state aid supervision is

---

[1] M Cini and L McGowan, *Competition Policy in the European Union* (Macmillan, Basingstoke, 1998) 135.

[2] Case C-39/94 *SFEI v La Poste* [1996] ECR I-3547, para 58.

[3] See Chapters 22–25, above.

[4] State Aid Action Plan, 'Less and Better Targeted State Aid: A Roadmap for State Aid Reform 2005–2009', COM(2005) 107 final, Commission press release IP/05/680, 7 June 2005.

[5] [2008] OJ L214/3.

a good litmus test of the EU's maturity as a legal order.[6] After years as a legal backwater of interest to only the most idiosyncratic practitioners and academics, state aid has become a mainstream political and legal issue. It took, for example, until 1999 for there to be a procedural and enforcement Regulation[7] in state aid matters to supply a counterpart to the 1962 Regulation in competition law more generally.[8] However, the regime of state aid control remains both distinctive and fraught with controversy. As will be seen from this chapter, some familiar questions arise—is market distortion measured by conceptual possibility or actual impact? Does financial support to services of general economic interest require justification? What is the most effective balance of public and private enforcement?

II – THE STRUCTURE OF ARTICLE 107 TFEU

Article 107 sets out the principles on the basis of which the compatibility of state aid with the internal market is to be judged.[9] Paragraph (1) of the Article lays down the general principle that state aid fulfilling certain broadly defined criteria is incompatible with the internal market. The paragraph does not expressly declare incompatible aids to be prohibited (*cf* the drafting of Articles 101 and 102 TFEU), but the European Court has accepted that it contains an implied prohibition, though neither absolute nor unconditional.[10]

The general principle in Article 107(1) is qualified by mandatory exceptions listed in paragraph (2) and discretionary exceptions listed in paragraph (3). If an aid is found to be within one of the categories in paragraph (2), it must, as a matter of law, be regarded as compatible with the internal market. On the other hand, the compatibility of aids falling within the categories in paragraph (3) is a discretionary matter, requiring an assessment of the positive and negative effects of the aid from the point of view of the Union as a whole. Under the machinery of Article 108 (see below) that discretion is exercised by the Commission, subject to reserve powers of the Council and the usual review criteria of the European Court. The latter's case law has also significantly enhanced the responsibilities of national courts in relation to the protection of individuals against failure by Member States to observe their duties under Article 108(3). Enabling legislation agreed by the Council in 1998[11] permits the Commission to adopt Regulations setting out block exemptions for certain types of aid.[12] Aid falling within a block exemption does not need to be notified. Aspects of state aid procedure and enforcement have been set out in detail by Regulation.[13]

---

[6] M Ross, 'State Aids: Maturing into a Constitutional Problem' (1995) 15 *YEL* 79.

[7] Regulation 659/1999 [1999] OJ L83.

[8] Regulation 17/62, replaced by Regulation 1/2003, see Chapter 25, above.

[9] For further comment, see C Quigley, *European State Aid Law and Policy*, 2nd edn (Oxford, Hart Publishing, 2009); A Biondi, P Eeckhout and J Flynn (eds), *The Law of State Aid in the European Union* (Oxford, Oxford University Press, 2004); K Bacon (ed), *European Community Law of State Aid* (Oxford, Oxford University Press, 2009).

[10] See the references to 'an aid which is prohibited' in Case 6/69 *Commission v France* [1969] ECR 523; [1970] CMLR 43 and 'the prohibition in [Art 87](1)' in Case 78/76 *Firma Steinike und Weinlig v Germany* [1977] ECR 595; [1977] 2 CMLR 688.

[11] Council Regulation 994/98; [1998] OJ L142/1.

[12] See GBER, above n 5; see also Regulation 1998/2006 on De Minimis Aid [2006] OJ L379/5

[13] Respectively, Regulation 659/1999, above n 7; Regulation 794/2004 [2004] OJ L140.

Article 107(1) provides:

Save as otherwise provided in the Treaties, any aid granted by a Member State or through State resources in any form whatsoever which distorts or threatens to distort competition by favouring certain undertakings or the production of certain goods shall, in so far as it affects trade between Member States, be incompatible with the internal market.

A general definition of state aid for the purposes of the Treaty was offered by the European Court in *Amministrazione delle finanze dello stato v Denkavit*,[14] where it said that paragraph (1) of the Article

refers to the decisions of Member States by which the latter, in pursuit of their own economic and social objectives give, by unilateral and autonomous decisions, undertakings or other persons resources or procure for them advantages intended to encourage the attainment of the economic or social objectives sought.[15]

State aid is thus to be understood in terms of its function as an instrument of national economic and social policy involving the provision of some kind of tangible benefit for specific undertakings.[16]

It is immaterial what form the benefit may take or what particular goal of policy it may be designed to serve. The European Court has repeatedly held that the prohibition in paragraph (1) does not distinguish between measures of state intervention by reference to their causes or aims but defines them in relation to their effects,[17] and extends to the following forms of aid: direct subsidies; exemption from duties and taxes; exemption from parafiscal charges; preferential interest rates; guarantees of loans on especially favourable terms; making land or buildings available either gratuitously or on especially favourable terms; provision of goods or services on preferential terms; indemnities against operating losses; deferred collection of fiscal or social contributions, direct and indirect state participation in share capital, and logistical or commercial assistance granted in return for unusually low consideration. This is not an exhaustive list, although it covers the forms of aid most frequently granted by the Member States. Since 2001, the Commission's website[18] has maintained a State Aid Scoreboard.

III – DEFINING STATE AID: THE CONDITIONS OF ARTICLE 107(1)

The concept of 'aid' provides the trigger for the application of Articles 107–109 and, therefore, the EU regime of supervision. According to the Court of Justice, Article 107(1) lays down the following conditions:

---

[14] Case 61/79 *Amministrazione delle finanze dello stato v Denkavit* [1980] ECR 1205; [1981] 3 CMLR 694.

[15] Ibid, [1980] ECR 1205, 1228; repeated by the Court of First Instance in Case T-351/02 *Deutsche Bahn v Commission* [2006] ECR II-1047; [2006] 2 CMLR 54.

[16] 'Undertakings' may include individuals if the usual tests of economic activity are satisfied; see Chapter 22, above; in the state aid context, see Case C-172/03 *Heiser* [2005] ECR I-1627, involving dental practitioners.

[17] Case 173/73 *Italy v Commission* [1974] ECR 709; [1974] 2 CMLR 593; Case C-241/94 *France v Commission* [1996] ECR 4551; [1997] 1 CMLR 983.

[18] See http://ec.europa.eu/competition/state_aid/studies_reports/studies_reports.html.

First, there must be an intervention by the State or through State resources. Second, the intervention must be liable to affect trade between Member States. Third, it must confer an advantage on the recipient. Fourth, it must distort or threaten to distort competition.'[19]

Although not always consistently identified and ordered in this way by either courts or commentators, these are cumulative requirements[20] and are discussed in turn below.

A – Intervention by the State or Through State Resources

To fall within the scope of Article 107(1) the aid must be granted 'by a Member State or through State resources'. Although the Court refers to this as one condition, it has also made it clear that it comprises two separate but cumulative elements.[21] Not only must the aid be granted directly or indirectly through state resources but it must be imputable to the state.[22] In other words, the phrase used in Article 107(1) is not as wide as might otherwise appear. The reference to 'or through State resources' serves to bring within the definition of aid, in addition to benefits granted directly by the state, those granted by a public or private body designated or established by the state. 'Secondly, those resources must be attributable to the State or to the relevant public body in such a way that it is able to exercise a sufficient degree of control over them.'[23] Clearly, the conditions will be satisfied by grants by regional or local authorities as well as by central government. Moreover, state resources do not always have to be under the control of the Treasury.[24]

However, the question of whether an alleged aid has come from state resources has proved controversial. Thus, in *Sloman Neptun*[25] German legislation created a shipping register which allowed ships flying under the German flag but employing non-EU crew to escape the full rigours of German labour law. Advocate General Darmon argued that the effect of reducing those shipowners' costs was equivalent to a state-authorised fund for their benefit. However, the Court rejected this view on the basis that there was no burden on state resources. It confirmed this approach in *Epifanio Viscido v Ente Poste Italiane*,[26] where the provision in question gave relief to Poste Italiane from the normal rule of Italian law that employment contracts were of indefinite duration. The flexibility of fixed-term contracts, whilst arguably conferring benefits or saved costs for the undertaking, did not involve any direct or indirect transfer of state resources to it.

Nevertheless, the value of the state resources test in its *Sloman Neptun* form continues to be criticised. In *Enirisorse v Sotacarbo*[27] Italian law provided that, in derogation from

---

[19] Case C-280/00 *Altmark GmbH v Nahverkehrsgesellschaft Altmark GmbH* ('*Altmark*')[2003] ECR I-7747, [2003] 3 CMLR 12, para 75. See also eg Case C-399/08 P *Commission v Deutsche Post AG* [2011] 1 CMLR 14.
[20] Case C-142/87 *Belgium v Commission* ('*Tubemeuse*') [1990] ECR I-959, para 25; Joined Cases C-278–80/92 *Spain v Commission* [1994] ECR I-4103, para 20; Case C-482/99 *France v Commission* ('*Stardust Marine*') [2002] ECR I-4397, para 68; *Altmark*, above n 19, para 74.
[21] *France v Commission* ('*Stardust Marine*'), above n 20, para 24.
[22] Case C-345/02 *Pearle v Hoofdbedrijfschap Ambachten* [2004] ECR I-7139, [2004] 3 CMLR 9, para 35.
[23] Opinion in *Pearle*, ibid, para 67.
[24] See Case C-379/98 *Preussen Elektra* [2001] ECR I-2099.
[25] Joined Cases C-72-73/91 *Firma Sloman Neptun Schiffahrts A-G v Seebetriebsrat Bodo Ziesmer, Sloman Neptun Schiffahrts AG* [1993] ECR I-887; [1995] 2 CMLR 97. A similar approach was taken in Case C-189/91 *Kirsammer-Hack v Sidal* [1993] ECR I-6185.
[26] Joined Cases C-52-54/97 *Epifanio Viscido v Ente Poste Italiane* [1998] ECR I-2629; [1998] 3 CMLR 184. See also *Preussen Elektra*, above n 24.
[27] Case C-237/04 *Enirisorse v Sotacarbo* [2006] ECR I-2843.

the general law,[28] members of a company controlled by the state could withdraw from that company on condition they relinquished all claims over that company's assets. Advocate General Poiares Maduro accepted that application of the *Sloman Neptun* approach would not treat the scenario as a transfer of state resources. However, he expressed strong dissatisfaction with the substance of that test, whilst accepting the legitimacy of a need to place Article 107(1) within limits.[29]

According to the Advocate General, a more workable and effects-based test would be one based on selective advantage.[30] The Court, however, adhered to the language of *Sloman Neptun* and observed that the national law merely prevented the company's budget from being burdened with a charge which, in a normal situation, would not have existed.[31]

For Article 107(1) to apply there must be imputability to the state. The way in which this is an additional requirement beyond the state resources element can be illustrated by the *Stardust Marine* case.[32] Here the financial measures which had been attacked as aid by the Commission were implemented by public undertakings. The Court insisted that it was necessary to go further and examine whether the public authorities had been involved, in one way or another, in the adoption of the aid measures. Without imposing a level of strictness which would demand proof of the state inciting a body to take particular measures, the Court listed factors which might indicate a sufficient degree of involvement. These included: the legal status of the public undertaking (whether subject to public law or company law, for example), the intensity of the supervision exercised by the public authorities over the management of the undertaking or deductions about state involvement to be drawn from the compass of the measures, their content or the conditions they contain. The Court accordingly annulled the Commission's decision.

The imputability test will clearly be satisfied if the state has chosen to act through the agency of some public or private body. EU law does not permit the rules on state aid to be circumvented merely through the creation of autonomous institutions charged with allocating aid.[33] However, where the state has enacted its obligations under an EU directive and an advantage results, this will not be treated as an aid imputed to the state.[34]

B – Liable to Affect Trade between Member States

The prohibition in Article 107(1) requires that the aid distorts or threatens to distort competition in so far as it affects trade between Member States. In *Philip Morris Holland v Commission*[35] the Court came close to enunciating a per se rule as to the effect on interstate trade which would result from aids designed to enable a cigarette manufacturer to close one of its two factories in the Netherlands and to expand production at the other. The Court said that:

---

[28] Whether in fact derogation was possible in the general law was not entirely clear, a point stressed by the Advocate General.

[29] Opinion, paras 44–45; see also *Pearle*, above n 22, para 36, also applying *Sloman Neptun*.

[30] The advantage condition is discussed separately, below.

[31] *Sloman Neptun*, above n 25, para 48.

[32] *France v Commission* ('*Stardust Marine*'), above n 20.

[33] Case T-358/94 *Air France v Commission* [1996] ECR II-2109, para 62; [1997] 1 CMLR 492.

[34] *Deutsche Bahn*, above n 15.

[35] Case 730/79 *Philip Morris Holland v Commission* [1980] ECR 2671; [1981] 2 CMLR 321.

When financial aid strengthens the position of an undertaking as compared with other undertakings competing in intra-Community trade the latter must be regarded as affected by that aid.[36]

Nevertheless, it is still the Court's formal position that there is no threshold or percentage below which it may be considered that trade between Member States is not affected.[37] Moreover, application of the condition does not depend on the local or regional character of the services supplied or on the scale of the field of activity concerned.[38] Whether aid is 'capable' of having an impact on trade between Member States remains the judicial test.[39]

The Court's approach thus does not sit entirely easily with the practice of the Commission, which has applied a de minimis policy since 1992.[40] This currently[41] means that aid of an amount less than €200,000 granted to an undertaking over a period of three years does not require notification for approval since it is deemed to have only negligible effects on competition and trade between Member States.

C – Conferring an Advantage on the Recipient

The third condition within the notion of aid is the requirement that it must 'favour' certain undertakings or the production of certain goods. This formulation suggests at least two ideas, advantage and selectivity, but the interplay between them has created difficulties in the case law. It impliedly requires some comparison to be made between the treatment accorded to the alleged beneficiary and the position of other undertakings.[42]

The notion of advantage has been expressed in a variety of ways, but all are driven by a quest to establish whether the transaction, activity or conduct amounts to a normal commercial transaction or rational market behaviour. Different contexts will demand nuanced tests, but two particular themes in the case law are sufficiently prevalent to merit closer discussion below. Firstly, there is a well-established principle that applies a hypothetical market investor (or creditor) test as the benchmark. However, there may be circumstances where this kind of comparison is impossible. Secondly, a discernible thread has arisen which is capable of denying the presence of an advantage where the alleged benefit can be described as 'inherent' in the scheme or system being investigated or challenged. This line of argument, if not carefully applied, runs the risk of conflating advantage and justification.

(i) Market/Private Investor/Creditor Tests

This approach had its origins in the cases of the 1980s which established that equity par-

---

[36] Ibid, para 11.
[37] *Heiser*, above n 16, para 32; see also para 35.
[38] Ibid, para 33; also *Altmark*, above n 19.
[39] eg Joined Cases T-195/01 and T-207/01 *Government of Gibraltar v Commission* [2002] ECR II-2309.
[40] *cf Belgium v Commission* ('*Tubemeuse*'), above n 20, para 43, where the Court expressly rejected the contention put forward by the Belgian government that the 5% threshold then used by the Commission in general competition matters should also apply to state aids.
[41] Commission Regulation 1998/2006 , above n 12.
[42] Case C-353/95P *Tiercé Ladbroke v Commission* [1997] ECR I-7007.

ticipation by the state in corporate financing could in principle amount to aid within the meaning of Article 107(1). Thus, in *Re Boch*[43] the Court observed:

> In the case of an undertaking whose capital is almost entirely held by the public authorities, the test is, in particular, whether in similar circumstances a private shareholder, having regard to the foreseeability of obtaining a return and leaving aside all social, regional policy and sectoral considerations, would have subscribed the capital in question.

In the wake of this judicial support, the market investor principle (now more commonly referred to as the 'private investor principle') was refined and elaborated beyond the context of capital investment. The key question has essentially become whether the recipient undertaking receives an economic advantage which it would not have obtained under normal market conditions.[44] Expressions of the principle can be found, for example, in relation to loans and interest rates thereon,[45] guarantees[46] and the renegotiation of credit terms.[47] Put shortly, the Court will only find that an aid exists if the state has been acting other than as an 'ordinary economic agent'.[48] This accordingly means that failure by the Commission to make proper assessments of costs, valuations and other economic criteria will undermine any allegation of aid.[49] The reference point for comparsion must be taken at the contemporaneous period of the financial support measures.[50] In *Italy v Commission*[51] the Court held that capital provided by a public investor who is not interested in profitability, even in the long term, must be regarded as an aid for the purposes of the EU rules.[52] However, the 'normal market conditions' comparison will break down if the operation in question is a universal service network which would never have been created by a private undertaking. This was the situation in *Chronopost*,[53] where La Poste held a monopoly in ordinary mail delivery in France. It had provided various logistical and commercial assistance to its subsidiary, Chronopost, providing the latter with access to its postal infrastructure for the collection and transport of Chronopost's express courier deliveries and access to La Poste's customers and enjoyment of its goodwill. The Commission had originally rejected the existence of aid, but this decision had been annulled by the Court of First Instance[54] on application by Chronopost's express courier delivery competitors. On appeal to the Court of Justice, the Court of First Instance's approach was held to have been flawed in law. In particular, an undertaking such as La Poste was in a situation 'very different' from that of a private undertaking acting under normal market conditions. Moreover, the provision of logistical and commercial assistance was inseparably linked to

---

[43] Case 40/85 *Re Boch: Belgium v Commission* [1986] ECR 2321; [1998] 2 CMLR 301. See also Joined Cases 296 and 318/82 *The Netherlands and Leeuwarder Papierwaren fabriek BV v Commission* [1985] ECR 809; [1985] 3 CMLR 380; *Spain v Commission*, above n 20.

[44] *SFEI v La Poste*, above n 2, para 60.

[45] Case T-214/95 *Vlaams Gewest v Commission* [1998] ECR II-717; Case T-16/96 *Cityflyer Express v Commission* [1998] ECR II-757; [1998] 2 CMLR 537.

[46] Joined Cases C-329/93 and C-62-63/95 *Germany v Commission, Hanseatische Industrie Beteiligungen GmbH v Commission, Bremer Vulkan Verbund A-G v Commission* [1996] ECRI-5151.

[47] Case C-256/97 *DMT* [1999] ECR I-3913.

[48] Case C-56/93 *Belgium v Commission* [1996] ECR I-723; see also Case T-196/04 *Ryanair Ltd v Commission* [2008] ECR II-3643; [2009] 2 CMLR 7.

[49] See Case T-98/00 *Linde AG v Commission* [2002] ECR II-3961.

[50] *France v Commission* ('*Stardust Marine*'), above n 20.

[51] Case C-303/88 *Italy v Commission* [1991] ECR I-1433; [1993] 2 CMLR 1.

[52] See also Case C-305/89 *Italy v Commission* [1991] ECR I-1603.

[53] Joined Cases C-83/01P, C-93/01P and C-94/01P *Chronopost v Ufex* [2003] ECR I-6993.

[54] Case T-613/97 *Ufex v Commission* [2000] ECR II-4055. Ufex was the successor to SFEI—see *SFEI v La Poste*, above n 2.

the La Poste network, since it consisted precisely in making available that network which had no equivalent on the market. Thus, according to the Court:

> [I]n the absence of any possibility of comparing the situation of La Poste with that of a private group of undertakings not operating in a reserved sector, normal market conditions, which are necessarily hypothetical, must be assessed by reference to the objective and verifiable elements which are available.

The Court accordingly referred the case back to the Court of First Instance for an assessment of how far payments by Chronopost covered La Poste's costs.

Judging whether aid exists because the state fails to demand money owed to it, or is prepared to delay its recovery, presents a further issue as to what is to be construed as 'normal'. Hence, and rather later than the invention of the market/private investor comparison, the case law has also spawned a 'hypothetical private creditor' approach. This may not always be easy to apply, as evidenced by *Spain v Commission*.[55] As Advocate General Poiares Maduro has since indicated, the hypothetical private creditor is a diligent and efficient market operator, capable of discerning and using the most appropriate means of achieving a certain result, ie the recovery of its debts.[56] In his view, choosing to waive a debt temporarily while the debtor continues its activities must satisfy three conditions to avoid constituting an aid: it must be possible in principle to make the undertaking economically viable and to improve its financial position; everything possible must be done to prevent further credit being run up and new debts accumulated; and the state must be able to rely on the recovery of the debts owed to it within a reasonable period.[57]

Having made some arrangement with a debtor over waiver, the creditor must exercise due diligence in monitoring and enforcing against further failures to try to recover at least a marginal amount of the money owed.[58]

(ii) Selectivity

Article 107(1) requires it to be determined whether, under a particular statutory scheme, a state measure is such as to favour 'certain undertakings or the production of certain goods' in comparison with others which, in the light of the objective pursued by the system in question, are in a comparable legal and factual situation.[59] A distinction is, therefore, drawn between general measures of economic policy, such as the easing of credit controls or a specific tax regime for the self-employed, which may very well improve the position of undertakings in the country concerned vis-à-vis their competitors elsewhere in the EU, and measures giving a competitive advantage to particular undertakings or industrial

---

[55] Case C-342/96 *Spain v Commission* [1999] ECR I-2459.

[56] Case C-276/02 *Spain v Commission* [2004] ECR I-8091, Opinion, para 36.

[57] Ibid, para 40. The Advocate General identified key differences between the investor and creditor models of comparsion for aid measurement at para 24.

[58] In *Spain v Commission*, above n 56, the Court annulled the Commission's decision because it had paid insufficient attention to evidence that the Spanish authorities had taken some steps for enforcement of tax and social security obligations. The Court of First Instance has subjected the Commission's application of the creditor tests to considerable scrutiny; see also Case T-152/99 *HAMSA v Commission* [2002] ECR II-3049; Joined Cases T-228/99 and T-233/99 *Westdeutsche Landesbank Girozentrale v Commission* [2003] ECR II-435.

[59] Case C-308/01 *GIL Insurance* [2004] ECR I-4777, citing Case C-143/99 *Adria-Wien Pipeline and Wietersdorfer & Peggauer Zementwerke* [2001] ECR I-836; Case C-409/00 *Spain v Commission* [2003] ECR I-1487; see also *Heiser*, above n 16, para 40; Case T-335/08 *BNP Paribas and Banca Nazionale del lavoro SpA (BNL) v Commission* [2011] ECR (nyr). See, for general discussion, A Bartosch, 'Is There a Need for a Rule of Reason in European State Aid Law? Or How to Arrive at a Coherent Concept of Material Selectivity' (2010) 47 *CMLRev* 730.

sectors.[60] The fact that the number of undertakings able to claim entitlement under the measure at issue is very large, or that they belong to different sectors of activity, is not sufficient to call into question its selective nature and thus rule out its classification as a state aid.[61] In *Commission v France*[62] the European Court held that a preferential discount rate for exports must be regarded as an aid falling within the Treaty supervisory regime, despite the fact that it applied to all national products without distinction. The explanation seems to be[63] that some undertakings would be producing solely for the domestic market so that not all undertakings would in fact be claiming the preferential entitlement.

This distinction between aids and general measures is sometimes slippery. Where the scope of the rules is defined by regional location, industrial sector or size of undertaking, selectivity is clearly present, but problems may arise where criteria for the provision of resources appear to be universal. The key indication in such cases is whether the application of the measure rests upon discretion. According to the Court in the *DMT* case:

> [Where the body granting financial assistance enjoys a degree of latitude which enables it to choose the beneficiaries or the conditions under which the financial assistance is provided, that assistance cannot be considered to be general in nature.[64]

The Court then left to the national court the question of whether the practices of the national social security office, which had included allowing payments from the undertaking to be postponed for eight years, were indeed part of a discretionary system. Examples of the interaction of selectivity criteria can be seen in cases involving the special insolvency procedure of Italian law.[65]

One effect of using the operation of discretionary rules as a measure of selectivity is to invite a closer scrutiny of national decision-making processes than is the case in relation to other, more self-evident, criteria such as those based upon membership of a particular industrial sector. The Court accepts that there is no selectivity where, although an advantage accrues to its recipient, a measure is justified by the nature or general scheme of the system of which it is part, provided the system in question has a legitimate purpose.[66]

However, the Court has been reluctant to allow the 'inherent' claim to succeed too readily. In *Adria-Wien*,[67] for example, the Court rejected the advice of Advocate General Mischo, who had taken the view that an Austrian tax rebate granted only to undertakings whose activity consisted primarily in the manufacture of goods was not an aid. In particular, the Court noted that undertakings supplying services could incur similar energy taxes yet not be able to claim the rebate. Ecological arguments were similarly undermined, since energy consumption by service providers was just as damaging to the environment;

---

[60] See eg Case T-233/04 *Netherlands v Commission* [2008] ECR II-591. See also B Kurcz and D Vallindas, 'Can General Measures Be Selective? Some Thoughts on the Interpretation of a State Aid Definition' (2008) 45 *CMLRev* 159.

[61] *Heiser*, above n 16, para 42 (in relation to VAT exemptions for medical practitioners).

[62] Cases 6 and 11/69 *Commission v France* [1969] ECR 523; [1970] CMLR 43.

[63] Following the Opinion of AG Roemer, 552. For a later example of aid covering a whole sector, see Case C-95/97 *Belgium v Commission* [1999] ECR I-3671.

[64] *DMT*, above n 47, para 27.

[65] Case C-200/97 *Ecotrade v AFS* [1998] ECR I-7907; [1999] 2 CMLR 833. See also Case C-295/97 *Piaggio* [1999] ECR I-3735, particularly at para 38. Although the wording of the ECSC Treaty was different, the notion of selectivity was treated as being the same as that for an aid under the EC Treaty.

[66] *Enirisorse v Sotacarbo*, above n 27, Opinion, para 52.

[67] *Adria-Wien Pipeline*, above n 59.

thus relief for one sector could not be justified. The Court has been equally robust in other contexts.[68]

D – Distortion of Competition

This is the fourth and final condition cited by the Court of Justice as necessary to establish an aid within the meaning of Article 107(1).[69] It is in practice linked closely with the question of effect on inter-state trade, discussed above. The Court has been relatively lax in relation to both requirements. Consequently, the amount of aid can be very little, yet still be held to distort competition.[70] For example, in *Vlaams Gewest*[71] the Court of First Instance swiftly dismissed a claim by the beneficiary airline that the measly amount of aid it had received, described as a few Belgian francs per passenger, could scarcely have enabled it to avoid increasing its fares or ward off insolvency. Nor can a beneficiary use the fact that other undertakings are receiving aids (even illegal ones) from their states to argue that its own aid is only neutralising other distortions.[72] Aid intended to relieve undertakings of all or part of the expenses that they would normally have had to bear in their day-to-day management or usual activities in principle distorts competition.[73] There are, however, instances where failure to identify the proper market has been fatal to a decision taken by the Commission.[74]

IV – JUSTIFICATIONS FOR AID: MANDATORY EXCEPTIONS UNDER ARTICLE 107(2)

Article 107(2) provides that the following categories of aid shall be compatible with the common market:

— (a) aid having a social character, granted to individual consumers, provided that such aid is granted without discrimination related to the origin of the products concerned.

The scope of this exception is limited, especially by the requirement that the aid must be for final consumers. Intervention by the state to buy wheat and then resell it at a discount to enable cheaper bread to be available for consumers might conceivably qualify.[75] A travel

---

[68] See *Spain v Commission*, above n 59; Case C-159/01 *Netherlands v Commission* [2004] ECR I-4461; the Court, however, accepted the argument in *GIL Insurance*, above n 59. For an example of its unsuccessful application before the CFI, see Joined Cases T-346/99, T-347/99 and T-348/99 *Disputación de álava* [2002] ECR II-4259, paras 58–64.

[69] For further discussion, see P Nicolaides, 'Distortion of Competition in the Field of State Aid: From Unnecessary Aid to Unnecessary Distortion' [2010] *ECLR* 402.

[70] *Spain v Commission*, above n 20, para 42.

[71] *Vlaams Gewest v Commission*, above n 45.

[72] *Ibid*.

[73] *Westdeutsche Landesbank Girozentrale*, above n 58.

[74] Case T-155/98 *SIDE v Commission* [2002] ECR II-1179; see also the rigorous approach to distorting competition taken by the Court of First Instance in Case T-93/02, *Confédération nationale du Crédit Mutuel* [2005] ECR II-143.

[75] Case 52/76 *Benedetti v Munari* [1977] ECR 163. However, as pointed out by AG Reischl at 190, the problem in this case was that the benefit appeared to go to the flour mills, not just the final consumers.

voucher subsidy scheme was held to fall outside the scope of the provision as it had not been made available to ultimate consumers on a non-discriminatory basis.[76]

— (b) aid to make good the damage caused by natural disasters or exceptional occurrences.

Aid to make good the damage caused by natural disasters is an obvious candidate for automatic exemption from the general principle in Article 107(1). Italian measures which the Commission has treated as falling under this heading were the assistance given in Liguria to repairs and reconstruction required as a result of the floods in 1977, and the provision in Friuli-Venezia Giulia of low-interest loans and subsidies for the reconstruction of industrial plant destroyed by the earthquake in 1976.[77] The aid must be to make good the damage, rather than just promote the industrial development of the area. However, the latter could still qualify for exemption under the discretionary provisions of Article 107(3)(a) or (c).

The notion of 'exceptional circumstances' is very vague, but is taken to extend the scope of Article 107(2)(b) to 'man-made' damage such as that caused by war, terrorism,[78] marine pollution or catastrophic transport accidents. On the other hand, its applicability in the case of difficulties of an exclusively economic nature is more doubtful. The exceptional aid measures adopted by the Member States in the face of the serious recession which began to affect the Community from the second half of 1974 onwards were dealt with by the Commission under the predecessor to Article 107(3)(b). There must be a sufficient causal link between the disaster or exceptional circumstance and the economic disadvantage sustained.[79]

— (c) aid granted to the economy of certain areas of the Federal Republic of Germany affected by the division of Germany, in so far as such aid is required in order to compensate for the economic disadvantage caused by that division.

Since the reunification of Germany in 1990[80] the state aid rules have applied with full effect throughout the state. The Commission has consistently taken the view that the exemption must now be applied restrictively[81] and that the provisions of the discretionary exemptions of Article 107(3) are adequate to deal with remaining problems.[82] However, this point was contested in the *Saxony* and *Volkswagen* cases.[83] It was submitted by VW and the government that as sub-paragraph (c) had been left intact by the Maastricht and Amsterdam Treaties, its modern purpose must extend to use in compensating disadvantages experienced by the East in its exposure to a market economy. The Court of First Instance rejected this argument, noting that the difficulties of economic transition were caused not by the division of Germany as such but, in particular, by the nature of the polit-

---

[76] Joined Cases T-116/01 and T-118/01 *P & O Ferries (Vizcaya) SA v Commission* [2003] ECR II-2957, para 167.

[77] [1978] Competition Report, point 164.

[78] Including compensation to airlines for the losses sustained as the result of the closure of US airspace and increased insurance premiums in the wake of the terrorist attacks on New York in September 2001.

[79] See Case C-278/00 *Greece v Commission* [2000] ECR I-8787, where there was insufficient connection between the Chernobyl nuclear disaster and a legal provision enabling Greece to settle a whole range of debts owed by agricultural co-operatives.

[80] Monetary union came into effect in Germany on 1 July 1990 and political union on 3 October 1990.

[81] eg in relation to investment aids for Volkswagen, Commission Decision 94/1068, [1994] OJ L385/1.

[82] *Aid to Buna* [1996] OJ L239/1; the Commission did not regard the difficulties facing companies of the former GDR in meeting the challenges of EU competitors as disadvantages caused by the division of Germany.

[83] Joined Cases T-132 and 143/96 *Freistaat Sachsen and Volkswagen v Commission* [1999] ECR II-3663.

ico-economic regime which then applied. The Commission, accordingly, had not erred in law in taking the view that new aid by investment in the car industry was to be assessed against the criteria of Article 107(3) rather than Article 107(2)(c).

The Court of Justice has maintained this position, emphasising that paragraph (c) only covers the economic disadvantages caused by the 1948 division stemming from the establishment of a physical frontier, such as the breaking of communication links or the loss of markets as a result of the breaking off of commercial relations between the two parts of German territory. The economic disadvantages suffered by the new Länder as a whole following division have not been directly caused by the geographical division of Germany within the meaning of Article 107(2)(c). Differences in development between the original and the new Länder are explained by causes other than the geographical rift caused by the division of Germany and in particular by the different politico-economic systems set up in each part of Germany.[84]

Article 107(2)(c) provides that: 'Five years after the entry into force of the Treaty of Lisbon, the Council, acting on a proposal from the Commission, may adopt a decision repealing this point.'

V – DISCRETIONARY EXCEPTIONS UNDER ARTICLE 107(3)

The discretion given to the Commission under Article 107(3) is a wide one. Advocate General Capotorti described it in *Philip Morris Holland* as 'implying an assessment of an economic, technical and policy nature'.[85] The Court said that the exercise of the discretion 'involves economic and social assessments which must be made in a Community context'.[86]

When applying the discretionary exceptions, the Commission seeks to ensure that aid measures are approved only if they both promote recognised EU objectives and do not frustrate the maintenance of the internal market. The Commission only has power to authorise aids which are necessary for the furtherance of one of the objectives listed in paragraph (3).

In more recent times the Commission has established detailed Communications and Guidelines covering a range of aid areas (eg training, R&D and innovation aid, rescue and restructuring aid). These documents, which are not explored in detail here, typically set out methods for the calculation of aid, the eligibility of recipients and the overall 'intensity' of permitted levels of aid.[87] Furthermore, the consolidated GBER, adopted in 2008, provides for a range of types of horizontal aid, some of which were already provided by existing individual block exemptions, for instance in relation to training and regional aid, in addition to extending the scope of existing block exemptions to, inter alia, environmental aid.

---

[84] Case C-156/98 *Germany v Commission* [2000] ECR I-6857; repeated in Case C-334/99 *Germany v Commission* [2003] ECR I-1139; Case C-277/00 *Germany v Commission* [2004] ECR I-3925.

[85] *Philip Morris Holland*, above n 35, [1980] ECR 2671, 2701.

[86] Ibid, 2691.

[87] See Commission website at http://ec.europa.eu/competition/state_aid/legislation/horizontal.html.

The categories of aid that the Commission may determine to be compatible with the internal market in accordance with Article 107(3) are as follows:

— (a) aid to promote the economic development of areas where the standard of living is abnormally low or where there is serious under-employment.

The Court has made it clear that the assessment to be made under paragraph (a) is not confined to whether the measures will contribute effectively to the economic development of the regions concerned, but must also evaluate the impact of the aid on trade between Member States, and in particular to assess the sectorial repercussions they may have at an EU level.[88]

— (b) aid to promote the execution of an important project of common European interest or to remedy a serious disturbance in the economy of a Member State.

The exception applies to two completely different types of aid. Originally seen as covering infrastructure or technological advancement,[89] it is now clear that there will be no common European interest in a scheme 'unless it forms part of a transnational European programme supported jointly by a number of governments of the Member States, or arises from concerted action by a number of Member States to combat a common threat such as environmental pollution'.[90] The Court has indicated that R&D projects do not per se qualify.[91]

As for the second category under Article 107(3)(b), serious disturbances, the Commission used it as a safety valve in the economic troubles besetting Member States which followed the energy crisis of 1974.[92] Disturbances must relate to the whole of a national economy, not just one region or sector.[93] In the latter case the appropriate tool is Article 107(3)(c).

In the wake of the economic and financial crisis in 2008, the Commission has introduced a number of measures under the aegis of this provision to effectively relax the application of the state aid rules in the financial sector and allow Member States to take action to avoid a widespread banking crisis disaster, and also to provide a temporary framework for state aid measures to support access to finance.[94] These generally allow notified measures to be treated by the Commission with extreme urgency.

— (c) aid to facilitate the development of certain economic activities or of certain economic

[88] Case C-114/00 *Spain v Commission* [2002] ECR I-7657, para 81.

[89] eg a common standard for the development of high-definition colour television: see [1989] Competition Report, point 151.

[90] Joined Cases 62/87 and 72/87 *Executif Regional Wallon and Glaverbel v Commission* [1988] ECR 1573; [1989] 2 CMLR 771.

[91] Ibid.

[92] See [1975] Competition Report, point 133.

[93] Case C-301/96 *Germany v Commission* [2003] ECR I-9919 where the German government merely referred to a serious disturbance in the economy of Saxony and made no allegation about serious disturbances for the German economy.

[94] See Commission website at http://ec.europa.eu/competition/state_aid/legislation/temporary.html and http://ec.europa.eu/competition/recovery/index.html. For further discussion, see eg D Zimmer and M Blaschzok, 'The Role of Competition in European State Aid Control During the Financial Markets Crisis' [2011] *ECLR* 9. See also H Gilliams, 'Stress Testing the Regulator: Review of State Aid to Financial Institutions after the Collapse of Lehman' (2011) 36 *ELRev* 3; H Gilliams, 'From Rescue to Restructuring: The Role of State Aid Control for the Financial Sector' (2010) 47 *CMLRev* 313; P Nicolaides and IE Rusu, 'The Conflicting Roles of State Aid Control: Support of Financial Institutions versus Safeguarding the Internal Market' (2010) 17 *Maastricht J* 223.

areas, where such aid does not adversely affect trading conditions to an extent contrary to the common interest.

This is the most important of the exceptions to the general principle in Article 107(1). The legal limits of the Commission's discretion under paragraph (c) are defined by the notion of facilitating the development of the activities or areas concerned and by the proviso that aid must not have an adverse effect on trading conditions 'to an extent contrary to the common interest'. It enables the Commission to authorise aids to particular industrial sectors, aids which promote certain 'horizontal' policies, and aids to particular regions of a Member State. Sectors to attract attention have been those in difficulties (eg textiles, shipbuilding, motor vehicles, coal and steel), those for which the EU has established policies (agriculture, fisheries and transport) and sectors which merit particular promotion (such as energy). 'Horizontal' policies address common themes and problems which may arise in any industry. The areas for which frameworks and guidelines have been developed include the following:[95] small and medium-sized enterprises (SMEs); research, development and innovation (R&D); environmental protection; training; and rescue and restructuring.[96] Aid schemes which might otherwise be deemed incompatible may be justified against these horizontal considerations. With the exception of rescue and restructuring aid, these various types of horizontal aid are provided for by the GBER.

— (d) aid to promote culture and heritage conservation where such aid does not affect trading conditions and competition in the Union to an extent that is contrary to the common interest.

This exception has been used by the Commission on a number of occasions, especially in relation to films and books.[97] However, its decisions approving aid to support the export of books in the French language to non-French-speaking countries were overturned by the Court of First Instance for errors in market assessment.[98] The proviso attached to paragraph (d) is the same as for paragraph (c), with the express addition of competition as a consideration pertinent to the common interest, presumably to take account of the particular impact that aids in the fields of broadcasting, media and other conduits of cultural expression might have.

— (e) Authorisation of aid by the Council.

The Council's powers to authorise state aids are limited, being confined to Article 107(3)(e) and Article 108(2) third sub-paragraph. The former represents the last in the list of express discretionary exceptions, namely: '(e) such other categories of aid as may be specified by decision of the Council acting by a qualified majority on a proposal from the Commission'. A series of directives on aids to shipbuilding in the Member States was adopted under this provision, although shipbuilding is now regulated by a 'standard' framework.[99]

Authorisation by the Council under Article 108(2) third sub-paragraph is expressly

---

[95] See http://ec.europa.eu/competition/state_aid/legislation/horizontal.html.

[96] See [2004] OJ C244/2.

[97] See E Psychogiopoulou, 'EC State Aid Control and Cultural Justifications' (2006) 33 *Legal IEI* 3.

[98] Case T-49/93 *SIDE v Commission* [1995] ECR II-2501; Case T-155/98 *SIDE v Commission* [2002] ECR II-1179.

[99] See Framework on Shipbuilding [2003] OJ C317, replacing Council Regulation 1540/98. This has subsequently been prolonged twice, most recently by Commission Communication adopted on 3 July 2008, [2008] OJ C173/3, extending the Framework to 31 December 2011.

reserved for exceptional circumstances, and has been described as one of the safety valves of the Treaty.[100] The case law interpreting this provision is limited, but most examples are to be found in the agricultural sector.

VI – ARTICLE 107 AND SERVICES OF GENERAL ECONOMIC INTEREST

Special mention should be made of the treatment in EU law of financial support granted by states to providers of services of general economic interest (SGEIs). Such undertakings are expressly mentioned in Article 106(2) TFEU.[101] In particular, that provision relaxes the full rigour of the competition rules where their application would constitute an obstacle to fulfilment of the tasks assigned. From 2000, the Court was confronted by the question of whether financial support to the providers of public services to offset the charges or losses incurred in meeting their obligations constituted aid. Two particular conceptual issues fell to be determined: firstly, whether such support was aid (hence notifiable under Article 107 and requiring justification) or compensation (taking it outside Article 107 altogether); secondly, what role, if any, was left to Article 106(2) in relation to such cases.

A – Aid or Compensation

The problem posed by the SGEI cases was not entirely novel. The notion of an aid as a 'gratuitous advantage'[102] had previously posed the question of what would happen where that advantage was effectively wiped out by the cost of meeting the criteria of eligibility.[103] However, the issue starkly resurfaced in *Ferring*,[104] a case concerning a special French sales tax applicable to pharmaceutical laboratories selling directly to pharmacies. Prima facie, this looked like a selective advantage in so far as it did not attach to wholesale distributors and thus was arguably a tax exemption in favour of the latter. However, the wholesale distributors had particular obligations imposed on them: in particular, they had to hold a permanent range of products to meet demands over a specific geographical area and to deliver requested supplies within a very short time throughout that area. The Court's judgment entertained the possibility that the sales tax imposed on the pharmaceutical distributors might be compensation for the services provided by the wholesalers if there was the necessary equivalence between the exemption and the additional costs of meeting the public service elements.

---

[100] AG Cosmas in Case C-122/94 *Commission v Council* [1996] ECR 881, para 62.

[101] See discussion further below in relation to Art 106(2). See eg Joined Cases T-309/04, T-317/04, T-329/04 and T-336/04 *TV 2/Danmark A/S v Commission* [2008] ECR II-02935, in relation to the classification of broadcasting services as services of general economic interest.

[102] See *Firma Steinike und Weinlig v Germany*, above n 10.

[103] See J Winter, 'Re(de)fining the Notion of State Aid in Art 87(1) of the EC Treaty' (2004) 41 *CMLRev* 475.

[104] Case C-53/00 *Ferring v ACOSS* [2001] ECR I-9067.

Advocate General Léger in *Altmark*[105] argued that the compensation approach under-mined Article 106(2) by conflating the questions of aid and justification at the Article 107(1) stage of analysis and disturbing the Commission's surveillance role. In his view, Article 106(2) was the 'central Treaty provision for reconciling Community objectives'.[106] A rather less strident approach was adopted by Advocate General Jacobs in *GEMO*,[107] argu-ing that some cases might be assessed under the aid rules and others could be properly treated as compensation, according to how clearly the entrusted obligation had been iden-tified and linked to the state support. Advocate General Stix-Hackl[108] described *Ferring* as a departure both from the Court's previous case law and the Commission's practice.

The Court in *Altmark*, however, took the opportunity to clarify the conditions neces-sary for compensation to escape classification as state aid:

> First, the recipient undertaking must actually have public service obligations to discharge, and the obligations must be clearly defined . . .
>
> Second, the parameters on the basis of which the compensation is calculated must be estab-lished in advance in an objective and transparent manner, to avoid it conferring an economic advantage which may favour the recipient undertaking over competing undertakings . . .
>
> Third, the compensation cannot exceed what is necessary to cover all or part of the costs incurred in the discharge of public service obligations, taking into account the relevant receipts and a reasonable profit for discharging those obligations. Compliance with such a condition is essential to ensure that the recipient undertaking is not given any advantage which distorts or threatens to distort competition by strengthening that undertaking's competitive position.
>
> Fourth, where the undertaking which is to discharge public service obligations, in a specific case, is not chosen pursuant to a public procurement procedure which would allow for the selection of the tenderer capable of providing those services at the least cost to the community, the level of compensation needed must be determined on the basis of an analysis of the costs which a typical undertaking, well run and adequately provided with means of transport so as to be able to meet the necessary public service requirements, would have incurred in discharging those obligations, taking into account the relevant receipts and a reasonable profit for discharging the obligations.[109]

These are cumulative criteria, so that failure to comply with any one of them will render the financial contribution an aid for the purposes of Article 107(1).[110]

These criteria provide a checklist for scrutiny that goes some way towards allaying fears that the Court might be prepared to jettison the entire supervisory regime of EU law in relation to SGEIs.[111] Post-*Altmark*, Commission decisions have been annulled for failing to apply the criteria adequately.[112] As will be discussed further below, national courts are empowered to determine whether a measure or package of measures amounts to aid and so will therefore need to apply the *Altmark* tests.[113]

[105] *Altmark*, above n 19.
[106] Ibid, Opinion, para 80.
[107] Case C-126/01 *GEMO* [2003] ECR I-13769.
[108] Case C-34/01 *Enirisorse v Amministrazione delle Finanze* [2003] ECR I-3609.
[109] *Altmark*, above n 19, paras 89–93.
[110] See eg Case C-140/09 *Fallimento Traghetti del Mediterraneo SpA v Presidenza del Consiglio dei Ministri* [2010] 3 CMLR 46.
[111] See the application of the *Altmark* criteria in Case T-289/03 *BUPA Insurance Ltd v Commission* [2008] ECR II-81; [2009] 2 CMLR 41.
[112] eg in Case T-157/01, *Danske Busvognmænd v Commission* [2004] ECR II-917; Case T-274/01 *Valmont Nederland BV v Commission* [2004] ECR; also *Confédération nationale du Crédit Mutuel*, above n 74 (although not exclusively decided upon compensation aspects).
[113] See eg Case C-451/03 *Servizi Ausiliari Dottori Commercialist v Calafiori* [2006] ECR I-2941; *Fallimento*

It is the fourth condition that is perhaps the most far-reaching, bearing upon the pro-cedural context in which 'compensation' payments are made by a state.[114] A certain degree of coercion is thus applied: either comply with the steps of *Altmark* or take the risk of having to justify an aid in a different forum.[115]

B – Article 106(2) after Altmark

The Court was conspicuously silent in *Altmark* as to where its pronouncements left Article 106(2). At first glance, since the tests were set up in relation to demarcating aid from compensation for the purposes of Article 107(1), a measure in relation to an entrusted undertaking that does not satisfy the criteria for compensation can still seek to take the benefit of Article 106(2). However, in *Heiser*,[116] the Court noted that:

> [T]he derogation provided for by [Article 106(2)] of the Treaty does not prevent a measure from being classified as State aid. . . . Nor could it, once such a classification has been made, allow the Member State concerned not to notify the measure pursuant to [Article 108(3)] of the Treaty.[117]

Moreover, it might be wondered how far the practicalities of a failure to meet the *Altmark* conditions would allow Article 106(2) to be applied in an undertaking's favour.[118] To clarify this, the Commission has adopted detailed measures, discussed below.

C – Legislation Post-Altmark in Relation to SGEIs

The real impact of *Altmark* was to trigger a legislative response from the Commission which sought to provide affirmation of the protection for compensation to provid-ers of SGEIs. In 2005 it adopted a package of measures, consisting of an amendment to the Transparency Directive,[119] a Decision on the conditions of compensation and a Framework for the measurement of compatibility with the aid rules for measures which go further than compensation. The Decision[120] specifies the conditions for qualification as compensation and applies to amounts of less than €30 million per year provided its beneficiaries have an annual turnover of less than €100 million. Compensation provided

---

Traghetti del Mediterraneo SpA, above n 110.

[114] *Servizi Ausiliari Dottori Commercialist*, above n 113. See also Case C-399/08 P *Commission v Deutsche Post AG* [2011] 1 CMLR 14; *Fallimento Traghetti del Mediterraneo SpA*, above n 110.

[115] See M Ross, 'The Europeanization of Public Services Supervision: Harnessing Competition and Citizenship?' (2004) 23 *YEL* 303; MT Karayigit, 'Under the Triangle Rules of Competition, State Aid and Public Procurement: Public Undertakings Entrusted with the Operation of Services of General Economic Interest' [2011] *ECLR* 542; D Cahill, 'The Ebb and Flow, the Doldrums and the Raging Tide: Single Market Law's Ebb and Flow over Services of General Economic Interest, the Legal Doldrums over Services of General Interest, and the Raging Tide of Art 106(2) (ex Art 86(2)) over State Aid and Public Procurement' (2010) 21 *EBLRev* 629.

[116] *Heiser*, above n 16.

[117] Ibid, para 51, citing Joined Cases C-261/01 and C-262/01 *Van Calster* [2003] ECR I-12249.

[118] See eg Case T-189/03 *ASM Brescia SpA v Commission*.

[119] Commission Directive 2006/111/EC [2006] OJ L318/17.

[120] Decision 2005/842 [2005] OJ L312/67 *On the Application of Art 86(2) to State Aid in the Form of Public Service Compensation Granted to Certain Undertakings Entrusted with the Operation of Services of General Economic Interest*. This was adopted on the basis of Art 106(3); see below.

to hospital and social housing for SGEIs is covered irrespective of amounts. Where the Decision applies, there is no need to notify the compensation since it does not constitute aid within the meaning of the Treaty.

The Commission's Framework,[121] on the other hand, governs public service compensation that does not take the benefit of Decision 2005/842 and which must therefore be notified as aid. The point of the Framework, without prejudice to Articles 101 and 102 TFEU and the public procurement rules, is to spell out the conditions under which such aid may be justified under Article 106(2). In particular, it requires the entrusting of SGEI responsibilities to specify the following: the precise nature and the duration of the public service obligations; the undertakings and territory concerned; the nature of any exclusive or special rights assigned to the undertaking; the parameters for calculating, controlling and reviewing the compensation; and the arrangements for avoiding and repaying any over-compensation.[122] Taking the fourth condition of the *Altmark* judgment as its departure point, the Framework fleshes out the notions of costs, compensation and reasonable profit. The Framework applies for six years to November 2011.[123] At the time of writing, the Commission has issued a Communication to launch the debate on the revision of the state aid package on SGEIs (the 'post-Altmark Package').[124] The main principles for reform focus on clarification of the key concepts in relation to state aid rules and SGEI and the adoption of a diversified and proportionate approach to different forms of SGEI, to maintain consistency with the overriding objective of EU state aid law and thereby ensure that any state aid implemented contributes to an objective of common interest.[125] In particular, the Commission is concerned with enhancing efficiency:

> Under the current Package, compensation granted for the provision of SGEI can cover the costs incurred by the provider and a reasonable profit margin. The current Package does not, however, take into account how the costs incurred by the provider of SGEI compare to those of a well-run undertaking. Some of the costs compensated by Member States to providers may thus be generated by low efficiency levels. Such a situation tends to distort the functioning of markets and may ultimately harm service quality and efficient delivery. In addition, it is misaligned with the general public policy objective of efficiency in public spending and correct resource allocation.[126]

It is anticipated that a new framework will be in place to broadly implement these proposals before the end of 2011.

---

[121] *Community Framework for State Aid in the Form of Public Service Compensation* [2005] OJ C297/4.

[122] Ibid, para 12.

[123] Note, in particular, the Commission Staff working document, 'Guide to the application of the European Union rules on state aid, public procurement and the internal market to services of general economic interest, and in particular to social services of general interest Brussels', 7 December 2010, SEC(2010) 1545 final. See also more generally, http://ec.europa.eu/services_general_interest/interest_en.htm and the Commission Communication on 'Services of general interest, including social services of general interest: a new European commitment', 20 November 2007, COM(2007) 725.

[124] Commission Communication on the Reform of the EU State Aid Rules on Services of General Economic Interest, Brussels, 23 March 2011, COM(2011) 146 final.

[125] Ibid, para 4.2.

[126] Ibid, para 4.2.2.2

VII – ENFORCEMENT OF STATE AID RULES: THE LEGISLATIVE MACHINERY

We have seen that state aid meeting the criteria in Article 107(1) is not automatically to be regarded as incompatible with the internal market, since it may fall within one of the excepted categories in paragraphs (2) and (3) of the Article, or be exempted using the special powers of the Council. Moreover, the application, in particular, of Article 107(3) entails a complex appreciation of economic and social factors in the light of the overall Union interest. The approach adopted by the Treaty is to make the EU institutions responsible in the first instance for giving concrete effect to the principles of Article 107, and machinery for this purpose has been provided in Articles 108 and 109.

The corollary of the provision of special machinery at Union level is that national courts may not rule on the compatibility of an aid with the internal market.[127] In this sense, Article 107 is not directly effective. However, it does not follow that national courts may not sometimes have to interpret Article 107, for example to decide whether a measure introduced by a Member State without obtaining clearance under Article 108(3) constitutes 'aid'. Such scrutiny forms part of the general obligation upon national courts to provide effective protection of individuals' rights conferred by these procedural requirements.[128] National courts are also empowered to determine whether an aid falls within the scope of a relevant block exemption.

Procedural legislation in the state aid field akin to that prevalent in general competition law matters took years to materialise. However, in 1999 the Council finally used its powers under Article 89 EC to adopt Regulation 659/1999, which came into force on 16 April 1999.[129] This ('Procedural') Regulation was aimed at codifying case law practices and making the procedural rules more transparent and accessible. A further Council ('Implementing') Regulation[130] was adopted in 2004 as part of the general modernisation package for EU competition law and deals with matters such as the forms for notification, the determination of time limits and the calculation of interest rates when pursuing recovery of aid. Finally, as part of the modernisation of state aid, in 2009 the Commission introduced a simplification package, consisting of a Notice and Best Practice Code, to accelerate state aid decisions in straightforward cases and thereby enhancing the effectiveness, transparency and predictability of its state aid decision-making processes.[131]

The 1999 Regulation distinguishes four different situations for procedural purposes: notified aid, unlawful aid, misuse of aid and existing aid schemes—each governed by a different chapter. These are discussed further below.

---

[127] *Firma Steinike und Weinlig v Germany*, above n 10.

[128] *SFEI v La Poste*, above n 2.

[129] Regulation 659/1999 [1999] OJ L83/1. See A Sinnaeve and P-J Slot, 'The New Regulation on State Aid Procedures' (1999) 36 *CMLRev* 1153; A Sinnaeve, 'State Aid Procedures: Developments Since the Entry into Force of the Procedural Regulation' (2007) 44 *CMLRev* 965.

[130] Regulation 794/2004, above n 13.

[131] See Commission press release IP/09/659, Brussels, 29 April 2009; Commission Notice on a Simplified Procedure for the Treatment of Certain Types of State Aid [2009] OJ C136/3 (and Corrigendum [2009] OJ C157/20); and Commission Notice on a Best Practices Code on the Conduct of State Aid Control Proceedings [2009] OJ C136/13.

A – Notified Aid

Article 108(3) of the Treaty provides:

> The Commission shall be informed, in sufficient time to enable it to submit its comments, of any plans to grant or alter aid. If it considers that any such plan is not compatible with the internal market having regard to Article 107, it shall without delay initiate the procedure provided for in paragraph 2. The Member State concerned shall not put its proposed measures into effect until this procedure has resulted in a final decision.

The paragraph establishes a system of prior control which is designed to prevent any aid incompatible with the internal market from being introduced. Member States are required to notify the Commission of plans to grant or alter aid sufficiently in advance of the date set for their implementation to enable it to examine the plans and form a view as to whether the procedure under Article 108(2) should be initiated against them. According to Article 2 of Regulation 659, the notification requirement relates to 'any plans to grant new aid', aid being defined in Article 1 as any measure fulfilling all the criteria laid down in Article 107(1) of the Treaty. This means that notification is not required for all measures which might constitute aid, but only for those which embrace each of the elements of Article 107(1). There is thus the capacity for 'existential' uncertainty[132] because of the potential gap between a Member State's view as to whether a measure, for example, affects inter-state trade or represents a sufficiently significant distortion of competition, compared to the Commission's ex post facto assessment of the situation. Aid falling within a block exemption need not be notified, nor in principle is notification required for individual applications of an approved aid scheme.[133] However, the principle of effectiveness requires that a Member State is required not only to notify the planned aid in the narrow sense but also the method of financing the aid inasmuch as that method is an integral part of the planned measure.[134]

The last sentence of Article 108(3) imposes a 'standstill' obligation upon the Member State proposing to introduce an aid.[135] This applies during the period of preliminary review by the Commission and, if the procedure under Article 108(2) is initiated, continues until a final decision is reached. A fortiori, a Member State is prohibited from putting an aid into effect without notifying it at all.[136]

Where aid is notified, Article 4 of Regulation 659 provides for three outcomes to be determined in the form of a decision by the Commission after conducting a preliminary examination. First, it may record that the notified measure does not constitute aid at all. Secondly, it may decide not to raise objections, specifying which exception of the Treaty has been applied. It does not appear that the Commission could attach conditions to such a finding, as these would imply incompatibility with the internal market requiring a formal investigation.[137] Thirdly, if doubts are raised as to the compatibility of the aid

---

[132] Sinnaeve and Slot, above n 129, 1165.

[133] Under Regulation 659, such an individual application constitutes 'existing aid'.

[134] *Van Calster*, above n 117. On the notion of 'integral', see Case C-175/02 *Pape* [2005] ECR I-127 and Case C-174/02 *Streekgewest Westelijk Noord-Brabant* [2005] ECR I-85.

[135] Case 84/82 *Germany v Commission* [1984] ECR 1451. This is now also stated in Art 3 of Regulation 659.

[136] Case C-204/97 *Portugal v Commission* [2001] ECR I-3175. See also Case C-400/99 *Italy v Commission* [2005] ECR I-3657.

[137] *cf* Art 7(3) of Regulation 659, and closure of the formal investigation procedure.

with the internal market, the Commission shall make a decision as to whether to initi-ate the formal investigation procedure of Article 108(2). Such a decision must be taken within two months, commencing the day following a complete notification.[138] Following the expiry of that period without a decision by the Commission the aid shall be deemed to have been authorised and the Member State may implement the measures after giving the Commission prior notice.[139]

Where an aid proposal is altered after having been notified to the Commission, the latter must be informed of the amendment, although this may be done in the course of consultations arising from the original notification.[140] Failure to bring amendments to the attention of the Commission will cause the standstill under Article 108(3) to remain in force against a scheme which has otherwise been found compatible with the common market. However, the Court recognises that not every technical modification to an exist-ing aid must be notified.[141] Detailed rules for the operation of the formal investigation procedure are set out in Article 6 of Regulation 659 Closure of the formal investigation procedure must follow the paths indicated by Article 7 of Regulation 659. Thus, as with the ending of the preliminary stage, the Commission may decide that no aid is involved. A second possibility is a positive decision confirming the aid and specifying which Treaty exception is being relied upon. The Commission has the power[142] to attach conditions to a positive decision. Finally, the Commission may adopt a negative decision, ruling that the notified aid is not compatible with the internal market.

Decisions taken under Article 7 are, as far as possible, to be taken by the Commission within a period of 18 months from the opening of the formal investigation procedure.[143] After the expiry of this period, the Member State may request the Commission to take a decision within two months. The overall length of the investigation period has been criticised,[144] not least because the necessity might be questioned of any aid project which takes almost two years to be approved.[145] The simplified Procedure and Best Practice Code adopted in 2009 may ameliorate this problem, at least in relation to straightforward cases.

B – Unlawful Aid

According to Article 1(f) of Regulation 659, unlawful aid is new aid put into effect in con-travention of Article 108(3) of the Treaty. Thus it covers not only aid that has not been notified at all, but also aid that is notified but implemented prior to authorisation and aid implemented in breach of the terms of authorisation. Where the Commission has in

[138] Art 4(5) of Regulation 659. Case law had established a two-month period as early as 1973 in Case 120/73 *Lorenz* [1973] ECR 1471.

[139] Art 4(6) of Regulation 659.

[140] Joined Cases 91 and 127/83 *Heineken Brouwerijen* [1984] ECR 2435; [1985] 1 CMLR 389.

[141] Case C-44/93 *Namur-Les Assurances du Crédit SA v Office National du Ducroire and Belgium* [1994] ECR I-3829.

[142] Art 7(4) of Regulation 659.

[143] Art 7(6) of Regulation 659. According to the General Court, a period of 22 months cannot be considered unreasonable merely because it exceeds 18 months, which is an objective to be observed and not a mandatory time-limit: Case T-190/00 *Regione Siciliana v Commission* [2003] ECR II-5015, para 139.

[144] See Sinnaeve and Slot, above n 129.

[145] At least two months for the preliminary stage, 18 months under Art 7(6) and the additional two months afterwards.

its possession information from whatever source regarding alleged unlawful aid, it shall examine that information without delay.[146] Although the time limits for the preliminary assessment of a properly notified aid do not apply, the Commission must still act within a reasonable time.[147]

Regulation 659 authorises three types of injunction for the Commission to use in the context of possible unlawful aid. First,[148] it can issue an injunction requiring a Member State to submit information, failure to comply giving the Commission the right to take a decision on the basis of the information it already has. Secondly,[149] the Commission may, after giving the Member State concerned the opportunity to submit its comments, adopt a decision requiring the Member State to suspend any unlawful aid until the Commission has taken a decision on the compatibility of the aid with the internal market. Thirdly,[150] the Commission has the power to issue a decision requiring the Member State provisionally to recover any unlawful aid until the Commission has taken a decision on the compatibility of the aid. Such an injunction can only be used, however, where according to established practice there are no doubts as to the aid character of the measure, there is an urgency to act and there is a serious risk of substantial and irreparable damage to a competitor. Where the Commission adopts a negative decision in cases of unlawful aid, it is obliged to issue a recovery decision requiring the Member State concerned to take all necessary measures to recover the aid from the beneficiary.[151] Whilst the power of the Commission to order recovery is well established in earlier case law,[152] the obligation to do so is a new feature established in Regulation 659. Article 14(2) provides that recovery shall not be required if this would be contrary to a general principle of EU law. However, this restriction is likely to apply only in exceptional situations. It is clear from the Court's previous case law that beneficiaries will not normally be able to invoke the protection of legitimate expectations as a reason for resisting recovery. The reason for this is that a diligent business person should normally be able to determine whether the procedural requirements of Article 108 of the Treaty have been observed.[153] Unjustified delays by the Commission in reaching decisions might give rise to legitimate expectations that the aid was not objectionable,[154] although the timetables introduced by the Regulation will usually pre-empt recourse to this route.

Any use by the Commission of its powers to order recovery is subject to a limitation period of ten years.[155] This runs from the day on which the unlawful aid is awarded to the beneficiary either as individual aid or as aid under an aid scheme. Any interruption, such as the result of the Commission making a request for information, starts the time period running afresh. There is no obligation to notify the beneficiary of such an interruption.[156]

---

[146] Art 10(1) of Regulation 659.

[147] Case T-95/96 *Gestevisión Telecinco v Commission* [1998] ECR II-3407; [1998] 3 CMLR 1112.

[148] Art 10(3) of Regulation 659.

[149] Art 11(1).

[150] Art 11(2).

[151] Art14(1).

[152] Case 70/72 *Commission v Germany* [1973] ECR 813; [1973] CMLR 741.

[153] Case 301/87 *France v Commission (Boussac)* [1990] ECR I-307, para 14; see also Case T-109/01 *Fleuren Compost* [2004] ECR II-127, paras 135–37.

[154] Case 223/85 *Rijn-Schelde-Verolme (RSV) Maschinefabrieken en Scheepswerven NV v Commission* [1987] ECR 4617; [1989] 2 CMLR 259, where the Commission delayed proceedings by 26 months.

[155] Art 15(1) of Regulation 659. This rule was inserted into the Regulation by the Council and did not form part of the Commission's original proposal.

[156] Case C-276/03P *Scott v Commission* [2005] ECR I-8437.

In any event the distortive effects of an aid which has operated undetected and without complaint for ten years must be open to doubt.

Once the Commission has made an order against a Member State seeking recovery, it is for the state to execute it using national laws and procedures. By Article 14(3) of Regulation 659 'recovery shall be effected without delay and in accordance with the procedures under the national law of the Member State concerned, provided that they allow the immediate and effective execution of the Commission's decision'. This provision, described as a 'real innovation',[157] allows the Commission to act against delaying procedures in Member States so that measures by national judges merely ordering suspensive effects of an aid could be seen as contrary to Regulation 659.

Prior to enactment of the Regulation, the Court had taken a strict view as to the nature of the obligation to repay in a line of cases following *Commission v Belgium*[158] where it emphasised the need to consider whether it was *impossible* for the Member State to comply with the Commission's decision. The mere fact that beneficiaries of the aid might suffer financial hardship from its revocation is not sufficient to thwart recovery.[159] Nor is conflict with national rules of company law in cases where undoing aid in the form of equity participation may run counter to standard principles about priorities between creditors and shareholders.[160] Apart from satisfying orthodox doctrines concerning the supremacy of Union law and the need to achieve effectiveness of enforcement, this position also makes clear that repayment is not a matter of countering improper benefits but is an absolute consequence of infringement of the obligations under the aids supervisory regime.[161] Impossibility is not for the State merely to assert; it must be demonstrated after an active search for a solution in the context of a dialogue between the Commission and the State concerned.[162] It is not enough where the Government in question merely informs the Commission of the legal, political or practical difficulties involved in recovery and without proposing to the Commission any alternative arrangements.[163]

C – Misuse of Aid

The notion of misuse appears in the Treaty itself in Article 108(2):

> If, after giving notice to the parties concerned to submit their comments, the Commission finds that aid granted by a State or through State resources is not compatible with the internal market having regard to Article 107, *or that such aid is being misused* [emphasis added], it shall decide that the State concerned shall abolish or alter such aid within a period of time to be determined by the Commission.

---

[157] Sinnaeve and Slot, above n 129.

[158] Case 52/84 *Commission v Belgium* [1986] ECR 89; [1987] 1 CMLR 710.

[159] Case 63/87 *Commission v Greece* [1988] ECR 2875; [1989] 3 CMLR 677.

[160] See *Belgium v Commission* ('*Tubemeuse*'), above n 20.

[161] Ibid. See also *France v Commission* (*Boussac*), above n 153.

[162] Case C-349/93 *Commission v Italy* [1995] ECR I-343. See also Case C-6/97 *Commission v Italy* [1999] ECR I-2981 where the fact that Italy had taken no steps to recover the tax credit in question meant that implementation of the recovery decision could not be shown to be impossible. See also case C-304/09 *Commission v Italy* (nyr) [2011] OJ C63/6.

[163] Case C-415/03 *Commission v Greece* [2005] ECR I-3875. Unsurprisingly, the Court did not view the transfer of assets of the beneficiary (Olympic Airways) to a new company (Olympic Airlines) to make recovery from the former impossible as acceptable!

Misuse is further defined in Article 1(g) of Regulation 659 as aid used by the beneficiary in contravention of a decision taken under the Regulation not to raise objections at the preliminary stage or a decision closing a formal investigation on the basis of either a positive or conditional approval. The key difference between misuse and unlawful aid is that in the former case it the beneficiary who has brought about the infringement, whereas the Member State is responsible for unlawful aid. Procedurally, the reference in Article 108(2) means that misuse cannot be addressed without opening a formal investigation. Subject to this important limitation, Regulation 659 adopts the same principles mutatis mutandis for enforcement against misuse as for unlawful aid. The only exception is that a provisional recovery injunction under Article 11(2) is not available to the Commission.

D – Existing Aids

Article 108(1) of the Treaty provides:

> The Commission shall, in co-operation with Member States, keep under constant review all systems of aid existing in those States. It shall propose to the latter any appropriate measures required by the progressive development or by the functioning of the internal market.

The notion of existing aid comprises the following categories: (i) all aid which existed prior to the entry into force of the Treaty in the respective Member States or before acceding to the Community or Union; (ii) aid schemes or individual aids authorised by the Commission or Council; (iii) aid authorised by default;[164] (iv) aid deemed to be existing by operation of the ten-year limitation period for recovery; (v) aid which is deemed to be an existing aid because it can be established that at the time when it was put into effect it did not constitute an aid, and subsequently became an aid due to the evolution of the internal market and without having been altered by the Member State.[165]

It would clearly make no sense for the maintenance of the single market if aids were only subject to controls at the time of their proposal. Article 108(1) thus provides for ongoing supervision and review of existing measures.[166]

VIII – RIGHTS OF INTERESTED PARTIES

In the absence of secondary legislation in the early days of state aid law, the rights of interested third parties developed in the case law as ad hoc responses to challenges to Commission decisions. However, the advent of Regulation 659 codified much of those principles. The Court summarised the development of its principles in *Commission v Aktionsgemeinschaft Recht und Eigentum*, as follows:

> 34 In the case of a Commission decision on state aid, it must be borne in mind that, in the context of the procedure for reviewing state aid provided for in Art [108], the preliminary stage

---

[164] eg using Art 4(6) of Regulation 659 where the Commission fails to comply with the two-month time limit to make a decision.

[165] Sinnaeve and Slot, above n 129, suggest that this might apply to an activity or product for which the state provides support and for which there is at the time no EU market or trade.

[166] See Arts 17 and 18 of Regulation 659.

of the procedure for reviewing aid under Art [108(3)], which is intended merely to allow the Commission to form a prima facie opinion on the partial or complete conformity of the aid in question, must be distinguished from the examination under Art [108(2)]. It is only in connection with the latter examination, which is designed to enable the Commission to be fully informed of all the facts of the case, that the [TFEU] imposes an obligation on the Commission to give the parties concerned notice to submit their comments (Cook at [??]; Matra v Commission (C-225/91): [1993] ECR I-3203 at [16]; and Commission v Sytraval and Brink's France (C-367/95 P): [1998] ECR I-1719 at [38]).

35 Where, without initiating the formal review procedure under Art [108(2)], the Commission finds, on the basis of Art [108(3)], that aid is compatible with the Common Market, the persons intended to benefit from those procedural guarantees may secure compliance therewith only if they are able to challenge that decision before the Community judicature (Cook at [23]; Matra at [17]; and Sytraval and Brink's France at [40]). For those reasons, the court declares to be admissible an action for the annulment of such a decision brought by a person who is concerned within the meaning of Art [108(2)] where he seeks, by instituting proceedings, to safeguard the procedural rights available to him under the latter provision (Cook at [23]–[26]; and Matra at [17]–[20]).

36 The parties concerned, within the meaning of Art [108(2)], who are thus entitled under the fourth paragraph of [263] to institute proceedings for *1235 annulment are those persons, undertakings or associations whose interests might be affected by the grant of the aid, in particular competing undertakings and trade associations (see, in particular, Sytraval and Brink's France at [41]).

37 On the other hand, if the applicant calls in question the merits of the decision appraising the aid as such, the mere fact that it may be regarded as concerned within the meaning of Art [108(2)] cannot suffice to render the action admissible. It must then demonstrate that it has a particular status within the meaning of the Plaumann v Commission case law. That applies in particular where the applicant's market position is substantially affected by the aid to which the decision at issue relates (see, to that effect, the judgment in Cofaz v Commission (169/84): [1986] ECR 391; [1986] 3 CMLR 385 at [22]–[25]; and the order in Sveriges Betodlares Centralförening and Henrikson (C-406/96 P): [1997] ECR I-7531 at [45]).[167]

In that case, on the basis that the relevant party was not seeking to contest a failure to initiate an Article 108(2) procedure, but was instead in reality seeking to have a contested decision annulled on substantive grounds, the Court applied the 'usual' *Plaumann* tests of locus standi.[168] The Court accordingly proceeded to set aside the Court of First Instance's judgment.[169] Even though members of the trade association concerned were economic operators who could be viewed as direct competitors of the beneficiaries of the aid, it did not follow that they were individually concerned for the purposes of *Plaumann* since all farmers in the European Union could be regarded as competitors of the beneficiaries of the land acquisition scheme.[170]

This judgment followed an Opinion from Advocate General Jacobs, who had described the case law up until that point as 'plainly unsatisfactory, being complex, apparently illogical, and inconsistent'.[171] He had canvassed a return to the terms of Article 263(4) TFEU and the tests of direct and individual concern, irrespective of the grounds on which the

---

[167] Case C-78/03 P *Commission v Aktionsgemeinschaft Recht und Eigentum* [2005] ECR I-10737, [2006] 2 CMLR 48.
[168] Case 25/62 *Plaumann v Commission* [1963] ECR 95; see Chapter X, above.
[169] Case T-114/00 *Aktionsgemeinschaft Recht und Eigentum v Commission* [2002] ECR II-5121.
[170] See also Case C-487/06P *British Aggregates Associaton v Commission (BAA)*[2009] 2 CMLR 10.
[171] *Commission v Aktionsgemeinschaft Recht und Eigentum*, above n 167, para 138.

action was brought, but without the strictness of *Plaumann*. The Court, instead, under-scored the earlier case law[172] distinctions whilst maintaining the view that Article 108(2) decisions require applicants to demonstrate a particular status whereby their market posi-tions are substantially affected.[173] Nonetheless, in *3F v Commission*[174] the Court set aside the earlier ruling of the CFI and held that a trade union (for seafarers) may be regarded as concerned within the meaning of Article 108(2), where the aid could have a real effect on it, or the workers it represented, for instance where the particular trade union could demonstrate that it was in competition with rival trade unions.

IX – THE ROLE OF NATIONAL COURTS

Although national courts are unable to rule on the compatibility of aid with the internal market, their role in the supervisory regime is highly significant because of the respon-sibilities placed upon them in relation to safeguarding the rights of individuals against non-observance by Member States of the procedural rules. As the previous discussion in this chapter has shown, the Court of Justice's case law requires four cumulative conditions to be established before an aid is present for the purposes of Article 107(1). Thus, to secure the necessary protection for individuals against a Member State's failure to notify, national courts must be able to evaluate the application of each of those criteria.

That the standstill clause of Article 108(3) could create directly effective rights was established as early as 1973 in the *Lorenz* case.[175] This was elaborated upon by the Court in its so-called *French Salmon* ruling,[176] stressing the fundamental difference between the central executive role performed by the Commission and the task of national courts. Whilst the Commission was required to examine the compatibility of the planned aid with the internal market, even in cases where the Member State infringed the prohibition of implementing aid measures, national courts merely safeguarded, pending a final decision by the Commission, the rights of individuals against any disregard by the state authorities of the prohibition contained in the last sentence of Article 108(3). It is clear that a find-ing by a national court that an aid has been granted in breach of Article 108(3) 'must in principle lead to its repayment in accordance with the procedural rules of domestic law'.[177] Even if the Commission subsequently declares the aid compatible with the internal mar-ket, this does not regularise a previous violation by the state of its notification obligations so that a national court's power to order repayment of aid already paid out is unaffected.[178] Recovery of the aid alone may not be sufficient to give effective protection for individuals.

---

[172] Case C-198/91 *Cook v Commission* [1993] ECR I-2487; Case C-225/91 *Matra v Commission* [1993] ECR I-3203; Case C-367/95P *Commission v Sytraval and Brink's Finance* [1998] ECR I-1719.

[173] See Case 169/84 *Cofaz v Commission* [1986] ECR 391.

[174] Case C-319/07 P *3F v Commission* [2009] ECR I-5963; [2009] 3 CMLR 40.

[175] Case 120/73 *Lorenz* [1973] ECR 1471.

[176] Case C-354/90 *Fédération Nationale du Commerce Extérieur des Produits Alimentaires v France* [1991] ECR I-5505

[177] Case C-39/94 *SFEI v La Poste*, above n 2.

[178] Nonetheless, the Court ruled in case C-199/06 *CELF and Ministre de la culture et de la Communication v SIDE* [2008] ECR I-469 that the national court faced with an illegal aid, subsequently held to be compatible by the Commission, is not bound to order recovery of the aid but only payment of the interest for the relevant period. However, the obligation to repay aid implemented contrary to Art 108(3) precludes national courts from staying proceedings until the Commission has declared on the compatibility of the aid, even where previous

Since the rights of individuals flow from the Member State's breach of the duty to notify under Article 108(3), claims for liability in damages may be available if the principles of *Francovich*[179] and *Brasserie du Pêcheur and Factortame*[180] are satisfied.[181]

It seems clear that where the obligation to notify includes the method of financing the aid, protection under Article 108(3) will extend in principle to reimbursement of charges or contributions levied specifically for that purpose.[182] Moreover, the Court's approach in the *Pape* and *Streekgewest Brabant* cases[183] confirms that national procedural rules may be challengeable if they represent obstacles to the effectiveness of state aid rules. Locus standi rules will thus have to address when an individual is sufficiently affected.

As discussed below, national courts may also incur responsibilities in the context of the application of the derogation set out in Article 106(2). Undertakings entrusted with services of general economic interest may invoke this provision to justify state aid in their favour.[184]

Finally, national courts cannot be used by disgruntled competitors where the real nature of the claim is one which should have been protected by recourse to Article 263 TFEU. In a case where the beneficiary of an aid had not used its undoubted position as an individually concerned undertaking to challenge an adverse decision addressed to the granting Member State,[185] the Court refused to allow the validity of the Commission's decision to be challenged via Article 267 TFEU in national proceedings arising from the recovery procedure.

X – INTRODUCTION TO ARTICLE 106 TFEU

The influence of the state in the economies of the European Union may appear in a variety of forms, whether as regulator,[186] participant or provider of resources.[187] This section concentrates upon the EU rules which apply in relation to undertakings which are state controlled or which enjoy a privileged legal status, normally in return for carrying out certain tasks deemed to be of public importance. Activities which have often been undertaken in this way to varying degrees in the Member States include energy utilities, railway and other transport services, postal and telecommunications services, broadcasting and

---

positive decisions have been annulled by the Community courts. See Case C-1/09 *CELF and Ministre de la culture et de la Communication v SIDE* (nyr) [2010] OJ C113/13.

[179] Joined Cases C-6, 9/90 *Francovich and another v Italy* [1991] ECR I-5357; [1993] 2 CMLR 66.

[180] Joined Cases C-46 and 48/93 *Brasserie du Pêcheur v Germany, R v Secretary of State for Transport, ex p Factortame* [1996] ECR I-1029; [1996] 1 CMLR 889.

[181] See AG Hernandez, 'The Principle of Non-contractual State Liability for Breaches of EC Law and its Application to State Aids' [1996] *ECLR* 355.

[182] *Van Calster*, above n 117, para 54.

[183] *Pape* and *Streekgewest Westelijk Noord-Brabant*, above n 134.

[184] Case C-174/97P *FFSA v Commission* [1998] ECR I-1303, extending Case C-387/92 *Banco Exterior de España* [1994] ECR I-877; [1994] 3 CMLR 473. See L Hancher and JL Buendia Sierra, 'Cross-Subsidization and EC Law' (1998) 35 *CMLRev* 901, esp 938–42; Cahill, above n 115.

[185] Case C-188/92 *TWD Textilwerke Deggendorf GmbH v Germany* [1994] ECR I-833; [1995] 2 CMLR 145.

[186] State measures of this type may, for example, fall within Art 34 TFEU; see Chapter 14, above.

[187] eg in the form of state aid; see above.

many other public services.[188] The organisation of Member State participation may be at national, regional or local level.

The extent to which the competition rules of the Treaty are applied to public or privileged undertakings has fundamental implications for the relationship between state and market. A number of approaches can be envisaged for the treatment of legal monopolies.[189] At one end of the spectrum, for example, the state might be said to have absolute sovereignty to grant exclusive rights. At the other, a paradigm of absolute competition could hold such exclusivity to be an infringement per se of the competition rules by creating a dominant position from which abuses could be pursued. The case law of the Court indicates a middle ground, sometimes favouring a limited form of sovereignty and intervening only when abuses necessarily flow from the grant of exclusivity, but on other occasions adopting a limited competition model in which the existence of a monopoly requires justification against higher interests recognised in EU law. Certainly, the Court recognises that the full force of the competition rules cannot always be applied. In the specific context of undertakings falling within the scope of Article 106(2) (see below), the Court has observed that Member States

> cannot be precluded, when defining the services of general economic interest which they entrust to certain undertakings, from taking account of objectives pertaining to their national policy or from endeavouring to attain them by means of obligations and constraints which they impose on such undertakings.[190]

Taking the Treaty at face value, the approach taken by EU law to public and privileged undertakings would seem that, while there can be no objection in principle to their special relationship with the state, whatever legal form this may take, their behaviour as market participants is governed by the same rules as those applicable to purely private undertakings, except where the Treaty itself specifically permits some derogation. The first limb of this proposition depends in part upon Article 345 TFEU, preserving intact the systems of property ownership in the Member States, which are therefore free to determine the extent and internal organisation of their public sectors; and in part upon the clear inference to be drawn from Article 106(1) that the conferment of special or exclusive rights upon an undertaking does not, in itself, constitute an infringement of any Treaty rule.[191] Support for the second limb of the general proposition can be found in the unqualified reference to 'undertakings' in Articles 101 and 102, and in the limited exemption contained in Article 106(2) for the benefit of entrusted undertakings and fiscal monopolies which would have been formulated differently if the rules of the Treaty did not normally apply to public undertakings.

However, this general proposition does not wholly encapsulate the case law developments, particularly since the 1990s as the tensions between market concerns, national

---

[188] This is not a Treaty term and is only used here as a general shorthand. The notion of 'services of general economic interest' is central to Art 106(2), discussed fully below. However, a number of Member States attach particular meaning to public services in national law, eg France (*ordre public*) and Italy (*servizio pubblico*). See T Prosser, *The Limits of Competition Law, Markets and Public Services* (Oxford, Oxford University Press, 2005) ch 5.

[189] See E Szyszczak, *The Regulation of the State in Competitive Markets in the European Union* (Oxford, Hart Publishing, 2007).

[190] Case C-157/94 *Commission v Netherlands* [1997] ECR I-5699, para 40.

[191] So held by the Court in Case 155/73 *Sacchi* [1974] ECR 409; [1974] 2 CMLR 177, and affirmed on numerous occasions since. See eg Case C-266/96 *Corsica Ferries France* [1998] ECR I-3949; [1998] 5 CMLR 402.

policy goals and other, non-economic, values in the Treaty have repeatedly come before the Court. Faced with these sensitive and highly politically charged choices, the Court has adopted a variety of approaches. One method has been to jettison jurisdiction by arguing that the activity, or the way it is organised, falls outside the scope of the Treaty's competition rules. It has already been seen[192] that the key concept of 'undertaking' can be used for this gatekeeping role in relation to some solidarity-based healthcare and welfare systems. However, this line-drawing can produce uncomfortable contortions as to whether something is 'economic' or not, and the extent to which some activities or functions can be severed from others.[193] A different approach is to apply the Treaty but to utilise the scope provided by Article 106(2) to mitigate the impact of the competition rules on a case-by-case basis. As will be seen below, the methodology adopted by the Court for the application of this provision has changed considerably over recent years. Whether Article 106(2) is accurately described now as an exception or a balancing exercise will be considered in more detail below. In addition, Article 14 TFEU (ex Article 16 EC), introduced by the TA, reinforces the particular position occupied by services of general economic interest in the values of the European Union, although the legal effects of this provision will not be dealt with in this brief overview.[194]

This section is primarily concerned with Article 106 TFEU. Another provision of the Treaty, Article 37 TFEU (ex Article 31 EC), relates to a particular category of public undertakings, namely state monopolies of a commercial character.[195] However, since Article 37 constitutes a specialised regime for the removal of obstacles to the free movement of goods which may be associated with the arrangements under which such monopolies operate, it was dealt with in Chapter 14, above. It should be remembered, however, that Article 106(2), discussed fully in this chapter, is applicable to Article 37 monopolies.[196]

Article 106 provides as follows:

1. In the case of public undertakings and undertakings to which Member States grant exclusive or special rights, Member States shall neither enact nor maintain in force any measure contrary to the rules contained in this Treaty, in particular to those rules provided for in Article 18 and Articles 101 to 109.

2. Undertakings entrusted with the operation of services of general economic interest or having the character of a revenue producing monopoly shall be subject to the rules contained in this Treaty, in particular to the rules on competition, insofar as the application of such rules does not obstruct the performance, in law or in fact, of the particular tasks assigned to them. The development of trade must not be affected to such an extent as would be contrary to the interests of the Union.

---

[192] See Chapter 22, above, particularly Case C-160/91 *Poucet and Pistre* [1993] ECR I-637; Case C-67/96 *Albany International BV v Stichting Bedrijfspensioenfonds Textielindustrie* [1999] ECR I-5751, [2000] 4 CMLR 446; Joined Cases C-180–84/98 *Pavlov* [2000] ECR I-6451, [2001] 4 CMLR 30; Joined Cases C-264/01, C-306/01, C-354/01 and C-355/01 *AOK Bundesverband* [2004] ECR I-2493; Case C-350/07 *Kattner Stahlbau GmbH v Maschinenbau- und Metall- Berufsgenossenschaft* [2009] ECR I-1513; [2009] 2 CMLR 51.

[193] See AG Poiares Maduro's Opinion in Case C-205/03P *FENIN v Commission* [2006] ECR I-6295; [2006] 5 CMLR 7.

[194] Referred to, for instance, in Commission Communication, above n 124. Cahill, above n 115.

[195] Arts 106 and 37 belong to a wider group of 'provisions relating to infringements of the normal functioning of the competition system by actions on the part of the States': see Case 94/74 *IGAV v ENCC* [1975] ECR 699; [1976] 2 CMLR 37. The Court also mentioned in this connection what are now Arts 107–09 (state aid) and Arts 116 and 117 (distortions in competition resulting from differences between Member States).

[196] Case C-438/02 *Hanner* [2005] ECR I-4551, para 47, citing *Commission v Netherlands*, above n 190. Revenue-producing monopolies are, in any event, expressly identified in the terms of Art 106(2).

3. The Commission shall ensure the application of the provisions of this Article and shall, where necessary, address appropriate directives or decisions to Member States.

The scheme of the Article contemplates state responsibility in the situations embraced by paragraph (1), relief from the obligations of the Treaty for the undertakings satisfying the criteria of paragraph (2), and a mechanism for supervision and enforcement using the legislative machinery provided by paragraph (3). As summarised by the Court of Justice, the provision

> concerns only undertakings for whose actions States must take special responsibility by reason of the influence which they may exert over such actions. It emphasises that such undertakings are subject to all the rules laid down in the Treaty, subject to the provisions contained in paragraph (2); it requires the Member States to respect those rules in their relations with those undertakings and in that regard imposes on the Commission a duty of surveillance which may, where necessary, be performed by the adoption of directives and decisions addressed to Member States.[197]

The use of Article 106 has changed drastically over time. Starting from a prolonged period in which the provision was hardly invoked at all, the influence of the single market imperative gave rise to a vigorous application of state responsibility and a flurry of legislative liberalisation activity. The position has now been reached where the rigour of paragraph (1) is seemingly tempered by a more generous use of paragraph (2). Examination of how readily the latter is applied (and the full rigour of market rules thus restrained), illuminates the extent of the European Union's evolution in its ordering of social and economic concerns.

XI – ARTICLE 106(1): THE RESPONSIBILITY OF MEMBER STATES

Article 106(1) constitutes a particular application of the general principle contained in the second paragraph of Article 4(3) TEU (ex Article 10 EC) that Member States are required to abstain from measures which are liable to jeopardise the attainment of the objectives of the Treaty.[198] The inclusion of a specific provision concerning the relationship between the state and public and privileged undertakings served both to highlight the particular seriousness of the problems which may arise, and to clarify the extensive nature of the responsibility imposed upon Member States in this situation.

A – The Categories of Undertaking in Article 106(1)

The effect of Article 106(1) is that undertakings for whose actions states must take special responsibility by reason of the influence which they may exert over such actions are subject to all the rules laid down in the Treaty, and in particular to the competition

---

[197] Joined Cases 188–190/80 *France, Italy and the United Kingdom v Commission* [1982] ECR 2545; [1982] 3 CMLR 144.

[198] Case 13/77 *INNO v ATAB* [1977] ECR 2115, 2144-2145; [1978] 1 CMLR 283.

provisions.[199] That responsibility arises in relation to public undertakings and undertakings to whom states grant special or exclusive rights. It will be recalled from the detailed discussion in Chapter 22 that the Court has formulated the notion of 'undertaking' in a number of ways.

As was seen, the Court has found the 'undertaking' requirement not to be satisfied in solidarity-based health and insurance schemes[200] and in relation to contexts where the body was acting qua state rather than undertaking.[201] Not surprisingly, the close interest and involvement of the state in many types of public services means that the application of Article 106 will often require an analysis of what constitutes an 'undertaking'.[202]

(i) Public Undertakings

Public undertakings are specifically mentioned in Article 106(1), but not defined therein. Clearly, there would be no consistency in application if it were necessary to rely upon the widely varying classifications of undertakings as 'public' or 'private' in national legal systems. The Commission adopted a definition for the purposes of the Transparency Directive[203] in 1980, and this was upheld by the Court of Justice when the legality of that measure was challenged.[204] According to Article 2 of that Directive and its successor Directive 2006/111,[205] a public undertaking is

> any undertaking over which the public authorities may exercise directly or indirectly a dominant influence by virtue of their ownership of it, their financial participation therein, or the rules which govern it.

The same provision also establishes certain presumptions, so that a 'dominant influence' will be taken to exist where the public authorities: hold the major part of the undertaking's subscribed capital; or control the majority of the votes attaching to shares issued by the undertaking; or can appoint more than half of the members of the undertaking's administrative, managerial or supervisory body. The Court held that this definition of a public undertaking did not amount to an abuse by the Commission of its powers under Article 106(3), since the financial criteria which the Directive adopted reflected the substantial forms of influence exerted by public authorities over the commercial decisions of public undertakings and were thus compatible with the Court's view of Article 106(1).[206]

A rather different form of words, but deriving its teleological support from the same notions of influence and opportunity, was used by Advocate General Ruiz-Jarabo Colomer in cases arising from so-called 'golden shares' cases involving privatised companies in strategically important parts of the economy:

---

[199] AG Stix-Hackl in Joined Cases C-34–38/01 *Enirisorse* [2003] ECR I-14243, Opinion para 38.

[200] See cases listed in n 192, above; also Case C-218/00 *Cisal* [2002] ECR I-691, [2002] 4 CMLR 24.

[201] See eg Case C-364/92 *Eurocontrol* [1994] ECR I-43, [1994] 5 CMLR 208.

[202] Case C-475/99 *Ambulanz Glöckner v Landkreis Sudwestpfalz* [2001] ECR I-8089; [2002] 4 CMLR 21, para 21. See also eg Case C-49/07 *Motoskyletistiki Omospondia Ellados Npid v Elliniko Dimosio* [2008] ECR I-4863; [2008] 5 CMLR 11.

[203] Directive 80/723 [1980] OJ L195/35.

[204] *France, Italy and the United Kingdom v Commission*, above n 197.

[205] Commission Directive 2006/111/EC of 16 November 2006 on the transparency of financial relations between Member States and public undertakings as well as on financial transparency within certain undertakings [2006] OJ L318/17.

[206] The Court has also applied this definition in Case 118/85 *Commission v Italy* [1987] ECR 2599. Joined Cases C-463/00 *Commission v Spain* and C-98/01 *Commission v United Kingdom* [2003] ECR I-4581, Opinion of AG Ruiz-Jarabo Colomer, para 56.

[I]t may be inferred from a purposive interpretation that the distinction between public and private undertakings, for the purposes of the Treaty, cannot be based merely on the identity of its various shareholders, but depends on the opportunity available to the State to impose specific economic policies other than the pursuit of the greatest financial gain which characterises private business.[207]

Public undertakings are always within the scope of application of Article 106(1), whether or not they have also been granted special or exclusive rights.[208]

(ii) Undertakings Granted Special or Exclusive Rights

The second category of undertakings referred to in Article 106(1) are those to which Member States grant special or exclusive rights. Such rights may be granted to public or private undertakings. The rationale behind the category is the fact that the state has deliberately intervened to relieve the undertaking concerned either wholly or partially from the discipline of competition, and must bear responsibility for the consequences. A right conferred by national legislation upon those carrying on an economic activity which is open to anyone, who thus form an indefinite class, is unlikely to be regarded as 'exclusive'.[209] Similarly, undertakings which are licensed to engage in an activity on the basis of their fulfilment of certain objective conditions (eg the financial safeguards imposed in the public interest upon insurance businesses) would be excluded from the category. The mode of granting the right (whether by an act under public law, eg a statute, regulation or administrative order, or by a private contract) is immaterial, again because formal differences between the legal systems of the various Member States cannot be allowed to interfere with the operation of Article 106(1).

Even though Article 345 TFEU, which preserves national systems of property ownership, presupposes the existence of undertakings which have special or exclusive rights, it does not follow that all such rights are necessarily compatible with the Treaty.[210] In particular, Article 345 does not have the effect of exempting the Member States' systems of property ownership from the fundamental rules of the Treaty.[211]

There is nothing in the wording of Article 106(1) to explain the notion of 'special or exclusive' rights. Early legislation adopted by the Commission failed to define such rights to the satisfaction of the Court.[212] However, in an amended version of the directive on competition in the markets for telecommunications services[213] the terms were defined, and these are now found in a revised version in the Directive on competition in the markets for electronic communications networks and services[214] as follows:

'[E]xclusive rights' shall mean the rights that are granted by a Member State to one undertaking through any legislative, regulatory or administrative instrument, reserving it the right to pro-

---

[207] *Commission v Spain* and *Commission v United Kingdom*, above n 206, Opinion, para 56.

[208] AG Stix-Hackl, Opinion in *Enirisorse*, above n 199.

[209] See *INNO v ATAB*, above n 198, 2146.

[210] Case C-202/88 *France v Commission* [1991] ECR I-1223; [1992] 5 CMLR 552, para 22.

[211] *Commission v Spain* and *Commission v United Kingdom*, above n 206, para 67 of Judgment.

[212] See proceedings arising from the Telecommunications Terminal Equipment Directive 88/301 [1988] OJ L131/73; *France v Commission*, above n 210. Also Joined Cases C-271, 281 and 289/90 *Spain v Commission* [1992] ECR I-5833 in relation to Directive 90/388 on the markets for telecommunications services.

[213] Directive 94/96; [1994] OJ L268/15, revising Directive 90/388/EC [1990] OJ L192/10.

[214] See Commission Directive 2002/77/ EC [2002] OJ L249/21, repealing Directive 90/388/EC.

vide an electronic communications service or undertake an electronic communications activity within a given geographical area.[215]

'[S]pecial rights' shall mean the rights that are granted by a Member State to a limited number of undertakings through any legislative, regulatory or administrative instrument which, within a given geographical area,

(a) designates or limits to two or more the number of such undertakings authorised to provide an electronic communications service or undertake an electronic communications activity, otherwise than according to objective, proportional and non-discriminatory criteria, or

(b) confers on any undertaking or undertakings, otherwise than according to such criteria, legal or regulatory advantages which substantially affect the ability of any other undertaking to provide the same electronic communications service or to undertake the same electronic communications activity in the same geographical area under substantially equivalent conditions.[216]

Examples of exclusive rights have included exclusive concessions to funeral enterprises in French communes,[217] statutory monopolies in the field of broadcasting,[218] the exclusive right of insemination centres authorised to serve defined areas,[219] and rights given to three undertakings to recover, and process, building waste produced within the municipality of Copenhagen.[220]

In relation to special rights, it now seems clear that not all the criteria set out in the legislative example above need to be satisfied for general classification. The reference to 'objective, proportional and non-discriminatory criteria' was not required by the Court in its *Ambulanz Glöckner* judgment.[221] Instead, it observed:

[T]he reservation of patient transport services to the medical aid organisations entrusted with the public ambulance service is sufficient for that measure to be characterised as a special or exclusive right within the meaning of [Article 106(1)] of the Treaty, for protection is conferred by a legislative measure on a limited number of undertakings which may substantially affect the ability of other undertakings to exercise the economic activity in question in the same geographical area under substantially equivalent conditions.

The mere allocation of funds does not make the recipient a holder of special or exclusive rights, since this ignores the influence on the market that such rights entail.[222]

B – The Scope of the Obligation Imposed on Member States under Article 106(1)

The phrase 'shall neither enact nor maintain in force any measure' is wide enough to cover any forms of positive action taken by a Member State, or the failure to remedy such

---

[215] Ibid, Art 1(5).
[216] Ibid, Art 1(6).
[217] Case 30/87 *Bodson v Pompes Funèbres des Régions Libérées SA* [1988] ECR 2479; [1989] 4 CMLR 984.
[218] *Sacchi*, above n 191.
[219] Case C-323/93 *Société Civile Agricole du Centre d'Insémination de la Crespelle v Coopérative d'Elevage et d'Insémination Artificielle du Département de la Mayenne* [1994] ECR I-5077.
[220] Case C-209/98 *FFAD v Københavns Kommune* [2000] ECR I-3743, [2001] 2 CMLR 936. Whether three undertakings may each have the same exclusive rights seems questionable, but in any event the 'special' threshold would be met.
[221] *Ambulanz Glöckner*, above n 202.
[222] AG Stix-Hackl, Opinion in *Enirisorse*, above n 199.

action previously taken. The notion of 'measure' is also open, and has been described by the Court as 'any law, regulation or administrative provision'.[223] Article 106(1) cannot be applied in isolation, but must always be used in tandem with another EU provision.

The first decision under Article 106(3) (see below) to challenge specific legislation of the type prohibited by Article 106(1) was issued by the Commission in 1985.[224] This related to a measure requiring all public property in Greece to be insured with a Greek state-owned insurance company, and also obliging state banks to recommend customers seeking a loan to take out associated insurance with a state-owned company. In the Commission's view, the preferential treatment accorded to domestic state-owned companies had the effect of excluding from large sections of the Greek insurance market not only Greek private insurers but also insurance companies from other Member States with subsidiaries or branches in the country. The legislation thus amounted to a restriction on freedom of establishment, enacted by Greece in contravention of Article 106(1).[225]

A literal view of Article 106(1) clearly embraces a standstill obligation upon Member States and the need to take positive action to undo prohibited measures. Additionally, the paragraph impliedly makes Member States accountable for the behaviour of public and privileged undertakings. In other words, responsibility under Article 106(1) does not presuppose positive action by the Member State itself: it suffices merely that a public undertaking or an undertaking granted special or exclusive rights has been guilty of conduct which, on the part of the state, would have involved a Treaty violation. In such a situation the Member State is under an obligation to take any remedial steps which may be necessary; and if its existing legal powers are inadequate, it may be required by the Commission to equip itself with additional powers.

Interpreting the notion of maintaining a measure in force in this way is consistent with the obligation to take general and particular measures imposed on Member States by Article 4(3) TFEU (ex Article 10 EC) and with the policy of Article 106(1). If state responsibility under this paragraph is derived, respectively, from the ability to influence public undertakings and from the assumption of the risk inherent in the deliberate distortion of competition by a grant of special or exclusive rights, it ought to make no difference whether the role of the state has been active, in imposing or encouraging certain behaviour, or passive, in failing to correct it.[226] As the Court has put it, the purpose of Article 106(1) is to prevent Member States from adopting or maintaining in force measures which deprive the Community's competition rules of their effectiveness.[227]

The responsibility of a Member State under Article 106(1) is independent of any violation of EU law by the undertaking in question: it is not based upon a theory of imputation, like the joint liability of a parent company for infringements of the competition rules by a subsidiary which it controls.[228] The undertaking's own conduct may be unimpeach-

---

[223] Case C-203/96 *Chemische Afvalstoffen Dusseldorp BV v Minister van Volkhuisvesting, Ruimtelijke Ordening en Milieubeheer* [1998] ECR I-4075, para 61; [1998] 3 CMLR 873; repeated in Case C-462/99 *Connect Austria Gesellschaft für Telekommunikation GmbH v Telekom-Control-Kommission* [2003] ECR I-5197. It is, of course, well established that 'state measures' for the purposes of Art 34 TFEU embrace single acts or administrative practices; see Case 249/81 *Commission v Ireland* [1982] ECR 4005, [1983] 2 CMLR 104.

[224] Decision 85/726 [1985] OJ L152/25.

[225] Greece did not comply with the Decision, giving rise to enforcement proceedings: Case 226/87 *Commission v Greece* [1988] ECR 3611.

[226] *cf* the position in relation to state measures and Art 101; discussed below.

[227] Case C-260/89 *ERT* [1991] ECR I-2925, para 35; [1994] 4 CMLR 540.

[228] See the discussion of 'undertaking' and the imputation of liability for infringements in Chapter 22, above.

able, for example where it has been compelled by the State to enter a cartel, so that the element of agreement required by Article 101 is missing. However, there must be a causal link between a Member State's legislative or administrative intervention on the one hand and anti-competitive behaviour of undertakings on the other.[229] The Court has held that in the context of Article 106(1) alleged abuses must be the 'direct consequence' of the national legal framework.[230]

One of the most difficult questions pertaining to the scope of the obligation in Article 106(1) is whether the mere grant of exclusive or special rights can itself constitute a 'measure' susceptible to challenge. In *Höfner v Macrotron*[231] the Court was asked whether a national law conferring exclusive rights over the placement of business executives constituted an abuse under Article 102. It was acknowledged that in practice some competition in the market for business placements was tolerated despite the legal monopoly. The Court observed in relation to Articles 102 and 106(1) that:

> A Member State is in breach of the prohibition contained in those two provisions only if the undertaking in question, merely by exercising the exclusive rights granted to it, cannot avoid abusing its dominant position.[232]

Albeit with some nuances in wording along the way,[233] this approach remains the one used by the Court.[234]

The idea that granting special or exclusive rights may, in some circumstances 'inevitably' bring about an abuse has been applied in a number of situations. Thus, in *Höfner* itself, the decisive feature was that the undertaking which had been granted an exclusive right was 'manifestly not in a position to satisfy demand' prevailing on the market for activities of that kind.[235] The fact that infringers of the monopoly had been able to set up in business and obtain clients made it rather easier to identify such failure, although this might not be so blatant in other cases. In *Ambulanz Glöckner*, Advocate General Jacobs attempted to set out some guidance for the national court when assessing this kind of 'manifest failure'. First, he suggested that a Member State should only be liable under Article 106(1) where there is a failure in the system which it has set up, ie where abuse is the consequence of its regulatory or decisional intervention. However, the Court in *Ambulanz Glöckner* made no comment about this suggested 'systemic' requirement.[236] Instead, it held that the German law, providing for prior consultation with the medical aid organisations in respect of any application from an independent operator for authorisation to provide non-emergency patient transport, gave an advantage to those organisations (which already held an exclusive right on the urgent transport market). This had the effect

---

[229] AG Jacobs in *Albany International*, above n 192, para 388 of Opinion.

[230] *Société Civile Agricole du Centre d'Insémination de la Crespelle*, above n 219.

[231] Case C-41/90 *Höfner and Elser v Macrotron* [1991] ECR I-1979; [1993] 4 CMLR 306.

[232] Ibid, para 29.

[233] The broadest standard being in the *Chemische Afvalstoffen Dusseldorp* Judgment, above n 223, where the Court said that a state would infringe Art 106(1) if it 'enabled' a privileged undertaking to abuse its dominant position.

[234] *Servizi Ausiliari Dottori Commercialisti v Calafiori*, above n 113, [2006] 2 CMLR 45; however, the Court ruled there was insufficient evidence supplied by the national court to determine whether either dominance or abuse were established. Note, para 23, citing *Ambulanz Glöckner*, above n 202. Similar formulations can be seen in *Corsica Ferries France*, above n 191, and *Albany International*, above n 192.

[235] *Höfner and Else*, above n 231, para 31. To similar effect, see Case C-55/96 *Job Centre Coop* [1997] ECR I-7119; [1998] 5 CMLR 167, paras 34-35.

[236] Similar claims for a 'systemic' test had been made by AG Fennelly in Case C-163/96 *Raso and others* [1998] ECR I-533; [1998] 5 CMLR 737, Opinion, para 66.

of limiting markets to the prejudice of consumers within the meaning of Article 102(b) of the Treaty by reserving to the medical aid organisations an ancillary transport activity which could be carried on by independent operators.

The scope of the notion of 'inevitable abuse' thus remains problematic, at least as regards the shades of difference between state measures which enable, induce or unavoidably lead to anti-competitive results. For example, the grant of exclusive rights to French insemination centres was not seen as necessarily leading them to charge excessive prices for their services.[237] However, on the other hand, it is clear that an extension of a monopoly by granting special or exclusive rights in an adjacent or ancillary market will be prohibited where there is no objective justification.[238] In such cases, a conflict of interest is certain to arise between the existing monopolist and the competitive situation in the allied market. Thus, in *ERT*[239] the monopolist was a broadcasting undertaking which not only held the exclusive right to broadcast its own programmes but also to retransmit foreign broadcasts. In the Court's view this created a situation in which the undertaking would be liable to infringe Article 102 by virtue of a discriminatory policy favouring its own programmes.[240] Quite clearly, if a Member State actually directly imposes abusive behaviour on an undertaking, there will be a breach of Article 106(1) by that Member State.[241]

The discussion above indicates that the weight of the case law, including even the *Höfner* thread where abuses 'inevitably' follow from privilege, restricts state responsibility under Article 106(1) to abuses caused by the state's privileging of the relevant undertakings. However, this reasoning does not seem to explain *Corbeau*,[242] one of the cases at the 'high-tide' of early 1990s case law in the wake of *Höfner*. The *Corbeau* case arose from a prosecution for violation of the monopoly rights of the Belgian postal service, the Régie des Postes. Corbeau had set up a private courier service which could undercut the monopoly on certain services. His defence to the criminal prosecution was to challenge the legality of the exclusivity conferred upon the Régie des Postes. At no point in the judgment, or the report, was there any discussion of what constituted the abuse. Instead, the focus of the Court's reasoning was upon the justifications that might exist for the monopoly under Article 106(2),[243] thus apparently reversing the burden of proof and implying that monopolies need justification to remain in existence. This is not the same as pointing to market failure as the evidence of abuse.

One should be careful not to exaggerate the significance of *Corbeau* in relation to the Article 106(1) discussion. A number of special factors may have applied, not least the fact that this was a 'Euro-defence' to a criminal charge rather than a claim from an abused complainant or injured competitor. The Court also treated the first two paragraphs of

---

[237] *Société Civile Agricole du Centre d'Insémination de la Crespelle*, above n 219. Similarly, in the *FAD* case, above n 220, there was no infringement where prices for waste processing were freely determined by the holders of the rights.

[238] Case C-18/88 *RTT v GB-Inno-BM* [1991] ECR I-5941; also *Ambulanz Glöckner*, above n 202.

[239] *ERT*, above n 227; see also Case C-179/90 *Merci Convenzionali Porto di Genova* [1991] ECR I-5889; [1994] 4 CMLR 422; *Raso*, above n 236.

[240] Similarly, see case C-49/07 *Motosykletistiki Omospondia Ellados Npid v Ellinko Dimosio* [2008] ECR I-4863; [2008] 5 CMLR 11, esp paras 51–52.

[241] eg the discriminatory tariffs applied as a result of a state administrative act by an airport authority holding exclusive rights in *Re Discount on Landing Fees at Zaventem*: Decision 95/364 [1995] OJ L216/8; also the situation where an exclusive right-holder is paid for services which it has not itself supplied: Case C-340/99 *TNT Traco v Poste Italiane* [2001] ECR I-4109. See also *Connect Austria*, above n 223, para 84.

[242] Case C-320/91 *Corbeau* [1993] ECR I-2533, [1995] 4 CMLR 621.

[243] Art 106(2) is discussed in detail in the next section.

Article 106 as interdependent, which might suggest that glossing over the foundations for responsibility under paragraph (1) was less important to it at the time than taking the opportunity for lengthier treatment of justifications under paragraph (2). If rationalisation of *Corbeau* is needed, then it is arguable that the 'basic' monopoly and special courier services are different markets and that the abuse strengthens dominance to cover an ancillary activity.[244] Similarly, Corbeau's activities might be proof of a *Höfner*-type market failure. But, it must be stressed, these perspectives were not discussed by the Court. However,[245] one lasting contribution of the Court's reasoning might be that part of a Member State's responsibilities under Article 106(1) is to keep changing market conditions under review—and take appropriate action.

XII – ARTICLE 106(2): ENTRUSTED UNDERTAKINGS AND FISCAL MONOPOLIES

Article 106(2) is drafted in terms which first emphasise that 'undertakings entrusted with the operation of services of general economic interest or having the character of a revenue-producing monopoly' are normally subject to the rules of the Treaty and then go on to exclude the application of the rules where the performance of the particular tasks assigned to the undertakings is liable to be obstructed. This is subject to a proviso which states that 'the development of trade must not be affected to such extent as would be contrary to the interests of the Union'. The case law of the Commission and Court initially showed a marked disinclination to accept the application of what was seen to be a derogation from the Treaty. However, the greater use of the competition rules to curb monopolies and public undertakings in the 1990s saw a corresponding development of arguments justifying the activities of such bodies by reference to Article 106(2). Obtaining the benefit of the provision is no longer the impossible task it once was, at least for undertakings charged with providing universal services of public interest. Indeed, from an analytical perspective, it may be that Article 106(2) should be viewed less as an exception to the Treaty to be narrowly construed but more as a particular regime to balance the delivery of effective public services in a modern Union with market economies.[246]

A – The Categories of Undertaking in Article 106(2)

There is nothing in the text of the Article that would restrict the categories of undertaking in the second paragraph to those covered by the first. However, undertakings called upon to perform services of the type envisaged by Article 106(2) are often either state controlled or given a quid pro quo in the form of special or exclusive rights. The more important

---

[244] This could be the Court's own explanation when distinguishing *Corbeau* in *Ambulanz Glöckner*, above n 202, although the remarks are in the context of Art 106(2) and purportedly to identify 'core' activity.

[245] L Hancher, casenote on *Corbeau* (1994) 31 *CMLRev* 105.

[246] In broad terms, the 'exception' approach was that taken by JL Buendía Sierra, *Exclusive Rights and State Monopolies under EC Law* (Oxford, Oxford University Press, 1999); the 'balancing' view was taken by J Baquero Cruz, 'Beyond Competition: Services of General Interest and European Community Law' in G de Búrca (ed), *EU Law and the Welfare State* (Oxford, Oxford University Press, 2005) 169.

of the two categories in Article 106(2) is that of entrusted undertakings. Because of the possible derogation which may be involved, the European Court said in an early case that the category must be strictly defined.[247]

It is immaterial whether the undertaking concerned is public or private, provided that the service has been *entrusted* to it 'by an act of the public authority'.[248] This does not imply that the act need be in any particular form;[249] the essential point is that the state must have taken legal steps to secure the provision of the service by the undertaking in question. Thus an undertaking created as a result of private initiative and managing the intellectual property rights of its members on an ordinary contractual basis could not be an entrusted undertaking, even if it happened to serve public purposes.[250] The same is true where legislation only *authorises* an undertaking to act, even though some supervision of those activities may be exercised by a public agency. Thus, in *GVL v Commission*[251] the Court held that the relevant German legislation did not confer the management of copyright and related rights on specific undertakings but defined in a general manner the rules applying to the activities of companies which intended to undertake the collective exploitation of such rights. Similarly, the fact that Member States had given express approval to the Eurocheque clearing system did not 'entrust' the banks concerned.[252]

The phrase 'operation of services' seems to have been chosen advisedly to indicate the organisation of some kind of regular performance, eg a public utility. It is generally agreed that the definition of 'services' in Article 57 TFEU, as a residual concept relating to types of performance not governed by the provisions on the free movement of goods, persons or capital, does not apply in the context of Article 106(2).

The requirement that there must be a SGEI[253] covers a wide range of activities[254] beyond the very obvious examples such as water companies,[255] energy,[256] and telecommunications[257] utilities and postal services.[258] Waste-management functions may also properly qualify, particularly where the service is designed to deal with an environmen-

---

[247] Case 127/73 *BRT v SABAM* [1974] ECR 313; [1974] 2 CMLR 238. See also *Motosykletistiki Omospondia Ellado*, above n 202, where it was held that the power to give consent to applications for authorisation to organise motorcycling events could not be classified as an economic activity and therefore, could not constitute a SGEI for the purposes of Art 106(2).

[248] [1974] ECR 313, 318.

[249] See also Case C-159/94 *Commission v France* [1997] ECR I-5815, para 66. In a slightly narrower context, the Commission's *Community Framework for State Aid in the Form of Public Service Compensation* (May 2004) refers to the need to assign a specific public service obligation 'by way of an official act that . . . may take the form of a legislative or regulatory act or a contract' (para 9).

[250] SABAM was such an undertaking.

[251] Case 7/82 *GVL v Commission* [1983] ECR 483; [1983] 3 CMLR 645.

[252] *Uniform Eurocheques* [1985] OJ L35/43, [1985] 3 CMLR 434.

[253] See discussion above in relation to the state aid provisions. Note, in particular, the Commission Staff working document, 'Guide to the application of the European Union rules on state aid', above n 123.

[254] See *BUPA Insurance*, above n 111, albeit in relation to the application of Art 107.

[255] *The Community v ANSEAU-NAVEWA* [1982] 2 CMLR 193; challenged on other issues in Joined Cases 96-102, 104-105, 108 and 110/82 *IAZ International Belgium v Commission* [1983] ECR 3369; [1984] 3 CMLR 276.

[256] eg Case C-393/92 *Almelo* [1994] ECR I-1477; Case C-19/93P *Rendo NV v Commission* [1995] ECR I-3319.

[257] *Telespeed Services v United Kingdom Post Office* [1982] OJ L360/36; [1983] 1 CMLR 457. The Commission's Decision was unsuccessfully challenged in Case 41/83 *Italy v Commission (British Telecom)* [1985] ECR 873, [1985] 2 CMLR 368; see also *RTT*, above n 238.

[258] *Corbeau*, above n 242.

tal problem.[259] In *Ahmed Saeed*[260] the Court noted that Article 106(2) may be applied to airline carriers who may be obliged, by the public authorities, to operate on routes which are not commercially viable but which it is necessary to operate for reasons of the general interest. This was also the view of the Court of First Instance in *Air Inter*[261] in the context of an airline running unprofitable routes to open up French cities and regions as part of regional development. In *Campus Oil*[262] the Court of Justice apparently did not dispute the Greek government's contention that a state-owned oil refinery could be an undertaking operating a SGEI.[263]

The general interest element can still be satisfied where the benefit of the service may be enjoyed by specific recipients.[264] On the other hand, a bank will not perform such a service when transferring customers' funds from one Member State to another.[265] In *Merci Convenzionali Porto di Genova*[266] the Court held that on the evidence submitted—dock work consisting of the loading, unloading, transhipment and storage of goods—was not necessarily of general economic interest. However, in *Corsica Ferries France*[267] the Court accepted that the provision of mooring services had special characteristics sufficient to bring them within the scope of Article 106(2). In particular, the grantees of the exclusive rights in question were obliged to provide at any time and to any user a universal mooring service, for reasons of safety in port waters.

Undertakings 'having the character of a revenue-producing monopoly', the second category in Article 106(2), are distinguished by the overriding purpose of raising revenue for the national exchequer through the exploitation of their exclusive right. They are normally combined with commercial monopolies, so that they must also satisfy the requirements of Article 37 TFEU.[268]

In the discussion that follows references to entrusted undertakings should be understood to include fiscal monopolies, unless the context indicates otherwise.

B – Application of the Conditions in Article 106(2)

The view that paragraph (2) is best categorised as an exception stems from the fact that it is capable of restricting the application of any Treaty provision, including Article 106(1). It makes no difference whether the rule in question is one designed primarily to influence the conduct of undertakings, eg Article 101 or Article 102, or that of states, eg Article 34

---

[259] *FFAD*, above n 220, para 75.

[260] Case 66/86 *Ahmed Saeed Flugreisen v Zentrale zur Bekampfung unlauteren Wettbewerbs* [1989] ECR 803; [1990] 4 CMLR 102.

[261] Case T-260/94 *Air Inter v Commission* [1997] ECR II-997; [1997] 5 CMLR 851, although the other conditions of the derogation were not actually made out.

[262] Case 72/83 *Campus Oil Ltd v Minister for Industry and Energy* [1984] ECR 2727; [1984] 3 CMLR 544.

[263] Ibid, paras 18–19.

[264] In Case 90/76 *Van Ameyde v UCI* [1977] ECR 1091; [1977] 2 CMLR 478 the Commission argued that the national insurers' bureau responsible for the settlement of claims in relation to damage caused by foreign vehicles in Italy did not qualify as an entrusted undertaking 'since its activities do not benefit the whole of the national economy', but this view seems too restrictive. The Court seems to have taken for granted that the bureau would so qualify: ibid, 1126.

[265] Nor was the bank 'entrusted'.

[266] *Merci Convenzionali Porto di Genova*, above n 239. The Court reiterated this view in Case C-242/95 *GT-Link A/S v De Danske Statsbaner* [1997] ECR I-4449; [1997] 5 CMLR 601.

[267] *Corsica Ferries France*, above n 191.

[268] See Chapter 14, above.

or Article 107.[269] To benefit from Article 106(2), an undertaking must show that application of the Treaty rules would obstruct the performance of the tasks assigned to it. This standard has been expressed in a variety of ways in the case law, although the strictest formulations tied to the impact upon the undertaking's economic viability have been relaxed in more recent years, at least in the context of undertakings entrusted with the provision of universal services for the public benefit.

Thus, early examples of restrictive interpretation include the Commission's declaration that Article 106(2) could only apply in the event that the undertaking concerned had no other technically and economically feasible means of performing its particular task.[270] The Court's original position[271] was that rules of the Treaty continued to apply so long as it was not shown that their prohibitions were 'incompatible' with the performance of the undertaking's tasks.

However, these approaches must now be read in the light of the Court's subsequent analysis of the scope of the exception in numerous cases involving the tension between the recognition of legitimate public service obligations imposed by states and the EU's drive towards liberalisation of sectors in pursuit of the single market. The flurry of cases expanding the scope of Article 106(1) (see above) brought in turn a reappraisal of the conditions needed to satisfy paragraph (2). Cases such as *Corbeau*[272] indicated that in principle there could be a 'core' monopoly activity worthy of relief from the full force of the competition rules, even though in that particular case the core provision of basic postal services was not actually threatened by the peripheral competition posed by Corbeau's specialised premium-rate services. Significantly, the Court recognised that the obligation to perform the relevant services in conditions of economic equilibrium presupposed that it would be possible to offset less profitable sectors against the profitable ones to some degree.

The limits to cross-subsidy were explored by the Court in *Ambulanz Glöckner*.[273] Comparing the two cases, the Court observed:

> It is true that, in paragraph 19 of *Corbeau*, the Court held that the exclusion of competition is not justified in certain cases involving specific services, severable from the service of general interest in question, if those services do not compromise the economic equilibrium of the service of general economic interest performed by the holder of the exclusive rights.
>
> However, that is not the case with the two services now under consideration, for two reasons in particular. First, unlike the situation in *Corbeau*, the two types of service in question, traditionally assumed by the medical aid organisations, are so closely linked that it is difficult to sever the non-emergency transport services from the task of general economic interest constituted by the provision of the public ambulance service, with which they also have characteristics in common.
>
> Second, the extension of the medical aid organisations' exclusive rights to the non-emergency transport sector does indeed enable them to discharge their general-interest task of providing emergency transport in conditions of economic equilibrium. The possibility which would be open to private operators to concentrate, in the non-emergency sector, on more profitable journeys could affect the degree of economic viability of the service provided by the medical aid organisations and, consequently, jeopardise the quality and reliability of that service.

---

[269] The application of Art 106(2) to the state aid rules was expressly recognised in *FFSA/Banco Exterior de España*, above n 194. State aid is discussed above.

[270] *Community v ANSEAU-NAVEWA*, above n 255.

[271] *Sacchi*, above n 191, and repeated in Case 311/84 *CBEM Télé-Marketing v Compagnie Luxembourgeoise de Télédiffusion and Information Publicité Benelux* [1985] ECR 3261; [1986] 2CMLR 558.

[272] *Corbeau*, above n 242.

[273] *Ambulanz Glöckner*, above n 202.

However, as the Advocate General explains in point 188 of his Opinion, it is only if it were established that the medical aid organisations entrusted with the operation of the public ambulance service were manifestly unable to satisfy demand for emergency ambulance services and for patient transport at all times that the justification for extending their exclusive rights, based on the task of general interest, could not be accepted.[274]

This benign view had also been visible a few months earlier in a ruling of the Court in relation to Italian postal services.[275] The Court found that it could be necessary not just to permit the universal service provider to engage in cross-subsidy but also to require suppliers of postal services not subject to those universal service obligations to contribute to the financing of the universal service and 'in that way' to enable the entrusted undertaking to perform its task.[276] Such amounts, however, must not exceed the losses incurred by the universal service undertaking.

To sum up, the focus of the Court's approach in its case law since *Corbeau* has been directed towards ensuring that the disturbances to the market and competitive conditions resulting from granting the protection of Article 106(2) are restricted to those necessary for performance of the legitimate service by the undertaking. Explicit confirmation that the derogation is not solely concerned with the economic viability of the undertaking was given by the Court in the 1997 energy cases[277] and applied subsequently in a non-utility context. Thus, dealing with the pension fund arrangements in *Albany International*,[278] the Court summarised its position regarding the conditions for Article 106(2) as follows:

> [I]t is not necessary . . . that the financial balance or economic viability of the undertaking entrusted with the operation of a service of general economic interest should be threatened. It is sufficient that, in the absence of the rights at issue, it would not be possible for the undertaking to perform the particular tasks entrusted to it, defined by reference to the obligations and constraints to which it is subject . . . or that maintenance of those rights is necessary to enable the holder of them to perform tasks of general economic interest which have been assigned to it under economically acceptable conditions.[279]

Although this approach is very much the standard, there are instances of different formulations.[280] Despite the greater scope for application of Article 106(2) as a result of the recent case law, the burden of proof remains on the undertaking (or state) to show that compliance with the Treaty would 'obstruct' the performance of the entrusted tasks.[281]

C – The Proviso to Article 106(2)

The proviso in the second sentence of Article 106(2) states that the development of trade must not be affected to such an extent as would be contrary to the interests of the Union. It thus identifies the point at which it still becomes necessary to apply the relevant provisions of EU law, even at the cost of preventing an entrusted undertaking or a fiscal monopoly

---

[274] Ibid, paras 59–62.
[275] *TNT Traco*, above n 241.
[276] Ibid, para 55.
[277] Case C-157/94 *Commission v Netherlands* [1997] ECR I-5699; Case C-158/94 *Commission v Italy* [1997] ECR I-5789; Case C-159/94 *Commission v France* [1997] ECR I-5815; Case C-160/94 *Commission v Spain* [1997] ECR I-5851, [1998] 2 CMLR 373.
[278] *Albany International*, above n 192.
[279] Ibid, para 107 of the Judgment.
[280] See eg *Chemische Afvalstoffen Dusseldorp*, above n 223.
[281] *Air Inter*, above n 261. *cf* 1997 energy cases, above n 277.

from performing its allotted task. However, the proviso has received remarkably little discrete interpretation, mainly because for many years attempts to rely on Article 106(2) were consistently rejected on other grounds. The Court in the 1997 energy cases[282] ruled that the Commission had failed to explain why the Community interest was adversely affected by the exclusive import and export rights which formed the subject-matter of the infringement proceedings. Evidence presented to the Court indicated that there had been increasing inter-state trade in electricity and natural gas despite the existence of the exclusive rights. Accordingly, the Commission was obliged to define the Community interest against which the development of trade was said to be affected. However, it had not done so; in particular, it had not shown why, in the absence of a common policy in the area concerned, development of direct trade between producers and consumers, in parallel with the development of trade between major networks, would have been possible having regard in particular to the existing capacity and arrangements for transmission and distribution.

D – Direct Effect of Article 106(2)

It has long been clear that a national court may decide whether an undertaking qualifies as 'entrusted' within the meaning of Article 106(2).[283] Any lingering doubts as to the powers of national courts in relation to whether undertakings are 'obstructed' in the performance of their tasks were removed by the Court's judgment in *ERT*.[284] National courts are accordingly competent to apply the first sentence of Article 106(2) either in favour of or against an undertaking. This does not, of course, diminish the complexity of the task involved in deciding the point at which relief from the full force of the competition rules is no longer necessary to secure the undertaking's entrusted aims. Nor are national courts assisted by different expressions in the European case law of the extent to which Article 106(2) requires a proportionality assessment.[285]

Strictly speaking, the applicability of the proviso contained in the second sentence of the exception still awaits definitive resolution by the Court. It is thus increasingly difficult to resist the conclusion that a national court is empowered in respect of every aspect of Article 106(2). The case is perhaps even more persuasive now that the provision seems to have been increasingly subjected to holistic interpretation.

E – Article 106(3): The Supervisory and Legislative Competence of the Commission

By Article 106(3) the Commission is both placed under an obligation to ensure the application of the Article and equipped with a special power to issue directives or decisions

---

[282] n 277 above.

[283] *BRT*, above n 247.

[284] *ERT*, above n 227.

[285] AG Léger in *Hanner*, above n 196, states that proportionality *and* necessity tests are applicable; obstacles to free competition are allowed only 'in so far as they are necessary in order to enable the undertaking entrusted with such a task of general interest to perform it. The proportionality test therefore means verifying whether the undertaking's specific task could be performed with less restrictive measures' (para 142).

for this purpose. Directives or decisions under Article 106(3) can only be addressed to Member States. However, where appropriate the Commission may have recourse to other powers, for example under Regulation 1/2003, against the undertaking concerned. There is, of course, nothing in Article 106 to prevent the Commission, if it so chooses, from issuing non-binding recommendations. The existence of a special enactment competence vested in the Commission sits uncomfortably against the other law-making processes of the Union.

Strengthened by early judicial support, the Commission sought liberalisation of particular sectors by measures adopted under Article 106(3).[286] However, there is no power to harmonise under Article 106(3) and so legislation has more recently been enacted by the Council and Parliament using other Treaty bases.[287]

XIII – NATIONAL LEGISLATION AND ARTICLE 101

Although the discussion of Article 101 in Chapter 23 focused on the collusive behaviour of undertakings, there is also a well-established strand of case law dealing with situations in which restrictive practices and distortions of competition are linked in some way to specific legislation or the general legal framework of a Member State. The Court of Justice has consistently maintained that although Article 101 is concerned solely with the conduct of undertakings, that provision, in conjunction with Article 10 EC, required the Member States not to introduce or maintain in force measures, even of a legislative or regulatory nature, which may render ineffective the competition rules applicable to undertakings.[288] Following the entry into force of the TL, similar provision is made in Article 4(3) TEU:

> Pursuant to the principle of sincere cooperation, the Union and the Member States shall, in full mutual respect, assist each other in carrying out tasks which flow from the Treaties.
>
> The Member States shall take any appropriate measure, general or particular, to ensure fulfilment of the obligations arising out of the Treaties or resulting from the acts of the institutions of the Union.
>
> The Member States shall facilitate the achievement of the Union's tasks and refrain from any measure which could jeopardise the attainment of the Union's objectives.

Accordingly, the principles developed by the Court under Article 10 EC continue to apply and, therefore generally in the context of their economic policy, the activities of the Member States must observe the principle of an open, competitive market economy.[289] However, it is clear from the case law that a Member State will not be made liable for

---

[286] See eg various early Directives such as Directive 90/388 on telecommunications services; [1990] OJ L192/10; Directive 95/51 on the use of cable television networks [1995] OJ L256/49; Directive 96/2 on mobile and personal communications; [1996] OJ L20/59.

[287] Note the possibility for measures to be introduced under Art 14 TEU (ex Art 16 EC).

[288] Case 267/86 *Van Eycke* [1988] ECR 4769; [1990] 4 CMLR 330, para 16; Case C-185/91 *Reiff* [1993] ECR I-5801, para 14; Case C-153/93 *Delta Schiffahrts- und Speditionsgesellschaft* [1994] ECR I-2517, para 15; Case C-35/96 *Commission v Italy (Re CNSD)* [1998] ECR I-3851, [1998] 5 CMLR 889; Case C-35/99 *Arduino* [2002] ECR I-1529, para 34; Case C-198/01 *Consorzio Industrie Fiammiferi (CIF) v Autorità Garante della Concorrenza e del Mercato* [2003] ECR I-8055, para 45.

[289] *CIF*, above n 288, para 47. See P Nebbia, case note (2004) 41 *CMLRev* 839.

every anti-competitive consequence of legislation, however tenuous or remote. Instead, the Court has indicated that liability can only attach to the Member State if either (a) it requires or favours the adoption of agreements, decisions or concerted practices contrary to Article 101, or reinforces their effects; or (b) deprives its own rules of the character of legislation by delegating to private economic operators responsibility for taking decisions affecting the economic sphere.[290] Each of these two tests is discussed further below.

A – Requiring or Favouring Anti-competitive Agreements, or Reinforcing their Effects

Although the Court repeatedly refers to this formula,[291] examples of direct influence are unusual. However, an enforcement action brought by the Commission against Italy in relation to its rules governing customs agents provides a case in point.[292] According to Italian Act No 1612/1960, the National Council of Customs Agents (CNSD) was made responsible for setting the tariff for services provided by customs agents. This tariff was compulsory and anyone contravening it was liable to disciplinary action, including suspension or removal from the register of customs agents. The Commission took action against Italy on the basis that the tariff-fixing was a decision of an association of undertakings, for which the Member State was responsible. The Court agreed. Having found that in adopting the tariff, the CNSD infringed Article 101,[293] it went on to condemn Italy's direct participation, observing:

> By adopting the national legislation in question, the Italian republic clearly not only required the conclusion of an agreement contrary to [Article 101] and declined to influence its terms, but also assists in ensuring compliance with that agreement.[294]

A more likely, if more problematic, application of the Court's formulation concerns the reinforcing of anti-competitive agreements since this could embrace looser forms of influence than those where the state directly requires anti-competitive conduct. However, it appears that the Court only entertains its application in relation to legislation that adopts or reinforces previous private arrangements. In *Van Eycke*,[295] for example, holders of certain Belgian savings accounts could get tax exemptions provided that the bank kept interest rates to below maximum levels specified in a royal decree. This decree was alleged to reinforce a previous arrangement between banks and financial institutions restricting interest rates. However, the Court of Justice left it to the national court to decide whether this was indeed the case.[296]

---

[290] See eg Case C-446/05 *Doulamis v Union des Dentistes et Stomatologistes de Belgique (UPR)* [2008] ECR I-1377; [2008] 5 CMLR 4 where national legislation prohibiting dental care services being advertised satisfied neither of these tests and was therefore not precluded by EU law.

[291] eg Case 229/83 *Leclerc v Sarl 'Au Blé Vert'* [1985] ECR 1; [1985] 2 CMLR 286, para 15; Joined Cases 209–13/84 *Ministère Public v Asjes* [1986] ECR 1425; [1986] 3 CMLR 173, para 72; Case 311/85 *VZW Vereniging van Vlaamse Reisbureaus v VZW Sociale Dienst* [1987] ECR 3801; [1989] 4 CMLR para 10; Case 254/87 *Syndicat des Libraires de Normandie v L'Aigle Distribution* [1988] ECR 4457.

[292] *Commission v Italy (Re CNSD)*, above n 288.

[293] The Court had no difficulty treating the activity of customs agent as economic and finding that the CNSD was an association of undertakings regardless of its national public law categorisation.

[294] [1998] ECR I-3851, para 55.

[295] *Van Eycke*, above n 288.

[296] The evidence of direct reinforcement was much clearer in *VZW Vereniging van Vlaamse Reisbureaus*, above n 291.

Subsequently, it proved difficult to persuade the Court of the reinforcing effects of national legislation. Thus, in *Meng*[297] the relevant German rules forbade insurance agents from sharing their commission with customers. Faced with the argument that this legislation restricted the competitiveness of agents, the Court declined to accept that it fell within the reach of Article 101 in combination with Article 10 EC. In its view, the measure was no more than regulation by the state of the insurance market. This reluctance on the part of the Court coincided with its drawing of lines in the sand in relation to other areas of market regulation under EU law.[298]

B – Legislation Deprived of its State Character by Delegation

Member States cannot absolve themselves of responsibility by simply delegating or transferring decision-making powers to private bodies. The question is whether the legislation is deprived of its state character, a conclusion that the Court again appears reluctant to draw. In *Reiff*,[299] for example, it was called upon to consider German legislation under which the rates for the carriage of goods by road were set by tariff boards made up of industry representatives appointed by the relevant minister. The Court noted that the industry representatives were not bound by instructions from the undertakings from which they were drawn, and as such were not representatives of those undertakings. Moreover, the Minister was able to take part in meetings of the tariff boards and held powers to substitute his own tariffs in substitution for those of the boards. These features, the Court concluded, meant that the system was not a delegation of the state's powers.[300]

The objection to states delegating their powers to private bodies is found in the scope thereby conferred for those bodies to take anti-competitive decisions in their own favour. Consequently, it seems there will be no breach by the state if the transfer includes requirements to take public interest considerations into account. In the Italian customs agents case,[301] for example, the Court noted that Italian Act 1612/90 neither obliged nor even encouraged the members of the CNSD to take into account not only the interests of the undertakings which appointed them but also the general interest and the interests of undertakings in other sectors or users of the services in question.[302] Instead, the legislation 'wholly relinquished'[303] to private economic operators the powers of the public authorities as regards the setting of tariffs, and the Italian Republic had accordingly failed to fulfil its obligations.

More recently, the case law on delegation has concerned the fixing of scales of lawyers' fees and has raised again the interaction of competition and free-movement provisions of the Treaty. Where, as in the *Arduino* case,[304] a Member State required a professional body to produce a draft tariff for minimum and maximum fees for lawyers' services, the Court

---

[297] Case C-2/91 *Meng* [1993] ECR I-5751; see also Case C-245/91 *Ohra* [1993] ECR 5851.
[298] Notably Cases C-267-268/91 *Keck and Mithouard* [1993] ECR I-6097; [1995] 1 CMLR 101. See N Reich, 'The "November Revolution" of the European Court of Justice: *Keck, Meng* and *Audi* Revisited' (1994) 31 CMLRev 459.
[299] *Reiff*, above n 288.
[300] See also Joined Cases C-140, 141, 142/94 *DIP v Commune di Bassano del Grappa* [1995] ECRI-3257.
[301] *Commission v Italy (Re CNSD)*, above n 288.
[302] Ibid, para 44.
[303] Ibid, para 57.
[304] *Arduino*, above n 288.

rejected the view that this constituted delegation. As a draft, the tariff could be reviewed by the appropriate minister and no approval could be given without opinions from two public bodies. The Court found that the legislation setting out the process 'does not contain either procedural arrangements or substantive requirements capable of ensuring, with reasonable probability, that, when producing the draft tariff the CNF [members of the Bar] conducts itself like an arm of the State working in the public interest'.[305]

This ruling proved contentious, and subsequent references were made by Italian courts on other aspects of the same legislation. In particular, they asked whether the *Arduino* ruling governed derogation from the fixed scales or their application to out-of-court services.[306] The Court ruled that Article 101 in conjunction with Article 10 EC did not preclude national measures approving a draft scale, produced by a professional body of lawyers, fixing a minimum fee for members of the legal profession. The statutory approval process ensured there was effective supervision by the state which had not delegated its powers to economic operators, and the draft and approval process did not require or encourage the adoption of any anti-competitive agreements.[307]

It should be noted that professional services constitute an area of particular difficulty for the purposes of application of the EU competition rules. The Court's treatment of *Wouters* displayed a retreat to a 'rule of reason' for justification, whilst its *Arduino* judgment also demonstrated a reluctance to apply the combined effects of Articles 101 and 10 EC without an obvious failure of state supervision in the legislative process.[308] The Commission adopted a Report on Competition in Professional Services in 2004 and a follow-up Report was adopted in 2005, whereby it invited professional organisations and Member States' authorities to undertake a voluntary review of existing professional rules on the basis of whether they are in the public interest, justified, necessary and proportionate.[309] No further subsequent action has been taken in this area by the Commission.

XIV – CONCLUDING REMARKS

As noted at the outset of this chapter, the State Action Plan of 2005 sought to modernise state aid law, and the GBER and other measures adopted should help in the aim to achieve less and better targeted horizontal aid. The Court jurisprudence over the last ten years also shows a tightening of the application of the rules, with a wide interpretation of what constitutes an advantage and the difficulties in disproving selectivity. Modernisation also involves the encouragement of greater reliance upon national level enforcement.[310] A study which reported in March 2006[311] identified the continuing difficulties and obsta-

---

[305] Ibid, para 39.

[306] Joined Cases C-94/04 *Cipolla v Fazari* and C-202/04 *Macrino, Capodarte v Meloni* [2006] ECR I-11421; [2007] 4 CMLR 8 .

[307] See paras 50–54 in particular.

[308] See also *Cipolla v Fazari*, above n 306, and *Macrino, Capodarte v Meloni*, above n 306.

[309] See 'Professional Services—Scope for More Reform' COM(2005) 405 final, which was a follow-up to the Commission's earlier 'Report on Competition in Professional Services' COM(2004) 83.

[310] On the difficulties in this process, see the early discussion by M Ross, 'State Aids and National Courts: Definitions and Other Problems—A Case of Premature Emancipation' (2000) 37 *CMLRev* 401.

[311] *Study on the Enforcement of State Aid Law at National Level*, co-ordinated by T Jestaedt, J Derenne and T Ottervanger). See the Commission's website at http://ec.europa.eu/competition/state_aid/studies_reports/studies_reports.html.

cles in this area, despite a significant increase in cases since the previous report made in 1999.[312] The 2009 update of that Report[313] highlighted the 'reasonably large' increase in the number of court cases in the interim period, and that this was not as a result of case law from 'new' Member States post-2004 accession. Most actions were brought against Member States, not against beneficiaries. Direct actions against competitors are still limited, and most of these result in injunctive relief to suspend aid. The authors of the report, and update, could find no examples of monetary damages being awarded on the basis of an illegal aid granted to a competitor. The 2006 Report particularly stressed the diversity of procedures and substantive rules at the level of national law as an explanation of the continued infancy of local enforcement of state aid law. On the basis of the evidence supplied by the 2006 Report, the inference is that the problem for decentralised enforcement by private action is now not so much a lack of awareness of state aid rules, but, rather, the obstacles in the national legal arena to effective enjoyment of the protection afforded by Article 108(3). The role of national courts, however, is still being prioritised despite their inability to rule on questions of compatibility of aid. In time, therefore, the balance between public and private enforcement may reflect more closely the model in other areas of EU law and developing in relation to Articles 101 and 102.

SGEIs are an increasingly important area of EU law, and considerable attention has been devoted in recent years to the ways and the extent to which Member States regulate the provision of public service obligations, both under state aid controls and Article 106, as discussed earlier in this chapter. It will be interesting to note how this area develops, in particular in the light of Article 14 TFEU (ex Article 16 EC) which refers to the shared Union values and the particular objectives of social and territorial cohesion which underlie the provision of SGEIs and make it a positive horizontal policy-shaping consideration for both Member States and the Community institutions. Article 14 captures the tension at the heart of the Union's current process of development: the balancing or prioritising of market-based considerations and those more concerned with cohesion and social solidarity.[314]

Further Reading

K Bacon (ed), *European Community Law of State Aid* (Oxford, Oxford University Press, 2009).

J Baquero Cruz, 'Beyond Competition: Services of General Interest and European Community Law' in G de Búrca (ed), *EU Law and the Welfare State* (Oxford, Oxford University Press, 2005) 169.

A Bartosch, 'Is There a Need for a Rule of Reason in European State Aid Law? Or How to Arrive at a Coherent Concept of Material Selectivity' (2010) 47 *CMLRev* 730.

A Biondi, 'The Rationale of State Aid Control: A Return to Orthodoxy' [2010] *Cambridge Yearbook of EU Law* 35.

C Bovis, 'Financing Services of General Interest in the EU: How Do Public Procurement and State Aids Interact to Demarcate between Market Forces and Protection?' (2005) 11 *ELJ* 79.

D Cahill, 'The Ebb and Flow, the Doldrums and the Raging Tide: Single Market Law's Ebb and Flow over Services of General Economic Interest, the Legal Doldrums over Services of General

---

[312] The 1999 study was considered in the 4th edn of this work, 706.

[313] http://ec.europa.eu/competition/state_aid/studies_reports/enforcement_study_2009.pdf.

[314] See M Krajewski, U Neergaard and J van de Gronden (eds), *The Changing Legal Framework for Services of General Interest in Europe* (The Hague, TMC Asser Press, 2009); and for earlier discussion, Freedland and Sciarra (eds), *Public Services and Citizenship in European Law* (Oxford, Clarendon Press, 1998).

Interest, and the Raging Tide of Art 106(2) (ex Art 86(2)) over State Aid and Public Procurement' (2010) 21 *EBLRev* 629.

M Krajewski, U Neergaard and J van de Gronden (eds), *The Changing Legal Framework for Services of General Interest in Europe* (The Hague, TMC Asser Press, 2009).

B Kurcz and D Vallindas, 'Can General Measures Be Selective? Some Thoughts on the Interpretation of a state Aid Definition' (2008) 45 *CMLRev* 159.

P Nicolaides, 'Distortion of Competition in the Field of State Aid: From Unnecessary Aid to Unnecessary Distortion' [2010] ECLR 402.

T Prosser, *The Limits of Competition Law, Markets and Public Services* (Oxford, Oxford University Press, 2005).

——, 'EU Competition Law and Public Services', in E Mossialos, G Permanand, R Baeten and TK Hervey (eds), *Health Systems Governance in Europe* (Cambridge, Cambridge University Press, 2010) 315–36.

C Quigley, *European State Aid Law and Policy*, 2nd edn (Oxford, Hart Publishing, 2009).

A Sinnaeve, 'State Aid Procedures: Developments Since the Entry into Force of the Procedural Regulation' (2007) 44 *CMLRev* 965.

E Szyszczak, *The Regulation of the State in Competitive Markets in the European Union* (Oxford, Hart Publishing, 2007).

P Vesterdorf and MU Nielsen, *State Aid Law of the European Union* (London: Sweet & Maxwell, 2008).

J Winter, 'Re(de)fining the Notion of State Aid in Article 87(1) of the EC Treaty' (2004) 41 *CMLRev* 475.

Part VI

External Relations

27

External Action

The Treaty of Lisbon has far-reaching effects on the law governing the external action of the European Union, more so than in any other policy area, except perhaps that of freedom, security and justice. In this chapter we begin by examining the constitutional framework of EU external action under the reorganised Treaties, which preserves the specificity of one area of external competence, that of the common foreign and security policy. We go on to consider the body of legal concepts, principles and mechanisms, largely developed in the case law of the Court of Justice, that constitute the general law of EU external action, focusing more particularly on the following: the express and implied conferral of external competence upon the Union; the factors that render EU external competence exclusive; the further constraints on Member States' powers of autonomous external action resulting from the duty of close co-operation with the Union, to which they are subject; the procedural code in Article 218 TFEU governing the negotiation and conclusion of international agreements on behalf of the Union; and so-called 'mixed agreements', to which the Union and also the Member States are parties. Finally, we turn our attention to the specific area in which the international role of the EU has historically been most prominent, that of the common commercial policy, which regulates trade between the Union and third countries. The important topic of the effect within the internal legal order of Union of provisions contained in international agreements to which the Union is party is treated in the following chapter.

I – THE CONSTUTIONAL FRAMEWORK

A – External Action Under the New Treaty Structure

Prior to the entry into force of the TL, the external action of the EU was conducted under three separate sets of constitutional arrangements, corresponding to the 'pillar structure' of the Union at the time. The 'First Pillar' competence of the European Community related, in broad terms, to the economic, social and environmental aspects of external relations, pursuant to legal bases contained in the EC Treaty. There was, in addition, competence over external action in matters falling within the scope of the ECSC Treaty, until its expiry in 2002;[1] as there was (and still is) in the matters to which the EURATOM Treaty applies.[2]

---

[1] Art ECSC. Competence for commercial policy was retained by the Member States.
[2] Art EURATOM.

Each of the European Communities had a distinct legal personality and entered into international agreements in its own name. Under the 'Second Pillar', governed by Title V of the TEU, competence for the common foreign and security policy (CFSP) was conferred upon the Union, as distinct from the Community; this covered the political, security and defence aspects of external relations, as defined by the then Article 11(1) TEU. Under the 'Third Pillar', the competence, once again of the Union, concerning the external dimension of police and judicial co-operation in criminal matters was governed by Title VI TEU. At one time it was controversial whether the Union enjoyed international legal personality, since there was nothing said about this in the TEU. However, the TA laid down a procedure for negotiating and concluding international agreements for the purposes of the Second and Third Pillars; and the practice developed of acting under this procedure in the name of the Union as such, implying recognition de facto by the Member States and by international partners of its international legal personality and Treaty-making power.[3] Pre-Lisbon, therefore, the Union used to act directly in external matters governed by Titles V and VI TEU, and in its Community persona in external matters governed by the EC Treaty.

As we have explained,[4] in the era of the TL the EU replaces and succeeds the European Community.[5] All competences to undertake external actions that are authorised by either the TEU or the TFEU are now exercisable by the Union, which enjoys explicitly conferred legal personality.[6]

We have also noted the disappearance of the 'Third Pillar' as a distinct legal sub-order, through the assimilation of police co-operation and of judicial co-operation in criminal matters into the Title of the TFEU relating to the area of freedom, security and justice (AFSJ), though decision-making on these matters retains some special features. The international aspect of the Union's activity in the field of criminal law is now, therefore, governed by the rules that apply generally to external EU competence arising under legal bases located in the TFEU.

In contrast, the regime applicable to the CFSP remains strongly differentiated from that of other fields of external action. The elements of this differentiation are more fully considered below. As we shall see, the issue whether a given external action of the Union should be organised on the basis of CFSP competence or on the basis of what, for convenience, may be termed 'TFEU external competences' remains a potential source of disputes.[7]

B – Part Five of the TFEU

An innovation of the TL is the gathering together in Part Five of the TFEU of provisions relating explicitly and specifically to external action by the Union, which either are new or were previously scattered about the EC Treaty. The legal bases authorising such action are:

---

[3] For a fuller analysis, see A Dashwood, 'Issues of Decision-making in the European Union after Nice' in A Arnull and D Wincott, *Accountability and Legitimacy in the European Union* (Oxford, Oxford University Press, 2002) 13, 14–21. See also P Eeckhout, *External Relations of the European Union: Legal and Constitutional Foundations* (Oxford, Oxford University Press, 2004) 154 –60.

[4] See Chapter 1.

[5] Art 1(3) TEU.

[6] Art 47 TEU.

[7] Discussed below, section I.D.

— Article 207 TFEU on the common commercial policy (CCP), which concerns the regulation of external trade.[8]

The Article confers exclusive competence upon the Union in all aspects of trade policy, including—besides the paradigm case of trade in goods—trade in services, the commercial aspects of intellectual property (IP) and foreign direct investment (FDI).

— Articles 208–11 TFEU on development co-operation; Articles 212 and 213 TFEU on economic, financial and technical co-operation with third countries (ie other than developing countries); and Article 214 TFEU on humanitarian aid, a new legal basis created by the TL.

The first two sets of provisions constitute the legal bases for all kinds of economic co-operation between the EU and different categories of third countries, as well as for action in matters such as the development of civil society, which help create the conditions for ensuring the success of such co-operation. The objectives of actions taken under those legal basis will typically be long-term ones, while Article 217 TFEU enables the Union to mount operations intended to provide ad hoc assistance and relief and protection for people in third countries who are victims of natural or man-made disasters. As we explain below, Union competence in these areas is exercised in parallel with that of the Member States.

— Article 215 TFEU on so-called 'restrictive measures'.

The Article provides a mechanism for the adoption of restrictive economic measures, implementing a decision taken within the framework of the CFSP. The purpose of such measures may be to put pressure on the governments of third countries, or particular members of a regime, in order to induce a change of policy; or to curb the activities of individuals or groups judged to be inimical to the EU, eg because of a link with international terrorism. The underlying CFSP decision embodies a judgement made on political and security grounds, while the measure adopted under Article 215 takes the necessary economic or financial measures, which will usually relate to matters falling within Union competence in respect of the internal market, the commercial policy or transport policy. Union restrictive measures are usually, though not invariably, adopted in order to give effect to resolutions of the UN Security Council.

— Article 217 TFEU on association agreements.

These agreements, the Court of Justice has said, create 'special, privileged links with a non-member country which must, at least to a certain extent, take part in the Community system'.[9] The degree of such participation is determined by the particular content of a given agreement. The special quality of association agreements is that they may relate to matters in respect of which the Treaties provide no substantive legal basis for external action, so long as there is a legal basis for internal action; an example would be the free movement of workers.[10] The Europe Agreements, designed to prepare the countries of Central and Eastern Europe for membership of the Union, were association agreements and so also is the Agreement creating the European Economic Area, between the EU and certain former member countries of EFTA.

— Article 219 TFEU on external currency arrangements for the eurozone.

— Article 220(1) relating to the establishment of 'all forms of appropriate cooperation' between the Union and various named (and other) international organisations.

---

[8] The common commercial policy is the subject of Part V of this chapter.
[9] Case 12/86 *Demirel* [1987] ECR 3719, para 9.
[10] Ibid, paras 9 et seq.

The organisations specifically mentioned are the UN and its specialised agencies, the Council of Europe, the Organisation for Security and Cooperation in Europe and the OECD.

In addition to these substantive legal bases, Part Five of the TFEU includes a provision identifying the situations in which the Union is authorised to enter into international agreements[11] and a procedural code governing the negotiation and conclusion of such agreements.[12] Those provisions are fully discussed below.

Although clearly focused on external action, the CFSP (except as regards the negotiation and conclusion of agreements) is conspicuously absent from Part Five.

It should also be noted that the provisions collected in Part Five are not the only ones in the TFEU that are relevant to the Union's activities in the international sphere. As we shall see, areas of policy primarily concerned with internal Union action—eg those relating to transport or the protection of the environment—may also have an external dimension.

C – The High Representative of the Union for Foreign Affairs and Security Policy

The creation of the post of High Representative of the Union for Foreign Affairs and Security Policy[13] is of such potential significance to the future of EU external action that it seems necessary to recall this innovation of the TL, even though the responsibilities of the office-holder have already been discussed in Part V of Chapter 3. As was explained there, the High Representative is required, at one and the same time, to fulfil the roles of mandatory of the Council in the development and implementation of the CFSP, Chair of the Foreign Affairs Council, and Vice-President of the Commission overseeing the performance of that body's responsibilities in the external relations field.[14] It was noted in Chapter 3 that the High Representative's duty of collegiality as a Commissioner, pursuant to Article 18(4) TEU, is qualified by the phrase, 'to the extent that this is consistent with paragraphs 2 and 3'. That provision may be thought to resolve, at least in a formal sense, any conflicts of loyalty that may arise from the 'double-hatting' of the High Representative, more particularly because Article 18(3) TEU refers to the chairing of the Foreign Affairs Council, whose remit covers the whole range of EU external action, not only the CFSP. Therefore at the definitive stage of the decision-making process on both CFSP matters and matters such as trade, development co-operation and international action on the environment, which are governed by the provisions of the TFEU, the High Representative is required to wear his/her Council hat. The trouble is that, if the High Representative were fully faithful to that principle, he/she would be liable to forfeit the confidence of other members of the Commission. A High Representative with sufficient authority to establish a measure of independence from both the Council and the Commission would be well

---

[11] Art 216(1) TFEU. Discussed below, section II.
[12] Art 218 TFEU. Discussed below.
[13] Hereinafter 'the High Representative'. See the discussion of the role of the High Representative in P Craig, *The Lisbon Treaty: Law, Politics, and Treaty Reform* (Oxford, Oxford University Press, 2010) 110–12.
[14] See Arts 18 and 27 TEU.

placed to promote the development of a properly coherent external policy and to avoid debilitating turf wars between the institutions.

At the time of writing, Baroness Ashton of Upholland had been in post as the first holder of the post of High Representative for a little over a year—much of this, it is understood, spent in handling the administrative complexity of setting up the European External Action Service, for which provision was also made by the TL.[15] According to the Treaty, the Service is to be composed of staff recruited from the General Secretariats of the Council and the Commission and also of officials seconded from national diplomatic services of the Member States. It will not be easy to form an effective EU diplomatic service, with a consistent approach to the great international issues of the day, from individuals of such disparate provenance.

As of now it is too soon after the entry into force of the TL to predict success or failure for this institutional venture; though, as has been said, the Union's genius for muddling through, and its long history of living with paradox, may perhaps give grounds for optimism.[16]

D – The General Treaty Provisions on the Union's External Action

As noted above, Title V of the TEU has a Chapter 1 headed, 'General provisions on the Union's external action'. Its location in the TEU, rather than the TFEU, is presumably explained by the decision to retain the specific provisions on the CFSP in that Treaty. Logic would dictate that general provisions, applicable to the CFSP as well as to TFEU external competences, should come before specific ones.

Article 21(1) TFEU sets out the principles (redolent of motherhood and apple pie) which are to guide the Union's action on the international scene. These—stated to have inspired the Union's own 'creation, development and enlargement'—comprise: democracy, the rule of law, the universality and indivisibility of human rights and fundamental freedoms, respect for human dignity, the principles of equality and solidarity, and respect for the principles of the UN Charter and international law. Rather more interesting is the commitment in the second subparagraph to, among other things, 'promote multilateral solutions to common problems'.

Article 21(2) TFEU provides:

The Union shall define and pursue common policies and actions, and shall work for a high degree of cooperation in all fields of international relations, in order to:

(a) safeguard its values, fundamental interests, security, independence and integrity;

(b) consolidate and support democracy, the rule of law, human rights and the principles of international law;

(c) preserve peace, prevent conflicts and strengthen international security, in accordance with the purposes and principles of the United Nations Charter, with the principles of the Helsinki Final Act, and with the aims of the Charter of Paris, including those relating to external borders;

---

[15] Art 27(3) TEU. See N Reslow and S Vanhoonacker, 'The European External Action Service: Living Forwards by Understanding Backwards' (2010) 15 *European Foreign Affairs Review* 1.

[16] A Dashwood and A Johnston, 'The Institutions of the Enlarged EU under the Regime of the Constitutional Treaty' (2004) 42 *CMLRev* 1481, 1503–04. cp one of these authors' much more critical reaction to the proposal for a post of 'Union Minister for Foreign Affairs' in A Dashwood, 'The Draft EU Constitution—First Impressions' (2002) 5 *CYELS* 395, 414–15.

(d) foster the sustainable economic, social and environmental development of developing countries, with the primary aim of eradicating poverty;

(e) encourage the integration of all countries into the world economy, including through the progressive abolition of restrictions on international trade;

(f) help develop international measures to preserve and improve the quality of the environment and the sustainable management of global natural resources, in order to ensure sustainable development;

(g) assist populations, countries and regions confronting natural or man-made disasters; and

(h) promote an international system based on stronger multilateral cooperation and good global governance.

That statement of objectives for the external action of the Union is rather heavily weighted towards matters which might be thought to belong to the domain of the CFSP. Items (a)–(c) and (h) correspond broadly to the list of specific CFSP objectives in the former Article 11(1) TEU, which has not been reproduced in the amended Treaty. Item (d) relates fairly directly to development co-operation, item (f) to the protection of the environment and item (g) to humanitarian aid, while item (e) seems, again, to be about development policy, with an oblique reference to trade liberalisation, which is only one aspect of the CCP. It is odd that the CCP should not figure more prominently, given its centrality to EU external relations activity, and that nothing should be said about the important contribution that could be made to the economic and social progress of EU citizens by increasing the Union's share of world trade.

Pursuant to Article 21(3) TFEU, the Union is bound to respect the principles and pursue the objectives set out in the preceding paragraphs 'in the development and implementation of the different areas of the Union's external action covered by this Title and by Part Five of the [TFEU], and of the external aspects of its other policies'. That wording might be thought to suggest that, whatever the external competence being exercised on a given occasion, all of the listed objectives are capable in principle of bearing some degree of relevance to the action taken. It cannot, of course, have been intended that they must all be considered to have the *same degree* of relevance to all legal bases, since that would undermine the principle of conferred powers. However, as we shall see, the establishment of this common list of objectives is liable to give rise to even more disputes than in the past, in situations where the choice between legal bases may have radically different legal consequences.[17]

A new power for the European Council to adopt decisions 'on the strategic interests and objectives of the Union' has been established by Article 22 TFEU. Such decisions, it is provided, 'may concern the relations of the Union with a specific country or region' or they may be 'thematic in approach'. Prior to the TL, the European Council was empowered by Article 13 TFEU to decide on what were then termed 'common strategies'. However, the fact that this power was exercisable under the Union's CFSP competence made its use for defining strategies extending to matters governed by the EC Treaty controversial. Article 22 TFEU lays down procedural arrangements that allow the same decision to cover matters falling within both the CFSP and the Union's TFEU external competences. Under the prescribed procedure, the European Council will act by unanimity (not consensus, so abstentions are possible), on a recommendation from the Council. When adopting such a recommendation, the Council must follow the procedures prescribed by the Treaties in

---

[17] See the discussion, below, of the choice between a CCP and an environment legal basis or between a CFSP and a development co-operation legal basis.

relation to the different elements it is intended the decision should comprise. Provision is made for the possibility of joint proposals to the Council, by the High Representative regarding CFSP elements and the Commission regarding elements belonging to other areas of external action. At the time of writing, no decisions had yet been adopted by the European Council pursuant to Article 22.

E – Continuing Particularity of the CFSP

(i) Scope of the CFSP

The scope of the CFSP is defined by Article 24(1), first subparagraph TEU as covering 'all areas of foreign policy and all questions relating to the Union's security, including the progressive framing of a common defence policy that might lead to a common defence'. Article 42(1) TEU complements that definition by elaborating on its security and defence aspects. The common security and defence policy is said to be an integral part of the CFSP. Its function is to 'provide the Union with an operational capacity drawing on civil and military assets'. These may be used 'on missions outside the Union for peace-keeping, conflict prevention and strengthening international security in accordance with the principles of the United Nations Charter'; such tasks to be 'undertaken using capabilities provided by the Member States'. According to Article 42(2), first subparagraph, the stage of a common defence will be reached only when the European Council, acting unanimously, so decides.

Despite the breadth of the definition in Article 24(1), the focus of the CFSP is foreign policy in its political, security and defence aspects, as distinct from its economic, social and environmental aspects. This follows from the multitude of legal bases in the TFEU available for pursuing the latter. The situation was clearer before the establishment of the list of common objectives in Article 21(2) TFEU and the abolition of the list specific to the CFSP in former Article 1 (1) TFEU; this, as we have seen, corresponded broadly to points (a)–(c) and (h) of the Article 21(2) list. The notion of a 'common defence' marks the limit of the present conferral of CFSP competence. It should probably be taken to mean the surrender by individual Member States of control over their armed forces to the authorities of the Union. The military ambitions of the Union for the time being are confined to the 'missions outside the Union' identified in Article 41(1).

Nothing could indicate more clearly the reason why the CFSP retains its particularity than the reference in Article 42(1) to the fact that the capabilities needed to 'provide the Union with an operational capacity drawing on civil and military assets' have to be furnished by the Member States. An even more brutal fact is that seriously useful military capabilities belong to relatively few of them. There is also an immense difference between the international influence, resulting from factors such as the spread of diplomatic representation, historic links with overseas countries and membership of international bodies, notably of the UN Security Council, which the Member States are able to deploy.

(ii) Elements of Particularity

The second subparagraph of Article 24(1) states explicitly that the CFSP 'is subject to specific rules and procedures' and goes on to summarise these differences. Expanding on the text of the paragraph, the elements of particularity that may be thought the most significant are the following.

(a) Retention of the CFSP in the TEU

There is, first, the retention of the specific provisions on the CFSP in Chapter 2 of Part V of the TEU, in contrast to all the other legal bases for Union external action, which are found in the TFEU, and the definition of CFSP competence in Article 2(4) TFEU. CFSP competence is identified as belonging to a special category, governed by the provisions of the TEU. The full significance of this will become clear when we consider the interaction between the Union's external competences and those of the Member States.

(b) The Institutions and Decision-making

As hitherto, the European Council and the Council retain their predominance in policy formation and decision-making on the CFSP.[18] The European Council identifies the Union's strategic interests, and determines the objectives of, and defines general guidelines for, the CFSP, and it now has formal decision-making power for this purpose.[19] On the basis of the policy lines established by the European Council, the Council frames the CFSP and takes the decisions necessary for defining and implementing it.[20] Any of the Member States or the High Representative may refer a question relating to the CFSP to the Council. Far from having a monopoly of the initiative, as it does in respect of TFEU external competences, the Commission has even lost its former independent right of referral to the Council, though it may 'support' an initiative taken by the High Representative.[21] It is the latter, acting under the Council's mandate, and not the Commission, that ensures the implementation of the decisions of the European Council and the Council, and represents the Union externally for matters relating to the CFSP.[22] Formerly, when those tasks were performed by the Presidency, the Commission had a right to be fully associated in them,[23] but that is no longer the case. The significance of this diminution of the Commission's direct involvement in the formation and conduct of the CFSP will emerge over time, in the light of the evolving relationship of the High Representative with the Council, on the one hand, and the Commission, on the other. As for the European Parliament, it plays no part in the adoption of particular decisions; it merely has a right to information and to have its views 'duly taken into consideration'.[24]

The general voting rule is that the basic decision on any CFSP matter must be adopted by unanimity, while QMV is available for implementing decisions, once a position has been taken on the issue of principle. The TL has created a new opportunity for QMV, where a proposal is presented by the High Representative, in response to a specific request by the European Council. However, since there would have to be consensus to make such a request, this does not constitute a real exception to the unanimity rule. Moreover, in situations where QMV is a possibility, there is an 'emergency brake' procedure, under which an objecting Member State would be able to force a referral of the matter to the European

---

[18] Craig, above n 13, 411–13.
[19] Art 26(1) TEU.
[20] Art 26(2) TEU.
[21] Art 22(1) TEU. cp the pre-Lisbon version of the same provision.
[22] Art 27(1) and (2) TEU.
[23] See former Art 18(4) TEU.
[24] Art 36 TEU.

Council, which would have to act by unanimity. Finally, QMV is completely excluded for decisions having military or defence implications.[25]

(iii) CFSP Instruments

Making and implementing foreign, security and defence policy is essentially an executive activity. It is expressly provided by Article 24(1), second subparagraph that '[t]he adoption of legislative acts shall be excluded'. In the interests of simplification, the TL abolished the two specialised forms of instrument that had formerly been provided for the CFSP: 'joint actions', the function of which was to organise CFSP operations; and 'common positions', which could be used to give binding force to an agreed point of view, eg the position of the Union on a matter of arms control.[26] Post-Lisbon, the only available instruments are decisions. However, the Treaty provides for the adoption of decisions under the same conditions, and with the same legal consequences, as applied previously. [27]

(iv) Jurisdiction of the Court of Justice

The Court of Justice has no jurisdiction with respect to the Treaty provisions on the CFSP, except for two purposes.[28] One of these is to ensure, pursuant to Article 40 TEU (of which more below), that CFSP competences do not encroach upon TFEU competences, or vice versa. The other jurisdiction, created by the TL, is to review the legality of CFSP decisions providing for restrictive measures against natural or legal persons. The conditions governing the standing of applicants are those of Article 263 TFEU. In a number of cases, there have been successful challenges to the legality of EU measures adopted for the purpose implementing CFSP decisions, under the 'cross-pillar' mechanism corresponding to the present Article 215 TFEU; however, there was previously no way of bringing a direct challenge against the underlying CFSP act.[29]

F – The Interface Between CFSP Competence and TFEU External Competences

The major differences between the institutional and procedural arrangements applicable to the CFSP and those applicable under the TFEU to other fields of external relations competence mean that choosing the appropriate legal basis for a given measure may be more bitterly contested than the choice between competing legal bases within the TFEU.

---

[25] On all these points, see Art 31TEU.

[26] See, as one example among many, Council Joint Action 2008/736/CFSP on the European Union Monitoring Mission in Georgia [2008] OJ L248/6; and Council Common Position relating to the Review Conference of the Biological and Toxic Weapons Convention [2006] OJ L88/65.

[27] cp present Arts 28 and 29 TEU with previous Arts 14 and 15 TEU.

[28] Art 24(1), second subpara TEU and Art 215 TFEU.

[29] The leading authority is Case T-315/01 *Kadi v Council and Commission* [2005] ECR II-3649; on appeal, Case C-402/05P [2008] ECR I-6321. The *Kadi* case has given rise to a voluminous literature. See, *ex abundantia*, annotations by Tomuschat (2006) 43 *CMLRev* 545, and by Gattini (2009) 46 *CMLRev* 213. See also P Eeckhout, 'EC Law and UN Security Council Resolutions—Finding the Right Fit' in A Dashwood and M Maresceau (eds), *The Law and Practice of EU External Relations* (Cambridge, Cambridge University Press, 2008) 104. Other authorities are: Case T-228/02 *OMPI v Council* [2006] ECR II-4665; annotated by Spaventa (2009) 46 *CMLRev* 1239; Case T-253/02 *Ayadi v Council* [2006] ECR II-2139; Case C-355/04P *Segi* [2007] I-1657.

The Commission and the European Parliament will usually have a strong preference for a TFEU legal basis, the Council for a CFSP legal basis. Under the pre-Lisbon Treaties, as interpreted by the Court of Justice, priority was given to legal bases in the EC Treaty. Former Article 47 TEU provided that 'nothing in this Treaty shall affect the [EC] Treaty'. The Court took that to mean that no measure should be adopted under a Second or Third Pillar competence if it was capable of being adopted under a First Pillar competence. The *ECOWAS* case provides an example.[30] This concerned a CFSP measure providing financial and technical assistance in support of the moratorium on the production of and trade in small arms and light weapons, which had been imposed by the Economic Community of West African States.[31] The Court of Justice found that the same measure was equally capable of serving the CFSP objective of arms control or the EC objective of development co-operation, and that the latter must prevail.[32]

Former Article 47 TEU has been replaced by Article 40 TEU, which provides:

> The implementation of the [CFSP] shall not affect the application of the procedures and the extent of the powers of the institutions laid down by the Treaties for the exercise of the Union competences referred to in Articles 3 to 6 of the [TFEU].
>
> Similarly, the implementation of the policies listed in those Articles shall not affect the application of the procedures and the extent of the powers of the institutions laid down by the Treaties for the exercise of the Union competences under this Chapter [ie the CFSP chapter of the TEU].

We note in passing the clear contrast that is drawn between CFSP competences and 'the competences referred to in Articles 3 to 6 [TFEU]', a point to which we shall return when considering whether supervening exclusivity pursuant to Article 3(2) TFEU applies in the area of the CFSP. In the present context, the important point is that TFEU competences are given no priority by the new Article 40 TEU over CFSP competence. The Article provides equal protection against mutual encroachment.

In future, therefore, if analysis of the aim and content of a measure shows that is capable of being adopted either under a TFEU legal basis or under the CFSP, the choice will have to be made on pragmatic policy grounds. A rough rule might be that CFSP competence should normally be resorted to, where the contemplated action, if performed within a Member State, would entail the exercise of state power. Other considerations would be the necessity for the exercise of political judgement, both at the initial stage and in the course of an operation, and the 'ownership' of the means employed. Such considerations would, for instance, amply justify the organisation as CFSP operations of civilian monitoring missions [33] or of police missions.[34]

Nevertheless, it is clear that cases of real or perceived overlap between CFSP competences and TFEU external competences are liable to occur even more frequently, now that Article 21(2) has established a common list of objectives for EU external action.

---

[30] Case C-91/05 *Commission v Council* [2008] ECR I-3651. See also Case C-170/96 *Commission v Council* [1998] ECR I-2763; annotation by Oliveira (1999) 36 *CMLRev* 149; Case C-176/03 *Commission v Council* [2005] ECR I-7879; annotation by Tobler (2006) 43 *CMLRev* 835; Case C-440/05 *Commission v Council* [2007] ECR I-9097.

[31] Council Decision 2004/833/CFSP OJ 2004 L359/65.

[32] For a fuller analysis of the legal position pre-Lisbon, see A Dashwood, 'Article 47 TEU and the Relationship between First and Second Pillar Competences' in Dashwood and Maresceau, above n 29, 102.

[33] eg Council Joint Action 2008/736/CFSP of 15 September 2008 on the European Union Monitoring Mission in Georgia [2008] OJ L248/26.

[34] eg Council Decision 2010/279/CFSP of 18 May 2010 on the European Union Police Mission in Afghanistan [2010] OJ L123/4.

II – EXPRESS AND IMPLIED EU EXTERNAL COMPETENCE

A – Two Fundamental Questions

There are two fundamental questions to which, in the pre-Lisbon era, the Treaties themselves provided only a partial answer. The Court of Justice has replied to those questions in a line of cases that began as early as 1970. The first of these questions we call 'the existence question'. It asks whether the Union is legally authorised to act in a given field of international relations. In other words, does competence exist for the Union to undertake the particular external action that is contemplated? The second question, which we call 'the exclusivity question', assumes that the Union is so competent, and asks whether its competence is exclusive. This will usually be because the Member States, or some of them, would like to be able to undertake the contemplated international action themselves, either instead of or alongside the Union, exercising the external powers they enjoy by virtue of their respective sovereignties. The TFEU now purports to provide answers at the level of primary law to both the existence and the exclusivity questions in Articles 216(1) and 3(2), respectively; however, as we shall see, it remains unclear for the time being how precisely those provisions reflect the subtleties and complexity of the case law.

Although frequently intertwined in the cases, the two questions are logically distinct, and the existence question has evident priority.

B – The Pre-Lisbon Case Law on Implied External Competence

Before turning to Article 216(1) TFEU, it is necessary to review the main elements of the case law on the existence question.

(i) The Rationale of EU Implied External Competence

The existence question is concerned with the application of the principle of conferral in the specific context of the Union's external action. As we have seen,[35] the principle of conferral (or principle of the attribution of powers) means, in the words of Article 5(2) TEU, that 'the Union shall act only within the limits of the competences conferred on it by the Member States in the treaties to attain the objectives set out therein'. In the pithier language of the Court of Justice (referring to the then EC), the Union 'has only those powers which have been conferred upon it'.[36] That principle, the Court went on to say, 'must be respected in both the internal action *and the international action* of the Community'.[37]

Just as in the case of internal action, competence for the Union to act internationally is conferred by a specific provision or provisions of the Treaty identifying what it is the institutions are being authorised to do, and/or the objectives they are being authorised to pursue ('the substantive legal basis'); and also the procedure the institutions are to follow in exercising the powers they have been given for this purpose ('the proce-

---

[35] See Chapter 5.
[36] Opinion 2/94, [1996] ECR I-1759, para 23.
[37] Ibid, para 24 (emphasis added).

dural legal basis'). However, where external action is contemplated, there is the additional requirement of the express or implied conferral of competence to enter into international agreements, or 'treaty-making power', in the jargon of public international law. The need for such conferral is due to the fact that, as we explain in Chapter 28, below, the provisions of international agreements concluded by the Union are automatically incorporated into the EU legal order and may, if they fulfil certain conditions, even produce direct effects that have to be recognised by Union and Member State courts.[38] In that sense, international agreements may be regarded as instruments for making EU law; and it is, therefore, a constitutional requirement that the Member States should have given their assent under the Treaties to this method of law-making in a given policy area, as they have to do with respect to internal legislation.

Historically, the conferral of competence on the Union to enter into international agreements became an issue for two reasons.

First, the EC Treaty contained an Article stating baldly that '[t]he Community shall have legal personality',[39] but no provision generally conferring treaty-making power in respect of matters for which which it enjoyed substantive competence. This was in contrast to the position under the EURATOM Treaty, Article 101(1) of which provides: 'The Community may, *within the limits of its powers and jurisdiction*, enter into obligations by concluding agreements or contracts with a third state, an international organisation or a national of a third state'.[40] Authorisation is thereby given for EURATOM to conclude international agreements, or indeed simple contracts with external parties, on any matter for which substantive competence has been conferred upon it.

Secondly, in the original version of the EC Treaty (or EEC Treaty, as it then was), there were only two legal bases that expressly authorised the Community to enter into international agreements. One was the provision that has become Article 207 TFEU on the CCP,[41] and the other the provision that has become Article 217 TFEU on association agreements.[42] In addition, the provision that has become Article 218 TFEU laid down some elements of the procedure for negotiating and concluding such agreements.[43] The Treaty also contained three provisions, which have now been brought together in Article 220 TFEU, on the establishment of appropriate forms of co-operation with the organs of the United Nations and its specialised agencies, the Council of Europe, the OECD and other international organisations, but without referring to the possibility of concluding international agreements to that end.[44] Apart from those provisions, all having a specifically external focus, the primordial EEC Treaty was silent as to the possibility for the then Community to pursue its objectives by action taken within the international legal order.

Did it follow that in other policy areas central to the realisation of the common market project, such as those of agriculture, fisheries, transport, competition, tax harmonisation and the general approximation of laws, the competences conferred upon the Community could only be exercised by way of the internal law-making instruments and procedures expressly mentioned in the relevant legal bases? If so, the attainment of the objectives

---

[38] Case 181/73 *Haegeman* [1974] ECR449; Case 12/86 *Demirel* [1987] ECR 3719.
[39] Former Art 281 EC.
[40] Emphasis added. See also Art 6(2) of the defunct ECSC Treaty.
[41] Then Art 113 EEC.
[42] Then Art 238 EEC.
[43] Then Art 228 EEC. The procedure has been set out much more fully by successive amending Treaties, including most recently the TL.
[44] Then Arts 229–31.

of the Community might have been seriously inhibited. But how could that conclusion be avoided, while still respecting the principle of conferral? A solution to this dilemma was provided by the Court of Justice, through the development of the doctrine of the Union's implied external competence.[45] The rationale of the doctrine was worked out in the Court's famous *AETR* judgment.[46]

The case arose out of a dispute over competence to negotiate and conclude the revised version of a multilateral agreement on the working conditions of the crews of commercial vehicles engaged in international road transport, which covered similar ground to an existing Community Regulation.[47] An arrangement reached within the Council that the negotiation and conclusion of the AETR would be undertaken by the Member States was challenged by the Commission, on the ground that not only was the Community competent to conclude the Agreement but, now that it had been exercised, this competence had become exclusive. For its part, the Council argued that, pursuant to the principle of conferral, Community competence to enter into the Agreement could not be assumed without express authorisation in the Treaty.

The Court of Justice observed that '[i]n the absence of specific provisions of the Treaty relating to the negotiation and conclusion of international agreements in the sphere of transport policy . . . one must turn to the general system of Community law in the sphere of relations with third countries'. It then cited Article 210 of the Treaty which, at the time, granted the Community legal personality,[48] and continued:

> This provision, placed at the head of Part Six of the Treaty, devoted to 'General and Final Provisions', means that in its external relations the Community enjoys the capacity to establish contractual links with third countries over the whole field of objectives defined in Part One of the Treaty, which Part Six supplements.
>
> To determine in a particular case the Community's authority to enter into international agreements, regard must be had to the whole scheme of the Treaty no less than to its substantive provisions.
>
> Such authority arises not only from an express conferment by the Treaty—as is the case with [Article 207 TFEU] for tariff and trade agreements and with [Article 217 TFEU] for association agreements—but may equally flow from other provisions of the Treaty and from measures adopted, within the framework of those provisions, by the Community institutions.[49]

Three important points are being made in that somewhat elliptical passage.

First, the Community (now, therefore, the Union) has capacity to conclude international agreements over the whole field of its objectives. This is inferred from the completely general grant of legal personality by the then Article 210 EEC and from the position of the latter as the first of the Treaty's 'Final Provisions', a fact which the Court interprets, with some boldness, as providing a cross-reference to Part One of the Treaty, where the objectives of the Community were defined.

Secondly, in the language of the judgement 'capacity' is contrasted with 'authority'

---

[45] There is a magisterial review of the case law in which the doctrine was developed in Eeckhout, above n 3, ch 3.

[46] Case 22/70 *Commission v Council (AETR)* [1971] ECR 263, para 16. AETR is the French acronym for the agreement in question, and more widely used than the English acronym, ERTA.

[47] Council Regulation No 543/69 on the harmonisation of certain social legislation relating to road transport [1969] OJ L77/49.

[48] Subsequently Art 281 EC. Now replaced by the conferral of legal personality upon the Union by Art 47 TEU.

[49] [1971] ECR 263, paras 14–16.

(or competence, in modern terminology[50]). This seems to be intended to accommodate the principle of conferral. The general capacity of the Community/Union[51] is merely an indication that competence to enter into international agreements must be understood as existing in instances other than those covered by the two legal bases of the original EEC Treaty that expressly provided for it. However, specifically conferred competence is needed, where the Community/Union is proposing to enter into an international agreement in particular circumstances. Therefore, while external action by the Community/Union may be authorised implicitly, identifying a specific legal basis for any such action remains a requirement.

In those few sentences, the Court of Justice effected a reconciliation between the principle of conferral and the availability of treaty-making power for the Community/Union to an extent commensurate with its far-reaching substantive competences. Confirmation of the reasoning in the *AETR* judgment was later provided in Opinion 2/94, where the Court of Justice said:

> The Community acts ordinarily on the basis of specific powers which, as the Court has held, are not necessarily the express consequence of specific provisions of the Treaty but may also be implied from them.
> Thus, in the field of international relations, at issue in this request for an Opinion, it is settled case-law that the competence of the Community to enter into international commitments may not only flow from express provisions of the Treaty but also be implied from those provisions.[52]

That was in a case that came to the Court of Justice under a special jurisdiction, now governed by Article 218(11) TFEU, which allows a request to be made for an opinion on the compatibility with the Treaties of an international agreement the Union is proposing to enter into.[53] The issue in Opinion 2/94 was the competence of the then Community to accede to the European Convention on the Protection of Human Rights and Fundamental Freedoms. The Court held that there was no provision of the EC Treaty conferring 'any general power to enact rules on human rights or to conclude international conventions in this field'.[54]

The third point in the passage cited from *AETR* is that, in order to identify those instances where EU external competence arises by implication, regard must be had to 'the whole scheme of the Treaty', competence may be found to flow from other Treaty provisions or from measures adopted by the institutions pursuant to such provisions. Corresponding to the two sources of implied external competence there mentioned, the case law shows that there are two principles of implication at work. These are the so-called *AETR* principle, which relates to external competence arising from the adoption of an EU measure, and the complementarity principle (other commentators prefer the term 'parallelism principle'), which relates to the external competence needed to enable the objectives of the internal competence expressly conferred by a Treaty provision to be fully achieved.

---

[50] The word used in the original French version of the *AETR* judgment is 'compétence'. The term 'authority' is simply a choice made by the translator.

[51] We use this phrase to indicate that what was then said about the Community applies equally to the Union, in contexts where references only to the latter would be jarring.

[52] [1996] ECR I-1759, paras 25 and 26.

[53] The equivalent provision at the time of Opinion 1/76 was former Art 228(1) EEC.

[54] [1996] ECR, para 27.

(ii) The AETR Principle

The principle that has come to bear its name is formulated twice in the *AETR* judgment. The more frequently cited formulation is found in paragraphs 17–19, which immediately follow the passage cited above:

> In particular, each time the Community, with a view to implementing a common policy envisaged by the Treaty, adopts provisions laying down common rules, whatever form these may take, the Member States no longer have the right, acting individually or even collectively, to undertake obligations with third countries which affect those rules.
>
> As and when such common rules come into being, the Community alone is in a position to assume and carry out contractual obligations towards third countries affecting the whole sphere of application of the Community legal system.
>
> With regard to the implementation of the provisions of the Treaty the system of internal Community measures may not therefore be separated from that of external relations.

The second formulation is at paragraph 22 of the judgment:

> [T]o the extent to which Community rules are promulgated for the attainment of the objectives of the Treaty, the Member States cannot, outside the framework of the Community institutions, assume obligations which might affect those rules or alter their scope.

The main difference between those passages, apart from the greater elaboration of the earlier one, is the phrase 'Community rules' in paragraph 22, whereas paragraph 17 refers to 'common rules' implementing 'a common policy envisaged by the Treaty'. The Court of Justice would subsequently confirm that the *AETR* principle is not confined to instances where the Community rules in question have been adopted in one of the areas where the Treaties refer to the establishment of a 'common policy' (agriculture and fisheries, transport, commercial policy and now also foreign and security policy).[55]

The thrust of the two formulations is the same: competence to enter into international agreements becomes the sole prerogative of the Community/Union, once measures have been adopted by the institutions pursuant to any provision of the Treaties, in so far as the acceptance of international commitments by the Member States would be liable to 'affect' those measures. That looks like a principle which is about the circumstances that deprive the Member States of the right to exercise their external powers in a certain matter, where previously they were free to act; in other words, it seems to answer the exclusivity question, and such, indeed, is one of the functions of the principle. However, as used in the *AETR* judgment, the principle serves first and foremost as a way of answering the existence question. This can clearly be seen from the location of paragraphs 17–19 in the development of the Court's reasoning. They represent the final step in the general justification of the view that external competence may exist even where express conferral is lacking. The *AETR* principle is put forward as a paradigm of how 'in a particular case the Community's authority to enter into international agreements' may, having regard to 'the whole scheme of the Treaty', be found to flow 'from measures adopted, within the framework of [its] provisions, by the Community institutions'. Similarly, in paragraph 22 the principle is invoked as the source of treaty-making power for the Community in the particular field of transport policy.

The *AETR* principle is explained by the Court of Justice as an application in the exter-

---

[55] See Opinion 2/91 on Convention No 170 of the ILO concerning safety in the use of chemicals at work [1993] ECR I-1061, para 10.

nal sphere of the principle of sincere co-operation, now found in Article 4(3) TFEU, which requires Member States

> on the one hand to take all appropriate measures to ensure fulfilment of the obligations arising out of the Treaty or resulting from action taken by the institutions and, on the other hand, to abstain from any measure which might jeopardise the attainment of the objectives of the Treaty.[56]

The underlying logic is, therefore, that of the primacy of EU law.[57] The pre-emptive effect of acts adopted by the institutions under expressly conferred internal powers fetters the external powers of Member States in the matters to which a given measure relates, leaving a gap that only the Union can fill. The automatic conferral of external competence in respect of those matters is an implication drawn from 'the whole scheme of the Treat[ies]'.

(iii) The Complementarity Principle

In *AETR* the Court's conclusion as to the existence of implied Community external competence, and its exclusivity, was based on the fact that the subject-matter of the AETR fell within the scope of Council Regulation 543/69 on the harmonisation of certain social legislation relating to road transport.[58] However, there is a hint in paragraphs 25–27 of the judgment that implied competence to conclude the Agreement might also have arisen independently of the actual exercise of the corresponding internal competence. After citing a provision contained in the legal basis for measures in the transport field, which refers to laying down 'common rules applicable to international transport to or from the territory of a Member State or passing across the territory of one or more Member States',[59] the Court of Justice went on:

> This provision is equally concerned with transport from or to third countries, as regards that part of the journey which takes place on Community territory.
> It thus assumes that the powers of the Community extend to relationships arising from international law, and hence involve the need in the sphere in question for agreements with the third countries concerned.

The logic of this passage is not that of primacy but rather of the *effet utile* of the Treaty provision in question. In order to be effective, 'common rules applicable to international transport' may have to regulate the parts of journeys that take place in third countries. That 'the powers of the Community . . . involve the need in the sphere in question for agreements with the third countries concerned' is accordingly said to be 'assumed' in that provision.

Why the Court of Justice failed to follow through that line of reasoning in *AETR* is unclear. Perhaps, in this first case on the external competence of the Community, it preferred to adopt the less potentially controversial position based on the existence of Regulation 543/69, while laying down a marker as to the approach it might be willing to take in future cases, where no common rules had yet been adopted.[60]

---

[56] [1971] ECR 263, para 21.
[57] See Chapter 8.
[58] [1971] ECR 263, paras 28–30.
[59] At the time, Art 75(1)(a) EEC; now Art 91(1)(a).
[60] This part of the *AETR* judgment is more fully considered in A Dashwood and J Heliskoski, 'The Classic Authorities Revisited', ch 1 of A Dashwood and C Hillion (eds), *The General Law of EC External Relations* (London, Sweet & Maxwell, 2000) 7–9.

Kramer was such a case.[61] Prosecutions were brought in the Netherlands against fishermen who were accused of having infringed catch limits imposed by the Dutch authorities pursuant to the North East Atlantic Fisheries Convention. The ingenious defence was put forward on behalf of the fishermen that competence in the matter of setting catch quotas had passed from the Member States to the Community. The legal basis for legislation on Community/Union fisheries policy was, and still is, the same as for agricultural policy; nothing is there said about the possibility of regulating fishing on the high seas or of concluding international agreements for this purpose.[62] There was a provision in the 1972 Act of Accession fixing a time limit for the adoption of measures on the conservation of marine biological resources[63] but, at the relevant time, no implementing legislation had been adopted. The Court of Justice, nevertheless, concluded from the relevant legal texts, as well as 'from the very nature of things', not only that the Community's internal legislative competence must be understood to extend to the high seas, but also that an effective conservation policy called for the Community to be competent 'to enter into international commitments for the conservation of the resources of the sea'.[64]

The *Kramer* decision was the earliest authority on the existence of implied Community external competent in the absence of common rules that were liable to be affected. However, there is no statement in the judgment of the principle the Court of Justice was applying. The formulation of the complementarity principle that has come to be regarded as standard was first provided by the Court in Opinion 1/76,[65] which—like *AETR*—concerned competence in transport matters. The subject of the request in Opinion 1/76 was a draft agreement between the Community and Switzerland relating to a scheme for the establishment of a laying-up fund for barges operating on the Rhine and the Moselle, which was designed to reduce surplus carrying capacity. One of the issues in the case was the competence of the Community to conclude the agreement, given that the internal legislation required to implement the scheme had not yet been adopted.

The Court of Justice gave its answer to that question in paragraphs 3 and 4 of the Opinion, which are couched in the terms of a statement of general principle:

> The power of the Community to conclude such an agreement is not expressly laid down in the Treaty. However, the Court has already had occasion to state, most recently in its judgment in [*Kramer*], that authority to enter into international commitments may not only arise from an express attribution by the Treaty, but equally may flow implicitly from its provisions. The Court has concluded *inter alia* that whenever Community law has created for the institutions of the Community powers within its internal system for the purpose of attaining a specific objective, the Community has authority to enter into the international commitments necessary for the attainment of that objective even in the absence of an express provision in that connection.
>
> This is particularly so in all cases in which internal power has already been used in order to adopt measures which come within the attainment of common policies. It is, however, not limited to that eventuality. Although the internal Community measures are only adopted when the international agreement is concluded and made enforceable, as is envisaged in the present case by the proposal for a regulation to be submitted to the Council by the Commission, the

---

[61] Joined Cases 3, 4 and 6/76 [1976] ECR 1279. Analysed in Dashwood and Heliskoski, ibid, 9–11.

[62] At the time, Art 43 EEC; now Art 43 TFEU. This is one of the Treaty provisions which, after being renumbered Art 37 EC by the TA, has reverted to its original numbering in the TFEU.

[63] Art 102.

[64] [1976] ECR 1279, para 33. On the aspect of the case relating to the exclusivity of the Community's competence, see below.

[65] [1977] ECR 741. Analysed in Dashwood and Heliskoski, above n 60, 11–14.

power to bind the Community *vis-a-vis* third countries nevertheless flows by implication from the provisions of the Treaty creating the internal power and in so far as the participation of the Community in the international agreement is, as here, necessary for the attainment of one of the objectives of the Community.

The logic of the principle stated in those paragraphs is that of effectiveness rather than primacy. We noted above that this was also the logic of paragraphs 25–27 of the *AETR* judgment. However, an element not present in that passage, though it did figure in the Court's reasoning in *Kramer*, is the emphasis placed upon the relationship between the express internal competence and the implication of external competence; the latter may be drawn, in so far as it is necessary for the attainment of the specific objective(s) for which the internal competence has been conferred. On this analysis, implied competence to enter into international commitments is explained as a necessary complement of the internal competence flowing from the relevant legal basis. Hence our designation of the principle formulated in Opinion 1/76 as 'the complementarity principle'.

Later cases have shown that the Court of Justice regards the complementarity principle as an expression of the normal (if not the only) way in which competence to enter into international agreements may arise for the Union in the absence of express conferral. This first became evident in Opinion 2/91,[66] where the request concerned competence to conclude Convention No 170 of the International Labour Organization (ILO) on safety in the use of chemicals at work, which the Commission contended belonged, in principle, exclusively to the then Community.[67] The Court prefaced its analysis of the substance of the case with a systematic restatement of the relevant rules of EC external relations law, including the complementarity principle as formulated in paragraph 3 of Opinion 1/76.[68] A reiteration of the principle as there formulated is also found in Opinion 2/94,[69] in a context that underlines its general applicability.

The paragraph of Opinion 1/76, which the Court of Justice cited on both those occasions as encapsulating the complementarity principle, was the third one, not the fourth. We respectfully share that preference, since the former paragraph is noticeably more precise in its language than the latter. In particular, the phrase, 'one of the objectives of the Community', at the end of paragraph 4, might be read as meaning that implied external competence may arise for the purpose of advancing Community objectives wider than those for the attainment of which the express internal competence has been conferred. In our submission, that cannot have been the Court's intention, since it would be inconsistent with the explanation that the external competence 'flows by implication from the provisions of the Treaty creating the internal power'. Indeed, it would undermine the rationale of the complementarity principle altogether. We note this point for future reference, because it was the fourth, rather than the third, paragraph of Opinion 1/76 that seems to have inspired the authors of Article 216(1) TFEU.

An important restriction upon the complementarity principle is that it does not have the effect of extending the substantive scope of the expressly conferred competence by adding to the range of things the Union is authorised to do. It is only about recognising

---

[66] [1993] ECR I-1061.

[67] We say 'in principle' because the Convention was only open to ratification by members of the ILO, whereas the Community's formal status in the Organisation was that of an observer. However, procedures had been created that allowed the effective exercise of Community competences within the ILO.

[68] [1993] ECR I-1061, para 7.

[69] [1996] ECR I-1759, para 26. The first sentence of the paragraph, referring to the possibility that competence to enter into international agreements may arise by implication, was quoted above, p 912.

the possibility for the Union to conclude international agreements in cases where competence to do so has not been conferred explicitly.[70]

The point may be illustrated by an issue that was debated in Opinion 1/94. The Commission had requested the Opinion of the Court of Justice as to whether the Community was exclusively competent to conclude the package of WTO Agreements. As we shall see, the Court held that exclusive EC competence for the CCP covered only very limited elements of the General Agreement on Trade in Services (GATS) and the Agreement on Trade Related Aspects of Intellectual Property (TRIPS).[71] In the alternative, the Commission had argued that the Community enjoyed implied competence, which in the circumstances must be exclusive, to conclude, among other things, the GATS. Its claim as to the existence of the competence was based on the provisions of the Treaty relating to the liberalisation of establishment and the supply of services within the internal market; from those provisions, the Commission contended, it could be inferred that parallel competence existed with respect to the liberalisation of establishment and services between the Community and third countries. That line of argument was rejected by the Court, which drew a contrast between the legal bases in the Treaty relating, respectively, to establishment and services and to transport. As to the latter, the Court recalled the passage of its *AETR* judgment, pointing out that substantive competence had been conferred on the Community to regulate the parts of a journey that took place in third countries. As to the former, the Court said:

> Unlike the chapter on transport, the chapters on the right of establishment and on freedom to provide services do not contain any provision expressly extending the competence of the Community to 'relationships arising from international law' . . . the sole objective of those chapters is to secure the right of establishment and freedom to provide services for nationals of the Member States.

In other words, the substantive legal bases relied upon the Commission did not authorise the contemplated action. Implied external competence could not arise in respect of matters that were not within the scope of the Community's expressly conferred internal competence.

A final point on the complementarity principle in the case law concerns the nature of the causal relationship entailed in the notion that conclusion of an international agreement is 'necessary' to attain the objectives of the Treaty provision in question. Must this criterion be equated with indispensability, in the sense that the expressly authorised internal action and implied external action are inextricably linked, because one could not achieve its purpose independently of the other? Such linkage existed in *Kramer*, owing to the nature of fisheries conservation, and in Opinion 1/76, because the proposed laying-up scheme for barges would not have been effective unless extended by an international agreement to cover Swiss operators. However, the general terms in which the principle was formulated in Opinion 1/76 seemed to indicate that the Court did not understand it to be confined to such exceptional situations. This was subsequently confirmed in Opinion 2/91, where implied competence to conclude ILO Convention No 170 was held to arise from the internal legislative competence of the Community in the area of social policy,

---

[70] See further A Dashwood, 'The Attribution of External Relations Competence' in Dashwood and Hillion, above n 60, 127–32.

[71] On the extension of the scope of the common commercial policy by the TN to cover trade in services and commercial aspects of intellectual property, a process which has now been completed by the TL, see below.

where it is certainly possible for the objectives of the Treaty to be pursued by actions that need not always have an international reach. It therefore appears that the term 'necessary' as applied under the complementarity principle can be understood in the broad sense of tending to facilitate an outcome. The test, it has been suggested, may be expressed thus: would the availability of implied external competence help to ensure, over time, optimal use of the expressly conferred internal competence?[72]

Nevertheless, as we shall see, the narrower sense of the term, as 'indispensable', has been used by the Court in dealing with the exclusivity issue, and this ambiguity has unfortunately found its way into the TL.

B – Article 216(1) TFEU

Although in its time controversial, by the mid-1990s when the Court of Justice rendered its Opinion 2/94 the existence question had become a matter of settled case law. Now, however, the conditions under which the Union is authorised to enter into international agreements have been enshrined in Article 216(1) TFEU as primary positive EU law.

Article 216(1) TFEU provides:

> The Union may conclude an agreement with one or more third countries or international organisations where the Treaties so provide or where the conclusion of an agreement is necessary in order to achieve, within the framework of the Union's policies, one of the objectives referred to in the Treaties, or is provided for in a legally binding Union act or is likely to affect common rules or alter their scope.

Four instances in which the Union enjoys competence to enter into international agreements are there identified:

(i)   where the Treaties so provide;
(ii) where the conclusion of an agreement is necessary in order to achieve, within the framework of the union's policies, one of the objectives referred to in the Treaties;
(iii) where the conclusion of an agreement is provided for in a legally binding Union act;
(iv) where the conclusion of an agreement is likely to affect common rules or alter their scope.

We examine those four instances in order, referring to them, where convenient, as 'instance (i)', 'instance (ii)', etc.

(i) Where the Treaties so provide

Instance (i) covers the straightforward situation where Treaty provisions expressly confer competence on the Union to enter into international agreements. There is no longer the same dearth of such provisions as in the primordial EEC Treaty. Explicit references to the possibility of concluding agreements with third countries or international organisations, or at least to co-operating with them, are found in several, though not all, of the substantive legal bases that have been created by the series of amending Treaties, from the Single European Act (SEA) to the TL.

In the opening section of this chapter, we noted the legal bases that specifically author-

---

[72] This is the test suggested in Dashwood and Heliskoski, above n 60, 16 and Dashwood, above n 70, 133.

ise action by the Union in the external sphere, now collected in Part Five of the TFEU. As might be expected, these explicitly confer treaty-making power, with the exception of Article 220(1), which only speaks of co-operation with international organisations, and Article 215 on restrictive measures, the latter being unilateral in nature. Outside Part Five, the legal bases for research and technological development[73] and for policy on the environment,[74] both established by the SEA, provide expressly for co-operation by the Union with third countries or international organisations, which may the subject of international agreements. The legal bases conferring tightly circumscribed 'supporting' Union competences[75] in the fields of education, vocational training, youth and sport, and those of culture and public health, which were brought into the EC Treaty by the TEU, impose a standard requirement that the Union 'foster cooperation with third countries and the competent international institutions';[76] while under the Treaty Title on the development of trans-European networks it is similarly provided that '[t]he Union may decide to cooperate with third countries to promote projects of mutual interest and to ensure the interoperability of networks'.[77] However, it is not expressly stipulated that international agreements may be concluded for the purposes of co-operation in those fields.

So far as concerns the CFSP, the TL has inserted into Chapter 2 of Title V of the TEU an Article 37, which provides: 'The Union may conclude agreements with one or more States or international organisations in areas covered by this Title.' There is thus now an express provision conferring general competence for the Union to enter into international agreements for any of the purposes for which it enjoys substantive CFSP competence. This is similar in its effect to Article 101(1) of the EURATOM Treaty, with which we contrasted the piecemeal approach of the EC Treaty.

Despite the Treaty amendments we have noted, there are policy areas central to the activity of the Union—in particular those of agriculture, fisheries, asylum and immigration, transport, competition, taxation, IP and social policy—for which express authorisation to enter into international agreements remains lacking. In those areas, the availability of external competence, where it may be needed to attain the objectives the Union has been authorised to pursue, depends on the remaining provisions of Article 216(1), which are somewhat loosely based on the doctrine of implied external competence, as developed by the Court of Justice.

(ii) Where the conclusion of an agreement is necessary in order to achieve, within the framework of the Union's policies, one of the objectives referred to in the Treaties

The scope of instance (ii) is far from clear. It seems unlikely that the intention of the provision can be to confer general treaty-making power in matters for which the Union enjoys substantive competence (along similar lines to Article 101(1) EURATOM, and indeed Article 37 TEU regarding the CFSP), because that would render the rest of Article 216(1) redundant. Could it be intended to enlarge the scope of the complementarity principle, by detaching the implication of external competence from the objectives specifically authorised by a given legal basis? This might account for the choice of the phrase 'one of the

---

[73] Arts 182 and 186 TFEU.
[74] Arts 191(4) and 192 TFEU.
[75] 'Supporting' in the sense of Art 2(5) and Art 6 TFEU.
[76] See, respectively, Art 165(3), Art 166(3), Art 167(3) and Art 168(3) TFEU.
[77] Art 171(3) TFEU.

objectives referred to in the Treaties', which reflects the language of the fourth paragraph of Opinion 1/76, rather than the more precise language of the third paragraph. So understood, the provision would authorise the conclusion of an agreement relating to matters which fell 'within the framework' of a Union policy, and could be seen as advancing 'one of the objectives referred to in the Treaties', but for the pursuit of which no competence to act by way of internal legislation had been specifically conferred.[78] For instance, there is a Union social policy and one of its objectives is the improvement of working conditions. However, the legislative competence conferred by Article 153(2)(b) TFEU is restricted to the adoption of minimum requirements, which means that Member States must always be left free to impose stricter ones. Would it now be open to the Union to enter into an international agreement on working conditions that purported to impose absolute standards? If the answer were 'yes', it would mean treating Article 216(1) as a free-standing substantive legal basis; but this cannot be correct, because it would be inconsistent with the inclusion of instance (i), which cross-refers to legal bases located elsewhere in the Treaties. In our view, the only viable interpretation of instance (ii) is that it represents a rather inept formulation of the complementarity principle, as this results from the case law.

(iii) Where the conclusion of an agreement is provided for in a legally binding Union act

At first sight, instance (iii) appears puzzling. Where competence to enter into international agreements does not already exist under the Treaties, either through express conferral or though implication pursuant to the complementarity principle or to the *AETR* principle, how can it be created by a Union act, which is secondary EU law?

As we shall see, a similar provision has found its way into Article 3(2) TFEU, where circumstances that render external competence exclusive are identified. The authors of the TL must have had in mind a passage found at paragraph 95 of Opinion 1/94, in which the Court of Justice said:

> Whenever the Community has included in its internal legislative acts provisions relating to the treatment of nationals of non-member countries *or expressly conferred on its institutions powers to negotiate with non-member countries*, it acquires exclusive external competence in the spheres covered by those acts.[79]

While that was evidently a statement about exclusivity (and we shall return to it as such, below),[80] the existence of external competence is assumed in the situations referred to. However, the significance of this instance of implied competence appears to have been misunderstood by those who saw fit to mention it in Article 216(1), owing to a failure to relate the statement cited above to its context in Opinion 1/94.

The statement follows a passage in which the Court of Justice remarked upon the fact that the internal market legal bases on establishment and the provision of services had frequently been used for the enactment of Directives containing provisions either regulating the treatment of third-country nationals within the Community or authorising

---

[78] This broad view seems to be taken by Paul Craig: see Craig, above n 13, 399–400.

[79] Emphasis added. See also Opinion 2/92, para 33.

[80] The Court of Justice has identified the two situations mentioned in para 95 of Opinion 1/94 as instances of an AETR effect leading to the exclusivity of EU competence: see Case C-467/98 *Commission v Denmark* (*Open Skies*) [2002] ECR I-9519, para 83; Opinion 1/03 *Lugano* [2006] ECR I-1145, para 121.

the institutions to negotiate agreements with third countries.[81] How could such 'external provisions', as the Court described them, be reconciled with the purely internal focus of the legal bases on establishment and the provision of services? The answer emerges from the Court's analysis of some of the measures in question, of which Directive 89/646[82] will serve as an example. The Directive established a system of uniform authorisation of credit institutions, coupled with the requirement of mutual recognition of national controls; having passed the test in one Member State, a credit institution would be able to operate in all the others, without seeking fresh authorisation. Under the Directive, the Commission was empowered to negotiate international agreements, in order to ensure that third countries whose institutions could gain access to the whole of the internal market, by securing authorisation for a subsidiary established in only one Member State,[83] would accord comparable market access to EU operators. The fact that authorisation by a single Member State would give third-country operators access to the markets of other Member States meant that reciprocal arrangements with non-Member States would have to be negotiated on a Union-wide basis.[84]

The external provisions in question were, therefore, an accessory and integral element of internal market measures. Properly understood, these were instances of the application of the complementarity principle at the level of secondary law. Particular policy choices made by the EU legislator in adopting measures that were firmly targeted on internal market objectives brought with them the necessity of entering into agreements with international partners.[85]

The inclusion of instance (iii) in Article 216(1) TFEU, therefore, appears redundant, because it is already covered by instance (ii), and misleading in so far as it may be understood to apply any more widely.

(iv) Where the conclusion of an agreement is likely to affect common rules or alter their scope

Instance (iv) is a reference to the *AETR* principle in its function as a source of competence for the Union to enter into international agreements where express conferral is lacking. The question may be asked whether a Treaty provision preserving the 'existence function' of the principle was strictly necessary at this time of day. Admittedly, with the expansion of the CCP into areas which, at the time of Opinion 1/94, it could not reach, it has become harder to think of examples where the complementarity principle would not apply, and external competence could arise only after internal competence has been exercised.[86] Nevertheless, the enshrinement of the *AETR* principle in Article 216(1) appears wise, since its 'existence function' is logically inseparable from its 'exclusivity function', and not to have acknowledged the former might have given rise to uncertainty.

---

[81] Paras 90–94 of Opinion 1/94.

[82] Second Council Directive on the coordination of laws, regulations and administrative provisions relating to the taking up and pursuit of the business of credit institutions and amending Directive 77/780/EEC [1989] OJ L386/1.

[83] See Art 54 TFEU.

[84] See the 20th recital of the preamble to the Directive.

[85] See further Dashwood, above n 70, 130–31.

[86] cp ibid, 134–36. The expansion of the common commercial policy to cover trade in services and commercial aspects of IP means that there is now expressly conferred external competence in areas where, as Opinion 1/94 showed, the complementarity principle was not applicable, so that external competence could only arise under the *AETR* principle.

C – Summing Up: The TL's Answer to the Existence Question

In the light of the foregoing it is only possible to express a tentative view as to the effect of the answer the TL purports to give by way of Article 216(1) TFEU to the existence question. It is submitted that Article 216(1) is capable of being interpreted consistently with the established case law on EU implied external competence arising under the complementarity principle and the *AETR* principle; and it should be so interpreted, to maintain the integrity of the principle of conferral, which has been a prime concern of the Court of Justice throughout the history of the doctrine of implied external competence, starting with the *AETR* judgment itself.

III – EXCLUSIVE EU EXTERNAL COMPETENCE

A – Exclusive External Competence Post-Lisbon

The nature of EU competences that the TL has provided in Articles 2–6 TFEU was discussed in general terms in Chapter 5. As was noted there, the regulatory powers of the Union have been classified into three main categories: exclusive Union competence; Union competence shared with the Member States ('shared competence'); and Union competence to support, co-ordinate or supplement Member State action ('supporting competence'). The categories are distinguished on the basis of the respective legal consequences their existence or exercise may have upon national regulatory powers in a given policy area. Where Union competence is exclusive in a specific area, the Union alone may legislate and adopt legally binding acts; Member States may do so only if empowered by the Union or when implementing Union acts.[87] In areas where competence is shared, the Union and the Member States may legislate and adopt legally binding acts; however, the Member States may do so only to the extent that the Union has not exercised its competence, or has ceased exercising it. The hallmark of supporting competence is that in the areas to which this applies any action that may be taken by the Union will not supersede the competence of the Member States.

Part of the TL's answer to the exclusivity question is found in Article 3(1) TFEU, which identifies the policy areas where Union competence is exclusive a priori, that is to say, because of the character of the activity in question, irrespective of whether or not the competence has been exercised. These are: the customs union; establishing the competition rules necessary for the functioning of the internal market; monetary policy for the Member States whose currency is the euro; the conservation of marine biological resources under the common fisheries policy; and the CCP. That exclusivity extends to the conclusion of international agreements follows from the reference in Article 2(1) TFEU to the adoption of legally binding acts. As pointed out in Chapter 5, the only novel item on the Article 3(1) list is competition law; the Court of Justice previously regarded this as a shared competence,[88] though it has now acknowledged the change to a competence

---

[87] Art 2(1) TFEU.
[88] Case 14/68 *Walt Wilhelm* [1969] ECR 1.

that is exclusive.[89] It was in Opinion 1/75,[90] which concerned the conclusion of an OECD understanding on the local costs it was permissible to cover with export credits, that the exclusive competence of the then Community for the CCP was first recognised. The scope of the Union's exclusive competence for the CCP has been significantly extended by the TL to trade in services, commercial aspects of IP and FDI.[91] Fisheries conservation is also a long-standing area of a priori Union exclusivity, recognised ever since the *Kramer* cases.[92]

The remaining part of the TL's answer to the exclusivity question consists of Article 3(2) TFEU, relating to what may be described as 'supervening external exclusivity', namely the circumstances that render Union competence to enter into international agreements exclusive in areas other than those listed in Article 3(1) TFEU, where the very nature of the activity does not in itself make this a necessity. Article 3(2) provides:

> The Union shall also have exclusive competence for the conclusion of an international agreement when its conclusion is provided for in a legislative act of the Union or is necessary to enable the Union to exercise its internal competence, or in so far as its conclusion may affect common rules or alter their scope.

There are issues that need to be addressed concerning the relationship of that provision to the established case law on supervening exclusivity, as well as to certain other provisions of the amended Treaties.

B – Article 3(2) TFEU and the Case Law on Supervening External Exclusivity

The three situations in which, in the terms of Article 3(2) TFEU, Union competence to enter into an international agreement is rendered exclusive are:

— when the conclusion of the agreement is provided for in a legislative act of the Union;
— the conclusion of the agreement is necessary to enable the Union to exercise its internal competence;
— in so far as the conclusion of the agreement may affect common rules or alter their scope.

Those situations will each be examined in the light of relevant case law.

(i) When the conclusion of the agreement is provided for in a legislative act of the Union

The inclusion of a similar provision in Article 216(1) TFEU, as one of the instances in which EU external competence arises, was described above as redundant and misleading, and mentioning it in Article 3(2) TFEU seems equally misconceived. The source of the provision was identified as paragraph 95 of Opinion 1/94, which refers to the Union's acquiring exclusive external competence through the inclusion in its internal legislative acts of 'provisions relating to the treatment of nationals of non-member countries', as

---

[89] Case C-550/07 P, *Akzo Nobel Chemicals*, Judgment of 14 September 2010.
[90] [1975] ECR 1355.
[91] See below.
[92] [1976] ECR 1279.

well as through the conferral on its institutions of 'powers to negotiate' with such coun-tries. Why it should have been thought appropriate to refer in Article 3(2) (and indeed in Article 216(1)) to the latter type of 'external provision' but not to the former is unclear. It is submitted that the better solution would have been to mention neither. The Court of Justice has made it abundantly clear that it regards the inclusion of such provisions in a legislative act, not as an independent basis for exclusive Union competence, but as trig-gering the *AETR* principle.[93]

(ii) When the conclusion of the agreement is necessary to enable the Union to exercise its internal competence

In Opinion 1/94 the Court of Justice appears to have accepted that EU external com-petence, derived by implication from explicitly conferred internal competence, may be rendered exclusive, without the existence of common rules liable to be affected under the *AETR* principle, in circumstances where the internal competence can only be effectively exercised at the same time as the external competence.[94] Opinion 1/76 was cited as author-ity for this proposition, and the facts of the case were recalled as illustrating the situation where it would apply. Owing to the participation of Swiss vessels in the inland waterways sector in question, the proposed scheme for laying-up barges could not have been estab-lished by autonomous common rules alone; to make the arrangement work, Switzerland had to be brought into it by means of an international agreement.[95] Conservation of marine biological resources was cited by the Court as a further illustration, since

> the restriction, by means of internal legislative measures, of fishing on the high seas by vessels flying the flag of a Member State would hardly be effective if the same restrictions were not to apply to vessels flying the flag of a non-member country bordering on the same seas.[96]

Those situations were contrasted with the subject-matter of the GATS. The Court noted:

> [A]ttainment of freedom of establishment and freedom to provide services for nationals of the Member States is not *inextricably linked* to the treatment to be afforded in the Community to nationals of non-member countries or in non-member countries to nationals of Member States of the Community.[97]

On that analysis, Opinion 1/76 is to be regarded as the origin of two distinct principles: one, the complementarity principle, of general application, providing the explanation as to how EU implied external competence normally arises; and the other identifying an excep-tional situation in which supervening exclusivity may arise independently of the exercise of internal Union competence. The curious thing is that there is no indication in Opinion 1/76 that the Court of Justice was consciously applying the latter principle; indeed, noth-ing at all is said about the exclusivity of the Community's competence to conclude the agreement with Switzerland. Nevertheless, the Court seems convinced that the principle exists, and that its origin was Opinion 1/76, as subsequent case law has confirmed.[98] For convenience, therefore, we refer to the principle as expressing 'Opinion 1/76 exclusivity'.

---

[93] See, besides para 95 of Opinion 1/94 and para 33 of Opinion 2/92, *Open Skies*, above n 80, para 81; Opinion 1/03 (*Lugano*), paras 121 and 122.
[94] [1994] ECR I-5267, para 89.
[95] Ibid, para 85.
[96] Ibid.
[97] Ibid, para 86 (emphasis added).
[98] See Opinion 2/92 [1995] ECR I-525, para 33; *Open Skies*, above n 80 para 57; Opinion 1/03, *New Lugano* [2006] ECR I-1145, para 115.

It is hard to understand the rationale of Opinion 1/76 exclusivity. If the internal Union competence is non-exclusive (as was the case in Opinion 1/76, since it concerned transport), and it has not yet been exercised, then why should the fact that, in the particular circumstances, such exercise could only achieve its purpose if combined with external action mean that EU external competence must be regarded as exclusive?[99] It has been pointed out that the six Member States interested in the laying-up scheme could perfectly well have established it without involving the Community, by taking internal national measures and themselves entering into an agreement with Switzerland.[100] The case of fisheries conservation is obviously different, because there exclusivity results a priori from the very nature of the activity.

An opportunity to clarify the principle of Opinion 1/76 exclusivity was provided by the *Open Skies* cases.[101] The dispute was about the legality of the so-called 'open skies' agreements relating to access for air carriers to the market for passenger services, which a number of Member States had concluded with the USA. Part of the Commission's case rested on a claim of Opinion 1/76 exclusivity for EU competence in this matter. The Commission argued, rather as it had done in Opinion 1/94, that such exclusivity was necessary to attain the objective of a properly functioning internal market; however, it sought to distinguish Opinion 1/94 by emphasising the international character of air transport, which made it impossible to keep the internal and external markets separate. This, the Commission contended, was borne out by the fact that it had been found necessary to include certain provisions relating to the treatment of third-country nationals in internal legislation on the air transport sector; and by the fact that the bilateral open sky agreements concluded with the United States had actually led to discrimination, the distortion of competition and the destabilisation of markets within the Union.

In his *Open Skies* Opinion, Advocate General Tizzano made a powerful case, in principle, against the Commission's understanding of Opinion 1/76 exclusivity.[102] His main criticism was its dependence upon an assessment as to whether or not, in given circumstances, an international agreement fulfilled the requirement of being 'necessary' to allow the corresponding internal competence to be exercised effectively. Individual Member States would have to make the assessment for themselves, when considering whether it was open to them to enter into an agreement; and, if they decided to proceed, the Commission would then have to assess whether they had been right to do so. 'To adopt the Commission's view, therefore', the Advocate General said 'would mean introducing serious elements of uncertainty and confusion into the system.' His conclusion was that, unless and until the necessity for an agreement had been duly and specifically recognised by the competent institutions and in accordance with the prescribed decision-making procedures, there could be no exclusive competence. In other words, supervening exclusivity can only ever arise as a consequence of the actual exercise of internal and/or external Union competence.

The Court of Justice did not follow the Advocate General down the route of effectively

---

[99] See the critique in Eeckhout, above n 3, 78 and 89–91.

[100] See Dashwood and Heliskoski, above n 60, 13; Eeckhout, above n 45, 78.

[101] Besides Case C-467/8, these were: Case C-466/98 *Commission v United Kingdom* [2002] ECR I-9427; Case C-468/98 *Commission v Sweden* [2002] ECR I-9575; Case C-469/98 *Commission v Finland* [2002] ECR I-9627; Case C-471/98 *Commission v Belgium* [2002] ECR I-9681; Case C-472/98 *Commission v Luxembourg* [2002] ECR I-9741; Case C-475/98 *Commission v Austria* [2002] ECR I-9797; Case C-478/98 *Commission v Germany* [2002] ECR I-9855.

[102] At paras 51–54. The Opinion is attached to Case C-466/98 [2002] ECR I-9427.

disowning Opinion 1/76 exclusivity.[103] Without resiling from the position of principle set forth in Opinion 1/94, it held, however, that the case did not disclose a situation in which internal competence could effectively be exercised only at the same time as external competence. In similar vein to Opinion 1/94, it pointed out that there was nothing to prevent the EU institutions from including, among the common rules they had laid down, provisions designed to mitigate any discrimination or distortions of competition that might result from commitments entered into by Member States under bilateral open skies agreements. Nor did it follow, from the inclusion in EU legislation on air transport of certain provisions relating to the treatment of third-country nationals, that the liberalisation of air transport services within the Union was inextricably linked to their liberalisation between the Union and non-Member States.

Thus, at the entry into force of the TL, it could be said that there was established authority for the principle of Opinion 1/76 exclusivity but that the Court of Justice had defined the conditions for its application so extremely narrowly as to deprive it of nearly all practical significance. There is cause for concern, therefore, that the principle has been enshrined in Article 3(2) TFEU in language that does not make it an explicit requirement, for exclusivity to arise, that the internal competence and the external competence be 'inextricably linked' or that the former be only capable of being exercised effectively 'at the same time as' the latter.

The problem lies in the ambiguous phrase, '*necessary* to enable the Union to exercise its internal competence'. Does 'necessary' have the same meaning here as in Article 216(1) TFEU, where case law on the complementarity principle would suggest that it connotes a tendency to facilitate, rather than indispensability? And, if so, would it follow that any situation giving rise to external competence under that principle, as enshrined in Article 216(1), would automatically trigger exclusivity under Article 3(2)? It surely cannot have been the intention of the authors of the TL to assimilate the two principles the Court of Justice has derived from Opinion 1/76, but which it has striven hard to keep separate. There is, moreover, a significant difference of wording between Article 216(1) and Article 3(2): enabling an internal competence to be exercised suggests a tighter causal relationship than furthering the attainment of one of the objectives referred to in the Treaties. Those considerations militate in favour of a suitably narrow interpretation of Opinion 1/76 exclusivity, as incorporated into Article 3(2) TFEU. Nevertheless, the imprecise drafting of the provision creates just the kind of uncertainty the Advocate General in *Open Skies* thought should be avoided, reopening the door to the argument on Opinion 1/76 exclusivity that the Commission put forward, and the Court rejected, in that case. It seems inevitable that this element of Article 3(2) TFEU will be the subject of future litigation.

(iii) In so far as the conclusion of the agreement may affect common rules or alter their scope

This is a clear reference to the *AETR* principle in its function as a source of the supervening exclusivity of external Union competence. It has become trite law that, once common rules have been adopted in relation to a certain matter, the Member States are prohibited from undertaking international commitments that might affect those particular rules. As noted above when the *AETR* case was being discussed, the reference to 'common rules' in paragraph 17 of the judgment must be understood to cover any rules adopted by EU

---

[103] *Open Skies*, above n 80, paras 57–62.

institutions, and not only those relating to the policy areas defined by the Treaties as having a discrete identity, such as the CAP.[104] The scope of the *AETR* principle, as now enshrined in Article 3(2) TFEU, is determined by what it means for existing EU rules to be 'affected'. It seems certain that, in interpreting this element of Article 3(2) the Court of Justice will be guided by its previous case law relating to '*AETR* effects', as we term them.

(a) No contradiction between the common rules and the provisions of the agreement

ILO Convention No 170, which was at issue in Opinion 1/91, included certain provisions establishing absolute safety standards for the handling of dangerous substances; the fact that these related to the same matters as existing EU Directives was found sufficient to trigger exclusivity, despite there being no contradiction between the two sets of rules.[105] The reasons for interpreting the operation of an *AETR* effect in this way were explained by Advocate General Tizzano in his *Open Skies* Opinion.[106] In the first place, the correspondence between the provisions of the agreement and the common rules would not guarantee that the latter would thereafter be uniformly applied; nor that amendments to the rules that might be adopted internally under EU legislation would be fully and immediately transposed into the agreement. In other words, there would be a risk of the common rules' being 'frozen' in their form at the time when the agreement was concluded, because changes would have to be negotiated with the third-country parties. Secondly, their 'reception' into the agreement would have the effect of distorting their nature and legal effect, and there would be the risk of their being protected against review by the Court of Justice.

(b) Relaxation of the test of an AETR effect—an area already covered to a large extent by EU rules

The provisions of ILO Convention No 170 on dangerous substances, referred to above, were broader in scope than the relevant EU Directives. Nevertheless, there was held to be an *AETR* effect with respect to the whole of that part of the Convention, because it was concerned with an area 'already covered to a large extent by Community rules progressively adopted since 1967 with a view to achieving an ever greater degree of harmonisation'. Subsequent cases have confirmed that it is not necessary, in order to produce an *AETR* effect, that an international agreement and existing EU rules be coextensive, so long as the test of coverage 'to a large extent' is satisfied.[107]

This apparent relaxation of the conditions under which the *AETR* principle applies met with criticism, because it introduced an element of considerable uncertainty; the vague notion of coverage 'to a considerable extent' made it hard to predict in what circumstances Member States would be deprived of their right to act autonomously in the international sphere.[108] The criticism appears justified. Through the operation of the *AETR* principle, exclusive external competence is acquired by the EU as a result of action taken by its own institutions. Unless it is governed by clear and precise criteria, the principle is liable to

---

[104] Opinion 2/91 [1993] ECR I-1061, para 10.

[105] Ibid, para 25. See also *Open Skies*, above n 80, para 82.

[106] [2002] ECR I-9427, paras 71 and 72. The *Open Skies* cases raised issues of *AETR* exclusivity as well as Opinion 1/76 exclusivity.

[107] *Open Skies*, above n 80, para 82.

[108] See D McGoldrick, *International Relations Law of the European Union* (Harlow, Longman, 1997) 74; O'Keeffe, 'Exclusive, Concurrent and Shared Competence' in Dashwood and Hillion, above n 60, 184.

conflict with the balance between Union and Member State powers under the Treaties, which is governed by the principle of conferral.

(c) Further relaxation of the test—nature and content of the EU rules and the future development of EU law

Far from responding to criticism of its relaxation of the test of an *AETR* effect, the Court of Justice went even further in Opinion 1/03.[109] The request for an Opinion concerned competence to conclude a new version of the so-called Lugano Convention,[110] which extended to certain third countries the principles of the Convention of 1968 on Jurisdiction and the Enforcement of Judgments in Civil and Commercial Matters; the latter had been replaced in 2001 by a Regulation, commonly referred to as 'the Brussels I Regulation',[111] following the creation by the TA of a legal basis in the EC Treaty for judicial co-operation in civil matters.[112] The main issue in the case was the applicability of the *AETR* principle, in the light of the fact that there was only a partial overlap between the Brussels I Regulation and New Lugano. While the rules of the respective instruments were similar in content, for the most part they pursued different objectives: those contained in the Regulation were designed to resolve conflicts of jurisdiction and to ensure 'free movement of judgements' within the EU; those contained in New Lugano, to resolve conflicts of jurisdiction and ensure 'free movement of judgments' between the EU and the third countries concerned, and also between those countries themselves. There was only a limited number of instances where rules contained in New Lugano would apply to matters governed by the Regulation.

The Court nevertheless reached the conclusion that the EU was exclusively competent to conclude New Lugano, by extrapolating from the notion of an area already covered to a large extent by EU rules. Where that test of an *AETR* effect is to be applied, the Court said:

> [T]he assessment must be based not only on the scope of the rules in question but also on their nature and content. It is also necessary to take into account not only the current state of Community law in the area in question but also its future development, in so far as that is foreseeable at the time of that analysis.[113]

The rationale of this wider test was 'to ensure a uniform and consistent application of the Community rules and the proper functioning of the system they establish in order to preserve the full effectiveness of Community law'. [114]

The new element in this reasoning is that the extent of the overlap between the rules of the envisaged agreement and those of EU law is not necessarily conclusive. An *AETR* effect may occur because of two other factors: the particular nature and content of the rules in question; and the possible impact on the future development of EU law.

As to the first of those factors, the Court of Justice evidently had in mind the risk that the operation under New Lugano of a set of rules closely parallel to those of the Brussels I Regulation might have an impact on the proper functioning of the system of rules the latter had established. It remains to be seen how the 'nature and content' test will apply outside the context of rules constituting a coherent code, such as the Regulation.

---

[109] [2006] ECR I-1145.
[110] Hereinafter, 'New Lugano'.
[111] Council Regulation No 44/2001/EC [2001] OJ L12/2.
[112] Now Art 81 TFEU; formerly Art 65 EC.
[113] [2006] ECR I-1145, para 126.
[114] Ibid, para 127.

The significance of the 'future development' test is even less clear. In support of this test, the Court of Justice cited the reference in Opinion 1/91, which is quoted above, to 'Community rules progressively adopted since 1967 with a view to achieving an ever greater degree of harmonisation'. The Court may have been making the point that autonomous international action by Member States must not be allowed to interfere with a systematic process of harmonisation which is under way in the policy area to which the envisaged agreement relates. If so, that raises questions as to how far the process must have been been taken, and how near it must be to achieving complete harmonisation of the area in question, before the *AETR* principle will be triggered.

There is, however, a definite limit to the 'new development test'. As the Court of Justice noted:

> [T]he Community enjoys only conferred powers and that, accordingly, any competence, especially where it is exclusive and not expressly conferred by the Treaty, must have its basis in *conclusions* drawn from a specific analysis of the relationship between the agreement envisaged *and the Community law in force* and from which it is clear that the conclusion of such an agreement is capable of affecting the Community rules.[115]

The *AETR* principle protects EU law in force at the time when the conclusion of the agreement is in prospect. The 'new development' test cannot, therefore, be invoked to prevent Member States from undertaking international commitments, simply because it is thought this may inhibit the future exercise of legislative powers by the Union's institutions. At most, it is submitted, the test will only be available to prevent the foreclosure of options for the development of already existing EU legislation.

Doubt has not been cast on that analysis by the so-called *BITs* cases,[116] in which clauses guaranteeing the free transfer of funds, which were contained in bilateral investment treaties concluded by certain Member States prior to their accession to the Union, were found to be incompatible with the EC Treaty, because they would be liable to constrain powers granted to the EU institutions, to restrict the movement of capital and payments under certain circumstances.[117] No actual decision had been adopted by the Council, which the transfer clauses would have interfered with; so the prohibited effect took the form of a possible restriction on the exercise of powers in the future. However, these were executive powers; the precise content of any decision that might be taken (imposition of restrictions on the movement of funds to third countries), and the conditions under which this might occur, were predefined by the Treaty, and therefore known to all Member States, including the parties to the offending BITs. It would be wrong to extrapolate from those cases to possible use of the 'new development test' of *AETR* exclusivity in order to prevent a Member State from entering into or maintaining international obligations, merely because they would be liable to pre-empt legislative choices the EU might, at some point, wish to make.

(d) The minimum standards rule

No *AETR* effect will occur where both the EU rules in question and the international

---

[115] Ibid, para 124 (emphasis added).
[116] Case C-205/06 *Commission v Austria* [2009] ECR I-1301; Case C-249/06 *Commission v Sweden* [2009] ECR I-1335; Case C-118/07 *Commission v Finland* [2009] ECR I-10889. On the incorporation into the common commercial policy of competence in the field of FDI, including competence to enter into BITs with third countries, see below.
[117] See Arts 64(2) and (3) and 66 TFEU.

agreement that is envisaged impose minimum standards. That was the situation in Opinion 1/91 with regard to the rules of ILO Convention No 170, other than those in the part of the Convention already considered, which related to the handling of dangerous substances. The rationale of the minimum standards rule, as explained by the Court of Justice in Opinion 1/91,[118] goes as follows. If, on the one hand, the EU decides to adopt rules that are less stringent than those of the agreement in question, Member States which have entered into the agreement will be free to comply with its more stringent requirements. If, on the other hand, the Union decides to adopt more stringent measures, there will be nothing to prevent the full application of those rules of EU law by the Member States, parties to the agreement. In Opinion 1/91, the Commission had argued that, because it might sometimes be difficult to determine whether a given measure is more protective than another, Member States could be tempted not to adopt provisions that were actually better suited to the social and technological conditions specific to the Union, thereby impairing the development of EU law. The Court brushed the argument aside on the ground that difficulties such as those referred to, which might arise for the legislative function of the Union, could not constitute the basis for exclusive EU competence.[119]

In *New Lugano* the minimum standards rule was cited by the Court as an established example of a situation where *AETR* exclusivity would not arise.[120]

(e) Parallel competence

In certain policy areas, the fact that legally binding acts have been adopted by the Union will not produce an *AETR* effect, owing to the nature of the activity in question. The examples for which authority can be found in the case law are the areas of humanitarian aid and development co-operation,[121] where the Union and the Member States are said to enjoy 'parallel competence'.[122] Action in those areas is essentially non-pre-emptive; the development co-operation activity of the Union does not need to be protected by the *AETR* principle, because parallel measures taken by the Member States will not impede the attainment of EU objectives.

The TL did not adopt the term 'parallel competence'. However, Union competence for development co-operation and humanitarian aid has been recognised as a special category of shared competence that is non-pre-emptive. Article 4(4) TFEU provides that the exercise of Union competence in these areas 'shall not result in Member States being prevented from exercising theirs'; and Article 4(3) confers similar 'parallel' status on competences in the areas of research, technological development and space. The relationship between these provisions and Article 3(2) TFEU is considered below.

(iv) Conclusion on Article 3(2) and the case law on supervening exclusivity

It seems likely that the Court of Justice will interpret Article 3(2) TFEU consistently with the case law on Opinion 1/76 exclusivity and on *AETR* exclusivity.

---

[118] [1993] ECR I-1061, para 18.

[119] Ibid, paras 19 and 20.

[120] [2006] ECR I-1145, para 123.

[121] Joined Cases C-181/91 and C-248/91 *European Parliament v Council (Bangladesh)* [1993] ECR I-3685; Case 316/91 *European Council v Parliament (EDF)* [1994] ECR I-625. See the analysis of these cases by A Ward, 'The Bangladesh and EDF Judgments' in Dashwood and Hillion, above n 60, 42.

[122] Authority for the use of this term can be found in the Opinion of AG Kokott in Case C-13/07 *Commission v Council (Vietnam)*, paras 67 and 68 (Opinion dated 26 March 2009).

As to the former, the Court may be called upon to resolve the issue whether the word 'necessary' in Article 3(2) can be understood in a different sense from in Article 216(1), requiring there to be an inextricable link between the conclusion of the agreement and the exercise of the Union's internal competence.

As to the latter, the reference in Article 3(2) to affecting common rules or altering their scope seems apt to bring into play the case law on the extensive test of an *AETR* effect, including on the limits to which the test is subject.

C – Article 3 (2) and Other Provisions of the Treaties

(i) The Treaty Provisions on Shared competence and on Supporting Competence

How does Article 3(2) TFEU relate to the Treaty provisions defining the other two main categories of Union competence?

With regard to supporting competence, the answer is straightforward. The areas in which the Union has competence to carry out actions to support, co-ordinate or supplement the actions of the Member States are, according to Article 6 TFEU: protection and improvement of human health; industry; culture; tourism; education, vocational training, youth and sport; civil protection; and administrative co-operation. None of the legal bases in those areas expressly confers competence to enter into international agreements, though several of them encourage co-operation between the Union and third countries or relevant international organisations. Presumably, were the conclusion of an agreement necessary to attain the Union's rather limited objectives in those fields, there would be competence for this purpose under Article 216(1). However, it is plain on the face of Article 2(5) TFEU that such competence would be non-exclusive in principle, because the adoption of internal measures could not have the consequence of 'superseding' the external competence of Member States.

Supervening exclusivity under the principles enshrined in Article 3(2) TFEU is, therefore, legally possible only in respect of the default category of shared competences. How, then, does Article 3(2) relate to the provisions of Article 2(2) TFEU and Article 4 TFEU? With regard to the former, it should be obvious from the foregoing analysis of Opinion 1/76 exclusivity and of *AETR* exclusivity that they curtail the right of Member States to act autonomously more drastically than the principle of Article 2 (2) that '[t]he Member States shall exercise their competence to the extent that the Union has not excised its competence'. If that principle applied to the conclusion of international agreements, it would effectively abolish Opinion 1/76 exclusivity and limit *AETR* effects to cases where the areas covered by the envisaged agreement and the EU legislation coincided fully. It was presumably to make crystal clear that this was not the desired outcome that Article 3 (2) was included in the Treaty. At all events, as the more general provision, Article 2(2) cannot be read as derogating from the more specific Article 3(2). With regard to Article 4 TFEU, it is equally clear that what is said in paragraphs (3) and (4), as to the a priori non-exclusivity of Union competence for research, technological development and space and for development co-operation and humanitarian aid, qualifies Article 3(2), both in the light of the case law and, once again, because it constitutes the more specific rule.

(ii) The Treaty Provisions on the CFSP

Does Article 3(2) TFEU apply to the Union's CFSP competence? It was suggested in Chapter 5 that the CFSP may have to be regarded as belonging to the default category of shared competences pursuant to Article 4(1) TFEU, since it is not one of the areas mentioned in either Articles 3 or 6. Be that as it may, it is submitted that the terms of Article 2(4) TFEU are perfectly clear: the Union is to 'have competence, in accordance with the provisions of the [TFEU], to define and implement a [CFSP]'. All of the provisions defining the nature and scope of this competence are, therefore, to be sought in the TEU, specifically in Chapter 2 of Title V. Apart from Article 2(4), which is simply a cross-reference to the TEU, CFSP competence is mentioned nowhere else in Title I of the TFEU. Moreover, Article 40 TEU, which has the purpose of preventing CFSP competence from encroaching upon the domain of TFEU external competence, and vice versa, draws a contrast between CFSP competence and 'the Union competences referred to in Articles 3 to 6 of the [TFEU]'. It follows from all this that the answer to the question posed in the opening sentence of the present paragraph must be 'No'. Supervening exclusivity will not arise under Article 3(2) TFEU in respect of the Union's CFSP competence. The impact of the adoption of a CFSP measure upon the freedom of Member States to conduct independent foreign, security and defence policies can only be determined in the light of the provisions of Chapter 2 of Title V TEU. These impose upon Member States a muscular duty to inform and consult within the European Council and the Council,[123] and the obligation to comply with any CFSP decisions that have been taken under Articles 28 or 29 TEU. There is no provision in the CFSP Chapter corresponding to Article 3(2) TFEU, and it would be astonishing if there were, given the subject-matter of the policy. The point is underlined by the new language of Article 4 concerning the duty of the Union to respect the Member States' essential state functions, and more particularly by the statement that 'national security remains the sole responsibility of each Member State'.

D – Lawful Member State Action in Areas of Exclusive EU Competence

Article 2(1) TFEU refers to the possibility of Member States' adopting legally binding acts in matters for which the EU is exclusively competent, 'if so empowered by the Union or for the implementation of Union acts'. This possibility—available irrespective of whether exclusivity arises a priori or through the operation of Article 3(2) TFEU—has its origin in case law going back as far as the *AETR* judgment. It was acknowledged by the Court of Justice in that case that third countries, which had originally negotiated the AETR with individual Member States might not be willing to accept the Community—then a relative newcomer on the international stage—as a party to the Agreement. Despite the exclusivity of Community competence, in principle, it was therefore held to be acceptable for the Member States to take on the task of negotiating and concluding the AETR; but they must do so 'in the interests and on behalf of the Community', in accordance with what is now recognised as the duty of sincere co-operation.[124] Similar pragmatism has been shown by the Court in other cases; for instance, though found in *Kramer* to be an area of exclusive Community competence, conservation of marine biological resources had to be carried

---

[123] Art 32.
[124] [1971] ECR 263, paras 81–88.

on by the Member States, including in its international aspect, as long as there was no conservation system in place within the framework of the common fisheries policy.[125] However, the Member States could only act with the authorisation and under the supervision of the Community institutions.

The use of the word 'empowered' in Article 2(1) TFEU is unfortunate, since it suggests that, where the Member States are called upon to act in matters for which the Union is exclusively competent, they require a grant of competence from the Union in order to do so. An analysis that chimes better with the constitutional principles articulated in Title I of the TEU, and is implicit in the case law, would be that acceptance of the exclusivity of EU external competence in the cases provided for by the Treaties has not deprived the Member States of the capacity they enjoy as full subjects of the international legal order, nor of the external powers derived from their respective sovereignties; they are, however, under an obligation to refrain from exercising that capacity and those powers by autonomously adopting legally binding acts, and more particularly by concluding international agreements, except in so far as they may be released from the obligation, because the Union needs them to act in its interests.

IV – SHARED COMPETENCE AND THE DUTY OF CLOSE CO-OPERATION

Where external relations competence is shared, the Court of Justice has said that 'it is essential to ensure close cooperation between the Member States and the [Union] institutions, both in the process of negotiation and conclusion and in the fulfilment of the commitments entered into', and that this obligation 'flows from the requirement of unity in the external representation of the Union'.[126] Like the *AETR* principle, the duty represents a particular application of the duty of sincere co-operation in Article 4(3) TEU. And like that principle, it is beginning to encroach—though somewhat less drastically—upon the freedom of the Member States to exercise their external powers autonomously.[127]

In recent cases, the duty of close co-operation has been acquiring a harder edge. Its content is being more precisely defined and the duty has been recognised as sufficiently concrete to found an infringement action.[128]

In infringement proceedings brought by the Commission against Luxembourg and Germany in 2003, it was held that failure by a Member State to co-operate and consult with the Commission, once the Council has formally authorised the opening of negotia-

---

[125] See Joined Cases 3, 4 and 6/76 *Kramer* [1976] ECR 12/79, paras 34–45; Case 61/77 *Commission v Ireland* [1978] ECR 417; Case 804/79 *Commission v United Kingdom* [1981] ECR 1045. See also Opinion 1/78, *Natural Rubber* [1979] ECR 1045. On the Court's pragmatic approach to such issues, see T Tridimas and P Eeckhout, 'The External Competence of the Community and the Case-law of the Court of Justice: Principle versus Pragmatism' (1994) 14 *YEL* 143.

[126] See (EURATOM) Ruling 1/78, *Physical Protection of Nuclear Materials* [1978] ECR 2151, paras 34–36; Opinion 2/91, *ILO* [1993] ECR I-1061, para 36; Opinion 1/94, *WTO* [1994] ECR I-5267, para 108.

[127] See Eeckhout, above n 3, 200–15; C Hillion, 'Mixity and Coherence: The Significance of the duty of Cooperation' in C Hillion and P Koutrakos (eds), *Mixed Agreements Revisited* (Oxford, Hart Publishing, 2010) 87.

[128] See E Nefrani, 'The Duty of Loyalty: Re-thinking its Scope through its Application in the Field of EU External Relations' (2010) 47 *CMLRev* 323.

tions with a view to the conclusion of an agreement with a third country, constitutes an infringement of the duty of sincere co-operation in Article 4(3) TEU. The complaint in Cases 266 and 433/03 was that Luxembourg and Germany had gone ahead with negotiating and concluding, or at any rate with ratifying and implementing, agreements with a group of third countries, even after the Commission had been formally authorised by the Council to open negotiations for a multilateral agreement, including with those countries. The Court of Justice said:

> The adoption of a decision authorising the Commission to negotiate a multilateral agreement on behalf of the Community marks the start of a coherent Community action at international level and requires, for that purpose, if not a duty of abstention on the part of the Member States, at the very least a duty of close cooperation between the latter and the Community institutions in order to facilitate the achievement of the Community tasks and to ensure the coherence and consistency of the action and its international representation.

Here, the factor that gave rise to the duty was a formal act adopted by the Council as an organ of the EU. Moreover, the Court used careful language in defining the content of the duty. It held back from asserting that the Member States concerned were required to abstain from concluding the offending agreements. The judgment could be read as implying that there would not have been an infringement if Luxembourg and Germany had shown the Commission the courtesy of making contact and discussing the situation.

The judgment in the more recent *PFOS* case might be thought to go considerably further, in fettering Member States' powers of external action. The complaint by the Commission was that Sweden had infringed the principle of close co-operation by unilaterally proposing the listing of a substance under the Stockholm Convention on Persistent Organic Pollutants (POPs), at a time when a concerted common strategy had been established by the Union, which involved not immediately making such a proposal. The reasons behind the strategy were partly economic, because the Union would have been required to make a contribution towards meeting the costs of compliance that would be incurred by developing countries. The Court of Justice agreed with the Commission that the initiative taken by Sweden amounted to an infringement of its duty of close co-operation.[129]

There were notable differences, as compared with Cases C-266 and 433/03—first and foremost, the absence of any formal act of an EU institution, even of a preparatory nature, such as authorisation by the Council to open treaty negotiations. At most, there was an informal understanding between national delegations and the Commission as to the course of action it was appropriate to pursue. Secondly, there was held to be a duty of abstention: Sweden was at fault in not refraining from taking unilateral action. The judgment raises a number of questions.

First, would the outcome have been different if Sweden had made explicitly clear that it was not able to rally to the common strategy that was found by the Court of Justice to have been agreed in 2005? It is not clear from either the Opinion or the judgment in the case exactly what position Sweden took at the crucial meeting of the Council's Working Party on International Environmental Issues on 6 July 2005. However, if Sweden had stated at that meeting that it was not willing to brook any delay in proposing the listing of PFOS, it is hard to see how it could be claimed that a concerted common strategy existed at the moment when its autonomous listing proposal was made on 14 July 2005. In the absence

---

[129] See Case C-246/07 *Commission v Sweden* (*PFOS*), Judgment of 20 April 2010, paras 69–105; Opinion of AG Poiares Maduro, paras 46–58.

of a formal decision governed by rules of procedure, decisions can only be taken by common accord, which means that everybody must agree.

Secondly, would it have made a difference if discussion within the Working Party had reached a complete stalemate? There are hints in the Opinion and the judgment that it would, indeed, have made a difference. For instance, the Advocate General spoke of there being a duty on Sweden to refrain from acting 'at least for a reasonable time';[130] while the Court said there was 'no decision-making vacuum or even a waiting period equivalent to the absence of a decision'.[131] It is submitted that in a 'decision-making vacuum' Sweden would have been perfectly justified in acting unilaterally, because there would then have been no Union position that could be jeopardised.

A third question arises from the fact that the POPs Convention had been concluded by the Community and the Member States as a mixed agreement. Would it have been different if Sweden's unilateral action had not taken place within an already established decision-making framework? It was surely relevant that the Member States and the Union had already committed themselves to a joint approach in the matter of the international control of POPs. This could be seen as strengthening the obligation to strive for a co-ordinated approach to the listing of particular substances. It is submitted that the case goes no further than establishing that a Member State is under a duty to abstain from exercising its autonomous external competence so as to dissociate itself from a concerted, though still informal, strategy reached within the context of an existing agreement.

The *POPs* case would appear to have no bearing on the more controversial issue of the possible operation of the duty of close co-operation at the pre-contractual stage, when the question is whether an international agreement (assuming there is no element of EU exclusivity) should be negotiated and concluded by the EU alone, by the EU and its Member States or by the Member States alone. The only guidance backed by judicial authority, so far received, as to how that issue should be resolved is disturbingly radical. In the proceedings brought by the Commission to contest the participation by the Member States in the decision establishing the Union's position on the accession of Vietnam to the WTO, the Council had argued that, in an area of shared competence, there was complete freedom to decide whether EU competence should be exercised, or whether it should be left to the Member States to act under their external powers. The shared competence in question, arising under former Article 133(5) EC, related to aspects of the CCP (trade in services and the commercial aspects of IP) which, at the time, had not yet been brought within the purview of the Union's exclusive competence. Responding to the Council's argument, Advocate General Kokott said:

> Contrary to the Council's view, it cannot voluntarily waive some or all of its powers under Article 133 (5) EC in favour of the Member States, but must take account of the Community interest in the most effective and coherent representation at international level as is possible and must make full use of its powers to that end. The Council must not allow the powers of the Community and its institutions, as formulated in the EC Treaty, to be distorted.
>
> Likewise, the Member States within the Council may not obstruct optimum efficacy of action by the Community with the object of themselves becoming involved alongside the Community... the duty of genuine cooperation [Article 4 (3) TFEU] requires the Member States to do everything possible to facilitate the exercise of the Community's powers and to abstain from any measure which could jeopardise the attainment of the objectives of the EC Treaty.[132]

---

[130] Opinion, para 49.
[131] Ibid, para 87.
[132] Case C-13/07 *Commission v Council* (*Vietnam*), Opinion of 26 March 2009, paras 83 and 84.

How the Court of Justice would have reacted to that reasoning is unknowable, because the case was withdrawn from the register before judgment. Advocate General Kokott appeared to be denying what is surely the purest orthodoxy, confirmed by the distinction which the TFEU itself now draws between exclusive and shared competence: namely that, in areas of shared competence, the choice as to whether the Member States or the Union should act, or whether they should act together, is a political one, and her view would exclude, in principle, the pragmatic choice of mixity. According to the Advocate General, 'the Union interest in the most effective and coherent representation at international level as is possible' may require the Council to exercise its powers to the full and the Member States to refrain from 'becoming involved alongside the [Union]'.

It is important to bear in mind that the case related to a corner of the CCP where, at the time, Union competence was not exclusive, though now it is. The view taken by the learned Advocate General may, perhaps, be distinguished on the ground that the duty of close co-operation would have applied with special stringency in that context. However, no such limitation appears on the face of the passage cited above.

To sum up where the law stands at present on the duty of close co-operation:

— When an EU position has been established (which, it seems, must have occurred, even if informally, within a Council body) the duty applies and may, in the circumstances, require Member States to refrain from autonomous action.
— It remains undecided, certainly by the Court of Justice itself, as to how the duty of co-operation might operate in the absence of an EU position: for instance, after the Commission has taken the initiative of putting forward a recommendation to open negotiations for an agreement with a third country, but before authorisation to do so has been given by the Council. The better view is that the duty would not be triggered in those circumstances. The alternative would imply that the Member States could be deprived of their right to exercise their external powers autonomously by a unilateral act of the Commission. There is no conceivable basis for this in the constitutional law of the Union.

V – THE PROCEDURAL CODE IN
ARTICLE 218 TFEU

Article 218 TFEU is the procedural legal basis for the negotiation and conclusion of international agreements between the EU and third countries or international organisations. The drafting practice that has become established over successive Treaty amendments is for the substantive legal bases that expressly confer treaty-making power upon the Union to cross-refer to this Article; though, as we shall see, Article 297 TFEU, the legal basis for the CCP, includes some additional procedural provisions.[133] The procedural code contained in Article 218 is not only the most elaborate to date but also the most complete, because its rules apply not only to the exercise of CFSP external competences but also to the exercise of CFSP competence.[134] It might have been thought that the need to accom-

---

[133] For an account of developments in the procedural arrangements of the EC Treaty up to the era of the TA, see Dashwood, above n 70, 124–27.

[134] Prior to the TL, the procedure for the negotiation and conclusion of international agreements for the purposes of both the Second and the Third Pillars was former Art 24 TEU.

modate the particularity of the CFSP would result in unacceptable complexity but the solutions arrived at are, in fact, rather elegant.

The right to initiate the process designed to lead eventually to the conclusion of an international agreement, and to conduct negotiations to that end, is dealt with in Article 218(3). As determined by the subject-matter of the envisaged agreement, the actors involved are, respectively, the High Representative and the Commission. If the envisaged agreement relates 'exclusively or principally' to the CFSP, it will be for the High Representative to submit recommendations to the Council; while in all other cases (including, presumably, where foreign and security policy is a significant but not the principal component of the agreement), the task will be for the Commission. That is a major change, as compared with the situation prior to the TL, when the exercise of CFSP and EC external competences was kept strictly separate. Paragraph (3) goes on to provide that the Council 'shall adopt a decision authorising the opening of negotiations and, depending on the subject of the agreement envisaged, nominating the Union's negotiator or the head of the Union's negotiating team'. The phrase 'depending on the subject of the agreement' must, it is submitted, be understood as referring to the same criteria as those that determine the right of initiative; so it will be the Commission that negotiates mixed CFSP/TFEU agreements, except those in which the CFSP element is predominant, where the High Representative will be the negotiator.[135]

As provided for by Article 218(2) and (4), and consistently with previous law and practice, it is the prerogative of the Council to authorise the opening of negotiations, to address directives to the negotiator, to designate a special committee in consultation with which the negotiations must be conducted, and at the end of the negotiating process to authorise the signing and the conclusion of any resulting agreement

Paragraphs (5) and (6) of Article 218 make the designated negotiator responsible for putting forward a proposal to the Council for the adoption of a decision authorising the signing of the agreement and, if necessary, its provisional application before entry into force; and subsequently a proposal for a decision by the Council authorising the conclusion of the agreement. The European Parliament has been given a formal role in the conclusion procedure in all cases except where the agreement relates *exclusively* to the CFSP. In respect of mixed CFSP/TFEU agreements, therefore, the situation of the Parliament will be the same as it would be if the agreement fell to be concluded purely on legal bases contained in the TFEU.

In accordance with point (a) of Article 218(6), the consent of the Parliament is required in the following cases:

(i)   association agreements;
(ii)   the projected agreement on the accession of the EU to the European Convention on the Protection of Human Rights and Fundamental Freedoms;
(iii) agreements establishing a specific institutional framework by organising co-operation procedures;
(iv)   agreements with important budgetary implications for the Union
(v)   agreements covering fields to which either the ordinary legislative procedure applies

---

[135] The inclusion of representatives of the European Parliament in the negotiating process is one of the elements of an Inter-Institutional Agreement adopted by the Parliament on 20 October 2010 and signed by the Presidents of the Parliament and the Commission, which has been the subject of a critical Opinion by the Legal Service of the Council: see EU Observer of 21 October 2010.

or the special legislative procedure where consent by the European Parliament is required.

The somewhat opaque description under (iii) presumably refers to instruments such as the WTO Agreement or the European Economic Area Agreement, which establish bodies with power to take legally binding Decisions An indication as to what is meant under (iv) by 'important budgetary implications' may be found in a case concerning an agreement for the purchase of fishing rights from Mauretania.[136] The Court of Justice took the view that it was unrealistic to compare the cost of the agreement with the overall Union budget. A better approach would be to consider its cost as a proportion of the total budgetary appropriations covering the Union's external action in a given year. The case under (iv) strengthens the Parliament's position; former Article 300(3) EC required the assent of the Parliament where an agreement would entail the amendment of a Union act adopted by co-decision. The implications of this new provision for the conclusion of agreements in the area of the common commercial policy are considered below. Point (b) of Article 218(6) provides that, in cases other than those listed under (a), the Parliament must be consulted. As previously, the Council has power to set a time limit for the delivery of the Parliament's opinion, depending on the urgency of the matter.

The voting rule for the Council is laid down by Article 218(8) TFEU. The normal rule of QMV is displaced, among other situations, 'when the agreement covers a field for which unanimity is required for the adoption of an act of the Union'. Hence, unless the CFSP elements of a mixed agreement fall within one of the derogations in Article 31(2) TEU that allow the Council to act by QMV, the agreement as a whole would have to be concluded by unanimity.

Decisions on the suspension of an agreement or establishing positions to be adopted on the Union's behalf in a body set up by an agreement, which is capable of acting with legal effects, are the subject of Article 218(9). Decisions of the latter kind automatically become part of the internal legal order of the Union,[137] so it is essential that its legislative organs should have given their approval in advance to any resulting commitments.[138] However, since both sorts of decision are likely, in practice, to require urgency, paragraph (9) provides for a simplified procedure, with no formal involvement of the European Parliament; although the right of the Parliament, pursuant to Article 218(10), to be kept immediately and fully informed, applies here as it does at all stages of decision-making under the Article. Again, the power of decision belongs to the Council, acting 'on a proposal from the Commission or the High Representative'. The text does not specify the circumstances in which one or the other of the latter has the right of initiative but should, it is submitted, be interpreted as a cross-referring to Article 218(3). The allocation of the task to either the Commission or the High Representative will therefore depend on the preponderance of elements within a CFSP/TFEU agreement.

The final provision of the procedural code, Article 218(11), provides for the jurisdiction under which the Court of Justice may be invited by a Member State, the European Parliament, the Council or the Commission to render an opinion on the compatibility

---

[136] Case C-189/97 *Parliament v Council* [1999] ECR 4741.

[137] Case 12/86 *Demirel* [1987] ECR 3719; Case C-192/89 *Sevince* [1990] ECR I-3461. See Chapter 28 below.

[138] The process of establishing such positions may lead to inter-institutional disputes that end in the Court of Justice. See the Opinion of AG Kokott of 26 March 2009 in Case C-13/07 *Commission v Council*, which concerned a decision on the admission of Vietnam to the WTO. No judgment was given in the case, which was removed from the register, following the entry into force of the TL. See also Opinion 1/08 [2009] ECR I-11129.

of an envisaged agreement with the Treaties. Such an opinion must be sought before the conclusion of the agreement concerned; thereafter, the only option for an institution or Member State wishing to raise the issue of compatibility with the Treaties is to bring an action under Article 263 TFEU challenging the validity, not of the agreement itself, because that would be a matter for international law, but of the Council decision by which it was concluded.[139] It will have become apparent that opinions sought pursuant to Article 218(11) have been a fertile source of case law on the Union's powers of external action.

VI – MIXED AGREEMENTS

The term 'mixed agreements' is applied to international agreements jointly concluded by the Union and the Member States, under their respective powers. The mixed agreement formula may be resorted to for two reasons.[140]

The formula is unavoidable where some of the matters it is envisaged to include in an agreement fall outside the competence of the EU. That would once have been the case, if provisions relating to political co-operation or to the field of criminal law were included in an agreement otherwise concerned with matters such as trade or development co-operation, which fell within the competence of the EC. The insertion into former Title V TEU of a procedural legal basis for negotiating and concluding international agreements[141] brought the possibility of combining Second and Third Pillar elements with First Pillar elements in a single instrument; hitherto, however 'cross-pillar mixity' does not seem to have been regarded as an attractive option, and 'classic mixity', with the Member States concluding the parts of agreements beyond the scope of what has become TFEU external competence, remains the norm.

More commonly in recent practice, mixity is the result of political choice. In areas of shared or parallel competence, there is no obligation for the Member States to stand aside and allow the Union to exercise its non-exclusive competence.[142] The Court of Justice was very clear in Opinion 1/94 that the Member States were only prevented from concluding the parts of the GATS and the TRIPS that fell within exclusive Community competence.[143]

It will sometimes be indicated in a Declaration of Competence, to what extent a mixed agreement has been concluded by the Union and the Member States, respectively. In the *Mox Plant* case, the Commission brought infringement proceedings against Ireland, as a result of that country's having initiated a claim against the UK for the alleged contravention of certain provisions of the UN Convention on the Law of the Sea. The complaint against Ireland was that, as part of an agreement which the Community had also con-

---

[139] See Case C-122/95 *Germany v Council* [1998] ECR I-973. See also Case C-327/91 *France v Commission* [1994] ECR I-3641.

[140] There is a voluminous literature on mixed agreements. See Hillion and Koutrakos, above n 127, the most up-to-date collection of scholarly studies at the time of writing. See also J Heliskoski, *Mixed Agreements as a Technique for Organising the International Relations of the European Community and its Member States* (The Hague, Kluwer, 2001) ch 7.

[141] Former Art 24 TEU.

[142] Except, of course, to the extent that AG Kokott may have been right in what she said about the operation of the duty of close cooperation in the *Vietnam* case, as discussed in Part IV, above.

[143] [1994] ECR I-5267.

cluded, the provisions in question had been incorporated into the EU legal order;[144] the initiation of international proceedings against the UK therefore amounted to a violation of the jurisdictional monopoly of the Court of Justice in disputes between Member States concerning the interpretation or application of the Treaties, as provided for by Article 344 TFEU. The provisions that were the subject of the Irish claim concerned marine pollution, where EU/Member State competence is shared, and it was necessary, therefore, to determine whether the Community had exercised its competence in relation to them. The answer was found in the Declaration of Competence, which identified the provisions concluded under Community competence as those belonging to areas in which Community rules existed, including where there was no *AETR* effect, because the rules established minimum standards. Ireland was found to be in breach of Article 344, because its claim against the UK related, in the main, to provisions in areas in which Community rules did indeed exist, so that, by becoming party to the Convention, the Community must be taken to have elected to exercise its competence with respect to those provisions.

However, it frequently happens that a mixed agreement fails to specify which parts have been concluded by the Union and which by the Member States. Such is the case with the WTO Agreement, as the Court of Justice has observed.[145] The silence may be deliberate, to avoid having to delay the conclusion of the Agreement, while disputes about competence are resolved. In the case of very wide-ranging agreements, such as those in the WTO package, the Member States will be alert to the danger that clear identification of the elements concluded by the Union might create opportunities for exorbitant claims of supervening exclusivity under the *AETR* principle. Where an indication is lacking as to which of the parties on the Union side of an agreement is accepting responsibility for its different elements, the issue, so far as it concerns third-country parties, will be a matter for public international law.[146]

Mixity has not been found to be problematic at the stage of negotiating agreements because the long-established practice is for the Member States to mandate the Commission to negotiate on their behalf, subject to a 'without prejudice' clause concerning competence. The conclusion of the agreement is a different matter. A mixed agreement must be concluded both by the Union and by all 27 of the Member States in accordance with their respective constitutional requirements. The process may be extremely lengthy, but it is possible to mitigate the inconvenience by taking advantage of the power under Article 218(5) TFEU to give the parts of the agreement falling within the competence of the Union provisional application. In theory it would be possible to introduce a Treaty amendment creating a simplified procedure for concluding mixed agreements simultaneously on behalf of the Union and the Member States, by a decision of the Council and the Representatives of the Governments of the Member States meeting within the Council, but no inclination has ever been shown for taking up this suggestion.

Where a mixed agreement establishes a decision-making body, it will be necessary for the Commission and the Member States to agree a code of conduct for operating within it. The Court of Justice has held that there is a legal obligation to comply with the rules of such a code, because they represent a concretisation of the duty of co-operation.[147]

---

[144] See Chapter 28.

[145] Case C-53/96 [1998] ECR I-3603.

[146] In Case C-316/91 *Parliament v Council* [1994] ECR I-625, AG Jacobs suggested that the Community and the Member States should be regarded as jointly liable, in the absence of an indication to the contrary.

[147] Case C-25/94 *Commission v Council* [1996] ECR I-1469. See Heliskoski, 'Internal Struggle for International Presence: The Exercise of Voting Rights within the FAO', in Dashwood and Hillion, above n 60, 7.

The effects of mixed agreements within the internal legal order of the Union are considered in Chapter 28; as also is the issue of the jurisdiction of the Court of Justice to respond to references for preliminary rulings under Article 267 TFEU on the interpretation of the provisions of such agreements, to which the same case law relates. Another issue is the Court's jurisdiction in proceedings brought by the Commission under Article 258 TFEU against a Member State for the infringement of a mixed agreement. The cases show that the Court will assert jurisdiction under Article 258, where the provisions in question concern matters within the competence of the Union, on two grounds, the relative weight of which is not entirely clear: that infringement of the agreement would attract international legal responsibility for the Union; and that the provisions in question fall within an area which is to a great extent covered by EU legislation, even if their precise subject-matter is not so covered.[148]

There is nothing in the TL that relates specifically to mixed agreements.[149] Of course, the scope for resorting to the mixity formula will be affected by the significant extension of the Union's exclusive competence in the area of the common commercial policy; as it would be, in the unlikely event of the Court's finding that Article 3(2) TFEU enlarges the scope of supervening exclusivity beyond that recognised in its case law. One other possible effect may be to encourage what would once have been described as cross-pillar mixity but which we should now call 'CFSP/TFEU mixity', as an alternative to classic mixity. One source of encouragement might be that there is now a single EU party, instead of, as formerly, the Union together with Community. Another might be the nicely judged procedural solutions provided by Article 218 TFEU, which ought to assuage concerns about possible problems in the negotiation and conclusion of mixed agreements

VII – THE COMMON COMMERCIAL POLICY

A – Introduction

The CCP comprises the arrangements organising the commercial relations between the EU and third countries. The focus of the CCP is external trade, in the wide modern sense of that notion, embracing the exchange of goods and services and the whole range of matters relevant to the regulation of such exchanges.

In the 1950s, when the European Communities were established, efforts to rationalise international economic relations were principally concerned with the liberalisation of trade in goods, through the progressive reduction of obstacles such as tariffs and quotas. This objective was reflected in the main international economic instrument of the time, the General Agreement on Tariffs and Trade (GATT), which was concluded in 1947. Later decades brought a new awareness of the special problems that free trade may pose for developing countries, heavily dependent on the production of commodities such as cocoa and natural rubber, the prices of which were liable to fluctuate widely; and the United Nations Conference on Trade and Development (UNCTAD), established in 1964, became

---

[148] Case C-13/00 *Commission v Ireland* (*Berne Convention*) [2002] ECR I-2923; Case C-239/03 *Commission v France* (*Etang de Berre*) [2004] ECR I-9325.

[149] The issues are canvassed by A Dashwood, 'Mixity in the Era of the Treaty of Lisbon' in Hillion and Koutrakos, above n 127.

a forum for addressing these issues. At the same time, the pattern of developed countries' trade was changing, with the supply of financial and other services gaining increasing importance in their economies. The outcome of the Uruguay Round of international trade negotiations, which was initiated in 1986 and brought to a successful conclusion at a conference held in Marrakesh in 1994, was the creation of a new international organisation, the WTO, with an extensive remit in the sphere of global economic relations. The WTO was based on a package of international agreements, the main elements of which were, besides the Agreement establishing the Organisation itself: a new version of the GATT, known as the 'GATT 1994', which replaced the GATT 1947; a General Agreement on Trade in Services (GATS); an Agreement on Trade-related Aspects of Intellectual Property (TRIPS); and an Understanding on Rules and Procedures Governing the Settlement of Disputes (DSU). At the time of writing, a fresh round of international trade negotiations, the so-called 'Dohar Round', had been initiated but remains stalled, as a result of fundamental disagreements between the groups representing different economic interests.[150]

We have seen that a legal basis was provided for the CCP by Article 113 of the original EEC Treaty. Post-Lisbon, the legal basis is Article 207 TFEU. The competence conferred on the Community enabled it, at an early stage, to assume the powers previously exercised by Member States in the area governed by the GATT, and it was recognised by GATT partners as a party to the Agreement.[151] The then Article 113, as interpreted by the Court of Justice, also proved sufficiently flexible to allow the participation of the Community in new forms of international instrument, such as commodity agreements including a price-stabilisation mechanism, which were designed to accommodate the concerns of developing countries.[152] However, when the moment came for the conclusion of the WTO package, the Court of Justice was not persuaded that a CFSP legal basis would serve for the Community to become a party to more than limited aspects of the GATS and the TRIPS.[153] The case law relating to these various developments will be discussed below. The text of what by then had become Article 133 EC was amended by the TN, in order to extend its scope to cover trade in services and commercial aspects of IP, but competence in these areas was still subjected to a regime significantly different from that of the CCP in general. It was left to the TL to complete the assimilation of the two areas into the CCP, and to extend competence to the important new area of FDI, under Article 207 TFEU.

The scope of the CCP has been, and remains, controversial, because of the nature of the competence conferred on the Union, and the procedure for its exercise. As noted above, the exclusivity of CCP competence was established in Opinion 1/75 as early as 1975, in the first Opinion rendered by the Court of Justice under what has become Article 218(11) TFEU.[154] The issue in the case was the competence of the Community to conclude a draft OECD Understanding that was designed to place a limit on the degree to which countries were permitted to subsidise their exports by financing local costs. After emphasising the breadth of CCP competence, the Court went on infer its exclusive character from the fact that the competence was conceived by the then Article 113 EEC 'in the context of the operation of the common market for the defence of the common interests of the

---

[150] For an account of these developments, explaining their significance to the evolution of the case law on the CCP, see Eeckhout, above n 3, ch 2.
[151] See the analysis of this process in Cases 21–24/72, *International Fruit Company* [1972] ECR 1219.
[152] See Opinion 1/78 *Natural Rubber* [1979] ECR 2871.
[153] Opinion 1/94 [1994] ECR I-5267.
[154] Opinion 1/75 [1975] ECR 1355.

Community, within which the particular interests of the Member States must endeavour to adapt to each other'.[155] In the Court's view, this conception was incompatible with concurrent powers on the part of the Member States to pursue their individual interests, at the risk of compromising the common interest. As to the decision-making procedure, prior to the introduction by the TL of the ordinary legislative procedure for the adoption of framework measures defining the framework for implementing the CCP (see below), the Council acted by QMV on a proposal from the Commission, with no formal involvement of the European Parliament. The combination of exclusive competence and QMV for Council decisions meant that control over trade policy had passed from individual Member States to the Community/Union, with the Commission taking a leadership role as the institution responsible for negotiating international agreements.[156] For the Member States, and therefore the Council, this sometimes made the choice of legal bases other than (current) Article 207 TFEU appear preferable; and this preference might be shared by the European Parliament, if it had a greater share in decision-making under the alternative legal basis. Over the years, therefore, there has been fertile ground for legal disputes, which have often ended in the Court of Justice.

B – Scope of the CCP

The present scope of the CCP is defined by Article 207 (1) TFEU. This provides:

> The common commercial policy shall be based on uniform principles, particularly in regard to changes in tariff rates, the conclusion of tariff and trade agreements relating to trade in goods and services, and the commercial aspects of intellectual property, foreign direct investment, the achievement of uniformity in measures of liberalisation, export policy and measures to protect trade such as those to be taken in the event of dumping or subsidies. The common commercial policy shall be conducted in the context of the principles and objectives of the Union's external action.

(i) The Choice of Article 207 TFEU as a Legal Basis

The principles determining the choice of the legal basis for legislation or for concluding an international agreement operate in relation to Article 207 TFEU in the same way as to any other Treaty provision.[157] The choice should not follow from the author's conviction but must rest on objective factors amenable to judicial review, notably the aim and content of the measure in question.[158] If examination of the measure reveals that it pursues a twofold purpose or that it has a twofold component, and if one of these is identifiable as the main or predominant purpose or component, whereas the other is merely incidental, the measure must be founded on the legal basis required by the former.[159] Only if the measure simultaneously pursues two or more objectives which are inseparably linked, without one being secondary or indirect in relation to the other(s), may a dual or multiple legal

---

[155] Opinion 1/75, 1363–64.
[156] See now Art 218(3) TFEU.
[157] Opinion 2/00 *Cartagena Protocol on Biosafety* [2001] ECR I-2793, paras 22 *et seq.*
[158] Ibid, para 22. See also Case C-269/97 *Commission v Council* [2000] ECR I-2257.
[159] Case C-187/93 *Parliament v Council* [1994] ECR I-2857, paras 19 and 21; Case 42/97 *Parliament v Council* [1999] ECR I-869, paras 39 and 40; Opinion 2/00, para 23.

basis be chosen.[160] In addition, the Court of Justice has recalled that, where the measure in question is an international agreement, account must be taken of Article 31 of the Vienna Convention on the Law of Treaties, which provides that 'a treaty shall be interpreted in good faith in accordance with the ordinary meaning to be given to the terms of the treaty in their context and in the light of its object and purpose'.[161]

Article 207 TFEU will, therefore, be the correct legal basis for concluding an international agreement (or adopting some other measure) if the preponderant purpose of the agreement, confirmed by its content, is to promote, facilitate or govern external trade.[162] If the agreement pursues several objectives, including the regulation of trade, which are inseparably linked without any of them being secondary and indirect in relation to the rest, then Article 207 will have to be included as part of a dual or multiple legal basis. Disputes arise because it is quite common for an agreement to contain provisions regulating some aspect of trade, which are designed to be the instrument for attaining objectives in some other policy area, such as development co-operation or the protection of the environment. Which should be seen as preponderant—the trade-related instrumentality or the ulterior purpose?

There have been cases in which the Council insisted, against the view of the Commission, that it was necessary to supplement the provision which has become Article 207 TFEU with a legal basis reflecting the fact that the measure in question had features intended to be of benefit to developing countries. This had a significant impact on the decision-making procedure, because at the time there was no specific legal basis for development co-operation; hence the provision corresponding to Article 352 TFEU, for the creation of supplementary powers, had to be used, which required the Council to act by unanimity. Opinion 1/78 concerned the International Agreement on Natural Rubber, which envisaged the establishment of a price-stabilisation mechanism in the form of a buffer stock.[163] Nearly a decade later, a similar disagreement gave rise to the so-called *GSP* case.[164] This related to Regulations adopted by the Council under an UNCTAD scheme that encouraged developed countries to operate a system of reduced tariffs that applied generally to imports from developing countries. Finding for the Commission in both cases, the Court of Justice stressed the evolutive character of the CCP. It had to be possible for the Community to be able to do business with new kinds of partners in international trade. Although the Court did not explicitly apply the predominant purpose and content test, which had not then become current, it is hard to deny that the test would have been satisfied, if it had done. The instruments in issue in both cases were essentially about regulating the international exchange of goods for money, and belonged to the domain of trade policy, even if some of the conditions governing the exchanges were determined by development policy objectives.

In another pair of cases, *Werner* and *Leifer*,[165] the Court of Justice found that a Member State's regime for controlling exports of dual-use goods (ie goods capable of being applied

---

[160] Case C-42/97, para 38; Opinion 2/00, para 23.
[161] Opinion 2/00, para 24.
[162] Ibid, para 37.
[163] [1979] ECR 2871.
[164] Case 45/86 *Commission v Council* [1987] ECR 1493. Because of the failure to agree on a legal basis, no specific Treaty Articles were cited in the Regulations. However, the judgment notes that the Council admitted at the hearing that the provisions it had in mind were (current) Art 207 TFEU and Art 352 TFEU. See the annotation by Steenbergen (1987) 24 *CMLRev* 731.
[165] Case C-70/94 *Werner* [1995] ECR I-3189; Case C-83/94 *Leifer* [1995] ECR 3231.

for both civilian and military ends) amounted to a trade measure within the scope of the Union's exclusive competence for the CCP. To avoid incompatibility with EU law, the regime would have to be justifiable under Article 11 of the EU Regulation governing exports to third countries, which provides for derogations from the general prohibition against restrictions on exports, including a derogation on grounds of national security.[166] Those cases were not, of course, about the choice of legal basis for a Union act. However, the Court's ruling was taken by the institutions to mean that the Union's own dual-use regime, when it was repealed and replaced soon afterwards, could be founded exclusively on the predecessor of Article 207 TFEU. The previous EU regime was based on a 'cross-pillar mechanism': the list of dual-use goods, the destinations affected by the controls and the guidelines to be taken into account by Member States when deciding whether to grant an export authorisation had been the subject of a CFSP act;[167] while all the detailed arrangements for controlling exports were laid down by an EC Regulation. Whether the abandonment of the cross-pillar mechanism was required by the *Werner* and *Leifer* judgments may perhaps be doubted. Deciding which countries are the 'bad guys', to which dual-use goods cannot safely be exported, is an entirely political decision, which it is proper to take within the CFSP framework; and there is nothing in the Court's reasoning to suggest that it should not be so taken. On the other hand, downstream of that decision, there cannot be any doubt that establishing a system of export controls for a particular category of goods is entirely a matter within the scope of the CCP.

More recent legal basis disputes have concerned the demarcation between the CFSP and policy on the environment. The cases show that, if examination of the context, aim and content of an international agreement establishes that its essential object is the protection of the environment, Article 192 TFEU, not Article 207 TFEU, should be the legal basis. That will be so even if the agreement contains provisions on controlling the transboundary movements of a dangerous product, and the bulk of those movements are likely to be in the course of trade; a relevant consideration would be that the provisions are wide enough to apply to 'unintentional' transboundary movements, as well as to movements for charitable or scientific purposes or those serving the public interest.[168] However, if the instrumentality of an agreement is largely based on trade-related measures, though the main concern of the authors was evidently the protection of the environment, the Court is likely to insist upon the inclusion of Article 207 as an additional legal basis.[169]

(ii) Trade in Services and Commercial Aspects of Intellectual Property

The tendency of earlier case law to emphasise the width and the evolutive character of CCP competence[170] might have aroused the expectation that the Court of Justice would

---

[166] See Regulation No 2603/69 [1969] OJ L234/25. Art 11 of the Regulation corresponds, in external trade, to Art 36 TFEU in intra-Union trade.

[167] See Council Decision 94/94/CFSP [1994] OJ L367/8. This was repealed by Council Decision 2000/402/CFSP [2000] OJ L159/218, which refers in recital (2) to the *Werner* and *Leifer* judgments.

[168] *Cartagena Protocol on Biosafety* [2001] ECR I-2793, paras 26–33, 37 and 38. See annotation by Dashwood (2002) 39 *CMLRev* 353. See also Case C-411/06 *Commission v European Parliament and Council* [2009] ECR I-7585.

[169] Case C-94/03 *Commission v Council (PIC Convention)* [2006] ECR I-107; Case C-178/03 *Commission v European Parliament and Council* [2006] ECR I-1. See the highly critical annotation by Koutrakos (2007) 44 *CMLRev* 171. For a very clear example of an agreement where the commercial object predominated over the environmental object, see Case C-281/01 *Commission v Council (Energy Star)* [2002] ECR I-12049.

[170] See above: Opinion 1/75, Opinion 1/78, Case C-45/86.

interpret the then legal basis, Article 113 EC, as extending to the subject-matter of the GATS and the TRIPS, given their inclusion in the WTO package of measures conceived as being broadly concerned with trade. Nevertheless, with a proper concern for the principle of conferral, in Opinion 1/94 the Court declined to do so.[171] The GATS identified four modes for the supply of services:

(1) cross-frontier supply, not involving any movement of persons;
(2) consumption abroad, where the consumer travels to the country of the service supplier;
(3) commercial presence (ie establishment) of a subsidiary or branch in the territory of a WTO member for the purpose of supplying a service; and
(4) 'the presence of natural persons', where a service supplier in one country sends staff to another country to provide services locally to recipients there.

Only mode (1) was found by the Court to be sufficiently similar to trade in goods for this to bring it within the scope of the CCP. The main reason given for holding differently in the case of the other three modes was that the treatment of third-country nationals on crossing the external frontiers of Member States was dealt with by the EC Treaty as an issue separate from commercial policy.[172] The same was true of policy on transport. As for the TRIPS, the Court said that '[i]ntellectual property rights do not relate specifically to international trade; they affect internal trade just as much as, if not more, than international trade'; and it went on to agree with the French government that the Agreement was essentially concerned with strengthening and harmonising the protection of IP.[173]

In an effort partially to reverse Opinion 1/94, a highly complex paragraph (5) was inserted into the then Article 133 EC by the TN. Agreements in the fields of trade in services and the commercial aspects of IP were brought within the scope of CCP competence, but subject to special conditions deviating from its most characteristic features. In particular, competence in these fields was not a priori exclusive and there was a range of situations in which the Council was required to act by unanimity instead of by the normal QMV. In addition, a new paragraph 6(2) identified a number of 'sensitive' service sectors (cultural and audiovisual services, educational services and social and human health services); in these sectors, the Union had no competence to conclude agreements on its own but could only act jointly with the Member States. Fortunately, it is no longer necessary to attempt to unravel the contorted language of these provisions.[174]

Pursuant to Article 207(1) TFEU, trade in services and the commercial aspects of IP are now fully within the scope of the CCP and therefore subject to the Union's exclusive competence—though, as we shall see, in the sensitive service sectors, unanimity remains the voting rule for the Council. A question that inevitably arises is how far the Member

---

[171] [1994] ECR I-5267. Opinion 1/94 met with a storm of criticism. Among the more measured commentaries, see: JHJ Bourgeois, 'The EC in the WTO and Advisory Opinion 1/94: An Ecternach Procession' (1995) 32 *CMLRev* 763; D de la Rochère, 'L'ère des competences partagées—à propos de l'etendue des competence extérieures de la CE', (1995) RMCUE 461; M Hilf, 'The ECJ's Opinion on the WTO—No Surprise, but Wise?' [1995] *EJIL* 245; T Tridimas, 'The WTO and OECD Opinions' in Dashwood and Hillion, above n 60, ch 4.

[172] Opinion 1/94, see paras 44–47.

[173] Paras 56–60.

[174] See M Cremona, 'A Policy of Bits and Pieces: The Common Commercial Policy after Nice' (2001) *CYELS* 61. Para (6) of former Art 133 EC was analysed by the Court of Justice in Opinion 1/08 [2009] ECR I-11129. See also the Opinion of AG Kokott of 26 March 2009 in Case C-13/07 *Commission v Council* (*Vietnam*), which analyses the provisions of para (5) of the Article. No judgment was given in the case, which was removed from the register, following the entry into force of the TL.

States remain individually competent in respect of the GATS and the TRIPS, which were concluded in 1994 as mixed agreements. The answer may lie in the wording of the new Article 207(1), which refers to 'the *conclusion* of . . . agreements relating to trade in goods and services'.[175] It is strongly arguable that Member States' competence remains unimpaired in the case of agreements already in existence when the TL entered into force. However, the issue will become urgent, and controversial, if the Dohar Round is ever completed and there is a new collection of trade agreements to be concluded.

'Commercial aspects of IP' remains an opaque notion, which the TL has done nothing to clarify. There is a great variety of international agreements relating to different forms of IP. Drawing a line between those that fall under Article 207, and therefore within the Union's exclusive competence, and those that do not, may not always be easy. A rule of thumb would be that only IP agreements concluded within a trade policy context, like the TRIPS as part of the WTO package, will belong to the CCP.

(iii) Foreign Direct Investment

FDI connotes a lasting financial interest, on the part of an entity resident in one economy in an enterprise resident in another economy, coupled with involvement in the management or control of the latter by the former; an example would be the building and operation of a car-assembly plant in South Africa by a UK company.[176] It is distinguished from portfolio investment, which connotes a purely financial interest, eg ownership of shares in an overseas enterprise. The practice has developed whereby governments negotiate a set of arrangements providing a mutual guarantee of protection in one country for investors from the other country. The generic term 'bilateral investment treaties' (BITs) is applied to such arrangements. Besides establishing standards for the protection of investors (typically, a guarantee of 'fair and equitable treatment', and against expropriation without compensation), BITs will normally give a right for the resolution, through arbitration before an independent international tribunal, of disputes between the investor and the host state, thereby avoiding the risk of possible bias in the latter's judicial process. It is also the practice of some countries to insist on the inclusion of provisions relating to the liberalisation of foreign investments in BITs that they negotiate.

However, FDI is not a term of art. Practice and possibly litigation will determine whether, for example, the concept enshrined in Article 207(1) extends to an investment in a foreign enterprise which does not secure a controlling interest;[177] or whether it covers liberalisation of investment, as well as the treatment of investors post-establishment. The uncertain scope of FDI competence under Article 207 seems likely to result in a preference for concluding BITs as mixed agreements.

Certain matters falling within the broad concept of FDI were subject to the non-exclusive competence of the EU, even before the TL. Thus the liberalisation of establishment for the purpose of supplying services under mode (3) of the GATS was brought within the scope of the CCP by paragraph (5) of former Article 133. Another example would be the Treaty rules on the free movement of capital and payments.[178] The general principle

---

[175] Emphasis added.
[176] Defined in the economic literature as 'the transfer of capital by a company in one country to another country to create or take over an establishment there which it wants to control': see W Molle, *The Economics of European Integration: Theory, Practice, Policy* (Aldershot, Ashgate, 2006) 125.
[177] An issue canvassed in the German Constitutional Court's ruling of 30 June 2009 relating to the TL.
[178] Arts 63–66 TFEU.

laid down by Article 63 is that all restrictions on the movement of capital and payments between Member States and between Member States and third countries is prohibited; however, there are powers for the EU institutions, under specified conditions, to impose restrictions on the movement of funds to third countries.[179] The overlap between Article 207 and those provisions is attested by the *BITs* cases, which were discussed above in the context of the 'new developments' test of *AETR* exclusivity. No guidance is provided by the Treaty as to which provisions have priority, but it is submitted that precedence should be given to the Articles on the movement of capital and payments, because they relate to one of the four basic EU freedoms.

The conferral on the Union of exclusive competence for FDI, an area in which its competence was formerly non-exclusive or non-existent, raises difficult issues.[180] As in the case of agreements on trade in services and the commercial aspects of IP, the status of pre-existing BITs has probably not been affected. For the future, it is very unlikely that, every time a BIT with a third country is mooted, the Union as a whole will be interested in participating. Arrangements will thus be needed to enable the 'blessing' of the Union to be given to future BITs concluded by individual Member States. There is a useful precedent in Regulation 847/2004 on the negotiation and implementation of air service agreements between Member States and third countries.[181] A Commission proposal, relating also (in our view, unnecessarily) to existing BITs, was before the Council at the time of writing, but appeared to be making little headway.[182] Another difficult issue is the status of intra-Union BITs, concluded at a time before one of the parties acceded to the EU. These are matters that call for extensive analysis, which is beyond the scope of the present volume.[183]

(iv) Transport

Pursuant to Article 207(5) TFEU, the negotiation and conclusion of international agreements in the field of transport remains outside scope of the CCP.

(v) The No-circumvention Rule

Article 207 (6) TFEU provides:

> The exercise of the competences conferred by this Article in the field of the common commercial policy shall not affect the delimitation of competences between the Union and the Member States, and shall not lead to harmonisation of legislative or regulatory provisions of the Member States insofar as the Treaties exclude such harmonisation.

This paragraph reformulates the principle enshrined in the first subparagraph of para-

---

[179] See Art 64(2) and (3) and Art 66 TFEU.

[180] See the Commission's Communication, 'Towards a Comprehensive European International Investment Policy' COM(2010) 343 final.

[181] Regulation No 847/2004/EC of the European Parliament and the Council [2004] OJ L157/7. The Regulation was adopted in the wake of the *Open Skies* cases, where some aspects of the air service agreements in question were found to be caught by the *AETR* principle. It established an authorisation procedure, allowing the practice of Member States' concluding such agreements to continue, under EU supervision.

[182] Commission Proposal for a Regulation of the European Parliament and of the Council establishing transitional arrangements for bilatral investment agreements between Member States and third countries COM(2010) 344 final.

[183] For a fuller analysis, see: FS Benyon, *Direct Investment, National Champions and EU Treaty Freedoms: From Maastricht to Lisbon* (Oxford, Hart Publishing, 2010); M Burgstaller, 'European Law and Investment Treaties' (2009) 26 *Journal of International Arbitration* 181; T Eilsmansberger (2009) 46 *CMLRev* 383; M Krajewski (2005) 42 *CMLRev* 114.

graph (6) of ex-Article 133 EC that, broad as its scope may be, the competence of the EU in the field of the CCP must not be used to circumvent the limits that are placed on Union competence elsewhere in the Treaties.

C – Procedure

Article 207(2) TFEU prescribes the ordinary legislative procedure for the adoption of 'measures defining the framework for implementing the common commercial policy'. This must be done by way of regulations.

The change in procedure is a significant one: previously, there was no formal requirement for the European Parliament to be involved in decision-making for the purposes of the CCP, although it was sometimes consulted on a non-mandatory basis. The notion of a 'framework measure' is not defined and is likely, in practice, to prove elusive. Presumably, it would cover all legislation establishing the general rules governing different aspects of commercial policy, such as any replacement to the Regulation setting up the EU regime for controlling exports of dual-use goods.[184] In contrast to Article 43(3) TFEU (ex-Article 37 EC) on the CAP, Article 207 does not provide specifically for the adoption by the Council, acting on a proposal from the Commission, of measures implementing CCP framework measures. Such measures will, therefore, fall to be adopted in accordance with the general rules on the implementation of legally binding Union acts, which are laid down by Article 291 TFEU. Pursuant to Article 291(2), implementing power can only be reserved for the Council in 'duly justified specific cases'.

The provisions of Article 207(3) relating to the negotiation and conclusion of international agreements in the area of the CCP add very little to those of the procedural code in Article 218 TFEU, to which they cross-refer. They are a survival from earlier versions of the legal basis for the CCP, dating back to the time when the procedural code was much less complete. An additional element is that the European Parliament has been given a legal right to receive regular reports from the Commission on the progress of negotiations.

An issue of some interest is the interaction between Article 207(2) and (3), on the one hand, and Article 218(6)(v), which requires the consent of the European Parliament to be obtained for the conclusion of agreements covering fields to which 'the ordinary legislative procedure applies', on the other. Does it follow that, because the ordinary legislative procedure has to be used in the case of measures that define the *framework* for implementing the CCP, Parliamentary consent is needed for all agreements in this policy area? That would involve a complete reversal of the position prior to the TL, when the relevant Treaty provision specifically excluded CCP agreements from the requirement even to consult the Parliament.[185] It cannot be said that an agreement relating to a particular aspect of the Union's commercial relations with a particular third country covers a field to which the ordinary legislative procedure applies. The better view is that the consent of the Parliament is required only for the conclusion of international agreements of a programmatic nature—a new version of the GATS would be an example of such an agreement. This is another of the results of Lisbon that may have to be litigated before it is settled.

The first subparagraph of Article 207(4) adopts the general rule of Article 218(8), first

---

[184] See Council Regulation (EC) No 428/2009 [2009] ECR L 134/1.
[185] Art 300(3), first subpara EC.

subparagraph, that the Council acts by QMV at the different stages in the negotiation and conclusion of CCP agreements; however, the political sensitivities that led to the establishment of the special regime contained in paragraphs (5) and (6) of former Article 133 EC are addressed by way of the retention of the unanimity rule in the cases referred to in the second and third subparagraphs. The second subparagraph relates to agreements In the fields of trade in services and the commercial aspects of IP, to which agreements relating to foreign direct investment have been added. Here the Council must act by unanimity, where an agreement includes provisions for which unanimity is required for the adoption of internal rules. The third subparagraph provides:

> The Council shall also act unanimously for the negotiation and conclusion of agreements:
> (a) in the field of trade in cultural or audiovisual services, where those agreements risk prejudicing the Union's cultural or linguistic diversity;
> (b) in the field of trade in social, education and health services, where these agreements risk seriously disturbing the national organisation of such services and prejudicing the responsibility of Member States to deliver them.

The sectors there referred to are the same ones as were the subject of the special arrangements provided for by former Article 133(6). The different sets of conditions governing the application of the unanimity rule in those sectors, identified respectively under (a) and (b), were presumably designed to limit the scope of this exception to the normal rule of QMV, but their highly discretionary nature will make it difficult, in practice, to resist claims that the conditions are satisfied.

D – Summing Up on the CCP

The CCP is likely to retain its central role in the external action of the Union. The exclusivity of Union competence and long-established practice mean that this is one policy area in which the EU does undoubtedly present a united front to the world. The new legal framework contained in Article 207 TFEU has removed much of the complexity of managing important areas of trade policy, which resulted from the limitations on the scope of the CCP that came to the fore in Opinion 1/94, and from the half-hearted attempt by the TN to remedy the situation. However, the precise limits of the refurbished and extended CCP remain to be determined. The interface between the CCP and other fields of international relations in which the Union is particularly active, notably that of environmental policy, will surely be contested for a considerable time to come.

VIII – CONCLUDING REMARKS

The TL has created a new constitutional framework for the external action of the European Union, while preserving the particularity of the arrangements applicable to the CFSP. The overlap between CFSP competence and TFEU external competences is likely to be extended, as a result of the suppression of the list of CFSP objectives in former Article 11 TEU and the substitution of a list of objectives common to the whole range of the Union's external action. Preventing turf wars at the interface between CFSP competence and TFEU external competences, such as that for development co-operation, will test the mettle of the newly appointed High Representative. Some provisions of the TFEU sit uneasily with judge-made law on EU implied external competence and on the conditions that render the Union's competence exclusive. It remains to be seen how the Court of Justice will reconcile the new Treaty provisions with its case law. Further constraints on the autonomous external action of Member States are being imposed as a result of recent developments in the duty of close co-operation, to which they are subject in policy areas where competence is shared. The reformed procedural code for the negotiation and conclusion of international agreements rather elegantly accommodates the continuing bipolarity of the organisation of Union external relations. Mixed agreements, jointly concluded by the Union and the Member States, have long been prominent in the practice of EU external relations, and they are likely to continue so in the Lisbon era.

Exclusive EU competence for the common commercial policy has been significantly extended by the TL, including into the economically important area of foreign direct investment, and this remains the field of external action in which the presence of the EU on the world stage is most visible.

The legal and institutional equipment for conducting a truly effective foreign policy for the European Union is in place, but some of it still needs to prove its worth in the heat of action.

Further Reading

P Craig, *The Lisbon Treaty* (Oxford, Oxford University Press, 2010) ch 10.

M Cremona, 'External Relations and External Competence: the Emergence of an Integrated Policy' in P Craig and G de Búrca, *The Evolution of EU Law* (Oxford, Oxford University Press, 1999).

M Cremona and B de Witte (eds), *EU Foreign Relations Law* (Oxford, Hart Publishing, 2008).

A Dashwood and C Hillion (eds), *The General Law of EC External Relations* (London, Sweet & Maxell, 2000).

A Dashwood and M Maresceau (eds), *The Law and Practice of EU External Relations* (Cambridge, Cambridge University Press, 2008).

G de Baere, *Constitutional Principles of EU External Relations* (Oxford, Oxford University Press, 2008).

P Eeckhout, *External Relations of the European Union* (Oxford, Oxford University Press, 2004).

J Heliskoski, *Mixed Agreements as a Technique for Organising the International Relations of the European Community and its Member States* (The Hague, Kluwer, 2001).

C Hillion and P Koutrakos (eds), *Mixed Agreements Revisited* (Oxford, Hart Publishing, 2010).

P Koutrakos, *EU International Relations Law* (Oxford, Hart Publishing, 2006).

R Schütze, 'Supremacy without Pre-emption? The Very Slowly Emergent Doctrine of Community Pre-emption' (2006) 43 *CMLRev* 1023.

——, *From Dual to Cooperative Federalism* (Oxford, Oxford University Press, 2009).

T Tridimas and P Eeckhout, 'The External Competence of the Community and the Case-law of the Court of Justice: Principle versus Pragmatism' (1994) 14 *YEL* 143.

P van Elsuwege, 'EU External Action after the Collapse of the Pillar Structure: In Search of a New Balance between Delimitation and Consistency' (2010) 47 *CMLRev* 987.

28

The Legal Effects of International Agreements

The TFEU makes provision for the EU to conclude international agreements with one or more third countries and with international organisations, and holds that such agreements are binding upon the institutions of the Union and the Member States. The Court of Justice has concluded that provisions of international agreements binding on the EU may be directly effective, and if so capable of being invoked before national courts against the authorities of Member States and other persons or bodies. International agreements that are directly effective may also be relied upon to invalidate incompatible EU secondary legislation. International agreements that lack direct effect may nevertheless be relied upon to invalidate incompatible EU secondary legislation if the secondary legislation in question indicates that such was the intention of the EU legislature. EU secondary legislation is to be interpreted as far as possible so as to be consistent with international agreements binding on the EU, as is national legislation implementing EU legislation.

I – THE DIRECT EFFECT OF INTERNATIONAL AGREEMENTS CONCLUDED BY THE EU

The TFEU makes provision for the conclusion of agreements between the EU and non-Member States.[1] Article 216(2) TFEU provides that: 'Agreements concluded by the Union are binding upon the institutions of the Union and on its Member States.' The stage has long been reached when it could be said that

> an agreement concluded by the Council of the European Union with a non-Member State in accordance with Articles 217 TFEU and 218 TFEU, constitutes, as far as the European Union is concerned, an act of one of the institutions of the Union, within the meaning of point (b) of the first paragraph of Article 267 TFEU; that, from the moment it enters into force, the provisions

---

[1] See generally, Chapter 27, and in particular Art 207 TFEU (common commercial policy), Art 216 TFEU (conclusion of agreements with one or more third countries or international organisations where the Treaties so provide or where the conclusion of an agreement is necessary in order to achieve, within the framework of the Union's policies, one of the objectives referred to in the Treaties, or is provided for in a legally binding Union act or is likely to affect common rules or alter their scope), Art 217 TFEU (association agreements with one or more third countries or international organisations), Art 218 TFEU (procedure for conclusion of agreements with one or more third countries or international organisations).

of such an agreement form an integral part of the legal order of the European Union; and that, within the framework of that legal order, the Court has jurisdiction to give preliminary rulings concerning the interpretation of such an agreement.[2]

Equally, decisions of a Council of Association adopted to give effect to the international agreement under which it was established are regarded as an integral part of the EU legal system.[3]

The Court nevertheless takes account of the international legal character of a treaty when interpreting its provisions and has held that

> an international treaty must be interpreted not solely by reference to the terms in which it is worded but also in the light of its objectives. Article 31 of the Vienna Convention on the Law of Treaties of 23 May 1969 provides in that respect that a treaty is to be interpreted in good faith in accordance with the ordinary meaning to be given to its terms in their context and in the light of its object and purpose.[4]

Appropriately worded provisions of an international agreement between the EU and a non-Member State may have direct effect, but the Court has pointed out that the institutions of the European Union, which have power to negotiate and conclude agreements with non-Member States, are free to agree with those states as to what effect the provisions of the agreement are to have in the internal legal order of the contracting parties. It is only if that question has not been settled by the agreement that it falls to be decided by the courts having jurisdiction in the matter, and in particular by the Court of Justice within the framework of its jurisdiction under the TFEU, in the same manner as any other question of interpretation relating to the application of the agreement in the EU.[5] The Court has held that a provision of an agreement concluded by the EU with non-Member States must be regarded as directly effective when, having regard to its wording and the purpose and nature of the agreement itself, the provision contains a clear and precise obligation which is not subject, in its implementation or effects, to the adoption of any subsequent measure.[6] This invariably involves an analysis of the spirit, general scheme and terms of that agreement.[7] It is irrelevant to the question of direct effect, however, whether an international agreement has been approved by means of a decision or by means of a regulation at the time of its conclusion by the EU.[8]

The Court has held provisions of various agreements between the EU and non-Member States to be directly effective.[9] This conclusion was not inevitable from a legal point of

---

[2] Case C-386/08 *Brita* (CJEU 25 February 2010), para 39; see also Case C-162/96 *Racke* [1998] ECR I-3655, para 41; Case 12/86 *Demirel* [1987] ECR 3719, para 14.

[3] Case 30/88 *Greece v Commission* [1989] ECR 3711, para 12; Case C-192/89 *Sevince* [1990] ECR I-3461, para 9; Case C-242/06 *Sahin* [2009] ECR I-8415, para 62.

[4] Case C-70/09 *Hengartner* (CJEU 15 July 2010), para 36, referring to 'settled case law' and citing, inter alia, Opinion 1/91 [1991] ECR I-6079, para 14; Case C-416/96 *El-Yassini* [1999] ECR I-1209, para 47; Case C-268/99 *Jany and Others* [2001] ECR I-8615, para 35. The Court has noted that 'though the Vienna Convention does not bind either the Community or all its Member States, a series of provisions in that convention reflect the rules of customary international law which, as such, are binding upon the Community institutions and form part of the Community legal order': Case C-386/08 *Brita* (CJEU 25 February 2010), para 42.

[5] Case C-160/09 *Katsivardas* (CJEU 20 May 2010), para 32.

[6] Case C-416/96 *El-Yassini* [1999] ECR I-1209, citing Case 12/86 *Demirel* [1987] ECR 3719, para 14; Case C-18/90 *Kziber* [1991] ECR I-199, para 15; and Case C-162/96 , *Racke* [1998] ECR I-3655, para 31.

[7] Case C-160/09 *Katsivardas* (CJEU 20 May 2010), para 33.

[8] Ibid, para 34.

[9] See eg Case 87/75 *Bresciani* [1976] ECR 129 (Art 2(1) of the Yaoundé Convention); Case 17/81 *Pabst & Richarz* [1982] ECR 1331 (Art 53(1) of the EEC–Greece Association Agreement); Case 104/81 *Kupferberg* [1982] ECR 3641 (Art 21 of the EEC–Portuguese Association Agreement); Case 12/86, *Demirel* [1987] ECR 3719 (Art

view and is open to criticism on policy grounds since it may place EU traders at a disadvantage compared with counterparts in non-Member States. While the latter may invoke provisions of international agreements in their favour before the courts of the Member States, EU traders might be unable to do likewise in those non-Member States which refuse to recognise that such international agreements have direct effect.

The Court of Justice has recognised that such an imbalance in implementation might exist, but has not regarded the failure of national courts in non-Member States to accord direct effect to the provisions of such agreements as amounting to a lack of reciprocity in implementing the agreements in question.[10] It will be seen that the Court has not taken this view of all international agreements to which the EU is a party, and in particular has taken a markedly different view as regards World Trade Organization (WTO) Agreements, and before that to the 1947 General Agreement on Tariffs and Trade (GATT 1947), which are discussed below. In referring to those international agreements, the provisions of which are capable of having direct effect in the EU legal order, the Court has on occasion contrasted those agreements with WTO Agreements, and referred to 'agreements concluded between the Community and non-member countries which introduce a certain asymmetry of obligations, or create special relations of integration with the Community'.[11] This statement of the Court is, however, to be read in context and does not imply that such international agreements are the only ones capable of having direct effect in the EU legal order.

In *Syndicat professionel coordination des pêcheurs de l'étang de Berre et de la région*[12] the Court considered whether a provision of the Protocol for the Protection of the Mediterranean Sea against Pollution from Land-based Sources was directly effective. The Article in issue provided that discharges into the Protocol area 'shall be strictly subject to the issue, by the competent national authorities, of an authorisation taking account of the provisions' of an Annex to the Protocol. In the national proceedings the Syndicat claimed that Electricité de France was discharging water from a hydroelectric power station without having obtained the prior authorisation referred to in the Protocol. The Court reasoned as follows:

> According to the settled case-law of the Court, a provision in an agreement concluded by the Community with a non-member country must be regarded as being directly applicable when, regard being had to its wording and to the purpose and nature of the agreement, the provision contains a clear and precise obligation which is not subject, in its implementation or effects, to the adoption of any subsequent measure.[13]

The Court concluded that the provision in question satisfied this test, was directly effective and could be relied upon by interested parties before the national courts.[14]

---

12 of the EEC–Turkey Association Agreement); Case C-192/89 *Sevince* [1990] ECR I-3461 (certain provisions of certain decisions of the Association Council); Case C-126/95 *Hallouzi-Choho* [1996] ECR I-4807 (Art 41(1) of the EEC–Morocco Cooperation Agreement); Case C-416/96 *El-Yassini* [1999] ECR I-1209 (Art 40(1) of the EEC–Morocco Cooperation Agreement); Case C-97/05 *Gattoussi* [2006] ECR I-11917 (Art 64(1) of the Euro-Mediterranean Agreement).

[10] See Case 104/81 *Kupferberg* [1982] ECR 3641, para 18.

[11] Case C-149/96 *Portugal v Council* [1999] ECR I-8395, citing as an example of such an agreement, the EEC–Portuguese Association Agreement in issue in *Kupferberg*, ibid.

[12] Case C-213/03 *Syndicat professionel coordination des pêcheurs de l'étang de Berre et de la région* [2004] ECR I-7357.

[13] Ibid, para 39.

[14] ibid, paras 40–47.

II – LIMITED LEGAL EFFECTS FOR THE GATT 1947 AND WTO AGREEMENTS

Policy reasons such as those referred to above, that is to say, the potential relative disadvantage of EU economic operators compared with counterparts in non-Member States if international agreements binding on the EU are enforceable in the EU legal order, seem to have carried some weight as regards the legal effects of GATT 1947 and of the WTO Agreements. The Court regarded GATT 1947 as binding on the Community, taking the view that under the EEC Treaty the Community assumed the powers previously exercised by Member States with respect to GATT 1947.[15] However, the Court rejected arguments that direct effect could be attributed to GATT 1947 as regards Article II, Article XI, the Protocols concluded within the framework of GATT 1947, and those provisions of GATT 1947 which determined the effect of those Protocols.[16] The fact that the provisions of GATT 1947 lacked direct effect led the Court to conclude both that individuals were precluded 'from invoking provisions of the GATT before the national courts of a Member State in order to challenge the application of national provisions',[17] and that such provisions could not be invoked to call in question the validity of Community acts.[18]

The Court first explained why provisions of GATT 1947 should not be held to be directly effective in *International Fruit Company*.[19] The Court considered 'the spirit, the general scheme and the terms of the General Agreement'.[20] It noted that the Agreement, which was based on the principle of negotiations, was characterised by the great flexibility of its provisions, in particular those conferring the possibility of derogation, the measures to be taken when confronted with exceptional difficulties, and the settlement of conflicts between the contracting parties.[21] The Court, after examining these features in some detail, concluded that the provision of the Agreement in issue (Article XI of GATT 1947) was not capable of conferring on individuals rights which they could invoke before national courts, and accordingly, that the validity of the Commission Regulations in issue in the national proceedings could not be affected by that provision.[22] Similar reasoning was adopted in subsequent cases.[23] In *Germany v Council (Bananas)* the Court insisted that the features of GATT 1947 which militated against its provisions having direct effect precluded not only those provisions being invoked before a national court to challenge the validity of an EU act, but also precluded such a challenge in a direct action before the European Court.[24]

The WTO Agreement of 1994 included the General Agreement on Trade in Services (GATS) and the Agreement on Trade Related Aspects of Intellectual Property Rights

---

[15] Cases 21-24/72 *International Fruit Company* [1972] ECR 1219; Case 9/73 *Schlüter* [1973] ECR 1135; Cases 267–69 *SPI and SAMI* [1983] ECR 801; Cases 290-291/81 *Compagnia Singer* [1983] ECR 847.

[16] Cases cited in previous footnote.

[17] Case C-469/93 *Chiquita Italia* [1995] ECR I-4533, para 29; see also Cases 267–69 *SPI and SAMI* [1983] ECR 801; Cases 290–91/81 *Compagnia Singer* [1983] ECR 847.

[18] Cases 21–24/72 *International Fruit Company* [1972] ECR 1219; Case 9/73 *Schlüter* [1973] ECR 1135.

[19] Cases 21–24/72 *International Fruit Company* [1972] ECR 1219.

[20] Ibid, para 20.

[21] Ibid, para 21.

[22] Ibid, para 27.

[23] See eg Case 9/73 *Schlüter* [1973] ECR 1135, paras 29, 30; Case C-280/93 *Germany v Council* [1994] ECR I-4973, paras 106–08.

[24] Case C-280/93 *Germany v Council* [1994] ECR I-4973, para 109; see also Case C-469/93 *Chiquita Italia* [1995] ECR I-4533, paras 26–29.

(TRIPs), in addition to GATT 1994 on goods. Council Decision 94/800/EC,[25] by which the EU approved the agreements reached in the Uruguay Round of multilateral nego- tiations, states in the 11th recital to its preamble that 'the Agreement establishing the World Trade Organization, including the Annexes thereto, is not susceptible to being directly invoked in Community or Member State courts'. While a reference in the pream- ble, unaccompanied by any indication to similar effect in the text of the Decision, cannot be of determinative legal significance, the preamble is certainly consistent with the view that neither the Community nor the Member States had any intention of establishing an international legal regime having direct effects.[26] As regards GATS, it should be noted that in their Schedule of Commitments the EU and its Member States have excluded direct effect.[27] It has been suggested that the language of the TRIPs Agreement lends itself to direct effect,[28] and in *Hermès* Advocate General Tesauro considered that the WTO Agreement could be given direct effect on the basis of reciprocity, and that Article 50(6) of TRIPs (concerning judicial revocation or cessation by lapse of time of provisional meas- ures of protection) had direct effect.[29]

In *Portugal v Council*[30] the Court of Justice held that the WTO Agreements are not in principle among the rules in the light of which the Court is to review the legality of meas- ures adopted by the EU institutions. The Court noted that while the WTO Agreements differ significantly from the provisions of GATT 1947, in particular by reason of the strengthening of the system of safeguards and the mechanism for resolving disputes, the system resulting from those agreements 'nevertheless accords considerable importance to negotiation between the parties'.[31] The Court noted that pursuant to the Understanding on Rules and Procedures Governing the Settlement of Disputes, inter alia, if a mem- ber of the WTO fails to fulfil its obligation to implement recommendations and rulings of the dispute-settlement body, it is, if so requested, and on the expiry of a reasonable period at the latest, to enter into negotiations with any party having invoked the dispute- settlement procedures, with a view to finding mutually acceptable compensation.[32] If the courts of members were required to refrain from applying rules of domestic law incon- sistent with the WTO Agreements, this would have the consequence of depriving the legislative or executive organs of the contracting parties of the possibility afforded by the Understanding of entering into negotiated arrangements, even on a temporary basis. The Court also noted that some of the contracting parties, which are among the most impor- tant commercial partners of the EU, have concluded from the subject-matter and purpose

---

[25] [1994] OJ L336/1.

[26] See the Opinion of AG Cosmas in Case C-183/95 *Affish* [1997] ECR I-4315, para 127 (reference in pream- ble not determinative but the Advocate General gives it some weight), and the Opinion of AG Elmer in Joined Cases C-364 /95 and C-365/95 95 *Port* [1998] ECR I-1023 (the Advocate General gives the recital some weight). AG Tesauro in Case C-53/96 *Hermès* [1998] ECR I-3603 states at para 24 of his Opinion that 'the statement in question appears only in the preamble to the Council Decision approving the WTO Agreements, not in the operative part of the Decision, and this significantly reduces its effect, in legal terms, of course'.

[27] The Introductory Note to the Schedule states that '[t]he rights and obligations arising from the GATS, including the schedule of commitments, shall have no self-executing effect and thus confer no rights directly to individual natural persons or juridical persons'. See P Eeckhout, 'The Domestic Legal Status of the WTO Agreement: Interconnecting Legal Systems' (1997) 34 *CMLRev* 11, 34.

[28] Eeckhout, ibid, 33.

[29] Opinion of AG Tesauro, above n 26, esp paras 34–37. The learned Advocate General considered that in the absence of reciprocity Community traders would be placed at a disadvantage compared with their foreign competitors; see para 31 of his Opinion.

[30] Case C-149/96 *Portugal v Council* [1999] ECR I-8395.

[31] Ibid, para 36.

[32] Ibid, paras 36–39.

of the WTO Agreements that they are not among the rules applicable by their courts when reviewing the legality of their rules of domestic law. Significantly, the Court added:

> To accept that the role of ensuring that Community law complies with those rules devolves directly on the Community judicature would deprive the legislative or executive organs of the Community of the scope for manoeuvre enjoyed by their counterparts in the Community's trading partners.[33]

It followed that the WTO Agreements could not be relied upon to review the legality of measures adopted by the EU institutions. The Court noted that the latter interpretation corresponded with the statement in the preamble to Decision 94/800, referred to above, according to which WTO Agreements and Annexes are not susceptible to being directly invoked in the EU or Member State courts.[34] In *Van Parys* the Court held that this conclusion held good even where the Dispute Settlement Body had found EU legislation to be incompatible with WTO rules.[35]

In *Dior*[36] the issue discussed in the Opinion of Advocate General Tesauro in *Hermès*—whether or not Article 50(6) of TRIPs was directly effective—arose for decision. The Court of Justice, referring to its reasoning in *Portugal v Council*, held that: '[T]he provisions of TRIPs, an annex to the WTO Agreement, are not such as to create rights upon which individuals may rely directly before the courts by virtue of Community law.'[37]

III – REVIEW OF EU MEASURES ON THE BASIS OF DIRECTLY EFFECTIVE INTERNATIONAL AGREEMENTS

In *Germany v Council (Bananas)* Germany argued that compliance with GATT 1947 was a condition of the lawfulness of EU acts, regardless of any question as to the direct effect of GATT 1947, and that the contested provision of the Regulation on the common organisation of the market in bananas infringed certain basic provisions of GATT 1947.[38] Advocate General Gulmann agreed that it was possible that an international agreement might be invoked in the context of an application under Article 263 TFEU in spite of the fact does it did not have direct effect. But he added that the position might also be that the reasons militating against the direct effect of an agreement also prevent the agreement from forming part of the legal basis for the Court's review of legality.[39] He thought that this was indeed so in the case of GATT 1947, and that the Court could not be criticised for referring in its previous case law[40] to the 'flexibility' of that agreement, as regards the possibility for contracting parties to negotiate exemptions, the existence of imprecise saving

---

[33] Ibid, para 46.
[34] Ibid, para 49.
[35] Case C-377/02 *Van Parys* [2005] ECR I-1465.
[36] Joined Cases C-300/98 and C-392/98 *Dior* [2000] ECR I-11307.
[37] Ibid, para 44; Case C-245/02 *Anheuser-Busch* [2004] ECR I-10989, para 54.
[38] Case C-280/93 *Germany v Council* [1994] ECR I-4973, para 103.
[39] Ibid, Opinion, para 137.
[40] Cases such as Joined Cases 21-24/72 *International Fruit Company* [1972] ECR1219; Case 9/73 *Schlüter* [1973] ECR 1135.

clauses, and the special rules for settling disputes.[41] In these circumstances he considered that GATT 1947 could not be directly relied upon in a challenge to validity under Article 263 TFEU. A contrary conclusion might alter the character of the obligations incumbent on the EU within the framework fixed by GATT 1947 itself.[42] The Court's judgment is framed in terms which suggest similar thinking to that of the Advocate General, that is to say, that the features of GATT 1947 which ruled out direct effect for its provisions, also ruled out those provisions providing a basis for review of the legality of EU acts. The Court, referring to its previous case law,[43] held:[44]

> Those features of GATT, from which the Court concluded that an individual within the Community cannot invoke it in a court to challenge the lawfulness of a Community act, also preclude the Court from taking provisions of GATT into consideration to assess the lawfulness of a regulation in an action brought by a Member State under the first paragraph of Article 173 of the Treaty.
>
> The special features noted above show that the GATT rules are not unconditional and that an obligation to recognize them as rules of international law which are directly applicable in the domestic legal systems of the contracting parties cannot be based on the spirit, general scheme or terms of GATT.

It will be recalled that the Court concluded in *Portugal v Council*, referred to above, that, having regard to their nature and structure, the WTO Agreements could not be relied upon to review the legality of measures adopted by the EU institutions. This case is susceptible to the same analysis as *Germany v Council*, namely that direct effect of an international agreement is not as such a precondition to invoking that agreement as a basis for review of an EU act, but the nature and structure of an agreement may rule out enforcement of its provisions within the EU legal order, whether such enforcement is sought, for example, by individuals in national proceedings seeking to challenge national rules, or by individuals or Member States seeking to challenge the validity of EU rules.

In *Netherlands v Parliament and Council (Biotech)* the Netherlands challenged a Directive on the legal protection of biotechnological inventions on a number of grounds, one of which was that the obligations created by the Directive for Member States were incompatible with those resulting from their international obligations, that is to say, certain WTO Agreements, and the Convention on Biological Diversity 1992 (CBD), which had been approved by the European Community by a Council Decision of 1993. The sole point of interest of this case for present purposes is the Court's response to the Council's argument that the legality of an EU act could only be called in question on grounds of a breach of an international agreement to which the Community was a party if the provisions of the agreement had direct effect, which was not the case as regards the WTO agreements and the CBD. Advocate General Jacobs argued in his Opinion that direct effect was perhaps not the correct test to apply and that

> it might be thought that it is in any event desirable as a matter of policy for the Court to be able to review the legality of Community legislation in the light of treaties binding the Community. There is no other court which is in a position to review Community legislation; thus if this Court

---

[41] Case C-280/93 *Germany v Council* [1994] ECR I-4973, Opinion, paras 138, 144.
[42] Ibid, Opinion, para 145.
[43] Cases such as Joined Cases 21-24/72 *International Fruit Company* [1972] ECR1219; Case 9/73 *Schlüter* [1973] ECR 1135.
[44] Case C-280/93 *Germany v Council* [1994] ECR I-4973, paras 109, 110.

is denied competence, Member States may be subject to conflicting obligations with no means of resolving them.[45]

He accordingly proposed to consider the substance of the Netherlands' arguments concerning the alleged infringement by the Directive of various international obligations of the Member States notwithstanding the Council's submission to the effect that the agreements in question were not directly effective.[46] The Court rejected the submissions of the Netherlands as regards the WTO Agreements on the basis of its previous case law to the effect that those agreements were not 'in principle, having regard to their nature and structure, among the rules in the light of which the Court is to review the lawfulness of measures adopted by the Community institutions'.[47] However, it dealt as follows with the argument as regards the CBD:

> Even if, as the Council maintains, the CBD contains provisions which do not have direct effect, in the sense that they do not create rights which individuals can rely on directly before the courts, that fact does not preclude review by the courts of compliance with the obligations incumbent on the Community as a party to that agreement.[48]

The Court examined on the merits the contention of the Netherlands, and of Norway, intervening, that the purpose of the Directive in issue ran counter to one of the objectives of the CBD, and concluded that the contention should be rejected. This case seems not so much to represent a change of course by the Court, to the effect that direct effect of an agreement is no longer a prerequisite for reliance upon that agreement to challenge the validity of an EU act, as a confirmation that an agreement might, by virtue of its nature and structure, provide a basis for the review of Community acts, even if the agreement lacks the characteristics of direct effect.

In *IATA* the Court considered the compatibility of Regulation (EC) No 261/2004 on compensation for airline passengers with certain provisions of the Montreal Convention for the Unification of Certain Rules for International Carriage by Air. The Court held that international agreements 'prevail over provisions of secondary legislation'[49] and that the Articles of the Montreal Convention in issue

> are among the rules in the light of which the Court reviews the legality of acts of the Community institutions since, first, neither the nature nor the broad logic of the Convention precludes this and, second those three articles appear, as regards their content, to be unconditional and sufficiently precise.[50]

Whether this formulation refers to criteria for assessing the legality of EU acts which are distinct from those which determine direct effect, or implies that those criteria are so similar to those which determine direct effect as to deprive the question of significance is not really clear.[51] The Court in the event found no inconsistency between the Regulation in issue and the Montreal Convention.

In *Intertanko* the Court considered whether an EC Directive dealing with ship-source

---

[45] Ibid, Opinion, para 147.
[46] ibid, Opinion, para 148.
[47] Case C-377/98 *Netherlands v Parliament and Council* [2001] ECR I-7079, para 52.
[48] Ibid, para 54.
[49] Case C-344/04 *IATA* [2006] ECR I-403, para 35.
[50] Ibid, para 39.
[51] For the former view, see M Mendez, 'The Enforcement of EU Agreements: Bolstering the Effectiveness of Treaty Law' (2010) 47 *CMLRev* 1719, 1748, citing K Lenaerts and T Corthaut, 'Of Birds and Hedges: The Role of Primacy in Invoking Norms of EU Law' (2006) 31 *ELRev* 287, 299.

pollution was compatible with provisions of the United Nations Convention on the Law of the Sea.[52] The Court noted that international agreements have primacy over EU secondary legislation, and that the validity of such legislation might be affected by incompatibility with such rules of international law,[53] in cases where the EU was bound by the rules of international law in question.[54] The Court repeated its formulation in *IATA* that the Court could examine the validity of EU legislation in the light of an international treaty only where the nature and broad logic of the latter do not preclude this and, in addition, the treaty's provisions appear, as regards their content, to be unconditional and sufficiently precise.[55] The Court proceeded to apply this analysis to the relevant provisions of UNCLOS. However, the Court found that:

> UNCLOS does not establish rules intended to apply directly and immediately to individuals and to confer upon them rights or freedoms capable of being relied upon against States, irrespective of the attitude of the ship's flag State.
>
> It follows that the nature and broad logic of UNCLOS prevent the Court from being able to assess the validity of a Community measure in the light of that Convention.[56]

Whatever the possible readings of the Court's previous case law, this judgment of the Grand Chamber in *Intertanko* makes it clear that international agreements can only be relied upon as a measure of the legality of EU acts if they give rise to rights in individuals—that is to say, if they are directly effective. Mendez comments that the 'general immunization of EU norms from review *vis-à-vis* UNCLOS, reflects badly on the EU's carefully cultivated image of fidelity to international law'.[57] Eeckhout favours a rights-based test in this context, though he does not think it is applied very persuasively in *Intertanko*. On the other hand, he thinks that the Court is right to be wary of allowing broad challenges to EU legislation based on alleged incompatibility with international law. He notes: 'In substance, judicial review of general legislation is constitutional in nature, and the institutional balance between the legislature and judiciary does not necessarily justify strict judicial review.'[58] The present writer would add that policy and indeed political considerations play a role in determinations by the EU institutions as to the freedom of action allowed to them by international agreements by which they are bound, and that this argues for an appropriate degree of judicial restraint on the part of the Court of Justice.

IV – THE *NAKAJIMA* EXCEPTION: REVIEW OF EU MEASURES ON THE BASIS OF NON-DIRECTLY EFFECTIVE INTERNATIONAL AGREEMENTS

Provisions of an international agreement which do not have direct effect may nevertheless be invoked to review the legality of an EU measure where EU legislation expressly or

---

[52] Case C-308/06 'Intertanko' [2008] ECR I-4057.
[53] Ibid, paras 42, 43.
[54] Ibid, para 44.
[55] Ibid, para 45.
[56] Ibid, 64, 65.
[57] Mendez, above n 51, 1751.
[58] P Eeckhout, 'Interntanko' (2009) 45 *CMLRev* 2054, 2055.

impliedly so provides. The cases which support this proposition have involved claims to invoke GATT 1947 or WTO Agreements but it would seem to be a proposition of general application. The Court held in *Fediol* that the definition in a common commercial policy Regulation of 'illicit commercial practices' as 'any international trade practices attributable to non-member countries which are incompatible with international law or with the generally accepted rules'[59] had the consequence that individuals could rely on provisions of the GATT in order to obtain a ruling on whether conduct contained in a complaint lodged under the relevant Regulation constituted an illicit commercial practice within the meaning of that Regulation. The Court noted that the 'GATT provisions form part of the rules of international law to which . . . that regulation refers, as is borne out by the second and fourth recitals in its preamble, read together'.[60] Again, in *Nakajima*, the Court held that where the EU adopts legislation in order to comply with the international obligations of the EU, such as GATT 1947 and its Anti-Dumping Code, the Court will regard provisions of that legislation which are inconsistent with those international obligations as being covered by the words 'infringement of this Treaty or of any rule of law relating to its application' which appear as a ground of annulment in Article 263 TFEU.[61] In *Germany v Council (Bananas)* the Court of Justice confirmed—citing *Fediol* and *Nakajima*—that since GATT 1947 lacked direct effect, it was only if the Community intended to implement a particular obligation entered into within the framework of GATT, or if the Community act expressly referred to specific provisions of GATT, that the Court could review the legality of the Community act in question from the point of view of the GATT rules.[62] The Court has applied similar reasoning as regards WTO Agreements.[63] The *Fediol/Nakajima* principle has been applied in a number of cases.[64] The Commission argued in *Egenberger*[65] that the Court should replace the '*Nakajima* exception' with the principle that Community measures should be interpreted consistently with international law. Advocate General Geelhoed rejected this argument. He considered that the scope of the exception was unclear. He thought it artificial to confine its application to cases where the preamble of EU legislation revealed an intent to implement a WTO obligation, and considered it should also apply where such an intent clearly appeared from a comparison between the content of the contested EU provision and that of the WTO obligation in issue.[66] The Court of Justice did not address the point.

---

[59] Art 2(1) of Council Regulation No 2641/84 on the strengthening of the common commercial policy with regard in particular to protection against illicit commercial practices [1984] OJ L252/1; repealed by Council Regulation No 3286/94 [1994] OJ L349/71.

[60] Case 70/87 *Fediol* [1989] ECR 1781, paras 19 and 20.

[61] Case C-69/89 *Nakajima* [1991] ECR I-2069, paras 29–31.

[62] Case C-280/93 *Germany v Council* [1994] ECR I-4973, para 111.

[63] Case C-149/96 *Portugal v Council* [1999] ECR I-8395, para 49; Case C-307/99 *OGT* [2001] ECR I-3159, para 27.

[64] See eg Case C-76/00 *Petrotub* [2003] ECR I-79 (validity of EU anti-dumping legislation in light of anti-dumping code); Case C-352/96 *Italy v Council* [1998] ECR I-6937 (legality of Council Regulation on tariff quotas for imports of rice in light of Art XXIV(6) of the GATT and the Understanding on the Interpretation of Art XXIV of the GATT).

[65] Case C-313/04 *Egenberger* [2006] ECR I-633.

[66] Ibid, Opinion, paras 62–66.

V – EXTENSION OF THE *NAKAJIMA* EXCEPTION TO THE REVIEW OF EU MEASURES ON THE BASIS OF CUSTOMARY INTERNATIONAL LAW

In *Racke*[67] the approach taken by the Court in *Nakajima*[68] (EU secondary legislation subject to an international agreement where this is the intention of the EU legislature) was extended to principles of customary international law reflected in the provisions of the Vienna Convention on the Law of Treaties. The plaintiff in the national proceedings challenged the validity of an EEC Regulation suspending trade concessions under the EEC–Yugoslavia Cooperation Agreement on the ground that such suspension was inconsistent with relevant provisions of the Vienna Convention on the Law of Treaties. These provisions referred to the doctrine of *rebus sic stantibus*, whereby a party may unilaterally terminate a treaty in the event of a fundamental change of circumstances. It appeared from the preamble to the suspension regulation that it was based on the conviction of the Council that a 'radical change in the conditions' under which the Co-operation Agreement had been concluded had occurred. The Court of Justice, purporting to apply *Nakajima* by analogy, denied that the case concerned the direct effect of rules of international law, and emphasised that the case concerned a regulation which had been taken pursuant to the relevant rules of international law, and could thus be challenged if the Council made manifest errors of assessment concerning the conditions for applying those rules; the Court concluded that no such manifest errors had been made. The present writer considers that *Racke* stretches the principles applied by the Court in *Nakajima* too far, even if the standard of review adopted by the Court was not excessively intrusive. The latter case can be justified on the basis of the proposition that non-directly effective provisions of international agreements may nevertheless govern the scope of EU legislation where that is the intention of the EU legislature. The reference to a 'radical change of conditions' in the preamble to the regulation is not of itself a convincing indication of a legislative intention to condition the efficacy of the regulation on a judicial assessment of its compatibility with international law. Moreover, the considerations referred to in *Portugal v Council*, above, and based in that case on the Understanding on Rules and Procedures Governing the Settlement of Disputes, to the effect that allowing reliance upon WTO Agreements to challenge the legality of measures adopted by the EU institutions would have the consequence of depriving legislative and executive organs of contracting parties of the possibility of entering into negotiated arrangements, are not without relevance to a context such as that in issue in *Racke*. Differences of opinion between states as regards their respective rights and obligations in international law are normally resolved by negotiation, unless the parties have consented in advance to international adjudication, or consent to such adjudication in the circumstances of the particular case. For the Court of Justice to act, in effect, as a form of compulsory international adjudication in such cases could place the EU and its Member States at a disadvantage when dealing with third countries with no comparable internal judicial constraints on their action.

---

[67] Case C-162/96 *Racke* [1998] ECR I-3655.
[68] Case C-69/89 *Nakajima* [1991] ECR I-2069.

VI – INTERPRETATION OF EU MEASURES IN LIGHT OF INTERNATIONAL AGREEMENTS AND CUSTOMARY INTERNATIONAL LAW

It is to be noted that provisions of international agreements, such as GATT 1947 and the WTO Agreements, which are not directly effective, may be taken into account in interpreting relevant provisions of EU legislation.[69] For example, in *Commission v Germany (IDA)* the Court of Justice considered an argument that provisions of an EC inward processing Regulation precluded the application of the measures provided for by the International Dairy Agreement, an agreement concluded under GATT 1947. The Court stated that:

> [T]he primacy of international agreements concluded by the Community over provisions of secondary Community legislation means that such provisions must, so far as is possible, be interpreted in a manner that is consistent with those agreements.[70]

Similarly, in *Retuerta*, the Court held that provisions of Regulation (EC) No 40/94 on the Community trade mark are to be interpreted, as far as possible, in the light of the wording of the TRIPs Agreement.[71]

The Court has also referred to principles of customary international law for the purpose of interpreting EU measures. In *Poulsen and Diva Navigation* the Court considered the terms of an EEC Regulation laying down technical measures on the conservation of fishery resources, noting that:

> As a preliminary point, it must be observed, first, that the European Community must respect international law in the exercise of its powers and that, consequently, Article 6 abovementioned must be interpreted, and its scope limited, in the light of the relevant rules of the international law of the sea.
>
> In this connexion, account must be taken of the Geneva Conventions of 29 April 1958 on the Territorial Sea and Contiguous Zone . . . and on Fishing and Conservation of the Living Resources of the High Seas . . . , in so far as they codify general rules recognized by international custom, and also of the United Nations Convention of 10 December 1982 on the Law of the Sea. . . . It has not entered into force, but many of its provisions are considered to express the current state of customary international maritime law.[72]

---

[69] Case 92/71 *Interfood* [1972] ECR 231, para 6 (GATT agreements relevant to interpretation of common external tariff); Case C-79/89 *Brown Boveri* [1991] ECR I-1853, paras 15–19 (decision of GATT Committee on Customs Valuation relevant to interpretation of EEC Regulation on customs value); Case C-70/94 *Werner* [1995] ECR I-3819, para 23; and Case C-83/94 *Leifer* [1995] ECR I-3231, para 24 (interpretation of EC Export Regulation under Common Commercial Policy in light of GATT).

[70] Case 61/94 *Commission v Germany* [1996] ECR I-3989, para 52; see also eg Case C-286/02 *Bellio Flli* [2004] ECR I-3465, para 33; Case C-311/04 *Algemene Scheeps Agentuur Dordrecht* [2006] ECR I-609, para 25; and Joined Cases C-447/05 and C-448/05 *Thomson and Vestel France* [2007] ECR I-2049, para 30.

[71] Case C-237/08 *Retuerta* (CJEU 11 May 2010), para 67; see also Case C-428/08 *Monsanto* (CJEU 6 July 2010) (interpretation of Art 9 of Directive 98/44/EC on the legal protection of biotechnological inventions in the light of the TRIPs Agreement).

[72] Case C-286/90 *Poulsen and Diva Navigation* [1992] ECR I-6019, paras 9, 10. The 1982 Convention has since entered into force, but the text of the judgment cited indicates that the Court of Justice is taking account of the Treaties cited as evidence of customary international law, and that it is the relevant principles of customary international law in light of which it is interpreting Community law.

VII – NATIONAL COURTS MUST INTERPRET NATIONAL LAW IN LIGHT OF NON-DIRECTLY EFFECTIVE PROVISIONS OF INTERNATIONAL AGREEMENTS BINDING ON THE EU

In *Hermès*[73] the Court applied by analogy the principle applied in *Poulsen and Diva Navigation* and *Commission v Germany (IDA)* to national rules implementing Community rules falling with the scope of the TRIPs Agreement. Article 50 of the latter Agreement provides that judicial authorities shall have the authority to order prompt and effective provisional measures. TRIPs is a 'mixed' agreement, falling with the scope of both Community competence and national competence, and was adopted by the Community and the Member States jointly. Article 50 only falls within EU competence to the extent that it covers subject-matter over which the EU has exercised internal competence. Under Article 99 of Regulation (EC) No 40/94 on the Community trade mark,[74] rights arising from a Community trade mark may be safeguarded by the adoption of 'provisional, including protective measures.' The Court reasoned as follows:

> [S]ince the Community is a party to the TRIPs Agreement and since the agreement applies to the Community trade mark, the courts referred to in Article 99 of Regulation (EC) No 40/94, when called upon to apply national rules with a view to ordering provisional measures for the protection of rights arising under a Community trade mark, are required to do so, as far as possible in the light of the wording and purpose of Article 50 of the TRIPs Agreement.[75]

In the above passage, the Court holds that the duty of consistent interpretation is incumbent upon national courts when they are protecting rights under *EU trade mark law*. The rationale is that since relevant EU rules must be interpreted in accordance with treaties such as TRIPs, national rules implementing those EU rules must be similarly interpreted by national courts. In *Dior*[76] the Court cites the above paragraph for a rather broader proposition—that the duty of consistent interpretation applies, not just in the field of the *Community* trade mark, but in *the field of trade marks*.[77] In *Schieving-Nijstad*[78] Advocate General Jacobs confessed that it is not easy to understand why EU law governs the effects of Article 50 of the TRIPs Agreement not only where a Community trade mark is involved but also in situations concerning national trade marks.[79] The Court's extension of its reasoning in *Hermès* to cover national trade marks has been criticised.[80]

In *Dior* the Court contrasted the duty of consistent interpretation of national courts in a field to which TRIPs applies and in respect of which the EU has already legislated ('as is the case with the field of trade marks') with their obligations in a field in which TRIPs applies but in respect of which the EU has not yet legislated and which consequently falls within the competence of Member States. In the latter situation:

---

[73] Case C-53/96 *Hermès* [1998] ECR I-3603.
[74] [1994] OJ L11/1.
[75] Case C-53/96 *Hermès* [1998] ECR I-3603, para 28.
[76] Joined Cases C-300/98 and C-392/98 *Dior* [2000] ECR I-11307.
[77] Ibid, para 47.
[78] Case C-89/99 *Schieving-Nijstad* [2001] ECR I-5851.
[79] Ibid, Opinion, para 40.
[80] P Eeckhout, *External Relations of the European Union* (Oxford, Oxford University Press, 2004) 242.

[T]he protection of intellectual property rights, and measures adopted for that purpose by the judicial authorities, do not fall within the scope of Community law. Accordingly, Community law neither requires nor forbids that the legal order of a Member State should accord to individuals the right to rely directly on the rule laid down by Article 50(6) of TRIPs or that it should oblige the courts to apply that rule of their own motion.

The above wording is a little curious. The contrast made by the Court is between the duty of national courts when acting within the scope of EU law on the one hand, and outside the scope of EU law on the other. As regards the first situation, the Court refers to the application of national rules in light of Article 50(6) of TRIPs; as regards the second situation the Court refers to the right of individuals to rely directly on Article 50(6) and the obligation of courts to apply that rule. The contrast is asymmetrical. Nevertheless, it seems that the conclusion which is to be drawn is that the legal effects of Article 50 of the TRIPs Agreement in a field in respect of which the Community has not yet legislated are to be determined by national law rather than Community law.[81] In *Merck Genéricos* the Court considered Article 33 of the TRIPs Agreement (a minimum 20 year period of patent protection), noted that no EU legislation existed in that field, and concluded that Member States were free to choose whether or not to give direct effect to that provision.[82]

VIII – THE JURISDICTION OF THE COURT OF JUSTICE TO INTERPRET MIXED AGREEMENTS

As noted at the beginning of this chapter, an agreement concluded by the Council with a non-Member State(s) in accordance with the TFEU is an act of an EU institution, and the provisions of such an agreement form an integral part of EU law. It follows that the Court of Justice has jurisdiction to interpret such agreements. As is apparent from the cases considered above, a potential difficulty in regarding all provisions of all international agreements between the EU and non-Member States as part of the EU legal order is that while some such agreements fall within the competence of the EU and the EU alone, others fall partly within EU competence and partly within national competence, and are concluded by both the EU and the Member States. The latter are described as mixed agreements. In *Demirel*[83] the Court considered the scope of a mixed agreement— the EEC–Turkey Association Agreement. Germany and the United Kingdom objected to the jurisdiction of the Court to interpret the provisions on freedom of movement for workers, since granting freedom of movement to nationals of non-Member States fell within national competence rather than Community competence. The Court rejected this argument on the ground that freedom of movement for workers fell within Community competence,[84] and the fact that it also involved the exercise of national competence did not exclude its jurisdiction to interpret the provisions in question. There must be a real

---

[81] Case C-89/99 *Schieving-Nijstad* [2001] ECR I-5851, Opinion of AG Jacobs, para 39; Eeckhout, above m 80, 243: 'In cases coming within the scope of national law, whether or not there is direct effect or consistent interpretation or any other type of effect, depends on national law.'

[82] Case C-431/05 *Merck Genéricos* [2007] ECR I-7001, paras 34, 35, 39, 40.

[83] Case 12/86 *Demirel* [1987] ECR 3719.

[84] Ibid, para 9 of the Court's judgment. An unconvincing argument, since the provisions of the Treaty on the free movement of workers apply only to nationals of Member States.

question as to the competence of the Court of Justice to interpret provisions of a mixed agreement falling solely within national competence, and in principle the Court of Justice lacks jurisdiction to interpret such provisions.[85]

The position is not, however, as simple as that. It follows from the reasoning in *Hermès* that where a provision of a mixed agreement could apply both to situations falling within the scope of national law, and to situations falling within the scope of EU law, the Court can interpret the provision, whatever the circumstances in which it is to apply.[86] And it follows from *Dior* that national courts and the EU courts, in pursuance of their duty of close mutual co-operation, must, for legal and practical reasons, give such provisions a uniform interpretation.[87] The Court adds that it is only the Court of Justice itself which 'acting in cooperation with the courts and tribunals of the Member States pursuant to Article [267 TFEU] is in a position to ensure such uniform interpretation'.[88] In *Merck Genéricos* the Court indicated that interpretation of a mixed agreement for the purpose of determining the sharing of competence between the EU and the Member States was a matter solely for the Court.[89]

IX – CONCLUDING REMARKS

International agreements concluded by the EU are treated by the Court as acts of institutions with the potential both to bind national authorities and other persons and bodies, and to invalidate incompatible EU legislation. However, the Court has felt it necessary to apply a fairly robust 'filter' to prevent too ready recourse to international agreements as a basis for challenging EU secondary legislation. The Court's case law has seemed at times to draw a distinction between the characteristics of an agreement which might permit reliance upon it to invalidate incompatible EU legislation, and the requirement that the agreement have direct effect. In *Intertanko*, however, the Court confirmed that the direct effect of an agreement, in the sense of a capacity to give rise to individual rights, is indeed a prerequisite to reliance upon that agreement to invalidate incompatible EU legislation. This clarification by the Court has been both welcomed and criticised, but some sort of 'filter' in this context is probably necessary, and a requirement of direct effect seems justified.

Further Reading

P Eeckhout, *External Relations of the European Union* (Oxford, Oxford University Press, 2004) esp chs 8 and 9.

——, 'Interntanko' (2009) 45 *CMLRev* 2054.

---

[85] For an interesting discussion, see AG Tesauro in Case C-53/96 *Hermès* [1998] ECR I-3603, paras 10–21 of his Opinion; a discussion of the position as regards TRIPs, but one which raises more general issues of principle.

[86] Case C-53/96 *Hermès* [1998] ECR I-3603, para 32. Ibid, para 38.

[87] Joined Cases C-300/98 and C-392/98 *Dior* [2000] ECR I-11307, para 37.

[88] Ibid, para 38.

[89] Case C-431/05 *Merck Genéricos* [2007] ECR I-7001, paras 34–37.

P Kuijper and M Bronckers, 'WTO Law in the European Court of Justice' (2005) 42 *CMLRev* 1313.

M Mendez, 'The Enforcement of EU Agreements: Bolstering the Effectiveness of Treaty Law' (2010) 47 *CMLRev* 1719.

Index

Introductory Note

References such as '178–9' indicate (not necessarily continuous) discussion of a topic across a range of pages. Wherever possible in the case of topics with many references, these have either been divided into sub-topics or only the most significant discussions of the topic are listed. Because the entire work is about 'EU law', the use of this term (and certain others which occur constantly throughout the book) as an entry point has been minimised. Information will be found under the corresponding detailed topics.

AAC (average avoidable cost) 785, 789, 796
abolition of restrictions 462, 470, 541–4, 558–9, 626, 631, 660
abstentions 45, 904, 934
abuse of dominance 706, 719, 754, 765–807
  definition of abuse 781–806
accession 10–11, 16–18, 30, 125–6, 340–2, 354, 528–9
  negotiations 17–18, 341–2, 354
accidents 191, 282, 473, 480, 505, 514, 716
accountability 19, 26, 53, 73, 95, 121, 900
accountants 601, 749
accounts, annual 576, 680–1, 685
actions for damages 64, 189–200, 308–9, 841
  case law after *Bergaderm* 195–8
  damage and causation 198–9
  and limitation 199–200
  Schöppenstedt formula 191–6
actions for failure to act 141, 159, 182–9, 205
  standing 185–7
acts, legality of 135, 153–4, 158, 225, 365, 957–61, 963
adaptation periods 633–4, 637–8, 640, 642, 644
administration of justice 156, 295, 299, 379, 642–3
administrative co-operation 83, 85, 104, 599–600, 931
  division of supervisory tasks 611–12
  Services Directive 611–19
administrative decisions 167, 272, 290–2, 313, 331, 832
administrative formalities 477–8
administrative phase 137, 141 *see also* pre-litigation procedure
administrative simplification, Services Directive 600, 616–19
advertising 107–8, 415–16, 423, 425–7, 444–5, 552, 621
  by regulated professions 610
  rules 423–4, 426
Advocates General, and fundamental rights 352–3
AETR 911–17, 920–2, 924, 926–33, 940, 948
AFSJ *see* Area of Freedom, Security and Justice agreements
  anti-competitive *see* anti-competitive agreements
  association 346, 553, 901, 910–11, 937, 953, 955

conclusion of 48, 84, 902, 938, 949–50, 953
  inter-institutional 12, 54, 59–60, 98, 937
  mixed 899, 935, 937–41, 947, 951, 965–7
  multilateral 719, 911, 934
  restrictive 706, 746, 756, 759, 763
agreements between undertakings 719, 729–30, 734–5
agricultural policy, common 8, 10, 167, 194, 196, 326, 331
agricultural products 146, 258, 333, 377, 449, 570
air transport 75–6, 795, 925–6
Altmark ruling 851, 853, 863–5
amendment, power of 78–9, 92
annual accounts 576, 680–1, 685
annulment 153–5, 157–67, 172–3, 177–8, 184, 186–8, 190–1
  effect 180–2
annulment actions 122, 147, 153–82
  acts susceptible of judicial review 156–60
  effect of annulment 180–2
  standing of non-privileged applicants 162–80
  standing of privileged and semi-privileged applicants 160–2
  time limit 155–6
anti-competitive agreements 253, 315, 730–63
  national legislation favouring 891–2
anti-competitive effects 741, 743–6, 772, 784, 786, 797, 806
anti-competitive objects 742–3, 784
applicants
  non-privileged 155, 160, 162, 172–3, 186–7
  privileged 155, 160–1, 202
  semi-privileged 155, 160–1
appreciable effects on competition and on trade between member states 752–4
aptitude tests 633–4, 636–7, 642, 644
Area of Freedom, Security and Justice (AFSJ) 32, 34, 44, 102, 126–7, 317, 900
assistance, mutual 4, 587, 607, 612, 614–15
association, freedom of 367, 374
association agreements 346, 553, 901, 910–11, 937, 953, 955
associations of undertakings 717, 729–30, 749, 816–17, 827, 891
  decisions of 734–5

attestations of competence 632–3
authorisation
    prior 367, 549, 564, 664, 667, 683, 694
    Services Directive 602–4
AVC *see* average variable cost
average avoidable cost *see* AAC
    average variable cost (AVC) 785, 788–9

balance, inter-institutional 65–7, 89, 95–6, 112, 131
barriers to market entry/expansion 777–8
benefit to consumers 757–8
best interests 373, 485, 689, 698
bidding companies 661, 694–7
binding acts 69, 100–1, 104, 157, 918, 922, 932–3
biological resources 100, 102–3, 915, 922, 924, 932
block exemptions 717–18, 729, 742, 755, 759–62,
    811–12, 848–9
branches 450, 532–4, 574–6, 592, 648–51, 660, 680–2
    networks of 551, 659
Budgetary Treaties 11
burden of proof 306, 316, 438, 440, 756, 771, 797
business activities 171–2, 283, 538, 549, 649–50, 674,
    818–19
    business secrets 739, 822–3

CAP *see* common agricultural policy
capacity, legal 237, 251, 652
capital movement 592, 595, 647, 662–3, 665–8, 670,
    673–4
capital requirements 87, 575, 650, 652–5
cartels 730–63
Cassis de Dijon ruling 102, 297, 407, 411–15, 418–
    19, 441–2, 459
causation, and damage 198–9
CCP *see* common commercial policy
CCT *see* common customs tariff
certainty, legal 36, 149–50, 181–2, 272–3, 298–301,
    327–9, 679–80
CFI *see* Court of First Instance
CFR *see* Charter of Fundamental Rights
CFSP *see* Common Foreign and Security Policy
charges having equivalent effect 4, 236, 245, 391–4,
    396, 401–2, 446
Charter of Fundamental Rights (CFR) 23, 33–5,
    340–1, 359–87, 809–10, 815–16, 832–3
    background 359–61
    horizontal provisions 382–6
    Preamble 362–3
    structure 361–2
    substantive provisions 363–82
    UK and Polish Protocol 386–7
children 368, 373, 376, 425, 476–7, 489–91, 525–8
citizens, inactive 466–8, 474–6, 482
citizenship, Union *see* Union citizenship
close co-operation, duty of 899, 933–6, 951
co-decision procedure 14, 16, 73, 76–8, 80, 89, 94–5
co-operation
    administrative *see* administrative co-operation
    close *see* close co-operation
    enhanced *see* enhanced co-operation
    judicial 18–19, 65, 72, 77, 120, 317, 900
    police 15, 211, 230, 900
co-operation agreements, and competition law 722–4

co-operation procedure 76–8, 112
co-ordination of national qualifications 625–45
    by Community rules 630–9
collective dominance 779–81
comitology system 87–91
commercial interests 172, 252, 495, 767, 789, 799
Commission 49–56, 59–61, 86–96, 135–61, 163–202,
    328–34, 392–404
    conduct of competition proceedings 814–26
    President 44, 52–3, 56, 60–1, 72
    right to alter/withdraw proposals 91–2
Committee of Permanent Representatives of the
    Governments of the Member States *see*
    COREPER
common agricultural policy (CAP) 8, 10, 167, 194,
    196, 326, 331
common commercial policy (CCP) 101, 901, 904,
    917, 921–3, 935–6, 941–51
common customs tariff (CCT) 8, 383, 392, 405
    and external relations 405–6
Common Foreign and Security Policy (CFSP) 33–4,
    55, 83–4, 128–9, 900–8, 932, 937
    and Treaty on European Union (TEU) 27–8
    High Representative *see* High Representative
common interest 724, 861, 865, 942–3
common market 4, 8, 109–10, 236, 720–2, 774–5,
    867–70
common market organisations 173, 177, 276, 325,
    333, 449, 718
common positions 70, 77, 269, 353, 907
common transport policy 8, 76, 185
Community institutions *see* institutions
Community interest 8, 136, 214, 228, 813, 889, 935
Community trade mark 450, 453, 964–5
companies 192, 575–6, 582–9, 647–74, 679–85, 690–
    2, 694–700 *see also* corporate establishment
    bidding 661, 694–7
    holding 588–9
    non-resident 583, 585–8
    offeree 683, 694–5, 697–8
    resident 583, 585, 588, 590, 595
company law 656–7, 668, 670–1, 673–4, 852, 870
    harmonisation 657, 660, 673, 677–701
    and competitiveness 688–90
    contribution to internal market 684–7
    and freedom of establishment 677–9
    obstacles to establishment addressed by 679–83
comparators 293, 299, 401
compensation 199–200, 288, 297, 307–8, 315, 518,
    522–3
    and aid 862–4
competence creep 105–11, 132, 386
competences 97–106, 908–13, 915–18, 920–2, 928–
    33, 939–42, 946–9
    exclusive 98, 100–1, 115, 128, 324, 922–33,
    945–8
    external *see* external competence
    implied 914, 916–17, 920
    internal 101, 912, 914, 916, 921, 923–6, 931
    legislative 109–10, 322, 889, 915, 917, 920
    national 251, 469, 965–7
    non-exclusive 127, 939, 947
    parallel 917, 930, 939

regulatory 102–3, 114, 124–5, 429, 623
shared 100–3, 105, 116, 922, 927, 930–3, 935–6
competition 399–401, 705–11, 716–20, 741–55, 758–9, 797–9, 803–6
  authorities, national 707, 709, 719, 809–15, 826, 838–9, 844
  distortion of 118–19, 730, 740–1, 841, 850–2, 857, 925–6
  intra-brand 760–1
  law 101, 253, 315, 351, 355, 379, 705–894
  cartels and anti-competitive agreements 730–63
  and co-operation agreements 722–4
  enforcement 351, 707, 785, 809–44
  fines 826–38
  and fundamental rights 351–2
  and global regulation/co-operation 724–5
  international context 722–5
  leniency policies/programmes 705, 708, 737, 810–11, 814, 833–4, 836
  material scope of rules 718
  personal scope of rules 713–18
  scope of EU rules 713–22
  settlements 836–8
  sources 705–9
  territorial scope of rules 718–22
  potential 743–4, 747, 760, 769, 771, 773
  price 749, 788, 791
  regulatory 654, 657, 687–8, 692
competitiveness 46, 597, 624, 640, 677–8, 699–700, 711
  and company law harmonisation 688–90
complementarity principle 912, 914–22, 924, 926
comprehensive health insurance 464–6, 474, 477
concertation 721, 737–9
concerted practices 719, 722, 729–30, 733–42, 755, 760, 762
concurrence of wills 729, 731–5
conditional rebates 795–6
conditions of employment 76, 369, 371, 509, 511, 514, 524
conferral principle 25, 97–115, 119, 123, 909, 911–12, 922
conferred powers 31–3, 904, 929
consent 10, 28–30, 80–2, 84–5, 453–8, 937–8, 949
  implied 458
  informed 363
consistent interpretation 148, 345, 966
  duty 239–44, 247–8, 250, 269, 282, 284–5, 965
Constitution for Europe see Constitutional Treaty
constitutional fundamentals 77, 233–387
constitutional order of states 67, 131–2
Constitutional Treaty (CT) 18–19, 28, 33, 35, 119–22, 278, 361
consular protection 360, 379, 494
consultation procedure 78–80, 84, 92, 94
consumer protection 31–2, 378, 412–13, 434–6, 442–5, 580, 622–3
continuous residence 479, 481
contracts of employment 294, 300, 502, 518, 522, 553, 820
COREPER (Committee of Permanent Representatives of the Governments of the Member States) 47–8, 92

corporate constitutions 647, 669–74
corporate control 673–4, 698
corporate establishment 531–2, 534, 647–61, 663, 665, 667, 673
  primary and secondary establishment of companies 649–58
corporate forms, national 692–3, 700
corporate governance 664, 677, 690, 693
Council 41–52, 75–96, 109–14, 126–31, 157–73, 176–90, 932–40
  European see European Council
  power of amendment 93–4
country of origin 370, 378, 410, 442, 486, 488, 539–40
Court of First Instance (CFI) 717, 720–2, 732–3, 744–6, 783–5, 793–5, 829–31 see also General Court
Court of Justice 60–5, 178–90, 193–205, 209–14, 216–30, 337–44, 347–54 see also Court of First Instance; General Court
credit institutions 118, 551, 610, 659, 921
criminal liability 242–4, 283, 380–1, 484
criminal sanctions 317, 351, 381, 613
cross-border acquisitions 647, 661–70
CT see Constitutional Treaty
currency, single 14, 21, 27, 34, 125–6, 391
customary international law 954, 963–4
customs duties 8, 245, 391–5, 401–2, 405, 446, 449
customs union 8, 100, 392–4, 922
  Czech Republic 17, 20, 48, 374, 386

damage, and causation 198–9
damages 160, 204–5, 223–4, 292, 306–15, 840–3, 858
  actions for 64, 189–200, 308–9, 841
  private law right to 314–15
Dassonville case 407, 409–10, 414–15, 417–18, 428, 459
de minimis 420, 428–9, 708, 741, 752
decentralised enforcement 235–9, 244, 254, 260–2, 284–5, 287–9, 296–7
decision-making powers 9, 34, 96, 99, 809, 844, 892
decision-making procedures 34, 69–96, 113, 125, 131
  adoption of legislative acts 71–83, 111, 907
  adoption of non-legislative acts 81, 83–91
  interaction between institutions 91–5
  legislative acts and non-legislative acts 69–71
decisions
  of associations of undertakings 729, 734, 734–5
  final 78, 184–5, 219, 272, 291, 294, 867
decisive influence 720–1
defendant institutions 177, 180–1, 188–9
delegated acts 71, 83, 90–1
  non-legislative acts adopted as 86–7
delegated powers 86–7, 327, 344, 708
delegation, legislation deprived of state character by 892–4
democratic principles 26, 368
  and Treaty on European Union (TEU) 26
democratic society 365–7, 384
Denmark 9–10, 126–7, 396–7, 401–2, 446, 575, 649–50
deposit guarantee schemes 36, 118

developing countries 10–11, 32, 79, 109, 377, 941–2, 944
development co-operation 13, 76, 103–4, 901–2, 904, 930–1, 944
dignity 24, 35, 338, 361, 363–4, 376, 572–3
diplomas 541, 615, 625–30 *see also* mutual recognition of diplomas, training and experience
diplomatic and consular protection 360, 379, 494
direct actions 64, 135–205, 209, 211, 225–6, 230, 304
    actions for damages 64, 189–200, 308–9, 841
    actions for failure to act 141, 159, 182–9, 205
    annulment actions 122, 147, 153–82
    illegality plea 200–3
    infringement actions 135–53, 205, 220, 933
    interim measures 203–4
    nonexistence of an act 200–3
direct and indirect discrimination on grounds of nationality, and right of establishment 545–7
direct discrimination 377, 397–8, 509, 545, 573, 579–80, 582
direct effect 143–4, 237–41, 277–81, 283–5, 296–7, 953–63, 966–7
    against whom 252–70
    directives 139, 255, 259, 261–3, 284
    horizontal 261, 265–6, 282, 315, 345, 840
    international agreements concluded by EU 953–5
    principle 37, 235, 244–70, 278–9, 282, 284
    and supremacy 278–84
    threshold criteria 245–8
    vertical 263, 267
    who may rely on 248–52
direct investment 662–3, 666–7, 948
direct universal suffrage 12, 56
directives
    adoption 380, 472, 507, 536–7, 877
    direct effect 139, 255, 259, 261–3, 284
directly elected European Parliament 12, 65
directors 402, 548, 575, 647, 652, 664–5, 669–72
disability 31, 137, 155, 266, 371, 374
disapplication of national provisions 264, 271, 273, 278, 280–1, 284, 296
disclosure 138, 192, 338, 576, 680–1, 804, 843
discounts 658, 757–8, 791–6, 824, 857
discretion 165, 194–6, 218–19, 308–9, 326–7, 436, 827
discretionary powers 69, 141, 153, 194–6, 326, 664, 666
discrimination 332–4, 371–3, 419–22, 435–7, 509–12, 560–3, 582–7
    direct 377, 397–8, 509, 545, 573, 579–80, 582
    on grounds of nationality 333, 452, 465, 562, 672
    on grounds of sex 371, 502
    indirect 397–8, 509, 515–17, 545–7, 552, 577–8, 581–3
    overt 515, 545, 626
    price 769, 791
    prohibition of 194, 266, 332–3, 370–1, 502, 547, 672
discriminatory internal taxation, and free movement of goods 395–401
discriminatory pricing 783, 790–1

discriminatory restrictions 407, 421, 428, 434, 520, 531, 548
discriminatory taxation 391–2, 396, 421
disguised restrictions 116, 410, 435, 437, 439–40, 452, 595
dismissals 222, 265, 345, 376–7, 506, 514
disposal of industrial waste 111–12
distortion of competition 118–19, 730, 740–1, 841, 850–2, 857, 925–6
distribution agreements 748, 760–1
distributors 448, 730, 733, 747, 760–2, 796, 862
doctors 533, 536, 625, 627, 629, 631, 636–7
domestic companies 662–3, 665
domestic products/goods 393–4, 396, 398–9, 402–4, 415–19, 423–6, 552
    similar 396–7, 401–2
dominance 706, 765, 767–9, 771–3, 775–9, 781–3, 799–801
    abuse of 706, 719, 754, 765–807
    joint or collective 779–81
dominant positions 766–8, 770–2, 775–7, 779, 781–4, 789, 794–6
dominant undertakings 706, 766–7, 777, 785–90, 792–3, 795, 799
downstream markets 774, 791, 798, 803, 805
dual nationality 468–9, 489–90, 501
    dual-use goods 944–5, 949

EAR *see* European Agency for Reconstruction
ECB *see* European Central Bank
ECJ *see* Court of Justice
ECN *see* European Competition Network
Economic and Social Committee 42, 71, 84, 106, 236, 659, 686
economic migrants 461, 463, 500, 503
economic policy 193–4, 435, 855, 879, 890
economically active citizens 473–4, 476, 508, 525
economically active migrants 461–3, 503
economically inactive citizens 466–8, 474–6, 482
ECS *see* European Company Statute
ECSC (European Coal and Steel Community), establishment 3–5
ECSC *see* European Coal and Steel Community
EDC *see* European Defence Community
education 104, 125, 277, 360, 368, 477, 505
    right to 525–7
EEA *see* European Economic Area
EEIGs *see* European Economic Interest Groupings
'by effect' restrictions of competition 744–50
effective judicial protection 173–5, 197, 205, 238–9, 299, 301–2, 317–19
effectiveness 238, 288–9, 304–5, 312–13, 315–16, 839–40, 842–3
    principle 289, 294–303, 305, 312, 318, 867
effects-based approach 712, 765–6, 806–7, 831
efficiency 709–12, 756, 759–61, 783, 786, 795, 842
    gains 747, 756–9
efficient competitor test 785–6, 789, 796
EFTA 9, 11, 212, 216, 615, 724, 901
elections 10, 12, 21, 35, 52–3, 56–8, 493
    municipal 379, 492–3
electronic means 532, 599, 609, 612, 618–19, 624
emanations of the state 263, 266–7

emergency brake mechanism 82–3
employee participation 683, 692, 700
employees 103, 106, 374–6, 510–11, 577–8, 660,
    691–2
employers 247, 251–2, 261–2, 374–5, 510–11, 513–
    14, 820
    private 254–5, 265, 315, 502
employment 255, 371–2, 374–6, 497–9, 505–11,
    521–4, 526–7
    conditions of 76, 369, 371, 509, 511, 514, 524
    contracts of 294, 300, 502, 518, 522, 553, 820
employment market 475, 482, 507–8, 522–4, 529
employment relationships 300, 502–3, 505, 820
enforcement
    competition law 351, 707, 785, 809–44
    decentralised 235–9, 244, 254, 260–2, 284–5,
        287–9, 296–7
    powers 809–11
    priorities 765–6, 776–7, 782–3, 785–7, 789, 796,
        805–6
    private 297, 315, 709, 712, 726, 809–10, 838–43
    public 812, 826–38, 840
    state aid rules 866–71
enhanced co-operation 19, 24, 27, 32, 81–3, 127–31,
    451
    passerelle clause 81–2
    system 27, 127, 129
enlargement 3, 14–17, 50–2, 57, 63, 528, 829
    6 to 15 9–11
    15 to 27 16–18
entrusted undertakings 707, 864, 875, 884–6, 888
environmental protection 27, 109, 167, 242, 377–8,
    384–5, 442–3
EPC see European Political Community
EPO see European Patent Office
equal rotation 46–7, 52
equal treatment 265–6, 371–3, 461–2, 475–6, 506–7,
    509–11, 527–9
    principle of 105, 255, 290–1, 371–3, 376, 464,
        548
    right to 461–2, 472, 475–6, 482, 489, 506–7, 509
equality, principle of 52, 332–3, 370, 372, 493, 514,
    608
equivalence, principle 287, 289, 292–4, 296, 312–13,
    318
equivalent effect 391–4, 401–3, 407–10, 417–18,
    431–3, 445–6, 459–60
equivalent protection 354–6
established market operators 551–2, 566, 659
established professional base 533, 556–7
establishment
    corporate 531–2, 534, 647–61, 663, 665, 667, 673
    freedom of see freedom of establishment
establishments, primary 534, 649, 651, 655
Estonia 17, 48, 126, 242, 349, 451, 553
ethnic origin 371–2, 376
EURATOM 7–8, 23, 191, 497, 899, 910, 919
EURES see European Employment Services
Eurocontrol 253, 714–15, 878
Europe Agreements 17, 901
European Agency for Reconstruction (EAR) 158
European Atomic Energy Community see
    EURATOM

European Central Bank (ECB) 27, 29, 41–2, 154,
    160–1, 182–3, 202
European Coal and Steel Community (ECSC) 8–9,
    12–13, 183, 337, 497, 724, 768
European Commission see Commission
European Company 654, 680, 691–3, 700
    Statute (ECS) 677–8, 683, 690–2, 700, 787–8
European Competition Network (ECN) 707, 709,
    725, 809–14, 826, 834, 839
European Cooperative Society 678, 700
European Council 14–15, 19–21, 26–30, 43–6, 52–7,
    81–4, 904–6
European Court of Justice see Court of Justice
European Defence Community (EDC) 5–7
European Economic Area (EEA) 66, 212, 216, 457–
    8, 724, 901
European Economic Interest Groupings (EEIGs) 678,
    685–7, 700
European Employment Services (EURES) 375
European External Action Service 55, 84, 903
European Parliament 26–30, 56–61, 69–73, 75–82,
    84–7, 89–92, 94–6
    directly elected 12, 65
    participation in decision-making 94–5
European Patent Office (EPO) 450–1
European Political Community (EPC) 5–7, 13, 337
European Private Company 654, 700
European Social Charter 340, 360, 374–5
evidence of formal qualifications 536, 542, 626, 630,
    632–3
exchange of information 104, 615, 733, 738, 750–2,
    755, 811
exclusionary effect 280, 282, 308, 605, 795
exclusive competence 98, 100–1, 115, 128, 324, 922–
    33, 945–8
exclusive rights 171, 447–9, 454, 458, 875, 878–84,
    886–9
exclusive territories 761–2
exclusivity 101, 115, 875, 914–15, 920, 924–7, 930–2
    supervening 908, 923–6, 930–2, 940–1
executive organs 90, 957–8, 963
exercise of official authority 492, 531, 568–71, 600
    occasional 570–1
exhaustion of rights
    patents 453–6
    principle 452–3
    trade marks 456–9
existence function 921
expansion, barriers to 777–8
exports 101, 167–8, 391–5, 404–5, 407–9, 432–6,
    459–60
    discriminatory tax treatment 404
    measures having equivalent effect to quantitative
        restrictions 432–4
external action 24, 27, 32, 46, 48, 55, 899–951
    common commercial policy (CCP) 101, 901,
        904, 917, 921–3, 935–6, 941–51
    constitutional framework 899–908
    exclusive EU external competence 920, 922–33
    express and implied EU external
        competence 909–22
    mixed agreements 937
    procedural code in Art 218 TFEU 936–9

external action – *continued*
  shared competence and duty of close
      co-operation 899, 936, 951
  and Treaty on European Union (TEU) 27–8
  under new Treaty structure 899–900
External Action Service, European 55, 84, 903
external competence 899, 903–4, 906–8, 933, 936–7,
      939, 950–1
  exclusive 920, 922–33
  express 909–22
  implied 909, 911–12, 916–17, 919, 922, 924, 951
  shared 933–6
external relations 13, 32, 44, 55, 101, 285, 899–967
  and common customs tariff (CCT) 405–6

failure to act, actions for 141, 159, 182–9, 205
fair and public hearing 289–90, 379, 821, 832–3
fair legal process 821–2
fair trial 173, 243, 270, 351–2, 379, 384, 815–16
families 365–6, 377, 462–4, 466–70, 472–3, 477–9,
      499–500
  workers' 520, 525–8
family circumstances 484, 584–5
family life 347–8, 365, 373, 468, 475, 485, 524
family members 462–3, 467–8, 470–82, 484–5, 487–
      8, 528, 572
  definition 468
  third-country national 471, 478–9, 481
fathers 373, 489–90, 517
FDI *see* foreign direct investment
fees 105, 393–5, 405, 476, 521–2, 555, 629
final decisions 78, 184–5, 219, 272, 291, 294, 867
financial institutions 662, 752, 860, 891
financial sanctions 149–50, 205
fines 181–2, 333, 381, 705, 708, 721, 809–12
  calculation 720, 827–8
  competition law enforcement 826–38
  infringement actions 149–53
Finland 10–11, 48, 51, 174, 427, 451, 553
First Pillar 14–15, 34, 69–70, 126, 269, 317, 356
fiscal barriers to free movement of goods 391–406
fiscal supervision 411–12, 441, 576
fixed-term contracts 255, 265, 502, 504, 506, 851
flexibility 46, 98, 141, 216, 579, 655, 830
  clause 28–9, 32, 78, 84, 106, 109, 111
  primary 125–7
  secondary 127–31
  Union competences 124–31
foreign companies 350, 551, 576, 652, 659, 679–81
foreign direct investment (FDI) 663–4, 901, 923,
      929, 942–3, 947, 950–1
foreign nationals 483, 510–11, 535, 538, 571–2, 626,
      648
foreign policy 6, 12–13, 905
formal notice, letters of 138–41, 149, 204
formal qualifications 536, 542, 626, 630–3, 636
formalities 167, 293, 328, 410, 471, 599, 616–19
  administrative 477–8
framework decisions 70, 155, 243, 269, 364, 381
France 4–5, 146–8, 151–2, 351–2, 430, 582–4, 666–7
Francovich right to reparation 307–14
free movement of capital 391, 589, 595, 656, 661–4,
      666–7, 669–73

free movement of goods 253–4, 409–12, 430–2, 434–
      41, 445–8, 450–3, 558–9
  and discriminatory internal taxation 395–401
  discriminatory tax treatment of exports 404
  fiscal barriers to 391–406
  quantitative restrictions and measures having
      equivalent effect 4, 8, 101, 391, 403,
      407–60
free movement of persons 14–15, 34, 213, 291, 350,
      431, 434
free movement of services 346, 427, 482, 501, 523,
      600, 602 *see also* freedom to provide services
  Services Directive 605–9
free movement of workers *see* freedom of movement
      for workers
freedom of association 367, 374
freedom of establishment 245–6, 532–600, 602,
      631–2, 652, 655–7, 659–61 *see also* right of
      establishment
  and company law harmonisation 677–9
  mergers and acquisitions as aspects of 660–1
  and Services Directive 602–5
freedom of movement for workers 17, 252, 262, 315,
      333, 497–529, 531–2
  access to employment and equal treatment 508–
      20
  ambit of Art 45 TFEU 500–2
  material scope of application of Art 45
      TFEU 508–25
  non-discriminatory restrictions 520–5
  personal scope of application of Art 45
      TFEU 503–8
  transitional arrangements for new Member
      States 528–9
  workers' families 520, 525–8
freedom to provide services 531–98, 634
  abolition of discriminatory restrictions 558–9
  case law 559–65
  and direct applicability of Art 56 TFEU 559
  and exercise of official authority 568–71
  general scope 554–8
  and imperative requirements in the general
      interest 573–81
  lawyers 639–40
  meaning 532–4
  national measures 558
  national measures to prevent
      circumvention 567–8
  and national tax measures 581–96
  prohibition of non discriminatory restrictions
      on 565–7
  public policy proviso 560, 571–3
frontier workers 480, 500
frontiers 391, 393–4, 471, 680, 685
functions, essential State 25, 97, 932
fundamental freedoms 340–2, 347–8, 573–7, 581,
      589–91, 596–7, 670–4
  exercise of 521, 540, 573–6, 591, 593, 665, 671
fundamental rights 23–5, 35–6, 43, 275–6, 337–59,
      430–1, 816–18
  and Advocate General role 352–3
  Charter of Fundamental Rights 359–87

and co-operation in criminal matters and
counter-terrorism 353–4
and competition law 351–2
EU and European Convention on Human
Rights 354–7
evolution of concept 337–9
and institutional structure of Union 351–4
as limit to acts of institutions 343–4
and Member States acting within the scope of
Union law 346–51
and Member States' implementing powers 344–5
political institutions' response 339–43
scope of application 343–57
and Treaty of Lisbon (TL) 340–3

gender reassignment 348, 372
general application 86, 164, 174–5, 178–9, 191–3,
200–1, 226
General Court 61–5, 153–4, 158–62, 166–8, 170–8,
202–3, 708 *see also* Court of First Instance
general derogation clause 383–4
general economic interest 378, 607, 847, 862, 864–5,
874–6, 886–8
services of 707, 876, 884, 887–8
general interest 41–2, 249–50, 512–14, 573–81, 590–
1, 864–5, 886–9 *see also* public interest
imperative requirements in the 573–81
mandatory requirements in the 441–6, 560, 591,
673
general meetings 115, 668–70, 673, 683–4, 694–5,
697–8
general principles of Union law 36–7, 253–6, 265–7,
321–37, 342–8, 387, 466–7
function and sources 321–2
legal certainty and legitimate expectation 328–32
non-discrimination 293, 332–4, 345
proportionality 325–8
sincere or loyal co-operation 322–4
subsidiarity 324–5
General Programmes 541–3, 554, 558–9, 626, 649,
679
geographic market 762, 773–5
Germany 4–5, 107–8, 438–9, 560–3, 651–4, 858–60,
958–9
Constitution 275–6, 338–9
Gibraltar 161, 355–6, 554, 853
golden shares 664, 666–7, 674, 878
good administration, rights to 318, 379, 492
good repute, information on 613–14
goods
domestic 402, 404, 411, 415, 417, 419, 437
free movement of *see* free movement of goods
imported 245, 396–7, 401–2, 412–14, 416, 420–1,
423–6
governance 96, 493, 725
corporate 664, 677, 690, 693
global 904
multi-level 66
Greece 140–2, 150–2, 398, 421–3, 558–9, 562–3, 881
groups of undertakings 374, 706, 855
guarantees 20, 682, 854
and Services Directive 610

hard-core restrictions 729, 753, 759, 761–2
harmonisation 99, 104, 106–7, 110, 316–17, 450,
684–5
complete 457, 929
minimum 103, 112, 130
positive 306, 413
head offices 657, 691–2
health 103, 118, 212, 367–8, 376–8, 435–8, 610–11
insurance 290, 464–6, 468, 474, 477–8, 525, 527
protection 107, 365, 367–8, 378, 435–6, 439
public 107–8, 411, 440–1, 485–7, 570–3, 628–9,
636–7
healthcare 263, 600, 607–8, 705, 715
hearing, fair 289–90, 379, 821, 832–3
hearing officers 821–2
High Representative 27–8, 49–50, 52–6, 128–9, 902–
3, 905–6, 937–8
home-country professional titles 634, 637–8, 640–5
horizontal agreements 742–3, 754, 760
horizontal application 282, 334, 502, 608, 672
horizontal direct effect 261, 265–6, 282, 315, 345,
840
horizontal disputes 253–5, 258, 261, 265–7, 282
horizontal effect 217, 501, 552–4, 673
hostile bidders 694–5
housing 360, 377, 508, 520, 544, 559
human dignity *see* dignity
human rights 5–6, 24–5, 109–10, 337–8, 340–2, 903,
912 *see also* fundamental rights
humanitarian aid 27, 32, 103–4, 901, 904, 930–1
hybrid settlements 837–8

ICN *see* International Competition Network
identity cards 246, 471, 478–9, 481
IGCs *see* Intergovernmental Conferences
illegality 174, 177, 191, 195–7, 228–9, 256, 831
plea 200–3
illness 473, 479–80, 494, 505, 629
ILO *see* International Labour Organization
immunity 583, 833–6
impartiality 228, 289–90, 367, 546, 603, 832–3
imperative requirements 486, 509, 516–17, 521, 540,
550, 638
in the general interest 573–81
implementing acts 71, 83, 86, 173, 176, 258
non-legislative acts adopted as 87–91
implementing legislation, national 147, 226, 257,
259–60, 304, 639
implementing measures 88–90, 142, 154, 162, 176,
186, 226
national 147, 226, 257, 260, 304, 639
implementing powers 88–90, 153, 176, 949
implied competence 914, 916–17, 920
implied consent 458
implied external competence 909, 911–12, 916–17,
919, 922, 924, 951
imported goods/products 245, 396–7, 401–2, 412–
14, 416, 420–1, 423–6
importers 166, 276, 391, 397–8, 410, 420–1, 459
imports 391–3, 395–8, 435–7, 439–43, 446–8, 450–3,
459–60
measures having equivalent effect to quantitative
restrictions 409–32

imports – *continued*
    parallel 431, 454–6, 459, 732–3, 737, 747, 791
inactive citizens *see* economically inactive citizens
incentives 53, 76–7, 104, 150–1, 453, 653, 803–5
incomes 246, 503, 516, 519, 584–5, 594–5
independence 42, 48, 51, 53, 62–3, 373–4, 902–3
independent legal effects 235, 244, 250, 256, 265–6
indirect discrimination 397–8, 509, 515–17, 545–7,
    552, 577–8, 581–3
individual rights 248–9, 257, 271, 297, 304, 353, 967
    creation 248–50, 284
individuals, private 205, 241, 253, 256, 261–2, 266–7,
    281
industrial action 349–50, 501
industrial waste, disposal of 111–12
influence, decisive 720–1
information
    exchange of 104, 615, 733, 738, 750–2, 755, 811
    from service providers 609
informed consent 363
infringement actions 135–53, 205, 220, 933
    fines and penalty payments 149–53
    procedure 137–43
    substantive issues 143–9
injunctions 251, 307, 316, 869
inspections 395, 405, 570, 612–13, 619, 817–19, 835
    targeted 834
institutions 41–67
    Article 13 TEU 41–3
    Commission *see* Commission
    Council *see* Council
    Court of First Instance *see* Court of First Instance
    Court of Justice *see* Court of Justice
    decision-making interaction between 91–5
    European Council *see* European Council
    European Parliament *see* European Parliament
    General Court *see* General Court
    High Representative *see* High Representative
    history 8–9
    and Treaty on European Union (TEU) 26–7
insurance
    health 290, 464–6, 468, 474, 477–8, 525, 527
    professional liability 610, 612, 641
insurance companies 561, 717, 840, 881
integration 4, 7, 125, 127, 130, 237, 640–1
    market 391, 412, 710, 741, 791
    negative 412–13, 725
    positive 412–13
intellectual property rights (IPRs) 408, 449–53, 798,
    802–3, 901, 942–3, 945–8
    and Articles 34-36 TFEU 449–59
intent/intention 30–1, 164–5, 458, 663, 783–4, 788–
    9, 962–3
inter-institutional agreements 12, 54, 59–60, 98, 937
inter-institutional balance 65–7, 89, 95–6, 112, 131
inter-state trade 394, 719, 767, 857, 867
interchangeability 768–71
interest, payment of 296–7, 301, 305, 583, 585, 659
interests
    best 373, 485, 689, 698
    commercial 172, 252, 495, 767, 789, 799
    general *see* general interest
    legitimate 384, 443, 577, 666, 822, 833

public *see* public interest
interference 5, 346–7, 349, 365–7, 451, 747, 798
Intergovernmental Conferences (IGCs) 15–16,
    18–19, 28–9, 35, 50–2, 98–100, 124–5
intergovernmentalism 66
interim measures 21, 175–6, 203–4, 227–8, 304–5,
    812, 823–4
    direct actions 203–4
interim orders 204, 225, 486–7
interim relief 204, 227–8, 238, 287, 289, 303–5, 318
    and national courts 303–5
internal competence 101, 912, 914, 916, 921, 923–6,
    931
    expressly conferred 917–18, 924
internal market 106–9, 412–16, 452–6, 598–624,
    677–80, 684–6, 718–19
Internal Market Information System 611, 615–16
internal security 47–8, 343
internal taxation 391, 395–6, 399, 401–5, 446, 448
international agreements 910–13, 915–21, 923–5,
    942–5, 953–5, 958–61, 963–4
    conclusion 32, 899, 911, 922, 931, 936, 948–9
    Court of Justice and mixed agreements 966–7
    direct effect of agreements concluded by
        EU 953–5
    interpretation of EU measures in light of
        international agreements and customary
        international law 964
    legal effects 953–67
    limited legal effects for GATT 1947 and WTO
        Agreements 956–8
    review of EU measures on the basis of directly
        effective international agreements 958–61
international commitments 313, 912–13, 915–16,
    926, 929
International Competition Network (ICN) 705, 724–
    5, 806, 812
International Labour Organization (ILO) 913, 916–
    17, 927, 930, 933
international law 24, 65, 236, 276–7, 720, 903, 961–4
    customary 954, 963–4
    new legal order of 236, 253
international obligations 270, 362, 484, 959, 962
international organisations 8, 32, 48, 355–6, 910,
    918–19, 953
internet 361, 424, 426, 434, 554, 601, 762
    sales 421, 424, 426, 762
interoperability 804, 824, 919
interpretation, consistent *see* consistent interpretation
intervention 5, 61, 136–7, 259, 298, 569, 851
intra-brand competition 760–1
intra-Community trade 404–7, 410, 415–17, 420,
    423–4, 427–30, 437–9
invalidity 180, 202, 226, 304, 322, 591, 840
inventors 451, 454–5, 714
investigations 43, 60, 192, 428–9, 612–13, 723,
    809–17
investments 5, 326, 344, 663–4, 668–9, 716–17, 947
    portfolio 647, 662–3, 947
investors 647, 656, 660, 665–6, 668–9, 680, 947
    direct 669, 674
    private 664, 670
involuntary unemployment 473, 480, 505

IP *see* intellectual property rights
IPRs *see* intellectual property rights
Ireland 10, 20, 126–7, 138–9, 141, 369–70, 939–41
irreparable damage 204, 227, 304, 869
    Italy 142–6, 257–8, 283–4, 393–8, 428, 512–15, 890–2

joint or collective dominance 779–81
judicial co-operation 18–19, 65, 72, 77, 120, 317, 900
judicial process 289–91, 295, 297–8, 318, 947
    fundamental right to 289–92
judicial protection 123, 174, 205, 225, 239, 267, 269
    domestic standards of 288–9, 295
    effective 173–5, 197, 205, 238–9, 299, 301–2, 317–19
    of Union rights before national courts 287–319
judicial remedies 210, 222–3, 225, 376
judicial review 86, 119, 121–2, 169, 226, 263–4, 486–8
    acts susceptible of 156–60
jurisdiction 153–5, 209–18, 339–43, 353, 355–7, 720–3, 966–7
    full 290, 343, 351, 353
    ultimate 275–6
justification 441–3, 552, 574–5, 578–82, 589–95, 622, 667
    objective 300, 334, 563, 574, 578, 790, 803–4

Keck and Mithouard ruling 407, 418–25, 427–8, 443, 522, 668, 892
knowledge 154–5, 510, 612–13, 626–7, 631–4, 642–3, 645
    linguistic 371, 510, 643–4
    professional 632–3

labelling requirements 280, 413–14, 417, 422, 443
labour 8, 10, 32–3, 282, 344, 375, 498–9
labour market 502, 506–8, 521, 523, 528–9, 553, 566
languages 32, 58, 83, 451, 617–19, 636, 643
    official 329, 413, 617, 636, 681
Latvia 17, 48, 528
lawyers
    freedom to provide services 639–40
    right of establishment 640–4
legal bases 81–4, 99–100, 105–7, 109–13, 904–6, 917–21, 942–6
    disputes 111–13, 945
    substantive 901–2, 909, 917–18, 936
legal capacity 237, 251, 652
legal certainty 36, 149–50, 181–2, 272–3, 298–301, 327–9, 679–80
legal effects 157–8, 181, 184, 202–3, 228–9, 268–9, 279–81
    independent 235, 244, 250, 256, 265–6
legal order 33–4, 61, 124–5, 129–30, 203, 312–14, 954–6
    domestic 28, 144, 209, 247, 256, 258, 278–9
    international 910, 933
    national 37, 235, 244, 250–1, 256, 262, 270
    new 66, 236, 253, 314, 322
legal personality 19, 24, 28, 160, 651–2, 656–7, 910–11

legal persons 85, 153–5, 160–4, 183–4, 186–7, 200–1, 549–50
legal remedies 158, 175, 184, 188, 215, 272, 313
legality 154–5, 200, 242–4, 275–6, 831, 958–9, 961–2
    of acts/measures adopted 135, 153–4, 158, 225, 365, 957–61, 963
    principle of 200, 242–3, 269–70, 833
legislative acts 80–3, 85–6, 93–5, 117, 122–3, 154–6, 176–7 *see also* legislative procedures
    adoption 71–83, 111, 907
    and non-legislative acts 69–71
legislative competence 109–10, 322, 889, 915, 917, 920
legislative procedures 12, 89, 113, 121, 131, 149, 153
    emergency brake mechanism 82–3
    initiation 72–3
    ordinary 63–4, 73–83, 90, 92–5, 112–13, 120–1, 129
    passerelle clauses 29, 48, 80–2, 84, 110, 129
    special 29, 56, 71, 77–83, 93–4, 110, 129
legislative process 13, 15, 54, 76, 78, 120–1, 694–6
    ordinary 81, 83
legislative proposals 34, 73, 78, 80, 85, 94–5, 122
legitimate expectations 36, 194, 272–3, 321, 327–32, 827, 869
    principle 300, 330–2
legitimate interests 384, 443, 577, 666, 822, 833
leniency
    applications 737, 833–6, 843
    policies/programmes 705, 708, 737, 810–11, 814, 833–4, 836
Leniency Notice 809, 830–1, 833–6
letters of formal notice 138–41, 149, 204
liability 145–6, 189–97, 199–200, 242, 306–10, 312–15, 720–1
    attribution of 741, 830–1
    non-contractual 32, 64, 135, 158, 189–90, 193–5, 197
    state 143, 190, 307–8, 314
licences 404, 433, 437, 439, 549, 603, 802
licensees 450, 453–4, 456
limitation
    and actions for damages 199–200
    periods 200, 272, 292–3, 299–300, 305, 822–3, 869
linguistic knowledge 371, 510, 643–4
links, real 466–7, 475, 482, 507–8
location 546, 582, 584, 604, 607, 648, 674
locus standi 154, 160, 172, 176–7, 205, 343, 872 *see also* standing
long-run average incremental cost (LRAIC) 785
lotteries 558, 563–4, 580
loyal co-operation 79, 87, 235, 239, 243, 269–70, 322–4
LRAIC *see* long-run average incremental cost
lump sums 149, 151–3, 517
    Luxembourg 230, 404, 444, 514–15, 519, 642–4, 933–4

main proceedings 217, 222, 347, 426, 522, 587, 629
maintenance grants 475–6, 482, 504–6
maintenance loans 475–6, 482
maladministration 59–60, 138

management 513, 519, 662–4, 666–7, 669, 672, 715–17
  central 554, 651
  procedure 89–90
mandatory references 222–5
mandatory requirements 411, 414, 434–5, 440–6, 560, 577, 673
  doctrine 327, 346–7, 407–8, 412–13, 420, 436
  in the general interest 441–6, 560, 591, 673
  and proportionality 445–6
  of public interest 412–14, 416, 422, 431, 442
manufacturers 438, 720, 723, 733, 748, 752, 770–2
margin squeezing 791–2, 798, 805
market
  common 4, 8, 109–10, 236, 720–2, 774–5, 867–70
  downstream 774, 791, 798, 803, 805
  geographic 762, 773–5
  internal *see* internal market
  national 433, 454, 551, 710, 744, 790, 861
  relevant 252, 535, 712, 731, 743–5, 751–2, 765–77
  secondary 803–4
  temporal 775
market access 419–21, 424–6, 428, 551–2, 659
  test 420, 425, 459
market definition 705, 769, 772–3
market entrants, new 459, 524, 551–2, 674
market entry 551, 659, 771, 777
  barriers to 777–8
market integration 391, 412, 710, 741, 791
market operators 550–2, 566, 597, 622, 670–2, 697, 840
  established 551–2, 566, 659
market power 706, 712, 765, 775–8, 780, 789, 806
market shares 445, 744, 753, 761, 765, 772, 776–8
  large 776, 778
market transparency 738–9
marriage 332, 366, 468, 470–1, 477, 480, 527
medical aid organisations 880, 882–3, 887–8
medicinal products 290, 425–6, 438, 716
Member States
  of establishment 562, 611–15, 629, 635–7, 659
  of incorporation 652, 656, 674, 691
  of origin 370, 454, 488–9, 526, 535–6, 538–41, 651
  of residence 31, 58, 493, 584–5, 594, 608–9
MEPs 21, 53, 57–9, 75–6, 82, 94–5, 129
mergers 642, 644, 647, 660–1, 663, 682, 723
  control 705, 707, 722, 782
  cross-border 683–4
migrant workers 76, 252–3, 331, 498–9, 516, 522–5, 621 *see also* freedom of movement for workers
migrants
  economic 461, 463, 500, 503
  non-economic 462
military service 364, 479, 514–15, 518–19
milk 196, 330, 344, 423, 770
  processed 421–3
minimum capital requirements 575, 650, 652–5
minimum harmonisation 103, 112, 130
minimum standards

of judicial protection 301, 312
  rule 929–30
misuse of aid 866, 870–1
misuse of powers 124, 154, 178, 180, 804
mixed agreements 899, 935, 937–41, 947, 951, 965–7
  and Court of Justice 966–7
mixity 933, 936, 939–41
mobility 375–6, 774
modernisation 677, 711, 725, 730, 763, 810, 838
  agenda 705, 709–10
  and state aid 848–9
monetary union 10, 14, 24, 43, 129, 790, 858
monopolies 72, 279, 447–9, 455, 776, 875–6, 882–4
  revenue-producing 884, 886
  state *see* state monopolies
mothers 469, 489–90, 517
movement
  capital 592, 595, 647, 662–3, 665–8, 670, 673–4
  freedom of *see* free movement of goods; freedom of movement for workers
multi-annual financial framework 12, 81
multi-level governance 66
municipal elections 379, 492–3
mutual assistance 4, 587, 607, 612, 614–15
mutual evaluation, Services Directive 619–20
mutual recognition 317, 412–13, 433, 443, 541, 921
  of diplomas, training and experience 625–45
  by Community rules 630–9
  direct applicability of Arts 49 and 56 TFEU 626–30
  principle 412–13

Nakajima exception 961–3
national competence 251, 469, 965–7
national competition authorities (NCAs) 707, 709, 719, 809–15, 826, 838–9, 844
national corporate forms 692–3, 700
national courts
  actions based directly upon Union law 303–15
  and effectiveness principle 294–302
  and equivalence principle 287, 289, 292–4, 296, 312–13, 318
  and Francovich right to reparation 307–14
  fundamental right to judicial process 289–92
  and interim relief 303–5
  and international agreements 965–6
  judicial protection of Union rights before 287–319
  private enforcement of competition law 838–43
  and private law right to damages 314–15
  and recovery of unlawfully levied charges 305–7
  and state aid 873–4
  and Union legislation concerning remedies and procedural rules 316–18
national frontiers 394, 439, 645–7
national implementing legislation/measures 147, 226, 257, 259–60, 304, 639
national law/legislation 146–9, 213–17, 237–41, 246–8, 266–71, 277–84, 374–8
national legal orders 37, 235, 244, 250–1, 256, 262, 270
national legal systems 28, 61, 244–5, 247–50, 267–9, 273, 278–9

national measures 138–40, 435–41, 521–2, 540–1, 565–7, 572–6, 578–81
national parliaments 18–19, 28–9, 71, 81–2, 84–5, 98, 360
    role 29, 81, 84, 120–1
    and subsidiarity 119–22
national procedural autonomy 288, 302–5, 318, 324, 842
national procedural rules 175, 300–1, 874
national proceedings 135, 173, 211, 222, 224, 536–7, 955–6
national qualifications, co-ordination of 625–45
national remedies 226, 289, 294–5, 298, 301–2, 317–18, 840–1
national rules 410–15, 442–3, 549–52, 561–8, 577–80, 594–7, 628–9
national security 25, 97, 290, 365, 367–8, 932, 945
national sovereignty *see* sovereignty
national tax measures, as restrictions on fundamental freedoms 581–96
national tax rules 534, 546, 581–5, 587–9, 591, 597
national territory 418–19, 422–4, 432–3, 516, 518–20, 560, 577
national treatment 537, 582, 920, 923
national workers 511, 514, 516–17, 519–20
nationality 468–71, 514–16, 518–26, 544–8, 560–3, 577–80, 582–3
    dual 468–9, 489–90, 501
    prohibition of discrimination on grounds of 333, 452, 465, 562, 672
nationals
    of member states 447–8, 462, 470, 518, 521, 534–5, 554
    of third countries 377, 556, 660
natural persons 84–5, 160, 162, 201, 582, 647–8, 813
naturalisation 469–70, 536
NCAs *see* national competition authorities
negative integration 412–13, 725
negative obligations 247–8
Netherlands 148, 363–4, 425–7, 548–9, 560, 586–90, 959–60
new development test 929
new legal order 66, 236, 253, 314, 322
new market entrants 459, 524, 551–2, 674
non bis in idem principle 815, 831, 833
non-contractual liability 32, 64, 135, 158, 189–90, 193–5, 197
non-discrimination
    as general principle of Union law 293, 332–4, 345
    principle 255, 321, 332–4, 345, 464, 466, 488–9
    and Services Directive 607–8, 620
non-discriminatory restrictions 435, 520, 531, 538, 547–8, 563–6, 574–5
non-economically active migrants 461–2, 503
non-exclusive competences 127, 939, 947
non-legislative acts 31, 48, 95, 176
    adopted as delegated acts 86–7
    adopted as implementing acts 87–91
    adopted directly under Treaties 83–5
    adoption 81, 83–91
    and legislative acts 69–71

non-member countries 17, 158, 405, 920–1, 924, 953–6, 966
non-nationals 452, 509, 512, 514–15, 517, 519, 539–40
non-privileged applicants 155, 160, 162, 172–3, 186–7
non-resident companies 583, 585–8
non-resident subsidiaries 588–9, 592, 595
non-residents 328, 489, 519, 583–5, 595, 597
non-wage-earning activities 542
Northern Ireland 469, 501, 513, 791
Norway 9–11, 457, 615, 653, 960
notified aid 866–9
    nurses 512–13, 625, 631, 636–7

by object restrictions of competition 742–4, 763
objections, statement of 721, 821–2, 825, 828, 837
objective criteria 333, 398, 400, 402, 608
objective differences 515, 583–5, 608, 626
objective justification 300, 334, 563, 574, 578, 790, 803–4
obligations
    international 270, 362, 484, 959, 962
    legal 94, 98, 252, 329, 467, 767, 940
    negative 247–8
    positive 209, 248, 296, 375, 449, 824
    of private parties inter se 281–2
    public service 713, 863, 865, 885, 894
    secondary 326–7
    substantive 253, 255, 258
    supplementary 730, 767, 796
observations 136–7, 149, 216, 221–2, 352, 620, 839
occasional exercise of official authority 570–1
occupational diseases 480, 716
offeree companies 683, 694–5, 697–8
offerors 683, 694–5
Office for Harmonisation in the Internal Market (OHIM) 450
official authority, exercise of 492, 531, 568–71, 600
official languages 329, 413, 617, 636, 681
official powers 569–70
officials 55, 59, 79, 190, 331–2, 615, 903
    national 47, 88, 90
OHIM *see* Office for Harmonisation in the Internal Market
oligopolistic markets 738, 751
Ombudsman 60, 62, 190, 377, 494–5
omissions 142, 191–2, 199–200, 205, 309, 313, 526
one-stop shops 599, 617–18, 834
opt-outs 27, 34, 125–7, 137, 155, 694, 699–701
ordinary legislative procedure 63–4, 73–83, 90, 92–5, 112–13, 120–1, 129
ordinary revision procedure 28–9, 35
'organic law' clause 80, 82
origin
    country of 370, 378, 410, 442, 486, 488, 539–40
    ethnic 371–2, 376
overriding reasons 435, 553, 577–81, 589–90, 596, 603–4, 610
overriding requirements 445, 531, 573–4, 576, 578–80, 603–5, 619–20
overt discrimination 515, 545, 626
    own-resources Decisions 12

parallel competence 917, 930, 939
parallel imports 431, 454–6, 459, 732–3, 737, 747, 791
parallel patents 454–5
parent companies 456, 585–9, 593–5, 655, 658–9, 718, 720–1
   non-resident 585–7
parents 105, 360, 373, 476–7, 491, 526–7, 720–1
Parliament, European see European Parliament
partnerships, registered 332, 470, 476, 480, 525
passerelle clauses 29, 48, 80–2, 84, 110, 129
patents 429, 449–51, 453–5, 629, 714, 966
   exhaustion of rights 453–6
   national 450–1, 454
   parallel 454–5
payment of interest 296–7, 301, 305, 583, 585, 659
penalties 150–3, 326, 328, 381, 484, 509, 812–13
   criminal 243, 381, 832
   custodial 484
penalty payments 149–53, 824, 826
   periodic 151–2, 708, 812, 824
pensioners 461–2, 474
pensions 330, 480, 516, 518, 591, 715
periodic penalty payments 151–2, 708, 812, 824
permanent residence 468, 479–82, 485, 509, 516, 528, 572
permanent residents 475, 479, 481–2, 486, 508
   rights 481–2
persistent organic pollutants (POPs) 934–5
personality, legal 19, 24, 28, 160, 651–2, 656–7, 910–11
persons
   employed 464, 503–4, 522, 539, 571
   free movement of 14–15, 34, 213, 291, 350, 431, 434
   legal 85, 153–5, 160–4, 183–4, 186–7, 200–1, 549–50
   natural 84–5, 160, 162, 201, 582, 647–8, 813
petitions 31, 60, 379, 494
pharmacies 420, 423, 426, 549, 576, 802, 862
physical qualities 407, 421–3
pillars
   First Pillar 14–15, 34, 69–70, 126, 269, 317, 356
   Second Pillar 27, 65, 70, 268, 900, 908
   Third Pillar 15, 70, 137, 243, 268–9, 351, 900
Plaumann test 166–7, 169–70, 172
points of single contact 599, 617–18 see also one-stop shops
Poland 4, 17, 20, 35, 48, 386, 616
police co-operation 15, 211, 230, 900
political parties 58, 76, 368
political rights 360–1, 369, 375, 492
political union 4, 499, 858
POPs see persistent organic pollutants
portfolio investment 647, 662–3, 947
Portugal 9–11, 427–8, 456, 549, 569–70, 669, 957–9
positive duties of member States in relation to free movement of goods 430–1
positive harmonisation 306, 413
positive integration 412–13
positive obligations 209, 248, 296, 375, 449, 824
posted workers 350, 479, 529, 556, 578, 607, 660
powers

of amendment 78–9, 92
conferred 31–3, 904, 929
decision-making 9, 34, 96, 99, 809, 844, 892
delegated 86–7, 327, 344, 708
discretionary 69, 141, 153, 194–6, 326, 664, 666
exclusive 709, 758, 809, 811
general 65, 93, 107, 109, 812, 912
implementing 88–90, 153, 176, 949
legislative 48, 72, 120, 847, 929
misuse of 124, 154, 178, 180, 804
official 569–70
regulatory 100, 102–4, 111–12, 131, 671, 706, 922
special 263, 665, 667, 866, 889
treaty-making 900, 910, 912–13, 919, 936
pre-emptive effects 102–4, 116, 914
pre-litigation procedure 137, 140, 142 see also administrative phase
precedence 144, 270, 339, 349, 372, 385, 411
predatory pricing 782–3, 787–9
pregnancy 377, 479, 555
preliminary rulings 64–5, 135–6, 153, 173, 308–9, 742–3, 751
   effects of Court of Justice ruling 228–30
   jurisdiction 210–11
   mandatory references 222–5
   national courts/tribunals 214–16
   procedure 175, 185, 212–13, 217–19, 225, 230
   questions that may be referred 211–14
   references for 209–31
   references on validity 225–8
   referral as discretion or duty 218–28
   relationship between Court of Justice and referring court 216–18
price competition 749, 788, 791
price discrimination 769, 791
pricing, predatory 782–3, 787–9
primacy 35, 61, 144, 209, 278–84, 914, 960–1
primary and secondary establishment of companies 649–58
primary establishments 534, 649, 651, 655
primary flexibility 125–7
primary law 3, 50, 57, 235, 253, 317, 356
   overview 23–37
   sundry written sources 34–6
   unwritten sources 36–7
primary obligations 326–7
prior authorisation 367, 549, 564, 664, 667, 683, 694
private creditors 573, 575, 650, 681–2
private employers 254–5, 265, 315, 502
private enforcement 297, 315, 709, 712, 726, 809–10, 838–43
private individuals 205, 241, 253, 256, 261–2, 266–7, 281
private limited companies 567, 586–7, 653, 681
private operators 8, 346, 608, 671–2, 887
private parties 162–6, 240–2, 253–6, 260–2, 264–6, 280–3, 344–5
private undertakings 188, 254, 262, 280, 715, 854, 879
privilege, professional 819–20
privileged applicants 155, 160–1, 202
privileged undertakings 875, 877, 881–2

procedural autonomy, national 288, 302–5, 318, 324, 842
procedural code 899, 902, 936, 938, 949
procedural guarantees 170, 365, 872
procedural requirements 83, 88, 114, 154, 178–9, 486, 833
procedural rules 238–9, 287–9, 292, 294–5, 298–9, 301–2, 316–18
processed milk 421–3
product requirements 407, 412, 418–23, 427–8, 443, 803–5
professional activities 535, 569, 625, 630–2, 634, 636–8, 641
professional bodies/organisations 554, 568, 601, 635, 637–9, 643–4, 892–3
professional conduct, rules of 638–43
professional knowledge 632–3
professional liability insurance 610, 612, 641
professional privilege 819–20
professional qualifications 534, 604, 607, 615, 626, 630–2, 635–8
Professional Qualifications Directive 615–16, 624, 630–2, 634–5, 637–9, 642, 645
professional rules 538, 561–2, 568, 577, 610, 757
professional secrecy 610, 640
professional titles, home-country 634, 637–8, 641, 643–4
professions, regulated 600, 610, 621, 630, 632–7
profits 198, 308, 313, 585–6, 588, 592–5, 686
    reasonable 863, 865
prohibited requirements, Services Directive 604, 606–7
proportionality 98, 116–17, 122–4, 321–2, 349–50, 437–9, 445
    assessment 123, 415, 490, 889
    as general principle of Union law 325–8
    as limit to actions of institutions 325–7
    as limit to actions of Member States 327–8
    and mandatory requirements 445–6
    principle 97–8, 121–4, 438–40, 445, 466–7, 564, 825–6
    review 575–6
    test 123, 580, 889
proposals, legislative 34, 73, 78, 80, 85, 94–5, 122
protected family members 478, 529
protectionist effect 393, 398–9, 401, 429
protectionist taxation 391, 396, 398–9
protective effect 400, 414, 429
providers 561–4, 568, 577–80, 599–614, 617–22, 635–6, 864–5
    information from 609
    information on good repute 613–14
provision of services *see* freedom to provide services
provisional measures 184, 957, 965
psychological difficulties 680–1, 685–6, 691
psychological obstacles 679, 685
public ambulance service 880, 887–8
public enforcement 812, 826–38, 840
public health 107–8, 411, 440–1, 485–7, 570–3, 628–9, 636–7
public hearing, fair and 289, 379, 832–3
public interest 249–50, 347, 415–16, 521–2, 577–81, 603–4, 622–3 *see also* general interest

mandatory requirements of 412–14, 416, 422, 431, 442
public law 167, 301, 313, 401, 512–14, 519, 569–71
public morality 35, 435–6, 440
public policy 76, 435–6, 482–8, 571–3, 604–6, 622, 662–4
public policy proviso 560, 571–3
public procurement 298, 309, 546–7, 596–7, 621, 864–5
public safety 290, 347, 365, 367–8
public security 435, 479, 482–7, 508, 570–3, 622, 662–4
public service contracts 247, 542, 546, 621
public service obligations 713, 863, 865, 885, 894
public services 263, 493, 511–14, 517, 707, 847, 875
public supply contracts 247, 542, 546, 621
public undertakings 664, 707, 852, 875–6, 878–9, 881, 884
    publicity 596, 603–4, 640

QMV *see* qualified majority, vote
qualifications 63, 101, 537–8, 577, 625–33, 635–9, 641–5
    formal 536, 542, 626, 630–3, 636
qualified majority, vote (QMV) 30, 45–6, 48–52, 81–5, 93, 128–9, 906–7
quality of services, and Services Directive 599–600, 609–10, 624
quantitative restrictions 4, 8, 101, 391, 403, 407–10, 432–3
    measures having equivalent effect
        exports 432–4
        imports 409–32
quantity discounts/rebates 793–5
    quotas 8, 10, 165, 330, 344, 392, 408

race 31, 294, 371–2, 774
ratification 5, 7, 10–11, 14–15, 19, 21, 29
    process 14–16, 19
raw materials 396–7, 404, 772, 799
real links 466–7, 475, 482, 507–8
real seat doctrine 651–2, 655, 657, 674, 692
reason, rule of 730, 743, 745–7, 749–50, 755, 757, 893
reasonable time 184, 289, 379, 506–7, 832–3, 869
reasoned opinions 111, 120–2, 136–7, 139–42, 189, 204
rebates 404, 765, 780, 791–4, 856
    conditional 795–6
    quantity 793
recidivism 720, 829–30
recipients of services 557, 599, 605, 616
    rights 607–9
reciprocity 237, 512, 694–6, 955, 957
recoupment 788–9
recovery 287, 289, 292–3, 332, 585, 855, 869–71
    of unlawfully levied charges, and national courts 305–7
references for preliminary rulings 209–31
    on validity 225–8
referenda 10–11, 14–16, 19–20, 33, 35, 51–2, 55
reflagging 349
reflection, period of 19, 51, 55

reforms 3, 15–16, 18, 49–51, 53, 69–70, 806
  institutional 15, 43, 55
refugees 369–70
refunds 167, 181, 293, 333, 583
refusals to supply 765, 782, 792, 797–8, 805
registered offices 216, 582, 584–5, 648, 650–2, 654–8, 691
registered partnerships 332, 470, 476, 480, 525
registration 427, 554, 568, 635–9, 641, 643, 692–3
regulated professions 600, 610, 621, 630, 632–7
  advertising and other forms of commercial communications 610
regulatory acts 154, 162, 173, 175–6, 186, 343, 687
regulatory competences 102–3, 114, 124–5, 429, 623
regulatory competition 654, 657, 687–8, 692
regulatory powers 100, 102–4, 111–12, 131, 671, 706, 922
relevant market 252, 535, 712, 731, 743–5, 751–2, 765–77
relief 136, 173, 227, 288, 296–7, 494, 592
religion 31, 266, 277, 366, 371, 532
remedies
  judicial 210, 222–3, 225, 376
  legal 158, 175, 184, 188, 215, 272, 313
  national 226, 289, 294–5, 298, 301–2, 317–18, 840–1
remuneration 182, 299, 503, 509, 550–1, 554–5, 659
reparation 195, 247, 267, 277, 289, 292, 297
  Francovich right to 307–14
repayment 293, 306, 404, 476, 516, 583, 587
reputation 198, 367, 456, 748, 799, 813
requirements
  labelling 280, 413–14, 417, 422, 443
  overriding 445, 531, 573–4, 576, 578–80, 603–5, 619–20
  Services Directive 601–2
resale at a loss 418–19
resale price maintenance 742, 749, 761
rescue 859–61
residence 461–4, 466–7, 470–3, 476–83, 491–3, 582–5, 608–9
  cards 471, 478–9, 481
  continuous 479, 481
  permanent 468, 479–82, 485, 509, 516, 528, 572
  permits 364, 464–5, 474–5, 518
Residence Directive 461, 467–88, 492
  abuse of rights 488
  administrative formalities 477–9
  derogations on the right of entry and residence on the grounds of public policy, public security and public health 482–8
  material scope 471–7
  personal scope 468–71
  right of permanent residence 479–81
  rights of residents and permanent residents 481–2
resident companies 583, 585, 588, 590, 595
resident subsidiaries 585, 587, 589–90, 592, 594
residents 60, 369, 464, 519, 583–5, 589, 595
  rights 481–2
  tax treatment of 524
residual rules 421, 427–8
resignation 60–1

resources 12, 29, 78, 80–2, 88, 468, 474
  biological 100, 102–3, 915, 922, 924, 932
  own 12, 44
  state 513, 847, 850–2, 870
  sufficient 377, 462–7, 473–5, 477–8, 525, 527
responsibilities 27, 53, 55–6, 140–1, 873–4, 877–9, 881
  special 717, 767, 798, 877
restrictions
  disguised 116, 410, 435, 437, 439–40, 452, 595
  by effect 744–50
  hard-core 729, 753, 759, 761–2
  non-discriminatory 435, 520, 531, 538, 547–8, 563–6, 574–5
  by object 742–4, 763
  territorial 481–2, 604, 619
restrictive agreements 706, 746, 756, 759, 763
restrictive effects 300, 411, 428, 438, 440, 672–3, 743–4
restrictive measures 84, 343, 353, 564, 901, 907, 919
retailers 338, 416, 440, 448, 745, 793
retroactive application 283, 329
retroactive effect 177, 300, 331
reverse discrimination 431
review, judicial see judicial review
revision procedure, ordinary 28–9, 35
revocation 86–7, 870
right of establishment 531–97
  abolition of restrictions on 541–3
  Art 18 TFEU and Arts 49 and 56 TFEU 547
  case law 535–41
  and direct and indirect discrimination on grounds of nationality 545–7
  and direct applicability of Art 49 TFEU 543–4
  and exercise of official authority 568–71
  general scope 534–5
  and imperative requirements in the general interest 573–81
  lawyers 640–4
  meaning 532–4
  national measures to prevent circumvention 567–8
  and national tax measures 581–96
  non-discriminatory restrictions on 547–52
  parallel interpretation of Arts 45, 49 and 56 TFEU and horizontal effect 552
  public policy proviso 560, 571–3
right to education 525–7
right to equal treatment 461–2, 472, 475–6, 482, 489, 506–7, 509
right to move 461–3, 465–6, 468, 489–91, 497, 506, 508
right to vote 58, 355, 379, 492–4, 500, 519
rights-holders, main 477–8, 480
Rome Treaties 7–9, 19
rotation, equal 46–7, 52
  rule of reason 730, 743, 745–7, 749–50, 755, 757, 893

safety 103, 263, 376–7, 610–11, 613, 635–7, 771
  public 290, 347, 365, 367–8
sales 412–14, 423–7, 444–5, 452–5, 457–9, 586, 761–2

passive 761–2
volume of 416–19, 429–30
sales promotion schemes 416–18, 444
sanctions 25, 65, 82, 472, 478, 488, 813–14
   criminal 317, 351, 381, 613
   financial 149–50, 205
Schengen Information System 471, 484–5
Schöppenstedt formula 191–6
Schuman Plan 3–5, 8
SEA *see* Single European Act
Second Pillar 27, 65, 70, 268, 900, 908
secondary flexibility 127–31
secondary legislation 42–3, 102–3, 251–2, 374–6,
   461–3, 465–7, 953
secondary obligations 326–7
secrecy, professional 610, 640
secrets, business 739, 822–3
security 6, 440, 485–8, 666–7, 694–5, 899–900,
   902–3
   internal 47–8, 343
   national 25, 97, 290, 365, 367–8, 932, 945
   policy 13, 27, 47, 54–5, 268, 899–900, 902
selective distribution 732, 748–9, 761–2
selectivity 748, 853, 855–6
self-employed activities 76–7, 248, 511, 532, 539,
   542, 559
self-employed persons 245, 461, 464, 473, 536, 541,
   553
selling arrangements 407, 418–29, 459, 522
semi-privileged applicants 155, 160–1
service activities 601–6, 608, 616–19, 624
service of general economic interest 707, 876, 884,
   887–8
service providers *see* providers
services 531–5, 553–69, 577–81, 599–617, 619–25,
   634–40, 883–7
   audiovisual 946, 950
   freedom to provide *see* freedom to provide
      services
   quality of 599–600, 609–10, 624
   recipients *see* recipients of services
   Services Directive 544, 599–624, 638–9, 641
   telecommunications 874, 879, 890
Services Directive 544, 599–624, 638–9, 641
   administrative co-operation 611–19
   administrative simplification 600, 616–19
   assessment 623–4
   authorisations 602–4
   case-by-case derogations 607
   free movement of services 605–9
   freedom for providers to provide services 605–7
   freedom of establishment for providers 602–5
   and guarantees 610
   and internal situations 621–2
   justifications excluded 622–3
   mutual evaluation 619–20
   and non-discrimination 607–8, 620
   prohibited requirements 604, 606–7
   and quality of services 599–600, 609–10, 624
   requirements 601–2
   requirements which must be amended if they
      cannot be justified 604–5
   rights of recipients of services 607–9

services covered 600–1
services of general economic interest (SGEIs) 378,
   707, 847, 862–5, 874–6, 884–6, 894
settlement procedures 836–7
settlement process 810–11, 838
sex discrimination 261–2, 348, 371–3
sexual orientation 31, 266, 294, 332, 348, 371, 470
SGEIs *see* services of general economic interest
shared competence 100–3, 105, 116, 922, 927, 930–3,
   935–6
shareholders 548, 587, 667–70, 672–4, 683–4, 693–4,
   697–9
shareholdings 647, 662, 668–71, 674
   controlling 670
shares 587–8, 647, 656–7, 662–3, 665–6, 670–2,
   694–5
   categories of 695–6
   special 664–7, 669, 671, 673
similar domestic products 396–7, 401–2
simplification, administrative 600, 616–19
sincere cooperation 25, 79, 87, 235, 269–70, 322–4,
   932–4
single contact, points of 599, 609, 617–19, 624
single currency 14, 21, 27, 34, 125–6, 391
Single European Act (SEA) 12–13, 19, 36, 43, 56,
   77–8, 340
single market 101, 107, 408, 413, 420, 650, 709–10
   see also internal market
Slovakia 17, 126
Slovenia 17, 48, 126, 451, 528, 696
social advantages 377, 464, 468, 504, 516, 518–19,
   527–8
social assistance 377, 462, 472–5, 477, 479, 482,
   505–8
social justice 24, 340, 711
social policy 29, 46, 81, 100, 125, 164, 919–20
   competences 85, 268
social protection 76, 377, 556, 578
social rights 32, 301, 350, 360–1, 365
social security 82, 377, 464, 498–9, 518, 521–2,
   636–7
social solidarity 894
solidarity 24, 350, 361, 374, 386, 467, 715–17
sovereign rights 66, 236–8, 253, 270
sovereignty 274, 277–8, 341, 356, 470, 490–1, 569
Spaak Report 7–8, 408, 498
Spain 47–9, 57–8, 151, 484, 493–4, 854–5, 878–9
special legislative procedures 29, 56, 71, 77–83, 93–4,
   110, 129
special powers 263, 665, 667, 866, 889
special relationship 25, 167, 512, 875
special shares 664–7, 669, 671, 673
specialised courts 42, 61, 63–4, 84
sporting competitions 523–4
spouses 131, 333, 470–1, 476–7, 519, 525, 539–40
stakeholders 689, 698–9
standing 71, 122, 154–5, 200–1, 225–6, 249–50,
   378–9 *see also* locus standi
   actions for failure to act 185–7

standing – *continued*
 of non-privileged applicants, annulment
  actions 162–80
 privileged and semi-privileged applicants,
  annulment actions 160–2
state, United 4–5, 159–60, 167, 458, 721, 769–70,
  800
state aid 10, 83, 135, 169, 225, 332, 848–94
 Art 106 TFEU 874–90
 and compensation 862–4
 definition 850–7
 discretionary exceptions 859–62
 enforcement of rules 866–71
 justifications for aid 857–9
 mandatory exceptions 857–9
 misuse of aid 866, 870–1
 and modernisation agenda 848–9
 national legislation and Art 101 890–3
 notified aid 866–9
 rights of interested parties 871–3
 role of national courts 873–4
 unlawful aid 847, 866, 868–9, 871
state liability 143, 190, 307–8, 314
state monopolies 8, 404, 724, 876, 884
 of a commercial character 447–9, 876
state regulation 705, 847–94
state resources 513, 847, 850–2, 870
statement of objections 721, 821–2, 825, 828, 837
statutory interest 296, 301–2
steel 4–6, 333, 861
students 105, 462–5, 475–6, 482, 526, 528
subsidiaries 532–3, 549–51, 584–9, 594–5, 648–50,
  658–60, 720–2
 non-resident 588–9, 592, 595
 resident 585, 587, 589–90, 592, 594
subsidiarity 33, 98, 124, 131, 321–2, 343, 690
 definition 114–16
 as general principle of Union law 324–5
 implementation 116–17, 119
 principle 25–6, 34, 71, 97–8, 114–23, 324–5,
  382–3
 role of national parliaments 119–22
 role of Union courts 117–19
 role of Union political institutions 116–17
 test 115–16, 119
 yellow card system 111, 120–2, 132
substantive legal bases 901–2, 909, 917–18, 936
sufficient resources 377, 462–7, 473–5, 477–8, 525,
  527
Sunday trading 415–17, 420, 422, 427, 443, 566
supervening exclusivity 908, 923–6, 930–2, 940–1
supervision 334, 512, 561, 568, 570, 577, 611–12
 fiscal 411–12, 441, 576
supplementary obligations 730, 767, 796
supply
 contracts 732, 799–800
 refusals to 765, 782, 792, 797–8, 805
supranationalism 66
supremacy 37, 237–9, 241, 243–5, 263–5, 283–5,
  296–7
 and direct effect 278–84
 principle 36, 235, 238, 270–80, 282, 284, 338
 Sweden 9–11, 51, 119, 126, 350, 399–400, 934–5

TA *see* Treaty of Amsterdam
takeover bids 661, 673, 683, 689, 693–700
targeted inspections 834
tax avoidance 572, 593–4
tax rules, national 534, 546, 581–5, 587–9, 591, 597
taxation
 discriminatory 391–2, 396, 421
 internal 391, 393–6, 399, 401–5, 446, 448
telecommunications 664–5, 885
temporal market 775
territoriality, principle 595, 722
TEU *see* Treaty on European Union
third parties 154, 156–8, 165, 306, 454–5, 680–3, 732
Third Pillar 15, 70, 137, 243, 268–9, 351, 900
threshold criteria, direct effect 245–8
titles, home-country 634, 637–8, 640–5
TN *see* Treaty of Nice
trade
 external 8, 101, 901, 941, 944–5
 intra-Community 404–7, 410, 415–17, 420, 423–
  4, 427–30, 437–9
trade associations 172–3, 734, 872
trade marks 170, 217–18, 450, 453, 456–9, 965
 Community 450, 453, 964–5
 exhaustion of rights 456–9
trade names 548–9, 658
trade policy 724, 901, 943–4, 950
trade unions 349–51, 367, 374–5, 434, 519–20, 553,
  581
training 104–5, 368, 504–5, 517, 521–2, 629–33,
  635–7
transit 243, 334, 395, 407–9, 435, 451
transitional arrangements 230, 456, 503, 528–9, 553
transitional periods 10–11, 18, 72, 124, 431, 448–9,
  543
transitional provisions 17, 45–6, 49, 57, 65, 70,
  268–9
transparency, market 738–9
transport 17, 185–7, 303, 817–18, 913–14, 917, 948
 policy, common 8, 76, 185
 services 185, 600, 874
transsexuals 348, 371
treaty-making power 900, 910, 912–13, 919, 936
Treaty of Amsterdam (TA) 12–13, 15–16, 72–3,
  76–8, 98, 124–7, 340 *see also Table of
  Legislation*
Treaty of Lisbon (TL) 19–21
Treaty of Nice (TN) 16, 18–19, 48–51, 63, 76–7, 101,
  340 *see also Table of Legislation*
Treaty on European Union (TEU) 13–15, 24–36,
  41–59, 79–84, 114–19, 121–9, 340–1
  see also Table of Legislation
 common provisions 24–5
 final provisions 28–30
 institutional provisions 26–7
 provisions on democratic principles 26
 provisions on enhanced co-operation 27
 provisions on external action and Common
  Foreign and Security Policy 27–8
 and Treaty on the Functioning of the European
  Union 33–4
Treaty on the Functioning of the European Union
  (TFEU) 30–2 *see also Table of Legislation*

and Treaty on European Union (TEU) 33–4
trigger models 279–82, 284
Turkey 17–18, 242, 363–4, 368

ultimate jurisdiction 275–6
ultra vires review 275–6
unanimity 47–8, 75–8, 81–5, 92–4, 128–30, 906–7,
    950
undertakings 713–20, 775–84, 814–23, 825–31, 834–
    8, 850–7, 874–90
    agreements between 719, 729–30, 734–5
    associations of *see* associations of undertakings
    and concurrence of wills 731–4
    conduct and performance 778
    entrusted 707, 864, 875, 884–6, 888
    parent *see* parent companies
    public 664, 707, 852, 875–6, 878–9, 881, 884
unemployment 497, 505–6, 528
    involuntary 473, 480, 505
uniform advertising concept 548–9, 658
uniform application of Union law 83, 209–10, 213,
    287–8, 295, 301, 304–5
Union citizens 58, 461–79, 481–3, 485, 487–9, 491–
    3, 524–6
Union citizenship 26, 31, 58, 391, 461–95, 500, 503
    evolution of case law 463–7
    history 461–3
    and Residence Directive 461, 467–88, 492
Union competences 31, 33, 324, 901, 908, 922–3,
    930–2 *see also* competences
    conferral principle 25, 97–115, 119, 123, 909,
        911–12, 922
    exclusive 100–1, 128, 922, 924
    proportionality principle *see* proportionality,
        principle
    subsidiarity principle *see* subsidiarity, principle
    system 97–132
United Kingdom 56–9, 125–7, 273–5, 355–6, 369–
    70, 386–7, 666–8
    courts 148, 213, 263, 843
United States 4–5, 159–60, 167, 458, 721, 769–70,
    800
    antitrust law 730, 745–6, 830
universal suffrage, direct 12, 56

unlawful aid 847, 866, 868–9, 871
    unlawfully levied charges, recovery 305–7

validity 147, 155, 173–5, 200–3, 209–12, 956, 959–63
    references on 225–8
vertical agreements 729, 742, 754–5, 760–1, 763
vertical direct effect 263, 267
vertical restraints 729, 741, 760–1, 828
veterinary surgeons 536–7, 631
veto 29, 81–2, 86–7, 128–9, 664–5, 667, 670–1
Vietnam 930, 935, 938–9, 946
visas 15, 72, 126, 471, 478, 484–5
vocational training 76, 104–5, 371, 376, 473, 479,
    505
votes 48–9, 51–3, 58, 120, 128–9, 355–6, 492–4
    qualified majority *see* qualified majority, vote
    weighting 16–17, 48–9
    voting rights 58, 340, 355, 379, 492–4, 500,
        694–5

weighting of votes 16–17, 48–9
welfare provision 463–4, 467, 474–5, 489, 497, 504,
    506
welfare tourism 463, 472, 506–7
wills, concurrence of 729, 733, 735
wine 170, 397, 399–400, 413–14, 433, 445
withdrawal
    proposals 92
    from Union 30, 84
women 24, 31, 53, 76, 290–1, 371–2, 376–7
work-seekers 473–5, 482, 505–8
workers *see also* freedom of movement for workers
    children 470, 526, 528
    definition 503–5
    families 520, 525–8
    posting of 479, 529, 660
    retention of worker status 505–6
working conditions 371, 376, 498, 911, 920
working time 103, 117–18, 123, 282–3, 376
World Trade Organization (WTO) 724, 933, 935,
    938, 942, 955, 957
    WTO *see* World Trade Organization

yellow card system 111, 120–2, 132